OXF Wo
Dictionary

OXFORD
UNIVERSITY PRESS

Great Clarendon Street, Oxford, OX2 6DP, United Kingdom

Oxford University Press is a department of the University of Oxford. It furthers the University's objective of excellence in research, scholarship, and education by publishing worldwide. Oxford is a registered trade mark of Oxford University Press in the UK and in certain other countries

First published 2012
2016 2015 2014 2013
10 9 8 7 6 5 4 3 2

The British National Corpus is a collaborative project involving Oxford University Press, Longman, Chambers, the Universities of Oxford and Lancaster and the British Library

ISBN: 978 0 19 439798 8 Book
ISBN: 978 0 19 439823 7 Book and CD-ROM Pack
ISBN: 978 0 19 439821 3 Book in Pack
ISBN: 978 0 19 439822 0 CD-ROM

Edited by Victoria Bull, assisted by Robert Duncan

Typeset by Data Standards Limited

Printed in China

ACKNOWLEDGEMENTS

The publisher would like to thank the following for their kind permission to reproduce photographs and other copyright material: Alamy Ltd 151 USB drive, 413 electric kettle, P3 computer games, model making, sailing, bowling, P6 hovercraft, P7 hatchback; Anton Balazh 413 kettle; Blend Images P3 stamp collecting; Brand X Pictures P3 sewing; Comstock P3 acting; Corbis P4 basketball, P5 table tennis; Corel 33, 112 castle, 173 calf, 194 buck, doe, 274, 280 firework, 433, 523, 528 glider, P2 carpenter, dentist, farmer, P4 cricket, hockey, rugby, skating, P5 boxing, racing, surfing, P6 ferry, helicopter, lifeboat, liner, oil tanker, submarine, yacht, P7 bus, lorry, train, P9 flats, farm, stately home, cottage, P16 burger, eggs, milkshake, pizza, beef, soup; Design Pics P2 plumber; Flying Images Ltd P2 nurse; Fotosearch P2 cook, teacher; Getty Images P2 pilot, P3 photography, P6 glider, P16 fish and chips; Getty Images/OJO Images P2 waiter; Getty Images/Stockbyte P3 Internet; Getty/Buccina Studios/PhotoDisc P1 pyjamas, P5 bungee; D Eaton 92, 139 coil, springs, 167, 280 fireplace, 285, 318, 413 key, 430, 517, 546, 759, 832, P8; Dennis Kitchen Studio 151 printer; Hemera Technologies Inc 6 concertina, 48 bagpipes, rackets, 49 (*not* briefcase, carrier bag), 50, 54 shopping basket, 65, 67, 78, 85, 91, 94, 103 camel, 104, 105, 117, 135, 148, 173 bull, cow, 183, 186, 206, 208, 221, 222, 231 (*not* duck), 232, 239, 241, 268, 292 football player, footballers, 295, 310 (*not* hoe), 317, 319, 344, 346, 352, 357 hinge, 362, 402, 406, 409, 411 canoe, kayak, 415, 419, 420, 439, 460, 473, 485 (*not* bassoon, double bass, kettledrum, oboe, piccolo, xylophone), 503 nutcrackers, 521 dungarees, overalls, 525, 527, 528 parachute, 538 penknife, 545, 547 pin, safety pin, 563 postbox, 566 pushchair, 629 (*not* tape), 646, 662 photos, 666, 667, 679, 683, 703, 713 (*not* correction fluid, highlighter, marker, ruler), 734, 737 dagger, sword, 745, 765, 767, 770, 776, 797, 838, P1 patterns, P7 (*not* lorry, hatchback, trains), P16 coffee, cereal, cheese, salad, tea, honey, ice cream, kebab, pancake, pasta, quiche, spaghetti, waffle; H Venning 240, 359, 363, 425, 431, 497, 548, 558, 585, 663 shake, 682, 765 sweaters, 812; Image Source P5 fencing; Ingram Publishing 28 antelope, 609, 647, 650 seal, P1 jacket; JB Illustrations 77 face, 107, 298; Jae Wagoner Artists Rep 123 chess; James Oliver/Digital Vision/ Getty Images/Photolibrary Group Ltd P4 athletics; John Foxx P16 jam; K Hiscock 123 chickens, 322, 357 hippo, rhino, 364, 405, 411 kangaroo, 417, 436, 476 gorilla, monkey, 506, 632, 688, 701 spider, 707, 831, P12–15; KJA-artists.com 49 carrier, 125 chips, crisps, 242, 418 label, price tag, ticket, 443, 476 chequebook, coins, credit card, note, 555, 593; K Jones 125 chips, crisps; K Maddison P10, P11; L Barnard/G White 108, 258, 641, 736; Leon Mason/Corbis P4 weightlifter; M Dunn 741; Meiklejohn Illustrations 52, 112 catapult, 706 (*not* squeeze); M Jones 689, 839; M Lonsdale/Hardlines 125 cups; M Shovel 34, 45, 62, 169, 175, 180 legs, 231 ducked, 234 looking, 292 footprints, 304, 337, 416, 426, 514 opposite, 521 overflowing, 552 sling, 584, 662 shadow, 672, 771, 795, 833, R16; M Woods 47, 58 beaver, 76, 99, 286, 418 shoelace, 448 magnet, 503 nuts, 550, 552 flower, 626, 775, 804; OUP/Fancy P6 plane; Photodisc/ Getty Images 282, 327, 485 bassoon, double bass, kettledrum, oboe, piccolo, xylophone, 521 apron, 821, P1 button, P2 doctor, police officer, P4 baseball, gymnastics, ice hockey, skiing, tennis, P5 abseiling, karate, waterskiing, rafting, windsurfing, P7 underground, P16 apple pie; Photolibrary Group Ltd 49 handbag, 151 PC, laptop, P3 climbing, gym, P5 golf; Polka Dot Images P7 painting; P Schramm 706; Punchstock P16 potato; Q2A Solutions 464, 537, 594; R Lewington 48 badger; Stockbyte/ Getty P16 noodles; V Luff 418 lace edge; all other pictures OUP

Cover: Corbis guitar/Radius Images, pizza/Susie M Eising, sky/ Paul Thompson, coffee/Ocean; Getty Images keyboard/William Andrew; OUP girl, Radcliffe Camera/Photolibary.com, cyclist

Although every effort has been made to trace and contact copyright holders before publication, this has not been possible in some cases. We apologise for any apparent infringement of copyright and, if notified, the publisher will be pleased to rectify any errors or omissions at the earliest possible opportunity.

Contents

Inside front cover Abbreviations, labels and symbols used in the dictionary

iv Guide to the dictionary

vi Phonetic spelling

1 – 839 **The Dictionary**

Study section

WT1 – WT16 Wordpower Writing Tutor

P1 – P16 Colour pages

R1 – R41 Reference section

R42 – R59 Wordpower Workout

R60 List of illustrations in the dictionary

R62 List of notes in the dictionary

Guide to the dictionary

Pronunciation in phonetic spelling

Part of speech (= *noun, verb, adjective*, etc.)

teacher /ˈtiːtʃə(r)/ *noun* [C] a person whose job is to teach, especially in a school or college: *He's a teacher at a primary school.* ◆ *a chemistry/music teacher*

Definition (= the meaning of the word) in simple English

Words with the same spelling divided into nouns, verbs, etc.

swot[1] /swɒt/ *noun* [C] (*informal*) a person who studies too hard

swot[2] /swɒt/ *verb* [I,T] (*informal*) (swo**tt**ing; swo**tt**ed) **swot (up) (for/on sth); swot sth up** to study sth very hard, especially to prepare for an exam: *She's swotting for her final exams.*

Irregular spelling and **irregular forms** clearly shown

I = intransitive verb
T = transitive verb

study[2] /ˈstʌdi/ *verb* (studying; studies; *pt, pp* studied) **1** [I,T] **study (sth/for sth)** to spend time learning about sth: *to study French at university* ◆ *Leon has been studying hard for his exams.*

Patterns that the word is used in

exam /ɪɡˈzæm/ (also *formal* **examination**) *noun* [C] a written, spoken or practical test of what you know or can do: *an English exam* ◆ *the exam results* ◆ *to* ***do/take/sit an exam*** ◆ *to* ***pass/fail an exam*** ◆ *to* ***revise for an exam*** ➲ note at **pass, study**

This word is used in **formal** English

Collocations (= words that go together) in bold

extra-curricular /ˌekstrə kəˈrɪkjələ(r)/ *adj* not part of the **curriculum** (= the normal course of studies in a school or college): *The school offers many extra-curricular activities such as sport, music, drama, etc.*

Difficult words in definitions are explained for you

The Oxford 3000™ marked with a key to show the most useful and important words in English

language /ˈlæŋɡwɪdʒ/ *noun*
➤ OF A COUNTRY **1** [C] the system of communication in speech and writing that is used by people of a particular country: *How many languages can you speak?* ◆ *What is your first language* (= your mother tongue)*?* ◆ *They fell in love in spite of* ***the language barrier*** (= having different first languages).
➤ COMMUNICATION **2** [U] the system of sounds and writing that people use to express their thoughts, ideas and feelings: *written/spoken language*

C = countable noun
U = uncountable noun

Short cuts take you quickly to the meaning you want

truant /ˈtruːənt/ *noun* [C] a child who stays away from school without permission
IDM **play truant**; (*AmE*) **play hooky** to stay away from school without permission

Idioms in a separate section

AmE shows **American English**

Stress marks show you how to pronounce compound words

ballpoint /ˈbɔːlpɔɪnt/ (also ˌballpoint ˈpen, *BrE also* Biro) *noun* [C] a pen with a very small metal ball at the end that rolls ink onto paper ➲ picture at **stationery**

Illustrations build your vocabulary and help with confusing words

vowel /ˈvaʊəl/ *noun* [C] a letter that represents a **vowel** sound. In English the vowels are *a*, *e*, *i*, *o* or *u* ➲ look at **consonant**

Look at related words to build your vocabulary

compulsory /kəmˈpʌlsəri/ *adj* that must be done, by law, rules, etc: *Maths and English are compulsory subjects on this course.* ♦ *It is compulsory to wear a hard hat on the building site.* SYN **obligatory** OPP **voluntary, optional**

Synonym (= a word with the same meaning)

Opposite (= a word with the opposite meaning)

clever /ˈklevə(r)/ *adj* cleverer; cleverest [You can also use **more clever** and **most clever**.] **1** able to learn, understand or do sth quickly and easily; intelligent: *a clever student* ♦ *How clever of you to mend my watch!* ➲ note at **intelligent** **2** (used about things, ideas, or sb's actions) showing skill or intelligence: *a clever device* ♦ *We made a clever plan.* ▶ **cleverly** *adv* ▶ **cleverness** *noun* [U]

Comparatives and superlatives of adjectives and adverbs are shown

Examples show you how to use the word

Derivative (= a word formed from another word)

note[2] /nəʊt/ *verb* [T] **1** to notice or pay careful attention to sth: *He noted a slight change in her attitude towards him.* ♦ *Please note that this office is closed on Tuesdays.* **2** to mention sth: *I'd like to note that the project has so far been extremely successful.* PHR V **note sth down** to write sth down so that you remember it

Phrasal verbs in a separate section

Topic notes give you the words you need to talk about everyday topics

TOPIC

E-book

You can buy an e-book **over the Internet** and read it on an **e-reader/e-book reader** (= a small electronic device that you carry with you). You can keep many books on one e-reader. It is also possible to buy an **app** (= computer application) that will allow you to **download** e-books **onto** your computer, smartphone, iPod, etc.

Exam tips give you helpful advice on how to prepare for and do exams

EXAM TIP

Paragraphs

When you write an essay, it is important to organize your writing into paragraphs to show how your ideas develop. Each paragraph should contain a separate idea and include at least two sentences that relate to this idea. You start each paragraph on a new line.

Other types of note

HELP	to avoid mistakes
MORE	to build your vocabulary
CULTURE	for information about Britain and America
GRAMMAR	for difficult grammar points
WRITING TIP	to help you improve your writing
OTHER WORDS FOR	for help choosing exactly the right word

Phonetic spelling

Vowels

iː	see /siː/	ʊ	put /pʊt/	aɪ	five /faɪv/
i	any /ˈeni/	uː	too /tuː/	aʊ	now /naʊ/
ɪ	sit /sɪt/	u	usual /ˈjuːʒuəl/	ɔɪ	join /dʒɔɪn/
e	ten /ten/	ʌ	cup /kʌp/	ɪə	near /nɪə/
æ	hat /hæt/	ɜː	fur /fɜː/	eə	hair /heə/
ɑː	arm /ɑːm/	ə	ago /əˈgəʊ/	ʊə	pure /pjʊə/
ɒ	got /gɒt/	eɪ	pay /peɪ/		
ɔː	saw /sɔː/	əʊ	home /həʊm/		

Consonants

p	pen /pen/	f	fall /fɔːl/	h	how /haʊ/
b	bad /bæd/	v	van /væn/	m	man /mæn/
t	tea /tiː/	θ	thin /θɪn/	n	no /nəʊ/
d	did /dɪd/	ð	then /ðen/	ŋ	sing /sɪŋ/
k	cat /kæt/	s	so /səʊ/	l	leg /leg/
g	got /gɒt/	z	zoo /zuː/	r	red /red/
tʃ	chin /tʃɪn/	ʃ	she /ʃiː/	j	yes /jes/
dʒ	June /dʒuːn/	ʒ	vision /ˈvɪʒn/	w	wet /wet/

A, a /eɪ/ *noun* [C,U] (*pl* As; A's; a's /eɪz/) **1** the first letter of the English alphabet: *'Andy' begins with (an) 'A'.* **2** the highest grade given for an exam or piece of work: *I got an 'A' for my essay.* **3** A (used about music) the sixth note in the scale of C major: *A major/minor* ◆ *A flat/sharp*

🔑 **a** /ə; *strong form* eɪ/ (also **an** /ən; *strong form* æn/) *indefinite article*

> **HELP** The form **an** is used before a vowel sound: *an apple* ◆ *an hour* ◆ *an MP*

1 one: *A cup of coffee, please.* ◆ *We've got an apple, a banana and two oranges.* **2** used when you talk about one example of sth for the first time: *I saw a dog chasing a cat this morning. The cat climbed up a tree.* ◆ *Have you got a dictionary* (= any dictionary)? **3** used for saying what kind of person or thing sb/sth is: *He's a doctor.* ◆ *She's a Muslim.* ◆ *You are a clever boy.* ◆ *'Is that an eagle?' 'No, it's a falcon.'* **4** (used when you are talking about a typical example of sth) any; every: *An elephant can live for up to eighty years.*

> **HELP** You can also use the plural in this sense: *Elephants can live for up to eighty years.*

5 (used with prices, rates, measurements) each: *I usually drink two litres of water a day.* ◆ *twice a week* ◆ *He was travelling at about 80 miles an hour.* **SYN** **per** **6** used with some expressions of quantity: *a lot of money* ◆ *a few cars* ℹ For more information about the indefinite article, look at the **Reference Section** at the back of this dictionary.

A2 (level) /ˌeɪ ˈtuː (levl)/ *noun* [C,U] a British exam usually taken in Year 13 of school or college (= the final year) when students are aged 18. Students must first have studied a subject at AS level before they can take an A2 exam. Together AS and A2 level exams form the A-level qualification, which is needed for entrance to universities: *A2 exams* ◆ *She's* ***doing an A2 (level)*** *in History.* ➲ look at **A level, AS (level)**

the AA /ˌeɪ ˈeɪ/ *abbr* (in Britain) the **Automobile Association**; an organization for drivers. If you are a member of the AA and your car breaks down, they will send sb to help you: *My car wouldn't start so I called the AA.*

A & E /ˌeɪ ənd ˈiː/ *abbr* = **accident and emergency**

aback /əˈbæk/ *adv*
PHR V **take sb aback** ➲ **take**

abacus /ˈæbəkəs/ *noun* [C] a frame with small balls which slide along wires. It is used as a tool or toy for counting.

🔑 **abandon** /əˈbændən/ *verb* [T] **1** to leave sb/sth that you are responsible for, usually permanently: *The bank robbers abandoned the car just outside the city.* **2** to stop doing sth without finishing it or without achieving what you wanted to do: *The search for the missing sailors was abandoned after two days.* ▸ **abandonment** *noun* [U]

abandoned /əˈbændənd/ *adj* **1** left and no longer wanted, used or needed: *an abandoned car/house* ◆ *The child was found abandoned but unharmed.* **2** (of people or their behaviour) wild; not following accepted standards

abashed /əˈbæʃt/ *adj* [not before a noun] feeling guilty and embarrassed because of sth that you have done: *'I'm sorry,' said Ali,* ***looking abashed.***

abate /əˈbeɪt/ *verb* [I,T] (*formal*) to become less strong; to make sth less strong: *The storm showed no signs of abating.*

abattoir /ˈæbətwɑː(r)/ (*BrE*) = **slaughterhouse**

abbey /ˈæbi/ *noun* [C] a large church together with a group of buildings where **monks** or **nuns** (= religious men or women who live away from other people) live or lived in the past

abbreviate /əˈbriːvieɪt/ *verb* [T] to make sth shorter, especially a word or phrase: *'Kilometre' is usually abbreviated to 'km'.* **SYN** **shorten** ➲ look at **abridge**

abbreviation /əˌbriːviˈeɪʃn/ *noun* [C] a short form of a word or phrase: *In this dictionary 'sth' is the abbreviation for 'something'.*

ABC /ˌeɪ biː ˈsiː/ *noun* [sing] **1** the alphabet; the letters of English from A to Z **2** the simple facts about sth: *an ABC of Gardening*

abdicate /ˈæbdɪkeɪt/ *verb* **1** [I] to give up being king or queen: *The Queen abdicated in favour of her son* (= her son became king). **2** [T] to give sth up, especially power or a position: *to* ***abdicate responsibility*** (= to refuse to be responsible for sth) ▸ **abdication** /ˌæbdɪˈkeɪʃn/ *noun* [C,U]

abdomen /ˈæbdəmən/ *noun* [C] a part of your body below the chest, in which the stomach is contained ▸ **abdominal** /æbˈdɒmɪnl/ *adj*

abduct /æbˈdʌkt/ *verb* [T] to take hold of sb and take them away illegally: *He has been abducted by a terrorist group.* ▸ **abduction** *noun* [C,U]

aberration /ˌæbəˈreɪʃn/ *noun* [C,U] (*formal*) a fact, an action or a way of behaving that is not usual, and that may be unacceptable

abet /əˈbet/ *verb* (**abetting**; **abetted**)
IDM **aid and abet** ➲ **aid**[2]

abhor /əbˈhɔː(r)/ *verb* [T] (**abhorring**; **abhorred**) to hate sth very much: *All civilized people abhor the use of torture.*

abhorrence /əbˈhɒrəns/ *noun* [U] a strong feeling of hate; disgust: *Protesters expressed their* ***abhorrence of*** *war.*

abhorrent /əbˈhɒrənt/ *adj* that makes you feel hate or disgust: *The idea of slavery is* ***abhorrent to*** *us nowadays.*

abide /əˈbaɪd/ *verb*
IDM **can't/couldn't abide sb/sth/doing sth** to hate sb/sth; to not like sb/sth at all **SYN** **stand**

A

PHR V **abide by sth** to obey a law, etc.; to do what sb has decided

ability /əˈbɪləti/ *noun* [C,U] (*pl* **abilities**) **the ability to do sth** the mental or physical power or skill that makes it possible to do sth: *the ability to make decisions* ◆ *students of mixed abilities* **OPP** **inability**

abject /ˈæbdʒekt/ *adj* (*formal*) **1** terrible and without hope: *abject poverty* **2** without any pride or respect for yourself: *an abject apology*

ablaze /əˈbleɪz/ *adj* [not before a noun] burning strongly; completely on fire: *Soldiers used petrol to* ***set*** *the building* ***ablaze****.*

able /ˈeɪbl/ *adj* (**abler**; **ablest**) [You can also use **more able** and **most able**.] **1** [used as a modal verb] **be able to do sth** to have the ability, power, opportunity, time, etc. to do sth: *Will you be able to come to a meeting next week?* ◆ *I was able to solve the problem quickly.* ◆ *Many men don't* ***feel able*** *to express their emotions.* **OPP** **unable**

HELP In the passive **can/could** are used, not **be able**: *The arrangement can't be changed.*

ⓘ For more information about modal verbs, look at the **Reference Section** at the back of this dictionary.
2 clever; doing your job well: *one of the ablest/most able students in the class* ◆ *an able politician* ▶ **ably** /ˈeɪbli/ *adv*

ˌable-ˈbodied *adj* physically healthy and strong; having full use of your body

abnormal /æbˈnɔːml/ *adj* different from what is normal or usual, in a way that worries you or that is unpleasant: *abnormal weather conditions* **OPP** **normal** ▶ **abnormally** /-məli/ *adv*: *abnormally high temperatures*

abnormality /ˌæbnɔːˈmæləti/ *noun* [C,U] (*pl* **abnormalities**) something that is not normal, especially in sb's body: *He was born with an abnormality of the heart.*

aboard /əˈbɔːd/ *adv, prep* on or onto a train, a ship, an aircraft or a bus: *The plane crashed, killing all 158 people aboard.* ◆ *We climbed aboard the train and found a seat.*

abode /əˈbəʊd/ *noun* [C, usually sing] (*written*) the place where you live
IDM **(of) no fixed abode/address** ➲ **fixed**

abolish /əˈbɒlɪʃ/ *verb* [T] to end a law or system officially: *When was capital punishment abolished here?*

abolition /ˌæbəˈlɪʃn/ *noun* [U] the act of ending a law or system officially: *the abolition of slavery in the US*

abominable /əˈbɒmɪnəbl/ *adj* very bad; shocking **SYN** **appalling** ▶ **abominably** /-əbli/ *adv*

Aboriginal /ˌæbəˈrɪdʒənl/ (also **Aborigine** /ˌæbəˈrɪdʒəni/) *noun* [C] a member of the race of people who were the first people to live in a country, especially Australia ▶ **aboriginal** *adj*: *aboriginal traditions*

abort /əˈbɔːt/ *verb* [T] **1** to make a **foetus** (= a baby that is developing in its mother's body) die before it is born **2** to end sth before it is complete: *The company aborted the project when they realized it was costing too much.*

abortion /əˈbɔːʃn/ *noun* [C,U] a medical operation that causes a baby to die inside its mother before it is fully developed: *to have an abortion* ◆ *Abortion is illegal in some countries.* ➲ look at **miscarriage**

abortive /əˈbɔːtɪv/ *adj* not completed successfully; failed: *He made two abortive attempts to escape from prison.* **SYN** **unsuccessful**

abound /əˈbaʊnd/ *verb* [I] to exist in large numbers: *Animals and birds abound in the forest.* ◆ *Rumours abound about the actor's arrest.*
PHR V **abound with sth** to contain large numbers of sth: *The lake abounds with fish.*

about[1] /əˈbaʊt/ *adv* **1** (also **around**) a little more or less than: *It's about three miles from here to the city centre.* ◆ *I got home at about half past seven.* **SYN** **approximately** **2** (*informal*) almost; nearly: *Dinner's just about ready.* **3** (also **around**) in many directions or places: *I could hear people moving about upstairs.* ◆ *Don't leave your clothes lying about all over the floor.* **4** (also **around**) [used after certain verbs] without doing anything in particular: *The kids spend most evenings* ***sitting about****, bored.* **5** (also **around**) present in a place; existing: *It was very late and there were few people about.* ◆ *There isn't much good music about these days.*
IDM **be about to do sth** to be going to do sth very soon: *The film's about to start.* ◆ *I was just about to explain when she interrupted me.*

about[2] /əˈbaʊt/ *prep* **1** on the subject of: *Let's talk about something else.* ◆ *What's your book about?* ◆ *He told me* ***all about*** *his family.* ◆ *I don't like it, but there's nothing I can do about it.* **2** in the character of sb/sth: *There's something about him that I don't quite trust.* ◆ *I like the food, the climate and everything else about this country.* **3** busy with sth; doing sth: *Everywhere people were going about their daily business.* **4** (also **around**) (*especially BrE*) in many directions or places; in different parts of sth: *We wandered about the town for an hour or two.* ◆ *Lots of old newspapers were scattered about the room.*
IDM **how/what about...?** **1** used when asking for information about sb/sth or for sb's opinion or wish: *How about Ruth? Have you heard from her lately?* ◆ *I'm going to have chicken. What about you?* **2** used when making a suggestion: *What about going to a film tonight?*

aˌbout-ˈturn (*AmE* aˌbout-ˈface) *noun* [C] a complete change of opinion, plan or behaviour: *The government did an about-turn over tax.* ➲ look at **U-turn**

above /əˈbʌv/ *prep, adv*
➤ HIGHER PLACE **1** in a higher place: *The coffee is in the cupboard above the sink.* ◆ *The people in the flat above make a lot of noise.* **OPP** **below**
➤ MORE THAN **2** more than a number, an amount, a price, etc: *children aged 11 and above* ◆ *A score of 70 and above will get you a grade B.* ◆ *You must get*

above 50% to pass. ◆ *above-average temperatures* **OPP** **below** ➲ look at **over**
➤AT WORK **3** with a higher position in an organization, etc: *The person above me is the department manager.* **OPP** **below**
➤PROUD **4** too proud to do sth: *He seems to think he's above helping with the cleaning.*
➤EARLIER PART **5** in an earlier part (of sth written): *Contact me at the above address/the address above.* **OPP** below
IDM **above all** (used to emphasize the main point) most importantly: *Above all, stay calm!*
above board (used especially about a business deal, etc.) honest and open

abrasive /əˈbreɪsɪv/ *adj* **1** rough and likely to scratch: *abrasive kitchen cleaners* **2** (used about a person) rude and rather aggressive

abreast /əˈbrest/ *adv* **abreast (of sb/sth)** next to or level with sb/sth and going in the same direction: *The soldiers marched two abreast.*
IDM **be/keep abreast of sth** to have all the most recent information about sth

abridge /əˈbrɪdʒ/ *verb* [T] to make sth (usually a book) shorter by removing parts of it ➲ look at **abbreviate**

⚷ **abroad** /əˈbrɔːd/ *adv* in or to another country or countries: *They found it difficult to get used to living abroad.* ◆ *My mother has never been abroad.* ◆ *She often **goes abroad** on business.*

abrupt /əˈbrʌpt/ *adj* **1** sudden and unexpected: *an abrupt change of plan* **2** seeming rude and unfriendly ▶ **abruptly** *adv* ▶ **abruptness** *noun* [U]

abscess /ˈæbses/ *noun* [C] a swelling on or in the body, containing **pus** (= a poisonous yellow liquid)

abscond /əbˈskɒnd/ *verb* [I] (*formal*) **abscond (from sth) (with sth)** to run away from a place where you should stay, sometimes with sth that you should not take: *to abscond from prison* ◆ *She absconded with all the company's money.*

abseil /ˈæbseɪl/ (*AmE* **rappel**) *verb* [I] **abseil (down, off, etc. sth)** to go down the side of a very steep, high rock or a building while you are tied to a rope, pushing against the surface with your feet ➲ picture on **page P5**

⚷ **absence** /ˈæbsəns/ *noun* **1** [C,U] a time when sb is away from somewhere; the fact of being away from somewhere: *Frequent absences due to illness meant he was behind with his work.* ◆ *I have to make all the decisions in my boss's absence.* **2** [U] the fact of sth/sb not being there; lack: ***In the absence of** a doctor, try to help the injured person yourself.* **OPP** for both meanings **presence**

⚷ **absent** /ˈæbsənt/ *adj* **1** **absent (from sth)** not present somewhere: *He was absent from work because of illness.* **OPP** **present** **2** thinking about sth else; not paying attention: *an absent stare* ▶ **absently** *adv*

absentee /ˌæbsənˈtiː/ *noun* [C] a person who is not in the place where they should be

absenteeism /ˌæbsənˈtiːɪzəm/ *noun* [U] the problem of workers or students often not going to work or school

absent-ˈminded *adj* often forgetting or not noticing things, because you are thinking about sth else **SYN** **forgetful** ▶ **absent-mindedly** *adv*

⚷ **absolute** /ˈæbsəluːt/ *adj* **1** complete; total: *a course for absolute beginners* ◆ *The whole trip was an absolute disaster.* ◆ *None of the political parties had **an absolute majority*** (= more votes, etc. than all the other parties together). **2** [only *before* a noun] used, especially in spoken English, to give emphasis to what you are saying: *There's absolute rubbish on television tonight!* **3** not measured in comparison with sth else: *Spending on the Health Service has increased **in absolute terms**.*

⚷ **absolutely** *adv* **1** /ˈæbsəluːtli/ completely: *It's absolutely freezing outside!* ◆ *I absolutely refuse to believe that.* ◆ *He made absolutely no effort* (= no effort at all) *to help me.* **2** /ˌæbsəˈluːtli/ (used when you are agreeing with sb) yes; certainly: *'It is a good idea, isn't it?' 'Oh, absolutely!'*

absolve /əbˈzɒlv/ *verb* [T] **absolve sb (from/of sth)** to say formally that sb does not have to take responsibility for sth: *The driver was absolved of any blame for the train crash.*

⚷ **absorb** /əbˈsɔːb; -ˈzɔːb/ *verb* [T]
➤LIQUID/HEAT **1** **absorb sth (into sth)** to take in and hold sth (a liquid, heat, etc.): *a drug that is quickly absorbed into the bloodstream* ◆ *Black clothes absorb the sun's heat.*
➤INTO STH LARGER **2** **absorb sth (into sth)** to take sth into sth larger, so that it becomes part of it: *Over the years many villages have been absorbed into the city.*
➤INFORMATION **3** to take sth into the mind and understand it: *I found it impossible to absorb so much information so quickly.*
➤INTEREST SB **4** to hold sb's attention completely or interest sb very much: *History is a subject that absorbs her.*
➤A HIT **5** to reduce the effect of a sudden violent knock, hit, etc: *The front of the car is designed to absorb most of the impact of a crash.* ▶ **absorption** /əbˈsɔːpʃn; -ˈzɔːp-/ *noun* [U]

absorbed /əbˈsɔːbd; -ˈzɔːbd/ *adj* **absorbed (in sth)** giving all your attention to sth: *He was absorbed in his work and didn't hear me come in.*

absorbent /əbˈsɔːbənt; -ˈzɔːb-/ *adj* able to take in and hold liquid: *an absorbent cloth*

absorbing /əbˈsɔːbɪŋ; -ˈzɔːb-/ *adj* holding all your interest and attention: *an absorbing book*

abstain /əbˈsteɪn/ *verb* [I] **1** (in a vote) to say that you are not voting either for or against sth: *Two people voted in favour, two voted against and one abstained.* ➲ noun **abstention** **2** (*formal*) **abstain (from sth/doing sth)** to stop yourself from doing sth that you enjoy: *The doctor said he should abstain from (eating) fatty foods until he was better.* ➲ noun **abstinence**

abstention /əbˈstenʃn/ *noun* [C,U] the act of not voting either for or against sth

abstinence /ˈæbstɪnəns/ *noun* [U] (*formal*) stopping yourself from having or doing sth that you

A

enjoy: *The doctor advised total abstinence from dairy products.* ➲ *verb* **abstain**

abstract[1] /ˈæbstrækt/ *adj* **1** existing only as an idea, not as a physical thing: *It is hard to imagine an abstract idea like 'eternity'.* OPP **concrete** **2** (used about art) not showing people and things as they really look: *an abstract painting*

abstract[2] /ˈæbstrækt/ *noun* [C] **1** an example of **abstract** art **2** a short piece of writing that tells you the main contents of a book, speech, etc. SYN **summary**

IDM **in the abstract** only as an idea, not in real life

absurd /əbˈsɜːd/ *adj* not at all logical or sensible: *It would be absurd to spend all your money on one pair of shoes.* ◆ *Don't be absurd! I can't possibly do all that in one day.* SYN **ridiculous** ▸ **absurdity** /əbˈsɜːdəti/ *noun* [C,U] (*pl* **absurdities**) ▸ **absurdly** *adv*

abundance /əˈbʌndəns/ *noun* [sing,U] a very large quantity of sth: *There is an abundance of wildlife in the forest.* ◆ *These flowers grow here **in abundance**.* SYN **profusion**

abundant /əˈbʌndənt/ *adj* existing in very large quantities; more than enough: *abundant supplies of food* ◆ *Fish are abundant in the lake.* SYN **plentiful** ▸ **abundantly** *adv*

⚷ **abuse**[1] /əˈbjuːs/ *noun* **1** [C,U] using sth in a bad or dishonest way: *an abuse of power* ◆ *the dangers of drug abuse* **2** [U] bad, usually violent treatment of sb: *He subjected his children to verbal and physical abuse.* ◆ *a victim of sexual abuse* **3** [U] rude words, used to insult another person: *The other driver leaned out of the car and **hurled abuse** at me.* ◆ *racial abuse*

⚷ **abuse**[2] /əˈbjuːz/ *verb* [T] **1** to use sth in a bad or dishonest way: *The politician was accused of abusing his position in order to become rich.* **2** to treat sb badly, often violently: *The girl had been physically abused.* **3** to say rude things to sb: *The goalkeeper got a red card for abusing the referee.* SYN **insult**

abusive /əˈbjuːsɪv/ *adj* using rude language to insult sb: *an abusive remark*

abysmal /əˈbɪzməl/ *adj* very bad; of very poor quality ▸ **abysmally** /-məli/ *adv*

abyss /əˈbɪs/ *noun* [C] a very deep hole that seems to have no bottom

a/c *abbr* = **account**[1] (1)

⚷ **academic**[1] /ˌækəˈdemɪk/ *adj* **1** connected with education, especially in schools and universities: *The academic year begins in September.* **2** connected with subjects of interest to the mind rather than technical or practical subjects: *academic subjects such as History* OPP **non-academic** **3** not connected with reality; not affecting the facts of a situation: *It's academic which one I prefer because I can't have either of them.* ▸ **academically** /-kli/ *adv*

academic[2] /ˌækəˈdemɪk/ *noun* [C] a person who teaches and/or does research at a university or college

academy /əˈkædəmi/ *noun* [C] (*pl* **academies**) **1** a school for special training: *a military academy* **2** **Academy** an official group of people who are important in art, science or literature: *the Royal Academy of Arts* **3** a school in England which has some independence from local authority control

accelerate /əkˈseləreɪt/ *verb* [I,T] to go faster; to make sth go faster or happen more quickly: *The driver slowed down for the bend then accelerated away.* ◆ *The government plans to accelerate the pace of reform.* ▸ **acceleration** /əkˌseləˈreɪʃn/ *noun* [U]

accelerator /əkˈseləreɪtə(r)/ *noun* [C] the control in a vehicle that you press with your foot in order to make it go faster ➲ picture at **car**

⚷ **accent** /ˈæksent; -sənt/ *noun* **1** [C,U] a particular way of pronouncing words that is connected with the country, area or social class that you come from: *He speaks with a strong Scottish accent.* **2** [C] the greater force that you give to a particular word or part of a word when you speak: *In the word 'because' the accent is on the second syllable.* SYN **stress** **3** [C] (in writing) a mark, usually above a letter, that shows that it has to be pronounced in a certain way: *Séance has an accent on the first 'e'.* **4** [C, usually sing] the particular importance that is given to sth: *In all our products the accent is on quality.* SYN **emphasis**

accentuate /əkˈsentʃueɪt/ *verb* [T] to make sth easier to notice: *She uses make-up to accentuate her beautiful eyes.*

⚷ **accept** /əkˈsept/ *verb* **1** [I,T] to say yes to sth or to agree to sth willingly: *Thank you for your invitation. I am happy to accept.* ◆ *He asked her to marry him and she accepted.* ◆ *She has accepted the job.* OPP **refuse** **2** [T] to agree to sth or approve of sth: *Do I have to pay in cash or will you accept a credit card?* ◆ *Why won't you accept my advice?* **3** [T] to admit or recognize that sth difficult or unpleasant is true: *They refused to accept responsibility for the accident.* ◆ *She didn't accept that I was telling the truth.* **4** [T] to make sb feel welcome or to allow sb to join a group or an organization: *The university has accepted me on the course.* ◆ *All children want to be accepted.* OPP **reject**

⚷ **acceptable** /əkˈseptəbl/ *adj* **1** that can be allowed: *One or two mistakes are acceptable but no more than that.* **2** good enough: *We hope that you will consider our offer acceptable.* ◆ *The food was acceptable, but no more* (= not very good, but good enough). SYN **satisfactory** OPP for both meanings **unacceptable** ▸ **acceptability** /əkˌseptəˈbɪləti/ *noun* [U] ▸ **acceptably** /əkˈseptəbli/ *adv*

acceptance /əkˈseptəns/ *noun* [C,U] the act of accepting or being accepted: *His ready acceptance of the offer surprised me.* ◆ *He quickly **gained acceptance** in the group* (= the other people thought of him as equal to them).

⚷ **access**[1] /ˈækses/ *noun* [U] **1** **access (to sth)** a way of entering or reaching a place: *Access to the garden is through the kitchen.* **2** **access (to sth)** the chance or right to use or have sth: *Do you have access to a personal computer?* **3** **access (to sb)** permission, especially legal or official, to see sb: *They are divorced, but he has regular access to the children.*

access² /ˈækses/ *verb* [T] to find information on a computer: *Click on the icon to access a file.*

accessible /əkˈsesəbl/ *adj* **1** possible to be reached or entered: *The island is only accessible by boat.* **2** easy to get, use or understand: *This TV programme aims to make history more accessible to children.* **OPP** for both meanings **inaccessible** ▸ **accessibility** /əkˌsesəˈbɪləti/ *noun* [U]: *Computers have given people greater accessibility to information.*

accession /ækˈseʃn/ *noun* [U] the act of taking a very high position, especially as ruler of a country or head of sth

accessory /əkˈsesəri/ *noun* [C] (*pl* accessories) **1** an extra item that is added to sth and is useful or attractive but not of great importance: *a wide range of car accessories, such as alloy wheels and roof racks* **2** [usually pl] a thing that you wear or carry that matches your clothes, for example a piece of jewellery, a bag, etc. **3** an accessory (to sth) (in law) a person who helps sb to do sth illegal

accident /ˈæksɪdənt/ *noun* [C] an unpleasant event that happens unexpectedly and causes damage, injury or death: *I hope they haven't had an accident.* ◆ *a car accident* ◆ *a fatal accident* (= when sb is killed) ◆ *I didn't mean to kick you, it was an accident.*
IDM **by accident** by chance; without intending to: *I knocked the vase over by accident as I was cleaning.* **OPP** **deliberately**

accidental /ˌæksɪˈdentl/ *adj* happening by chance; not planned: *Police do not know if the explosion was accidental or caused by a bomb.* ▸ **accidentally** /-təli/ *adv*: *As I turned around, I accidentally hit him in the face.*

ˌaccident and eˈmergency (also casualty) (*BrE*) *noun* [U] (*abbr* A & E) (*AmE* eˈmergency room) the part of a hospital where people who have been injured in accidents are taken for immediate treatment

ˈaccident-prone *adj* often having accidents

acclaim /əˈkleɪm/ *verb* [T, usually passive] acclaim sb/sth (as sth) to express a very high opinion of sb/sth: *a **highly acclaimed** new film* ◆ *The novel has been **acclaimed as** a modern classic.* ▸ **acclaim** *noun* [U]: *The film received widespread critical acclaim.*

acclimatize (also -ise) /əˈklaɪmətaɪz/ *verb* [I,T] acclimatize (yourself/sb/sth) (to sth) to get used to a new climate, situation, place, etc. so that it is not a problem any more ▸ **acclimatization** (also -isation) /əˌklaɪmətaɪˈzeɪʃn/ *noun* [U] ▸ **acclimatized** (also -ised) *adj*

accolade /ˈækəleɪd/ *noun* [C] a comment, prize, etc. that you receive which shows people's high opinion of sth you have done

accommodate /əˈkɒmədeɪt/ *verb* [T] **1** to provide sb with a place to stay, live or work: *During the conference, you will be accommodated in a nearby hotel.* **2** to have enough space for sb/sth, especially for a certain number of people: *Each apartment can accommodate up to six people.* **3** (*formal*) to do or provide what sb wants or needs

accommodating /əˈkɒmədeɪtɪŋ/ *adj* (used about a person) agreeing to do or provide what sb wants: *My boss is very accommodating when I need time off work.*

accommodation /əˌkɒməˈdeɪʃn/ *noun* [U] a place for sb to live or stay: *We lived in rented accommodation before buying this house.* ◆ *The price of the holiday includes flights and accommodation.*

GRAMMAR **Accommodation** is uncountable, so you CANNOT say 'an accommodation'. Sometimes it is better to use a different phrase instead: *I need to find somewhere to live.* ◆ *I'll help you find a place to stay.*

accompaniment /əˈkʌmpənimənt/ *noun* [C] something that goes together with another more important thing: *He only drinks wine as an accompaniment to food.*

accompany /əˈkʌmpəni/ *verb* [T] (accompanying; accompanies; *pt, pp* accompanied) **1** to go together with sb/sth: *He went to America accompanied by his wife and three children.* ◆ *Massive publicity accompanied the film's release.* **2** accompany sb (on sth) to play music for a singer or another instrument: *She accompanied him on the guitar.*

accomplice /əˈkʌmplɪs/ *noun* [C] an accomplice (to/in sth) a person who helps sb to do sth bad, especially a crime: *She was charged with being an accomplice to the murder.*

accomplish /əˈkʌmplɪʃ/ *verb* [T] to succeed in doing sth difficult that you planned to do: *I managed to accomplish my goal of sending twenty emails in an evening.*

accomplished /əˈkʌmplɪʃt/ *adj* highly skilled at sth: *an accomplished actor*

accomplishment /əˈkʌmplɪʃmənt/ *noun* **1** [C] something difficult that sb has succeeded in doing or learning **SYN** **achievement** **2** [U] (*formal*) the act of completing sth successfully: *the accomplishment of a plan*

accord¹ /əˈkɔːd/ *noun* [C] an agreement, especially between countries: *the Helsinki accords on human rights*
IDM **in accord (with sth/sb)** in agreement with sth/sb
of your own accord without being forced or asked: *He wasn't sacked from his job—he left of his own accord.*

accord² /əˈkɔːd/ *verb* (*formal*) **1** [T] to give sth to sb **2** [I] accord (with sth) to match; to agree with

accordance /əˈkɔːdns/ *noun*
IDM **in accordance with sth** in a way that follows or obeys sth: *to act in accordance with instructions*

accordingly /əˈkɔːdɪŋli/ *adv* **1** in a way that is suitable: *I realized that I was in danger and acted accordingly.* **2** (*formal*) therefore; for that reason

according to /əˈkɔːdɪŋ tə; *before vowels* tuː; tu/ *prep* **1** as stated by sb; as shown by sth: *According to Mick, it's a brilliant film.* ◆ *Standards of living are*

A

improving, according to the statistics. **2** in a way that matches, follows or depends on sth: *Everything went off **according to plan** (= as we had planned it).* ♦ *The salary will be fixed according to experience.*

accordion concertina

accordion /əˈkɔːdiən/ *noun* [C] a musical instrument that you hold in both hands and play by pulling the two sides apart and then pushing them together, while pressing the keys and/or buttons with your fingers

accost /əˈkɒst/ *verb* [T] to go up and talk to sb in a way that is surprising or rude

account¹ /əˈkaʊnt/ *noun* [C] **1** (*abbr* a/c) the arrangement by which a bank looks after your money for you: *a current/deposit account* ♦ *to open/close an account* ♦ *I have an account with/at Barclays.* ♦ *My salary is paid into my bank account every month.* ➲ note at **money** **2** [usually pl] a record of all the money that a person or business has received or paid out: *If you are self-employed you have to **keep** your own **accounts**.* **3** an arrangement with a shop, etc. that allows you to pay for goods or services at a later date: *Most customers **settle/pay** their **account** in full every month.* **4** sb's report or description of sth that has happened: *She gave the police a full account of the robbery.*

IDM **by all accounts** according to what everyone says: *By all accounts, she's a very good doctor.*

by your own account according to what you say yourself: *By his own account, Peter was not very good at his job.*

on account of because of: *Our flight was delayed on account of bad weather.*

on no account; not on any account not for any reason: *On no account should you walk home by yourself.*

take account of sth; take sth into account to consider sth, especially when deciding or judging sth: *We'll take account of your comments.* ♦ *We'll take your comments into account.*

account² /əˈkaʊnt/ *verb*

PHR V **account for sth** **1** to explain or give a reason for sth: *How can we account for these changes?* **2** to form the amount that is mentioned: *Sales to Europe accounted for 80% of our total sales last year.*

accountable /əˈkaʊntəbl/ *adj* expected to give an explanation of your actions, etc.; responsible: *She is too young to **be held accountable** for what she did.* ▶ **accountability** /əˌkaʊntəˈbɪləti/ *noun* [U]

accountancy /əˈkaʊntənsi/ *noun* [U] the work or profession of an **accountant**

accountant /əˈkaʊntənt/ *noun* [C] a person whose job is to keep or examine the financial accounts of a business, etc.

accredited /əˈkredɪtɪd/ *adj* officially recognized or approved: *a fully accredited course*

accumulate /əˈkjuːmjəleɪt/ *verb* **1** [T] to collect a number or quantity of sth over a period of time: *Over the years, I've accumulated hundreds of books.* **2** [I] to increase over a period of time: *Dust soon accumulates if you don't clean the house for a week or so.* ▶ **accumulation** /əˌkjuːmjəˈleɪʃn/ *noun* [C,U]

accurate /ˈækjərət/ *adj* exact and correct; without mistakes: *He gave the police an accurate description of the robbers.* ♦ *That clock isn't very accurate.* OPP **inaccurate** ▶ **accuracy** /ˈækjərəsi/ *noun* [U] OPP **inaccuracy** ▶ **accurately** *adv*: *It is difficult to estimate the age of these bones accurately.*

accusation /ˌækjuˈzeɪʃn/ *noun* [C,U] a statement saying that sb has done sth wrong

accuse /əˈkjuːz/ *verb* [T] **accuse sb (of sth/doing sth)** to say that sb has done sth wrong or broken the law: *I accused her of cheating.* ♦ *He was accused of murder.* ▶ **accuser** *noun* [C]

the accused /əˈkjuːzd/ *noun* [C] (*pl* **the accused**) (used in a court of law) the person who is said to have broken the law

accusing /əˈkjuːzɪŋ/ *adj* showing that you think sb has done sth wrong: *He gave me an accusing look.* ▶ **accusingly** *adv*

accustom /əˈkʌstəm/ *verb* [T] **accustom yourself/sb/sth to sth** to make yourself/sb/sth get used to sth: *It took him a while to accustom himself to the idea.*

accustomed /əˈkʌstəmd/ *adj* **1 accustomed to sth** if you are **accustomed** to sth, you are used to it and it is not strange for you: *She's accustomed to travelling a lot with her parents.* ♦ *It took a while for my eyes to get accustomed to the dark room.* SYN **used 2** (*formal*) usual; regular

ace /eɪs/ *noun* [C] **1** a playing card which has a single shape on it. An **ace** has either the lowest or the highest value in a game of cards: *the ace of spades* ➲ note at **card** ➲ picture at **card** **2** (in the sport of **tennis**) a **service** (= the first hit of the ball) that the person playing against you cannot hit back because it is too fast: *to serve an ace*

ache¹ /eɪk/ *verb* [I] to feel a continuous pain: *His legs ached after playing football.* ♦ *She was aching all over.*

ache² /eɪk/ *noun* [C] a pain that lasts for a long time: *to have toothache/earache/backache/stomach ache* ➲ note at **pain**

> **HELP** **Ache** is often used in compounds. In British English it is usually used without 'a' or 'an': *I've got toothache.* But we always use 'a' with 'headache': *I've got a bad headache.* In American English, **ache** is usually used with 'a' or 'an', especially when talking about a particular attack of pain: *I have an awful stomach ache.*

achieve /əˈtʃiːv/ *verb* [T] **1** to gain sth, usually by effort or skill: *You have achieved the success you* *deserve.* **2** to complete sth by hard work and skill: *They have achieved a lot in a short time.*

achievement /ə'tʃi:vmənt/ *noun* [C,U] something that you have done successfully, especially through hard work or skill: *She felt that winning the gold medal was her greatest achievement.* ♦ *He enjoys climbing mountains because it gives him* ***a sense of achievement.***

Achilles heel /əˌkɪli:z 'hi:l/ *noun* [C] a weak point or fault in sb/sth

acid[1] /'æsɪd/ *noun* [C,U] (in chemistry) a liquid substance that can dissolve metal and may burn your skin or clothes. **Acids** have a **pH** (= a measurement of the level of acid or alkali in sth) value of less than 7: *sulphuric acid* ➲ look at **alkali**

acid[2] /'æsɪd/ *adj* **1** (also **acidic** /ə'sɪdɪk/) containing an **acid**: *an acid solution* OPP **alkaline** **2** (used about a fruit, etc.) with a sour taste

acidity /ə'sɪdəti/ *noun* [U] the quality of being **acid**: *to measure the acidity of soil*

ˌacid 'rain *noun* [U] rain that has chemicals in it from factories, etc. and that causes damage to trees, buildings and rivers ➲ note at **environment**

acknowledge /ək'nɒlɪdʒ/ *verb* [T] **1** to accept or admit that sth is true or exists: *He* ***acknowledged (the fact) that*** *he had made a mistake.* ♦ *He is acknowledged to be the country's greatest writer.* **2** to show that you have seen or noticed sb/sth or received sth: *I would be grateful if you could acknowledge my application* (= tell me that you have received it).

acknowledgement /ək'nɒlɪdʒmənt/ *noun* **1** [U] the act of showing that you have seen or noticed sb/sth: *The president gave a smile of acknowledgement to the photographers.* **2** [C,U] a letter, etc. that says that sth has been received or noticed: *I haven't received (an) acknowledgement of my job application yet.* **3** [C] a few words of thanks that an author writes at the beginning or end of a book to the people who have helped them

acne /'ækni/ *noun* [U] a skin disease that usually affects young people. When you have **acne** you get a lot of spots on your face and neck.

acorn /'eɪkɔ:n/ *noun* [C] the small nut of the **oak** (= a large tree with hard wood), that grows in a base shaped like a cup

acoustic /ə'ku:stɪk/ *adj* **1** connected with sound or the sense of hearing **2** (of a musical instrument) not electric: *an acoustic guitar* ➲ picture at **music**

acoustics /ə'ku:stɪks/ *noun* [pl] the qualities of a room, etc. that make it good or bad for you to hear music, etc. in: *The theatre has excellent acoustics.*

acquaintance /ə'kweɪntəns/ *noun* **1** [C] a person that you know but who is not a close friend **2** [C,U] **acquaintance with sb/sth** a slight knowledge of sb/sth

acquainted /ə'kweɪntɪd/ *adj* [not before a noun] (*formal*) **1** **acquainted with sth** knowing sth: *I went for a walk to* ***get acquainted*** *with my new neighbourhood.* **2** **acquainted (with sb)** knowing sb, but usually not very closely

acquiesce /ˌækwi'es/ *verb* [I] (*written*) **acquiesce in/to sth** to accept sth without argument, although you may not agree with it ▸ **acquiescence** *noun* [U]

acquire /ə'kwaɪə(r)/ *verb* [T] (*formal*) to obtain or buy sth: *She has acquired a good knowledge of English.* ♦ *He's acquired a reputation for being difficult to work with.* ♦ *The company has acquired shares in a rival business.*

acquisition /ˌækwɪ'zɪʃn/ *noun* (*formal*) **1** [U] the act of obtaining or buying sth: *a study of language acquisition in children* **2** [C] something that you have obtained or bought: *This sculpture is the museum's latest acquisition.*

acquit /ə'kwɪt/ *verb* [T] (**acquitting**; **acquitted**) **1** **acquit sb (of sth)** to state formally that a person is not guilty of a crime: *The jury acquitted her of murder.* OPP **convict** **2** (*formal*) **acquit yourself ...** to behave in the way that is mentioned: *He* ***acquitted himself well*** *in his first match as a professional.* ▸ **acquittal** /ə'kwɪtl/ *noun* [C,U]

acre /'eɪkə(r)/ *noun* [C] a measure of land; 0.405 of a **hectare** (= 10000 square metres): *a farm of 20 acres/a 20-acre farm*

acrid /'ækrɪd/ *adj* having a strong, bitter smell or taste that is unpleasant: *acrid smoke*

acrimonious /ˌækrɪ'məʊniəs/ *adj* (*formal*) angry and full of strong feelings and words: *His parents went through an acrimonious divorce.* SYN **bitter**

acrobat /'ækrəbæt/ *noun* [C] a person who performs difficult movements of the body, especially in a **circus** (= a show that travels to different towns)

acrobatic /ˌækrə'bætɪk/ *adj* performing or involving difficult movements of the body: *an acrobatic dancer* ♦ *an acrobatic leap* ▸ **acrobatically** /-kli/ *adv*

acrobatics /ˌækrə'bætɪks/ *noun* [U] (the art of performing) difficult movements of the body

acronym /'ækrənɪm/ *noun* [C] **an acronym (for sth)** a short word that is made from the first letters of a group of words: *TEFL is an acronym for Teaching English as a Foreign Language.*

across /ə'krɒs/ *adv, prep* **1** from one side of sth to the other: *The stream was too wide to jump across.* ♦ *He walked across the field.* ♦ *A smile spread across his face.* ♦ *The river was about 20 metres across.* ♦ *The bank has 800 branches across* (= in all parts of) *the country.* **2** on the other side of sth: *There's a bank just across the road.* ♦ *The house* ***across*** *the road* ***from*** *us is for sale.*

HELP Across or over? We can use **across** or **over** to mean 'on or to the other side': *I ran across/over the road.* But when we talk about crossing something high, we usually use **over**: *I can't climb over that wall.* With 'room' we usually use **across**: *I walked across the room to the door.*

IDM **across the board** involving or affecting all groups, members, cases, etc.

A

acrylic /əˈkrɪlɪk/ *noun* [C,U] an artificial material that is used in making clothes and paint

act¹ /ækt/ *noun* [C]
➤STH YOU DO **1** a thing that you do: *In a typical act of generosity they refused to accept any money.* ◆ *to commit a violent act*

HELP **Act, action** or **activity**? **Act** and **action** can have the same meaning: *It was a brave act/action.* **Act**, not **action** can be followed by **of**: *It was an act of bravery.* **Activity** is used for something that is done regularly: *I like outdoor activities such as cycling and camping.*

➤LAW **2** *often* **Act** a law made by a government: *The government **passed an act** protecting the rights of tenants.*
➤BEHAVIOUR **3** behaviour that hides your true feelings: *She seems very happy but she's just **putting on an act**.*
➤IN PLAY **4** *often* **Act** one of the main divisions of a play or an **opera** (= a musical play): *How many scenes are there in Act 4?*
➤ENTERTAINMENT **5** a short piece of entertainment, especially as part of a show: *Did you enjoy the clowns' act?*
IDM **be/get in on the act** become involved in an activity that is becoming popular
get your act together to organize yourself so that you can do sth properly: *If he doesn't get his act together he's going to lose his job.*
a hard act to follow ➲ **hard¹**
in the act (of doing sth) while doing sth, especially sth wrong: *She caught him in the act of looking through the papers on her desk.*

act² /ækt/ *verb* **1** [I] **act (on sth)** to do sth; to take action: *The doctor knew he had to act quickly to save the child.* ◆ *I'm always giving my brother advice but he never acts on* (= as a result of) *it.* **2** [I] to behave in the way that is mentioned: *Stop **acting like** a child!* ◆ *Although she was trying to act cool, I could see she was really upset.* ◆ *Ali's acting strangely today—what's wrong with him?* **3** [I,T] to perform in a play or film: *I acted in a play at school.* ◆ *He's always wanted to act the part of Hamlet.* ◆ *He hasn't really hurt himself—he's just acting* (= pretending)! **4** [I] **act as sth** to perform a particular function: *The man we met on the plane to Tokyo was kind enough to act as our guide.* ◆ *The elephant's trunk acts as a nose, a hand and an arm.*

acting¹ /ˈæktɪŋ/ *noun* [U] the art or profession of performing in plays or films ➲ picture on **page P3**

acting² /ˈæktɪŋ/ *adj* [only *before* a noun] doing the job mentioned for a short time: *Jane Green will be the acting director while Henry King is away.*

action /ˈækʃn/ *noun*
➤DOING STH **1** [U] doing things, often for a particular purpose: *Now is the time for action.* ◆ *If we don't **take action** quickly it'll be too late!* **OPP** **inaction** **2** [C] something that you do: *The doctor's quick action saved the child's life.* ◆ *They should be judged by their actions, not by what they say.* ➲ note at **act**
➤IN COURT **3** [C,U] the process of settling an argument in a court of law: *He is going to **take legal action** against the hospital.*
➤IN WAR **4** [U] fighting in a war: *Their son was **killed in action**.*
➤IN STORY/FILM/PLAY **5** [sing] the most important events in a story, film or play: *The action takes place in London.*
➤EXCITING EVENTS **6** [U] exciting things that happen: *There's not much action in this boring town.* ◆ *I like films with lots of action.* ◆ *an **action-packed** film*
➤EFFECT **7** [sing] the effect that one substance has on another: *They're studying the **action of** sunlight **on** the skin.*
IDM **in action** in operation; while working or doing sth: *We shall have a chance to see their new team in action next week.*
into action into operation: *We'll put the plan into action immediately.*
out of action not able to do the usual things; not working: *The coffee machine's out of action again.*

activate /ˈæktɪveɪt/ *verb* [T] to make sth start working: *A slight movement can activate the car alarm.*

active /ˈæktɪv/ *adj* **1** involved in activity: *My grandfather is very active for his age.* ◆ *I have a very active social life.* ◆ *I was at the meeting but I didn't **take an active part** in the discussion.* **SYN** **lively** **OPP** **inactive** **2** that produces an effect; that is in operation: *an active volcano* (= one that can still explode) **3** used about the form of a verb or a sentence when the subject of the sentence performs the action of the verb: *In the sentence 'The dog bit him', the verb is active.*

HELP You can also say: 'The verb is in the active'.

➲ look at **passive** ▶ **actively** *adv*: *She is actively looking for a job.*

activist /ˈæktɪvɪst/ *noun* [C] a person who takes action to cause political or social change, usually as a member of a group: *a protest by environmental activists*

activity /ækˈtɪvəti/ *noun* (*pl* **activities**) **1** [U] a situation in which there is a lot of action or movement: *The house was full of activity on the morning of the wedding.* **OPP** **inactivity** **2** [C] something that you do, usually regularly and for enjoyment: *The hotel offers a range of leisure activities.* ➲ note at **act**

actor /ˈæktə(r)/ *noun* [C] a person whose job is to act in a play, film or on TV ➲ note at **theatre**: *one of the country's leading actors*

actress /ˈæktrəs/ *noun* [C] a woman whose job is to act in a play, film or on TV: *In 1940 he married actress Jane Wyman.*

MORE Many women now prefer to be called **actors**.

➲ note at **theatre**

actual /ˈæktʃuəl/ *adj* [only *before* a noun] real; that happened: *The actual damage to the car was not as great as we had feared.* ◆ *They seemed to be good friends but **in actual fact** they hated each other.*

A

actually /ˈæktʃuəli/ *adv* **1** really; in fact: *You don't actually believe her, do you?* ◆ *I can't believe that I'm actually going to America!* **2** although it may seem strange: *He actually expected me to cook his meal for him!*

HELP **Actually** is often used in conversation to get somebody's attention or to correct somebody politely: *Actually, I wanted to show you something. Have you got a minute?* ◆ *We aren't married, actually.* ◆ *I don't agree about the book. I think it's rather good, actually.*

HELP In English **actually** does **not** mean 'at the present time'. We use **currently, at present** or **at the moment** instead: *He's currently working on an article about China.* ◆ *I'm studying for my exams at present.*

acumen /ˈækjəmən/ *noun* [U] the ability to understand and decide things quickly and well: *business/commercial/financial acumen*

acupuncture /ˈækjupʌŋktʃə(r)/ *noun* [U] a way of treating an illness or stopping pain by putting thin needles into parts of the body

acute /əˈkjuːt/ *adj* **1** very serious; very great: *an acute shortage of food* ◆ *acute pain* **2** (used about an illness) becoming dangerous very quickly: *acute appendicitis* ➲ look at **chronic** **3** (used about feelings or the senses) very strong: *Dogs have an acute sense of smell.* ◆ *acute hearing* **4** showing that you are able to understand things easily: *The report contains some acute observations.* ▶ **acutely** *adv*

aˌcute ˈangle *noun* [C] an angle of less than 90° ➲ look at **obtuse angle, right angle**

AD /ˌeɪ ˈdiː/ *abbr* (from Latin) **anno domini**; used in dates to show the number of years after the time when Christians believe Jesus Christ was born: *in (the year) AD 44* ◆ *in 44 AD* ➲ look at **BC**

ad /æd/ *(informal)* = **advertisement**: *I saw your ad in the local paper.*

adage /ˈædɪdʒ/ *noun* [C] a common phrase expressing sth that is always true about people or the world

adamant /ˈædəmənt/ *adj (formal)* very sure; refusing to change your mind: *She was adamant that she would not come.* ▶ **adamantly** *adv*

Adam's apple /ˌædəmz ˈæpl/ *noun* [C] the lump at the front of the throat that sticks out, particularly in men, and moves up and down when you swallow

adapt /əˈdæpt/ *verb* **1** [T] **adapt sth (for sth)** to change sth so that you can use it in a different situation: *The bus was adapted for disabled people.* ◆ *The teacher adapts the coursebook to suit the needs of her students.* **2** [I,T] **adapt (yourself) (to sth)** to change your behaviour because the situation you are in has changed: *They were quick to adapt (themselves) to the new system.*

adaptable /əˈdæptəbl/ *adj* able to change to suit new situations

adaptation /ˌædæpˈteɪʃn/ *noun* **1** [C] a play or film that is based on a novel, etc: *a screen adaptation of Jane Austen's 'Pride and Prejudice'* **2** [U] the state or process of changing to suit a new situation

adapted /əˈdæptɪd/ *adj* having all the necessary qualities to do sth: *Chickens are poorly adapted for flight.*

adaptor (also **adapter**) /əˈdæptə(r)/ *noun* [C] **1** a device that allows you to connect more than one piece of electrical equipment to a **socket** (= an electricity supply point) **2** a device for connecting pieces of electrical equipment that were not designed to be fitted together

add /æd/ *verb* **1** [I,T] **add (sth) (to sth)** to put sth together with sth else, so that you increase the size, number, value, etc: *I added a couple more items to the shopping list.* ◆ *The noise of the crowd added to the excitement of the race.* **2** [I,T] to put numbers or amounts together so that you get a total: *If you **add** 3 **and** 3 **together**, you get 6.* ◆ ***Add** £8 **to** the total, to cover postage and packing.* ◆ *Ronaldo cost more than all the other players added together.* ◆ *Don't ask me to work it out—I can't add.* **OPP** **subtract**

MORE We often use the word **plus** when we add two numbers: *2 plus 2 is 4.*

3 [T] to say sth more: *'By the way, please don't tell anyone I phoned you,' she added.*
PHR V **add sth on (to sth)** to include sth: *10% will be added on to your bill as a service charge.*
add up to seem to be a true explanation: *I'm sorry, but your story just doesn't add up.*
add (sth) up to find the total of several numbers: *The waiter hadn't added up the bill correctly.*
add up to sth to have as a total: *How much does all the shopping add up to?*

added /ˈædɪd/ *adj* in addition to what is usual; extra: *milk with added vitamins*

ˈadded to *prep* in addition to sth; as well as

adder /ˈædə(r)/ *noun* [C] a small poisonous snake

addict /ˈædɪkt/ *noun* [C] a person who cannot stop taking or doing sth harmful: *a drug addict* ▶ **addicted** /əˈdɪktɪd/ *adj* **addicted (to sth)**: *He is addicted to computer games.* **SYN** **hooked** ▶ **addiction** *noun* [C,U]: *the problem of teenage drug addiction*

addictive /əˈdɪktɪv/ *adj* difficult to stop taking or doing: *Jogging is highly addictive.* ◆ *an addictive game*

addition /əˈdɪʃn/ *noun* **1** [U] adding sth, especially two or more numbers: *children learning addition and subtraction* ➲ look at **subtraction** **2** [C] **an addition (to sth)** a person or thing that is added to sth: *They've got a new addition to the family* (= another child).
IDM **in addition (to sth)** as well as: *She speaks five foreign languages in addition to English.*

A

additional /əˈdɪʃənl/ *adj* added: *a small additional charge for the use of the swimming pool* SYN **extra** ▶ **additionally** /-ʃənəli/ *adv*

additive /ˈædətɪv/ *noun* [C] a substance that is added to sth in small amounts for a special purpose: *food additives* (= to add colour or flavour)

address[1] /əˈdres/ *noun* [C] **1** the number of the building and the name of the street and place where sb lives or works: *Let me give you my home/business address.* ◆ *She no longer lives at this address.* ◆ *Please inform the office of any change of address.* ◆ *an address book* (= a small book where you keep the addresses of people you know or a computer file where you store email and Internet addresses) ➲ picture at **letter** **2** a series of words and/or numbers that tells you where you can find sth using a computer: *What's your email address?* **3** a formal speech that is given to an audience: *tonight's televised presidential address*
IDM **(of) no fixed abode/address** ➲ **fixed**

address[2] /əˈdres/ *verb* [T]
➤WRITE ON LETTER **1** address sth (to sb/sth) to write the name and address of the person you are sending a letter, etc. to: *The package was returned because it had been wrongly addressed.*
➤MAKE SPEECH **2** to make an important speech to an audience: *to address a meeting*
➤COMMUNICATE **3** (*formal*) address sth to sb make a comment, etc. to sb: *Kindly address any complaints you have to the manager.*
➤USE NAME **4** address sb as sth to talk or write to sb using a particular name or title: *She prefers to be addressed as 'Ms'.*
➤DEAL WITH PROBLEM **5** (*formal*) address (yourself to) sth to try to deal with a problem, etc: *The government is finally addressing the question of corruption.*

adept /əˈdept/ *adj* adept (at sth) very good or skilful at sth SYN **skilful** OPP **inept**

adequate /ˈædɪkwət/ *adj* **1** enough for what you need: *Make sure you take an adequate supply of water with you.* **2** just good enough; acceptable: *Your work is adequate but I'm sure you could do better.* OPP for both meanings **inadequate** ▶ **adequacy** /ˈædɪkwəsi/ *noun* [U] ▶ **adequately** *adv*: *The mystery has never been adequately explained.*

adhere /ədˈhɪə(r)/ *verb* [I] (*formal*) adhere (to sth) to stick firmly to sth: *Wash the wall first, or the paint will not adhere to the surface.*
PHR V **adhere to sth** to continue to support an idea, etc.; to follow a rule

adherent /ədˈhɪərənt/ *noun* [C] a person who supports a particular idea SYN **supporter** ▶ **adherence** *noun* [U]

adhesive[1] /ədˈhiːsɪv/ *noun* [C,U] a substance that makes things stick together: *a fast-drying adhesive*

adhesive[2] /ədˈhiːsɪv/ *adj* that can stick, or can cause two things to stick together: *He sealed the parcel with adhesive tape.* SYN **sticky**

ad hoc /ˌæd ˈhɒk/ *adj* made or done suddenly for a particular purpose: *They set up an ad hoc committee to discuss the matter.* ◆ *Staff training takes place occasionally* ***on an ad hoc basis.***

adjacent /əˈdʒeɪsnt/ *adj* adjacent (to sth) (used about an area, a place or a building) next to or close to sth: *She works in the office adjacent to mine.* ◆ *There was a fire in the adjacent building.*

adjectival /ˌædʒekˈtaɪvl/ *adj* that contains or is used like an adjective: *The adjectival form of 'smell' is 'smelly'.*

adjective /ˈædʒɪktɪv/ *noun* [C] a word that tells you more about a noun, for example *big* and *clever* in *a big house* and *a clever idea*

adjoining /əˈdʒɔɪnɪŋ/ *adj* next to or nearest to sth: *A scream came from the adjoining room.*

adjourn /əˈdʒɜːn/ *verb* [I,T] to stop a meeting, trial, etc. for a short time and start it again later: *The meeting adjourned for lunch.* ◆ *The trial was adjourned until the following week.* ▶ **adjournment** *noun* [C,U]

adjudicate /əˈdʒuːdɪkeɪt/ *verb* [I,T] (*written*) to act as an official judge in a competition or to decide who is right when two people or groups disagree about sth

adjudicator /əˈdʒuːdɪkeɪtə(r)/ *noun* [C] a person who acts as a judge, for example in a competition

adjust /əˈdʒʌst/ *verb* **1** [T] to change sth slightly, especially because it is not in the right position: *The brakes on my bicycle need adjusting.* ◆ *The seat can be adjusted to different positions.* **2** [I] adjust (to sth) to get used to new conditions or a new situation: *She found it hard to adjust to working at night.* ▶ **adjustment** *noun* [C,U]: *We'll just* ***make*** *a few* ***minor adjustments*** *and the room will look perfect.*

adjustable /əˈdʒʌstəbl/ *adj* that can be **adjusted**: *an adjustable chair*

ad lib /ˌæd ˈlɪb/ *adj, adv* done or spoken without preparation: *She had to speak ad lib because she couldn't find her notes.* ▶ **ad lib** *verb* [I] (ad li**bb**ing; ad li**bb**ed): *The singer forgot the words so he had to ad lib.*

administer /ədˈmɪnɪstə(r)/ *verb* [T] (*formal*) **1** to control or manage sth **2** to give sb sth, especially medicine

administration /ədˌmɪnɪˈstreɪʃn/ *noun* **1** (*BrE also informal* admin /ˈædmɪn/) [U] the process or act of managing sth, for example a system, an organization or a business: *The administration of a large project like this is very complicated.* ◆ *A lot of the teachers' time is taken up by admin.* **2** [sing] the group of people or part of a company that organizes or controls sth: *the hospital administration* **3** *often the* Administration [C] the government of a country, especially the US: *the Obama Administration*

administrative /ədˈmɪnɪstrətɪv/ *adj* connected with the organization of a country, business, etc., and the way in which it is managed: *London is still the most important administrative centre in Britain.*

A

administrator /əd'mɪnɪstreɪtə(r)/ *noun* [C] a person whose job is to organize or manage a system, business, etc.

admirable /'ædmərəbl/ *adj* (*formal*) that you admire; excellent ▶ **admirably** /-əbli/ *adv*: *She dealt with the problem admirably.*

admiral /'ædmərəl/ *noun* [C] the most important officer in the navy

⚷ **admiration** /ˌædmə'reɪʃn/ *noun* [U] admiration (for/of sb/sth) a feeling of liking and respecting sb/sth very much: *I have great admiration for what he's done.*

⚷ **admire** /əd'maɪə(r)/ *verb* [T] admire sb/sth (for sth/doing sth) to respect or like sb/sth very much; to look at sb/sth with pleasure: *Everyone admired the way he dealt with the problem.* ♦ *I've always admired her for being such a wonderful mother.* ♦ *We stopped at the top of the hill to admire the view.*

admirer /əd'maɪərə(r)/ *noun* [C] a person who admires sb/sth: *I've always been a great admirer of her books.*

admiring /əd'maɪərɪŋ/ *adj* feeling or expressing admiration ▶ **admiringly** *adv*

admissible /əd'mɪsəbl/ *adj* that can be allowed or accepted, especially in a court of law: *admissible evidence* OPP **inadmissible**

admission /əd'mɪʃn/ *noun* **1** [C,U] admission (to sth) the act of allowing sb to enter a school, club, public place, etc: *Admissions to British universities have increased by 15% this year.* ➲ look at **entrance** **2** [C] a statement that admits that sth is true **3** [U] the amount of money that you have to pay to enter a place: *The museum charges half-price admission on Mondays.*

⚷ **admit** /əd'mɪt/ *verb* (admitting; admitted) **1** [I,T] admit sth; admit to sth/doing sth; admit (that ...) to agree that sth unpleasant is true or that you have done sth wrong: *You should admit your mistake.* ♦ *After trying four times to pass the exam, I finally* ***admitted defeat***. ♦ *She admitted having broken the computer.* ♦ *He refused to admit to the theft.* ♦ *I have to admit (that) I was wrong.* OPP **deny** **2** [T] admit sb/sth (into/to sth) to allow sb/sth to enter; to take sb into a place: *He was admitted to hospital with suspected appendicitis.*

admittance /əd'mɪtns/ *noun* [U] (*formal*) being allowed to enter a place; the right to enter: *The journalist tried to gain admittance to the minister's office.*

admittedly /əd'mɪtɪdli/ *adv* it must be admitted (that ...): *The work is very interesting. Admittedly, I do get rather tired.*

ado /ə'du:/ *noun*
IDM **without further/more ado** (*old-fashioned*) without delaying; immediately

adolescence /ˌædə'lesns/ *noun* [U] the period of sb's life between being a child and becoming an adult, between the ages of about 13 and 17 SYN **puberty**

adolescent /ˌædə'lesnt/ *noun* [C] a young person who is no longer a child and not yet an adult, between the ages of about 13 and 17: *the problems of adolescents* ♦ *an adolescent daughter* ➲ look at **teenager**

⚷ **adopt** /ə'dɒpt/ *verb* **1** [I,T] to take a child into your family and treat them as your own child by law: *They couldn't have children so they adopted.* ♦ *They're hoping to adopt a child.* **2** [T] to take and use sth: *What approach did you adopt when dealing with the problem?* ▶ **adopted** *adj*: *an adopted child* ▶ **adoption** *noun* [C,U]: *The number of adoptions has risen in the past year* (= the number of children being adopted). ➲ note at **child**

adoptive /ə'dɒptɪv/ *adj* (used about parents) having legally taken a child to live with them as part of their family: *the baby's adoptive parents*

adorable /ə'dɔ:rəbl/ *adj* (used about children or animals) very attractive SYN **lovely**

adore /ə'dɔ:(r)/ *verb* [T] **1** to love and admire sb/sth very much: *Kim adores her older sister.* **2** to like sth very much: *I adore his music!* ▶ **adoration** /ˌædə'reɪʃn/ *noun* [U] ▶ **adoring** *adj*: *his adoring fans*

adorn /ə'dɔ:n/ *verb* [T] adorn sth (with sth) to add sth in order to make a thing or person more attractive or beautiful ▶ **adornment** *noun* [C,U]

adrenaline (also adrenalin) /ə'drenəlɪn/ *noun* [U] a substance that your body produces when you are very angry, frightened or excited and that makes your heart go faster

adrift /ə'drɪft/ *adj* [not before a noun] (used about a boat) not tied to anything or controlled by anyone

adulation /ˌædju'leɪʃn/ *noun* [U] (*formal*) admiration for sb, especially when this is greater than is necessary

⚷ **adult** /'ædʌlt; ə'dʌlt/ *noun* [C] a person or an animal that is fully grown: *This film is suitable for both adults and children.* SYN **grown-up** ▶ **adult** *adj*: *She was born in America but has spent her adult life in Chile.*

adultery /ə'dʌltəri/ *noun* [U] (*formal*) sex between a married person and sb who is not their wife/husband: *He was accused of* ***committing adultery***. ▶ **adulterous** /ə'dʌltərəs/ *adj*: *an adulterous relationship*

adulthood /'ædʌlthʊd; ə'dʌlt-/ *noun* [U] the time in your life when you are an adult

⚷ **advance**[1] /əd'vɑ:ns/ *noun* **1** [C, usually sing] forward movement: *the army's advance towards the border* OPP **retreat** **2** [C,U] progress in sth: *advances in computer technology* **3** [C] an amount of money that is paid to sb before the time when it is usually paid: *She asked for an advance on her salary.*
IDM **in advance (of sth)** before a particular time or event: *You should book tickets for the concert well in advance.*

⚷ **advance**[2] /əd'vɑ:ns/ *verb* **1** [I] to move forward: *The army advanced towards the city.* OPP **retreat** **2** [I,T] to make progress or help sth make progress: *Our research has not advanced much recently.*

A

advance³ /ədˈvɑːns/ *adj* [only *before* a noun] that happens before sth: *There was no advance warning of the earthquake.*

advanced /ədˈvɑːnst/ *adj* **1** highly developed: *a country that is not very advanced industrially* **2** of a high level: *an advanced English class*

adˈvanced level (*formal*) = **A level**

advancement /ədˈvɑːnsmənt/ *noun* (*formal*) **1** [U,C] the process of helping sth to make progress or succeed; the progress that is made: *the advancement of knowledge/education/science* **2** [U] progress in a job, social class, etc: *There are good opportunities for advancement if you have the right skills.*

advantage /ədˈvɑːntɪdʒ/ *noun* **1** [C] an advantage (over sb) something that may help you to do better than other people: *Her experience gave her an advantage over the other applicants.* ♦ *Living abroad means he* ***has the advantage of*** *being fluent in two languages.* ♦ *Some runners try to gain an unfair advantage by taking drugs.* **2** [C,U] something that helps you or that will bring you a good result: *Each of these systems has its advantages and disadvantages.* ♦ *The traffic is so bad here that* ***there is no advantage in*** *having a car.* ➲ look at **pro** OPP for both meanings **disadvantage**

IDM **take advantage of sb/sth 1** to make good or full use of sth: *We should take full advantage of these low prices while they last.* **2** to make use of sb/sth in a way that is unfair or dishonest in order to get what you want: *You shouldn't let him take advantage of you like this.*

advantageous /ˌædvənˈteɪdʒəs/ *adj* that will help you or bring you a good result

advent /ˈædvent/ *noun* **1** [sing] (*formal*) the advent of sth/sb the coming of an important event, person, new technology, etc. **2** Advent [U] (in the Christian year) the period that includes the four Sundays before Christmas

adventure /ədˈventʃə(r)/ *noun* [C,U] an experience or event that is very unusual, exciting or dangerous: *Our journey through the jungle was quite an adventure!* ♦ *She left home to travel, hoping for excitement and adventure.*

adventurous /ədˈventʃərəs/ *adj* **1** (used about a person) liking to try new things or have **adventures**: *I'm not an adventurous cook—I like to stick to recipes I know.* **2** involving **adventure**: *For a more adventurous holiday try mountain climbing.*

adverb /ˈædvɜːb/ *noun* [C] a word that adds more information about place, time, manner, cause or degree to a verb, an adjective, a phrase or another adverb: *In 'speak slowly', 'extremely funny', 'arrive late' and 'too quickly', 'slowly', 'extremely', 'late', 'too' and 'quickly' are adverbs.* ▶ **adverbial** /ædˈvɜːbiəl/ *adj*: *'Very quickly indeed' is an adverbial phrase.* ➲ note at **sudden**

adversary /ˈædvəsəri/ *noun* [C] (*pl* adversaries) (*formal*) an enemy, or an opponent in a competition

adverse /ˈædvɜːs/ *adj* (*formal*) making sth difficult for sb: *Our flight was cancelled because of adverse weather conditions.* OPP **favourable** ➲ look at **unfavourable** ▶ **adversely** *adv*

adversity /ədˈvɜːsəti/ *noun* [C,U] (*pl* adversities) (*formal*) difficulties or problems

advert /ˈædvɜːt/ (*BrE informal*) = **advertisement**: *adverts on television*

advertise /ˈædvətaɪz/ *verb* **1** [I,T] advertise sth (as sth) to put information in a newspaper, on the Internet, in a public place, on TV, etc. in order to persuade people to buy sth, to interest them in a new job, etc: *a poster advertising a new type of biscuit* ♦ *The job was advertised in the local newspapers.* ♦ *It's very expensive to advertise on TV.* **2** [I] advertise (for sb/sth) to say publicly in a newspaper, on a sign, etc. that you need sb to do a particular job, want to buy sth, etc: *The shop is advertising for a part-time sales assistant.* ▶ **advertiser** *noun* [C] ▶ **advertising** *noun* [U]: *The magazine gets a lot of money from advertising.* ♦ *an advertising campaign*

advertisement /ədˈvɜːtɪsmənt/ (also *informal* ad; advert) *noun* [C] a piece of information in a newspaper, on TV, a picture on a wall, etc. that tries to persuade people to buy sth, to interest them in a new job, etc: *an advertisement for a new brand of shampoo* ♦ *to put an advertisement in a newspaper*

advice /ədˈvaɪs/ *noun* [U] an opinion that you give sb about what they should do: *She* ***took*** *her teacher's* ***advice*** *and worked hard for the exam.* ♦ *Let me* ***give*** *you some* ***advice*** *...*

> **GRAMMAR** Advice is uncountable. We say a **piece of advice** (not 'an advice') and **a lot of** advice (not 'advices').

adˈvice columnist (*AmE*) = **agony aunt/uncle**

advisable /ədˈvaɪzəbl/ *adj* (*formal*) that is a good thing to do; sensible: *It is advisable to reserve a seat.* OPP **inadvisable**

advise /ədˈvaɪz/ *verb* **1** [I,T] advise sb (to do sth); advise (sb) (against sth/against doing sth) to tell sb what you think they should do: *I would strongly advise you to take the job.* ♦ *They advised us not to travel on a Friday.* ♦ *The newspaper article advised against eating too much meat.* ♦ *He did what the doctor advised.* ♦ *She advises the Government on economic affairs.* **2** [T] (*formal*) to officially tell sb sth: *We would like to advise you that the goods are now ready for collection.* SYN **inform**

adviser (*AmE* advisor) /ədˈvaɪzə(r)/ *noun* [C] a person who gives advice to a company, government, etc: *an adviser on economic affairs*

advisory /ədˈvaɪzəri/ *adj* giving advice only; not having the power to make decisions

advocate¹ /ˈædvəkeɪt/ *verb* [T] (*formal*) to recommend or say that you support a particular plan or action

advocate² /ˈædvəkət/ *noun* [C] **1** an advocate (of sth) a person who supports a particular plan or action, especially in public **2** a lawyer who defends sb in a court of law

aerial[1] /ˈeəriəl/ (*AmE* antenna) *noun* [C] a long metal stick on a building, car, etc. that receives radio or TV signals ➲ picture on **page P8**

aerial[2] /ˈeəriəl/ *adj* from or in the air: *an aerial photograph of the town*

aerobics /eəˈrəʊbɪks/ *noun* [U] physical exercises that people do to music: *I **do aerobics** twice a week to keep fit.*

aerodynamics /ˌeərəʊdaɪˈnæmɪks/ *noun* [U] the scientific study of the way that things move through the air ▸ **aerodynamic** *adj*: *the aerodynamic design of a racing car*

aeroplane /ˈeərəpleɪn/ *noun* [C] = **plane**[1] (1): *the noise of an aeroplane flying overhead*

aerosol /ˈeərəsɒl/ *noun* [C] a container in which a liquid substance is kept under pressure. When you press a button the liquid comes out in a fine spray. ➲ picture at **spray**

aerospace /ˈeərəʊspeɪs/ *noun* [U] the industry of building aircraft, vehicles and equipment to be sent into space

aesthetic (*AmE* also esthetic) /iːsˈθetɪk; es-/ *adj* concerned with beauty or art: *The columns are there for purely aesthetic reasons* (= only to look beautiful). ▸ **aesthetically** (*AmE* also esthetically) /-kli/ *adv*: *The design is **aesthetically pleasing** as well as practical.*

aesthetics (*AmE* also esthetics) /iːsˈθetɪks; es-/ *noun* [U] the study of beauty, especially in art

afar /əˈfɑː(r)/ *adv*
IDM from afar (*written*) from a long distance away

affable /ˈæfəbl/ *adj* pleasant, friendly and easy to talk to **SYN genial** ▸ **affably** /-əbli/ *adv*

affair /əˈfeə(r)/ *noun* **1** affairs [pl] important personal, business, national, etc. matters: *the minister for foreign affairs* ◆ *current affairs* (= the political and social events that are happening at the present time) **2** [C] an event or a situation: *The whole affair has been extremely unpleasant.* **3** [C] a sexual relationship between two people, usually when at least one of them is married to sb else: *She's **having an affair with** her boss.* **4** [sing] something private that you do not want other people to know about: *What happened between us is my affair. I don't want to discuss it.*
IDM state of affairs ➲ **state**[1]

affect /əˈfekt/ *verb* [T] **1** make sb/sth change in a particular way; to influence sb/sth: *Her personal problems seem to be affecting her work.* ◆ *This disease affects the brain.* ➲ note at **influence** **2** to make sb feel very sad, angry, etc: *The whole community was affected by the tragedy.*

> **HELP** Affect or effect? Notice that **affect** is a verb and **effect** is a noun: *Smoking can affect your health.* ◆ *Smoking can have a bad effect on your health.*

affected /əˈfektɪd/ *adj* (used about a person or their behaviour) not natural or sincere **OPP unaffected** ▸ **affectation** /ˌæfekˈteɪʃn/ *noun* [C,U]

affection /əˈfekʃn/ *noun* [C,U] (an) affection (for/towards sb/sth) a feeling of loving or liking sb/sth: *Mark felt great affection for his sister.*

affectionate /əˈfekʃənət/ *adj* showing that you love or like sb very much: *a very affectionate child* **SYN loving** ▸ **affectionately** *adv*

affidavit /ˌæfəˈdeɪvɪt/ *noun* [C] (*technical*) a written statement that you swear is true, and that can be used as evidence in court

affiliate /əˈfɪlieɪt/ *verb* [T, usually passive] affiliate sth (to sth) to connect an organization to a larger organization: *Our local club is affiliated to the national association.* ▸ **affiliated** *adj* ▸ **affiliation** /əˌfɪliˈeɪʃn/ *noun* [C,U]

affinity /əˈfɪnəti/ *noun* [C,U] (*pl* affinities) **1** (an) affinity (for/with sb/sth) a strong feeling that you like and understand sb/sth, usually because you feel similar to them or it in some way: *He had always had an affinity for wild and lonely places.* **2** (an) affinity (with sb/sth); (an) affinity (between A and B) a similar quality in two or more people or things

affirm /əˈfɜːm/ *verb* [T] (*formal*) to say formally or clearly that sth is true or that you support sth strongly ▸ **affirmation** /ˌæfəˈmeɪʃn/ *noun* [C,U]

affirmative /əˈfɜːmətɪv/ *adj* (*formal*) meaning 'yes': *an affirmative answer*

> **HELP** We can also say: *an answer in the affirmative*

OPP negative

affix /ˈæfɪks/ *noun* [C] a letter or group of letters added to the beginning or end of a word to change its meaning. The **prefix** *un-* in *unhappy* and the **suffix** *-less* in *careless* are both **affixes**.

afflict /əˈflɪkt/ *verb* [T, usually passive] (*formal*) afflict sb/sth (with sth) to cause sb/sth to suffer pain, sadness, etc: *He had been afflicted with the illness since childhood.* ▸ **affliction** *noun* [C,U]

affluent /ˈæfluənt/ *adj* having a lot of money: *Edward comes from a very affluent family.* **SYN wealthy** ▸ **affluence** *noun* [U]: *Increased exports have brought new affluence.*

afford /əˈfɔːd/ *verb* [T] [usually after *can*, *could* or *be able to*] afford sth/to do sth **1** to have enough money or time to be able to do sth: *We couldn't afford a car in those days.* ◆ *I've spent more than I can afford.* ➲ note at **loan** **2** to not be able to do sth or let sth happen because it would have a bad result for you: *The other team is very good so we can't afford to make any mistakes.* ▸ **affordable** *adj*: *affordable prices*

affront /əˈfrʌnt/ *noun* [C] an affront (to sb/sth) something that you say or do that is insulting to sb/sth ▸ **affront** *verb* [T, usually passive]: *She was affronted by his remarks.*

afield /əˈfiːld/ *adv*
IDM far/farther/further afield far away, especially from where you live or from where you are

A

staying: *We decided to hire a car in order to explore further afield.*

afloat /əˈfləʊt/ *adj* [not before a noun] **1** on the surface of the water; not sinking: *A life jacket helps you* ***stay afloat*** *if you fall in the water.* **2** (used about a business, an economy, etc.) having enough money to survive

afoot /əˈfʊt/ *adj* [not before a noun] being planned or prepared: *There are plans afoot to increase taxation.*

afraid /əˈfreɪd/ *adj* [not before a noun] **1** afraid (of sb/sth); afraid (of doing sth/to do sth) feeling fear; frightened: *Are you afraid of dogs?* ◆ *Ben is afraid of going out after dark.* ◆ *I was too afraid to answer the door.* **2** afraid (that ...); afraid (of doing sth) worried about sth: *We were afraid that you would be angry.* ◆ *to be afraid of offending somebody* **3** afraid for sb/sth worried that sb/sth will be harmed, lost, etc: *When I saw the gun I was afraid for my life.*

> **HELP** **Afraid** or **frightened**? You can only use **afraid** after a verb such as 'be', but you can use **frightened** before a noun or after a verb: *a frightened animal* ◆ *The animal was afraid/frightened.*

IDM **I'm afraid (that ...)** used for saying politely that you are sorry about sth: *I'm afraid I can't come on Sunday.* ◆ *'Is the factory going to close?' 'I'm afraid so.'* ◆ *'Is this seat free?' 'I'm afraid not/it isn't.'*

afresh /əˈfreʃ/ *adv* (*formal*) again, in a new way: *to start afresh*

ˌAfrican Aˈmerican *noun* [C] an American citizen whose family was originally from Africa ▶ **ˌAfrican Aˈmerican** *adj*

Afro-Caribbean /ˌæfrəʊ kærəˈbiːən/ *noun* [C] a person whose family came originally from Africa, and who was born or whose parents were born in the Caribbean ▶ **Afro-Caribbean** *adj*

after /ˈɑːftə(r)/ *prep, conj, adv* **1** at a later time; following sth: *Ian phoned just after 6 o'clock.* ◆ *the week after next* ◆ *I hope to arrive some time after lunch.* ◆ *They arrived at the station after the train had left.* ◆ *After we had finished our dinner, we went into the garden.* ◆ *I went out yesterday morning, and* ***after that*** *I was at home all day.* ◆ *That was in April. Soon after, I heard that he was ill.*

> **HELP** It is more common to use **afterwards** at the end of a sentence: *We played tennis and went to Angela's house afterwards.*

➲ note at **then** **2** ... after ... repeated many times or continuing for a long time: ***day after day*** *of hot weather* ◆ *I've told the children* ***time after time*** *not to do that.* **3** following or behind sb/sth: *Shut the door after you.* ◆ *C comes after B in the alphabet.* **4** as a result of sth: *After the way he behaved, I won't invite him here again.* **5** looking for or trying to catch or get sb/sth: *The police were after him.* ◆ *Nicky is after a job in advertising.* **6** used when sb/sth is given the name of another person or thing: *We called our son William after his grandfather.*

IDM **after all** **1** used when sth is different in reality to what sb expected or thought: *So you decided to come after all!* (= I thought you weren't going to come) **2** used for reminding sb of a certain fact: *She can't understand. After all, she's only two.*

ˈafter-effect *noun* [C] an unpleasant result of sth that comes some time later

aftermath /ˈɑːftəmæθ; -mɑːθ/ *noun* [sing] a situation that is the result of an important or unpleasant event

afternoon /ˌɑːftəˈnuːn/ *noun* [C,U] the part of a day between midday and about 6 o'clock: *I'll see you tomorrow afternoon.* ◆ *What are you doing this afternoon?* ◆ *I studied all afternoon.* ◆ *I usually go for a walk* ***in the afternoon***. ◆ *He goes swimming every afternoon.* ◆ *She arrived at 4 o'clock in the afternoon.* ◆ *Tom works two afternoons a week.* ◆ *Are you busy* ***on Friday afternoon***? ➲ note at **morning**

IDM **good afternoon** (*formal*) used when you see sb for the first time in the afternoon

> **HELP** Often we just say **Afternoon**: *'Good afternoon, Mrs Davies.' 'Afternoon, Jack.'*

aftershave /ˈɑːftəʃeɪv/ *noun* [C,U] a liquid with a pleasant smell that men put on their faces after shaving

afterthought /ˈɑːftəθɔːt/ *noun* [C, usually sing] something that you think of or add to sth else at a later time

afterwards /ˈɑːftəwədz/ (*AmE* also **afterward**) *adv* at a later time: *He was taken to hospital and died shortly afterwards.* ◆ *Afterwards, I realized I'd made a terrible mistake.*

again /əˈgen; əˈgeɪn/ *adv* **1** once more; another time: *Could you say that again, please?* ◆ *She's out at the moment, so I'll phone again later.* ◆ *Don't ever do that again!* **2** in the place or condition that sb/sth was in before: *It's great to be home again.* ◆ *I hope you'll soon be well again.* **3** in addition to sth: *'Is that enough?' 'No, I'd like* ***half as much again****, please'* (= one-and-a-half times the original amount).

IDM **again and again** many times: *He said he was sorry again and again, but she wouldn't listen.*

then/there again used to say that sth you have just said may not happen or be true: *She might pass her test, but then again she might not.*

yet again ➲ **yet**

against /əˈgenst; əˈgeɪnst/ *prep* **1** being an opponent to sb/sth in a game, competition, etc., or an enemy of sb/sth in a war or fight: *We played football against a school from another district.* **2** not agreeing with or supporting sb/sth: *Are you for or against the plan?* ◆ *She felt that everybody was against her.* **OPP** **for** **3** what a law, rule, etc. says you must not do: *It's* ***against the law*** *to buy cigarettes before you are sixteen.* **4** in order to protect yourself from sb/sth: *Take these pills as a precaution against malaria.* **5** in the opposite direction to sth: *We had to cycle against the wind.* **6** touching sb/sth for support: *I put the ladder against the wall.*

age[1] /eɪdʒ/ *noun* **1** [C,U] the length of time that sb has lived or that sth has existed: *Ali is seventeen* ***years***

of **age**. ♦ *She left school* **at the age of** *sixteen.* ♦ *Children of all ages will enjoy this film.* ♦ *He needs some friends of his own age.*

HELP When you want to ask about somebody's age, you usually say: *How old is she?* and the answer can be: *She's eighteen* or: *She's eighteen years old* (but NOT *She's eighteen years*). Here are some examples of other ways of talking about age: *I'm nearly nineteen.* ♦ *a girl of eighteen* ♦ *an eighteen-year-old girl* ♦ *The robber is of medium height and aged about 16 or 17.*

2 [C,U] a particular period in sb's life: *a problem that often develops in* **middle age** ♦ *Her sons will look after her in her* **old age**. **3** [C] a particular period of history: *the computer age* ♦ *the history of art through the ages* **4** [U] the state of being old: *a face lined with age* ♦ *The doctor said she* **died of old age**. ➲ look at **youth** **5** ages [pl] (*informal*) a very long time: *We had to wait (for) ages at the hospital.* ♦ *It's ages since I've done any exercise.*

IDM **the age of consent** the age at which sb can legally agree to have sex

at a tender age; at the tender age of ... ➲ **tender**[1]

come of age the age at which sb has an adult's rights and responsibilities in law: *My father gave me a watch when I came of age.*

feel your age ➲ **feel**[1]

under age not old enough by law to do sth

age[2] /eɪdʒ/ *verb* [I,T] (**ageing** *or* **aging**; *pt, pp* **aged** /eɪdʒd/) to become or look old; to cause sb to look old: *My father seems to have aged a lot recently.* ♦ *I could see her illness had aged her.* ♦ *an ageing aunt*

⚷ **aged** **1** /eɪdʒd/ *adj* [not before a noun] of the age mentioned: *The woman, aged 26, was last seen at Victoria Station.* **2 the aged** /ˈeɪdʒɪd/ *noun* [pl] very old people: *services for the sick and the aged*

ˈ**age group** *noun* [C] people of about the same age: *This club is very popular with the 20-30 age group.*

ageism (*AmE* also **agism**) /ˈeɪdʒɪzəm/ *noun* [U] unfair treatment of people because they are considered too old: *ageism in job advertisements* ▶ **ageist** /-ɪst/ *adj*: *ageist and sexist remarks* ▶ **ageist** *noun* [C]

⚷ **agency** /ˈeɪdʒənsi/ *noun* [C] (*pl* **agencies**) **1** a business or an organization that provides a particular service: *an advertising agency* ♦ *aid agencies caring for refugees* **2** (*especially AmE*) a government department: *the Central Intelligence Agency* (= the CIA)

agenda /əˈdʒendə/ *noun* [C] a list of matters that need to be discussed or dealt with: *The first item* **on the agenda** *at the meeting will be security.* ♦ *The government have* **set an agenda** *for reform over the next ten years.*

⚷ **agent** /ˈeɪdʒənt/ *noun* [C] **1** a person whose job is to do business for a company or for another person: *Our company's agent in Rio will meet you at the airport.* ♦ *Most actors and musicians have their own agents.* ♦ *a travel agent* ♦ *an estate agent* **2** = **secret agent**

aggravate /ˈæɡrəveɪt/ *verb* [T] **1** to make sth worse or more serious: *She aggravated her bad back by lifting a table.* **2** (*informal*) to make sb angry or annoyed: *What aggravates me is that she never listens.* ▶ **aggravation** /ˌæɡrəˈveɪʃn/ *noun* [C,U]

aggregate /ˈæɡrɪɡət/ *noun*

IDM **on aggregate** in total: *Our team won 3-1 on aggregate.*

aggression /əˈɡreʃn/ *noun* [U] **1** angry feelings or behaviour that make you want to attack other people: *People often react to this kind of situation with fear or aggression.* **2** the act of starting a fight or war without reasonable cause

⚷ **aggressive** /əˈɡresɪv/ *adj* **1** ready or likely to fight or argue: *an aggressive dog* ♦ *Some people get aggressive after drinking alcohol.* **2** using or showing force or pressure in order to succeed: *an aggressive salesman* ▶ **aggressively** *adv*: *The boys responded aggressively when I asked them to make less noise.*

aggressor /əˈɡresə(r)/ *noun* [C] a person or country that attacks sb/sth or starts fighting first

aggrieved /əˈɡriːvd/ *adj* (*formal*) upset or angry

aghast /əˈɡɑːst/ *adj* [not before a noun] **aghast (at sth)** filled with great fear and shock when you see or hear sth: *She stared aghast at the amount of blood.*

SYN **horrified**

agile /ˈædʒaɪl/ *adj* able to move quickly and easily: *Monkeys are extremely agile.* ▶ **agility** /əˈdʒɪləti/ *noun* [U]: *This sport is a test of both physical and mental agility.*

agism (*AmE*) = **ageism**

agitate /ˈædʒɪteɪt/ *verb* [I] **agitate (for/against sth)** to make other people feel very strongly about sth so that they want to help you achieve it: *to agitate for reform*

agitated /ˈædʒɪteɪtɪd/ *adj* worried or nervous ▶ **agitation** /ˌædʒɪˈteɪʃn/ *noun* [U]

AGM /ˌeɪ dʒiː ˈem/ *abbr* (*BrE*) **Annual General Meeting**; an important meeting which the members of an organization hold once a year

agnostic /æɡˈnɒstɪk/ *noun* [C] a person who is not sure whether God exists or not

⚷ **ago** /əˈɡəʊ/ *adv* in the past; back in time from now: *Paul left ten minutes ago* (= if it is 12 o'clock now, he left at ten to twelve). ♦ *That was* **a long time ago**. ♦ **How long ago** *did it happen?* ➲ note at **for**

GRAMMAR **Ago** is used with the past simple tense and not the present perfect tense: *I arrived in Britain three months ago.* Compare **ago** and **before**. **Ago** means 'earlier than now' and **before** means 'earlier than then' (that is earlier than a particular time in the past): *Anne married Simon two years ago.* ♦ *They had been at school together ten years before* (= ten years before she married Simon).

A

agonize (also -ise) /ˈæɡənaɪz/ *verb* [I] to worry or think about sth for a long time: *to agonize over a difficult decision*

agonized (also -ised) /ˈæɡənaɪzd/ *adj* showing extreme pain or worry: *an agonized cry*

agonizing (also -ising) /ˈæɡənaɪzɪŋ/ *adj* causing extreme worry or pain: *an agonizing choice* ◆ *an agonizing headache*

agony /ˈæɡəni/ *noun* [C,U] (*pl* **agonies**) great pain or suffering: *to be/scream in agony*

ˈagony aunt (*masc* ˈagony uncle) (*AmE* adˈvice columnist) *noun* [C] a person who writes in a newspaper or magazine giving advice in reply to people's questions about their personal problems

agoraphobia /ˌæɡərəˈfəʊbiə/ *noun* [U] fear of being in public places where there are a lot of people ▶ **agoraphobic** *adj*

🔑 **agree** /əˈɡriː/ *verb*

➤SHARE OPINION **1** [I] **agree (with sb/sth); agree (that ...)** to have the same opinion as sb/sth: *'I think we should talk to the teacher about this.' 'Yes, I agree.'* ◆ *I agree with Paul.* ◆ *Do you agree that we should travel by train?* ◆ *I'm afraid I don't agree.* OPP **disagree**

HELP Note that we say: *I agree* and: *I don't agree* NOT 'I am agree' or 'I am not agree'. This is incorrect.

➤SAY YES **2** [I] **agree (to sth/to do sth)** to say yes to sth: *I asked my boss if I could go home early and she agreed.* ◆ *Alkis has agreed to lend me his car for the weekend.* OPP **refuse**

➤ARRANGE **3** [I,T] **agree (to do sth); agree (on sth)** to make an arrangement or decide sth with sb: *They agreed to meet the following day.* ◆ *Can we agree on a price?* ◆ *We agreed a price of £500.*

➤APPROVE OF **4** [I] **agree with sth** to think that sth is right: *I don't agree with experiments on animals.* OPP **disagree**

➤BE THE SAME **5** [I] to be the same as sth: *The two accounts of the accident do not agree.* OPP **disagree**

IDM **not agree with sb** (used about food) to make sb feel ill: *I like spicy food but it doesn't agree with me.*

agreeable /əˈɡriːəbl/ *adj* **1** pleasant; nice OPP **disagreeable** **2** [not before a noun] (*formal*) ready to agree: *If you are agreeable, we would like to visit your offices on 21 May.* ▶ **agreeably** /-əbli/ *adv*: *I was agreeably surprised by the film.*

🔑 **agreement** /əˈɡriːmənt/ *noun* **1** [C] a contract or decision that two or more people have made together: *Please sign the agreement and return it to us.* ◆ *The leaders* ***reached an agreement*** *after five days of talks.* ◆ *We never* ***break an agreement.*** **2** [U] the state of agreeing with sb/sth: *She nodded her head in agreement.* ◆ *We* ***are*** *totally* ***in agreement with*** *what you have said.* OPP **disagreement**

agriculture /ˈæɡrɪkʌltʃə(r)/ *noun* [U] keeping animals and growing crops for food; farming: *the Minister of Agriculture* ▶ **agricultural** /ˌæɡrɪˈkʌltʃərəl/ *adj*

agritourism /ˈæɡrɪtʊərɪzəm/ *noun* [U] holidays in which tourists stay with local people who live in the countryside

aground /əˈɡraʊnd/ *adv* if a ship **runs/goes aground**, it touches the ground in water that is not deep enough and it cannot move: *The oil tanker* ***ran/went aground*** *off the Spanish coast.* ▶ **aground** *adj* [not before a noun]

ah /ɑː/ *exclam* used for expressing surprise, pleasure, understanding, etc: *Ah, there you are.*

aha /ɑːˈhɑː/ *exclam* used when you suddenly find or understand sth: *Aha! Now I understand.*

🔑 **ahead** /əˈhed/ *adv* **ahead (of sb/sth)** **1** in front of sb/sth: *I could see the other car about half a mile ahead of us.* ◆ *The path ahead looked narrow and steep.* ◆ *Look straight ahead and don't turn round!* **2** before or more advanced than sb/sth: *Inga and Nils arrived a few minutes ahead of us.* ◆ *London is about five hours ahead of New York.* ◆ *The Japanese are* ***way ahead*** *of us in their research.* **3** into the future: *He's got a difficult time ahead of him.* ◆ *We must* ***think ahead*** *and make a plan.* **4** winning in a game, competition, etc: *The goal* ***put*** *Italy 2-1* ***ahead*** *at half-time.* ➲ look at **behind**

IDM **ahead of your time** so modern that people do not understand you

streets ahead ➲ **street**

🔑 **aid**[1] /eɪd/ *noun* **1** [U] money, food, etc. that is sent to a country or to people in order to help them: *We sent aid to the earthquake victims.* ◆ *economic aid* **2** [U] help: *to walk* ***with the aid of*** *a stick* ◆ *He had to* ***go to the aid of*** *a child in the river.* ➲ look at **first aid** **3** [C] a person or thing that helps you: *a hearing aid* ◆ *dictionaries and other study aids*

IDM **in aid of sb/sth** in order to collect money for sb/sth, especially for a charity: *a concert in aid of Children in Need*

🔑 **aid**[2] /eɪd/ *verb* [T] (*formal*) to help sb/sth: *Sleep aids recovery from illness.*

IDM **aid and abet** to help sb to do sth that is not allowed by law

aide /eɪd/ *noun* [C] a person who helps another person, especially a politician, in their job

AIDS (also **Aids**) /eɪdz/ *noun* [U] **Acquired Immune Deficiency Syndrome**; an illness caused by **HIV** (= a virus which destroys the body's ability to fight infection): *He was HIV positive for three years before developing full-blown AIDS.* ◆ *to contract AIDS* ◆ *the AIDS virus*

ailing /ˈeɪlɪŋ/ *adj* not in good health; weak: *an ailing economy*

ailment /ˈeɪlmənt/ *noun* [C] (*formal*) any illness that is not very serious

🔑 **aim**[1] /eɪm/ *noun* **1** [C] something that you intend to do; a purpose: *Our aim is to open offices in Paris and Rome before the end of the year.* ◆ *His only aim in life is to make money.* **2** [U] the act of pointing sth at sb/sth before trying to hit them or it with it: *She picked up the gun,* ***took aim*** *and fired.* ◆ *Jo's aim was good and she hit the target.*

🔑 **aim**[2] /eɪm/ *verb* **1** [I] **aim to do sth; aim at/for sth** to intend to do or achieve sth: *We aim to leave after* breakfast. ◆ *The company is aiming at a 25% increase in profit.* ◆ *You should always aim for perfection in your work.* **2** [I,T] aim (sth) (at sb/sth) to point sth at sb/sth before trying to hit them or it with it: *She aimed (the gun) at the target and fired.* **3** [T] aim sth at sb/sth to direct sth at a particular person or group: *The advertising campaign is aimed at young people.*

IDM **be aimed at sth/doing sth** to be intended to achieve sth: *The new laws are aimed at reducing heavy traffic in cities.*

aimless /ˈeɪmləs/ *adj* having no purpose: *an aimless discussion* ▶ **aimlessly** *adv*

ain't /eɪnt/ (*informal*) *short for* **am not; is not; are not; has not; have not**

HELP Ain't is NOT considered to be correct English.

air[1] /eə(r)/ *noun* **1** [U] the mixture of gases that surrounds the earth and that people, animals and plants breathe: *the pure mountain air* ◆ *Open a window—I need some* ***fresh air***. ◆ *The air was polluted by smoke from the factory.* **2** [U] the space around and above things: *to throw a ball high* ***into the air*** ◆ ***in the open air*** (= outside) **3** [U] travel or transport in an aircraft: *to travel* ***by air*** ◆ *an air ticket* **4** [sing] an air (of sth) the particular feeling or impression that is given by sb/sth: *She has a confident air.*

IDM **a breath of fresh air** ➲ **breath**

clear the air ➲ **clear**[2]

in the air probably going to happen soon: *A feeling of change was in the air.*

in the open air ➲ **open**[1]

on/off (the) air (not) sending out programmes on the radio or TV: *This radio station is on the air 24 hours a day.*

vanish, etc. into thin air ➲ **thin**[1]

air[2] /eə(r)/ *verb* **1** [I,T] to put clothes, etc. in a warm place or outside in the fresh air to make sure they are completely dry; to become dry in this way: *Put the sheets on the washing line to air.* **2** [I,T] to make a room, etc. fresh by letting air into it; to become fresh in this way: *Open the window to air the room.* **3** [T] to tell people what you think about sth: *The discussion gave people a chance to* ***air their views***.

airbag /ˈeəbæg/ *noun* [C] a device in a car that fills with air if there is an accident. It protects the people sitting in the front.

airbase /ˈeəbeɪs/ *noun* [C] an airport for military aircraft

airborne /ˈeəbɔːn/ *adj* flying in the air

ˈair conditioning *noun* [U] the system that keeps the air in a room, building, etc. cool and dry ▶ **ˈair-conditioned** *adj*: *air-conditioned offices*

aircraft /ˈeəkrɑːft/ *noun* [C] (*pl* **aircraft**) any vehicle that can fly in the air, for example a plane ➲ picture on **page P6**

ˈaircraft carrier *noun* [C] a ship that carries military aircraft and that has a long flat area where they can take off and land

airfare /ˈeəfeə(r)/ *noun* [C] the money that you pay to travel by plane: *high/low/cheap airfares* ➲ look at **fare**

airfield /ˈeəfiːld/ *noun* [C] an area of land where aircraft can land or take off. An **airfield** is smaller than an airport.

ˈair force *noun* [C, with sing or pl verb] the part of a country's military organization that fights in the air ➲ note at **war** ➲ look at **army, navy**

ˈair hostess *noun* [C] (*old-fashioned*) a woman who looks after the passengers on a plane ➲ look at **cabin crew, flight attendant**

ˈairing cupboard *noun* [C] a warm cupboard that you put clothes, etc. in to make sure they are completely dry after being washed

airless /ˈeələs/ *adj* not having enough fresh air: *The room was hot and airless.*

airlift /ˈeəlɪft/ *noun* [C] an operation to take people, soldiers, food, etc. to or from an area by aircraft, especially in an emergency or when roads are closed or dangerous ▶ **airlift** *verb* [T]: *Two casualties* ***were airlifted to safety***.

airline /ˈeəlaɪn/ *noun* [C] a company that provides regular flights for people or goods in aircraft

airliner /ˈeəlaɪnə(r)/ *noun* [C] a large plane that carries passengers

airmail /ˈeəmeɪl/ *noun* [U] the system for sending letters, packages, etc. by plane: *I sent the parcel (by) airmail.*

airplane /ˈeəpleɪn/ (*AmE*) = **plane**[1](1)

airport /ˈeəpɔːt/ *noun* [C] a place where aircraft can land and take off and that has buildings for passengers to wait in ➲ note at **plane**: *Bologna airport* ◆ *waiting in the airport lounge*

ˈair raid *noun* [C] an attack by military aircraft

airsick /ˈeəsɪk/ *adj* feeling sick or **vomiting** (= bringing up food from the stomach) as a result of travelling on a plane ➲ look at **carsick, seasick, travel-sick**

airspace /ˈeəspeɪs/ *noun* [U] the part of the sky that is above a country and that belongs to that country by law

airstrip /ˈeəstrɪp/ (also **ˈlanding strip**) *noun* [C] a narrow piece of land where aircraft can take off and land

airtight /ˈeətaɪt/ *adj* that air cannot get into or out of

ˌair ˌtraffic conˈtroller *noun* [C] a person whose job is to organize routes for aircraft, and to tell pilots by radio when they can land and take off

airy /ˈeəri/ *adj* (**airier; airiest**) having a lot of fresh air inside

aisle /aɪl/ *noun* [C] a passage between the rows of seats in a church, theatre, etc., or between rows of shelves in a large shop

A

ajar /əˈdʒɑː(r)/ *adj* [not before a noun] (used about a door) slightly open

akin /əˈkɪn/ *adj (formal)* **akin to sth** similar to sth

à la carte /ˌɑː lɑː ˈkɑːt/ *adj, adv* (used about a meal in a restaurant) where each dish that is available has a separate price and there is not a fixed price for a complete meal

alarm[1] /əˈlɑːm/ *noun* **1** [U] a sudden feeling of fear or worry: *She jumped up* ***in alarm****.* **2** [sing] a warning of danger: *A small boy saw the smoke and* ***raised the alarm****.* **3** [C] a machine that warns you of danger, for example by ringing a loud bell: *The burglars* ***set off*** *the* ***alarm*** *when they broke the window.* ◆ *The* ***fire/burglar alarm*** *went off at 4 a.m.* **4** [C] = **alarm clock**

IDM **a false alarm** ➲ **false**

alarm[2] /əˈlɑːm/ *verb* [T] to make sb/sth feel suddenly frightened or worried: *The news of the escaped prisoner alarmed the local people.*

aˈlarm clock (also **alarm**) *noun* [C] a clock that you can set to make a noise at a particular time to wake you up: *She set the alarm clock for half past six.* ➲ picture at **clock**

alarmed /əˈlɑːmd/ *adj* [not before a noun] **alarmed (at/by sth)** frightened or worried: *She was alarmed at the thought of staying alone in the house.*

alarming /əˈlɑːmɪŋ/ *adj* that makes you frightened or worried: *The population of the world is increasing at an alarming rate.* ▶ **alarmingly** *adv*

alas /əˈlæs/ *exclam (formal)* used for expressing sadness about sth

albeit /ˌɔːlˈbiːɪt/ *conj (formal)* although: *He finally agreed to come, albeit unwillingly.*

albino /ælˈbiːnəʊ/ *noun* [C] (*pl* **albinos**) a person or an animal with very white skin, white hair and pink eyes

album /ˈælbəm/ *noun* [C] **1** a book in which you can keep stamps, photographs, etc. that you have collected **2** a collection of songs on a CD or on the Internet: *The band are about to release a new album.* ➲ note at **pop** ➲ look at **single**

alcohol /ˈælkəhɒl/ *noun* [U] **1** drinks such as beer, wine, etc. that can make people drunk: *He never drinks alcohol.* **2** the clear liquid in drinks such as beer and wine that can make you drunk: *low-alcohol beer*

alcoholic[1] /ˌælkəˈhɒlɪk/ *adj* containing alcohol: *alcoholic drinks* OPP **non-alcoholic**

> **MORE** Drinks without alcohol are also called **soft drinks**.

alcoholic[2] /ˌælkəˈhɒlɪk/ *noun* [C] a person who regularly drinks too much alcohol and cannot easily stop drinking

> **MORE** A person who does not drink alcohol at all is a **teetotaller**.

alcoholism /ˈælkəhɒlɪzəm/ *noun* [U] a medical condition that is caused by regularly drinking a large amount of alcohol and not being able to stop

alcove /ˈælkəʊv/ *noun* [C] a small area in a room where one part of the wall is further back than the rest of the wall

ale /eɪl/ *noun* [U,C] a type of beer

alert[1] /əˈlɜːt/ *adj* **alert (to sth)** watching, listening, etc. for sth with all your attention: *Security guards must be alert at all times.* ◆ *to be alert to possible changes*

alert[2] /əˈlɜːt/ *verb* [T] **alert sb (to sth)** to warn sb of danger or a problem

alert[3] /əˈlɜːt/ *noun* [C] a warning of possible danger: *a bomb alert*

IDM **on the alert (for sth)** ready or prepared for danger or an attack

ˈA level (also **adˈvanced level**) *noun* [C,U] a British exam taken in a particular subject, usually in the final year of school at the age of 18: *How many A levels have you got?* ◆ *I'm doing my A levels this summer.* ◆ *You need two passes at A level to get onto this course.* ➲ look at **A2, AS, GCSE**

algae /ˈældʒiː; ˈælgiː/ *noun* [pl, with sing or pl verb] very simple plants that grow mainly in water

algebra /ˈældʒɪbrə/ *noun* [U] a type of mathematics in which letters and symbols are used to represent numbers

alias[1] /ˈeɪliəs/ *adv* used for giving sb's false name: *Norma Jean Baker, alias Marilyn Monroe*

alias[2] /ˈeɪliəs/ *noun* [C] a false name, for example one that is used by a criminal: *Castorri is known to the police under several aliases.*

alibi /ˈæləbaɪ/ *noun* [C] (*pl* **alibis**) **an alibi (for sth)** a statement by sb that says you were in a different place at the time of a crime and so cannot be guilty of the crime: *He had a good alibi for the night of the robbery.*

alien[1] /ˈeɪliən/ *adj* **1 alien (to sb)** very strange and completely different from your normal experience **2** of another country; foreign: *an alien land*

alien[2] /ˈeɪliən/ *noun* [C] **1** *(formal)* a person who comes from another country **2** a creature that comes from another planet

alienate /ˈeɪliəneɪt/ *verb* [T] **1** to make people feel that they cannot share your opinions any more: *The Prime Minister's new policies on defence have alienated many of his supporters.* **2 alienate sb (from sb/sth)** to make sb feel that they do not belong somewhere or are not part of sth ▶ **alienation** /ˌeɪliəˈneɪʃn/ *noun* [U]

alight[1] /əˈlaɪt/ *adj* [not before a noun] on fire; burning: *A cigarette* ***set*** *the petrol* ***alight****.*

> **HELP** **Alight** or **burning**? You can only use **alight** after a verb such as 'be' but you can use **burning** before a noun: *The whole building was alight.* ◆ *a burning building*

alight[2] /əˈlaɪt/ *verb* [I] *(formal)* **alight (from sth)** to get off a bus, train, etc.

A

align /əˈlaɪn/ *verb* [T] align sth (with sth) to arrange things in a straight line or so that they are parallel to sth else: *The mechanic aligned the wheels of the car.*
PHR V **align yourself with sb/sth** to say that you support the opinions of a particular group, country, etc.

alignment /əˈlaɪnmənt/ *noun* **1** [U] arrangement in a straight line or parallel to sth else **2** [C,U] an agreement between political parties, countries, etc. to support the same thing

alike[1] /əˈlaɪk/ *adj* [not before a noun] very similar: *The two children are very alike.*

alike[2] /əˈlaɪk/ *adv* in the same way; equally: *We try to treat women and men alike in this company.* ♦ *The book is popular with adults and children alike.*

alimony /ˈælɪməni/ *noun* [U] money that you have to pay by law to your former wife or husband after getting divorced

ˈ**A-list** *adj* used to describe a group of people who are famous, successful or important: *He only invited **A-list celebrities** to his party.*

alive /əˈlaɪv/ *adj* [not before a noun] **1** not dead; living: *The young woman was still alive when the ambulance reached the hospital.* ♦ *The quick action of the doctors **kept** the child **alive**.*

> **HELP** **Alive** or **living**? **Alive** can only be used after a noun or a verb such as 'be', but you can use **living** before a noun: *Are her parents still alive?* ♦ *Does she have any living relatives?*

2 continuing to exist: *Many old traditions are very much alive in this area of the country.* **3** full of life: *In the evening the town really **comes alive**.*

alkali /ˈælkəlaɪ/ *noun* [C,U] a chemical substance that can burn skin when it is dissolved in water. An **alkali** has a **pH** (= a measurement of the level of acid or alkali in sth) value of more than 7. ➲ look at **acid** ▸ **alkaline** *adj*

all[1] /ɔːl/ *determiner, pron* **1** every one of a group: *All (of) my children can swim.* ♦ *My children can all swim.* ♦ *She's read all (of) these books.* ♦ *She's read them all.* ♦ *The people at the meeting all voted against the plan.* ♦ *All of them voted against the plan.* **2** the whole of a thing or of a period of time: *All (of) the food has gone.* ♦ *They've eaten all of it.* ♦ *They've eaten it all.* ♦ *This money is all yours.* ♦ *All of it is yours.* ♦ *all week/month/year* ♦ *He worked hard all his life.* **3** everything that; the only thing that: *I wrote down all I could remember.* ♦ *All I've eaten today is one banana.*
IDM **above all** ➲ **above**
after all ➲ **after**
for all **1** in spite of: *For all her wealth and beauty, she was never very happy.* **2** used to show that sth is not important or of no interest or value to you: ***For all I know**, he's probably remarried by now.* ➲ note at **altogether**
in all in total: *There were ten of us in all.*
not all that ... not very: *The film wasn't all that good.*
(not) at all in any way: *I didn't enjoy it at all.*
not at all used as a polite reply when sb thanks you for sth: *'Thanks very much for your help.' 'Not at all, it was a pleasure.'*

all[2] /ɔːl/ *adv* **1** completely; very: *He has lived all alone since his wife died.* ♦ *I didn't watch that programme—I forgot all about it.* ♦ *They got all excited about it.* **2** (in sport) for each side: *The score was two all.*
IDM **all along** from the beginning: *I knew you were joking all along.*
all the better, harder, etc. even better, harder, etc. than before: *It will be all the more difficult with two people missing.*
all/just the same ➲ **same**

Allah /ˈælə/ *noun* [sing] the Muslim name for God

allay /əˈleɪ/ *verb* [T] (*formal*) to make sth less strong

the ˌall-ˈclear *noun* [sing] a signal telling you that a situation is no longer dangerous

allege /əˈledʒ/ *verb* [T] (*formal*) to say that sb has done sth wrong, but without having any proof that this is true: *The woman alleged that Williams had attacked her with a knife.* ▸ **allegation** /ˌæləˈɡeɪʃn/ *noun* [C]: *to **make allegations** of police corruption* ▸ **alleged** /əˈledʒd/ *adj* [only *before* a noun] ▸ **allegedly** /əˈledʒɪdli/ *adv*: *The man was allegedly shot while trying to escape.*

allegiance /əˈliːdʒəns/ *noun* [U,C] (*formal*) support for a leader, government, belief, etc: *Many people **switched allegiance** and voted against the government.* SYN **loyalty**

allegory /ˈæləɡəri/ *noun* [C,U] (*pl* **allegories**) a story, play, picture, etc. in which each character or event is a symbol representing an idea or a quality, such as truth, evil, death, etc.; the use of such symbols ▸ **allegorical** /ˌæləˈɡɒrɪkl/ *adj*: *an **allegorical** figure/novel*

allergic /əˈlɜːdʒɪk/ *adj* **1** **allergic (to sth)** having an **allergy**: *I can't drink cow's milk. I'm allergic to it.* **2** caused by an **allergy**: *an allergic reaction to house dust*

allergy /ˈælədʒi/ *noun* [C] (*pl* **allergies**) **an allergy (to sth)** a medical condition that makes you ill when you eat, touch or breathe sth that does not normally make other people ill: *an allergy to cats/shellfish/pollen* ➲ note at **ill** ➲ look at **hay fever**

alleviate /əˈliːvieɪt/ *verb* [T] to make sth less strong or bad: *The doctor gave me an injection to alleviate the pain.* ▸ **alleviation** /əˌliːviˈeɪʃn/ *noun* [U]

alley /ˈæli/ (also **alleyway** /ˈæliweɪ/) *noun* [C] a narrow passage between buildings ➲ picture on **page P11**

alliance /əˈlaɪəns/ *noun* [C] an agreement between groups, countries, etc. to work together and support each other: *The two parties **formed an alliance**.* ➲ look at **ally**

allied *adj* **1** /ˈælaɪd/ [only *before* a noun] (used about organizations, countries, etc.) having an agreement to work together and support each other: *allied forces* **2** /əˈlaɪd/ **allied (to sth)** connect-

A

ed with; existing together with: *The newspaper is closely allied to the government.*

alligator /ˈælɪgeɪtə(r)/ *noun* [C] a large animal with a hard skin covered in scales, a long tail and a big mouth with sharp teeth. **Alligators** live in the lakes and rivers of America and China. ➲ look at **crocodile**

ˌall-ˈin *adj* [only *before* a noun] including everything: *an all-in price*

alliteration /əˌlɪtəˈreɪʃn/ *noun* [U] (*technical*) the use of the same letter or sound at the beginning of words that are close together, as in *sing a song of sixpence*

allocate /ˈæləkeɪt/ *verb* [T] allocate sth (to/for sb/sth) to give sth to sb as their share or to decide to use sth for a particular purpose: *The government has allocated half the budget for education.* ▸ **allocation** /ˌæləˈkeɪʃn/ *noun* [C,U]

⚷ **allot** /əˈlɒt/ *verb* [T] (allotting; allotted) allot sth (to sb/sth) to give a share of work, time, etc. to sb/sth: *Different tasks were allotted to each member of the class.* ◆ *We all finished the exam in the allotted time.*

allotment /əˈlɒtmənt/ *noun* [C] (*BrE*) a small area of land in a town that you can rent for growing vegetables on

ˌall ˈout *adj, adv* using all your strength, etc: *We're going all out for victory.* ◆ *an all-out effort*

⚷ **allow** /əˈlaʊ/ *verb* [T] **1** allow sb/sth to do sth; allow sth to give permission for sb/sth to do sth or for sth to happen: *You are not allowed to eat or drink on this bus.* ◆ *I'm afraid we don't allow people to bring dogs into this restaurant.* ◆ *Photography is not allowed inside the cathedral.* ◆ *You are allowed to bring two guests to the ceremony.* **2** allow sb sth to let sb have sth: *My contract allows me four weeks' holiday a year.* **3** to give permission for sb/sth to be or go somewhere: *No dogs allowed.* ◆ *I'm only allowed out on Friday and Saturday nights.* **4** to make sth possible: *Working part-time would allow me to spend more time with my family.* **5** allow sth (for sb/sth) to provide money, time, etc. for sb/sth: *You should allow about 30 minutes for each question.*
PHR V **allow for sb/sth** to think about possible problems when you are planning sth and include extra time, money, etc. for them: *The journey should take about two hours, allowing for heavy traffic.*

allowable /əˈlaʊəbl/ *adj* that is allowed, especially by law or by a set of rules

allowance /əˈlaʊəns/ *noun* [C] **1** an amount of money that you receive regularly to help you pay for sth that you need **2** an amount of sth that you are allowed: *Most flights have a 20kg baggage allowance.* **3** (*especially AmE*) = **pocket money**
IDM **make allowances for sb/sth** to judge a person or their actions in a kinder way than usual because they have a particular problem or disadvantage

alloy /ˈælɔɪ/ *noun* [C,U] a metal that is formed by mixing two types of metal together, or by mixing metal with another substance: *Brass is an alloy of copper and zinc.*

OTHER WORDS FOR
allow
Compare **allow, permit** and **let. Allow** can be used in both formal and informal English. The passive form **be allowed to** is especially common. **Permit** is a formal word and is usually used only in written English. **Let** is an informal word, and very common in spoken English. You **allow sb to do sth** but **let sb do sth** (no 'to'). **Let** cannot be used in the passive: *Visitors are not allowed/permitted to smoke in this area.* ◆ *Smoking is not allowed/permitted.* ◆ *I'm not allowed to smoke in my bedroom.* ◆ *My dad won't let me smoke in my bedroom.*

⚷ **ˌall ˈright** (also *informal* alright) *adj, adv, exclam* [not before a noun] **1** good enough: *Is everything all right?* **2** safe and well: *I hope the children are all right.* ◆ *Do you feel all right?* **3** showing you agree to do what sb has asked: *'Can you get me some stamps?' 'Yes, all right.'* SYN for all meanings **OK**

HELP You say 'That's all right,' when sb thanks you for sth or when sb says sorry for sth he/she has done: *'Thanks for the lift home.' 'That's (quite) all right.'* ◆ *'I'm so sorry I'm late.' 'That's all right. We haven't started yet anyway.'*

ˈall-round *adj* [only *before* a noun] able to do many different things well; good in many different ways: *a superb all-round athlete* ◆ *The school aims at the all-round development of the child.*

ˌall-ˈrounder *noun* [C] a person who can do many different things well

allude /əˈluːd/ *verb* [I] (*formal*) allude to sb/sth to speak about sb/sth in an indirect way ▸ **allusion** /əˈluːʒn/ *noun* [C,U]: *He likes to* **make allusions to** *the size of his salary.*

alluring /əˈlʊərɪŋ/ *adj* attractive in an exciting way: *an alluring smile* ▸ **alluringly** *adv*

⚷ **ally**[1] /ˈælaɪ/ *noun* [C] (*pl* allies) **1** a country that has an agreement to support another country, especially in a war: *France and its European allies* ➲ look at **alliance** **2** a person who helps and supports you, especially when other people are against you: *the Prime Minister's political allies*

⚷ **ally**[2] /əˈlaɪ/ *verb* [T] (allying; allies; *pt, pp* allied) ally (yourself) with sb/sth to give your support to another group or country: *The prince allied himself with the Scots.*

almighty /ɔːlˈmaɪti/ *adj* **1** having the power to do anything: *Almighty God* **2** [only *before* a noun] (*informal*) very great: *Suddenly we heard the most almighty crash.*

almond /ˈɑːmənd/ *noun* [C] a flat pale nut ➲ picture at **nut**

⚷ **almost** /ˈɔːlməʊst/ *adv* nearly; not quite: *By 9 o'clock almost everybody had arrived.* ◆ *Careful! I almost fell into the water then!* ◆ *The film has almost finished.* ◆ *She almost always cycles to school.*

A

◆ *There's almost nothing left.* ◆ *Almost all the students passed the exam.* SYN **nearly**

🔑 **alone** /ə'ləʊn/ *adj* [not before a noun] *adv* **1** without any other person: *The old man lives alone.* ◆ *Are you alone? Can I speak to you for a moment?* ◆ *I don't like walking home alone after dark.* **2** [after a noun or pronoun] only: *You alone can help us.* **3** [after a noun or pronoun] used to emphasize one particular thing: *The rent alone takes up most of my salary.*

IDM **go it alone** to start working on your own without the usual help

leave sb/sth alone ➲ **leave**[1]

let alone and certainly not: *We haven't decided where we're going yet, let alone booked the tickets.*

> OTHER WORDS FOR
>
> **alone**
>
> Alone and **lonely** both mean that you are not with other people. **Lonely** (*AmE* **lonesome**) means that you are unhappy about this, but **alone** does not usually suggest either happiness or unhappiness. **Alone** cannot be used before a noun. You can also use **on your own** and **by yourself** to mean 'alone'. These expressions are more informal and very common in spoken English.

🔑 **along** /ə'lɒŋ/ *prep, adv* **1** from one end to or towards the other end of sth: *I walked slowly along the road.* ◆ *David looked along the corridor to see if anyone was coming.* **2** on or beside sth long: *Wild flowers grew along both sides of the river.* ◆ *Our house is about halfway along the street.* **3** forward: *We moved along slowly with the crowd.* **4** (*informal*) with sb: *We're going for a walk. Why don't you* **come along** *too?*

IDM **all along** ➲ **all**[2]

along with sb/sth together with sb/sth

go along with sb/sth to agree with sb's ideas or plans

🔑 **alongside** /əˌlɒŋ'saɪd/ *prep, adv* **1** next to sb/sth or at the side of sth: *The boat moored alongside the quay.* ◆ *Nick caught up with me and rode alongside.* **2** together with sb/sth: *the opportunity to work alongside experienced musicians*

aloof /ə'lu:f/ *adj* not friendly or interested in other people: *Her shyness made her seem aloof.* SYN **distant**

🔑 **aloud** /ə'laʊd/ (also ˌ**out** '**loud**) *adv* in a normal speaking voice that other people can hear: *to read aloud from a book* OPP **silently**

🔑 **alphabet** /'ælfəbet/ *noun* [C] a set of letters in a fixed order that you use when you are writing a language: *There are 26 letters in the English alphabet.*

🔑 **alphabetical** /ˌælfə'betɪkl/ *adj* arranged in the same order as the letters of the alphabet: *The names are listed* **in alphabetical order.** ▶ **alphabetically** /-kli/ *adv*: *arranged/stored alphabetically*

alpine /'ælpaɪn/ *adj* of or found in high mountains: *alpine flowers*

🔑 **already** /ɔ:l'redi/ *adv* **1** used for talking about sth that has happened before now or before a particular time in the past: *'Would you like some lunch?' 'No, I've already eaten, thanks.'* ◆ *We got there at 6.30 but Marsha had already left.* ◆ *Sita was already awake when I went into her room.* **2** (used in negative sentences and questions for expressing surprise) so early; as soon as this: *Have you finished already?* ◆ *Surely you're not going already!*

alright /ɔ:l'raɪt/ (*informal*) = **all right**

🔑 **also** /'ɔ:lsəʊ/ *adv* [not with negative verbs] in addition; too: *He plays several instruments and also writes music.* ◆ *Bring summer clothing and also something warm to wear in the evenings.* ◆ *The food is wonderful, and also very cheap.*

IDM **not only ... (but) also** ➲ **not**

> OTHER WORDS FOR
>
> **also**
>
> Too and **as well** are less formal than **also** and are very common in spoken English. **Also** usually goes before a main verb or after 'is', 'are', 'were', etc: *He also enjoys reading.* ◆ *He has also been to Australia.* ◆ *He is also intelligent.* **Too** and **as well** usually go at the end of a phrase or sentence: *I really love this song, and I liked the first one too/as well.*

altar /'ɔ:ltə(r)/ *noun* [C] a high table that is the centre of a religious ceremony

🔑 **alter** /'ɔ:ltə(r)/ *verb* [I,T] to make sth different in some way, but without changing it completely; to become different: *We've altered our plan, and will now arrive at 7.00 instead of 8.00.* ◆ *The village seems to have altered very little in the last twenty years.*

alteration /ˌɔ:ltə'reɪʃn/ *noun* [C,U] (an) alteration (to/in sth) a small change in sb/sth: *We want to* **make** *a few* **alterations** *to the house before we move in.*

alternate[1] /'ɔ:ltəneɪt/ *verb* **1** [T] alternate A with B to cause two types of events or things to happen or follow regularly one after the other: *He alternated periods of work with periods of rest.* **2** [I] alternate with sth; alternate between A and B (used about two types of events, things, etc.) to happen or follow regularly one after the other: *Busy periods in the hospital alternate with times when there is not much to do.* ◆ *She seemed to alternate between hating him and loving him.* ▶ **alternation** /ˌɔ:ltə'neɪʃn/ *noun* [C,U]

alternate[2] /ɔ:l'tɜ:nət/ *adj* **1** (used about two types of events, things, etc.) happening or following regularly one after the other: *There will be alternate periods of sun and showers tomorrow.* **2** one of every two: *He works alternate weeks* (= he works the first week, he doesn't work the second week, he works again the third week, etc.). ▶ **alternately** *adv*: *The bricks were painted alternately white and red.*

🔑 **alternative**[1] /ɔ:l'tɜ:nətɪv/ *noun* [C] an alternative (to sth) one of two or more things that you can choose between: *What can I eat as an alternative to meat?* ◆ *There are several alternatives open to us at the moment.*

A

alternative² /ɔːlˈtɜːnətɪv/ *adj* [only *before* a noun] **1** that you can use, do, etc. instead of sth else: *The motorway was closed so we had to find an alternative route.* **2** different to what is usual or traditional: *alternative medicine* ▶ **alternatively** *adv*

although /ɔːlˈðəʊ/ *conj* **1** in spite of the fact that: *Although she was tired, she stayed up late watching TV.* ➲ note at **despite** **2** and yet; but: *I love dogs, although I wouldn't have one as a pet.* SYN for both meanings **though**

HELP **Though** and **although** are the same, but at the end of a sentence it is only possible to use **though**: *She knew all her friends would be at the party. She didn't want to go, though.* **Even though** can be used for emphasis: *She didn't want to go, although/though/even though she knew all her friends would be there.*

altitude /ˈæltɪtjuːd/ *noun* **1** [sing] the height of sth above sea level: *The plane climbed to an altitude of 10 000 metres.* **2** [C, usually pl] a place that is high above sea level: *You need to carry oxygen when you are climbing at high altitudes.*

alto /ˈæltəʊ/ *noun* [C] (*pl* **altos**) the lowest normal singing voice for a woman, the highest for a man; a woman or man with this voice

altogether /ˌɔːltəˈgeðə(r)/ *adv* **1** completely: *I don't altogether agree with you.* ♦ *At the age of 55 he stopped working altogether.* ♦ *This time the situation is altogether different.* **2** including everything; in total: *How much money will I need altogether?* ♦ *Altogether there were six of us.* **3** when you consider everything; generally: *Altogether, this town is a pleasant place to live.*

HELP **Altogether** or **all together**? **All together** means 'everything or everybody together': *Put your books all together on the table.* ♦ *Let's sing. All together now!*

altruistic /ˌæltruˈɪstɪk/ *adj* (*formal*) caring about the needs and happiness of other people more than your own: *altruistic behaviour* ▶ **altruism** /ˈæltruɪzəm/ *noun* [U]

aluminium /ˌæljəˈmɪniəm; ˌælə-/ (*AmE* **aluminum** /əˈluːmɪnəm/) *noun* [U] (*symbol* **Al**) a light silver-coloured metal that is used for making cooking equipment, etc: *aluminium saucepans*

always /ˈɔːlweɪz/ *adv* **1** at all times; regularly: *I always get up at 6.30.* ♦ *Why is the train always late when I'm in a hurry?* **2** all through the past until now: *Tony has always been shy.* ♦ *I've always liked music.* **3** for ever: *I shall always remember this moment.* **4** [only used with continuous tenses] again and again, usually in an annoying way: *She's always complaining about something.* **5** used with 'can' or 'could' for suggesting sth that sb could do, especially if nothing else is possible: *If you haven't got enough money, I could always lend you some.*

GRAMMAR **Always** does not usually go at the beginning of a sentence. It usually goes before the main verb or after 'is', 'are', 'were', etc: *He always wears those shoes.* ♦ *I have always wanted to visit Egypt.* ♦ *Fiona is always late.* However, **always** can go at the beginning of a sentence when you are telling somebody to do something: *Always stop and look before you cross the road.*

Alzheimer's disease /ˈæltshaɪməz dɪziːz/ *noun* [sing] a disease that affects the brain and makes you become more and more confused as you get older

AM /ˌeɪ ˈem/ *abbr* **amplitude modulation**; one of the systems of sending out radio signals

a.m. (*AmE* **A.M.**) /ˌeɪ ˈem/ *abbr* (from Latin) **ante meridiem**; before midday: *10 a.m.* (= 10 o'clock in the morning) ➲ look at **p.m.**

am /əm; *strong form* æm/ ➲ **be**

amalgamate /əˈmælgəmeɪt/ *verb* [I,T] (used especially about organizations, groups, etc.) to join together to form a single organization, group, etc. SYN **merge** ▶ **amalgamation** /əˌmælgəˈmeɪʃn/ *noun* [C,U]

amass /əˈmæs/ *verb* [T] to collect or put together a large quantity of sth: *We've amassed a lot of information on the subject.*

amateur¹ /ˈæmətə(r)/ *noun* [C] **1** a person who takes part in a sport or an activity for pleasure, not for money as a job: *Only amateurs can take part in the tournament.* OPP **professional** **2** (usually used in a critical way) a person who does not have skill or experience when doing sth

amateur² /ˈæmətə(r)/ *adj* **1** done, or doing sth, for pleasure (not for money as a job): *an amateur production of a play* ♦ *an amateur photographer* OPP **professional** **2** (also **amateurish** /-rɪʃ/) done without skill or experience: *The painting was an amateurish fake.*

amaze /əˈmeɪz/ *verb* [T] to surprise sb very much; to be difficult for sb to believe: *Sometimes your behaviour amazes me!* ♦ *It amazes me that anyone could be so stupid!*

amazed /əˈmeɪzd/ *adj* **amazed (at/by sb/sth); amazed (to do sth/that ...)** very surprised: *I was amazed by the change in his attitude.* ♦ *She was amazed to discover the truth about her husband.*

amazement /əˈmeɪzmənt/ *noun* [U] a feeling of great surprise: *He looked at me **in amazement**.* ♦ *To my **amazement**, he remembered me.*

amazing /əˈmeɪzɪŋ/ *adj* very surprising and difficult to believe: *She has shown amazing courage.* ♦ *I've got an amazing story to tell you.* SYN **incredible** ▶ **amazingly** *adv* ➲ note at **sudden**

ambassador /æmˈbæsədə(r)/ *noun* [C] an important person who represents their country in a foreign country: *the Spanish Ambassador to Britain* ➲ look at **consul**

MORE An ambassador lives and works in an **embassy**.

A

amber /ˈæmbə(r)/ *noun* [U] **1** a hard clear yellowish-brown substance used for making jewellery or objects for decoration **2** a yellowish-brown colour: *The three colours in traffic lights are red, amber and green.* ▶ **amber** *adj*

ambidextrous /ˌæmbiˈdekstrəs/ *adj* able to use the left hand and the right hand equally well

ambiguity /ˌæmbɪˈgjuːəti/ *noun* [C,U] (*pl* **ambiguities**) the possibility of being understood in more than one way; something that can be understood in more than one way

ambiguous /æmˈbɪgjuəs/ *adj* having more than one possible meaning: *That's a rather ambiguous remark—what exactly do you mean?* ▶ **ambiguously** *adv*

🔑 **ambition** /æmˈbɪʃn/ *noun* **1** [C] **ambition (to do/be sth); ambition (of doing sth)** something that you want to do or achieve very much: *It has always been her ambition to travel the world.* ◆ *He finally* ***achieved*** *his* ***ambition*** *of becoming a doctor.* **2** [U] a strong desire to be successful, to have power, etc: *One problem of young people today is their lack of ambition.*

ambitious /æmˈbɪʃəs/ *adj* **1 ambitious (to be/do sth)** having a strong desire to be successful, to have power, etc: *I'm not particularly ambitious—I'm content with my life the way it is.* ◆ *We are ambitious to succeed.* **2** difficult to achieve or do because it takes a lot of work or effort: *The company have announced ambitious plans for expansion.*

ambivalent /æmˈbɪvələnt/ *adj* having or showing a mixture of feelings or opinions about sth or sb ▶ **ambivalence** *noun* [C,U]

amble /ˈæmbl/ *verb* [I] to walk at a slow relaxed speed: *We ambled down to the beach.* **SYN** **stroll**

🔑 **ambulance** /ˈæmbjələns/ *noun* [C] a special vehicle for taking ill or injured people to and from hospital: *the ambulance service* ◆ *Call an ambulance!* ➲ note at **hospital**

ambush /ˈæmbʊʃ/ *noun* [C,U] a surprise attack from a hidden position: *He was killed in an enemy ambush.* ◆ *The robbers were waiting* ***in ambush***. ▶ **ambush** *verb* [T]

ameba (*AmE*) = **amoeba**

amen /ɑːˈmen; eɪˈmen/ *exclam* a word used at the end of prayers by Christians and Jews

amenable /əˈmiːnəbl/ *adj* happy to accept sth: *I'm amenable to any suggestions you may have.*

amend /əˈmend/ *verb* [T] to change sth slightly in order to make it better

amendment /əˈmendmənt/ *noun* **1** [C] a part that is added or a small change that is made to a piece of writing, especially to a law **2** [U] an act of **amending** sth

amends /əˈmendz/ *noun*

IDM **make amends** to do sth for sb, that shows that you are sorry for sth bad that you have done before

amenity /əˈmiːnəti/ *noun* [C] (*pl* **amenities**) something that makes a place pleasant or easy to live in: *Among the town's amenities are two cinemas and a sports centre.*

American /əˈmerɪkən/ *adj* from or connected with the US: *Have you met Bob? He's American.* ◆ *an American accent* ▶ **American** *noun* [C]: *Millions of Americans visit Britain each year.*

Aˌmerican ˈfootball (*AmE* **football**) *noun* [U] a game that is played in the US by two teams of eleven players with a ball shaped like an egg. The players wear **helmets** (= hard hats) and other protective clothing and try to carry the ball to the end of the field. ➲ note at **football** ➲ picture at **football**

Aˌmerican ˈIndian = **Native American**

amethyst /ˈæməθɪst/ *noun* [C,U] a purple stone, used in making jewellery: *an amethyst ring*

amiable /ˈeɪmiəbl/ *adj* friendly and pleasant ▶ **amiably** /-əbli/ *adv*

amicable /ˈæmɪkəbl/ *adj* made or done in a friendly way, without argument ▶ **amicably** /-əbli/ *adv*

amid /əˈmɪd/ (also **amidst** /əˈmɪdst/) *prep* (*written*) in the middle of; among

amiss /əˈmɪs/ *adj* [not before a noun] *adv* wrong; not as it should be: *When I walked into the room I could sense that something was amiss.*

IDM **not come/go amiss** to be useful or pleasant: *Things are fine, although a bit more money wouldn't come amiss.*

take sth amiss to be upset by sth, perhaps because you have understood it in the wrong way: *Please don't take my remarks amiss.*

ammonia /əˈməʊniə/ *noun* [U] (*symbol* NH_3) a gas with a strong smell; a clear liquid containing **ammonia** used for cleaning

ammunition /ˌæmjuˈnɪʃn/ *noun* [U] **1** the supply of bullets, etc. that you need to fire from a weapon: *The troops surrendered because they had run out of ammunition.* **2** facts or information that can be used against sb/sth

amnesia /æmˈniːziə/ *noun* [U] loss of memory

amnesty /ˈæmnəsti/ *noun* [C] (*pl* **amnesties**) **1** a time when a government forgives political crimes: *The government has announced an amnesty for all political prisoners.* **2** a time when people can give in illegal weapons without being arrested

amoeba (*AmE* also **ameba**) /əˈmiːbə/ *noun* [C] (*pl* **amoebas** *or* **amoebae** /-biː/) a very small living creature that consists of only one cell

amok /əˈmɒk/ *adv*

IDM **run amok** to suddenly become very angry or excited and start behaving violently, especially in a public place **SYN** **run riot**

🔑 **among** /əˈmʌŋ/ (also **amongst** /əˈmʌŋst/) *prep* **1** surrounded by; in the middle of: *I often feel nervous when I'm among strangers.* ◆ *I found the missing letter amongst a heap of old newspapers.* ➲ note at **between** ➲ picture at **between** **2** in or concerning a particular group of people or things: *Discuss it*

A

amongst yourselves and let me know your decision. ♦ *There is a lot of anger among students about the new law.* ♦ ***Among other things***, *the drug can cause headaches and sweating.* **3** to each one (of a group): *On his death, his money will be divided among his children.*

amoral /ˌeɪˈmɒrəl/ *adj* (used about people or their behaviour) not following any moral rules; not caring about right or wrong ➲ look at **moral, immoral**

amorous /ˈæmərəs/ *adj* showing sexual desire and love towards sb: *She rejected his amorous advances.* ▸ **amorously** *adv*

amount¹ /əˈmaʊnt/ *noun* [C] **1** total or sum of money: *You are requested to pay the full amount within seven days.* **2** the amount of sth is how much of it there is; quantity: *I spent an enormous amount of time preparing for the exam.* ♦ *I have a certain amount of sympathy with her.* ♦ *a large amount of money*

amount² /əˈmaʊnt/ *verb* [I] amount to sth **1** to add up to; to total: *The cost of the repairs amounted to £5000.* **2** to be the same as: *Whether I tell her today or tomorrow, it amounts to the same thing.*

amp /æmp/ *noun* [C] **1** (also *formal* ampere /ˈæmpeə(r)/) a measure of electric current **2** (*informal*) = **amplifier**

amphetamine /æmˈfetəmiːn/ *noun* [C,U] a drug, sometimes taken illegally, that makes you feel excited and full of energy

amphibian /æmˈfɪbiən/ *noun* [C] an animal with cold blood that can live on land and in water: *Frogs, toads and newts are all amphibians.* ➲ look at **reptile** ➲ picture on **page P13**

amphibious /æmˈfɪbiəs/ *adj* able to live or be used both on land and in water: *Frogs are amphibious.* ♦ *amphibious vehicles*

amphitheatre (*AmE* amphitheater) /ˈæmfɪθɪətə(r)/ *noun* [C] a round building without a roof and with rows of seats that rise in steps around an open space. **Amphitheatres** were used in ancient Greece and Rome for public entertainment.

ample /ˈæmpl/ *adj* **1** enough or more than enough: *We've got ample time to make a decision.* ♦ *I'm not sure how much the trip will cost, but I should think £1 000 will be ample.* **2** large: *There is space for an ample car park.* ▸ **amply** /ˈæmpli/ *adv*

amplifier /ˈæmplɪfaɪə(r)/ (also *informal* amp) *noun* [C] a piece of electrical equipment for making sounds louder or signals stronger ➲ picture at **music**

amplify /ˈæmplɪfaɪ/ *verb* [T] (amplifying; amplifies; *pt, pp* amplified) **1** to increase the strength of a sound, using electrical equipment **2** to add details to sth in order to explain it more fully ▸ **amplification** /ˌæmplɪfɪˈkeɪʃn/ *noun* [U]

amputate /ˈæmpjuteɪt/ *verb* [I,T] to cut off sb's arm, leg, etc. for medical reasons: *His leg was so badly injured that it had to be amputated from the knee down.* ▸ **amputation** /ˌæmpjuˈteɪʃn/ *noun* [C,U]

amuse /əˈmjuːz/ *verb* [T] **1** to make sb laugh or smile; to seem funny to sb: *Everybody laughed but I couldn't understand what had amused them.* **2** to make time pass pleasantly for sb; to stop sb from getting bored: *I did some crosswords to amuse myself on the journey.* ♦ *I've brought a few toys to amuse the children.*

amused /əˈmjuːzd/ *adj* thinking that sth is funny and wanting to laugh or smile: *I was amused to hear his account of what happened.*

IDM keep sb/yourself amused to do sth in order to pass time pleasantly and stop sb/yourself getting bored

amusement /əˈmjuːzmənt/ *noun* **1** [U] the feeling caused by sth that makes you laugh or smile, or by sth that entertains you: *Much to the pupils' amusement, the teacher fell off his chair.* **2** [C] something that makes time pass pleasantly; an entertainment: *The holiday centre offers a wide range of amusements, including golf and tennis.*

aˈmusement arcade = **arcade**(2)

aˈmusement park *noun* [C] a large park which has a lot of things that you can ride and play on and many different activities to enjoy

amusing /əˈmjuːzɪŋ/ *adj* causing you to laugh or smile: *He's a very amusing person and he makes me laugh a lot.* ♦ *The story was quite amusing.* ➲ note at **humour**

an ➲ **a**

anaemia (*AmE* anemia) /əˈniːmiə/ *noun* [U] a medical condition in which there are not enough red cells in the blood ▸ **anaemic** (*AmE* anemic) *adj*

anaesthetic (*AmE* anesthetic) /ˌænəsˈθetɪk/ *noun* [C,U] a substance that stops you feeling pain, for example when a doctor is performing a medical operation on you: *The dentist gave me a* ***local anaesthetic*** (= one that only affects part of the body and does not make you unconscious). ♦ *You'll need to be* ***under anaesthetic*** *for the operation.* ♦ *Did you have a* ***general anaesthetic*** (= one that makes you unconscious) *for your operation?*

anaesthetist (*AmE* anesthetist) /əˈniːsθətɪst/ *noun* [C] a person with the medical training necessary to give **anaesthetics** to patients

anaesthetize (also -ise; *AmE* anesthetize) /əˈniːsθətaɪz/ *verb* [T] to give an **anaesthetic** to sb

anagram /ˈænəɡræm/ *noun* [C] a word or phrase that is made by arranging the letters of another word or phrase in a different order: *'Worth' is an anagram of 'throw'.*

analogous /əˈnæləɡəs/ *adj* (*formal*) analogous (to/with sth) similar in some way; that you can compare

analogue (*AmE* analog) /ˈænəlɒɡ/ *adj* **1** (used about an electronic process) using a continuously changing range of physical quantities to measure or store data: *an* ***analogue circuit/computer/signal*** **2** (*BrE also* analog) (used about a clock or watch) showing the time using hands on a **dial** (= the round part) and not with a display of numbers ➲ look at **digital**

analogy /əˈnælədʒi/ *noun* [C] (*pl* **analogies**) **an analogy (between A and B)** a comparison between two things that shows a way in which they are similar: *You could make an analogy between the human body and a car engine.*
IDM **by analogy** by comparing sth to sth else and showing how they are similar

analyse (*AmE* **analyze**) /ˈænəlaɪz/ *verb* [T] to look at or think about the different parts or details of sth carefully in order to understand or explain it: *The water samples are now being analysed in a laboratory.* ◆ *to analyse statistics* ◆ *She analysed the situation and then decided what to do.*

analysis /əˈnæləsɪs/ *noun* (*pl* **analyses** /-siːz/) **1** [C,U] the careful examination of the different parts or details of sth: *Some samples of the water were sent to a laboratory* ***for analysis***. **2** [C] the result of a careful examination of sth: *Your analysis of the situation is different from mine.* **3** [U] = **psychoanalysis**

analyst /ˈænəlɪst/ *noun* [C] a person whose job is to examine sth carefully as an expert: *a food analyst* ◆ *a political analyst*

analytical /ˌænəˈlɪtɪkl/ (also **analytic** /ˌænəˈlɪtɪk/) *adj* using careful examination in order to understand or explain sth

analyze (*AmE*) = **analyse**

anarchic /əˈnɑːkɪk/ *adj* without rules or laws

anarchism /ˈænəkɪzəm/ *noun* [U] the political belief that there should be no government or laws in a country ▶ **anarchist** /-ɪst/ *noun* [C]

anarchy /ˈænəki/ *noun* [U] a situation in which people do not obey rules and laws; a situation in which there is no government in a country: *While the civil war went on, the country was in a state of anarchy.*

anatomy /əˈnætəmi/ *noun* (*pl* **anatomies**) **1** [U] the scientific study of the structure of human or animal bodies **2** [C] the structure of a living thing: *the anatomy of the frog* ▶ **anatomical** /ˌænəˈtɒmɪkl/ *adj*

ancestor /ˈænsestə(r)/ *noun* [C] a person in your family who lived a long time before you: *My ancestors settled in this country a hundred years ago.* ➲ look at **descendant** ▶ **ancestral** /ænˈsestrəl/ *adj*: *her ancestral home* (= that has belonged to her family for many years)

ancestry /ˈænsestri/ *noun* [U,C, usually sing] (*pl* **ancestries**) all of sb's **ancestors**: *He is* ***of*** *Scottish ancestry.*

anchor[1] /ˈæŋkə(r)/ *noun* [C,U] a heavy metal object at the end of a chain that you drop into the water from a boat in order to stop the boat moving

anchor[2] /ˈæŋkə(r)/ *verb* **1** [I,T] to drop an **anchor**; to stop a boat moving by using an **anchor** **2** [T] to fix sth firmly so that it cannot move

anchovy /ˈæntʃəvi/ *noun* [C,U] (*pl* **anchovies**) a small fish that has a strong taste of salt

ancient /ˈeɪnʃənt/ *adj* **1** belonging to a period of history that is thousands of years in the past: *ancient civilizations* ◆ *an ancient tradition* OPP **modern** **2** very old: *I can't believe he's only 30—he looks ancient!*

and /ənd; ən; *strong form* ænd/ *conj* **1** (used to connect words or parts of sentences) also; in addition to: *a boy and a girl* ◆ *Do it slowly and carefully.* ◆ *We were singing and dancing all evening.* ◆ *Come in and sit down.*

> **HELP** When the two things are closely linked, you do not need to repeat the 'a', etc: *a knife and fork* ◆ *my father and mother*

2 (used when you are saying numbers in sums) in addition to: *Twelve and six is eighteen.* SYN **plus**

> **HELP** When you are saying large numbers *and* is used after the word 'hundred': *We say 2264 as two thousand, two hundred and sixty-four.*

3 used instead of 'to' after certain verbs, for example 'go', 'come', 'try': *Go and answer the door for me, will you?* ◆ *Why don't you come and stay with us one weekend?* ◆ *I'll try and find out what's going on.* **4** used between repeated words to show that sth is increasing or continuing: *The situation is getting worse and worse.* ◆ *I shouted and shouted but nobody answered.*

anecdote /ˈænɪkdəʊt/ *noun* [C] a short interesting story about a real person or event

anemia (*AmE*) = **anaemia**

anesthetic (*AmE*) = **anaesthetic**

anesthetist (*AmE*) = **anaesthetist**

anesthetize (*AmE*) = **anaesthetize**

anew /əˈnjuː/ *adv* (*written*) again; in a new or different way: *I wish I could start my life anew!*

angel /ˈeɪndʒl/ *noun* [C] **1** a spirit who is believed to carry messages from God. In pictures **angels** are often dressed in white, with wings. **2** a person who is very kind

angelic /ænˈdʒelɪk/ *adj* looking or acting like an **angel** ▶ **angelically** /-kli/ *adv*

anger[1] /ˈæŋɡə(r)/ *noun* [U] the strong feeling that you have when sth has happened or sb has done sth that you do not like: *He could not hide his anger at the news.* ◆ *She was shaking with anger.*

anger[2] /ˈæŋɡə(r)/ *verb* [T] to make sb become angry

angle[1] /ˈæŋɡl/ *noun* [C] **1** the space between two lines or surfaces that meet, measured in degrees: *a* ***right angle*** (= an angle of 90°) ◆ *at an angle of 40°* ◆ *The three angles of a triangle add up to 180°.* ➲ picture on **page 26** **2** the direction from which you look at sth: *Viewed from this angle, the building looks bigger than it really is.*
IDM **at an angle** not straight

angle[2] /ˈæŋɡl/ *verb* [T] **1** to put sth in a position that is not straight: *Angle the lamp towards the desk.* **2 angle sth (at/to/towards sb)** to show sth from a particular point of view; to aim sth at a particular

A

angles

a right angle   an angle of 45°

person or group: *The new magazine is angled at younger viewers.*

PHR V **angle for sth** to try to make sb give you sth, without asking for it in a direct way: *She was angling for an invitation to our party.*

angler /ˈæŋglə(r)/ *noun* [C] a person who catches fish as a hobby ➲ look at **fisherman**

Anglican /ˈæŋglɪkən/ *noun* [C] a member of the Church of England or of a related church in another English-speaking country ▶ **Anglican** *adj*

angling /ˈæŋglɪŋ/ *noun* [U] fishing as a sport or hobby: *He **goes angling** at weekends.* ➲ look at **fishing**

Anglo- /ˈæŋgləʊ/ [in compounds] connected with England or Britain (and another country or countries): *Anglo-American relations*

Anglo-Saxon /ˌæŋgləʊ ˈsæksn/ *noun* **1** [C] a person whose family originally came from England **2** [C] a person who lived in England before the Norman Conquest (= the year 1066 when people originally from northern Europe defeated the English and then ruled the country) **3** (also ˌ**Old ˈEnglish**) [U] the English language before about 1150 ▶ ˌ**Anglo-ˈSaxon** *adj*

⚷ **angry** /ˈæŋgri/ *adj* (**angrier; angriest**) **angry (with sb) (at/about sth)** feeling or showing anger: *Calm down, there's no need to get angry.* ◆ *My parents will be angry with me if I get home late.* ◆ *He's always getting angry about something.* ▶ **angrily** *adv*

angst /æŋst/ *noun* [U] a feeling of worry about a situation, or about your life: *teenage angst*

anguish /ˈæŋgwɪʃ/ *noun* [U] (*written*) great mental pain or suffering ▶ **anguished** *adj*

angular /ˈæŋgjələ(r)/ *adj* with sharp points or corners

⚷ **animal** /ˈænɪml/ *noun* [C] a living creature that can move and feel: *the animal kingdom* ◆ *Humans are social animals.* ◆ *farm animals* ◆ *He studied the animals and birds of Southern Africa.* ➲ picture on page P12

HELP **Animal** is sometimes used to talk about only mammals.

animate /ˈænɪmət/ *adj* (*formal*) living; having life: *animate beings* **OPP** **inanimate**

animated /ˈænɪmeɪtɪd/ *adj* **1** interesting and full of energy: *an animated discussion* **2** (used about films) using a process or method which makes pictures or models appear to move: *an animated cartoon*

animation /ˌænɪˈmeɪʃn/ *noun* [U] **1** the state of being full of energy and enthusiasm **2** the method of making films, computer games, etc. with pictures or models that appear to move: *computer animation*

animosity /ˌænɪˈmɒsəti/ *noun* [C,U] (*pl* **animosities**) **animosity (toward(s) sb/sth); animosity (between A and B)** a strong feeling of disagreement, anger or hatred **SYN** **hostility**

⚷ **ankle** /ˈæŋkl/ *noun* [C] the part of your body where your foot joins your leg: *The water only came up to my ankles.* ➲ picture at **body**

annex /əˈneks/ *verb* [T] to take control of another country or region by force ▶ **annexation** /ˌænekˈseɪʃn/ *noun* [C,U]

annexe (*especially AmE* **annex**) /ˈæneks/ *noun* [C] a building that is joined to a larger one

annihilate /əˈnaɪəleɪt/ *verb* [T] to destroy or defeat sb/sth completely ▶ **annihilation** /əˌnaɪəˈleɪʃn/ *noun* [U]

⚷ **anniversary** /ˌænɪˈvɜːsəri/ *noun* [C] (*pl* **anniversaries**) a day that is exactly a year or a number of years after a special or an important event: *the hundredth anniversary of the country's independence* ◆ *a wedding anniversary* ➲ note at **birthday, jubilee**

annotated /ˈænəteɪtɪd/ *adj* (used about a book, etc.) with notes added to it that explain and give extra information about the contents

⚷ **announce** /əˈnaʊns/ *verb* [T] **1** to make sth known publicly and officially: *They announced that our train had been delayed.* ◆ *The winners will be announced in next week's paper.* **2** to say sth in a firm or serious way: *She stormed into my office and announced that she was leaving.*

announcement /əˈnaʊnsmənt/ *noun* **1** [C] a statement that tells people about sth: *Ladies and gentlemen, I'd like to **make an announcement**.* **2** [U] the act of telling people about sth

announcer /əˈnaʊnsə(r)/ *noun* [C] a person who introduces or gives information about programmes on radio or TV

⚷ **annoy** /əˈnɔɪ/ *verb* [T] to make sb angry or slightly angry: *It really annoys me when you act so selfishly.* ◆ *Close the door if the noise is annoying you.* **SYN** **irritate**

annoyance /əˈnɔɪəns/ *noun* **1** [U] the feeling of being annoyed **2** [C] something that annoys sb

⚷ **annoyed** /əˈnɔɪd/ *adj* **annoyed (with sb) (at/about sth); annoyed that ...** slightly angry: *I shall be extremely annoyed if he turns up late again.* ◆ *She's annoyed with herself for making such a stupid mistake.* ◆ *He's annoyed that nobody believes him.* ◆ *He got annoyed with me for being late.* **SYN** **irritated**

⚷ **annoying** /əˈnɔɪɪŋ/ *adj* making you feel angry or slightly angry: *It's so annoying that I can't come with you!* ◆ *His most annoying habit is always arriving late.*

A

annual[1] /ˈænjuəl/ *adj* **1** happening or done once a year or every year: *the company's annual report* ◆ *an annual festival* **2** for the period of one year: *What's the average annual salary for a nurse?* ◆ *the annual sales figures* ▶ **annually** /-juəli/ *adv*

annual[2] /ˈænjuəl/ *noun* [C] a book, especially one for children, that is published once each year: *the 2013 Football Annual*

annul /əˈnʌl/ *verb* [T] (annulling; annulled) to state officially that sth is no longer legally valid: *Their marriage was annulled after just six months.* ▶ **annulment** *noun* [C,U]

anomalous /əˈnɒmələs/ *adj* (*formal*) different from what is normal: *In a few anomalous cases, these drugs have made people ill.*

anomaly /əˈnɒməli/ *noun* [C] (*pl* anomalies) something that is different from what is normal or usual: *We discovered an anomaly in the sales figures for August.*

anon /əˈnɒn/ *abbr* **anonymous**; used to show that we do not know who did a piece of writing

anonymity /ˌænəˈnɪməti/ *noun* [U] the situation where sb's name is not known

anonymous /əˈnɒnɪməs/ *adj* **1** (used about a person) whose name is not known or made public: *An anonymous caller told the police that a robbery was going to take place.* **2** done, written, etc. by sb whose name is not known or made public: *He received an anonymous letter.* ▶ **anonymously** *adv*

anorak /ˈænəræk/ *noun* [C] (*BrE*) **1** a short coat with a covering for your head that protects you from rain, wind and cold **2** (*slang*) a person who enjoys learning boring facts: *He's a real anorak—he can name every player in the World Cup.*

anorexia /ˌænəˈreksiə/ (also anorexia nervosa /ˌænəˌreksiə nɜːˈvəʊsə/) *noun* [U] an illness, especially affecting young women, that makes them so afraid of being fat that they do not eat ➲ look at **bulimia** ▶ **anorexic** *adj, noun* [C]

another /əˈnʌðə(r)/ *determiner, pron* **1** one more person or thing of the same kind: *Would you like another drink?* ◆ *They've got three children already and they're having another.* **2** a different thing or person: *I'm afraid I can't see you tomorrow. Could we arrange another day?* ◆ *If you've already seen that film, we can go and see another.*
IDM **another/a different matter** ➲ **matter**[1]
one after another/the other ➲ **one**[1]
yet another ➲ **yet**

answer[1] /ˈɑːnsə(r)/ *noun* [C] an answer (to sb/sth) **1** something that you say, write or do as a reply: *The answer to your question is that I don't know.* ◆ *They've made me an offer and I have to* ***give*** *them* ***an answer*** *by Friday.* ◆ *I wrote to them two weeks ago and I'm still waiting for an answer.* ◆ *I knocked on the door and waited but there was no answer.* SYN **reply** **2** a solution to a problem: *I didn't have any money so the only answer was to borrow some.* **3** the correct reply to a question in a test or exam: *What was the answer to question 4?* **4** a reply to a question in a test or exam: *My answer to question 5 was wrong.* ◆ *How many answers did you get right?*
IDM **in answer (to sth)** as a reply (to sth)

answer[2] /ˈɑːnsə(r)/ *verb* [I,T] **1** to say or write sth back to sb who has asked you sth or written to you: *I asked her what the matter was but she didn't answer.* ◆ *I've asked you a question, now please answer me.* ◆ *Answer all the questions on the form.* ◆ *He hasn't answered my email yet* (= written an email back to me). ◆ *When I asked him how much he earned, he answered that it was none of my business.* ◆ *'No!' he answered angrily.* **2** to do sth as a reply: *to* ***answer the phone*** (= to pick up the phone when it rings) ◆ *I rang their doorbell but nobody answered.*
PHR V **answer back** to defend yourself against sth bad that has been written or said about you
answer (sb) back to reply rudely to sb
answer for sb/sth **1** to accept responsibility for sth/sb: *Somebody will have to answer for all the damage that has been caused.* **2** to speak in support of sb/sth: *I can certainly answer for her honesty.*

> OTHER WORDS FOR
>
> **answer**
>
> **Answer** and **reply** are the most common verbs used for speaking or writing in reaction to questions, letters, etc: *I asked him a question but he didn't answer.* ◆ *I sent my application but they haven't replied yet.* Note that you **answer** a person, a question, an email or a letter (no 'to') but you **reply to** an email or a letter. **Respond** is less common and more formal with this meaning: *Applicants must respond within seven days.* It is more commonly used with the meaning of 'reacting in a way that is desired': *Despite all the doctor's efforts the patient did not respond to treatment.*

answerable /ˈɑːnsərəbl/ *adj* [not before a noun] answerable to sb (for sth) having to explain and give good reasons for your actions to sb; responsible to sb

ˈ**answering machine** (*BrE also* answerphone /ˈɑːnsəfəʊn/) *noun* [C] a machine that answers the telephone and records messages from the people who call: *I rang him and left a message on his answering machine.*

ant /ænt/ *noun* [C] a very small insect that lives in large groups and works very hard ➲ picture on page P13

antagonism /ænˈtæɡənɪzəm/ *noun* [C,U] antagonism (towards sb/sth); antagonism (between A and B) a feeling of hate and of being against sb/sth ▶ **antagonistic** /ænˌtæɡəˈnɪstɪk/ *adj*

antagonize (also -ise) /ænˈtæɡənaɪz/ *verb* [T] to make sb angry or to annoy sb

the Antarctic /ænˈtɑːktɪk/ *noun* [sing] the most southern part of the world ➲ look at **the Arctic** ➲ picture at **earth**

A

Antarctic /æn'tɑːktɪk/ *adj* [only *before* a noun] connected with the coldest, most southern parts of the world: *an Antarctic expedition* ➲ look at **Arctic**

antelope /'æntɪləʊp/ *noun* [C] (*pl* **antelope** or **antelopes**) an African animal with horns and long, thin legs that can run very fast

antelope

antenatal /ˌænti'neɪtl/ *adj* [only *before* a noun] connected with the care of pregnant women: *an antenatal clinic* ♦ *antenatal care*

antenna /æn'tenə/ *noun* [C] **1** (*pl* **antennae** /-niː/) one of the two long thin parts on the heads of insects and some animals that live in shells. **Antennae** are used for feeling things. SYN **feeler** ➲ picture on **page P13** **2** (*pl* **antennas**) (*AmE*) = **aerial**[1]

anthem /'ænθəm/ *noun* [C] a song, especially one that is sung on special occasions: *the national anthem* (= the special song of a country)

anthology /æn'θɒlədʒi/ *noun* [C] (*pl* **anthologies**) a book that contains pieces of writing or poems, often on the same subject, by different authors: *an anthology of love poetry*

anthrax /'ænθræks/ *noun* [U] a serious disease that affects sheep, cows and sometimes people, and can cause death

anthropology /ˌænθrə'pɒlədʒi/ *noun* [U] the study of humans, especially of their origin, development, customs and beliefs ▸ **anthropological** /ˌænθrəpə'lɒdʒɪkl/ *adj* ▸ **anthropologist** /ˌænθrə'pɒlədʒɪst/ *noun* [C]

⚷ **anti-** /'ænti/ [in compounds] **1** against: *anti-tank weapons* ➲ look at **pro-** **2** the opposite of: *anticlimax* **3** preventing: *antifreeze*

antibiotic /ˌæntibaɪ'ɒtɪk/ *noun* [C, usually pl] a medicine which is used for destroying bacteria and curing infections

antibody /'æntibɒdi/ *noun* [C] (*pl* **antibodies**) a substance that the body produces in the blood to fight disease, or as a reaction when certain substances are put into the body

⚷ **anticipate** /æn'tɪsɪpeɪt/ *verb* [T] to expect sth to happen and prepare for it: *to anticipate a problem* ♦ *I anticipate that the situation will get worse.*

anticipation /ænˌtɪsɪ'peɪʃn/ *noun* [U] **1** the state of expecting sth to happen (and preparing for it): *The government has reduced tax **in anticipation of** an early general election.* **2** excited feelings about sth that is going to happen: *happy/eager/excited anticipation*

anticlimax /ˌænti'klaɪmæks/ *noun* [C,U] an event, etc. that is less exciting than you had expected or than what has already happened: *When the exams were over, we all had a sense of anticlimax.*

anticlockwise /ˌænti'klɒkwaɪz/ (*AmE* **counterclockwise**) *adv, adj* in the opposite direction to the movement of the hands of a clock: *Turn the lid anticlockwise/in an anticlockwise direction.* OPP **clockwise**

antics /'æntɪks/ *noun* [pl] funny, strange or silly ways of behaving

antidepressant /ˌæntidɪ'presnt/ *noun* [C] a drug used to treat **depression** (= unhappiness that lasts for a long time)

antidote /'æntidəʊt/ *noun* [C] **1** a medical substance that is used to prevent a poison or a disease from having an effect: *an antidote to snake bites* **2** anything that helps you to deal with sth unpleasant

antifreeze /'æntifriːz/ *noun* [U] a chemical that you add to the water in cars, etc. to stop it from freezing

antipathy /æn'tɪpəθi/ *noun* [C,U, usually sing] (*pl* **antipathies**) (*formal*) **antipathy (to/towards sb/sth)** a strong feeling of not liking sb/sth SYN **dislike**

antiperspirant /ˌænti'pɜːspərənt/ *noun* [C,U] a substance that people use, especially under the arms, to prevent or reduce sweat

antiquated /'æntɪkweɪtɪd/ *adj* old-fashioned and not suitable for the modern world

antique /æn'tiːk/ *adj* very old and therefore unusual and valuable: *an antique vase/table* ♦ *antique furniture/jewellery* ▸ **antique** *noun* [C]: *an antique shop* (= one that sells antiques) ♦ *That vase is an antique.*

antiquity /æn'tɪkwəti/ *noun* (*pl* **antiquities**) **1** [U] the ancient past, especially the times of the ancient Greeks and Romans **2** [U] the state of being very old or ancient **3** [C, usually pl] a building or object from ancient times: *Greek/Roman antiquities*

anti-Semitism /ˌænti 'semətɪzəm/ *noun* [U] unfair treatment of Jewish people ▸ **anti-Semitic** /ˌænti sə'mɪtɪk/ *adj*

antiseptic /ˌænti'septɪk/ *noun* [C,U] a liquid or cream that prevents a cut, etc. from becoming infected: *Put an antiseptic/some antiseptic on that scratch.* SYN **disinfectant** ▸ **antiseptic** *adj*: *antiseptic cream*

antisocial /ˌænti'səʊʃl/ *adj* **1** harmful or annoying to other people: *antisocial behaviour* **2** not liking to be with other people

antithesis /æn'tɪθəsɪs/ *noun* [C, usually sing] (*pl* **antitheses** /æn'tɪθəsiːz/) (*formal*) **1** the opposite of sth: *Love is the antithesis of hate.* **2** a difference between two things

antivirus /'æntivaɪrəs/ *adj* (used of software) designed to find and destroy computer viruses ➲ note at **cybercrime**

antler /'æntlə(r)/ *noun* [C, usually pl] a horn shaped like a branch on the head of some adult male animals: *a pair of antlers* ➲ picture at **deer**, **elk**, **reindeer** ➲ picture on **page P12**

antonym /ˈæntənɪm/ *noun* [C] (*technical*) a word that means the opposite of another word **SYN** **opposite** ➲ look at **synonym**

anus /ˈeɪnəs/ *noun* [C] the hole through which solid waste substances leave the body

🔑 **anxiety** /æŋˈzaɪəti/ *noun* [C,U] (*pl* **anxieties**) a feeling of worry or fear, especially about the future: *a feeling/state of anxiety* ◆ *There are anxieties over the effects of unemployment.*

🔑 **anxious** /ˈæŋkʃəs/ *adj* **1 anxious (about/for sb/sth)** worried and afraid: *I'm anxious about my exam.* ◆ *I began to get anxious when they still hadn't arrived at 9 o'clock.* ◆ *an anxious look/expression* **2** causing worry and fear: *For a few anxious moments we thought we'd missed the train.* **3 anxious to do sth; anxious for sth** wanting sth very much: *Police are anxious to find the owner of the white car.* ▶ **anxiously** *adv*: *'Are you all right?' he asked anxiously.*

🔑 **any** /ˈeni/ *determiner, pron, adv* **1** used instead of *some* in negative sentences and in questions: *We didn't have any lunch.* ◆ *I speak hardly any* (= almost no) *Spanish.* ◆ *Do you have any questions?* ◆ *I don't like any of his books.* ➲ note at **some** **2** used for saying that it does not matter which thing or person you choose: *Take any book you want.* ◆ *Come round any time—I'm usually in.* ◆ *I'll take any that you don't want.* **3** [used in negative sentences and questions] at all; to any degree: *I can't run any faster.* ◆ *Is your father any better?*

IDM **any moment, day, minute, second, etc. (now)** very soon: *She should be home any minute now.*

🔑 **anybody** /ˈenibɒdi/ (also **anyone**) *pron* **1** [usually in questions or negative statements] any person: *I didn't know anybody at the party.* ◆ *Is there anybody here who can speak Japanese?* ◆ *Would* ***anybody else*** (= any other person) *like to come with me?* ➲ note at **some, somebody**

> **HELP** The difference between **somebody** and **anybody** is the same as the difference between **some** and **any**.

2 any person, it does not matter who: *Anybody* (= all people) *can learn to swim.* ◆ *Can anybody come, or are there special invitations?*

anyhow /ˈenihaʊ/ *adv* **1** = **anyway** **2** in a careless way; with no order: *Don't throw your clothes down just anyhow!*

any ˈmore (*BrE*) (also **anymore**) *adv* often used at the end of negative sentences and at the end of questions, to mean 'any longer': *She doesn't live here any more.* ◆ *Why doesn't he speak to me any more?*

🔑 **anyone** /ˈeniwʌn/ = **anybody**

anyplace /ˈenipleɪs/ (*AmE*) = **anywhere**

🔑 **anything** /ˈeniθɪŋ/ *pron* **1** [usually in negative sentences and in questions] one thing (of any kind): *It was so dark that I couldn't see anything at all.* ◆ *There isn't anything interesting in the newspaper today.* ◆ *Did you buy anything?* ◆ *'I'd like a kilo of apples please.'* ***'Anything else?'*** (= any other thing?) ➲ note at **some**

> **HELP** The difference between **something** and **anything** is the same as the difference between **some** and **any**.

2 any thing or things: it does not matter what: *I'm very hungry—I'll eat anything!* ◆ *I'll do anything you say.*

IDM **anything but** not at all: *Their explanation was anything but clear.*

anything like sb/sth at all similar to sb/sth; nearly: *She isn't anything like her sister, is she?* ◆ *This car isn't anything like as fast as mine.*

as happy, quick, etc. as anything (*spoken*) very happy, quick, etc.

do nothing/not do anything by halves ➲ **half**[1]

like anything ➲ **like**[1]

not come to anything ➲ **come**

🔑 **anyway** /ˈeniweɪ/ (also **anyhow**) *adv* **1** (used to add an extra point or reason) in any case: *I don't want to go out tonight, and anyway I haven't got any money.* **SYN** **besides** **2** used when saying or writing sth which contrasts in some way with what has gone before: *I don't think we'll succeed, but anyway we can try.* ◆ *I'm afraid I can't come to your party, but thanks anyway.* **3** used after a pause in order to change the subject or go back to a subject being discussed before: *Anyway, that's enough about my problems. How are you?* **4** (used for correcting sth you have just said and making it more accurate) at least: *Everybody wants to be rich—well, most people anyway.*

🔑 **anywhere** /ˈeniweə(r)/ (*AmE* also **anyplace**) *adv* **1** [usually in negative sentences or in questions] in, at or to any place: *I can't find my keys anywhere.* ◆ *Is there a post office anywhere near here?* ◆ *You can't buy the book* ***anywhere else*** (= in another place). ➲ note at **some**

> **HELP** The difference between **somewhere** and **anywhere** is the same as the difference between **some** and **any**.

2 any place; it does not matter where: *You can sit anywhere you like.*

aorta /eɪˈɔːtə/ *noun* [C] the main **artery** that carries blood from the heart to the rest of the body

🔑 **apart** /əˈpɑːt/ *adv* **1** away from sb/sth or each other; not together: *The doors slowly slid apart.* ◆ *Stand with your feet apart.* ◆ *The houses are ten metres apart.* ◆ *I'm afraid our ideas are too far apart.* ◆ *I can't tell the twins apart.* (= I can't see the difference between them.) ➲ look at **tell**(7) **2** into pieces: *The material was so old that it just* ***fell/came apart*** *in my hands.*

IDM **take sth apart** to separate sth into pieces: *He took the whole bicycle apart.*

🔑 **aˈpart from** (*especially AmE* **aˈside from**) *prep* **1** except for: *I've answered all the questions apart from the last one.* ◆ *There's nobody here apart from me.* **2** as well as; in addition to: *Apart from music, she also loves painting.*

A

apartheid /əˈpɑːtaɪt/ *noun* [U] the former official government policy in South Africa of separating people of different races and making them live apart

apartment /əˈpɑːtmənt/ *noun* [C] **1** (*especially AmE*) = **flat**²(1) **2** a set of rooms rented for a holiday: *a self-catering apartment*

aˈpartment block *noun* [C] (*AmE*) (also aˈpartment building) a large building containing several apartments

apathetic /ˌæpəˈθetɪk/ *adj* lacking interest or desire to act: *Many students are apathetic about politics.*

apathy /ˈæpəθi/ *noun* [U] the feeling of not being interested in or enthusiastic about anything: *There is widespread apathy towards the elections.*

ape¹ /eɪp/ *noun* [C] a type of animal like a large **monkey** (= an animal that lives in hot countries and can climb trees) with no tail or only a very short tail: *Chimpanzees and gorillas are apes.*

ape² /eɪp/ *verb* [T] to copy sb/sth, especially in a ridiculous way: *The children were aping the teacher's way of walking.*

aperitif /əˌperəˈtiːf/ *noun* [C] an alcoholic drink that you have before a meal

aperture /ˈæpətʃə(r)/ *noun* [C] (*formal*) a small opening in sth, especially one that allows light into a camera

apex /ˈeɪpeks/ *noun* [C, usually sing] (*pl* **apexes**) the top or highest part of sth: *the apex of the roof*

apiece /əˈpiːs/ *adv* [used after a noun or number] each: *Rooney and Walcott scored a goal apiece.*

apologetic /əˌpɒləˈdʒetɪk/ *adj* feeling or showing that you are sorry for sth you have done: *He was most apologetic about his son's bad behaviour.* ♦ *I wrote him an apologetic letter.* ▶ **apologetically** /-kli/ *adv*

apologize (also -ise) /əˈpɒlədʒaɪz/ *verb* [I] apologize (to sb) (for sth) to say that you are sorry for sth that you have done: *You'll have to apologize to your teacher for being late.*

MORE When you apologize, the actual words you use are usually **'I'm sorry'**.

apology /əˈpɒlədʒi/ *noun* [C,U] (*pl* apologies) (an) apology (to sb) (for sth) a spoken or written statement that you are sorry for sth you have done, etc: *Please accept our apologies for the delay.* ♦ *a letter of apology*

apostrophe /əˈpɒstrəfi/ *noun* [C] **1** the sign (') used for showing that you have left a letter or letters out of a word as in *I'm, can't* or *we'll* **2** the sign (') used for showing who or what sth belongs to, as in *John's chair, the boy's room* or *Russia's President*

app /æp/ (also application) *noun* [C] a computer program that is designed to do a particular job, especially one that lets you see information about a particular subject, play games, etc. on your mobile phone: *I've got an English dictionary app on my phone.*

appal (*AmE* appall) /əˈpɔːl/ *verb* [T] (appa<u>ll</u>ing; appa<u>ll</u>ed) [usually passive] to shock sb very much: *We were appalled by the poverty and starvation we saw everywhere.* ▶ **appalling** *adj* ▶ **appallingly** *adv*

apparatus /ˌæpəˈreɪtəs/ *noun* [U] the set of tools, instruments or equipment used for doing a job or an activity

apparent /əˈpærənt/ *adj* **1** apparent (to sb) clear; easy to see: *It quickly became apparent to us that our teacher could not speak French.* **SYN** **obvious** **2** [only *before* a noun] that seems to be real or true but may not be: *His apparent interest in the proposal didn't last very long.*

apparently /əˈpærəntli/ *adv* according to what people say or to how sth appears, but perhaps not true: *Apparently, he's already been married twice.* ♦ *He was apparently undisturbed by the news.*

apparition /ˌæpəˈrɪʃn/ *noun* [C] the image of a dead person that a living person believes they can see

appeal¹ /əˈpiːl/ *noun* **1** [C] a formal request to sb in authority to change a decision: *The judge turned down the defendant's appeal.* **2** [U] the attraction or interesting quality of sth/sb: *I can't understand the appeal of stamp collecting.* **3** [C] a serious request for sth you need or want very much: *The police have made an urgent appeal for witnesses to come forward.* **4** [C] an appeal to sth a suggestion that tries to influence sb's feelings or thoughts so that they will do what you want: *an appeal to our sense of national pride*

appeal² /əˈpiːl/ *verb* [I] **1** appeal (against/for sth) to ask sb in authority to make or change a decision: *He decided to appeal against his conviction.* ♦ *The player fell down and appealed for a penalty.* **2** appeal (to sb) to be attractive or interesting to sb: *The idea of living in the country doesn't appeal to me at all.* **3** appeal to sb (for sth); appeal for sth to make a serious request for sth you need or want very much: *She appealed to the kidnappers to let her son go.* ♦ *Relief workers in the disaster area are appealing for more supplies.* **4** appeal to sth to influence sb's feelings or thoughts so that they will do sth you want: *We aim to appeal to people's generosity.*

appealing /əˈpiːlɪŋ/ *adj* **1** attractive or interesting: *The idea of a lying on a beach sounds very appealing!* **2** showing that you need help, etc: *an appealing look* ▶ **appealingly** *adv*

appear /əˈpɪə(r)/ *verb* [I] **1** appear to be/do sth; appear (that)... to seem: *She appears to be very happy in her job.* ♦ *It appears that you were given the wrong information.* ➲ *adjective* **apparent** **2** to suddenly be seen; to come into sight: *The bus appeared from round the corner.* **OPP** **disappear** **3** to begin to exist: *The disease is thought to have appeared in Africa.* **4** to be published or printed: *The article appeared in this morning's paper.* **5** to perform or speak where you are seen by a lot of people: *to appear on TV/in a play*

A

appearance /əˈpɪərəns/ *noun* **1** [U] the way that sb/sth looks or seems: *A different hairstyle can completely change your appearance.* ♦ *He gives the appearance of being extremely confident.* **2** [sing] the coming of sb/sth: *the appearance of TV in the home in the 1950s* **3** [C] an act of appearing in public, especially on stage, TV, etc: *His last appearance before his death was as Julius Caesar.*

appease /əˈpiːz/ *verb* [T] (*formal*) to give sb what they want in order to make them less angry or to give a country what it wants in order to avoid a war ▶ **appeasement** *noun* [U]

appendicitis /əˌpendəˈsaɪtɪs/ *noun* [U] an illness in which your **appendix** becomes extremely painful and usually has to be removed

appendix /əˈpendɪks/ *noun* [C] **1** (*pl* appendixes) a small organ inside your body near your stomach. In humans, the **appendix** has no real function. **2** (*pl* **appendices** /-dɪsiːz/) a section at the end of a book, etc. that gives extra information

appetite /ˈæpɪtaɪt/ *noun* [C,U] a strong desire for sth, especially food: *Some fresh air and exercise should give you an appetite* (= make you hungry). ♦ *He has a great* **appetite for** *work/life.* ♦ *loss of appetite*

IDM **whet sb's appetite** ➲ whet

appetizer (also -iser) /ˈæpɪtaɪzə(r)/ (*especially AmE*) = **starter**

appetizing (also -ising) /ˈæpɪtaɪzɪŋ/ *adj* (used about food, etc.) that looks or smells attractive; making you feel hungry: *an appetizing smell*

applaud /əˈplɔːd/ *verb* **1** [I,T] to hit your hands together many times in order to show that you like sb/sth: *The audience applauded loudly.* ♦ *The team was applauded as it left the field.* **2** [T, usually passive] to express approval of sth: *The decision was applauded by everybody.*

applause /əˈplɔːz/ *noun* [U] the noise made by a group of people hitting their hands together to show their approval and enjoyment: *Let's all give a big* **round of applause** *to the cook!*

apple /ˈæpl/ *noun* [C,U] a hard, round fruit with a smooth green, red or yellow skin: *apple juice* ♦ *an apple pie* ♦ *three apple trees* ➲ picture on **page P14**

appliance /əˈplaɪəns/ *noun* [C] a piece of equipment for a particular purpose in the house: *washing machines and other domestic appliances*

applicable /əˈplɪkəbl; ˈæplɪkəbl/ *adj* **applicable (to sb/sth)** that concerns sb/sth: *This part of the form is only applicable to married women.* SYN **relevant**

applicant /ˈæplɪkənt/ *noun* [C] a person who **applies** for sth, especially for a job, a place at a college, university, etc: *There were over 200 applicants for the job.*

application /ˌæplɪˈkeɪʃn/ *noun* **1** [C,U] **(an) application (to sb) (for sth)** a formal written request, especially for a job or a place in a school, club, etc: *Applications for the job should be made to the Personnel Manager.* ♦ *To become a member, fill in the* **application form**. ♦ *Further information is available* **on application** *to the principal.* ➲ note at **job** **2** [C,U] the practical use (of sth): *the application of technology in the classroom* **3** [C] a computer program designed to do a particular job: *a database application* **4** [C] = **app** **5** [U] hard work; effort: *Success as a writer demands great application.*

applied /əˈplaɪd/ *adj* (used about a subject) studied in a way that has a practical use OPP **pure**

apply /əˈplaɪ/ *verb* (applying; applies; *pt, pp* applied)

➤FOR JOB/COURSE **1** [I] **apply (to sb) (for sth)** to ask for sth in writing: *I've applied to that company for a job.* ♦ *She's applying for a place at university.*

➤USE **2** [T] **apply sth (to sth)** to make practical use of sth: *new technology which can be applied to solving problems in industry*

➤CREAM **3** [T] **apply sth (to sth)** to put or spread sth onto sth: *Apply the cream to the infected area twice a day.*

➤BE RELEVANT **4** [I] **apply (to sb/sth)** to concern or involve sb/sth: *This information applies to all children born after 2007.*

➤DESCRIBE **5** [T, usually passive] to use a word, a name, etc. to describe sb/sth: *I don't think the term 'music' can be applied to that awful noise.*

➤WORK HARD **6** [T] **apply yourself/sth (to sth/doing sth)** to make yourself give all your attention to sth: *to apply your mind to something*

appoint /əˈpɔɪnt/ *verb* [T] **1 appoint sb (to sth)** to choose sb for a job or position: *The committee have appointed a new chairperson.* ♦ *He's been appointed (as) assistant to Dr McMullen.* **2** (*formal*) **appoint sth (for sth)** to arrange or decide on sth: *the date appointed for the next meeting*

appointment /əˈpɔɪntmənt/ *noun* **1** [C,U] **an appointment (with sb)** an arrangement to see sb at a particular time: *I have an appointment with Dr Sula at 3 o'clock.* ♦ *I'd like to* **make an appointment** *to see the manager.* ♦ *I realized I wouldn't be able to* **keep the appointment** *so I cancelled it.* ♦ *Visits are* **by appointment only** (= at a time that has been arranged in advance). **2** [U] **appointment (to sth)** the act of choosing sb for a job: *Many people criticized the appointment of such a young man to the post.* **3** [C] a job or a position of responsibility: *a temporary/permanent appointment*

appraisal /əˈpreɪzl/ *noun* [C,U] (*formal*) a judgement about the value or quality of sb/sth

appraise /əˈpreɪz/ *verb* [T] (*formal*) to judge the value or quality of sb/sth

appreciable /əˈpriːʃəbl/ *adj* noticeable or important

appreciate /əˈpriːʃieɪt/ *verb* **1** [T] to enjoy sth or to understand the value of sb/sth: *My boss doesn't appreciate me.* ♦ *I don't appreciate good coffee—it all tastes the same to me.* **2** [T] to be grateful for sth: *Thanks very much. I really appreciate your help.* **3** [T] to understand a problem, situation, etc: *I appreciate your problem but I'm afraid I can't help you.* **4** [I] to increase in value: *Houses in this area have appreciated faster than elsewhere.*

A

appreciation /əˌpriːʃiˈeɪʃn/ *noun* [U] **1** understanding and enjoyment of the value of sth: *I'm afraid I have little appreciation of modern architecture.* **2** understanding of a situation, problem, etc. **3** the feeling of being grateful for sth: *We bought him a present to show our appreciation for all the work he had done.* **4** an increase in value

appreciative /əˈpriːʃətɪv/ *adj* **1** appreciative (of sth) grateful for sth: *He was very appreciative of our efforts to help.* **2** feeling or showing pleasure or admiration: *an appreciative audience*

apprehend /ˌæprɪˈhend/ *verb* [T] (*formal*) (used about the police) to catch sb and arrest them

apprehensive /ˌæprɪˈhensɪv/ *adj* worried or afraid that sth unpleasant may happen: *I'm feeling apprehensive about tomorrow's exam.* ▶ **apprehension** /ˌæprɪˈhenʃn/ *noun* [C,U]

apprentice /əˈprentɪs/ *noun* [C] a young person who works for a fixed period of time, in order to learn the skills needed in a particular job: *an apprentice electrician/chef/plumber*

apprenticeship /əˈprentɪʃɪp/ *noun* [C,U] the state or time of being an **apprentice**: *He served a two-year apprenticeship as a carpenter.*

⚷ **approach**[1] /əˈprəʊtʃ/ *verb* **1** [I,T] to come near or nearer to sb/sth: *The day of the exam approached.* ♦ *When you approach the village you will see a garage on your left.* **2** [T] to speak to sb usually in order to ask for sth: *I'm going to approach my bank manager about a loan.* **3** [T] to begin to deal with a problem, a situation, etc: *What is the best way to approach this problem?*

⚷ **approach**[2] /əˈprəʊtʃ/ *noun* **1** [C] a way of dealing with sb/sth: *Parents don't always know what approach to take with teenage children.* **2** [sing] the act of coming nearer (to sb/sth): *the approach of winter* **3** [C] a request for sth: *The club has* ***made an approach to*** *us for financial assistance.* **4** [C] a road or path leading to sth: *the approach to the village*

approachable /əˈprəʊtʃəbl/ *adj* **1** friendly and easy to talk to **2** [not before a noun] that can be reached **SYN** **accessible**

⚷ **appropriate**[1] /əˈprəʊpriət/ *adj* appropriate (for/to sth) suitable or right for a particular situation, person, use, etc: *The matter will be dealt with by the appropriate authorities.* ♦ *I don't think this film is appropriate for young children.* **OPP** **inappropriate** ▶ **appropriately** *adv*

appropriate[2] /əˈprəʊprieɪt/ *verb* [T] (*formal*) to take sth to use for yourself, usually without permission ▶ **appropriation** /əˌprəʊpriˈeɪʃn/ *noun* [U, sing]

⚷ **approval** /əˈpruːvl/ *noun* [U] feeling, showing or saying that you think sth is good; agreement: *Everybody* ***gave*** *their* ***approval to*** *the proposal.* **OPP** **disapproval**

⚷ **approve** /əˈpruːv/ *verb* **1** [I] approve (of sb/sth) to be pleased about sth; to like sb/sth: *His father didn't approve of him becoming a dancer.* ♦ *Her parents don't approve of her friends.* **OPP** **disapprove** **2** [T] to agree formally to sth or to say that sth is correct: *We need to get an accountant to approve these figures.*

⚷ **approving** /əˈpruːvɪŋ/ *adj* showing support or admiration for sth: *'I agree entirely,' he said with an approving smile.* ▶ **approvingly** *adv*

approx *abbr* (*written*) = **approximate, approximately**

⚷ **approximate** /əˈprɒksɪmət/ *adj* (*abbr* **approx**) almost correct but not completely accurate: *The approximate time of arrival is 3 o'clock.* ♦ *I can only give you an approximate idea of the cost.* **OPP** **exact**

⚷ **approximately** /əˈprɒksɪmətli/ *adv* (*abbr* approx) about: *It's approximately fifty miles from here.* **SYN** **roughly**

approximation /əˌprɒksɪˈmeɪʃn/ *noun* [C] a number, an answer, etc. which is nearly, but not exactly, right

Apr. *abbr* = **April**: *2 Apr. 2009*

apricot /ˈeɪprɪkɒt/ *noun* [C] a small, round, yellow or orange fruit with a large stone inside ➲ picture on **page P14**

⚷ **April** /ˈeɪprəl/ *noun* [U,C] (*abbr* **Apr.**) the 4th month of the year, coming after March ➲ note at **January**

ˌApril ˈFool's Day *noun* [sing] 1 April

CULTURE

On this day it is traditional for people to play tricks on each other, especially by inventing silly stories and trying to persuade other people that they are true. If somebody believes such a story, they are called an **April Fool**.

apron /ˈeɪprən/ *noun* [C] a piece of clothing that you wear over the front of your usual clothes in order to keep them clean, especially when cooking ➲ picture at **overall**

apt /æpt/ *adj* **1** suitable in a particular situation: *I thought 'difficult' was an apt description of the book.* **2** apt to do sth often likely to do sth

aptitude /ˈæptɪtjuːd/ *noun* [U,C] aptitude (for sth/for doing sth) natural ability or skill: *She has an aptitude for learning languages.*

aptly /ˈæptli/ *adv* in an appropriate way: *The winner of the race was aptly named Alan Speedy.* **SYN** **suitably**

aquamarine /ˌækwəməˈriːn/ *noun* **1** [C,U] a pale greenish-blue **precious** (= rare and valuable) stone **2** [U] a pale greenish-blue colour ▶ **aquamarine** *adj*: *the aquamarine sea*

aquarium /əˈkweəriəm/ *noun* [C] (*pl* **aquariums** *or* **aquaria** /-riə/) **1** a glass container filled with water, in which fish and water animals are kept **2** a building where people can go to see fish and other water animals

Aquarius /əˈkweəriəs/ *noun* [C,U] the 11th sign of the **zodiac** (= 12 signs which represent the posi-

A

tions of the sun, moon and planets), the Water Carrier; a person born under this sign: *I'm an Aquarius.* ➲ picture at **zodiac**

aquatic /əˈkwætɪk/ *adj* living or taking place in, on or near water: *aquatic plants* ◆ *windsurfing and other aquatic sports*

Arab /ˈærəb/ *noun* [C] a member of a people who lived originally in Arabia and who now live in many parts of the Middle East and North Africa ▶ **Arab** *adj*: *Arab countries*

Arabic /ˈærəbɪk/ *noun* [sing] the language of Arab people ▶ **Arabic** *adj*

arable /ˈærəbl/ *adj* (in farming) connected with growing crops for sale, not keeping animals: *arable land/farmers*

arbitrary /ˈɑːbɪtrəri/ *adj* not seeming to be based on any reason or plan: *The choice of players for the team seemed completely arbitrary.* ▶ **arbitrarily** /ˌɑːbɪˈtrerəli/ *adv*

arbitrate /ˈɑːbɪtreɪt/ *verb* [I,T] to officially settle an argument between two people or groups by finding a solution that both can accept ▶ **arbitration** /ˌɑːbɪˈtreɪʃn/ *noun* [U] ▶ **arbitrator** /ˈɑːbɪtreɪə(r)/ *noun* [C]

arc /ɑːk/ *noun* [C] a curved line, part of a circle

arcade /ɑːˈkeɪd/ *noun* [C] **1** a large covered passage or area with shops along one or both sides: *a shopping arcade* **2** (also aˈ**musement arcade**) a large room with machines and games that you put coins into to play

arch[1] /ɑːtʃ/ *noun* [C] **1** a curved structure with straight sides, often supporting a bridge or the roof of a large building, or it may be above a door or window ➲ look at **archway** **2** the curved part of the bottom of your foot

arch

arch

column

arch[2] /ɑːtʃ/ *verb* [I,T] to make a curve

archaeological (*AmE* **archeological**) /ˌɑːkiəˈlɒdʒɪkl/ *adj* connected with **archaeology**

archaeologist (*AmE* **archeologist**) /ˌɑːkiˈɒlədʒɪst/ *noun* [C] an expert in **archaeology**

archaeology (*AmE* **archeology**) /ˌɑːkiˈɒlədʒi/ *noun* [U] the study of the past, based on objects or parts of buildings that are found in the ground

archaic /ɑːˈkeɪɪk/ *adj* very old-fashioned; no longer used

archbishop /ˌɑːtʃˈbɪʃəp/ *noun* [C] a priest with a very high position, in some branches of the Christian Church, who is responsible for all the churches in a large area of a country: *the Archbishop of Canterbury* (= the head of the Church of England) ➲ look at **bishop**

archeological (*AmE*) = **archaeological**

archeologist (*AmE*) = **archaeologist**

archeology (*AmE*) = **archaeology**

archer /ˈɑːtʃə(r)/ *noun* [C] a person who shoots arrows through the air by pulling back a tight string on a **bow** (= a curved piece of wood) and letting go. In the past this was done in order to kill people, but it is now done as a sport.

archery /ˈɑːtʃəri/ *noun* [U] the sport of shooting arrows

architect /ˈɑːkɪtekt/ *noun* [C] a person whose job is to design buildings

architectural /ˌɑːkɪˈtektʃərəl/ *adj* connected with the design of buildings

architecture /ˈɑːkɪtektʃə(r)/ *noun* [U] **1** the study of designing and making buildings **2** the style or design of a building or buildings: *modern architecture*

archive /ˈɑːkaɪv/ *noun* [C] (also **archives** [pl]) a collection of historical documents, etc. which show the history of a place or an organization; the place where they are kept: *archive material on the First World War* ▶ **archive** *verb* [T]: *Do you want to archive these documents now?*

archway /ˈɑːtʃweɪ/ *noun* [C] a passage or entrance with an **arch** (= a curved structure) over it

the Arctic /ˈɑːktɪk/ *noun* [sing] the area around the North Pole ➲ look at **the Antarctic**

Arctic /ˈɑːktɪk/ *adj* [only *before* a noun] **1** connected with the region around the North Pole (the most northern point of the world) ➲ look at **Antarctic** **2 arctic** extremely cold

the ˌArctic ˈCircle *noun* [sing] a line that we imagine going around the cold area at the top of earth; the line of **latitude** (= a measurement of distance north or south) 66° 30′ North ➲ picture at **earth**

ardent /ˈɑːdnt/ *adj* showing strong feelings, especially a strong liking for sb/sth: *an ardent supporter of the local football team* ▶ **ardently** *adv*

arduous /ˈɑːdjuəs; -dʒu-/ *adj* full of difficulties; needing a lot of effort: *an arduous journey* ◆ *arduous work*

are /ə(r); *strong form* ɑː(r)/ ➲ **be**

⚷ **area** /ˈeəriə/ *noun* **1** [C] a part of a town, a country or the world: *Housing is very expensive in the Tokyo area.* ◆ *The wettest areas are in the West of the country.* ◆ *built-up areas* (= where there are a lot of buildings) ◆ *Forests cover a large area of the country.* **2** [C] a space used for a particular activity: *The shop has a children's play area.* **3** [C] a particular part of a subject or an activity: *Training is one area of the business that we could improve.* **4** [C,U] the size of a surface, that you can calculate by multiplying the length by the width: *The area of the room is 35 square metres.* ◆ *The room is 35 square metres* **in area**. ➲ look at **volume**

A

OTHER WORDS FOR

area

A **district** may be part of a town or country, and it may have fixed boundaries: *the district controlled by a council*. A **region** is larger, usually part of a country only and may not have fixed boundaries: *the industrial regions of the country*. An **area** is the most general term and is used with the same meaning as both **district** and **region**: *the poorer areas of a town* ◆ *an agricultural area of the country*. We use **part** more often when we are talking about a section of a town: *Which part of Paris do you live in?*

arena /əˈriːnə/ *noun* [C] **1** an area with seats around it where public entertainments (sports events, concerts, etc.) are held **2** an area of activity that concerns the public

aren't /ɑːnt/ *short for* **are not**

arguable /ˈɑːgjuəbl/ *adj* **1** probably true; that you can give reasons for: *It is arguable that all hospital treatment should be free.* **2** probably not true; that you can give reasons against ▶ **arguably** /-əbli/ *adv*: *'King Lear' is arguably Shakespeare's best play.*

⚷ **argue** /ˈɑːgjuː/ *verb* **1** [I] argue (with sb) (about/over sth) to say things, often angrily, that show that you do not agree with sb about sth: *The couple next door are always arguing.* ◆ *I never argue with my parents about money.* ➲ look at **fight**, **quarrel** **2** [I,T] argue that ...; argue (for/against sth) to give reasons that support your opinion about sth: *She argued that they needed more time to finish the project.* ◆ *He argued against buying a new computer.* ◆ *They argued for the right to strike.*

⚷ **argument** /ˈɑːgjumənt/ *noun* **1** [C,U] an argument (with sb) (about/over sth) an angry discussion between two or more people who disagree with each other: *Sue **had an argument** with her father about politics.* ◆ *He accepted the decision without argument.*

MORE A noisy, serious argument is a **row** /raʊ/. A **quarrel** is usually about something less serious.

2 [C] the reason(s) that you give to support your opinion about sth: *What are the **arguments for/against** lower taxes?*

argumentative /ˌɑːgjuˈmentətɪv/ *adj* often involved in or enjoying arguments

aria /ˈɑːriə/ *noun* [C] a song for one voice, especially in an **opera** (= a musical play)

arid /ˈærɪd/ *adj* (used about land or climate) very dry; with little or no rain

Aries /ˈeəriːz/ *noun* [C,U] the 1st of the 12 signs of the **zodiac** (= 12 signs which represent the positions of the sun, moon and planets), the Ram; a person born under this sign: *I'm an Aries.* ➲ picture at **zodiac**

⚷ **arise** /əˈraɪz/ *verb* [I] (*pt* arose /əˈrəʊz/; *pp* arisen /əˈrɪzn/) to begin to exist; to appear: *If any problems arise, let me know.* ◆ *A storm arose during the night.*

aristocracy /ˌærɪˈstɒkrəsi/ *noun* [C, with sing or pl verb] (*pl* aristocracies) the people of the highest social class who often have special titles **SYN** **nobility**

aristocrat /ˈærɪstəkræt/ *noun* [C] a member of the highest social class, often with a special title ▶ **aristocratic** /ˌærɪstəˈkrætɪk/ *adj*

arithmetic /əˈrɪθmətɪk/ *noun* [U] the kind of mathematics which involves counting with numbers (adding, **subtracting** (= taking away), multiplying and dividing): *I'm not very good at **mental arithmetic**.*

arm

arm in arm

arms folded/crossed

⚷ **arm**[1] /ɑːm/ *noun* [C] **1** the long part at each side of your body connecting your shoulder to your hand: *He was carrying a newspaper under his arm.* ➲ picture at **body** **2** the part of a piece of clothing that covers your arm; a sleeve: *He had a hole in the arm of his jumper.* **3** the part of a chair where you rest your arms

IDM **arm in arm** with your arm folded around sb else's arm: *The friends walked arm in arm.*

cross/fold your arms to cross your arms in front of your chest: *She folded her arms and waited.* ◆ *James was sitting with his arms crossed.*

twist sb's arm ➲ **twist**[1]

with open arms ➲ **open**[1]

⚷ **arm**[2] /ɑːm/ *verb* [I,T] to prepare sb/yourself to fight by supplying or getting weapons: *The country is beginning to arm itself for war.* ➲ look at **armed**, **arms**

armaments /ˈɑːməmənts/ *noun* [pl] weapons and military equipment

armband /ˈɑːmbænd/ *noun* [C] **1** a piece of cloth that you wear around your arm: *The captain of the team wears an armband.* **2** a plastic ring filled with air which you can wear on each of your arms when you are learning to swim

armchair /ˈɑːmtʃeə(r)/ *noun* [C] a soft comfortable chair with sides which support your arms ➲ picture at **chair**

⚷ **armed** /ɑːmd/ *adj* carrying a gun or other weapon; involving weapons: *All the terrorists were armed.* ◆ *armed robbery* ◆ *the armed forces* (= the army, navy and air force) **OPP** **unarmed**

armful /ˈɑːmfʊl/ *noun* [C] the amount that you can carry in your arms

armhole /ˈɑːmhəʊl/ *noun* [C] the opening in a piece of clothing where your arm goes through

armistice /ˈɑːmɪstɪs/ *noun* [C] an agreement between two countries who are at war that they will stop fighting

armour (*AmE* **armor**) /ˈɑːmə(r)/ *noun* [U] clothing, often made of metal, that soldiers wore in earlier times to protect themselves: *a suit of armour*

armoured (*AmE* **armored**) /ˈɑːməd/ *adj* (used about a vehicle) covered with metal to protect it in an attack

armpit /ˈɑːmpɪt/ *noun* [C] the part of the body under the arm at the point where it joins the shoulder ➲ picture at **body**

arms /ɑːmz/ *noun* [pl] **1** weapons, especially those that are used in war: *a reduction in nuclear arms* **2** = **coat of arms**

IDM **up in arms** protesting angrily about sth: *The workers were up in arms over the news that the factory was going to close.*

army /ˈɑːmi/ *noun* [C, with sing or pl verb] (*pl* armies) **1** the military forces of a country which are trained to fight on land: *the British Army* ◆ *She* ***joined the army*** *at the age of eighteen.* ◆ *The army is/are advancing towards the border.* ◆ *an army officer* ➲ note at **war** ➲ look at **air force**, **navy** **2** a large number of people, especially when involved in an activity together: *An army of children was helping to pick up the rubbish.*

ˈ**A-road** *noun* [C] (in Britain) a main road, usually not as wide as a **motorway** (= a wide road for fast traffic)

aroma /əˈrəʊmə/ *noun* [C] a smell, especially a pleasant one ➲ note at **smell**[2] ▸ **aromatic** /ˌærəˈmætɪk/ *adj* **SYN** **fragrant**

aromatherapy /əˌrəʊməˈθerəpi/ *noun* [U] the use of natural oils with a pleasant smell in order to control pain or make sb feel relaxed: *an aromatherapy massage* ▸ **aromatherapist** /-pɪst/ *noun* [C]

arose *past tense of* **arise**

around /əˈraʊnd/ *adv, prep* **1** (also **round**) in or to various places or directions: *This is our office—Victoria will show you around* (= show you the different parts of it). ◆ *They wandered around the town, looking at the shops.* **2** (also **round**) moving so as to face in the opposite direction: *Turn around and go back the way you came.* **3** (also **round**) on all sides; forming a circle: *The park has a wall all around.* ◆ *Gather around so that you can all see.* ◆ *We sat down around the table.* **4** (also **round**) near a place: *Is there a bank around here?* **5** (also **about**) present or available: *I went to the house but there was nobody around.* **6** (also **about**) approximately: *I'll see you around seven* (= at about 7 o'clock). **7** (also **about**) used for activities with no real purpose: *'What are you doing?' 'Nothing, just lazing around.'*

arouse /əˈraʊz/ *verb* [T] to cause a particular reaction in people: *to arouse somebody's curiosity/interest* ▸ **arousal** /əˈraʊzl/ *noun* [U]

arr. *abbr* **arrives**: *arr. York 07.15*

arrange /əˈreɪndʒ/ *verb* **1** [I,T] arrange (for) sth; arrange to do sth; arrange (sth) with sb to make plans and preparations so that sth can happen in the future: *We're arranging a surprise party for Mark.* ◆ *She arranged for her mother to look after the baby.* ◆ *He arranged to meet Stuart after work.* **2** [T] to put sth in order or in a particular pattern: *The books were arranged in alphabetical order.* ◆ *Arrange the chairs in a circle.* ◆ *She arranged the flowers in a vase.*

arrangement /əˈreɪndʒmənt/ *noun* **1** [C, usually pl] plans or preparations for sth that will happen in the future: *Come round this evening and we'll* ***make arrangements for*** *the party.* **2** [C,U] an agreement with sb to do sth: *They* ***have an arrangement*** *to share the cost of the food.* ◆ *We both need to use the computer so we'll have to* ***come to*** *some* ***arrangement****.* **3** [C] a group of things that have been placed in a particular pattern: *a flower arrangement*

array /əˈreɪ/ *noun* [C] a large collection of things, especially one that is impressive and is seen by other people

arrears /əˈrɪəz/ *noun* [pl] money that sb owes that they should have paid earlier

IDM **be in arrears; fall/get into arrears** to be late in paying money that you owe: *I'm in arrears with the rent.*

in arrears if money or a person is paid **in arrears** for work, the money is paid after the work has been done: *You will be paid monthly in arrears.*

arrest[1] /əˈrest/ *verb* [T] when the police arrest sb, they take them prisoner in order to question them about a crime: *The man was arrested for carrying a weapon.* ➲ note at **crime**

arrest[2] /əˈrest/ *noun* [C,U] the act of arresting sb: *The police* ***made*** *ten* ***arrests*** *after the riot.* ◆ *The wanted man is now* ***under arrest*** (= has been arrested).

arrival /əˈraɪvl/ *noun* **1** [U] reaching the place to which you were travelling: *On our arrival we were told that our rooms had not been reserved.* **OPP** **departure** **2** [C] people or things that have arrived: *We brought in extra chairs for the late arrivals.*

arrive /əˈraɪv/ *verb* [I] **1** arrive (at/in …) to reach the place to which you were travelling: *We arrived home at about midnight.* ◆ *What time does the train arrive in Newcastle?* ◆ *They arrived at the station ten minutes late.*

> **HELP** Be careful. We use **arrive in** with the name of a town, country, etc. and **arrive at** with a place, building, etc.

2 to come or happen: *The day of the wedding had finally arrived.*

PHR V **arrive at** to decide on or find sth, especially after discussion or thought: *We finally arrived at a decision.*

arrogant /ˈærəgənt/ *adj* thinking that you are better and more important than other people **SYN** **self-important** ▸ **arrogance** *noun* [U] ▸ **arrogantly** *adv*

A

arrow /ˈærəʊ/ *noun* [C] **1** a thin piece of wood or metal, with one pointed end and feathers at the other end, that is shot by pulling back the string on a **bow** (= a curved piece of wood) and letting go: *to fire an arrow at a target* ➲ look at **archer** **2** the sign (→) which is used to show direction: *The arrow is pointing left.*

arsenal /ˈɑːsənl/ *noun* [C] a large collection of weapons, or a building where they are made or stored

arsenic /ˈɑːsnɪk/ *noun* [U] (*symbol* As) a type of very strong poison

arson /ˈɑːsn/ *noun* [U] the crime of setting fire to a building on purpose

arsonist /ˈɑːsənɪst/ *noun* [C] a person who deliberately sets fire to a building

art /ɑːt/ *noun* **1** [U] the activity or skill of producing things such as paintings, designs, etc.; the objects that are produced: *an art class* ◆ *modern art* ◆ *I've never been good at art.* **2** [C,U] a skill or sth that needs skill: *There's* **an art to** *writing a good letter.* **3 the arts** [pl] art, literature, music, theatre, etc. when you think of them as a group: *The government has agreed to spend twice as much on the arts next year.* **4 arts** [pl] the subjects that you study at school or university that are not scientific, such as history or languages: *an arts degree*

MORE We usually contrast **arts** (or **arts subjects**) with **sciences** (or **science subjects**).

TOPIC

Art

An **artist** works in a **studio**. A **painter** paints **pictures**, for example **portraits** (= pictures of people), **landscapes** (= pictures of the countryside) or **abstract paintings** (= pictures that do not show people or things as they really look). A picture might be a **watercolour** or an **oil painting**. You put a picture in a **frame** and hang it on the wall. A **sculptor** makes **sculptures** of figures or objects in materials such as **marble** (= a type of stone) or **bronze** (= a type of metal). An **exhibition** is a collection of **works of art** which the public can go and see in an **art gallery**. A great work of art is called a **masterpiece**.

artefact /ˈɑːtɪfækt/ *noun* [C] an object that is made by a person

artery /ˈɑːtəri/ *noun* [C] (*pl* **arteries**) one of the tubes which take blood from the heart to other parts of the body ➲ look at **vein**

artful /ˈɑːtfl/ *adj* clever at getting what you want, sometimes by not telling the truth **SYN** **crafty**

arthritis /ɑːˈθraɪtɪs/ *noun* [U] a disease which causes swelling and pain when you bend your arms, fingers, etc. ▸ **arthritic** /ɑːˈθrɪtɪk/ *adj*

artichoke /ˈɑːtɪtʃəʊk/ (also ˌ**globe** ˈ**artichoke**) *noun* [C] a green vegetable with a lot of thick pointed leaves. You can eat the bottom part of the leaves and its centre. ➲ picture on **page P15**

article /ˈɑːtɪkl/ *noun* [C] **1** an object, especially one of a set: *articles of clothing* **2** a piece of writing in a newspaper or magazine: *There's an article about Mexico in today's paper.* **3** the words *a*, *an* (= the indefinite article) or *the* (= the definite article) ℹ For more information about articles, look at the **Reference Section** at the back of this dictionary.

articulate[1] /ɑːˈtɪkjuleɪt/ *verb* [I,T] to say sth clearly or to express your ideas or feelings: *She struggled to articulate her thoughts.* ▸ **articulation** /ɑːˌtɪkjuˈleɪʃn/ *noun* [U] (*formal*)

articulate[2] /ɑːˈtɪkjələt/ *adj* good at expressing your ideas clearly **OPP** **inarticulate**

articulated /ɑːˈtɪkjuleɪtɪd/ *adj* (*BrE*) (used about a large vehicle such as a lorry) made of two sections which are joined together

artificial /ˌɑːtɪˈfɪʃl/ *adj* not genuine or natural but made by people: *artificial flowers* ◆ *an artificial lake* ▸ **artificially** /-ʃəli/ *adv*

ˌ**artificial in**ˈ**telligence** *noun* [U] (the study of) the way in which computers can be made to copy the way humans think

artillery /ɑːˈtɪləri/ *noun* [U] large, heavy guns that are moved on wheels; the part of the army that uses them

artisan /ˌɑːtɪˈzæn/ *noun* [C] (*formal*) a person who makes things in a skilful way, especially with their hands **SYN** **craftsman**

artist /ˈɑːtɪst/ *noun* [C] a person who produces art, especially paintings or drawings: *I like that picture—who is the artist?* ◆ *a graphic artist* ◆ *Monet was a famous French artist.*

artiste /ɑːˈtiːst/ (also **artist**) *noun* [C] a person whose job is to perform, for example a singer or a dancer

artistic /ɑːˈtɪstɪk/ *adj* **1** [only *before* a noun] connected with art: *a work of great artistic merit* ◆ *the artistic director of the theatre* **2** showing a skill in art: *Elizabeth is very artistic—her drawings are excellent.* ▸ **artistically** /-kli/ *adv*

artistry /ˈɑːtɪstri/ *noun* [U] the skill of an artist

artwork /ˈɑːtwɜːk/ *noun* **1** [U] photographs, drawings, etc. that have been prepared for a book or magazine: *a piece of artwork* **2** [C] a work of art, especially one in a museum or a show

arty /ˈɑːti/ *adj* (*informal*) seeming or wanting to be very artistic or interested in the arts: *He can't really like all those boring arty films.*

as /əz; *strong form* æz/ *prep, adv, conj* **1** used for talking about sb/sth's job, role or function: *Think of me as your friend, not as your boss.*

HELP **As** or **like**? Before a noun, **as** refers to a job or function: *She works as a scientist.* ◆ *I used the jar as a vase.* **Like** means 'similar to': *He has blue eyes like his father.* **Like** (or formally, **such as**) also means 'for example': *I love sweet food, like chocolate.*

2 as ... as used for comparing people or things: *Lenka's almost as tall as me.* ♦ *Lenka's almost as tall as I am.* ♦ *It's not as cold as it was yesterday.* ♦ *I'd like an appointment **as soon as possible**.* ♦ *She earns **twice as much as** her husband.* ♦ *I haven't got as many books as you have.* ➲ note at **similarity** **3** while sth else is happening: *The phone rang just as I was leaving the house.* ♦ *As she walked along the road, she thought about her father.* **4** in a particular way, state, etc.; like: *Please do as I tell you.* ♦ *Leave the room **as it is**. Don't move anything.* **5** because: *I didn't buy the dress, as I decided it was too expensive.* ➲ note at **because** **6** used at the beginning of a comment about what you are saying: ***As you know**, I've decided to leave at the end of the month.*

IDM **as for** used when you are starting to talk about a different person or thing: *Gianni's upstairs. As for Tino, I've no idea where he is.*

as if; as though used for saying how sb/sth appears: *She looks as if/though she's just got out of bed.*

as it were used for saying that sth is only true in a certain way: *She felt, as it were, a stranger in her own house.*

as of; as from starting from a particular time: *As from next week, Tim Shaw will be managing this department.*

as to about a particular thing; concerning: *I was given no instructions as to how to begin.*

asap /ˌeɪ es eɪ ˈpiː/ *abbr* **as soon as possible**

asbestos /æsˈbestəs/ *noun* [U] a soft grey material that does not burn and was used in the past to protect against heat

ascend /əˈsend/ *verb* [I,T] (*formal*) to go up **OPP** **descend** ▶ **ascending** *adj*: *The questions are arranged in ascending order of difficulty* (= the most difficult ones are at the end).

ascent /əˈsent/ *noun* [C] **1** the act of climbing or going up: *the ascent of Everest* **2** a path or hill leading upwards: *There was a steep ascent before the path became flat again.* **OPP** for both meanings **descent**

ascertain /ˌæsəˈteɪn/ *verb* [T] (*formal*) to find sth out

ascribe /əˈskraɪb/ *verb* [T] **ascribe sth to sb/sth** **1** to say that sth was written by or belonged to sb: *Many people ascribe this play to Shakespeare.* **2** to say what caused sth: *He ascribed his forgetfulness to old age.*

asexual /ˌeɪˈsekʃuəl/ *adj* **1** (*technical*) not involving sex; not having sexual organs: *asexual reproduction* **2** not having sexual qualities; not interested in sex

ash /æʃ/ *noun* **1** [U,pl] the grey or black powder which is left after sth has burned: *cigarette ash* ♦ *the ashes of a fire* **2** **ashes** [pl] what is left after a dead person has been burned **3** [C] a type of forest tree that grows in cool countries

🔑 **ashamed** /əˈʃeɪmd/ *adj* [not before a noun] **ashamed (of sth/sb/yourself); ashamed that ...; ashamed to do sth** feeling guilty or embarrassed about sb/sth or because of sth you have done: *She was ashamed of her old clothes.* ♦ *How could you be so rude? I'm ashamed of you!* ♦ *She felt ashamed that she hadn't helped him.* **OPP** **unashamed**

ashen /ˈæʃn/ *adj* (used about sb's face) very pale; without colour because of illness or fear

ashore /əˈʃɔː(r)/ *adv* onto the land from the sea, a river, etc: *The passengers went ashore for an hour while the ship was in port.*

ashtray /ˈæʃtreɪ/ *noun* [C] a small dish for collecting **ash** (= the powder that is made as a cigarette is burned)

Asian /ˈeɪʃn; ˈeɪʒn/ *noun* [C] a person from Asia or whose family was originally from Asia ▶ **Asian** *adj*

🔑 **aside** /əˈsaɪd/ *adv* **1** on or to one side; out of the way: *We stood aside to let the man go past.* **2** to be kept separately, for a special purpose: *I try to **set aside** a little money each month.*

🔑 **aˈside from** (*especially AmE*) = **apart from**: *Aside from a few scratches, I'm OK.*

🔑 **ask** /ɑːsk/ *verb*

➤QUESTION **1** [I,T] **ask (sb) (about sb/sth); ask sb sth** to put a question to sb in order to find out some information: *We need to ask about tickets.* ♦ *Can I ask you a question?* ♦ *Ask him how old he is.* ♦ *She asked if I wanted tea or coffee.* ♦ *'What's the time?' he asked.* ♦ *He asked what the time was.* ♦ *He asked me the time.*

➤REQUEST **2** [I,T] **ask (sb) for sth; ask sth (of sb); ask sb to do sth** to request that sb gives you sth or does sth for you: *She sat down and asked for a cup of coffee.* ♦ *Don't ask Joe for money—he hasn't got any.* ♦ *You are asking too much of him—he can't possibly do all that!* ♦ *Ring this number and ask for Mrs Khan.* ♦ *I asked him if he would drive me home.* ♦ *I asked him to drive me home.*

➤PERMISSION **3** [I,T] to request permission to do sth: *I'm sure she'll let you go if you ask.* ♦ *Theo asked to use our phone.* ♦ *We asked the teacher if we could go home early.*

➤INVITE **4** [T] **ask sb (to sth)** to invite sb: *They asked six friends to dinner.*

➤MONEY **5** [T] to say the price that you want for sth: *How much are they asking for their car?*

IDM **ask for trouble/it** to behave in a way that will almost certainly cause you problems: *Driving when you're tired is just asking for trouble.*

if you ask me if you want my opinion

PHR V **ask after sb** to ask about sb's health or to ask for news of sb: *Tina asked after you today.*

ask sb out to invite sb to go out with you, especially as a way of starting a romantic relationship: *Harry's too shy to ask her out.*

ask sb round/over to invite sb to your home for a meal, to watch a DVD, etc.

askew /əˈskjuː/ *adv, adj* [not before a noun] not in a straight or level position

🔑 **asleep** /əˈsliːp/ *adj* [not before a noun] not awake; sleeping: *The baby is fast/sound asleep* (= very deeply asleep). ♦ *It didn't take me long to **fall asleep** last night.* **OPP** **awake** ➲ note at **sleep**[1]

A

HELP Asleep or sleeping? Notice that you can only use **asleep** after a noun or a verb such as 'be'. **Sleeping** can be used before the noun: *a sleeping child*

AS (level) /eɪ ˈes levl/ *noun* [C,U] **Advanced Subsidiary (level)**; a British exam usually taken in the year before the final year of school or college when students are aged 17. Together with A2 levels, AS levels form the A-level qualification, which is needed for entrance to universities: *Students will normally take four or five AS subjects.* ◆ *She's* ***doing an AS (level)*** *in French.* ➲ look at **A2 (level), A level**

asparagus /əˈspærəɡəs/ *noun* [U] a plant with green or white **stems** (= the long thin parts) that you cook and eat as a vegetable ➲ picture on **page P15**

🔑 **aspect** /ˈæspekt/ *noun* [C] one of the qualities or parts of a situation, an idea, a problem, etc: *What are the main aspects of your job?*

asphalt /ˈæsfælt/ *noun* [U] a thick black substance that is used for making the surface of roads

asphyxiate /əsˈfɪksieɪt/ *verb* [I,T] to make sb unable to breathe or to be unable to breathe: *He was asphyxiated by the smoke while he was asleep.* ▶ **asphyxiation** /əsˌfɪksiˈeɪʃn/ *noun* [U]

aspire /əˈspaɪə(r)/ *verb* [I] (*formal*) **aspire to sth/to do sth** to have a strong desire to have or do sth: *She aspired to become managing director.* ◆ *an aspiring actor* ▶ **aspiration** /ˌæspəˈreɪʃn/ *noun* [C,U]

aspirin /ˈæsprɪn; ˈæspərɪn/ *noun* [C,U] a drug used to reduce pain and a high temperature

ass /æs/ = **donkey**

assailant /əˈseɪlənt/ *noun* [C] (*formal*) a person who attacks sb

assassin /əˈsæsɪn/ *noun* [C] a person who kills a famous or important person for money or for political reasons ▶ **assassinate** /əˈsæsɪneɪt/ *verb* [T] ➲ note at **kill** ▶ **assassination** /əˌsæsɪˈneɪʃn/ *noun* [C,U]

assault /əˈsɔːlt/ *noun* [C,U] **assault (on sb/sth)** a sudden attack on sb/sth ▶ **assault** *verb* [T]: *He was charged with assaulting a police officer.*

assemble /əˈsembl/ *verb* **1** [I,T] to come together or bring sb/sth together in a group: *I've assembled all the information I need for my essay.* **2** [T] to fit the parts of sth together: *We spent hours trying to assemble our new bookshelves.*

assembly /əˈsembli/ *noun* (*pl* **assemblies**) **1** [C,U] a large group of people who come together for a particular purpose: *school assembly* (= a regular meeting for all the students and teachers of a school) **2** [U] the act of fitting the parts of sth together

asˈsembly line *noun* [C] a line of people and machines in a factory that fit the parts of sth together in a fixed order

assent /əˈsent/ *noun* [U] (*formal*) **assent (to sth)** official agreement to sth: *The committee* ***gave*** *their* ***assent*** *to the proposed changes.* ▶ **assent** *verb* [I] **assent (to sth)**

assert /əˈsɜːt/ *verb* [T] **1** to say sth clearly and firmly **2** to behave in a determined and confident way to make people listen to you or to get what you want: *You ought to assert yourself more.* ◆ *to assert your authority*

assertion /əˈsɜːʃn/ *noun* **1** [C] a statement that says you strongly believe that sth is true **2** [U] the act of showing, using or stating sth strongly

assertive /əˈsɜːtɪv/ *adj* expressing your opinion clearly and firmly so that people listen to you or do what you want ▶ **assertively** *adv* ▶ **assertiveness** *noun* [U]

assess /əˈses/ *verb* [T] **1** to judge or form an opinion about sth: *It's too early to assess the effects of the price rises.* **2 assess sth (at sth)** to guess or decide the amount or value of sth: *to assess the cost of repairs* ▶ **assessment** *noun* [C,U]: *I made a careful assessment of the risks involved.*

asset /ˈæset/ *noun* [C] **1 an asset (to sb/sth)** a person or thing that is useful to sb/sth: *She's a great asset to the organization.* **2** [usually pl] something of value that a person, company, etc. owns

assign /əˈsaɪn/ *verb* [T] **1 assign sth to sb/sth** to give sth to sb for a particular purpose: *We assigned 20% of our budget to the project.* **2 assign sb to sth** to give sb a particular job to do

assignment /əˈsaɪnmənt/ *noun* [C,U] a job or type of work that you are given to do: *The teacher gave us an assignment to do during the holidays.*

assimilate /əˈsɪməleɪt/ *verb* **1** [T] to learn and understand sth: *to assimilate new facts/information/ideas* **2** [I,T] **assimilate (sb/sth) (into sth)** to become or allow sb/sth to become part of a country, a social group, etc. ▶ **assimilation** /əˌsɪməˈleɪʃn/ *noun* [U]

🔑 **assist** /əˈsɪst/ *verb* [I,T] (*formal*) **assist (sb) in/with sth; assist (sb) in doing sth** to help: *Ben pays a student to assist him with his research.* ◆ *Volunteers assisted in searching for the boy.*

🔑 **assistance** /əˈsɪstəns/ *noun* [U] (*formal*) help or support: *financial assistance for poorer families* ◆ *She shouted for help but nobody came to her assistance.*

🔑 **assistant** /əˈsɪstənt/ *noun* [C] (*abbr* **Asst**) **1** a person who helps sb in a more important position: *The director is away today. Would you like to speak to her assistant?* ◆ *He's assistant to the Sales Manager.* **2** (*AmE* **clerk**) a person who sells things to people in a shop: *a shop/sales assistant* ▶ **assistant** *adj* [only *before* a noun]: *the assistant manager*

Assoc. *abbr* = **association**

🔑 **associate¹** /əˈsəʊʃieɪt/ *verb* **1** [T] **associate sb/sth (with sb/sth)** to make a connection between people or things in your mind: *I always associate the smell of the sea with my childhood.* **2** [I] **associate with sb** to spend time with sb: *I prefer not to associate with colleagues outside work.* **3** [T] **associate yourself with sth** to say that you support sth or agree with sth: *I do not wish to associate myself with any organ-*

ization that promotes violence. OPP for all meanings **dissociate**

associate² /əˈsəʊʃiət/ *noun* [C] a person that you meet and get to know through your work: *a business associate*

association /əˌsəʊʃiˈeɪʃn; -siˈeɪ-/ *noun* **1** [C] (*abbr* Assoc.) a group of people or organizations that work together for a particular purpose: *the National Association of Language Teachers* **2** [U] joining or working with another person or group: *We work* ***in association with*** *our New York office.* **3** [C,U] the act of connecting one person or thing with another in your mind: *The cat soon made the association between human beings and food.*

assorted /əˈsɔːtɪd/ *adj* of different types; mixed: *a bowl of assorted fruit*

assortment /əˈsɔːtmənt/ *noun* [C] a group of different things or of different types of the same thing: *You'll find a wide assortment of gifts in our shop.* SYN **mixture**

Asst *abbr* = **assistant**

assume /əˈsjuːm/ *verb* [T] **1** to accept or believe that sth is true even though you have no proof; to expect sth to be true: *I assume that you have the necessary documents.* ◆ *Everyone assumed Ralph was guilty.* ◆ *Everyone assumed Ralph to be guilty.* **2** to begin to use power or to have a powerful position: *to assume control of something* SYN **take 3** to pretend to have or be sb/sth: *to assume a false name*

assumption /əˈsʌmpʃn/ *noun* **1** [C] something that you accept is true even though you have no proof: *We'll work* ***on the assumption that*** *guests will be hungry when they arrive.* ◆ *It's unfair to* ***make assumptions about*** *somebody's character before you know them.* ◆ *a reasonable/ false assumption* **2** [U] **the assumption of sth** the act of taking power or of starting an important job

assurance /əˈʃʊərəns; -ʃɔːr-/ *noun* **1** [C] a promise that sth will certainly happen or be true: *They* ***gave me an assurance that*** *the work would be finished by Friday.* **2** (also ˌself-asˈsurance) [U] the belief that you can do or succeed at sth; confidence

assure /əˈʃʊə(r); -ʃɔː(r)/ *verb* [T] **1** to promise sb that sth will certainly happen or be true, especially if they are worried: *I assure you that it is perfectly safe.* ◆ *Let me assure you of my full support.* **2** to make sth sure or certain: *The success of the new product assured the survival of the company.*

assured /əˈʃʊəd; əˈʃɔːd/ (also ˌself-asˈsured) *adj* believing that you can do sth or succeed at sth; confident: *The doctor had a calm and assured manner.*

asterisk /ˈæstərɪsk/ *noun* [C] the symbol (*) that you use to make people notice sth in a piece of writing

asteroid /ˈæstərɔɪd/ *noun* [C] one of the very large rocks or small planets which go around the sun

asthma /ˈæsmə/ *noun* [U] a medical condition that makes breathing difficult

asthmatic /æsˈmætɪk/ *noun* [C] a person who has **asthma** ▸ **asthmatic** *adj*

astonish /əˈstɒnɪʃ/ *verb* [T] to surprise sb very much: *She astonished everybody by announcing her engagement.* SYN **amaze** ▸ **astonished** *adj*: *I was astonished by the decision.*

astonishing /əˈstɒnɪʃɪŋ/ *adj* very surprising SYN **amazing** ▸ **astonishingly** *adv*

astonishment /əˈstɒnɪʃmənt/ *noun* [U] very great surprise: *He stared* ***in astonishment.*** SYN **amazement**

astound /əˈstaʊnd/ *verb* [T, usually passive] to surprise sb very much: *We were astounded by how well he performed.* SYN **amaze**

astounded /əˈstaʊndɪd/ *adj* feeling or showing great surprise: *We sat in astounded silence.*

astounding /əˈstaʊndɪŋ/ *adj* causing sb to feel extremely surprised: *an astounding success*

astray /əˈstreɪ/ *adv*
IDM **go astray** to become lost or be stolen
lead sb astray ➲ **lead¹**

astride /əˈstraɪd/ *prep, adv* with one leg on each side of sth: *to sit astride a horse*

astrologer /əˈstrɒlədʒə(r)/ *noun* [C] a person who is an expert in **astrology**

astrology /əˈstrɒlədʒi/ *noun* [U] the study of the positions and movements of the stars and planets and the way that some people believe they affect people and events ➲ note at **zodiac** ➲ look at **horoscope**

astronaut /ˈæstrənɔːt/ *noun* [C] a person who works and travels in space

astronomer /əˈstrɒnəmə(r)/ *noun* [C] a person who studies **astronomy**

astronomical /ˌæstrəˈnɒmɪkl/ *adj* **1** connected with **astronomy** **2** extremely large: *astronomical house prices*

astronomy /əˈstrɒnəmi/ *noun* [U] the scientific study of the sun, moon, stars, etc.

astute /əˈstjuːt/ *adj* very clever; good at judging people or situations

asylum /əˈsaɪləm/ *noun* [U] protection that a government gives to people who have left their own country for political reasons: *to give somebody political asylum*

aˈsylum seeker *noun* [C] a person who has been forced to leave their own country because they are in danger and who arrives in another country asking to be allowed to stay there

at /ət; *strong form* æt/ *prep* **1** used to show where sb/sth is or where sth happens: *at the bottom/top of the page* ◆ *He was standing at the door.* ◆ *Change trains at Chester.* ◆ *We were at home all weekend.* ◆ *Are the children at school?* ◆ *'Where's Peter?' 'He's at Sue's.'* (= at Sue's house) **2** used to show when sth happens: *I start work at 9 o'clock.* ◆ *at the weekend* ◆ *at night* ◆ *at Easter* ◆ *She got married at 18* (= when she was 18). **3** in the direction of sb/sth: *What are you looking at?* ◆ *He pointed at the child* *with his pen.* ◆ *Don't shout at me!* **4** used to show what sb is doing or what is happening: *They were* ***hard at work.*** ◆ *The two countries were* ***at war.*** **5** used to show the price, rate, speed, etc. of sth: *We were travelling at about 50 miles per hour.* **6** because of sth: *I was surprised at her behaviour.* ◆ *We laughed at his jokes.* **7** used with adjectives that show how well sb/sth does sth: *She's not very* ***good at*** *French.* **8** the symbol (@) used in email addresses

ate *past tense of* **eat**

atheism /ˈeɪθiɪzəm/ *noun* [U] the belief that there is no God ▸ **atheist** /-ɪst/ *noun* [C]

athlete /ˈæθliːt/ *noun* [C] a person who can run, jump, etc. very well, especially one who takes part in sports competitions, etc.

athletic /æθˈletɪk/ *adj* **1** (used about a person) having a fit, strong and healthy body **2** [only *before* a noun] connected with **athletes** or **athletics**: *athletic ability*

athletics /æθˈletɪks/ *noun* [U] sports such as running, jumping, throwing, etc. ➲ note at **sport** ➲ picture on **page P4**

atishoo /əˈtɪʃuː/ *exclam* used to represent the sound that you make when you suddenly **sneeze** (= blow air out of your nose, for example because you have a cold)

atlas /ˈætləs/ *noun* [C] a book of maps: *a road atlas of Europe* ➲ note at **book**

ATM /ˌeɪ tiːˈem/ = **cash machine**

ATˈM card (*AmE*) = **cash card**

⚷ **atmosphere** /ˈætməsfɪə(r)/ *noun* **1 the atmosphere** [C, usually sing] the mixture of gases that surrounds the earth or any other star, planet, etc: *the earth's atmosphere* **2** [sing] the air in a place: *a smoky atmosphere* **3** [sing] the mood or feeling of a place or situation: *The atmosphere of the meeting was relaxed.*

atmospheric /ˌætməsˈferɪk/ *adj* **1** [only *before* a noun] connected with the earth's atmosphere **2** creating a particular feeling or emotion: *atmospheric music*

⚷ **atom** /ˈætəm/ *noun* [C] the smallest part into which a chemical element can be divided: *the splitting of the atom* ◆ *(figurative) There isn't an atom of* (= there is no) *truth in these rumours.* ➲ look at **molecule**

ˈatom bomb = **atomic bomb**

atomic /əˈtɒmɪk/ *adj* connected with an atom or atoms: *atomic physics* ➲ look at **nuclear**

aˌtomic ˈbomb (also **ˈatom bomb**) *noun* [C] a bomb that explodes using the energy that is produced when an atom or atoms are split

aˌtomic ˈenergy *noun* [U] the energy that is produced when an atom or atoms are split. **Atomic energy** can be used to produce electricity.

atrocious /əˈtrəʊʃəs/ *adj* extremely bad: *atrocious weather* **SYN** **terrible** ▸ **atrociously** *adv*

atrocity /əˈtrɒsəti/ *noun* [C,U] (*pl* **atrocities**) (an action of) very cruel treatment of sb/sth: *Both sides were accused of committing atrocities during the war.*

⚷ **attach** /əˈtætʃ/ *verb* [T] **1 attach sth (to sth)** to fasten or join sth to sth: *I attached a label to each bag.* **OPP** **detach** **2 attach sth to sb/sth** to think that sth has a particular quality: *Don't attach too much importance to what they say.* **3** [usually passive] **attach sb/sth to sb/sth** to make sb/sth join or belong to sb/sth: *The research centre is attached to the university.*

IDM **(with) no strings attached; without strings** ➲ **string**[1]

⚷ **attached** /əˈtætʃt/ *adj* **1** [not before a noun] **attached to sb/sth** liking sb/sth very much: *He's become very attached to you.* **2 attached to sth** joined to sth: *Please complete the attached application form.*

attachment /əˈtætʃmənt/ *noun* **1** [C,U] **attachment (to/for sb/sth)** the feeling of liking sb/sth very much: *emotional attachment* **2** [C] something that you can fit on sth else to make it do a different job: *an electric drill with a range of attachments* **3** [C] a document that you send to sb using email

⚷ **attack**[1] /əˈtæk/ *noun* **1** [C,U] **(an) attack (on sb/sth)** trying to hurt or defeat sb/sth by using force: *The rebel forces launched an attack on the capital.* ◆ *The town was* ***under attack from*** *all sides.* **2** [C,U] **(an) attack (on sb/sth)** an act of saying strongly that you do not like or agree with sb/sth: *an outspoken attack on government policy* **3** [C] a short period when you suffer badly from a disease, medical condition, etc: *an attack of asthma/flu/nerves* **4** [C] the act of trying to score a point in a game of sport: *The home team went* ***on the attack*** *again.*

⚷ **attack**[2] /əˈtæk/ *verb* **1** [I,T] to try to hurt or defeat sb/sth by using force: *The child was attacked by a dog.* **2** [T] to say strongly that you do not like or agree with sb/sth: *Steffi attacked Guy's right-wing political views.* **3** [T] to damage or harm sb/sth: *a virus that attacks the nervous system* **4** [I,T] to try to score a point in a game of sport: *This team attacks better than it defends.*

attacker /əˈtækə(r)/ *noun* [C] a person who tries to hurt sb using force: *The victim of the assault didn't recognize his attackers.*

attain /əˈteɪn/ *verb* [T] to succeed in getting or achieving sth, especially after a lot of effort

attainable /əˈteɪnəbl/ *adj* that can be achieved: *realistically attainable targets*

attainment /əˈteɪnmənt/ *noun* **1** [C] a skill or sth you have achieved **2** [U] the act of achieving sth: *the attainment of the government's objectives*

⚷ **attempt**[1] /əˈtempt/ *noun* [C] **1 an attempt (to do sth/at doing sth)** an act of trying to do sth: *The thief* ***made no attempt*** *to run away.* ◆ *I failed the exam once but passed* ***at the*** *second* ***attempt.*** ◆ *They failed* ***in*** *their* ***attempt*** *to reach the North Pole.* **2 an attempt (on sb/sth)** trying to attack or beat sb/sth: *an attempt on somebody's life* (= to try to kill sb)

IDM **a last-ditch attempt** ➲ **last**[1]

attempt² /əˈtempt/ *verb* [T] **attempt (to do) sth** to try to do sth that is difficult: *Don't attempt to make him change his mind.*

attempted /əˈtemptɪd/ *adj* [only *before* a noun] (used about a crime, etc.) that sb has tried to do but without success: *attempted rape/murder/robbery* ♦ *She was accused of attempted murder* (= she didn't succeed).

attend /əˈtend/ *verb* **1** [I,T] to go to or be present at a place: *The children attend the local school.* ♦ *We'd like as many people as possible to attend.* **2** [I] (*formal*) **attend to sb/sth** to give your care, thought or attention to sb/sth or look after sb/sth: *Please attend to this matter immediately.*

attendance /əˈtendəns/ *noun* **1** [U] being present somewhere: *Attendance at lectures is compulsory.* **2** [C,U] the number of people who go to or are present at a place: *There was a poor attendance at the meeting.*

attendant¹ /əˈtendənt/ *noun* [C] a person whose job is to serve or help people in a public place: *a car park attendant*

attendant² /əˈtendənt/ *adj* [only *before* a noun] (*formal*) that goes together with or results from sth: *unemployment and all its attendant social problems*

attention¹ /əˈtenʃn/ *noun* [U] **1** watching, listening to or thinking about sb/sth carefully: *I shouted in order to* ***attract*** *her* ***attention****.* ♦ *Shy people hate to be* ***the centre of attention*** (= the person that everyone is watching). ♦ *to hold somebody's attention* (= to keep them interested in sth) **2** special care or action: *The hole in the roof needs urgent attention.* ♦ *to require* ***medical attention*** **3** a position in which a soldier stands up straight and still: *to stand/come to attention*

IDM **catch sb's attention/eye** ➲ **catch¹**
draw (sb's) attention to sth ➲ **draw¹**
get/have sb's undivided attention; give your undivided attention (to sb/sth) ➲ **undivided**
pay attention ➲ **pay¹**

attention² /əˈtenʃn/ *exclam* used for asking people to listen to sth carefully: *Attention, please! The boat will be leaving in five minutes.*

attentive /əˈtentɪv/ *adj* **attentive (to sb/sth)** watching, listening to or thinking about sb/sth carefully: *The hotel staff were very attentive to our needs.* OPP **inattentive** ▶ **attentively** *adv*: *to listen attentively to something*

attest /əˈtest/ *verb* [I] (*formal*) **attest (to sth)** to show or prove that sth is true: *Her long fight against cancer attests to her courage.*

attic /ˈætɪk/ *noun* [C] the space or room under the roof of a house ➲ look at **loft** ➲ picture on **page P8**

attitude /ˈætɪtjuːd/ *noun* [C] **an attitude (to/towards sb/sth)** the way that you think, feel or behave: *People's attitude to marriage is changing.* ♦ *She has a positive attitude to her work.*

attn (also **attn.**) *abbr* (in writing) **for the attention of**: *Sales Dept, attn C Biggs*

attorney /əˈtɜːni/ (*AmE*) = **lawyer**

attract /əˈtrækt/ *verb* [T] **1** [usually passive] to cause sb to like sb/sth: *She was attracted by his sense of humour.* **2** to cause sb/sth to go to sth or give attention to sth: *I waved to attract the waiter's attention.* ♦ *Moths are attracted to light.* ♦ *The new film has attracted a lot of publicity.*

attraction /əˈtrækʃn/ *noun* **1** [U] a feeling of liking sb/sth: *sexual attraction* **2** [C] something that is interesting or enjoyable: *The city offers all kinds of tourist attractions.*

attractive /əˈtræktɪv/ *adj* **1** (used about a person) beautiful or nice to look at: *He found her very attractive.* ➲ note at **beautiful** **2** that pleases or interests you; that you like: *an attractive part of the country* ♦ *an attractive idea* OPP for both meanings **unattractive** ▶ **attractively** *adv* ▶ **attractiveness** *noun* [U]

attribute¹ /əˈtrɪbjuːt/ *verb* [T] **attribute sth to sb/sth** to believe that sth was caused or done by sb/sth: *Mustafa attributes his success to hard work.* ♦ *a poem attributed to Shakespeare*

attribute² /ˈætrɪbjuːt/ *noun* [C] a quality of sb/sth: *physical attributes* SYN **feature**

attributive /əˈtrɪbjətɪv/ *adj* (used about an adjective or a noun) used before a noun to describe it: *In 'the blue sky' and 'a family business', 'blue' and 'family' are attributive.* ➲ look at **predicative** ▶ **attributively** *adv*: *Some adjectives can only be used attributively.*

atypical /ˌeɪˈtɪpɪkl/ *adj* (*formal*) not typical of a particular type, group, etc: *atypical behaviour* OPP **typical** ➲ look at **untypical**

aubergine /ˈəʊbəʒiːn/ (*AmE* **eggplant**) *noun* [C,U] a long vegetable with dark purple skin ➲ picture on **page P15**

auburn /ˈɔːbən/ *adj* (used about hair) reddish-brown

auction¹ /ˈɔːkʃn/ *noun* [C,U] a public sale at which items are sold to the person who offers to pay the most money: *The house was sold* ***at/by auction****.*

auction² /ˈɔːkʃn/ *verb* [T] **auction sth (off)** to sell sth at an **auction**

auctioneer /ˌɔːkʃəˈnɪə(r)/ *noun* [C] a person who organizes the selling at an **auction**

audacious /ɔːˈdeɪʃəs/ *adj* (*formal*) willing to take risks or to do sth shocking: *an audacious decision* SYN **daring** ▶ **audaciously** *adv*

audacity /ɔːˈdæsəti/ *noun* [U] behaviour that shows courage but that is also rude or shocking: *He* ***had the audacity*** *to say I was too fat.* SYN **nerve**

audible /ˈɔːdəbl/ *adj* that can be heard: *Her speech was* ***barely audible****.* OPP **inaudible** ▶ **audibly** /-əbli/ *adv*

audience /ˈɔːdiəns/ *noun* [C] **1** [with sing or pl verb] all the people who are watching or listening to a play, concert, speech, the TV, etc: *The audience was/were wild with excitement.* ♦ *There were only about 200 people in the audience.* ➲ note at **theatre**

A

2 a formal meeting with a very important person: *He was granted an audience with the President.*

audio /ˈɔːdiəʊ/ *adj* [only *before* a noun] connected with the recording of sound: *audio equipment* ◆ *audio and video cassettes*

audio-ˈvisual *adj* using both sound and pictures

audit /ˈɔːdɪt/ *noun* [C] an official examination of the present state of sth, especially of a company's financial records: *to carry out an audit* ▶ **audit** *verb* [T]

audition¹ /ɔːˈdɪʃn/ *noun* [C] a short performance by a singer, an actor, etc. to find out if they are good enough to be in a play, show, etc.

audition² /ɔːˈdɪʃn/ *verb* [I,T] audition (sb) (for sth) to do or to watch sb do an **audition**: *I auditioned for a part in the play.* ◆ *They're auditioning singers for the band.*

auditor /ˈɔːdɪtə(r)/ *noun* [C] a person whose job is to examine a company's financial records

auditorium /ˌɔːdɪˈtɔːriəm/ *noun* [C] (*pl* auditoriums *or* auditoria /-riə/) the part of a theatre, concert hall, etc. where the audience sits

Aug. *abbr* = **August**: *10 Aug. 1957*

augment /ɔːgˈment/ *verb* [T] (*formal*) to increase the amount, value, size, etc. of sth ▶ **augmentation** /ˌɔːgmenˈteɪʃn/ *noun* [C,U]

augur /ˈɔːgə(r)/ *verb*
IDM **augur well/ill for sb/sth** (*formal*) to be a good/bad sign of what will happen in the future

August /ˈɔːgəst/ *noun* [U,C] (*abbr* Aug.) the 8th month of the year, coming after July ➲ note at **January**

aunt /ɑːnt/ (also *informal* auntie; aunty /ˈɑːnti/) *noun* [C] the sister of your father or mother; the wife of your uncle: *Aunt Ellen* ◆ *My aunt lives in Australia.*

au pair /ˌəʊ ˈpeə(r)/ *noun* (*BrE*) [C] a person, usually a girl, from another country who comes to live with a family in order to learn the language. An **au pair** helps to clean the house and look after the children.

aura /ˈɔːrə/ *noun* [C] (*formal*) the quality that sb/sth seems to have

aural /ˈɔːrəl/ *adj* connected with hearing and listening: *an aural comprehension test* ➲ look at **oral**

auspices /ˈɔːspɪsɪz/ *noun*
IDM **under the auspices of sb/sth** with the help and support of sb/sth

auspicious /ɔːˈspɪʃəs/ *adj* that seems likely to be successful in the future: *She made an auspicious start to her professional career when she won her first race.* OPP **inauspicious**

austere /ɒˈstɪə(r)/ *adj* **1** very simple; without decoration **2** (used about a person) very strict and serious **3** not having anything that makes your life more comfortable: *The nuns lead simple and austere lives.* ▶ **austerity** /ɒˈsterəti/ *noun* [U]

authentic /ɔːˈθentɪk/ *adj* **1** that you know is real or genuine: *an authentic Van Gogh painting* **2** true or accurate: *an authentic model of the building* ▶ **authenticity** /ˌɔːθenˈtɪsəti/ *noun* [U]

author /ˈɔːθə(r)/ *noun* [C] a person who writes a book, play, etc: *a well-known author of detective novels* ◆ *Who's your favourite author?* ▶ **authorship** *noun* [U]

authoritarian /ɔːˌθɒrɪˈteəriən/ *adj* not allowing people the freedom to decide things for themselves: *authoritarian parents*

authoritative /ɔːˈθɒrətətɪv/ *adj* **1** having authority; demanding or expecting that people obey you: *an authoritative tone of voice* **2** that you can trust and respect as true and correct: *They will be able to give you authoritative advice on the problem.*

authority /ɔːˈθɒrəti/ *noun* (*pl* authorities)
➤POWER **1** [U] the power and right to give orders and make others obey: *Children often begin to question their parents' authority at a very early age.* ◆ *You must get this signed by a person* ***in authority*** (= who has a position of power).
➤PERMISSION **2** [U] authority (to do sth) the right or permission to do sth: *The police* ***have the authority*** *to question anyone they wish.* ◆ *He was sacked for using a company vehicle* ***without authority.***
➤OFFICIAL GROUP **3** [C, usually pl] a person, group or government department that has the power to give orders, make official decisions, etc: *I have to report this to the authorities.*
➤KNOWLEDGE **4** [U] the power to influence people because they respect your knowledge or official position: *He spoke with authority and everybody listened.*
➤EXPERT **5** [C] an authority (on sth) a person with special knowledge: *He's an authority on criminal law.*

authorize (also -ise) /ˈɔːθəraɪz/ *verb* [T] to give official permission for sth or for sb to do sth: *He authorized his secretary to sign letters in his absence.* ▶ **authorization** (also -isation) /ˌɔːθəraɪˈzeɪʃn/ *noun* [U]

autistic /ɔːˈtɪstɪk/ *adj* having a serious mental illness which makes it very difficult to form relationships with other people

autobiography /ˌɔːtəbaɪˈɒgrəfi/ *noun* [C,U] (*pl* autobiographies) the story of a person's life, written by that person ➲ note at **book** ➲ look at **biography** ▶ **autobiographical** /ˌɔːtəˌbaɪəˈgræfɪkl/ *adj*

autograph /ˈɔːtəgrɑːf/ *noun* [C] a famous person's name, written by that person and given to sb: *The players stopped outside the stadium to* ***sign autographs.*** ▶ **autograph** *verb* [T]: *The whole team have autographed the football.*

automate /ˈɔːtəmeɪt/ *verb* [T, usually passive] to make sth operate by machine, without needing people

automatic¹ /ˌɔːtəˈmætɪk/ *adj* **1** (used about a machine) that can work by itself without direct human control: *an automatic washing machine* **2** done without thinking: *Practise this exercise until it becomes automatic.* **3** always happening as a result of a particular action or situation: *All the staff have an automatic right to a space in the car park.* ▶ **automatically** /-kli/ *adv*: *The lights will come on automatically when it gets dark.* ◆ *You will automat-*

A

ically receive a reminder when your next payment is due.

automatic² /ˌɔːtəˈmætɪk/ *noun* [C] an **automatic** machine, gun or car: *This car is an automatic* (= has automatic gears).

automation /ˌɔːtəˈmeɪʃn/ *noun* [U] the use of machines instead of people to do work

automobile /ˈɔːtəməbiːl/ (*AmE*) = **car**(1)

autonomy /ɔːˈtɒnəmi/ *noun* [U] the right of a person, an organization, a region, etc. to govern or control their or its own affairs ▶ **autonomous** /ɔːˈtɒnəməs/ *adj*: *The people in this region want to be completely autonomous.*

autopsy /ˈɔːtɒpsi/ *noun* [C] (*pl* autopsies) an examination of a dead body to find out the cause of death

🔑 **autumn** /ˈɔːtəm/ (*AmE usually* fall) *noun* [C,U] the season of the year that comes between summer and winter: *In autumn the leaves on the trees begin to fall.* ▶ **autumnal** /ɔːˈtʌmnəl/ *adj*

auxiliary /ɔːɡˈzɪliəri/ *adj* [only *before* a noun] giving extra help: *auxiliary nurses/troops/staff*

auˌxiliary ˈverb *noun* [C] a verb (for example *be, do* or *have*) that is used with a main verb to show tense, etc. or to form questions

avail /əˈveɪl/ *noun*
IDM **of little/no avail** not helpful; having little or no effect
to little/no avail without success: *They searched everywhere, but to no avail.*

availability /əˌveɪləˈbɪləti/ *noun* [U] the state of being available: *You will receive the colour you order, subject to availability* (= if it is available).

🔑 **available** /əˈveɪləbl/ *adj* **1** available (to sb) (used about things) that you can get, buy, use, etc: *This information is easily available to everyone at the local library.* ◆ *Refreshments are available at the snack bar.* **2** (used about people) free to be seen, talked to, etc: *The minister was not available for comment.*

avalanche /ˈævəlɑːnʃ/ *noun* [C] a very large amount of snow that slides quickly down the side of a mountain: *Two skiers are still missing after yesterday's avalanche.*

the avant-garde /ˌævɒŋ ˈɡɑːd/ *noun* [sing] extremely modern works of art, music or literature, or the artists who create these ▶ **avant-garde** *adj*

avarice /ˈævərɪs/ *noun* [U] (*formal*) extreme desire to be rich SYN **greed** ▶ **avaricious** /ˌævəˈrɪʃəs/ *adj*

avatar /ˈævətɑː(r)/ *noun* [C] **1** (in Hinduism and Buddhism) a god appearing in a physical form **2** a picture of a person or an animal that represents a particular user on a computer screen

Ave. *abbr* = **avenue**: *26 Elm Ave.*

avenge /əˈvendʒ/ *verb* [T] avenge sth; avenge yourself on sb to punish sb for hurting you, your family, etc. in some way: *He wanted to avenge his father's murder.* ◆ *He wanted to avenge himself on his father's murderer.* ➲ look at **revenge**

avenue /ˈævənjuː/ *noun* [C] **1** (*abbr* Ave.) a wide street, especially one with trees or tall buildings on each side: *I live on Kingsdown Avenue.* **2** a way of doing or getting sth: *We must explore every avenue open to us* (= try every possibility).

🔑 **average¹** /ˈævərɪdʒ/ *adj* **1** [only *before* a noun] (used about a number) found by calculating the **average²**(1): *What's the average age of your students?* **2** normal or typical: *children of* ***above/below average*** *intelligence*

🔑 **average²** /ˈævərɪdʒ/ *noun* **1** [C] the number you get when you add two or more figures together and then divide the total by the number of figures you added: *The average of 14, 3 and 1 is 6* (= 18 divided by 3 is 6). ◆ *He has scored 93 goals at* ***an average of*** *1.55 per game.* **2** [sing,U] the normal standard, amount or quality: ***On average****, I buy a newspaper about twice a week.*

average³ /ˈævərɪdʒ/ *verb* [T] to do, get, etc. a certain amount as an average: *If we average 50 miles an hour we should arrive at about 4 o'clock.*
PHR V **average out (at sth)** to result in an average (of sth)

averse /əˈvɜːs/ *adj* [not before a noun] (*formal*) [often with a negative] averse to sth against or not in favour of sth: *He is not averse to trying out new ideas.*

aversion /əˈvɜːʃn/ *noun* [C,usually sing] an aversion (to sb/sth) a strong feeling of not liking sb/sth: *Some people* ***have an aversion*** *to spiders.*

avert /əˈvɜːt/ *verb* [T] to prevent sth unpleasant: *The accident could have been averted.*

aviary /ˈeɪviəri/ *noun* [C] (*pl* aviaries) a large **cage** (= a box made of bars) or area in which birds are kept

aviation /ˌeɪviˈeɪʃn/ *noun* [U] the designing, building and flying of aircraft

avid /ˈævɪd/ *adj* **1** very enthusiastic about sth (usually a hobby): *an avid collector of antiques* SYN **keen** **2** avid for sth wanting to get sth very much: *Journalists crowded round the entrance, avid for news.* ▶ **avidly** *adv*: *He read avidly as a child.*

avocado /ˌævəˈkɑːdəʊ/ *noun* [C] (*pl* avocados) a tropical fruit that is wider at one end than the other, with a hard green skin and a large stone inside ➲ picture on **page P14**

🔑 **avoid** /əˈvɔɪd/ *verb* [T] **1** avoid sth/doing sth to prevent sth happening or to try not to do sth: *He always tried to avoid an argument if possible.* ◆ *She has to avoid eating fatty food.* **2** to keep away from sb/sth: *I leave home early to avoid the rush hour.* ▶ **avoidance** *noun* [U]

avoidable /əˈvɔɪdəbl/ *adj* that can be prevented; unnecessary OPP **unavoidable**

await /əˈweɪt/ *verb* [T] (*formal*) to wait for sb/sth: *We sat down to await the arrival of the guests.*

🔑 **awake¹** /əˈweɪk/ *adj* [not before a noun] not sleeping: *I was sleepy this morning but I'm* ***wide awake*** *now.* ◆ *They were so tired that they found it difficult to* *stay awake.* ♦ *I hope our singing didn't* ***keep*** *you* ***awake*** *last night.* OPP **asleep**

awake² /əˈweɪk/ *verb* [I,T] (*pt* awoke /əˈwəʊk/; *pp* awoken /əˈwəʊkən/) to wake up; to make sb/sth wake up: *I awoke to find that it was already 9 o'clock.* ♦ *A sudden loud noise awoke us.* ➲ A more common expression is **wake up.**

awaken /əˈweɪkən/ *verb* **1** [I,T] (*written*) to wake up; to make sb/sth wake up: *We were awakened by a loud knock at the door.* ➲ A much more common expression is **wake up. 2** [T] (*formal*) to produce a particular feeling, attitude, etc. in sb: *The film awakened memories of her childhood.*

PHR V **awaken sb to sth** to make sb notice or realize sth for the first time: *The letter awakened me to the seriousness of the situation.*

awakening /əˈweɪkənɪŋ/ *noun* [C, usually sing] **1** a moment when sb notices or realizes sth for the first time: *It was a rude* (= unpleasant) *awakening when I suddenly found myself unemployed.* **2** the act of starting to feel or understand sth; the start of a feeling, etc: *the awakening of an interest in the opposite sex*

⚷ **award¹** /əˈwɔːd/ *noun* [C] **1** a prize, etc. that sb gets for doing sth well: *This year the awards for best actor and actress went to two Americans.* **2** an amount of money given to sb as the result of a court decision: *She* ***received an award of*** *£5000 for damages.*

⚷ **award²** /əˈwɔːd/ *verb* [T] award sth (to sb) to give sth to sb as a prize, payment, etc: *She was awarded first prize in the gymnastics competition.* ♦ *The court awarded £10 000 each to the workers injured in the accident.*

⚷ **aware** /əˈweə(r)/ *adj* **1** [not before a noun] aware (of sb/sth); aware (that) knowing about or realizing sth; conscious of sb/sth: *I am* ***well aware*** *of the problems you face.* ♦ *I suddenly* ***became aware*** *that someone was watching me.* ♦ *There is no other entrance,* ***as far as I am aware.*** OPP **unaware 2** interested in and knowing about sth: *Many young people are very politically aware.*

awareness /əˈweənəs/ *noun* [U] knowledge or interest: *People's awareness of healthy eating has increased in recent years.* SYN **consciousness**

awash /əˈwɒʃ/ *adj* [not before a noun] awash (with sth) covered with water: (*figurative*) *The city was awash with rumours.*

⚷ **away** /əˈweɪ/ *adv* **1** away (from sth) at a particular distance from a place: *The village is two miles away from the sea.* ♦ *My parents live five minutes away.* **2** in the future: *Our summer holiday is only three weeks away.* **3** away (from sb/sth) to a different place or in a different direction: *Go away! I'm busy!* ♦ *I called his name, but he just walked away from me.* **4** into a place where sth is usually kept: *Put your books away now.* ♦ *They cleared the dishes away* (= off the table). ♦ *I'm going to throw my old clothes away* (= put them in the rubbish). **5** away (from sth) (used about people) not present: *My neighbours are away on holiday at the moment.* ♦ *Aki was away from school for two weeks with measles.* SYN **absent 6** continuously, without stopping: *They chatted away for hours.* **7** until sth disappears: *The crash of thunder slowly died away.* ♦ *He's given most of his money away.* **8** (used about a football, etc. match) on the other team's ground: *Our team's playing away on Saturday.* ♦ *an away match/game* OPP **home** ℹ For special uses with many verbs, for example **give away**, look at the verb entries.

IDM **do away with sb/sth** to get rid of sb/sth: *The government are going to do away with the tax on fuel.*

right/straight away immediately; without any delay: *I'll phone the doctor right away.*

awe /ɔː/ *noun* [U] feelings of respect and either fear or admiration: *We watched in awe as the rocket took off.*

IDM **be in awe of sb/sth** to admire sb/sth and be slightly afraid of them or it: *As a young boy he was very much in awe of his uncle.*

ˈ**awe-inspiring** *adj* causing a feeling of respect and fear or admiration

awesome /ˈɔːsəm/ *adj* **1** impressive and sometimes frightening: *an awesome task* **2** (*AmE slang*) very good; excellent

⚷ **awful** /ˈɔːfl/ *adj* **1** very bad or unpleasant: *We had an awful holiday. It rained every day.* ♦ *I feel awful—I think I'll go to bed.* ♦ *What an awful thing to say!* SYN **terrible** ➲ note at **bad 2** [only *before* a noun] (*informal*) very great: *We've got* ***an awful lot*** *of work to do.* **3** terrible; very serious: *I'm afraid there's been some awful news.*

⚷ **awfully** /ˈɔːfli/ *adv* (*informal*) very; extremely: *I'm awfully sorry.* SYN **terribly**

⚷ **awkward** /ˈɔːkwəd/ *adj* **1** embarrassed or embarrassing: *I often feel awkward in a group of people.* ♦ *There was an awkward silence.* **2** difficult to deal with: *That's an awkward question.* ♦ *You've put me in an awkward position.* ♦ *an awkward customer* ♦ *The box isn't heavy but it's awkward to carry.* SYN **difficult 3** not convenient: *My mother always phones at an awkward time.* ♦ *This tin-opener is very awkward to clean.* SYN **difficult 4** not using the body in the best way; not elegant or comfortable: *I was sitting with my legs in an awkward position.* ▶ **awkwardly** *adv* ▶ **awkwardness** *noun* [U]

awning /ˈɔːnɪŋ/ *noun* [C] a sheet of strong cloth that spreads out above a door or window to protect it from the sun or rain

awoke *past tense of* **awake²**

awoken *past participle of* **awake²**

awry /əˈraɪ/ *adv, adj* [not before a noun] wrong, not in the way that was planned; untidy

axe¹ (*especially AmE* ax) /æks/ *noun* [C] a tool with a wooden handle and a heavy metal head with a sharp edge, used for cutting wood, etc.

axe² (*especially AmE* ax) /æks/ *verb* [T] **1** (used especially in newspapers) to reduce sth by a great amount: *Budgets are to be axed.* **2** to remove sb/sth: *Hundreds of jobs have been axed.*

axis /ˈæksɪs/ *noun* [C] (*pl* axes /ˈæksiːz/) **1** a line we imagine through the middle of an object, around which the object turns: *The earth rotates on its axis.* ➲ picture at **earth** **2** a fixed line used for marking measurements on a **graph** (= a diagram with lines on it to show the relationship between two sets of numbers): *the horizontal/vertical axis*

axle /ˈæksl/ *noun* [C] a bar that connects a pair of wheels on a vehicle

azure /ˈæʒə(r); *BrE also* ˈæzjʊə(r)/ *adj, noun* [U] (of) a bright blue colour like the sky

B, b /biː/ *noun* [C,U] (*pl* Bs; B's; b's /biːz/) **1** the second letter of the English alphabet: *'Bicycle' begins with (a) 'B'.* **2** B (used about music) the seventh note in the scale of C major: *B major/minor* ◆ *B flat*

b. *abbr* = **born**[1]: *J S Bach, b. 1685*

BA /ˌbiː ˈeɪ/ *abbr* **Bachelor of Arts**; the degree that you receive when you complete a university or college course in an arts subject ➲ look at **BSc, MA**

baa /bɑː/ *noun* [sing] the sound that a sheep makes

babble[1] /ˈbæbl/ *noun* [sing] **1** the sound of many voices talking at the same time: *a babble of voices* **2** talking that is confused or silly and is difficult to understand: *I can't bear his constant babble.*

babble[2] /ˈbæbl/ *verb* [I] **1** to talk quickly or in a way that is difficult to understand **2** to make the sound of water running over stones

babe /beɪb/ *noun* [C] **1** (*old-fashioned*) a baby **2** (*especially AmE slang*) used when talking to sb, especially a girl or young woman: *It's OK, babe.* **3** (*slang*) an attractive young woman

baboon /bəˈbuːn/ *noun* [C] a large African or Asian **monkey** (= an animal that lives in hot countries and can climb trees) with a long face like a dog's

⚷ **baby** /ˈbeɪbi/ *noun* [C] (*pl* **babies**) **1** a very young child: *I'm going to* ***have a baby.*** ◆ *She's* ***expecting a baby*** *early next year.* ◆ *When's the baby* ***due?*** (= when will it be born?) ◆ *a baby boy/girl* **2** a very young animal or bird: *a baby rabbit* **3** (*AmE slang*) a person, especially a girl or young woman, that you like or love

TOPIC

Babies

A **pregnant** woman has a baby growing inside her; you can also say: *She's* ***having/expecting*** *a baby.* She **gives birth** and the baby **is born**, usually with the help of a **midwife**. If a baby is born early, it is **premature**. If a mother gives birth to two babies at the same time, they are **twins**. Parents **take care of** their baby by feeding it, bathing it and changing its **nappy**. A woman whose job is to look after other people's babies and children is a **nanny**. A baby sleeps in a **cot** and you take it outside in a **pram**. As a baby grows up and starts to walk it is called a **toddler**.

ˈ**baby boom** *noun* [C, usually sing] a time when more babies are born than usual

ˈ**baby carriage** (*AmE*) = **pram**

babyish /ˈbeɪbiɪʃ/ *adj* suitable for or behaving like a baby: *This book is a bit too babyish for Faruk now.*

babysit /ˈbeɪbisɪt/ *verb* [I] (**babysitting**; *pt, pp* **babysat**) to look after a child for a short time while the parents are out: *I sometimes babysit for our neighbours' children at weekends.* ▶ **babysitter** *noun* [C]

bachelor /ˈbætʃələ(r)/ *noun* [C] **1** a man who has not yet married ➲ look at **spinster**

MORE Nowadays **single** is the most usual word for describing a man who is not married: *a single man.*

2 a person who has a first university degree: *a Bachelor of Arts/Science*

back

⚷ **back**[1] /bæk/ *noun* [C] **1** the part of a person's or an animal's body between the neck and the bottom: *Do you sleep* ***on your back*** *or on your side?* ◆ *She was standing* ***with*** *her* ***back to*** *me so I couldn't see her face.* ◆ *A camel has a hump on its back.* **2** [usually sing] the part or side of sth that is furthest from the front: *I sat* ***at the back of*** *the class.* ◆ *The answers are* ***in the back of*** *the book.* ◆ *Write your address* ***on the back of*** *the cheque.* **3** the part of a chair that supports your upper body when you sit down: *He put his coat over the back of the chair.*

IDM **at/in the back of your mind** if sth is at the back of your mind, it is in your thoughts but is not the main thing that you are thinking about: *With next week's exam at the back of my mind, I couldn't relax and enjoy the film.*

back to front with the back where the front should be: *Wait a minute–you've got your jumper on back to front.* ➲ look at **way**[1](3)

behind sb's back without sb's knowledge or agreement: *They criticized her behind her back.* **OPP** **to sb's face**

get off sb's back (*informal*) to stop annoying sb, for example when you keep asking them to do sth: *I've told her I'll do the job by Monday, so I wish she'd get off my back!*

know sth like the back of your hand ➲ **know**[1]

a pat on the back ➲ **pat**[2]

B

turn your back on sb/sth to refuse to be involved with sb/sth: *He turned his back on his career and went to live in the country.*

⚷ **back²** /bæk/ *adj* [only *before* a noun] **1** furthest from the front: *Have you locked the back door?* ◆ *the back row of the theatre* ◆ *back teeth* **2** owed from a time in the past: *back pay/rent*
IDM **take a back seat** to allow sb to play a more important or active role than yourself in a particular situation

⚷ **back³** /bæk/ *adv* **1** away from the direction you are facing or moving in: *She walked away without **looking back**.* ◆ *Could everyone **move back** a bit, please?* **OPP** **forward** **2** away from sth; under control: *The police were unable to **keep** the crowds **back**.* ◆ *She tried to **hold back** her tears.* **3** in or to a place or state that sb/sth was in before: *I'm going out now—I'll **be back** about 6 o'clock.* ◆ *It started to rain so I **came back** home.* ◆ ***Go back** to sleep.* ◆ *Could I **have** my pen **back**, please?* ◆ *I've got to **take** these books **back** to the library.* **4** in or into the past; ago: *I met him a few years back, in Madrid.* ◆ ***Think back** to your first day at school.* **5** in return or in reply: *He said he'd **phone** me **back** in half an hour.*
IDM **back and forth** from one place to another and back again, all the time: *Travelling back and forth to work takes up a lot of time.*

⚷ **back⁴** /bæk/ *verb* **1** [I,T] to move backwards or to make sth move backwards: *She backed into her office and closed the door.* ◆ *He backed the car into the parking space.* **2** [T] to give help or support to sb/sth: *We can go ahead with the scheme if the bank will agree to back us.* **3** [T] to bet money that a particular horse, team, etc. will win in a race or game: *Which horse are you backing in the 2 o'clock race?* **4** [I] to face sth at the back: *Many of the colleges back onto the river.*
PHR V **back away (from sb/sth)** to move backwards because you are afraid, shocked, etc: *He began to back slowly away from the snake.*
back down to stop saying that you are right: *I think you are right to demand an apology. Don't back down now.*
back out (of sth) to decide not to do sth that you had promised to do: *You promised to come with me. You just can't back out of it now!*
back sb/sth up to support sb; to say or show that sth is true: *I'm going to say exactly what I think at the meeting. Will you back me up?* ◆ *All the evidence backed up what she had said.*
back (sth) up to move backwards, especially in a vehicle: *Back up a little so that the other cars can get past.*
back sth up to make a copy of a computer file, etc. that can be used if the original one is lost or damaged

ˌback ˈbench *noun* [C, usually pl] (in Britain) a seat in the House of Commons for an ordinary member of Parliament: *to sit on the back benches* ◆ *backbench MPs* ▶ **backbencher** *noun* [C]

backbone /ˈbækbəʊn/ *noun* **1** [C] the row of small bones that are connected together down the middle of your back **SYN** **spine** ➲ picture at **body** **2** [sing] the most important part of sth: *Agriculture is the backbone of their economy.*

backcloth /ˈbækklɒθ/ = **backdrop**

backdate /ˌbækˈdeɪt/ *verb* [T] to make a document, cheque or payment take effect from an earlier date: *The pay rise will be backdated to 1 April.*

backdrop /ˈbækdrɒp/ (also **backcloth**) *noun* [C] a painted piece of cloth that is hung at the back of the stage in a theatre

backer /ˈbækə(r)/ *noun* [C] a person, an organization or a company that gives support to sb, especially financial support

backfire /ˌbækˈfaɪə(r)/ *verb* [I] to have an unexpected and unpleasant result, often the opposite of what was intended

backgammon /ˈbækgæmən/ *noun* [U] a game for two people played by moving pieces around a board marked with long thin triangles

⚷ **background** /ˈbækgraʊnd/ *noun* **1** [C] the type of family and social class you come from and the education and experience you have: *We get on very well together in spite of our different backgrounds.* **2** [sing, U] the facts or events that are connected with a situation: *The talks are taking place against a background of increasing tension.* ◆ *I need some background information.* **3** [sing] the part of a view, scene, picture, etc. which is furthest away from the person looking at it: *You can see the mountains **in the background** of the photo.* **OPP** **foreground** **4** [sing] a position where sb/sth can be seen/heard, etc. but is not the centre of attention: *The film star's husband prefers to stay in the background.* ◆ *All the time I was speaking to her, I could hear a child crying **in the background**.* ◆ *I like to have **background music** when I'm studying.*

backhand /ˈbækhænd/ *noun* [sing] a way of hitting the ball in sports such as **tennis** that is made with the back of your hand facing forward **OPP** **forehand**

backing /ˈbækɪŋ/ *noun* [U] help or support to do sth, especially financial support: *financial backing* ◆ *a **backing group/singer/track*** (= one that accompanies the main singer or tune)

backlash /ˈbæklæʃ/ *noun* [sing] a strong negative reaction against a political or social event or development

backlog /ˈbæklɒg/ *noun* [C, usually sing] an amount of work, etc. that has not yet been done and should have been done already: *Because I've been off sick, I've got a backlog of work to catch up on.*

backpack¹ /ˈbækpæk/ (also **pack**, *BrE also* **rucksack**) *noun* [C] a large bag, often on a metal frame, that you carry on your back when you are travelling ➲ picture at **bag** ➲ picture on **page P1**

backpack² /ˈbækpæk/ *verb* [I] to go walking or travelling with your clothes, etc. in a **backpack** ➲ note at **holiday**

HELP **Go backpacking** is used when you are talking about spending time backpacking: *We went backpacking round Europe last summer.*

▸ **backpacker** *noun* [C]

backside /ˈbæksaɪd/ *noun* [C] (*informal*) the part of your body that you sit on **SYN** **bottom**

backslash /ˈbækslæʃ/ *noun* [C] a mark (\), used in computer commands ➲ look at **forward slash**

backstage /ˌbækˈsteɪdʒ/ *adv* in the part of a theatre where the actors get dressed, wait to perform, etc.

backstroke /ˈbækstrəʊk/ *noun* [U] a style of swimming that you do on your back: *Can you **do backstroke**?* ➲ picture at **swim**

backtrack /ˈbæktræk/ *verb* [I] **1** to go back the same way you came: *We got lost in the wood and had to backtrack.* **2** **backtrack (on sth)** to change your mind about a plan, promise, etc. that you have made: *Unions forced the company to backtrack on its plans to close the factory.*

backup /ˈbækʌp/ *noun* **1** [U] extra help or support that you can get if necessary: *The police officer requested urgent backup from the rest of the team.* **2** [C] a copy of a computer file, etc. that you can use if the original one is lost or damaged: *Always make a backup of your files.*

backward /ˈbækwəd/ *adj* **1** [only *before* a noun] directed towards the back: *a backward step/glance* **OPP** **forward** **2** slow to develop or learn: *Our teaching methods are backward compared to some countries.*

backwards /ˈbækwədz/ (*especially AmE* **backward**) *adv* **1** towards a place or a position that is behind: *Could everybody take a step backwards?* **2** in the opposite direction to usual: *Can you say the alphabet backwards?* **OPP** for both meanings **forwards**

IDM **backward(s) and forward(s)** first in one direction and then in the other, many times: *The dog ran backwards and forwards, barking loudly.*

backwater /ˈbækwɔːtə(r)/ *noun* [C] a place that is away from the places where most things happen and so is not affected by new ideas or outside events

backyard /ˌbækˈjɑːd/ *noun* [C] **1** (*BrE*) an area behind a house, with a hard surface and a wall or fence around it **2** (*AmE*) the whole area behind the house including the grass area and the garden

bacon /ˈbeɪkən/ *noun* [U] meat from the back or sides of a pig that has been **cured** (= treated with salt or smoke to keep it fresh), usually served in thin slices ➲ note at **meat** ➲ look at **gammon, ham, pork**

bacteria /bækˈtɪəriə/ *noun* [pl] very small living things that can only be seen with a **microscope** (= a piece of equipment that makes small objects look bigger). Bacteria exist in large numbers in air, water, soil, plants and the bodies of people and animals. Some bacteria cause disease. ➲ look at **virus** ▸ **bacterial** *adj*: *bacterial infections*

bad /bæd/ *adj* (**worse** /wɜːs/, **worst** /wɜːst/)

➤UNPLEASANT **1** not good; unpleasant: *bad weather* ◆ *I'm afraid I've got some bad news for you.* ◆ *It's bad enough losing your job, but to lose your house as well is awful.*

➤POOR QUALITY **2** of poor quality; of a low standard: *Many accidents are caused by bad driving.* ◆ *This isn't as bad as I thought.*

➤NOT SKILFUL **3** **bad (at sth/at doing sth)** not able to do sth well or easily: *a bad teacher/driver/cook* ◆ *I've always been bad at sport.* **SYN** **poor**

➤SERIOUS **4** serious: *The traffic was very bad on the way to work.* ◆ *She went home with a bad headache.* ◆ *That was a very bad mistake!*

➤NOT SUITABLE **5** [only *before* a noun] difficult or not suitable: *This is a bad time to phone—everyone's out to lunch.*

➤PERSON/BEHAVIOUR **6** not good; morally wrong: *He was not a bad man, just rather weak.*

➤HARMFUL **7** [not before a noun] **bad for sb/sth** likely to damage or hurt sb/sth: *Sugar is bad for your teeth.*

➤PART OF THE BODY **8** not healthy; painful: *He's always had a bad heart.* ◆ *Keith's off work with a bad back.*

➤FOOD **9** not fresh or suitable to eat: *These eggs will **go bad** if we don't eat them soon.*

IDM **not bad** (*informal*) quite good: *'What was the film like?' 'Not bad.'*

too bad (*informal*) used to show that nothing can be done to change a situation: *'I'd much rather stay at home.' 'Well that's just too bad. We've said we'll go.'* ℹ For other idioms containing **bad**, look at the entries for the nouns, adjectives, etc. For example, **go through a bad patch** is at **patch**.

> OTHER WORDS FOR
>
> **bad**
>
> You can say **awful, dreadful** or **terrible** instead of 'very bad'. **Horrible** describes somebody or something that is unpleasant or somebody who is unkind: *He's always saying horrible things to me.* We also say: ***poor** quality* ◆ *an **unpleasant** experience* ◆ *a **disgusting** smell* ◆ *a **serious** accident/illness/problem*

baddy /ˈbædi/ *noun* [C] (*pl* **baddies**) (*informal*) a bad person in a film, book, etc. **OPP** **goody**

badge /bædʒ/ *noun* [C] a small piece of metal, cloth or plastic with a design or words on it that you wear on your clothing: *The players all have jackets with the club badge on.*

badges

badge

badge

badger /ˈbædʒə(r)/ *noun* [C] an animal with black and white lines on its head that lives in holes in the ground and comes out at night ➲ picture on **page 48**

bad ˈlanguage *noun* [U] words that are used for swearing: *You'll get into trouble if you use bad language.*

badger

badly /ˈbædli/ *adv* (**worse** /wɜːs/, **worst** /wɜːst/) **1** in a way that is not good enough; not well: *'Can you speak French?' 'Only very badly.'* ♦ *She did badly in the exams.* OPP **well** **2** very much: *He badly needed a holiday.* **3** seriously; in a terrible way: *He was very badly hurt in the accident.*
IDM **well/badly off** ➲ **off**

badminton /ˈbædmɪntən/ *noun* [U] a game for two or four people in which players hit a **shuttlecock** (= a type of light ball with feathers) over a high net, using a **racket** (= a piece of equipment that is held in the hand)

badminton

ˌbad-ˈtempered *adj* often angry or impatient: *a bad-tempered old man* ♦ *Don't be so bad-tempered!*

baffle /ˈbæfl/ *verb* [T] to be impossible to understand; to confuse sb very much: *His illness baffled the doctors.* ▶ **baffled** *adj*: *The instructions were so complicated that I was absolutely baffled.* ▶ **baffling** *adj*: *I find it baffling how people can enjoy computer magazines.*

bag¹ /bæg/ *noun* **1** [C] a container made of paper or thin plastic that opens at the top: *She brought some sandwiches in a plastic bag.* ➲ picture at **container** **2** [C] a strong container made from cloth, plastic, leather, etc. usually with one or two handles, used to carry things in when travelling, shopping, etc: *a shopping bag* ♦ *Have you packed your bags yet?* ♦ *She took her purse out of her bag* (= handbag). ♦ *Don't forget your school bag.* **3** [C] the amount contained in a bag: *She's eaten a whole bag of sweets!* ♦ *a bag of crisps/sugar/flour* **4** [pl] (*BrE*) **bags (of sth)** a lot (of sth); plenty (of sth): *There's no hurry—we've got bags of time.* **5 bags** [pl] folds of skin under the eyes, often caused by lack of sleep: *I've got terrible bags under my eyes.*

bag² /bæg/ *verb* [T] (**bagging**; **bagged**) (*informal*) to try to get sth for yourself so that other people cannot have it: *Somebody's bagged the seats by the pool!*

bagel /ˈbeɪgl/ *noun* [C] a type of bread roll in the shape of a ring

baggage /ˈbægɪdʒ/ *noun* [U] bags, suitcases, etc. used for carrying sb's clothes and things on a journey: *excess baggage* (= baggage weighing more than the airline's allowed limit) ♦ *I went to wait for my suitcase at **baggage reclaim*** (= the area in an airport where baggage goes after being unloaded from a plane). SYN **luggage** ➲ note at **plane**

ˈbaggage room (*AmE*) = **left-luggage office**

baggy /ˈbægi/ *adj* (**baggier**; **baggiest**) (used about a piece of clothing) big; hanging on the body in a loose way: *a baggy sweater* OPP **tight**

bagpipes /ˈbægpaɪps/ *noun* [pl] a musical instrument, popular in Scotland, that is played by blowing air through a pipe into a bag and then pressing the bag so that the air comes out of other pipes

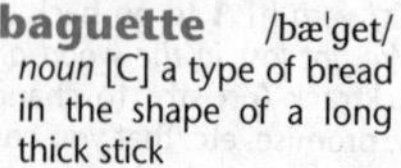
bagpipes

baguette /bæˈget/ *noun* [C] a type of bread in the shape of a long thick stick

bail¹ /beɪl/ *noun* [U] money that sb agrees to pay if a person accused of a crime does not appear in court on the day they are called. When **bail** has been arranged, the accused person can go free until that day: *She was **released on bail** of £2000.* ♦ *The judge **set bail** at £10 000.* ♦ *The judge felt that he was a dangerous man and **refused** him **bail**.* ♦ *She was **granted bail**.*

bail² /beɪl/ *verb* [T] to free sb on **bail¹**
PHR V **bail sb out** **1** to obtain sb's freedom by paying money to the court: *Her parents went to the police station and bailed her out.* **2** to rescue sb or sth from a difficult situation (especially by providing money): *If you get into trouble, don't expect me to bail you out again!*

bailiff /ˈbeɪlɪf/ *noun* [C] an officer whose job is to take the possessions and property of people who cannot pay money that they owe

bailout /ˈbeɪlaʊt/ *noun* [C] an act of giving money to a company, a foreign country, etc. that has very serious financial problems

bait /beɪt/ *noun* [U] **1** food or sth that looks like food that is put onto a hook to catch fish, or to catch animals or birds **2** something that is used for persuading or attracting sb: *Free offers are often used as bait to attract customers.*

bake /beɪk/ *verb* [I,T] **1** to cook in an oven in dry heat: *I could smell bread baking in the oven.* ♦ *On his birthday she baked him a cake.* ➲ note at **cook** **2** to become or to make sth hard by heating it: *The hot sun baked the earth.*

baked poˈtato = **jacket potato**

baker /ˈbeɪkə(r)/ *noun* **1** [C] a person who bakes bread, cakes, etc. to sell in a shop **2 the baker's** [sing] (*BrE*) a shop that sells bread, cakes, etc: *Get a loaf at the baker's.*

bakery /ˈbeɪkəri/ *noun* [C] (*pl* **bakeries**) a place where bread, cakes, etc. are baked and/or sold

baking /ˈbeɪkɪŋ/ *adj* very hot: *The workers complained of the baking heat in the office.*

ˈ**baking powder** *noun* [U] a mixture of powders that is used to make cakes rise and become light as they are baked

balance¹ /ˈbæləns/ *noun* **1** [sing] (a) balance (between A and B) a situation in which different or opposite things are of equal importance, size, etc: *The course provides a good balance between academic and practical work.* ◆ *Tourism has upset* ***the*** *delicate* ***balance of nature*** *on the island.* **2** [U] the ability to keep steady with an equal amount of weight on each side of the body: *to* ***lose*** *your* ***balance*** ◆ *It's very difficult to* ***keep*** *your* ***balance*** *when you start learning to ski.* ◆ *You need a good* ***sense of balance*** *to ride a motorbike.* **3** [C,usually sing] the amount that still has to be paid; the amount that is left after some has been used, taken, etc: *You can pay a 10% deposit now, with the balance due in one month.* ◆ *to check your* ***bank balance*** (= to find out how much money you have in your account) **4** [C] (*technical*) an instrument used for weighing things

IDM **in the balance** uncertain: *Following poor results, the company's future hangs in the balance.*

(catch/throw sb) off balance (to find or put sb) in a position that is not safe and from which it is easy to fall: *A strong gust of wind caught me off balance and I nearly fell over.*

on balance having considered all sides, facts, etc: *On balance, I've had a pretty good year.*

strike a balance (between A and B) ➲ **strike¹**

balance² /ˈbæləns/ *verb* **1** [I,T] to be or to put sb/sth in a steady position so that their/its weight is not heavier on one side than on the other: *I had to balance on the top step of the ladder to paint the ceiling.* ◆ *Carefully, she balanced a glass on top of the pile of plates.* **2** [I,T] balance (sth) (out) (with sth) to have or give sth equal value, importance, etc. in relation to other parts: *The loss in the first half of the year was balanced out by the profit in the second half.* **3** [T] balance sth against sth to consider and compare one matter in relation to another: *In planning the new road, we have to balance the benefit to motorists against the damage to the environment.* **4** [I,T] to have equal totals of money spent and money received: *I must have made a mistake—the accounts don't balance.* ◆ *She is always very careful to balance her weekly budget.*

balanced /ˈbælənst/ *adj* keeping or showing a balance so that different things, or different parts of things, exist in equal or correct amounts: *I like this newspaper because it gives a balanced view.* ◆ *A* ***balanced diet*** *plays an important part in good health.*

OPP **unbalanced**

ˌ**balance of ˈpayments** *noun* [sing] the difference between the amount of money one country receives from other countries for things it sells and the amount it pays other countries for things it buys, in a particular period of time

ˌ**balance of ˈpower** *noun* [sing] **1** a situation in which political power or military strength is divided between two countries or groups of countries **2** the power that a smaller political party has when the larger parties need its support because they do not have enough votes on their own

ˈ**balance sheet** *noun* [C] a written statement showing the amount of money and property that a company has, and how much has been received and paid out

balcony /ˈbælkəni/ *noun* [C] (*pl* **balconies**) **1** a platform built on an upstairs outside wall of a building, with a wall or rail around it **2** (*especially AmE*) = **circle¹** (3)

balcony

bald /bɔːld/ *adj* **1** (used about people) having little or no hair on your head: *I hope I*

B

bags

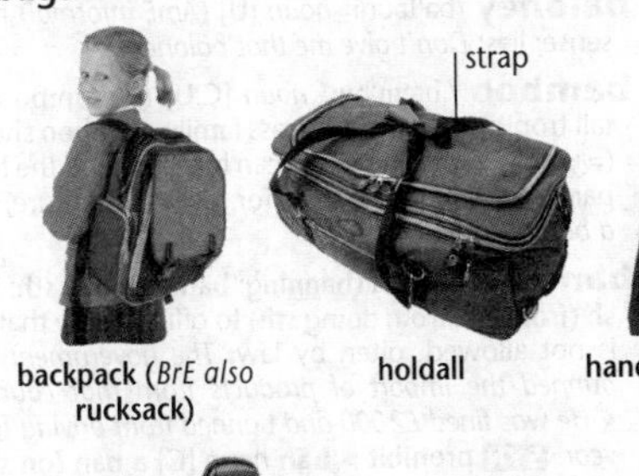

backpack (*BrE also* rucksack) holdall

handbag (*AmE* purse)

purse

suitcase (handle)

briefcase

carrier bag

bumbag (*AmE* fanny pack)

wallet (*AmE* billfold)

B

don't **go bald** *like my father did.* ♦ *He has a* **bald patch** *on the top of his head.* ➲ picture at **hair** **2** (used about sth that is said) simple; without extra words: *the bald truth*

balding /ˈbɔːldɪŋ/ *adj* starting to lose the hair on your head: *a balding man in his fifties*

baldly /ˈbɔːldli/ *adv* in a few words with nothing extra or unnecessary and without trying to be polite: *'You're lying,' he said baldly.*

bale /beɪl/ *noun* [C] a large quantity of sth pressed tightly together and tied up: *a bale of hay/cloth/paper*

balk (*especially AmE*) = **baulk**

⚷ **ball** /bɔːl/ *noun* [C]
➤ROUND OBJECT **1** a round object that you hit, kick, throw, etc. in games and sports: *a tennis/golf/rugby ball* ♦ *a football* ➲ picture at **pool** **2** a round object or a thing that has been formed into a round shape: *a ball of wool* ♦ *The children threw snowballs at each other.* ♦ *We had meatballs and pasta for dinner.*
➤THROW/KICK **3** one throw, kick, etc. of the ball in some sports: *That was a great ball from the defender.*
➤PART OF THE BODY **4** (*slang*) = **testicle**
➤DANCE **5** a large formal party at which people dance
IDM be on the ball (*informal*) to always know what is happening and be able to react to or deal with it quickly: *With so many new developments, you really have to be on the ball.*
set/start the ball rolling to start sth (an activity, a conversation, etc.) that involves or is done by a group: *I told a joke first, to set the ball rolling.*

ballad /ˈbæləd/ *noun* [C] a long song or poem that tells a story, often about love

ˌ**ball ˈbearing** *noun* [C] a ring of small metal balls used in a machine to enable the parts to turn smoothly; one of these small metal balls

ballerina /ˌbæləˈriːnə/ *noun* [C] a woman who dances in **ballets**

ballet /ˈbæleɪ/ *noun* **1** [U] a style of dancing that tells a story with music but without words: *He wants to be a* **ballet dancer.** **2** [C] a performance or work that consists of this type of dancing

ballet

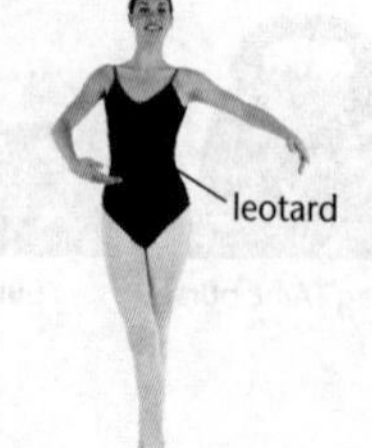

ballet dancer

ˈ**ball game** *noun* [C] **1** any game played with a ball **2** (*AmE*) a **baseball** match
IDM a (whole) new/different ball game something completely new or different: *I'm used to working outside, so sitting in an office all day is a whole new ball game for me.*

ballistic /bəˈlɪstɪk/ *adj*
IDM go ballistic (*informal*) to become very angry: *He went ballistic when I told him.*

balloon /bəˈluːn/ *noun* [C] **1** a small coloured object that you blow air into and use as a toy or for decoration: *to blow up/burst/pop a balloon* **2** (also **hot-ˈair balloon**) a large **balloon** made of cloth that is filled with gas or hot air so that it can fly through the sky, carrying people in a **basket** (= a container) underneath it

ballot /ˈbælət/ *noun* **1** [C,U] a secret written vote: *The union will* **hold a ballot** *on the new pay offer.* ♦ *The committee are elected by ballot every year.* **2** (*BrE also* ˈ**ballot paper**) [C] the piece of paper on which sb marks who they are voting for ▶ **ballot** *verb* [T] **ballot sb (about/on sth)**: *The union is balloting its members on strike action.*

ˈ**ballot box** *noun* **1** [C] the box into which people put the piece of paper with their vote on **2 the ballot box** [sing] the system of voting in an election: *People will express their opinion through the ballot box.*

ballpark /ˈbɔːlpɑːk/ *noun* [C] a place where the sport of **baseball** is played
IDM a ballpark figure/estimate a number, an amount, etc. that is approximately correct: *We asked the builders for a ballpark figure, to give us an idea of how much it would cost.*
in the ballpark (*informal*) (used about figures or amounts) that are within the same limits: *All the bids for the contract were in the same ballpark.*

ballpoint /ˈbɔːlpɔɪnt/ (also ˌ**ballpoint ˈpen**, *BrE also* **Biro™**) *noun* [C] a pen with a very small metal ball at the end that rolls ink onto paper ➲ picture at **stationery**

ballroom /ˈbɔːlruːm; -rʊm/ *noun* [C] a large room used for dancing on formal occasions

ˌ**ballroom ˈdancing** *noun* [U] a formal type of dance in which couples dance together using particular steps and movements

balm /bɑːm/ *noun* [U,C] a liquid, cream, etc. with a pleasant smell, used to make wounds less painful or skin softer: *lip balm*

baloney /bəˈləʊni/ *noun* [U] (*AmE informal*) nonsense; lies: *Don't give me that baloney!*

bamboo /ˌbæmˈbuː/ *noun* [C,U] (*pl* **bamboos**) a tall tropical plant of the grass family. **Bamboo shoots** (= young bamboo plants) can be eaten and the hard parts of the plant are used for making furniture, etc: *a bamboo chair*

⚷ **ban** /bæn/ *verb* [T] (**banning**; **banned**) **ban sth**; **ban sb (from sth/from doing sth)** to officially say that sth is not allowed, often by law: *The government has banned the import of products from that country.* ♦ *He was fined £2000 and banned from driving for a year.* **SYN prohibit** ▶ **ban** *noun* [C] **a ban (on sth)**: *There is a ban on mobile phones in the classroom.* ♦ *to impose/lift a ban*

banal /bəˈnɑːl/ *adj* not original or interesting: *a banal comment*

banana /bəˈnɑːnə/ *noun* [C,U] a curved fruit with yellow skin that grows in hot countries: *a bunch of bananas* ➲ picture on **page P14**
IDM go bananas (*slang*) to become angry, crazy or silly

B

band /bænd/ *noun* [C]
➤MUSICIANS **1** [with sing or pl verb] a small group of musicians who play popular music together, often with a singer or singers: *a rock/jazz band* ◆ *He plays the drums in a band.* ◆ *The band has/have announced that it/they is/are going to split up.* ➲ note at **pop**
➤GROUP OF PEOPLE **2** [with sing or pl verb] a group of people who do sth together or have the same ideas: *A small band of rebels is/are hiding in the hills.*
➤FOR FASTENING **3** a long thin piece or circle of material that is put round things to hold them together: *She rolled up the papers and put an* ***elastic band*** *round them.*
➤COLOUR **4** a line of colour or material on sth that contrasts with the background: *She wore a red pullover with a green band across the middle.*
➤RADIO WAVES **5** = **waveband**

bandage /ˈbændɪdʒ/ *noun* [C] a long piece of soft white cloth that you tie round a wound or an injury ▶ **bandage** *verb* [T] **bandage sth/sb (up)**: *The nurse bandaged my hand up.* ➲ picture at **plaster**

bandanna /bænˈdænə/ *noun* [C] a piece of brightly coloured cloth worn around the neck or head

B and B (also B & B) /ˌbiː ən ˈbiː/ *abbr* **bed and breakfast**

bandit /ˈbændɪt/ *noun* [C] a member of an armed group of thieves who attack people who are travelling

bandwagon /ˈbændwægən/ *noun*
IDM **climb/jump on the bandwagon** to copy what other people are doing because it is fashionable or successful

bandwidth /ˈbændwɪdθ/ *noun* [C,U] a measure of the amount of information that a group of connected computers or an Internet connection can send in a particular time

bang[1] /bæŋ/ *verb* [I,T] **1** to make a loud noise by hitting sth hard; to close sth or to be closed with a loud noise: *He banged his fist on the table and started shouting.* ◆ *Somewhere in the house, I heard a door bang.* SYN **slam** **2** to knock against sth by accident; to hit a part of the body against sth by accident: *As I was crossing the room in the dark I banged into a table.* ◆ *Be careful not to bang your head on the ceiling. It's quite low.*

bang[2] /bæŋ/ *noun* [C] **1** a sudden, short, very loud noise: *There was an enormous bang when the bomb exploded.* **2** a short, strong knock or hit, especially one that causes pain and injury: *a nasty bang on the head* **3** bangs (*AmE*) = **fringe**[1] (1)
IDM **with a bang** in a successful or exciting way: *Our team's season started with a bang when we won our first five matches.*

bang[3] /bæŋ/ *adv* (*especially BrE informal*) exactly; directly; right: *Our computers are* ***bang up to date.*** ◆ *The shot was bang on target.*
IDM **bang goes sth** (*informal*) used for expressing the idea that sth is now impossible: *'It's raining!' 'Ah well, bang goes our picnic!'*

bang[4] /bæŋ/ *exclam* used to sound like the noise of a gun, etc.

banger /ˈbæŋə(r)/ *noun* [C] (*BrE informal*) **1** a **sausage** (= meat formed in a long thin shape) **2** an old car that is in very bad condition: *I'm tired of driving around in that old banger.* **3** a small, noisy **firework** (= a device that burns or explodes, used for entertainment)

bangle /ˈbæŋgl/ *noun* [C] a circle of metal that is worn round the arm or wrist for decoration ➲ picture at **jewellery**

banish /ˈbænɪʃ/ *verb* [T] (*formal*) **1** to send sb away (especially out of the country), usually as a punishment: *They were banished from the country for demonstrating against the government.* SYN **exile** **2** to make sb/sth go away; to get rid of sb/sth: *She banished all hope of winning from her mind.*

banister (also bannister) /ˈbænɪstə(r)/ *noun* [C, often plural] the posts and rail at the side of a set of stairs: *The children loved sliding down the banister at the old house.* ➲ picture on **page P8**

banjo /ˈbændʒəʊ/ *noun* [C] (*pl* banjos) a musical instrument like a **guitar**, with a long thin neck, a round body and four or more strings ➲ picture at **music**

bank[1] /bæŋk/ *noun* [C]
➤FOR MONEY **1** an organization which keeps money safely for its customers; the office or building of such an organization. You can take money out, save, borrow or exchange money at a bank: *My salary is paid directly into my bank.* ◆ *I need to go to the bank to get some money out.* ◆ *a bank account/loan* ➲ note at **money**
➤STORE **2** a store of things, which you keep to use later: *a databank* ◆ *a blood bank in a hospital*
➤BESIDE A RIVER **3** the ground along the side of a river or **canal** (= an artificial river): *People were fishing along the banks of the river.*
➤HIGHER GROUND **4** a higher area of ground that goes down or up at an angle, often at the edge of sth or dividing sth: *There were grassy banks on either side of the road.*
➤CLOUD/SNOW **5** a mass of cloud, snow, etc: *The sun disappeared behind a bank of clouds.*

bank[2] /bæŋk/ *verb* [I] **bank (with/at ...)** to have an account with a particular bank: *I've banked with HSBC for years.*
PHR V **bank on sb/sth** to expect and trust sb to do sth, or sth to happen: *Our boss might let you have the morning off but I wouldn't bank on it.*

banker /ˈbæŋkə(r)/ *noun* [C] a person who owns or has an important job in a bank

ˌbank ˈholiday *noun* [C] (*BrE*) a public holiday (not a Saturday or Sunday)

banking /ˈbæŋkɪŋ/ *noun* [U] the type of business done by banks: *She decided on a career in banking.*

banknote /ˈbæŋknəʊt/ = **note**[1] (4)

bankrupt /ˈbæŋkrʌpt/ *adj* not having enough money to pay what you owe: *The company must cut its costs or it will* ***go bankrupt.*** ▶ **bankrupt** *verb*

[T]: *The failure of the new product almost bankrupted the firm.*

B

bankruptcy /ˈbæŋkrʌptsi/ *noun* [C,U] (*pl* **bankruptcies**) the state of being **bankrupt**: ***The company filed for bankruptcy*** (= asked to be officially bankrupt) *in 2011.*

ˈbank statement (also **statement**) *noun* [C] a printed list of all the money going into or out of your bank account during a certain period

banner /ˈbænə(r)/ *noun* [C] a long piece of cloth with words or signs on it, which can be hung up or carried on two poles: *The demonstrators carried banners saying 'Stop the War'.* ➲ picture at **placard**

bannister = **banister**

banquet /ˈbæŋkwɪt/ *noun* [C] a formal meal for a large number of people, usually as a special event at which speeches are made

banter /ˈbæntə(r)/ *noun* [U] friendly comments and jokes ▸ **banter** *verb* [I]

baptism /ˈbæptɪzəm/ *noun* [C,U] a ceremony in which a person becomes a member of the Christian Church by being held underwater for a short time or having drops of water put onto their head. Often they are also formally given a name. ➲ look at **christening** ▸ **baptize** (also **-ise**) /bæpˈtaɪz/ *verb* [T] ➲ look at **christen**

Baptist /ˈbæptɪst/ *noun* [C], *adj* (a member) of a Protestant Church that believes that **baptism** should only be for people who are old enough to understand the meaning of the ceremony and should be done by placing the person fully underwater

bars

a bar of soap

a bar of chocolate

bar¹ /bɑː(r)/ *noun* [C]

➤FOR DRINKS/FOOD **1** a place where you can buy and drink alcoholic and other drinks: *They had a drink in the bar before the meal.* **2** a long, narrow, high surface where drinks, etc. are served: *She went to the bar and ordered a drink.* ◆ *We sat on stools* ***at the bar.*** **3** [in compounds] a place where a particular type of food or drink is the main thing that is served: *a wine/coffee/sandwich bar*

➤SOAP/CHOCOLATE **4 a bar (of sth)** a small block of solid material, longer than it is wide: *a bar of soap/chocolate*

➤ON A WINDOW **5** a long, thin, straight piece of metal, often placed across a window or door to stop sb from getting through it: *They escaped by sawing through the bars of their prison cell.*

➤THAT PREVENTS YOU **6 a bar (to sth)** a thing that prevents you from doing sth: *Lack of education is not always a bar to success in business.*

➤IN MUSIC **7** one of the short, equal units of time into which music is divided: *If you sing a few bars of the song I might recognize it.*

IDM **behind bars** (*informal*) in prison: *The criminals are now safely behind bars.*

bar² /bɑː(r)/ *verb* [T] (**barring**; **barred**) **1** [usually passive] to close sth with a bar or bars: *All the windows were barred.* **2** to block a road, path, etc. so that nobody can pass: *A line of police officers barred the entrance.* **3 bar sb from sth/from doing sth** to say officially that sb is not allowed to do, use or enter sth: *He was barred from the club for fighting.*

bar³ /bɑː(r)/ *prep* except: *All the seats were taken, bar one.*

barbarian /bɑːˈbeəriən/ *noun* [C] a wild person with no culture, who behaves very badly

barbaric /bɑːˈbærɪk/ *adj* very cruel and violent: *barbaric treatment of prisoners* ▸ **barbarism** /ˈbɑːbərɪzəm/ *noun* [U]: *acts of barbarism committed in war* ▸ **barbarity** /bɑːˈbærəti/ *noun* [C,U] (*pl* **barbarities**)

barbecue /ˈbɑːbɪkjuː/ *noun* [C] (*abbr* **BBQ**) **1** a metal frame on which food is cooked outdoors over an open fire **2** an outdoor party at which food is cooked in this way: *Let's* ***have a barbecue*** *on the beach.* ➲ look at **roast** ▸ **barbecue** *verb* [T]: *barbecued steak* ➲ note at **cook**

ˌbarbed ˈwire /ˌbɑːbd ˈwaɪə(r)/ *noun* [U] strong wire with sharp points on it: *a barbed-wire fence*

barber /ˈbɑːbə(r)/ *noun* **1** [C] a man whose job is to cut men's hair and sometimes to shave them ➲ look at **hairdresser** **2 the barber's** [sing] (*BrE*) a shop where men go to have their hair cut

ˈbar code *noun* [C] a pattern of thick and thin lines that is printed on things you buy. It contains information that a computer can read.

bare /beə(r)/ *adj* (**barer**; **barest**) **1** (used about part of the body) not covered by clothing: *bare arms/feet/shoulders* ➲ look at **naked, nude** **2** without anything covering it or in it: *They had taken the pictures down, so the walls were bare.* **3** [only before a noun] just enough; the most basic or simple: *You won't pass your exams if you just do* ***the bare minimum.*** ◆ *I don't take much luggage when I travel, just* ***the bare essentials.***

IDM **with your bare hands** without weapons or tools: *She killed the snake with her bare hands.*

barefoot /ˈbeəfʊt/ *adj, adv* with nothing (for example shoes, socks, etc.) on your feet: *We walked barefoot along the beach.*

barely /ˈbeəli/ *adv* [used especially after *can* and *could* to emphasize that sth is difficult to do] only just; almost not: *I was so tired I could barely stand up.* ◆ *I earn barely enough money to pay my rent.* ➲ look at **hardly**

bargain¹ /ˈbɑːɡən/ *noun* [C] **1** something that is cheaper or at a lower price than usual: *At that price, it's an absolute bargain!* ◆ *I found a lot of bargains in the sale.* **2** an agreement between people or groups about what each of them will do for the other or others: *Let's* ***make a bargain****—I'll lend you the money*

if you'll help me with my work. ◆ *I lent him the money but he didn't* ***keep*** *his* ***side of the bargain.***
IDM **into the bargain** (used for emphasizing sth) as well; in addition; also: *They gave me free tickets and a free meal into the bargain.*
strike a bargain (with sb) ➲ **strike**[1]

bargain[2] /ˈbɑːɡən/ *verb* [I] **bargain (with sb) (about/over/for sth)** to discuss prices, conditions, etc. with sb in order to reach an agreement that suits each person: *I'm sure that if you bargain with him, he'll drop the price.* ◆ *They bargained over the price.*
PHR V **bargain for/on sth** [usually in negative sentences] to expect sth to happen and be ready for it: *When I agreed to help him I didn't bargain for how much it would cost me.*

barge[1] /bɑːdʒ/ *noun* [C] a long narrow boat with a flat bottom that is used for carrying goods or people on a **canal** (= an artificial river) or river

barge[2] /bɑːdʒ/ *verb* [I,T] to push people out of the way in order to get past them: *He barged (his way) angrily through the crowd.*

baritone /ˈbærɪtəʊn/ *noun* [C] a male singing voice that is fairly low; a man with this voice

MORE Baritone is between **tenor** and **bass**.

bark[1] /bɑːk/ *noun* **1** [U] the hard outer covering of a tree ➲ picture at **tree** **2** [C] the short, loud noise that a dog makes: *The dog next door has a very loud bark.*

bark[2] /bɑːk/ *verb* **1** [I] **bark (at sb/sth)** (used about dogs) to make a loud, short noise or noises **2** [I,T] **bark (sth) (out) (at sb)** to speak to sb in a loud voice in an angry or aggressive way: *The boss came in, barked out some orders and left again.*

barley /ˈbɑːli/ *noun* [U] **1** a plant that produces grain that is used for food or for making beer and other drinks **2** the grain produced by this plant

barman /ˈbɑːmən/ (*pl* -men /-mən/) (*fem* **barmaid** /ˈbɑːmeɪd/) (*AmE* **bartender**) *noun* [C] a person who serves drinks from behind a bar in a pub, etc.

bar mitzvah /ˌbɑː ˈmɪtsvə/ *noun* [C] a ceremony in the Jewish religion for a boy who is about 13 years old. After the ceremony, he is considered an adult. ➲ look at **bat mitzvah**

barn /bɑːn/ *noun* [C] a large building on a farm in which crops or animals are kept ➲ picture on **page P11**

barometer /bəˈrɒmɪtə(r)/ *noun* [C] **1** an instrument that measures air pressure and indicates changes in the weather **2** something that indicates the state of sth (a situation, a feeling, etc.): *Results of local elections are often a barometer of the government's popularity.*

baron /ˈbærən/ *noun* [C] **1** a man of a high social position **2** a person who controls a large part of a particular industry or type of business: *drug/oil barons*

baroness /ˈbærənəs/ *noun* [C] a woman of a high social position; the wife of a **baron**

baroque (also **Baroque**) /bəˈrɒk/ *adj* used to describe the highly decorated style of European art, buildings and music of the 17th and early 18th centuries: *baroque churches/music*

barracks /ˈbærəks/ *noun* [C, with sing or pl verb] (*pl* **barracks**) a building or group of buildings in which soldiers live: *Guards were on duty at the gate of the barracks.*

barrage /ˈbærɑːʒ/ *noun* [C] **1** a continuous attack on a place with a large number of guns **2** a large number of questions, comments, etc., directed at a person very quickly: *The minister faced a* ***barrage of questions*** *from reporters.*

barrel /ˈbærəl/ *noun* [C] **1** a large, round, wooden, plastic or metal container for liquids, that has a flat top and bottom and is wider in the middle: *a beer/wine barrel* ◆ *The price of oil is usually given per barrel.* **2** the long metal part of a gun like a tube through which the bullets are fired

barren /ˈbærən/ *adj* **1** (used about land or soil) not good enough for plants to grow on **2** (used about trees or plants) not producing fruit or seeds

barrette /bæˈret/ (*AmE*) = **hairslide**

barricade /ˌbærɪˈkeɪd/ *noun* [C] an object or line of objects that is placed across a road, an entrance, etc. to stop people getting through: *The demonstrators* ***put up barricades*** *to keep the police away.*
PHR V **barricade yourself in** to defend yourself by putting up a **barricade**: *Demonstrators took over the building and barricaded themselves in.*
▶ **barricade** *verb* [T]

barrier /ˈbæriə(r)/ *noun* [C] **1** an object that keeps people or things separate or prevents them moving from one place to another: *The crowd were all kept behind barriers.* ◆ *The mountains form a natural barrier between the two countries.* ➲ look at **crash barrier** **2** a **barrier (to sth)** something that causes problems or makes it impossible for sth to happen: *When you live in a foreign country, the* ***language barrier*** *can be a difficult problem to overcome.*

barring /ˈbɑːrɪŋ/ *prep* except for; if there is not/are not: *Barring any unforeseen problems, we'll be moving house in a month.*

barrister /ˈbærɪstə(r)/ *noun* [C] (in English law) a lawyer who is trained to speak for you in the higher courts ➲ note at **lawyer**

barrow /ˈbærəʊ/ *noun* [C] **1** (*BrE*) a small thing on two wheels on which fruit, vegetables, etc. are moved or sold in the street, especially in markets **2** = **wheelbarrow**

bartender /ˈbɑːtendə(r)/ (*AmE*) = **barman**

barter /ˈbɑːtə(r)/ *verb* [I,T] **barter sth (for sth); barter (with sb) (for sth)** to exchange goods, services, property, etc. for other goods, etc. without using money: *The farmer bartered his surplus grain for machinery.* ◆ *The prisoners bartered with the guards for writing paper and books.* ▶ **barter** *noun* [U]

B

base¹ /beɪs/ *noun* [C] **1** the lowest part of sth, especially the part on which it stands or at which it is fixed or connected to sth: *the base of a column/glass* ◆ *I felt a terrible pain* ***at the base of*** *my spine.* **2** an idea, a fact, etc. from which sth develops or is made: *With these ingredients* ***as a base****, you can create all sorts of interesting dishes.* ◆ *The country needs a strong economic base.* **3** a place used as a centre from which activities are done or controlled: *This hotel is an ideal base for touring the region.* **4** a military centre from which the armed forces operate: *an army base* **5** (in **baseball**) one of the four points that a runner must touch

base² /beɪs/ *verb* [T, usually passive] **base sb/sth in** ... to make one place the centre from which sb/sth can work or move around: *I'm based in New York, although my job involves a great deal of travel.* ◆ *a Cardiff-based company*
PHR V **base sth on sth** to form or develop sth from a particular starting point or source: *This film is based on a true story.*

baseball /ˈbeɪsbɔːl/ *noun* [U] a team game that is popular in the US in which players hit the ball with a **bat** (= a piece of wood or metal) and run around the four **bases** to score points ➲ picture on **page P4**

basement /ˈbeɪsmənt/ *noun* [C] a room or rooms in a building, partly or completely below ground level: *a basement flat* ➲ look at **cellar**

bases **1** *plural* of **basis** **2** *plural* of **base¹**

bash¹ /bæʃ/ *verb* (*informal*) **1** [I,T] to hit sb/sth very hard: *I didn't stop in time and bashed into the car in front.* **2** [T] to criticize sb/sth strongly: *The candidate continued to bash her opponent's policies.*

bash² /bæʃ/ *noun* [C] **1** a hard hit: *He gave Alex a bash on the nose.* **2** (*informal*) a large party or celebration: *Are you going to Gary's birthday bash?*
IDM **have a bash (at sth/at doing sth)** (*BrE spoken*) to try: *I'll get a screwdriver and have a bash at mending the light.*

bashful /ˈbæʃfl/ *adj* shy and embarrassed

basic /ˈbeɪsɪk/ *adj* **1** forming the part of sth that is most necessary and from which other things develop: *The basic question is, can we afford it?* ◆ *basic information/facts/ideas* **2** of the simplest kind or level; including only what is necessary without anything extra: *This course teaches basic computer skills.* ◆ *The* ***basic pay*** *is £300 a week–with extra for overtime.*

basically /ˈbeɪsɪkli/ *adv* used to say what the most important or most basic aspect of sb/sth is: *The two designs are basically the same.* **SYN** **essentially**

basics /ˈbeɪsɪks/ *noun* [pl] the simplest or most important facts or aspects of sth; things that you need the most: *So far, I've only learnt the basics of computing.*

basil /ˈbæzl/ *noun* [C] a **herb** (= a type of plant) with shiny green leaves that smell sweet and are used in cooking ➲ picture on **page P14**

basin /ˈbeɪsn/ *noun* [C] **1** = **washbasin** **2** a round open bowl often used for mixing or cooking food **3** an area of land from which water flows into a river: *the Amazon Basin*

basis /ˈbeɪsɪs/ *noun* (*pl* **bases** /ˈbeɪsiːz/) **1** [sing] the principle or reason which lies behind sth: *We made our decision* ***on the basis of*** *the reports which you sent us.* **2** [sing] the way sth is done or organized: *They meet* ***on a regular basis.*** ◆ *to employ somebody* ***on a*** *temporary/voluntary/part-time* ***basis*** **3** [C] a starting point, from which sth can develop: *She used her diaries as a basis for her book.*

bask /bɑːsk/ *verb* [I] **bask (in sth)** **1** to sit or lie in a place where you can enjoy the warmth: *The snake basked in the sunshine on the rock.* **2** to enjoy the good feelings you have when other people admire you, give you a lot of attention, etc: *The team was still* ***basking in the glory*** *of winning the cup.*

baskets

shopping basket   wicker basket

basket /ˈbɑːskɪt/ *noun* [C] **1** a container for carrying or holding things, made of thin pieces of material that bends easily, such as wood, plastic or wire: *a waste-paper basket* ◆ *a shopping basket* ◆ *a clothes/laundry basket* (= in which you put dirty clothes before they are washed) **2** (in **basketball**) a net that hangs from a metal ring high up at each end of a court ➲ picture on **page P4** **3** (in **basketball**) a score of one, two or three points, made by throwing the ball through one of the nets
IDM **put all your eggs in one basket** ➲ **egg¹**

basketball /ˈbɑːskɪtbɔːl/ *noun* [U] a game for two teams of five players in which you score points by throwing a large ball through the other team's **basket**(2) ➲ picture on **page P4**

bass /beɪs/ *noun* **1** [U] the lowest part in music **2** [C] the lowest male singing voice; a singer with this kind of voice ➲ look at **tenor**, **baritone** **3** [C] (also ˌ**bass gui'tar**) an electric **guitar** (= a musical instrument with strings) which plays very low notes ➲ note at **music** **4** = **double bass** ▶ **bass** *adj* [only before a noun]: *a bass drum* ◆ *Can you sing the bass part?*

bassoon /bəˈsuːn/ *noun* [C] a musical instrument that you blow which makes a very deep sound ➲ picture at **music**

baste /beɪst/ *verb* [T] to pour liquid, such as sauce, juice or wine, over meat, etc. while it is cooking

bat¹ /bæt/ *noun* [C] **1** a piece of wood for hitting the ball in sports such as **table tennis, cricket** or **baseball**: *a cricket bat* ➲ picture on **page P4**

B

MORE Some sports have special words for the type of bat that is used to hit the ball. In **tennis** and **badminton** you use a **racket**, in **hockey** you use a **stick** and in **golf** you use a **club**. In **snooker**, **pool** and **billiards** you hit the ball with a **cue**.

2 a small animal, like a mouse with wings, which flies and hunts at night ➲ picture on **page P12**
IDM off your own bat without anyone asking you or helping you

bat² /bæt/ *verb* [I] (**batting**; **batted**) (used about one player or a whole team) to have a turn hitting the ball in sports such as **cricket** or **baseball** ➲ look at **field**
IDM not bat an eyelid; (*AmE*) **not bat an eye** to show no surprise or embarrassment when sth unusual happens

batch /bætʃ/ *noun* [C] a number of things or people which belong together as a group: *The bus returned to the airport for the next batch of tourists.*

bated /ˈbeɪtɪd/ *adj*
IDM with bated breath excited or afraid, because you are waiting for sth to happen

bath¹ /bɑːθ/ *noun* **1** [C] (*especially AmE* also **bathtub**, *informal* **tub**) a large container for water in which you sit to wash your body: *Can you answer the phone? I'm in the bath!* ➲ picture on **page P8** **2** [sing] an act of washing the whole of your body when you sit or lie in a bath filled with water: *to **have a bath*** ◆ (*especially AmE*) *Would you prefer to **take a bath** or a shower?* **3 baths** [pl] (*BrE old-fashioned*) a public building where you can go to swim; a public place where people went in past times to have a wash or a bath: *Roman baths*

bath² /bɑːθ/ *verb* **1** [T] to give sb a bath: *bath the baby* **2** [I] (*old-fashioned*) to have a bath: *I prefer to bath in the mornings.*

bathe /beɪð/ *verb* **1** [T] to wash or put part of the body in water, often for medical reasons: *She bathed the wound with antiseptic.* **2** [I] (*old-fashioned*) to swim in the sea or in a lake or river ➲ look at **sunbathe**

bathed /beɪðd/ *adj* (*written*) [not before a noun] **bathed in sth** covered with sth: *The room was bathed in moonlight.*

bathrobe /ˈbɑːθrəʊb/ = **dressing gown**

bathroom /ˈbɑːθruːm; -rʊm/ *noun* [C] **1** a room where there is a bath and/or a shower, a **washbasin** (= a place to wash your hands) and often a toilet: *Go and wash your hands in the bathroom.* ➲ picture on **page P8** **2** (*AmE*) a room with a toilet: *I have to **go to the bathroom*** (= use the toilet). ➲ note at **toilet**

bathtub /ˈbɑːθtʌb/ = **bath¹**(1)

bat mitzvah /ˌbæt ˈmɪtsvə/ *noun* [C] a ceremony in the Jewish religion for a girl who is about 13 years old ➲ look at **bar mitzvah**

baton /ˈbætɒn/ *noun* [C] **1** = **truncheon** **2** a short thin stick used by the person who directs an **orchestra** (= a large group of musicians who play together) **3** a stick which a runner in a **relay** (= a race in which each member of the team runs one part of the race) passes to the next person in the team

batsman /ˈbætsmən/ *noun* [C] (*pl* **-men** /-mən/) (in the sport of **cricket**) one of the two players who hit the ball to score **runs** (= points scored by running from one end to the other) ➲ note at **cricket** ➲ picture on **page P4**

battalion /bəˈtæliən/ *noun* [C] a large unit of soldiers that forms part of a larger unit in the army

batter¹ /ˈbætə(r)/ *verb* [I,T] to hit sb/sth hard, many times: *The wind battered against the window.* ◆ *He battered the door down.*

batter² /ˈbætə(r)/ *noun* [U,C] a mixture of flour, eggs and milk used to cover food such as fish, vegetables, etc. before frying them

battered /ˈbætəd/ *adj* no longer looking new; damaged or out of shape: *a battered old hat*

battery /ˈbætəri; -tri/ *noun* (*pl* **batteries**) **1** [C] a device which provides electricity for a toy, radio, car, etc: *to recharge **a flat battery*** (= one that is no longer producing electricity) **2** [C] (*BrE*) a large number of very small **cages** (= boxes made of bars) in which chickens, etc. are kept on a farm: *a battery hen/farm* ➲ look at **free-range** **3** [U] the crime of attacking sb physically: *He was charged with **assault and battery**.*

battle¹ /ˈbætl/ *noun* **1** [C,U] a fight, especially between armies in a war: *the battle of Trafalgar* ◆ *to die/be killed **in battle*** **2** [C] **a battle (with sb) (for sth)** a competition, an argument or a fight between people or groups of people trying to win power or control: *a legal battle for custody of the children* **3** [C, usually sing] **a battle (against/for sth)** a determined effort to solve a difficult problem or to succeed in a difficult situation: *After three years she lost her battle against cancer.*
IDM a losing battle ➲ **lose**

battle² /ˈbætl/ *verb* [I,T] **battle (with/against sb/sth) (for sth)**; **battle (on)** to try very hard to achieve sth difficult or to deal with sth unpleasant or dangerous: *Mark is battling with his maths homework.* ◆ *The little boat battled against the wind.* ◆ *The two brothers were battling for control of the family business.* ◆ *Life is hard at the moment but we're battling on.* ◆ *The teams will **battle it out** in the final next week.*

battlefield /ˈbætlfiːld/ (also **battleground** /ˈbætlgraʊnd/) *noun* [C] the place where a battle is fought

battlements /ˈbætlmənts/ *noun* [pl] a low wall around the top of a castle with spaces in it that people inside could shoot through

battleship /ˈbætlʃɪp/ *noun* [C] a very large ship with big guns used in war

bauble /ˈbɔːbl/ *noun* [C] **1** a piece of cheap jewellery **2** a decoration in the shape of a ball that is hung on a Christmas tree

baulk (*especially AmE* **balk**) /bɔːk/ *verb* [I] **baulk (at sth)** to not want to do or agree to sth because it seems too difficult, dangerous or unpleasant: *She liked horses, but she baulked at riding one.*

bawl /bɔːl/ *verb* [I,T] to shout or cry loudly

B

bay /beɪ/ *noun* [C] **1** a part of the coast where the land goes in to form a curve: *the Bay of Bengal* ♦ *The harbour was in a sheltered bay.* ➲ picture on **page P10** **2** a part of a building, an aircraft or an area which has a particular purpose: *a parking/loading bay*
IDM **hold/keep sb/sth at bay** to stop sb dangerous from getting near you; to prevent a situation or problem from getting worse

bayonet /ˈbeɪənət/ *noun* [C] a knife that can be fixed to the end of a gun

bay ˈwindow *noun* [C] a window in a part of a room that sticks out from the wall of a house ➲ picture on **page P9**

bazaar /bəˈzɑː(r)/ *noun* [C] **1** (in some eastern countries) a market **2** (*BrE*) a sale where the money that is made goes to charity: *The school held a bazaar to raise money for the hospital.*

BBC /ˌbiː biː ˈsiː/ *abbr* **the British Broadcasting Corporation**; one of the national radio and TV companies in Britain: *a BBC documentary* ♦ *watch a programme on BBC1*

BBQ *abbr* = **barbecue**

BC /ˌbiː ˈsiː/ *abbr* **before Christ**; used in dates to show the number of years before the time when Christians believe Jesus Christ was born: *in (the year) BC 300* ➲ look at **AD**

be¹ /bi; *strong form* biː/ *verb* ⓘ For the forms of 'be', look at the irregular verbs section at the back of this dictionary. **1** [T] **there is/are** to exist; to be present: *I tried phoning them but there was no answer.* ♦ *There are some people outside.* ♦ *There are a lot of trees in our garden.* **2** [I] used to give the position of sb/sth or the place where sb/sth is: *Paula's in her office.* ♦ *Where are the scissors?* ♦ *The bus stop is five minutes' walk from here.* ♦ *St Tropez is on the south coast.* **3** [I] used to give the date or age of sb/sth or to talk about time: *My birthday is on April 24th.* ♦ *It's 6 o'clock.* ♦ *It was Tuesday yesterday.* ♦ *Sue'll be 21 in June.* ♦ *He's older than Miranda.* ♦ *It's ages since I last saw him.* **4** [I] used when you are giving the name of people or things, describing them or giving more information about them: *This is my father, John.* ♦ *I'm Alison.* ♦ *He's Italian. He's* **from** *Milan.* ♦ *He's a doctor.* ♦ *What's that?* ♦ *A lion is a mammal.* ♦ *'What colour is your car?' 'It's green.'* ♦ *How much was your ticket?* ♦ *The film was excellent.* ♦ *She's very friendly.* ♦ *'How is your wife?' 'She's fine, thanks.'* **5** [I] [only used in the perfect tenses] to go to a place (and return): *Have you ever* **been to** *Japan?* ➲ look at **been**
IDM **be yourself** to act naturally: *Don't be nervous; just be yourself and the interview will be fine.*
-to-be [in compounds] future: *his bride-to-be* ♦ *mothers-to-be* (= pregnant women)

be² /bi; *strong form* biː/ *auxiliary verb* **1** used with a past participle to form the passive; used with a present participle to form the continuous tenses: *He was killed in the war.* ♦ *Where were they made?* ♦ *The house was still being built.* ♦ *You will be told what to do.* ♦ *I am studying Italian.* ♦ *What have you been doing?* ⓘ For more information, look at the **Reference Section** at the back of this dictionary. **2 be to do sth** used to show that sth must happen or that sth has been arranged: *You are to leave here at 10 o'clock at the latest.* **3 if sb/sth were to do sth** used to show that sth is possible but not very likely: *If they were to offer me the job, I'd probably take it.*

beach /biːtʃ/ *noun* [C] an area of sand or small stones beside the sea: *to sit* **on the beach** ➲ picture on **page P10**

beacon /ˈbiːkən/ *noun* [C] a fire or light on a hill or tower, often near the coast, which is used as a signal

bead /biːd/ *noun* [C] **1** a small round piece of wood, glass or plastic with a hole in the middle for putting a string through to make jewellery, etc: *a string of glass beads* ➲ picture at **jewellery** **2** a drop of liquid: *There were* **beads of sweat** *on his forehead.*

beady /ˈbiːdi/ *adj* (used about eyes) small, round and bright; watching everything closely

beak /biːk/ *noun* [C] the hard pointed part of a bird's mouth: *The gull held the fish in its beak.* ➲ picture on **page P12**

beaker /ˈbiːkə(r)/ *noun* [C] **1** a plastic or paper drinking cup, usually without a handle **2** a glass container used in scientific experiments, etc. for pouring liquids

beam¹ /biːm/ *noun* [C] **1** a line of light: *the beam of a torch* ♦ *The car's headlights were* **on full beam** (= giving the most light possible and not directed downwards). ♦ *a laser beam* **2** a long piece of wood, metal, etc. that is used to support weight, for example in the floor or ceiling of a building **3** a happy smile

beam² /biːm/ *verb* **1** [I] **beam (at sb/sth)** to smile happily: *I looked at Sam and he beamed back at me.* **2** [T] to send out radio or TV signals: *The programme was beamed live by satellite to many different countries.* **3** [I] to send out light and warmth: *The sun beamed down on them.*

bean /biːn/ *noun* [C] **1** the seed or **pod** (= long thin seed container) from a climbing plant that is eaten as a vegetable: *soya beans* ♦ *a tin of baked beans* (= beans in a tomato sauce) ♦ *green beans* ➲ picture on **page P15** **2** similar seeds from other plants: *coffee beans*
IDM **full of beans/life** ➲ **full¹**
spill the beans ➲ **spill**

bear¹ /beə(r)/ *verb* (*pt* **bore** /bɔː(r)/; *pp* **borne** /bɔːn/)
➤ACCEPT **1** [T] [used with *can/could* in negative sentences or in questions] to be able to accept and deal with sth unpleasant: *I can't bear spiders.* ♦ *She couldn't bear the thought of anything happening to him.* ♦ *How can you bear to listen to that music?* ♦ *The pain was almost more than he could bear.* SYN **stand, endure**
➤NOT BE SUITABLE **2** [T] **not bear sth/doing sth** to not be suitable for sth; to not allow sth: *These figures won't bear close examination* (= when you look closely you will find mistakes). ♦ *What I would do if I lost my job* **doesn't bear thinking about** (= is too unpleasant to think about).
➤BE RESPONSIBLE **3** [T] (*formal*) to take responsibility

for sth: *Customers will bear the full cost of the improvements.*
➤FEEL **4** [T] to have a feeling, especially a negative feeling: *Despite what they did, she* ***bears*** *no* ***resentment*** *towards them.* ◆ *He's not the type to* ***bear a grudge*** *against anyone.*
➤SUPPORT **5** [T] to support the weight of sth: *Twelve pillars bear the weight of the roof.*
➤SHOW/CARRY **6** [T] (*formal*) to show sth; to carry sth so that it can be seen: *He still* ***bears the scars*** *of his accident.* ◆ *She* ***bore a*** *strong* ***resemblance*** *to her mother* (= she looked like her). ◆ *The waiters came in bearing trays of food.*
➤HAVE A CHILD **7** [T] (*formal*) to give birth to children: *She bore him four children, all sons.*

HELP A much more common expression is **have children**: *She had four children.* When you talk about sb's own birth you use **be born**: *Robert was born in 1996.*

➤TURN **8** [I] to turn or go in the direction that is mentioned: *Where the road forks, bear left.*
IDM **bear the brunt of sth** to suffer the main force of sth: *Her sons usually bore the brunt of her anger.*
bear fruit to be successful; to produce results: *At last our hard work is beginning to bear fruit.*
bear in mind (that); bear/keep sb/sth in mind ➲ **mind**[1]
bear witness (to sth) to show evidence of sth: *The burning buildings and empty streets bore witness to a recent attack.*
PHR V **bear down (on sb/sth)** **1** to move closer to sb/sth in a frightening way: *We could see the hurricane bearing down on the town.* **2** to push down hard on sb/sth
bear sb/sth out to show that sb is correct or that sth is true: *The evidence bears out my theory.*
bear up to be strong enough to continue at a difficult time: *How is he bearing up after his accident?*
bear with sb/sth to be patient with sb/sth: *Bear with me—I won't be much longer.*

bear[2] /beə(r)/ *noun* [C] a large, heavy wild animal with thick fur and sharp teeth: *a polar/grizzly/brown bear* ➲ look at **teddy bear**

bearable /ˈbeərəbl/ *adj* that you can accept or deal with, although unpleasant: *It was extremely hot but the breeze made it more bearable.* **OPP** **unbearable**

⚷ **beard** /bɪəd/ *noun* [C,U] the hair which grows on a man's cheeks and chin: *I'm going to* ***grow a beard.*** ➲ look at **goatee, moustache** ➲ picture at **hair**

bearded /ˈbɪədɪd/ *adj* with a beard

bearer /ˈbeərə(r)/ *noun* [C] a person who carries or brings sth: *I'm sorry to be the bearer of bad news.*

bearing /ˈbeərɪŋ/ *noun* **1** [U,sing] (a) **bearing on sth** a relation or connection to the subject being discussed: *Her comments* ***had*** *no* ***bearing*** *on our decision.* **2** [U,sing] the way in which sb stands or moves: *a man of dignified bearing* **3** [C] a direction measured from a fixed point using a **compass** (= an instrument that shows direction)
IDM **get/find your bearings** to become familiar with where you are
lose your bearings ➲ **lose**

beast /biːst/ *noun* [C] (*formal*) an animal, especially a large one: *a wild beast*

⚷ **beat**[1] /biːt/ *verb* (*pt* **beat**; *pp* **beaten** /ˈbiːtn/) **1** [T] **beat sb (at sth); beat sth** to defeat sb; to be better than sth: *He always beats me at tennis.* ◆ *We're hoping to beat the world record.* ◆ *If you want to keep fit, you can't beat swimming.* **2** [I,T] to hit many times, usually very hard: *The rain was beating on the roof of the car.* ◆ *The man was beating the donkey with a stick.* ➲ note at **hit** **3** [I,T] to make a regular sound or movement: *Her* ***heart beat*** *faster as she ran to pick up her child.* ◆ *We could hear the drums beating in the distance.* ◆ *The bird* ***beat its wings*** (= moved them up and down quickly). **4** [T] to mix quickly with a fork, etc: *Beat the eggs and sugar together.*
IDM **beat about/around the bush** to talk about sth for a long time without mentioning the main point: *Stop beating about the bush and tell me how much money you need.*
(it) beats me (*spoken*) I do not know: *It beats me where he's gone.* ◆ *'Why is she angry?' 'Beats me!'*
off the beaten track in a place where people do not often go
PHR V **beat sb/sth off** to fight until sb/sth goes away: *The thieves tried to take his wallet but he beat them off.*
beat sb to sth to get somewhere or do sth before sb else: *She beat me back to the house.* ◆ *I wanted to ring him first but Kate beat me to it.*
beat sb up to attack sb by hitting or kicking them many times: *He was badly beaten up at the bus stop last night.*

⚷ **beat**[2] /biːt/ *noun* **1** [C] a single hit on sth such as a drum or the movement of sth, such as your heart; the sound that this makes: *Her heart skipped a beat when she saw him.* **2** [sing] a series of regular hits on sth such as a drum, or of movements of sth; the sound that this makes: *the beat of the drums* ➲ look at **heartbeat** **3** [C] the strong rhythm that a piece of music has: *This type of music has a strong beat to it.* **4** [sing] the route along which a police officer regularly walks: *Having more policemen* ***on the beat*** *helps reduce crime.*

beating /ˈbiːtɪŋ/ *noun* [C] **1** a punishment that you give to sb by hitting them: *The boys got a beating when they were caught stealing.* **2** a defeat
IDM **take a lot of/some beating** to be so good that it would be difficult to find sth better: *Mary's cooking takes some beating.*

beautician /bjuːˈtɪʃn/ *noun* [C] a person whose job is to improve the way people look with beauty treatments, etc.

⚷ **beautiful** /ˈbjuːtɪfl/ *adj* very pretty or attractive; giving pleasure to the senses: *The view from the top of the hill was really beautiful.* ◆ *What a beautiful day —the weather's perfect!* ◆ *He has a beautiful voice.* ◆ *A beautiful perfume filled the air.* ◆ *a beautiful woman* ▶ **beautifully** /-fli/ *adv*: *He plays the piano beautifully.* ◆ *She was beautifully dressed.*

B

OTHER WORDS FOR

beautiful

Beautiful and **pretty** are usually used about women and girls. **Pretty** is especially used about young women or girls. **Good-looking** and **attractive** can be used for both men and women. **Handsome** is used most often to describe men. **Gorgeous** is an informal word for **very attractive**.

beauty /ˈbjuːti/ *noun* (*pl* **beauties**) **1** [U] the quality which gives pleasure to the senses; the state of being beautiful: *I was amazed by the beauty of the mountains.* ◆ *music of great beauty* **2** [C] a beautiful woman: *She grew up to be a beauty.* **3** [C] a particularly good example of sth: *Look at this tomato—it's a beauty!*

ˈ**beauty spot** *noun* [C] (*BrE*) a place in the countryside which is famous because it is beautiful

beaver /ˈbiːvə(r)/ *noun* [C] an animal with brown fur, a wide, flat tail and sharp teeth. It lives in water and on land and uses branches to build **dams** (= walls across rivers to hold back the water).

beaver

became *past tense* of **become**

WRITING TIP

Giving a reason

As, **because** and **so** are all words that you can use to give a reason for something: *I'm taking an umbrella, because it's starting to rain.* ◆ *As it was raining, I took an umbrella.* ◆ *It started to rain, so we decided to go back home.*

For more help with writing, look at **Wordpower Writing Tutor** at the back of this dictionary.

because /bɪˈkɒz/ *conj* for the reason that: *They didn't go for a walk, because it was too cold.* ◆ *I did it because he told me to.*

beˈcause of *prep* as a result of; on account of: *They didn't go for a walk because of the rain.* ◆ *They are here because of us.*

beck /bek/ *noun*

IDM **at sb's beck and call** always ready to obey sb's orders

beckon /ˈbekən/ *verb* [I,T] to show sb with a movement of your finger or hand that you want them to come closer: *She beckoned me over to speak to her.*

become /bɪˈkʌm/ *verb* [I] (*pt* **became** /bɪˈkeɪm/; *pp* **become**) to begin to be sth: *Mr Saito became Chairman in 2008.* ◆ *She wants to become a pilot.* ◆ *They became friends.* ◆ *She became nervous as the exam date came closer.* ◆ *He is becoming more like you every day.*

MORE **Get** is also used with adjectives in this sense: *She got nervous as the exam date came closer.* ◆ *He's getting more like you every day.* It is very common in conversation and is less formal than **become**.

PHR V **become of sb/sth** to happen to sb/sth: *What became of Alima? I haven't seen her for years!*

BEd /ˌbiː ˈed/ *abbr* **Bachelor of Education**; a degree in education for people who want to be teachers

bed[1] /bed/ *noun* **1** [C,U] a piece of furniture that you lie on when you sleep: *to* ***make the bed*** (= to arrange the sheets, etc. so that the bed is tidy and ready for sb to sleep in) ◆ *What time do you usually* ***go to bed?*** ◆ *She was lying* ***on the bed*** (= on top of the covers). ◆ *When he rang I was already* ***in bed*** (= under the covers). ◆ *It's late. It's* ***time for bed.*** ◆ *to get into bed* ◆ *to get out of bed* ➲ note at **sleep** ➲ picture on **page P8** **2 -bedded** having the type or number of beds mentioned: *a twin-bedded room* **3** [C] the ground at the bottom of a river or the sea: *the seabed* **4** [C] = **flower bed**

beds

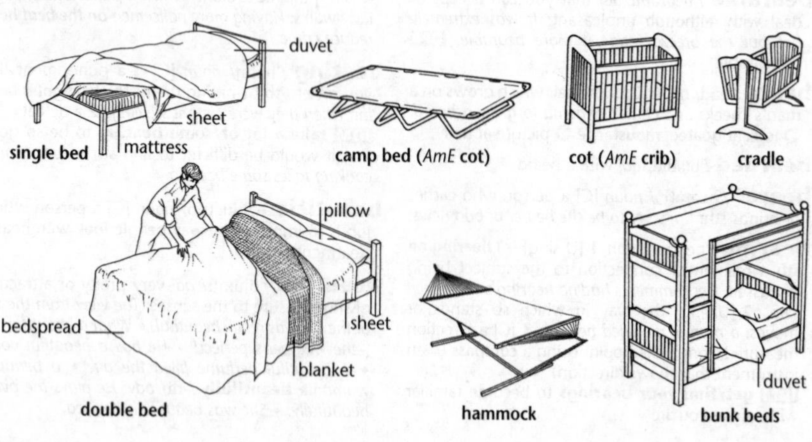

B

IDM **bed and ˈbreakfast**; ˌ**B and ˈB**; ˌ**B & ˈB** a place to stay in a private house or small hotel that consists of a room for the night and breakfast; a place that provides this ➲ note at **hotel**
go to bed with sb (*informal*) to have sex with sb

TOPIC

Beds

A bed for one person is called a **single bed** and a bed for a couple to share is a **double bed**. Two single beds next to each other in the same room are called **twin beds**. Rooms in hotels are called **double, single** or **twin-bedded/twin** rooms. Two single beds built as a unit with one above the other, used especially by children, are called **bunk beds**. A **futon** is a kind of mattress that can be used for sitting on or rolled out to make a bed.

bed² /bed/ *verb* [T] (bedding; bedded) to fix sth firmly in sth
PHR V **bed down** to sleep in a place where you do not usually sleep: *We couldn't find a hotel so we bedded down for the night in the van.*

bedclothes /ˈbedkləʊðz/ (*BrE also* ˈbedcovers) *noun* [pl] the sheets, covers, etc. that you put on a bed

bedding /ˈbedɪŋ/ *noun* [U] everything that you put on a bed and need for sleeping

bedraggled /bɪˈdrægld/ *adj* very wet and untidy or dirty: *bedraggled hair*

bedridden /ˈbedrɪdn/ *adj* being too old or ill to get out of bed

⚿ **bedroom** /ˈbedruːm; -rʊm/ *noun* [C] a room which is used for sleeping in: *You can sleep in the spare bedroom.* ♦ *a three-bedroom house* ➲ picture on **page P8**

bedside /ˈbedsaɪd/ *noun* [sing] the area that is next to a bed: *She sat at his bedside all night long.* ♦ *A book lay open on the* ***bedside table***. ➲ picture on **page P8**

bedsit /ˈbedsɪt/ (also ˈbedsitter) *noun* [C] (*BrE*) a room that a person rents which is used for both living and sleeping in

bedspread /ˈbedspred/ *noun* [C] an attractive cover for a bed that you put on top of the sheets and other covers ➲ picture at **bed**

bedtime /ˈbedtaɪm/ *noun* [U] the time that you normally go to bed

bee /biː/ *noun* [C] a black and yellow insect that lives in large groups and that makes **honey** (= a sweet substance that we eat) ➲ look at **beehive**, **wasp** ➲ picture on **page P13**

MORE A large number of bees together is a **swarm**. Bees **buzz** or **hum** when they make a noise. They may **sting** if they are angry.

beech /biːtʃ/ *noun* **1** (also ˈbeech tree) [C] a large tree that produces small nuts with three sides **2** [U] the wood from the **beech** tree

⚿ **beef** /biːf/ *noun* [U] the meat from a cow: *a joint of beef* ♦ *a slice of* ***roast beef*** ➲ note at **meat** ➲ picture on **page P16**

beefburger /ˈbiːfbɜːgə(r)/ (also **burger**; *especially AmE* **hamburger**) *noun* [C] **beef** that has been cut up small and pressed into a flat round shape

beefy /ˈbiːfi/ *adj* (beefier; beefiest) having a strong body with big muscles

beehive /ˈbiːhaɪv/ (also **hive**) *noun* [C] a type of box that people use for keeping **bees** (= black and yellow insects) in

been /biːn; bɪn/ *past participle* of **be, go¹**

GRAMMAR **Been** is used as the past participle of both **be** and **go**: *I've never been seriously ill.* ♦ *I've never been* ***to*** *Lisbon.* **Gone** is also a past participle of **go**. Note the difference in meaning: *I'm cold because I've just been outside* (= I'm here now). ♦ *Jim's not here, I'm afraid–he's just gone out* (= he's not here now).

beep /biːp/ *noun* [C] a short high noise, for example made by the horn of a car ▶ **beep** *verb* [I,T]: *I beeped my horn at the dog, but it wouldn't get off the road.*

beeper /ˈbiːpə(r)/ (*AmE*) = **bleeper**

⚿ **beer** /bɪə(r)/ *noun* **1** [U] a type of alcoholic drink that is made from grain: *a barrel/bottle/glass of beer* ➲ look at **wine** **2** [C] a type or glass of beer: *We went out for a couple of beers.*

MORE **Lager** is a type of light-coloured beer, which is drunk cold. **Bitter** is a darker beer, which is drunk at room temperature. **Shandy** is beer mixed with lemonade.

beet /biːt/ (*AmE*) = **beetroot**

beetle /ˈbiːtl/ *noun* [C] an insect, often large, shiny and black, with a hard case on its back covering its wings. There are many different types of **beetle**. ➲ picture on **page P13**

beetroot /ˈbiːtruːt/ (*AmE* **beet**) *noun* [C,U] a dark red vegetable which is the root of a plant. **Beetroot** is cooked and can be eaten hot or cold.

befall /bɪˈfɔːl/ *verb* [T] (*pt* **befell** /bɪˈfel/; *pp* **befallen** /bɪˈfɔːlən/) (*written*) (used about sth bad) to happen to sb

⚿ **before¹** /bɪˈfɔː(r)/ *prep, conj* **1** earlier than sb/sth; earlier than the time that: *You can call me any time before 10 o'clock.* ♦ *the week before last* ♦ *They should be here before long* (= soon). ♦ *Turn the lights off before you leave.* **2** (*formal*) in a position in front of sb/sth: *They knelt before the altar.* ♦ *You will appear before the judge tomorrow.* **3** in front of sb/sth (in an order): *'H' comes before 'N' in the alphabet.* ♦ *A very difficult task lies before us.* ♦ *a company that puts profit before safety* (= thinks profit is more important than being safe) **4** rather than: *I'd die before I apologized to him!*

B

before² /bɪˈfɔː(r)/ *adv* at an earlier time; already: *I think we've met somewhere before. ◆ It was fine yesterday but it rained the day before.* ➲ note at **ago**

beforehand /bɪˈfɔːhænd/ *adv* at an earlier time than sth: *If you visit us, phone beforehand to make sure we're in.*

befriend /bɪˈfrend/ *verb* [T] to become sb's friend; to be kind to sb

beg /beg/ *verb* [I,T] (**begging**; **begged**) **1 beg (sb) for sth; beg sth (of/from sb); beg (sb) to do sth** to ask sb for sth strongly, or with great emotion: *He begged for forgiveness. ◆ Can I beg a favour of you? ◆ We begged him to lend us the money.* **SYN entreat, implore** ➲ look at **plead 2 beg (for) sth (from sb)** to ask people for food, money, etc. because you are very poor: *People were begging for food in the streets.* **IDM I beg your pardon** (*formal*) **1** I am sorry: *I beg your pardon. I picked up your bag by mistake.* **2** used for asking sb to repeat sth because you did not hear it properly

began *past tense* of **begin**

beggar /ˈbegə(r)/ *noun* [C] a person who lives by asking people for money, food, etc. on the streets

begin /bɪˈgɪn/ *verb* (**beginning**; *pt* **began** /bɪˈgæn/; *pp* **begun** /bɪˈgʌn/) **1** [I,T] to start doing sth; to do the first part of sth: *Shall I begin or will you? ◆ I began* (= started reading) *this novel last month and I still haven't finished it. ◆ When did he begin his lesson? ◆ When do you begin work? ◆ We began writing to each other in 1992. ◆ The carpet is beginning to look dirty.* **2** [I] to start to happen or exist, especially from a particular time: *What time does the concert begin?* **3** [I] **begin (with sth)** to start in a particular way, with a particular event, or in a particular place: *My name begins with 'W' not 'V'. ◆ The fighting began with an argument about money. ◆ This is where the footpath begins.*

HELP **Begin** or **start**? **Begin** and **start** are very similar in meaning but **start** is more often used in informal speech. They can be followed by *to* or by the *-ing* form of a verb: *The baby began/started crying/to cry.* When **begin** or **start** are themselves in the *-ing* form they must be followed by *to*: *The baby was just beginning/starting to cry.* In some meanings only **start** can be used: *I couldn't start the car. ◆ We'll have to start* (= leave) *early if we want to be in Dover by 8 o'clock.*

IDM to begin with 1 at first: *To begin with they were very happy.* **2** used for giving your first reason for sth or to introduce your first point: *We can't possibly go. To begin with it's too far and we can't afford it either.*
▶ **beginner** *noun* [C]

beginning /bɪˈgɪnɪŋ/ *noun* [C] the first part of sth; the time when or the place where sth starts: *I've read the article **from beginning to end**. ◆ We're going away **at the beginning of** the school holidays.*

begrudge /bɪˈgrʌdʒ/ *verb* [T] **begrudge (sb) sth 1** to feel angry or upset because sb has sth that you think that they should not have: *He's worked hard. I don't begrudge him his success.* **2** to be unhappy that you have to do sth: *I begrudge paying so much money in tax each month.*

begun *past participle* of **begin**

behalf /bɪˈhɑːf/ *noun*
IDM on behalf of sb; on sb's behalf for sb; instead of sb: *I would like to thank you all on behalf of my colleagues and myself. ◆ Emma couldn't be present so her husband accepted the prize on her behalf.*

behave /bɪˈheɪv/ *verb* **1** [I] **behave well, badly, etc. (towards sb)** to act in a particular way: *Don't you think that Ellen has been behaving very strangely recently? ◆ I think you behaved very badly towards your father. ◆ He **behaves as if/though** he was the boss.* **2** [I,T] **behave (yourself)** to act in the correct or appropriate way: *I want you to behave yourselves while we're away.* **OPP misbehave 3 -behaved** [in compounds] behaving in the way mentioned: *a well-behaved child ◆ a badly-behaved class*

behaviour (*AmE* **behavior**) /bɪˈheɪvjə(r)/ *noun* [U] the way that you act or behave: *Her behaviour has been very strange recently. ◆ He was sent out of the class for bad behaviour.*

behead /bɪˈhed/ *verb* [T] to cut off sb's head, especially as a punishment **SYN decapitate**

behind /bɪˈhaɪnd/ *prep, adv* **1** in, at or to the back of sb/sth: *There's a small garden behind the house. ◆ The sun went behind a cloud. ◆ You go on ahead. I'll follow on behind. ◆ Look behind you before you drive off. ◆ He ran off but the police were close behind.* **2 behind (in/with) (sth)** later or less good than sb/sth; making less progress than sb/sth: *The train is twenty minutes behind schedule. ◆ Jane is behind the rest of the class in maths. ◆ We are a month behind with the rent.* ➲ look at **ahead 3** supporting or agreeing with sb/sth: *Whatever she decides, her family will be behind her.* **4** responsible for causing or starting sth: *What is the reason behind his sudden change of opinion?* **5** used to say that sth is in sb's past: *It's time you **put** your problems **behind you*** (= forgot about them). **6** in the place where sb/sth is or was: *Oh no! I've **left** the tickets **behind*** (= at home).

beige /beɪʒ/ *adj, noun* [U] (of) a light brown colour: *a beige coat*

being¹ ➲ **be**

being² /ˈbiːɪŋ/ *noun* **1** [U] the state of existing: *When did the organization **come into being**?* **SYN existence 2** [C] a living person or thing: *a human being*

belated /bɪˈleɪtɪd/ *adj* coming late: *a belated apology* ▶ **belatedly** *adv*: *They have realized, rather belatedly, that they have made a mistake.*

belch /beltʃ/ *verb* **1** [I] to let gas out from your stomach through your mouth with a sudden noise **SYN burp 2** [T] to send out a lot of smoke, etc: *The volcano belched smoke and ash.* ▶ **belch** *noun* [C]

belie /bɪˈlaɪ/ *verb* [T] (**belying**; **belies**; *pt, pp* **belied**) to give an idea of sth that is false: *His smiling face belied his true feelings.*

belief /bɪˈliːf/ *noun* **1** [sing,U] **belief in sb/sth** a feeling that sb/sth is true, morally good or right, or that sb/sth really exists: *She has lost her belief in God.* ➲ look at **disbelief** **2** [sing,U] (*formal*) **belief (that ...)** something you accept as true; what you believe: *It's my belief that people are basically good.* ◆ *There is a general belief that things will soon get better.* ◆ ***Contrary to popular belief*** (= in spite of what many people think) *the north of the country is not poorer than the south.* **3** [C] an idea about religion, politics, etc: *Divorce is contrary to their religious beliefs.*
IDM **beyond belief** (in a way that is) too great, difficult, etc. to be believed: *The amount of money we owe has increased beyond belief.*

believable /bɪˈliːvəbl/ *adj* that can be believed OPP **unbelievable**

believe /bɪˈliːv/ *verb* [not used in the continuous tenses] **1** [T] to feel sure that sth is true or that sb is telling the truth: *I don't believe you!* ◆ *He said he hadn't taken any money but I didn't believe him.* **2** [T] **believe (that) ...** to think that sth is true or possible, although you are not certain: *I believe they have moved to Italy.* ◆ *'Does Pat still work there?' 'I* ***believe so.****'* ◆ *The escaped prisoner is believed to be in this area.* ◆ *Four people are still missing, believed drowned.* **3** [T] **believe (that) ...** to have the opinion that sth is right or true: *The party believes (that) education is the most important issue facing the government.* ➲ note at **think** **4** [T] **don't/can't believe sth** used to show anger or surprise at sth: *I can't believe (that) you're telling me to do it again!* **5** [I] to have religious beliefs: *The god appears only to those who believe.*

HELP Although this verb is not used in the continuous tenses, it is common to see the present participle (= *-ing* form): *Believing the house to be empty, she quietly let herself in.*

IDM **believe it or not** it may be surprising but it is true: *Believe it or not, English food can sometimes be quite good.*
give sb to believe/understand (that) [often passive] to give sb the impression or idea that sth is true: *I was given to believe that I had got the job.*
PHR V **believe in sb/sth** to be sure that sb/sth exists: *Do you believe in God?* ◆ *Most young children believe in Father Christmas.*
believe in sb/sth; believe in doing sth to think that sb/sth is good or right: *They need a leader they can believe in.* ◆ *He doesn't believe in killing animals for their fur.*

believer /bɪˈliːvə(r)/ *noun* [C] a person who has religious beliefs
IDM **be a (great/firm) believer in sth** to think that sth is good or right: *He is a great believer in getting things done on time.*

belittle /bɪˈlɪtl/ *verb* [T] to make sb or the things they do seem unimportant or not very good

bell /bel/ *noun* [C] **1** a metal object, often shaped like a cup, that makes a ringing sound when it is hit by a small piece of metal inside it: *the sound of church bells* ◆ *Her voice came back* ***clear as a bell.*** ◆ *an animal with a bell round its neck* ➲ picture at goat **2** an electrical device that makes a ringing sound when the button on it is pushed; the sound that it makes: *Ring the doorbell and see if they're in.*
IDM **ring a bell** ➲ **ring**[2]

belligerent /bəˈlɪdʒərənt/ *adj* unfriendly and aggressive ▶ **belligerence** *noun* [U]

bellow /ˈbeləʊ/ *verb* **1** [I,T] **bellow (sth) (at sb)** to shout in a loud deep voice, especially because you are angry: *They bellowed at her to stop.* **2** [I] to make a deep low sound, like a **bull** (= an adult male cow) ▶ **bellow** *noun* [C]

belly /ˈbeli/ *noun* [C] (*pl* **bellies**) the stomach or the front part of your body between your chest and your legs

ˈbelly button (*informal*) = **navel**

belong /bɪˈlɒŋ/ *verb* [I] to have a right or usual place: *The plates belong in that cupboard.* ◆ *It took quite a long time before we felt we belonged in the village* (= until we felt comfortable).
PHR V **belong to sb** to be owned by sb: *Who does this pen belong to?* ◆ *Don't take anything that doesn't belong to you.*
belong to sth to be a member of a group or an organization: *Do you belong to any political party?*

belongings /bɪˈlɒŋɪŋz/ *noun* [pl] the things that you own that can be moved, that is, not land and buildings: *They lost all their belongings in the fire.*

beloved /bɪˈlʌvd; bɪˈlʌvɪd/ *adj* (*formal*) much loved: *They had always intended to return to their beloved Ireland.*

HELP When 'beloved' comes before a noun, the pronunciation is /bɪˈlʌvɪd/.

below /bɪˈləʊ/ *prep, adv* at or to a lower position or level than sb/sth: *Do not write below this line.* ◆ *The temperature fell below freezing during the night.* ◆ *Her marks in the exam were below average.* ◆ *I don't live on the top floor. I live on the floor below.* ◆ *temperatures of 30° and below* OPP **above** ➲ note at **under**

belt[1] /belt/ *noun* [C] **1** a thin piece of cloth, leather, etc. that you wear around your waist: *I need a belt to keep these trousers up.* ➲ look at **seat belt** ➲ picture on **page P1** **2** a long narrow piece of rubber, cloth, etc. in a circle, that is used for carrying things along or for making parts of a machine move: *The suitcases were carried round on a* ***conveyor belt.*** ◆ ***the fan belt*** *of a car* (= that operates the machinery that keeps a car engine cool) **3** an area of land that has a particular quality or where a particular group of people live: ***the green belt*** *around London* (= an area of countryside where you are not allowed to build houses, factories, etc.) ◆ *the commuter belt*
IDM **below the belt** (*informal*) unfair or cruel: *That remark was rather below the belt.*
tighten your belt ➲ **tighten**
under your belt (*informal*) that you have already done or achieved: *She's already got four tournament wins under her belt.*

B

belt² /belt/ *verb* (*informal*) **1** [T] to hit sb hard **2** [I] to run or go somewhere very fast: *I was belting along on my bicycle.*
PHR V **belt sth out** to sing, shout or play sth loudly: *In the restaurant, loudspeakers were belting out Spanish pop music.*
belt up (*slang*) used to tell sb rudely to be quiet: *Belt up! I can't think with all this noise.*

bemused /bɪˈmjuːzd/ *adj* confused and unable to think clearly

bench /bentʃ/ *noun* [C] **1** a long wooden or metal seat for two or more people, often outdoors: *a park bench* ➲ picture at **chair** **2** (in the British parliament) the seats where a particular group of politicians sit: *the Government* ***front bench*** ♦ *the Labour* ***back benches*** ➲ look at **back bench** **3** a long narrow table that people work at, for example in a factory

benchmark /ˈbentʃmɑːk/ *noun* [C] a standard that other things can be compared to: *These new safety features set a benchmark for other manufacturers to follow.*

bend

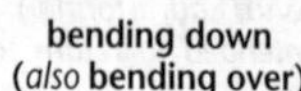
bending down (*also* **bending over**) **bending a spoon**

bend¹ /bend/ *verb* (*pt, pp* **bent** /bent/) **1** [I] to move your body forwards and downwards: *He* ***bent down*** *to tie up his shoelaces.* **2** [T] to make sth that was straight into a curved shape: *to bend a piece of wire into an S shape* ♦ *It hurts when I bend my knee.* **3** [I] to be or become curved: *The road bends to the left here.*
IDM **bend the rules** to do sth that is not normally allowed by the rules

bend² /bend/ *noun* [C] a curve or turn, for example in a road: *a sharp bend in the road*
IDM **round the bend** ➲ **round²**

beneath /bɪˈniːθ/ *prep, adv* **1** in, at or to a lower position than sb/sth; under: *The ship disappeared beneath the waves.* ♦ *His calm exterior hid the anger beneath.* ➲ note at **under** **2** not good enough for sb: *She felt that cleaning for other people was beneath her.*

benefactor /ˈbenɪfæktə(r)/ *noun* [C] a person who helps or gives money to a person or an organization

beneficial /ˌbenɪˈfɪʃl/ *adj* **beneficial (to sb/sth)** having a good or useful effect: *A good diet is beneficial to health.*

beneficiary /ˌbenɪˈfɪʃəri/ *noun* [C] (*pl* **beneficiaries**) **beneficiary (of sth)** **1** a person who gains as a result of sth: *Who will be the main beneficiary of the cuts in income tax?* **2** a person who receives money or property when sb dies

benefit¹ /ˈbenɪfɪt/ *noun* **1** [U,C] an advantage or useful effect that sth has: *A change in the law would be* ***to everyone's benefit.*** ♦ *I can't see* ***the benefit of*** *doing things this way.* ♦ *the benefits of modern technology* **2** [U,C] (*BrE*) money that the government gives to people who are ill, poor, unemployed, etc: *child/sickness/housing benefit* ♦ *I'm not entitled to unemployment benefit.* ♦ *to claim benefits* **3** [C, usually pl] advantages that you get from your company in addition to the money you earn: *a company car and other benefits*
IDM **for sb's benefit** especially to help, please, etc. sb: *For the benefit of the newcomers, I will start again.*
give sb the benefit of the doubt to believe what sb says although there is no proof that it is true

benefit² /ˈbenɪfɪt/ *verb* (**benefiting**; **benefited** *or* **benefitting**; **benefitted**) **1** [T] to produce a good or useful effect: *The new tax laws will benefit people on low wages.* **2** [I] **benefit (from sth)** to receive an advantage from sth: *Small businesses have benefited from the changes in the law.*

benevolent /bəˈnevələnt/ *adj* (*formal*) kind, friendly and helpful to others ▶ **benevolence** *noun* [U]

benign /bɪˈnaɪn/ *adj* **1** (used about people) kind or gentle: *a benign influence* **2** (used about a disease, etc.) not dangerous: *a benign tumour* OPP **malignant**

bent¹ *past tense, past participle of* **bend¹**

bent² /bent/ *adj* **1** not straight: *Do this exercise with your knees bent.* ♦ *This knife is bent.* ♦ *It was so funny we were* ***bent double*** *with laughter.* **2** (*BrE informal*) (used about a person in authority) dishonest: *a bent policeman* SYN **corrupt**
IDM **bent on sth/on doing sth** wanting to do sth very much; determined: *They seem bent on moving house, whatever the difficulties.*

bent³ /bent/ *noun* [sing] **a bent for sth/doing sth** a natural skill at sth or interest in sth: *She has a bent for music.*

bequeath /bɪˈkwiːð/ *verb* [T] (*formal*) **bequeath sth (to sb)** to arrange for sth to be given to sb after you have died: *He bequeathed £1 000 to his favourite charity.* ➲ A much more common word is **leave**.

bequest /bɪˈkwest/ *noun* [C] (*formal*) something that you arrange to be given to sb after you have died: *He left a bequest to each of his grandchildren.*

bereaved /bɪˈriːvd/ *adj* **1** having lost a relative or close friend who has recently died **2** **the bereaved** *noun* [pl] the people whose relative or close friend has died recently

bereavement /bɪˈriːvmənt/ *noun* (*formal*) **1** [U] the state of having lost a relative or close friend who has recently died **2** [C] the death of a relative or close friend: *There has been a bereavement in the family.*

bereft /bɪˈreft/ *adj* [not before a noun] (*formal*) **1** **bereft of sth** completely lacking sth; having lost sth: *bereft of ideas/hope* **2** (used about a person) sad and lonely because you have lost sth: *He was utterly bereft when his wife died.*

beret /ˈbereɪ/ *noun* [C] a soft flat round hat ➲ picture at **hat**

berry /ˈberi/ *noun* [C] (*pl* **berries**) a small soft fruit with seeds: *Those berries are poisonous.* ◆ *a raspberry/strawberry/blueberry*

berserk /bəˈzɜːk; -ˈsɜːrk/ *adj* [not before a noun] very angry; crazy: *If the teacher finds out what you've done he'll* ***go berserk***.

berth /bɜːθ/ *noun* [C] **1** a place for sleeping on a ship or train: *a cabin with four berths* **2** a place where a ship can stop and stay

beset /bɪˈset/ *verb* [T] (**besetting**; *pt, pp* **beset**) (*formal*) to affect sb/sth in a bad way: *The team has been beset by injuries all season.*

⚷ **beside** /bɪˈsaɪd/ *prep* at the side of, or next to sb/sth: *Come and sit beside me.* ◆ *He kept his bag close beside him at all times.*

IDM **beside the point** not connected with the subject you are discussing

beside yourself (with sth) not able to control yourself because of a very strong emotion: *Emily was almost beside herself with grief.*

besides /bɪˈsaɪdz/ *prep, adv* in addition to or as well as sb/sth; also: *There will be six people coming, besides you and David.* ◆ *I don't want to go out tonight. Besides, I haven't got any money.* ➲ look at **anyway**

besiege /bɪˈsiːdʒ/ *verb* [T] **1** to surround a place with an army **2** [usually passive] (used about sth unpleasant or annoying) to surround sb/sth in large numbers: *The actor was besieged by fans and reporters.*

besotted /bɪˈsɒtɪd/ *adj* [not before a noun] **besotted (with/by sb/sth)** so much in love with sb/sth that you cannot think or behave normally

⚷ **best**[1] /best/ *adj* [the superlative of *good*] of the highest quality or level; most suitable: *His latest book is by far his best.* ◆ *I'm going to wear my best shirt to the interview.* ◆ *Who in the class is* ***best at*** *maths?* ◆ ***It's best to*** *arrive early if you want a good seat.* ◆ *Who's your* ***best friend***? ◆ *What's the best way to get to York from here?*

IDM **your best bet** (*informal*) the most sensible or appropriate thing for you to do in a particular situation: *There's nowhere to park in the city centre. Your best bet is to go in by bus.*

the best/better part of sth ➲ **part**[1]

⚷ **best**[2] /best/ *adv* [the superlative of *well*] to the greatest degree; most: *He works best in the morning.* ◆ *Which of these dresses do you like best?* ◆ *one of Britain's best-loved TV stars*

IDM **as best you can** as well as you can even if it is not perfectly

⚷ **best**[3] /best/ **the best** *noun* [sing] the person or thing that is of the highest quality or level or better than all others: *When you pay that much for a meal you expect the best.* ◆ *Even the best of us make mistakes sometimes.* ◆ *I think James is the best!* ◆ *They are the best of friends.* ◆ *The best we can hope for is that the situation doesn't get any worse.* ➲ look at **second best**

IDM **all the best** (*informal*) used when you are saying goodbye to sb or ending a letter, to give sb your best wishes: *All the best! Keep in touch, won't you?*

at best if everything goes as well as possible; taking the most positive view: *We won't be able to deliver the goods before March, or, at best, the last week in February.*

at its/your best in its/your best state or condition: *This is an example of Beckett's work at its best.* ◆ *No one is at their best first thing in the morning.*

be (all) for the best used to say that although sth appears bad now, it will be good in the end: *I didn't get the job, but I'm sure it's all for the best.*

bring out the best/worst in sb to show sb's best/worst qualities: *The crisis really brought out the best in Tony.*

do/try your best to do all or the most that you can: *I did my best to help her.*

look your best ➲ **look**[1]

make the best of sth/a bad job to accept a difficult situation and try to be as happy as possible

ˌbest ˈman *noun* [sing] a man who helps and supports the **bridegroom** (= the man who is getting married) at a wedding ➲ note at **wedding**

bestow /bɪˈstəʊ/ *verb* [T] (*formal*) **bestow sth (on/upon sb)** to give sth to sb, especially to show how much they are respected: *It was a title bestowed upon him by the king.*

bestseller /ˌbestˈselə(r)/ *noun* [C] a book or other product that is bought by large numbers of people ▸ **ˈbestselling** *adj* [only before a noun]: *a bestselling novel*

⚷ **bet**[1] /bet/ *verb* [I,T] (**betting**; *pt, pp* **bet** or **betted**) **1 bet (sth) (on sth)** to risk money on a race or an event by trying to predict the result. If you are right, you win money: *I wouldn't bet on them winning the next election.* ◆ *I bet him £50 he couldn't beat me at tennis.* SYN **gamble, put money on sth** **2** (*informal*) used to say that you are almost certain that sth is true or that sth will happen: *I bet he arrives late—he always does.* ◆ *I bet you're worried about your exam, aren't you?*

IDM **I/I'll bet** (*spoken*) **1** used to show that you can understand what sb is feeling, describing, etc: *'I nearly died when he told me.' 'I bet!'* **2** used to tell sb that you do not believe what they have just said: *'I'm going to tell her what I think of her.' 'Yeah, I bet!'*

you bet (*spoken*) a way of saying 'Yes, of course!': *'Are you coming too?' 'You bet (I am)!'*

⚷ **bet**[2] /bet/ *noun* [C] **1** an act of betting: *Did you* ***have a bet*** *on that race?* ◆ *to win/lose a bet* **2** an opinion: *My bet is that he's missed the train.*

IDM **your best bet** ➲ **best**[1]

hedge your bets ➲ **hedge**[2]

betide /bɪˈtaɪd/ *verb*

IDM **woe betide sb** ➲ **woe**

betray /bɪˈtreɪ/ *verb* [T] **1** to give information about sb/sth to an enemy; to make a secret known:

She betrayed all the members of the group to the secret police. ♦ *He refused to betray their plans.* ♦ *to betray your country* ➲ note at **traitor** **2** to hurt sb who trusts you, especially by not being loyal or faithful to them: *If you take the money you'll* ***betray*** *her* ***trust***. ♦ *When parents get divorced the children often* ***feel betrayed***. **3** to show a feeling or quality that you would like to keep hidden: *Her steady voice did not betray the emotion she was feeling.* ▶ **betrayal** /bɪˈtreɪəl/ *noun* [C,U]

better¹ /ˈbetə(r)/ *adj* **1** [the comparative of *good*] **better than sb/sth** of a higher quality or level or more suitable than sb/sth: *I think her second novel was much better than her first.* ♦ *He's far better at English than me.* ♦ *It's a long way to drive. It would be better to take the train.* ♦ *You'd be better getting the train than driving.* **2** [the comparative of *well*] less ill; completely healthy again after an illness: *You can't go swimming until you're better.*

IDM **the bigger, smaller, faster, slower, etc. the better** used to say that sth should be as big, small, etc. as possible: *I love giving parties, the bigger the better.*

better² /ˈbetə(r)/ *adv* [the comparative of *well*] in a better way; to a greater or higher degree: *I think you could have done this better.* ♦ *Sylvie speaks English better than I do.*

IDM **(be) better off** [the comparative of *well off*] with more money: *We're much better off now I go out to work too.*

(be) better off (doing sth) to be in a more pleasant or suitable situation: *You look terrible. You'd be better off at home in bed.*

you, etc. had better you should; you ought to: *I think we'd better go before it gets dark.* ♦ *You'd better take a pen and paper—you might want to take notes.*

ⓘ For other idioms containing **better**, look at the entries for the nouns, adjectives, etc. For example **think better of (doing) sth** is at **think**.

better³ /ˈbetə(r)/ *noun* [sing] something that is of higher quality: *The hotel wasn't very good. I must say we'd expected better.*

IDM **a change for the better/worse** ➲ **change²**

get the better of sb/sth to defeat or be stronger than sb/sth: *When we have an argument she always gets the better of me.*

ˈ**betting shop** *noun* [C] a shop where you can go to put money on a race or an event ➲ look at **bookmaker**

between /bɪˈtwiːn/ *prep, adv* **1 between A and B; in between** in the space in the middle of two things, people, places etc: *I was sitting between Sam and Charlie.* ♦ *a village between Cambridge and Ely* ♦ *She was standing* ***in between*** *the desk* ***and*** *the wall.* **2 between A and B; in between** (used about two amounts, distances, ages, times, etc.) at a point that is greater or later than the first and smaller or earlier than the second; somewhere in the middle: *They said they would arrive between 4 and 5 o'clock.* ♦ *They've got this shirt in size 10 and size 16, but nothing in between.* **3** from one place to another and back again: *There aren't any direct trains between here and Manchester.* **4** involving or connecting two people, groups or things: *There's some sort of disagreement between them.* ♦ *There may be a connection between the two crimes.* **5** choosing one and not the other (of two things): *to choose between two jobs* ♦ *What's the difference between 'some' and 'any'?* **6** giving each person a share: *The money was divided equally between the two children.* ♦ *We ate all the chocolates between us.*

between

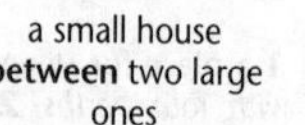

a small house **between** two large ones

a house **among** some trees

HELP **Between** or **among**? **Between** is usually used of two people or things: *sitting between her mother and father* ♦ *between the ages of 12 and 14.* However, **between** can sometimes be used of more than two when the people or things are being considered as individuals, especially when the meaning is that of number 6 (above): *We drank a bottle of wine between the three of us.* **Among** is always used of more than two people or things considered as a group rather than as individuals: *You're among friends here.*

7 by putting together the actions, efforts, etc. of two or more people: *Between us we saved up enough money to buy a car.*

beverage /ˈbevərɪdʒ/ *noun* [C] (*written*) a drink: *hot and cold beverages*

beware /bɪˈweə(r)/ *verb* [I] [only in the imperative or infinitive] **beware (of sb/sth)** (used for giving a warning) to be careful: *Beware of the dog!* (= written on a sign) ♦ *We were told to beware of strong currents in the sea.*

bewilder /bɪˈwɪldə(r)/ *verb* [T] to confuse and surprise: *I was completely bewildered by his sudden change of mood.* ▶ **bewildered** *adj*: *a bewildered expression* ▶ **bewildering** *adj*: *a bewildering experience* ▶ **bewilderment** *noun* [U]: *to stare at somebody* ***in bewilderment***

bewitch /bɪˈwɪtʃ/ *verb* [T] to attract and interest sb very much

beyond /bɪˈjɒnd/ *prep, adv* **1** on or to the other side of: *beyond the distant mountains* ♦ *We could see the mountains and the sea beyond.* **2** further than; later than: *Does the motorway continue beyond Birmingham?* ♦ *Most people don't go on working beyond the age of 65.* **3** more than sth: *The house was* ***far beyond*** *what I could afford.* ♦ *I haven't heard anything beyond a few rumours.* **4** used to say that sth is not possible: *The car was completely* ***beyond***

repair (= too badly damaged to repair). ♦ *The situation is* ***beyond*** *my* ***control****.* **5** too far or too advanced for sb/sth: *The activity was beyond the students' abilities.*
IDM be beyond sb (*informal*) to be impossible for sb to understand or imagine: *Why she wants to go and live there is quite beyond me.*

bias¹ /ˈbaɪəs/ *noun* **1** [C,U] a strong feeling of favour towards or against one group of people, or on one side in an argument, often not based on fair judgement or facts: *a bias against women drivers* ♦ *The BBC has been accused of* ***political bias****.* **2** [C, usually sing] an interest in one thing more than others; a special ability: *a course with a strong scientific bias*

bias² /ˈbaɪəs/ *verb* [T] (**biasing**; **biased** or **biassing**; **biassed**) to influence sb/sth, especially unfairly; to give an advantage to one group, etc: *Good newspapers should not be biased towards a particular political party.* ▶ **biased** *adj*: *a biased report*

bib /bɪb/ *noun* [C] a piece of cloth or plastic that a baby or small child wears under the chin to protect its clothes while it is eating

the Bible /ˈbaɪbl/ *noun* [sing] the book of great religious importance to Christian and Jewish people ▶ **biblical** /ˈbɪblɪkl/ *adj*

bibliography /ˌbɪbliˈɒɡrəfi/ *noun* [C] (*pl* **bibliographies**) **1** a list of the books and articles that a writer used when they were writing a particular book or article **2** a list of books on a particular subject

bicentenary /ˌbaɪsenˈtiːnəri/ *noun* [C] (*pl* **bicentenaries**) (*AmE* **bicentennial** /ˌbaɪsenˈteniəl/) the day or the year two hundred years after sth happened or began: *the bicentenary of the French Revolution*

biceps /ˈbaɪseps/ *noun* [C] (*pl* **biceps**) the large muscle at the front of the upper part of your arms

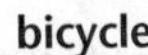
bicycle

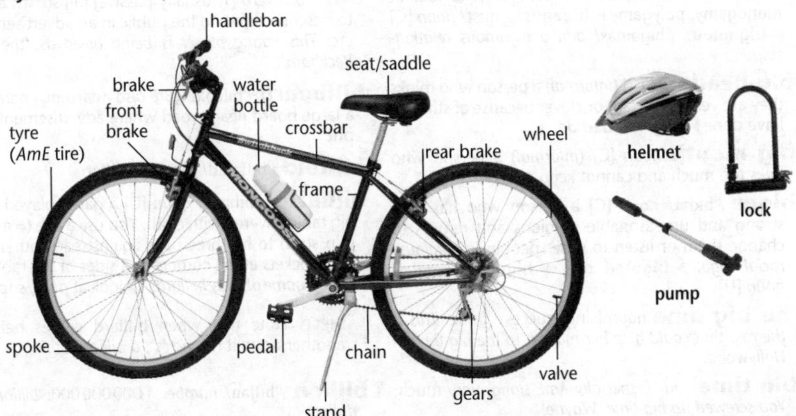

bicker /ˈbɪkə(r)/ *verb* [I] to argue about unimportant things: *The children are always bickering about something.*

bicycle /ˈbaɪsɪkl/ (also **bike**) *noun* [C] a vehicle with two wheels, which you sit on and ride by moving your legs: *Did you come by bicycle?* ♦ *He got on his bicycle and rode off.* ♦ *We went for a bicycle ride on Sunday.* ➲ note at **bike**

bid¹ /bɪd/ *verb* (**bidding**; *pt, pp* **bid**) **1 bid (sth) (for sth)** [I,T] to offer to pay a particular price for sth, especially at an **auction** (= a public sale where things are sold to the person who offers the most money): *Somebody bid £5000 for the painting.* ♦ *I wanted to buy the vase but another man was* ***bidding against*** *me.* **2** [I] to offer to do work or provide a service for a particular price, in competition with other companies, etc: *A French firm will be bidding for the contract.*

bid² /bɪd/ *noun* [C] **1** an offer by a person or a business company to pay a certain amount of money for sth: *Granada mounted a hostile* ***takeover bid*** (= when one company tries to buy another company) *for Forte.* ♦ *At the auction we* ***made a bid*** *of £100 for the chair.* **2** (*especially AmE*) = **tender²** **3 a bid (for sth)**; **a bid (to do sth)** an effort to do, obtain, etc. sth: *His bid for freedom had failed.* ♦ *Tonight the Ethiopian athlete will* ***make a bid*** *to break the world record.* **SYN attempt** ▶ **bidder** *noun* [C]: *The house was sold to the highest bidder* (= the person who offered the most money).

bide /baɪd/ *verb*
IDM bide your time to wait for a good opportunity: *I'll bide my time until the situation improves.*

bidet /ˈbiːdeɪ/ *noun* [C] a large bowl in the bathroom that you can sit on in order to wash your bottom

biennial /baɪˈeniəl/ *adj* happening once every two years

bifocals /ˌbaɪˈfəʊklz/ *noun* [pl] a pair of glasses with each **lens** (= a piece of glass) made in two parts. The upper part is for looking at things at a distance, and the lower part is for looking at things that are close to you. ▶ **bifocal** *adj*

big /bɪɡ/ *adj* (**bigger**; **biggest**) **1** large; not small: *a big house/town/salary* ◆ *This dress is too big for me.* OPP **small** **2** [only *before* a noun] (*informal*) older: *a big brother/sister* OPP **little** **3** great or important: *They had a big argument yesterday.* ◆ *That was the biggest decision I've ever had to make.* ◆ *some of the big names in Hollywood*
IDM **Big deal!** (*informal*) used to say that you think sth is not important or interesting: *'Look at my new bike!' 'Big deal! It's not as nice as mine.'*
a big deal/no big deal (*informal*) something that is (not) very important or exciting: *Birthday celebrations are a big deal in our family.* ◆ *A 2% pay increase is no big deal.*
give sb a big hand to hit your hands together to show approval, enthusiasm, etc: *The audience gave the girl a big hand when she finished her song.*
in a big/small way ➲ **way**[1]

OTHER WORDS FOR
big
Big and **large** can both be used when talking about size or number: *a big/large house* ◆ *a big baby.* **Large** is more formal and should be used in writing, unless it is in an informal style. **Large** is not usually used to describe people, except to avoid saying 'fat'. **Great** suggests importance, quality, etc: *a great occasion/musician.* In formal English, it is often used with uncountable nouns to mean 'a lot of': *great happiness/care/sorrow.* In informal English, **great** can be used to emphasize an adjective of size or quantity. Note also the phrases: *a large amount of* ◆ *a large number of* ◆ *a large quantity of* ◆ *a great deal of* ◆ *in great detail*

bigamy /ˈbɪɡəmi/ *noun* [U] the crime of being married to two people at the same time ➲ look at **monogamy, polygamy** ▶ **bigamist** /-mɪst/ *noun* [C] ▶ **bigamous** /ˈbɪɡəməs/ *adj*: *a bigamous relationship*

ˈ**big-head** *noun* [C] (*informal*) a person who thinks they are very important or clever because of sth they have done ▶ ˌ**big-ˈheaded** *adj*

ˈ**big mouth** *noun* [C] (*informal*) a person who talks too much and cannot keep a secret

bigot /ˈbɪɡət/ *noun* [C] a person who has very strong and unreasonable opinions and refuses to change them or listen to other people: *a religious/racial bigot* ▶ **bigoted** *adj* ▶ **bigotry** /ˈbɪɡətri/ *noun* [U]

the ˈbig time *noun* [sing] success; fame: *This is the role that could help her make it to the big time in Hollywood.*

ˈ**big time**[1] *adv* (*especially AmE slang*) very much: *You screwed up big time, Wayne!*

ˈ**big time**[2] *adj* [only *before* a noun] important or famous: *a big time politician/actor*

bike /baɪk/ *noun* [C] a bicycle or a motorbike: *Hasan's just learnt to* ***ride a bike.*** ➲ picture at **bicycle**

MORE Note that you **go on** a/your **bike** or **by bike**. You can also use the verbs **ride** and **cycle**. A **cyclist** is a person who rides a bike and a **motorcyclist** is a person who rides a motorbike.

bikini /bɪˈkiːni/ *noun* [C] (*pl* **bikinis**) a piece of clothing, in two pieces, that women wear for swimming

bilateral /ˌbaɪˈlætərəl/ *adj* **1** involving two groups of people or two countries: *bilateral relations/agreements/trade/talks* **2** involving both sides of the body or brain ➲ look at **multilateral, unilateral** ▶ **bilaterally** /-rəli/ *adv*

bile /baɪl/ *noun* [U] **1** a greenish brown liquid with a bitter unpleasant taste that is produced by your **liver** (= one of the body's main organs) to help your body break down the fats you eat **2** (*formal*) anger or hatred: *The critic's review of the play was just a paragraph of bile.*

bilingual /ˌbaɪˈlɪŋɡwəl/ *adj* **1** able to speak two languages equally well: *Our children are* ***bilingual in*** *English and Spanish.* **2** having or using two languages: *a bilingual dictionary* ➲ look at **monolingual**

bill[1] /bɪl/ *noun* **1** [C] a piece of paper that shows how much money you owe for goods or services: *an electricity bill* ◆ *to pay a bill* **2** (*AmE* **check**) [C] a piece of paper that shows how much you have to pay for the food and drinks you have had in a restaurant: *Can I have the bill, please?* ➲ note at **restaurant** **3** [C] (*AmE*) = **note**[1](4): *a ten-dollar bill* **4** [C] a plan for a possible new law: *The bill was passed/defeated.* **5** [sing] the programme of entertainment offered in a show, concert, etc: *Which bands are* ***on the bill*** *at the festival?* **6** [C] a bird's beak ➲ picture on **page P12**
IDM **foot the bill** ➲ **foot**[2]

bill[2] /bɪl/ *verb* [T, usually passive] **bill sb/sth as sth** to describe sb/sth to the public in an advertisement, etc: *This young player is being billed as 'the new Beckham'.*

billboard /ˈbɪlbɔːd/ (*BrE also* **hoarding**) *noun* [C] a large board near a road where advertisements are put

billfold /ˈbɪlfəʊld/ (*AmE*) = **wallet**

billiards /ˈbɪliədz/ *noun* [U] a game played on a big table covered with cloth. You use a **cue** (= a long thin stick) to hit three balls against each other and into pockets at the corners and sides of the table: *to have a game of/play billiards* ➲ look at **pool, snooker**

HELP Note that when **billiard** comes before another noun it has no 's': *a billiard table*

billion /ˈbɪljən/ *number* 1 000 000 000: *billions of dollars*

HELP Formerly, 'billion' was used with the meaning 'one million million'. We now say **trillion** for this. When you are counting, use billion without 's': *three billion yen*

ℹ For more information about numbers, look at the section on using numbers at the back of this dictionary.

billionaire /ˌbɪljəˈneə(r)/ *noun* [C] a person who has a billion pounds, dollars, etc.; an extremely rich person

billow /ˈbɪləʊ/ *verb* [I] **1** to fill with air and move in the wind: *curtains billowing in the breeze* **2** to move in large clouds through the air: *Smoke billowed from the chimneys.*

bins

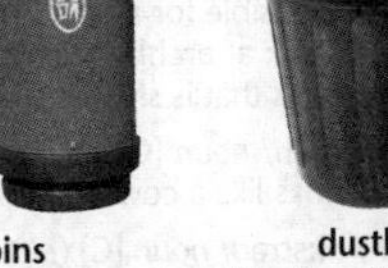

litter bins

dustbin (*AmE* **garbage can**)

bin /bɪn/ *noun* [C] **1** a container that you put rubbish in: *to throw something in the bin* ♦ *a litter bin* ♦ *The dustmen come to empty the bins on Wednesdays.* **2** a container, usually with a lid, for storing bread, flour, etc: *a bread bin*

binary /ˈbaɪnəri/ *adj* using only 0 and 1 as a system of numbers, used especially by computers: *the **binary system***

ˈ**bin bag** *noun* [C] (*informal*) (*BrE*) a large plastic bag for putting rubbish in ➲ look at **liner**

bind¹ /baɪnd/ *verb* [T] (*pt, pp* **bound** /baʊnd/) **1 bind sb/sth (to sb/sth); bind A and B (together)** to tie or fasten with string or rope: *They bound the prisoner's hands behind his back.* **2 bind A to B; bind A and B (together)** to unite people, organizations, etc. so that they live or work together more happily or with better effect: *The two countries are bound together by a common language.* **3 bind sb (to sth)** to force sb to do sth by making them promise to do it or by making it their duty to do it: *to be bound by a law/an agreement* ♦ *The contract binds you to completion of the work within two years.* **4** [usually passive] to fasten sheets of paper into a cover to form a book: *The book was bound in leather.*

bind² /baɪnd/ *noun* [sing] (*BrE informal*) something that you find boring or annoying: *I find housework a real bind.* **SYN** **nuisance**

binder /ˈbaɪndə(r)/ *noun* [C] a hard cover for holding sheets of paper, magazines, etc. together: *a ring binder* ➲ picture at **stationery**

binding¹ /ˈbaɪndɪŋ/ *adj* making it necessary for sb to do sth they have promised or to obey a law, etc: *This contract is **legally binding**.*

binding² /ˈbaɪndɪŋ/ *noun* **1** [C] a cover that holds the pages of a book together **2** [C,U] material that you fasten to the edge of sth to protect or decorate it **3 bindings** [pl] (in the activity of **skiing**) a device that fastens your boot to your **ski** (= a long, flat, narrow piece of wood or plastic)

binge¹ /bɪndʒ/ *noun* [C] (*informal*) a period of eating or drinking too much: *to go **on a binge***

binge² /bɪndʒ/ *verb* [I] (**bingeing** *or AmE* also **binging**) (*informal*) **binge (on sth)** to eat or drink too much, especially without being able to control yourself: *When she's depressed, she binges on chocolate.*

bingo /ˈbɪŋgəʊ/ *noun* [U] a game in which each player has a different card with numbers on it. The person in charge of the game calls numbers out and the winner is the first player to have all the numbers on their card called out.

binoculars

telescope

binoculars /bɪˈnɒkjələz/ *noun* [pl] an instrument with two **lenses** (= pieces of glass) which you look through in order to make objects in the distance seem nearer: *a **pair of binoculars***

biochemist /ˌbaɪəʊˈkemɪst/ *noun* [C] a person who studies **biochemistry**

biochemistry /ˌbaɪəʊˈkemɪstri/ *noun* [U] the study of the chemistry of living things

biodegradable /ˌbaɪəʊdɪˈgreɪdəbl/ *adj* that can be absorbed back into the earth naturally and so not harm the environment

biodiversity /ˌbaɪəʊdaɪˈvɜːsəti/ *noun* [U] the state of having a large number of different kinds of animals and plants which make a balanced environment

biofuel /ˈbaɪəʊfjuːəl/ *noun* [C,U] fuel made from plant or animal sources and used in engines

biogas /ˈbaɪəʊgæs/ *noun* [U] gas produced by natural waste, that can be used as fuel

biographer /baɪˈɒgrəfə(r)/ *noun* [C] a person who writes the story of sb else's life

biography /baɪˈɒgrəfi/ *noun* [C,U] (*pl* **biographies**) the story of sb's life written by sb else: *a biography of Napoleon* ♦ *I enjoy reading science fiction and biography.* ➲ note at **book** ➲ look at **autobiography** ▶ **biographical** /ˌbaɪəˈgræfɪkl/ *adj*

biological /ˌbaɪəˈlɒdʒɪkl/ *adj* **1** connected with the scientific study of animals, plants and other living things: *biological research* **2** involving the use of

B

living things to destroy or damage other living things: *biological weapons*

biology /baɪˈɒlədʒi/ *noun* [U] the scientific study of living things: *Biology is my favourite subject.* ➲ note at **science** ➲ look at **botany, zoology** ▸ **biologist** /-dʒɪst/ *noun* [C]

birch /bɜːtʃ/ *noun* **1** (also ˈ**birch tree**) [C] a type of tree with smooth thin branches **2** [U] the wood from the **birch** tree

bird /bɜːd/ *noun* [C] a creature that is covered with feathers and has two wings and two legs. Most birds can fly: *Gulls and sparrows are birds.* ♦ *I like to feed the birds in winter.* ➲ picture on **page P12**

> **MORE** Birds **fly** and **sing**. They build **nests** and lay eggs.

IDM **kill two birds with one stone** ➲ **kill**[1]

ˌ**bird of** ˈ**prey** *noun* [C] a bird that kills and eats other birds or small animals

birdwatcher /ˈbɜːdwɒtʃə(r)/ *noun* [C] a person who studies birds in their natural surroundings ➲ The formal word is **ornithologist.** ▸ **birdwatching** *noun* [U]

Biro™ /ˈbaɪrəʊ/ *noun* [C] (*pl* **Biros**) (*BrE*) = **ballpoint**

birth /bɜːθ/ *noun* **1** [C,U] being born; coming out of a mother's body: *It was a difficult birth.* ♦ *The baby weighed 3 kilos* **at birth** (= when it was born). ♦ *What's your* **date of birth**? (= the date on which you were born) **2** [sing] the beginning of sth: *the birth of an idea* **3** [U] the country you belong to: *She's always lived in England but she's German* **by birth.**

IDM **give birth (to sb)** to produce a baby: *She gave birth to her second child at home.* ➲ note at **baby**

ˈ**birth certificate** *noun* [C] an official document that states the date and place of sb's birth and the names of their parents

birth control *noun* [U] ways of limiting the number of children you have ➲ look at **contraception, family planning**

birthday /ˈbɜːθdeɪ/ *noun* [C] the day in each year which is the same date as the one when you were born: *My birthday's on November 15th.* ♦ *my eighteenth birthday* ♦ *a birthday present/card/cake*

> **TOPIC**
>
> **Birthdays**
>
> When it is somebody's birthday, we say **Happy Birthday**! If we know a person well, we send a special card to them or give them a present. They might have a birthday **party**, and a **birthday cake** with candles, one to represent each year of their age. Your 18th birthday is an important occasion when you legally become an adult. An **anniversary** is not the same as a **birthday**. It is the day in each year which is the same date as an important past event: *our wedding anniversary* ♦ *the anniversary of the end of the war*

birthmark /ˈbɜːθmɑːk/ *noun* [C] a red or brown mark on sb's body that has been there since they were born

birthplace /ˈbɜːθpleɪs/ *noun* **1** [C] the house or town where a person was born **2** [sing] the place where sth began: *Greece is the birthplace of the Olympic Games.*

ˈ**birth rate** *noun* [C] the number of babies born in a particular group of people during a particular period of time

biscuit /ˈbɪskɪt/ *noun* [C] **1** (*AmE* **cookie**) a type of small cake that is thin, hard and usually sweet: *a chocolate biscuit* ♦ *a packet of biscuits* ➲ picture at **cake 2** (*AmE*) a type of small simple cake that is not sweet

bisexual /ˌbaɪˈsekʃuəl/ *adj* sexually attracted to both men and women ➲ look at **heterosexual, homosexual**

bishop /ˈbɪʃəp/ *noun* [C] **1** a priest with a high position in some branches of the Christian Church, who is responsible for all the churches in a city or a district ➲ look at **archbishop 2** a piece used in the game of **chess** that is shaped like a **bishop's** hat

bison /ˈbaɪsn/ *noun* [C] (*pl* **bison**) a large wild animal that looks like a cow and is covered with hair

bistro /ˈbiːstrəʊ/ *noun* [C] (*pl* **bistros**) a small informal restaurant

bit[1] /bɪt/ *noun*

➤SMALL AMOUNT **1 a bit** [sing] slightly, a little: *I was a bit annoyed with him.* ♦ *I'm afraid I'll be a little bit late tonight.* ♦ *Could you be a bit quieter, please?* **2 a bit** [sing] a short time or distance: *Could you move forward a bit?* ♦ *I'm just going out for a bit.*

➤A LOT **3 a bit** [sing] (*informal*) a lot: *It must have rained* **quite a bit** *during the night.*

➤SMALL PART **4** [C] **a bit of sth** a small piece, amount or part of sth: *There were bits of broken glass all over the floor.* ♦ *Could you give me a bit of advice?* ♦ *Which bit of the film did you like best?*

➤COMPUTING **5** [C] the smallest unit of information that is stored in a computer's memory

➤FOR A HORSE **6** [C] a metal bar that you put in a horse's mouth when you ride it ➲ picture at **horse**

IDM **bit by bit** slowly or a little at a time: *Bit by bit we managed to get the information we needed.*

a bit much (*informal*) annoying or unpleasant: *It's a bit much expecting me to work on Sundays.*

a bit of a (*informal*) rather a: *I've got a bit of a problem …*

bits and pieces (*informal*) small things of different kinds: *I've finished packing except for a few bits and pieces.*

do your bit (*informal*) to do your share of sth; to help with sth: *It won't take long to finish if we all do our bit.*

not a bit not at all: *The holiday was not a bit what we had expected.*

to bits 1 into small pieces: *She angrily tore the letter to bits.* **2** very much: *I was* **thrilled to bits** *when I won the competition.*

bit[2] *past tense of* **bite**[1]

bitch[1] /bɪtʃ/ *verb* [I] (*informal*) **bitch (about sb/sth)** to say unkind and critical things about sb/sth, especially about sb who is not there: *She's not the kind of person who would bitch about you behind your back.*

bitch² /bɪtʃ/ *noun* [C] a female dog

bitchy /ˈbɪtʃi/ *adj* (**bitchier**; **bitchiest**) talking about other people in an unkind way: *a bitchy remark*

bite¹ /baɪt/ *verb* (*pt* **bit** /bɪt/; *pp* **bitten** /ˈbɪtn/) **1** [I,T] **bite (into sth)**; **bite (sb/sth)** to cut or attack sb/sth with your teeth: *He picked up the bread and bit into it hungrily.* ◆ *Don't worry about the dog–she never bites.* ◆ *The cat bit me.* ➲ picture at **lick** **2** [I,T] (used about some insects and animals) to push a sharp point into your skin and cause pain: *He was bitten by a snake/mosquito/spider.*

HELP Wasps, bees and jellyfish do not **bite** you. They **sting** you.

3 [I] to begin to have an unpleasant effect: *In the South the job losses are starting to bite.*
IDM **bite sb's head off** to answer sb in a very angry way
bite your 'tongue to stop yourself from saying sth that might upset sb or cause an argument, although you want to speak

bite² /baɪt/ *noun* **1** [C] a piece of food that you can put into your mouth: *She took a big bite of the apple.* **2** [sing] (*informal*) a a small meal: *Would you like* ***a bite to eat*** *before you go?* **SYN** **snack** **3** [C] a painful place on the skin made by an insect, a snake, a dog, etc: *I'm covered in mosquito bites.*

bitten *past participle* of **bite¹**

bitter¹ /ˈbɪtə(r)/ *adj* [**More bitter** and **most bitter** are the usual comparative and superlative forms, but **bitterest** can also be used.] **1** caused by anger or hatred: *a bitter quarrel* **2** **bitter (about sth)** (used about a person) very unhappy or angry about sth that has happened because you feel you have been treated unfairly: *She was very bitter about not getting the job.* **3** causing unhappiness or anger for a long time; difficult to accept: *Failing the exam was* ***a bitter disappointment*** *to him.* ◆ *I've learnt* ***from bitter experience*** *not to trust him.* **4** having a sharp, unpleasant taste; not sweet: *bitter coffee* ➲ look at **sour** **5** (used about the weather) very cold: *a bitter wind* ▶ **bitterness** *noun* [U]

bitter² /ˈbɪtə(r)/ *noun* [U,C] (*BrE*) a type of dark beer that is popular in Britain: *A pint of bitter, please.* ➲ note at **beer**

bitterly /ˈbɪtəli/ *adv* **1** in an angry and disappointed way: *'I've lost everything,' he said bitterly.* **2** (used for describing strong negative feelings or cold weather) extremely: *bitterly disappointed/resentful* ◆ *a bitterly cold winter/wind*

bitty /ˈbɪti/ *adj* (**bittier**; **bittiest**) (*informal*) made up of a lot of parts which do not seem to be connected: *Your essay is rather bitty.*

bizarre /bɪˈzɑː(r)/ *adj* very strange: *The story had a most bizarre ending.* **SYN** **weird** ▶ **bizarrely** *adv*: *bizarrely dressed*

bk *abbr* (*pl* **bks**) = **book¹**(1)

black¹ /blæk/ *adj* (**blacker**; **blackest**) **1** having the darkest colour, like night or coal: *a shiny black car* **2** belonging to a race of people with dark skins: *the black population of Britain* ◆ *black culture* **3** (used about coffee or tea) without milk or cream: *black coffee with sugar* **4** very angry: *to give somebody a* ***black look*** **5** (used about a situation) without hope: *The economic outlook for the coming year is rather black.* **SYN** **depressing** **6** funny in a cruel or unpleasant way: *The film was* ***a black comedy.***
IDM **black and blue** covered with **bruises** (= purple marks on the body) because you have been hit by sb/sth
black and white (used about TV, photographs, etc.) showing no colours except black, white and grey: *a film made in black and white*

black² /blæk/ *noun* **1** [U] the darkest colour, like night or coal: *People often* ***wear black*** (= black clothes) *at funerals.* **2** *usually* **Black** [C] a person who belongs to a race of people with dark skin

HELP Be careful. In this meaning **black** is more common in the plural. It can sound offensive in the singular.

IDM **be in the black** (*informal*) to have some money in the bank **OPP** **be in the red**
in black and white in writing or in print: *I won't believe I've passed the exam till I see it in black and white.*
▶ **blackness** *noun* [U]

black³ /blæk/ *verb*
PHR V **black out** to become unconscious for a short time **SYN** **faint**

BlackBerry™ /ˈblækbəri/ (*pl* **BlackBerrys**) *noun* [C] a very small computer that you hold in your hand and that you can use for phone calls, emails, looking at the Internet, etc: *While I'm away I'll check my emails on my BlackBerry.*

blackberry /ˈblækbəri/ (*pl* **blackberries**) *noun* [C] a small black fruit that grows wild on bushes ➲ picture on **page P14**

blackbird /ˈblækbɜːd/ *noun* [C] a common European bird. The male is black with a yellow beak and the female is brown.

blackboard /ˈblækbɔːd/ (*AmE* **chalkboard**) *noun* [C] a large dark board that teachers write on with **chalk** (= a small white or coloured stick)

blackcurrant /ˌblækˈkʌrənt; ˈblækkʌrənt/ *noun* [C] a small round black fruit that grows on bushes

blacken /ˈblækən/ *verb* **1** [I,T] to become black; to make sth black **2** [T] to make sb seem bad, by saying unpleasant things about them: *to blacken somebody's name*

ˌblack ˈeye *noun* [C] an area of dark-coloured skin around sb's eye where they have been hit: *He got a black eye in the fight.*

blackhead /ˈblækhed/ *noun* [C] a small spot on the skin with a black centre

B

ˌ**black ˈhole** *noun* [C] an area in outer space that pulls everything into it and from which nothing can escape

blacklist /ˈblæklɪst/ *noun* [C] a list of people, companies, etc. who are considered bad or dangerous: *to be on somebody's blacklist* ▶ **blacklist** *verb* [T]: *She was blacklisted by all the major Hollywood studios.*

ˌ**black ˈmagic** *noun* [U] a type of magic that is used for evil purposes

blackmail /ˈblækmeɪl/ *noun* [U] the crime of forcing a person to give you money or do sth for you, usually by threatening to make known sth which they want to keep secret ▶ **blackmail** *verb* [T] blackmail sb (into doing sth) ▶ **blackmailer** *noun* [C]

ˌ**black ˈmarket** *noun* [C, usually sing] the buying and selling of goods or foreign money in a way that is not legal: *to buy/sell something* ***on the black market***

blackout /ˈblækaʊt/ *noun* [C] **1** a period of time during a war, when all lights must be turned off or covered so that the enemy cannot see them **2** a period when you are unconscious for a short time: *to have a blackout*

blacksmith /ˈblæksmɪθ/ *noun* [C] a person whose job is to make and repair things made of iron

bladder /ˈblædə(r)/ *noun* [C] the part of your body where **urine** (= waste liquid) collects before leaving your body ➲ picture at **body**

⚷ **blade** /bleɪd/ *noun* [C] **1** the flat, sharp part of a knife, etc. ➲ picture at **garden**, **penknife**, **scissors**, **tool** **2** one of the flat, wide parts that turn round very quickly on an aircraft, etc: *the blades of a propeller* ➲ picture on **page P6** **3** the flat, wide part of an **oar** (= one of the long poles that you use to move a boat through water) **4** a long, thin leaf of grass: *a blade of grass*

blag /blæg/ *verb* [T] (**blagging**; **blagged**) (*BrE informal*) to persuade sb to give you sth, or to let you do sth, by talking to them in a clever or amusing way: *I blagged some tickets for the game.*

⚷ **blame¹** /bleɪm/ *verb* [T] blame sb (for sth); blame sth on sb/sth to think or say that a certain person or thing is responsible for sth bad that has happened: *The teacher blamed me for the accident.* ◆ *Some people blame the changes in the climate on pollution.*

IDM **be to blame (for sth)** to be responsible for sth bad: *The police say that careless driving was to blame for the accident.*

I don't blame you/her, etc. (for doing) to think that sb is not wrong to do sth; to understand sb's reason for doing sth: *I don't blame you for feeling fed up.*

shift the blame/responsibility (for sth) (onto sb) ➲ **shift¹**

⚷ **blame²** /bleɪm/ *noun* [U] blame (for sth) responsibility for sth bad: *The government must* ***take the blame*** *for the economic crisis.* ◆ *The report* ***put the blame*** *on rising prices.* ◆ *Why do I always* ***get the blame****?*

blameless /ˈbleɪmləs/ *adj* (*written*) not guilty; that should not be **blamed**: *He insisted that his wife was blameless and hadn't known about his crimes.* **SYN** **innocent**

blanch /blɑːntʃ/ *verb* **1** [I] (*formal*) blanch (at sth) to become pale because you are shocked or frightened **2** [T] to prepare food, especially vegetables, by putting it into boiling water for a short time

bland /blænd/ *adj* (**blander**; **blandest**) **1** ordinary or not very interesting: *a rather bland style of writing* **2** (used about food) mild or lacking in taste **3** not showing any emotion ▶ **blandly** *adv*

⚷ **blank¹** /blæŋk/ *adj* **1** empty, with nothing written, printed or recorded on it: *a blank CD/piece of paper/page* **2** without feelings, understanding or interest: *a blank expression on his face* ◆ *My mind* ***went blank*** *when I saw the exam questions* (= I couldn't think properly or remember anything). ▶ **blankly** *adv*: *She stared at me blankly, obviously not recognizing me.*

⚷ **blank²** /blæŋk/ *noun* [C] an empty space: ***Fill in the blanks*** *in the following exercise.* ◆ (*figurative*) *I couldn't remember his name—my mind was a complete blank.*

IDM **draw a blank** ➲ **draw¹**

ˌ**blank ˈcheque** *noun* [C] a cheque that has been signed but that has an empty space so that the amount to be paid can be written in later

blanket¹ /ˈblæŋkɪt/ *noun* [C] **1** a cover made of wool, etc. that is put on beds to keep people warm ➲ picture at **bed** **2** a thick layer or covering of sth: *a blanket of snow*

IDM **a wet blanket** ➲ **wet¹**

▶ **blanket** *verb* [T, often passive] blanket sth (in/with sth): *The countryside was blanketed in snow.*

blanket² /ˈblæŋkɪt/ *adj* [only *before* a noun] affecting everyone or everything: *There is a* ***blanket ban*** *on journalists reporting the case.*

blare /bleə(r)/ *verb* [I,T] blare (sth) (out) to make a loud, unpleasant noise: *Car horns were blaring in the street outside.* ◆ *The loudspeaker blared out pop music.* ▶ **blare** *noun* [sing]: *the blare of a siren*

blasphemy /ˈblæsfəmi/ *noun* [U] writing or speaking about God in a way that shows a lack of respect ▶ **blasphemous** /ˈblæsfəməs/ *adj*

blast¹ /blɑːst/ *noun* [C] **1** an explosion, especially one caused by a bomb **2** a sudden strong current of air: *a blast of cold air* **3** a loud sound made by a musical instrument, etc: *The driver gave a few blasts on his horn.*

blast² /blɑːst/ *verb* [T] **1** to make a hole, a tunnel, etc. in sth with an explosion: *They blasted a tunnel through the mountainside.* **2** to criticize sth very strongly: *Union leaders last night blasted the government's proposals.*

PHR V **blast off** (used about a **spacecraft**) to leave the ground; to take off

ˈ**blast-off** *noun* [U] the time when a **spacecraft** (= a vehicle that travels in space) leaves the ground

blatant /ˈbleɪtnt/ *adj* (used about actions which are considered bad) done in an obvious and open way without caring if people are shocked: *a blatant lie* ▶ **blatantly** *adv*

blaze[1] /bleɪz/ *verb* [I] **1** to burn with bright strong flames **2 blaze (with sth)** to be extremely bright; to shine brightly: *I woke up to find that the room was blazing with sunshine.* ◆ (*figurative*) *'Get out!' she shouted, her eyes blazing with anger.*

blaze[2] /bleɪz/ *noun* **1** [C] a large and often dangerous fire: *It took firefighters four hours to put out the blaze.* **2** [sing] **a blaze of sth** a very bright show of light or colour: *In the summer the garden was a blaze of colour.* ◆ *The new theatre was opened in **a blaze of publicity*** (= newspapers, etc. gave it a lot of attention).

blazer /ˈbleɪzə(r)/ *noun* [C] a jacket, especially one that has the colours or symbol of a school, club or team on it: *a school blazer*

bleach[1] /bliːtʃ/ *verb* [T] to make sth white or lighter in colour by using a chemical or by leaving it in the sun

bleach[2] /bliːtʃ/ *noun* [C,U] a strong chemical substance used for making clothes, etc. whiter or for cleaning things

bleak /bliːk/ *adj* (**bleaker**; **bleakest**) **1** (used about a situation) bad; without much hope: *a bleak future for the next generation* **2** (used about the weather) cold and grey: *a bleak winter's day* **3** (used about a place) cold, empty and grey: *the bleak Arctic landscape* ▶ **bleakly** *adv* ▶ **bleakness** *noun* [U]

bleary /ˈblɪəri/ *adj* (used about the eyes) red, tired and unable to see clearly: *We were all rather bleary-eyed after the overnight journey.* ▶ **blearily** *adv*

bleat /bliːt/ *verb* **1** [I] to make the sound of a sheep **2** [I,T] to speak in a weak or complaining voice ▶ **bleat** *noun* [C]

bleed /bliːd/ *verb* [I] (*pt, pp* **bled** /bled/) to lose blood ▶ **bleeding** *noun* [U]: *He wrapped a scarf around his arm to stop the bleeding.*

bleep[1] /bliːp/ *noun* [C] a short, high sound made by a piece of electronic equipment

bleep[2] /bliːp/ *verb* **1** [I] (used about machines) to make a short high sound: *Why is the computer bleeping?* **2** (*AmE* also **beep**) [T] to attract sb's attention using an electronic machine: *Please bleep the doctor on duty immediately.*

bleeper /ˈbliːpə(r)/ (*AmE* **beeper**) *noun* [C] a small piece of electronic equipment that **bleeps** to let a person (for example a doctor) know when sb is trying to contact them **SYN** **pager**

blemish /ˈblemɪʃ/ *noun* [C] a mark that spoils the way sth looks ▶ **blemish** *verb* [T] (*figurative*): *The defeat has blemished the team's perfect record.*

blend[1] /blend/ *verb* [T] **blend A with B; blend A and B (together)** to mix: *First blend the flour and the melted butter together.*

PHR V **blend (in) with sth** to combine with sth in an attractive or suitable way: *The new room is decorated to blend in with the rest of the house.*

blend (into sth) to match or be similar to the surroundings sb/sth is in: *These animals' ability to blend into their surroundings provides a natural form of defence.*

blend[2] /blend/ *noun* [C] a mixture: *He had the right blend of enthusiasm and experience.*

blender /ˈblendə(r)/ (*BrE also* **liquidizer**) *noun* [C] an electric machine that is used for making food into liquid ➲ picture at **mixer**

bless /bles/ *verb* [T] (*pt, pp* **blessed** /blest/) to ask for God's help and protection for sb/sth

IDM **be blessed with sth/sb** to be lucky enough to have sth/sb: *The West of Ireland is an area blessed with many fine sandy beaches.*

Bless you! what you say to a person who has just **sneezed** (= blown air noisily out of their nose, for example because they have a cold)

blessed /ˈblesɪd/ *adj* **1** having God's help and protection: *the Blessed Virgin Mary* **2** (in religious language) lucky: *Blessed are the pure in heart.* **SYN** **fortunate** **3** [only *before* a noun] (*formal*) giving great pleasure: *The cool breeze brought **blessed relief** from the heat.*

blessing /ˈblesɪŋ/ *noun* [C] **1** a thing that you are grateful for or that brings happiness: *It's a great blessing that we have two healthy children.* ◆ *Not getting that job was **a blessing in disguise*** (= sth which does not seem lucky but is a good thing in the end). **2** [usually sing] (a prayer asking for) God's help and protection: *The priest said a blessing.* **3** [usually sing] approval or support: *They got married without their parents' blessing.*

blew *past tense* of **blow[1]**

blight[1] /blaɪt/ *verb* [T] to spoil or damage sth: *His career has been blighted by injuries.*

blight[2] /blaɪt/ *noun* **1** [U,C] any disease that kills plants, especially crops: *potato blight* **2** [sing,U] **blight (on sb/sth)** something that has a bad effect on a situation, sb's life or the environment

⚷ **blind[1]** /blaɪnd/ *adj* (**blinder**; **blindest**) **1** unable to see: *a blind person* ◆ *to be completely/partially blind*

> **HELP** People who cannot see very well are sometimes described as **partially sighted** or **visually impaired** rather than **blind**.

2 blind (to sth) not wanting to notice or understand sth: *He was completely blind to her faults.* **3** without reason or thought: *He drove down the motorway in **a blind panic**.* **4** impossible to see round: *You should never overtake on **a blind corner**.*

IDM **turn a blind eye (to sth)** to pretend not to notice sth bad is happening so that you do not have to do anything about it

▶ **blindly** *adv* ▶ **blindness** *noun* [U]

blind[2] /blaɪnd/ *verb* [T] **1** to make sb unable to see: *Her grandfather had been blinded in an accident* (= permanently). ◆ *Just for a second I was blinded by the sun* (= for a short time). **2 blind sb (to sth)** to make sb unable to think clearly or behave in a sensible way

B

blind³ /blaɪnd/ *noun* **1** [C] a piece of cloth or other material that you pull down to cover a window ➲ picture at **curtain** **2 the blind** *noun* [pl] people who are unable to see

ˌblind ˈdate *noun* [C] an arranged meeting between a man and a woman who have never met before to see if they like each other enough to begin a romantic relationship

blindfold /ˈblaɪndfəʊld/ *noun* [C] a piece of cloth, etc. that is used for covering sb's eyes ▶ **blindfold** *verb* [T]

ˈblind spot *noun* [C] **1** the part of the road just behind you that you cannot see when driving a car **2** if you have a **blind spot** about sth, you cannot understand or accept it

bling /blɪŋ/ (also ˌ**bling-ˈbling**) *noun* [U] (*informal*) expensive shiny jewellery and fashionable clothes ▶ **bling** (also **bling-bling**) *adj*

blink /blɪŋk/ *verb* **1** [I, T] to shut your eyes and open them again very quickly: *Oh dear! You blinked just as I took the photograph!* ➲ look at **wink** **2** [I] (used about a light) to come on and go off again quickly ▶ **blink** *noun* [C]

blinker /ˈblɪŋkə(r)/ *noun* **1** [C] (*informal*) = **indicator**(2) **2 blinkers** [pl] pieces of leather that are placed at the side of a horse's eyes to stop it from looking sideways

blinkered /ˈblɪŋkəd/ *adj* not considering every aspect of a situation; not willing to accept different ideas about sth: *a blinkered policy/attitude/approach* **SYN** **narrow-minded**

blip /blɪp/ *noun* [C] **1** a light flashing on the screen of a piece of equipment, sometimes with a short high sound **2** a small problem that does not last for long

bliss /blɪs/ *noun* [U] perfect happiness ▶ **blissful** /ˈblɪsfl/ *adj* ▶ **blissfully** /-fəli/ *adv*

blister¹ /ˈblɪstə(r)/ *noun* [C] a small painful area of skin that looks like a bubble and contains clear liquid. **Blisters** are usually caused by rubbing or burning.

blister² /ˈblɪstə(r)/ *verb* [I,T] **1** to get or cause **blisters** **2** to swell and break open or to cause sth to do this: *The paint is starting to blister.*

blistering /ˈblɪstərɪŋ/ *adj* very strong or extreme: *the blistering midday heat* ◆ *The runners set off at a blistering pace.*

blitz /blɪts/ *noun* [C] **a blitz (on sth)** a sudden effort or attack on sb/sth: *The police are planning a blitz on vandalism.*

blizzard /ˈblɪzəd/ *noun* [C] a very bad storm with strong winds and a lot of snow ➲ note at **storm**

bloated /ˈbləʊtɪd/ *adj* unusually large and uncomfortable because of liquid, food or gas inside: *I felt a bit bloated after all that food.*

blob /blɒb/ *noun* [C] a small piece of a thick liquid: *a blob of paint/cream/ink*

bloc /blɒk/ *noun* [C, with sing or pl verb] a group of countries that work closely together because they have the same political interests

🔑 **block¹** /blɒk/ *noun* [C]

➤PIECE OF STH **1** a large, heavy piece of sth, usually with flat sides: *a block of wood* ◆ *huge concrete blocks*

➤BUILDING **2** a large building that is divided into separate flats or offices: *a block of flats* ➲ look at **apartment block, office block** ➲ picture on **page P9**

➤STREETS **3** a group of buildings in a town which has streets on all four sides: *The restaurant is three blocks away.*

➤AMOUNT **4** a quantity of sth or an amount of time that is considered as a single unit: *The class is divided into two blocks of fifty minutes.*

➤THAT STOPS YOU **5** [usually sing] a thing that makes movement or progress difficult or impossible: *a block to further progress in the talks* ➲ look at **roadblock**

IDM **have a block (about sth)** to be unable to think or understand sth properly: *I had a complete* ***mental block****. I just couldn't remember his name.*

🔑 **block²** /blɒk/ *verb* [T] **1 block sth (up)** to make it difficult or impossible for sb/sth to pass: *Many roads are completely blocked by snow.* **2** to prevent sth from being done: *The management tried to block the deal.* **3** to prevent sth from being seen by sb: *Get out of the way, you're blocking the view!*

PHR V **block sth off** to separate one area from another with sth solid: *This section of the motorway has been blocked off by the police.*

block sth out to try not to think about sth unpleasant: *She tried to block out the memory of the crash.*

blockade /blɒˈkeɪd/ *noun* [C] a situation in which a place is surrounded by soldiers or ships in order to prevent goods or people from reaching it ▶ **blockade** *verb* [T]

blockage /ˈblɒkɪdʒ/ *noun* [C] a thing that is preventing sth from passing; the state of being blocked: *a blockage in the drainpipe* ◆ *There are blockages on some major roads.*

blockbuster /ˈblɒkbʌstə(r)/ *noun* [C] a book or film with an exciting story which is very successful and popular

ˌblock ˈcapital *noun* [C, usually pl] a big letter such as 'A' (not 'a'): *Please write your name in block capitals.*

blog /blɒg/ (also **weblog**) *noun* [C] a personal record that sb puts on their website: *Have you seen his blog from the festival?* ▶ **blog** *verb* [I] (**blogging**; **blogged**): *I'll be blogging again on Tuesday.* ▶ **blogger** *noun* [C]

TOPIC

Blogs

A **blogger** is someone who writes a **blog** (or **weblog**) about things that interest them and about websites that they have visited. You visit someone's blog to read their **posts** (= messages) and you can **post comments** (= add messages) about what they have said. A popular **microblogging** site (= a service for very short blogs) is **Twitter™**, where you **follow** the people whose **tweets** (= short messages) you want to read.

bloke /bləʊk/ *noun* [C] (*BrE slang*) a man: *He's a really nice bloke.*

blonde (also **blond**) /blɒnd/ *adj* with fair or yellow hair: *Both my sisters have blonde hair.* ♦ *a small, blond boy* ▶ **blonde** *noun* [C]: *She's a blonde.* ➲ look at **brunette**

MORE When describing men the spelling **blond** is used: *He's tall and blond.* The noun is usually only used of women and is spelled **blonde**. It is sometimes considered offensive to refer to a woman in this way.

blood /blʌd/ *noun* [U] the red liquid that flows through your body: *The heart pumps blood around the body.* ➲ look at **bleed**
IDM in your blood a strong part of your character: *A love of the countryside was in his blood.*
in cold blood ➲ **cold**[1]
shed blood ➲ **shed**[2]
your (own) flesh and blood ➲ **flesh**

bloodbath /ˈblʌdbɑːθ/ *noun* [sing] an act of violently killing many people

ˈ**blood-curdling** *adj* very frightening: *a blood-curdling scream*

ˈ**blood donor** *noun* [C] a person who gives some of their blood for use in medical operations

ˈ**blood group** (also ˈ**blood type**) *noun* [C] any of several different types of human blood: *'What blood group are you?' 'Blood group/type O.'*

bloodless /ˈblʌdləs/ *adj* **1** without killing or violence: *a bloodless revolution* **2** (used about a part of the body) very pale

ˈ**blood pressure** *noun* [U] the force with which the blood travels round the body: *to **have high/low blood pressure***

bloodshed /ˈblʌdʃed/ *noun* [U] the killing or harming of people: *Both sides in the war want to avoid further bloodshed.*

bloodshot /ˈblʌdʃɒt/ *adj* (used about the white part of the eyes) full of red lines, for example when sb is tired

ˈ**blood sport** *noun* [C] a sport in which animals or birds are killed

bloodstain /ˈblʌdsteɪn/ *noun* [C] a mark or spot of blood on sth ▶ **bloodstained** *adj*

bloodstream /ˈblʌdstriːm/ *noun* [sing] the blood as it flows through the body: *drugs injected straight into the bloodstream*

bloodthirsty /ˈblʌdθɜːsti/ *adj* wanting to use violence or to watch scenes of violence

ˈ**blood transfusion** *noun* [C] the process of putting new blood into sb's body

ˈ**blood type** = **blood group**

ˈ**blood vessel** *noun* [C] any of the tubes in your body which blood flows through ➲ look at **artery**, **vein**

bloody /ˈblʌdi/ *adj* (**bloodier**; **bloodiest**) **1** involving a lot of violence and killing: *a bloody war* **2** covered with blood: *a bloody knife* **3** [only *before* a noun] *also adv* (*BrE slang*) a swear word used for emphasizing a comment or an angry statement: *What a bloody stupid thing to say!*

HELP Be careful. Many people find this word offensive.

bloom[1] /bluːm/ *noun* [C] a flower
IDM in bloom with its flowers open: *All the wild plants are in bloom.*

bloom[2] /bluːm/ *verb* [I] to produce flowers: *This shrub blooms in May.*

blossom[1] /ˈblɒsəm/ *noun* [C,U] a flower or a mass of flowers, especially on a fruit tree in the spring: *The apple tree is **in blossom**.* ➲ picture at **tree**

blossom[2] /ˈblɒsəm/ *verb* [I] **1** (used especially about trees) to produce flowers **2 blossom (into sth)** to become more healthy, confident or successful: *This young runner has blossomed into a top-class athlete.*

blot[1] /blɒt/ *verb* [T] (**blotting**; **blotted**) **1** to remove liquid from a surface by pressing soft paper or cloth on it **2** to make a spot or a mark on sth, especially ink on paper
PHR V blot sth out to cover or hide sth: *Fog blotted out the view completely.* ♦ *She tried to blot out the memory of what happened.*

blot[2] /blɒt/ *noun* [C] **1** a spot of sth, especially one made by ink on paper **SYN stain 2 a blot on sth** a thing that spoils your happiness or other people's opinion of you

blotch /blɒtʃ/ *noun* [C] a temporary mark or an area of different colour on skin, plants, cloth, etc: *The blotches on her face showed that she had been crying.* ▶ **blotchy** (also **blotched**) *adj*

ˈ**blotting paper** *noun* [U] soft paper that you use for drying wet ink after you have written sth on paper

blouse /blaʊz/ *noun* [C] a piece of clothing like a shirt, that women wear

blow[1] /bləʊ/ *verb* (*pt* **blew** /bluː/; *pp* **blown** /bləʊn/)
➤**WITH MOUTH 1** [I] to send air out of the mouth: *The policeman asked me to blow into the breathalyser.*
➤**WIND/AIR 2** [I,T] (used about wind, air, etc.) to be moving or to cause sth to move: *A gentle breeze was blowing.* **3** [I] to move because of the wind or a current of air: *The balloons blew away.* ♦ *My papers blew all over the garden.*
➤**INSTRUMENT 4** [I,T] to produce sound from a musical instrument, etc. by blowing air into it: *The referee's whistle blew for the end of the match.* ♦ *He blew a few notes on the trumpet.*

blow

blowing sucking

›MAKE STH **5** [T] to make or shape sth by blowing air out of your mouth: *to blow bubbles/smoke rings* ◆ *to blow (somebody) a kiss* (= to kiss your hand and pretend to blow the kiss towards sb)

›ELECTRICITY **6** [I,T] when a **fuse** (= a thin piece of wire in an electrical system) stops working suddenly because the electric current is too strong: *A fuse has blown.* ◆ *I think the kettle's blown a fuse.*

›MONEY **7** [T] (*informal*) **blow sth (on sth)** to spend or waste a lot of money on sth: *She blew all her savings on a trip to China.*

›OPPORTUNITY **8** [T] (*informal*) to waste an opportunity: *I think I've blown my chances of promotion.* ◆ *You had your chance and you blew it.*

IDM **blow your nose** to clear your nose by blowing strongly through it into a **handkerchief** (= a piece of cloth) or a **tissue** (= a piece of paper)

PHR V **blow sth apart** to completely destroy sth in an explosion

blow over to disappear without having a serious effect: *The scandal will soon blow over.*

blow up 1 to explode or to be destroyed in an explosion: *The car blew up when the door was opened.* **2** to start suddenly and strongly: *A storm blew up in the night.* ◆ *A huge row blew up about money.*

blow sth up 1 to make sth explode or to destroy sth in an explosion: *The terrorists tried to blow up the plane.* **2** to fill sth with air or gas: *to blow up a balloon* **3** to make a photograph bigger

blow up (at sb) (*informal*) to become very angry: *The teacher blew up when I said I'd forgotten my homework.*

⚷ **blow²** /bləʊ/ *noun* [C] **1** a hard hit from sb's hand, a weapon, etc: *She aimed a blow at me.* **2 a blow (to sb/sth)** a sudden shock or disappointment: *It was a blow when I didn't get the job.* **3** an act of blowing: *Give your nose a blow!*

IDM **a blow-by-blow account, description, etc. (of sth)** an account, etc. of an event that gives all the exact details of it

come to blows (with sb) (over sth) to start fighting or arguing (about sth)

deal sb/sth a blow; deal a blow to sb/sth ➲ **deal¹**

ˈ**blow-dry** *verb* [T] (**blow-drying**; **blow-dries**; *pt, pp* **blow-dried**) to dry and shape sb's hair using a **hairdryer** (= a machine that produces hot air) and a brush

blown *past participle* of **blow¹**

blowout /ˈbləʊaʊt/ *noun* [C] (*informal*) **1** a burst tyre: *We had a blowout on the motorway.* SYN **puncture 2** a very large meal at which people eat too much; a large party or social event

blubber /ˈblʌbə(r)/ *noun* [U] the fat of sea animals, such as whales

bludgeon /ˈblʌdʒən/ *verb* [T] **1** to hit sb several times with a heavy object **2 bludgeon sb (into sth/into doing sth)** to force sb to do sth, especially by arguing with them: *They tried to bludgeon me into joining their protest.*

⚷ **blue¹** /bluː/ *adj* (**bluer**; **bluest**) **1** having the colour of a clear sky when the sun shines: *His eyes were bright blue.* ◆ *light/dark blue* **2** (*informal*) (often used in songs) sad: *He'd been feeling blue all week.*

IDM **black and blue** ➲ **black¹**

once in a blue moon ➲ **once**

⚷ **blue²** /bluː/ *noun* **1** [C,U] the colour of a clear sky when the sun shines: *a deep blue* ◆ *dressed **in blue*** (= blue clothes) **2 the blues** [pl] a type of slow sad music: *a blues singer* **3 the blues** [pl] (*informal*) feelings of sadness: *to have the blues*

IDM **out of the blue** suddenly; unexpectedly: *I didn't hear from him for years and then this email came out of the blue.*

ˌ**blue-ˈchip** *adj* [only *before* a noun] a **blue-chip** investment is thought to be safe and likely to make a profit: *blue-chip companies*

ˌ**blue-ˈcollar** *adj* [only *before* a noun] doing or involving physical work with the hands rather than office work ➲ look at **white-collar**

blueish = **bluish**

blueprint /ˈbluːprɪnt/ *noun* [C] a photograph of a plan, or a description of how to make, build or achieve sth

bluff¹ /blʌf/ *verb* [I,T] to try to make people believe that sth is true when it is not, usually by appearing very confident: *Don't take any notice of him, he's just bluffing.*

IDM **bluff your way in, out, through, etc. sth** to trick sb in order to get into, out of a place, etc: *We managed to bluff our way into the stadium by saying we were journalists.*

bluff² /blʌf/ *noun* [U,C] making sb believe that you will do sth when you really have no intention of doing it, or that you know sth when, in fact, you do not know it

IDM **call sb's bluff** ➲ **call¹**

bluish (also **blueish**) /ˈbluːɪʃ/ *adj* (*informal*) slightly blue: *bluish green*

blunder¹ /ˈblʌndə(r)/ *noun* [C] a stupid mistake: *I'm afraid I've **made a** terrible **blunder**.*

blunder² /ˈblʌndə(r)/ *verb* [I] to make a stupid mistake

PHR V **blunder about, around, etc.** to move in an uncertain or careless way, as if you cannot see where you are going: *We blundered about in the dark, trying to find the light switch.*

blunt /blʌnt/ *adj* (**blunter**; **bluntest**) **1** (used about a knife, pencil, tool, etc.) without a sharp edge or point: *blunt scissors* OPP **sharp 2** (used about a person, comment, etc.) very direct; saying what you think without trying to be polite: *I'm sorry to be so blunt, but I'm afraid you're just not good enough.* ▶ **blunt** *verb* [T] ▶ **bluntly** *adv* ▶ **bluntness** *noun* [U]

blur[1] /blɜː(r)/ *noun* [C, usually sing] something that you cannot see clearly or remember well: *Without my glasses, their faces were just a blur.*

blur[2] /blɜː(r)/ *verb* [I,T] (blurring; blurred) to become or to make sth less clear: *The words on the page blurred as tears filled her eyes.* ▶ **blurred** *adj*

blurt /blɜːt/ *verb*
PHR V **blurt sth out** to say sth suddenly or without thinking: *We didn't want to tell Mum but Ann blurted the whole thing out.*

blush /blʌʃ/ *verb* [I] to become red in the face, especially because you are embarrassed or feel guilty: *She blushed with shame.* ▶ **blush** *noun* [C, usually sing]

blusher /ˈblʌʃə(r)/ (*AmE* also blush) *noun* [U,C] a coloured cream or powder that some people put on their cheeks to give them more colour

blustery /ˈblʌstəri/ *adj* (used to describe the weather) with strong winds: *The day was cold and blustery.*

BO /ˌbiː ˈəʊ/ *abbr* = **body odour**

boa constrictor /ˈbəʊə kənstrɪktə(r)/ (also boa) *noun* [C] a large South American snake that kills animals for food by wrapping its body around them and crushing them

boar /bɔː(r)/ *noun* [C] (*pl* boar *or* boars) **1** a wild pig **2** a male pig ➲ note at **pig**

🔑 **board**[1] /bɔːd/ *noun* **1** [C] a long, thin, flat piece of wood used for making floors, walls, etc: *The old house needed new* ***floorboards***. **2** [C] a thin flat piece of wood, etc. used for a particular purpose: *an ironing board* ♦ *a surfboard* ♦ *a noticeboard* ♦ *board games* (= games you play on a board) **3** [C, with sing or pl verb] a group of people who control an organization, company, etc: *The* ***board of directors*** *is/are meeting to discuss the firm's future.* ♦ *a board meeting* **4** [U] the meals that are provided when you stay in a hotel, etc: *The prices are for a double room and* ***full board*** (= all the meals).
IDM **above board** ➲ **above**
across the board ➲ **across**
on board on a ship or an aircraft: *All the passengers were safely on board.*

🔑 **board**[2] /bɔːd/ *verb* **1** [I,T] to get on a plane, ship, bus, etc: *We said goodbye and boarded the train.* **2** [I] be boarding when a plane or ship **is boarding**, it is ready for passengers to get on: *Flight LH7059 to Hamburg is now boarding at Gate 27.*
PHR V **board sth up** to cover with boards: *Nobody lives there now—it's all boarded up.*

boarder /ˈbɔːdə(r)/ *noun* [C] (*BrE*) **1** a child who lives at school and goes home for the holidays. **2** a person who pays to live at sb's house ➲ look at **lodger**

ˈ**boarding house** *noun* [C] a private house where you can pay to stay and have meals for a period of time

ˈ**boarding pass** (also ˈboarding card) *noun* [C] a document that you must show in order to get on a plane or ship

ˈ**boarding school** *noun* [C] a school that children live at while they are studying, going home only in the holidays

boardroom /ˈbɔːdruːm; -rʊm/ *noun* [C] the room where the **board of directors** (= the group of people in charge of a company or an organization) meets

boast /bəʊst/ *verb* **1** [I] to talk with too much pride about sth that you have or can do: *I wish she wouldn't boast about her family so much.* **2** [T] (used about a place) to have sth that it can be proud of: *The town boasts over a dozen restaurants.* ▶ **boast** *noun* [C]

boastful /ˈbəʊstfl/ *adj* (used about a person or the things that they say) showing too much pride

🔑 **boat** /bəʊt/ *noun* [C] **1** a small vehicle that is used for travelling across water: *The cave can only be reached* ***by boat***/ ***in a boat***. ♦ *a rowing/fishing boat* ➲ picture on **page 76** ➲ picture on **page P6** **2** any ship: *When does the next boat to France sail?*
IDM **rock the boat** ➲ **rock**[2]

TOPIC

Boats

A boat is smaller than a **ship**. A **liner** is used to carry people for long distances, called **voyages** or, if they are for pleasure, **cruises**. A **ferry** is used to carry people and sometimes cars for short distances, called **crossings**. A ship that carries goods from one place to another is a **freighter**. A large boat with sails is a **yacht**. **Lifeboat** has two meanings: it is a special boat that is used to rescue people who are in danger at sea, or it is a small boat that is kept on a ship and is used by people to escape if the ship is going to sink. A boat that you move by rowing with oars is a **rowing boat**.

The front of a boat is the **bow**, the back is the **stern**. When you are facing the front of a boat the side on the right is called **starboard**, the side on the left is called **port**. The people who work on a boat are its **crew**. The person in command is the **captain**.

bob /bɒb/ *verb* [I,T] (bobbing; bobbed) to move quickly up and down; to make sth do this: *The boats in the harbour were bobbing up and down in the water.* ♦ *She bobbed her head down below the top of the wall.*
PHR V **bob up** to appear suddenly from behind or under sth: *He disappeared and then bobbed up again on the other side of the pool.*

bobsleigh /ˈbɒbsleɪ/ (*AmE* bobsled /ˈbɒbsled/) *noun* [C] a racing vehicle for two or more people

boats

rowing boat (*AmE* rowboat)

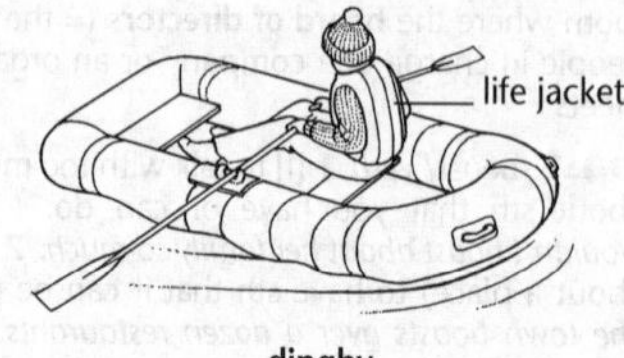

dinghy

that slides over snow along a track ➲ look at **sleigh, sledge, toboggan**

bode /bəʊd/ *verb*
IDM **bode well/ill (for sb/sth)** to be a sign that sb/sth will have a good/bad future

bodily[1] /ˈbɒdɪli/ *adj* [only *before* a noun] of the human body; physical: *First we must attend to their bodily needs* (= make sure that they have a home, enough to eat, etc.).

bodily[2] /ˈbɒdɪli/ *adv* by taking hold of the body: *She picked up the child and carried him bodily from the room.*

⚷ **body** /ˈbɒdi/ *noun* (*pl* **bodies**)
➤PERSON/ANIMAL **1** [C] the whole physical form of a person or an animal: *the human body* **2** [C] the part of a person that is not their legs, arms or head: *She had injuries to her head and body.* **3** [C] a dead person: *The police have found a body in the canal.*
➤MAIN PART **4** [sing] the main part of sth: *We agree with the body of the report, although not with certain details.*
➤GROUP OF PEOPLE **5** [C,with sing or pl verb] a group of people who work or act together, especially in an official way: *The governing body of the college meets/meet once a month.*
➤OBJECT **6** [C] (*formal*) an object: *The doctor removed a foreign body from the child's ear.*
IDM **in a body** all together

bodyboard /ˈbɒdibɔːd/ *noun* [C] a short light type of **surfboard** that you ride lying on your front ▶ **bodyboarding** *noun* [U]

bodybuilding /ˈbɒdibɪldɪŋ/ *noun* [U] making the muscles of the body stronger and larger by exercise ▶ **bodybuilder** *noun* [C]

bodyguard /ˈbɒdigɑːd/ *noun* [C] a person or group of people whose job is to protect sb

ˈ**body language** *noun* [U] showing how you feel by the way you move, stand, sit, etc., rather than by what you say: *I could tell by his body language that he was scared.*

ˈ**body odour** *noun* [U] (*abbr* **BO**) the unpleasant smell from sb's body, especially of sweat

bodywork /ˈbɒdiwɜːk/ *noun* [U] the main outside structure of a vehicle, usually made of painted metal

bog[1] /bɒg/ *noun* [C,U] an area of ground that is very soft and wet: *a peat bog*

bog[2] /bɒg/ *verb* (**bogging; bogged**)
PHR V **bog sb/sth down (in sth)** [usually passive] **1** (used about a vehicle) to make sth sink into mud or soft ground **2** (used about a person) to prevent sb from making any progress: *We got bogged down in a long discussion and didn't have time to make any decisions.*

bogey /ˈbəʊgi/ *noun* [C] **1** something that causes fear, often without reason **2** (*informal*) a piece of **mucus** (= the sticky substance that forms inside your nose)

boggle /ˈbɒgl/ *verb* [I] (*informal*) to be unable to imagine sth; impossible to imagine or believe: *'What will happen if his plan doesn't work?' '**The mind boggles!**'* ➲ look at **mind-boggling**

boggy /ˈbɒgi/ *adj* (**boggier; boggiest**) (used about land) soft and wet, so that your feet sink into it

bogus /ˈbəʊgəs/ *adj* pretending to be real or genuine: *a bogus policeman* SYN **false**

⚷ **boil**[1] /bɔɪl/ *verb* **1** [I] (used about a liquid) to reach a high temperature where bubbles rise to the surface and the liquid changes to a gas: *Water boils at 100°C.* ◆ *The kettle's boiling.* **2** [T] to heat a liquid until it boils and let it keep boiling: *Boil all drinking water for five minutes.* **3** [I,T] to cook (sth) in boiling water: *Put the potatoes on to boil, please.* ◆ *to boil an egg* ➲ note at **cook, recipe** **4** [I] (used about a person) to feel very angry: *She was boiling with rage.*
PHR V **boil down to sth** to have sth as the most important point: *What it all boils down to is that you don't want to spend too much money.*
boil over 1 (used about a liquid) to boil and flow over the sides of a pan: *You let the soup boil over.* **2** (used about an argument or sb's feelings) to become more serious or angry

boil[2] /bɔɪl/ *noun* **1** [sing] a period of boiling; the point at which a liquid boils: *You'll have to give those shirts a boil to get them clean.* **2** [C] a small, painful swelling under your skin, with a red or yellow top

boiler /ˈbɔɪlə(r)/ *noun* [C] a container in which water is heated to provide hot water or heating in a building or to produce steam in an engine

ˈ**boiler suit** *noun* [C] (*AmE* **coveralls**) a piece of clothing that you wear over your normal clothes to protect them when you are doing dirty work

boiling /ˈbɔɪlɪŋ/ (also ˌ**boiling** ˈ**hot**) *adj* (*informal*) very hot: *Open a window—it's boiling hot in here.* ◆ *Can I open a window? I'm boiling.* ➲ note at **cold**

ˈ**boiling point** *noun* [C] the temperature at which a liquid starts to boil

boisterous /ˈbɔɪstərəs/ *adj* (used about a person or their behaviour) noisy and full of energy: *Their children are very nice but they can get a bit too boisterous.*

The Human Body

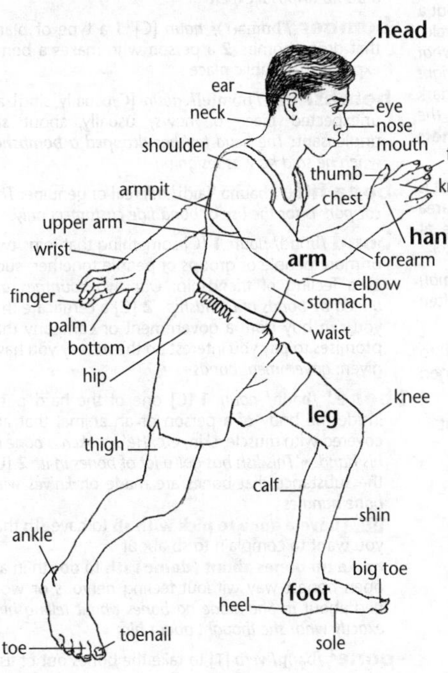

head
ear
neck
eye
nose
mouth
shoulder
fingernail
thumb
knuckle
armpit
chest
upper arm
hand
wrist
arm
forearm
elbow
finger
stomach
palm
waist
bottom
hip
knee
leg
thigh
calf
shin
ankle
big toe
foot
heel
toenail
toe
sole

the body

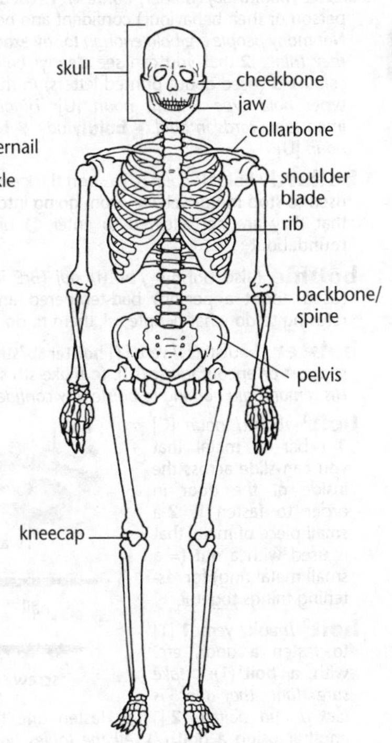

skull
cheekbone
jaw
collarbone
shoulder blade
rib
backbone/ spine
pelvis
kneecap

the skeleton

brain
throat
lung
heart
liver
stomach
kidney
small intestine
large intestine
bladder

internal organs

hair
forehead
temple
eyebrow
eyelid
eyelashes
cheek
nostril
gum
tongue
jaw
lip
tooth
throat
chin

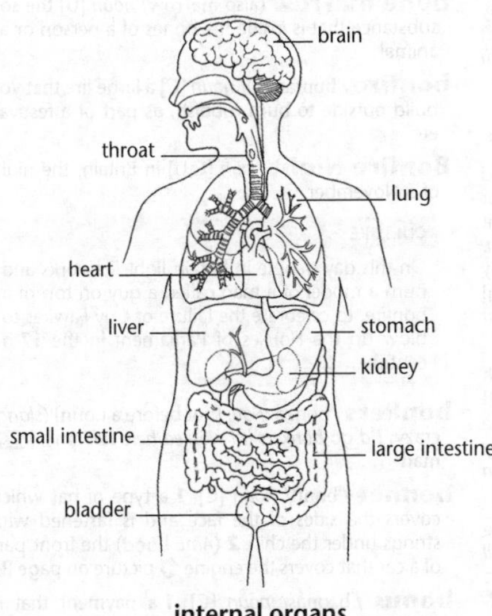

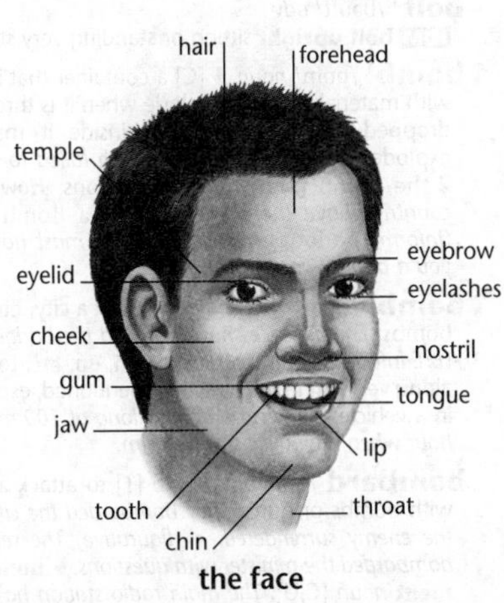

the face

B

bold /bəʊld/ *adj* (bolder; boldest) **1** (used about a person or their behaviour) confident and not afraid: *Not many people are bold enough to say exactly what they think.* **2** that you can see clearly: *bold, bright colours* **3** (used about printed letters) in thick, dark type: *bold type* ▶ **bold** *noun* [U]: *Highlight the important words **in bold**.* ▶ **boldly** *adv* ▶ **boldness** *noun* [U]

bollard /ˈbɒlɑːd/ *noun* [C] a short thick post that is used to stop motor vehicles from going into an area that they are not allowed to enter ➲ picture at **roundabout**

bolshie (also bolshy) /ˈbɒlʃi/ *adj* (*BrE informal*) (used about a person) bad-tempered and often refusing to do what people ask them to do

bolster /ˈbəʊlstə(r)/ *verb* [T] bolster sb/sth (up) to support or encourage sb/sth; to make sth stronger: *His remarks did nothing to bolster my confidence.*

bolt[1] /bəʊlt/ *noun* [C] **1** a bar of metal that you can slide across the inside of the door in order to fasten it **2** a small piece of metal that is used with a **nut** (= a small metal ring) for fastening things together

bolt | nut | washer | nail | screw

bolt[2] /bəʊlt/ *verb* **1** [T] to fasten a door, etc. with a **bolt**[1](1): *Make sure that the door is locked and bolted.* **2** [T] to fasten one thing to another using a **bolt**[1](2): *All the tables have been bolted to the floor so that nobody can steal them.* **3** [I] (used especially about a horse) to run away very suddenly, usually in fear **4** [T] bolt sth (down) to eat sth very quickly: *She bolted down a sandwich and dashed out of the house.*

bolt[3] /bəʊlt/ *adv*

IDM **bolt upright** sitting or standing very straight

bomb[1] /bɒm/ *noun* **1** [C] a container that is filled with material that will explode when it is thrown or dropped, or when a device inside it makes it explode: *Fortunately, the car bomb failed to **go off**.* **2** the bomb [sing] nuclear weapons: *How many countries have the bomb now?* **3** a bomb [sing] (*informal*) a lot of money: *That car must have cost you a bomb!*

bomb[2] /bɒm/ *verb* **1** [T] to attack a city, etc. with bombs: *Enemy forces have bombed the bridge.* **2** [I] (*BrE informal*) bomb along, down, up, etc. to move along very fast in the direction mentioned, especially in a vehicle: *He was bombing along at 100 miles an hour when the police stopped him.*

bombard /bɒmˈbɑːd/ *verb* [T] to attack a place with bombs or guns: *They bombarded the city until the enemy surrendered.* ◆ (*figurative*) *The reporters bombarded the minister with questions.* ▶ **bombardment** *noun* [C,U]: *The main radio station has **come under** enemy **bombardment**.*

ˈbomb disposal *noun* [U] the removing or exploding of bombs in order to make an area safe: *a bomb disposal expert*

bomber /ˈbɒmə(r)/ *noun* [C] **1** a type of plane that drops bombs **2** a person who makes a bomb explode in a public place

bombshell /ˈbɒmʃel/ *noun* [C, usually sing] an unexpected piece of news, usually about sth unpleasant: *The head teacher **dropped a bombshell** when he said he was resigning.*

bona fide /ˌbəʊnə ˈfaɪdi/ *adj* real or genuine: *This car park is for the use of bona fide customers only.*

bond /bɒnd/ *noun* **1** [C] something that joins two or more people or groups of people together, such as a feeling of friendship: *Our two countries are united by bonds of friendship.* **2** [C] a certificate that you can buy from a government or company that promises to pay you interest on the money you have given: *government bonds*

bone[1] /bəʊn/ *noun* **1** [C] one of the hard parts inside the body of a person or an animal that are covered with muscle, skin, etc: *He's broken a bone in his hand.* ◆ *This fish has got a lot of bones in it.* **2** [U] the substance that bones are made of: *knives with bone handles*

IDM **have a bone to pick with sb** to have sth that you want to complain to sb about

make no bones about (doing) sth to do sth in an open honest way without feeling nervous or worried about it: *She made no bones about telling him exactly what she thought about him.*

bone[2] /bəʊn/ *verb* [T] to take the bones out of fish or meat

ˌbone ˈdry *adj* completely dry: *Give that plant some water—it's bone dry.*

ˈbone marrow (also marrow) *noun* [U] the soft substance that is inside the bones of a person or an animal

bonfire /ˈbɒnfaɪə(r)/ *noun* [C] a large fire that you build outside to burn rubbish, as part of a festival, etc.

ˈBonfire Night *noun* [C,U] in Britain, the night of 5 November

CULTURE

On this day people in Britain light fireworks and burn a model of a man called a **guy** on top of a bonfire, to celebrate the failure of Guy Fawkes to blow up the Houses of Parliament in the 17th century.

bonkers /ˈbɒŋkəz/ *adj* [not before a noun] (*slang*) crazy: *I'd **go bonkers** if I worked here full-time.* SYN **mad**

bonnet /ˈbɒnɪt/ *noun* [C] **1** a type of hat which covers the sides of the face and is fastened with strings under the chin **2** (*AmE* hood) the front part of a car that covers the engine ➲ picture on **page P7**

bonus /ˈbəʊnəs/ *noun* [C] **1** a payment that is added to what is usual: *All our employees receive an annual bonus.* **2** something good that you get in addition to what you expect: *I enjoy my job, and having my own office is **an added bonus**.*

bony /ˈbəʊni/ *adj* (**bonier**; **boniest**) so thin that you can see the shape of the bones: *long bony fingers*

boo /buː/ *exclam, noun* [C] (*pl* **boos**) **1** a sound you make to show that you do not like sb/sth: *The band's act was met with boos from the audience.* **2** a sound you make to frighten or surprise sb: *He jumped out from behind the door and said 'boo'.* ▶ **boo** *verb* [I,T]

boob /buːb/ *noun* [C] **1** (*slang*) a woman's breast **2** (*informal*) a silly mistake ▶ **boob** *verb* [I] (*informal*): *I'm afraid I've boobed again.*

booby prize /ˈbuːbi praɪz/ *noun* [C] a prize that is given as a joke to the person or team that comes last in a competition

booby trap /ˈbuːbi træp/ *noun* [C] a device that will kill, injure or surprise sb when they touch the object that it is connected to ▶ **booby-trap** *verb* [T]

⚷ **book¹** /bʊk/ *noun* **1** [C] (*abbr* **bk**) a written work that is published as printed pages fastened together inside a cover, or in electronic form: *I'm reading a book on astrology.* ◆ *She's writing a book about her life abroad.* ◆ *Do you have any books by William Golding?* ◆ *hardback/paperback books* ➲ look at **e-book** **2** [C] a number of pieces of paper, fastened together inside a cover, for people to write or draw on: *Please write down all the new vocabulary in your exercise books.* ◆ *a notebook* ◆ *a sketch book* **3** [C] a number of things fastened together in the form of a book: *a book of stamps* ◆ *a chequebook* **4** **books** [pl] the records that a company, etc. keeps of the amount of money it spends and receives: *We employ an accountant to **keep the books**.*

IDM **be in sb's good/bad books** (*informal*) to have sb pleased/angry with you: *He's been in his girlfriend's bad books since he forgot her birthday.*

by the book exactly according to the rules: *A policeman must always do things by the book.*

(be) on sb's books (to be) on the list of an organization: *The employment agency has hundreds of qualified secretaries on its books.*

> TOPIC
>
> **Books**
>
> An **author** is a person who writes a book. The name of a book is its **title**. A **novel** is a book that tells a story, usually divided into **chapters**. The story of sb's life is called a **biography**, or an **autobiography** if a person writes their own life story. You use a **reference book**, for example a **dictionary**, an **atlas** or an **encyclopedia**, to look up information. Reference books usually have a **list of contents** at the front and an **index** at the back, to show you what information the book contains. A **hardback** has a hard **cover** and a **paperback** has a soft cover. Do you prefer reading **fiction** (= stories) or **non-fiction** (= facts)?

⚷ **book²** /bʊk/ *verb* **1** [I,T] to arrange to have or do sth at a particular time: *Have you booked a table, sir?* ◆ *to book a seat on a plane/train/bus* ◆ *I've booked a hotel room for you/I've booked you a hotel room.* ◆ *I'm sorry, but this evening's performance is fully booked* (= there are no seats left). ◆ *I forgot to book.* **2** [T] (*informal*) to officially write down the name of a person who has done sth wrong: *The police booked her for* (= charged her with) *dangerous driving.* ◆ *The player was booked for a foul and then sent off for arguing.*

PHR V **book in** to say that you have arrived at a hotel, etc., and sign your name on a list

book sb in to arrange a room for sb at a hotel, etc. in advance: *I've booked you in at the George Hotel.*

bookcase /ˈbʊkkeɪs/ *noun* [C] a piece of furniture with shelves to keep books on ➲ picture on **page P8**

bookie /ˈbʊki/ (*informal*) = **bookmaker**

booking /ˈbʊkɪŋ/ *noun* [C,U] the arrangement you make in advance to have a hotel room, a seat on a plane, etc: *Did you manage to **make a booking**?* ◆ *No advance booking is necessary.*

booking office *noun* [C] an office where you buy tickets

bookkeeping /ˈbʊkkiːpɪŋ/ *noun* [U] keeping the accounts of the money that a company, etc. spends or receives

booklet /ˈbʊklət/ *noun* [C] a small thin book, usually with a soft cover, that gives information about sth

bookmaker /ˈbʊkmeɪkə(r)/ (*also informal* **bookie**) *noun* **1** [C] a person whose job is to take bets on horse races, etc. **2** **the bookmaker's** [sing] a shop, etc. where you can bet money on a race or an event ➲ look at **betting shop**

bookmark /ˈbʊkmɑːk/ *noun* [C] **1** a narrow piece of card, etc. that you put between the pages of a book so that you can find the same place again easily **2** (*also* **favorite**) a file from the Internet that you have stored on your computer

bookseller /ˈbʊkselə(r)/ *noun* [C] a person whose job is selling books

bookshelf /ˈbʊkʃelf/ (*pl* **bookshelves** /ˈbʊkʃelvz/) *noun* [C] a shelf that you keep books on

bookshop /ˈbʊkʃɒp/ (*AmE* **bookstore**) *noun* [C] a shop that sells books ➲ look at **library**

bookstall /ˈbʊkstɔːl/ (*AmE* **ˈnews-stand**) *noun* [C] a type of small shop, which is open at the front, selling newspapers, magazines and books, for example at a station

bookstore /ˈbʊkstɔː(r)/ (*AmE*) = **bookshop**

bookworm /ˈbʊkwɜːm/ *noun* [C] a person who likes reading books very much

boom¹ /buːm/ *noun* [C] **1** a period in which sth increases or develops very quickly: *a boom in car sales* ➲ look at **slump** **2** [usually sing] a loud deep sound: *the distant boom of thunder*

boom² /buːm/ *verb* **1** [I,T] **boom (sth) (out)** to make a loud deep sound: *The loudspeaker boomed out instructions to the crowd.* **2** [I] to grow very quickly in size or value: *Business is booming in the computer industry.*

B

boomerang /ˈbuːməræŋ/ *noun* [C] a curved piece of wood that returns to you when you throw it in a particular way

boon /buːn/ *noun* [C] a thing that is very helpful and that you are grateful for

boost¹ /buːst/ *verb* [T] to increase sth in number, value or strength: *If we lower the price, that should boost sales.* ◆ *The good exam result boosted her confidence.*

boost² /buːst/ *noun* [C] something that encourages people; an increase: *The president's visit gave a boost to the soldiers' morale.* ◆ *The fall in the value of the pound has led to a boost in exports.*

⚷ **boot¹** /buːt/ *noun* [C] **1** a type of shoe that covers your foot and ankle and often part of your leg: *ski boots* ◆ *walking/climbing boots* ◆ *football boots* ➲ picture at **shoe** **2** (*AmE* **trunk**) the part of a car where you put luggage, usually at the back: *I'll put the luggage in the boot.* ➲ picture on **page P7**

boot² /buːt/ *verb* (*informal*) **1** [T] to kick sth/sb hard: *He booted the ball over the fence.* **2** [I,T] to make a computer ready for use when it is first switched on

PHR V **boot sb/sth out** to force sb/sth to leave a place: *The boys were booted out of the club for fighting.*

booth /buːð/ *noun* [C] a small place with thin walls that divide it from the rest of the room or area, where you can do sth that is private: *a phone booth*

booty /ˈbuːti/ *noun* [U] things that are taken by thieves or captured by soldiers in a war

booze¹ /buːz/ *noun* [U] (*informal*) alcohol

booze² /buːz/ *verb* [I] (*informal*) to drink a lot of alcohol: *He went out boozing with some friends on Saturday.*

⚷ **border¹** /ˈbɔːdə(r)/ *noun* [C] **1** a line that divides two countries, etc.; the land close to this line: *The refugees escaped **across/over the border**.* ◆ *the Moroccan border* ◆ *the border between France and Italy* ◆ *Italy's border with France* **2** a band or narrow line around the edge of sth, often for decoration: *a white tablecloth with a blue border*

OTHER WORDS FOR

border

We use **border** and **frontier** to talk about the line that divides two countries or states. We usually use **border** to talk about natural divisions: *The river forms the border between the two countries.* **Boundary** is usually used for the line that divides smaller areas: *the county boundary*

border² /ˈbɔːdə(r)/ *verb* [T] to form a border to an area; to be on the border of an area: *The road was bordered with trees.*

PHR V **border on sth** **1** to be almost the same as sth: *The dictator's ideas bordered on madness.* **2** to be next to sth: *Our garden borders on the railway line.*

borderline /ˈbɔːdəlaɪn/ *noun* [sing] the line that marks a division between two different cases, conditions, etc: *He's **a borderline case**–he may pass the exam or he may fail.*

⚷ **bore¹** /bɔː(r)/ *verb* **1** [T] to make sb feel bored, especially by talking too much: *I hope I'm not boring you.* **2** [I,T] to make a long deep hole with a tool: *This drill can bore (a hole) through solid rock.* **3** *past tense of* **bear¹**

bore² /bɔː(r)/ *noun* **1** [C] a person who talks a lot in a way that is not interesting **2** [sing] (*informal*) something that you have to do that you do not find interesting: *It's such a bore having to learn these lists of irregular verbs.*

⚷ **bored** /bɔːd/ *adj* **bored (with sth)** feeling tired and perhaps slightly annoyed because sth is not interesting or because you do not have anything to do: *I'm bored with eating the same thing every day.* ◆ *The children **get bored** on long journeys.* ◆ *He gave a bored yawn.* ◆ *The play was awful–we were **bored stiff*** (= extremely bored).

HELP If you have nothing to do, or if what you are doing does not interest you, then you are **bored**. The person or thing that makes you feel like this is **boring**.

boredom /ˈbɔːdəm/ *noun* [U] the state of being bored: *I sometimes eat out of boredom.*

⚷ **boring** /ˈbɔːrɪŋ/ *adj* not at all interesting: *a boring film/job/speech/man* **SYN** **dull**

⚷ **born¹** /bɔːn/ *verb* (*abbr* **b.**) **be born** to come into the world by birth; to start existing: *Where were you born?* ◆ *I was born in London, but I grew up in Leeds.* ◆ *I'm going to give up work after the baby is born.* ◆ *The idea of free education for all was born in the 19th century.* ◆ *His unhappiness was **born out of** a feeling of frustration.*

born² /bɔːn/ *adj* **1** [only *before* a noun] having a natural ability to do sth: *She's a born leader.* **2** **-born** [in compounds] born in the place or state mentioned: *This Kenyan-born athlete now represents Denmark.*

ˌborn-aˈgain *adj* [only *before* a noun] having found new, strong religious belief: *a born-again Christian*

borne *past participle of* **bear¹**

borough /ˈbʌrə/ *noun* [C] a town, or an area inside a large town, that has some form of local government

⚷ **borrow** /ˈbɒrəʊ/ *verb* [I,T] **borrow (sth) (from/off sb/sth)** **1** to take or receive sth from sb/sth that you intend to give back, usually after a short time: *I had to borrow from the bank to pay for my car.* ◆ *We'll have to borrow a lot of money to buy a car.* ◆ *Could I borrow your pen for a minute?* ◆ *He's always borrowing off his mother.* ◆ *I borrowed a book from the library.*

HELP Be careful not to confuse **borrow** with its opposite **lend**.

borrow/lend

She's **lending** her son some money.

He's **borrowing** some money from his mother.

2 to take sth and use it as your own; to copy sth: *That idea is borrowed from another book.*

borrower /ˈbɒrəʊə(r)/ *noun* [C] a person who borrows sth

bosom /ˈbʊzəm/ *noun* [sing] (*formal*) sb's chest, especially a woman's breasts: *She clutched the child to her bosom.*
IDM **in the bosom of sth** close to; with the protection of: *He was glad to be back in the bosom of his family.*

ˌ**bosom ˈfriend** *noun* [C] a very close friend

boss[1] /bɒs/ *noun* [C] (*informal*) **1** a person whose job is to give orders to others at work; an employer; a manager: *I'm going to ask the boss for a day off work.* ◆ *OK. You're the boss* (= you make the decisions). **2** a person who is in charge of a large organization: *the new boss at IBM* ◆ *Hospital bosses protested at the government's decision.*

boss[2] /bɒs/ *verb* [T] **boss sb (about/around)** to give orders to sb, especially in an annoying way: *I wish you'd stop bossing me around.*

bossy /ˈbɒsi/ *adj* (**bossier**; **bossiest**) liking to give orders to other people, often in an annoying way: *Don't be so bossy!* ▶ **bossily** *adv* ▶ **bossiness** *noun* [U]

botanist /ˈbɒtənɪst/ *noun* [C] a person who studies plants

botany /ˈbɒtəni/ *noun* [U] the scientific study of plants ➲ look at **biology**, **zoology** ▶ **botanical** /bəˈtænɪkl/ *adj*: *botanical gardens* (= a type of park where plants are grown for scientific study)

botch /bɒtʃ/ *verb* [T] (*informal*) **botch sth (up)** to do sth badly: *I've completely botched up this typing, I'm afraid.* SYN **mess sth up**

both /bəʊθ/ *determiner, pron* **1** the two; the one as well as the other: *Both women were French.* ◆ *Both the women were French.* ◆ *Both of the women were French.* ◆ *I liked them both.* ◆ *We were both very tired.* ◆ *Both of us were tired.* ◆ *I've got two sisters. They both live in London/Both of them live in London.*

HELP Note that we CANNOT say: *the both women* or: *my both sisters.*

2 both ... and ... not only ... but also ...: *Both he and his wife are vegetarian.* ➲ note at **similarity**

bother[1] /ˈbɒðə(r)/ *verb* **1** [I] [usually negative] **bother (to do sth/doing sth)**; **bother (about/with sth)** to make the effort to do sth: *'Shall I make you something to eat?' 'No, don't bother—I'm not hungry.'* ◆ *He didn't even bother to say thank you.* ◆ *Don't bother waiting for me—I'll catch you up later.* ◆ *Don't bother about the washing-up. I'll do it later.* **2** [T] to disturb, annoy or worry sb: *I'm sorry to bother you, but could I speak to you for a moment?* ◆ *Don't bother Geeta with that now—she's busy.* SYN **trouble**
IDM **be bothered (about sth)** (*especially BrE informal*) to think that sb/sth is important: *'What would you like to do this evening?' 'I'm not bothered really.'* ◆ *Sam doesn't seem too bothered about losing his job.*
can't be bothered (to do sth) used to say that you do not want to spend time or energy doing sth: *I can't be bothered to do my homework now. I'll do it tomorrow.*

bother[2] /ˈbɒðə(r)/ *noun* [U] trouble or difficulty: *Thanks for all your help. It's saved me a lot of bother.*

Botox™ /ˈbəʊtɒks/ *noun* [U] a substance that makes muscles relax. It is sometimes put under the skin around sb's eyes using a needle, in order to remove lines and make the skin look younger.

bottle[1] /ˈbɒtl/ *noun* [C] **1** a glass or plastic container with a narrow neck for keeping liquids in: *a beer bottle* ◆ *an empty bottle* ➲ picture at **bicycle** **2** the amount of liquid that a bottle can hold: *a bottle of lemonade* ➲ picture at **container**

bottle[2] /ˈbɒtl/ *verb* [T] to put sth into bottles: *After three or four months the wine is bottled.* ◆ *bottled water* (= that you can buy in bottles)
PHR V **bottle sth up** to not allow yourself to express strong emotions: *You'll make yourself ill if you keep your feelings bottled up.*

ˈ**bottle bank** *noun* [C] a large container in a public place where people can leave their empty bottles so that the glass can be **recycled** (= used again)

bottleneck /ˈbɒtlnek/ *noun* [C] **1** a narrow piece of road that causes traffic to slow down or stop **2** something that makes progress slower, especially in business or industry

bottom[1] /ˈbɒtəm/ *noun* **1** [C, usually sing] the lowest part of sth: *The house is* ***at the bottom*** *of a hill.* ◆ *I think I've got a pen* ***in the bottom*** *of my bag.* ◆ *The sea is so clear that you can see the bottom.* OPP **top** **2** [C] the flat surface on the outside of an object, on which it stands: *There's a label* ***on the bottom*** *of the box.* OPP **top** **3** [sing] the far end of sth: *The bus stop is* ***at the bottom*** *of the road.* OPP **top** **4** [sing] the lowest position in relation to other people, teams, etc: *I started* ***at the bottom*** *and now I'm the Managing Director.* OPP **top** **5** [C] the part of your body that you sit on: *He fell over and landed on his bottom.* ➲ picture at **body** **6 bottoms** [pl] the lower part of a piece of clothing that is in two parts: *pyjama bottoms* ◆ *track suit bottoms*

IDM **be at the bottom of sth** to be the cause of sth: *I'm sure Molly Potter is at the bottom of all this.*
from the (bottom of your) heart ➲ **heart**
get to the bottom of sth to find out the real cause of sth

🔑 **bottom²** /ˈbɒtəm/ *adj* [only *before* a noun] in the lowest position: *the bottom shelf* ♦ *I live on the bottom floor.*

bottomless /ˈbɒtəmləs/ *adj* very deep; without limit

ˌbottom ˈline *noun* [sing] **1 the bottom line** the most important thing to consider when you are discussing or deciding sth, etc: *A musical instrument should look and feel good, but the bottom line is how it sounds.* **2** the final profit or loss that a company has made in a particular period of time **3** the lowest price that sb will accept for sth

bough /baʊ/ *noun* [C] one of the main branches of a tree

bought *past tense, past participle* of **buy¹**

boulder /ˈbəʊldə(r)/ *noun* [C] a very large rock

boulevard /ˈbuːləvɑːd/ *noun* [C] a wide street in a city often with trees on each side

bounce /baʊns/ *verb* **1** [I,T] (used about a ball, etc.) to move away quickly after it has hit a hard surface; to make a ball do this: *The stone bounced off the wall and hit her on the head.* ♦ *A small boy came down the street, bouncing a ball.* **2** [I] to jump up and down continuously: *The children were bouncing on their beds.* ➲ picture at **hop** **3** [I,T] (used about a cheque) to be returned by a bank without payment because there is not enough money in the account **4** [I,T] **bounce (sth) (back)** (used about an email) to be returned to the person who sent it because the system cannot deliver it

PHR V **bounce back** to become healthy, successful or happy again after an illness, a failure, or a disappointment
▸ **bounce** *noun* [C]

bouncer /ˈbaʊnsə(r)/ *noun* [C] a person who is employed to stand at the entrance to a club, pub, etc. to stop people who are not wanted from going in, and to throw out people who are causing trouble inside

bouncy /ˈbaʊnsi/ *adj* (**bouncier**; **bounciest**) **1** that **bounces** well or that can make things **bounce**: *a bouncy ball/surface* **2** (used about a person) full of energy: *She's a very bouncy person.* SYN **lively**

🔑 **bound¹** /baʊnd/ *adj* [not before a noun] **1 bound to do sth** certain to do sth: *You've done so much work that you're bound to pass the exam.* **2 bound (by sth)(to do sth)** having a legal or moral duty to do sth: *The company is bound by UK employment law.* ♦ *She felt bound to refuse the offer.* **3 bound (for ...)** travelling to a particular place: *a ship bound for Australia*

IDM **bound up with sth** closely connected with sth

bound² /baʊnd/ *verb* [I] to run quickly with long steps: *She bounded out of the house to meet us.*
▸ **bound** *noun* [C]: *With a couple of bounds he had crossed the room.*

bound³ *past tense, past participle* of **bind¹**

boundary /ˈbaʊndri/ *noun* [C] (*pl* **boundaries**) a real or imagined line that marks the limits of sth and divides it from other places or things: *national boundaries* ♦ *The road is the boundary between the two districts.* ♦ *Scientists continue to push back the boundaries of human knowledge.* ➲ note at **border**

boundless /ˈbaʊndləs/ *adj* having no limit: *boundless energy*

bounds /baʊndz/ *noun* [pl] limits that cannot or should not be passed: *Price rises must be kept within reasonable bounds.*

IDM **out of bounds** (used about a place) where people are not allowed to go: *This area is out of bounds to all staff.*

bouquet /buˈkeɪ/ *noun* [C] a bunch of flowers that is arranged in an attractive way

bourbon /ˈbɜːbən/ *noun* [C,U] a type of **whisky** (= a strong alcoholic drink) that is made mainly in the US

bourgeois /ˈbʊəʒwɑː; ˌbʊəˈʒwɑː/ *adj* **1** belonging to the middle class **2** (disapproving) interested mainly in having more money and a higher social position: *bourgeois attitudes/ideas/values*

the bourgeoisie /ˌbʊəʒwɑːˈziː/ *noun* [sing, with sing or pl verb] the middle classes in society

bout /baʊt/ *noun* [C] **1** a short period of great activity: *a bout of hard work* **2** a period of illness: *I'm just recovering from a bout of flu.*

boutique /buːˈtiːk/ *noun* [C] a small shop that sells fashionable clothes or expensive presents
▸ **boutique** *adj* [only *before* a noun] (used about a business) small and offering products or services of a high quality to a small number of customers: *a boutique hotel in the old part of the city*

bovine /ˈbəʊvaɪn/ *adj* (*technical*) connected with cows: *bovine diseases*

bow¹ /baʊ/ *verb* [I,T] **bow (sth) (to sb)** to bend your head or the upper part of your body forward and down, as a sign of respect: *The speaker bowed to the guests and left the stage.* ♦ *He bowed his head respectfully.*

PHR V **bow out (of sth/as sth)** to leave an important position or stop taking part in sth: *After a long and successful career, she has decided to bow out of politics.* ♦ *He finally bowed out as chairman after ten years.*
bow to sb/sth to accept sth: *They finally bowed to pressure from the public.*

bow² /baʊ/ *noun* [C] **1** an act of **bowing¹**: *The director of the play came on stage to **take a bow**.* **2** the front part of a ship OPP **stern** ➲ note at **boat** ➲ picture on **page P6**

bow³ /bəʊ/ *noun* [C] **1** a weapon for shooting arrows. A **bow** is a curved piece of wood that is held in shape by a tight string. **2** a knot with two loose round parts and two loose ends that you use when you are tying shoes, etc: *He tied his laces **in a bow**.* ➲ picture at **loop** **3** a long thin piece of wood with hair stretched across it that you use for playing some musical instruments: *a violin bow* ➲ picture at **music**

bowel /ˈbaʊəl/ *noun* [C, usually pl] one of the tubes that carries waste food away from your stomach to the place where it leaves your body

bowl[1] /bəʊl/ *noun* [C] **1** a deep round dish without a lid that is used for holding food or liquid: *a soup bowl* ➲ look at **plate** ➲ picture on **page P16** **2** a large plastic container that is used for washing dishes, washing clothes, etc: *a washing-up bowl* **3** the amount of sth that is in a bowl: *I usually have a bowl of cereal for breakfast.*

bowl[2] /bəʊl/ *verb* [I,T] (in games such as **cricket**) to throw the ball in the direction of the person with the **bat** (= a piece of wood or metal)
PHR V bowl sb over 1 to knock sb down when you are moving quickly **2** to surprise sb very much in a pleasant way: *I was absolutely bowled over by the beautiful scenery.*

bow legs /ˌbəʊ ˈlegz/ *noun* [pl] legs that curve out at the knees ▸ **bow-legged** /ˌbəʊ ˈlegɪd/ *adj*

bowler /ˈbəʊlə(r)/ *noun* [C] **1** (in the sport of **cricket**) the player who throws the ball in the direction of the person with the **bat** (= a piece of wood or metal) ➲ note at **cricket** ➲ picture on **page P4** **2** (also ˌbowler ˈhat; *AmE* derby) a round hard black hat, usually worn by men ➲ picture at **hat**

bowling /ˈbəʊlɪŋ/ *noun* [U] a game in which you roll a heavy ball down a **lane** (= a special track) towards a group of **pins** (= wooden objects shaped like bottles) and try to knock them all down: *to go bowling*

ˈbowling alley *noun* [C] a building or part of a building where people can go **bowling**: *The complex contains a bowling alley, pool hall and indoor tennis courts.*

bowls /bəʊlz/ *noun* [U] a game in which you try to roll large wooden balls as near as possible to a smaller ball: *to play bowls*

bow tie /ˌbəʊ ˈtaɪ/ *noun* [C] a tie in the shape of a **bow**³(2), that is worn by men, especially on formal occasions

box[1] /bɒks/ *noun*
›CONTAINER **1** [C] a container made of wood, cardboard, metal, etc. with a flat stiff base and sides and often a lid: *a cardboard box* ♦ *a shoebox* ➲ picture at **container** **2** [C] a box and the things inside it: *a box of chocolates/matches/tissues*
›SMALL AREA **3** [C] a small area with walls on all sides that is used for a particular purpose: *a telephone box* ♦ *the jury/witness box* (= in a court of law)
›ON A FORM **4** [C] an empty square on a form in which you have to write sth: *Write your full name in the box below.*
›TV **5 the box** [sing] (*BrE informal*) TV: *What's on the box tonight?*

box[2] /bɒks/ *verb* **1** [I,T] to fight in the sport of **boxing** **2** [T] **box (sth) up** to put sth into a box
PHR V box sb/sth in to prevent sb from getting out of a small space: *Someone parked behind us and boxed us in.*
▸ **boxed** *adj*: *a boxed set of DVDs*

boxer /ˈbɒksə(r)/ *noun* [C] a person who does **boxing** as a sport ➲ picture on **page P5**

ˈboxer shorts (also boxers, *AmE* shorts) *noun* [pl] short trousers that men use as underwear

boxing /ˈbɒksɪŋ/ *noun* [U] a sport in which two people fight by hitting each other with their hands inside large gloves: *the world middleweight boxing champion* ♦ *boxing gloves* ➲ picture on **page P5**

ˈBoxing Day *noun* [C,U] (*BrE*) the day after Christmas Day; 26 December

ˈbox number *noun* [C] a number used as an address, especially in newspaper advertisements

ˈbox office *noun* [C] the place in a cinema, theatre, etc. where the tickets are sold

boy /bɔɪ/ *noun* [C] a male child or a young man: *They've got three children—two boys and a girl.* ♦ *I used to play here when I was a boy.* ♦ *Her eldest boy is at college.*

boycott /ˈbɔɪkɒt/ *verb* [T] to refuse to buy things from a particular company, take part in an event, etc. because you do not approve of it: *Several countries boycotted the Olympic Games in protest.* ♦ *We ask people to boycott companies that use child labour.*
▸ **boycott** *noun* [C]: *a boycott of the local elections*

boyfriend /ˈbɔɪfrend/ *noun* [C] a man or boy that sb has a romantic or sexual relationship with: *She has had a lot of boyfriends.*

boyhood /ˈbɔɪhʊd/ *noun* [U] the time of being a boy: *My father told me some of his boyhood memories.*

boyish /ˈbɔɪɪʃ/ *adj* like a boy: *a boyish smile*

bra /brɑː/ *noun* [C] a piece of clothing that women wear under their other clothes to support their breasts

brace[1] /breɪs/ *noun* **1** [C] (*AmE* braces [pl]) a metal frame that is fixed to a child's teeth in order to make them straight **2** braces (*AmE* suspenders) [pl] a pair of narrow pieces of **elastic** (= material that can stretch) that go over your shoulders to hold your trousers up

brace[2] /breɪs/ *verb* [T] brace sth/yourself (for sth) to prepare yourself for sth unpleasant: *You'd better brace yourself for some bad news.*

bracelet /ˈbreɪslət/ *noun* [C] a piece of jewellery, for example a metal chain or band, that you wear around your wrist or arm ➲ picture at **jewellery**

bracing /ˈbreɪsɪŋ/ *adj* making you feel healthy and full of energy: *bracing sea air*

bracket[1] /ˈbrækɪt/ *noun* [C] **1** (*especially AmE* parenthesis) [usually pl] one of two marks, () or [ ], that you put round extra information in a piece of writing: *A translation of each word is given **in brackets**.* **2** age, income, price, etc. bracket ages, prices, etc. which are between two limits: *to be in a* *high income bracket* **3** a piece of metal or wood that is fixed to a wall and used as a support for a shelf, lamp, etc.

bracket² /ˈbrækɪt/ *verb* [T] **1** to put a word, number, etc. between **brackets¹**(1) **2 bracket A and B (together); bracket A with B** to think of two or more people or things as similar in some way

brag /bræg/ *verb* [I] (**bragging; bragged**) **brag (to sb) (about/of sth)** to talk in a very proud way about sth: *She's always bragging to her friends about how clever she is.*

braid /breɪd/ *noun* **1** [U] thin coloured rope that is used to decorate military uniforms, etc. **2** (*AmE*) = **plait 3** (*AmE*) = **pigtail**

Braille /breɪl/ *noun* [U] a system of printing, using little round marks that are higher than the level of the paper they are on and which people who cannot see can read by touching them: *The signs were written **in Braille**.*

⚷ **brain** /breɪn/ *noun* **1** [C] the part of your body inside your head that controls your thoughts, feelings and movements: *damage to the brain* ◆ *a brain tumour* ◆ *a brain surgeon* ➲ picture at **body 2** [C,U] the ability to think clearly; intelligence: *She has a very quick brain and learns fast.* ◆ *He hasn't got the brains to be a doctor.* **3** [C,usually pl] (*informal*) a very clever person: *He's one of the best brains in the country.* **4 the brains** [sing] the person who plans or organizes sth: *She's the real brains in the organization.*

IDM have sth on the brain (*informal*) to think about sth all the time: *I've had that song on the brain all day.*

rack your brains ➲ **rack²**

brainchild /ˈbreɪntʃaɪld/ *noun* [sing] the idea, plan, design, etc. of a particular person: *The music festival was the brainchild of a young teacher.*

ˌ**brain-dead** *adj* **1** having serious brain damage and needing a machine to stay alive **2** (*informal*) unable to think clearly; stupid: *He's brain-dead from watching too much TV.*

brainless /ˈbreɪnləs/ *adj* (*informal*) very silly; stupid

brainstorm¹ /ˈbreɪnstɔːm/ *noun* [C] **1** a moment of sudden confusion: *I **had a brainstorm** in the exam and couldn't answer any questions.* **2** (*AmE*) = **brainwave**

brainstorm² /ˈbreɪnstɔːm/ *verb* [I,T] to solve a problem or make a decision by thinking of as many ideas as possible in a short time: *We'll spend five minutes brainstorming on how we can raise money.* ◆ *Brainstorm as many ideas as possible before you start to write your answer.* ➲ note at **mind map**

brainwash /ˈbreɪnwɒʃ/ *verb* [T] **brainwash sb (into doing sth)** to force sb to believe sth by using strong mental pressure: *TV advertisements try to brainwash people into buying things that they don't need.* ▸ **brainwashing** *noun* [U]

brainwave /ˈbreɪnweɪv/ (*AmE* **brainstorm**) *noun* [C] (*informal*) a sudden clever idea: *If I **have a brainwave**, I'll let you know.*

brainy /ˈbreɪni/ *adj* (**brainier; brainiest**) (*informal*) intelligent

braise /breɪz/ *verb* [T] to cook meat or vegetables slowly in a little liquid in a covered dish

brake¹ /breɪk/ *noun* [C] **1** the part of a vehicle that makes it go slower or stop: *She put her foot on the brake and just managed to stop in time.* ➲ picture at **bicycle, car 2** something that makes sth else slow down or stop: *The Government must try to **put a brake on** inflation.*

brake² /breɪk/ *verb* [I] to make a vehicle go slower or stop by using the **brakes**: *If the driver hadn't braked in time, the car would have hit me.*

bran /bræn/ *noun* [U] the brown outer covering of grains that is left when the grain is made into flour

⚷ **branch¹** /brɑːntʃ/ *noun* [C] **1** one of the main parts of a tree that grows out of the **trunk** (= the thick central part): *He climbed the tree and sat on a branch.* ➲ picture at **tree 2** an office, a shop, etc. that is part of a larger organization: *The company I work for has branches in Paris, Milan and New York.* **3** a part of an academic subject: *Psychiatry is a branch of medicine.*

branch² /brɑːntʃ/ *verb*

PHR V branch off (used about a road) to leave a larger road and go off in another direction: *A bit further on, the road branches off to the left.*

branch out (into sth) to start doing sth new and different from the things you usually do: *The band has recently branched out into acting.*

⚷ **brand¹** /brænd/ *noun* [C] **1** the name of a product that is made by a particular company: *a well-known brand of coffee* **2** a particular type of sth: *a strange brand of humour*

brand² /brænd/ *verb* [T] **1 brand sb (as sth)** to say that sb has a bad character so that people have a bad opinion of them: *She was branded as a troublemaker after she complained about her long working hours.* **2** to mark an animal with a hot iron to show who owns it

branding /ˈbrændɪŋ/ *noun* [U] the activity of giving a particular name and image to goods and services so that people will be attracted to them and want to buy them

brandish /ˈbrændɪʃ/ *verb* [T] to wave sth in the air in an aggressive or excited way: *The robber was brandishing a knife.*

brand ˈ**new** *adj* completely new

brandy /ˈbrændi/ *noun* [U,C] (*pl* **brandies**) a strong alcoholic drink that is made from wine

brash /bræʃ/ *adj* too confident and direct: *Her brash manner makes her unpopular with strangers.* ▸ **brashness** *noun* [U]

brass /brɑːs/ *noun* **1** [U] a hard yellow metal that is a mixture of **copper** (= a reddish-brown metal) and **zinc** (= a silver-grey metal): *brass buttons on a uniform* **2** [U,sing,with sing or pl verb] the group of musical instruments that are made of **brass**: *the* *brass section in an orchestra* ➲ note at **instrument** ➲ picture at **music**

brat /bræt/ *noun* [C] a child who behaves badly and annoys you

bravado /brəˈvɑːdəʊ/ *noun* [U] a confident way of behaving that is intended to impress people, sometimes as a way of hiding a lack of confidence

brave¹ /breɪv/ *adj* (**braver**; **bravest**) **1** ready to do things that are dangerous or difficult without showing fear: *the brave soldiers who fought in the war* ◆ *'This may hurt a little, so try and be brave,' said the dentist.* **2** needing or showing courage: *a brave decision* ◆ *a brave fight against cancer* ▶ **bravely** *adv*: *The men bravely defended the town for three days.*

brave² /breɪv/ *verb* [T] to face sth unpleasant, dangerous or difficult without showing fear: *She braved the rain and went out into the street.*

bravery /ˈbreɪvəri/ *noun* [U] actions that are **brave**: *After the war he received a medal for bravery.* SYN **courage**

bravo /ˌbrɑːˈvəʊ/ *exclam* a word that people shout to show that they have enjoyed sth that sb has done, for example a play

brawl /brɔːl/ *noun* [C] a noisy fight among a group of people, usually in a public place ▶ **brawl** *verb* [I]: *We saw some football fans brawling in the street.*

brawn /brɔːn/ *noun* [U] physical strength: *To do this kind of job you need more brawn than brain (= you need to be strong rather than clever).* ▶ **brawny** *adj*: *He folded his brawny arms across his chest.*

brazen /ˈbreɪzn/ *adj* without embarrassment, especially in a way which shocks people: *Don't believe a word she says—she's a brazen liar!* ▶ **brazenly** *adv*: *He brazenly admitted he'd been having an affair.*

brazil /brəˈzɪl/ (also **braˈzil nut**) *noun* [C] a nut that we eat, with a very hard shell that has three sides ➲ picture at **nut**

breach¹ /briːtʃ/ *noun* **1** [C,U] **breach (of sth)** an act that breaks an agreement, a law, etc: *Giving private information about clients is a breach of confidence.* ◆ *The company was found to be* ***in breach of*** *contract.* **2** [C] a break in friendly relations between people, groups, etc: *The incident caused a breach between the two countries.* **3** [C] an opening in a wall, etc. that defends or protects sb/sth: *The waves made a breach in the sea wall.*

breach² /briːtʃ/ *verb* [T] **1** to break an agreement, a law, etc: *He accused the Government of breaching international law.* **2** to make an opening in a wall, etc. that defends or protects sb/sth

bread /bred/ *noun* [U] a type of food made from flour, water and usually **yeast** (= a substance which makes the bread rise) mixed together and baked in an oven: *We had bread and cheese for lunch.* ◆ *Would you like some bread and butter?*

GRAMMAR **Bread** is uncountable, so we say **a piece/slice of bread** or **some bread** (not 'a bread').

bread

a loaf of bread

a bread roll

MORE A **loaf** of bread is bread that has been shaped and cooked in one piece. A **roll** is bread baked in a round shape for one person to eat. **Wholemeal** bread is made from flour that contains all the grain.

breadcrumbs /ˈbredkrʌmz/ *noun* [pl] very small pieces of bread that are used in cooking

breadth /bredθ/ *noun* [U] **1** the distance between the two sides of sth: *We measured the length and breadth of the garden.* SYN **width** **2** the wide variety of things, subjects, etc. that sth includes: *I was amazed by the breadth of her knowledge.* ➲ *adjective* **broad**

IDM **the length and breadth of sth** ➲ **length**

breadwinner /ˈbredwɪnə(r)/ *noun* [C, usually sing] the person who earns most of the money that their family needs: *When his dad died, Steve became the breadwinner.*

break¹ /breɪk/ *verb* (*pt* **broke** /brəʊk/; *pp* **broken** /ˈbrəʊkən/)

➤IN PIECES **1** [I,T] to separate, or make sth separate, into two or more pieces: *She dropped the vase onto the floor and it broke.* ◆ *He broke his leg in a car accident.* ➲ picture at **chip**

➤STOP WORKING **2** [I,T] (used about a machine, etc.) to stop working; to stop a machine, etc. working: *The photocopier has broken.* ◆ *Be careful with my camera—I don't want you to break it.*

➤LAW/PROMISE **3** [T] to do sth that is against the law, or against what has been agreed or promised: *to break the law/rules/speed limit* ◆ *Don't worry—I never break my promises.*

➤STOP **4** [I,T] to stop doing sth for a short time: *Let's break for coffee now.* ◆ *We decided to break the journey and stop for lunch.*

➤END STH **5** [T] to make sth end: *Once you start smoking it's very difficult to* ***break the habit***. ◆ *Suddenly, the silence was broken by the sound of a bird singing.*

➤BEGIN **6** [I] to begin: *Day was breaking as I left the house.* ◆ *We ran indoors when the storm broke.*

➤OF NEWS **7** [I] if a piece of news **breaks**, it becomes known: *When the story broke in the newspapers, nobody could believe it.* ➲ look at **break the news**

➤OF A WAVE **8** [I] to reach its highest point and begin to fall: *I watched the waves breaking on the rocks.*

➤OF THE VOICE **9** [I] to change suddenly: *Most boys' voices break when they are 13 or 14 years old.* ◆ *His voice was breaking with emotion as he told us the awful news.*

➤OF A RECORD **10** [T] to do sth better, faster, etc. than anyone has ever done it before: *She had broken the world 100 metres record.* ⓘ For idioms containing

break, look at the entries for the nouns, adjectives, etc. For example, **break even** is at **even**.

B

PHR V **break away (from sb/sth) 1** to escape suddenly from sb who is holding you **2** to leave a political party, state, etc. in order to form a new one

break down 1 (used about a vehicle or machine) to stop working: *Akram's car broke down on the way to work this morning.* ➲ note at **car 2** (used about a system, discussion, etc.) to fail: *Talks between the two countries have completely broken down.* **3** to lose control of your feelings and start crying: *He broke down in tears when he heard the news.*

break sth down 1 to destroy sth by using force: *The police had to break down the door to get into the house.* **2** to make a substance separate into parts or change into a different form in a chemical process: *Food is broken down in our bodies by the digestive system.*

break in to enter a building by force, usually in order to steal sth: *Burglars broke in and stole cash, credit cards and a laptop.*

break in (on sth) to interrupt when sb else is speaking: *She longed to break in on their conversation but didn't want to appear rude.*

break into sth 1 to enter a place that is closed: *Thieves broke into his car and stole the radio.* ◆ (*figurative*) *The company is trying to break into the Japanese market.* **2** to start doing sth suddenly: *to break into song/a run*

break off to suddenly stop doing or saying sth: *He started speaking and then broke off in the middle of a sentence.*

break (sth) off to remove a part of sth by force; to be removed in this way: *Could you break off another bit of chocolate for me?*

break sth off to end a relationship suddenly: *After a bad argument, they decided to **break off** their **engagement**.*

break out (used about fighting, wars, fires, etc.) to start suddenly: *They left the city when war broke out in 1939.*

break out in sth to suddenly have a skin problem: *to break out in spots/a rash*

break out (of sth) to escape from a prison, etc.

break through (sth) to manage to get past sth that is stopping you: *The protesters were trying to break through the line of police.*

break up 1 to separate into smaller pieces: *The ship broke up on the rocks.* **2** (used about events that involve a group of people) to end or finish: *The meeting broke up just before lunch.* **3** (*BrE*) to start school holidays: *When do you break up for the summer holidays?* **4** when a person who is talking on a mobile phone **breaks up**, you can no longer hear them clearly because the signal has been interrupted

break sth up 1 to make sth separate into smaller pieces: *The ship was broken up for scrap metal.* **2** to make people leave sth or stop doing sth, especially by using force: *The police arrived and broke up the fight.*

break up (with sb) to end a relationship with sb: *She's broken up with her boyfriend.*

break with sth to end a relationship or connection with sb/sth: *to break with tradition/the past*

break² /breɪk/ *noun* [C]

➤SHORT REST **1** a short period of rest: *We worked all day without a break.* ◆ *to **take a break*** ➲ note at **interval**

➤HOLIDAY **2** a short holiday: *a weekend break in Prague*

➤CHANGE **3 break (in sth)**; **break (with sb/sth)** a change from what usually happens or an end to sth: *The incident led to a break in diplomatic relations.* ◆ *She wanted to make a complete break with the past.*

➤SPACE **4** an opening or a space in sth: *Wait for a break in the traffic before you cross the road.*

➤BROKEN PART **5** a place where sth has been broken: *The X-ray showed there was no break in his leg.*

➤GOOD LUCK **6** (*informal*) a piece of good luck: *to give somebody a break* (= to help sb by giving him/her a chance to be successful)

IDM **break of day** (*written*) the time when light first appears in the morning **SYN** **dawn**

give sb a break 1 used to tell sb to stop saying things that are annoying or not true: *Give me a break and stop nagging, OK!* **2** (*especially AmE*) to be fair to sb

breakage /ˈbreɪkɪdʒ/ *noun* [C, usually pl] something that has been broken: *Customers must pay for any breakages.*

breakaway /ˈbreɪkəweɪ/ *adj* [only *before* a noun] (used about a political group, an organization, or a part of a country) that has separated from a larger group or country ▶ **breakaway** *noun* [C]

breakdown /ˈbreɪkdaʊn/ *noun* [C] **1** a time when a vehicle, machine, etc. stops working: *I hope we don't **have a breakdown** on the motorway.* **2** the failure or end of sth: *The breakdown of the talks means that a strike is likely.* **3** a list of all the details of sth: *I would like a full breakdown of how the money was spent.* **4** = **nervous breakdown**

breakfast /ˈbrekfəst/ *noun* [C,U] the meal which you have when you get up in the morning: *to **have breakfast*** ◆ *What do you usually have **for breakfast**?* ◆ *to eat a big breakfast* ➲ note at **meal**

CULTURE

In a hotel, an **English** breakfast means cereal, fried eggs, bacon, sausages, tomatoes, toast, etc. A **Continental** breakfast means bread and jam with coffee.

IDM **bed and breakfast** ➲ **bed¹**

ˈbreak-in *noun* [C] the act of entering a building by force, especially in order to steal sth: *The police say there have been several break-ins in this area.*

breakneck /ˈbreɪknek/ *adj* [only *before* a noun] very fast and dangerous: *He drove her to the hospital **at breakneck speed**.*

breakthrough /ˈbreɪkθruː/ *noun* [C] **a breakthrough (in sth)** an important discovery or development: *Scientists are hoping to **make a breakthrough** in cancer research.*

break-up *noun* [C] **1** the end of a relationship between two people: *the break-up of a marriage* **2** the process or result of a group or an organization separating into smaller parts: *the break-up of the Soviet Union*

breast /brest/ *noun* [C] **1** one of the two soft round parts of a woman's body that can produce milk: *She put the baby to her breast.* ♦ *breast cancer* ♦ *breast milk* **2** a word used especially in literature for the top part of the front of your body, below the neck: *to clasp somebody to your breast* SYN **chest** **3** the front part of the body of a bird: *breast feathers* ♦ *The robin has a red breast.* ➲ picture on **page P12**

breastfeed /ˈbrestfiːd/ *verb* [I,T] (*pt, pp* breast-fed) to feed a baby with milk from the breast

breaststroke /ˈbreststrəʊk/ *noun* [sing,U] a style of swimming on your front in which you start with your hands together, push both arms forward and then move them out and back through the water: *to **do (the) breaststroke*** ➲ look at **backstroke, butterfly, crawl** ➲ picture at **swim**

breath /breθ/ *noun* **1** [U] the air that you take into and blow out of your lungs: *His breath smelt of garlic.* ♦ *to **have bad breath*** (= breath which smells unpleasant) **2** [C] an act of taking air into or blowing air out of your lungs: *Take a few deep breaths before you start running.*

IDM **a breath of fresh air** the clean air which you breathe outside, especially when compared to the air inside a room or building: *Let's go for a walk. I need a breath of fresh air.* ♦ (*figurative*) *The child's happy face was like a breath of fresh air on that miserable day.*

catch your breath ➲ **catch**[1]

get your breath (again/back) to rest after physical exercise so that your breathing returns to normal

hold your breath to stop breathing for a short time, for example when you are swimming or because of fear or excitement: *We all held our breath as we waited for her reply.*

(be/get) out of/short of breath (to be/start) breathing very quickly, for example after physical exercise: *She was out of breath after climbing the stairs.*

say sth, speak, etc. under your breath to say sth very quietly, usually because you do not want people to hear you

take your breath away to be very surprising or beautiful: *The spectacular view took our breath away.* ➲ *adjective* **breathtaking**

take a deep breath ➲ **deep**[1]

with bated breath ➲ **bated**

breathalyse (*AmE* breathalyze) /ˈbreθəlaɪz/ *verb* [T] to test the breath of a driver with a **breathalyser**

breathalyser (also Breathalyzer™) /ˈbreθəlaɪzə(r)/ *noun* [C] a device used by the police to measure the amount of alcohol in a driver's breath

breathe /briːð/ *verb* [I,T] to take air, etc. into your lungs and blow it out again: ***Breathe out** as you lift the weight and **breathe in** as you lower it.* ♦ *None of us want to breathe (in) exhaust fumes from heavy traffic.*

IDM **(not) breathe a word (of/about sth) (to sb)** to (not) tell sb about sth that is secret: *If you breathe a word of this to my mother, I'll never speak to you again!*

▶ **breathing** *noun* [U]: *heavy/irregular breathing* ♦ *These deep breathing exercises will help you relax.*

breather /ˈbriːðə(r)/ *noun* [C] (*informal*) a short rest: *to **have/take a breather***

breathless /ˈbreθləs/ *adj* **1** having difficulty breathing: *I was hot and breathless when I got to the top of the hill.* **2** not able to breathe because you are so excited, frightened, etc: *to be breathless with excitement* ▶ **breathlessly** *adv*

breathtaking /ˈbreθteɪkɪŋ/ *adj* extremely surprising, beautiful, etc: *breathtaking scenery*

ˈ**breath test** *noun* [C] a test by the police on the breath of a driver to measure how much alcohol he or she has drunk ➲ look at **breathalyse**

breed[1] /briːd/ *verb* (*pt, pp* bred /bred/) **1** [I] (used about animals) to have sex and produce young animals: *Many animals won't breed in zoos.* SYN **mate** **2** [T] to keep animals or plants in order to produce young from them: *These cattle are bred to produce high yields of milk.* **3** [T] to cause sth: *This kind of thinking breeds intolerance.* ▶ **breeding** *noun* [U]

breed[2] /briːd/ *noun* [C] a particular variety of an animal: *a breed of cattle/dog*

breeder /ˈbriːdə(r)/ *noun* [C] a person who breeds animals or plants: *a dog breeder*

ˈ**breeding ground** *noun* [C] **1** a place where wild animals go to breed **2** a place where sth can develop: *a breeding ground for crime*

breeze[1] /briːz/ *noun* [C] a light wind: *A warm breeze was blowing.*

breeze[2] /briːz/ *verb* [I] breeze along, in, out, etc. to move in a confident and relaxed way: *He just breezed in twenty minutes late without a word of apology.*

breezy /ˈbriːzi/ *adj* (breezier; breeziest) **1** with a little wind **2** happy and relaxed: *You're **bright and breezy** this morning!*

brevity /ˈbrevəti/ *noun* [U] the state of being short or quick ➲ *adjective* **brief**

brew /bruː/ *verb* **1** [T] to make beer **2** [T] to make a drink of tea or coffee by adding hot water: *to brew a pot of tea* **3** [I] (used about tea) to stand in hot water before it is ready to drink: *Leave it to brew for a few minutes.*

IDM **be brewing** (used about sth bad) to develop or grow: *There's **trouble brewing**.*

brewery /ˈbruːəri/ *noun* [C] (*pl* breweries) a place where beer is made

bribe /braɪb/ *noun* [C] money, etc. that is given to sb such as an official to persuade them to do sth to help you that is wrong or dishonest: *to **accept/take bribes*** ▶ **bribe** *verb* [T] bribe sb (with sth): *They got a visa by bribing an official.* ▶ **bribery** /ˈbraɪbəri/ *noun* [U]

bric-a-brac /ˈbrɪk ə bræk/ *noun* [U] small items of little value, for decoration in a house

B

brick /brɪk/ *noun* [C,U] a hard block of baked **clay** (= a type of earth) that is used for building houses, etc: *a lorry carrying bricks* ♦ *a house built of red brick*

bricklayer /ˈbrɪkleɪə(r)/ *noun* [C] a person whose job is to build walls with bricks

brickwork /ˈbrɪkwɜːk/ *noun* [U] the part of a building that is made of bricks

bridal /ˈbraɪdl/ *adj* [only *before* a noun] connected with a **bride**

bride /braɪd/ *noun* [C] a woman on or just before her wedding day: *a* ***bride-to-be*** (= a woman whose wedding is soon) ♦ *the bride and groom* ➲ note at **wedding**

bridegroom /ˈbraɪdgruːm/ (also **groom**) *noun* [C] a man on or just before his wedding day ➲ note at **wedding**

bridesmaid /ˈbraɪdzmeɪd/ *noun* [C] a woman or girl who helps the **bride** on her wedding day ➲ note at **wedding**

bridge[1] /brɪdʒ/ *noun* **1** [C] a structure that carries a road or railway across a river, valley, road or railway: *a bridge over the River Danube* ➲ picture on **page P10** **2 the bridge** [sing] the high part of a ship where the captain and the people who control the ship stand **3** [U] a card game for four people

bridge[2] /brɪdʒ/ *verb* [T] to build a bridge over sth
IDM bridge a/the gap to fill a space between two people, groups or things or to bring them closer together: *Baby food bridges the gap between milk and solid food.*

bridle /ˈbraɪdl/ *noun* [C] the narrow pieces of leather that you put around a horse's head so that you can control it when you are riding it ➲ picture at **horse**

brief[1] /briːf/ *adj* (**briefer**; **briefest**) short or quick: *a brief description* ♦ *Please be brief. We don't have much time.* ➲ *noun* **brevity**
IDM in brief using only a few words: *In brief, the meeting was a disaster.*

brief[2] /briːf/ *noun* [C] instructions or information about a job or task: *He was given the brief of improving the image of the organization.*

brief[3] /briːf/ *verb* [T] to give sb information or instructions about sth: *The minister has been fully briefed on what questions to expect.*

briefcase /ˈbriːfkeɪs/ *noun* [C] a flat case that you use for carrying papers, etc., especially when you go to work ➲ picture at **bag** ➲ picture on **page P1**

briefing /ˈbriːfɪŋ/ *noun* [C,U] instructions or information that you are given before sth happens: *a press/news briefing* (= where information is given to journalists)

briefly /ˈbriːfli/ *adv* **1** for a short time; quickly: *She glanced briefly at the letter.* **2** using only a few words: *I'd like to comment very briefly on that last statement.*

briefs /briːfs/ *noun* [pl] men's or women's underwear: *a pair of briefs*

brigade /brɪˈgeɪd/ *noun* [C] **1** a large group of soldiers that forms a unit in the army **2** a group of people who work together for a particular purpose: *the fire brigade*

brigadier /ˌbrɪgəˈdɪə(r)/ *noun* [C] an important officer in the army

bright /braɪt/ *adj* (**brighter**; **brightest**)
➤FULL OF LIGHT **1** having a lot of light: *a bright, sunny day* ♦ *eyes bright with happiness*
➤OF A COLOUR **2** strong and easy to see: *a bright yellow jumper*
➤HAPPY **3** happy: *to feel bright and cheerful*
➤INTELLIGENT **4** intelligent; able to learn things quickly: *a bright child* ♦ *a* ***bright idea*** ➲ note at **intelligent**
➤POSITIVE **5** likely to be pleasant or successful: *The future looks bright.*
IDM look on the bright side ➲ **look[1]**
▶ **brightly** *adv*: *brightly coloured clothes* ▶ **brightness** *noun* [U]

brighten /ˈbraɪtn/ *verb* [I,T] **brighten (sth) (up)** to become brighter or happier; to make sth brighter: *His face brightened when he saw her.* ♦ *to brighten up somebody's day* (= make it happier)

brilliant /ˈbrɪliənt/ *adj* **1** very clever, skilful or successful: *a brilliant young scientist* ♦ *That's a brilliant idea!* **2** having a lot of light; very bright: *brilliant sunshine* **3** (*informal*) very good: *That was a brilliant film!* ➲ note at **good** ▶ **brilliance** *noun* [U] ▶ **brilliantly** *adv*

brim[1] /brɪm/ *noun* [C] **1** the top edge of a cup, glass, etc: *The cup was full to the brim.* **2** the bottom part of a hat that is wider than the rest ➲ picture at **hat**

brim[2] /brɪm/ *verb* [I] (**brimming**; **brimmed**) **brim (with sth)** to be full of sth: *His eyes were brimming with tears.*
PHR V brim over (with sth) (used about a cup, glass, etc.) to have more liquid than it can hold: *The bowl was brimming over with water.* ♦ (*figurative*) *to be brimming over with health/happiness*

brine /braɪn/ *noun* [U] salt water that is used especially to keep food in good condition

bring /brɪŋ/ *verb* [T] (*pt, pp* **brought** /brɔːt/)
➤CARRY **1** to carry or take sb/sth to a place with you: *Is it all right if I bring a friend to the party?* ♦ *Could you bring us some water, please?* ♦ *My sister went to Spain on holiday and brought me back a T-shirt.* ♦ (*figurative*) *He will bring valuable skills and experience to the team.*
➤CAUSE **2** to cause or result in sth: *The sight of her brought a smile to his face.* ♦ *Money doesn't always bring happiness.* **3** to cause sb/sth to be in a certain place or condition: *Their screams brought people running from all directions.* ♦ *Add water to the mixture and bring it to the boil.* ♦ *An injury can easily* ***bring*** *an athlete's career* ***to an end.***
➤MOVE **4** to move sth somewhere: *She brought the book down off the shelf.* ♦ *Louis brought a photo out of his wallet and showed it to us.*
➤FORCE YOURSELF **5 bring yourself to do sth** to force yourself to do sth: *The film was so horrible that I couldn't bring myself to watch it.* ℹ For idioms containing **bring**, look at the entries for the nouns,

B

bring/fetch/take

Bring the newspaper.

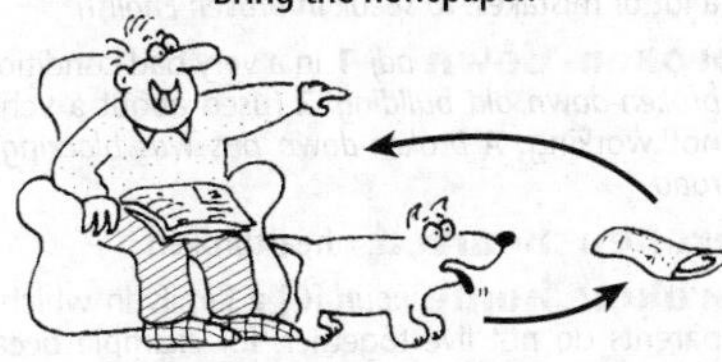
Fetch the newspaper.

Take the newspaper.

adjectives, etc. For example **bring up the rear** is at **rear**.

PHR V **bring sth about** to cause sth to happen: *to bring about changes in people's lives*

bring sth back **1** to cause sb to remember sth: *The photographs brought back memories of his childhood.* **2** to cause sth that existed before to be introduced again: *Nobody wants to bring back the days of child labour.*

bring sb/sth down to defeat sb/sth; to make sb/sth lose a position of power: *to bring down the government*

bring sth down to make sth lower in level: *to bring down the price of something*

bring sth forward **1** to move sth to an earlier time: *The date of the meeting has been brought forward by two weeks.* **OPP** **put sth back** **2** to suggest sth for discussion

bring sb in to ask or employ sb to do a particular job: *A specialist was brought in to set up the new computer system.*

bring sth in to introduce sth: *The government have brought in a new law on dangerous dogs.*

bring sth off to manage to do sth difficult: *The team brought off an amazing victory.*

bring sth on to cause sth: *Her headaches are brought on by stress.*

bring sth out to produce sth or cause sth to appear: *When is the company bringing out its next new model?*

bring sb round (also **bring sb to**) to make sb become conscious again: *I splashed cold water on his face to try to bring him round.*

bring sb round (to sth) to persuade sb to agree with your opinion: *After a lot of discussion we finally brought them round to our point of view.*

bring sth round to sth to direct a conversation to a particular subject: *I finally brought the conversation round to the subject of money.*

bring sb up to look after a child until they are an adult and to teach them how to behave: *After her parents were killed the child was brought up by her uncle.* ◆ *a well-brought-up child*

bring sth up **1** to introduce sth into a discussion or conversation: *I intend to bring the matter up at the next meeting.* **2** to be sick so that food comes up from the stomach and out of the mouth **SYN** **vomit**

brink /brɪŋk/ *noun* [sing] **the brink (of sth)** if you are on the **brink** of sth, you are almost in a very new, exciting or dangerous situation: *Just when the band were* ***on the brink*** *of becoming famous, they split up.*

brisk /brɪsk/ *adj* (**brisker** *no superlative*) **1** quick or using a lot of energy; busy: *They set off* ***at a brisk pace.*** ◆ *Trading has been brisk this morning.* **2** confident and practical; wanting to get things done quickly ▶ **briskly** *adv* ▶ **briskness** *noun* [U]

bristle[1] /ˈbrɪsl/ *noun* [C] **1** a short thick hair: *The bristles on my chin hurt the baby's face.* **2** one of the short thick hairs of a brush

bristle[2] /ˈbrɪsl/ *verb* [I] **1** **bristle (with sth) (at sb/sth)** to show that you are angry **2** (used about hair or an animal's fur) to stand up straight because of fear, anger, cold, etc.

PHR V **bristle with sth** to be full of sth

Brit /brɪt/ *noun* [C] (*informal*) a British person

Britain /ˈbrɪtn/ = **Great Britain**

British /ˈbrɪtɪʃ/ *adj* **1** of the United Kingdom (= Great Britain and Northern Ireland): *British industry* ◆ *to hold a British passport* **2** **the British** *noun* [pl] the people of the United Kingdom

the ˌBritish ˈIsles *noun* [pl] Great Britain and Ireland with all the islands that are near their coasts

> **HELP** Note that the British Isles is only a geographical unit, not a political unit. ➲ note at **United Kingdom**

Briton /ˈbrɪtn/ *noun* [C] a person who comes from Great Britain

> **MORE** This is normally only used in newspapers, or when talking about the inhabitants of Britain in earlier times: *Three Britons killed in air crash.* ◆ *the Ancient Britons*. Otherwise we say 'a British man', 'a British woman'.

brittle /ˈbrɪtl/ *adj* hard but easily broken: *The bones become brittle in old age.*

broach /brəʊtʃ/ *verb* [T] to start talking about a particular subject, especially one which is difficult or embarrassing: *How will you **broach the subject** of the money he owes us?*

B

ˈ**B-road** *noun* [C] (in Britain) a road that is not as wide or important as an **A-road** (= a main road) or a **motorway** (= a wide road for fast traffic): *We drove the whole way on B-roads.*

broad /brɔːd/ *adj* (**broader**; **broadest**) **1** wide: *a broad street/river* ◆ *broad shoulders* ◆ *a broad smile* ➲ *noun* **breadth** OPP **narrow**

HELP **Wide** is more often used than **broad** when you are talking about the distance between one side of something and the other: *The gate is four metres wide.*

2 including many different people or things: *We sell a **broad range** of products.* **3** [only *before* a noun] without a lot of detail; general: *I'll explain the new system **in broad terms**.* **4** (used about the way sb speaks) very strong: *She has a broad Somerset accent.*

IDM **(in) broad daylight** during the day, when it is easy to see: *He was attacked in broad daylight.*

broadband /ˈbrɔːdbænd/ *noun* [U] a way of connecting a computer to the Internet, which allows you to receive information, including pictures, etc., very quickly: *We have broadband at home now.*

ˌ**broad** ˈ**bean** *noun* [C] a type of large flat green **bean** (= seed from a plant) that can be cooked and eaten as a vegetable

broadcast /ˈbrɔːdkɑːst/ *verb* [I,T] (*pt, pp* **broadcast**) to send out radio or TV programmes: *The Olympics are **broadcast live** around the world (= at the same time as they take place).* ▶ **broadcast** *noun* [C]: *We watched a **live broadcast** of the speech (= one that was made at the same time as the speech was made).*

broadcaster /ˈbrɔːdkɑːstə(r)/ *noun* [C] a person who speaks on the radio or on TV

broaden /ˈbrɔːdn/ *verb* [I,T] **broaden (sth) (out)** to become wider; to make sth wider: *The river broadens out beyond the bridge.* ◆ (*figurative*) *Travel broadens the mind* (= it makes you understand other people better).

broadly /ˈbrɔːdli/ *adv* **1** generally: ***Broadly speaking**, the scheme will work as follows ...* **2** (used to describe a way of smiling) with a big, wide smile: *He smiled broadly as he shook everyone's hand.*

ˌ**broad-ˈminded** *adj* happy to accept beliefs and ways of life that are different from your own OPP **narrow-minded**

broccoli /ˈbrɒkəli/ *noun* [U] a thick green plant with green or purple flower heads that can be cooked and eaten as a vegetable ➲ picture on **page P15**

brochure /ˈbrəʊʃə(r)/ *noun* [C] a small book with pictures and information about sth

broil /brɔɪl/ (*especially AmE*) = **grill**²(1)

broke¹ *past tense* of **break**¹

broke² /brəʊk/ *adj* [not before a noun] (*informal*) having no money: *I can't come out tonight—I'm absolutely broke.*

broken¹ *past participle* of **break**¹

broken² /ˈbrəʊkən/ *adj* **1** damaged or in pieces; not working: *The washing machine's broken.* ◆ *Watch out! There's broken glass on the floor.* ◆ *a broken leg* ◆ *How did the window **get broken**?* ➲ picture at **chip**²(1) **2** (used about a promise or an agreement) not kept **3** not continuous; interrupted: *a broken line* ◆ *a broken night's sleep* **4** [only *before* a noun] (used about a foreign language) spoken slowly with a lot of mistakes: *to speak in broken English*

ˌ**broken-ˈdown** *adj* **1** in a very bad condition: *a broken-down old building* **2** (used about a vehicle) not working: *A broken-down bus was blocking the road.*

ˌ**broken-ˈhearted** = **heartbroken**

ˌ**broken ˈhome** *noun* [C] a family in which the parents do not live together, for example because they are divorced: *Many of the children came from broken homes.*

broker /ˈbrəʊkə(r)/ *noun* [C] a person who buys and sells things, for example shares in a business, for other people: *an insurance broker* ➲ look at **stockbroker**

brolly /ˈbrɒli/ (*pl* **brollies**) (*BrE informal*) = **umbrella**

bronchitis /brɒŋˈkaɪtɪs/ *noun* [U] an illness of the **bronchial tubes** (= tubes leading to the lungs) that causes a very bad cough

bronze /brɒnz/ *noun* **1** [U] a dark brown metal that is made by mixing tin with **copper** (= a reddish-brown metal) **2** = **bronze medal** ▶ **bronze** *adj*

bronzed /brɒnzd/ *adj* having skin that has been turned brown, in an attractive way, by the sun ➲ look at **tan**

ˌ**bronze ˈmedal** (also **bronze**) *noun* [C] a round piece of **bronze** that you get as a prize for coming third in a race or a competition ➲ look at **gold medal, silver medal**

brooch /brəʊtʃ/ *noun* [C] a piece of jewellery with a pin at the back that women wear on their clothes ➲ picture at **jewellery**

brood¹ /bruːd/ *verb* [I] **1 brood (on/over/about sth)** to worry, or to think a lot about sth that makes you worried or sad: *to brood on a failure* **2** (used about a female bird) to sit on her eggs

brood² /bruːd/ *noun* [C] all the young birds that belong to one mother

broody /ˈbruːdi/ *adj* **1** (used about a woman) wanting to have a baby **2** (used about a female bird) ready to have or sit on eggs: *a broody hen*

brook /brʊk/ *noun* [C] a small narrow river SYN **stream**

broom /bruːm/ *noun* [C] a brush with a long handle that you use for removing dirt from the floor ➲ picture at **brush**

broomstick /ˈbruːmstɪk/ *noun* [C] the handle of a **broom**

B

Bros *abbr* **Brothers** (used in the name of companies): *Wentworth Bros Ltd*

broth /brɒθ/ *noun* [U] thick soup: *chicken broth*

brothel /ˈbrɒθl/ *noun* [C] a place where men can go and pay to have sex with a **prostitute** (= a woman who earns money in this way)

brother /ˈbrʌðə(r)/ *noun* [C] **1** a man or boy who has the same parents as another person: *Michael and Jim are brothers.* ◆ *Michael is Jim's brother.* ◆ *a younger/older brother* ◆ *brothers and sisters* ◆ *Michael and Jim are Maria's brothers.* ➲ look at **half-brother**, **stepbrother**

HELP **Siblings** means 'both brothers and sisters' but it is very formal, so we usually say: *Have you got any brothers and sisters?* ◆ *I haven't got any brothers or sisters.*

2 a man who is a member of a Christian religious community: *Brother Luke* **3** (*informal*) a man who you feel close to because he is a member of the same society, group, etc. as you: *He was greatly respected by his brother officers.*

brotherhood /ˈbrʌðəhʊd/ *noun* **1** [U] a feeling of great friendship and understanding between people: *the brotherhood of man* (= a feeling of friendship between all the people in the world) **2** [C, with sing or pl verb] an organization which is formed for a particular, often religious, purpose

ˈ**brother-in-law** *noun* [C] (*pl* **brothers-in-law**) **1** the brother of your husband or wife **2** the husband of your sister

brotherly /ˈbrʌðəli/ *adj* showing feelings of love and kindness that you would expect a brother to show: *brotherly love/advice*

brought *past tense, past participle of* **bring**

brow /braʊ/ *noun* [C] **1** = **forehead** **2** [usually pl] = **eyebrow** **3** [sing] the top part of a hill: *Suddenly a car came over the brow of the hill.*

brown[1] /braʊn/ *adj* (**browner**; **brownest**) *noun* **1** [C,U] (of) the colour of earth or wood: *brown eyes/hair* ◆ *the yellows and browns of the trees in autumn* ◆ *You don't look nice in brown* (= in brown clothes). **2** having skin that the sun has made darker: *Although I often sunbathe, I never seem to* **go** *brown.*

brown[2] /braʊn/ *verb* [I,T] to become or make sth become brown: *First, brown the meat in a frying pan.*

brownie /ˈbraʊni/ *noun* [C] **1** a type of heavy chocolate cake that often contains nuts **2** **Brownie** a young girl who is a member of the lowest level of the Girl Guides organization

ˌ**brown** ˈ**paper** *noun* [U] strong, thick paper used for putting round packages, etc: *I wrapped the books in brown paper and tied the package with string.*

browse /braʊz/ *verb* **1** [I] to spend time pleasantly in a shop, looking at a lot of things rather than looking for one particular thing: *I spent hours browsing in the local bookshop.* **2** [I] **browse through sth** to look through a book or magazine without reading every part or studying it carefully: *I enjoyed browsing through the catalogue but I didn't order anything.* **3** [T] to look for and read information on a computer: *I've just been browsing the Internet for information on Iceland.* ▶ **browse** *noun* [sing]

browser /ˈbraʊzə(r)/ *noun* [C] a computer program that lets you look at words and pictures from other computer systems by receiving information through telephone wires: *an Internet browser*

bruise /bruːz/ *noun* [C] a blue, brown or purple mark that appears on the skin after sb has fallen, been hit, etc.

MORE A bruise around your eye is a **black eye**.

▶ **bruise** *verb* [I,T]: *I fell over and bruised my arm.* ◆ *Handle the fruit carefully or you'll bruise it.* ◆ *I've got the sort of skin that bruises easily.*

brunette /bruːˈnet/ *noun* [C] a white woman with dark brown hair ➲ look at **blonde**

brunt /brʌnt/ *noun*
IDM **bear the brunt of sth** ➲ **bear**[1]

brushes

brush[1] /brʌʃ/ *noun* **1** [C] an object that is used for cleaning things, painting, tidying your hair, etc: *I took a brush and swept the snow from the path.* ◆ *a toothbrush* ◆ *a paintbrush* ◆ *a hairbrush* **2** [sing] an act of cleaning, tidying the hair, etc. with a brush: *The floor needs a brush.*

IDM **(have) a brush with sb/sth** (to have or almost have) an unpleasant meeting with sb/sth: *My only brush with the law was when I was stopped for speeding.*

brush[2] /brʌʃ/ *verb* **1** [T] to clean, tidy, etc. sth with a brush: *Make sure you* **brush** *your* **teeth** *twice a day.* ◆ **Brush** *your* **hair** *before you go out.* ➲ note at **clean**[2] **2** [I,T] to touch sb/sth lightly when passing: *Her hand brushed his cheek.* ◆ *Leaves brushed against the car as we drove along the narrow road.*

PHR V **brush sb/sth aside** **1** to refuse to pay attention to sb/sth: *She brushed aside the protests and continued with the meeting.* **2** to push past sb/sth: *He hurried through the crowd, brushing aside the reporters and photographers who tried to stop him.*

brush sth off (sth)/away to remove sth with a brush or with the hand, as if using a brush: *I brushed the dust off my jacket.*
brush sth up/brush up on sth to study or practise sth in order to get back knowledge or skill that you had before and have lost: *She took a course to brush up her Spanish.*

ˈbrush-off *noun*
IDM give sb the brush-off (*informal*) to refuse to be friendly to sb: *I'd ask her to go out with me but I'm scared she'd give me the brush-off.*

brusque /bruːsk/ *adj* using very few words and sounding rude: *He gave a brusque 'No comment!' and walked off.* ▶ **brusquely** *adv*

Brussels sprout /ˌbrʌslz ˈspraʊt/ (also **sprout**) *noun* [C, usually pl] a round green vegetable that looks like a very small **cabbage** (= a large round vegetable with thick green leaves) ➲ picture on **page P15**

brutal /ˈbruːtl/ *adj* very cruel and/or violent: *a brutal murder* ♦ *a brutal dictatorship* ▶ **brutally** /-təli/ *adv*: *He was brutally honest and told her that he didn't love her any more.*

brutality /bruːˈtæləti/ *noun* [C,U] (*pl* **brutalities**) very cruel and violent behaviour

brute¹ /bruːt/ *noun* [C] **1** a cruel, violent man **2** a large strong animal: *That dog of theirs is an absolute brute.*

brute² /bruːt/ *adj* [only *before* a noun] using strength to do sth rather than thinking about it: *I think you'll have to use* **brute force** *to get this window open.*

BSc /ˌbiː es ˈsiː/ *abbr* **Bachelor of Science**; the degree that you receive when you complete a university or college course in a science subject ➲ look at **BA**, **MSc**

BSE /ˌbiː es ˈiː/ (also *informal* ˌ**mad** ˈ**cow disease**) *noun* [U] **bovine spongiform encephalopathy**; a disease of cows which affects their brains and usually kills them ➲ look at **CJD**

BST /ˌbiː es ˈtiː/ *noun* [U] **British Summer Time**; the time used in Britain between March and October, which is one hour ahead of GMT

BTEC /ˈbiːtek/ *noun* [C] an exam for young people who have left secondary school and are training in commercial or technical subjects: *She's doing a BTEC in design.*

BTW *abbr* used in emails, etc. to mean 'by the way'

bubble¹ /ˈbʌbl/ *noun* [C] a ball of air or gas, in liquid or floating in the air: *You can* **blow bubbles** *with washing-up liquid.* ♦ *We knew where there were fish because of the bubbles on the surface.*

bubble² /ˈbʌbl/ *verb* [I] **1** to produce bubbles or to rise with bubbles: *Cook the pizza until the cheese starts to bubble.* ♦ *The clear water bubbled up out of the ground.* **2 bubble (over) (with sth)** to be full of happy feelings

ˈbubble bath *noun* [U] a liquid that you can add to the water in a bath to produce a mass of white bubbles

bubblegum /ˈbʌblɡʌm/ *noun* [U] a sticky sweet that you eat but do not swallow and that can be blown into bubbles out of the mouth ➲ look at **chewing gum**

bubbly /ˈbʌbli/ *adj* (**bubblier**; **bubbliest**) **1** full of bubbles **2** (used about a person) happy and full of energy

buck¹ /bʌk/ *noun* [C] **1** (*AmE informal*) a US dollar: *Could you lend me a few bucks?* **2** (*pl* **buck** *or* **bucks**) a male **rabbit** (= a small animal with long ears) or **deer** (= a large wild animal that eats grass) ➲ note at **deer** ➲ picture at **deer** ➲ picture on **page P12**
IDM pass the buck ➲ **pass¹**

buck² /bʌk/ *verb* [I] (used about a horse) to jump into the air or to kick the back legs in the air
PHR V buck (sb/sth) up (*informal*) to feel or to make sb feel better or happier: *Drink this—it'll buck you up.* ♦ *Unless you buck your ideas up* (= become more sensible and serious), *you'll never pass the exam.*

bucket /ˈbʌkɪt/ *noun* [C] **1** a round, open container, usually made of metal or plastic, with a handle, that is used for carrying sth **2** (also **bucketful** /-fʊl/) the amount that a **bucket** contains: *How many buckets of water do you think we'll need?*
IDM a drop in the bucket ➲ **drop²**

buckle¹ /ˈbʌkl/ *verb* [I,T] **1** to fasten or be fastened with a **buckle** **2** to become crushed or bent because of heat, force, weakness, etc.; to crush or bend sth in this way: *Some railway lines buckled in the heat.*

buckle² /ˈbʌkl/ *noun* [C] a piece of metal or plastic at the end of a belt or other narrow piece of material that is used for fastening it ➲ picture at **button** ➲ picture on **page P1**

bud /bʌd/ *noun* [C] a small lump on a tree or plant that opens and develops into a flower or leaf: *rosebuds* ➲ picture at **plant**, **tree**

IDM **nip sth in the bud** ➲ **nip**

Buddhism /ˈbʊdɪzəm/ *noun* [U] an Asian religion that was started in India by Siddharta Gautama (Buddha)

Buddhist /ˈbʊdɪst/ *noun* [C] a person whose religion is **Buddhism** ▶ **Buddhist** *adj*: *a Buddhist temple*

budding /ˈbʌdɪŋ/ *adj* [only *before* a noun] wanting or starting to develop and be successful: *Have you got any tips for budding young photographers?*

buddy /ˈbʌdi/ *noun* [C] (*pl* **buddies**) (*informal*) a friend: *an old college buddy of mine*

budge /bʌdʒ/ *verb* [I,T] **1** to move or make sth move a little: *I tried as hard as I could to loosen the screw but it simply wouldn't budge.* ♦ *We just couldn't budge the car when it got stuck in the mud.* **2** to change or make sb change a firm opinion: *Neither side in the dispute is prepared to budge.*

budgerigar /ˈbʌdʒərigɑː(r)/ (also *informal* **budgie**) *noun* [C] a small, brightly coloured bird that people often keep as a pet in a **cage** (= a box made of bars) ➲ note at **pet**

budget¹ /ˈbʌdʒɪt/ *noun* **1** [C,U] a plan of how to spend an amount of money over a particular period of time; the amount of money that is mentioned: *What's your monthly budget for food?* ♦ *a country's defence budget* ♦ *The work was finished on time and* ***within budget.*** ♦ *The builders are already 20%* ***over budget.*** **2 Budget** [C, usually sing] a statement by a government saying how much money it plans to spend on particular things in the next year and how it plans to collect money: *Do you think taxes will go up in this year's budget?*

budget² /ˈbʌdʒɪt/ *verb* [I,T] **budget (sth) (for sth)** to plan carefully how much money to spend on sth: *The government has budgeted £10 billion for education.*

budget³ /ˈbʌdʒɪt/ *adj* [only *before* a noun] (*informal*) (used in advertisements) very cheap: *budget holidays*

budgie /ˈbʌdʒi/ (*informal*) = **budgerigar**

buff¹ /bʌf/ *noun* [C] (*informal*) a person who knows a lot about a particular subject and is very interested in it: *a film/computer buff*

buff² /bʌf/ *adj* (*slang*) physically fit and attractive with big muscles

buffalo /ˈbʌfələʊ/ *noun* [C] (*pl* **buffalo** *or* **buffaloes**) a large wild animal that looks like a cow with long curved horns: *a herd of buffalo*

buffer /ˈbʌfə(r)/ *noun* [C] **1** a thing or person that reduces the unpleasant effects of sth or prevents violent contact between two things, people, etc: *UN forces are acting as a buffer between the two sides in the war.* **2** a flat round piece of metal with a spring behind it that is on the front or back of a train or at the end of a railway track. **Buffers** reduce the shock when sth hits them.

buffet¹ /ˈbʊfeɪ; ˈbʌfeɪ/ *noun* [C] **1** a meal (usually at a party or a special occasion) at which food is placed on a long table and people serve themselves: *Lunch was a cold buffet.* ♦ *a buffet lunch* **2** part of a train or a place at a station where passengers can buy food and drinks

buffet² /ˈbʌfɪt/ *verb* [T] to knock or push sth in a rough way from side to side: *The boat was buffeted by the rough sea.*

bug¹ /bʌg/ *noun* **1** [C] (*especially AmE*) any small insect **2** [C] an illness that is not very serious and that people get from each other: *I don't feel very well —I think I've got the bug that's going round.* **3** *usually* **the ... bug** [sing] (*informal*) a sudden interest in sth: *They've been bitten by the golf bug.* **4** [C] a very small **microphone** (= a device used for recording sounds) that is hidden and used to secretly listen to and record people's conversations **5** [C] something wrong in a system or machine, especially a computer: *There's a bug in the software.*

bug² /bʌg/ *verb* [T] (**bugging**; **bugged**) **1** to hide a very small **microphone** (= a device used for recording sounds) somewhere so that people's conversations can be recorded secretly: *Be careful what you say. This room is bugged.* **2** (*informal*) to annoy or worry sb: *It bugs him that he's not as successful as his brother.*

buggy /ˈbʌgi/ (*pl* **buggies**) (*BrE*) = **pushchair**

build¹ /bɪld/ *verb* (*pt, pp* **built** /bɪlt/) **1** [T] to make sth by putting pieces, materials, etc. together: *They've built a new bridge across the river.* ♦ *The house is built of stone.* **2** [I] to use land for building on: *There's plenty of land to build on around here.* **3** [T] to develop or increase sth: *The government is trying to build a more modern society.* ♦ *This book claims to help people to build their self-confidence.*

PHR V **build sth in/on; build sth into/onto sth** to make sth a part of sth else: *They've made sure that a large number of checks are built into the system.* ♦ *We're planning to build two more rooms onto the back of the house.*

build on sth to use sth as a base from which you can make further progress: *Now that we're beginning to make a profit, we must build on this success.*

build sth on sth to base sth on sth: *a society built on the principle of freedom and democracy*

build up (to sth) to become greater in amount or number; to increase: *The traffic starts to build up at this time of day.*

build sth up 1 to make sth seem more important or greater than it really is: *I don't think it's a very serious matter, it's just been built up in the newspapers.* **2** to increase or develop sth over a period: *You'll need to build up your strength again slowly after the operation.*

build² /bɪld/ *noun* [C,U] the shape and size of sb's body: *She* ***has a*** *very athletic* ***build.***

> **HELP** **Build** or **figure**? **Build** usually describes size in connection with strength and muscle and is used for both men and women. **Figure** usually describes shape, especially whether it is attractive or not, and is usually used only for women.

B

builder /ˈbɪldə(r)/ *noun* [C] a person whose job is to build houses and other buildings

🔑 **building** /ˈbɪldɪŋ/ *noun* **1** [C] a structure, such as a house, shop or school, that has a roof and walls: *There are a lot of very old buildings in this town.* **2** [U] the process or business of making buildings: *the building of the school* ◆ *building materials* ◆ *the building industry*

ˈ**building site** *noun* [C] an area of land on which a building is being built

ˈ**building society** *noun* [C] (*BrE*) an organization like a bank with which people can save money and which lends money to people who want to buy a house

ˈ**build-up** *noun* [C, usually sing] **1** a build-up (of sth) an increase of sth over a period: *The build-up of tension in the area has made war seem more likely.* **2** a build-up (to sth) a period of preparation or excitement before an event: *The players started to get nervous in the build-up to the big game.*

built[1] /bɪlt/ [in compounds] made in the particular way that is mentioned: *a newly built station* ◆ *The man was tall and well built.*

built[2] *past tense, past participle of* **build**

ˌ**built-ˈin** *adj* [only *before* a noun] that is a part of sth and cannot be removed: *built-in cupboards*

ˌ**built-ˈup** *adj* covered with buildings, roads, etc: *a built-up area*

bulb /bʌlb/ *noun* [C] **1** (also ˈlight bulb) the glass part of an electric lamp that gives out light: *The bulb's gone* (= it no longer works) *in this lamp.* ➲ picture at **lamp** **2** the round root of certain plants: *a tulip bulb* ➲ picture at **plant**

bulbous /ˈbʌlbəs/ *adj* fat, round and ugly: *a bulbous red nose*

bulge[1] /bʌldʒ/ *verb* [I] **1** bulge (with sth) to be full of sth: *His bags were bulging with presents for the children.* **2** to stick out in a lump from sth that is usually flat: *My stomach is starting to bulge. I must get more exercise.*

bulge[2] /bʌldʒ/ *noun* [C] a round lump that sticks out on sth

bulging /ˈbʌldʒɪŋ/ *adj* sticking out: *He had a thin face and rather bulging eyes.*

bulimia /buˈlɪmiə/ (also bulimia nervosa /buˌlɪmiə nɜːˈvəʊsə/) *noun* [U] an illness in which a person eats too much and then forces himself or herself to **vomit** (= bring up food from the stomach) ➲ look at **anorexia** ▸ **bulimic** *adj, noun* [C]

bulk /bʌlk/ *noun* **1** [sing] the bulk (of sth) the main part of sth; most of sth: *The bulk of the work has been done, so we should finish this week.* **2** [U] the size, quantity or weight of sth large: *The cupboard isn't especially heavy—what makes it hard to move is its bulk.* ◆ *He slowly lifted his vast bulk out of the chair.*

IDM **in bulk** in large quantities: *If you buy in bulk, it's 10% cheaper.*

bulky /ˈbʌlki/ *adj* (bulkier; bulkiest) large and heavy and therefore difficult to move or carry: *a bulky parcel*

bull /bʊl/ *noun* [C] **1** an adult male of the cow family ➲ note at **cow** ➲ picture at **cow** **2** a male **whale** (= a very large sea animal) or **elephant** (= a large grey animal with a long nose)

bulldog /ˈbʊldɒɡ/ *noun* [C] a strong dog with short legs, a large head and a short, thick neck

ˈ**Bulldog clip™** *noun* [C] (*BrE*) a metal device for holding papers together ➲ picture at **stationery**

bulldoze /ˈbʊldəʊz/ *verb* [T] to make ground flat or to knock down a building with a **bulldozer**: *The old buildings were bulldozed and new ones were built.*

bulldozer

bulldozer /ˈbʊldəʊzə(r)/ *noun* [C] a large, powerful vehicle with a wide piece of metal at the front, used for clearing ground or knocking down buildings

🔑 **bullet** /ˈbʊlɪt/ *noun* [C] a small metal object that is fired from a gun: *The bullet hit her in the arm.* ◆ *a bullet wound*

bulletin /ˈbʊlətɪn/ *noun* [C] **1** a short news report on TV or radio; an official statement about a situation: *The next* **news bulletin** *on this channel is at 9 o'clock.* **2** a short newspaper that a club or an organization produces: *As a member of the fan club, she receives a monthly bulletin.*

ˈ**bulletin board** *noun* [C] **1** (*AmE*) = **noticeboard** **2** a place in a computer system where you can write or read messages ➲ note at **netiquette**

bulletproof /ˈbʊlɪtpruːf/ *adj* made of a strong material that stops bullets from passing through it

bullfight /ˈbʊlfaɪt/ *noun* [C] a traditional public entertainment, especially in Spain, Portugal and Latin America, in which a **bull** (= an adult male cow) is fought and usually killed ▸ **bullfighter** *noun* [C] ▸ **bullfighting** *noun* [U]

bullion /ˈbʊliən/ *noun* [U] bars of gold or silver: *The dollar price of gold bullion has risen by more than 10%.*

bullseye /ˈbʊlzaɪ/ *noun* [C] the centre of the round object that you shoot or throw things at in certain sports; a shot that hits this

bully[1] /ˈbʊli/ *noun* [C] (*pl* bullies) a person who uses their strength or power to hurt or frighten people who are weaker

bully[2] /ˈbʊli/ *verb* [T] (bullying; bullies; *pt, pp* bullied) bully sb (into doing sth) to use your strength or power to hurt or frighten sb who is weaker or to make them do sth: *Don't try to bully me into making*

B

a decision. ▶ **bullying** *noun* [U]: *Bullying is a serious problem in many schools.*

bum /bʌm/ *noun* [C] (*informal*) **1** (*BrE*) the part of your body on which you sit **SYN** **bottom** **2** (*especially AmE*) an insulting word for a person who lives on the street **3** (*especially AmE*) a lazy or useless person

bumbag /ˈbʌmbæg/ (*AmE* ˈ**fanny pack**) *noun* [C] (*informal*) a small bag worn around the waist to keep money, etc. in ➲ picture at **bag**

bump¹ /bʌmp/ *verb* **1** [I] **bump against/into sb/sth** to hit sb/sth by accident when you are moving: *She bumped into a lamp post because she wasn't looking where she was going.* **2** [T] **bump sth (against/on sth)** to hit sth against or on sth by accident: *I bumped my knee on the edge of the table.* **3** [I] to move along over a rough surface: *The car bumped along the track to the farm.*
PHR V **bump into sb** to meet sb by chance: *I bumped into an old friend on the bus today.*
bump sb off (*slang*) to murder sb
bump sth up (*informal*) to increase or make sth go up: *All this publicity will bump up sales of our new product.*

bump² /bʌmp/ *noun* [C] **1** the action or sound of sth hitting a hard surface: *She fell and hit the ground with a bump.* **2** a lump on the body, often caused by a hit **3** a part of a surface that is higher than the rest of it: *There are a lot of bumps in the road, so drive carefully.*

bumper¹ /ˈbʌmpə(r)/ *noun* [C] the bar fixed to the front and back of a motor vehicle to protect it if it hits sth ➲ picture on **page P7**

bumper² /ˈbʌmpə(r)/ *adj* [only *before* a noun] larger than usual: *The unusually fine weather has produced a bumper harvest this year.*

bumpy /ˈbʌmpi/ *adj* (**bumpier**; **bumpiest**) not flat or smooth: *a bumpy road* ♦ *Because of the stormy weather, it was a very bumpy flight.* **OPP** **smooth**

bun /bʌn/ *noun* [C] **1** a small round sweet cake: *a currant bun* ➲ picture at **cake** **2** a small soft bread roll: *a hamburger bun* **3** hair fastened tightly into a round shape at the back of the head: *She wears her hair **in a bun**.* ➲ picture at **hair**

🔑 **bunch¹** /bʌntʃ/ *noun* **1** [C] a number of things, usually of the same type, fastened or growing together: *He bought her a bunch of flowers.* ♦ *a bunch of bananas/grapes* ♦ *a bunch of keys* **2** [C, with sing or pl verb] (*informal*) a group of people: *My colleagues are the best bunch of people I've ever worked with.* **3 bunches** [pl] long hair that is tied on each side of the head: *She wore her hair in bunches.* ➲ picture at **hair**

bunch² /bʌntʃ/ *verb* [I,T] **bunch (sth/sb) (up/together)** to stay together in a group; to form sth into a group or bunch: *The runners bunched up as they came round the final bend.* ♦ *He kept his papers bunched together in his hand.*

bundle¹ /ˈbʌndl/ *noun* [C] **1** a number of things tied or folded together: *a bundle of letters with an elastic band round them* **2** a number of things that belong, or are sold together: *a bundle of graphics packages for your PC*

bundle² /ˈbʌndl/ *verb* [T] to put or push sb or sth quickly and in a rough way in a particular direction: *He was arrested and bundled into a police car.*
PHR V **bundle sth up; bundle sth together** to make or tie a number of things together: *I bundled up the old newspapers and threw them away.*

bung¹ /bʌŋ/ *verb* [T] (*BrE informal*) to put or throw sth somewhere in a rough or careless way: *We bunged the suitcases into the car and drove away.*

bung² /bʌŋ/ *noun* [C] a round piece of wood or rubber that is used for closing the hole in a container such as a **barrel**

bungalow /ˈbʌŋgələʊ/ *noun* [C] (*BrE*) a house that is all on one level, without stairs ➲ picture on **page P9**

bunged ˈ**up** *adj* (*informal*) blocked, so that nothing can get through: *I feel terrible—I've got a cold and my nose is all bunged up.*

bungee jumping /ˈbʌndʒi dʒʌmpɪŋ/ *noun* [U] a sport in which you jump from a high place, for example a bridge, with a thick **elastic** (= material that can stretch) rope tied round your feet ➲ picture on **page P5**

bungle /ˈbʌŋgl/ *verb* [T] to do sth badly or fail to do sth: *a bungled robbery*

bunk /bʌŋk/ *noun* [C] **1** a bed that is fixed to a wall, especially on a ship or train **2** (also **bunk bed**) one of a pair of single beds built as a unit with one above the other ➲ note at **bed** ➲ picture at **bed**
IDM **do a bunk** (*BrE informal*) to run away or escape; to leave without telling anyone

bunker /ˈbʌŋkə(r)/ *noun* [C] **1** a strong underground building that gives protection in a war **2** a hole filled with sand on a **golf course** (= the large area of land on which you hit a small ball into a number of holes)

bunny /ˈbʌni/ *noun* [C] (*pl* **bunnies**) a child's word for **rabbit** (= a small animal with long ears)

Bunsen burner /ˌbʌnsn ˈbɜːnə(r)/ *noun* [C] an instrument used in scientific work that produces a hot gas flame

buoy¹ /bɔɪ/ *noun* [C] an object that floats on the sea or a river that shows the places where it is dangerous for boats to go

buoy² /bɔɪ/ *verb* [T] **buoy sb/sth (up)** **1** to keep sb happy and confident: *His encouragement buoyed her up during that difficult period.* **2** to keep sth at a high level: *Share prices were buoyed by news of a takeover.*

buoyant /ˈbɔɪənt/ *adj* **1** (used about prices, business activity, etc.) staying at a high level or increasing, so that people make more money: *Despite the recession, the property market remained buoyant.* **2** happy and confident: *The team were in buoyant mood after their win.* **3** (used about a material) floating or able to float ▶ **buoyancy** /-ənsi/ *noun* [U]: *the buoyancy of the German economy*

burden[1] /ˈbɜːdn/ *noun* [C] **1** a responsibility or difficult task that causes a lot of work or worry: *Having to make all the decisions is a terrible burden for me.* ◆ *I don't want to be a burden to my parents.* **2** something that is heavy and difficult to carry

burden[2] /ˈbɜːdn/ *verb* [T] **burden sb/yourself (with sth)** to give sb/yourself a responsibility or task that causes a lot of work or worry

bureau /ˈbjʊərəʊ/ *noun* [C] (*pl* **bureaux** *or* **bureaus** /-rəʊz/) **1** (*BrE*) a writing desk with drawers and a lid **2** an organization that provides information: *a tourist information bureau* **3** (*especially AmE*) one of certain government departments: *the Federal Bureau of Investigation*

bureaucracy /bjʊəˈrɒkrəsi/ *noun* (*pl* **bureaucracies**) **1** [U] (often used in a critical way) the system of official rules that an organization has for doing sth, that people often think is too complicated: *Getting a visa involves a lot of unnecessary bureaucracy.* **2** [C,U] a system of government by a large number of officials who are not elected; a country with this system ▸ **bureaucratic** /ˌbjʊərəˈkrætɪk/ *adj*: *You have to go through a complex bureaucratic procedure if you want to get your money back.*

bureaucrat /ˈbjʊərəkræt/ *noun* [C] (often used in a critical way) an official in an organization or government department

bureau de change /ˌbjʊərəʊ də ˈʃɑːnʒ/ *noun* [C] (*pl* **bureaux de change**) an office at an airport, in a hotel, etc. where you can change the money of one country to the money of another country

burger /ˈbɜːgə(r)/ **1** (also **beefburger**, *especially AmE* **hamburger**) **beef** that has been cut up small, pressed into a flat round shape and cooked. A **burger** is often eaten in a bread roll. **2** something that is cooked like and looks like a **burger**, but is made of sth else: *a veggie burger*

burglar /ˈbɜːglə(r)/ *noun* [C] a person who enters a building illegally in order to steal: *The burglars broke in by smashing a window.* ➲ note at **thief** ▸ **burgle** /ˈbɜːgl/ (*AmE* **burglarize** /ˈbɜːgləraɪz/) *verb* [T]: *Our flat was burgled while we were out.*

ˈ**burglar alarm** *noun* [C] a piece of equipment, usually fixed on a wall, that makes a loud noise if a thief enters a building

burglary /ˈbɜːgləri/ *noun* [C,U] (*pl* **burglaries**) the crime of entering a building illegally in order to steal: *There was a burglary next door last week.* ◆ *He is in prison for burglary.*

burgundy /ˈbɜːgəndi/ *noun* **1 Burgundy** [U,C] (*pl* **Burgundies**) a red or white wine from the Burgundy area of eastern France **2** [U] a dark red colour ▸ **burgundy** *adj*

burial /ˈberiəl/ *noun* [C,U] the ceremony when a dead body is buried in the ground: *The burial took place on Friday.* ➲ note at **funeral**

burka (also **burkha**) /ˈbʊəkə; ˈbɜːkə/ *noun* [C] a long loose piece of clothing that covers the whole body and that is worn by Muslim women in some countries

burly /ˈbɜːli/ *adj* (**burlier**; **burliest**) (used about a person or their body) strong and heavy

⚷ **burn**[1] /bɜːn/ *verb* (*pt, pp* **burnt** /bɜːnt/ *or* **burned** /bɜːnd/) **1** [I] to be on fire: *Firemen raced to the burning building.* ➲ note at **alight** **2** [T] to destroy, damage or injure sb/sth with fire or heat: *We took all the rubbish outside and burned it.* ◆ *It was a terrible fire and the whole building was burnt to the ground* (= completely destroyed). ◆ *If you get too close to the fire you'll burn yourself.* ◆ *The people inside the building couldn't get out and they were all burnt to death.* **3** [I] to be destroyed, damaged or injured by fire or heat: *If you leave the cake in the oven for much longer, it will burn.* ◆ *I can't spend too much time in the sun because I burn easily.* ◆ *They were trapped by the flames and they burned to death.* **4** [T] to produce a hole or mark in or on sth by burning: *He dropped the match and it burned a hole in the carpet.* **5** [T] to use sth as fuel: *an oil-burning lamp* **6** [I] to feel very hot and painful: *You have a temperature—your forehead's burning.* **7** [I] to produce light: *I don't think he went to bed at all—I could see his light burning all night.* **8** [T] to put information onto a CD, etc. **9** [I] **burn (with sth)** to be filled with a very strong feeling: *She was burning with indignation.*

IDM **sb's ears are burning** ➲ **ear**

PHR V **burn down** (used about a building) to be completely destroyed by fire: *The fire could not be brought under control and the school burned down.*

burn sth down to completely destroy a building by fire: *The house was burnt down in a fire some years ago.*

burn (sth) off to remove sth or to be removed by burning

burn sth out [usually passive] to completely destroy sth by burning: *the burnt-out wreck of a car*

burn (yourself) out to work, etc., until you have no more energy or strength and feel extremely tired: *I've been studying so hard recently I feel completely burned out.*

burn (sth) up to destroy or to be destroyed by fire or strong heat: *The space capsule burnt up on its re-entry into the earth's atmosphere.*

burn[2] /bɜːn/ *noun* [C] damage or an injury caused by fire or heat: *He was taken to hospital with minor burns.* ◆ *There's a cigarette burn on the carpet.*

burner /ˈbɜːnə(r)/ (*AmE*) = **ring**[1](5)

burning /ˈbɜːnɪŋ/ *adj* [only *before* a noun] **1** (used about a feeling) extremely strong: *a burning ambition/desire* **2** very important or urgent: *a burning issue/question* **3** feeling very hot: *the burning sun*

burnt *past tense, past participle* of **burn**

burp /bɜːp/ *verb* [I] to make a noise with the mouth when air rises from the stomach and is forced out: *He sat back when he had finished his meal and burped loudly.* ▸ **burp** *noun* [C]

burrow[1] /ˈbʌrəʊ/ *verb* [I] to dig a hole in the ground, to make a tunnel or to look for sth: *These* *animals burrow for food.* ◆ (*figurative*) *She burrowed in her handbag for her keys.*

burrow[2] /ˈbʌrəʊ/ *noun* [C] a hole in the ground made by certain animals, for example **rabbits** (= small animals with long ears), in which they live

bursar /ˈbɜːsə(r)/ *noun* [C] the person who manages the financial matters of a school, college or university

bursary /ˈbɜːsəri/ *noun* [C] (*pl* **bursaries**) a sum of money given to a specially chosen student to pay for his or her studies at a college or university ➲ look at **scholarship**

burst[1] /bɜːst/ *verb* (*pt, pp* **burst**) **1** [I,T] to break open suddenly and violently, usually because there is too much pressure inside; to cause this to happen: *The ball burst when I kicked it.* ◆ *You'll burst that tyre if you blow it up any more.* ◆ (*figurative*) *If I eat any more I'll burst!* ◆ *If it rains much more, the river will burst its banks.* **2** [I] **burst into, out of, through, etc.** (**sth**) to move suddenly in a particular direction, often using force: *She burst into the manager's office and demanded to speak to him.*
IDM be bursting (with sth) to be very full of sth: *I packed so many clothes that my suitcase was bursting.* ◆ *She was bursting with pride when she won the race.*
be bursting to do sth to want to do sth very much: *I'm bursting to tell someone the news but it's a secret.*
burst (sth) open to open or make sth open suddenly or violently: *Suddenly the doors burst open and five police officers rushed in.*
PHR V burst in on sb/sth to interrupt sb/sth by arriving suddenly: *The police burst in on the gang as they were counting the money.*
burst into sth to start doing sth suddenly: *On hearing the news she* ***burst into tears*** (= started crying). ◆ *The lorry hit a wall and* ***burst into flames*** (= started burning).
burst out 1 to start doing sth suddenly: *He looked so ridiculous that I* ***burst out laughing***. **2** to say sth suddenly and with strong feeling: *She burst out, 'I can't stand it any more!'*

burst[2] /bɜːst/ *noun* [C] **1** a short period of a particular activity, that often starts suddenly: *a burst of energy/enthusiasm/speed* ◆ *a burst of applause/gunfire* ◆ *He prefers to work* ***in short bursts***. **2** an occasion when sth bursts or explodes; a crack or hole caused by this: *a burst in a water pipe*

bury /ˈberi/ *verb* [T] (**burying**; **buries**; *pt, pp* **buried**) **1** to put a dead body in the ground: *She was buried in Highgate Cemetery.* **2** to put sth in a hole in the ground and cover it: *Our dog always buries its bones in the garden.* **3** [usually passive] to cover or hide sth/sb: *At last I found the photograph, buried at the bottom of a drawer.* ◆ (*figurative*) *Aisha was buried in a book and didn't hear us come in.*

bus /bʌs/ *noun* [C] a big public vehicle which takes passengers along a fixed route and stops regularly to let people get on and off: *Where do you usually get on/off the bus?* ◆ *We'll have to hurry up if we want to* ***catch the*** *9 o'clock* ***bus***. ◆ *We'd better run or we'll* ***miss the bus***. ➲ picture on **page P7**

TOPIC

Travelling by bus

You can get on or off a bus at a **bus stop** and the place where most bus routes start is the **bus station**. The **bus driver** will probably take the money (your **fare**) and give you your **ticket**, or there may be a **conductor** who collects the fares. You can buy a **single** (= to your destination but not back) or a **return** ticket (= to your destination and back). A bus **pass** allows you to travel in a particular area for a fixed period of time. In British English a comfortable bus used for long journeys is called a **coach**. Note that we travel **on the bus** or **by bus**: *'How do you get to work?' 'On the bus.'*

bush /bʊʃ/ *noun* **1** [C] a plant like a small, thick tree with many low branches: *a rose bush* ◆ *The house was surrounded by thick bushes.* ➲ picture on **page P11** **2** *often* **the bush** [U] wild land that has not been cleared, especially in Africa and Australia
IDM beat about/around the bush ➲ **beat**[1]

bushy /ˈbʊʃi/ *adj* (**bushier**; **bushiest**) growing closely together in large numbers; thick: *bushy hair/eyebrows*

busier, busiest, busily ➲ **busy**[1]

business /ˈbɪznəs/ *noun*
➤TRADE **1** [U] buying and selling as a way of earning money: *She's planning to* ***set up in business*** *as a hairdresser.* ◆ *I'm going to* ***go into business*** *with my brother.* ◆ *They are very easy to* ***do business with***.
➤WORK **2** [U] the work that you do as your job: *The manager will be away* ***on business*** *next week.* ◆ *a business trip*
➤CUSTOMERS **3** [U] the number of customers that a person or company has had: *Business has been good for the time of year.*
➤COMPANY **4** [C] a firm, a shop, a factory, etc. which produces or sells goods or provides a service: *She aims to* ***start a business*** *of her own.* ◆ *Small businesses are finding it hard to survive at the moment.*
➤RESPONSIBILITY **5** [U] something that concerns a particular person: *The friends I choose are my business, not yours.* ◆ *Our business is to collect the information, not to comment on it.* ◆ *'How much did it cost?' 'It's* ***none of your business***!*'* (= I don't want to tell you. It's private.)
➤IMPORTANT MATTERS **6** [U] important matters that need to be dealt with or discussed: *First we have some unfinished business from the last meeting to deal with.*
➤EVENT **7** [sing] a situation or an event, especially one that is strange or unpleasant: *The divorce was an awful business.* ◆ *I found the whole business very depressing.*
IDM get down to business to start the work that has to be done: *Let's just have a cup of coffee before we get down to business.*
go out of business to have to close because there is no more money available: *The shop went out of business because it couldn't compete with the new supermarket.*
have no business to do sth/doing sth to have no

right to do sth: *You have no business to read/reading my letters without asking me.*
mind your own business ➲ **mind**[2]
monkey business ➲ **monkey**

businesslike /ˈbɪznəslaɪk/ *adj* dealing with matters in a direct and practical way, without trying to be friendly: *She has a very businesslike manner.*

🔑 **businessman** /ˈbɪznəsmæn; -mən/, **businesswoman** /ˈbɪznəswʊmən/ *noun* [C] (*pl* -men /-men/, -women /-wɪmɪn/) **1** a person who works in business, especially in a top position: *a millionaire businessman* **2** a person who is skilful at dealing with money: *I should have got a better price for the car, but I'm not much of a businessman.*

ˈ**business person** *noun* [C] (*pl* -people /-piːpl/) a person who works in business, especially in a top position ➲ look at **businessman**

ˈ**business studies** *noun* [U] the study of how to control and manage a company: *a course in business studies*

busk /bʌsk/ *verb* [I] to sing or play music in the street so that people will give you money

busker /ˈbʌskə(r)/ *noun* [C] a street musician ➲ picture on **page P11**

bust[1] /bʌst/ *verb* (*pt, pp* bust *or* busted) (*informal*) **1** [T] to break or damage sth so that it cannot be used **2** [T] to arrest sb: *He was busted for possession of heroin.*

bust[2] /bʌst/ *noun* [C] **1** a model in stone, etc. of a person's head, shoulders and chest **2** a woman's breasts; the measurement round a woman's chest: *This blouse is a bit too tight around the bust.* **3** (*informal*) an unexpected visit by the police in order to arrest people for doing sth illegal: *a drugs bust*

bust[3] /bʌst/ *adj* [not before a noun] (*informal*) broken or not working: *The zip on these trousers is bust.*
IDM go bust (*informal*) (used about a business) to close because it has lost so much money: *During the recession thousands of businesses went bust.* **SYN go bankrupt**

bustle[1] /ˈbʌsl/ *verb* **1** [I,T] to move in a busy, noisy or excited way; to make sb move somewhere quickly: *He bustled about the kitchen making tea.* ◆ *They bustled her out of the room before she could see the body.* **2** [I] bustle (with sth) to be full of people, noise or activity: *The streets were bustling with shoppers.*

bustle[2] /ˈbʌsl/ *noun* [U] excited and noisy activity: *She loved the bustle of city life.*

ˈ**bust-up** *noun* [C] (*informal*) an argument: *He had a bust-up with his boss over working hours.*

🔑 **busy**[1] /ˈbɪzi/ *adj* (busier; busiest) **1** busy (with sth); busy (doing sth) having a lot of work or tasks to do; not free; working on sth: *Mr Khan is busy until 4 o'clock but he could see you after that.* ◆ *Don't disturb him. He's busy.* ◆ *She's busy with her preparations for the party.* ◆ *We're busy decorating the spare room before our visitors arrive.* **2** (used about a period of time) full of activity and things to do: *I've had rather a busy week.* **3** (used about a place) full of people, movement and activity: *The town centre was so busy that you could hardly move.* **4** (*especially AmE*) (used about a telephone) being used: *The line's busy at the moment. I'll try again later.*
IDM get busy to start working: *We'll have to get busy if we're going to be ready in time.*
▶ **busily** *adv*: *When I came in, she was busily writing something at her desk.*

busy[2] /ˈbɪzi/ *verb* [T] (busying; busies; *pt, pp* busied) busy yourself with sth; busy yourself doing sth to keep yourself busy; to find sth to do

busybody /ˈbɪzibɒdi/ *noun* [C] (*pl* busybodies) a person who is too interested in other people's private lives

🔑 **but**[1] /bət; *strong form* bʌt/ *conj* **1** used for introducing an idea which contrasts with or is different from what has just been said: *The weather will be sunny but cold.* ◆ *Theirs is not the first but the second house on the left.* ◆ *James hasn't got a car but his sister has.* **2** however; and yet: *By the end of the day we were tired but happy.* ◆ *I'd love to come but I can't make it till 8 o'clock.* **3** used when you are saying sorry for sth: *Excuse me, but is your name David Harries?* ◆ *I'm sorry, but I can't stay any longer.* **4** used for introducing a statement that shows that you are surprised or annoyed or that you disagree: *'Here's the book you lent me.' 'But it's all dirty and torn!'* ◆ *'But that's not possible!'*
IDM but then however; on the other hand: *We could go swimming. But then perhaps it's too cold.* ◆ *He's brilliant at the piano. But then so was his father* (= however, this is not surprising because ...).

but[2] /bət; *strong form* bʌt/ *prep* except: *I've told no one but you about this.* ◆ *We've had nothing but trouble with this washing machine!*
IDM but for sb/sth except for or without sb/sth: *We wouldn't have managed but for your help.*

butcher[1] /ˈbʊtʃə(r)/ *noun* [C] **1** a person who sells meat: *The butcher cut me four lamb chops.* ➲ note at **meat** **2** the butcher's [sing] a shop that sells meat: *She went to the butcher's for some sausages.* **3** a person who kills a lot of people in a cruel way

butcher[2] /ˈbʊtʃə(r)/ *verb* [T] to kill a lot of people in a cruel way

butchery /ˈbʊtʃəri/ *noun* [U] **1** cruel killing **2** the work of preparing meat to be sold

butler /ˈbʌtlə(r)/ *noun* [C] a person who works in a very large house, whose duties include organizing and serving food and wine

butt[1] /bʌt/ *verb* [T] to hit sb/sth with the head
PHR V butt in (on sb/sth) to interrupt sb/sth or to join in sth without being asked: *I'm sorry to butt in but could I speak to you urgently for a minute?*

butt[2] /bʌt/ *noun* [C] **1** the thicker, heavier end of a weapon or tool: *the butt of a rifle* **2** a short piece of a cigarette which is left when it has been smoked **3** ((*especially AmE informal*) the part of your body that you sit on; your bottom: *Get up off your butt and do some work!* **4** the act of hitting sb with your head
IDM be the butt of sth a person who is often

laughed at or talked about in an unkind way: *Fat children are often the butt of other children's jokes.*

butter[1] /ˈbʌtə(r)/ *noun* [U] a soft yellow fat that is made from cream and used for spreading on bread, etc. or in cooking: *Do you prefer butter or low-fat spread?* ♦ *First, melt a little butter in the pan.* ➲ look at **margarine**

butter[2] /ˈbʌtə(r)/ *verb* [T] to spread butter on bread, etc: *I'll cut the bread and you butter it.* ♦ *hot buttered toast*

butterfly /ˈbʌtəflaɪ/ *noun* **1** [C] (*pl* **butterflies**) an insect with a long, thin body and four brightly coloured wings: *Caterpillars develop into butterflies.* ➲ picture on **page P13** **2** [sing,U] a style of swimming in which both arms are brought over the head at the same time, and the legs move up and down together ➲ picture at **swim**

IDM **have butterflies (in your stomach)** (*informal*) to feel very nervous before doing sth

buttermilk /ˈbʌtəmɪlk/ *noun* [U] the liquid that is left when butter is separated from milk

buttock /ˈbʌtək/ *noun* [C,usually pl] one of the two parts of your body which you sit on

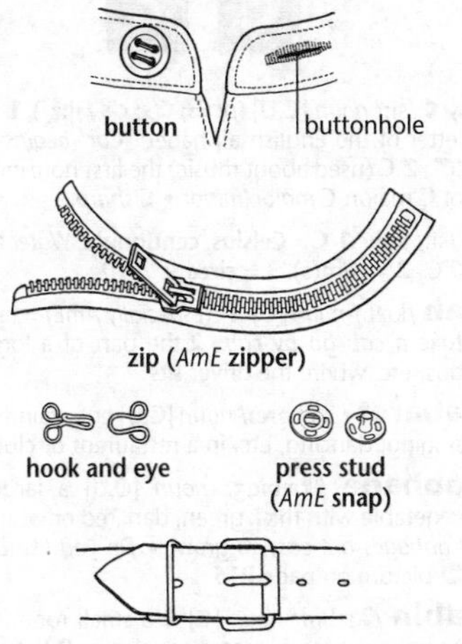

button /ˈbʌtn/ *noun* [C] **1** a small, often round, piece of plastic, wood or metal that you use for fastening your clothes: *One of the buttons on my jacket has come off.* ♦ *This blouse is too tight–I can't fasten the buttons.* ➲ picture on **page P1** **2** a small part of a machine, etc. that you press in order to operate sth: ***Press the button** to ring the bell.* ♦ *To dial the same number again, **push the** 'redial' button.* ♦ *Which button turns the volume down?* ♦ *Double click the right mouse button.* ➲ picture at **handle** **3** a small area on a computer screen that you click on in order to do sth: *To print a file, simply click on the 'print' button.*

buttonhole /ˈbʌtnhəʊl/ *noun* [C] **1** a hole in a piece of clothing that you push a button through in order to fasten it ➲ picture at **button** **2** (*BrE*) a flower worn in the **buttonhole** of a coat or jacket

buttress[1] /ˈbʌtrəs/ *noun* [C] a stone or brick structure that supports a wall

buttress[2] /ˈbʌtrəs/ *verb* [T] (*formal*) to support or give strength to sb/sth: *The sharp increase in crime seems to buttress the argument for more police officers on the street.*

buy[1] /baɪ/ *verb* [T] (*pt, pp* **bought** /bɔːt/) **buy sth (for sb)**; **buy sb sth** to get sth by paying money for it: *I'm going to buy a new dress for the party.* ♦ *We bought this book for you in London.* ♦ *Can I buy you a coffee?* ♦ *He bought the car from a friend.* ♦ *Did you buy your car new or second-hand?* ♦ *He bought the necklace as a present for his wife.* ➲ note at **shopping** OPP **sell**

IDM **buy time** to do sth in order to delay an event, a decision, etc: *He took a few days' holiday in order to buy some time before giving them his final decision.*

PHR V **buy sb off** (*informal*) to pay sb money, especially dishonestly, to stop them from doing sth you do not want them to do: *They tried to buy me off with a large discount.*

buy sb out to pay sb for their share in a house, business, etc. in order to get full control of it yourself: *After the divorce, she bought him out and kept the house for herself.*

buy[2] /baɪ/ *noun* [C] an act of buying sth or a thing that you can buy: *I think your camera was a very good buy* (= worth the money you paid).

buyer /ˈbaɪə(r)/ *noun* [C] **1** a person who is buying sth or may buy sth: *I think I've found a buyer for my car.* OPP **seller** **2** a person whose job is to choose and buy goods to be sold in a large shop

buyout /ˈbaɪaʊt/ *noun* [C] the act of buying enough or all of the shares in a company in order to get control of it

buzz[1] /bʌz/ *verb* **1** [I] to make the sound that a **bee** (= a black and yellow insect) makes when flying: *A large fly was buzzing against the windowpane.* ♦ *The doorbell buzzed loudly.* **2** [I] **buzz (with sth)** to be full of excitement, activity, thoughts, etc: *Her head was buzzing with questions that she wanted to ask.* ♦ *The room was buzzing with activity.* **3** [I,T] to call sb by using an electric bell, etc: *The doctor will buzz for you when he's ready.*

buzz[2] /bʌz/ *noun* **1** [C,usually sing] the sound that a **bee** (= a black and yellow insect), etc. makes when flying: *the buzz of insects* **2** [sing] the low sound made by many people talking at the same time: *I could hear the buzz of conversation in the next room.* **3** [sing] (*informal*) a strong feeling of excitement or pleasure: *a buzz of expectation* ♦ *Parachuting **gives me a real buzz**.* ♦ *She **gets a buzz out of** shopping for expensive clothes.*

buzzer /ˈbʌzə(r)/ *noun* [C] a piece of equipment that makes a **buzzing** sound: *Press your buzzer if you know the answer to a question.*

buzzword /ˈbʌzwɜːd/ *noun* [C] a word or phrase, especially one connected with a particular subject, that has become fashionable and popular: *Empowerment is the current buzzword.*

by /baɪ/ *prep, adv* **1** beside; very near: *Come and sit by me.* ♦ *We stayed in a cottage by the sea.* ♦ *The shops are close by.* **2** used after a passive verb for showing who or what did or caused sth: *She was knocked down by a car.* ♦ *The event was organized by local people.* ♦ *I was deeply shocked by the news.* ♦ *Who was the book written by?/Who is the book by?* **3** through doing or using sth; by means of sth: *You can get hold of me by phoning this number.* ♦ *Will you be paying by cash or card?* ♦ *The house is heated by electricity.* ♦ *'How do you go to work?' 'By train, usually.'* ♦ *by bus/car/plane/bicycle* ♦ *We went in by the back door.* **4** as a result of sth: *I got on the wrong bus by mistake/accident.* ♦ *I met an old friend by chance.* **5** not later than; before: *I'll be home by 7 o'clock.* ♦ *He should have telephoned by now/by this time.* **6** past: *He walked straight by me without speaking.* ♦ *We stopped to let the ambulance get by.* **7** [usually without *the*] during a period of time; in a particular situation: *By day we covered about thirty miles and by night we rested.* ♦ *The electricity went off so we had to work by candlelight.* **8** to the amount mentioned: *Prices have gone up by 10 per cent.* ♦ *I missed the bus by a few minutes.* **9** according to sth; concerning sth: *It's 8 o'clock by my watch.* ♦ *By law you have to attend school from the age of five.* ♦ *She's French by birth.* ♦ *He's a doctor by profession.* **10** (used with a part of the body or an article of clothing) holding: *He grabbed me by the arm.* **11** [often used with *the*] in the quantity or period mentioned: *You can rent a car by the day, the week or the month.* ♦ *Copies of the book have sold by the million.* ♦ *They came in one by one.* ♦ *Day by day she was getting better.* **12** used for showing the measurements of an area: *The table is six feet by three feet* (= six feet long and three feet wide). **13** used for multiplying or dividing: *4 multiplied by 5 is 20.* ♦ *6 divided by 2 is 3.*
IDM by and large ➲ large
by the way ➲ way[1]

bye /baɪ/ (also ˌbye-ˈbye) *exclam* (*informal*) goodbye: *Bye! See you tomorrow.* ♦ *She waved bye-bye and got into the car.*

ˈby-election *noun* [C] an election to choose a new Member of Parliament for a particular **constituency** (= town or area). It is held when the former member has died or left suddenly. ➲ note at **election**

bygone /ˈbaɪɡɒn/ *adj* [only *before* a noun] that happened a long time ago: *a bygone era*

bygones /ˈbaɪɡɒnz/ *noun*
IDM let bygones be bygones to decide to forget disagreements or arguments that happened in the past

bypass[1] /ˈbaɪpɑːs/ *noun* [C] **1** a road which traffic can use to go round a town, instead of through it ➲ look at **ring road** **2** an operation on the heart to send blood along a different route so that it does not go through a part which is damaged or blocked: *a triple bypass operation* ♦ *heart bypass surgery*

bypass[2] /ˈbaɪpɑːs/ *verb* [T] to go around or to avoid sth using a **bypass**: *Let's try to bypass the city centre.* ♦ (*figurative*) *It's no good trying to bypass the problem.*

ˈby-product *noun* [C] **1** something that is formed during the making of sth else **2** something that happens as the result of sth else

bystander /ˈbaɪstændə(r)/ *noun* [C] a person who is standing near and sees sth that happens, without being involved in it: *Several **innocent bystanders** were hurt when the two gangs attacked each other.*

byte /baɪt/ *noun* [C] a unit of information stored in a computer, equal to 8 **bits**. Computer memory is measured in **bytes**.

byword /ˈbaɪwɜːd/ *noun* [C, usually sing] **1** a byword for sth a person or a thing that is a typical or well-known example of a particular quality: *A limousine is a byword for luxury.* **2** (*especially AmE*) a word or phrase that is often used

C, c /siː/ *noun* [C,U] (*pl* Cs; C's; c's /siːz/) **1** the third letter of the English alphabet: *'Car' begins with (a) 'C'.* **2** C (used about music) the first note in the scale of C major: *C major/minor* ♦ *C sharp*

C /siː/ *abbr* **1** C = **Celsius, centigrade**: *Water freezes at 0°C.* **2** = **cent(s)** **3** = **circa**: *c 1770*

cab /kæb/ *noun* [C] **1** (*especially AmE*) = **taxi[1]**: *Let's take a cab/go by cab.* **2** the part of a lorry, train, bus, etc. where the driver sits

cabaret /ˈkæbəreɪ/ *noun* [C,U] entertainment with singing, dancing, etc. in a restaurant or club

cabbage /ˈkæbɪdʒ/ *noun* [C,U] a large round vegetable with thick green, dark red or white leaves: *Cabbages are easy to grow.* ♦ *Do you like cabbage?* ➲ picture on **page P15**

cabin /ˈkæbɪn/ *noun* [C] **1** a small room in a ship or boat, where a passenger sleeps **2** the part of a plane where the passengers sit **3** a small wooden house: *a log cabin*

ˈcabin crew *noun* [C, with sing or pl verb] the people whose job is to take care of passengers on a plane

cabinet /ˈkæbɪnət/ *noun* [C] **1 the Cabinet** [with sing or pl verb] the most important ministers in a government, who decide and advise on policy and have regular meetings: *The Cabinet is/are meeting today to discuss the crisis.* **2** a cupboard with shelves or drawers, used for storing things: *a medicine cabinet* ♦ *a filing cabinet* ➲ picture on **page P8**

cable /ˈkeɪbl/ *noun* **1** [C] a thick strong metal rope **2** [C,U] a set of wires covered with plastic, etc., for carrying electricity or signals: *underground/overhead cables* ♦ *a telephone cable* ♦ *two metres of cable* **3** = **cable television**

ˈ**cable car** *noun* [C] a vehicle like a box that hangs on a moving metal **cable** and carries passengers up and down a mountain

ˌ**cable ˈtelevision** (also cable) *noun* [U] a system of sending out TV programmes along wires instead of by radio signals

cache[1] /kæʃ/ *noun* [C] **1** a hidden store of things such as weapons: *an arms cache* **2** a part of a computer's memory that stores copies of data that is often needed while a program is running. This data can be found very quickly.

cache[2] /kæʃ/ *verb* [T] **1** to store things in a secret place, especially weapons **2** to store data in a **cache[1]** on a computer: *This page is cached.*

cackle /ˈkækl/ *verb* [I] to laugh in a loud, unpleasant way ▶ **cackle** *noun* [C]

cactus /ˈkæktəs/ *noun* [C] (*pl* cactuses *or* cacti /ˈkæktaɪ/) a type of plant that grows in hot, dry areas, especially deserts. A **cactus** has a thick **stem** (= the central part) and sharp points but no leaves.

cadet /kəˈdet/ *noun* [C] a young person who is training to be in the army, navy, air force or police

cadge /kædʒ/ *verb* [I,T] (*informal*) cadge (sth) (from/off sb) to try to persuade sb to give or lend you sth: *He's always trying to cadge money off me.*

Caesarean (also Caesarian; *AmE* also cesarean, cesarian) /siˈzeəriən/ *noun* [C] a medical operation in which an opening is cut in a mother's body in order to take out the baby when a normal birth would be impossible or dangerous: *to have a Caesarean*

MORE This operation is also called a **Caesarean section** or in American English a **C-section.**

cafe /ˈkæfeɪ/ *noun* [C] a small restaurant that serves drinks and light meals ➲ picture on **page P11**

CULTURE

In Britain a cafe does not normally serve alcoholic drinks. People go to a **pub** or **bar** to drink wine, beer etc.

cafeteria /ˌkæfəˈtɪəriə/ *noun* [C] a restaurant, especially one for workers, where people collect their meals themselves and carry them to their tables ➲ look at **canteen**

caffeine /ˈkæfiːn/ *noun* [U] the substance found in coffee and tea that makes you feel more active ➲ look at **decaffeinated**

cage /keɪdʒ/ *noun* [C] a box made of bars or wire, or a space surrounded by wire or metal bars, in which a bird or an animal is kept so that it cannot escape: *a birdcage* ▶ **cage** *verb* [T] ▶ **caged** *adj*: *He felt like a caged animal in the tiny office.*

cagey /ˈkeɪdʒi/ *adj* (cagier; cagiest) (*informal*) cagey (about sth) not wanting to give information or to talk about sth

cagoule /kəˈguːl/ *noun* [C] a long jacket with a **hood** (= a part that covers your head) that protects you from the rain or wind

cajole /kəˈdʒəʊl/ *verb* [T,I] cajole sb (into sth/into doing sth); cajole sth out of sb to persuade sb to do sth by talking to them and being very nice: *He cajoled me into agreeing to do the work.* ◆ *I managed to cajole their address out of him.* ◆ *Her voice was soft and cajoling.* **SYN** coax

cakes

cake[1] /keɪk/ *noun* **1** [C,U] a sweet food made by mixing flour, eggs, butter, sugar, etc. together and baking the mixture in the oven: *to make/bake a cake* ◆ *a wedding cake* ◆ *a piece/slice of birthday cake* ◆ *Would you like some more cake?* **2** [C] a mixture of other food, cooked in a round, flat shape: *fish/potato cakes*

IDM have your cake and eat it to enjoy the advantages of sth without its disadvantages; to have both things that are available: *You can't go out every night and pass your exams. You can't have your cake and eat it.*

a piece of cake ➲ **piece[1]**

cake[2] /keɪk/ *verb* [T, usually passive] cake sth (in/with sth) to cover sth with a thick layer of sth that becomes hard when it dries: *boots caked in mud*

calamity /kəˈlæməti/ *noun* [C,U] (*pl* calamities) a terrible event that causes a lot of damage or harm **SYN** disaster

calcium /ˈkælsiəm/ *noun* [U] (*symbol* Ca) a chemical element that is found in food such as milk or cheese. It helps to make teeth and bones strong.

calculate /ˈkælkjuleɪt/ *verb* [T] **1** to find sth out by using mathematics; to work sth out: *It's difficult to calculate how long the project will take.* **2** to consider or expect sth: *We calculated that the advantages would be greater than the disadvantages.*

IDM be calculated to do sth to be intended or designed to do sth: *His remark was clearly calculated to annoy me.*

calculating /ˈkælkjuleɪtɪŋ/ *adj* planning things in a very careful way in order to achieve what you want, without considering other people: *Her cold, calculating approach made her many enemies.*

calculation /ˌkælkjuˈleɪʃn/ *noun* **1** [C,U] finding an answer by using mathematics: *I'll have to* ***do*** *a few* ***calculations*** *before telling you how much I can afford.* ◆ *Calculation of the exact cost is impossible.* **2** [U] (*formal*) careful planning in order to achieve what you want, without considering other people: *His actions were the result of deliberate calculation.*

calculator /ˈkælkjuleɪtə(r)/ *noun* [C] a small electronic machine used for calculating figures: *a pocket calculator*

caldron (*especially AmE*) = **cauldron**

calendar /ˈkælɪndə(r)/ *noun* [C] **1** a list that shows the days, weeks and months of a particular year

> **HELP** **Calendar** or **diary**? A **calendar** is often hung on a wall and may have a separate page for each month, sometimes with a picture or photograph. A **diary** is a little book which you can carry around with you and which has spaces next to the dates so that you can write in appointments, etc.

2 a list of dates and events in a year that are important in a particular area of activity: *Wimbledon is a major event in the sporting calendar.* **3** a system for dividing time into fixed periods and for marking the beginning and end of a year: *the Muslim calendar*

ˌcalendar ˈmonth = **month**(1)

ˌcalendar ˈyear = **year**(1)

calf /kɑːf/ *noun* [C] (*pl* **calves** /kɑːvz/) **1** the back of your leg, between your ankle and your knee: *I've strained a calf muscle.* ➲ picture at **body** **2** a young cow ➲ note at **cow, meat** ➲ picture at **cow** **3** the young of some other animals, for example **elephants** (= large grey animals with long noses)

calibre (*AmE* caliber) /ˈkælɪbə(r)/ *noun* [sing, U] the quality or ability of a person or thing: *The company's employees are of (a) high calibre.*

CALL /kɔːl/ *abbr* **computer-assisted language learning**

call¹ /kɔːl/ *verb*

➤NAME **1 be called** to have as your name: *His wife is called Silvia.* ◆ *What was that village called?* **2** [T] to name or describe a person or thing in a certain way: *They called the baby Freddie.* ◆ *It was very rude to call her fat.* ◆ *Are you calling me a liar?*

➤SHOUT **3** [I,T] **call (out) to sb; call (sth) (out)** to say sth loudly or to shout in order to attract attention: *'Hello, is anybody there?' she called.* ◆ *He called out the names and the winners stepped forward.* ◆ *I could hear a man calling his dog.* ◆ *She called out to her father for help.*

➤TELEPHONE **4** [I,T] (*especially AmE*) = **ring²**(1): *Who's calling, please?* ◆ *I'll call you tomorrow.* ◆ *We're just in the middle of dinner. Can I call you back later?* ➲ note at **telephone**

➤ORDER SB TO COME **5** [T] to order or ask sb to come to a certain place: *Can you call everybody in for lunch?* ◆ *I think we had better call the doctor.*

➤VISIT **6** [I] **call (in/round) (on sb/at ...)** to make a short visit to a person or place: *I called in on Mike on my way home.* ◆ *We called at his house but there was nobody in.*

➤STOP **7** [I] **call at ...** (used about a train, ship, etc.) to stop at the places mentioned: *This is the express service to London, calling at Manchester and Birmingham.*

➤MEETING **8** [T] to arrange for sth to take place at a certain time: *to call a meeting/an election/a strike*

IDM **bring/call sb/sth to mind** ➲ **mind¹**

call sb's bluff to tell sb to actually do what they are threatening to do (believing that they will not risk doing it)

call it a day (*informal*) to decide to stop doing sth: *Let's call it a day. I'm exhausted.*

call sb names to use insulting words about sb

call the shots/tune (*informal*) to be in a position to control a situation and make decisions about what should be done

PHR V **call by** (*informal*) to make a short visit to a place or person as you pass: *I'll call by to pick up the book on my way to work.*

call for sb (*BrE*) to collect sb in order to go somewhere together: *I'll call for you when it's time to go.*

call for sth to demand or need sth: *The crisis calls for immediate action.* ◆ *This calls for a celebration!*

call sth off to cancel sth: *The football match was called off because of the bad weather.*

call sb out to ask sb to come, especially to an emergency: *We had to call out the doctor in the middle of the night.*

call sb up 1 (*especially AmE*) to telephone sb: *He called me up to tell me the good news.* **2** to order sb to join the army, navy or air force: *All men under 30 were called up to fight in the war.*

call sth up to look at sth that is stored in a computer: *The bank clerk called up my account details on screen.*

call² /kɔːl/ *noun*

➤TELEPHONE **1** (also **ˈphone call**) [C] an act of telephoning or a conversation on the telephone: *Were there any calls for me while I was out?* ◆ *I'll* ***give*** *you* ***a call*** *at the weekend.* ◆ *to* ***make a*** *local* ***call*** ◆ *a long-distance call*

➤SHOUT **2** [C] a loud sound that is made to attract attention; a shout: *a call for help* ◆ *That bird's call is easy to recognize.*

➤VISIT **3** [C] a short visit, especially to sb's house: *The doctor has several calls to make this morning.* ◆ (*old-fashioned*) *We could* ***pay a call*** *on Dave on our way home.*

➤DEMAND **4** [C] a request, demand for sth: *There have been calls for the President to resign.* **5** [C,U] **call for sth** a need for sth: *The doctor said there was no call for concern.*

IDM **at sb's beck and call** ➲ **beck**

(be) on call to be ready to work if necessary: *Dr Young will be on call this weekend.*

ˈcall box = **telephone box**

ˈcall centre (*AmE* ˈcall center) *noun* [C] an office in which many people work using telephones, for example taking customers' orders or answering questions

caller /ˈkɔːlə(r)/ *noun* [C] a person who telephones or visits sb

callous /ˈkæləs/ *adj* not caring about the suffering of other people **SYN** **cruel**

calm¹ /kɑːm/ *adj* (**calmer**; **calmest**) **1** not excited, worried or angry; quiet: *Try to **keep calm**—there's no need to panic.* ◆ *She spoke in a calm voice.* ◆ *The city is calm again after last night's riots.* **2** without big waves: *a calm sea* **OPP** **rough** **3** without much wind: *calm weather* ▶ **calmly** *adv* ▶ **calmness** *noun* [U]

calm² /kɑːm/ *verb* [I,T] **calm (sb/sth) (down)** to become or to make sb quiet or calm: *Calm down! Shouting at everybody won't help.* ◆ *I did some breathing exercises to calm my nerves.*

calm³ /kɑːm/ *noun* [C,U] a period of time or a state when everything is peaceful: *After living in the city, I enjoyed the calm of country life.*

Calor gas™ /ˈkælə gæs/ *noun* [U] gas that is kept in special bottles and used for cooking, heating, etc.

calorie /ˈkæləri/ *noun* [C] a measure of the energy value of food: *A fried egg contains about 100 calories.* ◆ *a low-calorie drink/yogurt/diet*

calves *plural* of **calf**

camcorder /ˈkæmkɔːdə(r)/ *noun* [C] a camera that you can carry around and use for recording pictures and sound on a video ➲ picture at **camera**

came *past tense* of **come**

camel /ˈkæml/ *noun* [C] an animal that lives in the desert and has a long neck and either one or two **humps** (= large masses of fat) on its back. It is used for carrying people and goods.

camel

cameo /ˈkæmiəʊ/ *noun* [C] (*pl* **cameos**) **1** a small part in a film or play that is usually played by a famous actor: *Sean Connery plays a cameo role as the dying king.* **2** a piece of jewellery that has a design in one colour and a background in a different colour

camera

digital camera
camcorder
tripod

camera /ˈkæmərə/ *noun* [C] a piece of equipment that you use for taking photographs or moving pictures: *Just point the camera and press the button.* ◆ *a video/TV camera*

TOPIC

Cameras

You use a camera to **take photos** (*formal* **photographs**). You adjust the **lens** to make sure that the image is **in focus** (= clear and sharp), not **out of focus** (= not clear). You need a **zoom lens** to take pictures of things that are a long distance away. If there is not much light or you are indoors you will probably need to use the **flash**. **Digital cameras** allow you to take digital photos which you can download and store on your computer. Some people like to put their photos into **albums** to look at them, others prefer to just view them on their computer. If you want to **pose** for a photo and ask sb to take it with your camera, you can say *'Could you take a photo of me, please?'*

cameraman /ˈkæmrəmæn/ *noun* [C] (*pl* **-men** /-men/) a person whose job is to operate a camera for a film or a TV company ➲ look at **photographer**

camouflage /ˈkæməflɑːʒ/ *noun* [U] **1** materials or colours that soldiers use to make themselves and their equipment difficult to see **2** the way in which an animal's colour or shape matches its surroundings and makes it difficult to see ▶ **camouflage** *verb* [T]

camp¹ /kæmp/ *noun* [C,U] a place where people live in tents or simple buildings away from their usual home: *a holiday camp* ◆ *a refugee camp* ◆ *an army training camp* ◆ *The climbers set up camp at the foot of the mountain.*

camp² /kæmp/ *verb* [I] **camp (out)** to sleep without a bed, especially outside in a tent: *We camped next to a river.*

HELP **Go camping** is a common way of talking about camping for pleasure: *They went camping in France last year.*

campaign¹ /kæmˈpeɪn/ *noun* [C] **1** a plan to do a number of things in order to achieve a special aim: *to launch an advertising/election campaign* ◆ *a campaign to reduce road accidents* **2** a planned series of attacks in a war

campaign² /kæmˈpeɪn/ *verb* [I] **campaign (for/against sb/sth)** to take part in a planned series of activities in order to make sth happen or to prevent sth: *Local people are campaigning for lower speed limits in the town.* ▶ **campaigner** *noun* [C]: *an animal rights campaigner*

ˈcamp bed (*AmE* **cot**) *noun* [C] a light, narrow bed that you can fold up and carry easily ➲ picture at **bed**

camper /ˈkæmpə(r)/ *noun* [C] **1** a person who stays in a tent on holiday **2** (also **ˈcamper van**, *AmE* **RV**; **recreˌational ˈvehicle**) a motor vehicle in which you can sleep, cook, etc. when you are on holiday ➲ picture at **camping**

camping /ˈkæmpɪŋ/ *noun* [U] sleeping or having a holiday in a tent, **camper**, etc: *Camping is cheaper than staying in hotels.* ♦ *to go on a camping holiday*

camping

camper

caravan (*AmE* **trailer**)

tent

campsite /ˈkæmpsaɪt/ *noun* [C] a place where you can stay in a tent

campus /ˈkæmpəs/ *noun* [C,U] the area of land where the main buildings of a college or university are: *the college campus*

can¹ /kən; *strong form* kæn/ *modal verb* (*negative* **cannot** /ˈkænɒt/; *short form* **can't** /kɑːnt/; *pt* **could** /kəd/; *strong form* /kʊd/; *negative* **could not**; *short form* **couldn't** /ˈkʊdnt/)

➤ABILITY **1** used for showing that it is possible for sb/sth to do sth or that sb/sth has the ability to do sth: *Can you ride a bike?* ♦ *He can't speak French.*

> **GRAMMAR** **Can** has no infinitive or participle forms. To make the future and perfect tenses, we use **be able to**: *One day people will be able to travel to Mars.* **Could have** is used when we say that somebody had the ability or opportunity to do something but did not do it: *She could have passed the exam but she didn't really try.*

➤SENSES **2** used with the verbs 'feel', 'hear', 'see', 'smell', 'taste': *I can smell something burning.*

➤PERMISSION **3** used to ask for or give permission: *Can I have a drink, please?* ♦ *He asked if he could have a drink.*

> **GRAMMAR** When we are talking about general permission in the past **could** is used: *I could do anything I wanted when I stayed with my grandma.* When we are talking about one particular occasion we do not use **could**: *They were allowed to visit him in hospital yesterday.*

➤OFFER **4** used for offering to do sth: *Can I help at all?*

➤REQUEST **5** used to ask sb to do sth: *Can you help me carry these books?*

➤PROBABILITY **6** used in the negative for saying that you are sure sth is not true: *That can't be Maria—she's in London.* ♦ *Surely you can't be hungry. You've only just had lunch.*

➤POSSIBILITY **7** used to talk about sb's typical behaviour or of a typical effect: *You can be very annoying.* ♦ *Wasp stings can be very painful.* ⓘ For more information about modal verbs, look at the **Reference Section** at the back of this dictionary.

can² /kæn/ *noun* [C] **1** a metal or plastic container that is used for holding or carrying liquid: *an oil can* ♦ *a watering can* **2** a metal container in which food or drink is kept without air so that it stays fresh: *a can of sardines* ♦ *a can of coke* ➲ picture at **container**

> **HELP** **Can** or **tin**? In British English we usually use the word **tin** when it contains food. **Can** is used for drinks.

can³ /kæn/ *verb* [T] (**canning**; **canned**) to put food, drink, etc. into a can in order to keep it fresh for a long time: *canned fruit*

canal /kəˈnæl/ *noun* [C] **1** a deep cut that is made through land and filled with water for boats or ships to travel along; a smaller cut used for carrying water to fields, crops, etc: *the Panama Canal* **2** one of the tubes in the body through which food, air, etc. passes

caˈnal boat *noun* [C] a long narrow boat used on canals

canary /kəˈneəri/ *noun* [C] (*pl* **canaries**) a small yellow bird that sings and is often kept in a **cage** (= a box made of bars) as a pet

cancel /ˈkænsl/ *verb* [T] (**cancelling**; **cancelled**, *AmE* **canceling**; **canceled**) **1** to decide that sth that has been planned or arranged will not happen: *All flights have been cancelled because of the bad weather.* ➲ look at **postpone** **2** to stop sth that you asked for or agreed to: *to cancel a reservation* ♦ *I wish to cancel my order for these books.*

PHR V **cancel (sth) out** to be equal or have an equal effect: *What I owe you is the same as what you owe me, so our debts cancel each other out.*

cancellation /ˌkænsəˈleɪʃn/ *noun* [C,U] the act of cancelling sth: *We had to make a last-minute cancellation.*

Cancer /ˈkænsə(r)/ *noun* [C,U] the 4th sign of the **zodiac** (= 12 signs which represent the positions of the sun, moon and planets), the Crab; a person born under this sign: *I'm a Cancer.* ➲ picture at **zodiac**

cancer /ˈkænsə(r)/ *noun* [C,U] a very serious disease in which lumps grow in the body: *She has lung cancer.* ♦ *He died of cancer.*

cancerous /ˈkænsərəs/ *adj* (used especially about a part of the body or sth growing in the body) having cancer: *a cancerous growth* ♦ *cancerous cells*

candid /ˈkændɪd/ *adj* saying exactly what you think: *a candid interview* SYN **frank** ➲ *noun* **candour** ▶ **candidly** *adv*

candidacy /ˈkændɪdəsi/ *noun* [U] the fact of being a **candidate**

candidate /ˈkændɪdət/ *noun* [C] **1** a person who makes a formal request to be considered for a job or wants to be elected to a particular position: *We have some very good candidates for the post.* ➲ note at **election** **2** a person who is taking an exam: *There are 12 candidates for FCE this month.*

candle /ˈkændl/ *noun* [C] a round stick of **wax** (= solid oil or fat) with a **wick** (= a piece of string) through the middle that you can burn to give light: *to light/blow out a candle*

candlelight /ˈkændllaɪt/ *noun* [U] light that comes from a candle: *They had dinner by candlelight.*

wick
candle

candlestick /ˈkændlstɪk/ *noun* [C] an object for holding a **candle** or **candles**: *a silver candlestick*

candlestick
candle

candour (*AmE* candor) /ˈkændə(r)/ *noun* [U] the quality of being honest; saying exactly what you think ➲ *adjective* **candid**

⚷ **candy** /ˈkændi/ *noun* [C,U] (*pl* candies) (*AmE*) = **sweet**[2](1): *You eat too much candy.*

cane /keɪn/ *noun* **1** [C,U] the long central part of certain plants, for example **bamboo** (= a tall tropical plant), that is like a tube and is used as a material for making furniture, etc: *sugar cane* ◆ *a cane chair* **2** [C] a stick that is used to help sb walk

canine /ˈkeɪnaɪn/ *adj* connected with dogs

canister /ˈkænɪstə(r)/ *noun* [C] a small round metal container: *a gas canister*

cannabis /ˈkænəbɪs/ *noun* [U] a drug made from **hemp** (= a type of plant) that some people smoke for pleasure, but which is illegal in many countries

cannibal /ˈkænɪbl/ *noun* [C] a person who eats human flesh ▸ **cannibalism** /ˈkænɪbəlɪzəm/ *noun* [U]

cannon /ˈkænən/ *noun* [C] (*pl* cannon *or* cannons) **1** a large, simple gun that was used in the past for firing **cannon balls** (= large stone or metal balls) **2** a large gun on a ship, an army vehicle, an aircraft, etc.

⚷ **cannot** ➲ **can**[1]

canoe /kəˈnuː/ *noun* [C] a light, narrow boat for one or two people that you can move through the water using a **paddle** (= a flat piece of wood) ➲ look at **kayak** ➲ picture at **kayak** ▸ **canoe** *verb* [I] (canoeing; canoes; *pt, pp* canoed): *They canoed down the river.*

> **HELP** When we are talking about spending time in a canoe it is more usual to say **go canoeing**: *We're going canoeing on the river tomorrow.*

canon /ˈkænən/ *noun* [C] a Christian priest who works in a **cathedral** (= a large church)

ˈ**can opener** (*especially AmE*) = **tin opener**

canopy /ˈkænəpi/ *noun* [C] (*pl* **canopies**) a cover that hangs or spreads above sth: *The highest branches in the rainforest form a dense canopy.* ◆ *a parachute canopy*

can't *short for* **cannot**

canteen /kænˈtiːn/ *noun* [C] the place in a school, a factory, an office, etc. where the people who work there can get meals: *the staff canteen* ➲ look at **cafeteria**

canter /ˈkæntə(r)/ *verb* [I] (used about a horse and its rider) to run fairly fast but not very fast: *We cantered along the beach.* ➲ look at **gallop, trot** ▸ **canter** *noun* [sing]

canvas /ˈkænvəs/ *noun* **1** [U] a type of strong cloth that is used for making sails, bags, tents, etc. **2** [C] a piece of strong cloth for painting a picture on

canvass /ˈkænvəs/ *verb* **1** [I,T] **canvass (sb/sth) (for sth)** to try to persuade people to vote for a particular person or party in an election or to support sb/sth: *to canvass for votes* ◆ *He's canvassing for the Conservative Party.* ◆ *She's been to trying to canvass support for the plan.* **2** [T] to find out what people's opinions are about sth

canyon /ˈkænjən/ *noun* [C] a deep valley with very steep sides

⚷ **cap**[1] /kæp/ *noun* [C] **1** a hat that has a part sticking out at the front: *a baseball cap* ➲ picture at **hat** **2** a soft hat that is worn for a particular purpose: *a shower cap* **3** a hat that is given to a player who is chosen to play for their country: *He won his first cap against France.* **4** a covering for the end or top of sth: *Please put the cap back on the bottle.* ➲ note at **top**[1] ➲ picture at **container**

cap[2] /kæp/ *verb* [T] (**capping**; **capped**) **1** to cover the top of sth: *mountains capped with snow* **2** to limit the amount of money that can be spent on sth **3** to follow sth with sth bigger or better **4** to choose a player to represent their country in a sport **IDM** **to cap it all** (*informal*) as a final piece of bad luck: *I had a row with my boss, my bike was stolen, and now to cap it all I've lost my keys!*

capability /ˌkeɪpəˈbɪləti/ *noun* [C,U] (*pl* **capabilities**) **capability (to do sth/of doing sth)** the quality of being able to do sth: *Animals in the zoo have lost the capability to catch/of catching food for themselves.* ◆ *I tried to fix the computer, but it was* ***beyond my capabilities***.

⚷ **capable** /ˈkeɪpəbl/ *adj* **1 capable of (doing) sth** having the ability or qualities necessary to do sth: *He's capable of passing the exam if he tries harder.* ◆ *That car is capable of 180 miles per hour.* ◆ *I do not believe that she's capable of stealing.* **2** having a lot of skill; good at doing sth: *She's a very capable teacher.* **OPP** **incapable** ▸ **capably** /-əbli/ *adv*

⚷ **capacity** /kəˈpæsəti/ *noun* (*pl* **capacities**) **1** [sing, U] the amount that a container or space can hold: *The tank has a capacity of 1 000 litres.* ◆ *The stadium was* ***filled to capacity***. **2** [sing] **a capacity (for sth/for doing sth)**; **a capacity (to do sth)** the ability to understand or do sth: *That book is beyond the capacity of young children.* ◆ *a capacity for hard work/for learning languages* ◆ *Babies are born with the capacity to swim underwater.* **3** [C] the official position that sb has: ***In his capacity as*** *chairman of the council ...* **SYN** **role** **4** [U, sing] the amount that a factory or machine can produce: *The power station is working* ***at full capacity***.

cape /keɪp/ *noun* [C] **1** a piece of clothing with no sleeves that hangs from your shoulders ➲ look at cloak **2** a piece of high land that sticks out into the sea: *the Cape of Good Hope*

capital¹ /ˈkæpɪtl/ *noun* **1** (also ˌcapital ˈcity) [C] the town or city where the government of a country is: *Rome is the capital of Italy.* **2** [C] a place that is well known for a particular thing: *Niagara Falls is the honeymoon capital of the world.* **3** [U] an amount of money that you use to start a business or to put in a bank, etc. so that you earn interest on it: *When she had enough capital, she bought a shop.* **4** (also ˌcapital ˈletter) [C] the large form of a letter of the alphabet: *Write your name in capitals.* ➲ note at **letter**

capital² /ˈkæpɪtl/ *adj* [only *before* a noun] **1** connected with punishment by death: *Murder is a capital offence in some countries.* **2** (used about letters of the alphabet) written in the large form: *'David' begins with a capital 'D'.*

ˌcapital inˈvestment *noun* [U] money that a business spends on buildings, equipment, etc.

capitalism /ˈkæpɪtəlɪzəm/ *noun* [U] the economic system in which businesses are owned and run for profit by individuals and not by the state ➲ look at **communism, Marxism, socialism** ▶ **capitalist** /-ɪst/ *noun* [C], *adj*

capitalize (also -ise) /ˈkæpɪtəlaɪz/ *verb*
PHR V capitalize on sth to use sth to your advantage: *We can capitalize on the mistakes that our rivals have made.*

ˌcapital ˈletter = capital¹(4)

ˌcapital ˈpunishment *noun* [U] punishment by death for serious crimes ➲ look at **corporal punishment, death penalty**

capitulate /kəˈpɪtʃuleɪt/ *verb* [I] (*formal*) to stop fighting and accept that you have lost; to give in to sb ▶ **capitulation** /kəˌpɪtʃuˈleɪʃn/ *noun* [C,U]

capricious /kəˈprɪʃəs/ *adj* changing behaviour suddenly in a way that is difficult to predict: *a capricious actor* **SYN unpredictable**

Capricorn /ˈkæprɪkɔːn/ *noun* [C,U] the 10th sign of the **zodiac** (= 12 signs which represent the positions of the sun, moon and planets), the Goat; a person born under this sign: *I'm a Capricorn.* ➲ picture at **zodiac**

capsize /kæpˈsaɪz/ *verb* [I,T] (used about boats) to turn over in the water: *The canoe capsized.* ◆ *A big wave capsized the yacht.*

capsule /ˈkæpsjuːl/ *noun* [C] **1** a very small closed tube of medicine that you swallow ➲ picture at **medicine** **2** a container that is closed so that air, water, etc. cannot enter

captain¹ /ˈkæptɪn/ *noun* [C] (*abbr* capt.) **1** the person who is in command of a ship or an aircraft: *The captain gave the order to abandon ship.* ◆ *Captain Cook* ➲ note at **boat** **2** a person who is the leader of a group or team: *Who's (the) captain of the French team?* **3** an officer at a middle level in the army or navy

captain² /ˈkæptɪn/ *verb* [T] to be the captain of a group or team

caption /ˈkæpʃn/ *noun* [C] the words that are written above or below a picture, photograph, etc. to explain what it is about

captivate /ˈkæptɪveɪt/ *verb* [T] to attract and hold sb's attention ▶ **captivating** *adj*

captive¹ /ˈkæptɪv/ *adj* kept as a prisoner; (used about animals) kept in a **cage** (= a box made of bars), etc: (*figurative*) *a* ***captive audience*** (= listening because they cannot leave)
IDM hold/take sb captive/prisoner to keep sb as a prisoner and not allow them to escape

captive² /ˈkæptɪv/ *noun* [C] a prisoner

captivity /kæpˈtɪvəti/ *noun* [U] the state of being kept in a place that you cannot escape from: *Wild animals are often unhappy when kept* ***in captivity.***

captor /ˈkæptə(r)/ *noun* [C] a person who takes or keeps a person as a prisoner

capture¹ /ˈkæptʃə(r)/ *verb* [T] **1** to take a person or an animal prisoner: *The lion was captured and taken back to the zoo.* **SYN catch** **2** to take control of sth: *The town has been captured by the rebels.* ◆ *The company has captured 90% of the market.* **3** to make sb interested in sth: *The story captured the children's imagination/interest/attention.* **SYN catch** **4** to succeed in representing or recording sth in words, pictures, etc: *This poem captures the atmosphere of the carnival.* ◆ *The robbery was captured on video.*

capture² /ˈkæptʃə(r)/ *noun* [U] the act of capturing sth or being captured: *the capture of enemy territory* ◆ *data capture*

car /kɑː(r)/ *noun* [C] **1** (*AmE* also **automobile**) a road vehicle with four wheels that can carry a small number of people: *a new/second-hand car* ◆ *Where can I park the car?* ◆ *They had a car crash.* ◆ *to get into/out of a car* ➲ note at **driving, parking, road** ➲ picture on **page P7**

HELP Note that we go **in the car** or **by car**. You can also use the verb **drive**: *I come to work in the car/by car.* ◆ *I drive to work.*

2 (*BrE*) a section of a train that is used for a particular purpose: *a dining/sleeping car* **3** (*AmE*) = **carriage**(1) **4** (*AmE*) = **truck**

TOPIC

Cars

You **fill up** your car with **petrol** or **diesel** at a **petrol station**. Many cars run on **unleaded** petrol. If your car **breaks down** (= stops working), it might need to be **towed** (= pulled by another vehicle) to a **garage** so that you can **have it repaired** by a **mechanic**.

carafe /kəˈræf/ *noun* [C] a glass container like a bottle with a wide neck, in which wine or water is served ➲ picture at **jug**

caramel /ˈkærəmel/ *noun* **1** [C,U] a type of sticky sweet that is made from boiled sugar, butter and milk **2** [U] burnt sugar that is used to add flavour and colour to food

carat (*AmE* **karat**) /ˈkærət/ *noun* [C] a measure of how pure gold is or how heavy **jewels** (= valuable stones) are: *a 20-carat gold ring*

caravan /ˈkærəvæn/ *noun* [C] **1** (*AmE* **trailer**) a large vehicle that is pulled by a car or a horse. You can sleep, cook, etc. in a **caravan** when you are travelling or on holiday. ➲ picture at **camping**

HELP When we are talking about using a caravan for holidays we say **go caravanning**.

2 a group of people and animals that travel together, for example across a desert

carbohydrate /ˌkɑːbəʊˈhaɪdreɪt/ *noun* [C,U] one of the substances in food, for example sugar, that gives your body energy: *Athletes need a diet that is high in carbohydrate.*

carbon /ˈkɑːbən/ *noun* [U] (*symbol* C) a chemical substance that is found in all living things, and also in diamonds, coal, petrol, etc.

ˌcarbon ˈcopy *noun* [C] **1** a copy of a letter, etc. that was made using **carbon paper** **2** a person or a thing that is very similar to sb/sth else

ˈcarbon credit *noun* [C] a measure of the amount of **carbon dioxide** and other gases that a country or an organization is allowed to produce and that can be traded ➲ look at **carbon trading**

carbon dioxide /ˌkɑːbən daɪˈɒksaɪd/ *noun* [U] (*symbol* CO_2) a gas that has no colour or smell that people and animals breathe out of their lungs

ˌcarbon ˈfootprint *noun* [C] a measure of the amount of **carbon dioxide** that is produced by the daily activities of a person or company: *Companies are looking at ways to* ***reduce*** *their* ***carbon footprints***.

carbon monoxide /ˌkɑːbən məˈnɒksaɪd/ *noun* [U] (*symbol* CO) a poisonous gas. Motor vehicles produce a lot of **carbon monoxide**.

ˌcarbon ˈneutral *adj* producing no **carbon dioxide** or an amount that is balanced by actions that protect the environment: *We need to use more fuels that are renewable and carbon neutral.* **SYN** **zero-carbon**

ˌcarbon ˈoffset *noun* [C,U] a way for a company or person to reduce the level of **carbon dioxide** (= a gas) for which they are responsible. They pay money to a company that works to reduce the total amount produced in the world, for example by planting trees: *Wind energy companies sell carbon offsets.*

ˈcarbon paper *noun* [U] thin paper with a dark substance on one side that you put between two sheets of paper to make a copy of what you are writing

ˈcarbon trading *noun* [U] a system that gives countries and organizations the right to produce a particular amount of **carbon dioxide** and other gases that cause **global warming** (= the increase in the temperature of the earth's atmosphere), and allows them to sell this right ➲ look at **carbon credit**

car

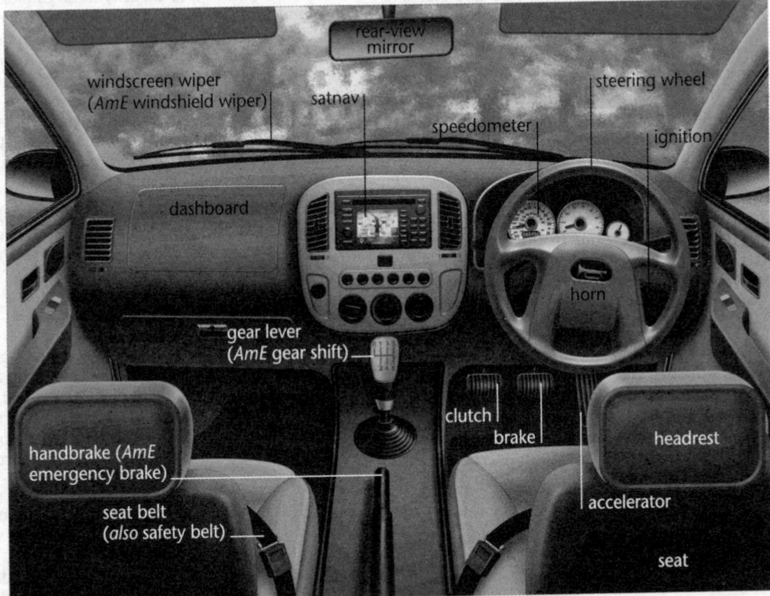

C

ˌcar ˈboot sale *noun* [C] (*BrE*) an outdoor sale where people sell things they do not want from the back of their cars

carburettor (*AmE* **carburetor**) /ˌkɑːbəˈretə(r)/ *noun* [C] the piece of equipment in a car's engine that mixes petrol and air

carcass /ˈkɑːkəs/ *noun* [C] the dead body of an animal ➲ look at **corpse**

cards

card /kɑːd/ *noun* **1** [U] thick stiff paper: *a piece of card* **2** [C] a small piece of card or plastic that has information on it: *Here is my business card in case you need to contact me.* ◆ *a membership/an identity/a credit card* ➲ picture at **money** **3** (also ˈ**greetings card**) [C] a piece of card with a picture on it that you use for sending a special message to sb: *a Christmas/birthday card* ◆ *a get-well card* (= one that you send to sb who is ill) ➲ picture at **letter** **4** [C] = **postcard** **5** (also ˈ**playing card**) [C] one of a set of 52 small pieces of card with shapes or pictures on them that are used for playing games: *a pack of cards* **6 cards** [pl] games that are played with cards: *Let's play cards.* ◆ *Let's have a game of cards.* ◆ *I never win at cards!*

IDM on the cards; (*AmE* **in the cards**) (*informal*) likely to happen: *Their marriage break-up has been on the cards for some time now.*

TOPIC

Playing cards

A **pack** of cards is divided into four **suits**, two red (**hearts** and **diamonds**) and two black (**clubs** and **spades**). Each suit has an **ace**, a **king**, a **queen**, a **jack** and nine other cards, numbered from 2 to 10. Before we play cards we **shuffle**, **cut** and **deal** the cards. A popular card game, often played for money, is **poker**.

cardboard /ˈkɑːdbɔːd/ *noun* [U] very thick paper that is used for making boxes, etc: *The goods were packed in cardboard boxes.*

cardiac /ˈkɑːdiæk/ *adj* [only *before* a noun] (*formal*) connected with the heart: *cardiac surgery* ◆ *a cardiac arrest* (= when the heart stops temporarily or permanently)

cardigan /ˈkɑːdɪɡən/ *noun* [C] a warm piece of clothing, often made of wool, which you wear on the top half of your body. **Cardigans** have long sleeves and fasten at the front, usually with buttons. ➲ note at **sweater**

cardinal /ˈkɑːdɪnl/ *noun* [C] **1** a priest at a high level in the Roman Catholic Church **2** (also ˌ**cardinal** ˈ**number**) a whole number, for example 1, 2, 3, that shows quantity ➲ look at **ordinal**

ˈ**card index** (also **index**) *noun* [C] (*pl* **card indexes**) a box of cards with information on them, such as names, books, subjects, etc., arranged in order from A-Z

care¹ /keə(r)/ *noun* **1** [U] **care (for sb)** the process of looking after sb/sth and providing what they need for their health or protection: *All the children in their care were healthy and happy.* ◆ *This hospital provides free medical care.* ◆ *She's in intensive care* (= the part of the hospital for people who are very seriously ill). ◆ *skin/hair care products* **2** [U] **care (over sth/in doing sth)** thinking about what you are doing so that you do it well or do not make a mistake: *You should **take** more **care** over your homework.* ◆ *This box contains glasses—please handle it **with care**.* **3** [C,U] something that makes you feel worried or unhappy: *Since Charlie retired he **doesn't have a care in the world**.* ◆ *It was a happy life, free from care.*

IDM in care (used about children) living in a home which is organized by the government, and not with their parents: *They were taken into care after their parents died.*

take care (that .../to do sth) to be careful: *Goodbye and take care!* ◆ *Take care that you don't spill your tea.* ◆ *He took care not to arrive too early.*

take care of sb/sth to deal with sb/sth; to organize or arrange sth: *I'll take care of the food for the party.* ➲ note at **care²**

take care of yourself/sb/sth to keep yourself/sb/sth safe from injury, illness, damage, etc.; to look after sb/sth: *My mother took care of me when I was ill.* ◆ *She always takes great care of her books.*

care² /keə(r)/ *verb* [I,T] **care (about sb/sth)** to be worried about or interested in sb/sth: *Money is the thing that she cares about most.* ◆ *He really cares about his staff.* ◆ *I don't care what you do.*

HELP **Care about** or **take care of?**: *She really **cares about** the environment* (= she is interested in it and thinks it is important). ◆ *He has to **take care of/look after** his sick wife* (= be with her and help her). ◆ *You can borrow my camera, but please take care of/look after it* (= keep it in good condition). **Take care of** can also mean 'be responsible for': *I'll take care of the travel arrangements.*

IDM I, etc. couldn't care less (*informal*) it does not matter to me, etc. at all: *I couldn't care less what Barry thinks.*

not care/give a damn (about sb/sth) ➲ **damn³**

who cares? (*informal*) nobody is interested; it is not

important to anyone: *'I wonder who'll win the match.' 'Who cares?'*
would you care for .../to do sth (*formal*) a polite way to ask if sb would like sth or would like to do sth
PHR V care for sb to look after sb: *Who cared for her while she was ill?*
care for sb/sth to like or love sb/sth: *She still cares for Liam, although he married someone else.* ◆ *I don't care for that colour very much.*

career[1] /kəˈrɪə(r)/ *noun* [C] **1** the series of jobs that sb has in a particular area of work: *Sarah is considering a career in engineering.* ◆ *a successful career in politics* **2** the period of your life that you spend working: *She spent most of her career working in India.*

career[2] /kəˈrɪə(r)/ *verb* [I] to move quickly and in a dangerous way: *The car careered off the road and crashed into a wall.*

carefree /ˈkeəfriː/ *adj* with no problems or worries

careful /ˈkeəfl/ *adj* **1** careful (of/with sth); careful (to do sth) thinking about what you are doing so that you do not have an accident or make mistakes, etc: ***Be careful!*** *There's a car coming.* ◆ *Please be very careful of the traffic.* ◆ *Be careful with that knife—it's very sharp.* ◆ *That ladder doesn't look very safe. Be careful you don't fall.* ◆ *I was careful not to say anything about the money.* ◆ *a careful driver* **OPP careless** **2** giving a lot of attention to details to be sure sth is right: *I'll need to give this matter some careful thought.* ◆ *a careful worker* ▶ **carefully** /-fəli/ *adv*: *Please listen carefully. It's important that you remember all this.*

caregiver /ˈkeəgɪvə(r)/ (*AmE*) = **carer**

careless /ˈkeələs/ *adj* **1** careless (about/with sth) not thinking enough about what you are doing so that you make mistakes: *Jo's very careless.* ◆ *The accident was caused by careless driving.* **OPP careful** **2** resulting from a lack of thought or attention to detail: *a careless mistake* ▶ **carelessly** *adv*: *She threw her coat carelessly on the chair.* ▶ **carelessness** *noun* [U]

carer /ˈkeərə(r)/ (*AmE* **caregiver**) *noun* [C] a person who regularly looks after a sick or an old person at home

caress /kəˈres/ *verb* [T] to touch sb/sth in a gentle and loving way ▶ **caress** *noun* [C]

caretaker /ˈkeəteɪkə(r)/ (*AmE* **janitor**) *noun* [C] a person whose job is to look after a large building, for example a school or a block of flats

cargo /ˈkɑːgəʊ/ *noun* [C,U] (*pl* **cargoes**, *AmE* also **cargos**) the goods that are carried in a ship or an aircraft: *Luggage is carried in the cargo hold of the plane.* ◆ *a cargo ship*

ˈcargo pants (also **cargoes**, *BrE also* **combats**) *noun* [pl] loose trousers that have pockets in various places, for example on the side of the leg above the knee ➲ picture on **page P1**

the Caribbean /ˌkærɪˈbiːən; kəˈrɪbiən/ *noun* [sing] the area in the Caribbean Sea where the group of islands called the West Indies is found ▶ **Caribbean** *adj*

caricature /ˈkærɪkətʃʊə(r)/ *noun* [C] a picture or description of sb that makes their appearance or behaviour funnier and more extreme than it really is: *Many of the people in the book are caricatures of the author's friends.*

caring /ˈkeərɪŋ/ *adj* showing that you care about other people: *We must work towards a more caring society.*

carnage /ˈkɑːnɪdʒ/ *noun* [U] the violent killing of a large number of people: *a scene of carnage* **SYN slaughter**

carnation /kɑːˈneɪʃn/ *noun* [C] a white, pink or red flower with a pleasant smell

carnival /ˈkɑːnɪvl/ *noun* [C] a public festival that takes place in the streets with music and dancing: *the carnival in Rio*

carnivore /ˈkɑːnɪvɔː(r)/ *noun* [C] any animal that eats meat ▶ **carnivorous** /kɑːˈnɪvərəs/ *adj*: *Tigers are carnivorous animals.*

carol /ˈkærəl/ (also **ˌChristmas ˈcarol**) *noun* [C] a Christian religious song that people sing at Christmas

carousel /ˌkærəˈsel/ *noun* [C] **1** (*AmE*) = **merry-go-round** **2** a moving belt at an airport that carries luggage for passengers to collect

ˈcar park (*AmE* **ˈparking lot**) *noun* [C] an area or building where you can leave your car: *a multi-storey car park*

carpenter /ˈkɑːpəntə(r)/ *noun* [C] a person whose job is to make things from wood ➲ note at **house** ➲ look at **joiner** ➲ picture on **page P2**

carpentry /ˈkɑːpəntri/ *noun* [U] the skill or work of a **carpenter**

carpet /ˈkɑːpɪt/ *noun* **1** [C,U] (a piece of) thick material that is used for covering floors and stairs: *a fitted carpet* (= one that is cut to the exact shape of a room) ◆ *a square metre of carpet* ➲ look at **rug** ➲ picture on **page P8** **2** [C] a thick layer of sth that covers the ground: *a carpet of snow* ▶ **carpeted** *adj*: *The rooms are carpeted.*

carriage /ˈkærɪdʒ/ *noun* [C] **1** (also **coach**; *AmE* **car**) one of the separate parts of a train where people sit: *a first-class carriage* ➲ picture on **page P7** **2** a vehicle with wheels that is pulled by horses ➲ look at **coach**

carriageway /ˈkærɪdʒweɪ/ *noun* [C] (*BrE*) one of the two sides of a **motorway** (= a wide road for fast traffic) or main road, used by vehicles travelling in one direction only: *the southbound carriageway of the motorway* ➲ look at **dual carriageway**

carrier /ˈkæriə(r)/ *noun* [C] **1** (in business) a company that transports people or goods: *the Dutch carrier, KLM* **2** a military vehicle or ship that is used for transporting soldiers, planes, weapons, etc: *an aircraft carrier* **3** a person or an animal that can give an infectious disease to others but does not show the signs of the disease: *Some insects are carriers of tropical diseases.* **4** (*BrE*) = **carrier bag**

C

ˈcarrier bag (*BrE also* **carrier**) *noun* [C] a plastic or paper bag for carrying shopping ➲ picture at **bag**

carrot /ˈkærət/ *noun* **1** [C,U] a long thin orange vegetable that grows under the ground: *A pound of carrots, please.* ◆ *grated carrot* ➲ picture on page **P15** **2** [C] something attractive that is offered to sb in order to persuade them to do sth: *The management have offered them the carrot of a £500 bonus if they agree to work extra hours.*

carry /ˈkæri/ *verb* (**carrying**; **carries**; *pt, pp* **carried**) **1** [T] to hold sb/sth in your hand, arms or on your back while you are moving from one place to another: *Could you carry this bag for me? It's terribly heavy.* ◆ *She was carrying a rucksack on her back.*

HELP **Carry** or **wear**? You use **wear**, not **carry**, to talk about having clothes, jewellery, etc. on your body: *He was wearing a black jacket.*

2 [T] to have sth with you as you go somewhere: *I never carry much money with me when I go to London.* ◆ *Do the police carry guns in your country?* **3** [T] to transport sb/sth from one place to another: *A train carrying hundreds of passengers crashed yesterday.* ◆ *Strong winds carried the boat off course.* **4** [T] to have an infectious disease that can be given to others, usually without showing any signs of the disease yourself: *Rats carry all sorts of diseases.* **5** [I] (used about a sound) to reach a long distance: *You'll have to speak louder if you want your voice to carry to the back of the room.* **6** [T, usually passive] to officially approve of sth in a meeting, etc., because the largest number of people vote for it: *The motion was carried by 12 votes to 9.*

IDM **be/get carried away** to be so excited that you forget what you are doing: *I got so carried away watching the race that I forgot how late it was.*

carry weight to have influence on the opinion of sb else: *Nick's views carry a lot of weight with our manager.*

PHR V **carry it/sth off** to succeed in doing sth difficult: *He felt nervous before he started his speech but he carried it off very well.*

carry on (with sth/doing sth) to continue: *They ignored me and carried on with their conversation.* ◆ *She intends to carry on studying after the course has finished.*

carry on sth to do an activity: *to carry on a conversation/a business*

carry sth out **1** to do sth that you have been ordered to do: *The soldiers carried out their orders without question.* **2** to do a task, repair, etc: *to carry out tests/an investigation*

carrycot /ˈkærikɒt/ *noun* [C] a small bed, like a box with handles, that you can carry a baby in

ˈcarry-on bag *noun* [C] (*AmE*) = **hand luggage**

ˈcarry-out (*AmE*) = **takeaway**

carsick /ˈkɑːsɪk/ *adj* feeling sick or **vomiting** (= bringing up food from the stomach) as a result of travelling in a car: *to get/feel/be carsick* ➲ look at **airsick, seasick, travel-sick**

cart[1] /kɑːt/ *noun* [C] **1** a vehicle with wheels that is used for transporting things: *a horse and cart* **2** = **trolley**(1)

cart[2] /kɑːt/ *verb* [T] (*informal*) to take or carry sth/sb somewhere, often with difficulty: *We left our luggage at the station because we didn't want to cart it around all day.*

cartilage /ˈkɑːtɪlɪdʒ/ *noun* [C,U] a strong substance in the places where your bones join

carton /ˈkɑːtn/ *noun* [C] a small container made of cardboard or plastic: *a carton of milk/orange juice* ➲ picture at **container**

cartoon /kɑːˈtuːn/ *noun* [C] **1** a funny drawing, especially in a newspaper or magazine **2** a film that tells a story by using moving drawings instead of real people and places

cartoonist /kɑːˈtuːnɪst/ *noun* [C] a person who draws **cartoons**

cartridge /ˈkɑːtrɪdʒ/ *noun* [C] **1** a small tube that contains powder that can explode and a bullet. You put a **cartridge** into a gun when you want to fire it. **2** a closed container that holds sth that is used in a machine, for example film for a camera, ink for printing, etc. **Cartridges** can be removed and replaced when they are finished or empty.

cartwheel /ˈkɑːtwiːl/ *noun* [C] a fast physical movement in which you turn in a circle sideways by putting your hands on the ground and bringing your legs, one at a time, over your head: *to* ***do/turn*** ***cartwheels***

carve /kɑːv/ *verb* **1** [I,T] **carve (sth) (out of sth)** to cut wood or stone in order to make an object or to put a pattern or writing on it: *The statue is carved out of marble.* ◆ *He carved his name on the desk.* **2** [T] to cut a piece of cooked meat into slices: *to carve a chicken*

carving /ˈkɑːvɪŋ/ *noun* [C,U] an object or a design that has been **carved**: *There are ancient carvings on the walls of the cave.*

cascade[1] /kæˈskeɪd/ *noun* [C] **1** a small **waterfall** (= water that falls down the side of a mountain, etc.) **2** a large quantity of sth that falls or hangs down: *a cascade of blond hair*

cascade[2] /kæˈskeɪd/ *verb* [I] to fall or hang down, especially in large amounts or in stages: *Water cascaded from the roof.*

case /keɪs/ *noun*

➤ **SITUATION** **1** [C] a particular situation or example of sth: ***In some cases***, *people have had to wait two weeks for a doctor's appointment.* ◆ *Most of us travel to work by tube—or,* ***in Jim's case***, *by train and tube.* ◆ *Cases of the disease are very unusual in this country.* **2** **the case** [sing] the true situation: *The man said he worked in Cardiff, but we discovered later that this was not the case.*

➤ **LEGAL MATTER** **3** [C] a crime or legal matter: *The police deal with hundreds of murder cases a year.* ◆ *The case will come to court in a few months.*

➤ **REASONS** **4** [C, usually sing] the facts and reasons that support one side in a discussion or legal matter: *She tried to* ***make a case for*** *shorter working hours, but the others disagreed.*

➤CONTAINER **5** [C] [in compounds] a container or cover for sth: *a pencil case* ◆ *a pillowcase* ◆ *a bookcase* ◆ *She put her glasses back in the case.* **6** = **suitcase**: *Would you like me to carry your case?*
IDM **(be) a case of sth/doing sth** a situation in which sth is needed: *There's no secret to success in this business. It's just a case of hard work.*
in any case whatever happens or has happened: *I don't care how much the tickets cost, I'm going in any case.* **SYN** **anyway**
(just) in case because sth might happen: *I think I'll take an umbrella in case it rains.* ◆ *I wasn't intending to buy anything but I took my credit card just in case.*

> **HELP** **In case** or **if**? In British English, **in case** and **if** have a different meaning. Compare: *You should buy insurance, in case you are robbed.* ◆ *If you are robbed, you should call the police.*

in case of sth (*formal*) if sth happens: *In case of fire, break this glass.*
in that case if that is the situation: *'I'm busy on Tuesday.' 'Oh well, in that case we'll have to meet another day.'*

ˈcase study *noun* [C] a detailed study of a person, group, situation, etc. over a period of time

cash¹ /kæʃ/ *noun* [U] **1** money in the form of coins or notes and not cheques, plastic cards, etc: *Would you prefer me to pay **in cash** or by credit card?* ◆ *How much cash have you got with/on you?* ➲ note at **money**

> **HELP** We use **cash** when we are talking about coins and notes, but **change** when we are talking about coins only.

2 (*informal*) money in any form: *I'm a bit short of cash this month so I can't afford to go out much.* ➲ picture at **money**

cash² /kæʃ/ *verb* [T] to exchange a cheque, etc. for coins and notes: *I'm just going to the bank to cash a cheque.*
PHR V **cash in (on sth)** to take advantage of a situation

cashback /ˈkæʃbæk/ *noun* [U] **1** if you ask for **cashback** when you are paying for goods in some shops with a **debit card** (= a plastic card that takes money directly from your bank account), you get a sum of money in cash, that is added to your bill **2** an offer of money as a present that is made by some banks, companies selling cars, etc. in order to persuade customers to do business with them

ˈcash card (*AmE* ˌATˈM card) *noun* [C] a plastic card given by a bank to its customers so that they can get money from a **cash machine** (= a special machine in or outside a bank) ➲ look at **cheque card**, **credit card**

ˈcash desk *noun* [C] the place in a large shop where you pay for things

ˈcash dispenser = **cash machine**

cashew /ˈkæʃuː; kæˈʃuː/ (also ˈcashew nut) *noun* [C] a small curved nut that we eat ➲ picture at **nut**

ˈcash flow *noun* [sing] the movement of money into and out of a business as goods are bought and sold: *The company had cash-flow problems and could not pay its bills.*

cashier /kæˈʃɪə(r)/ *noun* [C] the person in a bank, shop, etc. that customers pay money to or get money from

ˈcash machine (also ˈcash dispenser; Cashpoint™) *noun* [C] a machine inside or outside a bank, etc., that you can get money from at any time of day by putting in a **cash card** (= a special card that is given to you by your bank) ➲ note at **money**

cashmere /ˈkæʃmɪə(r)/ *noun* [U] a type of wool that is very fine and soft

Cashpoint™ /ˈkæʃpɔɪnt/ = **cash machine**

ˈcash register = **till²**

casing /ˈkeɪsɪŋ/ *noun* [C,U] a cover that protects sth: *a camera with a waterproof casing*

casino /kəˈsiːnəʊ/ *noun* [C] (*pl* **casinos**) a place where people play card games, etc. in which you can win or lose money

cask /kɑːsk/ *noun* [C] a large wooden container in which alcoholic drinks, etc. are stored

casket /ˈkɑːskɪt/ (*AmE*) = **coffin**

cassava /kəˈsɑːvə/ (also **manioc**) *noun* [U] **1** a tropical plant with many branches and long roots that you can eat **2** the roots of this plant, which can be cooked or made into flour

casserole /ˈkæsərəʊl/ *noun* **1** [C,U] a type of food made by cooking meat and vegetables in liquid for a long time in the oven: *chicken casserole* **2** [C] (also ˈcasserole dish) a large dish with a lid for cooking **casseroles** in

cassette /kəˈset/ *noun* [C] a small flat plastic case containing tape for playing or recording music or sound: *to put on/play/listen to a cassette* ◆ ***a cassette player/recorder*** ➲ look at **video**

cast¹ /kɑːst/ *verb* (*pt, pp* **cast**) **1** [I,T] to throw a fishing line or net into the water: *He cast his line into the river and waited.* **2** [T, often passive] to choose an actor for a particular role in a play, film, etc: *She always seems to be cast in the same sort of role.*
IDM **cast doubt on sth** to make people less sure about sth: *New evidence casts doubt on the truth of the Prime Minister's statement.*
cast an eye/your eye(s) over sb/sth to look at sb/sth quickly
cast light on sth to help to explain sth: *Can you cast any light on the problem?*
cast your mind back to make yourself remember sth: *She cast her mind back to the day she met her husband.*
cast a shadow (across/over sth) to cause an area of shade to appear somewhere: (*figurative*) *The accident cast a shadow over the rest of the holiday* (= stopped people enjoying it fully).
cast a/your vote to vote: *Cast your vote for the winner by calling this phone number now.*
PHR V **cast around/about for sth** to try to find sth: *Jack cast around desperately for a solution to the problem.*

C

cast² /kɑːst/ *noun* **1** [C, with sing or pl verb] all the actors in a play, film, etc: *The entire cast was/were excellent.* **2** [C] a container that you use to make an object in a particular shape by pouring hot liquid metal, etc. into it; an object that is made in this way SYN **mould**

castaway /ˈkɑːstəweɪ/ *noun* [C] a person who is left alone somewhere after their ship has sunk

caste /kɑːst/ *noun* [C,U] a social class or group based on your position in society, how much money you have, family origin, etc.; the system of dividing people in this way: *Hindu society is based on a caste system.*

ˌcast ˈiron *noun* [U] a hard type of iron that is shaped by pouring the hot liquid metal into a **mould** (= a specially shaped container): *a bridge made of cast iron* ◆ *(figurative) a cast-iron alibi* (= one that people cannot doubt) ➲ look at **wrought iron**

castle /ˈkɑːsl/ *noun* [C] **1** a large building with high walls and towers that was built in the past to defend people against attack: *a medieval castle* ◆ *Edinburgh Castle* **2** (in the game of **chess**) any of the four pieces placed in the corner squares of the board at the start of the game, usually made to look like a **castle**

castle

ˈcast-off *noun* [C, usually pl] a piece of clothing that you no longer want and that you give to sb else or throw away: *When I was little I had to wear my sister's cast-offs.*

castrate /kæˈstreɪt/ *verb* [T] to remove part of the sexual organs of a male animal so that it cannot produce young ➲ look at **neuter** ▶ **castration** /kæˈstreɪʃn/ *noun* [U]

casual /ˈkæʒuəl/ *adj* **1** relaxed and not worried; not showing great effort or interest: *I'm not happy about your casual attitude to your work.* ◆ *It was only a casual remark so I don't know why he got so angry.* **2** (used about clothes) not formal: *I always change into casual clothes as soon as I get home from work.* **3** (used about work) done only for a short period; not regular or permanent: *Most of the building work was done by casual labour.* ◆ *a casual job* ▶ **casually** /ˈkæʒuəli/ *adv*: *She walked in casually and said, 'I'm not late, am I?'* ◆ *Dress casually—it won't be a formal party.*

casualty /ˈkæʒuəlti/ *noun* (*pl* casualties) **1** [C] a person who is killed or injured in a war or an accident: *After the accident the casualties were taken to hospital.* **2** [C] a person or thing that suffers as a result of sth else: *Many small companies became casualties of the economic crisis.* SYN **victim** **3** [C,U] (also ˈ**casualty department**) = **accident and emergency**

cat /kæt/ *noun* [C] **1** a small animal with soft fur that people often keep as a pet: *cat food* ➲ note at pet **2** a wild animal of the cat family: *the big cats* (= lions, tigers, etc.)

> **MORE** A young cat is called a **kitten**. A male cat is called a **tom**, although **cat** is often used for both males and females. When a cat makes a soft sound of pleasure, it **purrs**. When it makes a louder sound, it **miaows**.

catalogue (*AmE* **catalog**) /ˈkætəlɒg/ *noun* [C] **1** a list of all the things that you can buy, see, etc. somewhere **2** a series, especially of bad things: *a catalogue of disasters/errors/injuries* ▶ **catalogue** (*AmE* **catalog**) *verb* [T]: *She started to catalogue all the new library books.*

catalyst /ˈkætəlɪst/ *noun* [C] **1** (in chemistry) a substance that makes a reaction happen faster without being changed itself **2** catalyst (for sth) a person or thing that causes a change: *I see my role as being a catalyst for change.*

catalytic converter /ˌkætəˌlɪtɪk kənˈvɜːtə(r)/ *noun* [C] a device used in motor vehicles to reduce the damage caused to the environment by poisonous gases

catamaran /ˌkætəməˈræn/ *noun* [C] a fast sailing boat with two **hulls** (= bottom parts that go in the water)

catapult¹ /ˈkætəpʌlt/ (*AmE* **slingshot**) *noun* [C] a Y-shaped stick with a piece of **elastic** (= material that can stretch) tied to each side that is used by children for shooting stones

catapult

catapult² /ˈkætəpʌlt/ *verb* [T] to throw sb/sth suddenly and with great force: *When the car crashed the driver was catapulted through the windscreen.* ◆ *(figurative) The success of his first film catapulted him to fame.*

cataract /ˈkætərækt/ *noun* [C] a white area that grows over the eye as a result of disease

catarrh /kəˈtɑː(r)/ *noun* [U] a thick liquid that forms in the nose and throat when you have a cold

catastrophe /kəˈtæstrəfi/ *noun* [C] **1** a sudden disaster that causes great suffering or damage: *major catastrophes such as floods and earthquakes* **2** an event that causes great difficulty, disappointment, etc: *It'll be a catastrophe if I fail the exam again.* ▶ **catastrophic** /ˌkætəˈstrɒfɪk/ *adj*: *The war had a catastrophic effect on the whole country.*

catch¹ /kætʃ/ *verb* (*pt, pp* caught /kɔːt/)

➤HOLD **1** [T] to take hold of sth that is moving, usually with your hand or hands: *The dog caught the ball in its mouth.*

➤CAPTURE **2** [T] to capture sb/sth that you have been following or looking for: *Two policemen ran after the thief and caught him at the end of the street.* ◆ *to catch a fish*

➤DISCOVER **3** [T] to notice or see sb doing sth bad: *I caught her taking money from my purse.*

➤BE IN TIME **4** [T] to be in time for sth; not to miss sb/sth: *We arrived just in time to catch the beginning of* the film. ♦ *I'll phone her now. I might just catch her before she leaves the office.*

➤GET BUS, ETC. **5** [T] to get on a bus, train, plane, etc: *I caught the train from Bari to Lecce.* **OPP** **miss**

➤ILLNESS **6** [T] to get an illness: *to catch a cold/flu/measles*

➤GET STUCK **7** [I,T] to become or cause sth to become accidentally connected to or stuck in sth: *His jacket caught on a nail and ripped.* ♦ *If we leave early we won't get caught in the traffic.*

➤HIT **8** [T] to hit sb/sth: *The branch caught him on the head.*

➤HEAR/UNDERSTAND **9** [T] to hear or understand sth that sb says: *I'm sorry, I didn't quite catch what you said. Could you repeat it?*

IDM **catch sb's attention/eye** to make sb notice sth: *I tried to catch the waiter's eye so that I could get the bill.*

catch your breath **1** to breathe in suddenly because you are surprised **2** to rest after physical exercise so that your breathing returns to normal: *I had to sit down at the top of the hill to catch my breath.*

catch your death (of cold) to get very cold: *Don't go out without a coat–you'll catch your death!*

catch fire to start burning, often accidentally: *Nobody knows how the building caught fire.*

catch sb red-handed to find sb just as they are doing sth wrong: *The police caught the burglars red-handed with the stolen jewellery.*

catch sight of sb/sth to see sb/sth for a moment: *I caught sight of the man at the end of the street.*

catch the sun (*informal*) (used about people) to become red or brown because of spending time in the sun: *Your face looks red. You've really caught the sun, haven't you?*

PHR V **be/get caught up in sth** to be or get involved in sth, usually without intending to: *I seem to have got caught up in a rather complicated situation.*

catch on (*informal*) **1** to become popular or fashionable: *The idea has never really caught on in this country.* **2** to understand or realize sth: *She's sometimes a bit slow to catch on.*

catch sb out to cause sb to make a mistake by asking a clever question: *Ask me anything you like–you won't catch me out.*

catch up (with sb); **catch sb up** to reach sb who is in front of you: *Sharon's missed so much school she'll have to work hard to catch up with the rest of the class.* ♦ *Go on ahead, I'll catch you up in a minute.*

catch up on sth to spend time doing sth that you have not been able to do for some time: *I'll have to go into the office at the weekend to catch up on my work.*

catch² /kætʃ/ *noun* [C] **1** an act of catching sth, for example a ball **2** the amount of fish that sb has caught: *The fishermen brought their catch to the harbour.* **3** a device for fastening sth and keeping it closed: *I can't close my suitcase–the catch is broken.* ♦ *a window catch* **4** a hidden disadvantage or difficulty in sth that seems attractive: *It looks like a good offer, but I'm sure there must be a catch in it.*

catching /ˈkætʃɪŋ/ *adj* [not before a noun] (used about a disease or an emotion) passing easily or quickly from one person to another **SYN** **infectious**

catchment area /ˈkætʃmənt eəriə/ *noun* [C] the area from which a school gets its students, a hospital gets its patients, etc.

catchphrase /ˈkætʃfreɪz/ *noun* [C] a phrase that becomes famous for a while because it is used by a famous person

catchy /ˈkætʃi/ *adj* (**catchier**; **catchiest**) (used about a tune or song) easy to remember

categorical /ˌkætəˈɡɒrɪkl/ *adj* very definite: *The answer was a categorical 'no'.* ▶ **categorically** /-kli/ *adv*: *The Minister categorically denied the rumour.*

categorize (also **-ise**) /ˈkætəɡəraɪz/ *verb* [T] to divide people or things into groups; to say that sb/sth belongs to a particular group

⚷ **category** /ˈkætəɡəri/ *noun* [C] (*pl* **categories**) a group of people or things that are similar to each other: *This painting won first prize in the junior category.* ♦ *These books are* ***divided into categories*** *according to subject.*

cater /ˈkeɪtə(r)/ *verb* [I] **1** **cater (for sb/sth)** to provide and serve food and drink at an event or in a place that a lot of people go to: *Our firm caters for the 5 000 staff and visitors at the festival.* **2** **cater for sb/sth**; **cater to sth** to provide what sb/sth needs or wants: *We need a hotel that caters for small children.* ♦ *The menu caters to all tastes.*

caterer /ˈkeɪtərə(r)/ *noun* [C] a person or business that provides food and drink at events or in places that a lot of people go to

catering /ˈkeɪtərɪŋ/ *noun* [U] the activity or business of providing food and drink at events or in places that a lot of people go to: *the hotel and catering industry* ♦ *Who's going to* ***do the catering*** *at the wedding?*

caterpillar /ˈkætəpɪlə(r)/ *noun* [C] a small animal with a long body and a lot of legs, which eats the leaves of plants. A **caterpillar** later becomes a **butterfly** (= an insect with large brightly coloured wings) or a **moth** (= an insect similar to a butterfly). ➲ picture on **page P13**

cathedral /kəˈθiːdrəl/ *noun* [C] a large church that is the most important one in a district

Catholic /ˈkæθlɪk/ = **Roman Catholic** ▶ **Catholicism** /kəˈθɒləsɪzəm/ = **Roman Catholicism**

cattle /ˈkætl/ *noun* [pl] male and female cows that are kept as farm animals for their milk or meat: *a herd (= a group) of cattle* ➲ note at **cow**

caught *past tense, past participle of* **catch¹**

cauldron (*especially AmE* **caldron**) /ˈkɔːldrən/ *noun* [C] a large, deep, metal pot that is used for cooking things over a fire

cauliflower /ˈkɒliflaʊə(r)/ *noun* [C,U] a large vegetable with green leaves and a round white centre that you eat when it is cooked ➲ picture on **page P15**

⚷ **cause¹** /kɔːz/ *noun* **1** [C] a thing or person that makes sth happen: *The police do not know the cause of the accident.* ♦ *Smoking is one of the causes of heart* disease. **2** [U] cause (for sth) reason for feeling sth or behaving in a particular way: *The doctor assured us that there was no **cause for concern**.* ◆ *I don't think you have any real **cause for complaint**.* **3** [C] an idea or organization that a group of people believe in and support: *We are all committed to the cause of racial equality.*

IDM be for/in a good cause to be worth doing because it will help other people

a lost cause ➲ **lost²**

🔑 **cause²** /kɔːz/ *verb* [T] to make sth happen: *The fire was caused by an electrical fault.* ◆ *High winds caused many trees to fall during the night.* ◆ *Is your leg causing you any pain?*

'cause (*BrE informal*) = **cos**

causeway /ˈkɔːzweɪ/ *noun* [C] a raised road or path across water or wet ground

caustic /ˈkɔːstɪk/ *adj* **1** (used about a substance) able to burn or destroy things by chemical action **2** critical in a cruel way: *a caustic remark*

caution¹ /ˈkɔːʃn/ *noun* **1** [U] great care, because of possible danger: *Any advertisement that asks you to send money should be treated **with caution**.* **2** [C] a spoken warning that a judge or police officer gives to sb who has committed a crime that is not too serious

caution² /ˈkɔːʃn/ *verb* **1** [I,T] caution (sb) against sth to warn sb not to do sth: *The president's advisers have cautioned against calling an election too early.* **2** [T] to give sb an official warning: *Dixon was cautioned by the referee for wasting time.*

cautionary /ˈkɔːʃənəri/ *adj* [only *before* a noun] giving a warning: *The teacher told us a **cautionary tale** about a girl who cheated in her exams.*

cautious /ˈkɔːʃəs/ *adj* taking great care to avoid possible danger or problems: *I'm very cautious about expressing my opinions in public.* ▶ **cautiously** *adv*

cavalry /ˈkævlri/ *noun* [sing, with sing or pl verb] the part of the army that fought on horses in the past; the part of the modern army that uses heavily protected vehicles

cave¹ /keɪv/ *noun* [C] a large hole in the side of a cliff (= a high steep area of rock) or hill, or under the ground: *When it started to rain, we ran to shelter in a cave.*

cave² /keɪv/ *verb*

PHR V cave in 1 to fall in: *The roof of the tunnel had caved in and we could go no further.* **2** to suddenly stop arguing or being against sth: *He finally caved in and agreed to the plan.*

cavern /ˈkævən/ *noun* [C] a large, deep hole in the side of a hill or under the ground; a big **cave¹**

caviar (also caviare) /ˈkæviɑː(r)/ *noun* [U] the eggs of a **sturgeon** (= a large fish) that you can eat. Caviar is usually very expensive.

cavity /ˈkævəti/ *noun* [C] (*pl* cavities) an empty space inside sth solid: *a cavity in a tooth* ◆ *a wall cavity*

CBI /ˌsiː biː ˈaɪ/ *abbr* **the Confederation of British Industry**; an employers' association

cc /ˌsiː ˈsiː/ *abbr* **1 carbon copy** (used on business letters and emails to show that a copy is being sent to another person) **2 cubic centimetre(s)**: *a 1200cc engine*

CCTV /ˌsiː siː tiː ˈviː/ *abbr* = **closed-circuit television**

🔑 **CD** /ˌsiː ˈdiː/ (also ˌcompact ˈdisc) *noun* [C] a small, round, flat piece of hard plastic on which sound or information is recorded ➲ look at **CD player**.

ˌCˈD burner (also ˌCˈD writer) *noun* [C] a piece of equipment used for copying sound or information from a computer onto a CD

ˌCˈD player *noun* [C] a piece of equipment that you use for playing CDs

CD-ROM /ˌsiː diː ˈrɒm/ *noun* [C] a CD on which large amounts of information, sound and pictures can be stored, for use on a computer ➲ picture at **computer**

🔑 **cease** /siːs/ *verb* [I,T] (*formal*) to stop or end: *Fighting in the area has now ceased.* ◆ *That organization has ceased to exist.*

ceasefire /ˈsiːsfaɪə(r)/ *noun* [C] an agreement between two groups to stop fighting each other ➲ look at **truce**

ceaseless /ˈsiːsləs/ *adj* continuing for a long time without stopping ▶ **ceaselessly** *adv*

cedar /ˈsiːdə(r)/ *noun* **1** [C] a tall tree that has hard red wood and wide spreading branches and that stays green all year **2** [U] the wood from the **cedar** tree

cede /siːd/ *verb* [T] (*written*) to give land or control of sth to another country or person

🔑 **ceiling** /ˈsiːlɪŋ/ *noun* [C] **1** the top surface of the inside of a room: *a room with a high/low ceiling* **2** a top limit: *The Government has put a 10% ceiling on wage increases.*

celeb /səˈleb/ (*informal*) = **celebrity**

🔑 **celebrate** /ˈselɪbreɪt/ *verb* [I,T] to do sth to show that you are happy about sth that has happened or because it is a special day: *When I got the job we celebrated by going out for a meal.* ◆ *Gloria celebrated her 18th birthday yesterday.* ▶ **celebratory** /ˌseləˈbreɪtəri/ *adj*: *We went out for a celebratory meal after the match.*

celebrated /ˈselɪbreɪtɪd/ *adj* (*formal*) famous: *a celebrated poet*

🔑 **celebration** /ˌselɪˈbreɪʃn/ *noun* [C,U] the act or occasion of doing sth enjoyable because sth good has happened or because it is a special day: *birthday celebrations* ◆ *I think this is an occasion for celebration!*

celebrity /səˈlebrəti/ (also *informal* celeb) *noun* [C] (*pl* celebrities) a famous person: *a TV celebrity* **SYN personality**

celery /ˈseləri/ *noun* [U] a vegetable with long green and white sticks that can be eaten without being cooked: *a stick of celery* ➲ picture on **page P15**

celibate /ˈselɪbət/ *adj* (*formal*) never having sexual relations, often because of religious beliefs ▸ **celibacy** /ˈselɪbəsi/ *noun* [U]

🔑 **cell** /sel/ *noun* [C] **1** a small room in a prison or police station in which a prisoner is locked **2** the smallest living part of an animal or a plant: *The human body consists of millions of cells.* ◆ *red blood cells*

cellar /ˈselə(r)/ *noun* [C] an underground room that is used for storing things ➲ look at **basement** ➲ picture on **page P8**

cellist /ˈtʃelɪst/ *noun* [C] a person who plays the **cello**

cello /ˈtʃeləʊ/ *noun* [C] (*pl* cellos) a large musical instrument with strings. You sit down to play it and hold it between your knees. ➲ note at **music** ➲ picture at **music**

Cellophane™ /ˈseləfeɪn/ *noun* [U] a transparent plastic material used for wrapping things

🔑 **cellphone** /ˈselfəʊn/ (also ˌcellular ˈphone) (*especially AmE*) = **mobile phone**

cellular /ˈseljələ(r)/ *adj* consisting of cells: *cellular tissue*

Celsius /ˈselsiəs/ (also centigrade) *adj* (*abbr* C) the name of a scale for measuring temperatures, in which water freezes at 0° and boils at 100°: *The temperature tonight will fall to 7°C* (= 'seven degrees Celsius'). ➲ look at **Fahrenheit**

Celtic /ˈkeltɪk/ *adj* connected with the Celts (= the people who lived in Wales, Scotland, Ireland and Brittany in ancient times) or with their culture

cement[1] /sɪˈment/ *noun* [U] a grey powder, that becomes hard after it is mixed with water and left to dry. It is used in building for sticking bricks or stones together or for making very hard surfaces.

cement[2] /sɪˈment/ *verb* [T] **1** to join two things together using **cement[1]**, or a strong sticky substance **2** to make a relationship, an agreement, etc. very strong: *This agreement has cemented the relationship between our two countries.*

cemetery /ˈsemətri/ *noun* [C] (*pl* cemeteries) a place where dead people are buried, especially a place that does not belong to a church ➲ look at **graveyard, churchyard**

censor[1] /ˈsensə(r)/ *noun* [C] an official who **censors[2]** books, films, etc: *All films have to be examined by the board of film censors.*

censor[2] /ˈsensə(r)/ *verb* [T] to remove the parts of a book, film, etc. that might offend people or that are considered to be immoral or a political threat: *News reports from the area have been censored.* ▸ **censorship** *noun* [U]: *state censorship of radio and TV programmes*

censure /ˈsenʃə(r)/ *verb* [T] (*written*) to tell sb, in a strong and formal way, that they have done sth wrong: *The attorney was censured for not revealing the information earlier.* ▸ **censure** *noun* [U]

census /ˈsensəs/ *noun* [C] an official count of the people who live in a country, including information about their ages, jobs, etc.

🔑 **cent** /sent/ *noun* [C] (*abbr* c, ct) a unit of money that is worth 100th part of the main unit of money in many countries, for example of the US dollar or of the euro: *The price of a stamp goes up by 10 cents today.* ➲ look at **per cent**

centenary /senˈtiːnəri/ *noun* [C] (*pl* centenaries) (*AmE* centennial /senˈteniəl/) the year that comes exactly one hundred years after an important event or the beginning of sth: *2001 was the centenary of Disney's birth.*

center (*AmE*) = **centre**

centigrade /ˈsentɪgreɪd/ = **Celsius**

centilitre (*AmE* centiliter) /ˈsentiliːtə(r)/ *noun* [C] (*abbr* cl) a measure of liquid. There are 100 **centilitres** in a litre.

🔑 **centimetre** (*AmE* centimeter) /ˈsentɪmiːtə(r)/ *noun* [C] (*abbr* cm) a measure of length. There are 100 centimetres in a metre: *The insect was about two centimetres long.*

centipede /ˈsentɪpiːd/ *noun* [C] a small creature like an insect, with a long thin body and many legs

🔑 **central** /ˈsentrəl/ *adj* **1** most important; main: *The film's central character is a fifteen-year-old girl.* **2** [only *before* a noun] having control over all other parts: *central government* (= the government of a whole country, not local government) ◆ *the central nervous system* **3** in the centre of sth: *a map of central Europe* ◆ *Our flat is very central* (= near the centre of the city and therefore very convenient).

ˌcentral ˈheating *noun* [U] a system for heating a building from one main point. Air or water is heated and carried by pipes to all parts of the building.

centralize (also -ise) /ˈsentrəlaɪz/ *verb* [T, usually passive] to give control of all the parts of a country or an organization to a group of people in one place: *Our education system is becoming increasingly centralized.* ▸ **centralization** (also -isation) /ˌsentrəlaɪˈzeɪʃn/ *noun* [U]

centrally /ˈsentrəli/ *adv* in or from the centre: *a centrally located hotel* (= near the centre of the town)

🔑 **centre[1]** (*AmE* center) /ˈsentə(r)/ *noun* **1** [C, usually sing] the middle point or part of sth: *I work in the centre of London.* ◆ *Which way is the town centre, please?* ◆ *She hit the target dead centre* (= exactly in the centre). ➲ note at **middle** **2** [C] a place where sb/sth is collected together; the point towards which sth is directed: *major urban/industrial centres* ◆ *She always likes to be* ***the centre of attention.*** ◆ *You should bend your legs to keep a low* ***centre of gravity.*** **3** [C] a building or place where a particular activity or service is based: *a sports/health/shopping centre* ◆ *This university is a centre of excellence for medical research.* **4** [sing, with sing or pl verb] a political position that is not extreme: *a party of the centre*

centre² (*AmE* center) /ˈsentə(r)/ *verb*
PHR V **centre on/around sb/sth** to have sb/sth as its centre: *My aunt's life centres on the home and family.*

-centric /ˈsentrɪk/ [in compounds] concerned with or interested in the thing mentioned: *Eurocentric policies* (= concerned with Europe)

century /ˈsentʃəri/ *noun* [C] (*pl* **centuries**) **1** a particular period of 100 years that is used for giving dates: *We live in the 21st century* (= the period between the years 2000 and 2099). **2** any period of 100 years: *People have been making wine in this area for centuries.*
IDM **the turn of the century/year** ➲ **turn²**

ceramic /səˈræmɪk/ *adj* made of **clay** (= a type of earth) that has been baked: *ceramic tiles* ▶ **ceramic** *noun* [C, usually pl]: *an exhibition of ceramics by Picasso*

cereal /ˈsɪəriəl/ *noun* [C,U] **1** any type of grain that can be eaten or made into flour, or the grass that the grain comes from: *Wheat, barley and rye are cereals.* **2** a food that is made from grain, often eaten for breakfast with milk: *a bowl of cereal* ➲ picture on **page P16**

cerebral /ˈserəbrəl/ *adj* of the brain

ceremonial /ˌserɪˈməʊniəl/ *adj* connected with a ceremony: *a ceremonial occasion* ▶ **ceremonially** /-niəli/ *adv*

ceremony /ˈserəməni/ *noun* (*pl* **ceremonies**) **1** [C] a formal public or religious event: *the opening ceremony of the Olympic Games* ◆ *a wedding ceremony* **2** [U] formal behaviour, speech, actions, etc. that are expected on special occasions: *The new hospital was opened **with great ceremony**.*

certain /ˈsɜːtn/ *adj* **1** certain (that ...); certain (to do sth) sure to happen or to do sth; definite: *It is almost certain that unemployment will increase this year.* ◆ *The director is certain to agree.* ◆ *We must rescue them today, or they will face certain death.* ➲ note at **sure** **2** [not before a noun] certain (that ...); certain (of sth) completely sure; without any doubts: *I'm absolutely certain that there was somebody outside my window.* ◆ *We're not quite certain what time the train leaves.* ◆ *I'm certain of one thing—he didn't take the money.* **OPP** **uncertain** **3** [only *before* a noun] used for talking about a particular thing or person without naming it or them: *You can only contact me at certain times of the day.* ◆ *There are certain reasons why I'd prefer not to meet him again.* **4** [only *before* a noun] (*formal*) used before sb's name to show that you do not know them: *I received a letter from a certain Mrs Berry.* **5** [only *before* a noun] some, but not very much: *I suppose I have **a certain amount of** respect for Mr Law.* **6** [only *before* a noun] noticeable but difficult to describe: *There was a certain feeling of autumn in the air.*
IDM **for certain** without doubt: *I don't know for certain what time we'll arrive.*
make certain (that ...) **1** to do sth in order to be sure that sth else happens: *They're doing everything they can to make certain that they win.* **2** to do sth in order to be sure that sth is true: *We'd better phone Akram before we go to make certain he's expecting us.*

certainly /ˈsɜːtnli/ *adv* **1** without doubt; definitely: *The number of students will certainly increase after 2015.* **2** (used in answer to questions) of course: *'Do you think I could borrow your notes?' 'Certainly.'*

certainty /ˈsɜːtnti/ *noun* (*pl* **certainties**) **1** [U] the state of being completely sure about sth: *We can't say with certainty that there is life on other planets.* **OPP** **uncertainty** **2** [C] something that is sure to happen: *It's now almost a certainty our team will win the league.*

certificate /səˈtɪfɪkət/ *noun* [C] **1** an official piece of paper that says that sth is true or correct: *a birth/marriage/medical certificate* **2** an official document that students gain by successfully completing a course of study or by passing an exam: *First Certificate in English* ➲ note at **degree**

certify /ˈsɜːtɪfaɪ/ *verb* [T] (**certifying**; **certifies**; *pt, pp* **certified**) **1** to say formally that sth is true or correct: *We need someone to certify that this is her signature.* **2** to give sb a certificate to show that they have successfully completed a course of training for a particular profession: *a certified accountant*

cesarean (*AmE*) = **Caesarean**

cf. *abbr* **compare**

CFC /ˌsiː ef ˈsiː/ *noun* [C,U] **chlorofluorocarbon**; a type of gas, found for example in cans of spray, which is harmful to the earth's atmosphere ➲ look at **ozone layer**

ch *abbr* = **chapter**

chador /ˈtʃɑːdɔː(r)/ *noun* [C] a large piece of cloth that covers a woman's head and upper body so that only the face can be seen, worn by some Muslim women

chain¹ /tʃeɪn/ *noun* **1** [C,U] a line of metal rings that are joined together: *a bicycle chain* ◆ *She was wearing a silver chain round her neck.* ◆ *a length of chain* ➲ picture at **bicycle, jewellery, key, padlock** **2** [C] a series of connected things or people: *a chain of mountains/a mountain chain* ◆ *The book examines the complex **chain of events** that led to the Russian Revolution.* ◆ *The Managing Director is at the top of the **chain of command**.* **3** [C] a group of shops, hotels, etc. that are owned by the same company: *a chain of supermarkets* ◆ *a fast-food chain*

chain² /tʃeɪn/ *verb* [T] chain sb/sth (to sth); chain sb/sth (up) to fasten sb/sth to sth else with a chain: *The dog is kept chained up outside.*

chainsaw /ˈtʃeɪnsɔː/ *noun* [C] a tool for cutting wood that has a chain with sharp teeth

ˈchain-smoke *verb* [I] to smoke continuously, lighting one cigarette after another ▶ **ˈchain-smoker** *noun* [C]

ˈchain store *noun* [C] one of a number of similar shops that are owned by the same company

chair¹ /tʃeə(r)/ *noun* **1** [C] a piece of furniture for one person to sit on, with a seat, a back and four legs: *a kitchen chair* ◆ *an armchair* **2** [sing] the person who is controlling a meeting: *Please address*

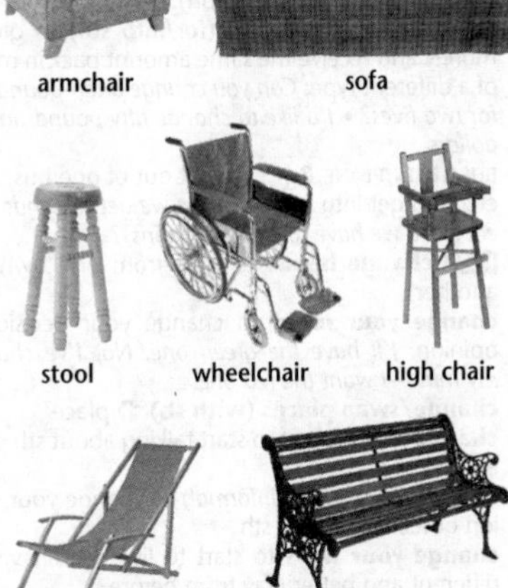

your questions to the chair. **3** [C] the position of being in charge of a department in a university: *She holds the chair of economics at London University.*

chair[2] /tʃeə(r)/ *verb* [T] to be the chairperson of a meeting: *Who's chairing today's meeting?*

🔑 **chairman** /ˈtʃeəmən/, **chairwoman** /ˈtʃeəwʊmən/, **chairperson** /ˈtʃeəpɜːsn/ (*pl* -persons) *noun* [C] (*pl* -men /-mən/, -women /-wɪmɪn/) **1** a person who controls a meeting **2** the head of a company or other organization ▶ **chairmanship** *noun* [sing]

chalet /ˈʃæleɪ/ *noun* [C] a wooden house, especially one built in a mountain area or used by people on holiday

chalk[1] /tʃɔːk/ *noun* **1** [U] a type of soft white rock: *chalk cliffs* **2** [C,U] a small stick of soft white or coloured rock that is used for writing or drawing

chalk[2] /tʃɔːk/ *verb* [I,T] to write or draw sth with chalk: *Somebody had chalked a message on the wall.*
PHR V **chalk sth up** to succeed in getting sth: *The team has chalked up five wins this summer.*

chalkboard /ˈtʃɔːkbɔːd/ (*AmE*) = **blackboard**

🔑 **challenge**[1] /ˈtʃælɪndʒ/ *noun* [C] **1** something new and difficult that forces you to make a lot of effort: *Rob found his new job an exciting challenge.* ◆ *The school will have to* **face** *many* **challenges** *in the coming year.* ◆ *How will this government* **meet the challenge** *of rising unemployment?* **2** **a challenge (to sb) (to do sth)** an invitation from sb to fight, play, argue, etc. against them: *The school team accepted the challenge and fixed a match for the following week.*

🔑 **challenge**[2] /ˈtʃælɪndʒ/ *verb* [T] **1** to question if sth is true, right, etc. or not: *She hates anyone challenging her authority.* **2** **challenge sb (to sth/to do sth)** to invite sb to fight, play, argue, etc. against you: *They've challenged us to a football match this Saturday.*

challenger /ˈtʃælɪndʒə(r)/ *noun* [C] a person who invites you to take part in a competition, because they want to win a title or position that you hold

challenging /ˈtʃælɪndʒɪŋ/ *adj* forcing you to make a lot of effort: *a challenging job*

🔑 **chamber** /ˈtʃeɪmbə(r)/ *noun* [C] **1** an organization that makes important decisions, or the room or building where it meets: *a council chamber* ◆ *Parliament consists of an upper chamber and a lower chamber.* **2** a room that is used for a particular purpose: *a burial chamber* **3** a closed space in the body, a machine, etc: *the four chambers of the heart*

chambermaid /ˈtʃeɪmbəmeɪd/ *noun* [C] a woman whose job is to clean and tidy hotel bedrooms

ˈ**chamber music** *noun* [U] a type of **classical music** (= traditional Western music) that is written for a small group of instruments

chameleon /kəˈmiːliən/ *noun* [C] a small **lizard** (= an animal with four legs, dry skin and a long tail) that can change colour according to its surroundings

champagne /ʃæmˈpeɪn/ *noun* [U,C] a French white wine which has a lot of bubbles in it and is often very expensive

champion[1] /ˈtʃæmpiən/ *noun* [C] **1** a person, team, etc. that has won a competition: *a world champion* ◆ *a champion swimmer* **2** a person who speaks and fights for a particular group, idea, etc: *a champion of free speech*

champion[2] /ˈtʃæmpiən/ *verb* [T] to support or fight for a particular group or idea: *to champion the cause of human rights*

championship /ˈtʃæmpiənʃɪp/ *noun* [C, often plural] a competition or series of competitions to find the best player or team in a sport or game: *the World Hockey Championships*

🔑 **chance**[1] /tʃɑːns/ *noun* **1** [C] **a chance of (doing) sth; a chance (that …)** a possibility: *Is there any chance of getting tickets for tonight's concert?* ◆ *I think we* **stand a** *good* **chance** *of winning the competition.* ◆ *I think there's a good chance that she'll be the next team manager.* ◆ *to have a slim/an outside chance of success* **2** [C] **chance (of doing sth/to do sth)** an opportunity: *If somebody invited me to America, I'd jump at the chance* (= accept with enthusiasm). ◆ *Be quiet and* **give** *her* **a chance** *to explain.* ◆ *I think you should tell him now. You may not* **get** *another* **chance**.
➲ note at **occasion** **3** [C] a risk: *We may lose some money but we'll just have to take that chance.* ◆ *Fasten your seat belt—you shouldn't take (any) chances.* ◆ *I didn't want to* **take a chance on** *anyone seeing*

me, so I closed the curtains. **4** [U] luck; the way that some things happen without any cause that you can see or understand: *We have to plan every detail—I don't want to* ***leave*** *anything* ***to chance.*** ◆ *We met* ***by chance*** (= we had not planned to meet) *as I was walking down the street.*

IDM **by any chance** (used for asking sth politely) perhaps or possibly: *Are you, by any chance, going into town this afternoon?*

the chances are (that)... (*informal*) it is probable that ...: *The chances are that it will rain tomorrow.*

no chance (*informal*) there is no possibility of that happening: *'Perhaps your mother will give you the money.' 'No chance!'*

on the off chance in the hope that sth might happen, although it is not very likely: *I didn't think you'd be at home, but I just called in on the off chance.*

chance² /tʃɑːns/ *verb* **1** [T] (*informal*) chance sth/ doing sth to risk sth: *It might be safe to leave the car here, but I'm not going to* ***chance it.*** **2** [I] (*formal*) chance to do sth to do sth without planning or trying to do it: *I chanced to see the letter on his desk.*

chance³ /tʃɑːns/ *adj* [only *before* a noun] not planned: *a chance meeting*

chancellor /ˈtʃɑːnsələ(r)/ *noun* [C] **1** the head of the government in some countries: *the German chancellor* **2** (also ˌChancellor of the Exˈchequer) (*BrE*) the government minister who makes decisions about taxes and government spending

chandelier /ˌʃændəˈlɪə(r)/ *noun* [C] a large round frame with many branches for lights or **candles** (= tall sticks that you burn to give light), that hangs from the ceiling and is decorated with small pieces of glass

change¹ /tʃeɪndʒ/ *verb*

➤BECOME/MAKE DIFFERENT **1** [I,T] to become different or to make sb/sth different: *This town has changed a lot since I was young.* ◆ *Our plans have changed—we leave in the morning.* ◆ *His lottery win has not changed him at all.* **SYN** **alter** **2** [I,T] change (sb/ sth) to/into sth; change (from A) (to/into B) to become a different thing; to make sb/sth take a different form: *to change from a caterpillar into a butterfly* ◆ *They changed the spare bedroom into a study. The traffic lights changed from green to red.*

➤REPLACE **3** [T] change sth (for sth) to take, have or use sth instead of sth else: *Could I change this shirt for a larger size?* ◆ *to change jobs* ◆ *to change a wheel on a car* ◆ *to change direction* ◆ *Can I change my appointment from Wednesday to Thursday?*

➤EXCHANGE **4** [T] [used with a plural noun] to change sth (with sb) to exchange sth with sb, so that you have what they had, and they have what you had: *The teams change ends at half-time.* ◆ *If you want to sit by the window I'll change seats with you.* **SYN** **swap**

➤CLOTHES **5** [I,T] change (out of sth) (into sth) to take off your clothes and put different ones on: *He's changed his shoes.* ◆ *I had a shower and changed before going out.* ◆ *She changed out of her work clothes and into a clean dress.*

HELP **Get changed** is a common expression meaning 'to change your clothes': *You can get changed in the bedroom.*

➤CLEAN THINGS **6** [T] to put clean things onto sb/sth: *The baby's nappy needs changing.* ◆ *to change the bed* (= to put clean sheets on)

➤MONEY **7** [T] change sth (for/into sth) to give sb money and receive the same amount back in money of a different type: *Can you change a ten-pound note for two fives?* ◆ *I'd like to change fifty pounds into US dollars.*

➤BUS/TRAIN/PLANE **8** [I,T] to get out of one bus, train, etc. and get into another: *Can we get to London direct or do we have to change (trains)?*

IDM **change hands** to pass from one owner to another

change your mind to change your decision or opinion: *I'll have the green one. No, I've changed my mind—I want the red one.*

change/swap places (with sb) ➲ **place¹**

change the subject to start talking about sth different

change your tune (*informal*) to change your opinion or feelings about sth

change your ways to start to live or behave in a different and better way from before

chop and change ➲ **chop¹**

PHR V **change over (from sth) (to sth)** to stop doing or using one thing and start doing or using sth else: *The theatre has changed over to a new booking system.*

change² /tʃeɪndʒ/ *noun* **1** [C,U] change (in/to sth) the process of becoming or making sth different: *There was little change in the patient's condition overnight.* ◆ *After two hot summers, people were talking about a change in the climate.* **2** [C] a change (of sth) something that you take, have or use instead of sth else: *We must notify the bank of our change of address.* ◆ *I packed my toothbrush and a change of clothes.* **3** [U] the money that you get back if you pay more than the amount sth costs: *If a postcard costs 60p and you pay with a pound coin, you will get 40p change.* **4** [U] coins of low value: *He needs some change for the phone.* ◆ *Have you got change for a twenty-pound note?* (= coins or notes of lower value that together make 20 pounds) ➲ note at **cash**

IDM **a change for the better/worse** a person, thing or situation that is better/worse than the one before

a change of heart a change in your opinion or the way that you feel

for a change in order to do sth different from usual: *I usually cycle to work, but today I decided to walk for a change.*

make a change used to say that an activity is enjoyable or pleasant because it is different from what you usually do

changeable /ˈtʃeɪndʒəbl/ *adj* likely to change; often changing: *English weather is very changeable.*

changeover /ˈtʃeɪndʒəʊvə(r)/ *noun* [C] a change from one system to another

ˈ**changing room** *noun* [C] a room for changing clothes in, for example before or after playing sport ➲ look at **fitting room**

channel[1] /ˈtʃænl/ *noun* [C] **1** a TV station: *Which channel is the film on?* ➲ look at **station** **2** a band of radio waves used for sending out radio or TV programmes: *digital/satellite channels* **3** a way or route along which news, information, etc. is sent: *a channel of communication* ◆ *You have to order new equipment through the official channels.* **4** an open passage along which liquids can flow: *drainage channels in the rice fields* **5** the part of a river, sea, etc. which is deep enough for boats to pass through **6 the Channel** (also **the ˌEnglish ˈChannel**) the sea between England and France: *a cross-channel ferry*

channel[2] /ˈtʃænl/ *verb* [T] (**channelling; channelled**, (*AmE* also) **channeling; channeled**) to make sth move along a particular path or route: *Water is channelled from the river to the fields.* ◆ (*figurative*) *You should channel your energies into something constructive.*

the ˌChannel ˈTunnel *noun* [sing] the tunnel under the sea that connects England and France

chant[1] /tʃɑːnt/ *noun* **1** [C] a word or phrase that is sung or shouted many times: *A chant of 'we are the champions' went round the stadium.* **2** [C,U] a religious song with only a few notes that are repeated many times

chant[2] /tʃɑːnt/ *verb* [I,T] to sing or shout a word or phrase many times: *The protesters marched by, chanting slogans.*

chaos /ˈkeɪɒs/ *noun* [U] a state of great confusion and lack of order: *The country was* ***in chaos*** *after the war.* ◆ *The heavy snow has* ***caused chaos*** *on the roads.*

chaotic /keɪˈɒtɪk/ *adj* in a state of **chaos**: *With no one in charge the situation became chaotic.*

chap /tʃæp/ *noun* [C] (*especially BrE old-fashioned informal*) a man or boy

chapel /ˈtʃæpl/ *noun* [C,U] a small building or room that is used by some Christians as a church or for prayer: *a Methodist chapel*

chaperone /ˈʃæpərəʊn/ *noun* [C] in the past, an older person, usually a woman, who went to public places with a young woman who was not married, to look after her and to make sure that she behaved correctly ▶ **chaperone** *verb* [T]

chaplain /ˈtʃæplɪn/ *noun* [C] a Christian priest who is responsible for the religious needs of people in prison, hospital, the army, etc. ➲ look at **priest**

chapter /ˈtʃæptə(r)/ *noun* [C] (*abbr* **ch**) one of the parts into which a book is divided: *Please read Chapter 2 for homework.* ◆ (*figurative*) *The last few years have been a difficult chapter in the country's history.*

character /ˈkærəktə(r)/ *noun*

➤QUALITIES **1** [C,U] the qualities that make sb/sth different from other people or things; the nature of sb/sth: *The new shopping centre has changed the character of the town.* ◆ *Although they are twins, their characters are quite different.* ◆ *These two songs are very different* ***in character.*** **2** [U] strong personal qualities: *The match developed into a test of character rather than just physical strength.* **3** [U] qualities that make sb/sth interesting: *Modern houses often seem to lack character.*

➤GOOD OPINION **4** [U] the good opinion that people have of you: *The article was a vicious attack on the president's character.*

➤PERSON **5** [C] (*informal*) an interesting or amusing person; a strange or an unpleasant person: *Neil's quite a character—he's always making us laugh.* ◆ *I saw a suspicious-looking character outside the bank, so I called the police.* **6** [C] a person in a book, story, etc: *The main character in the film is a boy who meets an alien.*

➤SYMBOL/LETTER **7** [C] a letter or sign that you use when you are writing or printing: *Chinese characters*

IDM **in/out of character** typical/not typical of sb/sth: *Emma's rude reply was completely out of character.*

characteristic[1] /ˌkærəktəˈrɪstɪk/ *adj* **characteristic of (sb/sth)** very typical of sb/sth: *The flat landscape is characteristic of this part of the country.* OPP **uncharacteristic** ▶ **characteristically** /-kli/ *adv*: *'No' he said, in his characteristically direct manner.*

characteristic[2] /ˌkærəktəˈrɪstɪk/ *noun* [C] a **characteristic of (sb/sth)** a quality that is typical of sb/sth and that makes them or it different from other people or things: *The chief characteristic of fish is that they live in water.*

characterize (also **-ise**) /ˈkærəktəraɪz/ *verb* [T] (*formal*) **1** [often passive] to be typical of sb/sth: *the tastes that characterize Indian cooking* **2 characterize sb/sth (as sth)** to describe what sb/sth is like: *The president characterized the meeting as friendly and positive.*

charade /ʃəˈrɑːd/ *noun* **1** [C] a situation or an event that is clearly false but in which people pretend to do or be sth: *They pretend to be friends but it's all a charade. Everyone knows they hate each other.* **2 charades** [U] a party game in which people try to guess the title of a book, film, etc. that one person must represent using actions but not words

charcoal /ˈtʃɑːkəʊl/ *noun* [U] a black substance that is produced from burned wood. It can be used for drawing or as a fuel.

charge[1] /tʃɑːdʒ/ *noun*

➤MONEY **1** [C,U] the price that you must pay for sth: *The hotel makes a small charge for changing currency.* ◆ *We deliver* ***free of charge****.* ➲ note at **price**

➤CRIME **2** [C,U] a statement that says that sb has done sth illegal or bad: *He was arrested* ***on a charge of*** *murder.* ◆ *She was released* ***without charge****.* ◆ *The writer dismissed the charge that his books were childish.*

➤RESPONSIBILITY **3** [U] a position of control over sb/sth; responsibility for sb/sth: *Who is* ***in charge of*** *the school while Mrs Webb's away?* ◆ *The assistant manager had to* ***take charge of*** *the team when the manager resigned.*

➤ELECTRICITY **4** [C] the amount of electricity that is put into a battery or carried by a substance: *a positive/negative charge*

➤ATTACK **5** [C] a sudden attack where sb/sth runs straight at sb/sth else: *He led the charge down the field.*

IDM bring/press charges (against sb) to formally accuse sb of a crime so that there can be a trial in a court of law

reverse the charges ➲ **reverse**[1]

C

🔑 **charge**[2] /tʃɑːdʒ/ *verb* **1** [T,I] **charge (sb/sth) for** sth to ask sb to pay a particular amount of money: *We charge £65 per night for a single room.* ◆ *They forgot to charge us for the drinks.* ◆ *Do you charge for postage and packing?* ➲ look at **overcharge 2** [T] **charge sb (with sth)** to accuse sb officially of doing sth which is against the law: *Three men have been charged with attempted robbery.* **3** [I,T] to run straight at sb/sth, or in a particular direction, in an aggressive or noisy way: *The bull put its head down ready to charge (us).* ◆ *The children charged into the room.* **4** [T] to put electricity into sth: *to charge a battery* ➲ look at **recharge**

IDM charge/pay the earth ➲ **earth**[1]

charger /ˈtʃɑːdʒə(r)/ *noun* [C] a piece of equipment for loading a battery with electricity: *a mobile phone charger*

chariot /ˈtʃæriət/ *noun* [C] an open vehicle with two wheels that was pulled by a horse or horses in ancient times

charisma /kəˈrɪzmə/ *noun* [U] a powerful personal quality that some people have to attract and influence other people: *The president is not very clever, but he has great charisma.* ▶ **charismatic** /ˌkærɪzˈmætɪk/ *adj*

charitable /ˈtʃærətəbl/ *adj* **1** connected with a charity **2** kind; generous: *Some people accused him of lying, but a more charitable explanation was that he had made a mistake.*

🔑 **charity** /ˈtʃærəti/ *noun* (*pl* **charities**) **1** [C,U] an organization that collects money to help people who are poor, sick, etc. or to do work that is useful to society: *We cycled round Africa to* ***raise money for charity***. ➲ note at **money 2** [U] kindness towards other people: *to act out of charity*

ˈcharity shop *noun* [C] a shop that sells clothes, books, etc. given by people to make money for charity

charlatan /ˈʃɑːlətən/ *noun* [C] a person who pretends to have knowledge or skills that they do not really have

charm[1] /tʃɑːm/ *noun* **1** [C,U] a quality that pleases and attracts people: *The charm of the island lies in its unspoilt beauty.* ◆ *Alison still finds it hard to resist Frank's charms.* **2** [C] something that you wear because you believe it will bring you good luck: *a lucky charm* ➲ picture at **jewellery**

charm[2] /tʃɑːm/ *verb* [T] **1** to please and attract sb: *Her drawings have charmed children all over the world.* **2** to protect sb/sth as if by magic: *He has led a charmed life, surviving serious illness and a plane crash.*

charming /ˈtʃɑːmɪŋ/ *adj* very pleasing or attractive: *a charming old house* ▶ **charmingly** *adv*

charred /tʃɑːd/ *adj* burnt black by fire

🔑 **chart**[1] /tʃɑːt/ *noun* **1** [C] a drawing which shows information in the form of a diagram, etc: *a temperature chart* ◆ *This chart shows the company's sales for this year.* ➲ look at **pie chart**, **flow chart 2** [C] a map of the sea or the sky: *navigation charts* **3 the charts** [pl] an official list of the songs or CDs, etc. that have sold the most in a particular week: *The album went straight into the charts at number 1.*

🔑 **chart**[2] /tʃɑːt/ *verb* [T] **1** to follow or record sth carefully and in detail: *This TV series charts the history of the country since independence.* **2** to make a map of one area of the sea or sky: *Cook charted the coast of New Zealand in 1768.*

charter[1] /ˈtʃɑːtə(r)/ *noun* [C,U] **1** a written statement of the rights, beliefs and purposes of an organization or a particular group of people: *The club's charter does not permit women to become members.* **2** the renting of a ship, plane, etc. for a particular purpose or for a particular group of people: *a charter airline*

charter[2] /ˈtʃɑːtə(r)/ *verb* [T] to rent a ship, plane, etc. for a particular purpose or for a particular group of people: *As there was no regular service to the island we had to charter a boat.*

chartered /ˈtʃɑːtəd/ *adj* [only *before* a noun] (used about people in certain professions) fully trained; having passed all the necessary exams: *a chartered accountant*

ˈcharter flight *noun* [C] a flight in which all seats are paid for by a travel company and then sold to their customers, usually at a lower price than normal: *Is it a charter flight or a scheduled flight?*

🔑 **chase**[1] /tʃeɪs/ *verb* **1** [I,T] **chase (after) sb/sth** to run after sb/sth in order to catch them or it: *The dog chased the cat up a tree.* ◆ *The police car chased after the stolen van.* **2** [I] to run somewhere fast: *The kids were chasing around the park.*

🔑 **chase**[2] /tʃeɪs/ *noun* [C] the act of following sb/sth in order to catch them or it: *an exciting car chase*

IDM give chase to begin to run after sb/sth in order to try to catch them or it: *The robber ran off and the policeman gave chase.*

chasm /ˈkæzəm/ *noun* [C] **1** a deep hole in the ground **2** a wide difference of feelings, interests, etc. between two people or groups

chassis /ˈʃæsi/ *noun* [C] (*pl* **chassis** /-siz/) the metal frame of a vehicle onto which the other parts fit

chaste /tʃeɪst/ *adj* (*old-fashioned*) **1** not having sex with anyone; only having sex with your husband/wife **2** not involving thoughts and feelings about sex: *a chaste kiss on the cheek* ▶ **chastity** /ˈtʃæstəti/ *noun* [U]

chastise /tʃæˈstaɪz/ *verb* [T] (*formal*) **chastise sb (for sth/for doing sth)** to criticize or punish sb for doing sth wrong ▶ **chastisement** *noun* [U]

🔑 **chat**[1] /tʃæt/ *verb* [I] (**chatting**; **chatted**) **chat (with/to sb) (about sth) 1** to talk to sb in an informal, friendly way: *The two grandmothers sat chatting about the old days.* ◆ *Helen chats away for hours on the phone to her friends.* **2** to exchange messages with other people on the Internet, especially in a chat room: *He's been on the computer all morning, chatting with his friends.*

PHR V **chat sb up** (*BrE informal*) to talk to sb in a friendly way because you are sexually attracted to them

chat² /tʃæt/ *noun* [C,U] **1** a friendly informal conversation: *I'll **have a chat** with Jim about the arrangements.* **2** communication between people on the Internet: *Fans are invited to an online chat.* ♦ *Internet chat services*

ˈchat room *noun* [C] an area on the Internet where you can join in a discussion ➲ note at **Internet**

TOPIC

Chat room

You can take part in an **online discussion** in a **chat room** by **posting a message** or **following a thread** (= adding your comments). You can use chat rooms to communicate with people that share your interests. **Online chat** is a way of communicating by exchanging messages with people in the same chat room as you **in real time** (= at the same time as the messages are sent). When you take part in online chat, you can sometimes use **webcams** (= video cameras connected to the Internet) to see other people in the chat room. Chat rooms usually have rules that their users should follow. In some chat rooms **moderators** check that the comments are appropriate and respond to complaints. Messages that people deliberately send to make other users angry are called **trolls**.

ˈchat show *noun* [C] a TV or radio programme on which well-known people are invited to talk about themselves

chatter /ˈtʃætə(r)/ *verb* [I] **1** to talk quickly or for a long time about sth unimportant: *The children were all laughing and chattering excitedly.* **2** (used about your teeth) to knock together because you are cold or frightened ▶ **chatter** *noun* [U]

chatty /ˈtʃæti/ *adj* (**chattier**; **chattiest**) **1** talking a lot in a friendly way **2** in an informal style: *a chatty letter*

chauffeur /ˈʃəʊfə(r)/ *noun* [C] a person whose job is to drive a car for sb else: *a chauffeur-driven limousine* ▶ **chauffeur** *verb* [T]

chauvinism /ˈʃəʊvɪnɪzəm/ *noun* [U] **1** the belief that your country is better than all others **2** (also **male ˈchauvinism**) the belief that men are better than women ▶ **chauvinist** /-ɪst/ *noun* [C]

cheap¹ /tʃiːp/ *adj* (**cheaper**; **cheapest**) **1** low in price, costing little money: *Oranges are cheap at the moment.* ♦ *Computers are getting cheaper all the time.* SYN **inexpensive** OPP **dear**, **expensive** **2** charging low prices: *a cheap hotel/restaurant* SYN **inexpensive** OPP **expensive** **3** low in price and quality and therefore not attractive: *The clothes in that shop look cheap.*

IDM **dirt cheap** ➲ **dirt**

cheap² /tʃiːp/ *adv* (*informal*) for a low price: *I got this coat cheap in the sale.*

IDM **be going cheap** (*informal*) be on sale at a lower price than usual

cheapen /ˈtʃiːpən/ *verb* [T] **1** to make sb lose respect for himself or herself: *She felt cheapened by their treatment of her.* **2** to make sth lower in price **3** to make sth appear to have less value: *The film was accused of cheapening human life.*

cheaply /ˈtʃiːpli/ *adv* for a low price: *You can travel quickly and cheaply all over the town by bus.*

cheat¹ /tʃiːt/ *verb* **1** [T] to trick sb, or to make them believe sth that is not true, especially when that person trusts you: *The shopkeeper cheated customers by giving them too little change.* **2** [I] **cheat (at sth)** to act in a dishonest or unfair way in order to get an advantage for yourself: *Paul was caught cheating in the exam.* ♦ *to cheat at cards* **3** [I] **cheat (on sb)** to not be faithful to your husband, wife or regular partner by having a secret sexual relationship with sb else

PHR V **cheat sb (out) of sth** to take sth from sb in a dishonest or unfair way: *They tried to cheat the old lady out of her savings.*

cheat² /tʃiːt/ *noun* [C] a person who cheats: *The man's a liar and a cheat!*

check¹ /tʃek/ *verb* **1** [I,T] **check (sth) (for sth)** to examine or test sth in order to make sure that it is safe or correct, in good condition, etc: *Check your work for mistakes before you hand it in.* ♦ *The doctor X-rayed me to check for broken bones.* **2** [I,T] **check (sth) (with sb)** to find out if sth/sb is there, correct or true, or if sth is how you think it is: *You'd better check with Tim that it's OK to borrow his bike.* ♦ *I'll phone and check what time the bus leaves.* ♦ *I need to check my email.* **3** [T] to stop or make sb/sth stop or go more slowly: *She almost told her boss what she thought of him, but checked herself in time.* ♦ *Phil checked his pace as he didn't want to tire too early.* **4** [T] (*AmE*) = **tick¹**(2)

PHR V **check in (at …)**; **check into …** to go to a desk in a hotel or an airport and tell an official that you have arrived: *Passengers should check in two hours before their departure time.* ➲ note at **hotel**, **plane**

check sth off to mark names or items on a list: *The boxes were all checked off as they were unloaded.*

check (up) on sb/sth to find out how sb/sth is: *We call my grandmother every evening to check up on her.*

check out (of …) to pay for your room, etc. and leave a hotel ➲ note at **hotel**: *What time do we need to check out in the morning?*

check sb/sth out **1** to find out more information about sb/sth, especially to find out if sth is true or not: *We need to check out these rumours of possible pay cuts.* **2** (*slang*) to look at sb/sth, especially to find out if you like them or it: *I'm going to check out that new club tonight.*

check up on sb/sth to make sure that sb/sth is working correctly, behaving well, etc., especially if you think he/she/it is not: *My mother's always checking up on me to see if I've done my homework.*

EXAM TIP

Checking your work

Before the exam, practise checking your work before you hand it in. Read it through several times: once to look at spellings, once to check that you have used the correct grammatical constructions and that the forms of the verbs and plurals of nouns are correct, and once to make sure that you have not missed anything out that you wanted to say. Use your dictionary to help you check. Make a note of useful points and add them to your **last-minute list** (= a list that you check just before your exam).

C

check[2] /tʃek/ *noun* **1** [C] **a check (on sth)** a close look at sth to make sure that it is safe, correct, in good condition, etc: *We* ***carry out/do*** *regular* ***checks*** *on our products to make sure that they are of high quality.* ♦ *I don't go to games, but I like to* ***keep a check*** *on my team's results.* **2** [C,U] a pattern of squares, often of different colours: *a check jacket* ♦ *a pattern of blue and red checks* **3** [U] the position in **chess** (= a game for two players played on a black and white board) in which a player's king (= the most important piece) can be directly attacked by the other player's pieces: *There, you're in check.* ➲ look at **checkmate** **4** (*AmE*) = **bill**[1](2) **5** (*AmE*) = **cheque** **6** (*AmE*) = **tick**[2](1) ➲ look at **rain check**
IDM **hold/keep sth in check** to keep sth under control so that it does not get worse: *government measures to keep inflation in check*

checkbook (*AmE*) = **chequebook**

checked /tʃekt/ *adj* with a pattern of squares: *a red-and-white checked tablecloth* ➲ picture on **page P1**

checkers /ˈtʃekəz/ (*AmE*) = **draught**[1](2)

ˈcheck-in *noun* [C,U] **1** the place where you go first when you arrive at an airport to show your ticket, etc. **2** the act of checking in at an airport: *Our check-in time is 10.30 a.m.*

ˈchecking account (*AmE*) = **current account**

checklist /ˈtʃeklɪst/ *noun* [C] a list of things that you must remember to do

ˈcheck mark (*AmE*) = **tick**[2](1)

checkmate /ˌtʃekˈmeɪt/ (also **mate**) *noun* [U] the position in **chess** (= a game for two players played on a black and white board) in which one player cannot prevent their king (= the most important piece) from being captured and so loses the game ➲ look at **check**[2](3)

checkout /ˈtʃekaʊt/ *noun* [C] the place in a large shop or on a website where you pay

checkpoint /ˈtʃekpɔɪnt/ *noun* [C] a place where all people and vehicles must stop and be checked: *an army checkpoint*

ˈcheck-up *noun* [C] a general medical examination to make sure that you are healthy: *to* ***go for/have*** *a check-up*

Cheddar /ˈtʃedə(r)/ *noun* [U] a type of hard yellow cheese

cheek /tʃiːk/ *noun* **1** [C] either side of the face below your eyes: *Tears rolled down her cheeks.* ➲ picture at **body** **2** [U, sing] (*BrE*) rude behaviour; lack of respect: *He's got a cheek, asking to borrow money again!*
IDM **(with) tongue in cheek** ➲ **tongue**

cheekbone /ˈtʃiːkbəʊn/ *noun* [C] the bone below your eye ➲ picture at **body**

cheeky /ˈtʃiːki/ *adj* (**cheekier**; **cheekiest**) (*BrE*) not showing respect; rude: *Don't be so cheeky! Of course I'm not fat!* ▶ **cheekily** *adv*

cheer[1] /tʃɪə(r)/ *noun* [C] a loud shout to show that you like sth or to encourage sb who is taking part in a competition, sport, etc: *The crowd* ***gave a cheer*** *when the team scored.* ➲ look at **hip**

cheer[2] /tʃɪə(r)/ *verb* **1** [I,T] to shout to show that you like sth or to encourage sb who is taking part in competition, sport, etc: *Everyone cheered the winner as he crossed the finishing line.* **2** [T] to make sb happy or to give hope: *They were all cheered by the good news.*
PHR V **cheer sb on** to shout in order to encourage sb in a race, competition, etc: *As the runners started the last lap, the crowd cheered them on.*
cheer (sb/sth) up to become or to make sb happier; to make sth look more attractive: *Cheer up! Things aren't that bad.* ♦ *A few pictures would cheer this room up a bit.*

cheerful /ˈtʃɪəfl/ *adj* **1** feeling happy; showing that you are happy: *Caroline is always very cheerful.* ♦ *a cheerful smile* **2** giving you a feeling of happiness: *walls painted in cheerful colours* ➲ note at **happy** ▶ **cheerfully** /-fəli/ *adv*: *to laugh/nod/whistle cheerfully* ▶ **cheerfulness** *noun* [U]

cheerio /ˌtʃɪəriˈəʊ/ *exclam* (*BrE informal*) goodbye: *Cheerio! See you later.*

cheerleader /ˈtʃɪəliːdə(r)/ *noun* [C] (in the US) one of a group of girls or women at a sports match who wear special uniforms and shout, dance, etc. in order to encourage people to support the players

cheers /tʃɪəz/ *exclam* (*informal*) **1** used to express good wishes before having an alcoholic drink: *'Cheers,' she said, raising her wine glass.* **2** (*BrE*) goodbye **3** (*BrE*) thank you

cheery /ˈtʃɪəri/ *adj* (**cheerier**; **cheeriest**) happy and smiling: *a cheery remark/wave/smile* ▶ **cheerily** *adv*

cheese /tʃiːz/ *noun* **1** [U] a type of food made from milk. Cheese is usually white or yellow in colour and can be soft or hard: *a piece of cheese* ♦ *a cheese sandwich* ♦ *a chunk/piece/slice of cheese* ➲ picture on **page P16** **2** [C] a type of cheese: *a wide selection of cheeses*

cheesecake /ˈtʃiːzkeɪk/ *noun* [C,U] a type of cake that is made from soft cheese and sugar on a **pastry** (= a mixture of flour, fat and water) or biscuit base, often with fruit on top

cheesy /ˈtʃiːzi/ *adj* (**cheesier**; **cheesiest**) (*informal*) of low quality and without style: *an incredibly cheesy love song*

cheetah /ˈtʃiːtə/ *noun* [C] a large wild cat with black spots that can run very fast ➲ picture at **lion**

chef /ʃef/ *noun* [C] a professional cook, especially the head cook in a hotel, restaurant, etc.

chemical¹ /ˈkemɪkl/ *adj* connected with chemistry; involving changes to the structure of a substance: *a chemical reaction* ♦ *the chemical industry* ♦ *chemical weapons/warfare* ▸ **chemically** /-kli/ *adv*

chemical² /ˈkemɪkl/ *noun* [C] a substance that is used or produced in a chemical process: *Sulphuric acid is a dangerous chemical.*

chemist /ˈkemɪst/ *noun* [C] **1** (also **pharmacist**; *AmE* also **druggist**) a person who prepares and sells medicines **2 the chemist's** (*AmE* **drugstore**) [sing] a shop that sells medicines, soap, camera film, etc: *I got my tablets from the chemist's.* ♦ *Take this prescription to the chemist's.* **3** a person who studies chemistry: *My daughter is a research chemist.*

chemistry /ˈkemɪstri/ *noun* [U] **1** the scientific study of the structure of substances and what happens to them in different conditions or when mixed with each other: *We did an experiment in the chemistry lesson.* ➲ note at **science 2** the structure of a particular substance: *The patient's blood chemistry was monitored regularly.*

cheque (*AmE* **check**) /tʃek/ *noun* [C,U] a piece of paper printed by a bank that you sign and use to pay for things: *She wrote out a cheque for £50.* ♦ *I went to the bank to* ***cash a cheque***. ♦ *Can I* ***pay by cheque***? ➲ picture at **money**

chequebook (*AmE* **checkbook**) /ˈtʃekbʊk/ *noun* [C] a book of cheques ➲ picture at **money**

ˈcheque card *noun* [C] (*BrE*) a small plastic card that you show when you pay with a cheque to prove that your bank will pay the amount on the cheque ➲ look at **cash card, credit card, debit card**

cherish /ˈtʃerɪʃ/ *verb* [T] **1** to love sb/sth and look after them or it carefully: *The ring was her most cherished possession.* **2** to keep a thought, feeling, etc. in your mind and think about it often: *She cherished the memory of those days in Paris.*

cherry /ˈtʃeri/ *noun* [C] (*pl* **cherries**) **1** a small round black or red fruit that has a stone inside it ➲ picture on **page P14 2** (also ˈ**cherry tree**) the tree that produces **cherries**

cherub /ˈtʃerəb/ *noun* [C] (in art) a type of **angel** (= a being who is believed to live in heaven), shown as an attractive child with wings ▸ **cherubic** /tʃəˈruːbɪk/ *adj* (*formal*): *a cherubic face* (= looking round and innocent, like a small child's)

chess /tʃes/ *noun* [U] a game for two people that is played on a **chessboard** (= a board with 64 black and white squares). Each player has 16 pieces which can be moved according to fixed rules: *Can you* ***play chess***?

chest /tʃest/ *noun* [C] **1** the top part of the front of your body: *a muscular chest* ♦ *a chest infection* ➲ picture at **body 2** a large strong box that is used for storing or carrying things: *We packed all our books into a chest.* ♦ *a treasure chest*

chess

IDM **get sth off your chest** (*informal*) to talk about sth that you have been thinking or worrying about

chestnut /ˈtʃesnʌt/ *noun* [C] **1** (also ˈ**chestnut tree**) a tree with large leaves that produces smooth brown nuts in shells with sharp points on the outside **2** a smooth brown nut from the **chestnut** tree. You can eat some types of **chestnut**. ➲ look at **horse chestnut** ➲ picture at **nut**

ˌchest of ˈdrawers (*AmE* **dresser**) *noun* [C] a piece of furniture with drawers in it that is used for storing clothes, etc. ➲ picture on **page P8**

chew /tʃuː/ *verb* [I,T] **1** to break up food in your mouth with your teeth before you swallow it: *You should chew your food thoroughly.* **2 chew (on) sth** to bite sth continuously with the back teeth: *The dog was chewing on a bone.*

ˈchewing gum (also **gum**) *noun* [U] a sweet sticky substance that you **chew** in your mouth but do not swallow ➲ look at **bubblegum**

chewy /ˈtʃuːi/ *adj* (**chewier**; **chewiest**) (used about food) difficult to break up with your teeth before it can be swallowed: *chewy meat/toffee*

chic /ʃiːk/ *adj* fashionable and elegant SYN **stylish** ▸ **chic** *noun* [U]

chick /tʃɪk/ *noun* [C] **1** a baby bird, especially a young chicken ➲ picture at **chicken 2** (*old-fashioned, slang*) a way of referring to a young woman

chickens

chicken¹ /ˈtʃɪkɪn/ *noun* **1** [C] a bird that people often keep for its eggs and its meat: *free-range chickens* **2** [U] the meat of this bird: *chicken soup*

MORE Chicken is the general word for the bird and its meat. A male chicken is called a **cock** (*US* **rooster**), a female is called a **hen** and a young bird is called a **chick**.

C

IDM Don't count your chickens (before they're hatched) ➲ **count**[1]

chicken[2] /ˈtʃɪkɪn/ *verb*
PHR V chicken out (of sth) (*informal*) to decide not to do sth because you are afraid: *Mark chickened out of swimming across the river when he saw how far it was.*

chickenpox /ˈtʃɪkɪnpɒks/ *noun* [U] a disease, especially of children. When you have **chickenpox** you feel very hot and get red spots on your skin that make you want to scratch.

chickpea /ˈtʃɪk piː/ (*AmE usually* **garbanzo**) *noun* [C] a round brown seed that can be dried and used in cooking: *leek and chickpea stew*

chicory /ˈtʃɪkəri/ (*AmE* **endive**) *noun* [U] a small pale green plant with bitter leaves that can be eaten cooked or not cooked

⚷ **chief**[1] /tʃiːf/ *adj* [only *before* a noun] **1** most important; main: *One of the chief reasons for his decision was money.* **2** of the highest level or position: *the chief executive of a company*

⚷ **chief**[2] /tʃiːf/ *noun* [C] **1** the person who has command or control over an organization: *the chief of police* **2** the leader of a **tribe** (= a group of people with the same language and customs): *African tribal chiefs*

chiefly /ˈtʃiːfli/ *adv* mostly: *His success was due chiefly to hard work.* **SYN mainly**

chiffon /ˈʃɪfɒn/ *noun* [U] a very thin, transparent type of cloth used for making clothes, etc.

chilblain /ˈtʃɪlbleɪn/ *noun* [C] a painful red area on your foot, hand, etc. that is caused by cold weather

⚷ **child** /tʃaɪld/ *noun* [C] (*pl* **children** /ˈtʃɪldrən/) **1** a young boy or girl who is not yet an adult: *A group of children were playing in the park.* ◆ *a six-year-old child* **2** a son or daughter of any age: *She has two children but both are married and have moved away.*

TOPIC

Children

An **only child** is a child who has no brothers or sisters. A child whose parents have died is an **orphan**. A person may **adopt** a child who is not his/her own son or daughter. A **foster child** is looked after for a certain period of time by a family that is not his/her own. If your husband or wife has children from a previous marriage, they are your **stepchildren**. Parents are responsible for **bringing up** their children (= looking after them until they are adults and teaching them how to behave).

childbirth /ˈtʃaɪldbɜːθ/ *noun* [U] the act of giving birth to a baby: *His wife died* ***in childbirth.***

childcare /ˈtʃaɪldkeə(r)/ *noun* [U] the job of looking after children, especially while the parents are at work: *Some employers provide childcare facilities.*

childhood /ˈtʃaɪldhʊd/ *noun* [C,U] the time when you are a child: *Harriet had a very unhappy childhood.* ◆ *childhood memories*

childish /ˈtʃaɪldɪʃ/ *adj* like a child **SYN immature** **OPP mature**

HELP **Childish** or **childlike?** If you say that people or their behaviour are **childlike**, you mean that they are like children in some way: *His childlike enthusiasm delighted us all.* If you say that an adult's behaviour is **childish**, you are criticizing it because you think it is silly: *Don't be so childish! You can't always have everything you want.*

▶ **childishly** *adv*

childless /ˈtʃaɪldləs/ *adj* having no children

childlike /ˈtʃaɪldlaɪk/ *adj* like a child ➲ note at **childish**

childminder /ˈtʃaɪldmaɪndə(r)/ *noun* [C] (*BrE*) a person whose job is to look after a child while his or her parents are at work ➲ look at **babysitter**

children *plural* of **child**

ˈ**children's home** *noun* [C] an institution where children live whose parents cannot look after them

chili (*AmE*) = **chilli**

chill[1] /tʃɪl/ *noun* **1** [sing] an unpleasant cold feeling: *There's a chill in the air.* ◆ (*figurative*) *A chill of fear went down my spine.* **2** [C] (*informal*) a common illness that affects your nose and throat; a cold: *to catch a chill*

chill[2] /tʃɪl/ *verb* **1** [I,T] to become or to make sb/sth colder: *Let the pudding chill for an hour in the fridge.* **2** *verb* [I] (*informal*) to spend time relaxing: *We went home and chilled in front of the television.*
PHR V chill out (*informal*) to relax and stop feeling angry or nervous about sth: *Sit down and chill out!*

chilli (*AmE* **chili**) /ˈtʃɪli/ *noun* [C,U] (*pl* **chillies**, *AmE* **chilies**) a small green or red vegetable that has a very strong hot taste: *chilli powder* ➲ picture on **page P15**

chilling /ˈtʃɪlɪŋ/ *adj* frightening: *a chilling ghost story*

chilly /ˈtʃɪli/ *adj* (**chillier**; **chilliest**) (used about the weather but also about people) too cold to be comfortable: *It's a chilly morning. You need a coat on.* ◆ *They gave us a very chilly* (= unfriendly) *reception.*

chime /tʃaɪm/ *verb* [I,T] (used about a bell or clock) to ring
PHR V chime in (with sth) (*informal*) to interrupt a conversation and add your own comments
▶ **chime** *noun* [C]

chimney /ˈtʃɪmni/ *noun* [C] a structure through which smoke or steam is carried up and out through the roof of a building: *Smoke poured out of the factory chimneys.* ➲ picture on **page P8**

ˈ**chimney pot** *noun* [C] a short wide pipe that is placed on top of a **chimney**

ˈ**chimney sweep** *noun* [C] a person whose job is to clean the inside of **chimneys** with long brushes

chimpanzee /ˌtʃɪmpænˈziː/ (also *informal* chimp /tʃɪmp/) *noun* [C] a small intelligent **ape** (= an animal that lives in hot countries and can climb trees) ➲ look at **monkey**

🔑 **chin** /tʃɪn/ *noun* [C] the part of your face below your mouth: *He sat listening, his chin resting on his hand.* ♦ *a **strong/weak/pointed chin*** ♦ *a **double chin** (= fat under sb's chin that looks like another chin)* ➲ picture at **body**

IDM (keep your) chin up (*informal*) used to tell sb to try to stay cheerful even though they are in a difficult or unpleasant situation

china /ˈtʃaɪnə/ *noun* [U] **1** white **clay** (= a type of earth) of good quality that is used for making cups, plates, etc: *a china vase* **2** cups, plates, etc. that are made from **china**

chink /tʃɪŋk/ *noun* [C] a small narrow opening: *Daylight came in through a chink between the curtains.*

chintz /tʃɪnts/ *noun* [U] a shiny cotton cloth with a printed design, usually of flowers, which is used for making curtains, covering furniture, etc.

chips (*esp AmE* **French fries**)   crisps (*AmE* **chips**)

🔑 **chip¹** /tʃɪp/ *noun* [C] **1** the place where a small piece of stone, glass, wood, etc. has broken off sth: *This dish has a chip in it.* **2** a small piece of stone, glass, wood, etc. that has broken off sth: *chips of wood* **3** (*especially AmE* ˌFrench ˈfry; fry) [usually pl] a thin piece of potato that is fried in hot fat or oil: *Would you prefer boiled potatoes or chips?* ➲ note at **fish** **4** (*AmE*) = **crisp²** **5** = **microchip** **6** a flat round piece of plastic that you use instead of money when you are playing some games

IDM have a chip on your shoulder (about sth) (*informal*) to feel angry about sth that happened a long time ago because you think it is unfair: *My dad still has a chip on his shoulder about being thrown out of school.*

chip² /tʃɪp/ *verb* [I,T] (**chipping**; **chipped**) **1** to break a small piece off the edge or surface of sth: *They chipped the paint trying to get the table through the door.* **2** (in sport) to kick or hit a ball a short distance through the air

PHR V chip in (with sth) (*informal*) **1** to interrupt when sb else is talking **2** to give some money as part of the cost of sth: *We all chipped in and bought him a present when he left.*

chip

chip   crack

chipped   **cracked**   **broken**

ˈ**chip shop** (*BrE informal* **chippy** /ˈtʃɪpi/; *pl* chippies) *noun* [C] (in Britain) a shop that cooks and sells fish and chips and other fried food to take away and eat

chiropodist /kɪˈrɒpədɪst/ (also **podiatrist**) *noun* [C] a person whose job is to look after people's feet
▶ **chiropody** (also **podiatry**) *noun* [U]

chirp /tʃɜːp/ *verb* [I] (used about small birds and some insects) to make short high sounds

chisel /ˈtʃɪzl/ *noun* [C] a tool with a sharp end that is used for cutting or shaping wood or stone ➲ picture at **tool**

chivalry /ˈʃɪvəlri/ *noun* [U] polite and kind behaviour by men which shows respect towards women
▶ **chivalrous** /ˈʃɪvlrəs/ *adj*

chives /tʃaɪvz/ *noun* [pl] the long thin leaves of a plant that tastes like onion and is used in cooking

chlorine /ˈklɔːriːn/ *noun* [U] (*symbol* Cl) a greenish-yellow gas with a strong smell, that is used for making water safe to drink or to swim in

chlorophyll /ˈklɒrəfɪl/ *noun* [U] the green substance in plants that absorbs light from the sun to help them grow

chock-a-block /ˌtʃɒk ə ˈblɒk/ *adj* (*BrE informal*) [not before a noun] completely full: *The High Street was chock-a-block with shoppers.*

chocoholic /ˌtʃɒkəˈhɒlɪk/ *noun* [C] (*informal*) a person who loves chocolate and eats a lot of it

🔑 **chocolate** /ˈtʃɒklət/ *noun* **1** [U] a sweet brown substance made from **cocoa beans** (= seeds of a tropical tree) that you can eat as a sweet or use to give flavour to food and drinks: *a bar of **milk/plain chocolate*** ♦ *a chocolate milkshake* ➲ picture at **bar** **2** [C] a small sweet that is made from or covered with chocolate: *a box of chocolates* **3** [C,U] a drink made from chocolate powder with hot milk or water: *a mug of **hot chocolate*** **4** [U] a dark brown colour

🔑 **choice¹** /tʃɔɪs/ *noun* **1** [C] a choice (between A and B) an act of choosing between two or more people or things: *David was forced to **make a choice** between moving house and losing his job.* **2** [U] the right or chance to choose: *There is a rail strike so we **have no choice** but to cancel our trip.* ♦ *to have freedom of choice* ➲ look at **option** **3** [C] a person or thing that is chosen: *Barry would be my choice as team captain.* **4** [C,U] two or more things from

which you can or must choose: *This cinema offers a choice of six different films every night.* ➲ *verb* **choose**
IDM **out of/from choice** because you want to; of your own free will: *I wouldn't have gone to London out of choice. I was sent there on business.*

C

choice² /tʃɔɪs/ *adj* (choicer; choicest) [only *before* a noun] of very good quality: *choice beef*

choir /ˈkwaɪə(r)/ *noun* [C, with sing or pl verb] a group of people who sing together in churches, schools, etc.

choke¹ /tʃəʊk/ *verb* **1** [I,T] choke (on sth) to be or to make sb unable to breathe because sth is stopping air getting into the lungs: *She was choking on a fish bone.* ◆ *The smoke choked us.* ➲ look at **strangle** **2** [T, usually passive] choke sth (up) (with sth) to fill a passage, space, etc., so that nothing can pass through: *The roads to the coast were choked with traffic.*
PHR V **choke sth back** to hide or control a strong emotion: *to choke back tears/anger*

choke² /tʃəʊk/ *noun* [C] **1** the device in a car, etc. that controls the amount of air going into the engine. If you pull out the **choke** it makes it easier to start the car. **2** an act or the sound of sb **choking**: *A tiny choke of laughter escaped her.*

cholera /ˈkɒlərə/ *noun* [U] a serious disease that causes stomach pains and **vomiting** (= bringing up food from the stomach) and can cause death. **Cholera** is most common in hot countries and is carried by water.

cholesterol /kəˈlestərɒl/ *noun* [U] a substance that is found in the blood, etc. of people and animals. Too much **cholesterol** can cause heart disease.

⚷ **choose** /tʃuːz/ *verb* [I,T] (*pt* chose /tʃəʊz/; *pp* chosen /ˈtʃəʊzn/) **1** choose (between A and/or B); choose (A) (from B); choose sb/sth as sth to decide which thing or person you want out of the ones that are available: *Choose carefully before you make a final decision.* ◆ *Amy had to choose between getting a job or going to college.* ◆ *The viewers chose this programme as their favourite.* **2** choose (to do sth) to decide or prefer to do sth: *You are free to leave whenever you choose.* ◆ *They chose to resign rather than work for the new manager.* ➲ *noun* **choice**
IDM **pick and choose** ➲ **pick¹**

choosy /ˈtʃuːzi/ *adj* (choosier; choosiest) (*informal*) (used about a person) difficult to please

⚷ **chop¹** /tʃɒp/ *verb* [T] (chopping; chopped) chop sth (up) (into sth) to cut sth into pieces with a knife, etc: *finely chopped herbs* ◆ *Chop the onions up into small pieces.*
IDM **chop and change** to change your plans or opinions several times
PHR V **chop sth down** to cut a tree, etc. at the bottom so that it falls down: *It's a shame to chop a cherry tree down.*
chop sth off (sth) to remove sth from sth by cutting it with a knife or a sharp tool: *to chop a branch off a tree*

chop² /tʃɒp/ *noun* [C] **1** a thick slice of meat with a piece of bone in it: *a pork/lamb chop* ➲ look at **steak** **2** an act of **chopping** sth: *a karate chop*

chopper /ˈtʃɒpə(r)/ (*informal*) = **helicopter**

ˈ**chopping board** *noun* [C] a piece of wood or plastic used for cutting meat or vegetables on ➲ picture at **kitchen**

choppy /ˈtʃɒpi/ *adj* (choppier; choppiest) (used about the sea) with a lot of small waves; not calm

chopsticks /ˈtʃɒpstɪks/ *noun* [pl] two thin sticks made of wood or plastic, that people use for picking up food to eat, especially in some Asian countries

choral /ˈkɔːrəl/ *adj* (used about music) that is written for or involves a **choir** (= a group of singers)

chord /kɔːd/ *noun* [C] two or more musical notes that are played at the same time

chore /tʃɔː(r)/ *noun* [C] a job that is not interesting but that you must do: *household chores*

choreograph /ˈkɒriəɡrɑːf/ *verb* [T] to design and arrange the movements of a dance ▸ **choreographer** /ˌkɒriˈɒɡrəfə(r)/ *noun* [C]

choreography /ˌkɒriˈɒɡrəfi/ *noun* [U] the arrangement of movements for a dance performance

chorus¹ /ˈkɔːrəs/ *noun* **1** [C] the part of a song that is repeated SYN **refrain** ➲ look at **verse** **2** [C] a piece of music, usually part of a larger work, that is written for a large **choir** (= a group of singers) **3** [C, with sing or pl verb] a large group of people who sing together **4** [C, with sing or pl verb] the singers and dancers in a musical show who do not play the main parts **5** [sing] a chorus of sth something that a lot of people say together: *a chorus of cheers/criticism/disapproval*

chorus² /ˈkɔːrəs/ *verb* [T] (used about a group of people) to sing or say sth together: *'That's not fair!' the children chorused.*

chose *past tense* of **choose**

chosen *past participle* of **choose**

Christ /kraɪst/ (also Jesus; Jesus ˈChrist) *noun* [sing] the man who Christians believe is the son of God and on whose ideas and beliefs the Christian religion is based

christen /ˈkrɪsn/ *verb* [T] **1** to give a person, usually a baby, a name during a Christian ceremony in which they are made a member of the Church: *The baby was christened Simon Mark.* ➲ look at **baptize** **2** to give sb/sth a name: *The area has been christened 'Britain's last wilderness'.*

christening /ˈkrɪsnɪŋ/ *noun* [C] the church ceremony in the Christian religion in which a baby is given a name ➲ look at **baptism**

Christian /ˈkrɪstʃən/ *noun* [C] a person whose religion is Christianity ▸ **Christian** *adj*

Christianity /ˌkrɪstiˈænəti/ *noun* [U] the religion that is based on the ideas taught by Jesus Christ

Christmas /ˈkrɪsməs/ *noun* [C,U] **1** ˌChristmas ˈDay a public holiday on 25 December. It is the day on which Christians celebrate the birth of Christ each year. **2** the period of time before and after 25 December: *We wish you a merry Christmas.* ◆ *Where are you spending Christmas this year?*

MORE Christmas is sometimes written as **Xmas** in informal English.

ˈChristmas card *noun* [C] a card with a picture on the front and a message inside that people send to their friends and relatives at Christmas

ˌChristmas ˈcarol = **carol**

ˌChristmas ˈcracker = **cracker(2)**

ˌChristmas ˈdinner *noun* [C,U] the traditional meal eaten on Christmas Day: *We had a traditional Christmas dinner that year, with roast turkey, Christmas pudding and all the trimmings.*

ˌChristmas ˈEve *noun* [C,U] 24 December, the day before Christmas Day

ˌChristmas ˈpudding *noun* [C,U] a sweet dish made from dried fruit and eaten hot with sauce at Christmas

ˈChristmas tree *noun* [C] a real or an artificial tree, which people bring into their homes and cover with coloured lights and decorations at Christmas

chrome /krəʊm/ (also **chromium** /ˈkrəʊmiəm/) *noun* [U] (*symbol* **Cr**) a hard shiny metal that is used for covering other metals

chromosome /ˈkrəʊməsəʊm/ *noun* [C] a part of a cell in living things that decides the sex, character, shape, etc. that a person, an animal or a plant will have

chronic /ˈkrɒnɪk/ *adj* (used about a disease or a problem) that continues for a long time: *chronic bronchitis* ◆ *There is a chronic shortage of housing in the city.* ➲ look at **acute** ▶ **chronically** /-kli/ *adv*

chronicle /ˈkrɒnɪkl/ *noun* [C, often plural] a written record of historical events describing them in the order in which they happened

chronological /ˌkrɒnəˈlɒdʒɪkl/ *adj* arranged in the order in which the events happened: *This book describes the main events in his life **in chronological order**.* ▶ **chronologically** /-kli/ *adv*

chrysalis /ˈkrɪsəlɪs/ *noun* [C] the form of a **butterfly** (= an insect with large brightly coloured wings) or a **moth** (= an insect similar to a butterfly) while it is changing into an adult inside a hard case, which is also called a chrysalis ➲ picture on **page P13**

chrysanthemum /krɪˈsænθəməm/ *noun* [C] a large garden flower which is brightly coloured and shaped like a ball

chubby /ˈtʃʌbi/ *adj* (**chubbier**; **chubbiest**) slightly fat in an attractive way: *a baby with chubby cheeks* ➲ note at **fat**

chuck /tʃʌk/ *verb* [T] (*informal*) to throw sth in a careless way: *You can chuck those old shoes in the bin.*

PHR V chuck sth in to give sth up: *He's chucked his job in because he was fed up.*

chuck sb out (of sth) to force sb to leave a place: *They were chucked out of the cinema for making too much noise.*

chuckle /ˈtʃʌkl/ *verb* [I] to laugh quietly: *Bruce chuckled to himself as he read the letter.* ▶ **chuckle** *noun* [C]

chug /tʃʌg/ *verb* [I] (**chugging**; **chugged**) to move making the sound of an engine running slowly: *The train chugged out of the station.*

chunk /tʃʌŋk/ *noun* [C] a large or thick piece of sth: *chunks of bread and cheese*

chunky /ˈtʃʌŋki/ *adj* (**chunkier**; **chunkiest**) **1** thick and heavy: *chunky jewellery* **2** (used about a person) short and strong: *He was a short man with chunky legs.* **3** (used about food) containing thick pieces: *chunky banana milkshake*

🔑 **church** /tʃɜːtʃ/ *noun* **1** [C,U] a building where Christians go to worship: *Services are held in this church every Sunday morning at 10.* ◆ *Do you go to church regularly?*

HELP Notice that when you are talking about going to a ceremony (a service) in a church you say 'in church', 'to church' or 'at church' without 'a' or '**the**': *Was Mrs Stevens at church today?*

2 Church [C] a particular group of Christians: *the Anglican/Catholic/Methodist/Church* **3 (the) Church** [sing] the ministers or the institution of the Christian religion: *the conflict between Church and State*

churchgoer /ˈtʃɜːtʃgəʊə(r)/ *noun* [C] a person who goes to church regularly

the ˌChurch of ˈEngland (*abbr* **C. of E.**) *noun* [sing] the Protestant Church, which is the official church in England, whose leader is the Queen or King ➲ look at **Anglican**

churchyard /ˈtʃɜːtʃjɑːd/ *noun* [C] the area of land that is around a church ➲ look at **cemetery**, **graveyard**

churn /tʃɜːn/ *verb* **1** [I,T] **churn (sth) (up)** to move, or to make water, mud, etc. move around violently: *The dark water churned beneath the huge ship.* ◆ *Vast crowds had churned the field into a sea of mud.* **2** [I,T] if your stomach **churns** or sth makes it **churn**, you feel sick because you are disgusted or nervous: *Reading about the murder in the newspaper made my stomach churn.* **3** [T] to make butter from milk or cream

PHR V churn sth out (*informal*) (often disapproving) to produce large numbers of sth very quickly

chute /ʃuːt/ *noun* [C] a tube or passage down which people or things can slide: *a laundry/rubbish chute* (= from the upper floors of a high building) ◆ *a water chute* (= at a swimming pool)

chutney /ˈtʃʌtni/ *noun* [U,C] a thick sweet sauce that is made from fruit or vegetables. You eat **chutney** cold with cheese or meat.

CIA /ˌsiː aɪ ˈeɪ/ *abbr* **the Central Intelligence Agency**; the US government organization that tries to discover secret information about other countries

ciabatta /tʃəˈbætə/ *noun* [U,C] a type of Italian bread made in a long flat shape; a **loaf** (= a whole piece of baked bread) of this

cider /ˈsaɪdə(r)/ *noun* [U,C] **1** (*BrE*) an alcoholic drink made from apples: *dry/sweet cider* **2** (*AmE*) a drink made from apples that does not contain alcohol

cigar /sɪˈgɑː(r)/ *noun* [C] a thick roll of **tobacco** (= a type of dried leaf) that people smoke. **Cigars** are larger than cigarettes

cigarette /ˌsɪgəˈret/ *noun* [C] a thin tube of white paper filled with **tobacco** (= a type of dried leaf) that people smoke: *a packet/pack of cigarettes*

ciga'rette lighter (also lighter) *noun* [C] an object which produces a small flame for lighting cigarettes, etc.

cinder /ˈsɪndə(r)/ *noun* [C] a very small piece of burning coal, wood, etc.

cinema /ˈsɪnəmə/ *noun* **1** [C] (*BrE*) a place where you go to see a film: *What's on at the cinema this week?*

> **HELP** In American English, you use **movie theater** to talk about the building where films are shown but **the movies** when you are talking about going to see a film there: *There are five movie theaters in this town.* ♦ *Let's go to the movies this evening.*

2 [U] films in general; the film industry: *one of the great successes of British cinema* ➲ note at **film**

cinnamon /ˈsɪnəmən/ *noun* [U] a sweet brown powder that is used as a spice in cooking ➲ picture on **page P14**

circa /ˈsɜːkə/ *prep* (*abbr* c) (*written*) (used with dates) about; approximately: *The vase was made circa 600 AD.*

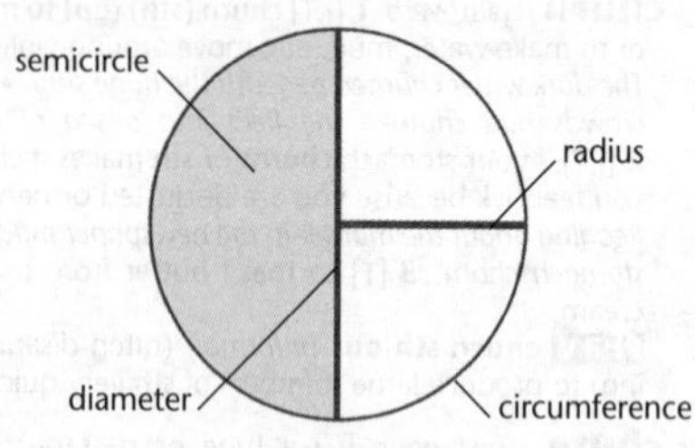

circle

circle¹ /ˈsɜːkl/ *noun* **1** [C] a flat, round area: *She cut out a circle of paper.* ➲ picture at **shape** **2** [C] a round shape like a ring: *The children were drawing circles and squares on a piece of paper.* ♦ *We all stood in a circle and held hands.* **3 the (dress) circle** (also **balcony**) [sing] an area of seats that is upstairs in a cinema, theatre, etc: *We've booked seats in the front row of the circle.* **4** [C] a group of people who are friends, or who have the same interest or profession: *He has a large circle of friends.* ♦ *Her name was well known in artistic circles.*

IDM a vicious circle ➲ **vicious**

circle² /ˈsɜːkl/ *verb* **1** [I,T] to move, or to move round sth, in a circle: *The plane circled the town several times before it landed.* **2** [T] to draw a circle round sth: *There are three possible answers to each question. Please circle the correct one.*

circuit /ˈsɜːkɪt/ *noun* **1** [C] a journey, route or track that forms a circle: *The cars have to complete ten circuits of the track.* **2** [C] the complete path of wires and equipment that an electric current flows around **3** [sing] a series of sports competitions, meetings or other organized events that are regularly visited by the same people: *She's one of the best players on the tennis circuit.*

circular¹ /ˈsɜːkjələ(r)/ *adj* **1** round and flat; shaped like a circle: *a circular table* **2** (used about a journey, etc.) moving round in a circle: *a circular tour of Munich*

circular² /ˈsɜːkjələ(r)/ *noun* [C] a printed letter, notice or advertisement that is sent to a large number of people

circulate /ˈsɜːkjəleɪt/ *verb* [I,T] **1** (used about a substance) to move or make sth move round continuously: *Blood circulates round the body.* **2** to go or be passed from one person to another: *Rumours were circulating about the Minister's private life.* ♦ *We've circulated a copy of the report to each department.*

circulation /ˌsɜːkjəˈleɪʃn/ *noun* **1** [U] the movement of blood around the body: *If you have bad circulation, your hands and feet get cold easily.* **2** [U] the passing of sth from one person or place to another: *the circulation of news/information/rumours* ♦ *Those coins are no longer in circulation* (= being used by people). **3** [C] the number of copies of a newspaper, magazine, etc. that are sold each time it is produced: *This newspaper has a circulation of over a million.*

circumcise /ˈsɜːkəmsaɪz/ *verb* [T] **1** to remove the skin at the end of the **penis** (= the male sexual organ) of a boy or man for religious or medical reasons **2** to cut off part of the sex organs of a girl or woman ▸ **circumcision** /ˌsɜːkəmˈsɪʒn/ *noun* [C,U]

circumference /səˈkʌmfərəns/ *noun* [C,U] the distance round a circle or sth in the shape of a circle: *The Earth is about 40 000 kilometres **in circumference**.* ➲ look at **diameter, radius** ➲ picture at **circle**

circumspect /ˈsɜːkəmspekt/ *adj* (*formal*) thinking very carefully about sth before doing it, because there may be risks involved **SYN cautious**

circumstance /ˈsɜːkəmstəns/ *noun* **1** [C, usually pl] the facts and events that affect what happens in a particular situation: *Police said there were no **suspicious circumstances** surrounding the boy's death.* ♦ *In normal circumstances I would not have accepted the job, but at that time I had very little money.* **2 circumstances** [pl] (*formal*) the amount of money that you have: *The company has promised to repay the money when its financial circumstances improve.*

IDM **in/under the circumstances** as the result of a particular situation: *It's not an ideal solution, but it's the best we can do in the circumstances.* ♦ *My father was ill at that time, so under the circumstances I decided not to go on holiday.*
in/under no circumstances never; not for any reason: *Under no circumstances should you enter my office.*

circumstantial /ˌsɜːkəmˈstænʃl/ *adj* (used in connection with the law) containing details and information that strongly suggest sth is true but are not actual proof of it: *They had only circumstantial evidence.*

circus /ˈsɜːkəs/ *noun* [C] a show performed in a large tent by a company of people and animals

CIS /ˌsiː aɪ ˈes/ *abbr* **the Commonwealth of Independent States** (a group of independent countries that were part of the Soviet Union until 1991)

cistern /ˈsɪstən/ *noun* [C] a container for storing water, especially one that is connected to a toilet

cite /saɪt/ *verb* [T] (*formal*) to mention sth or use sb's exact words as an example to support, or as proof of, what you are saying: *She cited a passage from the president's speech.* ▶ **citation** /saɪˈteɪʃn/ *noun* [C,U]

⚷ **citizen** /ˈsɪtɪzn/ *noun* [C] **1** a person who is legally accepted as a member of a particular country: *She was born in Japan, but became an American citizen in 1981.* **2** a person who lives in a town or city: *the citizens of Paris* ➲ look at **senior citizen**

citizenship /ˈsɪtɪzənʃɪp/ *noun* [U] the state of being a citizen of a particular country: *After living in Spain for twenty years, he decided to apply for Spanish citizenship.*

citrus /ˈsɪtrəs/ *adj* used to describe fruit such as oranges and lemons

⚷ **city** /ˈsɪti/ *noun* (*pl* cities) **1** [C] a large and important town: *Venice is one of the most beautiful cities in the world.* ♦ *Many people are worried about housing conditions in Britain's inner cities* (= the central parts where there are often social problems). ♦ *the city centre* ♦ *the country's* ***capital city*** ➲ picture on **page P11** **2 the City** [sing] the oldest part of London, which is now Britain's financial centre: *a City stockbroker*

TOPIC

City life

Life in the **city** can be **hectic** (= very busy). People are often **in a hurry** and the **streets** are **crowded** and **noisy**. There is a lot of **traffic** (= cars, buses, etc.) so the air is **polluted**. Many people live in **flats**, and if you live in the **suburbs** (= areas outside the city), you spend a lot of time **commuting** (= travelling to and from work). But cities are also **lively** places (= full of energy). There are restaurants, shops, theatres, museums and **sports facilities** (such as stadiums and swimming pools). Many cities are **cosmopolitan** (= full of people from all over the world).

civic /ˈsɪvɪk/ *adj* officially connected with a city or town: *civic pride* (= feeling proud because you belong to a particular town or city) ♦ *civic duties* ♦ *the civic centre* (= the area where the public buildings are in a town)

⚷ **civil** /ˈsɪvl/ *adj* **1** [only *before* a noun] connected with the people who live in a country: *civil disorder* (= involving groups of people within the same country) **2** [only *before* a noun] connected with the state, not with the army or the Church: *a civil wedding* (= not a religious one) ♦ *civil engineering* (= the designing and building of roads, railways, bridges, etc.) **3** [only *before* a noun] (in law) connected with the personal legal matters of ordinary people, and not criminal law: *civil courts* **4** polite, but not very friendly: *I know you don't like the director, but do try and be civil to him.* ▶ **civilly** /ˈsɪvəli/ *adv*

civilian /səˈvɪliən/ *noun* [C] a person who is not in the army, navy, air force or police force: *Two soldiers and one civilian were killed when the bomb exploded.*

civilization (also -isation) /ˌsɪvəlaɪˈzeɪʃn/ *noun* **1** [U] an advanced state of social and cultural development, or the process of reaching this state: *the civilization of the human race* **2** [C,U] a society which has its own highly developed culture and way of life: *the civilizations of ancient Greece and Rome* ♦ *Western civilization* **3** [U] all the people in the world and the societies they live in considered as a whole: *Global warming poses a threat to the whole of civilization.*

civilize (also -ise) /ˈsɪvəlaɪz/ *verb* [T] to educate and improve a person or a society; to make sb's manners or behaviour better

civilized (also -ised) /ˈsɪvəlaɪzd/ *adj* **1** (used about a society) well organized; having a high level of social and cultural development **2** polite and reasonable: *a civilized conversation*

ˌcivil ˈrights (also ˌcivil ˈliberties) *noun* [pl] sb's legal right to freedom and equal treatment in society, whatever their sex, race or religion: *the civil rights leader Martin Luther King*

ˌcivil ˈservant *noun* [C] a person who works for **the civil service**

the ˌcivil ˈservice *noun* [sing] all the government departments, except for the armed forces, and all the people who work in them

ˌcivil ˈwar *noun* [C,U] a war between groups of people who live in the same country

CJD /ˌsiː dʒeɪ ˈdiː/ *abbr* **Creutzfeldt-Jakob disease**; a disease of the brain caused by eating infected meat ➲ look at **BSE**

cl *abbr* = **centilitre**

clad /klæd/ *adj* [not before a noun] (*formal*) dressed (in); wearing a particular type of clothing: *The children were warmly clad in coats, hats and scarves.*

⚷ **claim**[1] /kleɪm/ *verb* **1** [T] **claim (that); claim (to be sth)** to say that sth is true, without having any proof: *Colin claims (that) the book belongs to him.* ♦ *The woman claims to be the oldest person in Britain.*

2 [I,T] claim (for sth) to ask for sth from the government, a company, etc. because you think it is your legal right to have it, or it belongs to you: *The police are keeping the animal until somebody claims it.* ◆ *Don't forget to claim for your travel expenses when you get back.* ◆ (*figurative*) *No one has claimed responsibility for the bomb attack.* **3** [T] to cause death: *The earthquake claimed thousands of lives.*

claim² /kleɪm/ *noun* [C] **1** a claim (that) a statement that sth is true, which does not have any proof: *I do not believe the Government's claim that they can reduce unemployment by the end of the year.* **2** a claim (to sth) the right to have sth: *You will have to prove your claim to the property in a court of law.* **3** a claim (for sth) a demand for money that you think you have a right to, especially from the government, a company, etc: *to make an insurance claim* ◆ *After the accident he decided to put in a claim for compensation.*
IDM **stake a/your claim** ➲ **stake²**

claimant /ˈkleɪmənt/ *noun* [C] a person who believes they have the right to have sth: *The insurance company refused to pay the claimant any money.*

clairvoyant /kleəˈvɔɪənt/ *noun* [C] a person who some people believe has special mental powers and can see what will happen in the future

clam¹ /klæm/ *noun* [C] a **shellfish** (= a creature with a shell that lives in water) that you can eat ➲ picture at **shellfish**

clam² /klæm/ *verb* (clamming; clammed)
PHR V **clam up (on sb)** (*informal*) to stop talking and refuse to speak, especially when sb asks you about sth

clamber /ˈklæmbə(r)/ *verb* [I] clamber up, down, out etc. to move or climb with difficulty, usually using both your hands and feet: *She managed to clamber up and over the wall.*

clammy /ˈklæmi/ *adj* (clammier; clammiest) cold, slightly wet and sticky in an unpleasant way: *clammy hands*

clamour (*AmE* clamor) /ˈklæmə(r)/ *verb* [I] clamour for sth to demand sth in a loud or angry way: *The public are clamouring for an answer to all these questions.* ▶ **clamour** (*AmE* clamor) *noun* [sing]: *the clamour of angry voices*

clamp¹ /klæmp/ *verb* [T] **1** clamp A and B (together); clamp A to B to fasten two things together with a **clamp**: *The metal rods were clamped together.* ◆ *Clamp the wood to the table so that it doesn't move.* **2** to hold sth very firmly in a particular position: *Her lips were clamped tightly together.* **3** (*BrE*) to fix a metal object to the wheel of a vehicle that has been parked illegally, so that it cannot move: *Oh no! My car's been clamped.*
PHR V **clamp down on sb/sth** (*informal*) to take strong action in order to stop or control sth: *The police are clamping down on people who drink and drive.* ➲ look at **clampdown**

clamp² /klæmp/ *noun* [C] **1** a tool that you use for holding two things together very tightly **2** (also ˈwheel clamp) (*BrE*) a metal object that is fixed to the wheel of a car that has been parked illegally, so that it cannot drive away

clampdown /ˈklæmpdaʊn/ *noun* [C] strong action to stop or control sth: *a clampdown on tax evasion*

clan /klæn/ *noun* [C, with sing or pl verb] a group of families who are related to each other, especially in Scotland

clandestine /klænˈdestɪn; ˈklændəstaɪn/ *adj* (*formal*) secret and often not legal: *a clandestine meeting*

clang /klæŋ/ *verb* [I,T] to make or cause sth metal to make a loud ringing sound: *The iron gates clanged shut.* ▶ **clang** *noun* [C]

clank /klæŋk/ *verb* [I,T] to make or cause sth metal to make a loud unpleasant sound: *The lift clanked its way up to the seventh floor.* ▶ **clank** *noun* [C]

clap¹ /klæp/ *verb* (clapping; clapped) **1** [I,T] to hit your hands together many times, usually to show that you like sth: *The audience clapped as soon as the singer walked onto the stage.* ◆ *Everybody was clapping their hands in time to the music.* **2** [T] to put sth onto sth quickly and firmly: *'Oh no, I shouldn't have said that,' she said, clapping a hand over her mouth.* ▶ **clapping** *noun* [U]

clap² /klæp/ *noun* [C] **1** an act of clapping: *Let's have a big clap for our next performer!* **2** a sudden loud noise: *a clap of thunder*

claret /ˈklærət/ *noun* **1** [C,U] a red wine from Bordeaux in France **2** [U] a dark red colour

clarification /ˌklærəfɪˈkeɪʃn/ *noun* [U,C] an act of making sth clear and easier to understand: *We'd like some clarification of exactly what the new exam will be like.* ➲ look at **clarity**

clarify /ˈklærəfaɪ/ *verb* [T] (*formal*) (clarifying; clarifies; *pt, pp* clarified) to make sth become clear and easier to understand: *I hope that what I say will clarify the situation.* ➲ *adjective* **clear**

clarinet /ˌklærəˈnet/ *noun* [C] a musical instrument that is made of wood. You play a **clarinet** by blowing through it. ➲ look at **woodwind** ➲ note at **music** ➲ picture at **music**

clarity /ˈklærəti/ *noun* [U] the quality of being clear and easy to understand: *clarity of expression* ➲ look at **clarification**

clash¹ /klæʃ/ *verb* **1** [I] clash (with sb) (over sth) to fight or disagree seriously about sth: *A group of demonstrators clashed with police outside the Town Hall.* **2** [I] clash (with sth) (used about two events) to happen at the same time: *It's a pity the two concerts clash. I wanted to go to both of them.* **3** [I] clash (with sth) (used about colours, etc.) to not match or look nice together: *I don't think you should wear that tie—it clashes with your shirt.* **4** [I,T] (used about two metal objects) to hit together with a loud noise; to cause two metal objects to do this: *She clashed the cymbals.*

clash² /klæʃ/ *noun* [C] **1** a fight or serious disagreement: *a clash between police and demonstrators* **2** a big difference: *a clash of opinions* ◆ *There was a per-*

sonality clash between the two men (= they did not get well on together or like each other). **3** a loud noise, made by two metal objects hitting each other: *the clash of cymbals*

clasp¹ /klɑːsp/ *verb* [T] to hold sb/sth tightly: *Kevin clasped the child in his arms.*

clasp² /klɑːsp/ *noun* [C] an object, usually of metal, which fastens or holds sth together: *the clasp on a necklace/brooch/handbag* ➲ picture at **jewellery**

class¹ /klɑːs/ *noun*
➤SCHOOL **1** [C, with sing or pl verb] a group of students who are taught together: *Jane and I are in the same class at school.* ♦ *The whole class is/are going to the theatre tonight.* **2** [C,U] a lesson: *Classes begin at 9 o'clock in the morning.* ♦ *We watched an interesting video in class* (= during the lesson) *yesterday.*
➤SOCIETY **3** [U,C] the way people are divided into social groups; one of these groups: *The idea of class still divides British society.* ♦ *class differences* ♦ *the working/middle/upper class*
➤GROUP **4** [C] (*technical*) a group of animals, plants, words, etc. of a similar type: *There are several different classes of insects.*
➤QUALITY **5** [U] (*informal*) high quality or style: *Pele was a football player of great class.* **6** [C] [in compounds] of a certain level of quality: *a first-class carriage on a train* ♦ *Are you travelling economy class or business class on this flight?*
➤UNIVERSITY DEGREE **7** [C] [in compounds] (*BrE*) a mark that you are given when you pass your final university exam: *a first-/second-/third-class degree*

class² /klɑːs/ *verb* [T] **class sb/sth (as sth)** to put sb/sth in a particular group or type: *Certain animals and plants are now classed as 'endangered species'.*

classic¹ /ˈklæsɪk/ *adj* **1** (used about a book, play, etc.) important and having a value that will last: *the classic film 'Gone With The Wind'* **2** typical: *It was a classic case of bad management.* **3** elegant but traditional in style or design: *a classic grey suit*

classic² /ˈklæsɪk/ *noun* **1** [C] a famous book, play, etc. which has a value that will last: *All of Charles Dickens' novels are classics.* **2 Classics** [U] the study of ancient Greek and Roman language and literature: *a degree in Classics* ➲ note at **literature**

classical /ˈklæsɪkl/ *adj* **1** traditional, not modern: *classical ballet* ♦ *the classical theory of unemployment* **2** connected with ancient Greece or Rome: *classical architecture* **3** (used about music) serious and having a value that lasts: *I prefer classical music to pop.* ♦ *a classical composer/violinist* ➲ note at **music** ▶ **classically** /-kli/ *adv*

classified /ˈklæsɪfaɪd/ *adj* officially secret: *classified information*

ˌclassified adˈvertisement (*BrE informal* ˌclassified ˈad; ˈsmall ad) *noun* [C, usually pl] a small advertisement that you put in a newspaper if you want to buy or sell sth, employ sb, find a flat, etc.

classify /ˈklæsɪfaɪ/ *verb* [T] (**classifying**; **classifies**; *pt, pp* **classified**) **classify sb/sth (as sth)** to put sb/sth into a group with other people or things of a similar type: *Would you classify it as an action film or a thriller?* ▶ **classification** /ˌklæsɪfɪˈkeɪʃn/ *noun* [C,U]: *the classification of the different species of butterfly*

classmate /ˈklɑːsmeɪt/ *noun* [C] a person who is in the same class as you at school or college

classroom /ˈklɑːsruːm; -rʊm/ *noun* [C] a room in a school, college, etc. where lessons are taught: *classroom activities* ♦ *technology in the classroom*

classy /ˈklɑːsi/ *adj* (*informal*) (**classier**; **classiest**) (*informal*) of high quality or style; expensive and fashionable: *a classy restaurant*

clatter /ˈklætə(r)/ *verb* [I,T] to make or cause sth hard to make a series of short loud repeated sounds: *The horses clattered down the street.* ▶ **clatter** *noun* [usually sing]

clause /klɔːz/ *noun* [C] **1** a group of words that includes a subject and a verb. A **clause** is usually only part of a sentence: *The sentence 'After we had finished eating, we watched a film.' contains two clauses.* **2** one of the sections of a legal document that says that sth must or must not be done

claustrophobia /ˌklɔːstrəˈfəʊbiə/ *noun* [U] fear of being in a small space with walls on all sides

claustrophobic /ˌklɔːstrəˈfəʊbɪk/ *adj* **1** extremely afraid of small spaces with walls on all sides: *Hilary always feels claustrophobic in lifts.* **2** used about sth that makes you feel afraid in this way: *a claustrophobic little room*

clavicle /ˈklævɪkl/ (*formal*) = **collarbone**

claw¹ /klɔː/ *noun* [C] **1** one of the long curved nails on the end of an animal's or a bird's foot ➲ picture on **page P12** **2** one of a pair of long, sharp fingers that certain types of **shellfish** (= creatures with shells that live in water) have. They use them for holding things or picking things up: *the claws of a crab* ➲ picture at **shellfish**

claw² /klɔː/ *verb* [I,T] **claw (at) sb/sth** to scratch or tear sb/sth with **claws** or with your nails: *The cat was clawing at the furniture.*

clay /kleɪ/ *noun* [U] heavy earth that is soft and sticky when it is wet and becomes hard when it is baked or dried: *clay pots*

clean¹ /kliːn/ *adj* (**cleaner**; **cleanest**) **1** not dirty: *The whole house was beautifully clean.* ♦ *Cats are very clean animals.* OPP **dirty** ➲ *noun* **cleanliness** **2** free from harmful or unpleasant substances: *clean air* ♦ *clean drinking water* **3** (used about humour) not about sex: *a clean joke* OPP **dirty** **4** having no record of offences or crimes: *a clean driving licence*
IDM **a clean sweep** a complete victory in a sports competition, an election, etc. that you get by winning all the different parts of it: *The Russians made a clean sweep of all the gymnastics events.*

clean² /kliːn/ *verb* [I,T] to make sth free from dust or dirt by washing or rubbing it: *to clean the windows* ♦ *Don't forget to clean your teeth!* ♦ *Linda comes in to clean after office hours.* ➲ look at **dry-clean**, **spring-clean**

HELP **Do the cleaning** is often used instead of clean: *I do the cleaning once a week.*

C

PHR V **clean sth out** to clean the inside of sth: *I'm going to clean out all the cupboards next week.*
clean (sth) up to remove all the dirt from a place that is particularly dirty: *I'm going to clean up the kitchen before Mum and Dad get back.* ◆ *Oh no, you've spilt coffee on the new carpet! Can you clean it up?*

OTHER WORDS FOR

clean

Clean is a general word for removing dirt from something. If you **wash** something you clean it with water and often soap. You can **wipe** a surface by rubbing it with a wet cloth; you **dust** a surface by rubbing it with a dry cloth. If you **brush** something you clean it with a brush that has a short handle; if you **sweep** the floor you use a brush with a long handle. When you clean or tidy your home, you **do the housework**.

clean³ /kliːn/ *adv* (*informal*) completely: *I clean forgot it was your birthday.*
IDM **come clean (with sb) (about sth)** (*informal*) to tell the truth about sth that you have been keeping secret: *She decided to come clean with her father about the money she owed.*
go clean out of your mind to be completely forgotten

cleaner /ˈkliːnə(r)/ *noun* **1** [C] a person whose job is to clean the rooms and furniture inside a house or other building: *an office cleaner* **2** [C] a substance or a special machine that you use for cleaning sth: *liquid floor cleaners* ◆ *a carpet cleaner* ➲ look at **vacuum cleaner** **3 the cleaner's** = **dry-cleaner's**

cleanliness /ˈklenlinəs/ *noun* [U] being clean or keeping things clean: *High standards of cleanliness are important in a hotel kitchen.*

cleanly /ˈkliːnli/ *adv* easily or smoothly in one movement: *The knife cut cleanly through the rope.*

cleanse /klenz/ *verb* [T] to clean your skin or a wound ➲ look at **ethnic cleansing**

cleanser /ˈklenzə(r)/ *noun* [C,U] a substance that you use for cleaning your skin, especially your face

ˌclean-ˈshaven *adj* a man who is **clean-shaven** does not have a beard or other hair growing on his face

clear¹ /klɪə(r)/ *adj* (**clearer**; **clearest**)
➤WITHOUT DOUBT **1 clear (to sb)** easy to understand and not causing any confusion: *There are clear advantages to the second plan.* ◆ *It was clear to me that he was not telling the truth.* ◆ *She gave me clear directions on how to get there.* ➲ *verb* **clarify**
➤SURE **2 clear (about/on sth)** sure or definite; without any doubts or confusion: *I'm not quite clear about the arrangements for tomorrow.* ➲ *verb* **clarify**
➤EASY TO HEAR, ETC. **3** easy to see or hear: *His voice wasn't very clear on the telephone.*
➤TRANSPARENT **4** easy to see through: *The water was so clear that we could see the bottom of the lake.*
➤NOT MARKED **5** free from marks: *a clear sky* (= without clouds) ◆ *a clear skin* (= without spots)
➤NOT BLOCKED **6 clear (of sth)** free from things that are blocking the way: *The police say that most roads are now clear of snow.*
➤NOT GUILTY **7** not guilty: *It wasn't your fault. You can have a completely clear conscience.*
IDM **make yourself clear**; **make sth clear/plain (to sb)** to speak so that there can be no doubt about what you mean: *'I do not want you to go to that concert,' said my mother. 'Do I make myself clear?'* ◆ *He made it quite clear that he was not happy with the decision.*

clear² /klɪə/ *verb*
➤REMOVE **1** [T] to remove sth that is not wanted or needed: *to clear the roads of snow/to clear snow from the roads* ◆ *It's your turn to clear the table* (= to take away the dirty plates, etc. after a meal). **2** [T] to make people leave a place: *After the bomb warning, police cleared the streets.*
➤OF WEATHER/WATER **3** [I] (used about smoke, etc.) to disappear: *The fog slowly cleared and the sun came out.* **4** [I] (used about the sky, the weather or water) to become free of clouds, rain or mud: *After a cloudy start, the weather will clear during the afternoon.*
➤FIND SB NOT GUILTY **5** [T] **clear sb (of sth)** to provide proof that sb is innocent of sth: *The man has finally been cleared of murder.*
➤GIVE PERMISSION **6** [T] to give official permission for a plane, ship, etc. to enter or leave a place: *At last the plane was cleared for take-off.* **7** [T] **clear sth (with sb)** to get official approval for sth to be done: *I'll have to clear it with the manager before I can refund your money.*
➤MONEY **8** [I] (used about a cheque) to go through the system that moves money from one account to another: *The cheque will take three days to clear.*
➤GET OVER/PAST **9** [T] to jump over or get past sth without touching it: *The horse cleared the first jump but knocked down the second.*
IDM **clear the air** to improve a difficult or tense situation by talking honestly about worries, doubts, etc: *I'm sure if you discuss your feelings with her it will help to clear the air between you.*
clear your throat to cough slightly in order to make it easier to speak
PHR V **clear off** (*informal*) used to tell sb to go away
clear sth out to tidy sth and throw away things that you do not want: *I really must clear out the kitchen cupboards.*
clear up (used about the weather or an illness) to get better: *We can go out for a walk if it clears up later on.* ◆ *The doctor told him to stay at home until his cold cleared up.*
clear (sth) up to make sth tidy: *Make sure you clear up properly before you leave.*
clear sth up to find the solution to a problem, cause of confusion, etc: *There's been a slight misunderstanding but we've cleared it up now.*

clear³ /klɪə(r)/ *adv* **1** in a way that is easy to see or hear: *We can hear the telephone loud and clear from here.* **2 clear (of sth)** away from sth; not touching sth: *Stand clear of the doors* (= on a train).
IDM **keep/stay/steer clear (of sb/sth)** to avoid

sb/sth because they or it may cause problems: *It's best to keep clear of the town centre during the rush hour.*

clearance /ˈklɪərəns/ *noun* [U] **1** the removing of sth that is old or not wanted: *The shop is having a clearance sale* (= selling everything quickly by offering it at a low price). **2** the distance between an object and something that is passing under or beside it, for example a ship or vehicle: *There was not enough clearance for the bus to pass under the bridge safely.* **3** official permission for sb/sth to do sth: *She was given clearance to work at the nuclear research establishment.*

ˌclear-ˈcut *adj* definite and easy to see or understand

ˌclear-ˈheaded *adj* able to think clearly, especially if there is a problem

clearing /ˈklɪərɪŋ/ *noun* [C] a small area without trees in the middle of a wood or forest

clearly /ˈklɪəli/ *adv* **1** in a way that is easy to see, hear or understand: *It was so foggy that we couldn't see the road clearly.* **2** in a way that is not confused: *I'm so tired that I can't think clearly.* **3** without doubt: *She clearly doesn't want to speak to you any more.* SYN **obviously**

ˌclear-ˈsighted *adj* understanding or thinking clearly; able to make good decisions and judgements

cleavage /ˈkliːvɪdʒ/ *noun* [C,U] the space between a woman's breasts

clef /klef/ *noun* [C] (in music) a sign (𝄞, 𝄢) at the beginning of a line of written music that shows the area of sound that the notes are in: *the bass/treble clef*

clementine /ˈkleməntiːn/ *noun* [C] a type of fruit like a small orange

clench /klentʃ/ *verb* [T] to close or hold tightly: *She clenched her fists and looked as if she was going to hit him.*

clergy /ˈklɜːdʒi/ *noun* [pl] the people who perform religious ceremonies in the Christian church: *a member of the clergy*

clergyman /ˈklɜːdʒimən/ *noun* [C] (*pl* -men /-mən/) a male member of the **clergy**

clergywoman /ˈklɜːdʒiwʊmən/ *noun* [C] (*pl* -women /-wɪmɪn/) a female member of the **clergy**

clerical /ˈklerɪkl/ *adj* **1** connected with the work of a **clerk** in an office: *clerical work* **2** connected with the **clergy**

clerk /klɑːk/ *noun* [C] **1** a person whose job is to do written work or look after records or accounts in an office, a bank, a court of law, etc: *an office clerk* ◆ *a Town Clerk* **2** (*AmE*) = **shop assistant**

clever /ˈklevə(r)/ *adj* (cleverer; cleverest) [You can also use **more clever** and **most clever**.] **1** able to learn, understand or do sth quickly and easily; intelligent: *a clever student* ◆ *How clever of you to mend my watch!* ➲ note at **intelligent** **2** (used about things, ideas or sb's actions) showing skill or intelligence: *a clever device* ◆ *We made a clever plan.* ▶ **cleverly** *adv* ▶ **cleverness** *noun* [U]

cliché /ˈkliːʃeɪ/ *noun* [C] a phrase or an idea that has been used so many times that it no longer has any real meaning or interest: *She trotted out the old cliché that 'a problem shared is a problem halved'.*

click¹ /klɪk/ *verb* **1** [I,T] to make a short sharp sound; to cause sth to do this: *The door clicked shut.* ◆ *He clicked his fingers at the waiter.* **2** [I,T] **click (on sth)** to press one of the buttons on a computer mouse: *To open a file, click on the menu.* ◆ *Position the pointer and* **double click** *the left-hand mouse button* (= press it twice very quickly). **3** [I] (*informal*) (used about a problem, etc.) to become suddenly clear or understood: *Once I'd found the missing letter, everything* **clicked into place**. **4** [I] (*BrE informal*) (used about two people) to become friendly immediately: *We met at a party and just clicked.*

click² /klɪk/ *noun* [C] **1** a short sharp sound: *the click of a switch* **2** the act of pressing the button on a computer mouse

client /ˈklaɪənt/ *noun* [C] **1** a person who receives a service from a professional person, for example a lawyer: *to act on behalf of a client* **2** a computer that is connected to a **server** (= the main computer that stores shared information)

> **HELP** Client or customer? **Client** cannot be used for people in shops or restaurants. Those people are **customers**.

clientele /ˌkliːənˈtel/ *noun* [U] all the customers, guests or **clients** who regularly go to a particular shop, hotel, organization, etc. ➲ Less formal words are **customers** or **guests**.

cliff /klɪf/ *noun* [C] a high, very steep area of rock, especially one next to the sea: *the white cliffs of Dover* ➲ picture on **page P10**

climate /ˈklaɪmət/ *noun* [C] **1** the normal weather conditions of a particular region: *a dry/humid/tropical climate* **2** an area with particular weather conditions: *They wanted to move to a warmer climate.* **3** the general opinions, etc. that people have at a particular time: *What is the current* **climate of opinion** *regarding the death penalty?* ◆ *the political climate*

ˈclimate change *noun* [U] changes in the earth's weather, including changes in temperature, wind patterns and **rainfall** (= the total amount of rain that falls in a particular place during a month, year, etc.), especially the increase in the temperature of the earth's atmosphere that is caused by the increase of particular gases, especially **carbon dioxide**: *the threat of global climate change* ➲ look at **global warming**

climatic /klaɪˈmætɪk/ *adj* [only *before* a noun] connected with the climate

climax /ˈklaɪmæks/ *noun* [C] the most important and exciting part of a book, play, piece of music, an event, etc: *The novel* **reaches a dramatic climax** *in the final chapter.* ▶ **climax** *verb* [I]

climb[1] /klaɪm/ *verb* **1** [I,T] **climb (up) (sth)** to move up towards the top of sth: *to climb a tree/mountain/rope* ◆ *She climbed the stairs to bed.* ◆ *to climb up a ladder* **2** [I] to move, with difficulty or effort, in the direction mentioned: *I managed to climb out of the window.* ◆ *The prisoners climbed over the wall.* **3** [I] to go up mountains, etc. as a sport

HELP **Go climbing** is a common way of talking about climbing for pleasure: *I go climbing in the Alps most summers.*

4 [I] to rise to a higher position: *The plane climbed steadily.* ◆ *The road climbed steeply up the side of the mountain.* ◆ (*figurative*) *The value of the dollar climbed against the pound.*

IDM **climb/jump on the bandwagon** ➲ **band-wagon**

PHR V **climb down (over sth)** (*informal*) to admit that you have made a mistake; to change your opinion about sth in an argument ➲ look at **climbdown**

climb[2] /klaɪm/ *noun* [C] an act of climbing or a journey made by climbing: *The monastery could only be reached by a three-hour climb.*

climbdown /ˈklaɪmdaʊn/ *noun* [C] an act of admitting you have been wrong; a change of opinion in an argument: *a government climbdown*

climber /ˈklaɪmə(r)/ *noun* [C] a person who climbs mountains as a sport

climbing /ˈklaɪmɪŋ/ *noun* [U] the sport or activity of climbing rocks or mountains: *to **go climbing*** ◆ *a climbing accident* ➲ picture on **page P3**

clinch /klɪntʃ/ *verb* [T] (*informal*) to finally manage to get what you want in an argument or a business agreement: *to clinch a deal*

cling /klɪŋ/ *verb* [I] (*pt, pp* **clung** /klʌŋ/) **1 cling (on) to sb/sth; cling together** to hold on tightly to sb/sth: *She clung to the rope with all her strength.* ◆ *They clung together for warmth.* **2 cling to sb/sth** to stick firmly to sth: *Her wet clothes clung to her.* **3 cling (on) to sth** to continue to believe sth, often when it is not reasonable to do so: *They were still clinging to the hope that the girl would be found alive.* ▶ **clingy** *adj*: *a clingy child* (= that does not want to leave its parents) ◆ *a clingy sweater*

ˈ**cling film** *noun* [U] thin transparent plastic used for covering food to keep it fresh

clinic /ˈklɪnɪk/ *noun* [C] **1** a small hospital or a part of a hospital where you go to receive special medical treatment: *He's being treated at a private clinic.* **2** a time when a doctor sees patients and gives special treatment or advice: *Dr Greenall's clinic is from 2 to 4 on Mondays.* ◆ *An antenatal clinic is held every Friday.*

clinical /ˈklɪnɪkl/ *adj* **1** [only *before* a noun] connected with the examination and treatment of patients at a **clinic** or hospital: *Clinical trials of the new drug have proved successful.* **2** (used about a person) cold and not emotional ▶ **clinically** /-kli/ *adv*: *clinically dead* (= *judged to be dead from the condition of the body*)

clink /klɪŋk/ *noun* [sing] the short sharp ringing sound that objects made of glass, metal, etc. make when they touch each other: *the clink of glasses* ▶ **clink** *verb* [I,T]

clip[1] /klɪp/ *noun* [C] **1** a small object, usually made of metal or plastic, used for holding things together: *a paper clip* ◆ *a hair clip* ➲ picture at **stationery** **2** an act of cutting sth **3** a small section of a film that is shown so that people can see what the rest of the film is like ➲ look at **trailer** **4** (*informal*) a quick hit with the hand: *She gave the boy a clip round the ear.*

clip[2] /klɪp/ *verb* (**clipping**; **clipped**) **1** [I,T] to be fastened with a **clip**; to fasten sth to sth else with a **clip**: *Clip the photo to the letter, please.* **2** [T] to cut sth, especially by cutting small parts off: *Andy will clip the hedge tomorrow.* **3** [T] to hit sb/sth quickly: *My wheel clipped the pavement and I fell off my bike.*

clipboard /ˈklɪpbɔːd/ *noun* [C] **1** a small board with a **clip** at the top for holding papers, used by sb who wants to write while standing or moving around ➲ picture at **stationery** **2** a place where information from a computer file is stored for a time until it is added to another file

clippers /ˈklɪpəz/ *noun* [pl] a small metal tool used for cutting things, for example hair or nails: *a pair of nail clippers* ➲ picture at **scissors**

clipping /ˈklɪpɪŋ/ (*AmE*) = **cutting**[1](1)

clique /kliːk/ *noun* [C] a small group of people with the same interests who do not want others to join their group ▶ **cliquey** *adj*: *The office can be a very cliquey place.*

clitoris /ˈklɪtərɪs/ *noun* [C] the small part of the female sex organs which becomes larger when a woman is sexually excited

cloak /kləʊk/ *noun* **1** [C] a type of loose coat without sleeves that was more common in former times ➲ look at **cape** **2** [sing] a thing that hides sth else: (*figurative*) *a cloak of mist*

cloakroom /ˈkləʊkruːm/ *noun* [C] a room near the entrance to a building where you can leave your coat, bags, etc.

clobber /ˈklɒbə(r)/ *verb* [T] (*BrE informal*) to hit sb hard

clock[1] /klɒk/ *noun* [C] **1** an instrument that shows you what time it is: *an alarm clock* ◆ *a church clock* ➲ look at **watch** **2** (*informal*) = **milometer**: *My car has only 10 000 miles on the clock.*

IDM **against the clock** to do sth fast in order to finish it before a certain time: *It was a race against the clock to get the building work finished on time.*

around/round the clock all day and all night: *They are working round the clock to repair the bridge.*

put the clock/clocks forward/back to change the time, usually by one hour, at the beginning/end of summer

clock[2] /klɒk/ *verb*

PHR V **clock in/on; clock off** to record the time that you arrive at or leave work, especially by putting a card into a type of clock

clock sth up to achieve a certain number or total: *Our car clocked up over 2 000 miles while we were on holiday.*

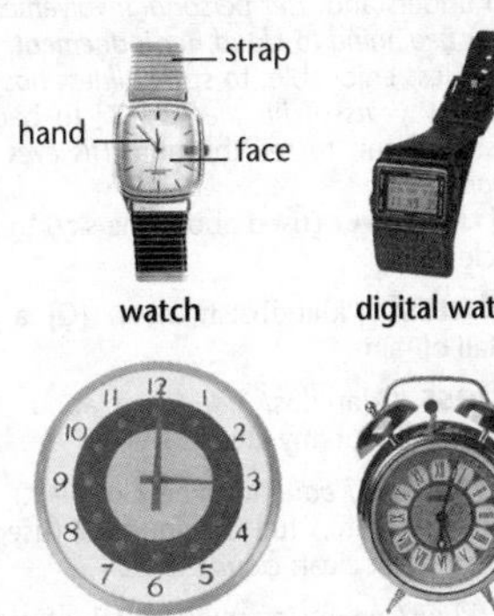

clockwise /ˈklɒkwaɪz/ *adv, adj* in the same direction as the hands of a clock: *Turn the handle clockwise.* ◆ *to move in a clockwise direction* OPP **anticlockwise, counterclockwise**

clockwork /ˈklɒkwɜːk/ *noun* [U] a type of machinery found in certain toys, etc. that you operate by turning a key: *a clockwork toy* ◆ *The plan went* **like clockwork** (= smoothly and without any problems).

clog[1] /klɒg/ *verb* [I,T] (clogging; clogged) **clog (sth) (up) (with sth)** to block or become blocked: *The drain is always clogging up.* ◆ *The roads were clogged with traffic.*

clog[2] /klɒg/ *noun* [C] a type of shoe made completely of wood or with a thick wooden base

cloister /ˈklɔɪstə(r)/ *noun* [C, usually pl] a covered passage around a square garden, usually forming part of a religious building

clone[1] /kləʊn/ *noun* [C] an exact copy of a plant or an animal that is produced from one of its cells by scientific methods

clone[2] /kləʊn/ *verb* [T] **1** to produce an exact copy of a plant or an animal from one of its cells: *A team from the UK were the first to successfully clone an animal.* **2** to illegally copy information from sb's credit card or mobile phone so that you can use it but the owner of the card or phone receives the bill

⚷ **close**[1] /kləʊz/ *verb* [I,T] **1** to shut: *The door closed quietly.* ◆ *to close a door/window* ◆ *Close your eyes—I've got a surprise.* ◆ *Close your books.* **2** to be, or to make sth, not open to the public: *What time do the shops close?* ◆ *The police have closed the road to traffic.* **3** to end or to bring sth to an end: *The meeting closed at 10pm.* ◆ *Detectives have closed the case on the missing girl.* OPP for all meanings **open**

PHR V **close (sth) down** to stop all business or work permanently at a shop or factory: *The factory has had to close down.* ◆ *Health inspectors have closed the restaurant down.*

close in (on sb/sth) to come nearer and gradually surround sb/sth, especially in order to attack: *The army is closing in on the enemy troops.*

close sth off to prevent people from entering a place or an area: *The police closed off the city centre because of a bomb alert.*

close[2] /kləʊz/ *noun* [sing] the end, especially of a period of time or an activity: *the close of the 20th century* ◆ *The speaker* **brought** *the lecture* **to a close.** ◆ *The guests began to leave as the evening* **drew to a close.**

⚷ **close**[3] /kləʊs/ *adj, adv* **1** [not before a noun] **close (to sb/sth); close (together)** near: *Is our hotel close to the beach?* ◆ *The tables are quite close together.* ◆ *to follow close behind someone* ◆ *I held her close* (= tightly). **2** (used about a friend, etc.) known very well and liked: *They invited only close friends to the wedding.* **3** [only *before* a noun] near in a family relationship: *a close relative* OPP **distant** **4** careful; thorough: *On close examination, you could see that the banknote was a forgery.* **5** (used about a competition, etc.) only won by a small amount: *a close match* ➲ note at **near**[1] **6** (used about the weather, etc.) heavy and with little movement of air: *It's so close today that there might be a storm.*

IDM **at close quarters** at or from a position that is very near

close by (sb/sth) at a short distance from sb/sth: *She lives close by.*

close on nearly; almost: *He was born close on a hundred years ago.*

a close shave/thing a bad thing that almost happened: *I wasn't injured, but it was a close shave.*

close/dear/near to sb's heart ➲ **heart**

close up (to sb/sth) at or from a very short distance to sb/sth: *You can't tell it's a forgery until you look at it close up.*

come close (to sth/to doing sth) to almost do sth: *We didn't win but we came close.*

▶ **closely** *adv*: *to watch somebody closely* ◆ *The insect closely resembles a stick.*

▶ **closeness** *noun* [U]

close[4] /kləʊs/ *noun* [C] a street that is closed at one end: *5 Devon Close*

⚷ **closed** /kləʊzd/ *adj* not open; shut: *Keep your mouth closed.* ◆ *The supermarket is closed.* ◆ *The museum is closed on Mondays.* ◆ (*figurative*) *a closed mind* OPP **open**

ˌclosed-ˌcircuit ˈtelevision (*abbr* CCTV) *noun* [C,U] a television system used in a limited area, for example a shopping centre, to protect it from crime

⚷ **closet** /ˈklɒzɪt/ *noun* [C] (*especially AmE*) a large cupboard that is built into a room: *a walk-in closet*

close-up /ˈkləʊs ʌp/ *noun* [C] a photograph or film of sb/sth that you take from a very short distance away: *Here's a close-up of Mike.*

ˈclosing time *noun* [C] the time when a shop, pub, etc. closes

closure /ˈkləʊʒə(r)/ *noun* [C,U] the permanent closing, for example of a business: *The firm is threatened with closure.*

clot[1] /klɒt/ *noun* [C] a lump formed by blood as it dries: *They removed a blood clot from his brain.*

clot² /klɒt/ *verb* [I,T] (clotting; clotted) to form or cause blood to form thick lumps: *a drug that stops blood from clotting during operations*

cloth /klɒθ/ *noun* (*pl* cloths /klɒθs/) **1** [U] a material made of cotton, wool, etc. that you use for making clothes, curtains, etc: *a metre of cloth* SYN **fabric** **2** [C] a piece of material that you use for a particular purpose: *a tablecloth* ♦ *Where can I find a cloth to wipe this water up?* ➲ picture at **bucket**

clothe /kləʊð/ *verb* [T] to provide clothes for sb: *to feed and clothe a child*

clothed /kləʊðd/ *adj* **clothed (in sth)** dressed; wearing sth: *He was clothed in black from head to foot.*

clothes /kləʊðz/ *noun* [pl] the things that you wear, for example trousers, shirts, dresses, coats, etc: *to put on/take off your clothes* ♦ *She was wearing new clothes.* ➲ picture on **page P1**

GRAMMAR There is no singular form of **clothes**. An **article**/an **item**/a **piece of clothing** is used to describe a single thing that you wear: *A kilt is **an item of clothing** worn in Scotland.*

TOPIC

Clothes

Before buying new clothes, you can **try** them **on** to see if they **fit** (= are the right shape and **size** for you). **Well-dressed** people **wear** clothes which **suit** them (= make them look good). When we say that a **style** of clothing is **in fashion, fashionable** or **trendy** we mean that it is popular at the moment. Many people wear **smart** clothes, such as a suit, at work. Others wear a **uniform**: *a police/schooluniform*. People usually **get changed** into **casual** (= comfortable, informal) clothes when they come home from work or school.

ˈclothes line *noun* [C] a thin rope that you hang clothes on so that they can dry

ˈclothes peg (*AmE* clothespin) = **peg¹**(3)

clothing /ˈkləʊðɪŋ/ *noun* [U] the clothes that you wear, especially for a particular activity: *You will need waterproof/outdoor/winter clothing.* ➲ **Clothing** is a more formal word than **clothes**.

ˌclotted ˈcream *noun* [U] a type of thick rich cream

cloud¹ /klaʊd/ *noun* **1** [C,U] a mass of very small drops of water that floats in the sky and is usually white or grey: *The sun disappeared behind a cloud.* ♦ *A band of thick cloud is spreading from the west.* ➲ picture on **page P10** **2** [C] a mass of smoke, dust, sand, etc: *Clouds of smoke were pouring from the burning building.*

IDM **every cloud has a silver lining** even a very bad situation has a positive side

under a cloud with the disapproval of the people around you: *She left her job under a cloud because she'd been accused of stealing.*

cloud² /klaʊd/ *verb* **1** [T] to make sth less clear or easy to understand: *Her personal involvement in the case was beginning to **cloud her judgement**.* **2** [T] to make sth less enjoyable; to spoil: *Illness has clouded the last few years of his life.* **3** [I,T] to become or make sth difficult to see through: *His eyes clouded with tears.*

PHR V **cloud over** (used about the sky) to become full of clouds

cloudburst /ˈklaʊdbɜːst/ *noun* [C] a sudden heavy fall of rain

cloudless /ˈklaʊdləs/ *adj* (used about the sky, etc.) clear; without any clouds

cloudy /ˈklaʊdi/ *adj* (cloudier; cloudiest) **1** (used about the sky, etc.) full of clouds **2** (used about liquids, etc.) not clear: *cloudy water*

clout /klaʊt/ *noun* (*informal*) **1** [U] influence and power: *He's an important man—he has a lot of clout in the town.* **2** [C] a hard hit, usually with the hand: *to give someone a clout*

clove /kləʊv/ *noun* [C] **1** the small dried flower of a tropical tree, used as a spice in cooking ➲ picture on **page P14** **2** one of the small separate sections of **garlic** (= a vegetable of the onion family with a strong taste and smell)

clover /ˈkləʊvə(r)/ *noun* [U] a small plant with pink or white flowers and leaves with three parts to them

CULTURE

Sometimes clover leaves have four parts and it is thought to be very lucky if you find one of these.

clown¹ /klaʊn/ *noun* [C] **1** a person who wears funny clothes and a big red nose and does silly things to make people (especially children) laugh **2** a person who makes jokes and does silly things to make the people around them laugh: *At school, Jan was always the class clown.*

clown² /klaʊn/ *verb* [I] **clown (about/around)** to act in a funny or silly way: *Stop clowning around and get some work done!*

cloze test /ˈkləʊz test/ *noun* [C] a type of test in which you have to put suitable words in spaces in a text where words have been left out

EXAM TIP

Doing a cloze test

To find the correct word, look very carefully at the words on either side of the gap. Think about which words **collocate** (= go with) each other. Try to hear natural speech patterns in your head. When you know which word to use, make sure it is in the right tense and form. When you are practising for this type of exam, you can use the grammatical information and example sentences in your dictionary to help you.

club¹ /klʌb/ *noun* **1** [C] a group of people who meet regularly to share an interest, do sport, etc.; the place where they meet: *to join a club* ♦ *to be a member of a club* ♦ *a tennis/football/golf club* **2** (also nightclub) [C] a place where you can go to dance and drink late at night: *the club scene in Ibiza* **3** [C] a heavy stick, usually with one end that is thicker than the other, used as a weapon **4** [C] = **golf club** **5** clubs [pl] in a pack of playing cards, the **suit** (= one of the four sets) with black three-leafed shapes on them: *the two/ace/queen of clubs* ➲ note at **card** ➲ picture at **card** **6** [C] one of the cards from this suit: *I played a club.*

club² /klʌb/ *verb* (clu**bb**ing; clu**bb**ed) **1** [T] to hit sb/sth hard with a heavy object **2** [I] go clubbing to go dancing and drinking in a club: *She goes clubbing every Saturday.*
PHR V **club together (to do sth)** to share the cost of sth, for example a present: *We clubbed together to buy him a leaving present.*

cluck /klʌk/ *noun* [C] the noise made by a chicken ▸ **cluck** *verb* [I]

clue /klu:/ *noun* [C] a clue (to sth) a piece of information that helps you solve a problem or a crime, answer a question, etc: *The police were looking for clues to his disappearance.* ◆ *the clues for solving a crossword puzzle*
IDM **not have a clue** (*informal*) to know nothing about sth

clued-up /ˌklu:d ˈʌp/ (*AmE* also ˌclued-ˈin) *adj* clued-up (on sth) knowing a lot about sth: *I'm not really clued-up on the technical details.*

clueless /ˈklu:ləs/ *adj* (*informal*) not able to understand; stupid: *Many politicians are clueless about the lives of ordinary people.*

clump /klʌmp/ *noun* [C] a small group of plants or trees, growing together

clumsy /ˈklʌmzi/ *adj* (clumsier; clumsiest) **1** (used about a person) careless and likely to knock into, drop or break things: *I spilt your coffee. Sorry—that was clumsy of me.* **2** (used about a comment, etc.) likely to upset or offend people: *He made a clumsy apology.* **3** large, difficult to use and not attractive in design: *a clumsy piece of furniture* ▸ **clumsily** *adv* ▸ **clumsiness** *noun* [U]

clung *past tense, past participle of* **cling**

cluster¹ /ˈklʌstə(r)/ *noun* [C] a group of people, plants or things that stand or grow close together: *a cluster of schoolchildren*

cluster² /ˈklʌstə(r)/ *verb*
PHR V **cluster around sb/sth** to form a group around sb/sth: *The tourists clustered around their guide.*

clutch¹ /klʌtʃ/ *verb* [T] to hold sth tightly, especially because you are in pain, afraid or excited: *He clutched his mother's hand in fear.*
PHR V **clutch at sth** to try to take hold of sth: *She clutched at the money but the wind blew it away.*

clutch² /klʌtʃ/ *noun* **1** [C] the part of a vehicle, etc. that you press with your foot when you are driving in order to change the **gear** (= the machinery that changes engine power into movement); the part of the engine that it is connected to: *to press/release the clutch* ➲ picture at **car** **2** clutches [pl] power or control over sb: *He fell* **into** *the enemy's clutches.*

clutter¹ /ˈklʌtə(r)/ *verb* [T] clutter sth (up) to cover or fill sth with a lot of objects in an untidy way: *Don't leave those books there—they're cluttering up the table.*

clutter² /ˈklʌtə(r)/ *noun* [U] things that are where they are not wanted or needed and make a place untidy: *Who left all this clutter on the floor?* ▸ **cluttered** *adj*: *a cluttered desk*

🔑 **cm** *abbr* = **centimetre**

Co. /kəʊ/ *abbr* **1** = **company**: *W Smithson & Co.* **2** (*written*) = **County**: *Co. Down*

c/o *abbr* (used for addressing a letter to sb who is staying at another person's house); **care of**: *Andy Kirkham, c/o Mrs Potter*

🔑 **coach¹** /kəʊtʃ/ *noun* [C] **1** a person who trains people to compete in certain sports: *a tennis coach* **2** (*BrE*) a comfortable bus used for long journeys: *It's cheaper to travel* **by coach** *than by train.* ➲ note at **bus** ➲ picture on **page P7** **3** = **carriage** **4** a large vehicle with four wheels pulled by horses, used in the past for carrying passengers ➲ look at **carriage**, **car**

coach² /kəʊtʃ/ *verb* [T] coach sb (in/for sth) to train or teach sb, especially to compete in a sport or pass an exam: *She is being coached for the Olympics by a former champion.*

🔑 **coal** /kəʊl/ *noun* **1** [U] a type of black mineral that is dug from the ground and burnt to give heat: *a lump of coal* ◆ *a coal fire* ◆ *a coal mine* **2** a piece of coal: *A hot coal fell out of the fire and burnt the carpet.* ➲ picture at **fireplace**

coalition /ˌkəʊəˈlɪʃn/ *noun* [C, with sing or pl verb] a government formed by two or more political parties working together: *to form a coalition* ◆ *a coalition government*

ˈcoal mine (also pit) *noun* [C] a place, usually underground, where coal is dug from the ground ➲ look at **colliery**

ˈcoal miner (also miner) *noun* [C] a person whose job is to dig coal from the ground

coarse /kɔ:s/ *adj* (coarser; coarsest) **1** consisting of large pieces; rough, not smooth: *coarse salt* ◆ *coarse cloth* **OPP** **fine, smooth** **2** (used about a person or their behaviour) rude, likely to offend people; having bad manners: *His coarse remarks about women offended her.* ▸ **coarsely** *adv*: *Chop the onion coarsely* (= into pieces which are not too small). ◆ *He laughed coarsely.*

coarsen /ˈkɔ:sn/ *verb* [I,T] to become or to make sth **coarse**

🔑 **coast¹** /kəʊst/ *noun* [C] the area of land that is next to or close to the sea: *After sailing for an hour we could finally see the coast.* ◆ *Ancona is* **on the** *east* **coast**. ➲ picture on **page P10**

coast² /kəʊst/ *verb* [I] **1** to travel in a car, on a bicycle, etc. (especially down a hill) without using power **2** to achieve sth without much effort: *They coasted to victory.*

coastal /ˈkəʊstl/ *adj* on or near a coast: *a coastal path*

C

coastguard /ˈkəʊstgɑːd/ *noun* [C] a person or group of people whose job is to watch the sea near the coast in order to help people or ships that are in danger or to stop illegal activities

coastline /ˈkəʊstlaɪn/ *noun* [C] the edge or shape of a coast: *a rocky coastline*

⚷ **coat**[1] /kəʊt/ *noun* [C] **1** a piece of clothing that you wear over your other clothes to keep warm when you are outside: *Put your coat on—it's cold outside.* ➲ look at **overcoat**, **raincoat** ➲ picture on **page P1** **2** the fur or hair covering an animal's body: *a dog with a smooth coat* ➲ picture on **page P12** **3** a layer of sth covering a surface: *The walls will probably need two coats of paint.*

coat[2] /kəʊt/ *verb* [T] **coat sth (with/in sth)** to cover sth with a layer of sth: *biscuits coated with milk chocolate*

ˈ**coat hanger** = **hanger**

coating /ˈkəʊtɪŋ/ *noun* [C] a thin layer of sth that covers sth else: *wire with a plastic coating*

ˌ**coat of** ˈ**arms** (also **arms**) *noun* [C] a design that is used as the symbol of a family, a town, a university, etc.

coax /kəʊks/ *verb* [T] **coax sb (into/out of sth/doing sth)**; **coax sth out of/from sb** to persuade sb gently: *The child wasn't hungry, but his mother coaxed him into eating a little.* ◆ *At last he coaxed a smile out of her.*

cobalt /ˈkəʊbɔːlt/ *noun* [U] **1** (*symbol* Co) a hard silver-white metal that is often mixed with other metals and used to give a deep bluish-green colour to glass **2** (also ˌ**cobalt** ˈ**blue**) a deep bluish-green colour

cobble /ˈkɒbl/ *verb*

PHR V **cobble sth together** to make sth or put sth together quickly and without much care

cobbler /ˈkɒblə(r)/ *noun* [C] (*old-fashioned*) a person who repairs shoes

cobbles /ˈkɒblz/ (also **cobblestones** /ˈkɒblstəʊnz/) *noun* [pl] small round stones used (in the past) for covering the surface of streets ▶ **cobbled** *adj*

cobra /ˈkəʊbrə/ *noun* [C] a poisonous snake that can spread out the skin at the back of its neck. **Cobras** live in India and Africa.

cobweb /ˈkɒbweb/ *noun* [C] a net of threads made by a spider in order to catch insects

cocaine /kəʊˈkeɪn/ (also *informal* **coke**) *noun* [U] a dangerous drug that some people take for pleasure but which is **addictive** (= difficult to stop using)

cock[1] /kɒk/ *noun* [C] **1** (*AmE* **rooster**) an adult male chicken ➲ note at **chicken** ➲ picture at **chicken** **2** an adult male bird of any type

cock[2] /kɒk/ *verb* [T] to hold up a part of the body: *The horse cocked its ears on hearing the noise.*

PHR V **cock sth up** (*BrE slang*) to do sth very badly and spoil sth ➲ look at **cock-up**

cock-a-doodle-doo /ˌkɒk ə ˌduːdl ˈduː/ *noun* [sing] the noise made by an adult male chicken

cockerel /ˈkɒkərəl/ *noun* [C] a young male chicken

cockney /ˈkɒkni/ *noun* **1** [C] a person who was born and grew up in the East End of London **2** [U] the way of speaking English that is typical of people living in this area: *a cockney accent*

cockpit /ˈkɒkpɪt/ *noun* [C] the area in a plane, boat or racing car where the pilot or driver sits

cockroach /ˈkɒkrəʊtʃ/ (*AmE* **roach**) *noun* [C] a large dark brown insect, usually found in dirty or slightly wet places

cocktail /ˈkɒkteɪl/ *noun* [C] **1** a drink made from a mixture of alcoholic drinks and fruit juices **2** a mixture of small pieces of food that is served cold: *a prawn cocktail*

ˈ**cock-up** *noun* [C] (*slang*) something that was badly done; a mistake that spoils sth

cocoa /ˈkəʊkəʊ/ *noun* **1** [U] a dark brown powder made from the seeds of a tropical tree and used in making chocolate **2** [C,U] a hot drink made from this powder mixed with milk or water; a cup of this drink: *a cup of cocoa*

coconut /ˈkəʊkənʌt/ *noun* [C,U] a large tropical fruit with a hard shell that is covered with hair ➲ picture on **page P14**

cocoon[1] /kəˈkuːn/ *noun* [C] **1** a covering of silk threads that some insects make to protect themselves before they become adults **2** a soft covering that wraps all around sb/sth and keeps them safe: (*figurative*) *the cocoon of a caring family*

cocoon[2] /kəˈkuːn/ *verb* [T] **cocoon sb/sth (in sth)** to surround sb/sth completely with sth for protection

cod /kɒd/ *noun* [C,U] (*pl* **cod**) a large sea fish with white flesh that you can eat

⚷ **code**[1] /kəʊd/ *noun* **1** [C,U] a system of words, letters, numbers, etc. that are used instead of the real letters or words to make a message or information secret: *They managed to break/crack the enemy code* (= find out what it means). ◆ *a security code* ◆ *They wrote letters to each other* **in code**. ➲ look at **decode** **2** [C] a group of numbers, letters, etc. that is used for identifying sth: *What's the code* (= the telephone number) *for Stockholm?* ➲ look at **bar code** **3** [U] a system of computer programming instructions **4** [C] a set of rules for behaviour: *a code of practice* (= a set of standards agreed and accepted by a particular profession) ◆ *the Highway Code* (= the rules for driving on the roads)

code[2] /kəʊd/ *verb* [T] **1** to use a particular system for identifying things: *The files are colour-coded: blue for Europe, green for Africa.* **2** (also **encode**) to put or write sth in code: *coded messages* OPP **decode**

C

ˌ**co-eduˈcational** (also *informal* coed /ˌkəʊˈed/) *adj* (used about a school) where girls and boys are taught together SYN **mixed**

coerce /kəʊˈɜːs/ *verb* [T] (*formal*) coerce sb (into sth/doing sth) to force sb to do sth, for example by threatening them ▶ **coercion** /kəʊˈɜːʃn/ *noun* [U]

coexist /ˌkəʊɪgˈzɪst/ *verb* [I] to live or be together at the same time or in the same place as sb/sth ▶ **coexistence** *noun* [U]

C. of E. /ˌsiː əv ˈiː/ *abbr* = **Church of England**

⚷ **coffee** /ˈkɒfi/ *noun* **1** [U] **coffee beans** (= seeds of a tropical bush) that are cooked, made into powder and used for making a drink: *Coffee is the country's biggest export.* ◆ *a jar of coffee* **2** [U] a drink made by adding hot water to this powder: *Would you prefer tea or coffee?* ◆ *a cup of coffee* **3** [C] a cup of this drink: *Two coffees please.* ➲ picture on **page P16**

TOPIC

Coffee

Black coffee is made without milk; **white coffee** is with milk. **Decaffeinated coffee** has had the **caffeine** (= the substance that makes you feel more awake and full of energy) taken out. Coffee can be **weak** or **strong**. **Instant coffee** is sold in a jar and made by pouring hot water or milk onto coffee powder in a cup. **Fresh coffee** is made in a coffee pot from coffee beans that have just been ground (= crushed into a powder). **Filter coffee** is made in a special machine. You can buy different kinds of coffee ready to drink at a **coffee bar/shop**.

ˈ**coffee bar** (also ˈcoffee shop) *noun* [C] (*BrE*) a place in a hotel, a large shop, etc. where simple food, coffee, tea and other drinks without alcohol are served

ˈ**coffee pot** *noun* [C] a container in which coffee is made and served

ˈ**coffee table** *noun* [C] a small low table for putting magazines, cups, etc. on ➲ picture on **page P8**

coffin /ˈkɒfɪn/ *noun* [C] (*AmE* casket) a box in which a dead body is buried in the ground or **cremated** (= burnt) ➲ note at **funeral**

cog /kɒg/ *noun* [C] **1** one of a series of teeth on the edge of a wheel that fit between the teeth on the next wheel and cause it to move **2** = **cogwheel**

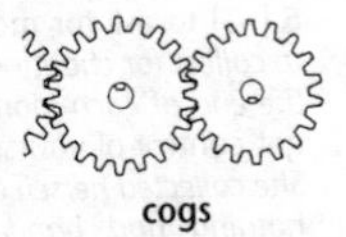

cogs

cognac /ˈkɒnjæk/ *noun* **1** [U] a type of **brandy** (= a strong alcoholic drink made from wine) that is made in France **2** [C] a glass of this drink

cogwheel /ˈkɒgwiːl/ (also cog) *noun* [C] a wheel with a series of teeth on its edge that fit into the teeth in the next wheel and cause it to move

cohabit /kəʊˈhæbɪt/ *verb* [I] (*formal*) (used about a couple) to live together as if they are married

coherent /kəʊˈhɪərənt/ *adj* clear and easy to understand OPP **incoherent** ▶ **coherence** *noun* [U] ▶ **coherently** *adv*

cohesion /kəʊˈhiːʒn/ *noun* [U] the ability to stay or fit together well: *What the team lacks is cohesion—all the players play as individuals.*

coil[1] /kɔɪl/ *verb* [I,T] to make sth into a round shape: *a snake coiled under a rock*

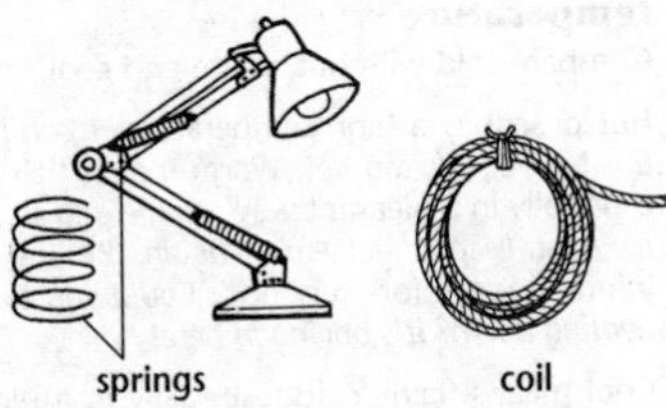

springs coil

coil[2] /kɔɪl/ *noun* [C] a length of rope, wire, etc. that has been made into a round shape: *a coil of rope*

⚷ **coin**[1] /kɔɪn/ *noun* [C] a piece of money made of metal: *a pound coin* ➲ picture at **money**

coin[2] /kɔɪn/ *verb* [T] to invent a new word or phrase: *Who was it who coined the phrase 'less is more'?*

coincide /ˌkəʊɪnˈsaɪd/ *verb* [I] coincide (with sth) **1** (used about events) to happen at the same time as sth else: *The Queen's visit is timed to coincide with the country's centenary celebrations.* **2** to be exactly the same or very similar: *Our views coincide completely.*

coincidence /kəʊˈɪnsɪdəns/ *noun* [C,U] two or more similar things happening at the same time by chance, in a surprising way: *We hadn't planned to meet, it was just coincidence.*

coincidental /kəʊˌɪnsɪˈdentl/ *adj* resulting from two similar or related events happening at the same time by chance ▶ **coincidentally** /-təli/ *adv*

coke /kəʊk/ *noun* [U] **1** (*informal*) = **cocaine** **2** a solid black substance produced from coal and used as a fuel

Col. *abbr* = **Colonel**

cola /ˈkəʊlə/ *noun* [C,U] a sweet brown drink that does not contain alcohol; a glass or can of this

colander /ˈkʌləndə(r)/ *noun* [C] a metal or plastic bowl with a lot of small holes in it that is used for removing water from food that has been boiled or washed ➲ picture at **kitchen**

⚷ **cold**[1] /kəʊld/ *adj* (colder; coldest) **1** having a low temperature; not hot or warm: *Shall we put the heating on? I'm cold.* ◆ *Take your coat. It's cold outside.* ◆ *I'm not going into the sea—the water's too cold.* **2** (used about food or drink) not heated or cooked; having become cold after being heated or cooked: *a cold drink* ◆ *Have your soup before it gets cold.* **3** (used about a person or sb's behaviour) very unfriendly; not showing kindness, understanding, etc: *She gave him a cold, hard look.*

IDM **cold turkey** suddenly and completely, without getting used to sth gradually: *I gave up smoking cold turkey.*

get/have cold feet (*informal*) to become/be afraid

to do sth: *She started to get cold feet as her wedding day approached.*
in cold blood in a cruel way and without pity: *to kill somebody in cold blood*

C

OTHER WORDS FOR

temperature

Compare **cold** with **hot, warm** and **cool.**

Hot describes a high temperature: *I can't drink this tea yet, it's too hot.* **Warm** means 'fairly hot, especially in a pleasant way': *Come and sit by the fire, you'll soon get warm again.* **Boiling** is an informal word for 'very hot': *Could you turn the heating down? It's boiling in here!*

Cool means 'fairly cold, especially in a pleasant way': *It's hot outside but it's nice and cool in here.* **Freezing** means 'extremely cold': *It's absolutely freezing outside.* It can mean that the temperature is below 0° Celsius.

cold[2] /kəʊld/ *noun* **1** [sing,U] lack of heat; low temperature; cold weather: *We walked home in the snow, shivering with cold.* ◆ *Come on, let's get out of the cold and go indoors.* **2** [C,U] a common illness of the nose and throat. When you have a cold you have a sore throat and often cannot breathe through your nose: *I think I'm getting a cold.* ◆ *Wear some warm clothes when you go out or you'll* ***catch cold.*** ➲ note at ill

ˌcold-ˈblooded *adj* **1** cruel; having or showing no pity: *cold-blooded killers* **2** (used about animals, for example fish or snakes) having a blood temperature that changes with the temperature of the surroundings: *Reptiles are cold-blooded.* ➲ look at **warm-blooded**

ˌcold-ˈhearted *adj* unkind; showing no kindness, understanding, etc.

coldly /ˈkəʊldli/ *adv* in an unfriendly way; in a way that shows no kindness or understanding: *'Stop crying immediately,' she said coldly.*

coldness /ˈkəʊldnəs/ *noun* [U] the lack of warm feelings; unfriendly behaviour

colic /ˈkɒlɪk/ *noun* [U] severe pain in the stomach area, which especially babies get

collaborate /kəˈlæbəreɪt/ *verb* [I] **1** collaborate (with sb) (on sth) to work together (with sb), especially to create or produce sth: *She collaborated with another author on the book.* **2** collaborate (with sb) (disapproving) to help the enemy forces who have taken control of your country ▶ **collaboration** /kəˌlæbəˈreɪʃn/ *noun* [U] ▶ **collaborator** /kəˈlæbəreɪtə(r)/ *noun* [C]

collage /ˈkɒlɑːʒ/ *noun* [C,U] a picture made by fixing pieces of paper, cloth, photographs, etc. onto a surface; the art of making a picture like this

collapse[1] /kəˈlæps/ *verb* [I] **1** to fall down or break into pieces suddenly: *A lot of buildings collapsed in the earthquake.* **2** (used about a person) to fall down and often become unconscious, usually because you are very ill: *The winner collapsed at the end of the race.* **3** (used about a business, plan, etc.) to fail suddenly or completely: *The company collapsed, leaving hundreds of people out of work.* **4** to fold sth or be folded into a shape that uses less space: *a chair that collapses for easy storage*

collapse[2] /kəˈlæps/ *noun* **1** [C,U] the sudden or complete failure of sth, such as a business, plan, etc: *The peace talks were on the brink/verge of collapse.* **2** [sing,U] (used about a building) a sudden fall: *the collapse of the motorway bridge* **3** [sing,U] (used about a person) a medical condition when a person becomes very ill and suddenly falls down: *She was taken to hospital after her collapse at work.*

collapsible /kəˈlæpsəbl/ *adj* that can be folded into a shape that makes sth easy to store: *a collapsible bed*

collar[1] /ˈkɒlə(r)/ *noun* [C] **1** the part of a shirt, coat, dress, etc. that fits round the neck and is often folded over: *a coat with a fur collar* ➲ look at **blue-collar, dog collar, white-collar** ➲ picture at **lace** ➲ picture on **page P1** **2** a band of leather that is put round an animal's neck (especially a dog)

collar[2] /ˈkɒlə(r)/ *verb* [T] (*informal*) to catch hold of sb who does not want to be caught: *The police officer collared the thief.*

collarbone /ˈkɒləbəʊn/ (also *formal* clavicle) *noun* [C] one of the two bones that connect your chest bones to your shoulder ➲ picture at **body**

collateral /kəˈlætərəl/ *noun* [U] property or sth valuable that you agree to give if you cannot pay back money that you have borrowed

colleague /ˈkɒliːɡ/ *noun* [C] a person who works at the same place as you: *We were friends and colleagues for many years.*

collect[1] /kəˈlekt/ *verb* **1** [T] to bring a number of things together: *All the exam papers will be collected at the end.* **2** [T] to get and keep together a number of objects of a particular type over a period of time as a hobby: *He used to collect stamps.* ➲ picture on **page P3** **3** [I] to come together: *A crowd collected to see what was going on.* **SYN** **gather** **4** [T] (*especially BrE*) to go and get sb/sth from a particular place; to pick sb/sth up: *to collect the children from school* **5** [I,T] to ask for money from a number of people: *to collect for charity* ◆ *The landlord collects the rent at the end of each month.* **6** [T] collect yourself/sth to get control of yourself, your feelings, thoughts, etc: *She collected herself and went back into the room as if nothing had happened.* ◆ *I tried to* ***collect my thoughts*** *before the exam.*

collect[2] /kəˈlekt/ *adj, adv* (*AmE*) (used about a telephone call) to be paid for by the person who receives the call: *a collect call* ◆ *She called me collect.*

HELP In British English, we **make a reverse-charge call** or **reverse the charges.**

collected /kəˈlektɪd/ *adj* [not before a noun] calm and in control of yourself, your feelings, thoughts, etc: *She felt cool, calm and collected before the interview.*

collection /kəˈlekʃn/ *noun* **1** [C] a group of objects of a particular type that sb has collected as a hobby: *a stamp collection* **2** [C,U] the act of getting sth from a place or from people: *rubbish collections* **3** [C] a group of people or things: *a large collection of papers on the desk* **4** [C] a number of poems, stories, letters, etc. published together in one book: *a collection of modern poetry* **5** [C] the act of asking for money from a number of people (for charity, in church, etc.): *a collection for the poor* **6** [C] a variety of new clothes or items for the home that are specially designed and sold at a particular time: *Armani's stunning new autumn collection*

collective[1] /kəˈlektɪv/ *adj* shared by a group of people together; not individual: *collective responsibility* ▶ **collectively** *adv*: *We took the decision collectively at a meeting.*

collective[2] /kəˈlektɪv/ *noun* [C, with sing or pl verb] an organization or a business that is owned and controlled by the people who work in it

collector /kəˈlektə(r)/ *noun* [C] [in compounds] a person who collects things as a hobby or as part of their job: *a stamp collector* ◆ *a ticket/rent/tax collector*

college /ˈkɒlɪdʒ/ *noun* **1** [C,U] an institution where you can study after you leave school (at the age of 16): *an art college* ◆ *a sixth-form college* (= an institution where students aged 16 to 18 can prepare for A Levels) ◆ *She's studying Spanish at the college of further education* (= a college that provides education and training for people over 16).

> **HELP** We talk about **college**, without **the**, when we mean that somebody is attending a college or university as a student: *He's at college in York.* ◆ *She's going to college in October.* We use **the** if somebody goes there for any other reason: *I went to an art exhibition at the college last night.*

2 [C] (in the US) a university, or part of one, where students can study for a degree **3** [C] (in Britain) one of the separate institutions into which certain universities are divided: *King's College, London* ◆ *a tour of Oxford colleges*

collide /kəˈlaɪd/ *verb* [I] collide (with sb/sth) to crash; to hit sb/sth very hard while moving: *He ran along the corridor and collided with his music teacher.*

colliery /ˈkɒliəri/ *noun* [C] (*pl* collieries) (*especially BrE*) a coal mine and its buildings

collision /kəˈlɪʒn/ *noun* [C,U] an occasion when things or people **collide**: *It was a* ***head-on collision*** *and the driver was killed instantly.*

IDM be on a collision course (with sb/sth) 1 to be in a situation which is certain to end in a disagreement or an argument: *I'm not surprised they're arguing—they've been on a collision course over money all week.* **2** to be moving in a direction which is certain to cause a crash: *The ship was on a collision course with an iceberg.*

collocation /ˌkɒləˈkeɪʃn/ *noun* [C,U] a combination of words in a language, that happens very often and more frequently than would happen by chance; the fact that these combinations happen: *'Resounding success' and 'crying shame' are English collocations.* ◆ *Students need to be aware of the importance of collocation.*

> EXAM TIP
>
> **Collocations**
>
> When you learn a new word, learn the words that go with it. This expands your vocabulary and helps you to write and speak natural English. For example, if you look at the entry for **fashion**, you will find sentences that include the expressions *the latest fashion*, *in fashion*, *come back into fashion* and *out of fashion*. You can even learn more by looking up familiar words. For example, is it better to say 'strong rain' or 'heavy rain'?

colloquial /kəˈləʊkwiəl/ *adj* (used about words, phrases, etc.) used in spoken conversation, not in formal situations ▶ **colloquially** /-kwiəli/ *adv*

colloquialism /kəˈləʊkwiəlɪzəm/ *noun* [C] a **colloquial** word or phrase

collusion /kəˈluːʒn/ *noun* [U] (*formal*) secret agreement, especially in order to do sth dishonest: *The police were corrupt and were acting* ***in collusion with*** *the criminals.*

cologne /kəˈləʊn/ = **eau de cologne**

colon /ˈkəʊlən/ *noun* [C] the mark (:) used before a list, an explanation, an example, etc.

colonel /ˈkɜːnl/ *noun* [C] (*abbr* Col.) an officer of a high level in the army

colonial /kəˈləʊniəl/ *adj* connected with or belonging to a **colony** (= a country that is controlled by another country): *Spain used to be a major colonial power.*

colonialism /kəˈləʊniəlɪzəm/ *noun* [U] the practice by which a powerful country controls another country or countries, in order to become richer

colonist /ˈkɒlənɪst/ *noun* [C] a person who goes to live in a country that has become a **colony**

colonize (also -ise) /ˈkɒlənaɪz/ *verb* [T] to take control of another country or place and make it a **colony** ▶ **colonization** (also -isation) /ˌkɒlənaɪˈzeɪʃn/ *noun* [U]

colony /ˈkɒləni/ *noun* [C] (*pl* colonies) **1** a country or an area that is ruled by another, more powerful country **2** [with sing or pl verb] a group of people who go to live permanently in another country but keep their own habits and customs **3** a group of the same type of animals, insects or plants living or growing in the same place: *a colony of ants*

colossal /kəˈlɒsl/ *adj* extremely large: *a colossal building* ◆ *a colossal amount of money*

colour[1] (*AmE* color) /ˈkʌlə(r)/ *noun* **1** [C,U] the fact that sth is red, green, yellow, blue, etc: *'What colour is your car?' 'Red.'* ◆ *What colours do the Swedish team play in?* ◆ *a dark/deep colour* ◆ *a bright colour* ◆ *a light/pale colour* ◆ *Those flowers certainly give the room a bit of colour.*

HELP We say 'I like the colour blue' NOT 'I like blue colour'. Also, we say that a thing **is** a certain colour, not that it **has** a colour.

C

2 [U] the use of all the colours, not just black and white: *All the pictures in the book are* ***in colour.*** ♦ *colour printing* **3** [U] a red or pink colour in your face, particularly when it shows how healthy you are or that you are embarrassed: *You look much better now, you've got a bit more colour.* ♦ *Colour flooded her face when she thought of what had happened.* **4** [U] interesting or exciting details: *It's a busy area, full of activity and colour.*
IDM **off colour** ill
with flying colours ➲ **flying**

colour² (*AmE* color) /ˈkʌlə(r)/ *verb* [T] **1** to put colour on sth, for example by painting it: *Colour the picture with your crayons.* ♦ *The area coloured yellow on the map is desert.* **2** to influence thoughts, opinions, etc: *You shouldn't let one bad experience at school colour your attitude to education.*
PHR V **colour sth in** to fill a shape, a picture, etc. with colour using pencils, paint, etc: *The children were colouring in pictures of animals.*

ˈ**colour-blind** *adj* unable to see certain colours, especially red and green

coloured (*AmE* colored) /ˈkʌləd/ *adj* **1** having colour or a particular colour: *a coffee-coloured dress* ♦ *brightly coloured lights* **2** (used about a person) belonging to a race that does not have white skin

HELP This word is considered offensive nowadays. To refer to a person belonging to a particular racial group, you should use black, Asian, etc. as appropriate.

colourful (*AmE* colorful) /ˈkʌləfl/ *adj* **1** with bright colours; full of colour: *Gary wore a colourful shirt.* **2** full of interest or excitement: *a colourful story* ♦ *He has a rather colourful past.*

colouring (*AmE* coloring) /ˈkʌlərɪŋ/ *noun* **1** [C,U] a substance that is used to give a particular colour to sth, especially food **2** [U] the colour of a person's hair, skin, etc: *to have fair/dark colouring*

colourless (*AmE* colorless) /ˈkʌlələs/ *adj* **1** without any colour: *a colourless liquid, like water* **2** not interesting or exciting **SYN** **dull**

ˈ**colour scheme** *noun* [C] the way in which colours are arranged, especially in a room

colt /kəʊlt/ *noun* [C] a young male horse

column /ˈkɒləm/ *noun* [C]
➤STONE **1** a tall solid vertical post made of stone, supporting or decorating a building or standing alone: *Nelson's Column is a monument in London.* ➲ picture at **arch**
➤SHAPE **2** something that has the shape of a column: *a column of smoke* (= smoke rising straight up)
➤ON PAGE **3** one of the vertical sections into which a printed page, especially in a newspaper, is divided: *a column of text*
➤IN NEWSPAPER **4** a piece of writing in a newspaper or magazine that is part of a regular series or always written by the same writer: *the travel/gossip column*
➤NUMBERS **5** a series of numbers written one under the other: *to add up a column of figures*
➤PEOPLE/VEHICLES **6** a long line of people, vehicles, etc., one following behind another: *a column of troops*

columnist /ˈkɒləmnɪst/ *noun* [C] a journalist who writes regular articles in a newspaper or magazine: *a gossip columnist*

coma /ˈkəʊmə/ *noun* [C] a deep unconscious state, often lasting for a long time and caused by serious illness or injury

comatose /ˈkəʊmətəʊs/ *adj* **1** deeply unconscious; in a **coma** **2** (*informal*) deeply asleep: *After a large dinner, Mum was comatose on the sofa.*

comb¹ /kəʊm/ *noun* [C] **1** a flat piece of metal or plastic with teeth that you use for making your hair tidy **2** [usually sing] an act of **combing** the hair: *Give your hair a comb before you go out.*

comb² /kəʊm/ *verb* [T] **1** to make your hair tidy using a **comb** **2** comb sth (for sb/sth) to search an area carefully: *Police are combing the woodland for the murder weapon.*

combat¹ /ˈkɒmbæt/ *noun* [C,U] a fight, especially in war: *unarmed combat* (= without weapons)

combat² /ˈkɒmbæt/ *verb* [T] to fight against sth; to try to stop or defeat sth: *to combat terrorism* ♦ *new medicines to combat heart disease*

combatant /ˈkɒmbətənt/ *noun* [C] a person who takes part in fighting, especially in war

combats /ˈkɒmbæts/ (also ˈcombat trousers) *noun* [pl] (*BrE*) = **cargo pants**

combination /ˌkɒmbɪˈneɪʃn/ *noun* [C,U] a number of people or things mixed or joined together; a mixture: *The team manager still hasn't found the right combination of players.* ♦ *On this course, you may study French* ***in combination with*** *Spanish or Italian.*

combine /kəmˈbaɪn/ *verb* **1** [I,T] combine (sth) (with sb/sth) to join or mix two or more things together: *The two organizations combined to form one company.* ♦ *Bad weather, combined with illness, led to the picnic being cancelled.* **2** [T] combine A and/with B to do or have two or more things at the same time: *to combine business with pleasure* ♦ *This car combines speed and reliability.*

combined /kəmˈbaɪnd/ *adj* done by a number of people joining together, resulting from the joining of two or more things: *The* ***combined efforts*** *of the emergency services prevented a major disaster.*

combine harvester /ˌkɒmbaɪn ˈhɑːvɪstə(r)/ (also combine) *noun* [C] a large farm machine that both cuts a crop and separates the grain from the rest of the plant ➲ look at **harvest**

combustible /kəmˈbʌstəbl/ *adj* able to begin burning easily: *combustible material/gases* **SYN** **inflammable**

combustion /kəmˈbʌstʃən/ *noun* [U] the process of burning

C

come /kʌm/ *verb* [I] (*pt* came /keɪm/; *pp* come) **1** to move to or towards the person who is speaking or the place that sb is talking about: *Come here, please.* ♦ *Come and see what I've found.* ♦ *I hope you can come to my party.* ♦ *They're coming to stay for a week.* ♦ *The children came running into the room.* **2** come (to ...) to arrive somewhere or reach a particular place or time: *What time are you coming home?* ♦ *Has the newspaper come yet?* ♦ *After a few hours in the jungle, we came to a river* ♦ *Her hair comes down to her waist.* ♦ *The water in the pool came up to our knees.* ♦ *The time has come to say goodbye.* **3** to be in a particular position in a series: *March comes after February.* ♦ *Charlie came second in the exam.* ♦ *I can't wait to find out what comes next in the story.* **4** come in sth to be available: *This blouse comes in a choice of four colours.* ♦ *Do these trousers come in a larger size?* **5** to be produced by or from sth: *Wool comes from sheep.* **6** to become open or loose: *Your blouse has come undone.* ♦ *Her hair has come untied.* **7** come to do sth used for talking about how, why or when sth happened: *How did you come to lose your passport?* **8** come to/into sth to reach a particular state: *We were all sorry when the holiday came to an end.* ♦ *The military government came to power in a coup d'état.*

IDM **come and go** to be present for a short time and then go away: *The pain in my ear comes and goes.*

come easily, naturally, etc. to sb to be easy, natural, etc. for sb to do: *Apologizing does not come easily to her.*

come to nothing; not come to anything to fail; to not be successful: *Unfortunately, all his efforts came to nothing.*

How come? (*informal*) why or how: *'I think you owe me some money.' 'How come?* ♦ *How come you're back so early?*

to come [used after a noun] in the future: *You'll regret it in years to come.*

when it comes to sth/to doing sth when it is a question of sth: *When it comes to value for money, these prices are hard to beat.* ℹ For other idioms containing **come**, look at the entries for the nouns, adjectives, etc. For example **come to a head** is at **head**.

PHR V **come about** to happen: *How did this situation come about?*

come across/over (as sth) to make an impression of a particular type: *Elizabeth comes across as being rather shy.*

come across sb/sth to meet or find sb/sth by chance: *I came across this book in a second-hand shop.*

come along 1 to arrive or appear: *An old man was coming along the road.* **2** = **come on**(2) **3** = **come on**(3)

come apart to break into pieces: *This old coat is coming apart at the seams.*

come away (from sth) to become separated from sth: *The wallpaper is coming away from the wall in the corner.*

come away with sth to leave a place with a particular opinion or feeling: *We came away with a very favourable impression of Lisbon.*

come back 1 to return: *I don't know what time I'll be coming back.* **2** to become popular or fashionable again: *Flared trousers are coming back again.*

come back (to sb) to be remembered: *When I went to Italy again, my Italian started to come back to me.*

come before sb/sth to be more important than sb/sth else: *Mark feels his family comes before his career.*

come between sb and sb to damage the relationship between two people: *Arguments over money came between the two brothers.*

come by sth to manage to get sth: *Fresh vegetables are hard to come by in the winter.*

come down 1 to fall down: *The power lines came down in the storm.* **2** (used about an aircraft, etc.) to land: *The helicopter came down in a field.* **3** (used about prices) to become lower: *The price of land has come down in the past year.*

come down to sth/to doing sth (*informal*) to be able to be explained by a single important point: *It all comes down to having the right qualifications.*

come down with sth to become ill with sth: *I think I'm coming down with flu.*

come forward to offer help: *The police are asking witnesses to come forward.*

come from ... to live in or have been born in a place: *Where do you come from originally?*

come from (doing) sth to be the result of sth: *'I'm tired.' 'That comes from all the late nights you've had.'*

come in 1 to enter a place: *Come in and sit down.* **2** (used about the **tides** (= the regular movements of the sea)) to move towards the land and cover the beach ➲ look at **tide** **3** to become popular or fashionable: *Punk fashions came in during the seventies.* **4** (used about news or information) to be received: *Reports are coming in of fighting in Beirut.*

come in for sth to receive sth, especially sth unpleasant: *The government came in for a lot of criticism.*

come of sth/of doing sth to be the result of sth: *We've written to several companies asking for help but nothing has come of it yet.*

come off 1 to be able to be removed: *Does the hood come off?* **2** (*informal*) to be successful: *The deal seems unlikely to come off.* **3** [before an adverb] (*informal*) to be in a good, bad, etc. situation as a result of sth: *Unfortunately, Dennis came off worst in the fight.*

come off (sth) 1 to fall off sth: *Kim came off her bicycle and broke her leg.* **2** to become removed from sth: *One of the legs has come off this table.*

come off it (*spoken*) used to say that you do not believe sb/sth or that you strongly disagree with sb: *'I thought it was quite a good performance.' 'Oh, come off it—it was awful!'*

come on 1 to start to act, play in a game of sport, etc: *The audience jeered every time the villain came on.* ♦ *The substitute came on in the second half.* **2** (also come along) to make progress or to improve: *Your English is coming on nicely.* **3** (also Come along!) used to tell sb to hurry up, try harder, etc: *Come on or we'll be late!* **4** to begin: *I've got a cold coming on.*

come out 1 to appear; to be published: *The rain*

stopped and the sun came out. ◆ *The report came out in 1998.* **2** to become known: *It was only after David's death that the truth came out.* **3** if a person **comes out,** they tell family, friends, etc. that they are **homosexual** (= sexually attracted to people of the same sex)

come out (of sth) to be removed from sth: *Red wine stains don't come out easily.*

come out against sth to say in public that you do not like or agree with sth: *The Prime Minister came out against capital punishment.*

come out in sth to become covered in spots, etc: *Heat makes him come out in a rash.*

come out with sth to say sth unexpectedly: *The children came out with all kinds of stories.*

come over = **come across/over**

come over (to ...) (from ...) to visit people or a place a long way away: *They've invited us to come over to Australia for a holiday.*

come over sb (used about a feeling) to affect sb: *A feeling of despair came over me.*

come round 1 (also come to) to become conscious again: *She hasn't come round from the anaesthetic yet.* OPP **pass out 2** (used about an event that happens regularly) to happen: *The end of the holidays always comes round very quickly.*

come round (to ...) to visit a person or place not far away: *Do you want to come round for lunch on Saturday?*

come round (to sth) to change your opinion so that you agree with sb/sth: *They finally came round to our way of thinking.*

come through (used about news, information, etc.) to arrive: *The football results are just coming through.*

come through (sth) to escape injury or death in a dangerous situation, illness, etc: *She was lucky to come through the operation.*

come to = **come round**(1)

come to sth 1 to equal or total a particular amount: *The bill for the meal came to £35.* **2** to result in a bad situation: *We will sell the house to pay our debts if we have to but we hope it won't come to that.*

come under sth to be included in a particular section, department, etc: *Garages that sell cars come under 'car dealers' in the telephone book.*

come up 1 (used about a plant) to appear above the soil **2** (used about the sun and moon) to rise **3** to happen or be going to happen in the future: *Something's come up at work so I won't be home until late tonight.* **4** to be discussed or mentioned: *The subject of religion came up.*

come up against sb/sth to find a problem or difficulty that you have to deal with: *We came up against a very strong team in the first match.*

come up to sth to be as good as usual or as necessary: *This piece of work does not come up to your usual standard.*

come up with sth to find an answer or a solution to sth: *Engineers have come up with new ways of saving energy.*

comeback /ˈkʌmbæk/ *noun* [C] a return to a position of strength or importance that you had before: *The former world champion is hoping to make a comeback.*

comedian /kəˈmiːdiən/ (also comic) *noun* [C] a person whose job is to entertain people and make them laugh, for example by telling jokes

comedown /ˈkʌmdaʊn/ *noun* [sing] (*informal*) a loss of importance or social position: *It's **a bit of a comedown** for her having to move to a smaller flat.*

comedy /ˈkɒmədi/ *noun* (*pl* comedies) **1** [C] an amusing play, film, etc. that has a happy ending: *a romantic comedy* ➲ look at **tragedy 2** [U] the quality of being amusing or making people laugh: *There is a hint of comedy in all her novels.* SYN **humour**

comet /ˈkɒmɪt/ *noun* [C] an object in space that looks like a bright star with a tail and that moves around the sun

comfort¹ /ˈkʌmfət/ *noun* **1** [U] the state of having everything your body needs, or of having a pleasant life: *Most people expect to live **in comfort** in their old age.* ◆ *to travel in comfort* **2** [U] the feeling of being physically relaxed and in no pain: *This car has been specially designed for extra comfort.* OPP **discomfort 3** [U] help or kindness to sb who is suffering: *I tried to offer a few words of comfort.* **4** [sing] be a comfort (to sb) a person or thing that helps you when you are very sad or worried: *You've been a real comfort to me.* **5** [C] something that makes your life easier or more pleasant: *the comforts of home*

comfort² /ˈkʌmfət/ *verb* [T] to try to make sb feel less worried or unhappy: *to comfort a crying child*

comfortable /ˈkʌmftəbl/ *adj* **1** (also *informal* comfy /ˈkʌmfi/) that makes you feel physically relaxed and in no pain; that provides you with everything your body needs: *a comfortable temperature* (= not too hot or too cold) ◆ *Sit down and make yourselves comfortable.* ◆ *a comfortable pair of shoes* OPP **uncomfortable 2** not having or causing worry, difficulty, etc: *He did not feel comfortable in the presence of so many women.* **3** having or providing enough money for all your needs: *My parents are not wealthy but they're quite comfortable.* ▶ **comfortably** /-əbli/ *adv*: *Jon was sitting comfortably in the armchair.* ◆ *You can't live comfortably on such low wages.*

comic¹ /ˈkɒmɪk/ *adj* that makes you laugh; connected with amusing entertainment: *a comic scene in a play*

comic² /ˈkɒmɪk/ *noun* [C] **1** = **comedian 2** (*especially AmE* ˈcomic book) a magazine for children that tells stories through pictures

comical /ˈkɒmɪkl/ *adj* that makes you laugh; funny ▶ **comically** /-kli/ *adv*

ˈcomic book (*especially AmE*) = **comic²**(2)

ˈcomic strip (also ˈstrip cartoon) *noun* [C] a short series of pictures that tell a funny story, for example in a newspaper

coming /ˈkʌmɪŋ/ *noun* [sing] the moment when sth new arrives or begins: *The coming of the computer meant the loss of many jobs.* ▶ **coming** *adj* [only *before* a noun]: *We've got a lot of plans for the coming year.*

C

comma /ˈkɒmə/ *noun* [C] the mark (,) used for dividing parts of a sentence or items in a list

command¹ /kəˈmɑːnd/ *noun* **1** [C] an order: *The captain's commands must be obeyed without question.* **2** [C] an instruction given to a computer **3** [U] control over sb/sth: *Who is* ***in command of*** *the expedition?* ◆ *to* ***take command of*** *a situation* **4** [sing] the state of being able to do or use sth well: *She has a good command of French.*

IDM **at/by sb's command** (*formal*) because you were ordered by sb: *At the command of their officer the troops opened fire.*

be at sb's command to be ready to obey sb: *I'm completely at your command.*

command² /kəˈmɑːnd/ *verb* [T] **1** (*formal*) **command (sb to do sth)** to tell or order sb to do sth: *I command you to leave now!* **2 command sb/sth** to control or be in charge of sb/sth: *to command an army/a regiment/a ship* **3** to deserve and get sth: *The old man commanded great respect.*

commandant /ˈkɒməndænt/ *noun* [C] the officer in charge of a particular group of people or institution

commandeer /ˌkɒmənˈdɪə(r)/ *verb* [T] to take control or possession of sth for military or police use

commander /kəˈmɑːndə(r)/ *noun* [C] **1** a person who controls or is in charge of a military organization or group **2** (*BrE*) an officer at a fairly high level in the navy

commanding /kəˈmɑːndɪŋ/ *adj* **1** [only *before* a noun] in charge or having control of sb/sth: *Who is your commanding officer?* **2** strong or powerful: *to speak in a commanding tone of voice*

commandment (also **Commandment**) /kəˈmɑːndmənt/ *noun* [C] (*formal*) one of the ten important laws that Christian people should obey

commando /kəˈmɑːndəʊ/ *noun* [C] (*pl* **commandos**) one of a group of soldiers who is trained to make sudden attacks in enemy areas

commemorate /kəˈmeməreɪt/ *verb* [T] to exist or take place in order to make people remember a special event: *a statue commemorating all the soldiers who died in the last war* ▶ **commemoration** /kəˌmeməˈreɪʃn/ *noun* [C,U]: *The concerts were held* ***in commemoration*** *of the 200th anniversary of Mozart's death.*

commence /kəˈmens/ *verb* [I,T] (*formal*) **commence sth/doing sth** to start or begin ▶ **commencement** *noun* [C,U]

commend /kəˈmend/ *verb* [T] (*formal*) to say officially that sb/sth is very good: *Dean was commended for his excellent work.*

commendable /kəˈmendəbl/ *adj* (*formal*) that people think is good: *She acted with commendable honesty and fairness.*

comment¹ /ˈkɒment/ *noun* [C,U] **comment (on sth)** something that you say or write that gives your opinion or feeling about sth: *The chancellor was not available for comment.* ◆ *I heard someone* ***make a*** *rude* ***comment*** *about my clothes.* ➲ look at **observation**, **remark**

IDM **no comment** used in reply to a question when you do not want to say anything at all: *'Mr President, how do you feel about these latest developments?' 'No comment.'*

comment² /ˈkɒment/ *verb* [I] **comment (on sth)** to say what you think or feel about sth: *Several people commented on how ill David looked.* ◆ *He refused to comment until after the trial.*

commentary /ˈkɒməntri/ *noun* (*pl* **commentaries**) **1** [C,U] a spoken description on the radio or TV of sth as it is happening: *a sports commentary* **2** [C] a written explanation or discussion of sth such as a book or play **3** [C] something that shows what sth is like: *This drug scandal is a sad commentary on the state of the sport.* ◆ *These petty quarrels are a sad commentary on the state of the government.*

commentate /ˈkɒmənteɪt/ *verb* [I] **commentate (on sth)** to give a spoken description on the radio or TV of sth as it is happening

commentator /ˈkɒmənteɪtə(r)/ *noun* [C] **1** a person who gives their opinion about sth on the radio, on TV or in a newspaper: *a political commentator* **2** a person who gives a spoken description on radio or TV of sth as it is happening: *a sports commentator*

commerce /ˈkɒmɜːs/ *noun* [U] the business of buying and selling things

commercial¹ /kəˈmɜːʃl/ *adj* **1** connected with buying and selling goods and services: *commercial law* **2** selling sth or sold in large quantities to the public: *commercial airlines* ◆ *commercial products* **3** [only *before* a noun] making or trying to make money: *Although it won a lot of awards, the film was not a commercial success.* ▶ **commercially** /-ʃəli/ *adv*: *The factory was closed down because it was no longer commercially viable.*

commercial² /kəˈmɜːʃl/ *noun* [C] an advertisement on TV or the radio: *a commercial break* (= a space between TV programmes when commercials are shown)

commercialism /kəˈmɜːʃəlɪzəm/ *noun* [U] the attitude that making money is more important than anything else

commercialize (also -ise) /kəˈmɜːʃəlaɪz/ *verb* [T] to try to make money out of sth, even if it means spoiling it: *Christmas has become very commercialized over recent years.* ▶ **commercialization** (also -isation) /kəˌmɜːʃəlaɪˈzeɪʃn/ *noun* [U]

commiserate /kəˈmɪzəreɪt/ *verb* [I] (*formal*) **commiserate (with sb) (on/over/for sth)** to feel sorry for and show understanding towards sb who is unhappy or in difficulty: *I commiserated with Debbie over losing her job.*

commission¹ /kəˈmɪʃn/ *noun* **1** *often* **Commission** [C] an official group of people who are asked to find out about sth: *A Commission was appointed to investigate the causes of the accident.* **2** [C,U] money that you get for selling sth: *Agents get 10% commission on everything they sell.* **3** [C,U] money that a bank, etc. charges for providing a particular service: *The bureau de change charges 5% commission.* **4** [C] a formal request to an artist, a writer, etc. to produce a piece of work: *He received a commission to write a play for the festival.*

C

commission² /kəˈmɪʃn/ *verb* [T] commission sb (to do sth); commission sth (from sb) to ask an artist, a writer, etc. to do a piece of work: *to commission an architect to design a building*

commissioner /kəˈmɪʃənə(r)/ *noun* [C] the head of the police or of a government department in some countries

commit /kəˈmɪt/ *verb* [T] (committing; committed) **1** to do sth bad or illegal: *to commit a crime* **2** to kill yourself deliberately: *to **commit suicide*** **3** commit sb/yourself (to sth/to doing sth) to make a definite agreement or promise to do sth: *I can't commit myself to helping you tomorrow.* **4** commit yourself (on sth) to make a decision or give an opinion publicly so that it is then difficult to change it: *I'm not going to commit myself on who will win the election.* ➲ look at **non-committal** **5** (*formal*) to decide to use money or time in a certain way: *The government has committed £2 billion to education.* **6** (*formal*) commit sb to sth to send sb to a prison, mental hospital, etc: *She was committed to a psychiatric hospital.*

commitment /kəˈmɪtmənt/ *noun* **1** [C,U] a promise or an agreement to do sth; a responsibility: *When I **make a commitment** I always stick to it.* ◆ *Helen now works fewer hours because of family commitments.* **2** [U] commitment (to sth) being prepared to give a lot of your time and attention to sth because you believe it is right or important: *I admire Gary's commitment to protecting the environment.*

committed /kəˈmɪtɪd/ *adj* committed (to sth) prepared to give a lot of your time and attention to sth because you believe it is right or important: *The company is committed to providing quality products.*

committee /kəˈmɪti/ *noun* [C, with sing or pl verb] a group of people who have been chosen to discuss sth or decide sth: *to be/sit on a committee* ◆ *The planning committee meets/meet twice a week.*

commodity /kəˈmɒdəti/ *noun* [C] (*pl* commodities) a product or material that can be bought and sold: *Salt was once a very valuable commodity.*

common¹ /ˈkɒmən/ *adj* (commoner; commonest) [**More common** and **most common** are more frequent.] **1** happening or found often or in many places; usual: *Pilot error is the commonest/most common cause of plane crashes.* ◆ *The daisy is a common wild flower.* OPP **uncommon** **2** common (to sb/sth) shared by or belonging to two or more people or groups; shared by most or all people: *This type of behaviour is common to most children of that age.* ◆ *We have a common interest in gardening.* **3** [only *before* a noun] not special; ordinary: *The officers had much better living conditions than the common soldiers.* **4** (*BrE informal*) having or showing a lack of education: *Don't speak like that. It's common!*

IDM **be common/public knowledge** ➲ **knowledge**

common² /ˈkɒmən/ *noun* [C] an area of open land that anyone can use

IDM **have sth in common (with sb/sth)** to share sth with sb/sth else: *to have a lot in common with somebody*

in common with sb/sth (*formal*) in the same way as sb/sth else; like sb/sth: *This company, in common with many others, is losing a lot of money.*

ˌcommon ˈground *noun* [U] beliefs, interests, etc. that two or more people or groups share

ˌcommon ˈlaw *noun* [U] laws in England that are based on decisions that judges have made, not laws that were made by Parliament

commonly /ˈkɒmənli/ *adv* normally; usually: *commonly held opinions* ◆ *Christopher is commonly known as Kit.*

commonplace /ˈkɒmənpleɪs/ *adj* not exciting or unusual; ordinary: *Foreign travel has become commonplace in recent years.*

ˈcommon room *noun* [C] a room in a school, university, etc. where students or teachers can go to relax when they are not in class

the Commons /ˈkɒmənz/ = The House of Commons

ˌcommon ˈsense *noun* [U] the ability to make good sensible decisions or to behave in a sensible way

the Commonwealth /ˈkɒmənwelθ/ *noun* [sing] the group of countries that once formed the British Empire and that work together in a friendly way

commotion /kəˈməʊʃn/ *noun* [sing,U] great noise or excitement

communal /kəˈmjuːnl; ˈkɒmjənl/ *adj* shared by a group of people: *a communal kitchen*

commune /ˈkɒmjuːn/ *noun* [C, with sing or pl verb] a group of people, not from the same family, who live together and share their property and responsibilities

communicate /kəˈmjuːnɪkeɪt/ *verb* **1** [I,T] to share and exchange information, ideas or feelings with sb: *Parents often have difficulty communicating with their teenage children.* ◆ *Our boss is good at communicating her ideas to the team.* **2** [T, usually passive] (*formal*) to pass a disease from one person or animal to another: *The disease is communicated though dirty drinking water.* **3** [I] to lead from one place to another: *two rooms with a communicating door*

communication /kəˌmjuːnɪˈkeɪʃn/ *noun* **1** [U] the act of sharing or exchanging information, ideas or feelings: *Radio is the only means of communication in remote areas.* ◆ *We are **in regular communication with** our head office in New York.* **2** communications [pl] the methods that are used for travelling to and from a place or for sending messages between places: *The telephone lines are down so communications are very difficult.* **3** [C] (*formal*) a message: *a communication from head office*

communicative /kəˈmjuːnɪkətɪv/ *adj* willing and able to talk and share ideas, etc: *Paolo has excellent communicative skills.*

communion /kəˈmjuːniən/ *noun* [U] **1** Communion a Christian church ceremony in which people share bread and wine **2** (*formal*) the sharing of thoughts or feelings

communiqué /kəˈmjuːnɪkeɪ/ *noun* [C] an official statement, especially from a government, a political group, etc.

communism /ˈkɒmjunɪzəm/ *noun* [U] the political system in which the state owns and controls all factories, farms, services, etc. and aims to treat everyone equally ➲ look at **capitalism**, **Marxism**, **socialism**

communist (also Communist) /ˈkɒmjənɪst/ *noun* [C] a person who believes in or supports **communism**; a member of the **Communist** Party ▶ **communist** (also Communist) *adj*: *communist sympathies*

⚷ **community** /kəˈmjuːnəti/ *noun* (*pl* communities) **1** the community [sing] all the people who live in a particular place, area, etc. when considered as a group: *Recent increases in crime have disturbed the whole community.* **2** [C, with sing or pl verb] a group of people who have sth in common: *the Asian community in Britain* ◆ *the business community* **3** [U] the feeling of belonging to a group in the place where you live: *There is a strong sense of community in the neighbourhood.*

comˈmunity centre (*AmE* comˈmunity center) *noun* [C] a building that local people can use for meetings, classes, sports, etc.

commute /kəˈmjuːt/ *verb* [I] to travel by bus, train, car, etc. from home to work and back every day: *A lot of people commute to London from nearby towns.* ▶ **commuter** *noun* [C]

compact /kəmˈpækt; ˈkɒmpækt/ *adj* small and easy to carry: *a compact camera*

ˌcompact ˈdisc = CD

companion /kəmˈpæniən/ *noun* [C] a person or an animal who you spend a lot of time or go somewhere with: *a travelling companion*

companionship /kəmˈpæniənʃɪp/ *noun* [U] the pleasant feeling of having a friendly relationship with sb and not being alone

⚷ **company** /ˈkʌmpəni/ *noun* (*abbr* Co.) (*pl* companies) **1** [C, with sing or pl verb] a business organization selling goods or services: *The company is/are planning to build a new factory.*

> **HELP** In names, **company** is written with a capital letter. The abbreviation is **Co.**: *the Walt Disney Company* ◆ *Milton & Co.*

2 [C, with sing or pl verb] a group of actors, singers, dancers, etc: *a ballet company* ◆ *the Royal Shakespeare Company* **3** [U] being with a person: *I always enjoy Rachel's company.* ◆ *Jeffrey is very good company* (= pleasant to be with). **4** [U] a visitor or visitors: *Sorry, I wouldn't have called if I'd known you had company.*

IDM **keep sb company** to go or be with sb so that they are not alone: *She was nervous, so I went with her to keep her company.*

part company ➲ **part**[2]

comparable /ˈkɒmpərəbl/ *adj* comparable (to/with sb/sth) of a similar standard or size; that can be compared with sth: *The population of Britain is comparable to that of France.* ◆ *A comparable flat in my country would be a lot cheaper.*

comparative[1] /kəmˈpærətɪv/ *adj* **1** that compares things of the same kind: *a comparative study of systems of government* **2** compared with sth else or with what is usual or normal: *He had problems with the written exam, but passed the practical exam with comparative ease.* **3** (used about the form of an adjective or adverb) expressing a greater amount, quality, size, etc: *'Hotter' and 'more quickly' are the comparative forms of 'hot' and 'quickly'.*

comparative[2] /kəmˈpærətɪv/ *noun* [C] the form of an adjective or adverb that expresses a greater amount, quality, size, etc: *'Bigger' is the comparative of 'big'.*

comparatively /kəmˈpærətɪvli/ *adv* when compared with sth else or with what is usual; fairly: *Fortunately, the disease is comparatively rare nowadays.*

⚷ **compare** /kəmˈpeə(r)/ *verb* **1** [T] (*abbr* cf.) compare A and B; compare A with/to B to consider people or things in order to see how similar or how different they are: *When the police compared the two letters, they realized that they had been written by the same person.* ◆ *I'm quite a patient person,* **compared with** *him.* ◆ **Compared to** *the place where I grew up, this town is exciting.* **2** [I] compare (with/to sb/sth) to be as good as sb/sth: *Her last film was brilliant but this one simply doesn't compare.* ◆ *There is nothing to compare with the taste of bread fresh from the oven.* **3** [T] compare A to B to say that sb/sth is similar to sb/sth else: *When it was built, people compared the stadium to a spaceship.*

IDM **compare notes (with sb)** to discuss your opinions, ideas, experiences, etc. with sb else: *At the beginning of term we met and compared notes about the holidays.*

⚷ **comparison** /kəmˈpærɪsn/ *noun* [C,U] an act of comparing; a statement in which people or things are compared: *Put the new one and the old one side by side,* **for comparison**. ◆ *It's hard to* **make comparisons** *between two athletes from different sports.*

IDM **by/in comparison (with sb/sth)** when compared: *In comparison with many other people, they're quite well off.*

compartment /kəmˈpɑːtmənt/ *noun* [C] **1** one of the separate sections which railway **carriages** (= the parts of a train) are divided into: *a first-class compartment* **2** one of the separate sections into which certain containers are divided: *the* **glove compartment** (= the space where you can keep maps, etc. in a car)

compass /ˈkʌmpəs/ *noun* [C] **1** an instrument for finding direction, with a needle that always points

compasses

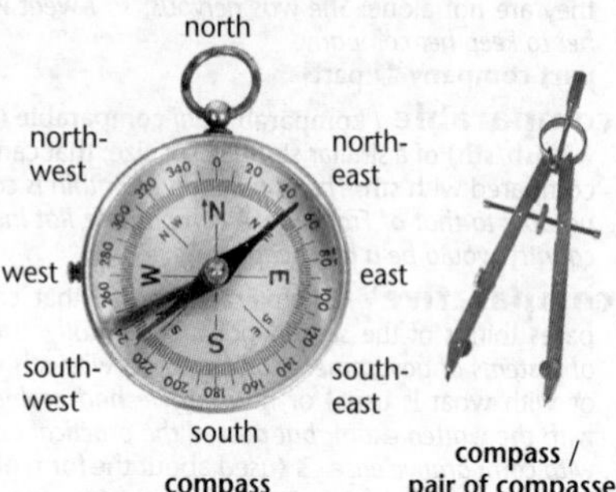

north: *the points of the compass* (= North, South, East, West, etc.) ◆ *They had to find their way back to the camp using a map and a compass.* **2 compasses** [pl] a V-shaped instrument that is used for drawing circles: *Use a pair of compasses.*

compassion /kəm'pæʃn/ *noun* [U] **compassion (for sb)** understanding or pity for sb who is suffering: *to have/feel/show compassion* ▶ **compassionate** /kəm'pæʃənət/ *adj*

compatible /kəm'pætəbl/ *adj* **compatible (with sb/sth)** able to be used together, or to live or exist together: *These two computer systems are not compatible.* ◆ *Lee's diet is not compatible with his active lifestyle.* **OPP incompatible** ▶ **compatibility** /kəm,pætə'bɪləti/ *noun* [U]

compatriot /kəm'pætriət/ *noun* [C] a person who comes from the same country as you

compel /kəm'pel/ *verb* [T] (**compelling**; **compelled**) (*formal*) **compel sb to do sth** to force sb to do sth: *I felt compelled to tell her what I really thought of her.*

compelling /kəm'pelɪŋ/ *adj* that forces or persuades you to do or to believe sth: *compelling evidence* ➲ *noun* **compulsion**

compensate /'kɒmpenseɪt/ *verb* **1** [I] **compensate (for sth)** to remove or reduce the bad effect of sth: *His willingness to work hard compensates for his lack of skill.* **2** [I,T] **compensate (sb) (for sth)** to pay sb money because you have injured them or lost or damaged their property: *The airline offered to compensate me for losing my luggage.*

compensation /,kɒmpen'seɪʃn/ *noun* **1** [U] **compensation (for sth)** money that you pay to sb because you have injured them or lost or damaged their property: *I got £5000 (in) compensation for my injuries.* **2** [C,U] a fact or an action that removes or reduces the bad effect of sth: *City life can be very tiring but there are compensations* (= good things about it).

compère /'kɒmpeə(r)/ *noun* [C] (*BrE*) a person who entertains the audience and introduces the different people who perform in a show ▶ **compère** *verb* [T]: *Who compèred the show?*

compete /kəm'pi:t/ *verb* [I] **compete (in sth) (against/with sb) (for sth)** to try to win or achieve sth, or to try to be better than sb else: *The world's best athletes compete in the Olympic Games.* ◆ *We'll be competing against seven other teams for the trophy.* ◆ *As children, they always used to compete with each other.* ◆ *Supermarkets have such low prices that small shops just can't compete.*

competence /'kɒmpɪtəns/ *noun* [U] the fact of having the ability or skill that is needed for sth: *She quickly proved her competence in her new position.* **OPP incompetence**

competent /'kɒmpɪtənt/ *adj* **1** having the ability or skill needed for sth: *a highly competent player* ◆ *Isobel is competent at her job.* **OPP incompetent** **2** good enough, but not excellent: *The singer gave a competent, but not particularly exciting, performance.* ▶ **competently** *adv*

competition /,kɒmpə'tɪʃn/ *noun* **1** [U] a situation where two or more people or organizations are trying to achieve, obtain, etc. the same thing or to be better than sb else: *He is **in competition with** three other people for promotion.* ◆ *There was **fierce competition** among the players for places in the team.* **2** [C] an organized event in which people try to win sth: *to **take part in/go in for/enter a competition*** ◆ *They **hold a competition** every year to find the best young artist.* ◆ *He came second in an international piano competition.* **3 the competition** [sing, with sing or pl verb] the other people, companies, etc. who are trying to achieve the same as you: *If we are going to succeed, we must offer a better product than the competition.*

competitive /kəm'petətɪv/ *adj* **1** involving people or organizations competing against each other: *The travel industry is a highly competitive business.* ◆ *competitive sports* **2** able to be as successful as or more successful than others: *They are trying to make the company competitive in the international market.* ◆ *Our prices are highly competitive* (= as low as or lower than those of the others). **3** (used about people) wanting very much to win or to be more successful than others: *She's a very competitive player.* ▶ **competitively** *adv*: *Their products are competitively priced.* ▶ **competitiveness** *noun* [U]

competitor /kəm'petɪtə(r)/ *noun* [C] a person or an organization that is competing against others: *There are ten competitors in the first race.* ◆ *Two local companies are our main competitors.*

compilation /,kɒmpɪ'leɪʃn/ *noun* **1** [C] a collection of pieces of music, writing, film, etc. that are taken from different places and put together: *A compilation CD of the band's greatest hits.* **2** [U] the act of **compiling** sth

compile /kəm'paɪl/ *verb* [T] to collect information and arrange it in a list, book, etc: *to compile a dictionary/a report/a list*

complacent /kəm'pleɪsnt/ *adj* feeling too satisfied with yourself or with a situation, so that you think that there is no need to worry: *He had won his matches so easily that he was in danger of becoming complacent.* ▶ **complacency** /kəm'pleɪsnsi/ *noun* [U] ▶ **complacently** *adv*

complain /kəmˈpleɪn/ *verb* [I] **complain (to sb) (about sth/that ...)** to say that you are not satisfied with or happy about sth: *We complained to the hotel manager that the room was too noisy.* ♦ *People are always complaining about the weather.* ➲ note at **protest**

PHR V **complain of sth** to say that you have a pain or illness: *He went to the doctor, complaining of headaches.*

complaint /kəmˈpleɪnt/ *noun* **complaint (about sth); complaint (that ...)** **1** [C] a statement that you are not satisfied with sth: *You should* ***make a complaint*** *to the company that made the machine.* **2** [U] the act of complaining: *I wrote a* ***letter of complaint*** *to the manager about the terrible service I had received.* ♦ *Jim's behaviour never gave the teachers* ***cause for complaint.*** **3** [C] an illness or a disease: *a serious heart complaint*

complement¹ /ˈkɒmplɪmənt/ *noun* [C] (*formal*) **1** a thing that goes together well with sth else: *A cream sauce is the perfect complement to this dessert.* **2** the total number that makes a group complete: *Without a full complement of players, the team will not be able to take part in the match.* **3** a word or words, especially a noun or an adjective, used after a verb such as 'be' or 'become' and describing the subject of that verb: *In 'I'm angry' and 'He became a teacher', 'angry' and 'teacher' are complements.*

complement² /ˈkɒmplɪment/ *verb* [T] to go together well with: *The colours of the furniture and the carpet complement each other.*

complementary /ˌkɒmplɪˈmentri/ *adj* going together well with sb/sth; adding sth which the other person or thing does not have: *They work well together because their skills are complementary: he's practical and she's creative.*

complete¹ /kəmˈpliːt/ *adj* **1** [only *before* a noun] as great as possible; in every way: *It was a complete waste of time.* ♦ *The room is a complete mess.* ♦ *We were in complete agreement.* SYN **total** **2** having or including all parts; with nothing missing: *I gave a complete list of the stolen items to the police.* ♦ *The book explains the complete history of the place.* OPP **incomplete** **3** [not before a noun] **complete (with sth)** including sth extra, in addition to what is expected: *The computer* ***comes complete*** *with instruction manual and printer.* **4** [not before a noun] finished or ended: *The repair work should be complete by Friday.* OPP **incomplete** ▶ **completeness** *noun* [U]

complete² /kəmˈpliːt/ *verb* [T] **1** to finish sth; to bring sth to an end: *When the building has been completed, it will look impressive.* ♦ *He completed his teacher training course in June 2005.* **2** to write all the necessary information on sth (for example a form): *Please complete the following in capital letters.* **3** to make sth whole: *We need two more players to complete the team.*

completely /kəmˈpliːtli/ *adv* in every way; fully: *The building was completely destroyed by fire.* ♦ *I've completely forgotten her name.* SYN **totally**

completion /kəmˈpliːʃn/ *noun* [U] (*formal*) the act of finishing sth or the state of being finished: *You will be paid on completion of the work.* ♦ *The new motorway is due for completion within two years.*

complex¹ /ˈkɒmpleks/ *adj* made up of several connected parts and often difficult to understand: *a complex system of taxation* ♦ *a complex problem/subject* SYN **complicated**

complex² /ˈkɒmpleks/ *noun* [C] **1** a group of connected things, especially buildings: *a shopping/sports complex* **2** **a complex (about sth)** a mental problem that makes sb worry a lot about sth: *He's got a complex about his height.* ♦ *an inferiority complex*

complexion /kəmˈplekʃn/ *noun* [C] **1** the natural colour and quality of the skin on your face: *a dark/fair complexion* ♦ *a healthy complexion* **2** [usually sing] the general nature or character of sth: *These recent announcements* ***put a different complexion on*** *our situation.*

complexity /kəmˈpleksəti/ *noun* (*pl* **complexities**) **1** [U] the state of being **complex** and difficult to understand: *an issue of great complexity* **2** [C] one of the many details that make sth complicated: *I haven't time to explain the complexities of the situation now.*

compliant /kəmˈplaɪənt/ *adj* (*formal*) **compliant (with sth)** working or done in agreement with particular rules, orders, etc: *All new products must be compliant with EU specifications.* ▶ **compliance** *noun* [U]: *A hard hat must be worn at all times* ***in compliance with*** *safety regulations.*

complicate /ˈkɒmplɪkeɪt/ *verb* [T] to make sth difficult to understand or deal with: *Let's not complicate things by adding too many details.*

complicated /ˈkɒmplɪkeɪtɪd/ *adj* made of many different things or parts that are connected; difficult to understand: *a novel with a very complicated plot* ♦ *The instructions look very complicated.* SYN **complex**

complication /ˌkɒmplɪˈkeɪʃn/ *noun* [C] **1** something that makes a situation hard to understand or to deal with: *Unless there are any unexpected complications, I'll be arriving next month.* **2** a new illness that you get when you are already ill: *She developed complications after the operation.*

complicity /kəmˈplɪsəti/ *noun* [U] (*formal*) the fact of being involved with sb else in a crime

compliment¹ /ˈkɒmplɪmənt/ *noun* **1** [C] **a compliment (on sth)** a statement or action that shows admiration for sb: *People often* ***pay*** *her* ***compliments*** *on her piano playing.* **2** **compliments** [pl] (*formal*) used to say that you like sth or to thank sb for sth: *Tea and coffee are provided with the compliments of the hotel management* (= without charge).

compliment² /ˈkɒmplɪment/ *verb* [T] **compliment sb (on sth)** to say that you think sb/sth is very good: *She complimented them on their smart appearance.*

C

complimentary /ˌkɒmplɪˈmentri/ *adj* **1** given free of charge: *a complimentary theatre ticket* **2** showing that you think sb/sth is very good: *He made several complimentary remarks about her work.*

comply /kəmˈplaɪ/ *verb* [I] (**complying; complies;** *pt, pp* **complied**) (*formal*) **comply (with sth)** to obey an order or a request: *All school buildings must comply with the fire and safety regulations.*

component /kəmˈpəʊnənt/ *noun* [C] one of several parts of which sth is made: *The human eye has two main components.* ◆ *the components of a machine/system* ▶ **component** *adj* [only *before* a noun]: *the component parts of an engine*

compose /kəmˈpəʊz/ *verb* **1** [T] to be the parts that together form sth: *the parties that compose the coalition government* **2** [I,T] to write music: *Mozart composed forty-one symphonies.* **3** [T] to produce a piece of writing, using careful thought: *I sat down and composed a letter of reply.* **4** [T] to make yourself, your feelings, etc. become calm and under control: *The news came as such a shock that it took me a while to* ***compose myself.***

composed /kəmˈpəʊzd/ *adj* **1 composed of sth** made or formed from several different parts, people, etc: *The committee is composed of politicians from all parties.* **2** calm, in control of your feelings: *Although he felt very nervous, he managed to appear composed.*

composer /kəmˈpəʊzə(r)/ *noun* [C] a person who writes music

composite /ˈkɒmpəzɪt/ *adj* [only *before* a noun] consisting of different parts or materials ▶ **composite** *noun* [C]

composition /ˌkɒmpəˈzɪʃn/ *noun* **1** [U] the parts that form sth; the way in which the parts of sth are arranged: *the chemical composition of a substance* ◆ *the composition of the population* **2** [C] a piece of music that has been written by sb: *Chopin's best-known compositions* ➲ note at **music** **3** [U] the act or skill of writing a piece of music or text: *She studied both musical theory and composition.* **4** [C] a short piece of writing done at school, in an exam, etc: *Write a composition of about 300 words on one of the following subjects.*

compost /ˈkɒmpɒst/ *noun* [U] a mixture of dead plants, old food, etc. that is added to soil to help plants grow ▶ **compost** *verb* [T]

composure /kəmˈpəʊʒə(r)/ *noun* [U] the state of being calm and having your feelings under control: *The goalkeeper couldn't regain his composure after his mistake.*

compound¹ /ˈkɒmpaʊnd/ *noun* [C] **1** something that consists of two or more things or substances combined together: *a chemical compound* **2** a word or phrase consisting of two or more parts that combine to make a single meaning: *'Car park' and 'bad-tempered' are compounds.* **3** an area of land with a group of buildings on it, surrounded by a wall or fence

compound² /kəmˈpaʊnd/ *verb* [T] to make sth such as a problem worse

comprehend /ˌkɒmprɪˈhend/ *verb* [T] (*formal*) to understand sth completely: *She's too young to comprehend what has happened.*

comprehensible /ˌkɒmprɪˈhensəbl/ *adj* easy to understand: *The book is written in language that is clear and comprehensible.* OPP **incomprehensible**

comprehension /ˌkɒmprɪˈhenʃn/ *noun* **1** [U] (*formal*) the ability to understand: *The horror of war is* ***beyond comprehension.*** OPP **incomprehension** **2** [C,U] an exercise that tests how well you understand spoken or written language: *a listening comprehension* ➲ note at **skim**

comprehensive¹ /ˌkɒmprɪˈhensɪv/ *adj* **1** including everything or nearly everything that is connected with a particular subject: *a guide book giving comprehensive information on the area* **2** (*BrE*) (used about education) teaching children of all levels of ability in the same school: *a comprehensive education system*

comprehensive² /ˌkɒmprɪˈhensɪv/ (also **compreˈhensive school**) *noun* [C] (*BrE*) a secondary school in which children of all levels of ability are educated: *My sister went to the local comprehensive.*

comprehensively /ˌkɒmprɪˈhensɪvli/ *adv* completely SYN **thoroughly**

compreˈhensive school (*BrE*) = **comprehensive²**

compress /kəmˈpres/ *verb* [T] **compress sth (into sth)** to make sth fill less space than usual: *Divers breathe compressed air from tanks.* ◆ *He found it hard to compress his ideas into a single page.* ▶ **compression** /kəmˈpreʃn/ *noun* [U]

comprise /kəmˈpraɪz/ *verb* [T] **1** to consist of; to have as parts or members: *a house comprising three bedrooms, kitchen, bathroom and a living room* **2** to form or be part of sth: *Women comprise 62% of the staff.*

compromise¹ /ˈkɒmprəmaɪz/ *noun* [C,U] **a compromise (between/on sth)** an agreement that is reached when each person gets part, but not all, of what they wanted: *to* ***reach a compromise*** ◆ *Both sides will have to be prepared to* ***make compromises.***

compromise² /ˈkɒmprəmaɪz/ *verb* **1** [I] **compromise (with sb) (on sth)** to accept less than you want or are aiming for, especially in order to reach an agreement: *Unless both sides are prepared to compromise, there will be no peace agreement.* ◆ *The company never compromises on the quality of its products.* **2** [T] **compromise sb/sth/yourself** to put sb/sth/yourself in a bad or dangerous position, especially by doing sth that is not very sensible: *He compromised himself by accepting money from them.*

compulsion /kəmˈpʌlʃn/ *noun* **1** [U] the act of forcing sb to do sth or being forced to do sth: *There is no compulsion to take part. You can decide yourself.* ➲ *verb* **compel** **2** [C] a strong desire that you cannot control, often to do sth that you should not do:

Though I knew it was wrong, I felt a strong compulsion to laugh. SYN **urge**

compulsive /kəmˈpʌlsɪv/ *adj* **1** (used about a bad or harmful habit) caused by a strong desire that you cannot control: *compulsive eating* **2** (used about a person) having a bad habit that they cannot control: *a compulsive gambler/shoplifter* **3** so interesting or exciting that you cannot take your attention away from it: *This book makes compulsive reading.* ▶ **compulsively** *adv*

compulsory /kəmˈpʌlsəri/ *adj* that must be done, by law, rules, etc: *Maths and English are compulsory subjects on this course.* ◆ *It is compulsory to wear a hard hat on the building site.* SYN **obligatory** OPP **optional, voluntary**

compute /kəmˈpjuːt/ *verb* [T] (*formal*) to calculate sth

⚷ **computer** /kəmˈpjuːtə(r)/ *noun* [C] an electronic machine that can store, find and arrange information, calculate amounts and control other machines: *The bills are all done* ***by computer.*** ◆ *a computer program* ◆ *a home/personal computer* ◆ *computer software/games* ◆ *First of all, the details are fed into a computer.* ➲ note at **Internet**

TOPIC

Computers

Most people use their **computers** for sending and receiving **emails** and for **word processing** (= writing letters, reports, etc.). You can also use **the Internet**, play **computer games** or watch **DVDs**. You **log in/on** with your **username** and **password**. You **type in** words on a **keyboard** and **print out** documents on a **printer**. Information is displayed on the **screen** and you select the **icons** (= small pictures or symbols) using a **mouse**. **Data** (= information) is stored in **files** on the **hard disk**, or on a **flash drive** or **CD-ROM**. The **programs** that are used to operate a computer are called **software**. A computer that you use at work or home is a **PC** or **desktop**. A **laptop** is a small computer that you can carry around with you and a **tablet** is a very small, flat computer that you work by touching the screen.

computerize (also -ise) /kəmˈpjuːtəraɪz/ *verb* [T] to use computers to do a job or to store information: *The whole factory has been computerized.* ◆ *We*

computer

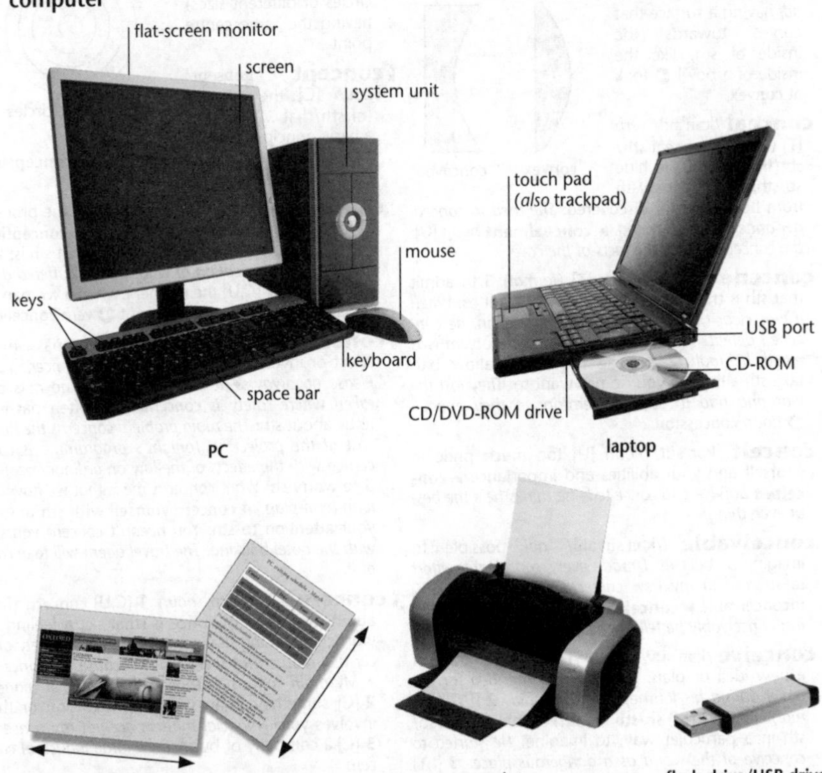

have now computerized the library catalogue. ▶ **computerization** (also -isation) /kəm,pjuːtəraɪ'zeɪʃn/ *noun* [U]

com,puter-'literate *adj* able to use a computer

computing /kəm'pjuːtɪŋ/ *noun* [U] the use of computers: *She did a course in computing.*

comrade /'kɒmreɪd/ *noun* [C] **1** a person who is a member of the same political party as the person speaking **2** (*old-fashioned*) a friend or other person that you work with, especially as soldiers during a war: *They were old army comrades.* ▶ **comradeship** *noun* [U]

Con *abbr* = **Conservative**²(2)

con¹ /kɒn/ *noun* [C] (*informal*) a trick, especially in order to cheat sb out of some money
IDM **the pros and cons** ➲ **pro**

con² /kɒn/ *verb* [T] (conning; conned) (*informal*) con sb (into doing sth/out of sth) to cheat sb, especially in order to get money: *He conned her into investing in a company that didn't really exist.* ♦ *The old lady was conned out of her life savings.*

concave /kɒn'keɪv/ *adj* having a surface that curves towards the inside of sth, like the inside of a bowl ➲ look at **convex**

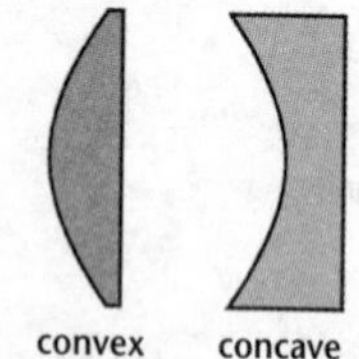

conceal /kən'siːl/ *verb* [T] (*formal*) conceal sth/sb (from sb/sth) to hide sb/sth; to prevent sb/sth from being seen or discovered: *She tried to conceal her anger from her friend.* ▶ **concealment** *noun* [U]: *the concealment of the facts of the case*

concede /kən'siːd/ *verb* [T] (*formal*) **1** to admit that sth is true although you do not want to: *When it was clear that he would lose the election, he conceded defeat.* ♦ *She conceded that the problem was mostly her fault.* **2** concede sth (to sb) to allow sb to take sth although you do not want to: *They lost the war and had to concede territory to their enemy.* ➲ *noun* **concession**

conceit /kən'siːt/ *noun* [U] too much pride in yourself and your abilities and importance ▶ **conceited** *adj*: *He's so conceited—he thinks he's the best at everything!*

conceivable /kən'siːvəbl/ *adj* possible to imagine or believe: *I made every conceivable effort to succeed in my new career.* **SYN** **possible** **OPP** **inconceivable** ▶ **conceivably** /-əbli/ *adv*: *She might just conceivably be telling the truth.*

conceive /kən'siːv/ *verb* **1** [T] (*formal*) to think of a new idea or plan: *He conceived the idea for the novel during his journey through India.* **2** [I,T] (*formal*) conceive (of) sb/sth (as sth) to think about sb/sth in a particular way; to imagine: *He started to conceive of the world as a dangerous place.* **3** [I,T] to become pregnant ➲ *noun* **conception**

⚷ **concentrate** /'kɒnsntreɪt/ *verb* [I,T] **1** concentrate (sth) (on sth/doing sth) to give all your attention or effort to sth: *I need to concentrate on passing this exam.* ♦ *I tried to concentrate my thoughts on the problem.* **2** to come together or to bring people or things together in one place: *Most factories are concentrated in one small area of the town.*

concentrated /'kɒnsntreɪtɪd/ *adj* **1** showing determination: *With one concentrated effort we can finish the work by tonight.* **2** made stronger by removing some liquid: *This is concentrated orange juice. You have to add water before you drink it.*

⚷ **concentration** /,kɒnsn'treɪʃn/ *noun* **1** [U] concentration (on sth) the ability to give all your attention or effort to sth: *This type of work requires total concentration.* ♦ *Don't lose (your) concentration or you might make a mistake.* **2** [C] concentration (of sth) a large amount of people or things in one place: *There is a high concentration of chemicals in the drinking water here.*

,concen'tration camp *noun* [C] a prison (usually a number of buildings inside a high fence) where political prisoners are kept in very bad conditions

concentric /kən'sentrɪk/ *adj* (used about circles of different sizes) having the same centre point

concentric circles

⚷ **concept** /'kɒnsept/ *noun* [C] the concept (of sth/that ...) an idea; a basic principle: *It is difficult to* ***grasp the concept*** *of eternity.* ▶ **conceptual** /kən'septʃuəl/ *adj*

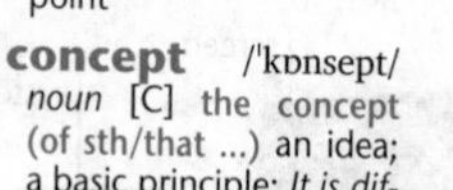

conception /kən'sepʃn/ *noun* **1** [U] the process of forming an idea or a plan **2** [C,U] (a) conception (of sth) an understanding of how or what sth is: *We have no real conception of what people suffered during the war.* **3** [C,U] the moment when a woman or female animal becomes pregnant ➲ *verb* **conceive**

⚷ **concern**¹ /kən'sɜːn/ *verb* [T] **1** [often passive] to affect or involve sb/sth: *This does not concern you. Please go away.* ♦ *It is important that no risks are taken* ***where*** *safety* ***is concerned.*** **2** [often passive] to be about sth: *The main problem concerns the huge cost of the project.* ♦ *Tonight's programme is concerned with the effects of the law on ordinary people.* **3** to worry sb: *What concerns me is that we have no long-term plan.* **4** concern yourself with sth to give your attention to sth: *You needn't concern yourself with the hotel booking. The travel agent will take care of it.*

⚷ **concern**² /kən'sɜːn/ *noun* **1** [C,U] concern (for/about/over sb/sth); concern (that ...) a feeling of worry; something that causes worry: *The safety officer assured us that there was no* ***cause for concern.*** ♦ *My main concern is that we'll run out of money.* **2** [C] something that is important to you or that involves you: *Financial matters are not my concern.* **3** [C] a company or business: *a large industrial concern*
IDM **a going concern** ➲ **going**²

concerned /kən'sɜːnd/ *adj* concerned (about/ for sth); concerned (that ...) worried and feeling concern about sth: *If you are concerned about your baby's health you should consult a doctor immediately.* OPP **unconcerned**

concerning /kən'sɜːnɪŋ/ *prep* about; on the subject of: *She refused to answer questions concerning her private life.*

concert /'kɒnsət/ *noun* [C] a performance of music: *The band is on tour doing concerts all over the country.* ♦ *a concert of music by Bach* ♦ *a concert **hall/pianist*** ➲ look at **recital**

IDM **in concert (with sb/sth)** (*formal*) working together with sb/sth

concerted /kən'sɜːtɪd/ *adj* [only *before* a noun] done by a group of people working together: *We must all **make a concerted effort** to finish the work on time.*

concertina /ˌkɒnsə'tiːnə/ *noun* [C] a musical instrument that you hold in your hands and play by pressing the ends together and pulling them apart ➲ look at **accordion** ➲ picture at **accordion**

concerto /kən'tʃɜːtəʊ/ *noun* [C] (*pl* **concertos**) a piece of music for an **orchestra** (= a large group of musicians who play together) and one instrument playing a **solo** (= an important part on its own): *Mozart's second piano concerto*

concession /kən'seʃn/ *noun* **1** [C,U] (a) concession (to sb/sth) something that you agree to do in order to end an argument: *Employers have been forced to **make concessions** to the union.* ➲ *verb* **concede** **2** [C] a lower price for certain groups of people: *Concessions are available for students and pensioners.*

concessionary /kən'seʃənəri/ *adj* having a lower price for certain groups of people: *a concessionary fare*

conciliation /kənˌsɪli'eɪʃn/ *noun* [U] the process of ending an argument or a disagreement: *All attempts at conciliation have failed and civil war seems inevitable.*

conciliatory /kən'sɪliətəri/ *adj* that tries to end an argument or a disagreement: *a conciliatory speech/gesture*

concise /kən'saɪs/ *adj* giving a lot of information in a few words: *He gave a clear and concise summary of what had happened.* SYN **brief** ▶ **concisely** *adv* ▶ **conciseness** *noun* [U]

conclude /kən'kluːd/ *verb* **1** [T] conclude sth from sth to form an opinion as the result of thought or study: *From the man's strange behaviour I concluded that he was drunk.* **2** [I,T] (*formal*) to end or to bring sth to an end: *The prince concluded his tour by attending a charity concert.* **3** [T] conclude sth (with sb) to formally arrange or agree to sth: *conclude a business deal/treaty*

conclusion /kən'kluːʒn/ *noun* **1** [C] the conclusion (that ...) an opinion that you reach after thinking about sth carefully: *After trying to phone Bob for days, I **came to the conclusion** that he was on holiday.* ♦ *Have you **reached** any **conclusions** from your studies?* **2** [C, usually sing] (*formal*) an end to sth: *Let us hope the peace talks **reach a** successful **conclusion**.* **3** [U] an act of arranging or agreeing to sth formally: *The summit ended with the conclusion of an arms-reduction treaty.*

IDM **a foregone conclusion** ➲ **foregone**

in conclusion finally: *In conclusion, I would like to wish you continued success in the future.*

jump to conclusions ➲ **jump**[1]

conclusive /kən'kluːsɪv/ *adj* that shows sth is definitely true or real: *The blood tests gave conclusive proof of Roy's guilt.* OPP **inconclusive** ▶ **conclusively** *adv*

concoct /kən'kɒkt/ *verb* [T] **1** to make sth unusual by mixing different things together **2** to make up or invent sth (an excuse, a story, etc.) ▶ **concoction** *noun* [C]

concourse /'kɒŋkɔːs/ *noun* [C] a large hall or space inside a building such as a station or an airport

concrete[1] /'kɒŋkriːt/ *adj* **1** made of concrete: *a concrete floor/bridge* **2** based on facts, not on ideas or guesses: ***concrete evidence/proposals/proof*** ♦ *Can you give me a concrete example of what you mean?* OPP **abstract** ▶ **concretely** *adv*

concrete[2] /'kɒŋkriːt/ *noun* [U] a hard substance made from **cement** (= a grey powder) mixed with sand, water and small stones, which is used in building: *a modern office building of glass and concrete*

concrete[3] /'kɒŋkriːt/ *verb* [T] concrete sth (over) to cover sth with concrete

concur /kən'kɜː(r)/ *verb* [I] (**concurring**; **concurred**) (*formal*) to agree

concurrent /kən'kʌrənt/ *adj* existing or happening at the same time as sth else ▶ **concurrently** *adv*: *The semi-finals are played concurrently, so it is impossible to watch both.*

concuss /kən'kʌs/ *verb* [T, usually passive] to injure sb's brain by hitting their head: *I was slightly concussed when I fell off my bicycle.* ▶ **concussion** /kən'kʌʃn/ *noun* [U]

condemn /kən'dem/ *verb* [T] **1** condemn sb/sth (for/as sth) to say strongly that you think sb/sth is very bad or wrong: *A government spokesman condemned the bombing as a cowardly act of terrorism.* **2** condemn sb (to sth/to do sth) to say what sb's punishment will be; to sentence sb: *The murderer was condemned to death.* ♦ (*figurative*) *Their poor education condemns them to a series of low-paid jobs.* **3** condemn sth (as sth) to say officially that sth is not safe enough to use: *The building was condemned as unsafe and was demolished.*

condemnation /ˌkɒndem'neɪʃn/ *noun* [C,U] the act of **condemning** sth; a statement that **condemns**: *The bombing brought condemnation from all around the world.*

condensation /ˌkɒnden'seɪʃn/ *noun* [U] small drops of liquid that are formed when warm air touches a cold surface

condense /kən'dens/ *verb* **1** [I,T] to change or make sth change from gas to liquid: *Steam con-*

C

C

denses into water when it touches a cold surface. ➲ look at **evaporate** **2** [T] condense sth (into sth) to make sth smaller or shorter so that it fills less space: *We'll have to condense these three chapters into one.*

condescend /ˌkɒndɪˈsend/ *verb* [I] **1** condescend (to do sth) to do sth that you believe is below your level of importance: *Celia only condescends to speak to me when she wants me to do something for her.* **2** condescend (to sb) to behave towards sb in a way that shows that you think you are better or more important than them SYN **patronize** ▶ **condescending** *adj*: *a condescending smile* ▶ **condescension** /ˌkɒndɪˈsenʃn/ *noun* [U]

condition[1] /kənˈdɪʃn/ *noun* **1** [U,sing] the state that sb/sth is in: *to be in poor/good/excellent condition* ◆ *He looks really ill. He is certainly not in a condition to drive home.* **2** [C] a medical problem that you have for a long time: *to have a heart/lung condition* **3** conditions [pl] the situation or surroundings in which people live, work or do things: *The prisoners were kept* ***in*** *terrible* ***conditions***. ◆ *poor living/housing/working conditions* **4** [C] something that must happen so that sth else can happen or be possible: *One of the conditions of the job is that you agree to work on Sundays.* ◆ *He said I could borrow his bike* ***on one condition****—that I didn't let anyone else ride it.* ◆ *I agreed to help* ***on condition that*** *I got half the profit.*
IDM **on no condition** (*formal*) not for any reason: *On no condition must the press find out about this.*
out of condition not physically fit

condition[2] /kənˈdɪʃn/ *verb* [T] to affect or control the way that sb/sth behaves: *Boys are conditioned to think that they are stronger than girls.*

conditional /kənˈdɪʃənl/ *adj* **1** conditional (on/upon sth) that only happens if sth else is done or happens first: *My university place is conditional on my getting good marks in the exams.* OPP **unconditional** **2** [only *before* a noun] describing a situation that must exist before sth else can happen. A **conditional** sentence often contains the word 'if': *'If you don't study, you won't pass the exam' is a conditional sentence.* ℹ For more information about conditional sentences, look at the **Reference Section** at the back of this dictionary. ▶ **conditionally** /-ʃənəli/ *adv*

conditioner /kənˈdɪʃənə(r)/ *noun* [C,U] a substance that keeps sth in a good condition: *Do you use conditioner on your hair?*

condo /ˈkɒndəʊ/ (*informal*) = **condominium**

condolence /kənˈdəʊləns/ *noun* [pl,U] an expression of how sorry you feel for sb whose relative or close friend has just died: *offer your condolences* ◆ *a message of condolence*

condom /ˈkɒndɒm/ (also *informal* rubber) *noun* [C] a thin rubber covering that a man wears over his sexual organ during sex to prevent the woman from becoming pregnant or as protection against disease

condominium /ˌkɒndəˈmɪniəm/ (also *informal* condo) *noun* [C] (*AmE*) a flat or block of flats owned by the people who live in them

condone /kənˈdəʊn/ *verb* [T] to accept or agree with sth that most people think is wrong: *I can never condone violence—no matter what the circumstances are.*

conducive /kənˈdjuːsɪv/ *adj* (*formal*) conducive (to sth) helping or making sth happen: *This hot weather is not conducive to hard work.*

conduct[1] /kənˈdʌkt/ *verb* [T] **1** (*formal*) to organize and do sth, especially research: *to conduct tests/a survey/an inquiry* **2** to stand in front of an **orchestra** (= a large group of musicians who play together) and direct the musicians: *a concert by the Philharmonic Orchestra, conducted by Sir Colin Davis* **3** (*formal*) conduct yourself well, badly, etc. to behave in a particular way: *He conducted himself far better than expected.* **4** to allow heat or electricity to pass along or through sth: *Rubber does not conduct electricity.*

conduct[2] /ˈkɒndʌkt/ *noun* [U] **1** sb's behaviour: *His conduct has always been of the highest standard.* ◆ *a code of conduct* (= a set of rules for behaviour) **2** (*formal*) conduct of sth the act of controlling or organizing sth: *She was criticized for her conduct of the bank's affairs.*

conductor /kənˈdʌktə(r)/ *noun* [C] **1** a person who stands in front of an **orchestra** (= a large group of musicians who play together), a group of singers, etc. and directs their performance **2** (*AmE*) = **guard**[1](5) **3** (*BrE*) a person whose job is to collect money from passengers on a bus or to check their tickets **4** a substance that allows heat or electricity to pass through or along it

cone /kəʊn/ *noun* [C] **1** a shape or an object that has a round base and a point at the top: *traffic cones* ◆ *an ice cream cone* ➲ *adjective* **conical** ➲ picture at **cube** **2** the hard fruit of a **pine** tree or a **fir** tree (= trees with thin sharp leaves which stay green all through the year) ➲ look at **conifer** ➲ picture at **tree**

confectionery /kənˈfekʃənəri/ *noun* [U] sweets, cakes, chocolates, etc.

confederacy /kənˈfedərəsi/ *noun* [C] a group of people, states or political parties with the same aim

confederation /kənˌfedəˈreɪʃn/ *noun* [C,U] an organization of smaller groups which have joined together: *a confederation of independent republics*

confer /kənˈfɜː(r)/ *verb* (conferring; conferred) **1** [I] confer (with sb) (on/about sth) to discuss sth with sb before making a decision: *The president is conferring with his advisers.* **2** [T] (*written*) confer sth (on sb) to give sb a special right or advantage

conference /ˈkɒnfərəns/ *noun* [C] a large official meeting, often lasting several days, at which members of an organization, a profession, etc. meet to discuss important matters: *Political parties usually* ***hold a conference*** *once a year.* ◆ *an international conference on climate change* ◆ *a conference room/centre/hall*

confess /kənˈfes/ *verb* [I,T] confess (to sth/to doing sth); confess (sth) (to sb) to admit that you have done sth bad or wrong: *The young woman confessed to the murder of her boyfriend/to murdering her boyfriend.* ◆ *They confessed to their mother that they* *had spent all the money on sweets.* ➲ A less formal expression is **own up (to sth)**.

confession /kənˈfeʃn/ *noun* [C,U] an act of admitting that you have done sth bad or wrong: *The police persuaded the man to make a full confession.*

confetti /kənˈfeti/ *noun* [U] small pieces of coloured paper that people throw over a man and woman who have just got married

confide /kənˈfaɪd/ *verb* [T] confide sth to sb to tell sb sth that is secret: *She did not confide her love to anyone—not even to her best friend.*

PHR V **confide in sb** to talk to sb that you trust about sth secret or private

⚷ **confidence** /ˈkɒnfɪdəns/ *noun* [U] **1** confidence (in sb/sth) trust or strong belief in sb/sth: *The public is losing confidence in the present government.* ◆ *I have every confidence in Emily's ability to do the job.* **2** the feeling that you are sure about your own abilities, opinion, etc: *I didn't **have the confidence** to tell her I thought she was wrong.* ◆ *to be **full of confidence*** ◆ *'Of course we will win,' the team captain said **with confidence**.* ➲ look at **self-confidence** **3** a feeling of trust in sb to keep sth a secret: *The information was given to me **in strict confidence**.* ◆ *It took a while to **win/gain her confidence**.*

ˈ**confidence trick** *noun* [C] a way of getting money by cheating sb

⚷ **confident** /ˈkɒnfɪdənt/ *adj* confident (of sth/that ...); confident (about sth) feeling or showing that you are sure about your own abilities, opinions, etc: *Kate feels confident of passing/that she can pass the exam.* ◆ *to be confident of success* ◆ *You should feel confident about your own abilities.* ◆ *Dillon has a very confident manner.* ➲ look at **self-confident** ▶ **confidently** *adv*: *She stepped confidently onto the stage and began to sing.*

confidential /ˌkɒnfɪˈdenʃl/ *adj* secret; not to be shown or told to other people: *The letter was marked 'private and confidential'.* ▶ **confidentiality** /ˌkɒnfɪˌdenʃiˈæləti/ *noun* [U] ▶ **confidentially** /-ʃəli/ *adv*

configuration /kənˌfɪgəˈreɪʃn/ *noun* [C,U] **1** (*formal*) the way in which the parts of sth, or a group of things, are arranged **2** the equipment and programs that form a computer system and the particular way that these are arranged

configure /kənˈfɪgə(r)/ *verb* [T, usually passive] to arrange sth in a particular way, especially computer equipment

⚷ **confine** /kənˈfaɪn/ *verb* [T] **1** confine sb/sth/yourself to sth to stay within the limits of sth: *Please confine your questions to the topic we are discussing.* SYN **restrict** **2** confine sb/sth (in/to sth) to keep a person or an animal in a particular, usually small, place: *The prisoners are confined to their cells for long periods at a time.*

⚷ **confined** /kənˈfaɪnd/ *adj* (used about a space) very small: *Sailors on submarines must get used to living in confined spaces.*

confinement /kənˈfaɪnmənt/ *noun* [U] being kept in a small space: *to be kept **in solitary confinement*** (= in a prison and separated from other people)

confines /ˈkɒnfaɪnz/ *noun* [pl] (*formal*) the limits of sth: *Patients are not allowed beyond the confines of the hospital grounds.*

⚷ **confirm** /kənˈfɜːm/ *verb* [T] **1** to say or show that sth is true; to make sth definite: *Seeing the two of them together confirmed our suspicions.* ◆ *Can you confirm that you will be able to attend?* **2** to accept sb as a full member of a Christian Church in a special ceremony: *He was confirmed at the age of thirteen.* ▶ **confirmation** /ˌkɒnfəˈmeɪʃn/ *noun* [C,U]: *We are waiting for confirmation of the report.* ◆ *You will receive a written confirmation of your reservation.* ◆ (*formal*): *We are **awaiting confirmation**.*

confirmed /kənˈfɜːmd/ *adj* [only before a noun] fixed in a particular habit or way of life: *a confirmed bachelor*

confiscate /ˈkɒnfɪskeɪt/ *verb* [T] to take sth away from sb as a punishment: *Any cigarettes found in school will be confiscated.* ▶ **confiscation** /ˌkɒnfɪˈskeɪʃn/ *noun* [C,U]

⚷ **conflict**[1] /ˈkɒnflɪkt/ *noun* [C,U] **1** (a) conflict with sb/sth (over sth) a fight or an argument: *an armed conflict* ◆ *The new laws have brought the Government **into conflict** with the unions over pay increases.* **2** a difference between two or more ideas, wishes, etc: *Many women have to cope with the conflict between their career and their family.* ◆ *a conflict of interests*

⚷ **conflict**[2] /kənˈflɪkt/ *verb* [I] A and B conflict; A conflicts with B to disagree with or be different from sb/sth: *The statements of the two witnesses conflict.* ◆ *John's statement conflicts with yours.* ◆ *conflicting results*

conform /kənˈfɔːm/ *verb* [I] conform (to sth) **1** to behave in the way that other people and society expect you to behave: *Children are under a lot of pressure to conform when they first start school.* **2** to obey a rule or law: *This building does not conform to fire regulations.* ▶ **conformity** /kənˈfɔːməti/ *noun* [U] (*formal*)

conformist /kənˈfɔːmɪst/ *noun* [C] a person who behaves in the way that people are expected to behave by society OPP **nonconformist**

⚷ **confront** /kənˈfrʌnt/ *verb* [T] **1** confront sth; confront sb (with sb/sth) to think about, or to make sb think about, sth that is difficult or unpleasant: *to confront a problem/a difficulty/an issue* ◆ *When the police confronted him with the evidence, he confessed.* **2** to stand in front of sb, for example because you want to fight them: *The unarmed demonstrators were confronted by a row of soldiers.*

confrontation /ˌkɒnfrʌnˈteɪʃn/ *noun* [C,U] a fight or an argument

⚷ **confuse** /kənˈfjuːz/ *verb* [T] **1** to make sb unable to think clearly or to know what to do: *He confused everybody with his pages of facts and figures.* **2** confuse A and/with B to mistake sb/sth for sb/sth else: *I* *often confuse Lee with his brother. They look very much alike.* **3** to make sth complicated: *The situation is confused by the fact that so many organizations are involved.*

C

confused /kən'fju:zd/ *adj* **1** not able to think clearly: *When he regained consciousness he was dazed and confused.* **2** difficult to understand: *The article is very confused—I don't know what the main point is.* ▶ **confusedly** /kən'fju:zɪdli/ *adv*

confusing /kən'fju:zɪŋ/ *adj* difficult to understand: *Her instructions were contradictory and confusing.* ▶ **confusingly** *adv*

confusion /kən'fju:ʒn/ *noun* [U] **1** the state of not being able to think clearly or not understanding sth: *He stared* ***in confusion*** *at the exam paper.* ◆ *There is still a great deal of confusion as to the true facts.* **2** the act of mistaking sb/sth for sb/sth else: *To avoid confusion, all luggage should be labelled with your name and destination.* **3** a lack of order: *Their unexpected visit threw all our plans into confusion.*

congeal /kən'dʒi:l/ *verb* [I,T] (used about a liquid) to become solid; to make a liquid solid: *congealed blood*

congenial /kən'dʒi:niəl/ *adj* (*formal*) pleasant: *We spent an evening in congenial company.*

congenital /kən'dʒenɪtl/ *adj* (used about a disease) beginning at and continuing since birth

congested /kən'dʒestɪd/ *adj* so full of sth that nothing can move: *The streets of London are congested with traffic.* ▶ **congestion** /kən'dʒestʃən/ *noun* [U]: *severe traffic congestion*

conglomerate /kən'glɒmərət/ *noun* [C] a large firm made up of several different companies

conglomeration /kənˌglɒmə'reɪʃn/ *noun* [C] a group of many different things that have been brought together

congratulate /kən'grætʃuleɪt/ *verb* [T] congratulate sb (on sth) to tell sb that you are pleased about sth they have done: *Colin congratulated Sue on passing her driving test.*

congratulations /kənˌgrætʃu'leɪʃnz/ *noun* [pl] used for telling sb that you are pleased about sth they have done: *Congratulations on the birth of your baby boy!* ◆ *Congratulations! Your painting has won first prize.* ◆ *to offer/send your congratulations*

congregate /'kɒŋgrɪgeɪt/ *verb* [I] to come together in a crowd or group

congregation /ˌkɒŋgrɪ'geɪʃn/ *noun* [C, with sing or pl verb] the group of people who attend a particular church

congress /'kɒŋgres/ *noun* [C] **1** a large formal meeting or series of meetings: *a medical congress* **2** Congress the name in some countries (for example the US) for the group of people who are elected to make the laws: *Congress will vote on the proposals tomorrow.*

CULTURE

The US Congress consists of the **Senate** and the **House of Representatives.**

congressional /kən'greʃənl/ *adj* [only *before* a noun] connected with a **congress** or **Congress**

Congressman /'kɒŋgresmən/, **Congresswoman** /'kɒŋgreswʊmən/ *noun* [C] (*pl* -men /-mən/, -women /-wɪmɪn/) (also Congressperson /-pɜ:sn/) a member of Congress in the US, especially the House of Representatives

conical /'kɒnɪkl/ *adj* having a round base and getting narrower towards a point at the top ➲ *noun* cone

conifer /'kɒnɪfə(r)/ *noun* [C] a tree with needles that stays green all through the year and that has cones (= hard brown fruit) ▶ **coniferous** /kə'nɪfərəs/ *adj*

conjecture /kən'dʒektʃə(r)/ *verb* [I,T] (*formal*) to guess about sth without real proof or evidence ▶ **conjecture** *noun* [C,U]

conjugal /'kɒndʒəgl/ *adj* [only *before* a noun] (*formal*) connected with marriage

conjugate /'kɒndʒəgeɪt/ *verb* [T] to give the different forms of a verb ▶ **conjugation** /ˌkɒndʒu'geɪʃn/ *noun* [C,U]

conjunction /kən'dʒʌŋkʃn/ *noun* [C] a word that is used for joining other words, phrases or sentences: *'And', 'but' and 'or' are conjunctions.*
IDM **in conjunction with sb/sth** together with sb/sth

conjure /'kʌndʒə(r)/ *verb* [I] to do tricks by clever, quick hand movements, that appear to be magic
PHR V **conjure sth up 1** to cause an image to appear in your mind: *Hawaiian music conjures up images of sunshine, flowers and sandy beaches.* **2** to make sth appear quickly or suddenly: *Mum can conjure up a meal out of almost anything.*
▶ **conjuring** *noun* [U]

conjuror (also conjurer) /'kʌndʒərə(r)/ *noun* [C] a person who does clever tricks that appear to be magic ➲ look at **magician**

conker /'kɒŋkə(r)/ (*BrE informal*) = **horse chestnut**(2)

connect /kə'nekt/ *verb* **1** [I,T] connect (sth) (up) (to/with sth) to be joined to sth; to join sth to sth else: *The tunnels connect (up) ten metres further on.* ◆ *The printer is connected to the computer.* ◆ *This motorway connects Cadiz with Seville.* ➲ look at **disconnect 2** [T] connect sb/sth (with sb/sth) to have an association with sb/sth else; to realize or show that sb/sth is involved with sb/sth else: *There was no evidence that she was connected with the crime.* **3** [I] connect (with sth) (used about a bus, train, plane, etc.) to arrive at a particular time so that passengers can change to another bus, train, plane, etc: *a connecting flight*

connection /kə'nekʃn/ *noun* **1** [C,U] a connection between A and B; a connection with/to sth an association or a relationship between two or more people or things: *Is there any connection between the* *two organizations? ◆ What's your connection with Brazil? Have you worked there? ◆ I'm having problems with my Internet connection.* **2** [C] a place where two wires, pipes, etc. join together: *The radio doesn't work. There must be a loose connection somewhere.* **3** [C] a bus, train, plane, etc. that leaves soon after another arrives: *Our bus was late, so we missed our connection.*

IDM **in connection with sb/sth** (*formal*) about or concerning: *I am writing to you in connection with your application.*
in this/that connection (*formal*) about or concerning this/that

connive /kəˈnaɪv/ *verb* [I] connive at sth; connive (with sb) (to do sth) to work secretly with sb to do sth that is wrong; to do nothing to stop sb doing sth wrong: *The two parties connived to get rid of the president.*

connoisseur /ˌkɒnəˈsɜː(r)/ *noun* [C] a person who knows a lot about art, good food, wine, music, etc.

connotation /ˌkɒnəˈteɪʃn/ *noun* [C] an idea expressed by a word in addition to its main meaning: *'Spinster' means a single woman, but it has negative connotations.*

conquer /ˈkɒŋkə(r)/ *verb* [T] **1** to take control of a country or city and its people by force, especially in a war: *Napoleon's ambition was to conquer Europe.* ◆ (*figurative*) *The young singer conquered the hearts of audiences all over the world.* **2** to succeed in controlling or dealing with a strong feeling, problem, etc: *She's trying to conquer her fear of flying.*

conqueror /ˈkɒŋkərə(r)/ *noun* [C] a person who has **conquered**(1) sth

conquest /ˈkɒŋkwest/ *noun* **1** [C,U] an act of **conquering** sth: *the Norman conquest* (= of England in 1066) ◆ *the conquest of Mount Everest* **2** [C] an area of land that has been taken in a war

conscience /ˈkɒnʃəns/ *noun* [C,U] the part of your mind that tells you if what you are doing is right or wrong: *a clear/a guilty conscience*

IDM **have sth on your conscience** to feel guilty because you have done sth wrong

conscientious /ˌkɒnʃiˈenʃəs/ *adj* (used about people) careful to do sth correctly and well: *He's a conscientious worker.* ▶ **conscientiously** *adv*

ˌconscientious obˈjector *noun* [C] a person who refuses to join the army, etc. because they believe it is morally wrong to kill other people

🔑 **conscious** /ˈkɒnʃəs/ *adj* **1** [not before a noun] conscious (of sth/that ...) noticing or realizing that sth exists: *She didn't seem conscious of the danger.* ◆ *Bill suddenly became conscious that someone was following him.* SYN **aware** **2** able to see, hear, feel, etc. things; awake: *The injured driver was still conscious when the ambulance arrived.* OPP **unconscious** **3** that you do on purpose or for a particular reason: *We made a conscious effort to treat both children equally.*

MORE Deliberate has a similar meaning.

▶ **consciously** *adv*

consciousness /ˈkɒnʃəsnəs/ *noun* **1** [U] the state of being able to see, hear, feel, etc: *As he fell, he hit his head and* ***lost consciousness.*** ◆ *She* ***regained consciousness*** *after two weeks in a coma.* **2** [U,sing] consciousness (of sth) the state of realizing or noticing that sth exists: *There is (a) growing consciousness of the need to save energy.*

conscript[1] /kənˈskrɪpt/ *verb* [T] to make sb join the army, navy or air force ▶ **conscription** *noun* [U]

conscript[2] /ˈkɒnskrɪpt/ *noun* [C] a person who has been **conscripted** ➲ look at **volunteer**

conscription /kənˈskrɪpʃn/ (*especially AmE* the draft) *noun* [U] the system of making sb join the army, etc.

consecrate /ˈkɒnsɪkreɪt/ *verb* [T] to state formally in a special ceremony that a place or an object can be used for religious purposes ▶ **consecration** /ˌkɒnsɪˈkreɪʃn/ *noun* [C,U]

consecutive /kənˈsekjətɪv/ *adj* coming or happening one after the other: *This is the team's fourth consecutive win.* ▶ **consecutively** *adv*

consensus /kənˈsensəs/ *noun* [sing,U] (a) consensus (among/between sb) (on/about sth) agreement among a group of people: *to* ***reach a consensus*** ◆ *There is no consensus among experts about the causes of climate change.*

consent[1] /kənˈsent/ *verb* [I] consent (to sth) to agree to sth; to allow sth to happen

consent[2] /kənˈsent/ *noun* [U] agreement; permission: *The child's parents had to give their consent to the operation.*

IDM **the age of consent** ➲ **age**[1]

🔑 **consequence** /ˈkɒnsɪkwəns/ *noun* **1** [C] something that happens or follows as a result of sth else: *Many people may lose their jobs* ***as a consequence of*** *recent poor sales.* **2** [U] (*formal*) importance: *It is of no consequence.*

consequent /ˈkɒnsɪkwənt/ *adj* [only *before* a noun] (*formal*) following as the result of sth else: *The lack of rain and consequent poor harvests have led to food shortages.* ▶ **consequently** *adv*: *She didn't work hard enough, and consequently failed the exam.* ➲ note at **therefore**

conservation /ˌkɒnsəˈveɪʃn/ *noun* [U] **1** the protection of the natural world: *Conservation groups are protesting against the plan to build a road through the forest.* **2** not allowing sth to be wasted, damaged or destroyed: *the conservation of energy* ➲ *verb* **conserve**

conservationist /ˌkɒnsəˈveɪʃənɪst/ *noun* [C] a person who believes in protecting the natural world

conservatism /kənˈsɜːvətɪzəm/ *noun* [U] **1** the disapproval of new ideas and change **2** *usually* Conservatism the beliefs of the Conservative Party

🔑 **conservative**[1] /kənˈsɜːvətɪv/ *adj* **1** Conservative connected with the British Conservative Party: *Conservative voters* **2** not liking change; traditional: *This design is too modern for them. They have very*

C

conservative tastes. **3** (used when you are guessing how much sth costs) lower than the real figure or amount: *Even **a conservative estimate** would put the damage at about £4000 to repair.* ▶ **conservatively** *adv*

conservative² /kən'sɜːvətɪv/ *noun* [C] **1** a person who does not like change **2** *usually* Conservative (*abbr* Con) a member of the British Conservative Party

the Con'servative Party *noun* [sing, with sing or pl verb] one of the main political parties in Britain. The Conservative Party supports a free market and is against the state controlling industry. ➲ note at **party** ➲ look at **the Labour Party, the Liberal Democrats**

conservatory /kən'sɜːvətri/ *noun* [C] (*pl* conservatories) (*BrE*) a room with glass walls and a glass roof that is built onto the outside of a house

conserve /kən'sɜːv/ *verb* [T] to avoid wasting sth: *to conserve water* ➲ *noun* **conservation**

⚷ **consider** /kən'sɪdə(r)/ *verb* [T] **1** consider sb/sth (for/as sth); consider doing sth to think about sth carefully, often before making a decision: *They are considering him for the part of Romeo.* ◆ *She had never considered nursing as a career.* ◆ *We're considering going to Spain for our holidays.* **2** consider sb/sth (as/to be) sth; consider that ... to think about sb/sth in a particular way: *He considered the risk (to be) too great.* ◆ *He considered that the risk was too great.* ◆ *Jane considers herself an expert on the subject.* **3** to remember or pay attention to sth, especially sb's feelings: *I can't just move abroad. I have to consider my family.*

⚷ **considerable** /kən'sɪdərəbl/ *adj* great in amount or size: *A considerable number of people preferred the old building to the new one.* ▶ **considerably** /-əbli/ *adv* (*formal*): *This flat is considerably larger than our last one.* SYN **significantly**

considerate /kən'sɪdərət/ *adj* considerate (of sb) (to do sth); considerate (towards sb) careful not to upset people; thinking of others: *It was very considerate of you to offer to drive me home.* SYN **thoughtful** OPP **inconsiderate**

⚷ **consideration** /kənˌsɪdə'reɪʃn/ *noun* **1** [U] (*formal*) an act of thinking about sth carefully or for a long time: *I have given some consideration to the idea but I don't think it would work.* **2** [C] something that you think about when you are making a decision: *If he changes his job, the salary will be an important consideration.* **3** [U] consideration (for sb/sth) the quality of thinking about what other people need or feel: *Most drivers show little consideration for cyclists.*

IDM **take sth into consideration** to think about sth when you are forming an opinion or making a decision

considering /kən'sɪdərɪŋ/ *prep, conj* (used for introducing a surprising fact) when you think about or remember sth: *Considering you've only been studying for a year, you speak English very well.*

consign /kən'saɪn/ *verb* [T] (*formal*) consign sb/sth to sth to put or send sb/sth somewhere, especially in order to get rid of them or it: *I think I can consign this junk mail straight to the bin.*

consignment /kən'saɪnmənt/ *noun* [C] goods that are being sent to sb/sth: *a new consignment of books*

⚷ **consist** /kən'sɪst/ *verb* [not used in the continuous tenses]

PHR V **consist in sth** (*formal*) to have sth as its main point: *Her job consisted in welcoming the guests as they arrived.*

consist of sth to be formed or made up of sth: *The band consists of a singer, two guitarists and a drummer.*

> **HELP** Although this verb is not used in the continuous tenses, it is common to see the present participle (= *-ing* form): *It's a full-time course consisting of six different modules.*

consistency /kən'sɪstənsi/ *noun* (*pl* consistencies) **1** [U] the quality of always having the same standard, opinions, behaviour, etc: *Your work lacks consistency. Sometimes it's excellent but at other times it's full of mistakes.* OPP **inconsistency** **2** [C,U] how thick or smooth a liquid substance is: *The mixture should have a thick, sticky consistency.*

consistent /kən'sɪstənt/ *adj* **1** always having the same opinions, standard, behaviour, etc.; not changing **2** consistent (with sth) agreeing with or similar to sth: *I'm afraid your statement is not consistent with what the other witnesses said.* OPP for both meanings **inconsistent** ▶ **consistently** *adv*: *We must try to maintain a consistently high standard.*

consolation /ˌkɒnsə'leɪʃn/ *noun* [C,U] a thing or person that makes you feel better when you are sad SYN **comfort**: *It was some consolation to me to know that I wasn't the only one who had failed the exam.*

console¹ /kən'səʊl/ *verb* [T] to make sb happier when they are very sad or disappointed SYN **comfort**

console² /'kɒnsəʊl/ *noun* [C] a flat surface which contains all the controls and switches for a machine, a piece of electronic equipment, etc: *a **games console***

consolidate /kən'sɒlɪdeɪt/ *verb* [I,T] to become or to make sth firmer or stronger: *We're going to consolidate what we've learnt so far by doing some revision exercises today.* ▶ **consolidation** /kənˌsɒlɪ'deɪʃn/ *noun* [U]

consonant /'kɒnsənənt/ *noun* [C] any of the letters of the English alphabet except *a, e, i, o* and *u*: *The letters 't', 'm', 's' and 'b' are all consonants.* ➲ look at **vowel**

consortium /kən'sɔːtiəm/ *noun* [C] (*pl* consortiums *or* consortia /-tiə/) a group of companies that work closely together for a particular purpose

conspicuous /kən'spɪkjuəs/ *adj* easily seen or noticed OPP **inconspicuous** ▶ **conspicuously** *adv*

conspiracy /kənˈspɪrəsi/ *noun* [C,U] (*pl* conspiracies) a secret plan by a group of people to do sth bad or illegal: *a conspiracy against the president*

conspirator /kənˈspɪrətə(r)/ *noun* [C] a member of a group of people who are planning to do sth bad or illegal

conspire /kənˈspaɪə(r)/ *verb* [I] **1** conspire (with sb) (to do sth) to plan to do sth bad or illegal with a group of people: *A group of terrorists were conspiring to blow up the plane.* **2** conspire (against sb/sth) (used about events) to seem to work together to make sth bad happen: *When we both lost our jobs in the same week, we felt that everything was conspiring against us.*

constable /ˈkʌnstəbl/ = **police constable**

constabulary /kənˈstæbjələri/ *noun* [C] (*pl* constabularies) the police force of a particular area: *the West Yorkshire Constabulary*

constant /ˈkɒnstənt/ *adj* **1** happening or existing all the time or again and again: *The constant noise gave me a headache.* **2** that does not change: *You use less petrol if you drive at a constant speed.*

constantly /ˈkɒnstəntli/ *adv* always; again and again: *The situation is constantly changing.*

constellation /ˌkɒnstəˈleɪʃn/ *noun* [C] a group of stars that forms a pattern and has a name

consternation /ˌkɒnstəˈneɪʃn/ *noun* [U] a feeling of shock or worry: *We stared at each other **in consternation**.*

constipated /ˈkɒnstɪpeɪtɪd/ *adj* not able to empty waste from your body ▶ **constipation** /ˌkɒnstɪˈpeɪʃn/ *noun* [U]: *to suffer from/have constipation*

constituency /kənˈstɪtjuənsi/ *noun* [C] (*pl* constituencies) a district and the people who live in it that a politician represents ➲ note at **election**

constituent /kənˈstɪtjuənt/ *noun* [C] **1** a person who lives in the district that a politician represents **2** one of the parts that form sth: *Hydrogen and oxygen are the constituents of water.*

constitute /ˈkɒnstɪtjuːt/ *verb* [T] [not used in the continuous tenses] (*formal*) **1** to be considered as sth; to be equal to sth: *The presence of the troops constitutes a threat to peace.* **2** to be one of the parts that form sth: *Women constitute a high proportion of part-time workers.*

HELP Although this verb is not used in the continuous tenses, it is common to see the present participle (= *-ing* form): *Management has to fix a maximum number of hours as constituting a day's work.*

constitution /ˌkɒnstɪˈtjuːʃn/ *noun* **1** [C] the basic laws or rules of a country or an organization: *the United States constitution* **2** [U] the way the parts of sth are put together; the structure of sth: *the constitution of DNA*

constitutional /ˌkɒnstɪˈtjuːʃənl/ *adj* connected with or allowed by the **constitution** of a country, etc: *It is not constitutional to imprison a person without trial.*

constrain /kənˈstreɪn/ *verb* [T] (*formal*) constrain sb/sth (to do sth) to limit sb/sth; to force sb/sth to do sth: *The company's growth has been constrained by high taxes.*

constraint /kənˈstreɪnt/ *noun* [C,U] something that limits you SYN **restriction**: *There are always some financial constraints on a project like this.*

constrict /kənˈstrɪkt/ *verb* [I,T] **1** to become or make sth tighter, narrower or less: *She felt her throat constrict with fear.* ◆ *The valve constricts the flow of air.* **2** to limit sb's freedom to do sth ▶ **constriction** *noun* [C,U]

construct /kənˈstrʌkt/ *verb* [T] **1** to build or make sth: *Early houses were constructed out of mud and sticks.* ➲ **Construct** is more formal than **build**. **2** to form sth by putting different things together: *You must learn how to construct a logical argument.*

construction /kənˈstrʌkʃn/ *noun* **1** [U] the act or method of building or making sth: *A new bridge is now **under construction**.* ◆ *He works in the construction industry.* **2** [C] (*formal*) something that has been built or made; a building: *The new pyramid was a construction of glass and steel.* **3** [C] the way that words are used together in a phrase or sentence: *a difficult grammatical construction*

constructive /kənˈstrʌktɪv/ *adj* useful or helpful: *constructive suggestions/criticisms/advice* ▶ **constructively** *adv*

construe /kənˈstruː/ *verb* [T] (*formal*) construe sth (as sth) to understand the meaning of sth in a particular way: *Her confident manner is sometimes construed as arrogance.* ➲ look at **misconstrue**

consul /ˈkɒnsl/ *noun* [C] an official who works in a foreign city helping people from his or her own country who are living or visiting there: *the British consul in Miami* ➲ look at **ambassador** ▶ **consular** /ˈkɒnsjələ(r)/ *adj*

consulate /ˈkɒnsjələt/ *noun* [C] the building where a **consul** works ➲ look at **embassy**

consult /kənˈsʌlt/ *verb* **1** [T] consult sb/sth (about sth) to ask sb for some information or advice, or to look for it in a book, etc: *If the symptoms continue, consult your doctor.* **2** [I] consult (with sb) to discuss sth with sb: *Harry consulted with his sisters before selling the family business.* ◆ *I expect to be consulted on major issues.*

consultancy /kənˈsʌltənsi/ *noun* (*pl* consultancies) **1** [C] a company that gives expert advice on a particular subject **2** [U] expert advice that sb is paid to provide on a particular subject

consultant /kənˈsʌltənt/ *noun* [C] **1** a person who gives advice to people on business, law, etc: *a firm of management consultants* **2** (*BrE*) a hospital doctor who is an expert in a particular area of medicine: *a consultant psychiatrist*

consultation /ˌkɒnslˈteɪʃn/ *noun* [C,U] **1** a discussion between people before a decision is taken:

Diplomats met for consultations on the hostage crisis. ◆ *The measures were introduced without consultation.* **2** (*formal*) meeting sb to get information or advice, or looking for it in a book: *a consultation with a doctor*

consume /kən'sjuːm/ *verb* [T] (*formal*) **1** to use sth such as fuel, energy or time: *This car consumes a lot of petrol.* **2** to eat or drink sth: *Wrestlers can consume up to 10 000 calories in a day.* ➲ *noun* **consumption** **3** (used about an emotion) to affect sb very strongly: *She was consumed with rage after he left her.* ◆ *consumed with anger/curiousity/grief/rage* **4** (used about fire) to destroy sth

🔑 **consumer** /kən'sjuːmə(r)/ *noun* [C] a person who buys things or uses services: *Consumers should complain if they are not satisfied with the service they receive.*

consuming /kən'sjuːmɪŋ/ *adj* [only *before* a noun] that takes up a lot of your time and attention: *Sport is her consuming passion.*

consummate[1] /'kɒnsəmət/ *adj* [only *before* a noun] (*formal*) extremely skilled; a perfect example of sth: *a consummate performer/performance/professional*

consummate[2] /'kɒnsəmeɪt/ *verb* [T] (*formal*) to make a marriage or relationship complete by having sex ▶ **consummation** /ˌkɒnsə'meɪʃn/ *noun* [C,U]

consumption /kən'sʌmpʃn/ *noun* [U] **1** the act of using, eating, etc. sth: *The meat was declared unfit for human consumption* (= for people to eat). **2** the amount of fuel, etc. that sth uses: *a car with low fuel consumption* ➲ *verb* **consume**

cont. (also contd) *abbr* **continued**: *cont. on p 9*

🔑 **contact**[1] /'kɒntækt/ *noun* **1** [U] contact (with sb/sth) meeting, talking to or writing to sb else: *They are trying to* ***make contact*** *with the kidnappers.* ◆ *We* ***keep in contact*** *with our office in New York.* ◆ *It's a pity to* ***lose contact*** *with old school friends.* **2** [U] contact (with sb/sth) the state of touching sb/sth: *This product should not* ***come into contact*** *with food.* **3** [C] a person that you know who may be able to help you: *business contacts*

🔑 **contact**[2] /'kɒntækt/ *verb* [T] to telephone or write to sb: *Is there a phone number where I can contact you?* ▶ **contactable** /'kɒntæktəbl/ *adj*: *I'll be contactable on this number ...*

ˈ**contact lens** *noun* [C] a small piece of plastic that fits onto your eye to help you to see better ➲ picture at **glasses**

contagious /kən'teɪdʒəs/ *adj* (used about a disease) that you can get by touching sb/sth: *Measles is a highly contagious disease.* ◆ (*figurative*) *Her laugh is contagious.* ➲ look at **infectious** ▶ **contagion** /kən'teɪdʒən/ *noun* [U]

🔑 **contain** /kən'teɪn/ *verb* [T] [not used in the continuous tenses] **1** to have sth inside or as part of itself: *Each box contains 24 tins.*

HELP Although this verb is not used in the continuous tenses, it is common to see the present participle (= *-ing* form): *food containing nuts*

2 to keep sth within limits; to control sth: *efforts to contain inflation* ◆ *She found it hard to contain her anger.*

HELP **Contain** or **include**? We use **contain** to talk about objects which have other things inside them: *a jar containing olives* ◆ *This film contains violent scenes.* We use **include** to show that sb/sth forms part of a whole or belongs to something: *a team of seven people including a cameraman and a doctor* ◆ *The price of the holiday includes accommodation.*

🔑 **container** /kən'teɪnə(r)/ *noun* [C] **1** a box, bottle, bag, etc. in which sth is kept: *a plastic container* **2** a large metal box that is used for transporting goods by sea, road or rail: *a container lorry/ship*

contaminate /kən'tæmɪneɪt/ *verb* [T] to add a substance which will make sth dirty or harmful: *The town's drinking water was contaminated with poisonous chemicals.* ▶ **contamination** /kənˌtæmɪ'neɪʃn/ *noun* [U]

contd = **continued**

contemplate /'kɒntəmpleɪt/ *verb* [T] **1** to think carefully about sth or the possibility of doing sth: *Before her illness she had never contemplated retiring.* **SYN** **consider** **2** to look at sb/sth, often quietly or for a long time ▶ **contemplation** /ˌkɒntəm'pleɪʃn/ *noun* [U]

🔑 **contemporary**[1] /kən'temprəri/ *adj* **1** belonging to the same time as sb/sth else: *The programme includes contemporary film footage of the First World War.* **2** of the present time: *contemporary music/art/society* **SYN** **modern**

contemporary[2] /kən'temprəri/ *noun* [C] (*pl* contemporaries) a person who lives or does sth at the same time as sb else: *The Beatles and their contemporaries changed popular music in the 60s.*

contempt /kən'tempt/ *noun* [U] contempt (for sb/sth) the feeling that sb/sth does not deserve any respect or is without value: *The teacher treated my question* ***with contempt***. ▶ **contemptuous** /kən'temptʃuəs/ *adj*: *The boy just gave a contemptuous laugh when I asked him to be quiet.*

contemptible /kən'temptəbl/ *adj* (*formal*) not deserving any respect at all: *contemptible behaviour* **SYN** **despicable**

contend /kən'tend/ *verb* **1** [T] (*formal*) to say or argue that sth is true: *The young man contended that he was innocent.* **2** [I] contend (for sth) to compete against sb to win or gain sth: *Two athletes are contending for first place.* **3** [I] contend with/against sb/sth to have to deal with a problem or a difficult situation: *She's had a lot of problems to contend with.*

contender /kən'tendə(r)/ *noun* [C] a person who may win a competition: *There are only two serious contenders for the leadership.*

🔑 **content**[1] /'kɒntent/ *noun* **1** contents [pl] the thing or things that are inside sth: *Add the contents* *of this packet to a pint of cold milk and mix well.* **2** [sing] the main subject, ideas, etc. of a book, an article, a TV programme, etc: *The content of the essay is good, but there are too many grammatical mistakes.* **3** [sing] the amount of a particular substance that sth contains: *Many processed foods have a high sugar content.*

content² /kən'tent/ *adj* [not before a noun] content (with sth); content to do sth happy or satisfied with what you have or do: *I don't need a new car—I'm perfectly content with this one.*

content³ /kən'tent/ *verb* [T] content yourself with sth to accept sth even though it was not exactly what you wanted: *The restaurant was closed, so we had to content ourselves with a sandwich.*

content⁴ /kən'tent/ *noun*
IDM to your heart's content ➲ **heart**

contented /kən'tentɪd/ *adj* happy or satisfied: *The baby gave a contented chuckle.* ▶ **contentedly** *adv*

contention /kən'tenʃn/ *noun* **1** [U] (*formal*) arguing; disagreement **2** [C] (*formal*) your opinion; something that you say is true: *The government's contention is that unemployment will start to fall next year.*
IDM in contention (for sth) having a chance of winning a competition: *Four teams are still in contention for the cup.*

contentious /kən'tenʃəs/ *adj* likely to cause argument: *a contentious issue*

contentment /kən'tentmənt/ *noun* [U] a feeling of happiness and satisfaction

contest¹ /'kɒntest/ *noun* [C] **1** a competition to find out who is the best, strongest, most beautiful, etc: *I've decided to* **enter** *that writing* **contest**. **2** a struggle to gain control or power: *a contest for the leadership of the party*

contest² /kən'test/ *verb* [T] **1** to take part in a competition or try to win sth: *Twenty-four teams will contest next year's World Cup.* **2** to say that sth is wrong or that it was not done properly: *They contested the decision, saying that the judges had not been fair.*

contestant /kən'testənt/ *noun* [C] a person who takes part in a **contest**: *Four contestants appear on the quiz show each week.*

context /'kɒntekst/ *noun* [C,U] **1** the situation in which sth happens or that caused sth to happen: *To* **put** *our company* **in context**, *we are now the third largest in the country.* **2** the words that come before or after a word, phrase or sentence that help you to understand its meaning: *You can often guess the meaning of a word from its context.* ♦ *Taken* **out of context**, *his comment made no sense.*

continent /'kɒntɪnənt/ *noun* **1** [C] one of the seven main areas of land on the Earth: *Asia, Africa and Antarctica are continents.* **2 the Continent** [sing] (*BrE*) the main part of Europe not including

containers

C

Britain or Ireland: *We're going to spend a weekend on the Continent.*

continental /ˌkɒntɪˈnentl/ *adj* **1** (*BrE*) connected with the main part of Europe not including Britain or Ireland: *continental holidays* **2** connected with or typical of a continent: *Moscow has a continental climate: hot summers and cold winters.*

contingency /kənˈtɪndʒənsi/ *noun* [C] (*pl* contingencies) a possible future situation or event: *We'd better make* ***contingency plans*** *just in case something goes wrong.* ◆ *We've tried to prepare for every possible contingency.*

contingent /kənˈtɪndʒənt/ *noun* [C, with sing or pl verb] **1** a group of people from the same country, organization, etc. who are attending an event: *the Irish contingent at the conference* **2** a group of armed forces forming part of a larger force

continual /kənˈtɪnjuəl/ *adj* [only *before* a noun] happening again and again: *His continual phone calls started to annoy her.* ➲ look at **incessant** ▶ **continually** /-juəli/ *adv*

continuation /kənˌtɪnjuˈeɪʃn/ *noun* [sing, U] something that continues or follows sth else; the act of making sth continue: *The team are hoping for a continuation of their recent good form.* ◆ *Continuation of the current system will be impossible.*

🔑 **continue** /kənˈtɪnjuː/ *verb* **1** [I] to keep happening or existing without stopping: *If the pain continues, see your doctor.* **2** [I,T] continue (doing/to do sth); continue (with sth) to keep doing sth without stopping: *They ignored me and continued their conversation.* ◆ *He continued working/to work late into the night.* ◆ *Will you continue with the lessons after the exam?* **3** [I,T] to go further in the same direction: *The next day we continued our journey.* **4** [I,T] to begin to do or say sth again after you had stopped: *The meeting will continue after lunch.* ◆ *I'm sorry I interrupted. Please continue.* ◆ *We'll continue the meeting later.*

continued /kənˈtɪnjuːd/ (*abbr* cont.; contd) *adj* [only *before* a noun] going on without stopping: *We are grateful for your continued support.*

continuity /ˌkɒntɪˈnjuːəti/ *noun* [U] the fact of continuing without stopping or of staying the same: *The pupils will have the same teacher for two years to ensure continuity.*

🔑 **continuous** /kənˈtɪnjuəs/ *adj* **1** happening or existing without stopping: *There was a continuous line of cars stretching for miles.* **2** (*informal*) repeated many times: *For four days the town suffered continuous attacks.* ▶ **continuously** *adv*: *It has rained continuously here for three days.*

the conˈtinuous tense (also the proˈgressive tense) *noun* [C] the form of a verb such as 'I am waiting', 'I was waiting' or 'I have been waiting' which is made from a part of 'be' and a verb ending in '-ing' and is used to describe an action that continues for a period of time ℹ For more information about the continuous tense, look at the **Reference Section** at the back of this dictionary.

contort /kənˈtɔːt/ *verb* [I,T] to move or to make sth move into a strange or unusual shape: *His face contorted/was contorted with pain.* ▶ **contortion** *noun* [C]

contour /ˈkɒntʊə(r)/ *noun* [C] **1** the shape of the outer surface of sth: *I could just make out the contours of the house in the dark.* **2** (also contour line) a line on a map joining places of equal height

contra- /ˈkɒntrə/ [in nouns, verbs and adjectives] against; opposite: *contraflow* ◆ *contradict*

contraband /ˈkɒntrəbænd/ *noun* [U] goods that are illegally taken into or out of a country: *contraband cigarettes* ◆ *to smuggle contraband*

contraception /ˌkɒntrəˈsepʃn/ *noun* [U] the ways of preventing a woman from becoming pregnant: *a reliable form of contraception* ➲ look at **birth control, family planning**

contraceptive /ˌkɒntrəˈseptɪv/ *noun* [C] a drug or a device that prevents a woman from becoming pregnant ▶ **contraceptive** *adj* [only *before* a noun]

🔑 **contract**[1] /ˈkɒntrækt/ *noun* [C] a written legal agreement: *They* ***signed a*** *three-year* ***contract with*** *a major record company.* ◆ *a temporary contract*

🔑 **contract**[2] /kənˈtrækt/ *verb* **1** [I,T] to become or to make sth smaller or shorter: *Metals contract as they cool.* OPP **expand** **2** [T] to get an illness or disease, especially a serious one: *to contract pneumonia* **3** [I,T] to make a written legal agreement with sb to do sth: *His firm has been contracted to supply all the furniture for the new building.*

PHR V **contract sth out (to sb)** to arrange for work to be done by sb outside your own company

contraction /kənˈtrækʃn/ *noun* **1** [U] the process of becoming or of making sth become smaller or shorter: *the expansion and contraction of a muscle* **2** [C] a strong movement of the muscles that happens to a woman as her baby is born **3** [C] a shorter form of a word or words: *'Mustn't' is a contraction of 'must not'.*

EXAM TIP

Using contractions

Think carefully before you use a contraction in an exam, as they are not usually used in formal writing. You can use contractions in some types of writing, for example a letter or an email to a friend, or an article for a student magazine, but be careful. Make sure you are still using proper English. You should never use words like 'gonna' or 'wanna', which are only used in spoken English.

contractor /kənˈtræktə(r)/ *noun* [C] a person or company that has a contract to do work or provide goods or services for another company

contractual /kənˈtræktʃuəl/ *adj* connected with or included in a contract

contradict /ˌkɒntrəˈdɪkt/ *verb* [T] to say that sth is wrong or not true; to say the opposite of sth: *These instructions seem to contradict previous ones.*

contradiction /ˌkɒntrəˈdɪkʃn/ *noun* [C,U] a statement, a fact or an action that is opposite to or different from another one: *There were a number of contradictions in what he told the police.* ♦ *This letter is* ***in*** *complete* ***contradiction to*** *their previous one.*

contradictory /ˌkɒntrəˈdɪktəri/ *adj* being opposite to or not matching sth else: *Contradictory reports appeared in the newspapers.*

contraflow /ˈkɒntrəfləʊ/ *noun* [C] (*BrE*) the system that is used when one half of a wide road is closed for repairs, and traffic going in both directions has to use the other side

contralto /kənˈtræltəʊ/ *noun* [C,U] (*pl* **contraltos**) the lowest female singing voice; a woman with this voice

contraption /kənˈtræpʃn/ *noun* [C] a strange or complicated piece of equipment: *The first aeroplanes were dangerous contraptions.*

contrary[1] /ˈkɒntrəri/ *adj* **1** [only *before* a noun] completely different: *I thought it was possible, but she took the contrary view.* **OPP** **opposite** **2 contrary to** completely different from; opposite to; against: ***Contrary to popular belief*** (= to what many people think)*, not all boxers are stupid.*

contrary[2] /ˈkɒntrəri/ *noun*

IDM **on the contrary** the opposite is true; certainly not: *'You look as if you're not enjoying yourself.' 'On the contrary, I'm having a great time.'*

to the contrary (*formal*) saying the opposite: *Unless I hear anything to the contrary, I shall assume that the arrangements haven't changed.*

contrast[1] /ˈkɒntrɑːst/ *noun* **1** [U] comparison between two people or things that shows the differences between them: ***In contrast to*** *previous years, we've had a very successful summer.* **2** [C,U] (a) **contrast (to/with sb/sth)**; (a) **contrast (between A and B)** a clear difference between two things or people that is seen when they are compared: *There is a tremendous contrast between the climate in the valley and the climate in the hills.* **3** [C] something that is clearly different from sth else when the two things are compared: *The work you did today is quite a contrast to what you did last week.*

WRITING TIP

How to show contrast 1

To show contrast between positive and negative aspects of a subject, we often use **however, nevertheless, nonetheless** or **on the one hand ... on the other hand**: *Smartphones are very useful.* ***However,*** *they are very expensive.* ♦ *Smartphones are very expensive.* ***Nevertheless/Nonetheless,*** *they are very useful.* ♦ ***On the one hand*** *smartphones are very useful, but* ***on the other hand,*** *they are very expensive.* ➲ note at **despite**

ℹ For more help with writing, look at **Wordpower Writing Tutor** at the back of this dictionary.

contrast[2] /kənˈtrɑːst/ *verb* **1** [T] **contrast (A and/with B)** to compare people or things in order to show the differences between them: *The film contrasts his poor childhood with his later life as a millionaire.* **2** [I] **contrast with sb/sth** to be clearly different when compared: *This comment contrasts sharply with his previous remarks.*

contrasting /kənˈtrɑːstɪŋ/ *adj* very different in style, colour or attitude: *bright, contrasting colours* ♦ *contrasting opinions*

contravene /ˌkɒntrəˈviːn/ *verb* [T] (*formal*) to break a law or a rule ▶ **contravention** /ˌkɒntrəˈvenʃn/ *noun* [C,U]

contribute /kənˈtrɪbjuːt; ˈkɒntrɪbjuːt/ *verb* **contribute (sth) (to/towards sth)** **1** [I,T] to give a part of the total, together with others: *Would you like to contribute towards our collection for famine relief?* ♦ *The research has contributed a great deal to our knowledge of cancer.* **2** [I] to be one of the causes of sth: *It is not known whether the bad weather contributed to the accident.* **3** [I,T] to write articles for a magazine or newspaper: *She contributed a number of articles to the magazine.*

contribution /ˌkɒntrɪˈbjuːʃn/ *noun* [C] **a contribution (to/towards sth)** something that you give, especially money or help, or do together with other people: *If we all* ***make a*** *small* ***contribution,*** *we'll be able to buy Ray a good present.* ♦ *I'd like to thank everyone for their contribution towards clearing up after the party.*

contributor /kənˈtrɪbjətə(r)/ *noun* [C] a person who **contributes** to sth

contributory /kənˈtrɪbjətəri/ *adj* helping to cause or produce sth: *Tiredness is a contributory factor in many road accidents.*

contrive /kənˈtraɪv/ *verb* [T] **1** to manage to do sth, although there are difficulties: *If I can contrive to get off work early, I'll see you later.* **2** to plan or invent sth in a clever and/or dishonest way: *He contrived a scheme to cheat insurance companies.*

contrived /kənˈtraɪvd/ *adj* hard to believe; not natural or realistic: *The ending of the film seemed rather contrived.*

control[1] /kənˈtrəʊl/ *noun* **1** [U] **control (of/over sb/sth)** power and ability to make sb/sth do what you want: *Rebels managed to* ***take control*** *of the radio station.* ♦ *Some teachers find it difficult to* ***keep control*** *of their class.* ♦ *He* ***lost control*** *of the car and crashed.* ♦ *I was late because of circumstances* ***beyond my control.*** **2** [C,U] (a) **control (on/over sth)** a limit on sth; a way of keeping sb/sth within certain limits: *price controls* ♦ *The faults forced the company to review its* ***quality control*** *procedures.* **3** [C] one of the parts of a machine that is used for operating it: *the controls of an aeroplane/a TV* ♦ *a control panel* ♦ *Hold down the* ***control key*** (= a key on a computer keyboard used for performing a particular operation) *and click.* ♦ *a* ***control pad*** (= used for playing computer games) **4** [sing] the place from which sth is operated or where sth is checked: *We went through passport control and then got onto the plane.*

IDM **be in control (of sth)** to direct or manage a situation: *The police are again in control of the area following last night's violence.*

be/get out of control to be/become impossible to deal with: *The demonstration got out of control and fighting broke out.*

under control being dealt with successfully: *It took several hours to bring the fire under control.*

control² /kən'trəʊl/ *verb* [T] (controlling; controlled) **1** to have power and ability to make sb/sth do what you want: *One family controls the company.* ♦ *Police struggled to control the crowd.* ♦ *I couldn't control myself any longer and burst out laughing.* **2** to keep sth within certain limits: *measures to control price rises* ▶ **controller** *noun* [C]: *air traffic controllers*

con'trol freak *noun* [C] (*informal*) (used in a critical way) a person who always wants to be in control of their own and other people's lives, and to organize how things are done

controlled /kən'trəʊld/ *adj* **1** done or arranged in a very careful way: *a controlled explosion* **2** limited, or managed by law or by rules: *controlled airspace* **3 -controlled** [in compounds] managed by a particular group or in a particular way: *a British-controlled company* ♦ *computer-controlled systems* **4** remaining calm and not getting angry or upset: *She remained quiet and controlled.* ➲ look at **uncontrolled**

controversial /ˌkɒntrə'vɜːʃl/ *adj* causing public discussion and disagreement: *a controversial issue/decision/plan*

controversy /'kɒntrəvɜːsi; kən'trɒvəsi/ *noun* [C,U] (*pl* **controversies**) public discussion and disagreement about sth: *The plans for changing the city centre caused much controversy.*

conurbation /ˌkɒnɜː'beɪʃn/ *noun* [C] a very large area of houses and other buildings where towns have grown and joined together

convalesce /ˌkɒnvə'les/ *verb* [I] to rest and get better over a period of time after an illness ▶ **convalescence** *noun* [sing,U] ▶ **convalescent** /ˌkɒnvə'lesnt/ *adj*

convene /kən'viːn/ *verb* [I,T] (*formal*) to come together or to bring people together for a meeting, etc.

convenience /kən'viːniəns/ *noun* **1** [U] the quality of being easy, useful or suitable for sb: *a building designed* **for the convenience of** *disabled people* ♦ **For convenience**, *you can pay for everything at once.* **2** [C] something that makes things easier, quicker or more comfortable: *houses with all the modern conveniences* (= central heating, hot water, etc.) **3** [C] (*BrE*) a public toilet

con'venience food *noun* [C,U] food that you buy frozen or in a box or can, that you can prepare very quickly and easily

convenient /kən'viːniənt/ *adj* **1** suitable or practical for a particular purpose; not causing difficulty: *I'm willing to meet you on any day that's convenient for you.* ♦ *It isn't convenient to talk at the moment, I'm in the middle of a meeting.* OPP **inconvenient** **2** close to sth; in a useful position: *Our house is convenient for the shops.* ▶ **conveniently** *adv*

convent /'kɒnvənt/ *noun* [C] a place where **nuns** (= religious women) live together in a community ➲ look at **monastery**

convention /kən'venʃn/ *noun* **1** [C,U] a traditional way of behaving or of doing sth: *A speech by the bride's father is one of the conventions of a wedding.* ♦ *The film shows no respect for convention.* **2** [C] a large meeting of the members of a profession, political party, etc: *the Democratic Party Convention* SYN **conference** **3** [C] a formal agreement, especially between different countries: *the Geneva Convention*

conventional /kən'venʃənl/ *adj* **1** always behaving in a traditional or normal way: *conventional attitudes* ♦ *I quite like him but he's so conventional* (= boring, because of this). **2** following what is traditional or the way sth has been done for a long time: *You can cook it in a microwave or in a conventional oven.* ▶ **conventionally** /-ʃənəli/ *adv*

converge /kən'vɜːdʒ/ *verb* [I] converge (on sb/sth) (used about two or more people or things) to move towards each other or meet at the same point from different directions: *Fans from all over the country converge on the village during the annual music festival.* OPP **diverge**

conversant /kən'vɜːsnt/ *adj* (*formal*) conversant with sth knowing about sth; familiar with sth: *All employees should be conversant with basic accounting.*

conversation /ˌkɒnvə'seɪʃn/ *noun* [C,U] a talk between two or more people: *I* **had a** *long* **conversation** *with her about her plans for the future.* ♦ *His job is his only* **topic of conversation**. ♦ *She finds it difficult to make conversation* (= to think of things to say).

IDM **deep in thought/conversation** ➲ **deep¹**

▶ **conversational** /-ʃənl/ *adj*

converse /kən'vɜːs/ *verb* [I] (*formal*) to talk to sb; to have a conversation

conversely /'kɒnvɜːsli/ *adv* (*formal*) in a way that is opposite to sth: *People who earn a lot of money have little time to spend it. Conversely, many people with limitless time do not have enough money to do what they want.*

conversion /kən'vɜːʃn/ *noun* [C,U] (a) conversion (from sth) (into/to sth) **1** the act or process of changing from one form, system or use to another: *a conversion table for miles and kilometres* **2** becoming a member of a different religion

convert¹ /kən'vɜːt/ *verb* [I,T] **1** convert (sth) (from sth) (into/to sth) to change from one form, system or use to another: *a sofa that converts into a double bed* ♦ *How do you convert pounds into kilos?* **2** convert (sb) (from sth) (to sth) to change or to persuade sb to change to a different religion: *As a young man he converted to Islam.* ♦ *to convert people to Christianity*

convert² /'kɒnvɜːt/ *noun* [C] a convert (to sth) a person who has changed their religion

convertible¹ /kən'vɜːtəbl/ *adj* able to be changed into another form: *convertible currencies*

(= ones that can be exchanged for those of other countries)

convertible² /kənˈvɜːtəbl/ *noun* [C] a car with a roof that can be folded down or taken off

convex /ˈkɒnveks/ *adj* having a surface that curves towards the outside of sth, like an eye: *a convex lens* ➲ look at **concave** ➲ picture at **concave**

convey /kənˈveɪ/ *verb* [T] **1** convey sth (to sb) to make ideas, thoughts, feelings, etc. known to sb: *The film conveys a lot of information but in an entertaining way.* ◆ *Please convey my sympathy to her at this sad time.* **2** (*formal*) to take sb/sth from one place to another, especially in a vehicle

conˈveyor belt *noun* [C] a moving belt that carries objects from one place to another, for example in a factory

convict¹ /kənˈvɪkt/ *verb* [T] convict sb (of sth) to say officially in a court of law that sb is guilty of a crime: *He was convicted of armed robbery and sent to prison.* **OPP** **acquit**

convict² /ˈkɒnvɪkt/ *noun* [C] a person who has been found guilty of a crime and put in prison

conviction /kənˈvɪkʃn/ *noun* **1** [C,U] the act of finding sb guilty of a crime in a court of law: *He has several previous convictions for burglary.* **2** [C] a very strong opinion or belief: *religious convictions* **3** [U] the feeling of being certain about what you are doing: *He played without conviction and lost easily.*

convince /kənˈvɪns/ *verb* [T] **1** convince sb (of sth/that ...) to succeed in making sb believe sth: *She convinced him of the need to go back.* ◆ *I couldn't convince her that I was right.* **2** convince sb (to do sth) to persuade sb to do sth: *I tried to convince him to see a doctor.*

convinced /kənˈvɪnst/ *adj* [not before a noun] completely sure about sth: *He's convinced of his ability to win.*

convincing /kənˈvɪnsɪŋ/ *adj* **1** able to make sb believe sth: *Her explanation for her absence wasn't very convincing.* **2** (used about a victory) complete; clear: *a convincing win* ▶ **convincingly** *adv*

convoy /ˈkɒnvɔɪ/ *noun* [C,U] a group of vehicles or ships travelling together: *a convoy of lorries* ◆ *warships travelling* ***in convoy***

convulse /kənˈvʌls/ *verb* [I,T] to make sudden violent movements that you cannot control; to cause sb to move in this way: *He was convulsed with pain.*

convulsion /kənˈvʌlʃn/ *noun* [C, usually pl] a sudden violent movement that you cannot control: *Children sometimes have convulsions when they are ill.* ▶ **convulsive** /kənˈvʌlsɪv/ *adj*: *Her breath came in convulsive gasps.*

coo /kuː/ *verb* [I] **1** to make a soft low sound like a dove (= a white bird, often used as a sign of peace) **2** to speak in a soft, gentle voice: *He went to the cot and cooed over the baby.*

cook¹ /kʊk/ *verb* **1** [I,T] to prepare food for eating by heating it: *My mother taught me how to cook.* ◆ *The sauce should be cooked on low heat for twenty minutes.* ◆ *He cooked us a meal.* **2** [I] (used about food) to be prepared for eating by being heated: *I could smell something delicious cooking in the kitchen.* ➲ note at **recipe** ➲ picture on **page P11**

PHR V **cook sth up** (*informal*) to invent sth that is not true: *She cooked up an excuse for not arriving on time.*

C

TOPIC

Cooking

Food can be cooked in various ways. You can **boil** or **steam** vegetables with water in a **saucepan** and you can **fry** meat, fish and vegetables in oil in a **frying pan**. You **roast** meat or **bake** bread and cakes in the **oven**. You can **grill** meat or fish under the **grill**, but **toast** is usually made in a **toaster**. If you want an easy meal you can **microwave** a **ready meal** (= a complete meal bought from a supermarket) in a special oven called a **microwave**. In the summer you can **barbecue** burgers, etc. on an outside grill, also called a **barbecue**.

cook² /kʊk/ *noun* [C] a person who cooks: *My sister is an excellent cook.* ➲ picture on **page P2**

cookbook /ˈkʊkbʊk/ (*BrE also* ˈcookery book) *noun* [C] a book that gives instructions on cooking and contains **recipes** (= instructions on how to cook individual dishes) ➲ note at **recipe**

cooker /ˈkʊkə(r)/ (*especially AmE* stove) *noun* [C] a large piece of kitchen equipment for cooking using gas or electricity. It consists of an oven, a flat top on which pans can be placed and often a **grill** (= a device which heats the food from above). ➲ picture on **page P8**

cookery /ˈkʊkəri/ *noun* [U] the skill or activity of preparing and cooking food: *Chinese/French/Italian cookery*

ˈcookery book = cookbook

cookie /ˈkʊki/ **1** (*AmE*) = **biscuit** **2** a computer file with information that shows the user's preferences and that is stored each time that person uses the Internet

cooking /ˈkʊkɪŋ/ *noun* [U] **1** the preparation of food for eating: *Cooking is one of her hobbies.* ◆ *In our house, I do the cleaning and my husband* ***does the cooking***. **2** food produced by cooking: *He missed his mother's cooking when he left home.*

cool¹ /kuːl/ *adj* **1** fairly cold; not hot or warm: *It was a cool evening so I put on a pullover.* ◆ *What I'd like is a long cool drink.* ➲ note at **cold¹** **2** calm; not excited or angry: *She always manages to remain cool under pressure.* **3** unfriendly; not showing interest: *When we first met, she was rather cool towards me, but later she became friendlier.* **4** (*informal*) very good or fashionable: *Those are cool shoes you're wearing!* **5** (*informal*) people say **Cool!** or **That's cool** to show that they approve of sth or agree to a suggestion: *'We're meeting in town and then going to see a film.' 'Cool!'*

cool² /kuːl/ *verb* **1** [I,T] cool (sth/sb) (down/off) to lower the temperature of sth; to become cool¹(1): *Let the soup cool (down).* ◆ *After the game we needed* *to cool off.* ◆ *A nice cold drink will soon cool you down.* **2** [I] (used about feelings) to become less strong: *Relations between them have definitely cooled.*

PHR V **cool (sb) down/off** to become or make sb calmer

cool³ /kuːl/ *noun* **the cool** [sing] a cool temperature or place; the quality of being cool: *We sat in the cool of a cafe, out of the sun.*

IDM **keep/lose your cool** to stay calm/to stop being calm and become angry, nervous, etc.

ˌcooling-ˈoff period *noun* [C] a period of time when sb can think again about a decision that they have made

coolly /ˈkuːlli/ *adv* in a calm way; without showing much interest or excitement: *At first she was very angry; then she explained the problem coolly.*

coolness /ˈkuːlnəs/ *noun* [U] the quality or state of being cool: *the coolness of the water* ◆ *his coolness under stress* ◆ *their coolness towards strangers*

coop /kuːp/ *verb*

PHR V **coop sb/sth up (in sth)** to keep sb/sth inside a small space: *The children were cooped up indoors all day because the weather was so terrible.*

cooperate (*BrE also* **co-operate**) /kəʊˈɒpəreɪt/ *verb* [I] **cooperate (with sb/sth) 1** to work with sb else to achieve sth: *Our company is cooperating with an Italian firm on this project.* **2** to be helpful by doing what sb asks you to do: *If everyone cooperates by following the instructions, there will be no problem.*

cooperation (*BrE also* **co-operation**) /kəʊˌɒpəˈreɪʃn/ *noun* [U] **1 cooperation (with sb)** working together with sb else to achieve sth: *Schools are working in close cooperation with parents to improve standards.* **2** help that you give by doing what sb asks you to do: *The police asked the public for their cooperation in the investigation.*

cooperative¹ (*BrE also* **co-operative**) /kəʊˈɒpərətɪv/ *adj* **1** done by people working together: *a cooperative business venture* **2** helpful; doing what sb asks you to do: *My firm were very cooperative and allowed me to have time off.*

cooperative² (*BrE also* **co-operative**) /kəʊˈɒpərətɪv/ *noun* [C] a business or an organization that is owned and run by all of the people who work for it: *a workers' cooperative*

coordinate¹ (*BrE also* **co-ordinate**) /kəʊˈɔːdɪneɪt/ *verb* [T] to organize different things or people so that they work together: *It is her job to coordinate the various departments.*

coordinate² (*BrE also* **co-ordinate**) /kəʊˈɔːdɪnət/ *noun* [C] one of the two sets of numbers and/or letters that are used for finding the position of a point on a map

Coˌordinated Uniˈversal Time *noun* [U] (*abbr* **UTC**) the time based on **atomic clocks** (= very accurate and scientific clocks), used as the basis of legal time in most countries ➲ look at **GMT**

coordination (*BrE also* **co-ordination**) /kəʊˌɔːdɪˈneɪʃn/ *noun* [U] **1** the organization of different things or people so that they work together **2** the ability to control the movements of your body properly: *Children's coordination improves as they get older.*

coordinator (*BrE also* **co-ordinator**) /kəʊˈɔːdɪneɪtə(r)/ *noun* [C] a person who is responsible for organizing different things or people so that they work together

cop¹ /kɒp/ (*also* **copper**) *noun* [C] (*informal*) a police officer

cop² /kɒp/ *verb* (**copping**; **copped**)

PHR V **cop out (of sth)** (*informal*) to avoid sth that you should do, because you are afraid or lazy: *She was going to help me with the cooking but she copped out at the last minute.*

🔑 **cope** /kəʊp/ *verb* [I] **cope (with sb/sth)** to deal successfully with a difficult matter or situation: *She finds it difficult to cope with the pressure of exams.* SYN **manage**

copier /ˈkɒpiə(r)/ (*especially AmE*) = **photocopier**

copious /ˈkəʊpiəs/ *adj* in large amounts: *She made copious notes at the lecture.* ▶ **copiously** *adv*

ˈcop-out *noun* [C] (*informal*) a way of avoiding sth that you should do

copper /ˈkɒpə(r)/ *noun* **1** [U] (*symbol* **Cu**) a common reddish-brown metal: *water pipes made of copper* **2** [C] (*BrE*) a coin of low value made of brown metal: *I only had a few coppers left.* **3** = **cop¹**

copse /kɒps/ *noun* [C] a small area of trees or bushes

copulate /ˈkɒpjuleɪt/ *verb* [I] (*formal*) (used especially about animals) to have sex ▶ **copulation** /ˌkɒpjuˈleɪʃn/ *noun* [U]

🔑 **copy¹** /ˈkɒpi/ *noun* [C] (*pl* **copies**) **1** something that is made to look exactly like sth else: *I kept a copy of the letter I wrote.* ◆ *the master copy* (= the original piece of paper from which copies are made) ◆ *to make a copy of a computer file* ➲ look at **photocopy** **2** one book, newspaper, record, etc. of which many have been printed or produced: *I managed to buy the last copy of the book left in the shop.*

🔑 **copy²** /ˈkɒpi/ *verb* (**copying**; **copies**; *pt, pp* **copied**) **1** [T] to make sth exactly the same as sth else: *The children copied pictures from a book.* ◆ *It is illegal to copy videos.* **2** [T] **copy sth (down/out)** to write down sth exactly as it is written somewhere else: *I copied down the address on the brochure.* ◆ *I copied out the letter more neatly.* **3** [T] to do or try to do the same as sb else: *She copies everything her friends do.* SYN **imitate** **4** [I] **copy (from sb)** to cheat in an exam or a test by writing what sb else has written: *He was caught copying from another student in the exam.* **5** [T] = **photocopy**

copyright /ˈkɒpiraɪt/ *noun* [C,U] the legal right to be the only person who may print, copy, perform, etc. a piece of original work, such as a book, a song or a computer program: *Who owns the copyright?*

EXAM TIP

Copying

When you are doing a written exam, try not to copy the words exactly as they are used in the instructions. You will gain marks if you use your own words and expressions instead.

You should never copy anyone else's work in an exam. This is cheating, and, if you are caught, you will get no marks for that exam.

coral /ˈkɒrəl/ *noun* [U] a hard red, pink or white substance that forms in the sea from the bones of very small sea animals: *a coral reef* (= a line of rock in the sea formed by coral)

cord /kɔːd/ *noun* **1** [C,U] (a piece of) strong, thick string ➲ picture at **rope** **2** (*especially AmE*) = **flex**² **3** **cords** [pl] trousers made of **corduroy** (= a thick soft cotton cloth with raised lines on it)

cordial /ˈkɔːdiəl/ *adj* (*formal*) pleasant and friendly: *a cordial greeting/smile* ▶ **cordially** /-diəli/ *adv*

cordless /ˈkɔːdləs/ *adj* not connected to its power supply by wires: *a cordless phone/kettle/iron*

cordon¹ /ˈkɔːdn/ *noun* [C] a line or ring of police or soldiers that prevents people from entering an area

cordon² /ˈkɔːdn/ *verb*

PHR V **cordon sth off** to stop people entering an area by surrounding it with a ring of police or soldiers: *The street where the bomb was discovered was quickly cordoned off.*

corduroy /ˈkɔːdərɔɪ/ *noun* [U] a thick soft cotton cloth with lines on it, used for making clothes: *a corduroy jacket*

⚷ **core** /kɔː(r)/ *noun* **1** [C] the hard centre of certain fruits, containing seeds: *an apple core* ➲ picture on **page P14** **2** [C] the central part of a planet: *the earth's core* **3** [sing] the central or most important part of sth: *the core curriculum* (= the subjects that all students have to study) ◆ *What's the core issue here?*

IDM **to the core** completely; in every way: *The news shook him to the core* (= shocked him very much).

cork /kɔːk/ *noun* **1** [U] a light soft material which comes from the outside of a type of tree: *cork floor tiles* **2** [C] a round piece of **cork** that you push into the end of a bottle to close it, especially a bottle of wine ➲ picture at **container**

corkscrew /ˈkɔːkskruː/ *noun* [C] a tool that you use for pulling **corks** out of bottles ➲ picture at **kitchen**

corn /kɔːn/ *noun* **1** [U] (*especially BrE*) any plant that is grown for its grain, such as **wheat**; the seeds from these plants: *a field of corn* ◆ *a cornfield* **2** [U] (*AmE*) = **maize** **3** [U] (*AmE*) = **sweetcorn** **4** [C] a small, painful area of hard skin on the foot, especially the toe

⚷ **corner**¹ /ˈkɔːnə(r)/ *noun* [C] **1** a place where two lines, edges, surfaces or roads meet: *Put the lamp* ***in the corner*** *of the room.* ◆ *Write your address in the top right-hand corner.* ◆ *The shop is* ***on the corner*** *of Wall Street and Long Road.* ◆ *He went* ***round the corner*** *at*

corners

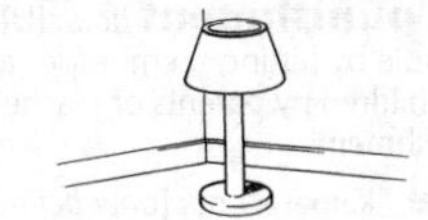

The lamp is **in** the corner.

The bank is **on** the corner.

top speed. **2** a quiet or secret place or area: *a remote corner of Scotland* **3** a difficult situation from which you cannot escape: *to get yourself into a corner* **4** (in football) a free kick from the corner of the field: *to take a corner*

IDM **cut corners** to do sth quickly and not as well as you should

(just) round the corner very near: *There's a phone box just round the corner.*

corner² /ˈkɔːnə(r)/ *verb* [T] **1** to get a person or an animal into a position from which they or it cannot escape: *He cornered me at the party and started telling me all his problems.* **2** to get control in a particular area of business so that nobody else can have any success in it: *That company's really* ***cornered the market*** *in health foods.*

cornflakes /ˈkɔːnfleɪks/ *noun* [pl] food made of small pieces of dried **corn** and eaten with milk for breakfast

cornflour /ˈkɔːnflaʊə(r)/ *noun* [U] very fine flour often used to make sauces, etc. thicker

ˌ**corn on the ˈcob** *noun* [U] **sweetcorn** (= a type of vegetable) that is cooked with all the yellow grains still on the inner part and eaten ➲ picture on **page P15**

corny /ˈkɔːni/ *adj* (**cornier**; **corniest**) (*informal*) too ordinary or familiar to be interesting or amusing: *a corny joke*

coronary¹ /ˈkɒrənri/ *adj* connected with the heart

coronary² /ˈkɒrənri/ *noun* [C] (*pl* **coronaries**) a type of heart attack

coronation /ˌkɒrəˈneɪʃn/ *noun* [C] an official ceremony at which sb is made a king or queen

coroner /ˈkɒrənə(r)/ *noun* [C] a person whose job is to find out the causes of death of people who have died in violent or unusual ways

Corp. *abbr* (*AmE*) = **corporation**(1): *West Coast Motor Corp.*

C

corporal /ˈkɔːpərəl/ *noun* [C] a person at a low level in the army or air force

ˌcorporal ˈpunishment *noun* [U] the punishment of people by hitting them, especially the punishment of children by parents or teachers ➲ look at **capital punishment**

corporate /ˈkɔːpərət/ *adj* [only *before* a noun] of or shared by all the members of a group or an organization: *corporate responsibility*

corporation /ˌkɔːpəˈreɪʃn/ *noun* [C, with sing or pl verb] **1** (*abbr* Corp.) a large business company: *multinational corporations* ◆ *the British Broadcasting Corporation* **2** (*BrE*) a group of people elected to govern a particular town or city

corps /kɔː(r)/ *noun* [C, with sing or pl verb] (*pl* corps /kɔːz/) **1** a part of an army with special duties: *the medical corps* **2** a group of people involved in a special activity: *the diplomatic corps*

corpse /kɔːps/ *noun* [C] a dead body, especially of a person ➲ look at **carcass**

⚷ **correct**[1] /kəˈrekt/ *adj* **1** with no mistakes; right or true: *Well done! All your answers were correct.* ◆ *Have you got the correct time, please?* **2** (used about behaviour, manners, dress, etc.) suitable, proper or right: *What's the correct form of address for a judge?* **OPP** for both meanings **incorrect** ▶ **correctly** *adv* ▶ **correctness** *noun* [U]

⚷ **correct**[2] /kəˈrekt/ *verb* [T] **1** to make a mistake, fault, etc. right or better: *to correct a spelling mistake* ◆ *to correct a test* (= mark the mistakes in it) **2** to tell sb what mistakes they are making or what faults they have: *He's always correcting me when I'm talking to people.*

correction /kəˈrekʃn/ *noun* **1** [C] a change that makes a mistake, fault, etc. right or better: *I've made a few small corrections to your report.* ◆ *The paper had to publish a correction to the story.* **2** [U] the act or process of correcting sth: *There are some programming errors that need correction.*

corrective /kəˈrektɪv/ *adj* intended to make sth right that is wrong: *to take corrective action*

correlate /ˈkɒrəleɪt/ *verb* [I,T] to have or to show a relationship or connection between two or more things ▶ **correlation** /ˌkɒrəˈleɪʃn/ *noun* [C,U]: *There is a correlation between a person's diet and height.*

correspond /ˌkɒrəˈspɒnd/ *verb* [I] **1** correspond (to/with sth) to be the same as or equal to sth; to match: *Does the name on the envelope correspond with the name inside the letter?* **2** (*formal*) correspond (with sb) to write letters to and receive them from sb: *They corresponded for a year before they got married.*

correspondence /ˌkɒrəˈspɒndəns/ *noun* **1** [U, sing] (*formal*) the act of writing letters; the letters themselves: *There hasn't been any correspondence between them for years.* **2** [C,U] a close connection or relationship between two or more things: *There is no correspondence between the two sets of figures.*

correspondent /ˌkɒrəˈspɒndənt/ *noun* [C] **1** a person who provides news or writes articles for a newspaper, etc., especially from a foreign country: *our Middle East correspondent* **2** a person who writes letters to sb

corresponding /ˌkɒrəˈspɒndɪŋ/ *adj* [only *before* a noun] related or similar to sth: *Sales are up 10% compared with the corresponding period last year.* **SYN** **equivalent** ▶ **correspondingly** *adv*

corridor /ˈkɒrɪdɔː(r)/ *noun* [C] a long narrow passage in a building or train, with doors that open into rooms, etc.

corroborate /kəˈrɒbəreɪt/ *verb* [T] (*formal*) to support a statement, an idea, etc. by providing new evidence: *The witness corroborated Mr Patton's statement about the night of the murder.* ▶ **corroboration** /kəˌrɒbəˈreɪʃn/ *noun* [U]

corrode /kəˈrəʊd/ *verb* [I,T] (used about metals) to become weak or to be destroyed by chemical action; to cause a metal to do this: *Parts of the car were corroded by rust.* ▶ **corrosion** /kəˈrəʊʒn/ *noun* [U] ▶ **corrosive** /kəˈrəʊsɪv/ *adj*

corrugated /ˈkɒrəgeɪtɪd/ *adj* (used about metal or cardboard) shaped into folds

corrugated

corrugated iron

corrupt[1] /kəˈrʌpt/ *adj* **1** doing or involving illegal or dishonest things in exchange for money, etc: *corrupt officials who accept bribes* ◆ *corrupt business practices* **2** containing changes or faults, and no longer in the original state: *corrupt software*

corrupt[2] /kəˈrʌpt/ *verb* **1** [T] to cause sb/sth to start behaving in a dishonest or an immoral way: *Too many people are corrupted by power.* **2** [I,T] [often passive] to change the original form of sth or to cause mistakes to appear, especially in a computer file: *The program has somehow corrupted the system files.* ◆ *corrupted data*

corruption /kəˈrʌpʃn/ *noun* [U] **1** dishonest or immoral behaviour or activities: *There were accusations of corruption among senior police officers.* **2** the process of making sb/sth **corrupt**

corset /ˈkɔːsɪt/ *noun* [C] a piece of clothing worn especially in the past to make a woman's waist look smaller

cos (also **'cos, 'cause, coz**) /kəz; *BrE also* kɒz/ *conj* (*BrE informal*) because: *I can't come to the party cos I've got too much homework.*

HELP Do NOT use **cos** in formal written English.

cosmetic[1] /kɒzˈmetɪk/ *noun* [C, usually pl] a substance that you put on your face or hair to make yourself look more attractive ➲ look at **make-up**

cosmetic[2] /kɒzˈmetɪk/ *adj* **1** done in order to improve only the appearance of sth, without changing it in any other way: *changes in government policy which are purely cosmetic* **2** used or done in order to make your face or body more attractive: *cosmetic products* ♦ *cosmetic surgery*

cosmic /ˈkɒzmɪk/ *adj* connected with space or the universe

cosmonaut /ˈkɒzmənɔːt/ *noun* [C] an **astronaut** (= a person who works and travels in space) from the former Soviet Union

cosmopolitan /ˌkɒzməˈpɒlɪtən/ *adj* **1** containing people from all over the world: *a cosmopolitan city* **2** influenced by the culture of other countries: *a cosmopolitan and sophisticated young woman*

the cosmos /ˈkɒzmɒs/ *noun* [sing] the universe

🔑 **cost**[1] /kɒst/ *noun* **1** [C,U] the money that you have to pay for sth: *The cost of petrol has gone up again.* ♦ *The hospital was built* ***at a cost of*** *£10 million.* ♦ *The damage will have to be repaired regardless of cost.* ➲ note at **price** **2** [sing,U] what you have to give or lose in order to obtain sth else: *He achieved great success but only* ***at the cost of*** *a happy family life.* **3 costs** [pl] the amount of money that the losing side has to pay for lawyers, etc. in a court of law: *a £2500 fine and £1000 costs*
IDM at all costs/at any cost using whatever means are necessary to achieve sth: *We must win at all costs.*
cover the cost (of sth) ➲ **cover**[1]
to your cost in a way that is unpleasant or bad for you: *Life can be lonely at university, as I found out to my cost.*

🔑 **cost**[2] /kɒst/ *verb* [T] (*pt, pp* **cost**) **1** to have the price of: *How much does a return ticket to London cost?* ♦ *We'll take the bus—it won't cost much.* ♦ (*informal*) *How much did your bike cost you?* **2** to make you lose sth: *That one mistake cost him his job.*
IDM cost the earth/a fortune to be very expensive

co-star /ˈkəʊstɑː(r)/ *verb* (**co-starring**; **co-starred**) **1** [T] (used about a film, play, etc.) to have two or more famous actors as its stars: *a film co-starring Ryan Gosling and Emma Stone* **2** [I] (used about actors) to be one of two or more stars in a film, play, etc: *Emma Stone co-stars with Ryan Gosling in the film.*
▶ **co-star** *noun* [C]: *His co-star was Marilyn Monroe.*

costly /ˈkɒstli/ *adj* (**costlier**; **costliest**) **1** costing a lot of money; expensive: *a costly repair bill* **2** involving great loss of time, effort, etc: *a costly mistake*

costume /ˈkɒstjuːm/ *noun* [C,U] **1** a set or style of clothes worn by people in a particular country or in a particular historical period: *17th-century costume* ♦ *Welsh national costume* **2** clothes that an actor, etc. wears in order to look like sth else: *One of the children was dressed in a pirate's costume.* ♦ *The last rehearsal of the play will be done in costume.* **3** (*BrE*) = **swimsuit**

cosy (*AmE* **cozy**) /ˈkəʊzi/ *adj* (**cosier**; **cosiest**) warm and comfortable: *The room looked cosy and inviting in the firelight.*

cot /kɒt/ *noun* [C] **1** (*AmE* **crib**) a bed with high sides for a baby **2** (*AmE*) = **camp bed** ➲ picture at **bed**

🔑 **cottage** /ˈkɒtɪdʒ/ *noun* [C] a small and usually old house, especially in the country: *a country cottage with roses round the door* ♦ *We rented a holiday cottage by the sea.* ➲ picture on **page P9**

ˌcottage ˈcheese *noun* [U] a type of soft white cheese in small wet lumps

🔑 **cotton** /ˈkɒtn/ *noun* [U] **1** a natural cloth or thread made from the thin white hairs of the cotton plant: *a cotton shirt* ♦ *a reel of cotton* **2** (*AmE*) = **cotton wool**

ˌcotton ˈwool *noun* [U] a soft mass of cotton, used for cleaning the skin, cuts, etc.

couch[1] /kaʊtʃ/ *noun* [C] a long seat, often with a back and arms, for sitting or lying on: *They were sitting on the couch in the living room.*

couch[2] /kaʊtʃ/ *verb* [T, usually passive] (*formal*) to express a thought, an idea, etc. in the way mentioned: *His reply was couched in very polite terms.*

ˈcouch potato *noun* [C] (*informal*) a person who spends a lot of time sitting and watching television

cough

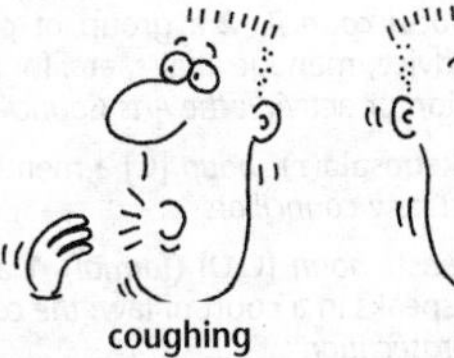
coughing

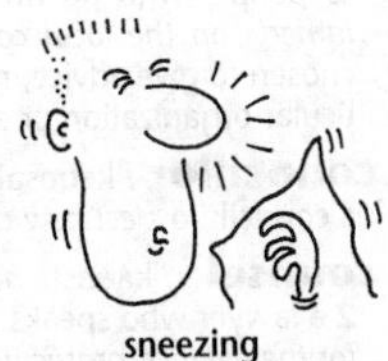
sneezing

🔑 **cough**[1] /kɒf/ *verb* **1** [I] to send air out of your throat and mouth with a sudden loud noise, especially when you have a cold, have sth in your throat, etc: *The smoke from the fire made me cough.* ➲ note at **ill** **2** [T] **cough (up) sth** to send sth out of your throat and mouth with a sudden loud noise: *When I started coughing (up) blood I called the doctor.*
PHR V cough (sth) up (*informal*) to give money when you do not want to: *Come on, cough up what you owe me!*
▶ **coughing** *noun* [U]: *a fit of coughing*

🔑 **cough**[2] /kɒf/ *noun* [C] **1** an act or the sound of coughing: *He gave a nervous cough before he started to speak.* **2** an illness or infection that makes you cough a lot: *Kevin's got a bad cough.*

🔑 **could** /kəd; *strong form* kʊd/ *modal verb* (*negative* **could not**; *short form* **couldn't** /ˈkʊdnt/)
➤ **ABILITY/PERMISSION** **1** used as the past tense of can: *I could run three miles without stopping when I was younger.* ♦ *Elena said we could stay at her house.*

GRAMMAR If something was possible on one occasion in the past, use **was/were able to** or **managed to**: *The firemen were able to/managed to rescue the children.* But in negative sentences **could not** can be used, too: *The firemen couldn't rescue the children.*

➤ **REQUEST** **2** used for asking permission politely: *Could I possibly borrow your car?* **3** used for asking sb politely to do sth for you: *Could you open the door? My hands are full.*

➤POSSIBILITY **4** used for saying that sth may be or may have been possible: *I could do it now if you like.* ♦ *She could be famous one day.* ♦ *He could have gone to university but he didn't want to.* ♦ *You could have said you were going to be late!* (= I'm annoyed that you didn't)
➤SUGGESTION **5** used for making a suggestion: *'What do you want to do tonight?' 'We could go to the cinema or we could just stay in.'*
➤SENSES **6** used with the verbs 'feel', 'hear', 'see', 'smell', 'taste': *We could hear/see children playing outside.* ℹ For more information about modal verbs, look at the **Reference Section** at the back of this dictionary.
IDM **could do with sth** to want or need sth: *I could do with a holiday.*

⚷ **council** (also Council) /ˈkaʊnsl/ *noun* [C, with sing or pl verb] **1** a group of people who are elected to govern an area such as a town, city, etc: *The county council has/have decided to build a new road.* ♦ *a council house* (= one that a council owns and lets to people who do not have much money) ♦ *My father's on the local council.* **2** a group of people chosen to give advice, manage affairs, etc. for a particular organization or activity: *the Arts Council*

councillor /ˈkaʊnsələ(r)/ *noun* [C] a member of a **council**: *to elect new councillors*

counsel¹ /ˈkaʊnsl/ *noun* [C,U] (*formal*) **1** advice **2** a lawyer who speaks in a court of law: *the counsel for the defence/prosecution*

counsel² /ˈkaʊnsl/ *verb* [T] (counselling; counselled, (*AmE*) counseling; counseled) **1** to give professional advice and help to sb with a problem **2** (*formal*) to tell sb what you think they should do; to advise: *Mr Dean's lawyers counselled him against making public statements.*

counselling (*AmE* counseling) /ˈkaʊnsəlɪŋ/ *noun* [U] professional advice and help given to people with problems: *Many students come to us for counselling.*

counsellor (*AmE* counselor) /ˈkaʊnsələ(r)/ *noun* [C] a person whose job is to give advice: *a marriage counsellor*

⚷ **count¹** /kaʊnt/ *verb* **1** [I] to say numbers one after another in order: *Close your eyes and count (up) to 20.* **2** [T] count sth to calculate the total number or amount of sth: *The teacher counted the children as they got on the bus.* **3** [T] to include sb/sth when you are calculating an amount or a number: *There were thirty people on the bus, not counting the driver.* **4** [I] count (for sth) to be important or valuable: *I sometimes think my opinion counts for nothing at work.* **5** [I] count (as sth) to be valid or accepted: *The referee had already blown his whistle so the goal didn't count.* ♦ *Will my driving licence count as identification?* **6** [I,T] to consider sb/sth in a particular way: *You should count yourself lucky to have a good job.* ♦ *On this airline, children over 12 count/are counted as adults.*
IDM **Don't count your chickens (before they're hatched)** used to say that you should not be too confident that sth will be successful because sth might still go wrong
PHR V **count against sb** to be considered as a disadvantage: *Do you think my age will count against me?*
count on sb/sth to expect sth with confidence; to depend on sb/sth: *Can I count on you to help me tonight?*
count sb/sth out 1 to count things slowly, one by one: *She carefully counted out the money into my hand.* **2** (*informal*) to not include sb/sth: *If you're going swimming, you can count me out!*

count² /kaʊnt/ *noun* [C] **1** [usually sing] an act of counting or a number that you get after counting: *At the last count, there were nearly 2 million unemployed.* ♦ *Raise your leg and hold for a count of ten.* **2** [usually pl] a point that is made in a discussion, an argument, etc: *I proved her wrong **on** all **counts**.*
IDM **keep/lose count (of sth)** to know/not know how many there are of sth: *I've lost count of the number of times he's told that joke!*

countable /ˈkaʊntəbl/ *adj* that can be counted: *'Chair' is a countable noun, but 'sugar' isn't.* ♦ *Countable nouns are marked '[C]' in this dictionary.* OPP **uncountable** ℹ For more information about countable nouns, look at the **Reference Section** at the back of this dictionary.

countdown /ˈkaʊntdaʊn/ *noun* [C] the act of saying numbers backwards to zero just before sth important happens: *the countdown to the lift-off of a rocket* ♦ (*figurative*) *The countdown to this summer's Olympic Games has started.*

countenance¹ /ˈkaʊntənəns/ *noun* [C] (*formal*) sb's face or expression

countenance² /ˈkaʊntənəns/ *verb* [T] (*formal*) to support sth or agree to sth happening: *The committee refused to countenance Harding's proposals.*

⚷ **counter¹** /ˈkaʊntə(r)/ *noun* [C] **1** a long, flat surface in a shop, bank, etc. where customers are served: *The man **behind the counter** in the bank was very helpful.* **2** a small object (usually round and made of plastic) that is used in some games to show where a player is on the board **3** an electronic device for counting sth: *The needle on the rev counter soared.* **4** (*AmE*) = **worktop**

counter² /ˈkaʊntə(r)/ *verb* **1** [I,T] to reply or react to criticism: *He countered our objections with a powerful defence of his plan.* **2** [T] to try to reduce or prevent the bad effects of sth: *The shop has installed security cameras to counter theft.*

counter³ /ˈkaʊntə(r)/ *adv* counter to sth in the opposite direction to sth: *The results of these experiments **run counter to** previous findings.*

counter- /ˈkaʊntə(r)/ [in compounds] **1** against; opposite: *counterterrorism* ♦ *counter-argument* **2** related or similar to sth: *counterpart/countersign*

counteract /ˌkaʊntərˈækt/ *verb* [T] to reduce the effect of sth by acting against it: *measures to counteract traffic congestion*

ˈ**counter-attack** *noun* [C] an attack made in reaction to an enemy or opponent's attack ▶ **counter-attack** *verb* [I,T]

counterclockwise /ˌkaʊntəˈklɒkwaɪz/ (*AmE*) = **anticlockwise**

counterfeit /ˈkaʊntəfɪt/ *adj* not genuine, but copied so that it looks like the real thing: *counterfeit money*

counterfoil /ˈkaʊntəfɔɪl/ *noun* [C] the part of a cheque, ticket, etc. that you keep when you give the other part to sb else

counterpart /ˈkaʊntəpɑːt/ *noun* [C] a person or thing that has a similar position or function in a different country or organization: *the French president and his Italian counterpart* (= the Italian president)

counterproductive /ˌkaʊntəprəˈdʌktɪv/ *adj* having the opposite effect to the one you want: *It can be counterproductive to punish children.* ➲ look at **productive**

countless /ˈkaʊntləs/ *adj* [only *before* a noun] very many: *I've tried to phone him countless times but he's not there.*

⚷ **country** /ˈkʌntri/ *noun* (*pl* **countries**) **1** [C] an area of land with its own people, government, etc: *France, Spain and other European countries* ◆ *There was snow over much of the country during the night.* **2** [U] an area of land: *We looked down over miles of open country.* ◆ *hilly country* SYN **terrain** **3 the country** [sing] the people who live in a country: *a survey to find out what the country really thinks* **4 the country** [sing] land which is away from towns and cities: *Do you live in a town or* ***in the country****?* ➲ note at **scenery** ➲ look at **countryside** **5** [U] = **country and western**

OTHER WORDS FOR

country

Nation is another word for country, or the people who live in a country: *The entire nation, it seemed, was watching TV*. **State** is used for talking about a country as an organized political community controlled by one government. It can also mean the government itself: *a politically independent state* ◆ *the member states of the EU* ◆ *You get a pension from the state when you retire.* ◆ *state education* **Land** is more formal or literary: *explorers who set out to discover new lands*

ˌ**country and** ˈ**western** (also **country**) *noun* [U] a type of music based on traditional music from the southern and western US

countryman /ˈkʌntrimən/ *noun* [C] (*pl* **-men** /-mən/) a person from your own country: *The Italian Castorri beat his* ***fellow countryman*** *Rossi in the final.*

⚷ **the countryside** /ˈkʌntrisaɪd/ *noun* [U, sing] land which is away from towns and cities, where there are fields, woods, etc: *From the hill there is a magnificent view of the surrounding countryside.* ➲ look at **country** ➲ note at **nature, scenery** ➲ picture on **page P11**

⚷ **county** /ˈkaʊnti/ *noun* [C] (*abbr* **Co.**) (*pl* **counties**) an area in Britain, Ireland or the US which has its own local government: *the county of Nottinghamshire* ◆ *Orange County, California* ➲ look at **province, state**

coup /kuː/ *noun* [C] **1** (also **coup d'état** /ˌkuː deɪˈtɑː/) a sudden, illegal and often violent change of government: *a coup to overthrow the President* ◆ *an attempted coup* (= one which did not succeed) **2** a clever and successful thing to do: *Getting that promotion was a real coup.*

⚷ **couple**[1] /ˈkʌpl/ *noun* [C, with sing or pl verb] two people who are together because they are married or in a relationship: *a married couple* ◆ *Is/Are that couple over there part of our group?* ➲ look at **pair**
IDM **a couple of people, things, etc.** **1** two people, things, etc: *I need a couple of plates.* **2** a few: *I last saw her a couple of months ago.*

couple[2] /ˈkʌpl/ *verb* [T, usually passive] to join or connect sb/sth to sb/sth else: *The fog, coupled with the amount of traffic on the roads, made driving very difficult.*

coupon /ˈkuːpɒn/ *noun* [C] **1** a small piece of paper which you can use to buy goods at a lower price, or which you can collect and then exchange for goods: *a coupon worth 10% off your next purchase* **2** a printed form in a newspaper or magazine which you use to order goods, enter a competition, etc.

⚷ **courage** /ˈkʌrɪdʒ/ *noun* [U] the ability to control fear in a situation that may be dangerous or unpleasant: *It took real courage to go back into the burning building.* ◆ *She* ***showed*** *great* ***courage*** *all through her long illness.* SYN **bravery**
IDM **pluck up courage** ➲ **pluck**[1]
▶ **courageous** /kəˈreɪdʒəs/ *adj*

courgette /kʊəˈʒet; kɔːˈʒet/ (*AmE* **zucchini**) *noun* [C] a long vegetable with dark green skin that is white inside ➲ picture on **page P15**

courier /ˈkʊriə(r)/ *noun* [C] **1** a person whose job is to carry letters, important papers, etc., especially when they are urgent: *The package was delivered by motorcycle courier.* **2** a person whose job is to look after a group of tourists

⚷ **course** /kɔːs/ *noun* **1** [C] **a course (in/on sth)** a complete series of lessons or studies: *I've decided to* ***enrol on a*** *computer* ***course****.* ◆ *I'm going to* ***take/do a course*** *in French.* **2** [C,U] the route or direction that sth, especially an aircraft, a ship or a river, takes: *The hijackers forced the captain to* ***change course*** *and head for Cuba.* ◆ *to be* ***on/off course*** (= going in the right/wrong direction) ◆ (*figurative*) *I'm on course* (= making the right amount of progress) *to finish this work by the end of the week.* ◆ *The road follows the course of the river.* **3** (also ˌ**course of** ˈ**action**) [C] a way of dealing with a particular situation: *In that situation, resignation was the only course open to him.* **4** [sing] the development of sth over a period of time: *events that changed* ***the course of history*** ◆ *In the normal course of events* (= the way things normally happen) *such problems do not arise.* **5** [C] any of the separate parts of a meal: *a three-course lunch* ◆ *I had chicken for the* ***main course.*** ➲ note at **restaurant 6** [C] an area where **golf** (= a game in which you hit a small ball into a number of holes) is played or where certain types of race take place: *a golf course* ◆ *a racecourse* **7** [C] **a course (of sth)** a series of medical treatments: *The doctor put her on a course of tablets.*

IDM be on a collision course (with sb/sth) ➲ collision

in the course of sth during sth: *He mentioned it in the course of conversation.*

in the course of time when enough time has passed **SYN eventually**

in due course ➲ **due**[1]

a matter of course ➲ **matter**[1]

of course naturally; certainly: *Of course, having children has changed their lives a lot.* ◆ *'Can I use your phone?' 'Of course (you can).'* ◆ *'You're not annoyed with me, are you?' 'Of course (I'm) not.'*

coursebook /ˈkɔːsbʊk/ *noun* [C] a book for studying from that is used regularly in class

ˌcourse of ˈaction = course(3)

coursework /ˈkɔːswɜːk/ *noun* [U] work that students do during a course of study, not in exams, that is included in their final grade: *Coursework accounts for 40% of the final marks.*

court[1] /kɔːt/ *noun* **1** [C,U] (also ˌ**court of ˈlaw**; *BrE also* ˈ**law court**) the place where legal trials take place and crimes, etc. are judged: *the* ***civil/criminal*** *courts* ◆ *A man has been charged and will* ***appear in court*** *tomorrow.* ◆ *Bill's company are refusing to pay him so he's decided to* ***take*** *them* ***to court.*** **2 the court** [sing] the people in a court, especially those taking part in the trial: *Please tell the court exactly what you saw.* **3** [C,U] an area where certain ball games are played: *a tennis/squash/badminton court* ➲ look at **pitch** ➲ picture on **page P4**

> **TOPIC**
>
> **Court**
>
> The **accused** (= a person charged with a crime) has the right to a **trial** which is held in a **court**. All trials have a **judge** and some have a **jury** (= a group of members of the public), who **try** the **case**. One group of lawyers (the **prosecution**) tries to prove the guilt of the accused (= to show that he did it), while another group (the **defence**) tries to defend him. They examine the **evidence** to see if there is **proof** that he committed the crime. They may hear evidence from **witnesses** (= people who saw the crime being committed). At the end of the trial the judge or the jury will reach a **verdict** and decide if he is **guilty** or **not guilty**. If the accused is found guilty he will receive a **sentence**. He may be **fined** (= forced to pay money) or sent to **jail/prison**.

court[2] /kɔːt/ *verb* [T] (*formal*) **1** to try to gain sb's support by paying special attention to them: *Politicians from all parties will be courting voters this week.* **2** to do sth that might have a very bad effect: *Britain is courting ecological disaster if it continues to dump waste in the North Sea.*

courteous /ˈkɜːtiəs/ *adj* polite and pleasant, showing respect for other people **OPP discourteous**
▶ **courteously** *adv*

courtesy /ˈkɜːtəsi/ *noun* (*pl* **courtesies**) **1** [U] polite and pleasant behaviour that shows respect for other people: *She didn't even* ***have the courtesy*** *to say that she was sorry.* **2** [C] (*formal*) a polite thing that you say or do when you meet people in formal situations: *The two presidents exchanged courtesies before their meeting.*

IDM (by) courtesy of sb (*formal*) with the permission or because of the kindness of sb: *These pictures are being shown by courtesy of BBC TV.*

ˌcourt ˈmartial *noun* [C,U] (*pl* **courts martial**) a military court that deals with matters of military law; a trial that takes place in such a court: *His case will be heard by a court martial.*
▶ **court-martial** *verb* [T]

ˌcourt of ˈlaw *noun* [C] (*pl* **courts of law**) = **court**[1](1)

courtship /ˈkɔːtʃɪp/ *noun* [C,U] (*old-fashioned*) the relationship between a man and a woman before they get married

courtyard /ˈkɔːtjɑːd/ *noun* [C] an area of ground, without a roof, that has walls or buildings around it, for example in a castle or between houses or flats

cousin /ˈkʌzn/ (also ˌ**first ˈcousin**) *noun* [C] the child of your aunt or uncle: *Paul and I are cousins.*

> **MORE** The same word is used for both male and female cousins. A **second cousin** is the child of your mother's or father's cousin.

cove /kəʊv/ *noun* [C] a small area of the coast where the land curves round so that it is protected from the wind, etc: *a sandy cove*

cover[1] /ˈkʌvə(r)/ *verb*

➤ **HIDE/PROTECT 1** [T] **cover sb/sth (up/over) (with sth)** to put sth on or in front of sth to hide or protect it: *Could you cover the food and put it in the fridge?* ◆ *She couldn't look any more and covered her eyes.* ◆ *I covered the floor with newspaper before I started painting.* ◆ (*figurative*) *Paula laughed to cover (= hide) her embarrassment.* **OPP uncover**

➤ **SPREAD OVER SURFACE 2** [T] **cover sb/sth in/with sth** to be on the surface of sth; to make sth do this: *A car went through the puddle and covered me with mud.* ◆ *Graffiti covered the walls.* ◆ *The eruption of the volcano covered the town in a layer of ash.* **3** [T] to fill or spread over a certain area: *The floods cover an area of about 15 000 square kilometres.*

➤ **INCLUDE 4** [T] to include or to deal with sth: *All the papers covered the election in depth.* ◆ *The course covered both British and European naval history.*

➤ **MONEY 5** [T] to be enough money for sth: *We'll give you some money to cover your expenses.*

➤ **TRAVEL 6** [T] to travel a certain distance: *We covered about 500 kilometres that day.*

➤ **DO SB'S JOB 7** [I] **cover (for sb)** to do sb's job while they are away from work: *Matt's phoned in sick today so we'll have to find someone to cover (for him).*

›INSURANCE **8** [T] **cover sb/sth against/for sth** to protect sb/sth with insurance: *The insurance policy covers us for any damage to our property.*

IDM cover the cost (of sth) to have or make enough money to pay for sth: *We made so little money at our school dance that we didn't even cover the cost of the band.*

PHR V cover sth up to prevent people hearing about a mistake or sth bad: *The police have been accused of trying to cover up the facts of the case.*
cover up for sb to hide sb's mistakes or crimes in order to protect them: *His wife covered up for him to the police.*

cover² /ˈkʌvə(r)/ *noun*
›PROTECTION **1** [C] something that is put on or over sth, especially in order to protect it: *a plastic cover for a computer* ◆ *a duvet cover* **2** [U] protection from the weather, damage, etc: *When the storm started we had to* **take cover** *in a shop doorway.* ◆ *When the gunfire started everyone* **ran for cover**. **SYN shelter**
›OF BOOK, ETC. **3** [C] the outside part of a book or magazine: *I read the magazine from cover to cover* (= from beginning to end).
›INSURANCE **4** [U] **cover (against sth)** insurance against sth: *The policy* **provides cover** *against theft.*
›ON BED **5 the covers** [pl] the sheets, etc. on a bed: *She threw back the covers and leapt out of bed.*
›HIDING STH **6** [C,U] **a cover (for sth)** something that hides what sb is really doing: *The whole company was just a cover for all kinds of criminal activities.* ◆ *police officers working* **under cover**
›OF JOB **7** [U] doing sb's job for them while they are away from work: *Joe's off next week so we'll have to arrange cover.*

IDM under (the) cover of sth hidden by sth: *They attacked under cover of darkness.*

coverage /ˈkʌvərɪdʒ/ *noun* [U] **1** the act or amount of reporting on an event in newspapers, on TV, etc: *TV coverage of the Olympic Games was excellent.* **2** the amount or quality of information included in a book, magazine, etc: *The grammar section provides coverage of all the most problematic areas.*

coveralls /ˈkʌvərɔːlz/ *noun* [pl] (*AmE*) **1** = **overall²(2) 2** = **boiler suit**

covered /ˈkʌvəd/ *adj* **1 covered in/with sth** having a layer or a large amount of sth on sb/sth: *She was covered in mud/sweat/dust.* ◆ *nuts covered with chocolate* **2** having a cover, especially a roof: *a covered shopping centre*

covering /ˈkʌvərɪŋ/ *noun* [C] something that covers the surface of sth: *There was a thick covering of dust over everything.*

ˌcovering ˈletter (*AmE* ˈ**cover letter**) *noun* [C] a letter containing extra information that you send with sth: *To apply for the job, send your CV with a covering letter.*

covert /ˈkʌvət; ˈkəʊvɜːt/ *adj* (*formal*) done secretly: *a covert police operation* **OPP overt** ▶ **covertly** *adv*

ˈcover-up *noun* [C] an act of preventing sth bad or dishonest from becoming known: *Several newspapers have claimed that there has been a government cover-up.*

covet /ˈkʌvət/ *verb* [T] (*formal*) to want to have sth very much (especially sth that belongs to sb else)

cow /kaʊ/ *noun* [C] **1** a large female animal that is kept on farms to produce milk or beef: *to milk a cow* ◆ *dairy cows* (= cows kept for their milk) ➲ note at **meat**

> **MORE** Cow is often used for both the male and female animal. A male cow is called a **bull** and a young cow is a **calf**. A group of cows is a **herd**. An ox is a male that cannot produce young and which is used for pulling heavy loads. Cows and bulls that are kept as farm animals can be called **cattle**. The noise that cows make is **moo**.

2 the adult female of certain large animals, for example **elephants** (= large grey animals with a long nose) **3** (*slang*) an insulting word for a woman

coward /ˈkaʊəd/ *noun* [C] a person who has no courage and is afraid in dangerous or unpleasant situations: *I hate going to the dentist's because I'm a terrible coward.* ▶ **cowardly** *adj*

cowardice /ˈkaʊədɪs/ *noun* [U] a lack of courage; behaviour that shows that you are afraid

cowboy /ˈkaʊbɔɪ/ *noun* [C] **1** a man whose job is to look after cows (usually on a horse) in certain parts of the US **2** (*BrE informal*) a person in business who is not honest or who does work badly: *a cowboy builder*

cower /ˈkaʊə(r)/ *verb* [I] to move back or into a low position because of fear: *The dog cowered under the table when the storm started.*

coy /kɔɪ/ *adj* **1** pretending to be shy or innocent: *She lifted her head a little and gave him a coy smile.* **2** not wanting to give information about sth or to answer questions that tell people too much about you: *Don't be coy, tell me how much you earn.* ▶ **coyly** *adv*

coz (*BrE informal*) = **cos**

cozy (*AmE*) = **cosy**

crab /kræb/ *noun* **1** [C] a sea animal with a flat shell and ten legs that moves sideways. The front two legs have **pincers** (= long curved points) on them. ➲ picture on **page P13** **2** [U] the meat from a crab

crack¹ /kræk/ *verb*
➤BREAK **1** [I,T] to break or to make sth break so that a line appears on the surface, but without breaking into pieces: *Don't put boiling water into that glass—it'll crack.* ◆ *The stone cracked the windscreen but didn't break it.* ➲ picture at **chip** **2** [T] to break sth open: *Crack two eggs into a bowl.*
➤HIT **3** [T] to hit a part of your body against sth; to hit sb with sth: *She stood up and cracked her head on the cupboard door.* ◆ *She cracked the thief over the head with her umbrella.*
➤MAKE SOUND **4** [I,T] to make a sudden loud, sharp sound; to cause sth to make this sound: *to crack a whip/your knuckles*
➤VOICE **5** [I] (used about sb's voice) to suddenly change in a way that is not controlled: *Her voice cracked as she spoke about her father's death.*
➤UNDER PRESSURE **6** [I] to no longer be able to deal with pressure and so lose control: *He cracked under the strain of all his problems.*
➤FIND SOLUTION **7** [T] (*informal*) to solve a problem: *to crack a code* ◆ *The police have cracked an international diamond-smuggling ring.*
➤JOKE **8** [T] to tell or make a joke: *Stop cracking jokes and do some work!*
IDM **get cracking** (*BrE informal*) to start doing sth immediately: *I have to finish this job today so I'd better get cracking.*
PHR V **crack down (on sb/sth)** (used about people in authority) to start dealing strictly with bad or illegal behaviour: *The police have started to crack down on street crime.*
crack up **1** (*informal*) to be unable to deal with pressure and so lose control and become mentally ill: *He cracked up when his wife left him.* **2** (*slang*) to suddenly start laughing, especially when you should be serious

crack² /kræk/ *noun*
➤BREAK **1** [C] a line on the surface of sth where it has broken, but not into separate pieces: *a pane of glass with a crack in it* ◆ (*figurative*) *They had always seemed happy together, but then cracks began to appear in their relationship.* ➲ picture at **chip²**(1)
➤OPENING **2** [C] a narrow opening: *a crack in the curtains*
➤SOUND **3** [C] a sudden loud, sharp sound: *There was a loud crack of thunder as the storm broke.*
➤HIT **4** [C] a hard hit on a part of the body: *Suddenly a golf ball gave him a nasty crack on the head.*
➤DRUG **5** [U] a dangerous and illegal drug that some people take for pleasure and cannot then stop taking: *a crack addict*
➤JOKE **6** [C] (*informal*) an amusing, often critical, comment; a joke: *She* ***made a crack*** *about his bald head and he got angry.*
IDM **the crack of dawn** very early in the morning
have a crack (at sth/at doing sth) (*informal*) to try to do sth: *I'm not sure how to play but I'll have a crack at it.*

crack³ /kræk/ *adj* [only *before* a noun] (used about soldiers or sports players) very well trained and skilful: *crack troops* ◆ *He's a crack shot* (= very accurate at shooting) *with a rifle.*

crackdown /ˈkrækdaʊn/ *noun* [C] action to stop bad or illegal behaviour: *Fifty people have been arrested in a police crackdown on street crime.*

cracked /krækt/ *adj* damaged with lines in its surface but not completely broken: *a cracked mirror/mug* ◆ *He suffered cracked ribs and bruising.* ➲ picture at **chip**

cracker /ˈkrækə(r)/ *noun* [C] **1** a thin dry biscuit that is often eaten with cheese **2** (also ˌ**Christmas ˈcracker**) a cardboard tube covered in coloured paper and containing a small present. **Crackers** are pulled apart by two people, each holding one end, at Christmas parties. They make a loud noise as they break. **3** (*BrE informal*) a very good example of sth: *That story he told was a real cracker.*

crackle /ˈkrækl/ *verb* [I] to make a series of short, sharp sounds: *The radio started to crackle and then it stopped working.* ▶ **crackle** *noun* [sing]: *the crackle of dry wood burning*

cradle¹ /ˈkreɪdl/ *noun* [C] a small bed for a baby. **Cradles** can often be moved from side to side. ➲ picture at **bed**

cradle² /ˈkreɪdl/ *verb* [T] to hold sb/sth carefully and gently in your arms

craft /krɑːft/ *noun* **1** [C,U] a job or an activity for which you need skill with your hands: *an arts and crafts exhibition* ◆ *I studied craft and design at school.* ➲ look at **handicraft** **2** [C] any job or activity for which you need skill: *He regards acting as a craft.* **3** [C] (*pl* **craft**) (*formal*) a boat, an aircraft or a **spacecraft** (= a vehicle that travels in space): *a pleasure craft*

craftsman /ˈkrɑːftsmən/ *noun* [C] (*pl* **-men** /-mən/) a person who makes things in a skilful way, especially with their hands

craftsmanship /ˈkrɑːftsmənʃɪp/ *noun* [U] the skill used by sb to make sth of high quality with their hands

crafty /ˈkrɑːfti/ *adj* (**craftier**; **craftiest**) clever at getting or achieving things by using unfair or dishonest methods ▶ **craftily** *adv*

crag /kræg/ *noun* [C] a steep, rough mass of rock on a hill or mountain

craggy /ˈkrægi/ *adj* **1** having a lot of steep rough rock: *a craggy coastline* **2** (used about a man's face) strong and with deep lines, especially in an attractive way

cram /kræm/ *verb* (**cramming**; **crammed**) **1** [T] **cram sb/sth in (sth)**; **cram sb/sth into/onto sth** to push people or things into a small space: *We only spent two days in Dublin but we managed to cram a lot of sightseeing in.* ◆ *I managed to cram all my clothes into the bag but I couldn't close it.* **2** [I] **cram in (sth)**; **cram into/onto sth** to move, with a lot of other people, into a small space: *He only had a small car but they all managed to cram in.* **3** [I] to study very hard and learn a lot in a short time before an exam: *She's cramming for her exams.*

crammed /kræmd/ *adj* very or too full: *That book is crammed with useful information.*

cramp /kræmp/ *noun* [U,C] a sudden pain that you get in a muscle, that makes it difficult to move

cramped /kræmpt/ *adj* not having enough space: *The flat was terribly cramped with so many of us living there.*

cranberry /ˈkrænbəri/ *noun* [C] (*pl* **cranberries**) a small round red fruit that tastes sour and is used in cooking: *cranberry sauce*

crane[1] /kreɪn/ *noun* [C] a large machine with a long metal arm that is used for moving or lifting heavy objects ➲ picture on **page P11**

crane[2] /kreɪn/ *verb* [I,T] to stretch your neck forward in order to see or hear sth: *We all craned forward to get a better view.*

crank /kræŋk/ *noun* [C] a person with strange ideas or who behaves in a strange way: *Lots of cranks phoned the police confessing to the man's murder.*

cranny /ˈkræni/ *noun* [C] (*pl* **crannies**) a small opening in a wall, rock, etc.
IDM every nook and cranny ➲ **nook**

crap /kræp/ *noun* [U] (*slang*) a rude word meaning nonsense or rubbish ▸ **crappy** /ˈkræpi/ *adj* (**crappier; crappiest**) [usually before a noun] (*slang*)

HELP Be careful. Some people find this word offensive.

crash[1] /kræʃ/ *noun* [C] **1** an accident when a car or other vehicle hits sth and is damaged: *a car/plane crash* **2** a sudden loud noise made by sth breaking, hitting sth, etc: *I heard a crash and ran outside.* **3** (used about money or business) a sudden fall in the value or price of sth: *the Stock Market crash of 1987* **4** a sudden failure of a machine, especially a computer

crash[2] /kræʃ/ *verb* **1** [I,T] to have an accident in a vehicle; to drive a vehicle into sth: *He braked too late and crashed into the car in front.* **2** [I] to hit sth hard, making a loud noise: *The tree crashed to the ground.* **3** [I] to make a loud noise: *I could hear thunder crashing outside.* **4** [I] (used about money or business) to suddenly lose value or fail: *Share prices crashed to an all-time low yesterday.* **5** [I] (used about a computer) to suddenly stop working: *We lost the data when the computer crashed.*

crash[3] /kræʃ/ *adj* [only *before* a noun] done in a very short period of time: *She did a* **crash course** *in Spanish before going to work in Madrid.*

ˈcrash barrier *noun* [C] a strong low fence or wall at the side of a road or between two halves of a major road

ˈcrash helmet *noun* [C] a hard hat worn by motorbike riders, racing drivers, etc. ➲ picture at **hat**

ˌcrash-ˈland *verb* [I,T] to land a plane in a dangerous way in an emergency ▸ **ˌcrash ˈlanding** *noun* [C]: *to make a crash landing*

crass /kræs/ *adj* stupid, showing that you do not understand sth: *It was a crass comment to make, when he knew how upset she was.*

crate /kreɪt/ *noun* [C] a large box in which goods are carried or stored

crater /ˈkreɪtə(r)/ *noun* [C] **1** the hole in the top of a **volcano** (= a mountain that explodes), through which hot gases and liquid rock are forced ➲ picture at **volcano** **2** a large hole in the ground: *The bomb left a large crater.* ◆ *craters on the moon*

cravat /krəˈvæt/ *noun* [C] a wide piece of cloth that some men tie around their neck and wear inside the **collar** (= the folded part around the neck) of their shirt

crave /kreɪv/ *verb* [I,T] **crave (for) sth** to want and need to have sth very much: *Sometimes I really crave for some chocolate.* ◆ *He craves attention from other people.*

craving /ˈkreɪvɪŋ/ *noun* [C] a strong desire for sth: *When she was pregnant she used to* **have cravings for** *all sorts of peculiar food.*

crawl[1] /krɔːl/ *verb* [I] **1** to move slowly with your body on or close to the ground, or on your hands and knees: *Their baby has just started to crawl.* ◆ *An insect crawled across the floor.* **2** (used about vehicles) to move very slowly: *The traffic crawls through the centre of town in the rush hour.* **3** (*informal*) **crawl (to sb)** to be very polite or pleasant to sb in order to be liked or to gain sth: *He only got promoted because he crawled to the manager.*

The baby is crawling.

IDM be crawling with sth to be completely full of or covered with unpleasant animals: *The kitchen was crawling with insects.* ◆ (*figurative*) *The village is always crawling with tourists at this time of year.*

crawl[2] /krɔːl/ *noun* **1** [sing] a very slow speed: *The traffic slowed to a crawl.* **2** *often* **the crawl** [sing,U] a style of swimming which you do on your front. When you do the **crawl**, you move first one arm and then the other over your head, turn your face to one side so that you can breathe and kick up and down with your legs. ➲ picture at **swim**

crayon /ˈkreɪən/ *noun* [C,U] a soft, thick, coloured pencil that is used for drawing or writing, especially by children ▸ **crayon** *verb* [I,T]

craze /kreɪz/ *noun* [C] **a craze (for sth)** **1** a strong interest in sth, that usually only lasts for a short time: *There was a craze for that kind of music last year.* **2** something that a lot of people are very interested in: *Knitting is the latest craze among Hollywood celebrities.*

crazy /ˈkreɪzi/ *adj* (**crazier; craziest**) (*informal*) **1** not sensible; stupid: *You must be crazy to turn down such a wonderful offer.* **2** very angry: *She* **goes crazy** *when people criticize her.* **3** showing great excitement: *The fans* **went crazy** *when their team scored the first goal.* **4 crazy about sb/sth** liking sb/sth very much: *He's always been crazy about horses.* ▶ **crazily** *adv* ▶ **craziness** *noun* [U]

C

creak /kriːk/ *verb* [I] to make the noise of wood bending or of sth not moving smoothly: *The floorboards creaked when I walked across the room.* ▶ **creak** *noun* [C] ▶ **creaky** *adj*: *creaky stairs*

cream¹ /kriːm/ *noun* **1** [U] the thick yellowish-white liquid that rises to the top of milk: *coffee with cream* ◆ *whipped cream* (= cream that has been beaten) ➲ picture on **page P16** **2** [C,U] a substance that you rub into your skin to keep it soft **3** = **ointment**: *(an) antiseptic cream* **4 the cream** [sing] the best part of sth or the best people in a group: *the cream of New York society*

cream² /kriːm/ *adj, noun* [U] (of) a yellowish-white colour: *cream linen trousers*

cream³ /kriːm/ *verb*
PHR V cream sb/sth off to take away the best people or part from sth for a particular purpose: *The big clubs cream off the country's best young players.*

creamy /ˈkriːmi/ *adj* (**creamier**; **creamiest**) **1** containing cream; thick and smooth like cream: *a creamy sauce* **2** having a light colour like cream: *creamy skin*

crease¹ /kriːs/ *noun* [C] **1** an untidy line on paper, material, a piece of clothing, etc. that should not be there: *Your shirt needs ironing, it's full of creases.* ◆ *When I unrolled the poster, there was a crease in it.* **2** a tidy straight line that you make in sth, for example when you fold it: *He had a sharp crease in his trousers.*

crease² /kriːs/ *verb* [I,T] to get **creases**; to make sth get **creases**: *Hang up your jacket or it will crease.* ◆ *Crease the paper carefully down the middle.*

create /kriˈeɪt/ *verb* [T] **1** to cause sth new to happen or exist: *a plan to create new jobs in the area* **2** to produce a particular feeling: *William created a bad impression at the interview.*

creation /kriˈeɪʃn/ *noun* **1** [U] the act of causing sth new to happen or exist: *the creation of new independent states* **2** [C] something new that sb has made or produced: *This dish is a new creation—I didn't use a recipe.* **3** *usually* **the Creation** [sing] the act of making the whole universe, as described in the Bible

creative /kriˈeɪtɪv/ *adj* **1** using skill or imagination to make or do new things: *She's a fantastic designer—she's so creative.* **2** connected with producing new things: *the company's creative team* ▶ **creatively** *adv*

creativity /ˌkriːeɪˈtɪvəti/ *noun* [U] the ability to make or produce new things using skill or imagination: *We want teaching that encourages children's creativity.*

creator /kriˈeɪtə(r)/ *noun* [C] a person who makes or produces sth new: *He was the creator of some of the best-known characters in literature.*

creature /ˈkriːtʃə(r)/ *noun* [C] a living thing such as an animal, a bird, a fish or an insect, but not a plant: *a living creature* ◆ *sea creatures*

crèche /kreʃ/ *noun* [C] a place where small children are looked after while their parents are working, shopping, etc.

credentials /krəˈdenʃlz/ *noun* [pl] **1** the qualities, experience, etc. that make sb suitable for sth: *He has the perfect credentials for the job.* **2** a document that is proof that you have the training, education, etc. necessary to do sth, or proof that you are who you say you are

credibility /ˌkredəˈbɪləti/ *noun* [U] the quality that sb has that makes people believe or trust them: *The Prime Minister had lost all credibility and had to resign.*

credible /ˈkredəbl/ *adj* **1** that you can believe: *It's hardly credible that such a thing could happen without him knowing it.* **OPP incredible** **2** that seems possible: *We need to think of a credible alternative to nuclear energy.*

credit¹ /ˈkredɪt/ *noun*
➤PAYING LATER **1** [U] a way of buying goods or services and not paying for them until later: *I bought the TV* **on credit**.
➤MONEY BORROWED **2** [U] a sum of money that a bank, etc. lends to sb: *The company was not able to get any further credit and went bankrupt.*
➤MONEY IN ACCOUNT **3** [U] having money in an account **3**: *No bank charges are made if your account remains* **in credit**. ◆ *I've run out of credit on my mobile phone.* **4** [C] a payment made into an account: *There have been several credits to her account over the last month.* **OPP debit**
➤PRAISE **5** [U] an act of saying that sb has done sth well: *He* **got all the credit** *for the success of the project.* ◆ *I can't* **take** *any* **credit**; *the others did all the work.* ◆ *She didn't do very well but at least* **give** *her* **credit for** *trying.*
➤PERSON **6** [sing] **a credit to sb/sth** a person or thing that you should be proud of: *She is a credit to her school.*
➤IN FILM/ON TV **7 the credits** [pl] the list of the names of the people who made a film or TV programme, shown at the beginning or end of the film/programme
➤AT UNIVERSITY **8** [C] (*AmE*) a part of a course at a college or university that a student has completed successfully
IDM do sb credit (used about sb's qualities or successes) to be so good that people should be proud of them: *His courage and optimism do him credit.*
have sth to your credit to have finished sth that is successful: *He has three best-selling novels to his credit.*
(be) to sb's credit used for showing that you approve of sth that sb has done, although you have criticized them for sth else: *The company, to its credit, apologized and refunded my money.*

credit² /ˈkredɪt/ *verb* [T] **1** to add money to an account: *Has the payment been credited to my bank* *account yet?* **2 credit sb/sth with sth; credit sth to sb/sth** to believe or say that sb/sth has a particular quality or has done sth well: *Of course I wouldn't do such a stupid thing—credit me with a bit more sense than that!* **3** [usually in negative sentences and questions] to believe sth: *I simply cannot credit that he has made the same mistake again!*

creditable /ˈkredɪtəbl/ *adj* of a quite good standard that cannot be criticized, though not excellent: *It was a creditable result considering that three players were injured.*

ˈcredit card *noun* [C] a small plastic card that you can use to buy goods or services and pay for them later: *Can I pay by credit card?* ➲ look at **cash card, cheque card, debit card** ➲ picture at **money**

ˈcredit crunch *noun* [usually sing] a time when it suddenly becomes difficult to borrow money from a bank

creditor /ˈkredɪtə(r)/ *noun* [C] a person or company from whom you have borrowed money: *He went abroad to avoid his creditors.*

creed /kriːd/ *noun* [C] a set of beliefs or principles (especially religious ones) that strongly influence sb's life

creek /kriːk/ *noun* [C] **1** (*BrE*) a narrow piece of water where the sea flows into the land **2** (*AmE*) a small river **SYN** **stream**

creep[1] /kriːp/ *verb* [I] (*pt, pp* **crept** /krept/) **1** to move very quietly and carefully so that nobody will notice you: *She crept into the room so as not to wake him up.* **2** to move forward slowly: *The traffic was only creeping along.*

IDM **make your flesh creep** ➲ **flesh**

PHR V **creep in** to begin to appear: *All sorts of changes are beginning to creep into the education system.*

creep[2] /kriːp/ *noun* [C] (*informal*) a person that you do not like because they try too hard to be liked by people in authority

IDM **give sb the creeps** (*informal*) to make sb feel frightened or nervous: *There's something about him that gives me the creeps.*

creeper /ˈkriːpə(r)/ *noun* [C] a plant that grows up trees or walls or along the ground

creepy /ˈkriːpi/ *adj* (**creepier**; **creepiest**) (*informal*) that makes you feel nervous or frightened **SYN** **spooky**

cremate /krəˈmeɪt/ *verb* [T] to burn the body of a dead person as part of a funeral service ➲ note at **funeral** ▶ **cremation** /krəˈmeɪʃn/ *noun* [C,U]

crematorium /ˌkreməˈtɔːriəm/ *noun* [C] (*pl* **crematoria** /-ˈtɔːriə/ *or* **crematoriums**) a building in which the bodies of dead people are burned

Creole (also **creole**) /ˈkriːəʊl/ *noun* **1** [C] a person of mixed European and African race, especially one who lives in the West Indies **2** [C] a person whose relatives were among the first Europeans to live in the West Indies and South America, or among the first French or Spanish people to live in the southern states of the US: *the Creole cooking of New Orleans* **3** [C,U] a language that was originally a mixture of a European language and a local, especially African, language

crept *past tense, past participle of* **creep**[1]

crescendo /krəˈʃendəʊ/ *noun* [C] (*pl* **crescendos**) a noise or piece of music that gets louder and louder

crescent /ˈkresnt/ *noun* [C] **1** a curved shape that is pointed at both ends, like the moon in its first and last stages ➲ picture at **shape** **2** a street that is curved

cress /kres/ *noun* [U] a small plant with very small green leaves that does not need to be cooked and is eaten in salads and **sandwiches** (= two slices of bread with food between them)

crest /krest/ *noun* [C] **1** the top of a hill or a wave **2** a design used as a symbol of a particular family or organization: *the university crest* **3** a group of feathers on the top of a bird's head

crestfallen /ˈkrestfɔːlən/ *adj* disappointed or sad because you have failed and did not expect to

crevasse /krəˈvæs/ *noun* [C] a deep crack in a very thick layer of ice

crevice /ˈkrevɪs/ *noun* [C] a narrow crack in a rock, wall, etc.

crew /kruː/ *noun* [C, with sing or pl verb] **1** all the people who work on a ship, an aircraft, etc. ➲ note at **boat** **2** a group of people who work together: *a camera crew* (= people who film things for TV, etc.)

crib[1] /krɪb/ (*AmE*) = **cot**

crib[2] /krɪb/ *verb* [I,T] (**cribbing**; **cribbed**) **crib (sth) (from/off sb)** to copy sb else's work and pretend it is your own

crick /krɪk/ *noun* [sing] a pain in your neck, back, etc. that makes it difficult for you to move easily ▶ **crick** *verb* [T]: *I've cricked my neck.*

cricket /ˈkrɪkɪt/ *noun* **1** [U] a game that is played with a ball and a **bat** (= a piece of wood) on a large area of grass by two teams of eleven players ➲ picture on **page P4**

> **MORE** In cricket, the **bowler** bowls (= throws) the ball to the **batsman** who tries to hit it with a **bat** and then score a **run** by running from one **wicket** to the other.

2 [C] an insect that makes a loud noise by rubbing its wings together

cricketer /ˈkrɪkɪtə(r)/ *noun* [C] a person who plays **cricket**

crime /kraɪm/ *noun* **1** [U] illegal behaviour or activities: *There has been an increase in car crime recently.* ◆ *to fight crime* **2** [C] something which is illegal and which people are punished for, for example by being sent to prison: *to* ***commit a crime*** ➲ look at **cybercrime** **3** *usually* **a crime** [sing] something that is morally wrong: *It is a crime to waste food when people are starving.*

TOPIC

Crime

A crime is **illegal** or **against the law**. A person who **commits** a crime is a **criminal.** There are different words for particular crimes and the people who commit them. A **murderer** commits **murder** (= kills sb). A **kidnapper kidnaps** sb (= takes sb away by force and asks for money for them to be returned). **Terrorists** use violence for political reasons and commit acts of **terrorism**. For example, they sometimes **hijack** planes (= take control of them using violence). **Vandals** commit **vandalism** (= destroy people's property for no reason).

It is the job of the police to **investigate** crimes and try to catch the criminal. If the police think sb may have committed a crime, that person is a **suspect.** When they have enough **evidence** the police can **arrest** and **charge** them **with** the crime (= officially accuse them). If the suspect **confesses** to the crime, they admit that they did it. If they **deny** the charge, they say that they did not do it.

criminal¹ /ˈkrɪmɪnl/ *adj* **1** [only *before* a noun] connected with crime: *Deliberate damage to public property is a **criminal offence**.* ♦ *criminal law* **2** morally wrong: *a criminal waste of taxpayers' money* ▶ **criminally** /-nəli/ *adv*: *criminally insane*

criminal² /ˈkrɪmɪnl/ *noun* [C] a person who has done sth illegal: *CCTV in the city centre has helped to deter criminals.*

crimson /ˈkrɪmzn/ *adj, noun* [U] (of) a dark red colour

cringe /krɪndʒ/ *verb* [I] **1** to move away from sb/sth because you are frightened: *The dog cringed in terror when the man raised his arm.* **2** to feel embarrassed: *awful family photographs which **make** you cringe*

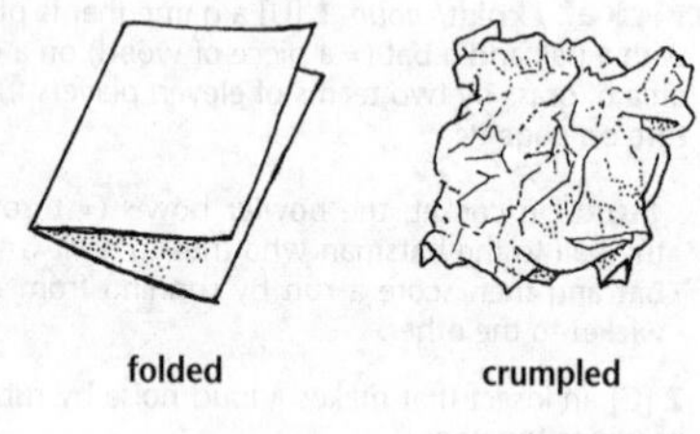
folded crumpled

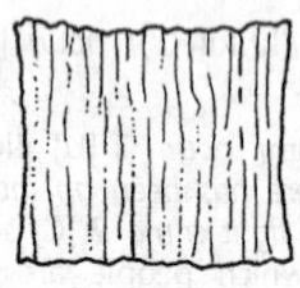
crinkled

crinkle /ˈkrɪŋkl/ *verb* [I,T] **crinkle (sth) (up)** to have, or to make sth have, thin folds or lines in it: *He crinkled the silver paper up into a ball.* ▶ **crinkly** /ˈkrɪŋkli/ *adj*: *crinkly material*

cripple /ˈkrɪpl/ *verb* [T] to damage sth badly: *The recession has crippled the motor industry.*

crippling /ˈkrɪplɪŋ/ *adj* that causes very great damage or has a very bad effect: *They had crippling debts and had to sell their house.*

crisis /ˈkraɪsɪs/ *noun* [C,U] (*pl* **crises** /-siːz/) a time of great danger or difficulty; the moment when things change and either improve or get worse: *the international crisis caused by the invasion* ♦ *a friend you can rely on in times of crisis*

crisp¹ /krɪsp/ *adj* (**crisper**; **crispest**) **1** pleasantly hard and dry: *Store the biscuits in a tin to keep them crisp.* **2** firm and fresh or new: *a crisp salad/apple* ♦ *a crisp cotton dress* **3** (used about the air or weather) cold and dry: *a crisp winter morning* **4** (used about the way sb speaks) quick, clear but not very friendly: *a crisp reply* ▶ **crisply** *adv*: *'I disagree,' she said crisply.* ▶ **crispy** *adj* (*informal*) = **crisp**

crisp² /krɪsp/ (*BrE also* poˌtato ˈcrisp; *AmE* **chip**; poˈtato **chip**) *noun* [C] a very thin piece of potato that is fried in oil, then dried and eaten cold. Crisps are sold in small plastic bags and usually have salt or another flavouring on them: *a packet of crisps* ➲ picture at **chip**

criss-cross /ˈkrɪs krɒs/ *adj* [only *before* a noun] with many straight lines that cross over each other: *a criss-cross pattern* ▶ **criss-cross** *verb* [I,T]: *Many footpaths criss-cross the countryside in Suffolk.*

criterion /kraɪˈtɪəriən/ *noun* [C] (*pl* **criteria** /-riə/) the standard that you use when you make a decision or form an opinion about sb/sth: *The main criterion is value for money.* ♦ *What are the criteria for deciding who gets a place on the course?*

critic /ˈkrɪtɪk/ *noun* [C] **1** a person whose job is to give their opinion about a play, film, book, work of art, etc: *a film/restaurant/art critic* **2** a person who says what is bad or wrong with sb/sth: *He is a long-standing critic of the council's transport policy.*

critical /ˈkrɪtɪkl/ *adj* **1 critical (of sb/sth)** saying what is wrong with sb/sth: *The report was very critical of safety standards on the railways.* ♦ *You're always so critical!* **2** very important; at a time when things can suddenly become better or worse: *The talks between the two leaders have **reached a critical stage**.* **3** dangerous or serious: *The patient is **in a critical condition**.* **4** [only *before* a noun] describing the good and bad points of a play, film, book, work of art, etc: *a critical guide to this month's new films* ▶ **critically** /-kli/ *adv*: *a critically ill patient* ♦ *It was a critically important decision.*

criticism /ˈkrɪtɪsɪzəm/ *noun* **1** [C,U] (an expression of) what you think is bad about sb/sth: *The council has **come in for** severe **criticism** over the plans.* **2** [U] the act of describing the good and bad points of a play, film, book, work of art, etc: *literary criticism*

criticize (also **-ise**) /ˈkrɪtɪsaɪz/ *verb* [I,T] **criticize (sb/sth) (for sth)** to say what is bad or wrong with sb/sth: *The doctor was criticized for not sending the patient to hospital.* OPP **praise**

critique /krɪˈtiːk/ *noun* [C] a piece of writing that describes the good and bad points of sb/sth

croak /krəʊk/ *verb* [I] to make a rough low sound like a **frog** (= a small animal that lives in or near water, with long back legs that it uses for jumping) ▶ **croak** *noun* [C]

crochet /ˈkrəʊʃeɪ/ *noun* [U] a way of making clothes, cloth, etc. by using wool or cotton and a needle with a hook at one end ▶ **crochet** *verb* [I,T] (*pt, pp* crocheted /-ʃeɪd/) ➲ look at **knit**

crockery /ˈkrɒkəri/ *noun* [U] cups, plates and dishes ➲ look at **cutlery**

crocodile /ˈkrɒkədaɪl/ *noun* [C] a large animal with a hard skin covered in scales, a long tail and a big mouth with sharp teeth. **Crocodiles** live in rivers and lakes in hot countries. ➲ look at **alligator**

crocus /ˈkrəʊkəs/ *noun* [C] a small yellow, purple or white flower that grows in early spring

croissant /ˈkrwæsɒ̃/ *noun* [C] a type of bread roll, shaped in a curve, that is often eaten with butter for breakfast

crony /ˈkrəʊni/ *noun* [C] (*pl* cronies) (*informal*) (often used in a critical way) a friend

crook /krʊk/ *noun* [C] **1** (*informal*) a dishonest person; a criminal **2** a bend or curve in sth: *the crook of your arm* (= the inside of your elbow)

crooked /ˈkrʊkɪd/ *adj* **1** not straight or even: *That picture is crooked.* ♦ *crooked teeth* **2** (*informal*) not honest: *a crooked accountant*

⚷ **crop**[1] /krɒp/ *noun* **1** [C, usually pl] plants that are grown on farms for food: *Rice and soya beans are the main crops here.* **2** [C] all the grain, fruit, vegetables, etc. of one type that are grown on a farm at one time: *a crop of apples* **3** [sing] a number of people or things which have appeared at the same time: *the recent crop of movies about aliens*

crop[2] /krɒp/ *verb* (cropping; cropped) **1** [T] to cut sth very short: *cropped hair* **2** [T] to cut off part of a photograph or picture **3** [I] to produce a crop
PHR V **crop up** to appear suddenly, when you are not expecting it: *We should have finished this work yesterday but some problems cropped up.*

cropper /ˈkrɒpə(r)/ *noun*
IDM **come a cropper** (*informal*) **1** to fall over or have an accident **2** to fail

croquet /ˈkrəʊkeɪ/ *noun* [U] a game that you play on grass. When you play **croquet** you use **mallets** (= long wooden hammers) to hit balls through **hoops** (= curved pieces of metal).

⚷ **cross**[1] /krɒs/ *noun* [C] **1** a mark that you make by drawing one line across another (X). The sign is used for showing the position of sth, for showing that sth is not correct, etc: *I drew a cross on the map to show where our house is.* ♦ *Incorrect answers were marked with a cross.* ➲ look at **noughts and crosses** ➲ picture at **tick** **2** *often* the Cross the two pieces of wood in the shape of a cross on which people were killed as a punishment in the past, or sth in this shape that is used as a symbol of the Christian religion: *She wore a gold cross round her neck.* ➲ look at **crucifix** **3** [usually sing] a cross (between A and B) something (especially a plant or an animal) that is a mixture of two different types of thing: *a fruit which is a cross between a peach and an apple* **4** (in sports such as football) a kick or hit of the ball that goes across the front of the goal: *Silva's cross was headed into the goal by Tevez.*

⚷ **cross**[2] /krɒs/ *verb*
➤GO/PUT ACROSS **1** [I,T] cross (over) (from sth/to sth) to go from one side of sth to the other: *to cross the road* ♦ *Where did you cross the border?* ♦ *We crossed from Dover to Calais.* ♦ *I waved and she crossed over.* **2** [I] (used about lines, roads, etc.) to pass across each other: *The two roads cross just north of the village.* **3** [T] to put sth across or over sth else: *to cross your arms/legs*
➤OPPOSE **4** [T] to make sb angry by refusing to do what they want you to do: *He's an important man. It could be dangerous to cross him.*
➤MIX **5** [T] cross sth with sth to produce a new type of plant or animal by mixing two different types: *If you cross a horse with a donkey, you get a mule.*
➤IN SPORT **6** [I,T] (in sports such as football and **hockey**) to pass the ball across the front of the goal: *Owen crossed (the ball) for Cole to head into the goal.*
IDM **cross/fold your arms** ➲ **arm**[1] ➲ picture at **arm**
cross your fingers; keep your fingers crossed ➲ **finger**[1]
cross my heart (and hope to die) (*spoken*) used for emphasizing that what you are saying is true: *I won't tell a soul. Cross my heart!*
cross your mind (used about a thought, an idea, etc.) to come into your mind: *It never once crossed my mind that she was lying.*
PHR V **cross sth off (sth)** to remove sth from a list, etc. by drawing a line through it: *Cross Dave's name off the guest list—he can't come.*
cross sth out to draw a line through sth that you have written because you have made a mistake, etc: *to cross out a spelling mistake*

cross[3] /krɒs/ *adj* (*informal*) cross (with sb) (about/for sth) angry or annoyed: *I was really cross with her for leaving me with all the work.* ➲ **Cross** is less formal than **angry**. ▶ **crossly** *adv*: *'Be quiet,' Dad said crossly.*

crossbar /ˈkrɒsbɑː(r)/ *noun* [C] **1** the piece of wood over the top of a goal in football, etc. **2** the metal bar that joins the front and back of a bicycle ➲ picture at **bike**

ˌcross-ˈcountry *adj, adv* across fields and natural land; not using roads or tracks: *We walked 10 miles cross-country before we saw a village.*

ˌcross-eˈxamine *verb* [T] to ask sb questions in a court of law, etc. in order to find out the truth about sth: *The witness was cross-examined for an hour.* ▶ **ˌcross-eˌxamiˈnation** *noun* [C,U]

ˌcross-ˈeyed *adj* having one or both your eyes looking towards your nose

crossfire /ˈkrɒsfaɪə(r)/ *noun* [U] a situation in which guns are being fired from two or more different directions: *The journalist was killed in crossfire.*

C

♦ (*figurative*) *When my parents argued, I sometimes got* ***caught in the crossfire.***

crossing /ˈkrɒsɪŋ/ *noun* [C] **1** a place where you can cross over sth: *You should cross the road at the pedestrian crossing.* ♦ *a border crossing* ➲ look at **level crossing 2** a journey from one side of a sea or river to the other: *We had a rough crossing.*

with her legs crossed

cross-legged

cross-legged /ˌkrɒs ˈlegd; -ˈlegɪd/ *adj, adv* sitting on the floor with your legs pulled up in front of you and with one leg or foot over the other: *to sit cross-legged*

ˌcross ˈpurposes *noun*

IDM at cross purposes a state of confusion between people who are talking about different things but think they are talking about the same thing: *I think we're talking at cross purposes; that's not what I meant at all.*

ˌcross ˈreference *noun* [C] a note in a book that tells you to look in another place in the book for more information

crossroads /ˈkrɒsrəʊdz/ *noun* [C] (*pl* **crossroads**) a place where two or more roads cross each other: *When you come to the next crossroads turn right.* ➲ picture at **roundabout**

ˌcross section *noun* [C] **1** a picture of what the inside of sth would look like if you cut through it: *a cross section of the human brain* **2** a number of people, etc. that come from the different parts of a group, and so can be considered to represent the whole group: *The families we studied were chosen to represent a cross section of society.*

crosswalk /ˈkrɒswɔːk/ (*AmE*) = **pedestrian crossing**

sudoku

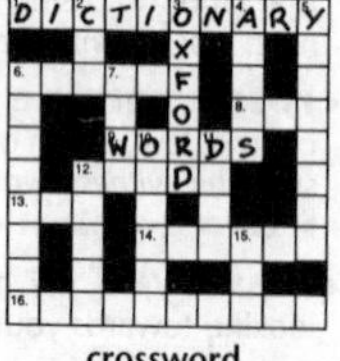

crossword

crossword /ˈkrɒswɜːd/ (also **ˈcrossword puzzle**) *noun* [C] a word game in which you have to write the answers to **clues** (= questions) in square spaces, which are arranged in a pattern: *Every morning I try to* ***do the crossword*** *in the newspaper.*

crotch /krɒtʃ/ (also **crutch**) *noun* [C] the place where your legs, or the legs of a pair of trousers, join at the top

crouch /kraʊtʃ/ *verb* [I] **crouch (down)** to bend your legs and body so that you are close to the ground: *He crouched down behind the sofa.* ➲ picture at **kneel**

crow¹ /krəʊ/ *noun* [C] a large black bird that makes a loud noise

IDM as the crow flies (used for describing distances) in a straight line: *It's a kilometre as the crow flies but three kilometres by road.*

crow² /krəʊ/ *verb* [I] **1** to make a loud noise like a **cock** (= an adult male chicken) **2** (*informal*) to speak in a very proud way about sth **SYN boast**

crowbar /ˈkrəʊbɑː(r)/ *noun* [C] a long iron bar that is used for forcing sth open

crowd¹ /kraʊd/ *noun* **1** [C, with sing or pl verb] a large number of people in one place: *The crowd was/were extremely noisy.* ♦ *He pushed his way through the crowd.* ♦ *I go shopping early in the morning to avoid the crowds.* **2** [C, with sing or pl verb] (*informal*) a group of people who know each other: *John, Linda and Barry will be there–all the usual crowd.* **3 the crowd** [sing] ordinary people: *He wears weird clothes because he wants to* ***stand out from the crowd.***

crowd² /kraʊd/ *verb* [T] (used about a lot of people) to fill an area: *Groups of tourists crowded the main streets.* ♦ (*figurative*) *Memories crowded her mind.*

PHR V crowd around/round (sb) (used about a lot of people) to stand in a large group around sb/sth: *Fans crowded round the singer hoping to get his autograph.*

crowd into sth; crowd in to go into a small place and make it very full: *Somehow we all crowded into their small living room.*

crowd sb/sth into sth; crowd sb/sth in to put a lot of people into a small place: *Ten prisoners were crowded into one small cell.*

crowd sth out; crowd sb out (of sth) to completely fill a place so that nobody else can enter: *Students crowd out the cafe at lunchtimes.* ♦ *Smaller companies are being crowded out of the market.*

crowded /ˈkraʊdɪd/ *adj* full of people: *a crowded bus* ♦ *people living in poor and crowded conditions*

crown¹ /kraʊn/ *noun* **1** [C] a circle made of gold and **jewels** (= valuable stones), that a king or queen wears on his or her head on official occasions **2 the Crown** [sing] the state as represented by a king or queen: *an area of land belonging to the Crown* **3** [sing] the top of your head or of a hat ➲ picture at **hat 4** [sing] the top of a hill

crown² /kraʊn/ *verb* [T] **1** to put a crown on the head of a new king or queen in an official ceremony: *Elizabeth was crowned in 1953.* ♦ (*figurative*) *the newly crowned British champion*

MORE The ceremony at which someone is made king or queen is called a **coronation.**

2 [often passive] crown sth (with sth) to have or put sth on the top of sth: *The mountain was crowned with snow.* ♦ (*figurative*) *Her years of hard work were finally crowned with success.*

crowning /ˈkraʊnɪŋ/ *adj* [only *before* a noun] the best or most important: *Winning the World Championship was the crowning moment of her career.*

crucial /ˈkruːʃl/ *adj* crucial (to/for sth) extremely important: *Early diagnosis of the illness is crucial for successful treatment.* **SYN** **vital** ▸ **crucially** /-ʃəli/ *adv*

crucifix /ˈkruːsəfɪks/ *noun* [C] a small model of a cross with a figure of Jesus on it

crucifixion /ˌkruːsəˈfɪkʃn/ *noun* [C,U] the act of killing sb by fastening them to a cross: *the Crucifixion of Christ*

crucify /ˈkruːsɪfaɪ/ *verb* [T] (crucifying; crucifies; *pt, pp* crucified) to kill sb by fastening them to a cross

crude /kruːd/ *adj* (cruder; crudest) **1** simple and basic, without much detail, skill, etc: *The method was crude but very effective.* ♦ *She explained how the system worked* ***in crude terms.*** **2** referring to sex or the body in a way that would offend many people: *He's always telling crude jokes.* **3** in its natural state, before it has been treated with chemicals: *crude oil* ▸ **crudely** *adv*: *a crudely drawn face*

cruel /kruːəl/ *adj* (crueller; cruellest) causing physical or mental pain or suffering to sb/sth: *I think it's cruel to keep animals in cages.* ♦ *a cruel punishment* **OPP** **kind** ▸ **cruelly** /ˈkruːəli/ *adv*

cruelty /ˈkruːəlti/ *noun* (*pl* cruelties) **1** [U] cruelty (to sb/sth) cruel behaviour: *cruelty to children* **OPP** **kindness** **2** [C, usually pl] a cruel act: *the cruelties of war*

cruise¹ /kruːz/ *noun* [C] a holiday in which you travel on a ship and visit a number of different places: *They're planning to* ***go on a cruise.***

cruise² /kruːz/ *verb* [I] **1** to travel by boat, visiting a number of places, as a holiday: *to cruise around the Caribbean* ➲ note at **holiday, journey** **2** to stay at the same speed in a car, plane, etc: *cruising at 80 kilometres an hour*

cruiser /ˈkruːzə(r)/ *noun* [C] **1** a large fast ship used in a war **2** a motorboat which has room for people to sleep in it

crumb /krʌm/ *noun* [C] a very small piece of bread, cake or biscuit

crumble /ˈkrʌmbl/ *verb* [I,T] crumble (sth) (up) to break or make sth break into very small pieces: *The walls of the church are beginning to crumble.* ♦ *We crumbled up the bread and threw it to the birds.* ♦ (*figurative*) *Support for the government is beginning to crumble.* ▸ **crumbly** /ˈkrʌmbli/ *adj*: *This cheese has a crumbly texture.*

crumple /ˈkrʌmpl/ *verb* [I,T] crumple (sth) (into sth); crumple (sth) (up) to be pressed or to press sth into an untidy shape: *The front of the car crumpled when it hit the wall.* ♦ *She crumpled the letter into a ball and threw it away.* ➲ picture at **crinkle, squeeze**

crunch¹ /krʌntʃ/ *noun* [sing] an act or the noise of **crunching**: *the crunch of feet on gravel*

IDM **if/when it comes to the crunch** if/when you are in a difficult situation and must make a difficult decision: *If it comes to the crunch, I'll stay and fight.*

crunch² /krʌntʃ/ *verb* **1** [T] crunch sth (up) to make a loud noise when you are eating sth hard: *to crunch an apple* **2** [I] to make a loud noise like the sound of sth being crushed: *We crunched through the snow.* ▸ **crunchy** *adj*: *a crunchy apple*

crusade /kruːˈseɪd/ *noun* [C] **1** a fight for sth that you believe to be good or against sth that you believe to be bad: *a crusade for justice* ♦ *a crusade against drugs* **SYN** **campaign** **2** Crusade one of the wars fought in Palestine by European Christians against Muslims in the Middle Ages ▸ **crusader** *noun* [C]

crush¹ /krʌʃ/ *verb* [T] **1** to press sb/sth hard so that he/she/it is broken, damaged or injured: *She sat on my hat and crushed it.* ♦ *He was crushed to death by a lorry.* **2** crush sth (up) to break sth into very small pieces or a powder: *Crush the garlic and fry in oil.* ➲ picture at **squeeze** **3** to defeat sb/sth completely: *The army was quickly sent in to crush the rebellion.*

crush² /krʌʃ/ *noun* **1** [sing] a large group of people in a small space: *There was such a crush that I couldn't get near the bar.* **2** [C] (*informal*) a crush (on sb) a strong feeling of love for sb that only usually lasts for a short time: *Maria* ***had a huge crush*** *on her teacher.*

crushing /ˈkrʌʃɪŋ/ *adj* [only *before* a noun] that defeats sb/sth completely; very bad: *a crushing defeat*

crust /krʌst/ *noun* [C,U] **1** the hard part on the outside of a piece of bread, a **pie** (= a type of baked food), etc. **2** a hard layer on the outside of sth: *the earth's crust*

crustacean /krʌˈsteɪʃn/ *noun* [C] (*technical*) a creature with a hard shell and a soft body that is divided into sections, such as a **crab, lobster** or **shrimp.** Most **crustaceans** live in water. ➲ look at **shellfish**

crusty /ˈkrʌsti/ *adj* (crustier; crustiest) **1** (used about food) having a hard part on the outside: *crusty bread* **2** (*informal*) bad-tempered and impatient: *a crusty old man*

crutch /krʌtʃ/ *noun* [C] **1** a type of stick that you put under your arm to help you walk when you have hurt your leg or foot: *She was* ***on crutches*** *for two months after she broke her ankle.* ➲ look at **walking stick** ➲ picture at **plaster** **2** = **crotch**

crux /krʌks/ *noun* [sing] the most important or difficult part of a problem: ***The crux of the matter*** *is how to stop this from happening again.*

cry¹ /kraɪ/ *verb* (crying; cries; *pt, pp* cried) **1** [I] to make a noise and produce tears in your eyes, for example because you are unhappy or have hurt

yourself: *The baby never stops crying.* ◆ *The child was crying for* (= because she wanted) *her mother.* ◆ *'It's all right. Don't cry.'* **2** [I,T] cry (out) to shout or make a loud noise: *We could hear someone crying for help.* ◆ *'Look,' he cried, 'There they are.'*
IDM **cry your eyes out** to cry a lot for a long time
a shoulder to cry on ➲ **shoulder**[1]
PHR V **cry out for sth** to need sth very much: *Birmingham is crying out for a new transport system.*

cry[2] /kraɪ/ *noun* (*pl* cries) **1** [C] a shout or loud high noise: *the cries of the children in the playground* ◆ *We heard Adam give a cry of pain as the dog bit him.* ◆ (*figurative*) *Her suicide attempt was really **a cry for help**.* **2** [sing] an act of crying: *After a good cry I felt much better.*
IDM **a far cry from sth/from doing sth** ➲ **far**[1]
hue and cry ➲ **hue**

crying /ˈkraɪɪŋ/ *adj* [only *before* a noun] (used to talk about a bad situation) very great: *There's a crying need for more doctors.* ◆ *It's **a crying shame** that so many young people can't find jobs.*

crypt /krɪpt/ *noun* [C] a room that is under a church, where people were sometimes buried in the past

cryptic /ˈkrɪptɪk/ *adj* having a hidden meaning that is not easy to understand: *a cryptic message/remark/smile* SYN **mysterious** ▶ **cryptically** /-kli/ *adv*

crystal /ˈkrɪstl/ *noun* **1** [C] a regular shape that some mineral substances form when they become solid: *salt crystals* **2** [U] a clear mineral that can be used in making jewellery **3** [U] glass of very high quality: *a crystal vase*

ˌcrystal ˈball *noun* [C] a glass ball in which some people say you can see what will happen in the future

ˌcrystal ˈclear *adj* **1** (used about water, glass, etc.) that you can see through perfectly **2** very easy to understand: *The meaning is crystal clear.*

crystallize (also -ise) /ˈkrɪstəlaɪz/ *verb* [I,T] **1** (used about thoughts, plans, etc.) to become or to make clear and fixed: *Our ideas began to crystallize into a definite plan.* ◆ *The final chapter crystallizes all the main issues.* **2** (*technical*) to form or to make sth form into **crystals**: *The salt crystallizes as the water evaporates.*

ct *abbr* = **cent**

cu. *abbr* = **cubic**: *a volume of 3 cu. ft*

cub /kʌb/ *noun* **1** [C] a young animal, for example a bear, lion, etc. ➲ note at **fox** ➲ picture at **lion** **2 the Cubs** [pl] the part of the Boy Scout organization that is for younger boys **3 Cub** (also **Cub ˈScout**) [C] a member of the **Cubs**

cube[1] /kjuːb/ *noun* [C] **1** a solid shape that has six equal square sides **2** the number that you get if you multiply a number by itself twice: *The cube of 5* (5^3) *is 125* (= 5 x 5 x 5).

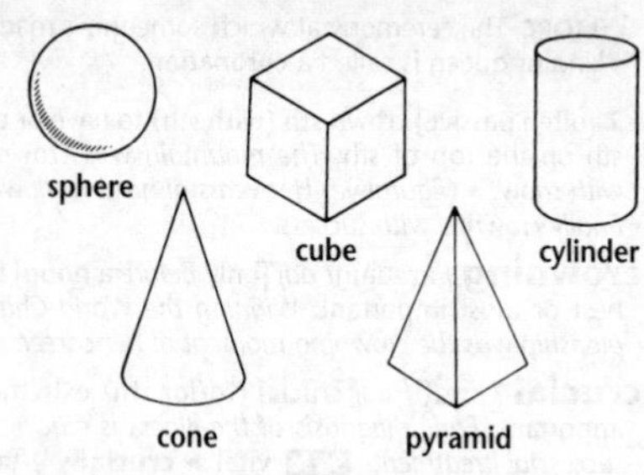

cube[2] /kjuːb/ *verb* [T, usually passive] to multiply a number by itself twice: *Four cubed* (4^3) *is 64* (= 4 x 4 x 4).

cubic /ˈkjuːbɪk/ *adj* [only *before* a noun] (*abbr* cu.) used to show that a measurement is the **volume** (= the amount of space that sth contains or fills) of sth, that is the height multiplied by the length and the width: *If a box is 4cm long, 4cm wide and 4cm high, its volume is 64 cubic centimetres.* ◆ *The lake holds more than a million cubic metres of water.*

cubicle /ˈkjuːbɪkl/ *noun* [C] a small room that is made by separating off part of a larger room: *There are cubicles at the swimming pool for changing your clothes.*

Cub ˈScout = **cub**(3)

cuckoo /ˈkʊkuː/ *noun* [C] (*pl* cuckoos) a bird which makes a sound like its name and which leaves its eggs in another bird's nest

cucumber /ˈkjuːkʌmbə(r)/ *noun* [C,U] a long, thin vegetable with a dark green skin that does not need to be cooked ➲ picture on **page P15**

cuddle /ˈkʌdl/ *verb* [I,T] to hold sb/sth closely in your arms: *The little girl was cuddling her favourite doll.*
PHR V **cuddle up (to/against sb/sth); cuddle up (together)** to move close to sb and sit or lie in a comfortable position: *They cuddled up together for warmth.*
▶ **cuddle** *noun* [C]: *He **gave** the child **a cuddle** and kissed her goodnight.*

cuddly /ˈkʌdli/ *adj* (cuddlier; cuddliest) soft and pleasant to hold close to you: *a cuddly toy*

cue /kjuː/ *noun* [C] **1** a word or movement that is the signal for sb else to say or do sth, especially in a play: *When Julia puts the tray on the table, that's your cue to come on stage.* **2** a long, thin wooden stick used to hit the ball in the games of **snooker, billiards** or **pool** (= similar games where players try to hit balls into pockets around a special table) ➲ picture at **pool**
IDM **(right) on cue** at exactly the moment expected: *Just as I was starting to worry about Stan, he phoned right on cue.*
take your cue from sb/sth to copy what sb/sth else does as an example of how to behave: *I'm not sure how to behave at a Japanese wedding, so I'll **take** my **cue from** the hosts.*

cuff /kʌf/ *noun* [C] **1** the end part of a sleeve, which often fastens at the wrist ➲ picture on **page P1**

2 cuffs [pl] = **handcuffs** **3** a light hit with the open hand

IDM **off the cuff** (used about sth you say) without thought or preparation before that moment: *I haven't got the figures here, but, off the cuff, I'd say the rise is about 10%.*

cufflink /ˈkʌflɪŋk/ *noun* [C, usually pl] one of a pair of small objects used instead of a button to fasten a shirt sleeve together at the wrist

cuisine /kwɪˈziːn/ *noun* [U] the style of cooking of a particular country, restaurant, etc: *Italian cuisine*

cul-de-sac /ˈkʌl də sæk/ *noun* [C] (*pl* cul-de-sacs) a street that is closed at one end

culinary /ˈkʌlɪnəri/ *adj* [only *before* a noun] (*formal*) connected with cooking

cull[1] /kʌl/ *verb* [T] to kill a number of animals in a group to prevent the group from becoming too large

PHR V **cull sth from sth** to collect information, ideas, etc., from different places: *I managed to cull some useful addresses from the Internet.*

cull[2] /kʌl/ *noun* [C] the act of killing some animals in order to stop a group becoming too large: *a deer cull*

culminate /ˈkʌlmɪneɪt/ *verb* [I] (*formal*) culminate in sth to reach a final result: *The team's efforts culminated in victory in the championships.* ▶ **culmination** /ˌkʌlmɪˈneɪʃn/ *noun* [sing]: *The joint space mission was the culmination of years of research.*

culpable /ˈkʌlpəbl/ *adj* (*formal*) responsible for sth bad that has happened

culprit /ˈkʌlprɪt/ *noun* [C] a person who has done sth wrong

cult /kʌlt/ *noun* [C] **1** a person or thing that has become popular with a particular group of people: *cult movies* **2** a type of religion or religious group, especially one that is considered unusual

cultivate /ˈkʌltɪveɪt/ *verb* [T] **1** to prepare and use land for growing plants for food or to sell: *to cultivate the soil* **2** to grow plants for food or to sell: *Olives have been cultivated for centuries in Mediterranean countries.* **3** to try to develop a friendship with sb: *He cultivated links with colleagues abroad.* ▶ **cultivation** /ˌkʌltɪˈveɪʃn/ *noun* [U]

cultivated /ˈkʌltɪveɪtɪd/ *adj* **1** well educated, with good manners **2** (used about land) used for growing plants for food or to sell **3** (used about plants) grown on a farm, not wild

cultural /ˈkʌltʃərəl/ *adj* **1** connected with the customs, ideas, beliefs, etc. of a society or country: *The country's cultural diversity is a result of taking in immigrants from all over the world.* ➲ look at **multicultural** **2** connected with art, music, literature, etc: *The city has a rich cultural life, with many theatres, concert halls and art galleries.* ▶ **culturally** /-rəli/ *adv*

culture /ˈkʌltʃə(r)/ *noun* **1** [C,U] the customs, ideas, beliefs, etc. of a particular society, country, etc: *the language and culture of the Aztecs* ◆ *people from many different cultures* **2** [U] art, literature, music, etc: *London has always been a centre of culture.*

cultured /ˈkʌltʃəd/ *adj* well educated and showing a good knowledge of art, music, literature, etc.

ˈ**culture shock** *noun* [U] a feeling of confusion, etc. that you may have when you go to live in or visit a country that is very different from your own

cumbersome /ˈkʌmbəsəm/ *adj* **1** heavy and difficult to carry, use, wear, etc. **2** (used about a system, etc.) slow and complicated: *cumbersome legal procedures*

cumulative /ˈkjuːmjələtɪv/ *adj* increasing steadily in amount, degree, etc: *a cumulative effect*

cunning /ˈkʌnɪŋ/ *adj* clever in a dishonest or bad way: *He was as cunning as a fox.* ◆ *a cunning trick* **SYN** sly, wily ▶ **cunning** *noun* [U] ▶ **cunningly** *adv*

cups

cup and saucer **mug**

cup[1] /kʌp/ *noun* [C] **1** a small container usually with a handle, used for drinking liquids: *a teacup* ◆ *a cup of coffee* **2** an object shaped like a cup: *an eggcup* **3** (in sport) a large metal cup given as a prize; the competition for such a cup: *Our team won the cup in the basketball tournament.* ◆ *the World Cup* ➲ picture at **medal**

IDM **not sb's cup of tea** not what sb likes or is interested in: *Horror films aren't my cup of tea.*

cup[2] /kʌp/ *verb* [T] (cupping; cupped) to form sth, especially your hands, into the shape of a cup; to hold sth with your hands shaped like a cup: *I cupped my hands to take a drink from the stream.*

cupboard /ˈkʌbəd/ *noun* [C] a piece of furniture, usually with shelves inside and a door or doors at the front, used for storing food, clothes, etc: *a kitchen cupboard* ◆ *built-in cupboards* ➲ picture on **page P8**

cupful /ˈkʌpfʊl/ *noun* [C] the amount that a cup will hold: *two cupfuls of water*

curable /ˈkjʊərəbl/ *adj* (used about a disease) that can be made better **OPP** **incurable**

curate /ˈkjʊərət/ *noun* [C] (in the Church of England) an assistant to a priest

curator /kjʊəˈreɪtə(r)/ *noun* [C] a person whose job is to look after the things that are kept in a museum

curb[1] /kɜːb/ *verb* [T] to limit or control sth, especially sth bad: *He needs to learn to curb his anger.*

curb² /kɜːb/ *noun* [C] **1** a curb (on sth) a control or limit on sth: *a curb on local government spending* **2** (*especially AmE*) = **kerb**

curdle /ˈkɜːdl/ *verb* [I,T] (used about liquids) to turn sour or to separate into different parts; to make sth do this: *She heated the sauce for too long and it curdled.* ➲ look at **blood-curdling**

cure¹ /kjʊə(r)/ *verb* [T] **1** cure sb (of sth) to make sb healthy again after an illness: *The treatment cured him of cancer.* **2** to make an illness, injury, etc. end or disappear: *It is still not possible to cure the common cold.* ♦ (*figurative*) *The plumber cured the problem with the central heating.* **3** to make certain types of food last longer by drying them, or treating them with smoke or salt: *cured ham*

cure² /kjʊə(r)/ *noun* [C] a cure (for sth) **1** a medicine or treatment that can cure an illness, etc: *There is no cure for this illness.* **2** a return to good health; the process of being cured: *The new drug brought about a miraculous cure.*

curfew /ˈkɜːfjuː/ *noun* [C] **1** a time after which people are not allowed to go outside their homes, for example during a war: *The government imposed a dusk-to-dawn curfew.* **2** (*AmE*) a time when children must arrive home in the evening: *She has a 10 o'clock curfew.*

curiosity /ˌkjʊəriˈɒsəti/ *noun* (*pl* curiosities) **1** [U] a desire to know or learn: *I was full of curiosity about their plans.* ♦ ***Out of curiosity**, he opened her letter.* **2** [C] an unusual and interesting person or thing: *The museum was full of historical curiosities.*

curious /ˈkjʊəriəs/ *adj* **1** curious (about sth); curious (to do sth) wanting to know or learn sth: *They were very curious about the people who lived upstairs.* ♦ *He was curious to know how the machine worked.* **2** unusual or strange: *It was curious that she didn't tell anyone about the incident.* ▶ **curiously** *adv*

curl¹ /kɜːl/ *verb* **1** [I,T] to form or to make sth form into a curved or round shape: *Does your hair curl naturally?* **2** [I] to move round in a curve: *The snake curled around his arm.* ♦ *Smoke curled up into the sky.* PHR V **curl up** to pull your arms, legs and head close to your body: *The cat curled up in front of the fire.*

curl² /kɜːl/ *noun* [C] **1** a piece of hair that curves round: *Her hair fell in curls round her face.* **2** a thing that has a curved round shape: *a curl of blue smoke*

curler /ˈkɜːlə(r)/ *noun* [C] a small plastic or metal tube that you roll your hair around in order to make it curly

curly /ˈkɜːli/ *adj* (curlier; curliest) full of **curls**; shaped like a **curl**: *He's got curly hair.* ♦ *a dog with a curly tail* OPP **straight** ➲ picture at **hair**

currant /ˈkʌrənt/ *noun* [C] **1** a very small dried **grape** (= a small fruit that grows in bunches) used to make cakes, etc. **2** [in compounds] a small black, red or white fruit that grows in bunches on bushes: *blackcurrants*

currency /ˈkʌrənsi/ *noun* (*pl* currencies) **1** [C,U] the system or type of money that a particular country uses: *The currency of Argentina is the peso.* ♦ *foreign currency* ♦ *a weak/strong/stable currency* **2** [U] the state of being believed, accepted or used by many people: *The new ideas soon **gained currency**.*

current¹ /ˈkʌrənt/ *adj* **1** [only *before* a noun] of the present time; happening now: *current fashions/events* **2** generally accepted; in common use: *Is this word still current?*

current² /ˈkʌrənt/ *noun* **1** [C] a continuous flowing movement of water, air, etc: *to swim **against/with the current*** ♦ (*figurative*) *a current of anti-government feeling* **2** [C,U] the flow of electricity through a wire, etc: *Turn off the current before cleaning the machine.*

ˌcurrent acˈcount (*AmE* ˈchecking account) *noun* [C] a bank account that you can take money out of at any time, and that provides you with a cheque book and **cash card** (= a special card that is given to you by your bank) ➲ look at **deposit account**

ˌcurrent afˈfairs *noun* [pl] important political or social events that are happening at the present time

currently /ˈkʌrəntli/ *adv* at present; at the moment: *He is currently working in Spain.* ➲ note at **actually**

curriculum /kəˈrɪkjələm/ *noun* [C] (*pl* curriculums *or* curricula /-lə/) all the subjects that are taught in a school, college or university; the contents of a particular course of study: *Latin is not **on the curriculum** at our school.* ➲ look at **syllabus**

curriculum vitae /kəˌrɪkjələm ˈviːtaɪ/ = **CV**

curry /ˈkʌri/ *noun* [C,U] (*pl* curries) an Indian dish of meat, vegetables, etc. containing a lot of spices, usually served with rice: *a hot/mild curry* ▶ **curried** *adj*: *curried chicken*

ˈcurry powder *noun* [U] a fine mixture of strongly flavoured spices that is used to make **curry**

curse¹ /kɜːs/ *noun* [C] **1** a word used for expressing anger; a swear word **2** a word or words expressing a wish that sth terrible will happen to sb: *The family seemed to be under a curse* (= a lot of bad things happened to them). **3** something that causes great harm: *the curse of poverty*

curse² /kɜːs/ *verb* **1** [I,T] curse (sb/sth) (for sth) to swear at sb/sth; to use rude language to express your anger: *He dropped the box, cursing himself for his clumsiness.* **2** [T] to use a magic word or phrase against sb because you wish them harm: *She cursed his family.*

cursor /ˈkɜːsə(r)/ *noun* [C] a small sign on a computer screen that shows the position you are at

cursory /ˈkɜːsəri/ *adj* quick and short; done in a hurry: *a cursory glance*

curt /kɜːt/ *adj* short and not polite: *She gave him a curt reply and slammed the phone down.* ▶ **curtly** *adv* ▶ **curtness** *noun* [U]

curtail /kɜːˈteɪl/ *verb* [T] (*formal*) to make sth shorter or smaller; to reduce sth: *I had to curtail my* answer as I was running out of time. ▶ **curtailment** noun [C,U]

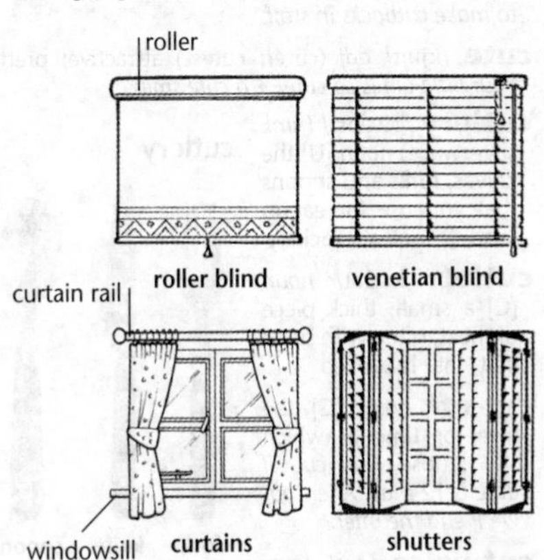

curtain /ˈkɜːtn/ noun [C] **1** (AmE also **drape**) a piece of cloth that you can move to cover a window, etc: *Could you* ***draw the curtains****, please?* (= Could you open/close the curtains?) ◆ *a pair of curtains* ◆ *lace curtains* ◆ *a shower curtain* ◆ *The curtain goes up at 7pm* (= in a theatre, the play begins). **2** a thing that covers or hides sth: *a curtain of mist*

curtsy (also curtsey) /ˈkɜːtsi/ noun [C] (pl curtsies or curtseys) a movement made by a woman as a sign of respect, done by bending the knees, with one foot behind the other ▶ **curtsy** (also curtsey) verb [I]: *She curtsied to the Queen.*

curve[1] /kɜːv/ noun [C] a line that bends round: *a curve on a graph* ◆ *a pattern of straight lines and curves* ➲ picture at **line**

curve[2] /kɜːv/ verb [I,T] to bend or to make sth bend in a curve: *The bay curved round to the south.* ▶ **curved** adj: *a curved blade* ➲ picture at **line**

cushion[1] /ˈkʊʃn/ noun [C] **1** a bag filled with soft material, for example feathers, which you put on a chair, etc. to make it more comfortable ➲ picture on **page P8**

MORE A cushion on a bed is a **pillow**.

2 something that acts or is shaped like a **cushion**: *A hovercraft rides on a cushion of air.* ➲ picture at **pool**

cushion[2] /ˈkʊʃn/ verb [T] **1** to make a fall, hit, etc. less painful: *The snow cushioned his fall.* **2** to reduce the unpleasant effect of sth: *She spent her childhood on a farm, cushioned from the effects of the war.*

cushy /ˈkʊʃi/ adj (cushier; cushiest) (informal) too easy, needing little effort (in a way that seems unfair to others): *a cushy job*

custard /ˈkʌstəd/ noun [U] a sweet yellow sauce made from milk, eggs and sugar. In Britain it is eaten hot or cold with sweet dishes: *apple pie and custard*

custodian /kʌˈstəʊdiən/ noun [C] **1** (formal) a person who looks after or protects sth, such as a museum, library, etc. **2** (AmE) = **caretaker**

custody /ˈkʌstədi/ noun [U] **1** the legal right or duty to take care of sb/sth: *After the divorce, the mother* ***had custody of*** *the children.* **2** the state of being guarded, or kept in prison temporarily, especially by the police: *The man was* ***kept in custody*** *until his trial.*

custom /ˈkʌstəm/ noun **1** [C,U] a way of behaving which a particular group or society has had for a long time: *It's the custom in Britain for a bride to throw her bouquet to the wedding guests.* ◆ *according to* ***local custom*** ➲ note at **habit** **2** [sing] (formal) something that a person does regularly: *It was her custom to rise early in the morning.* **3** [U] (BrE) commercial activity; the practice of people buying things regularly from a particular shop, etc: *The local shop lost a lot of custom when the new supermarket opened.* ➲ look at **customs**

customary /ˈkʌstəməri/ adj according to custom; usual: *Is it customary to send cards at Christmas in your country?*

customer /ˈkʌstəmə(r)/ noun [C] **1** a person who buys goods or services in a shop, restaurant, etc: *a regular customer* ◆ *The shop assistant was serving a customer.* ➲ note at **client** **2** (informal, old-fashioned) [after certain adjectives] a person: *a tough/an awkward/an odd customer*

customs (also Customs) /ˈkʌstəmz/ noun [pl] **1** the government department that collects taxes paid on goods from other countries: *a customs officer* **2** the place at a port or an airport where your bags are checked to make sure you are not bringing goods into the country illegally: *to go through customs and passport control* ➲ look at **excise**

cut[1] /kʌt/ verb (cutting; pt, pp cut)

➤HOLE **1** [I,T] to make an opening, a wound or a mark in sth using a sharp tool, for example a pair of scissors or a knife: *Be careful not to cut yourself on that broken glass!* ◆ *This knife doesn't cut very well.*

➤REMOVE **2** [T] cut sth (from sth) to remove sth or a part of sth, using a knife, etc: *She cut two slices of bread (from the loaf).*

➤DIVIDE **3** [T] cut sth (in/into sth) to divide sth into pieces with a knife, etc: *She cut the cake into eight (pieces).* ◆ *He cut the rope in two.*

➤MAKE SHORTER **4** [T] to make sth shorter by using scissors, etc: *I cut my own hair.* ◆ *to have your hair cut* (= at the hairdresser's) ◆ *to cut the grass*

➤SHAPE/FORM **5** [T] to make or form sth by removing material with a sharp tool: *She cut a hole in the card and pushed the string through.* ◆ *They cut a path through the jungle.*

➤REDUCE/REMOVE **6** [T] to reduce sth or make it shorter; to remove sth: *to cut taxes/costs/spending* ◆ *Several violent scenes in the film were cut.*

➤COMPUTING **7** [T] to remove a piece of text from the screen: *Use the* ***cut and paste*** *buttons to change the order of the paragraphs.*

➤GO ACROSS **8** [I] cut across, along, through, etc. (sth) to go across, etc. sth, in order to make your route shorter: *It's much quicker if we cut across the field.*

C

›STOP **9** [T] (*spoken*) to stop sth: *Cut the chat and get on with your work!*

›UPSET **10** [T] to deeply offend sb or hurt their feelings: *His cruel remarks cut her deeply.* ℹ For idioms containing **cut**, look at the entries for the nouns, adjectives, etc. For example **cut corners** is at **corner**.

PHR V **be cut out for sth; be cut out to be sth** to have the qualities needed to do sth; to be suitable for sth/sb: *You're not cut out to be a teacher.*

cut across sth to affect or be true for different groups that usually remain separate: *The question of aid for the earthquake victims cuts across national boundaries.*

cut sth back; cut back (on sth) to reduce sth: *to cut back on public spending*

cut sth down 1 to make sth fall down by cutting it: *to cut down a tree* **2** to make sth shorter: *I have to cut my essay down to 2000 words.*

cut sth down; cut down (on sth) to reduce the quantity or amount of sth; to do sth less often: *You should cut down on fatty foods.*

cut in (on sb/sth) to interrupt sb/sth: *She kept cutting in on our conversation.*

cut sb off [often passive] to stop or interrupt sb's telephone conversation: *We were cut off before I could give her my message.*

cut sb/sth off [often passive] to stop the supply of sth to sb: *The electricity/gas/water has been cut off.*

cut sth off to block a road, etc. so that nothing can pass: *We must cut off all possible escape routes.*

cut sth off (sth) to remove sth from sth larger by cutting: *Be careful you don't cut your fingers off using that electric saw.*

cut sb/sth off (from sb/sth) [often passive] to prevent sb/sth from moving from a place or contacting people outside: *The farm was cut off from the village by heavy snow.*

cut sth open to open sth by cutting: *She fell and cut her head open.*

cut sth out 1 to remove sth or to form sth into a particular shape by cutting: *He cut the job advertisement out of the newspaper.* **2** to not include sth: *Cut out all the boring details!* **3** (*especially AmE informal*) to stop saying or doing sth that annoys sb: *Cut that out and leave me alone!* **4** (*informal*) to stop doing or using sth: *You'll only lose weight if you cut out sweet things from your diet.*

cut sth up to cut sth into small pieces with a knife, etc: *He cut up the meat on his plate.*

cut[2] /kʌt/ *noun* [C]

›INJURY **1** an injury or opening in the skin made with a knife, etc: *He had a deep cut on his forehead.*

›OF HAIR **2** an act of cutting: *to have a cut and blow-dry* (= at the hairdresser's)

›REDUCTION **3** a cut (in sth) a reduction in size, amount, etc: *a cut in government spending* ◆ *a power cut* (= when the electric current is stopped temporarily)

›MONEY **4** (*informal*) a share of the profits from sth, especially sth dishonest: *They were rewarded with a cut of 5% from the profits.*

›MEAT **5** a piece of meat from a particular part of an animal: *cheap cuts of lamb* ➲ look at **short cut**

cutback /ˈkʌtbæk/ *noun* [C] a reduction in amount or number: *The management were forced to make cutbacks in staff.*

cute /kjuːt/ *adj* (cuter; cutest) attractive; pretty: *Your little girl is so cute!* ◆ *a cute smile*

cutlery /ˈkʌtləri/ (*AmE* silverware) *noun* [U] the knives, forks and spoons that you use for eating food ➲ look at **crockery**

cutlet /ˈkʌtlət/ *noun* [C] a small, thick piece of meat, often with bone in it, that is cooked

ˈcut-off *noun* [C] the level or time at which sth stops: *The cut-off date is 12 May. After that we'll end the offer.*

ˈcut-price (*AmE* ˈcut-rate) *adj* [only *before* a noun] sold at a reduced price; selling goods at low prices: *cut-price offers* ◆ *a cut-price store*

cutters /ˈkʌtəz/ *noun* [pl] a tool that you use for cutting through sth, for example metal: *a pair of wire cutters*

ˈcut-throat *adj* caring only about success and not worried about hurting anyone: *cut-throat business practices*

cutting[1] /ˈkʌtɪŋ/ *noun* [C] **1** (*AmE* clipping) a piece cut out from a newspaper, etc: *press cuttings* **2** a piece cut off from a plant that you use for growing a new plant

cutting[2] /ˈkʌtɪŋ/ *adj* (used about sth you say) unkind; meant to hurt sb's feelings: *a cutting remark*

cutting ˈedge *noun* [sing] **1** the cutting edge (of sth) the newest, most advanced stage in the development of sth: *working at the cutting edge of computer technology* **2** an aspect of sth that gives it an advantage: *We're relying on him to give the team a cutting edge.*

CV /ˌsiː ˈviː/ (*AmE* résumé) *noun* [C] **curriculum vitae**; a formal list of your education and work experience, often used when you are trying to get a new job ➲ note at **job**

cwt. *abbr* = **hundredweight**

cyanide /ˈsaɪənaɪd/ *noun* [U] a poisonous chemical

cyberbully /ˈsaɪbəbʊli/ *noun* [C] (*pl* cyberbullies) a person who uses the Internet to threaten and frighten sb else with unpleasant messages ➲ look at **bully** ▶ **cyberbullying** *noun* [U]

cybercafe /ˈsaɪbəkæfeɪ/ *noun* [C] a place with computers where customers can pay to use the Internet ➲ note at **Internet**

cybercrime /ˈsaɪbəkraɪm/ *noun* [U,C] crime that is committed using the Internet, for example by stealing sb's bank details or sending a virus to sb's computer

TOPIC

Cybercrime

Be careful when you **download** (= copy) **a file**, as it may **contain a virus**. It is important that you install **antivirus software** (= a program that finds and destroys viruses) and a **firewall** (= a program that prevents people from making changes to your computer without your permission). Your **email account** should have **a filter** to stop any **junk emails/spam** reaching your inbox. There is also the danger of **phishing**. This is when criminals send emails to try to make you give them information that will allow them to steal money from you.

cyberspace /ˈsaɪbəspeɪs/ *noun* [U] a place that is not real, where electronic messages exist while they are being sent from one computer to another

cycle¹ /ˈsaɪkl/ *noun* [C] **1** a bicycle or motorbike: *a cycle shop* SYN **bike** **2** a series of events, etc. that happen again and again in the same order: *the life cycle of a frog*

cycle² /ˈsaɪkl/ *verb* [I] to ride a bicycle: *Leonie usually cycles to work.*

HELP **Go cycling** is a common way of talking about cycling for pleasure: *We go cycling most weekends.*

cyclic /ˈsaɪklɪk/ (also **cyclical** /ˈsɪklɪkl/) *adj* following a repeated pattern

cyclist /ˈsaɪklɪst/ *noun* [C] a person who rides a bicycle

cyclone /ˈsaɪkləʊn/ *noun* [C] a large, violent storm in which strong winds move in a circle ➲ note at **storm**

cygnet /ˈsɪɡnət/ *noun* [C] a young **swan** (= a large white bird with a long neck)

cylinder /ˈsɪlɪndə(r)/ *noun* [C] **1** an object shaped like a tube ➲ picture at **cube** **2** a part of an engine shaped like a tube, for example in a car ▸ **cylindrical** /səˈlɪndrɪkl/ *adj*

cymbal /ˈsɪmbl/ *noun* [C, usually pl] one of a pair of round metal plates used as a musical instrument. **Cymbals** make a loud ringing sound when you hit them together or with a stick. ➲ picture at **music**

cynic /ˈsɪnɪk/ *noun* [C] a person who believes that people only do things for themselves, rather than to help others: *Don't be such a cynic. He did it to help us, not for the money.* ▸ **cynical** /-kl/ *adj*: *a cynical remark* ▸ **cynically** /-kli/ *adv* ▸ **cynicism** /ˈsɪnɪsɪzem/ *noun* [U]

Cyrillic /səˈrɪlɪk/ *noun* [U] the alphabet that is used in languages such as Russian

cyst /sɪst/ *noun* [C] a swelling or a lump filled with liquid in the body or under the skin

czar, czarina = **tsar, tsarina**

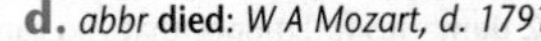

D, d /diː/ *noun* [C,U] (*pl* **Ds; D's; d's** /diːz/) **1** the fourth letter of the English alphabet: *'December' begins with (a) 'D'.* **2 D** (used about music) the second note in the scale of C major: *D major/minor* ◆ *D flat/sharp*

d. *abbr* **died**: *W A Mozart, d. 1791*

dab¹ /dæb/ *verb* [I,T] (**dabbing; dabbed**) to touch sth lightly, usually several times: *He dabbed the cut with some cotton wool.*

PHR V **dab sth on/off (sth)** to put sth on or to remove sth lightly: *to dab some antiseptic on a wound*

dab² /dæb/ *noun* [C] **1** a small quantity of sth that is put on a surface: *a dab of paint/perfume* **2** a light touch: *She gave her eyes a dab with a handkerchief.*

dabble /ˈdæbl/ *verb* **1** [I] to become involved in sth in a way that is not very serious: *to dabble in politics* **2** [T] to put your hands, feet, etc. in water and move them around: *We sat on the bank and dabbled our toes in the river.*

dad /dæd/ *noun* [C] (*informal*) father: *Is that your dad?* ◆ *Come on, Dad!*

daddy /ˈdædi/ *noun* [C] (*pl* **daddies**) (*informal*) (used by children) father: *I want my daddy!*

daffodil /ˈdæfədɪl/ *noun* [C] a tall yellow flower that grows in the spring

daft /dɑːft/ *adj* (**dafter; daftest**) (*informal*) silly: *Don't be daft.* ◆ *a daft idea*

dagger /ˈdæɡə(r)/ *noun* [C] a type of knife used as a weapon, especially in past times ➲ picture at **sword**

daily¹ /ˈdeɪli/ *adj* [only *before* a noun] *adv* done, made or happening every day: *a daily routine/delivery/newspaper* ◆ *Our airline flies to Japan daily.* ➲ note at **routine**

daily² /ˈdeɪli/ *noun* [C] (*pl* **dailies**) (*informal*) a newspaper that is published every day except Sunday

dainty /ˈdeɪnti/ *adj* (**daintier; daintiest**) **1** small and pretty: *a dainty lace handkerchief* **2** (used about sb's movements) very careful in a way that tries to show good manners: *Veronica took a dainty bite of her cucumber sandwich.* ▸ **daintily** *adv*

dairy¹ /ˈdeəri/ *noun* [C] (*pl* **dairies**) **1** a place on a farm where milk is kept and butter, cheese, etc. are made **2** a company which sells milk, butter, eggs, etc.

dairy² /ˈdeəri/ *adj* [only *before* a noun] **1** made from milk: *dairy products/produce* (= milk, butter, cheese, etc.) **2** connected with the production of milk: *dairy cattle* ◆ *a dairy farm*

D

daisy /ˈdeɪzi/ *noun* [C] (*pl* **daisies**) a small white flower with a yellow centre, which usually grows wild in grass

dam /dæm/ *noun* [C] a wall built across a river to hold back the water and form a **reservoir** (= a lake) behind it ▶ **dam** *verb* [T] (**damming**; **dammed**)

D

damage¹ /ˈdæmɪdʒ/ *noun* **1** [U] **damage (to sth)** harm or injury caused when sth is broken or spoiled: *Earthquakes can* **cause** *terrible* **damage** *in urban areas.* ◆ *It will take weeks to* **repair the damage** *done by the vandals.* **2 damages** [pl] money that you can ask for if sb damages sth of yours or hurts you: *Mrs Rees, who lost a leg in the crash, was awarded damages of £100000.*

damage² /ˈdæmɪdʒ/ *verb* [T] to spoil or harm sth, for example by breaking it: *The roof was damaged by the storm.* ▶ **damaging** *adj*: *These rumours could be damaging to her reputation.*

dame /deɪm/ *noun* **Dame** [C] (*BrE*) a title given to a woman as an honour because of sth special that she has done: *Dame Agatha Christie*

damn¹ /dæm/ (also **damned** /dæmd/) *adj, adv* (*slang*) **1** a swear word that people use to show that they are angry: *Some damn fool has parked too close to me.* **2** (a swear word that people use for emphasizing what they are saying) very: *Read it! It's a damn good book.*

damn² /dæm/ *verb* [I,T] (*slang*) a swear word that people use to show that they are angry: *Damn (it)! I've left my money behind.*

damn³ /dæm/ *noun*

IDM not care/give a damn (about sb/sth) (*slang*) not care at all: *I don't give a damn what he thinks about me.*

damning /ˈdæmɪŋ/ *adj* that criticizes sth very much: *There was a damning article about the book in the newspaper.*

damp¹ /dæmp/ *adj* (**damper**; **dampest**) a little wet: *The house had been empty and felt rather damp.* ▶ **damp** *noun* [U]: *She hated the damp and the cold of the English climate.* ➲ note at **wet**

damp² /dæmp/ *verb* [T] **damp sth (down) 1** to make sth less strong or urgent: *He tried to damp down their expectations in case they failed.* **2** to make a fire burn less strongly or stop burning: *He tried to damp (down) the flames.*

dampen /ˈdæmpən/ *verb* [T] **1** to make sth a little wet: *He dampened his hair to try to stop it sticking up.* **2** to make sth less strong or urgent: *Even the awful weather did not dampen their enthusiasm for the trip.*

dance¹ /dɑːns/ *noun* **1** [C] a series of steps and movements which you do to music: *The only dance I can do is the tango.* **2** [U] dancing as a form of art or entertainment: *She's very interested in modern dance.* **3** [C] (*old-fashioned*) a social meeting at which people dance with each other: *My parents met at a dance.*

dance² /dɑːns/ *verb* **1** [I,T] to move around to the rhythm of music by making a series of steps: *I can't dance very well.* ◆ *to dance the samba* **2** [I] to jump and move around with energy: *She was dancing up and down with excitement.*

dancer /ˈdɑːnsə(r)/ *noun* [C] a person who dances, often as a job: *a ballet dancer* ◆ *She's a good dancer.* ➲ picture at **ballet**

dancing /ˈdɑːnsɪŋ/ *noun* [U] the act of moving to music: *I'm hopeless at dancing—I've got no sense of rhythm.* ◆ *Will there be dancing at the party?*

dandelion /ˈdændɪlaɪən/ *noun* [C] a small wild plant with a bright yellow flower

dandruff /ˈdændrʌf/ *noun* [U] small pieces of dead skin in the hair, that look like white powder

danger /ˈdeɪndʒə(r)/ *noun* **1** [U,C] the chance that sb/sth may be hurt, killed or damaged or that sth bad may happen: *When he saw the men had knives, he realized his life was* **in danger**. ◆ *The men kept on running until they thought they were* **out of danger**. ◆ *If things carry on as they are,* **there's a danger that** *the factory may have to close.* **2** [C] **a danger (to sb/sth)** a person or thing that can cause injury, pain or damage to sb: *Drunk drivers are a danger to everyone on the road.*

dangerous /ˈdeɪndʒərəs/ *adj* likely to cause injury or damage: *a dangerous animal/road/illness* ◆ *Police warn that the man is highly dangerous.* ▶ **dangerously** *adv*: *He was standing dangerously close to the cliff edge.*

dangle /ˈdæŋɡl/ *verb* [I,T] to hang freely; to hold sth so that it hangs down in this way: *She sat on the fence with her legs dangling.* ◆ *The police dangled a rope from the bridge and the man grabbed it.*

dank /dæŋk/ *adj* wet, cold and unpleasant

dare¹ /deə(r)/ *verb* **1** [I] [usually in negative sentences] **dare (to) do sth** to have enough courage to do sth: *Nobody dared (to) speak.* ◆ *I daren't ask her to lend me any more money.* ◆ *We were so frightened that we didn't dare (to) go into the room.*

> **GRAMMAR** The negative is **dare not** (usually **daren't** /deənt/) or **do not/does not (= don't/doesn't) dare**. In the past tense it is **did not (didn't) dare**. In the present tense the negative is used without *to*: *I daren't move.*

2 [T] **dare sb (to do sth)** to ask or tell sb to do sth in order to see if they have the courage to do it: *Can you jump off that wall? Go on, I dare you!* ◆ *He dared his friend to put a mouse in the teacher's bag.*

IDM don't you dare used for telling sb very strongly not to do sth: *Don't you dare tell my parents about this!*

how dare you used when you are angry about sth that sb has done: *How dare you speak to me like that!*

I dare say used when you are saying sth is probable: *'I think you should accept the offer.' 'I dare say you're right.'*

dare² /deə(r)/ *noun* [C, usually sing] something dangerous that sb asks you to do, to see if you have the courage to do it: *'Why did you try to swim across the river?'* **'For a dare.'**

daredevil /ˈdeədevl/ *noun* [C] a person who likes to do dangerous things

daring /ˈdeərɪŋ/ *adj* involving or taking risks: *a daring attack* SYN **brave** ▶ **daring** *noun* [U]: *The climb required skill and daring.*

🔑 **dark**[1] /dɑːk/ *adj* (**darker**; **darkest**) **1** with no light or very little light: *It was a dark night, with no moon.* ◆ *What time does it* ***get dark*** *in winter?* **2** (used about a colour) not light; nearer black than white: *dark blue* OPP **light, pale** **3** (*especially BrE*) (used about sb's hair, skin or eyes) brown or black; not fair: *She was small and dark with brown eyes.* OPP **fair** ➲ look at **skin**[1](2) **4** [only *before* a noun] hidden and frightening: *He seemed friendly, but there was a dark side to his character.* SYN **mysterious** **5** [only *before* a noun] sad; without hope: *the dark days of the recession*

🔑 **dark**[2] /dɑːk/ *noun* **the dark** [sing] the state of having no light: *He's afraid of the dark.* ◆ *Why are you sitting alone* ***in the dark****?*
IDM **before/after dark** before/after the sun goes down in the evening
(be/keep sb) in the dark (about sth) (be/keep sb) in a position of not knowing about sth: *Don't keep me in the dark. Tell me!*

darken /ˈdɑːkən/ *verb* [I,T] to become or to make sth darker: *The sky suddenly darkened and it started to rain.*

ˌdark ˈglasses = **sunglasses**

darkly /ˈdɑːkli/ *adv* **1** in a threatening or an unpleasant way: *He hinted darkly that all was not well.* **2** showing a dark colour

darkness /ˈdɑːknəs/ *noun* [U] the state of being dark: *We sat* ***in total darkness****, waiting for the lights to come back on.*

darkroom /ˈdɑːkruːm; -rʊm/ *noun* [C] a room that can be made completely dark so that film can be taken out of a camera and photographs can be produced there

darling /ˈdɑːlɪŋ/ *noun* [C] a word that you say to sb you love

darn /dɑːn/ *verb* [I,T] to repair a hole in clothes by sewing across it in one direction and then in the other: *I hate darning socks.*

dart[1] /dɑːt/ *noun* **1** [C] an object like a small arrow. It is thrown in a game or shot as a weapon: *The keeper fired a tranquillizer dart into the tiger to send it to sleep.* **2** **darts** [U] a game in which you throw **darts** at a **dartboard**

dart[2] /dɑːt/ *verb* [I,T] to move or make sth move suddenly and quickly in a certain direction: *A rabbit darted across the field.* ◆ *She darted an angry glance at me.*

dartboard /ˈdɑːtbɔːd/ *noun* [C] a round board used in the game of **darts**

dash[1] /dæʃ/ *noun* **1** [sing] an act of going somewhere suddenly and quickly: *Suddenly the prisoner made a dash for the door.* **2** [C, usually sing] a small amount of sth that you add to sth else: *Add a dash of lemon juice.* **3** [C] a small horizontal line (–) used in writing, especially for adding extra information ➲ look at **hyphen**

dash[2] /dæʃ/ *verb* **1** [I] to go somewhere suddenly and quickly: *We all dashed for shelter when it started to rain.* ◆ *I must dash—I'm late.* **2** [I,T] to hit sth with great force; to throw sth so that it hits sth else very hard: *She dashed her racket to the ground.*
IDM **dash sb's hopes (of sth/of doing sth)** to completely destroy sb's hopes of doing sth: *The accident dashed his hopes of becoming a pianist.*
PHR V **dash sth off** to write or draw sth very quickly: *I dashed off a note to my boss and left.*

dashboard /ˈdæʃbɔːd/ *noun* [C] the part in a car in front of the driver where most of the switches, etc. are ➲ picture at **car**

🔑 **data** /ˈdeɪtə; ˈdɑːtə/ *noun* [U,pl] facts or information: *to gather/collect data* ◆ *data capture/retrieval* (= ways of storing and looking at information on a computer)

database /ˈdeɪtəbeɪs/ *noun* [C] a large amount of data that is stored in a computer and can easily be used, added to, etc.

🔑 **date**[1] /deɪt/ *noun* **1** [C] a particular day of the month or year: *What's the date today?/What date is it today?/What's today's date?* ◆ *What's your* ***date of birth****?* ◆ *We'd better* ***fix a date*** *for the next meeting.* **2** [sing] a particular time: *We can discuss this* ***at a later date****.* ➲ look at **sell-by date** **3** [C] an arrangement to meet sb, especially a boyfriend or girlfriend: *Shall we* ***make a date*** *to have lunch together?* ◆ *I've got a date with her on Friday night.* ➲ look at **blind date** **4** [C] a small, sweet, dark brown fruit that comes from a tree which grows in hot countries
IDM **out of date** **1** not fashionable; no longer useful: *out-of-date methods/machinery* **2** no longer able to be used: *I must renew my passport. It's out of date.*
to date (*formal*) until now: *We've had very few complaints to date.*
up to date **1** completely modern: *The new kitchen will be right up to date, with all the latest gadgets.* **2** with all the most recent information; having done everything that you should: *In this report we'll bring you up to date with the latest news from the area.*

🔑 **date**[2] /deɪt/ *verb* **1** [T] to write the day's date on sth: *The letter is dated 24 March, 2012.* **2** [T] to discover or guess how old sth is: *The skeleton has been dated at about 3000 BC.* **3** [I] to seem, or to make sb/sth seem old-fashioned: *We chose a simple style so that it wouldn't date as quickly.*
PHR V **date back to ...; date from ...** to have existed since ...: *The house dates back to the 17th century.* ◆ *We found photographs dating from before we were born.*

dated /ˈdeɪtɪd/ *adj* not fashionable: *This sort of jacket looks rather dated now.*

daub /dɔːb/ *verb* [T] **daub A on B; daub B with A** to spread a lot of a substance such as paint, mud, etc. carelessly onto sth: *The walls of the building were daubed with red paint.*

🔑 **daughter** /ˈdɔːtə(r)/ *noun* [C] a female child: *I have two sons and one daughter.* ◆ *Janet's daughter is a doctor.*

D

ˈ**daughter-in-law** *noun* [C] (*pl* **daughters-in-law**) the wife of your son

daunt /dɔːnt/ *verb* [T, usually passive] to frighten or to worry sb by being too big or difficult: *Don't be daunted by all the controls—in fact it's a simple machine to use.* ▶ **daunting** *adj*: *a daunting task*

dawdle /ˈdɔːdl/ *verb* [I] to go somewhere very slowly: *Stop dawdling! We've got to be at school by eight.*

dawn[1] /dɔːn/ *noun* **1** [U,C] the early morning, when light first appears in the sky: *before/at dawn* ◆ *Dawn was breaking* (= it was starting to get light) *as I set off to work.* ➲ look at **daybreak** **2** [sing] the beginning: *the dawn of civilization*
IDM **the crack of dawn** ➲ **crack**[2]

dawn[2] /dɔːn/ *verb* [I] **1** (*formal*) to begin to grow light, after the night: *The day dawned bright and cold.* ◆ (*figurative*) *A new era of peace is dawning.* **2** **dawn (on sb)** to become clear (to sb): *Suddenly it dawned on her. 'Of course!' she said. 'You're Mike's brother!'*

🔑 **day** /deɪ/ *noun* **1** [C] a period of 24 hours. Seven days make up a week: *'What day is it today?' 'Tuesday.'* ◆ *We went to Italy for ten days.* ◆ *We're meeting again* ***the day after tomorrow/in two days' time.*** ◆ *The* ***next/following day*** *I saw Mark again.* ◆ *I'd already spoken to him* ***the day before/the previous day.*** ◆ *I have to take these pills twice* ***a day.*** ◆ *I work* ***six days a week.*** *Sunday's my day off* (= when I do not work). **2** [C,U] the time when the sky is light; not night: *The days were warm but the nights were freezing.* ◆ *It's been raining all day (long).* ◆ *Owls sleep* ***by day*** (= during the day) *and hunt at night.* **3** [C] the hours of the day when you work: *She's expected to work a seven-hour day.* **4** [C] *often* **days** a particular period of time in the past: *in Shakespeare's day* ◆ *There weren't so many cars* ***in those days***
IDM **at the end of the day** ➲ **end**[1]
break of day ➲ **break**[2]
call it a day ➲ **call**[1]
day by day every day; as time passes: *Day by day, she was getting a little bit stronger.*
day in, day out every day, without any change: *Frank sits at his desk working, day in, day out.*
day-to-day happening as a normal part of each day; usual
from day to day; from one day to the next within a short period of time: *Things change so quickly that we never know what will happen from one day to the next.*
have a field day ➲ **field day**
it's early days (yet) ➲ **early**
make sb's day (*informal*) to make sb very happy
one day; some day at some time in the future: *One day we'll go back and see all our old friends.*
the other day, morning, week, etc. ➲ **other**
the present day ➲ **present**[1]
these days in the present age SYN **nowadays**

daybreak /ˈdeɪbreɪk/ *noun* [U] the time in the early morning when light first appears SYN **dawn**

daydream /ˈdeɪdriːm/ *noun* [C] thoughts that are not connected with what you are doing; often pleasant scenes in your imagination: *The child stared out of the window, lost in a daydream.* ▶ **daydream** *verb* [I]: *Don't just sit there daydreaming—do some work!*

daylight /ˈdeɪlaɪt/ *noun* [U] the light that there is during the day: *The colours look quite different* ***in daylight.*** ◆ *daylight hours*
IDM **(in) broad daylight** ➲ **broad**

ˌ**day reˈturn** *noun* [C] (*BrE*) a train or bus ticket for going somewhere and coming back on the same day. It is cheaper than a normal return ticket.

daytime /ˈdeɪtaɪm/ *noun* [U] the time when it is light; not night: *These flowers open* ***in the daytime*** *and close again at night.* ◆ *daytime TV*

daze /deɪz/ *noun*
IDM **in a daze** unable to think or react normally; confused

dazed /deɪzd/ *adj* unable to think or react normally; confused: *He had a dazed expression on his face.*

dazzle /ˈdæzl/ *verb* [T, usually passive] **1** (used about a bright light) to make sb unable to see for a short time: *She was dazzled by the other car's headlights.* **2** to impress sb very much: *He had been dazzled by her beauty.* ▶ **dazzling** *adj*: *a dazzling light*

🔑 **dead**[1] /ded/ *adj* **1** no longer alive: *My father's dead. He died two years ago.* ◆ *Police found a dead body under the bridge.* ◆ *The man was shot dead by a masked gunman.* ◆ *dead leaves* ➲ *noun* **death**, *verb* **die** **2** no longer used; finished: *Latin is a dead language.* OPP **living** **3** [not before a noun] (used about a piece of equipment) no longer working: *I picked up the telephone but the line was dead.* ◆ *This battery's dead.* **4** without movement, activity or interest: *This town is completely dead after 11 o'clock at night.* **5** [not before a noun] (used about a part of the body) no longer able to feel anything: *Oh no, my foot's* ***gone dead.*** *I was sitting on it for too long.* SYN **numb** **6** [only *before* a noun] complete or exact: *a dead silence/calm* ◆ *The arrow hit the dead centre of the target.*
IDM **a dead end** **1** a street that is only open at one end **2** a point, situation, etc. from which you can make no further progress: *a dead-end job* (= one that offers no chance of moving to a higher position)
drop dead ➲ **drop**[1]

dead[2] /ded/ **the dead** *noun* [pl] people who have died: *A church service was held in memory of the dead.*
IDM **in/at the dead of night** in the middle of the night, when it is very dark and quiet

dead[3] /ded/ *adv* completely, exactly or very: *The car made a strange noise and then stopped dead.* ◆ *He's dead keen to start work.*

deaden /ˈdedn/ *verb* [T] to make sth less strong, painful, etc: *They gave her drugs to try and deaden the pain.*

ˌ**dead ˈheat** *noun* [C] the result of a race when two people, etc. finish at exactly the same time

deadline /ˈdedlaɪn/ *noun* [C] a time or date before which sth must be done or finished: *I usually* *set myself* ***a deadline*** *when I have a project to do.* ◆ *A journalist is used to having to* ***meet deadlines****.*

deadlock /ˈdedlɒk/ *noun* [sing,U] a situation in which two sides cannot reach an agreement: *Talks have reached (a) deadlock.* ◆ *to try to break the deadlock*

deadly /ˈdedli/ *adj, adv* (**deadlier**; **deadliest**) **1** causing or likely to cause death: *a deadly poison/weapon/disease* **2** [adjective only *before* a noun] very great; complete: *They're deadly enemies.* **3** extremely accurate, so that no defence is possible: *That player is deadly when he gets in front of the goal.* **4** completely; extremely: *I'm not joking. In fact I'm deadly serious.*

deadpan /ˈdedpæn/ *adj* without any expression on your face or in your voice: *He told the joke with a completely deadpan face.*

deaf /def/ *adj* (**deafer**; **deafest**) **1** unable to hear anything or unable to hear very well: *You'll have to speak louder. My father's a bit deaf.* ◆ *to go deaf* **2 the deaf** *noun* [pl] people who cannot hear: *sign language for the deaf* **3 deaf to sth** not wanting to listen to sth: *I've told her what I think but she's deaf to my advice.* ▶ **deafness** *noun* [U]

deafen /ˈdefn/ *verb* [T, usually passive] to make sb unable to hear by making a very loud noise: *We were deafened by the loud music.* ▶ **deafening** *adj*: *deafening music*

deal[1] /diːl/ *verb* (*pt, pp* **dealt** /delt/) **1** [I,T] **deal (sth) (out)**; **deal (sth) (to sb)** to give cards to players in a game of cards: *Start by dealing seven cards to each player.* ◆ *Whose turn is it to deal?* **2** [I,T] (*informal*) to buy and sell illegal drugs

IDM deal sb/sth a blow; **deal a blow to sb/sth** **1** to give sb a shock, etc: *This news dealt a terrible blow to my father.* **2** to hit sb/sth: *He was dealt a nasty blow to the head in the accident.*

PHR V deal in sth to buy and sell a particular product: *He deals in second-hand cars.*

deal sth out to give sth to a number of people: *The profits will be dealt out among us.*

deal with sb/sth **1** to do business with a person or an organization: *Our firm deals with customers all over the world.* **2** to take suitable action in a particular situation in order to solve a problem, etc: *He's a difficult man. Nobody quite knows how to deal with him.* ◆ *My secretary will deal with my correspondence while I'm away.* **3** to have sth as its subject: *This chapter deals with letter-writing.*

deal[2] /diːl/ *noun* [C] **1** an agreement or arrangement, especially in business: *We're hoping to* ***do a deal*** *with an Italian company.* ◆ *Let's* ***make a deal*** *not to criticize each other's work.* ◆ *'I'll help you with your essay if you'll fix my bike.' 'OK,* ***it's a deal!****'* **2** the way that sb is treated: *With high fares and unreliable services, rail users are* ***getting a raw deal****.* ◆ *The new law aims to give pensioners* ***a fair deal****.* **3** the act of giving cards to players in a card game

IDM a big deal/no big deal ➲ **big**

a good/great deal (of sth) a lot (of sth): *I've spent a great deal of time on this report.*

dealer /ˈdiːlə(r)/ *noun* [C] **1** a person whose business is buying and selling things: *a dealer in gold and silver* ◆ *an art dealer* **2** the person who gives the cards to the players in a game of cards

dealing /ˈdiːlɪŋ/ *noun* **1 dealings** [pl] relations, especially in business: *We had some dealings with that firm several years ago.* **2** [U] buying and selling: *share dealing*

dealt *past tense, past participle* of **deal**[1]

dean /diːn/ *noun* [C] **1** a priest who is responsible for a large church or a number of small churches **2** an important official at some universities or colleges

dear[1] /dɪə(r)/ *adj* (**dearer**; **dearest**) **1 dear (to sb)** loved by or important to sb: *It was a subject that was very dear to him.* ◆ *She's one of my dearest friends.* **2 Dear** used at the beginning of a letter before the name or title of the person you are writing to: *Dear Sarah, …* ◆ *Dear Mr. Dawson, …* ◆ *Dear Sir or Madam, …*

> **MORE** Use **Dear Sir or Madam** if you do not know the name of the person you are writing to, and end your letter with **Yours faithfully.**

➲ note at **sincere** **3** (*BrE*) expensive: *How can people afford to drive when petrol is so dear?*

IDM close/dear/near to sb's heart ➲ **heart**

dear[2] /dɪə(r)/ *exclam* **1** used for expressing disappointment, sadness, surprise, etc: *Dear me! Aren't you ready?* **2** (*old-fashioned*) used when speaking to sb you know well: *Would you like a cup of tea, dear?*

dearly /ˈdɪəli/ *adv* **1** very much: *I'd dearly like to go there again.* **2** (*formal*) in a way that causes damage or suffering, or costs a lot of money: *I've already paid dearly for that mistake.*

dearth /dɜːθ/ *noun* [sing] **a dearth (of sb/sth)** a lack of sth; not enough of sth: *There's a dearth of young people in the village.*

death /deθ/ *noun* **1** [C,U] the end of sb/sth's life; dying: *There were two deaths and many other people were injured in the accident.* ◆ *The police do not know the* ***cause of death****.* ◆ *There was no food and people were* ***starving to death****.* ➲ *adjective* **dead**, *verb* **die** **2** [U] the end (of sth): *the death of communism*

IDM catch your death (of cold) ➲ **catch**[1]

a matter of life and/or death ➲ **matter**[1]

put sb to death [usually passive] (*formal*) to kill sb as a punishment, in past times

sick to death of sb/sth ➲ **sick**[1]

sudden death ➲ **sudden**

deathly /ˈdeθli/ *adj, adv* like death: *There was a deathly silence.*

ˈdeath penalty *noun* [sing] the legal punishment of being killed for a crime ➲ look at **capital punishment**

ˈdeath toll *noun* [C] the number of people killed in a disaster, a war, an accident, etc.

debase /dɪˈbeɪs/ *verb* [T, usually passive] (*formal*) to reduce the quality or value of sth

debatable /dɪˈbeɪtəbl/ *adj* not certain; that you could argue about: *It's debatable whether people have a better lifestyle these days.*

debate¹ /dɪˈbeɪt/ *noun* **1** [C] a formal argument or discussion of a question at a public meeting or in Parliament: *a debate on educational reform* **2** [U] general discussion about sth expressing different opinions: *There's been a lot of debate about the cause of acid rain.*

D

debate² /dɪˈbeɪt/ *verb* **1** [I,T] to discuss sth in a formal way or at a public meeting: *Politicians will be debating the bill later this week.* **2** [T] to think about or discuss sth before deciding what to do: *They debated whether to go or not.*

debauched /dɪˈbɔːtʃt/ *adj* a **debauched** person is immoral in their sexual behaviour, drinks a lot of alcohol, takes drugs, etc. SYN **depraved** ▶ **debauchery** /dɪˈbɔːtʃəri/ *noun* [U]

debit¹ /ˈdebɪt/ *noun* [C] an amount of money paid out of a bank account OPP **credit** ➲ look at **direct debit**

debit² /ˈdebɪt/ *verb* [T] to take an amount of money out of a bank account, etc. usually as a payment; to record this

ˈ**debit card** *noun* [C] a plastic card that can be used to take money directly from your bank account when you pay for sth ➲ look at **credit card**

debris /ˈdebriː/ *noun* [U] pieces from sth that has been destroyed, especially in an accident

debt /det/ *noun* **1** [C] an amount of money that you owe to sb: *Teresa borrowed a lot of money and she's still paying off the debt.* ➲ note at **loan** **2** [U] the state of owing money: *After he lost his job, he **got into debt**.* **3** [C, usually sing] (*formal*) something that you owe sb, for example because they have helped or been kind to you: *In his speech he acknowledged his debt to his family and friends for their support.*

IDM **be in/out of debt** to owe/not owe money
be in sb's debt (*formal*) to feel grateful to sb for sth that they have done for you

debtor /ˈdetə(r)/ *noun* [C] a person who owes money

debug /ˌdiːˈbʌg/ *verb* [T] (debugging; debugged) to look for and remove the faults in a computer program

debut (also début) /ˈdeɪbjuː/ *noun* [C] a first appearance in public of an actor, etc: *She **made** her **debut** in London in 1989.*

Dec. *abbr* = **December**: *5 Dec. 2012*

decade /ˈdekeɪd; dɪˈkeɪd/ *noun* [C] a period of ten years: *the last decade of the 20th century*

decadence /ˈdekədəns/ *noun* [U] behaviour, attitudes, etc. that show low moral standards ▶ **decadent** /ˈdekədənt/ *adj*: *a decadent society*

decaffeinated /ˌdiːˈkæfɪneɪtɪd/ *adj* (used about coffee or tea) with most or all of the **caffeine** (= the substance that makes you feel awake) removed ➲ note at **coffee**

decapitate /dɪˈkæpɪteɪt/ *verb* [T] (*formal*) to cut off sb's head SYN **behead**

decay¹ /dɪˈkeɪ/ *noun* [U] the process or state of being slowly destroyed: *tooth decay* ◆ *The old farm was in a terrible state of decay.*

decay² /dɪˈkeɪ/ *verb* [I] **1** to go bad or be slowly destroyed: *the decaying carcass of a dead sheep* SYN **rot** **2** to become weaker or less powerful: *His business empire began to decay.* ▶ **decayed** *adj*: *a decayed tooth*

the deceased /dɪˈsiːst/ *noun* [sing] (*formal*) a person who has died, especially one who has died recently: *Many friends of the deceased were present at the funeral.* ▶ **deceased** *adj*

deceit /dɪˈsiːt/ *noun* [U] dishonest behaviour; trying to make sb believe sth that is not true: *Their marriage eventually broke up because she was tired of his lies and deceit.*

deceitful /dɪˈsiːtfl/ *adj* dishonest; trying to make sb believe sth that is not true ▶ **deceitfully** /-fəli/ *adv* ▶ **deceitfulness** *noun* [U]

deceive /dɪˈsiːv/ *verb* [T] deceive sb/yourself (into doing sth) to try to make sb believe sth that is not true: *He deceived his mother into believing that he had earned the money, not stolen it.* ◆ *You're deceiving yourself if you think there's an easy solution to the problem.* ➲ *noun* **deception** *or* **deceit**

December /dɪˈsembə(r)/ *noun* [U,C] (*abbr* Dec.) the 12th month of the year, coming after November ➲ note at **January**

decency /ˈdiːsnsi/ *noun* [U] moral or correct behaviour: *She **had the decency to** admit that it was her fault.*

decent /ˈdiːsnt/ *adj* **1** of a good enough standard: *All she wants is a decent job with decent wages.* **2** (used about people or behaviour) honest and fair; treating people with respect **3** not likely to offend or shock sb: *I can't come to the door, I'm not decent* (= I'm not dressed). OPP **indecent** ▶ **decently** *adv*

deception /dɪˈsepʃn/ *noun* [C,U] making sb believe or being made to believe sth that is not true: *He had obtained the secret papers **by deception**.* ➲ *verb* **deceive**

deceptive /dɪˈseptɪv/ *adj* likely to make you believe sth that is not true: *The water is deceptive. It's much deeper than it looks.* ▶ **deceptively** *adv*: *She made the task sound deceptively easy.*

decibel /ˈdesɪbel/ *noun* [C] a measure of how loud a sound is

decide /dɪˈsaɪd/ *verb* **1** [I,T] decide (to do sth); decide against (doing) sth; decide about/on sth; decide that ... to think about two or more possibilities and choose one of them: *There are so many to choose from—I can't decide!* ◆ *We've decided not to invite Isabel.* ◆ *She decided against borrowing the money.* ◆ *They decided on a name for the baby.* ◆ *He decided that it was too late to go.* ◆ *The date hasn't been decided yet.* **2** [T] to influence sth so that it produces a particular result: *Your votes will decide* *the winner.* **3** [T] to cause sb to make a decision: *What finally decided you to leave?* ➲ *noun* **decision**, *adjective* **decisive**

decided /dɪˈsaɪdɪd/ *adj* [only *before* a noun] clear; definite: *There has been a decided improvement in his work.* ▶ **decidedly** *adv*

deciduous /dɪˈsɪdʒuəs/ *adj* (used about a tree) of a type that loses its leaves every autumn ➲ look at **evergreen**

decimal¹ /ˈdesɪml/ *adj* based on or counted in units of ten: *decimal currency*

decimal² /ˈdesɪml/ *noun* [C] part of a number, written after a **decimal point** (= a small round mark): *A quarter expressed as a decimal is 0.25.*

decimate /ˈdesɪmeɪt/ *verb* [T] to destroy or badly damage a large number of people or things: *The rabbit population was decimated by the disease.*

decipher /dɪˈsaɪfə(r)/ *verb* [T] to succeed in reading or understanding sth that is not clear: *It's impossible to decipher his handwriting.*

⚷ **decision** /dɪˈsɪʒn/ *noun* **1** [C,U] a decision (to do sth); a decision on/about sth; a decision that ... a choice or judgement that you make after thinking about various possibilities: *Have you* ***made a decision*** *yet?* ♦ *I realize now that I made the wrong decision.* ♦ *There were good reasons for his decision to leave.* ♦ *I* ***took the decision*** *that I believed to be right.* **2** [U] being able to decide clearly and quickly: *We are looking for someone with decision for this job.* ➲ *verb* **decide**

decisive /dɪˈsaɪsɪv/ *adj* **1** making sth certain or final: *the decisive battle of the war* **2** having the ability to make clear decisions quickly: *It's no good hesitating. Be decisive.* OPP **indecisive** ➲ *verb* **decide** ▶ **decisively** *adv* ▶ **decisiveness** *noun* [U]

deck /dek/ *noun* [C] **1** one of the floors of a ship or bus **2** (*AmE*) = **pack²**(6): *a deck of cards* **3** part of a machine that records and/or plays sounds
IDM **on deck** on the part of a ship which you can walk on outside: *I'm going out on deck for some fresh air.*

deckchair /ˈdektʃeə(r)/ *noun* [C] a chair that you use outside, especially on the beach. You can fold it up and carry it. ➲ picture at **chair**

declaration /ˌdekləˈreɪʃn/ *noun* **1** [C,U] an official statement about sth: *In his speech he made a strong declaration of support for free education.* ♦ *the declaration of war* **2** [C] a written statement giving information on goods or money you have earned, on which you have to pay tax: *a customs declaration*

⚷ **declare** /dɪˈkleə(r)/ *verb* [T] **1** to state sth publicly and officially or to make sth known in a firm, clear way: *to* ***declare war*** *on another country* ♦ *I declare that the winner of the award is Jenni Taylor.* **2** to give information about goods or money you have earned, on which you have to pay tax: *You must declare all your income on this form.*

⚷ **decline¹** /dɪˈklaɪn/ *noun* [C,U] (a) decline (in sth) a process or period of becoming weaker, smaller or less good: *a decline in sales* ♦ *As an industrial power, the country is* ***in decline.***

⚷ **decline²** /dɪˈklaɪn/ *verb* **1** [I] to become weaker, smaller or less good: *declining profits* ♦ *The standard of education has declined in this country.* **2** [I,T] (*formal*) to refuse, usually politely: *Thank you for the invitation but I'm afraid I have to decline.*

D

decode /ˌdiːˈkəʊd/ *verb* [T] to find the meaning of a secret message OPP **encode**

decoder /ˌdiːˈkəʊdə(r)/ *noun* [C] a device that changes electronic signals into a form that can be understood: *a satellite/video decoder*

decompose /ˌdiːkəmˈpəʊz/ *verb* [I,T] to slowly be destroyed by natural chemical processes: *The body was so badly decomposed that it couldn't be identified.* ▶ **decomposition** /ˌdiːkɒmpəˈzɪʃn/ *noun* [U]

decor /ˈdeɪkɔː(r)/ *noun* [U, sing] the style in which the inside of a building is decorated

⚷ **decorate** /ˈdekəreɪt/ *verb* **1** [T] decorate sth (with sth) to add sth in order to make a thing more attractive to look at: *Decorate the cake with cherries and nuts.* **2** [I,T] (*especially BrE*) to put paint and/or coloured paper onto walls, ceilings and doors in a room or building: *I think it's about time we decorated the living room.*

⚷ **decoration** /ˌdekəˈreɪʃn/ *noun* **1** [C,U] something that is added to sth in order to make it look more attractive: *Christmas decorations* ♦ *the elaborate decoration on the carved wooden door* **2** [U] the process of decorating a room or building; the style in which sth is decorated: *The house is in need of decoration.*

⚷ **decorative** /ˈdekərətɪv/ *adj* attractive or pretty to look at: *The cloth had a decorative lace edge.*

decorator /ˈdekəreɪtə(r)/ *noun* [C] a person whose job is to paint and decorate houses and buildings

decoy /ˈdiːkɔɪ/ *noun* [C] a person or an object that is used in order to trick sb/sth into doing what you want, going where you want, etc. ▶ **decoy** *verb* [T]

⚷ **decrease¹** /dɪˈkriːs/ *verb* [I,T] to become or to make sth smaller or less: *Profits have decreased by 15%.* ♦ *Decrease speed when you are approaching a road junction.* OPP **increase**

⚷ **decrease²** /ˈdiːkriːs/ *noun* [C,U] (a) decrease (in sth) the process of becoming or making sth smaller or less; the amount that sth is reduced by: *a 10% decrease in sales*

decree /dɪˈkriː/ *noun* [C] an official order given by a government, a ruler, etc. ▶ **decree** *verb* [T] (*pt, pp* decreed)

decrepit /dɪˈkrepɪt/ *adj* (used about a thing or person) old and in very bad condition or poor health

dedicate /ˈdedɪkeɪt/ *verb* [T] **1** dedicate sth to sth to give all your energy, time, efforts, etc. to sth: *He dedicated his life to helping the poor.* **2** dedicate sth to sb to say that sth is specially for sb: *He dedicated the book he had written to his brother.*

dedicated /ˈdedɪkeɪtɪd/ *adj* giving a lot of your energy, time, efforts, etc. to sth that you believe to be important: *dedicated nurses and doctors*

dedication /ˌdedɪˈkeɪʃn/ *noun* **1** [U] wanting to give your time and energy to sth because you feel it is important: *I admire her dedication to her career.* **2** [C] a message at the beginning of a book or piece of music saying that it is for a particular person

D

deduce /dɪˈdjuːs/ *verb* [T] to form an opinion using the facts that you already know: *From his name I deduced that he was Polish.* ➲ *noun* **deduction**

deduct /dɪˈdʌkt/ *verb* [T] **deduct sth (from sth)** to take sth such as money or points away from a total amount: *Marks will be deducted for untidy work.*

deduction /dɪˈdʌkʃn/ *noun* [C,U] **1** something that you work out from facts that you already know; the ability to think in this way: *It was a brilliant piece of deduction by the detective.* ➲ *verb* **deduce** **2 deduction (from sth)** taking away an amount or number from a total; the amount or number taken away from the total: *What is your total income after deductions?* (= when tax, insurance, etc. are taken away) ➲ *verb* **deduct**

deed /diːd/ *noun* [C] **1** (*formal*) something that you do; an action: *a brave/good/charitable deed* **2** a legal document that shows that you own a house or building: *The deeds of our house are kept at the bank.*

deem /diːm/ *verb* [T] (*formal*) to have a particular opinion about sth: *He did not even deem it necessary to apologize.*

deep[1] /diːp/ *adj* (**deeper**; **deepest**)
➤TOP TO BOTTOM **1** going a long way down from the surface: *to dig a deep hole* ◆ *That's a deep cut.* ◆ *a coat with deep pockets* ➲ *noun* **depth** ➲ picture at **shallow**
➤FRONT TO BACK **2** going a long way from front to back: *deep shelves*
➤MEASUREMENT **3** measuring a particular amount from top to bottom or from front to back: *The water is only a metre deep at this end of the pool.* ◆ *shelves 40 centimetres deep*
➤SOUNDS **4** low: *a deep voice*
➤COLOURS **5** dark; strong: *a deep red* OPP **light**
➤SLEEP **6** not easy to wake from: *I was in a deep sleep and didn't hear the phone ringing for ages.* OPP **light**
➤EMOTION **7** strongly felt: *He felt a very deep love for the child.*
➤THOROUGH **8** dealing with difficult subjects or details: *His books show a deep understanding of human nature.* SYN **profound**
IDM **deep in thought/conversation** thinking very hard or giving sb/sth your full attention
take a deep breath to breathe in a lot of air, especially in preparation for doing sth difficult: *He took a deep breath then walked on stage.*
▶ **the deep** *noun* [U]: *She awoke in the deep of the night* (= in the middle of the night). ◆ *the deep* (= a way in literature of referring to the sea)
▶ **deeply** *adv*: *a deeply unhappy person* ◆ *to breathe deeply*

deep[2] /diːp/ *adv* a long way down or inside sth: *He gazed deep into her eyes.* ◆ *He dug his hands deep into his pockets.*
IDM **deep down** in what you really think or feel: *I tried to appear optimistic but deep down I knew there was no hope.*
dig deep ➲ **dig**[1]

deepen /ˈdiːpən/ *verb* [I,T] to become or to make sth deep or deeper: *The river deepens here.*

ˌdeep ˈfreeze = **freezer**

ˌdeep-ˈrooted (also **ˌdeep-ˈseated**) *adj* strongly felt or believed and therefore difficult to change: *deep-rooted fears*

ˌdeep vein thromˈbosis *noun* [C,U] (*abbr* **DVT**) a serious condition caused by a **clot** (= a thick mass of blood) forming in a tube that carries blood to the heart: *Passengers on long-haul flights are being warned about the risks of deep vein thrombosis.*

deer

deer /dɪə(r)/ *noun* [C] (*pl* **deer**) a large wild animal that eats grass. The male has **antlers** (= large horns shaped like branches) on its head.

> **MORE** A male deer is called a **buck** or, especially if it has fully-grown antlers, a **stag**. The female is a **doe** and a young deer is a **fawn**. **Venison** is the meat from deer.

deface /dɪˈfeɪs/ *verb* [T] to spoil the way sth looks by writing on or marking its surface

defamation /ˌdefəˈmeɪʃn/ *noun* [U,C] (*formal*) the act of damaging the opinion that people have of sb by saying or writing bad or false things about them: *He sued for defamation of character.*

default[1] /dɪˈfɔːlt; ˈdiːfɔːlt/ *noun* [sing] a course of action taken by a computer when it is not given any other instruction
IDM **by default** because nothing happened, not because of successful effort: *They won by default, because the other team didn't turn up.*

default[2] /dɪˈfɔːlt; ˈdiːfɔːlt/ *verb* [I] **1 default (on sth)** to not do sth that you should do by law: *If you* *default on the credit payments* (= you don't pay them), *the car will be taken back.* **2 default (to sth)** (used about a computer) to take a particular course of action when no other command is given

defeat[1] /dɪˈfiːt/ *verb* [T] **1** to win a game, a fight, a vote, etc. against sb: *The army defeated the rebels after three days of fighting.* ◆ *In the last match France defeated Wales.* SYN **beat** **2** to be too difficult for sb to do or understand: *I've tried to work out what's wrong with the car but it defeats me.* **3** to prevent sth from succeeding: *The local residents are determined to defeat the council's building plans.*

defeat[2] /dɪˈfiːt/ *noun* **1** [C] an occasion when sb fails to win or be successful against sb else: *This season they have had two victories and three defeats.* **2** [U] the act of losing or not being successful: *She refused to* ***admit defeat*** *and kept on trying.*

defeatism /dɪˈfiːtɪzəm/ *noun* [U] the attitude of expecting sth to end in failure

defeatist /dɪˈfiːtɪst/ *adj* expecting not to succeed: *a defeatist attitude/view* ▶ **defeatist** *noun* [C]: *Don't be such a defeatist, we haven't lost yet!*

defecate /ˈdefəkeɪt/ *verb* [I] (*formal*) to get rid of waste from the body; to go to the toilet

defect[1] /ˈdiːfekt/ *noun* [C] sth that is wrong with or missing from sb/sth: *a speech defect* ◆ *defects in the education system* ▶ **defective** /dɪˈfektɪv/ *adj*

defect[2] /dɪˈfekt/ *verb* [I] to leave your country, a political party, etc. and join one that is considered to be the enemy ▶ **defection** *noun* [C,U] ▶ **defector** /dɪˈfektə(r)/ *noun* [C]

defence (*AmE* **defense**) /dɪˈfens/ *noun*

➤PROTECTION **1** [U] something that you do or say to protect sb/sth from attack, bad treatment, criticism, etc: *Would you fight* ***in defence of*** *your country?* ◆ *When her brother was criticized she* ***leapt to his defence.*** ◆ *I must say* ***in her defence*** *that I have always found her a very reliable employee.* ➲ look at **self-defence** **2** [C] **a defence (against sth)** something that protects sb/sth from sth, or that is used to fight against attack: *the body's defences against disease* **3** [U] the military equipment, forces, etc. for protecting a country: *Spending on defence needs to be reduced.*

➤IN LAW **4** [C] an argument in support of the accused person in a court of law: *His defence was that he was only carrying out orders.* **5 the defence** [sing, with sing or pl verb] the lawyer or lawyers who are acting for the accused person in a court of law: *The defence claims/claim that many of the witnesses were lying.* ➲ note at **court** ➲ look at **the prosecution**

➤IN SPORT **6** *usually* **the defence** [sing, U] action to prevent the other team scoring; the players who try to do this: *She plays in defence.*

defenceless /dɪˈfensləs/ *adj* unable to defend yourself against attack

defend /dɪˈfend/ *verb*

➤PROTECT **1** [T] **defend sb/sth/yourself (against/from sb/sth)** to protect sb/sth from harm or danger: *Would you be able to defend yourself if someone attacked you in the street?*

➤SUPPORT **2** [T] **defend sb/sth/yourself (against/from sb/sth)** to say or write sth to support sb/sth that has been criticized: *The minister went on TV to defend the government's policy.*

➤IN SPORT **3** [I,T] to try to stop the other team or player scoring: *They defended well and managed to hold onto their lead.*

➤IN COMPETITIONS **4** [T] to take part in a competition that you won before and try to win it again: *She successfully defended her title.* ◆ *He is the defending champion.*

➤IN LAW **5** [T] to speak for sb who is accused of a crime in a court of law: *He has employed one of the UK's top lawyers to defend him.*

defendant /dɪˈfendənt/ *noun* [C] a person who is accused of a crime in a court of law

defender /dɪˈfendə(r)/ *noun* [C] a person who defends sb/sth, especially in sport

defense (*AmE*) = **defence**

defensive[1] /dɪˈfensɪv/ *adj* **1** that protects sb/sth from attack: *The troops took up a defensive position.* OPP **offensive** **2** showing that you feel that sb is criticizing you: *When I asked him about his new job, he became very defensive and tried to change the subject.*

defensive[2] /dɪˈfensɪv/ *noun*

IDM **on the defensive** acting in a way that shows that you expect sb to attack or criticize you: *My questions about her past immediately put her on the defensive.*

defer /dɪˈfɜː(r)/ *verb* [T] (**deferring**; **deferred**) (*formal*) to leave sth until a later time: *She deferred her place at university for a year.*

deference /ˈdefərəns/ *noun* [U] polite behaviour that you show towards sb/sth, usually because you respect them

IDM **in deference to sb/sth** because you respect and do not wish to upset sb: *In deference to her father's wishes, she didn't mention the subject again.*

defiance /dɪˈfaɪəns/ *noun* [U] open refusal to obey sb/sth: *an* ***act of defiance*** ◆ *She married Jack* ***in defiance of*** *her parents' wishes.* ➲ *verb* **defy**

defiant /dɪˈfaɪənt/ *adj* showing open refusal to obey sb/sth ➲ *verb* **defy** ▶ **defiantly** *adv*

deficiency /dɪˈfɪʃnsi/ *noun* (*pl* **deficiencies**) **deficiency (in/of sth)** **1** [C,U] the state of not having enough of sth; a lack: *a deficiency of vitamin C* **2** [C] a fault or a weakness in sb/sth: *The problems were caused by deficiencies in the design.*

deficient /dɪˈfɪʃnt/ *adj* **1 deficient (in sth)** not having enough of sth: *food that is deficient in minerals* **2** not good enough or not complete

deficit /ˈdefɪsɪt/ *noun* [C] the amount by which the money you receive is less than the money you have spent: *a trade deficit*

define /dɪˈfaɪn/ *verb* [T] **1** to say exactly what a word or an idea means: *How would you define 'happiness'?* **2** to explain the exact nature of sth clearly: *We need to define the problem before we can attempt to solve it.*

defining /dɪˈfaɪnɪŋ/ *adj* **1** (used about clauses) explaining which particular person or thing you are talking about rather than giving extra information about them ℹ For more information, look at the **Reference Section** at the back of this dictionary. **2** a set of carefully chosen words used to write the explanations in some dictionaries: *This dictionary uses a* ***defining vocabulary*** *of 3000 words.*

D

⚷ **definite** /ˈdefɪnət/ *adj* **1** fixed and unlikely to change; certain: *I'll give you a definite decision in a couple of days.* OPP **indefinite** **2** clear; easy to see or notice: *There has been a definite change in her attitude recently.*

the ˌdefinite ˈarticle *noun* [C] the name used for the word 'the' ➲ look at **the indefinite article** ℹ For more information about the definite article, look at the **Reference Section** section at the back of this dictionary.

⚷ **definitely** /ˈdefɪnətli/ *adv* certainly; without doubt: *I'll definitely consider your advice.*

⚷ **definition** /ˌdefɪˈnɪʃn/ *noun* [C,U] a description of the exact meaning of a word or an idea: *Wordpower is a dictionary with clear, simple definitions.*

definitive /dɪˈfɪnətɪv/ *adj* in a form that cannot be changed or that cannot be improved: *This is the definitive version.* ◆ *the definitive performance of Hamlet* ▶ **definitively** *adv*

deflate /dɪˈfleɪt; ˌdiː-/ *verb* **1** [I,T] to become or to make sth smaller by letting the air or gas out of it: *The balloon slowly deflated.* OPP **inflate** **2** [T] to make sb feel less confident, proud or excited: *I felt really deflated when I got my exam results.*

deflect /dɪˈflekt/ *verb* **1** [I,T] to change direction after hitting sb/sth; to make sth change direction in this way: *The ball deflected off a defender and into the goal.* **2** [T] to turn sb's attention away from sth: *Nothing could deflect her from her aim.*

deflection /dɪˈflekʃn/ *noun* [C,U] a change of direction after hitting sb/sth

deforestation /ˌdiːˌfɒrɪˈsteɪʃn/ *noun* [U] cutting down trees over a large area ➲ note at **environment**

deform /dɪˈfɔːm/ *verb* [T] to change or spoil the natural shape of sth

deformed /dɪˈfɔːmd/ *adj* having a shape that is not normal because it has grown wrongly

deformity /dɪˈfɔːməti/ *noun* [C,U] (*pl* **deformities**) the condition of having a part of the body that is an unusual shape because of disease, injury, etc: *The disease causes facial deformities.*

defraud /dɪˈfrɔːd/ *verb* [T] **defraud sb (of sth)** to get sth from sb in a dishonest way: *He defrauded the company of millions.*

defrost /ˌdiːˈfrɒst/ *verb* **1** [I,T] (used about frozen food) to return to a normal temperature; to make food do this: *Defrost the chicken thoroughly before cooking.* **2** [T] to remove the ice from sth: *to defrost a fridge* ➲ look at **de-ice**

deft /deft/ *adj* (used especially about movements) skilful and quick ▶ **deftly** *adv*

defunct /dɪˈfʌŋkt/ *adj* no longer existing or in use

defuse /ˌdiːˈfjuːz/ *verb* [T] **1** to make a situation calmer or less dangerous: *She defused the tension by changing the subject.* **2** to remove part of a bomb so that it cannot explode: *Army experts defused the bomb safely.*

defy /dɪˈfaɪ/ *verb* [T] (**defying**; **defies**; *pt, pp* **defied**) **1** to refuse to obey sb/sth: *She defied her parents and continued seeing Brendan.* ➲ *adjective* **defiant**, *noun* **defiance** **2** to make sth impossible or very difficult: *It's such a beautiful place that it defies description.*
IDM **defy sb to do sth** to ask sb to do sth that you believe to be impossible: *I defy you to prove me wrong.*

degenerate¹ /dɪˈdʒenəreɪt/ *verb* [I] to become worse, lower in quality, etc: *The calm discussion degenerated into a nasty argument.* ▶ **degeneration** /dɪˌdʒenəˈreɪʃn/ *noun* [U]

degenerate² /dɪˈdʒenərət/ *adj* having moral standards that have fallen to a very low level

degradation /ˌdegrəˈdeɪʃn/ *noun* [U] **1** the act of making sb be less respected; the state of being less respected: *the degradation of being in prison* **2** causing the condition of sth to become worse: *environmental degradation*

degrade /dɪˈgreɪd/ *verb* [T] to make people respect sb less: *It's the sort of film that really degrades women.* ▶ **degrading** *adj*

⚷ **degree** /dɪˈgriː/ *noun* **1** [C] a measurement of angles: *a forty-five degree (45°) angle* ◆ *An angle of 90 degrees is called a right angle.* **2** [C] a measurement of temperature: *Water boils at 100 degrees Celsius (100°C).* ◆ *three degrees below zero/minus three degrees (-3°)* **3** [C,U] (used about feelings or qualities) a certain amount or level: *There is always* ***a degree of*** *risk involved in mountaineering.* ◆ *I sympathize with her* ***to some degree.*** **4** [C] an official document that students gain by successfully completing a course at university or college: *Michael's got* ***a degree in*** *Philosophy.* ◆ *to* ***do a*** *Chemistry* ***degree*** ◆ *a first-class degree*

TOPIC

Qualifications

In Britain **degree** is the usual word for the qualification you get when you complete and pass a university course. You can study for a **diploma** or a **certificate** at other types of college. The courses may be shorter and more practical than degree courses. The best result you can get in a British university degree is a **first**, followed by a **two-one**, a **two-two**, a **third**, a **pass** and a **fail**.

dehydrate /diːˈhaɪdreɪt; ˌdiːhaɪˈdreɪt/ *verb* **1** [T, usually passive] to remove all the water from sth: *Dehydrated vegetables can be stored for months.* **2** [I,T] to lose or make sb lose too much water from the body: *If you run for a long time in the heat, you start to dehydrate.* ▶ **dehydration** /ˌdiːhaɪˈdreɪʃn/ *noun* [U]: *Several of the runners were suffering from severe dehydration.*

de-ice /ˌdiː ˈaɪs/ *verb* [T] to remove the ice from sth: *The car windows need de-icing.* ➲ look at **defrost**

deign /deɪn/ *verb* [T] **deign to do sth** to do sth although you think you are too important to do it: *He didn't even deign to look up when I entered the room.*

deity /ˈdeɪəti/ *noun* [C] (*pl* **deities**) (*formal*) a god

dejected /dɪˈdʒektɪd/ *adj* very unhappy, especially because you are disappointed: *The fans went home dejected after watching their team lose once more.* ▶ **dejectedly** *adv* ▶ **dejection** /dɪˈdʒekʃn/ *noun* [U]

⚷ **delay¹** /dɪˈleɪ/ *noun* [C,U] a situation or period of time where you have to wait: *Delays are likely on the roads because of heavy traffic.* ◆ *If you smell gas, you should report it* **without delay** (= immediately).

⚷ **delay²** /dɪˈleɪ/ *verb* **1** [T] to make sb/sth slow or late: *The plane was delayed for several hours because of bad weather.* **2** [I,T] **delay (sth/doing sth)** to decide not to do sth until a later time: *I was forced to delay the trip until the following week.*

delegate¹ /ˈdelɪɡət/ *noun* [C] a person who has been chosen to speak or take decisions for a group of people, especially at a meeting

delegate² /ˈdelɪɡeɪt/ *verb* [I,T] to give sb with a lower job or position a particular task to do: *You can't do everything yourself. You must learn how to delegate.*

delegation /ˌdelɪˈɡeɪʃn/ *noun* **1** [C, with sing or pl verb] a group of people who have been chosen to speak or take decisions for a larger group of people, especially at a meeting: *The British delegation walked out of the meeting in protest.* **2** [U] the process of giving sb work or responsibilities that would usually be yours

delete /dɪˈliːt/ *verb* [T] to remove sth that is written: *Your name has been deleted from the list.* ▶ **deletion** /dɪˈliːʃn/ *noun* [C,U]

⚷ **deliberate¹** /dɪˈlɪbərət/ *adj* **1** done on purpose; planned: *Was it an accident or was it deliberate?* **SYN** **intentional** **2** done slowly and carefully, without hurrying: *She spoke in a calm, deliberate voice.*

deliberate² /dɪˈlɪbəreɪt/ *verb* [I,T] (*formal*) to think about or discuss sth fully before making a decision: *The judges deliberated for an hour before announcing the winner.*

⚷ **deliberately** /dɪˈlɪbərətli/ *adv* **1** in a way that was planned, not by chance: *I didn't break it deliberately, it was an accident.* **SYN** **purposely** **OPP** **by accident** **2** slowly and carefully, without hurrying: *He packed up his possessions slowly and deliberately.*

deliberation /dɪˌlɪbəˈreɪʃn/ *noun* (*formal*) **1** [C,U] discussion or thinking about sth in detail: *After much deliberation I decided to reject the offer.* **2** [U] the quality of being very slow and careful in what you say and do: *He spoke with great deliberation.*

delicacy /ˈdelɪkəsi/ *noun* (*pl* **delicacies**) **1** [U] the quality of being easy to damage or break **2** [U] great care; a gentle touch: (*figurative*) *Be tactful! It's a matter of some delicacy.* **3** [C] a type of food that is considered particularly good: *Try this dish, it's a local delicacy.*

⚷ **delicate** /ˈdelɪkət/ *adj* **1** easy to damage or break: *delicate skin* ◆ *the delicate mechanisms of a watch* **2** often ill or hurt: *He was a delicate child and often in hospital.* **3** needing skilful treatment and care: *Repairing this is going to be a very delicate operation.* **4** (used about colours, flavours, etc.) light and pleasant; not strong: *a delicate shade of pale blue* ▶ **delicately** *adv*: *She stepped delicately over the broken glass.*

delicatessen /ˌdelɪkəˈtesn/ *noun* [C] a shop that sells special, unusual or foreign foods, especially cold cooked meat, cheeses, etc.

delicious /dɪˈlɪʃəs/ *adj* having a very pleasant taste or smell: *This soup is absolutely delicious.*

⚷ **delight¹** /dɪˈlaɪt/ *noun* **1** [U] great pleasure: *She laughed with delight as she opened the present.* **SYN** **joy** **2** [C] something that gives sb great pleasure: *The story is a delight to read.* ▶ **delightful** /-fl/ *adj*: *a delightful view of the sea* ▶ **delightfully** /-fəli/ *adv*

⚷ **delight²** /dɪˈlaɪt/ *verb* [T] to give sb great pleasure: *She delighted the audience by singing all her old songs.*

PHR V **delight in sth/in doing sth** to get great pleasure from sth: *He delights in playing tricks on people.*

⚷ **delighted** /dɪˈlaɪtɪd/ *adj* **delighted (at/with/about sth); delighted to do sth/that ...** extremely pleased: *She was delighted at getting the job/that she got the job.* ◆ *They're absolutely delighted with their baby.* ➲ note at **happy**

delinquency /dɪˈlɪŋkwənsi/ *noun* [U] (*formal*) bad or criminal behaviour, especially among young people

delinquent /dɪˈlɪŋkwənt/ *adj* (*formal*) (usually used about a young person) behaving badly and often breaking the law ▶ **delinquent** *noun* [C]: *a juvenile delinquent*

delirious /dɪˈlɪriəs/ *adj* **1** speaking or thinking in a crazy way, often because of illness **2** extremely happy: *I was absolutely delirious when I passed the exam.* ▶ **deliriously** *adv*

⚷ **deliver** /dɪˈlɪvə(r)/ *verb* **1** [I,T] to take sth (goods, letters, etc.) to the place requested or to the address on it: *Your order will be delivered within five days.* ◆ *We deliver free within the local area.* **2** [T] (*formal*) to say sth formally: *to deliver a speech/lecture/warning* **3** [I] (*informal*) **deliver (on sth)** to do or give sth that you have promised: *The new leader has made a lot of promises, but can he deliver on them?* **4** [T] to help a mother to give birth to her baby: *to deliver a baby*

IDM **come up with/deliver the goods** ➲ **goods**

⚷ **delivery** /dɪˈlɪvəri/ *noun* (*pl* **deliveries**) **1** [U] the act of taking sth (goods, letters, etc.) to the place or person who has ordered it or whose address is on it: *Please allow 28 days for delivery.* ◆ *a delivery van* **2** [C] an occasion when sth is delivered: *Is there a*

D

delivery here on Sundays? **3** [C] something (goods, letters, etc.) that is **delivered**: *The shop is waiting for a new delivery of apples.* **4** [C] the process of giving birth to a baby: *an easy/difficult delivery*

delta /ˈdeltə/ *noun* [C] an area of flat land shaped like a triangle where a river divides into smaller rivers as it goes into the sea

D

delude /dɪˈluːd/ *verb* [T] to make sb believe sth that is not true: *If he thinks he's going to get rich quickly, he's deluding himself.* ➲ *noun* **delusion**

deluge[1] /ˈdeljuːdʒ/ *noun* [C] **1** a sudden very heavy fall of rain **2 a deluge (of sth)** a very large number of things that happen or arrive at the same time: *The programme was followed by a deluge of complaints from the public.* SYN **flood**

deluge[2] /ˈdeljuːdʒ/ *verb* [T, usually passive] to send or give sb/sth a very large quantity of sth, all at the same time: *They were deluged with applications for the job.* SYN **flood**

delusion /dɪˈluːʒn/ *noun* [C,U] a false belief: *He seems to be* ***under the delusion*** *that he's popular.* ➲ *verb* **delude**

de luxe /ˌdə ˈlʌks/ *adj* of extremely high quality and more expensive than usual: *a de luxe hotel*

delve /delv/ *verb* [I] **delve into sth** to search inside sth: *She delved into the bag and brought out a tiny box.* ♦ *(figurative) We must delve into the past to find the origins of the custom.*

Dem /dem/ *abbr* = **democrat**(2), **Democratic Party**

demand[1] /dɪˈmɑːnd/ *noun* **1** [C] **a demand (for sth/that ...)** a strong request or order that must be obeyed: *a demand for changes in the law* ♦ *I was amazed by their demand that I should leave immediately.* **2 demands** [pl] something that sb/sth makes you do, especially sth that is difficult or tiring: *Running a marathon* ***makes*** *huge* ***demands*** *on the body.* **3** [U,sing] **demand (for sth/sb)** the desire or need for sth among a group of people: *We no longer sell that product because there is no demand for it.*

IDM **in demand** wanted by a lot of people: *I'm in demand this weekend—I've had three invitations!*

on demand at any time that you ask for it: *This treatment is available from your doctor on demand.*

demand[2] /dɪˈmɑːnd/ *verb* [T] **1 demand to do sth/that ...; demand sth** to ask for sth in an extremely firm or aggressive way: *I walked into the office and demanded to see the manager.* ♦ *She demanded that I pay her immediately.* ♦ *Your behaviour was disgraceful and I demand an apology.* **2** to need sth: *a sport that demands skill as well as strength*

demanding /dɪˈmɑːndɪŋ/ *adj* **1** (used about a job, task, etc.) needing a lot of effort, care, skill, etc: *It will be a demanding schedule—I have to go to six cities in six days.* **2** (used about a person) always wanting attention or expecting very high standards of people: *Young children are very demanding.* ♦ *a demanding boss*

demise /dɪˈmaɪz/ *noun* [sing] **1** the end or failure of sth: *Poor business decisions led to the company's demise.* **2** *(formal)* the death of a person

demo /ˈdeməʊ/ *noun* [C] (*pl* **demos**) *(informal)* **1** *(especially BrE)* = **demonstration**(1): *They all went on the demo.* **2** = **demonstration**(2): *I'll* ***give you a demo.*** **3** a record or tape with an example of sb's music on it: *a demo tape*

democracy /dɪˈmɒkrəsi/ *noun* (*pl* **democracies**) **1** [U] a system in which the government of a country is elected by the people **2** [C] a country that has this system **3** [U] the right of everyone in an organization, etc. to be treated equally and to vote on matters that affect them: *There is a need for more democracy in the company.*

democrat /ˈdeməkræt/ *noun* [C] **1** a person who believes in and supports **democracy** **2 Democrat** (*abbr* **Dem**) a member of, or sb who supports, the Democratic Party of the US ➲ look at **Republican**

democratic /ˌdeməˈkrætɪk/ *adj* **1** based on the system of **democracy**: *democratic elections* ♦ *a democratic government* ➲ note at **politics** **2** having or supporting equal rights for all people: *a democratic decision* (= made by all the people involved) ▸ **democratically** /-kli/ *adv*: *a democratically elected government*

the ˌDemoˈcratic Party *noun* [sing] (*abbr* **Dem**) one of the two main political parties of the US ➲ look at **the Republican Party**

demographics /ˌdeməˈgræfɪks/ *noun* [pl] data relating to the population and different groups within it: *the demographics of radio listeners* ▸ **demographic** *adj*: ***demographic*** *changes/trends/factors* ▸ **demographically** /-kli/ *adv*

demolish /dɪˈmɒlɪʃ/ *verb* [T] to destroy sth, for example a building: *The old shops were demolished and a supermarket was built in their place.* ♦ *(figurative) She demolished his argument in one sentence.* ▸ **demolition** /ˌdeməˈlɪʃn/ *noun* [C,U]

demon /ˈdiːmən/ *noun* [C] an evil spirit

demonic /diˈmɒnɪk/ *adj* connected with, or like, a **demon**

demonstrate /ˈdemənstreɪt/ *verb* **1** [T] **demonstrate sth (to sb)** to show sth clearly by giving proof: *Using this chart, I'd like to demonstrate to you what has happened to our sales.* **2** [I,T] **demonstrate sth (to sb)** to show and explain to sb how to do sth or how sth works: *The crew demonstrated the use of life jackets just after take-off.* ♦ *I'm not sure what you mean—could you demonstrate?* **3** [I] **demonstrate (against/for sb/sth)** to take part in a public protest for or against sb/sth: *Enormous crowds have been demonstrating against the government.* SYN **protest**

demonstration /ˌdemənˈstreɪʃn/ *noun* **1** *(especially BrE informal* **demo**) [C] **a demonstration (against/for sb/sth)** a public protest for or against sb/sth: *demonstrations against a new law* **2** (also *informal* **demo**) [C,U] an act of showing or explaining to sb how to do sth or how sth works: *The salesman gave me a demonstration of what the computer could do.* **3** [C,U] something that shows clearly that sth exists or is true: *This accident is a clear demonstration of the system's faults.*

demonstrative /dɪˈmɒnstrətɪv/ *adj* (used about a person) showing feelings, especially loving feelings, in front of other people

demonstrator /ˈdemənstreɪtə(r)/ *noun* [C] a person who takes part in a public protest SYN **protester**

demoralize (also -ise) /dɪˈmɒrəlaɪz/ *verb* [T] to make sb lose confidence or the courage to continue doing sth: *Repeated defeats completely demoralized the team.* ▶ **demoralization** (also -isation) /dɪˌmɒrəlaɪˈzeɪʃn/ *noun* [U] ▶ **demoralizing** (also -ising) *adj*: *Constant criticism can be extremely demoralizing.*

demote /ˌdiːˈməʊt/ *verb* [T] demote sb (from sth) (to sth) to move sb to a lower position or less important job, often as a punishment OPP **promote** ▶ **demotion** /ˌdiːˈməʊʃn/ *noun* [C,U]

demure /dɪˈmjʊə(r)/ *adj* (used especially about a girl or young woman) shy, quiet and polite

den /den/ *noun* [C] **1** the place where certain wild animals, such as **lions** live **2** a secret place, especially for illegal activities: *a gambling den*

denial /dɪˈnaɪəl/ *noun* **1** [C] a statement that sth is not true: *The minister issued a denial that he was involved in the scandal.* **2** [C,U] (a) denial (of sth) refusing to allow sb to have or do sth: *a denial of personal freedom* **3** [U] a refusal to accept that sth unpleasant or painful has happened: *He's been **in denial** ever since the accident.* ➲ *verb* **deny**

denim /ˈdenɪm/ *noun* [U] a thick cotton cloth (often blue) that is used for making clothes, especially jeans: *a denim jacket* ➲ picture on **page P1**

denomination /dɪˌnɒmɪˈneɪʃn/ *noun* [C] one of the different religious groups that you can belong to

denote /dɪˈnəʊt/ *verb* [T] to mean or be a sign of sth: *In algebra the sign x always denotes an unknown quantity.*

denounce /dɪˈnaʊns/ *verb* [T] to say publicly that sth is wrong; to be very critical of a person in public: *The well-known actor has been denounced as a bad influence on young people.* ➲ *noun* **denunciation**

dense /dens/ *adj* (denser; densest) **1** containing a lot of things or people close together: *dense forests* ◆ *areas of dense population* **2** difficult to see through: *dense fog* **3** (*informal*) not intelligent; stupid ▶ **densely** *adv*: *densely populated areas*

density /ˈdensəti/ *noun* (*pl* densities) **1** [U] the number of things or people in a place in relation to its area: *There is a high density of wildlife in this area.* **2** [C,U] (*technical*) the relation of the weight of a substance to its size: *Lead has a high density.*

dent¹ /dent/ *verb* [T] to damage a flat surface by hitting it but not breaking it: *I hit a wall and dented the front of the car.*

dent² /dent/ *noun* [C] a place where a flat surface, especially metal, has been hit and damaged but not broken: *This tin's got a dent in it.*

dental /ˈdentl/ *adj* [only *before* a noun] connected with teeth: *dental care/treatment*

ˈdental floss *noun* [U] a type of thread that is used for cleaning between the teeth

🔑 **dentist** /ˈdentɪst/ *noun* **1** [C] a person whose job is to look after people's teeth: *an appointment with the dentist* ➲ note at **tooth** ➲ picture on **page P2** **2 the dentist's** [sing] the place where a dentist works: *I have to go to the dentist's today.*

dentistry /ˈdentɪstri/ *noun* [U] **1** the medical study of the teeth and mouth **2** the work of a dentist

dentures /ˈdentʃəz/ = **false teeth**

denunciation /dɪˌnʌnsiˈeɪʃn/ *noun* [C,U] an expression of strong disapproval of sb/sth in public ➲ *verb* **denounce**

🔑 **deny** /dɪˈnaɪ/ *verb* [T] (denying; denies; *pt, pp* denied) **1** deny sth/doing sth; deny that ... to state that sth is not true; to refuse to admit or accept sth: *In court he denied all the charges.* ◆ *She denied telling lies/that she had told lies.* OPP **admit** **2** (*formal*) deny sb sth; deny sth (to sb) to refuse to allow sb to have sth: *She was denied permission to remain in the country.* ➲ *noun* **denial**

deodorant /diˈəʊdərənt/ *noun* [C,U] a chemical substance that you put onto your body to prevent bad smells

dep. *abbr* **departs**: *dep. London 15.32*

depart /dɪˈpɑːt/ *verb* [I,T] (*formal*) to leave a place, usually at the beginning of a journey: *Ferries depart for Spain twice a day.* ◆ *The next train to the airport departs from platform 2.* ➲ note at **leave¹** ➲ *noun* **departure**

🔑 **department** /dɪˈpɑːtmənt/ *noun* [C] (*abbr* Dept) **1** one of the sections into which an organization, for example a school or a business, is divided: *the Modern Languages department* ◆ *She works in the accounts department.* **2** a division of the government responsible for a particular subject: *the Department of Health* ➲ look at **ministry**

departmental /ˌdiːpɑːtˈmentl/ *adj* [only *before* a noun] connected with a department: *There is a departmental meeting once a month.*

deˈpartment store *noun* [C] a large shop that is divided into sections selling different types of goods

🔑 **departure** /dɪˈpɑːtʃə(r)/ *noun* [C,U] **1** leaving or going away from a place: *Helen's sudden departure meant I had to do her job as well as mine.* ◆ *Passengers should check in at least one hour before departure.* OPP **arrival** ➲ *verb* **depart** **2** a departure (from sth) an action which is different from what is usual or expected: *a departure from normal practice*

🔑 **depend** /dɪˈpend/ *verb*

IDM **that depends; it (all) depends** [used alone or at the beginning of a sentence] used to say that you are not certain of sth until other things have been considered: *'Can you lend me some money?' 'That depends. How much do you want?'* ◆ *I don't*

D

know whether I'll see him. It depends what time he gets here.

PHR V **depend on sb/sth** to be able to trust sb/sth to do sth: *If you ever need any help, you know you can depend on me.* ♦ *You can't depend on the trains. They're always late.* ♦ *I was depending on getting the money today.* **SYN** **rely on**

depend on sb/sth (for sth) to need sb/sth to provide sth: *Our organization depends on donations from the public.*

depend on sth to be decided or influenced by sb/sth: *His whole future depends on these exams.*

dependable /dɪˈpendəbl/ *adj* that can be trusted: *The bus service is very dependable.* **SYN** **reliable**

dependant (*especially AmE* dependent) /dɪˈpendənt/ *noun* [C] a person who depends on sb else for money, a home, food, etc: *insurance cover for you and all your dependants*

dependence /dɪˈpendəns/ *noun* [U] dependence on sb/sth the state of needing sb/sth: *The country wants to reduce its dependence on imported oil.* **OPP** **independence**

dependency /dɪˈpendənsi/ *noun* [U] the state of being **dependent** on sb/sth; the state of being unable to live without sth, especially a drug

dependent /dɪˈpendənt/ *adj* **1** dependent (on sb/sth) needing sb/sth to support you: *The industry is heavily dependent on government funding.* ♦ *Do you have any dependent children?* **2** dependent on sb/sth influenced or decided by sth: *The price you pay is dependent on the number in your group.* **OPP** for both meanings **independent**

depict /dɪˈpɪkt/ *verb* [T] **1** to show sb/sth in a painting or drawing: *a painting depicting a country scene* **2** to describe sb/sth in words: *The novel depicts rural life a century ago.*

deplete /dɪˈpliːt/ *verb* [T] to reduce the amount of sth so that there is not much left: *Wealthy nations are depleting the world's natural resources.* ▶ **depletion** /dɪˈpliːʃn/ *noun* [U]

deplorable /dɪˈplɔːrəbl/ *adj* (*formal*) morally bad and deserving disapproval: *They are living in deplorable conditions.* ▶ **deplorably** /-əbli/ *adv*

deplore /dɪˈplɔː(r)/ *verb* [T] (*formal*) to feel or say that sth is morally bad: *I deplore such dishonest behaviour.*

deploy /dɪˈplɔɪ/ *verb* [T] **1** to put soldiers or weapons in a position where they are ready to fight **2** to use sth in a useful and successful way ▶ **deployment** *noun* [U,C]: *the deployment of troops*

deport /dɪˈpɔːt/ *verb* [T] to force sb to leave a country because they have no legal right to be there: *A number of illegal immigrants have been deported.* ▶ **deportation** /ˌdiːpɔːˈteɪʃn/ *noun* [C,U]

depose /dɪˈpəʊz/ *verb* [T] to remove a ruler or leader from power: *There was a revolution and the dictator was deposed.*

deposit[1] /dɪˈpɒzɪt/ *noun* [C] **1** a deposit (on sth) a sum of money which is the first payment for sth, with the rest of the money to be paid later: *Once you have paid a deposit, the booking will be confirmed.* **2** [usually sing] a deposit (on sth) a sum of money that you pay when you rent sth and get back when you return it without damage: *Boats can be hired for £15 an hour, plus £30 deposit.* **3** a sum of money paid into a bank account **4** a substance that has been left on a surface or in the ground as the result of a natural or chemical process: *mineral deposits*

deposit[2] /dɪˈpɒzɪt/ *verb* [T] **1** to put sth down somewhere: *He deposited his bags on the floor and sat down.* **2** (used about liquid or a river) to leave sth lying on a surface, as the result of a natural or chemical process: *mud deposited by a flood* **3** to put money into an account at a bank: *He deposited £20 a week into his savings account.* **4** deposit sth (in sth); deposit sth (with sb/sth) to put sth valuable in an official place where it is safe until needed again: *Valuables can be deposited in the hotel safe.*

deˈposit account *noun* [C] (*BrE*) a type of bank account where your money earns interest. You cannot take money out of a **deposit account** without arranging it first with the bank. ➲ look at **current account**

depot /ˈdepəʊ/ *noun* [C] **1** a place where large amounts of food, goods or equipment are stored **2** a place where large numbers of vehicles (buses, lorries, etc.) are kept when not in use **3** (*AmE*) a small bus or railway station

depraved /dɪˈpreɪvd/ *adj* (*formal*) morally bad: *This is the work of a depraved mind.* **SYN** **wicked**, **evil** ▶ **depravity** /dɪˈprævəti/ *noun* [U] **SYN** **wickedness**

depreciate /dɪˈpriːʃieɪt/ *verb* [I] to become less valuable over a period of time: *New cars start to depreciate the moment they are on the road.* ▶ **depreciation** /dɪˌpriːʃiˈeɪʃn/ *noun* [C,U]

depress /dɪˈpres/ *verb* [T] **1** to make sb unhappy and without hope or enthusiasm: *All this wet weather really depresses me.* **2** (used about business) to cause sth to become less successful: *The reduction in the number of tourists has depressed local trade.* **3** (*formal*) to press sth down on a machine, etc: *To switch off the machine, depress the lever.* ▶ **depressing** *adj*: *The thought of growing old alone is very depressing.* ▶ **depressingly** *adv*

depressed /dɪˈprest/ *adj* **1** very unhappy, often for a long period of time: *He's been very depressed since he lost his job.* ➲ note at **sad** **2** (used about a place or an industry) without enough businesses or jobs: *an attempt to create employment in depressed areas*

depression /dɪˈpreʃn/ *noun* **1** [U] a feeling of unhappiness that lasts for a long time. **Depression** can be a medical condition and may have physical signs, for example being unable to sleep, etc: *clinical/post-natal depression* **2** [C,U] a period when the economic situation is bad, with little business activity and many people without a job: *The country was in the grip of (an) economic depression.* **3** [C] a part of a surface that is lower than the parts around it: *Rainwater collects in shallow depressions in the ground.*

deprive /dɪˈpraɪv/ *verb* [T] **deprive sb/sth of sth** to prevent sb/sth from having sth; to take away sth from sb: *The prisoners were deprived of food.* ▶ **deprivation** /ˌdeprɪˈveɪʃn/ *noun* [U]

deprived /dɪˈpraɪvd/ *adj* not having enough of the basic things in life, such as food, money, etc: *He came from a deprived background.*

Dept *abbr* = **department**: *the Sales Dept*

depth /depθ/ *noun* **1** [C,U] the distance down from the top to the bottom of sth: *The hole should be 3 cm in depth.* **2** [C,U] the distance from the front to the back of sth: *the depth of a shelf* ➲ picture at **length** **3** [U] the amount of emotion, knowledge, etc. that a person has: *He tried to convince her of the depth of his feelings for her.* **4** [C, usually pl] the deepest, most extreme or most serious part of sth: ***in the depths of** winter* (= when it is coldest) ➲ *adjective* **deep**

IDM **in depth** looking at all the details; in a thorough way: *to discuss a problem in depth* ◆ *an in-depth report*

out of your depth **1** (*BrE*) in water that is too deep for you to stand up in: *If you're not a very strong swimmer, don't go out of your depth.* **2** in a situation that is too difficult for you: *When they start discussing politics I soon get out of my depth.*

deputation /ˌdepjuˈteɪʃn/ *noun* [C, with sing or pl verb] a group of people sent to sb to act or speak for others

deputize (also -ise) /ˈdepjutaɪz/ *verb* [I] **deputize (for sb)** to act for sb in a higher position, who is away or unable to do sth

deputy /ˈdepjuti/ *noun* [C] (*pl* **deputies**) the second most important person in a particular organization, who does the work of their manager if the manager is away: *the deputy head of a school*

derail /dɪˈreɪl/ *verb* [T] to cause a train to come off a railway track

derailment /dɪˈreɪlmənt/ *noun* [C,U] an occasion when sth causes a train to come off a railway track

deranged /dɪˈreɪndʒd/ *adj* thinking and behaving in a way that is not normal, especially because of mental illness

derby /ˈdɑːbi/ *noun* [C] (*pl* **derbies**) **1** (*BrE*) a race or sports competition: *a motorcycle derby* **2 the Derby** (*BrE*) a horse race which takes place every year at Epsom **3** (*AmE*) = **bowler**(2)

derelict /ˈderəlɪkt/ *adj* no longer used and in bad condition: *a derelict house*

deride /dɪˈraɪd/ *verb* [T] to say that sb/sth is ridiculous; to laugh at sb/sth in a cruel way ▶ **derision** /dɪˈrɪʒn/ *noun* [U]: *Her comments were met with derision.* ▶ **derisive** /dɪˈraɪsɪv/ *adj*: *'What rubbish!' he said with a derisive laugh.*

derisory /dɪˈraɪsəri/ *adj* too small or of too little value to be considered seriously: *Union leaders rejected the derisory pay offer.*

derivation /ˌderɪˈveɪʃn/ *noun* [C,U] the origin from which a word or phrase has developed

derivative /dɪˈrɪvətɪv/ *noun* [C] a form of sth (especially a word) that has developed from the original form: *'Sadness' is a derivative of 'sad.'*

derive /dɪˈraɪv/ *verb* **1** [T] (*formal*) **derive sth from sth** to get sth (especially a feeling or an advantage) from sth: *I derive great satisfaction from my work.* **2** [I,T] (used about a name or word) to come from sth; to have sth as its origin: *The town derives its name from the river on which it was built.*

derogatory /dɪˈrɒɡətri/ *adj* expressing a lack of respect for, or a low opinion of, sth: *derogatory comments about the standard of my work*

descend /dɪˈsend/ *verb* [I,T] (*formal*) to go down to a lower place; to go down sth: *The plane started to descend and a few minutes later we landed.* ◆ *She descended the stairs slowly.* OPP **ascend**

IDM **be descended from sb** to have sb as a relative in past times: *He says he's descended from a Russian prince.*

descendant /dɪˈsendənt/ *noun* [C] a person who belongs to the same family as sb who lived a long time ago: *Her family are descendants of one of the first Englishmen to arrive in America.* ➲ look at **ancestor**

descent /dɪˈsent/ *noun* **1** [C] a movement down to a lower place: *The pilot informed us that we were about to begin our descent.* OPP **ascent** **2** [U] sb's family origins: *He is **of** Italian **descent**.* SYN **ancestry**

describe /dɪˈskraɪb/ *verb* [T] **describe sb/sth (to/for sb); describe sb/sth (as sth)** to say what sb/sth is like, or what happened: *Can you describe the bag you lost?* ◆ *It's impossible to describe how I felt.* ◆ *The thief was described as tall, thin, and aged about twenty.*

description /dɪˈskrɪpʃn/ *noun* **1** [C,U] a picture in words of sb/sth or of sth that happened: *The man gave the police a detailed description of the burglar.* **2** [C] a type or kind of sth: *It must be a tool **of some description**, but I don't know what it's for.*

descriptive /dɪˈskrɪptɪv/ *adj* that describes sb/sth, especially in a skilful or an interesting way: *a piece of descriptive writing* ◆ *She gave a highly descriptive account of the journey.*

desecrate /ˈdesɪkreɪt/ *verb* [T] to damage a thing or place of religious importance or to treat it without respect: *desecrated graves* ▶ **desecration** /ˌdesɪˈkreɪʃn/ *noun* [U]

desert[1] /ˈdezət/ *noun* [C,U] a large area of land, usually covered with sand, that is hot and has very little water and very few plants: *the Gobi Desert*

desert[2] /dɪˈzɜːt/ *verb* **1** [T] to leave sb/sth, usually for ever: *Many people have deserted the countryside and moved to the towns.* **2** [I,T] (used especially about sb in the armed forces) to leave without permission: *He deserted because he didn't want to fight.* ▶ **desertion** *noun* [C,U]

deserted /dɪˈzɜːtɪd/ *adj* empty, because all the people have left: *a deserted house* ◆ *deserted streets* SYN **abandoned**

deserter /dɪˈzɜːtə(r)/ *noun* [C] a person who leaves the armed forces without permission

ˌdesert ˈisland *noun* [C] an island, especially a tropical one, where nobody lives

deserve /dɪˈzɜːv/ *verb* [T] [not used in the continuous tenses] to earn sth, either good or bad, because of sth that you have done: *We've done a lot of work and we deserve a break.* ♦ *He deserves to be punished severely for such a crime.*

HELP Although this verb is not used in the continuous tenses, it is common to see the present participle (= *-ing* form): *There are other aspects of the case deserving attention.*

deservedly /dɪˈzɜːvɪdli/ *adv* in a way that is right because of what sb has done: *He deservedly won the Best Actor award.*

deserving /dɪˈzɜːvɪŋ/ *adj* **deserving (of sth)** that you should give help, money, etc. to: *This charity is a most deserving cause.*

design¹ /dɪˈzaɪn/ *noun* **1** [U] the way in which sth is planned and made or arranged: *Design faults have been discovered in the car.* **2** [U] the process and skill of making drawings that show how sth should be made, how it will work, etc: *to study industrial design* ♦ *graphic design* **3** [C] **a design (for sth)** a drawing or plan that shows how sth should be made, built, etc: *The architect showed us her design for the new theatre.* **4** [C] a pattern of lines, shapes, etc. that decorate sth: *a T-shirt with a geometric design on it* **SYN** **pattern**

design² /dɪˈzaɪn/ *verb* **1** [I,T] to plan and make a drawing of how sth will be made: *to design cars/dresses/houses* **2** [T] to invent, plan and develop sth for a particular purpose: *The bridge wasn't designed for such heavy traffic.*

designate /ˈdezɪgneɪt/ *verb* [T, often passive] (*formal*) **1 designate sth (as) sth** to give sth a name to show that it has a particular purpose: *This has been designated (as) a conservation area.* **2 designate sb (as) sth** to choose sb to do a particular job or task: *Who has she designated (as) her deputy?* **3** to show or mark sth: *These arrows designate the emergency exits.*

designer /dɪˈzaɪnə(r)/ *noun* [C] a person whose job is to make drawings or plans showing how sth will be made: *a fashion designer* ▶ **designer** *adj* [only *before* a noun]: *designer jeans*

desirable /dɪˈzaɪərəbl/ *adj* **1** wanted, often by many people; worth having: *Experience is desirable but not essential for this job.* **OPP** **undesirable** **2** sexually attractive

desire¹ /dɪˈzaɪə(r)/ *noun* [C,U] **(a) desire (for sth/to do sth)** **1** the feeling of wanting sth very much; a strong wish: *the desire for a peaceful solution to the crisis* ♦ *I have no desire to visit that place again.* **2** the wish for a sexual relationship with sb: *She felt a surge of love and desire for him.*

desire² /dɪˈzaɪə(r)/ *verb* [T] **1** [not used in the continuous tenses] (*formal*) to want; to wish for: *They have everything they could possibly desire.* ♦ *The service in the restaurant left a lot to be desired* (= was very bad). **2** to find sb/sth sexually attractive: *He still desired her.*

HELP Although this verb is not used in the continuous tenses, it is common to see the present participle (= *-ing* form): *Not desiring another argument, she turned away.*

desk /desk/ *noun* [C] **1** a type of table, often with drawers, that you sit at to write or work: *The students put their books on their desks.* ♦ *He used to be a pilot but now he has **a desk job*** (= he works in an office). **2** a table or place in a building where a particular service is provided: *an information desk* ♦ *Take your suitcases and tickets to the check-in desk.*

desktop /ˈdesktɒp/ *noun* [C] **1** the top of a desk **2** a computer screen on which you can see **icons** (= symbols) showing the programs, information, etc. that are available to be used **3** (also **desktop comˈputer**) a computer that can fit on a desk ➲ look at **laptop**

ˌdesktop ˈpublishing *noun* [U] (*abbr* **DTP**) the use of a small computer and a machine for printing, to produce books, magazines and other printed material

desolate /ˈdesələt/ *adj* **1** (used about a place) empty in a way that seems very sad: *desolate wasteland* **2** (used about a person) lonely, very unhappy and without hope ▶ **desolation** /ˌdesəˈleɪʃn/ *noun* [U]: *a scene of desolation.* ♦ *He felt utter desolation when his wife died.*

despair¹ /dɪˈspeə(r)/ *noun* [U] the state of having lost all hope: *I felt like giving up **in despair**.* ▶ **despairing** *adj*: *a despairing cry* ➲ look at **desperate**

despair² /dɪˈspeə(r)/ *verb* [I] **despair (of sb/sth)** to lose all hope that sth will happen: *We began to despair of ever finding somewhere to live.*

despatch (*BrE*) = **dispatch**

desperate /ˈdespərət/ *adj* **1** out of control and ready to do anything to change the situation you are in because it is so terrible: *She became desperate when her money ran out.* **2** done with little hope of success, as a last thing to try when everything else has failed: *I made a desperate attempt to persuade her to change her mind.* **3 desperate (for sth/to do sth)** wanting or needing sth very much: *Let's go into a cafe. I'm desperate for a drink.* **4** terrible, very serious: *There is a desperate shortage of skilled workers.* ▶ **desperately** *adv*: *She was desperately* (= extremely) *unlucky not to win.* ▶ **desperation** /ˌdespəˈreɪʃn/ *noun* [U]

despicable /dɪˈspɪkəbl/ *adj* very unpleasant or evil: *a despicable act of terrorism*

despise /dɪˈspaɪz/ *verb* [T] to hate sb/sth very much: *I despise him for lying to me.*

despite /dɪˈspaɪt/ *prep* without being affected by the thing mentioned: *Despite having very little money, they enjoy life.* ♦ *The scheme went ahead despite public opposition.* ♦ *She was good at physics,* *despite the fact that* she found it boring. **SYN** in spite of

WRITING TIP

How to show contrast 2

To show that there is something surprising or unexpected in the contrast between the two points, we can use **despite, in spite of** or **although:** *In spite of/Despite knowing about the dangers of smoking, large numbers of young people continue to smoke.* ◆ *In spite of/Despite the fact that smoking is dangerous, large numbers of young people continue to smoke.* ◆ *Although smoking is dangerous, large numbers of young people continue to smoke.*

➲ note at **contrast** ℹ For more help with writing, look at **Wordpower Writing Tutor** at the back of this dictionary.

despondent /dɪˈspɒndənt/ *adj* **despondent (about/over sth)** without hope; expecting no improvement: *She was becoming increasingly despondent about finding a job.* ▶ **despondency** /dɪˈspɒndənsi/ *noun* [U]

despot /ˈdespɒt/ *noun* [C] a ruler with great power, especially one who uses it in a cruel way ▶ **despotic** /dɪˈspɒtɪk/ *adj*

dessert /dɪˈzɜːt/ *noun* [C,U] something sweet that is eaten after the main part of a meal: *What would you like* ***for dessert****—ice cream or fresh fruit?* ➲ note at **restaurant** ➲ look at **pudding**

dessertspoon /dɪˈzɜːtspuːn/ *noun* [C] a spoon used for eating sweet food after the main part of a meal ➲ picture at **spoon**

destabilize (also **-ise**) /ˌdiːˈsteɪbəlaɪz/ *verb* [T] to make a system, government, country, etc. become less safe and successful: *Terrorist attacks were threatening to destabilize the government.* ➲ look at **stabilize**

destination /ˌdestɪˈneɪʃn/ *noun* [C] the place where sb/sth is going: *I finally reached my destination two hours late.* ◆ *popular holiday destinations like the Bahamas*

destined /ˈdestɪnd/ *adj* **1 destined for sth/to do sth** having a future that has been decided or planned at an earlier time: *I think she is destined for success.* ◆ *He was destined to become one of the country's leading politicians.* **2 destined for ...** travelling towards a particular place: *I boarded a bus destined for New York.*

destiny /ˈdestəni/ *noun* (*pl* **destinies**) **1** [C] the things that happen to you in your life, especially things that you cannot control: *She felt that it was her destiny to be a great singer.* **2** [U] a power that people believe controls their lives **SYN** for both meanings **fate**

destitute /ˈdestɪtjuːt/ *adj* without any money, food or a home ▶ **destitution** /ˌdestɪˈtjuːʃn/ *noun* [U]

⚷ **destroy** /dɪˈstrɔɪ/ *verb* [T] **1** to damage sth so badly that it can no longer be used or no longer exists: *The building was destroyed by fire.* ◆ *The defeat destroyed his confidence.* **2** to kill an animal, especially because it is injured or dangerous: *The horse broke its leg and had to be destroyed.*

destroyer /dɪˈstrɔɪə(r)/ *noun* [C] **1** a small ship that is used in war **2** a person or thing that destroys sth

⚷ **destruction** /dɪˈstrʌkʃn/ *noun* [U] the act of destroying sth: *The war brought death and destruction to the city.* ◆ *the destruction of the rainforests*

destructive /dɪˈstrʌktɪv/ *adj* causing a lot of harm or damage: *destructive weapons* ◆ *the destructive effects of a poor diet*

detach /dɪˈtætʃ/ *verb* [T] **detach sth (from sth)** to separate sth from sth it is connected to: *Detach the form at the bottom of the page and send it to this address ...* **OPP** attach

detachable /dɪˈtætʃəbl/ *adj* that can be separated from sth it is connected to: *a coat with a detachable hood*

detached /dɪˈtætʃt/ *adj* **1** (used about a house) not joined to any other house ➲ picture on **page P9** **2** not being or not feeling personally involved in sth; without emotion

detachment /dɪˈtætʃmənt/ *noun* **1** [U] the fact or feeling of not being personally involved in sth **2** [C] a group of soldiers who have been given a particular task away from the main group

⚷ **detail¹** /ˈdiːteɪl/ *noun* [C,U] one fact or piece of information: *Just give me the basic facts. Don't worry about the details.* ◆ *On the application form you should give details of your education and experience.* ◆ *The work involves close attention to detail.*

IDM go into detail(s) to talk or write about the details of sth; to explain sth fully: *I can't go into detail now because it would take too long.*

in detail including the details: *We haven't discussed the matter in great detail yet.* **SYN** thoroughly

▶ **detailed** *adj*: *a detailed description*

detail² /ˈdiːteɪl/ *verb* [T] to give a full list of sth; to describe sth completely: *He detailed all the equipment he needed for the job.*

detain /dɪˈteɪn/ *verb* [T] to stop sb from leaving a place; to delay sb: *A man has been detained by the police for questioning* (= kept at the police station). ◆ *Don't let me detain you if you're busy.* ➲ look at **detention**

detainee /ˌdiːteɪˈniː/ *noun* [C] a person who is kept in prison, usually because of his or her political opinions

detect /dɪˈtekt/ *verb* [T] to notice or discover sth that is difficult to see, feel, etc: *I detected a slight change in his attitude.* ◆ *Traces of blood were detected on his clothes.* ▶ **detection** *noun* [U]: *The crime escaped detection* (= was not discovered) *for many years.*

detective /dɪˈtektɪv/ *noun* [C] a person, especially a police officer, who tries to solve crimes

de'tective story *noun* [C] a story about a crime in which sb tries to find out who the guilty person is

detector /dɪˈtektə(r)/ *noun* [C] a machine that is used for finding or noticing sth: *a smoke/metal/lie detector*

detention /dɪˈtenʃn/ *noun* [U,C] **1** the act of stopping a person leaving a place, especially by keeping them in prison: *They were kept* ***in detention*** *for ten days.* **2** the punishment of being kept at school for a time after other students have gone home ➲ *verb* **detain**

deter /dɪˈtɜː(r)/ *verb* [T] (**deterring**; **deterred**) **deter sb (from doing sth)** to make sb decide not to do sth, especially by telling them that it would have bad results: *The council is trying to deter visitors from bringing their cars into the city centre.* ➲ *noun* **deterrent**

detergent /dɪˈtɜːdʒənt/ *noun* [C,U] a chemical liquid or powder that is used for cleaning things

deteriorate /dɪˈtɪəriəreɪt/ *verb* [I] to become worse: *The political tension is deteriorating into civil war.* ▸ **deterioration** /dɪˌtɪəriəˈreɪʃn/ *noun* [C,U]

⚷ **determination** /dɪˌtɜːmɪˈneɪʃn/ *noun* [U] **1 determination (to do sth)** the quality of having firmly decided to do sth, even if it is very difficult: *her determination to win* ◆ *You need great determination to succeed in business.* **2** (*formal*) the process of deciding sth officially: *the determination of future government policy*

⚷ **determine** /dɪˈtɜːmɪn/ *verb* [T] (*formal*) **1** to discover the facts about sth: *We need to determine what happened immediately before the accident.* **2** to make sth happen in a particular way or be of a particular type: *The results of the tests will determine what treatment you need.* ◆ *Age and experience will be* ***determining factors*** *in our choice of candidate.* **3** to decide sth officially: *A date for the meeting has yet to be determined.*

⚷ **determined** /dɪˈtɜːmɪnd/ *adj* **determined (to do sth)** having firmly decided to do sth or to succeed, even if it is difficult: *He is determined to leave school, even though his parents want him to stay.* ◆ *She's a very determined athlete.*

determiner /dɪˈtɜːmɪnə(r)/ *noun* [C] a word that comes before a noun to show how the noun is being used: *'Her', 'most' and 'those' are all determiners.*

deterrent /dɪˈterənt/ *noun* [C] something that should stop you doing sth: *Their punishment will be a deterrent to others.* ➲ *verb* **deter** ▸ **deterrent** *adj*

detest /dɪˈtest/ *verb* [T] to hate or not like sb/sth at all: *They absolutely detest each other.* SYN **loathe**

detonate /ˈdetəneɪt/ *verb* [I,T] to explode or to make a bomb, etc. explode

detonator /ˈdetəneɪtə(r)/ *noun* [C] a device for making a bomb explode

detour /ˈdiːtʊə(r)/ *noun* [C] **1** a longer route from one place to another that you take in order to avoid sth/sb or in order to see or do sth: *Because of the accident we had to make a five-kilometre detour.* **2** (*AmE*) = **diversion**(3)

detox /ˈdiːtɒks/ *noun* [U] (*informal*) **1** the process of removing harmful substances from your body by only eating and drinking particular things **2** = **detoxification** ▸ **detoxify** /ˌdiːˈtɒksɪfaɪ/ *verb* [I,T]

detoxification /diːˌtɒksɪfɪˈkeɪʃn/ (also *informal* detox) *noun* [U] treatment given to people to help them stop drinking alcohol or taking drugs

detract /dɪˈtrækt/ *verb* [I] **detract from sth** to make sth seem less good or important: *These criticisms in no way detract from the team's achievements.*

detriment /ˈdetrɪmənt/ *noun*

IDM **to the detriment of sb/sth** harming or damaging sb/sth: *Doctors claim that the changes will be to the detriment of patients.*

▸ **detrimental** /ˌdetrɪˈmentl/ *adj*: *Too much sugar is* ***detrimental to*** *your health.*

deuce /djuːs/ *noun* [U] a score of 40 points to each player in a game of **tennis**

devalue /ˌdiːˈvæljuː/ *verb* [T] **1** to reduce the value of the money of one country in relation to the value of the money of other countries: *The pound has been devalued against the dollar.* **2** to reduce the value or importance of sth: *The refusal of the top players to take part devalues this competition.* ▸ **devaluation** /ˌdiːˌvæljuˈeɪʃn/ *noun* [U]

devastate /ˈdevəsteɪt/ *verb* [T] **1** to destroy sth or damage it badly: *a land devastated by war* **2** to make sb extremely upset and shocked: *This tragedy has devastated the community.* ▸ **devastation** /ˌdevəˈsteɪʃn/ *noun* [U]: *a scene of total devastation*

devastated /ˈdevəsteɪtɪd/ *adj* extremely shocked and upset: *They were devastated when their baby died.*

devastating /ˈdevəsteɪtɪŋ/ *adj* **1** that destroys sth completely: *a devastating explosion* **2** that shocks or upsets sb very much: *The closure of the factory was a devastating blow to the workers.*

⚷ **develop** /dɪˈveləp/ *verb*

➤GROW **1** [I,T] to grow slowly, increase, or change into sth else; to make sb/sth do this: *to develop from a child into an adult* ◆ *a scheme to help pupils develop their natural talents* ◆ *Scientists have developed crops that are resistant to disease.* ◆ *Over the years, she's developed her own unique singing style.*

➤PROBLEM/DISEASE **2** [I,T] to begin to have a problem or disease; to start to affect sth: *to develop cancer/AIDS* ◆ *Trouble is developing along the border.*

➤BUILD HOUSES **3** [T] to build houses, shops, factories, etc. on a piece of land: *This site is being developed for offices.*

➤IDEA/STORY **4** [T] to make an idea, a story, etc. clearer or more detailed by writing or talking about it more: *She went on to develop this theme later in the lecture.*

➤PHOTOGRAPHS **5** [T] to make pictures from a piece of film by using special chemicals: *to develop a film*

developed /dɪˈveləpt/ *adj* of a good level or standard: *a highly developed economy*

developer /dɪˈveləpə(r)/ (also ˈproperty developer) *noun* [C] a person or company that builds houses, shops, etc. on a piece of land

developing /dɪˈveləpɪŋ/ *adj* [only *before* a noun] (used about a poor country) that is trying to develop or improve its economy: *a developing country* ♦ *the developing world*

development /dɪˈveləpmənt/ *noun* **1** [U] the process of becoming bigger, stronger, better, etc., or of making sb/sth do this: *a child's intellectual development* ♦ *the development of tourism in Cuba* **2** [U,C] the process of creating sth more advanced; a more advanced product: *She works in* ***research and development*** *for a software company.* ♦ *the latest developments in space technology* **3** [C] a new event that changes a situation: *This week has seen a number of new developments in the Middle East.* **4** [C,U] a piece of land with new buildings on it; the process of building on a piece of land: *a new housing development* ♦ *The land has been bought for development.*

deviate /ˈdiːvieɪt/ *verb* [I] **deviate (from sth)** to change or become different from what is normal or expected: *He never once deviated from his original plan.*

deviation /ˌdiːviˈeɪʃn/ *noun* [C,U] a difference from what is normal or expected, or from what is approved of by society: *a deviation from our usual way of doing things*

device /dɪˈvaɪs/ *noun* [C] **1** a tool or piece of equipment made for a particular purpose: *a security device which detects any movement* ♦ *labour-saving devices such as washing machines and vacuum cleaners* ➲ note at **tool** **2** a clever method for getting the result you want: *Critics dismissed the speech as a political device for winning support.*

devil /ˈdevl/ *noun* [C] **1 the Devil** the most powerful evil being, according to the Christian, Jewish and Muslim religions ➲ look at **Satan** **2** an evil being; a spirit **3** (*spoken*) a word used to show pity, anger, etc. when you are talking about a person: *The poor devil died in hospital two days later.* ♦ *Those kids can be little devils sometimes.*

IDM be a devil used to encourage sb to do sth that they are not sure about doing: *Go on, be a devil—buy both of them.*

speak/talk of the devil used when the person who is being talked about appears unexpectedly

devious /ˈdiːviəs/ *adj* clever but not honest or direct: *I wouldn't trust him—he can be very devious.* ♦ *a devious trick/plan* ▶ **deviously** *adv*

devise /dɪˈvaɪz/ *verb* [T] to invent a new way of doing sth: *They've devised a plan for keeping traffic out of the city centre.*

devoid /dɪˈvɔɪd/ *adj* (*formal*) **devoid of sth** not having a particular quality; without sth: *devoid of hope/ambition/imagination*

devolution /ˌdiːvəˈluːʃn/ *noun* [U] the movement of political power from central to local government

devote /dɪˈvəʊt/ *verb* [T] **devote yourself/sth to sb/sth** to give a lot of time, energy, etc. to sb/sth: *She gave up work to devote herself full-time to her music.* ♦ *Schools should devote more time to science subjects.*

devoted /dɪˈvəʊtɪd/ *adj* **devoted (to sb/sth)** loving sb/sth very much; completely loyal to sb/sth: *Neil's absolutely devoted to his wife.*

devotee /ˌdevəˈtiː/ *noun* [C] **a devotee (of sb/sth)** a person who likes sb/sth very much: *Devotees of science fiction will enjoy this new film.*

devotion /dɪˈvəʊʃn/ *noun* [U] **devotion (to sb/sth)** **1** great love for sb/sth: *a mother's devotion to her children* **SYN dedication** **2** the act of giving a lot of your time, energy, etc. to sb/sth: *devotion to duty* **SYN dedication** **3** very strong religious feeling

devour /dɪˈvaʊə(r)/ *verb* [T] **1** to eat sth quickly because you are very hungry **2** to do or use sth quickly and completely: *Lisa devours two or three novels a week.*

devout /dɪˈvaʊt/ *adj* very religious: *a devout Muslim family* ▶ **devoutly** *adv*

dew /djuː/ *noun* [U] small drops of water that form on plants, leaves, etc. during the night

dexterity /dekˈsterəti/ *noun* [U] skill at doing things, especially with your hands

diabetes /ˌdaɪəˈbiːtiːz/ *noun* [U] a serious disease in which sb's body cannot control the level of sugar in the blood

diabetic¹ /ˌdaɪəˈbetɪk/ *adj* connected with **diabetes** or **diabetics**: *diabetic chocolate* (= safe for diabetics)

diabetic² /ˌdaɪəˈbetɪk/ *noun* [C] a person who suffers from **diabetes**

diagnose /ˈdaɪəgnəʊz/ *verb* [T] **diagnose sth (as sth); diagnose sb as/with sth** to find out and say exactly what illness a person has or what the cause of a problem is: *His illness was diagnosed as bronchitis.* ♦ *I've been diagnosed as (a) diabetic/with diabetes.* ♦ *After a couple of minutes I diagnosed the trouble—a flat battery.*

diagnosis /ˌdaɪəgˈnəʊsɪs/ *noun* [C,U] (*pl* **diagnoses** /-siːz/) the act of saying exactly what illness a person has or what the cause of a problem is: *to* ***make a diagnosis***

diagnostic /ˌdaɪəgˈnɒstɪk/ *adj* (*technical*) connected with identifying sth, especially an illness: *to carry out* ***diagnostic tests***

diagonal /daɪˈægənl/ *adj* (used about a straight line) joining two sides of sth at an angle that is not 90° or vertical or horizontal: *Draw a diagonal line from one corner of the square to the opposite corner.* ➲ picture at **line** ▶ **diagonally** /-nəli/ *adv*

diagram /ˈdaɪəgræm/ *noun* [C] a simple picture that is used to explain how sth works or what sth looks like: *a diagram of the body's digestive system*

dial¹ /ˈdaɪəl/ *noun* [C] **1** the round part of a clock, watch, control on a machine, etc. that shows a measurement of time, amount, temperature, etc: *a dial for showing air pressure* **2** the round control on a radio, cooker, etc. that you turn to change sth

D

3 the round part with holes in it on some older telephones that you turn to call a number

dial² /ˈdaɪəl/ *verb* [I,T] (**dialling**; **dialled**, (*AmE*) **dialing**; **dialed**) to push the buttons or move the **dial** on a telephone in order to call a telephone number: *You can now dial direct to Singapore.* ◆ *to dial the wrong number*

D

dialect /ˈdaɪəlekt/ *noun* [C,U] a form of a language that is spoken in one part of a country: *a local dialect*

ˈdialog box (*BrE also* ˈ**dialogue box**) *noun* [C] a box that appears on a computer screen asking the user to choose what they want to do next

dialogue (*AmE* **dialog**) /ˈdaɪəlɒɡ/ *noun* [C,U] **1** (a) conversation between people in a book, play, etc: *This movie is all action, with very little dialogue.* ◆ *On the tape you will hear a short dialogue between a shop assistant and a customer.* **2** (a) discussion between people who have different opinions: *(a) dialogue between the major political parties*

diameter /daɪˈæmɪtə(r)/ *noun* [C] a straight line that goes from one side to the other of a circle, passing through the centre ➲ look at **circumference**, **radius** ➲ picture at **circle**

🔑 **diamond** /ˈdaɪəmənd/ *noun* **1** [C,U] a hard, bright **precious** (= rare and valuable) stone which is very expensive and is used for making jewellery. A diamond usually has no colour: *a diamond ring* **2** (also **lozenge**) [C] a flat shape that has four sides of equal length and points at two ends ➲ picture at **shape** **3** **diamonds** [pl] in a pack of playing cards, the **suit** (= one of the four sets) with red shapes like diamonds (2) on them: *the seven of diamonds* ➲ note at **card** ➲ picture at **card** **4** [C] one of the cards from this suit: *I haven't got any diamonds.* **5** [U] celebrating the 60th anniversary of sth: *This year's their diamond wedding.* ➲ look at **golden, silver**

diaper /ˈdaɪəpə(r)/ (*AmE*) = **nappy**

diaphragm /ˈdaɪəfræm/ *noun* [C] **1** the muscle between your lungs and your stomach that helps you to breathe **2** a rubber device that a woman puts inside her body before having sex to prevent her from becoming pregnant

diarrhoea (*AmE* **diarrhea**) /ˌdaɪəˈrɪə/ *noun* [U] an illness that causes you to get rid of **faeces** (= solid waste) from your body very often and in a more liquid form than usual

🔑 **diary** /ˈdaɪəri/ *noun* [C] (*pl* **diaries**) **1** a book in which you write down things that you have to do, remember, etc: *I'll just check in my diary to see if I'm free that weekend.* ➲ note at **calendar** **2** a book in which you write down what happens to you each day: *Do you* ***keep a*** *diary?*

dice /daɪs/ *noun* [C] (*pl* **dice**) a small solid square object with six sides and a different number of spots (from one to six) on each side, used in certain games: ***Throw the dice*** *to see who goes first.*

dice

dictate /dɪkˈteɪt/ *verb* **1** [I,T] **dictate (sth) (to sb)** to say sth in a normal speaking voice so that sb else can write or type it: *to dictate a letter to a secretary* **2** [I,T] **dictate (sth) (to sb)** to tell sb what to do in a way that seems unfair: *Parents can't dictate to their children how they should run their lives.* **3** [T] to control or influence sth: *The kind of house people live in is usually dictated by how much they earn.*

dictation /dɪkˈteɪʃn/ *noun* [C,U] spoken words that sb else must write or type: *We had a dictation in English today* (= a test in which we had to write down what the teacher said).

dictator /dɪkˈteɪtə(r)/ *noun* [C] a ruler who has total power in a country, especially one who rules the country by force ▶ **dictatorship** *noun* [C,U]: *a military dictatorship* ▶ **dictatorial** /ˌdɪktəˈtɔːriəl/ *adj*: *dictatorial behaviour*

🔑 **dictionary** /ˈdɪkʃənri/ *noun* [C] (*pl* **dictionaries**) **1** a book that contains a list of the words in a language in the order of the alphabet and that tells you what they mean, in the same or another language: *to look up a word in a dictionary* ◆ *a bilingual/monolingual dictionary* **2** a book that lists the words connected with a particular subject and tells you what they mean: *a dictionary of idioms* ◆ *a medical dictionary* ➲ note at **book**

did /dɪd/ *past tense* of **do**

didn't /ˈdɪdnt/ *short for* **did not**

🔑 **die** /daɪ/ *verb* (**dying**; **dies**; *pt, pp* **died**) **1** [I,T] **die (from/of sth)** to stop living: *My father died when I was three.* ◆ *Thousands of people have died from this disease.* ◆ *to die of hunger* ◆ *to die for what you believe in* ◆ *to die a natural/violent death* ➲ *adjective* **dead**, *noun* **death** **2** [I] to stop existing; to disappear: *The old customs are dying.* ◆ *Our love will never die.*

IDM **be dying for sth/to do sth** (*spoken*) to want sth/to do sth very much: *I'm dying for a cup of coffee.*

die hard to change or disappear only slowly or with difficulty: *Old attitudes towards women die hard.*

die laughing to find sth very funny: *I thought I'd die laughing when he told that joke.*

to die for (*informal*) if you think that sth is to die for, you really want it and would do anything to get it: *She was wearing a dress to die for.*

PHR V **die away** to slowly become weaker before stopping or disappearing: *The sound of the engine died away as the car drove into the distance.*

die down to slowly become less strong: *Let's wait until the storm dies down before we go out.*

die off to die one by one until there are none left

die out to stop happening or disappear: *The use of horses on farms has almost died out in this country.*

diesel /ˈdiːzl/ *noun* **1** [U] a type of heavy oil used in some engines instead of petrol: *a diesel engine* ◆ *a taxi that runs on diesel* **2** [C] a vehicle that uses diesel: *My new car's a diesel.* ➲ look at **petrol**

🔑 **diet¹** /ˈdaɪət/ *noun* **1** [C,U] the food that a person or an animal usually eats: *They* ***live on a diet of*** *rice and vegetables.* ◆ *I always try to have a healthy, balanced diet* (= including all the different types of food

that the body needs). ◆ *Poor diet is a cause of ill health.* **2** [C] certain foods that a person who is ill or who wants to lose weight is allowed to eat: *a low-fat diet* ◆ *a sugar-free diet*
IDM **be/go on a diet** to eat only certain foods or a small amount of food because you want to lose weight
▸ **dietary** /ˈdaɪətəri/ *adj*: *dietary habits*

diet² /ˈdaɪət/ *verb* [I] to try to lose weight by eating less food or only certain kinds of food: *You've lost some weight. Have you been dieting?*

differ /ˈdɪfə(r)/ *verb* [I] **1** differ (from sb/sth) to be different: *How does this car differ from the more expensive model?* **2** differ (with sb) (about/on sth) to have a different opinion: *I'm afraid I differ with you on that question.*

difference /ˈdɪfrəns/ *noun* **1** [C] a difference (between A and B) the way that people or things are not the same or the way that sb/sth has changed: *What's the difference between this computer and that cheaper one?* ◆ *From a distance it's hard to* ***tell the difference*** *between the twins.* OPP **similarity** **2** [C,U] difference (in sth) (between A and B) the amount by which people or things are not the same or by which sb/sth has changed: *There's an age difference of three years between the two children.* ◆ *There's very little difference in price since last year.* ◆ *We gave a 30% deposit and must* ***pay the difference*** *when the work is finished* (= the rest of the money). **3** [C] a disagreement that is not very serious: *All couples* ***have*** *their* ***differences*** *from time to time.* ◆ *There was* ***a difference of opinion*** *over how much we owed.*
IDM **make a, some, etc. difference (to sb/sth)** to have an effect (on sb/sth): *Marriage made a big difference to her life.*
make no difference (to sb/sth); not make any difference to not be important (to sb/sth); to have no effect: *It makes no difference to us if the baby is a girl or a boy.*
split the difference ➲ split¹

WRITING TIP

How to compare different things

To show how two things, people, etc. are different, we can use comparative adjectives: *Australia is bigger than England.* ◆ *Enthusiasm is more important than experience.* You can also use the following expressions; **Unlike X, Y ...**: *Unlike Jim, Mike likes playing sports* (= Mike likes playing sports, but Jim does not), **X is different from Y (in that) ...**: *Tablet computers are different from laptops in that a tablet has a touchscreen* (= a tablet has a touchscreen, but a laptop does not), **While X ..., Y ...**: *While Brian enjoys going out with his friends, Simon prefers to stay at home* or **X ..., while Y ...**: *Brian enjoys going out with his friends, while Simon prefers to stay at home* (= Brian is very sociable, but Simon is not).

➲ note at **similarity** ℹ For more help with writing, look at **Wordpower Writing Tutor** at the back of this dictionary.

different /ˈdɪfrənt/ *adj* **1** different (from/to sb/sth) not the same: *The play was different from anything I had seen before.* ◆ *The two houses are very different in style.* ◆ *You'd look completely different with short hair.* ◆ *When Ulf started school in this country, the other kids were cruel to him because he was different.* OPP **similar**

HELP In American English **different than** is also used.

2 [only *before* a noun] separate; individual: *This coat is available in three different colours.*
IDM **another/a different matter** ➲ matter¹
a (whole) new/different ball game ➲ **ball game**
▸ **differently** *adv*: *I think you'll feel differently about it tomorrow.*

differentiate /ˌdɪfəˈrenʃieɪt/ *verb* **1** [I,T] differentiate between A and B; differentiate A (from B) to see or show how things are different: *It is hard to differentiate between these two types of seed.* **2** [T] differentiate sth (from sth) to make one thing different from another: *The coloured feathers differentiate the male bird from the plain brown female.* **3** [T] to treat one person or group differently from another: *We don't differentiate between the two groups—we treat everybody alike.* SYN **distinguish** ▸ **differentiation** /ˌdɪfəˌrenʃiˈeɪʃn/ *noun* [U]

difficult /ˈdɪfɪkəlt/ *adj* **1** difficult (for sb) (to do sth) not easy to do or understand: *a difficult test/problem* ◆ *I* ***find it difficult to*** *get up early in the morning.* ◆ *It was difficult for us to hear the speaker.* ◆ *I'm in a difficult situation. Whatever I do, somebody will be upset.* **2** (used about a person) not friendly, reasonable or helpful: *a difficult customer* SYN **awkward**

difficulty /ˈdɪfɪkəlti/ *noun* (*pl* difficulties) **1** [U,C] difficulty (in sth/in doing sth) a problem; a situation that is hard to deal with: *I'm sure you won't* ***have*** *any* ***difficulty*** *getting a visa for America.* ◆ *We* ***had no difficulty*** *selling our car.* ◆ *We found a hotel* ***without difficulty.*** ◆ ***With difficulty,*** *I managed to persuade Alice to lend us the money.* ◆ *I could see someone* ***in difficulty*** *in the water so I went to help them.* ◆ *If you borrow too much money you may* ***get into*** *financial* ***difficulties.*** **2** [U] how hard sth is to do or to deal with: *The questions start easy and then increase in difficulty.*

diffident /ˈdɪfɪdənt/ *adj* not having confidence in your own strengths or abilities: *He has a very diffident manner.* ▸ **diffidence** *noun* [U]

dig¹ /dɪɡ/ *verb* [I,T] (digging; *pt, pp* dug /dʌɡ/) to move earth and make a hole in the ground: *The children are busy digging in the sand.* ◆ *to dig a hole*
IDM **dig deep** to try harder, give more, go further, etc. than is usually necessary: *Charities for the homeless are asking people to dig deep into their pockets in this cold weather.*
dig your heels in to refuse to do sth or to change your mind about sth: *The union dug its heels in and waited for a better pay offer.*
PHR V **dig (sth) in; dig sth into sth** to push or press (sth) into sb/sth: *My neck is all red where my*

collar is digging in. ♦ *He dug his hands deep into his pockets.*

dig sb/sth out (of sth) **1** to get sb/sth out of sth by moving the earth, etc. that covers them or it: *Rescue workers dug the survivors out of the rubble.* **2** to get or find sb/sth by searching: *I dug out some old photos from the attic.*

dig sth up **1** to remove sth from the earth by digging: *to dig up potatoes* **2** to make a hole or take away soil by digging: *Workmen are digging up the road in front of our house.* **3** to find information by searching or studying: *Newspapers have dug up some embarrassing facts about his private life.*

spade

dig

dig² /dɪg/ [C], *noun* **1** a hard push: *to give somebody a dig in the ribs* (= with your elbow) **2** something that you say to upset sb: *The others kept **making digs** at him because of the way he spoke.* **3** an occasion or a place where a group of people try to find things of historical or scientific interest in the ground in order to study them: *an archaeological dig*

digest /daɪˈdʒest/ *verb* [T] **1** to change food in your stomach so that it can be used by the body: *I'm not going to go swimming until I've digested my lunch.* **2** to think about new information so that you understand it fully: *The lecture was interesting, but too much to digest all at once.*

digestion /daɪˈdʒestʃən/ *noun* [C,U] the process of changing food in your stomach so that it can be used by the body ▶ **digestive** /daɪˈdʒestɪv/ *adj*: *the digestive system*

digit /ˈdɪdʒɪt/ *noun* [C] any of the numbers from 0 to 9: *a six-digit telephone number*

digital /ˈdɪdʒɪtl/ *adj* **1** using an electronic system that uses the numbers 1 and 0 to record sound or store information, and that gives results of a high quality: *a digital camera* ♦ *digital television/radio* **2** showing information by using numbers: *a digital watch* ➲ picture at **clock**

dignified /ˈdɪgnɪfaɪd/ *adj* behaving in a calm, serious way that makes other people respect you: *dignified behaviour* OPP **undignified**

dignity /ˈdɪgnəti/ *noun* [U] **1** calm, serious behaviour that makes other people respect you: *to behave **with dignity*** **2** the quality of being serious and formal: *the quiet dignity of the funeral service*

digress /daɪˈgres/ *verb* [I] (*formal*) to stop talking or writing about the main subject under discussion and start talking or writing about another less important one ▶ **digression** /daɪˈgreʃn/ *noun* [C,U]

dike = dyke

dilapidated /dɪˈlæpɪdeɪtɪd/ *adj* (used about buildings, furniture, etc.) old and broken ▶ **dilapidation** /dɪˌlæpɪˈdeɪʃn/ *noun* [U]

dilate /daɪˈleɪt/ *verb* [I,T] to become or to make sth larger, wider or more open: *Her eyes dilated with fear.* ♦ *dilated pupils/nostrils* OPP **contract** ▶ **dilation** /daɪˈleɪʃn/ *noun* [U]

dilemma /dɪˈlemə/ *noun* [C] a situation in which you have to make a difficult choice between two or more things: *Doctors **face a** moral **dilemma** of when to keep patients alive artificially and when to let them die.* ♦ *to be **in a dilemma***

diligent /ˈdɪlɪdʒənt/ *adj* (*formal*) showing care and effort in your work or duties: *a diligent student/worker* ▶ **diligently** *adv*

dilute /daɪˈluːt/ *verb* [T] dilute sth (with sth) to make a liquid weaker by adding water or another liquid ▶ **dilute** *adj*

dim¹ /dɪm/ *adj* (dimmer; dimmest) **1** not bright or easy to see; not clear: *The light was too dim to read by.* ♦ *a dim shape in the distance* ♦ *My memories of my grandmother are quite dim.* **2** (*informal*) not very clever; stupid: *He's a bit dim.* **3** (*informal*) (used about a situation) without much hope: *The prospects of the two sides reaching an agreement look dim.* ▶ **dimly** *adv*

dim² /dɪm/ *verb* [I,T] (dimming; dimmed) to become or make sth less bright or clear: *The lights dimmed.* ♦ *to dim the lights*

dime /daɪm/ *noun* [C] a coin used in the US and Canada that is worth ten cents

dimension /daɪˈmenʃn/ *noun* **1** [C,U] a measurement of the length, width or height of sth **2** **dimensions** [pl] the size of sth including its length, width and height: *to measure the dimensions of a room* ♦ (*figurative*) *The full dimensions of this problem are only now being recognized.* **3** [C] something that affects the way you think about a problem or situation: *to add a new dimension to a problem/situation* **4** **-dimensional** /-ʃənl/ [in compounds] having the number of **dimensions** mentioned: *a three-dimensional model*

diminish /dɪˈmɪnɪʃ/ *verb* [I,T] (*formal*) to become or to make sth smaller or less important: *The world's rainforests are diminishing fast.* ♦ *The bad news did nothing to diminish her enthusiasm for the plan.* SYN **decrease**

diminutive /dɪˈmɪnjətɪv/ *adj* (*formal*) much smaller than usual

dimple /ˈdɪmpl/ *noun* [C] a round area in the skin on your cheek, etc. which often only appears when you smile

din /dɪn/ *noun* [sing] a lot of unpleasant noise that continues for some time

dine /daɪn/ *verb* [I] (*formal*) to eat a meal, especially in the evening: *We dined at an exclusive French restaurant.*

PHR V **dine out** to eat in a restaurant

diner /ˈdaɪnə(r)/ *noun* [C] **1** a person who is eating at a restaurant **2** (*AmE*) a restaurant that serves simple, cheap food

dinghy /ˈdɪŋgi/ *noun* [C] (*pl* **dinghies**) **1** a small boat that you sail ➲ look at **yacht** **2** a small open boat, often used to take people to land from a larger boat ➲ picture at **boat**

dingy /ˈdɪndʒi/ *adj* (**dingier**; **dingiest**) dirty and dark: *a dingy room/hotel*

ˈ**dining room** *noun* [C] a room where you eat meals ➲ picture on **page P8**

⚷ **dinner** /ˈdɪnə(r)/ *noun* **1** [C,U] the main meal of the day, eaten either at midday or in the evening: *Would you like to* **go out for/to dinner** *one evening?* ♦ *I never eat a big dinner.* ♦ *What's for dinner, Mum?* ➲ note at **meal** **2** [C] a formal occasion in the evening during which a meal is served: *The club is holding its annual dinner next week.*

ˈ**dinner jacket** (*AmE* **tuxedo**) *noun* [C] a black or white jacket that a man wears on formal occasions. A **dinner jacket** is usually worn with a **bow tie** (= a special kind of tie).

dinosaur /ˈdaɪnəsɔː(r)/ *noun* [C] one of a number of very large animals that became **extinct** (= disappeared from the earth) millions of years ago: *dinosaur fossils*

Dip *abbr* = **diploma**

dip[1] /dɪp/ *verb* (**dipping**; **dipped**) **1** [T] **dip sth (into sth); dip sth (in)** to put sth into liquid and immediately take it out again: *Julie dipped her toe into the pool to see how cold it was.* **2** [I,T] to go down or make sth go down to a lower level: *The road suddenly dipped down to the river.* ♦ *Sales have dipped disastrously this year.*

PHR V **dip into sth** **1** to use part of an amount of sth that you have: *Tim had to dip into his savings to pay for his new car.* **2** to read parts, but not all, of sth: *I've only dipped into the book. I haven't read it all the way through.*

dip[2] /dɪp/ *noun* **1** [C] (*informal*) a short swim: *We went for a dip before breakfast.* **2** [C] a fall to a lower level, especially for a short time: *a dip in sales/temperature* **3** [C] an area of lower ground: *The cottage was hidden in a dip in the hills.* **4** [C,U] a thick sauce into which you **dip** biscuits, vegetables, etc. before eating them: *a cheese/chilli dip*

diphtheria /dɪfˈθɪəriə/ *noun* [U] a serious disease of the throat that makes it difficult to breathe

diphthong /ˈdɪfθɒŋ/ *noun* [C] two vowel sounds that are pronounced together to make one sound, for example the /aɪ/ sound in 'fine'

diploma /dɪˈpləʊmə/ *noun* [C] (*abbr* **Dip**) a **diploma (in sth)** a certificate that you receive when you complete a course of study, often at a college: *I'm studying for a diploma in hotel management.* ➲ note at **degree**

diplomacy /dɪˈpləʊməsi/ *noun* [U] **1** the activity of managing relations between different countries: *If diplomacy fails, there is a danger of war.* **2** skill in dealing with people without upsetting or offending them: *He handled the tricky situation with tact and diplomacy.*

diplomat /ˈdɪpləmæt/ *noun* [C] an official who represents their country in a foreign country: *a diplomat at the embassy in Rome*

diplomatic /ˌdɪpləˈmætɪk/ *adj* **1** connected with **diplomacy**(1): *to break off diplomatic relations* **2** skilful at dealing with people: *He searched for a diplomatic reply so as not to offend her.* SYN **tactful**
▸ **diplomatically** /-kli/ *adv*

dire /ˈdaɪə(r)/ *adj* (**direr**; **direst**) (*formal*) very bad or serious; terrible: *dire consequences/poverty*

IDM **be in dire straits** to be in a very difficult situation: *The business is in dire straits financially and may go bankrupt.*

⚷ **direct**[1] /dəˈrekt; daɪ-/ *adj, adv* **1** with nobody/nothing in between; not involving anyone/anything else: *The British Prime Minister is* **in direct contact with** *the US President.* ♦ *a direct attack on the capital* ♦ *As a* **direct result** *of the new road, traffic jams in the centre have been reduced.* ♦ *You should protect your skin from direct sunlight.* OPP **indirect** **2** going from one place to another without turning or stopping; straight: *a direct flight to Hong Kong* ♦ *This bus goes direct to London.* OPP **indirect** **3** saying what you mean; clear: *She sometimes offends people with her direct way of speaking.* ♦ *Politicians never give a* **direct answer** *to a* **direct question**. OPP **indirect** **4** [only before a noun] complete; exact: *What she did was in direct opposition to my orders.*

⚷ **direct**[2] /dəˈrekt; daɪ-/ *verb* [T] **1** **direct sth to/towards sb/sth; direct sth at sb/sth** to point or send sth towards sb/sth or in a particular direction: *In recent weeks the media's attention has been directed towards events abroad.* ♦ *The advert is directed at young people.* ♦ *The actor directed some angry words at a photographer.* **2** to manage or control sb/sth: *A policeman was in the middle of the road, directing the traffic.* ♦ *to direct a play/film* **3** (*formal*) to tell or order sb to do sth: *Take the medicine as directed by your doctor.* **4** **direct sb (to …)** to tell or show sb how to get somewhere: *I was directed to an office at the end of the corridor.* ➲ note at **lead**[1]

diˌrect ˈdebit *noun* [C,U] an order to your bank that allows sb else to take a particular amount of money out of your account on certain dates

⚷ **direction** /dəˈrekʃn; daɪ-/ *noun* **1** [C,U] the path, line or way along which a person or thing is moving, looking, pointing, developing, etc: *A woman was seen running* **in the direction of** *the station.* ♦ *We met him coming* **in the opposite direction**. ♦ *I think the new speed limit is still too high, but it's* **a step in the right direction**. ♦ *I think the wind has* **changed direction**. ♦ *I've got such a hopeless* **sense of direction** *—I'm always getting lost.* **2** [C,U] a purpose; an aim: *I want a career that gives me a (sense of) direction in life.* **3** [usually pl] information or instructions about how to do sth or how to get to a place: *I'll* **give** *you* **directions** *to my house.* **4** [U] the act of managing or controlling sth: *This department is under the direction of Mrs Walters.*

TOPIC

Asking for and giving directions

Excuse me, is there a bank near here?

Can you tell me the way to the (nearest) station?

Turn right at the T-junction.

Turn left at the crossroads.

Go straight on at the traffic lights.

Take the third exit at the roundabout.

Take the second left.

It's on the right, next to the museum.

It's opposite the library.

You can't miss it!

D

directive /də'rektɪv; daɪ-/ *noun* [C] an official order to do sth: *an EU directive on safety at work*

directly[1] /də'rektli; daɪ-/ *adv* **1** in a direct line or way: *The bank is directly opposite the supermarket.* ◆ *He refused to answer my question directly.* ◆ *Lung cancer is directly related to smoking.* **2** immediately; very soon: *Wait where you are. I'll be back directly.*

directly[2] /də'rektli; daɪ-/ *conj* as soon as: *I phoned him directly I heard the news.*

di,rect 'object *noun* [C] a noun or phrase that is affected by the act of a verb: *In the sentence 'Anna bought a record', 'a record' is the direct object.* ➲ look at **indirect object** ℹ For more information about direct objects, look at the **Reference Section** at the back of this dictionary.

director /də'rektə(r); daɪ-/ *noun* [C] **1** a person who manages or controls a company or an organization: *the managing director of Rolls Royce* ◆ *She's on the board of directors* (= the group of directors) *of a large computer company.* **2** a person who is responsible for a particular activity or department in a company, a college, etc: *He's the director of studies of a language school.* **3** a person who tells the actors, etc. what to do in a film, play, etc: *a film/theatre director*

directory /də'rektəri; daɪ-/ *noun* [C] (*pl* **directories**) **1** a list of names, addresses and telephone numbers in the order of the alphabet: *the telephone directory* ◆ *I tried to look up Joe's number but he's ex-directory* (= he has chosen not to be listed in the telephone directory). **2** a file containing a group of other files or programs in a computer

di,rect 'speech *noun* [U] the actual words that a person said ➲ look at **reported speech** ℹ For more information about direct speech, look at the **Reference Section** at the back of this dictionary.

dirt /dɜːt/ *noun* [U] **1** a substance that is not clean, such as dust or mud: *His face and hands were covered in dirt.* **2** earth or soil: *a dirt track* **3** damaging information about sb: *The press are always trying to* **dig up dirt** *on the minister's love life.*

IDM **dirt cheap** extremely cheap

dirty[1] /'dɜːti/ *adj* (**dirtier**; **dirtiest**) **1** not clean: *Your hands are dirty. Go and wash them!* ◆ *Gardening is dirty work* (= it makes you dirty). OPP **clean** **2** referring to sex in a way that may upset or offend people: *to tell a dirty joke* **3** unpleasant or dishonest: *He's a dirty player.* ◆ *I'm not going to tell her you don't want to go. You* **do** *your own* **dirty work**.

IDM **a dirty word** an idea or thing that you do not like or agree with: *Work is a dirty word to Frank.*

play dirty (*informal*) to behave or to play a game in an unfair or dishonest way

▶ **dirty** *adv*

dirty[2] /'dɜːti/ *verb* [I,T] (**dirtying**; **dirties**; *pt, pp* **dirtied**) to become or to make sth dirty OPP **clean**

disability /,dɪsə'bɪləti/ *noun* (*pl* **disabilities**) **1** [C] something that makes you unable to use a part of your body properly: *Because of his disability, he needs constant care.* **2** [U] the state of being unable to use a part of your body properly, usually because of injury or disease: *physical/mental disability*

disable /dɪs'eɪbl/ *verb* [T, often passive] to make sb unable to use part of their body properly, usually because of injury or disease: *Many soldiers were disabled in the war.*

disabled /dɪs'eɪbld/ *adj* **1** unable to use a part of your body properly: *A car accident left her permanently disabled.* **2 the disabled** *noun* [pl] people who are **disabled**: *The hotel has improved facilities for the disabled.*

disadvantage /,dɪsəd'vɑːntɪdʒ/ *noun* [C] **1** something that may make you less successful than other people: *Your qualifications are good. Your main disadvantage is your lack of experience.* **2** something that is not good or that causes problems: *The main disadvantage of the job is the long hours.* ◆ *What are the advantages and disadvantages of nuclear power?* OPP for both meanings **advantage**

IDM **put sb/be at a disadvantage** to put sb or be in a situation where they or you may be less successful than other people: *The fact that you don't speak the language will put you at a disadvantage in France.*

to sb's disadvantage (*formal*) not good or helpful for sb: *The agreement will be to your disadvantage—don't accept it.*

disadvantaged /,dɪsəd'vɑːntɪdʒd/ *adj* in a bad social or economic situation; poor: *disadvantaged groups/children*

disadvantageous /,dɪsædvæn'teɪdʒəs/ *adj* causing sb to be in a worse situation compared to other people

disagree /,dɪsə'griː/ *verb* [I] **1 disagree (with sb/sth) (about/on sth)** to have a different opinion from sb/sth; to not agree: *Stephen often disagrees with his father about politics.* ◆ *They strongly disagreed with my idea.* ◆ *'We have to tell him.' 'No, I disagree. I don't think we should tell him at all.'* **2** to be different: *These two sets of statistics disagree.* OPP for both meanings **agree**

PHR V **disagree with sb** (used about sth you have eaten or drunk) to make you feel ill; to have a bad effect on you

disagreeable /ˌdɪsəˈgriːəbl/ *adj* (*formal*) unpleasant OPP **agreeable** ▸ **disagreeably** /-əbli/ *adv*

🔑 **disagreement** /ˌdɪsəˈgriːmənt/ *noun* [C,U] **disagreement (with sb) (about/on/over sth)** a situation in which people have a different opinion about sth and often also argue: *It's normal for couples to* ***have disagreements.*** ◆ *Mandy resigned after a disagreement with her boss.* ◆ *The conference ended in disagreement.* OPP **agreement**

disallow /ˌdɪsəˈlaʊ/ *verb* [T] to not allow or accept sth: *The goal was disallowed because the player was offside.*

🔑 **disappear** /ˌdɪsəˈpɪə(r)/ *verb* [I] **1** to become impossible to see or to find: *He walked away and disappeared into a crowd of people.* ◆ *My purse was here a moment ago and now it's disappeared.* **2** to stop existing: *Plant and animal species are disappearing at an alarming rate.* SYN for both meanings **vanish** OPP for both meanings **appear** ▸ **disappearance** *noun* [C,U]: *The mystery of her disappearance was never solved.*

🔑 **disappoint** /ˌdɪsəˈpɔɪnt/ *verb* [T] to make sb sad because what they had hoped for has not happened or is less good, interesting, etc. than they had hoped: *I'm sorry to disappoint you but I'm afraid you haven't won the prize.*

🔑 **disappointed** /ˌdɪsəˈpɔɪntɪd/ *adj* **disappointed (about/at sth); disappointed (in/with sb/sth); disappointed that …** sad because you/sb/sth did not succeed or because sth was not as good, interesting, etc. as you had hoped: *Lucy was deeply disappointed at not being chosen for the team.* ◆ *We were disappointed with our hotel.* ◆ *I'm disappointed in you. I thought you could do better.* ◆ *They are very disappointed that they can't stay longer.* ◆ *I was disappointed to hear that you can't come to the party.*

🔑 **disappointing** /ˌdɪsəˈpɔɪntɪŋ/ *adj* making you feel sad because sth was not as good, interesting, etc. as you had hoped: *It has been a disappointing year for the company.* ▸ **disappointingly** *adv*

🔑 **disappointment** /ˌdɪsəˈpɔɪntmənt/ *noun* **1** [U] the state of being disappointed: ***To his*** *great* ***disappointment*** *he failed to get the job.* **2** [C] **a disappointment (to sb)** a person or thing that disappoints you: *She has suffered many disappointments in her career.*

🔑 **disapproval** /ˌdɪsəˈpruːvl/ *noun* [U] a feeling that sth is bad or that sb is behaving badly: *She shook her head* ***in disapproval.***

🔑 **disapprove** /ˌdɪsəˈpruːv/ *verb* [I] **disapprove (of sb/sth)** to think that sb/sth is bad, silly, etc: *His parents strongly disapproved of his decision to leave college before he had finished his course.* OPP **approve**

🔑 **disapproving** /ˌdɪsəˈpruːvɪŋ/ *adj* showing that you think sth is bad, silly, etc: *After he had told the joke there was a disapproving silence.* ▸ **disapprovingly** *adv*: *David frowned disapprovingly when I arrived late.*

disarm /dɪsˈɑːm/ *verb* **1** [T] to take weapons away from sb: *The police caught and disarmed the terrorists.* **2** [I] (used about a country) to reduce the number of weapons it has **3** [T] to make sb feel less angry: *Jenny could always disarm the teachers with a smile.*

disarmament /dɪsˈɑːməmənt/ *noun* [U] reducing the number of weapons that an army or a country has: *nuclear disarmament*

disassociate /ˌdɪsəˈsəʊʃieɪt; -ˈsəʊs-/ = **dissociate**

🔑 **disaster** /dɪˈzɑːstə(r)/ *noun* **1** [C] an event that causes a lot of harm or damage: *earthquakes, floods and other natural disasters* **2** [C,U] a terrible situation or event: *Losing your job is unfortunate, but it's not a disaster.* ◆ *This year's lack of rain could* ***spell disaster*** *for many farmers.* **3** [C,U] (*informal*) a complete failure: *The school play was an absolute disaster. Everything went wrong.*

disastrous /dɪˈzɑːstrəs/ *adj* terrible, harmful or failing completely: *Our mistake had disastrous results.* ▸ **disastrously** *adv*: *The plan went disastrously wrong.*

disband /dɪsˈbænd/ *verb* [I,T] to stop existing as a group; to separate

disbelief /ˌdɪsbɪˈliːf/ *noun* [U] the feeling of not believing sb/sth: *'It can't be true!' he shouted* ***in disbelief.***

disbelieve /ˌdɪsbɪˈliːv/ *verb* [T] to think that sth is not true or that sb is not telling the truth: *I have no reason to disbelieve her.* OPP **believe**

🔑 **disc** (*especially AmE* **disk**) /dɪsk/ *noun* [C] **1** a round flat object: *He wears an identity disc around his neck.* **2** = **CD** **3** = **disk**(2) **4** one of the pieces of **cartilage** (= thin strong material) between the bones in your back: *a slipped disc* (= one that has moved from its correct position, causing pain)

discard /dɪsˈkɑːd/ *verb* [T] (*formal*) to throw sth away because it is not useful

discern /dɪˈsɜːn/ *verb* [T] (*formal*) to see or notice sth with difficulty: *I discerned a note of anger in his voice.* ▸ **discernible** *adj*: *The shape of a house was just discernible through the mist.*

discerning /dɪˈsɜːnɪŋ/ *adj* able to recognize the quality of sb/sth: *The discerning music lover will appreciate the excellence of this recording.*

discharge¹ /dɪsˈtʃɑːdʒ/ *verb* [T] **1** to allow sb officially to leave; to send sb away: *to discharge somebody from hospital* **2** to send sth out (a liquid, gas, etc.): *Smoke and fumes are discharged from the factory.* **3** to do sth that you have to do: *to discharge a duty/task*

discharge² /ˈdɪstʃɑːdʒ/ *noun* [C,U] **1** a substance that has come out of somewhere: *yellowish discharge from a wound* **2** the act of sending sb/sth out or away: *The wounded soldier was given a medical discharge.* ◆ *The discharge of oil from the leaking tanker could not be prevented.*

disciple /dɪˈsaɪpl/ *noun* [C] a person who follows a teacher, especially a religious one SYN **follower**

disciplinary /ˈdɪsəplɪnəri; ˌdɪsəˈplɪnəri/ *adj* connected with punishment for breaking rules

D

discipline[1] /ˈdɪsəplɪn/ *noun* **1** [U] the practice of training people to obey rules and behave well: *A good teacher must be able to* ***maintain discipline*** *in the classroom.* **2** [U] the practice of training your mind and body so that you control your actions and obey rules; a way of doing this: *It takes a lot of* ***self-discipline*** *to study for three hours a day.* ♦ *Having to get up early every day is good discipline for a child.* **3** [C] a subject of study: *academic disciplines*

D

discipline[2] /ˈdɪsəplɪn/ *verb* [T] **1** to train sb to obey and to behave in a controlled way: *You should discipline yourself to practise the piano every morning.* **2** to punish sb: *The player was disciplined for using racist language.*

ˈ**disc jockey** = **DJ**

disclaim /dɪsˈkleɪm/ *verb* [T] to say that you do not have sth: *to disclaim responsibility/knowledge* SYN **deny**

disclose /dɪsˈkləʊz/ *verb* [T] (*formal*) to tell sth to sb or to make sth known publicly: *The newspapers did not disclose the victim's name.* SYN **reveal**

disclosure /dɪsˈkləʊʒə(r)/ *noun* [C,U] making sth known; the facts that are made known: *the disclosure of secret information* ♦ *He resigned following disclosures about his private life.* SYN **revelation**

disco /ˈdɪskəʊ/ *noun* [C] (*pl* **discos**) (*old-fashioned*) a place, party, etc. where people dance to recorded music: *Are you going to the school disco?* ➲ look at **club**

discolour (*AmE* **discolor**) /dɪsˈkʌlə(r)/ *verb* [I,T] to change or to make sth change colour (often by the effect of light, age or dirt)

discomfort /dɪsˈkʌmfət/ *noun* [U] **1** a slight feeling of pain: *There may be some discomfort after the operation.* **2** a feeling of embarrassment: *I could sense John's discomfort when I asked him about his job.*

disconcert /ˌdɪskənˈsɜːt/ *verb* [T, usually passive] to make sb feel confused or worried: *She was disconcerted when everyone stopped talking and looked at her.* ▸ **disconcerting** *adj* ▸ **disconcertingly** *adv*

disconnect /ˌdɪskəˈnekt/ *verb* [T] **1** to stop a supply of water, gas or electricity going to a piece of equipment or a building: *If you don't pay your gas bill your supply will be disconnected.* **2** to separate sth from sth: *The brake doesn't work because the cable has become disconnected from the lever.*

discontent /ˌdɪskənˈtent/ (also **discontentment** /ˌdɪskənˈtentmənt/) *noun* [U] the state of being unhappy with sth: *The management could sense growing discontent among the staff.* ▸ **discontented** *adj*: *to be/feel discontented*

discontinue /ˌdɪskənˈtɪnjuː/ *verb* [T] (*formal*) to stop sth or stop producing sth

discord /ˈdɪskɔːd/ *noun* [U] (*formal*) disagreement or argument

discordant /dɪsˈkɔːdənt/ *adj* that spoils a general feeling of agreement: *Her criticism was the only discordant note in the discussion.*

discount[1] /ˈdɪskaʊnt/ *noun* [C,U] a lower price than usual: *Staff get 20% discount on all goods.* ♦ *Do you give a discount for cash?* SYN **reduction**

discount[2] /dɪsˈkaʊnt/ *verb* [T] to consider sth not true or not important: *I think we can discount that idea. It's just not practical.*

discourage /dɪsˈkʌrɪdʒ/ *verb* [T] **discourage sb (from doing sth)** to stop sb doing sth, especially by making them realize that it would not be successful or a good idea: *I tried to discourage Jake from giving up his job.* ♦ *Don't let these little problems discourage you.* OPP **encourage** ▸ **discouraged** *adj*: *After failing the exam again Paul felt very discouraged.* ▸ **discouraging** *adj*: *Constant criticism can be very discouraging.*

discouragement /dɪsˈkʌrɪdʒmənt/ *noun* [C,U] a thing that makes you not want to do sth; the act of trying to stop sb from doing sth: *the government's discouragement of smoking* ♦ *the government's discouragement of political protest*

discourse /ˈdɪskɔːs/ *noun* [C,U] (*formal*) a long and serious discussion of a subject in speech or writing

discourteous /dɪsˈkɜːtiəs/ *adj* not polite or showing respect for people SYN **impolite** OPP **courteous**

discover /dɪˈskʌvə(r)/ *verb* [T] **1** to find or learn sth that nobody had found or knew before: *Who discovered the lost city of Machu Picchu?* ♦ *Scientists are hoping to discover the cause of the epidemic.* **2** to find sb/sth that was hidden and that you did not expect to find: *The police discovered the painting hidden under the floor.* **3** to find out about sth; to find some information about sth: *I think I've discovered why the computer won't print out.* ▸ **discoverer** *noun* [C]: *Parkinson's disease was named after its discoverer.*

discovery /dɪˈskʌvəri/ *noun* (*pl* **discoveries**) **1** [U] the act of finding sth: *The discovery of X-rays changed the history of medicine.* **2** [C] something that has been found or learnt about for the first time: *scientific discoveries*

discredit /dɪsˈkredɪt/ *verb* [T] to make people stop respecting or believing sb/sth: *Journalists are trying to discredit the president by inventing stories about his love life.* ▸ **discredit** *noun* [U]

discreet /dɪˈskriːt/ *adj* careful in what you say and do so as not to cause embarrassment or difficulty for sb: *I don't want anyone to find out about this, so please be discreet.* OPP **indiscreet** ➲ *noun* **discretion** ▸ **discreetly** *adv*

discrepancy /dɪsˈkrepənsi/ *noun* [C,U] (*pl* **discrepancies**) a difference between two things that should be the same: *Something is wrong here. There is a discrepancy between these two sets of figures.*

discretion /dɪˈskreʃn/ *noun* [U] **1** the freedom and power to make decisions by yourself: *You must decide what is best. Use your discretion.* **2** care in what you say and do so as not to cause embarrassment or difficulty for sb: *This is confidential but I know I can rely on your discretion.* ➲ *adjective* **discreet**

IDM **at sb's discretion** depending on what sb thinks or decides: *Pay increases are awarded at the discretion of the director.*

discriminate /dɪˈskrɪmɪneɪt/ *verb* **1** [I,T] **discriminate (between A and B)** to see or make a difference between two people or things: *The immigration law discriminates between political and economic refugees.* **2** [I] **discriminate (against sb)** to treat one person or group worse than others: *It is illegal to discriminate against any ethnic or religious group.*

discriminating /dɪˈskrɪmɪneɪtɪŋ/ *adj* able to judge the good quality of sth: *a discriminating audience/customer* SYN **discerning**

discrimination /dɪˌskrɪmɪˈneɪʃn/ *noun* [U] **1 discrimination (against sb)** treating one person or group worse than others: *sexual/racial/religious discrimination* ◆ *Discrimination against disabled people is illegal.* **2** (*formal*) the state of being able to see a difference between two people or things: *discrimination between right and wrong*

discus /ˈdɪskəs/ *noun* **1** [C] a heavy round flat object that is thrown as a sport **2 the discus** [sing] the sport or event of throwing a **discus** as far as possible

discuss /dɪˈskʌs/ *verb* [T] **discuss sth (with sb)** to talk or write about sth seriously or formally: *I must discuss the matter with my parents before I make a decision.* ◆ *The article discusses the need for a change in the law.*

discussion /dɪˈskʌʃn/ *noun* [C,U] the process of talking about sth seriously or deeply: *We had a long discussion about art.* ◆ *After much discussion we all agreed to share the cost.*

IDM **under discussion** being talked about: *Plans to reform the Health Service are under discussion in Parliament.*

disdain /dɪsˈdeɪn/ *noun* [U] the feeling that sb/sth is not good enough to be respected: *Monica felt that her boss always* ***treated*** *her ideas* ***with disdain.*** ▶ **disdainful** /-fl/ *adj* ▶ **disdainfully** /-fəli/ *adv*

disease /dɪˈziːz/ *noun* [C,U] an illness of the body in humans, animals or plants: *an infectious/contagious disease* ◆ *These children* ***suffer from a*** *rare* ***disease.*** ◆ *Rats and flies* ***spread disease.*** ◆ *Smoking causes heart disease.* ◆ *Obesity causes heart disease.* ▶ **diseased** *adj*: *His diseased kidney had to be removed.* ➲ note at **ill**

HELP **Disease** or **illness**? A **disease** is a medical problem which has a name and may be caused by bacteria, viruses, etc. Diseases can often be caught and passed on to other people. An **illness** can be either a medical problem or a period of ill health.

disembark /ˌdɪsɪmˈbɑːk/ *verb* [I] (*formal*) to get off a ship or an aircraft OPP **embark** ▶ **disembarkation** /ˌdɪsˌembɑːˈkeɪʃn/ *noun* [U]

disenchanted /ˌdɪsɪnˈtʃɑːntɪd/ *adj* having lost your good opinion of sb/sth: *Fans are already becoming disenchanted with the new team manager.* ▶ **disenchantment** *noun* [U]

disentangle /ˌdɪsɪnˈtæŋgl/ *verb* [T] to free sb/sth that had become connected to sb/sth else in a confused and complicated way: *My coat got caught up in some bushes and I couldn't disentangle it.* ◆ (*figurative*) *Listening to her story, I found it hard to disentangle the truth from the lies.*

disfigure /dɪsˈfɪgə(r)/ *verb* [T] to spoil the appearance of sb/sth: *His face was permanently disfigured by the fire.*

disgrace[1] /dɪsˈgreɪs/ *noun* **1** [U] the state of not being respected by other people, usually because you have behaved badly: *She left the company* ***in disgrace*** *after admitting stealing from colleagues.* **2** [sing] **a disgrace (to sb/sth)** a person or thing that gives a very bad impression and makes you feel sorry and embarrassed: *The streets are covered in litter. It's a disgrace!* ◆ *Politicians who tell lies are a disgrace to their profession.*

disgrace[2] /dɪsˈgreɪs/ *verb* [T] to behave badly in a way that makes you or other people feel sorry and embarrassed: *My brother disgraced himself by starting a fight at the wedding.*

disgraceful /dɪsˈgreɪsfl/ *adj* very bad, making other people feel sorry and embarrassed: *The behaviour of the team's fans was absolutely disgraceful.* ▶ **disgracefully** /-fəli/ *adv*

disgruntled /dɪsˈgrʌntld/ *adj* disappointed and annoyed

disguise[1] /dɪsˈgaɪz/ *verb* [T] **disguise sb/sth (as sb/sth)** to change the appearance, sound, etc. of sb/sth so that people cannot recognize them or it: *They disguised themselves as fishermen and escaped in a boat.* ◆ (*figurative*) *His smile disguised his anger.*

disguise[2] /dɪsˈgaɪz/ *noun* [C,U] a thing that you wear or use to change your appearance so that nobody recognizes you: *The robbers were wearing heavy disguises so that they could not be identified.* ◆ *She is so famous that she has to go shopping* ***in disguise.***

disgust[1] /dɪsˈgʌst/ *noun* [U] **disgust (at sth)** a strong feeling of not liking or approving of sth/sb that you feel is unacceptable, or that looks, smells, etc. unpleasant: *The film was so bad that we walked out* ***in disgust.*** ◆ ***Much to my disgust,*** *I found a hair in my soup.*

disgust[2] /dɪsˈgʌst/ *verb* [T] **1** to cause a strong feeling of not liking or approving of sb/sth: *Cruelty towards animals absolutely disgusts me.* **2** to make sb feel ill: *The way he eats with his mouth open completely disgusts me.*

disgusted /dɪsˈgʌstɪd/ *adj* **disgusted (at/with sb/sth)** not liking or approving of sb/sth at all: *We were disgusted at the standard of service we received.*

disgusting /dɪsˈgʌstɪŋ/ *adj* very unpleasant: *What a disgusting smell!* SYN **revolting**

disgustingly /dɪsˈɡʌstɪŋli/ *adv* **1** extremely (often used to show that you would like to have what sb else has): *Our neighbours are disgustingly rich.* **2** in a way that you do not like or approve of or that makes you feel sick: *The kitchen was disgustingly dirty.*

D

dish¹ /dɪʃ/ *noun* **1** [C] a round container for food that is deeper than a plate: *Is this dish ovenproof?* **2 the dishes** [pl] all the plates, cups, etc. that you use during a meal: *I'll cook and you can wash the dishes.* **3** [C] a type of food prepared in a particular way: *The* ***main dish*** *was curry. It was served with a selection of* ***side dishes***. ♦ *Paella is a typical Spanish dish, made with rice and shellfish.* **4** = **satellite dish**

dish² /dɪʃ/ *verb*
PHR V dish sth out (*informal*) to give away a lot of sth: *to dish out advice*
dish sth up (*informal*) to serve food

dishcloth /ˈdɪʃklɒθ/ *noun* [C] a cloth for washing dishes

dishearten /dɪsˈhɑːtn/ *verb* [T, usually passive] to make sb lose hope or confidence **OPP hearten SYN discourage** ▶ **disheartened** /dɪsˈhɑːtnd/ *adj* ▶ **disheartening** /dɪsˈhɑːtnɪŋ/ *adj*: *a disheartening experience*

dishevelled (*AmE* **disheveled**) /dɪˈʃevld/ *adj* (used about sb's appearance) very untidy **SYN unkempt**

dishonest /dɪsˈɒnɪst/ *adj* that you cannot trust; likely to lie, steal or cheat: *Beware of dishonest traders in tourist areas.* **OPP honest** ▶ **dishonestly** *adv* ▶ **dishonesty** *noun* [U] **OPP honesty**

dishonour¹ (*AmE* **dishonor**) /dɪsˈɒnə(r)/ *noun* [U, sing] (*formal*) the state of no longer being respected, especially because you have done sth bad: *Her cheating in exams has* ***brought dishonour on*** *the school.* **OPP honour** ▶ **dishonourable** *adj* **OPP honourable**

dishonour² (*AmE* **dishonor**) /dɪsˈɒnə(r)/ *verb* [T] (*formal*) to do sth bad that makes people stop respecting you or sb/sth close to you

dishwasher /ˈdɪʃwɒʃə(r)/ *noun* [C] a machine that washes plates, cups, knives, forks, etc. ➲ picture on **page P8**

disillusion /ˌdɪsɪˈluːʒn/ *verb* [T] to destroy sb's belief in or good opinion of sb/sth ▶ **disillusion** (also **disillusionment**) *noun* [U]: *I feel increasing disillusion with the government.*

disillusioned /ˌdɪsɪˈluːʒnd/ *adj* disappointed because sb/sth is not as good as you first thought: *She's disillusioned with nursing.*

disillusionment /ˌdɪsɪˈluːʒnmənt/ = **disillusion**

disinfect /ˌdɪsɪnˈfekt/ *verb* [T] to clean sth with a liquid that destroys bacteria: *to disinfect a wound* ▶ **disinfection** *noun* [U]

disinfectant /ˌdɪsɪnˈfektənt/ *noun* [C,U] a substance that destroys bacteria and is used for cleaning

disintegrate /dɪsˈɪntɪɡreɪt/ *verb* [I] to break into many small pieces: *The plane disintegrated as it fell into the sea.* ▶ **disintegration** /dɪsˌɪntɪˈɡreɪʃn/ *noun* [U]: *the gradual disintegration of traditional values*

disinterested /dɪsˈɪntrəstɪd/ *adj* fair, not influenced by personal feelings: *Let me give you some disinterested advice.*

HELP Be careful. **Uninterested** has a different meaning.

disjointed /dɪsˈdʒɔɪntɪd/ *adj* (used especially about ideas, writing or speech) not clearly connected and therefore difficult to follow ▶ **disjointedly** *adv*

disk /dɪsk/ *noun* [C] **1** (*especially AmE*) = **disc 2** a flat piece of plastic that stores information for use by a computer ➲ note at **computer** ➲ look at **floppy disk, hard disk**

ˈdisk drive *noun* [C] a piece of electrical equipment that passes information to or from a computer disk

diskette /dɪsˈket/ = **floppy disk**

dislike¹ /dɪsˈlaɪk/ *verb* [T] (*formal*) **dislike (doing) sth** to not like sb/sth: *I really dislike flying.* ♦ *What is it that you dislike about living here?* **OPP like**

OTHER WORDS FOR

dislike

Dislike is rather formal, so in conversation we use **don't like**: *I don't like (doing) sport.* You can also say 'I don't **spend much time** doing sport', 'I'm **not** very **keen on** (doing) sport', or 'I'm **not** very **interested in** sport'. If you dislike sth very much, you can use **hate, really don't like** or **can't stand**: *I hate/really don't like/can't stand (doing) sport.*

dislike² /dɪsˈlaɪk/ *noun* [U, sing] **(a) dislike (of/for sb/sth)** the feeling of not liking sb/sth: *She couldn't hide her dislike for him.* ♦ *He seems to have a strong dislike of hard work.*
IDM take a dislike to sb/sth to start **disliking** sb/sth: *He took an instant dislike to his boss.*

dislocate /ˈdɪsləkeɪt/ *verb* [T] to put sth (usually a bone) out of its correct position: *He dislocated his shoulder during the game.* ▶ **dislocation** /ˌdɪsləˈkeɪʃn/ *noun* [C,U]

dislodge /dɪsˈlɒdʒ/ *verb* [T] **dislodge sth (from sth)** to make sb/sth move from its correct fixed position: *The strong wind dislodged several tiles from the roof.*

disloyal /dɪsˈlɔɪəl/ *adj* **disloyal (to sb/sth)** not supporting your friends, family, country, etc.; doing sth that will harm them: *It was disloyal to your friends to repeat their conversation to Peter.* **OPP loyal** ▶ **disloyalty** /-ˈlɔɪəlti/ *noun* [C,U] (*pl* **disloyalties**)

dismal /ˈdɪzməl/ *adj* **1** causing or showing sadness: *dismal surroundings* **SYN miserable 2** (*informal*) of low quality; poor: *a dismal standard of work*

dismantle /dɪsˈmæntl/ *verb* [T] to take sth to pieces; to separate sth into the parts it is made from: *The photographer dismantled his equipment and packed it away.*

dismay /dɪsˈmeɪ/ *noun* [U] a strong feeling of disappointment and sadness: *I realized **to my dismay** that I was going to miss the plane.* ▸ **dismay** *verb* [T]: *Their reaction dismayed him.* ▸ **dismayed** *adj* dismayed (at/by sth); dismayed to find, hear, see, etc: *I was dismayed to find that the train had already left.*

dismember /dɪsˈmembə(r)/ *verb* [T] to cut a dead body into pieces

⚷ **dismiss** /dɪsˈmɪs/ *verb* [T] **1** dismiss sb/sth (as sth) to decide not to think about sth/sb: *He dismissed the idea as nonsense.* **2** dismiss sb (from sth) to order an employee to leave his or her job: *He was dismissed from his post for refusing to obey orders.* SYN **fire**, **sack** ➲ note at **job** **3** to send sb away: *The lesson ended and the teacher dismissed the class.* **4** (used in law) to say that a trial or court case should not continue, usually because there is not enough evidence: *The case was dismissed.* ▸ **dismissal** /dɪsˈmɪsl/ *noun* [C,U]: *She was hurt at their dismissal of her offer of help.* ◆ *a case of unfair dismissal*

dismissive /dɪsˈmɪsɪv/ *adj* dismissive (of sb/sth) saying or showing that you think that sb/sth is not worth considering seriously: *The boss was dismissive of all the efforts I had made.* ▸ **dismissively** *adv*

dismount /dɪsˈmaʊnt/ *verb* [I] to get off sth that you ride (a horse, a bicycle, etc.) OPP **mount**

disobedient /ˌdɪsəˈbiːdiənt/ *adj* refusing or failing to obey OPP **obedient** ▸ **disobedience** *noun* [U]

disobey /ˌdɪsəˈbeɪ/ *verb* [I,T] to refuse to do what you are told to do: *He was punished for disobeying orders.* OPP **obey**

disorder /dɪsˈɔːdə(r)/ *noun* **1** [U] an untidy, confused or badly organized state: *His financial affairs are **in complete disorder**.* OPP **order** **2** [U] violent behaviour by a large number of people: *Disorder broke out on the streets of the capital.* **3** [C,U] an illness in which the mind or a part of the body is not working properly: *treatment for **eating disorders** such as anorexia* ◆ *a kind of **mental disorder***

disordered /dɪsˈɔːdəd/ *adj* untidy, confused or badly organized

disorderly /dɪsˈɔːdəli/ *adj* **1** (used about people or behaviour) out of control and violent; causing trouble in public: *They were arrested for being **drunk and disorderly**.* **2** untidy OPP **orderly**

disorganization (also -isation) /dɪsˌɔːɡənaɪˈzeɪʃn/ *noun* [U] a lack of careful planning and order OPP **organization**

disorganized (also -ised) /dɪsˈɔːɡənaɪzd/ *adj* badly planned; not able to plan well OPP **organized**

disorientate /dɪsˈɔːriənteɪt/ (*especially AmE* disorient /dɪsˈɔːrient/) *verb* [T] to make sb become confused about where they are: *The road signs were very confusing and I soon became disorientated.* ▸ **disorientation** /dɪsˌɔːriənˈteɪʃn/ *noun* [U]

disown /dɪsˈəʊn/ *verb* [T] to say that you no longer want to be connected with or responsible for sb/sth: *When he was arrested, his family disowned him.*

disparage /dɪˈspærɪdʒ/ *verb* [T] (*formal*) to talk about sb/sth in a critical way; to say that sb/sth is of little value or importance ▸ **disparaging** *adj*: *disparaging remarks*

disparity /dɪˈspærəti/ *noun* [U,C] (*pl* disparities) (*formal*) a difference, especially one connected with unfair treatment: *the wide disparity between rich and poor*

dispatch (*BrE also* despatch) /dɪˈspætʃ/ *verb* [T] (*formal*) to send sb/sth to a place: *Your order will be dispatched within 7 days.*

dispel /dɪˈspel/ *verb* [T] (dispelling; dispelled) to make sth, especially a feeling or a belief, disappear: *His reassuring words dispelled all her fears.*

dispensable /dɪˈspensəbl/ *adj* not necessary: *I suppose I'm dispensable. Anybody could do my job.* OPP **indispensable**

dispense /dɪˈspens/ *verb* [T] (*formal*) to give or provide people with sth: *a machine that dispenses hot and cold drinks*

PHR V **dispense with sb/sth** to get rid of sb/sth that is not necessary: *They decided to dispense with luxuries and live a simple life.*

dispenser /dɪˈspensə(r)/ *noun* [C] a machine or container from which you can get sth: *a cash dispenser at a bank* ◆ *a soap dispenser* ➲ picture at **stationery**

disperse /dɪˈspɜːs/ *verb* [I,T] to separate and go in different directions; to make sb/sth do this: *When the meeting was over, the group dispersed.* ◆ *The police arrived and quickly dispersed the crowd.* ▸ **dispersal** /dɪˈspɜːsl/ *noun* [U,C]

dispirited /dɪˈspɪrɪtɪd/ *adj* having lost confidence or hope SYN **depressed**

displace /dɪsˈpleɪs/ *verb* [T] **1** to remove and take the place of sb/sth: *She hoped to displace Seles as the top tennis player in the world.* **2** to force sb/sth to move from the usual or correct place: *refugees displaced by the war* ▸ **displacement** *noun* [U]

⚷ **display**[1] /dɪˈspleɪ/ *verb* [T] **1** to put sth in a place where people will see it or where it will attract attention: *Posters for the concert were displayed throughout the city.* **2** to show signs of sth (for example a feeling or a quality): *She displayed no interest in the discussion.*

⚷ **display**[2] /dɪˈspleɪ/ *noun* [C] **1** an arrangement of things in a public place for people to see: *a window display in a shop* **2** a public event in which sth is shown in action: *a firework display* **3** behaviour that shows a particular feeling or quality: *a sudden display of aggression* **4** words, pictures, etc. that can be seen on a computer screen

IDM **on display** in a place where people will see it and where it will attract attention: *Treasures from the sunken ship were put on display at the museum.*

displease /dɪsˈpliːz/ *verb* [T] (*formal*) to annoy sb or to make sb angry or upset ▸ **displeased** *adj* OPP **pleased**

displeasure /dɪsˈpleʒə(r)/ *noun* [U] (*formal*) the feeling of being annoyed or not satisfied: *I wrote to*

D

express my displeasure at not having been informed sooner.

disposable /dɪˈspəʊzəbl/ *adj* made to be thrown away after being used once or for a short time: *a disposable razor*

disposal /dɪˈspəʊzl/ *noun* [U] the act of getting rid of sth or throwing sth away: *the disposal of dangerous chemical waste* ♦ *bomb disposal*
IDM **at sb's disposal** available for sb to use at any time: *They put their house at my disposal.*

D

dispose /dɪˈspəʊz/ *verb*
PHR V **dispose of sb/sth** to throw away or sell sth; to get rid of sb/sth that you do not want

disposition /ˌdɪspəˈzɪʃn/ *noun* [C, usually sing] the natural qualities of sb's character or the way they usually behave: *to have a cheerful disposition* ♦ *people of a nervous disposition* **SYN** **temperament**

disproportionate /ˌdɪsprəˈpɔːʃənət/ *adj* disproportionate (to sth) too large or too small when compared to sth else: *Her salary is disproportionate to the amount of work she has to do.* ▶ **disproportionately** *adv*

disprove /ˌdɪsˈpruːv/ *verb* [T] to show that sth is not true **OPP** **prove**

dispute¹ /dɪˈspjuːt; ˈdɪspjuːt/ *noun* [C,U] (a) dispute (between A and B) (over/about sth) a disagreement or argument between two people, groups or countries: *a pay dispute* ♦ *There was some dispute between John and his boss about whose fault it was.*
IDM **in dispute** in a situation of arguing or being argued about: *He is in dispute with the tax office about how much he should pay.*

dispute² /dɪˈspjuːt/ *verb* [T] to argue about sth and to question if it is true or right: *The player disputed the referee's decision.*

disqualify /dɪsˈkwɒlɪfaɪ/ *verb* [T] (disqualifying; disqualifies; *pt, pp* disqualified) disqualify sb (from sth/doing sth); disqualify sb (for sth) to officially prevent sb from doing sth or taking part in sth, usually because they have broken a rule or law: *He was disqualified from driving for two years.* ♦ *The team were disqualified for cheating.* ▶ **disqualification** /dɪsˌkwɒlɪfɪˈkeɪʃn/ *noun* [C,U]

disregard /ˌdɪsrɪˈɡɑːd/ *verb* [T] to take no notice of sb/sth; to treat sth as unimportant: *These are the latest instructions. Please disregard any you received before.* ▶ **disregard** *noun* [U, sing] disregard (for sb/sth): *He rushed into the burning building with complete disregard for his own safety.*

disrepair /ˌdɪsrɪˈpeə(r)/ *noun* [U] the state of being in bad condition because repairs have not been made: *Over the years the building **fell into disrepair**.*

disreputable /dɪsˈrepjətəbl/ *adj* not to be trusted; well known for being bad or dishonest: *disreputable business methods* **OPP** **respectable**

disrepute /ˌdɪsrɪˈpjuːt/ *noun* [U] the situation when people no longer respect sb/sth: *The players' bad behaviour **brings** the game **into disrepute**.*

disrespect /ˌdɪsrɪˈspekt/ *noun* [U] disrespect (for/to sb/sth) a lack of respect for sb/sth that is shown in what you do or say **OPP** **respect** ▶ **disrespectful** /-fl/ *adj* **OPP** **respectful** ▶ **disrespectfully** /-fəli/ *adv*

disrupt /dɪsˈrʌpt/ *verb* [T] to stop sth happening as or when it should: *The strike severely disrupted flights to Spain.* ▶ **disruption** *noun* [C,U] ▶ **disruptive** /dɪsˈrʌptɪv/ *adj*

dissatisfaction /ˌdɪsˌsætɪsˈfækʃn/ *noun* [U] dissatisfaction (with/at sb/sth) the feeling of not being satisfied or pleased: *There is some dissatisfaction among teachers with the plans for the new exam.* **OPP** **satisfaction**

dissatisfied /dɪsˈsætɪsfaɪd/ *adj* dissatisfied (with sb/sth) not satisfied or pleased: *complaints from dissatisfied customers* **OPP** **satisfied**

dissect /dɪˈsekt/ *verb* [T] to cut up a dead body, a plant, etc. in order to study it ▶ **dissection** *noun* [C,U]

dissent¹ /dɪˈsent/ *noun* [U] (*formal*) disagreement with official or generally agreed ideas or opinions: *There is some dissent within the Labour Party on these policies.*

dissent² /dɪˈsent/ *verb* [I] (*formal*) dissent (from sth) to have opinions that are different to those that are officially held ▶ **dissenting** *adj*: *dissenting groups/opinions/views*

dissertation /ˌdɪsəˈteɪʃn/ *noun* [C] a long piece of writing on sth that you have studied, especially as part of a university degree ➲ look at **thesis**

disservice /dɪsˈsɜːvɪs/ *noun*
IDM **do (a) disservice to sb/sth** to do sth that harms sb and the opinion other people have of them: *The minister's comments do the teaching profession a great disservice.*

dissident /ˈdɪsɪdənt/ *noun* [C] a person who strongly disagrees with and criticizes their government, especially in a country where it is dangerous to do this: *left-wing dissidents* ▶ **dissidence** /ˈdɪsɪdəns/ *noun* [U]

dissimilar /dɪˈsɪmɪlə(r)/ *adj* dissimilar (from/to sb/sth) not the same; different: *Your situation is **not dissimilar** (= is similar) to mine.* **OPP** **similar**

dissociate /dɪˈsəʊʃieɪt; -ˈsəʊs-/ (also disassociate) *verb* [T] dissociate sb/sth/yourself (from sth) to show that you are not connected with or do not support sb/sth; to show that two things are not connected with each other: *She dissociated herself from the views of the extremists in her party.* **OPP** **associate**

⚷ **dissolve** /dɪˈzɒlv/ *verb* [I,T] (used about a solid) to become or to make sth become part of a liquid: *Sugar dissolves in water.* ♦ *Dissolve two tablets in cold water.*

dissuade /dɪˈsweɪd/ *verb* [T] dissuade sb (from doing sth) to persuade sb not to do sth: *I tried to dissuade her from spending the money, but she insisted.* **OPP** **persuade**

⚷ **distance**¹ /ˈdɪstəns/ *noun* **1** [C,U] the amount of space between two places or things: *The map tells you the distances between the major cities.* ♦ *We can* walk home from here; it's no distance* (= it isn't far). ♦ *The house is **within walking distance** of the shops.* **2** [sing] a point that is a long way from sb/sth: *At this distance I can't read the number on the bus.* ♦ *From a distance the village looks quite attractive.*

IDM **in the distance** far away: *I could just see Paul in the distance.*

keep your distance to stay away from sb/sth: *Rachel's got a bad cold, so I'm keeping my distance until she gets better.*

within striking distance ➲ strike[1]

distance[2] /ˈdɪstəns/ *verb* [T] **distance yourself from sb/sth** to become less involved or connected with sb/sth: *She was keen to distance herself from the views of her colleagues.*

distant /ˈdɪstənt/ *adj* **1** a long way away in space or time: *travel to distant parts of the world* ♦ *in the not-too-distant future* (= quite soon) **2** [only *before* a noun] (used about a relative) not closely related: *a distant cousin* **3** not very friendly: *He has a rather distant manner and it's hard to get to know him well.* **4** seeming to be thinking about sth else: *She had a distant look in her eyes and clearly wasn't listening to me.*

distaste /dɪsˈteɪst/ *noun* [U, sing] not liking sth; the feeling that sb/sth is unpleasant or offends you: *He looked at the dirty room with distaste.*

distasteful /dɪsˈteɪstfl/ *adj* (*formal*) unpleasant or causing offence: *a distasteful remark*

distil (*AmE* **distill**) /dɪˈstɪl/ *verb* [T] (**distilling**; **distilled**) to make a liquid pure by heating it until it becomes a gas and then collecting the liquid that forms when the gas cools ▶ **distillation** /ˌdɪstɪˈleɪʃn/ *noun* [C,U]

distillery /dɪˈstɪləri/ *noun* [C] (*pl* **distilleries**) a factory where strong alcoholic drink is made by the process of **distilling**

distinct /dɪˈstɪŋkt/ *adj* **1** clear; easily seen, heard or understood: *There has been a distinct improvement in your work recently.* ♦ *I had **the distinct impression** that she was lying.* **2** **distinct (from sth)** clearly different: *Her books fall into two distinct groups: the novels and the travel stories.* ♦ *This region, as distinct from other parts of the country, relies heavily on tourism.* OPP **indistinct**

distinction /dɪˈstɪŋkʃn/ *noun* **1** [C,U] (a) **distinction (between A and B)** a clear or important difference between things or people: *We must **make a distinction** between classical and popular music here.* **2** [U] the quality of being excellent; fame for what you have achieved: *a violinist **of distinction*** **3** [C,U] the highest mark that is given to students in some exams for excellent work: *James got a distinction in maths.* ➲ *verb* ➲ **distinguish**

IDM **draw a distinction between sth and sth** ➲ draw[1]

distinctive /dɪˈstɪŋktɪv/ *adj* clearly different from others and therefore easy to recognize: *The soldiers were wearing their distinctive red berets.* ▶ **distinctively** *adv*

distinctly /dɪˈstɪŋktli/ *adv* **1** clearly: *I distinctly heard her say that she would be here on time.* **2** very; particularly: *His behaviour has been distinctly odd recently.*

🔑 **distinguish** /dɪˈstɪŋɡwɪʃ/ *verb* **1** [I,T] **distinguish between A and B; distinguish A from B** to recognize the difference between two things or people: *He doesn't seem able to distinguish between what's important and what isn't.* ♦ *People who are colour-blind often can't distinguish red from green.* SYN **differentiate** **2** [T] **distinguish A (from B)** to make sb/sth different from others: *distinguishing features* (= things by which sb/sth can be recognized) ♦ *The power of speech distinguishes humans from animals.* **3** [T] to see, hear or recognize with effort: *I listened carefully but they were too far away for me to distinguish what they were saying.* **4** [T] **distinguish yourself** to do sth which causes you to be noticed and admired: *She distinguished herself in the exams.* ➲ *verb* ➲ **distinction**

distinguishable /dɪˈstɪŋɡwɪʃəbl/ *adj* **1** possible to recognize as different from sb/sth else: *The male bird is distinguishable from the female by the colour of its beak.* **2** possible to see, hear or recognize with effort: *The letter is so old that the signature is barely distinguishable.* OPP for both meanings **indistinguishable**

distinguished /dɪˈstɪŋɡwɪʃt/ *adj* important, successful and respected by other people: *a distinguished guest*

distort /dɪˈstɔːt/ *verb* [T] **1** to change the shape or sound of sth so that it seems strange or is not clear: *Her face was distorted with grief.* ♦ *The kidnapper used a device to distort his voice over the telephone.* **2** to change sth and show it a way that is not correct or true: *Foreigners are often given a distorted view of this country.* ▶ **distortion** *noun* [C,U]

distract /dɪˈstrækt/ *verb* [T] **distract sb (from sth)** to take sb's attention away from sth: *Could you stop talking please? You're distracting me from my work.*

distracted /dɪˈstræktɪd/ *adj* unable to give your full attention to sth because you are worried or thinking about sth else

distraction /dɪˈstrækʃn/ *noun* [C,U] something that takes your attention away from what you were doing or thinking about: *I find it hard to work at home because there are so many distractions.*

IDM **to distraction** with the result that you become upset, excited or angry and unable to think clearly: *The noise of the traffic outside at night is driving me to distraction.*

distraught /dɪˈstrɔːt/ *adj* extremely upset and anxious

distress[1] /dɪˈstres/ *noun* [U] **1** the state of being very upset or of suffering great pain or difficulty: *She was **in** such **distress** that I didn't want to leave her on her own.* **2** the state of being in great danger and needing immediate help: *The ship's captain radioed that it was **in distress**.*

distress[2] /dɪˈstres/ *verb* [T] to make sb very upset or unhappy: *Try not to say anything to distress the patient further.* ▶ **distressed** *adj*: *She was too dis-*

D

tressed to talk. ▶ **distressing** *adj*: *a distressing experience/illness*

distribute /dɪˈstrɪbjuːt; ˈdɪstrɪbjuːt/ *verb* [T] **1 distribute sth (to/among sb/sth)** to give things to a number of people: *Tickets will be distributed to all club members.* ◆ *They distributed emergency food supplies to the areas that were most in need.* **2** to transport and supply goods to shops, companies, etc: *Which company distributes this product in your country?* **3** to spread sth equally over an area: *Make sure that the weight is **evenly distributed**.*

D

distribution /ˌdɪstrɪˈbjuːʃn/ *noun* **1** [C,U] the way sth is shared out; the pattern in which sth is found: *a map to show the distribution of rainfall in Africa* **2** [U] the act of giving sth to a number of people: *the distribution of food parcels to the refugees* **3** [U] the system of transporting and delivering goods: *worldwide distribution systems*

distributor /dɪˈstrɪbjətə(r)/ *noun* [C] a person or company that transports and supplies goods to a number of shops and companies

district /ˈdɪstrɪkt/ *noun* [C] **1** a part of a town or country that is special for a particular reason or is of a particular type: *rural districts* ◆ *the financial district of the city* **2** an official division of a town or country: *the district council* ◆ *postal districts* ➲ note at **area**

distrust /dɪsˈtrʌst/ *noun* [U, sing] **(a) distrust (of sb/sth)** the feeling that you cannot believe sb/sth; a lack of trust ▶ **distrust** *verb* [T]: *She distrusts him because he lied to her once before.* ➲ look at **mistrust** ▶ **distrustful** /-fl/ *adj*

disturb /dɪˈstɜːb/ *verb* [T] **1** to interrupt sb while they are doing sth or sleeping; to spoil a peaceful situation: *I'm sorry to disturb you but there's a phone call for you.* ◆ *Their sleep was disturbed by a loud crash.* **2** to move sth or change its position: *I noticed a number of things had been disturbed and realized that there had been a burglary.* **3** to cause sb to worry: *It disturbed her to think that he might be unhappy.*

disturbance /dɪˈstɜːbəns/ *noun* [C,U] something that makes you stop what you are doing, or that upsets the normal condition of sth: *They were arrested for causing a disturbance* (= fighting) *in the town centre.* ◆ *emotional disturbance*

disturbed /dɪˈstɜːbd/ *adj* **1** having mental or emotional problems: *a school for disturbed young people* **2** very anxious and unhappy about sth: *I was deeply disturbed by the news of his accident.*

disturbing /dɪˈstɜːbɪŋ/ *adj* making you worried or upset: *I found the film about AIDS very disturbing.*

disuse /dɪsˈjuːs/ *noun* [U] the state of not being used any more: *The farm buildings had been allowed to **fall into disuse**.*

disused /ˌdɪsˈjuːzd/ *adj* not used any more: *a disused railway line*

ditch[1] /dɪtʃ/ *noun* [C] a long narrow hole that has been dug into the ground, especially along the side of a road or field for water to flow along

IDM **a last-ditch attempt** ➲ **last**[1]

ditch[2] /dɪtʃ/ *verb* [T] (*informal*) to get rid of or leave sb/sth: *She ditched her old friends when she became famous.*

dither /ˈdɪðə(r)/ *verb* [I] to be unable to decide sth: *Stop dithering and make up your mind!* SYN **hesitate**

ditto /ˈdɪtəʊ/ *noun* [C] (*symbol* ") the same; used, especially in a list, underneath a particular word or phrase, to show that it is repeated and to avoid having to write it again ▶ **ditto** *adv*: *'I'm starving.' 'Ditto* (= me too).*'*

divan /dɪˈvæn/ *noun* [C] (*BrE*) a type of bed with a thick base and a mattress

dive[1] /daɪv/ *verb* [I] (*pt* **dived**, *AmE* also **dove** /dəʊv/; *pp* **dived**) **1 dive (off/from sth) (into sth)**; **dive in** to jump into water with your arms and head first: *In Acapulco, men dive off the cliffs into the sea.* ◆ *A passer-by dived in and saved the drowning man.* **2** to swim under the surface of the sea, a lake, etc: *people diving for pearls* ◆ *I'm hoping to **go diving** on holiday.* **3** to move quickly and suddenly downwards: *He dived under the table and hid there.* ◆ *The engines failed and the plane dived.*

PHR V **dive into sth** to put your hand quickly into a pocket or bag in order to find or get sth: *She dived into her bag and brought out an old photograph.*

dive[2] /daɪv/ *noun* [C] **1** the act of **diving** into water **2** a quick and sudden downwards movement: *Despite a desperate dive, the goalkeeper couldn't stop the ball.*

diver /ˈdaɪvə(r)/ *noun* [C] **1** a person who swims under the surface of water using special equipment **2** a person who jumps into water with their arms and head first

diverge /daɪˈvɜːdʒ/ *verb* [I] (*formal*) **diverge (from sth)** **1** (used about roads, lines, etc.) to separate and go in different directions: *The paths suddenly diverged and they didn't know which one to take.* **2** to be or become different: *Attitudes among teachers diverge on this question.* OPP for both meanings **converge**

diverse /daɪˈvɜːs/ *adj* very different from each other: *people from diverse social backgrounds* ◆ *My interests are very diverse.* ➲ noun **diversity**

diversify /daɪˈvɜːsɪfaɪ/ *verb* [I,T] (**diversifying**; **diversifies**; *pt, pp* **diversified**) **diversify (sth) (into sth)** to increase or develop the number or types of sth: *To remain successful in the future, the company will have to diversify.* ◆ *Latin diversified into several different languages.* ▶ **diversification** /daɪˌvɜːsɪfɪˈkeɪʃn/ *noun* [C,U]

diversion /daɪˈvɜːʃn/ *noun* **1** [C,U] the act of changing the direction or purpose of sth, especially in order to solve or avoid a problem: *We made a short diversion to go and look at the castle.* ◆ *the diversion of government funds to areas of greatest need* **2** [C] something that takes your attention away from sth: *Some prisoners created a diversion while others escaped.* **3** [C] (*AmE* **detour**) a different route which traffic can take when a road is closed: *For London, follow the diversion.*

diversity /daɪˈvɜːsəti/ *noun* [C,U] the wide variety of sth: *cultural and ethnic diversity*

divert /daɪˈvɜːt/ *verb* [T] divert sb/sth (from sth) (to sth); divert sth (away from sth) to change the direction or purpose of sb/sth, especially to avoid a problem: *During the road repairs, all traffic is being diverted.* ◆ *Government money was diverted from defence to education.* ◆ *Politicians often criticise each other to divert attention away from their own mistakes.*

divide¹ /dɪˈvaɪd/ *verb*
➤SEPARATE INTO PARTS **1** [I,T] divide (sth) (up) (into sth) to separate into different parts: *The egg divides into two cells.* ◆ *Where the path divides, keep right.* ◆ *The house was divided up into flats.* **2** [T] divide sth (out/up) (between/among sb) to separate sth into parts and give a part to each of a number of people: *The robbers divided the money out between themselves.* ◆ *When he died, his property was divided up among his children.* **3** [T] divide sth (between A and B) to use different parts or amounts of sth for different purposes: *They divide their time between their two homes.* **4** [T] to separate two places or things: *The river divides the old part of the city from the new.*
➤CAUSE DISAGREEMENT **5** [T] to cause people to disagree: *The question of immigration has divided the country.* SYN **split**
➤MATHEMATICS **6** [T] divide sth by sth to calculate how many times a number will go into another number: *10 divided by 5 is 2.* OPP **multiply**

divide² /dɪˈvaɪd/ *noun* [C, sing] a divide (between A and B) a difference between two groups of people that separates them from each other: *a divide between the rich and the poor*

diˌvided ˈhighway (*AmE*) = **dual carriageway**

dividend /ˈdɪvɪdend/ *noun* [C] a part of a company's profits that is paid to the people who own shares in the company

divine /dɪˈvaɪn/ *adj* connected with God or a god

diving /ˈdaɪvɪŋ/ *noun* [U] the activity or sport of jumping into water or swimming under the surface of the sea, a lake, etc. ➲ picture at **swim**

ˈdiving board *noun* [C] a board at the side of a swimming pool from which people can jump into the water

divisible /dɪˈvɪzəbl/ *adj* [not before a noun] that can be divided: *12 is divisible by 3.*

division /dɪˈvɪʒn/ *noun*
➤INTO SEPARATE PARTS **1** [U,sing] division (of sth) (into sth); division (of sth) (between A and B) the process or result of separating sth into different parts; the sharing of sth between different people, groups, places, etc: *an unfair division of the profits* ◆ *There is a growing economic division between the north and south of the country.*
➤MATHEMATICS **2** [U] dividing one number by another: *the teaching of multiplication and division*
➤DISAGREEMENT **3** [C,U] a division (in/within sth); a division (between A and B) a disagreement or difference of opinion between sb/sth: *deep divisions within the Labour Party*
➤PART OF ORGANIZATION **4** [C] a part or section of an organization: *the company's sales division* ◆ *the First Division* (= one of the groups of teams in a sports competition)
➤BORDER **5** [C] a line that separates sth; a border: *The river marks the division between the two counties.*

divisive /dɪˈvaɪsɪv/ *adj* (*formal*) likely to cause disagreements or arguments between people: *a divisive policy*

D

divorce¹ /dɪˈvɔːs/ *noun* [C,U] the legal end of a marriage: *to* ***get a divorce*** ◆ *Two in five marriages end in divorce.*

divorce² /dɪˈvɔːs/ *verb* **1** [I,T] to legally end your marriage to sb: *My parents* ***got divorced*** *when I was three.* ◆ *She divorced him a year after their marriage.* **2** [T] divorce sb/sth from sth to separate sb/sth from sth: *Sometimes these modern novels seem completely divorced from everyday life.* ▶ **divorced** *adj*

MORE If a couple are still legally married but not living together any more, they are **separated**.

divorcee /dɪˌvɔːˈsiː/ *noun* [C] a person who is divorced, especially a woman

divulge /daɪˈvʌldʒ/ *verb* [T] (*formal*) to tell sth that is secret: *The phone companies refused to divulge details of their costs.*

Diwali /diːˈwɑːli/ *noun* [sing] a Hindu festival that takes place in October or November, in which people decorate their homes with lights

DIY /ˌdiː aɪ ˈwaɪ/ *abbr* **do-it-yourself**; the activity of making, repairing or decorating things in the home yourself, instead of paying sb to do it: *a DIY store* (= where you can buy materials for DIY) ➲ note at **house**

dizzy /ˈdɪzi/ *adj* (dizzier; dizziest) **1** feeling as if everything is turning round and that you might fall: *I* ***feel/get dizzy*** *in high places.* **2** very great; extreme: *the dizzy pace of life in London* ◆ *The following year, the band's popularity reached* ***dizzy heights***. ▶ **dizziness** *noun* [U]

DJ /ˈdiː dʒeɪ/ (also ˈ**disc jockey**) *noun* [C] a person who plays and talks about recorded music on radio or television or at a club

DNA /ˌdiː en ˈeɪ/ *noun* [U] the chemical in the cells of animals and plants that controls what characteristics that animal or plant has: *a DNA test*

do¹ /duː/ *verb* ⓘ For the forms of 'do', look at the **Reference section** at the back of this dictionary. **1** [T] to perform an action, activity or job: *What are you doing?* ◆ *What is the government doing about pollution* (= what action are they taking)? ◆ *What do you do* (= what is your job)? ◆ *Have you done your homework?* ◆ *I do twenty minutes' exercise every morning.* ◆ *to do the cooking/cleaning/ironing* ◆ *to do judo/aerobics/windsurfing* ◆ *What did you* ***do with*** *the keys* (= where did you put them)? **2** [I,T] to make progress or develop; to improve sth: *'How's your daughter doing at school?' 'She's doing well.'* ◆ *Last week's win has* ***done wonders for*** *the team's confidence.* ◆ *This latest scandal will* ***do nothing for*** (= will harm) *this government's reputation.* **3** [T] to make or produce sth: *The photocopier does 60 copies a minute.* ◆ *to do a painting/drawing* **4** [T] to study sth or find the answer to sth: *to do French/a course/a degree* ◆ *I can't do question three.* **5** [T] to travel a certain distance or at a certain speed: *I normally do about five miles when I go running.* ◆ *This car does 120 miles per hour.* **6** [T] to provide a service: *Do you do eye tests here?* **7** [I,T] to be enough or suitable: *If you haven't got a pen, a pencil will do.* ◆ *This room will do me nicely.* **8** [T] to have a particular effect: *A holiday will do you good.* ◆ *The storm did a lot of damage.*

D

IDM be/have (got) (sth) to do with sb/sth to be connected with sb/sth: *I'm not sure what Paola's job is, but I think it's got something to do with animals.* ◆ *'How much do you earn?' 'It's nothing to do with you!'*

that does it (*informal*) used to show that you will not accept sth any longer: *That does it—I'm leaving! I won't put up with you swearing at me any longer.*

that's done it (*informal*) used to say that an accident, a mistake, etc. has spoiled or ruined sth: *That's done it. You've broken it now.* ℹ For other idioms containing **do**, look at the entries for the nouns, adjectives, etc. For example, **do sb credit** is at **credit**.

PHR V do away with sth to get rid of sth: *Most European countries have done away with their royal families.*

do sb out of sth to prevent sb having sth in an unfair way; to cheat sb: *They've done me out of my share of the money!*

do sth up 1 to fasten a piece of clothing: *Hurry up. Do up your jacket and we can go!* **OPP undo 2** to repair a building and make it more modern: *They're doing up the old cottage.* ➲ note at **house**

do without (sth) to manage without having sth: *If there isn't any coffee left, we'll just have to do without.*

🔑 **do²** /də; *strong form* duː/ *auxiliary verb* **1** used with other verbs to form questions and negative sentences, also in short answers and **question tags** (= short questions at the end of a sentence): *I don't like fish.* ◆ *Does she speak Italian?* ◆ *He doesn't work here, does he?* ℹ For more information, look at the **Reference section** at the back of this dictionary. **2** used to avoid repeating the main verb: *He earns a lot more than I do.* ◆ *She's feeling much better than she did last week.* **3** used for emphasizing the main verb: *I can't find the receipt now but I'm sure I did pay the phone bill.*

do³ /duː/ *noun* [C] (*pl* **dos** /duːz/) (*informal*) a party or other social event: *We're having a bit of a do to celebrate Tim's birthday.*

IDM dos and don'ts things that you should and should not do: *the dos and don'ts of mountain climbing*

docile /ˈdəʊsaɪl/ *adj* (used about a person or an animal) quiet and easy to control

dock¹ /dɒk/ *noun* **1** [C,U] an area of a port where ships stop to be loaded, repaired, etc. **2 docks** [pl] a group of **docks** with all the buildings, offices, etc. that are around them: *He works down at the docks.* **3** (*AmE*) = **jetty 4** [C, usually sing] the place in a court of law where the person who is accused sits or stands

dock² /dɒk/ *verb* **1** [I,T] (used about a ship) to sail into a port and stop at the **dock**: *The ship had docked/was docked at Lisbon.* **2** [T] to take away part of the money sb earns, especially as a punishment: *They've docked £20 off my wages because I was late.*

ˈ**docking station** *noun* [C] a device to which you can connect a small computer in order to use it like a larger one; a device with speakers that you can connect to some types of small equipment for listening to music ➲ note at **iPod™**, **smartphone**

🔑 **doctor¹** /ˈdɒktə(r)/ *noun* (*abbr* **Dr**) **1** [C] a person who has been trained in medicine and who treats people who are ill: *Our family doctor is Dr Laing.* ◆ *I've got a doctor's appointment at 10 o'clock.* ➲ note at **disease, hospital, ill** ➲ picture on **page P2 2 the doctor's** [sing] a doctor's **surgery** (= the place where a doctor sees patients): *I'm going to the doctor's today.* **3** [C] a person who has a **doctorate** (= the highest degree from a university): *a Doctor of Philosophy*

TOPIC

Going to the doctor

In Britain a **doctor** who looks after general health problems is called a **GP** (/ˌdʒiː ˈpiː/). He/She works in **a surgery**. When you **go to the doctor's**, you describe your **symptoms**: *My head* ***hurts***. ◆ ***I've got*** *stomach* ***ache***. The doctor may **prescribe** a particular **medicine**. This is written on an official piece of paper called a **prescription**, which you take to a **chemist's** and show when you buy the medicine. If you are feeling very **ill** or if you are in a lot of **pain**, the doctor may send you to **hospital** for more **treatment**.

doctor² /ˈdɒktə(r)/ *verb* [T] **1** to change sth that should not be changed in order to gain an advantage: *The results of the survey had been doctored.* **2** to add sth harmful to food or drink

doctorate /ˈdɒktərət/ *noun* [C] the highest university degree

doctrine /ˈdɒktrɪn/ *noun* [C,U] a set of beliefs that is taught by a church, political party, etc.

🔑 **document** /ˈdɒkjumənt/ *noun* [C] **1** an official piece of writing which gives information, proof or evidence: *Her lawyer asked her to read and sign a number of documents.* **2** a computer file that contains writing, etc: *Save the document before closing.*

documentary /ˌdɒkjuˈmentri/ *noun* [C] (*pl* **documentaries**) a film or TV or radio programme that gives facts or information about a particular subject: *Did you see that documentary on Sri Lanka?*

doddle /ˈdɒdl/ *noun* [sing] (*BrE informal*) something that is very easy to do: *The exam was an absolute doddle!*

dodge¹ /dɒdʒ/ *verb* **1** [I,T] to move quickly in order to avoid sb/sth: *I had to dodge between the cars to cross the road.* **2** [T] to avoid doing sth that you should do: *Don't try to dodge your responsibilities!*

dodge² /dɒdʒ/ *noun* [C] (*informal*) a clever way of avoiding sth: *The man had been involved in a massive tax dodge.*

dodgy /ˈdɒdʒi/ *adj* (**dodgier**; **dodgiest**) (*BrE informal*) involving risk; not honest or not to be trusted: *This meat looks a bit dodgy—when did we buy it?* ◆ *a dodgy business deal*

doe /dəʊ/ *noun* [C] a female **deer** (= a large wild animal that eats grass) or **rabbit** (= a small animal with long ears) ➲ note at **deer** ➲ picture at **deer**

does /dʌz/ ➲ **do**

doesn't /ˈdʌznt/ *short for* **does not**

⚷ **dog¹** /dɒg/ *noun* [C] **1** an animal that many people keep as a pet, or for working on farms, hunting, etc: *dog food* ➲ note at **pet** **2** a male dog or male **fox** (= a wild animal like a dog with reddish fur and a thick tail): *If you're getting a puppy, bitches are gentler than dogs.*

TOPIC

Dogs

When you **take** your dog **for a walk**, you control it with a long piece of leather, rope, etc. called a **lead**. You might put a **muzzle** over its nose and mouth so that it cannot **bite**. When a dog makes a noise it **barks** (written as **woof**) and when it is excited, it **wags** its **tail**. A young dog is called a **puppy**. Dogs that are **trained** to help the blind (= people who cannot see) are called **guide dogs**.

dog² /dɒg/ *verb* [T] (**dogging**; **dogged**) to follow sb closely: *A shadowy figure was dogging their every move.* ◆ (*figurative*) *Bad luck and illness have dogged her career from the start.*

ˈ**dog collar** *noun* [C] (*informal*) a white band that is worn around the neck by some priests in the Christian church

ˈ**dog-eared** *adj* (used about a book or piece of paper) in bad condition with untidy corners and edges because it has been used a lot

dogged /ˈdɒgɪd/ *adj* refusing to give up even when sth is difficult: *I was impressed by his* ***dogged determination*** *to succeed.* ▶ **doggedly** *adv*: *She doggedly refused all offers of help.*

dogma /ˈdɒgmə/ *noun* [C,U] a belief or set of beliefs that people are expected to accept as true without questioning

dogmatic /dɒgˈmætɪk/ *adj* being certain that your beliefs are right and that others should accept them, without considering other opinions or evidence ▶ **dogmatically** /-kli/ *adv*

dogsbody /ˈdɒgzbɒdi/ *noun* [C] (*pl* **dogsbodies**) (*BrE informal*) a person who has to do the boring or unpleasant jobs that nobody else wants to do and who is considered less important than other people

the doldrums /ˈdɒldrəmz/ *noun*

IDM **in the doldrums** **1** unhappy: *He's been in the doldrums ever since she left him.* **2** not active or busy: *Business has been in the doldrums recently.*

the dole /dəʊl/ *noun* [sing] (*BrE informal*) money that the State gives every week to people who are unemployed: *I lost my job and had to go* ***on the dole***.

dole /dəʊl/ *verb*

PHR V **dole sth out** (*informal*) to give sth, especially food, money, etc. in small amounts to a number of people

doleful /ˈdəʊlfl/ *adj* sad or unhappy: *She looked at him with large doleful eyes.* ▶ **dolefully** /-fəli/ *adv*

doll /dɒl/ *noun* [C] a child's toy that looks like a small person or a baby

⚷ **dollar** /ˈdɒlə(r)/ *noun* **1** [C] (*symbol* $) a unit of money in some countries, for example the US, Canada and Australia: *Can I pay in US dollars?*

MORE There are 100 **cents** in a dollar.

2 [C] a note or coin that is worth one dollar: *a dollar bill* **3 the dollar** [sing] the value of the US dollar on international money markets: *The dollar fell against the pound.*

dollop /ˈdɒləp/ *noun* [C] (*informal*) a lump of sth soft, especially food: *a dollop of ice cream*

dolphin

shark

dolphin /ˈdɒlfɪn/ *noun* [C] an animal that lives in the sea and looks like a large fish. **Dolphins** usually swim in **schools** (= large groups).

domain /dəˈmeɪn; dəʊ-/ *noun* [C] **1** an area of knowledge or activity: *I don't know—that's outside my domain.* ◆ *This issue is now in the public domain* (= the public knows about it). **2** a set of websites on the Internet which end with the same group of letters, for example '.com', '.org'

dome /dəʊm/ *noun* [C] a round roof on a building: *the dome of St Paul's in London* ➲ picture on **page P11** ▶ **domed** *adj*: *a domed roof/forehead*

⚷ **domestic** /dəˈmestɪk/ *adj* **1** not international; only within one country: *domestic affairs/flights/politics* **2** [only *before* a noun] connected with the home or family: *domestic chores/tasks* ◆ *the growing* *problem of* ***domestic violence*** (= violence between members of the same family) ◆ *domestic water/gas/electricity supplies* **3** (used about a person) enjoying doing things in the home, such as cooking and cleaning: *I'm not a very domestic sort of person.* **4** (used about animals) kept as pets or on farms; not wild: *domestic animals such as cats, dogs and horses*

D

domesticated /də'mestɪkeɪtɪd/ *adj* **1** (used about animals) happy being near people and being controlled by them **2** (used about people) to be good at cleaning the house, cooking, etc:

dominance /'dɒmɪnəns/ *noun* [U] control or power: *Japan's dominance of the car industry*

dominant /'dɒmɪnənt/ *adj* more powerful, important or noticeable than others: *His mother was the dominant influence in his life.*

dominate /'dɒmɪneɪt/ *verb* **1** [I,T] to be more powerful, important or noticeable than others: *The Italian team dominated throughout the second half of the game.* ◆ *She always tends to dominate the conversation.* **2** [T] (used about a building or place) to be much higher than everything else: *The cathedral dominates the area for miles around.* ▶ **domination** /ˌdɒmɪ'neɪʃn/ *noun* [U]

domineering /ˌdɒmɪ'nɪərɪŋ/ *adj* having a very strong character and wanting to control other people SYN **overbearing**

dominion /də'mɪniən/ *noun* (*formal*) **1** [U] the power to rule and control: *to have dominion over an area* **2** [C] an area controlled by one government or ruler: *the dominions of the Roman empire*

domino /'dɒmɪnəʊ/ *noun* [C] (*pl* **dominoes**) one of a set of small flat pieces of wood or plastic, marked on one side with two groups of spots representing numbers, that are used for playing a game called **dominoes**

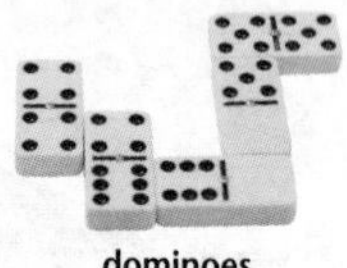

dominoes

donate /dəʊ'neɪt/ *verb* [T] **donate sth (to sb/sth)** **1** to give money or goods to an organization, especially one for people or animals who need help: *She donated a large sum of money to Cancer Research.* **2** to allow doctors to remove blood or a body organ in order to help sb who needs it

donation /dəʊ'neɪʃn/ *noun* [pl] money, etc. that is given to a person or an organization such as a charity, in order to help people or animals in need

done[1] *past participle* of **do**[1]

done[2] /dʌn/ *adj* [not before a noun] **1** finished: *I've got to go out as soon as this job is done.* **2** (used about food) cooked enough: *The meat's ready but the vegetables still aren't done.*

IDM **over and done with** completely finished; in the past

done[3] /dʌn/ *exclam* used for saying that you accept an offer: *'I'll give you twenty pounds for it.' 'Done!'*

donkey /'dɒŋki/ *noun* [C] (also **ass**) an animal like a small horse, with long ears

IDM **donkey's years** (*BrE informal*) a very long time: *We've known each other for donkey's years.*

donkey

donor /'dəʊnə(r)/ *noun* [C] **1** a person who gives money or goods to an organization that helps people or animals **2** a person who gives blood or a part of their own body for medical use: *a blood/kidney donor*

don't /dəʊnt/ *short for* **do not**

donut (*AmE*) = **doughnut**

doodle /'du:dl/ *verb* [I] to draw lines, patterns, etc. without thinking, especially when you are bored ▶ **doodle** *noun* [C]

doom /du:m/ *noun* [U] death or a terrible event in the future which you cannot avoid: *a sense of impending doom* (= that sth bad is going to happen) ◆ *Don't listen to her. She's always full of* ***doom and gloom*** (= expecting bad things to happen). ▶ **doomed** *adj*: *The plan was doomed from the start.*

door /dɔ:(r)/ *noun* [C] **1** a piece of wood, glass, etc. that you open and close to get in or out of a room, building, car, etc: *to open/shut/close the door* ◆ *to answer the door* (= to open the door when sb knocks or rings the bell) ◆ *There's somebody at the door. Could you see who it is?* ◆ *Have you bolted/locked the door?* ◆ *I could hear someone knocking on the door.* ◆ *the front/back door* ◆ *the fridge door* ➲ picture on **page P7** **2** the entrance to a building, room, car, etc: *I looked through the door and saw her sitting there.*

IDM **(from) door to door** (from) house to house: *The journey takes about five hours, door to door.* ◆ *a door-to-door salesman* (= a person who visits people in their homes to try and sell them things)

next door (to sb/sth) in the next house, room, etc: *Do you know the people who live next door?*

out of doors outside: *Shall we eat out of doors today?* SYN **outdoors** OPP **indoors**

doorbell /'dɔ:bel/ *noun* [C] a bell with a button outside a house that you push to let the people inside know that you are there

doorman /'dɔ:mən/ *noun* [C] (*pl* **-men** /-mən/) a man, often in uniform, whose job is to stand at the entrance to a large building such as a hotel or a theatre, and open the door for visitors, find them taxis, etc.

doormat /'dɔ:mæt/ *noun* [C] **1** a piece of material on the floor in front of a door which you can clean your shoes on before going inside **2** (*informal*) a person who allows other people to treat them badly without complaining

doorstep /'dɔ:step/ *noun* [C] a step in front of a door outside a building

IDM **on your/the doorstep** very near to you: *The sea was right on our doorstep.*

doorway /ˈdɔːweɪ/ *noun* [C] an opening filled by a door leading into a building, room, etc: *She was standing in the doorway.*

dope[1] /dəʊp/ *noun* (*informal*) **1** [U] an illegal drug, such as **cannabis** **2** [C] a stupid person: *What a dope!*

dope[2] /dəʊp/ *verb* [T] to give a drug secretly to a person or an animal, especially to make them sleep

dopey /ˈdəʊpi/ *adj* (**dopier**; **dopiest**) (*informal*) **1** stupid; not intelligent **2** tired and not able to think clearly, especially because of drugs, alcohol or lack of sleep

dorm = **dormitory**

dormant /ˈdɔːmənt/ *adj* not active for some time: *a dormant volcano*

dormitory /ˈdɔːmətri/ *noun* [C] (*pl* **dormitories**) (also **dorm** /dɔːm/) **1** a large bedroom with a number of beds in it, especially in a school, etc. **2** (*AmE*) = **hall of residence**

dosage /ˈdəʊsɪdʒ/ *noun* [C, usually sing] the amount of a medicine you should take over a period of time: *The recommended dosage is one tablet every four hours.*

dose[1] /dəʊs/ *noun* [C] **1** an amount of medicine that you take at one time: *Take a dose of the medicine before going to bed.* ➲ look at **overdose** **2** an amount of sth, especially sth unpleasant: *a dose of the flu* ◆ *I can only stand him in small doses.*

dose[2] /dəʊs/ *verb* [T] to give sb/yourself some medicine or a drug: *She dosed herself with aspirin and went to work.*

doss /dɒs/ *verb* (*BrE informal*)

PHR V **doss about/around** to waste time not doing very much: *We just dossed about in class yesterday.*

doss (down) to lie down to sleep, without a proper bed: *Do you mind if I doss down on your floor tonight?*

⚷ **dot**[1] /dɒt/ *noun* [C] **1** a small, round mark, like a full stop: *a white dress with black dots* ◆ *The letters i and j have dots above them.*

> **HELP** We use **dot** when we say a person's email address. For the address written as **ann@smithuni.co.uk** we would say 'Ann **at** smithuni **dot** co **dot** uk'.

2 something that looks like a **dot**: *He watched until the aeroplane was just a dot in the sky.*

IDM **on the dot** (*informal*) at exactly the right time or at exactly the time mentioned: *Lessons start at 9 o'clock on the dot.*

dot[2] /dɒt/ *verb* [T] (**dotting**; **dotted**) **1** to mark with a **dot** **2** [usually passive] to spread things or people over an area; to be spread over an area: *The countryside was* **dotted with** *small villages.* ◆ *There are restaurants* **dotted about** *all over the centre of town.* ◆ *Small villages dot the countryside.*

dot-com (also **dotcom**) /ˌdɒt ˈkɒm/ *noun* [C] a company that sells products and services on the Internet: *The weaker dot-coms have collapsed.* ◆ *a dot-com millionaire*

dote /dəʊt/ *verb* [I] **dote on sb/sth** to have or show a lot of love for sb/sth and ignore their faults: *He's always doted on his eldest son.* ▶ **doting** *adj*: *doting parents*

dotted ˈline *noun* [C] a line of **dots** which show where sth is to be written on a form, etc: *Sign on the dotted line.* ➲ picture at **line**

D

⚷ **double**[1] /ˈdʌbl/ *adj, determiner* **1** twice as much or as many (as usual): *His income is double his wife's.* ◆ *We'll need double the amount of wine.* **2** having two equal or similar parts: *double doors* ◆ *Does 'necessary' have (a) double 's'?* ◆ *My phone number is two four double three four (= 24334).* **3** made for or used by two people or things: *a double garage* ➲ note at **bed**[1] ➲ picture at **bed**

⚷ **double**[2] /ˈdʌbl/ *adv* in pairs or two parts: *When I saw her with her twin sister I thought I was* **seeing double**.

⚷ **double**[3] /ˈdʌbl/ *noun* **1** [U] twice the (usual) number or amount: *When you work overtime, you get paid double.* **2** [C] a glass of strong alcoholic drink containing twice the usual amount **3** [C] a person who looks very much like another: *I thought it was you I saw in the supermarket. You must have a double.* **4** [C] an actor who replaces another actor in a film to do dangerous or other special things **5** [C] a bedroom for two people in a hotel, etc: *Would you like a single or a double?* ➲ look at **single** **6** **doubles** [U, with sing or pl verb] (in some sports, for example **tennis**) with two pairs playing: *the Men's Doubles final* ➲ look at **single**

⚷ **double**[4] /ˈdʌbl/ *verb* **1** [I,T] to become or to make sth twice as much or as many; to multiply by two: *The price of houses has almost doubled.* ◆ *Think of a number and double it.* **2** [I] **double (up) as sth** to have a second use or function: *The small room doubles (up) as a study.*

PHR V **double (sb) up/over** (to cause sb) to bend the body: *to be doubled up with pain/laughter*

ˌdouble ˈbass (also **bass**) *noun* [C] the largest musical instrument with strings, that you can play either standing up or sitting down ➲ picture at **music**

ˌdouble-ˈbreasted *adj* (used about a coat or jacket) having two rows of buttons down the front

ˌdouble-ˈcheck *verb* [I,T] to check sth again, or with great care

ˌdouble-ˈclick *verb* [I,T] ~ (**on sth**) to choose a particular function or item on a computer screen by pressing one of the buttons on a mouse twice quickly: *To run an application, just double-click on the icon.*

ˌdouble-ˈcross *verb* [T] to cheat sb who believes that they can trust you after you have agreed to do sth dishonest together

ˌdouble-ˈdecker *noun* [C] a bus with two floors

ˌdouble ˈDutch *noun* [U] (*BrE*) conversation or writing that you cannot understand at all: *The listening comprehension in the exam was really hard. It all sounded like double Dutch to me!*

ˌ**double ˈfigures** (*AmE* ˌdouble ˈdigits) *noun* [U] (*BrE*) a number that is more than nine and less than 100: *Inflation is* ***in double figures***.

ˌ**double ˈglazing** *noun* [U] two layers of glass in a window to keep a building warm or quiet ▶ ˌ**double-ˈglazed** *adj*

D

doubly /ˈdʌbli/ *adv* **1** more than usually: *Pete made doubly sure that the door was locked.* **2** in two ways: *He was doubly blessed with both good looks and talent.*

doubt¹ /daʊt/ *noun* [C,U] **doubt (about sth); doubt that …; doubt as to sth** a feeling of being uncertain about sth: *If you have any doubts about the job, feel free to ring me and discuss them.* ◆ *There's some doubt that Jan will pass the exam.*
IDM cast doubt on sth ➲ **cast¹**
give sb the benefit of the doubt ➲ **benefit¹**
in doubt not sure or definite
no doubt 1 used when you are saying that sth is probable: *No doubt she'll write when she has time.* **2** used when you are saying that sth is certainly true: *He's made some great movies. There's no doubt about it.*
without (a) doubt definitely: *It was, without doubt, the coldest winter for many years.*

doubt² /daʊt/ *verb* [T] to think sth is unlikely or to feel uncertain (about sth): *She never doubted that he was telling the truth.* ◆ *I doubt whether/if I'll have time to go to the shops today.* ◆ *He had never doubted her support.*

doubtful /ˈdaʊtfl/ *adj* **1 doubtful (about sth/about doing sth)** (used about a person) not sure: *John still felt doubtful about his decision.* **2** unlikely or uncertain: *It's doubtful whether/if we'll finish in time.* ◆ *It was doubtful that he was still alive.* ▶ **doubtfully** /-fəli/ *adv*: *'I suppose it'll be all right,' she said doubtfully.*

doubtless /ˈdaʊtləs/ *adv* almost certainly: *Doubtless she'll have a good excuse for being late!*

dough /dəʊ/ *noun* [U] **1** a mixture of flour, water, etc. used for baking into bread, etc. **2** (*slang*) money

doughnut (*AmE* **donut**) /ˈdəʊnʌt/ *noun* [C] a small cake in the shape of a ball or a ring, often filled with jam, etc., made from a sweet **dough** cooked in very hot oil ➲ picture at **cake**

dour /dʊə(r)/ *adj* (used about sb's manner or expression) cold and unfriendly

douse /daʊs/ (also **dowse** /daʊz/) *verb* [T] **1 douse sth (with sth)** to stop a fire from burning by pouring liquid over it: *The firefighters managed to douse the flames.* **2 douse sb/sth (in/with sth)** to cover sb/sth with liquid: *to douse yourself in perfume* (= wear too much of it)

dove¹ /dʌv/ *noun* [C] a type of white bird, often used as a sign of peace

dove² /dəʊv/ (*AmE*) *past tense of* **dive¹**

dowdy /ˈdaʊdi/ *adj* (**dowdier; dowdiest**) (used about a person or the clothes they wear) not attractive or fashionable

down¹ /daʊn/ *adv, prep* **1** to or at a lower level or place; from the top towards the bottom of sth: *Can you get that book down from the top shelf?* ◆ *'Where's Mary?' 'She's down in the basement.'* ◆ *Her hair hung down her back.* ◆ *The rain was running down the window.* **2** from a standing or vertical position to a sitting or horizontal one: *I think I'll sit/lie down.* **3** used for showing that the level, amount, strength, etc. of sth is less or lower: *Do you mind if I turn the heating down a bit?* **4** to or in the south: *We went down to Devon for our holiday.* **5** on paper: *Put these dates down in your diary.* **6** along: *We sailed down the river towards the sea.* ◆ *'Where's the nearest garage?' 'Go down this road and take the first turning on the right.'* **7 down to sb/sth** even including: *We had everything planned down to the last detail.*
IDM be down to sb to be sb's responsibility: *When my father died it was down to me to look after the family's affairs.*
be down to sth to have only the amount mentioned left: *I need to do some washing—I'm down to my last shirt.*
down and out having no money, job or home
down in the dumps unhappy or sad
down under (*informal*) (in) Australia

down² /daʊn/ *verb* [T] (*informal*) to finish a drink quickly: *She* ***downed*** *her drink* ***in one*** (= she drank the whole glass without stopping).

down³ /daʊn/ *adj* [not before a noun] **1** sad: *You're looking a bit down today.* **2** (used about computers) not working: *I can't access the file as our computers have been down all morning.* **3** lower than before: *Unemployment figures are down again this month.*

down⁴ /daʊn/ *noun* [U] very soft feathers: *a duvet filled with duck down*
IDM ups and downs ➲ **ups**

ˈ**down-and-out** *noun* [C] a person who has got no money, job or home

downcast /ˈdaʊnkɑːst/ *adj* **1** (used about a person) sad and without hope **2** (used about eyes) looking down

downfall /ˈdaʊnfɔːl/ *noun* [sing] a loss of sb's money, power, social position, etc.; the thing that causes this: *The government's downfall seemed inevitable.* ◆ *Greed was her downfall.*

downgrade /ˌdaʊnˈɡreɪd/ *verb* [T] **downgrade sb/sth (from sth) (to sth)** to reduce sb/sth to a lower level or position of importance: *Tom's been downgraded from manager to assistant manager.*

downhearted /ˌdaʊnˈhɑːtɪd/ *adj* [not before a noun] sad

downhill /ˌdaʊnˈhɪl/ *adj, adv* (going) downwards; towards the bottom of a hill: *It's an easy walk. The road runs downhill most of the way.* **OPP uphill**
IDM go downhill to get worse: *Their relationship has been going downhill for some time now.*

download /ˌdaʊnˈləʊd/ *verb* [T] to copy a computer file, etc. from a large computer system to a smaller one OPP **upload** ▶ **download** /ˈdaʊnləʊd/ *noun* [C]

downmarket /ˌdaʊnˈmɑːkɪt/ *adj* cheap and of low quality: *a downmarket newspaper* OPP **upmarket** ▶ **downmarket** *adv*

ˌdown ˈpayment *noun* [C] a sum of money that is given as the first part of a larger payment: *We're saving to* ***make a down payment on*** *a new car.*

downpour /ˈdaʊnpɔː(r)/ *noun* [C] a heavy, sudden fall of rain

downright /ˈdaʊnraɪt/ *adj* [only *before* a noun] (used about sth bad or unpleasant) complete: *The holiday was a downright disaster.* ▶ **downright** *adv*: *The way he spoke to me was downright rude!*

downside /ˈdaʊnsaɪd/ *noun* [C, usually sing] the disadvantages or negative aspects of sth: *All good ideas have a downside.*

Down's syndrome /ˈdaʊnz sɪndrəʊm/ *noun* [U] a medical condition in which a person is born with a flat, wide face and lower than average intelligence

⚷ **downstairs** /ˌdaʊnˈsteəz/ *adv, adj* towards or on a lower floor of a house or building: *He fell downstairs and broke his arm.* ◆ *Dad's downstairs, in the kitchen.* ◆ *a downstairs toilet* OPP **upstairs** ▶ **downstairs** *noun* [sing]: *We're painting the downstairs.* OPP **upstairs**

downstream /ˌdaʊnˈstriːm/ *adv* in the direction in which a river flows: *We were rowing downstream.* OPP **upstream**

ˌdown to ˈearth *adj* (used about a person) sensible, realistic and practical

downtrodden /ˈdaʊntrɒdn/ *adj* (used about a person) made to suffer bad treatment or living conditions by people in power, but being too tired, poor, ill, etc. to change this

downturn /ˈdaʊntɜːn/ *noun* [C, usually sing] a **downturn (in sth)** a drop in the amount of business that is done; a time when the economy becomes weaker: *a downturn in sales/trade/business* OPP **upturn**

⚷ **downward** /ˈdaʊnwəd/ *adj* [only *before* a noun] towards the ground or a lower level: *a downward movement* ▶ **downwards** /ˈdaʊnwədz/ *adv*: *She laid the picture face downwards on the table.* OPP **upward(s)**

dowry /ˈdaʊri/ *noun* [C] (*pl* **dowries**) money and/or property which, in some countries, a woman's family gives to the man she is marrying, or that a husband must pay to his wife's family

dowse = **douse**

doze /dəʊz/ *verb* [I] to sleep lightly and/or for a short time: *He was dozing in front of the TV.*

PHR V **doze off** to go to sleep, especially during the day: *I'm sorry—I must have dozed off for a minute.* ▶ **doze** *noun* [sing]

⚷ **dozen** /ˈdʌzn/ *noun* [C] (*abbr* **doz.**) (*pl* **dozen**) twelve or a group of twelve: *A dozen eggs, please.* ◆ *half a dozen* (= six) ◆ *two dozen sheep*

IDM **dozens (of sth)** (*informal*) very many: *I've tried phoning her dozens of times.*

dozy /ˈdəʊzi/ *adj* **1** wanting to sleep; not feeling awake: *The wine had made her rather dozy.* **2** (*BrE informal*) stupid: not intelligent: *You dozy thing—look what you've done!*

Dr *abbr* = **Doctor**[1]: *Dr Ruchira Paranjape*

drab /dræb/ *adj* (**drabber**; **drabbest**) not interesting or attractive: *a drab grey office building*

⚷ **draft**[1] /drɑːft/ *noun* **1** [C] a piece of writing, etc. which will probably be changed and improved; not the final version: *the first draft of a speech/essay* **2** [C] a written order to a bank to pay money to sb: *All payments must be made* ***by bank draft***. **3 the draft** [sing] (*especially AmE*) = **conscription** **4** [C] (*AmE*) = **draught**[1] (1)

⚷ **draft**[2] /drɑːft/ *verb* [T] **1** to make a first or early copy of a piece of writing: *I'll draft a letter and show it to you before I send it.* **2** to choose people and send them somewhere for a special task: *Extra police are being drafted in to control the crowds.* **3** [usually passive] (*AmE*) to force sb to join the armed forces: *He was drafted into the army.*

draftsman /ˈdræftsmən/ (*AmE*) = **draughtsman**

drafty (*AmE*) = **draughty**

⚷ **drag**[1] /dræg/ *verb* (**dragging**; **dragged**) **1** [T] to pull sb/sth along with difficulty: *The box was so heavy we had to drag it along the floor.* **2** [T] to make sb come or go somewhere: *She's always trying to drag me along to museums, but I'm not interested.* **3** [I] **drag (on)** to be boring or to seem to last a long time: *The speeches dragged on for hours.* **4** [T] to move sth across the screen of the computer using the mouse: *Click on the file and drag it into the new folder.*

PHR V **drag sth out** to make sth last longer than necessary: *Let's not drag this decision out—shall we go or not?*

drag sth out (of sb) to force or persuade sb to give you information

drag[2] /dræg/ *noun* **1** [sing] (*informal*) a person or thing that is boring or annoying: *'The car's broken down.' 'Oh no! What a drag!'* **2** [C] an act of breathing in cigarette smoke: *He took a long drag on his cigarette.* **3** [U] women's clothes worn by a man, especially as part of a show, etc: *men* ***in drag***

ˌdrag-and-ˈdrop *adj* relating to the moving of **icons** (= small pictures or symbols that represents programs), etc. on a screen using the mouse

dragon /ˈdrægən/ *noun* [C] (in stories) a large animal with wings, which can breathe fire

dragonfly /ˈdrægənflaɪ/ *noun* [C] (*pl* **dragonflies**) an insect with a long thin body and two pairs of wings, often seen near water ➲ picture on page P13

D

drain¹ /dreɪn/ *verb* **1** [I,T] to become empty or dry as liquid flows away and disappears; to make sth dry or empty in this way: *Leave the dishes to drain.* ◆ *The whole area will have to be drained before it can be used for farming.* ◆ *Drain the pasta and add the sauce.* **2** [I,T] **drain (sth) (from/out of sth); drain (sth) (away/off)** to flow away; to make a liquid flow away: *The sink's blocked—the water won't drain away at all.* ◆ *The plumber had to drain the water from the heating system.* ◆ (*figurative*) *He felt all his anger begin to drain away.* **3** [T] to drink all the liquid in a glass, cup, etc: *He drained his glass in one gulp.* **4** [T] **drain sb/sth (of sth)** to make sb/sth weaker, poorer, etc. by slowly using all the strength, money, etc. available: *Her hospital expenses were slowly draining my funds.* ◆ *The experience left her **emotionally drained**.*

drain² /dreɪn/ *noun* [C] a pipe or hole in the ground that dirty water, etc. goes down to be carried away

IDM **(go) down the drain** (*informal*) (to be) wasted: *All that hard work has gone down the drain.*
a drain on sb/sth something that uses up time, money, strength, etc: *The cost of travelling is a great drain on our budget.*

drainage /ˈdreɪnɪdʒ/ *noun* [U] a system used for making water, etc. flow away from a place

ˈ**draining board** (*AmE* ˈdrain board) *noun* [C] the place in the kitchen where you put plates, cups, knives, etc. to dry after washing them

drainpipe /ˈdreɪnpaɪp/ *noun* [C] a pipe which goes down the side of a building and carries water from the roof into a **drain** ➲ picture on **page P8**

drake /dreɪk/ *noun* [C] a male **duck** (= a bird that lives on or near water) ➲ note at **duck** ➲ picture at **duck**

drama /ˈdrɑːmə/ *noun* **1** [C] a play for the theatre, radio or TV: *a contemporary drama* **2** [U] plays as a form of writing; the performance of plays: *He wrote some drama, as well as poetry.* ➲ note at **literature** **3** [C,U] an exciting event; exciting things that happen: *a real-life courtroom drama*

dramatic /drəˈmætɪk/ *adj* **1** noticeable or sudden and often surprising: *a dramatic change/increase/fall/improvement* **2** exciting or impressive: *the film's dramatic opening scene* **3** connected with plays or the theatre: *Shakespeare's dramatic works* **4** (used about a person or their behaviour) showing feelings, etc. in a very obvious way because you want other people to notice you: *Calm down. There's no need to be so dramatic about everything!* ▶ **dramatically** /-kli/ *adv*

dramatist /ˈdræmətɪst/ *noun* [C] a person who writes plays for the theatre, radio or TV SYN **playwright**

dramatize (also -ise) /ˈdræmətaɪz/ *verb* **1** [T] to make a book, an event, etc. into a play: *The novel has been dramatized for TV.* **2** [I,T] to make sth seem more exciting or important than it really is: *The newspaper was accused of dramatizing the facts.* ▶ **dramatization** (also -isation) /ˌdræmətaɪˈzeɪʃn/ *noun* [C,U]

drank *past tense* of **drink²**

drape /dreɪp/ *verb* [T] **1 drape sth round/over sth** to put a piece of cloth, clothing, etc. on sth in a loose way: *He draped his coat over the back of his chair.* **2** [usually passive] **drape sb/sth (in/with sth)** to cover sb/sth (with cloth, etc.): *The furniture was draped in dust sheets.* ▶ **drape** *noun* (*AmE*) = **curtain**(1)

drastic /ˈdræstɪk/ *adj* extreme, and having a sudden very strong effect: *a drastic rise in crime* ▶ **drastically** /-kli/ *adv*

draught¹ /drɑːft/ *noun* **1** (*AmE* draft) [C] a flow of cold air that comes into a room: *Can you shut the door? There's a draught in here.* **2 draughts** (*AmE* **checkers**) [U] a game for two players that you play on a black and white board using round black and white pieces ▶ **draughty** (*AmE* drafty) *adj* (**draughtier; draughtiest**)

draught² /drɑːft/ *adj* (*BrE*) (used about beer, etc.) served from a **barrel** (= a large round container) rather than a bottle: *draught beer*

draughtsman (*AmE* draftsman) /ˈdrɑːftsmən/ *noun* [C] (*pl* **-men** /-mən/) a person whose job is to do technical drawings

draw¹ /drɔː/ *verb* (*pt* **drew** /druː/; *pp* **drawn** /drɔːn/)

➤PICTURE **1** [I,T] to make a picture or diagram of sth with a pencil, pen, etc. but not paint: *I'm good at painting but I can't draw.* ◆ *Shall I draw you a map of how to get there?*

➤PULL **2** [T] to pull sth/sb into a new position or in the direction mentioned: *She drew the letter out of her pocket and handed it to me.* ◆ *to draw* (= open or close) *the curtains* ◆ *He drew me by the hand into the room.*

➤MOVE **3** [I] to move in the direction mentioned: *The train drew into the station* ◆ *I became more anxious as my exams drew nearer.*

➤GET/TAKE **4** [T] **draw sth (from sb/sth)** to get or take sth from sb/sth: *He draws the inspiration for his stories from his family.*

➤ATTRACT **5** [T] **draw sth (from sb); draw sb (to sb/sth)** to make sb react to or be interested in sb/sth: *The advertisement has drawn criticism from people all over the country.* ◆ *The musicians drew quite a large crowd.*

➤LEARN **6** [T] **draw sth (from sth)** to learn or decide sth as a result of study, research or experience: *Can we **draw** any **conclusions** from this survey?* ◆ *There are important **lessons to be drawn** from this tragedy.*

➤GAME **7** [I,T] to finish a game, competition, etc. with equal scores so that neither person or team wins: *The two teams drew.* ◆ *The match was drawn.*

IDM **bring sth/come/draw to an end** ➲ **end¹**
draw (sb's) attention to sth to make sb notice sth: *The article draws attention to the problem of homelessness.*
draw a blank to get no result or find no answer: *Detectives investigating the case have drawn a blank so far.*
draw a distinction between sth and sth to show how two things are different

draw the line at sth/doing sth to say 'no' to sth even though you are happy to help in other ways: *I do most of the cooking but I draw the line at washing up as well!*
draw lots to decide sth by chance: *They drew lots to see who should stay behind.*
PHR V draw in to get dark earlier as winter arrives: *The days/nights are drawing in.*
draw out to become lighter in the evening as summer gets nearer
draw sth out to take money out of a bank account: *How much cash do I need to draw out?*
draw up (used about a car, etc.) to drive up and stop in front of or near sth: *A police car drew up outside the building.*
draw sth up to prepare and write a document, list, etc: *Our solicitor is going to draw up the contract.*

draw² /drɔː/ *noun* [C] **1** an act of deciding sth by chance by pulling out names or numbers from a bag, etc: *a prize draw* **2** a result of a game or competition in which both players or teams get the same score so that neither of them wins: *The match **ended in a draw**.*

drawback /ˈdrɔːbæk/ *noun* [C] a disadvantage or problem: *His lack of experience is a major drawback.* **SYN disadvantage**

drawbridge /ˈdrɔːbrɪdʒ/ *noun* [C] a bridge that can be pulled up, for example to stop people from entering a castle: *to **raise/lower the drawbridge***

drawer /drɔː(r)/ *noun* [C] a container which forms part of a piece of furniture such as a desk, that you can pull out to put things in: *There's some paper in the top drawer of my desk.*

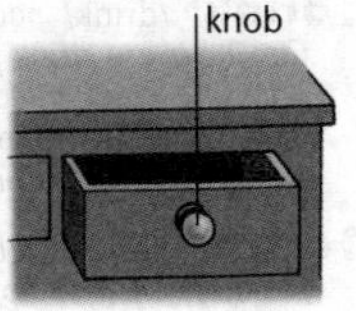

drawer

drawing /ˈdrɔːɪŋ/ *noun* **1** [C] a picture made with a pencil, pen, etc. but not paint: *He **did a drawing** of the building.* ➲ note at **painting** **2** [U] the art of drawing pictures: *She's good at drawing and painting.*

ˈdrawing pin (*AmE* **thumbtack**) *noun* [C] a short pin with a flat top, used for fastening paper, etc. to a board or wall ➲ picture at **pin**, **stationery**

ˈdrawing room *noun* [C] (*old-fashioned*) a living room, especially in a large house

drawl /drɔːl/ *verb* [I,T] to speak slowly, making the vowel sounds very long ▶ **drawl** *noun* [sing]: *to speak with a drawl*

drawn¹ *past participle of* **draw¹**

drawn² /drɔːn/ *adj* (used about a person or their face) looking tired, worried or ill: *He looked pale and drawn after the long journey.*

ˌdrawn-ˈout *adj* lasting longer than necessary: *long drawn-out negotiations*

dread¹ /dred/ *verb* [T] to be very afraid of or worried about sth: *I'm dreading the exams.* ◆ *She dreaded having to tell him what had happened.* ◆ *I **dread to think** what my father will say.* ▶ **dreaded** *adj*

dread² /dred/ *noun* [U,sing] great fear: *He lived **in dread of** the same thing happening to him.*

dreadful /ˈdredfl/ *adj* very bad or unpleasant: *We had a dreadful journey—traffic jams all the way!* ◆ *I'm afraid there's been a dreadful* (= very serious) *mistake.* **SYN terrible** ➲ note at **bad**

dreadfully /ˈdredfəli/ *adv* **1** very; extremely: *I'm dreadfully sorry, I didn't mean to upset you.* **2** very badly: *The party went dreadfully and everyone left early.*

dreadlocks /ˈdredlɒks/ *noun* [pl] hair worn in long thick pieces, especially by some black people

dream¹ /driːm/ *noun* **1** [C] a series of events or pictures which happen in your mind while you are asleep: *I **had** a strange **dream** last night.* ◆ *That horror film has given me **bad dreams**.* ➲ look at **nightmare** **2** [C] something that you want very much to happen, although it is not likely: *His dream was to give up his job and live in the country.* ◆ *My dream house would have a huge garden and a swimming pool.* ◆ *Becoming a professional dancer was **a dream come true** for Nicola.* **3** [sing] a state of mind in which you are not thinking about what you are doing: *You've been in a dream all morning!*

dream² /driːm/ *verb* (*pt, pp* **dreamt** /dremt/ *or* **dreamed**) **1** [I,T] **dream (about sb/sth)** to see or experience pictures and events in your mind while you are asleep: *I dreamt about the house that I lived in as a child.* ◆ *I dreamed that I was running but I couldn't get away.* ➲ look at **daydream** **2** [I] **dream (about/of sth/doing sth)** to imagine sth that you would like to happen: *I've always dreamt about winning lots of money.* **3** [I] **dream (of doing sth/that ...)** to imagine that sth might happen: *I **wouldn't dream of** telling Stuart that I don't like his music.* ◆ *When I watched the Olympics on TV, I **never dreamt** that one day I'd be here competing!*
PHR V dream sth up (*informal*) to think of a plan, an idea, etc., especially sth strange: *Which of you dreamt up that idea?*

dreamer /ˈdriːmə(r)/ *noun* [C] a person who thinks a lot about ideas, plans, etc. which may never happen instead of thinking about real life

dreamt *past tense, past participle of* **dream**

dreamy /ˈdriːmi/ *adj* (**dreamier**; **dreamiest**) looking as though you are not paying attention to what you are doing because you are thinking about sth else: *a dreamy look/expression* ▶ **dreamily** *adv*

dreary /ˈdrɪəri/ *adj* (**drearier**; **dreariest**) not at all interesting or attractive; boring: *His dreary voice sends me to sleep.*

dredge /dredʒ/ *verb* [T] to clear the mud, etc. from the bottom of a river, **canal** (= an artificial river), etc. using a special machine
PHR V dredge sth up to mention sth unpleasant from the past that sb would like to forget: *The newspaper had dredged up all sorts of embarrassing details about her private life.*

D

dregs /dregz/ *noun* [pl] **1** the last drops in a container of liquid, containing small pieces of solid waste **2** the worst and most useless part of sth: *These people were regarded as the dregs of society.*

drench /drentʃ/ *verb* [T, usually passive] to make sb/sth completely wet: *Don't go out while it's raining so hard or you'll **get drenched**.*

D

dress[1] /dres/ *noun* **1** [C] a piece of clothing worn by a girl or a woman. It covers the body from the shoulders to the knees or below: *a wedding dress* **2** [U] clothes for either men or women: *formal/casual dress* ◆ *He was wearing Bulgarian national dress.*

dress[2] /dres/ *verb* **1** [I,T] to put clothes on sb or yourself: *He dressed quickly and left the house.* ◆ *My husband dressed the children while I got breakfast ready.* ◆ *Hurry up! Aren't you dressed yet?* OPP **undress** ➲ note at **routine** ➲ **Get dressed** is more common than **dress**. **2** [I] to put or have clothes on, in the way or style mentioned: *to dress well/badly/casually* ◆ *to be well dressed/badly dressed/casually dressed* **3** [T] to put a clean covering on the place on sb's body where they have been hurt: *to dress a wound*

IDM **(be) dressed in sth** wearing sth: *The people at the funeral were all dressed in black.*

PHR V **dress up** **1** to put on special clothes, especially in order to look like sb/sth else: *The children decided to dress up as pirates.* **2** to put on formal clothes, usually for a special occasion: *You don't need to dress up for the party.*

dresser /ˈdresə(r)/ *noun* [C] **1** (*BrE*) a piece of furniture with cupboards at the bottom and shelves above. It is used for holding dishes, cups, etc. **2** (*AmE*) = **chest of drawers**

dressing /ˈdresɪŋ/ *noun* **1** [C,U] a sauce for food, especially for salads **2** [C] a covering that you put on a part of sb's body that has been hurt to protect it and keep it clean

ˈ**dressing gown** (*AmE* **bathrobe**; **robe**) *noun* [C] a piece of clothing like a loose coat with a belt, which you wear before or after a bath, before you get dressed in the morning, etc.

ˈ**dressing table** *noun* [C] a piece of furniture in a bedroom, which has drawers and a mirror

drew *past tense* of **draw**[1]

dribble /ˈdrɪbl/ *verb* **1** [I] to allow **saliva** (= liquid that is produced in the mouth) to run out of the mouth: *Small children often dribble.* **2** [I,T] (used about a liquid) to move downwards in a thin flow; to make a liquid move in this way: *The paint dribbled slowly down the side of the pot.* **3** [I] (used in ball games) to make a ball move forward by using many short kicks or hits: *Ronaldo dribbled round the goalkeeper and scored.*

dried[1] *past tense, past participle* of **dry**[2]

dried[2] /draɪd/ *adj* (used about food) with all the liquid removed from it: *dried milk/fruit*

drier = **dryer**

drift[1] /drɪft/ *noun* **1** [C] a slow movement towards sth: *the country's drift into economic decline* **2** [C] a pile of snow or sand that was made by wind or water **3** [sing] the general meaning of sth: *I don't understand all the details of the plan but I **get the drift**.*

drift[2] /drɪft/ *verb* [I] **1** to move slowly or without any particular purpose: *He drifted from room to room.* ◆ *Helena drifted into acting almost by accident.* **2** (used about snow or sand) to be moved into piles by wind or water: *The snow drifted up to two metres deep in some places.* **3** to be carried or moved along by wind or water: *The boat drifted out to sea.*

PHR V **drift apart** to slowly become less close or friendly with sb

drill[1] /drɪl/ *noun* **1** [C] a tool or machine that is used for making holes in things: *a dentist's drill* ➲ picture at **tool** **2** [C] something that you repeat many times in order to learn sth **3** [C,U] practice for what you should do in an emergency: *a fire drill* **4** [U] exercise in marching, etc. that soldiers do

drill[2] /drɪl/ *verb* [I,T] **1** to make a hole in sth with a **drill**: *to drill for oil* ◆ *to drill a hole in something* **2** [T] to teach sb by making them repeat sth many times

drily (also **dryly**) /ˈdraɪli/ *adv* (used about the way sb says sth) in an amusing way that sounds serious: *'I can hardly contain my excitement,' Peter said drily* (= he was not excited at all).

drink[1] /drɪŋk/ *noun* [C,U] **1** liquid for drinking: *Can I **have a drink** please?* ◆ *a drink of milk* ◆ *soft drinks* (= cold drinks without alcohol) ◆ *food and drink* ➲ picture on **page P16** **2** (an) alcoholic drink: *Shall we **go for a drink**?*

drink[2] /drɪŋk/ *verb* (*pt* **drank** /dræŋk/; *pp* **drunk** /drʌŋk/) **1** [I,T] to take liquid into your body through your mouth: *Would you like anything to drink?* ◆ *We sat drinking coffee and chatting for hours.* ◆ *Sam stopped drinking and put the cup down.* **2** [I,T] to drink alcohol: *I never **drink and drive** so I'll have an orange juice.* ◆ *What do you drink—beer or wine?* ◆ *Her father used to **drink heavily** but he's teetotal now.*

PHR V **drink to sb/sth** to wish sb/sth good luck by holding your glass up in the air before you drink: *We all drank to the future of the bride and groom.* ➲ look at **toast**

drink (sth) up to finish drinking sth: *Drink up your tea—it's getting cold.*

ˌ**drink-ˈdriver** (*AmE* ˌ**drunk ˈdriver**) *noun* [C] a person who drives after drinking too much alcohol ▶ ˌ**drink-ˈdriving** (*AmE* ˌ**drunk ˈdriving**) *noun* [U]: *He was convicted of drink-driving and was banned for two years.* ➲ note at **driving**

drinker /ˈdrɪŋkə(r)/ *noun* [C] a person who drinks a lot of sth, especially alcohol: *a heavy drinker* ◆ *I'm not a big coffee drinker.*

drinking /ˈdrɪŋkɪŋ/ *noun* [U] drinking alcohol: *Her drinking became a problem.*

ˈ**drinking water** *noun* [U] water that is safe to drink

drip[1] /drɪp/ *verb* (**dripping**; **dripped**) **1** [I] (used about a liquid) to fall in small drops: *Water was dripping down through the roof.* **2** [I,T] to produce drops of liquid: *The tap is dripping.* ♦ *Her finger was dripping blood.*

drip[2] /drɪp/ *noun* **1** [sing] the act or sound of water dripping **2** [C] a drop of water that falls down from sb/sth: *We put a bucket under the hole in the roof to catch the drips.* **3** [C] a piece of medical equipment, like a tube, that is used for putting liquid food or medicine straight into sb's blood: *She's* ***on a drip.***

drive[1] /draɪv/ *verb* (*pt* **drove** /drəʊv/; *pp* **driven** /ˈdrɪvn/)
➤VEHICLE **1** [I,T] to control or operate a car, train, bus, etc: *Can you drive?* ♦ *to drive a car/train/bus/lorry* **2** [I,T] to go or take sb somewhere in a car, etc: *I usually drive to work.* ♦ *We drove Maki to the airport.*
➤MACHINE **3** [T] to make a machine work, by giving it power: *What drives the wheels in this engine?*
➤MAKE SB DO STH **4** [T] to cause sb to be in a particular state or to do sth: *His constant stupid questions* ***drive me mad.*** ♦ *to drive somebody to despair* **5** [T] to make sb/sth work very hard: *You shouldn't drive yourself so hard.*
➤MAKE SB/STH MOVE **6** [T] to force people or animals to move in a particular direction: *The dogs drove the sheep into the field.*
➤HIT STH **7** [T] to force sth into a particular position by hitting it: *to drive a post into the ground*
IDM **be driving at** (*informal*) to want to say sth; to mean: *I'm afraid I don't understand what you're driving at.*
drive sth home (to sb) to make sth clear so that people understand it
PHR V **drive off** (used about a car, driver, etc.) to leave
drive sb/sth off to make sb/sth go away: *They kept a large dog outside to drive off burglars.*

drive[2] /draɪv/ *noun*
➤IN VEHICLE **1** [C] a journey in a car: *The supermarket is only a five-minute drive away.* ♦ *Let's* ***go for a drive.*** **2** [U] the equipment in a vehicle that takes power from the engine to the wheels: *a car with four-wheel drive*
➤OUTSIDE HOUSE **3** (also **driveway**) [C] a wide path or short road that leads to the door of a house: *We keep our car on the drive.*
➤EFFORT **4** [C] a big effort by a group of people in order to achieve sth: *The company is launching a big sales drive.*
➤ENERGY **5** [U] the energy and determination you need to succeed in doing sth: *You need lots of drive to run your own company.*
➤DESIRE **6** [C,U] a strong natural need or desire: *a strong sex drive*
➤IN SPORT **7** [C] a long hard hit: *This player has the longest drive in golf.*
➤COMPUTING **8** [C] the part of a computer that reads and stores information: *a 200 GB hard drive* ♦ *a CD drive* ➲ look at **disk drive** ➲ picture at **computer**
➤ROAD **9** [C] a street, usually where people live: *They live at 23 Woodlands Drive.*

ˈdrive-by *adj* [only *before* a noun] (*AmE*) (used about a shooting) done from a moving car: *drive-by killings*

ˈdrive-in *noun* [C] a place where you can eat, watch a film, etc. in your car

driven *past participle* of **drive**[1]

driver /ˈdraɪvə(r)/ *noun* [C] a person who drives a vehicle: *a bus/train driver*

ˈdrive-through *noun* [C] (*especially AmE*) a restaurant, bank, etc. where you can be served without getting out of your car

D

driving[1] /ˈdraɪvɪŋ/ *noun* [U] the action or skill of controlling a car, etc: *She was arrested for dangerous driving.* ♦ *Joe's having* ***driving lessons.*** ♦ *She works as a* ***driving instructor.*** ♦ *a* ***driving school*** ➲ note at **car, road**
IDM **be in the driving seat** to be the person, group, etc. that has the most powerful position in a particular situation

TOPIC

Driving

You cannot **drive** unless you have passed your **driving test** and have a **driving licence. Motorists** should not **break the speed limit** (= drive too fast) or **drink and drive** (= drive a car after drinking alcohol). You can offer to take a person somewhere in your car by asking: *'Can I* ***give you a lift****?'* The **driver** and **passengers** (= people travelling in a **vehicle**) should wear **seatbelts**, in case there is an **accident**/a **crash**. If the road is **congested**, for example during **rush hour**, you will probably find yourself stuck in a **traffic jam**.

driving[2] /ˈdraɪvɪŋ/ *adj* [only *before* a noun] very strong: *driving rain* ♦ *driving ambition* ♦ *Who's the driving force behind this plan?*

ˈdriving licence (*AmE* **ˈdriver's license**) *noun* [C] an official document that shows that you are allowed to drive

drizzle /ˈdrɪzl/ *noun* [U] light rain with very small drops ▶ **drizzle** *verb* [I] ➲ note at **weather**

drone /drəʊn/ *verb* [I] to make a continuous low sound: *the sound of the tractors droning away in the fields*
PHR V **drone on** to talk in a flat or boring voice: *We had to listen to the chairman drone on about sales for hours.*
▶ **drone** *noun* [sing]

drool /druːl/ *verb* [I] **1** to let **saliva** (= liquid) come out from the mouth, usually at the sight or smell of sth good to eat **2 drool (over sb/sth)** to show in a silly or exaggerated way that you want sth or admire sb/sth very much: *teenagers drooling over photographs of their favourite pop stars*

droop /druːp/ *verb* [I] to bend or hang downwards, especially because of weakness or because you are tired: *The flowers were drooping without water.* ▶ **drooping** *adj*: *a drooping moustache*

drop[1] /drɒp/ *verb* (**dropping**; **dropped**) **1** [T] to let sth fall: *That vase was very expensive. Whatever you do, don't drop it!* **2** [I] to fall: *The parachutist* dropped safely to the ground. ◆ At the end of the race she dropped to her knees exhausted. **3** [I,T] to become lower; to make sth lower: *The temperature will drop to minus 3 overnight.* ◆ *They ought to drop their prices.* ◆ *to drop your voice* (= speak more quietly) **4** [T] **drop sb/sth (off)** to stop your car, etc. so that sb can get out, or in order to take sth out: *Drop me off at the traffic lights, please.* ◆ *I'll drop the parcel at your house.* **5** [T] **drop sb/sth (from sth)** to no longer include sb/sth in sth: *Joe has been dropped from the team.* **6** [T] to stop doing sth: *I'm going to drop geography next term* (= stop studying it).

drop

IDM **drop dead** (*informal*) to die suddenly
drop sb a line (*informal*) to write a letter or an email to sb: *Do drop me a line when you've time.*

PHR V **drop back; drop behind (sb)** to move into a position behind sb else, because you are moving more slowly: *Towards the end of the race she dropped behind the other runners.*
drop by; drop in (on sb) to go to sb's house on an informal visit or without having told them you were coming: *We were in the area so we thought we'd drop in and see you.*
drop off (*informal*) to fall into a light sleep: *I dropped off in front of the TV.*
drop out (of sth) to leave or stop doing sth before you have finished: *His injury forced him to drop out of the competition.*

drop² /drɒp/ *noun* **1** [C] a very small amount of liquid that forms a round shape: *a drop of blood/rain* **2** [C, usually sing] a small amount of liquid: *I just have a drop of milk in my coffee.* **3** [sing] a fall to a smaller amount or level: *The job is much more interesting but it will mean a drop in salary.* ◆ *a drop in prices/temperature* **4** [sing] a distance down from a high point to a lower point: *a sheer drop of 40 metres to the sea* **5 drops** [pl] liquid medicine that you put into your eyes, ears or nose: *The doctor prescribed me drops to take twice a day.*

IDM **at the drop of a hat** immediately; without having to stop and think about it
a drop in the ocean; (*AmE* **a drop in the bucket**) an amount of sth that is too small or unimportant to make any real difference to a situation: *The money we made was a drop in the ocean compared to the amount we need.*

ˈdrop-dead *adv* (*informal*) used before an adjective to emphasize how attractive sb/sth is: *She's drop-dead gorgeous.*

ˌdrop-down ˈmenu *noun* [C] a list which appears on your computer screen and that stays there until you choose one of the functions on it

dropout /ˈdrɒpaʊt/ *noun* [C] **1** a person who leaves school, university, etc. before finishing their studies: *a university with a high dropout rate* **2** a person who does not accept the ideas and ways of behaving of the rest of society

droppings /ˈdrɒpɪŋz/ *noun* [pl] waste material from the bodies of small animals or birds

drought /draʊt/ *noun* [C,U] a long period without rain: *two years of severe drought*

drove *past tense of* **drive¹**

drown /draʊn/ *verb* **1** [I,T] to die in water because it is not possible to breathe; to make sb die in this way: *The girl fell into the river and drowned.* ◆ *Twenty people were drowned in the floods.* **2** to make sth very wet; to completely cover sth in water or another liquid: *The fruit was drowning in cream.* **3** [T] **drown sb/sth (out)** (used about a sound) to be so loud that you cannot hear sb/sth else: *His answer was drowned out by the music.*

drowsy /ˈdraʊzi/ *adj* (**drowsier**; **drowsiest**) tired and almost asleep: *The heat made me feel drowsy.* ▶ **drowsily** *adv* ▶ **drowsiness** *noun* [U]

drudgery /ˈdrʌdʒəri/ *noun* [U] hard and boring work

drug¹ /drʌg/ *noun* [C] **1** a chemical which people use to give them pleasant or exciting feelings. It is illegal in many countries to use drugs: *He doesn't drink or* ***take drugs.*** ◆ *She suspected her son was* ***on drugs.*** ◆ ***hard drugs*** *such as heroin and cocaine* ◆ ***soft drugs*** **2** a chemical which is used as a medicine: *drug companies* ◆ *Some drugs can only be obtained with a prescription from a doctor.*

drug² /drʌg/ *verb* [T] (**drugging**; **drugged**) **1** to give a person or an animal a chemical to make them or it go to asleep or become unconscious: *The lion was drugged before the start of the journey.* **2** to put a drug into food or drink: *I think his drink was drugged.*

ˈdrug addict *noun* [C] a person who cannot stop taking drugs ▶ **ˈdrug addiction** *noun* [U]

druggist /ˈdrʌgɪst/ (*AmE*) = **chemist**(1)

drugstore /ˈdrʌgstɔː(r)/ (*AmE*) = **chemist**(2)

drum¹ /drʌm/ *noun* [C] **1** a musical instrument like an empty container with plastic or skin stretched across the ends. You play a drum by hitting it with your hands or with sticks: *She plays the drums in a band.* ➲ note at **music** ➲ picture at **music** **2** a round container: *an oil drum*

drum² /drʌm/ *verb* (**drumming**; **drummed**) **1** [I] to play a drum or drums **2** [I,T] to make a noise like a drum by hitting sth many times: *to drum your fingers on the table* (= because you are annoyed, impatient, etc.)

PHR V **drum sth into sb** to make sb remember sth by repeating it many times: *The importance of road safety should be drummed into children from an early age.*
drum sth up to try to get support or business: *to drum up more custom*

drummer /ˈdrʌmə(r)/ *noun* [C] a person who plays a drum or drums

drumstick /ˈdrʌmstɪk/ *noun* [C] **1** a stick used for playing the drums **2** the lower part of the leg of a chicken or similar bird that we cook and eat

drunk¹ /drʌŋk/ *adj* [not before a noun] having drunk too much alcohol: *to get drunk* OPP **sober**
▸ **drunk** (also *old-fashioned* **drunkard** /ˈdrʌŋkəd/) *noun* [C]: *There was a drunk asleep on the bench.*

drunk² *past participle of* **drink²**

ˌdrunk ˈdriver = **drink-driver**

drunken /ˈdrʌŋkən/ *adj* [only *before* a noun] **1** having drunk too much alcohol: *drunken drivers* **2** showing the effects of too much alcohol: *drunken singing* ▸ **drunkenly** *adv* ▸ **drunkenness** *noun* [U]

dry¹ /draɪ/ *adj* (**drier**; **driest**)
➤NOT WET **1** without liquid in it or on it: *The washing isn't dry yet.* ♦ *The paint is dry now.* ♦ *Rub your hair dry with a towel.* OPP **wet**
➤WITHOUT RAIN **2** having little or no rain: *a hot, dry summer* ♦ *a dry climate* OPP **wet**
➤HAIR/SKIN **3** not having enough natural oil: *a shampoo for dry hair*
➤WINE **4** not sweet: *a crisp dry white wine*
➤HUMOUR **5** (used about what sb says, or sb's way of speaking) amusing, although it sounds serious: *a dry sense of humour*
➤BORING **6** not interesting: *dry legal documents*
➤WITHOUT ALCOHOL **7** where no alcohol is allowed: *a dry country/state*
IDM **be left high and dry** ➲ **leave¹**
▸ **dryness** *noun* [U]

dry² /draɪ/ *verb* [I,T] (**drying**; **dries**; *pt, pp* **dried**) to become dry; to make sth dry: *I hung my shirt in the sun to dry.* ♦ *to dry your hands on a towel*
PHR V **dry (sth) out** to become or make sth become completely dry: *Don't allow the soil to dry out.*
dry up 1 (used about a river, etc.) to have no more water in it **2** to stop being available: *Because of the recession, offers of work have begun to dry up.* **3** to forget what you were going to say, for example because you are very nervous: *When he came on stage and saw the audience, he dried up completely.*
dry (sth) up (*BrE*) to dry plates, knives, forks, etc. with a small piece of cloth after they have been washed

ˌdry-ˈclean *verb* [T] to clean clothes using special chemicals, without using water

ˌdry-ˈcleaner's (also **cleaner's**) *noun* [C] the shop where you take your clothes to be cleaned

dryer (also **drier**) /ˈdraɪə(r)/ *noun* [C] [often in compounds] a machine that you use for drying sth: *a hairdryer*

ˌdry ˈland *noun* [U] land, not the sea: *I was glad to be back* **on dry land** *again.*

dryly = **drily**

DTP /ˌdiː tiː ˈpiː/ *abbr* = **desktop publishing**

dual /ˈdjuːəl/ *adj* [only *before* a noun] having two parts: *to have dual nationality*

ˌdual ˈcarriageway (*AmE* **diˌvided ˈhighway**) *noun* [C] a wide road that has an area of grass or a fence in the middle to separate the traffic going in one direction from the traffic going in the other direction

dub /dʌb/ *verb* [T] (**dubbing**; **dubbed**) **1** to give sb/sth a new or amusing name: *Margaret Thatcher was dubbed 'the Iron Lady'.* **2 dub sth (into sth)** to change the sound in a film so that what the actors said originally is spoken by actors using a different language: *I don't like foreign films when they're dubbed into English. I prefer subtitles.* ➲ look at **subtitle** **3** to make a piece of music by mixing different pieces of recorded music together

dubious /ˈdjuːbiəs/ *adj* **1 dubious (about sth/about doing sth)** not sure or certain: *I'm very dubious about whether we're doing the right thing.* **2** that may not be honest or safe: *dubious financial dealings*
▸ **dubiously** *adv*

duchess /ˈdʌtʃəs/ *noun* [C] a woman who has the same position as a **duke** (= a man of high social position), or who is the wife of a **duke**

ducks

duck¹ /dʌk/ *noun* (*pl* **ducks** *or* **duck**) **1** [C] a common bird that lives on or near water. **Ducks** have short legs, **webbed feet** (= with pieces of skin between the toes) for swimming and a wide beak. **2** [C] a female **duck**

MORE **Duck** is often used for both males and females. A male duck is called a **drake** and a young duck is a **duckling**. The sound a duck makes is a **quack**.

3 [U] the meat of a **duck**: *roast duck with orange sauce*

duck² /dʌk/ *verb* **1** [I, T] to move your head down quickly so that you are not seen or hit by sb/sth: *The boys ducked out of sight behind a high hedge.* ♦ *I had to duck my head down to avoid the low doorway.* **2** [I,T] (*informal*) **duck (out of) sth** to try to avoid sth difficult or unpleasant: *She tried to duck out of apologizing.* ♦ *The President is trying to duck responsibility for the crisis.* **3** [T] to push sb's head underwater for

duck

He ducked.

D

a short time, especially when playing: *The kids were ducking each other in the pool.*

duckling /ˈdʌklɪŋ/ *noun* [C,U] a young **duck**; the meat of a young **duck** ➲ note at **duck** ➲ picture at **duck**

duct /dʌkt/ *noun* [C] a tube that carries liquid, gas, etc: *They got into the building through the air duct.* ◆ *tear ducts* (= in the eye)

dud /dʌd/ *noun* [C] (*informal*) a thing that cannot be used because it is not real or does not work properly: *a dud note/coin/firework*

dude /duːd/ *noun* [C] (*especially AmE slang*) a man

due¹ /djuː/ *adj* [not before a noun]

➤CAUSED BY **1 due to sb/sth** caused by or because of sb/sth: *His illness is probably due to stress.*

➤EXPECTED **2** expected or planned to happen or arrive: *The conference is due to start in four weeks' time.* ◆ *What time is the next train due (in)?* ◆ *The baby is due in May.*

➤OWED **3** having to be paid: *The rent is due on the fifteenth of each month.* **4 due (to sb)** that is owed to you because it is your right to have it: *Make sure you claim all the benefits that are due to you.* **5 due for sth** expecting sth or having the right to sth: *I think that I'm due for a pay rise.*

IDM **in due course** at some time in the future, quite soon: *All applicants will be informed of our decision in due course.*

due² /djuː/ *adv* [used before *north, south, east* and *west*] exactly: *The plane was flying due east.*

due³ /djuː/ *noun*

IDM **give sb his/her due** to be fair to a person: *She doesn't work very quickly, but to give Sarah her due, she is very accurate.*

duel /ˈdjuːəl/ *noun* [C] a formal type of fight with guns or other weapons which was used in the past to decide an argument between two men

duet /djuˈet/ (also **duo**) *noun* [C] a piece of music for two people to sing or play ➲ look at **solo**

duffel coat (also **duffle coat**) /ˈdʌfl kəʊt/ *noun* [C] a coat made of thick wool cloth with a **hood** (= a part that covers your head). A duffel coat has **toggles** (= special long buttons).

dug *past tense, past participle of* **dig¹**

duke (also **Duke**) /djuːk/ *noun* [C] a man of the highest social position ➲ look at **duchess**

dull /dʌl/ *adj* (**duller**; **dullest**) **1** not interesting or exciting; boring: *Miss Potter's lessons are always so dull.* **2** not bright: *a dull and cloudy day* **3** not loud, sharp or strong: *Her head hit the floor with a dull thud.* ◆ *a dull pain* OPP **sharp** ▶ **dullness** *noun* [U] ▶ **dully** *adv*

duly /ˈdjuːli/ *adv* (*formal*) in the correct or expected way: *We all duly assembled at 7.30 as agreed.*

dumb /dʌm/ *adj* (**dumber**; **dumbest**) **1** not able to speak: *to be deaf and dumb* ◆ (*figurative*) *They were* ***struck dumb*** *with amazement.* **2** (*informal*) stupid: *What a dumb thing to do!*

PHR V **dumb (sth) down** to make sth less accurate and of worse quality, by trying to make it easier for people to understand: *The BBC denies that its broadcasting has been dumbed down.*

▶ **dumbly** *adv*: *Ken did all the talking, and I just nodded dumbly.*

dumbfounded /dʌmˈfaʊndɪd/ *adj* very surprised

dummy /ˈdʌmi/ *noun* [C] (*pl* **dummies**) **1** a model of a person, used especially when making clothes or for showing them in a shop window: *a tailor's dummy* **2** something that is made to look like sth else but that is not the real thing: *The robbers used dummy handguns in the raid.* **3** (*informal*) a stupid person: *Don't just stand there like a dummy—help me!* **4** (*AmE* **pacifier**) a rubber object that you put in a baby's mouth to keep them quiet and happy

dummy

dump¹ /dʌmp/ *verb* [T] **1** to get rid of sth that you do not want, especially in a place which is not suitable: *Nuclear waste should not be dumped in the sea.* ◆ (*figurative*) *I wish you wouldn't keep dumping all the extra work on me.* **2** to put sth down quickly or in a careless way: *The children dumped their coats and bags in the hall and ran off to play.* **3** (*informal*) to end a relationship with sb: *Did you hear that Laura dumped Chris last night?*

dump² /dʌmp/ *noun* [C] **1** a place where rubbish or waste material from factories, etc. is left: *a rubbish dump* **2** (*informal*) a place that is very dirty, untidy or unpleasant: *The flat is cheap but it's a real dump.* SYN for both meanings **tip**

IDM **down in the dumps** ➲ **down¹**

dumpling /ˈdʌmplɪŋ/ *noun* [C] a small ball of **dough** (= a mixture of flour and water) that is cooked and usually eaten with meat

dune /djuːn/ (also ˈ**sand dune**) *noun* [C] a hill of sand by the sea or in the desert ➲ picture on **page P10**

dung /dʌŋ/ *noun* [U] waste material from the bodies of large animals: *cow dung*

dungarees /ˌdʌŋɡəˈriːz/ (*AmE* **overalls**) *noun* [pl] a piece of clothing, similar to trousers, but covering your chest as well as your legs and with narrow pieces of cloth that go over the shoulders: *a pair of dungarees* ➲ picture at **overall**

dungeon /ˈdʌndʒən/ *noun* [C] an old underground room used as a prison, especially in a castle

duo /ˈdjuːəʊ/ *noun* [C] (*pl* **duos**) **1** two people playing music or singing together **2** = **duet**

dupe /djuːp/ *verb* [T] to lie to sb in order to make them believe sth or do sth: *He was duped into giving them his credit card.*

duplicate¹ /ˈdjuːplɪkeɪt/ *verb* [T] **1** to make an exact copy of sth **2** to do sth that has already been done: *We don't want to duplicate the work of other departments.* ▶ **duplication** /ˌdjuːplɪˈkeɪʃn/ *noun* [U]

duplicate² /ˈdjuːplɪkət/ *noun* [C] something that is exactly the same as sth else

IDM **in duplicate** with two copies (for example of an official piece of paper) that are exactly the same: *The contract must be in duplicate.*

▶ **duplicate** *adj* [only before a noun]: *a duplicate key*

durable /ˈdjʊərəbl/ *adj* that can last a long time: *a durable fabric* ▶ **durability** /ˌdjʊərəˈbɪləti/ *noun* [U]

duration /djuˈreɪʃn/ *noun* [U] (*formal*) the time that sth lasts: *Please remain seated for the duration of the flight.*

duress /djuˈres/ *noun* [U] (*formal*) threats or force that are used to make sb do sth: *He signed the confession* ***under duress****.*

⚷ **during** /ˈdjʊərɪŋ/ *prep* within the period of time mentioned: *During the summer holidays we went swimming every day.* ♦ *Grandpa was taken ill during the night.*

HELP **During** or **for**? Notice that you use **during** to refer to the period of time in which something happens and **for** to say how long something lasts: *I went shopping during my lunch break. I was out for about 25 minutes.*

dusk /dʌsk/ *noun* [U] the time in the evening when the sun has already gone down and it is nearly dark ➲ look at **dawn, twilight**

⚷ **dust¹** /dʌst/ *noun* [U] very small pieces of dry dirt, sand, etc. in the form of a powder: *a thick layer of dust* ♦ *chalk/coal dust* ♦ *The tractor came up the track in a cloud of dust.* ♦ *a speck* (= a small piece) *of dust* ▶ **dusty** *adj* (**dustier; dustiest**): *This shelf has got very dusty.*

⚷ **dust²** /dʌst/ *verb* [I,T] to clean a room, furniture, etc. by removing dust with a cloth: *Let me dust those shelves before you put the books on them.* ➲ note at **clean²**

dustbin /ˈdʌstbɪn/ (*AmE* ˈ**garbage can**; ˈ**trash can**) *noun* [C] a large container for rubbish that you keep outside your house ➲ picture at **bin**

duster /ˈdʌstə(r)/ *noun* [C] a soft dry cloth that you use for cleaning furniture, etc. ➲ picture at **bucket**

dustman /ˈdʌstmən/ *noun* [C] (*pl* **-men** /-mən/) a person whose job is to take away the rubbish that people put in **dustbins**

dustpan /ˈdʌstpæn/ *noun* [C] a flat container with a handle into which you brush dirt from the floor: *Where do you keep your* ***dustpan and brush****?* ➲ picture at **brush**

Dutch /dʌtʃ/ *adj* from the Netherlands ❶ For more information, look at the section on geographical names at the back of this dictionary.

dutiful /ˈdjuːtɪfl/ *adj* happy to respect and obey sb: *a dutiful son* ▶ **dutifully** /-fəli/ *adv*

⚷ **duty** /ˈdjuːti/ *noun* (*pl* **duties**) **1** [C,U] something that you have to do because people expect you to do it or because you think it is right: *A soldier must* ***do his duty****.* ♦ *a sense of moral duty* **2** [C,U] the tasks that you do when you are at work: *the duties of a policeman* ♦ *Which nurses are on night duty this week?* **3** [C,U] a tax that you pay, especially on goods that you bring into a country: *import duty*

IDM **on/off duty** (used about doctors, nurses, police officers, etc.) to be working/not working: *The porter's on duty from 8 till 4.* ♦ *What time does she go off duty?*

ˌ**duty-ˈfree** *adj* (used about goods) that you can bring into a country without paying tax: *an airport duty-free shop*

▶ ˌ**duty-ˈfree** *adv*: *I bought this wine duty-free.* ➲ look at **tax-free**

duvet /ˈduːveɪ/ *noun* [C] a thick cover filled with feathers or another soft material that you sleep under to keep warm in bed ➲ look at **eiderdown, quilt** ➲ picture at **bed**

DVD /ˌdiː viː ˈdiː/ *noun* [C] **digital videodisc** or **digital versatile disc**; a disk on which large amounts of information, especially photographs and video, can be stored, for use in a computer or **DVD player**: *Is it available* ***on DVD*** *yet?* ♦ *a DVD-ROM drive* ➲ picture at **computer**

ˌ**DVˈD burner** (also ˌ**DVˈD writer**) *noun* [C] a piece of equipment used for copying sound or information from a computer onto a **DVD**

ˌ**DVˈD player** *noun* [C] a piece of equipment that you use for playing **DVDs**

DVT /ˌdiː viː ˈtiː/ *abbr* = **deep vein thrombosis**

dwarf¹ /dwɔːf/ *noun* [C] (*pl* **dwarfs** or **dwarves** /dwɔːvz/) **1** (in children's stories) a very small person with magic powers **2** a person, animal or plant that is much smaller than the usual size

dwarf² /dwɔːf/ *verb* [T] (used about a large object) to make sth seem very small in comparison: *The skyscraper dwarfs all the other buildings around.*

dwell /dwel/ *verb* [I] (*pt, pp* **dwelt** /dwelt/ *or* **dwelled**) (*old-fashioned, formal*) to live or stay in a place

PHR V **dwell on/upon sth** to think or talk a lot about sth that it would be better to forget: *I don't want to dwell on the past. Let's think about the future.*

dweller /ˈdwelə(r)/ *noun* [C] [in compounds] a person or an animal that lives in the place mentioned: *city dwellers*

dwelling /ˈdwelɪŋ/ *noun* [C] (*formal*) the place where a person lives; a house or flat

dwelt *past tense, past participle of* **dwell**

dwindle /ˈdwɪndl/ *verb* [I] **dwindle (away)** to become smaller or weaker: *Their savings dwindled away to nothing.*

dye¹ /daɪ/ *verb* [T] (**dyeing; dyes;** *pt, pp* **dyed**) to make sth a different colour: *Does she dye her hair?* ♦ *I'm going to dye this blouse black.*

dye² /daɪ/ *noun* [C,U] a substance that is used to change the colour of sth

dyke (also **dike**) /daɪk/ *noun* [C] **1** a long thick wall that is built to prevent the sea or a river from covering low land with water **2** (*BrE*) a long narrow space dug in the ground and used for taking water away from land

dynamic /daɪˈnæmɪk/ *adj* **1** (used about a person) full of energy and ideas; active **2** (used about a force or power) that causes movement ▶ **dynamism** /ˈdaɪnəmɪzəm/ *noun* [U]

dynamics /daɪˈnæmɪks/ *noun* **1** [pl] the way in which people or things behave and react to each other in a particular situation **2** [U] the scientific study of the forces involved in movement: *fluid dynamics*

dynamite /ˈdaɪnəmaɪt/ *noun* [U] **1** a powerful substance which can explode **2** a thing or person that causes great excitement, shock, etc: *His news was dynamite.*

dynamo /ˈdaɪnəməʊ/ *noun* [C] (*pl* **dynamos**) a device that changes energy from the movement of sth such as wind or water into electricity

dynasty /ˈdɪnəsti/ *noun* [C] (*pl* **dynasties**) a series of rulers who are from the same family: *the Ming dynasty in China*

dysentery /ˈdɪsəntri/ *noun* [U] a serious disease which causes you to have **diarrhoea** (= the need to get rid of waste material from your body very often) and to lose blood

dyslexia /dɪsˈleksiə/ *noun* [U] a difficulty that some people have with reading and spelling ▶ **dyslexic** *noun* [C], *adj*

E, e /iː/ *noun* [C,U] (*pl* **Es**; **E's**; **e's** /iːz/) **1** the fifth letter of the English alphabet: *'Egg' begins with (an) 'E'.* **2** E (used about music) the third note in the scale of C major: *E major/minor* ◆ *E flat*

E *abbr* = **east**[1], **eastern**(1): *E Asia*

e- /iː/ [in compounds] connected with the use of electronic communication, especially the Internet, for sending information, doing business, etc: *e-commerce* ◆ *e-business* ◆ *an e-ticket*

each other

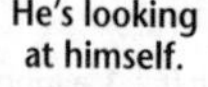

He's looking at himself.

They're looking at each other.

each /iːtʃ/ *determiner, pron* every individual person or thing: *Each lesson lasts an hour.* ◆ *Each of the lessons lasts an hour.* ◆ *The lessons each last an hour.* ◆ *These T-shirts are £5 each.*

each ˈother *pron* used for saying that A does the same thing to B as B does to A: *Emma and Dave love each other very much* (= Emma loves Dave and Dave loves Emma). ◆ *We looked at each other.*

eager /ˈiːgə(r)/ *adj* **eager (to do sth); eager (for sth)** full of desire or interest: *We're all eager to start work on the new project.* ◆ *eager for success* SYN **keen** ▶ **eagerly** *adv* ▶ **eagerness** *noun* [U]

eagle /ˈiːgl/ *noun* [C] a very large bird that can see very well. It eats small birds and animals.

eagle

ear /ɪə(r)/ *noun* **1** [C] one of the two parts of the body of a person or an animal that are used for hearing: *He pulled his hat down over his ears.* ➲ picture at **body** ➲ picture on **page P12** **2** [sing] **an ear (for sth)** an ability to recognize and repeat sounds, especially in music or language: *Kimiko has a good ear for languages.* **3** [C] the top part of a plant that produces grain: *an ear of corn*

IDM **sb's ears are burning** used when a person thinks that other people are talking about them, especially in an unkind way

go in one ear and out the other (*informal*) (used about information, etc.) to be forgotten quickly: *Everything I tell him seems to go in one ear and out the other.*

play (sth) by ear to play a piece of music that you have heard without using written notes: *She can read music, but she can also play by ear.*

play it by ear (*informal*) to decide what to do as things happen, instead of planning in advance: *We don't know what Alan's reaction will be, so we'll just have to play it by ear.*

prick up your ears ➲ **prick**[1]

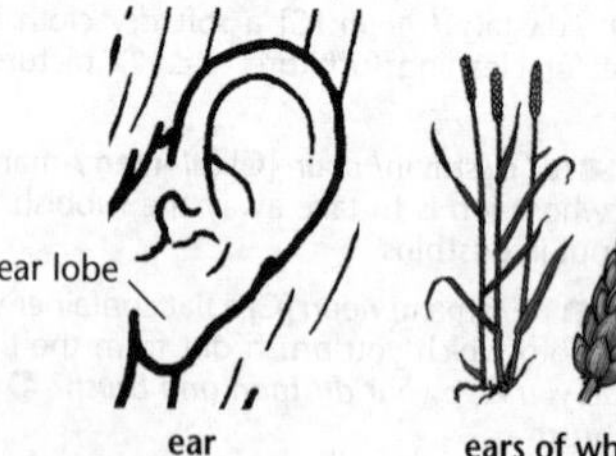

ear　　ears of wheat

earache /ˈɪəreɪk/ *noun* [C,U] a pain in your ear: *I've got earache.* ➲ note at **ache**

eardrum /ˈɪədrʌm/ *noun* [C] a thin piece of skin inside the ear that is tightly stretched and that allows you to hear sound

earl /ɜːl/ *noun* [C] a British man of a high social position

ˈear lobe *noun* [C] the round soft part at the bottom of your ear

early /ˈɜːli/ *adj, adv* (**earlier; earliest**) **1** near the beginning of a period of time, a piece of work, a series, etc: *I have to get up early on weekday mornings.* ◆ *I think John's in his early twenties.* ◆ *The project is still only in its early stages.* **2** before the usual or expected time: *She arrived five minutes early for her interview.* OPP for both meanings **late**
IDM **at the earliest** not before the date or time mentioned: *I can repair it by Friday at the earliest.*
the early hours very early in the morning, in the hours after midnight
an early/a late night ➲ **night**
early on soon after the beginning: *He achieved fame early on in his career.*
an early riser a person who usually gets up early in the morning
it's early days (yet) (*BrE*) used to say that it is too soon to know how a situation will develop

earmark /ˈɪəmɑːk/ *verb* [T] **earmark sb/sth (for sth/sb)** to choose sb/sth to do sth in the future: *The shop has been earmarked for closure.*

earn /ɜːn/ *verb* **1** [I,T] to get money by working: *How much does a dentist earn?* ◆ *I earn £20000 a year.* ◆ *It's hard to* ***earn a living*** *as an artist.* **2** [T] to get money as profit or interest on money you lend, have in a bank, etc: *Your money would earn more in a high-interest account.* **3** [T] to win the right to sth, for example by working hard: *The team's victory today has earned them a place in the final.*

earnest /ˈɜːnɪst/ *adj* serious or determined: *He's such an earnest young man—he never makes a joke.* ◆ *They were having a very earnest discussion.*
IDM **in earnest 1** happening more seriously or with more force than before: *After two weeks work began in earnest on the project.* **2** serious and sincere about what you are going to do: *He was in earnest about wanting to leave university.*
▶ **earnestly** *adv*

earnings /ˈɜːnɪŋz/ *noun* [pl] the money that a person earns by working: *Average earnings have increased by 5%.*

earphones /ˈɪəfəʊnz/ = **headphones**

earring /ˈɪərɪŋ/ *noun* [C] a piece of jewellery that is worn in or on the lower part of the ear: *Are these clip-on earrings or are they for pierced ears?* ➲ picture at **jewellery**

earshot /ˈɪəʃɒt/ *noun*
IDM **(be) out of/within earshot** (be) where a person cannot/can hear: *Wait until he's out of earshot before you say anything about him.*

earth[1] /ɜːθ/ *noun* **1 the earth; the Earth** [sing] the world; the planet on which we live: *life on earth* ◆ *The earth goes round the sun.* ➲ note at **space** ➲ picture at **eclipse** **2** [U,sing] the surface of the world; land: *The spaceship fell towards earth.* ◆ *I could feel the earth shake when the earthquake started.* **3** [U] the substance that plants grow in; soil: *The earth around here is very fertile.* ➲ note at **ground** **4** [C, usually sing] (*AmE* **ground**) a wire that makes a piece of electrical equipment safer by connecting it to the ground: *The green and yellow wire is the earth.*
IDM **charge/pay the earth** (*BrE informal*) to charge/pay a very large amount of money: *Dan must have paid the earth for that new car.*
cost the earth/a fortune ➲ **cost**[2]
how/why/where/who etc. on earth (*informal*) used for emphasizing sth or expressing surprise: *Where on earth have you been?*

the earth

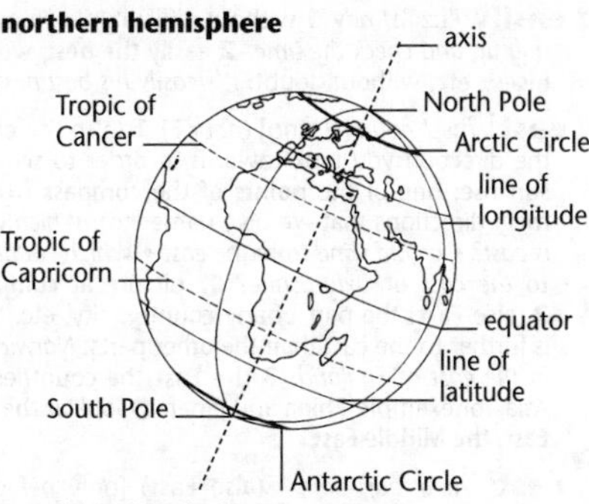

earth[2] /ɜːθ/ (*AmE* **ground**) *verb* [T] to make a piece of electrical equipment safer by connecting it to the ground with a wire: *Make sure the plug is earthed.*

earthenware /ˈɜːθnweə(r)/ *adj* made of very hard baked **clay** (= a type of earth): *an earthenware bowl* ▶ **earthenware** *noun* [U]

earthly /ˈɜːθli/ *adj* (often in questions or negatives) possible: *What earthly use is a gardening book to me? I haven't got a garden!* ◆ *There's* ***no earthly reason*** *why you shouldn't go.*

earthquake /ˈɜːθkweɪk/ (also *informal* **quake**) *noun* [C] sudden, violent movement of the earth's surface

earthworm /ˈɜːθwɜːm/ *noun* [C] a small, long, thin animal with no legs or eyes that lives in the soil

ease[1] /iːz/ *noun* [U] a lack of difficulty: *She answered the questions* ***with ease***. ➲ *adjective* **easy**
IDM **(be/feel) at (your) ease** to be/feel comfortable, relaxed, etc: *They were all so kind and friendly that I felt completely at ease.*

ease[2] /iːz/ *verb* **1** [T] to move sth slowly and gently: *He eased the key into the lock.* **2** [I,T] to become or make sth less painful or serious: *The pain should ease by this evening.* ◆ *This money will ease their financial problems a little.* ➲ *adjective* **easy**
IDM **ease sb's mind** to make sb feel less worried: *The doctor tried to ease her mind about her son's illness.*
PHR V **ease off** to become less strong or unpleasant: *Let's wait until the rain eases off.*
ease up to work less hard: *Ease up a bit or you'll make yourself ill!*

E

easel /ˈiːzl/ *noun* [C] a wooden frame that holds a picture while it is being painted

easily /ˈiːzəli/ *adv* **1** without difficulty: *I can easily ring up and check the time.* **2 easily the best, worst, nicest, etc.** without doubt: *It's easily his best novel.*

east¹ /iːst/ *noun* [U,sing] (*abbr* E) **1** (also **the east**) the direction you look towards in order to see the sun rise; one of the **points of the compass** (= the main directions that we give names to): *Which way is east?* ♦ *a cold wind from the east* ♦ *Which county is* **to the east of** *Oxfordshire?* ➲ picture at **compass 2** (also **East**) the part of any country, city, etc. that is further to the east than the other parts: *Norwich is in the east of England.* **3 the East** the countries of Asia, for example China and Japan ➲ look at **the Far East, the Middle East**

east² /iːst/ *adj, adv* **1** (also **East**) [only *before* a noun] in the east: *the east coast* ♦ *East Africa* **2** (used about a wind) coming from the east **3** to or towards the east: *They headed east.* ♦ *We live east of the city.*

eastbound /ˈiːstbaʊnd/ *adj* travelling or leading towards the east: *The eastbound carriageway of the motorway is blocked.*

Easter /ˈiːstə(r)/ *noun* [U] a festival on a Sunday in March or April when Christians celebrate Christ's return to life; the time before and after **Easter** Sunday: *the Easter holidays* ♦ *Are you going away* **at** *Easter?*

ˈEaster egg *noun* [C] an egg, usually made of chocolate, that you give as a present at **Easter**

easterly /ˈiːstəli/ *adj* **1** [only *before* a noun] towards or in the east: *They travelled in an easterly direction.* **2** (used about winds) coming from the east: *cold easterly winds*

eastern (also **Eastern**) /ˈiːstən/ *adj* **1** [only *before* a noun] (*abbr* E) of, in or from the east of a place: *Eastern Scotland* ♦ *the eastern shore of the lake* **2** from or connected with the countries of the East: *Eastern cookery* (= that comes from Asia)

eastwards /ˈiːstwədz/ (also **eastward**) *adv* towards the east: *The Amazon flows eastwards.* ▶ **eastward** *adj*: *to travel in an eastward direction*

easy¹ /ˈiːzi/ *adj* (**easier**; **easiest**) **1** not difficult: *an easy question* ♦ *It isn't easy to explain the system.* ♦ *The system isn't easy to explain.* **OPP hard 2** comfortable, relaxed and not worried: *an easy life* ♦ *My mind's easier now.* **OPP uneasy** ➲ *noun, verb* **ease**
IDM free and easy ➲ **free¹**
I'm easy (*informal*) used to say that you do not have a strong opinion when sb offers you a choice: *'Do you want to watch this or the news?' 'I'm easy. It's up to you.'*

easy² /ˈiːzi/ *adv* (**easier**; **easiest**)
IDM easier said than done (*spoken*) more difficult to do than to talk about: *'You should get her to help you.' 'That's easier said than done.'*
go easy on sb/on/with sth (*informal*) **1** to be gentle or less strict with sb: *Go easy on him; he's just a child.* **2** to avoid using too much of sth: *Go easy on the salt; it's bad for your heart.*
take it/things easy to relax and not work too hard or worry too much

easy ˈchair *noun* [C] a large comfortable chair with arms

ˌeasy-ˈgoing *adj* (used about a person) calm, relaxed and not easily worried or upset by what other people do: *Her parents are very easy-going. They let her do what she wants.* **SYN laid-back**

eat /iːt/ *verb* (*pt* **ate** /et; eɪt/; *pp* **eaten** /ˈiːtn/) **1** [I,T] to put food into your mouth, then chew and swallow it: *Who ate all the biscuits?* ♦ *Eat your dinner up, Joe* (= finish it all). ♦ *She doesn't eat properly. No wonder she's so thin.* ♦ *Do you want something to eat?* **2** [I] to have a meal: *What time shall we eat?* ♦ *We ate at a pizzeria near our hotel.*
IDM have sb eating out of your hand to have control and power over sb
have your cake and eat it ➲ **cake¹**
PHR V eat sth away/eat away at sth to damage or destroy sth slowly over a period of time: *The sea had eaten away at the cliff.*
eat out to have a meal in a restaurant: *Would you like to eat out tonight?*

eater /ˈiːtə(r)/ *noun* [C] a person who eats in a particular way: *My uncle's a big eater* (= he eats a lot). ♦ *We're not great meat eaters in our family.*

eau de cologne /ˌəʊ də kəˈləʊn/ (also **cologne**) *noun* [U] a type of **perfume** (= a pleasant-smelling liquid) that is not very strong

eaves /iːvz/ *noun* [pl] the edges of a roof that stick out over the walls: *There's a bird's nest under the eaves.*

eavesdrop /ˈiːvzdrɒp/ *verb* [I] (**eavesdropping**; **eavesdropped**) **eavesdrop (on sb/sth)** to listen secretly to other people talking: *They caught her eavesdropping on their conversation.*

the ebb /eb/ *noun* [sing] the time when sea water flows away from the land

> **MORE** The movement of sea water twice a day is called the **tide**. The opposite of **ebb tide** is **high tide**.

IDM the ebb and flow (of sth) (used about a situation, noise, feeling, etc.) a regular increase and decrease in the progress or strength of sth

eBay™ /ˈiːbeɪ/ *noun* [U] a website on the Internet where people can **auction** goods (= sell them to the person who offers the most money for them): *He buys rare baseball cards on eBay.*

> **TOPIC**
> **eBay™**
> You can buy or sell things on an **auction website**. You **bid** (= say how much you want to pay) for the item you want. The person who offers the most money **wins the auction** and gets the item.

ebb /eb/ *verb* [I] **1** (used about sea water) to flow away from the land, as happens twice a day **SYN go out 2 ebb (away)** (used about a feeling, etc.) to become weaker: *The crowd's enthusiasm began to ebb.*

ebony /ˈebəni/ *noun* [U] a hard black wood

ˈ**e-book** *noun* [C] a book that you can read on a computer screen or on an electronic device that you hold in your hand: *You can download unlimited e-books for free.* ➲ look at **e-reader**

TOPIC

E-books

You can buy an e-book **over the Internet** and read it on an **e-reader/e-book reader** (= a small electronic device that you carry with you). You can keep many books on one e-reader. It is also possible to buy an **app** (= computer application) that will allow you to **download** e-books **onto** your computer, smartphone, iPod™, etc.

ˈ**e-book reader** = ˈe-reader

eccentric /ɪkˈsentrɪk/ *adj* (used about people or their behaviour) strange or unusual: *People said he was mad but I think he was just slightly eccentric.* ▶ **eccentric** *noun* [C]: *She's just an old eccentric.* ▶ **eccentricity** /ˌeksenˈtrɪsəti/ *noun* [C,U] (*pl* **eccentricities**)

ecclesiastical /ɪˌkli:ziˈæstɪkl/ *adj* connected with or belonging to the Christian Church: *ecclesiastical law*

echo[1] /ˈekəʊ/ *noun* [C] (*pl* **echoes**) a sound that is repeated as it is sent back off a surface such as the wall of a tunnel: *I could hear the echo of footsteps somewhere in the distance.*

echo[2] /ˈekəʊ/ *verb* **1** [I] (used about a sound) to be repeated; to come back as an **echo**: *Their footsteps echoed in the empty church.* **2** [I,T] **echo sth (back)**; **echo (with/to sth)** to repeat or send back a sound; to be full of a particular sound: *The tunnel echoed back their calls.* ◆ *The hall echoed with their laughter.* **3** [T] to repeat what sb has said, done or thought: *The child echoed everything his mother said.* ◆ *The newspaper article echoed my views completely.*

eclair /ɪˈkleə(r)/ *noun* [C] a type of long thin cake, usually filled with cream and covered with chocolate ➲ picture at **cake**

eclipse

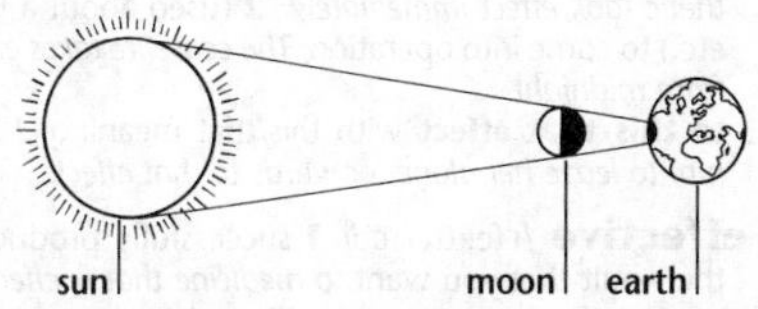

eclipse[1] /ɪˈklɪps/ *noun* [C] an occasion when the moon or the sun seems to completely or partly disappear, because one of them is passing between the other and the earth: *a total/partial eclipse of the sun*

eclipse[2] /ɪˈklɪps/ *verb* [T] (used about the moon, etc.) to cause an **eclipse** of the sun, etc.

eco-friendly /ˌikəʊ ˈfrendli/ *adj* not harmful to the environment: *eco-friendly products/fuel*

ecologist /iˈkɒlədʒɪst/ *noun* [C] a person who studies or is an expert in **ecology**

ecology /iˈkɒlədʒi/ *noun* [U] the relationship between living things and their surroundings; the study of this subject ▶ **ecological** /ˌi:kəˈlɒdʒɪkl/ *adj*: *The oil spill caused an ecological disaster.* ▶ **ecologically** /-kli/ *adv*

⚷ **economic** /ˌi:kəˈnɒmɪk; ˌekə-/ *adj* **1** [only *before* a noun] connected with the supply of money, business, industry, etc: *The country faces growing economic problems.* **2** producing a profit: *The mine was closed because it was not economic.* **OPP** **uneconomic**

HELP Be careful. **Economical** has a different meaning.

economical /ˌi:kəˈnɒmɪkl; ˌekə-/ *adj* that costs or uses less time, money, fuel, etc. than usual: *The new model is a very economical car to run.* **OPP** **uneconomical** ▶ **economically** /-kli/ *adv*: *The train service could be run more economically.*

ˌ**economic** ˈ**migrant** *noun* [C] a person who moves from their own country to a new country in order to find work or have a better standard of living

economics /ˌi:kəˈnɒmɪks; ˌekə-/ *noun* [U] the study or principles of the way money, business and industry are organized: *a degree in economics* ◆ *the economics of a company*

economist /ɪˈkɒnəmɪst/ *noun* [C] a person who studies or is an expert in **economics**

economize (also -ise) /ɪˈkɒnəmaɪz/ *verb* [I] **economize (on sth)** to save money, time, fuel, etc.; to use less of sth

⚷ **economy** /ɪˈkɒnəmi/ *noun* (*pl* **economies**) **1** the **economy** [C] the operation of a country's money supply, commercial activities and industry: *There are signs of improvement in the economy.* ◆ *the economies of America and Japan* **2** [C,U] careful spending of money, time, fuel, etc.; trying to save, not waste sth: *Our department is* ***making economies*** *in the amount of paper it uses.* ◆ *economy class* (= the cheapest class of air travel)

ecosystem /ˈi:kəʊsɪstəm/ *noun* [C] all the plants and living creatures in a particular area considered in relation to their physical environment

ecotourism /ˈi:kəʊtʊərɪzəm; -tɔ:r-/ *noun* [U] holidays that are organized so that tourists can visit beautiful areas without harming the natural environment ▶ **ecotourist** /-ɪst/ *noun* [C]

ecstasy /ˈekstəsi/ *noun* [C,U] (*pl* **ecstasies**) a feeling or state of great happiness: *to be* ***in ecstasy*** ◆ *She* ***went into ecstasies*** *about the ring he had bought her.*

ecstatic /ɪkˈstætɪk/ *adj* extremely happy

eczema /ˈeksɪmə/ *noun* [U] a disease which makes your skin red and dry so that you want to scratch it

ed. (also **Ed.**) *abbr* = **edition**(1), **editor**

eddy /ˈedi/ *noun* [C] (*pl* eddies) a movement of air, water or dust in a circle

edge¹ /edʒ/ *noun* [C] **1** the place where sth, especially a surface, ends: *the edge of a table* ♦ *The leaves were brown and curling at the edges.* ♦ *I stood at the water's edge.* **2** the sharp cutting part of a knife, etc.
IDM **an/the edge on/over sb/sth** a small advantage over sb/sth: *She knew she had the edge over the other candidates.*
(be) on edge to be nervous, worried or quick to become upset or angry: *I'm a bit on edge because I get my exam results today.*

edge² /edʒ/ *verb* **1** [I,T] edge (your way/sth) across, along, away, back, etc. to move yourself/sth somewhere slowly and carefully: *We edged closer to get a better view.* ♦ *She edged her chair up to the window.* **2** [T, usually passive] edge sth (with sth) to put sth along the edge of sth else: *The cloth was edged with lace.*

edgeways /ˈedʒweɪz/ (also edgewise /-waɪz/) *adv*
IDM **not get a word in edgeways** ➲ **word¹**

edgy /ˈedʒi/ *adj* (edgier; edgiest) (*informal*) nervous, worried or quick to become upset or angry: *You seem very edgy. What's bothering you?*

edible /ˈedəbl/ *adj* good or safe to eat: *Are these mushrooms edible?* OPP **inedible**

edifice /ˈedɪfɪs/ *noun* [C] (*formal*) a large impressive building

edit /ˈedɪt/ *verb* [T] **1** to prepare a piece of writing to be published, making sure that it is correct, the right length, etc. **2** to make changes to text or data on screen on a computer **3** to prepare a film, TV or radio programme by cutting and arranging recorded material in a particular order **4** to be the editor of a newspaper, magazine, etc.

edition /ɪˈdɪʃn/ *noun* [C] **1** (*abbr* ed.) the form in which a book is published; all the books, newspapers, etc. published in the same form at the same time: *a paperback/hardback edition* ♦ *the online edition of 'Il Pais'* **2** one of a series of newspapers, magazines, TV or radio programmes: *And now for this week's edition of 'Panorama'...*

editor /ˈedɪtə(r)/ *noun* [C] (*abbr* ed.) also (*abbr* Ed.) **1** the person who is in charge of all or part of a newspaper, magazine, etc. and who decides what should be included: *the financial editor* ♦ *Who is the editor of 'The Times'?* **2** a person whose job is to prepare a book or other material to be published by checking for mistakes and correcting the text: *an online/web editor* **3** a person whose job is to prepare a film, TV programme, etc. for showing to the public by cutting and putting the recorded material in the correct order

editorial /ˌedɪˈtɔːriəl/ *adj* connected with the task of preparing sth such as a newspaper, magazine or TV or radio programme to be published or broadcast: *the magazine's editorial staff* ♦ *an editorial decision* ▶ **editorial** *noun* [C] an article in a newspaper, usually written by the editor, giving an opinion on an important subject

educate /ˈedʒukeɪt/ *verb* [T] to teach or train sb, especially in school: *Young people should be educated to care for their environment.* ♦ *All their children were educated at private schools.*

educated /ˈedʒukeɪtɪd/ *adj* having studied and learnt a lot of things to a high standard: *a highly educated woman* ♦ *He spoke in an educated voice.*

education /ˌedʒuˈkeɪʃn/ *noun* [U,sing] **1** the teaching or training of people, especially in schools: *primary/secondary/higher/adult education* ♦ *She received an excellent education.* ➲ note at **school**, **study** **2** [U] Education the subject of study that deals with how to teach; the institutions or people involved in this: *a Bachelor of Education degree* ♦ *the Education Department* ▶ **educational** /-ʃənl/ *adj*: *an educational toy/visit/experience*

eel /iːl/ *noun* [C] a long fish that looks like a snake

eerie (also eery) /ˈɪəri/ *adj* strange and frightening: *an eerie noise* ▶ **eerily** /ˈɪərəli/ *adv* ▶ **eeriness** *noun* [U]

effect /ɪˈfekt/ *noun* **1** [C,U] (an) effect (on sb/sth) a change that is caused by sth; a result: *the effects of acid rain on the lakes and forests* ♦ *Her shouting* ***had little or no effect*** *on him.* ♦ *Despite her terrible experience, she seems to have suffered no* ***ill effects***. ➲ note at **affect** ➲ look at **after-effect**, **side effect** **2** [C,U] a particular look, sound or impression that an artist, writer, etc. wants to create: *How does the artist* ***create the effect of*** *moonlight?* ♦ *He likes to say things just for effect* (= to impress people). **3 effects** [pl] (*formal*) your personal possessions: *The insurance policy covers all baggage and personal effects.*
IDM **bring/put sth into effect** to cause sth to come into use: *The recommendations will soon be put into effect.*
come into effect (used especially about laws or rules) to begin to be used
in effect 1 in fact; for all practical purposes: *Though they haven't made an official announcement, she is, in effect, the new director.* **2** (used about a rule, a law, etc.) in operation; in use: *The new rules will be in effect from next month.*
take effect 1 (used about a drug, etc.) to begin to work; to produce the result you want: *The anaesthetic took effect immediately.* **2** (used about a law, etc.) to come into operation: *The ceasefire takes effect from midnight.*
to this/that effect with this/that meaning: *I told him to leave her alone, or words to that effect.*

effective /ɪˈfektɪv/ *adj* **1** successfully producing the result that you want: *a medicine that is effective against the common cold* ♦ *That picture would look more effective on a dark background.* OPP **ineffective** **2** [only *before* a noun] real or actual, although perhaps not official: *The soldiers gained effective control of the town.* ▶ **effectiveness** *noun* [U]

effectively /ɪˈfektɪvli/ *adv* **1** in a way that successfully produces the result you wanted: *She dealt with the situation effectively.* **2** in fact; in reality: *It meant that, effectively, they had lost.*

effeminate /ɪˈfemɪnət/ *adj* (used about a man or his behaviour) like a woman

effervescent /ˌefəˈvesnt/ *adj* **1** (used about people and their behaviour) excited, enthusiastic and full of energy SYN **bubbly** **2** (used about a liquid) having or producing small bubbles of gas SYN **fizzy** ▸ **effervescence** *noun* [U]

efficient /ɪˈfɪʃnt/ *adj* able to work well without making mistakes or wasting time and energy: *Our secretary is very efficient.* ◆ *You must find a more efficient way of organizing your time.* OPP **inefficient** ▸ **efficiency** /ɪˈfɪʃnsi/ *noun* [U] ▸ **efficiently** *adv*

effigy /ˈefɪdʒi/ *noun* [C] (*pl* **effigies**) **1** a statue of a famous or religious person, often shown lying down: *stone effigies in the church* **2** a model of a person that makes them look ugly: *The demonstrators burned a crude effigy of the president.*

effluent /ˈefluənt/ *noun* [U] (*formal*) liquid waste, especially chemicals produced by factories

effort /ˈefət/ *noun* **1** [C,U] the physical or mental strength or energy that you need to do sth; something takes a lot of energy: *They have* ***put a lot of effort into*** *their studies this year.* ◆ *It's a long climb to the top, but well worth the effort.* **2 an effort (to do sth)** [C] an attempt to do sth, especially when it is difficult to do: *I didn't feel like going out, but I'm glad I* ***made the effort.*** ◆ *He* ***made no effort*** *to contact his parents.* ◆ *It was a real effort to stay awake in the lecture.* ◆ *The project was a joint effort.*

effortless /ˈefətləs/ *adj* needing little or no effort so that sth seems easy ▸ **effortlessly** *adv*

EFL /ˌiː ef ˈel/ *abbr* **English as a Foreign Language**

e.g. /ˌiː ˈdʒiː/ *abbr* **for example**: *popular sports, e.g. football, tennis, swimming*

egalitarian /iˌɡælɪˈteəriən/ *adj* (used about a person, system, society, etc.) following the principle that everyone should have equal rights

egg¹ /eɡ/ *noun* **1** [C] an almost round object with a hard shell that contains a young bird, insect or **reptile** (= an animal that has skin covered in scales): *crocodile eggs*

egg

MORE A female bird **lays** her eggs, often in a **nest**, and then **sits on** them until they **hatch**.

2 [C,U] a bird's egg, especially one from a chicken, etc., that we eat: *egg yolks/whites* ➲ picture on **page P16**

MORE Eggs may be **boiled, fried, poached** or **scrambled**.

3 [C] (in women and female animals) the small cell that can join with a **sperm** (= a male seed) to make a baby: *an egg donor*

IDM **put all your eggs in one basket** to risk everything by depending completely on one thing, plan, etc. instead of giving yourself several possibilities

egg² /eɡ/ *verb*

PHR V **egg sb on (to do sth)** to encourage sb to do sth, especially sth that they should not do

ˈ**egg cup** *noun* [C] a small cup for holding a boiled egg

eggplant /ˈeɡplɑːnt/ (*AmE*) = **aubergine**

eggshell /ˈeɡʃel/ *noun* [C,U] the hard outside part of an egg ➲ picture at **egg**

ego /ˈiːɡəʊ; ˈeɡəʊ/ *noun* [C] (*pl* **egos**) the (good) opinion that you have of yourself: *It was a blow to her ego when she lost her job.*

egocentric /ˌeɡəʊˈsentrɪk; ˌiːɡ-/ *adj* thinking only about yourself and not what other people need or want SYN **selfish**

egoism /ˈeɡəʊɪzəm; ˈiːɡ-/ (also **egotism** /ˈeɡətɪzəm; ˈiːɡ-/) *noun* [U] the fact of thinking that you are better or more important than anyone else ▸ **egoist** /ˈeɡəʊɪst; ˈiːɡ-/ (also **egotist** /ˈeɡətɪst; ˈiːɡə-/) *noun* [C]: *I hate people who are egoists.* ▸ **egoistic** /ˌeɡəʊˈɪstɪk; ˌiːɡ-/ (also **egotistical** /ˌeɡəˈtɪstɪkl; ˌiːɡə-/) *adj*

eh /eɪ/ *exclam* (*BrE informal*) **1** used for asking sb to repeat sth: *'Did you like the film?' 'Eh?' 'I asked if you liked the film!'* **2** used for asking sb to agree with you: *'Good party, eh?'*

Eid (also **Id**) /iːd/ *noun* [sing] one of the two main Muslim festivals, especially one that celebrates the end of Ramadan (= a month when people do not eat during the day)

eiderdown /ˈaɪdədaʊn/ *noun* [C] (*BrE*) a covering for a bed filled with soft feathers, usually used on top of other coverings for the bed ➲ look at **duvet**

eight /eɪt/ *number* **1** 8 ➲ note at **six** **2 eight-** [in compounds] having eight of sth: *an eight-sided shape*

eighteen /ˌeɪˈtiːn/ *number* 18 ➲ note at **six** ▸ **eighteenth** /ˌeɪˈtiːnθ/ *ordinal number, noun* ➲ note at **sixth**

eighth¹ /eɪtθ/ *ordinal number* 8th ➲ note at **sixth**

eighth² /eɪtθ/ *noun* [C] ⅛; one of eight equal parts of sth

eighty /ˈeɪti/ *number* 80 ➲ note at **sixty** ▸ **eightieth** /ˈeɪtiəθ/ *ordinal number, noun* ➲ note at **sixth**

either¹ /ˈaɪðə(r); ˈiːðə(r)/ *determiner, pron* **1** one or the other of two; it does not matter which: *You can choose either soup or salad, but not both.* ◆ *You can ask either of us for advice.* ◆ *Either of us is willing to help.* **2** both: *It is a pleasant road, with trees on either side.*

either² /ˈaɪðə(r); ˈiːðə(r)/ *adv* **1** [used after two negative statements] also: *I don't like Pat and I don't like Nick much either.* ◆ *'I can't remember his name.' 'I can't either.'*

MORE We can also say **neither can I**. Look at **too** for agreement with positive statements.

2 used for emphasizing a negative statement: *The*

restaurant is quite good. And it's not expensive, either. **3 either ... or ...** used when you are giving a choice, usually of two things: *I can meet you either Thursday or Friday.* ◆ *Either you leave or I do.* ◆ *You can either write or phone.* ➲ note at **neither, too**

ejaculate /iˈdʒækjuleɪt/ *verb* **1** [I] to send out **semen** (= liquid) from the **penis** (= the male sexual organ) **2** [I,T] (*old-fashioned*) to say sth suddenly ▸ **ejaculation** /iˌdʒækjuˈleɪʃn/ *noun* [C,U]

E

eject /iˈdʒekt/ *verb* **1** [T, often passive] (*formal*) **eject sb (from sth)** to push or send sb/sth out of a place (usually with force): *The protesters were ejected from the building.* **2** [I] to escape from an aircraft that is going to crash **3** [I,T] to remove a disk from a machine, usually by pressing a button: *To eject the CD, press this button.* ◆ *After recording for three hours, the DVD will eject automatically.*

eke /iːk/ *verb*

PHR V eke sth out to make a small amount of sth last a long time

elaborate¹ /ɪˈlæbərət/ *adj* very complicated; done or made very carefully: *an elaborate pattern* ◆ *elaborate plans* ▸ **elaborately** *adv*: *an elaborately decorated room*

elaborate² /ɪˈlæbəreɪt/ *verb* [I] (*formal*) **elaborate (on sth)** to give more details about sth: *Could you elaborate on that idea?*

elapse /ɪˈlæps/ *verb* [I] (*formal*) (used about time) to pass

elastic¹ /ɪˈlæstɪk/ *noun* [U] material with rubber in it which can stretch

elastic² /ɪˈlæstɪk/ *adj* **1** (used about material, etc.) that returns to its original size and shape after being stretched **2** that can be changed; not fixed: *Our rules are quite elastic.*

eˌlastic ˈband = **rubber band**

elasticity /ˌiːlæˈstɪsəti; ˌelæ-; ɪˌlæ-/ *noun* [U] the quality that sth has of being able to stretch and return to its original size and shape

elated /iˈleɪtɪd/ *adj* very happy and excited ▸ **elation** /iˈleɪʃn/ *noun* [U]

elbow¹ /ˈelbəʊ/ *noun* [C] **1** the place where the bones of your arm join and your arm bends: *She jabbed him with her elbow.* ➲ picture at **body** **2** the part of the sleeve of a coat, jacket, etc. that covers the elbow: *His old jacket was worn at the elbows.*

elbow² /ˈelbəʊ/ *verb* [T] to push sb with your elbow: *He elbowed her out of the way.* ➲ look at **nudge**

ˈelbow room *noun* [U] (*informal*) enough space to move freely

elder¹ /ˈeldə(r)/ *adj* **1** [only *before* a noun] older (of two members of a family): *My elder daughter is at university now but the other one is still at school.* ◆ *an elder brother/sister* **2 the elder** [sing] the older of two people: *Who is the elder of the two?*

elbow

He elbowed past.

She nudged her.

elder² /ˈeldə(r)/ *noun* **1 my, etc. elder** [sing] a person who is older than me, etc: *He is her elder by several years.* **2 elders** [pl] older people: *Do children still respect the opinions of their elders?*

elderly /ˈeldəli/ *adj* **1** (used about a person) old: *elderly relatives*

HELP This is a polite way of saying 'old'.

2 the elderly *noun* [pl] old people in general: *The elderly need special care in winter.* ➲ look at **old**

eldest /ˈeldɪst/ *adj, noun* [C] (the) oldest (of three or more members of a family): *Their eldest child is a boy.* ◆ *John's got 4 boys. The eldest has just gone to university.*

elect /ɪˈlekt/ *verb* [T] **1 elect sb (to sth); elect sb (as sth)** to choose sb to have a particular job or position by voting for them: *He was elected to Parliament in 2010.* ◆ *The committee elected her as their representative.* **2** (*formal*) **elect to do sth** to decide to do sth: *Many people elect to work from home.*

election /ɪˈlekʃn/ *noun* [C,U] (the time of) choosing a Member of Parliament, President, etc. by voting: *In America, presidential elections are held every four years.* ◆ *If you're interested in politics why not* ***stand for election*** *yourself?* ➲ note at **politics**

CULTURE

In Britain **general elections** are held about every five years. Sometimes **by-elections** are held at other times. In each region (**constituency**) voters must choose one person from a list of **candidates**.

elector /ɪˈlektə(r)/ *noun* [C] a person who has the right to vote in an election ➲ A more common word is **voter**. ▸ **electoral** /ɪˈlektərəl/ *adj*: *the electoral register/roll* (= the list of electors in an area)

electorate /ɪˈlektərət/ *noun* [C, with sing or pl verb] all the people who can vote in a region, country, etc.

electric /ɪˈlektrɪk/ *adj* **1** producing or using electricity: *an electric current* ◆ *an electric kettle* **2** very exciting: *The atmosphere was electric.*

electrical /ɪˈlektrɪkl/ *adj* of or about electricity: *an electrical appliance* (= a machine that uses electricity) ◆ *an electrical engineer* (= a person who designs electrical systems and equipment)

the eˌlectric ˈchair *noun* [sing] a chair used in some countries for killing criminals with a very strong electric current

electrician /ɪˌlekˈtrɪʃn/ *noun* [C] a person whose job is to connect and repair electrical systems and equipment ➲ note at **house**

electricity /ɪˌlekˈtrɪsəti/ *noun* [U] a type of energy that we use to make heat, light and power to work machines, etc: *Turn that light off. We don't want to waste electricity.*

> **MORE** Electricity is usually **generated** in **power stations**. It may also be produced by **generators** or **batteries**.

eˌlectric ˈrazor = **shaver**

eˌlectric ˈshock (also **shock**) *noun* [C] a sudden painful feeling that you get if electricity goes through your body

electrify /ɪˈlektrɪfaɪ/ *verb* [T] (**electrifying**; **electrifies**; *pt, pp* **electrified**) **1** to supply sth with electricity: *The railways are being electrified.* **2** to make sb very excited: *Ronaldo electrified the crowd with his pace and skill.*

electrocute /ɪˈlektrəkjuːt/ *verb* [T] to kill sb with electricity that goes through the body ▶ **electrocution** /ɪˌlektrəˈkjuːʃn/ *noun* [U]

electrode /ɪˈlektrəʊd/ *noun* [C] one of two points where an electric current enters or leaves a battery, etc.

electron /ɪˈlektrɒn/ *noun* [C] part of an atom, that carries a negative electric charge ➲ look at **neutron**, **proton**

electronic /ɪˌlekˈtrɒnɪk/ *adj* **1** using **electronics**: *electronic equipment* ◆ *This dictionary is available in electronic form* (= on a computer disk). **2** done using a computer: *electronic banking/shopping* ▶ **electronically** /-kli/ *adv*

electronics /ɪˌlekˈtrɒnɪks/ *noun* [U] the technology used to produce computers, radios, etc.; the study of this technology: *the electronics industry*

elegant /ˈelɪɡənt/ *adj* attractive and of good style or design: *She looked very elegant in her new dress.* ◆ *an elegant coat* **SYN** **stylish** ▶ **elegance** *noun* [U] ▶ **elegantly** *adv*

element /ˈelɪmənt/ *noun*

➤ PART/AMOUNT **1** [C] one important part of sth: *Cost is an important element when we're thinking about holidays.* **2** [C, usually sing] **an element of sth** a small amount of sth: *There was an element of truth in what he said.*

➤ GROUP OF PEOPLE **3** [C] people of a certain type: *The criminal element at football matches causes a lot of trouble.*

➤ CHEMISTRY **4** [C] one of the simple chemical substances, for example iron, gold, etc.

➤ ELECTRICAL PART **5** [C] the metal part of a piece of electrical equipment that produces heat: *The kettle needs a new element.*

➤ WEATHER **6 the elements** [pl] (bad) weather: *to be exposed to the elements*

➤ BASIC PRINCIPLES **7 elements** [pl] the basic principles of a subject that you have to learn first **SYN** **basics**: *He taught me the elements of map-reading.*

IDM **in/out of your element** in a situation where you feel comfortable/uncomfortable: *Bill's in his element speaking to a large group of people, but I hate it.*

elementary /ˌelɪˈmentri/ *adj* **1** connected with the first stages of learning sth: *an elementary course in English* ◆ *a book for elementary students* **2** basic; not difficult: *elementary physics*

ˌeleˈmentary school *noun* [C] (*AmE*) a school for children aged 5 to 12

elephant

elephant /ˈelɪfənt/ *noun* [C] a very large grey animal with big ears, two **tusks** (= long curved teeth) and a **trunk** (= a very long nose) ➲ picture on **page P12**

elevate /ˈelɪveɪt/ *verb* [T] (*formal*) to move sb/sth to a higher place or more important position: *an elevated platform* ◆ *He was elevated to the Board of Directors.* **SYN** **raise**

elevation /ˌelɪˈveɪʃn/ *noun* **1** [C,U] (*formal*) the process of moving to a higher place or more important position: *his elevation to the presidency* **2** [C] the height of a place above sea level: *The city is* ***at an elevation of*** *2000 metres.*

elevator /ˈelɪveɪtə(r)/ (*AmE*) = **lift²**(1): *It's on the fifth floor, so we'd better take the elevator.*

eleven /ɪˈlevn/ *number* 11 ➲ note at **six** ▶ **eleventh** /ɪˈlevnθ/ *ordinal number, noun* ➲ note at **sixth**

elf /elf/ *noun* [C] (*pl* **elves** /elvz/) (in stories) a small creature with pointed ears who has magic powers

elicit /iˈlɪsɪt/ *verb* [T] (*formal*) **elicit sth (from sb)** to manage to get information, facts, a reaction, etc. from sb

eligible /ˈelɪdʒəbl/ *adj* **eligible (for sth/to do sth)** having the right to do or have sth: *In Britain, you are eligible to vote when you are eighteen.* **OPP** **ineligible**

eliminate /ɪˈlɪmɪneɪt/ *verb* [T] **1** to remove sb/sth that is not wanted or needed: *We must try and eliminate the problem.* **2** [often passive] to stop sb going further in a competition, etc: *The school team was eliminated in the first round of the competition.* ▶ **elimination** /ɪˌlɪmɪˈneɪʃn/ *noun* [C,U]

elite /eɪˈliːt/ *noun* [C, with sing or pl verb] a social group that is thought to be the best or most important because of its power, money, intelligence, etc:

an intellectual elite ▸ **elite** *adj*: *an elite group of artists*

elitism /ɪˈliːtɪzəm/ *noun* [U] the belief that some people should be treated in a special way: *Many people believe that private education encourages elitism.* ▸ **elitist** /-ɪst/ *noun* [C], *adj*

elk /elk/ (*AmE* **moose**) *noun* [C] a very large **deer** (= a large wild animal that eats grass) with large flat **antlers** (= horns shaped liked branches) on its head

elk

ellipse /ɪˈlɪps/ *noun* [C] (*technical*) a regular **oval** (= shaped like an egg) shape

elliptical /ɪˈlɪptɪkl/ *adj* **1** with a word or words left out of a sentence deliberately: *He made an elliptical remark* (= one that suggests more than is actually said). **2** (also **elliptic** /ɪˈlɪptɪk/) connected with or in the form of an **ellipse** ▸ **elliptically** /-kli/ *adv*: *to speak/write elliptically*

elm /elm/ (also **ˈelm tree**) *noun* [C] a tall tree with large leaves

elocution /ˌeləˈkjuːʃn/ *noun* [U] the ability to speak clearly and pronounce words correctly, especially in public

elongated /ˈiːlɒŋgeɪtɪd/ *adj* long and thin in a way that is not normal

elope /ɪˈləʊp/ *verb* [I] **elope (with sb)** to run away secretly to get married

eloquent /ˈeləkwənt/ *adj* (*formal*) able to use language and express your opinions well, especially when you speak in public ▸ **eloquence** *noun* [U] ▸ **eloquently** *adv*

🔑 **else** /els/ *adv* [used after words formed with *any-*, *every-*, *no-*, *some-* and after question words] another, different person, thing or place: *This isn't mine. It must be **someone else's**.* ◆ *Was it you who phoned me, or **somebody else**?* ◆ ***Everybody else** is allowed to stay up late.* ◆ *You'll have to pay. **Nobody else** will.* ◆ ***What else** would you like?* ◆ *I'm tired of that cafe—shall we go **somewhere else** for a change?*
IDM **or else** otherwise; if not: *You'd better go to bed now or else you'll be tired in the morning.* ◆ *He either forgot or else decided not to come.*

🔑 **elsewhere** /ˌelsˈweə(r)/ *adv* in or to another place: *He's travelled a lot—in Europe and elsewhere.*

ELT /ˌiː el ˈtiː/ *abbr* **English Language Teaching**

elude /iˈluːd/ *verb* [T] (*formal*) **1** to manage to avoid being caught by sb: *The escaped prisoner eluded the police for three days.* **2** to be difficult or impossible for sb to remember: *I remember his face but his name eludes me.*

elusive /iˈluːsɪv/ *adj* not easy to catch, find or remember

elves *plural of* **elf**

emaciated /ɪˈmeɪʃieɪtɪd; ɪˈmeɪsieɪtɪd/ *adj* extremely thin and weak because of illness, lack of food, etc. ▸ **emaciation** /ɪˌmeɪsiˈeɪʃn/ *noun* [U]

🔑 **email** (also **e-mail**) /ˈiːmeɪl/ *noun* **1** [U] a way of sending electronic messages and data from one computer to another: *to send a message by email* **2** [C,U] a message or messages sent by email: *I'll **send** you **an email** tomorrow.* ◆ *to **receive/get/open** an email* ▸ **email** *verb* [T]: *I'll email the information to you.* ◆ *I'll email her the documents.*

TOPIC

Email

Enter your username (= the name you use on your computer) and **password** (= a secret word) to **access your email account.** First, you might want to **check your inbox** to see if anyone has **sent** you **an email**. When you **receive an email**, you can **open it**, read it, and then **reply to** it. You can also **forward** (= send) it to someone else, or **delete** (= remove) it. If you want to send someone a file, for example a photo or other document, you can **add it as an attachment**.

emanate /ˈeməneɪt/ *verb* [T] (*formal*) to produce or show sth: *He emanates confidence.*
PHR V **emanate from sth** to come from sth or somewhere: *The sound of loud music emanated from the building.*

emancipate /ɪˈmænsɪpeɪt/ *verb* [T] (*formal*) to give sb the same legal, social and political rights as other people ▸ **emancipated** *adj*: *Are women now fully emancipated (= with the same rights and opportunities as men)?* ▸ **emancipation** /ɪˌmænsɪˈpeɪʃn/ *noun* [U]

embalm /ɪmˈbɑːm/ *verb* [T] to prevent a dead body from decaying by treating it with special substances ▸ **embalmer** *noun* [C]

embankment /ɪmˈbæŋkmənt/ *noun* [C] a wall of stone or earth that is built to stop a river from spreading into an area that should be dry, or to carry a road or railway

embargo /ɪmˈbɑːgəʊ/ *noun* [C] (*pl* **embargoes**) an official order to stop doing business with another country: *to impose an embargo on arms sales* ◆ *to lift/remove an embargo*

embark /ɪmˈbɑːk/ *verb* [I] to get on a ship: *Passengers with cars and caravans must embark first.* **OPP** **disembark**
PHR V **embark on sth** (*formal*) to start sth (new): *I'm embarking on a new career.*
▸ **embarkation** /ˌembɑːˈkeɪʃn/ *noun* [C,U]

🔑 **embarrass** /ɪmˈbærəs/ *verb* [T] **1** to make sb feel uncomfortable or shy: *Don't ever embarrass me in front of my friends again!* **2** to cause problems or difficulties for sb: *The Minister's mistake embarrassed the government.*

🔑 **embarrassed** /ɪmˈbærəst/ *adj* **embarrassed (about/at sth); embarrassed (to do sth)** feeling uncomfortable or shy because of sth silly you have done, because people are looking at you, etc: *He's embarrassed about his height.* ♦ *Some women are too embarrassed to consult their doctor about the problem.*

embarrassing /ɪmˈbærəsɪŋ/ *adj* making you feel uncomfortable or shy: *an embarrassing question/mistake* ▶ **embarrassingly** *adv*

embarrassment /ɪmˈbærəsmənt/ *noun* **1** [U] the feeling you have when you are embarrassed: *I nearly died of embarrassment when he said that.* **2** [C] a person or thing that makes you embarrassed

embassy /ˈembəsi/ *noun* [C] (*pl* **embassies**) (the official building of) a group of **diplomats** (= officials who represent their country) and the **ambassador** (= the official with the highest position), who represent their government in a foreign country ➲ look at **consulate**

embed /ɪmˈbed/ *verb* [T] (**embedding**; **embedded**) [usually passive] to fix sth firmly and deeply (in sth else): *The axe was embedded in the piece of wood.*

embellish /ɪmˈbelɪʃ/ *verb* [T] (*formal*) **1** to make sth more beautiful by adding decoration to it SYN **decorate** **2** to make a story more interesting by adding details that are not always true ▶ **embellishment** *noun* [U,C]

ember /ˈembə(r)/ *noun* [C, usually pl] a piece of wood or coal that is not burning, but is still red and hot after a fire has died

embezzle /ɪmˈbezl/ *verb* [T] to steal money that you are responsible for or that belongs to your employer ▶ **embezzlement** *noun* [U]

emblem /ˈembləm/ *noun* [C] an object or symbol that represents sth: *The dove is the emblem of peace.*

embody /ɪmˈbɒdi/ *verb* [T] (**embodying**; **embodies**; *pt, pp* **embodied**) (*formal*) **1** to be a very good example of sth: *To me she embodies all the best qualities of a teacher.* **2** to include or contain sth: *This latest model embodies many new features.* ▶ **embodiment** *noun* [C]: *She is the embodiment of a caring mother.*

embrace /ɪmˈbreɪs/ *verb* **1** [I,T] to put your arms around sb as a sign of love, happiness, etc. **2** [T] (*formal*) to accept sth with enthusiasm: *She embraced Christianity in her later years.* **3** [T] (*formal*) to include: *His report embraced all the main points.* ▶ **embrace** *noun* [C]: *He held her in a warm embrace.*

embroider /ɪmˈbrɔɪdə(r)/ *verb* **1** [I,T] to decorate cloth by sewing a pattern or picture on it: *an embroidered blouse* **2** [T] to add details that are not true to a story to make it more interesting ▶ **embroidery** /ɪmˈbrɔɪdəri/ *noun* [U]

embryo /ˈembriəʊ/ *noun* [C] (*pl* **embryos** /-əʊz/) a baby, an animal or a plant in the early stages of development before birth ➲ look at **foetus** ▶ **embryonic** /ˌembriˈɒnɪk/ *adj*

emerald /ˈemərəld/ *noun* [C] a bright green **precious stone** (= one that is rare and valuable): *a ring studded with diamonds and emeralds* ▶ **emerald** (also ˌ**emerald ˈgreen**) *adj*: *an emerald green dress*

emerge /iˈmɜːdʒ/ *verb* [I] **emerge (from sth)** **1** to appear or come out from somewhere: *A man emerged from the shadows.* ♦ (*figurative*) *The country emerged from the war in ruins.* **2** to become known: ***It emerged that** she was lying about her age.* ▶ **emergence** *noun* [U]: *the emergence of new technologies*

emergency /iˈmɜːdʒənsi/ *noun* [C,U] (*pl* **emergencies**) a serious event that needs immediate action: *In an emergency phone 999 for help.* ♦ *The government has declared **a state of emergency*** (= a time when special plans or actions can be put into effect) *following the earthquake.* ♦ *an emergency exit*

eˈmergency brake (*AmE*) = **handbrake**

eˈmergency room *noun* [C] (*abbr* **ER**) (*AmE*) = **accident and emergency**

emigrant /ˈemɪɡrənt/ *noun* [C] a person who has gone to live in another country ➲ look at **immigrant**

emigrate /ˈemɪɡreɪt/ *verb* [I] **emigrate (from …) (to …)** to leave your own country to go and live in another: *They emigrated from Ireland to Australia twenty years ago.* ▶ **emigration** /ˌemɪˈɡreɪʃn/ *noun* [C,U] ➲ look at **immigrant, immigration, migrate**

eminent /ˈemɪnənt/ *adj* (*formal*) (used about a person) famous and important: *an eminent scientist*

eminently /ˈemɪnəntli/ *adv* (*formal*) very; extremely: *She is eminently suitable for the job.*

emit /iˈmɪt/ *verb* [T] (**emitting**; **emitted**) (*formal*) to send out sth, for example a smell, a sound, smoke, heat or light: *The animal emits a powerful smell when scared.* ▶ **emission** /iˈmɪʃn/ *noun* [C,U]: *sulphur dioxide emissions from power stations*

emoticon /ɪˈməʊtɪkɒn/ *noun* [C] a symbol that shows your feelings when you send an email or text message. For example :-) represents a smiling face.

emotion /ɪˈməʊʃn/ *noun* [C,U] a strong feeling such as love, anger, fear, etc: *to control/express your emotions* ♦ *His voice was filled with emotion.* ♦ *Brown showed no emotion as the police took him away.*

emotional /ɪˈməʊʃənl/ *adj* **1** connected with people's feelings: *emotional problems* **2** causing strong feelings: *an emotional issue* **3** having strong emotions and showing them in front of people: *Kelly gave an emotional speech.* ♦ *He always **gets** very **emotional** when I leave.* ▶ **emotionally** /-ʃənəli/ *adv*: *She felt physically and emotionally drained after giving birth.*

emotive /iˈməʊtɪv/ *adj* causing strong feelings: *emotive language* ♦ *an emotive issue*

empathy /ˈempəθi/ *noun* [C,U] **empathy (with/for sb/sth)**; **empathy (between A and B)** the ability to imagine how another person is feeling and so understand their mood: *Some adults **have** (a) great **empathy** with children.* ▶ **empathize** (also **-ise**) /ˈempəθaɪz/ *verb* [I] **empathize (with sb/sth)**: *He's a popular teacher because he empathizes with his students.*

E

emperor /ˈempərə(r)/ *noun* [C] the ruler of an empire

emphasis /ˈemfəsɪs/ *noun* [C,U] (*pl* emphases /-siːz/) **1** emphasis (on sth) (giving) special importance or attention (to sth): *There's a lot of emphasis on science at our school.* ◆ *You should* **put** *a greater* **emphasis** *on quality rather than quantity when you write.* **2** the force that you give to a word or phrase when you are speaking; a way of writing a word to show that it is important: *In the word 'photographer' the emphasis is on the second syllable.* ◆ *I underlined the key phrases of my letter for emphasis.* SYN for both meanings **stress**

emphasize (also -ise) /ˈemfəsaɪz/ *verb* [T] emphasize (that ...) to put **emphasis** on sth: *They emphasized that healthy eating is important.* ◆ *They emphasized the importance of healthy eating.* SYN **stress**

emphatic /ɪmˈfætɪk/ *adj* said or expressed in a strong way: *an emphatic refusal/denial* ▶ **emphatically** /-kli/ *adv*

empire /ˈempaɪə(r)/ *noun* [C] **1** a group of countries that is governed by one country: *the Roman Empire* ➲ look at **emperor, empress 2** a very large company or group of companies: *a business empire*

empirical /ɪmˈpɪrɪkl/ *adj* (*formal*) based on experiments and practical experience, not on ideas: *empirical evidence*

employ /ɪmˈplɔɪ/ *verb* [T] **1** employ sb (in/on sth); employ sb (as sth) to pay sb to work for you: *They employ 600 workers.* ◆ *Three people are employed on the task of designing a new computer system.* ◆ *He is employed as a lorry driver.* ➲ look at **unemployed 2** (*formal*) employ sth (as sth) to use: *In an emergency, an umbrella can be employed as a weapon.*

employee /ɪmˈplɔɪiː/ *noun* [C] a person who is paid to work for sb: *The factory has 500 employees.* ➲ note at **job**

employer /ɪmˈplɔɪə(r)/ *noun* [C] a person or company that employs other people: *The car factory is the largest employer in this town.*

employment /ɪmˈplɔɪmənt/ *noun* [U] **1** the state of having a paid job: *to be in/out of employment* ◆ *This bank can* **give employment to** *ten extra staff.* ◆ *It is difficult to* **find employment** *in the north of the country.* ➲ note at **work** ➲ look at **unemployment 2** (*formal*) the use of sth: *the employment of force*

emˈployment agency *noun* [C] a company that helps people to find work and other companies to find workers

empower /ɪmˈpaʊə(r)/ *verb* [T, usually passive] (*formal*) to give sb power or authority (to do sth) ▶ **empowerment** *noun* [U]: *the empowerment of the individual*

empress /ˈemprəs/ *noun* [C] **1** a woman who rules an empire **2** the wife of an **emperor** (= a man who rules an empire)

empty[1] /ˈempti/ *adj* (emptier; emptiest) **1** having nothing or nobody inside it: *an empty box* ◆ *The bus was half empty.* **2** without meaning or value: *It was an empty threat* (= it was not meant seriously). ◆ *My life feels empty now the children have left home.* SYN **hollow** ▶ **emptiness** *noun* [U]

empty[2] /ˈempti/ *verb* (emptying; empties; *pt, pp* emptied) **1** [T] empty sth (out/out of sth) to remove everything that is inside a container, etc: *I've emptied a wardrobe for you to use.* ◆ *Luke emptied everything out of his desk and left.* **2** [I] to become empty: *The cinema emptied very quickly once the film was finished.*

ˌempty-ˈhanded *adj* without getting what you wanted; without taking sth to sb: *The robbers fled empty-handed.*

EMU /ˌiː em ˈjuː/ *abbr* **Economic and Monetary Union** (of the countries of the European Union) ➲ look at **euro**

emulate /ˈemjuleɪt/ *verb* [T] (*formal*) to try to do sth as well as, or better than, sb ➲ A less formal word is **copy**.

emulsion /ɪˈmʌlʃn/ *noun* [C,U] **1** a mixture of liquids that do not normally mix together, such as oil and water **2** (also eˈmulsion paint) (*BrE*) a type of paint used on walls and ceilings that dries without leaving a shiny surface

enable /ɪˈneɪbl/ *verb* [T] enable sb/sth to do sth to make it possible for sb/sth to do sth: *The software enables you to access the Internet in seconds.* SYN **allow**

enamel /ɪˈnæml/ *noun* [U] **1** a hard shiny substance used for protecting or decorating metal, etc: *enamel paint* **2** the hard white outer covering of a tooth

enchanted /ɪnˈtʃɑːntɪd/ *adj* **1** (in stories) affected by magic powers **2** (*formal*) pleased or very interested: *The audience was enchanted by her singing.*

enchanting /ɪnˈtʃɑːntɪŋ/ *adj* very nice or pleasant; attractive SYN **delightful**

encircle /ɪnˈsɜːkl/ *verb* [T] (*formal*) to make a circle round sth; to surround: *London is encircled by the M25 motorway.*

encl. (also enc.) *abbr* **enclosed**; used on business letters to show that another document is being sent in the same envelope

enclose /ɪnˈkləʊz/ *verb* [T] **1** [usually passive] enclose sth (in sth) to surround sth with a wall, fence, etc.; to put one thing inside another: *The garden is enclosed by a high hedge.* ◆ *The jewels were enclosed in a strong box.* **2** to put sth in an envelope, package, etc. with sth else: *Can I enclose a letter with this parcel?*

enclosed /ɪnˈkləʊzd/ *adj* **1** with walls, etc. all around: *He gets very nervous in enclosed spaces.* **2** sent with a letter, etc: *Please complete the enclosed application form* ◆ ***Please find enclosed*** *my completed form.*

enclosure /ɪnˈkləʊʒə(r)/ *noun* [C] **1** a piece of land inside a wall, fence, etc. that is used for a particular purpose: *a wildlife enclosure* **2** something that is placed inside an envelope together with the letter

encode /ɪnˈkəʊd/ = **code**²(2)

encore¹ /ˈɒŋkɔː(r)/ *noun* [C] a short, extra performance at the end of a concert, etc.

encore² /ˈɒŋkɔː(r)/ *exclam* called out by an audience that wants the people who perform in a concert, etc. to sing or play sth extra

encounter¹ /ɪnˈkaʊntə(r)/ *verb* [T] **1** to experience sth (a danger, difficulty, etc.): *I've never encountered any discrimination at work.* SYN **meet with sth** **2** (*formal*) to meet sb unexpectedly; to experience or find sth unusual or new: *She was the most remarkable woman he had ever encountered.* ➲ look at **come across**

encounter² /ɪnˈkaʊntə(r)/ *noun* [C] **an encounter (with sb/sth); an encounter (between A and B)** an unexpected (often unpleasant) meeting or event: *I've had a number of* ***close encounters*** (= situations which could have been dangerous) *with bad drivers.*

encourage /ɪnˈkʌrɪdʒ/ *verb* [T] **1 encourage sb/sth (in sth/to do sth)** to give hope, support or confidence to sb: *The teacher encouraged her students to ask questions.* ♦ *They will encourage students in their pursuit of higher education.* **2** to make sth happen more easily: *The government wants to encourage new businesses to start up in the area.* OPP for both meanings **discourage** ▶ **encouragement** *noun* [C, U] ▶ **encouraging** *adj*

encroach /ɪnˈkrəʊtʃ/ *verb* [I] (*formal*) **encroach (on/upon sth)** to use more of sth than you should: *I do hope that I am not encroaching too much upon your free time.*

encyclopedia (also **encyclopaedia**) /ɪnˌsaɪkləˈpiːdiə/ *noun* [C] (*pl* **encyclopedias**) a book or set of books that gives information about very many subjects, arranged in the order of the alphabet (= from A to Z) ➲ note at **book**

end¹ /end/ *noun* [C] **1** the furthest or final part of sth; the place or time where sth stops: *My house is* ***at the end of*** *the street.* ♦ *I live in the end house.* ♦ *There are some seats* ***at the far end of*** *the room.* ♦ *I'm going on holiday* ***at the end of*** *October.* ♦ *He promised to give me an answer by the end of the week.* ♦ *She couldn't wait to hear the end of the story.*

> **HELP** **In the end** or **at the end**? The idiom **in the end** refers to time and means 'finally': *We were too tired to cook, so in the end we decided to eat out.* **At the end of sth** refers to the last part of a book, film, class, etc., at the point where it is about to finish: *At the end of the meal we had an argument about who should pay for it.*

2 (*formal*) an aim or purpose: *They were prepared to do anything to achieve their ends.* **3** a little piece of sth that is left after the rest has been used: *a cigarette end*

IDM **at an end** (*formal*) finished or used up: *Her career is at an end.*

at the end of the day (*BrE informal*) used to say the most important fact in a situation: *At the end of the day, you have to make the decision yourself.*

at the end of your tether feeling that you cannot deal with a difficult situation any more, because you are too tired, worried, etc.

at a loose end ➲ **loose¹**

at your wits' end ➲ **wit**

bring sth/come/draw to an end (to cause sth) to finish: *His stay in England was coming to an end.*

a dead end ➲ **dead¹**

end to end in a line with the ends touching: *They put the tables end to end.*

in the end at last; finally: *He wanted to get home early but in the end it was midnight before he left.*

make ends meet to have enough money for your needs: *It's hard for us to make ends meet.*

make sb's hair stand on end ➲ **hair**

a means to an end ➲ **means**

no end of sth (*informal*) too many or much; a lot of sth: *She has given us no end of trouble.*

odds and ends ➲ **odds**

on end (used about time) continuously: *He sits and reads for hours on end.*

put an end to sth to stop sth from happening any more

end² /end/ *verb* [I,T] **end (in/with sth)** (to cause sth) to finish: *The road ends here.* ♦ *How does this story end?* ♦ *The match ended in a draw.* ♦ *I think we'd better end this conversation now.*

PHR V **end up (as sth); end up (doing sth)** to find yourself in a place/situation that you did not plan or expect: *We got lost and ended up in the centre of town.* ♦ *She had always wanted to be a writer but ended up as a teacher.* ♦ *There was nothing to eat at home so we ended up getting a takeaway.*

endanger /ɪnˈdeɪndʒə(r)/ *verb* [T] to cause danger to sb/sth: *Smoking seriously endangers your health.* ♦ *Pollution from the factory endangers public safety.*

endangered /ɪnˈdeɪndʒəd/ *adj* (used about animals, plants, etc.) in danger of becoming **extinct** (= no longer alive in the world): *The giant panda is* ***an endangered species.*** ➲ note at **environment**

endear /ɪnˈdɪə(r)/ *verb* [T] (*formal*) **endear sb/yourself to sb** to make sb/yourself liked by sb: *She managed to endear herself to everybody by her kindness.* ▶ **endearing** *adj*: *an endearing habit* ▶ **endearingly** *adv*

endeavour (*AmE* **endeavor**) /ɪnˈdevə(r)/ *verb* [I] (*formal*) **endeavour to do sth** to try hard to do sth: *She endeavoured to finish her work on time.* ▶ **endeavour** (*AmE* **endeavor**) *noun* [C,U]

endemic /enˈdemɪk/ *adj* **endemic (in/to ...)** regularly found in a particular place or among a particular group of people and difficult to get rid of: *Malaria is endemic in many hot countries.* ♦ *the endemic problem of racism*

ending /ˈendɪŋ/ *noun* [C] **1** the end (of a story, play, film, etc.): *That film made me cry but I was pleased that it had* ***a happy ending.*** **2** the last part

E

of a word, which can change: *When nouns end in -ch or -sh or -x, the plural ending is -es not -s.*

endive /ˈendaɪv/ (*AmE*) = **chicory**

endless /ˈendləs/ *adj* **1** very large in size or amount and seeming to have no end: *The possibilities are endless.* **2** lasting for a long time and seeming to have no end: *Our plane was delayed for hours and the wait seemed endless.* SYN **interminable** ▶ **endlessly** *adv*

E

endorse /ɪnˈdɔːs/ *verb* [T] **1** to say publicly that you give official support or agreement to a plan, statement, decision, etc: *Members of all parties endorsed a ban on firearms.* **2** [usually passive] (*BrE*) to add a note to sb's **driving licence** (= the document which allows sb to drive a vehicle) to say that the driver has broken the law ▶ **endorsement** *noun* [C,U]

endow /ɪnˈdaʊ/ *verb* [T] to give a large sum of money to an institution such as a school or college PHR V **be endowed with sth** to naturally have a particular characteristic, quality, etc: *She was endowed with intelligence and wit.*

endowment /ɪnˈdaʊmənt/ *noun* [C,U] money that is given to a school, college, etc.; the act of giving this money

ˈ**end product** *noun* [C] something that is produced by a particular process or activity

endurance /ɪnˈdjʊərəns/ *noun* [U] the ability to continue doing sth painful or difficult for a long period of time without complaining

endure /ɪnˈdjʊə(r)/ *verb* (*formal*) **1** [T] to suffer sth painful or uncomfortable, usually without complaining: *She endured ten years of loneliness.* SYN **bear 2** [I] to continue SYN **last** ▶ **enduring** *adj*

ˌ**end-ˈuser** *noun* [C] a person who actually uses a product rather than one who makes or sells it, especially sb who uses a product connected with computers

enemy /ˈenəmi/ *noun* (*pl* **enemies**) **1** [C] a person who hates and tries to harm you: *They used to be friends but became* ***bitter enemies.*** ♦ *He has* ***made*** *several* ***enemies*** *during his career.* ➲ *noun* **enmity**. **2 the enemy** [sing, with sing or pl verb] the army or country that your country is fighting against: *The enemy is/are approaching.* ♦ *enemy forces*

energetic /ˌenəˈdʒetɪk/ *adj* full of or needing energy and enthusiasm: *Jogging is a very energetic form of exercise.* ▶ **energetically** /-kli/ *adv*

energy /ˈenədʒi/ *noun* (*pl* **energies**) **1** [U] the ability to be very active or do a lot of work without getting tired: *Children are usually* ***full of energy.*** **2 energies** [pl] the effort and attention that you give to doing sth: *She devoted all her energies to helping the blind.* **3** [U] the power that comes from coal, electricity, gas, etc. that is used for producing heat, driving machines, etc: *nuclear energy*

enforce /ɪnˈfɔːs/ *verb* [T] to make people obey a law or rule or do sth that they do not want to: *How will they enforce the new law?* ▶ **enforced** *adj*: *enforced redundancies* ▶ **enforcement** *noun* [U]

engage /ɪnˈgeɪdʒ/ *verb* [T] (*formal*) **1** to interest or attract sb: *You need to engage the students' attention right from the start.* **2 engage sb (as sth)** to give work to sb: *They engaged him as a cook.* **3 engage (with sth)** to make parts of a machine fit together: *Engage the clutch before selecting a gear.*
PHR V **engage in sth** to take part in sth: *I don't engage in that kind of gossip!*

engaged /ɪnˈgeɪdʒd/ *adj* **1** (*formal*) **engaged (in/on sth)** (used about a person) busy doing sth: *They are engaged in talks with the Irish government.* **2 engaged (to sb)** having agreed to get married: *We've just* ***got engaged.*** ♦ *Susan is engaged to Jim.* **3** (*especially AmE* **busy**) (used about a telephone) in use: *I can't get through—the line is engaged.* **4** (*BrE*) (used about a public toilet) in use OPP **vacant**

engagement /ɪnˈgeɪdʒmənt/ *noun* [C] **1** an agreement to get married; the time when you are engaged: *He broke off their engagement.* **2** (*formal*) an arrangement to go somewhere or do sth at a fixed time: *I can't come on Tuesday as I have a* ***prior engagement.*** SYN **appointment**

enˈ**gagement ring** *noun* [C] a ring, usually with **precious stones** (= ones that are rare and valuable) in it, that a man gives to a woman when they agree to get married: *a diamond engagement ring*

engine /ˈendʒɪn/ *noun* [C] **1** the part of a vehicle that produces power to make the vehicle move: *This engine runs on diesel.* ♦ *a car/jet engine* ➲ note at **motor 2** (also **locomotive**) a vehicle that pulls a railway train

ˈ**engine driver** (also ˈ**train driver**; *AmE* **engineer**) *noun* [C] a person whose job is to drive a railway engine

engineer[1] /ˌendʒɪˈnɪə(r)/ *noun* [C] **1** a person whose job is to design, build or repair engines, machines, etc: *a civil/chemical/electrical/mechanical engineer* **2** (*AmE*) = **engine driver**

engineer[2] /ˌendʒɪˈnɪə(r)/ *verb* [T] (*formal*) to arrange for sth to happen by careful secret planning: *Her promotion was engineered by her father.*

engineering /ˌendʒɪˈnɪərɪŋ/ *noun* [U] (the study of) the work that is done by an engineer: *mechanical/civil/chemical engineering*

English[1] /ˈɪŋglɪʃ/ *noun* **1** [U] the language that is spoken in Britain, the US, Australia, etc: *Do you speak English?* ♦ *I've been learning English for 5 years.* **2 the English** [pl] the people of England

English[2] /ˈɪŋglɪʃ/ *adj* belonging to England, the English people, the English language, etc: *English history* ♦ *the English countryside* ➲ note at **United Kingdom**

CULTURE

Be careful. The people of Scotland (the Scots) and of Wales (the Welsh) are **British**, not English.

the ˌ**English** ˈ**Channel** = **channel**[1] (6)

Englishman /ˈɪŋglɪʃmən/, **Englishwoman** /ˈɪŋglɪʃwʊmən/ *noun* [C] (*pl* -men

/-mən/, -women /-wɪmɪn/) a person who comes from England or whose parents are English

HELP We normally say: *I'm English* not *I'm an Englishman.*

ˌEnglish ˈmuffin (*AmE*) = **muffin**(1)

engrave /ɪnˈɡreɪv/ *verb* [T] engrave A with B; engrave B on A to cut words or designs on metal, stone, etc: *The cup is engraved with his name.* ♦ *His name is engraved on the cup.*

engraving /ɪnˈɡreɪvɪŋ/ *noun* **1** [C] a design that is cut into a piece of metal or stone; a picture made from this **2** [U] the art or process of cutting designs into wood, metal, etc.

engrossed /ɪnˈɡrəʊst/ *adj* engrossed (in/with sth) so interested in sth that you give it all your attention: *She was completely engrossed in her book.*

enhance /ɪnˈhɑːns/ *verb* [T] (*formal*) to improve sth or to make sth look better ▶ **enhanced** *adj*: *enhanced efficiency* ▶ **enhancement** *noun* [C,U]: *the enhancement of sound quality*

enigma /ɪˈnɪɡmə/ *noun* [C] (*pl* enigmas) a person, thing or situation that is difficult to understand ▶ **enigmatic** /ˌenɪɡˈmætɪk/ *adj*

⚷ **enjoy** /ɪnˈdʒɔɪ/ *verb* [T] **1** enjoy sth/enjoy doing sth to get pleasure from sth: *I really enjoyed that meal.* ♦ *He enjoys listening to music while he's driving.* ➲ note at **like 2** enjoy yourself to be happy; to have a good time: *I enjoyed myself at the party last night.*

⚷ **enjoyable** /ɪnˈdʒɔɪəbl/ *adj* giving pleasure: *We spent an enjoyable few days in Scotland.* ▶ **enjoyably** /-əbli/ *adv*: *The evening passed enjoyably.*

⚷ **enjoyment** /ɪnˈdʒɔɪmənt/ *noun* [U,C] pleasure or a thing which gives pleasure: *She gets a lot of enjoyment from teaching.* ♦ *One of her main enjoyments is foreign travel.*

enlarge /ɪnˈlɑːdʒ/ *verb* [I,T] to make sth bigger or to become bigger: *I'm going to have this photo enlarged.*
PHR V **enlarge on sth** (*formal*) to say or write more about sth

enlargement /ɪnˈlɑːdʒmənt/ *noun* [U,C] making sth bigger or sth that has been made bigger: *an enlargement of a photo* OPP **reduction**

enlighten /ɪnˈlaɪtn/ *verb* [T] (*formal*) to give sb information so that they understand sth better

enlightened /ɪnˈlaɪtnd/ *adj* having an understanding of people's needs, a situation, etc. that is not based on old-fashioned ideas

enlist /ɪnˈlɪst/ *verb* **1** [T] to get help, support, etc: *We need to enlist your support.* **2** [I,T] to join the army, navy or air force; to make sb a member of the army, etc: *They enlisted as soon as war was declared.*

enmity /ˈenməti/ *noun* [U] the feeling of hatred towards an enemy

enormity /ɪˈnɔːməti/ *noun* [sing] (*formal*) the very great size, effect, etc. of sth; the fact that sth is very serious: *the enormity of a task/decision/problem*

⚷ **enormous** /ɪˈnɔːməs/ *adj* very big or very great: *an enormous building* ♦ *enormous pleasure* SYN **huge** ▶ **enormously** *adv*

⚷ **enough¹** /ɪˈnʌf/ *determiner, pron* **1** as much or as many of sth as necessary: *We've saved enough money to buy a house.* ♦ *Not everybody can have a book—there aren't enough.* ♦ *If enough of you are interested, we'll arrange a trip to the theatre.* **2** as much or as many as you want: *I've had enough of living in a city* (= I don't want to live in a city any more). ♦ *Don't give me any more books. I've got* **quite enough** *already.*

⚷ **enough²** /ɪˈnʌf/ *adv* [used *after* verbs, adjectives and adverbs] **1** to the necessary amount or degree: *You don't practise enough.* ♦ *He's old enough to travel alone.* ♦ *Does she speak Italian well enough to get the job?* SYN **sufficiently** ➲ picture at **too 2** quite, but not very: *She plays well enough, for a beginner.*
IDM **fair enough** ➲ **fair¹**
funnily, strangely, etc. enough it is funny, etc. that …: *Funnily enough, I thought exactly the same myself.*
sure enough ➲ **sure**

enquire (also inquire) /ɪnˈkwaɪə(r)/ *verb* [I,T] (*formal*) enquire (about sb/sth) to ask for information about sth: *Could you enquire when the trains to Cork leave?* ♦ *We need to enquire about hotels in Vienna.*
PHR V **enquire after sb** to ask about sb's health
enquire into sth to study sth in order to find out all the facts: *The journalist enquired into the politician's financial affairs.*

enquirer (also inquirer) /ɪnˈkwaɪərə(r)/ *noun* [C] (*formal*) a person who asks for information

enquiring (also inquiring) /ɪnˈkwaɪərɪŋ/ *adj* **1** interested in learning new things: *We should encourage children to have enquiring minds.* **2** asking for information: *He gave me an enquiring look.* ▶ **enquiringly** (also inquiringly) *adv*

⚷ **enquiry** (also inquiry) /ɪnˈkwaɪəri/ *noun* (*pl* enquiries) **1** [C] (*formal*) an enquiry (about/concerning/into sb/sth) a request for information about sth; a question that you ask about sth: *a telephone enquiry* ♦ *I'll* **make** *some* **enquiries** *into English language courses in Oxford.* **2** [U] the act of asking about sth: *After weeks of enquiry he finally found what he was looking for.* **3** [C] an enquiry (into sth) an official process to find out the cause of sth: *After the accident there was an enquiry into safety procedures.*

enrage /ɪnˈreɪdʒ/ *verb* [T] (*formal*) [usually passive] to make sb very angry

enrich /ɪnˈrɪtʃ/ *verb* [T] **1** to improve the quality, flavour, etc. of sth: *These cornflakes are enriched with vitamins.* **2** to make sb/sth rich or richer OPP **impoverish** ▶ **enrichment** *noun* [U]

enrol (*AmE* enroll) /ɪnˈrəʊl/ *verb* [I,T] (enro<u>l</u>ling; enro<u>l</u>led) to become or to make sb a member of a club, school, etc: *I've enrolled on an Italian course.* ♦ *They enrolled 100 new students last year.* ▶ **enrol-**

ment (*AmE* enrollment) *noun* [C,U]: *Enrolment for the course will take place next week.*

en route /ˌɒ̃ ˈruːt/ *adv* en route (from ...) (to ...); en route (for ...) on the way; while travelling from/to a place: *The car broke down when we were en route for Dover.*

ensemble /ɒnˈsɒmbl/ *noun* **1** [C, with sing or pl verb] a small group of musicians, dancers or actors who perform together: *a brass/wind/string ensemble* ◆ *The ensemble is/are based in Lyon.* **2** [C, usually sing] a set of clothes that are worn together

ensue /ɪnˈsjuː/ *verb* [I] (*formal*) to happen after (and often as a result of) sth else

en suite /ˌɒ̃ ˈswiːt/ *adj, adv* (used about a bedroom and bathroom) forming one unit: *The bedroom has a bathroom en suite.*

🔑 **ensure** (*AmE* insure) /ɪnˈʃʊə(r); -ˈʃɔː(r)/ *verb* [T] to make sure that sth happens or is definite: *Please ensure that the door is locked before you leave.*

entail /ɪnˈteɪl/ *verb* [T] (*formal*) to make sth necessary; to involve sth: *The job sounds interesting but I'm not sure what it entails.*

entangled /ɪnˈtæŋgld/ *adj* caught in sth else: *The bird was entangled in the net.* ◆ *(figurative) She didn't want to get emotionally entangled (= involved) with him.*

🔑 **enter** /ˈentə(r)/ *verb*
➤COME/GO IN **1** [I,T] (*formal*) to come or go into a place: *Don't enter without knocking.* ◆ *They all stood up when he entered the room.* ➲ Much more common expressions are **come into** and **go into**. ➲ *nouns* **entrance, entry**
➤BECOME MEMBER **2** [T] to become a member of sth, especially a profession or an institution: *She entered the legal profession in 2008.* ◆ *to enter school/college/university* ➲ *noun* **entrant**
➤BEGIN ACTIVITY **3** [T] to begin or become involved in an activity, a situation, etc: *When she entered the relationship, she had no idea he was already married.* ◆ *We have just entered a new phase in international relations.*
➤EXAM/COMPETITION **4** [I,T] enter (for) sth; enter sb (in/for sth) to put your name or sb's name on the list for an exam, race, competition, etc: *I entered a competition in the Sunday paper and I won £200!*
➤WRITE INFORMATION **5** [T] enter sth (in/into/on/onto sth) to put names, numbers, details, etc. in a list, book, computer, etc: *Enter your password and press return.* ◆ *I've entered all the data onto the computer.*
PHR V **enter into sth** **1** to start to think or talk about sth: *I don't want to enter into details now.* **2** to be part of sth; to be involved in sth: *This is a business matter. Friendship doesn't enter into it.*
enter into sth (with sb) to begin sth: *The government has entered into negotiations with the unions.*

enterprise /ˈentəpraɪz/ *noun* **1** [C] a company or business: *a new industrial enterprise* **2** [C] a large project, especially one that is difficult: *It's a very exciting new enterprise.* ◆ *a joint enterprise* SYN **venture** **3** [U] the ability to think of new projects or create new businesses and make them successful: *We need men and women of enterprise and energy.*

enterprising /ˈentəpraɪzɪŋ/ *adj* having or showing the ability to think of new projects or new ways of doing things and make them successful: *One enterprising farmer opened up his field as a car park and charged people to park there.*

🔑 **entertain** /ˌentəˈteɪn/ *verb* **1** [I,T] to welcome sb as a guest, especially to your home; to give sb food and drink: *They entertain a lot.* ◆ *Barbeques are a favourite way of entertaining friends.* **2** [T] entertain (sb) (with sth) to interest and amuse sb in order to please them: *I find it very hard to keep my class entertained on a Friday afternoon.*

🔑 **entertainer** /ˌentəˈteɪnə(r)/ *noun* [C] a person whose job is to amuse people, for example by singing, dancing or telling jokes: *a street entertainer*

🔑 **entertaining** /ˌentəˈteɪnɪŋ/ *adj* interesting and amusing: *an entertaining speech* ◆ *She was always so funny and entertaining.*

🔑 **entertainment** /ˌentəˈteɪnmənt/ *noun* [U,C] film, music, etc. used to interest and amuse people: *There isn't much entertainment for young people in this town.* ◆ *There's a full programme of entertainments every evening.*

enthral (*AmE* enthrall) /ɪnˈθrɔːl/ *verb* [T] (enthralling; enthralled) [usually passive] to hold sb's interest and attention completely: *He was enthralled by her story.* ▶ **enthralling** *adj*

🔑 **enthusiasm** /ɪnˈθjuːziæzəm/ *noun* [U] enthusiasm (for/about sth/doing sth) a strong feeling of excitement or interest in sth and a desire to become involved in it: *Jan showed great enthusiasm for the new project.*

enthusiast /ɪnˈθjuːziæst/ *noun* [C] a person who is very interested in an activity or subject

🔑 **enthusiastic** /ɪnˌθjuːziˈæstɪk/ *adj* enthusiastic (about sth/doing sth) full of excitement and interest in sth: *The kids are very enthusiastic about sport.* ▶ **enthusiastically** /-kli/ *adv*: *The film was received enthusiastically by the critics.*

entice /ɪnˈtaɪs/ *verb* [T] entice sb (into sth/doing sth) to persuade sb to do sth or to go somewhere by offering them sth nice: *Advertisements try to entice people into buying more things than they need.* ▶ **enticement** *noun* [C,U]

enticing /ɪnˈtaɪsɪŋ/ *adj* attractive and interesting

🔑 **entire** /ɪnˈtaɪə(r)/ *adj* [only *before* a noun] whole or complete: *He managed to read the entire book in two days.* SYN **whole** ▶ **entirely** *adv*: *I entirely agree with Michael.* ▶ **entirety** /ɪnˈtaɪərəti/ *noun* [U] (*formal*): *We must consider the problem in its entirety (= as a whole).*

🔑 **entitle** /ɪnˈtaɪtl/ *verb* [T, usually passive] entitle sb (to sth) to give sb the right to have or do sth: *I think I'm entitled to a day's holiday—I've worked hard enough.*

🔑 **entitled** /ɪnˈtaɪtld/ *adj* (used about books, plays, etc.) with the title: *Gloria read a poem entitled 'Salt'.*

entitlement /ɪnˈtaɪtlmənt/ *noun* (*formal*) **1** [U] entitlement (to sth) the official right to have or do sth: *This may affect your entitlement to compensation.* **2** [C] something that you have an official right to; the amount that you have the right to receive: *Your contributions will affect your pension entitlements.*

entity /ˈentəti/ *noun* [C] (*pl* entities) something that exists separately from sth else and has its own identity: *The kindergarten and the school are in the same building but they're really* ***separate entities.***

entrance /ˈentrəns/ *noun* **1** [C] the entrance (to/of sth) the door, gate or opening where you go into a place: *I'll meet you at the entrance to the theatre.* OPP **exit** **2** [C] entrance (into/onto sth) the act of coming or going into a place, especially in a way that attracts attention: *He made a dramatic entrance onto the stage.* SYN **entry** OPP **exit** **3** [U] entrance (to sth) the right to enter a place: *They were refused entrance to the club because they were wearing trainers.* ♦ *an entrance fee* SYN **entry** ➲ look at **admission, admittance** **4** [U] entrance (into/to sth) permission to join a club, society, university, etc: *You don't need to take an entrance exam to get into university.* ➲ look at **admission**

entrant /ˈentrənt/ *noun* [C] a person who enters a profession, competition, exam, university, etc.

entreat /ɪnˈtriːt/ *verb* [T] (*formal*) to ask sb to do sth, often in an emotional way SYN **beg**

entrepreneur /ˌɒntrəprəˈnɜː(r)/ *noun* [C] a person who makes money by starting or running businesses, especially when this involves taking financial risks ▸ **entrepreneurial** /ˌɒntrəprəˈnɜːriəl/ *adj*: *entrepreneurial skills*

entrust /ɪnˈtrʌst/ *verb* [T] (*formal*) entrust A with B/entrust B to A to make sb responsible for sth: *I entrusted Rachel with the arrangements for the party.* ♦ *I entrusted the arrangements for the party to Rachel.*

entry /ˈentri/ *noun* (*pl* entries)
➤GOING IN **1** [C] the act of coming or going into a place: *The thieves forced an entry into the building.* SYN **entrance** **2** [U] entry (to/into sth) the right to enter a place: *The immigrants were refused entry at the airport.* ♦ *The sign says 'No Entry'.* ♦ *an entry visa* SYN **entrance** ➲ look at **admission, admittance**
➤JOINING GROUP **3** [U] the right to take part in sth or become a member of a group: *countries seeking entry into the European Union*
➤IN COMPETITION **4** [C] a person or thing that is entered for a competition, etc: *There were fifty entries for the Eurovision song contest.* ♦ *The winning entry is number 45!*
➤WRITTEN INFORMATION **5** [C] one item that is written down in a list, account book, dictionary, etc: *an entry in a diary* ♦ *You'll find 'ice-skate' after the entry for 'ice'.* **6** [U] an act of recording information in a computer, book, etc: *More keyboarding staff are required for data entry.*
➤DOOR **7** [C] (*AmE*) a door, gate, passage, etc. where you enter a building, etc. SYN **entrance**

envelop /ɪnˈveləp/ *verb* [T] (*formal*) to cover or surround sb/sth completely (in sth): *The hills were enveloped in mist.*

envelope /ˈenvələʊp; ˈɒn-/ *noun* [C] the paper cover for a letter: *Have you written his address on the envelope?* ➲ look at **stamped addressed envelope** ➲ picture at **letter**

enviable /ˈenviəbl/ *adj* something that is **enviable** is the sort of thing that is good and that other people want to have too: *He is in the* ***enviable position*** *of having two job offers to choose from.* ➲ *verb and noun* **envy**

envious /ˈenviəs/ *adj* envious (of sb/sth) wanting sth that sb else has: *She was envious of her sister's success.* SYN **jealous** ➲ *verb and noun* **envy** ▸ **enviously** *adv*

environment /ɪnˈvaɪrənmənt/ *noun* **1** [C,U] the conditions in which you live, work, etc: *a pleasant working environment* **2** the environment [sing] the natural world, for example the land, air and water, in which people, animals and plants live: *We need stronger laws to protect the environment.* ➲ look at **surroundings** ▸ **environmental** /ɪnˌvaɪrənˈmentl/ *adj*: *environmental science* ▸ **environmentally** /-təli/ *adv*: *environmentally damaging*

> TOPIC
>
> **The environment**
>
> The environment is being damaged by air and water **pollution**. Many **species** of wildlife are **endangered**, partly as a result of **deforestation**, and trees and rivers are damaged by **acid rain**. **Environmentalists** are also concerned about **global warming** and the hole in the **ozone layer**.
>
> We can **conserve** the Earth's **resources** (= coal, oil, etc.) by **recycling** more **waste**, and by using **renewable energy** such as **solar power** (= from the sun) and **hydroelectric power** (= from water).

environmentalist /ɪnˌvaɪrənˈmentəlɪst/ *noun* [C] a person who wants to protect the environment

enˌvironmentally ˈfriendly (also enˌvironment-ˈfriendly) *adj* (used about products) not harming the environment: *environmentally-friendly packaging*

envisage /ɪnˈvɪzɪdʒ/ *verb* [T] (*formal*) to think of sth as being possible in the future; to imagine: *I don't envisage any problems with this.*

envoy /ˈenvɔɪ/ *noun* [C] a person who is sent by a government with a message to another country

envy¹ /ˈenvi/ *noun* [U] envy (of sb); envy (at/of sth) the feeling that you have when sb else has sth that you want: *It was difficult for her to hide her envy of her friend's success.* ➲ look at **enviable, envious**
IDM **be the envy of sb** to be the person or thing that causes sb to feel **envy**: *The city's transport system is the envy of many of its European neighbours.*

envy² /ˈenvi/ *verb* [T] (envying; envies; *pt, pp* envied) envy (sb) (sth) to want sth that sb else has; to feel **envy**: *I've always envied your good luck.* ♦ *I don't envy you that job* (= I wouldn't like to have it).

E

enzyme /ˈenzaɪm/ *noun* [C] (*technical*) a substance, produced by all living things, that helps a chemical change happen or happen more quickly, without being changed itself

ephemeral /ɪˈfemərəl/ *adj* (*formal*) lasting or used for only a short time **SYN** **short-lived**

epic /ˈepɪk/ *adj* very long and exciting: *an epic struggle/journey* ▶ **epic** *noun* [C]: *The film 'Glory' is an American Civil War epic.*

epidemic /ˌepɪˈdemɪk/ *noun* [C] a large number of cases of people or animals suffering from the same disease at the same time

epilepsy /ˈepɪlepsi/ *noun* [U] a disease of the brain that can cause a person to become unconscious (sometimes with violent movements that they cannot control)

epileptic /ˌepɪˈleptɪk/ *noun* [C] a person who suffers from **epilepsy** ▶ **epileptic** *adj*: *an epileptic fit*

epilogue /ˈepɪlɒg/ *noun* [C] a short piece that is added at the end of a book, play, etc. and that comments on what has gone before ➲ look at **prologue**

episode /ˈepɪsəʊd/ *noun* [C] **1** one separate event in sb's life, a novel, etc: *That's an episode in my life I'd rather forget.* **2** one part of a TV or radio story that is shown or told in several parts

epitaph /ˈepɪtɑːf/ *noun* [C] words that are written or said about a dead person, especially words written on a stone where they are buried

epitome /ɪˈpɪtəmi/ *noun* [sing] **the epitome (of sth)** a perfect example of sth: *Her clothes are the epitome of good taste.*

epitomize (also **-ise**) /ɪˈpɪtəmaɪz/ *verb* [T] to be typical of sth: *This building epitomizes modern trends in architecture.*

epoch /ˈiːpɒk/ *noun* [C] a period of time in history (that is important because of special events, characteristics, etc.)

⚷ **equal¹** /ˈiːkwəl/ *adj* **1** **equal (to sb/sth)** the same in size, amount, value, number or level: *This animal is equal in weight to a small car.* ◆ *They are equal in weight.* ◆ *They are of equal weight.* ◆ *Divide it into two equal parts.* **OPP** **unequal** **2** having the same rights or being treated the same as other people: *This company has an equal opportunities policy* (= does not consider age, race, sex, etc. when employing sb). **3** (*formal*) **equal to sth** having the strength, ability, etc. to do sth: *I'm afraid Bob just isn't equal to the job.*

IDM **be on equal terms (with sb)** to have the same advantages and disadvantages as sb else

⚷ **equal²** /ˈiːkwəl/ *noun* [C] a person who has the same ability, rights, etc. as you do: *to treat somebody as an equal*

⚷ **equal³** /ˈiːkwəl/ *verb* [T] (**equalling**; **equalled**, (*AmE*) **equaling**; **equaled**) **1** (used about numbers, etc.) to be the same as sth: *44 plus 17 equals 61 is written: 44 + 17 = 61.* **2** to be as good as sb/sth: *He ran an excellent race, equalling the world record.*

equality /iˈkwɒləti/ *noun* [U] the situation in which everyone has the same rights and advantages: *racial equality* (= between people of different races) **OPP** **inequality**

equalize (also **-ise**) /ˈiːkwəlaɪz/ *verb* [I] (in sport) to reach the same number of points as your opponent: *Wales equalized in the 87th minute to make the score two all.* ▶ **equalizer** (also **-iser**) *noun* [C]: *Rooney scored the equalizer.*

⚷ **equally** /ˈiːkwəli/ *adv* **1** to the same degree or amount: *They both worked equally hard.* **2** in equal parts: *His money was divided equally between his children.* **3** (*formal*) (used when you are comparing two ideas or commenting on what you have just said) at the same time; but/and also: *I do not think what he did was right. Equally, I can understand why he did it.*

equate /iˈkweɪt/ *verb* [T] **equate sth (with sth)** to consider one thing as being the same as sth else: *Some parents equate education with exam success.*

equation /ɪˈkweɪʒn/ *noun* [C] (in mathematics) a statement that two quantities are equal: *2x + 5 = 11 is an equation.*

the equator (also **the Equator**) /ɪˈkweɪtə(r)/ *noun* [sing] the imagined line around the earth at an equal distance from the North and South Poles: *north/south of the Equator* ◆ *The island is on the equator.* ➲ picture at **earth** ▶ **equatorial** /ˌekwəˈtɔːriəl/ *adj*: *equatorial rainforests* ◆ *an equatorial climate*

equestrian /ɪˈkwestriən/ *adj* (*formal*) connected with horse riding

equilibrium /ˌiːkwɪˈlɪbriəm; ˌek-/ *noun* [U, sing] **1** a state of balance, especially between opposite forces or influences: *The point at which the solid and the liquid are* ***in equilibrium*** *is called the freezing point.* ◆ *We have achieved economic equilibrium.* **2** a calm state of mind and a balance of emotions

equip /ɪˈkwɪp/ *verb* [T] (**equipping**; **equipped**) **equip sb/sth (with sth)** **1** [usually passive] to supply sb/sth with what is needed for a particular purpose: *We shall equip all schools with new computers over the next year.* ◆ *The flat has a* ***fully-equipped*** *kitchen.* **2** to prepare sb for a particular task: *The course equips students with all the skills necessary to become a chef.*

⚷ **equipment** /ɪˈkwɪpmənt/ *noun* [U] the things that are needed to do a particular activity: *office/sports/computer equipment*

> **GRAMMAR** **Equipment** is uncountable. We say a **piece of equipment** if we are talking about one item: *a very useful piece of kitchen equipment.*

⚷ **equivalent** /ɪˈkwɪvələnt/ *adj* **equivalent (to sth)** equal in value, amount, meaning, importance, etc: *The British House of Commons is roughly equivalent to the American House of Representatives.* ▶ **equivalent** *noun* [C]: *There is no English equivalent to the French 'bon appétit'.*

ER /ˌiː ˈɑː(r)/ *abbr* (*AmE*) **emergency room**

er /ɜː(r)/ *exclam* used in writing to show the sound that sb makes when they cannot decide what to say next

era /ˈɪərə/ *noun* [C] a period of time in history (that is special for some reason): *The composer's death marked the* ***end of an era.***

eradicate /ɪˈrædɪkeɪt/ *verb* [T] (*formal*) to destroy or get rid of sth completely: *Some diseases, such as smallpox, have been completely eradicated.* ▶ **eradication** /ɪˌrædɪˈkeɪʃn/ *noun* [U]

erase /ɪˈreɪz/ *verb* [T] (*formal*) to remove sth completely (a pencil mark, a computer file, etc.): (*figurative*) *He tried to erase the memory of those terrible years from his mind.* ➲ We usually say **rub out** a pencil mark. ▶ **eraser** (*especially AmE*) = **rubber**(2)

ˈe-reader (also ˈe-book reader) *noun* [C] a device on which you can read electronic books, newspapers, etc. ➲ note at **e-book**

erect[1] /ɪˈrekt/ *adj* **1** standing straight up: *He stood with his head erect.* **2** (used about the male sexual organ) hard and standing up because of sexual excitement

erect[2] /ɪˈrekt/ *verb* [T] (*formal*) to build sth or to stand sth straight up: *Huge TV screens were erected above the stage.* ♦ *to erect a statue*

erection /ɪˈrekʃn/ *noun* **1** [C] if a man has an **erection**, his **penis** (= his sexual organ) becomes hard and stands up because he is sexually excited: *to get/have an erection* **2** [U] (*formal*) the act of building sth or standing sth straight up

erode /ɪˈrəʊd/ *verb* [T, usually passive] (used about the sea, the weather, etc.) to destroy sth slowly: *The cliff has been eroded by the sea.* ▶ **erosion** /ɪˈrəʊʒn/ *noun* [U]: *the erosion of rocks by the sea*

erotic /ɪˈrɒtɪk/ *adj* causing sexual excitement: *an erotic film/poem/dream*

err /ɜː(r)/ *verb* [I] (*formal*) to be or do wrong; to make mistakes

IDM **err on the side of sth** to do more of sth than is necessary in order to avoid the opposite happening: *It is better to err on the side of caution* (= it is better to be too careful rather than not careful enough).

errand /ˈerənd/ *noun* [C] (*old-fashioned*) a short journey to take or get sth for sb, for example to buy sth from a shop

erratic /ɪˈrætɪk/ *adj* (used about sb's behaviour, or about the quality of sth) changing without reason; that you can never be sure of: *Marc Jones is a talented player but he's very erratic* (= sometimes he plays well, sometimes badly). ▶ **erratically** /-kli/ *adv*

erroneous /ɪˈrəʊniəs/ *adj* (*formal*) not correct; based on wrong information: *erroneous conclusions/assumptions* ▶ **erroneously** *adv*

> **HELP** **Error** or **mistake**? **Error** is more formal than **mistake**. There are some expressions such as *error of judgement, human error* where only **error** can be used.

🔑 **error** /ˈerə(r)/ *noun* **1** [C] (*formal*) a mistake: *The telephone bill was too high because of a* ***computer error.*** ♦ *an* ***error of judgement*** ♦ *to* ***make an error*** ➲ note at **mistake** **2** [U] the state of being wrong: *The letter was sent to you* ***in error.*** ♦ *The accident was the result of* ***human error.***

IDM **trial and error** ➲ **trial**

ˈerror message *noun* [C] a message that appears on a computer screen which tells you that you have done sth wrong or that the program cannot do what you want it to do

erupt /ɪˈrʌpt/ *verb* [I] **1** (used about a **volcano**) to explode and throw out fire, burning rocks, smoke, etc. **2** (used about violence, shouting, etc.) to start suddenly: *The demonstration erupted into violence.* **3** (used about a person) to suddenly become very angry: *George erupted when he heard the news.* ▶ **eruption** *noun* [C,U]: *a volcanic eruption*

E

escalate /ˈeskəleɪt/ *verb* [I,T] **1** escalate (sth) (into sth) (to cause sth) to become stronger or more serious: *The demonstrations are escalating into violent protest in all the major cities.* ♦ *The terrorist attacks escalated tension in the capital.* **2** (to cause sth) to become greater or higher; to increase: *The cost of housing in the south has escalated in recent years.* ▶ **escalation** /ˌeskəˈleɪʃn/ *noun* [C,U]

escalator /ˈeskəleɪtə(r)/ *noun* [C] moving stairs that carry people between different floors of a shop, etc.

escapade /ˌeskəˈpeɪd/ *noun* [C] an exciting experience that may be dangerous

🔑 **escape**[1] /ɪˈskeɪp/ *verb* **1** [I] escape (from sb/sth) to manage to get away from a place where you do not want to be; to get free: *They managed to escape from the burning building.* ♦ *Two prisoners have escaped.* **2** [I,T] to manage to avoid sth dangerous or unpleasant: *The two men in the other car escaped unhurt in the accident.* ♦ *David Smith escaped injury when his car skidded off the road.* ♦ *to escape criticism/punishment* **3** [T] to be forgotten or not noticed by sb: *His name escapes me.* ♦ *to escape somebody's notice* **4** [I] (used about gases or liquids) to come or get out of a container, etc: *There's gas escaping somewhere.* ▶ **escaped** *adj*: *The police have caught the escaped prisoner.*

🔑 **escape**[2] /ɪˈskeɪp/ *noun* **1** [C,U] escape (from sth) the act of escaping: *There have been twelve escapes from the prison this year.* ♦ *She had* ***a narrow/lucky escape*** *when a lorry crashed into her car.* ♦ *When the guard fell asleep they were able to* ***make*** *their* ***escape.*** ➲ look at **fire escape** **2** [U, sing] something that helps you forget your normal life: *For him, listening to music is a means of escape.* ♦ *an escape from reality*

escapism /ɪˈskeɪpɪzəm/ *noun* [U] an activity, a form of entertainment, etc. that helps you avoid or forget unpleasant or boring things: *For John, reading is a* ***form of escapism.*** ▶ **escapist** /-ɪst/ *adj*

escort[1] /ˈeskɔːt/ *noun* **1** [C,U, with sing or pl verb] one or more people or vehicles that go with and protect sb/sth, or that go with sb/sth as an honour: *an armed escort* ♦ *He arrived* ***under police escort.***

2 [C] (*formal*) a person who takes sb to a social event **3** [C] a person, especially a woman, who is paid to go out socially with sb: *an escort agency*

escort[2] /ɪsˈkɔːt/ *verb* [T] to go with sb to protect them or to show them the way: *The President's car was escorted by several police cars.* ♦ *Philip escorted her to the door.*

Eskimo /ˈeskɪməʊ/ *noun* [C] (*pl* **Eskimo** *or* **Eskimos**) a member of a race of people from northern Canada, and parts of Alaska, Greenland and Siberia.

E

> **HELP** Be careful. Some of these people prefer to be called **Inuit**.

ESL /ˌiː es ˈel/ *abbr* **English as a Second Language**

ESOL /ˈiːsɒl/ *abbr* **English for speakers of other languages**; the teaching of English as a foreign language to people who are living in the UK or Ireland

ESP *abbr* /ˌiː es ˈpiː/ **English for Specific/Special Purposes**; the teaching of English to people who need it for a special reason, such as scientific study, a technical job, etc.

esp. *abbr* = **especially**(1)

especial /ɪˈspeʃl/ *adj* [only *before* a noun] (*formal*) not usual; special: *This will be of especial interest to you.*

especially /ɪˈspeʃəli/ *adv* **1** (*abbr* **esp.**) more than other things, people, situations, etc.; particularly: *She loves animals, especially dogs.* ♦ *Teenage boys, especially, can be very competitive.* ♦ *He was very disappointed with his mark in the exam, especially as he had worked so hard for it.* **SYN** **particularly** **2** for a particular purpose or person: *I made this especially for you.* ➲ A less formal word is **specially**. **3** very (much): *It's not an especially difficult exam.* ♦ *'Do you like jazz?' 'Not especially.'* **SYN** **particularly**

espionage /ˈespiənɑːʒ/ *noun* [U] the act of finding out secret information about another country or organization ➲ *verb* **spy**

Esq. *abbr* (*especially BrE formal*) **Esquire**; used when you are writing a man's name on an envelope: *Edward Hales, Esq.*

> **HELP** This is old-fashioned and many people now prefer to write: *Mr Edward Hales.*

essay /ˈeseɪ/ *noun* [C] an essay (on/about sth) a short piece of writing on one subject: *a 1000-word essay on tourism* ♦ *write an essay* ♦ ***hand in*** *an essay*

essence /ˈesns/ *noun* **1** [U] the basic or most important quality of sth: *The essence of the problem is that there is not enough money available.* ♦ *Although both parties agree* ***in essence****, some minor differences remain.* **2** [C,U] a substance (usually a liquid) that is taken from a plant or food and that has a strong smell or taste of that plant or food: *coffee/vanilla essence*

essential /ɪˈsenʃl/ *adj* completely necessary; that you must have or do: *essential services* ♦ *essential medical supplies* ♦ *Maths is essential for a career in computers.* ♦ *It is essential that all school-leavers should have a qualification.* ➲ note at **important**
▸ **essential** *noun* [C,usually pl]: *food, and other essentials such as clothing and heating*

essentially /ɪˈsenʃəli/ *adv* when you consider the basic or most important part of sth: *The problem is essentially one of money.* **SYN** **basically**

establish /ɪˈstæblɪʃ/ *verb* [T] **1** to start or create an organization, a system, etc: *The school was established in 1875.* ♦ *Before we start on the project, we should establish some rules.* **2** to make sth exist (especially a formal relationship with sb/sth): *The government is trying to establish closer links between the two countries.* **3** establish sb/sth (as sth) to cause sb/sth to be accepted: *She has been trying to establish herself as a novelist for years.* **4** to discover or find proof of the facts of a situation: *The police have not been able to establish the cause of the crash.*

establishment /ɪˈstæblɪʃmənt/ *noun* **1** [C] (*formal*) an organization, a large institution or a hotel: *an educational establishment* **2 the Establishment** [sing] the people in positions of power in a country, who usually do not support change **3** [U] the act of creating or starting a new organization, system, etc: *the establishment of new laws on taxes*

estate /ɪˈsteɪt/ *noun* [C] **1** a large area of land in the countryside that is owned by one person or family: *He owns a large estate in Scotland.* **2** (*BrE*) an area of land that has a lot of houses or factories of the same type on it: *an industrial estate* (= where there are a lot of factories) ♦ *a housing estate* **3** all the money and property that sb leaves when they die: *Her estate was left to her daughter.*

eˈstate agent (*AmE* **realtor**™; **real estate agent**) *noun* [C] a person whose job is to buy and sell houses and land for other people ➲ note at **house**

eˈstate car (*AmE* **station wagon**) *noun* [C] a car with a door at the back and a long area for luggage behind the back seat

esteem /ɪˈstiːm/ *noun* [U] (*formal*) great respect; a good opinion of sb

esthetic (*AmE*) = **aesthetic**

esthetics (*AmE*) = **aesthetics**

estimate[1] /ˈestɪmət/ *noun* [C] **1** an estimate (of sth) a guess or judgement about the size, cost, etc. of sth, before you have all the facts and figures: *Can you give me* ***a rough estimate*** *of how many people will be at the meeting?* ♦ ***At a conservative estimate*** (= the real figure will probably be higher), *the job will take six months to complete.* **2** an estimate (for sth/doing sth) a written statement from a person who is going to do a job for you, for example a builder, telling you how much it will probably cost: *They gave me an estimate for repairing the roof.* ➲ look at **quotation**
IDM **a ballpark figure/estimate** ➲ **ballpark**

estimate[2] /ˈestɪmeɪt/ *verb* [T] estimate sth (at sth); estimate that ... to calculate the size, cost, etc. of sth approximately, before you have all the facts and figures: *The police estimated the crowd at 10 000.* ♦ *She estimated that the work would take three months.*

estimation /ˌestɪˈmeɪʃn/ *noun* [U] (*formal*) opinion or judgement: *Who is to blame, **in your estimation**?*

estranged /ɪˈstreɪndʒd/ *adj* **1** no longer living with your husband/wife: *her estranged husband* **2** estranged (from sb) no longer friendly or in contact with sb who was close to you: *He became estranged from his family following an argument.*

estuary /ˈestʃuəri/ *noun* [C] (*pl* estuaries) the wide part of a river where it joins the sea ➲ picture on page P10

🔑 **etc.** *abbr* **et cetera**; and so on, and other things of a similar kind: *sandwiches, biscuits, cakes, etc.*

eternal /ɪˈtɜːnl/ *adj* **1** without beginning or end; existing or continuing for ever: *Some people believe in eternal life* (= after death). **2** [only *before* a noun] happening too often; seeming to last for ever: *I'm tired of these eternal arguments!* ▶ **eternally** /-nəli/ *adv*: *I'll be **eternally grateful** if you could help.*

eternity /ɪˈtɜːnəti/ *noun* **1** [U] time that has no end; the state or time after death **2 an eternity** [sing] (*informal*) a period of time that never seems to end: *It seemed like an eternity before the ambulance arrived.*

ethical /ˈeθɪkl/ *adj* **1** connected with beliefs about what is right or wrong: *That is an ethical problem.* **2** morally correct: *Although she didn't break the law, her behaviour was certainly not ethical.* ▶ **ethically** /-kli/ *adv*

ethics /ˈeθɪks/ *noun* **1** [pl] beliefs about what is morally correct or acceptable: *The medical profession has its own **code of ethics**.* **2** [U] the study of what is right and wrong in human behaviour

ethnic /ˈeθnɪk/ *adj* connected with or typical of a particular race or people that share a cultural tradition: *ethnic minorities* ◆ *ethnic food/music/clothes*

ˌethnic ˈcleansing *noun* [U] the policy of forcing people of a certain race or religion to leave an area or country

etiquette /ˈetɪket/ *noun* [U] the rules of polite and correct behaviour: *professional etiquette* ➲ look at **netiquette**

etymology /ˌetɪˈmɒlədʒi/ *noun* (*pl* etymologies) **1** [U] the study of the origins and history of words and their meanings **2** [C] an explanation of the origin and history of a particular word

EU /ˌiː ˈjuː/ *abbr* = **European Union**

euphemism /ˈjuːfəmɪzəm/ *noun* [C,U] using a polite word or expression instead of a more direct one when you are talking about sth that is unpleasant or embarrassing; a word used in this way: *'Pass away' is a euphemism for 'die'.* ▶ **euphemistic** /ˌjuːfəˈmɪstɪk/ *adj*

euphoria /juːˈfɔːriə/ *noun* [U] (*formal*) a feeling of great happiness ▶ **euphoric** /juːˈfɒrɪk/ *adj*: *My euphoric mood could not last.*

🔑 **euro** /ˈjʊərəʊ/ *noun* [C] (*symbol* €) (*pl* euros *or* euro) (since 1999) a unit of money used in some countries of the European Union: *The price is given in dollars or euros.* ➲ look at **EMU**

European[1] /ˌjʊərəˈpiːən/ *adj* of or from Europe: *European languages*

European[2] /ˌjʊərəˈpiːən/ *noun* [C] a person from a European country

the ˌEuropean ˈUnion *noun* [sing] (*abbr* EU) an economic and political association of certain European countries

euthanasia /ˌjuːθəˈneɪziə/ *noun* [U] the practice (illegal in most countries) of killing without pain sb who wants to die because they are suffering from a disease that cannot be cured

evacuate /ɪˈvækjueɪt/ *verb* [I,T] to move people from a dangerous place to somewhere safer; to leave a place because it is dangerous: *Thousands of people were evacuated from the war zone.* ◆ *The village had to be evacuated when the river burst its banks.* ◆ *Locals were told to evacuate.* ▶ **evacuation** /ɪˌvækjuˈeɪʃn/ *noun* [C,U]

evade /ɪˈveɪd/ *verb* [T] **1** to manage to escape from or to avoid meeting sb/sth: *They managed to evade capture and escaped to France.* **2** to avoid dealing with or doing sth: *to evade responsibility* ◆ *I asked her directly, but she evaded the question.* ➲ *noun* **evasion**

evaluate /ɪˈvæljueɪt/ *verb* [T] (*formal*) to study the facts and then form an opinion about sth: *We evaluated the situation very carefully before we made our decision.* ▶ **evaluation** /ɪˌvæljuˈeɪʃn/ *noun* [C,U]

evangelical /ˌiːvænˈdʒelɪkl/ *adj* of or belonging to a Christian group that emphasizes the authority of the Bible and the importance of people being saved through faith

evaporate /ɪˈvæpəreɪt/ *verb* **1** [I,T] (used about a liquid) to change into steam or gas and disappear: *The water evaporated in the sunshine.* ➲ look at **condense** **2** [T] to disappear completely: *All her confidence evaporated when she saw the exam paper.* ▶ **evaporation** /ɪˌvæpəˈreɪʃn/ *noun* [U]

evasion /ɪˈveɪʒn/ *noun* [C,U] **1** the act of avoiding sth that you should do: *He has been sentenced to two years' imprisonment for **tax evasion**.* ◆ *an evasion of responsibility* **2** a statement that avoids dealing with a question or subject in a direct way: *The President's reply was full of evasions.* ➲ *verb* **evade**

evasive /ɪˈveɪsɪv/ *adj* trying to avoid sth; not direct: *Ann gave an evasive answer.*

eve /iːv/ *noun* [C] the day or evening before a religious festival, important event, etc: *New Year's Eve* ◆ *He injured himself on the eve of the final.*

🔑 **even**[1] /ˈiːvn/ *adj* **1** flat, level or smooth: *The game must be played on an even surface.* OPP **uneven** **2** not changing; regular: *He's very **even-tempered**—in fact I've never seen him angry.* **3** (used about a competition, etc.) equal, with one side being as good as the other: *The contest was very even until the last few minutes of the game.* OPP **uneven** **4** (used about numbers) that can be divided by two: *2, 4, 6, 8, 10, etc. are even numbers.* OPP **odd**

IDM be/get even (with sb) (*informal*) to hurt or harm sb who has hurt or harmed you
break even to make neither a loss nor a profit

even² /ˈiːvn/ *adv* **1** used for emphasizing sth that is surprising: *It isn't very warm here even in summer.* ♦ *He didn't even open the letter.* **2 even more, less, bigger, nicer, etc.** used when you are comparing things, to make the comparison stronger: *You know even less about it than I do.* ♦ *It is even more difficult than I expected.* ♦ *We are even busier than yesterday.*
IDM even if used for saying that what follows 'if' makes no difference: *I wouldn't ride a horse, even if you paid me.*
even so (used for introducing a new idea, fact, etc. that is surprising) in spite of that: *There are a lot of spelling mistakes; even so it's quite a good essay.* **SYN nevertheless**
even though although: *I like her very much even though she can be very annoying.* ➲ note at **although**

evening /ˈiːvnɪŋ/ *noun* [C,U] the part of the day between the afternoon and the time that you go to bed: *What are you doing this evening?* ♦ *We were out yesterday evening.* ♦ *I went to the cinema on Saturday evening.* ♦ *Tom usually goes swimming on Wednesday evenings.* ♦ *Most people watch TV* ***in the evening.*** ♦ *an evening class* (= a course of lessons for adults that takes place in the evening) ➲ note at **morning**
IDM good evening (*formal*) used when you see sb for the first time in the evening

HELP Often we just say **Evening**: *'Good evening, Mrs Wilson.' 'Evening, Mr Mills.'*

evenly /ˈiːvnli/ *adv* in a smooth, regular or equal way: *The match was very evenly balanced.* ♦ *Spread the cake mixture evenly in the tin.*

event /ɪˈvent/ *noun* [C] **1** something that happens, especially sth important or unusual: *a historic event* ♦ *The events of the past few days have made things very difficult for the Government.* **2** a planned public or social occasion: *a fund-raising event* **3** one of the races, competitions, etc. in a sports programme: *The next event is the 800 metres.*
IDM at all events/in any event whatever happens: *I hope to see you soon, but in any event I'll phone you on Sunday.*
in the event of sth (*formal*) if sth happens: *In the event of fire, leave the building as quickly as possible.*

eventful /ɪˈventfl/ *adj* full of important, dangerous or exciting things happening

eventual /ɪˈventʃuəl/ *adj* [only *before* a noun] happening at the end of a period of time or a process: *It is impossible to say what the eventual cost will be.*

eventually /ɪˈventʃuəli/ *adv* in the end; finally: *He eventually managed to persuade his parents to let him buy a motorbike.* **SYN finally**

ever /ˈevə(r)/ *adv* **1** (used in questions and negative sentences, and in sentences with *if*) at any time: *Do you ever wish you were famous?* ♦ *Nobody ever comes to see me.* ♦ *She* ***hardly ever*** (= almost never) *goes out.* ♦ *If you ever visit England, you must come and stay with us.* ♦ *Have you ever been to Spain?* **2** when you are comparing things: *Today is hotter* ***than ever.*** ♦ *This is the best meal I have ever had.* **3** used with a question that begins with 'when', 'where', 'who', 'how', etc. to show that you are surprised or shocked: ***How ever*** *did he get back so quickly?* ♦ ***What ever*** *were you thinking about when you wrote this?* ➲ look at **whatever, whenever, however**
IDM (as) bad, good, etc. as ever (as) bad, good, etc. as usual or as always: *In spite of his problems, Andrew is as cheerful as ever.*
ever after (used especially at the end of stories) from that moment on for always: *The prince married the princess and they lived happily ever after.*
ever since ... all the time from ... until now: *She has had a car ever since she was at university.*
ever so/ever such (a) (*BrE informal*) very: *He's ever so kind.* ♦ *He's ever such a kind man.*
for ever ➲ **forever**

ever- /ˈevə(r)/ [in compounds] always; continuously: *the ever-growing problem of pollution*

evergreen /ˈevəgriːn/ *noun* [C], *adj* (a tree or bush) with green leaves all through the year ➲ look at **deciduous**

everlasting /ˌevəˈlɑːstɪŋ/ *adj* (*formal*) continuing for ever; never changing: *everlasting life/love*

every /ˈevri/ *determiner* **1** [used with singular nouns] all of the people or things in a group of three or more: *She knows every student in the school.* ♦ *There are 200 students in the school, and she knows every one of them.* ♦ *I've read every book in this house.* ♦ *You were out every time I phoned.* ➲ note at **everybody** **2** all that is possible: *You have every chance of success.* ♦ *She had every reason to be angry.* **3** used for saying how often sth happens: *We see each other* ***every day.*** ♦ *Take the medicine every four hours* (= at 8, 12, 4 o'clock, etc.). ♦ *I work* ***every other day*** (= on Monday, Wednesday, Friday, etc.). ♦ ***One in every*** *three marriages ends in divorce.*

everybody /ˈevribɒdi/ (also **everyone** /ˈevriwʌn/) *pron* [with sing verb] every person; all people: *Is everybody here?* ♦ *The police questioned everyone who was at the party.* ♦ *I'm sure everybody else* (= all the other people) *will agree with me.* ➲ note at **somebody**

HELP Everyone is only used about people and is not followed by 'of'. **Every one** means 'each individual person or thing' and is often followed by 'of': ***Every one of*** *his records has been successful.*

everyday /ˈevrideɪ/ *adj* [only *before* a noun] normal or usual: *The Internet is now part of everyday life.*

everyone = **everybody**

everyplace (*AmE*) = **everywhere**

everything /ˈevriθɪŋ/ *pron* [with sing verb] **1** each thing; all things: *Sam lost everything in the fire.* ♦ *Everything is very expensive in this shop.* ♦ *We can leave* ***everything else*** (= all the other things) *until* *tomorrow.* **2** the most important thing: *Money isn't everything.*

everywhere /ˈevriweə(r)/ (*AmE* also **everyplace** /ˈevripleɪs/) *adv* in or to every place: *I've looked everywhere.*

evict /ɪˈvɪkt/ *verb* [T] to force sb (officially) to leave the house or land which they are renting: *They were evicted for not paying the rent.* ▶ **eviction** *noun* [C,U]

evidence /ˈevɪdəns/ *noun* [U] **evidence (of/for sth); evidence that ...** the facts, signs, etc. that make you believe that sth is true: *There was no evidence of a struggle in the room.* ◆ *You have absolutely no evidence for what you're saying!* ◆ *There was not enough evidence to prove him guilty.* ◆ *Her statement to the police was **used in evidence** against him.* ◆ *The witnesses to the accident will be asked to **give evidence** in court.* ➲ note at **court** ➲ look at **proof**

> **GRAMMAR** Evidence is uncountable, so you cannot say 'an evidence', you must say 'a piece of evidence': *One **piece of evidence** is not enough to prove somebody guilty.*

IDM (to be) in evidence that you can see; present in a place: *When we arrived, there was no ambulance in evidence.*

evident /ˈevɪdənt/ *adj* clear (to the eye or mind); obvious: *It was evident that the damage was very serious.*

evidently /ˈevɪdəntli/ *adv* **1** clearly; in a way that can be easily seen or understood: *She was evidently extremely shocked at the news.* **2** according to what people say: *Evidently he has decided to leave.*

evil[1] /ˈiːvl/ *adj* morally bad; causing trouble or harming people: *In the play, Richard is portrayed as an evil king.* **OPP good**

evil[2] /ˈiːvl/ *noun* [U,C] a force that causes bad or harmful things to happen: *The play is about the good and evil in all of us.* ◆ *Drugs and alcohol are two of the evils of modern society.* **OPP good**

IDM the lesser of two evils ➲ **lesser**

evocative /ɪˈvɒkətɪv/ *adj* **evocative (of sth)** making you think of or remember a strong image or feeling, in a pleasant way: *evocative smells/sounds/music* ◆ *Her new book is wonderfully evocative of village life.*

evoke /ɪˈvəʊk/ *verb* [T] (*formal*) to produce a memory, feeling, etc. in sb in a pleasant way: *For me, that music always evokes hot summer evenings.* ◆ *Her novel evoked a lot of interest.*

evolution /ˌiːvəˈluːʃn; ˌev-/ *noun* [U] **1** the gradual development of plants, animals, etc. over many years as they adapt to changes in their environment: *Darwin's theory of evolution* **2** the process of change and development of sth that happens gradually: *Political evolution is a slow process.*

evolve /iˈvɒlv/ *verb* **1** [I,T] (*formal*) to develop or to make sth develop gradually, from a simple to a more advanced form: *His style of painting has evolved gradually over the past 20 years.* **2** [I] **evolve (from sth)** (used about plants, animals, etc.) to develop over many thousands of years from simple forms to more advanced ones

ewe /juː/ *noun* [C] a female sheep ➲ note at **sheep** ➲ picture at **goat**

ex- /eks/ [prefix] [in nouns] former: *ex-wife* ◆ *ex-president*

exacerbate /ɪɡˈzæsəbeɪt/ *verb* [T] (*formal*) to make sth worse, especially a disease or problem: *The symptoms may be exacerbated by stress.* **SYN aggravate** ▶ **exacerbation** /ɪɡˌzæsəˈbeɪʃn/ *noun* [C,U]

exact[1] /ɪɡˈzækt/ *adj* **1** (completely) correct; accurate: *He's in his mid-fifties. Well, 56 **to be exact**.* ◆ *I can't tell you the exact number of people who are coming.* ◆ *She's **the exact opposite** of her sister.* **2** able to work in a way that is completely accurate: *You need to be very exact when you calculate the costs.* ▶ **exactness** *noun* [U]

exact[2] /ɪɡˈzækt/ *verb* [T] (*formal*) **exact sth (from sb)** to demand and get sth from sb

exacting /ɪɡˈzæktɪŋ/ *adj* needing a lot of care and attention; difficult: *exacting work*

exactly /ɪɡˈzæktli/ *adv* **1** (used to emphasize that sth is correct in every way) just: *You've arrived at exactly the right moment.* ◆ *I found exactly what I wanted.* **2** used to ask for, or give, completely correct information: *He took exactly one hour to finish.* **3** (*spoken*) (used for agreeing with a statement) yes; you are right: *'I don't think she's old enough to travel on her own.' 'Exactly.'* **SYN** for all meanings **precisely**

IDM not exactly (*spoken*) **1** (used when you are saying the opposite of what you really mean) not really; not at all: *He's not exactly the most careful driver I know.* **2** used as an answer to say that sth is almost true: *'So you think I'm wrong?' 'No, not exactly, but ...'*

exaggerate /ɪɡˈzædʒəreɪt/ *verb* [I,T] to make sth seem larger, better, worse, etc. than it really is: *Don't exaggerate. I was only two minutes late, not twenty.* ◆ *The problems have been greatly exaggerated.* ▶ **exaggerated** *adj*: *exaggerated claims* ▶ **exaggeration** /ɪɡˌzædʒəˈreɪʃn/ *noun* [C,U]: *It's rather an exaggeration to say that all the students are lazy.*

exam /ɪɡˈzæm/ (also *formal* **examination**) *noun* [C] a written, spoken or practical test of what you know or can do: *an English exam* ◆ *the exam results* ◆ *to **do/take/sit an exam*** ◆ *to **pass/fail an exam*** ◆ *to **revise for an exam*** ➲ note at **pass, study**

> **HELP** Exam or test? A **test** is usually shorter and less important than an exam.

ℹ There are many notes in this dictionary to help you to prepare for exams. A list at the back of the dictionary shows you where to find them.

examination /ɪɡˌzæmɪˈneɪʃn/ *noun* **1** [C] (*formal*) = **exam** **2** [C,U] the act of looking at sb/sth carefully, especially to see if there is anything wrong or to find the cause of a problem: *a medical examination* ◆ ***On close examination**, it was found that the passport was false.*

E

examine /ɪɡˈzæmɪn/ *verb* [T] **1** to consider or study an idea, a subject, etc. very carefully: *These theories will be examined in more detail later on in the lecture.* **2 examine sb/sth (for sth)** to look at sb/sth carefully in order to find out sth: *The doctor examined me, but she couldn't find anything wrong* ◆ *The detective examined the room for clues.* **3** (*formal*) **examine sb (in/on sth)** to test what sb knows or can do: *You will be examined on everything that has been taught in the course.*

examiner /ɪɡˈzæmɪnə(r)/ *noun* [C] a person who tests sb in an exam

example /ɪɡˈzɑːmpl/ *noun* [C] **1 an example (of sth)** something such as an object, a fact or a situation which shows, explains or supports what you say: *I don't quite understand you. Can you* ***give me an example of*** *what you mean?* ◆ *This is* ***a typical example of*** *a Victorian house.* **2 an example (to sb)** a person or thing or a type of behaviour that is good and should be copied: *Joe's bravery should be an example to us all.*

IDM **follow sb's example/lead** ➲ **follow**

for example [The abbreviation for this is **e.g.**] used for giving a fact, situation, etc. which explains or supports what you are talking about: *In many countries, for example Spain, family life is much more important than here.* ◆ *popular pets, e.g. cats and dogs*

WRITING TIP

Giving examples

When you are writing, giving examples helps to support your argument. You can use any of these phrases: *There is a similar word in many languages,* ***for example*** *in French and Italian.* ◆ *The report is incomplete; it does not include sales in France,* ***for instance****.* ◆ *It is possible to combine Computer Science with other subjects* ***such as*** *Physics.*

ℹ For more help with writing, look at **Wordpower Writing Tutor** at the back of this dictionary.

set a(n) (good/bad) example (to sb) to behave in a way that should/should not be copied: *Parents should always take care when crossing roads in order to set a good example to their children.*

exasperate /ɪɡˈzæspəreɪt/ *verb* [T] to make sb angry; to annoy sb very much: *This lack of progress exasperates me.* ▶ **exasperated** *adj*: *She was becoming exasperated with all their questions.* ▶ **exasperating** *adj*: *an exasperating problem* ▶ **exasperation** /ɪɡˌzæspəˈreɪʃn/ *noun* [U]: *He finally threw the book across the room* ***in exasperation****.*

excavate /ˈekskəveɪt/ *verb* [I,T] to dig in the ground to look for old objects or buildings that have been buried for a long time; to find sth by digging in this way: *A Roman villa has been excavated in a valley near the village.* ▶ **excavation** /ˌekskəˈveɪʃn/ *noun* [C,U]: *Excavations on the site have revealed Saxon objects.*

exceed /ɪkˈsiːd/ *verb* [T] **1** to be more than a particular number or amount: *The weight should not exceed 20 kilos.* **2** to do more than the law, a rule, an order, etc. allows you to do: *He was stopped by the police for exceeding the speed limit* (= driving faster than is allowed). ➲ look at **excess, excessive**

exceedingly /ɪkˈsiːdɪŋli/ *adv* (*formal*) very: *an exceedingly difficult problem*

excel /ɪkˈsel/ *verb* (**excelling**; **excelled**) (*formal*) **1** [I] **excel (in/at sth/doing sth)** to be very good at doing sth: *Regina excels at sports.* **2** [T] (*BrE*) **excel yourself** to do sth even better than you usually do: *Rick's cooking is always good but this time he really excelled himself.*

excellence /ˈeksələns/ *noun* [U] the quality of being very good: *The head teacher said that she wanted the school to be a centre of academic excellence.*

excellent /ˈeksələnt/ *adj* very good; of high quality: *He speaks excellent French.* ➲ note at **good** ▶ **excellently** *adv*

except[1] /ɪkˈsept/ *prep* **except (for) sb/sth; except that ...** not including sb/sth; apart from the fact that: *The museum is open every day except Mondays.* ◆ *I can answer all of the questions except for the last one.* ◆ *It was a good hotel except that it was rather noisy.*

except[2] /ɪkˈsept/ *verb* [T, often passive] (*formal*) **except sb/sth (from sth)** to leave sb/sth out; to not include sb/sth: *Nobody is excepted from helping with the housework.* ▶ **excepting** *prep*: *I swim every day excepting Sundays.*

exception /ɪkˈsepʃn/ *noun* [C] a person or thing that is not included in a general statement: *Most of his songs are awful but this one is an exception.* ◆ *Everybody was poor as a student and I was* ***no exception****.*

IDM **make an exception (of sb/sth)** to treat sb/sth differently: *We don't usually allow children under 14 but we'll make an exception in your case.*

with the exception of except for; apart from: *He has won every major tennis championship with the exception of Wimbledon.*

without exception in every case; including everyone/everything: *Everybody without exception must take the test.*

exceptional /ɪkˈsepʃənl/ *adj* **1** very unusual: *You will only be allowed to leave early in exceptional circumstances.* **2** unusually good: *We have had a really exceptional summer.* SYN **outstanding** ▶ **exceptionally** /-ʃənəli/ *adv*: *The past year has been exceptionally difficult for us.*

excerpt /ˈeksɜːpt/ *noun* [C] a short piece taken from a book, film, piece of music, etc.

excess[1] /ɪkˈses/ *noun* [sing] **an excess (of sth)** more of sth than is necessary or usual; too much of sth: *An excess of fat in your diet can lead to heart disease.*

IDM **in excess of** more than: *Her debts are in excess of £1 000.* ➲ *verb* **exceed**

excess[2] /ˈekses/ *adj* [only *before* a noun] more than is usual or allowed; extra: *Cut any excess fat off the meat.* ➲ *verb* **exceed**

ˌexcess ˈbaggage *noun* [U] bags, cases, etc. taken on to a plane that weigh more than the amount each passenger is allowed to carry without paying extra: *Her luggage was over 23 kilos, and she had to pay excess baggage charges.*

excessive /ɪk'sesɪv/ *adj* too much; too great or extreme: *He was driving at excessive speed when he crashed.* ▶ **excessively** *adv*

⚷ **exchange**[1] /ɪks'tʃeɪndʒ/ *noun* **1** [C,U] giving or receiving sth in return for sth else: *a useful exchange of information* ♦ *We can offer free accommodation* ***in exchange for*** *some help in the house.* **2** [U] the relation in value between kinds of money used in different countries: *What's the* ***exchange rate/rate of exchange*** *for dollars?* ➲ look at **foreign exchange**, **stock exchange** **3** [C] a visit by a group of students or teachers to another country and a return visit by a similar group from that country: *She went on an exchange to Germany when she was sixteen.* **4** [C] an angry conversation or argument: *She had a* ***heated exchange*** *with her neighbours about the noise the night before.* **5** [C] = **telephone exchange**

⚷ **exchange**[2] /ɪks'tʃeɪndʒ/ *verb* [T] **exchange sth for sth; exchange sth (with sb)** to give or receive sth in return for sth else: *I would like to exchange this skirt for a bigger size.* ♦ *Claire and Molly exchanged phone numbers with the boys.* ♦ *They exchanged glances* (= they looked at each other). ➲ note at **shopping**

excise /'eksaɪz/ *noun* [U] a government tax on certain goods that are produced or sold inside a country, for example cigarettes, alcohol, etc. ➲ look at **customs**

excitable /ɪk'saɪtəbl/ *adj* easily excited

⚷ **excite** /ɪk'saɪt/ *verb* [T] **1** to make sb feel happy and enthusiastic or nervous: *Don't excite the baby too much or we'll never get him off to sleep.* **2** to make sb react in a particular way: *The programme excited great interest.*

⚷ **excited** /ɪk'saɪtɪd/ *adj* **excited (about/at/by sth)** feeling or showing happiness and enthusiasm; not calm: *Are you getting excited about your holiday?* ♦ *We're all very excited at the thought of moving house.* ▶ **excitedly** *adv*

⚷ **excitement** /ɪk'saɪtmənt/ *noun* [U] the state of being excited, especially because sth interesting is happening or will happen: *There was* ***great excitement*** *as the winner's name was announced.* ♦ *The match was* ***full of excitement*** *until the very last minute.*

⚷ **exciting** /ɪk'saɪtɪŋ/ *adj* causing strong feelings of pleasure and interest: *That's very exciting news.* ♦ *Berlin is one of the most exciting cities in Europe.*

exclaim /ɪk'skleɪm/ *verb* [I,T] to say sth suddenly and loudly because you are surprised, angry, etc: *'I just don't believe it!' he exclaimed.*

exclamation /ˌekskləˈmeɪʃn/ *noun* [C] a short sound, word or phrase that you say suddenly because of a strong emotion, pain, etc: *'Ouch!' is an exclamation.* SYN **interjection**

ˌexcla'mation mark (*AmE* ˌexcla'mation point) *noun* [C] a mark (!) that is written after an **exclamation**

⚷ **exclude** /ɪk'sklu:d/ *verb* [T] [not used in the continuous tenses] **1** to leave out; not include: *The price excludes all extras such as drinks or excursions.* OPP **include** **2 exclude sb/sth (from sth)** to prevent sb/sth from entering a place or taking part in sth: *Women are excluded from the temple.* ♦ *Jake was excluded from the game for cheating.* OPP **include** **3** to decide that sth is not possible: *The police had* ***excluded the possibility*** *that the child had run away.*

⚷ **excluding** /ɪk'sklu:dɪŋ/ *prep* leaving out; without: *Lunch costs £10 per person excluding drinks.* OPP **including**

exclusion /ɪk'sklu:ʒn/ *noun* [U] keeping or leaving sb/sth out

exclusive[1] /ɪk'sklu:sɪv/ *adj* **1** [only *before* a noun] only to be used by or given to one person, group, etc.; not to be shared: *This car is for the Director's exclusive use.* ♦ *Tonight we are showing an exclusive interview with the new leader of the Labour Party* (= on only one TV or radio station). **2** expensive and not welcoming people who are thought to be of a lower social class: *an exclusive restaurant* ♦ *a flat in an exclusive part of the city* **3 exclusive of sb/sth** not including sb/sth; without: *Lunch costs £10 per person exclusive of drinks.*

exclusive[2] /ɪk'sklu:sɪv/ *noun* [C] a newspaper story that is given to and published by only one newspaper

exclusively /ɪk'sklu:sɪvli/ *adv* only; not involving anyone/anything else: *The swimming pool is reserved exclusively for members of the club.*

excrement /'ekskrɪmənt/ *noun* [U] (*formal*) the solid waste material that you get rid of from your body when you go to the toilet SYN **faeces**

excrete /ɪk'skri:t/ *verb* [T] (*formal*) to get rid of solid waste material from the body

excruciating /ɪk'skru:ʃieɪtɪŋ/ *adj* extremely painful

excursion /ɪk'skɜ:ʃn/ *noun* [C] a short journey or trip that a group of people make for pleasure: *to* ***go on an excursion*** *to the seaside* ➲ note at **travel**

excusable /ɪk'skju:zəbl/ *adj* that you can forgive: *an excusable mistake* OPP **inexcusable**

⚷ **excuse**[1] /ɪk'skju:s/ *noun* [C] **an excuse (for sth/doing sth)** a reason (that may or may not be true) that you give in order to explain your behaviour: *There's* ***no excuse for*** *rudeness.* ♦ *He always* ***finds an excuse*** *for not helping with the housework.* ♦ *to* ***make an excuse***

⚷ **excuse**[2] /ɪk'skju:z/ *verb* [T] **1 excuse sb/sth (for sth/for doing sth)** to forgive sb for sth they have done wrong that is not very serious: *Please excuse the interruption but I need to talk to you.* ➲ Note on **page 258** **2** to explain sb's bad behaviour and make it seem less bad: *Nothing can excuse such behaviour.* **3 excuse sb (from sth)** to free sb from a duty, responsibility, etc: *She excused herself* (= asked if she could leave) *and left the meeting early.*

HELP The expression **excuse me** is used when you interrupt somebody or when you want to start talking to somebody that you don't know: *Excuse me, can you tell me the way to the station?* In American English, and occasionally in British English, **excuse me** is used when you apologize for something: *Did I tread on your toe? Excuse me.*

E

execute /ˈeksɪkjuːt/ *verb* [T] **1** [usually passive] **execute sb (for sth)** to kill sb as an official punishment: *He was executed for murder.* **2** (*formal*) to perform a task, etc. or to put a plan into action ▶ **execution** /ˌeksɪˈkjuːʃn/ *noun* [C,U]

executioner /ˌeksɪˈkjuːʃənə(r)/ *noun* [C] a person whose job is to **execute** criminals

executive¹ /ɪɡˈzekjətɪv/ *noun* **1** [C] a person who has an important position as a manager of a business or an organization: *She's a senior executive in a computer company.* **2** [C, with sing or pl verb] the group of people who are in charge of an organization or a company: *The executive has/have yet to reach a decision.* **3 the executive** [sing, with sing or pl verb] the part of a government responsible for putting new laws into effect ➲ look at **judiciary**, **legislature**

executive² /ɪɡˈzekjətɪv/ *adj* [only *before* a noun] **1** (used in connection with people in business, government, etc.) concerned with managing, making plans, decisions, etc: *an executive director of the company* ◆ *executive decisions/jobs/duties* **2** (used about goods, buildings, etc.) designed to be used by important business people: *an executive briefcase*

exemplary /ɪɡˈzempləri/ *adj* very good; that can be an example to other people: *exemplary behaviour*

exemplify /ɪɡˈzemplɪfaɪ/ *verb* [T] (**exemplifying**; **exemplifies**; *pt, pp* **exemplified**) to be a typical example of sth

exempt¹ /ɪɡˈzempt/ *adj* [not before a noun] **exempt (from sth)** free from having to do sth or pay for sth: *Children under 16 are exempt from dental charges.*

exempt² /ɪɡˈzempt/ *verb* [T] (*formal*) **exempt sb/sth (from sth)** to say officially that sb does not have to do sth or pay for sth ▶ **exemption** *noun* [C,U]

exercise¹ /ˈeksəsaɪz/ *noun*

➤ACTIVITY **1** [U] physical or mental activity that keeps you healthy and strong: *The doctor advised Sebastian to* ***take regular exercise.*** ◆ *Swimming is a good form of exercise.* **2** [C, often plural] a movement or activity that you do in order to stay healthy or to become skilled at sth: *I* ***do*** *keep-fit* ***exercises*** *every morning.* ◆ *breathing/stretching/relaxation exercises*

➤STUDY **3** [C] a piece of work that is intended to help you learn or practise sth: *an exercise on phrasal verbs*

➤USE OF POWER, ETC. **4** [U] (*formal*) **exercise of sth** the use of sth, for example a power, right, etc: *the exercise of patience/judgement/discretion* ◆ *the exercise of power by the government*

➤FOR PARTICULAR RESULT **5** [C] **an exercise in sth** an activity or a series of actions that have a particular aim: *The project is an exercise in getting the best results at a low cost.*

➤FOR SOLDIERS **6** [C, usually pl] a series of activities by soldiers to practise fighting: *military exercises*

exercise

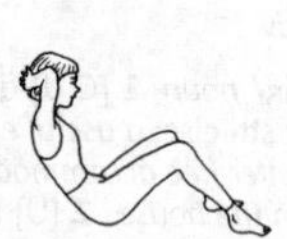
She's doing sit-ups.

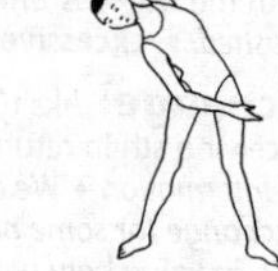
She's stretching.

He's doing press-ups (*AmE* **push-ups**).

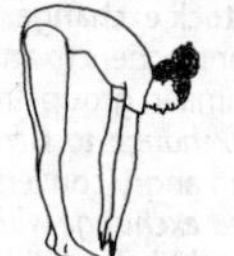
She's touching her toes.

exercise² /ˈeksəsaɪz/ *verb* **1** [T] to make use of sth, for example a power, right, etc: *You should exercise your right to vote.* **2** [I] to do some form of physical activity in order to stay fit and healthy: *It is important to exercise regularly.*

ˈ**exercise book** (*AmE* **notebook**) *noun* [C] a small book for students to write their work in

exert /ɪɡˈzɜːt/ *verb* [T] **1** to make use of sth, for example influence, strength, etc., to affect sb/sth: *Parents exert a powerful influence on their children's opinions.* **2 exert yourself** to make a big effort: *You won't make any progress if you don't exert yourself a bit more.*

exertion /ɪɡˈzɜːʃn/ *noun* [U,C] using your body in a way that takes a lot of effort; something that you do that makes you tired: *At his age physical exertion was dangerous.* ◆ *I'm tired after the exertions of the past few days.*

exhale /eksˈheɪl/ *verb* [I,T] (*formal*) to breathe out so that air leaves your lungs **OPP** **inhale** ▶ **exhalation** /ˌekshəˈleɪʃn/ *noun* [C,U]

exhaust¹ /ɪɡˈzɔːst/ *noun* **1** [U] the waste gas that comes out of a vehicle, an engine or a machine: *car exhaust fumes/emissions* **2** [C] (also **exˈhaust pipe**; *AmE* **tailpipe**) a pipe (particularly at the back of a car) through which waste gas escapes from an engine or machine ➲ picture on **page P7**

exhaust² /ɪɡˈzɔːst/ *verb* [T] **1** to make sb very tired: *The long journey to work every morning exhausted him.* **2** to use sth up completely; to finish sth: *All the supplies of food have been exhausted.* **3** to say everything you can about a subject: *Well, I think we've exhausted that topic.*

exhausted /ɪɡˈzɔːstɪd/ *adj* very tired

exhausting /ɪɡˈzɔːstɪŋ/ *adj* making sb very tired: *Teaching young children is exhausting work.*

exhaustion /ɪɡˈzɔːstʃən/ *noun* [U] the state of being very tired

exhaustive /ɪɡˈzɔːstɪv/ *adj* including everything possible: *This list is certainly not intended to be exhaustive.*

exˈhaust pipe = exhaust[1] (2)

exhibit[1] /ɪɡˈzɪbɪt/ *verb* [T] **1** to show sth in a public place for people to enjoy or to give them information: *His paintings have been exhibited in the local art gallery.* **2** (*formal*) to show clearly that you have a particular quality, feeling, etc: *The refugees are exhibiting signs of exhaustion and stress.*

exhibit[2] /ɪɡˈzɪbɪt/ *noun* [C] an object that is shown in a museum, etc. or as a piece of evidence in a court of law

exhibition /ˌeksɪˈbɪʃn/ *noun* **1** [C] a collection of objects, for example works of art, that are shown to the public: *an exhibition of photographs at the Mall Gallery* **2** [C] an occasion when a particular skill is shown to the public: *We saw an exhibition of Scottish dancing last night.* **3** [sing] (*formal*) the act of showing a quality, feeling, etc: *The game was a superb exhibition of football at its best.*

exhibitor /ɪɡˈzɪbɪtə(r)/ *noun* [C] a person or a company that shows their work or products to the public

exhilarate /ɪɡˈzɪləreɪt/ *verb* [T, usually passive] to make sb feel very excited and happy: *We felt exhilarated by our walk along the beach.* ▶ **exhilarating** *adj* ▶ **exhilaration** /ɪɡˌzɪləˈreɪʃn/ *noun* [U]

exile /ˈeksaɪl/ *noun* **1** [U] the state of being forced to live outside your own country (especially for political reasons): *The leader was deposed and driven into exile in 2009.* ♦ *They lived **in exile** in London for many years.* **2** [C] a person who is forced to live outside their own country (especially for political reasons) ➲ look at **refugee** ▶ **exile** *verb* [T, usually passive]: *After the revolution the king was exiled.*

exist /ɪɡˈzɪst/ *verb* [I] **1** [not used in the continuous tenses] to be real; to be found in the real world; to live: *Dreams only exist in our imagination.* ♦ *Fish cannot exist out of water.* **2 exist (on sth)** to manage to live: *I don't know how she exists on the wage she earns.*

existence /ɪɡˈzɪstəns/ *noun* **1** [U] the state of existing: *This is the oldest human skeleton **in existence**.* ♦ *How did the universe **come into existence**?* **2** [sing] a way of living, especially when it is difficult: *The family endured a miserable existence living in one small room together.*

existing /ɪɡˈzɪstɪŋ/ *adj* [only *before* a noun] that is already there or being used; present: *Under the existing law you are not allowed to work in this country.*

exit[1] /ˈeksɪt; ˈeɡzɪt/ *noun* [C] **1** a door or way out of a public building or vehicle: *The emergency exit is at the back of the bus.* OPP **entrance** **2** the act of leaving sth: *If I see her coming I'll make a quick exit.* ♦ *an exit visa* (= one that allows you to leave a country) **3** a place where traffic can leave a road or a **motorway** (= a wide road for fast traffic) to join another road: *At the roundabout take the third exit.*

exit[2] /ˈeksɪt; ˈeɡzɪt/ *verb* [I,T] (*formal*) **1** to leave a place: *He exited through the back door.* **2** to finish using a computer program: *I exited the database and switched off the computer.*

exodus /ˈeksədəs/ *noun* [sing] ~ (from ...) (to ...) (*formal*) a situation in which many people leave a place at the same time: *the **mass exodus** from Paris to the country in the summer*

exonerate /ɪɡˈzɒnəreɪt/ *verb* [T, often passive] (*formal*) to say officially that sb was not responsible for sth bad that happened

exorbitant /ɪɡˈzɔːbɪtənt/ *adj* (*formal*) (used about the cost of sth) much more expensive than it should be

exotic /ɪɡˈzɒtɪk/ *adj* unusual or interesting because it comes from a different country or culture: *exotic plants/animals/fruits*

expand /ɪkˈspænd/ *verb* [I,T] to become or to make sth bigger: *Metals expand when they are heated.* ♦ *We hope to expand our business this year.* OPP **contract**

PHR V **expand on sth** to give more details of a story, plan, idea, etc.

expanse /ɪkˈspæns/ *noun* [C] a large open area (of land, sea, sky, etc.): *I lay on my back and stared up at the vast expanse of blue sky.*

expansion /ɪkˈspænʃn/ *noun* [U] the act of becoming bigger or of making sth become bigger: *The rapid expansion of the university has caused a lot of problems.*

expansive /ɪkˈspænsɪv/ *adj* (*formal*) (used about a person) talking a lot in an interesting way; friendly

expatriate /ˌeksˈpætriət/ (also *informal* **expat** /ˌeksˈpæt/) *noun* [C] a person who lives outside their own country: *American expatriates in London*

expect /ɪkˈspekt/ *verb* [T] **1** to think or believe that sb/sth will come or that sth will happen: *She was expecting a letter from the bank this morning but it didn't come.* ♦ *I expect that it will rain this afternoon.* ♦ *I know the food's not so good, but what did you expect from such a cheap restaurant?* (= it's not surprising) ♦ *She's expecting a baby in the spring* (= she's pregnant). ➲ note at **wait[1]** **2 expect sth (from sb); expect sb to do sth** to feel confident that you will get sth from sb or that they will do what you want: *He expects a high standard of work from everyone.* ♦ *Factory workers are often expected to work at nights.* **3** [not used in the continuous tenses] (*BrE*) to think that sth is true or correct; to suppose: *'Whose is this suitcase?' 'Oh it's Angela's, I expect.'* ♦ *'Will you be able to help me later?' '**I expect so**.'*

expectancy /ɪkˈspektənsi/ *noun* [U] the state of expecting sth, especially sth good, to happen; hope: *a look/feeling of expectancy* ➲ look at **life expectancy**

expectant /ɪkˈspektənt/ *adj* **1** hoping for sth good and exciting: *an expectant audience* ♦ *expect-*

E

ant faces **2** having a baby soon: *an expectant mother/father* ▶ **expectantly** *adv*

🔑 **expectation** /ˌekspekˈteɪʃn/ *noun* (*formal*) **1** [C,U] **expectation (of sth)** the belief that sth will happen or come: *The dog was sitting under the table **in expectation** of food.* **2** [C, usually pl] hope for the future: *They had great expectations for their son, but he didn't really live up to them.*

IDM against/contrary to (all) expectation(s) very different to what was expected: *Contrary to all expectations, Val won first prize.*

not come up to (sb's) expectations to not be as good as expected

expected /ɪkˈspektɪd/ *adj* that you think will happen: *Double the expected number of people came to the meeting.* **OPP unexpected**

expedient /ɪkˈspiːdiənt/ *adj* (*formal*) (used about an action) convenient or helpful for a purpose, but possibly not completely honest or moral: *The government decided that it was expedient not to increase taxes until after the election.* ▶ **expediency** /ɪkˈspiːdiənsi/ *noun* [U]

expedition /ˌekspəˈdɪʃn/ *noun* [C] **1** a long journey for a special purpose: *a scientific expedition to Antarctica* **2** a short journey that you make for pleasure: *a fishing expedition*

expel /ɪkˈspel/ *verb* [T] (**expelling**; **expelled**) **1** to force sb to leave a country, school, club, etc: *The government has expelled all foreign journalists.* ◆ *The boy was expelled from school for smoking.* ◆ *The boy was expelled from school for fighting.* **2** (*technical*) to send sth out by force: *to expel air from the lungs* ➲ *noun* **expulsion**

expend /ɪkˈspend/ *verb* [T] (*formal*) **expend sth (on sth)** to spend or use money, time, care, etc. in doing sth: *I have expended a lot of time and energy on that project.*

expendable /ɪkˈspendəbl/ *adj* (*formal*) not considered important enough to be saved: *In a war human life is expendable.*

expenditure /ɪkˈspendɪtʃə(r)/ *noun* [U, sing] (*formal*) the act of spending money; the amount of money that is spent: *Government expenditure on education has been cut.*

🔑 **expense** /ɪkˈspens/ *noun* **1** [C,U] the cost of sth in time or money: *Running a car is a great expense.* ◆ *The movie was filmed in Tahiti **at great expense**.* **2 expenses** [pl] money that is spent for a particular purpose: *You can claim back your travelling expenses.*

IDM at sb's expense 1 with sb paying; at sb's cost: *My trip is at the company's expense.* **2** against sb, so that they look silly: *They were always making jokes at Paul's expense.*

at the expense of sth harming or damaging sth: *He was a successful businessman, but it was at the expense of his family life.*

🔑 **expensive** /ɪkˈspensɪv/ *adj* costing a lot of money: *Houses are very expensive in this area.* **OPP inexpensive, cheap** ▶ **expensively** *adv*

🔑 **experience¹** /ɪkˈspɪəriəns/ *noun* **1** [U] the things that you have done in your life; the knowledge or skill that you get from seeing or doing sth: *We all learn **by experience**.* ◆ *She has five years' teaching experience.* ◆ *I know **from experience** what will happen.* **2** [C] something that has happened to you (often sth unusual or exciting): *She wrote a book about her experiences in Africa.*

🔑 **experience²** /ɪkˈspɪəriəns/ *verb* [T] to have sth happen to you; to feel: *It was the first time I'd ever experienced failure.* ◆ *to experience pleasure/pain/difficulty*

🔑 **experienced** /ɪkˈspɪəriənst/ *adj* having the knowledge or skill that is necessary for sth: *He's an experienced diver.* **OPP inexperienced**

🔑 **experiment¹** /ɪkˈsperɪmənt/ *noun* [C,U] a scientific test that is done in order to get proof of sth or to get new knowledge: *to carry out/perform/conduct/do an experiment* ◆ *We need to prove this theory **by experiment**.*

🔑 **experiment²** /ɪkˈsperɪmənt/ *verb* [I] **experiment (on/with sth)** to do tests to see if sth works or to try to improve it: *Is it really necessary to experiment on animals?* ◆ *We're experimenting with a new timetable this month.*

experimental /ɪkˌsperɪˈmentl/ *adj* connected with experiments or trying new ideas: *We're still at the experimental stage with the new product.* ◆ *experimental drama* ▶ **experimentally** /-təli/ *adv*

🔑 **expert** /ˈekspɜːt/ *noun* [C] **an expert (at/in/on sth)** a person who has a lot of special knowledge or skill: *a computer expert* ◆ *Let me try—I'm an expert at parking cars in small spaces.* ◆ *She's a leading expert in the field of genetics.* ▶ **expert** *adj*: *He's an expert cook.* ◆ *I think we should get expert advice on the problem.* ▶ **expertly** *adv*

expertise /ˌekspɜːˈtiːz/ *noun* [U] a high level of special knowledge or skill: *Mr Dixon has many years of expertise in employment matters.*

expire /ɪkˈspaɪə(r)/ *verb* [I] (used about an official document, agreement, etc.) to come to the end of the time when you can use it or in which it has effect: *My passport's expired. I'll have to renew it.* **SYN run out**

expiry /ɪkˈspaɪəri/ *noun* [U] the end of a period when you can use sth: *What's the expiry date on your credit card?*

🔑 **explain** /ɪkˈspleɪn/ *verb* [I,T] **explain (sth) (to sb)** **1** to make sth clear or easy to understand: *She explained how I should fill in the form.* ◆ *I don't understand. Can you explain it to me?*

> **HELP** Note that you have to say 'Explain **it to me**' NOT 'Explain me it'.

2 to give a reason for sth: *'This work isn't very good.' 'I wasn't feeling very well.' 'Oh, that explains it then.'* ◆ *The manager explained to the customers why the goods were late.*

IDM explain yourself 1 to give reasons for your behaviour, especially when it has upset sb **2** to say what you mean in a clear way

PHR V explain sth away to give reasons why sth is not your fault or is not important

🔑 **explanation** /ˌekspləˈneɪʃn/ *noun* **1** [C,U] an explanation (for sth) a statement, fact or situation that gives a reason for sth: *He could not **give an explanation** for his behaviour.* **2** [C] a statement or a piece of writing that makes sth easier to understand: *For a full explanation of how the machine works, turn to page 5.*

explanatory /ɪkˈsplænətri/ *adj* giving an explanation: *There are some explanatory notes at the back of the book.* ◆ *Those instructions are self-explanatory* (= they don't need explaining).

explicable /ɪkˈsplɪkəbl; ˈeksplɪkəbl/ *adj* that can be explained: *Barry's strange behaviour is only explicable in terms of the stress he is under.* OPP **inexplicable**

explicit /ɪkˈsplɪsɪt/ *adj* **1** clear, making sth easy to understand: *I gave you explicit instructions not to touch anything.* ◆ *She was quite explicit about her feelings on the subject.* ➲ look at **implicit** **2** not hiding anything: *Some of the sex scenes in that play were very explicit.* ▶ **explicitly** *adv*: *He was explicitly forbidden to stay out later than midnight.*

🔑 **explode** /ɪkˈspləʊd/ *verb* [I,T] to burst or to make sth burst with a loud noise: *The bomb exploded without warning.* ◆ *The army exploded the bomb at a safe distance from the houses.* ◆ *(figurative) My father exploded* (= became very angry) *when I told him how much the car would cost to repair.* ➲ *noun* **explosion**

exploit¹ /ɪkˈsplɔɪt/ *verb* [T] **1** to use sth or to treat sb unfairly for your own advantage: *Some employers exploit foreign workers, making them work long hours for low pay.* **2** to develop sth or make the best use of sth: *This region has been exploited for oil for fifty years.* ◆ *Solar energy is a source of power that needs to be exploited more fully.* ▶ **exploitation** /ˌeksplɔɪˈteɪʃn/ *noun* [U]: *They're making you work 80 hours a week? That's exploitation!*

exploit² /ˈeksplɔɪt/ *noun* [C] something exciting or interesting that sb has done

exploration /ˌekspləˈreɪʃn/ *noun* [C,U] the act of travelling around a place in order to learn about it: *space exploration*

exploratory /ɪkˈsplɒrətri/ *adj* done in order to find sth out: *The doctors are doing some exploratory tests to try and find out what's wrong.*

🔑 **explore** /ɪkˈsplɔː(r)/ *verb* [I,T] to travel around a place, etc. in order to learn about it: *I've never been to Paris before—I'm going out to explore.* ◆ *They went on an expedition to explore the River Amazon.* ◆ *(figurative) We need to explore* (= look carefully at) *all the possibilities before we decide.*

explorer /ɪkˈsplɔːrə(r)/ *noun* [C] a person who travels round a place in order to learn about it

🔑 **explosion** /ɪkˈspləʊʒn/ *noun* [C] **1** the sudden loud noise when sth like a bomb bursts violently: *Two people were killed in the explosion.* **2** a sudden and often surprising increase in sth: *the population explosion* ➲ *verb* **explode**

explosive¹ /ɪkˈspləʊsɪv/ *adj* **1** capable of exploding and therefore dangerous: *Hydrogen is highly explosive.* **2** causing strong feelings or having dangerous effects: *The situation is explosive. We must do all we can to calm people down.*

explosive² /ɪkˈspləʊsɪv/ *noun* [C,U] a substance that is used for causing explosions

exponent /ɪkˈspəʊnənt/ *noun* [C] **1** a person who supports an idea, a belief, etc. and persuades others that it is good: *She was **a leading exponent** of free trade during her political career.* **2** a person who is able to perform a particular activity with skill: *the most famous exponent of the art of mime*

🔑 **export¹** /ɪkˈspɔːt/ *verb* [I,T] **1** to send goods, etc. to another country, usually for sale: *India exports tea and cotton.* **2** to move information from one computer program to another OPP for both meanings **import**

🔑 **export²** /ˈekspɔːt/ *noun* **1** [U] sending goods to another country for sale: *Most of our goods are produced for export.* ◆ *the export trade* **2** [C, usually pl] a product or service that is sent to another country for sale: *What are Brazil's main exports?* OPP for both meanings **import** ▶ **exporter** *noun* [C]: *the world's largest exporter of cars* OPP **importer**

🔑 **expose** /ɪkˈspəʊz/ *verb* [T] **1** expose sth (to sb); expose sb/sth (as sth) to show sth that is usually hidden; to tell sth that has been kept secret: *She didn't want to expose her true feelings to her family.* ◆ *The politician was exposed as a liar on TV.* **2** expose sb/sth to sth to put sb/sth or yourself in a situation that could be difficult or dangerous: *to be exposed to radiation/danger* **3** **expose sb to sth** to give sb the chance to experience sth: *I like jazz because I was exposed to it as a child.*

exposed /ɪkˈspəʊzd/ *adj* (used about a place) not protected from the wind and bad weather

exposure /ɪkˈspəʊʒə(r)/ *noun* **1** [U] being allowed or forced to experience sth: *TV can give children exposure to other cultures from an early age.* ◆ *Exposure to radiation is almost always harmful.* **2** [U,C] the act of making sth public; the thing that is made public: *The new movie has been given a lot of exposure in the media.* ◆ *The politician resigned because of the exposures about his private life.* **3** [U] a harmful condition when a person becomes very cold because they have been outside in very bad weather: *The climbers all died of exposure.*

🔑 **express¹** /ɪkˈspres/ *verb* [T] **1** to show sth such as a feeling or an opinion by words or actions: *I found it very hard to express what I felt about her.* ◆ *to express fears/concern about something* **2** **express yourself** to say or write your feelings, opinions, etc: *I don't think she expresses herself very well in that article.*

🔑 **express²** /ɪkˈspres/ *adj* [only before a noun] **1** going or sent quickly: *an express coach* **2** (used about a command, wish, etc.) clearly and definitely stated: *It was her express wish that he should have the picture after her death.* ▶ **express** *adv*: *We'd better* *send the parcel express if we want it to get there on time.*

express³ /ɪk'spres/ (also ex'press train) *noun* [C] a fast train that does not stop at all stations

expression /ɪk'spreʃn/ *noun* **1** [U,C] something that you say that shows your opinions or feelings: *Freedom of expression is a basic human right.* ◆ *an expression of gratitude/sympathy/anger* **2** [C] the look on sb's face that shows what they are thinking or feeling: *He had a puzzled expression on his face.* **3** [C] a word or phrase with a particular meaning: *'I'm starving' is an expression meaning 'I'm very hungry'.* ◆ *a slang/an idiomatic expression*

expressive /ɪk'spresɪv/ *adj* showing feelings or thoughts: *That is a very expressive piece of music.* ◆ *Philippa has a very expressive face.* ▶ **expressively** *adv*

expressly /ɪk'spresli/ *adv* **1** clearly; definitely: *I expressly told you not to do that.* **2** for a special purpose; specially: *These scissors are expressly designed for left-handed people.*

expressway /ɪk'spresweɪ/ (*AmE*) = **motorway**

expulsion /ɪk'spʌlʃn/ *noun* [C,U] the act of making sb leave a place or an institution: *There have been three expulsions from school this year.* ➲ *verb* **expel**

exquisite /'ekskwɪzɪt; ɪk'skwɪzɪt/ *adj* extremely beautiful and pleasing: *an exquisite piece of craftsmanship* ◆ *I think that ring is exquisite.* ▶ **exquisitely** *adv*

ext. *abbr* = **extension**(3): *ext. 3492*

extend /ɪk'stend/ *verb* **1** [T] to make sth longer or larger (in space or time): *We're planning to extend the back of the house to give us more space.* ◆ *Since my injury I can't extend this leg fully* (= make it completely straight). ◆ *Could you extend your visit for a few days?* **2** [I,T] to cover the area or period of time mentioned: *The desert extends over a huge area of the country.* ◆ *The company is planning to extend its operations into Asia.* **3** [T] (*formal*) to offer sth to sb: *to extend hospitality/a warm welcome/an invitation to somebody*

extension /ɪk'stenʃn/ *noun* [C] **1** a part that is added to a building: *They're building an extension on the hospital.* **2** an extra period of time that you are allowed for sth: *I've applied for an extension to my work permit.* **3** (*abbr* ext.) a telephone that is connected to a central telephone in a house or to a **switchboard** (= a central point where all telephone calls are answered) in a large office building: *What's your extension number?* ◆ *Can I have extension 4342, please?*

extensive /ɪk'stensɪv/ *adj* large in area or amount: *The house has extensive grounds.* ◆ *Most of the buildings suffered extensive damage.* ▶ **extensively** *adv*

extent /ɪk'stent/ *noun* [sing,U] **the extent of sth** the length, area, size or importance of sth: *I was amazed at the extent of his knowledge.* ◆ *The* **full extent of** *the damage is not yet known.*

IDM **to a certain/to some extent** used to show that sth is only partly true: *I agree with you to a certain extent but there are still a lot of points I disagree with.*

to what extent how far; how much: *I'm not sure to what extent I believe her.*

exterior¹ /ɪk'stɪəriə(r)/ *noun* [C] the outside of sth; the appearance of sb/sth: *The exterior of the house is fine but inside it isn't in very good condition.* ◆ *Despite his calm exterior, Steve suffers badly from stress.*

exterior² /ɪk'stɪəriə(r)/ *adj* on the outside: *the exterior walls of a house* OPP **interior**

exterminate /ɪk'stɜːmɪneɪt/ *verb* [T] to kill a large group of people or animals: *Once rats infest a building, they are very hard to exterminate.* ▶ **extermination** /ɪkˌstɜːmɪ'neɪʃn/ *noun* [U]

external /ɪk'stɜːnl/ *adj* **1** connected with the outside of sth: *The cream is for external use only* (= to be used on the skin). **2** coming from another place: *You will be tested by an external examiner.* OPP for both meanings **internal** ▶ **externally** /-nəli/ *adv*: *The building has been restored externally and internally.* ◆ *The university has many externally funded research projects.* OPP **internally**

extinct /ɪk'stɪŋkt/ *adj* **1** (used about a type of animal, plant, etc.) no longer existing: *Tigers are nearly extinct in the wild.* **2** (used about a **volcano**) no longer active ▶ **extinction** *noun* [U]: *The giant panda is in danger of extinction.*

extinguish /ɪk'stɪŋgwɪʃ/ *verb* [T] (*formal*) to cause sth to stop burning: *The fire was extinguished very quickly.* ➲ A less formal expression is **put out**. ▶ **extinguisher** = **fire extinguisher**

extort /ɪk'stɔːt/ *verb* [T] (*formal*) **extort sth (from sb)** to get sth by using threats or violence: *The gang were found guilty of extorting money from small businesses.* ▶ **extortion** *noun* [U]

extortionate /ɪk'stɔːʃənət/ *adj* (used especially about prices) much too high

extra¹ /'ekstrə/ *adj, adv* more than is usual, expected, or than exists already: *I'll need some extra money for the holidays.* ◆ *'What size is this sweater?' 'Extra large.'* ◆ *Is wine included in the price of the meal or is it extra?* ◆ *I tried to be extra nice to him yesterday because it was his birthday.* ➲ look at **additional**

extra² /'ekstrə/ *noun* [C] **1** something that costs more, or that is not normally included: *The price of the holiday is all-inclusive, with no* **hidden extras**. **2** a person in a film, etc. who has a small unimportant part, for example in a crowd

extract¹ /'ekstrækt/ *noun* [C] a part of a book, piece of music, etc., that has often been specially chosen to show sth: *The newspaper published extracts from the controversial novel.*

extract² /ɪk'strækt/ *verb* [T] (*formal*) to take sth out, especially with difficulty: *I think this tooth will have to be extracted.* ◆ *I wasn't able to extract an apology from her.*

extraction /ɪk'strækʃn/ *noun* (*formal*) **1** [U,C] the act of taking sth out: *extraction of salt from the* *sea* ◆ *Dentists report that children are requiring fewer extractions* (= of teeth). **2** [U] family origin: *He's an American but he's of Italian extraction.*

extra-curricular /ˌekstrə kəˈrɪkjələ(r)/ *adj* not part of the **curriculum** (= the normal course of studies in a school or college): *The school offers many extra-curricular activities such as sport, music, drama, etc.*

extradite /ˈekstrədaɪt/ *verb* [T] to send a person who may be guilty of a crime from the country in which they are living to the country which wants to put them on trial for the crime: *The suspected terrorists were captured in Spain and extradited to France.* ▶ **extradition** /ˌekstrəˈdɪʃn/ *noun* [C,U]

⚷ **extraordinary** /ɪkˈstrɔːdnri/ *adj* not what you would expect in a particular situation; very strange or unusual: *That was extraordinary behaviour for a teacher!* ◆ *She has an extraordinary ability to whistle and sing at the same time.* **SYN** **incredible** ▶ **extraordinarily** /ɪkˈstrɔːdnrəli/ *adv*: *He was an extraordinarily talented musician.*

extrapolate /ɪkˈstræpəleɪt/ *verb* [I,T] (*formal*) extrapolate (sth) (from/to sth) to form an opinion or make a judgement about a new situation by using facts that you know from a different situation: *The figures were obtained by extrapolating from past trends.* ◆ *We have extrapolated these results from research in other countries.* ▶ **extrapolation** /ɪkˌstræpəˈleɪʃn/ *noun* [U,C]

extraterrestrial /ˌekstrətəˈrestriəl/ *noun* [C] (in stories) a creature that comes from another planet; a creature that may exist on another planet ▶ **extraterrestrial** *adj*: *extraterrestrial beings/life*

extravagant /ɪkˈstrævəgənt/ *adj* **1** spending or costing too much money: *He's terribly extravagant—he travels everywhere by taxi.* ◆ *an extravagant present* **2** exaggerated; more than is usual, true or necessary: *the extravagant claims of advertisers* ▶ **extravagance** *noun* [C,U] ▶ **extravagantly** *adv*

⚷ **extreme** /ɪkˈstriːm/ *adj* **1** [only *before* a noun] the greatest or strongest possible: *You must take extreme care when driving at night.* ◆ *extreme heat/difficulty/poverty* **2** much stronger than is considered usual, acceptable, etc: *Her extreme views on immigration are shocking to most people.* **3** [only *before* a noun] as far away as possible from the centre in the direction mentioned: *There could be snow in the extreme north of the country.* ◆ *politicians on the extreme left of the party* ➲ look at **moderate, radical** ▶ **extreme** *noun* [C]: *Alex used to be very shy but now she's gone to the opposite extreme.*

⚷ **extremely** /ɪkˈstriːmli/ *adv* very: *Listen carefully because this is extremely important.*

extreme ˈsport *noun* [C] a very dangerous sport or activity which some people do for fun: *He enjoys extreme sports, such as bungee jumping and hang-gliding.* ➲ picture on **page P5**

extremist /ɪkˈstriːmɪst/ *noun* [C] a person who has extreme political opinions ➲ look at **moderate, radical** ▶ **extremism** /ɪkˈstriːmɪzəm/ *noun* [U]

extremity /ɪkˈstreməti/ *noun* [C] (*pl* **extremities**) the part of sth that is furthest from the centre

extricate /ˈekstrɪkeɪt/ *verb* [T] to manage to free sb/sth from a difficult situation or position: *I finally managed to extricate myself from the meeting by saying that I had a train to catch.*

extrovert /ˈekstrəvɜːt/ *noun* [C] a person who is confident and full of life and who prefers being with other people to being alone **OPP** **introvert**

exuberant /ɪgˈzjuːbərənt/ *adj* (used about a person or their behaviour) full of energy and excitement ▶ **exuberance** *noun* [U]

⚷ **eye**[1] /aɪ/ *noun* [C] **1** one of the two organs of your body that you use to see with: *She opened/closed her eyes.* ◆ *He's got blue eyes.* ➲ look at **black eye** ➲ picture at **body**

> **MORE** When you close both eyes and open them again quickly, you **blink**. ➲ picture at **blink** If you do this with only one eye, you **wink**. People with poor **eyesight** (= who cannot see well) usually wear **glasses** or use **contact lenses**. ➲ picture at **glasses**

2 the ability to see sth: *He has **sharp eyes*** (= he can see very well). ◆ *She has **an eye for detail*** (= she notices small details). **3** the hole at one end of a needle that the thread goes through

IDM **as far as the eye can see** ➲ **far**[2]

be up to your eyes in sth (*informal*) to have more of sth than you can easily do or manage: *I can't come out with you tonight—I'm up to my eyes in work.*

before sb's very eyes in front of sb so that they can clearly see what is happening

cast an eye/your eye(s) over sb/sth ➲ **cast**[1]

catch sb's attention/eye ➲ **catch**[1]

cry your eyes out ➲ **cry**[1]

an eye for an eye used to say that you should punish sb by doing to them what they have done to sb else

have (got) your eye on sb to watch sb carefully to make sure that they do nothing wrong

have (got) your eye on sth to be thinking about buying sth: *I've got my eye on a suit that I saw in the sales.*

in the eyes of sb/in sb's eyes in the opinion of sb: *She was still a child in her mother's eyes.*

in the public eye ➲ **public**[1]

keep an eye on sb/sth to make sure that sb/sth is safe; to look after sb/sth: *Please could you keep an eye on the house while we're away?*

keep an eye open/out (for sb/sth) to watch or look out for sb/sth: *I've lost my ring—could you keep an eye out for it?*

keep your eyes peeled/skinned (for sb/sth) (*informal*) to watch carefully for sb/sth: *Keep your eyes peeled for the turning to the village.*

look sb in the eye ➲ **look**[1]

the naked eye ➲ **naked**

not bat an eye ➲ **bat**[2]

see eye to eye (with sb) ➲ **see**

set eyes on sb/sth to see sb/sth: *He loved the house the moment he set eyes on it.*

there is more to sb/sth than meets the eye ➲ **meet**

turn a blind eye ➲ **blind**[1]
with your eyes open knowing what you are doing: *You went into the new job with your eyes open, so you can't complain now.*

eye[2] /aɪ/ *verb* [T] (eyeing *or* eying; *pt, pp* eyed) to look at sb/sth closely: *She eyed the stranger with suspicion.*

eyeball /ˈaɪbɔːl/ *noun* [C] the whole of your eye (including the part which is hidden inside the head)

eyebrow /ˈaɪbraʊ/ (also **brow**) *noun* [C] the line of hair that is above your eye ➲ picture at **body**
IDM **raise your eyebrows** ➲ **raise**

ˈ**eye-catching** *adj* (used about a thing) attracting your attention immediately because it is interesting, bright or pretty

eyeglasses /ˈaɪɡlɑːsɪz/ (*AmE*) = **glasses**

eyelash /ˈaɪlæʃ/ (also **lash**) *noun* [C] one of the hairs that grow on the edges of your **eyelids** ➲ picture at **body**

ˈ**eye level** *noun* at the same height as sb's eyes when they are standing up: *Computer screens should be at eye level.* ◆ *an eye-level grill*

eyelid /ˈaɪlɪd/ (also **lid**) *noun* [C] the piece of skin that can move to cover your eye ➲ picture at **body**
IDM **not bat an eyelid** ➲ **bat**[2]

eyeliner /ˈaɪlaɪnə(r)/ *noun* [U] a substance that you use to draw a dark line around your eyes to make them look more attractive

ˈ**eye-opener** *noun* [C] something that makes you realize the truth about sth: *That TV programme about the inner cities was a real eye-opener.*

eyeshadow /ˈaɪʃædəʊ/ *noun* [U] colour that is put on the skin above the eyes to make them look more attractive

eyesight /ˈaɪsaɪt/ *noun* [U] the ability to see: *good/poor eyesight*

eyesore /ˈaɪsɔː(r)/ *noun* [C] something that is ugly and unpleasant to look at: *All this litter in the streets is a real eyesore.*

eyewitness /ˈaɪwɪtnəs/ = **witness**[1] (1)

F, f /ef/ *noun* [C,U] (*pl* Fs; F's; f's /efs/) **1** the 6th letter of the English alphabet: *'Five' begins with (an) 'F'.* **2 F** (used about music) the fourth note in the scale of C major: *F major/minor* ◆ *F sharp*

F *abbr* = **Fahrenheit**: *Water freezes at 32°F*

f *abbr* **1** = **female** **2** = **feminine**

FA /ˌef ˈeɪ/ *abbr* (*BrE*) **the Football Association**: *the FA Cup*

fable /ˈfeɪbl/ *noun* [C] a short story that teaches a moral lesson and that often has animals as the main characters: *Aesop's fables*

fabric /ˈfæbrɪk/ *noun* **1** [C,U] (a type of) cloth or soft material that is used for making clothes, curtains, etc: *cotton fabrics* **2** [sing] the basic structure of a building or system: *The Industrial Revolution changed the fabric of society.*

fabulous /ˈfæbjələs/ *adj* **1** very good; excellent: *It was a fabulous concert.* **2** very great: *fabulous wealth/riches/beauty*

facade /fəˈsɑːd/ *noun* [C] **1** the front wall of a large building that you see from the outside **2** [usually sing] the way sb/sth appears to be, which is different from the way sb/sth really is: *His good humour was just a facade.*

⚷ **face**[1] /feɪs/ *noun* [C] **1** the front part of your head; the expression that is shown on it: *Go and wash your face.* ◆ *She has a very pretty face.* ◆ *He came in with a smile on his face.* ◆ *Her face lit up* (= showed happiness) *when John came into the room.* ➲ picture at **body** **2 -faced** [in compounds] having the type of face or expression mentioned: *a red-faced man* ◆ *round-faced/pale-faced* **3** the front or one side of sth: *the north face of the mountain* ◆ *He put the cards* **face up/down** *on the table.* ◆ *a clock face* ➲ picture at **clock**
IDM **face to face (with sb/sth)** close to and looking at sb/sth
keep a straight face ➲ **straight**[2]
lose face ➲ **lose**
make/pull faces/a face (at sb/sth) to make an expression that shows that you do not like sb/sth: *When she saw what was for dinner she pulled a face.*
make/pull faces to make rude expressions with your face: *The children made faces behind the teacher's back.*
save face ➲ **save**[1]
to sb's face if you say sth to sb's face, you do it when that person is with you: *I wanted to say that I was sorry to her face, not on the phone.* **OPP** **behind sb's back**

⚷ **face**[2] /feɪs/ *verb* **1** [I,T] to have your face or front pointing towards sb/sth or in a particular direction: *The garden faces south.* ◆ *Can you all face the front, please?* **2** [T] to need attention or action from sb: *There are several problems facing the government.* ◆ *We are faced with a difficult decision.* **3** [T] to have to deal with sth unpleasant or difficult: *I can't face another argument.* ◆ *He couldn't face going to work yesterday—he felt too ill.*
IDM **let's face it** (*informal*) we must accept it as true: *Let's face it, we can't afford a holiday this year.*
PHR V **face up to sth** to accept a difficult or unpleasant situation and do sth about it: *She had to face up to the fact that she was wrong.*

Facebook™ /ˈfeɪsbʊk/ *noun* [sing] a **social networking site** (= a website for people who share your interests) ➲ note at **social networking**

facecloth /ˈfeɪsklɒθ/ (also **flannel**) *noun* [C] a small square piece of cloth that is used for washing the face, hands, etc.

faceless /ˈfeɪsləs/ *adj* without individual character or identity: *faceless civil servants*

facelift /ˈfeɪslɪft/ *noun* [C] a medical operation that makes your face look younger ➲ look at **plastic surgery**

facet /ˈfæsɪt/ *noun* [C] **1** one part or particular aspect of sth: *There are many facets to this argument* (= points that must be considered). **2** one side of a **precious** (= rare and valuable) stone

facetious /fəˈsiːʃəs/ *adj* trying to be amusing about a subject at a time that is not appropriate so that other people become annoyed: *He kept making facetious remarks during the lecture.* ▶ **facetiously** *adv*

ˌface ˈvalue *noun* [U, sing] the cost or value that is shown on the front of stamps, coins, etc.
IDM take sb/sth at (his, her, its) face value to accept sb/sth as he/she/it appears to be: *Don't take his story at face value. There's something he hasn't told us yet.*

facial /ˈfeɪʃl/ *adj* connected with a person's face: *a facial expression* ◆ *facial hair*

facile /ˈfæsaɪl/ *adj* (used about a comment, argument, etc.) not carefully thought out

facilitate /fəˈsɪlɪteɪt/ *verb* [T] (*formal*) to make sth possible or easier

facility /fəˈsɪləti/ *noun* (*pl* **facilities**) **1 facilities** [pl] services, buildings, equipment, etc. that make it possible to do sth: *Our town has excellent sports facilities* (= a swimming pool, football ground, etc.). **2** [C] an extra function or ability that a machine, etc. may have: *a facility for checking spelling*

facsimile /fækˈsɪməli/ *noun* [C,U] an exact copy of a picture, piece of writing, etc.

fact /fækt/ *noun* **1** [C] something that you know has happened or is true: *It is a scientific fact that light travels faster than sound.* ◆ *We need to know all the facts before we can decide.* ◆ *I know* **for a fact** *that Peter wasn't ill yesterday.* ◆ ***The fact that*** *I am older than you makes no difference at all.* ◆ *You must* **face facts** *and accept that he has gone.* **2** [U] true things; reality: *The film is based on fact.* **OPP fiction**
IDM as a matter of fact ➲ **matter**[1]
the fact (of the matter) is (that)... the truth is that ...: *I would love a car, but the fact is that I just can't afford one.*
a fact of life something unpleasant that you must accept because you cannot change it: *Most people now see unemployment as just another fact of life.*
facts and figures detailed information: *Before we make a decision, we need some more facts and figures.*
the facts of life the details of sexual behaviour and how babies are born
hard facts ➲ **hard**[1]
in (actual) fact 1 used for introducing more detailed information: *It was cold. In fact it was freezing.* **2** (used for emphasizing that sth is true) really; actually: *I thought the lecture would be boring but in actual fact it was rather interesting.*

faction /ˈfækʃn/ *noun* [C] a small group of people within a larger one, whose members have some different aims and beliefs to those of the larger group: *rival factions within the administration*

factor /ˈfæktə(r)/ *noun* [C] **1** one of the things that influences a decision, situation, etc: *His unhappiness at home was a major factor in his decision to go abroad.* **2** (*technical*) (in mathematics) a whole number (except 1) by which a larger number can be divided: *2, 3, 4 and 6 are factors of 12.*

factory /ˈfæktri; -təri/ *noun* [C] (*pl* **factories**) a building or group of buildings where goods are made in large quantities by machine

ˈfactory farm *noun* [C] a type of farm where animals live inside in small spaces and eat special food so that they produce a large amount of meat, milk, etc. as quickly and cheaply as possible ▶ **ˈfactory farming** *noun* [U]

factual /ˈfæktʃuəl/ *adj* based on or containing things that are true or real: *a factual account of the events* ➲ look at **fictional**

faculty /ˈfæklti/ *noun* [C] (*pl* **faculties**) **1** one of the natural abilities of a person's body or mind: *the faculty of hearing/sight/speech* **2** (also **Faculty**) one department in a university, college, etc: *the Faculty of Law/Arts* **3** [with sing or pl verb] all the teachers in a **faculty** of a university, college, etc: *The Faculty has/have been invited to the meeting.*

fad /fæd/ *noun* [C] (*informal*) a fashion, interest, etc. that will probably not last long

fade /feɪd/ *verb* **1** [I,T] to become or make sth become lighter in colour or less strong or fresh: *Jeans fade when you wash them.* ◆ *Look how the sunlight has faded these curtains.* **2** [I] **fade (away)** to disappear slowly (from sight, hearing, memory, etc.): *The cheering of the crowd faded away.* ◆ *The smile faded from his face.*

faeces (*AmE* **feces**) /ˈfiːsiːz/ *noun* [pl] (*technical*) the solid waste material that you get rid of from your body when you go to the toilet

fag /fæg/ *noun* [C] (*BrE slang*) a cigarette

Fahrenheit /ˈfærənhaɪt/ *noun* [U] (*abbr* F) the name of a scale which measures temperatures: *Water freezes at 32° Fahrenheit (32°F).* ➲ look at **Celsius**

fail[1] /feɪl/ *verb* **1** [I,T] to not be successful in sth: *She failed her driving test.* ◆ *I feel that I've failed—I'm 25 and I still haven't got a steady job.* ➲ look at **pass, succeed 2** [I] **fail to do sth** to not do sth: *She never fails to do her homework.* **3** [T] to decide that sb is not successful in a test, exam, etc: *The examiners failed half of the candidates.* **OPP pass 4** [I] to stop working: *My brakes failed on the hill but I managed to stop the car.* **5** [I] (used about health, etc.) to become weak: *His eyesight is failing.* **6** [I,T] to not be enough or not do what people are expecting or wanting: *If the crops fail, people will starve.* ◆ *I think the government has failed us.*

fail[2] /feɪl/ *noun* [C] the result of an exam in which sb is not successful **OPP pass**
IDM without fail always, even if there are difficulties: *She spends an hour in the gym each day without fail.*

failing[1] /ˈfeɪlɪŋ/ *noun* [C] a weakness or fault: *She's not very patient—that's her only failing.*

failing[2] /ˈfeɪlɪŋ/ *prep* if sth is not possible: *Ask Jackie to go with you, or failing that, try Anne.*

failure /ˈfeɪljə(r)/ *noun* **1** [U] lack of success: *All my efforts ended in failure.* OPP **success** **2** [C] a person or thing that is not successful: *His first attempt at skating was a miserable failure.* OPP **success** **3** [C,U] **failure to do sth** not doing sth that people expect you to do: *I was very disappointed at his failure to come to the meeting.* **4** [C,U] an example of sth not working properly: *She died of heart failure.* ◆ *There's been a failure in the power supply.*

F

faint[1] /feɪnt/ *adj* (**fainter**; **faintest**) **1** (used about things that you can see, hear, feel, etc.) not strong or clear: *a faint light/sound* ◆ *There is still a faint hope that they will find more people alive.* **2** (used about actions, etc.) done without much effort: *He made a faint protest.* **3** [not before a noun] (used about people) likely to become unconscious; very weak: *I **feel faint**—I'd better sit down.*
IDM **not have the faintest/foggiest (idea)** (*informal*) to not know at all: *I haven't the faintest idea where they've gone.*
▶ **faintly** *adv*: *She smiled faintly.* ◆ *He looked faintly embarrassed.*

faint[2] /feɪnt/ *verb* [I] to become unconscious for a short time SYN **pass out** OPP **come round/to**

fair[1] /feə(r)/ *adj* (**fairer**; **fairest**) **1** appropriate and acceptable in a particular situation: *That's a fair price for that house.* ◆ *I think **it's fair to say that** the number of homeless people is increasing.* OPP **unfair** **2** **fair (to/on sb)** treating each person or side equally, according to the law, the rules, etc: *That's not fair—he got the same number of mistakes as I did and he's got a better mark.* ◆ *It wasn't fair on her to ask her to stay so late.* ◆ *a fair trial* OPP **unfair** **3** quite good, large, etc: *They have a fair chance of success.* **4** (used about the skin or hair) light in colour: *Chloe has fair hair and blue eyes.* OPP **dark** ➲ look at **skin** (2) **5** (used about the weather) good, without rain: *a fair and breezy autumn day*
IDM **fair enough** (*spoken*) used to show that you agree with what sb has suggested
fair play equal treatment of both/all sides according to the rules: *The referee is there to ensure fair play during the match.*
(more than) your fair share of sth (more than) the usual or expected amount of sth: *We've had more than our fair share of trouble this year.*

fair[2] /feə(r)/ *noun* [C] **1** (*BrE also* **funfair**) a type of entertainment in a field or park. At a **fair** you can ride on machines or try and win prizes at games. **Fairs** usually travel from town to town. **2** a large event where people, businesses, etc. show and sell their goods: *a trade fair* ◆ *the Frankfurt book fair*

fairground /ˈfeəgraʊnd/ *noun* [C] a large outdoor area where **fairs** are held

ˌfair-ˈhaired *adj* with light-coloured hair SYN **blonde**

fairly /ˈfeəli/ *adv* **1** quite, not very: *He is fairly tall.* ➲ note at **rather** **2** in an acceptable way; in a way that treats people equally or according to the law, rules, etc: *I felt that the teacher didn't treat us fairly.* OPP **unfairly**

fairness /ˈfeənəs/ *noun* [U] treating people equally or according to the law, rules, etc.

ˌfair-ˈtrade *adj* involving trade which helps to pay fair prices to workers in poor countries: *We buy 10% of our bananas from fair-trade sources.*

fairy /ˈfeəri/ *noun* [C] (*pl* **fairies**) (in stories) a small creature with wings and magic powers

ˈfairy tale (also **ˈfairy story**) *noun* [C] a story that is about **fairies**, magic, etc.

faith /feɪθ/ *noun* **1** [U] **faith (in sb/sth)** strong belief (in sb/sth); trust: *I've got great/little faith in her ability to do the job.* ◆ *I have **lost faith** in him.* **2** [U] strong religious belief: *a man of great faith* **3** [C] a particular religion: *the Jewish faith*
IDM **in good faith** with honest reasons for doing sth: *I bought the car in good faith. I didn't know it was stolen.*

faithful /ˈfeɪθfl/ *adj* **1** **faithful (to sb/sth)** always staying with and supporting a person, an organization or a belief; loyal: *He was always faithful to his wife* (= he didn't have sexual relations with anyone else). ◆ *Peter has been a faithful friend.* OPP **unfaithful** **2** true to the facts; accurate: *a faithful description*
▶ **faithfully** /-fəli/ *adv*

> MORE **Yours faithfully** is used to end formal letters that you have started *Dear Sir or Madam*.

➲ note at **sincere** ▶ **faithfulness** *noun* [U] ➲ look at **fidelity**

fake[1] /feɪk/ *noun* [C] **1** a work of art, etc. that seems to be real or genuine but is not **2** a person who is not really what they appear to be ▶ **fake** *adj*: *a fake passport*

fake[2] /feɪk/ *verb* [T] **1** to copy sth and try to make people believe it is the real thing: *He faked his father's signature.* **2** to make people believe that you are feeling sth that you are not: *I faked surprise when he told me the news.*

falcon /ˈfɔːlkən/ *noun* [C] a bird with long pointed wings that kills and eats other animals. **Falcons** can be trained to hunt.

fall[1] /fɔːl/ *verb* [I] (*pt* **fell** /fel/; *pp* **fallen** /ˈfɔːlən/)
➤DROP DOWN **1** to drop down towards the ground: *He fell off the ladder onto the grass.* ◆ *The rain was falling steadily.* **2** **fall (down/over)** to suddenly stop standing and drop to the ground: *She slipped on the ice and fell.* ◆ *The little boy fell over and hurt his knee.*
➤OF HAIR/CLOTH **3** to hang down: *Her hair fell down over her shoulders.*
➤DECREASE **4** to become lower or less: *The temperature is falling.* ◆ *The price of coffee has fallen again.* OPP **rise**
➤BE DEFEATED **5** to be defeated or captured: *The Government fell because of the scandal.*
➤DIE IN WAR **6** (*written*) to be killed (in battle): *Millions of soldiers fell in the war.*
➤BECOME **7** to change into a different state; to

become: *He* ***fell asleep*** *on the sofa.* ◆ *They* ***fell in love*** *with each other in Spain.* ◆ *I must get some new shoes —these ones are* ***falling to pieces.***

➤HAPPEN **8** (*formal*) to come or happen: *My birthday falls on a Sunday this year.*

➤BELONG TO GROUP **9** to belong to a particular group, type, etc: *Animals fall into two groups, those with backbones and those without.*

IDM **fall flat** ➲ **flat**[1]

fall foul of sb/sth to get in trouble with sb/sth because you have done sth wrong: *At sixteen she fell foul of the law for the first time.*

fall/get into arrears ➲ **arrears**

fall/slot into place ➲ **place**[1]

fall/land on your feet ➲ **foot**[1]

fall short (of sth) to not be enough; to not reach sth: *The pay rise fell short of what they had asked for.*

PHR V **fall apart** to break (into pieces): *My car is falling apart.*

fall back on sb/sth to use sb/sth when you are in difficulty: *When the electricity was cut off we fell back on candles.*

fall for sb (*informal*) to be strongly attracted to sb; to fall in love with sb

fall for sth (*informal*) to be tricked into believing sth that is not true: *He makes excuses and she falls for them every time.*

fall out (with sb) (*BrE*) to argue and stop being friendly (with sb)

fall through to fail or not happen: *Our trip to Japan has fallen through.*

fall[2] /fɔːl/ *noun*

➤DOWN/OFF STH **1** [C] an act of falling down or off sth: *She* ***had a*** *nasty* ***fall*** *from her horse.*

➤AMOUNT/DISTANCE **2** [C] **a fall (of sth)** the amount of sth that has fallen or the distance that sth has fallen: *We have had a heavy fall of snow.* ◆ *a fall of four metres*

➤WATER **3 falls** [pl] a large amount of water falling down from a height: *Niagara Falls* SYN **waterfall**

➤AUTUMN **4** [C] (*AmE*) = **autumn**

➤DECREASE **5** [C] **a fall (in sth)** a decrease (in value, quantity, etc.): *There has been a sharp fall in interest rates.* SYN **drop** OPP **rise**

➤DEFEAT **6** [sing] **the fall of sth** a (political) defeat; a failure: *the fall of the Roman Empire*

IDM **sb's fall from grace** a situation in which sb loses the respect that people had for them by doing sth wrong or immoral

fallacy /ˈfæləsi/ *noun* [C,U] (*pl* **fallacies**) (*formal*) a false belief or a wrong idea: *It's a fallacy that money brings happiness* (= it's not true).

fallen *past participle of* **fall**[1]

fallible /ˈfæləbl/ *adj* able or likely to make mistakes: *Even our new computerized system is fallible.* OPP **infallible**

fallout /ˈfɔːlaʊt/ *noun* [U] dangerous waste that is carried in the air after a nuclear explosion

false /fɔːls/ *adj* **1** not true; not correct: *I think the information you have been given is false.* ◆ *I got a completely false impression of him from our first meeting.* OPP **true** **2** not real; artificial: *false hair/eyelashes* OPP **real, natural** **3** not genuine, but made to look real in order to trick people: *This suitcase has a false bottom.* ◆ *a false name/passport* **4** (used about sb's behaviour or expression) not sincere or honest: *a false smile* ◆ *false modesty*

IDM **a false alarm** a warning about a danger that does not happen

a false friend a word in another language that looks similar to a word in your own but has a different meaning

on/under false pretences pretending to be or to have sth in order to trick people: *She got into the club under false pretences—she isn't a member at all!*

▶ **falsely** *adv*: *He was falsely accused of theft.* ◆ *She smiled falsely at his joke.*

ˌfalse ˈteeth (also **dentures**) *noun* [pl] artificial teeth that are worn by sb who has lost their natural teeth

falsify /ˈfɔːlsɪfaɪ/ *verb* [T] (**falsifying**; **falsifies**; *pt, pp* **falsified**) (*formal*) to change a document, information, etc. so that it is no longer true in order to trick sb: *to falsify data/records/accounts*

falter /ˈfɔːltə(r)/ *verb* [I] **1** to become weak or move in a way that is not steady: *The engine faltered and stopped.* **2** to lose confidence and determination: *Murray faltered and missed the ball.*

fame /feɪm/ *noun* [U] being known or talked about by many people because of what you have achieved: *Pop stars achieve fame at a young age.* ◆ *The town's only* ***claim to fame*** *is that George Eliot was born there.*

famed /feɪmd/ *adj* **famed (for sth)** very well known (for sth): *Welsh people are famed for their singing.* ➲ A more common word is **famous**.

familiar /fəˈmɪliə(r)/ *adj* **1 familiar (to sb)** known to you; often seen or heard and therefore easy to recognize: *to look/sound familiar* ◆ *Chinese music isn't very familiar to people in Europe.* ◆ *It was a relief to see a familiar face in the crowd.* OPP **unfamiliar** **2 familiar with sth** having a good knowledge of sth: *People in Europe aren't very familiar with Chinese music.* OPP **unfamiliar** **3 familiar (with sb)** (used about sb's behaviour) too friendly and informal: *I was annoyed by the waiter's familiar behaviour.*

familiarity /fəˌmɪliˈærəti/ *noun* [U] **1 familiarity (with sth)** having a good knowledge of sth: *His familiarity with the area was an advantage.* **2** being too friendly and informal

familiarize (also **-ise**) /fəˈmɪliəraɪz/ *verb* [T] **familiarize sb/yourself (with sth)** to teach sb about sth or learn about sth until you know it well: *I want to familiarize myself with the plans before the meeting.*

family /ˈfæməli/ *noun* (*pl* **families**) **1** [C, with sing or pl verb] a group of people who are related to each other: *I have quite a large family.* ◆ *a family of four* ◆ *the Dawson family*

MORE Sometimes we use **family** to mean 'parents and their children' (a **nuclear family**); sometimes we use it to include other relatives, for example grandparents, aunts, uncles, etc. (an **extended family**).

GRAMMAR **Family** is used with a singular verb when we are thinking of it as a unit: *Almost every family in the country owns a TV.* A plural verb is used when we are thinking of the members of a family as individuals: *My family are all very tall.*

2 [C,U] children: *We are planning to* ***start a family*** *next year* (= to have our first baby). ◆ *to bring up/raise a family* ◆ *Do you have any family?* **3** [C] a group of animals, plants, etc. that are of a similar type; a group of related things, especially languages: *Lions belong to the cat family.*

IDM **run in the family** to be found very often in a family: *Red hair runs in the family.*

▶ **family** *adj*: *a family car* (= suitable for a family with children)

EXAM TIP

Word families

When you learn a word, make a note of other words in the same family. For example, if you learn the word **rely**, you will see a note in the dictionary that points you to the noun **reliance** and the adjectives **reliable** and **reliant**. Learn word families to help you with exam questions where you have to rewrite a sentence changing the part of speech, but not the meaning.

ˈfamily name *noun* [C] the name that is shared by members of a family **SYN** **surname** ➲ note at **name**

ˌfamily ˈplanning *noun* [U] controlling the number of children you have by using birth control ➲ look at **contraception**

ˌfamily ˈtree *noun* [C] a diagram that shows the relationships between different members of a family over a long period of time: *How far back can you trace your family tree?*

famine /ˈfæmɪn/ *noun* [C,U] a lack of food over a long period of time in a large area that can cause the death of many people: *There is a severe famine in many parts of Africa.* ◆ *The long drought* (= a lack of rain or water) *was followed by famine.*

famished /ˈfæmɪʃt/ *adj* [not before a noun] (*informal*) very hungry: *When's lunch? I'm famished!*

⚷ **famous** /ˈfeɪməs/ *adj* **famous** (**for sth**) known about by many people: *a famous singer* ◆ *Glasgow is famous for its museums and art galleries.* ◆ *One day, I'll be rich and famous.*

MORE **Infamous** and **notorious** mean 'famous for being bad'.

famously /ˈfeɪməsli/ *adv* in a way that is famous: *the words Nelson famously uttered just before he died*

IDM **get on/along famously** to have a very good relationship with sb, especially from the first meeting: *My girlfriend and my father got on famously.*

fans

⚷ **fan**[1] /fæn/ *noun* [C] **1** a person who admires and is very enthusiastic about a sport, a film star, a singer, etc: *football fans* ◆ *She's a Madonna fan.* ◆ *fan mail* (= letters from fans to the person they admire) **2** a machine with parts that turn around very quickly to create a current of cool or warm air: *an electric fan* ◆ *a fan heater* **3** an object in the shape of half a circle made of paper, feathers, etc. that you wave in your hand to create a current of cool air

fan[2] /fæn/ *verb* [T] (fa<u>nn</u>ing; fa<u>nn</u>ed) **1** to make air blow on sb/sth by waving a fan, your hand, etc. in the air: *She used a newspaper to fan her face.* **2** to make a fire burn more strongly by blowing on it: *The strong wind really fanned the flames.*

PHR V **fan out** to spread out: *The police fanned out across the field.*

fanatic /fəˈnætɪk/ *noun* [C] a person who is very enthusiastic about sth and may have extreme or dangerous opinions (especially about religion or politics): *a health-food fanatic* ➲ look at **freak** ▶ **fanatical** /-kl/ (also **fanatic**) *adj*: *He's fanatical about keeping things tidy.* ▶ **fanatically** /-kli/ *adv* ▶ **fanaticism** /fəˈnætɪsɪzəm/ *noun* [C,U]

ˈfan belt *noun* [C] the belt that operates the machinery that cools a car engine

⚷ **fancy**[1] /ˈfænsi/ *verb* [T] (**fancying; fancies;** *pt, pp* **fancied**) **1** (*BrE informal*) to like the idea of having or doing sth; to want sth or to want to do sth: *What do you fancy to eat?* ◆ *I don't fancy going out in this rain.* **2** (*BrE informal*) to be sexually attracted to sb: *Jack keeps looking at you. I think he fancies you.* **3** **fancy yourself (as) sth** to think that you would be good at sth; to think that you are sth (although this may not be true): *He fancied himself (as) a poet.*

fancy[2] /ˈfænsi/ *noun*

IDM **take sb's fancy** (*informal*) to attract or please sb: *If you see something that takes your fancy I'll buy it for you.*

take a fancy to sb/sth (*informal*) to start liking sb/sth: *I think that Laura's really taken a fancy to you.*

⚷ **fancy**[3] /ˈfænsi/ *adj* (**fancier; fanciest**) not simple or ordinary: *My father doesn't like fancy food.* ◆ *I just want a pair of black shoes—nothing fancy.* **OPP** **plain**

ˌfancy ˈdress *noun* [U] special clothes that you wear to a party at which people dress up to look like a different person (for example from history or a story): *We've been invited to a fancy dress party—I'm going as Napoleon.* ◆ *It was a Halloween party and everyone went* ***in fancy dress.***

fanfare /ˈfænfeə(r)/ *noun* [C] a short loud piece of music that is used for introducing sb important, for example a king or queen

fang /fæŋ/ *noun* [C] a long sharp tooth of a dog, snake, etc. ➲ picture on **page P12**

fanny pack /ˈfæni pæk/ (*AmE*) = **bumbag**

fantasize (also -ise) /ˈfæntəsaɪz/ *verb* [I,T] to imagine sth that you would like to happen: *He liked to fantasize that he had won a gold medal at the Olympics.*

fantastic /fænˈtæstɪk/ *adj* **1** (*informal*) very good; excellent: *She's a fantastic swimmer.* ➲ note at **good** **2** (*informal*) very large or great: *A Rolls Royce costs a fantastic amount of money.* **3** strange and difficult to believe: *a story full of fantastic creatures from other worlds* ▶ **fantastically** /-kli/ *adv*

fantasy /ˈfæntəsi/ *noun* [C,U] (*pl* **fantasies**) a situation that you imagine but that is not true: *I have a fantasy about going to live in the Bahamas.* ◆ *They live in a world of fantasy.* ➲ note at **imagination**

fanzine /ˈfænziːn/ *noun* [C] a magazine that is written by and for people who like a particular sports team, singer, etc.

FAQ /ˌef eɪ ˈkjuː/ *abbr* used in writing to mean **frequently asked questions**

⚷ **far¹** /fɑː(r)/ *adj* (**farther** /ˈfɑːðə(r)/ *or* **further** /ˈfɜːðə(r)/, **farthest** /ˈfɑːðɪst/ *or* **furthest** /ˈfɜːðɪst/) **1** a long distance away: *Let's walk—it's not far.* **2** [only *before* a noun] more distant (of two or more things): *the far side of the river* **3** [only *before* a noun] a long way from the centre in the direction mentioned: *politicians from the far left of the party*
IDM **a far cry from sth/from doing sth** an experience that is very different from sth/doing sth

⚷ **far²** /fɑː(r)/ *adv* (**farther** /ˈfɑːðə(r)/ *or* **further** /ˈfɜːðə(r)/, **farthest** /ˈfɑːðɪst/ *or* **furthest** /ˈfɜːðɪst/) **1** (at) a distance: *London's not far from here.* ◆ *How far did we walk yesterday?* ◆ *If we sit too far away from the screen, I won't be able to see the film.* ◆ *I can't swim as far as you.* ◆ *How much further is it?*

> **HELP** **Far** or **a long way**? **Far** in this sense is usually used in negative sentences and questions. In positive sentences we say **a long way**: *It's a long way from here to the sea.* **Far** can also be used in sentences that have a negative meaning although they are positive in form: *Let's get a bus. It's much too far to walk.*

2 very much: *She's far more intelligent than I thought.* ◆ *There's far too much salt in this soup.* **3** (to) a certain degree: *How far have you got with your homework?* ◆ *The company employs local people as far as possible.* **4** a long time: *We danced far into the night.*
IDM **as far as** to the place mentioned but not further: *We walked as far as the river and then turned back.*
as/so far as used for giving your opinion or judgement of a situation: ***As far as I know**, she's not coming, but I may be wrong.* ◆ ***As far as** school work **is concerned**, he's hopeless.* ◆ ***As far as I'm concerned**, this is the most important point.* ◆ ***As far as I can see**, the accident was John's fault, not Ann's.*
as far as the eye can see to the furthest place you can see
by far (used for emphasizing comparative or superlative words) by a large amount: *Carmen is by far the best student in the class.*
far afield ➲ **afield**
far from sth almost the opposite of sth; not at all: *He's far from happy* (= he's very sad or angry).
far from doing sth instead of doing sth: *Far from enjoying the film, he fell asleep in the middle.*
far from it (*informal*) certainly not; just the opposite: *'Did you enjoy your holiday?' 'No, far from it. It was awful.'*
few and far between ➲ **few**
go far **1** to be enough: *This food won't go very far between three of us.* **2** to be successful in life: *Dan is very talented and should go far.*
go too far to behave in a way that causes trouble or upsets other people: *He's always been naughty but this time he's gone too far.*
so far until now: *So far the weather has been good but it might change.*
so far so good (*spoken*) everything has gone well until now

faraway /ˈfɑːrəweɪ/ *adj* [only *before* a noun] **1** (*written*) a great distance away: *He told us stories of faraway countries.* **2** (used about a look in sb's eyes) as if you are thinking of sth else: *She stared out of the window with a faraway look in her eyes.*

farce /fɑːs/ *noun* **1** [C,U] something important or serious that is not organized well or treated with respect: *The meeting was a farce—everyone was shouting at the same time.* **2** [C] a funny play for the theatre full of ridiculous situations ▶ **farcical** /ˈfɑːsɪkl/ *adj*

fare¹ /feə(r)/ *noun* [C] the amount of money you pay to travel by bus, train, taxi, etc: *What's the fare to Birmingham?* ◆ *Adults pay **full fare**, children pay **half fare**.* ➲ look at **airfare**

fare² /feə(r)/ *verb* [I] (*formal*) to be successful or not successful in a particular situation: *How did you fare in your examination* (= did you do well or badly)*?*

the ˌFar ˈEast *noun* [sing] China, Japan and other countries in East and South East Asia ➲ look at **the Middle East**

farewell /ˌfeəˈwel/ *exclam* (*old-fashioned*) goodbye ▶ **farewell** *noun* [C]: *He said his farewells and left.*

ˌfar-ˈfetched *adj* not easy to believe: *It's a good book but the story's too far-fetched.*

⚷ **farm¹** /fɑːm/ *noun* [C] an area of land with fields and buildings that is used for growing crops and keeping animals: *to work **on a farm*** ◆ *farm buildings/workers/animals* ➲ picture on **page P9**, **page P11**

farm² /fɑːm/ *verb* [I,T] to use land for growing crops or keeping animals: *She farms 200 acres.*

farmer /ˈfɑːmə(r)/ *noun* [C] a person who owns or manages a farm ➲ picture on **page P2**

farmhouse /ˈfɑːmhaʊs/ *noun* [C] the house on a farm where the farmer lives ➲ picture on **page P11**

farming /ˈfɑːmɪŋ/ *noun* [U] managing a farm or working on it: *farming methods/areas*

farmyard /ˈfɑːmjɑːd/ *noun* [C] an outside area near a **farmhouse** surrounded by buildings or walls ➲ picture on **page P11**

ˌfar-ˈreaching *adj* having a great influence on a lot of other things: *far-reaching changes*

ˌfar-ˈsighted *adj* **1** being able to see what will be necessary in the future and making plans for it **2** (*AmE*) = **long-sighted**

fart /fɑːt/ *verb* [I] (*informal*) to suddenly let gas from the stomach escape from your bottom

HELP Be careful. Some people find this word offensive. A more polite way of saying this is 'to break wind'.

▶ **fart** *noun* [C]

farther /ˈfɑːðə(r)/ ➲ **far** ➲ note at **further**

farthest /ˈfɑːðɪst/ ➲ **far**

fascinate /ˈfæsɪneɪt/ *verb* [T] to attract or interest sb very much: *Chinese culture has always fascinated me.* ▶ **fascinating** *adj* ▶ **fascination** /ˌfæsɪˈneɪʃn/ *noun* [C,U]

fascism (also **Fascism**) /ˈfæʃɪzəm/ *noun* [U] an extreme **right-wing** political system which is in favour of strong central government and does not allow anyone to speak against it ▶ **fascist** (also **Fascist**) /-ɪst/ *noun* [C], *adj*

fashion /ˈfæʃn/ *noun* **1** [C,U] the style of dressing or behaving that is the most popular at a particular time: *What is **the latest fashion** in hairstyles?* ◆ *a fashion show/model/magazine* ◆ *Jeans are always **in fashion**.* ◆ *I think hats will **come back into fashion**.* ◆ *That colour is **out of fashion** this year.* ➲ note at **clothes** **2** [sing] the way you do sth: *Watch him. He's been behaving **in a** very strange **fashion**.*

fashionable /ˈfæʃnəbl/ *adj* **1** popular or in a popular style at the time: *fashionable clothes* ◆ *a fashionable area/opinion* OPP **unfashionable** ➲ look at **old-fashioned** **2** considering fashion to be important: *fashionable society* ▶ **fashionably** /-əbli/ *adv*

fast¹ /fɑːst/ *adj* (**faster**; **fastest**) **1** able to move or act at great speed: *a fast car/worker/runner/reader* ➲ note at **quick** **2** [not before a noun] (used about a clock or watch) showing a time that is later than the real time: *The clock is five minutes fast.* OPP **slow** **3** [only *after* a noun] firmly fixed: *He made the boat fast* (= he tied it to sth) *before he got out.* ◆ *Do you think the colour in this T-shirt is fast* (= will not come out when washed)?

IDM **fast and furious** very fast and exciting
hard and fast ➲ **hard¹**

fast² /fɑːst/ *adv* (**faster**; **fastest**) **1** quickly: *The dog ran very fast.* **2** firmly or deeply: *Sam was **fast asleep** by 10 o'clock.* ◆ *Our car was stuck fast in the mud.*

fast³ /fɑːst/ *verb* [I] to eat no food for a certain time, usually for religious reasons: *Muslims fast during Ramadan.* ▶ **fast** *noun* [C]

fasten /ˈfɑːsn/ *verb* **1** [I,T] **fasten sth (up)** to close or join the two parts of sth; to become closed or joined: *Please fasten your seat belts.* ◆ *Fasten your coat up—it's cold outside.* ◆ *My dress fastens at the back.* OPP **unfasten** **2** [T] to close or lock sth firmly so that it will not open: *Close the window and fasten it securely.* OPP **unfasten** **3** [T] **fasten sth (on/to sth); fasten A and B (together)** to fix or tie sth to sth, or two things together: *Fasten this badge on your jacket.* ◆ *How can I fasten these pieces of wood together?*

fastener /ˈfɑːsnə(r)/ (also **fastening** /ˈfɑːsnɪŋ/) *noun* [C] something that fastens things together

ˌfast ˈfood *noun* [U] food that can be served very quickly in special restaurants and is often taken away to be eaten in the street: *a fast food restaurant*

ˌfast-ˈforward *verb* [T] to make a tape or video go forward quickly without playing it ▶ **fast ˈforward** *noun* [U]: *Press fast forward to advance the video.* ◆ *the fast-forward button* ➲ look at **rewind**

fastidious /fæˈstɪdiəs/ *adj* difficult to please; wanting everything to be perfect

fat¹ /fæt/ *adj* (**fatter**; **fattest**) **1** (used about people's or animal's bodies) weighing too much; covered with too much fat: *You'll **get fat** if you eat too much.* ◆ *fat legs, arms, etc.* OPP **thin** **2** (used about a thing) thick or full: *a fat wallet/book*

OTHER WORDS FOR

fat

It is not polite to describe sb as **fat**. **Large** and **overweight** are sometimes used instead: *She's a rather large lady.* ◆ *I'm a bit overweight.* Generally it is not polite to refer to sb's weight when you talk to him/her. **Chubby** is mainly used to describe babies and children who are slightly fat in a pleasant way: *a baby with chubby cheeks.* Doctors use the word **obese** to describe people who are very fat in a way that is not healthy.

fat² /fæt/ *noun* **1** [U] the soft white substance under the skins of animals and people: *I don't like meat with lots of fat on it.* ➲ *adjective* **fatty** **2** [C,U] the substance containing oil that we obtain from animals, plants or seeds and use for cooking: *Cook the onions in a little fat.*

fatal /ˈfeɪtl/ *adj* **1** causing or ending in death: *a fatal accident/disease/crash* ➲ look at **mortal** **2** causing trouble or a bad result: *She made the fatal mistake of trusting him.* ▶ **fatally** /-təli/ *adv*: *fatally injured*

fatality /fəˈtæləti/ *noun* [C] (*pl* **fatalities**) sb's death caused by an accident, in war, etc: *There were no fatalities in the fire.*

fate /feɪt/ *noun* **1** [C] your future; something that happens to you: *Both men suffered the same fate—*

they both lost their jobs. **2** [U] the power that some people believe controls everything that happens: *It was fate that brought them together again after twenty years.*

fateful /ˈfeɪtfl/ *adj* having an important effect on the future: *a fateful decision*

father¹ /ˈfɑːðə(r)/ *noun* [C] **1** sb's male parent: *John looks exactly like his father.* **2 Father** the title of certain priests: *Father O'Reilly*

father² /ˈfɑːðə(r)/ *verb* [T] to become a father by making a woman pregnant: *to father a child*

ˌFather ˈChristmas (*especially AmE* ˈSanta Claus) *noun* [C] (*BrE*) an imaginary old man with a red coat and a long white beard who, children believe, brings presents at Christmas

fatherhood /ˈfɑːðəhʊd/ *noun* [U] the state of being a father

ˈfather-in-law *noun* [C] (*pl* ˈfathers-in-law) the father of your husband or wife

fatherly /ˈfɑːðəli/ *adj* like or typical of a father: *Would you like a piece of fatherly advice?*

Father's Day *noun* [C] a day when fathers receive cards and gifts from their children, usually the third Sunday in June

fathom /ˈfæðəm/ *verb* [T] [usually in the negative] to understand sth: *I can't fathom what he means.*

fatigue /fəˈtiːg/ *noun* [U] **1** the feeling of being extremely tired: *He was suffering from mental and physical fatigue.* SYN **exhaustion** **2** weakness in metals caused by a lot of use: *The plane crash was caused by metal fatigue in a wing.*

fatten /ˈfætn/ *verb* [T] **fatten sb/sth (up)** to make sb/sth fatter: *He's fattening the pigs up for market.*

fattening /ˈfætnɪŋ/ *adj* (used about food) that makes people fat: *Chocolate is very fattening.*

fatty /ˈfæti/ *adj* (**fattier**; **fattiest**) (used about food) having a lot of fat in or on it

faucet /ˈfɔːsɪt/ (*AmE*) = **tap²**(1)

fault¹ /fɔːlt/ *noun* **1** [C] something wrong or not perfect in sb's character or in a thing: *One of my faults is that I'm always late.* ➲ note at **mistake** **2** [U] responsibility for a mistake: *It will be your* ***own fault*** *if you don't pass your exams.* ♦ *It wasn't my fault!*

IDM **be at fault** to be wrong or responsible for a mistake: *The other driver was at fault—he didn't stop at the traffic lights.*

find fault (with sb/sth) ➲ **find¹**

fault² /fɔːlt/ *verb* [T] to find sth wrong with sb/sth: *It was impossible to fault her English.*

faultless /ˈfɔːltləs/ *adj* without any mistakes: *The pianist gave a faultless performance.* SYN **perfect**

faulty /ˈfɔːlti/ *adj* (used especially about electricity or machinery) not working properly: *a faulty switch* ♦ *faulty goods*

fauna /ˈfɔːnə/ *noun* [U] all the animals of an area or a period of time: *the flora and fauna of South America* ➲ look at **flora**

faux pas /ˌfəʊ ˈpɑː/ *noun* [C] (*pl* **faux pas** /ˌfəʊ ˈpɑːz/) something you say or do that is embarrassing or offends people: *to* ***make a faux pas***

favorite (*AmE*) = **favourite**

favoritism (*AmE*) = **favouritism**

favour¹ (*AmE* **favor**) /ˈfeɪvə(r)/ *noun* **1** [C] something that helps sb: *Would you* ***do me a favour*** *and post this letter for me?* ♦ *Could I* ***ask you a favour****?* ♦ *Are they paying you for the work, or are you doing it* ***as a favour****?* **2** [U] **favour (with sb)** liking or approval: *I'm afraid I'm* ***out of favour*** *with my neighbour since our last argument.* ♦ *The new boss's methods didn't* ***find favour*** *with the staff.*

IDM **in favour of sb/sth** in agreement with: *Are you in favour of private education?*

in sb's favour to the advantage of sb: *The committee decided in their favour.*

favour² (*AmE* **favor**) /ˈfeɪvə(r)/ *verb* [T] **1** to support sb/sth; to prefer: *Which suggestion do you favour?* **2** to treat one person very well and so be unfair to others: *Parents must try not to favour one of their children.*

favourable (*AmE* **favorable**) /ˈfeɪvərəbl/ *adj* **1** showing liking or approval: *He made a favourable impression on the interviewers.* **2** (often used about the weather) suitable or helpful: *Conditions are favourable for skiing today.* OPP for both meanings **unfavourable** ▶ **favourably** (*AmE* **favorably**) /-əbli/ *adv*

favourite¹ (*AmE* **favorite**) /ˈfeɪvərɪt/ *adj* liked more than any other: *What is your favourite colour?* ♦ *Who is your favourite singer?*

favourite² (*AmE* **favorite**) /ˈfeɪvərɪt/ *noun* [C] **1** a person or thing that you like more than any others: *The other kids were jealous of Rose because she was the teacher's favourite.* **2 favourite (for sth/to do sth)** the horse, team, person, etc. that is expected to win: *Mimms is the hot favourite for the leadership of the party.* OPP **outsider** **3 favorite** = **bookmark**

favouritism (*AmE* **favoritism**) /ˈfeɪvərɪtɪzəm/ *noun* [U] giving unfair advantages to the person or people that you like best: *The referee was accused of* ***showing favouritism*** *to the home side.*

fawn¹ /fɔːn/ *adj, noun* [U] (of) a light yellowish-brown colour

fawn² /fɔːn/ *noun* [C] a young **deer** (= a large wild animal that eats grass) ➲ note at **deer** ➲ picture at **deer**

fax¹ /fæks/ *noun* **1** [C,U] a copy of a letter, etc. that you can send by telephone lines using a special machine: *They need an answer today so I'll* ***send a fax.*** ♦ *The company contacted us* ***by fax.*** **2** [C] (*also* ˈ**fax machine**) the machine that you use for sending faxes: *Have you got a fax?* ♦ *What's your fax number?*

fax² /fæks/ *verb* [T] **fax sth (to sb)**; **fax sb (sth)** to send sb a **fax**: *We will fax our order to you tomorrow.* ♦ *I've faxed her a copy of the letter.*

faze /feɪz/ *verb* [T] (*informal*) to make sb worried or nervous: *He doesn't get fazed by things going wrong.*

FBI /ˌef biː ˈaɪ/ *abbr* (*AmE*) **Federal Bureau of Investigation**; a section of the US government which deals with crimes that affect more than one state of the US, such as **terrorism** (= violent acts for political purposes)

FC /ˌef ˈsiː/ *abbr* (*BrE*) **Football Club**: *Everton FC*

FCO /ˌef siː ˈəʊ/ *abbr* = **Foreign and Commonwealth Office**

FE /ˌef ˈiː/ *abbr* = **further education**

F

⚷ **fear[1]** /fɪə(r)/ *noun* [C,U] the feeling that you have when sth dangerous, painful or frightening might happen: *He was shaking* ***with fear*** *after the accident.* ◆ *People in this area live* ***in*** *constant* ***fear*** *of crime.* ◆ *She showed no fear.* ◆ *This book helped me overcome my fear of dogs.* ◆ *My fears for his safety were unnecessary.*

IDM **no fear** (*spoken*) (used when answering a suggestion) certainly not

⚷ **fear[2]** /fɪə(r)/ *verb* [T] **1** to be afraid of sb/sth or of doing sth: *We all fear illness and death.* **2** to feel that sth bad might happen or might have happened: *The government fears that it will lose the next election.* ◆ *Thousands of people are feared dead in the earthquake.*

PHR V **fear for sb/sth** to be worried about sb/sth: *Parents often fear for the safety of their children.*

fearful /ˈfɪəfl/ *adj* (*formal*) **1 fearful (of sth/doing sth); fearful that ...** afraid or worried about sth: *You should never be fearful of starting something new.* ◆ *They were fearful that they would miss the plane.* ➲ Much more common words are **frightened**, **scared** and **afraid**. **2** [only *before* a noun] terrible: *the fearful consequences of war* ▶ **fearfully** /-fəli/ *adv* ▶ **fearfulness** *noun* [U]

fearless /ˈfɪələs/ *adj* never afraid ▶ **fearlessly** *adv* ▶ **fearlessness** *noun* [U]

feasible /ˈfiːzəbl/ *adj* possible to do: *a feasible plan* ▶ **feasibility** /ˌfiːzəˈbɪləti/ *noun* [U]

feast /fiːst/ *noun* [C] a large, special meal, especially to celebrate sth ▶ **feast** *verb* [I] **feast (on sth)**: *They feasted on exotic dishes.*

feat /fiːt/ *noun* [C] something you do that shows great strength, skill or courage: *That new bridge is a remarkable feat of engineering.* ◆ *Persuading Helen to give you a pay rise was* ***no mean feat*** (= difficult to do).

⚷ **feather** /ˈfeðə(r)/ *noun* [C] one of the light, soft things that grow in a bird's skin and cover its body ➲ picture on **page P12**

⚷ **feature[1]** /ˈfiːtʃə(r)/ *noun* [C] **1** an important or noticeable part of sth: *Mountains and lakes are the main features of the landscape of Wales.* ◆ *Noise is a feature of city life.* **2** a part of the face: *Her eyes are her best feature.* **3 a feature (on sth)** a special article or programme about sth in a newspaper, on TV, etc: *There's a feature on kangaroos in this magazine.* **4** (*old-fashioned*) (also ˈ**feature film**) a long film that tells a story

⚷ **feature[2]** /ˈfiːtʃə(r)/ *verb* **1** [T] to include sb/sth as an important part: *The film features many well-known actors.* **2** [I] **feature in sth** to have a part in sth: *Does marriage feature in your future plans?* **SYN** **figure**

featureless /ˈfiːtʃələs/ *adj* without any qualities or noticeable characteristics: *a dull, featureless landscape*

Feb. *abbr* = **February**: *18 Feb. 2012*

⚷ **February** /ˈfebruəri/ *noun* [U,C] (*abbr* **Feb.**) the 2nd month of the year, coming after January ➲ note at **January**

feces (*AmE*) = **faeces**

fed *past tense, past participle of* **feed[1]**

⚷ **federal** /ˈfedərəl/ *adj* **1** organized as a **federation**: *a federal system of rule* **2** connected with the central government of a **federation**: *That is a federal not a state law.*

federation /ˌfedəˈreɪʃn/ *noun* [C] a group of states, etc. that have joined together to form a single group

ˌ**fed** ˈ**up** *adj* [not before a noun] (*informal*) **fed up (with/of sb/sth/doing sth)** bored or unhappy; tired of sth: *What's the matter? You look really fed up.* ◆ *I'm fed up with waiting for the phone to ring.*

⚷ **fee** /fiː/ *noun* [C] **1** [usually plural] the money you pay for professional advice or service from private doctors, lawyers, schools, universities, etc: *We can't afford private school fees.* ◆ *Does the bank* ***charge a fee****?* **2** the cost of an exam, the cost of becoming a member of a club, the amount you pay to go into certain buildings, etc: *How much is the entrance fee?* ➲ note at **pay[2]**

feeble /ˈfiːbl/ *adj* (**feebler**; **feeblest**) **1** with no energy or power; weak: *a feeble old man* ◆ *a feeble cry* **2** not able to make sb believe sth: *a feeble argument/excuse* ▶ **feebly** /ˈfiːbli/ *adv*

⚷ **feed[1]** /fiːd/ *verb* (*pt, pp* **fed** /fed/) **1** [T] **feed sb/sth (on) (sth)** to give food to a person or an animal: *Don't forget to feed the cat.* ◆ *I can't come yet. I haven't fed the baby.* ◆ *Some of the snakes in the zoo are fed (on) rats.* **2** [I] **feed (on sth)** (used about animals or babies) to eat: *What do horses feed on in the winter?* ◆ *Bats feed at night.* **3** [T] **feed A (with B); feed B into/to/through A** to supply sb/sth with sth; to put sth into sth else: *This channel feeds us with news and information 24 hours a day.* ◆ *Metal sheets are fed through the machine one at a time.*

feed[2] /fiːd/ *noun* **1** [C] a meal for an animal or a baby: *When's the baby's next feed due?* **2** [U] food for animals: *cattle feed*

feedback /ˈfiːdbæk/ *noun* [U] information or comments about sth that sb has done which tells them how good or bad it is: *The teacher spent five minutes with each of us to* ***give us feedback on*** *our homework.* ◆ *We like to get feedback from our customers.*

⚷ **feel[1]** /fiːl/ *verb* (*pt, pp* **felt** /felt/) **1** [I] [usually with an adjective] to be in the state that is mentioned: *to feel cold/sick/tired/happy* ◆ *How are you feeling today?* ◆ *You'll feel better in the morning.* **2** [T] to notice or experience sth physical or emotional: *It was so cold that she could not feel her toes.* ♦ *I felt something crawling up my back.* ♦ *I don't feel any sympathy for Matt at all.* ♦ *You could feel the tension in the courtroom.* **3** [I] used to say how sth seems to you when you touch, see, smell, experience, etc. it: *My new coat feels like leather but it's not.* ♦ *He* ***felt as if*** *he had been there before.* ♦ *My head* ***feels as though*** *it will burst.* ♦ *I felt (that) it was a mistake not to ask her advice.*

MORE 'It' is often used as the subject of **feel** in this sense: *It feels as if it is going to snow soon.*

4 [T] to touch sth in order to find out what it is like: *Feel this material. Is it cotton or silk?* ♦ *I felt her forehead to see if she had got a temperature.* **5** [T] to be affected by sth: *Do you feel the cold in winter?* ♦ *She felt it badly when her mother died.* **6** [I] **feel (about) (for sb/sth)** to try to find sth with your hands instead of your eyes: *She felt about in the dark for the light switch.*

IDM be/feel like jelly ➲ **jelly**
be/feel out of it ➲ **out of**
be/feel sorry for sb ➲ **sorry**[1]
feel free (to do sth) (*informal*) used to tell sb they are allowed to do sth: *Feel free to use the phone.*
feel like sth/doing sth to want sth or to want to do sth: *Do you feel like going out?*
feel your age to realize that you are getting old, especially compared to other younger people around you
have/feel a lump in your throat ➲ **lump**[1]
not feel yourself to not feel healthy or well
PHR V feel for sb to understand sb's feelings and situation and feel sorry for them: *I really felt for him when his wife died.*
feel up to sth/to doing sth to have the strength and the energy to do or deal with sth: *I really don't feel up to eating a huge meal.*

feel[2] /fiːl/ *noun* [sing] **1** an act of touching sth in order to learn about it: *Let me have a feel of that material.* **2** the impression sth gives you when you touch it; the impression that a place or situation gives you: *You can tell it's wool by the feel.* ♦ *The town has a friendly feel.*

feeler /ˈfiːlə(r)/ *noun* [C, usually pl] either of the two long thin parts on the heads of some insects and of some animals that live in shells that they use to feel and touch things with **SYN antenna**
IDM put out feelers (*informal*) to try to find out what people think about sth before you do it

feeling /ˈfiːlɪŋ/ *noun* **1** [C] **a feeling (of sth)** something that you feel in your mind or body: *a feeling of hunger/happiness/fear/helplessness* ♦ *I've got a funny feeling in my leg.* **2** [sing] a belief or idea that sth is true or is likely to happen: *I* ***get the feeling*** *that Ian doesn't like me much.* ♦ *I* ***have a*** *nasty* ***feeling*** *that Jan didn't get our message.* **3** [C,U] **feeling(s) (about/on sth)** an attitude or opinion about sth: *What are your feelings on this matter?* ♦ *My own feeling is that we should postpone the meeting.* ♦ *Public feeling seems to be against the new road.* **4** [U,C, usually pl] strong emotion; sb's emotions: *Let's practise that song again, this time* ***with feeling.*** ♦ *I have to tell Jeff his work's not good enough but I don't want to* ***hurt*** *his* ***feelings.*** **5** [C,U] **(a) feeling/feelings (for sb/sth)** love or understanding for sb/sth: *She doesn't have much (of a) feeling for music.* ♦ *He still has feelings for his ex-wife.* **6** [U] the ability to feel in your body: *After the accident he lost all feeling in his legs.*

IDM bad/ill feeling unhappy relations between people: *The decision caused a lot of bad feeling at the factory.*
no hard feelings ➲ **hard**[1]

feet *plural* of **foot**[1]

feisty /ˈfaɪsti/ *adj* (**feistier; feistiest**) (*informal*) (used about people) strong, determined and not afraid to argue

feline /ˈfiːlaɪn/ *adj* connected with an animal of the cat family; like a cat

fell[1] *past tense* of **fall**[1]

fell[2] /fel/ *verb* [T] to cut down a tree

fellow[1] /ˈfeləʊ/ *noun* [C] **1** (*old-fashioned*) a man: *What's that fellow over there doing?* **2** a person who is paid to study a particular thing at a university: *Lisa Jones is a research fellow in the biology department.* **3** a member of an academic or professional organization, or of certain universities: *a fellow of New College, Oxford*

fellow[2] /ˈfeləʊ/ *adj* [only *before* a noun] another or others like yourself in the same situation: *Her fellow students were all older than her.* ♦ *fellow workers/passengers/citizens*

fellowship /ˈfeləʊʃɪp/ *noun* **1** [U] a feeling of friendship between people who share an interest **2** [C] a group or society of people who share the same interest or belief **3** [C] the position of a college or university fellow

felon /ˈfelən/ *noun* [C] (*especially AmE*) a person who has committed a **felony**

felony /ˈfeləni/ *noun* [C,U] (*pl* **felonies**) (*especially AmE*) the act of committing a serious crime, such as murder; a crime of this type ➲ look at **misdemeanour**

felt[1] *past tense, past participle* of **feel**[1]

felt[2] /felt/ *noun* [U] a type of soft cloth made from wool, etc. which has been pressed tightly together: *a felt hat*

ˌfelt-tip ˈpen (also **felt ˈtip**) *noun* [C] a type of pen with a point made of felt ➲ picture at **stationery**

female[1] /ˈfiːmeɪl/ *adj* **1** being a woman or a girl: *a female artist/employer/student* ➲ look at **feminine** **2** being of the sex that can produce eggs or give birth to babies: *a female cat* **3** (used about plants and flowers) that can produce fruit **OPP** for all meanings **male**

female[2] /ˈfiːmeɪl/ *noun* [C] **1** an animal that can produce eggs or give birth to babies; a plant that can produce fruit: *Is your mouse a male or a female?* **2** a woman or a girl: *More females than males become teachers.* ➲ look at **male**

F

feminine /ˈfemənɪn/ *adj* **1** typical of or looking like a woman; connected with women: *My daughter always dresses like a boy. She hates looking feminine.* ➲ note at **masculine** ➲ look at **female** **2** (in English) of the forms of words used to describe females: *'Lioness' is the feminine form of 'lion'.* **3** (in the grammar of some languages) belonging to a certain class of nouns, adjectives or pronouns: *The German word for a flower is feminine.* ➲ look at **masculine, neuter** ▶ **femininity** /ˌfeməˈnɪnəti/ *noun* [U]

feminism /ˈfemənɪzəm/ *noun* [U] the belief that women should have the same rights and opportunities as men ▶ **feminist** /-ɪst/ *noun* [C], *adj*

F

fence

wall

⚷ **fence**[1] /fens/ *noun* [C] a line of wooden or metal posts joined by wood, wire, metal, etc. to divide land or to keep animals in, or to keep people and animals out

IDM **sit on the fence** ➲ **sit** ➲ picture on **page P11**

fence[2] /fens/ *verb* **1** [T] to surround land with a fence **2** [I] to fight with a **foil** (= a long thin pointed weapon) as a sport

PHR V **fence sth/sb in 1** to surround sth with a fence: *They fenced in their garden to make it more private.* **2** to limit sb's freedom: *She felt fenced in by so many responsibilities.*

fence sth off to separate one area from another with a fence

fencing /ˈfensɪŋ/ *noun* [U] the sport of fighting with **foils** (= long thin pointed weapons) ➲ picture on **page P5**

fend /fend/ *verb*

PHR V **fend for yourself** to look after yourself without help from anyone else: *It's time Ben left home and learnt to fend for himself.*

fend sb/sth off to defend yourself from sb/sth that is attacking you: *Politicians usually manage to fend off awkward questions.*

fender /ˈfendə(r)/ *noun* [C] **1** (*AmE*) = **wing**(4) **2** a low metal frame in front of an open fire that stops coal or wood falling out

feng shui /ˌfeŋ ˈʃuːi; ˌfʊŋ ˈʃweɪ/ *noun* [U] a Chinese system for deciding the right position for a building and for placing objects inside a building in order to make people feel comfortable and happy

fennel /ˈfenl/ *noun* [U] a vegetable that has a thick round part at the base of the leaves with a strong taste. The seeds and leaves are also used in cooking.

ferment[1] /fəˈment/ *verb* [I,T] to change or make the chemistry of sth change, especially sugar changing to alcohol: *The wine is starting to ferment.* ▶ **fermentation** /ˌfɜːmenˈteɪʃn/ *noun* [U]

ferment[2] /ˈfɜːment/ *noun* [U] a state of political or social excitement and change: *The country is* ***in ferment*** *and nobody's sure what will happen next.*

fern /fɜːn/ *noun* [C] a green plant with no flowers and a lot of long thin leaves

ferocious /fəˈrəʊʃəs/ *adj* very aggressive and violent: *a ferocious beast/attack/storm/war* ▶ **ferociously** *adv*

ferocity /fəˈrɒsəti/ *noun* [U] violence; cruel and aggressive behaviour ➲ *adjective* **fierce**

ferret[1] /ˈferɪt/ *noun* [C] a small animal with a long thin body, kept as a pet or for hunting other animals

ferret[2] /ˈferɪt/ *verb* [I] (*informal*) ferret (about/around) (for sth) to search for sth that is lost or hidden among a lot of things: *She opened the drawer and ferreted around for her keys.*

PHR V **ferret sb/sth out** (*informal*) to discover information or to find sb/sth by searching thoroughly, asking a lot of questions, etc.

ferry[1] /ˈferi/ *noun* [C] (*pl* **ferries**) a boat that carries people, vehicles or goods across a river or across a narrow part of the sea: *a car ferry* ➲ note at **boat** ➲ picture on **page P6**

ferry[2] /ˈferi/ *verb* [T] (**ferrying**; **ferries**; *pt, pp* **ferried**) to carry people or goods in a boat or other vehicle from one place to another, usually for a short distance: *Could you ferry us across to the island?* ◆ *We share the job of ferrying the children to school.*

fertile /ˈfɜːtaɪl/ *adj* **1** (used about land or soil) that plants grow well in OPP **infertile** **2** (used about people, animals or plants) that can produce babies, fruit or new plants OPP **infertile** ➲ look at **sterile** **3** (used about sb's mind) full of ideas: *She has a fertile imagination.* ▶ **fertility** /fəˈtɪləti/ *noun* [U]: *Nowadays women can take drugs to increase their fertility* (= their chances of having a child). OPP **infertility**

fertilize (also -ise) /ˈfɜːtəlaɪz/ *verb* [T] **1** (*technical*) to put a male seed into an egg, a plant or a female animal so that a baby, fruit or a young animal starts to develop **2** to put natural or artificial substances on soil in order to make plants grow better ▶ **fertilization** (also -isation) /ˌfɜːtəlaɪˈzeɪʃn/ *noun* [U]

fertilizer (also -iser) /ˈfɜːtəlaɪzə(r)/ *noun* [C,U] a natural or chemical substance that is put on land or soil to make plants grow better ➲ look at **manure**

fervent /ˈfɜːvənt/ *adj* having or showing very strong feelings about sth: *She's a fervent believer in women's rights.* ◆ *a fervent belief/hope/desire* ▶ **fervently** *adv*

fervour (*AmE* fervor) /ˈfɜːvə(r)/ *noun* [U] very strong feelings about sth SYN **enthusiasm**

fester /ˈfestə(r)/ *verb* [I] **1** (used about a cut or an injury) to become infected: *a festering sore/wound* **2** (used about an unpleasant situation, feeling or thought) to become more unpleasant because you do not deal with it successfully

⚷ **festival** /ˈfestɪvl/ *noun* [C] **1** a series of plays, films, musical performances, etc. often held regularly in one place: *the Cannes Film Festival* ◆ *a jazz festival* **2** a day or time when people celebrate sth (especially a religious event): *Christmas is an important Christian festival.*

festive /ˈfestɪv/ *adj* happy, because people are enjoying themselves celebrating sth: *the festive season* (= Christmas)

festivity /feˈstɪvəti/ *noun* (*pl* **festivities**) **1** [pl] happy events when people celebrate sth: *The festivities went on until dawn.* **2** [U] being happy and celebrating sth: *The wedding was followed by three days of festivity.*

fetch /fetʃ/ *verb* [T] **1** (*especially BrE*) to go to a place and bring back sb/sth: *Shall I fetch you your coat?* ◆ *Shall I fetch your coat for you?* ➲ picture at **bring** **2** (used about goods) to be sold for the price mentioned: *'How much will your car fetch?' 'It should fetch about £2000.'*

fete (also **fête**) /feɪt/ *noun* [C] (*BrE*) an outdoor event with competitions, entertainment and things to buy, often organized to make money for a particular purpose: *the school/village/church fete*

fetus (*AmE*) = **foetus**

feud /fjuːd/ *noun* [C] **a feud (between A and B); a feud (with sb) (over sb/sth)** an angry and serious argument between two people or groups that continues over a long period of time: *a family feud* (= within a family or between two families) ▶ **feud** *verb* [I]

feudal /ˈfjuːdl/ *adj* connected with the system of **feudalism**: *the feudal system*

feudalism /ˈfjuːdəlɪzəm/ *noun* [U] the social system which existed in the Middle Ages in Europe, in which people worked and fought for a person who owned land and received land and protection from them in return

fever /ˈfiːvə(r)/ *noun* **1** [C,U] a condition of the body when it is too hot because of illness: *He has a high fever.* ➲ note at **ill** ➲ look at **temperature** **2** [sing] **a fever (of sth)** a state of nervous excitement: *a fever of impatience*

feverish /ˈfiːvərɪʃ/ *adj* **1** suffering from or caused by a fever: *a feverish cold/dream* **2** showing great excitement ▶ **feverishly** *adv*

few /fjuː/ *determiner* (**fewer**; **fewest**) *adj, pron* [used with a plural countable noun and a plural verb] **1** not many: *Few people live to be 100.* ◆ *There are fewer cars here today than yesterday.* ◆ *Few of the players played really well.* **2** **a few** a small number of; some: *a few people* ◆ *a few hours/days/years* ◆ *I'll meet you later. I've got a few things to do first.* ◆ *I knew a few of the people there.* ➲ note at **less**

IDM **few and far between** not happening very often; not common: *Pubs are a bit few and far between in this area.*

a good few; quite a few a fairly large amount or number: *It's been a good few years since I saw him last.*

fiancé (*fem* **fiancée**) /fiˈɒnseɪ/ *noun* [C] a person who has promised to marry sb: *This is my fiancée Liz. We got engaged a few weeks ago.*

fiasco /fiˈæskəʊ/ *noun* [C] (*pl* **fiascos**, *AmE* also **fiascoes**) an event that does not succeed, often in a way that causes embarrassment: *Our last party was a complete fiasco.* **SYN** **disaster**

fib /fɪb/ *noun* [C] (*informal*) something you say that is not true: *Please don't tell fibs.* **SYN** **lie** ▶ **fib** *verb* [I] (**fibbing**; **fibbed**) **HELP** **Fib** is used when the lie does not seem very important.

fibre (*AmE* **fiber**) /ˈfaɪbə(r)/ *noun* **1** [U] parts of plants that you eat which are good for you because they help to move food quickly through your body: *Wholemeal bread is* ***high in fibre.*** **2** [C,U] a material or a substance that is made from natural or artificial threads

> **MORE** **Natural** fibres are, for example, cotton and wool. **Man-made** or **synthetic** fibres are **nylon, polyester**, etc.

3 [C] one of the thin threads which form a natural or artificial substance: *cotton/wood/nerve/muscle fibres*

fibreglass (*AmE* **fiberglass**) /ˈfaɪbəɡlɑːs/ (also **glass ˈfibre**) *noun* [U] a material made from small threads of plastic or glass, used for making small boats, parts of cars, etc.

fickle /ˈfɪkl/ *adj* always changing your mind or your feelings so you cannot be trusted: *a fickle friend*

fiction /ˈfɪkʃn/ *noun* [U] stories, novels, etc. which describe events and people that are not real: *I don't read much fiction.* **OPP** **non-fiction** ➲ note at **literature** ➲ look at **fact**

fictional /ˈfɪkʃənl/ *adj* not real or true; only existing in stories, novels, etc: *fictional characters* ➲ look at **factual**

fictitious /fɪkˈtɪʃəs/ *adj* invented; not real: *The novel is set in a fictitious town called Eden.*

fiddle¹ /ˈfɪdl/ *verb* **1** [I] **fiddle (about/around) (with sth)** to play with sth carelessly, because you are nervous or not thinking: *Tristram sat nervously, fiddling with a pencil.* **2** [T] (*informal*) to change the details or facts of sth (business accounts, etc.) in order to get money dishonestly: *She fiddled her expenses form.*

fiddle² /ˈfɪdl/ *noun* [C] (*informal*) **1** = **violin** **2** (*BrE*) a dishonest action, especially one connected with money: *a tax fiddle*

fiddler /ˈfɪdlə(r)/ *noun* [C] a person who plays the **violin** (= a musical instrument with strings), especially to play **folk music** (= traditional music)

fiddly /ˈfɪdli/ *adj* (**fiddlier**; **fiddliest**) (*informal*) difficult to do or manage with your hands (because small or complicated parts are involved)

fidelity /fɪˈdeləti/ *noun* [U] **1** (*formal*) **fidelity (to sb/sth)** the quality of being faithful, especially to a wife or husband by not having a sexual relationship with anyone else ➲ A less formal word is **faithfulness.** **OPP** **infidelity** **2** the quality of being accurate or close to the original: *the fidelity of the translation to the original text* ➲ look at **hi-fi**

fidget /ˈfɪdʒɪt/ *verb* [I] **fidget (with sth)** to keep moving your body, hands or feet because you are

F

nervous, bored, excited, etc: *She fidgeted nervously with her keys.* ▶ **fidgety** *adj*

⚷ **field**[1] /fiːld/ *noun* [C] **1** an area of land on a farm, usually surrounded by fences or walls, used for growing crops or keeping animals in ➲ picture on **page P11** **2** an area of land used for sports, games or some other activity: *a football field* ♦ *an airfield* (= where planes land and take off) ♦ *a battlefield* ➲ look at **pitch** **3** an area of land where oil, coal or other minerals are found: *a North Sea oilfield* ♦ *a coalfield* **4** an area of study or knowledge: *He's an expert in the field of economics.* ♦ *That question is outside my field* (= not one of the subjects that I know about). **5** an area affected by or included in sth: *a magnetic field* ♦ *It's outside my field of vision* (= I can't see it).

F

field[2] /fiːld/ *verb* **1** [T] to choose a team for games such as football, **cricket**, etc: *New Zealand is fielding an excellent team for the next match.* **2** [I,T] (in sports such as **cricket**, **baseball**, etc.) to (be ready to) catch and throw back the ball after sb has hit it

MORE When one team is **fielding**, the other is **batting**.

ˈ**field day** *noun*
IDM **have a field day** to get the opportunity to do sth you enjoy, especially sth other people do not approve of: *The newspapers always have a field day when there's a political scandal.*

fielder /ˈfiːldə(r)/ *noun* [C] (in sports such as **cricket** and **baseball**) a player who is trying to catch the ball rather than hit it

ˈ**field event** *noun* [C] a sport, such as jumping and throwing, that is not a race and does not involve running ➲ look at **track event**

ˈ**field hockey** (*AmE*) = **hockey**(1)

ˈ**field trip** *noun* [C] a journey made to study sth in its natural environment: *We went on a geography field trip.*

fieldwork /ˈfiːldwɜːk/ *noun* [U] practical research work done outside school, college, etc.

fiend /fiːnd/ *noun* [C] **1** a very cruel person **2** (*informal*) a person who is very interested in one particular thing: *My dad's a real crossword fiend.*

fiendish /ˈfiːndɪʃ/ *adj* **1** very unpleasant or cruel **2** (*informal*) clever and complicated: *a fiendish plan* ▶ **fiendishly** *adv*

fierce /fɪəs/ *adj* (**fiercer**; **fiercest**) **1** angry, aggressive and frightening: *The house was guarded by fierce dogs.* **2** very strong; violent: *fierce competition for jobs* ♦ *a fierce attack* ➲ noun **ferocity** ▶ **fiercely** *adv*

fiery /ˈfaɪəri/ *adj* (**fierier**; **fieriest**) **1** looking like fire: *She has fiery red hair.* **2** quick to become angry: *a fiery temper* **SYN** **passionate**

⚷ **fifteen** /ˌfɪfˈtiːn/ *number* 15 ➲ note at **six** ▶ **fifteenth** /ˌfɪfˈtiːnθ/ *ordinal number, noun* [C] ➲ note at **sixth**

⚷ **fifth**[1] /fɪfθ/ *ordinal number* 5th ➲ note at **sixth**

⚷ **fifth**[2] /fɪfθ/ *noun* [C] ⅕; one of five equal parts of sth

⚷ **fifty** /ˈfɪfti/ *number* 50 ➲ note at **sixty** ▶ **fiftieth** /ˈfɪftiəθ/ *ordinal number, noun* [C] ➲ note at **sixth**

ˌ**fifty-ˈfifty** *adj, adv* equal or equally (between two people, groups, etc.): *You've got **a fifty-fifty chance** of winning.* ♦ *We'll divide the money fifty-fifty.*

fig /fɪɡ/ *noun* [C] (a type of tree with) a soft sweet fruit full of seeds that grows in warm countries and is often eaten dried ➲ picture on **page P14**

fig. *abbr* = **figure**[1](7): *See diagram at fig. 2.*

⚷ **fight**[1] /faɪt/ *verb* (*pt, pp* **fought** /fɔːt/) **1** [I,T] **fight (against sb/sth)** to use physical strength, guns, weapons, etc. against sb/sth: *My younger brothers were always fighting.* ♦ *They gathered soldiers to fight the invading army.* **2** [I,T] **fight (against sth)** to try very hard to stop or prevent sth: *to fight a fire/a decision/prejudice* ♦ *to fight against crime/disease* **3** [I] **fight (for sth/to do sth)** to try very hard to get or keep sth: *to fight for your rights* **4** [I] **fight (with sb) (about/over sth)** to argue: *It's not worth fighting about money.* ➲ look at **argue, quarrel**
PHR V **fight back** to attack sb who has attacked you: *If he hits you again, fight back!*
▶ **fighting** *noun* [U]: *Fighting broke out in the city last night.*

⚷ **fight**[2] /faɪt/ *noun* **1** [C] **a fight (with sb/sth); a fight (between A and B)** the act of using physical force against sb/sth: *Don't **get into a fight** at school, will you?* ♦ *Fights broke out between rival groups of fans.* **2** [sing] **a fight (against/for sth) (to do sth)** the work done trying to destroy, prevent or achieve sth: *Protesters won their fight against the airport expansion.* **3** [C] (*especially AmE*) **a fight (with sb/sth) (about/over sth)** an argument about sth: *I **had a fight** with my mum over what time I had to be home.* **4** [U] the desire to continue trying or fighting: *I've had some bad luck but I've still got plenty of fight in me.*
IDM **pick a fight** ➲ **pick**[1]

fighter /ˈfaɪtə(r)/ *noun* [C] **1** (also ˈ**fighter plane**) a small fast military aircraft used for attacking enemy aircraft: *a fighter pilot* ♦ *a jet fighter* **2** a person who fights in a war or a **boxer** (= sb who fights with their hands in sport)

figurative /ˈfɪɡərətɪv/ *adj* (used about a word or an expression) not used with its exact meaning but in a way that is different to give a special effect: *'He exploded with rage' is a figurative use of the verb 'to explode'.* ➲ look at **literal, metaphor** ▶ **figuratively** *adv*

⚷ **figure**[1] /ˈfɪɡə(r)/ *noun*
➤NUMBER **1** [C] an amount (in numbers) or a price: *The unemployment figures are lower this month.* ♦ *What sort of figure are you thinking of for your house?* **2** [C] a written sign for a number (0 to 9): *Write the numbers in figures, not words.* ♦ *He has a six-figure income/an income in six figures* (= £100 000 or more). ♦ *Interest rates are now down to single figures* (= less than 10%). ♦ *double figures* (= 10 to 99) **3** **figures** [pl] (*informal*) mathematics: *I don't **have a head for figures*** (= I'm not very good with numbers).
➤PERSON **4** [C] an important person: *an important*

political figure **5** [C] the shape of the human body, especially a woman's body that is attractive: *She's got a beautiful slim figure.* ➲ note at **build²** **6** [C] a person that you cannot see very clearly or do not know: *Two figures were coming towards us in the dark.* ♦ *There were two figures on the right of the photo that I didn't recognize.*

➤PICTURE **7** [C] (*abbr* fig.) a diagram or picture used in a book to explain sth: *Figure 3 shows the major cities of Peru.*

IDM **a ballpark figure/estimate** ➲ **ballpark**
facts and figures ➲ **fact**
in round figures/numbers ➲ **round¹**

figure² /ˈfɪɡə(r)/ *verb* **1** [I] figure (as sth) (in/among sth) to be included in sth; to be an important part of sth: *Women don't figure much in his novels.* SYN **feature** **2** [T] (*especially AmE*) figure (that) to think or decide that sth is true: *I figured he was here because I saw his car outside.*

IDM **it/that figures** (*informal*) that is what I expected; that makes sense

PHR V **figure on sth/on doing sth** (*especially AmE*) to include sth in your plans: *I figure on arriving in New York on Wednesday.*
figure sb/sth out to find an answer to sth or to understand sb: *I can't figure out why she married him in the first place.*

ˌfigure of ˈeight (*AmE* ˌfigure ˈeight) *noun* [C] (*pl* ˌfigures of ˈeight) (*AmE* ˌfigure ˈeights) something in the shape of the number 8

ˌfigure of ˈspeech *noun* [C] (*pl* ˌfigures of ˈspeech) a word or expression used in a different way from its usual meaning in order to make a special effect

file¹ /faɪl/ *noun* [C] **1** a box or a cover that is used for keeping papers together: *a box file* ➲ picture at **stationery** **2** a collection of information that is stored together in a computer, with a particular name: *to open/close a file* ♦ *to create/delete/save/copy a file* **3** a file (on sb/sth) a collection of papers or information about sb/sth kept inside a file: *The police are now keeping a file on all known football hooligans.* **4** a metal tool with a rough surface used for shaping hard substances or for making surfaces smooth: *a nail file* ➲ picture at **tool**

IDM **in single file** ➲ **single¹**
on file kept in a file: *We have all the information you need on file.*
the rank and file ➲ **rank¹**

file² /faɪl/ *verb* **1** [T] file sth (away) to put and keep documents, etc. in a particular place so that you can find them easily; to put sth into a file: *I filed the letters away in a drawer.* **2** [I] file in, out, past, etc. to walk or march in a line: *The children filed out of the classroom at the end of the lesson.* **3** [T] file sth (away, down, etc.) to shape sth hard or make sth smooth with a file: *to file your nails*

ˈfile sharing *noun* [U] the practice of sharing computer files with other people over the Internet or another computer network: *illegal file sharing of music*

ˈfiling cabinet (*AmE* ˈfile cabinet) *noun* [C] a piece of office furniture with deep drawers for storing files

fill /fɪl/ *verb* **1** [I,T] fill (sth/sb) (with sth) to make sth full or to become full: *Can you fill the kettle for me?* ♦ *The news filled him with excitement.* ♦ *The room filled with smoke within minutes.* **2** [T] to do a job: *I'm afraid that teaching post has just been filled* (= sb has got the job). **3** [T] to use up your time doing sth: *How do you fill your day now that you're retired?*

PHR V **fill sth in** **1** (*AmE* also fill sth out) to complete a form, etc. by writing information on it: *Could you fill in the application form, please?* **2** to fill a hole or space completely to make a surface flat: *You had better fill in the cracks in the wall before you paint it.*
fill (sth) up to become or to make sth completely full: *The room soon filled up.*

fillet (*AmE* filet) /ˈfɪlɪt/ *noun* [C,U] a piece of meat or fish with the bones taken out

filling¹ /ˈfɪlɪŋ/ *noun* **1** [C] the material that a dentist uses to fill a hole in a tooth: *a gold filling* ➲ note at **tooth** **2** [C,U] the food inside a **sandwich** (= two slices of bread with food between them), cake, **pie** (= a type of baked food), etc. ➲ picture on **page P16**

filling² /ˈfɪlɪŋ/ *adj* (used about food) that makes you feel full: *Pasta is very filling.*

film¹ /fɪlm/ *noun*
➤MOVING PICTURES **1** (*AmE* **movie**) [C] a story, play, etc. shown in moving pictures at the cinema or on TV: *Let's go to the cinema—there's a good film on this week.* ♦ *to* **watch a film** *on TV* ♦ *to* **see a film** *at the cinema* ♦ *a horror/documentary/feature film* ♦ *a film director/producer/critic* **2** [U] the art or business of making films: *She's studying film and theatre.* ♦ *the film industry* **3** [U] moving pictures of real events: *The programme included film of the town one hundred years ago.*
➤IN CAMERA **4** [C,U] a roll of thin plastic that you use in some types of camera to take photographs: *to have a film developed* ➲ note at **camera**
➤THIN LAYER **5** [C, usually sing] a thin layer of a substance or material: *The oil forms a film on the surface of the water.*

TOPIC

Films

My favourite **film** is **set** in Rome. It is **based on** a book and it **stars** several famous **actors**. The **dialogue** is in Italian, but there are English **subtitles**. **Critics** gave the film good **reviews** and praised the director (= the person who tells the actors what to do). The person who wrote the **script** won an award for the best **screenplay**. There is a **sequel** coming out next year. I saw the film at the **cinema** but it is also available on **DVD**. You can buy the **soundtrack** (= the music) on CD or as a **download** (= computer file).

film² /fɪlm/ *verb* [I,T] to record moving pictures of an event, story, etc. with a camera: *They're filming in Oxford today.* ♦ *The man was filmed stealing from the shop.*

F

'film star *noun* [C] a person who is a famous actor in films

filter¹ /ˈfɪltə(r)/ *noun* [C] **1** a device for holding back substances from a liquid or gas that passes through it: *a coffee filter* ◆ *an oil filter* **2** a piece of coloured glass used with a camera to hold back some types of light

filter² /ˈfɪltə(r)/ *verb* **1** [T] to pass a liquid through a **filter**: *Do you normally filter your water?* **2** [I] **filter in, out, through, etc.** to move slowly and/or in small amounts: *Sunlight filtered into the room through the curtains.* ◆ (*figurative*) *News of her illness filtered through to her friends.*

PHR V **filter sb/sth out (of sth)** to remove sth that you do not want from a liquid, light, etc. using a special device or substance: *This chemical filters impurities out of the water.* ◆ (*figurative*) *This test is designed to filter out weaker candidates before the interview stage.*

filth /fɪlθ/ *noun* [U] **1** unpleasant dirt: *The room was covered in filth.* **2** sexual words or pictures that cause offence

filthy /ˈfɪlθi/ *adj* (**filthier**; **filthiest**) **1** very dirty **2** (used about language, books, films, etc.) connected with sex in a way that causes offence

fin /fɪn/ *noun* [C] **1** one of the parts of a fish that it uses for swimming ➲ picture on **page P13** **2** a flat, thin part that sticks out of an aircraft, a vehicle, etc. to improve its balance and movement through the air or water

final¹ /ˈfaɪnl/ *adj* **1** [only *before* a noun] last (in a series): *This will be the final lesson of our course.* ◆ *I don't want to miss the final episode of that series.* **2** not to be changed: *The judge's decision is always final.* ◆ *I'm not lending you the money, and that's final!*

IDM **the last/final straw** ➲ **straw**

final² /ˈfaɪnl/ *noun* [C] the last game or match in a series of competitions or sports events: *The first two runners in this race go through to the final.* ◆ *the 2010 World Cup Finals* (= the last few games in the competition) ➲ look at **semi-final** **2** **finals** [pl] the exams you take in your last year at university: *I'm taking my finals in June.*

finale /fɪˈnɑːli/ *noun* [C] the last part of a piece of music, a show, etc.

finalist /ˈfaɪnəlɪst/ *noun* [C] a person who is in the final of a competition ➲ look at **semi-finalist**

finalize (also **-ise**) /ˈfaɪnəlaɪz/ *verb* [T] to make firm decisions about plans, dates, etc: *Have you finalized your holiday arrangements yet?*

finally /ˈfaɪnəli/ *adv* **1** after a long time or delay: *It was getting dark when the plane finally took off.* SYN **eventually** **2** used to introduce the last in a list of things: *Finally, I would like to say how much we have all enjoyed this evening.* SYN **lastly** **3** in a definite way so that sth will not be changed: *We haven't decided finally who will get the job yet.*

finance¹ /ˈfaɪnæns; fəˈnæns/ *noun* **1** [U] the money you need to start or support a business, etc: *How will you raise the finance to start the project?* **2** [U] the activity of managing money: *Who is the new Minister of Finance?* ◆ *an expert in finance* **3 finances** [pl] the money a person, company, country, etc. has to spend: *What are our finances like at the moment* (= how much money have we got)?

finance² /ˈfaɪnæns; fəˈnæns/ *verb* [T] to provide the money to pay for sth: *Your trip will be financed by the company.*

financial /faɪˈnænʃl; fəˈn-/ *adj* connected with money: *The business got into financial difficulties.* ▸ **financially** *adv* /-ʃəli/

finch /fɪntʃ/ *noun* [C] a small bird with a short strong beak

find¹ /faɪnd/ *verb* [T] (*pt, pp* **found** /faʊnd/)

➤BY CHANCE **1** to discover sth by chance: *I've found a piece of glass in this milk.* ◆ *We went into the house and found her lying on the floor.* ◆ *This particular species can be found* (= exists) *all over the world.*

➤BY SEARCHING **2** to discover sth that you want or that you have lost after searching for it: *After six months she finally found a job.* ◆ *Scientists haven't yet found a cure for colds.* ◆ *I hope you find an answer to your problem.* ◆ *Did you find the pen you lost?*

> **MORE** Notice the expressions **find the time, find the money**: *I never seem to find the time to read the newspaper these days.* ◆ *We'd like to go on holiday but we can't find the money.*

➤FROM EXPERIENCE **3** to have an opinion about sth because of your own experience: *I find that book very difficult to understand.* ◆ *We didn't find the film at all funny.* ◆ *How are you finding life as a student?*

➤REALIZE **4** to suddenly realize or discover sth: *I got home to find that I'd left the tap on all day.* ◆ *Ben turned a corner and suddenly found himself in the port.*

➤REACH **5** to arrive somewhere naturally: *These birds* ***find their way*** *to Africa every winter.*

IDM **find fault (with sb/sth)** to look for things that are wrong with sb/sth and complain about them: *Monica wouldn't make a good teacher because she's always finding fault with people.*

find your feet to become confident and independent in a new situation: *Don't worry if the job seems difficult at first—you'll soon find your feet.*

get/find your bearings ➲ **bearing**

PHR V **find (sth) out** to get some information; to discover a fact: *Have you found out how much the tickets cost?* ◆ *I later found out that Will had been lying to me.*

find sb out to discover that sb has done sth wrong: *He had used a false name for years before they found him out.*

find² /faɪnd/ *noun* [C] a thing or a person that has been found, especially one that is valuable or useful: *Archaeologists made some interesting finds when they dug up the field.* ◆ *This new young player is quite a find!*

finder /ˈfaɪndə(r)/ *noun* [C] a person or thing that finds sth

finding /ˈfaɪndɪŋ/ *noun* [C, usually pl] information that is discovered as a result of research into sth: *the findings of a survey/report/committee*

fine¹ /faɪn/ *adj* (finer; finest)
➤GOOD QUALITY **1** [usually *before* a noun] of very good quality, with great beauty or detail: *a fine piece of work* ◆ *fine detail/carving/china*
➤IN GOOD HEALTH **2** in good health, or happy and comfortable: *'How are you?' '**Fine, thanks.**'* ◆ *'Do you want to change places?' 'No, I'm fine here, thanks.'*
➤ACCEPTABLE **3** good enough; acceptable: *'Do you want some more milk in your coffee?' 'No, **that's fine**, thanks.'* ◆ *Don't cook anything special—a sandwich will be fine.* ◆ *The hotel rooms were fine but the food was awful.*

HELP We do not use meanings **2** and **3** in questions or in the negative form, so you CANNOT say 'Are you fine?' or 'This isn't fine'.

➤WEATHER **4** bright with sun; not raining: *Let's hope it stays fine for the match tomorrow.*
➤VERY THIN **5** very thin or narrow: *That hairstyle's no good for me—my hair's too fine.* ◆ *You must use a fine pencil for the diagrams.* **OPP thick**
➤DETAIL **6** difficult to notice or understand: *I couldn't understand **the finer points** of his argument.* ◆ *There's **a fine line between** being reserved and being unfriendly.*
➤WITH SMALL GRAINS **7** made of very small pieces, grains, etc: *Salt is finer than sugar.* **OPP coarse**
▶ **fine** *adv* in a way that is good enough: *Keep going like that—you're doing fine.*

fine² /faɪn/ *noun* [C] a sum of money that you have to pay for breaking a law or rule: *a parking fine* ◆ *You'll **get a fine** if you park your car there.* ▶ **fine** *verb* [T] **fine sb (for sth/doing sth)**: *He was fined £100 for driving without lights.* ➲ note at **court**

finely /ˈfaɪnli/ *adv* **1** into small pieces: *The onions must be finely chopped for this recipe.* **2** very accurately: *a finely tuned instrument*

the ˌfine ˈprint (*AmE*) = **the small print**

finger¹ /ˈfɪŋɡə(r)/ *noun* [C] one of the five parts at the end of each hand: *little finger, ring finger, middle finger, forefinger (or index finger), thumb* ➲ picture at **body**

MORE Sometimes we think of the **thumb** as one of the fingers, sometimes we contrast it: *Hold the pen between your finger and thumb.* The five parts at the end of each foot are called **toes**.

IDM cross your fingers; keep your fingers crossed to hope that sb/sth will be successful or lucky: *There's nothing more we can do now—just cross our fingers and hope for the best.* ◆ *I'll keep my fingers crossed for you in your exams.*
have green fingers ➲ **green¹**
snap your fingers ➲ **snap¹**

finger² /ˈfɪŋɡə(r)/ *verb* [T] to touch or feel sth with your fingers

fingermark /ˈfɪŋɡəmɑːk/ *noun* [C] a mark on sth made by a dirty finger

fingernail /ˈfɪŋɡəneɪl/ (also **nail**) *noun* [C] the thin hard layer that covers the outer end of each finger ➲ picture at **body**

fingerprint /ˈfɪŋɡəprɪnt/ *noun* [C] the mark that is made by the pattern of lines on the tip of sb's finger: *The burglar left his fingerprints all over the house.*

fingertip /ˈfɪŋɡətɪp/ *noun* [C] the end of your finger
IDM have sth at your fingertips to have sth ready for quick and easy use: *They asked some difficult questions but luckily I had all the facts at my fingertips.*

finish¹ /ˈfɪnɪʃ/ *verb* **1** [I,T] **finish (sth/doing sth)** to complete sth or reach the end of sth: *What time does the film finish?* ◆ *Haven't you finished yet? You've taken ages!* ◆ *The Ethiopian runner won and the Kenyans finished second and third.* ◆ *Finish your work quickly!* ◆ *Have you finished writing that report?* **2** [T] **finish sth (off/up)** to eat, drink or use the last part of sth: *Finish up your milk, Tony!* ◆ *Who finished off all the bread?* **3** [T] **finish sth (off)** to complete the last details of sth or make sth perfect: *She stayed up all night to finish off the article she was writing.* ◆ *He's just **putting the finishing touches to** his painting.*
PHR V finish sb/sth off (*informal*) to kill sb/sth; to be the thing that makes sb unable to continue: *The cat played with the mouse before finishing it off.* ◆ *I was very tired towards the end of the race, and that last hill finished me off.*
finish with sth to stop needing or using sth: *I'll borrow that book when you've finished with it.*
finish with sb (*informal*) to end a relationship with sb: *Sally's not going out with David any more—she finished with him last week.*

finish² /ˈfɪnɪʃ/ *noun* [C] **1** the last part or end of sth: *There was a dramatic finish to the race when two runners fell.* ◆ *I enjoyed the film **from start to finish**.* **2** the last covering of paint, polish, etc. that is put on a surface to make it look good: *a gloss/matt finish*

finished /ˈfɪnɪʃt/ *adj* **1** [not before a noun] **finished (with sb/sth)** having stopped doing sth, using sth or dealing with sb/sth: *'Are you using the computer?' 'Yes, I won't be finished with it for another hour or so.'* **2** [not before a noun] not able to continue: *The business is finished—there's no more money.* **3** made; completed: *the finished product/article*

finite /ˈfaɪnaɪt/ *adj* having a definite limit or a fixed size: *The world's resources are finite.* **OPP infinite**

fir /fɜː(r)/ (also **ˈfir tree**) *noun* [C] a tree with leaves like needles, that do not fall off in winter

ˈfir cone *noun* [C] the fruit of the **fir** tree

fire¹ /ˈfaɪə(r)/ *noun* **1** [C,U] burning and flames, especially when it destroys and is out of control: *Firemen struggled for three hours to **put out the fire**.* ◆ *It had been a dry summer so there were many forest fires.* ◆ *In very hot weather, dry grass can **catch fire*** (= start burning). ◆ *Did someone **set fire to** that pile of* *wood?* ◆ *Help! The frying pan's* ***on fire!*** **2** [C] burning wood or coal used for warming people or cooking food: *They tried to* ***light a fire*** *to keep warm.* ◆ *It's cold —don't let the fire go out!* **3** [C] a machine for heating a room, etc: *a gas/an electric fire* **4** [U] shooting from guns: *The soldiers came* ***under fire*** *from all sides.* ◆ *I heard machine-gun fire in the distance.*

IDM come/be under fire be strongly criticized: *The government has come under fire from all sides for its foreign policy.*

get on/along like a house on fire ➲ **house**[1]

open fire ➲ **open**[2]

fire[2] /ˈfaɪə(r)/ *verb* **1** [I,T] fire (sth) (at/on/into sb/sth) to shoot bullets, etc. from a gun or other weapon: *Can you hear the guns firing?* ◆ *She fired an arrow at the target.* ◆ *(figurative) If you stop firing questions at me, I might be able to answer!* ◆ *The soldiers fired on the crowd, killing twenty people.* **2** [T] = **sack**[2]: *He was fired for always being late.* **3** [T] fire sb with sth to produce a strong feeling in sb: *Her speech fired me with determination.*

ˈfire alarm *noun* [C] a bell or other signal to warn people that there is a fire

firearm /ˈfaɪərɑːm/ *noun* [C] a gun that you can carry

ˈfire brigade (*AmE* ˈ**fire department**) *noun* [C, with sing or pl verb] an organization of people trained to deal with fires

-fired /ˈfaɪəd/ [in compounds] using the fuel mentioned: *gas-fired central heating*

ˈfire department (*AmE*) = **fire brigade**

ˈfire engine *noun* [C] a special vehicle that carries equipment for dealing with large fires

ˈfire escape *noun* [C] a special set of stairs on the outside of a building that people can go down if there is a fire

ˈfire extinguisher (also **extinguisher**) *noun* [C] a metal container with water or chemicals inside that you use for stopping small fires

firefighter /ˈfaɪəfaɪtə(r)/ *noun* [C] a person whose job is to stop fires

firelight /ˈfaɪəlaɪt/ *noun* [U] the light that comes from a fire

fireman /ˈfaɪəmən/ *noun* [C] (*pl* -men /-mən/) a man whose job is to stop fires

fireplace /ˈfaɪəpleɪs/ *noun* [C] the open place in a room where you light a fire

fireside /ˈfaɪəsaɪd/ *noun* [sing] the part of a room beside the fire: *Come and sit by the fireside.*

ˈfire station *noun* [C] a building where **firefighters** (= people who stop fires) wait to be called, and where the vehicles that they use are kept

firewall /ˈfaɪəwɔːl/ *noun* [C] a part of a computer system that prevents people from getting at information without permission, but still allows them to receive information that is sent to them ➲ note at **cybercrime**

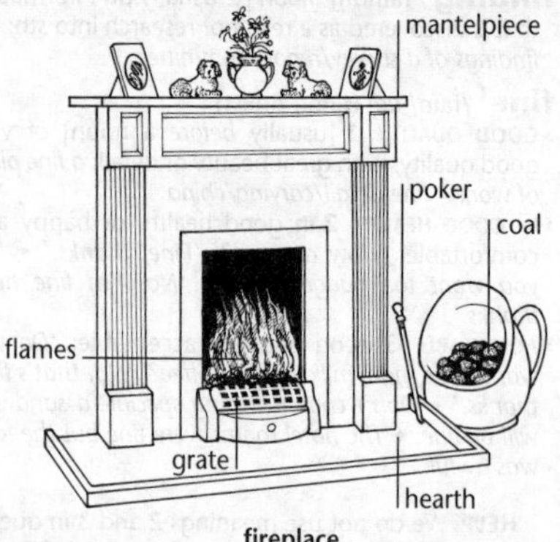

fireplace

firewood /ˈfaɪəwʊd/ *noun* [U] wood used for burning on fires

firework /ˈfaɪəwɜːk/ *noun* [C] a small object that burns or explodes with coloured lights and loud sounds, used for entertainment

firework

ˈfiring squad *noun* [C] a group of soldiers who have been ordered to shoot and kill a prisoner

firm[1] /fɜːm/ *noun* [C] a business company: *Which firm do you work for?* ◆ *a firm of solicitors*

firm[2] /fɜːm/ *adj* (**firmer**; **firmest**) **1** able to stay the same shape when pressed; quite hard: *a firm mattress* ◆ *firm muscles* **2** strong and steady or not likely to change: *She kept a firm grip on her mother's hand.* ◆ *a firm commitment/decision/offer* **3 firm (with sb)** strong and in control: *He's very firm with his children.* ◆ *You have to show the examiner that you have a firm grasp* (= good knowledge) *of grammar.*

IDM a firm hand strong control or discipline: *Those children need a teacher with a firm hand.*

▶ **firmly** *adv* ▶ **firmness** *noun* [U]

first[1] /fɜːst/ *determiner, ordinal number* coming before all others; that has not happened before: *the first half of the game* ◆ *You've won first prize!* ◆ *King Charles I* (= King Charles the First) ◆ *What were your first impressions of this country when you arrived?* ◆ *She's expecting her first baby.* ➲ note at **sixth** ➲ look at **one**

IDM at first glance/sight when first seen or examined: *The task seemed impossible at first glance, but it turned out to be quite easy.*

first/last thing ➲ **thing**

first[2] /fɜːst/ *adv* **1** before any others: *Sue arrived first at the party.* ◆ *Mike's very competitive—he gets upset if he doesn't* ***come first*** *in every game.* ◆ *Do you want to* ***go first*** *or second?* **2** before doing anything else: *I'll come out later. I've got to finish my homework first.* **3** the time before all the other times; for the first time: *Where did you first meet your husband?* **4** used for introducing the first thing in a list: *There* are several people I would like to thank: *First, my mother.* SYN **firstly** **5** at the beginning: *When I first started my job I hated it.*

IDM **at first** at the beginning: *At first I thought he was joking, but then I realized he was serious.*

come first to be more important to sb than anything else: *Although she enjoys her job, her family has always come first.*

first and foremost more than anything else; most importantly: *He worked in TV but he was a stage actor first and foremost.*

first come, first served (*informal*) people will be dealt with, served, seen, etc. strictly in the order in which they arrive: *Tickets can be bought here on a first come, first served basis.*

first of all as the first thing (to be done or said): *In a moment I'll introduce our guest speaker, but first of all, let me thank you all for coming.*

first off (*informal*) before anything else: *First off, let's decide who does what.*

head first ➲ **head**[1]

first[3] /fɜːst/ *noun* **1 the first** [C] (*pl* **the first**) the first person or thing, people or things: *Are we the first to arrive?* ♦ *They enjoyed the holiday—their first for ten years.* **2 a first** [sing] an important event that is happening for the first time: *This operation is a first in medical history.* **3** [C] **a first (in sth)** the highest level of degree given by a university in the UK: *He **got a first** in History at Liverpool.*

IDM **from the (very) first** from the beginning: *They hated each other from the first.*

ˌfirst ˈaid *noun* [U] medical help that you give to sb who is hurt or ill before the doctor arrives: *a first-aid kit/course* ♦ *to give somebody first aid*

ˌfirst ˈclass *noun* [U] **1** the best and most expensive seats on a train, ship or plane: *There is more room in first class.* **2** (*BrE*) the way of sending letters, etc. that is faster but more expensive than **second class**

▶ **ˌfirst ˈclass** *adv*: *to travel first class* ♦ *to send a letter first class*

ˌfirst-ˈclass *adj* **1** of the best quality; of the highest standard: *a first-class player* ♦ *This book is really first-class.* SYN **excellent** **2** [only *before* a noun] used about the best and most expensive seats on a train, ship or plane: *a first-class cabin/seat/ticket* **3** [only *before* a noun] (*BrE*) used about the way of sending letters, etc. that is faster but more expensive than **second-class**: *first-class mail/letters/stamps* **4** [only *before* a noun] (used about a university degree in the UK) of the highest level: *a first-class honours degree in geography*

ˌfirst ˈcousin = **cousin**

the ˌfirst ˈfloor *noun* [C] **1** (*BrE*) the floor of a building above the **ground floor** (= the one on street level): *I live in a flat **on the first floor**.* ♦ *a first-floor flat* **2** (*AmE*) = **ground floor**

ˌfirst ˈgear *noun* [C] the lowest gear on a car, bicycle, etc: *To move off, **put** the car **into first gear** and slowly release the clutch.*

ˌfirst-ˈhand *adj* (used about information, experience, a story, etc.) heard, seen or learnt by yourself, not from other people: *He gave me a first-hand account of the accident* (= he had seen it).

▶ **ˌfirst-ˈhand** *adv*: *I've experienced the problem first-hand, so I know how you feel.*

firstly /ˈfɜːstli/ *adv* used to introduce the first point in a list: *They were angry firstly because they had to pay extra, and secondly because no one had told them about it.* SYN **first**

ˈfirst name *noun* [C] the first of your names that come before your family name: *'What's Mr Vilimek's first name?' 'Petr, I think.'* ➲ note at **name**[1]

the ˌfirst ˈperson *noun* [sing] **1** the words such as 'I', 'me', 'we', and the verb forms that go with them: *'I am' is the first person singular of the verb 'to be'.* **2** the style of telling a story as if it happened to you: *The author writes in the first person.*

ˌfirst-ˈrate *adj* excellent; of the best quality

ˈfir tree = **fir**

fish[1] /fɪʃ/ *noun* (*pl* **fish** *or* **fishes**) **1** [C] an animal that lives and breathes in water and swims: *How many fish have you caught?* ♦ *I went diving on holiday—it was fantastic to see so many different fishes* (= types of fish). ➲ note at **saltwater** ➲ picture on **page P13**

> **HELP** The plural form **fish** is more common. **Fishes** is used when we are talking about different types of fish.

2 [U] fish as food: *We're having fish for dinner.* ➲ picture on **page P16**

> **CULTURE**
>
> In Britain a common type of fast food is **fish and chips**, which we buy at a **fish and chip shop**.

fish[2] /fɪʃ/ *verb* [I] **1 fish (for sth)** to try to catch fish: *He's fishing for trout.* ♦ *They often **go fishing** at weekends.* **2 fish (around) (in sth) (for sth)** to search for sth in water or in a deep or hidden place: *She fished (around) for her keys in the bottom of her bag.*

PHR V **fish for sth** to try to get sth you want in an indirect way: *to fish for an invitation*

fish sth out (of sth) to take or pull sth out (of sth) especially after searching for it: *After the accident they fished the car out of the canal.*

fishcake /ˈfɪʃkeɪk/ *noun* [C] (*especially BrE*) pieces of fish mixed with potato that are made into a flat round shape, covered with **breadcrumbs** (= very small pieces of bread) and fried

fisherman /ˈfɪʃəmən/ *noun* [C] (*pl* **-men** /-mən/) a person who catches fish either as a job or as a sport ➲ look at **angler**

ˌfish ˈfinger (*AmE* **ˌfish ˈstick**) *noun* [C] a narrow piece of fish covered with **breadcrumbs** (= very small pieces of bread) or **batter** (= a mixture of flour, eggs and milk), usually frozen and sold in packs

fishing /ˈfɪʃɪŋ/ *noun* [U] catching fish as a job, sport or hobby: *Fishing is a major industry in Iceland.* ➲ look at **angling**

ˈfishing rod *noun* [C] a long thin stick with a line and a hook on it for catching fish

fishmonger /ˈfɪʃmʌŋgə(r)/ *noun* (*BrE*) **1** [C] a person whose job is to sell fish **2 the fishmonger's** [sing] a shop that sells fish

fishy /ˈfɪʃi/ *adj* (**fishier**; **fishiest**) **1** (*informal*) seeming wrong, dishonest or illegal: *The police thought the man's story sounded extremely fishy.* SYN **suspicious** **2** tasting or smelling like a fish: *a fishy smell*

fist /fɪst/ *noun* [C] a hand with the fingers closed together tightly: *She* ***clenched*** *her* ***fists*** *in anger.*

fist

fit¹ /fɪt/ *verb* (**fitting**; **fitted**) **1** [I,T] to be the right size or shape for sb/sth: *These jeans fit very well.* ◆ *This dress doesn't fit me any more.* ◆ *This key doesn't fit in the lock.* **2** [T] **fit (sb/sth) in/into/on/onto sth** to find or have enough space for sb/sth: *I can't fit into these trousers any more.* ◆ *Can you fit one more person in the car?* ◆ *I can't fit all these books onto the shelf.* **3** [T] to put or fix sth in the right place: *The builders are fitting new windows today.* ◆ *I can't fit these pieces of the model together.* **4** [T] to be or make sb/sth right or suitable: *I don't think Tom's fitted for such a demanding job.* ◆ *The description fits Jo perfectly.*

PHR V **fit sb/sth in**; **fit sb/sth in/into sth** to find time to see sb or to do sth: *The doctor managed to fit me in this morning.* ◆ *You're tired because you're trying to fit too much into one day.*

fit in (with sb/sth) to be able to live, work, etc. in an easy and natural way (with sb/sth): *The new girl found it difficult to fit in (with the other children) at school.* ◆ *I will happily change my plans to fit in with yours.*

fit² /fɪt/ *adj* (**fitter**; **fittest**) **1 fit (for sth/to do sth)** strong and in good physical health (especially because of exercise): *Swimming is a good way to* ***keep fit.*** ◆ *My dad's almost recovered from his illness, but he's still not fit enough for work.* ◆ *She goes to keep-fit classes.* OPP **unfit** **2 fit (for sb/sth)**; **fit to do sth** good enough; suitable: *Do you think she is fit for the job?* ◆ *These houses are not fit (for people) to live in.* **3** (*BrE informal*) sexually attractive

fit³ /fɪt/ *noun* **1** [C] a sudden attack of an illness, in which sb becomes unconscious and their body may make violent movements: *to have fits* **2** [C] a sudden short period of coughing, laughing, etc. that you cannot control: *a fit of laughter/anger* **3** [sing] [usually after an adjective] the way in which sth (for example a piece of clothing) fits: *a good/bad/tight/loose fit*

fitness /ˈfɪtnəs/ *noun* [U] **1** the condition of being strong and healthy: *Fitness is important in most sports.* **2 fitness for sth/to do sth** the quality of being suitable: *The directors were not sure about his fitness for the job.*

fitted /ˈfɪtɪd/ *adj* [only *before* a noun] made or cut to fit a particular space and fixed there: *a fitted carpet* ◆ *a fitted kitchen* (= one with fitted cupboards)

fitting¹ /ˈfɪtɪŋ/ *adj* **1** (*formal*) right; suitable: *It is only fitting that this great team should play on one of the finest pitches in the world.* **2 -fitting** used in compounds to describe how clothes, etc. fit: *a tight-fitting dress* ◆ *loose-fitting trousers*

fitting² /ˈfɪtɪŋ/ *noun* [C,usually pl] the things that are fixed in a building or on a piece of furniture but that can be changed or moved if necessary ➲ look at **fixture**

ˈfitting room *noun* [C] a room in a shop where you can put on clothes to see how they look ➲ look at **changing room**

five /faɪv/ *number* **1** 5 ➲ note at **six** ➲ look at **fifth** **2 five-** [in compounds] having five of the thing mentioned: *a five-day week*

IDM **nine to five** ➲ **nine**

fiver /ˈfaɪvə(r)/ *noun* [C] (*BrE informal*) £5 or a five-pound note: *Can you lend me a fiver?*

fix¹ /fɪks/ *verb* [T]

➤FASTEN **1** to put sth firmly in place so that it will not move: *Can you fix this new handle to the door?* ◆ (*figurative*) *I found it difficult to keep my mind fixed on my work.*

➤ARRANGE **2 fix sth (up)** to decide or arrange sth: *We need to fix the price.* ◆ *Have you fixed (up) a date for the party?*

➤FOOD/DRINK **3** (*especially AmE*) **fix sth (for sb)** to prepare sth (especially food or drink): *Can I fix you a drink/a drink for you?*

➤REPAIR **4** to repair sth: *The electrician's coming to fix the cooker.*

➤RESULT **5** [usually passive] (*informal*) to arrange the result of sth in a way that is not honest or fair: *Fans of the losing team suspected that the match had been fixed.*

PHR V **fix sb up (with sth)** (*informal*) to arrange for sb to have sth: *I can fix you up with a place to stay.*

fix sth (up) to get sth ready: *They're fixing up their spare room for the new baby.*

fix² /fɪks/ *noun* [C] **1** a solution to a problem, especially one that is easy or temporary: *There's no* ***quick fix*** *to this problem.* **2** [usually sing] (*informal*) a difficult situation: *I was* ***in a*** *real* ***fix***—*I'd forgotten my keys.* **3** [usually sing] (*informal*) a result that is dishonestly arranged

fixation /fɪkˈseɪʃn/ *noun* [C] **a fixation (with sth)** an interest in sth that is too strong and not normal: *I'm tired of James's fixation with football.*

fixed /fɪkst/ *adj* **1** staying the same: *a fixed date/price/rent* OPP **movable** **2** (of ideas, etc.) not changing: *He has such fixed ideas that you can't discuss anything with him.*

IDM **(of) no fixed abode/address** (*formal*) (with) no permanent place to live: *Daniel Stephens, of no fixed abode, was found guilty of robbery.*

how are you, etc. fixed (for sth)? (*informal*) used to ask how much of sth a person has, or to ask about arrangements: *How are you fixed for cash?* ◆ *How are you fixed for Sunday* (= have you arranged anything to do)?

fixture /ˈfɪkstʃə(r)/ *noun* [C] **1** a sports event arranged for a particular day: *to arrange/cancel/play* *a fixture* **2** [usually pl] a piece of furniture or equipment that is fixed in a house or building and sold with it: *Does the price of the house include fixtures and fittings?* ➲ look at **fitting**

fizz /fɪz/ *noun* [U] the bubbles in a liquid and the sound they make: *This lemonade's lost its fizz.* ▶ **fizz** *verb* [I]

fizzle /ˈfɪzl/ *verb*
PHR V fizzle out to end in a weak or disappointing way: *The game started well but it fizzled out in the second half.*

fizzy /ˈfɪzi/ *adj* (**fizzier**; **fizziest**) (used about a drink) containing many small bubbles of gas ➲ look at **still**

HELP Wine or mineral water that contains bubbles is usually described as **sparkling**, not **fizzy**.

ˌfizzy ˈdrink (*AmE* **soda**) *noun* [C] a sweet drink without alcohol that contains many small bubbles: *The only fizzy drinks I've got are cola and lemonade.*

fjord /ˈfjɔːd/ *noun* [C] a long narrow piece of sea between **cliffs** (= high steep areas of rock), especially in Norway

flabbergasted /ˈflæbəgɑːstɪd/ *adj* (*informal*) extremely surprised and/or shocked

flabby /ˈflæbi/ *adj* (**flabbier**; **flabbiest**) having too much soft fat instead of muscle: *a flabby stomach*

flag[1] /flæg/ *noun* [C] a piece of cloth with a special design on it that may be the symbol of a country, club, etc. or may have a particular meaning. A flag can be tied to a pole or held in the hand: *the French flag* ◆ *the flag of France* ◆ *The flag is flying for the Queen's birthday.* ◆ *The train will leave when the guard waves his flag.* ➲ picture on **page P11**

flag[2] /flæg/ *verb* [I] (**flagging**; **flagged**) to become tired or less strong
PHR V flag sb/sth down to wave to sb in a car to make them stop: *to flag down a taxi*

flagrant /ˈfleɪgrənt/ *adj* [only *before* a noun] (used about an action) shocking because it is done in a very obvious way and shows no respect for people, laws, etc.

flail /fleɪl/ *verb* [I,T] to wave or move about without control: *The insect's legs were flailing in the air.* ◆ *Don't flail your arms about like that—you might hurt someone.*

flair /fleə(r)/ *noun* **1** [sing] **(a) flair for sth** a natural ability to do sth well: *She has a flair for languages.* **2** [U] the quality of being interesting or having style: *That poster is designed with her usual flair.*

flak /flæk/ *noun* [U] (*informal*) criticism: *He'll get some flak for missing that goal.*

flake[1] /fleɪk/ *noun* [C] a small thin piece of sth: *snowflakes* ◆ *flakes of paint*

flake[2] /fleɪk/ *verb* [I] **flake (off)** to come off in **flakes**: *This paint is very old—it's beginning to flake (off).*

flaky /ˈfleɪki/ *adj* **1** tending to break into small, thin pieces: *dry flaky skin* **2** (*especially BrE informal*) that does not work well: *I found the software a bit flaky.* **3** (*AmE informal*) (of a person) behaving in a strange way

flamboyant /flæmˈbɔɪənt/ *adj* **1** (used about a person) acting in a loud, confident way that attracts attention: *a flamboyant gesture/style/personality* **2** bright and easily noticed: *flamboyant colours* ▶ **flamboyance** *noun* [U] ▶ **flamboyantly** *adv*

flame /fleɪm/ *noun* [C,U] an area of bright burning gas that comes from sth that is on fire: *The flame of the candle flickered by the open window.* ◆ *The house was* **in flames** *when the fire engine arrived.* ◆ *The piece of paper* **burst into flames** *in the fire* (= suddenly began to burn strongly). ◆ *a sheet of flame* ➲ picture at **fireplace**

flaming /ˈfleɪmɪŋ/ *adj* [only *before* a noun] **1** (used about anger, an argument, etc.) violent: *We had a flaming argument over the bills.* **2** burning brightly **3** (*slang*) used as a mild swear word: *I can't get in—I've lost the flaming key.* **4** (used about colours, especially red) very bright: *flaming red hair* ◆ *a flaming sunset*

flamingo /fləˈmɪŋgəʊ/ *noun* [C] a large pink bird that has long legs and stands in water

flammable /ˈflæməbl/ *adj* able to burn easily

HELP Be careful. **Inflammable** has the same meaning and is more common.

flan /flæn/ *noun* [C,U] (*BrE*) a round open **pie** (= a type of baked food) that is filled with eggs and cheese, fruit, etc.

flank[1] /flæŋk/ *noun* [C] **1** the left or right side of an army during a battle, or a sports team during a game **2** the side of an animal's body

flank[2] /flæŋk/ *verb* [T, usually passive] to be placed at the side or sides of: *The road was flanked by trees.*

flannel /ˈflænl/ *noun* **1** [U] a type of soft cloth made of wool **2** [C] = **facecloth**

flap[1] /flæp/ *noun* [C] a piece of cloth, paper, etc. that is fixed to sth at one side only, often covering an opening: *the flap of an envelope*
IDM be in/get into a flap (*informal*) to be in/get into a state of worry or excitement

flap[2] /flæp/ *verb* (**flapping**; **flapped**) **1** [I,T] to move (sth) up and down or from side to side, especially in the wind: *The sails were flapping in the wind.* ◆ *The bird flapped its wings and flew away.* **2** [I] (*informal*) to become worried or excited: *Stop flapping—it's all organized!*

flare[1] /fleə(r)/ *verb* [I] to burn for a short time with a sudden bright flame
PHR V flare up 1 (used about a fire) to suddenly burn more strongly **2** (used about violence, anger, etc.) to start suddenly or to become suddenly worse

flare[2] /fleə(r)/ *noun* **1** [sing] a sudden bright light or flame **2** [C] a thing that produces a bright light or flame, used especially as a signal

flared /fleəd/ *adj* (used about trousers and skirts) becoming wider towards the bottom edge

flash¹ /flæʃ/ *verb* **1** [I,T] to produce or make sth produce a sudden bright light for a short time: *The neon sign above the door flashed on and off all night.* ◆ *That lorry driver's flashing his lights at us* (= in order to tell us sth). **2** [T] to show sth quickly: *The detective flashed his card and went straight in.* **3** [I] to move very fast: *I saw something flash past the window.* ◆ *Thoughts kept flashing through my mind and I couldn't sleep.* **4** [T] to send sth by radio, TV, etc: *The news of the disaster was flashed across the world.*
PHR V **flash back** (used about sb's thoughts) to return suddenly to a time in the past: *Something he said made my mind flash back to my childhood.*

flash² /flæʃ/ *noun* **1** [C] a sudden bright light that comes and goes quickly: *a flash of lightning* **2** [C] a flash (of sth) a sudden strong feeling or idea: *a flash of inspiration* ◆ *The idea came to me in a flash.* **3** [C,U] a bright light that you use with a camera for taking photographs when it is dark; the device for producing this light: *a camera with a built-in flash* ➲ picture at **camera**
IDM **in/like a flash** very quickly
(as) quick as a flash ➲ **quick¹**

flashback /ˈflæʃbæk/ *noun* [C] **1** a part of a film, play, etc. that shows sth that happened before the main story **2** a sudden, clear memory of sth that happened in the past: *a flashback to childhood*

ˈflash drive (also ˈmemory stick; ˈpen drive; ˌUSˈB drive) *noun* [C] a small memory device that can be used to store data from a computer and to move it from one computer to another ➲ picture at **computer**

flashlight /ˈflæʃlaɪt/ (*AmE*) = **torch**(1)

flashy /ˈflæʃi/ *adj* (flashier; flashiest) attracting attention by being very big, bright and expensive: *a flashy sports car*

flask /flɑːsk/ *noun* [C] **1** a bottle with a narrow neck that is used for storing and mixing chemicals in scientific work **2** (*BrE*) = **Thermos™**

flat¹ /flæt/ *adj, adv* (flatter; flattest)
➤LEVEL **1** smooth and level, with no parts that are higher than the rest: *The countryside in Essex is quite flat* (= there are not many hills). ◆ *I need a flat surface to write this letter on.* ◆ *a flat roof* ◆ *She lay flat on her back in the sunshine.*
➤NOT HIGH **2** not high or deep: *You need flat shoes for walking.* ◆ *a flat dish*
➤NOT EXCITING **3** without much interest or energy: *Things have been a bit flat since Alex left.*
➤REFUSAL **4** [only *before* a noun] (used about sth that you say or decide) that will not change; firm: *He answered our request with a flat 'No!'*
➤IN MUSIC **5** half a note lower than the stated note OPP **sharp** **6** lower than the correct note: *That last note was flat. Can you sing it again?* ◆ *You're singing flat.* OPP **sharp**
➤DRINK **7** not fresh because it has lost its bubbles: *Open a new bottle. That lemonade has **gone flat**.*
➤BATTERY **8** (*BrE*) no longer producing electricity; not working: *We couldn't start the car because the battery was completely flat.*
➤TYRE **9** without enough air in it: *This tyre looks flat—has it got a puncture?*
➤PRICE **10** that is the same for everyone; that is fixed: *We charge a flat fee of £20, however long you stay.*
➤TIME **11** (used for emphasizing how quickly sth is done) in exactly the time mentioned and no longer: *She can get up and out of the house in ten minutes flat.*
IDM **fall flat** (used about a joke, a story, an event, etc.) to fail to produce the effect that you wanted
fall flat on your face to fall so that you are lying on your front: *He **fell flat on his face** in the mud.*
flat out as fast as possible; without stopping: *He's been working flat out for two weeks and he needs a break.*

flat² /flæt/ *noun* **1** [C] (*especially AmE* **apartment**) a set of rooms that is used as a home (usually in a large building): *Do you rent your flat or have you bought it?* ◆ *That old house has been divided into luxury flats.* ➲ note at **house** ➲ picture on **page P9**

> **HELP** **Apartment** is the normal word in American English. In British English we say **apartment** when talking about a flat we are renting for a holiday, etc. rather than to live in: *We're renting an apartment in the South of France.*

2 [sing] the flat (of sth) the flat part or side of sth: *the flat of your hand* **3** [C] (*symbol* ♭) a note which is half a note lower than the note with the same letter ➲ look at **sharp** **4** [C] (*especially AmE*) a tyre on a vehicle that has no air in it: *We had to stop to fix a flat.*

> TOPIC
>
> **Living in a flat**
>
> A tall building that contains many **flats** is called a **block of flats**. Blocks of flats are divided into **floors** (= levels): *I live in a second-floor flat.* If you **rent** a flat, you are the **tenant** and you pay money to the **landlord/landlady** (= the owner). The money that you pay every month is the **rent**. A **deposit** is money that you pay before you move in, but get back when you move out, if you have not damaged anything. Your flat may be **furnished** or **unfurnished**. People who share a flat with you but are not your family are called your **flatmates**.

flatly /ˈflætli/ *adv* **1** in a direct way; absolutely: *He flatly denied the allegations.* **2** in a way that shows no interest or emotion

flatmate /ˈflætmeɪt/ *noun* [C] (*BrE*) a person who shares a flat with one or more other people

ˌflat-ˈscreen (also flat-ˈpanel) *adj* [only *before* a noun] (used about a television or computer monitor) very thin when compared with the traditional type ➲ picture at **computer**

flatten /ˈflætn/ *verb* [I,T] flatten (sth) (out) to become or make sth flat: *The countryside flattens out as you get nearer the sea.* ◆ *The storms have flattened crops all over the country.*

flatter /ˈflætə(r)/ *verb* [T] **1** to say nice things to sb, often in a way that is not sincere, because you want to please them or because you want to get an advantage for yourself **2** flatter yourself (that) to choose to believe sth good about yourself although other people may not think the same: *He flatters himself that he speaks fluent French.* **3** [usually passive] to give pleasure or honour to sb: *I felt very flattered when they gave me the job.*

flattering /ˈflætərɪŋ/ *adj* making sb look or sound more attractive or important than they really are

flattery /ˈflætəri/ *noun* [U] saying good things about sb/sth that you do not really mean

flaunt /flɔːnt/ *verb* [T] to show sth that you are proud of so that other people will admire it

flautist /ˈflɔːtɪst/ (*AmE* **flutist**) *noun* [C] a person who plays the **flute** (= a musical instrument that you hold sideways and blow into)

flavour¹ (*AmE* flavor) /ˈfleɪvə(r)/ *noun* [C,U] **1** the taste (of food): *ten different flavours of yogurt* ◆ *yogurt in ten different flavours* ◆ *Do you think a little salt would improve the flavour?* **2** [sing] an idea of the particular quality or character of sth: *The website will give you a flavour of what the city is like.*

flavour² (*AmE* flavor) /ˈfleɪvə(r)/ *verb* [T] to give flavour to sth: *Add a little nutmeg to flavour the sauce.* ◆ *strawberry-flavoured milkshake*

flavouring (*AmE* flavoring) /ˈfleɪvərɪŋ/ *noun* [C, U] something that you add to food or drink to give it a particular taste: *This orange juice contains no artificial flavourings.*

flaw /flɔː/ *noun* [C] **1** a flaw (in sth) a mistake in sth that makes it not good enough or causes it not to function as it should: *There are some flaws in her argument.* **2** a mark or crack in an object that means that it is not perfect **3** a flaw (in sb/sth) a bad quality in sb's character: *His only real flaw is impatience.* ▶ **flawed** *adj*: *I think your plan is flawed.*

flawless /ˈflɔːləs/ *adj* with no faults or mistakes: *a flawless diamond* SYN **perfect**

flea /fliː/ *noun* [C] a very small jumping insect without wings that lives on animals, for example cats and dogs. **Fleas** bite people and animals and make them scratch. ➲ picture on **page P13**

ˈflea market *noun* [C] a market, often in a street, that sells old and used goods

fleck /flek/ *noun* [C, usually pl] a very small mark on sth; a very small piece of sth: *After painting the ceiling, her hair was covered with flecks of blue paint.*

flee /fliː/ *verb* [I,T] (*pt, pp* fled /fled/) flee (to .../into ...); flee (from) sb/sth to run away or escape from sth: *The robbers fled the country with £100 000.*

fleece¹ /fliːs/ *noun* **1** [C] the wool coat of a sheep ➲ picture at **goat** **2** [U,C] a type of soft warm cloth that feels like sheep's wool; a warm piece of clothing made from this cloth, which you wear on the top half of your body: *a fleece lining* ◆ *a bright red fleece* ➲ note at **sweater**

fleece² /fliːs/ *verb* [T] (*informal*) to take a lot of money from sb by charging them too much: *Some local shops have been fleecing tourists.* SYN **rip sb off**

fleet /fliːt/ *noun* [C, with sing or pl verb] **1** a group of ships or boats that sail together: *a fishing fleet* **2** a fleet (of sth) a group of vehicles (especially taxis, buses or aircraft) that are travelling together or owned by one person or organization

flesh /fleʃ/ *noun* [U] **1** the soft part of a human or animal body (between the bones and the skin): *Tigers are flesh-eating animals.*

> **MORE** The flesh of animals that we eat is called **meat**.

2 the part of a fruit or vegetable that is soft and can be eaten ➲ picture on **page P14**

IDM **your (own) flesh and blood** a member of your family

in the flesh in person, not on TV, in a photograph, etc.

make your flesh creep to make you feel disgusted and/or nervous: *The way he smiled made her flesh creep.*

flew *past tense* of **fly¹**

flex¹ /fleks/ *verb* [T] to bend or move a leg, arm, muscle, etc. in order to exercise it

flex² /fleks/ (*BrE*) (*especially AmE* **cord**) *noun* [C,U] (a piece of) wire inside a plastic tube, used for carrying electricity to electrical equipment ➲ picture at **rope**

> **MORE** At the end of a flex there is a **plug** which you fit into a **socket/power point**.

flexible /ˈfleksəbl/ *adj* **1** that can be changed easily: *flexible working hours* **2** able to bend or move easily without breaking OPP for both meanings **inflexible** ▶ **flexibility** /ˌfleksəˈbɪləti/ *noun* [U]

flick /flɪk/ *verb* **1** [T] flick sth (away, off, onto, etc.) to hit sth lightly and quickly with your finger or hand in order to move it: *She flicked the dust off her jacket.* ◆ *Please don't flick ash on the carpet.* **2** [I,T] flick (sth) (away, off, out, etc.) to move, or to make sth move, with a quick sudden movement: *She flicked the switch and the light came on.*

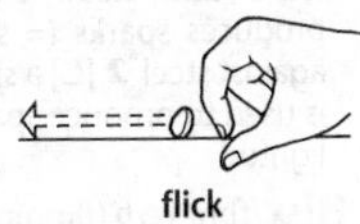
flick

PHR V **flick/flip through sth** to turn over the pages of a book, magazine, etc. quickly without reading everything
▶ **flick** *noun* [C]

flicker¹ /ˈflɪkə(r)/ *verb* [I] **1** (used about a light or a flame) to keep going on and off as it burns or shines: *The candle flickered and went out.* **2** (used about a feeling, thought, etc.) to appear for a short time: *A smile flickered across her face.* **3** to move lightly and quickly up and down: *His eyelids flickered for a second and then he lay still.*

flicker² /ˈflɪkə(r)/ *noun* [C, usually sing] **1** a light that shines on and off quickly: *the flicker of the TV/flames* **2** a feeling of sth that only lasts for a short time: *a flicker of hope/interest/doubt* **3** a small, sudden movement of part of the body

flier = flyer

flies ➲ fly

flight /flaɪt/ *noun* **1** [C] a journey by air: *to book a flight* ◆ *a direct/scheduled/charter flight* ◆ *They met **on a flight** to Australia.* ◆ *a manned space flight to Mars* ➲ note at **journey, plane** **2** [C] an aircraft that takes you on a particular journey: *Flight BA4351 from London to New York is boarding now* (= is ready for passengers to get on it). **3** [U] the act of flying: *It's unusual to see swans **in flight*** (= when they are flying). **4** [C] a number of stairs or steps going up or down: *a flight of stairs* **5** [C,U] the act of running away or escaping from a dangerous or difficult situation: *the refugees' flight from the war zone*

ˈflight attendant *noun* [C] a person whose job is to serve and take care of passengers on an aircraft

flimsy /ˈflɪmzi/ *adj* (**flimsier**; **flimsiest**) **1** not strong; easily broken or torn: *a flimsy bookcase* ◆ *a flimsy blouse* **2** weak; not making you believe that sth is true: *He gave a **flimsy excuse** for his absence.*

flinch /flɪntʃ/ *verb* [I] **flinch (at sth)**; **flinch (away)** to make a sudden movement backwards because of sth painful or frightening: *She couldn't help flinching away as the dentist came towards her with the drill.*

PHR V **flinch from sth/doing sth** to avoid doing sth because it is unpleasant: *She didn't flinch from telling him the whole truth.*

fling¹ /flɪŋ/ *verb* [T] (*pt, pp* **flung** /flʌŋ/) to throw sb/sth suddenly and carelessly or with great force: *He flung his coat on the floor.*

fling² /flɪŋ/ *noun* [C] a short period of fun and pleasure

flint /flɪnt/ *noun* **1** [U] very hard grey stone that produces **sparks** (= small flames) when you hit it against steel **2** [C] a small piece of **flint** or metal that is used to produce **sparks** (for example in a cigarette lighter)

flip /flɪp/ *verb* (**flipping**; **flipped**) **1** [I,T] to turn (sth) over with a quick movement: *She flipped the book open and started to read.* **2** [T] to throw sth into the air and make it turn over: *Let's flip a coin to see who starts.* **3** [I] (*spoken*) **flip (out)** to become very angry or excited: *When his father saw the damage to the car he flipped.*

PHR V **flick/flip through sth** ➲ flick

ˈflip chart *noun* [C] large sheets of paper that can be turned over, used to give information at meetings

ˈflip-flop (*AmE* **thong**) *noun* [C, usually pl] a simple open shoe with a narrow piece of material that goes between your big toe and the toe next to it ➲ picture at **shoe**

flippant /ˈflɪpənt/ (also *informal* **flip**) *adj* not serious enough about things that are important

flipper /ˈflɪpə(r)/ *noun* [C] **1** a flat arm that is part of the body of some sea animals and that they use for swimming: *Seals have flippers.* ➲ picture at **seal** ➲ picture on **page P13** **2** a rubber shoe shaped like an animal's **flipper** that people wear so that they can swim better, especially underwater: *a pair of flippers* ➲ picture at **snorkel**

flipping /ˈflɪpɪŋ/ *adj, adv* (*slang*) used as a mild way of swearing: *When's the flipping bus coming?*

flirt¹ /flɜːt/ *verb* [I] **flirt (with sb)** to behave in a way that suggests you find sb attractive and are trying to attract them: *Who was that boy Irene was flirting with at the party?* ◆ (*figurative*) *to flirt with death/danger/disaster*

PHR V **flirt with sth** to think about doing sth (but not very seriously): *She had flirted with the idea of becoming a teacher for a while.*

flirt² /flɜːt/ *noun* [C] a person who often **flirts** with people

flirtatious /flɜːˈteɪʃəs/ *adj* behaving in a way that shows a sexual attraction to sb that is not serious: *a flirtatious smile* ▶ **flirtatiously** *adv*

flit /flɪt/ *verb* [I] (**flitting**; **flitted**) **flit (from A to B)**; **flit (between A and B)** to fly or move quickly from one place to another without staying anywhere for long: *She flits from one job to another.*

float

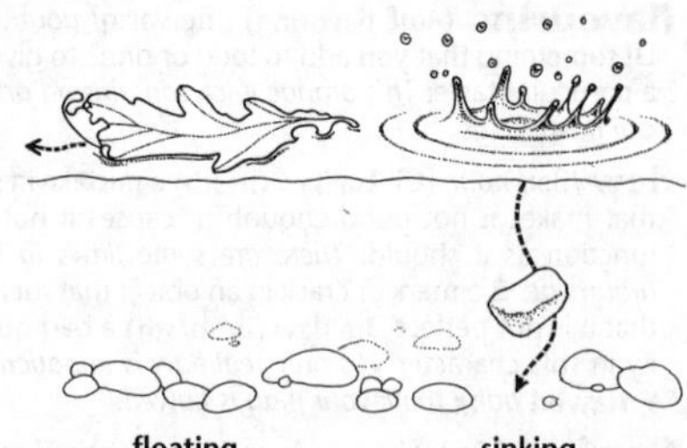

float¹ /fləʊt/ *verb* **1** [I] to move slowly through air or on water: *Boats were floating gently down the river.* ◆ *The smell of freshly baked bread floated in through the window.* **2** [I] **float (in/on sth)** to stay on the surface of a liquid and not sink: *Wood floats in water.* **3** [T] to sell shares in a company or business for the first time: *The company was floated on the stock market in 2009.* **4** [I,T] (used in **economics**) if a government **floats** its country's money or allows it to **float**, it allows its value to change freely according to the value of the money of other countries

float² /fləʊt/ *noun* [C] **1** a lorry or other vehicle that is decorated and used in a celebration that travels through the streets: *a carnival float* **2** a light object used in fishing that moves on the water when a fish has been caught **3** a light object used for helping people to learn to swim

floating /ˈfləʊtɪŋ/ *adj* not fixed; not living permanently in one place: *a floating population*

flock¹ /flɒk/ *noun* [C] **1** a group of sheep or birds ➲ look at **herd** **2** a large number of people: *Flocks of tourists visit Barcelona every summer.*

flock² /flɒk/ *verb* [I] (used about people) to go or meet somewhere in large numbers: *People are flocking to her latest exhibition.*

flog /flɒg/ *verb* [T] (**flogging**; **flogged**) **1** [usually passive] to hit sb hard several times with a stick or a **whip** (= a long thin piece of rope or leather) as a punishment **2** (*BrE informal*) to sell sth

flogging /ˈflɒgɪŋ/ *noun* [C,U] the act of hitting sb several times with a stick or a **whip** (= a long thin piece of rope or leather) as a punishment

flood¹ /flʌd/ *verb* **1** [I,T] to fill a place with water; to be filled or covered with water: *I left the taps on and flooded the bathroom.* ♦ *The River Trent floods almost every year.* **2** [I] **flood in/into/out of sth** to go somewhere in large numbers: *Since the TV programme was shown, phone calls have been flooding into the studio.* **3** [I,T] (used about a thought, feeling, etc.) to fill sb's mind suddenly: *At the end of the day all his worries came flooding back.*

flood² /flʌd/ *noun* [C] **1** a large amount of water that has spread from a river, the sea, etc. and that covers an area which should be dry: *Many people have been forced to leave their homes because of the floods.* **2 a flood (of sth)** a large number or amount: *She received a flood of letters after the accident.*

floodlight /ˈflʌdlaɪt/ *noun* [C] a powerful light that is used for lighting places where sports are played, the outside of public buildings, etc.

floodlit /ˈflʌdlɪt/ *adj* lit by **floodlights**: *a floodlit hockey match*

floor¹ /flɔː(r)/ *noun* **1** [C, usually sing] the flat surface that you walk on inside a building: *Don't come in—there's broken glass* ***on the floor!*** ♦ *a wooden/concrete/marble floor* ➲ note at **ground** **2** [C] all the rooms that are on the same level of a building: *My office is* ***on the*** *second* ***floor.***

HELP In Britain, the **ground floor** is the floor at street level, and the floor above is the **first floor**. In American English the **first floor** is the floor at street level.

3 [C, usually sing] the ground or surface at the bottom of the sea, a forest, etc: *the ocean/valley/cave/forest floor*

floor² /flɔː(r)/ *verb* [T] (*informal*) to surprise or confuse sb completely with a question or a problem: *Some of the questions I was asked in the interview completely floored me.*

floorboard /ˈflɔːbɔːd/ *noun* [C] one of the long wooden boards used to make a floor ➲ picture on **page P8**

flop¹ /flɒp/ *verb* [I] (**flopping**; **flopped**) **1 flop into/onto sth; flop (down/back)** to sit or lie down in a sudden and careless way because you are very tired: *I was so tired that all I could do was flop onto the sofa and watch TV.* **2 flop around, back, over, etc.** to move, hang or fall in an awkward way without control: *Her hair flopped over her eyes.* **3** (used about a book, film, album, etc.) to be a complete failure with the public

flop² /flɒp/ *noun* [C] (used about a film, play, party, etc.) something that is not a success; a failure: *Her first novel was very successful but her second was a flop.* ♦ *a box-office flop*

floppy /ˈflɒpi/ *adj* (**floppier**; **floppiest**) soft and hanging downwards; not hard and stiff: *a floppy hat*

ˌfloppy ˈdisk (also **floppy** (*pl* **floppies**) *or* **diskette**) *noun* [C] a square piece of plastic that can store information from a computer ➲ look at **hard disk**

flora /ˈflɔːrə/ *noun* [pl] all the plants growing in a particular area: *He's studying the* ***flora and fauna*** (= the plants and animals) *of South America.* ➲ look at **fauna**

floral /ˈflɔːrəl/ *adj* decorated with a pattern of flowers, or made with flowers: *wallpaper with a floral design*

florist /ˈflɒrɪst/ *noun* **1** [C] a person who has a shop that sells flowers **2 a florist's** [sing] a shop that sells flowers

floss /flɒs/ = **dental floss**

flotation /fləʊˈteɪʃn/ *noun* **1** [C,U] the process of selling shares in a company to the public for the first time in order to make money: *plans for (a) flotation on the stock exchange* ♦ *a stock-market flotation* **2** [U] the act of floating on or in water

flounder /ˈflaʊndə(r)/ *verb* [I] **1** to find it difficult to speak or act (usually in a difficult or embarrassing situation): *The questions they asked her at the interview had her floundering helplessly.* **2** to have a lot of problems and be in danger of failing completely: *By the end of the year, the business was floundering.* **3** to struggle to move or get somewhere in water, mud, etc.

flour /ˈflaʊə(r)/ *noun* [U] a very thin powder made from a type of grain such as **wheat** and used for making bread, cakes, biscuits, etc.

flourish¹ /ˈflʌrɪʃ/ *verb* **1** [I] to be strong and healthy; to develop in a successful way: *a flourishing business* **2** [T] to wave sth in the air so that people will notice it: *He proudly flourished two tickets for the concert.*

flourish² /ˈflʌrɪʃ/ *noun* [C] an exaggerated movement: *He opened the door for her with a flourish.*

flout /flaʊt/ *verb* [T] to refuse to obey or accept sth: *to flout the rules of the organization* ♦ *to flout somebody's advice*

flow¹ /fləʊ/ *noun* [C, usually sing, U] **a flow (of sth/sb)** **1** a steady, continuous movement of sth/sb: *Press hard on the wound to stop the flow of blood.* **2** a supply of sth: *the flow of information between the school and the parents* **3** the way in which words, ideas, etc. are joined together smoothly: *Once Charlie's* ***in full flow****, it's hard to stop him talking.*

IDM the ebb and flow (of sth) ➲ **the ebb**

flow² /fləʊ/ *verb* [I] **1** to move in a smooth and continuous way (like water): *This river flows south into the English Channel.* ♦ *a fast-flowing stream* ♦ *Traffic began to flow normally again after the accident.* **2** (used about words, ideas, actions, etc.) to be joined together smoothly: *As soon as we sat down*

F

at the table, the conversation began to flow. **3** (used about hair and clothes) to hang down in a loose way: *a long flowing dress*

ˈflow chart (also **ˈflow diagram**) *noun* [C] a diagram that shows the connections between different stages of a process or parts of a system

flower¹ /ˈflaʊə(r)/ *noun* [C] **1** the coloured part of a plant or tree from which seeds or fruit grow: *The plant has a beautiful red flower.* ◆ *The roses are* **in flower** *early this year.* ➲ picture at **plant** **2** a plant that is grown for its flowers: *to grow flowers* ◆ *a bunch of flowers*

> **MORE** A flower has thin soft coloured **petals**. It grows from a **bud** on the end of a **stem**. We **pick** flowers or buy them at the **florist's** (= flower shop), then **arrange** them in a **vase**. Flowers that are given or carried on a special occasion are called a **bouquet**.

flower² /ˈflaʊə(r)/ *verb* [I] to produce flowers: *This plant flowers in late summer.*

ˈflower bed (also **bed**) *noun* [C] a piece of ground in a garden or park where flowers are grown ➲ picture on **page P8**

flowerpot /ˈflaʊəpɒt/ *noun* [C] a pot in which a plant can be grown

flowery /ˈflaʊəri/ *adj* **1** covered or decorated with flowers: *a flowery dress/hat/pattern* ➲ picture on **page P1** **2** (used about a style of speaking or writing) using long, difficult words when they are not necessary

flown *past participle of* **fly¹**

fl oz *abbr* = **fluid ounce**

flu /fluː/ (also *formal* **influenza**) *noun* [U] an illness that is like a bad cold but more serious. You usually feel very hot and your arms and legs hurt.

fluctuate /ˈflʌktʃueɪt/ *verb* [I] **fluctuate (between A and B)** (used about prices and numbers, or people's feelings) to change many times from one thing to another: *The number of students fluctuates between 100 and 150.* ▶ **fluctuation** /ˌflʌktʃuˈeɪʃn/ *noun* [C,U]

fluent /ˈfluːənt/ *adj* **1** **fluent (in sth)** able to speak or write a foreign language easily and accurately: *After a year in France she was fluent in French.* **2** (used about speaking, reading or writing) expressed in a smooth and accurate way: *He speaks fluent German.* ▶ **fluency** /ˈfluːənsi/ *noun* [U]: *My knowledge of Japanese grammar is good but I need to work on my fluency.* ▶ **fluently** *adv*

fluff /flʌf/ *noun* [U] **1** very small pieces of wool, cotton, etc. that form into balls and collect on clothes and other surfaces **2** the soft new fur on young animals or birds

fluffy /ˈflʌfi/ *adj* (**fluffier**; **fluffiest**) **1** covered in soft fur: *a fluffy kitten* **2** that looks or feels very soft and light: *fluffy clouds/towels*

fluid¹ /ˈfluːɪd/ *noun* [C,U] a substance that can flow; a liquid: *The doctor told her to drink plenty of fluids.* ◆ *cleaning fluid* ◆ *correction fluid*

fluid² /ˈfluːɪd/ *adj* **1** able to flow smoothly like a liquid: (*figurative*) *I like her fluid style of dancing.* **2** (used about plans, etc.) able to change or likely to be changed

ˌfluid ˈounce *noun* [C] (*abbr* **fl oz**) a measure of liquid; in the UK, 0.0284 of a litre; in the US, 0.0295 of a litre. ❶ For more information about measurements, look at the section on using numbers at the back of this dictionary.

fluke /fluːk/ *noun* [C, usually sing] (*informal*) a surprising and lucky result that happens by accident, not because you have been clever or skilful: *The result was no fluke. The better team won.*

flung *past tense, past participle of* **fling¹**

fluorescent /ˌflɔːˈresnt; ˌflʊəˈr-/ *adj* **1** producing a bright white light: *fluorescent lighting* **2** very bright; seeming to shine: *fluorescent pink paint*

fluoride /ˈflɔːraɪd/ *noun* [U] a chemical that can be added to water or **toothpaste** (= a substance you use to clean your teeth) to help prevent bad teeth

flurry /ˈflʌri/ *noun* [C] (*pl* **flurries**) **1** a short time in which there is suddenly a lot of activity: *a flurry of excitement/activity* **2** a sudden short fall of snow or rain

flush¹ /flʌʃ/ *verb* **1** [I] (used about a person or their face) to go red: *Susan flushed and could not hide her embarrassment.* ➲ A more common word is **blush**. **2** [I,T] when a toilet **flushes** or you **flush** it, water passes through it to clean it, after a handle, etc. has been pressed: *Please remember to flush the toilet after use.* ◆ *The toilet won't flush.* **3** [T] **flush sth away, down, etc.** to get rid of sth in a flow of water

flush² /flʌʃ/ *noun* [C, usually sing] **1** a hot feeling or red colour that you have in your face when you are embarrassed, excited, angry, etc: *The cold wind brought a flush to our cheeks.* ◆ *a flush of anger* **2** the act of cleaning a toilet with a quick flow of water; the system for doing this

flushed /flʌʃt/ *adj* with a hot red face: *You look very flushed. Are you sure you're all right?*

fluster /ˈflʌstə(r)/ *verb* [T, usually passive] to make sb feel nervous and confused (because there is too much to do or not enough time): *Don't get flustered —there's plenty of time.* ▶ **fluster** *noun* [sing]: *I always get* **in a fluster** *before exams.*

flute /fluːt/ *noun* [C] a musical instrument like a pipe that you hold sideways and play by blowing over a hole at one side ➲ note at **music** ➲ picture at **music** ▶ **flutist** /ˈfluːtɪst/ (*AmE*) = **flautist**

flutter¹ /ˈflʌtə(r)/ *verb* **1** [I,T] to move or make sth move quickly and lightly, especially through the air: *The flags were fluttering in the wind.* ◆ *The bird fluttered its wings and tried to fly.* **2** [I] your heart or stomach **flutters** when you feel nervous and excited

flutter² /ˈflʌtə(r)/ *noun* [C, usually sing] a quick, light movement: *the flutter of wings/eyelids*

flux /flʌks/ *noun* [U] continuous movement and change: *Our society is* **in a state of flux**.

fly[1] /flaɪ/ *verb* (**flying**; **flies**; *pt* **flew** /fluː/; *pp* **flown** /fləʊn/)

➤OF BIRD, AIRCRAFT, ETC. **1** [I,T] to move through the air: *This bird has a broken wing and can't fly.* ♦ *How long does it take to fly the Atlantic?*

➤PLANE **2** [I,T] to travel or carry sb/sth in an aircraft, etc: *My daughter is flying (out) to Singapore next week.* ♦ *Supplies of food were flown (in) to the starving people.* **3** [I,T] (used about a pilot) to control an aircraft: *You have to have special training to fly a jumbo jet.*

➤MOVE QUICKLY **4** [I] to move quickly or suddenly, especially through the air: *A large stone* ***came flying*** *through the window.* ♦ *I slipped and my shopping* ***went flying*** *everywhere.* ♦ *Suddenly the door* ***flew open*** *and Mark came running in.* ♦ (*figurative*) *The weekend has just* ***flown by*** *and now it's Monday again.*

➤MOVE IN AIR **5** [I,T] to move about or to make sth move about in the air: *The flags are flying.* ♦ *to fly a flag/kite* ➲ *noun* **flight**

IDM **as the crow flies** ➲ **crow**[1]

fly off the handle (*informal*) to become very angry in an unreasonable way

let fly (at sb/sth) **1** to shout angrily at sb: *My parents really let fly at me when I got home late.* **2** to hit sb in anger: *She let fly at him with her fists.*

fly[2] /flaɪ/ *noun* [C] **1** (*pl* **flies**) a small insect with two wings: *Flies buzzed round the dead cow.* ➲ picture on **page P13** **2** (also **flies** [pl]) an opening down the front of a pair of trousers that fastens with buttons or a **zip** (= a device for fastening clothes, with two rows of metal or plastic teeth) and is covered with a narrow piece of cloth: *Henry, your flies are undone.* ➲ picture on **page P1**

IDM **a fly on the wall** a person who watches others without being noticed: *I'd love to be a fly on the wall when he tells her the news.*

not harm/hurt a fly to be kind and gentle and unwilling to cause unhappiness

flyer (also **flier**) /ˈflaɪə(r)/ *noun* [C] **1** a person who travels in a plane as a pilot or a passenger: *frequent flyers* ♦ *I'm a nervous flyer.* **2** a small sheet of paper that advertises a product or an event and is given to a large number of people

flying /ˈflaɪɪŋ/ *adj* [only *before* a noun] able to fly: *flying insects*

IDM **get off to a flying start** to begin sth well; to make a good start

with flying colours with great success; very well: *Martin passed the exam with flying colours.*

▶ **flying** *noun* [U]: *I'm scared of flying.*

ˌflying ˈsaucer *noun* [C] a round **spacecraft** (= a vehicle that travels in space) that some people say they have seen and believe comes from another planet ➲ look at **UFO**

ˌflying ˈvisit *noun* [C] a very quick visit: *I can't stop. This is just a flying visit.*

flyover /ˈflaɪəʊvə(r)/ (*AmE* **overpass**) *noun* [C] a type of bridge that carries a road over another road

FM /ˌef ˈem/ *abbr* **frequency modulation**; one of the systems of sending out radio signals

foal /fəʊl/ *noun* [C] a young horse ➲ note at **horse**

foam[1] /fəʊm/ *noun* [U] **1** (also ˌ**foam ˈrubber**) a light rubber material that is used inside seats, etc. to make them comfortable: *a foam mattress* **2** a mass of small air bubbles that form on the surface of a liquid: *white foam on the tops of the waves* **3** an artificial substance that is between a solid and a liquid and is made from very small bubbles: *shaving foam*

foam[2] /fəʊm/ *verb* [I] to produce **foam**: *We watched the foaming river below.*

fob /fɒb/ *verb* (**fobbing**; **fobbed**)

PHR V **fob sb off (with sth)** **1** to try to stop sb asking questions or complaining by telling them sth that is not true: *Don't let them fob you off with any more excuses.* **2** to try to give sb sth that they do not want: *Don't try to fob me off with that old car—I want a new one.*

focal point /ˈfəʊkl pɔɪnt/ *noun* [sing] the centre of interest or activity

focus[1] /ˈfəʊkəs/ *verb* [I,T] (**focusing**; **focused** *or* **focussing**; **focussed**) **focus (sth) (on sth)** **1** to give all your attention to sth: *to focus on a problem* **2** (used about your eyes or a camera) to change or be changed so that things can be seen clearly: *Gradually his eyes focused.* ♦ *I focussed (the camera) on the person in the middle of the group.*

focus[2] /ˈfəʊkəs/ *noun* [C, usually sing] the centre of interest or attention; special attention that is given to sb/sth: *The school used to be the focus of village life.*

IDM **in focus/out of focus** (used about a photograph or sth in a photograph) clear/not clear: *This picture is so badly out of focus that I can't recognize anyone.*

ˈfocus group *noun* [C] a small group of people who are asked to discuss a particular subject. The information obtained is used for research into people's choices and preferences: *A focus group of 100 teachers considered new methods were an improvement.*

fodder /ˈfɒdə(r)/ *noun* [U] food that is given to farm animals

foe /fəʊ/ *noun* [C] (*written*) an enemy

foetus (*AmE* **fetus**) /ˈfiːtəs/ *noun* [C] a young human or animal that is still developing in its mother's body

> **MORE** An **embryo** is at an earlier stage of development.

fog /fɒɡ/ *noun* [U,C] thick white cloud that forms close to the land or sea and is difficult to see through: *Patches of dense fog are making driving dangerous.* ♦ *Bad fogs are common in November.* ➲ note at **weather**

> **MORE** **Fog** is thicker than **mist**. **Haze** is caused by heat. **Smog** is caused by pollution.

foggy /ˈfɒɡi/ *adj* (**foggier**; **foggiest**) used to describe the weather when there is **fog**

IDM **not have the faintest/foggiest (idea)** ➲ **faint**[1]

foil[1] /fɔɪl/ *noun* **1** (also tinfoil) [U] metal that has been made into very thin sheets, used for putting around food: *aluminium foil* **2** [C] a long, thin, pointed weapon used in the sport of **fencing** ➲ picture on **page P5**

foil[2] /fɔɪl/ *verb* [T] to prevent sb from succeeding, especially with a plan; to prevent a plan from succeeding: *The prisoners were foiled in their attempt to escape.*

F

foist /fɔɪst/ *verb*

PHR V **foist sth on/upon sb** to force sb to accept sth that they do not want: *Jeff had a lot of extra work foisted on him when his boss was away.*

fold[1] /fəʊld/ *verb* **1** [T] fold sth (up) to bend one part of sth over another part in order to make it smaller, tidier, etc: *He folded the letter into three before putting it into the envelope.* ◆ *Fold up your clothes neatly and put them away please.* **OPP** **unfold** ➲ picture at **crinkle** **2** [I] fold (up) to be able to be made smaller in order to be carried or stored more easily: *This table folds up flat.* ◆ *a folding bed* **3** [T] fold A in B; fold B round/over A to put sth around sth else: *I folded the photos in a sheet of paper and put them away.* **4** [I] (used about a business, a play in the theatre, etc.) to close because it is a failure

IDM **cross/fold your arms** ➲ **arm**[1] ➲ picture at **arm**

▶ **folding** *adj* [only *before* a noun]: *a folding chair*

fold[2] /fəʊld/ *noun* [C] **1** a curved shape that is made when there is more material, etc. than is necessary to cover sth: *the folds of a curtain/dress* **2** the mark or line where sth has been folded **3** a small area inside a fence where sheep are kept together in a field

folder /ˈfəʊldə(r)/ *noun* [C] **1** a cardboard or plastic cover that is used for holding papers, etc. ➲ picture at **stationery** **2** a collection of files on one subject that is stored in a computer or on a disk

foliage /ˈfəʊliɪdʒ/ *noun* [U] (*formal*) all the leaves of a tree or plant

folk[1] /fəʊk/ *noun* **1** (*AmE* folks /fəʊks/) [pl] (*informal*) people in general: *Some folk are never satisfied.* **2** [pl] a particular type of people: *Old folk often don't like change.* ◆ *country/city folk* **3** folks [pl] (*informal*) used as a friendly way of addressing more than one person: *What shall we do today, folks?* **4** folks [pl] (*informal*) your parents or close relatives: *How are your folks?* **5** [U] music in the traditional style of a country or community: *Do you like Irish folk?*

folk[2] /fəʊk/ *adj* [only *before* a noun] traditional in a community; of a traditional style: *Robin Hood is an English folk hero.* ◆ *folk music* ◆ *a folk song*

folklore /ˈfəʊklɔː(r)/ *noun* [U] traditional stories and beliefs

follow /ˈfɒləʊ/ *verb*

➤GO AFTER **1** [I,T] to come, go or happen after sb/sth: *You go first and I'll follow (on) later.* ◆ *The dog followed her (around) wherever she went.* ◆ *I'll have soup followed by spaghetti.*

➤BE RESULT **2** [I] follow (on) (from sth) to be the logical result of sth; to be the next logical step after sth: *It doesn't follow that old people can't lead active lives.* ◆ *Intermediate Book One follows on from Elementary Book Two.*

➤ROAD/PATH **3** [T] to go along a road, etc.; to go in the same direction as sth: *Follow this road for a mile and then turn right at the station.* ◆ *The road follows the river for a few miles.*

➤INSTRUCTIONS **4** [T] to do sth or to happen according to instructions, an example, what is usual, etc: *When lighting fireworks, it is important to* ***follow the instructions*** *carefully.* ◆ *The day's events followed the usual pattern.*

➤UNDERSTAND **5** [I,T] to understand the meaning of sth: *The children couldn't follow the plot of that film.*

➤KEEP WATCHING **6** [T] to keep watching or listening to sth as it happens or develops: *The film follows the career of a young dancer.* ◆ *Have you been following the tennis championships?*

➤INTERNET SITE **7** [T] to regularly read the messages that sb writes on an Internet site: *Follow us at @OUPELTGlobal on Twitter.*

IDM **a hard act to follow** ➲ **hard**[1]

as follows used for introducing a list: *The names of the successful candidates are as follows ...*

follow in sb's footsteps to do the same job as sb else who did it before you: *He followed in his father's footsteps and joined the army.*

follow sb's example/lead to do what sb else has done or decided to do

follow suit to do the same thing that sb else has just done

follow your nose to go straight forward: *Turn right at the lights and after that just follow your nose until you get to the village.*

PHR V **follow sth through** to continue doing sth until it is finished

follow sth up **1** to take further action about sth: *You should follow up your email with a phone call.* **2** to find out more about sth: *We need to follow up the story about the school.*

follower /ˈfɒləʊə(r)/ *noun* [C] **1** a person who follows or supports a person, belief, etc. **2** a person who regularly reads the messages that sb writes on an Internet site: *a celebrity with thousands of followers on Facebook*

following[1] /ˈfɒləʊɪŋ/ *adj* **1** next (in time): *He became ill on Sunday and died the following day.* **2** that are going to be mentioned next: *Please could you bring the following items to the next meeting ...*

following[2] /ˈfɒləʊɪŋ/ *noun* **1** [sing] a group of people who support or admire sth: *The Brazilian team has a large following in all parts of the world.* **2** the following [sing, pl] the person or thing (or people or things) that you will mention next: *The following is a summary of events.* ◆ *The following are the winners of the competition ...*

following[3] /ˈfɒləʊɪŋ/ *prep* after; as a result of: *Following the riots, many students have been arrested.*

ˈ**follow-up** *noun* [C] something that is done as a second stage to continue or develop sth: *As a follow-up to the TV series, the BBC is publishing a book.*

folly /ˈfɒli/ *noun* [C,U] (*pl* **follies**) (*formal*) an act that is not sensible and may have a bad result: *It would be folly to ignore their warnings.*

fond /fɒnd/ *adj* (**fonder**; **fondest**) **1** [not before a noun] **fond of sb/sth; fond of doing sth** liking a person or thing, or liking doing sth: *Teachers often* ***grow fond*** *of their students.* ◆ *Elephants are very fond of bananas.* ◆ *I'm not fond of getting up early.* **2** [only *before* a noun] kind and loving: *I have* ***fond memories*** *of my grandmother.*

fondle /ˈfɒndl/ *verb* [T] to touch sb/sth gently in a loving or sexual way

fondly /ˈfɒndli/ *adv* in a loving way: *Miss Murphy will be fondly remembered by all her former students.*

fondness /ˈfɒndnəs/ *noun* [U,sing] **(a) fondness (for sb/sth)** a liking for sb/sth: *I've always had a fondness for cats.* ◆ *My grandmother talks about her schooldays* ***with fondness.***

font /fɒnt/ *noun* [C] **1** a large stone bowl in a church that holds water for a **baptism** (= a ceremony in which a person becomes a member of the Christian Church) **2** the particular size and style of a set of letters that are used in printing, on a computer screen, etc.

food /fuːd/ *noun* **1** [U] the things that people or animals eat: *Food and drink will be provided after the meeting.* ◆ *There is a shortage of food in some areas.* **2** [C,U] a particular type of food that you eat: *My favourite food is pasta.* ◆ *Have you ever had Japanese food?* ◆ *baby food* ◆ *dog food* ◆ *health foods* ➲ note at **restaurant** ➲ picture on **page P16**

foodie /ˈfuːdi/ *noun* [C] (*informal*) a person who is very interested in cooking and eating different kinds of food

ˈ**food mile** *noun* [C] a measurement of the distance that food travels from the producer to the consumer and the fuel that this uses

ˈ**food poisoning** *noun* [U] an illness that is caused by eating food that is bad for you

ˈ**food processor** *noun* [C] an electric machine that can mix food and also cut food into small pieces ➲ picture at **mixer**

foodstuff /ˈfuːdstʌf/ *noun* [C, usually pl] a substance that is used as food: *There has been a sharp rise in the cost of basic foodstuffs.*

fool[1] /fuːl/ *noun* [C] a person who is silly or who acts in a silly way: *I felt such a fool when I realized my stupid mistake.* **SYN** **idiot** ➲ look at **April Fool's Day**
IDM **make a fool of sb/yourself** to make sb/yourself look **foolish** or silly: *Sheila got drunk and made a complete fool of herself.*

fool[2] /fuːl/ *verb* **1** [T] **fool sb (into doing sth)** to trick sb: *Don't be fooled into believing everything that the salesman says.* **2** [I] to speak without being serious: *You didn't really believe me when I said I was going to America, did you? I was only fooling.*
PHR V **fool about/around** to behave in a silly way: *Stop fooling around with that knife or someone will get hurt!*

foolhardy /ˈfuːlhɑːdi/ *adj* taking unnecessary risks

foolish /ˈfuːlɪʃ/ *adj* **1** not sensible: *I was foolish enough to trust him.* **2** looking silly or feeling embarrassed: *I felt a bit foolish when I couldn't remember the man's name.* **SYN** for both meanings **silly, stupid** ▶ **foolishly** *adv*: *I foolishly agreed to lend him money.* ▶ **foolishness** *noun* [U]

foolproof /ˈfuːlpruːf/ *adj* not capable of going wrong or being wrongly used: *Our security system is absolutely foolproof.*

foot[1] /fʊt/ *noun* (*pl* **feet** /fiːt/)
➤PART OF BODY **1** [C] the lowest part of the body, at the end of the leg, on which a person or an animal stands: *People usually* ***get to their feet*** (= stand up) *for the national anthem.* ◆ *I usually go to school* ***on foot*** (= walking). ◆ *I need to sit down—I've been* ***on my feet*** *all day.* ◆ *There's broken glass on the floor, so don't walk around* ***in bare feet*** (= without shoes and socks). ◆ *She sat by the fire and the dog sat at her feet.* ◆ *a foot brake/pedal/pump* (= one that is operated by your foot) ➲ picture at **body**
➤-FOOTED **2** [in compounds] having or using the type of foot or number of feet mentioned: *There are no left-footed players in the team.* ◆ *a four-footed creature*
➤PART OF SOCK **3** [C] the part of a sock, etc. that covers the foot
➤BOTTOM **4** [sing] **the foot of sth** the bottom of sth: *There's a note at the foot of the page.* ◆ *the foot of the stairs* ◆ *the foot of the bed* **OPP** **top**
➤MEASUREMENT **5** [C] (*abbr* **ft**) a measure of length; 30.48 centimetres. There are 3 feet in a yard: *'How tall are you?' 'Five foot six (inches).'* ◆ *a six-foot high wall* ℹ For more information about measurements, look at the section on using numbers at the back of this dictionary.
IDM **be rushed/run off your feet** to be extremely busy; to have too many things to do: *Over Christmas we were rushed off our feet at work.*
fall/land on your feet to be lucky in finding yourself in a good situation, or in getting out of a difficult situation: *I really landed on my feet getting such a good job with so little experience.*
find your feet ➲ **find**[1]
get/have cold feet ➲ **cold**[1]
get/start off on the right/wrong foot (with sb) (*informal*) to start a relationship well/badly: *I seem to have got off on the wrong foot with the new boss.*
have one foot in the grave (*informal*) to be so old or ill that you are not likely to live much longer
(back) on your feet completely healthy again after an illness or a time of difficulty
put your feet up to sit down and relax, especially with your feet off the floor and supported: *I'm so tired that I just want to go home and put my feet up.*
put your foot down (*informal*) to say firmly that sth must (not) happen: *I put my foot down and told Andy he couldn't use our car any more.*

put your foot in it (*informal*) to say or do sth that makes sb embarrassed or upset
set foot in/on sth to visit, enter or arrive at/in a place: *No woman has ever set foot in the temple.*
stand on your own (two) feet to take care of yourself without help; to be independent
under your feet in the way; stopping you from working, etc: *Would somebody get these children out from under my feet and take them to the park?*

foot² /fʊt/ *verb*
IDM **foot the bill (for sth)** (*informal*) to pay (for sth)

F

footage /ˈfʊtɪdʒ/ *noun* [U] part of a film showing a particular event: *The documentary included footage of the assassination of Kennedy.*

football

footballers
(*AmE* **soccer players**)

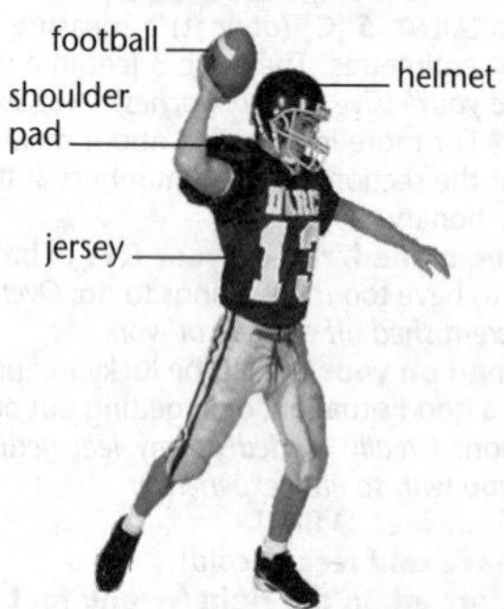

American football player
(*AmE* **football player**)

football /ˈfʊtbɔːl/ *noun* **1** (*especially AmE* **soccer**) [U] a game that is played by two teams of eleven players who try to kick a round ball into a goal: *a football pitch/match* ◆ *Tom plays football every Saturday.* ➲ note at **sport** **2** [C] the large round ball that is used in this game

footballer /ˈfʊtbɔːlə(r)/ (*especially AmE* **soccer player**) *noun* [C] a person who plays football: *a talented footballer*

HELP In the US **soccer** is the usual word for the game, since Americans use the word **football** to refer to **American Football**.

foothold /ˈfʊthəʊld/ *noun* [C] (*figurative*) **1** a place where you can safely put your foot when you are climbing **2** a strong position in a business or profession from which sb can progress: *We need to get a foothold in the European market.*

footing /ˈfʊtɪŋ/ *noun* [sing] **1** being able to stand firmly on a surface: *Climbers usually attach themselves to a rope in case they* **lose their footing**. **2** the basis on which sth is established or organized: *The company is now* **on a firm footing** *and should soon show a profit.* **3** the level or position of sb/sth (in relation to sb/sth else): *to be* **on an equal footing** *with somebody*

footnote /ˈfʊtnəʊt/ *noun* [C] an extra piece of information that is added at the bottom of a page in a book

footpath /ˈfʊtpɑːθ/ *noun* [C] a path for people to walk on, especially in the country: *a footpath through the woods* ➲ picture on **page P11**

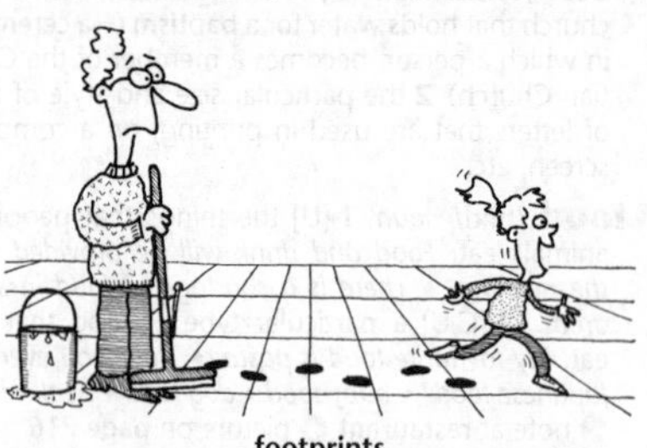

footprints

footprint /ˈfʊtprɪnt/ *noun* [C] a mark that is left on the ground by a foot or a shoe ➲ look at **track**

footstep /ˈfʊtstep/ *noun* [C] the sound of sb walking: *I heard his footsteps in the hall.*
IDM **follow in sb's footsteps** ➲ **follow**

footwear /ˈfʊtweə(r)/ *noun* [U] boots or shoes

for¹ /fə(r); *strong form* fɔː(r)/ *prep* **1** showing the person that will use or have sth: *Here is a letter for you.* ◆ *He made lunch for them.* ◆ *It's a book for children.* **2** in order to help sb/sth: *What can I do for you?* ◆ *You should take some medicine for your cold.* ◆ *Doctors are fighting for his life.* ◆ *shampoo for dry hair* **3** meaning sth or representing sb/sth: *What's the 'C' for in 'BBC'?* ◆ *What's the Russian for 'window'?* ◆ *She plays hockey for England.* **4** in support of (sb/sth): *Are you for or against shops opening on Sundays?* **5** in order to do, have or get sth: *What's this gadget for?* ◆ *What did you do that for?* (= Why did you do that?) ◆ *Are you learning English for your job or for fun?* ◆ *She asked me for help.* ◆ *Phone now for information.* ◆ *to go for a walk/swim/drink* **6** (showing a reason) as a result of: *Ben didn't want to come for some reason.* ◆ *He was sent to prison for robbery.* ◆ *I couldn't speak for laughing.* **7** (showing the price or value of sth) in exchange for: *I bought this car for £2000.* ◆ *You get one point for each correct answer.* ◆ *I want to exchange this sweater* *for a larger one.* ◆ *The officer was accused of giving secret information for cash.* **8** [after an adjective] showing how usual, suitable, difficult, etc. sb/sth is in relation to sb/sth else: *She's tall for her age.* ◆ *It's quite warm for January.* ◆ *It's unusual for Alex to be late.* ◆ *I think Sandra is perfect for this job.* **9** showing the place that sb/sth will go to: *Is this the train for Glasgow?* ◆ *They set off for the shops.* **10** showing a length of time: *I'm going away for a few days.* ◆ *for a while/a long time/ages* ◆ *They have left the town* ***for good*** (= they will not return). ◆ *He was in prison for 20 years* (= he is not in prison now). ◆ *He has been in prison for 20 years* (= he is still in prison). ➲ note at **during, since**

GRAMMAR **Since** is used with a point in time and usually a perfect tense for showing when something began: *He has been in prison since 2008.* **Ago** is usually used with a past tense for showing when something began: *He went to prison 20 years ago.*

11 at a particular, fixed time: *What did they give you for your birthday?* ◆ *Shall we have eggs for breakfast?* ◆ *I'm going to my parents' for Christmas.* ◆ *The appointment is for 10.30.* **12** showing how many times sth has happened: *I'm warning you for the last time.* ◆ *I met him for the second time yesterday.* **13** showing a distance: *He walked for ten miles.*

IDM **be (in) for it** (*BrE informal*) to be going to get into trouble or be punished: *If you arrive late again you'll be in for it.*

for all in spite of: *For all his money, he's a very lonely man.*

for ever ➲ **forever**

for² /fə(r); *strong form* fɔː(r)/ *conj* (*formal*) because: *The children soon lost their way, for they had never been in the forest alone before.*

forage /ˈfɒrɪdʒ/ *verb* [I] **forage (for sth)** (used especially about animals) to search for food

forbid /fəˈbɪd/ *verb* [T] (**forbidding**; *pt* **forbade** /fəˈbeɪd/ *or* **forbad** /fəˈbæd/; *pp* **forbidden** /fəˈbɪdn/) **1** **forbid sb to do sth** to order sb not to do sth: *My parents forbade me to see Tim again.* **OPP** **allow** **2** [usually passive] to not allow sth: *Smoking is forbidden anywhere in the building.* ◆ *Photography is forbidden anywhere in the building.* **SYN** **prohibit** **OPP** for both meanings **allow**

forbidding /fəˈbɪdɪŋ/ *adj* looking unfriendly or frightening: *The coast near the village is rather grey and forbidding.*

force¹ /fɔːs/ *noun* **1** [U] physical strength or power: *The force of the explosion knocked them to the ground.* ◆ *The police* ***used force*** *to break up the demonstration.* **2** [U] power and influence: *the force of public opinion* **3** [C] a person or thing that has power or influence: *Britain is no longer a major force in international affairs.* ◆ *Julia has been* ***the driving force*** *behind the company's success.* **4** [C] a group of people who are trained for a particular purpose: *a highly trained workforce* ◆ *the police force* **5** [usually plural] the soldiers and weapons that an army, etc. has: *the armed forces* **6** [C,U] (*technical*) a power that can cause change or movement: *the force of gravity*

IDM **bring sth/come into force** to start using a new law, etc.; to start being used: *The government want to bring new anti-pollution legislation into force next year.*

force of habit if you do sth from or out of **force of habit**, you do it in a particular way because you have always done it that way in the past

in force **1** (used about people) in large numbers: *The police were present in force at the football match.* **2** (used about a law, rule, etc.) being used: *The new speed limit is now in force.*

join forces (with sb) ➲ **join¹**

force² /fɔːs/ *verb* [T] **1** **force sb (to do sth); force sb (into sth/doing sth)** to make sb do sth that they do not want to do: *She forced herself to speak to him.* ◆ *The President was forced into resigning.* **2** to use physical strength to do sth or to move sth: *The window had been forced (open).* ◆ *We had to force our way through the crowd.* **3** to make sth happen when it will not happen naturally: *to force a smile/laugh* ◆ *To force the issue, I gave him until midday to decide.*

forceful /ˈfɔːsfl/ *adj* having the power to persuade people: *He has a very forceful personality.* ◆ *a forceful speech*

forceps /ˈfɔːseps/ *noun* [pl] a special instrument that looks like a pair of scissors but is not sharp. **Forceps** are used by doctors for holding things firmly: *a pair of forceps*

forcible /ˈfɔːsəbl/ *adj* [only *before* a noun] done using (physical) force: *The police made a forcible entry into the building.* ▶ **forcibly** /-əbli/ *adv*: *The squatters were forcibly removed by the police.*

ford /fɔːd/ *noun* [C] a place in a river where you can walk or drive across because the water is not deep

fore /fɔː(r)/ *noun*

IDM **be/come to the fore** to be in or get into an important position so that you are noticed by people; to play an important part

forearm /ˈfɔːrɑːm/ *noun* [C] the part of your arm between your elbow and your wrist ➲ picture at **body**

foreboding /fɔːˈbəʊdɪŋ/ *noun* [U,sing] a strong feeling that danger or trouble is coming: *She was filled with* ***a sense of foreboding.***

forecast /ˈfɔːkɑːst/ *verb* [T] (*pt, pp* **forecast** *or* **forecasted**) to say (with the help of information) what will probably happen in the future: *The Chancellor did not forecast the sudden rise in inflation.* ◆ *Rain has been forecast for tomorrow.* ▶ **forecast** *noun* [C]: *a sales forecast for the coming year* ➲ look at **weather forecast**

forecourt /ˈfɔːkɔːt/ *noun* [C] a large open area in front of a building such as a hotel or petrol station

forefinger /ˈfɔːfɪŋɡə(r)/ (also ˈ**index finger**) *noun* [C] the finger next to the thumb

forefront /ˈfɔːfrʌnt/ *noun* [sing] the leading position; the position at the front: *Our department is right* ***at the forefront of*** *scientific research.*

forego = **forgo**

foregone[1] *past participle* of **forgo**

foregone[2] /ˈfɔːɡɒn/ *adj*
IDM **a foregone conclusion** a result that is or was certain to happen: *Her promotion was a foregone conclusion.*

foreground /ˈfɔːɡraʊnd/ *noun* [sing] **1** the part of a view, picture, photograph, etc. that appears closest to the person looking at it: *Notice the artist's use of colour* ***in the foreground*** *of the picture.* **2** a position where you will be noticed most: *He likes to be in the foreground at meetings.* OPP for both meanings **background**

forehand /ˈfɔːhænd/ *noun* [C] a way of hitting the ball in sports such as **tennis**, that is made with the inside of your hand facing forward OPP **backhand**

forehead /ˈfɔːhed; ˈfɒrɪd/ (also **brow**) *noun* [C] the part of sb's face above the eyes and below the hair ➲ picture at **body**

foreign /ˈfɒrən/ *adj* **1** belonging to or connected with a country that is not your own: *a foreign country/coin/accent* ◆ *to learn a foreign language* **2** [only *before* a noun] dealing with or involving other countries: *foreign policy* (= government decisions concerning other countries) ◆ *foreign affairs/news/trade* ◆ *the French Foreign Minister* **3** (used about an object or a substance) not being where it should be: *The X-ray showed up a* ***foreign body*** (= object) *in her stomach.*

the ˌForeign and ˈCommonwealth Office *noun* [sing, with sing or pl verb] (*abbr* FCO) the British government department that deals with relations with other countries

CULTURE
Many people still refer to this department by its old name **the Foreign Office.**

foreigner /ˈfɒrənə(r)/ *noun* [C] a person who belongs to a country that is not your own

ˌforeign exˈchange *noun* [U,C] the system of buying and selling money from a different country; the place where it is bought and sold

the ˌForeign ˈSecretary *noun* [C] the person in the government who is responsible for dealing with foreign countries ➲ look at **Home Secretary**

foreleg /ˈfɔːleg/ *noun* [C] either of the two front legs of an animal that has four legs ➲ note at **hind** ➲ picture on **page P12**

foreman /ˈfɔːmən/, **forewoman** /ˈfɔːwʊmən/ *noun* [C] (*pl* -men /-mən/, -women /-wɪmɪn/) a worker who is in charge of a group of other factory or building workers

foremost /ˈfɔːməʊst/ *adj* most famous or important; best: *Laurence Olivier was among the foremost actors of the last century.*
IDM **first and foremost** ➲ **first**[2]

forename /ˈfɔːneɪm/ *noun* [C] (*formal*) your first name, that is given to you when you are born ➲ note at **name**

forensic /fəˈrensɪk; -ˈrenzɪk/ *adj* [only *before* a noun] using scientific methods to find out about a crime: *The police are carrying out forensic tests to try and find out the cause of death.*

forerunner /ˈfɔːrʌnə(r)/ *noun* [C] a forerunner (of sb/sth) a person or thing that is an early example or a sign of sth that appears or develops later: *Country music was undoubtedly one of the forerunners of rock and roll.*

foresee /fɔːˈsiː/ *verb* [T] (*pt* foresaw /fɔːˈsɔː/; *pp* foreseen /fɔːˈsiːn/) to know or guess that sth is going to happen in the future: *Nobody could have foreseen the result of the election.* ➲ look at **unforeseen**

foreseeable /fɔːˈsiːəbl/ *adj* that can be expected; that you can guess will happen: *These problems were foreseeable.* ◆ *The weather won't change* ***in the foreseeable future*** (= as far into the future as we can see).

foreseen *past participle* of **foresee**

foresight /ˈfɔːsaɪt/ *noun* [U] the ability to see what will probably happen in the future and to use this knowledge to make careful plans: *My neighbour had the foresight to move house before the new motorway was built.* ➲ look at **hindsight**

foreskin /ˈfɔːskɪn/ *noun* [C] the piece of skin that covers the end of the male sexual organ

forest /ˈfɒrɪst/ *noun* [C,U] a large area of land covered with trees: *a tropical forest* ◆ *a forest fire* ➲ picture on **page P10**

MORE A **forest** is larger than a **wood**. A **jungle** is a forest in a tropical part of the world.

forestall /fɔːˈstɔːl/ *verb* [T] to take action to prevent sb from doing sth or sth from happening

forestry /ˈfɒrɪstri/ *noun* [U] the science of planting and taking care of trees in forests

forethought /ˈfɔːθɔːt/ *noun* [U] careful thought about, or preparation for, the future: *With forethought, most accidents can be avoided.* ◆ *With a little forethought, healthy eating at work can be quite easy.*

forever /fərˈevə(r)/ *adv* **1** (also **for ever**) for all time; permanently: *I wish the holidays would last forever!* ◆ *I realized that our relationship had finished forever.* **2** [only used with continuous tenses] very often; in a way which is annoying: *Our neighbours are forever having noisy parties.*

forewent *past tense* of **forgo**

foreword /ˈfɔːwɜːd/ *noun* [C] a piece of writing at the beginning of a book that introduces the book and/or its author

forfeit /ˈfɔːfɪt/ *verb* [T] to lose sth or have sth taken away from you, usually because you have done sth wrong: *Because of his violent behaviour he forfeited the right to visit his children.* ▶ **forfeit** *noun* [C]

forgave *past tense* of **forgive**

forge[1] /fɔːdʒ/ *verb* [T] **1** to put a lot of effort into making sth strong and successful: *Our school has forged links with a school in Romania.* **2** to make an illegal copy of sth: *to forge a signature/banknote/passport* ➲ look at **counterfeit**
PHR V **forge ahead** to go forward or make progress quickly: *I think it's now time to forge ahead with our plans to open a new shop.*

forge[2] /fɔːdʒ/ *noun* [C] a place where objects are made by heating and shaping metal

forgery /ˈfɔːdʒəri/ *noun* (*pl* **forgeries**) **1** [U] the crime of illegally copying a document, painting, etc. **2** [C] a document, picture, etc. that is a copy of the real one

⚷ **forget** /fəˈget/ *verb* (*pt* **forgot** /fəˈgɒt/; *pp* **forgotten** /fəˈgɒtn/) **1** [T] **forget (doing) sth** to not be able to remember sth: *I've forgotten what I was going to say.* ◆ *I've forgotten her telephone number.* ◆ *He forgot that he had invited her to the party.* ◆ *I'll never forget meeting my husband for the first time.* **2** [I,T] **forget (about) sth; forget to do sth** to fail to remember to do sth that you ought to have done: *'Why didn't you come to the party?' 'Oh dear! I completely forgot about it!'* ◆ *'Did you feed the cat?' 'Sorry, I forgot.'* ◆ *Don't forget to do your homework!* **3** [T] to fail to bring sth with you: *When my father got to the airport he realized he'd forgotten his passport.*

> **HELP** **Forget** or **leave**? When you are talking about something you have forgotten, and you want to say **where** it is, use the word **leave**. You CANNOT say: *'He forgot his passport at home.'* You have to say: *'He left his passport at home.'*

4 [I,T] **forget (about) sb/sth; forget about doing sth** to make an effort to stop thinking about sb/sth; to stop thinking that sth is possible: *Forget about your work and enjoy yourself!* ◆ *'I'm sorry I shouted at you.' 'Forget it (= don't worry about it).'* ◆ *Let's forget about cooking tonight and get a takeaway instead.*

forgetful /fəˈgetfl/ *adj* often forgetting things: *My mother's nearly 80 and she's starting to get a bit forgetful.* SYN **absent-minded**

forgivable /fəˈgɪvəbl/ *adj* that can be forgiven

⚷ **forgive** /fəˈgɪv/ *verb* [T] (*pt* **forgave** /fəˈgeɪv/; *pp* **forgiven** /fəˈgɪvn/) **1 forgive sb/yourself (for sth/for doing sth)** to stop being angry towards sb for sth that they have done wrong: *I can't forgive his behaviour last night.* ◆ *I can't forgive him for his behaviour last night.* ◆ *I will never forgive him for behaving like that last night.* **2 forgive me (for doing sth)** used for politely saying sorry: *Forgive me for asking, but where did you get that dress?* ▶ **forgiveness** *noun* [U]: *He **begged for forgiveness** for what he had done.*

forgiving /fəˈgɪvɪŋ/ *adj* **forgiving (of sth)** ready and able to forgive

forgo (also **forego**) /fɔːˈgəʊ/ *verb* [T] (**forgoes** /-ˈgəʊz/; *pt* **forwent** /-ˈwent/; *pp* **forgone** /-ˈgɒn/) (*formal*) to decide not to have or do sth that you want

forgot *past tense* of **forget**

forgotten *past participle* of **forget**

⚷ **fork**[1] /fɔːk/ *noun* [C] **1** a small metal object with a handle and two or more **prongs** (= long pointed parts) that you use for lifting food to your mouth when eating: *a knife and fork* ➲ picture at **cutlery** **2** a large tool with a handle and three or more **prongs** (= long pointed parts) that you use for digging the ground: *a garden fork* ➲ picture at **garden** **3** a place where a road, river, etc. divides into two parts; one of these parts: *After about two miles you'll come to a fork in the road.*

fork[2] /fɔːk/ *verb* [I] **1** (used about a road, river, etc.) to divide into two parts: *Bear right where the road forks.* **2** to go along the left or right fork of a road: *Fork right up the hill.*
PHR V **fork out (for sth)** (*informal*) to pay for sth when you do not want to: *I forked out over £20 for that book.*

forked /fɔːkt/ *adj* with one end divided into two parts, like the shape of the letter 'Y': *a bird with a forked tail* ◆ *the forked tongue of a snake*

forklift truck /ˌfɔːklɪft ˈtrʌk/ (also **ˈforklift**) *noun* [C] a vehicle with special equipment on the front for moving and lifting heavy objects

forklift truck

forlorn /fəˈlɔːn/ *adj* lonely and unhappy; not cared for

⚷ **form**[1] /fɔːm/ *noun*
➤TYPE **1** [C] a particular type or variety of sth or a way of doing sth: *Swimming is a good form of exercise.* ◆ *We never eat meat **in any form**.*
➤SHAPE **2** [C,U] the shape of sb/sth; the way sth is presented: *He could just make out a shadowy form.* ◆ *The articles were published **in book form**.*
➤DOCUMENT **3** [C] an official document with questions on it and spaces where you give answers and personal information: *an **entry form** for a competition* ◆ *Please fill in an **application form**.* ◆ *an **order form*** (= a form that is filled in by sb ordering goods from a factory, shop, etc.)
➤BEING FIT **4** [U] (of a sports player, team, etc.) the state of being fit and strong: *to be **in/out of form***
➤PERFORMANCE **5** [U] how well sb/sth is performing at a particular time, for example in sport or business: *to be **on/off form*** ◆ *On present form the Italian team should win easily.*
➤IN SCHOOL **6** [C] (*BrE old-fashioned*) a class in a school: *Who's your form teacher?*

> **CULTURE**
> In Britain, the years at secondary school used to be called **first/second/third**, etc. **form**, but now they are usually called **Year 7** to **Year 11**. However the last two years of school (for pupils aged between 16 and 18) are still referred to as **the sixth form**.

➤OF WORD **7** [C] a way of spelling or changing a word in a sentence: *the irregular forms of the verbs* ◆ *The plural form of 'mouse' is 'mice'.*
IDM **true to form** ➲ **true**

form² /fɔːm/ *verb*
➤START TO EXIST **1** [I,T] to begin to exist or to make sth exist: *A pattern was beginning to form in the monthly sales figures.* ◆ *These tracks were formed by rabbits.* **2** [T] to begin to have or think sth: *I haven't formed an opinion about the new boss yet.* ◆ *to form a friendship*
➤MAKE **3** [T] to make or organize sth: *to form a government* ◆ *In English we usually form the past tense by adding '-ed'.*
➤MAKE SHAPE **4** [T] to become or make a particular shape: *The police formed a circle around the house.* ◆ *to form a line/queue*
➤HAVE FUNCTION **5** [T] to be the thing mentioned: *Seminars form the main part of the course.* ◆ *The survey **formed part of** a larger programme of market research.*

formal /ˈfɔːml/ *adj* **1** (used about language or behaviour) used when you want to appear serious or official and in situations in which you do not know the other people very well: *'Yours faithfully' is a formal way of ending a letter.* ◆ *She has a very formal manner–she doesn't seem to be able to relax.* ◆ *a formal occasion* (= one where you must behave politely and wear the clothes that people think are suitable) OPP **informal**

HELP In this dictionary some words and phrases are marked *(formal)* or *(informal)*. This will help you to choose the right word for a particular situation. Often there is an informal or neutral (= neither formal nor informal) word with a similar meaning to a more formal one.

2 official: *I shall make **a formal complaint** to the hospital about the way I was treated.* ▶ **formally** /-məli/ *adv*

formality /fɔːˈmæləti/ *noun* (*pl* **formalities**) **1** [C] an action that is necessary according to custom or law: *There are certain formalities to attend to before we can give you a visa.* **2** [C] a thing that you must do as part of an official process, but which has little meaning and will not affect what happens: *Michael already knows he has the job so the interview is **just a formality**.* **3** [U] careful attention to rules of language and behaviour

EXAM TIP

Exam format

Find out what the exam will be like. How many parts are there? What are the different question types? What are the **time limits** and **word limits**? Find out how much time you will have to read the questions before a listening test begins. If your answers need to be written on an answer sheet, practise using one and check how much time, if any, you will have at the end of the exam to transfer your answers onto it. ➲ note at **limit**

format¹ /ˈfɔːmæt/ *noun* [C] the shape of sth or the way it is arranged or produced: *It's the same book but in a different format.*

format² /ˈfɔːmæt/ *verb* [T] (**formatting**; **formatted**) **1** to prepare a computer disk so that data can be recorded on it: *to format a disk* **2** to arrange text on a page or a screen: *to format a document*

formation /fɔːˈmeɪʃn/ *noun* **1** [U] the act of making or developing sth: *the formation of a new government* **2** [C,U] an arrangement or pattern (especially of soldiers, ships, etc.): *A number of planes flew over **in formation**.* **3** [C] a thing that is formed; the particular way in which it is formed: *cloud/rock formations*

formative /ˈfɔːmətɪv/ *adj* [only *before* a noun] having an important and lasting influence (on sb's character and opinions): *A child's early years are thought to be the most formative ones.*

former /ˈfɔːmə(r)/ *adj* [only *before* a noun] of an earlier time; belonging to the past: *Bill Clinton, the former American president* ◆ *In former times people often had larger families.*

the former /ˈfɔːmə(r)/ *noun* [sing] the first (of two people or things just mentioned): *Of the two hospitals in the town–the General and the Royal–the former* (= the General) *has the better reputation.* ➲ look at **the latter**

formerly /ˈfɔːməli/ *adv* in the past; before now: *Namibia, formerly known as South-West Africa* ◆ *The hotel was formerly a castle.*

HELP **Used to be** is a more common way of saying **was formerly**: *The hotel used to be a castle.*

formidable /ˈfɔːmɪdəbl/ *adj* **1** causing you to be quite frightened: *His mother is a rather formidable lady.* **2** difficult to deal with; needing a lot of effort: *Reforming the education system will be a formidable task.*

formula /ˈfɔːmjələ/ *noun* [C] (*pl* **formulas** *or* **formulae** /-liː/) **1** (*technical*) a group of signs, letters or numbers used in science or mathematics to express a general law or fact: *What is the formula for converting miles to kilometres?* **2** a list of (often chemical) substances used for making sth; the instructions for making sth: *The formula for the new vaccine has not yet been made public.* **3** **a formula for (doing) sth** a plan of how to get or do sth: *What is her formula for success?* ◆ *Unfortunately, there's no **magic formula** for a perfect marriage.*

formulate /ˈfɔːmjuleɪt/ *verb* [T] **1** to prepare and organize a plan or ideas for doing sth: *to formulate a plan* **2** to express sth (clearly and exactly): *She struggled to formulate a simple answer to his question.*

forsake /fəˈseɪk/ *verb* [T] (*pt* **forsook** /fəˈsʊk/; *pp* **forsaken** /fəˈseɪkən/) **forsake sb/sth (for sb/sth)** (*formal*) **1** to leave sb/sth, especially when you have a responsibility to stay: *He had made it clear to his wife that he would never forsake her.* SYN **abandon** **2** to stop doing sth, or leave sth, especially sth that you enjoy: *She forsook the glamour of the city and went to live in the wilds of Scotland.* SYN **renounce**

fort /fɔːt/ *noun* [C] a strong building that is used for military defence

forth /fɔːθ/ *adv*
IDM and so forth and other things like those just mentioned: *The sort of job that you'll be doing is taking messages, making tea and so forth.*
back and forth ➲ **back**[3]

forthcoming /ˌfɔːθˈkʌmɪŋ/ *adj* **1** that will happen or appear in the near future: *Look at our website for a list of **forthcoming events**.* **2** [not before a noun] offered or given: *If no money is forthcoming, we shall not be able to continue the project.* **3** [not before a noun] (used about a person) ready to be helpful, give information, etc: *Kate isn't very forthcoming about her job, so I don't know what she does exactly.*

forthright /ˈfɔːθraɪt/ *adj* saying exactly what you think in a clear and direct way

fortieth ➲ **forty**

fortification /ˌfɔːtɪfɪˈkeɪʃn/ *noun* [C, usually pl] walls, towers, etc., built especially in the past to protect a place against attack

fortify /ˈfɔːtɪfaɪ/ *verb* [T] (**fortifying**; **fortifies**; *pt, pp* **fortified**) **1** to make a place ready to defend itself in an attack: *to fortify a city* **2** to make sb/yourself feel stronger, braver, etc: *He fortified himself against the cold with a hot drink.*

fortnight /ˈfɔːtnaɪt/ *noun* [C, usually sing] (*BrE*) two weeks: *We're going on holiday for a fortnight.* ◆ *School finishes in a fortnight/in a fortnight's time* (= two weeks from now).

fortnightly /ˈfɔːtnaɪtli/ *adj, adv* (happening or appearing) once every two weeks: *This magazine is published fortnightly.*

fortress /ˈfɔːtrəs/ *noun* [C] a castle or other large strong building that it is not easy to attack

fortunate /ˈfɔːtʃənət/ *adj* lucky: *It was fortunate that he was at home when you phoned.* **OPP unfortunate**

fortunately /ˈfɔːtʃənətli/ *adv* by good luck: *Fortunately the traffic wasn't too bad so I managed to get to the meeting on time.* **SYN luckily**

⚷ **fortune** /ˈfɔːtʃuːn/ *noun* **1** [U] chance or the power that affects what happens in sb's life; luck: *Fortune was not on our side that day* (= we were not lucky). **SYN fate** **2** [C,U] a very large amount of money: *I always **spend a fortune** on presents at Christmas.* ◆ *She went to Hollywood in search of **fame and fortune**.* ➲ note at **money** **3** [C, usually pl] the things (both good and bad) that happen to a person, family, country, etc: *The country's fortunes depend on its industry being successful.* **4** [C] what is going to happen to a person in the future: *Show me your hand and I'll try to **tell your fortune**.* **SYN fate, destiny**
IDM cost the earth/a fortune ➲ **cost**[2]

ˈ**fortune-teller** *noun* [C] a person who tells people what will happen to them in the future

⚷ **forty** /ˈfɔːti/ *number* 40 ➲ note at **sixty**
IDM forty winks (*informal*) a short sleep, especially during the day
▶ **fortieth** /ˈfɔːtiəθ/ *ordinal number, noun* ➲ note at **sixth**

forum /ˈfɔːrəm/ *noun* [C] **a forum (for sth)** a place or meeting where people can exchange and discuss ideas: *TV is now an important forum for political debate.*

⚷ **forward**[1] /ˈfɔːwəd/ *adv* **1** (also **forwards**) in the direction that is in front of you; towards the front, end or future: *Keep going forward and try not to look back.* **2** in the direction of progress: *The discovery of a new form of treatment is a big step forward in the fight against cancer.* **SYN** for both meanings **ahead** **OPP** for both meanings **back, backward(s)** ❶ **Forward** is used after many verbs, for example **bring, come, look, put**. For the meaning of the expressions, look at the verb entries.
IDM backward(s) and forward(s) ➲ **backwards**

⚷ **forward**[2] /ˈfɔːwəd/ *adj* **1** [only *before* a noun] towards the front or future: *forward planning* **2** having developed earlier than is normal or expected; advanced: *Children who read before they are five are considered very forward.* **OPP backward** **3** behaving towards sb in a way that is too confident or too informal: *I hope you don't think I'm being too forward, asking you so many questions.*

forward[3] /ˈfɔːwəd/ *verb* [T] **1** to send a letter, etc. received at one address to a new address: *The post office is forwarding all our mail.* ◆ *I'm forwarding this email to my manager.* **2** to help to improve sth or to make sth progress: *I'm trying to forward my career in publishing.*

forward[4] /ˈfɔːwəd/ *noun* [C] an attacking player in a sport such as football

ˈ**forwarding address** *noun* [C] a new address to which letters, etc. should be sent: *The previous owners didn't leave a forwarding address.*

ˈ**forward-looking** *adj* thinking about or planning for the future; having modern ideas

ˈ**forwards** *adj* = **forward**[1] (1)

ˈ**forward slash** *noun* [C] a mark (/) used in computer commands and in Internet addresses ➲ look at **backslash**

forwent *past tense* of **forgo**

fossil /ˈfɒsl/ *noun* [C] (part of) an animal or plant that lived thousands of years ago and which has turned into rock

ˈ**fossil fuel** *noun* [C,U] fuel such as coal or oil, that was formed over millions of years from the remains of animals or plants

fossilize (also **-ise**) /ˈfɒsəlaɪz/ *verb* [I,T] **1** [usually passive] to become or make sth become a **fossil**: *fossilized bones* **2** to become or make sb/sth become fixed and unable to change or develop

foster /ˈfɒstə(r)/ *verb* [T] **1** to help or encourage the development of sth (especially feelings or ideas): *to foster somebody's friendship/trust* **2** (*especially BrE*) to take a child who needs a home into your

F

family and to take care of them without becoming the legal parent: *to foster a child*

MORE The people who do this are **foster parents**. The child is a **foster child**.

➲ note at **child** ➲ look at **adopt**

fought *past tense, past participle of* **fight**[1]

foul[1] /faʊl/ *adj* (**fouler**; **foulest**) **1** that smells or tastes disgusting: *a foul-smelling cigar* ◆ *This coffee tastes foul!* **2** (*especially BrE*) very bad or unpleasant: *Careful what you say—he's* ***in a foul temper/mood.*** ◆ *The* ***foul weather*** *prevented our plane from taking off.* **3** (used about language) very rude; full of swearing: *foul language*
IDM **fall foul of sb/sth** ➲ **fall**[1]

foul[2] /faʊl/ *verb* **1** [I,T] (used in sports) to do sth, or to do sth to sb, that is against the rules of the game: *Rooney was fouled inside the box and the referee awarded his team a penalty.* **2** [T] to make sth dirty (with rubbish, waste, etc.): *Do not allow your dog to foul the pavement.*

foul[3] /faʊl/ *noun* [C] (used in sports) an action that is against the rules: *He was sent off for a foul on the goalkeeper.*

ˌfoul ˈplay *noun* [U] **1** violence or crime that causes sb's death: *The police suspect foul play.* **2** action that is against the rules of a sport

found[1] *past tense, past participle of* **find**[1]

found[2] /faʊnd/ *verb* [T] **1** to start an organization, institution, etc: *This museum was founded in 1683.* **2** to be the first to start building and living in a town or country: *Liberia was founded by freed American slaves.* **3** [usually passive] **be founded on (sth)** to base sth on sth: *The book was founded on real life.*

foundation /faʊnˈdeɪʃn/ *noun* **1 foundations** [pl] a layer of bricks, etc. under the surface of the ground that forms the solid base of a building: *The builders have only just started to* ***lay the foundations*** *of the new school.* **2** [C,U] the idea, principle, or fact on which sth is based: *This coursebook aims to give students a solid foundation in grammar.* ◆ *That rumour is completely without foundation* (= it is not true). **3** [C] an organization that provides money for a special purpose: *The British Heart Foundation* **4** [U] the act of starting a new institution or organization: *The organization has grown enormously since its foundation in 1995.*

founˈdation course *noun* [C] a general course at a college that prepares students for longer or more difficult courses

founder /ˈfaʊndə(r)/ *noun* [C] a person who starts a new institution or organization: *a portrait of the founder of our school*

ˌfounder ˈmember *noun* [C] one of the original members of a club, an organization, etc.

foundry /ˈfaʊndri/ *noun* [C] (*pl* **foundries**) a place where metal or glass is melted and shaped into objects

fountain /ˈfaʊntən/ *noun* [C] **1** a decoration (in a garden or in a square in a town) that sends a flow of water into the air; the water that comes out of a fountain ➲ picture on **page P11** **2** a strong flow of liquid or another substance that is forced into the air: *a fountain of blood/sparks* **3** a person or thing that provides a large amount of sth: *Ed's* ***a fountain of information*** *on football.*

ˈfountain pen *noun* [C] a type of pen that you fill with ink ➲ picture at **stationery**

four /fɔː(r)/ *number* **1** 4 ➲ note at **six** **2 four-** [in compounds] having four of the thing mentioned: *four-legged animals*
IDM **on all fours** bent over with your hands and knees on the ground: *The children went through the tunnel on all fours.*

ˌfour-letter ˈword *noun* [C] a swear word that shocks or offends people (often with four letters)

fourteen /ˌfɔːˈtiːn/ *number* 14 ➲ note at **six**
▶ **fourteenth** /ˌfɔːˈtiːnθ/ *ordinal number, noun* ➲ note at **sixth**

fourth /fɔːθ/ *ordinal number* 4th ➲ note at **sixth**

MORE For ¼ we use the word **quarter**: *a quarter of an hour* (= 15 minutes)

ˌfour-wheel ˈdrive *noun* [U,C] an engine that turns all four wheels of a vehicle; a vehicle with this type of engine

four-ˈwheeler (*AmE*) = **quad bike**

fowl /faʊl/ *noun* [C] (*pl* **fowl** *or* **fowls**) a bird, especially a chicken, that is kept on a farm

fox

fox /fɒks/ *noun* [C] a wild animal like a small dog with reddish-brown fur, a pointed nose and a thick tail

MORE A fox is often described as **sly** or **cunning**. A female fox is a **vixen**, a young fox is a **cub**.

foyer /ˈfɔɪeɪ/ *noun* [C] an entrance hall in a cinema, theatre, hotel, etc. where people can meet or wait

fracking /ˈfrækɪŋ/ *noun* [U] the process or industry of getting gas out of the ground by using high pressure and fluid

fraction /ˈfrækʃn/ *noun* [C] **1** a small part or amount: *For a fraction of a second I thought the car was going to crash.* **2** a division of a number: *½ and ¼ are fractions.*

fractionally /ˈfrækʃənəli/ *adv* to a very small degree; slightly: *fractionally faster/taller/heavier*

fracture /ˈfræktʃə(r)/ *noun* [C,U] a break in a bone or other hard material ▸ **fracture** *verb* [I,T]: *She fell and fractured her ankle.* ◆ *A water pipe fractured and flooded the bathroom.*

fragile /ˈfrædʒaɪl/ *adj* easily damaged or broken: *This bowl is very fragile. Please handle it carefully.*

fragment[1] /ˈfrægmənt/ *noun* [C] a small piece that has broken off or that comes from sth larger: *The builders found fragments of Roman pottery on the site.* ◆ *I heard only a fragment of their conversation.*

fragment[2] /frægˈment/ *verb* [I,T] (*formal*) to break (sth) into small pieces: *The country is becoming increasingly fragmented by civil war.*

fragrance /ˈfreɪgrəns/ *noun* [C,U] a pleasant smell ➲ note at **smell[2]**

fragrant /ˈfreɪgrənt/ *adj* having a pleasant smell

frail /freɪl/ *adj* (**frailer**; **frailest**) weak or not healthy: *My aunt is still very frail after her accident.*

frailty /ˈfreɪlti/ *noun* [C,U] (*pl* **frailties**) weakness of sb's body or character

⚷ **frame[1]** /freɪm/ *noun* [C] **1** a border of wood or metal that goes around the outside of a door, picture, window, etc: *a picture frame* **2** the basic strong structure of a piece of furniture, building, vehicle, etc. which gives it its shape: *the frame of a bicycle/an aircraft* ➲ picture at **bike** **3** [usually pl] a structure made of plastic or metal that holds the two **lenses** (= pieces of glass) in a pair of glasses: *gold-rimmed frames* ➲ picture at **glasses** **4** [usually sing] the basic shape of a human or animal body: *He has a large frame but he's not fat.*

IDM **frame of mind** a particular state or condition of your feelings; the mood you are in: *I'm not in the right frame of mind for a party. I'd prefer to be on my own.*

⚷ **frame[2]** /freɪm/ *verb* [T] **1** to put a border around sth (especially a picture or photograph): *Let's have this photograph framed.* **2** [usually passive] to give false evidence against sb in order to make them seem guilty of a crime: *The man claimed that he had been framed by the police.* **3** (*formal*) to express sth in a particular way: *The question was very carefully framed.*

framework /ˈfreɪmwɜːk/ *noun* [C] **1** the basic structure of sth that gives it shape and strength: *A greenhouse is made of glass panels fixed in a metal framework.* ◆ *(figurative) the basic framework of society* **2** a system of rules or ideas which help you decide what to do: *The plan may be changed but it will provide a framework on which we can build.*

franc /fræŋk/ *noun* [C] the unit of money that is used in Switzerland and several other countries (replaced in 2002 in France, Belgium and Luxembourg by the euro)

franchise /ˈfræntʃaɪz/ *noun* **1** [C,U] official permission to sell a company's goods or services in a particular area; a business or a service that is run in this way: *They have the franchise to sell this product in Cyprus.* ◆ *Most fast-food restaurants are operated* ***under franchise.*** ◆ *Most fast-food restaurants are franchises.* **2** [U] (*formal*) the right to vote in elections

frank /fræŋk/ *adj* (**franker**; **frankest**) [**More frank** is also common.] showing your thoughts and feelings clearly; saying what you mean: *To be perfectly frank with you, I don't think you'll pass your driving test.* ▸ **frankly** *adv*: *Please tell me frankly what you think about my idea.* ▸ **frankness** *noun* [U]

frankfurter /ˈfræŋkfɜːtə(r)/ (*AmE* also **wiener**) *noun* [C] a type of small smoked **sausage** (= meat formed in a long thin shape)

frantic /ˈfræntɪk/ *adj* **1** very busy or done in a hurry: *Things are frantic in the office at this time of year.* ◆ *a frantic search for the keys* **SYN** **hectic** **2** extremely worried or frightened: *She went frantic when she couldn't find her child.* ◆ *frantic cries for help* ▸ **frantically** /-kli/ *adv*

fraternal /frəˈtɜːnl/ *adj* (*formal*) connected with the relationship that exists between brothers; like a brother: *fraternal love/rivalry*

fraternity /frəˈtɜːnəti/ *noun* (*pl* **fraternities**) **1** [C] a group of people who share the same work or interests: *the medical fraternity* **2** [U] the feeling of friendship and support between people in the same group

fraud /frɔːd/ *noun* **1** [C,U] (an act of) cheating sb in order to get money, etc. illegally: *The accountant was sent to prison for fraud.* ◆ *Massive amounts of money are lost every year in credit card frauds.* **2** [C] a person who tricks sb by pretending to be sb else

fraudulent /ˈfrɔːdjələnt/ *adj* (*formal*) done in order to cheat sb; dishonest: *the fraudulent use of stolen cheques*

fraught /frɔːt/ *adj* **1** **fraught with sth** filled with sth unpleasant: *a situation fraught with danger/difficulty* **2** (used about people) worried and nervous; (used about a situation) very busy so that people become nervous: *Things are usually fraught at work on Mondays.*

fray /freɪ/ *verb* [I,T] **1** if cloth, etc. **frays** or becomes **frayed**, some of the threads at the end start to come apart: *This shirt is beginning to fray at the cuffs.* ◆ *She frayed the bottom of her jeans.* **2** if sb's nerves, etc. **fray** or become **frayed**, they start to get annoyed: *Tempers began to fray towards the end of the match.*

freak[1] /friːk/ *noun* [C] **1** (*informal*) a person who has a very strong interest in sth: *a fitness/computer freak* **SYN** **fanatic** **2** a very unusual and strange event, person, animal, etc: *The other kids think Ally's a freak because she doesn't watch TV.* ▸ **freak** *adj*: *a freak accident/storm/result*

freak[2] /friːk/ *verb* [I,T] (*informal*) **freak (sb) (out)** if sb **freaks** or sth **freaks** them, they react very strongly to sth that makes them suddenly feel shocked, surprised, frightened, etc: *She freaked out when she heard the news.* ◆ *The film 'Snakes on a Plane' really freaked me out.*

freckle /ˈfrekl/ *noun* [C,usually pl] a small brown spot on your skin: *A lot of people with red hair have got freckles.* ➲ look at **mole** ▸ **freckled** *adj*

F

free[1] /friː/ *adj* (freer; freest) *adv*
➤NOT CONTROLLED **1** free (to do sth) not controlled by the government, rules, etc: *There is free movement of people across the border.* ◆ *free speech/a free press*
➤NOT IN PRISON **2** not in prison or in a **cage** (= a box made of bars), etc.; not held or controlled: *The government **set** 6 political prisoners **free** last year.* ◆ *There is nowhere around here where dogs can run free.*
➤NO PAYMENT **3** costing nothing: *Admission to the museum is **free of charge**.* ◆ *Children under five usually travel free on trains.*
➤WITHOUT STH **4** free from/of sth not having sth dangerous, unpleasant, etc: *free of worries/responsibility* ◆ *free from pain*
➤AVAILABLE **5** not busy or being used: *I'm afraid Mr Spencer is not free this afternoon.* ◆ *I don't get much **free time**.* ◆ *Is this seat free?*
IDM **feel free** ➲ feel[1]
free and easy informal or relaxed: *The atmosphere in our office is very free and easy.*
get, have, etc. a free hand to get, have, etc. permission to make your own decisions about sth: *I had a free hand in designing the course.*
of your own free will because you want to, not because sb forces you

free[2] /friː/ *verb* [T] **1** free sb/sth (from sth) to let a person or an animal leave or escape from a place where he/she/it is held: *to free a prisoner* ◆ *The protesters freed the animals from their cages.* SYN **release** **2** free sb/sth of/from sth to take away sth that is unpleasant from sb: *The medicine freed her from pain for a few hours.* **3** free sb/sth (up) for sth; free sb/sth (up) to do sth to make sth available so that it can be used; to put sb in a position in which they can do sth: *If I cancel my trip, that will free me to see you on Friday.*

ˌ**free ˈagent** *noun* [C] a person who can do what they want because nobody else has the right to tell them what to do

freedom /ˈfriːdəm/ *noun* **1** [C,U] the right or ability to do or say what you want: *You have the freedom to come and go as you please.* ◆ *freedom of speech* ◆ *the rights and freedoms of the individual* ➲ look at **liberty** **2** [U] the state of not being held prisoner or controlled by sb else: *The opposition leader was given his freedom after 25 years.* **3** [U] freedom from sth the state of not being affected by sth unpleasant: *freedom from fear/hunger/pain* **4** [U] the freedom of sth the right to use sth without restriction: *You can have the freedom of the ground floor, but please don't go upstairs.*

ˈ**freedom fighter** *noun* [C] a name to describe a person who uses violence to try to remove a government from power, by people who support this

ˌ**free ˈenterprise** *noun* [U] the operation of business without government control

freehand /ˈfriːhænd/ *adj* [only *before* a noun] *adv* (used about a drawing) (done) by hand, without the help of any instruments: *a freehand sketch* ◆ *to draw freehand*

ˌ**free ˈkick** *noun* [C] (in the sports of football or **rugby**) a situation in which a player of one team is allowed to kick the ball because a member of the other team has broken a rule

freelance /ˈfriːlɑːns/ *adj, adv* earning money by selling your services or work to different organizations rather than being employed by a single company: *a freelance journalist* ◆ *She works freelance.* ▶ **freelance** (also **freelancer** /ˈfriːlɑːnsə(r)/) *noun* [C] ▶ **freelance** *verb* [I]: *I left my full-time job because I can earn more by freelancing.*

freely /ˈfriːli/ *adv* **1** in a way that is not controlled or limited: *He is the country's first freely elected president for 40 years.* **2** without trying to avoid the truth even though it might be embarrassing; in an honest way: *I freely admit that I made a mistake.*

Freemason /ˈfriːmeɪsn/ (also **mason**) *noun* [C] a man who belongs to an international secret society whose members help each other and who recognize each other by secret signs

ˌ**free-ˈrange** *adj* (used about a system of farming) kept or produced in a place where animals can move around freely: *free-range hens/turkeys* ◆ *We always buy free-range eggs.* ➲ look at **battery**

ˌ**free ˈspeech** *noun* [U] the right to express any opinion in public

freeway /ˈfriːweɪ/ (*AmE*) = **motorway**

freeze[1] /friːz/ *verb* (*pt* **froze** /frəʊz/; *pp* **frozen** /ˈfrəʊzn/)
➤BECOME ICE **1** [I,T] to become hard (and often change into ice) because of extreme cold; to make sth do this: *Water freezes at 0° Celsius.* ◆ *The ground was **frozen solid** for most of the winter.* ◆ *frozen peas/fish/food*
➤WEATHER **2** [I] used with 'it' to describe extremely cold weather when water turns into ice: *I think it's going to freeze tonight.*
➤BE VERY COLD **3** [I,T] to be very cold or to die from cold: *It was so cold on the mountain that we thought we would **freeze to death**.* ◆ *Turn the heater up a bit—I'm **frozen stiff**.*
➤STOP MOVING **4** [I] to stop moving suddenly and completely because you are frightened or in danger: *The terrible scream made her freeze with terror.* ◆ *Suddenly the man pulled out a gun and shouted 'Freeze!'* **5** [I] when a computer screen **freezes** you cannot move any of the images, etc. on it, because there is a problem with the system
➤PRICES **6** [T] to keep the money people earn, prices, etc. at a fixed level for a certain period of time: *Spending on defence has been frozen for one year.*

freeze[2] /friːz/ *noun* [C] **1** the fixing of the money people earn, prices, etc. at one level for a certain period of time **2** a period of weather when the temperature stays below freezing point (0° Celsius)

freezer /ˈfriːzə(r)/ (also ˌ**deep ˈfreeze**) *noun* [C] a large box or cupboard in which you can store food for a long time at a temperature below freezing point (0° Celsius) so that it stays frozen ➲ look at **fridge** ➲ picture on **page P8**

freezing[1] /ˈfriːzɪŋ/ *adj* (*informal*) very cold: *I'm freezing!* ◆ *It's absolutely freezing outside.* ➲ note at **cold**

freezing² /ˈfriːzɪŋ/ (also ˈ**freezing point**) *noun* [U] the temperature at which water freezes: *Last night the temperature fell to six degrees below freezing.*

freight /freɪt/ *noun* [U] goods that are carried from one place to another by ship, lorry, etc.; the system for carrying goods in this way: *a freight train* ♦ *Your order will be sent by air freight.*

freight car (*AmE*) = **wagon**

freighter /ˈfreɪtə(r)/ *noun* [C] a ship or an aircraft that carries only goods and not passengers ➲ note at **boat**

ˌ**French** ˈ**bread** *noun* [U] white bread in the shape of a long thick stick

ˌ**French** ˈ**fry** (*especially AmE*) = **chip¹**(3)

ˌ**French** ˈ**window** (*AmE* ˌFrench ˈdoor) *noun* [C] one of a pair of glass doors that open onto a garden

frenzied /ˈfrenzid/ *adj* that is wild and out of control: *a frenzied attack* ♦ *frenzied activity*

frenzy /ˈfrenzi/ *noun* [sing,U] a state of great emotion or activity that is not under control: *The crowd was* **in a frenzy** *at the speaker's words.* ♦ *I could hear a frenzy of activity in the kitchen.*

frequency /ˈfriːkwənsi/ *noun* (*pl* frequencies) **1** [U] the number of times sth happens in a particular period: *Fatal accidents have decreased in frequency in recent years.* **2** [U] the fact that sth happens often: *The frequency of child deaths from cancer near the nuclear power station is being investigated.* **3** [C,U] the rate at which a sound wave or radio wave **vibrates** (= moves up and down): *a high/low frequency*

🔑 **frequent¹** /ˈfriːkwənt/ *adj* happening often: *His visits became less frequent.* **OPP** **infrequent** ▶ **frequently** *adv*

frequent² /friˈkwent/ *verb* [T] (*formal*) to go to a place often: *He spent most of his evenings in Paris frequenting bars and clubs.*

🔑 **fresh** /freʃ/ *adj* (**fresher**; **freshest**)
➤FOOD **1** (used especially about food) produced or picked very recently; not frozen or in a tin: *fresh bread/fruit/flowers* ➲ look at **stale**
➤NEW **2** left somewhere or experienced recently: *fresh blood/footprints* ♦ *Write a few notes while the lecture is still* **fresh in** *your* **mind**. **3** new and different: *They have decided to* **make a fresh start** *in a different town.* ♦ *I'm sure he'll have some fresh ideas on the subject.*
➤CLEAN **4** pleasantly clean or bright: *Open the window and let some* **fresh air** *in.*
➤WATER **5** without salt; not sea water: *a shortage of fresh water*
➤NOT TIRED **6** full of energy: *I'll think about the problem again in the morning when I'm fresh.*
➤JUST FINISHED **7** **fresh from/out of sth** having just finished sth: *Life isn't easy for a young teacher fresh from university.*
IDM **break fresh/new ground** ➲ **ground¹**
▶ **freshly** *adv*: *freshly baked bread* ▶ **freshness** *noun* [U]

freshen /ˈfreʃn/ *verb* [T] **freshen sth (up)** to make sth cleaner or brighter: *Some new curtains and wallpaper would freshen up this room.*
PHR V **freshen up** to wash and make yourself clean and tidy

fresher /ˈfreʃə(r)/ *noun* [C] (*BrE*) a student who has just started his or her first term at university

ˌ**fresh-faced** *adj* having a young, healthy-looking face: *fresh-faced kids*

freshman /ˈfreʃmən/ *noun* [C] (*pl* -men /-mən/) (*AmE*) a student who is in their first year at college, high school, university, etc.

freshwater /ˈfreʃwɔːtə(r)/ *adj* [only *before* a noun] living in water or having water that is not salty: *freshwater fish* ♦ *a freshwater lake*

fret¹ /fret/ *verb* [I] (**fretting**; **fretted**) **fret (about/at/over sth)** to be worried and unhappy about sth: *I was awake for hours fretting about my exams.*

fret² /fret/ *noun* [C] one of the bars across the long thin part of a **guitar** (= a musical instrument with strings), etc. that show you where to put your fingers to produce a particular sound ➲ picture at **music**

Fri. *abbr* = **Friday**: *Fri. 27 May*

friction /ˈfrɪkʃn/ *noun* [U] **1** the rubbing of one surface or thing against another: *You have to put oil in the engine to reduce friction between the moving parts.* **2** **friction (between A and B)** disagreement between people or groups: *There is a lot of friction between the older and younger members of staff.*

🔑 **Friday** /ˈfraɪdeɪ; -di/ *noun* [C,U] (*abbr* **Fri.**) the day of the week after Thursday ➲ note at **Monday**

🔑 **fridge** /frɪdʒ/ (also *formal* **refrigerator**; *AmE* **icebox**) *noun* [C] a metal container with a door in which food, etc. is kept cold (but not frozen) so that it stays fresh ➲ look at **freezer** ➲ picture on **page P8**

TOPIC

Friends

People often **get to know** each other through work or school, and then **become friends**. A common informal word for friend is **mate**: *I'm going out with my mates.* **Friendly** people **get on well** (= have a good relationship) with lots of people. They usually find it easy to **make friends**. If you and a friend are very **close**, you can **chat** (= talk) about anything. Even if you don't see each other very often, you can **keep in touch** (for example by phone or email). When you **meet up/get together** again, you can **catch up on** (= find out about) each other's news.

🔑 **friend** /frend/ *noun* [C] **1** a person that you know and like (not a member of your family), and who likes you: *Dalibor and I are* **old friends**. *We were at school together.* ♦ *We're only inviting* **close friends** *and relatives to the wedding.* ♦ *Carol's my* **best friend**. ♦ *A friend of mine told me about this restaurant.* ♦ *One of my friends told me about this restaurant.* ➲ look at **boyfriend**, **girlfriend**, **penfriend** **2** a **friend of/to sth** a person who supports an organization, a charity, etc., especially by giving money; a person who supports a particular idea, etc: *the*

Friends of the Churchill Hospital **3** a person you communicate with using a **social networking site** (= a website for people who share your interests): *She's got 150 friends on Facebook.* ➲ note at **social networking**

IDM **be/make friends (with sb)** to be/become a friend (of sb): *Tony is rather shy and finds it hard to make friends.*

a false friend ➲ **false**

friendly¹ /ˈfrendli/ *adj* (friendlier; friendliest) **1** friendly (to/toward(s) sb) behaving in a kind and open way: *Everyone here has been very friendly towards us.* OPP **unfriendly** ➲ note at **nice** **2** showing kindness in a way that makes people feel happy and relaxed: *a friendly smile/atmosphere* OPP **unfriendly** **3** friendly with sb treating sb as a friend: *Nick's **become** quite **friendly** with the boy next door.* ◆ *Are you **on friendly terms** with your neighbours?* **4** [in compounds] helpful to sb/sth; not harmful to sth: *This software is extremely **user-friendly**.* ◆ *ozone-friendly sprays* **5** in which the people, teams, etc. taking part are not competing seriously: *a friendly argument* ◆ *I've organized a friendly match against my brother's team.* ▶ **friendliness** *noun* [U]

friendly² /ˈfrendli/ *noun* [C] (*pl* friendlies) a sports match that is not part of an important competition

friendship /ˈfrendʃɪp/ *noun* **1** [C] a friendship (with sb); a friendship (between A and B) a relationship between people who are friends: *a close/lasting/lifelong friendship* **2** [U] the state of being friends: *Our relationship is based on friendship, not love.*

fright /fraɪt/ *noun* [C,U] a sudden feeling of fear or shock: *I hope I didn't **give** you **a fright** when I shouted.* ◆ *The child cried out **in fright** when she saw a dark shadow at the window.*

frighten /ˈfraɪtn/ *verb* [T] to make sb/sth afraid or shocked: *That programme about the rise in the crime rate really frightened me.*

PHR V **frighten sb/sth away/off** to cause a person or an animal to go away by frightening them or it: *Walk quietly so that you don't frighten the birds away.*

frightened /ˈfraɪtnd/ *adj* **1** full of fear or worry: *Frightened children were calling for their mothers.* ◆ *I was frightened that they would think that I was rude.* **2** frightened of sb/sth afraid of a particular person, thing or situation: *When I was young I was frightened of spiders.* ➲ note at **afraid**

frightening /ˈfraɪtnɪŋ/ *adj* making you feel afraid or shocked: *a frightening experience* ◆ *It's frightening that time passes so quickly.*

frightful /ˈfraɪtfl/ *adj* (*old-fashioned*) **1** (used for emphasizing sth) very bad or great: *We're in a frightful rush.* **2** very bad or unpleasant: *The weather this summer has been frightful.* SYN for both meanings **awful, terrible**

frightfully /ˈfraɪtfəli/ *adv* (*old-fashioned*) very: *I'm frightfully sorry.*

frigid /ˈfrɪdʒɪd/ *adj* **1** (usually used about a woman) unable to enjoy sex **2** not showing any emotion

frill /frɪl/ *noun* [C] **1** a decoration for the edge of a dress, shirt, etc. which is made by forming many folds in a narrow piece of cloth **2** [usually pl] something that is added that you feel is not necessary: *We just want a plain simple meal—no frills.* ▶ **frilly** *adj*: *a frilly dress*

fringe¹ /frɪndʒ/ *noun* [C] **1** (*AmE* bangs [pl]) the part of your hair that is cut so that it hangs over your **forehead** (= the part of your face above your eyes): *Your hair looks better with a fringe.* ➲ picture at **hair** **2** a border for decoration on a piece of clothing, etc. that is made of a lot of hanging threads **3** (*BrE*) the outer edge of an area or a group that is a long way from the centre or from what is usual: *Some people **on the fringes of** the socialist party are opposed to the policy on Europe.*

fringe² /frɪndʒ/ *verb*

IDM **be fringed with sth** to have sth as a border or around the edge: *The lake was fringed with pine trees.*

ˈfringe benefit *noun* [C, usually pl] an extra thing that is given to an employee in addition to the money he or she earns: *The fringe benefits of this job include a car and free health insurance.* ➲ A more informal word is **perk**.

frisk /frɪsk/ *verb* **1** [T] to pass your hands over sb's body in order to search for hidden weapons, drugs, etc. **2** [I] (used about an animal or child) to play and jump about happily and with a lot of energy

frisky /ˈfrɪski/ *adj* (friskier; friskiest) full of life and wanting to play

fritter /ˈfrɪtə(r)/ *verb*

PHR V **fritter sth away (on sth)** to waste time or money on things that are not important

frivolity /frɪˈvɒləti/ *noun* [U] silly behaviour (especially when you should be serious)

frivolous /ˈfrɪvələs/ *adj* not serious; silly

frizzy /ˈfrɪzi/ *adj* (frizzier; frizziest) (used about hair) very curly

fro /frəʊ/ *adv*

IDM **to and fro** ➲ **to**

frog /frɒg/ *noun* [C] a small animal with smooth skin and long back legs that it uses for jumping. **Frogs** live in or near water: *Our pond is full of frogs in the spring.* ➲ picture on **page P13**

frogman /ˈfrɒgmən/ *noun* [C] (*pl* -men /-mən/) a person whose job is to work under the surface of water wearing special rubber clothes and using breathing equipment: *Police frogmen searched the river.*

frogspawn /ˈfrɒgspɔːn/ *noun* [U] a clear substance that looks like jelly and contains the eggs of a **frog** ➲ picture on **page P13**

from /frəm; *strong form* frɒm/ *prep* **1** showing the place, direction or time that sb/sth starts or started: *She comes home from work at 7 o'clock.* ◆ *a cold wind from the east* ◆ *Water was dripping from the tap.* ◆ *Peter's on holiday from next Friday.* ◆ *The supermarket is open **from** 8 a.m. **till** 8 p.m. every day.* **2** showing the person who sent or gave sth: *I borrowed this jacket from my sister.* ♦ *a phone call from my father* **3** showing the origin of sb/sth: *'Where do you come from?' 'I'm from Australia.'* ♦ *cheeses from France and Italy* ♦ *quotations from Shakespeare* **4** showing the material which is used to make sth: *Paper is* ***made from*** *wood.* ♦ *This sauce is made from cream and wine.*

HELP **Made of** tells us the material the object actually consists of: *a table made of wood* ♦ *a house made of bricks*

5 showing the distance between two places: *The house is five miles from the town centre.* ♦ *I work not far from here.* **6** showing the point at which a series of prices, figures, etc. starts: *Tickets cost from £3 to £11.* **7** showing the state of sb/sth before a change: *The time of the meeting has been changed* ***from*** *7* ***to*** *8 o'clock.* ♦ *The article was translated* ***from*** *Russian* ***into*** *English.* ♦ *Things have gone* ***from*** *bad* ***to*** *worse.* **8** showing that sb/sth is taken away, removed or separated from sb/sth else: *Children don't like being separated from their parents for a long period.* ♦ *(in mathematics) 8 from 12 leaves 4.* **9** showing sth that you want to avoid: *There was no shelter from the wind.* ♦ *This game will stop you from getting bored.* **10** showing the cause of sth: *People in the camps are suffering from hunger and cold.* **11** showing the reason for making a judgement or forming an opinion: *You can tell quite a lot from somebody's handwriting.* **12** showing the difference between two people, places or things: *Can you tell margarine from butter?* ♦ *Is Portuguese very different from Spanish?*
IDM **from ... on** starting at a particular time and continuing for ever: *She never spoke to him again* ***from that day on.*** ♦ ***From now on*** *you must earn your own living.*

front[1] /frʌnt/ *noun*
➤FORWARD PART/POSITION **1 the front** [C, usually sing] the side or surface of sth/sb that faces forward: *a dress with buttons down the front* ♦ *The front of a building was covered with ivy.* ♦ *a card with flowers* ***on the front*** ♦ *She slipped on the stairs and spilt coffee all down her front.* **2 the front** [sing] the most forward part of sth; the area that is just outside of or before sb/sth: *Young children should not travel* ***in the front of*** *the car.* ♦ *There is a small garden* ***at the front of*** *the house.*

HELP **On the front, in front or at the front?**
On the front of means 'on the front surface of sth': *The number is shown on the front of the bus.*

In front (of sth) means 'further forward than another person or thing'; before sb/sth else: *A car has stopped in front of the bus.* ♦ *There were three people in front of me in the queue.*

At/In the front (of sth) means 'in the most forward part inside sth': *The driver sits at the front of the bus.* Look at these sentences too: *The teacher usually stands in front of the class.* ♦ *The noisy children were asked to sit at the front of the class* (= in the front seats).

➤IN WAR **3 the front** [C, usually sing] the line or area where fighting takes place in a war: *to be sent to the front*
➤AREA OF ACTIVITY **4** [C] a particular area of activity: *Things are difficult* ***on the*** *political/economic* ***front*** *at the moment.* ♦ *Progress has been made* ***on all fronts.***
➤HIDING FEELINGS **5** [sing] a way of behaving that hides your true feelings: *His brave words were just a front. He was really feeling very nervous.*
➤WEATHER **6** [C] a line or area where warm air and cold air meet: *A* ***cold front*** *is moving in from the north.*
IDM **back to front** ➲ back[1]
in front further forward than sb/sth: *Some of the children ran on in front.* ♦ *After three laps the Kenyan runner was in front.* **SYN** **ahead**
in front of sb/sth **1** in a position further forward than but close to sb/sth: *The bus stops right in front of our house.* ♦ *Don't stand in front of the TV.* ♦ *The book was open in front of her on the desk.* ➲ picture at **opposite**

HELP Be careful. **In front of** does not mean the same as **opposite.**

2 if you do sth in front of sb, you do it when that person is there in the same room or place as you: *Don't do that in front of the children.*
up front (*informal*) as payment before sth is done: *I want half the money up front and half when the job is finished.*

front[2] /frʌnt/ *adj* [only *before* a noun] on or at the front: *the front garden/room* ♦ *Open the front door.* ♦ *sit in the front row* ♦ *front teeth* ♦ *Have you seen the front page of today's paper?*

frontal /ˈfrʌntl/ *adj* [only *before* a noun] from the front: *a frontal attack*

frontier /ˈfrʌntɪə(r)/ *noun* **1** [C] **the frontier (between A and B)** the line where one country joins another; border: *the end of frontier controls in Europe* ➲ note at **border** **2 the frontiers** [pl] the limit between what we do and do not know: *Scientific research is constantly* ***pushing back the frontiers of*** *our knowledge about the world.*

ˌfront-ˈpage *adj* [only *before* a noun] interesting or important enough to appear on the front page of a newspaper: *front-page news/headlines*

frost[1] /frɒst/ *noun* [C,U] the weather condition when the temperature falls below freezing point (0° Celsius) and a thin layer of ice forms on the ground and other surfaces, especially at night: *a* ***hard frost*** ♦ *a chilly night with some* ***ground frost***

frost[2] /frɒst/ *verb* [T] (*especially AmE*) = **ice**[2]
PHR V **frost over/up** to become covered with a thin layer of ice: *The window has frosted over/up.* ➲ look at **defrost**

frostbite /ˈfrɒstbaɪt/ *noun* [U] a serious medical condition of the fingers, toes, etc. that is caused by very low temperatures: *All the climbers were suffering from frostbite.*

F

frosted /ˈfrɒstɪd/ *adj* [only *before* a noun] (used about glass or a window) with a special surface so you cannot see through it

frosting /ˈfrɒstɪŋ/ (*especially AmE*) = icing

frosty /ˈfrɒsti/ *adj* (frostier; frostiest) **1** very cold, with **frost** (= ice on the ground): *a cold and frosty morning* **2** cold and unfriendly: *a frosty welcome*

froth[1] /frɒθ/ *noun* [U] a mass of small white bubbles on the top of a liquid, etc. ▶ **frothy** *adj*: *frothy beer* ◆ *a frothy cappuccino*

F

froth[2] /frɒθ/ *verb* [I,T] to have or produce a mass of white bubbles: *The mad dog was frothing at the mouth.*

frown /fraʊn/ *verb* [I] to show you are angry, serious, etc. by making lines appear on your **forehead** (= the part of your face above your eyes)

frown

PHR V **frown on/upon sth** to think that sth is not good or suitable: *Smoking is very much frowned upon these days.* ◆ *Performing experiments on animals is very much frowned upon these days.* ◆ *Her parents frowned on her plans to go backpacking alone.* SYN **disapprove**

▶ **frown** *noun* [C]

froze *past tense of* **freeze**[1]

frozen[1] *past participle of* **freeze**[1]

frozen[2] /ˈfrəʊzn/ *adj* **1** (used about food) stored at a low temperature in order to keep it for a long time: *frozen meat/vegetables* **2** (*informal*) (used about people and parts of the body) very cold: *My feet are frozen!* ◆ *I was* ***frozen stiff.*** SYN **freezing** **3** (used about water) with a layer of ice on the surface: *The pond is frozen. Let's go skating.*

frugal /ˈfruːgl/ *adj* **1** using only as much money or food as is necessary: *a frugal existence/life* OPP **extravagant** **2** (used about meals) small, simple and not costing very much: *a frugal lunch of bread and cheese* SYN **meagre** ▶ **frugality** /fruˈgæləti/ *noun* [U] ▶ **frugally** /ˈfruːgəli/ *adv*: *to live/eat frugally*

fruit /fruːt/ *noun* **1** [C,U] the part of a plant or tree that contains seeds and that we eat: *Try and eat more* ***fresh fruit*** *and vegetables.* ◆ *Marmalade is made with* ***citrus fruit*** (= oranges, lemons, etc.). ◆ *Is a tomato a fruit or a vegetable?* ◆ *fruit juice* ◆ *fruit salad* ➲ picture on **page P14**

HELP We can use the countable form of 'fruit' to talk about types of fruit: *The papaya is a tropical fruit.* ◆ *Most big supermarkets sell all sorts of tropical fruits.* When talking about an individual piece of fruit we usually use the name of the fruit: *Would you like an apple?* or we use the uncountable form: *Would you like some fruit?*

2 [C] the part of any plant in which the seed is formed **3** [pl] **the fruits (of sth)** a good result or success from work that you have done: *It will be years before we see the fruits of this research.*

IDM **bear fruit** ➲ **bear**[1]

fruitful /ˈfruːtfl/ *adj* producing good results; useful: *fruitful discussions*

fruition /fruˈɪʃn/ *noun* [U] (*formal*) the time when a plan, etc. starts to be successful: *After months of hard work, our efforts were* ***coming to fruition.***

fruitless /ˈfruːtləs/ *adj* producing poor or no results; not successful: *a fruitless search* ◆ *It's fruitless to keep trying—she'll never agree to it.*

frustrate /frʌˈstreɪt/ *verb* [T] **1** to cause a person to feel annoyed or impatient because they cannot do or achieve what they want: *It's the lack of money that really frustrates him.* **2** (*formal*) to prevent sb from doing sth or sth from happening: *The rescue work has been frustrated by bad weather conditions.* ▶ **frustrated** *adj*: *He felt very frustrated at his lack of progress in learning Chinese.* ▶ **frustrating** *adj*

frustration /frʌˈstreɪʃn/ *noun* [C,U] a feeling of anger because you cannot get what you want; something that causes you to feel like this: *He felt anger and frustration at no longer being able to see very well.* ◆ *Every job has its frustrations.*

fry[1] /fraɪ/ *verb* [I,T] (frying; fries; *pt, pp* fried) to cook sth or to be cooked in hot fat or oil: *to fry an egg* ◆ *a fried egg* ◆ *I could smell bacon frying in the kitchen.* ➲ note at **cook, recipe**

fry[2] /fraɪ/ *noun* [C] (*pl* fries) (*especially AmE*) = **chip**[1] (3)

frying pan (*AmE* frypan /ˈfraɪpæn/) *noun* [C] a flat pan with a long handle that is used for frying food

ft *abbr* = **foot**[1] (5): *a room 10 ft by 6 ft*

fudge /fʌdʒ/ *noun* [U] a type of soft brown sweet made from sugar, butter and milk

fuel[1] /ˈfjuːəl/ *noun* **1** [U] material that is burned to produce heat or power: *What's the car's fuel consumption?* **2** [C] a type of fuel: *I think gas is the best fuel for central heating.*

fuel[2] /ˈfjuːəl/ *verb* [T] (fuelling; fuelled, (*AmE*) fueling; fueled) **1** to put petrol into a vehicle **2** to make sb feel an emotion more strongly: *Her interest in the Spanish language was fuelled by a visit to Spain.*

fugitive /ˈfjuːdʒətɪv/ *noun* [C] a person who is running away or escaping (for example from the police) ➲ look at **refugee**

fulfil (*AmE* fulfill) /fʊlˈfɪl/ *verb* [T] (fulfilling; fulfilled) **1** to make sth that you wish for happen; to achieve a goal: *He finally fulfilled his childhood dream of becoming a doctor.* ◆ *to fulfil your ambition/potential* **2** to do or have everything that you should or that is necessary: *to fulfil a duty/obligation/promise/need* ◆ *The conditions of entry to university in this country are quite difficult to fulfil.* **3** to have a particular role or purpose: *Italy fulfils a very important role within the European Union.* **4** to make sb feel completely happy and satisfied: *I need a job that really fulfils me.* ▶ **fulfilled** *adj*: *When I had my baby*

I felt totally fulfilled. ▸ **fulfilling** *adj*: *I found working abroad a very fulfilling experience.*

fulfilment (*AmE* **fulfillment**) /fʊlˈfɪlmənt/ *noun* [U] the act of achieving a goal; the feeling of satisfaction that you have when you have done sth: *the fulfilment of your dreams/hopes/ambitions* ◆ *to find personal/emotional fulfilment*

⚷ **full¹** /fʊl/ *adj* (**fuller**; **fullest**)
▸WITH NO SPACE **1** holding or containing as much or as many as possible: *The bin needs emptying. It's **full up*** (= completely full). ◆ *a full bottle* ◆ *The bus was full so we had to wait for the next one.* ◆ (*figurative*) *We need a good night's sleep because we've got a full* (= busy) *day tomorrow.*
▸HAVING A LOT **2** **full of sb/sth** containing a lot of sb/sth: *The room was full of people.* ◆ *His work was full of mistakes.* ◆ *The children are full of energy.*
▸WITH FOOD **3** **full (up)** having had enough to eat and drink: *No more, thank you. I'm full (up).*
▸COMPLETE **4** [only *before* a noun] complete; not leaving anything out: *I should like **a full report** on the accident, please.* ◆ ***Full details** of today's TV programmes are on page 20.* ◆ *He took **full responsibility** for what had happened.* ◆ *Please give your **full name and address**.*
▸MAXIMUM **5** [only *before* a noun] the highest or greatest possible: *She got **full marks** in her French exam.* ◆ *The train was travelling **at full speed**.*
▸TALKING A LOT **6** **full of sb/sth/yourself** pleased about or proud of sb/sth/yourself: *When she got back from holiday she was full of everything they had seen.* ◆ *He's **full of himself*** (= thinks that he is very important) *since he got that new job.*
▸FAT **7** round or rather fat in shape: *She's got quite **a full figure**.* ◆ *He's quite **full in the face**.*
▸CLOTHES **8** (used about clothes) made with plenty of cloth: *a full skirt*

IDM **at full strength** (used about a group) having all the people it needs or usually has: *Nobody is injured, so the team will be at full strength for the game.*

at full stretch working as hard as possible: *When the factory is operating at full stretch, it employs 800 people.*

full of beans/life with a lot of energy and enthusiasm: *They came back from their holiday full of beans.*

have your hands full ➲ **hand¹**

in full with nothing missing; completely: *Your money will be refunded in full* (= you will get all your money back). ◆ *Please write your name in full.*

in full swing at the stage when there is the most activity: *When we arrived the party was already in full swing.*

in full view (of sb/sth) in a place where you can easily be seen: *In full view of the guards, he tried to escape over the prison wall.*

to the full as much as possible: *to enjoy life to the full*

full² /fʊl/ *adv* **full in/on (sth)** straight; directly: *John hit him full in the face.* ◆ *The two cars crashed full on.*

ˌfull-ˈblown *adj* [only *before* a noun] fully developed: *Her anger turned into a full-blown tantrum.*

ˌfull ˈboard *noun* [U] (in a hotel, etc.) including all meals ➲ note at **hotel** ➲ look at **half board, bed and breakfast**

full-fledged (*AmE*) = **fully fledged**

ˌfull-ˈlength *adj* [only *before* a noun] **1** (used about a picture, mirror, etc.) showing a person from head to foot **2** not made shorter: *a full-length film* **3** (used about a dress, skirt, etc.) reaching the feet

ˌfull ˈmoon *noun* [sing] the moon when it appears as a complete circle

ˌfull-ˈscale *adj* [only *before* a noun] **1** using every thing or person that is available: *The police have started a full-scale murder investigation.* **2** (used about a plan, drawing, etc.) of the same size as the original object: *a full-scale plan/model*

ˌfull ˈstop (*especially AmE* **period**) *noun* [C] a mark (.) that is used in writing to show the end of a sentence

ˌfull-ˈtime *adj, adv* (done or working) for all the normal period of work: *He has a full-time job.* ◆ *He works full-time.* ◆ *We employ 800 full-time staff.* ➲ look at **part-time**

⚷ **fully** /ˈfʊli/ *adv* completely; to the highest possible degree: *I'm fully aware of the problem.* ◆ *All our engineers are fully trained.*

ˌfully ˈfledged (*AmE* also **full-ˈfledged**) *adj* completely trained or completely developed: *My sister is now a fully fledged solicitor.*

fumble /ˈfʌmbl/ *verb* [I] to try to find or take hold of sth with your hands in a nervous or careless way: *'It must be here somewhere,' she said, fumbling in her pocket for her key.*

fume /fjuːm/ *verb* [I] to be very angry about sth

fumes /fjuːmz/ *noun* [pl] smoke or gases that smell unpleasant and that can be dangerous to breathe in: *diesel/petrol/exhaust fumes*

⚷ **fun¹** /fʌn/ *noun* [U] pleasure and enjoyment; an activity or a person that gives you pleasure and enjoyment: *We **had** a lot of **fun** at the party last night.* ◆ *The party was **great fun**.* ◆ *Have fun* (= enjoy yourself)! ◆ ***It's no fun** having to get up at 4 o'clock every day.*

IDM **(just) for fun/for the fun of it** (just) for entertainment or pleasure; not seriously: *I don't need English for my work. I'm learning it for fun.*

in fun as a joke: *It was said in fun. They didn't mean to upset you.*

make fun of sb/sth to laugh at sb/sth in an unkind way; to make other people do this: *The older children are always making fun of him because of his accent.*

poke fun at sb/sth ➲ **poke**

⚷ **fun²** /fʌn/ *adj* amusing or enjoyable: *to have a fun time/day out* ◆ *Brett's a fun guy.*

> **HELP** **Fun or funny? Fun** is not the same as **funny**: *The party was fun* (= it was enjoyable). ◆ *The film was funny* (= it made me laugh). **Funny** can also mean 'strange'.

F

function[1] /ˈfʌŋkʃn/ *noun* [C] **1** the purpose or special duty of a person or thing: *The function of the heart is to pump blood through the body.* ♦ *to perform/fulfil a function* **2** an important social event, ceremony, etc: *The princess attends hundreds of official functions every year.*

function[2] /ˈfʌŋkʃn/ *verb* [I] to work correctly; to be in action: *Only one engine was still functioning.* SYN **operate**

functional /ˈfʌŋkʃənl/ *adj* **1** practical and useful rather than attractive: *cheap functional furniture* **2** working; being used: *The system is now fully functional.*

functionality /ˌfʌŋkʃəˈnæləti/ *noun* (*pl* functionalities) **1** [U] the quality in sth of being very suitable for the purpose it was designed for SYN **practicality** **2** [U] the purpose that sth is designed for: *Manufacturing processes may be affected by the functionality of the product.* **3** [C,U] the functions that a computer or other electronic system can perform: *new software with additional functionality*

ˈ**function key** *noun* [C] one of several keys on a computer, each marked with 'F' and a number, that can be used to perform a particular operation

fund[1] /fʌnd/ *noun* **1** [C] a sum of money that is collected for a particular purpose: *They contributed £100 to the disaster relief fund.* **2** funds [pl] money that is available and can be spent: *The hospital is trying to* ***raise funds*** *for a new kidney machine.*

fund[2] /fʌnd/ *verb* [T] to provide a project, school, charity, etc. with money: *education programmes funded by the UN*

fundamental /ˌfʌndəˈmentl/ *adj* basic and important; from which everything else develops: *There will be fundamental changes in the way the school is run.* ♦ *There is a fundamental difference between your opinion and mine.* ➲ look at **essential** ▶ **fundamentally** /-təli/ *adv*: *The government's policy on this issue has changed fundamentally.*

fundamentalist /ˌfʌndəˈmentəlɪst/ *noun* [C] a person who follows the basic rules and teachings of any religion very strictly ▶ **fundamentalist** *adj*: *Christian fundamentalist teaching* ▶ **fundamentalism** /-ɪzəm/ *noun* [U]

fundamentals /ˌfʌndəˈmentlz/ *noun* [pl] basic facts or principles

ˈ**fund-raiser** *noun* [C] a person whose job is to find ways of collecting money for a charity or an organization ▶ ˈ**fund-raising** *noun* [U]: *fund-raising events*

funeral /ˈfjuːnərəl/ *noun* [C] a ceremony (often a religious one) for burying or burning a dead person: *The funeral will be held next week.*

> **MORE** The body of the dead person is carried in a **coffin**, on which there are often **wreaths** of flowers. The coffin is buried in a **grave** or is **cremated** (= burned).

ˈ**funeral director** = **undertaker**

funfair /ˈfʌnfeə(r)/ = **fair**[2](1)

fungus /ˈfʌŋgəs/ *noun* [C,U] (*pl* fungi /ˈfʌŋgiː; -gaɪ/ *or* funguses) **1** a type of plant without leaves, flowers or green colouring, such as a **mushroom**. Some **fungi** can be harmful. ➲ note at **mushroom** ➲ look at **toadstool** **2** a substance like a wet powder that grows on old wood or food, walls, etc. ➲ look at **mould** ▶ **fungal** /ˈfʌŋgl/ *adj*: *a fungal disease/infection/growth*

funnel /ˈfʌnl/ *noun* [C] **1** an object that is wide at the top and narrow at the bottom, used for pouring liquid, powder, etc. into a small opening **2** the metal pipe which takes smoke or steam out of a ship, an engine, etc.

funnily /ˈfʌnəli/ *adv* in a strange or unusual way: *She's walking very funnily.*
IDM **funnily enough** used for expressing surprise at sth strange that has happened: *Funnily enough, my parents weren't at all cross about it.*

funny /ˈfʌni/ *adj* (funnier; funniest) **1** that makes you smile or laugh: *a funny story* ♦ *He's an extremely funny person.* ♦ *That's the funniest thing I've heard in ages!* **2** strange or unusual; difficult to explain or understand: *Oh dear, the engine is making a funny noise.* ♦ *It's funny that they didn't phone to let us know they couldn't come.* ♦ ***That's funny****—he was here a moment ago and now he's gone.* SYN **peculiar** ➲ note at **fun**[2], **humour** **3** (*informal*) slightly ill: *Can I sit down for a minute? I* ***feel*** *a bit* ***funny***.

fur /fɜː(r)/ *noun* **1** [U] the soft thick hair that covers the bodies of some animals ➲ picture on **page P12** **2** [C,U] the skin and hair of an animal that is used for making clothes, etc.; a piece of clothing that is made from this: *a fur coat*

furious /ˈfjʊəriəs/ *adj* **1** furious (with sb); furious (at sth) very angry: *He was furious with her for losing the car keys.* ♦ *She was furious at having to walk home.* ➲ *noun* **fury** **2** very strong; violent: *They had a furious argument.*
IDM **fast and furious** ➲ **fast**[1]
▶ **furiously** *adv*

furnace /ˈfɜːnɪs/ *noun* [C] a large, very hot fire, surrounded on all sides by walls, that is used for melting metal, burning rubbish, etc.

furnish /ˈfɜːnɪʃ/ *verb* [T] to put furniture in a room, house, etc: *The room was comfortably furnished.* ▶ **furnished** *adj*: *She's renting a furnished room in Birmingham.*

furnishings /ˈfɜːnɪʃɪŋz/ *noun* [pl] the furniture, carpets, curtains, etc. in a room, house, etc.

furniture /ˈfɜːnɪtʃə(r)/ *noun* [U] the things that can be moved, for example tables, chairs, beds, etc. in a room, house or office: *modern/antique/second-hand furniture* ♦ *garden/office furniture*

> **GRAMMAR** **Furniture** is uncountable: *They only got married recently and they haven't got much furniture.* We say **a piece of furniture** if we are talking about one item: *The only nice* ***piece of furniture*** *in the room was an old-fashioned desk.*

furrow /ˈfʌrəʊ/ *noun* [C] **1** a line in a field that is made by a **plough** (= a farming machine that turns the earth) for planting seeds in **2** a deep line in the skin on sb's face ➲ look at **wrinkle**

furry /ˈfɜːri/ *adj* (furrier; furriest) having fur: *a small furry animal*

further¹ /ˈfɜːðə(r)/ *adj, adv* **1** (also farther) [the comparative of *far*] at or to a greater distance in time or space: *It's not safe to go any further.* ◆ *I can't remember any further back than 1970.* **2** more; to a greater degree: *Are there* ***any further questions?*** ◆ *Please let us know if you require any* ***further information.*** ◆ *I have* ***nothing further to say*** *on the subject.* ◆ *The museum is closed* ***until further notice*** (= until we say that it is open again). ◆ *Can I have time to consider the matter further?*

HELP **Further or farther? Further** and **farther** can both be used when you are talking about distance: *Bristol is further/farther from London than Oxford is.* ◆ *I jumped further/farther than you did.* In other senses only **further** can be used: *We need a further week to finish the job.*

IDM **further afield** ➲ **afield**

further² /ˈfɜːðə(r)/ *verb* [T] (*formal*) to help sth to develop or be successful: *to further the cause of peace*

ˌfurther eduˈcation *noun* [U] (*abbr* FE) (*BrE*) education that is provided for people after leaving school, but not at a university ➲ look at **higher education**

furthermore /ˌfɜːðəˈmɔː(r)/ *adv* also; in addition

furthest /ˈfɜːðɪst/ ➲ **far**

furtive /ˈfɜːtɪv/ *adj* secret, acting as though you are trying to hide sth because you feel guilty: *a furtive glance at the letter* ▶ **furtively** *adv*

fury /ˈfjʊəri/ *noun* [U] very great anger: *She was speechless with fury.* ➲ *adjective* **furious**

fuse¹ /fjuːz/ *noun* [C] **1** a small piece of wire in an electrical system, machine, etc. that melts and breaks if there is too much power. This stops the flow of electricity and prevents fire or damage: *A fuse has blown—that's why the house is in darkness.* ◆ *That plug needs a 15 amp fuse.* **2** a piece of rope, string, etc. or a device that is used to make a bomb, etc. explode at a particular time

fuse² /fjuːz/ *verb* [I,T] **1** (used about two things) to join together to become one; to make two things do this: *As they heal, the bones will fuse together.* ◆ *The two companies have been fused into one large organization.* **2** to stop working because a **fuse**¹(1) has melted; to make a piece of electrical equipment do this: *The lights have fused.* ◆ *I've fused the lights.*

fuselage /ˈfjuːzəlɑːʒ/ *noun* [C] the main part of a plane (not the engines, wings or tail)

fusion /ˈfjuːʒn/ *noun* [U, sing] the process or the result of joining different things together to form one: *the fusion of two political systems*

fuss¹ /fʌs/ *noun* [sing, U] a time when people behave in an excited, a nervous or an angry way, especially about sth unimportant: *Mum always makes a fuss about my untidy bedroom.* ◆ *What's all the fuss about?* ◆ *It was all a fuss about nothing.*

IDM **make/kick up a fuss (about/over sth)** to complain strongly

make a fuss of/over sb/sth to pay a lot of attention to sb/sth: *My grandmother used to make a big fuss of me when she visited.*

fuss² /fʌs/ *verb* [I] **1** fuss (over sb/sth) to pay too much attention to sb/sth: *Stop fussing over all the details.* **2** to be worried or excited about small things: *Stop fussing. We're not going to be late.*

IDM **not be fussed (about sb/sth)** (*BrE informal*) to not care very much: *'Where do you want to go for lunch?' 'I'm not fussed.'*

fussy /ˈfʌsi/ *adj* (fussier; fussiest) **1** fussy (about sth) (used about people) giving too much attention to small details and therefore difficult to please: *He is very fussy about food* (= there are many things which he does not eat). ➲ look at **particular, picky** **2** having too much detail or decoration: *I don't like that pattern. It's too fussy.*

futile /ˈfjuːtaɪl/ *adj* (used about an action) having no success; useless: *They made a last futile attempt to make him change his mind.* ▶ **futility** /fjuːˈtɪləti/ *noun* [U]

futon /ˈfuːtɒn/ *noun* [C] a Japanese **mattress** (= the soft part of a bed), often on a wooden frame, that can be used for sitting on or rolled out to make a bed ➲ note at **bed**

future /ˈfjuːtʃə(r)/ *noun* **1** the future [sing] the time that will come after the present: *Who knows what will happen* ***in the future?*** ◆ *in the near/distant future* (= soon/not soon) **2** [C] what will happen to sb/sth in the time after the present: *Our children's futures depend on a good education.* ◆ *The company's future does not look very hopeful.* **3** [U] the possibility of being successful: *I could see no future in this country so I left to work abroad.* **4** the future (tense) [sing] the form of a verb that expresses what will happen after the present ℹ For more information about the future tense, look at the **Reference Section** at the back of this dictionary.

IDM **in future** from now on: *Please try to be more careful in future.*

▶ **future** *adj* [only *before* a noun]: *She met her future husband when she was still at school.* ◆ *You can keep that book for future reference* (= to look at again later).

fuzzy /ˈfʌzi/ *adj* (fuzzier; fuzziest) not clear: *The photo was a bit fuzzy but I could just make out my mother in it.*

FYI /ˌef waɪ ˈaɪ/ *abbr* (*written*) **for your information**

F

G

G, g /dʒiː/ *noun* [C,U] (*pl* Gs; G's; g's /dʒiːz/) **1** the 7th letter of the English alphabet: *'Gentleman' begins with (a) 'G'.* **2** G (used about music) the fifth note in the scale of C major: *G major/minor* ♦ *G sharp*

g *abbr* = **gram**

gable /ˈgeɪbl/ *noun* [C] the pointed part at the top of an outside wall of a house between two parts of the roof

gadget /ˈgædʒɪt/ *noun* [C] (*informal*) a small device, tool or machine that has a particular but usually unimportant purpose: *This car has all the latest gadgets.*

Gaelic /ˈgeɪlɪk; ˈgælɪk/ *adj, noun* [U] (of) the Celtic language and the culture of Ireland or Scotland

gag¹ /gæg/ *noun* [C] **1** a piece of cloth, etc. that is put in or over sb's mouth in order to stop them from talking **2** a joke

gag² /gæg/ *verb* [T] (gagging; gagged) to put a **gag** in or over sb's mouth

gage /geɪdʒ/ (*AmE*) = **gauge¹**

gaily /ˈgeɪli/ *adv* **1** in a bright and attractive way: *a gaily decorated room* **2** happily: *She waved gaily to the crowd.* **3** without thinking or caring about the effect of your actions on other people: *She gaily announced that she was leaving.*

⚷ **gain¹** /geɪn/ *verb* **1** [T] to gradually get more of sth: *The train was gaining speed.* ♦ *to gain weight/confidence* OPP **lose** **2** [T] to obtain or win sth, especially sth that you need or want: *They managed to gain access to secret information.* ♦ *The country gained its independence ten years ago.* **3** [I,T] gain (sth) (by/from sth/doing sth) to get an advantage: *I've got **nothing to gain** by staying in this job.* OPP **lose**

IDM **gain ground** to make progress; to become stronger or more popular

PHR V **gain in sth** to gradually get more of sth: *He's gained in confidence in the past year.*

gain on sb/sth to get closer to sb/sth that you are trying to catch: *I saw the other runners were gaining on me so I increased my pace.*

⚷ **gain²** /geɪn/ *noun* [C,U] an increase, improvement or advantage in sth: *We hope to **make a gain*** (= get more money than we paid) *when we sell our house.* ♦ *a **gain in weight** of one kilo* ♦ *He will do anything for **personal gain**, even if it means treating people badly.* OPP **loss**

gait /geɪt/ *noun* [sing] the way that sb/sth walks

gal. *abbr* = **gallon**

gala /ˈgɑːlə/ *noun* [C] a special social occasion or sports event: *a swimming gala*

galaxy /ˈgæləksi/ *noun* **1** [C] (*pl* galaxies) a large group of stars and planets in space **2** the Galaxy; the ˌMilky ˈWay [sing] the system of stars that contains our sun and its planets, seen as a bright band in the night sky

gale /geɪl/ *noun* [C] a very strong wind: *Several trees blew down in the gale.* ➲ look at **storm**

gallant /ˈgælənt/ *adj* (*formal*) **1** showing courage in a difficult situation: *gallant men/soldiers/heroes* ♦ *He made a gallant attempt to speak French, but nobody could understand him.* SYN **brave** **2** (used about men) polite to and showing respect for women

gallantry /ˈgæləntri/ *noun* [U] **1** courage, especially in battle **2** polite behaviour towards women by men

gallery /ˈgæləri/ *noun* [C] (*pl* galleries) **1** a building or room where works of art are shown to the public: *an art gallery* ➲ picture on **page P11** **2** an upstairs area at the back or sides of a large hall or theatre where people can sit

galley /ˈgæli/ *noun* [C] **1** a long flat ship with sails, especially one used by the ancient Greeks or Romans in war **2** the kitchen on a ship or plane

⚷ **gallon** /ˈgælən/ *noun* [C] (*abbr* gal.) a measure of liquid; 4.5 litres

MORE There are 8 **pints** in a gallon. An American gallon is the same as 3.8 litres.

ℹ For more information about measurements, look at the section on using numbers at the back of this dictionary.

gallop /ˈgæləp/ *verb* [I] (used about a horse or a rider) to go at the fastest speed ➲ look at **canter**, **trot** ▶ **gallop** *noun* [sing]

gallows /ˈgæləʊz/ *noun* [C] (*pl* gallows) a wooden frame used in the past on which people were killed by hanging

galore /gəˈlɔː(r)/ *adv* [only *after* a noun] in large numbers or amounts: *There will be prizes galore at our children's party on Saturday.*

galvanize (also -ise) /ˈgælvənaɪz/ *verb* [T] **1** galvanize sb (into sth/into doing sth) to make sb take action by shocking them or by making them excited: *The urgency of his voice **galvanized them into action**.* **2** (*technical*) to cover metal with **zinc** (= a silver-grey metal) in order to protect it from being damaged by water: *a galvanized bucket* ♦ *galvanized steel*

⚷ **gamble¹** /ˈgæmbl/ *verb* [I,T] gamble (sth) (on sth) to bet money on the result of a card game, horse race, etc: *to gamble on horses* ♦ *She gambled all her money on the last race.* SYN **bet**

PHR V **gamble on sth/on doing sth** to act in the hope that sth will happen although it may not: *I wouldn't gamble on the weather staying fine.*

▶ **gambler** *noun* [C]: *He's a compulsive gambler.*

▶ **gambling** *noun* [U]: *Some people want to ban Internet gambling.*

⚷ **gamble²** /ˈgæmbl/ *noun* [C] something you do that is a risk: *Setting up this business was a bit of a gamble.*

⚷ **game¹** /geɪm/ *noun* **1** [C] a game (of sth) a form of play or sport with rules; a time when you play it:

Shall we ***play a game****? ♦ Let's* ***have a game*** *of chess. ♦ a game of football/rugby/tennis ♦ 'Monopoly' is a very popular* ***board game****. ♦ a new computer game ♦ Tonight's game is between Holland and Italy. ♦ The game ended in a draw.* **2** games [pl] an important sports competition: *Where were the last Olympic Games held?* **3** [C] (in sports such as **tennis**) a section of a match that forms a unit in scoring: *two games all* (= both players have won two games) **4** [C] how well sb plays a sport: *My new racket has really improved my game.* **5** [C] an activity that you do to have fun: *Some children were playing a game of hide-and-seek.* **6** [C] (*informal*) a secret plan or trick: *Stop* ***playing games*** *with me and tell me where you've hidden my bag.* **7** [U] wild animals or birds that are killed for sport or food: *big game* (= lions, tigers, etc.)

IDM give the game away to tell a person sth that you are trying to keep secret: *It was the expression on her face that gave the game away.*

game² /geɪm/ *adj* (used about a person) ready to try sth new, unusual, difficult, etc: *I've never been sailing before but I'm game to try.*

gamekeeper /ˈgeɪmkiːpə(r)/ *noun* [C] a person who is responsible for the birds and animals that are kept on private land for people to hunt

ˈgame show *noun* [C] a television programme in which people play games or answer questions to win prizes ➲ look at **quiz**

gammon /ˈgæmən/ *noun* [U] (*BrE*) meat from the back leg or side of a pig that has been **cured** (= treated with salt or smoke to keep it fresh), usually served in thick slices ➲ look at **bacon, ham, pork**

gander /ˈgændə(r)/ *noun* [C] a male **goose** (= a bird like a large duck with a long neck)

gang¹ /gæŋ/ *noun* [C, with sing or pl verb] **1** an organized group of criminals **2** a group of young people who cause trouble, fight other groups, etc: *The woman was robbed by a gang of youths. ♦ gang warfare/violence* **3** (*informal*) a group of friends who meet regularly

gang² /gæŋ/ *verb*

PHR V gang up on sb (*informal*) to join together with other people in order to act against sb: *She's upset because she says the other kids are ganging up on her.*

gangrene /ˈgæŋgriːn/ *noun* [U] the death of a part of the body because the blood supply to it has been stopped as a result of disease or injury ▶ **gangrenous** /ˈgæŋgrɪnəs/ *adj*

gangster /ˈgæŋstə(r)/ *noun* [C] a member of a group of criminals

gangway /ˈgæŋweɪ/ *noun* [C] **1** (*BrE*) a passage between rows of seats in a cinema, an aircraft, etc. **2** a bridge that people use for getting on or off a ship

gaol, gaoler (*BrE*) = **jail, jailer**

🔑 **gap** /gæp/ *noun* [C] **1** a gap (in/between sth) an empty space in sth or between two things: *The sheep got out through a gap in the fence.* **2** a period of time when sth stops, or between two events: *I returned to tennis after a gap of about two years. ♦ a gap in the conversation* **3** a difference between people or their ideas: *The gap between the rich and the poor is getting wider.* **4** a part of sth that is missing: *In this exercise you have to fill (in) the gaps in the sentences. ♦ I think our new product should fill* ***a gap in the market****.*

IDM bridge a/the gap ➲ **bridge²**

gape /geɪp/ *verb* [I] **1** gape (at sb/sth) to look at sb/sth for a long time with your mouth open because you are surprised, shocked, etc: *We gaped in astonishment when we saw what Amy was wearing.* **2** gape (open) to be or become wide open: *a gaping hole/wound*

ˈgap year *noun* [C] (*BrE*) a year that a young person spends working and/or travelling, often between leaving school and starting university: *I'm planning to take a gap year and go backpacking in India.*

🔑 **garage** /ˈgærɑːʒ; -rɪdʒ/ *noun* [C] **1** a small building where a car, etc. is kept: *The house has a double garage* (= with space for two cars). **2** a place where vehicles are repaired and/or petrol is sold: *a garage mechanic* ➲ look at **petrol station**

🔑 **garbage** /ˈgɑːbɪdʒ/ (*especially AmE*) = **rubbish**

ˈgarbage can (*AmE*) = **dustbin**

garbled /ˈgɑːbld/ *adj* (used about a message, story, etc.) difficult to understand because it is not clear

🔑 **garden¹** /ˈgɑːdn/ *noun* [C] **1** (*AmE* yard) a piece of land next to a house where flowers and vegetables can be grown, usually with a **lawn** (= an area of grass): *Let's have lunch in the garden. ♦ the back/front garden ♦ garden flowers ♦ garden chairs* (= for using in the garden) ➲ note at **yard** ➲ picture on **page P8** ➲ picture on **page 310** **2** gardens [pl] a public park: *the Botanical Gardens*

garden² /ˈgɑːdn/ *verb* [I] to work in a garden: *She's been gardening all afternoon.*

ˈgarden centre *noun* [C] a place where plants, seeds, garden equipment, etc. are sold

gardener /ˈgɑːdnə(r)/ *noun* [C] a person who works in a garden as a job or for pleasure

gardening /ˈgɑːdnɪŋ/ *noun* [U] looking after a garden: *I'm going to* ***do*** *some* ***gardening*** *this afternoon. ♦ gardening tools/gloves*

ˈgarden party *noun* [C] a formal social event that takes place outside usually in a large garden in summer

gargle /ˈgɑːgl/ *verb* [I] to wash your throat with a liquid (which you do not swallow)

garish /ˈgeərɪʃ/ *adj* too bright or decorated and therefore unpleasant **SYN gaudy**

garlic /ˈgɑːlɪk/ *noun* [U] a plant of the onion family with a strong taste and smell that is used in cooking: *Chop two* ***cloves of garlic*** *and fry in oil.* ➲ picture on **page P15**

garment /ˈgɑːmənt/ *noun* [C] (*formal*) one piece of clothing ➲ look at **clothes**

G

garden equipment

garnish /ˈɡɑːnɪʃ/ *verb* [T] to decorate a dish of food with a small amount of another food: *Garnish the soup with a little parsley before serving.* ▶ **garnish** *noun* [U,C]

garrison /ˈɡærɪsn/ *noun* [C] a group of soldiers who are living in and guarding a town or building

⚷ **gas**[1] /ɡæs/ *noun* (*pl* gases; gasses) **1** [C,U] a substance like air that is not a solid or a liquid: *Hydrogen and oxygen are gases.* **2** [U] a particular type of gas or mixture of gases that is used for heating or cooking: *a gas cooker* **3** [U] (*AmE*) = **petrol**

gas[2] /ɡæs/ *verb* [T] (gassing; gassed) to poison or kill sb with gas

ˈ**gas chamber** *noun* [C] a room that can be filled with poisonous gas in order to kill animals or people

gash /ɡæʃ/ *noun* [C] a long deep cut or wound: *He had a nasty gash in his arm.* ▶ **gash** *verb* [T]

ˈ**gas mask** *noun* [C] an piece of equipment that is worn over the face to protect against poisonous gas

ˈ**gas meter** *noun* [C] an instrument that measures the amount of gas that you use in your home

⚷ **gasoline** /ˈɡæsəliːn/ (*AmE*) = **petrol**

gasp /ɡɑːsp/ *verb* [I,T] **1** gasp (at sth) to take a sudden loud breath with your mouth open, usually because you are surprised or in pain: *She gasped in surprise at the news.* **2** to have difficulty breathing: *I pulled the boy out of the pool and he lay there gasping for breath.* ▶ **gasp** *noun* [C]: *to give a gasp of surprise/pain/horror*

ˈ**gas station** (*AmE*) = **petrol station**

gastric /ˈɡæstrɪk/ *adj* [only *before* a noun] (*technical*) connected with the stomach: *a gastric ulcer* ◆ *gastric juices* (= the liquid in your stomach)

gastronomic /ˌɡæstrəˈnɒmɪk/ *adj* [only *before* a noun] connected with good food

⚷ **gate** /ɡeɪt/ *noun* [C] **1** the part of a fence, wall, etc. like a door that can be opened to let people or vehicles through: *Please keep the garden gate closed.* ➲ picture at **fence** **2** (also gateway) the space in a wall, fence, etc. where the gate is: *Drive through the gates and you'll find the car park on the right.* **3** the place at an airport where you get on or off a plane: *Lufthansa Flight 139 to Geneva is now boarding at gate 16.*

gateau /ˈɡætəʊ/ *noun* [C] (*pl* gateaux /ˈɡætəʊz/) a large cake that is usually decorated with cream, fruit, etc: *a strawberry gateau*

gatecrash /ˈɡeɪtkræʃ/ *verb* [I,T] to go to a private party without being invited ▶ **gatecrasher** *noun* [C]

gateway /ˈɡeɪtweɪ/ *noun* [C] **1** = gate(2) **2** [sing] the gateway to sth the place which you must go through in order to get to somewhere else: *The port of Dover is England's gateway to Europe.* ◆ (*figurative*) *A good education can be the gateway to success.*

⚷ **gather** /ˈɡæðə(r)/ *verb*

➤COME/BRING TOGETHER **1** [I,T] gather (round) (sb/sth); gather sb/sth (round) (sb/sth) (used about people) to come or be brought together in a group: *A crowd soon gathered at the scene of the accident.* ◆ *We all gathered round and listened to what the guide was saying.* ◆ *The children were gathered around the teacher's desk.* **2** [T] gather sth (together/up) to bring many things together: *He gathered up all his papers and put them away.* ◆ *They have gathered together a lot of information on the subject.*

➤COLLECT **3** [T] (*formal*) to pick wild flowers, fruit, etc. from a wide area: *to gather mushrooms*

➤UNDERSTAND **4** [I,T] to understand or find out sth

(from sb/sth): *I gather from your letter that you have several years' experience of this kind of work.* ◆ *'She's been very ill recently.' 'So I gather.'*
➤INCREASE **5** [I,T] to gradually become greater; to increase: *I gathered speed as I cycled down the hill.*

gathering /ˈɡæðərɪŋ/ *noun* [C] a time when people come together; a meeting: *a social/family gathering*

gaudy /ˈɡɔːdi/ *adj* (gaudier; gaudiest) too bright or decorated and therefore unpleasant **SYN garish**

gauge[1] (*AmE* also gage) /ɡeɪdʒ/ *noun* [C] **1** an instrument for measuring the amount of sth: *a fuel/temperature/pressure gauge* **2** (*technical*) a measurement of the width of sth or of the distance between two things: *a narrow-gauge railway* **3** a gauge (of sth) a fact that you can use to judge a situation, sb's feelings, etc.

gauge[2] /ɡeɪdʒ/ *verb* [T] **1** to make a judgement or to calculate sth by guessing: *It was difficult to gauge the mood of the audience.* **2** to measure sth accurately using a special instrument

gaunt /ɡɔːnt/ *adj* (used about a person) very thin because of illness, worry or not having enough food

gauze /ɡɔːz/ *noun* [U] a thin material like a net, that is used for covering an area of skin that you have hurt or cut

gave *past tense* of **give**[1]

gawp /ɡɔːp/ *verb* [I] (*informal*) gawp (at sb/sth) to look for a long time in a stupid way because you are surprised, shocked, etc: *Lots of drivers slowed down to gawp at the accident.*

gay[1] /ɡeɪ/ *adj* **1** sexually attracted to people of the same sex: *the gay community of New York* ◆ *a gay bar/club* (= for gay people) ◆ *Is she gay?* ➲ *noun* **gayness** **SYN homosexual** **OPP straight** **2** (gayer; gayest) (*old-fashioned*) happy and full of fun ➲ *noun* **gaiety**

gay[2] /ɡeɪ/ *noun* [C] a person, especially a man, who is sexually attracted to people of the same sex: *lesbians and gays* **SYN homosexual** **OPP straight**

gaze /ɡeɪz/ *verb* [I] to look steadily for a long time: *She sat at the window gazing dreamily into space.*
▶ **gaze** *noun* [sing]

GB *abbr* **1** /ˌdʒiː ˈbiː/ = **Great Britain** **2** = **gigabyte**

Gb (also Gbit) *abbr* (*written*) = **gigabit**

GCSE /ˌdʒiː siː es ˈiː/ *abbr* **General Certificate of Secondary Education**; an examination that students in England, Wales and Northern Ireland take when they are about 16. They often take **GCSEs** in five or more subjects. For Scottish examinations, look at SCE. ➲ look at **A level**

GDP /ˌdʒiː diː ˈpiː/ *abbr* **gross domestic product**; the total value of all goods and services produced by a country in one year ➲ look at **GNP**

⚷ **gear**[1] /ɡɪə(r)/ *noun* **1** [C] the machinery in a vehicle that turns engine power into a movement forwards or backwards: *Most cars have four or five forward gears and a reverse.* ➲ picture at **bicycle** **2** [U] a particular position of the gears in a vehicle: *first/second/top/reverse gear* ◆ *to change gear* **3** [U] equipment or clothing that you need for a particular activity, etc: *camping/fishing/sports gear* **4** [U] (*informal*) clothes: *wearing the latest gear* **5** [U] a piece of machinery that is used for a particular purpose: *the landing gear of an aeroplane* ◆ *lifting gear*

gear[2] /ɡɪə(r)/ *verb*
PHR V **gear sth to/towards sb/sth** [often passive] to make sth suitable for a particular purpose or person: *There is a special course geared towards the older learner.*
gear up (for sb/sth); gear sb/sth up (for sb/sth) to get ready or to make sb/sth ready

gearbox /ˈɡɪəbɒks/ *noun* [C] the metal case that contains the gears of a car, etc.

ˈ**gear lever** (also ˈgearstick /ˈɡɪəstɪk/ (*AmE*) ˈgear shift) *noun* [C] a stick that is used for changing gear in a car, etc. ➲ picture at **car**

gee /dʒiː/ *exclam* (*AmE*) used for expressing surprise, pleasure, etc.

geek /ɡiːk/ *noun* [C] (*informal*) a person who is not popular or fashionable: *a computer geek* **SYN nerd**
▶ **geeky** *adj*

geese *plural* of **goose**

gel /dʒel/ *noun* [C,U] [in compounds] a thick substance that is between a liquid and a solid: *hair gel* ◆ *shower gel*

gelatin /ˈdʒelətɪn/ (also gelatine /ˈdʒelətiːn/) *noun* [U] a clear substance that is made by boiling animal bones and is used in many products, especially in cooking, to make liquid thick or firm

gelignite /ˈdʒelɪɡnaɪt/ *noun* [U] a substance that is used for making explosions

gem /dʒem/ *noun* [C] **1** a rare and valuable stone that is used in jewellery **2** a person or thing that is especially good

Gemini /ˈdʒemɪnaɪ/ *noun* [C,U] the 3rd sign of the **zodiac** (= 12 signs which represent the positions of the sun, moon and planets), the Twins; a person born under this sign: *I'm a Gemini.* ➲ picture at **zodiac**

Gen. *abbr* = **General**[2]

gender /ˈdʒendə(r)/ *noun* [C,U] **1** (*formal*) the fact of being male or female **SYN sex** **2** (in some languages) the division of nouns, pronouns, etc. into classes (**masculine, feminine, neuter**); one of these classes

gene /dʒiːn/ *noun* [C] a unit of information inside a cell which controls what a living thing will be like. **Genes** are passed from parents to children. ➲ look at **genetics**

genera *plural* of **genus**

⚷ **general**[1] /ˈdʒenrəl/ *adj* **1** affecting all or most people, places, things, etc: *Dishwashers were once a luxury, but now they are in general use.* ◆ *a matter of general interest* ◆ *the general public* (= most ordinary people) **2** [only *before* a noun] referring to or describing the main part of sth, not the details: *Your general health is very good.* ◆ *The introduction gives* *you a general idea of what the book is about.* ♦ *As a* ***general rule****, the most common verbs in English tend to be irregular.* **3** not limited to one subject, use or activity: *Children need a good general education.* ♦ *The quiz tests your* ***general knowledge****.* **4** [in compounds] with responsibility for the whole of an organization: *a general manager*

IDM in general 1 in most cases; usually: *In general, standards of hygiene are good.* **2** as a whole: *I'm interested in Spanish history in general, and the civil war in particular.*

general² /ˈdʒenrəl/ *noun* [C] (*abbr* Gen.) an army officer in a very high position

G

ˌgeneral eˈlection *noun* [C] an election in which all the people of a country vote to choose a government ➲ note at **election**

generalization (also -isation) /ˌdʒenrəlaɪˈzeɪʃn/ *noun* [C,U] a general statement that is based on only a few facts or examples; the act of making such a statement: *You can't* ***make*** *sweeping* ***generalizations about*** *French people if you've only been to France for a day!*

generalize (also -ise) /ˈdʒenrəlaɪz/ *verb* [I] generalize (about sth) to form an opinion or make a statement using only a small amount of information instead of looking at the details: *You can't generalize about English food after only two days.* ♦ *You're generalizing. Every case is different.*

⚷ **generally** /ˈdʒenrəli/ *adv* **1** by or to most people: *He is generally considered to be a good doctor.* **2** usually: *She generally cycles to work.* **3** without discussing the details of sth: *Generally speaking, houses in America are bigger than houses in this country.*

⚷ **generate** /ˈdʒenəreɪt/ *verb* [T] to produce or create sth: *to generate heat/power/electricity*

⚷ **generation** /ˌdʒenəˈreɪʃn/ *noun* **1** [C,with sing or pl verb] all the people in a family, group or country who were born at about the same time: *We should look after the planet for future generations.* ♦ *This photograph shows three generations of my family* (= children, parents and grandparents).

GRAMMAR In the singular, **generation** is used with a singular or plural verb: *The younger generation only seem/seems to be interested in money.*

2 [C] the average time that children take to grow up and have children of their own, usually considered to be about 25–30 years: *A generation ago foreign travel was still only possible for a few people.* **3** [U] the production of sth, especially heat, power, etc: *the generation of electricity by water power*

the ˌgeneˈration gap *noun* [sing] the difference in behaviour, and the lack of understanding, between young people and older people

generator /ˈdʒenəreɪtə(r)/ *noun* [C] a machine that produces electricity

generic /dʒəˈnerɪk/ *adj* **1** shared by, including or typical of a whole group of things: *'Vine fruit' is the* ***generic term*** *for currants and raisins.* **2** (used about a product, especially a drug) not using the name of the company that made it ▸ **generically** /-kli/ *adv*

generosity /ˌdʒenəˈrɒsəti/ *noun* [U] the quality of being generous

⚷ **generous** /ˈdʒenərəs/ *adj* **1** happy to give more money, help, etc. than is usual or expected: *It was very generous of your parents to lend us all that money.* **2** larger than usual: *a generous helping of pasta* ▸ **generously** *adv*: *People gave very generously to our appeal for the homeless.*

genetic /dʒəˈnetɪk/ *adj* connected with **genes** (= the units in the cells of a living thing that control what it is like), or with **genetics**: *The disease is caused by a genetic defect.* ▸ **genetically** /-kli/ *adv*

geˌnetically ˈmodified *adj* (*abbr* GM) (used about food, plants, etc.) that has been grown from cells whose **genes** (= the units in the cells of a living thing that control what it is like) have been changed in an artificial way

geˌnetic engiˈneering *noun* [U] the science of changing the way a human, animal or plant develops by changing the information in its **genes** (= the units in the cells of a living thing that control what it is like)

genetics /dʒəˈnetɪks/ *noun* [U] the scientific study of the ways in which different characteristics are passed from each generation of living things to the next ➲ look at **gene**

genial /ˈdʒiːniəl/ *adj* (used about a person) pleasant and friendly

genie /ˈdʒiːni/ *noun* [C] (in stories) a spirit with magic powers, especially one that lives in a bottle or a lamp

genitals /ˈdʒenɪtlz/ (also *formal* genitalia /ˌdʒenɪˈteɪliə/) *noun* [pl] the parts of sb's sex organs that are outside the body ▸ **genital** *adj*

genius /ˈdʒiːniəs/ *noun* **1** [U] very great and unusual intelligence or ability: *Her idea was* ***a stroke of genius****.* **2** [C] a person who has very great and unusual ability, especially in a particular subject: *Einstein was a mathematical genius.* ➲ look at **prodigy** **3** [sing] a genius for (doing) sth a very good natural skill or ability

genocide /ˈdʒenəsaɪd/ *noun* [U] the murder of all the people of a particular race, religion, etc.

genome /ˈdʒiːnəʊm/ *noun* [C] the complete set of genes (= units of information) in a cell or living thing: *the human genome*

genre /ˈʒɒ̃rə; ˈʒɒnrə/ *noun* [C] (*formal*) a particular type or style of literature, art, film or music

gent (*informal*) = **gentleman**

genteel /dʒenˈtiːl/ *adj* behaving in a very polite and quiet way, often in order to make people think that you are from a high social class ▸ **gentility** /dʒenˈtɪləti/ *noun* [U]

⚷ **gentle** /ˈdʒentl/ *adj* (**gentler**; **gentlest**) **1** (used about people) kind and calm; touching or treating people or things in a careful way so that they are not hurt: *'I'll try and be as gentle as I can,' said the den-*

tist. **2** not strong, violent or extreme: *gentle exercise* ◆ *a gentle slope/curve* ▶ **gentleness** *noun* [U] ▶ **gently** /ˈdʒentli/ *adv*

gentleman /ˈdʒentlmən/ *noun* [C] (*pl* -men /-mən/) (also *informal* gent) /dʒent/ **1** a man who is polite and who behaves well towards other people: *Everyone likes and respects Joe because he's a real gentleman.* **2** (*formal*) used when speaking to or about a man or men in a polite way: ***Ladies and gentlemen*** (= at the beginning of a speech) ◆ *Mrs Flinn, there is a gentleman here to see you.* **3** (*old-fashioned*) a rich man with a high social position: *a country gentleman*

the gents (also the Gents) *noun* [sing] (*BrE informal*) a public toilet for men ➲ note at **toilet**

genuine /ˈdʒenjuɪn/ *adj* **1** real; true: *He thought that he had bought a genuine Rolex watch but it was a cheap fake.* ➲ look at **imitation** **2** sincere and honest; that can be trusted: *a very genuine person* ▶ **genuinely** *adv*

genus /ˈdʒiːnəs/ *noun* [C] (*pl* genera /ˈdʒenərə/) (*technical*) a group into which animals, plants, etc. that have similar characteristics are divided ➲ look at **class, family, species**

geographer /dʒiˈɒɡrəfə(r)/ *noun* [C] an expert in, or a student of, geography

geography /dʒiˈɒɡrəfi/ *noun* [U] **1** the study of the world's surface, physical qualities, climate, countries, products, population, etc: *human/physical/economic geography* **2** the physical arrangement of a place: *We're studying the geography of Asia.* ▶ **geographical** /ˌdʒiːəˈɡræfɪkl/ *adj* ▶ **geographically** /-kli/ *adv*

geologist /dʒiˈɒlədʒɪst/ *noun* [C] a student of or an expert in **geology**

geology /dʒiˈɒlədʒi/ *noun* [U] the study of rocks, and of the way they are formed ▶ **geological** /ˌdʒiːəˈlɒdʒɪkl/ *adj*

geometric /ˌdʒiːəˈmetrɪk/ (also **geometrical** /-ɪkl/) *adj* **1** connected with **geometry** **2** consisting of regular shapes and lines: *a geometric design/pattern* ▶ **geometrically** /-kli/ *adv*

geometry /dʒiˈɒmətri/ *noun* [U] the study in mathematics of lines, shapes, curves, etc.

geothermal /ˌdʒiːəʊˈθɜːml/ *adj* connected with the natural heat of rock deep in the ground: *geothermal energy*

geriatrics /ˌdʒeriˈætrɪks/ *noun* [U] the medical care of old people ▶ **geriatric** *adj*

germ /dʒɜːm/ *noun* **1** [C, usually pl] a very small living thing that causes disease ➲ look at **bacteria, virus** **2** [sing] the germ of sth the beginning of sth that may develop: *the germ of an idea*

German measles /ˌdʒɜːmən ˈmiːzlz/ (also rubella) *noun* [U] a mild disease that causes red spots all over the body. If a woman catches it when she is pregnant, it may harm the baby.

germinate /ˈdʒɜːmɪneɪt/ *verb* [I,T] (used about a seed) to start growing; to cause a seed to do this ▶ **germination** /ˌdʒɜːmɪˈneɪʃn/ *noun* [U]

gerund /ˈdʒerənd/ *noun* [C] a noun, ending in -ing, that has been made from a verb: *In the sentence 'His hobby is collecting stamps', 'collecting' is a gerund.*

gestation /dʒeˈsteɪʃn/ *noun* [U, sing] the period of time that a baby human or animal develops inside its mother's body; the process of developing inside the mother's body: *The **gestation period** of a horse is about eleven months.*

gesticulate /dʒeˈstɪkjuleɪt/ *verb* [I] to make movements with your hands and arms in order to express sth

gesture[1] /ˈdʒestʃə(r)/ *noun* [C] **1** a movement of the hand, head, etc. that expresses sth: *I saw the boy **make a** rude **gesture** at the policeman before running off.* **2** something that you do that shows other people what you think or feel

gesture[2] /ˈdʒestʃə(r)/ *verb* [I,T] to point at sth, to make a sign to sb: *She asked them to leave and gestured towards the door.*

get /ɡet/ *verb* (getting; *pt* got /ɡɒt/; *pp* got, *AmE* gotten /ˈɡɒtn/) **1** [T] [no passive] to receive, obtain or buy sth: *I got a letter from my sister.* ◆ *Did you get a present for your mother?* ◆ *Did you get your mother a present?* ◆ *She got a job in a travel agency.* ◆ *Louise got 75% in the maths exam.* ◆ *I'll come if I can get time off work.* ◆ *How much did you get for your old car* (= when you sold it)? ◆ *to get a shock/surprise* **2** [T] have got sth to have sth: *I've got a lot to do today.* ◆ *Lee's got blond hair.* ◆ *Have you got a spare pen?* **3** [T] [no passive] to go to a place and bring sth back: ***Go and get** me a pen, please.* ◆ *Sam's gone to get his mother from the station.* **SYN** **fetch** **4** [T] to catch or have an illness, pain, etc: *I think I'm getting a cold.* ◆ *He gets really bad headaches.* ◆ *Teenagers often get acne.* **5** [I,T] to become; to reach a particular state or condition; to make sb/sth be in a particular state or condition: *It's getting dark.* ◆ *to get angry/bored/annoyed* ◆ *to get fat* ◆ *I can't **get used to** my new bed.* ◆ *to **get dressed*** ◆ *When did you **get married**?* ◆ *to get (sb) pregnant* ◆ *Just give me five minutes to **get ready**.* ◆ *He's always **getting into trouble** with the police.* ◆ *Don't get your dress dirty!* ◆ *She's shy, but she's great fun once you **get to know** her.* **6** [I] used instead of 'be' in the passive: *She got bitten by a dog.* ◆ *Don't leave your wallet on the table or it'll get stolen.* **7** [T] get sb/sth to do sth to make or persuade sb/sth to do sth: *I got him to agree to the plan.* ◆ *I can't get the TV to work.* **8** [T] get sth done to cause sth to be done: *Let's get this work done, then we can go out.* ◆ *I'm going to **get my hair cut**.* ◆ *I had to get the car repaired.* **9** [T] [used with verbs in the -ing form] to start doing sth: *We don't have much time so we'd better get working.* ◆ *I got talking to a woman on the bus.* ◆ *We'd better **get going** if we don't want to be late.* **10** [I] get to do sth to have the chance to do sth: *Did you get to try the new smartphone?* **11** [I] to arrive at or reach a place: *We should get to London at about ten.* ◆ *Can you tell me how to get to the hospital?* ◆ *What time do you usually **get home**?* ◆ *I got half way up the mountain then gave up.* ◆ *How far have you got with your book?*

➲ look at **get in** **12** [I,T] to move or go somewhere; to move or put sth somewhere: *I can't swim so I couldn't get across the river.* ◆ *My grandmother's 92 and she doesn't get out of the house much.* ◆ *We couldn't get the piano upstairs.* ◆ *My foot was swollen and I couldn't get my shoe off.* **13** [T] to use a form of transport: *Shall we walk or get the bus?* **14** [T] get (sb) sth; get sth (for sb) to prepare food: *Can I get you anything to eat?* ◆ *Joe's in the kitchen getting breakfast for everyone.* **15** [T] to hit, hold or catch sb/sth: *He got me by the throat and threatened to kill me.* ◆ *A boy threw a stone at me but he didn't get me.* **16** [T] to hear or understand sth: *I'm sorry, I didn't get that. Could you repeat it?* ◆ *Did you get that* **joke** *that Karen told?*

G

IDM **get somewhere/nowhere (with sb/sth)** to make/not make progress: *I'm getting nowhere with my research.*

be getting at sth (*informal*) to try to say sth without saying it in a direct way; to suggest: *I'm not quite sure what you're getting at—am I doing something wrong?*

be getting on (for) **1** to be getting old or late: *He's getting on—he's over 70, I'm sure.* **2** to be nearly a particular time, age or number: *Time's getting on—we don't want to be late.* ◆ *I'm not sure how old she is, but she must be getting on for 50.* ℹ For other idioms containing **get**, look at the entries for the nouns, adjectives, etc. For example, **get rid of** is at **rid**.

PHR V **get about/around/round** (used about news, a story, etc.) to become known by many people: *The rumour got around that Freddie wore a wig.*

get sth across (to sb) to succeed in making people understand sth: *The party failed to get its policies across to the voters.*

get ahead to progress and be successful in sth, especially a career

get along **1** [usually used in the continuous tenses] (*informal*) to leave a place: *I'd love to stay, but I should be getting along now.* **2** = **get on**

get around **1** (*BrE also* get about) to move or travel from place to place: *My grandmother needs a stick to get around these days.* **2** = **get about/around/round**

get around sb/sth = **get round sb/sth**

get around to sth/doing sth = **get round to sth/doing sth**

get at sb to criticize sb a lot: *The teacher's always getting at me about my spelling.*

get at sb/sth to be able to reach sb/sth; to have sb/sth available for immediate use: *The files are locked away and I can't get at them.*

get away (from ...) to succeed in leaving or escaping from sb or a place: *He kept talking to me and I couldn't get away from him.* ◆ *The thieves got away in a stolen car.*

get away with sth/doing sth to do sth bad and not be punished for it: *He lied, but he got away with it.*

get back to return to the place where you live or work: *When did you get back from Italy?*

get sth back to be given sth that you had lost or lent: *Can I borrow this book? You'll get it back next week, I promise.*

get back to sb to speak to, write to, email or phone sb later, especially in order to give an answer: *I'll get back to you on prices when I've got some more information.*

get back to sth to return to doing sth or talking about sth: *I woke up early and couldn't get back to sleep.* ◆ *Let's get back to the point you raised earlier.*

get behind (with sth) to fail to do, pay sth, etc. on time, and so have more to do, pay, etc. the next time: *to get behind with your work/rent*

get by (on/in/with sth) to manage to live or do sth with difficulty: *It's very hard to get by on such a low income.* ◆ *My Italian is good and I can get by in Spanish.*

get sb down to make sb unhappy

get down to sth/doing sth to start working on sth: *We'd better stop chatting and get down to work.* ◆ *I must get down to answering these letters.*

get in to reach a place: *What time does your train get in?*

get in; get into sth **1** to climb into a car: *We all got in and Tim drove off.* **2** to be elected to a political position: *Who do you think will get in at the next election?*

get sb in to call sb to your house to do a job: *We had to get a plumber in to fix the pipes.*

get sth in **1** to collect or bring sth inside; to buy a supply of sth: *It's going to rain—I'd better get the washing in from outside.* **2** to manage to find an opportunity to say or do sth: *He talked all the time and I couldn't get a word in.*

get in on sth to become involved in an activity

get into sb (*informal*) (used about a feeling or attitude) to start affecting sb strongly, causing them to behave in an unusual way: *I wonder what's got into him—he isn't usually unfriendly.*

get into sth **1** to put on a piece of clothing with difficulty: *I've put on so much weight I can't get into my trousers.* **2** to start a particular activity; to become involved in sth: *How did you first get into the music business?* ◆ *She has got into the habit of turning up late.* ◆ *We got into an argument about politics.* **3** to become more interested in or familiar with sth: *I've been getting into yoga recently.* ◆ *It's taking me a while to get into my new job.*

get off (sb/sth) used especially to tell sb to stop touching you/sb/sth: *Get off (me) or I'll call the police!* ◆ *Get off that money, it's mine!*

get off (sth) **1** to leave a bus, train, etc.; to climb down from a bicycle, horse, etc. **2** to leave work with permission at a particular time: *I might be able to get off early today.*

get off (with sth) to be lucky to receive no serious injuries or punishment: *to get off with just a warning*

get on to progress or become successful in life, in a career, etc: *After leaving university she was determined to get on.*

get on/along to have a particular amount of success: *'How did you get on at your interview?' 'I got the job!'* ◆ *How are you getting along on your course?*

get on/onto sth to climb onto a bus, train, bicycle, horse, etc: *I got on just as the train was about to leave.*

get on to sb (about sth) to speak or write to sb about a particular matter
get on/along with sb; get on/along (together) to have a friendly relationship with sb: *Do you get on well with your colleagues?* ◆ *We're not close friends but we get on together quite well.*
get on/along with sth to make progress with sth that you are doing: *How are you getting on with that essay?*
get on with sth to continue doing sth, especially after an interruption: *Stop talking and get on with your work!*
get out (used about a piece of information) to become known, after being secret until now
get sth out (of sth) to take sth from its container: *I got my keys out of my bag.*
get out of sth/doing sth to avoid a duty or doing sth that you have said you will do
get sth out of sb to persuade or force sb to give you sth: *His parents finally got the truth out of him.*
get sth out of sb/sth to gain sth from sb/sth: *I get a lot of pleasure out of music.*
get over sth 1 to deal with a problem successfully: *We'll have to get over the problem of finding somewhere to live first.* **2** to feel normal again after being ill or having an unpleasant experience: *He still hasn't got over his wife's death.*
get sth over with (*informal*) to do and complete sth unpleasant that has to be done: *I'll be glad to get my visit to the dentist's over with.*
get round = **get about/around/round**
get round/around sb (*informal*) to persuade sb to do sth or agree with sth: *My father says he won't lend me the money but I think I can get round him.*
get round/around sth to find a way of avoiding or dealing with a problem
get round/around to sth/doing sth to find the time to do sth, after a delay: *I've been meaning to read that book for ages but I haven't got round to it yet.*
get through sth to use or complete a certain amount or number of sth: *I got through a lot of money at the weekend.* ◆ *I got through an enormous amount of work today.*
get (sb) through (sth) to manage to complete sth difficult or unpleasant; to help sb to do this: *She got through her final exams easily.*
get through (to sb) 1 to succeed in making sb understand sth: *They couldn't get through to him that he was completely wrong.* **2** to succeed in speaking to sb on the phone: *I couldn't get through to them because their phone was engaged all day.*
get to sb (*informal*) to affect sb in a bad way: *Public criticism is beginning to get to the team manager.*
get sb/sth together to collect people or things in one place: *I'll just get my things together and then we'll go.*
get together (with sb) to meet socially or in order to discuss or do sth: *Let's get together and talk about it.* ➲ look at **meet up**
get up to stand up: *He got up to let an elderly woman sit down.*
get (sb) up to get out of bed or make sb get out of bed: *What time do you have to get up in the morning?* ◆ *Could you get me up at 6 tomorrow?* ➲ note at **routine**
get up to sth 1 to reach a particular point or stage in sth: *We've got up to the last section of our grammar book.* **2** to be busy with sth, especially sth secret or bad: *I wonder what the children are getting up to?*

getaway /ˈgetəweɪ/ *noun* [C] an escape (after a crime): *to **make a getaway*** ◆ *a getaway car/driver*

ˈ**get-together** *noun* [C] (*informal*) an informal social meeting or party: *We're going to have a get-together on Saturday evening.*

ghastly /ˈgɑːstli/ *adj* (**ghastlier**; **ghastliest**) extremely unpleasant or bad: *a ghastly accident* **SYN** **terrible**

ghetto /ˈgetəʊ/ *noun* [C] (*pl* **ghettoes**) a part of a town where many people of the same race, religion, etc. live in poor conditions

ghost /gəʊst/ *noun* [C] the spirit of a dead person that a living person believes they can see or hear: *I don't believe in ghosts.* ◆ *a ghost story* ➲ look at **apparition**, **spectre**

ghostly /ˈgəʊstli/ *adj* (**ghostlier**; **ghostliest**) looking or sounding like a **ghost**; full of **ghosts**: *ghostly noises*

ˈ**ghost town** *noun* [C] a town that used to be busy and have people living in it, but is now empty

ghostwriter /ˈgəʊstraɪtə(r)/ *noun* [C] a person who writes a book, etc. for a famous person (whose name appears as the author)

🔑 **giant** /ˈdʒaɪənt/ *noun* [C] **1** an extremely large, strong person: *a giant of a man* **2** something that is very large: *the multinational oil giants* (= very large companies) ▶ **giant** *adj* [only *before* a noun]: *a giant new shopping centre*

gibberish /ˈdʒɪbərɪʃ/ *noun* [U] words that have no meaning or that are impossible to understand: *I was so nervous in my interview I just spoke gibberish.*

giddy /ˈgɪdi/ *adj* (**giddier**; **giddiest**) having the feeling that everything is going round and that you are going to fall: *I feel giddy. I must sit down.* **SYN** **dizzy**

🔑 **gift** /gɪft/ *noun* [C] **1** something that you give to sb; a present: *This watch was a gift from my mother.* ◆ *This week's magazine contains a **free gift** of some make-up.* ◆ *The company **made a gift of** a computer to a local school.* **SYN** **present 2** a gift (for sth/doing sth) natural ability: *I'd love to **have a gift** for languages like Mike has.* **SYN** **talent**

gifted /ˈgɪftɪd/ *adj* having natural ability or great intelligence

gig /gɪg/ *noun* [C] (*informal*) an event where a musician or band is paid to perform: *The band are doing gigs all around the country.*

gigabit /ˈgɪgəbɪt/ (*abbr* **Gb**; **Gbit**) *noun* [C] a unit of computer memory, equal to 2^{30} **bits** (= small units of information)

gigabyte /ˈgɪgəbaɪt/ (*abbr* **GB**) *noun* [C] a unit of computer memory, equal to 2^{30} **bytes** (= small units of information)

G

gigantic /dʒaɪˈgæntɪk/ *adj* extremely big **SYN** **enormous, huge**

giggle /ˈgɪgl/ *verb* [I] to laugh in a silly way that you can't control, because you are amused or nervous ▶ **giggle** *noun* [C]: *I've* ***got the giggles*** (= I can't stop laughing).

gill /gɪl/ *noun* [C, usually pl] one of the parts on the side of a fish's head that it breathes through ➲ picture on **page P13**

gilt /gɪlt/ *noun* [U] a thin covering of gold

gimmick /ˈgɪmɪk/ *noun* [C] an unusual idea to attract attention or to persuade people to buy sth: *New magazines often use free gifts or other gimmicks to get people to buy them.*

G

gin /dʒɪn/ *noun* [C,U] a strong, alcoholic drink with no colour

ginger /ˈdʒɪndʒə(r)/ *noun* [U], *adj* **1** a root that tastes hot and is used as a spice in cooking: *ground ginger* ◆ *ginger biscuits* ➲ picture on **page P14** **2** (of) a light brownish-orange colour: *ginger hair*

ˌginger ˈale *noun* [U] a drink that does not contain alcohol and is flavoured with **ginger**. It does not contain alcohol but is often mixed with alcoholic drinks.

ˌginger ˈbeer *noun* [U] a drink that is flavoured with **ginger**. Some types of ginger beer contain a small amount of alcohol.

gingerbread /ˈdʒɪndʒəbred/ *noun* [U] a sweet cake or soft biscuit flavoured with **ginger**: *a gingerbread man* (= a gingerbread biscuit in the shape of a person)

gingerly /ˈdʒɪndʒəli/ *adv* very slowly and carefully so as not to cause harm, make a noise, etc: *I removed the bandage very gingerly and looked at the cut.*

Gipsy = Gypsy

giraffe /dʒəˈrɑːf/ *noun* [C] (*pl* **giraffe** *or* **giraffes**) a large African animal with a very long neck, long legs, and big dark spots on its skin

girder /ˈgɜːdə(r)/ *noun* [C] a long, heavy piece of iron or steel that is used in the building of bridges, large buildings, etc.

⚷ **girl** /gɜːl/ *noun* [C] **1** a female child: *Is the baby a boy or a girl?* ◆ *There are more boys than girls in the class.* **2** a daughter: *They have two boys and a girl.* **3** (sometimes offensive) a young woman: *The girl at the cash desk was very helpful.* **4 girls** [pl] a woman's female friends of any age: *a night out with the girls*

⚷ **girlfriend** /ˈgɜːlfrend/ *noun* [C] **1** a girl or woman with whom sb has a romantic and/or sexual relationship: *Has Frank got a girlfriend?* **2** (*especially AmE*) a girl or woman's female friend: *I had lunch with a girlfriend.*

Girl ˈGuide (*old-fashioned*) = **guide**[1] (5)

girlhood /ˈgɜːlhʊd/ *noun* [U] the time when sb is a girl

girlish /ˈgɜːlɪʃ/ *adj* looking, sounding or behaving like a girl: *a girlish figure/giggle*

giro /ˈdʒaɪrəʊ/ *noun* (*pl* **giros**) (*BrE*) [U] a system for moving money from one bank, etc. to another

girth /gɜːθ/ *noun* [U,C] the measurement around sth, especially sb's waist: *a man of enormous girth* ◆ *a tree one metre in girth/with a girth of one metre*

gist /dʒɪst/ *noun* [sing] **the gist (of sth)** the general meaning of sth rather than all the details: *I know a little Spanish so I was able to* ***get the gist*** *of what he said.*

⚷ **give**[1] /gɪv/ *verb* (*pt* **gave** /geɪv/; *pp* **given** /ˈgɪvn/) **1** [T] **give sb sth; give sth to sb** to let sb have sth, especially sth that they want or need: *I gave Jackie a book for her birthday.* ◆ *Give me that book a minute—I just want to check something.* ◆ *I gave my bag to my friend to look after.* ◆ *I'll give you my phone number.* ◆ *The doctor gave me this cream for my skin.* ◆ *He was thirsty so I gave him a drink.* ◆ *Just phone and I'll give you all the help you need.* **2** [T] **give sb sth; give sth to sb** to make sb have sth, especially sth they do not want: *Mr Johns gives us too much homework.* ◆ *If you go to school with the flu, you'll give it to everyone.* **3** [T] to make sb have a particular feeling, idea, etc: *Swimming always gives me a good appetite.* ◆ *to give somebody a surprise/shock/fright* ◆ *What gives you the idea that he was lying?* **4** [T] **give (sb) sth; give sth to sb** to let sb have your opinion, decision, judgement, etc: *Can you give me some advice?* ◆ *My boss has given me permission to leave early.* ◆ *The judge gave him five years in prison.* **5** [T] **give (sb) sth; give sth (to sb)** to speak to people in a formal situation: *to give a speech/talk/lecture* ◆ *The officer was called to give evidence in court.* ◆ *Sarah's going to give me a cooking lesson.* **6** [T] **give (sb) sth for sth; give (sb) sth (to do sth)** to pay in order to have sth: *How much did you give him for fixing the car?* ◆ (*figurative*) *I'd give anything* (= I would love) *to be able to sing like that.* **7** [T] to spend time dealing with sb/sth: *We need to give some thought to this matter urgently.* **8** [T] **give (sb/sth) sth** to do sth to sb/sth; to make a particular sound or movement: *to give somebody a kiss/push/hug/bite* ◆ *to give something a clean/wash/polish* ◆ ***Give me a call*** *when you get home.* ◆ *She opened the door and gave a shout of horror.* **9** [T] to perform or organize sth for people: *The company gave a party to celebrate its 50th anniversary.* **10** [I] to bend or stretch under pressure: *The branch began to give under my weight.*

IDM **give or take** more or less the number mentioned: *It took us two hours to get here, give or take five minutes.* ❶ For other idioms containing **give**, look at the entries for the nouns, adjectives, etc. For example, **give way** is at **way**.

PHR V **give sth away** to give sth to sb without wanting money in return: *When she got older she gave all her toys away.* ◆ *We are giving away a free DVD with this month's issue.*

give sth/sb away to show or tell the truth about sth/sb which was secret: *He smiled politely and didn't give away his real feelings.*

give sth back to return sth to the person that you took or borrowed it from: *I lent him some books months ago and he still hasn't given them back to me.*

give sth in to give sth to the person who is collecting it: *I've got to give this essay in to my teacher by Friday.*

give in (to sb/sth) to stop fighting against sb/sth; to accept that you have been defeated

give off sth to send sth (for example smoke, a smell, heat, etc.) out into the air: *Cars give off poisonous fumes.*

give out (used about a machine, etc.) to stop working: *His heart gave out and he died.*

give sth out to give one of sth to each person: *Please give out these books to the class.*

give up to stop trying to do sth; to accept that you cannot do sth: *They gave up once the other team had scored their third goal.* ◆ *I give up. What's the answer?*

give sb up; give up on sb to stop expecting sb to arrive, succeed, improve, etc: *I'd almost given him up, when he arrived, full of apologies.* ◆ *Her work was so poor that all her teachers gave up on her.*

give sth up; give up doing sth to stop doing or having sth that you did or had regularly before: *Don't give up hope. Things are bound to improve.* ◆ *I've tried many times to give up smoking.*

give yourself/sb up (to sb) to go to the police when they are trying to catch you; to tell the police where sb is

give sth up (to sb) to give sth to sb who needs or asks for it: *He gave up his seat on the bus to an elderly woman.*

give² /ɡɪv/ *noun* [U] the quality of being able to bend or stretch a little

IDM give and take a situation in which two people, groups, etc., respect each other's rights and needs: *There has to be some give and take for a marriage to succeed.*

giveaway /ˈɡɪvəweɪ/ *noun* [C] (*informal*) **1** a thing that is included free when you buy sth: *There's usually some giveaway with that magazine.* **2** something that makes you guess the truth about sb/sth: *She said she didn't know about the money but her face was **a dead** (= complete) **giveaway**.*

given¹ *past participle of* **give¹**

given² /ˈɡɪvn/ *adj* [only *before* a noun] already stated or decided: *At any given time, up to 200 people are using the library.*

given³ /ˈɡɪvn/ *prep* considering sth: *Given that you had very little help, I think you did very well.*

ˈgiven name (*especially AmE*) = **first name**

glacial /ˈɡleɪʃl; ˈɡleɪsiəl/ *adj* **1** (*technical*) connected with, or caused by, **glaciers**: *a glacial landscape* ◆ *glacial deposits/erosion* **2** very cold: *glacial winds/temperatures* **SYN icy**

glacier /ˈɡlæsiə(r)/ *noun* [C] a large mass of ice that moves slowly down a valley ➲ picture on **page P10**

🔑 **glad** /ɡlæd/ *adj* **1** [not before a noun] **glad (about sth); glad to do sth/that ...** happy; pleased: *Are you glad about your new job?* ◆ *I'm glad to hear he's feeling better.* ◆ *I'm glad (that) he's feeling better.* ◆ *I'll be glad when these exams are over.* ➲ note at **happy 2 glad (of sth); glad (if ...)** grateful for sth: *If you are free, I'd be glad of some help.* ◆ *I'd be glad if you could help me.* ▶ **gladness** *noun* [U]

glade /ɡleɪd/ *noun* [C] a small open area of grass in a wood or forest

gladiator /ˈɡlædieɪtə(r)/ *noun* [C] (in ancient Rome) a man who fought against another man or a wild animal in a public show

gladly /ˈɡlædli/ *adv* used for politely agreeing to a request or accepting an invitation: *'Could you help me carry these bags?' 'Gladly.'* ◆ *She gladly accepted the invitation to stay the night.*

glamorize (also **-ise**) /ˈɡlæməraɪz/ *verb* [T] to make sth appear more attractive or exciting than it really is: *TV tends to glamorize violence.*

glamour (*AmE* also **glamor**) /ˈɡlæmə(r)/ *noun* [U] the quality of seeming to be more exciting or attractive than ordinary things or people: *Young people are often attracted by the glamour of city life.* ▶ **glamorous** /ˈɡlæmərəs/ *adj*: *the glamorous world of opera* ▶ **glamorously** *adv*

glance¹ /ɡlɑːns/ *verb* [I] to look quickly at sb/sth: *She glanced round the room to see if they were there.* ◆ *He glanced at her and smiled.* ◆ *The receptionist glanced down the list of names.*

PHR V glance off (sth) to hit sth at an angle and move off again in another direction: *The ball glanced off his knee and into the net.*

glance² /ɡlɑːns/ *noun* [C] a quick look: *to take/have a glance at the newspaper headlines*

IDM at a (single) glance with one look: *I could tell at a glance that something was wrong.*

at first glance/sight ➲ **first¹**

gland /ɡlænd/ *noun* [C] any of the organs inside your body that produce chemical substances for your body to use: *sweat glands* ▶ **glandular** /ˈɡlændjulə(r)/ *adj*: *glandular fever* (= an infectious disease)

glare¹ /ɡleə(r)/ *verb* [I] **1 glare (at sb/sth)** to look at sb in a very angry way **2** to shine with strong light that hurts your eyes

glare² /ɡleə(r)/ *noun* **1** [C] a very angry look **2** [U] strong light that hurts your eyes: *the glare of the sun/a car's headlights*

glaring /ˈɡleərɪŋ/ *adj* **1** very easy to see; shocking: *a glaring mistake/injustice* **2** (used about a light) too strong and bright **3** angry: *glaring eyes* ▶ **glaringly** *adv*: *a **glaringly obvious** mistake*

glasses

wine glass tumbler beer mug

🔑 **glass** /ɡlɑːs/ *noun* **1** [U] a hard substance that you can usually see through that is used for making windows, bottles, etc: *He cut himself on broken glass.* ◆ *a* *sheet/pane of glass* ♦ *a glass jar/dish/vase* **2** [C] a drinking container made of glass; the amount of liquid it contains: *a wine glass* ♦ *a brandy glass* ♦ *Could I have a glass of water, please?*

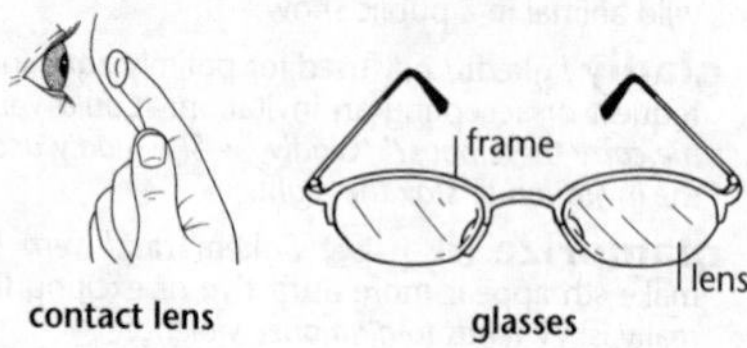

contact lens **glasses**

G

glasses /ˈɡlɑːsɪz/ (also spectacles (*informal* specs; *AmE* also eyeglasses) *noun* [pl] two **lenses** (= pieces of glass or plastic) in a frame that a person wears in front of their eyes in order to be able to see better: *My sister has to* ***wear glasses.*** ♦ *I need* ***a*** *new* ***pair of glasses.*** ♦ *I need some new glasses.* ♦ *reading glasses* ♦ *dark glasses*

glass ˈfibre = **fibreglass**

glasshouse /ˈɡlɑːshaʊs/ *noun* [C] a building with glass sides and a glass roof, for growing plants in ➲ look at **greenhouse**

glassy /ˈɡlɑːsi/ *adj* (glassier; glassiest) **1** looking like glass **2** (used about the eyes) showing no interest or expression

glaze[1] /ɡleɪz/ *verb* [T] **1** to fit a sheet of glass into a window, etc. ➲ look at **double glazing** **2** glaze sth (with sth) to cover a pot, brick, **pie** (= a type of baked food), etc. with a shiny transparent substance (before it is put into an oven)

PHR V **glaze over** (used about the eyes) to show no interest or expression

glaze[2] /ɡleɪz/ *noun* [C,U] (a substance that gives) a shiny transparent surface on a pot, brick, **pie** (= a type of baked food), etc.

glazed /ɡleɪzd/ *adj* (used about the eyes, etc.) showing no interest or expression

glazier /ˈɡleɪziə(r)/ *noun* [C] a person whose job is to fit glass into windows, etc.

gleam /ɡliːm/ *noun* [C, usually sing] **1** a soft light that shines for a short time: *the gleam of moonlight on the water* **2** a small amount of sth: *a faint gleam of hope* **3** a sudden expression of an emotion in sb's eyes: *I saw a gleam of amusement in his eyes.* ▶ **gleam** *verb* [I]: *gleaming white teeth* ♦ *The children's eyes gleamed with enthusiasm.*

glean /ɡliːn/ *verb* [T] glean sth (from sb/sth) to obtain information, knowledge etc., sometimes with difficulty and often from various different places: *These figures have been gleaned from a number of studies.*

glee /ɡliː/ *noun* [U] a feeling of happiness, usually because sth good has happened to you or sth bad has happened to sb else: *She couldn't hide her glee when her rival came last in the race.* ▶ **gleeful** /ˈɡliːfl/ *adj* ▶ **gleefully** /-fəli/ *adv*

glen /ɡlen/ *noun* [C] a deep, narrow valley, especially in Scotland or Ireland

glib /ɡlɪb/ *adj* using words in a way that is clever and quick, but not sincere: *a glib salesman/politician* ♦ *a glib answer/excuse* ▶ **glibly** *adv* ▶ **glibness** *noun* [U]

glide /ɡlaɪd/ *verb* [I] **1** to move smoothly without noise or effort: *The dancers glided across the floor.* **2** to fly in a **glider**

glider /ˈɡlaɪdə(r)/ *noun* [C] a light aircraft without an engine that flies using air currents ➲ look at **hang-glider** ➲ picture on **page P6**

gliding /ˈɡlaɪdɪŋ/ *noun* [U] the sport of flying in a glider: *I've always wanted to* ***go gliding.***

glimmer /ˈɡlɪmə(r)/ *noun* [C] **1** a weak light that is not steady: *I could see a faint glimmer of light in one of the windows.* **2** a small sign of sth: *a glimmer of hope* ▶ **glimmer** *verb* [I]

glimpse /ɡlɪmps/ *noun* [C] **1** a glimpse (at/of sth) a very quick and not complete view of sb/sth: *I just managed to* ***catch a glimpse*** *of the fox's tail as it ran down a hole.* **2** a glimpse (into/of sth) a short experience of sth that helps you understand it: *The programme gives us an interesting glimpse into the life of the cheetah.* ▶ **glimpse** *verb* [T]

glint /ɡlɪnt/ *verb* [I] to shine with small bright flashes of light: *His eyes glinted at the thought of all that money.* ▶ **glint** *noun* [C]

glisten /ˈɡlɪsn/ *verb* [I] (used about wet surfaces) to shine: *Her eyes glistened with tears.* ♦ *Tears glistened in her eyes.*

glitter /ˈɡlɪtə(r)/ *noun* [U] **1** a shiny appearance consisting of many small flashes of light: *the glitter of jewellery* **2** the exciting quality that sth appears to have: *the glitter of a career in show business* **3** very small, shiny pieces of thin metal or paper, used as a decoration: *The children decorated their pictures with glitter.* ▶ **glitter** *verb* [I]

glittering /ˈɡlɪtərɪŋ/ *adj* **1** very impressive or successful: *a glittering event/career/performance* **2** shining brightly with many small flashes of light

glitz /ɡlɪts/ *noun* [U] the quality of appearing very attractive, exciting and impressive, in a way that is not always genuine ▶ **glitzy**: *a glitzy, Hollywood-style occasion*

gloat /ɡləʊt/ *verb* [I] gloat (about/over sth) to show that you are happy about your own success or sb else's failure, in an unpleasant way

global /ˈɡləʊbl/ *adj* **1** affecting the whole world: *the global effects of pollution* **2** considering or including all parts: *We must take a global view of the problem.* ▶ **globally** /-bəli/ *adv*

globalization (also -isation) /ˌɡləʊbəlaɪˈzeɪʃn/ *noun* [U] the fact that different cultures and economic systems around the world are becoming connected and similar to each other because of the influence of large companies and of improved communication

globalize (also -ise) /ˈɡləʊbəlaɪz/ *verb* [I,T] if sth, for example a company, **globalizes** or is **globalized**, it operates all around the world

the ˌglobal ˈvillage *noun* [sing] the world considered as a single community connected by computers, phones, the Internet, etc.

ˌglobal ˈwarming *noun* [sing] the increase in the temperature of the earth's atmosphere, caused by the increase of certain gases ➲ note at **environment** ➲ look at **greenhouse effect**

globe /gləʊb/ *noun* **1** [C] a round object with a map of the world on it **2 the globe** [sing] the earth: *to travel all over the globe* **3** [C] any object shaped like a ball

ˌglobe ˈartichoke = **artichoke**

globetrotter /ˈgləʊbtrɒtə(r)/ *noun* [C] (*informal*) a person who travels to many countries

globule /ˈglɒbjuːl/ *noun* [C] a very small drop of a liquid: *There were globules of fat in the soup.*

gloom /gluːm/ *noun* [U] **1** a feeling of being sad and without hope: *The news brought deep gloom to the village.* **2** the state of being almost totally dark

gloomy /ˈgluːmi/ *adj* (**gloomier**; **gloomiest**) **1** dark in a way that makes you feel sad: *This dark paint makes the room very gloomy.* **2** sad and without much hope: *Don't be so gloomy—cheer up!* ▸ **gloomily** *adv*: *He stared gloomily at the phone.* ▸ **gloominess** *noun* [U]

glorified /ˈglɔːrɪfaɪd/ *adj* [only *before* a noun] described in a way that makes sb/sth seem better, bigger, more important, etc. than he/she/it really is

glorify /ˈglɔːrɪfaɪ/ *verb* [T] (**glorifying**; **glorifies**; *pt*, *pp* **glorified**) to make sb/sth appear better or more important than he/she/it really is: *His biography does not attempt to glorify his early career.*

glorious /ˈglɔːriəs/ *adj* **1** having or deserving fame or success: *a glorious victory* **2** very beautiful or impressive: *a glorious day/view* ▸ **gloriously** *adv*

glory¹ /ˈglɔːri/ *noun* [U] **1** fame or honour that you get for achieving sth: *The winning team was welcomed home **in a blaze of glory**.* **2** great beauty

glory² /ˈglɔːri/ *verb* (**glorying**; **glories**; *pt*, *pp* **gloried**)
PHR V glory in sth to take (too much) pleasure or pride in sth: *He gloried in his sporting successes.*

gloss¹ /glɒs/ *noun* [U, sing] (a substance that gives sth) a smooth, shiny surface: *gloss paint* ◆ *gloss photographs* ➲ look at **matt**

gloss² /glɒs/ *verb*
PHR V gloss over sth to avoid talking about a problem, mistake, etc. in detail

glossary /ˈglɒsəri/ *noun* [C] (*pl* **glossaries**) a list of special or unusual words and their meanings, usually at the end of a text or book

glossy /ˈglɒsi/ *adj* (**glossier**; **glossiest**) smooth and shiny: *glossy hair* ◆ *a glossy magazine* (= printed on shiny paper)

⚷ **glove** /glʌv/ *noun* [C] a piece of clothing that covers your hand and has five separate parts for the fingers: *I need a new pair of gloves for the winter.* ◆ *leather/suede/woollen gloves* ◆ ***rubber gloves*** ➲ look at **mitten** ➲ picture at **bucket**

glow /gləʊ/ *verb* [I] **1** to produce light and/or heat without smoke or flames: *The cat's eyes glowed in the dark.* **2 glow (with sth)** to be warm or red because of excitement, exercise, etc: *to glow with health/enthusiasm/pride/pleasure* ▸ **glow** *noun* [sing]: *the glow of the sky at sunset*

glower /ˈglaʊə(r)/ *verb* [I] **glower (at sb/sth)** to look angrily (at sb/sth)

glowing /ˈgləʊɪŋ/ *adj* saying that sb/sth is very good: *His teacher wrote a glowing report about his work.* ▸ **glowingly** *adv*

glucose /ˈgluːkəʊs/ *noun* [U] a type of sugar that is found in fruit

⚷ **glue¹** /gluː/ *noun* [U] a thick sticky liquid that is used for joining things together: *You can make glue from flour and water.* ◆ *Stick the picture to the card with glue.*

⚷ **glue²** /gluː/ *verb* [T] (**gluing**) **glue A (to/onto B)**; **glue A and B (together)** to join a thing or things together with glue: *Do you think you can glue the handle back onto the teapot?*
IDM glued to sth (*informal*) giving all your attention to sth and not wanting to leave it: *He just sits there every evening glued to the TV.*

glum /glʌm/ *adj* sad and quiet ▸ **glumly** *adv*

glut /glʌt/ *noun* [C, usually sing] more of sth than is needed: *The glut of coffee has forced down the price.*

glutton /ˈglʌtn/ *noun* [C] **1** a person who eats too much **2** (*informal*) **a glutton for sth** a person who enjoys having or doing sth difficult, unpleasant, etc: *She's a glutton for punishment—she never stops working.*

gluttony /ˈglʌtəni/ *noun* [U] the habit of eating and drinking too much

GM /ˌdʒiː ˈem/ *abbr* = **genetically modified**

gm *abbr* = **gram**

GMT /ˌdʒiː em ˈtiː/ *abbr* **Greenwich Mean Time**; the exact time at Greenwich in England, used in the past for calculating time everywhere in the world ➲ look at **Coordinated Universal Time**

gnarled /nɑːld/ *adj* rough and having grown into a strange shape, because of old age or hard work: *a gnarled oak tree* ◆ *The old man had gnarled fingers.*

gnash /næʃ/ *verb*
IDM **gnash your teeth** to feel very angry and upset about sth

gnat /næt/ *noun* [C] a type of very small fly that bites **SYN** **midge**

gnaw /nɔː/ *verb* **1** [I,T] gnaw (away) (at/on) sth to bite sth many times: *The dog lay on the carpet gnawing away on its bone.* **2** [I] gnaw (away) at sb to make sb feel worried or frightened over a long period of time: *Fear of the future gnawed away at her all the time.*

G

gnome /nəʊm/ *noun* [C] (in children's stories, etc.) a little old man with a beard and a pointed hat who lives under the ground

GNP /ˌdʒiː en ˈpiː/ *abbr* **gross national product**; the total value of all the goods and services produced by a country in one year, including money received from foreign countries ➲ look at **GDP**

go[1] /gəʊ/ *verb* [I] (going; goes /gəʊz/; *pt* went /went/; *pp* gone /gɒn/) **1** to move or travel from one place to another: *She always goes home by bus.* ◆ *We're going to London tomorrow.* ◆ *We've still got 50 miles to go.* ◆ *How fast does this car go?* ◆ *Caroline threw the ball and the dog went running after it.*

> **GRAMMAR** **Been** is used as the past participle of **go** when somebody has travelled to a place and has returned. **Gone** means that somebody has travelled to a place but has not yet returned: *I've just been to Berlin. I got back this morning.* ◆ *John's gone to Peru. He'll be back in two weeks.*

2 to travel to a place to take part in an activity or do sth: *Are you going to Dave's party?* ◆ *Shall we go swimming this afternoon?* ◆ *to go for a swim/drive/drink/walk/meal* ◆ *We went on a school trip to a museum.* ◆ *They've gone on holiday.* ◆ *We went to watch the match.* ◆ *I'll go and make the tea.* ◆ *He went to the cinema yesterday.* **3** to leave a place: *I have to go now. It's nearly 4 o'clock.* ◆ *What time does the train go?* **4** to belong to or stay in an institution: *Which school does Ralph go to?* ◆ *to go to hospital/prison/college/university* **5** to lead to or reach a place or time: *Where does this road go to?* **6** to be put or to fit in a particular place: *Where does this vase go?* ◆ *My clothes won't all go in one suitcase.* **7** to happen in a particular way; to develop: *How's the new job going?* **8** to become; to reach a particular state: *Her hair is going grey.* ◆ *to go blind/deaf/bald/senile/mad* ◆ *The baby has gone to sleep.* **9** to stay in the state mentioned: *Many mistakes go unnoticed.* **10** to have certain words or a certain tune: *How does that song go?* **11** to make a sound: *The bell went early today.* ◆ *Cats go 'miaow'.* **12** (*spoken, informal*) used for saying what a person said: *I said, 'How are you, Jim?' and he goes, 'It's none of your business!'* **13** to start an activity: *Everybody ready to sing? Let's go!* **14** to work correctly: *This clock doesn't go.* ◆ *Is your car going at the moment?* **15** to be removed, lost, used, etc.; to disappear: *I like the furniture, but that carpet will have to go.* ◆ *About half my salary goes on rent.* ◆ *Has your headache gone yet?* ◆ *Jeans will never go out of fashion.* **16** to become worse or stop working correctly: *The brakes on the car have gone.* ◆ *His sight/voice/mind has gone.* **17** [only used in the continuous tenses] (*informal*) to be available: *Are there any jobs going in your department?* **18** (used about time) to pass: *The last hour went very slowly.* **19** (*informal*) used for saying that you do not want sb to do sth bad or stupid: *You can borrow my bike again, but don't go breaking it this time!* ◆ *I hope John doesn't go and tell everyone about our plan.*

IDM **as people, things, etc. go** compared to the average person or thing: *As Chinese restaurants go, it wasn't bad.*

be going to do sth 1 used for showing what you plan to do in the future: *We're going to sell our car.* **2** used for saying that you think sth will happen: *It's going to rain soon.* ◆ *Oh no! He's going to fall!*

go all out for sth; go all out to do sth to make a great effort to do sth

go for it (*informal*) to do sth after not being sure about it: *'Do you think we should buy it?' 'Yeah, let's go for it!'*

have a lot going for you to have many advantages

Here goes! said just before you start to do sth difficult or exciting

to go 1 that is/are left before sth ends: *How long (is there) to go before the end of the lesson?* **2** (*spoken*) that you can take away to eat or drink: *Two coffees to go, please.* ⓘ For other idioms containing **go**, look at the entries for the nouns, adjectives, etc. For example, **go astray** is at **astray**.

PHR V **go about** = **go round/around/about**

go about sth/doing sth to start trying to do sth difficult: *I wouldn't have any idea how to go about building a house.*

go about with sb = **go round/around/about with sb**

go after sb/sth to try to catch or get sb/sth: *I went after the boy who stole my wallet but he was too fast for me.*

go against sb to not be in sb's favour or not be to sb's advantage: *The referee's decision went against him.*

go against sb/sth to do sth that sb/sth says you should not do: *She went against her parents' wishes and married him.*

go ahead 1 to travel in front of other people in your group and arrive before them: *I'll go ahead and tell them you're coming.* **2** to take place after being delayed or in doubt: *Although several members were missing, the meeting went ahead without them.*

go ahead (with sth) to do sth after not being sure that it was possible: *We decided to go ahead with the match in spite of the heavy rain.* ◆ *'Can I take this chair?' 'Sure, go ahead.'*

go along to continue; to progress: *The course gets more difficult as you go along.*

go along with sb/sth to agree with sb/sth; to do what sb else has decided: *I'm happy to go along with whatever you suggest.*

go around = **go round/around/about**

go around with sb = **go round/around/about with sb**

go away 1 to disappear or leave: *I've got a head-*

ache that just won't go away. ◆ *Just go away and leave me alone!* **2** to leave home for a period of time, especially for a holiday: *We're going away to the coast this weekend.*
go back (to sth) 1 to return to a place: *It's a wonderful city and I'd like to go back there one day.* **2** to return to an earlier matter or situation: *Let's go back to the subject we were discussing a few minutes ago.* **3** to have its origins in an earlier period of time: *A lot of the buildings in the village go back to the 15th century.*
go back on sth to break a promise, an agreement, etc: *I promised to help them and I can't go back on my word.*
go back to sth/doing sth to start doing again sth that you had stopped doing: *When the children got a bit older she went back to full-time work.*
go by 1 (used about time) to pass: *As time went by, her confidence grew.* **2** to pass a place: *He stood at the window watching people go by.*
go by sth to use particular information, rules, etc. to help you decide your actions or opinions: *She'll be late if past experience **is anything to go by**.*
go down 1 (used about a ship, etc.) to sink **2** (used about the sun) to disappear from the sky **3** to become lower in price, level, etc.; to fall: *The number of people out of work went down last month.*
go down (with sb) [used with adverbs, especially 'well' or 'badly' or in questions beginning with 'how'] to be received in a particular way by sb: *The film went down well with the critics.*
go down with sth to catch an illness; to become ill with sth
go for sb to attack sb
go for sb/sth 1 to be true for a particular person or thing: *We've got financial problems but I suppose the same goes for a great many people.* **2** to choose sb/sth: *I think I'll go for the roast chicken.*
go in (used about the sun) to disappear behind a cloud
go in for sth to enter or take part in an exam or competition
go in for sth/doing sth to do or have sth as a hobby or interest
go into sth 1 to hit sth while travelling in/on a vehicle: *I couldn't stop in time and went into the back of the car in front.* **2** to start working in a certain type of job: *When she left school she went into nursing.* **3** to look at or describe sth in detail: *I haven't got time to go into all the details now.*
go off 1 to explode: *A bomb has gone off in the city centre.* **2** to make a sudden loud noise: *I woke up when my alarm clock went off.* **3** (used about lights, heating, etc.) to stop working: *There was a power cut and all the lights went off.* **4** (used about food and drink) to become too old to eat or drink; to go bad **5** (*BrE*) to become worse in quality: *I used to like that band but they've gone off recently.*
go off sb/sth to stop liking or being interested in sb/sth: *I went off spicy food after I was ill last year.*
go off (with sb) to leave (with sb): *I don't know where Sid is—he went off with John an hour ago.*
go off with sth to take sth that belongs to sb else
go on 1 (used about lights, heating, etc.) to start working: *I saw the lights go on in the house opposite.* **2** (used about time) to pass: *As time went on, she became more and more successful.* **3** [used especially in the continuous tenses] to happen or take place: *Can anybody tell me what's going on here?* **4** (used about a situation) to continue without changing: *This is a difficult period but it won't go on forever.* **5** to continue speaking after stopping for a moment: *Go on. What happened next?* **6** used for encouraging sb to do sth: *Oh go on, let me borrow your car. Just for tonight.*
go on sth to use sth as information so that you can understand a situation: *There were no witnesses to the crime, so the police had very little to go on.*
go on (about sb/sth) to talk about sb/sth for a long time in a boring or annoying way: *He went on and on about the people he works with.*
go/be on (at sb) (about sth) to keep complaining about sth: *She's always (going) on at me to mend the roof.*
go on (doing sth) to continue doing sth without stopping or changing: *We don't want to go on living here for the rest of our lives.*
go on (with sth) to continue doing sth, perhaps after a pause or break: *He ignored her and went on with his meal.*
go on to do sth to do sth after completing sth else
go out 1 to leave the place where you live or work for a short time, especially in order to do sth enjoyable: *Let's go out for a meal tonight* (= to a restaurant). ◆ *I'm just going out for a walk, I won't be long.* ◆ *He goes out with his friends a lot.* ➲ look at **socialize** **2** to stop being fashionable or in use: *That kind of music went out in the seventies.* **3** (used about the sea) to move away from the land: *Is the tide coming in or going out?* **SYN** **ebb** **4** to stop shining or burning: *Suddenly all the lights went out.*
go out (with sb); go out (together) to spend time with sb and have a romantic and/or sexual relationship with them: *Is Fiona going out with anyone?* ◆ *They went out together for five years before they got married.*
go over sth to look at, think about or discuss sth carefully from beginning to end: *Go over your work before you hand it in.*
go over to sth to change to a different side, system, habit, etc.
go round [used especially after 'enough'] to be shared among all the people: *In this area, there aren't enough jobs to go round.*
go round/around/about (used about a story, an illness, etc.) to pass from person to person: *There's a rumour going round that he's going to resign.* ◆ *There's a virus going round at work.*
go round (to ...) to visit sb's home, usually a short distance away: *I'm going round to Jo's for dinner tonight.*
go round/around/about with sb to spend time and go to places regularly with sb: *Her parents don't like the people she has started going round with.*
go through to be completed successfully: *The deal went through as agreed.*
go through sth 1 to look in or at sth carefully, especially in order to find sth: *I always start the day by going through my email.* ◆ *I went through all my pockets but I couldn't find my wallet.* **2** to look at,

G

think about or discuss sth carefully from beginning to end: *We'll start the lesson by going through your homework.* **3** to have an unpleasant experience: *I'd hate to go through such a terrible ordeal again.*

go through with sth to do sth unpleasant or difficult that you have decided, agreed or threatened to do: *Do you think she'll go through with her threat to leave him?*

go together [used about two or more things] **1** to belong to the same set or group **2** to look or taste good together

go towards sth to be used as part of the payment for sth: *The money I was given for my birthday went towards my new bike.*

go under 1 to sink below the surface of some water **2** (*informal*) (used about a company) to fail and close: *A lot of firms are going under in the recession.*

go up 1 to become higher in price, level, amount, etc: *The birth rate has gone up by 10%.* **SYN rise 2** to start burning suddenly and strongly: *The car crashed into a wall and went up in flames.* **3** to be built: *New buildings are going up all over town.*

go with sth 1 to be included with sth; to happen as a result of sth: *Pressure goes with the job.* **2** to look or taste good with sth else: *What colour carpet would go with the walls?* **SYN match**

go without (sth) to choose or be forced to not have sth: *They went without sleep night after night while the baby was ill.*

go² /gəʊ/ *noun* [C] (*pl* **goes** /gəʊz/) **1** a turn to play in a game, etc: *Whose go is it?* ◆ *Hurry up—it's your go.* **SYN turn 2** (*informal*) **a go (at sth/doing sth)** an occasion when you try to do sth: *Shall I* ***have a go*** *at fixing it for you?* ◆ *I've never played this game before, but I'll* ***give it a go.*** ◆ *Andrew passed his driving test* ***first go.*** **SYN attempt**

IDM be on the go (*informal*) to be very active or busy: *I've been on the go all day and now I'm exhausted.*

have a go at sb (*informal*) to criticize sb/sth: *Dad's always having a go at me about my hair.*

make a go of sth (*informal*) to be successful at sth: *The work is hard, but I'm determined to make a go of it.*

goad /gəʊd/ *verb* [T] **goad sb/sth (into sth/doing sth)** to cause sb to do sth by making them angry

ˈgo-ahead¹ *noun* [sing] **the go-ahead (for sth)** permission to do sth: *It looks like the council will* ***give*** *us* ***the go-ahead*** *for the new building.*

ˈgo-ahead² *adj* enthusiastic to try new ways of doing things

goal /gəʊl/ *noun* [C] **1** (in sports such as football, **hockey, rugby**) the area between two posts into which the ball must be kicked, hit, etc. for a point or points to be scored: *He crossed the ball in front of the goal.* ➲ picture on **page P4 2** the act of kicking or hitting the ball into the goal: *Everton won by three goals to two.* ◆ *to score a goal* **3** your purpose or aim: *This year I should* ***achieve*** *my* ***goal*** *of visiting all the capital cities of Europe.*

goalkeeper /ˈgəʊlkiːpə(r)/ (also *informal* **goalie** /ˈgəʊli/ *or* **keeper**) *noun* [C] (in sports such as football, etc.) the player who stands in front of the goal and tries to stop the other team from scoring: *The goalkeeper made a magnificent save.*

goalless /ˈgəʊlləs/ *adj* with no goals scored: *a goalless draw* ◆ *The match finished goalless.*

goalpost /ˈgəʊlpəʊst/ *noun* [C] (in sports such as football, etc.) one of the two posts that form the sides of a goal.

goats

sheep

goat /gəʊt/ *noun* [C] a small animal with horns which lives in mountain areas or is kept on farms for its milk and meat

goatee /gəʊˈtiː/ *noun* [C] a small pointed beard on a man's chin

gobble /ˈgɒbl/ *verb* [I,T] (*informal*) **gobble sth (up/down)** to eat quickly and noisily

gobbledegook (also **gobbledygook**) /ˈgɒbldiguːk/ *noun* [U] (*informal*) complicated language that is hard to understand

ˈgo-between *noun* [C] a person who takes messages between two people or groups

goblin /ˈgɒblɪn/ *noun* [C] (in stories) a small ugly creature who tricks people

gobsmacked /ˈgɒbsmækt/ *adj* (*informal*) so surprised that you are unable to speak

god /gɒd/ *noun* **1 God** [sing] [not used with *the*] the being or spirit in Christianity, Islam and Judaism who people say prayers to and who people believe created the universe: *Do you believe in God?* ◆ *Muslims worship God in a mosque.* **2** (*fem* **goddess** /ˈgɒdes/) [C] a being or spirit that people believe has power over a particular part of nature or that represents a particular quality: *Mars was the Roman god of war and Venus was the goddess of love.*

> **HELP** **God** is used in a number of expressions. Be careful. Some people think that it is wrong to use God's name in this way. *Oh my God!* expresses surprise or shock: *Oh my God! I've won the lottery!* We use *thank God* when we are happy and relieved about something: *Thank God you've*

arrived—I was beginning to think you'd had an accident. We use *for God's sake* when we are asking somebody to do something and want to sound more urgent, or when we are angry with somebody: *For God's sake, shut up!* **Heaven** or **goodness** are used in some of these expressions in order to avoid using the word **God**.

godchild /ˈgɒdtʃaɪld/ (also ˈgod-daughter /ˈgɒdˌdɔːtə(r)/, godson /ˈgɒdsʌn/) *noun* [C] a child who has a **godparent**

goddess /ˈgɒdes/ *noun* [C] a female god

godforsaken /ˈgɒdfəseɪkən/ *adj* [only *before* a noun] (used about a place) not interesting or attractive in any way

godparent /ˈgɒdpeərənt/ (also godfather /ˈgɒdfɑːðə(r)/, godmother /ˈgɒdmʌðə(r)/) *noun* [C] a person chosen by a child's family who promises to help the child and to make sure they are educated as a Christian

godsend /ˈgɒdsend/ *noun* [sing] something unexpected that is very useful because it comes just when it is needed

goggles /ˈgɒglz/ *noun* [pl] special glasses that you wear to protect your eyes from water, wind, dust, etc. ➲ look at **mask**

going[1] /ˈgəʊɪŋ/ *noun* **1** [sing] (*formal*) the act of leaving a place: *We were all saddened by his going.* SYN **departure** **2** [U] the rate or speed of travel, progress, etc: *Three children in four years? That's **not bad going**!* **3** [U] how difficult it is to make progress: *The path up the mountain was **rough going**.* ♦ *It'll be **hard going** if we need to finish this by Friday!*
IDM **get out, go, leave, etc. while the going is good** to leave a place or stop doing sth while it is still easy to do so

going[2] /ˈgəʊɪŋ/ *adj*
IDM **a going concern** a successful business
the going rate (for sth) the usual cost (of sth): *What's the going rate for an office cleaner?*

ˌgoing-ˈover *noun* [sing] (*informal*) **1** a very careful examination of sth: ***Give the car a good going-over** before deciding to buy it.* **2** a serious physical attack on sb

ˌgoings-ˈon *noun* [pl] (*informal*) unusual things that are happening

go-kart /ˈgəʊ kɑːt/ *noun* [C] a vehicle like a very small car with no roof or doors, used for racing ▶ **ˈgo-karting** *noun* [U] the sport or activity of riding a **go-kart**: *We **went go-karting** yesterday.*

gold /gəʊld/ *noun* **1** [U] (*symbol* Au) a rare and valuable yellow metal that is used for making coins, jewellery, etc: *Is your bracelet made of solid gold?* ♦ *22 carat gold* ♦ *a gold chain/watch* **2** [C] = **gold medal**
IDM **(as) good as gold** very well behaved
have a heart of gold ➲ **heart**
▶ **gold** *adj*: *The invitation was written in gold letters.*

golden /ˈgəʊldən/ *adj* **1** made of gold or having a bright yellow colour like gold: *a golden crown* ♦ *golden hair/sand* **2** best, most important, most liked, etc: *a golden opportunity* **3** celebrating the 50th anniversary of sth: *The couple celebrated their golden wedding last year.* ➲ look at **silver, diamond**
IDM **the golden rule (of sth)** the most important principle to follow when doing sth in order to be successful: *When you run a marathon, the golden rule is: don't start too fast.*

goldfish /ˈgəʊldfɪʃ/ *noun* [C] (*pl* **goldfish**) a small orange fish, often kept as a pet in a bowl ➲ note at **pet**

ˌgold ˈmedal (also gold) *noun* [C] the prize for first place in a sports competition: *How many gold medals did we win in the 2012 Olympics?* ➲ look at **silver medal, bronze medal**

ˌgold ˈmedallist *noun* [C] the winner of a **gold medal**

ˈgold mine *noun* [C] **1** a place where gold is taken from the ground **2** a gold mine (of sth) a place, person or thing that provides a lot of sth: *This website is a gold mine of information.*

golf /gɒlf/ *noun* [U] a game that is played outdoors on a **golf course** and in which you use a **golf club** to hit a small hard ball into a series of holes (usually 18): *to play a round of golf* ➲ picture on **page P5**

ˈgolf club *noun* [C] a long metal stick that is specially shaped at one end and used for hitting a ball when playing **golf** ➲ look at **bat, racket, stick** ➲ picture on **page P5**

ˈgolf course *noun* [C] a large area of land that is designed for playing **golf** on

golfer /ˈgɒlfə(r)/ *noun* [C] a person who plays **golf** ➲ picture on **page P5**

golly /ˈgɒli/ *exclam* (*old-fashioned, informal*) used for expressing surprise

gone[1] *past participle* of **go**[1]

gone[2] /gɒn/ *adj* [not before a noun] not present any longer; completely used or finished: *He stood at the door for a moment, and then he was gone.* ♦ *Can I have some more ice cream, please, or is it all gone?*

GRAMMAR *Gone* meaning 'disappeared' or 'finished' is used with the verb *be*, as in the examples above. When we are thinking about where something has disappeared to, we use *have*: *Nobody knows where John has gone.*

gone[3] /gɒn/ *prep* later than: *Hurry up! It's gone six already!*

gonna /ˈgənə/ (*informal*) a way of writing 'going to' to show that sb is speaking in an informal way: *'What's he gonna do now?' she asked.* ➲ note at **contraction**

EXAM TIP
Do not write 'gonna' yourself (unless you are copying somebody's accent) because it might be marked as a mistake.

goo /guː/ *noun* [U] (*informal*) a sticky wet substance SYN **slime**

good[1] /gʊd/ *adj* (better; best) **1** of a high quality or standard: *a good book/film/actor* ◆ *That's a really good idea!* ◆ *The hotel was quite good, but not fantastic.* **2** pleasant or enjoyable: *It's good to be home again.* ◆ *good news/weather* ◆ ***Have a good time*** *at the party!* **3** (used about a reason, etc.) acceptable and easy to understand: *a good excuse/explanation/reason* ◆ *She has good reason to be pleased—she's just been promoted.* **4** good at sth; good with sb/sth able to do sth or deal with sb/sth well: *Jane's really good at science subjects but she's* ***no good at*** *languages.* ◆ *He's very good with children.* ◆ *Are you any good at drawing?* **5** morally right or well behaved: *She was a very good person—she spent her whole life trying to help other people.* ◆ *Were the children good while we were out?* **6** good (to sb); good of sb (to do sth) kind; helpful: *They were good to me when I was ill.* ◆ *It was good of you to come.* **7** good (for sb/sth) having a positive effect on sb/sth's health or condition: *Green vegetables are very good for you.* ◆ *This cream is good for burns.* **8** good (for sb/sth) suitable or convenient: *This beach is very good for surfing.* ◆ *I think Paul would be a good person for the job.* ◆ *'When shall we meet?' 'Thursday would be a good day for me.'* **9** used when you are pleased about sth: *'Lisa's invited us to dinner next week.' 'Oh, good!'* **10** a good ... great in number, amount, etc: ***a good many/a good few*** *people* (= a lot of people) ◆ *a good distance* (= a long way) ◆ *a good* (= at least) *ten minutes/three miles* ◆ *Take a good* (= long and careful) *look at this photograph.* ◆ *What you need is a good rest.* ◆ *Give the fruit a good wash before you eat it.* **11** good (for sth) that can be used or can provide sth: *I've only got one good pair of shoes.* ◆ *This ticket's good for another three days.*
IDM **as good as** almost: *The project is as good as finished.* SYN **virtually**
good for you, him, her, etc. (*informal*) used to show that you are pleased that sb has done sth clever: *'I passed my driving test!' 'Well done! Good for you!'* ℹ For other idioms containing **good,** look at the entries for the nouns, adjectives, etc. For example, **in good faith** is at **faith.**

OTHER WORDS FOR

good

In informal English you can say **brilliant, fantastic** or **great** instead of 'very good'. **Excellent** and **wonderful** are more formal words: *an excellent example/opportunity*. We use particular words to describe particular things that are good: ***delicious/tasty*** *food* ◆ *a* ***talented*** *artist/player/writer* ◆ *an* ***outstanding*** *achievement/performance/piece of work.*

good[2] /gʊd/ *noun* [U] **1** behaviour that is morally right or acceptable: *the difference between good and evil* ◆ *I'm sure there's some good in everybody.* **2** something that will help sb/sth; advantage: *She did it* ***for the good of*** *her country.* ◆ *I know you don't want to go into hospital, but it's* ***for your own good.*** ◆ ***What's the good of*** *learning French if you have no chance of using it?* ➲ look at **goods**
IDM **be no good (doing sth)** to be of no use or value: *It's no good standing here in the cold. Let's go home.* ◆ *This sweater isn't any good. It's too small.*
do you good to help or be useful to you: *It'll do you good to meet some new people.*
for good for ever: *I hope they've gone for good this time!*
not much good (*informal*) bad or not useful: *'How was the party?' 'Not much good.'*
do sb a/the world of good ➲ **world**

goodbye /ˌgʊdˈbaɪ/ *exclam* said when sb goes or you go: *Goodbye! See you tomorrow!* ◆ *We said goodbye to Steven at the airport.*

MORE Other informal ways to say 'goodbye' are **bye** and **see you.**

▸ **goodbye** *noun* [C]: *We said our goodbyes and left.*

ˌGood ˈFriday *noun* [C] the Friday before Easter when Christians remember the death of Christ

ˌgood-ˈhumoured *adj* pleasant and friendly

goodie (*informal*) = **goody**

goodies /ˈgʊdiz/ *noun* [pl] (*informal*) exciting things that are provided or given: *There were lots of cakes and other goodies on the table.*

ˌgood-ˈlooking *adj* (usually used about a person) attractive OPP **ugly** ➲ note at **beautiful**

ˌgood-ˈnatured *adj* friendly or kind

goodness /ˈgʊdnəs/ *noun* [U] **1** the quality of being good SYN **virtue** **2** the part of sth that has a good effect, especially on sb/sth's health: *Wholemeal bread has more goodness in it than white bread.*

HELP **Goodness** is used in a number of expressions. We say *Goodness (me)!* to show that we are surprised. *Thank goodness* expresses happiness and relief: *Thank goodness it's stopped raining!* We say *For goodness' sake* when we are asking somebody to do something and want to sound more urgent or when we are angry with somebody: *For goodness' sake, hurry up!*

goodnight /ˌgʊdˈnaɪt/ *exclam* said late in the evening, before you go home or before you go to sleep: *Goodnight! See you in the morning!*

goods /gʊdz/ *noun* [pl] **1** things that are for sale: *a wide range of consumer goods* ◆ *electrical goods* ◆ *stolen goods* **2** (*BrE*) things that are carried by train or lorry: *a goods train* ◆ *a heavy goods vehicle* (= HGV) ➲ look at **freight**
IDM **come up with/deliver the goods** (*informal*) to do what you have promised to do

ˌgood ˈsense *noun* [U] good judgement or intelligence: *He had the good sense to refuse the offer.*

goodwill /ˌgʊdˈwɪl/ *noun* [U] friendly, helpful feelings towards other people: *The visit was designed to promote friendship and goodwill.*

goody (also **goodie**) /ˈgʊdi/ *noun* [C] (*pl* **goodies**) (*informal*) a good person in a film, book, etc. OPP **baddy**

ˈ**goody-goody** *noun* [C] (usually used in a critical way) a person who always behaves well to please people such as parents or teachers

gooey /ˈguːi/ *adj* (*informal*) soft and sticky: *gooey cakes*

goof /guːf/ *verb* [I] (*especially AmE informal*) to make a silly mistake

google /ˈguːgl/ *verb* [T,I] to type words into the **search engine** Google® in order to find information about sb/sth: *'Do you know who directed the last Harry Potter film?' 'No, I don't. Have you tried googling it?'*

goose /guːs/ *noun* [C] (*pl* geese /giːs/) a large bird with a long neck that lives on or near water. **Geese** are kept on farms for their meat and eggs. ➲ picture at **swan**

> **MORE** Goose is the general word for the bird and its meat. A male goose is called a **gander** and a young goose is a **gosling**.

gooseberry /ˈgʊzbəri/ *noun* [C] (*pl* gooseberries) a small green fruit that is covered in small hairs and has a sour taste ➲ picture on **page P14**
IDM **play gooseberry** (*BrE*) to be with two people who have a romantic relationship and who want to be alone together

ˈ**goose pimples** (also goosebumps /ˈguːsbʌmps/) *noun* [pl] small points or lumps which appear on your skin because you are cold or frightened

gore¹ /gɔː(r)/ *noun* [U] thick blood that comes from a wound ➲ *adjective* **gory**

gore² /gɔː(r)/ *verb* [T] (used about an animal) to wound a person or another animal with a horn, etc: *She was gored to death by a bull.*

gorge¹ /gɔːdʒ/ *noun* [C] a narrow valley with steep sides and a river running through it

gorge² /gɔːdʒ/ *verb* [I,T] **gorge (yourself) (on/with sth)** to eat a lot of food

gorgeous /ˈgɔːdʒəs/ *adj* (*informal*) extremely pleasant or attractive: *What gorgeous weather!* ◆ *You look gorgeous in that dress.* ➲ note at **beautiful** ▶ **gorgeously** *adv*

gorilla /gəˈrɪlə/ *noun* [C] a large black African **ape** (= an animal like a monkey without a tail) ➲ picture at **monkey**

gory /ˈgɔːri/ *adj* (**gorier**; **goriest**) full of violence and blood: *a gory film*

gosh /gɒʃ/ *exclam* (*old-fashioned, informal*) used for expressing surprise, shock, etc.

gosling /ˈgɒzlɪŋ/ *noun* [C] a young **goose** (= a bird like a large duck with a long neck)

gospel /ˈgɒspl/ *noun* **1 Gospel** [C] one of the four books in the Bible that describe the life of Jesus Christ and the ideas which he taught: *St Matthew's/Mark's/Luke's/John's Gospel* **2** (also ˌgospel ˈtruth) [U] the truth: *You can't take what he says as gospel.* **3** (also ˈgospel music) [U] a style of religious music developed by African Americans

gossip /ˈgɒsɪp/ *noun* **1** [U] informal talk about other people and their private lives, that is often unkind or not true: *Matt phoned me up to tell me the latest gossip.* **2** [C] an informal conversation about other people's private lives: *The two neighbours were having a good gossip over the fence.* **3** [C] a person who enjoys talking about other people's private lives ▶ **gossip** *verb* [I]

ˈ**gossip column** *noun* [C] a part of a newspaper or magazine where you can read about the private lives of famous people ➲ note at **newspaper**

got *past tense, past participle* of **get**

gotta /ˈgɒtə/ (*AmE informal*) a way of writing 'got to' or 'got a' to show that sb is speaking in an informal way: *I gotta go* (= I have got to go). ◆ *Gotta* (= have you got a) *minute?*

> **HELP** Do not write 'gotta' yourself (unless you are copying somebody's accent) because it might be marked as a mistake.

gotten (*AmE*) *past participle* of **get**

gouge /gaʊdʒ/ *verb* [T] to make a hole in a surface using a sharp object in a rough way
PHR V **gouge sth out** to remove or form sth by digging into a surface

gourmet /ˈgʊəmeɪ/ *noun* [C] a person who enjoys food and wine and knows a lot about it

⚷ **govern** /ˈgʌvn/ *verb* **1** [I,T] to rule or control the public affairs of a country, city, etc: *The UK is governed by the Prime Minister and the Cabinet.* **2** [T, often passive] to influence or control sb/sth: *Our decision will be governed by the amount of money we have to spend.*

⚷ **government** /ˈgʌvənmənt/ *noun* **1** *often* **the Government** [C, with sing or pl verb] the group of people who rule or control a country: *He has resigned from the Government.* ◆ *The foreign governments involved are meeting in Geneva.* ◆ *government policies/money/ministers/officials* ➲ note at **politics** ➲ look at **opposition**

> **GRAMMAR** **Government** is used with a singular verb when we are thinking of it as a unit: *The Government welcomes the proposal.* A plural verb is used when we are thinking about all the individual members of the government: *The Government are still discussing the problem.*

2 [U] the activity or method of controlling a country, city, etc: *weak/strong/corrupt government* ◆ *communist/democratic/totalitarian government* ◆ *Which party is* **in government**? ▶ **governmental** /ˌgʌvnˈmentl/ *adj*

⚷ **governor** /ˈgʌvənə(r)/ *noun* [C] **1** a person who rules or controls a region or state (especially in the US): *the Governor of New York State* **2** the leader or a member of a group of people who control an organization: *the governor of the Bank of England* ◆ *school governors*

G

gown /gaʊn/ *noun* [C] **1** a woman's long formal dress for a special occasion: *a ball gown* **2** a long loose piece of clothing that is worn by judges, doctors performing operations, etc.

GP /ˌdʒiː ˈpiː/ *abbr* **general practitioner**; a doctor who treats all types of illnesses and works in the community, not in a hospital

GPS /ˌdʒiː piː ˈes/ *abbr* **global positioning system**; a system by which signals are sent from **satellites** (= electronic devices that move round the earth) to a special device, used to show the position of a person or thing on the surface of the earth very accurately: *The drivers all have GPS in their vans.* ◆ *I got a GPS for my birthday.* ➲ look at **satnav**

G

grab /græb/ *verb* (**grabbing**; **grabbed**) **1** [I,T] **grab sth (from sb)** to take sth with a sudden movement: *Helen grabbed the toy car from her little brother.* ◆ ***Grab hold of** his arm in case he tries to run!* ◆ *Someone had arrived before us and grabbed all the seats.* ◆ *Don't grab—there's plenty for everybody.* ◆ (*figurative*) *He grabbed the opportunity of a free trip to America.* ◆ (*figurative*) *I'll try to grab the waitress's attention.* ➲ look at **snatch** **2** [I] **grab at/for sth** to try to get or catch sb/sth: *Jonathan grabbed at the ball but missed.* **3** [T] to get sth quickly because you are in a hurry: *I'll just grab something to eat and then we'll go.* ▶ **grab** /græb/ *noun* [C]: *She made a grab for the boy but she couldn't stop him falling.*

grace /greɪs/ *noun* [U] **1** the ability to move in a smooth and controlled way **2** extra time that is allowed for sth **3** a short prayer of thanks to God before or after a meal: *to say grace*

IDM **sb's fall from grace** ➲ **fall**[2]

have the grace to do sth to be polite enough to do sth

with good grace in a pleasant and reasonable way, without complaining: *He accepted the refusal with good grace.*

graceful /ˈgreɪsfl/ *adj* **1** moving in a smooth, attractive way or having a smooth, attractive form: *a graceful dancer* ◆ *graceful curves* **2** polite and kind in a difficult situation

HELP **Gracious** has a different meaning.

▶ **gracefully** /-fəli/ *adv*: *The goalkeeper rose gracefully to catch the ball.* ◆ *She accepted the decision gracefully* (= without showing her disappointment). ▶ **gracefulness** *noun* [U]

graceless /ˈgreɪsləs/ *adj* **1** not knowing how to be polite to people **2** (used about a movement or a shape) ugly and not elegant ▶ **gracelessly** *adv*

gracious /ˈgreɪʃəs/ *adj* **1** (used about a person or their behaviour) kind, polite and generous: *a gracious smile* **2** [only *before* a noun] showing the easy comfortable way of life that rich people can have: *gracious living*

HELP **Graceful** has a different meaning.

IDM **Good gracious!** used for expressing surprise: *Good gracious! Is that the time?*

▶ **graciously** *adv* ▶ **graciousness** *noun* [U]

grade[1] /greɪd/ *noun* [C] **1** the quality or the level of ability, importance, etc. that sb/sth has: *We need to use high-grade materials for this job.* **2** a mark that is given for school work, etc. or in an exam: *He got good/poor grades this term.* ◆ *Very few students pass the exam with a grade A.* **3** (*AmE*) a class or classes in a school in which all the children are of a similar age: *My daughter is in the third grade.*

IDM **make the grade** (*informal*) to reach the expected standard; to succeed: *She wanted to be a professional tennis player, but she didn't make the grade.*

grade[2] /greɪd/ *verb* [T, often passive] to put things or people into groups according to their quality, ability, size, etc: *I've graded their work from 1 to 10.* ◆ *Eggs are graded by size.*

gradient /ˈgreɪdiənt/ *noun* [C] the degree at which a road, etc. goes up or down: *The hill has a gradient of 1 in 4 (= 25%).* ◆ *a steep gradient*

gradual /ˈgrædʒuəl/ *adj* happening slowly or over a long period of time; not sudden: *There has been a gradual increase in the number of people without jobs.* OPP **sudden** ▶ **gradually** /-dʒuəli/ *adv*: *After the war life gradually got back to normal.*

graduate[1] /ˈgrædʒuət/ *noun* [C] **1** **a graduate (in sth)** a person who has a first degree from a university, etc: *a law graduate/a graduate in law* ◆ *a graduate of London University/a London University graduate* ➲ look at **postgraduate, undergraduate, bachelor, student** **2** (*AmE*) a person who has completed a course at a school, college, etc: *a high-school graduate*

graduate[2] /ˈgrædʒueɪt/ *verb* [I] **1** **graduate (in sth) (from sth)** to get a (first) degree from a university, etc: *She graduated in History from Cambridge University.* **2** (*AmE*) **graduate (from sth)** to complete a course at a school, college, etc. **3** **graduate (from sth) to sth** to change (from sth) to sth more difficult, important, expensive, etc: *She's graduated from being a classroom assistant to becoming a teacher.*

graduation /ˌgrædʒuˈeɪʃn/ *noun* **1** [U] the act of successfully completing a university degree or (in the US) studies at a high school **2** [sing] a ceremony in which certificates are given to people who have **graduated**

graffiti /grəˈfiːti/ *noun* [U,pl] pictures or writing on a wall, etc. in a public place: *The wall was covered in graffiti.*

graft /grɑːft/ *noun* [C] **1** a piece of a living plant that is fixed onto another plant so that it will grow **2** a piece of living skin, bone, etc. that is fixed onto a damaged part of a body in an operation: *a skin graft* ▶ **graft** *verb* [T] **graft sth onto sth**: *Skin from his leg was grafted onto the burnt area of his face.* ➲ look at **transplant**

grain /greɪn/ *noun* **1** [U,C] the seeds of food plants such as rice, etc.; a single seed of such a plant: *The US is a major producer of grain.* ◆ *grain exports* ◆ *a few grains of rice* **2** [C] **a grain of sth** a very small piece of sth: *a grain of sand/salt/sugar* ◆ (*figurative*)

graffiti

*There isn't **a grain of truth** in the rumour.* **3** [U] the natural pattern of lines that can be seen or felt in wood, rock, stone, etc: *to cut a piece of wood along/across the grain*

IDM (be/go) against the grain to be different from what is usual or natural

gram (also **gramme**) /græm/ *noun* [C] (*abbr* **g, gm**) a measure of weight. There are 1 000 grams in a kilogram. ℹ For more information about weights, look at the section on using numbers at the back of this dictionary.

grammar /ˈgræmə(r)/ *noun* **1** [U] the rules of a language, for example for forming words or joining words together in sentences: *Russian grammar can be difficult for foreign learners.* **2** [U] the way in which sb uses the rules of a language: *You have a good vocabulary, but your grammar needs improvement.* **3** [C] a book that describes and explains the rules of a language: *a French grammar*

ˈgrammar school *noun* [C] (in Britain, especially in the past) a type of secondary school for children from 11–18 who are good at academic subjects

grammatical /grəˈmætɪkl/ *adj* **1** connected with grammar: *the grammatical rules for forming plurals* **2** following the rules of a language: *The sentence is not grammatical.* ▶ **grammatically** /-kli/ *adv*

gramme = **gram**

gran /græn/ (*BrE informal*) = **grandmother**

grand¹ /grænd/ *adj* (**grander**; **grandest**) **1** impressive and large or important (also used in names): *Our house isn't very grand, but it has a big garden.* ◆ *She thinks she's very grand because she drives a Porsche.* ◆ *the Grand Canyon* ◆ *the Grand Hotel* ➲ *noun* **grandeur** **2** (*informal*) very good or pleasant: *You've done a grand job!* ▶ **grandly** *adv* ▶ **grandness** *noun* [U]

grand² /grænd/ *noun* [C] (*pl* **grand**) (*slang*) 1 000 pounds or dollars

grandad (also **granddad**) /ˈgrændæd/ (*BrE informal*) = **grandfather**

grandchild /ˈgræntʃaɪld/ *noun* [C] the daughter or son of your child

granddaughter /ˈgrændɔːtə(r)/ *noun* [C] a daughter of your child ➲ look at **grandson**

grandeur /ˈgrændʒə(r)/ *noun* [U] (*formal*) **1** the quality of being large and impressive: *the grandeur of the Swiss Alps* **2** the feeling of being important

grandfather /ˈgrænfɑːðə(r)/ *noun* [C] the father of your father or mother ➲ look at **grandmother**

> **MORE** In spoken or informal English more common words are **grandad** or **grandpa.**

ˈgrandfather clock *noun* [C] a clock that stands on the floor in a tall wooden case

grandiose /ˈgrændiəʊs/ *adj* bigger or more complicated than necessary

grandma /ˈgrænmɑː/ (*informal*) = **grandmother**

grandmother /ˈgrænmʌðə(r)/ *noun* [C] the mother of your father or mother ➲ look at **grandfather**

> **MORE** In spoken or informal English more common words are **gran, granny, grandma** or **nan.**

grandpa /ˈgrænpɑː/ (*informal*) = **grandfather**

grandparent /ˈgrænpeərənt/ *noun* [C] the mother or father of one of your parents: *This is a picture of two of my great-grandparents* (= the parents of one of my grandparents).

> **MORE** If you need to make it clear which grandfather or grandmother you are talking about, you can say: *My maternal/paternal grandfather/grandmother* or *my mother's/father's father/mother.*

ˌgrand piˈano *noun* [C] a large flat piano (with horizontal strings) ➲ picture at **piano**

ˌgrand ˈslam *noun* [C] winning all of a set of important matches or competitions in a particular sport, for example **tennis** or **rugby**

grandson /ˈgrænsʌn/ *noun* [C] a son of your child ➲ look at **granddaughter**

grandstand /ˈgrænstænd/ *noun* [C] rows of seats, usually covered by a roof, from which you get a good view of a sports competition, etc.

ˌgrand ˈtotal *noun* [C] the amount that you get when you add several totals together

granite /ˈgrænɪt/ *noun* [U] a hard grey rock

granny /ˈgræni/ *noun* (*pl* **grannies**) (*informal*) = **grandmother**

grant¹ /grɑːnt/ *verb* [T] **1** (*formal*) to (officially) give sb what they have asked for: *He was granted permission to leave early.* **2** to agree (that sth is true): *I grant you that New York is an interesting place but I still wouldn't want to live there.*

IDM take sb/sth for granted to be so used to sb/sth that you forget their true value and are not grateful: *In developed countries we take running water for granted.*

take it for granted to accept sth as being true: *She*

takes it for granted that I'll help her with her homework.

grant² /grɑːnt/ *noun* [C] money that is given by the government, etc. for a particular purpose: *a student grant* (= to help pay for university education) ◆ *to apply for/be awarded a grant*

granted /ˈgrɑːntɪd/ *adv* used for saying that sth is true, before you make a comment about it: *'You could have done more to help.' 'Granted, but you didn't ask me until yesterday.'*

granulated sugar /ˌgrænjuleɪtɪd ˈʃʊgə(r)/ *noun* [U] white sugar in the form of small grains

granule /ˈgrænjuːl/ *noun* [C] a small hard piece of sth: *instant coffee granules*

grape /greɪp/ *noun* [C] a small soft green or purple fruit that grows in bunches on a **vine** (= a climbing plant) and that is used for making wine: *a bunch of grapes* ➲ picture on **page P14**

MORE Green grapes are usually called 'white' and purple grapes are usually called 'black'. Grapes that have been dried are called **raisins**, **currants** or **sultanas**.

IDM sour grapes ➲ **sour**

grapefruit /ˈgreɪpfruːt/ *noun* [C] (*pl* **grapefruit** *or* **grapefruits**) a large round yellow fruit with a thick skin and a sour taste ➲ picture on **page P14**

the grapevine /ˈgreɪpvaɪn/ *noun* [sing] the way that news is passed from one person to another: *I heard* ***on/through the grapevine*** *that you're moving.*

graphs

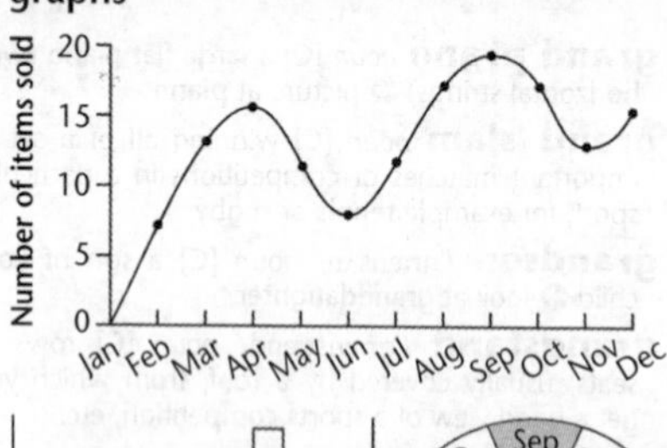

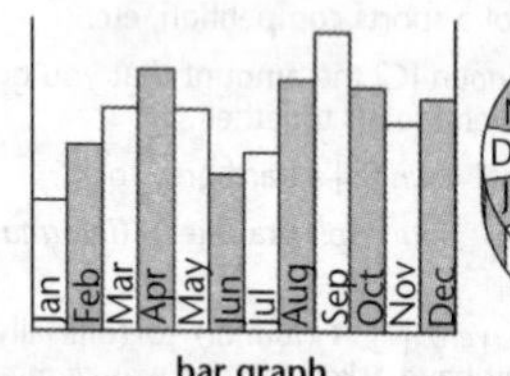

bar graph

pie chart

graph /grɑːf/ *noun* [C] a diagram in which a line or a curve shows the relationship between two quantities, measurements, etc: *a graph showing/to show the number of cars sold each month*

graphic /ˈgræfɪk/ *adj* **1** [only *before* a noun] connected with drawings, diagrams, etc: *graphic design* ◆ *a graphic artist* **2** (used about descriptions) clear and giving a lot of detail, especially about sth unpleasant: *She described the accident in graphic detail.* ▶ **graphically** /-kli/ *adv*

graphics /ˈgræfɪks/ *noun* [pl] designs, diagrams, etc. that are used especially in the production of books, magazines, etc: *computer graphics*

graphite /ˈgræfaɪt/ *noun* [U] a soft black mineral that is used in pencils

grapple /ˈgræpl/ *verb* [I] **1** grapple (with sb) to get hold of sb and fight with or try to control them **2** grapple (with sth/to do sth) to try to find a solution to a problem

grasp¹ /grɑːsp/ *verb* [T] **1** to take hold of sb/sth suddenly and firmly: *Lisa grasped the child firmly by the hand before crossing the road.* ◆ (*figurative*) *to grasp an opportunity/a chance* **2** to understand sth completely: *I don't think you've grasped how serious the situation is.*

PHR V grasp at sth to try to take hold of sth

grasp² /grɑːsp/ *noun* [sing,U] **1** a firm hold of sb/sth: *Get a good grasp on the rope before pulling yourself up.* ◆ *I grabbed the boy, but he slipped from my grasp.* **2** sb's understanding of a subject or of difficult facts: *He has* ***a good grasp of*** *English grammar.* **3** the ability to get or achieve sth: *Finally their dream was* ***within*** *their* ***grasp***.

grasping /ˈgrɑːspɪŋ/ *adj* wanting very much to have a lot more money, power, etc.

grass /grɑːs/ *noun* **1** [U] the common green plant with thin leaves which covers fields and parts of gardens. Cows, sheep, horses, etc. eat grass: *Don't walk on the grass.* ◆ *I must cut the grass at the weekend.* ◆ *a blade* (= one leaf) *of grass*

MORE An area of grass in a garden is called a **lawn**.

2 [C] one type of grass: *an arrangement of dried flowers and grasses*

grasshopper /ˈgrɑːshɒpə(r)/ *noun* [C] an insect that lives in long grass or trees and that can jump high in the air. **Grasshoppers** make sounds with their legs. ➲ picture on **page P13**

ˌgrass ˈroots *noun* [pl] the ordinary people in an organization, not those who make decisions: *the grass roots of the party*

grassy /ˈgrɑːsi/ *adj* (grassier; grassiest) covered with grass

grate¹ /greɪt/ *noun* [C] the metal frame that holds the wood, coal, etc. in a **fireplace** (= the open place in a room where you light a fire) ➲ picture at **fireplace**

grate² /greɪt/ *verb* **1** [T] to rub food into small pieces using a **grater**: *grated cheese/carrot* **2** [I] grate (on sb) to annoy sb **SYN irritate** **3** [I] grate (against/on sth) to make a sharp unpleasant sound (when two metal surfaces rub against each other)

grateful /ˈgreɪtfl/ *adj* grateful (to sb) (for sth); grateful (that ...) feeling or showing thanks (to sb): *We are very grateful to you for all the help you have given us.* ◆ *He was very grateful that you did as he* *asked.* OPP **ungrateful** ➲ *noun* **gratitude** ▶ **gratefully** /-fəli/ *adv*

grater /ˈgreɪtə(r)/ *noun* [C] a kitchen tool that is used for cutting food (for example cheese) into small pieces by rubbing it across its rough surface ➲ picture at **kitchen**

gratify /ˈgrætɪfaɪ/ *verb* [T] (**gratifying**; **gratifies**; *pt*, *pp* **gratified**) [usually passive] (*formal*) to give sb pleasure and satisfaction ▶ **gratifying** *adj*

grating /ˈgreɪtɪŋ/ *noun* [C] a frame made of metal bars that is fixed over a hole in the road, a window, etc.

gratitude /ˈgrætɪtjuːd/ *noun* [U] **gratitude (to sb) (for sth)** the feeling of being grateful or of wanting to give your thanks: *We should like to express our gratitude to David for all his help.* OPP **ingratitude**

gratuity /grəˈtjuːəti/ *noun* [C] (*pl* **gratuities**) (*formal*) money that you give to sb who has provided a service for you SYN **tip**

⚷ **grave**[1] /greɪv/ *noun* [C] the place where a dead body is buried: *I put some flowers on my grandmother's grave.* ➲ note at **funeral** ➲ look at **tomb**
IDM **have one foot in the grave** ➲ **foot**[1]

⚷ **grave**[2] /greɪv/ *adj* (*formal*) **1** bad or serious: *These events could have* ***grave consequences*** *for us all.* ◆ *The children were* ***in grave danger***. **2** (used about people) sad or serious: *He was looking extremely grave.* ➲ *noun* **gravity**. ➲ A much more common word for both senses is **serious**. ▶ **gravely** *adv*: *gravely ill*

gravel /ˈgrævl/ *noun* [U] very small stones that are used for making roads, paths, etc.

gravestone /ˈgreɪvstəʊn/ *noun* [C] a stone in the ground that shows the name, dates, etc. of the dead person who is buried there SYN **headstone**, **tombstone**

graveyard /ˈgreɪvjɑːd/ *noun* [C] an area of land, often next to a church, where dead people are buried ➲ look at **cemetery**, **churchyard**

gravity /ˈgrævəti/ *noun* [U] **1** the natural force that makes things fall to the ground when you drop them: *the force of gravity* **2** (*formal*) importance ➲ A more common word is **seriousness**. ➲ *adjective* **grave**

gravy /ˈgreɪvi/ *noun* [U] a thin sauce that is made from the juices that come out of meat while it is cooking ➲ look at **sauce**

gray (*especially AmE*) = **grey**

grayish (*especially AmE*) = **greyish**

graze[1] /greɪz/ *verb* **1** [I] (used about cows, sheep, etc.) to eat grass (that is growing in a field): *There were cows grazing by the river.* **2** [T] to break the surface of your skin by rubbing it against sth rough: *The child fell and grazed her knee.* **3** [T] to pass sth and touch it lightly: *The bullet grazed his shoulder.*

graze[2] /greɪz/ *noun* [C] a slight injury where the surface of the skin has been broken by being rubbed against sth rough

grease[1] /griːs/ *noun* [U] **1** any thick substance containing oil, especially one that is used to make machines run smoothly: *Her hands were covered with oil and grease.* **2** the fat that comes from cooking meat: *You'll need very hot water to get all the grease off those pans.*

grease[2] /griːs/ *verb* [T] to rub **grease** or fat on or in sth: *Grease the tin thoroughly to stop the cake from sticking.*

greasy /ˈgriːsi/ *adj* (**greasier**; **greasiest**) covered with or containing a lot of **grease**: *greasy skin/hair* ◆ *greasy food*

⚷ **great**[1] /greɪt/ *adj* (**greater**; **greatest**)
➤LARGE **1** large in amount, degree, size, etc.; a lot of: *We had great difficulty in solving the problem.* ◆ *The party was a great success.*
➤PLEASANT **2** (*informal*) good; wonderful: *We had* ***a great time*** *in Paris.* ◆ ***It's great*** *to see you again.* ➲ note at **good**, **nice**
➤IMPORTANT **3** particularly important; of unusually high quality: *Einstein was perhaps the greatest scientist of the century.* ➲ note at **big**
➤VERY **4** [only *before* a noun] (*informal*) (used to emphasize adjectives of size, quantity, etc.) very; very good: *There was a* ***great big*** *dog in the garden.* ◆ *They were great friends.*
➤FAMILY **5** **great-** used before a noun to show a family relationship

> **HELP** **Great-** can be added to words for family members to show another generation: *your* ***great-aunt*** (= the aunt of your mother or father) ◆ *your* ***great-grandchild*** (= the son or daughter of one of your grandchildren) ◆ *your* ***great-grandparents*** (= the parents of your grandparents) ◆ *your* ***great-great-grandfather*** (= the grandfather of one of your grandparents).

IDM **go to great lengths** to make more effort than usual in order to achieve sth: *I went to great lengths to find this book for you.*
a good/great deal ➲ **deal**[2]
make great strides to make very quick progress
▶ **greatness** *noun* [U]

great[2] /greɪt/ *noun* [C, usually pl] (*informal*) a person or thing of special ability or importance: *That film is one of the all-time greats.*

Great ˈBritain (also **Britain**) *noun* [U] (*abbr* **GB**) England, Wales and Scotland ➲ note at **United Kingdom**

⚷ **greatly** /ˈgreɪtli/ *adv* very much

greed /griːd/ *noun* [U] **greed (for sth)** a strong desire for more food, money, power, etc. than you really need

greedy /ˈgriːdi/ *adj* (**greedier**; **greediest**) **greedy (for sth)** wanting more food, money, power, etc. than you really need: *Don't be so greedy—you've had three pieces of cake already.* ▶ **greedily** *adv* ▶ **greediness** *noun* [U]

⚷ **green**[1] /griːn/ *adj* (**greener**; **greenest**) **1** having the colour of grass or leaves: *dark/light/pale green* **2** connected with protecting the environment or the natural world: *the Green party* ◆ *green products*

(= that do not damage the environment) **3** (*informal*) with little experience of life or a particular job: *I'm not so green as to believe that!* **4** a strange, pale colour (because you feel sick): *At the sight of all the blood he* ***turned green*** *and fainted.*

IDM give sb/get the green light (*informal*) to give sb/get permission to do sth

green with envy wanting to have what sb else has got: *He was green with envy when he saw his neighbour's new car.* **SYN jealous**

have green fingers; (*AmE* **have a green thumb**) (*informal*) to have the ability to make plants grow well

G

green² /griːn/ *noun*

➤COLOUR **1** [C,U] the colour of grass or leaves: *They were dressed in green.* ♦ *The room was decorated in greens and blues.*

➤VEGETABLES **2 greens** [pl] green vegetables that are usually eaten cooked: *For a healthy diet you should eat more cabbage, spinach, broccoli and other greens.*

➤AREA OF GRASS **3** [C] (*BrE*) an area of grass in the centre of a village: *the village green* ➲ picture on **page P11** **4** [C] a flat area of very short grass used in games such as **golf**: *the green at the 18th hole*

➤POLITICS **5 Green** [C] a member of a green political party

ˌgreen ˈbelt *noun* [C,U] (*BrE*) an area of open land around a city where building is not allowed

ˈgreen card *noun* [C] a document that allows sb from another country to live and work legally in the US

greenery /ˈgriːnəri/ *noun* [U] attractive green leaves and plants

greengrocer /ˈgriːngrəʊsə(r)/ *noun* (*BrE*) **1** [C] a person who has a shop that sells fruit and vegetables ➲ look at **grocer** **2 the greengrocer's** [sing] a shop that sells fruit and vegetables

greenhouse /ˈgriːnhaʊs/ *noun* [C] a small building made of glass in which plants are grown ➲ look at **glasshouse, hothouse**

the ˈgreenhouse effect *noun* [sing] the warming of the earth's atmosphere as a result of harmful gases, etc. in the air ➲ look at **global warming**

greenish /ˈgriːnɪʃ/ *adj* slightly green

greet /griːt/ *verb* [T] **1 greet sb (with sth)** to welcome sb when you meet them; to say hello to sb: *He greeted me with a friendly smile.* ♦ (*figurative*) *As we entered the house we were greeted by the smell of cooking.* **2** [usually passive] **greet sb/sth (as/with sth)** to react to sb or receive sth in a particular way: *The news was greeted with a loud cheer.*

greeting /ˈgriːtɪŋ/ *noun* [C] the first words you say when you meet sb or write to them: *'Hello' and 'Hi' are informal greetings.*

gregarious /grɪˈgeəriəs/ *adj* liking to be with other people **SYN sociable**

grenade /grəˈneɪd/ *noun* [C] a small bomb that is thrown by hand or fired from a gun

grew *past tense of* **grow**

grey¹ (*especially AmE* **gray**) /greɪ/ *adj* (**greyer**; **greyest**) **1** having the colour between black and white: *dark/light/pale grey* ♦ *He was wearing a grey suit.* **2** having grey hair: *He's* ***going grey.*** **3** (used about the weather) full of cloud; not bright: *grey skies* ♦ *a grey day* **4** boring and sad; without interest or variety: *Life seems grey and pointless without him.*

grey² (*especially AmE* **gray**) /greɪ/ *noun* [C,U] the colour between black and white: *dressed in grey*

greyhound /ˈgreɪhaʊnd/ *noun* [C] a large thin dog that can run very fast and that is used for racing: *greyhound racing*

greyish (*especially AmE* **grayish**) /ˈgreɪɪʃ/ *adj* slightly grey

grid /grɪd/ *noun* [C] **1** a pattern of straight lines that cross each other to form squares: *She drew a grid to show how the students had scored in each part of the test.* **2** a frame of parallel metal or wooden bars, usually covering a hole in sth **3** a system of squares that are drawn on a map so that the position of any place can be described or found: *a grid reference* **4** the system of electricity wires, etc. taking power to all parts of a country: *the National Grid*

gridlock /ˈgrɪdlɒk/ *noun* [U,C] a situation in which there are so many cars in the streets of a town that the traffic cannot move at all ▶ **gridlocked** *adj*

grief /griːf/ *noun* [U] great sadness (especially because of the death of sb you love)

IDM Good grief! (*spoken*) used for expressing surprise or shock: *Good grief! Whatever happened to you?*

grievance /ˈgriːvəns/ *noun* [C] **a grievance (against sb)** something that you think is unfair and that you want to complain or protest about

grieve /griːv/ *verb* **1** [I,T] **grieve (for sb)** to feel great sadness (especially about the death of sb you love) **2** [T] (*formal*) to cause unhappiness

grill¹ /grɪl/ *noun* [C] **1** (*BrE*) a part of a cooker where the food is cooked by heat from above **2** a metal frame that you put food on to cook over an open fire **3 = grille**

grill² /grɪl/ *verb* [T] **1** (*especially AmE* **broil**) to cook under or on a **grill**: *grilled steak/chicken/fish* ➲ note at **cook** **2** (*informal*) **grill sb (about sth)** to question sb for a long time

grille (also **grill**) /grɪl/ *noun* [C] a metal frame that is placed over a window, a piece of machinery, etc.

grim /grɪm/ *adj* (**grimmer**; **grimmest**) **1** (used about a person) very serious; not smiling **2** (used about a situation, news, etc.) unpleasant or worrying: *The news is grim, I'm afraid.* **3** (used about a place) unpleasant to look at; not attractive: *a grim block of flats* **4** [not before a noun] (*BrE informal*) ill: *I was feeling grim yesterday, but I managed to get to work.* ▶ **grimly** *adv*

grimace /ˈgrɪməs; grɪˈmeɪs/ *noun* [C] an ugly expression on your face that shows that you are angry, disgusted or that sth is hurting you: *a grimace of pain* ▶ **grimace** *verb* [I]: *She grimaced with pain.*

grime /graɪm/ *noun* [U] a thick layer of dirt

grimy /ˈgraɪmi/ *adj* (**grimier**; **grimiest**) very dirty ➲ look at **filthy**

grin /grɪn/ *verb* [I] (**grinning**; **grinned**) **grin (at sb)** to give a wide smile (so that you show your teeth): *She grinned at me as she came into the room.* ▶ **grin** *noun* [C]

grind¹ /graɪnd/ *verb* [T] (*pt, pp* **ground** /graʊnd/) **1 grind sth (down/up)**; **grind sth (to/into sth)** to press and break sth into very small pieces or into a powder between two hard surfaces or in a special machine: *Wheat is ground into flour.* ◆ *ground pepper* **2** to make sth sharp or smooth by rubbing it on a rough hard surface: *to grind a knife on a stone* **3 grind sth in/into sth** to press or rub sth into a surface: *He ground his cigarette into the ashtray.* **4** to rub sth together or make sth rub together, often producing an unpleasant noise: *Some people **grind** their **teeth** while they're asleep.*

IDM grind to a halt/standstill to go slower and then stop

grind² /graɪnd/ *noun* [sing] (*informal*) an activity that is tiring and boring and that takes a lot of time: *the **daily grind** of working life*

grinder /ˈgraɪndə(r)/ *noun* [C] a machine for **grinding**: *a coffee grinder*

grip¹ /grɪp/ *noun* **1** [sing] **a grip (on sb/sth)** a firm hold (on sb/sth): *I relaxed my grip and he ran away.* ◆ *The climber slipped and lost her grip.* ◆ (*figurative*) *The teacher kept a firm grip on the class.* **2** [sing] **a grip (on sth)** an understanding of sth **3** [C] the person whose job it is to move the cameras while a film is being made

IDM come/get to grips with sth to start to understand and deal with a problem

get/keep/take a grip/hold (on yourself) (*informal*) to try to behave in a calmer or more sensible way; to control yourself

in the grip of sth experiencing sth unpleasant that cannot be stopped: *a country in the grip of recession*

grip² /grɪp/ *verb* (**gripping**; **gripped**) **1** [I,T] to hold sb/sth tightly: *She gripped my arm in fear.* **2** [T] to interest sb very much; to hold sb's attention: *The book grips you from start to finish.* ➲ *adjective* **gripping**

gripe /graɪp/ *noun* [C] (*informal*) a statement complaining about sth **SYN complaint** ▶ **gripe** *verb* [I]

gripping /ˈgrɪpɪŋ/ *adj* exciting; holding your attention: *a gripping film/book*

grisly /ˈgrɪzli/ *adj* (**grislier**; **grisliest**) extremely unpleasant and frightening and usually connected with death and violence: *a grisly crime/death/murder* ➲ look at **gruesome**

gristle /ˈgrɪsl/ *noun* [U] a hard substance in a piece of meat that is unpleasant to eat: *a lump of gristle* ▶ **gristly** /ˈgrɪstli/ *adj*

grit¹ /grɪt/ *noun* [U] **1** small pieces of stone or sand: *I've got a piece of grit in my shoe.* **2** (*informal*) courage; determination that makes it possible for sb to continue doing sth difficult or unpleasant

grit² /grɪt/ *verb* [T] (**gritting**; **gritted**) to spread **grit** or salt on a road that is covered with ice

IDM grit your teeth 1 to bite your teeth tightly together: *She gritted her teeth against the pain as the doctor examined her injured foot.* **2** to use your courage or determination in a difficult situation

groan /grəʊn/ *verb* [I] **groan (at/with sth)** to make a deep sad sound because you are in pain, or to show that you are unhappy about sth: *He groaned with pain.* ◆ *They were all **moaning and groaning** (= complaining) about the amount of work they had to do.* ▶ **groan** *noun* [C]

grocer /ˈgrəʊsə(r)/ *noun* **1** [C] a person who has a shop that sells food and other things for the home ➲ look at **greengrocer** **2 the grocer's** [sing] a shop that sells food and other things for the home

G

⚷ **groceries** /ˈgrəʊsəriz/ *noun* [pl] food and other things for the home that you buy regularly: *Can you help me unload the groceries from the car, please?*

groggy /ˈgrɒgi/ *adj* (**groggier**; **groggiest**) (*informal*) weak and unable to walk steadily because you feel ill, have not had enough sleep, etc: *She felt a bit groggy when she came round from the operation.*

groin /grɔɪn/ *noun* [C] the front part of your body where it joins your legs

groom¹ /gruːm/ *verb* [T] **1** to clean or look after an animal by brushing, etc: *to groom a horse/dog/cat* **2** [usually passive] **groom sb (for/as sth)** to choose and prepare sb for a particular career or job

groom² /gruːm/ *noun* [C] **1** a person who looks after horses, especially by cleaning and brushing them **2** = **bridegroom**

groove /gruːv/ *noun* [C] a long deep line that is cut in the surface of sth

grope /grəʊp/ *verb* **1** [I] **grope (about/around) (for sth)** to search for sth or find your way using your hands because you cannot see: *He groped around for the light switch.* **2** [T] (*informal*) to touch sb sexually, especially when they do not want you to

gross /grəʊs/ *adj* **1** [only *before* a noun] being the total amount before anything is taken away: *gross income* (= before tax, etc. is taken away) ➲ look at **net** **2** [only *before* a noun] (*formal*) very great or serious: *gross indecency/negligence/misconduct* **3** very rude and unpleasant **4** very fat and ugly: *She's not just fat, she's positively gross!* **5** (*informal*) very unpleasant **SYN disgusting**

grossly /ˈgrəʊsli/ *adv* very: *grossly unfair*

grotesque /grəʊˈtesk/ *adj* strange or ugly in a way that is not natural

grotty /ˈgrɒti/ *adj* (**grottier**; **grottiest**) (*BrE informal*) unpleasant; of poor quality: *She lives in a grotty flat.*

⚷ **ground¹** /graʊnd/ *noun*

➤ SURFACE OF EARTH **1 the ground** [sing] the solid surface of the earth: *We sat on the ground to eat our picnic.* ◆ *He slipped off the ladder and fell to the ground.*

➤ SOIL **2** [U] an area or type of soil: *solid/marshy/stony ground*

➤ AREA OF LAND **3** [C] a piece of land that is used for a

particular purpose: *a sports ground* ◆ *a playground* ℹ An area of land that is not being used is called *waste ground*.
➤GARDENS **4 grounds** [pl] land or gardens surrounding a large building: *the grounds of the palace*
➤AREA OF INTEREST **5** [U] an area of interest, study, discussion, etc: *The lecture went over **the same old ground** /covered a lot of **new ground**.* ◆ *to be on dangerous ground* (= saying sth likely to cause anger)
➤REASON **6** [C, usually pl] **grounds (for sth/doing sth)** a reason for sth: *She retired **on medical grounds**.* ◆ *grounds for divorce*
➤ELECTRICAL WIRE **7** (*AmE*) = **earth**[1](4)
IDM **above/below ground** above/below the surface of the earth
break fresh/new ground to make a discovery or introduce a new method or activity
gain ground ➲ **gain**[1]
get (sth) off the ground (used about a business, project, etc.) to make a successful start
give/lose ground (to sb/sth) to allow sb to have an advantage; to lose an advantage for yourself: *They are not prepared to give ground on tax cuts.* ◆ *The Conservatives lost a lot of ground to the Liberal Democrats at the election.*
hold/keep/stand your ground to refuse to change your opinion or to be influenced by pressure from other people
thin on the ground ➲ **thin**[1]

OTHER WORDS FOR
ground
The **Earth** is the name of the planet where we live. **Land** is the opposite of sea: *The sailors sighted land.* ◆ *The astronauts returned to Earth.* **Land** is also something that you can buy or sell: *The price of land in Tokyo is extremely high.* When you are outside, the surface under your feet is called **the ground**. When you are inside it is called **the floor**: *Don't sit on the ground. You'll get wet.* ◆ *Don't sit on the floor. I'll get another chair.* Plants grow in **earth** or **soil**.

ground[2] /graʊnd/ *verb* [T] **1** [usually passive] to force an aircraft, etc. to stay on the ground: *to be grounded by fog* **2** [usually passive] to punish a child by not allowing them to go out with friends for a period of time: *Emma was grounded for a whole week after she stayed out late without asking permission.* **3** (*AmE*) = **earth**[2]

ground[3] *past tense, past participle of* **grind**[1]

ˌground ˈbeef (*AmE*) = **mince**

ˈground crew (also **ˈground staff**) *noun* [C,U] the people in an airport whose job it is to look after an aircraft while it is on the ground

ˌground ˈfloor (*AmE* ˌ**first** ˈ**floor**) *noun* [C] the floor of a building that is at ground level: *a ground-floor flat* ➲ note at **floor**

grounding /ˈgraʊndɪŋ/ *noun* [sing] **a grounding (in sth)** the teaching of the basic facts or principles of a subject: *This book provides a good grounding in grammar.*

groundless /ˈgraʊndləs/ *adj* having no reason or cause: *Our fears were groundless.*

groundnut /ˈgraʊndnʌt/ = **peanut**

ˈground staff = **ground crew**

groundwork /ˈgraʊndwɜːk/ *noun* [U] work that is done in preparation for further work or study

group[1] /gruːp/ *noun* [C] **1** [with sing or pl verb] a number of people or things that are together in the same place or that are connected in some way: *a group of girls/trees/houses* ◆ *Students were standing **in groups** waiting for their exam results.* ◆ *He is in the 40–50 **age group**.* ◆ *Many young people dress as they do because of pressure from their peer group* (= the people of the same age). ◆ *people of many different social groups* ◆ *a pressure group* (= a political group that tries to influence the government) ◆ *Which **blood group*** (for example A, O, etc.) *do you belong to?* ◆ *Divide the class into groups.*

GRAMMAR In the singular, **group** can be used with a singular or plural verb: *Our discussion group **is/are** meeting this week.* But if you are thinking of the members of the group as individuals who have come together, a plural verb is more common: *A group of us **are** planning to meet for lunch.*

2 (used in business) a number of companies that are owned by the same person or organization: *a newspaper group* **3** (*old-fashioned*) a number of people who play music together: *a pop group* **SYN band** ➲ note at **pop**

group[2] /gruːp/ *verb* [I,T] **group (sb/sth) (around/round sb/sth); group (sb/sth) (together)** to put sb/sth or to form into one or more groups: *Group these words according to their meaning.*

grove /grəʊv/ *noun* [C] a small group of trees, especially of one particular type: *an olive grove*

grovel /ˈgrɒvl/ *verb* [I] (**grovelling; grovelled**, (*AmE*) **groveling; groveled**) **1 grovel (to sb) (for sth)** to try too hard to please sb who is more important than you or who can give you sth that you want: *to grovel for forgiveness* **2 grovel (around/about) (for sth)** to move around on your hands and knees (usually when you are looking for sth) ▶ **grovelling** *adj*: *I wrote a grovelling letter of apology.*

grow /grəʊ/ *verb* (*pt* **grew** /gruː/; *pp* **grown** /grəʊn/) **1** [I] **grow (in sth)** to increase in size or number; to develop into an adult form: *a growing child* ◆ *She's growing in confidence all the time.* ◆ *You must invest if you want your business to grow.* ◆ *Plants grow from seeds.* ◆ *Kittens soon grow into cats.* **2** [I,T] (used about plants) to exist and develop in a particular place; to make plants grow by giving them water, etc: *Palm trees don't grow in cold climates.* ◆ *We grow vegetables in our garden.* **3** [T] to allow your hair or nails to grow: *Claire's growing her hair long.* ◆ *to grow a beard/moustache* **4** [I] to gradually change from one state to another; to become: *It began to grow dark.* ◆ *to grow older/wiser/taller/*

bigger • *The teacher was growing more and more impatient.* ➲ A less formal word is **get**.

PHR V grow into sth 1 to gradually develop into a particular type of person: *She has grown into a very elegant woman.* **2** to become big enough to fit into clothes, etc: *The coat is too big for him, but he will soon grow into it.*

grow on sb to become more pleasing: *I didn't like ginger at first, but it's a taste that grows on you.*

grow out of sth to become too big or too old for sth: *She's grown out of that dress I made her last year.*

grow (sth) out (used about the style in which you have your hair cut) to disappear gradually as your hair grows; to allow your hair to grow in order to change the style

grow up 1 to develop into an adult: *What do you want to be when you grow up?* (= what job do you want to do later?) • *She grew up* (= lived when she was a child) *in Spain.* **2** (used about a feeling, etc.) to develop or become strong: *A close friendship has grown up between them.*

grower /ˈɡrəʊə(r)/ *noun* [C] a person or company that grows plants, fruit or vegetables to sell: *a tobacco grower*

growing /ˈɡrəʊɪŋ/ *adj* [only *before* a noun] increasing: *A growing number of people are becoming vegetarian these days.*

growl /ɡraʊl/ *verb* [I] growl (at sb/sth) (used about dogs and other animals) to make a low noise in the throat to show anger or to give a warning ▸ **growl** *noun* [C]

grown[1] *past participle of* **grow**

grown[2] /ɡrəʊn/ *adj* [only *before* a noun] physically an adult: *a fully-grown elephant*

ˌgrown-ˈup[1] *adj* physically or mentally adult: *She's very grown-up for her age.* **SYN mature**

ˈgrown-up[2] *noun* [C] (used by children) an adult person **SYN adult**

⚷ **growth** /ɡrəʊθ/ *noun* **1** [U] the process of growing and developing: *A good diet is very important for children's growth.* • *a growth industry* (= one that is growing) **2** [U, sing] an increase (in sth): *population growth* **3** [C] a lump caused by a disease that grows in a person's or an animal's body: *a cancerous growth* **4** [U] something that has grown: *several days' growth of beard*

grub /ɡrʌb/ *noun* **1** [C] the first form that an insect takes when it comes out of the egg. **Grubs** are short, fat and white. **2** [U] (*informal*) food

grubby /ˈɡrʌbi/ *adj* (**grubbier**; **grubbiest**) (*informal*) dirty after being used and not washed

grudge[1] /ɡrʌdʒ/ *noun* [C] a grudge (against sb) unfriendly feelings towards sb, because you are angry about what has happened in the past: *to* ***bear a grudge*** *against somebody*

grudge[2] /ɡrʌdʒ/ *verb* [T] grudge sb sth; grudge doing sth to be unhappy that sb has sth or that you have to do sth: *I don't grudge him his success—he deserves it.* • *I grudge having to pay so much tax.* ➲ look at **begrudge**

grudging /ˈɡrʌdʒɪŋ/ *adj* given or done although you do not want to: *grudging thanks* ▸ **grudgingly** *adv*

gruelling (*AmE* **grueling**) /ˈɡruːəlɪŋ/ *adj* very tiring and long: *a gruelling nine-hour march*

gruesome /ˈɡruːsəm/ *adj* very unpleasant or shocking, and usually connected with death or injury ➲ look at **grisly**

gruff /ɡrʌf/ *adj* (used about a person or a voice) rough and unfriendly ▸ **gruffly** *adv*

grumble /ˈɡrʌmbl/ *verb* [I] to complain in a bad-tempered way; to keep saying that you do not like sth: *The students were always grumbling about the standard of the food.* ➲ look at **complain**, **moan** ▸ **grumble** *noun* [C]

grumpy /ˈɡrʌmpi/ *adj* (**grumpier**; **grumpiest**) (*informal*) bad-tempered ▸ **grumpily** *adv*

grunt /ɡrʌnt/ *verb* [I,T] to make a short low sound in the throat. People **grunt** when they do not like sth or are not interested and do not want to talk: *I tried to find out her opinion but she just grunted.* ▸ **grunt** *noun* [C]

⚷ **guarantee**[1] /ˌɡærənˈtiː/ *noun* [C] **1** a firm promise that sth will be done or that sth will happen: *The refugees are demanding guarantees about their safety before they return home.* **2** a written promise by a company that it will repair or replace a product if it breaks in a certain period of time: *The watch comes with a year's guarantee.* • *Is the computer still* ***under guarantee***? ➲ look at **warranty 3** something that makes sth else certain to happen: *If you don't have a reservation there's no guarantee that you'll get a seat on the train.*

⚷ **guarantee**[2] /ˌɡærənˈtiː/ *verb* [T] **1** to promise that sth will be done or will happen: *They have guaranteed delivery within one week.* **2** to give a written promise to repair or replace a product if anything is wrong with it: *This washing machine is guaranteed for three years.* **3** to make sth certain to happen: *Tonight's win guarantees the team a place in the final.*

⚷ **guard**[1] /ɡɑːd/ *noun*

➤PROTECTING **1** [C] a person who protects a place or people, or who stops prisoners from escaping: *a security guard* ➲ look at **warder**, **bodyguard 2** [U] the state of being ready to prevent attack or danger: *Soldiers* ***keep guard*** *at the gate.* • *Who is* ***on guard***? • *The prisoner arrived* ***under*** *armed* ***guard***. • *a guard dog*

➤SOLDIERS **3** [sing, with sing or pl verb] a group of soldiers, police officers, etc. who protect sb/sth: *The president always travels with an armed guard.*

➤COVER **4** [C] [in compounds] something that covers sth dangerous or protects sth: *a fireguard* • *a mudguard* (= over the wheel of a bicycle)

➤ON TRAIN **5** (*AmE* **conductor**) [C] a person who is in charge of a train but does not drive it

➤IN SPORT **6** [U] a position that you take to defend yourself, especially in sports such as **boxing**: (*figurative*) *She doesn't trust journalists, and never* ***lets*** *her* ***guard drop*** *during interviews.*

IDM on/off (your) guard ready/not ready for an attack, surprise, mistake, etc: *The question caught me off (my) guard and I didn't know what to say.*

guard² /gɑːd/ *verb* [T] **1** to keep sb/sth safe from other people; protect: *The building was guarded by men with dogs.* ◆ (*figurative*) *a closely guarded secret* **2** to be ready to stop prisoners from escaping: *The prisoner was closely guarded on the way to court.*
PHR V guard against sth to try to prevent sth or stop sth happening

guarded /ˈgɑːdɪd/ *adj* (used about an answer, statement, etc.) careful; not giving much information or showing what you feel: *a guarded reply* **OPP unguarded** ▶ **guardedly** *adv*

G

guardian /ˈgɑːdiən/ *noun* [C] **1** a person or institution that guards or protects sth: *The police are the guardians of law and order.* **2** a person who is legally responsible for the care of another person, especially of a child whose parents are dead

guerrilla (also guerilla) /gəˈrɪlə/ *noun* [C] a member of a small military group which is not part of an official army and which makes surprise attacks on the enemy

guess¹ /ges/ *verb* **1** [I,T] guess (at sth) to try and give an answer or make a judgement about sth without being sure of all the facts: *I'd guess that he's about 45.* ◆ *I tried to guess how much her new phone cost.* ◆ *If you're not sure of an answer, guess.* ◆ *We can only guess at her reasons for leaving.* **2** [I,T] to guess correctly; to give the correct answer when you are not sure about it: *I guessed the answer straightaway.* ◆ *You'll never guess what Adam just told me!* ◆ *Did I guess right?* **3** [T] (*especially AmE informal*) to imagine that sth is probably true or likely; to suppose: *I guess you're tired after your long trip.* **4** [T] used to show that you are going to say sth surprising or exciting: *Guess what! I'm getting married!*

guess² /ges/ *noun* [C] an effort you make to imagine a possible answer or give an opinion when you cannot be sure if you are right: *If you don't know the answer, then **have a guess**!* ◆ *I don't know how far it is, but **at a guess** I'd say about 50 miles.* ◆ *I'd say it'll take about four hours, but that's just **a rough guess**.*
IDM anybody's/anyone's guess something that nobody can be certain about: *What's going to happen next is anybody's guess.*
your guess is as good as mine I do not know: *'Where's Ron?' 'Your guess is as good as mine.'*

guesswork /ˈgeswɜːk/ *noun* [U] the process of guessing: *I arrived at the answer **by pure guesswork**.*

guest /gest/ *noun* [C] **1** a person who is invited to a place or to a special event: *We've got guests this weekend.* ◆ *wedding guests* ◆ *Who is the guest speaker at the conference?* **2** a person who is staying at a hotel, etc: *This hotel has accommodation for 500 guests.*
IDM be my guest (*informal*) used to give sb permission to do sth that they have asked to do: *'Could I have a look at your newspaper?' 'Be my guest!'*

ˈguest house *noun* [C] a small hotel, sometimes in a private house

guidance /ˈgaɪdns/ *noun* [U] guidance (on sth) help or advice: *The centre offers guidance for unemployed people on how to find work.*

guide¹ /gaɪd/ *noun* [C]
➤BOOK/MAGAZINE **1** a book, magazine, etc. that gives information or help on a subject: *Your Guide to Using the Internet* ◆ *Have we got a TV guide for this week?* **2** (also guidebook /ˈgaɪdbʊk/) a book that gives information about a place to tourists or people who are travelling: *The guide says that it was built 500 years ago.*
➤PERSON **3** a person who shows tourists or people who are travelling where to go: *She works as a **tour guide** in Venice.*
➤STH THAT HELPS **4** something that helps you to judge or plan sth: ***As a rough guide**, use twice as much water as rice.*
➤GIRL **5 Girl Guide** a member of an organization called **the Guides** that teaches girls practical skills and organizes activities such as camping ➲ look at **Scout**

guide² /gaɪd/ *verb* [T] **1** to help a person or a group of people to find the way to a place; to show sb a place that you know well: *He guided us through the busy streets to our hotel.* ◆ *We were guided around the museum by a young student.* ➲ note at **lead 2** to have an influence on sb/sth: *I was guided by your advice.* **3** to help sb deal with sth difficult or complicated: *The manual will guide you through every step of the procedure.* **4** to carefully move sb/sth or to help sb/sth to move in a particular direction: *A crane lifted the piano and two men carefully guided it through the window.*

guided /ˈgaɪdɪd/ *adj* led by a guide: *a guided tour/walk*

ˈguide dog *noun* [C] a dog trained to guide a person who is unable to see

guideline /ˈgaɪdlaɪn/ *noun* [C] **1** [usually pl] official advice or rules on how to do sth **2** something that can be used to help you make a decision or form an opinion: *These figures are a useful guideline when buying a house.*

guild /gɪld/ *noun* [C, with sing or pl verb] an organization of people who do the same job or who have the same interests or aims: *the Screen Actors' Guild*

guillotine /ˈgɪlətiːn/ *noun* [C] **1** a machine that was used in France in the past for cutting people's heads off **2** a machine used for cutting paper ▶ **guillotine** *verb* [T]

guilt /gɪlt/ *noun* [U] **1** guilt (about/at sth) the unpleasant feelings that you have when you know or think that you have done sth bad: *I sometimes feel guilt about not spending more time with my children.* **2** the fact of having broken a law: *We took his refusal to answer questions as an admission of guilt.* **OPP innocence** **3** the responsibility for doing sth wrong or for sth bad that has happened: *It's difficult to say whether the guilt lies with the parents or the children.* **SYN blame**

guilty /ˈgɪlti/ *adj* (guiltier; guiltiest) **1** guilty (about sth) having an unpleasant feeling because you have done sth bad: *I* ***feel*** *really* ***guilty*** *about lying to Sam.* ◆ *It's hard to sleep with* ***a guilty conscience.*** **2 guilty (of sth)** having broken a law; being responsible for doing sth wrong: *She* ***pleaded guilty/not guilty*** *to the crime.* ◆ *to be guilty of murder* ◆ *The jury* ***found*** *him* ***guilty*** *of fraud.* OPP **innocent** ▶ **guiltily** *adv*

guinea pig /ˈɡɪni pɪɡ/ *noun* [C] **1** a small animal with no tail that is often kept as a pet ➲ note at **pet** **2** a person who is used in an experiment: *I volunteered to act as a guinea pig in their research into dreams.*

guise /ɡaɪz/ *noun* [C] a way in which sb/sth appears, which is often different from usual or hides the truth: *The President was at the meeting* ***in*** *his* ***guise as*** *chairman of the charity.* ◆ *His speech presented racist ideas* ***under the guise of*** *nationalism.*

guitar /ɡɪˈtɑː(r)/ *noun* [C] a type of musical instrument with strings that you play with your fingers or with a **plectrum** (= a small piece of plastic) ➲ note at **music** ➲ picture at **music**

guitarist /ɡɪˈtɑːrɪst/ *noun* [C] a person who plays the **guitar**

gulf /ɡʌlf/ *noun* **1** [C] a part of the sea that is almost surrounded by land: *the Gulf of Mexico* **2 the Gulf** [sing] the Persian Gulf, the area of sea between Arabia and Iran **3** [C] an important or serious difference between people in the way they live, think or feel: *the gulf between rich and poor*

gull /ɡʌl/ (also **seagull**) *noun* [C] a white or grey bird that makes a loud noise and lives near the sea

gullible /ˈɡʌləbl/ *adj* (used about a person) believing and trusting people too easily, and therefore easily tricked

gulp¹ /ɡʌlp/ *verb* **1** [I,T] **gulp sth (down)**; **gulp (for) sth** to swallow large amounts of food, drink, etc. quickly: *He gulped down his breakfast and went out.* **2** [I] to make a swallowing movement because you are afraid, surprised, etc. **3** to breathe quickly and deeply, because you need more air: *She finally came to the surface, desperately gulping (for) air.*

gulp² /ɡʌlp/ *noun* [C] **1 a gulp (of sth)** the amount that you swallow when you **gulp** **2** the act of breathing in or swallowing sth: *I drank my coffee* ***in one gulp*** *and ran out of the door.*

gum /ɡʌm/ *noun* **1** [C] either of the firm pink parts of your mouth that hold your teeth ➲ picture at **body** **2** [U] a substance that you use to stick things together (especially pieces of paper) **3** = **chewing gum**

gun¹ /ɡʌn/ *noun* [C] **1** a weapon that is used for shooting: *The robber held a gun to the bank clerk's head.*

> MORE Verbs often used with 'gun' are **load, unload, point, aim, fire.** Different types of gun include **machine gun, pistol, revolver, rifle, shotgun.**

2 a tool that uses pressure to send out a substance or an object: *a grease gun* ◆ *a staple gun*
IDM **jump the gun** ➲ **jump¹**

gun² /ɡʌn/ *verb* [T] (gu<u>nn</u>ing; gu<u>nn</u>ed)
PHR V **gun sb down** (*informal*) to shoot and kill or seriously injure sb

gunboat /ˈɡʌnbəʊt/ *noun* [C] a small ship used in war that carries heavy guns

gunfight /ˈɡʌnfaɪt/ *noun* [C] a fight between people using guns

gunfire /ˈɡʌnfaɪə(r)/ *noun* [U] the repeated firing of guns; the sound of guns firing: *We could hear gunfire.*

gunman /ˈɡʌnmən/ *noun* [C] (*pl* -men /-mən/) a man who uses a gun to steal from or kill people

gunpoint /ˈɡʌnpɔɪnt/ *noun*
IDM **at gunpoint** threatening to shoot sb: *He held the hostages at gunpoint.*

gunpowder /ˈɡʌnpaʊdə(r)/ *noun* [U] a powder that can explode and is used in guns, etc.

gunshot /ˈɡʌnʃɒt/ *noun* [C] the firing of a gun or the sound that it makes

gurgle /ˈɡɜːɡl/ *verb* [I] **1** to make a sound like water flowing quickly through a narrow space: *a gurgling stream* **2** if a baby **gurgles**, it makes a noise in its throat because it is happy ▶ **gurgle** *noun* [C]

guru /ˈɡʊruː/ *noun* [C] **1** a spiritual leader or teacher in the Hindu or Sikh religion **2** a person whose opinions you admire and respect, and whose ideas you follow: *a management/fashion guru*

gush /ɡʌʃ/ *verb* **1** [I] **gush (out of/from/into sth)**; **gush out/in** (used about a liquid) to flow out suddenly and in great quantities: *Blood gushed from the wound.* ◆ *I turned the tap on and water gushed out.* **2** [T] (used about a container/vehicle, etc.) to produce large amounts of a liquid: *The broken pipe was gushing water all over the road.* **3** [I,T] to express pleasure or admiration so much that it does not sound sincere ▶ **gush** *noun* [C]: *a sudden gush of water*

gust /ɡʌst/ *noun* [C] a sudden strong wind ▶ **gust** *verb* [I]

gusto /ˈɡʌstəʊ/ *noun*
IDM **with gusto** with great enthusiasm: *They sang with great gusto.*

gut¹ /ɡʌt/ *noun* **1** [C] the tube in the body that food passes through when it leaves the stomach

> MORE A more technical word is **intestine.**

2 guts [pl] the organs in and around the stomach, especially of an animal **3** [C] a person's fat stomach **4 guts** [pl] (*informal*) courage and determination: *It* ***takes guts*** *to admit that you are wrong.* ◆ *I don't* ***have the guts*** *to tell my boss what he's doing wrong.*

gut² /ɡʌt/ *verb* [T] (gu<u>tt</u>ing; gu<u>tt</u>ed) **1** to destroy the inside of a building: *The warehouse was gutted by fire.* **2** to remove the organs from inside an animal, fish, etc.

G

gut[3] /gʌt/ *adj* [only *before* a noun] based on feelings and emotions rather than thought and reason: *a gut feeling/reaction* ♦ *My gut instinct is to say no.*

gutter /ˈgʌtə(r)/ *noun* **1** [C] a long piece of metal or plastic with a curved bottom that is fixed to the edge of a roof to carry away the water when it rains ➲ picture on **page P8** **2** [C] a lower part at the edge of a road along which the water flows away when it rains **3** [sing] the very lowest level of society: *She rose from the gutter to become a great star.*

⚷ **guy** /gaɪ/ *noun* **1** [C] (*informal*) a man or a boy: *He's a nice guy.* **2 guys** [pl] (*informal*) used when speaking to a group of people of either sex: *What do you guys want to eat tonight?* **3** [sing] (*BrE*) a model of a man that is burned on 5 November in memory of Guy Fawkes ➲ look at **Bonfire Night**

H

guzzle /ˈgʌzl/ *verb* [I,T] (*informal*) to eat or drink too fast and too much

gym /dʒɪm/ *noun* **1** (also *formal* gymnasium /dʒɪmˈneɪziəm/; *pl* gymnasiums *or* gymnasia /-zɪə/) [C] a room or hall with equipment for doing physical exercise: *The school has built a new gym.* **2** [C] = **health club**: *I work out at the gym twice a week.* **3** [U] physical exercises done in a **gym**: *Do you like gym?* ♦ *gym shoes* ➲ picture on **page P3**

gymnast /ˈdʒɪmnæst/ *noun* [C] a person who does **gymnastics** ➲ picture on **page P4**

gymnastics /dʒɪmˈnæstɪks/ *noun* [U] physical exercises that are done inside a building, often using special equipment such as bars and ropes: *She won a gold medal in gymnastics.* ➲ picture on **page P4**

gynaecology (*AmE* gynecology) /ˌgaɪnəˈkɒlədʒi/ *noun* [U] the study and treatment of the diseases and medical problems of women ▸ **gynaecological** (*AmE* gynecological) /ˌgaɪnəkəˈlɒdʒɪkl/ *adj* ▸ **gynaecologist** (*AmE* gynecologist) /ˌgaɪnəˈkɒlədʒɪst/ *noun* [C]

Gypsy (also Gipsy) /ˈdʒɪpsi/ *noun* [C] (*pl* Gypsies) a member of a race of people who traditionally spend their lives travelling around from place to place, living in **caravans** (= homes with wheels that can be pulled by a car or by a horse) ➲ look at **traveller**

> **MORE** Some people find the word **Gypsy** offensive and prefer **Romani.**

H, h /eɪtʃ/ *noun* [C,U] (*pl* Hs; H's; h's /ˈeɪtʃɪz/) the 8th letter of the English alphabet: *'Hat' begins with (an) 'H'.*

ha[1] /hɑː/ *exclam* **1** used for showing that you are surprised or pleased: *Ha! I knew he was hiding something!* **2 ha! ha!** used in written language to show that sb is laughing

ha[2] *abbr* = **hectare**

⚷ **habit** /ˈhæbɪt/ *noun* **1** [C] a/the habit (of doing sth) something that you do often and almost without thinking, especially sth that is hard to stop doing: *I'm trying to* ***get into the habit*** *of hanging up my clothes every night.* ♦ *I'm trying to* ***break the habit*** *of staying up too late.* ➲ *adjective* **habitual**

> **HELP** **Habit** or **custom**? A **habit** is usually something that is done by one person. A **custom** is something that is done by a group, community or nation: *the custom of giving presents at Christmas*

2 [U] usual behaviour: *I sometimes think I only drink coffee* ***out of habit*** *now—I don't really enjoy it.*
IDM **force of habit** ➲ **force**[1]
kick the habit ➲ **kick**[1]

habitable /ˈhæbɪtəbl/ *adj* (used about buildings) suitable to be lived in **OPP** **uninhabitable**

habitat /ˈhæbɪtæt/ *noun* [C] the natural home of a plant or an animal: *I've seen wolves in the zoo, but not in their natural habitat.*

habitation /ˌhæbɪˈteɪʃn/ *noun* [U] (*formal*) the act of living in a place

habitual /həˈbɪtʃuəl/ *adj* **1** which you always have or do; usual: *He had his habitual nap after lunch.* **2** [only *before* a noun] doing sth very often: *a habitual criminal/drinker/liar* ▸ **habitually** /-tʃuəli/ *adv*

hack /hæk/ *verb* [I,T] **1 hack (away) (at) sth** to cut sth in a rough way with a tool such as a large knife: *He hacked away at the bushes.* **2** (*informal*) **hack (into) (sth)** to use a computer to look at and/or change information that is stored on another computer without permission ➲ look at **phone hacking**

hacker /ˈhækə(r)/ *noun* [C] (*informal*) a person who secretly looks at and/or changes information on sb else's computer system without permission

had[1] /hæd; həd/ *past tense, past participle* of **have**

had[2] /hæd/ *adj*
IDM **be had** (*informal*) to be tricked: *I've been had. This watch I bought doesn't work.*

hadn't /ˈhædnt/ *short for* **had not**

haemophilia (*AmE* hemophilia) /ˌhiːməˈfɪliə/ *noun* [U] a disease that causes a person to lose a lot of blood even from very small injuries because the blood does not **clot** (= stop flowing)

haemophiliac (*AmE* hemophiliac) /ˌhiːməˈfɪliæk/ *noun* [C] a person who suffers from **haemophilia**

haemorrhage (*AmE* **hemorrhage**) /ˈhemərɪdʒ/ *noun* [C,U] the loss of a lot of blood from inside the body ▸ **haemorrhage** (*AmE* **hemorrhage**) *verb* [I]

haemorrhoids (*especially AmE* **hemorrhoids**) /ˈhemərɔɪdz/ (also **piles**) *noun* [pl] a medical condition in which the **veins** (= tubes that carry blood) near the **anus** (= the opening where waste food leaves the body) swell and become painful

haggard /ˈhæɡəd/ *adj* (used about a person) looking tired or worried

haggle /ˈhæɡl/ *verb* [I] **haggle (with sb) (over/about sth)** to argue with sb until you reach an agreement, especially about the price of sth: *In the market, some tourists were haggling over the price of a carpet.*

hail[1] /heɪl/ *verb* **1** [T] **hail sb/sth as sth** to say in public that sb/sth is very good or very special: *The book was hailed as a masterpiece.* **2** [T] to call or wave to sb/sth: *to hail a taxi* **3** [I] when it **hails**, small balls of ice fall from the sky like rain ➲ note at **weather**

hail[2] /heɪl/ *noun* **1** [U] small balls of ice, called **hailstones**, that fall from the sky like rain **2** [sing] **a hail of sth** a large amount of sth that is aimed at sb in order to harm them: *a hail of bullets/stones/abuse*

⚷ **hair** /heə(r)/ *noun* **1** [U,C] the mass of long thin things that grow on the head and body of people and animals; one of these things: *He has got short black hair.* ◆ *Dave's losing his hair* (= going bald). ◆ *The dog left hairs all over the furniture.* ➲ picture at **body 2 -haired** *adj* [in compounds] having the type of hair mentioned: *a dark-haired woman* ◆ *a long-haired dog* **3** a thing that looks like a very thin thread that grows on the surface of some plants: *The leaves and stem are covered in fine hairs.*

IDM **keep your hair on** (*spoken*) (used to tell sb to stop shouting and become less angry) calm down

let your hair down (*informal*) to relax and enjoy yourself after being formal

make sb's hair stand on end to frighten or shock sb

not turn a hair to not show any reaction to sth that many people would find surprising or shocking

split hairs ➲ **split**[1]

TOPIC

Hair

Light-coloured hair is called **blonde/blond** or **fair**, and reddish-brown hair is called **ginger, auburn** or **red**. As people get older they might **go grey**. In order to make your hair tidy or to **style** it, you **brush** or **comb** it. You wash it with **shampoo** and use a **hairdryer** to **blow-dry** it. You can **part** it/have a **parting** in the middle or on one side, and you might have a **fringe** (= a short piece of hair at the front). When you **go to the hairdresser's** you can **have your hair cut** or **trimmed** (= a small amount cut off). You might also **have it permed** (= made curly) or **straightened** (= made straight). You can also have your hair **coloured**, or ask the hairdresser for **highlights** (= areas of hair that are lighter than the rest). People who want to have longer hair sometimes **get extensions** (= artificial hair that is attached to a person's real hair). A **barber** is a hairdresser who only cuts men's hair.

hairbrush /ˈheəbrʌʃ/ *noun* [C] a brush that you use on your hair ➲ picture at **brush**

haircut /ˈheəkʌt/ *noun* [C] **1** the act of sb cutting your hair: *You need (to have) a haircut.* **2** the style in which your hair has been cut: *That haircut really suits you.*

hairdo /ˈheədu:/ (*informal*) = **hairstyle**

⚷ **hairdresser** /ˈheədresə(r)/ *noun* **1** [C] a person whose job is to cut, shape, colour, etc. hair ➲ look at **barber 2 the hairdresser's** [sing] the place where you go to have your hair cut: *I've made an appointment at the hairdresser's for 10 o'clock.*

hair

hairdryer (also hairdrier) /ˈheədraɪə(r)/ *noun* [C] a machine that dries hair by blowing hot air through it

hairgrip /ˈheəgrɪp/ (*AmE* ˈbobby pin) *noun* [C] a piece of wire that is folded in the middle and used for holding hair in place ➲ look at **hairpin**

hairless /ˈheələs/ *adj* without hair ➲ look at **bald**

hairline[1] /ˈheəlaɪn/ *noun* [C] the edge of sb's hair, especially at the front

hairline[2] /ˈheəlaɪn/ *adj* (used about a crack in sth) very thin: *a hairline fracture of the leg*

hairpin /ˈheəpɪn/ *noun* [C] a piece of wire, shaped like a U, used for holding hair in place ➲ look at **hairgrip**

ˌhairpin ˈbend (*AmE* ˌhairpin ˈcurve; ˌhairpin ˈturn) *noun* [C] a very sharp bend in a road, especially a mountain road

ˈhair-raising *adj* that makes you very frightened: *a hair-raising experience*

hairslide /ˈheəslaɪd/ (also slide; *AmE* barrette) *noun* [C] a small decorative piece of metal or plastic used for holding hair in place

hairspray /ˈheəspreɪ/ *noun* [U,C] a substance you spray onto your hair to hold it in place **SYN** **lacquer**

hairstyle /ˈheəstaɪl/ (also *informal* hairdo) *noun* [C] the style in which your hair has been cut or arranged

hairstylist /ˈheəstaɪlɪst/ (also stylist) *noun* [C] a person whose job it is to cut and shape sb's hair

hairy /ˈheəri/ *adj* (hairier; hairiest) **1** having a lot of hair **2** (*slang*) dangerous or worrying

hajj (also haj) /hædʒ/ *noun* [sing] the **pilgrimage** (= religious journey) to Mecca that many Muslims make

halal /ˈhælæl/ *adj* [only *before* a noun] (used about meat) from an animal that has been killed according to Muslim law

🔑 **half**[1] /hɑːf/ *determiner, pron, noun* [C] (*pl* halves /hɑːvz/) one of two equal parts of sth: *three and a half kilos of potatoes* ◆ *Two halves make a whole.* ◆ *half an hour* ◆ *an hour and a half* ◆ *The second half of the book is more exciting.* ◆ *Giggs scored in the first half* (= of a match). ◆ *Half of this money is yours.* ◆ *Half the people in the office leave at 5.* ➲ *verb* **halve**

IDM **break, cut, etc. sth in half** to break, etc. sth into two parts

go half and half/go halves with sb (*BrE*) to share the cost of sth with sb

do nothing/not do anything by halves to do whatever you do completely and properly

🔑 **half**[2] /hɑːf/ *adv* not completely: *half full* ◆ *The hotel was only **half finished**.* ◆ *He's half German* (= one of his parents is German).

IDM **half past ...** (in time) 30 minutes past an hour: *half past six* (= 6.30)

HELP In spoken British English people also say **half six** to mean 6.30.

not half as much, many, good, bad, etc. much less: *This episode wasn't half as good as the last.*

ˌhalf-ˈbaked *adj* (*informal*) not thought about or planned well: *a half-baked idea/scheme*

ˌhalf ˈboard *noun* [U] (*BrE*) a price for a room in a hotel, etc. which includes breakfast and an evening meal ➲ note at **hotel** ➲ look at **full board, bed and breakfast**

ˈhalf-brother *noun* [C] a brother with whom you share one parent ➲ look at **stepbrother**

ˌhalf-ˈhearted *adj* without interest or enthusiasm ▶ **half-heartedly** *adv*

ˌhalf-ˈprice *adj* costing half the usual price: *a half-price ticket* ▶ **ˌhalf-ˈprice** *adv*: *Children aged under four go half-price.*

ˈhalf-sister *noun* [C] a sister with whom you share one parent ➲ look at **stepsister**

ˌhalf-ˈterm *noun* [C] (*BrE*) a short holiday in the middle of one of the periods into which a school year is divided

ˌhalf-ˈtime *noun* [U] (in sport) the period of time between the two halves of a match

halfway /ˌhɑːfˈweɪ/ *adj, adv* at an equal distance between two places; in the middle of a period of time: *They have a break halfway through the morning.* **SYN** **midway**

🔑 **hall** /hɔːl/ *noun* [C] **1** (also hallway) a room or passage that is just inside the front entrance of a house or public building: *There is a public telephone in the **entrance hall** of this building.* ➲ picture on **page P8** **2** a building or large room in which meetings, concerts, dances, etc. can be held: *a concert hall* ➲ look at **town hall**

hallmark /ˈhɔːlmɑːk/ *noun* [C] **1** a characteristic that is typical of sb: *The ability to motivate students is the hallmark of a good teacher.* **2** a mark that is put on objects made of valuable metals, giving information about the quality of the metal and when and where the object was made

hallo = **hello**

ˌhall of ˈresidence *noun* [C] (*pl* halls of residence) (*AmE* dormitory) (in colleges, universities, etc.) a building where students live

Halloween (also Hallowe'en) /ˌhæləʊˈiːn/ *noun* [sing] the night of October 31st when in the past people believed that dead people appeared from their graves

CULTURE

Halloween is the time when people say that witches and ghosts appear. Children now dress up as witches, etc. and play tricks on people. They go to people's houses and say **'trick or treat'** and people give them sweets.

hallucination /həˌluːsɪˈneɪʃn/ *noun* [C,U] seeing or hearing sth that is not really there (because you are ill or have taken a drug): *Was the figure real* *or just a hallucination?* ♦ *to suffer from/have hallucinations*

hallway /ˈhɔːlweɪ/ = **hall**(1)

halo /ˈheɪləʊ/ *noun* [C] (*pl* **halos** *or* **haloes**) the circle of light that is drawn around the head of a holy person in a painting

halt /hɔːlt/ *noun* [sing] a stop (that does not last very long): *Work* ***came to a halt*** *when the machine broke down.*
IDM **grind to a halt/standstill** ➲ **grind**[1]
▸ **halt** *verb* [I,T] (*formal*): *An accident halted the traffic in the town centre for half an hour.*

halve /hɑːv/ *verb* **1** [I,T] to reduce by a half; to make sth reduce by a half: *Shares in the company have halved in value.* ♦ *We aim to halve the number of people on our waiting list in the next six months.* **2** [T] to divide sth into two equal parts: *First halve the peach and then remove the stone.*

halves *plural of* **half**

ham /hæm/ *noun* [U] meat from a pig's back leg that has been **cured** (= treated with salt or smoke to keep it fresh) ➲ note at **meat** ➲ look at **bacon, gammon, pork**

hamburger /ˈhæmbɜːɡə(r)/ **1** (*especially AmE*) = **burger 2** (*AmE*) = **mince**

hamlet /ˈhæmlət/ *noun* [C] a very small village

hammer[1] /ˈhæmə(r)/ *noun* [C] a tool with a heavy metal head that is used for hitting nails, etc. ➲ picture at **tool**

hammer[2] /ˈhæmə(r)/ *verb* **1** [I,T] hammer sth (in/into/onto sth) to hit with a hammer: *She hammered the nail into the wall.* **2** [I,T] to hit sth several times, making a loud noise: *He hammered on the door until somebody opened it.*
IDM **hammer sth into sb** to force sb to remember sth by repeating it many times
hammer sth out to succeed in making a plan or agreement after a lot of discussion

hammering /ˈhæmərɪŋ/ *noun* **1** [U] the noise that is made by sb using a hammer or by sb hitting sth many times **2** [C] (*BrE informal*) a very bad defeat

hammock /ˈhæmək/ *noun* [C] a bed, made of rope or strong cloth, which is hung up between two trees or poles ➲ picture at **bed**

hamper[1] /ˈhæmpə(r)/ *verb* [T, usually passive] to make sth difficult: *The building work was hampered by bad weather.*

hamper[2] /ˈhæmpə(r)/ *noun* [C] a large **basket** (= a container) with a lid that is used for carrying food

hamster /ˈhæmstə(r)/ *noun* [C] a small animal that is kept as a pet. **Hamsters** are like mice but are fatter and do not have a tail. They store food in the sides of their mouths. ➲ note at **pet**

hand[1] /hænd/ *noun*
▸PART OF BODY **1** [C] the part of your body at the end of your arm which has five fingers: *He* ***took*** *the child* ***by the hand.*** ♦ *She was on her hands and knees* (= crawling on the floor) *looking for an earring.* ➲ picture at **body**
▸-HANDED **2 -handed** *adj* [in compounds] having, using or made for the type of hand(s) mentioned: *heavy-handed* (= clumsy and careless) ♦ *right-handed/left-handed*
▸HELP **3 a hand** [sing] (*informal*) some help: *I'll give you a hand with the washing up.* ♦ *Do you want/need a hand?*
▸ON CLOCK **4** [C] the part of a clock or watch that points to the numbers: *the hour/minute/second hand* ➲ picture at **clock**
▸WORKER **5** [C] a person who does physical work on a farm, in a factory, etc: *farmhands*
▸CARDS **6** [C] the set of playing cards that sb has been given in a game of cards: *to be dealt a good/bad hand*
IDM **(close/near) at hand** (*formal*) near in space or time: *Help is close at hand.*
be an old hand (at sth) ➲ **old**
by hand 1 done by a person and not by machine: *I had to do all the sewing by hand.* **2** not by post: *The letter was delivered by hand.*
catch sb red-handed ➲ **catch**[1]
change hands ➲ **change**[1]
a firm hand ➲ **firm**[2]
(at) first hand (used about information that you have received) from sb who was closely involved: *Did you get this information first hand?* ➲ look at **second-hand**
get, have, etc. a free hand ➲ **free**[1]
get, have, etc. the upper hand ➲ **upper**
get/lay your hands on sb/sth (*informal*) to catch sb: *Just wait till I get my hands on that boy!*
get/lay your hands on sth to find or obtain sth: *I need to get my hands on a good dictionary.*
give sb a big hand ➲ **big**
hand in hand 1 holding each other's hands: *The couple walked hand in hand along the beach.* **2** usually happening together; closely connected: *Drought and famine usually go hand in hand.*
your hands are tied to not be in a position to do as you would like because of rules, promises, etc: *I'd like to help but my hands are tied.*
hands off (sb/sth) (*informal*) used for ordering sb not to touch sb/sth
hands up 1 used in a school, etc. for asking people to lift one hand and give an answer: *Hands up who'd like to go on the trip this afternoon?* **2** used by a person with a gun to tell other people to put their hands in the air
have sb eating out of your hand ➲ **eat**
have a hand in sth to take part in or share sth: *Even members of staff had a hand in painting and decorating the new office.*
have your hands full to be very busy or too busy to do sth else
a helping hand ➲ **help**[1]
hold sb's hand to give sb support in a difficult situation: *I'll come to the dentist's with you to hold your hand.*
hold hands (with sb) (used about two or more people) to hold each other's hands
in hand 1 (used about money, etc.) not yet used: *If*

you have time in hand at the end of the exam, check what you have written. **2** being dealt with at the moment; under control: *The situation is in hand.* OPP **out of hand**

in your hands; in the hands of sb in your possession, control or care: *The document is no longer in my hands.* ◆ *The matter is in the hands of a solicitor.*

in safe hands ➲ **safe**[1]

keep your hand in to do an activity from time to time so that you do not forget how to do it or lose the skill: *I play tennis from time to time just to keep my hand in.*

know sth like the back of your hand ➲ **know**[1]

lend (sb) a hand/lend a hand (to sb) ➲ **lend**

off your hands not your responsibility any more

on hand available to help or to be used: *There is always an adult on hand to help when the children are playing outside.*

on your hands being your responsibility: *We seem to have a problem on our hands.*

on the one hand ... on the other (hand) used for showing opposite points of view: *On the one hand, of course, cars are very useful. On the other hand, they cause a huge amount of pollution.* ➲ note at **contrast**

(get) out of hand not under control: *Violence at football matches is getting out of hand.* OPP **in hand**

out of your hands not in your control; not your responsibility: *I can't help you, I'm afraid. The matter is out of my hands.*

shake sb's hand/shake hands (with sb)/shake sb by the hand ➲ **shake**[1]

to hand near or close to you: *I'm afraid I haven't got a pen to hand.*

try your hand at sth ➲ **try**[1]

turn your hand to sth to have the ability to do sth: *She can turn her hand to all sorts of jobs.*

wash your hands of sb/sth ➲ **wash**[1]

with your bare hands ➲ **bare**

hand[2] /hænd/ *verb* [T] hand sb sth; hand sth to sb to give or pass sth to sb

IDM **have (got) to hand it to sb** used to show admiration and approval of sb's work or efforts: *You've got to hand it to Rita—she's a great cook.*

PHR V **hand sth back (to sb)** to give or return sth to the person who owns it or to where it belongs

hand sth down (to sb) **1** to pass customs, etc. from older people to younger ones: *These stories have been handed down from generation to generation.* **2** to pass clothes, toys, etc. from older children to younger ones in the family

hand sth in (to sb) to give sth to sb in authority, especially a piece of work or sth that is lost: *I found a wallet and handed it in to the police.*

hand sth on (to sb) to send or give sth to another person: *When you have read the article, please hand it on to another student.*

hand sth out (to sb) to give sth to many people in a group: *Food was handed out to the starving people.*

hand (sth) over (to sb) to give sb else your position of power or the responsibility for sth: *She resigned as chairperson and handed over to one of her younger colleagues.*

hand (sb) over to sb (used at a meeting or on the TV, radio, telephone, etc.) to let sb speak or listen to another person: *I'm handing you over now to our foreign correspondent.*

hand sb/sth over (to sb) to give sb/sth (to sb): *People were tricked into handing over large sums of money.*

hand sth round to pass sth, especially food and drinks, to all the people in a group

handbag /ˈhændbæg/ (*AmE* **purse**) *noun* [C] a small bag in which women carry money, keys, etc. SYN **shoulder bag** ➲ picture at **bag**

handbook /ˈhændbʊk/ *noun* [C] a small book that gives instructions on how to use sth or advice and information about a particular subject ➲ look at **manual**[2]

handbrake /ˈhændbreɪk/ (*AmE* eˈmergency brake; ˈparking brake) *noun* [C] a device that is operated by hand to stop a car from moving when it is parked ➲ picture at **car**

handcuffs /ˈhændkʌfs/ (also **cuffs**) *noun* [pl] a pair of metal rings that are joined together by a chain and put around the wrists of prisoners

handful /ˈhændfʊl/ *noun* **1** [C] **a handful (of sth)** as much or as many of sth as you can hold in one hand: *a handful of sand* **2** [sing] **a handful (of sth)** a small number (of sb/sth): *Only a handful of people came to the meeting.* **3 a handful** [sing] (*informal*) a person or an animal that is difficult to control: *The little girl is quite a handful.*

handgun /ˈhændgʌn/ *noun* [C] a small gun that you can hold and fire with one hand

ˌ**hand-ˈheld** *adj* [usually before a noun] small enough to be held in the hand while being used: *a hand-held camera/computer/device*

handicap[1] /ˈhændikæp/ *noun* **1** (*old-fashioned*) = **disability**

> **HELP** Be careful. Many people now find this word offensive.

2 [C] something that makes doing sth more difficult; a disadvantage: *Not speaking French is going to be a bit of a handicap in my new job.* **3** a disadvantage that is given to the strongest people competing in a sports event, etc. so that the weaker people have more chance

handicap[2] /ˈhændikæp/ *verb* [T] (**handicapping**; **handicapped**) [usually passive] to give or be a disadvantage to sb: *They were handicapped by their lack of education.*

handicapped /ˈhændikæpt/ *adj* (*old-fashioned*) = **disabled**

> **HELP** Be careful. Many people now find this word offensive.

handicraft /ˈhændikrɑːft/ *noun* **1** [C] an activity that needs skill with the hands as well as artistic ability, for example sewing **2 handicrafts** [pl] the objects that are produced by this activity

handiwork /ˈhændiwɜːk/ *noun* [U] **1** a thing that you have made or done, especially using your artistic skill: *We admired her exquisite handiwork.*

2 something done by a particular person or group, especially sth bad: *This looks like the handiwork of criminals.*

handkerchief /ˈhæŋkətʃɪf; -tʃiːf/ *noun* [C] (*pl* **handkerchiefs** *or* **handkerchieves** /-tʃiːvz/) a square piece of cloth or soft thin paper that you use for clearing your nose

HELP A more informal word is **hanky** or **hankie**. A handkerchief that is made of soft thin paper is also called a **paper handkerchief** or a **tissue**.

handle¹ /ˈhændl/ *verb* [T] **1** to deal with or to control sb/sth: *This port handles 100 million tons of cargo each year.* ◆ *I have a problem at work and I don't really know how to handle it.* **2** to touch or hold sth with your hand(s): *Wash your hands before you handle food.* ▶ **handler** *noun* [C]: *baggage/dog/food handlers*

handles

knobs

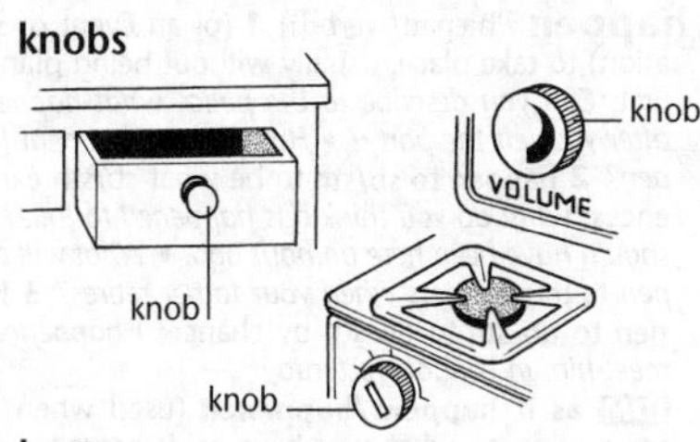

buttons

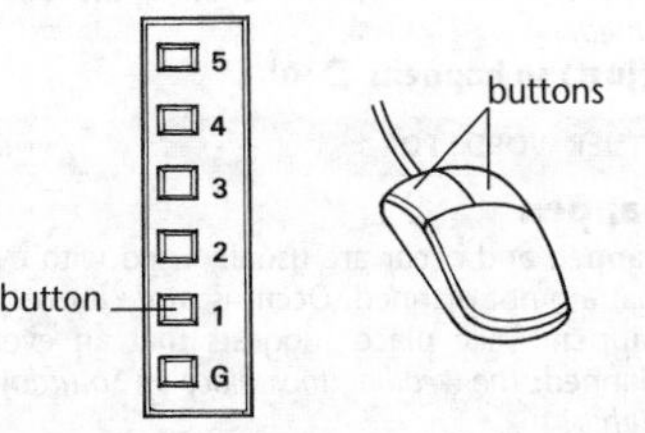

handle² /ˈhændl/ *noun* [C] a part of sth that is used for holding or opening it: *She turned the handle and opened the door.* ➲ picture at **garden, bag, cup**
IDM **fly off the handle** ➲ **fly¹**

handlebar /ˈhændlbɑː(r)/ *noun* [C, usually pl] the metal bar at the front of a bicycle that you hold when you are riding it ➲ picture at **bicycle**

ˈ**hand luggage** *noun* [U] (*AmE* ˈ**carry-on bag**) small bags, etc. that you can keep with you on a plane: *You can only take one piece of hand luggage on this flight.*

handmade /ˌhændˈmeɪd/ *adj* made by hand and of very good quality, not by machine

handout /ˈhændaʊt/ *noun* [C] **1** food, money, etc. given to people who need it badly **2** a document that is given to a lot of people, to advertise sth or explain sth, for example in a class

ˌ**hand-ˈpicked** *adj* carefully or personally chosen for a special purpose

handrail /ˈhændreɪl/ *noun* [C] a bar which you can hold to stop you from falling (on stairs, from a building, etc.): *Hold on to the handrail—these steps are very slippery.*

handset /ˈhændset/ *noun* [C] **1** a mobile phone, especially the main part of the phone not including the battery or **SIM card** (= a plastic card that stores phone numbers, etc.): *handset manufacturers* **2** a device that you hold in your hand to operate a television, etc. ➲ look at **remote control** **3** = **receiver**

ˈ**hands-free** *adj* if a telephone, etc. is **hands-free**, you can use it without needing to hold it in your hand: *Are hands-free mobile phones really safe to use when driving?*

handshake /ˈhændʃeɪk/ *noun* [C] the act of shaking sb's right hand with your own when you meet them

handsome /ˈhænsəm/ *adj* (**handsomer**; **handsomest**) [**More handsome** and **most handsome** are more common.] **1** (used about a man) attractive ➲ note at **beautiful** **2** (used about money, an offer, etc.) large or generous: *a handsome profit* ▶ **handsomely** *adv*: *Her efforts were handsomely rewarded.*

ˌ**hands-ˈon** *adj* involving doing sth yourself, rather than watching sb else do it; practical: *She needs some hands-on computer experience.*

handwriting /ˈhændraɪtɪŋ/ *noun* [U] a person's style of writing by hand

handwritten /ˌhændˈrɪtn/ *adj* written by hand, not typed or printed

handy /ˈhændi/ *adj* (**handier**; **handiest**) **1** easy to use: *a handy tip* ◆ *a handy gadget* **SYN** **useful** **2** **handy (for sth/doing sth)** within easy reach of sth; in a convenient place: *Always keep a first-aid kit handy for emergencies.* **3** (*informal*) skilful in using your hands or tools to make or repair things: *Jane is very handy around the house.*
IDM **come in handy** to be useful at some time: *Don't throw that box away. It may come in handy.*

handyman /ˈhændimæn/ *noun* [sing] a man who is good at doing practical jobs inside and outside the house, either as a hobby or as a job

hang¹ /hæŋ/ *verb* (*pt, pp* **hung** /hʌŋ/) **1** [I,T] to fasten sth or be fastened at the top so that the lower part is free or loose: *Hang your coat on the hook.* ◆ *I left the washing hanging on the line all day.* ◆ *She hung the picture over the fireplace.* **2** [I,T] to bend or let sth bend downwards: *The dog's tongue was* *hanging out.* ♦ *He hung his head in shame.* **3** [I,T] (*pt, pp* **hanged**) to kill sb/yourself by putting a rope around the neck and allowing the body to drop downwards: *He was hanged for murder.* **4** [I] **hang (above/over sb/sth)** to stay in the air in a way that is unpleasant or threatening: *Smog hung in the air over the city.*

IDM be/get hung up (about/on sb/sth) to think about sb/sth all the time in a way that is not healthy or good: *She's really hung up about her parents' divorce.*

hang (on) in there (*spoken*) to have courage and keep trying, even though a situation is difficult: *The worst part is over now. Just hang on in there and be patient.*

PHR V hang about/around (*informal*) to stay in or near a place not doing very much

hang back 1 to not want to do or say sth, often because you are shy or not sure of yourself **2** to stay in a place after other people have left it

hang on 1 to hold sth tightly: *Hang on, don't let go!* **2** (*informal*) to wait for a short time: *Hang on a minute. I'm nearly ready.*

hang on sth to depend on sth: *A lot hangs on this decision.*

hang on to sth 1 to hold sth tightly: *He hung on to the child's hand as they crossed the street.* **2** (*informal*) to keep sth: *Let's hang on to the car for another year.*

hang out (*informal*) to spend a lot of time in a place: *The local kids hang out at the park.*

hang sth out to put washing, etc. on a clothes line so that it can dry

hang over sb to be present or about to happen in a way which is unpleasant or threatening: *This essay has been hanging over me for days.*

hang sth up to put sth on a nail, hook, etc: *Hang your coat up over there.*

hang up to end a telephone conversation and put the telephone down

hang up on sb (*informal*) to end a telephone conversation without saying goodbye because you are angry

hang[2] /hæŋ/ *noun*

IDM get the hang of (doing) sth (*informal*) to learn how to use or do sth: *It took me a long time to get the hang of the new system.*

hangar /ˈhæŋə(r)/ *noun* [C] a big building where planes are kept

hanged *past tense, past participle* of **hang**[1] (3)

hanger /ˈhæŋə(r)/ (also ˈ**coat hanger**; ˈ**clothes hanger**) *noun* [C] a metal, plastic or wooden object with a hook that is used for hanging up clothes in a cupboard ➲ picture at **hook**

ˌhanger-ˈon *noun* [C] (*pl* ˌ**hangers-ˈon**) a person who tries to be friendly with sb who is rich or important

ˈhang-glider *noun* [C] a type of frame covered with cloth, which a person holds and flies through the air with as a sport ➲ look at **glider** ➲ picture at parachute ▶ ˈ**hang-gliding** *noun* [U]: *to go hang-gliding*

hanging /ˈhæŋɪŋ/ *noun* [C,U] death as a form of punishment for a crime, caused by putting a rope around a person's neck and letting the body drop downwards

hangman /ˈhæŋmən/ *noun* **1** [C] a person whose job is to kill criminals as a form of punishment by hanging them with a rope **2** [U] a word game where the aim is to guess all the letters of a word before a picture of a person hanging is completed

hangover /ˈhæŋəʊvə(r)/ *noun* [C] the headache and sick feeling that you have if you have drunk too much alcohol the night before

ˈhang-up *noun* [C] (*informal*) **a hang-up (about sb/sth)** an emotional problem about sth that makes you embarrassed or worried: *He has a real hang-up about his height.*

hanker /ˈhæŋkə(r)/ *verb* [I] **hanker (after/for/to do sth)** to want sth very much (often sth that you cannot easily have)

hanky (also **hankie**) /ˈhæŋki/ *noun* [C] (*pl* **hankies**) (*informal*) = **handkerchief**

Hanukkah /ˈhænʊkə/ *noun* [U] an eight-day Jewish festival and holiday in November or December

haphazard /hæpˈhæzəd/ *adj* with no particular order or plan; badly organized ▶ **haphazardly** *adv*

happen /ˈhæpən/ *verb* [I] **1** (of an event or situation) to take place, usually without being planned first: *Can you describe to the police what happened after you left the party?* ♦ *How did the accident happen?* **2 happen to sb/sth** to be what sb/sth experiences: *What do you think has happened to Julie? She should have been here an hour ago.* ♦ *What will happen to the business when your father retires?* **3 happen to do sth** to do sth by chance: *I happened to meet him in London yesterday.*

IDM as it happens/happened (used when you are adding to what you have said) actually: *As it happens, I did remember to bring the book you wanted.*

it (just) so happens ➲ **so**[1]

> OTHER WORDS FOR
>
> **happen**
>
> **Happen** and **occur** are usually used with events that are not planned. **Occur** is more formal than **happen**. **Take place** suggests that an event is planned: *The wedding took place on Saturday July 20th.*

happening /ˈhæpənɪŋ/ *noun* [C, usually pl] a thing that happens; an event (that is usually strange or difficult to explain): *Strange happenings have been reported in that old hotel.*

happily /ˈhæpɪli/ *adv* **1** in a happy way: *children playing happily on the beach* **2** it is lucky that: *The police found my handbag and, happily, nothing had been stolen.* **SYN fortunately 3** willingly: *I would happily give up my job if I didn't need the money.*

happy /ˈhæpi/ *adj* (happier; happiest)
➤FEELING/GIVING PLEASURE **1** happy (to do sth); happy for sb; happy that … feeling or showing pleasure; pleased: *I was really happy to see Mark again yesterday.* ◆ *You look very happy today.* ◆ *Congratulations! I'm very happy for you.* OPP **unhappy, sad** **2** giving or causing pleasure: *a happy marriage/memory/childhood* ◆ *The film is sad but it has **a happy ending**.*
➤GREETING **3** **Happy** used to wish sb an enjoyable time: *Happy Birthday!*
➤SATISFIED **4** happy (with/about sb/sth) satisfied that sth is good and right; not worried: *I'm not very happy with what you've done.* ◆ *I'm not too happy about her living alone.*
➤WILLING **5** [not before a noun] happy to do sth ready to do sth; pleased: *I'll be happy to see you any day next week.*
➤LUCKY **6** [only *before* a noun] lucky: *a happy coincidence.* SYN **fortunate** ▶ **happiness** *noun* [U]

OTHER WORDS FOR
happy
You are usually **glad** or **pleased** about a particular event or situation. **Happy** is used for describing a state, condition of mind, etc. and it can also be used before the noun it describes: *This kind of music always makes me feel happy.* ◆ *She's such a happy child—she's always laughing.* **Delighted** means very happy about something: *I was delighted to meet her.* A **cheerful** person is happy and shows it in their behaviour or expression: *a cheerful, hard-working employee*

ˌhappy-go-ˈlucky *adj* not caring or worried about life and the future

ˈhappy hour *noun* [C,usually sing] a time, usually in the evening, when a pub or bar sells alcoholic drinks at lower prices than usual

harass /ˈhærəs; həˈræs/ *verb* [T] to annoy or worry sb by doing unpleasant things to them, especially over a long time: *The court ordered him to stop harassing his ex-wife.* ▶ **harassment** *noun* [U]: *sexual harassment*

harassed /ˈhærəst; həˈræst/ *adj* tired and worried because you have too much to do

harbour[1] (*AmE* harbor) /ˈhɑːbə(r)/ *noun* [C,U] a place on the coast where ships can be tied up and protected from the sea and bad weather ➲ picture on **page P10**

harbour[2] (*AmE* harbor) /ˈhɑːbə(r)/ *verb* [T] **1** to hide or protect sb/sth that is bad: *They were accused of harbouring terrorists.* **2** to keep feelings or thoughts secret in your mind for a long time: *She began to **harbour doubts** about the decision.*

hard[1] /hɑːd/ *adj* (harder; hardest)
➤NOT SOFT **1** not soft to touch; not easy to break or bend: *The bed was so hard that I couldn't sleep.* ◆ *Diamonds are the hardest known mineral.* OPP **soft**
➤NOT EASY **2** hard (for sb) (to do sth) difficult to do or understand; not easy: *The first question in the exam was very hard.* ◆ *This book is hard to understand./It is a hard book to understand.* ◆ *It's hard for young people to find good jobs nowadays.* ◆ *I find her attitude very **hard to take*** (= difficult to accept). SYN **tough** OPP **easy** **3** needing or using a lot of physical strength or mental effort: *It's a hard climb to the top of the hill.* ◆ ***Hard work** is said to be good for you.* ◆ *He's a hard worker.* **4** (used about conditions) full of difficulty: *She had a hard time when her parents died.* ◆ *to have a hard day/life/childhood*
➤NOT KIND **5** not feeling or showing kindness or pity; not gentle: *You have to be hard to succeed in business.* OPP **soft, lenient**
➤WEATHER **6** very cold: *The forecast is for a hard winter/frost.* OPP **mild**
➤WATER **7** containing particular minerals so that soap does not make many bubbles: *a **hard water** area* OPP **soft**
IDM **a hard act to follow** a person or a thing that it is difficult to do better than
be hard at it to be working very hard doing sth
be hard on sb/sth **1** to treat sb/sth in a very strict or unkind way: *Don't be too hard on her—she's only a child.* **2** to be difficult for or unfair to sb/sth: *Managing with very little money can be hard on students.*
give sb a hard time (*informal*) to make a situation unpleasant, embarrassing or difficult for sb
hard and fast (used about rules, etc.) that cannot be changed: *There are no hard and fast rules about this.*
hard facts information that is true, not just people's opinions
hard luck! ➲ **luck**
hard of hearing unable to hear well
have a hard job doing/to do sth; **have a hard time doing sth** to do sth with great difficulty
learn the hard way ➲ **learn**
no hard feelings (*spoken*) used to tell sb you do not feel angry after an argument, etc: *'No hard feelings, I hope,' he said, offering me his hand.*
take a hard line (on sth) to deal with sth in a very serious way that you will not allow anyone to change: *The government has taken a hard line on people who drink and drive.*
▶ **hardness** *noun* [U]

hard[2] /hɑːd/ *adv* **1** with great effort, energy or attention: *He worked hard all his life.* ◆ *You'll have to try a bit harder than that.* **2** with great force; heavily: *It was raining/snowing hard.* ◆ *He hit her hard across the face.*

HELP **Hard or hardly?** Do not confuse **hard** with **hardly**. **Hardly** is an adverb meaning 'almost not': *I hardly ever go to concerts.* ◆ *I can hardly wait for my birthday.*

IDM **be hard pressed/pushed/put to do sth** to find sth very difficult to do: *He was hard pressed to explain her sudden disappearance.*
be hard up (for sth) to have too few or too little of sth, especially money
die hard ➲ **die**
hard done by (*BrE*) not fairly treated: *He felt very hard done by when he wasn't chosen for the team.*

hardback /ˈhɑːdbæk/ *noun* [C] a book that has a hard cover: *This book is only available **in hardback**.* ➲ look at **paperback**

H

ˌhard-ˈboiled *adj* (used about an egg) boiled until it is solid inside

ˌhard ˈcore *noun* [sing, with sing or pl verb] the members of a group who are the most active

ˌhard ˈcurrency *noun* [U] money belonging to a particular country that is easy to exchange and not likely to fall in value

ˌhard ˈdisk *noun* [C] a piece of hard plastic that is fixed inside a computer and is used for storing data and programs permanently ➲ look at **floppy disk**

ˈhard drive *noun* [C, usually sing] a part of a computer that reads data on a **hard disk**

TOPIC

Hard drive

Sometimes your computer may **crash** and you have to **reboot** it (= switch it off and on again). If your **hard drive fails**, you may lose all the data that you had **stored on** it, so it's a good idea to **back up your files** (= make copies of them), possibly on an **external hard drive** (= one that is not part of your computer).

ˌhard ˈdrug *noun* [C, usually pl] a powerful and illegal drug that some people take for pleasure and can become **addicted** to (= unable to stop taking or using it): *Heroin and cocaine are hard drugs.* ➲ look at **soft**

harden /ˈhɑːdn/ *verb* **1** [I,T] to become or to make sth hard or less likely to change: *The concrete will harden in 24 hours.* ◆ *The firm has hardened its attitude on this question.* **2** [I] (used about sb's face, voice, etc.) to become serious and unfriendly **3** [T, usually passive] **harden sb/sth/yourself** to make sb less kind or less easily shocked: *a hardened criminal* ◆ *War reporters get hardened to seeing suffering.*

ˌhard-ˈheaded *adj* determined and not allowing yourself to be influenced by emotions: *a hard-headed businessman*

ˌhard-ˈhearted *adj* not kind to other people and not considering their feelings OPP **soft-hearted**

ˌhard-ˈhitting *adj* that talks about or criticizes sb/sth in an honest and very direct way: *a hard-hitting campaign/speech/report*

🔑 **hardly** /ˈhɑːdli/ *adv* **1** almost no; almost not; almost none: *There's* ***hardly any*** *coffee left.* ◆ *We* ***hardly ever*** *go out nowadays.* ◆ *I hardly spoke any English when I first came here.* ➲ look at **almost** **2** used especially after 'can' and 'could' and before the main verb to emphasize that sth is difficult to do: *Speak up—I can hardly hear you.* **3** (used to say that sth has just begun, happened, etc.) only just: *She'd* ***hardly*** *gone to sleep* ***before/when*** *it was time to get up again.*

HELP Note that if 'hardly' is at the beginning of a sentence, the verb follows immediately. This use is found in formal writing: *Hardly had she gone to sleep when it was time to get up again.*

4 (used to suggest that sth is unlikely or unreasonable) not really: *You can hardly expect me to believe that excuse!* ➲ note at **hard** ➲ look at **barely**, **scarcely**

ˌhard-ˈnosed *adj* not affected by feelings or emotions when trying to get what you want: *hard-nosed journalists/politicians*

hardship /ˈhɑːdʃɪp/ *noun* [C,U] a situation that is difficult or unpleasant because you do not have enough money, food, etc: *This new tax is going to cause a lot of hardship.*

ˌhard ˈshoulder (*AmE* shoulder) *noun* [C] a narrow section of road at the side of a **motorway** (= a wide road for fast traffic) where cars are allowed to stop in an emergency

hardware /ˈhɑːdweə(r)/ *noun* [U] **1** the machinery and electronic parts of a computer system ➲ look at **software** **2** tools and equipment that are used in the house and garden: *a hardware shop*

ˌhard-ˈwearing *adj* (*BrE*) (used about materials, clothes, etc.) strong and able to last for a long time

ˌhard-ˈworking *adj* working with effort and energy: *a hard-working man*

hardy /ˈhɑːdi/ *adj* (**hardier**; **hardiest**) strong and able to survive difficult conditions and bad weather: *a hardy plant*

hare /heə(r)/ *noun* [C] an animal like a **rabbit** (= a small animal with long ears) but bigger and with longer ears and legs ➲ picture at **rabbit**

harem /ˈhɑːriːm/ *noun* [C] a number of women living with one man, especially in Muslim societies. The part of the building the women live in is also called a **harem**.

🔑 **harm¹** /hɑːm/ *noun* [U] damage or injury: *Peter ate some of those berries but they didn't* ***do*** *him* ***any harm.*** ◆ *Experienced staff watch over the children to make sure they don't* ***come to any harm.***

IDM **no harm done** (*informal*) used to tell sb that they have not upset anyone or caused any damage or injury: *'Sorry about what I said to you last night.' 'That's all right, Jack, no harm done!'*

out of harm's way in a safe place: *Put the medicine out of harm's way where the children can't reach it.*

there is no harm in doing sth; it does no harm (for sb) to do sth there's nothing wrong in doing sth (and sth good may result): *I'm sure he'll say no, but there's no harm in asking.*

🔑 **harm²** /hɑːm/ *verb* [T] to cause injury or damage; hurt: *Too much sun can harm your skin.*

🔑 **harmful** /ˈhɑːmfl/ *adj* **harmful (to sb/sth)** causing harm: *Traffic fumes are harmful to the environment.*

🔑 **harmless** /ˈhɑːmləs/ *adj* **1** not able or not likely to cause damage or injury; safe: *You needn't be frightened—these insects are totally harmless.* **2** not likely to upset people: *The children can watch that film—it's quite harmless.*

▶ **harmlessly** *adv*

harmonica /hɑːˈmɒnɪkə/ (also **mouth organ**) *noun* [C] a small musical instru-

harmonica

ment that you play by moving it across your lips while you are blowing

harmonious /hɑːˈməʊniəs/ *adj* **1** friendly, peaceful and without disagreement **2** (used about musical notes, colours, etc.) producing a pleasant effect when heard or seen together ▶ **harmoniously** *adv*

harmonize (also -ise) /ˈhɑːmənaɪz/ *verb* [I] **1** harmonize (with sth) (used about two or more things) to produce a pleasant effect when seen, heard, etc. together **2** harmonize (with sb/sth) to sing or play music that sounds good combined with the main tune ▶ **harmonization** (also -isation) /ˌhɑːmənaɪˈzeɪʃn/ *noun* [U]

harmony /ˈhɑːməni/ *noun* (*pl* harmonies) **1** [U] a state of agreement or of living together in peace: *We need to live more **in harmony with** our environment.* **2** [C,U] a pleasing combination of musical notes, colours, etc: *There are some beautiful harmonies in that music.*

harness¹ /ˈhɑːnɪs/ *noun* [C] **1** a set of narrow pieces of leather that is put around a horse's neck and body so that it can pull sth **2** a set of narrow pieces of material for fastening sth to sb's body or for stopping sb from moving around, falling, etc: *a safety harness*

harness² /ˈhɑːnɪs/ *verb* [T] **1** harness sth (to sth) to put a **harness** on a horse, etc. or to tie a horse, etc. to sth using a **harness**: *Two ponies were harnessed to the cart.* **2** to control the energy of sth in order to produce power or to achieve sth: *to harness the sun's rays as a source of energy*

harp /hɑːp/ *noun* [C] a large musical instrument which has many strings stretching from the top to the bottom of a frame. You play the **harp** with your fingers. ➲ picture at **music** ▶ **harpist** /-pɪst/ *noun* [C]

harpoon /hɑːˈpuːn/ *noun* [C] a long thin weapon with a sharp pointed end and a rope tied to it that is used to catch **whales** (= very large sea animals) and large fish ▶ **harpoon** *verb* [T]

harrowing /ˈhærəʊɪŋ/ *adj* making people feel very sad or upset: *The programme showed harrowing scenes of the victims of the war.*

harsh /hɑːʃ/ *adj* (harsher; harshest) **1** very strict and unkind: *a harsh punishment/criticism* ◆ *The judge had some **harsh words** for the journalist's behaviour.* ➲ look at **severe** **2** unpleasant and difficult to live in, look at, listen to, etc: *She grew up in the harsh environment of London's East End.* ◆ *a harsh light/voice* **3** too strong or rough and likely to damage sth: *This soap is too harsh for a baby's skin.* ▶ **harshly** *adv* ▶ **harshness** *noun* [U]

harvest /ˈhɑːvɪst/ *noun* **1** [C,U] the time of year when the grain, fruit, etc. is collected on a farm; the act of collecting the grain, fruit, etc: *Farmers always need extra help with the harvest.* **2** [C] the amount of grain, fruit, etc. that is collected: *This year's wheat harvest was very poor.* ▶ **harvest** *verb* [I,T]: *to harvest crops* ➲ look at **combine harvester**

has /həz; *strong form* hæz/ ➲ **have**

ˈ**has-been** *noun* [C] (*informal*) a person or thing that is no longer as famous, successful or important as before

hash /hæʃ/ *noun* **1** [U] a hot dish of meat mixed together with potato and fried **2** [U] (*informal*) = **hashish** **3** (also ˈhash sign) (*BrE*) [C] the symbol (#), especially one on a telephone
IDM **make a hash of sth** (*informal*) to do sth badly

hashish /ˈhæʃiːʃ/ (also *informal* hash) *noun* [U] a drug made from **hemp** (= a type of plant) that some people smoke for pleasure and which is illegal in many countries **SYN** **cannabis**

ˈ**hash sign** = hash(3)

ˈ**hashtag** /ˈhæʃtæg/ *noun* [C] a word or phrase with the symbol # in front of it, that is used in messages sent on the Internet to help people find the subjects that interest them: *I searched for the hashtags '#jobs' and '#teaching' on Twitter.*

hasn't /ˈhæznt/ *short for* **has not**

hassle¹ /ˈhæsl/ *noun* (*informal*) **1** [C,U] a thing or situation that is annoying because it is complicated or involves a lot of effort: *It's going to be a hassle having to change trains with all this luggage.* **2** [U] disagreeing or arguing: *I've decided what to do—please don't give me any hassle about it.*

hassle² /ˈhæsl/ *verb* [T] (*informal*) to annoy sb, especially by asking them to do sth many times: *I wish he'd stop hassling me about decorating the house.* **SYN** **bother**

haste /heɪst/ *noun* [U] speed in doing sth, especially because you do not have enough time: *The letter had clearly been written **in haste**.*

hasten /ˈheɪsn/ *verb* (*formal*) **1** [I] hasten to do sth to be quick to do or say sth: *She hastened to apologize.* **2** [T] to make sth happen or be done earlier or more quickly

hasty /ˈheɪsti/ *adj* (hastier; hastiest) **1** said or done too quickly: *He said a hasty 'goodbye' and left.* **2** hasty (in doing sth/to do sth) (used about a person) acting or deciding too quickly or without enough thought: *Maybe I was too hasty in rejecting her for the job.* ▶ **hastily** *adv*

🔑 **hat** /hæt/ *noun* [C] a covering that you wear on your head, usually when you are outside: *to wear a hat* ◆ *a sun hat* ➲ picture on **page 346**
IDM **at the drop of a hat** ➲ **drop²**

hatch¹ /hætʃ/ *verb* **1** [I] hatch (out) (used about a baby bird, insect, fish, etc.) to come out of an egg: *Ten chicks hatched out this morning.* **2** [T] to make a baby bird, etc. come out of an egg **3** [T] hatch sth (up) to think of a plan (usually to do sth bad): *He hatched a plan to avoid paying any income tax.*

hatch² /hætʃ/ *noun* [C] **1** an opening in the **deck** (= the floor) of a ship or the bottom of an aircraft through which goods are passed **2** an opening in the wall between a kitchen and another room that is used for passing food through **3** the door in a plane or **spacecraft** (= a vehicle that travels in space)

H

hatchback /ˈhætʃbæk/ *noun* [C] a car with a large door at the back that opens upwards ➲ picture on **page P7**

hatchet /ˈhætʃɪt/ *noun* [C] a small **axe** (= a tool with a short handle and a metal head with a sharp edge used for cutting wood)

hate¹ /heɪt/ *verb* [T] **1 hate (sb/sth); hate (doing/to do sth)** to have a very strong feeling of not liking sb/sth at all: *I hate grapefruit.* ♦ *I hate it when it's raining like this.* ♦ *I hate to see the countryside spoilt.* ♦ *He hates driving at night.* ➲ note at **dislike**

> **MORE** Detest and loathe express a stronger feeling than hate.

2 used when saying sth you would prefer not to have to say or as a polite way of saying sorry for sth: *I hate to say it, but I think she's failed the exam.* ♦ *I hate to bother you, but did you pick up my keys by mistake?*

hate² /heɪt/ *noun* **1** [U] a very strong feeling of not liking sb/sth at all: *Jan gave her a look of pure hate.* **SYN** hatred **2** [C] a thing that you do not like at all: *Plastic flowers are one of my* ***pet hates*** (= the things that I particularly do not like).

hateful /ˈheɪtfl/ *adj* **hateful (to sb)** extremely unpleasant: *It was a hateful thing to say.*

hatred /ˈheɪtrɪd/ *noun* [U] **hatred (for/of sb/sth)** a very strong feeling of not liking sb/sth; hate

ˈhat-trick *noun* [C] three points, goals, etc. scored by one player in the same game; three successes achieved by one person: *to score a hat-trick*

haughty /ˈhɔːti/ *adj* (**haughtier**; **haughtiest**) proud, and thinking that you are better than other people: *She gave me a haughty look.* ▶ **haughtily** *adv*

haul¹ /hɔːl/ *verb* [T] to pull sth with a lot of effort or difficulty: *A lorry hauled the car out of the mud.*

haul² /hɔːl/ *noun* **1** [C, usually sing] **a haul (of sth)** a large amount of sth that has been stolen, caught, collected, etc: *The fishermen came back with a good haul of fish.* **2** [sing] a distance to be travelled: *It seemed* ***a long haul*** *back home.*

haulage /ˈhɔːlɪdʒ/ *noun* [U] (*BrE*) the transport of goods by road, rail, etc.; the money charged for this

haunt¹ /hɔːnt/ *verb* [T] **1** [often passive] if a **ghost** (= the spirit of a dead person) **haunts** a place, people say that they have seen it there: *The house is said to be haunted.* **2** (used about sth unpleasant or sad) to be always in your mind: *His unhappy face has haunted me for years.*

haunt² /hɔːnt/ *noun* [C] a place that you visit regularly: *This cafe has always been a favourite haunt of mine.*

haunting /ˈhɔːntɪŋ/ *adj* having a quality that stays in your mind: *a haunting song*

have¹ /hæv/ *verb* [T] ℹ For the forms of 'have', look at the irregular verbs section at the back of this dictionary.

➤**OWN/HOLD 1** (*BrE also* **have got**) [not used in the continuous tenses] to own or to hold sth: *I've got a new camera.* ♦ *The flat has two bedrooms.* ♦ *He's got short dark hair.* ♦ *to have patience/enthusiasm/skill* ♦ *Have you got any brothers and sisters?* ♦ *Do you have time to check my work?* ➲ look at **possess**

➤**DUTY 2** (also **have got**) [not used in the continuous tenses] to have a particular duty or plan: *Do you have any homework tonight?* ♦ *I've got a few things to do this morning, but I'm free later.*

➤**HOLD/KEEP IN POSITION 3** (also **have got**) [not used in the continuous tenses] to hold sb/sth; to keep sth in a particular place: *The dog had me by the leg.* ♦ *We've got our TV up on a shelf.*

➤**ILLNESS 4** (also **have got**) [not used in the continuous tenses] to be ill with sth: *She's got a bad cold.* ♦ *to have flu/a headache/cancer/AIDS*

➤**EXPERIENCE 5** to experience sth: *to have fun* ♦ *to have problems/difficulties* ♦ *to have an idea/an impression/a feeling* ♦ *to have an accident* **6** to suffer the effect of what sb else does to you: *She had her bag stolen on the underground.*

➤**DO STH 7** used with many nouns to talk about doing sth: *What time do you have breakfast?* ♦ *to have a*

hats

cowboy hat · bowler (*AmE* derby) · top hat · sun hat · hood · hard hat · crash helmet · baseball cap · woolly hat · beret · cap

drink/something to eat ◆ I'll just have a shower then we'll go. ◆ to have an argument/talk/chat

➤CAUSE **8** to cause sb/sth to do sth or to be in a particular state: *The music soon had everyone dancing.* ◆ *I'll have dinner ready when you get home.*

➤HAVE STH DONE **9** to arrange for sb to do sth: *I have my hair cut every six weeks.* ◆ *You should have your eyes tested.*

➤ENTERTAIN **10** to look after or entertain sb: *We're having some people to dinner tomorrow.*

IDM **have had it** (*informal*) used about things that are completely broken, or dead: *This TV has had it. We'll have to buy a new one.* ℹ For other idioms containing **have**, look at the entries for the nouns, adjectives, etc. For example, **not have a clue** is at **clue**.

PHR V **have sb on** to trick sb as a joke: *Don't listen to what Jim says—he's only having you on.*

have (got) sth on 1 to be wearing sth: *She's got a green jumper on.* **2** (*informal*) to have an arrangement to do sth: *I've got a lot on this week* (= I'm very busy).

have sth out to have part of your body removed: *to have a tooth/your appendix out*

have² /həv; *strong form* hæv/ *auxiliary verb* used for forming the perfect tenses ℹ For more information, look at the **Reference Section** at the back of this dictionary.

haven /ˈheɪvn/ *noun* [C] **a haven (of sth); a haven (for sb/sth)** a place where people or animals can be safe and rest: *a haven of peace* ◆ *The lake is a haven for water birds.* ◆ *a* **tax haven** (= a country where income tax is low)

haven't /ˈhævnt/ *short for* **have not**

have to /ˈhæv tə; ˈhæf tə; *strong form and before vowels* ˈhæv tuː; ˈhæf tuː/ (*also* **have got to**) *modal verb* used for saying that sb must do sth or that sth must happen: *He usually has to work on Saturday mornings.* ◆ *Do you have to have a visa to go to America?* ◆ *We don't have to* (= it's not necessary to) *go to the party if you don't want to* ◆ *We had to do lots of boring exercises.* ◆ *She's got to go to the bank this afternoon.* ◆ *There has to be a reason for his strange behaviour.* ➲ A more common, less formal expression in British English is **have got to.** ➲ note at **must** ℹ For more information about modal verbs, look at the **Reference Section** at the back of this dictionary.

havoc /ˈhævək/ *noun* [U] a situation in which there is a lot of damage or confusion: *The rail strikes will* **cause havoc** *all over the country.* ➲ look at **wreak**

hawk /hɔːk/ *noun* [C] a type of large bird that catches and eats small animals and birds. **Hawks** can see very well.

MORE Hawks are a type of **bird of prey**.

hay /heɪ/ *noun* [U] grass that has been cut and dried for use as animal food

ˈhay fever *noun* [U] an illness that affects the eyes, nose and throat and is caused by breathing in **pollen** (= the powder produced by some plants) ➲ look at **allergy**

haywire /ˈheɪwaɪə(r)/ *adj*

IDM **be/go haywire** (*informal*) to be or become out of control: *I can't do any work because the computer's gone haywire.*

hazard¹ /ˈhæzəd/ *noun* [C] a danger or risk: *Smoking is a serious health hazard.* ◆ *Pollution is a serious health hazard.*

hazard² /ˈhæzəd/ *verb* [T] to make a guess or to suggest sth even though you know it may be wrong: *I don't know what he paid for the house but I could* **hazard a guess.**

hazardous /ˈhæzədəs/ *adj* involving risk or danger

haze /heɪz/ *noun* **1** [C,U] air that is difficult to see through because of heat, dust or smoke ➲ note at **fog 2** [sing] a mental state in which you cannot think clearly

hazel¹ /ˈheɪzl/ *noun* [C] a small tree or bush that produces nuts

hazel² /ˈheɪzl/ *adj* (used especially about eyes) light brown in colour

hazelnut /ˈheɪzlnʌt/ *noun* [C] a small brown nut that we eat ➲ picture at **nut**

hazy /ˈheɪzi/ *adj* (**hazier; haziest**) **1** not clear, especially because of heat: *The fields were hazy in the early morning sun.* **2** difficult to remember or understand clearly: *a hazy memory* **3** (used about a person) uncertain, not expressing things clearly: *She's a bit hazy about the details of the trip.*

HD /ˌeɪtʃ ˈdiː/ *abbr* = **high-definition**

he¹ /hiː/ *pron* (the subject of a verb) the male person mentioned earlier: *I spoke to John before he left.* ◆ *Look at that boy—he's going to fall in!*

GRAMMAR If you want to refer to a person who could be either male or female, there are several ways to do this: **He or she, him or her, his or her,** and in writing **he/she** or **s/he** can be used: *If you are not sure, ask your doctor. He/She can give you further information.* It is now common to use **they, them** or **their**: *Everybody knows what they want.* ◆ *When somebody asks me a question I always try to give them a quick answer.* **They, them** and **their** are used in this way in this dictionary. However, it is also possible to make the sentence plural: *A baby cries when s/he is tired* ◆ *Babies cry when they are tired.*

he² /hiː/ *noun* [sing] a male animal: *Is your cat a he or a she?*

head¹ /hed/ *noun*

➤PART OF BODY **1** [C] the part of your body above your neck: *She turned her head to look at him.* ➲ picture at **body**

➤-HEADED **2** [in compounds] having the type of head mentioned: *a bald-headed man*

➤MIND **3** [C] a person's mind, brain or mental ability: *Use your head!* (= Think!) ◆ *A horrible thought entered my head.*

➤IN CHARGE **4** [C,U] the person in charge of a group of people: *the head of the family* ◆ *Several* ***heads of state*** (= official leaders of countries) *attended the funeral.* ◆ *the head waiter* **5** (also ˌ**head 'teacher**) [C] the teacher in charge of a school: *Who is going to be the new head?*
➤SIDE OF COIN **6 heads** [U] the side of a coin with the head of a person on it: *Heads or tails? Heads I go first, tails you do.*
➤TOP PART **7** [C,sing] the top, front or most important part: *to sit at the head of the table* ◆ *the head of a nail* ◆ *the head of the queue*
IDM bite sb's head off ➲ **bite**[1]
come to a head; bring sth to a head if a situation comes to a head or if you bring it to a head, it suddenly becomes very bad and you have to deal with it immediately
do sb's head in (*BrE informal*) to make sb upset and confused
get sth into your head; put sth into sb's head to start or to make sb start believing or thinking sth: *Barry's got it into his head that glasses would make him more attractive.*
go to sb's head 1 to make sb drunk: *Wine always goes straight to my head.* **2** to make sb too proud: *If you keep telling him how clever he is, it will go to his head!*
have a head for sth 1 to be good at sth: *to have a head for business/figures* **2** if sb does not **have a head for heights**, they feel nervous and think they are going to fall when they look down from a high place: *You need a good head for heights if you live on the top floor!*
a/per head for each person: *How much will the meal cost a head?*
head first 1 with your head before the rest of your body: *Don't go down the slide head first.* **2** too quickly or suddenly: *Don't rush head first into a decision.*
head over heels (in love) loving sb very much: *Jane's fallen head over heels in love with Andy.*
hit the nail on the head ➲ **hit**[1]
keep your head to stay calm
keep your head above water to just manage to survive in a difficult situation, especially one in which you do not have enough money
keep your head down to try not to be noticed
laugh, scream, etc. your head off to laugh, shout, etc. very loudly and for a long time
lose your head ➲ **lose**
make head or tail of sth to understand sth: *I can't make head or tail of this exercise.*
off the top of your head ➲ **top**[1]
out of/off your head (*informal*) crazy, often because of the effects of drugs or alcohol
put/get your heads together to make a plan with sb
a roof over your head ➲ **roof**
shake your head ➲ **shake**[1]
take it into your head to do sth to suddenly decide to do sth that other people consider strange: *I don't know why Kevin took it into his head to enter that marathon!*

H

head[2] /hed/ *verb*
➤MOVE TOWARDS **1** [I] to move in the direction mentioned: *The ship headed towards the harbour.* ◆ *Where are you heading?*
➤BE IN CHARGE **2** [T] to be in charge of or to lead sth: *Do you think that he has the experience necessary to head a government?*
➤BE FIRST **3** [T] to be at the front of a line, top of a list, etc: *to head a procession*
➤WRITE TITLE **4** [T, often passive] to give a title at the top of a piece of writing: *The report was headed 'The State of the Market'.*
➤FOOTBALL **5** [T] to hit the ball with your head: *He headed the ball into the net.*
PHR V head for to move towards a place: *It's getting late—I think it's time to head for home.*

headache /ˈhedeɪk/ *noun* [C] **1** a pain in your head: *I've got a splitting* (= very bad) *headache.* ➲ note at **ache 2** a person or thing that causes worry or difficulty: *Paying the bills is a constant headache.*

heading /ˈhedɪŋ/ *noun* [C] the words written as a title at the top of a page or a piece of writing: *The company's aims can be grouped under three main headings.*

headlamp = **headlight**

headland /ˈhedlənd; -lænd/ *noun* [C] a narrow piece of land that sticks out into the sea ➲ picture on **page P10**

headlight /ˈhedlaɪt/ (also **headlamp** /ˈhedlæmp/) *noun* [C] one of the two large bright lights at the front of a vehicle ➲ picture on **page P7**

headline /ˈhedlaɪn/ *noun* **1** [C] the title of a newspaper article printed in large letters above the story **2 the headlines** [pl] the main items of news read on TV or radio

headlong /ˈhedlɒŋ/ *adv, adj* **1** with your head before the rest of your body: *I tripped and fell headlong into the road.* **2** too quickly; without enough thought: *He rushed headlong into buying the business.*

headmaster /ˌhedˈmɑːstə(r)/ (*fem* **headmistress** /ˌhedˈmɪstrəs/) *noun* [C] (*BrE old-fashioned*) (*AmE usually* **principal**) a teacher who is in charge of a school, especially a private school

ˌ**head-'on** *adj* [only *before* a noun] *adv* with the front of one car, etc. hitting the front of another: *a head-on crash*

headphones /ˈhedfəʊnz/ (also **earphones**) *noun* [pl] a piece of equipment worn over or in the ears that makes it possible to listen to music, the radio, etc. without other people hearing it ➲ note at **listen**

headquarters /ˌhedˈkwɔːtəz/ *noun* [U,with sing or pl verb] (*abbr* **HQ**) the place from where an organization is controlled; the people who work there: *Where is/are the firm's headquarters?*

headrest /ˈhedrest/ *noun* [C] the part of a seat or chair that supports a person's head, especially on the front seat of a car

headscarf /ˈhedskɑːf/ *noun* [C] (*pl* **headscarves**) a square piece of cloth worn by women to cover the head

headset /ˈhedset/ *noun* [C] a pair of **headphones** (= a piece of equipment for listening that you wear over or in your ears), especially one with a **microphone** (= a device for speaking into) fixed to it: *The pilot was talking into his headset.*

headstand /ˈhedstand/ *noun* [C] a position in which a person has their head on the ground and their feet straight up in the air

ˌhead ˈstart *noun* [sing] an advantage that you have from the beginning: *Being able to speak English gave her a head start at school.*

headstone /ˈhedstəʊn/ *noun* [C] a large stone with writing on, used to mark where a dead person is buried SYN **gravestone, tombstone**

headstrong /ˈhedstrɒŋ/ *adj* doing what you want, without listening to advice from other people

ˌhead ˈteacher = **head**[1] (5)

headway /ˈhedweɪ/ *noun*
IDM **make headway** to go forward or make progress in a difficult situation

heal /hiːl/ *verb* [I,T] **heal (over/up)** to become healthy again; to make sth healthy again: *The cut will heal up in a few days.* ◆ (*figurative*) *Nothing he said could heal the damage done to their relationship.*

health /helθ/ *noun* [U] **1** the condition of sb's body or mind: *Fresh fruit is good for your health.* ◆ *in good/poor health* ◆ (*figurative*) *the health of your marriage/finances* **2** the state of being well and free from illness: *As long as you have your health, nothing else matters.* **3** the work of providing medical care: *health insurance* ◆ *health and safety regulations* ◆ *the rising costs of* ***health care***

ˈhealth centre *noun* [C] a building where a group of doctors see their patients

ˈhealth club (also **gym**) *noun* [C] a private club where people go to do physical exercise in order to stay or become healthy and fit

ˈhealth food *noun* [C,U] food that does not contain any artificial substances and is therefore thought to be good for your health

the ˈhealth service *noun* [C] the organization of the medical services of a country ➲ look at **the National Health Service**

healthy /ˈhelθi/ *adj* (**healthier**; **healthiest**) **1** not often ill; strong and well: *a healthy child/animal/plant* **2** helping to produce good health: *a healthy climate/diet/lifestyle* **3** showing good health (of body or mind): *healthy skin and hair* **4** normal and sensible: *There was plenty of healthy competition between the brothers.* OPP for all meanings **unhealthy** ▶ **healthily** *adv*

heap[1] /hiːp/ *noun* [C] **1** **a heap (of sth)** an untidy pile of sth: *a heap of books/papers* ◆ *All his clothes are* ***in a heap*** *on the floor!* ➲ note at **pile** ➲ look at **scrapheap** **2** (*informal*) **a heap (of sth)**; **heaps (of sth)** a large number or amount; plenty: *I've got a heap of work to do.* ◆ *There's heaps of time before the train leaves.*
IDM **heaps better, more, older, etc.** (*informal*) much better, etc.

heap[2] /hiːp/ *verb* [T] **1** **heap sth (up)** to put things in a pile: *I'm going to heap all the leaves up over there.* ◆ *Add six heaped tablespoons of flour (= in a recipe).* **2** **heap A on/onto B; heap B with A** to put a large amount of sth on sth/sb: *He heaped food onto his plate.* ◆ *The press heaped the team with praise.*

hear /hɪə(r)/ *verb* (*pt, pp* **heard** /hɜːd/) **1** [I,T] [not used in the continuous tenses] to receive sounds with your ears: *Can you speak a little louder—I can't hear very well.* ◆ *I didn't hear you go out this morning.* ◆ *Did you hear what I said?* ➲ note at **smell**[1]

> HELP **Hear** or **listen**? Often, **hear** means to receive a sound without necessarily trying to; to **listen** is to make a conscious or active effort to hear something: *I always wake up when I hear the birds singing.* ◆ *I love listening to music in the evening.* ◆ *Listen—I've got something to tell you.* Sometimes, **hear** can have a similar meaning to 'listen to': *We'd better hear what they have to say.*

2 [T] [not used in the continuous tenses] to be told about sth: *I hear that you've been offered a job in Canada.* ◆ *'I passed my test!'* ***'So I've heard****—well done!'* ◆ *I was sorry to hear about your mum's illness.*

> HELP Although this verb is not used in the continuous tenses, it is common to see the present participle (= *-ing* form): *Not hearing what he'd said over the noise of the machines, she just nodded and smiled.*

3 [T] (used about a judge, a court, etc.) to listen to the evidence in a trial in order to make a decision about it: *Your case will be heard this afternoon.*
IDM **Hear! Hear!** used for showing that you agree with what sb has just said, especially in a meeting
won't/wouldn't hear of sth to refuse to allow sth: *I wanted to go to art school but my parents wouldn't hear of it.*
PHR V **hear from sb** to receive a letter, email, telephone call, etc. from sb
hear of sb/sth to know about sb/sth because you have already been told about them/it: *Have you heard of the Bermuda Triangle?*

hearing /ˈhɪərɪŋ/ *noun* **1** [U] the ability to hear: *Her hearing isn't very good so you need to speak louder.* **2** [C] a time when evidence is given to a judge in a court of law: *a court/disciplinary hearing* **3** [sing] a chance to give your opinion or explain your position: *to get/give somebody a fair hearing*
IDM **hard of hearing** ➲ **hard**[1]
in/within sb's hearing near enough to sb that they can hear what is being said

ˈhearing aid *noun* [C] a small device for people who cannot hear well that fits inside the ear and makes sounds louder

hearsay /ˈhɪəseɪ/ *noun* [U] things you have heard another person or other people say, which may or may not be true

H

hearse /hɜːs/ *noun* [C] a large car used for carrying a dead person to their funeral

heart /hɑːt/ *noun*
➤PART OF BODY **1** [C] the organ inside your chest that sends blood round your body: *When you exercise your heart beats faster.* ◆ *heart disease/failure* ➲ picture at **body**
➤FEELINGS/EMOTIONS **2** [C] the centre of sb's feelings and emotions: *She has a kind heart* (= she is kind and gentle). ◆ *They say he died of a broken heart* (= unhappiness caused by sb he loved).
➤-HEARTED **3** [in compounds] having the type of feelings or character mentioned: *kind-hearted* ◆ *cold-hearted*
➤CENTRE **4** [sing] **the heart (of sth)** the most central or important part of sth; the middle: *Rare plants can be found* ***in the heart of*** *the forest.* ◆ *Let's get straight to* ***the heart of the matter***.
➤SHAPE **5** [C] a symbol that is shaped like a heart, often red or pink and used to show love: *He sent her a card with a big red heart on it.*
➤IN CARD GAMES **6** **hearts** [pl] in a pack of playing cards, the **suit** (= one of the four sets) with red shapes like hearts on them: *the queen of hearts* ➲ note at **card** ➲ picture at **card** **7** [C] one of the cards from this **suit**: *Play a heart, if you've got one.*
IDM **after your own heart** (used about people) similar to yourself or of the type you like best
at heart really; in fact: *My father seems strict but he's a very kind man at heart.*
break sb's heart to make sb very sad
(off) by heart by remembering exactly; from memory: *Learning lists of words off by heart isn't a good way to increase your vocabulary.*
a change of heart ➲ **change**[2]
close/dear/near to sb's heart having a lot of importance and interest for sb: *a subject that is very dear to my heart*
cross my heart ➲ **cross**[2]
from the (bottom of your) heart in a way that is true and sincere: *I mean what I said from the bottom of my heart.*
have a heart of gold to be a very kind person
have/with sb's (best) interests at heart ➲ **interest**[1]
heart and soul with a lot of energy and enthusiasm
your heart is not in sth used to say that you are not very interested in or enthusiastic about sth: *It's hard to do a job if your heart isn't in it.*
your heart sinks to suddenly feel disappointed or sad: *When I saw the queues of people in front of me, my heart sank.*
in your heart (of hearts) used to say that you know that sth is true although you do not want to admit or believe it: *She knew in her heart of hearts that she was making the wrong decision.*
lose heart ➲ **lose**
not have the heart (to do sth) to be unable to do sth unkind: *I don't really have the time to help her, but I didn't have the heart to say no.*
pour your heart out (to sb) ➲ **pour**
set your heart on sth; have your heart set on sth to decide you want sth very much; to be determined to do or have sth
take heart (from sth) to begin to feel more positive (because of sth)
take sth to heart to be deeply affected or upset by sth
to your heart's content as much as you want
with all your heart; with your whole heart completely: *I hope with all my heart that things work out for you.*
young at heart ➲ **young**[1]

heartache /ˈhɑːteɪk/ *noun* [U] great sadness or worry

ˈ**heart attack** *noun* [C] a sudden serious illness when the heart stops working correctly, sometimes causing death: *She's had a heart attack.*

heartbeat /ˈhɑːtbiːt/ *noun* [C] the regular movement or sound of the heart as it sends blood round the body

heartbreak /ˈhɑːtbreɪk/ *noun* [U] very great sadness

heartbreaking /ˈhɑːtbreɪkɪŋ/ *adj* making you feel very sad

heartbroken /ˈhɑːtbrəʊkən/ (also ˌbroken-ˈhearted) *adj* extremely sad because of sth that has happened: *Mary was heartbroken when John left her.*

hearten /ˈhɑːtn/ *verb* [T, usually passive] to encourage sb; to make sb feel happier OPP **dishearten**

heartening /ˈhɑːtnɪŋ/ *adj* encouraging; making you believe that sth good will happen OPP **disheartening**

heartfelt /ˈhɑːtfelt/ *adj* deeply felt; sincere: *a heartfelt apology*

hearth /hɑːθ/ *noun* [C] the place where you have an open fire in the house; the area in front of an open fire ➲ picture at **fireplace**

heartily /ˈhɑːtɪli/ *adv* **1** with obvious enthusiasm and enjoyment: *He joined in heartily with the singing.* **2** very much; completely

heartland /ˈhɑːtlænd/ *noun* [C] the most central or important part of a country, area, etc.

heartless /ˈhɑːtləs/ *adj* unkind; cruel ▸ **heartlessly** *adv* ▸ **heartlessness** *noun* [U]

ˈ**heart-rending** *adj* making you feel very sad: *The mother of the missing boy made a heart-rending appeal on TV.*

ˌ**heart-to-ˈheart** *noun* [C] a conversation in which you say exactly what you really feel or think: *John's teacher had a heart-to-heart with him to find out what was worrying him.*

hearty /ˈhɑːti/ *adj* (**heartier**; **heartiest**) **1** showing warm and friendly feelings: *a hearty welcome* **2** loud, happy and full of energy: *a hearty laugh* **3** [only *before* a noun] (used about a meal) large; making you feel full: *a hearty breakfast* **4** showing that you feel strongly about sth: *He nodded his head in hearty agreement.* ◆ *Hearty congratulations to everyone involved.*

heat¹ /hi:t/ *noun* ▸FEELING HOT **1** [U, sing] the feeling of sth hot: *This fire doesn't **give out** much **heat**.* ♦ *The fire gave out a fierce heat.* **2** [sing] [often with *the*] hot weather: *I like the English climate because I can't stand the heat.* **3** [sing] a thing that produces heat: *Remove the pan from the heat* (= the hot part of the cooker). ▸STRONG FEELINGS **4** [U] a state or time of anger or excitement: ***In the heat of the moment**, she threatened to resign.* ▸RACE **5** [C] one of the first parts of a race or competition. The winners of the heats compete against other winners until the final result is decided: *He won his heat and went through to the final.*

IDM **be on heat** (used about some female animals) to be ready to have mate

heat² /hi:t/ *verb* [I,T] **heat (sth) (up)** to become or to make sth hot or warm: *Wait for the oven to heat up before you put the pie in.* ♦ *The meal is already cooked but it will need heating up.*

heated /ˈhi:tɪd/ *adj* (used about a person or discussion) angry or excited: *a heated argument/debate* ▸ **heatedly** *adv*

heater /ˈhi:tə(r)/ *noun* [C] a machine used for making water or the air in a room, car, etc. hotter: *an electric/gas heater* ♦ *a water heater*

heath /hi:θ/ *noun* [C] an area of open land that is not used for farming and that is often covered with rough grass and other wild plants

heather /ˈheðə(r)/ *noun* [U] a low wild plant that grows especially on hills and land that is not farmed and has small purple, pink or white flowers

heating /ˈhi:tɪŋ/ *noun* [U] a system for making rooms and buildings warm: *Our heating goes off at 10 p.m. and comes on again in the morning.* ➲ look at **central heating**

heatwave /ˈhi:tweɪv/ *noun* [C] a period of unusually hot weather

heave¹ /hi:v/ *verb* **1** [I,T] to lift, pull or throw sb/sth heavy with one big effort: *Take hold of this rope and heave!* ♦ *We heaved the cupboard up the stairs.* **2** [I] **heave (with sth)** to move up and down or in and out in a heavy but regular way: *His chest was heaving with the effort of carrying the cooker.* **3** [I] to experience the tight feeling you get in your stomach when you are just about to **vomit** (= bring up food from the stomach): *The sight of all that blood made her stomach heave.*

IDM **heave a sigh** to breathe out slowly and loudly: *He heaved a sigh of relief when he heard the good news.*

heave² /hi:v/ *noun* [C] a strong pull, push, throw, etc.

heaven /ˈhevn/ *noun* **1** [U] (also **Heaven**) the place where, in some religions, it is believed that God lives and where good people go when they die: *to go to/be in heaven* OPP **hell** ➲ note at **God** **2** [U, sing] a place or a situation in which you are very happy: *It was **heaven on earth** spending all winter skiing.* **3 the heavens** [pl] (used in poetry and literature) the sky: *The stars shone brightly in the heavens that night.*

heavenly /ˈhevnli/ *adj* **1** [only *before* a noun] connected with heaven or the sky: *heavenly bodies* (= the sun, moon, stars, etc.) **2** (*informal*) very pleasant; wonderful

heavy /ˈhevi/ *adj* (**heavier**; **heaviest**) **1** weighing a lot; difficult to lift or move: *This box is too heavy for me to carry.* **2** used when asking or stating how much sb/sth weighs: ***How heavy** is your suitcase?* **3** larger, stronger or more than usual: *heavy rain* ♦ *heavy traffic* ♦ *a heavy smoker/drinker* (= sb who smokes/drinks a lot) ♦ *The sound of his heavy* (= loud and deep) *breathing told her that he was asleep.* ♦ *a heavy sleeper* (= sb who is difficult to wake) ♦ *a heavy meal* **4** (used about a material or substance) solid or thick: *heavy soil* ♦ *a heavy coat* OPP **light** **5** full of hard work; (too) busy: *a heavy day/schedule/timetable* **6** serious, difficult or boring: *His latest novel makes **heavy reading**.* ♦ *Things got a bit heavy when she started talking about her failed marriage.*

IDM **make heavy weather of sth** to make sth seem more difficult than it really is

take a heavy toll/take its toll (on sth) ➲ **toll** ▸ **heavily** *adv* ▸ **heaviness** *noun* [U]

ˌheavy-ˈduty *adj* [only *before* a noun] not easily damaged and therefore suitable for regular use or for hard physical work: *a heavy-duty tyre/carpet*

ˌheavy-ˈhanded *adj* **1** not showing much understanding of other people's feelings: *a heavy-handed approach* **2** using unnecessary force: *heavy-handed police methods*

ˌheavy ˈindustry *noun* [C,U] industry that uses large machinery to produce metal, coal, vehicles, etc.

ˌheavy ˈmetal *noun* [U] a style of very loud rock music that is played on electric instruments

heavyweight /ˈheviweɪt/ *noun* [C] a person who is in the heaviest weight group in certain fighting sports: *the world heavyweight boxing champion*

heckle /ˈhekl/ *verb* [I,T] to interrupt a speaker at a public meeting with difficult questions or rude comments ▸ **heckler** /ˈheklə(r)/ *noun* [C]

hectare /ˈhekteə(r)/ *noun* [C] (*abbr* ha) a measure of land; 10 000 square metres

hectic /ˈhektɪk/ *adj* very busy with of a lot of things that you have to do quickly ▸ **hectically** /-kli/ *adv*

he'd /hi:d/ *short for* **he had; he would**

hedge¹ /hedʒ/ *noun* [C] a row of bushes or trees planted close together at the edge of a garden or field to separate one piece of land from another ➲ picture on **page P11**

hedge² /hedʒ/ *verb* [I] to avoid giving a direct answer to a question

IDM **hedge your bets** to protect yourself against losing or making a mistake by supporting more than one person or opinion

H

hedgehog /ˈhedʒhɒg/ *noun* [C] a small brown animal covered with **spines** (= sharp needles)

hedgehog

hedgerow /ˈhedʒrəʊ/ *noun* [C] a row of bushes, etc. especially at the side of a country road or around a field

heed¹ /hiːd/ *verb* [T] (*formal*) to pay attention to advice, a warning, etc.

heed² /hiːd/ *noun*
IDM **take heed (of sb/sth); pay heed (to sb/sth)** (*formal*) to pay careful attention to what sb says: *You should take heed of your doctor's advice.*

H

heel¹ /hiːl/ *noun* [C] **1** the back part of your foot below your ankle: *These shoes rub against my heels.* ➲ picture at **body** **2** the part of a sock, etc. that covers your **heel** **3** the higher part of a shoe under the **heel** of your foot: *High heels* (= shoes with high heels) *are not practical for long walks.* ➲ picture at **shoe** **4** -heeled having the type of **heel** mentioned: *high-heeled/low-heeled shoes*
IDM **dig your heels in** ➲ **dig¹**
head over heels ➲ **head¹**

heel² /hiːl/ *verb* [T] to repair the heel of a shoe

hefty /ˈhefti/ *adj* (**heftier**; **heftiest**) (*informal*) big and strong or heavy: *a hefty young man*

height /haɪt/ *noun* **1** [C,U] the measurement from the bottom to the top of a person or thing: *The nurse is going to check your height and weight.* ♦ *We need a fence that's about two metres* **in height**. ➲ note at **tall** ➲ picture at **length** ➲ *adjective* **high** **2** [U] the fact that sb is tall or sth is high: *He looks older than he is because of his height.* **3** [C,U] the distance that sth is above the ground: *We are now flying at a height of 10 000 metres.* ♦ *The plane* **lost/gained height** *steadily.* ➲ When talking about aeroplanes a more formal word for height is **altitude**. **4** [C, usually pl] a high place or area: *I can't go up there. I'm afraid of heights.* **5** [sing] the strongest or most important part of sth: *the height of summer*

heighten /ˈhaɪtn/ *verb* [I,T] to become or to make sth greater or stronger: *I'm using yellow paint to heighten the sunny effect of the room.*

heir /eə(r)/ *noun* [C] **heir (to sth)** the person with the legal right to **inherit** (= receive) money, property or a title when the owner dies: *He's the heir to a large fortune.*

MORE A female heir is often called an **heiress**.

heirloom /ˈeəluːm/ *noun* [C] something valuable that has belonged to the same family for many years

held *past tense, past participle of* **hold¹**

helicopter /ˈhelɪkɒptə(r)/ (also *informal* **chopper**) *noun* [C] a small aircraft that can go straight up into the air. **Helicopters** have **blades** (= long thin metal parts that go round very fast) on top. ➲ picture on **page P6**

helium /ˈhiːliəm/ *noun* [U] (*symbol* **He**) a gas which is lighter than air and which does not burn

hell /hel/ *noun* **1** [sing] (also **Hell**) the place where, in some religions, it is believed that bad people go to when they die: *to go to/be in hell* ➲ look at **heaven** **2** [U, sing] (*informal*) a situation or place that is very unpleasant or painful: *He went through hell when his wife left him.* **3** [U] (*slang*) used as a swear word to show anger: *Oh hell, I've left my phone at home!*

HELP Be careful. Some people find this sense of hell offensive.

4 **the hell** (*slang*) used as a swear word in questions to show anger or surprise: *Why the hell didn't you tell me this before?*
IDM **all hell broke loose** (*informal*) there was suddenly a lot of noise and confusion
(just) for the hell of it (*informal*) for fun
give sb hell (*informal*) to speak to sb very angrily or to be very strict with sb
a/one hell of a ... (*informal*) used to make an expression stronger or to mean 'very': *He got into a hell of a fight* (= a terrible fight).
like hell ➲ **like¹**

he'll /hiːl/ *short for* **he will**

hellish /ˈhelɪʃ/ *adj* terrible; very unpleasant: *a hellish experience*

hello (*BrE also* **hallo**) /həˈləʊ/ *exclam, noun* used when you meet sb, for attracting sb's attention or when you are using the telephone ➲ note at **introduce**

MORE Other informal ways to say 'hello' are **hi** and **hiya**.

helm /helm/ *noun* [C] a handle or a wheel used for steering a boat or ship
IDM **at the helm** in charge of an organization, group of people, etc.

helmet /ˈhelmɪt/ *noun* [C] a type of hard hat that you wear to protect your head: *a crash helmet* ➲ picture at **bicycle**

help¹ /help/ *verb* **1** [I,T] **help (sb) (with sth)**; **help (sb) (to) do sth**; **help sb (across, over, out of, into, etc.)** to do sth for sb in order to be useful or to make sth easier for them: *Can I help?* ♦ *Could you help me with the cooking?* ♦ *I helped her to organize the day.* ♦ *My son's helping in our shop at the moment.* ♦ *She helped her grandmother up the stairs* (= supported her as she climbed the stairs). **2** [I] (*spoken*) used to get sb's attention when you are in danger or difficulty: *Help! I'm going to fall!* **3** [I,T] to make sth better or easier: *If you apologize to him it might help.* ♦ *This medicine should help your headache.* **4** [T] **help yourself (to sth)** to take sth (especially food and drink) that is offered to you: *Help yourself to a drink!* ♦ *'Can I borrow your pen?' 'Yes, help yourself.'* **5** [T] **help yourself to sth** to take sth without asking permission; to steal: *Don't just help yourself to my money!*
IDM **can/can't/could(n't) help (doing) sth/**

yourself be able/not be able to stop or avoid doing sth: *It was so funny I couldn't help laughing.* ♦ *I just couldn't help myself—I had to laugh.*

a helping hand some help: *My neighbour is always ready to give me a helping hand.*

PHR V **help (sb) out** to help sb in a difficult situation; to give money to help sb

help² /help/ *noun* **1** [U] **help (with sth)** the act of helping: *Do you need any help with that?* ♦ *This map isn't much help.* ♦ *She stopped smoking **with the help of** her family and friends.* ♦ *He repaired his car **with the help of** his father.* ♦ *Run and **get help**—my son's fallen in the river!* **2** [sing] **a help (to sb)** a person or thing that helps: *Your directions were a great help—we found the place easily.*

helper /ˈhelpə(r)/ *noun* [C] a person who helps (especially with work)

helpful /ˈhelpfl/ *adj* giving help: *helpful advice* ▶ **helpfully** /-fəli/ *adv* ▶ **helpfulness** *noun* [U]

helping /ˈhelpɪŋ/ *noun* [C] the amount of food that is put on a plate at one time: *After two helpings of pasta, I couldn't eat any more.* ➲ look at **portion**

helpless /ˈhelpləs/ *adj* unable to take care of yourself or do things without the help of other people: *a helpless baby* ▶ **helplessly** *adv*: *They watched helplessly as their house went up in flames.* ▶ **helplessness** *noun* [U]

hem¹ /hem/ *noun* [C] the edge at the bottom of a piece of cloth (especially on a skirt, dress or trousers) that has been turned up and sewn

hem² /hem/ *verb* [T] (**hemming**; **hemmed**) to turn up and sew the bottom of a piece of clothing or cloth

PHR V **hem sb in** to surround sb and prevent them from moving away: *We were hemmed in by the crowd and could not leave.*

hemisphere /ˈhemɪsfɪə(r)/ *noun* [C] **1** one half of the earth: *the northern/southern/eastern/western hemisphere* ➲ picture at **earth** **2** the shape of half a ball

hemophilia, hemophiliac (*AmE*) = **haemophilia, haemophiliac**

hemorrhage (*AmE*) = **haemorrhage**

hemorrhoids (*AmE*) = **haemorrhoids**

hemp /hemp/ *noun* [U] a plant that is used for making rope and rough cloth and for producing **cannabis** (= a drug which is illegal in many countries)

hen /hen/ *noun* [C] **1** a female bird that is kept for its eggs or its meat ➲ note at **chicken** ➲ picture at **chicken** **2** the female of any type of bird: *a hen pheasant* ➲ look at **cock**

hence /hens/ *adv* (*formal*) for this reason: *I've got some news to tell you—hence the letter.*

henceforth /ˌhensˈfɔːθ/ (also **henceforward** /ˌhensˈfɔːwəd/) *adv* (*formal*) from now on; in future

henchman /ˈhentʃmən/ *noun* [C] (*pl* -men /-mən/) a person who is employed by sb to protect them and who may do things that are illegal or violent

ˈ**hen party** (also ˈ**hen night**) *noun* [C] (*BrE*) a party that a woman who will soon be getting married has with her female friends ➲ look at **stag night**

henpecked /ˈhenpekt/ *adj* used to describe a husband who always does what his wife tells him to do

hepatitis /ˌhepəˈtaɪtɪs/ *noun* [U] a serious disease of the **liver** (= one of the body's main organs)

her¹ /hɜː(r)/ *pron* (the object of a verb or preposition) the woman or girl that was mentioned earlier: *He told Sue that he loved her.* ♦ *I've got a letter for your mother. Could you give it to her, please?* ➲ note at **he** ➲ look at **she**

her² /hɜː(r)/ *determiner* of or belonging to the woman or girl mentioned earlier: *That's her book. She left it there this morning.* ♦ *Fiona has broken her leg.* ➲ look at **hers**

herald /ˈherəld/ *verb* [T] (*written*) to be a sign that sb/sth is going to happen soon: *The minister's speech heralded a change of policy.*

herb /hɜːb/ *noun* [C] a plant whose leaves, seeds, etc. are used in medicine or in cooking: *Add some herbs, such as rosemary and thyme.* ➲ look at **spice** ➲ picture on **page P14**

herbal /ˈhɜːbl/ *adj* made of or using **herbs**: *herbal medicine/remedies*

herd¹ /hɜːd/ *noun* [C] a large number of animals that live and feed together: *a herd of cattle/deer/elephants* ➲ note at **cow** ➲ look at **flock**

herd² /hɜːd/ *verb* [T] to move people or animals somewhere together in a group: *The prisoners were herded onto the train.*

here¹ /hɪə(r)/ *adv* **1** [after a verb or a preposition] in, at or to the place where you are or which you are pointing to: *Come (over) here.* ♦ *The school is a mile from here.* ♦ *Please sign here.* **2** at this point in a discussion or a piece of writing: *Here the speaker stopped and looked around the room.* **3** used at the beginning of a sentence to introduce or draw attention to sb/sth: *Here is the 10 o'clock news.* ♦ *Here comes the bus.* ♦ *Here we are* (= we've arrived).

> **HELP** Note the word order in the last example. We say *Here are the children.* but with a pronoun we say *Here they are.*

4 used for emphasizing a noun: *I think you'll find this book here very useful.*

IDM **here and there** in various places

here goes (*informal*) used to say that you are about to do sth exciting, dangerous, etc: *I've never done a backward dive before, but here goes!*

here's to sb/sth used for wishing for the health, success, etc. of sb/sth while holding a drink: *Here's to a great holiday!*

here you are; here you go (*informal*) used when you are giving sth to sb: *Here you are—this is that book I was talking about.*

neither here nor there not important: *My opinion*

H

is neither here nor there. If you like the dress then buy it.

here² /hɪə(r)/ *exclam* used for attracting sb's attention, when offering help or when giving sth to sb: *Here, let me help!*

hereabouts /ˌhɪərəˈbaʊts/ (*AmE* **hereabout**) *adv* near this place

hereafter /ˌhɪərˈɑːftə(r)/ *adv* (*written*) (used in legal documents, etc.) from now on

hereditary /həˈredɪtri/ *adj* passed on from parent to child: *a hereditary disease*

heredity /həˈredəti/ *noun* [U] the process by which physical or mental qualities pass from parent to child

H

heresy /ˈherəsi/ *noun* [C,U] (*pl* **heresies**) a (religious) opinion or belief that is different from what is generally accepted to be true

heretic /ˈherətɪk/ *noun* [C] a person whose religious beliefs do not agree with what is generally accepted ▶ **heretical** /həˈretɪkl/ *adj*

heritage /ˈherɪtɪdʒ/ *noun* [C, usually sing] the customs, qualities and culture of a country that have existed for a long time and that have great importance for the country

hermit /ˈhɜːmɪt/ *noun* [C] a person who prefers to live alone, without contact with other people, often for religious reasons

hernia /ˈhɜːniə/ (also **rupture**) *noun* [C,U] the medical condition in which an organ inside the body, for example the stomach, pushes through the wall of muscle which surrounds it

⚷ **hero** /ˈhɪərəʊ/ *noun* [C] (*pl* **heroes**) **1** a person who is admired, especially for having done sth difficult or good: *The team were given a* ***hero's welcome*** *on their return home.* **2** the most important male character in a book, play, film, etc: *The hero of the film is a little boy.* ➲ look at **heroine, villain**

heroic /həˈrəʊɪk/ *adj* (used about people or their actions) having a lot of courage: *a heroic effort* ▶ **heroically** /-kli/ *adv*

heroin /ˈherəʊɪn/ *noun* [U] a powerful illegal drug that some people take for pleasure and then cannot stop taking

heroine /ˈherəʊɪn/ *noun* [C] **1** a woman who is admired, especially for having done sth difficult or good **2** the most important female character in a book, play, film, etc. ➲ look at **hero**

heroism /ˈherəʊɪzəm/ *noun* [U] great courage

herring /ˈherɪŋ/ *noun* [C,U] (*pl* **herring** *or* **herrings**) a fish that swims in **shoals** (= large groups) in cold seas and is used for food

IDM **a red herring** ➲ **red**

⚷ **hers** /hɜːz/ *pron* of or belonging to her: *I didn't have a pen, but Helen lent me hers.*

⚷ **herself** /hɜːˈself/ *pron* **1** used when the female who does an action is also affected by it: *She hurt herself quite badly when she fell downstairs.* ◆ *Irene looked at herself in the mirror.* **2** used to emphasize the female who does the action: *She told me the news herself.* ◆ *Has Rosy done this herself?* (= or did sb else do it for her?)

IDM **(all) by herself** **1** alone: *She lives by herself.* ➲ note at **alone** **2** without help: *I don't think she needs any help—she can change a tyre by herself.*

(all) to herself without having to share: *Julie has the bedroom to herself now her sister's left home.*

he's /hiːz/ *short for* **he is; he has**

hesitant /ˈhezɪtənt/ *adj* **hesitant (to do/about doing sth)** slow to speak or act because you are not sure if you should or not: *I'm very hesitant about criticizing him too much.* ▶ **hesitancy** /ˈhezɪtənsi/ *noun* [U] ▶ **hesitantly** *adv*

⚷ **hesitate** /ˈhezɪteɪt/ *verb* [I] **1 hesitate (about/over sth)** to pause before you do sth or before you take a decision, usually because you are uncertain or worried: *He hesitated before going into her office.* ◆ *She's still hesitating about whether to accept the job or not.* **2 hesitate (to do sth)** to not want to do sth because you are not sure that it is right: *Don't hesitate to phone if you have any problems.* ▶ **hesitation** /ˌhezɪˈteɪʃn/ *noun* [C,U]: *She agreed without a moment's hesitation.*

heterosexual /ˌhetərəˈsekʃuəl/ *adj* sexually attracted to people of the opposite sex ➲ look at **bisexual, homosexual** ▶ **heterosexual** *noun* [C]

het up /ˌhet ˈʌp/ *adj* [not before a noun] (*informal*) **het up (about/over sth)** worried or excited about sth

hexagon /ˈheksəgən/ *noun* [C] a shape with six sides ▶ **hexagonal** /heksˈægənl/ *adj*

hey /heɪ/ *exclam* (*informal*) used to attract sb's attention or to show that you are surprised or interested: *Hey, what are you doing?*

IDM **hey presto** people sometimes say **'hey presto'** when they have done sth so quickly that it seems like magic

heyday /ˈheɪdeɪ/ *noun* [sing] the period when sb/sth was most powerful, successful, rich, etc.

HGV /ˌeɪtʃ dʒiː ˈviː/ *abbr* (*BrE*) **heavy goods vehicle**; a large vehicle such as a lorry

⚷ **hi** /haɪ/ *exclam* (*informal*) used to say hello: *Hi guys!*

hibernate /ˈhaɪbəneɪt/ *verb* [I] (used about animals) to spend the winter in a state like deep sleep ▶ **hibernation** /ˌhaɪbəˈneɪʃn/ *noun* [U]

hiccup (also **hiccough**) /ˈhɪkʌp/ *noun* **1** [C] a sudden, usually repeated sound that is made in the throat and that you cannot control **2 (the) hiccups** [pl] a series of **hiccups**: *Don't eat so fast or you'll* ***get hiccups!*** ◆ *If you* ***have the hiccups****, try holding your breath.* **3** [C] a small problem or difficulty: *There's been a slight hiccup in our holiday arrangements but I've got it sorted out now.* ▶ **hiccup** (also **hiccough**) *verb* [I]

⚷ **hide¹** /haɪd/ *verb* (*pt* **hid** /hɪd/; *pp* **hidden** /ˈhɪdn/) **1** [T] to put or keep sb/sth in a place where they or it cannot be seen; to cover sth so that it cannot be seen: *Where shall I hide the money?* ◆ *You couldn't see Bill in the photo—he was hidden behind John.* **2** [I] to be or go in a place where you cannot be seen or found: *Quick, run and hide!* ♦ *The child was hiding under the bed.* **3** [T] **hide sth (from sb)** to keep sth secret, especially your feelings: *She tried to hide her disappointment from them.*

hide² /haɪd/ *noun* **1** [C] a place from which people can watch wild animals, birds, etc. without being seen **2** [C,U] the skin of a large animal, especially when it is used for leather

ˌhide-and-ˈseek *noun* [U] a children's game in which one person hides and the others try to find them

hideous /ˈhɪdiəs/ *adj* very ugly or unpleasant: *a hideous sight* ♦ *a hideous crime* ♦ *That new dress she's got is hideous.* ▶ **hideously** *adv*

hiding /ˈhaɪdɪŋ/ *noun* **1** [U] the state of being hidden: *The escaped prisoners are believed to be* ***in hiding*** *somewhere in London.* ♦ *to go into hiding* **2** [C, usually sing] (*informal*) a punishment involving being hit hard many times: *You deserve a good hiding for what you've done.*

hierarchy /ˈhaɪərɑːki/ *noun* [C] (*pl* **hierarchies**) a system or an organization that has many levels from the lowest to the highest ▶ **hierarchical** /ˌhaɪəˈrɑːkɪkl/ *adj*

hieroglyphics /ˌhaɪərəˈglɪfɪks/ *noun* [pl] the system of writing that was used in ancient Egypt in which a small picture represents a word or sound

hi-fi /ˈhaɪ faɪ/ *noun* [C,U] equipment for playing recorded music that produces high quality sound ▶ **hi-fi** *adj*: *a hi-fi system*

higgledy-piggledy /ˌhɪgldi ˈpɪgldi/ *adv, adj* (*informal*) not in any order; mixed up together

high¹ /haɪ/ *adj* (**higher**; **highest**)
➤FROM BOTTOM TO TOP **1** (used about things) having a large distance between the bottom and the top: *high cliffs* ♦ *What's the highest mountain in the world?* ♦ *high heels* (on shoes) ♦ *The garden wall was so high that we couldn't see over it.* **OPP** **low** ➲ note at **tall** ➲ *noun* **height** **2** having a particular height: *The hedge is one metre high.* ♦ *knee-high boots*
➤FAR FROM GROUND **3** at a level which is a long way from the ground, or from sea level: *a high shelf* ♦ *The castle was built on high ground.* **OPP** **low**
➤MORE THAN USUAL **4** above the usual or normal level or amount: *high prices* ♦ *at high speed* ♦ *a high level of unemployment* ♦ *He's got a high temperature.* ♦ *Oranges are high in vitamin C.* **OPP** **low**
➤BETTER THAN USUAL **5** better than what is usual: *high-quality goods* ♦ *Her work is of a very high standard.* ♦ *He has a high opinion of you.* **OPP** **poor**
➤IMPORTANT **6** having an important position: *Sam only joined the company three years ago, but she's already quite high up.*
➤GOOD **7** morally good: *high ideals*
➤SOUND **8** not deep or low: *Dogs can hear very high sounds.* ♦ *Women usually have higher voices than men.* **OPP** **low**
➤ON DRUGS **9** [not before a noun] (*informal*) **high (on sth)** under the influence of drugs, alcohol, etc.
➤IN CAR **10** (used about a gear in a car) that allows a faster speed **OPP** **low**
IDM **be left high and dry** ➲ **leave¹**
a high/low profile ➲ **profile**
It's about/high time ➲ **time¹**

high² /haɪ/ *noun* [C] **1** a high level or point: *Profits reached an all-time high last year.* **OPP** **low** **2** an area of high air pressure **OPP** **low** **3** (*informal*) a feeling of great pleasure or happiness that sb gets from doing sth exciting or being successful: *He was* ***on a high*** *after passing all his exams.* ♦ *She talked about the* ***highs and lows*** *of her career.* **OPP** **low** **4** (*informal*) a feeling of great pleasure or happiness that may be caused by a drug, alcohol, etc.
IDM **on high** (*formal*) (in) a high place, the sky or heaven: *The order came from on high.*

high³ /haɪ/ *adv* **1** at or to a high position or level: *The sun was high in the sky.* ♦ *I can't jump any higher.* ♦ *The plane flew high overhead.* ➲ *noun* **height** **2** at a high level: *How high can you sing?* **OPP** for both meanings **low**
IDM **high and low** everywhere: *We've searched high and low for the keys.*
run high (used about the feelings of a group of people) to be especially strong: *Emotions are running high in the neighbourhood where the murders took place.*

highbrow /ˈhaɪbraʊ/ *adj* interested in or concerned with matters that many people would find too serious to be interesting: *highbrow newspapers/TV programmes*

ˈhigh chair *noun* [C] a special chair with long legs and a table, for a small child to sit in when eating ➲ picture at **chair**

ˌhigh-ˈclass *adj* of especially good quality: *a high-class restaurant*

ˌHigh ˈCourt *noun* [C] the most important court of law in some countries

ˌhigh-defiˈnition *adj* (*abbr* **HD**) [only *before* a noun] using or produced by a system that gives very clear detailed images: *high-definition television*

ˌhigher eduˈcation *noun* [U] education and training at a college or university, especially to degree level ➲ look at **further education**

the ˈhigh jump *noun* [sing] the sport in which people try to jump over a bar in order to find out who can jump the highest ➲ look at **long jump**

highland /ˈhaɪlənd/ *adj* [only *before* a noun] **1** in or connected with an area of land that has mountains: *highland streams* ➲ look at **lowland** **2** [pl] in or connected with the Highlands (= the part of Scotland where there are mountains)

ˌhigh-ˈlevel *adj* involving important people: *high-level talks*

highlight¹ /ˈhaɪlaɪt/ *verb* [T] **1** to emphasize sth so that people give it special attention: *The report highlighted the need for improved safety at football grounds.* **2** to mark part of a text with a different colour or to mark an area on a computer screen so that people give it more attention: *I've highlighted the important passages in yellow.*

H

highlight² /ˈhaɪlaɪt/ *noun* **1** [C] the best or most interesting part of sth: *The highlights of the match will be shown on TV tonight.* **2 highlights** [pl] areas of lighter colour that are put in sb's hair

highlighter /ˈhaɪlaɪtə(r)/ (also ˈ**highlighter pen**) *noun* [C] a special pen used for marking words in a text in bright colours ➲ picture at **stationery**

highly /ˈhaɪli/ *adv* **1** to a high degree; very: *highly trained/educated/developed* ◆ *a highly paid job* ◆ *It's highly unlikely that anyone will complain.* **2** with admiration: *I think very highly of your work.*

ˌ**highly** ˈ**strung** *adj* nervous and easily upset

Highness /ˈhaɪnəs/ *noun* **your/his/her Highness** [C] a title used when speaking about or to a member of a royal family

ˌ**high-**ˈ**powered** *adj* **1** (used about people) important and successful: *high-powered executives* **2** (used about things) having great power: *a high-powered engine*

ˈ**high-rise** *adj* [only *before* a noun] (used about a building) very tall and having a lot of floors

ˈ**high school** *noun* [C,U] a school for students between the ages of 11 and 18 in Britain, or 14 and 18 in some other countries

ˈ**high street** *noun* [C] (*BrE*) (often used in names) the main street of a town: *The Post Office is in the High Street.*

high-tech (also **hi-tech**) /ˌhaɪ ˈtek/ *adj* using the most modern methods and machines, especially electronic ones: *high-tech industries/hospitals* **OPP low-tech**

ˌ**high** ˈ**tide** *noun* [U] the time when the sea comes furthest onto the land **OPP low tide** ➲ look at **the ebb**

highway /ˈhaɪweɪ/ *noun* [C] (*especially AmE*) a main road (between towns) ➲ look at **motorway**

hijab /hɪˈdʒɑːb/ *noun* [C] a head covering worn in public by some Muslim women

hijack /ˈhaɪdʒæk/ *verb* [T] **1** to take control of a plane, etc. by force, usually for political reasons: *The plane was hijacked on its flight to Sydney.* ➲ note at **crime** ➲ look at **kidnap 2** to take control of a meeting, an event, etc. in order to force people to pay attention to sth: *The rally was hijacked by right-wing extremists.* ▶ **hijack** *noun* [C]: *The hijack was ended by armed police.* ▶ **hijacker** *noun* [C] ▶ **hijacking** *noun* [C,U]

hike /haɪk/ *noun* [C] a long walk in the country: *We went on a ten-mile hike at the weekend.* ▶ **hike** *verb* [I] ▶ **hiker** *noun* [C]

hiking /ˈhaɪkɪŋ/ *noun* [U] the activity of going for long walks in the country for pleasure

> **HELP** **Go hiking** is used when you are talking about spending time hiking: *They went hiking in Wales for their holiday.*

hilarious /hɪˈleəriəs/ *adj* extremely funny ➲ note at **humour** ▶ **hilariously** *adv*

hilarity /hɪˈlærəti/ *noun* [U] the state of finding sth very funny, which causes people to laugh loudly

hill /hɪl/ *noun* [C] **1** a high area of land that is not as high as a mountain: *There was a wonderful view from the top of the hill.* ➲ picture on **page P11 2** a slope on a road: *Take care when driving down steep hills.* ➲ look at **uphill, downhill**

hillside /ˈhɪlsaɪd/ *noun* [C] the side of a hill

hilltop /ˈhɪltɒp/ *noun* [C] the top of a hill

hilly /ˈhɪli/ *adj* (**hillier**; **hilliest**) having a lot of hills: *The country's very hilly around here.*

hilt /hɪlt/ *noun* [C] the handle of a knife or a **sword** (= a long metal weapon)
IDM to the hilt to a high degree; completely: *I'll defend you to the hilt.*

him /hɪm/ *pron* (the object of a verb or preposition) the man or boy who was mentioned earlier: *Helen told Ian that she loved him.* ◆ *I've got a letter for your father—can you give it to him, please?* ➲ note at **he**

himself /hɪmˈself/ *pron* **1** used when the male who does an action is also affected by it: *He cut himself when he was shaving.* ◆ *John looked at himself in the mirror.* ➲ picture at **each other 2** used to emphasize the male who does the action: *He told me the news himself.* ◆ *Did he write this himself?* (= or did sb else do it for him?)
IDM (all) by himself 1 alone: *He lives by himself.* ➲ note at **alone 2** without help: *He should be able to cook a meal by himself.*
(all) to himself without having to share: *Charlie has the bedroom to himself now his brother's left home.*

hind /haɪnd/ *adj* [only *before* a noun] (used about an animal's legs, etc.) at the back ➲ picture on **page P12**

> **MORE** We also say **back legs.** The legs at the front are the **front legs** or **forelegs.**

hinder /ˈhɪndə(r)/ *verb* [T] to make it more difficult for sb/sth to do sth: *A lot of scientific work is hindered by lack of money.*

hindrance /ˈhɪndrəns/ *noun* [C] a person or thing that makes it difficult for you to do sth

hindsight /ˈhaɪndsaɪt/ *noun* [U] the understanding that you have of a situation only after it has happened: ***With hindsight,*** *I wouldn't have lent him the money.* ➲ look at **foresight**

Hindu /ˈhɪnduː; ˌhɪnˈduː/ *noun* [C] a person whose religion is Hinduism ▶ **Hindu** *adj*: *Hindu beliefs*

Hinduism /ˈhɪnduːɪzəm/ *noun* [U] the main religion of India that includes the worship of one or more gods and the belief that, after death, people will return to life in a different form.

hinge¹ /hɪndʒ/ *noun* [C] a piece of metal that joins two sides of a box, door, etc. together and allows it to be opened or closed

hinge² /hɪndʒ/ *verb*
PHR V **hinge on sth** to depend on sth: *The future of the project hinges on the meeting today.*

hinge

hint¹ /hɪnt/ *noun* **1** [C] something that you suggest in an indirect way: *If you keep mentioning parties, maybe they'll **take the hint** and invite you.* **2** [C] something that suggests what will happen in the future: *The first half of the match **gave** no **hint** of the excitement to come.* **SYN** **sign** **3** [usually sing] a small amount of sth: *There was a hint of sadness in his voice.* **SYN** **suggestion** **4** [C] a piece of advice or information: *helpful hints* **SYN** **tip**

hint² /hɪnt/ *verb* [I,T] **hint (at sth); hint that ...** to suggest sth in an indirect way: *They only hinted at their great disappointment.* ♦ *He hinted that he might be moving to Greece.*

hip¹ /hɪp/ *noun* [C] the part of the side of your body above your legs and below your waist: *He stood there angrily with his hands on his hips.* ➲ picture at **body**

hip² /hɪp/ *exclam*
IDM **hip, hip, hurray/hurrah** shouted three times when a group wants to show that it is pleased with sb or with sth that has happened

ˈhip hop *noun* [U] a type of dance music with spoken words and a steady beat played on electronic instruments

hippie (also **hippy**) /ˈhɪpi/ *noun* [C] (*pl* **hippies**) a person who rejects the usual values and way of life of western society. Especially in the 1960s, **hippies** showed that they were different by wearing brightly coloured clothes, having long hair and taking drugs.

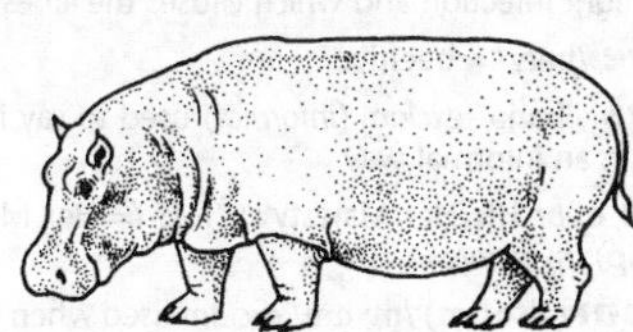
hippopotamus (*also* **hippo**)

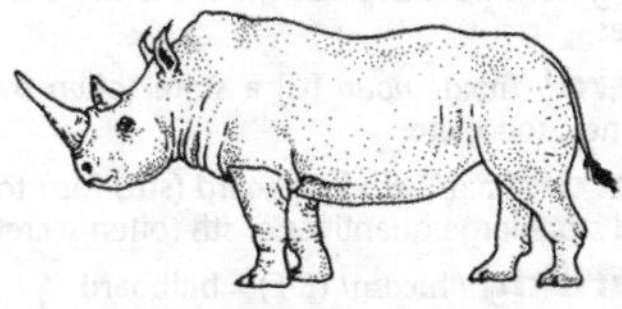
rhinoceros (*also* **rhino**)

hippopotamus /ˌhɪpəˈpɒtəməs/ *noun* [C] (*pl* **hippopotamuses** /-məsɪz/ *or* **hippopotami** /-maɪ/) (also *informal* **hippo**) a large African animal with a large head and short legs that lives in or near rivers

hire¹ /ˈhaɪə(r)/ *verb* [T] **1** (*AmE* **rent**) **hire sth (from sb)** to have the use of sth for a short time by paying for it

> **HELP** **Hire** or **rent**? In British English, you **hire** something for a short time: *We hired a car for the day.* You **rent** something if the period of time is longer: *to rent a house/flat/TV.* In American English **rent** is used in both situations.

2 to give sb a job for a short time: *We'll have to hire somebody to mend the roof.*

> **HELP** In American English **hire** is also used for talking about permanent jobs: *We just hired a new secretary.*

PHR V **hire sth (out) (to sb)** (*AmE* **rent**) to allow sb to use sth for a short fixed period in exchange for money: *We hire (out) our vans by the day.*

> **HELP** In British English, **rent** or **let** is used if the period of time is longer: *Mrs Higgs rents out rooms to students.* ♦ *We let our house while we were in France for a year.*

hire² /ˈhaɪə(r)/ *noun* [U] the act of paying to use sth for a short time: *Car hire is expensive in this country.* ♦ *Do you have bicycles **for hire**?*

ˌhire ˈpurchase *noun* [U] (*BrE*) (*abbr* **h.p.**) a way of buying goods. You do not pay the full price immediately but by **instalments** (= small regular payments) until the full amount is paid: *a hire purchase agreement for a car*

his¹ /hɪz/ *determiner* of or belonging to the man or boy who was mentioned earlier: *Peter has sold his car.* ♦ *He hurt his shoulder skiing.*

his² /hɪz/ *pron* of or belonging to him: *This is my book so that one must be his.* ➲ note at **he**

hiss /hɪs/ *verb* **1** [I,T] to make a sound like a very long 's' to show that you are angry or do not like sth: *The cat hissed at me.* ♦ *The speech was hissed and booed.* **2** [T] to say sth in a quiet angry voice: *'Stay away from me!' she hissed.* ▶ **hiss** *noun* [C]

historian /hɪˈstɔːriən/ *noun* [C] a person who studies or who is an expert in history

historic /hɪˈstɒrɪk/ *adj* famous or important in history: *The ending of apartheid was a historic event.* ➲ note at **important**

historical /hɪˈstɒrɪkl/ *adj* that really lived or happened; connected with real people or events in the past: *historical events/records/research* ▶ **historically** /-kli/ *adv*

history /ˈhɪstri/ *noun* (*pl* **histories**) **1** [U] all the events of the past: *an important moment in history* ➲ look at **natural history** **2** [C, usually sing] the series of events or facts that is connected with sb/sth: *He has a history of violence.* ♦ *a patient's medical history* **3** [U] the study of past events: *a degree in history* ♦ *History was my favourite subject at school.* **4** [C] a written description of past events: *She's writing a new history of Europe.*

H

HELP History or **story**? **History** is something true that really happened. A **story** is a description of a series of events that may or may not have happened.

IDM go down in/make history to be or do sth so important that it will be recorded in history: *She made history by becoming the first woman President.*
the rest is history ➲ **rest**[2]

hit[1] /hɪt/ *verb* [T] (hi**tt**ing; *pt, pp* hit) **1** to make sudden, violent contact with sb/sth: *The bus left the road and hit a tree.* ◆ *to hit somebody in the eye/across the face/on the nose* **2 hit sth (on/against sth)** to knock a part of your body, etc. against sth: *Peter hit his head on the low beam.* **3** to have a bad or unpleasant effect on sb/sth: *Inner city areas have been badly hit by unemployment.* ◆ *Her father's death has hit her very hard.* **4** to reach a place or a level: *If you follow this road you should hit the motorway in about ten minutes.* ◆ *The price of oil hit a new high yesterday.* **5** to experience sth unpleasant or difficult: *Things were going really well until we hit this problem.* **6** to suddenly come into sb's mind; to make sb realize or understand sth: *I thought I recognized the man's face and then it hit me—he was my old maths teacher!*
IDM hit it off (with sb) (*informal*) to like sb when you first meet them: *When I first met Tony's parents, we didn't really hit it off.*
hit the nail on the head to say sth that is exactly right
hit the jackpot to win a lot of money or have a big success
hit the roof (*informal*) to become very angry
PHR V hit back (at sb/sth) to attack (with words) sb who has attacked you: *The Prime Minister hit back at his critics.*
hit on sth to suddenly find sth by chance: *I finally hit on a solution to the problem.*
hit out (at sb/sth) to attack sb/sth: *The man hit out at the policeman.*

OTHER WORDS FOR

hit

Strike is a more formal word than **hit**. **Beat** means to hit many times: *He was badly beaten in the attack.* **Punch** means to hit somebody or something hard with your hand closed, for example when two people are fighting: *She punched him in the face.* **Smack** means to hit somebody with your hand flat, especially as a punishment: *I think it's wrong to smack children.*

hit[2] /hɪt/ *noun* [C] **1** the act of hitting sth: *The ship took a* **direct hit** *and sank.* ◆ *She gave her brother a hard hit on the head.* **2** a person or thing that is very popular or successful: *The album was a big hit.* **3** a result of a search on a computer, especially on the Internet
IDM make a hit (with sb) (*informal*) to make a good impression on sb: *The new teacher seems to have made a hit with the students.*

ˌhit-and-ˈmiss (also ˌhit-or-ˈmiss) *adj* (*informal*) not well organized; careless: *This method is a bit hit-or-miss, but it usually works.*

ˌhit-and-ˈrun *adj* [only *before* a noun] (used about a road accident) caused by a driver who does not stop to help

hitch[1] /hɪtʃ/ *verb* **1** [I,T] (*informal*) to get a free ride in a person's car; to travel around in this way by waiting by the side of a road and trying to get passing cars to stop: *I managed to hitch to Paris in just six hours.* ◆ *We missed the bus so we had to* **hitch a lift**. ➲ look at **hitchhike 2** [T] to fasten sth to sth else: *to hitch a trailer to the back of a car*

hitch[2] /hɪtʃ/ *noun* [C] a small problem or difficulty: *a technical hitch*

hitchhike /ˈhɪtʃhaɪk/ (also *informal* **hitch**) *verb* [I] to travel by waiting by the side of a road and holding out your hand or a sign until a driver stops and takes you in the direction you want to go: *He hitchhiked across Europe.*

MORE Hitchhike is usually used to talk about travelling long distances in this way for pleasure. **Hitch** can be used to mean the same, but it is also used to talk about travelling short distances in this way, for example because your car has broken down or you have missed a bus. **Hitch** can also be used transitively: *I hitched a lift/ride to the nearest petrol station.* **Thumb a lift** means the same.

▶ **hitchhiker** *noun* [C]

hi-tech = **high-tech**

hitherto /ˌhɪðəˈtuː/ *adv* (*formal*) until now

ˌhit-or-ˈmiss = **hit-and-miss**

HIV /ˌeɪtʃ aɪ ˈviː/ *noun* [U] **human immunodeficiency virus**; a virus which destroys the body's ability to fight infection and which causes the illness **AIDS**

hive /haɪv/ = **beehive**

hiya /ˈhaɪjə/ *exclam* (*informal*) used to say hello to sb in an informal way

HM *abbr* **His/Her Majesty's**: *HMS* (= Her Majesty's Ship) *Invincible*

hmm (also **hm**) /m; hm/ *exclam* used when you are not sure or when you are thinking about sth

ˌHM ˌRevenue and ˈCustoms *noun* [sing] the government department in the UK that collects taxes

hoard[1] /hɔːd/ *noun* [C] a store (often secret) of money, food, etc.

hoard[2] /hɔːd/ *verb* [I,T] **hoard (sth) (up)** to collect and store large quantities of sth (often secretly)

hoarding /ˈhɔːdɪŋ/ (*BrE*) = **billboard**

hoarse /hɔːs/ *adj* (used about a person or their voice) sounding rough and quiet, especially because of a sore throat: *a hoarse whisper* ▶ **hoarsely** *adv*

hoax /həʊks/ *noun* [C] a trick to make people believe sth that is not true, especially sth unpleasant: *The fire brigade answered the call, but found that it was a hoax.*

hob /hɒb/ (*AmE* **stovetop**) *noun* [C] the surface on the top of a cooker that is used for boiling, frying, etc.

hobble /ˈhɒbl/ *verb* [I] to walk with difficulty because your foot or leg is hurt: *He hobbled home on his twisted ankle.*

hobby /ˈhɒbi/ *noun* [C] (*pl* **hobbies**) something that you do regularly for pleasure in your free time: *Danesh's hobbies are flower arranging and mountain biking.* SYN **pastime** ➲ picture on **page 352**

hockey /ˈhɒki/ *noun* [U] **1** (*BrE*) a game that is played on a field by two teams of eleven players who try to hit a small hard ball into a goal with a curved wooden stick ➲ picture on **page P4**

HELP In the US **hockey** is usually called **field hockey** to show that it is not **ice hockey**.

2 (*AmE*) = **ice hockey**

hoe /həʊ/ *noun* [C] a garden tool with a long handle that is used for turning the soil and for removing plants that you do not want ➲ picture at **garden**

hog¹ /hɒg/ *noun* [C] a male pig that is kept for its meat

IDM **go the whole hog** (*informal*) to do sth as completely as possible: *Instead of getting a taxi, why not go the whole hog and hire a limousine for the evening?*

hog² /hɒg/ *verb* [T] (**hogging**; **hogged**) (*informal*) to take or keep too much or all of sth for yourself: *The red car was hogging the middle of the road so no one could overtake.*

Hogmanay /ˈhɒgməneɪ/ *noun* [U] the Scottish name for New Year's Eve (31 December) and the celebrations that take place then

hoist /hɔɪst/ *verb* [T] to lift or pull sth up, often by using ropes, etc: *to hoist a flag/sail*

hold¹ /həʊld/ *verb* (*pt*, *pp* **held** /held/)

hold

They held hands.

➤IN HANDS **1** [T] to take sb/sth and keep them or it in your hand, etc: *He held a book in his hand.* ◆ *The woman was holding a baby in her arms.* ◆ *Hold my hand. This is a busy road.* ◆ *They are* ***holding hands*** (= holding each other's hands).

➤IN POSITION **2** [T] to keep sth in a certain position: *Hold your head up straight.* ◆ *Hold the camera still or you'll spoil the picture.* ◆ *These two screws hold the shelf in place.*

➤SUPPORT **3** [T] to take the weight of sb/sth: *Are you sure that branch will be strong enough to hold you?*

➤CONTAIN **4** [T] to contain or have space for a particular amount: *The car holds five people.* ◆ *How much does this bottle hold?*

➤SB PRISONER **5** [T] to keep a person in a position or place by force: *The terrorists are* ***holding*** *three men* ***hostage***. ◆ *A man is being held at the police station.*

➤STAY SAME **6** [I] to remain the same: *I hope this weather holds till the weekend.* ◆ *What I said still holds—nothing has changed.*

➤OWN **7** [T] to have sth, usually in an official way: *Does he* ***hold a*** *British* ***passport***? ◆ *She holds the world record in the 100 metres.*

➤OPINION **8** [T] to have an opinion, etc: *They* ***hold the view*** *that we shouldn't spend any more money.* **9** [T] to believe that sth is true about a person: *I* ***hold*** *the parents* ***responsible*** *for the child's behaviour.*

➤EVENT, MEETING, ETC. **10** [T] to organize an event; to have a meeting, an election, a concert, etc: *They're holding a party for his fortieth birthday.* ◆ *The Olympic Games are held every four years.*

➤CONVERSATION **11** [T] to have a conversation: *It's impossible to* ***hold a conversation*** *with all this noise.*

➤ON TELEPHONE **12** [I,T] to wait until the person you are calling is ready: *I'm afraid his phone is engaged. Will you* ***hold the line***?

IDM **Hold it!** (*spoken*) Stop! Do not move! ℹ For other idioms containing **hold**, look at the entries for the nouns, adjectives, etc. For example, **hold your own** is at **own**.

PHR V **hold sth against sb** to not forgive sb because of sth they have done

hold sb/sth back 1 to prevent sb from making progress **2** to prevent sb/sth from moving forward: *The police tried to hold the crowd back.*

hold sth back 1 to refuse to give some of the information that you have: *The police are sure that she is holding something back. She knows much more than she is saying.* **2** to control an emotion and stop yourself from showing what you really feel: *He fought to hold back tears of anger and frustration.*

hold off (sth/doing sth) to delay sth

hold on 1 to wait or stop for a moment: *Hold on. I'll be with you in a minute.* **2** to manage in a difficult or dangerous situation: *They managed to hold on until a rescue party arrived.*

hold onto sb/sth to hold sb/sth tightly: *The boy held onto his mother because he didn't want her to go.*

hold onto sth to keep sth; to not give or sell sth: *They've offered me a lot of money for this painting, but I'm going to hold onto it.*

hold out to last (in a difficult situation): *How long will our supply of water hold out?*

hold sth out to offer sth by moving it towards a person or animal in your hand: *He held out a carrot to the horse.*

hold out for sth (*informal*) to cause a delay while you continue to ask for sth: *Union members are holding out for a better pay offer.*

hold sb/sth up to make sb/sth late; to cause a delay: *We were held up by the traffic.*

hold up sth to steal from a bank, shop, vehicle, etc. using a gun

hold² /həʊld/ *noun* **1** [C] the act or manner of having sb/sth in your hand(s): *to have a firm hold on the rope* ◆ *judo/wrestling holds* **2** [sing] **a hold (on/over sb/sth)** influence or control: *The new government has strengthened its hold on the country.* **3** [C] the part of a ship or an aircraft where goods are stored: *Five men were found hiding in the ship's hold.*

H

IDM catch, get, grab, take, etc. hold (of sb/sth) **1** to take sb/sth in your hands: *I managed to catch hold of the dog before it ran out into the road.* **2** to take control of sb/sth; to start to have an effect on sb/sth: *Mass hysteria seemed to have taken hold of the crowd.*
get/keep/take a grip/hold (on yourself) ➲ grip[1]
get hold of sb to find sb or make contact with sb: *I've been trying to get hold of the complaints department all morning.*
get hold of sth to find sth that will be useful: *I must try and get hold of a good second-hand bicycle.*
on hold **1** delayed until a later time or date: *We'll have to put our holiday plans on hold until we've saved enough money.* **2** if a person on the telephone is put **on hold**, they have to wait until the person that they want to talk to is free: *I'll just pop you on hold.*

holdall /ˈhəʊldɔːl/ *noun* [C] a large bag that is used for carrying clothes, etc. when you are travelling ➲ picture at **bag**

holder /ˈhəʊldə(r)/ *noun* [C] [in compounds] **1** a person who has or holds sth: *a season-ticket holder* ◆ *the world record holder in the 100 metres* ◆ *holders of European passports* **2** something that contains or holds sth: *a toothbrush holder*

ˈ**hold-up** *noun* [C] **1** a delay: *'What's the hold-up?' 'There's been an accident ahead of us.'* **2** the act of stealing from a bank, etc. using a gun: *The gang have carried out three hold-ups of high street banks.*

⚷ **hole** /həʊl/ *noun* [C] **1** an opening; an empty space in sth solid: *The pavement is full of holes.* ◆ *There are holes in my socks.* ◆ *I've got a hole in my tooth.* **2** the place where an animal lives in the ground or in a tree: *a mouse hole* **3** (in the sport of **golf**) the hole in the ground that you must hit the ball into. Each section of the **golf course** (= the large area of grass where you play) is also called a hole: *an eighteen-hole golf course*

⚷ **holiday** /ˈhɒlədeɪ/ *noun* **1** (*AmE* **vacation**) [C,U] a period of rest from work or school (often when you go and stay away from home): *We're going to Italy **for our** summer **holidays** this year.* ◆ *How much holiday do you get a year in your new job?* ◆ *Mr Phillips isn't here this week. He's away **on holiday**.* ◆ *I'm going to **take a** week's **holiday** in May and spend it at home.* ◆ *the school/Christmas/Easter/summer holidays* **2** [C] a day of rest when many people do not go to work, school, etc. often for religious or national celebrations: *Next Monday is a holiday.* ◆ *New Year's Day is a **bank/public holiday** in Britain.*

> **MORE** **Holiday** in this sense is used in both British and American English. A day when you choose not go to work is also called a **day off**: *I'm having two days off next week when we move house.* **Leave** is time when you do not go to work for a special reason: *sick leave* ◆ *maternity leave* (= for a mother with a new baby) ◆ *unpaid leave.*

> **TOPIC**
> **Holidays**
> You can choose your holiday from a **brochure** and book it at a **travel agent's** or you can do it yourself online. Some people do a lot of **sightseeing** when they **go on holiday**. They **look round** historical buildings and **take photographs**. Others prefer to **sunbathe** on a **beach** and **go swimming** or **snorkelling**. Many people go on a **package holiday** which is organized by a company, and they pay a fixed price that includes their travel, accommodation, etc. They might stay in a large hotel in a holiday **resort**. Other people **go backpacking** (= travel cheaply, carrying their clothes in a backpack), **go on safari** (= take a trip to see wild animals, especially in East Africa), or go on a **cruise** (= a holiday on a large ship). Most people like to buy some **souvenirs** before they go home.

ˈ**holiday camp** *noun* [C] (*BrE*) a place that provides a place to stay and organized entertainment for people on holiday

holidaymaker /ˈhɒlədeɪmeɪkə(r); -dimeɪ-/ *noun* [C] (*BrE*) a person who is away from home on holiday

⚷ **hollow**[1] /ˈhɒləʊ/ *adj* **1** with a hole or empty space inside: *a hollow tree* **2** (used about parts of the face) sinking deep into the face: *hollow cheeks* ◆ *hollow-eyed* **3** (used about a sound) seeming to come from a **hollow** place: *hollow footsteps* **4** not sincere: *a hollow laugh/voice* ◆ *hollow promises/threats*

hollow[2] /ˈhɒləʊ/ *noun* [C] an area that is lower than the land around it

hollow[3] /ˈhɒləʊ/ *verb*
PHR V hollow sth out to take out the inside part of sth

holly /ˈhɒli/ *noun* [U] a plant that has shiny dark green leaves with sharp points and red **berries** (= small round fruit) in the winter. It is often used as a Christmas decoration.

holocaust /ˈhɒləkɔːst/ *noun* [C] a situation where a great many things are destroyed and a great many people die: *a nuclear holocaust*

hologram /ˈhɒləɡræm/ *noun* [C] an image or picture which appears to stand out from the flat surface it is on when light falls on it

holster /ˈhəʊlstə(r)/ *noun* [C] a leather case used for carrying a gun that is fixed to a belt or worn under the arm

⚷ **holy** /ˈhəʊli/ *adj* (**holier**; **holiest**) **1** connected with God or with religion and therefore very special or important: *the Holy Bible* ◆ *holy water* ◆ *The Koran is the holy book of Islam.* **2** (used about a person) good in a moral and religious way: *a holy life/man*
▸ **holiness** *noun* [U]

homage /ˈhɒmɪdʒ/ *noun* [U,C,usually sing] (*formal*) **homage (to sb/sth)** something that is said or done to show respect publicly for sb: *to **pay/do homage** to the dead leader*

home[1] /həʊm/ *noun* **1** [C,U] the place where you live or where you feel that you belong: *She **left home*** (= left her parents' house and began an independent life) *at the age of 21.* ◆ *Children from **broken homes*** (= whose parents are divorced) *sometimes have learning difficulties.* ◆ *That old house would make an ideal **family home**.* ➲ note at **house** ➲ picture on **page P9**

HELP Be careful. The preposition *to* is not used before 'home': *It's time to **go home**.* ◆ *She's usually tired when she gets/arrives home.* If you want to talk about somebody else's home you have to say: *at Jane and Andy's* or: *at Jane and Andy's place/house.*

2 [C] a place that provides care for a particular type of person or for animals: *a children's home* (= for children who have no parents to look after them) ◆ *an **old people's home*** **3** [sing] **the home of sth** the place where sth began: *Greece is said to be the home of democracy.*

IDM at home 1 in your house, flat, etc: *Is anybody at home?* ◆ *Tomorrow we're staying at home all day.*

HELP In American English **home** is often used without the preposition *at*: *Is anybody home?*

2 comfortable, as if you were in your own home: *Please make yourself at home.* ◆ *I felt quite at home on the ship.* **3** (used in sport) played in the town to which the team belongs: *Liverpool are playing at home on Saturday.* **OPP away**

romp home/to victory ➲ **romp**

home[2] /həʊm/ *adj* [only *before* a noun] **1** connected with home: *home cooking* ◆ *your home address/town* ◆ *a happy home life* (= with your family) **2** (*especially BrE*) connected with your own country, not with a foreign country: *The **Home Secretary** is responsible for **home affairs**.* **3** (used in sport) connected with a team's own sports ground: *The home team has a lot of support.* ◆ *a home game* **OPP away**

home[3] /həʊm/ *adv* at, in or to your home or home country: *We must be getting home soon.* ◆ *She'll be flying home for New Year.*

IDM bring sth home to sb to make sb understand sth fully

drive sth home (to sb) ➲ **drive**[1]

home[4] /həʊm/ *verb*

PHR V home in on sb/sth to move towards sb/sth: *The police homed in on the house where the thieves were hiding.*

homecoming /ˈhəʊmkʌmɪŋ/ *noun* [C,U] the act of returning home, especially when you have been away for a long time

ˌhome-ˈgrown *adj* (used about fruit and vegetables) grown in your own garden

homeland /ˈhəʊmlænd/ *noun* [sing] the country where you were born or that your parents came from, or to which you feel you belong: *Many refugees have been forced to leave their homeland.*

homeless /ˈhəʊmləs/ *adj* **1** having no home **2 the homeless** *noun* [pl] people who have no home ▸ **homelessness** *noun* [U]

homely /ˈhəʊmli/ *adj* (**homelier**; **homeliest**) (*BrE*) (used about a place) simple but also pleasant or welcoming

ˌhome-ˈmade *adj* made at home; not bought in a shop: *home-made cakes*

the ˈHome Office *noun* [sing] the department of the UK government that is responsible for the law, the police and prisons within the UK and for decisions about who can enter the country

homeopath (*BrE also* **homoeopath**) /ˈhəʊmiəpæθ/ *noun* [C] a person who treats sick people using **homeopathy**

homeopathy (*BrE also* **homoeopathy**) /ˌhəʊmiˈɒpəθi/ *noun* [U] the treatment of a disease by giving very small amounts of a drug that would cause the disease if given in large amounts ▸ **homeopathic** (*BrE also* **homoeopathic**) /ˌhəʊmiəˈpæθɪk/ *adj*: *homeopathic medicine*

ˈhome page *noun* [C] the first of a number of pages of information on the Internet that belongs to a person or an organization. A **home page** contains connections to other pages of information.

the ˌHome ˈSecretary *noun* [C] (*BrE*) the minister who is in charge of the Home Office ➲ look at **the Foreign Secretary**

homesick /ˈhəʊmsɪk/ *adj* **homesick (for sb/sth)** sad because you are away from home and you miss it: *She was very homesick for Canada.* ▸ **homesickness** *noun* [U]

hometown /ˈhəʊmtaʊn/ *noun* [C] the place where you were born or lived as a child

homeward /ˈhəʊmwəd/ *adj*, *adv* (*also* **homewards**) going towards home: *the homeward journey* ◆ *to travel homewards*

homework /ˈhəʊmwɜːk/ *noun* [U] work that is given by teachers for students to do at home: *Have we got any homework?* ◆ *We've got a translation to do **for homework**.* ◆ *I haven't **done my homework** yet.* ➲ note at **study** ➲ look at **housework**

GRAMMAR Homework is uncountable, so we have to say **a piece of homework** (not 'a homework') and **a lot of homework** (not 'homeworks').

homicidal /ˌhɒmɪˈsaɪdl/ *adj* likely to murder sb: *a homicidal maniac*

homicide /ˈhɒmɪsaɪd/ *noun* [C,U] (*especially AmE*) the illegal killing of one person by another; murder

homoeopath, homoeopathy (*BrE*) = **homeopath, homeopathy**

homonym /ˈhɒmənɪm/ *noun* [C] a word that is spelt or pronounced like another word but that has a different meaning

homophobia /ˌhɒməˈfəʊbiə; ˌhəʊm-/ *noun* [U] a strong dislike and fear of **homosexual** people ▸ **homophobic** *adj*

H

homophone /ˈhɒməfəʊn/ *noun* [C] a word that is pronounced the same as another word but that has a different spelling and meaning: *'Flower' and 'flour' are homophones.*

homosexual /ˌhəʊməˈsekʃuəl; ˌhɒm-/ *adj* sexually attracted to people of the same sex ➲ look at **bisexual, gay, heterosexual, lesbian** ▶ **homosexual** *noun* [C] ▶ **homosexuality** /ˌhəʊməˌsekʃuˈæləti; ˌhɒm-/ *noun* [U]

Hon *abbr* **1** = **Honorary**(2): *Hon President* **2** = **Honourable**(2)

honest /ˈɒnɪst/ *adj* **1** (used about a person) telling the truth and never stealing or cheating: *Just be honest—do you like this skirt or not?* ◆ ***To be honest,*** *I don't think that's a very good idea.* **2** showing honest qualities: *an honest face* ◆ *I'd like your honest opinion, please.* **OPP** for both meanings **dishonest** ▶ **honesty** *noun* [U] **OPP** **dishonesty**

honestly /ˈɒnɪstli/ *adv* **1** in an honest way: *He tried to answer the lawyer's questions honestly.* **2** used for emphasizing that what you are saying is true: *I honestly don't know where she has gone.* **3** used for expressing disapproval: *Honestly! What a mess!*

honey /ˈhʌni/ *noun* **1** [U] the sweet sticky substance that is made by **bees** (= black and yellow insects) and that people eat ➲ picture on **page P16** **2** [C] (*informal*) a person that you like or love; a way of addressing sb that you like or love: *He's a real honey—always ready to help.* ◆ *Honey, I'm home.*

honeycomb /ˈhʌnikəʊm/ *noun* [C,U] a structure of shapes with six sides, in which bees keep their eggs and **honey**

honeymoon /ˈhʌnimuːn/ *noun* [C] a holiday that is taken by two people who have just got married: *We had our first argument while we were on our honeymoon.*

honk /hɒŋk/ *verb* [I,T] to sound the horn of a car; to make this sound

honorable (*AmE*) = **honourable**

honorary /ˈɒnərəri/ *adj* **1** given as an honour (without the person needing the usual certificates, etc.): *to be awarded an honorary degree* **2** often **Honorary** (*abbr* **Hon**) not paid: *He is the Honorary President.*

honour¹ (*AmE* **honor**) /ˈɒnə(r)/ *noun* **1** [U] the respect from other people that a person, country, etc. gets because of high standards of behaviour and moral character: *the guest of honour* (= the most important one) ➲ look at **dishonour** **2** [sing] (*formal*) something that gives pride or pleasure: *It was a great honour to be asked to speak at the conference.* **3** [U] the quality of doing what is morally right: *I give you my word of honour.* **4** **Honours** [pl] (*abbr* **Hons**) a university course that is of a higher level than a basic course: *a First Class Honours degree* **5** (also **honours**) [pl] if you pass an exam **with honours**, you receive a special mark for having achieved a very high standard

IDM **in honour of sb/sth; in sb/sth's honour** out of respect for sb/sth: *A party was given in honour of the guests from Bonn.*

honour² (*AmE* **honor**) /ˈɒnə(r)/ *verb* [T] **1** **honour sb/sth (with sth)** to show great (public) respect for sb/sth or to give sb pride or pleasure: *I am very honoured by the confidence you have shown in me.* **2** to do what you have agreed or promised

honourable (*AmE* **honorable**) /ˈɒnərəbl/ *adj* **1** acting in a way that makes people respect you; having or showing honour **OPP** **dishonourable** **2** [only *before* a noun] **the Honourable** (*abbr* **the Hon**) a title that is given to some high officials and to Members of Parliament when they are speaking to each other ▶ **honourably** /-əbli/ *adv*

Hons /ɒnz/ *abbr* = **Honours¹**(4): *John North BSc (Hons)*

hood /hʊd/ *noun* [C] **1** the part of a coat, etc. that you pull up to cover your head and neck in bad weather ➲ picture at **hat** **2** a piece of cloth that covers sb's head so that they cannot be recognized or so that they cannot see **3** (*especially BrE*) a folding cover for a car, etc: *We drove all the way with the hood down.* **4** (*AmE*) = **bonnet**(2)

hoody (also **hoodie**) /ˈhʊdi/ *noun* [C] (*pl* **hoodies**) (*BrE informal*) a jacket or **sweatshirt** (= a warm piece of clothing with long sleeves) with a **hood** ➲ picture on **page P1**

hoof /huːf/ *noun* [C] (*pl* **hoofs** or **hooves** /huːvz/) the hard part of the foot of horses and some other animals ➲ look at **paw** ➲ picture at **horse** ➲ picture on **page P12**

hooks

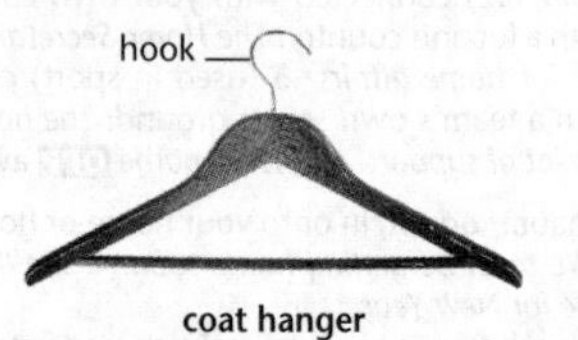

coat hanger

coat hook

hook¹ /hʊk/ *noun* [C] **1** a curved piece of metal, plastic, etc. that is used for hanging things on, catching fish with, etc: *Put your coat on the hook over there.* ◆ *a fish hook* **2** (used in boxing) a way of hitting sb that is done with the arm bent: *a right hook* (= with the right arm)

IDM **off the hook** (used about the top part of a telephone) not in position, so that telephone calls cannot be received

get/let sb off the hook (*informal*) to free yourself or sb else from a difficult situation or punishment: *My father paid the money I owed and got me off the hook.*

hook² /hʊk/ *verb* **1** [I,T] to fasten or catch sth with a hook or sth in the shape of a hook; to be fastened in this way: *We hooked the trailer to the back of the car.* ◆ *The curtain simply hooks onto the rail.* **2** [T] to put sth around sth else so that you can hold on to it or move it: *Hook the rope through your belt.*

PHR V **hook (sth) up (to sth)** to connect sb/sth to

a piece of electronic equipment or to a power supply

ˌhook and ˈeye *noun* [C] a thing that is used for fastening clothes ➲ picture at **button**

hooked /hʊkt/ *adj* **1** shaped like a hook: *a hooked nose* **2** [not before a noun] (*informal*) **hooked (on sth)** needing sth that is bad for you, especially drugs: *to be hooked on gambling* SYN **addicted** **3** [not before a noun] (*informal*) **hooked (on sth)** enjoying sth very much, so that you want to do it, see it, etc. as much as possible: *Suzi is hooked on computer games.*

hooky /ˈhʊki/ (*AmE*)
IDM **play hooky** (*old-fashioned, informal*) = **play truant**

hooligan /ˈhuːlɪɡən/ *noun* [C] a person who behaves in a violent and aggressive way in public places: *football hooligans* ➲ look at **lout**, **yob** ▶ **hooliganism** /ˈhuːlɪɡənɪzəm/ *noun* [U]

hoop /huːp/ *noun* [C] a large metal or plastic ring

hooray = **hurray**

hoot¹ /huːt/ *verb* [I,T] (*BrE*) to sound the horn of a car or to make a loud noise: *The driver hooted (his horn) at the dog but it wouldn't move.* ♦ *They hooted with laughter at the suggestion.*

hoot² /huːt/ *noun* **1** [C] (*especially BrE*) a short loud laugh or shout: *hoots of laughter* **2** [sing] (*spoken*) a situation or a person that is very funny: *Bob is a real hoot!* **3** [C] (*BrE*) the loud sound that is made by the horn of a vehicle **4** [C] the cry of an **owl** (= a bird with large round eyes that hunts animals at night)

hoover /ˈhuːvə(r)/ *verb* [I,T] (*BrE*) to clean a carpet, etc. with a machine that sucks up the dirt: *The bedroom carpet needs hoovering.* SYN **vacuum** ▶ **Hoover™** *noun* [C] SYN **vacuum cleaner**

hooves *plural* of **hoof**

hop

He's hopping. She's jumping.

The ball is bouncing.

hop¹ /hɒp/ *verb* [I] (**hopping**; **hopped**) **1** (used about a person) to jump on one leg: *I twisted my ankle so badly I had to hop all the way back to the car.* **2** (used about an animal or a bird) to jump with both or all feet together **3 hop (from sth to sth)** to change quickly from one activity or subject to another
IDM **Hop it!** (*slang*) Go away!
PHR V **hop in/into sth**; **hop out/out of sth** (*informal*) to get in or out of a car, etc. (quickly)
hop on/onto sth; **hop off sth** (*informal*) to get onto/off a bus, etc. (quickly)

hop² /hɒp/ *noun* **1** [C] a short jump by a person on one leg or by a bird or an animal with its feet together **2** [C] a tall climbing plant with flowers **3 hops** [pl] the flowers of this plant that are used in making beer

hope¹ /həʊp/ *verb* [I,T] **hope that ...**; **hope to do sth**; **hope (for sth)** to want sth to happen or be true: *I hope that you feel better soon.* ♦ *Hoping to hear from you soon* (= at the end of a letter or email). ♦ *'Is it raining?' '**I hope not**. I haven't got a coat with me.'* ♦ *'Are you coming to London with us?' 'I'm not sure yet but **I hope so**.'*

hope² /həʊp/ *noun* **1** [C,U] **(a) hope (of/for sth)**; **(a) hope of doing sth**; **(a) hope that ...** the feeling of wanting sth to happen and thinking that it will: *What hope is there for the future?* ♦ *There is **no hope** of finding anybody else alive.* ♦ *David has **high hopes** of becoming a jockey* (= is very confident about it). ♦ *She never **gave up hope** that a cure for the disease would be found.* **2** [sing] a person, a thing or a situation that will help you get what you want: *Please can you help me? You're my **last hope**.*
IDM **dash sb's hopes (of sth/of doing sth)** ➲ **dash²**
in the hope of sth/that ... because you want sth to happen: *I came here in the hope that we could talk privately.*
pin (all) your hopes on sb/sth ➲ **pin²**
a ray of hope ➲ **ray**

hopeful /ˈhəʊpfl/ *adj* **1 hopeful (about sth)**; **hopeful that ...** believing that sth that you want will happen: *He's very hopeful about the success of the business.* ♦ *The ministers seem hopeful that an agreement will be reached.* SYN **optimistic** **2** making you think that sth good will happen: *a hopeful sign* SYN **promising**

hopefully /ˈhəʊpfəli/ *adv* **1** (*informal*) used to say what you hope will happen: *Hopefully, we'll be finished by 6 o'clock.* **2** showing hope: *She smiled hopefully at me, waiting for my answer.*

hopeless /ˈhəʊpləs/ *adj* **1** giving no hope that sth/sb will be successful or get better: *It's hopeless. There is nothing we can do.* **2** (*informal*) **hopeless (at sth)** (used about a person) often doing things wrong; very bad at doing sth: *I'm absolutely hopeless at tennis.* ▶ **hopelessly** *adv*: *They were hopelessly lost.* ▶ **hopelessness** *noun* [U]

horde /hɔːd/ *noun* [C] a very large number of people

horizon /həˈraɪzn/ *noun* **1** [sing] the line where the earth and sky appear to meet: *The ship appeared* on/disappeared over the horizon. ➲ picture on **page P10** **2 horizons** [pl] the limits of your knowledge or experience: *Foreign travel is a good way of expanding your horizons.*

IDM **on the horizon** likely to happen soon: *There are further job cuts on the horizon.*

horizontal /ˌhɒrɪˈzɒntl/ *adj* going from side to side, not up and down; flat or level: *horizontal lines* ◆ *The gymnasts were exercising on the horizontal bars.* ➲ look at **vertical, perpendicular** ➲ picture at **line** ▶ **horizontally** /-təli/ *adv*

hormone /ˈhɔːməʊn/ *noun* [C] a substance in your body that influences how you grow and develop

horn /hɔːn/ *noun* [C] **1** one of the hard pointed things that some animals have on their heads ➲ picture at **goat** ➲ picture on **page P12** **2** one of the group of metal musical instruments that you play by blowing into them: *the French horn* ➲ picture at **music** **3** the thing in a car, etc. that gives a loud warning sound: *Don't sound your horn late at night.* ➲ picture at **car**

horoscope /ˈhɒrəskəʊp/ *noun* [C] (also **stars** [pl]) a statement about what is going to happen to a person in the future, based on the position of the stars and planets when they were born: *What does my horoscope for next week say?* ➲ note at **zodiac** ➲ look at **astrology**

horrendous /hɒˈrendəs/ *adj* (*informal*) very bad or unpleasant: *The queues were absolutely horrendous.* ▶ **horrendously** *adv*

horrible /ˈhɒrəbl/ *adj* **1** (*informal*) bad or unpleasant: *This coffee tastes horrible!* ◆ *Don't be so horrible* (= unkind)*!* ◆ *I've got **a horrible feeling** that I've forgotten something.* ➲ note at **bad** **2** shocking and/or frightening: *a horrible murder/death/nightmare* SYN for both meanings **terrible** ▶ **horribly** /-əbli/ *adv*

horrid /ˈhɒrɪd/ *adj* (*informal*) very unpleasant or unkind: *horrid weather* ◆ *I'm sorry that I was so horrid last night.* SYN **horrible**

horrific /həˈrɪfɪk/ *adj* **1** extremely bad and shocking or frightening: *a horrific murder/accident/attack* **2** (*informal*) very bad or unpleasant ▶ **horrifically** /-kli/ *adv*: *horrifically expensive*

horrify /ˈhɒrɪfaɪ/ *verb* [T] (**horrifying; horrifies**; *pt, pp* **horrified**) to make sb feel extremely shocked, disgusted or frightened ▶ **horrified** *adj*: *He was horrified when he discovered the truth.* ▶ **horrifying** *adj*

horror /ˈhɒrə(r)/ *noun* **1** [U, sing] a feeling of great fear or shock: *They watched **in horror** as the building collapsed.* **2** [C,U] something that makes you feel frightened or shocked: *a horror film/story* ◆ *the horrors of war*

horse /hɔːs/ *noun* **1** [C] a large animal that is used for riding on or for pulling or carrying heavy loads: *a horse and cart*

horse

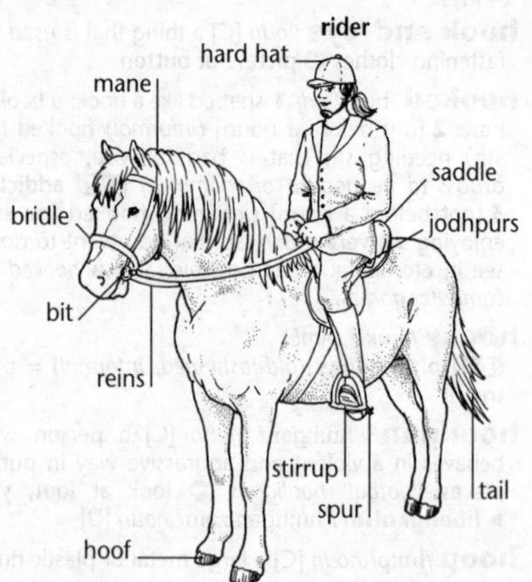

MORE **Horse** is often used for both males and females. A male horse is a **stallion**, a female horse is a **mare** and a young horse is a **foal**.

2 the horses [pl] (*informal*) horse racing: *He won some money on the horses.*

IDM **on horseback** sitting on a horse

MORE Police officers who ride horses are called **mounted police**.

ˈ**horseback riding** (*AmE*) = **riding**

horse ˈchestnut *noun* [C] **1** a large tall tree with pink or white flowers, and nuts that grow inside cases that are covered with sharp points **2** (also *informal* **conker**) the smooth brown nut from this tree

horseman /ˈhɔːsmən/ *noun* [C] (*pl* **-men** /-mən/) a man who rides a horse: *an experienced horseman*

horsepower /ˈhɔːspaʊə(r)/ *noun* [C] (*pl* **horsepower**) (*abbr* **h.p.**) a measure of the power of an engine

ˈ**horse racing** (also **racing**) *noun* [U] the sport in which a **jockey** rides a horse in a race to win money

MORE Horse racing takes place at a **racecourse**. People often **bet** on the results of horse races.

➲ picture on **page P5**

horseshoe /ˈhɔːsʃuː/ (also **shoe**) *noun* [C] a piece of metal in the shape of a U that is fixed to the bottom of a horse's foot. ❶ Some people believe that horseshoes bring good luck.

horsewoman /ˈhɔːswʊmən/ *noun* [C] (*pl* **-women** /-wɪmɪn/) a woman who rides a horse

horticulture /ˈhɔːtɪkʌltʃə(r)/ *noun* [U] the study or practice of growing flowers, fruit and vegetables: *a college of agriculture and horticulture* ▶ **horticultural** /ˌhɔːtɪˈkʌltʃərəl/ *adj*

hose /həʊz/ (also **hosepipe** /ˈhəʊzpaɪp/) *noun* [C, U] a long rubber or plastic tube that water can flow through ➲ picture at **garden**

hospice /ˈhɒspɪs/ *noun* [C] a special hospital where people who are dying are cared for

hospitable /hɒˈspɪtəbl; ˈhɒspɪtəbl/ *adj* (used about a person) friendly and kind to visitors **OPP** **inhospitable**

hospital /ˈhɒspɪtl/ *noun* [C] a place where ill or injured people are treated: *He was rushed **to hospital** in an ambulance.* ♦ *to be admitted to/discharged from hospital* ♦ *a psychiatric/mental hospital* ➲ note at **disease, doctor, hurt**

HELP If a person goes **to hospital** or is **in hospital** (without 'the' in British English), he/she is a patient receiving treatment there: *His mother's in hospital.* ♦ *She cut her hand and had to go to hospital.* 'The hospital' refers to one particular hospital, or indicates that the person is only visiting the building temporarily: *He went to the hospital to visit Jana.*

TOPIC

Hospitals

If somebody has an **accident**, they may need to go to **hospital** (**the hospital** in American English) for medical **treatment**. Dial *999* and call an **ambulance**. They will be taken first to **A & E** (= the accident and emergency department). If you **cut** yourself very badly, you might need **stitches** (= small lines of thread used to sew your skin together). If your arm, ankle, etc. is **painful** and **swollen**, a doctor might take an **X-ray** to see if it is **broken**. A person who is being treated in a hospital by **doctors** and **nurses** is a **patient**. If people **have an operation/have surgery**, it is performed by a **surgeon** in an **operating theatre**. Patients sleep in a **ward** (= a room shared with other patients). The fixed times during the day when you are allowed to visit somebody in hospital are called **visiting hours**.

hospitality /ˌhɒspɪˈtæləti/ *noun* [U] looking after guests and being friendly and welcoming towards them

host /həʊst/ *noun* [C] **1** a person who invites guests to their house, etc. and provides them with food, drink, etc: *It's polite to write a thank-you letter to your host.* ♦ *I'll be staying with a **host family** while I study English in the UK.* ➲ look at **hostess** **2** a person who introduces a TV or radio show and talks to the guests: *a game show host* **3 a host of sth** a large number of people or things: *I've got a whole host of things I want to discuss with him.* ▶ **host** *verb* [T]: *The city is aiming to host the Olympic Games in ten years' time.*

hostage /ˈhɒstɪdʒ/ *noun* [C] a person who is caught and kept prisoner by a person or group. He or she may be killed or injured if the person or group who is holding them does not get what they are asking for: *The gunmen tried to **take** the staff **hostage**.* ♦ *The hijackers say they will **hold** the passengers **hostage** until their demands are met.* ➲ look at **ransom**

hostel /ˈhɒstl/ *noun* [C] **1** a place like a cheap hotel where people can stay when they are living away from home: *a youth hostel* ♦ *a student hostel* **2** (*BrE*) a building where people who have no home can stay for a short time

hostess /ˈhəʊstəs; -es/ *noun* [C] **1** a woman who invites guests to her house, etc. and provides them with food, drink, etc. ➲ look at **host** **2** a woman who introduces a TV or radio show and talks to the guests

hostile /ˈhɒstaɪl/ *adj* **hostile (to/towards sb/sth)** having very strong feelings against sb/sth: *a hostile crowd* ♦ *They are very hostile to any change.*

hostility /hɒˈstɪləti/ *noun* **1** [U] **hostility (to/towards sth)** very strong feelings against sb/sth: *She didn't say anything but I could sense her hostility.* **2 hostilities** [pl] fighting in a war

hot[1] /hɒt/ *adj* (hotter; hottest) **1** having a high temperature: *Can I open the window? I'm really hot.* ♦ *It's hot today, isn't it?* ♦ *It was **boiling hot** (= very hot) on the beach.* ♦ *Be careful—the plates are hot.* ♦ *a hot meal* (= one that has been cooked) ➲ note at **cold** ➲ look at **humid** **2** (used about food) causing a burning feeling in your mouth: *hot curry* **SYN** **spicy** **3** (*informal*) difficult or dangerous to deal with: *The defenders found the Italian strikers **too hot to handle**.* **4** (*informal*) exciting and popular: *This band is **hot stuff**!*

IDM **in hot pursuit** following sb who is moving fast

hot[2] /hɒt/ *verb* (hotting; hotted)

PHR V **hot up** (*BrE informal*) to become more exciting: *The election campaign has really hotted up in the past few days.*

ˌhot-ˈair balloon = **balloon**(2)

ˈhot dog *noun* [C] a hot **sausage** (= meat formed in a long thin shape) in a soft bread roll ➲ picture on **page P16**

hotel /həʊˈtel/ *noun* [C] a place where you pay to stay when you are on holiday or travelling: *to stay in/at a hotel* ♦ *I've booked a double room at the Grand Hotel.* ♦ *a two-star hotel*

TOPIC

Hotels

You make a **reservation** for a **double**, **single** or **twin-bedded/twin** (= with two single beds) room at a hotel. When you arrive you **check in** or **register** at **reception** and when you leave you **check out**. If your accommodation is **full board**, all your meals are included, and **half board** includes breakfast and an evening meal. If you stay in a **motel**, you can park your car near your room. A **bed and breakfast** (**B and B**) is a private house which provides a room for the night and breakfast.

hotelier /həʊˈteliə(r); -lieɪ/ *noun* [C] a person who owns or manages a hotel

hothouse /ˈhɒthaʊs/ *noun* [C] a heated glass building where plants are grown ➲ look at **greenhouse**

hotline /ˈhɒtlaɪn/ *noun* [C] a special telephone line to a business or an organization

hotlink /ˈhɒtlɪŋk/ = **hyperlink**

hotly /ˈhɒtli/ *adv* **1** in an angry or excited way: *They have hotly denied the newspaper reports.* **2** closely and with determination: *The dog ran off, hotly pursued by its owner.*

ˌhot-ˈwater bottle *noun* [C] a rubber container that is filled with hot water and put in a bed to warm it

H

hound¹ /haʊnd/ *noun* [C] a type of dog that is used for hunting or racing

hound² /haʊnd/ *verb* [T] to follow and disturb sb: *Many famous people complain of being hounded by the press.*

hour /ˈaʊə(r)/ *noun* **1** [C] (*abbr* hr) a period of 60 minutes: *He studies* **for** *three* **hours** *most evenings.* ♦ *The programme lasts about* **half an hour**. ♦ *I'm going shopping now. I'll be back in about an hour.* ♦ *In two* **hours' time** *I'll be having lunch.* ♦ *a four-hour journey* ♦ *Japan is eight hours ahead of the UK.* ♦ *I get paid* **by the hour**. ♦ *How much do you get paid* **per/an hour**? **2** [C] the distance that you can travel in about 60 minutes: *London is only two hours away.* **3** [C] a period of about an hour when sth particular happens: *I'm going shopping in my* **lunch hour**. ♦ *The traffic is very bad in* **the rush hour**. **4 hours** [pl] the period of time when sb is working or a shop, etc. is open: *Employees are demanding shorter* **working hours**. **5 hours** [pl] a long time: *He went on speaking* **for hours** *and hours.* **6 the hour** [sing] the time when a new hour starts (= 1 o'clock, 2 o'clock, etc.): *Buses are* **on the hour** *and at twenty past the hour.*

IDM at/till all hours at/until any time: *She stays out till all hours* (= very late).

at an unearthly hour ➲ **unearthly**

the early hours ➲ **early**

hourly /ˈaʊəli/ *adj* [only *before* a noun] *adv* **1** (done, happening, etc.) every hour: *an hourly news bulletin* ♦ *Trains run hourly.* **2** for one hour: *What is your hourly rate of pay?*

house¹ /haʊs/ *noun* [C] (*pl* houses /ˈhaʊzɪz/)
➤BUILDING **1** a building that is made for people to live in: *We live in a three-bedroom/three-bedroomed house* ➲ look at **bungalow, cottage, flat** ➲ picture on **page P8, page P9**

> **HELP House** or **home**? Your **home** is the place where you live, even if it is not a house: *Let's go home to my flat.* Your home is also the place where you feel that you belong. A **house** is just a building: *We've only just moved into our new house and it doesn't feel like home yet.*

2 [usually sing] all the people who live in one house: *Don't shout. You'll wake the whole house up.* **3** a building that is used for a particular purpose: *a warehouse*
➤COMPANY **4** a large firm involved in a particular kind of business: *a fashion/publishing house*
➤RESTAURANT **5** a restaurant, usually that sells one particular type of food: *a curry/spaghetti house* ♦ *house wine* (= the cheapest wine in a restaurant)
➤PARLIAMENT **6 House** a group of people who meet to make a country's laws: *the House of Commons* ♦ *the Houses of Parliament* ➲ note at **Parliament**
➤IN THEATRE, ETC. **7** [usually sing] the audience at a theatre or cinema, or the area where they sit: *There was a full house for the play this evening.*

IDM get on/along like a house on fire (*informal*) to immediately become good friends with sb

on the house paid for by the pub, restaurant, etc. that you are visiting; free: *Your first drink is on the house.*

> TOPIC
>
> **Houses**
>
> If you want to **move house** (= leave your home and go to live in a different one) you go to an **estate agent**, who is a person whose job is to sell **property** (= houses, land, etc.). The money that you borrow in order to buy a house is called a **mortgage**. A party given by somebody who has just **moved into** (= started living in) a house is called a **house-warming**.
>
> You can **extend** your house to make it bigger. You **do up/renovate** your house by repairing and decorating it. If you do the work yourself it is called **DIY** (= do it yourself): *They're spending the weekend doing DIY.* Otherwise you may need a **plumber** (to fit or repair water pipes, bathrooms, etc.), an **electrician** (to connect or repair the electrical system) or a **carpenter** (to make or repair wooden structures).

house² /haʊz/ *verb* [T] **1** to provide sb with a place to live: *The Council must house homeless families.* **2** to contain or keep sth: *Her office is housed in a separate building.*

houseboat /ˈhaʊsbəʊt/ *noun* [C] a boat on a river, etc. where sb lives and which usually stays in one place

housebound /ˈhaʊsbaʊnd/ *adj* unable to leave your house because you are old or ill

household /ˈhaʊshəʊld/ *noun* [C] all the people who live in one house and the work, money, organization, etc. that is needed to look after them: *Most households now own at least one car.* ▶ **household** *adj* [only *before* a noun]: *household expenses*

householder /ˈhaʊshəʊldə(r)/ *noun* [C] a person who rents or owns the house that they live in

ˈhouse husband *noun* [C] a man who stays at home to cook, clean, take care of the children, etc. while his wife or partner goes out to work ➲ look at **housewife**

housekeeper /ˈhaʊskiːpə(r)/ *noun* [C] a person who is paid to look after sb else's house and organize the work in it

housekeeping /ˈhaʊskiːpɪŋ/ *noun* [U] **1** the work involved in looking after a house **2** the money that you need to manage a house

the ˌHouse of ˈCommons (also the Commons) *noun* [with sing or pl verb] (in the UK and Canada) the part of Parliament whose members are elected by the people of the country ➲ note at **Parliament**

the House of ˈLords (also the Lords) *noun* [with sing or pl verb] the group of people (who are not elected) who meet to discuss the laws that have been suggested by the House of Commons ➲ note at **Parliament**

the ˌHouse of ˌRepreˈsentatives *noun* [sing] the group of people who are elected to make new laws in the US ➲ look at **Congress, the Senate**

ˈhouse-proud *adj* paying great attention to the care, cleaning, etc. of your house

ˌhouse-to-ˈhouse *adj* [only *before* a noun] going to each house: *The police are making house-to-house enquiries.*

ˈhouse-warming *noun* [C] a party that you have when you have just moved into a new home

housewife /ˈhaʊswaɪf/ *noun* [C] (*pl* **housewives**) a woman who does not have a job outside the home and who spends her time cleaning the house, cooking, looking after her family, etc. ➲ look at **house husband**

housework /ˈhaʊswɜːk/ *noun* [U] the work that is needed to take care of a home and family, for example cleaning and cooking: *to do the housework* ➲ note at **clean**

> **HELP** Be careful. **Homework** (not **housework**) is work that is given by teachers for students to do at home.

⚷ **housing** /ˈhaʊzɪŋ/ *noun* [U] houses, flats, etc. for people to live in: *poor housing conditions* ◆ *a housing shortage*

ˈhousing estate *noun* [C] (*BrE*) an area where there are a large number of similar houses that were built at the same time

hover /ˈhɒvə(r)/ *verb* [I] **1** (used about a bird, etc.) to stay in the air in one place **2** (used about a person) to wait near sb/sth: *He hovered nervously outside the office.*

hovercraft /ˈhɒvəkrɑːft/ *noun* [C] (*pl* **hovercraft**) a type of boat that can move over land or water, held up by air being forced downwards ➲ picture on **page P6**

⚷ **how** /haʊ/ *adv, conj* **1** (often used in questions) in what way: *How do you spell your name?* ◆ *Can you show me how to use this machine?* ◆ *I can't remember how to get there.* ◆ ***How ever** did you manage to find me here?* ➲ look at **however 2** used when you are asking about sb's health or feelings: *'How is your mother?' 'She's much better, thank you.'* ◆ *How are you feeling today?* ◆ *How do you feel about your son joining the army?*

> **HELP** You use 'how' only when you are asking about a person's health. When you are asking about a person's character or appearance you say **what ... like?**: *'What are your new neighbours like?' 'They seem very friendly and quiet.'*

3 used when you are asking about sb's opinion of a thing or a situation: *How was the weather?* ◆ *How is your meal?* ◆ ***How** did the interview **go**?* **4** used in questions when you are asking about the degree, amount, age, etc. of sb/sth: *How old are you?* ◆ *How much is that?* **5** used for expressing surprise, pleasure, etc: *She's gone. How strange!* ◆ *I can't believe how expensive it is!*

IDM how/what about ...? ➲ **about**[2]

How come? ➲ **come**

How do you do? (*formal*) used when meeting sb for the first time ➲ note at **introduce**

> **HELP** Be careful. **How are you?** and **How do you do?** are answered differently: *'How do you do?'* is answered with the same words: *'How do you do?'* The answer to *'How are you?'* depends on how you are feeling: *'I'm fine.'/'Very well.'/'Much better.'*

⚷ **however** /haʊˈevə(r)/ *adv, conj* **1** (*formal*) (used for adding a comment to what you have just said) although sth is true: *Sales are poor this month. There may, however, be an increase before Christmas.*

> **HELP** When **ever** is used to emphasize **how**, meaning 'in what way' it is written as a separate word: ***How ever** could he afford a car like that?*

➲ note at **contrast 2** in whatever way: *However I sat I couldn't get comfortable.* ◆ *You can dress however you like.* **3** [before an adjective or adverb] to whatever degree: *He won't wear a hat however cold it is.* ◆ *You can't catch her however fast you run.*

howl /haʊl/ *verb* [I] to make a long loud sound: *I couldn't sleep because there was a dog howling all night.* ◆ *The wind howled around the house.* ▶ **howl** *noun* [C]

h.p. /ˌeɪtʃ ˈpiː/ (also HP) *abbr* **1** = **horsepower** **2** (*BrE*) = **hire purchase**

HQ /ˌeɪtʃ ˈkjuː/ *abbr* = **headquarters**

HR /ˌeɪtʃ ˈɑː(r)/ *abbr* = **human resources**

hr *abbr* (*pl* **hrs**) = **hour**(1): *3 hrs 15 mins*

HRH /ˌeɪtʃ ɑːr ˈeɪtʃ/ *abbr* **His/Her Royal Highness**: *HRH Prince Harry*

hub /hʌb/ *noun* [C, usually sing] **1 the hub (of sth)** the central and most important part of a place or an activity: *the commercial hub of the city* **2** the central part of a wheel

hubbub /ˈhʌbʌb/ *noun* [sing, U] **1** the noise made by a lot of people talking at the same time: *I couldn't hear the announcement over the hubbub.* **2** a

H

situation in which there is a lot of noise, excitement and activity: *the hubbub of city life*

huddle[1] /ˈhʌdl/ *verb* [I] **huddle (up) (together)** **1** to get close to other people because you are cold or frightened: *The campers huddled together around the fire.* **2** to make your body as small as possible because you are cold or frightened: *She huddled up in her sleeping bag and tried to get some sleep.* ▶ **huddled** *adj*: *We found the children lying huddled together on the ground.*

huddle[2] /ˈhʌdl/ *noun* [C] a small group of people or things that are close together: *They all stood* ***in a huddle****, laughing and chatting.*

hue /hjuː/ *noun* [C] (*written*) a colour; a particular shade of a colour

IDM **hue and cry** strong public protest about sth: *There was a hue and cry about the new taxes.*

huff /hʌf/ *noun*

IDM **in a huff** (*informal*) in a bad mood because sb has annoyed or upset you: *Did you see Sam* ***go off in a huff*** *when he wasn't chosen for the team?*

hug /hʌg/ *verb* [T] (**hugging**; **hugged**) **1** to put your arms around sb, especially to show that you love them: *He hugged his mother and sisters and got on the train.* **2** to hold sth close to your body: *She hugged the parcel to her chest as she ran.* **3** (used about a ship, car, road, etc.) to stay close to sth: *to hug the coast* ▶ **hug** *noun* [C]: *Noel's crying—I'll go and* ***give*** *him* ***a hug****.*

huge /hjuːdʒ/ *adj* very big: *a huge amount/quantity/sum/number* ◆ *a huge building* ◆ *The film was a huge success.* ◆ *This is a huge problem for us.* SYN **enormous** ▶ **hugely** *adv*: *hugely successful/popular/expensive*

huh /hʌ/ *exclam* (*informal*) used for expressing anger, surprise, etc. or for asking a question: *They've gone away, huh? They didn't tell me.*

hull /hʌl/ *noun* [C] the main part of a ship

hullabaloo /ˌhʌləbəˈluː/ *noun* [sing] a lot of loud noise, for example made by people shouting

hum /hʌm/ *verb* (**humming**; **hummed**) **1** [I,T] to sing with your lips closed: *You can hum the tune if you don't know the words.* **2** [I] to make a continuous low noise: *The machine began to hum as I switched it on.* ▶ **hum** *noun* [sing]: *the hum of machinery/distant traffic*

human[1] /ˈhjuːmən/ *adj* connected with people, not with animals, machines or gods; typical of people: *the human body* ◆ *The disaster was caused by* ***human error****.* ▶ **humanly** *adv*: *They did all that was humanly possible to rescue him* (= everything that a human being could possibly do).

human[2] /ˈhjuːmən/ (also ˌ**human** ˈ**being**) *noun* [C] a person: *Dogs can hear much better than humans.*

humane /hjuːˈmeɪn/ *adj* having or showing kindness or understanding, especially to a person or an animal that is suffering: *Animals must be kept in humane conditions.* OPP **inhumane** ▶ **humanely** *adv*

humanitarian /hjuːˌmænɪˈteəriən/ *adj* concerned with trying to make people's lives better and reduce suffering: *Many countries have sent* ***humanitarian aid*** *to the earthquake victims.*

humanity /hjuːˈmænəti/ *noun* **1** [U] all the people in the world, thought of as a group: *crimes against humanity* SYN **the human race** **2** [U] the quality of being kind and understanding: *The prisoners were treated with humanity.* OPP **inhumanity** **3 (the) humanities** [pl] the subjects of study that are concerned with the way people think and behave, for example literature, history, etc. ➲ look at **science**

ˌ**human** ˈ**nature** *noun* [U] feelings, behaviour, etc. that all people have in common

the ˌ**human** ˈ**race** *noun* [sing] all the people in the world, when thought of as a group SYN **humanity**

ˌ**human re**ˈ**sources** *noun* [U, with sing or pl verb] (*abbr* **HR**) the department in a company that deals with employing and training people SYN **personnel**

ˌ**human** ˈ**rights** *noun* [pl] the basic freedoms that all people should have, for example the right to say what you think, to travel freely, etc.

humble[1] /ˈhʌmbl/ *adj* (**humbler**; **humblest**) **1** not thinking that you are better or more important than other people; not proud: *He became very rich and famous but he always remained a very humble man.* ➲ look at **modest** ➲ *noun* **humility** **2** not special or important: *She comes from a humble background.* ▶ **humbly** /ˈhʌmbli/ *adv*: *He apologized very humbly for his behaviour.*

humble[2] /ˈhʌmbl/ *verb* [T] to make sb feel that they are not as good or important as they thought

humid /ˈhjuːmɪd/ *adj* (used about the air or climate) warm and feeling slightly wet: *Hong Kong is hot and humid in summer.* ▶ **humidity** /hjuːˈmɪdəti/ *noun* [U]

humiliate /hjuːˈmɪlieɪt/ *verb* [T] to make sb feel ashamed or stupid: *I felt humiliated when the teacher laughed at my work.* ▶ **humiliating** *adj*: *a humiliating defeat* ▶ **humiliation** /hjuːˌmɪliˈeɪʃn/ *noun* [C,U]

humility /hjuːˈmɪləti/ *noun* [U] the quality of not thinking that you are better than other people ➲ *adjective* **humble**

hummus (also **houmous**) /ˈhʊməs; ˈhuːməs/ *noun* [U] a type of food originally from the Middle East that is a soft mixture of **chickpeas**, **sesame** seeds, oil, lemon juice and **garlic**

humorless (*AmE*) = **humourless**

humorous /ˈhjuːmərəs/ *adj* amusing or funny *He gave a humorous account of their trip to Spain.* ▶ **humorously** *adv*

humour[1] (*AmE* **humor**) /ˈhjuːmə(r)/ *noun* [U] **1** the funny or amusing qualities of sb/sth: *It is sometimes hard to understand the humour* (= the jokes) *of another country.* **2** being able to see when sth is funny and to laugh at things: *I can't stand* *people with no* ***sense of humour****.* **3 -humoured** (*AmE* **-humored**) [in compounds] having or showing a particular mood: *good-humoured*

TOPIC

Humour

Do you have a **good sense of humour**? What do you find **funny/amusing**? When something is **hilarious**, do you **burst out laughing**? Some people are **witty** (= use words in a clever way). **Clowns** do **slapstick** (= for example, falling over or covering people with water). A **practical joke** is something you do to make a person look silly. **Comedians** tell **jokes** and may use **satire** to **make fun of** people such as politicians.

humour² (*AmE* **humor**) /ˈhjuːmə(r)/ *verb* [T] to keep sb happy by doing what they want

humourless (*AmE* **humorless**) /ˈhjuːmələs/ *adj* having no sense of fun; serious

hump /hʌmp/ *noun* [C] a large lump that sticks out above the surface of sth, for example on the back of a **camel** (= an animal that lives in the desert) ➲ picture at **camel**

hunch¹ /hʌntʃ/ *verb* [I,T] to bend your back and shoulders forward into a round shape

hunch² /hʌntʃ/ *noun* [C] (*informal*) a thought or an idea that is based on a feeling rather than on facts or information: *I've got a hunch that she'll be back soon.*

hunchback /ˈhʌntʃbæk/ *noun* [C] a person with a back that has a round lump on it

⚷ **hundred** /ˈhʌndrəd/ *number* **1** (*pl* **hundred**) 100: *two hundred* ◆ *There were a/one hundred people in the room.* ◆ *She's a hundred today.*

HELP Note that when we are saying a number, for example 1 420, we put 'and' after the word **hundred**: *one thousand four hundred* ***and*** *twenty*

2 hundreds (*informal*) a lot; a large amount: *I've got hundreds of things to do today.* ℹ For more information about numbers, look at the section on using numbers at the back of this dictionary.

⚷ **hundredth¹** /ˈhʌndrədθ/ *ordinal number* 100th ➲ note at **sixth**

⚷ **hundredth²** /ˈhʌndrədθ/ *noun* [C] ¹⁄₁₀₀; one of a hundred equal parts of sth

hundredweight /ˈhʌndrədweɪt/ *noun* [C] (*abbr* **cwt.**) a measure of weight, about 50.8 kilograms ℹ For more information about weights, look at the section on using numbers at the back of this dictionary.

hung *past tense, past participle* of **hang¹**

hunger¹ /ˈhʌŋgə(r)/ *noun* **1** [U] the state of not having enough food to eat, especially when this causes illness or death: *Many people die of hunger every day in the camp.* **2** [U] the feeling caused by a need to eat: *Hunger is one reason why babies cry.*

HELP Be careful. You cannot say *I have hunger* in English. You must say *I am hungry*.

3 [sing] **hunger (for sth)** a strong desire for sth: *a hunger for knowledge/fame/success* ➲ look at **thirst**

hunger² /ˈhʌŋgə(r)/ *verb*
PHR V hunger for/after sth (*formal*) to have a strong desire for sth

ˈ**hunger strike** *noun* [C,U] a time when sb (especially a prisoner) refuses to eat because they are protesting about sth: *to be/go* ***on hunger strike***

⚷ **hungry** /ˈhʌŋgri/ *adj* (**hungrier**; **hungriest**) **1** wanting to eat: *I'm hungry. Let's eat soon.* ◆ *There were hungry children begging for food in the streets.* ➲ look at **thirsty** **2 hungry for sth** wanting sth very much: *People were hungry for change.*
IDM go hungry to not have any food
▶ **hungrily** *adv*

hunk /hʌŋk/ *noun* [C] **1** a large piece of sth: *a hunk of bread/cheese/meat* **2** (*informal*) a man who is big, strong and attractive

⚷ **hunt¹** /hʌnt/ *verb* [I,T] **1 hunt (for) (sb/sth)** to try to find sb/sth: *The police are still hunting the murderer.* **2** to run after wild animals, etc. in order to catch or kill them either for sport or for food: *Owls hunt at night.* ◆ *Are tigers still being hunted in India?*

HELP We often use the expression **go hunting** when we are talking about people spending time hunting.

hunt² /hʌnt/ *noun* [C] **1** the act of hunting wild animals, etc: *a fox hunt* **2** [usually sing] **a hunt (for sb/sth)** the act of looking for sb/sth that is difficult to find: *The police have launched a hunt for the missing child.*

hunter /ˈhʌntə(r)/ *noun* [C] a person that hunts wild animals for food or sport; an animal that hunts its food

⚷ **hunting** /ˈhʌntɪŋ/ *noun* [U] the act of following and killing wild animals or birds as a sport or for food ➲ look at **shoot**

hurdle¹ /ˈhɜːdl/ *noun* **1** [C] a type of light fence that a person or a horse jumps over in a race: *to clear a hurdle* (= to jump over it successfully) **2 the hurdles** [pl] a race in which runners or horses have to jump over **hurdles**: *the 200 metres hurdles* **3** [C] a problem or difficulty that you must solve or deal with before you can achieve sth

hurdle² /ˈhɜːdl/ *verb* [I,T] **hurdle (over sth)** to jump over sth while you are running

hurl /hɜːl/ *verb* [T] to throw sth with great force

hurray (also **hooray**) /həˈreɪ/ (also **hurrah** /həˈrɑː/) *exclam* used for expressing great pleasure, approval, etc: *Hurray! We've won!*
IDM hip, hip, hurray/hurrah ➲ **hip²**

hurricane /ˈhʌrɪkən/ *noun* [C] a violent storm with very strong winds ➲ note at **storm**

hurried /ˈhʌrid/ *adj* done (too) quickly: *a hurried meal* ▶ **hurriedly** *adv*

H

hurry[1] /ˈhʌri/ *verb* (**hurrying**; **hurries**; *pt, pp* **hurried**) **1** [I] to move or do sth quickly because there is not much time: *Don't hurry. There's plenty of time.* ◆ *They hurried back home after school.* ◆ *Several people hurried to help.* **2** [T] **hurry sb (into sth/doing sth)** to cause sb/sth to do sth, or sth to happen, more quickly: *Don't hurry me. I'm going as fast as I can.* ◆ *He was hurried into a decision.* **3** [T, usually passive] to do sth too quickly: *Good food should never be hurried.* **SYN** for all meanings **rush**
PHR V **hurry up (with sth)** (*informal*) to move or do sth more quickly: *Hurry up or we'll miss the train.*

hurry[2] /ˈhʌri/ *noun* [U] the need or wish to do sth quickly: *Take your time. There's* **no hurry**. **SYN** **rush**
IDM **in a hurry** quickly: *She got up late and left in a hurry.*
in a hurry (to do sth) wanting to do sth soon; impatient: *They are in a hurry to get the job done before the winter.*
in no hurry (to do sth); not in any hurry (to do sth) **1** not needing or wishing to do sth quickly: *We weren't in any hurry so we stopped to admire the view.* **2** not wanting to do sth: *I am in no hurry to repeat that experience.*

hurt[1] /hɜːt/ *verb* (*pt, pp* **hurt**) **1** [T,I] to cause sb/yourself physical pain or injury: *Did he hurt himself?* ◆ *I fell and hurt my arm.* ◆ *No one was seriously hurt in the accident.* ◆ *These shoes hurt; they're too tight.* **2** [I] to feel painful: *My leg hurts.* ◆ ***It hurts** when I lift my leg.* ◆ *Where exactly does it hurt?* **3** [T] to make sb unhappy; to upset sb: *His unkind remarks hurt her deeply.* ◆ *I didn't want to **hurt** his **feelings**.*
IDM **it won't/wouldn't hurt (sb/sth) (to do sth)** (*informal*) used to say that sb should do sth: *It wouldn't hurt you to help with the housework occasionally.*

> OTHER WORDS FOR
>
> **hurt**
>
> A person may be **wounded** by a knife, sword, gun, etc., usually as a result of fighting: *a wounded soldier*. People are usually **injured** in an accident: *Five people were killed in the crash and twelve others were injured.* **Hurt** and **injured** are similar in meaning but **hurt** is more often used when the damage is not very great: *I hurt my leg when I fell off my bike.*

hurt[2] /hɜːt/ *adj* **1** injured physically: *None of the passengers were **badly/seriously hurt**.* **2** upset and offended by sth that sb has said or done: *She was **deeply hurt** that she had not been invited to the party.*

hurt[3] /hɜːt/ *noun* [U] a feeling of unhappiness because sb has been unkind or unfair to you: *There was hurt and real anger in her voice.*

hurtful /ˈhɜːtfl/ *adj* **hurtful (to sb)** making sb feel upset and offended **SYN** **unkind**

hurtle /ˈhɜːtl/ *verb* [I] to move with great speed, perhaps causing danger: *The lorry **came hurtling** towards us.*

husband /ˈhʌzbənd/ *noun* [C] a man that a woman is married to: *Her ex-husband sees the children once a month.*

hush[1] /hʌʃ/ *verb* [I] (*spoken*) used to tell sb to be quiet, to stop talking or crying: *Hush now and try to sleep.*
PHR V **hush sth up** to hide information to stop people knowing about sth; to keep sth secret

hush[2] /hʌʃ/ *noun* [sing] no noise or sound at all

ˌhush-ˈhush *adj* (*informal*) very secret

husk /hʌsk/ *noun* [C] the dry outer covering of nuts, fruits and seeds, especially of grain: *Brown rice has not had the husks removed.*

husky[1] /ˈhʌski/ *adj* (**huskier**; **huskiest**) (used about a person or their voice) sounding rough and quiet

husky[2] /ˈhʌski/ *noun* [C] (*pl* **huskies**) a strong dog with thick fur that is used in teams for pulling heavy loads over snow

hustle /ˈhʌsl/ *verb* [T] to push or move sb in a way that is not gentle

hut /hʌt/ *noun* [C] a small building with one room, usually made of wood or metal: *a beach hut* ◆ *a wooden/mud hut*

hutch /hʌtʃ/ *noun* [C] a wooden box with a front made of wire, that is used for keeping **rabbits** (= small animals with long ears) or other animals in

hybrid /ˈhaɪbrɪd/ *noun* [C] **1** an animal or a plant that has parents of different types: *A mule is a hybrid of a male donkey and a female horse.* **2** **hybrid (between/of A and B)** something that is the product of mixing two or more different things: *The music was a hybrid of Western pop and traditional folk song.* **SYN** **mixture**

hydrant /ˈhaɪdrənt/ *noun* [C] a pipe in a street from which water can be taken for stopping fires, cleaning the streets, etc.

hydraulic /haɪˈdrɔːlɪk/ *adj* operated by water or another liquid moving through pipes, etc. under pressure: *hydraulic brakes*

hydroelectric /ˌhaɪdrəʊɪˈlektrɪk/ *adj* using the power of water to produce electricity; produced by the power of water: *a hydroelectric dam/plant* ◆ *hydroelectric power* ➲ note at **environment**

hydrogen /ˈhaɪdrədʒən/ *noun* [U] (*symbol* **H**) a light gas with no colour. **Hydrogen** and **oxygen** (= another gas) form water (H_2O).

hygiene /ˈhaɪdʒiːn/ *noun* [U] (the rules of) keeping yourself and things around you clean, in order to prevent disease: *High standards of hygiene are essential when you are preparing food.* ◆ *personal hygiene*

hygienic /haɪˈdʒiːnɪk/ *adj* clean, without the bacteria that cause disease: *hygienic conditions* **OPP** **unhygienic** ▶ **hygienically** /-kli/ *adv*

hymn /hɪm/ *noun* [C] a religious song that Christians sing together in church, etc.

hype[1] /haɪp/ *noun* [U] (*informal*) advertisements that tell you how good and important a new product, film, etc. is: *Don't believe all the hype—the book is rubbish!*

hype² /haɪp/ *verb* [T] **hype sth (up)** to exaggerate how good or important sth is: *His much-hyped new movie is released next week.*

hyperactive /ˌhaɪpərˈæktɪv/ *adj* (used especially about children and their behaviour) too active and only able to keep quiet and still for short periods ▶ **hyperactivity** /ˌhaɪpəræk'tɪvəti/ *noun* [U]

hyperlink /'haɪpəlɪŋk/ (also **hotlink**) *noun* [C] a place in an electronic document on a computer that is connected to another electronic document: *Click on the hyperlink.*

hypermarket /'haɪpəmɑːkɪt/ *noun* [C] (*BrE*) a very large shop outside a town that sells a wide variety of goods

hyphen /'haɪfn/ *noun* [C] the mark (-) used for joining two words together (for example *left-handed*, *red-hot*) or to show that a word has been divided and continues on the next line ➲ look at **dash**

hyphenate /'haɪfəneɪt/ *verb* [T] to join two words together with a **hyphen** ▶ **hyphenation** /ˌhaɪfə'neɪʃn/ *noun* [U]

hypnosis /hɪp'nəʊsɪs/ *noun* [U] (the producing of) an unconscious state where sb's mind and actions can be controlled by another person: *She was questioned* ***under hypnosis.***

hypnotize (also **-ise**) /'hɪpnətaɪz/ *verb* [T] to put sb into an unconscious state where the person's mind and actions can be controlled ▶ **hypnotic** /hɪp'nɒtɪk/ *adj* ▶ **hypnotism** /'hɪpnətɪzəm/ *noun* [U] ▶ **hypnotist** /-tɪst/ *noun* [C]

hypochondriac /ˌhaɪpə'kɒndriæk/ *noun* [C] a person who is always worried about their health and believes they are ill, even when there is nothing wrong

hypocrisy /hɪ'pɒkrəsi/ *noun* [U] behaviour in which sb does not act according to the moral standards that they claim to have

hypocrite /'hɪpəkrɪt/ *noun* [C] a person who pretends to have moral standards or opinions which they do not really have. **Hypocrites** say one thing and do another: *What a hypocrite! She says she's against the hunting of animals but she's wearing a fur coat.* ▶ **hypocritical** /ˌhɪpə'krɪtɪkl/ *adj* ▶ **hypocritically** /-kli/ *adv*

hypodermic /ˌhaɪpə'dɜːmɪk/ *noun* [C] a medical instrument with a long needle that is used for giving sb an **injection** (= putting a drug under the skin) ▶ **hypodermic** *adj: a hypodermic needle/syringe*

hypothesis /haɪ'pɒθəsɪs/ *noun* [C] (*pl* **hypotheses** /-siːz/) an idea that is suggested as the possible explanation for sth but has not yet been found to be true or correct

hypothetical /ˌhaɪpə'θetɪkl/ *adj* based on situations that have not yet happened, not on facts: *That's a hypothetical question because we don't know what the situation will be next year.* ▶ **hypothetically** /-kli/ *adv*

hysteria /hɪ'stɪəriə/ *noun* [U] a state in which a person or a group of people cannot control their emotions, for example cannot stop laughing, crying, shouting, etc: *mass hysteria*

hysterical /hɪ'sterɪkl/ *adj* **1** very excited and unable to control your emotions: *hysterical laughter* ♦ *She was hysterical with grief.* **2** (*informal*) very funny ▶ **hysterically** /-kli/ *adv*

hysterics /hɪ'sterɪks/ *noun* [pl] **1** an expression of extreme fear, excitement or anger that makes sb lose control of their emotions: *She* ***went into hysterics*** *when they told her the news.* ♦ (*informal*) *My father would* ***have hysterics*** (= be very angry) *if he knew I was with you.* **2** (*informal*) a state of being unable to stop laughing: *The comedian had the audience* ***in hysterics.***

Hz /hɜːts/ *abbr* **hertz**; (used in radio) a measure of **frequency** (= the rate at which a sound wave moves up and down)

I, i /aɪ/ *noun* [C,U] (*pl* **Is; I's; i's** /aɪz/) the 9th letter of the English alphabet: *'Ice' begins with (an) 'I'.*

I /aɪ/ *pron* (the subject of a verb) the person who is speaking or writing: *I phoned and said that I was busy.* ♦ *I'm not going to fall, am I?*

ice¹ /aɪs/ *noun* [U] water that has frozen and become solid: *Do you want ice in your orange juice?* ♦ *I slipped on a patch of ice.* ♦ *black ice* (= ice on roads, that cannot be seen easily) ➲ picture on **page P10**

IDM **break the ice** to say or do sth that makes people feel more relaxed, especially at the beginning of a party or meeting: *She smiled to break the ice.*

cut no ice (with sb) to have no influence or effect on sb: *His excuses cut no ice with me.*

on ice 1 (used about wine, etc.) kept cold by being surrounded by ice: *The table is set, the candles are lit and the champagne is on ice.* **2** (used about a plan, etc.) waiting to be dealt with later; delayed: *We've had to put our plans to go to Australia on ice for the time being.*

ice² /aɪs/ (*especially AmE* **frost**) *verb* [T] to decorate a cake by covering it with a mixture of sugar, butter, chocolate, etc. ➲ look at **icing**

PHR V **ice (sth) over/up** to cover sth or become covered with ice: *The windscreen of the car had iced over in the night.*

iceberg /'aɪsbɜːg/ *noun* [C] a very large block of ice that floats in the sea

IDM **the tip of the iceberg** ➲ **tip¹**

icebox /'aɪsbɒks/ (*AmE*) = **fridge**

'ice cap *noun* [C] a layer of ice that permanently covers parts of the earth: *Are the* ***polar ice caps*** (= at the North and South Poles) *in danger of melting?*

ˌice-'cold *adj* very cold: *ice-cold beer* ♦ *Your hands are ice-cold.*

ice 'cream *noun* **1** [U] a frozen sweet food that is made from cream: *Desserts are served with cream or ice cream.* ➲ picture on **page P16** **2** [C] an amount of **ice cream** that is served to sb, often in a **cone** (= a special container that you can eat): *a strawberry ice cream*

'ice cube *noun* [C] a small block of ice that you put in a drink to make it cold

iced /aɪst/ *adj* (used about drinks) very cold: *iced tea*

'ice hockey (*AmE* **hockey**) *noun* [U] a game that is played on ice by two teams who try to hit a **puck** (= small flat rubber object) into a goal with long wooden sticks ➲ note at **hockey** ➲ picture on **page P4**

ˌice 'lolly *noun* [C] (*AmE* **Popsicle™**) a piece of flavoured ice on a stick ➲ look at **lollipop**

'ice rink (also **rink**, **'skating rink**) *noun* [C] a large area of ice, or a building containing a large area of ice, which is used for **skating** (= moving on the ice wearing special boots)

'ice skate = **skate²(1)**

'ice-skate = **skate¹**

'ice skating = **skating(1)**

icicle /'aɪsɪkl/ *noun* [C] a pointed piece of ice that is formed by water freezing as it falls or runs down from sth

icing /'aɪsɪŋ/ (*AmE* **frosting**) *noun* [U] a mixture of sugar, butter, chocolate, etc. that is used to decorate cakes ➲ picture at **cake**

icon /'aɪkɒn/ *noun* [C] **1** a small picture or symbol on a computer screen that represents a program: *Click on the printer icon with the mouse.* **2** a person or thing that is considered to be a symbol of sth: *Madonna and other pop icons of the 1980s* **3** (also **ikon**) a painting or statue of a holy person that is also thought of as a holy object

iconic /aɪ'kɒnɪk/ *adj* acting as a sign or symbol of sth: *iconic images of New York, such as the Empire State Building*

ICT /ˌaɪ siː 'tiː/ *noun* [U] (*BrE*) **information and communications technology**; the study of the use of computer, the Internet, video and other technology as a subject in British schools

icy /'aɪsi/ *adj* (**icier**; **iciest**) **1** very cold: *icy winds/water/weather* **SYN** **freezing** **2** covered with ice: *icy roads*

ID /ˌaɪ 'diː/ *abbr* (*informal*) = **identification(2)**, **identity**: *You must carry ID at all times.*

Id = **Eid**

I'd /aɪd/ *short for* **I had; I would**

I'D card = **identity card**

idea /aɪ'dɪə/ *noun* **1** [C] **an idea (for sth)**; **an idea (of sth/of doing sth)** a plan, thought or suggestion, especially about what to do in a particular situation: *That's a good idea!* ◆ *He's* ***got an idea*** *for a new play.* ◆ *I had the* ***bright idea*** *of getting Jane to help me with my homework.* ◆ *Has anyone got any ideas of how to tackle this problem?* ◆ *It was your idea to invite so many people to the party.* **2** [sing] **an idea (of sth)** a picture or impression in your mind: *You have no idea* (= you can't imagine) *how difficult it was to find a time that suited everybody.* ◆ *The programme* ***gave a good idea*** *of what life was like before the war.* ◆ *Staying in to watch the football on TV is not my idea of a good time.* **3** [C] **an idea (about sth)** an opinion or belief: *She has her own ideas about how to bring up children.* **4 the idea** [sing] **the idea (of sth/of doing sth)** the aim or purpose of sth: *The idea of the course is to teach the basics of car maintenance.*

IDM **get the idea** to understand the aim or purpose of sth: *Right! I think I've got the idea.*

get the idea that ... to get the feeling or impression that ...: *Where did you get the idea that I was paying for this meal?*

have an idea that ... to feel or think that ...: *I'm not sure but I have an idea that they've gone on holiday.*

not have the faintest/foggiest (idea) ➲ **faint¹**

ideal¹ /aɪ'diːəl/ *adj* **ideal (for sb/sth)** the best possible; perfect: *She's the ideal candidate for the job.* ◆ ***In an ideal world*** *there would be no poverty.* ◆ *It would be an* ***ideal opportunity*** *for you to practise your Spanish.*

ideal² /aɪ'diːəl/ *noun* [C] **1** an idea or principle that seems perfect to you and that you want to achieve: *She finds it hard to live up to her parents' high ideals.* ◆ *political/moral/social ideals* **2** [usually sing] **an ideal (of sth)** a perfect example of a person or thing: *It's my ideal of what a family home should be.*

idealism /aɪ'diːəlɪzəm/ *noun* [U] the belief that a perfect life, situation, etc. can be achieved, even when this is not very likely: *Young people are usually full of idealism.* ➲ look at **realism** ▶ **idealist** /-ɪst/ *noun* [C]: *Most people are idealists when they are young.* ▶ **idealistic** /ˌaɪdiə'lɪstɪk/ *adj*

idealize (also **-ise**) /aɪ'diːəlaɪz/ *verb* [T] to imagine or show sb/sth as being better than he/she/it really is: *Old people often idealize the past.*

ideally /aɪ'diːəli/ *adv* **1** perfectly: *They are ideally suited to each other.* **2** in an ideal situation: *Ideally, no class should be larger than 25.*

identical /aɪ'dentɪkl/ *adj* **1** **identical (to/with sb/sth)** exactly the same as; similar in every detail: *I can't see any difference between these two pens—they look identical to me.* ◆ *That watch is identical to the one I lost yesterday.* **2 the identical** [only *before* a noun] the same: *This is the identical room we stayed in last year.* ▶ **identically** /-kli/ *adv*

iˌdentical 'twin *noun* [C] either of two children born at the same time from the same mother who have developed from a single egg. **Identical twins** are of the same sex and look very similar.

identification /aɪˌdentɪfɪ'keɪʃn/ *noun* **1** [U,C] the process of showing, recognizing or giving proof of who or what sb/sth is: *The identification of the bodies of those killed in the explosion was very difficult.* **2** (*abbr* **ID**) [U] an official paper, document, etc. that is proof of who you are: *Do you have any identification?* **3** [U,C] **identification (with sb/sth)** a strong feeling of understanding or sharing the same feelings as sb/sth: *children's identification with TV heroes*

identify /aɪˈdentɪfaɪ/ *verb* [T] (**identifying; identifies;** *pt, pp* **identified**) **identify sb/sth (as sb/sth)** to recognize or be able to say who or what sb/sth is: *The police need someone to identify the body.* ◆ *We must identify the cause of the problem before we look for solutions.*

PHR V **identify sth with sth** to think or say that sth is the same as sth else: *You can't identify nationalism with fascism.*

identify with sb to feel that you understand and share what sb else is feeling: *I found it hard to identify with the woman in the film.*

identify (yourself) with sb/sth to support or be closely connected with sb/sth: *She became identified with the new political party.*

identity /aɪˈdentəti/ *noun* [C,U] (*pl* **identities**) (*abbr* **ID**) who or what a person or thing is: *There are few clues to the identity of the killer.* ◆ *The region has its own* ***cultural identity.*** ◆ *The arrest was a case of mistaken identity* (= the wrong person was arrested).

iˈdentity card (also **IˈD card**) *noun* [C] a card with your name, photograph, etc. that is proof of who you are

ideology /ˌaɪdiˈɒlədʒi/ *noun* [C,U] (*pl* **ideologies**) a set of ideas that a political or economic system is based on: *Marxist ideology* ▶ **ideological** /ˌaɪdiəˈlɒdʒɪkl/ *adj*

idiom /ˈɪdiəm/ *noun* [C] an expression whose meaning is different from the meanings of the individual words in it: *The idiom 'bring something home to somebody' means 'make somebody understand something'.*

idiomatic /ˌɪdiəˈmætɪk/ *adj* **1** using language that contains expressions that are natural to sb who has spoken that language from birth: *He speaks good idiomatic English.* **2** containing an **idiom**: *an idiomatic expression*

idiosyncrasy /ˌɪdiəˈsɪŋkrəsi/ *noun* [C,U] (*pl* **idiosyncrasies**) a person's particular way of behaving, thinking, etc., especially when it is unusual: *Wearing a raincoat, even on a hot day, is one of her idiosyncrasies.* ▶ **idiosyncratic** /ˌɪdiəsɪŋˈkrætɪk/ *adj*: *His teaching methods are idiosyncratic but successful.*

idiot /ˈɪdiət/ *noun* [C] (*informal*) a very stupid person: *I was an idiot to forget my passport.* ▶ **idiotic** /ˌɪdiˈɒtɪk/ *adj* ▶ **idiotically** /-kli/ *adv*

idle /ˈaɪdl/ *adj* **1** not wanting to work hard: *He has the ability to succeed but he is just* ***bone idle*** (= very lazy). SYN **lazy** **2** not doing anything; not being used: *She can't bear to be idle.* ◆ *The factory* ***stood idle*** *while the machines were being repaired.* **3** [only *before* a noun] not to be taken seriously because it will not have any result: *an idle promise/threat* ◆ *idle chatter/curiosity* ▶ **idleness** *noun* [U] ▶ **idly** /ˈaɪdli/ *adv*

idol /ˈaɪdl/ *noun* [C] **1** a person (such as a film star) who is admired or loved: *a pop/football/teen/screen idol* **2** a statue that people treat as a god

idolize (also **-ise**) /ˈaɪdəlaɪz/ *verb* [T] to love or admire sb very much or too much: *He is an only child and his parents idolize him.*

idyllic /ɪˈdɪlɪk/ *adj* very pleasant and peaceful; perfect: *an idyllic holiday*

i.e. /ˌaɪ ˈiː/ *abbr* that is; in other words: *deciduous trees, i.e. those which lose their leaves in autumn*

if /ɪf/ *conj* **1** used in sentences in which one thing only happens or is true when another thing happens or is true: *If you see him, give him this letter.* ◆ *We won't go to the beach if it rains.* ◆ *If I had more time, I would learn another language.* ◆ *I might see her tomorrow. If not, I'll see her at the weekend.* ➲ note at **case, when** **2** when; every time: *If I try to phone her she just hangs up.* ◆ *If metal gets hot it expands.* **3** used after verbs such as 'ask', 'know', 'remember': *They asked if we would like to go too.* ◆ *I can't remember if I posted the letter or not.* ➲ note at **whether** **4** used when you are asking sb to do sth or suggesting sth politely: *If you could just come this way, sir.* ◆ *If I might suggest something ...*

IDM **as if** ➲ **as**

even if ➲ **even²**

if I were you used when you are giving sb advice: *If I were you, I'd leave now.*

if it wasn't/weren't for sb/sth if a particular person or situation did not exist or was not there; without sb/sth: *If it wasn't for him, I wouldn't stay in this country.*

if only used for expressing a strong wish: *If only I could drive.* ◆ *If only he'd write.*

igloo /ˈɪɡluː/ *noun* [C] (*pl* **igloos**) a small house that is built from blocks of hard snow

ignite /ɪɡˈnaɪt/ *verb* [I,T] (*formal*) to start burning or to make sth start burning: *A spark from the engine ignited the petrol.*

ignition /ɪɡˈnɪʃn/ *noun* **1** [C, usually sing] the electrical system that starts the engine of a car: *to turn the ignition on/off* ◆ *First of all, put the key in the ignition.* ➲ picture at **car** **2** [U] the act of starting to burn or making sth start to burn

ignominious /ˌɪɡnəˈmɪniəs/ *adj* (*formal*) making you feel embarrassed: *The team suffered an ignominious defeat.* ▶ **ignominiously** *adv*

ignorance /ˈɪɡnərəns/ *noun* [U] **ignorance (of/about sth)** a lack of information or knowledge: *The workers were* ***in complete ignorance*** *of the management's plans.*

ignorant /ˈɪɡnərənt/ *adj* **1** **ignorant (of/about sth)** not knowing about sth: *Many people are ignorant of their rights.* **2** (*informal*) having or showing bad manners: *an ignorant person/remark* ➲ look at **ignore**

ignore /ɪɡˈnɔː(r)/ *verb* [T] to pay no attention to sb/sth: *I said hello to Debbie but she totally ignored me* (= acted as though she hadn't seen me). ◆ *Alison ignored her doctor's advice about getting more exercise.*

HELP Be careful. **Ignore** and **be ignorant** are different in meaning.

I

ikon = icon(3)

I'll /aɪl/ *short for* **I will; I shall**

ill¹ /ɪl/ *adj* **1** [not before a noun] (*AmE* **sick**) not in good health; not well: *I can't drink milk because it makes me* ***feel ill.*** ◆ *My mother was* ***taken ill*** *suddenly last week.* ◆ *My grandfather is* ***seriously ill*** *in hospital.* ➲ note at **doctor** **2** [only *before* a noun] bad or harmful: *He resigned because of* ***ill health.*** ◆ *I'm glad to say I suffered no* ***ill effects*** *from all that rich food.* ➲ *noun* **illness**

TOPIC

Feeling ill

If you are **suffering from** an **illness**, you feel **ill**. If you have a **fever**, for example when you have **flu**, you have a high **temperature**. If you catch a **cold**, you will start **sneezing**. You might also have a **cough** and a **sore throat**. If you **come down with chickenpox** or **measles**, your skin is covered in red **spots**. If you become ill when you eat, touch or breathe in something that does not normally make other people ill, you have an **allergy**, for example **hay fever**. You might come out in a **rash** (= an area of small red spots). A disease that moves easily from one person to another is **infectious** or **contagious** (= passed by touch). If your illness is not serious, you will quickly **get better**. When somebody is ill, we usually wish them **'Get well soon!'**

ill² /ɪl/ *adv* **1** [in compounds] badly or wrongly: *You would be* ***ill-advised*** *to drive until you have fully recovered.* **2** (*formal*) only with difficulty; not easily: *They could ill afford the extra money for better heating.*

IDM **augur well/ill for sb/sth** ➲ **augur**
bode well/ill (for sb/sth) ➲ **bode**
bad/ill feeling ➲ **feeling**

illegal /ɪˈliːɡl/ *adj* not allowed by the law: *It is illegal to drive a car without insurance.* ◆ *illegal drugs/immigrants/activities* OPP **legal** ▶ **illegally** /-ɡəli/ *adv*

illegality /ˌɪliˈɡæləti/ *noun* (*pl* **illegalities**) **1** [U] the state of being illegal **2** [C] an illegal act ➲ look at **legality**

illegible /ɪˈledʒəbl/ *adj* difficult or impossible to read: *Your handwriting is quite illegible.* OPP **legible** ▶ **illegibly** /-əbli/ *adv*

illegitimate /ˌɪləˈdʒɪtəmət/ *adj* **1** (*old-fashioned*) (used about a child) born to parents who are not married to each other **2** not allowed by law; against the rules: *the illegitimate use of company money* OPP for both meanings **legitimate** ▶ **illegitimacy** /ˌɪləˈdʒɪtəməsi/ *noun* [U] ▶ **illegitimately** *adv*

ˌill-ˈfated *adj* not lucky: *the ill-fated ship, the Titanic*

illicit /ɪˈlɪsɪt/ *adj* (used about an activity or substance) not allowed by law or by the rules of society: *the illicit trade in ivory* ◆ *They were having an illicit affair.*

illiterate /ɪˈlɪtərət/ *adj* **1** not able to read or write OPP **literate** **2** (used about a piece of writing) very badly written **3** [usually after a noun or adverb] not knowing much about a particular subject: *computer illiterate* ▶ **illiteracy** /ɪˈlɪtərəsi/ *noun* [U]: *adult illiteracy* OPP **literacy**

illness /ˈɪlnəs/ *noun* **1** [U] the state of being physically or mentally ill: *He's missed a lot of school through illness.* ◆ *There is a history of mental illness in the family.* **2** [C] a type or period of physical or mental ill health: *a* ***minor/serious*** *illness* ◆ *He died after a short illness.* ➲ note at **disease** ➲ *adjective* **ill**

illogical /ɪˈlɒdʒɪkl/ *adj* not sensible or reasonable: *It seems illogical to me to pay somebody to do work that you could do yourself.* OPP **logical** ▶ **illogicality** /ɪˌlɒdʒɪˈkæləti/ *noun* [C,U] (*pl* **illogicalities**) ▶ **illogically** /ɪˈlɒdʒɪkli/ *adv*

ˌill-ˈtreat *verb* [T] to treat sb/sth badly or in an unkind way: *This cat has been ill-treated.* ▶ **ill-ˈtreatment** *noun* [U]

illuminate /ɪˈluːmɪneɪt/ *verb* [T] (*formal*) **1** to shine light on sth or to decorate sth with lights: *The palace was illuminated by spotlights.* **2** to explain sth or make sth clear

illuminating /ɪˈluːmɪneɪtɪŋ/ *adj* helping to explain sth or make sth clear: *an illuminating discussion*

illumination /ɪˌluːmɪˈneɪʃn/ *noun* **1** [U,C] light or the place where a light comes from: *The only illumination in the room came from the fire.* **2** **illuminations** [pl] (*BrE*) brightly coloured lights that are used for decorating a street, town, etc: *Christmas illuminations*

illusion /ɪˈluːʒn/ *noun* **1** [C,U] a false idea, belief or impression: *I* ***have no illusions*** *about the situation —I know it's serious.* ◆ *I think Peter's* ***under the illusion*** *that he'll be the new director.* **2** [C] something that your eyes tell you is there or is true but in fact is not: *That line looks longer, but in fact the lines are the same length. It's an* ***optical illusion.*** ➲ picture at **optical illusion**

illusory /ɪˈluːsəri/ *adj* (*formal*) not real, although seeming to be: *The profits they had hoped for proved to be illusory.*

illustrate /ˈɪləstreɪt/ *verb* [T] **1** to add pictures, diagrams, etc. to a book or magazine: *Most cookery books are illustrated.* **2** to explain or make sth clear by using examples, pictures or diagrams: *These statistics* ***illustrate the point*** *that I was making very well.*

illustration /ˌɪləˈstreɪʃn/ *noun* **1** [C] a drawing, diagram or picture in a book or magazine: *colour illustrations* **2** [U] the activity or art of illustrating **3** [C] an example that makes a point or an idea clear: *Can you give me an illustration of what you mean?*

illustrator /ˈɪləstreɪtə(r)/ *noun* [C] a person who draws or paints pictures for books, etc.

illustrious /ɪˈlʌstriəs/ *adj* (*formal*) famous and successful

I'm /aɪm/ *short for* **I am**

image /ˈɪmɪdʒ/ *noun* [C] **1** the general impression that a person or an organization gives to the public:

When you meet him, he's very different from his public image. **2** a mental picture or idea of sb/sth: *I have an image of my childhood as always sunny and happy.* **3** a picture or description that appears in a book, film or painting: *horrific images of war* **4** a copy or picture of sb/sth seen in a mirror, through a camera, on TV, computer, etc: *A perfect image of the building was reflected in the lake.* ◆ *(figurative) He's* ***the (spitting) image of*** *his father* (= he looks exactly like him).

imagery /ˈɪmɪdʒəri/ *noun* [U] language that produces pictures in the minds of the people reading or listening: *poetic imagery*

imaginable /ɪˈmædʒɪnəbl/ *adj* that you can imagine: *Sophie made all the excuses imaginable when she was caught stealing.* ◆ *His house was equipped with every imaginable luxury.*

⚷ **imaginary** /ɪˈmædʒɪnəri/ *adj* existing only in the mind; not real: *Many children have imaginary friends.*

⚷ **imagination** /ɪˌmædʒɪˈneɪʃn/ *noun* **1** [U,C] the ability to create mental pictures or new ideas: *He has a lively imagination.* ◆ *She's very clever but she doesn't* ***have*** *much* ***imagination****.*

> **HELP** **Imagination or fantasy? Imagination** is a creative quality that a person has. **Fantasy** refers to thoughts, stories, etc. that are not related to reality.

2 [C] the part of the mind that uses this ability: *If you* ***use*** *your* ***imagination****, you should be able to guess the answer.*

imaginative /ɪˈmædʒɪnətɪv/ *adj* having or showing imagination: *She's always full of imaginative ideas.* ▸ **imaginatively** *adv*

⚷ **imagine** /ɪˈmædʒɪn/ *verb* [T] **1 imagine that …; imagine sb/sth (doing/as sth)** to form a picture or idea in your mind of what sth/sb might be like: *Imagine that you're lying on a beach.* ◆ *It's not easy to imagine your brother as a doctor.* ◆ *I can't imagine myself cycling 20 miles a day.* **2** to see, hear or think sth that is not true or does not exist: *She's always imagining that she's ill but she's fine really.* ◆ *I thought I heard someone downstairs, but I must have been* ***imagining things****.* **3** to think that sth is probably true **SYN** **suppose**: *I imagine he'll be coming by car.*

imam /ɪˈmɑːm/ *noun* [C] (in Islam) a religious man who leads the prayers in a **mosque** (= a building where Muslims meet and worship)

imbalance /ɪmˈbæləns/ *noun* [C] **an imbalance (between A and B); an imbalance (in/of sth)** a difference; not being equal: *an imbalance in the numbers of men and women teachers*

imbecile /ˈɪmbəsiːl/ *noun* [C] a stupid person **SYN** **idiot**

IMF /ˌaɪ em ˈef/ *abbr* the **International Monetary Fund**; the organization within the United Nations which is concerned with trade and economic development

imitate /ˈɪmɪteɪt/ *verb* [T] **1** to copy sb/sth: *Small children learn by imitating their parents.* **2** to copy the speech or actions of sb/sth, often in order to make people laugh: *She could imitate her mother perfectly.*

imitation /ˌɪmɪˈteɪʃn/ *noun* **1** [C] a copy of sth real: *Some artificial flowers are good imitations of real ones.* ➲ look at **genuine** **2** [U] the act of copying sb/sth: *Good pronunciation of a language is best learnt* ***by imitation****.* **3** [C] the act of copying the way sb talks and behaves, especially in order to make people laugh: *Can you* ***do*** *any* ***imitations*** *of politicians?*

immaculate /ɪˈmækjələt/ *adj* **1** perfectly clean and tidy: *immaculate white shirts* **2** without any mistakes **SYN** **perfect**: *an immaculate performance* ▸ **immaculately** *adv*

immaterial /ˌɪməˈtɪəriəl/ *adj* **immaterial (to sb/sth)** not important: *It's immaterial to me whether we go today or tomorrow.*

immature /ˌɪməˈtjʊə(r)/ *adj* **1** (used about a person) behaving in a way that is not sensible and is typical of people who are much younger: *He's too immature to take his work seriously.* **2** not fully grown or developed: *an immature body* **OPP** for both meanings **mature**

immeasurable /ɪˈmeʒərəbl/ *adj* (*formal*) too large, great, etc. to be measured: *to cause immeasurable harm* ▸ **immeasurably** /-əbli/ *adv*: *Housing standards improved immeasurably after the war.*

immediacy /ɪˈmiːdiəsi/ *noun* [U] (*formal*) the quality of being available or seeming to happen close to you and without delay: *Letters do not have the same immediacy as email.*

⚷ **immediate** /ɪˈmiːdiət/ *adj* **1** happening or done without delay: *I'd like an immediate answer to my proposal.* ◆ *The government responded with immediate action.* **2** [only *before* a noun] existing now and needing urgent attention: *Tell me what your immediate needs are.* **3** [only *before* a noun] nearest in time, position or relationship: *They won't make any changes in* ***the immediate future****.* ◆ *He has left most of his money to his immediate family* (= wife, parents, children, brothers and sisters).

⚷ **immediately** /ɪˈmiːdiətli/ *adv, conj* **1** at once; without delay: *Can you come home immediately after work?* ◆ *I couldn't immediately see what he meant.* **2** nearest in time or position: *Who's the girl immediately in front of Simon?* ◆ *What did you do immediately after you left school?* **3** very closely; directly: *He wasn't immediately involved in the crime.* **4** (*BrE*) as soon as: *I opened the letter immediately I got home.*

immense /ɪˈmens/ *adj* very big or great: *immense difficulties/importance/power* ◆ *She gets immense pleasure from her garden.*

immensely /ɪˈmensli/ *adv* extremely; very much: *immensely enjoyable* ◆ *'Did you enjoy the party?' 'Yes, immensely.'*

immensity /ɪˈmensəti/ *noun* [U] an extremely large size: *the immensity of the universe*

immerse /ɪˈmɜːs/ *verb* [T] **1 immerse sth (in sth)** to put sth into a liquid so that it is covered: *Make*

I

sure the spaghetti is fully immersed in the boiling water. **2** immerse yourself (in sth) to involve yourself completely in sth so that you give it all your attention: *Rachel's usually immersed in a book.* ▸ **immersion** /ɪˈmɜːʃn/ *noun* [U]: *Immersion in cold water resulted in rapid loss of heat.* ◆ *a two-week immersion course in French* (= in which the student will hear and use only French)

immigrant /ˈɪmɪgrənt/ *noun* [C] a person who has come into a foreign country to live there permanently: *The government plans to tighten controls to prevent* ***illegal immigrants***. ◆ *London has a high immigrant population.*

MORE A society with many immigrant communities is a **multicultural society**. Groups of immigrants or children of immigrants who share a common cultural tradition are an **ethnic minority**.

immigrate /ˈɪmɪgreɪt/ *verb* [I] (*especially AmE*) to come and live permanently in a country after leaving your own country

HELP In British English it is more common to use the verb **emigrate**, which is used in connection with the place that somebody has come from: *My parents emigrated to this country from Jamaica.*

immigration /ˌɪmɪˈgreɪʃn/ *noun* [U] **1** the process of coming to live permanently in a country that is not your own; the number of people who do this: *There are greater controls on immigration than there used to be.* **2** (also immiˈgration control) the control point at an airport, port, etc. where the official documents of people who want to come into a country are checked: *When you leave the plane you have to go through customs and immigration.* ➲ look at **emigrate, emigrant, emigration**

imminent /ˈɪmɪnənt/ *adj* (usually used about sth unpleasant) almost certain to happen very soon: *Heavy rainfall means that flooding is imminent.* ▸ **imminently** *adv*

immobile /ɪˈməʊbaɪl/ *adj* not moving or not able to move: *The hunter stood immobile until the lion had passed.* OPP **mobile** ▸ **immobility** /ˌɪməˈbɪləti/ *noun* [U]

immobilize (also -ise) /ɪˈməʊbəlaɪz/ *verb* [T] to prevent sb/sth from moving or working normally: *The railways have been completely immobilized by the strike.* ◆ *This device immobilizes the car to prevent it being stolen.*

immobilizer (also -iser) /ɪˈməʊbəlaɪzə(r)/ *noun* [C] a device in a vehicle that prevents thieves from starting the engine when the vehicle is parked

🔑 **immoral** /ɪˈmɒrəl/ *adj* (used about people or their behaviour) considered wrong or not honest by most people: *It's immoral to steal.* OPP **moral**

HELP Be careful. **Amoral** has a different meaning.

▸ **immorality** /ˌɪməˈræləti/ *noun* [U] OPP **morality**
▸ **immorally** /ɪˈmɒrəli/ *adv*

immortal /ɪˈmɔːtl/ *adj* living or lasting for ever: *Nobody is immortal—we all have to die some time.* OPP **mortal** ▸ **immortality** /ˌɪmɔːˈtæləti/ *noun* [U]

immortalize (also -ise) /ɪˈmɔːtəlaɪz/ *verb* [T] to give lasting fame to sb/sth: *He immortalized their relationship in a poem.*

immune /ɪˈmjuːn/ *adj* **1** immune (to sth) having natural protection against a certain disease or illness: *You should be immune to measles if you've had it already.* ◆ *These vitamins help to strengthen your* ***immune system***. **2** immune (to sth) not affected by sth: *You can say what you like—I'm immune to criticism!* **3** immune (from sth) protected from a danger or punishment: *Young children are immune from prosecution.*

immunity /ɪˈmjuːnəti/ *noun* [U] the ability to avoid or not be affected by disease, criticism, punishment by law, etc: *In many countries people have no immunity to diseases like measles.* ◆ *Ambassadors to other countries receive* ***diplomatic immunity*** (= protection from being arrested, etc.)

immunize (also -ise) /ˈɪmjunaɪz/ *verb* [T] to protect sb from a disease, usually by putting a **vaccine** (= a substance that protects the body) into their blood: *Before visiting certain countries you will need to be immunized against cholera.* ➲ look at **inoculate, vaccinate** ▸ **immunization** (also -isation) /ˌɪmjunaɪˈzeɪʃn/ *noun* [C,U]

imp /ɪmp/ *noun* [C] (in stories) a small creature like a little man, who has magic powers and behaves badly

🔑 **impact** /ˈɪmpækt/ *noun* **1** [C,usually sing] an impact (on/upon sb/sth) a powerful effect or impression: *I hope this anti-smoking campaign will* ***make/have an impact*** *on young people.* ◆ *I hope this road safety campaign will* ***make/have an impact*** *on drivers.* **2** [C,U] the action or force of one object hitting another: *The impact of the crash threw the passengers out of their seats.* ◆ *The bomb exploded* ***on impact***.

impair /ɪmˈpeə(r)/ *verb* [T] (*formal*) to damage sth or make it weaker: *Ear infections can result in impaired hearing.*

impale /ɪmˈpeɪl/ *verb* [T] impale sb/sth (on sth) to push a sharp pointed object through sb/sth: *The boy fell out of the tree and impaled his leg on some railings.*

impart /ɪmˈpɑːt/ *verb* [T] (*formal*) **1** impart sth (to sb) to pass information, knowledge, etc. to other people: *He rushed home eager to impart the good news.* **2** impart sth (to sth) to give a certain quality to sth: *The low lighting imparted a romantic atmosphere to the room.*

impartial /ɪmˈpɑːʃl/ *adj* not supporting one person or group more than another; fair: *The referee must be impartial.* ▸ **impartiality** /ˌɪmˌpɑːʃiˈæləti/ *noun* [U] OPP **partiality** ▸ **impartially** /ɪmˈpɑːʃəli/ *adv*

impassable /ɪmˈpɑːsəbl/ *adj* (used about a road, etc.) impossible to travel on because it is blocked: *Flooding and fallen trees have made many roads impassable.* OPP **passable**

impassioned /ɪm'pæʃnd/ *adj* (used especially about a speech) showing strong feelings about sth: *an impassioned plea/speech/defence*

impassive /ɪm'pæsɪv/ *adj* (used about a person) showing no emotion or reaction ▶ **impassively** *adv*

⚷ **impatient** /ɪm'peɪʃnt/ *adj* **1** impatient (at sth/with sb) not able to stay calm and wait for sb/sth; easily annoyed by sb/sth that seems slow: *The passengers are getting impatient at the delay.* ◆ *It's no good being impatient with small children.* OPP **patient** **2** impatient for/to do sth wanting sth to happen soon: *By the time they are sixteen many young people are impatient to leave school.* ▶ **impatience** *noun* [U]: *He began to explain for the third time with growing impatience.* OPP **patience** ▶ **impatiently** *adv* OPP **patiently**

impeccable /ɪm'pekəbl/ *adj* without any mistakes or faults; perfect: *impeccable behaviour* ◆ *His accent is impeccable.* ▶ **impeccably** /-əbli/ *adv*

impede /ɪm'piːd/ *verb* [T] (*formal*) to make it difficult for sb/sth to move or go forward: *The completion of the new motorway has been impeded by bad weather conditions.*

impediment /ɪm'pedɪmənt/ *noun* [C] (*formal*) **1** an impediment (to sth) something that makes it difficult for a person or thing to move or progress: *The high rate of tax is a major impediment to new businesses.* **2** something that makes speaking difficult: *Jane had a speech impediment*

impending /ɪm'pendɪŋ/ *adj* [only *before* a noun] (usually used about sth bad) that will happen soon: *There was a feeling of impending disaster in the air.*

impenetrable /ɪm'penɪtrəbl/ *adj* **1** impossible to enter or go through: *The jungle was impenetrable.* **2** impossible to understand: *an impenetrable mystery*

imperative /ɪm'perətɪv/ *adj* (*formal*) very important or urgent: *It's imperative that you see a doctor immediately.*

the imperative /ɪm'perətɪv/ *noun* [sing] the form of the verb that is used for giving orders: *In 'Shut the door!' the verb is in the imperative.*

imperceptible /ˌɪmpə'septəbl/ *adj* too small to be seen or noticed: *The difference between the original painting and the copy was almost imperceptible.* OPP **perceptible** ▶ **imperceptibly** /-əbli/ *adv*: *Almost imperceptibly winter was turning into spring.*

imperfect /ɪm'pɜːfɪkt/ *adj* with mistakes or faults: *an imperfect system* OPP **perfect** ▶ **imperfectly** *adv*

imperfection /ˌɪmpə'fekʃn/ *noun* [C,U] a fault or weakness in sb/sth: *They learned to live with each other's imperfections.*

imperial /ɪm'pɪəriəl/ *adj* [only *before* a noun] **1** connected with an empire or its ruler: *the imperial palace* **2** connected with the system for measuring length, weight and volume that, in the past, was used for all goods in the UK and is still used for some ➲ look at **inch, foot, yard, ounce, pound, pint, gallon, metric**

imperialism /ɪm'pɪəriəlɪzəm/ *noun* [U] a political system in which a rich and powerful country has **colonies** (= countries that it controls) ▶ **imperialist** /-ɪst/ *adj, noun* [C]

impersonal /ɪm'pɜːsənl/ *adj* **1** not showing friendly human feelings; cold in feeling or atmosphere: *My hotel room was very impersonal.* **2** not referring to any particular person: *Can we try to keep the discussion as impersonal as possible, please?*

impersonate /ɪm'pɜːsəneɪt/ *verb* [T] to copy the behaviour and way of speaking of a person or to pretend to be a different person: *a comedian who impersonates politicians* ▶ **impersonation** /ɪmˌpɜːsə'neɪʃn/ *noun* [C,U] ▶ **impersonator** /ɪm'pɜːsəneɪtə(r)/ *noun* [C]

impertinent /ɪm'pɜːtɪnənt/ *adj* (*formal*) not showing respect; rude: *I do apologize. It was impertinent of my son to speak to you like that.*

> **HELP** The opposite is NOT **pertinent**. It is **polite** or **respectful**.

▶ **impertinence** *noun* [U]: *He had the impertinence to ask my age.* ▶ **impertinently** *adv*

imperturbable /ˌɪmpə'tɜːbəbl/ *adj* (*formal*) not easily worried by a difficult situation

impervious /ɪm'pɜːviəs/ *adj* impervious (to sth) **1** not affected or influenced by sth: *She was impervious to criticism.* **2** (*technical*) not allowing water, etc. to pass through

impetuous /ɪm'petʃuəs/ *adj* acting or done quickly and without thinking: *an impetuous decision* ➲ A more common word is **impulsive**. ▶ **impetuously** *adv*

impetus /'ɪmpɪtəs/ *noun* [U,sing] (an) impetus (for sth); (an) impetus (to do sth) something that encourages sth else to happen: *This scandal provided the main impetus for changes in the rules.* ◆ *I need fresh impetus to start working on this essay again.*

impinge /ɪm'pɪndʒ/ *verb* [I] (*formal*) impinge on/upon sth to have a noticeable effect on sth, especially a bad one: *I'm not going to let my job impinge on my home life.*

implant /'ɪmplɑːnt/ *noun* [C] something that is put into a person's body in a medical operation: *dental implants* ➲ look at **transplant**

implausible /ɪm'plɔːzəbl/ *adj* not easy to believe: *an implausible excuse* OPP **plausible**

implement[1] /'ɪmplɪment/ *verb* [T] to start using a plan, system, etc: *Some teachers are finding it difficult to implement the government's educational reforms.* ▶ **implementation** /ˌɪmplɪmen'teɪʃn/ *noun* [U]

implement[2] /'ɪmplɪmənt/ *noun* [C] a tool or instrument (especially for work outdoors): *farm implements* ➲ note at **tool**

implicated /'ɪmplɪkeɪt/

IDM **be implicated in sth** to be involved in sth

unpleasant, especially a crime: *A well-known politician was implicated in the scandal.*

implication /ˌɪmplɪˈkeɪʃn/ *noun* **1** [C, usually pl] **implications (for/of sth)** the effect that sth might have on sth else in the future: *The new law will **have** serious **implications** for our work.* **2** [C,U] something that is suggested or said in a way that is not direct: *The implication of what she said was that we had made a bad mistake.* ➲ *verb* **imply 3** [U] **implication (in sth)** the fact of being involved, or of involving sb, in sth unpleasant, especially a crime: *The player's implication in this scandal could affect his career.* ➲ *verb* **implicate**

implicit /ɪmˈplɪsɪt/ *adj* **1** not expressed in a direct way but understood by the people involved: *We had an implicit agreement that we would support each other.* ➲ look at **explicit 2** complete; total: *I have implicit faith in your ability to do the job.* ▶ **implicitly** *adv*

implore /ɪmˈplɔː(r)/ *verb* [T] (*formal*) to ask sb with great emotion to do sth, because you are in a very serious situation: *She implored him not to leave her alone.* SYN **beg**

imply /ɪmˈplaɪ/ *verb* [T] (**implying**; **implies**; *pt, pp* **implied**) to suggest sth in an indirect way or without actually saying it: *He didn't say so—but he implied that I was lying.* ➲ *noun* **implication**

impolite /ˌɪmpəˈlaɪt/ *adj* rude: *I think it was impolite of him to ask you to leave.* SYN **rude, discourteous** OPP **polite** ▶ **impolitely** *adv*

import¹ /ˈɪmpɔːt/ *noun* **1** [C, usually pl] a product or service that is brought into one country from another: *What are your country's major imports?* OPP **export 2** [U] (also **importation**) the act of bringing goods or services into a country: *new controls on the import of certain goods from abroad*

import² /ɪmˈpɔːt/ *verb* [T] **1** **import sth (from ...)** to buy goods, etc. from a foreign country and bring them into your own country: *imported goods* ◆ *Britain imports wine from France/Italy/Spain.* ◆ (*figurative*) *We need to import some extra help from somewhere fast.* OPP **export 2** to move information into a computer program from another program ▶ **importer** *noun* [C] OPP **exporter**

importance /ɪmˈpɔːtns/ *noun* [U] the quality of being important: *The decision was **of great importance** to the future of the business.*

important /ɪmˈpɔːtnt/ *adj* **1** **important (to sb); important (for sb/sth) (to do sth); important that ...** having great value or influence; very necessary: *an important meeting/decision/factor* ◆ *This job is very important to me.* ◆ *It's important not to be late.* ◆ *It's important for people to see the results of what they do.* ◆ *It was important to me that you were there.* **2** (used about a person) having great influence or authority: *Milton was one of the most important writers of his time.* ▶ **importantly** *adv*

OTHER WORDS FOR

important

Essential and **vital** both mean 'very important or completely necessary': *It is essential/vital that our children get the best possible education.* ◆ *Fresh fruit and vegetables are **an essential/a vital part** of a healthy diet.* We also say **play a vital/key role in** ... *The police play a key role in our society.* Something that is important in history is **historic**: *a historic decision/event/occasion.*

importation /ˌɪmpɔːˈteɪʃn/ = **import¹** (2)

impose /ɪmˈpəʊz/ *verb* **1** [T] **impose sth (on/upon sb/sth)** to make a law, rule, opinion, etc. be accepted by using your power or authority: *A new tax will be imposed on wine and spirits.* ◆ *Parents should try not to impose their own ideas on their children.* **2** [I] **impose (on/upon sb/sth)** to ask or expect sb to do sth that may cause extra work or trouble: *I hate to impose on you but can you lend me some money?* ▶ **imposition** /ˌɪmpəˈzɪʃn/ *noun* [U,C]: *the imposition of military rule*

imposing /ɪmˈpəʊzɪŋ/ *adj* big and important; impressive: *They lived in a large, imposing house near the park.*

impossible /ɪmˈpɒsəbl/ *adj* **1** not able to be done or to happen: *It's impossible for me to be there before 12.* ◆ *I find it almost impossible to get up in the morning!* ◆ *That's impossible!* (= I don't believe it!) OPP **possible 2** very difficult to deal with: *This is an impossible situation!* ◆ *He's always been an impossible child.* ▶ **the impossible** *noun* [sing]: *Don't attempt the impossible!* ▶ **impossibility** /ɪmˌpɒsəˈbɪləti/ *noun* [C,U] (*pl* **impossibilities**): *What you are suggesting is a complete impossibility!*

impossibly /ɪmˈpɒsəbli/ *adv* extremely: *impossibly complicated*

impostor /ɪmˈpɒstə(r)/ *noun* [C] a person who pretends to be sb else in order to trick other people

impotent /ˈɪmpətənt/ *adj* **1** without enough power to influence a situation or to change things SYN **powerless 2** (used about a man) not capable of having sex ▶ **impotence** *noun* [U]

impoverish /ɪmˈpɒvərɪʃ/ *verb* [T] (*formal*) to make sb/sth poor or lower in quality OPP **enrich**

impractical /ɪmˈpræktɪkl/ *adj* **1** not sensible or realistic: *It would be impractical to take our bikes on the train.* **2** (used about a person) not good at doing ordinary things that involve using your hands; not good at organizing or planning things: *He's clever but completely impractical.* OPP for both meanings **practical**

imprecise /ˌɪmprɪˈsaɪs/ *adj* not clear or exact: *imprecise instructions* OPP **precise**

impress /ɪmˈpres/ *verb* [T] **1** **impress sb (with sth); impress sb that...** to make sb feel admiration and respect: *She's always trying to impress people with her new clothes.* ◆ *It impressed me that he understood immediately what I meant.* **2** (*formal*) **impress sth on/upon sb** to make the importance of sth very clear to sb: *You should impress on John that he must pass these exams.*

impressed /ɪmˈprest/ *adj* impressed (by/with sb/sth) feeling admiration for sb/sth because you think they are particularly good, interesting, etc: *I must admit I am impressed.* ♦ *We were all impressed by her enthusiasm.*

⚷ **impression** /ɪmˈpreʃn/ *noun* [C] **1** an idea, a feeling or an opinion that you get about sb/sth: *What's your* ***first impression*** *of the new director?* ♦ *I'm not sure but I* ***have/get the impression*** *that Jane's rather unhappy.* ♦ *I was* ***under the impression*** (= I believed, but I was wrong) *that you were married.* **2** the effect that a person or thing produces on sb else: *She* ***gives the impression*** *of being older than she really is.* ♦ *Do you think I* ***made a good impression on*** *your parents?* **3** an amusing copy of the way sb acts or speaks: *My brother can do a good impression of the Prime Minister.* SYN **impersonation** **4** a mark that is left when an object has been pressed hard into a surface

impressionable /ɪmˈpreʃənəbl/ *adj* easy to influence: *Sixteen is a very impressionable age.*

⚷ **impressive** /ɪmˈpresɪv/ *adj* causing a feeling of admiration and respect because of the importance, size, quality, etc. of sth: *an impressive building/speech* ♦ *The way he handled the situation was most impressive.*

imprint /ˈɪmprɪnt/ *noun* [C] a mark made by pressing an object on a surface: *the imprint of a foot in the sand*

imprison /ɪmˈprɪzn/ *verb* [T, often passive] to put or keep sb in prison: *He was imprisoned for armed robbery.* ▶ **imprisonment** *noun* [U]: *She was sentenced to five years' imprisonment.*

improbable /ɪmˈprɒbəbl/ *adj* not likely to be true or to happen: *an improbable explanation* ♦ *It is* ***highly improbable*** *that Alexandra will arrive tonight.* SYN **unlikely** OPP **probable** ▶ **improbability** /ɪmˌprɒbəˈbɪləti/ *noun* [U] ▶ **improbably** /ɪmˈprɒbəbli/ *adv*

impromptu /ɪmˈprɒmptjuː/ *adj* (done) without being prepared or organized: *an impromptu party*

improper /ɪmˈprɒpə(r)/ *adj* (*formal*) **1** illegal or dishonest: *It seems that she had been involved in improper business deals.* **2** not suitable for the situation; rude in a sexual way: *It would be improper to say anything else at this stage.* ♦ *He lost his job for making improper suggestions to several of the women.* OPP for both meanings **proper** ▶ **improperly** *adv* OPP **properly**

impropriety /ˌɪmprəˈpraɪəti/ *noun* [U,C] (*pl* improprieties) (*formal*) behaviour or actions that are morally wrong or not appropriate: *She was unaware of the impropriety of her remark.*

⚷ **improve** /ɪmˈpruːv/ *verb* [I,T] to become or to make sth better: *Your work has greatly improved.* ♦ *I hope the weather will improve later on.* ♦ *Your vocabulary is excellent but you could improve your pronunciation.*

PHR V **improve on/upon sth** to produce sth that is better than sth else: *Nobody will be able to improve on that score* (= nobody will be able to make a higher score).

⚷ **improvement** /ɪmˈpruːvmənt/ *noun* [C,U] (an) improvement (on/in sth) (a) change which makes the quality or condition of sb/sth better: *Your written work is in need of some improvement.* ♦ *There's been (a) considerable* ***improvement in*** *your mother's condition.* ♦ *These marks are an* ***improvement on*** *your previous ones.*

improvise /ˈɪmprəvaɪz/ *verb* [I,T] **1** to make, do, or manage sth without preparation, using what you have: *If you can't find the equipment you need, you'll have to improvise.* **2** to play music, speak or act using your imagination instead of written or remembered material: *It was obvious that the actor had forgotten his lines and was trying to improvise.* ▶ **improvisation** /ˌɪmprəvaɪˈzeɪʃn/ *noun* [C,U]

impudent /ˈɪmpjədənt/ *adj* (*formal*) very rude; lacking respect and not polite ➲ A more informal word is **cheeky**. ▶ **impudently** *adv* ▶ **impudence** *noun* [U]

impulse /ˈɪmpʌls/ *noun* [C] **1** [usually sing] an impulse (to do sth) a sudden desire to do sth without thinking about the results: *Her first impulse was to run away.* **2** (*technical*) a force or movement of energy that causes a reaction: *nerve/electrical impulses*

IDM **on (an) impulse** without thinking or planning and not considering the results: *When I saw the child fall in the water, I just acted on impulse and jumped in after her.*

impulsive /ɪmˈpʌlsɪv/ *adj* likely to act suddenly and without thinking; done without careful thought: *He is an impulsive character.* ▶ **impulsively** *adv* ▶ **impulsiveness** *noun* [U]

impure /ɪmˈpjʊə(r)/ *adj* **1** not pure or clean; consisting of more than one substance mixed together (and therefore not of good quality): *impure metals* **2** (*old-fashioned*) (used about thoughts and actions connected with sex) not moral; bad OPP for both meanings **pure**

impurity /ɪmˈpjʊərəti/ *noun* (*pl* **impurities**) **1** [C, usually pl] a substance that is present in small amounts in another substance, making it dirty or of poor quality: *People are being advised to filter their water to remove impurities.* **2** [U] (*old-fashioned*) the state of being morally bad ➲ look at **purity**

⚷ **in**[1] /ɪn/ *adv, prep* **1** (used to show place) inside or to a position inside a particular area or object: *a country in Africa* ♦ *islands in the Pacific* ♦ *in a box* ♦ *I read about it in the newspaper.* ♦ *He lay* ***in bed.*** ♦ *She put the keys in her pocket.* ♦ *His wife's* ***in hospital.*** ♦ *She opened the door and went in.* ♦ *My suitcase is full. I can't get any more in.* ♦ *When does the train get in* (= to the station)? **2** at home or at work: *I knocked at the door, but he wasn't in.* ♦ *She won't* ***be in*** *till late today.* OPP **out** **3** contained in; forming the whole or part of sth: *What's in this casserole?* ♦ *There are 31 days in January.* **4** (showing time) during a period of time: *My birthday is in August.* ♦ *in spring/summer/autumn/winter* ♦ *He was born in 1980.* ♦ *You could walk there in about an hour* (= it would take that long to walk there). **5** (showing time) after a period of

I

time: *I'll be finished in ten minutes.* **6** wearing sth: *They were all dressed in black for the funeral.* ◆ *I've never seen you in a suit before.* ◆ *a woman in a yellow dress* **7** showing the condition or state of sb/sth: *My father is in poor health.* ◆ *This room is* ***in a mess!*** ◆ *Richard's* ***in love.*** ◆ *He's in his mid-thirties.* **8** used with feelings: *I watched* ***in horror*** *as the plane crashed to the ground.* ◆ *He was* ***in such a rage*** *I didn't dare to go near him.* **9** showing sb's job or the activity sb is involved in: *He's got a good job in advertising.* ◆ *All her family are in politics* (= they are politicians). ◆ *He's in the army.* **10** used for saying how things are arranged: *We sat in a circle.* ◆ *She had her hair in plaits.* **11** used for saying how sth is written or expressed: *Please write in pen.* ◆ *They were talking* ***in Italian/French/Polish.*** ◆ *to work in groups/teams* **12** used for giving the rate of sth and for talking about numbers: ***One*** *family* ***in four*** *in the UK owns a cat.* **13** received by sb official: *All applications must* ***be in*** *by 20 March.* **14** (used about the sea) at the highest point, when the water is closest to the land: *The tide's coming in.* ⓘ For special uses with many verbs and nouns, for example **in time**, **give in**, look at the verb and noun entries.

IDM **be in for it/sth** (*informal*) to be going to experience sth unpleasant: *He'll be in for a shock when he gets the bill.* ◆ *You'll be in for it when Mum sees what you've done.*

be/get in on sth (*informal*) to be included or involved in sth: *I'd like to be in on the new project.*

have (got) it in for sb (*informal*) to be unpleasant to sb because they have done sth to upset you: *John's had it in for me ever since I missed his party.*

in² /ɪn/ *adj* (*informal*) fashionable at the moment: *the in place to go* ◆ *The colour grey is very in this season.*

in³ /ɪn/ *noun*

IDM **the ins and outs (of sth)** the details and difficulties (involved in sth): *Will somebody explain the ins and outs of the situation to me?*

in. *abbr* = **inch¹**

⚷ **inability** /ˌɪnəˈbɪləti/ *noun* [sing] inability (to do sth) lack of ability, power or skill: *He has a complete inability to listen to other people's opinions.* OPP **ability** ➲ *adjective* **unable**

inaccessible /ˌɪnækˈsesəbl/ *adj* very difficult or impossible to reach or contact: *That beach is inaccessible by car.* OPP **accessible** ▶ **inaccessibility** /ˌɪnækˌsesəˈbɪləti/ *noun* [U]

inaccurate /ɪnˈækjərət/ *adj* not correct or accurate; with mistakes: *an inaccurate report/description/statement* OPP **accurate** ▶ **inaccuracy** /ɪnˈækjərəsi/ *noun* [C,U] (*pl* **inaccuracies**): *There are always some inaccuracies in newspaper reports.* ▶ **inaccurately** *adv*

inaction /ɪnˈækʃn/ *noun* [U] doing nothing; lack of action: *The crisis was blamed on the government's earlier inaction.* OPP **action**

inactive /ɪnˈæktɪv/ *adj* doing nothing; not active: *The virus remains inactive in the body.* OPP **active** ▶ **inactivity** /ˌɪnækˈtɪvəti/ *noun* [U] OPP **activity**

inadequate /ɪnˈædɪkwət/ *adj* **1** inadequate (for sth/to do sth) not enough; not good enough: *the problem of inadequate housing* OPP **adequate** **2** (used about a person) not able to deal with a problem or situation; not confident: *There was so much to learn in the new job that for a while I felt totally inadequate.* ▶ **inadequately** *adv* ▶ **inadequacy** /ɪnˈædɪkwəsi/ *noun* [C,U] (*pl* inadequacies): *his inadequacy as a parent*

inadmissible /ˌɪnədˈmɪsəbl/ *adj* (*formal*) that cannot be allowed or accepted, especially in a court of law: *inadmissible evidence* OPP **admissible**

inadvertently /ˌɪnədˈvɜːtəntli/ *adv* without thinking, not on purpose: *She had inadvertently left the letter where he could find it.* SYN **unintentionally** ▶ **inadvertent** *adj*

inadvisable /ˌɪnədˈvaɪzəbl/ *adj* (*formal*) not sensible; not showing good judgement: *It is inadvisable to go swimming after a meal.* OPP **advisable**

inane /ɪˈneɪn/ *adj* without any meaning; silly: *an inane remark* ▶ **inanely** *adv*

inanimate /ɪnˈænɪmət/ *adj* not alive: *A rock is an inanimate object.* OPP **animate**

inappropriate /ˌɪnəˈprəʊpriət/ *adj* not suitable: *Isn't that dress rather inappropriate for the occasion?* OPP **appropriate**

inarticulate /ˌɪnɑːˈtɪkjələt/ *adj* **1** (used about a person) not able to express ideas and feelings clearly **2** (used about speech) not clear or well expressed OPP for both meanings **articulate** ▶ **inarticulately** *adv*

inasmuch as /ˌɪnəzˈmʌtʃ əz/ *conj* (*formal*) because of the fact that: *We felt sorry for the boys inasmuch as they had not realized that what they were doing was wrong.*

inattention /ˌɪnəˈtenʃn/ *noun* [U] lack of attention: *The tragic accident was the result of a moment's inattention.* OPP **attention**

inattentive /ˌɪnəˈtentɪv/ *adj* not paying attention: *One inattentive student can disturb the whole class.* OPP **attentive**

inaudible /ɪnˈɔːdəbl/ *adj* not loud enough to be heard OPP **audible** ▶ **inaudibly** /-əbli/ *adv*

inaugurate /ɪˈnɔːgjəreɪt/ *verb* [T] **1** to introduce a new official, leader, etc. at a special formal ceremony: *He will be inaugurated as President next month.* **2** to start, introduce or open sth new, often at a special formal ceremony ▶ **inaugural** /ɪˈnɔːgjərəl/ *adj* [only *before* a noun]: *the President's inaugural speech* ▶ **inauguration** /ɪˌnɔːgjəˈreɪʃn/ *noun* [C,U]

inauspicious /ˌɪnɔːˈspɪʃəs/ *adj* (*formal*) showing signs that the future will not be good or successful: *He made an inauspicious start.* OPP **auspicious**

inbox /ˈɪnbɒks/ *noun* [C] the place on a computer where you can see new email messages: *I have a stack of emails in my inbox.*

Inc. (also inc) /ɪŋk/ *abbr* (*AmE*) = **incorporated**: *Manhattan Drugstores Inc.*

incalculable /ɪnˈkælkjələbl/ *adj (formal)* very great; too great to calculate: *an incalculable risk*

incapable /ɪnˈkeɪpəbl/ *adj* **1** incapable of sth/doing sth not able to do sth: *She is incapable of hard work/working hard.* ♦ *He's quite incapable of unkindness* (= too nice to be unkind). **2** not able to do, manage or organize anything well: *As a doctor, she's totally incapable.* OPP for both meanings **capable**

incapacitate /ˌɪnkəˈpæsɪteɪt/ *verb* [T] *(formal)* to make sb/sth unable to live or work normally: *They were completely incapacitated by the heat in Spain.*

incarcerate /ɪnˈkɑːsəreɪt/ *verb* [T] *(formal)* incarcerate sb (in sth) to put sb in prison or in another place from which they cannot escape SYN **imprison** ▶ **incarceration** /ɪnˌkɑːsəˈreɪʃn/ *noun* [U]

incarnation /ˌɪnkɑːˈneɪʃn/ *noun* [C] **1** (in some religions) one of a series of lives in a particular form: *He believed he was a prince in a previous incarnation.* ➲ look at **reincarnation** **2** the incarnation of sth (a person that is) a perfect example of a particular quality: *She is the incarnation of goodness.*

incendiary /ɪnˈsendiəri/ *adj* [only *before* a noun] that causes a fire: *an incendiary bomb/device*

incense /ˈɪnsens/ *noun* [U] a substance that produces a sweet smell when burnt, used especially in religious ceremonies

incensed /ɪnˈsenst/ *adj* incensed (by/at sth) very angry SYN **furious**

incentive /ɪnˈsentɪv/ *noun* [C,U] (an) incentive (for/to sb/sth) (to do sth) something that encourages you (to do sth): *There's no incentive for young people to do well at school because there aren't any jobs when they leave.*

incessant /ɪnˈsesnt/ *adj* never stopping (and usually annoying): *incessant rain/noise/chatter* SYN **constant** ➲ look at **continual** ▶ **incessantly** *adv*

incest /ˈɪnsest/ *noun* [U] illegal sex between members of the same family, for example brother and sister

incestuous /ɪnˈsestjuəs/ *adj* **1** involving illegal sex between members of the same family: *an incestuous relationship* **2** (used about a group of people and their relationships with each other) too close; not open to anyone outside the group: *Life in a small community can be very incestuous.*

🔑 **inch**[1] /ɪntʃ/ *noun* [C] *(abbr* in.) a measure of length; 2.54 centimetres. There are 12 **inches** in a foot: *He's 5 foot 10 inches tall.* ♦ *Three inches of rain fell last night.* ⓘ For more information about measurements, look at the section on using numbers at the back of this dictionary.

inch[2] /ɪntʃ/ *verb* [I,T] inch forward, past, through, etc. to move slowly and carefully in the direction mentioned: *He inched (his way) forward along the cliff edge.*

incidence /ˈɪnsɪdəns/ *noun* [sing] *(formal)* incidence of sth the number of times sth (usually unpleasant) happens; the rate of sth: *a high incidence of crime/disease/unemployment*

🔑 **incident** /ˈɪnsɪdənt/ *noun* [C] *(formal)* something that happens (especially sth unusual or unpleasant): *There were a number of incidents after the football match.* ♦ *a diplomatic incident* (= a dangerous or unpleasant situation between countries)

incidental /ˌɪnsɪˈdentl/ *adj* incidental (to sth) happening as part of sth more important: *The book contains various themes that are incidental to the main plot.*

incidentally /ˌɪnsɪˈdentli/ *adv* used to introduce extra news, information, etc. that the speaker has just thought of: *Incidentally, that new restaurant you told me about is excellent.* ➲ A less formal expression is **by the way**.

incinerate /ɪnˈsɪnəreɪt/ *verb* [T] *(formal)* to destroy sth completely by burning

incinerator /ɪnˈsɪnəreɪtə(r)/ *noun* [C] a container or machine for burning rubbish, etc.

incision /ɪnˈsɪʒn/ *noun* [C] *(formal)* a cut carefully made into sth (especially into a person's body as part of a medical operation)

incisive /ɪnˈsaɪsɪv/ *adj* **1** showing clear thought and good understanding of what is important, and having the ability to express this: *an incisive mind* ♦ *incisive comments* **2** showing sb's ability to take decisions and act quickly and directly: *an incisive move*

incite /ɪnˈsaɪt/ *verb* [T] incite sb (to sth); incite sth to encourage sb to do sth by making them very angry or excited: *He was accused of inciting the crowd to violence.* ▶ **incitement** *noun* [C,U]: *He was guilty of incitement to violence.*

incl. *abbr* = **including, inclusive**: *total £59.00 incl. tax*

inclination /ˌɪnklɪˈneɪʃn/ *noun* [C,U] inclination (to do sth); inclination (towards/for sth) a feeling that makes sb want to behave in a particular way: *He did not show* ***the slightest inclination*** *to help.* ♦ *She had no inclination for a career in teaching.*

incline[1] /ɪnˈklaɪn/ *verb* **1** [I] *(formal)* incline to/towards sth to tend to behave in a particular way or make a particular choice: *I don't know what to choose, but I'm inclining towards the fish.* **2** [T] *(formal)* to bend (your head) forward: *He inclined his head in agreement.* **3** [I] incline towards sth to be at an angle in a particular direction: *The land inclines towards the shore.*

incline[2] /ˈɪnklaɪn/ *noun* [C] *(formal)* a slight hill: *a steep/slight incline* SYN **slope**

inclined /ɪnˈklaɪnd/ *adj* **1** [not before a noun] inclined (to do sth) tending to do sth: *I know Amir well, so I'm* ***inclined to believe*** *what he says.* **2** inclined to do sth likely to do sth: *She's inclined to change her mind very easily.* **3** having a natural ability in the subject mentioned: *to be musically inclined*

🔑 **include** /ɪnˈkluːd/ *verb* [T] [not used in the continuous tenses] **1** to have as one part; to contain (among other things): *The price of the holiday includes the flight, the hotel and car hire.* ♦ *The crew included one woman.* ➲ note at **contain** **2** include

I

sb/sth (as/in/on sth) to make sb/sth part (of another group, etc.): *The children immediately included the new girl in their games.* ♦ *Everyone was disappointed, myself included.* OPP for both meanings **exclude** ▸ **inclusion** /ɪnˈkluːʒn/ *noun* [U]: *The inclusion of all that violence in the film was unnecessary.*

including /ɪnˈkluːdɪŋ/ *prep* (*abbr* incl.) having as a part: *It costs £17.99, including postage and packing.* OPP **excluding**

inclusive /ɪnˈkluːsɪv/ *adj* (*abbr* incl.) **1** inclusive (of sth) (used about a price, etc.) including or containing everything; including the thing mentioned: *Is that an inclusive price or are there some extras?* ♦ *The rent is inclusive of electricity.* **2** [only *after* a noun] including the dates, numbers, etc. mentioned: *You are booked at the hotel from Monday to Friday inclusive* (= including Monday and Friday).

HELP When talking about time, **through** is often used in American English instead of **inclusive**: *We'll be away (from) Friday through Sunday.*

I

incognito /ˌɪnkɒɡˈniːtəʊ/ *adv* hiding your real name and identity (especially if you are famous and do not want to be recognized): *to travel incognito*

incoherent /ˌɪnkəʊˈhɪərənt/ *adj* not clear or easy to understand; not saying sth clearly: *incoherent mumbling* OPP **coherent** ▸ **incoherence** *noun* [U] ▸ **incoherently** *adv*

income /ˈɪnkʌm; -kəm/ *noun* [C,U] the money you receive regularly as payment for your work or as interest on money you have saved, etc: *It's often difficult for a family to live on one income.* ➲ note at **pay**

MORE We talk about a **monthly** or an **annual** income. An income may be **high** or **low**. Your **gross** income is the amount you earn before paying tax. Your **net** income is your income after tax.

ˈ**income tax** *noun* [U] the amount of money you pay to the government according to how much you earn

incoming /ˈɪnkʌmɪŋ/ *adj* [only *before* a noun] **1** arriving or being received: *incoming flights/passengers* ♦ *incoming phone calls* **2** new; recently elected: *the incoming government*

incomparable /ɪnˈkɒmprəbl/ *adj* so good or great that it does not have an equal: *incomparable beauty* ➲ *verb* **compare**

incompatible /ˌɪnkəmˈpætəbl/ *adj* incompatible with sb/sth very different and therefore not able to live or work happily with sb or exist with sth: *The hours of the job are incompatible with family life.* OPP **compatible** ▸ **incompatibility** /ˌɪnkəmˌpætəˈbɪləti/ *noun* [C,U] (*pl* incompatibilities)

incompetent /ɪnˈkɒmpɪtənt/ *adj* lacking the necessary skill to do sth well: *He is completely incompetent at his job.* ♦ *an incompetent teacher/manager* OPP **competent** ▸ **incompetent** *noun* [C]: *She's a total incompetent at basketball.* ▸ **incompetence** *noun* [U] ▸ **incompetently** *adv*: *The business was run incompetently.*

incomplete /ˌɪnkəmˈpliːt/ *adj* having a part or parts missing; not total: *Unfortunately the jigsaw puzzle was incomplete.* OPP **complete** ▸ **incompletely** *adv*

incomprehensible /ɪnˌkɒmprɪˈhensəbl/ *adj* impossible to understand: *an incomprehensible explanation* ♦ *Her attitude is totally incomprehensible to the rest of us.* OPP **comprehensible, understandable** ▸ **incomprehension** /ɪnˌkɒmprɪˈhenʃn/ *noun* [U]

inconceivable /ˌɪnkənˈsiːvəbl/ *adj* impossible or very difficult to believe or imagine: *It's inconceivable that he would have stolen anything.* OPP **conceivable**

inconclusive /ˌɪnkənˈkluːsɪv/ *adj* not leading to a definite decision or result: *an inconclusive discussion* ♦ *inconclusive evidence* (= that doesn't prove anything) OPP **conclusive** ▸ **inconclusively** *adv*

incongruous /ɪnˈkɒŋɡruəs/ *adj* strange and out of place; not suitable in a particular situation: *That huge table looks rather incongruous in such a small room.* ▸ **incongruously** *adv* ▸ **incongruity** /ˌɪnkɒnˈɡruːəti/ *noun* [U]

inconsiderate /ˌɪnkənˈsɪdərət/ *adj* (used about a person) not thinking or caring about the feelings, or needs of other people: *It was inconsiderate of you not to offer her a lift.* SYN **thoughtless** OPP **considerate** ▸ **inconsiderately** *adv* ▸ **inconsiderateness** *noun* [U]

inconsistent /ˌɪnkənˈsɪstənt/ *adj* **1** inconsistent (with sth) (used about statements, facts, etc.) not the same as sth else; not matching, so that one thing must be wrong or not true: *The witnesses' accounts of the event are inconsistent.* ♦ *These new facts are inconsistent with the earlier information.* **2** (used about a person) likely to change (in attitude, behaviour, etc.) so that you cannot depend on them: *She's so inconsistent—sometimes her work is good and sometimes it's really awful.* OPP for both meanings **consistent** ▸ **inconsistency** /ˌɪnkənˈsɪstənsi/ *noun* [C,U] (*pl* inconsistencies): *There were far too many inconsistencies in her argument.* OPP **consistency** ▸ **inconsistently** *adv*

inconspicuous /ˌɪnkənˈspɪkjuəs/ *adv* not easily noticed: *I tried to **make** myself as **inconspicuous** as possible so that no one would ask me a question.* OPP **conspicuous** ▸ **inconspicuously** *adv*

incontinent /ɪnˈkɒntɪnənt/ *adj* unable to control the passing of **urine** (= liquid waste) and **faeces** (= solid waste) from the body ▸ **incontinence** *noun* [U]

inconvenience /ˌɪnkənˈviːniəns/ *noun* [U,C] trouble or difficulty, especially when it affects sth that you need to do; a person or thing that causes this: *We apologize for any inconvenience caused by the delays.* ▸ **inconvenience** *verb* [T] SYN **put sb out**

inconvenient /ˌɪnkənˈviːniənt/ *adj* causing trouble or difficulty, especially when it affects sth that you need to do: *It's a bit inconvenient at the* *moment—could you phone again later?* OPP **convenient** ▶ **inconveniently** *adv*

incorporate /ɪnˈkɔːpəreɪt/ *verb* [T] **incorporate sth (in/into/within sth)** to make sth a part of sth else; to have sth as a part: *I'd like you to incorporate this information into your report.* SYN **include** ▶ **incorporation** /ɪnˌkɔːpəˈreɪʃn/ *noun* [U]

incorporated /ɪnˈkɔːpəreɪtɪd/ *adj* (*abbr* **Inc.**) (following the name of a company) formed into a **corporation** (= an organization that is recognized by law)

incorrect /ˌɪnkəˈrekt/ *adj* not right or true: *Incorrect answers should be marked with a cross.* OPP **correct** ▶ **incorrectly** *adv*

incorrigible /ɪnˈkɒrɪdʒəbl/ *adj* (used about a person or their behaviour) very bad; too bad to be corrected or improved: *an incorrigible liar*

⚷ **increase**[1] /ɪnˈkriːs/ *verb* [I,T] **increase (sth) (from A) (to B); increase (sth) (by sth)** to become or to make sth larger in number or amount: *She increased her speed to overtake the lorry.* ◆ *My employer would like me to increase my hours of work from 25 to 30.* ◆ *The rate of inflation has increased by 1% to 7%.* OPP **decrease, reduce**

⚷ **increase**[2] /ˈɪŋkriːs/ *noun* [C,U] **(an) increase (in sth)** a rise in the number, amount or level of sth: *There has been a* ***sharp increase*** *of nearly 50% on last year's figures.* ◆ *Doctors expect some further increase in the spread of the disease.* ◆ *They are demanding a large wage increase.* OPP **decrease, reduction**
IDM **on the increase** becoming greater or more common; increasing: *Attacks by dogs on children are on the increase.*

⚷ **increasingly** /ɪnˈkriːsɪŋli/ *adv* more and more: *increasingly difficult/important/dangerous* ◆ *It's becoming increasingly clear that Sam is doing no work in this subject.*

incredible /ɪnˈkredəbl/ *adj* **1** impossible or very difficult to believe: *I found Jacqueline's account of the event incredible.* SYN **unbelievable** OPP **credible** **2** (*informal*) extremely good or big: *He earns an incredible salary.* ▶ **incredibly** /-əbli/ *adv*: *We have had some incredibly strong winds recently.*

increment /ˈɪŋkrəmənt/ *noun* [C] (*formal*) an increase in a number or an amount, especially a regular pay increase: *a salary of £25 000 with annual increments* ▶ **incremental** /ˌɪŋkrəˈmentl/ *adj*: *incremental costs* ▶ **incrementally** /-təli/ *adv*

incriminate /ɪnˈkrɪmɪneɪt/ *verb* [T] to provide evidence that sb is guilty of a crime: *The police searched the house but found nothing to incriminate the man.*

incubate /ˈɪŋkjubeɪt/ *verb* **1** [T] to keep an egg at the right temperature so that it can develop and break open **2** [I,T] (used about a disease) to develop without showing signs; (used about a person or an animal) to carry a disease without showing signs: *Some viruses incubate for weeks.*

incubation /ˌɪŋkjuˈbeɪʃn/ *noun* **1** [U] the process of **incubating** eggs **2** [C] (also ˌ**incuˈbation period**) the period between catching a disease and the time when signs of it appear

incubator /ˈɪŋkjubeɪtə(r)/ *noun* [C] **1** a heated machine used in hospitals for keeping small or weak babies alive **2** a heated machine for keeping eggs warm until the young birds are born

incur /ɪnˈkɜː(r)/ *verb* [T] (**incurred; incurring**) (*formal*) to suffer the unpleasant results of a situation that you have caused: *to incur debts/somebody's anger*

incurable /ɪnˈkjʊərəbl/ *adj* that cannot be cured or made better: *an incurable disease* OPP **curable** ▶ **incurably** /-əbli/ *adv*: *incurably ill/romantic*

indebted /ɪnˈdetɪd/ *adj* **indebted (to sb) (for sth)** very grateful to sb: *I am deeply indebted to my family and friends for all their help.*

indecent /ɪnˈdiːsnt/ *adj* shocking to many people in society, especially because sth involves sex or the body: *indecent photos/behaviour/language* ◆ *Those tiny swimming trunks are indecent!* OPP **decent** ▶ **indecency** /ɪnˈdiːsnsi/ *noun* [U,sing] ▶ **indecently** *adv*

indecision /ˌɪndɪˈsɪʒn/ (also **indecisiveness**) *noun* [U] the state of being unable to decide: *This indecision about the future is really worrying.*

indecisive /ˌɪndɪˈsaɪsɪv/ *adj* not able to make decisions easily OPP **decisive** ▶ **indecisively** *adv*: *He stood at the crossroads indecisively, wondering which way to go.* ▶ **indecisiveness** *noun* = **indecision**

⚷ **indeed** /ɪnˈdiːd/ *adv* **1** (used for emphasizing a positive statement or answer) really; certainly: *'Have you had a good holiday?' 'We have indeed.'* **2** used after 'very' with an adjective or adverb to emphasize the quality mentioned: *Thank you very much indeed.* ◆ *She's very happy indeed.* **3** (used for adding information to a statement) in fact: *It's important that you come at once. Indeed, it's essential.* **4** used for showing interest, surprise, anger, etc: *'They were talking about you last night.' 'Were they indeed!'*

indefensible /ˌɪndɪˈfensəbl/ *adj* (used about behaviour, etc.) completely wrong; that cannot be defended or excused

indefinable /ˌɪndɪˈfaɪnəbl/ *adj* difficult or impossible to describe: *She has that indefinable quality that makes an actress a star.* ▶ **indefinably** /-əbli/ *adv*

indefinite /ɪnˈdefɪnət/ *adj* not fixed or clear: *She will be away for the indefinite future.* OPP **definite**

the inˌdefinite ˈarticle *noun* [C] the name used for the words *a* and *an* ➲ look at **the definite article** ⓘ For more information about the indefinite article, look at the **Reference Section** at the back of this dictionary.

indefinitely /ɪnˈdefɪnətli/ *adv* for a period of time that has no fixed end: *The meeting was postponed indefinitely.*

indelible /ɪnˈdeləbl/ *adj* that cannot be removed or washed out: *indelible ink* ◆ (*figurative*) *The experience made an indelible impression on me.* ▶ **indelibly** /-əbli/ *adv*

I

indent /ɪnˈdent/ *verb* [T] to start a line of writing further away from the edge of the page than the other lines

independence /ˌɪndɪˈpendəns/ *noun* [U] independence (from sb/sth) (used about a person, country, etc.) the state of being free and not controlled by another person, country, etc: *In 1947 India achieved independence from Britain.* ◆ *financial independence*

CULTURE

On **Independence Day** (4 July) Americans celebrate the day in 1776 when America declared itself independent from Britain.

independent /ˌɪndɪˈpendənt/ *adj* **1** independent (of/from sb/sth) free from and not controlled by another person, country, etc: *Most former colonies are now independent nations.* ◆ *independent schools/TV* (= not supported by government money) **2** not influenced by or connected with sb/sth: *Complaints against the police should be investigated by an independent body.* ◆ *Two independent opinion polls have obtained similar results.* **3** independent (of sb/sth) not needing or wanting help: *I got a part-time job because I wanted to be financially independent of my parents.* OPP **dependent** ▶ **independently** *adv* independently (of sb/sth): *Scientists working independently of each other have had very similar results.*

indescribable /ˌɪndɪˈskraɪbəbl/ *adj* too good or bad to be described: *indescribable poverty/luxury/noise* ▶ **indescribably** /-əbli/ *adv*

indestructible /ˌɪndɪˈstrʌktəbl/ *adj* that cannot be easily damaged or destroyed

index /ˈɪndeks/ *noun* [C] (*pl* indexes) **1** a list in order from A to Z, usually at the end of a book, of the names or subjects that are referred to in the book: *If you want to find all the references to London, look it up in the index.* **2** (*BrE*) = **card index** **3** (*pl* indexes *or* indices /ˈɪndɪsiːz/) a way of showing how the price, value, rate, etc. of sth has changed: *the cost-of-living index* ▶ **index** *verb* [T]: *The books in the library are indexed by subject and title.*

ˈ**index finger** = forefinger

Indian /ˈɪndiən/ *noun* [C], *adj* **1** (a person) from the Republic of India: *Indian food is hot and spicy.* **2** (*old-fashioned*) = **Native American**: *The Sioux were a famous Indian tribe.* ➲ look at **West Indian**

indicate /ˈɪndɪkeɪt/ *verb* **1** [T] to show that sth is probably true or exists: *Recent research indicates that children are getting too little exercise.* **2** [T] to say sth in an indirect way: *The spokesman indicated that an agreement was likely soon.* **3** [T] to make sb notice sth, especially by pointing to it: *The receptionist indicated where I should sign.* ◆ *The boy seemed to be indicating that I should follow him.* **4** [I,T] (*BrE*) to signal that your car, etc. is going to turn: *The lorry indicated left but turned right.*

indication /ˌɪndɪˈkeɪʃn/ *noun* [C,U] an indication (of sth/doing sth); an indication that ... something that shows sth; a sign: *There was no indication of a struggle.* ◆ *There is every indication that he will make a full recovery.*

indicative /ɪnˈdɪkətɪv/ *adj* (*formal*) being or giving a sign of sth: *Is the unusual weather indicative of climatic changes?*

indicator /ˈɪndɪkeɪtə(r)/ *noun* [C] **1** something that gives information or shows sth; a sign: *The indicator showed that we had plenty of petrol.* ◆ *The unemployment rate is a reliable indicator of economic health.* **2** (*AmE* ˈ**turn signal**, *informal* **blinker**) the flashing light on a car, etc. that shows that it is going to turn right or left ➲ picture on **page P7**

indices *plural* of **index**(3)

indictment /ɪnˈdaɪtmənt/ *noun* [C] **1** an indictment (of sth) something that shows how bad sth is: *The fact that many children leave school with no qualifications is an indictment of our education system.* **2** a written paper that officially accuses sb of a crime

indie /ˈɪndi/ *adj* [only *before* a noun] (used about a company, person or product) not part of a large organization; independent: *an indie publisher* ◆ *indie music*

indifference /ɪnˈdɪfrəns/ *noun* [U] indifference (to sb/sth) a lack of interest or feeling towards sb/sth: *He has always shown indifference to the needs of others.*

indifferent /ɪnˈdɪfrənt/ *adj* **1** indifferent (to sb/sth) not interested in or caring about sb/sth: *The manager of the shop seemed indifferent to our complaints.* **2** not very good: *The standard of football in the World Cup was rather indifferent.* ▶ **indifferently** *adv*

indigenous /ɪnˈdɪdʒənəs/ *adj* (used about people, animals or plants) living or growing in the place where they are from originally

indigestible /ˌɪndɪˈdʒestəbl/ *adj* (used about food) difficult or impossible for the stomach to deal with

indigestion /ˌɪndɪˈdʒestʃən/ *noun* [U] pain in the stomach that is caused by difficulty in dealing with food: *Peppers give me indigestion.*

indignant /ɪnˈdɪɡnənt/ *adj* indignant (with sb) (about/at sth); indignant (that) ... shocked or angry because sb has said or done sth that you do not like and do not agree with: *They were indignant that they had to pay more for worse services.* ▶ **indignantly** *adv*

indignation /ˌɪndɪɡˈneɪʃn/ *noun* [U] indignation (at/about sth); indignation that ... shock and anger because sth is unfair or unreasonable: *commuters' indignation at the rise in fares*

indignity /ɪnˈdɪɡnəti/ *noun* [U,C] (*pl* indignities) indignity (of sth/of doing sth) a situation that makes you feel embarrassed because you are not treated with respect; an act that causes this feeling: *the daily indignities of imprisonment* SYN **humiliation**

indigo /ˈɪndɪɡəʊ/ *adj* very dark blue in colour ▶ **indigo** *noun* [U]

indirect /ˌɪndəˈrekt; -daɪˈr-/ *adj* **1** not being the direct cause of sth; not having a direct connection with sth: *an indirect result* **2** that avoids saying sth in an obvious way: *an indirect answer to a question* **3** not going in a straight line or using the shortest route: *We came the indirect route to avoid driving through London.* OPP for all meanings **direct** ▶ **indirectly** *adv* OPP **directly** ▶ **indirectness** *noun* [U]

ˌindirect ˈobject *noun* [C] a person or thing that an action is done to or for: *In the sentence, 'I sent him an email', 'him' is the indirect object.* ➲ look at **direct object** ℹ For more information about indirect objects, look at the **Reference Section** at the back of this dictionary.

ˌindirect ˈspeech = **reported speech**

indiscreet /ˌɪndɪˈskriːt/ *adj* not careful or polite in what you say or do OPP **discreet** ▶ **indiscreetly** *adv*

indiscretion /ˌɪndɪˈskreʃn/ *noun* [C,U] behaviour that is not careful or polite, and that might cause embarrassment or offence

indiscriminate /ˌɪndɪˈskrɪmɪnət/ *adj* done or acting without making sensible judgement or caring about the possible harmful effects: *Martin is indiscriminate in his choice of friends.* ▶ **indiscriminately** *adv*

indispensable /ˌɪndɪˈspensəbl/ *adj* very important, so that it is not possible to be without it: *A car is indispensable nowadays if you live in the country.* SYN **essential** OPP **dispensable**

indisputable /ˌɪndɪˈspjuːtəbl/ *adj* definitely true; that cannot be shown to be wrong

indistinct /ˌɪndɪˈstɪŋkt/ *adj* not clear: *indistinct figures/sounds/memories* OPP **distinct** ▶ **indistinctly** *adv*

indistinguishable /ˌɪndɪˈstɪŋgwɪʃəbl/ *adj* **indistinguishable (from sth)** appearing to be the same: *From a distance the two colours are indistinguishable.* OPP **distinguishable**

individual¹ /ˌɪndɪˈvɪdʒuəl/ *adj* **1** [only *before* a noun] considered separately rather than as part of a group: *Each individual animal is weighed and measured before being set free.* **2** for or from one person: *an individual portion of butter* ◆ *Children need individual attention when they are learning to read.* **3** typical of one person in a way that is different from other people: *I like her individual style of dressing.*

individual² /ˌɪndɪˈvɪdʒuəl/ *noun* [C] **1** one person, considered separately from others or a group: *Are the needs of society more important than the rights of the individual?* **2** (*informal*) a person of the type that is mentioned: *She's a strange individual.*

individuality /ˌɪndɪˌvɪdʒuˈæləti/ *noun* [U] the qualities that make sb/sth different from other people or things: *People often try to express their individuality by the way they dress.*

individually /ˌɪndɪˈvɪdʒuəli/ *adv* separately; one by one: *The teacher talked to each member of the class individually.*

indivisible /ˌɪndɪˈvɪzəbl/ *adj* that cannot be divided or split into smaller pieces

indoctrinate /ɪnˈdɒktrɪneɪt/ *verb* [T] to force sb to accept particular beliefs without allowing them to consider others: *For 20 years the people have been indoctrinated by the government.* ▶ **indoctrination** /ɪnˌdɒktrɪˈneɪʃn/ *noun* [U]

indoor /ˈɪndɔː(r)/ *adj* [only *before* a noun] done or used inside a building: *indoor games* ◆ *an indoor swimming pool* OPP **outdoor**

indoors /ˌɪnˈdɔːz/ *adv* in or into a building: *Oh dear! I've left my sunglasses indoors.* ◆ *Let's go indoors.* OPP **outdoors, out of doors**

induce /ɪnˈdjuːs/ *verb* [T] (*formal*) **1** to make or persuade sb to do sth: *Nothing could induce him to change his mind.* **2** to cause or produce sth: *herbal tea that induces sleep*

inducement /ɪnˈdjuːsmənt/ *noun* [C,U] something that is offered to sb to make them do sth: *financial inducements to mothers to stay at home*

induction /ɪnˈdʌkʃn/ *noun* [U,C] the process of introducing sb to a new job, skill, organization, etc.; an event at which this takes place: *an induction day for new students*

indulge /ɪnˈdʌldʒ/ *verb* **1** [I,T] **indulge (yourself) (in sth)** to allow yourself to have or do sth for pleasure: *I'm going to indulge myself and go shopping for some new clothes.* ◆ *Maria never indulges in gossip.* ◆ *At the weekends he indulges his passion for fishing.* **2** [T] to give sb/sth what he/she/it wants or needs: *You shouldn't indulge that child. It will make him very selfish.*

indulgence /ɪnˈdʌldʒəns/ *noun* **1** [U] the state of having or doing whatever you want: *to lead a life of indulgence* ◆ *Over-indulgence in chocolate makes you fat.* **2** [C] something that you have or do because it gives you pleasure: *The holiday was an extravagant indulgence.*

indulgent /ɪnˈdʌldʒənt/ *adj* allowing sb to have or do whatever they want: *indulgent parents* ▶ **indulgently** *adv*

industrial /ɪnˈdʌstriəl/ *adj* **1** [only *before* a noun] connected with industry: *industrial development* ◆ *industrial workers* **2** having a lot of factories, etc: *an industrial region/country/town*

inˌdustrial ˈaction *noun* [U] action that workers take, especially stopping work, in order to protest about sth to their employers: *to threaten (to take) industrial action* SYN **strike**

industrialist /ɪnˈdʌstriəlɪst/ *noun* [C] a person who owns or manages a large **industrial** company

industrialize (also -ise) /ɪnˈdʌstriəlaɪz/ *verb* [I, T] to develop industries in a country: *Japan industrialized rapidly at the end of the 19th century.* ▶ **industrialization** (also -isation) /ɪnˌdʌstriəlaɪˈzeɪʃn/ *noun* [U]

industrious /ɪnˈdʌstriəs/ *adj* always working hard SYN **hard-working**

I

industry /ˈɪndəstri/ *noun* (*pl* industries) **1** [U] the production of goods in factories: *Is British industry being threatened by foreign imports?* ◆ *heavy/light industry* **2** [C] the people and activities involved in producing sth, providing a service, etc: *the tourist/catering/entertainment industry* ◆ *the steel industry*

inedible /ɪnˈedəbl/ *adj* (*formal*) not suitable to be eaten: *an inedible plant* OPP **edible**

ineffective /ˌɪnɪˈfektɪv/ *adj* not producing the effect or result that you want OPP **effective**

inefficient /ˌɪnɪˈfɪʃnt/ *adj* not working or producing results in the best way, so that time or money is wasted: *Our heating system is very old and extremely inefficient.* ◆ *an inefficient secretary* OPP **efficient** ▶ **inefficiency** /ˌɪnɪˈfɪʃənsi/ *noun* [U] ▶ **inefficiently** *adv*

ineligible /ɪnˈelɪdʒəbl/ *adj* ineligible (for/to do sth) without the necessary certificates, etc. to do or get sth: *ineligible to vote* OPP **eligible** ▶ **ineligibility** /ɪnˌelɪdʒəˈbɪləti/ *noun* [U]

inept /ɪˈnept/ *adj* inept (at sth) not able to do sth well: *She is totally inept at dealing with people.* OPP **adept**

inequality /ˌɪnɪˈkwɒləti/ *noun* [C,U] (*pl* inequalities) (a) difference between groups in society because one has more money, opportunities, etc. than the other: *There will be problems as long as inequality between the races exists.* OPP **equality**

inert /ɪˈnɜːt/ *adj* (*formal*) not able to move or act

inertia /ɪˈnɜːʃə/ *noun* [U] **1** a lack of energy; not being able to move or change **2** the physical force that keeps things where they are or keeps them moving in the direction they are travelling

inescapable /ˌɪnɪˈskeɪpəbl/ *adj* (*formal*) that cannot be avoided: *an inescapable conclusion*

inevitable /ɪnˈevɪtəbl/ *adj* that cannot be avoided or prevented from happening: *With more cars on the road, traffic jams are inevitable.* ▶ **the inevitable** *noun* [sing]: *They fought to save the firm from closure, but eventually had to accept the inevitable.* ▶ **inevitability** /ɪnˌevɪtəˈbɪləti/ *noun* [U] ▶ **inevitably** /ɪnˈevɪtəbli/ *adv*

inexcusable /ˌɪnɪkˈskjuːzəbl/ *adj* that cannot be allowed or forgiven: *Their behaviour was quite inexcusable.* OPP **excusable**

inexhaustible /ˌɪnɪɡˈzɔːstəbl/ *adj* that cannot be finished or used up completely: *Our energy supplies are not inexhaustible.*

inexpensive /ˌɪnɪkˈspensɪv/ *adj* low in price: *an inexpensive camping holiday* SYN **cheap** OPP **expensive** ▶ **inexpensively** *adv*

inexperience /ˌɪnɪkˈspɪəriəns/ *noun* [U] not knowing how to do sth because you have not done it before: *The mistakes were all due to inexperience.* OPP **experience** ▶ **inexperienced** *adj*: *He's too young and inexperienced to be given such responsibility.*

inexplicable /ˌɪnɪkˈsplɪkəbl/ *adj* that cannot be explained: *Her sudden disappearance is quite inexplicable.* OPP **explicable** ▶ **inexplicably** /-əbli/ *adv*

infallible /ɪnˈfæləbl/ *adj* **1** (used about a person) never making mistakes or being wrong: *Even the most careful editor is not infallible.* **2** always doing what you want it to do; never failing: *No computer is infallible.* OPP for both meanings **fallible** ▶ **infallibility** /ɪnˌfæləˈbɪləti/ *noun* [U]

infamous /ˈɪnfəməs/ *adj* (*formal*) infamous (for sth) famous for being bad: *The area is infamous for crime.* SYN **notorious** ➲ look at **famous**

infancy /ˈɪnfənsi/ *noun* [U] the time when you are a baby or young child: (*figurative*) *Research in this field is still in its infancy.*

infant /ˈɪnfənt/ *noun* [C] (*formal*) **1** a baby or very young child: *There is a high rate of infant mortality* (= many children die when they are still babies). ➲ In spoken or informal English more common words are **baby**, **toddler** and **child**. **2** (in Britain and Australia) a child at school between the ages of 4 and 7: *Mrs Davies teaches infants.*

infantile /ˈɪnfəntaɪl/ *adj* (used about behaviour) typical of, or connected with, a baby or very young child and therefore not appropriate for adults or older children: *infantile jokes*

infantry /ˈɪnfəntri/ *noun* [U, with sing or pl verb] soldiers who fight on foot: *The infantry was/were supported by heavy gunfire.*

ˈinfant school *noun* [C] (in Britain and Australia) a school for children between the ages of 4 and 7 ➲ look at **primary school**

infatuated /ɪnˈfætʃueɪtɪd/ *adj* infatuated (with sb/sth) having a very strong feeling of love or attraction for sb/sth that usually does not last long and makes you unable to think about anything else: *The young girl was infatuated with one of her teachers.* ▶ **infatuation** /ɪnˌfætʃuˈeɪʃn/ *noun* [C,U]

infect /ɪnˈfekt/ *verb* [T] **1** [usually passive] infect sb/sth (with sth) to cause sb/sth to have a disease or illness: *We must clean the wound before it becomes infected.* ◆ *Many thousands of people have been infected with the virus.* **2** to make people share a particular feeling or emotion: *Paul's happiness infected the whole family.*

infected /ɪnˈfektɪd/ *adj* containing harmful bacteria: *The wound from the dog bite had become infected.* ◆ *an infected water supply*

infection /ɪnˈfekʃn/ *noun* **1** [U] the act of becoming or making sb ill: *A dirty water supply can be a source of infection.* ◆ *There is a danger of infection.* **2** [C] a disease or illness that is caused by harmful bacteria, etc. and affects one part of your body: *She is suffering from a chest infection.* ◆ *an ear infection*

MORE Infections can be caused by **bacteria** or **viruses**. An informal word for these is **germs**.

infectious /ɪnˈfekʃəs/ *adj* (used about a disease, illness, etc.) that can be easily passed on to another person: *Flu is a highly infectious disease.* ◆ (*figurative*) *infectious laughter* ➲ look at **contagious**

infer /ɪnˈfɜː(r)/ *verb* [T] (*formal*) (**inferring**; **inferred**) **infer sth (from sth)** to form an opinion or decide that sth is true from the information you have: *I inferred from our conversation that he was unhappy with his job.* ▸ **inference** /ˈɪnfərəns/ *noun* [C,U]

inferior /ɪnˈfɪəriə(r)/ *adj* **inferior (to sb/sth)** low or lower in social position, importance, quality, etc: *This material is obviously inferior to that one.* ◆ *Don't let people make you* ***feel inferior****.* **OPP** **superior** ▸ **inferior** *noun* [C]: *She always treats me as her intellectual inferior.* ▸ **inferiority** /ɪnˌfɪəriˈɒrəti/ *noun* [U]

inˌferiˈority complex *noun* [C] the state of feeling less important, clever, successful, etc. than other people

infertile /ɪnˈfɜːtaɪl/ *adj* **1** (used about a person or an animal) not able to have babies or produce young **2** (used about land) not able to grow strong healthy plants **OPP** for both meanings **fertile** ▸ **infertility** /ˌɪnfɜːˈtɪləti/ *noun* [U]: *infertility treatment* **OPP** **fertility**

infested /ɪnˈfestɪd/ *adj* **infested (with sth)** (used about a place) with large numbers of unpleasant animals or insects in it: *The warehouse was infested with rats.*

infidelity /ˌɪnfɪˈdeləti/ *noun* [U,C] (*pl* **infidelities**) the act of not being faithful to your wife, husband or partner, by having a sexual relationship with sb else ➲ A less formal word is **unfaithfulness**.

infiltrate /ˈɪnfɪltreɪt/ *verb* [I,T] to enter an organization, etc. secretly so that you can find out what it is doing: *The police managed to infiltrate the gang of terrorists.* ▸ **infiltration** /ˌɪnfɪlˈtreɪʃn/ *noun* [C,U] ▸ **infiltrator** /ˈɪnfɪltreɪtə(r)/ *noun* [C]

infinite /ˈɪnfɪnət/ *adj* **1** very great: *You need infinite patience for this job.* **2** without limits; that never ends: *Supplies of oil are not infinite.* **OPP** for both meanings **finite**

infinitely /ˈɪnfɪnətli/ *adv* very much: *Your English is infinitely better than my German.*

infinitive /ɪnˈfɪnətɪv/ *noun* [C] the basic form of a verb

> **GRAMMAR** The infinitive is sometimes used with *to* and sometimes without *to*, depending on what comes before it: *He can sing.* ◆ *He wants to sing.*

infinity /ɪnˈfɪnəti/ *noun* **1** [U] space or time without end: *The ocean seemed to stretch over the horizon into infinity.* **2** [U,C] (*symbol* ∞) (in mathematics) the number that is larger than any other

infirmary /ɪnˈfɜːməri/ *noun* [C] (*pl* **infirmaries**) (used mainly in names) a hospital: *The Manchester Royal Infirmary*

inflamed /ɪnˈfleɪmd/ *adj* (used about a part of the body) red and swollen or painful because of an infection or injury

inflammable /ɪnˈflæməbl/ *adj* that burns easily: *Petrol is highly inflammable.*

> **HELP** Be careful. **Flammable** has the same meaning but is less common.

inflammation /ˌɪnfləˈmeɪʃn/ *noun* [C,U] a condition in which a part of the body becomes red, sore and swollen because of infection or injury

inflatable /ɪnˈfleɪtəbl/ *adj* that can or must be filled with air: *an inflatable dinghy/mattress*

inflate /ɪnˈfleɪt/ *verb* [I,T] to fill sth with air; to become filled with air ➲ A less formal word is **blow up**: *Can you help me blow up some balloons for the party?* **OPP** **deflate**

inflation /ɪnˈfleɪʃn/ *noun* [U] a general rise in prices; the rate at which prices rise: *the inflation rate/rate of inflation* ◆ *Inflation now stands at 3%.*

inflection (also **inflexion**) /ɪnˈflekʃn/ *noun* [C,U] **1** a change in the form of a word, especially its ending, that changes its function in the grammar of the language, for example *-ed*, *-est* **2** the rise and fall of your voice when you are talking **SYN** **intonation**

I

inflexible /ɪnˈfleksəbl/ *adj* **1** that cannot be changed or made more suitable for a particular situation **2** (of people or organizations) unwilling to change their opinions, decisions or the way in which they do things: *He has a very inflexible attitude to change.* **3** (used about a material) difficult or impossible to bend **SYN** for all meanings **rigid** **OPP** for all meanings **flexible** ▸ **inflexibility** /ɪnˌfleksəˈbɪləti/ *noun* [U] ▸ **inflexibly** /ɪnˈfleksəbli/ *adv*

inflict /ɪnˈflɪkt/ *verb* [T] **inflict sth (on sb)** to force sb to have sth unpleasant or that they do not want: *Don't inflict your problems on me—I've got enough of my own.*

ˈin-flight *adj* [only *before* a noun] happening or provided during a journey in a plane: *in-flight entertainment*

🔑 **influence¹** /ˈɪnfluəns/ *noun* **1** [U,C] **(an) influence (on/upon sb/sth)** the power to affect, change or control sb/sth: *TV can have a strong influence on children.* ◆ *Nobody should drive while they are* ***under the influence of*** *alcohol.* **2** [C] **an influence (on sb/sth)** a person or thing that affects or changes sb/sth: *His new girlfriend has been a good influence on him.* ◆ *cultural/environmental influences*

🔑 **influence²** /ˈɪnfluəns/ *verb* [T] to have an effect on or power over sb/sth so that he/she/it changes: *You must decide for yourself. Don't let anyone else influence you.* ◆ *Her style of painting has been influenced by Japanese art.*

> **HELP** **Influence** or **affect**? **Affect** and **influence** are often very similar in meaning. **Affect** is usually used when the change is physical and **influence** is more often used to describe a change of opinion or attitude: *Drinking alcohol can affect your ability to drive.* ◆ *TV advertisements have influenced my attitude towards the homeless.*

influential /ˌɪnfluˈenʃl/ *adj* **influential (in sth/in doing sth)** having power or influence: *an influential* *politician* ♦ *He was influential in getting the hostages set free.*

influenza /ˌɪnfluˈenzə/ (*formal*) = **flu**

influx /ˈɪnflʌks/ *noun* [C, usually sing] an influx (of sb/sth) (into ...) large numbers of people or things arriving suddenly: *the summer influx of visitors from abroad*

⚷ **inform** /ɪnˈfɔːm/ *verb* [T] inform sb (of/about sth) to give sb information (about sth), especially in an official way: *You should inform the police of the accident.* ♦ *I have not been informed when the ceremony will take place.*

PHR V **inform on sb** to give information to the police, etc. about what sb has done wrong: *The wife of the killer informed on her husband.* ➲ look at **informed**

⚷ **informal** /ɪnˈfɔːml/ *adj* relaxed and friendly or suitable for a relaxed occasion: *Don't get dressed up for the party—it'll be very informal.* ♦ *The two leaders had informal discussions before the conference began.* **OPP** **formal**

> **HELP** Some words and expressions in this dictionary are described as *(informal)*. This means that you can use them when you are speaking to friends or people that you know well but that you should not use them in written work, official letters, etc.

▸ **informality** /ˌɪnfɔːˈmæləti/ *noun* [U]: *an atmosphere of informality* ▸ **informally** /-məli/ *adv*: *I was told informally* (= not officially) *that our plans had been accepted.*

informant /ɪnˈfɔːmənt/ *noun* [C] a person who gives secret knowledge or information about sb/sth to the police or a newspaper: *The journalist refused to name his informant.* ➲ look at **informer**

⚷ **information** /ˌɪnfəˈmeɪʃn/ *noun* [U] information (on/about sb/sth) knowledge or facts: *For further information please see our website.* ♦ *Can you give me some information about evening classes in Italian, please?* ♦ *a tourist information centre* ➲ look at **FYI**

> **GRAMMAR** The word **information** is uncountable. When we are talking about a single item, we say a **bit/piece of information** (not 'an information').

inforˌmation techˈnology *noun* [U] (*abbr* IT) the study or use of electronic equipment, especially computers, for collecting, storing and sending out information

informative /ɪnˈfɔːmətɪv/ *adj* giving useful knowledge or information

informed /ɪnˈfɔːmd/ *adj* having knowledge or information about sth: *Consumers cannot make informed choices unless they are told all the facts.* ♦ *Do **keep** me **informed** of any changes.* ♦ *They are not **fully informed** about the situation yet.*

informer /ɪnˈfɔːmə(r)/ *noun* [C] a criminal who gives the police information about other criminals ➲ look at **informant**

infrared /ˌɪnfrəˈred/ *adj* (used about light) that produces heat but that you cannot see: *infrared radiation* ♦ *an infrared lamp* ➲ look at **ultraviolet**

infrastructure /ˈɪnfrəstrʌktʃə(r)/ *noun* [C,U] the basic systems and services that are necessary for a country or an organization to run smoothly, for example transport, and water and power supplies

infrequent /ɪnˈfriːkwənt/ *adj* not happening often **OPP** **frequent** ▸ **infrequently** *adv*

infringe /ɪnˈfrɪndʒ/ *verb* (*formal*) **1** [T] to break a rule, law, agreement, etc: *The material can be copied without infringing copyright.* **2** [I] infringe on/upon sth to reduce or limit sb's rights, freedom, etc: *She refused to answer questions that infringed on her private affairs.* ▸ **infringement** *noun* [C,U]

infuriate /ɪnˈfjʊərieɪt/ *verb* [T] to make sb very angry ▸ **infuriating** *adj*: *an infuriating habit* ▸ **infuriatingly** *adv*

infuse /ɪnˈfjuːz/ *verb* [T] **1** [T] (*formal*) to have an effect on all parts of sth: *Politics infuses all aspects of our lives.* ♦ *Her novels are infused with sadness.* **2** [I,T] if you infuse **herbs** (= certain types of plant), etc. or they infuse, you put them in hot water until their flavour has passed into the water

ingenious /ɪnˈdʒiːniəs/ *adj* **1** (used about a thing or an idea) made or planned in a clever way: *an ingenious plan for making lots of money* ♦ *an ingenious device/experiment/invention* **2** (used about a person) full of new ideas and clever at finding solutions to problems or at inventing things ▸ **ingeniously** *adv* ▸ **ingenuity** /ˌɪndʒəˈnjuːəti/ *noun* [U]

ingrained /ɪnˈgreɪnd/ *adj* ingrained (in sb/sth) (used about a habit, an attitude, etc.) that has existed for a long time and is therefore difficult to change: *ingrained prejudices/beliefs*

ingratiate /ɪnˈgreɪʃieɪt/ *verb* [T] (*formal*) ingratiate yourself (with sb) to make yourself liked by doing or saying things that will please people, especially people who might be useful to you: *He was always trying to ingratiate himself with his teachers.* ▸ **ingratiating** *adj*: *an ingratiating smile* ▸ **ingratiatingly** *adv*

ingratitude /ɪnˈgrætɪtjuːd/ *noun* [U] (*formal*) the state of not showing or feeling thanks for sth that has been done for you; not being grateful **OPP** **gratitude**

⚷ **ingredient** /ɪnˈgriːdiənt/ *noun* [C] **1** one of the items of food you need to make sth to eat: *Mix all the ingredients together in a bowl.* **2** one of the qualities necessary to make sth successful: *The film has all the ingredients of success.*

inhabit /ɪnˈhæbɪt/ *verb* [T] to live in a place: *Are the Aran Islands inhabited* (= do people live there)?

inhabitant /ɪnˈhæbɪtənt/ *noun* [C, usually pl] a person or an animal that lives in a place: *The local* *inhabitants protested at the plans for a new motorway.*

HELP When you want to know how many people live in a particular place, you say: *What is the population of ...?* NOT: *How many inhabitants are there in ...?* However, when you answer this question you can say: *The population is 10 000.* OR: *It has 10 000 inhabitants.*

inhale /ɪnˈheɪl/ *verb* [I,T] to breathe in: *Be careful not to inhale the fumes from the paint.* **OPP** **exhale**

inherent /ɪnˈhɪərənt/ *adj* **inherent (in sb/sth)** that is a basic or permanent part of sb/sth and that cannot be removed: *The risk of collapse is inherent in any business.* ▶ **inherently** *adv*: *No matter how safe we make them, cars are inherently dangerous.*

inherit /ɪnˈherɪt/ *verb* [T] **inherit sth (from sb)** **1** to receive property, money, etc. from sb who has died: *I inherited quite a lot of money from my mother. She left me $12 000 when she died.*

MORE The person who inherits from sb is that person's **heir**.

2 to receive a quality, characteristic, etc. from your parents or family: *She has inherited her father's gift for languages.*

inheritance /ɪnˈherɪtəns/ *noun* [C,U] the act of **inheriting**; the money, property, etc. that you **inherit**: *inheritance tax*

inhibit /ɪnˈhɪbɪt/ *verb* [T] **1** to prevent sth or make sth happen more slowly: *a drug to inhibit the growth of tumours* **2** **inhibit sb (from sth/from doing sth)** to make sb nervous and embarrassed so that they are unable to do sth: *The fact that her boss was there inhibited her from saying what she really felt.* ▶ **inhibited** *adj*: *The young man felt shy and inhibited in the roomful of women.* **OPP** **uninhibited**

inhibition /ˌɪnhɪˈbɪʃn; ˌɪnɪˈb-/ *noun* [C,U] a shy or nervous feeling that stops you from saying or doing what you really want: *After the first morning of the course, people started to **lose** their **inhibitions**.*

inhospitable /ˌɪnhɒˈspɪtəbl/ *adj* **1** (used about a place) not pleasant to live in, especially because of the weather: *the inhospitable Arctic regions* **2** (used about a person) not friendly or welcoming to guests **OPP** for both meanings **hospitable**

ˌin-ˈhouse *adj* [only *before* a noun] existing or happening within a company or an organization: *an in-house magazine*

inhuman /ɪnˈhjuːmən/ *adj* **1** very cruel and without pity: *inhuman treatment/conditions* **2** not seeming to be human and therefore frightening: *an inhuman noise*

inhumane /ˌɪnhjuːˈmeɪn/ *adj* very cruel; not caring if people or animals suffer: *the inhumane conditions in which animals are kept on some large farms* **OPP** **humane**

inhumanity /ˌɪnhjuːˈmænəti/ *noun* [U] very cruel behaviour: *The 20th century was full of examples of man's inhumanity to man.* **OPP** **humanity**

⚷ **initial**[1] /ɪˈnɪʃl/ *adj* [only *before* a noun] happening at the beginning; first: *My initial reaction was to refuse, but I later changed my mind.* ♦ *the initial stages of our survey*

⚷ **initial**[2] /ɪˈnɪʃl/ *noun* [C, usually pl] the first letter of a name: *Alison Elizabeth Wilson's initials are A.E.W.*

initial[3] /ɪˈnɪʃl/ *verb* [T] (**initialling**; **initialled**, (*AmE*) **initialing**; **initialed**) to mark or sign sth with your initials: *Any changes made on the document should be initialled by you.*

⚷ **initially** /ɪˈnɪʃəli/ *adv* at the beginning; at first: *I liked the job initially, but it soon got quite boring.*

initiate /ɪˈnɪʃieɪt/ *verb* [T] **1** (*formal*) to start sth: *to initiate peace talks* **2** **initiate sb (into sth)** to explain sth to sb or make them experience sth for the first time: *I wasn't initiated into the joys of skiing until I was 30.* **3** **initiate sb (into sth)** to bring sb into a group by means of a special ceremony: *to initiate somebody into a secret society* ▶ **initiation** /ɪˌnɪʃiˈeɪʃn/ *noun* [U]: *All the new students had to go through a strange **initiation ceremony**.*

⚷ **initiative** /ɪˈnɪʃətɪv/ *noun* **1** [C] a new plan for solving a problem or improving a situation: *a new government initiative to help people start small businesses* **2** [U] the ability to see and do what is necessary without waiting for sb to tell you: *Don't keep asking me how to do it. Use your initiative.* **3** **the initiative** [sing] the power or opportunity to act and gain an advantage before other people do: *to take/lose the initiative*

IDM **on your own initiative** without being told by sb else what to do

take the initiative to be first to act to influence a situation: *Let's take the initiative and start organizing things now.*

inject /ɪnˈdʒekt/ *verb* [T] **1** to put a drug under the skin of a person's or an animal's body with a **syringe** (= a needle) **2** **inject sth (into sth)** to add sth: *They injected a lot of money into the business.*

injection /ɪnˈdʒekʃn/ *noun* **1** [C,U] **(an) injection (of sth) (into sb/sth)** the act of **injecting** a drug or other substance: *to give somebody an injection of penicillin* ♦ *a tetanus injection* ♦ *An anaesthetic was administered **by injection**.* **SYN** **jab** **2** [C] a large amount of sth that is added to sth to help it: *The theatre needs a huge **cash injection** if it is to stay open.* **3** [U,C] the act of forcing liquid into sth: *fuel injection*

injunction /ɪnˈdʒʌŋkʃn/ *noun* [C] **an injunction (against sb)** an official order from a court of law to do/not do sth: *An injunction prevented the programme from being shown on TV.*

⚷ **injure** /ˈɪndʒə(r)/ *verb* [T] to harm or hurt yourself or sb else physically, especially in an accident: *The goalkeeper seriously injured himself when he hit the goalpost.* ♦ *She fell and injured her back.* ➲ note at **hurt**

⚷ **injured** /ˈɪndʒəd/ *adj* **1** physically or mentally hurt: *an injured arm/leg* ♦ *injured pride* **2** the injured *noun* [pl] people who have been hurt: *The injured were rushed to hospital.*

injury /ˈɪndʒəri/ *noun* [C,U] (*pl* injuries) (an) injury (to sb/sth) harm done to a person's or an animal's body, especially in an accident: *They escaped from the accident with only* ***minor injuries.*** ◆ *serious injury/injuries*

ˈ**injury time** *noun* [U] (*BrE*) time that is added to the end of a football, etc. match when there has been time lost because of injuries to players

injustice /ɪnˈdʒʌstɪs/ *noun* [U,C] the fact of a situation being unfair; an unfair act: *racial/social injustice* ◆ *People are protesting about the injustice of the new tax.*

IDM **do sb an injustice** to judge sb unfairly: *I'm afraid I've done you both an injustice.*

I

ink /ɪŋk/ *noun* [U,C] coloured liquid that is used for writing, drawing, etc: *Please write* ***in ink****, not pencil.*

inkling /ˈɪŋklɪŋ/ *noun* [C, usually sing] an inkling (of sth/that ...) a slight feeling (about sth): *I had an inkling that something was wrong.*

ˈ**ink-pad** *noun* [C] a thick piece of soft material full of ink, used with a rubber stamp ➲ picture at **stationery**

inky /ˈɪŋki/ *adj* covered in ink; very dark: *inky fingers* ◆ *an inky night sky*

inland /ˈɪnlænd/ *adj* /ˌɪnˈlænd/ *adv* away from the coast or borders of a country: *inland areas* ◆ *The village lies twenty miles inland.* ◆ *Goods are carried inland along narrow mountain roads.*

ˈ**in-laws** *noun* [pl] (*informal*) your husband's or wife's mother and father or other relatives: *My in-laws are coming to lunch on Sunday.*

inlet /ˈɪnlet/ *noun* [C] **1** a narrow area of water that stretches into the land from the sea or a lake, or between islands **2** an opening through which liquid, air or gas can enter a machine: *a fuel inlet* OPP **outlet**

inmate /ˈɪnmeɪt/ *noun* [C] one of the people living in an institution such as a prison

inn /ɪn/ *noun* [C] (*BrE*) a small hotel or old pub usually in the country

innate /ɪˈneɪt/ *adj* (used about an ability or quality) that you have when you are born: *the innate ability to learn*

inner /ˈɪnə(r)/ *adj* [only *before* a noun] **1** (of the) inside; towards or close to the centre of a place: *The inner ear is very delicate.* ◆ *an inner courtyard* OPP **outer 2** (used about a feeling, etc.) that you do not express or show to other people; private: *Everyone has inner doubts.*

ˌ**inner** ˈ**city** *noun* [C] the poor parts of a large city, near the centre, that often have a lot of social problems: *There are huge problems in our inner cities.* ◆ *Inner-city schools often have difficulty in attracting good teachers.*

innermost /ˈɪnəməʊst/ *adj* [only *before* a noun] **1** (used about a feeling or thought) most secret or private: *She never told anyone her innermost thoughts.* **2** nearest to the centre or inside of sth: *the innermost shrine of the temple*

innings /ˈɪnɪŋz/ *noun* [C] (*pl* innings) a period of time in a game of **cricket** when it is the turn of one player or team to **bat** (= hit the ball)

innocence /ˈɪnəsns/ *noun* [U] **1** the fact of not being guilty of a crime, etc: *The accused man* ***protested*** *his* ***innocence*** *throughout his trial.* OPP **guilt 2** lack of knowledge and experience of the world, especially of bad things: *the innocence of childhood*

innocent /ˈɪnəsnt/ *adj* **1** innocent (of sth) not having done wrong: *An innocent man was arrested by mistake.* ◆ *to be innocent of a crime* SYN **blameless** OPP **guilty 2** [only *before* a noun] being hurt or killed in a crime, war, etc. although not directly involved in it: ***innocent victims*** *of a bomb blast* ◆ *He was an innocent bystander.* **3** not wanting to cause harm or upset sb: *He got very aggressive when I asked an* ***innocent question*** *about his past life.* **4** not knowing the bad things in life; believing everything you are told: *She was so innocent as to believe that politicians never lie.* SYN **naive** ▶ **innocently** *adv*: *'What are you doing here?' she asked innocently* (= pretending she did not know the answer).

innocuous /ɪˈnɒkjuəs/ *adj* (*formal*) not meant to cause harm or upset sb: *I made an* ***innocuous remark*** *about teachers and she got really angry.* SYN **harmless**

innovate /ˈɪnəveɪt/ *verb* [I] to create new things, ideas or ways of doing sth ▶ **innovation** /ˌɪnəˈveɪʃn/ *noun* [C,U] (an) innovation (in sth) [C]: *technological innovations in industry* ▶ **innovative** /ˈɪnəvətɪv; ˈɪnəveɪtɪv/ *adj*: *innovative methods/designs/products* ▶ **innovator** /ˈɪnəveɪtə(r)/ *noun* [C]

innuendo /ˌɪnjuˈendəʊ/ *noun* [C,U] (*pl* innuendoes *or* innuendos) an indirect way of talking about sb/sth, usually suggesting sth bad or rude: *His speech was full of sexual innuendo.*

innumerable /ɪˈnjuːmərəbl/ *adj* too many to be counted

inoculate /ɪˈnɒkjuleɪt/ *verb* [T] inoculate sb (against sth) to protect a person or an animal from a disease by giving them a mild form of the disease with an **injection** (= putting a substance under their skin with a needle): *The children have been inoculated against tetanus.* ➲ look at **immunize, vaccinate** ▶ **inoculation** /ɪˌnɒkjuˈleɪʃn/ *noun* [C,U]

inoffensive /ˌɪnəˈfensɪv/ *adj* not likely to offend or upset sb: *a gentle and inoffensive man* SYN **harmless** OPP **offensive**

inopportune /ɪnˈɒpətjuːn/ *adj* (*formal*) happening at a bad time SYN **inappropriate, inconvenient** OPP **opportune**

inordinate /ɪnˈɔːdɪnət/ *adj* (*formal*) much greater than usual or expected: *They spent an* ***inordinate amount*** *of time and money on the production.* ▶ **inordinately** *adv*

inorganic /ˌɪnɔːˈɡænɪk/ *adj* not made of or coming from living things: *Rocks and metals are inorganic substances.* OPP **organic**

input[1] /ˈɪnpʊt/ *noun* **1** [C,U] input (of sth) (into/to sth) what you put into sth to make it successful: *We need some input from teachers into this book.* **2** [U] the act of putting information into a computer: *The computer breakdown means we have lost the whole day's input.* ➲ look at **output**

input[2] /ˈɪnpʊt/ *verb* [T] (inputting; *pt, pp* input *or* inputted) to put information into a computer: *to input text/data/figures*

inquest /ˈɪŋkwest/ *noun* [C] an official investigation to find out how sb died: *to hold an inquest*

inquire, inquirer, inquiring, inquiry = enquire, enquirer, enquiring, enquiry

inquisitive /ɪnˈkwɪzətɪv/ *adj* **1** too interested in finding out about what other people are doing: *Don't be so inquisitive. It's none of your business.* SYN **nosy** **2** interested in finding out about many different things: *You need an inquisitive mind to be a scientist.* SYN **curious** ▶ **inquisitively** *adv* ▶ **inquisitiveness** *noun* [U]

insane /ɪnˈseɪn/ *adj* **1** seriously mentally ill **2** not showing sensible judgement: *You must be insane to leave such a great job.* ➲ look at **mad** ▶ **insanely** *adv*: *insanely jealous* ▶ **insanity** /ɪnˈsænəti/ *noun* [U]

insanitary /ɪnˈsænətri/ *adj* (*formal*) dirty and likely to cause disease: *The restaurant was closed because of the insanitary condition of the kitchen.* ➲ look at **sanitary**

insatiable /ɪnˈseɪʃəbl/ *adj* that cannot be satisfied; very great: *an insatiable desire for knowledge* ◆ *an insatiable appetite*

inscribe /ɪnˈskraɪb/ *verb* [T] (*formal*) inscribe A (on/in B); inscribe B (with A) to write sth on sth or cut words into the surface of sth: *The names of all the previous champions are inscribed on the cup.* ◆ *The book was inscribed with the author's name.*

inscription /ɪnˈskrɪpʃn/ *noun* [C] words that are written or cut on sth: *There was a Latin inscription on the tombstone.*

🔑 **insect** /ˈɪnsekt/ *noun* [C] a small animal with six legs, two pairs of wings and a body which is divided into three parts: *Ants, flies, beetles, butterflies and mosquitoes are all insects.* ◆ *an insect bite/sting* ➲ picture on **page P13**

> **HELP** Some other small animals, for example spiders, are often also called insects although this is not strictly correct.

insecticide /ɪnˈsektɪsaɪd/ *noun* [C,U] a substance that is used for killing insects ➲ look at **pesticide**

insecure /ˌɪnsɪˈkjʊə(r)/ *adj* **1** insecure (about sb/sth) not confident about yourself or your relationships with other people: *Many teenagers are insecure about their appearance.* **2** not safe or protected: *This ladder feels a bit insecure.* ◆ *The future of the company looks very insecure.* OPP for both meanings **secure** ▶ **insecurely** *adv* ▶ **insecurity** /ˌɪnsɪˈkjʊərəti/ *noun* [U]: *Their aggressive behaviour is a sign of insecurity.* OPP **security**

insensitive /ɪnˈsensətɪv/ *adj* insensitive (to sth) **1** not knowing or caring how another person feels and therefore likely to hurt or upset them: *Some insensitive reporters tried to interview the families of the accident victims.* ◆ *an insensitive remark* **2** not able to feel or react to sth: *insensitive to pain/cold/criticism* OPP for both meanings **sensitive** ▶ **insensitively** *adv* ▶ **insensitivity** /ɪnˌsensəˈtɪvəti/ *noun* [U]

inseparable /ɪnˈseprəbl/ *adj* that cannot be separated from sb/sth: *inseparable friends* OPP **separable**

🔑 **insert** /ɪnˈsɜːt/ *verb* [T] (*formal*) to put sth into sth or between two things: *I decided to insert a paragraph in the text.* ◆ *Position the cursor where you want to insert a word.* ▶ **insertion** *noun* [C,U]

inshore *adj* /ˈɪnʃɔː(r)/ *adv* /ˌɪnˈʃɔː(r)/ in or towards the part of the sea that is close to the land: *inshore fishermen* ◆ *Sharks don't often come inshore.*

🔑 **inside**[1] /ˌɪnˈsaɪd/ *prep, adj* [only *before* a noun] *adv* **1** in, on or to the inner part or surface of sth: *Is there anything inside the box?* ◆ *It's safer to be inside the house in a thunderstorm.* ◆ *We'd better stay inside until the rain stops.* ◆ *It's getting cold. Let's go inside.* ◆ *the inside pages of a newspaper* OPP **outside** **2** (*formal*) (used about time) in less than; within: *Your prescription will be ready inside an hour.* **3** known or done by sb in a group or an organization: *The robbers seemed to have had some inside information about the bank's security system.* **4** (*slang*) in prison: *He was sentenced to three years inside.*

🔑 **inside**[2] /ˌɪnˈsaɪd/ *noun* **1** [C] the inner part or surface of sth: *The door was locked from the inside.* ◆ *There's a label somewhere* ***on the inside***. OPP **outside** **2** insides [pl] (*informal*) the organs inside the body: *The coffee warmed his insides.*

IDM **inside out** with the inner surface on the outside: *You've got your jumper on inside out.* ➲ picture at **back**

know sth inside out ➲ **know**[1]

insider /ɪnˈsaɪdə(r)/ *noun* [C] a person who knows a lot about a group or an organization because they are a part of it: *The book gives us an insider's view of how government works.*

insidious /ɪnˈsɪdiəs/ *adj* (*formal*) spreading gradually or without being noticed, but causing serious harm: *the insidious effects of polluted water supplies* ▶ **insidiously** *adv*

insight /ˈɪnsaɪt/ *noun* [C,U] (an) insight (into sth) an understanding of what sb/sth is like: *The book gives a good insight into the lives of the poor.*

insignia /ɪnˈsɪgniə/ *noun* [C] (*pl* insignia) the symbol or sign that shows sb's position, or that they are a member of a group or an organization: *the royal insignia* ◆ *His uniform bore the insignia of a captain.*

insignificant /ˌɪnsɪgˈnɪfɪkənt/ *adj* of little value or importance: *an insignificant detail* ◆ *Working in such a big company made her feel insignificant.* OPP **significant** ▶ **insignificance** *noun* [U] ▶ **insignificantly** *adv*

insincere /ˌɪnsɪn'sɪə(r)/ *adj* saying or doing sth that you do not really believe: *His apology sounded insincere.* ♦ *Dan gave an insincere smile.* OPP **sincere** ▶ **insincerely** *adv* ▶ **insincerity** /ˌɪnsɪn'serəti/ *noun* [U] OPP **sincerity**

insinuate /ɪn'sɪnjueɪt/ *verb* [T] to suggest sth unpleasant in an indirect way: *She seemed to be insinuating that our work was below standard.* ▶ **insinuation** /ɪnˌsɪnju'eɪʃn/ *noun* [C,U]: *to* ***make insinuations*** *about somebody's honesty*

insipid /ɪn'sɪpɪd/ *adj* having almost no taste or flavour; not interesting or exciting

insist /ɪn'sɪst/ *verb* [I] **1** insist (on sth/doing sth); insist that ... to say strongly that you must have or do sth, or that sb else must do sth: *He always insists on the best.* ♦ *Dan insisted on coming too.* ♦ *My parents insist that I come home by taxi.* ♦ *'Have another drink.' 'Oh all right, if you insist.'* **2** insist (on sth); insist that ... to say firmly that sth is true (when sb does not believe you): *She insisted on her innocence.* ♦ *Benjamin insisted that the accident wasn't his fault.* ▶ **insistence** *noun* [U]

I

insistent /ɪn'sɪstənt/ *adj* **1** insistent (on sth/doing sth); insistent that ... saying strongly that you must have or do sth, or that sb else must do sth: *Doctors are insistent on the need to do more exercise.* ♦ *She was most insistent that we should all be there.* **2** continuing for a long time in a way that cannot be ignored: *the insistent ringing of the telephone* ▶ **insistently** *adv*

insolent /'ɪnsələnt/ *adj* (*formal*) lacking respect; rude: *insolent behaviour* ▶ **insolence** *noun* [U] ▶ **insolently** *adv*

insoluble /ɪn'sɒljəbl/ *adj* **1** that cannot be explained or solved: *We faced almost insoluble problems.* **2** that cannot be dissolved in a liquid OPP for both meanings **soluble**

insomnia /ɪn'sɒmniə/ *noun* [U] the condition of being unable to sleep: *Do you ever suffer from insomnia?* ➲ look at **sleepless**

insomniac /ɪn'sɒmniæk/ *noun* [C] a person who cannot sleep

inspect /ɪn'spekt/ *verb* [T] **1** inspect sb/sth (for sth) to look at sth closely or in great detail: *The detective inspected the room for fingerprints.* SYN **examine** **2** to make an official visit to make sure that rules are being obeyed, work is being done properly, etc: *All food shops should be inspected regularly.* ▶ **inspection** *noun* [C,U]: *The fire prevention service will* ***carry out an inspection*** *of the building next week.* ♦ ***On inspection****, the passport turned out to be false.*

inspector /ɪn'spektə(r)/ *noun* [C] **1** an official who visits schools, factories, etc. to make sure that rules are being obeyed, work is being done properly, etc: *a health and safety inspector* **2** (*BrE*) a police officer with quite an important position **3** a person whose job is to check passengers' tickets on buses or trains **4** (*AmE*) = **surveyor**(2)

inspiration /ˌɪnspə'reɪʃn/ *noun* **1** [C,U] an inspiration (to/for sb); inspiration (to do/for sth) a feeling, person or thing that makes you want to do sth or gives you exciting new ideas: *The beauty of the mountains was a great* ***source of inspiration*** *to the writer.* ♦ *What gave you the inspiration to become a dancer?* **2** [C,U, usually sing] (*informal*) a sudden good idea: *I've had an inspiration—why don't we go to that new club?* ♦ *The answer came to me in a* ***flash of inspiration****.*

inspire /ɪn'spaɪə(r)/ *verb* [T] **1** inspire sth; inspire sb (to do sth) to make sb want to do or create sth: *Nelson Mandela's autobiography inspired her to go into politics.* ♦ *The attack was inspired by racial hatred.* **2** inspire sb (with sth); inspire sth (in sb) to make sb feel, think, etc. sth: *to be inspired with enthusiasm* ♦ *The guide's nervous manner did not* ***inspire*** *much* ***confidence*** *in us.* ▶ **inspiring** *adj*: *an inspiring speech.*

inspired /ɪn'spaɪəd/ *adj* **1** having excellent qualities or abilities: *The pianist gave an inspired performance.* **2** (in compounds) used to form adjectives to show how sth has been influenced: *a politically-inspired killing*

instability /ˌɪnstə'bɪləti/ *noun* [U] the state of being likely to change: *There are growing signs of political instability.* OPP **stability** ➲ *adjective* **unstable**

install (*AmE* also instal) /ɪn'stɔːl/ *verb* [T] **1** to put a piece of equipment, etc. in place so that it is ready to be used: *We are waiting to have our new washing machine installed.* ♦ *to install a computer system* SYN **put sth in** **2** install sb (as sth) to put sb or yourself in a position or place: *He was installed as President yesterday.* ▶ **installation** /ˌɪnstə'leɪʃn/ *noun* [C,U]: *a military/nuclear installation* ♦ *the installation of a new chairman*

instalment (*AmE* installment) /ɪn'stɔːlmənt/ *noun* [C] **1** one of the regular payments that you make for sth until you have paid the full amount: *to pay for something* ***in instalments*** **2** one part of a story that is shown or published as a series: *Don't miss next week's exciting instalment of this new drama.*

instance /'ɪnstəns/ *noun* [C] an instance (of sth) an example or case (of sth): *There have been several instances of racial attacks in the area.* ♦ *In most instances the drug has no side effects.*

IDM **for instance** for example: *There are several interesting places to visit around here—Warwick, for instance.* ➲ note at **example**

instant[1] /'ɪnstənt/ *adj* **1** happening immediately: *The film was an instant success.* ♦ *She took an instant dislike to me.* ♦ *A new government cannot bring about instant change.* SYN **immediate** **2** [only *before* a noun] (used about food) that can be prepared quickly and easily, usually by adding hot water: *instant coffee*

instant[2] /'ɪnstənt/ *noun* [C, usually sing] **1** a very short period of time: *Alex thought* ***for an instant*** *and then agreed.* **2** a particular point in time: ***At that instant*** *I realized I had been tricked.* ♦ *Stop doing that* *this instant* (= now)! **SYN** for both meanings **moment**

instantaneous /ˌɪnstənˈteɪniəs/ *adj* happening immediately or extremely quickly ▶ **instantaneously** *adv*

instantly /ˈɪnstəntli/ *adv* without delay; immediately: *I asked him a question and he replied instantly.*

ˌinstant ˈmessaging *noun* [U] a system on the Internet that allows people to exchange written messages with each other very quickly

TOPIC

Instant messaging

If you want to **chat with** someone on the Internet you can use **instant messaging** to exchange short written messages. When you **log on**, you can show that you are **online** and **available to chat**.

⚷ **instead** /ɪnˈsted/ *adv, prep* instead (of sb/sth/doing sth) in the place of sb/sth: *I couldn't go so my husband went instead.* ♦ *Instead of 7.30 could I come at 8.00?* ♦ *You should play football instead of just watching it on TV.*

instigate /ˈɪnstɪɡeɪt/ *verb* [T] (*formal*) to make sth start to happen ▶ **instigation** /ˌɪnstɪˈɡeɪʃn/ *noun* [U]

instil (*AmE* instill) /ɪnˈstɪl/ *verb* [T] (instilling; instilled) instil sth (in/into sb) to make sb think or feel sth: *Parents should try to instil a sense of responsibility into their children.*

instinct /ˈɪnstɪŋkt/ *noun* [C,U] the natural tendency that causes a person or an animal to behave in a particular way without thinking or learning about it: *Birds learn to fly* ***by instinct.*** ♦ *In a situation like that you don't have time to think—you just* ***act on instinct.*** ▶ **instinctive** /ɪnˈstɪŋktɪv/ *adj*: *Your instinctive reaction is to run from danger.* ▶ **instinctively** *adv*

⚷ **institute**[1] /ˈɪnstɪtjuːt/ *noun* [C] an organization that has a particular purpose; the building used by this organization: *the Institute of Science and Technology* ♦ *institutes of higher education*

institute[2] /ˈɪnstɪtjuːt/ *verb* [T] (*formal*) to introduce a system, policy, etc., or start a process: *The government has instituted a new scheme for youth training.*

⚷ **institution** /ˌɪnstɪˈtjuːʃn/ *noun* **1** [C] a large, important organization that has a particular purpose, such as a bank, a university, etc: *the financial institutions in the City of London* **2** [C] a building where certain people with special needs live and are looked after: *a mental institution* (= a hospital for the mentally ill) ♦ *She's been in institutions all her life.* **3** [C] a social custom or habit that has existed for a long time: *the institution of marriage* **4** [U] the act of introducing a system, policy, etc., or of starting a process: *the institution of new safety procedures*

institutional /ˌɪnstɪˈtjuːʃənl/ *adj* connected with an institution: *The old lady is in need of institutional care.*

instruct /ɪnˈstrʌkt/ *verb* [T] **1** instruct sb (to do sth) to give an order to sb; to tell sb to do sth: *The soldiers were instructed to shoot above the heads of the crowd.* **2** (*formal*) instruct sb (in sth) to teach sb sth: *Children must be instructed in road safety before they are allowed to ride a bike on the road.*

⚷ **instruction** /ɪnˈstrʌkʃn/ *noun* **1** instructions [pl] detailed information on how you should use sth, do sth, etc: *Read the instructions on the back of the packet carefully.* ♦ *You should always* ***follow the instructions.*** **2** [C] an instruction (to do sth) an order that tells you what to do or how to do sth: *The guard was* ***under*** *strict* ***instructions*** *not to let anyone in or out.* **3** [U] (*formal*) instruction (in sth) the act of teaching sth to sb: *The staff need instruction in the use of the new booking system.*

instructive /ɪnˈstrʌktɪv/ *adj* giving useful information ▶ **instructively** *adv*

instructor /ɪnˈstrʌktə(r)/ *noun* [C] a person whose job is to teach a practical skill or sport: *a driving/fitness/golf instructor*

⚷ **instrument** /ˈɪnstrəmənt/ *noun* [C] **1** a tool that is used for doing a particular job or task: *surgical/optical/precision instruments* ➲ note at **tool** **2** something that is used for playing music: *Do you play an instrument?* ➲ note at **music** **3** something that is used for measuring speed, distance, temperature, etc. in a car, plane or ship: *the instrument panel of a plane* **4** (*formal*) something that sb uses in order to achieve sth: *The press should be more than an instrument of the government.*

TOPIC

Musical instruments

Musical instruments may be **stringed** (*violins, guitars, etc.*), **brass** (*horns, trumpets, etc.*), **woodwind** (*flutes, clarinets, etc.*) or **keyboard** (*piano, organ, synthesizer, etc.*). **Percussion** instruments include drums and cymbals.

instrumental /ˌɪnstrəˈmentl/ *adj* **1** instrumental in doing sth helping to make sth happen: *She was instrumental in getting him the job.* **2** for musical instruments without voices: *instrumental music*

insubordinate /ˌɪnsəˈbɔːdɪnət/ *adj* (*formal*) (used about a person or behaviour) not obeying rules or orders ▶ **insubordination** /ˌɪnsəˌbɔːdɪˈneɪʃn/ *noun* [U]: *He was dismissed from the army for insubordination.*

insubstantial /ˌɪnsəbˈstænʃl/ *adj* (*formal*) not large, solid or strong: *a hut built of insubstantial materials* **OPP** **substantial**

insufferable /ɪnˈsʌfrəbl/ *adj* (*formal*) (used about a person or behaviour) extremely unpleasant or annoying

insufficient /ˌɪnsəˈfɪʃnt/ *adj* insufficient (for sth/to do sth) not enough: *The students complained that they were given insufficient time for the test.* **OPP** **sufficient** ▶ **insufficiently** *adv*

insular /ˈɪnsjələ(r)/ *adj* only interested in your own country, ideas, etc. and not in those from outside ▶ **insularity** /ˌɪnsjuˈlærəti/ *noun* [U]

insulate /ˈɪnsjuleɪt/ *verb* [T] **insulate sth (against/from sth)** to protect sth with a material that prevents electricity, heat or sound from passing through: *The walls are insulated against noise.* ▶ **insulation** /ˌɪnsjuˈleɪʃn/ *noun* [U]

insult[1] /ɪnˈsʌlt/ *verb* [T] to speak or act rudely to sb: *I felt very insulted when I didn't even get an answer to my letter.* ◆ *He was thrown out of the hotel for insulting the manager.*

insult[2] /ˈɪnsʌlt/ *noun* [C] a rude comment or action: *The drivers were standing in the road yelling insults at each other.*

insulting /ɪnˈsʌltɪŋ/ *adj* **insulting (to sb/sth)** making sb feel offended: *insulting behaviour/remarks* ◆ *That poster is insulting to women.*

insuperable /ɪnˈsuːpərəbl/ *adj* (*formal*) (used about a problem, etc.) impossible to solve

insurance /ɪnˈʃʊərəns; -ˈʃɔːr-/ *noun* **1** [U] **insurance (against sth)** an arrangement with a company in which you pay them regular amounts of money and they agree to pay the costs if, for example, you die or are ill, or if you lose or damage sth: *life/car/travel/household insurance* ◆ *an insurance policy* ◆ *to **take out insurance** against fire and theft* **2** [U] the business of providing insurance: *He works in insurance.* **3** [U,sing] **(an) insurance (against sth)** something you do to protect yourself (against sth unpleasant): *Many people take vitamin pills as an insurance against illness.*

insure /ɪnˈʃʊə(r); -ˈʃɔː(r)/ *verb* [T] **1 insure sb/sth (against/for sth)** to buy or to provide insurance: *They insured the painting for £10 000 against damage or theft.* **2** (*AmE*) = **ensure**

insurgent /ɪnˈsɜːdʒənt/ *noun* [C, usually pl] (*formal*) a person fighting against the government or armed forces of their own country **SYN** **rebel** ▶ **insurgent** *adj* **SYN** **rebellious**

insurmountable /ˌɪnsəˈmaʊntəbl/ *adj* (*formal*) (used about a problem, etc.) impossible to solve

insurrection /ˌɪnsəˈrekʃn/ *noun* [C,U] (*formal*) violent action against the rulers of a country or the government

intact /ɪnˈtækt/ *adj* [not before a noun] complete; not damaged: *Very few of the buildings **remain intact** following the earthquake.*

intake /ˈɪnteɪk/ *noun* [C, usually sing] **1** the amount of food, drink, etc. that you take into your body: *My doctor told me to reduce my salt intake.* **2** the (number of) people who enter an organization or institution during a certain period: *This year's intake of students is down 10%.* **3** the act of taking sth into your body, especially breath

intangible /ɪnˈtændʒəbl/ *adj* difficult to describe, understand or measure: *The benefits of good customer relations are intangible.* **OPP** **tangible**

integral /ˈɪntɪɡrəl; ɪnˈteɡral/ *adj* **1 integral (to sth)** necessary in order to make sth complete: *Spending a year in France is **an integral part of** the university course.* **2** included as part of sth: *The car has an integral solar panel.*

integrate /ˈɪntɪɡreɪt/ *verb* **1** [T] **integrate sth (into sth); integrate A and B/integrate A with B** to join things so that they become one thing or work together: *The two small schools were integrated into one large one.* ◆ *These programs can be integrated with your existing software.* **2** [I,T] **integrate (sb) (into/with sth)** to join in and become part of a group or community, or to make sb do this: *It took Amir a while to integrate into his new school.* ➲ look at **segregate** ▶ **integration** /ˌɪntɪˈɡreɪʃn/ *noun* [U]: *racial integration* ➲ look at **segregation**

integrity /ɪnˈteɡrəti/ *noun* [U] the quality of being honest and having strong moral principles: *He's a person **of great integrity** who will say exactly what he thinks.*

intellect /ˈɪntəlekt/ *noun* **1** [U] the power of the mind to think and to learn: *a woman of considerable intellect* **2** [C] an extremely intelligent person: *He was one of the most brilliant intellects of his time.*

intellectual[1] /ˌɪntəˈlektʃuəl/ *adj* **1** [only *before* a noun] connected with sb's ability to think, reason and understand things: *The boy's intellectual development was very advanced for his age.* **2** (used about a person) well educated and enjoying activities in which you have to think seriously about things ▶ **intellectually** /-tʃuəli/ *adv*

intellectual[2] /ˌɪntəˈlektʃuəl/ *noun* [C] a person who is well educated and enjoys thinking seriously about things

intelligence /ɪnˈtelɪdʒəns/ *noun* [U] **1** the ability to understand, learn and think: *a person of normal intelligence* ◆ *an intelligence test* **2** important information about a person or country: *to receive intelligence about somebody* ◆ *enemy intelligence*

intelligent /ɪnˈtelɪdʒənt/ *adj* having or showing the ability to understand, learn and think; clever: *All their children are very intelligent.* ◆ *an intelligent question* ▶ **intelligently** *adv*

OTHER WORDS FOR

intelligent

Bright, **clever** and (especially in US English) **smart** all mean 'intelligent'. **Bright** is used especially to talk about young people: *She's the brightest girl in the class.* People who are **clever** or **smart** are able to understand and learn things quickly: *He's smarter than his brother.* **Clever** and **smart** can also describe actions or ideas that show intelligence: *What a clever idea!* ◆ *a smart career move* (= an action that will help your career).

intelligible /ɪnˈtelɪdʒəbl/ *adj* (used especially about speech or writing) possible or easy to understand **SYN** **understandable** **OPP** **unintelligible**

intend /ɪnˈtend/ *verb* [T] **1 intend to do sth/doing sth** to plan or mean to do sth: *I'm afraid I spent more money than I had intended.* ◆ *I certainly don't intend to wait here all day!* ◆ *They had intended staying in Wales for two weeks but the weather was so bad that they left after one.* ➲ *noun* **intention** **2 intend sth for sb/sth; intend sb to do sth** to plan, mean or make sth for a particular person or purpose: *You shouldn't have read that letter–it wasn't intended for you.* ◆ *I didn't intend you to have all the work.*

intended /ɪnˈtendɪd/ *adj* **1** [only *before* a noun] that you are trying to achieve or reach: *the intended purpose* ◆ *The bullet missed its intended target.* **2** intended for sb/sth; intended as sth; intended to be/do sth planned or designed for sb/sth: *The book is intended for children.* ◆ *The notes are intended as an introduction to the course.* ◆ *The lights are intended to be used in the garden.*

intense /ɪnˈtens/ *adj* very great, strong or serious: *intense heat/cold/pressure* ◆ *intense anger/interest/desire* ▶ **intensely** *adv*: *They dislike each other intensely.* ▶ **intensity** /ɪnˈtensəti/ *noun* [U]: *I wasn't prepared for the intensity of his reaction to the news.*

intensify /ɪnˈtensɪfaɪ/ *verb* [I,T] (intensifying; intensifies; *pt, pp* intensified) to become or to make sth greater or stronger: *The government has intensified its campaign against obesity.* ◆ *Fighting in the region has intensified.* ▶ **intensification** /ɪnˌtensɪfɪˈkeɪʃn/ *noun* [U]

intensive /ɪnˈtensɪv/ *adj* **1** involving a lot of work or care in a short period of time: *an intensive investigation/course* **2** (used about methods of farming) aimed at producing as much food as possible from the land or money available: *intensive agriculture* ▶ **intensively** *adv*

inˌtensive ˈcare *noun* [U] special care in hospital for patients who are very seriously ill or injured; the department that gives this care: *She was in intensive care for a week after the crash.*

intent¹ /ɪnˈtent/ *adj* **1** intent (on/upon sth) showing great attention: *She was so intent upon her work that she didn't hear me come in.* **2** intent on/upon sth/doing sth determined to do sth: *He's always been intent on making a lot of money.* ▶ **intently** *adv*

intent² /ɪnˈtent/ *noun* [U] (*formal*) what sb intends to do; intention: *He was charged with possession of a gun* ***with intent to*** *commit a robbery.* ◆ *to do something with evil/good intent*

IDM **to/for all intents and purposes** in effect, even if not completely true: *When they scored their fourth goal the match was, to all intents and purposes, over.*

intention /ɪnˈtenʃn/ *noun* [C,U] (an) intention (of doing sth/to do sth) what sb intends or means to do; a plan or purpose: *Our intention was to leave early in the morning.* ◆ *I* ***have no intention of*** *staying indoors on a nice sunny day like this.* ◆ *I borrowed the money* ***with the intention of*** *paying it back the next day.*

intentional /ɪnˈtenʃənl/ *adj* done on purpose, not by chance: *I'm sorry I took your jacket–it wasn't intentional!* SYN **deliberate** OPP **unintentional** ▶ **intentionally** /-ʃənəli/ *adv*: *I can't believe the boys broke the window intentionally.*

interact /ˌɪntərˈækt/ *verb* [I] **1** interact (with sb) (used about people) to communicate or mix with sb, especially while you work, play or spend time together: *He is studying the way children interact with each other at different ages.* **2** (used about two things) to have an effect on each other

▶ **interaction** *noun* [U,C] interaction (between/with sb/sth) [U]: *interaction between the two departments*

interactive /ˌɪntərˈæktɪv/ *adj* **1** that involves people working together and having an influence on each other: *The college uses interactive language-learning techniques.* **2** involving direct communication both ways, between a computer, etc. and the person using it: *interactive TV/computer games* ➲ picture on **page P3**

ˌinteractive ˈwhiteboard (*abbr* IWB) *noun* [C] a piece of classroom equipment using a computer connected to a large screen that you can write on or use to control the computer by touching it with your finger or a pen: *Nearly every classroom has an* ***interactive whiteboard***.

intercept /ˌɪntəˈsept/ *verb* [T] to stop or catch sb/sth that is moving from one place to another: *Detectives intercepted him at the airport.* ▶ **interception** *noun* [U,C]

interchangeable /ˌɪntəˈtʃeɪndʒəbl/ *adj* interchangeable (with sth) able to be used in place of each other without making any difference to the way sth works: *Are these two words interchangeable (= do they have the same meaning)?* ▶ **interchangeably** /-əbli/ *adv*

intercom /ˈɪntəkɒm/ *noun* [C] a system of communication by radio or telephone inside an office, plane, etc.; the device you press or switch on to start using this system

interconnect /ˌɪntəkəˈnekt/ *verb* [I,T] interconnect (A) (with B); interconnect A and B to connect similar things; to be connected to similar things: *electronic networks which interconnect thousands of computers around the world*

intercontinental /ˌɪntəˌkɒntɪˈnentl/ *adj* between continents: *intercontinental flights*

intercourse /ˈɪntəkɔːs/ (*formal*) = **sex**(3)

interdependent /ˌɪntədɪˈpendənt/ *adj* depending on each other: *Exercise and good health are generally interdependent.* ◆ *interdependent economies/organizations* ▶ **interdependence** *noun* [U]

interest¹ /ˈɪntrəst/ *noun* **1** [U, sing] an interest (in sb/sth) a desire to learn or hear more about sb/sth or to be involved with sb/sth: *She's begun to* ***show*** *a great* ***interest*** *in politics.* ◆ *I wish he'd* ***take*** *more* ***interest in*** *his children.* ◆ *Don't* ***lose interest*** *now!* **2** [U] the quality that makes sth interesting: *I thought this article might* ***be of interest to*** *you.* ◆ *Computers* ***hold no interest for*** *me.* ◆ *places of historical interest* **3** [C, usually pl] something that you enjoy doing or learning about: *What are your interests and hobbies?* **4** [U] interest (on sth) the money that you pay for borrowing money from a bank, etc. or the money that you earn when you keep money in a bank, etc: *We pay 6% interest on our mortgage at the moment.* ◆ *The* ***interest rate*** *has never been so high/low.* ◆ *Some companies offer* ***interest-free*** *loans.* ➲ note at **loan**

IDM **have/with sb's (best) interests at heart** to want sb to be happy and successful, even though

your actions may not show it: *Don't be angry with your father—you know he has your best interests at heart.*
in sb's interest(s) to sb's advantage: *Using less water is in the public interest.*
in the interest(s) of sth in order to achieve or protect sth: *In the interest(s) of safety, please fasten your seat belts.*

interest² /ˈɪntrəst/ *verb* [T] to make sb want to learn or hear more about sth or to become involved in sth: *It might interest you to know that I didn't accept the job.* ♦ *The subject of the talk was one that interests me greatly.*
PHR V **interest sb in sth** to persuade sb to buy, have, do sth: *Can I interest you in our new brochure?*

interested /ˈɪntrəstɪd/ *adj* **1** [not before a noun] **interested (in sth/sb); interested in doing sth; interested to do sth** wanting to know or hear more about sth/sb; enjoying or liking sth/sb: *They weren't interested in my news at all!* ♦ *I'm really not interested in going to university.* ♦ *I was interested to hear that you've got a new job. Where is it?* OPP **uninterested**
➲ note at **like**

> **HELP** If you like what you are doing, and want to know or hear more, then you are **interested** in it. The person or thing that makes you feel like this is **interesting.**

2 [only *before* a noun] involved in or affected by sth; in a position to gain from sth: *As an interested party* (= sb who is directly involved), *I was not allowed to vote.* OPP **disinterested**

interesting /ˈɪntrəstɪŋ; -trest-/ *adj* **interesting (to do sth); interesting that ...** enjoyable and entertaining; holding your attention: *an interesting person/book/idea/job* ♦ *It's always interesting to hear about the customs of other societies.* ♦ *It's interesting that Luisa chose Peru for a holiday.* ▶ **interestingly** *adv*

interface /ˈɪntəfeɪs/ *noun* [C] **1** the way a computer program gives information to a user or receives information from a user, in particular the appearance of the screen: *the user interface* **2** a connection or computer program that joins one device or system to another: *the interface between computer and printer* **3 the interface (between A and B)** the point where two people, things, systems, etc. meet and affect each other: *the interface between manufacturing and sales*

interfere /ˌɪntəˈfɪə(r)/ *verb* [I] **1 interfere (in sth)** to get involved in a situation which does not involve you and where you are not wanted: *You shouldn't interfere in your children's lives—let them make their own decisions.* **2 interfere (with sth)** to prevent sth from succeeding or being done or happening as planned: *Every time the telephone rings it interferes with my work.* ♦ *She never lets her private life interfere with her career.* **3 interfere (with sth)** to touch or change sth without permission: *Many people feel that scientists shouldn't interfere with nature.* ▶ **interfering** *adj*

interference /ˌɪntəˈfɪərəns/ *noun* [U] **1 interference (in sth)** the act of getting involved in a situation that does not involve you and where you are not wanted: *I resented my mother's interference in my affairs.* **2** extra noise (because of other signals or bad weather) that prevents you from receiving radio, TV or telephone signals clearly

interim¹ /ˈɪntərɪm/ *adj* [only *before* a noun] not final or lasting; temporary until sb/sth more permanent is found: *an interim arrangement* ♦ *The deputy head teacher took over in **the interim period** until a replacement could be found.*

interim² /ˈɪntərɪm/ *noun*
IDM **in the interim** in the time between two things happening; until a particular event happens

interior /ɪnˈtɪəriə(r)/ *noun* **1** [C, usually sing] the inside part of sth: *I'd love to see the interior of the castle.* ♦ *the earth's interior* OPP **exterior** **2 the interior** [sing] the central part of a country or continent that is a long way from the coast: *an expedition into the interior of Australia* **3 the Interior** [sing] a country's own news and affairs that do not involve other countries: *the Department of the Interior* ▶ **interior** *adj* [only *before* a noun]: *interior walls*

inˌterior deˈsign *noun* [U] the art or job of choosing colours, furniture, carpets, etc. to decorate the inside of a house ▶ **inˌterior deˈsigner** *noun* [C]

interjection /ˌɪntəˈdʒekʃn/ *noun* [C] a word or phrase that is used to express surprise, pain, pleasure, etc. (for example *Oh!*, *Hurray!* or *Wow!*) SYN **exclamation**

interlude /ˈɪntəluːd/ *noun* [C] a period of time between two events or activities: *They finally met again after an interlude of several years.* ♦ *Their stay in Karnak was a pleasant interlude in their busy lives.*
➲ note at **interval**

intermarry /ˌɪntəˈmæri/ *verb* [I] (**intermarrying; intermarries;** *pt, pp* **intermarried**) to marry sb from a different religion, culture, country, etc. ▶ **intermarriage** /ˌɪntəˈmærɪdʒ/ *noun* [U]

intermediary /ˌɪntəˈmiːdiəri/ *noun* [C] (*pl* **intermediaries**) **an intermediary (between A and B)** a person or an organization that helps two people or groups to reach an agreement, by being a means of communication between them

intermediate /ˌɪntəˈmiːdiət/ *adj* **1** in between two things in position, level, etc: *an intermediate step/stage in a process* **2** having more than a basic knowledge of sth but not yet advanced; suitable for sb who is at this level: *an intermediate student/book/level*

interminable /ɪnˈtɜːmɪnəbl/ *adj* lasting for a very long time and therefore boring or annoying: *an interminable delay/speech* ♦ *The wait seemed interminable.* SYN **endless** ▶ **interminably** /-əbli/ *adv*

intermission /ˌɪntəˈmɪʃn/ *noun* [C] (*especially AmE*) a short period of time separating the parts of a film, play, etc. ➲ note at **interval**

intermittent /ˌɪntəˈmɪtənt/ *adj* stopping for a short time and then starting again several times:

There will be intermittent showers. ▶ **intermittently** *adv*

intern /ɪnˈtɜːn/ *verb* [T, usually passive] (*formal*) **intern sb (in sth)** to keep sb in prison for political reasons, especially during a war ▶ **internment** *noun* [U]

⚷ **internal** /ɪnˈtɜːnl/ *adj* **1** [only *before* a noun] of or on the inside (of a place, person or object): *internal injuries/organs* **2** happening or existing inside a particular organization: *an internal exam* (= one arranged and marked inside a particular school or college) ◆ *an internal police inquiry* **3** (used especially about political or economic affairs) inside a country: *a country's internal affairs/trade/markets* ◆ *an internal flight* **OPP** for all meanings **external** ▶ **internally** /-nəli/ *adv*: *This medicine is not to be taken internally* (= not swallowed). **OPP** **externally**

⚷ **international** /ˌɪntəˈnæʃnəl/ *adj* involving two or more countries: *an international agreement/flight/football match* ◆ *international trade/law/sport* ➲ look at **local**, **national**, **regional** ▶ **internationally** /-ʃənəli/ *adv*

⚷ **Internet** /ˈɪntənet/ *usually* **the Internet** (also *informal* **the Net**) *noun* [sing] the international system of computers that makes it possible for you to see information from all around the world on your computer and to send information to other computers: *I read about it* ***on the Internet.*** ◆ *Do you have Internet access?* ➲ look at **intranet**, **ISP**, **Wi-Fi™**

TOPIC

The Internet

If you want to **use the Internet**, you need a computer. If you don't have **Internet access** at home, you can go to an **Internet cafe** to **surf the Net**. In order to visit a **website**, you need to type in a **URL/web address** (for example, www.oup.com/elt, which we say as 'double-U double-U double-U dot o-u-p dot com slash e-l-t'). If you want to find information about something **on the Internet**, but you don't know where to **look it up**, you can **do a search** using a **search engine**. You can buy things **online**, join a discussion in a **chat room**, **post** questions on a **message board**, or **download** music (but be careful you don't get a **virus**!)

internship /ˈɪntɜːnʃɪp/ *noun* [C] (*AmE*) **1** a period of time during which sb, especially a student, gets practical experience in a job, for example during the summer holiday: *a 6-week internship at a television station* ➲ look at **work experience** **2** a job that an advanced student of medicine, whose training is nearly finished, does in a hospital to get further practical experience

⚷ **interpret** /ɪnˈtɜːprɪt/ *verb* **1** [T] **interpret sth (as sth)** to explain or understand the meaning of sth: *Your silence could be interpreted as rudeness.* ◆ *How would you interpret this part of the poem?* **OPP** **misinterpret** **2** [I] **interpret (for sb)** to translate what sb is saying into another language as you hear it: *He can't speak English so he'll need somebody to interpret for him.*

⚷ **interpretation** /ɪnˌtɜːprɪˈteɪʃn/ *noun* [C,U] **1** an explanation or understanding of sth: *What's your interpretation of these statistics?* ◆ *What he meant by that remark is* ***open to interpretation*** (= it can be explained in different ways). **2** the way an actor or musician chooses to perform or understand a character or piece of music: *a modern interpretation of 'Hamlet'*

interpreter /ɪnˈtɜːprɪtə(r)/ *noun* [C] a person whose job is to translate what sb is saying immediately into another language: *The President spoke to the crowd through an interpreter.* ➲ look at **translator**

interrelate /ˌɪntərɪˈleɪt/ *verb* [I,T] [usually passive] (*formal*) (used about two or more things) to connect or be connected very closely so that each has an effect on the other ▶ **interrelated** *adj*

interrogate /ɪnˈterəɡeɪt/ *verb* [T] **interrogate sb (about sth)** to ask sb a lot of questions over a long period of time, especially in an aggressive way: *The prisoner was interrogated for six hours.* ▶ **interrogator** /ɪnˈterəɡeɪtə(r)/ *noun* [C] ▶ **interrogation** /ɪnˌterəˈɡeɪʃn/ *noun* [C,U]: *The prisoner broke down* ***under interrogation*** *and confessed.*

interrogative[1] /ˌɪntəˈrɒɡətɪv/ *adj* **1** (*formal*) asking a question; having the form of a question: *an interrogative tone/gesture/remark* **2** (in grammar) used in questions: *an interrogative sentence/pronoun/determiner/adverb*

interrogative[2] /ˌɪntəˈrɒɡətɪv/ *noun* [C] a question word: *'Who', 'what' and 'where' are interrogatives.*

⚷ **interrupt** /ˌɪntəˈrʌpt/ *verb* **1** [I,T] **interrupt (sb/sth) (with sth)** to say or do sth that makes sb stop what they are saying or doing: *He kept interrupting (me) with silly questions.* **2** [T] to stop the progress of sth for a short time: *The programme was interrupted by an important news flash.*

⚷ **interruption** /ˌɪntəˈrʌpʃn/ *noun* [U,C] the act of interrupting sb/sth; the thing that interrupts sb/sth: *I need to work for a few hours without interruption.* ◆ *I've had so many interruptions this morning that I've done nothing!*

intersect /ˌɪntəˈsekt/ *verb* [I,T] (used about roads, lines, etc.) to meet or cross each other: *The lines intersect at right angles.*

intersection /ˌɪntəˈsekʃn/ *noun* [C] the place where two or more roads, lines, etc. meet or cross each other

intersperse /ˌɪntəˈspɜːs/ *verb* [T, usually passive] to put things at various points in sth: *His speech was interspersed with jokes.*

intertwine /ˌɪntəˈtwaɪn/ *verb* [I,T] if two things **intertwine** or if you **intertwine** them, they become very closely connected and difficult to separate: *His interests in business and politics were closely intertwined.*

⚷ **interval** /ˈɪntəvl/ *noun* [C] **1** a period of time between two events: *There was a long interval*

I

between sending the letter and getting a reply. **2** a short break separating the different parts of a play, film, concert, etc: *There will be two 15-minute intervals, when the bar will be open.* **3** [usually pl] a short period during which sth different happens from what is happening for the rest of the time: *There'll be a few* ***sunny intervals*** *between the showers today.*
IDM **at intervals** with time or spaces between: *I visit my grandparents* ***at regular intervals.*** ♦ *Plant the trees at two-metre intervals.*

OTHER WORDS FOR

interval

Some words that have a similar meaning to interval are **intermission, break, recess, interlude** and **pause**. In British English we use **interval** for a break in a performance. The US word is **intermission.** A **break** is especially used in connection with periods of work or study, for example a **lunch/tea break** in an office, factory or school: *The children play outside in the breaks at school.* ♦ *You've worked so hard you've earned a break.* In American English a break at school is called **(a) recess**. In British English **recess** is a longer period of time when work or business stops, especially in Parliament or the law courts: *Parliament is in recess.* ♦ *the summer recess.* An **interlude** is a short period of time that passes between two events, during which something different happens: *a peaceful interlude in the fighting*, and a **pause** is a short temporary stop in action or speech: *After a moment's pause, she answered.*

intervene /ˌɪntəˈviːn/ *verb* [I] **1** intervene (in sth) to become involved in a situation in order to improve it: *She would have died if the neighbours hadn't intervened.* ♦ *to intervene in a dispute* **2** to interrupt sb who is speaking in order to say sth **3** (used about events, etc.) to happen in a way that delays sth or stops it from happening: *If no further problems intervene, we should be able to finish in time.* ▸ **intervention** /ˌɪntəˈvenʃn/ *noun* [U,C] intervention (in sth): *military intervention in the crisis*

intervening /ˌɪntəˈviːnɪŋ/ *adj* [only *before* a noun] coming or existing between two events, dates, objects, etc: *the intervening years/days/months*

interview¹ /ˈɪntəvjuː/ *noun* [C] **1** an interview (for sth) a meeting at which sb is asked questions to find out if they are suitable for a job, course of study, etc: *to attend an interview* ➲ note at **job** **2** an interview (with sb) a meeting at which a journalist asks sb questions in order to find out their opinion, etc: *There was an interview with the Prime Minister on TV last night.* ♦ *The actress refused to* ***give an interview*** (= answer questions).

interview² /ˈɪntəvjuː/ *verb* [T] **1** interview sb (for sth) to ask sb questions to find out if they are suitable for a job, course of study, etc: *How many applicants did you interview for the job?* **2** interview sb (about sth) to ask sb questions about their opinions, private life, etc. especially on the radio or TV or for a newspaper, magazine, etc: *Next week, I will be interviewing Spielberg about his latest movie.* **3** interview sb (about sth) to ask sb questions at a private meeting: *The police are waiting to interview the injured girl.*

interviewee /ˌɪntəvjuːˈiː/ *noun* [C] a person who is questioned in an interview

interviewer /ˈɪntəvjuːə(r)/ *noun* [C] a person who asks the questions in an interview

intestine /ɪnˈtestɪn/ *noun* [C, usually pl] the tube in your body that carries food away from your stomach to the place where it leaves your body ➲ A less formal word is **gut**. ➲ picture at **body** ▸ **intestinal** /ɪnˈtestɪnl; ˌɪnteˈstaɪnl/ *adj*

intimacy /ˈɪntɪməsi/ *noun* [U] the state of having a close personal relationship with sb: *Their intimacy grew over the years.*

intimate /ˈɪntɪmət/ *adj* **1** (used about people) having a very close relationship: *They're intimate friends.* **2** very private and personal: *They told each other their most intimate secrets.* **3** (used about a place, an atmosphere, etc.) quiet and friendly: *I know an intimate little restaurant we could go to.* **4** very detailed: *He's lived here all his life and has an* ***intimate knowledge*** *of the area.* ▸ **intimately** *adv*

intimidate /ɪnˈtɪmɪdeɪt/ *verb* [T] intimidate sb (into sth/doing sth) to frighten or threaten sb, often in order to make them do sth: *She refused to be intimidated by their threats.* ▸ **intimidating** *adj*: *The teacher had rather an intimidating manner.* ▸ **intimidation** /ɪnˌtɪmɪˈdeɪʃn/ *noun* [U]: *The rebel troops controlled the area by intimidation.*

into /ˈɪntə; *before vowels* ˈɪntu; *strong form* ˈɪntuː/ *prep* **1** moving to a position inside or in sth: *Come into the house.* ♦ *I'm going into town.* OPP **out of** **2** in the direction of sth: *Please speak into the microphone.* ♦ *At this point we were driving into the sun and had to shade our eyes.* **3** to a point at which you hit sth: *I backed the car into a wall.* ♦ *She walked into a glass door.* **4** showing a change from one thing to another: *We're turning the spare room into a study.* ♦ *She changed into her jeans.* ♦ *Translate the passage into German.* **5** concerning or involving sth: *an inquiry into safety procedures* **6** used when you are talking about dividing numbers: *7 into 28 goes 4 times.*
IDM **be into sth** (*spoken, informal*) to be very interested in sth, for example as a hobby: *I'm really into canoeing.* ➲ note at **like**

intolerable /ɪnˈtɒlərəbl/ *adj* too bad, unpleasant or difficult to bear or accept: *The living conditions were intolerable.* ♦ *intolerable pain* SYN **unbearable** OPP **tolerable** ➲ *verb* **tolerate** ▸ **intolerably** /-əbli/ *adv*

intolerant /ɪnˈtɒlərənt/ *adj* intolerant (of sb/sth) not able to accept behaviour or opinions that are different from your own; finding sb/sth too unpleasant to bear: *She's very intolerant of young children.* OPP **tolerant** ▸ **intolerance** *noun* [U] OPP **tolerance** ▸ **intolerantly** *adv*

intonation /ˌɪntəˈneɪʃn/ *noun* [C,U] the rise and fall of your voice while you are speaking SYN **inflection**

intoxicated /ɪnˈtɒksɪkeɪtɪd/ *adj (formal)* **1** having had too much alcohol to drink; drunk **2** very excited and happy: *She was intoxicated by her success.* ▶ **intoxication** /ɪnˌtɒksɪˈkeɪʃn/ *noun* [U]

intranet /ˈɪntrənet/ *noun* [C] a system of computers inside an organization that makes it possible for people who work there to look at the same information and to send information to each other ➲ look at **the Internet**

intransitive /ɪnˈtrænsətɪv/ *adj* (used about a verb) used without an object. **Intransitive** verbs are marked '[I]' in this dictionary. OPP **transitive** ℹ For more information about intransitive verbs, look at the **Reference Section** at the back of this dictionary. ▶ **intransitively** *adv*: *The verb is being used intransitively.*

intrepid /ɪnˈtrepɪd/ *adj (formal)* without any fear of danger: *an intrepid climber*

intricacy /ˈɪntrɪkəsi/ *noun* **1** intricacies [pl] the intricacies of sth the complicated parts or details of sth: *It's difficult to understand all the intricacies of the situation.* **2** [U] the quality of having complicated parts, details or patterns

intricate /ˈɪntrɪkət/ *adj* having many small parts or details put together in a complicated way: *an intricate pattern* ◆ *The story has an intricate plot.* ▶ **intricately** *adv*

intrigue[1] /ɪnˈtriːɡ/ *verb* [T] to make sb very interested and wanting to know more: *I was intrigued by the way he seemed to know all about us already.* ▶ **intriguing** *adj*: *an intriguing story*

intrigue[2] /ˈɪntriːɡ/ *noun* [C,U] secret plans to do sth, especially sth bad: *The film is about political intrigues against the government.* ◆ *His new novel is full of intrigue and suspense.*

intrinsic /ɪnˈtrɪnsɪk; -zɪk/ *adj* [only *before* a noun] belonging to sth as part of its nature; basic: *The object is of no intrinsic value* (= the material it is made of is not worth anything). ▶ **intrinsically** /-kli/ *adv*

⚷ **introduce** /ˌɪntrəˈdjuːs/ *verb* [T]
➤PEOPLE **1** introduce sb (to sb) to tell two or more people who have not met before what each other's names are: *'Who's that girl over there?' 'Come with me and I'll introduce you to her.'* **2** introduce yourself (to sb) to tell sb you have met for the first time what your name is: *He came over and introduced himself to me.*
➤RADIO/TV PROGRAMME **3** to be the first or main speaker on a radio or TV programme telling the audience who is going to speak, perform, etc: *May I introduce my first guest on the show tonight ...*
➤NEW EXPERIENCE **4** introduce sb to sth to make sb begin to learn about sth or do sth for the first time: *This page will introduce you to the basic aims of our society.*
➤NEW PRODUCT/LAW **5** introduce sth (in/into sth) to bring in sth new, use sth, or take sth to a place for the first time: *The new law was introduced in 2010.* ◆ *The company is introducing a new range of cars this summer.* ◆ *a newly-introduced ban on mobile phones in schools* ◆ *Goats were first introduced to the island in the 17th century.*

TOPIC

Introducing people

In Britain there are a number of different ways of introducing one person to another, depending on the occasion. In a formal introduction, we use a person's title followed by the surname. In an informal situation, or when introducing children, we use first names. In both formal and informal introductions we say **this is,** when referring to the people we are introducing, NOT 'he/she is' and NOT 'here is' *(formal) 'May I introduce you. Dr Waters, **this is** Mr Jones. Mr Jones, Dr Waters.'* ◆ *(informal) 'Mrs Smith, **this is** my daughter, Jane.'* ◆ *(informal) 'John, meet Mary.'* An informal response to an introduction is **Hello** or **Nice to meet you.** A formal response is **How do you do?** The other person also replies: 'How do you do?' When people are introduced, they often **shake hands.**

⚷ **introduction** /ˌɪntrəˈdʌkʃn/ *noun*
➤STH NEW **1** [U] introduction of sth (into sth) the act of bringing in sth new; using sth or taking sth to a place for the first time: *the introduction of new teaching methods*
➤PEOPLE **2** [C, usually pl] the act of telling two or more people each other's names for the first time: *I think I'll get my father to **make/do the introductions**—he's better at remembering names!*
➤FIRST EXPERIENCE **3** [sing] an introduction to sth the first experience of sth: *My first job—in a factory—was not a pleasant introduction to work.*
➤OF BOOK/SPEECH **4** [C] the first part of a book, a piece of written work or a talk which gives a general idea of what is going to follow: *a brief introduction*
➤TO SUBJECT **5** [C] an introduction (to sth) a book for people who are beginning to study a subject: *'An Introduction to English Grammar'*

introductory /ˌɪntrəˈdʌktəri/ *adj* **1** happening or said at the beginning in order to give a general idea of what will follow: *an introductory speech/chapter/remark* SYN **opening** **2** intended as an introduction to a subject or an activity: *introductory courses* **3** offered for a short time only, when a product is first on sale: *an **introductory price/offer***

introvert /ˈɪntrəvɜːt/ *noun* [C] a quiet, shy person who prefers to be alone than with other people OPP **extrovert** ▶ **introverted** *adj*

intrude /ɪnˈtruːd/ *verb* [I] intrude (on/upon sb/sth) to enter a place or situation without permission or when you are not wanted: *I'm sorry to intrude on your Sunday lunch but ...*

intruder /ɪnˈtruːdə(r)/ *noun* [C] a person who enters a place without permission and often secretly

intrusion /ɪnˈtruːʒn/ *noun* [C,U] (an) intrusion (on/upon/into sth) something that disturbs you or your life when you want to be private: *This was another example of press intrusion into the affairs of the royals.* ▶ **intrusive** /ɪnˈtruːsɪv/ *adj*

intuition /ˌɪntjuˈɪʃn/ *noun* [C,U] the feeling or understanding that makes you believe or know sth is true without being able to explain why: *She knew, by intuition, about his illness although he never mentioned it.* ▶ **intuitive** /ɪnˈtjuːɪtɪv/ *adj* ▶ **intuitively** *adv*: *Intuitively, she knew that he was lying.*

Inuit /ˈɪnjuɪt/ *noun* [pl] a race of people from northern Canada and parts of Greenland and Alaska ▶ **Inuit** *adj* ➲ look at **Eskimo**

inundate /ˈɪnʌndeɪt/ *verb* [T, usually passive] **1** inundate sb (with sth) to give or send sb so many things that they cannot deal with them all: *We were inundated with applications for the job.* SYN **swamp** **2** (*formal*) to cover an area of land with water: *After the heavy rains the fields were inundated.* ➲ A less formal word is **flood**.

invade /ɪnˈveɪd/ *verb* **1** [I,T] to enter a country with an army in order to attack and take control of it: *When did the Romans invade Britain?* ➲ note at **war** **2** [T] to enter in large numbers, often where sb/sth is not wanted: *The whole area has been invaded by tourists.* ➲ *noun* **invasion** ▶ **invader** *noun* [C]

invalid[1] /ɪnˈvælɪd/ *adj* **1** not legally or officially acceptable: *I'm afraid your passport is invalid.* **2** not correct according to reason; not based on all the facts: *an invalid argument* **3** (used about an instruction, etc.) of a type that the computer cannot recognize: *an invalid command* OPP for all meanings **valid**

invalid[2] /ˈɪnvəlɪd/ *noun* [C] a person who has been very ill for a long time and needs other people to take care of them

invalidate /ɪnˈvælɪdeɪt/ *verb* [T] (*formal*) **1** to prove that an idea, a story, an argument, etc. is wrong: *This new piece of evidence invalidates his version of events.* **2** to make a document, contract, election, etc. no longer legally or officially valid or acceptable OPP for both meanings **validate** ▶ **invalidation** /ɪnˌvælɪˈdeɪʃn/ *noun* [U]

invaluable /ɪnˈvæljuəbl/ *adj* invaluable (to/for sb/sth) extremely useful: *invaluable help/information/support*

HELP Be careful. **Invaluable** is not the opposite of valuable. The opposite of valuable is **valueless** or **worthless**.

invariable /ɪnˈveəriəbl/ *adj* not changing

invariably /ɪnˈveəriəbli/ *adv* always: *She invariably arrives late.*

invasion /ɪnˈveɪʒn/ *noun* [C,U] **1** the act of entering another country with your army in order to take control of it: *the threat of invasion* **2** the act of entering a place where you are not wanted and disturbing sb: *Such questions are an* ***invasion of privacy****.* ➲ *verb* **invade**

invent /ɪnˈvent/ *verb* [T] **1** to think of or make sth for the first time: *When was the camera invented?* **2** to say or describe sth that is not true: *I realized that he had invented the whole story.* ▶ **inventor** *noun* [C]

invention /ɪnˈvenʃn/ *noun* **1** [C] a thing that has been made or designed by sb for the first time: *The electric car is a useful invention.* **2** [U] the action or process of making or designing sth for the first time: *Books had to be written by hand before the invention of printing.* **3** [C,U] telling a story or giving an excuse that is not true: *It was obvious that his story about being robbed was (an) invention.*

inventive /ɪnˈventɪv/ *adj* having clever and original ideas ▶ **inventiveness** *noun* [U]

inventory /ˈɪnvəntri/ *noun* [C] (*pl* **inventories**) a detailed list, for example of all the furniture in a house, goods in a shop, etc: *The landlord is coming to* ***make an inventory*** *of the contents of the flat.*

invert /ɪnˈvɜːt/ *verb* [T] (*formal*) to put sth in the opposite order or position to the way it usually is: *What you see in a mirror is an inverted image of yourself.*

inˌverted ˈcommas (*BrE*) = **quotation marks**: *to put something* ***in inverted commas***

invest /ɪnˈvest/ *verb* [I,T] invest (sth) (in sth) **1** to put money into a bank, business, property, etc. in the hope that you will make a profit: *Many firms have invested heavily in this project.* ◆ *I've invested all my money in the company.* ➲ note at **money** **2** to spend money, time or energy on sth that you think is good or useful: *I'm thinking of investing in a new guitar.* ◆ *You have to invest a lot of time if you really want to learn a language well.* ▶ **investor** *noun* [C]

investigate /ɪnˈvestɪɡeɪt/ *verb* [I,T] to try to find out all the facts about sth: *A murder was reported and the police were sent to investigate.* ◆ *A group of experts are investigating the cause of the crash.* ▶ **investigator** *noun* [C]

investigation /ɪnˌvestɪˈɡeɪʃn/ *noun* [C,U] (an) investigation (into sth) an official examination of the facts about a subject, situation, problem, etc: *The airlines are going to* ***carry out an investigation*** *into security procedures at airports.* ◆ *The matter is still* ***under investigation*** *by the police.*

investigative /ɪnˈvestɪɡətɪv/ *adj* trying to find out all the facts about sb/sth: *investigative journalism*

investment /ɪnˈvestmənt/ *noun* **1** [U,C] (an) investment (in sth) the act of putting money in a bank, business, property, etc.; the amount of money that you put in: *investment in local industry* ◆ *The company will have to* ***make an*** *enormous* ***investment*** *to update their computer systems.* **2** [C] a thing that is worth buying: *This coat has been a good investment—I've worn it for three years.*

invigilate /ɪnˈvɪdʒɪleɪt/ *verb* [I,T] (*BrE*) to watch the people taking an exam to make sure that nobody is cheating ▶ **invigilator** *noun* [C]

invigorate /ɪnˈvɪɡəreɪt/ *verb* [T, often passive] to make sb feel healthy, fresh and full of energy: *I felt invigorated after my run.* ▶ **invigorating** *adj*

invincible /ɪnˈvɪnsəbl/ *adj* too strong or powerful to be defeated

invisible /ɪnˈvɪzəbl/ *adj* invisible (to sb/sth) that cannot be seen: *Bacteria are invisible to the naked* eye. OPP visible ▶ **invisibility** /ɪnˌvɪzəˈbɪləti/ *noun* [U] ▶ **invisibly** /ɪnˈvɪzəbli/ *adv*

invitation /ˌɪnvɪˈteɪʃn/ *noun* **1** [C] **an invitation to sb/sth (to sth/to do sth)** a written or spoken request to go somewhere or do sth: *Did you get an invitation to the conference?* ◆ *a wedding invitation*

> **MORE** You may **accept** an invitation, or you may **turn it down** or **decline** it.

2 [U] the act of inviting sb or being invited: *Entry is by invitation only.* ◆ *a letter of invitation*

invite /ɪnˈvaɪt/ *verb* [T] **1 invite sb (to/for sth)** to ask sb to come somewhere or to do sth: *We invited all the family to the wedding.* ◆ *Successful applicants will be invited for interview next week.* **2** to make sth unpleasant likely to happen: *You're inviting trouble if you carry so much money around.*

PHR V **invite sb back 1** to ask sb to return with you to your home: *Shall we invite the others back for coffee after the meeting?* **2** to ask sb to come to your home a second time, or after you have been a guest at their home

invite sb in to ask sb to come into your home

invite sb out to ask sb to go out somewhere with you: *We've been invited out to the theatre by my aunt and uncle.*

invite sb over/round (*informal*) to ask sb to come to your home: *I've invited Marco and his family round for lunch on Sunday.*

> **MORE** Note that **ask** can be used instead of invite in all senses.

inviting /ɪnˈvaɪtɪŋ/ *adj* attractive and pleasant: *The smell of cooking was very inviting.*

invoice /ˈɪnvɔɪs/ *noun* [C] an official paper that lists goods or services that you have received and says how much you have to pay for them

involuntary /ɪnˈvɒləntri/ *adj* done without wanting or meaning to: *She gave an involuntary gasp of pain as the doctor inserted the needle.* OPP **voluntary, deliberate** ▶ **involuntarily** /ɪnˈvɒləntrəli/ *adv*

involve /ɪnˈvɒlv/ *verb* [T] **1** [not used in the continuous tenses] to make sth necessary: *The job involves a lot of travelling.* **2** [not used in the continuous tenses] if a situation, an event or an activity involves sb, they take part in it: *The story involves a woman who cycled to India with her child.* ◆ *More than 100 people were involved in the project.* **3 involve sb/sth in (doing) sth** to cause sb/sth to take part in or be concerned with sth: *Please don't involve me in your family arguments.*

involved /ɪnˈvɒlvd/ *adj* **1** [not before a noun] **involved (in sth)** closely connected with sth; taking an active part in sth: *I'm very involved in local politics.* **2** [not before a noun] **involved (with sb)** having a sexual relationship with sb: *She is involved with an older man.* **3** difficult to understand; complicated: *The book has a very involved plot.*

involvement /ɪnˈvɒlvmənt/ *noun* [C,U] the act of taking part in sth: *They deny any involvement in the robbery.*

inward /ˈɪnwəd/ *adv, adj* **1** (also **inwards**) towards the inside or centre: *Stand in a circle facing inwards.* **2** [only *before* a noun] inside your mind, not shown to other people: *my inward feelings* OPP for both meanings **outward**

inwardly /ˈɪnwədli/ *adv* in your mind; secretly: *He was inwardly relieved that they could not come to the party.*

iodine /ˈaɪədiːn/ *noun* [U] (*symbol* I) a substance that is found in sea water. A liquid containing **iodine** is sometimes used to clean cuts in your skin.

IOU /ˌaɪ əʊ ˈjuː/ *abbr* **I owe you**; a piece of paper that you sign showing that you owe sb some money

IPA /ˌaɪ piː ˈeɪ/ *abbr* the **International Phonetic Alphabet**; an alphabet that is used to show the pronunciation of words in any language

iPod™ /ˈaɪpɒd/ *noun* [C] a type of **MP3 player** (= a small piece of equipment that can store information taken from the Internet and that you carry with you): *Gary listens to his iPod when he's training.* ➲ note at **podcast**

> **TOPIC**
>
> **iPods**
>
> You can listen to music on your **iPod™** wherever you are, using **headphones**. You can **download** music from the Internet or copy it from a CD, **flash drive**, etc. to your computer's **hard drive**, and then **load tracks** (= put songs) **onto** your iPod™. There are also **podcasts** (= recordings of radio broadcasts or videos, taken from the Internet) that you can load onto your iPod™. At home you can plug it into a **docking station** (= a device with speakers) to hear the music aloud.

IQ /ˌaɪ ˈkjuː/ *abbr* **intelligence quotient**; a measure of how intelligent sb is: *have a high/low IQ* ◆ *an IQ of 120*

IRA /ˌaɪ ɑːr ˈeɪ/ *abbr* the **Irish Republican Army**; an illegal organization which has fought for Northern Ireland to be united with the Republic of Ireland

irate /aɪˈreɪt/ *adj* (*formal*) very angry

iris /ˈaɪrɪs/ *noun* [C] the coloured part of your eye ➲ look at **pupil**

Irish /ˈaɪrɪʃ/ *adj* from Ireland ℹ For more information, look at the section on geographical names at the back of this dictionary.

iron¹ /ˈaɪən/ *noun* **1** [U] (*symbol* Fe) a hard strong metal that is used for making steel and is found in small quantities in food and in blood: *an iron bar* ◆ *iron ore* ◆ *The doctor gave me iron tablets.* ◆ (*figurative*) *The general has an iron* (= very strong) *will.* ➲ picture at **corrugated** **2** [C] an electrical instrument with a flat bottom that is heated and used to smooth clothes after you have washed and dried them: *a steam iron*

iron² /ˈaɪən/ *verb* [I,T] to use an iron to make clothes, etc. smooth: *Could you iron this dress for me?*

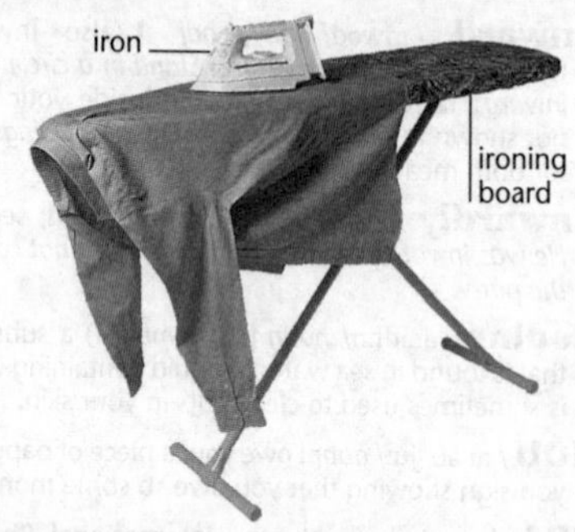

HELP Do the ironing is often used instead of iron: *I usually do the ironing on Sunday.*

PHR V **iron sth out** to get rid of any problems or difficulties that are affecting sth

ironic /aɪˈrɒnɪk/ (also ironical /aɪˈrɒnɪkl/) *adj* **1** meaning the opposite of what you say: *Jeff sometimes offends people with his ironic sense of humour.* ➲ look at **sarcastic** **2** (used about a situation) strange or amusing because it is unusual or unexpected: *It is ironic that the busiest people are often the most willing to help.* ▸ **ironically** /-kli/ *adv*

ironing /ˈaɪənɪŋ/ *noun* [U] clothes, etc. that you have just ironed or that you need to iron: *a large pile of ironing*

ˈ**ironing board** *noun* [C] a special narrow table covered with cloth that you iron clothes on ➲ picture at **iron**

irony /ˈaɪrəni/ *noun* (*pl* **ironies**) **1** [C,U] an unusual or unexpected part of a situation, etc. that seems strange or amusing: *The irony was that when he finally got the job, he discovered that he didn't like it.* **2** [U] a way of speaking that shows you are joking or that you mean the opposite of what you say: *'The English are such good cooks,' he said with heavy irony.*

irrational /ɪˈræʃənl/ *adj* not based on reason or clear thought: *an irrational fear of spiders* ▸ **irrationality** /ɪˌræʃəˈnæləti/ *noun* [U] ▸ **irrationally** /ɪˈræʃənəli/ *adv*

irreconcilable /ɪˌrekənˈsaɪləbl/ *adj* (*formal*) (used about people or their ideas and beliefs) so different that they cannot be made to agree ▸ **irreconcilably** /-əbli/ *adv*

irregular /ɪˈregjələ(r)/ *adj* **1** not having an even, smooth shape or pattern: *an irregular outline* **OPP** **regular** **2** happening at times that you cannot predict: *His visits became more and more irregular.* **OPP** **regular** **3** not allowed according to the rules or social customs: *It is highly irregular for a doctor to give information about patients without their permission.* **4** not following the usual rules of grammar: *'Caught' is an irregular past tense form.* **OPP** **regular** ▸ **irregularity** /ɪˌregjəˈlærəti/ *noun* [C,U] (*pl* irregularities) ▸ **irregularly** *adv*

irrelevant /ɪˈreləvənt/ *adj* not connected with sth or important to it: *That evidence is irrelevant to the case.* **OPP** **relevant** ▸ **irrelevance** (also irrelevancy; *pl* irrelevancies) *noun* [U,C] ▸ **irrelevantly** *adv*

irreparable /ɪˈrepərəbl/ *adj* that cannot be repaired: *Irreparable damage has been done to the ancient forests of Eastern Europe.* ▸ **irreparably** /-əbli/ *adv*

irreplaceable /ˌɪrɪˈpleɪsəbl/ *adj* (used about sth very valuable or special) that cannot be replaced **OPP** **replaceable**

irrepressible /ˌɪrɪˈpresəbl/ *adj* full of life and energy: *young people full of irrepressible good humour* ▸ **irrepressibly** /-əbli/ *adv*

irresistible /ˌɪrɪˈzɪstəbl/ *adj* **1** so strong that it cannot be stopped or prevented: *an irresistible urge to laugh* **2** irresistible (to sb) very attractive: *He seems to think he's irresistible to women.* ➲ verb **resist** ▸ **irresistibly** /-əbli/ *adv*

irrespective of /ˌɪrɪˈspektɪv əv/ *prep* not affected by: *Anybody can take part in the competition, irrespective of age.*

irresponsible /ˌɪrɪˈspɒnsəbl/ *adj* not thinking about the effect your actions will have; not sensible: *It is irresponsible to let small children go out alone.* **OPP** **responsible** ▸ **irresponsibility** /ˌɪrɪˌspɒnsəˈbɪləti/ *noun* [U] ▸ **irresponsibly** /ˌɪrɪˈspɒnsəbli/ *adv*

irreverent /ɪˈrevərənt/ *adj* not feeling or showing respect: *This comedy takes an irreverent look at the world of politics.* ▸ **irreverence** *noun* [U] ▸ **irreverently** *adv*

irreversible /ˌɪrɪˈvɜːsəbl/ *adj* that cannot be stopped or changed: *an irreversible decision* ♦ *The disease can do irreversible damage to the body.* ▸ **irreversibly** /-əbli/ *adv*

irrigate /ˈɪrɪgeɪt/ *verb* [T] to supply water to an area of land so that crops will grow: *irrigated land/crops* ▸ **irrigation** /ˌɪrɪˈgeɪʃn/ *noun* [U]: *irrigation channels*

irritable /ˈɪrɪtəbl/ *adj* becoming angry easily: *to be/feel/get irritable* **SYN** **bad-tempered** ▸ **irritability** /ˌɪrɪtəˈbɪləti/ *noun* [U] ▸ **irritably** /ˈɪrɪtəbli/ *adv*

irritate /ˈɪrɪteɪt/ *verb* [T] **1** to make sb angry: *It really irritates me the way he keeps repeating himself.* **SYN** **annoy** **2** to cause a part of the body to be painful or sore: *I don't use soap because it irritates my skin.* ▸ **irritating** *adj*: *I found her extremely irritating* ▸ **irritation** /ˌɪrɪˈteɪʃn/ *noun* [C,U]

irritated /ˈɪrɪteɪtɪd/ *adj* irritated (at/by/with sth) annoyed or angry: *She was getting more and more irritated at his comments.*

is /ɪz/ ➲ **be**

-ish [in compounds] **1** from the country mentioned: *Turkish* ♦ *Irish* **2** having the nature of; like: *childish* **3** fairly; approximately: *reddish* ♦ *thirtyish*

Islam /ˈɪzlɑːm; ɪzˈlɑːm/ *noun* [U] the religion of Muslim people. Islam teaches that there is only one God and that Muhammad is His Prophet. ▶ **Islamic** /ɪzˈlæmɪk/ *adj*: *Islamic law*

🔑 **island** /ˈaɪlənd/ *noun* [C] **1** a piece of land that is surrounded by water: *the islands of the Caribbean* ◆ *the Greek islands* ◆ *life on a small island* ➲ picture on **page P10** **2** (*BrE*) = **traffic island**

islander /ˈaɪləndə(r)/ *noun* [C] a person who lives on a small island

isle /aɪl/ *noun* [C] an island: *the Isle of Wight* ◆ *the British Isles*

> **HELP** Isle is most commonly used in names.

isn't /ˈɪznt/ *short for* **is not**

isolate /ˈaɪsəleɪt/ *verb* [T] isolate sb/sth (from sb/sth) to put or keep sb/sth separate from other people or things: *Some farms were isolated by the heavy snowfalls.* ◆ *We need to isolate all the animals with the disease so that the others don't catch it.*

isolated /ˈaɪsəleɪtɪd/ *adj* **1** isolated (from sb/sth) alone or apart from other people or things: *an isolated village deep in the countryside* ◆ *I was kept isolated from the other patients.* **2** not connected with others; happening once: *an isolated case of food poisoning*

isolation /ˌaɪsəˈleɪʃn/ *noun* [U] isolation (from sb/sth) the state of being separate and alone; the act of separating sb/sth: *He lived* ***in*** *complete* ***isolation*** *from the outside world.* ◆ ***In isolation*** *each problem does not seem bad, but together they are quite worrying.* ➲ look at **loneliness, solitude**

ISP /ˌaɪ es ˈpiː/ *abbr* **Internet Service Provider**; a company that provides you with an Internet connection and services such as email, etc.

🔑 **issue**[1] /ˈɪʃuː; ˈɪsjuː/ *noun* **1** [C] a problem or subject for discussion: *I want to* ***raise the issue*** *of overtime pay at the meeting.* ◆ *The government cannot avoid the issue of homelessness any longer.* ◆ *If you* ***have any issues with*** *the new timetable, ring our helpline.* **2** [C] one in a series of things that are published or produced: *Do you have last week's issue of this magazine?* **3** [U] the act of publishing or giving sth to people: *the issue of blankets to the refugees*
IDM **make an issue (out) of sth** to give too much importance to a small problem: *OK, we disagree on this but let's not make an issue of it.*

🔑 **issue**[2] /ˈɪʃuː; ˈɪsjuː/ *verb* **1** [T] to give or say sth to sb officially: *The new employees were issued with uniforms.* ◆ *to issue a visa* ◆ *The police will issue a statement later today.* **2** [T] to produce sth such as a magazine or article: *We issue a monthly newsletter for students.*
PHR V **issue from sth** (*formal*) to come or go out: *An angry voice issued from the loudspeaker.*

IT /ˌaɪ ˈtiː/ *abbr* = **information technology**

🔑 **it** /ɪt/ *pron* **1** [used as the subject or object of a verb, or after a preposition] the animal or thing mentioned earlier: *Look at that car. It's going much too fast.* ◆ *The children went up to the dog and patted it.*

> **HELP** It can also refer to a baby whose sex you do not know: *Is it a boy or a girl?*

2 used for identifying a person: *It's your Mum on the phone.* ◆ *'Who's that?' 'It's the postman.'* ◆ *It's me!* ◆ *It's him!* **3** used in the position of the subject or object of a verb when the real subject or object is at the end of the sentence: *It's hard for them to talk about their problems.* ◆ *I think it doesn't really matter what time we arrive.* **4** used in the position of the subject of a verb when you are talking about time, the date, distance, the weather, etc: *It's nearly half past eight.* ◆ *It's Tuesday today.* ◆ *It's about 100 kilometres from London.* ◆ *It was very cold at the weekend.* ◆ *It's raining.* **5** used when you are talking about a situation: *It gets very crowded here in the summer.* ◆ *I'll come at 7 o'clock if it's convenient.* ◆ *It's a pity they can't come to the party.* **6** used for emphasizing a part of a sentence: *It was Jerry who said it, not me.* ◆ *It's your health I'm worried about, not the cost.*
IDM **that/this is it** **1** that/this is the answer or the main point: *That's it! You've solved the puzzle!* **2** that/this is the end: *That's it, I've had enough! I'm going home!*

italics /ɪˈtælɪks/ *noun* [pl] a type of writing or printing in which the letters do not stand straight up: *All the example sentences in the dictionary are printed* ***in italics.*** ▶ **italic** *adj*

itch /ɪtʃ/ *noun* [C] the feeling on your skin that makes you want to rub or scratch it: *I've got an itch on my back.* ▶ **itch** *verb* [I]: *My whole body is itching.* ▶ **itchy** *adj*: *This shirt is itchy.* ◆ *My skin is all itchy.*

it'd /ˈɪtəd/ *short for* **it had; it would**

🔑 **item** /ˈaɪtəm/ *noun* [C] **1** one single thing on a list or in a collection: *Some items arrived too late to be included in the catalogue.* ◆ *What is the first item on the agenda?* **2** one single article or object: *Can I pay for each item separately?* ◆ *an item of clothing* **3** a single piece of news: *There was an interesting item about Spain in yesterday's news.*

itemize (also -ise) /ˈaɪtəmaɪz/ *verb* [T] to make a list of all the separate items in sth: *an itemized telephone bill*

itinerant /aɪˈtɪnərənt/ *adj* (*formal*) [only before a noun] travelling from place to place: *an itinerant circus family*

itinerary /aɪˈtɪnərəri/ *noun* [C] (*pl* itineraries) a plan of a journey, including the route and the places that you will visit

it'll /ˈɪtl/ *short for* **it will**

🔑 **its** /ɪts/ *determiner* of or belonging to a thing: *The club held its Annual General Meeting last night.* ➲ note at it's

it's /ɪts/ *short for* **it is; it has**

> **HELP** Be careful. **It's** is a short way of saying *it is* or *it has.* **Its** means 'belonging to it' and does not have an apostrophe: *The bird has broken its wing.*

I

itself /ɪtˈself/ *pron* **1** used when the animal or thing that does an action is also affected by it: *The cat was washing itself.* ♦ *The company has got itself into financial difficulties.* **2** used to emphasize sth: *The building itself is beautiful, but it's in a very ugly part of town.*
IDM **(all) by itself 1** without being controlled by a person; automatically: *The central heating comes on by itself before we get up.* **2** alone: *The house stood all by itself on the hillside.* ➲ note at **alone**

ITV /ˌaɪ tiː ˈviː/ *abbr* (*BrE*) **Independent Television**; a group of TV companies in the UK that are paid for by advertising: *to watch a film on ITV*

I've /aɪv/ *short for* **I have**

ivory /ˈaɪvəri/ *noun* [U] the hard white substance that the **tusks** (= long teeth) of an elephant are made of

ivy /ˈaɪvi/ *noun* [U] a climbing plant that has dark leaves with three or five points

J

J, j /dʒeɪ/ *noun* [C,U] (*pl* Js; J's; j's /dʒeɪz/) the 10th letter of the English alphabet: *'Jam' begins with (a) 'J'.*

jab¹ /dʒæb/ *verb* [I,T] jab sb/sth (with sth); jab sth into sb/sth to push at sb/sth with a sudden, rough movement, usually with sth sharp: *She jabbed me in the ribs with her elbow.* ♦ *The robber jabbed a gun into my back and ordered me to move.*

jab² /dʒæb/ *noun* [C] **1** a sudden rough push with sth sharp: *He **gave me a jab** in the ribs with the stick.* **2** (*BrE informal*) the act of putting a drug, etc. under sb's skin with a needle: *I'm going to the doctor's to **have a** flu **jab** today.* SYN **injection**

jack¹ /dʒæk/ *noun* [C] **1** a piece of equipment for lifting a car, etc. off the ground, for example in order to change its wheel **2** the card between the ten and the queen in a pack of cards ➲ note at **card** ➲ picture at **card**

jack² /dʒæk/ *verb*
PHR V **jack sth in** (*slang*) to stop doing sth: *Jerry got fed up with his job and jacked it in.*
jack sth up to lift a car, etc. using a **jack**: *We jacked the car up to change the wheel.*

jacket /ˈdʒækɪt/ *noun* [C] a short coat with sleeves: *a denim/leather jacket* ♦ *Do you have to wear a jacket and tie to work?* ➲ look at **life jacket** ➲ picture on **page P1**

jacket poˈtato (also ˌ**baked poˈtato**) *noun* [C] a potato that is cooked in the oven in its skin ➲ picture on **page P16**

jackknife /ˈdʒæknaɪf/ *verb* [I] (used about a lorry that is in two parts) to go out of control and bend suddenly in a dangerous way

the jackpot /ˈdʒækpɒt/ *noun* [C] the largest money prize that you can win in a game
IDM **hit the jackpot** ➲ **hit¹**

Jacuzzi™ /dʒəˈkuːzi/ *noun* [C] a large bath in which the water moves around, giving you a pleasant feeling

jade /dʒeɪd/ *noun* [U] **1** a hard stone that is usually green and is used in making jewellery **2** a bright green colour ▶ **jade** *adj*

jaded /ˈdʒeɪdɪd/ *adj* tired and bored after doing the same thing for a long time without a break

jagged /ˈdʒægɪd/ *adj* rough with sharp points: *jagged rocks*

jaguar /ˈdʒægjuə(r)/ *noun* [C] a large wild cat with black spots that comes from Central and South America

jail¹ /dʒeɪl/ = **prison**: *She was **sent to jail** for ten years.*

jail² /dʒeɪl/ *verb* [T] to put sb in prison: *She was jailed for ten years.*

jailer /ˈdʒeɪlə(r)/ *noun* [C] (*old-fashioned*) a person whose job is to guard prisoners

jam¹ /dʒæm/ *noun* **1** [U] a sweet substance that you spread on bread, made by boiling fruit and sugar together: *a jar of raspberry jam* ➲ look at **jelly** ➲ picture on **page P16**

> **MORE** Jam made from oranges or lemons is called **marmalade**.

2 [C] a situation in which you cannot move because there are too many people or vehicles: *a traffic jam* **3** [C, sing] (*informal*) a difficult situation: *We're **in a** bit of **a jam** without our passports or travel documents.*

jam² /dʒæm/ *verb* (jamming; jammed) **1** [T] jam sb/sth in, under, between, etc. sth to push or force sb/sth into a place where there is not much room: *She managed to jam everything into her suitcase.* **2** [I, T] jam (sth) (up) to become or to make sth unable to move so that it does not work: *Something is jamming (up) the machine.* ♦ *The paper keeps jamming in the photocopier.* ♦ *I can't open the door. The lock's jammed.* **3** [T, usually passive] jam sth (up) (with sb/sth) to fill sth with too many people or things: *The cupboard was **jammed full** of old newspapers and magazines.* ♦ *The suitcase was **jam-packed with** (= completely full of) designer clothes.* ♦ *The switchboard was jammed with hundreds of calls from unhappy customers.* **4** [T] to send out signals in order to stop radio programmes, etc. from being received or heard clearly
PHR V **jam on the brakes/jam the brakes on** to stop a car suddenly by pushing hard on the **brake** (= the device for making a vehicle stop) with your foot

Jan. *abbr* = **January**: *1 Jan. 2013*

jangle /ˈdʒæŋgl/ *verb* [I,T] to make a noise like metal hitting against metal; to move sth so that it makes this noise: *The baby smiles if you jangle your keys.* ▶ **jangle** *noun* [U]

janitor /ˈdʒænɪtə(r)/ (*AmE*) = **caretaker**

January /ˈdʒænjuəri/ *noun* [U,C] (*abbr* Jan.) the 1st month of the year, coming after December

HELP Note how the names of the months are used in sentences: *We're going skiing* ***in January****.* ♦ *last/next January* ♦ *We first met* ***on January 31st****, 2009.* ♦ *Our wedding anniversary is at the end of January.* ♦ *January mornings can be very dark in Britain.* ♦ *Michael's birthday is (on) January 17.* We say 'on January the seventeenth' or 'on the seventeenth of January' or, in American English, 'January seventeenth'. In both British and American English, the months of the year are always written with a capital letter.

jar[1] /dʒɑː(r)/ *noun* [C] **1** a container with a lid, usually made of glass and used for keeping food, etc. in: *a jam jar* ♦ *a large storage jar for flour* ➲ picture at **container 2** the food that a **jar** contains: *a jar of honey/jam/coffee*

jar[2] /dʒɑː(r)/ *verb* (jarring; jarred) **1** [T] to hurt or damage sth as a result of a sharp knock: *He fell and jarred his back.* **2** [I] jar (on sb/sth) to have an unpleasant or annoying effect: *The dripping tap jarred on my nerves.*

jargon /ˈdʒɑːɡən/ *noun* [U] special or technical words that are used by a particular group of people in a particular profession and that other people do not understand: *medical/scientific/legal/computer jargon*

jaundice /ˈdʒɔːndɪs/ *noun* [U] a disease that makes your skin and eyes yellow

jaundiced /ˈdʒɔːndɪst/ *adj* **1** not expecting sb/sth to be good or useful, especially because of experiences that you have had in the past: *He had a jaundiced view of life.* ♦ *She looked on politicians with a jaundiced eye.* **2** suffering from **jaundice**

javelin /ˈdʒævlɪn/ *noun* **1** [C] a long stick with a pointed end that is thrown in sports competitions **2** the javelin [sing] the event or sport of throwing the **javelin** as far as possible

jaw /dʒɔː/ *noun* **1** [C] either of the two bones in your face that contain your teeth: *the lower/upper jaw* ➲ picture at **body 2** jaws [pl] the mouth (especially of a wild animal): *The lion came towards him with its jaws open.*

jazz[1] /dʒæz/ *noun* [U] a style of music with a strong rhythm, originally of African-American origin: *modern/traditional jazz* ➲ look at **classical, pop, rock**

jazz[2] /dʒæz/ *verb*
PHR V jazz sth up (*informal*) to make sth brighter, more interesting or exciting

jealous /ˈdʒeləs/ *adj* **1** feeling upset or angry because you think that sb you like or love is showing interest in sb else: *Tim seems to get jealous whenever Sue speaks to another boy!* **2** jealous (of sb/sth) feeling angry or sad because you want to be like sb else or because you want what sb else has: *He's always been jealous of his older brother.* ♦ *I'm very jealous of your new car—how much did it cost?* **SYN envious** ▶ **jealously** *adv* ▶ **jealousy** *noun* [C,U] (*pl* jealousies)

jeans /dʒiːnz/ *noun* [pl] trousers made of **denim** (= strong, usually blue, cotton cloth): *These jeans are a bit too tight.* ♦ *a pair of jeans* ➲ picture on **page P1**

Jeep™ /dʒiːp/ *noun* [C] a small, strong vehicle suitable for travelling over rough ground

jeer /dʒɪə(r)/ *verb* [I,T] jeer (at) sb/sth to laugh or shout rude comments at sb/sth to show your lack of respect for them or it: *The spectators booed and jeered at the losing team.* ▶ **jeer** *noun* [C, usually pl]: *The Prime Minister was greeted with jeers in the House of Commons today.*

jelly /ˈdʒeli/ *noun* (*pl* jellies) (*AmE* Jell-O™ /ˈdʒeləʊ/) **1** [C,U] a soft, solid brightly coloured food that shakes when it is moved. **Jelly** is made from sugar and fruit juice and is eaten cold at the end of a meal, especially by children: *raspberry jelly and ice cream* **2** [U] a type of jam that does not contain any solid pieces of fruit: *blackcurrant jelly*
IDM be/feel like jelly (used especially about the legs or knees) to feel weak because you are nervous, afraid, etc: *My legs felt like jelly before the exam.*
turn to jelly (used about the legs and knees) to suddenly become weak because of fear

jellyfish /ˈdʒelifɪʃ/ *noun* [C] (*pl* jellyfish) a sea animal with a soft transparent body and long thin parts that can sting you

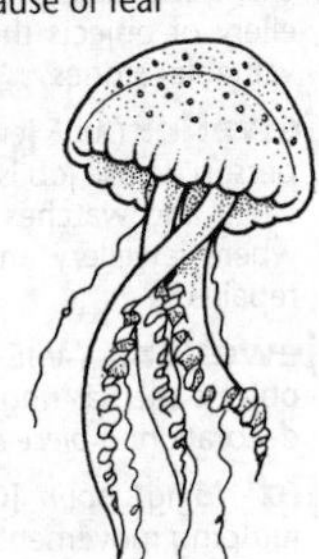
jellyfish

jeopardize (also -ise) /ˈdʒepədaɪz/ *verb* [T] to risk harming or destroying sth: *He would never do anything to jeopardize his career.*

jeopardy /ˈdʒepədi/ *noun*
IDM in jeopardy in a dangerous position and likely to be lost or harmed: *The future of the factory and 15 000 jobs are in jeopardy.*

jerk[1] /dʒɜːk/ *verb* [I,T] to move or make sb/sth move with a sudden sharp movement: *She jerked the door open.* ♦ *His head jerked back as the car set off.* ▶ **jerky** *adj* ▶ **jerkily** /-kɪli/ *adv*

jerk[2] /dʒɜːk/ *noun* [C] **1** a sudden sharp movement **2** (*(especially AmE slang)* a stupid or annoying person

jersey /ˈdʒɜːzi/ *noun* **1** [C] a piece of clothing made of wool that you wear over a shirt **SYN jumper, pullover** ➲ note at **sweater 2** [C] a shirt worn by sb playing a sports game ➲ picture at **football 3** [U] soft thin cloth made of cotton or wool that is used for making clothes

Jesus /ˈdʒiːzəs/ (also Jesus ˈChrist) = **Christ**

jet[1] /dʒet/ *noun* [C] **1** a fast plane **2** a fast, thin current of water, gas, etc. coming out of a small hole

jet[2] /dʒet/ (jetting; jetted) *verb* [I] (*informal*) jet off to fly somewhere in a plane

jet ˈblack *adj* very dark black in colour

ˈjet engine *noun* [C] a powerful engine that makes planes fly by pushing out a current of hot air and gases at the back

jet lag *noun* [U] the tired feeling that people often have after a long journey in a plane to a place where the local time is different ▸ **ˈjet-lagged** *adj*

the ˈjet set *noun* [sing] the group of rich, successful and fashionable people (especially those who travel around the world a lot)

ˈJet Ski™ *noun* [C] a vehicle with an engine, like a motorbike, for riding across water ▸ **ˈjet-skiing** *noun* [U]

jetty /ˈdʒeti/ *noun* [C] (*pl* **jetties**) (also **ˈlanding stage**; *AmE* **dock**) a stone wall or wooden platform built out into the sea or a river where boats are tied and where people can get on and off them

Jew /dʒuː/ *noun* [C] a person whose family originally came from the ancient Hebrew people of Israel and/or whose religion is Judaism ▸ **Jewish** *adj*

jewel /ˈdʒuːəl/ *noun* **1** [C] a valuable stone (for example a diamond) **SYN gem** **2** [pl] pieces of jewellery or objects that contain **precious** (= rare and valuable) stones

jeweller (*AmE* **jeweler**) /ˈdʒuːələ(r)/ *noun* **1** [C] a person whose job is to buy, sell, make or repair jewellery and watches **2 the jeweller's** [sing] a shop where jewellery and watches are made, sold and repaired

⚷ **jewellery** (*AmE* **jewelry**) /ˈdʒuːəlri/ *noun* [U] objects such as rings, etc. that are worn as personal decoration: *a piece of jewellery*

jig¹ /dʒɪɡ/ *noun* [C] a type of quick dance with jumping movements; the music for this dance

jig² /dʒɪɡ/ *verb* [I] (**jigging**; **jigged**) **jig about/around** to move about in an excited or impatient way

jiggle /ˈdʒɪɡl/ *verb* [T] (*informal*) to move sth quickly from side to side: *She jiggled her car keys to try to distract the baby.*

jigsaw /ˈdʒɪɡsɔː/ (also **ˈjigsaw puzzle**) *noun* [C] a picture on cardboard or wood that is cut into small pieces and has to be fitted together again

jingle¹ /ˈdʒɪŋɡl/ *noun* **1** [sing] a ringing sound like small bells, made by metal objects gently hitting each other: *the jingle of coins* **2** [C] a short simple tune or song that is easy to remember and is used in advertising on TV or radio

jingle² /ˈdʒɪŋɡl/ *verb* [I,T] to make or cause sth to make a pleasant gentle sound like small bells ringing: *She jingled the coins in her pocket.*

jinx /dʒɪŋks/ *noun* [C,sing] (*informal*) bad luck; a person or thing that people believe brings bad luck to sb/sth ▸ **jinx** *verb* [T] ▸ **jinxed** *adj*: *After my third accident in a month, I began to think I was jinxed.*

the jitters /ˈdʒɪtəz/ *noun* [pl] (*informal*) feelings of fear or worry, especially before an important event or before having to do sth difficult: *Just thinking about the exam **gives me the jitters!***

jewellery

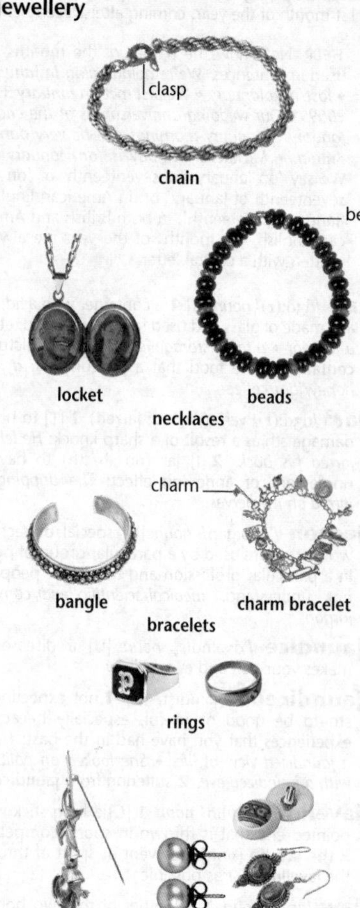

jittery /ˈdʒɪtəri/ *adj* (*informal*) nervous or worried: *She felt jittery and tense.*

⚷ **job** /dʒɒb/ *noun* [C] **1** the work that you do regularly to earn money: *She **took/got a job** as a waitress.* ◆ *A lot of people will **lose** their **jobs** if the factory closes.* ➲ note at **office**, **pay**, **retire**, **work** ➲ picture on page P2

> **HELP** **Post** and **position** are formal words for job: *I would like to apply for the post/position of Marketing Manager.*

2 a task or a piece of work: *I always have a lot of jobs to do in the house at weekends.* ◆ *The garage has **done a good/bad job on** our car.* **3** [usually sing] a duty or responsibility: *It's not his job to tell us what we can and can't do.*

IDM do the job/trick (*informal*) to get the result that is wanted: *This extra strong glue should do the job.*
have a hard job doing/to do sth ➲ **hard**[1]
it's a good job (*BrE spoken*) it is a good or lucky thing: *It's a good job you reminded me—I had completely forgotten!*
just the job/ticket (*informal*) exactly what is needed in a particular situation: *This dress will be just the job for Helen's party.*
make a bad, good, etc. job of sth to do sth badly, well, etc.
make the best of sth/a bad job ➲ **best**[3]
out of a job without paid work ➲ A more formal word is **unemployed**.

TOPIC

Jobs

When you **apply for a job**, you usually **fill in an application form** or send your **CV** with a **covering letter** (= a letter containing extra information about yourself). Then you **have an interview**. If it goes well and the employer is satisfied with your **references** (= letters that describe your character and abilities, often from a former employer), you will **get the job**. You **sign the contract** and become an **employee**. A job can be **well paid/highly paid** or **badly paid/low-paid**. A job can be **full-time** or **part-time**, **permanent** or **temporary**. If your **working conditions** are good and you have the chance to **be promoted** (= be given a more important job), then you will probably get a lot of **job satisfaction**.

TOPIC

Leaving a job

If you want to **leave your job**, you **resign** or **hand in** your **resignation/notice**. If a company no longer needs an employee, it will **make** him/her **redundant**. If an employee's work is not good enough, the company may **dismiss** him/her. In less formal English we use the verbs **fire** or **sack**, or the noun **the sack**: *Her boss fired/sacked her.* ◆ *Her boss gave her the sack.* ◆ *She got the sack.* When you stop working because you have reached a certain age (usually 60 or 65), you **retire**.

jobless /ˈdʒɒbləs/ *adj* **1** (usually used about large numbers of people) without paid work **SYN unemployed** **2 the jobless** *noun* [pl] people without paid work ▶ **joblessness** *noun* [U] **SYN unemployment**

jockey /ˈdʒɒki/ *noun* [C] a person who rides horses in races, especially as a profession ➲ look at **DJ** ➲ picture on **page P5**

jodhpurs /ˈdʒɒdpəz/ *noun* [pl] special trousers that you wear for riding a horse ➲ picture at **horse**

jog[1] /dʒɒg/ *verb* (**jogging**; **jogged**) **1** [I] to run slowly, especially as a form of exercise

HELP When we talk about jogging for pleasure or exercise, it is more usual to say **go jogging**: *I go jogging most evenings.*

2 [T] to push or knock sb/sth slightly: *He jogged my arm and I spilled the milk.* **SYN nudge**
IDM jog sb's memory to say or do sth that makes sb remember sth

jog[2] /dʒɒg/ *noun* [sing] **1** a slow run as a form of exercise: *She* ***goes for a jog*** *before breakfast.* **2** a slight push or knock **SYN nudge**

jogger /ˈdʒɒgə(r)/ *noun* [C] a person who goes **jogging** for exercise

⚷ **join**[1] /dʒɔɪn/ *verb*
➤CONNECT **1** [T] **join A to B; join A and B (together)** to fasten or connect one thing to another: *The Channel Tunnel joins Britain to France.* ◆ *The two pieces of wood had been carefully joined together.* ◆ *We've knocked down the wall and joined the two rooms into one.*
➤BECOME ONE **2** [I,T] **join (up) (with sb/sth)** to meet or unite (with sb/sth) to form one thing or group: *Do the two rivers join (up) at any point?* ◆ *Where does this road join the motorway?* ◆ *Would you like to join us for a drink?* ◆ *We'll join up with the other class later.*
➤CLUB **3** [I,T] to become a member of a club or an organization: *I've joined an aerobics class.* ◆ *He joined the company three months ago.*
➤TAKE PART **4** [T] to take your place in sth or to take part in sth: *We'd better go and join the queue if we want to see the film.* ◆ *Come downstairs and join the party.* **5** [I,T] **join (with) sb in sth/in doing sth/to do sth; join together in doing sth/to do sth** to take part with sb (often in doing sth for sb else): *Everybody here joins me in wishing you the best of luck in your new job.* ◆ *The whole school joined together to sing the school song.*
IDM join forces (with sb) to work together in order to achieve a shared goal: *The two companies joined forces to win the contract.*
PHR V join in (sth/doing sth) to take part in an activity: *Everyone started singing but Frank refused to join in.*
join up to become a member of the army, navy or air force

join[2] /dʒɔɪn/ *noun* [C] a place where two things are fixed or connected: *He glued the handle back on so cleverly that you couldn't see the join.*

joiner /ˈdʒɔɪnə(r)/ *noun* [C] a person whose job is to make the wooden parts of a building ➲ look at **carpenter**

⚷ **joint**[1] /dʒɔɪnt/ *adj* [only *before* a noun] shared or owned by two or more people: *Have you and your husband got a* ***joint account*** (= a shared bank account)? ◆ *a joint decision* ▶ **jointly** *adv*

⚷ **joint**[2] /dʒɔɪnt/ *noun* [C] **1** a part of the body where two bones fit together and are able to bend: *the knee joint* **2** the place where two or more things are fastened or connected together, especially to form a corner **3** (*BrE*) a large piece of meat that you cook whole in the oven: *a joint of lamb*

joke[1] /dʒəʊk/ *noun* **1** [C] something said or done to make you laugh, especially a funny story: *to tell/crack jokes* ◆ *a dirty joke* (= about sex) ◆ *I'm sorry, I didn't* ***get the joke*** (= understand it). ➲ note at **humour** **2** [sing] a ridiculous person, thing or situation: *The salary he was offered was a joke!*
IDM **make a joke of sth** to laugh about sth that is serious or should be taken seriously: *It's unkind to make jokes about people.*
play a joke/trick on sb to trick sb in order to amuse yourself or other people
see the joke ➲ see
take a joke to be able to laugh at a joke against yourself: *The trouble with Pete is he can't take a joke.*

joke[2] /dʒəʊk/ *verb* [I] **1 joke (with sb) (about sth)** to say sth to make people laugh; to tell a funny story: *She spent the evening laughing and joking with her old friends.* **2** to say sth that is not true because you think it is funny: *I never joke about religion.* ◆ *Don't get upset. I was* ***only joking!***
IDM **you must be joking; you're joking** (*spoken*) (used to express great surprise) you cannot be serious

joker /ˈdʒəʊkə(r)/ *noun* [C] **1** a person who likes to tell jokes or play tricks **2** an extra card which can be used instead of any other one in some card games ➲ picture at **card**

jolly /ˈdʒɒli/ *adj* (jollier; jolliest) happy

jolt[1] /dʒəʊlt/ *verb* [I,T] to move or make sb/sth move in a sudden rough way: *The lorry jolted along the bumpy track.* ◆ *The crash jolted all the passengers forward.*

jolt[2] /dʒəʊlt/ *noun* [usually sing] **1** a sudden movement: *The train stopped with a jolt.* **2** a sudden surprise or shock: *His sudden anger gave her quite a jolt.*

jostle /ˈdʒɒsl/ *verb* [I,T] to push hard against sb in a crowd

jot /dʒɒt/ *verb* (jo<u>tt</u>ing; jo<u>tt</u>ed)
PHR V **jot sth down** to make a quick short note of sth: *Let me jot down your address.*

journal /ˈdʒɜːnl/ *noun* [C] **1** a newspaper or a magazine, especially one in which all the articles are about a particular subject or profession: *a medical/scientific journal* **2** a written record of the things you do, see, etc. each day: *Have you read his journal of the years he spent in India?* ➲ look at **diary**

journalism /ˈdʒɜːnəlɪzəm/ *noun* [U] the profession of collecting and writing about news in newspapers and magazines or talking about it on the TV or radio

journalist /ˈdʒɜːnəlɪst/ *noun* [C] a person whose job is to collect and write about news in newspapers and magazines or to talk about it on the TV or radio ➲ note at **newspaper** ➲ look at **reporter**

journey /ˈdʒɜːni/ *noun* [C] an act of travelling from one place to another, usually on land: *Did you have a good journey?* ◆ *a two-hour journey* ◆ *The journey to work takes me 45 minutes.* ◆ *We'll have to break the journey* (= stop for a rest). ➲ note at **travel**

> **MORE** A journey can include both air and sea travel. To refer specifically to a journey by air we say a **flight** and by sea we say a **voyage** or, if it is for pleasure, a **cruise**.

jovial /ˈdʒəʊviəl/ *adj* (used about a person) happy and friendly

joy /dʒɔɪ/ *noun* **1** [U] a feeling of great happiness: *We'd like to wish you joy and success in your life together.* **2** [C] a person or thing that gives you great pleasure: *the joys of fatherhood* ◆ *That class is a joy to teach.* **3** [U] [used in questions and negative sentences] (*BrE informal*) success or satisfaction: *'I asked again if we could have seats with more legroom but* ***got no joy*** *from the check-in clerk.'*
IDM **jump for joy** ➲ **jump**[1]
sb's pride and joy ➲ **pride**[1]

joyful /ˈdʒɔɪfl/ *adj* very happy: *a joyful occasion* ▸ **joyfully** /-fəli/ *adv* ▸ **joyfulness** *noun* [U]

joyless /ˈdʒɔɪləs/ *adj* unhappy: *The couple had a joyless marriage.*

joyriding /ˈdʒɔɪraɪdɪŋ/ *noun* [U] the crime of stealing a car and driving it for pleasure, usually in a fast and dangerous way ▸ **joyride** *noun* [C] ▸ **joyrider** *noun* [C]

joystick /ˈdʒɔɪstɪk/ *noun* [C] a stick with a handle that is used to control movement on a computer, aircraft, machine, etc.

JP /ˌdʒeɪ ˈpiː/ *abbr* = **Justice of the Peace**

Jr /ˈdʒuːniə(r)/ *abbr* (*AmE*) = **Junior**[1] (3): *Samuel P Carson, Jr*

Jr = **Junior**[1] (3)

jubilant /ˈdʒuːbɪlənt/ *adj* (*formal*) extremely happy, especially because of a success: *The football fans were jubilant at their team's victory in the cup.*

jubilation /ˌdʒuːbɪˈleɪʃn/ *noun* [U] (*formal*) great happiness because of a success

jubilee /ˈdʒuːbɪliː/ *noun* [C] a special anniversary of an event that took place a certain number of years ago, and the celebrations that go with it: *It's the company's* ***golden jubilee*** *this year* (= it is 50 years since it was started).

> **MORE** An anniversary or jubilee can be **silver** (25 years), **golden** (50 years) or **diamond** (60 years).

Judaism /ˈdʒuːdeɪɪzəm/ *noun* [U] the religion of the Jewish people

judge[1] /dʒʌdʒ/ *noun* [C] **1** a person in a court of law whose job is to decide how criminals should be punished and to make legal decisions: *The judge sentenced the man to seventeen years in prison.* ➲ note at **court** **2** a person who decides who has won a competition: *a panel of judges* **3** [usually sing] **a judge of sth** a person who has the ability or knowledge to give an opinion about sth: *You're a good judge of character–what do you think of him?*

judge² /dʒʌdʒ/ *verb* **1** [I,T] to form or give an opinion about sb/sth based on the information you have: ***Judging by/from*** *what he said, his work is going well.* ◆ *It's difficult to judge how long the project will take.* ◆ *The party was judged a great success by everybody.* **2** [I,T] to decide the result or winner of a competition: *The head teacher will judge the competition.* **3** [I,T] to form an opinion about sb/sth, especially when you do not approve of them or it: *Don't judge him too harshly—he's had a difficult time.* **4** [T] to decide if sb is guilty or innocent in a court of law: *It was the hardest case he had ever had to judge.*

judgement (also **judgment**) /ˈdʒʌdʒmənt/ *noun* **1** [U] the ability to form opinions or to make sensible decisions: *He always shows excellent judgement in his choice of staff.* ◆ *to have good/poor/sound judgement* **2** [C,U] an opinion that you form after carefully considering the information you have: *What,* ***in your judgement****, would be the best course of action?* **3 judgment** [C,U] an official decision made by a judge or a court of law: *The man collapsed when the judgment was read out in court.*

judicial /dʒuˈdɪʃl/ *adj* connected with a court of law, a judge or a legal judgment: *the judicial system*

judiciary /dʒuˈdɪʃəri/ *noun* **the judiciary** [C, with sing or pl verb] (*pl* **judiciaries**) the judges of a country or a state, when they are considered as a group: *an independent judiciary* ➲ look at **executive, legislature**

judicious /dʒuˈdɪʃəs/ *adj* (*formal*) (used about a decision or an action) sensible and carefully considered; showing good judgement ▶ **judiciously** *adv*

judo /ˈdʒuːdəʊ/ *noun* [U] a sport from Asia in which two people fight and try to throw each other to the ground ➲ look at **martial arts**

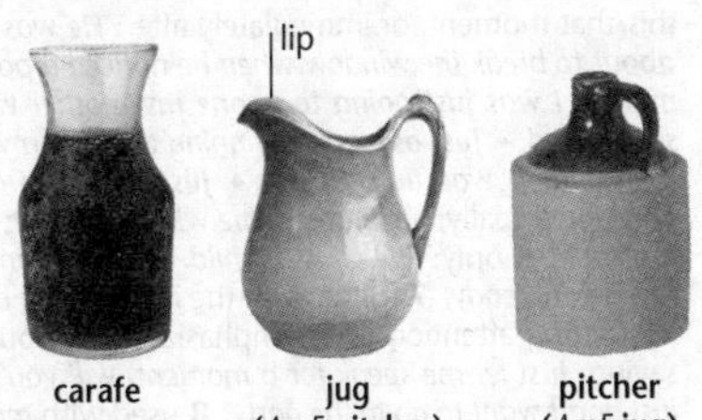

carafe jug (*AmE* **pitcher**) pitcher (*AmE* **jug**)

jug /dʒʌg/ (*AmE* **pitcher**) *noun* [C] a container with a handle used for holding or pouring liquids: *a milk jug* ◆ *a jug of water*

juggle /ˈdʒʌgl/ *verb* [I,T] **1 juggle (with sth)** to keep three or more objects such as balls in the air at the same time by throwing them one at a time and catching them quickly **2 juggle sth (with sth)** to try to deal with two or more important jobs or activities at the same time

juggler /ˈdʒʌglə(r)/ *noun* [C] a person who juggles to entertain people

juice /dʒuːs/ *noun* [C,U] **1** the liquid that comes from fruit and vegetables: *carrot/grapefruit/lemon juice* ◆ *I'll have an orange juice, please.* **2** the liquid that comes from a piece of meat when it is cooked: *You can use the juices of the meat to make gravy.* **3** the liquid in your stomach that helps you break down the food you eat: *gastric/digestive juices*

juggler

juicy /ˈdʒuːsi/ *adj* (**juicier; juiciest**) **1** containing a lot of juice: *juicy oranges* **2** (*informal*) (used about information) interesting because it is shocking: *juicy gossip*

jukebox /ˈdʒuːkbɒks/ *noun* [C] a machine in a bar, etc. that plays music when money is put in

Jul. *abbr* = **July**: *4 Jul. 2012*

July /dʒuˈlaɪ/ *noun* [U,C] (*abbr* **Jul.**) the 7th month of the year, coming after June ➲ note at **January**

jumble¹ /ˈdʒʌmbl/ *verb* [T, usually passive] **jumble sth (up/together)** to mix things together in a confused and untidy way: *I must sort my clothes out—they're all jumbled up in the drawer.*

jumble² /ˈdʒʌmbl/ *noun* **1** [sing] an untidy group of things: *a jumble of papers/ideas* SYN **mess** **2** [U] (*BrE*) a collection of old things for a **jumble sale**: *Have you got any jumble you don't want?*

ˈjumble sale (*AmE* **ˈrummage sale**) *noun* [C] a sale of old things that people do not want any more. Clubs, churches, schools and other organizations hold **jumble sales** to get money.

jumbo¹ /ˈdʒʌmbəʊ/ *noun* [C] (*pl* **jumbos**) (also **ˌjumbo ˈjet**) a very large aircraft that can carry several hundred passengers

jumbo² /ˈdʒʌmbəʊ/ *adj* [only *before* a noun] (*informal*) very large

jump¹ /dʒʌmp/ *verb*

▸MOVE OFF GROUND **1** [I] to move quickly into the air by pushing yourself up with your legs and feet, or by stepping off a high place: *to jump into the air/off a bridge/onto a chair* ◆ *How high can you jump?* ◆ *Jump up and down to keep warm.* ➲ picture at **hop**

▸GO OVER **2** [T] to get over sth by jumping: *The dog jumped the fence and ran off down the road.*

▸MOVE QUICKLY **3** [I] to move quickly and suddenly: *The phone rang and she jumped up to answer it.* ◆ *A taxi stopped and we jumped in.*

▸FROM SURPRISE/FEAR **4** [I] to make a sudden movement because of surprise or fear: *'Oh, it's only you—you made me jump,' he said.*

▸INCREASE **5** [I] **jump (from sth) to sth; jump (by) (sth)** to increase suddenly by a very large amount: *His salary jumped from £20 000 to £28 000 last year.* ◆ *Prices jumped (by) 50% in the summer.*

▸CHANGE SUDDENLY **6** [I] **jump (from sth) to sth** to go suddenly from one point in a series, a story, etc. to another: *The book kept jumping from the present to the past.*

IDM **climb/jump on the bandwagon** ➲ **bandwagon**

J

jump for joy to be extremely happy about sth
jump the gun to do sth too soon, before the proper time
jump the queue (*BrE*) to go to the front of a line of people without waiting for your turn
jump to conclusions to decide that sth is true without thinking about it carefully enough
PHR V jump at sth to accept an opportunity, offer, etc. with enthusiasm: *Of course I jumped at the chance to work in New York for a year.*

jump² /dʒʌmp/ *noun* [C] **1** an act of jumping: *With a huge jump the horse cleared the hedge.* ◆ *to do a parachute jump* ➲ look at **high jump, long jump** **2** a thing to be jumped over: *The third jump consisted of a five-bar gate.* ◆ *a ski jump* **3 a jump (in sth)** a sudden increase in amount, price or value: *a 20% jump in profits*

jumper /ˈdʒʌmpə(r)/ *noun* [C] **1** (*BrE*) a piece of clothing with long sleeves, usually made of wool, that you wear on the top part of your body **SYN jersey, pullover** ➲ note at **sweater** ➲ picture on **page P1** **2** a person or an animal that jumps

jumpy /ˈdʒʌmpi/ *adj* (*informal*) nervous or worried: *I always get a bit jumpy if I'm travelling by plane.*

Jun. *abbr* = **June**: *10 Jun. 2012*

junction /ˈdʒʌŋkʃn/ *noun* [C] a place where roads, railway lines, etc. meet

June /dʒuːn/ *noun* [U,C] (*abbr* **Jun.**) the 6th month of the year, coming after May ➲ note at **January**

jungle /ˈdʒʌŋgl/ *noun* [C,U] a thick forest in a hot tropical country: *the jungles of Africa and South America* ➲ note at **forest**

junior¹ /ˈdʒuːniə(r)/ *adj* **1 junior (to sb)** having a low or lower position (than sb) in an organization, etc: *a junior officer/doctor/employee* ◆ *A lieutenant is junior to a captain in the army.* **2** [only *before* a noun] (*BrE*) of or for children below a particular age: *the junior athletics championships* **3 Junior** (*abbr* **Jr**) (*especially AmE*) used after the name of a son who has the same first name as his father: *Sammy Davis, Junior* ➲ look at **senior**

junior² /ˈdʒuːniə(r)/ *noun* **1** [C] a person who has a low position in an organization, etc: *office juniors* **2** [sing] [with *his, her, your,* etc.] a person who is younger than sb else by the number of years mentioned: *She's two years his junior/his junior by two years.* **3** [C] (in Britain) a child who goes to **junior school**: *The juniors are having an outing to a museum today.* ➲ look at **senior**

ˌjunior ˈhigh school (also ˌjunior ˈhigh) *noun* [C,U] (in the US) a school for young people between the ages of 12 and 14 ➲ look at **senior high school**

ˈjunior school *noun* [C,U] (in Britain) a school for children between the ages of 7 and 11 ➲ look at **primary school**

junk /dʒʌŋk/ *noun* [U] (*informal*) things that are old or useless or do not have much value: *There's an awful lot of junk up in the attic.*

ˈjunk food *noun* [U] (*informal*) food that is not very good for you but that is ready to eat or quick to prepare

junkie /ˈdʒʌŋki/ *noun* [C] (*informal*) a person who is unable to stop taking dangerous drugs **SYN addict**

ˈjunk mail *noun* [U] advertising material that is sent to people who have not asked for it ➲ look at **spam**

junta /ˈdʒʌntə/ *noun* [C, with sing or pl verb] a group, especially of military officers, who rule a country by force

Jupiter /ˈdʒuːpɪtə(r)/ *noun* [sing] the planet that is fifth in order from the sun

jurisdiction /ˌdʒʊərɪsˈdɪkʃn/ *noun* [U] legal power or authority; the area in which this power can be used: *That question is outside the jurisdiction of this council.*

juror /ˈdʒʊərə(r)/ *noun* [C] a member of a **jury**

jury /ˈdʒʊəri/ *noun* [C, with sing or pl verb] (*pl* **juries**) **1** a group of members of the public in a court of law who listen to the facts about a crime and decide if sb is guilty or not guilty: *Has/Have the jury reached a verdict?* ➲ note at **court** **2** a group of people who decide who is the winner in a competition: *The jury is/are about to announce the winners.*

just¹ /dʒʌst/ *adv* **1** exactly: *It's just 8 o'clock.* ◆ *That's just what I meant.* ◆ *You're* ***just as*** *clever as he is.* ◆ *The room was too hot before, but now it's just right.* ◆ *He looks* ***just like*** *his father.* ◆ *My arm hurts just here.* **2** almost not: *I could* ***only just*** *hear what she was saying.* ◆ *We got to the station* ***just in time****.* **3** a very short time before: *She's just been to the shops.* ◆ *He'd just returned from France when I saw him.* ◆ *They came here just before Easter.* **4** at exactly this/that moment, or immediately after: *He was* ***just about to*** *break the window when he noticed a policeman.* ◆ *I was* ***just going to*** *phone my mother when she arrived.* ◆ ***Just as*** *I was beginning to enjoy myself, John said it was time to go.* ◆ ***Just then*** *the door opened.* **5** really; absolutely: *The whole day was just fantastic!* **6** only: *She's just a child.* ◆ *Just a minute! I'm nearly ready.* **7** [often with the imperative] used for getting attention or to emphasize what you are saying: *Just let me speak for a moment, will you?* ◆ *I just don't want to go to the party.* **8** used with *might, may* or *could* to express a slight possibility: *This might just/just might be the most important decision of your life.*
IDM all/just the same ➲ **same**
it is just as well (that ...) it is a good thing: *It's just as well you remembered to bring your umbrella!*
just about almost or approximately: *I've just about finished.* ◆ *Karen's plane should be taking off just about now.*
just now **1** at this exact moment or during this exact period: *I can't come with you just now—can you wait 20 minutes?* **2** a very short time ago: *I saw Tony just now.*
just so exactly right
not just yet not now, but probably quite soon

just² /dʒʌst/ *adj* fair and right; reasonable: *I don't think that was a very just decision.* ▸ **justly** *adv*

justice /ˈdʒʌstɪs/ *noun* **1** [U] the fair treatment of people: *a struggle for justice* **2** [U] the quality of being fair or reasonable: *Everybody realized the justice of what he was saying.* **3** [U] the law and the way it is used: *the criminal justice system* **4** (also Justice) [C] (*AmE*) a judge in a court of law
IDM **do justice to sb/sth; do sb/sth justice** to treat sb/sth fairly or to show the real quality of sb/sth: *The review doesn't do justice to her talents.* ◆ *I don't like him, but to do him justice, he's a very clever man.*
a miscarriage of justice ➲ **miscarriage**

ˌJustice of the ˈPeace *noun* [C] (*abbr* JP) a person who judges less serious cases in a court of law

justifiable /ˈdʒʌstɪfaɪəbl; ˌdʒʌstɪˈfaɪəbl/ *adj* that you can accept because there is a good reason for it: *His action was entirely justifiable.* ▶ **justifiably** /-əbli/ *adv*

justification /ˌdʒʌstɪfɪˈkeɪʃn/ *noun* [C,U] (a) justification (for sth/doing sth) (a) good reason: *I can't see any justification for tax rises.*

justify /ˈdʒʌstɪfaɪ/ *verb* [T] (justifying; justifies; *pt, pp* justified) to give or be a good reason for sth: *Can you justify your decision?*

jut /dʒʌt/ *verb* [I] (jutting; jutted) jut (out) (from/into/over sth) to stick out further than the surrounding surface, objects, etc: *rocks that jut out into the sea*

juvenile /ˈdʒuːvənaɪl/ *adj* **1** [only *before* a noun] (*formal*) of, for or involving young people who are not yet adults: *juvenile crime* **2** silly and more typical of a child than an adult: *Patrick's twenty but he is still quite juvenile.* SYN **childish** ▶ **juvenile** *noun* [C]

ˌjuvenile deˈlinquent *noun* [C] a young person who is guilty of committing a crime

juxtapose /ˌdʒʌkstəˈpəʊz/ *verb* [T] (*formal*) to put two people, things, etc. very close together, especially in order to show how they are different: *The artist achieves a special effect by juxtaposing light and dark.* ▶ **juxtaposition** /ˌdʒʌkstəpəˈzɪʃn/ *noun* [C,U]

K, k /keɪ/ *noun* [C,U] (*pl* Ks; K's; k's /keɪz/) the 11th letter of the English alphabet: *'Kate' begins with (a) 'K'.*

K /keɪ/ *abbr* **1** (*informal*) one thousand: *She earns 22K (= £22000) a year.* **2** = **kilometre(s)** **3** = **kilobyte**

kaleidoscope /kəˈlaɪdəskəʊp/ *noun* **1** [C] a toy that consists of a tube containing mirrors and small pieces of coloured glass. When you look into one end of the tube and turn it, you see changing patterns of colours. **2** [sing] a situation, pattern, etc. containing a lot of different parts that are always changing

kangaroo /ˌkæŋɡəˈruː/ *noun* [C] (*pl* kangaroos) an Australian animal that moves by jumping on its strong back legs and that carries its young in a **pouch** (= a pocket of skin) on its stomach

pouch

kangaroo

karaoke /ˌkæriˈəʊki/ *noun* [U] a type of entertainment in which a machine plays only the music of popular songs so that people can sing the words themselves

karat (*AmE*) = **carat**

karate /kəˈrɑːti/ *noun* [U] a style of fighting originally from Japan in which the hands and feet are used as weapons ➲ look at **martial arts** ➲ picture on **page P5**

kart /kɑːt/ = **go-kart**

kayak

canoe

kayak /ˈkaɪæk/ *noun* [C] a light narrow boat for one person in which the part where you sit is covered over ➲ look at **canoe** ▶ **kayaking** *noun* [U]: *I'm going to **go kayaking** in Wales.*

KB (also K) *abbr* = **kilobyte**

Kb (also Kbit) *abbr* = **kilobit**

kebab /kɪˈbæb/ *noun* [C] small pieces of meat, vegetables, etc. that are cooked on a **skewer** (= a stick) ➲ picture on **page P16**

keel¹ /kiːl/ *noun* [C] a long piece of wood or metal on the bottom of a boat that stops it falling over sideways in the water

keel² /kiːl/ *verb*
PHR V **keel over** to fall over

keen /kiːn/ *adj* (keener; keenest) **1** keen (to do sth/on doing sth/that ...) very interested in sth; wanting to do sth: *They are both keen gardeners.* ◆ *I failed the first time but I'm keen to try again.* ◆ *I wasn't too keen on going camping.* ◆ *She was keen that we should all be there.* ➲ note at **like 2** (used about one of the senses, a feeling, etc.) good or strong: *Foxes have a keen sense of smell.*

IDM keen on sb/sth very interested in or having a strong desire for sb/sth: *He's very keen on jazz.*

▶ **keenly** *adv*

▶ **keenness** *noun* [U]

keep[1] /ki:p/ *verb* (*pt, pp* **kept** /kept/)

➤STAY **1** [I] to continue to be in a particular state or position: *You must keep warm.* ◆ *That child can't keep still.* ◆ *I still keep in touch with my old school friends.* **2** [T] to make sb/sth stay in a particular state, place or condition: *Please keep this door closed.* ◆ *He kept his hands in his pockets.* ◆ *I'm sorry to keep you waiting.*

➤CONTINUE **3** [I] **keep doing sth** to continue doing sth or to repeat an action many times: *Keep going until you get to the church and then turn left.* ◆ *She keeps asking me silly questions.*

➤DELAY **4** [T] to delay sb/sth; to prevent sb from leaving: *Where's the doctor? What's keeping him?*

➤NOT GIVE BACK/SAVE **5** [T] to continue to have sth; to save sth for sb: *You can keep that book—I don't need it any more.* ◆ *Can I keep the car until next week?* ◆ *Can you keep my seat for me till I get back?*

➤PUT/STORE **6** [T] to have sth in a particular place: *Where do you keep the matches?* ◆ *Keep your passport in a safe place.*

➤ANIMALS **7** [T] to have and look after animals: *They keep ducks on their farm.*

➤FOOD **8** [I] to stay fresh: *Drink up all the milk—it won't keep in this weather.*

➤PROMISE/ARRANGEMENT **9** [T] to do what you promised or arranged: *Can you keep a promise?* ◆ *She didn't keep her appointment at the dentist's.* ◆ *to keep a secret* (= not tell it to anyone)

➤DIARY/RECORD **10** [T] to write down sth that you want to remember: *Keep a record of how much you spend.* ◆ *to keep a diary*

➤SUPPORT **11** [T] to support sb with your money: *You can't keep a family on the money I earn.*

IDM keep going to make an effort, especially when you are in a difficult situation: *You just have to keep yourself busy and keep going.* ◆ *Keep going, Sarah, you're nearly there.*

keep it up to continue doing sth as well as you are doing it now ⓘ For other idioms containing **keep**, look at the entries for the nouns, adjectives, etc. For example, **keep count** is at **count**.

PHR V keep at it/sth to continue to work on/at sth: *Keep at it—we should be finished soon.*

keep away from sb/sth to not go near sb/sth: *Keep away from the town centre this weekend.*

keep sb/sth back to prevent sb/sth from moving forwards: *The police tried to keep the crowd back.*

keep sth back (from sb) to refuse to tell sb sth: *I know he's keeping something back; he knows much more than he says.*

keep sth down to make sth stay at a low level, to stop sth increasing: *Keep your voice down.*

keep sb from sth/from doing sth to prevent sb from doing sth

keep sth from sb to refuse to tell sb sth

keep off sth to not go near or on sth: *Keep off the grass!*

keep sth off (sb/sth) to stop sth touching or going on sb/sth: *I'm trying to keep the flies off the food.*

keep on (doing sth) to continue doing sth or to repeat an action many times, especially in an annoying way: *He keeps on interrupting me.*

keep on (at sb) (about sb/sth) to continue talking to sb in an annoying or complaining way: *She kept on at me about my homework until I did it.*

keep (sb/sth) out (of sth) to not enter sth; to stop sb/sth entering sth: *They put up a fence to keep people out of their garden.*

keep to sth to not leave sth; to do sth in the usual, agreed or expected way: *Keep to the path!* ◆ *He didn't keep to our agreement.*

keep sth to/at sth to not allow sth to rise above a particular level: *We're trying to keep costs to a minimum.*

keep sth up 1 to prevent sth from falling down **2** to make sth stay at a high level: *We want to keep up standards of education.* **3** to continue doing sth: *How long can the baby keep up that crying?*

keep up (with sb) to do sth at the same speed as sb: *Can't you walk a bit slower? I can't keep up with you.* ◆ *Some students struggle to keep up when they move to a new school.*

keep up (with sth) to know about what is happening: *You have to read the latest magazines if you want to keep up.*

keep[2] /ki:p/ *noun* [U] food, clothes and all the other things that you need to live

IDM for keeps (*informal*) for always: *Take it. It's yours for keeps.*

keeper /ˈki:pə(r)/ *noun* [C] **1** a person who guards or looks after sth: *a zookeeper* **2** (*informal*) = **goalkeeper**

keeping /ˈki:pɪŋ/ *noun*

IDM in/out of keeping (with sth) 1 that does/does not look good with sth: *That modern table is out of keeping with the style of the room.* **2** in/not in agreement with a rule, belief, etc: *The Council's decision is in keeping with government policy.*

keg /keg/ *noun* [C] a round metal or wooden container, used especially for storing beer

kennel /ˈkenl/ *noun* [C] a small house for a dog

kept *past tense, past participle* of **keep**[1]

kerb (*AmE* **curb**) /kɜ:b/ *noun* [C] the edge of the raised path at the side of a road, usually made of long pieces of stone: *They stood on the kerb waiting to cross the road.* ➲ picture at **roundabout**

kernel /ˈkɜ:nl/ *noun* [C] **1** the inner part of a nut or seed **2** the most important part of an idea or a subject

kerosene /ˈkerəsi:n/ (*AmE*) = **paraffin**

ketchup /ˈketʃəp/ *noun* [U] a thick cold sauce made from tomatoes that is eaten with hot or cold food

kettle /ˈketl/ *noun* [C] a container with a lid, used for boiling water: *an electric kettle*

kettledrum /ˈketldrʌm/ *noun* [C] a large metal drum with a round bottom and a thin plastic top that can be made looser or tighter to produce

kettles

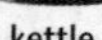

kettle

electric kettle

different musical notes. A set of **kettledrums** is usually called **timpani**. ➲ picture at **music**

key¹ /kiː/ *noun* [C]

➤TOOL FOR LOCKING **1** a metal object that is used for locking a door, starting a car, etc: *Have you seen my car keys anywhere?* ◆ *We need a spare key to the front door.* ◆ *a bunch of keys*

➤MOST IMPORTANT PART **2** [usually sing] **the key (to sth)** something that helps you achieve or understand sth: *A good education is the key to success.*

➤ON PIANO/COMPUTER **3** one of the parts of a piano, computer, etc. that you press with your fingers to make it work: *Press the return key to enter the information.* ➲ picture at **computer, music**

key

lock

key

chain

➤IN MUSIC **4** a set of musical notes that is based on one particular note: *The concerto is in the key of A minor.*

➤ANSWERS **5** a set of answers to exercises or problems: *an answer key*

➤ON MAP **6** a list of the symbols and signs used in a map or book, showing what they mean

IDM under lock and key ➲ **lock²**

key² /kiː/ *verb* [T] **key sth (in)** to put information into a computer or give it an instruction by typing: *Have you keyed that report yet?* ◆ *First, key in your password.*

key³ /kiː/ *adj* [usually *before* a noun] very important: *Tourism is a key industry in Spain.* ◆ *a* **key issue/factor/point** ➲ note at **important**

keyboard /ˈkiːbɔːd/ *noun* [C] **1** the set of keys on a piano, computer, etc: *Arianne was tapping away at her keyboard.* ➲ picture at **computer, piano** **2** an electrical musical instrument like a small piano: *The recording features Herbie Hancock on keyboard.* ➲ picture at **music**

keyhole /ˈkiːhəʊl/ *noun* [C] the hole in a lock where you put the key

ˌkeyhole ˈsurgery *noun* [U] (*especially BrE*) medical operations which involve only a very small cut being made in the patient's body

keypad /ˈkiːpæd/ *noun* [C] a small set of buttons with numbers on that you press when you use a telephone, computer, etc.

ˈkey ring *noun* [C] a ring on which you keep keys

keyword /ˈkiːwɜːd/ *noun* [C] **1** a word that tells you about the main idea or subject of sth: *When you're studying a language, the keyword is patience.* **2** a word or phrase that is used to give an instruction to a computer

kg *abbr* = **kilo**: *weight 10kg*

khaki /ˈkɑːki/ *adj, noun* [U] (of) a pale brownish-yellow or brownish-green colour: *the khaki uniforms of the desert soldiers*

kHz /ˈkɪləhɜːts/ *abbr* **kilohertz**; (used in radio) a measure of **frequency** (= the rate at which a sound wave moves up and down)

kibibit /ˈkɪbibɪt/ (*abbr* **Kib**; **Kibit**) = **kilobit**(2)

kibibyte /ˈkɪbibaɪt/ = **kilobyte**(2)

kick¹ /kɪk/ *verb* **1** [I,T] to hit or move sb/sth with your foot: *He kicked the ball wide of the net.* ◆ *The police kicked the door down.* **2** [I,T] to move your foot or feet: *You must kick harder if you want to swim faster.*

IDM kick the habit to stop doing sth harmful that you have done for a long time

kick yourself to be annoyed with yourself because you have done sth stupid, missed an opportunity, etc.

PHR V kick off to start sth, especially a game of football

kick sb out (of sth) (*informal*) to force sb to leave a place: *to be kicked out of university*

kick² /kɪk/ *noun* [C] **1** an act of kicking: *She gave the door a kick and it closed.* **2** (*informal*) a feeling of great pleasure, excitement, etc: *He seems to* ***get a real kick out of*** *driving fast.*

ˈkick-off *noun* [C] the start of a game of football: *Kick-off is at 2.30.*

kid¹ /kɪd/ *noun* **1** [C] (*informal*) a child or young person: *How are your kids?* **2** **kid brother/sister** [C] (*especially AmE informal*) younger brother/sister **3** [C,U] a young **goat** (= a small animal with horns that lives in mountain areas) or its skin: *a kid jacket* ➲ picture at **goat**

kid² /kɪd/ *verb* [I,T] (**kidding**; **kidded**) (*informal*) to trick sb/yourself by saying sth that is not true; to make a joke about sth: *I didn't mean it. I was only kidding.*

kiddie (also **kiddy**) /ˈkɪdi/ *noun* [C] (*pl* **kiddies**) (*informal*) a child

kidnap /ˈkɪdnæp/ *verb* [T] (**kidnapping**; **kidnapped**) to take sb away by force and demand money for their safe return: *The child was kidnapped and £50 000 ransom was demanded for her release.* ➲ look at **hijack** ▶ **kidnapper** *noun* [C]: *The kidnappers demanded £50 000.* ▶ **kidnapping** *noun* [C,U] ➲ note at **crime**

kidney /ˈkɪdni/ *noun* **1** [C] one of the two parts of your body that separate waste liquid from your blood ➲ picture at **body** **2** [U,C] the **kidneys** of an animal when they are cooked and eaten as food: *steak and kidney pie*

🔑 **kill¹** /kɪl/ *verb* **1** [I,T] to make sb/sth die: *Smoking kills.* ♦ *She was killed instantly in the crash.* **2** [T] (*spoken*) to be very angry with sb: *My mum will kill me when she sees this mess.* **3** [T] to cause sth to end or fail: *The minister's opposition killed the idea stone dead.* **4** [T] (*informal*) to cause sb pain; to hurt: *My feet are killing me.* **5** [T] (*informal*) **kill yourself/sb** to make yourself/sb laugh a lot: *We were **killing ourselves laughing**.*

IDM **kill time, an hour, etc.** to spend time doing sth that is not interesting or important while you are waiting for sth else to happen

kill two birds with one stone to do one thing which will achieve two results

PHR V **kill sth off** to cause sth to die or to not exist any more

> **OTHER WORDS FOR**
>
> **kill**
>
> **Murder** means to kill a person on purpose: *This was no accident. The old lady was murdered.* **Assassinate** means to kill for political reasons: *President Kennedy was assassinated.* **Slaughter** and **massacre** mean to kill a large number of people: *Hundreds of people were massacred when the army opened fire on the crowd.* **Slaughter** is also used of killing an animal for food.

kill² /kɪl/ *noun* [usually sing] **1** the act of killing: *Lions often make a kill in the evening.* **2** an animal or animals that have been killed: *The eagle took the kill back to its young.*

killer /ˈkɪlə(r)/ *noun* [C] a person, animal or thing that kills: *a killer disease* ♦ *He's a dangerous killer who may strike again.*

🔑 **killing** /ˈkɪlɪŋ/ *noun* [C] act of killing a person on purpose; a murder: *There have been a number of brutal killings in the area recently.*

IDM **make a killing** (*informal*) to make a large profit quickly

kiln /kɪln/ *noun* [C] a type of large oven for baking pots, bricks, etc. that are made of **clay** (= a type of earth) to make them hard

kilo /ˈkiːləʊ/ *noun* [C] (*pl* **kilos**) = **kilogram**

kilobit /ˈkɪləbɪt/ *noun* [C] (*abbr* **Kb**; **Kbit**) **1** a unit of computer memory, equal to 1 000 **bits** (= the smallest units of information) **2** (also **kibibit**) a unit of computer memory, equal to 1 024 **bits** (= the smallest units of information)

kilobyte /ˈkɪləbaɪt/ *noun* [C] (*abbr* **K**; **KB**) **1** a unit of computer memory, equal to 1 000 **bytes** (= small units of information) **2** (also **kibibyte**) a unit of computer memory, equal to 1 024 **bytes** (= small units of information)

🔑 **kilogram** (also **kilogramme** /ˈkɪləgræm/ **kilo**) *noun* [C] (*abbr* **kg**) a measure of weight; 1 000 grams: *a kilogram of rice* ♦ *I bought two kilos of potatoes.* ℹ For more information about weights, look at the section on using numbers at the back of this dictionary.

🔑 **kilometre** (*AmE* **kilometer**) /ˈkɪləmiːtə(r); kɪˈlɒmɪtə(r)/ *noun* [C] (*abbr* **k**, **km**) a measure of length; 1 000 metres: *They live 100 km from Paris.*

kilowatt /ˈkɪləwɒt/ *noun* [C] (*abbr* **kW**; **kw**) a measure of electric power; 1 000 **watts**

kilt /kɪlt/ *noun* [C] a skirt that is worn by men as part of the national dress of Scotland; a similar skirt worn by women

kin /kɪn/ ➲ **next of kin**

🔑 **kind¹** /kaɪnd/ *noun* [C] a type of person or thing: *The concert attracted people **of all kinds**.* ♦ *The concert attracted **all kinds of** people.* ♦ ***What kind of** car have you got?* ♦ *Many kinds of plant and animal are being lost every year.* ♦ *In the evenings I listen to music, write letters, that **kind of thing**.* **SYN** **sort**, **type**

> **GRAMMAR** Remember that **kind** is countable, so you CANNOT say: *I like all kind of music.* You should say: *I like all kinds of music. Kinds of* may be followed by a singular or plural noun: *There are so many kinds of camera/cameras on the market that it's hard to know which is best.*

IDM **a kind of** (*informal*) used for describing sth in a way that is not very clear: *I had a kind of feeling that something would go wrong.* ♦ *There's a funny kind of smell in here.*

kind of (*spoken*) slightly; a little: *I'm kind of worried about the interview.*

of a kind **1** of poor quality: *The village has a bus service of a kind—two buses a week!* **2** the same: *The friends were two of a kind—very similar in so many ways.*

🔑 **kind²** /kaɪnd/ *adj* (**kinder**; **kindest**) **kind (to sb)**; **kind (of sb) (to do sth)** caring about others; friendly and generous: *Everyone's been so kind to us since we came here!* ♦ *It was kind of you to offer, but I don't need any help.* **OPP** **unkind**

kindergarten /ˈkɪndəgɑːtn/ *noun* [C] a school for children aged from about 2 to 5 **SYN** **nursery school**

ˌkind-ˈhearted *adj* kind and generous

🔑 **kindly** /ˈkaɪndli/ *adv* **1** in a kind way: *The nurse smiled kindly.* **2** (*old-fashioned, informal*) (used for asking sb to do sth) please: *Would you kindly wait a moment?* ▸ **kindly** *adj* [only before a noun]: *a kindly face*

🔑 **kindness** /ˈkaɪndnəs/ *noun* [C,U] the quality of being kind; a kind act: *Thank you very much for all your kindness.*

🔑 **king** /kɪŋ/ *noun* [C] **1** (the title of) a man who rules a country. A king is usually the son or close relative of the former ruler: *The new king was crowned in Westminster Abbey.* ♦ *King Edward VII* (= the seventh) ♦ (*figurative*) *The lion is the king of the jungle.* ➲ look at **queen**, **prince**, **princess** **2** the most important piece used in the game of **chess**, that can move one square in any direction **3** one of the four playing cards in a pack with a picture of a king: *the king of spades* ➲ note at **card** ➲ picture at **card**

kingdom /ˈkɪŋdəm/ *noun* [C] **1** a country that is ruled by a king or queen: *the United Kingdom* **2** one of the parts of the natural world: *the animal kingdom*

ˈ**king-size** (also ˈ**king-sized**) *adj* bigger than usual: *a king-size bed*

kink /kɪŋk/ *noun* [C] a turn or bend in sth that should be straight

kiosk /ˈkiːɒsk/ *noun* [C] a very small building in the street where newspapers, sweets, cigarettes, etc. are sold

kip /kɪp/ *verb* [I] (**kipping**; **kipped**) (*BrE informal*) to sleep: *You could kip on the sofa if you like.* ▶ **kip** *noun* [sing,U]: *I'm going to have a kip.* ◆ *I didn't get much kip last night.*

kipper /ˈkɪpə(r)/ *noun* [C] a type of fish that has been kept for a long time in salt, and then smoked

⚷ **kiss** /kɪs/ *verb* [I,T] to touch sb with your lips to show love or friendship, or when saying hello or goodbye: *They sat in the back row of the cinema, kissing and cuddling.* ◆ *He kissed her on the cheek.* ◆ *They kissed each other goodbye.* ▶ **kiss** *noun* [C]: *a kiss on the lips/cheek*

kit¹ /kɪt/ *noun* **1** [C] a set of parts that you buy and put together in order to make sth: *a kit for a model aeroplane* **2** [C,U] a set of tools, equipment or clothes that you need for a particular purpose, sport or activity: *a tool kit* ◆ *a drum kit* ◆ *football/gym kit*

kit² /kɪt/ *verb* (**kitting**; **kitted**)
PHR V kit sb/yourself out/up (in/with sth) to give sb all the necessary clothes, equipment, tools, etc. for sth

⚷ **kitchen** /ˈkɪtʃɪn/ *noun* [C] a room where food is prepared and cooked: *We usually eat in the kitchen.* ➲ picture on **page P8**

kite /kaɪt/ *noun* [C] a toy which consists of a light frame covered with paper or cloth. **Kites are flown in** the wind on the end of a long piece of string: *to fly a kite*

kitesurfing /ˈkaɪtsɜːfɪŋ/ (also **kiteboarding** /ˈkaɪtbɔːdɪŋ/) *noun* [U] the sport of riding on water while standing on a short wide board and being pulled along by wind power, using a large **kite**

kitten /ˈkɪtn/ *noun* [C] a young cat ➲ note at **cat**

kitty /ˈkɪti/ *noun* [C] (*pl* **kitties**) **1** a sum of money that is collected from a group of people and used for a particular purpose: *All the students in the flat put £20 a week into the kitty.* **2** (*spoken*) a way of calling or referring to a cat

kiwi /ˈkiːwiː/ *noun* [C] (*pl* **kiwis**) **1** a New Zealand bird with a long beak and short wings that cannot fly **2** (also ˈ**kiwi fruit**) a fruit with brown skin that is green inside with black seeds ➲ picture on **page P14**

km *abbr* = **kilometre**

knack /næk/ *noun* [sing] (*informal*) **knack (of/for doing sth)** skill or ability to do sth (difficult) that you have naturally or you can learn: *Knitting isn't difficult once you've got the knack of it.*

knead /niːd/ *verb* [T] to press and squeeze **dough** (= a mixture of flour and water) with your hands in order to make bread, etc.

⚷ **knee** /niː/ *noun* [C] **1** the place where your leg bends in the middle: *Angie fell and grazed her knee.* ◆ *She was **on her hands and knees** on the floor looking for her earrings.* ◆ *Come and sit on my knee.* ➲ picture at **body** **2** the part of a pair of trousers, etc. that covers the knee: *There's a hole in the knee of those jeans.*

kneecap /ˈniːkæp/ *noun* [C] the bone that covers the front of the knee ➲ picture at **body**

ˌ**knee-ˈdeep** *adj, adv* up to your knees: *The water was knee-deep in places.*

kneel /niːl/ *verb* [I] (*pt, pp* **knelt** /nelt/; *AmE* also **kneeled**) **kneel (down)** to rest on one or both knees: *She knelt down to talk to the child.* ➲ picture on **page 416**

K

kitchen utensils

kneel

She's kneeling. He's squatting.

He's crouching.

knew *past tense* of **know**[1]

knickers /ˈnɪkəz/ (*AmE* **panties**) *noun* [pl] a piece of underwear for women that covers the area between the waist and the top of the legs: *a pair of knickers*

knife[1] /naɪf/ *noun* [C] (*pl* **knives** /naɪvz/) a sharp blade with a handle. A knife is used for cutting things or as a weapon: *The carving knife is very blunt/sharp.* ♦ *a knife and fork* ♦ *a penknife/pocket knife/bread knife* ➲ picture at **cutlery, kitchen**

knife[2] /naɪf/ *verb* [T] to deliberately injure sb with a knife **SYN** **stab**

knight /naɪt/ *noun* [C] **1** a soldier who fought on a horse in the Middle Ages **2** a man who has been given a title of honour by a king or queen and who can use *Sir* in front of his name **3** a piece used in the game of **chess** that is shaped like a horse's head ▶ **knighthood** /ˈnaɪthʊd/ *noun* [C]: *He received a knighthood.*

knit /nɪt/ *verb* [I,T] (**knitting**; *pt, pp* **knitted** *or AmE* **knit**) **1** to make sth (for example an article of clothing) with wool using two long needles or a special machine: *I'm knitting a sweater for my nephew.* ➲ look at **crochet** ➲ picture at **sew** **2 knit** [only used in this form] joined closely together: *a **closely/tightly knit** village community* ▶ **knitting** *noun* [U]: *I usually do some knitting while I'm watching TV.* ♦ *Where's my knitting?*

ˈ**knitting needle** = **needle**(2)

knitwear /ˈnɪtweə(r)/ *noun* [U] articles of clothing that have been knitted: *the knitwear department*

knives *plural* of **knife**

knob /nɒb/ *noun* [C] **1** a round switch on a machine (for example a TV) that you press or turn: *the volume control knob* **2** a round handle on a door, drawer, etc. ➲ picture at **drawer** ➲ picture at **handle**

knock[1] /nɒk/ *verb* **1** [I] **knock (at/on sth)** to make a noise by hitting sth firmly with your hand: *Is that someone knocking at the door?* ♦ *I knocked on the window but she didn't hear me.* **2** [T] **knock sth (on/against sth)** to hit sb/sth hard, often by accident: *He knocked the vase onto the floor.* ♦ *Be careful not to knock your head on the shelf when you get up.* ♦ *to knock somebody unconscious* **3** [T] (*informal*) to say bad things about sb/sth; to criticize sb/sth: *'I hate this town.' 'Don't knock it—there are far worse places to live.'*

IDM **knock on wood** ➲ **wood**

PHR V **knock about/around** (*informal*) to be in a place; to travel and live in various places: *Is last week's newspaper still knocking about?*

knock sb down to hit sb causing them to fall to the ground: *The old lady was knocked down by a cyclist.*

knock sth down to destroy a building, etc: *They knocked down the old factory because it was unsafe.*

knock off (sth) (*spoken*) to stop working: *What time do you knock off?*

knock sth off **1** (*informal*) to reduce a price by a certain amount: *He agreed to knock £10 off the price.* **2** (*slang*) to steal sth

knock sb out **1** to hit sb so that they become unconscious or cannot get up again for a while: *The punch on the nose knocked him out.* **2** (used about a drug, alcohol, etc.) to cause sb to sleep or become unconscious: *Those three glasses of vodka really knocked her out.*

knock sb out (of sth) to beat a person or team in a competition so that they do not play any more games in it: *Belgium was knocked out of the European Cup by France.*

knock sb/sth over to cause sb/sth to fall over: *Be careful not to knock over the drinks.*

knock[2] /nɒk/ *noun* [C] a sharp hit from sth hard or the sound it makes: *a nasty knock on the head* ♦ *I thought I heard a knock at the door.* ♦ (*figurative*) *She has suffered some hard knocks* (= bad experiences) *in her life.*

knocker /ˈnɒkə(r)/ *noun* [C] a piece of metal fixed to the outside of a door that you hit against the door to attract attention ➲ picture on **page P8**

ˈ**knock-on** *adj* (*especially BrE*) causing other events to happen one after the other: *An increase in the price of oil has **a knock-on effect** on other goods.*

knockout /ˈnɒkaʊt/ *noun* [C] **1** a hard hit that causes sb to become unconscious or to be unable to get up again for a while **2** a competition in which the winner of each game goes on to the next part but the person who loses plays no more games

knot[1] /nɒt/ *noun* [C] **1** a place where two ends or pieces of rope, string, etc. have been tied together: *to tie/untie a knot* ➲ picture at **loop** **2** a measure of the speed of a ship; approximately 1.8 kilometres per hour

knot² /nɒt/ *verb* [T] (knotting; knotted) to fasten sth together with a knot

know¹ /nəʊ/ *verb* (*pt* knew /njuː/; *pp* known /nəʊn/) [not used in the continuous tenses]
➤HAVE INFORMATION **1** [I,T] know (about sth); know (that) ... to have knowledge or information in your mind: *I don't know much about sport.* ◆ *Did you know that she was coming?* ◆ *Do you know where this bus stops?* ◆ *Do you know their telephone number?* ◆ *'You've got a flat tyre.' 'I know.'* ◆ *Do you* ***know the way*** *to the restaurant?*
➤FEEL SURE **2** [T,I] to feel certain; to be sure of sth: *I just know you'll pass the exam!* ◆ ***As far as I know*** (= I think it is true but I am not absolutely sure), *the meeting is next Monday afternoon.*
➤BE FAMILIAR **3** [T] to be familiar with a person or a place; to have met sb or been somewhere before: *We've known each other for years.* ◆ *I don't know this part of London well.*

MORE You can use **meet** to talk about the first time you see and talk to someone, or are introduced to someone: *Rahul and I met at university in 2008.* After you meet someone and gradually become friends, you **get to know** him/her: *Kevin's wife seems very interesting. I'd like to get to know her better.*

➤GIVE NAME **4** [T, often passive] know sb/sth as sth to give sth a particular name; to recognize sb/sth as sth: *Istanbul was previously known as Constantinople.*
➤SKILL **5** [T] know how to do sth to have learnt sth and be able to do it: *Do you know how to make pancakes?*

HELP Be careful. In front of a verb you must use **how to**. You CANNOT say: *I know make pancakes.*

➤EXPERIENCE **6** [T] to have personal experience of sth: *Many people in western countries don't know what it's like to be hungry.* **7** [T] [only in the past and perfect tenses] to have seen, heard, or experienced sth: *I've known him go a whole day without eating.* ◆ *It's been known to snow in June.*

HELP Although this verb is not used in the continuous tenses, it is common to see the present participle (= *-ing* form): *Knowing how he'd react if he ever found out about it, she kept quiet.*

IDM God, goodness, Heaven, etc. knows 1 I do not know: *They've ordered a new car but goodness knows how they're going to pay for it.* **2** used for emphasizing sth: *I hope I get an answer soon. Goodness knows, I've waited long enough.* ➲ note at **God**
I might have known ➲ **might¹**
know better (than that/than to do sth) to have enough sense to realize that you should not do sth: *I thought you knew better than to go out in the rain with no coat on.*
know sth inside out/like the back of your hand (*informal*) to be very familiar with sth
know what you are talking about (*informal*) to have knowledge of sth from your own experience: *I've lived in London so I know what I'm talking about.*
know what's what (*informal*) to have all the important information about sth; to fully understand sth
let sb know to tell sb about sth: *Could you let me know what time you're arriving?*
show sb/know/learn the ropes ➲ **rope¹**
you know used when the speaker is thinking of what to say next, or to remind sb of sth: *Well, you know, it's rather difficult to explain.* ◆ *I've just met Marta. You know—Jim's ex-wife.*
you never know (*spoken*) you cannot be certain: *Keep those empty boxes. You never know, they might come in handy one day.*
PHR V know of sb/sth to have information about or experience of sb/sth: *Do you know of any pubs around here that serve food?*

know² /nəʊ/ *noun*
IDM in the know (*informal*) having information that other people do not

ˈknow-all (also ˈknow-it-all) *noun* [C] an annoying person who behaves as if they know everything

ˈknow-how *noun* [U] (*informal*) practical knowledge of or skill in sth

knowing /ˈnəʊɪŋ/ *adj* showing that you know about sth that is thought to be secret: *a knowing look*

knowingly /ˈnəʊɪŋli/ *adv* **1** on purpose; deliberately: *I've never knowingly lied to you.* **2** in a way that shows that you know about sth that is thought to be secret: *He smiled knowingly at her.*

ˈknow-it-all = **know-all**

knowledge /ˈnɒlɪdʒ/ *noun* **1** [U, sing] knowledge (of/about sth) information, understanding and skills that you have gained through learning or experience: *I have* ***a working knowledge*** *of French* (= enough to be able to make myself understood). **2** [U] the state of knowing about a particular fact or situation: *He* ***denied all knowledge*** *of the affair.* ◆ *She did it* ***without my knowledge*** (= I did not know about it).
IDM be common/public knowledge to be sth that everyone knows
to (the best of) your knowledge from the information you have, although you may not know everything: *To the best of my knowledge they are still living there.*

knowledgeable /ˈnɒlɪdʒəbl/ *adj* having a lot of knowledge: *She's very knowledgeable about history.* ▶ **knowledgeably** /-əbli/ *adv*

known *past participle of* **know¹**

knuckle /ˈnʌkl/ *noun* [C] the bones where your fingers join the rest of your hand ➲ picture at **body**

koala /kəʊˈɑːlə/ *noun* [C] an Australian animal with thick grey fur that lives in trees and looks like a small bear

koala

the Koran (also Qur'an) /kəˈrɑːn/ *noun*

K

[sing] the most important book in the Islamic religion

kosher /ˈkəʊʃə(r)/ *adj* (used about food) prepared according to the rules of Jewish law

kph /ˌkeɪ piː ˈeɪtʃ/ *abbr* **kilometres per hour**

kung fu /ˌkʌŋ ˈfuː/ *noun* [U] a Chinese style of fighting using the feet and hands as weapons ➲ look at **martial arts**

kW (also kw) *abbr* = **kilowatt**: *a 2kW electric heater*

L, l /el/ *noun* [C,U] (*pl* Ls; L's; l's /elz/) the 12th letter of the English alphabet: *'Language' begins with (an) 'L'.*

l *abbr* **1** [in writing] l = **litre** **2** L (*BrE*) used on a sign on a car to show that the driver is learning to drive **3** L large (size): *S, M and L* (= small, medium and large)

Lab *abbr* (in British politics) **Labour**

lab /læb/ (*informal*) = **laboratory**

price tag label ticket

label¹ /ˈleɪbl/ *noun* [C] **1** a piece of paper, etc. that is fixed to sth and which gives information about it: *There is a list of all the ingredients on the label.* **2** a company that produces and sells music, CDs, etc: *It's his first release for a major label.*

label² /ˈleɪbl/ *verb* [T] (**labelling**; **labelled**, (*AmE*) **labeling**; **labeled**) **1** [usually passive] to fix a **label** or write information on sth **2** **label sb/sth (as) sth** to describe sb/sth in a particular way, especially unfairly

laboratory /ləˈbɒrətri/ *noun* [C] (*pl* **laboratories**) (also *informal* **lab**) a room or building that is used for scientific research, testing, experiments, etc. or for teaching about science: *The blood samples were sent to the laboratory for analysis.* ♦ *a physics laboratory* ➲ look at **language laboratory**

laborious /ləˈbɔːriəs/ *adj* needing a lot of time and effort: *a laborious task/process/job* ▶ **laboriously** *adv*

labour¹ (*AmE* labor) /ˈleɪbə(r)/ *noun* **1** [U] work, usually of a hard, physical kind: *manual labour* (= work using your hands) **2** [U] workers, when thought of as a group: *There is a shortage of skilled labour.* **3** [U,C, usually sing] the process of giving birth to a baby: *She* ***went into labour*** *in the early hours of this morning.* ♦ *She was* ***in labour*** *for ten hours.* ♦ *She had a difficult labour.* **4** = **the Labour Party**

labour² (*AmE* labor) /ˈleɪbə(r)/ *verb* [I] **1** **labour (away)** to work hard at sth: *She laboured on her book for two years.* **2** to move or do sth with difficulty and effort

laboured (*AmE* labored) /ˈleɪbəd/ *adj* done slowly or with difficulty: *laboured breathing*

labourer (*AmE* laborer) /ˈleɪbərə(r)/ *noun* [C] a person whose job involves hard physical work: *unskilled/farm labourers*

the ˈLabour Party (also Labour) *noun* [sing, with sing or pl verb] one of the main political parties in Britain. The **Labour Party** supports the interests of working people: *He has always voted Labour.* ♦ *a Labour MP* ➲ note at **party** ➲ look at **the Conservative Party, the Liberal Democrats**

ˈlabour-saving *adj* reducing the amount of work needed to do sth: *labour-saving devices such as washing machines and dishwashers*

labyrinth /ˈlæbərɪnθ/ *noun* [C] a complicated set of paths and passages, which is difficult to find your way through: *a labyrinth of corridors* SYN **maze**

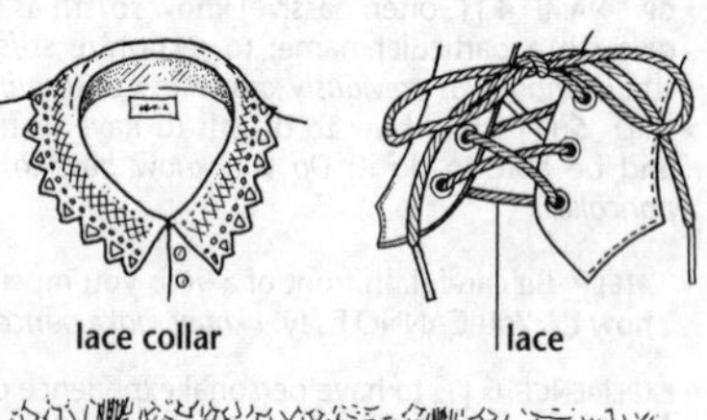
lace collar lace

lace

lace¹ /leɪs/ *noun* **1** [U] cloth that is made of very thin threads sewn in patterns with small holes in between: *lace curtains* ♦ *a collar made of lace* ➲ *adjective* **lacy** **2** = **shoelace**: *Do up your laces or you'll trip over them.*

lace² /leɪs/ *verb* [I,T] **lace (sth) (up)** to tie or fasten sth with a **lace¹**(2): *She was sitting on the end of the bed lacing up her boots.* ▶ **lace-up** *adj, noun* [C]: *lace-up shoes* ♦ *a pair of lace-ups*

lack¹ /læk/ *noun* [U, sing] **a lack (of sth)** the state of not having sth or not having enough of sth: *A lack of food forced many people to leave their homes.* ♦ *The trip was cancelled through lack of interest.*

lack² /læk/ *verb* [T] to have none or not enough of sth: *She seems to lack the will to succeed.*

lacking /ˈlækɪŋ/ *adj* [not before a noun] **1** **lacking in sth** not having enough of sth: *He's certainly not lacking in intelligence.* **2** not present or available: *I feel there is something lacking in my life.*

lacklustre /ˈlæklʌstə(r)/ *adj* not interesting or exciting: *a lacklustre performance* SYN **dull**

laconic /ləˈkɒnɪk/ *adj* (*formal*) using only a few words to say sth ▸ **laconically** /-kli/ *adv*

lacquer /ˈlækə(r)/ *noun* [U] **1** a type of transparent paint that is put on wood, metal, etc. to give it a hard, shiny surface **2** (*old-fashioned*) a liquid that you put on your hair to keep it in place SYN **hairspray**

lacy /ˈleɪsi/ *adj* made of or looking like **lace** (= material made of thin threads with small holes that form a pattern)

lad /læd/ *noun* (*BrE informal*) **1** [C] (*old-fashioned*) a boy or young man: *School has changed since I was a lad.* **2 the lads** [pl] a group of friends that a man spends time with: *a night out with the lads*

ladder /ˈlædə(r)/ *noun* [C] **1** a piece of equipment that is used for climbing up sth. A **ladder** consists of two long pieces of metal, wood or rope with steps fixed between them: (*figurative*) *to climb the ladder of success* ➲ look at **stepladder 2** (*AmE* **run**) a long hole in **tights** or **stockings** (= the thin pieces of clothing that women wear to cover their legs), where the threads have broken: *Oh no! I've got a ladder in my tights.* ▸ **ladder** *verb* [T]

laden /ˈleɪdn/ *adj* [not before a noun] **laden (with sth)** having or carrying a lot of sth: *The travellers were laden down with luggage.* ◆ *The orange trees were laden with fruit.*

the ˈLadies *noun* [sing] (*BrE informal*) a public toilet for women ➲ note at **toilet**

ladle[1] /ˈleɪdl/ *noun* [C] a large deep spoon with a long handle, used especially for serving soup ➲ picture at **kitchen**

ladle[2] /ˈleɪdl/ *verb* [T] to serve food with a **ladle**

lady /ˈleɪdi/ *noun* [C] (*pl* **ladies**) **1** a polite way of saying 'woman', especially when you are referring to an older woman: *The old lady next door lives alone.* **2** (*formal*) used when speaking to or about a woman or women in a polite way: ***Ladies and gentlemen*** (= at the beginning of a speech) ◆ *Mrs Flinn, there's a lady here to see you.* **3** a title that is used before the name of a woman who has a high social position: *Lady Elizabeth Groves* ➲ look at **Lord**

ladybird /ˈleɪdibɜːd/ (*AmE* **ladybug** /ˈleɪdibʌg/) *noun* [C] a small insect that is red or yellow with black spots ➲ picture on **page P13**

lag[1] /læg/ *verb* [I] (**lagging**; **lagged**) **lag (behind)**; **lag (behind sb/sth)** to move or develop more slowly than sb/sth: *James has missed a lot of classes and is lagging behind the others at school.*

lag[2] /læg/ (also ˈ**time lag**) *noun* [C] a period of time between two events; a delay ➲ look at **jet lag**

lager /ˈlɑːgə(r)/ *noun* [C,U] (*BrE*) a type of light beer that is a gold colour: *Three pints of lager, please.* ➲ note at **beer**

lagoon /ləˈguːn/ *noun* [C] a lake of salt water that is separated from the sea by sand or rock

laid *past tense, past participle of* **lay**[1]

laid-back /ˌleɪd ˈbæk/ *adj* (*informal*) calm and relaxed; seeming not to worry about anything SYN **easy-going**

lain *past participle of* **lie**[2]

lake /leɪk/ *noun* [C] a large area of water that is surrounded by land: *They've gone sailing **on the lake**.* ◆ *We all swam **in the lake**.* ◆ *Lake Constance* ➲ picture on **page P10**

OTHER WORDS FOR

lake

A **lake** is usually big enough to sail on: *Lake Como*. A **pond** may be big enough for animals to drink from or may be a very small area of water in a garden: *We have a fish pond in our garden.* A **pool** is a much smaller area of water: *When the tide went out, pools of water were left among the rocks.* An artificial pool, however, can be larger: *a swimming pool*. A **puddle** is a small pool of water made by the rain.

lamb /læm/ *noun* **1** [C] a young sheep ➲ note at **sheep** ➲ picture at **goat 2** [U] the meat of a young sheep: *lamb chops* ➲ note at **meat**

lame /leɪm/ *adj* **1** (used mainly about animals) not able to walk properly because of an injury to the leg or foot: *The horse is lame and cannot work.* **2** (used about an excuse, argument, etc.) not easily believed; weak

lament /ləˈment/ *noun* [C] (*formal*) a song, poem or other expression of sadness for sb who has died or for sth that has ended ▸ **lament** *verb* [T]

laminated /ˈlæmɪneɪtɪd/ *adj* **1** (used about wood, plastic, etc.) made by sticking several thin layers together: *laminated glass* **2** covered with thin transparent plastic for protection

lamp /læmp/ *noun* [C] a device that uses electricity, gas or oil to produce light: *a street lamp* ◆ *a table/desk/bicycle lamp* ◆ *a sunlamp* ➲ picture on **page 420**

ˈ**lamp post** *noun* [C] a tall pole at the side of the road with a light on the top ➲ look at **street light** ➲ picture on **page P11**

lamps

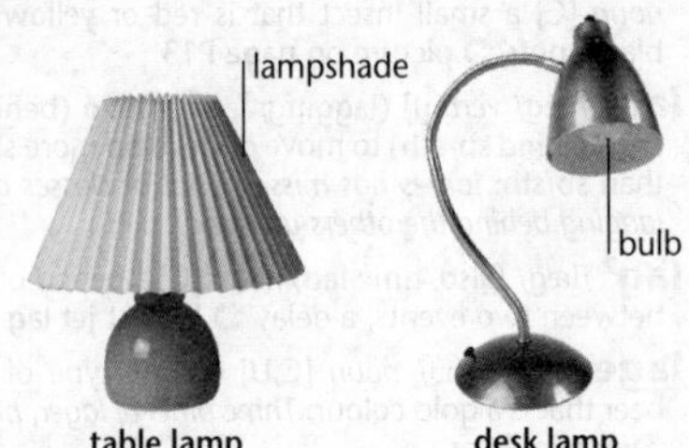

lampshade /ˈlæmpʃeɪd/ *noun* [C] a cover for a lamp that makes it look more attractive and makes the light softer ➲ picture at **lamp**

LAN /læn/ *abbr* **local area network**; a system that connects computers inside a single building or buildings in the same area ➲ look at **WAN**

land¹ /lænd/ *noun* **1** [U] the solid part of the surface of the earth (= not sea): *Penguins can't move very fast* ***on land***. OPP **sea** ➲ note at **ground 2** [U] an area of ground: *The land rose to the east.* ◆ *She owns 500 acres of land in Scotland.* **3** [U] ground, soil or earth of a particular kind: *The land is rich and fertile.* ◆ *arid/barren land* ◆ *arable/agricultural/industrial land* **4** [C] (*written*) a country or region: *She died far from her native land.* ◆ *to travel to distant lands* ➲ note at **country**

L

land² /lænd/ *verb* **1** [I,T] to come down from the air or to bring sth down to the ground: *The bird landed on the roof.* ◆ *He fell off the ladder and landed on his back.* ◆ *The pilot landed the aeroplane safely.* ◆ *His flight is due to land at 3 o'clock.* OPP **take off 2** [I,T] to go onto land or put sth onto land from a ship: *to land cargo* **3** [T] to succeed in getting sth, especially sth that a lot of people want: *The company has just landed a million-dollar contract.*

IDM **fall/land on your feet** ➲ **foot¹**

PHR V **land up (in ...)** (*BrE informal*) to finish in a certain position or situation: *He landed up in a prison cell for the night.*

land sb with sb/sth (*informal*) to give sb sth unpleasant to do, especially because nobody else wants to do it

landfill /ˈlændfɪl/ *noun* **1** [C,U] an area of land where large amounts of waste material are buried **2** [U] waste material that will be buried; the burying of waste material

landing /ˈlændɪŋ/ *noun* [C] **1** the area at the top of a set of stairs in a house, or between one set of stairs and another in a large building **2** the act of coming down onto the ground (in an aircraft): *The plane made an* ***emergency landing*** *in a field.* ◆ *a crash landing* ◆ *a safe landing* OPP **take-off** ➲ picture at **take-off**

ˈlanding card *noun* [C] a form on which you have to write details about yourself when flying to a foreign country

ˈlanding gear = undercarriage

ˈlanding stage = jetty

ˈlanding strip = airstrip

landline /ˈlændlaɪn/ *noun* [C] a telephone connection that uses wires carried on poles or under the ground ➲ look at **mobile phone**

landlord /ˈlændlɔːd/ (*fem* **landlady** /ˈlændleɪdi/; *pl* **landladies**) *noun* [C] **1** a person who rents a house or room to people for money **2** (*BrE*) a person who owns or manages a pub, small hotel, etc.

landmark /ˈlændmɑːk/ *noun* [C] **1** an object (often a building) that can be seen easily from a distance and will help you to recognize where you are: *Big Ben is one of the landmarks on London's skyline.* **2 a landmark (in sth)** an important stage or change in the development of sth

landmine /ˈlændmaɪn/ *noun* [C] a bomb placed on or under the ground, which explodes when sb moves or drives over it

landscape¹ /ˈlændskeɪp/ *noun* **1** [C, usually sing] everything you can see when you look across a large area of land: *an urban/industrial landscape* ➲ note at **scenery** ➲ picture on **page P10 2** [C,U] a picture or a painting that shows a view of the countryside; this style of painting: *one of Constable's landscapes* **3** [U] (*technical*) the way of printing a document in which the top of the page is one of the longer sides: *Select the landscape option when printing the file.* ➲ look at **portrait** ➲ picture at **computer**

landscape² /ˈlændskeɪp/ *verb* [T] to improve the appearance of an area of land by changing its design and planting trees, flowers, etc.

landslide /ˈlændslaɪd/ *noun* [C] **1** the sudden fall of a mass of earth, rocks, etc. down the side of a mountain: *Part of the railway line was buried beneath a landslide.* **2** a great victory for one person or one political party in an election

lane /leɪn/ *noun* [C] **1** a narrow road in the country: *We found a route through country lanes to avoid the traffic jam on the main road.* ➲ picture on **page P11 2** used in the names of roads: *Crossley Lane* **3** a section of a wide road that is marked by painted white lines to keep lines of traffic separate: *a four-lane motorway* ◆ *the inside/middle/fast/outside lane* **4** a section of a sports track, swimming pool, etc. for one person to go along: *The British athlete is in lane two.* ➲ picture on **page P4 5** a route or path that is regularly used by ships or aircraft: *the busy* ***shipping lanes*** *of the English Channel*

language /ˈlæŋgwɪdʒ/ *noun*

➤OF A COUNTRY **1** [C] the system of communication in speech and writing that is used by people of a particular country: *How many languages can you speak?* ◆ *What is your first language* (= your mother tongue)? ◆ *They fell in love in spite of* ***the language barrier*** (= having different first languages).

➤COMMUNICATION **2** [U] the system of sounds and writing that people use to express their thoughts, ideas and feelings: *written/spoken language*

➤STYLE OF SPEAKING/WRITING **3** [U] words of a particular type or words that are used by a particular

person or group: *bad (= rude) language* ◆ *legal language* ◆ *the language of Shakespeare*
➤SIGNS/SYMBOLS **4** [U] any system of signs, symbols, movements, etc. that is used to express sth: *sign language* (= using your hands, not speaking) ➲ look at **body language**
➤COMPUTING **5** [C,U] a system of symbols and rules that is used to operate a computer: *BASIC is a common computer language.*

ˈlanguage laboratory *noun* [C] (*pl* **language laboratories**) a room in a school or college that contains special equipment to help students to learn foreign languages by listening to CDs or tapes, watching DVDs or videos, recording themselves, etc.

lanky /ˈlæŋki/ *adj* (**lankier**; **lankiest**) (used about a person) very tall and thin

lantern /ˈlæntən/ *noun* [C] a type of light that can be carried, with a metal frame, glass sides and a light or **candle** (= a tall stick that you burn) inside

lanyard /ˈlænjɑːd; -jəd/ *noun* [C] a string or wire that you wear around your neck or wrist for holding sth: *I carry my ID card on a lanyard round my neck.* ◆ *The lanyard keeps your iPod around your neck so your music is always available.*

lap¹ /læp/ *noun* [C] **1** the flat area that is formed by the upper part of your legs when you are sitting down: *The child sat quietly on his mother's lap.* **2** one journey around a running track, etc: *There are three more laps to go in the race.* **3** one part of a long journey

lap² /læp/ *verb* (**lapping**; **lapped**) **1** [I] (used about water) to make gentle sounds as it moves against sth: *The waves lapped against the side of the boat.* **2** [T] **lap sth (up)** (usually used about an animal) to drink sth using the tongue: *The cat lapped up the cream.* **3** [T] to pass another person in a race who has been round the track fewer times than you
PHR V **lap sth up** (*informal*) to accept sth with great enjoyment without stopping to think if it is good, true, etc.

lapel /ləˈpel/ *noun* [C] one of the two parts of the front of a coat or jacket that are folded back

lapse¹ /læps/ *noun* [C] **1** a short time when you cannot remember sth or you are not thinking about what you are doing: *a lapse of memory* ◆ *The crash was the result of a temporary lapse in concentration.* **2** a period of time between two things that happen: *She returned to work after a lapse of ten years bringing up her family.* ➲ look at **elapse** **3** a piece of bad behaviour from sb who usually behaves well

lapse² /læps/ *verb* [I] **1** (used about a contract, an agreement, etc.) to finish or stop, often by accident: *My membership has lapsed because I forgot to renew it.* **2** to become weaker or stop for a short time: *My concentration lapsed during the last part of the exam.*
PHR V **lapse into sth** to gradually pass into a worse or less active state or condition; to start speaking or behaving in a less acceptable way: *to lapse into silence/a coma*

laptop /ˈlæptɒp/ *noun* [C] a small computer that is easy to carry and that can use batteries for power: *Moira took her laptop to Korea.* ➲ note at **computer** ➲ picture at **computer**

lard /lɑːd/ *noun* [U] hard white fat that is used in cooking

larder /ˈlɑːdə(r)/ *noun* [C] a large cupboard or small room that is used for storing food **SYN** **pantry**

large /lɑːdʒ/ *adj* (**larger**; **largest**) greater in size, amount, etc. than usual; big: *a large area/house/family/appetite* ◆ *a large number of people* ◆ *I'd like a large coffee, please.* ◆ *We have this shirt in small, medium or large.* ➲ note at **big, fat**
IDM **at large 1** as a whole; in general: *He is well known to scientists but not to the public at large.* **2** (used about a criminal, animal, etc.) not caught; free: *One of the escaped prisoners is still at large.*
by and large mostly; in general: *By and large the school is very efficient.*

largely /ˈlɑːdʒli/ *adv* mostly: *His success was largely due to hard work.*

ˌlarge-ˈscale *adj* happening over a large area or affecting a lot of people: *large-scale production/unemployment*

lark /lɑːk/ *noun* [C] a small brown bird with a pleasant song

larva /ˈlɑːvə/ *noun* [C] (*pl* **larvae** /ˈlɑːviː/) an insect that has just come out of its egg and has a short fat soft body with no legs ➲ picture on **page P13**

laryngitis /ˌlærɪnˈdʒaɪtɪs/ *noun* [U] a mild illness of the throat that makes it difficult to speak

laser /ˈleɪzə(r)/ *noun* [C] a device that produces a controlled line of very powerful light

lash¹ /læʃ/ *verb* **1** [I,T] (used especially about wind, rain and storms) to hit sth with great force: *The rain lashed against the windows.* **2** [T] to hit sb with a piece of rope, leather, etc.; to move sth like a piece of rope, leather, etc. violently **3** [T] **lash A to B; lash A and B together** to tie two things together firmly with rope, etc: *The two boats were lashed together.*
PHR V **lash out (at/against sb/sth)** to suddenly attack sb/sth (with words or by hitting them or it): *The actor lashed out at a photographer outside his house.*

lash² /læʃ/ *noun* [C] **1** = **eyelash** **2** a hit with a **whip** (= a long thin piece of rope or leather)

lass /læs/ (also **lassie** /ˈlæsi/) *noun* [C] (*informal*) a girl or young woman

HELP Lass is most commonly used in Scotland and the North of England.

lasso /læˈsuː/ *noun* [C] (*pl* **lassos** or **lassoes**) a long rope that is tied in a circle at one end and is used for catching cows and horses ▶ **lasso** *verb* [T]

last¹ /lɑːst/ *determiner, adj, adv, noun* [C] (*pl* **the last**) **1** at the end; after all the others: *December is the last month of the year.* ◆ *Would the last person to leave please turn off the lights?* ◆ *Our house is the last one on the left.* ◆ *She lived alone for the last years of her life.* ◆ *The British athlete came in last.* ◆ *Her name is last on the list.* ◆ *Alex was the last to finish.* ◆ *They were the last to arrive.* **2** used about a time, period,

L

event, etc. in the past that is nearest to the present: *last night/week/Saturday/summer* ♦ *We have been working on the book for the last six months.* ♦ ***The last time** I saw her was in London.* ♦ *We'll win this time, because they beat us **last time**.* ♦ *When did you last have your eyes checked?* ♦ *When I saw her last she seemed very happy.*

HELP **Last** or **latest**? **The latest** means 'most recent' or 'newest'. **The last** means the one before the present one: *His last novel was a huge success, but the latest one is much less popular.*

3 final: *This is my last chance to take the exam.* ♦ *Alison's retiring—tomorrow is her last day at work.* ♦ *We finished **the last of the** bread at breakfast so we'd better get some more.* **4** [only *before* a noun] not expected or not suitable: *He's the last person I thought would get the job.*

IDM **at (long) last** in the end; finally: *After months of separation they were together at last.*

first/last thing ➲ **thing**

have the last laugh to be the person, team, etc. who is successful in the end

have, etc. the last word to be the person who makes the final decision or the final comment

in the last resort; (as) a last resort when everything else has failed; the person or thing that helps when everything else has failed: *In the last resort my grandad could play in the match.*

last but not least (used before the final item in a list) just as important as all the other items

last/next but one, two, etc. one, two, etc. away from the last/next: *I live in the next house but one on the right.* ♦ *X is the last letter but two of the alphabet* (= the third letter from the end).

a last-ditch attempt a final effort to avoid sth unpleasant or dangerous

the last minute/moment the final minute/ moment before sth happens: *We arrived at the last minute to catch the train.* ♦ *a last-minute change of plan*

the last/final straw ➲ **straw**

▸ **lastly** *adv*: *Lastly, I would like to thank the band who played this evening.* **SYN** **finally**

L

⚷ **last²** /lɑːst/ *verb* [not used in the continuous tenses] **1** [T] to continue for a period of time: *The exam lasts three hours.* ♦ *How long does a cricket match last?* ♦ *The flight seemed to last forever.* **2** [I,T] to continue to be good or to function: *Do you think this weather will last till the weekend?* ♦ *It's only a cheap radio but it'll probably last a year or so.* **3** [I,T] to be enough for what sb needs: *This money won't last me till the end of the month.*

HELP Although this verb is not used in the continuous tenses, it is common to see the present participle (= *-ing* form): *An earthquake lasting approximately 20 seconds struck the city last night.*

lasting /ˈlɑːstɪŋ/ *adj* continuing for a long time: *The book left a lasting impression on me.*

ˌlast-ˈminute *adj* done, decided or organized just before sth happens or before it is too late: *a last-minute holiday*

EXAM TIP

Last-minute learning

In the weeks before your exam, keep a note of any points that are particularly difficult and make a list of things to check over the evening before your exam. These might be notes in the dictionary about words that you often get confused, or verb tenses (look at the note at **tense**), or groups of words about a particular topic. Keep your last-minute list short!

ˈlast name = **surname**

latch¹ /lætʃ/ *noun* [C] **1** a small metal bar that is used for fastening a door or a gate. You have to lift the **latch** in order to open the door. **2** (*especially BrE*) a type of lock for a door that you open with a key from the outside

latch² /lætʃ/ *verb*

PHR V **latch on (to sth)** (*informal*) to understand sth: *It took them a while to latch on to what she was talking about.*

⚷ **late** /leɪt/ *adj* (**later**; **latest**) *adv* **1** near the end of a period of time: *in the late afternoon/summer/20th century* ♦ *in the late morning* ♦ *His mother's in her late fifties* (= between 55 and 60). ♦ *in late May/late in May* ♦ *We got back home late in the evening.* **OPP** **early** **2** after the usual or expected time: *I'm sorry I'm late.* ♦ *She was ten minutes late for school.* ♦ *The ambulance arrived too late to save him.* ♦ *to be late with the rent* ♦ *The buses are running late today.* ♦ *to stay up late* **OPP** **early** **3** near the end of the day: *It's getting late—let's go home.* **OPP** **early** **4** [only *before* a noun] no longer alive; dead: *his late wife*

IDM **an early/a late night** ➲ **night**

later on at a later time: *Later on you'll probably wish that you'd worked harder at school.* ♦ *Bye—I'll see you a bit later on.*

sooner or later ➲ **soon**

latecomer /ˈleɪtkʌmə(r)/ *noun* [C] a person who arrives or starts sth late

lately /ˈleɪtli/ *adv* in the period of time up until now; recently: *What have you been doing lately?* ♦ *Hasn't the weather been dreadful lately?* ➲ note at **recently**

latent /ˈleɪtnt/ *adj* existing, but not yet very noticeable, active or well developed: *latent defects/disease* ♦ *latent talent*

⚷ **later¹** /ˈleɪtə(r)/ *adv* at a time in the future; after the time you are talking about: *See you later.* ♦ *I met her again three years later.* ➲ note at **then**

⚷ **later²** /ˈleɪtə(r)/ *adj* coming after sth else or at a time in the future: *The game has been postponed to a later date.*

lateral /ˈlætərəl/ *adj* connected with the side of sth or with movement to the side: *the lateral branches of a tree* ♦ *lateral eye movements* ▸ **laterally** /-rəli/ *adv*

latest /ˈleɪtɪst/ *adj* [only *before* a noun] very recent or new: *the latest fashions* ◆ *the latest news* ◆ *the terrorists' latest attack on the town* ➲ note at **last**[1]

the latest *noun* [sing] (*informal*) the most recent or the newest thing or piece of news: *This is the very latest in computer technology.* ◆ *This is the latest in a series of attacks by this terrorist group.*
IDM **at the latest** no later than the time or the date mentioned: *You need to hand your projects in by Friday at the latest.*

lather /ˈlɑːðə(r)/ *noun* [U] a white mass of bubbles that are produced when you mix soap with water

Latin /ˈlætɪn/ *noun* [U] the language that was used in ancient Rome ▶ **Latin** *adj*: *Latin poetry* ◆ *Spanish, Italian and other Latin languages* (= that developed from Latin)

ˌLatin Aˈmerican *noun* [C], *adj* (a person who comes) from Latin America (the parts of Central and South America where Spanish or Portuguese is spoken): *Latin American music*

latitude /ˈlætɪtjuːd/ *noun* [U] the distance of a place north or south of the **equator** (= the line around the middle of the earth) ➲ look at **longitude** ➲ picture at **earth**

MORE Latitude is measured in **degrees**.

latter /ˈlætə(r)/ *adj* [only *before* a noun] (*formal*) nearer to the end of a period of time; later: *Interest rates should fall in the latter half of the year.* ▶ **latterly** *adv*

the latter /ˈlætə(r)/ *noun* [sing], *pron* the second (of two people or things that are mentioned): *The options were History and Geography. I chose the latter.*

MORE The first of two people or things that are mentioned is **the former**.

laugh[1] /lɑːf/ *verb* [I] to make the sounds that show you are happy or amused: *His jokes always make me laugh.* ◆ *to laugh out loud* ➲ note at **humour**
IDM **die laughing** ➲ **die**
PHR V **laugh at sb/sth 1** to show, by laughing, that you think sb/sth is funny: *The children laughed at the clown.* **2** to show that you think sb is ridiculous: *Don't laugh at him. He can't help the way he speaks.*

laugh[2] /lɑːf/ *noun* [C] **1** the sound or act of laughing: *Her jokes got a lot of laughs.* ◆ *We all had a good laugh at what he'd written.* **2 a laugh** [sing] (*informal*) an occasion or a person that is very funny: *The party was a good laugh.*
IDM **for a laugh** as a joke
have the last laugh ➲ **last**[1]

laughable /ˈlɑːfəbl/ *adj* deserving to be laughed at; of very poor quality; ridiculous

ˈlaughing stock *noun* [C] a person or thing that other people laugh at (in an unpleasant way)

laughter /ˈlɑːftə(r)/ *noun* [U] the sound or act of laughing: *Everyone roared with laughter.*

launch[1] /lɔːntʃ/ *verb* [T] **1** to start sth new or to show sth for the first time: *to launch a new product onto the market* **2** to send sth such as a **spacecraft** (= a vehicle that travels in space), weapon, etc. into space, into the sky or through the water: *to launch a missile* ◆ *The lifeboat was launched immediately.*

launch[2] /lɔːntʃ/ *noun* [C] **1** [usually sing] the act of **launching** a ship, **spacecraft** (= a vehicle that travels in space), new product, etc: *The official launch date for our newest product is 10 May.* **2** a large motorboat

launder /ˈlɔːndə(r)/ *verb* [T] **1** (*formal*) to wash, dry and iron clothes, etc: *freshly laundered sheets* **2** to move money that has been obtained illegally into foreign bank accounts or legal businesses so that it is difficult for other people to know where the money came from

launderette (also **laundrette**) /lɔːnˈdret/ (*AmE* Laundromat™ /ˈlɔːndrəmæt/) *noun* [C] a type of shop where you pay to wash and dry your clothes in machines

laundry /ˈlɔːndri/ *noun* (*pl* **laundries**) **1** [U] clothes, etc. that need washing or that are being washed: *dirty laundry* ➲ A more common expression is **the washing**. **2** [C] a business where you send sheets, clothes, etc. to be washed and dried

lava /ˈlɑːvə/ *noun* [U] hot liquid rock that comes out of a **volcano** (= a mountain that explodes) ➲ picture at **volcano**

lavatory /ˈlævətri/ *noun* [C] (*pl* **lavatories**) (*formal*) **1** a toilet **2** a room that contains a toilet, a place to wash your hands, etc: *Where's the ladies' lavatory, please?* ➲ note at **toilet**

lavender /ˈlævəndə(r)/ *noun* [U] a garden plant with purple flowers that smells very pleasant

lavish[1] /ˈlævɪʃ/ *adj* **1** large in amount or number: *a lavish meal* **2** giving or spending a large amount of money: *She was always very lavish with her presents.*

lavish[2] /ˈlævɪʃ/ *verb*
PHR V **lavish sth on sb/sth** to give a lot of sth, often too much, to sb/sth

law /lɔː/ *noun* **1 the law** [U] all the laws in a country or state: *Stealing is* ***against the law****.* ◆ *to break the law* ◆ *to obey the law* ➲ look at **legal 2** [C] an official rule of a country or state that says what people may or may not do: *There's a new law about the use of mobile phones while driving.* ➲ note at **rule 3** [U] the law as a subject of study or as a profession: *She is studying law.* ◆ *My brother works for* ***a law firm*** *in Brighton.* ➲ look at **legal 4** [C] (in science) a statement of what always happens in certain situations or conditions: *the laws of mathematics/gravity*
IDM **law and order** a situation in which the law is obeyed ➲ note at **court, crime**

ˈlaw-abiding *adj* (used about a person) obeying the law: *law-abiding citizens*

lawbreaker /ˈlɔːbreɪkə(r)/ *noun* [C] a person who does not obey the law; a criminal

ˈlaw court *noun* [C] (*BrE*) = **court**[1](1)

lawful /ˈlɔːfl/ *adj* allowed or recognized by law: *We shall use all lawful means to obtain our demands.* ➲ look at **legal, legitimate**

lawless /ˈlɔːləs/ *adj* (used about a person or their actions) breaking the law ▶ **lawlessness** *noun* [U]

lawn /lɔːn/ *noun* [C,U] an area of grass in a garden or park that is regularly cut ➲ picture on **page P9**

lawnmower /ˈlɔːnməʊə(r)/ *noun* [C] a machine that is used for cutting the grass in a garden ➲ picture at **garden**

lawsuit /ˈlɔːsuːt/ *noun* [C] a legal argument in a court of law that is between two people or groups and not between the police and a criminal: *to file a lawsuit*

⚷ **lawyer** /ˈlɔːjə(r)/ *noun* [C] a person who is trained and qualified to advise people about the law: *to consult a lawyer*

> **MORE** A **solicitor** is a lawyer who gives legal advice, prepares legal documents, arranges the buying or selling of land, etc. A **barrister** is a lawyer who speaks for you in a court of law. The American term is **attorney**.

L

lax /læks/ *adj* not having high standards; not strict: *Their security checks are rather lax.* **SYN** **careless**

laxative /ˈlæksətɪv/ *noun* [C] a medicine, food or drink that makes the body get rid of solid waste material easily ▶ **laxative** *adj*

⚷ **lay**[1] /leɪ/ *verb* [T] (*pt, pp* laid /leɪd/)

➤PUT DOWN **1** to put sb/sth carefully in a particular position or on a surface: *Before they started, they laid newspaper on the floor.* ◆ *He laid the child gently down on her bed.* ◆ *'Don't worry,' she said, laying her hand on my shoulder.* ➲ note at **lie**[2] **2** to put sth in the correct position for a particular purpose: *They're laying new electricity cables in our street.*

➤EGGS **3** to produce eggs: *Hens lay eggs.*

➤PREPARE **4** to prepare sth for use: *The police have laid a trap for him and I think they'll catch him this time.* ◆ *Can you **lay the table** please* (= put the knives, forks, plates, etc. on it)?

➤WITH NOUN **5** (used with some nouns to give a similar meaning to a verb) to put: *They laid all the blame on him* (= they said he was responsible). ◆ *to lay emphasis on something* (= emphasize it)

IDM **get/lay your hands on sb/sth** ➲ **hand**[1]

PHR V **lay sth down** to give sth as a rule: *It's all laid down in the rules of the club.*

lay off (sb) (*informal*) to stop annoying sb: *Can't you lay off me for a bit?*

lay sb off to stop giving work to sb: *They've laid off 500 workers at the car factory.*

lay sth on (*informal*) to provide sth: *They're laying on a trip to London for everybody.*

lay sth out **1** to spread out a number of things so that you can see them easily or so that they look nice: *All the food was laid out on a table in the garden.* **2** to arrange sth in a planned way: *The new shopping centre is very attractively laid out.*

lay[2] /leɪ/ *adj* [only *before* a noun] **1** without special training in or knowledge of a particular subject **2** (used about a religious teacher) who has not been officially trained as a priest: *a lay preacher*

lay[3] *past tense* of **lie**[2]

layabout /ˈleɪəbaʊt/ *noun* [C] (*BrE informal*) a person who is lazy and does not do much work

ˈlay-by (*pl* lay-bys) (*AmE* ˈrest area; ˈrest stop) *noun* [C] an area at the side of a road where vehicles can stop for a short time

⚷ **layer** /ˈleɪə(r)/ *noun* [C] a piece or quantity of sth that is on sth else or between other things: *A thin layer of dust covered everything in the room.* ◆ *It's very cold. You'll need several layers of clothing.* ◆ *the top/bottom layer* ◆ *the inner/outer layer*

layman /ˈleɪmən/ *noun* [C] (*pl* -men /-mən/) (also **layperson**) a person who does not have special training in or knowledge of a particular subject: *a medical reference book for the layman*

layout /ˈleɪaʊt/ *noun* [C, usually sing] the way in which the parts of sth are arranged: *The magazine has a new page layout.*

laze /leɪz/ *verb* [I] **laze (about/around)** to do very little; to rest or relax

⚷ **lazy** /ˈleɪzi/ *adj* (**lazier**; **laziest**) **1** (used about a person) not wanting to work: *Don't be lazy. Come and give me a hand.* **2** making you feel that you do not want to do very much: *a lazy summer's afternoon* **3** moving slowly or without much energy: *a lazy smile* ▶ **lazily** *adv* ▶ **laziness** *noun* [U]

lb *abbr* **pound(s)**; a measure of weight

⚷ **lead**[1] /liːd/ *verb* (*pt, pp* led /led/)

➤SHOW THE WAY **1** [T] to go with or in front of a person or an animal to show the way or to make them or it go in the right direction: *The teacher led the children out of the hall and back to the classroom.* ◆ *She led the horse into its stable.* ◆ *The receptionist **led the way** to the boardroom.* ◆ *to lead somebody by the hand*

> **HELP** **Lead, guide** or **direct**? You usually **guide** a tourist or somebody who needs special help, by going with them: *to guide visitors around Oxford* ◆ *He guided the blind woman to her seat.* If you **direct** somebody, you explain with words how to get somewhere: *Could you direct me to the nearest Post Office, please?*

➤ROAD/PATH **2** [I] to go to a place: *I don't think this path leads anywhere.*

➤CAUSE **3** [I] **lead to sth** to have sth as a result: *Eating too much sugar can lead to all sorts of health problems.* **4** [T] **lead sb to do sth** to influence what sb does or thinks: *He led me to believe he really meant what he said.*

➤LIFE **5** [T] to have a particular type of life: *They lead a very busy life.* ◆ *to lead a life of crime*

➤BE BEST/FIRST **6** [I,T] to be winning or in first place in front of sb: *The champion is leading (her rival) by 18 seconds.* ◆ *The department led the world in cancer research.*

➤BE IN CONTROL **7** [I,T] to be in control or the leader of sth: *to lead a discussion*

IDM lead sb astray to make sb start behaving or thinking in the wrong way

PHR V lead up to sth to be an introduction to or cause of sth

lead² /li:d/ *noun*

➤FIRST PLACE **1 the lead** [sing] the first place or position in front of other people or organizations: *The French athlete has gone **into the lead**.* ◆ *Who is **in the lead**?* ◆ *Britain has **taken the lead** in developing computer software for that market.* **2** [sing] the distance or amount by which sb/sth is in front of another person or thing: *The company has a lead of several years in the development of the new technology.*

➤INFORMATION **3** [C] a piece of information that may help to give the answer to a problem: *The police are **following** all possible **leads** to track down the killer.*

➤ACTOR **4** [C] the main part in a play, show or other situation: *Who's playing the lead in the new film?* ◆ *Jill played **a lead role** in getting the company back into profit.*

➤FOR DOG **5** [C] a long piece of leather, chain or rope that is used for controlling a dog. The **lead** is connected to a **collar** (= a band that is put around the neck): *All dogs must be **kept on a lead**.*

➤FOR ELECTRICITY **6** [C] a piece of wire that carries electricity to a piece of equipment: *The lead on this stereo isn't long enough.*

IDM follow sb's example/lead ➲ **follow**

lead³ /led/ *noun* **1** [U] (*symbol* **Pb**) a soft heavy grey metal. Lead is used in pipes, roofs, etc. **2** [C, U] the black substance inside a pencil that makes a mark when you write ➲ picture at **stationery**

leader /ˈli:də(r)/ *noun* [C] **1** a person who is a manager or in charge of sth: *a strong leader* ◆ *She is a natural leader* (= she knows how to tell other people what to do). **2** the person or thing that is best or in first place: *The leader has just finished the third lap.* ◆ *The new shampoo soon became a market leader.*

leadership /ˈli:dəʃɪp/ *noun* **1** [U] the state or position of being a manager or the person in charge: *Who will take over the leadership of the party?* **2** [U] the qualities that a leader should have: *She's got good leadership skills.* **3** [C, with sing or pl verb] the people who are in charge of a country, an organization, etc.

leading /ˈli:dɪŋ/ *adj* [only *before* a noun] **1** best or most important: *He's one of the leading experts in this field.* ◆ *She played a leading role in getting the business started.* **2** that tries to make sb give a particular answer: *The lawyer was warned not to ask the witness **leading questions**.*

lead story /ˈli:d stɔ:ri/ *noun* [C] (*pl* **lead stories**) the most important piece of news in a newspaper or on a news programme

leaf¹ /li:f/ *noun* [C] (*pl* **leaves** /li:vz/) one of the thin, flat, usually green parts of a plant or tree: *The trees lose their leaves in autumn.* ➲ picture at **plant**, **tree**

leaf² /li:f/ *verb*

PHR V leaf through sth to turn the pages of a book, etc. quickly and without looking at them carefully

leaflet /ˈli:flət/ *noun* [C] a printed piece of paper that gives information about sth. **Leaflets** are usually given free of charge: *I picked up a leaflet advertising a new club.*

leafy /ˈli:fi/ *adj* (**leafier**; **leafiest**) **1** having many leaves: *leafy green vegetables* **2** (used about a place) with many trees

league /li:g/ *noun* [C] **1** a group of sports clubs that compete with each other for a prize: *the football league* ◆ *Which team is top of the league at the moment?* ➲ look at **rugby** **2** a level of quality, ability, etc: *He is so much better than the others. They're just not in the same league.* **3** a group of people, countries, etc. that join together for a particular purpose: *the Women's League for Peace*

IDM in league (with sb) having a secret agreement (with sb)

leak¹ /li:k/ *verb* **1** [I,T] to allow liquid or gas to get through a hole or crack: *The boat was leaking badly.* **2** [I] (used about liquid or gas) to get out through a hole or crack: *Water is leaking in through the roof.* **3** [T] **leak sth (to sb)** to give secret information to sb: *The committee's findings were leaked to the press before the report was published.*

PHR V leak out (used about secret information) to become known

leak² /li:k/ *noun* [C] **1** a small hole or crack which liquid or gas can get through: *There's a leak in the pipe.* ◆ *The roof has sprung a leak.* **2** the liquid or gas that gets through a hole: *a gas leak* **3** the act of giving away information that should be kept secret ▶ **leaky** *adj*

leakage /ˈli:kɪdʒ/ *noun* [C,U] the act of coming out of a hole or crack; the liquid or gas that comes out: *a leakage of dangerous chemicals*

lean

She is leaning against a tree. He is leaning out of a window.

lean¹ /li:n/ *verb* (*pt, pp* **leant** /lent/ *or* **leaned** /li:nd/) **1** [I] to move the top part of your body and head forwards, backwards or to the side: *He leaned across the table to pick up the phone.* ◆ *She leaned out of the window and waved.* ◆ *Just lean back and relax.* **2** [I] to be in a position that is not straight or vertical: *That wardrobe leans to the right.* **3** [I,T] lean (sth) against/on sth to rest against sth so that it gives support; to put sth in this position: *She stopped and leant on the gate.* ♦ *Please don't lean bicycles against this window.*

lean² /liːn/ *adj* **1** (used about a person or an animal) thin and in good health **2** (used about meat) having little or no fat **3** not producing much: *a lean harvest*

leap¹ /liːp/ *verb* [I] (*pt, pp* leapt /lept/ *or* leaped /liːpt/) **1** to jump high or a long way: *The horse leapt over the wall.* ♦ *A fish suddenly leapt out of the water.* ♦ *We all leapt into the air when they scored the goal.* ♦ *(figurative) Share prices leapt to a record high yesterday.* **2** to move quickly: *I looked at the clock and leapt out of bed.* ♦ *She leapt back when the pan caught fire.*
PHR V **leap at sth** to accept a chance or offer with enthusiasm: *She leapt at the chance to work in TV.*

leap² /liːp/ *noun* [C] **1** a big jump: *He took* ***a flying leap*** *at the wall but didn't get over it.* ♦ *(figurative) My heart gave a leap when I heard the news.* **2** a sudden large change or increase in sth: *The development of penicillin was a great* ***leap forward*** *in the field of medicine.*

L

leapfrog /ˈliːpfrɒg/ *noun* [U] a children's game in which one person bends over and another person jumps over their back

leapfrog

leapt *past tense, past participle of* **leap¹**

ˈ**leap year** *noun* [C] one year in every four, in which February has 29 days instead of 28

learn /lɜːn/ *verb* (*pt, pp* learnt /lɜːnt/ *or* learned /lɜːnd/) **1** [I,T] learn (sth) (from sb/sth) to get knowledge, a skill, etc. (from sb/sth): *I'm not very good at driving yet—I'm still learning.* ♦ *We're learning about China at school.* ♦ *Debbie is learning to play the piano.* ♦ *to learn a foreign language/a musical instrument* ♦ *Where did you learn how to swim?* ➲ note at **study** **2** [I] learn (of/about) sth to get some information about sth; to find out: *I was sorry to learn about your father's death.* **3** [T] to study sth so that you can repeat it from memory: *The teacher said we have to learn the poem for tomorrow.* **4** [I] to understand or realize: *We should have learned by now that we can't rely on her.* ♦ *It's important to learn from your mistakes.*
IDM **learn the hard way** to understand or realize sth by having an unpleasant experience rather than by being told
learn your lesson to understand what you must do/not do in the future because you have had an unpleasant experience
show sb/know/learn the ropes ➲ **rope¹**

learned /ˈlɜːnɪd/ *adj* having a lot of knowledge from studying; for people who have a lot of knowledge: *a learned scholar* ♦ *a learned journal*

learner /ˈlɜːnə(r)/ *noun* [C] a person who is learning: *a learner driver* ♦ *textbooks for young learners*

learning /ˈlɜːnɪŋ/ *noun* [U] **1** the process of learning sth: *new methods of language learning* **2** knowledge that you get from studying

learnt *past tense, past participle of* **learn**

lease /liːs/ *noun* [C] a legal agreement that allows you to use a building or land for a fixed period of time in return for rent: *The lease on the flat runs out/expires next year.* ▶ **lease** *verb* [T]: *They lease the land from a local farmer.* ♦ *Part of the building is leased out to tenants.*

least /liːst/ *determiner, pron, adv* **1** [used as the superlative of *little*] smallest in size, amount, degree, etc: *He's got the least experience of all of us.* ♦ *You've done the most work, and I'm afraid John has done the least.* **2** less than anyone/anything else; less than at any other time: *He's the person who needs help least.* ♦ *I bought the least expensive tickets.* ♦ *My uncle always appears when we're least expecting him.*
OPP for both meanings **most**
IDM **at least 1** not less than, and probably more: *It'll take us at least two hours to get there.* **2** even if nothing else is true or you do nothing else: *It may not be beautiful but at least it's cheap.* ♦ *You could at least say you're sorry!* **3** used for correcting sth that you have just said: *I saw him—at least I think I saw him.*
at the (very) least not less and probably much more: *It'll take six months to build, at the very least.*
last but not least ➲ **last¹**
least of all especially not: *Nobody should be worried, least of all you.*
not in the least (bit) not at all: *It doesn't matter in the least.* ♦ *I'm not in the least bit worried.*
to say the least ➲ **say¹**

leather /ˈleðə(r)/ *noun* [U] the skin of animals which has been specially treated. Leather is used to make shoes, bags, coats, etc: *a leather jacket*

leave¹ /liːv/ *verb* (*pt, pp* left /left/)
➤ GO AWAY **1** [I,T] to go away from sb/sth: *We should leave now if we're going to get there by 8 o'clock.* ♦ *I felt sick in class so I left the room.* ♦ *At what age do most people leave school in your country?* ♦ *Hal left his wife for another woman.*

> **HELP** **Leave** or **depart**? If you **leave** sb/sth it may be permanently or just for a short time: *He leaves the house at 8.00 every morning.* ♦ *He left New York and went to live in Canada.* **Depart** is a more formal word and is used about boats, trains, aeroplanes, etc: *The 6.15 train for Bath departs from Platform 3.*

➤ LET STH STAY **2** [T] to cause or allow sb/sth to stay in a particular place or condition; to not deal with sth: *Leave the door open, please.* ♦ *Don't leave the iron on when you are not using it.* ♦ *Why do you always leave your homework till the last minute?*
➤ PUT **3** [T] to put sth somewhere: *Val left a message on her answerphone.* ♦ *I left him a note.*
➤ CAUSE **4** [T] to make sth happen or stay as a result: *Don't put that cup on the table. It'll leave a mark.*

➤REMAIN **5** [T] to not use sth: *Leave some milk for me, please.*
➤FORGET **6** [T] **leave sth (behind)** to forget to bring sth with you: *I'm afraid I've left my homework at home. Can I give it to you tomorrow?* ◆ *I can't find my glasses. Maybe I left them behind at work.* ➲ note at **forget**
➤AFTER DEATH **7** [T] to give sth to sb when you die: *In his will he left everything to his three sons.*
➤RESPONSIBILITY **8** [T] to give the care of or responsibility for sb/sth to another person: *I'll **leave it to** you to organize all the food.*
IDM be left high and dry to be left without help in a difficult situation
leave sb/sth alone to not touch, annoy or speak to sb/sth
leave go (of sth) to stop touching or holding sth: *Leave go of my arm—you're hurting me!*
leave sb in the lurch to leave sb without help in a difficult situation
leave sth on one side ➲ **side**[1]
PHR V leave sb/sth out (of sth) to not include sb/sth: *This doesn't make sense. I think you've left out a word.*

leave[2] /liːv/ *noun* [U] a period of time when you do not go to work: *Diplomats working abroad usually get a month's home leave each year.* ◆ *annual leave* ◆ *sick leave* ◆ *Molly's not working—she's **on** maternity **leave**.* ➲ note at **holiday**

leaves *plural* of **leaf**[1]

lecture /ˈlektʃə(r)/ *noun* [C] **1** a lecture (on/about sth) a talk that is given to a group of people to teach them about a particular subject, especially as part of a university course: *The college has asked a journalist to come and **give a lecture** on the media.* ◆ *a course of lectures* ➲ note at **university** **2** a serious talk to sb that explains what they have done wrong or how they should behave: *We got a lecture from a policeman about playing near the railway.* ▶ **lecture** *verb* [I,T]: *Alex lectures in European Studies at London University.* ◆ *The policeman lectured the boys about playing ball games in the road.*

lecturer /ˈlektʃərə(r)/ *noun* [C] a person who gives talks to teach people about a subject, especially as a job in a university

led *past tense, past participle* of **lead**[1]

ledge /ledʒ/ *noun* [C] a narrow shelf underneath a window, or a narrow piece of rock that sticks out on the side of a **cliff** (= a high steep area of rock) or mountain

leech /liːtʃ/ *noun* [C] a small creature with a soft body and no legs that usually lives in water and that fastens itself to other creatures and sucks their blood

leek /liːk/ *noun* [C] a long thin vegetable that is white at one end with thin green leaves ➲ picture on **page P15**

left[1] *past tense, past participle* of **leave**[1]

left[2] /left/ *adj* **1** [only *before* a noun] on the side where your heart is in the body: *I've broken my left arm.* **OPP right** **2** still available after everything else has been taken or used: ***Is** there any bread **left**?* ◆ *How much time do we **have left**?* ◆ *If there's any money **left over**, we'll have a cup of coffee.*

left[3] /left/ *adv* to or towards the left: *Turn left just past the Post Office.* **OPP right**

left[4] /left/ *noun* [sing] **1** the left side: *In Britain we drive **on the left**.* ◆ *Our house is just **to/on the left of** that tall building.* ◆ *If you look **to your left** you'll see one of the city's most famous landmarks.* **OPP right** **2 the Left** [with sing or pl verb] political parties or groups that support **socialism** (= the political idea that everyone is equal and that money should be equally divided): *The Left is/are losing popularity.* ➲ look at **left wing**

ˈleft-hand *adj* [only *before* a noun] of or on the left: *the left-hand side of the road* ◆ *a left-hand drive car* **OPP right-hand**

ˌleft-ˈhanded *adj, adv* **1** using the left hand rather than the right hand: *Are you left-handed?* ◆ *I write left-handed.* **2** made for **left-handed** people to use: *left-handed scissors* **OPP right-handed**

ˌleft-ˈluggage office (*AmE* ˈbaggage room) *noun* [C] the place at a railway station, etc. where you can leave your luggage for a short time

leftovers /ˈleftəʊvəz/ *noun* [pl] food that has not been eaten when a meal has finished

left ˈwing *noun* [sing] **1** [with sing or pl verb] the members of a political party, group, etc. that want more social change than the others in their party: *the left wing of the Labour Party* **2** the left side of the field in some team sports: *He plays on the left wing for Manchester United.* ▶ **left-wing** *adj* **OPP right wing**

leg /leg/ *noun* [C] **1** one of the parts of the body on which a person or an animal stands or walks: *A spider has eight legs.* ◆ *She sat down and crossed her legs.* ➲ picture at **body** **2** the part of a pair of trousers, etc. that covers the leg: *There's a hole in the leg of my trousers/my trouser leg.* **3** one of the parts of a chair, table etc. on which it stands: *the leg of a chair/table* ◆ *a chair/table leg* **4** one part or section of a journey, competition, etc: *The band are in Germany on the first leg of their world tour.*
IDM pull sb's leg ➲ **pull**[1]
stretch your legs ➲ **stretch**[1]

legacy /ˈlegəsi/ *noun* [C] (*pl* **legacies**) money or property that is given to you after sb dies, because they wanted you to have it: *He received a large legacy from his grandmother.*

legal /ˈliːgl/ *adj* **1** [only *before* a noun] using or connected with the law: *legal advice* ◆ *to take legal action against somebody* ◆ *the legal profession* **2** allowed by law: *It is not legal to drive a car without insurance.* **OPP illegal** ➲ look at **lawful**, **legitimate** ▶ **legally** /ˈliːgəli/ *adv*: *Schools are legally responsible for the safety of their pupils.*

legality /liːˈgæləti/ *noun* [U] the state of being legal **OPP illegality**

legalize (also **-ise**) /ˈliːgəlaɪz/ *verb* [T] to make sth legal

legend /ˈledʒənd/ *noun* **1** [C,U] an old story or group of stories that may or may not be true; this

L

type of story: *the legend of Robin Hood* ◆ *According to legend, Robin Hood lived in Sherwood Forest.* **SYN** **myth** **2** [C] a famous person or event: *a movie/jazz/baseball legend* ➲ look at **star** ▸ **legendary** /ˈledʒəndri/ *adj*: *the legendary heroes of Greek myths* ◆ *Michael Jordan, the legendary basketball star*

leggings /ˈlegɪŋz/ *noun* [pl] a piece of women's clothing that fits tightly over both legs from the waist to the feet, like a very thin pair of trousers

legible /ˈledʒəbl/ *adj* that is clear enough to be read easily: *His writing is so small that it's barely legible.* ◆ *legible handwriting* **OPP** **illegible** ➲ look at **readable** ▸ **legibility** /ˌledʒəˈbɪləti/ *noun* [U] ▸ **legibly** /ˈledʒəbli/ *adv*

legislate /ˈledʒɪsleɪt/ *verb* [I] **legislate (for/against sth)** to make a law or laws

legislation /ˌledʒɪsˈleɪʃn/ *noun* [U] **1** a group of laws: *The government is introducing new legislation to help small businesses.* **2** the process of making laws

legislative /ˈledʒɪslətɪv/ *adj* [only *before* a noun] (*formal*) connected with the act of making and passing laws: *a legislative assembly/body/council*

legislature /ˈledʒɪsleɪtʃə(r)/ *noun* [C] (*formal*) a group of people who have the power to make and change laws: *the national/state legislature* ➲ look at **executive**, **judiciary**

legitimate /lɪˈdʒɪtɪmət/ *adj* **1** reasonable or acceptable: *a legitimate excuse/question/concern* **2** allowed by law: *Could he earn so much from legitimate business activities?* **OPP** **illegitimate** ➲ look at **lawful**, **legal** **3** (*old-fashioned*) (used about a child) having parents who are married to each other **OPP** **illegitimate** ▸ **legitimacy** /lɪˈdʒɪtɪməsi/ *noun* [U] ▸ **legitimately** *adv*

leisure /ˈleʒə(r)/ *noun* [U] the time when you do not have to work; free time: *Shorter working hours mean that people have more leisure.* ◆ *leisure activities* ➲ picture on **page P3**

IDM **at your leisure** (*formal*) when you have free time: *Take this document home and read it at your leisure.*

ˈ**leisure centre** *noun* [C] a public building where you can do sports and other activities in your free time

leisurely /ˈleʒəli/ *adj* without hurry: *a leisurely Sunday breakfast* ◆ *I always cycle at a leisurely pace.*

lemon /ˈlemən/ *noun* [C,U] a yellow fruit with sour juice that is used for giving flavour to food and drink: *a slice of lemon* ◆ *Add the juice of 2 lemons.* ➲ note at **rind** ➲ picture on **page P14**

lemonade /ˌleməˈneɪd/ *noun* [C,U] **1** (*BrE*) a sweet lemon drink with a lot of bubbles in it **2** a drink that is made from fresh lemon juice, sugar and water

lend /lend/ *verb* [T] (*pt*, *pp* **lent** /lent/) **1 lend sb sth; lend sth to sb** to allow sb to use sth for a short time or to give sb money that must be paid back after a certain period of time: *Could you lend me £10 until Friday?* ◆ *He lent me his bicycle.* ◆ *He lent his bicycle to me.* ➲ picture at **borrow**

HELP Be careful not to confuse **lend** with its opposite **borrow**.

2 (*formal*) **lend sth (to sth)** to give or add sth: *to lend advice/support* ◆ *This evidence lends weight to our theory.*

IDM **lend (sb) a hand/lend a hand (to sb)** to help sb

PHR V **lend itself to sth** to be suitable for sth

lender /ˈlendə(r)/ *noun* [C] a person or an organization that lends sth, especially money

length

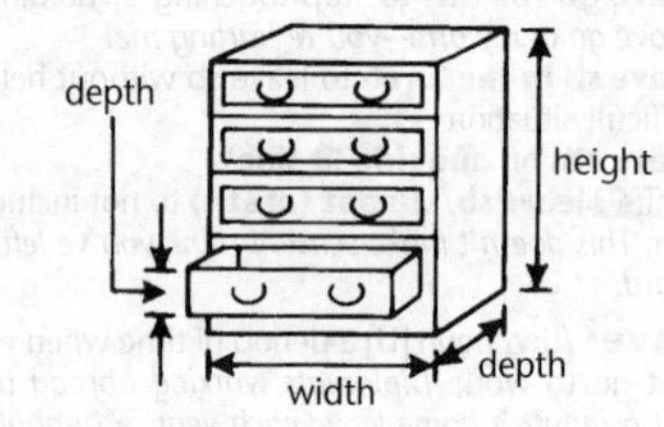

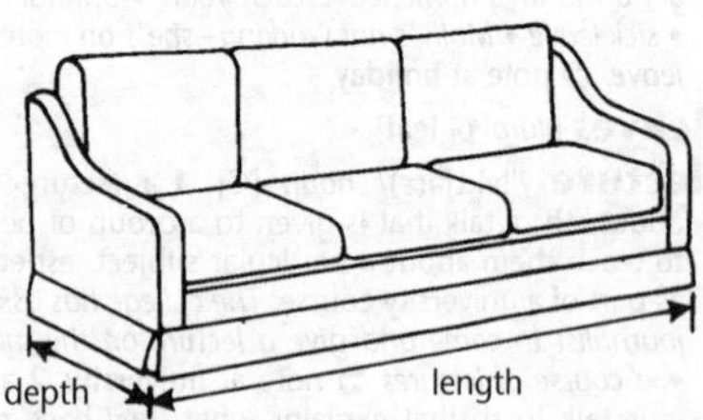

length /leŋθ/ *noun*

▸ SIZE/MEASUREMENT **1** [U,C] how long sth is; the size of sth from one end to the other: *to measure the length of a room* ◆ *It took an hour to walk the length of Oxford Street.* ◆ *The tiny insect is only one millimetre* ***in length***. ◆ *This snake can grow to a length of two metres.* ➲ look at **width**, **breadth**

▸ TIME **2** [U] the amount of time that sth lasts: *Many people complained about the* ***length of time*** *they had to wait.* ◆ *the length of a class/speech/film*

▸ OF BOOK, ETC. **3** [U] the number of pages in a book, a letter, etc: *Her novels vary in length.*

▸ OF SWIMMING POOL **4** [C] the distance from one end of a swimming pool to the other: *I can swim a length in thirty seconds.*

▸ LONG THIN PIECE **5** [C] a piece of sth long and thin: *a length of material/rope/string*

IDM **at length** for a long time or in great detail: *We discussed the matter at great length.*

go to great lengths ➲ **great**[1]

the length and breadth of sth to or in all parts of sth: *They travelled the length and breadth of India.*

lengthen /ˈleŋθən/ *verb* [I,T] to become longer or to make sth longer

lengthways /ˈleŋθweɪz/ (also **lengthwise** /ˈleŋθwaɪz/) *adv* in a direction from one end to the other of sth: *Fold the paper lengthwise.*

lengthy /ˈleŋθi/ *adj* (lengthier; lengthiest) very long

lenient /ˈliːniənt/ *adj* (used about a punishment or person who punishes) not as strict as expected ▸ **leniency** /ˈliːniənsi/ (also lenience) *noun* [U] ▸ **leniently** *adv*

lens /lenz/ *noun* [C] **1** a curved piece of glass that makes things look bigger, clearer, etc. when you look through it ➲ picture at **camera**

MORE Some people wear **contact lenses** to help them see better. You may use a **zoom** or **telephoto lens** on your camera.

2 = **contact lens** ➲ picture at **glasses**

Lent /lent/ *noun* [U] a period of 40 days starting in February or March, when some Christians stop doing or eating certain things for religious reasons: *I'm giving up smoking for Lent.* ♦ *I'm giving up chocolate for Lent.*

lent *past tense, past participle* of **lend**

lentil /ˈlentl/ *noun* [C] a small brown, orange or green seed that can be dried and used in cooking: *lentil soup/stew*

Leo /ˈliːəʊ/ *noun* [C,U] (*pl* Leos) the 5th sign of the **zodiac** (= 12 signs which represent the positions of the sun, moon and planets), the Lion; a person born under this sign: *I'm a Leo.* ➲ picture at **zodiac**

leopard /ˈlepəd/ *noun* [C] a large wild animal of the cat family that has yellow fur with dark spots. **Leopards** live in Africa and Southern Asia. ➲ picture at **lion**

MORE A female leopard is called a **leopardess** and a baby is called a **cub**.

leotard /ˈliːətɑːd/ *noun* [C] a piece of clothing that fits the body tightly from the neck down to the tops of the legs. **Leotards** are worn by dancers or women doing certain sports. ➲ picture at **ballet**

leper /ˈlepə(r)/ *noun* [C] a person who suffers from **leprosy**

leprosy /ˈleprəsi/ *noun* [U] a serious infectious disease that affects the skin, nerves, etc. and can cause parts of the body to fall off

lesbian /ˈlezbiən/ *noun* [C] a woman who is sexually attracted to other women ▸ **lesbian** *adj*: *a lesbian relationship* ♦ *the lesbian and gay community* ▸ **lesbianism** /ˈlezbiənɪzəm/ *noun* [U] ➲ look at **gay, homosexual**

🔑 **less¹** /les/ *determiner, pron, adv* **1** [used with uncountable nouns] a smaller amount (of): *It took less time than I thought.* ♦ *I'm too fat—I must try to eat less.* ♦ *It's not far—it'll take less than an hour to get there.* **OPP** **more**

GRAMMAR Some people use **less** with plural nouns: *less cars*, but **fewer** is the form which is still considered to be correct: *fewer cars.*

2 not so much (as): *He's less intelligent than his brother.* ♦ *It rains less in London than in Manchester.* ♦ *People work less well when they're tired.*

IDM **I, etc. couldn't care less** ➲ **care²**
less and less becoming smaller and smaller in amount or degree
more or less ➲ **more²**

less² /les/ *prep* taking a certain number or amount away: *You'll earn £10 an hour, less tax.* **SYN** **minus**

lessen /ˈlesn/ *verb* [I,T] to become less; to make sth less

lesser /ˈlesə(r)/ *adj, adv* [only *before* a noun] not as great/much as: *He is guilty and so, **to a lesser extent**, is his wife.* ♦ *a lesser-known artist*

IDM **the lesser of two evils** the better of two bad things

🔑 **lesson** /ˈlesn/ *noun* [C] **1** a period of time when you learn or teach sth: *She gives piano lessons.* ♦ *I want to have/take extra lessons in English conversation.* ♦ *a driving lesson* **2** something that is intended to be or should be learnt: *I'm sure we can all learn some lessons from this disaster.*

IDM **learn your lesson** ➲ **learn**

🔑 **let** /let/ *verb* [T] (letting; *pt, pp* let)

➤ALLOW **1** to allow sth to happen: *He's let the dinner burn again!* ♦ *Don't let the fire go out.* **2 let sb/sth do sth** to allow sb/sth to do sth; to make sb/sth able to do sth: *My parents let me stay out till 11 o'clock.* ♦ *I wanted to borrow Dave's bike but he wouldn't let me.* ♦ *This ticket lets you travel anywhere in the city for a day.* ➲ note at **allow**

HELP You cannot use **let** in the passive here. You must use **allow** or **permit** and **to**: *They let him take the exam again.* ♦ *He was allowed to take the exam again.*

3 to allow sb/sth to go somewhere: *Open the windows and let some fresh air in.* ♦ *She was let out of prison yesterday.*

➤MAKING SUGGESTIONS **4** used for making suggestions about what you and other people can do: *'Let's go to the cinema tonight.' 'Yes, let's.'*

HELP The negative is **let's not** or (in British English only) **don't let's**: *Let's not/Don't let's go to that awful restaurant again.*

➤OFFERING HELP **5** used for offering help to sb: *Let me help you carry your bags.*

➤HOUSE/ROOM **6 let sth (out) (to sb)** to allow sb to use a building, room, etc. in return for rent: *They let out two rooms to students.* ♦ *There's a flat to let in our block.* ➲ note at **hire**

IDM **let sb/sth go; let go of sb/sth** to stop holding sb/sth: *Let me go. You're hurting me!* ♦ *Hold the rope and don't let go of it.*

let yourself go **1** to relax without worrying what other people think: *After work I like to go out with friends and let myself go.* **2** to allow yourself to become untidy, dirty, etc: *He used to be so smart but after he got married he just let himself go.* ℹ For other idioms containing **let**, look at the entries for the nouns, adjectives, etc. For example, **let sth slip** is at **slip**.

L

PHR V let sb down to not do sth that you promised to do for sb; to disappoint sb: *Bob really let me down when he didn't finish the work on time.*
let on (about sth) (to sb) to tell sb a secret: *He didn't let on how much he'd paid for the vase.*
let sb off to not punish sb, or to give sb less of a punishment than expected: *He expected to go to prison but they let him off with a fine.*
let sth out to make a sound with your voice: *to let out a scream/sigh/groan/yell*

lethal /ˈliːθl/ *adj* that can cause death or great damage: *a lethal weapon/drug* ▶ **lethally** /ˈliːθəli/ *adv*

lethargy /ˈleθədʒi/ *noun* [U] the feeling of being very tired and not having any energy ▶ **lethargic** /ləˈθɑːdʒɪk/ *adj*

letters and cards

letter /ˈletə(r)/ *noun* [C] **1** a written or printed message that you send to sb: *I got a letter from Matthew this morning.* ◆ *I'm writing **a thank-you letter** to my uncle for the flowers he sent.* ➲ note at **post 2** a written or printed sign that represents a sound in a language: *'Z' is the last letter of the English alphabet.*

MORE Letters may be written or printed as **capitals** or **small letters**: *Is 'east' written with a capital or a small 'e'?*

ˈletter box *noun* [C] **1** a hole in a door or wall for putting letters, etc. through ➲ picture on **page P8** **2** (*AmE* **mailbox**) a small box near the main door of a building or by the road in which letters are left for the owner to collect **3** = **postbox**

lettuce /ˈletɪs/ *noun* [C,U] a plant with large green leaves which are eaten cold in salads: *a lettuce leaf* ➲ picture on **page P15**

leukaemia (*AmE* **leukemia**) /luːˈkiːmiə/ *noun* [U] a serious disease of the blood which often results in death

level¹ /ˈlevl/ *noun* [C] **1** the amount, size or number of sth (compared to sth else): *a low level of unemployment* ◆ *high stress/pollution levels* **2** the height, position, standard, etc. of sth: *He used to play tennis at a high level.* ◆ *intermediate-level students* ◆ *top-level discussions* **3** a way of considering sth: ***on a** spiritual/personal/professional **level*** **4** a flat surface or layer: *a multi-level shopping centre*

level² /ˈlevl/ *adj* **1** with no part higher than any other; flat: *Make sure the shelves are level before you fix them in position.* ◆ *Put the tent up on level ground.* ◆ *a level teaspoon of sugar* **2 level (with sb/sth)** at the same height, standard or position: *The boy's head was level with his father's shoulder.* ◆ *The teams are level on 34 points.*
IDM a level playing field a situation in which everyone has an equal chance of success

level³ /ˈlevl/ *verb* [T] (**levelling**; **levelled**, (*AmE*) **leveling**; **leveled**) to make sth flat, equal or level: *The ground needs levelling before we lay the patio.* ◆ *Juventus levelled the score with a late goal.* ◆ *Many buildings were levelled* (= destroyed) *in the earthquake.*
PHR V level sth at sb/sth to aim sth at sb/sth: *They levelled serious criticisms at the standard of teaching.*
level off/out to become flat, equal or level

ˌlevel ˈcrossing (*AmE* **ˈrailroad crossing**) *noun* [C] a place where a railway crosses the surface of a road

ˌlevel-ˈheaded *adj* calm and sensible; able to make good decisions in a difficult situation

lever /ˈliːvə(r)/ *noun* [C] **1** a handle that you pull or push in order to make a machine, etc. work: *Pull the lever towards you.* ◆ *the gear lever in a car* **2** a bar or tool that is used to lift or open sth when you put pressure or force on one end: *You need to get the tyre off with a lever.* ▶ **lever** *verb* [T]: *The police had to lever the door open.*

leverage /ˈliːvərɪdʒ/ *noun* [U] **1** the act of using a **lever** (= a bar or tool) to lift or open sth; the force needed to do this **2** (*formal*) the ability to influence what people do: *diplomatic leverage*

levy /ˈlevi/ *verb* [T] (**levying**; **levies**; *pt, pp* **levied**) (*written*) **levy sth (on sb)** to officially demand and collect money, etc: *to levy a tax*

liability /ˌlaɪəˈbɪləti/ *noun* (*pl* **liabilities**) **1** [U] **liability (for sth)** the state of being responsible for sth: *The company cannot accept liability for damage to cars in this car park.* **2** [C] (*informal*) a person or thing that can cause a lot of problems, cost a lot of money, etc.

liable /ˈlaɪəbl/ *adj* [not before a noun] **1 liable (for sth)** (in law) responsible for sth **2 liable to do sth** likely to do sth: *We're all liable to have accidents when we are very tired.* **3 liable to sth** likely to have or suffer from sth: *The area is liable to floods.*

liaise /li'eɪz/ *verb* [I] liaise (with sb/sth) to work closely with a person, group, etc. and give them or it regular information about what you are doing

liaison /li'eɪzn/ *noun* **1** [U, sing] liaison (between A and B) communication between two or more people or groups that work together **2** [C] a secret sexual relationship

liar /'laɪə(r)/ *noun* [C] a person who does not tell the truth: *She called me a liar.* ➲ look at **lie**[1]

Lib Dem /ˌlɪb 'dem/ *abbr* = **Liberal Democrat**

libel /'laɪbl/ *noun* [C,U] the act of printing a statement about sb that is not true and would give people a bad opinion of them: *The singer is suing the newspaper for libel.* ▶ **libel** *verb* [T] (libelling; libelled, (*AmE*) libeling; libeled): *He claims he was libelled in the magazine article.*

liberal /'lɪbərəl/ *adj* **1** accepting different opinions or kinds of behaviour: *He has very liberal parents.* **SYN** **tolerant** **2** (in politics) believing in or based on principles of commercial freedom, freedom of choice, and avoiding extreme social and political change: *liberal policies/politicians* **3** not strictly limited in amount or variety ▶ **liberal** *noun* [C]: *Charles has always considered himself a liberal.* ▶ **liberalism** /'lɪbərəlɪzəm/ *noun* [U]

the ˌLiberal 'Democrats *noun* [pl] (*abbr* Lib Dems) a political party in Britain that represents views that are not extreme

liberally /'lɪbərəli/ *adv* freely or in large amounts

liberate /'lɪbəreɪt/ *verb* [T] liberate sb/sth (from sth) to allow sb/sth to be free: *France was liberated in 1945.* ▶ **liberation** /ˌlɪbə'reɪʃn/ *noun* [U]

liberated /'lɪbəreɪtɪd/ *adj* free from the restrictions of traditional opinions or ways of behaving

liberty /'lɪbəti/ *noun* [C,U] (*pl* liberties) the freedom to go where you want, do what you want, etc: *We must defend our civil liberties at all costs.* ➲ look at **freedom**
IDM **at liberty (to do sth)** free or allowed to do sth: *You are at liberty to leave when you wish.*

Libra /'liːbrə/ *noun* [C,U] the 7th sign of the **zodiac** (= 12 signs which represent the positions of the sun, moon and planets), the Scales; a person born under this sign: *I'm a Libra.* ➲ picture at **zodiac**

librarian /laɪ'breəriən/ *noun* [C] a person who works in or is in charge of a library

library /'laɪbrəri; 'laɪbri/ *noun* [C] (*pl* libraries) **1** a room or building that contains a collection of books, etc. that can be looked at or borrowed: *My library books are due back tomorrow.* ➲ look at **bookshop** **2** a private collection of books, etc: *a new edition to add to your library*

lice *plural* of **louse**

licence (*AmE* license) /'laɪsns/ *noun* **1** [C] a licence (for sth/to do sth) an official paper that shows you are allowed to do or have sth: *You need a licence for this software.* ◆ *The company has applied for a licence to import goods into China.* ➲ look at **driving licence** **2** [U] (*formal*) licence (to do sth) permission or freedom to do sth: *The soldiers were given licence to kill if they were attacked.*

license[1] /'laɪsns/ *verb* [T] to give official permission for sth: *The new drug hasn't been licensed in the US.*

license[2] (*AmE*) = **licence**

licensee /ˌlaɪsən'siː/ *noun* [C] (*BrE*) a person who is officially allowed to sell alcoholic drinks

'license plate (*AmE*) = **number plate**

'licensing laws *noun* [pl] (*BrE*) the laws that control when and where alcoholic drinks can be sold

lick

licking

biting

swallowing

lick /lɪk/ *verb* [T] to move your tongue across sth: *The child licked the spoon clean.* ◆ *I licked the envelope and stuck it down.* ▶ **lick** *noun* [C]

licorice (*especially AmE*) = **liquorice**

lid /lɪd/ *noun* [C] **1** the top part of a box, pot, etc. that can be lifted up or taken off: *I can't get the lid off this jar.* ➲ picture at **container, piano, teapot** **2** = **eyelid**

lie[1] /laɪ/ *verb* [I] (lying; *pt, pp* lied) lie (to sb) (about sth) to say or write sth that you know is not true: *He lied about his age in order to join the army.* ◆ *How could you lie to me?* ▶ **lie** *noun* [C]: *to tell a lie* ◆ *That story about his mother being ill was just **a pack of lies**.* ➲ look at **fib, liar**

> **MORE** You tell a **white lie** in order not to hurt sb's feelings.

lie[2] /laɪ/ *verb* [I] (lying; *pt* lay /leɪ/; *pp* lain /leɪn/) **1** to be in or move into a flat or horizontal position (so that you are not standing or sitting): *He lay on the sofa and went to sleep.* ◆ *to lie on your back/side/front* ◆ *The book lay open in front of her.*

> **HELP** **Lie or lay?** Do not confuse **lie**[2] and **lay**. **Lie** does not have an object: *He is lying on the beach.* The past simple is **lay**: *She was tired so she lay on the bed.* **Lay** has an object: *He is laying a carpet in our new house.* The past simple is **laid**: *She laid her child on the bed.*

2 to be or stay in a certain state or position: *Snow lay thick on the ground.* ◆ *The hills lie to the north of the town.* ◆ *They are young and their whole lives **lie ahead** of them.* **3** lie (in sth) to exist or to be found somewhere: *The problem lies in deciding when to stop.*
IDM **lie in wait (for sb)** to hide somewhere waiting to attack, surprise or catch sb
lie low to try not to attract attention to yourself
PHR V **lie about/around** to relax and do nothing

lie back to relax and do nothing while sb else works, etc.
lie behind sth to be the real hidden reason for sth: *We may never know what lay behind his decision to resign.*
lie down (used about a person) to be in or move into a flat or horizontal position so that you can rest

MORE We also say **have a lie-down.**

lie in (*informal*) to stay in bed later than usual because you do not have to get up

MORE We also say **have a lie-in.**

➲ look at **oversleep**
lie with sb (to do sth) (*formal*) to be sb's responsibility to do sth

ˈlie detector *noun* [C] a piece of equipment that can show if a person is telling the truth or not

Lieut. *abbr* = **Lieutenant**

lieutenant /lefˈtenənt (*especially AmE*) luːˈtenənt/ *noun* [C] (*abbr* **Lieut.**; **Lt**) an officer at a middle level in the army, navy or air force

L

life /laɪf/ *noun* (*pl* lives /laɪvz/)
➤BEING ALIVE **1** [U] the quality that people, animals or plants have when they are not dead: *Do you believe in life after death?* ♦ *to bring somebody/come back to life* **2** [C,U] the state of being alive as a human being: *Would you* ***risk*** *your* ***life*** *to protect your property?* ♦ *Doctors fought all night to* ***save*** *her* ***life.***
➤LIVING THINGS **3** [U] living things: *Life on earth began in a very simple form.* ♦ *No life was found on the moon.* ♦ *There was no sign of life in the deserted house.* ♦ *plant life*
➤PERIOD OF TIME **4** [C,U] the period during which sb/sth is alive or exists: *I've lived in this town* ***all*** *my* ***life.*** ♦ *I spent my early life in London.* ♦ *to have a short/long/exciting life*
➤EXPERIENCE/ACTIVITIES **5** [U] the things that you may experience while you are alive: *Life can be hard for a single parent.* ♦ *I'm not happy with the situation, but I suppose* ***that's life.*** **6** [C,U] a way of living: *They went to America to* ***start a new life.*** ♦ *They* ***lead a*** *busy* ***life.*** ♦ *married life*
➤ENERGY **7** [U] energy; activity: *Young children are* ***full of life.*** ♦ *These streets* ***come to life*** *in the evenings.*
➤REALITY **8** [U] something that really exists and is not just a story, a picture, etc: *I wonder what that actor's like* ***in real life.*** ♦ *Do you draw people* ***from life*** *or from photographs?*
IDM **a fact of life** ➲ fact
the facts of life ➲ fact
full of beans/life ➲ full[1]
get a life (*spoken*) used to tell sb to stop being boring and do sth more interesting
have the time of your life ➲ time[1]
lose your life ➲ lose
a matter of life and/or death ➲ matter[1]
take your (own) life to kill yourself
a walk of life ➲ walk[2]
a/sb's way of life ➲ way[1]

ˌlife-and-ˈdeath (also ˌlife-or-ˈdeath) *adj* [only *before* a noun] very serious or dangerous: *a life-and-death struggle/matter/decision*

lifebelt /ˈlaɪfbelt/ (also **lifebuoy**) *noun* [C] (*BrE*) a ring that is made from light material which will float. A **lifebelt** is thrown to a person who has fallen into water to stop them from sinking.

lifeboat /ˈlaɪfbəʊt/ *noun* [C] **1** a special boat that is used for rescuing people who are in danger at sea ➲ picture on **page P6** **2** a small boat that is carried on a large ship and that is used to escape from the ship if it is in danger of sinking ➲ note at **boat**

lifebuoy /ˈlaɪfbɔɪ/ = **lifebelt**

ˈlife coach *noun* [C] a person who is employed by sb to give them advice about how to achieve the things they want in their life and work

ˈlife cycle *noun* [C] the series of forms into which a living thing changes as it develops

ˈlife expectancy *noun* [C,U] (*pl* **life expectancies**) the number of years that a person is likely to live

lifeguard /ˈlaɪfɡɑːd/ *noun* [C] a person at a beach or swimming pool whose job is to rescue people who are in difficulty in the water

ˈlife jacket (*especially AmE* ˈ**life vest**) *noun* [C] a plastic or rubber jacket without sleeves that can be filled with air. A life jacket is used to make sb float if they fall into water. ➲ picture at **boat**

lifeless /ˈlaɪfləs/ *adj* **1** dead or appearing to be dead **2** without energy or interest SYN **dull**

lifelike /ˈlaɪflaɪk/ *adj* looking like a real person or thing: *The flowers are made of silk but they are very lifelike.*

lifeline /ˈlaɪflaɪn/ *noun* [C] something that is very important for sb and that they depend on: *For many old people their telephone is a lifeline.*

lifelong /ˈlaɪflɒŋ/ *adj* [only *before* a noun] for all of your life: *a lifelong friend*

ˌlife-or-ˈdeath = **life-and-death**

ˈlife-size (also ˈ**life-sized**) *adj* of the same size as the real person or thing: *a life-sized statue*

lifespan /ˈlaɪfspæn/ *noun* [C] the length of time that sth is likely to live, work, last, etc: *A mosquito has a lifespan of only a few days.*

ˈlife story *noun* [C] (*pl* **life stories**) the story of sb's life

lifestyle /ˈlaɪfstaɪl/ *noun* [C] the way that you live

lifetime /ˈlaɪftaɪm/ *noun* [C] the period of time that sb is alive

ˈlife vest (*especially AmE*) = **life jacket**

lift[1] /lɪft/ *verb*
➤RAISE **1** [T] **lift sb/sth (up)** to move sb/sth to a higher level or position: *He lifted the child up onto his shoulders.* ♦ *Lift your arm very gently and see if it hurts.* ♦ *It took two men to lift the piano.*
➤MOVE SB/STH **2** [T] to move sb/sth from one place or position to another: *She lifted the suitcase down from the rack.*

➤REMOVE LAW **3** [T] to end or remove a rule, law, etc: *The ban on public meetings has been lifted.*
➤MAKE SB HAPPY **4** [I,T] to become or make sb happier: *The news lifted our spirits.*
➤CLOUDS, FOG, ETC. **5** [I] to rise up and disappear: *The mist lifted towards the end of the morning.*
➤COPY **6** [T] (*informal*) **lift sth (from sb/sth)** to steal or copy sth: *Most of his essay was lifted straight from the textbook.* ➲ look at **shoplifting**
PHR V lift off (used about a **spacecraft**) to rise straight up from the ground ➲ look at **lift-off**

lift² /lɪft/ *noun* **1** (*AmE* **elevator**) [C] a machine in a large building that is used for carrying people or goods from one floor to another: *It's on the third floor so we'd better* **take the lift**. **2** [C] a free ride in a car, etc: *Can you* **give** *me* **a lift** *to the station, please?* ◆ *I got a lift from a passing car.* **3** [sing] (*informal*) a feeling of being happier or more confident than before: *Passing the exam gave him a real lift.* **4** [sing] the act of moving or being moved to a higher position: *Her only reaction was a slight lift of one eyebrow.*
IDM thumb a lift/ride ➲ **thumb²**

ˈ**lift-off** *noun* [C] the start of the flight of a **spacecraft** (= a vehicle that travels in space) when it leaves the ground

ligament /ˈlɪɡəmənt/ *noun* [C] a short, strong part inside the body that joins a bone to another bone ➲ look at **tendon**

light¹ /laɪt/ *noun* **1** [U,C] the energy from the sun, a lamp, etc. that allows you to see things: *a beam/ray of light* ◆ *The light was too dim for us to read by.* ◆ *Strong light is bad for the eyes.* ◆ *We could see strange lights in the sky.*

> **MORE** You may see things by **sunlight, moonlight, firelight, candlelight** or **lamplight.**

2 [C] something that produces light, for example an electric lamp: *Suddenly all the lights went out/came on.* ◆ *the lights of the city in the distance* ◆ *If the lights* (= traffic lights) *are red, stop!* ◆ *That car hasn't got its lights on.*

> **MORE** A light may be **on** or **off**. You **put, switch** or **turn** a light **on, off** or **out**: *Shall I put the light on? It's getting dark in here.* ◆ *Please turn the lights out before you leave.*

3 [C] something, for example a match, that can be used to light a cigarette, start a fire, etc: *Have you got a light?*
IDM bring sth/come to light to make sth known or to become known
cast light on sth ➲ **cast¹**
give sb/get the green light ➲ **green¹**
in a good, bad, etc. light (used about the way that sth is seen or described by other people) well, badly, etc: *The newspapers often portray his behaviour in a bad light.*
in the light of because of; considering
set light to sth to cause sth to start burning
shed light on sth ➲ **shed²**

light² /laɪt/ *adj* (**lighter**; **lightest**)
➤FULL OF LIGHT **1** having a lot of light: *In summer it's still light at 10 o'clock.* ◆ *a light room* **OPP dark**
➤COLOUR **2** pale: *a light-blue sweater* **OPP dark**
➤NOT HEAVY **3** not of great weight: *Carry this bag—it's the lightest.* ◆ *I've lost weight—I'm five kilos lighter than I used to be.* ◆ *light clothes* (= for summer) **OPP heavy**
➤GENTLE **4** not using much force: *a light touch on the shoulder*
➤EASY **5** not tiring or difficult: *light exercise* ◆ *light entertainment/reading*
➤SMALL AMOUNT **6** not great in amount, degree, etc: *Traffic in London is light on a Sunday.* ◆ *a light prison sentence* ◆ *a light wind* ◆ *a light breakfast*
➤SLEEP **7** [only *before* a noun] (used about sleep) not deep: *I'm a light sleeper, so the slightest noise wakes me.* ▶ **lightness** *noun* [U]

light³ /laɪt/ *verb* (*pt, pp* **lit**) **HELP Lighted** is also used as the past tense and past participle, especially before nouns: *The church was full of lighted candles.*
1 [I,T] to begin or to make sth begin to burn: *The gas cooker won't light.* ◆ *to light a fire* ◆ *Candles were lit in memory of the dead.* **2** [T] to give light to sth: *The street is well/badly lit at night.* ◆ *We only had a small torch to light our way through the forest.*
PHR V light (sth) up 1 to start smoking a cigarette: *Several people got off the train and lit up immediately.* **2** to make sth bright with light: *The fireworks lit up the whole sky.* **3** (used about sb's face, eyes, etc.) to become bright with happiness or excitement

light⁴ /laɪt/ *adv* without much luggage: *I always travel light.*

ˈ**light bulb** = **bulb**(1)

lighted *past tense, past participle of* **light³**

lighten /ˈlaɪtn/ *verb* [I,T] **1** to become or to make sth brighter **2** to become lighter in weight or to make sth lighter

lighter /ˈlaɪtə(r)/ = **cigarette lighter**

ˌ**light-ˈheaded** *adj* not in complete control of your thoughts and movements

ˌ**light-ˈhearted** *adj* **1** intended to be funny and enjoyable **2** happy and without problems

lighthouse /ˈlaɪthaʊs/ *noun* [C] a tall building with a light at the top to warn ships of danger near the coast

lighthouse

lighting /ˈlaɪtɪŋ/ *noun* [U] the quality or type of lights used in a room, building, etc.

lightly /ˈlaɪtli/ *adv* **1** gently; with very little force: *He touched her lightly on the arm.* **2** only a little; not much: *lightly cooked/spiced/whisked* **3** not seriously; without serious thought: *We do not take our customers' complaints lightly.*

IDM get off/be let off lightly to avoid serious punishment or trouble

lightning¹ /ˈlaɪtnɪŋ/ *noun* [U] a bright flash of light that appears in the sky during a storm: *The tree was* ***struck by lightning*** *and burst into flames.* ♦ *a flash of lightning* ➲ note at **storm** ➲ look at **thunder**

lightning² /ˈlaɪtnɪŋ/ *adj* [only *before* a noun] very quick or sudden: *a lightning attack*

lightweight /ˈlaɪtweɪt/ *noun* [C], *adj* **1** a person who is in one of the lightest weight groups in certain fighting sports: *a lightweight boxing champion* **2** (a thing) weighing less than usual: *a lightweight suit for the summer*

likable = **likeable**

like¹ /laɪk/ *prep, conj*

➤SIMILAR TO **1** similar to sb/sth: *You* ***look*** *very/just/exactly* ***like*** *your father.* ♦ *Those two singers* ***sound like*** *cats!* ♦ *Your house is* ***nothing like*** *how I imagined it.* ➲ note at **how**

> **HELP** If you want a description of sb/sth, you ask, **'What is he/she/it like?'**: *Tell me about your town. What's* (= what is) *it like?* ♦ *What was it like being interviewed on TV?* Notice that we do NOT use **like** in the answer to these questions: *'What's your brother like?' 'He's tall and fair, and rather serious.'* If you only want to ask about the appearance of sb/sth, you can say, **'What does he/she/it look like?'**: *'What does your brother look like?' 'He's tall and fair, with blue eyes.'*

L

2 [in compounds] in the manner of; similar to: *child-like innocence/simplicity* ♦ *a very lifelike statue*

➤TYPICAL **3** typical of a particular person: *It was just like Maria to be late.*

➤SAME AS **4** in the same way as sb/sth: *Stop behaving like children.* ♦ *That's not right. Do it like this.* ♦ *She can't draw like her sister can.* ♦ *She behaves like she owns the place.* ➲ note at **as**

➤FOR EXAMPLE **5** for example; such as: *They enjoy most team games, like football and rugby.* ➲ note at **as**

➤SAY **6** (*slang*) (used before saying what sb said, how sb felt, etc.): *When I saw the colour of my hair I was like 'Wow, I can't believe it!'*

IDM like anything (*spoken*) very much, fast, hard, etc: *We had to pedal like anything to get up the hill.*

like hell (*informal*) very much; with a lot of effort: *I'm working like hell at the moment.*

nothing like ➲ **nothing**

that's more like it used to say that sth is better than before: *The sun's coming out now—that's more like it!*

like² /laɪk/ *verb* [T] **1 like sb/sth; like doing sth; like to do sth; like sth about sb/sth** to find sb/sth pleasant; to enjoy sth: *He's nice. I like him a lot.* ♦ *Do you like their new flat?* ♦ *How do you like John's new girlfriend?* ♦ *I like my coffee strong.* ♦ *I like playing tennis.* ♦ *I like to go to the cinema on Thursdays.* ♦ *What is it you like about Sarah so much?* ♦ *She didn't like it when I shouted at her.* ♦ *I don't like him borrowing my things without asking.* ♦ *The job seems strange at first, but you'll* ***get to like*** *it.* ♦ *I don't* ***like the look/sound/idea/thought of*** *that.* **OPP dislike** ➲ note at **dislike**

> **GRAMMAR** If you **like doing sth**, you enjoy it: *I like listening to music.* If you **like to do sth**, you might not enjoy it, but you do it because it is a habit, or because you think it is a good idea: *I like to go to the dentist every six months.*

2 to want: *Do what you like. I don't care.* ♦ *We can go whenever you like.* ♦ *I didn't like to disturb you while you were eating.*

> **HELP Would like** is a more polite way to say 'want': *Would you like something to eat?* ♦ *I'd like to speak to the manager.* ♦ *We'd like you to come to dinner on Sunday.* ♦ *How would you like to come to Scotland with us?* **Would like** is followed by the infinitive with *to*, not by the *-ing* form.

IDM I like that! (*BrE old-fashioned informal*) used for saying that sth is not true or not fair

if you like used for agreeing with sb or suggesting sth in a polite way: *'Shall we stop for a rest?' 'Yes, if you like.'*

like the look/sound of sb/sth to have a good impression of sb/sth after seeing or hearing about them or it

> **OTHER WORDS FOR**
>
> **like**
>
> If you **like** doing sth very much, you can say 'I **enjoy/spend a lot of time** doing ...': *She enjoys playing tennis.* You can also say 'I **love** (playing) tennis', 'I'm really **keen on** (playing) tennis', or 'I'm really **into** tennis'. If you like studying sth or finding out about sth, use **interested in**: *He's very interested in the history of tennis.*

like³ /laɪk/ *noun* **1 likes** [pl] things that you like: *Tell me about some of your* ***likes and dislikes.*** **2** [sing] a person or thing that is similar to sb/sth else: *I enjoy going round castles, old churches* ***and the like.*** ♦ *She was a great singer, and we may never see her like/the like of her again.* ▸ **like** *adj* (*formal*)

likeable (also **likable**) /ˈlaɪkəbl/ *adj* (used about a person) easy to like; pleasant

likelihood /ˈlaɪklihʊd/ *noun* [U] the chance of sth happening; how likely sth is to happen: *There seems very little likelihood of success.* **SYN probability**

likely /ˈlaɪkli/ *adj, adv* (**likelier**; **likeliest**) **1 likely (to do sth)** probable or expected: *Do you think it's likely to rain?* ♦ *The boss is not likely to agree.* ♦ *It's not likely that the boss will agree.* ➲ note at **probable** **2** probably suitable: *a likely candidate for the job* **OPP** for both meanings **unlikely**

IDM not likely! (*informal*) certainly not

liken /ˈlaɪkən/ *verb* [T] (*formal*) **liken sb/sth to sb/sth** to compare one person or thing with another: *This young artist has been likened to Picasso.*

likeness /ˈlaɪknəs/ *noun* [C,U] the fact of being similar in appearance; an example of this: *The witness's drawing turned out to be* ***a good likeness of*** *the attacker.*

likewise /ˈlaɪkwaɪz/ *adv* (*formal*) the same; in a similar way: *I intend to send a letter of apology and suggest that you do likewise.*

liking /ˈlaɪkɪŋ/ *noun* [sing] **a liking (for sb/sth)** the feeling that you like sb/sth: *I have a liking for spicy food.*
IDM **too ... for your liking** that you do not like because he/she/it has too much of a particular quality: *The music was a bit too loud for my liking.*

lilac /ˈlaɪlək/ *noun* **1** [C,U] a tree or large bush that has large purple or white flowers in spring **2** [U] a pale purple colour ▶ **lilac** *adj*

lilo (also **Li-lo™**) /ˈlaɪləʊ/ *noun* [C] (*pl* **lilos**) (*BrE*) a plastic or rubber bed that you fill with air when you want to use it. A **lilo** is used on the beach or for camping.

lily /ˈlɪli/ *noun* [C] (*pl* **lilies**) a type of plant that has large white or coloured flowers in the shape of a bell

limb /lɪm/ *noun* [C] **1** a leg or an arm of a person **2** one of the main branches of a tree
IDM **out on a limb** without the support of other people

lime /laɪm/ *noun* **1** [U] a white substance that is used in traditional building methods and also to help plants grow **2** [C] a fruit that looks like a small green lemon ➲ picture on **page P14** **3** [U] (also **ˌlime ˈgreen**) a yellowish-green colour

the limelight /ˈlaɪmlaɪt/ *noun* [U] the centre of public attention: *to be in/out of the limelight*

⚷ **limit¹** /ˈlɪmɪt/ *noun* [C] **1** the greatest or smallest amount of sth that is allowed or possible: *a speed/age/time limit* ◆ *He was fined for exceeding the speed limit.* ◆ *There's a limit to the amount of time I'm prepared to spend on this.* **2** the outside edge of a place or area: *the city limits* ◆ *Lorries are not allowed within a two-mile limit of the town centre.*
IDM **off limits** (used about a place) where people are not allowed to go
within limits only up to a reasonable point or amount

EXAM TIP

Word limit

In a **writing exam** you are told how many words you must write for each task. Practise writing the correct number before the exam. Knowing how many words you usually write on a line will help you to count as you write. You will lose marks if you are **over** or **under the word limit** (= write too many or too few words).

⚷ **limit²** /ˈlɪmɪt/ *verb* [T] **limit sb/sth (to sth)** to keep sb/sth within or below a certain amount, size, degree or area: *I'm limiting myself to one cup of coffee a day.*

limitation /ˌlɪmɪˈteɪʃn/ *noun* **1** [C,U] **(a) limitation (on sth)** the act of limiting or controlling sth; a condition that puts a limit on sth: *There are no limitations on what we can do.* **2 limitations** [pl] things that you cannot do: *It is important to know your own limitations.*

⚷ **limited** /ˈlɪmɪtɪd/ *adj* small in number, amount, etc: *Book early for the show because there are only a limited number of seats available.* OPP **unlimited**

limited ˈcompany *noun* [C] (*abbr* **Ltd**) a company whose owners only have to pay a limited amount of the money that they owe if the company fails

limousine /ˈlɪməziːn; lɪməˈziːn/ (also *informal* **limo** /ˈlɪməʊ/) *noun* [C] a large expensive car that usually has a sheet of glass between the driver and the passengers in the back

limp¹ /lɪmp/ *adj* not firm or strong: *You should put those flowers in water before they go limp.*

limp² /lɪmp/ *verb* [I] to walk with difficulty because you have hurt your leg or foot: *The goalkeeper limped off the field with a twisted ankle.* ▶ **limp** *noun* [sing]: *to walk with a limp*

lines

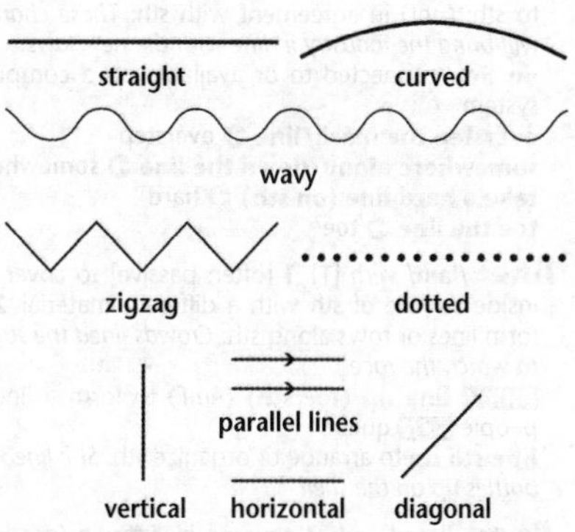

⚷ **line¹** /laɪn/ *noun*
▸LONG THIN MARK **1** [C] a long thin mark on the surface of sth or on the ground: *to draw a line* ◆ *a straight/wiggly/dotted line* ◆ *The old lady had lines on her forehead.* ◆ *The ball was definitely over the line.* ◆ *the finishing line of a race*
▸DIVISION **2** [C] a border or limit between one place or thing and another: *to cross state lines* ◆ *There's a thin line between showing interest and being nosy.*
▸ROW **3** [C] a row of people, things, words on a page, etc: *There was a long line of people waiting at the Post Office.* ◆ *a five-line poem* ◆ *Start each paragraph on a new line.*
▸SERIES **4** [C] a series of people in a family, or of things or events that follow each other in time: *He comes from* ***a long line of*** *musicians.*
▸WORDS **5 lines** [pl] the words that are spoken by an actor in a play, etc: *to learn your lines*
▸STRING **6** [C] a piece of rope or string: *Hang out the clothes on the (washing) line, please.* ◆ *a fishing line*
▸TELEPHONE **7** [C] a telephone or electricity wire or connection: *I'm sorry—the line is engaged. Can you try again later?* ◆ *I'll just check for you. Can you* ***hold the line*** (= wait)*?*

L

➤RAILWAY **8** [C] a section of railway track: *The accident was caused by a cow on the line.*

➤DIRECTION **9** [C, usually sing] a direction or course of movement, thought or action: *He was so drunk he couldn't walk **in a straight line**.* ◆ *The answer's not quite correct, but you're **on the right lines**.* ◆ *The two countries' economies are developing **along** similar **lines**.*

➤ACTIVITY **10** [C] something that you do as a job, do well, or enjoy doing: *What **line of business/work** are you in?*

➤PRODUCT **11** [sing] one type of goods in a shop, etc: *a new line in environment-friendly detergents*

➤TRANSPORT **12** [C] a company that provides transport by air, ship, etc: *an airline*

➤ARMY **13** [C] the place where an army is fighting: *There's renewed fighting on **the front line**.*

IDM **draw the line at sth/doing sth** ➲ draw[1]
drop sb a line ➲ drop[1]
in line for sth likely to get sth: *You could be in line for promotion if you keep working like this.*
in line with sth; out of line with sth (not) similar to sth; (not) in agreement with sth: *These changes will bring the industry in line with the new laws.*
on line connected to or available on a computer system
overstep the mark/line ➲ overstep
somewhere along/down the line ➲ somewhere
take a hard line (on sth) ➲ hard[1]
toe the line ➲ toe[2]

line[2] /laɪn/ *verb* [T] **1** [often passive] to cover the inside surface of sth with a different material **2** to form lines or rows along sth: *Crowds lined the streets to watch the race.*
PHR V **line up (for sth)** (*AmE*) to form a line of people SYN **queue**
line sth up to arrange or organize sth: *She lined the bottles up on the shelf.*

lined /laɪnd/ *adj* **1** covered in lines: *a face lined with age* ◆ *lined paper* **2 -lined** [in compounds] having the object mentioned all along the side(s); having the inside surface covered with the material mentioned: *a tree-lined avenue* ◆ *fur-lined boots*

linen /ˈlɪnɪn/ *noun* [U] **1** a type of strong cloth that is made from a natural substance from a plant **2** sheets and other types of cloth used in the house to cover beds, tables, etc: *bedlinen*

liner /ˈlaɪnə(r)/ *noun* [C] **1** a large ship that carries people, etc. long distances ➲ note at **boat** ➲ picture on **page P6** **2** something that is put inside sth else to keep it clean or protect it. A **liner** is usually thrown away after it has been used: *a dustbin liner*

linger /ˈlɪŋgə(r)/ *verb* [I] **linger (on)** to stay somewhere or do sth for longer than usual: *His eyes lingered on the money in her bag.*

lingerie /ˈlænʒəri/ *noun* [U] (used in shops, etc.) women's underwear

linguist /ˈlɪŋgwɪst/ *noun* [C] a person who is good at learning foreign languages; a person who studies or teaches language(s)

linguistic /lɪŋˈgwɪstɪk/ *adj* connected with language or the study of language

linguistics /lɪŋˈgwɪstɪks/ *noun* [U] the scientific study of language

lining /ˈlaɪnɪŋ/ *noun* [C,U] material that covers the inside surface of sth: *I've torn the lining of my coat.*
IDM **every cloud has a silver lining** ➲ cloud[1]

link[1] /lɪŋk/ *noun* [C] **1 a link (between A and B); a link (with sb/sth)** a connection or relationship between two or more people or things: *There is a strong link between smoking and heart disease.* ◆ *There is a strong link between obesity and heart disease.* **2** a means of travelling or communicating between two places: *To visit similar websites to this one, click on the links at the bottom of the page.* **3** one ring of a chain ➲ picture at **padlock**

link[2] /lɪŋk/ *verb* [T] **link A to/with B; link A and B (together)** to make a connection between two or more people or things: *The new bridge will link the island to the mainland.* ◆ *The computers are linked together in a network.*
PHR V **link up (with sb/sth)** to join together (with sb/sth): *The bands have linked up for a charity concert.*

ˈlink-up *noun* [C] the joining together or connection of two or more things

linoleum /lɪˈnəʊliəm/ (also *informal* lino /ˈlaɪnəʊ/) *noun* [U] a type of strong material with a hard shiny surface, used for covering floors

lion /ˈlaɪən/ *noun* [C] a large animal of the cat family that lives in Africa and parts of southern Asia. Male **lions** have a **mane** (= hair around their head and neck).

MORE A female lion is called a **lioness** and a young lion is called a **cub**. The noise a lion makes is a **roar**.

IDM the lion's share (of sth) (*BrE*) the largest or best part of sth when it is divided

lip /lɪp/ *noun* [C] **1** either of the two soft edges at the opening of your mouth: *to kiss somebody on the lips* ➲ picture at **body**

MORE You have a **top/upper** lip and a **bottom/** lower lip.

2 -lipped [in compounds] having the type of lips mentioned: *thin-lipped* **3** the edge of a cup or sth that is shaped like a cup ➲ picture at **jug**
IDM purse your lips ➲ **purse²**

ˈlip gloss *noun* [U,C] a substance that is put on your lips to make them look shiny

ˈlip-read *verb* [I,T] (*pt, pp* **lip-read** /-red/) to understand what sb is saying by looking at the movements of their lips

lipstick /ˈlɪpstɪk/ *noun* [U,C] a substance that is used for giving colour to your lips: *to put on some lipstick* ♦ *a new lipstick*

liqueur /lɪˈkjʊə(r)/ *noun* [C,U] a strong sweet alcoholic drink that is often drunk in small quantities after a meal

liquid /ˈlɪkwɪd/ *noun* [C,U] a substance, for example water, that is not solid or a gas and that can flow or be poured ▸ **liquid** *adj*

liquidate /ˈlɪkwɪdeɪt/ *verb* [T] **1** to close a business because it has no money left **2** to destroy or remove sb/sth that causes problems ▸ **liquidation** /ˌlɪkwɪˈdeɪʃn/ *noun* [U]: *If the company doesn't receive a big order soon, it will have to* ***go into liquidation.***

liquidize (also **-ise**) /ˈlɪkwɪdaɪz/ *verb* [T] to cause sth to become liquid ▸ **liquidizer** (also **-iser**) (*BrE*) = **blender**

liquor /ˈlɪkə(r)/ *noun* [U] (*AmE*) strong alcoholic drinks; spirits

liquorice (*AmE* **licorice**) /ˈlɪkərɪʃ/ *noun* [U] a black substance, made from a plant, that is used in some sweets

ˈliquor store (*AmE*) = **off-licence**

lisp /lɪsp/ *noun* [C] a speech fault in which 's' is pronounced as 'th': *He speaks with a slight lisp.* ▸ **lisp** *verb* [I,T]

list /lɪst/ *noun* [C] a series of names, figures, items, etc. that are written, printed or said one after another: *a checklist of everything that needs to be done* ♦ *a waiting list* ♦ *Your name is third* ***on the list.*** ➲ note at **last-minute** ▸ **list** *verb* [T]: *to list items in alphabetical order*

listen /ˈlɪsn/ *verb* [I] **1 listen (to sb/sth)** to pay attention to sb/sth in order to hear them or it: *Now please listen carefully to what I have to say.* ♦ *to listen to music/the radio* ➲ note at **hear 2 listen to sb/sth** to take notice of or believe what sb says: *You should listen to your parents' advice.*
PHR V listen (out) for sth to wait to hear sth: *to listen (out) for a knock on the door*
listen in (on/to sth) to listen to sb else's private conversation: *Have you been listening in on my phone calls?*

TOPIC

Listening to music

A **hi-fi** or **stereo** is a machine used for listening to CDs, etc. When you want to listen to music, you **put** a CD **on** (= make it start playing). If you want to make the music louder, you **turn** the volume **up.** If you want to make it quieter, you **turn** it **down.** A small music player that you carry around with you is called an **MP3 player** or **iPod™**.

➲ note at **iPod™**
▸ **listen** *noun* [usually sing] (*informal*): ***Have a listen*** *and see if you can hear anything.*

listener /ˈlɪsənə(r)/ *noun* [C] a person who listens: *When I'm unhappy I always phone Charlie—he's such a good listener.* ♦ *The new radio show has attracted a record number of listeners.*

listless /ˈlɪstləs/ *adj* tired and without energy ▸ **listlessly** *adv*

lit *past tense, past participle* of **light³**

liter (*AmE*) = **litre**

literacy /ˈlɪtərəsi/ *noun* [U] the ability to read and write **OPP illiteracy** ➲ look at **numeracy**

literal /ˈlɪtərəl/ *adj* **1** (used about the meaning of a word or phrase) original or basic: *The adjective 'big-headed' is hardly ever used in its literal sense.* ➲ look at **figurative, metaphor 2** (used when translating, etc.) dealing with each word separately without looking at the general meaning: *A literal translation is not always accurate.*

literally /ˈlɪtərəli/ *adv* **1** according to the basic or original meaning of the word, etc: *You can't translate these idioms literally.* **2** (*informal*) used for emphasizing sth: *We were literally frozen to death* (= we were very cold).

literary /ˈlɪtərəri/ *adj* of or concerned with literature: *literary criticism* ♦ *a literary journal*

literate /ˈlɪtərət/ *adj* **1** able to read and write **OPP illiterate** ➲ look at **numerate** ➲ *noun* **literacy 2** having education or knowledge in a particular area: *computer-literate* (= able to use a computer)

literature /ˈlɪtrətʃə(r)/ *noun* [U] **1** writing that is considered to be a work of art: *French literature* ♦ *a great work of literature* **2 literature (on sth)** printed material about a particular subject: *promotional literature*

TOPIC

Literature

If you study **literature** at school or university, you study **poetry** (= collections of poems), **drama** (= plays) and **fiction** (= novels). A person who writes plays is a **playwright** and someone who writes poetry is a **poet**. A great work of literature is called a **classic**: *'Alice in Wonderland' is a childhood classic.* The study of Greek and Latin literature is called **classics**.

L

litigation /ˌlɪtɪˈɡeɪʃn/ *noun* [U] the process of taking legal action in a court of law: *The company has been in litigation with its previous auditors for a year.*

litre (*AmE* **liter**) /ˈliːtə(r)/ *noun* [C] (*abbr* **l**) a measure of liquid: *ten litres of petrol* ◆ *a litre bottle of wine* ℹ For more information about measurements, look at the section on using numbers at the back of this dictionary.

litter /ˈlɪtə(r)/ *noun* **1** [U] pieces of paper, rubbish, etc. that are left in a public place **2** [C] all the young animals that are born to one mother at the same time: *a litter of six puppies* ▶ **litter** *verb* [T]: *The streets were littered with rubbish.*

ˈ**litter bin** (*AmE* ˈ**trash can**) *noun* [C] a container to put rubbish in, in the street or a public building ➲ picture at **bin**

little¹ /ˈlɪtl/ *adj* [The forms **littler** and **littlest** are rare. It is more common to use **smaller** and **smallest**.] **1** not big; small: *a little bag of sweets* ◆ *Do you want the big one or the little one?* ◆ *a little mistake/problem* ➲ note at **small**

> **HELP** **Little** is often used with another adjective: *a little old lady* ◆ *a cute little kitten* ◆ *What a funny little shop!*

2 young: *a little girl/boy* ◆ *my little* (= younger) *brother* ◆ *I was very naughty when I was little.* **3** (used about distance or time) short: *Do you mind waiting **a little while**?* ◆ *We only live **a little way** from here.* ◆ *It's only a little further.*

little² /ˈlɪtl/ *adv, pron, determiner* **1** [also as a noun after *the*] not much or not enough: *I slept very little last night.* ◆ *a little-known author* ◆ *They have very little money.* ◆ *There is little hope that she will recover.* ➲ look at **less, least** **2 a little** a small amount; to a small degree: *I like a little sugar in my tea.* ◆ *Could I have a little help, please?* ◆ *'Is there any butter left?' 'Yes, just a little.'* ◆ *This skirt is a little too tight.*

> **MORE** **A little bit** or **a bit** is often used instead of 'a little': *I was feeling a little bit tired so I decided not to go out.*

IDM **little by little** slowly: *After the accident her strength returned little by little.*

live¹ /lɪv/ *verb* **1** [I] to have your home in a particular place: *Where do you live?* ◆ *He still lives with his parents.* **2** [I] to be or stay alive: *She hasn't got long to live.* ◆ *to live to a great age* **3** [I,T] to pass or spend your life in a certain way: *to live a quiet life* ◆ *to live in comfort/poverty* **4** [I] to enjoy all the opportunities of life fully: *I want to live a bit before settling down.*
IDM **live/sleep rough** ➲ **rough⁴**
PHR V **live by sth** to follow a particular belief or set of principles
live by doing sth to get the money, food, etc. you need by doing a particular activity: *They live by hunting and fishing.*
not live sth down to be unable to make people forget sth bad or embarrassing that you have done
live for sb/sth to consider sb/sth to be the most important thing in your life: *He felt he had nothing to live for after his wife died.*
live off sb/sth to depend on sb/sth in order to live: *Barry lives off tinned food.* ◆ *She could easily get a job but she still lives off her parents.*
live on to continue to live or exist: *Mozart is dead but his music lives on.*
live on sth **1** to have sth as your only food: *to live on bread and water* **2** to manage to buy what you need to live: *I don't know how they live on so little money!*
live out sth **1** to actually do sth that you only imagined doing before: *to live out your dreams/fantasies* **2** to spend the rest of your life in a particular way: *They lived out their last few years in Peru.*
live through sth to survive an unpleasant experience: *She lived through two wars.*
live together to live in the same house, etc. as sb and have a sexual relationship with them
live it up to enjoy yourself in an exciting way, usually spending a lot of money
live up to sth to be as good as expected: *Children sometimes find it hard to live up to their parents' expectations.*
live with sb = **live together**
live with sth to accept sth unpleasant that you cannot change: *It can be hard to live with the fact that you are getting older.*

live² /laɪv/ *adj, adv*
➤ NOT DEAD **1** having life; not dead: *Have you ever touched a **real live** snake?*
➤ RADIO/TV PROGRAMME **2** seen or heard as it is happening: *live coverage of the Olympic Games* ◆ *This programme is coming live from the Millennium Stadium.* ◆ *to go out live on TV*
➤ PERFORMANCE **3** given or made when people are watching or listening; not recorded: *The cafe has live music on Saturdays.*
➤ ELECTRICITY **4** (used about a wire, etc.) carrying electricity: *That cable is live.*
➤ BOMB, ETC. **5** (used about a bomb, bullet, etc.) that has not yet exploded: *live ammunition*

livelihood /ˈlaɪvlihʊd/ *noun* [C, usually sing] the way that you earn money: *When the factory closed he lost his livelihood.*

lively /ˈlaɪvli/ *adj* (**livelier**; **liveliest**) full of energy, interest, excitement, etc: *lively children* ◆ *The town is quite lively at night.*

liven /ˈlaɪvn/ *verb*
PHR V **liven (sb/sth) up** to become or make sb/sth become more interesting and exciting: *Once the band began to play the party livened up.*

liver /ˈlɪvə(r)/ *noun* **1** [C] the part of your body that cleans your blood ➲ picture at **body** **2** [U] the **liver** of an animal when it is cooked and eaten as food: *fried liver and onions*

lives *plural of* **life**

livestock /ˈlaɪvstɒk/ *noun* [U] animals that are kept on a farm, such as cows, pigs, sheep, etc.

living¹ /ˈlɪvɪŋ/ *adj* **1** alive now: *He has no living relatives.* ➲ note at **alive** **2** [only *before* a noun] still used or practised now: *living languages/traditions* **OPP** for both meanings **dead**

living² /ˈlɪvɪŋ/ *noun* **1** [C,usually sing] money to buy things that you need in life: *What do you do **for a living**?* **2** [U] your way or quality of life: *The **cost of living** has risen in recent years.* ◆ *The **standard of living** is very high in that country.*

ˈ**living room** (*BrE also* ˈsitting room) *noun* [C] the room in a house where people sit, relax, watch TV, etc. together ➲ picture on **page P8**

lizard /ˈlɪzəd/ *noun* [C] a small animal with four legs, dry skin and a long tail

lizard

🔑 **load¹** /ləʊd/ *noun* [C] **1** something (heavy) that is being or is waiting to be carried: *a truck carrying a load of sand* ➲ picture at **pulley** **2** [in compounds] the quantity of sth that can be carried: *bus loads of tourists* **3** **loads (of sth)** [pl] (*informal*) a lot (of sth): *There are loads of things to do in Dublin in the evenings.*
IDM **a load of rubbish, etc.** (*informal*) nonsense

🔑 **load²** /ləʊd/ *verb* **1** [I,T] **load (sth/sb) (up) (with sth)**; **load (sth/sb) (into/onto sth)** to put a large quantity of sth into or onto sb/sth: *Have you finished loading yet?* ◆ *They loaded the plane (up) with supplies.* ◆ *Load the washing into the machine.* **2** [I] to receive a load: *The ship is still loading.* **3** [T] to put sth into a machine, a weapon, etc. so that it can be used: *to load film into a camera* ◆ *to load a gun* **4** [T] to put data or a program into a computer: *Have you loaded the software?* OPP for all meanings **unload**

loaded /ˈləʊdɪd/ *adj* **1** **loaded (with sth)** carrying a load; full and heavy **2** [not before a noun] (*informal*) having a lot of money; rich **3** giving an advantage: *The system is loaded in their favour.* **4** (used especially about a gun or a camera) containing a bullet, a film, etc.

loaf /ləʊf/ *noun* [C] (*pl* **loaves** /ləʊvz/) bread baked in one piece: *a loaf of bread* ➲ picture at **bread**

> TOPIC
>
> **Loans**
>
> If you **can't afford** (= don't have enough money for) sth, you can **take out** a **loan**, for example from a bank. You can say: *I'm going to **borrow** some money **from** the bank* or: *The bank is going to **lend** me some money*. You will then **owe** the money and you will have to **pay** it **back**: *I'm paying back the £1000 that I owe in instalments—£50 every month*. The money you owe is called a **debt** (/det/): *I've got lots of debts*. When you borrow from a bank you also have to pay extra money called **interest**. The money that you borrow in order to buy a house, etc. is a **mortgage** (/ˈmɔːɡɪdʒ/).

🔑 **loan** /ləʊn/ *noun* **1** [C] money, etc. that sb/sth lends you: *to **take out a** bank **loan*** ◆ *to pay off a loan* ➲ note at **money** ➲ look at **borrow** **2** [U] the act of lending sth or the state of being lent: *The books are **on loan** from the library.* ▶ **loan** *verb* [T] (*formal*) **loan sth (to sb)**

> HELP In American English **loan** as a verb is less formal and more common.

loath (also **loth**) /ləʊθ/ *adj* (*formal*) **loath to do sth** not willing to do sth: *He was loath to admit his mistake.*

loathe /ləʊð/ *verb* [T] [not used in the continuous tenses] to hate sb/sth SYN **detest**

> HELP Although this verb is not used in the continuous tenses, it is common to see the present participle (= *-ing* form): *Loathing the thought of having to apologize, she knocked on his door.*

▶ **loathing** *noun* [U] ▶ **loathsome** /ˈləʊðsəm/ *adj*: *a loathsome place*

loaves *plural* of **loaf**

lob /lɒb/ *verb* [I,T] (**lobbing**; **lobbed**) (in sport) to hit, kick or throw a ball high into the air, so that it lands behind your opponent ▶ **lob** *noun* [C]

lobby¹ /ˈlɒbi/ *noun* [C] (*pl* **lobbies**) **1** the area that is just inside a large building, where people can meet and wait: *a hotel lobby* **2** [with sing or pl verb] a group of people who try to influence politicians to do or not do sth: *the anti-gun lobby*

lobby² /ˈlɒbi/ *verb* [I,T] (**lobbying**; **lobbies**; *pt, pp* **lobbied**) to try to influence a politician or the government to do or not do sth

lobe /ləʊb/ *noun* [C] **1** = **ear lobe** ➲ picture at **ear** **2** one part of an organ of the body, especially the brain or lungs

lobster /ˈlɒbstə(r)/ *noun* **1** [C] a large sea creature with eight legs. A **lobster** is bluish-black but it turns red when it is cooked. ➲ picture at **shellfish** **2** [U] meat from a **lobster** eaten as food

🔑 **local¹** /ˈləʊkl/ *adj* of a particular place (near you): *local newspapers/radio* ◆ *the local doctor/policeman/plumber* ➲ look at **international, national, regional** ▶ **locally** /ˈləʊkəli/ *adv*: *I do most of my shopping locally.*

local² /ˈləʊkl/ *noun* [C] **1** [usually pl] a person who lives in a particular place: *The locals seem very friendly.* **2** (*BrE informal*) a pub that is near your home where you often go to drink

localize (also -ise) /ˈləʊkəlaɪz/ *verb* [T] to limit sth to a particular place or area

ˈ**local time** *noun* [U] the time at a particular place in the world: *We arrive in Singapore at 2 o'clock in the afternoon, local time.*

🔑 **locate** /ləʊˈkeɪt/ *verb* [T] **1** to find the exact position of sb/sth: *The damaged ship has been located two miles off the coast.* **2** to put or build sth in a particular place: *They located their headquarters in Swindon.* ▶ **located** *adj*: *Where exactly is your office located?*

🔑 **location** /ləʊˈkeɪʃn/ *noun* **1** [C] a place or position: *Several locations have been suggested for the new office block.* **2** [U] the act of finding where sb/

sth is: *Police enquiries led to the location of the terrorists' hideout.*
IDM **on location** (used about a film, TV programme, etc.) made in a suitable place away from the building where films, etc. are usually made: *The series was filmed on location in Thailand.*

loch /lɒk/ *noun* [C] the Scottish word for a lake: *the Loch Ness monster*

lock[1] /lɒk/ *verb* **1** [I,T] to close or fasten (sth) so that it can only be opened with a key: *The door won't lock.* ◆ *Have you locked the car?* OPP **unlock** **2** [T] to put sb/sth in a safe place and lock it: *Lock your passport in a safe place.* **3** [T] **be locked in sth** to be involved in an angry argument, etc. with sth, or to be holding sb very tightly: *The two sides were locked in a bitter dispute.* ◆ *They were locked in a passionate embrace.*
PHR V **lock sth away** to keep sth in a safe or secret place that is locked
lock sb in/out to lock a door so that a person cannot get in/out: *I locked myself out of the house and had to climb in through the window.*
lock (sth) up to lock all the doors, windows, etc. of a building: *Make sure that you lock up before you leave.*
lock sb up to put sb in prison

lock[2] /lɒk/ *noun* [C] **1** something that is used for fastening a door, lid, etc. so that you need a key to open it again: *to turn the key in the lock* ➲ look at **padlock** ➲ picture at **key** **2** a device with a key that prevents a vehicle or machine from being used: *a bicycle lock* ◆ *a steering lock* ➲ picture at **bicycle** **3** a part of a river or a **canal** (= an artificial river) where the level of water changes. Locks have gates at each end and are used to allow boats to move to a higher or lower level.
IDM **pick a lock** ➲ **pick**[1]
under lock and key in a locked place

locker /ˈlɒkə(r)/ *noun* [C] a small cupboard that can be locked in a school or sports centre, where you can leave your clothes, books, etc.

locket /ˈlɒkɪt/ *noun* [C] a piece of jewellery that you wear on a chain around your neck and which opens so that you can put a picture, etc. inside ➲ picture at **jewellery**

locksmith /ˈlɒksmɪθ/ *noun* [C] a person who makes and repairs locks

locomotive /ˌləʊkəˈməʊtɪv/ = **engine**(2)

locust /ˈləʊkəst/ *noun* [C] a flying insect from Africa and Asia that moves in very large groups, eating and destroying large quantities of plants

lodge[1] /lɒdʒ/ *noun* [C] **1** a small house in the country **2** a room at the entrance to a large building such as a college or factory

lodge[2] /lɒdʒ/ *verb* **1** [T] (*formal*) **lodge sth (with sb) (against sb/sth)** to make a statement complaining about sth to a public organization or authority: *They lodged a compensation claim against the factory.* **2** [I] to pay to live in sb's house with them: *He lodged with a family for his first term at university.* **3** [I,T] to become firmly fixed or to make sth do this

lodger /ˈlɒdʒə(r)/ *noun* [C] a person who pays rent to live in a house as a member of the family ➲ look at **boarder**

lodging /ˈlɒdʒɪŋ/ *noun* **1** [C,U] a place where you can stay: *The family offered full board and lodging* (= a room and all meals) *in exchange for English lessons.* **2 lodgings** [pl] (*old-fashioned*) a room or rooms in sb's house where you can pay to stay

loft /lɒft/ *noun* [C] the room or space under the roof of a house or other building ➲ look at **attic** ➲ picture on **page P8**

log[1] /lɒg/ *noun* [C] **1** a thick piece of wood that has fallen or been cut from a tree ➲ picture at **tree** ➲ picture on **page P10** **2** (also **logbook**) the official written record of a ship's or an aircraft's journey: *to keep a log*

log[2] /lɒg/ *verb* [T] (**logging**; **logged**) to keep an official written record of sth
PHR V **log in/on** to perform the actions that allow you to start using a computer system: *You need to key in your password to log on.* ➲ note at **computer**
log off/out to perform the actions that allow you to finish using a computer system

logarithm /ˈlɒgərɪðəm/ (also *informal* **log**) *noun* [C] one of a series of numbers arranged in lists that allow you to solve problems in mathematics by adding or taking away numbers instead of multiplying or dividing

logbook /ˈlɒgbʊk/ = **log**[1](2)

loggerheads /ˈlɒgəhedz/ *noun*
IDM **at loggerheads (with sb)** strongly disagreeing (with sb)

logic /ˈlɒdʒɪk/ *noun* [U] **1** a sensible reason or way of thinking: *There is no logic in your argument.* **2** the science of using reason: *the rules of logic*

logical /ˈlɒdʒɪkl/ *adj* **1** seeming natural, reasonable or sensible: *There is only one logical conclusion.* OPP **illogical** **2** thinking in a sensible way: *a logical mind* ▸ **logically** /-kli/ *adv*

login /ˈlɒgɪn/ *noun* **1** [U] (also **logon** /ˈlɒgɒn/) the act of starting to use a computer system, usually by typing a name or word that you choose to use: *If you've forgotten your login ID, click this link.* **2** [C] the name that you use to enter a computer system: *Enter your login and password and press 'go'.*

logo /ˈləʊgəʊ/ *noun* [C] (*pl* **logos**) a printed symbol or design that a company or an organization uses as its special sign: *the company/brand logo*

loiter /ˈlɔɪtə(r)/ *verb* [I] to stand or walk around somewhere for no obvious reason

lollipop /ˈlɒlipɒp/ (also **lolly** /ˈlɒli/; *pl* **lollies**) *noun* [C] a sweet on a stick ➲ look at **ice lolly**

lone /ləʊn/ *adj* [only *before* a noun] **1** without any other people; alone: *a lone swimmer* SYN **solitary** **2** (used about a parent) single; without a partner

lonely /ˈləʊnli/ *adj* (**lonelier**; **loneliest**) **1** unhappy because you are not with other people: *to feel sad and lonely* **2** (used about a situation or a period of time) sad and spent alone: *lonely nights in front of the TV* **3** [only *before* a noun] far from other people and places where people live: *a lonely house in the hills* ➲ note at **alone** ▸ **loneliness** *noun* [U] ➲ look at **solitude, isolation**

loner /ˈləʊnə(r)/ *noun* [C] (*informal*) a person who prefers being alone to being with other people

lonesome /ˈləʊnsəm/ *adj* (*AmE*) lonely or making you feel lonely ➲ note at **alone**

long¹ /lɒŋ/ *adj* (**longer** /ˈlɒŋɡə(r)/, **longest** /ˈlɒŋɡɪst/) measuring a large amount in distance or time: *She has lovely long hair.* ♦ *We had to wait a long time.* ♦ *a very long journey/book/corridor* ♦ *Nurses work very long hours.* ♦ *I walked **a long way** today.* **OPP** **short** ➲ note at **far** ➲ picture at **hair** ➲ *noun* **length**

> **HELP** **Long** is also used when you are asking for or giving information about how much something measures in length, distance or time: ***How long** is the film?* ♦ *The insect was only 2 millimetres long.* ♦ *a five-mile-long traffic jam*

IDM **a long shot** a person or thing that probably will not succeed, win, etc.
at the longest not longer than the stated time: *It will take a week at the longest.*
go a long way (used about money, food, etc.) to be used for buying a lot of things, feeding a lot of people, etc.
have a long way to go to need to make a lot more progress before sth can be achieved
in the long run after a long time; in the end
in the long/short term ➲ **term¹**
▸ **long** *noun* [U]: *I'm sorry I haven't written to you for so long.* ♦ *This shouldn't take long.*

long² /lɒŋ/ *adv* (**longer** /lɒŋɡə(r)/, **longest** /lɒŋɡɪst/) **1** for a long time: *She didn't stay long.* ♦ *You shouldn't have to wait long.* ♦ *I hope we don't have to wait much longer.* ♦ *They won't be gone **for long**.* ♦ *Just wait here—I won't be long.* ♦ *'How long will it take to get there?' 'Not long.'*

> **HELP** **Long or a long time? Long** and **a long time** are both used as expressions of time. In positive sentences **a long time** is usually used: *They stood there for a long time.* **Long** is only used in positive sentences with another adverb, for example 'too', 'enough', 'ago', etc: *We lived here long ago.* ♦ *I've put up with this noise long enough. I'm going to make a complaint.* Both **long** and **a long time** can be used in questions: *Were you away long/a long time?* In negative sentences there is sometimes a difference in meaning between **long** and **a long time**: *I haven't been here long* (= I arrived only a short time ago). ♦ *I haven't been here for a long time* (= it is a long time since I was last here).

2 a long time before or after a particular time or event: *We got married **long before** we moved here.* ♦ *Don't worry—they'll be here **before long**.* ♦ *All that happened long ago.* **3** for the whole of the time that is mentioned: *The baby cried **all night long**.*
IDM **as/so long as** on condition that: *As long as no problems arise we should get the job finished by Friday.* **SYN** **provided (that)**
no/not any longer not any more: *They no longer live here.* ♦ *They don't live here any longer.*

long³ /lɒŋ/ *verb* [I] **long for sth; long (for sb) to do sth** to want sth very much, especially sth that is not likely: *She longed to return to Greece.* **SYN** **yearn** ▸ **longing** *noun* [C,U]: *a longing for peace* ▸ **longingly** *adv*

ˌlong-ˈdistance *adj* [only *before* a noun] (used about travel or communication) between places that are far from each other: *a long-distance lorry driver* ▸ **long distance** *adv*

ˈlong-haul *adj* [only *before* a noun] connected with the transport of people or goods over long distances: *a long-haul flight*

longitude /ˈlɒŋɡɪtjuːd/ *noun* [U] the distance of a place east or west of a line from the North Pole to the South Pole that passes through Greenwich in London. **Longitude** is measured in degrees. ➲ look at **latitude** ➲ picture at **earth**

the ˈlong jump *noun* [sing] the sport in which people try to jump as far as possible ➲ look at **high jump**

ˌlong-ˈlife *adj* made to last for a long time: *a long-life battery* ♦ *long-life milk*

ˌlong-ˈlived *adj* that has lived or lasted for a long time: *a long-lived dispute*

ˈlong-range *adj* [only *before* a noun] **1** that can go or be sent over long distances: *long-range nuclear missiles* **2** of or for a long period of time starting from the present: *the long-range weather forecast*

ˌlong-ˈsighted (*AmE* ˌ**far-ˈsighted**) *adj* able to see things clearly only when they are quite far away **OPP** **short-sighted, nearsighted**

ˌlong-ˈstanding *adj* that has lasted for a long time: *a long-standing arrangement*

ˌlong-ˈsuffering *adj* (used about a person) having a lot of troubles but not complaining

ˌlong-ˈterm *adj* of or for a long period of time: *long-term planning*

ˌlong-ˈwinded *adj* (used about sth that is written or spoken) boring because it is too long

loo /luː/ *noun* [C] (*pl* **loos**) (*BrE informal*) toilet ➲ note at **toilet**

look¹ /lʊk/ *verb*
➤ USE EYES **1** [I,T] **look (at sth)** to turn your eyes in a particular direction (in order to pay attention to sb/sth): *Sorry, I wasn't looking. Can you show me again?* ♦ *Look carefully at this picture.* ♦ *to look out of the window* ♦ *She blushed and looked away.* ♦ *Look who's come to see us.* ♦ *Look where you're going!*
➤ SEARCH **2** [I] **look (for sb/sth)** to try to find (sb/sth): *We've been looking for you everywhere. Where have you been?* ♦ *to look for work* ♦ *'I can't find my shoes.' 'Have you looked under the bed?'*
➤ SEEM/APPEAR **3** [I] **look (like sb/sth) (to sb); look (to sb) as if .../as though ...** to seem or appear: *You look*

very smart in that shirt. ♦ to look tired/ill/sad/well/happy ♦ The boy looks like his father. ♦ That film looks good—I might go and see it. ♦ You look (to me) as if/as though you need some sleep.

➤LISTEN **4** [I] used for asking sb to listen to what you are saying: *Look, Will, I know you are busy but could you give me a hand?*

➤FACE DIRECTION **5** [I] to face a particular direction: *This room looks south so it gets the sun all day.*

➤INTEND **6** [I] **look to do sth** to aim to do sth: *We are looking to double our profits over the next five years.*

HELP **Look, watch** or **see**? If you **look** at sth, you pay attention to it: *Look carefully. Can you see anything strange?* When you look at sth for a time, paying attention to what happens, you **watch** it: *Watch what I do, then you try.* If you become conscious of sth, you **see** it: *I saw a girl riding past on a bicycle.* **See** can also mean 'to watch a film, play, TV programme': *We went to see a movie last night.*

IDM **look bad; not look good** to be considered bad manners: *It'll look bad if we get there an hour late.*

look your best to look as beautiful or attractive as possible

look down your nose at sb/sth (*especially BrE informal*) to think that you are better than sb else; to think that sth is not good enough for you

look good to seem to be encouraging: *This year's sales figures are looking good.*

look sb in the eye to look straight at sb without feeling embarrassed or afraid

(not) look yourself to (not) look as well or healthy as usual

look on the bright side (of sth) to be positive about a bad situation, thinking of the advantages and not the disadvantages

never/not look back to become and continue being successful

PHR V **look after sb/sth/yourself** to be responsible for or take care of sb/sth/yourself: *I want to go back to work if I can find somebody to look after the children.* ♦ *The old lady's son looked after all her financial affairs.* ➲ note at **care²**

look ahead to think about or plan for the future

look at sth **1** to examine or study sth: *My tooth aches. I think a dentist should look at it.* ♦ *The government is looking at ways of reducing unemployment.* ♦ *Could I look at* (= read) *the newspaper when you've finished with it?* **2** to consider sth: *Different races and nationalities look at life differently.*

look back (on sth) to think about sth in your past

look down on sb/sth to think that you are better than sb/sth

look forward to sth/doing sth to wait with pleasure for sth to happen: *I'm really looking forward to the weekend.*

look into sth to study or try to find out sth: *A committee was set up to look into the causes of the accident.*

look on to watch sth happening without taking any action: *All we could do was look on as the house burned.*

look on sb/sth as sth; look on sb with sth to think of sb/sth in a particular way: *They seem to look on me as someone who can advise them.*

look out to be careful or to pay attention to sth dangerous: *Look out! There's a bike coming.*

look out (for sb/sth) to pay attention in order to see, find or avoid sb/sth: *Look out for thieves!*

look round **1** to turn your head in order to see sb/sth **2** to look at many things (before buying sth): *She looked round but couldn't find anything she liked.*

look round sth to walk around a place looking at things: *to look round a town/shop/museum*

look through sth to read sth quickly

look to sb for sth; look to sb to do sth to expect sb to do or to provide sth: *He always looked to his father for advice.*

look up **1** to move your eyes upwards to look at sb/sth: *She looked up and smiled.* **2** (*informal*) to improve: *Business is looking up.*

look sth up to search for information in a book: *to look up a word in a dictionary*

look up to sb to respect and admire sb

look² /lʊk/ *noun*

➤USING EYES **1** [C] the act of looking: ***Have a look*** *at this article.* ♦ ***Take a*** *close* ***look*** *at the contract before you sign it.*

➤SEARCH **2** [C, usually sing] a look (for sb/sth) a search: *I'll* ***have a*** *good* ***look*** *for that book later.*

➤EXPRESSION **3** [C] the expression on sb's face: *He had a worried look on his face.*

➤APPEARANCE **4** **looks** [pl] sb's appearance: *He's lucky—he's got good looks and intelligence.*

➤FASHION **5** [C] a fashion or style: *The shop has a new look to appeal to younger customers.*

IDM **by/from the look of sb/sth** judging by the appearance of sb/sth: *It's going to be a fine day by the look of it.*

like the look/sound of sb/sth ➲ **like²**

ˈlook-in *noun*

IDM **(not) give sb a look-in; (not) get/have a look-in** (*informal*) to (not) give sb, or to (not) have a chance to do sth: *Tina doesn't get a look-in when Ben's playing on the computer.*

-looking /ˈlʊkɪŋ/ [in compounds] having the appearance mentioned: *an odd-looking building* ♦ *He's very good-looking.*

lookout /ˈlʊkaʊt/ *noun* [C] (a person who has) the responsibility of watching to see if danger is coming; the place this person watches from: *One of the gang acted as lookout.*

IDM **be on the lookout for sb/sth; keep a lookout for sb/sth** to pay attention in order to see, find or avoid sb/sth

loom¹ /luːm/ *verb* [I] **loom (up)** to appear as a shape that is not clear and in a way that seems frightening: *The mountain loomed (up) in the distance.*

loom² /luːm/ *noun* [C] a piece of equipment that is used for **weaving** (= making cloth by passing pieces of thread over and under other pieces)

loony /ˈluːni/ *noun* [C] (*pl* **loonies**) (*slang*) a person who is crazy ▶ **loony** *adj*: *I'm tired of his loony ideas.*

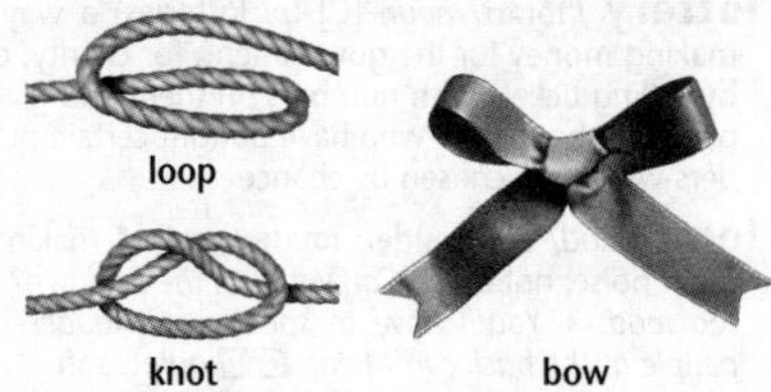

loop /luːp/ *noun* [C] a curved or round shape made by a line curving round and joining or crossing itself: *a loop in a rope* ◆ *The road goes around the lake in a loop.*
IDM **in the loop/out of the loop** (*informal*) part of a group of people that is dealing with sth important/not part of this group
▶ **loop** *verb* [I,T]: *He was trying to loop a rope over the horse's head.*

loophole /ˈluːphəʊl/ *noun* [C] a way of avoiding sth because the words of a rule or law are badly chosen

loose[1] /luːs/ *adj*
➤NOT TIED/FIXED **1** not tied up or shut in sth; free: *The horse managed to **get loose** and escape.* ◆ *I take the dog to the woods and **let** him **loose**.* ◆ *She wore her long hair loose.* **2** not firmly fixed: *I've got a loose tooth* ◆ *The saucepan handle is a bit loose so be careful.* **3** not contained in sth or joined together: *loose change* (= coins) ◆ *some loose sheets of paper*
➤CLOTHES **4** not fitting closely; not tight: *These trousers don't fit. They're much too loose round the waist.* OPP **tight**
➤NOT EXACT **5** not completely accurate or the same as sth: *a loose translation*
IDM **all hell broke loose** ➲ **hell**
at a loose end having nothing to do and feeling bored
▶ **loosely** *adv*: *The film is loosely based on the life of Beethoven.*

loose[2] /luːs/ *noun*
IDM **on the loose** escaped and dangerous: *a lion on the loose from a zoo*

ˌloose ˈcannon *noun* [C] a person, usually a public figure, who often behaves in a way that nobody can predict

ˌloose-ˈleaf *adj* (used about a book, file, etc.) with pages that can be removed or added separately: *a loose-leaf binder*

loosen /ˈluːsn/ *verb* [I,T] to become or make sth less tight: *The rope holding the boat loosened.* ◆ *to loosen your tie/belt* ◆ *Don't loosen your grip on the rope or you'll fall.*
PHR V **loosen (sb/sth) up** to relax or move more easily: *These exercises will help you to loosen up.*

loot /luːt/ *verb* [I,T] to steal things during a war or period of fighting

lop /lɒp/ *verb* [T] (**lopping**; **lopped**) to cut branches off a tree
PHR V **lop sth off/away** to cut sth off/away

lopsided /ˌlɒpˈsaɪdɪd/ *adj* with one side lower or smaller than the other: *a lopsided smile*

lord /lɔːd/ *noun* [C] **1** a man with a very high position in society: *the Lord Mayor of London* ◆ *Lord and Lady Derby* **2 the Lord** [sing] God; Christ **3 the Lords** [with sing or pl verb] (*BrE*) (members of) the House of Lords: *The Lords has/have voted against the bill.*

lorry /ˈlɒri/ *noun* [C] (*pl* **lorries**) (*BrE*) (*especially AmE* **truck**) a large strong motor vehicle that is used for carrying goods by road ➲ note at **van** ➲ picture on **page P7**

lose /luːz/ *verb* (*pt, pp* **lost** /lɒst/) **1** [T] to become unable to find sth: *I've lost my purse. I can't find it anywhere.* **2** [T] to no longer have sb/sth: *She lost a leg in the accident.* ◆ *He lost his wife last year* (= she died). ◆ *to lose your job* **3** [T] to have less of sth: *to lose weight/interest/patience* ◆ *The company is losing money all the time.* OPP **gain** **4** [T] (*informal*) to cause sb not to understand sth: *You've totally lost me! Please explain again.* **5** [I,T] to not win; to be defeated: *We played well but we lost 2-1.* ◆ *to lose a court case/an argument* ◆ *Parma lost to Milan in the final.* **6** [I,T] to become poorer (as a result of sth): *The company lost on the deal.* **7** [T] to waste time, a chance, etc: *Hurry up! There's **no time to lose**.*
IDM **give/lose ground (to sb/sth)** ➲ **ground**[1]
keep/lose your cool ➲ **cool**[3]
keep/lose count (of sth) ➲ **count**[2]
keep/lose your temper ➲ **temper**
keep/lose track of sb/sth ➲ **track**[1]
lose your bearings to become confused about where you are
lose face to lose the respect of other people
lose your head to become confused or very excited
lose heart to stop believing that you will be successful in sth you are trying to do
lose it (*spoken*) to go crazy or suddenly become unable to control your emotions
lose your life to be killed
lose sight of sb/sth to no longer be able to see sb/sth: *We eventually lost sight of the animal in some trees.* ◆ (*figurative*) *We mustn't lose sight of our original aim.*
lose your touch to lose a special skill or ability
lose touch (with sb/sth) to no longer have contact (with sb/sth): *I've lost touch with a lot of my old school friends.*
a losing battle a competition, fight, etc. in which it seems that you will fail to be successful
win/lose the toss ➲ **toss**
PHR V **lose out (on sth/to sb)** (*informal*) to be at a disadvantage: *If a teacher pays too much attention to the brightest students in the class, the others lose out.*

loser /ˈluːzə(r)/ *noun* [C] **1** a person who is defeated: *He is a bad loser. He always gets angry if I beat him.* **2** a person who is never successful **3** a person who suffers because of a particular situation, decision, etc.

loss /lɒs/ *noun* **1** [C,U] (a) **loss (of sth)** the state of no longer having sth or not having as much as before; the act of losing sth: *loss of blood/sleep*

L

◆ *weight/hair loss* ◆ *Have you reported the loss of your wallet?* ◆ *The plane crashed with great* ***loss of life***. **2** [C] a loss (of sth) the amount of money which is lost by a business: *The firm* ***made a loss*** *of £5 million.* ➲ look at **profit** **3** [C] a loss (to sb) the disadvantage that is caused when sb/sth leaves or is taken away; the person or thing that causes this disadvantage: *If she leaves, it/she will be a big loss to the school.*

IDM **at a loss** not knowing what to do or say

cut your losses to stop wasting time or money on sth that is not successful

lost[1] *past tense, past participle* of **lose**

lost[2] /lɒst/ *adj* **1** unable to find your way; not knowing where you are: *This isn't the right road—we're completely lost!* ◆ *If you* ***get lost****, stop and ask someone the way.* **2** that cannot be found or that no longer exists: *The letter must have* ***got lost*** *in the post.* **3** unable to deal with a situation or to understand sth: *Sorry, I'm lost. Could you explain the last part again?* **4** lost on sb not noticed or understood by sb: *The humour of the situation was completely lost on Joe.*

IDM **get lost** (*slang*) used to rudely tell sb to go away

a lost cause a goal or an aim that cannot be achieved

lost for words not knowing what to say

ˌlost ˈproperty *noun* [U] things that people have lost or left in a public place and that are kept in a special office for the owners to collect

lot[1] /lɒt/ *pron, determiner* a lot (of); lots (of) a large amount or number (of things or people): *'How many do you need?' 'A lot.'* ◆ *I've got* ***a lot to do*** *today.* ◆ *Have some more cake. There's lots left.* ◆ ***An awful lot*** *of* (= very many) *people will be disappointed if the concert is cancelled.* ◆ *There seem to be* ***quite a lot*** *of new shops opening.* ◆ *Sit here—there's lots of room.* ◆ *Lots of love, Billy* (= an informal ending for a letter).

> **GRAMMAR** In negative statements and questions, **much** and **many** are more usual: *A lot of girls go to dancing classes, but not many boys.* ◆ *'How much would a car like that cost?' 'A lot!'*

lot[2] /lɒt/ *adv* (*informal*) **1** a lot; lots [before an adjective or adverb] very much: *a lot bigger/better/faster* ◆ *They see lots more of each other than before.* **2** a lot very much or often: ***Thanks a lot****—that's very kind.* ◆ *It generally rains a lot at this time of year.*

lot[3] /lɒt/ *noun* [sing, with sing or pl verb] (*informal*) all of sth; the whole of a group of things or people: *When we opened the bag of potatoes* ***the whole lot*** *was/were bad.* ◆ *The manager has just sacked* ***the lot of them****!* ◆ *Just one more suitcase and* ***that's the lot****!* ◆ *'How many of these books shall we take?'* ***'The lot.'*** ◆ *You count those kids and I'll count* ***this lot****.*

IDM **draw lots** ➲ **draw**[1]

lo-tech = low-tech

loth = loath

lotion /ˈləʊʃn/ *noun* [C,U] liquid that you use on your hair or skin: *suntan lotion*

lottery /ˈlɒtəri/ *noun* [C] (*pl* **lotteries**) a way of making money for the government, for charity, etc. by selling tickets with numbers on them and giving prizes to the people who have bought certain numbers which are chosen by chance

loud /laʊd/ *adj* (**louder**; **loudest**) *adv* **1** making a lot of noise; not quiet: *Can you turn the TV down? It's too loud.* ◆ *You'll have to speak a bit louder—the people at the back can't hear.* **OPP** **quiet, soft**

> **HELP** **Loud** or **noisy**? **Loud** is usually used to describe the sound itself or the thing producing the sound: *a loud noise/bang* ◆ *loud music.* **Noisy** is used to describe a person, animal, place, event, etc. that is very loud or too loud: *a noisy road/party/engine/child*

2 (used about clothes or colours) too bright: *a loud shirt*

IDM **out loud** so that people can hear it: *Shall I read this bit out loud to you?*

▶ **loudly** *adv* ▶ **loudness** *noun* [U]

loudspeaker /ˌlaʊdˈspiːkə(r)/ *noun* [C] **1** a piece of electrical equipment for speaking, playing music, etc. to a lot of people **2** = **speaker**(3)

lounge[1] /laʊndʒ/ *noun* [C] **1** the part of an airport where passengers wait: *the departure lounge* **2** (*BrE*) a comfortable room in a house or hotel where you can sit and relax **SYN** **living room**

lounge[2] /laʊndʒ/ *verb* [I] lounge (about/around) to sit, stand or lie in a lazy way

louse /laʊs/ *noun* [C] (*pl* **lice** /laɪs/) a small insect that lives on the bodies of animals and people

lousy /ˈlaʊzi/ *adj* (**lousier**; **lousiest**) (*informal*) very bad: *We had lousy weather on holiday.*

lout /laʊt/ *noun* [C] a young man who behaves in a rude, rough or stupid way ➲ look at **hooligan, yob**

lovable (also **loveable**) /ˈlʌvəbl/ *adj* having a character or appearance that is easy to love: *a lovable little boy*

love[1] /lʌv/ *noun*

➤AFFECTION **1** [U] a strong feeling that you have when you like sb/sth very much: *a mother's love for her children* ◆ *to* ***fall in love*** *with somebody* ◆ *It was* ***love at first sight****. They got married two months after they met!* ◆ *He's* ***madly in love*** *with her.* ◆ *a love song/story*

➤ENJOYMENT **2** [U, sing] a strong feeling of interest in or enjoyment of sth: *a love of adventure/nature/sport*

➤SB/STH YOU LIKE **3** [C] a person, a thing or an activity that you like very much: *His great love was always music.* ◆ *Who was your first love?*

➤FRIENDLY NAME **4** [C] (*BrE informal*) used as a friendly way of speaking to sb, often sb you do not know: *'Hello, love. What can I do for you?'*

➤IN TENNIS **5** [U] a score of zero: *The score is forty-love.*

IDM **give/send sb your love** to give/send sb a friendly message: *Give Maria my love when you next see her.*

(lots of) love (from) used at the end of a letter to a

friend or a member of your family: *See you soon. Love, Jim*
make love (to sb) to have sex

love² /lʌv/ *verb* [T] **1** [not used in the continuous tenses] to like sb/sth in the strongest possible way: *I split up from my girlfriend last year, but I still love her.* ◆ *She loves her children.* **2** to like or enjoy sth very much: *I love the summer!* ◆ *I really love swimming in the sea.* ◆ *'What do you think of this music?' 'I love it!'* **3 would love sth/to do sth** used to say that you would very much like sth/to do sth: *'Would you like to come?' 'I'd love to.'* ◆ *'What about a drink?' 'I'd love one.'* ◆ *We'd love you to come and stay with us.*

ˈlove affair *noun* [C] **1** a romantic and/or sexual relationship between two people who are in love and not married to each other: *She had a love affair with her tennis coach.* **2** a great enthusiasm for sth

lovely /ˈlʌvli/ *adj* (**lovelier**; **loveliest**) **1** beautiful or attractive: *a lovely room/voice/expression* ◆ *You look lovely with your hair short.* **2** enjoyable or pleasant; very nice: *We had a lovely holiday.* ➲ note at **nice**
IDM lovely and warm, peaceful, fresh, etc. used for emphasizing how good sth is because of the quality mentioned: *These blankets are lovely and soft.* ▶ **loveliness** *noun* [U]

lover /ˈlʌvə(r)/ *noun* [C] **1** a partner in a sexual relationship with sb who they are not married to: *He discovered that his wife had a lover.* ◆ *The park was full of young lovers holding hands.* **2** a person who likes or enjoys the thing mentioned: *a music lover* ◆ *an animal lover*

loving /ˈlʌvɪŋ/ *adj* **1** feeling or showing love or care: *She's very loving towards her brother.* ◆ *a loving family* **SYN affectionate** **2** [in compounds] **-loving** loving the thing or activity mentioned: *a fun-loving girl* ▶ **lovingly** *adv*

low¹ /ləʊ/ *adj* (**lower**; **lowest**) *adv*
➤NOT HIGH/TALL **1** close to the ground or to the bottom of sth: *Hang that picture a bit higher, it's much too low!* ◆ *That plane is flying very low.*
➤LEVEL/VALUE **2** below the usual or normal level or amount: *Temperatures were very low last winter.* ◆ *The price of fruit is lower in the summer.* ◆ *low wages* ◆ *low-fat yogurt* **3** below what is normal or acceptable in quality, importance or development: *a low standard of living* ◆ *low status*
➤SOUND/VOICE **4** deep or quiet: *His voice is already lower than his father's.* ◆ *A group of people in the library were speaking in low voices.*
➤UNHAPPY **5** not happy and lacking energy: *He's been **feeling** a bit **low** since his illness.*
➤LIGHT/HEAT **6** (used about a light, an oven, etc.) made to produce only a little light or heat: *Cook the rice on a low heat for 20 minutes.* ◆ *The low lighting adds to the restaurant's atmosphere.*
➤IN CAR **7** (used about a gear in a car) that allows a slower speed **OPP high**
IDM high and low ➲ **high³**
a high/low profile ➲ **profile**
lie low ➲ **lie²**
run low (on sth) to start to have less of sth than you need; to start to be less than is needed: *We're running low on coffee–shall I go and buy some?*

low² /ləʊ/ *noun* [C] a low point, level, figure, etc: *Unemployment has fallen to a new low.* **OPP high**

ˈlow-down *noun*
IDM give sb/get the low-down (on sb/sth) (*informal*) to tell sb/be told the true facts or secret information (about sb/sth)

lower¹ /ˈləʊə(r)/ *adj* [only *before* a noun] below sth or at the bottom of sth: *She bit her lower lip.* ◆ *the lower deck of a ship* **OPP upper**

lower² /ˈləʊə(r)/ *verb* [T] **1** to make or let sb/sth go down: *They lowered the boat into the water.* ◆ *to lower your head/eyes* **2** to make sth less in amount, quality, etc: *The virus lowers resistance to other diseases.* ◆ *Could you **lower** your **voice** slightly? I'm trying to sleep.* **OPP** for both meanings **raise**

ˌlower ˈcase *noun* [U] letters that are written or printed in their small form; not in capital letters: *The text is all in lower case.* ◆ *lower-case letters* **OPP upper case**

ˌlow-ˈkey *adj* quiet and not wanting to attract a lot of attention: *The wedding will be very low-key. We're only inviting ten people.*

lowland /ˈləʊlənd/ *noun* [C, usually pl] a flat area of land at about sea level: *the lowlands near the coast* ◆ *lowland areas*

ˌlow-ˈlying *adj* (used about land) near to sea level; not high

low-tech (also **lo-tech**) /ˌləʊ ˈtek/ *adj* (*informal*) not using the most modern technology or methods **OPP high-tech**

ˌlow ˈtide *noun* [U] the time when the sea is at its lowest level: *At low tide you can walk out to the island.* **OPP high tide**

loyal /ˈlɔɪəl/ *adj* (used about a person) not changing in your friendship or beliefs: *a loyal friend/supporter* **SYN faithful** **OPP disloyal** ▶ **loyally** *adv* ▶ **loyalty** /ˈlɔɪəlti/ *noun* [C,U] (*pl* **loyalties**)

lozenge /ˈlɒzɪndʒ/ *noun* [C] **1** = **diamond**(2) **2** a sweet that you suck if you have a cough or a sore throat

L-plate /ˈel pleɪt/ *noun* [C] a sign with a large red letter L (for 'learner') on it, that you fix to a car to show that the driver is learning to drive

Lt *abbr* = **Lieutenant**

Ltd /ˈlɪmətɪd/ *abbr* (*BrE*) = **limited company**: *Pierce and Co. Ltd*

lubricant /ˈluːbrɪkənt/ *noun* [C,U] a substance, for example oil, that makes the parts of a machine work easily and smoothly

lubricate /ˈluːbrɪkeɪt/ *verb* [T] to put oil, etc. onto or into sth so that it works smoothly ▶ **lubrication** /ˌluːbrɪˈkeɪʃn/ *noun* [U]

lucid /ˈluːsɪd/ *adj* (*formal*) **1** (used about sth that is said or written) clear and easy to understand: *a lucid style/description* **2** (used about sb's mind) not confused; clear and normal ▶ **lucidity** /luːˈsɪdəti/ *noun* [U] ▶ **lucidly** *adv*

L

luck /lʌk/ *noun* [U] **1** success or good things that happen by chance: *We'd like to **wish** you lots of **luck** in your new career.* ◆ *He says this necklace will **bring** you **luck**.* ◆ *I could hardly believe my luck when they offered me the job.* ◆ ***With** a bit of **luck**, we'll finish this job today.* **2** chance; the force that people believe makes things happen: *There's no skill in this game—it's all luck.* ◆ *to have good/bad luck* ➲ look at **fortune**

IDM **Bad luck!**; **Hard luck!** used to show pity for sb: *'Bad luck! Maybe you'll win next time.'*

be in/out of luck to be lucky/to not be lucky: *I was in luck—they had one ticket left!*

Good luck (to sb)! used to wish that sb is successful: *Good luck! I'm sure you'll get the job.*

push your luck ➲ **push**[1]

worse luck ➲ **worse**

lucky /ˈlʌki/ *adj* (**luckier**; **luckiest**) **1** (used about a person) having good luck: *He's lucky to be alive after an accident like that.* ◆ *With so much unemployment, I **count myself lucky** that I've got a job.* ◆ *'I'm off on holiday next week.' 'Lucky you!'* **2** (used about a situation, event, etc.) having a good result: *It's lucky I got here before the rain started.* ◆ *a lucky escape* **3** (used about a thing) bringing success or good luck: *a lucky number* ◆ *It was not my lucky day.* OPP **unlucky**

IDM **you'll be lucky** used to tell sb that sth they are expecting will probably not happen: *You're hoping for a ticket for Sunday's match? You'll be lucky!*

▶ **luckily** /ˈlʌkɪli/ *adv*: *Luckily, I remembered to bring some money.* ➲ note at **sudden**

lucrative /ˈluːkrətɪv/ *adj* (*formal*) allowing sb to earn a lot of money: *a lucrative contract/business/market*

ludicrous /ˈluːdɪkrəs/ *adj* very silly: *What a ludicrous idea!* SYN **ridiculous** ▶ **ludicrously** *adv*: *a ludicrously expensive project*

lug /lʌg/ *verb* [T] (**lugging**; **lugged**) (*informal*) to carry or pull sth very heavy with great difficulty

luggage /ˈlʌgɪdʒ/ *noun* [U] bags, suitcases, etc. used for carrying sb's clothes and things on a journey: *'How much luggage are you taking with you?' 'Only one suitcase.'* ◆ *You're only allowed one piece of **hand luggage*** (= a bag that you carry with you on the plane). SYN **baggage**

ˈ**luggage rack** *noun* [C] a shelf above the seats in a train or bus for putting your bags, etc. on ➲ picture at **rack**

lukewarm /ˌluːkˈwɔːm/ *adj* **1** (used about liquids) only slightly warm **2** **lukewarm (about sb/sth)** not showing much interest or desire

lull[1] /lʌl/ *noun* [C, usually sing] **a lull (in sth)** a short period of quiet between times of activity

lull[2] /lʌl/ *verb* [T] **1** to make sb relaxed and calm: *She sang a song to **lull** the children **to sleep**.* **2** **lull sb into sth** to make sb feel safe, and not expecting anything bad to happen: *Our success **lulled** us **into a false sense of security**.*

lullaby /ˈlʌləbaɪ/ *noun* [C] (*pl* **lullabies**) a gentle song that you sing to help a child to go to sleep

lumber[1] /ˈlʌmbə(r)/ (*especially AmE*) = **timber**(1)

lumber[2] /ˈlʌmbə(r)/ *verb* **1** [I] to move in a slow, heavy way: *A family of elephants lumbered past.* **2** [T, usually passive] (*informal*) **lumber sb (with sb/sth)** to give sb a responsibility or job that they do not want

luminous /ˈluːmɪnəs/ *adj* that shines in the dark: *a luminous watch*

lump[1] /lʌmp/ *noun* [C] **1** a piece of sth solid of any size or shape: *The sauce was full of lumps.* ◆ *a lump of coal/cheese/wood* **2** a swelling under the skin: *You'll have a bit of a lump on your head where you banged it.*

IDM **have/feel a lump in your throat** to feel pressure in your throat because you are about to cry

lump[2] /lʌmp/ *verb* [T] **lump A and B together**; **lump A (in) with B** to put or consider different people or things together in the same group

IDM **lump it** (*informal*) to accept sth unpleasant because you have no choice: *That's the deal—like it or lump it.*

ˈ**lump sum** *noun* [C] an amount of money paid all at once rather than in several smaller amounts

lumpy /ˈlʌmpi/ *adj* full of or covered with lumps: *This bed is very lumpy.* OPP **smooth**

lunacy /ˈluːnəsi/ *noun* [U] behaviour that is very stupid: *It was lunacy to drive so fast in that terrible weather.* SYN **madness**

lunar /ˈluːnə(r)/ *adj* connected with the moon: *a lunar spacecraft/eclipse/landscape*

lunatic[1] /ˈluːnətɪk/ *noun* [C] (*informal*) a person who behaves in a stupid way doing crazy and often dangerous things SYN **madman, maniac**

lunatic[2] /ˈluːnətɪk/ *adj* stupid; crazy: *a lunatic idea*

lunch /lʌntʃ/ *noun* [C,U] a meal that you have in the middle of the day: *Hot and cold lunches are served between 12 and 2.* ◆ *What would you like for lunch?* ➲ note at **meal** ▶ **lunch** *verb* [I] (*formal*)

> **MORE** A **packed lunch** is food that you prepare at home and take to school or work. People at a **business lunch/working lunch** eat lunch together while continuing to discuss business. In Britain lunches served to children at school are called **school dinners.**

ˈ**lunch hour** *noun* [C, usually sing] the time around the middle of the day when you stop work or school to have **lunch**: *I went to the shops in my lunch hour.*

lunchtime /ˈlʌntʃtaɪm/ *noun* [C,U] the time around the middle of the day when **lunch** is eaten: *I'll meet you at lunchtime.*

lung /lʌŋ/ *noun* [C] one of the two organs of your body that are inside your chest and are used for breathing ➲ picture at **body**

lunge /lʌndʒ/ *noun* [C, usually sing] **a lunge (at sb)**; **a lunge (for sb/sth)** a sudden powerful forward movement of the body, especially when trying to attack sb/sth: *She made a lunge for the ball.* ▶ **lunge** *verb* [I]: *He lunged towards me with a knife.*

lurch /lɜːtʃ/ *noun* [C, usually sing] a sudden movement forward or to one side

IDM leave sb in the lurch ➲ **leave**[1]

▶ **lurch** *verb* [I]: *Suddenly the horse lurched to one side and the child fell off.*

lure[1] /lʊə(r)/ *verb* [T] to persuade or trick sb to go somewhere or do sth, usually by offering them sth nice: *Young people are lured to the city by the prospect of a job and money.*

lure[2] /lʊə(r)/ *noun* [C] the attractive qualities of sth: *the lure of money/fame/adventure*

lurid /ˈlʊərɪd; ˈljʊər-/ *adj* **1** having colours that are too bright, in a way that is not attractive: *a lurid purple and orange dress* **2** (used about a story or a piece of writing) deliberately shocking, especially because of violent or unpleasant detail ▶ **luridly** *adv*

lurk /lɜːk/ *verb* [I] to wait somewhere secretly especially in order to do sth bad or illegal: *I thought I saw somebody lurking among the trees.*

luscious /ˈlʌʃəs/ *adj* (used about food) tasting very good: *luscious fruit*

lush /lʌʃ/ *adj* (used about plants or gardens) growing well, with a lot of healthy grass and plants close together

lust[1] /lʌst/ *noun* **1** [U] **lust (for sb)** strong sexual desire **2** [C,U] **(a) lust (for sth)** (a) very strong desire to have or get sth: *a lust for power* ◆ *(a) lust for life* (= enjoyment of life)

lust[2] /lʌst/ *verb* [I] **lust (after sb)**; **lust (after/for sth)** to feel a very strong desire for sb/sth: *to lust for power/success/fame*

lustful /ˈlʌstfl/ *adj* full of sexual desire: *lustful thoughts* ▶ **lustfully** /-fəli/ *adv*

luxurious /lʌgˈʒʊəriəs/ *adj* very comfortable; full of expensive and beautiful things: *a luxurious hotel* ▶ **luxuriously** *adv*

luxury /ˈlʌkʃəri/ *noun* (*pl* **luxuries**) **1** [U] the enjoyment of expensive and beautiful things; great comfort and pleasure: *They are said to be* ***living in luxury*** *in Barbados.* ◆ *to lead* ***a life of luxury*** ◆ *a luxury hotel/car/yacht* **2** [C] something that is enjoyable and expensive that you do not really need: *She bought flowers, chocolates and other luxuries.* **3** [U, sing] a pleasure which you do not often have: *It was (an) absolute luxury to do nothing all weekend.*

LW *abbr* (*especially BrE*) **long wave**; a band of radio waves with a length of more than 1000 metres: *1 500m LW*

lynch /lɪntʃ/ *verb* [T] (used about a crowd of people) to kill, usually by hanging, sb who is thought to be guilty of a crime without a legal trial in a court of law

lyric /ˈlɪrɪk/ *adj* (used about poetry) expressing personal feelings and thoughts: *lyric poems*

lyrical /ˈlɪrɪkl/ *adj* like a song or a poem, expressing strong personal feelings

lyrics /ˈlɪrɪks/ *noun* [pl] the words of a song

M, m /em/ *noun* [C,U] (*pl* **Ms; M's; m's** /emz/) the 13th letter of the English alphabet: *'Mark' begins with (an) 'M'.*

M *abbr* **1** (also **med**) = **medium**[1] **2** /em/ (*BrE*) = **motorway**: *heavy traffic on the M25*

m *abbr* **1** m = **metre**: *a 500m race* **2** m = **million**: *population 10m*

MA /ˌem ˈeɪ/ *abbr* **Master of Arts**; a second degree that you receive when you complete a more advanced course or piece of research in an arts subject at university or college ➲ look at **BA, MSc**

mac /mæk/ (also **mackintosh**) *noun* [C] (*especially BrE*) a coat that is made to keep out the rain

macabre /məˈkɑːbrə/ *adj* unpleasant and frightening because it is connected with death: *a macabre tale/joke/ritual*

macaroni /ˌmækəˈrəʊni/ *noun* [U] a type of **pasta** (= Italian food made from flour and water) in the shape of short tubes

machete /məˈʃeti/ *noun* [C] a wide heavy knife used as a cutting tool and as a weapon

machine /məˈʃiːn/ *noun* [C] [often in compounds] a piece of equipment with moving parts that is designed to do a particular job. A machine usually needs electricity, gas, steam, etc. in order to work: *a washing/sewing/knitting machine* ◆ *a machine for making pasta* ➲ note at **tool**

maˈchine gun *noun* [C] a gun that fires bullets very quickly and continuously ➲ note at **gun**

machinery /məˈʃiːnəri/ *noun* [U] machines in general, especially large ones; the moving parts of a machine: *farm/agricultural/industrial machinery*

macho /ˈmætʃəʊ/ *adj* (*informal*) (used about a man or his behaviour) having qualities typical of men, like strength and courage, but using them in an aggressive way: *He's too macho to ever admit he was wrong and apologize.*

mackintosh /ˈmækɪntɒʃ/ = **mac**

mad /mæd/ *adj* (**madder**; **maddest**)

➤ILL **1** having a mind that does not work normally; mentally ill: *They realized that he had* ***gone mad.***

HELP **Mentally ill** is the polite way of describing a person who is not mentally normal.

➤STUPID **2** (*BrE*) not at all sensible; stupid: *You must be mad to drive in this weather.*

➤ANGRY **3** [not before a noun] **mad (at/with sb) (about sth)** very angry: *His laziness* ***drives me mad!*** ◆ ((*especially AmE*) *Don't* ***get/go mad*** *at him. He didn't mean to do it.*

➤VERY INTERESTED **4** (*informal*) **mad about/on sb/sth** liking sb/sth very much: *He's mad on computer games at the moment.* ◆ *Steve's mad about Jane.*

M

▸WILD **5** not controlled; wild or very excited: *The audience was cheering and clapping like mad* (= very hard). ◆ *When Brad Pitt appeared on the hotel balcony his fans* ***went mad.***

madam /ˈmædəm/ *noun* [sing] **1** (*formal*) used as a polite way of speaking to a woman, especially to a customer in a shop or restaurant: *Can I help you, madam?* ➲ look at **sir** **2** **Madam** used for beginning a formal letter to a woman when you do not know her name: *Dear Madam, I am writing in reply …*

ˌmad ˈcow disease (*informal*) = BSE

maddening /ˈmædnɪŋ/ *adj* that makes you very angry or annoyed: *She has some really maddening habits.* ▸ **maddeningly** *adv*

made *past tense, past participle* of **make**[1]

madly /ˈmædli/ *adv* **1** in a wild or crazy way: *They were rushing about madly.* **2** (*informal*) very; extremely: *They're madly in love.*

madman /ˈmædmən/ *noun* [C] (*pl* -men /-mən/) a person who behaves in a wild or crazy way **SYN** **lunatic**

madness /ˈmædnəs/ *noun* [U] crazy or stupid behaviour that could be dangerous: *It would be madness to take a boat out on the sea in such rough weather.*

M

⚷ **magazine** /ˌmægəˈziːn/ (also *informal* **mag** /mæg/) *noun* [C] a type of large thin book with a paper cover that you can buy every week or month containing articles, photographs, etc. often on a particular topic: *a fashion/computer/gardening magazine* ➲ note at **newspaper**

magenta /məˈdʒentə/ *adj* reddish-purple in colour ▸ **magenta** *noun* [U]

maggot /ˈmægət/ *noun* [C] a young insect before it grows wings and legs and becomes a fly ➲ picture at **worm**

⚷ **magic**[1] /ˈmædʒɪk/ *noun* [U] **1** a secret power that some people believe can make strange or impossible things happen by saying special words or doing special things: *The witch had used her magic to turn the children into frogs.* ➲ look at **black magic** **2** the art of doing tricks that seem impossible, in order to entertain people **3** a special quality that makes sth seem wonderful: *I'll never forget the magic of that moment.*

⚷ **magic**[2] /ˈmædʒɪk/ *adj* **1** used in or using magic: *a magic spell/potion/charm/trick* ◆ *There is no magic formula for passing exams—just hard work.* **2** having a special quality that makes sth seem wonderful: *Respect is the magic ingredient in our relationship.*

magical /ˈmædʒɪkl/ *adj* **1** that seems to use magic: *a herb with magical powers to heal* **2** wonderful and exciting: *Our holiday was absolutely magical.* ▸ **magically** /-kli/ *adv*

magician /məˈdʒɪʃn/ *noun* [C] **1** a person who performs magic tricks to entertain people ➲ look at **conjuror** **2** (in stories) a man who has magic powers ➲ look at **wizard**

ˌmagic ˈwand = wand

magistrate /ˈmædʒɪstreɪt/ *noun* [C] an official who acts as a judge in cases involving less serious crimes

magnanimous /mægˈnænɪməs/ *adj* kind, generous and forgiving (especially towards an enemy or opponent)

magnate /ˈmægneɪt/ *noun* [C] a person who is rich, powerful and successful, especially in business: *a media/property/shipping magnate*

magnesium /mægˈniːziəm/ *noun* [U] (*symbol* Mg) a light, silver-white metal that burns with a bright white flame

magnet /ˈmægnət/ *noun* [C] a piece of iron, steel, etc. that can attract and pick up other metal objects

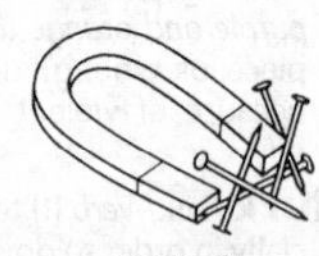
magnet

magnetic /mægˈnetɪk/ *adj* **1** having the ability to attract metal objects: *magnetic fields* ◆ *a magnetic tape/disk* (= containing electronic information that can be read by a computer or other machine) **2** having a quality that strongly attracts people: *a magnetic personality* ▸ **magnetism** /ˈmægnətɪzəm/ *noun* [U]: *Nobody could resist his magnetism.*

magnificent /mægˈnɪfɪsnt/ *adj* extremely impressive and attractive: *What a magnificent castle!* **SYN** **splendid** ▸ **magnificence** /-ˈnɪfɪsns/ *noun* [U] ▸ **magnificently** *adv*

magnify

magnify /ˈmægnɪfaɪ/ *verb* [T] (**magnifying**; **magnifies**; *pt, pp* **magnified**) **1** to make sth look bigger than it is, usually using a special piece of equipment: *to magnify something under a microscope* **SYN** **enlarge** **2** to make sth seem more important than it really is: *to magnify a problem* **SYN** **exaggerate** ▸ **magnification** /ˌmægnɪfɪˈkeɪʃn/ *noun* [U]

ˈmagnifying glass *noun* [C] a round piece of glass, usually with a handle, that is used for making things look bigger than they are ➲ picture at **magnify**

magnitude /ˈmægnɪtjuːd/ *noun* [U] the great size or importance of sth

mahogany /məˈhɒgəni/ *noun* [U] the hard dark reddish-brown wood from a tropical tree that is used especially for making furniture

maid /meɪd/ *noun* [C] a woman whose job is to clean in a hotel or large house ➲ look at **chambermaid**

maiden name /ˈmeɪdn neɪm/ *noun* [C] a woman's family name before marriage ➲ note at **name** ➲ look at **née**

maiden voyage /ˌmeɪdn ˈvɔɪɪdʒ/ *noun* [C] the first journey of a new ship

mail /meɪl/ (*BrE also* **post**) *noun* [U] **1** the system for collecting and sending letters and packages: *to send a parcel by airmail/surface mail* ➲ note at **post** **2** the letters, etc. that you receive: *There isn't much mail today.* **3** = **email** ▸ **mail** *verb* [T] (*especially AmE*)

mailbox /ˈmeɪlbɒks/ *noun* [C] **1** (*AmE*) = **letter box**(2) **2** (*AmE*) = **postbox** **3** a computer program that receives and stores email

ˈ**mailing list** *noun* [C] a list of the names and addresses of people to whom advertising material or information is regularly sent by a business or an organization

mailman /ˈmeɪlmæn/ *noun* (*pl* -men /-men/) (*AmE*) = **postman**

ˌ**mail ˈorder** *noun* [U] a method of shopping. You choose what you want from a **catalogue** (= a book or Internet site showing goods for sale) and the goods are sent to you by post. ➲ note at **online**

maim /meɪm/ *verb* [T] to hurt sb so badly that part of their body can no longer be used

main[1] /meɪn/ *adj* [only *before* a noun] most important: *My main reason for wanting to learn English is to get a better job.* ◆ *a busy main road* ◆ *He doesn't earn very much but he's happy, and that's* ***the main thing.*** **SYN** **chief**

IDM **in the main** (*formal*) generally; mostly: *We found English people very friendly in the main.*

main[2] /meɪn/ *noun* **1** [C] a large pipe or wire that carries water, gas or electricity between buildings: *The water main has burst.* **2 the mains** [pl] (*BrE*) the place where the supply of gas, water or electricity to a building starts; the system of providing these services to a building: *Turn the water off at the mains.* ◆ *mains gas/water/electricity*

mainframe /ˈmeɪnfreɪm/ (*also* ˌ**mainframe comˈputer**) *noun* [C] a large powerful computer, usually the centre of a system that is shared by many users ➲ look at **PC**

mainland /ˈmeɪnlænd/ *noun* [sing] the main part of a country or continent, not including the islands around it: *mainland Greece*

mainly /ˈmeɪnli/ *adv* mostly: *The students here are mainly from Japan.*

mainstay /ˈmeɪnsteɪ/ *noun* [C] a person or thing that is the most important part of sth, which makes it possible for it to exist or to be successful: *Cocoa is the mainstay of the country's economy.*

mainstream /ˈmeɪnstriːm/ *noun* [sing] the ideas and opinions that are considered normal because they are shared by most people; the people who hold these opinions and beliefs: *The Green Party is not* ***in the mainstream*** *of British politics.*

maintain /meɪnˈteɪn/ *verb* [T] **1** to make sth continue at the same level, standard, etc: *We need to maintain the quality of our goods but not increase the price.* ◆ *to maintain law and order* **2** to keep sth in good condition by checking and repairing it regularly: *to maintain a road/building/machine* ◆ *The house is large and expensive to maintain.* **3** to keep saying that sth is true even when others disagree or do not believe it: *I still maintain that I was right to sack him.* ◆ *She has always maintained her innocence.* **4** to support sb with your own money: *He has to maintain a child from his previous marriage.*

maintenance /ˈmeɪntənəns/ *noun* [U] **1** keeping sth in good condition: *This house needs a lot of maintenance.* ◆ *car maintenance* **2** (*BrE*) money that sb must pay regularly to a former wife, husband or partner especially when they have had children together: *He has to pay maintenance to his ex-wife.*

maisonette /ˌmeɪzəˈnet/ *noun* [C] (*BrE*) a flat on two floors that is part of a larger building

maize /meɪz/ (*AmE* **corn**) *noun* [U] a tall plant which produces yellow grains in a large mass that are cooked and eaten ➲ look at **sweetcorn**

Maj. *abbr* = **major**[2](1)

majestic /məˈdʒestɪk/ *adj* impressive because of its size or beauty: *a majestic mountain landscape* ▸ **majestically** /-kli/ *adv*

M

majesty /ˈmædʒəsti/ *noun* (*pl* **majesties**) **1** [U] the impressive and attractive quality that sth has: *the splendour and majesty of the palace and its gardens* **2 His/Her/Your Majesty** [C] (*formal*) used when speaking to or about a royal person: *Her Majesty the Queen*

major[1] /ˈmeɪdʒə(r)/ *adj* **1** [only *before* a noun] very large, important or serious: *The patient needs major heart surgery.* ◆ *There haven't been any major problems.* **OPP** **minor** **2** of one of the two types of **key**[1](4) in which music is usually written: *the key of D major* ➲ look at **minor**

major[2] /ˈmeɪdʒə(r)/ *noun* **1** (*abbr* **Maj.**) [C] an officer of a middle level in the army or the US air force **2** [C] (*AmE*) the main subject or course of a student at college or university; the student who studies it: *Her major is French.*

major[3] /ˈmeɪdʒə(r)/ *verb*

PHR V **major in sth** (*AmE*) to study sth as your main subject at college or university

ˌ**major ˈgeneral** *noun* [C] an officer of a high level in the army

majority /məˈdʒɒrəti/ *noun* (*pl* **majorities**) **1** [sing, with sing or pl verb] **majority (of sb/sth)** the largest number or part of a group of people or things: *The majority of students in the class come/comes from Japan.* ◆ *This treatment is not available in* ***the vast majority*** *of hospitals.* **OPP** **minority** **2** [C, usually sing] **majority (over sb)** (in an election) the difference in the number of votes for the person/party who came first and the person/party who came second: *He was elected by/with a majority of almost 5000 votes.*

MORE If you have an **overall majority**, you got more votes than all the other people/parties added together.

IDM be in the/a majority to form the largest number or part of sth: *Women are in the majority in the teaching profession.*

make¹ /meɪk/ *verb* [T] (*pt, pp* made /meɪd/)
➤CREATE **1** to produce or create sth: *to make bread* ◆ *This model is **made of** steel, and that one is **made out of** used matches.* ◆ *Cheese is **made from** milk.* ◆ *Those cars are **made in** Slovakia.* ◆ *Shall I make you a sandwich/make a sandwich for you?* ◆ *to make breakfast* ◆ *to make a hole in something* ◆ *to make a law/rule* ◆ *to make a movie*
➤PERFORM ACTION **2** [used with nouns] to perform a certain action: *to make a mistake/noise* ◆ *to make a guess/comment/statement/suggestion* ◆ *to make progress* ◆ *I've made an appointment to see the doctor.*

HELP **Make** can be used like this with a number of different nouns. Often there is a verb with a similar form, for example **make a decision** = **decide.** But if you use 'make' + noun, you can use an adjective with it: *He made the right decision.* ◆ *They made a generous offer.*

➤CAUSE **3** to cause a particular effect, feeling, situation, etc: *The film made me cry.* ◆ *Flying makes him nervous.* ◆ *Her remarks made the situation worse.* ◆ *I'll **make it clear** to him that we won't pay.* ◆ ***Make sure** you lock the car.* ◆ *You don't need to know much of a language to **make yourself understood**.* ◆ *to make trouble/a mess/a noise*
➤BECOME **4** to make sb/sth become sth; to have the right qualities to become sth: *She was made* (= given the job of) *President.* ◆ *You can borrow some money this time, but don't **make a habit of** it.* ◆ *Karen explains things very clearly—she'd make a good teacher.* **5** to become sth; to achieve sth: *I'm hoping to make head of the department by the time I'm thirty.*
➤FORCE **6 make sb do sth** to force sb/sth to do sth: *You can't make her come with us if she doesn't want to.* ◆ *They made me repeat the whole story.*

GRAMMAR In the passive we must use **to**: *He was **made to wait** at the police station.*

➤MONEY/NUMBERS/TIME **7** used with money, numbers and time: *How much do you think he makes* (= earns) *a month?* ◆ *to make a lot of money* ◆ *5 and 7 make 12.* ◆ *'What's the time?' 'I make it 6.45.'*
➤GET TO **8** to manage to reach a place or go somewhere: *We should make Bristol by about 10.* ◆ *I can't make the meeting next week.*

IDM make do with sth to use sth that is not good enough because nothing better is available: *If we can't get limes, we'll have to make do with lemons.*
make it to manage to do sth; to succeed: *She'll never make it as an actress.* ◆ *He's badly injured—it looks like he might not make it* (= survive). ⓘ For other idioms containing **make**, look at the entries for the nouns, adjectives, etc. For example, **make amends** is at **amends**.

PHR V be made for sb/each other to be well matched to sb/each other: *Jim and Alice seem made for each other.*
make for sb/sth to move towards sb/sth
make for sth to help or allow sth to happen: *Arguing all the time doesn't make for a happy marriage.*
make sb/sth into sb/sth to change sb/sth into sb/sth: *She made her spare room into an office.*
make sth of sb/sth to understand the meaning or nature of sb/sth: *What do you make of Colin's letter?*
make off (with sth) (*informal*) to leave or escape in a hurry, for example after stealing sth: *Someone's made off with my wallet!*
make sb/sth out 1 to understand sb/sth: *I just can't make him out.* **2** to be able to see or hear sb/sth; to manage to read sth: *I could just make out her signature.*
make out that ... ; make yourself out to be sth to say that sth is true and try to make people believe it: *He made out that he was a millionaire.* ◆ *She's not as clever as she makes herself out to be.*
make (yourself/sb) up to put powder, colour, etc. on your/sb's face to make it look attractive
make sth up 1 to form sth: *the different groups that make up our society* **2** to invent sth, often sth that is not true: *to make up an excuse* **3** to make a number or an amount complete; to replace sth that has been lost: *We need one more person to make up our team.*
make up for sth to do sth that corrects a bad situation: *Her enthusiasm makes up for her lack of experience.*
make it up to sb (*informal*) to do sth that shows that you are sorry for what you have done to sb or that you are grateful for what they have done for you: *You've done me a big favour. How can I make it up to you?*
make (it) up (with sb) to become friends again after an argument: *Has she made it up with him yet?*

make² /meɪk/ *noun* [C] the name of the company that produces sth: *'What make of car does he drive?' 'A Ford, I think.'*

IDM on the make always trying to make money for yourself, especially in a dishonest way: *The country is being ruined by politicians on the make.*

ˈmake-believe *noun* [U] things that sb imagines or invents that are not real

makeover /ˈmeɪkəʊvə(r)/ *noun* [C,U] the process of improving the appearance of a person or a place, or of changing the impression that sth gives

maker /ˈmeɪkə(r)/ *noun* [C] a person, company or machine that makes sth: *a film-maker* ◆ *If it doesn't work, send it back to the maker.* ◆ *an ice cream maker*

makeshift /ˈmeɪkʃɪft/ *adj* made to be used for a short time until there is sth better: *They slept in makeshift shelters made from old cardboard boxes.*

ˈmake-up *noun* **1** [U] powder, cream, etc. that you put on your face to make yourself more attractive. Actors use **make-up** to change their appearance when they are acting: *to put on/take off make-up* ➲ look at **cosmetic** ➲ *verb* **make (yourself/sb) up**

2 [sing] sb's character: *He can't help his temper. It's part of his make-up.*

making /ˈmeɪkɪŋ/ *noun* [sing] the act of doing or producing sth; the process of being made: *bread-making* ◆ *This movie has been three years in the making.*
IDM be the making of sb to be the reason that sb is successful: *University was the making of Gina.*
have the makings of sth to have the necessary qualities for sth: *The book has the makings of a good film.*

maladjusted /ˌmæləˈdʒʌstɪd/ *adj* (used about a person) not able to behave well with other people

malaria /məˈleəriə/ *noun* [U] a serious disease in hot countries that you get from the bite of a **mosquito** (= a small flying insect)

male¹ /meɪl/ *adj* belonging to the sex that does not give birth to babies or produce eggs: *a male goat* ◆ *a male model/nurse/colleague* ➲ look at **masculine**, **female**

male² /meɪl/ *noun* [C] a male person or animal ➲ look at **female**: *the body of a white male aged about 40*

male ˈchauvinism = **chauvinism**(2)

malice /ˈmælɪs/ *noun* [U] a wish to hurt other people ▶ **malicious** /məˈlɪʃəs/ *adj* ▶ **maliciously** *adv*

malignant /məˈlɪɡnənt/ *adj* (used about a disease) likely to cause death if not controlled: *He has a malignant brain tumour.* ◆ *malignant cells* **OPP benign**

mall /mæl; mɔːl/ (also ˈ**shopping mall**) (*especially AmE*) a large building or covered area that has many shops, restaurants, etc. inside it: *Some teenagers were hanging out at the mall.* ➲ look at **shopping centre**

malleable /ˈmæliəbl/ *adj* **1** (used about metal or plastic) that can be hit or pressed into different shapes easily without breaking **2** (used about people or ideas) easily influenced or changed ▶ **malleability** /ˌmæliəˈbɪləti/ *noun* [U]

mallet /ˈmælɪt/ *noun* [C] a heavy wooden hammer ➲ picture at **tool**

malnutrition /ˌmælnjuːˈtrɪʃn/ *noun* [U] bad health that is the result of not having enough food or enough of the right kind of food ▶ **malnourished** /ˌmælˈnʌrɪʃt/ *adj*: *The children were badly malnourished.*

malt /mɔːlt/ *noun* [U] grain that is used for making beer and **whisky** (= a strong alcoholic drink)

maltreat /ˌmælˈtriːt/ *verb* [T] (*formal*) to treat a person or an animal in a cruel or unkind way ▶ **maltreatment** *noun* [U]

mammal /ˈmæml/ *noun* [C] an animal of the type that gives birth to live babies, not eggs, and feeds its young on milk from its own body: *Whales, dogs and humans are mammals.* ➲ picture on **page P12**

mammoth /ˈmæməθ/ *adj* very big

man¹ /mæn/ *noun* (*pl* **men** /men/) **1** [C] an adult male person: *men, women and children* **2** [U] humans as a group; the human race: *Early man lived by hunting.* ◆ *the damage man has caused to the environment* **3** [C] a person of either sex, male or female: *All men are equal.* ◆ *No man could survive long in such conditions.* **4** [C] [in compounds] a man who comes from a particular place; a man who has a particular job or interest: *a Frenchman* ◆ *a businessman* ◆ *sportsmen and women*
IDM the man in the street an ordinary man or woman
the odd man/one out ➲ **odd**

man² /mæn/ *verb* [T] (**manning**; **manned**) to operate sth or to provide people to operate sth: *The telephones are manned 24 hours a day.*

manage /ˈmænɪdʒ/ *verb* **1** [I,T] [often with *can* or *could*] to succeed in doing or dealing with sth difficult; to be able to do sth: *However did you manage to find us here?* ◆ *I can't manage this suitcase. It's too heavy.* ◆ *Paula can't manage next Tuesday* (= she can't come then) *so we'll meet another day.* ➲ note at **could 2** [I] **manage (without/with sb/sth)**; **manage (on sth)** to deal with a difficult situation; to continue in spite of difficulties: *My grandmother couldn't manage without her neighbours.* ◆ *Can you manage with just one assistant?* ◆ *It's hard for a family to manage on just one income.* **3** [T] to be in charge or control of sth: *She manages a small advertising business.* ◆ *You need to manage your time more efficiently.*

manageable /ˈmænɪdʒəbl/ *adj* not too big or too difficult to deal with

management /ˈmænɪdʒmənt/ *noun* **1** [U] the control or organization of sth: *Good classroom management is vital with large groups of children.* **2** [C,U, with sing or pl verb] the people who control a business or company: *The hotel is now* ***under new management.***

GRAMMAR In the singular, **management** is used with a singular or plural verb: *The management is/are considering making some workers redundant.*

manager /ˈmænɪdʒə(r)/ *noun* [C] **1** a man or woman who controls an organization or part of an organization: *a bank manager* **2** a person who looks after the business affairs of a singer, actor, etc. **3** a person who is in charge of a sports team: *the England manager*

manageress /ˌmænɪdʒəˈres/ *noun* [C] (*old-fashioned*) a woman who is in charge of a shop or restaurant

managerial /ˌmænəˈdʒɪəriəl/ *adj* connected with the work of a manager: *Do you have any managerial experience?*

ˌmanaging diˈrector *noun* [C] a person who controls a business or company

mandarin /ˈmændərɪn/ *noun* [C] a type of small orange

M

mandate /ˈmændeɪt/ *noun* [usually sing] the power that is officially given to a group of people to do sth, especially after they have won an election: *The union leaders had a clear mandate from their members to call a strike.*

mandatory /ˈmændətəri; mænˈdeɪtəri/ *adj* (*formal*) that you must do, have, obey, etc: *a mandatory life sentence* SYN **compulsory**

mane /meɪn/ *noun* [C] the long hair on the neck of some animals ➲ picture at **horse, lion** ➲ picture on **page P12**

maneuver (*AmE*) = **manoeuvre**

mangle /ˈmæŋɡl/ *verb* [T, usually passive] to damage sth so badly that it is difficult to see what it looked like originally: *The motorway was covered with the mangled wreckage of cars.*

mango /ˈmæŋɡəʊ/ *noun* [C] (*pl* **mangoes** *or* **mangos**) a tropical fruit that has a yellow and red skin and is yellow inside ➲ picture on **page P14**

manhole /ˈmænhəʊl/ *noun* [C] a hole in the street with a lid over it through which sb can go to look at the pipes, etc. that are underground

manhood /ˈmænhʊd/ *noun* [U] the state of being a man rather than a boy

mania /ˈmeɪniə/ *noun* **1** [C] (*informal*) a great enthusiasm for sth: *World Cup mania is sweeping the country.* **2** [U] a serious mental illness that may cause sb to be very excited or violent

maniac /ˈmeɪniæk/ *noun* [C] **1** a person who behaves in a wild and stupid way: *to drive like a maniac* SYN **lunatic, madman** **2** a person who has a stronger love of sth than is normal: *a football/sex maniac*

manic /ˈmænɪk/ *adj* **1** full of nervous energy or excited activity: *His behaviour became more manic as he began to feel stressed.* **2** connected with **mania**(2)

manicure /ˈmænɪkjʊə(r)/ *noun* [C,U] treatment to make your hands and nails look attractive: *to have a manicure*

manifest /ˈmænɪfest/ *verb* [I,T] (*formal*) **manifest (sth/itself) (in/as sth)** to show sth or to be shown clearly: *Mental illness can manifest itself in many forms.* ▶ **manifest** *adj*: *manifest failure/anger* ▶ **manifestly** *adv*: *manifestly unfair*

manifestation /ˌmænɪfeˈsteɪʃn/ *noun* [C,U] (*formal*) a sign that sth is happening

manifesto /ˌmænɪˈfestəʊ/ *noun* [C] (*pl* **manifestos**) a written statement by a political party that explains what it hopes to do if it becomes the government in the future

manioc /ˈmænɪɒk/ = **cassava**

manipulate /məˈnɪpjuleɪt/ *verb* [T] **1** to influence sb so that they do or think what you want: *Clever politicians know how to manipulate public opinion.* **2** to use, move or control sth with skill ▶ **manipulation** /məˌnɪpjuˈleɪʃn/ *noun* [C,U]

manipulative /məˈnɪpjələtɪv/ *adj* **1** able to influence sb or force sb to do what you want, often in an unfair way: *manipulative behaviour* **2** (*formal*) connected with the ability to handle objects with skill

mankind /mænˈkaɪnd/ *noun* [U] all the people in the world: *A nuclear war would be a threat to all mankind.*

manly /ˈmænli/ *adj* (**manlier**; **manliest**) typical of or suitable for a man: *a deep manly voice* ▶ **manliness** *noun* [U]

ˌman-ˈmade *adj* made by people, not formed in a natural way; artificial: *man-made fabrics such as nylon and polyester*

⚷ **manner** /ˈmænə(r)/ *noun* **1** [sing] the way that you do sth or that sth happens: *Stop arguing! Let's try to act **in a** civilized **manner**.* **2** [sing] the way that sb behaves towards other people: *to have an aggressive/a relaxed/a professional manner* **3** **manners** [pl] a way of behaving that is considered acceptable in your country or culture: *Their children **have no manners*** (= behave very badly). ◆ *In some countries it is **bad manners** to show the soles of your feet.*
IDM **all manner of ...** every kind of ...: *You meet all manner of people in my job.*

mannerism /ˈmænərɪzəm/ *noun* [C] sb's particular way of speaking or a particular movement they often do

manoeuvre[1] (*AmE* **maneuver**) /məˈnuːvə(r)/ *noun* **1** [C] a movement that needs care or skill: *Parking the car in such a small space would be a tricky manoeuvre.* **2** [C,U] something clever that you do in order to win sth, trick sb, etc: *political manoeuvre(s)* SYN **move** **3** **manoeuvres** [pl] a way of training soldiers when large numbers of them practise fighting in battles

manoeuvre[2] (*AmE* **maneuver**) /məˈnuːvə(r)/ *verb* [I,T] to move (sth) to a different position using skill: *The driver was manoeuvring his lorry into a narrow gateway.*

manor /ˈmænə(r)/ (also ˈ**manor house**) *noun* [C] a large house in the country that has land around it

manpower /ˈmænpaʊə(r)/ *noun* [U] the people that you need to do a particular job: *There is a shortage of skilled manpower in the computer industry.*

mansion /ˈmænʃn/ *noun* [C] a very large house

manslaughter /ˈmænslɔːtə(r)/ *noun* [U] the crime of killing sb without intending to do so ➲ look at **murder**

mantelpiece /ˈmæntlpiːs/ *noun* [C] a narrow shelf above the space in a room where a fire goes ➲ picture at **fireplace**

manual[1] /ˈmænjuəl/ *adj* using your hands; operated by hand: *Office work can sometimes be more tiring than **manual work**.* ◆ *a skilled **manual worker*** ◆ *Does your car have a manual or an automatic gearbox?* ▶ **manually** /-juəli/ *adv*

manual[2] /ˈmænjuəl/ *noun* [C] a book that explains how to do or operate sth: *a training manual* ◆ *a car manual*

🔑 **manufacture** /ˌmænjuˈfæktʃə(r)/ *verb* [T] to make sth in large quantities using machines: *a local factory that manufactures furniture* SYN **produce** ▶ **manufacture** *noun* [U]: *The manufacture of chemical weapons should be illegal.*

🔑 **manufacturer** /ˌmænjuˈfæktʃərə(r)/ *noun* [C] a person or company that makes sth: *a car manufacturer* ◆ *Always follow the manufacturer's instructions.*

manufacturing /ˌmænjuˈfæktʃərɪŋ/ *noun* [U] the business or industry of producing goods in large quantities in factories, etc: *Many jobs in manufacturing were lost during the recession.*

manure /məˈnjʊə(r)/ *noun* [U] the waste matter from animals that is put on the ground in order to make plants grow better: *horse manure* ➲ look at **fertilizer**

manuscript /ˈmænjuskrɪpt/ *noun* [C] **1** a copy of a book, piece of music, etc. before it has been printed **2** a very old book or document that was written by hand

🔑 **many** /ˈmeni/ *determiner, pron* [used with plural nouns or verbs] **1** a large number of people or things: *Have you made many friends at school yet?* ◆ *Not many of my friends smoke.* ◆ *Not many of my friends drive.* ◆ *Many of the mistakes were just careless.* ◆ *There are* **too many** *mistakes in this essay.* ◆ *I've known her for* **a good/great many** (= very many) *years.*

HELP **Many or a lot of? Many** in positive sentences sounds quite formal: *Many people have smartphones nowadays.* When speaking or writing informally we usually use **a lot of:** *A lot of people have smartphones nowadays.* In negative sentences and questions, however, **many** can always be used without sounding formal: *I don't know many cheap places to eat.* ◆ *Are there many hotels in this town?*

2 used to ask about the number of people or things, or to refer to a known number: ***How many*** *children have you got?* ◆ *How many came to the meeting?* ◆ *I don't work* **as many** *hours* **as** *you.* ◆ *There are* ***half/twice as many*** *boys as girls in the class.* **3** [in compounds] having a lot of the thing mentioned: *a many-sided shape* **4 many a** [used with a singular noun and verb] a large number of: *I've heard him say that many a time.*

Maori /ˈmaʊri/ *noun* [C] (*pl* **Maori** *or* **Maoris**) a member of the race of people who were the original people to live in New Zealand ▶ **Maori** *adj*

🔑 **map** /mæp/ *noun* [C] a drawing or plan of (part of) the surface of the earth that shows countries, rivers, mountains, roads, etc: *a map of the world* ◆ *a road/street map* ◆ *I can't find Cambridge* **on the map**. ◆ *to read a map* ➲ look at **atlas** ▶ **map** *verb* [T] (**mapping; mapped**): *The region is so remote it has not yet been mapped.*

maple /ˈmeɪpl/ *noun* [C] a tree that has leaves with five points and that produces a very sweet liquid that you can eat: *maple syrup*

Mar. *abbr* = **March**: *17 Mar. 1956*

marathon /ˈmærəθən/ *noun* [C] **1** a long running race, in which people run about 42 kilometres: *Have you ever run a marathon?* **2** an activity that lasts much longer than expected: *The interview was a real marathon.*

marble /ˈmɑːbl/ *noun* **1** [U] a hard attractive stone that is used to make statues and parts of buildings: *a marble statue* **2** [C] a small ball of coloured glass that children play with **3 marbles** [pl] the children's game that you play by rolling **marbles** along the ground trying to hit other **marbles**

🔑 **March** /mɑːtʃ/ *noun* [U,C] (*abbr* **Mar.**) the 3rd month of the year, coming after February ➲ note at **January**

🔑 **march**[1] /mɑːtʃ/ *verb* **1** [I] to walk with regular steps (like a soldier): *The President saluted as the troops marched past.* **2** [I] to walk in a determined way: *She marched up to the manager and demanded an apology.* **3** [T] to make sb walk or march somewhere: *The prisoner was marched away.* **4** [I] to walk in a large group to protest about sth: *The demonstrators marched through the centre of town.*

🔑 **march**[2] /mɑːtʃ/ *noun* [C] **1** an organized walk by a large group of people who are protesting about sth: *a peace march* ➲ look at **demonstration** **2** a journey made by marching: *The soldiers were tired after their long march.*

mare /meə(r)/ *noun* [C] a female horse ➲ note at **horse**

margarine /ˌmɑːdʒəˈriːn/ *noun* [U] a food that is similar to butter, made of animal or vegetable fats

margin /ˈmɑːdʒɪn/ *noun* [C] **1** the empty space at the side of a page in a book, etc. **2** [usually sing] the amount of space, time, votes, etc. by which you win sth: *He won by a wide/narrow/comfortable margin.* **3** the amount of profit that a company makes on sth **4** [usually sing] an amount of space, time, etc. that is more than you need: *It is a complex operation with little* ***margin for error***. **5** the area around the edge of sth: *the margins of the Pacific Ocean*

marginal /ˈmɑːdʒɪnl/ *adj* small in size or importance: *The differences are marginal.* ▶ **marginally** /-nəli/ *adv*: *In most cases costs will increase only marginally.*

marijuana /ˌmærəˈwɑːnə/ *noun* [U] a drug that is smoked and is illegal in many countries

marina /məˈriːnə/ *noun* [C] a place where pleasure boats can be tied up and protected from the sea and bad weather

marinade /ˌmærɪˈneɪd/ *noun* [C,U] a mixture of oil, wine, spices, etc. in which meat or fish is left before it is cooked in order to make it softer or to give it a particular flavour

marinate /ˈmærɪneɪt/ (also **marinade**) *verb* [I,T] if you **marinate** food or it **marinates**, you leave it in a **marinade** before cooking it

marine[1] /məˈriːn/ *adj* [only *before* a noun] **1** connected with the sea: *marine life* **2** connected with ships or sailing: *marine insurance*

M

marine² /məˈriːn/ *noun* [C] a soldier who has been trained to fight on land or at sea

marital /ˈmærɪtl/ *adj* [only *before* a noun] connected with marriage: *marital problems*

ˌmarital ˈstatus *noun* [U] (*written*) (used on official documents) if you are married, single, divorced, etc.

maritime /ˈmærɪtaɪm/ *adj* connected with the sea or ships: *a maritime museum*

mark¹ /mɑːk/ *verb* [T]

➤WRITE **1** to put a sign on sth: *We marked the price on all items in the sale.* ◆ *I'll mark all the boxes I want you to move.*

➤SPOIL **2** to spoil the appearance of sth by making a mark on it: *The white walls were dirty and marked.*

➤SHOW POSITION **3** to show where sth is or where sth happened: *The route is marked in red.* ◆ *Flowers mark the spot where he died.*

➤CELEBRATE **4** to celebrate or officially remember an important event: *The ceremony marked the fiftieth anniversary of the opening of the school.*

➤SHOW CHANGE **5** to be a sign that sth new is going to happen: *This decision marks a change in government policy.*

➤GIVE GRADE **6** to look at sb's schoolwork, etc., show where there are mistakes and give it a number or letter to show how good it is: *Why did you mark that answer wrong?* ◆ *He has 100 exam papers to mark.*

➤IN SPORT **7** to stay close to a player of the opposite team so that they cannot play easily: *Hughes was marking Taylor.*

PHR V **mark sb/sth down as/for sth** to decide that sb/sth is of a particular type or suitable for a particular use: *From the first day of school, the teachers marked Fred down as a troublemaker.*

mark sth out to draw lines to show the position of sth: *Spaces for each car were marked out in the car park.*

mark sth up/down to increase/decrease the price of sth that you are selling: *All goods have been marked down by 15%.*

mark² /mɑːk/ *noun* [C]

➤SPOT/DIRT **1** a spot or line that spoils the appearance of sth: *There's a dirty mark on the front of your shirt.* ◆ *If you put a hot cup down on the table it will* ***leave a mark***. ➲ look at **birthmark** **2** something that shows who or what sb/sth is, especially by making them or it different from others: *My horse is the one with the white mark on its face.*

➤SYMBOL **3** a written or printed symbol that is a sign of sth: *a question/punctuation/exclamation mark*

➤SIGN **4** a sign of a quality or feeling: *They stood in silence for two minutes as* ***a mark of respect***.

➤GRADE **5** a number or letter you get for school work that tells you how good your work was: *She got very good marks in the exam.* ◆ *The* ***pass mark*** *is 60 out of 100.* ◆ *to get full marks* (= everything correct)

➤LEVEL **6** the level or point that sth/sb has reached: *The race is almost at the half-way mark.*

➤EFFECT **7** an effect that people notice and will remember: *The time he spent in prison* ***left its mark*** ***on*** *him.* ◆ *He was only eighteen when he first* ***made*** *his* ***mark*** *in politics.*

➤MODEL/TYPE **8** a particular model or type of sth: *the new SL 53 Mark III*

HELP Be careful. You cannot use **mark** to talk about the product itself, or the company that makes it. Instead, use **brand** or, especially for cars and electrical goods, **make**: *What brand of coffee do you buy?* ◆ *What make is your car?*

➤TARGET **9** (*formal*) a person or an object towards which sth is directed: *The arrow hit/missed its mark.* ◆ *His judgement of the situation is* ***wide of the mark*** (= wrong). **SYN** **target**

➤MONEY **10** the former unit of money in Germany (replaced in 2002 by the euro)

IDM **on your marks, get set, go!** used at the start of a sports race

overstep the mark/line ➲ **overstep**

quick, slow, etc. off the mark quick, slow, etc. in reacting to a situation

marked /mɑːkt/ *adj* clear; noticeable: *There has been a marked increase in vandalism in recent years.* ► **markedly** /ˈmɑːkɪdli/ *adv*: *Her background is markedly different from mine.*

marker /ˈmɑːkə(r)/ *noun* [C] something that shows the position of sth: *I've highlighted the important sentences with a marker pen.*

market¹ /ˈmɑːkɪt/ *noun* **1** [C] a place where people go to buy and sell things: *a market stall/trader/town* ◆ *a cattle/fish/meat market* ➲ note at **shop** ➲ look at **flea market, hypermarket, supermarket** ➲ picture on **page P11** **2** [C] business or commercial activity; the amount of buying and selling of a particular type of goods: *The company currently has a 10% share of the market.* ◆ *the property/job market* **3** [C,U] a country, an area or a group of people that buys sth; the number of people who buy sth: *The company is hoping to expand into the European Market.* ◆ *There's no market for very large cars when petrol is so expensive.* ➲ look at **black market, stock market**

IDM **on the market** available to buy: *This is one of the best cameras on the market.*

market² /ˈmɑːkɪt/ *verb* [T] to sell sth with the help of advertising: *It is marketed as a healthy snack.*

marketable /ˈmɑːkɪtəbl/ *adj* that can be sold easily because people want it

marketing /ˈmɑːkɪtɪŋ/ *noun* [U] the activity of showing and advertising a company's products in the best possible way: *Effective marketing will lead to increased sales.* ◆ *the international marketing department*

marketplace /ˈmɑːkɪtpleɪs/ *noun* **1 the marketplace** [sing] the activity of competing with other companies to buy and sell goods, services, etc. **2** [C] the place in a town where a market is held

ˌmarket reˈsearch (also ˌmarket ˈresearch) *noun* [U] the study of what people want to buy and why: *to carry out/do market research*

marking /ˈmɑːkɪŋ/ *noun* [C, usually pl] shapes, lines and patterns of colour on an animal or a bird, or painted on a road, vehicle, etc.

marksman /ˈmɑːksmən/ *noun* [C] (*pl* -men /-mən/) a person who can shoot very well with a gun

marmalade /ˈmɑːməleɪd/ *noun* [U] a type of jam that is made from oranges or lemons

maroon /məˈruːn/ *adj, noun* [U] (of) a dark brownish-red colour

marooned /məˈruːnd/ *adj* in a place that you cannot leave: *The sailors were marooned on a desert island.*

marquee /mɑːˈkiː/ *noun* [C] a very large tent that is used for parties, shows, etc.

marriage /ˈmærɪdʒ/ *noun* **1** [C,U] the state of being husband and wife: *They are getting divorced after five years of marriage.* ♦ *a happy marriage* **2** [C] a wedding ceremony: *The marriage took place at a registry office.* ➲ note at **wedding** ➲ *verb* **get married (to sb)** *or* **marry (sb)**

married /ˈmærid/ *adj* **1** **married (to sb)** having a husband or wife: *a married man/woman/couple* ♦ *Sasha's married to Mark.* ♦ *They're planning to* ***get married*** *in summer.* **OPP** **unmarried, single** **2** [only *before* a noun] connected with marriage: *How do you like married life?*

marrow /ˈmærəʊ/ *noun* **1** = **bone marrow** **2** [C, U] (*BrE*) a large vegetable with green skin that is white inside ➲ picture on **page P15**

marry /ˈmæri/ *verb* (**marrying**; **marries**; *pt, pp* **married**) **1** [I,T] to take sb as your husband or wife: *They married when they were very young.* ♦ *When did he ask you to marry him?* ➲ note at **wedding** ➲ look at **divorce**

> **HELP** **Get married** is more commonly used than **marry**: *When are Jo and Mark getting married?* ♦ *We got married in 2003.* Note that we say 'get married **to** sb', NOT 'with' sb.

2 [T] to join two people together as husband and wife: *We asked the local vicar to marry us.* ➲ *noun* **marriage**

Mars /mɑːz/ *noun* [sing] the red planet, that is fourth in order from the sun ➲ look at **Martian**

marsh /mɑːʃ/ *noun* [C,U] an area of soft wet land ▶ **marshy** *adj*

marshal /ˈmɑːʃl/ *noun* [C] **1** a person who helps to organize or control a large public event: *Marshals are directing traffic in the car park.* **2** (*AmE*) an officer of a high level in the police or fire department or in a court of law

marsupial /mɑːˈsuːpiəl/ *noun* [C] any animal that carries its young in a **pouch** (= a pocket of skin) on the mother's stomach: *Kangaroos and koalas are marsupials.*

martial /ˈmɑːʃl/ *adj* [only *before* a noun] (*formal*) connected with war

ˌmartial ˈarts *noun* [pl] fighting sports such as **karate** or **judo**, in which you use your hands and feet as weapons

Martian /ˈmɑːʃn/ *noun* [C] (in stories) a creature that comes from the planet Mars

martyr /ˈmɑːtə(r)/ *noun* [C] **1** a person who is killed because of what they believe **2** a person who tries to make people feel sorry for them: *Don't be such a martyr! You don't have to do all the housework.* ▶ **martyrdom** /ˈmɑːtədəm/ *noun* [U]

marvel /ˈmɑːvl/ *noun* [C] a person or thing that is wonderful or that surprises you: *The new building is a marvel of modern technology.* ▶ **marvel** *verb* [I] (**marvelling**; **marvelled**, (*AmE*) **marveling**; **marveled**) (*formal*) **marvel (at sth)**: *We marvelled at how much they had managed to do.*

marvellous (*AmE* **marvelous**) /ˈmɑːvələs/ *adj* very good; wonderful: *a marvellous opportunity* **SYN** **fantastic** ▶ **marvellously** (*AmE* **marvelously**) *adv*

Marxism /ˈmɑːksɪzəm/ *noun* [U] the political and economic thought of Karl Marx ➲ look at **communism, socialism, capitalism** ▶ **Marxist** /-ɪst/ *noun* [C], *adj*: *Marxist ideology*

marzipan /ˈmɑːzɪpæn/ *noun* [U] a food that is made of sugar, egg and **almonds** (= a type of nut). Marzipan is used to make sweets or to put on cakes.

masc *abbr* = **masculine**

mascara /mæˈskɑːrə/ *noun* [U] a beauty product that is used to make your **eyelashes** (= the hairs around your eyes) dark and attractive

mascot /ˈmæskət/ *noun* [C] a person, animal or thing that is thought to bring good luck

masculine /ˈmæskjəlɪn/ *adj* **1** with the qualities that people think are typical of men: *a deep, masculine voice* ♦ *Her short hair makes her look quite masculine.* ➲ look at **feminine, male, manly** **2** (in English) of the forms of words used to describe males **3** (in the grammar of some languages) belonging to a certain class of nouns, adjectives or pronouns: *The French word for 'sun' is masculine.*

> **MORE** In English grammar **masculine** words refer to male people or animals: *'He' is a masculine pronoun.* **Feminine** words refer to female people or animals: *'She' is a feminine pronoun.* In some other languages all nouns are given a **gender**; usually **masculine, feminine** or **neuter**.

▶ **masculinity** /ˌmæskjuˈlɪnəti/ *noun* [U]

mash /mæʃ/ *verb* [T] to mix or crush sth until it is soft: *mashed potatoes*

mask¹ /mɑːsk/ *noun* [C] something that you wear that covers your face or part of your face. People wear **masks** in order to hide or protect their faces or to make themselves look different: *a surgical/Halloween mask* ➲ look at **gas mask, goggles** ➲ picture at **snorkel** ➲ picture on **page P5**

M

mask² /mɑːsk/ *verb* [T] to hide a feeling, smell, fact, etc: *He masked his anger with a smile.*

masked /mɑːskt/ *adj* wearing a **mask**: *a masked gunman*

masochism /ˈmæsəkɪzəm/ *noun* [U] the enjoyment of pain, or of what most people would find unpleasant: *He swims in the sea even in winter—that's sheer masochism!* ➲ look at **sadism** ▶ **masochist** /-ɪst/ *noun* [C] ▶ **masochistic** /ˌmæsəˈkɪstɪk/ *adj*

mason /ˈmeɪsn/ *noun* [C] **1** a person who makes things from stone **2** = **Freemason**

masonry /ˈmeɪsənri/ *noun* [U] the parts of a building that are made of stone

masquerade /ˌmæskəˈreɪd; ˌmɑːsk-/ *noun* [C] a way of behaving that hides the truth or sb's true feelings ▶ **masquerade** *verb* [I] **masquerade as sth**: *Two people, masquerading as doctors, knocked at the door and asked to see the child.*

🔑 **mass¹** /mæs/ *noun* **1** [C] **a mass (of sth)** a large amount or number of sth: *a dense mass of smoke* ◆ *(informal) There were masses of people at the market today.* **2 the masses** [pl] ordinary people when considered as a political group: *a TV programme that brings science to the masses* **3** [U] (in physics) the quantity of material that sth contains: *the mass of a planet* **4 Mass** [C,U] the ceremony in some Christian churches when people eat bread and drink wine in order to remember the last meal that Christ had before he died: *to go to Mass*

🔑 **mass²** /mæs/ *adj* [only *before* a noun] involving a large number of people or things: *a mass murderer* ◆ *mass unemployment*

mass³ /mæs/ *verb* [I,T] to come together or bring people or things together in large numbers: *The students massed in the square.*

massacre /ˈmæsəkə(r)/ *noun* [C] the killing of a large number of people or animals ➲ note at **kill** ▶ **massacre** *verb* [T]

massage /ˈmæsɑːʒ/ *noun* [C,U] the act of rubbing and pressing sb's body in order to reduce pain or to help them relax: *to give somebody a massage* ▶ **massage** *verb* [T]

🔑 **massive** /ˈmæsɪv/ *adj* very big: *the massive walls of the castle* ◆ *He suffered a massive heart attack.* ◆ *a massive increase in prices* **SYN** **huge** ▶ **massively** *adv*

ˌmass-ˈmarket *adj* [only *before* a noun] (used about goods, etc.) produced for very large numbers of people

ˌmass ˈmedia *noun* [pl] newspapers, TV and radio that reach a large number of people

ˌmass-proˈduce *verb* [T] to make large numbers of similar things by machine in a factory: *mass-produced goods* ▶ **mass production** *noun* [U]

mast /mɑːst/ *noun* [C] **1** a tall wooden or metal pole for holding a ship's sails or a flag ➲ picture on **page P6** **2** a tall pole that is used for sending out radio or TV signals

🔑 **master¹** /ˈmɑːstə(r)/ *noun* [C] **1** a person who has great skill at doing sth: *a master builder* ◆ *an exhibition of work by French masters* (= artists) **2** (*BrE old-fashioned*) a male teacher (usually in a private school): *the chemistry master* **3** a film or tape from which copies can be made: *the master copy*

master² /ˈmɑːstə(r)/ *verb* [T] **1** to learn how to do sth well: *It takes years of study to master a foreign language.* **2** to control sth: *to master a situation*

mastermind /ˈmɑːstəmaɪnd/ *noun* [C] a very clever person who has planned or organized sth: *The mastermind behind the robbery was never caught.* ▶ **mastermind** *verb* [T]: *The police failed to catch the man who masterminded the robbery.*

masterpiece /ˈmɑːstəpiːs/ *noun* [C] a work of art, music, literature, etc. that is of the highest quality

ˈmaster's degree (also **master's**) *noun* [C] a second or higher university degree. You usually get a **master's degree** by studying for one or two years after your first degree: *Master of Arts (MA)* ◆ *Master of Science (MSc)*

mastery /ˈmɑːstəri/ *noun* [U] **1 mastery (of sth)** great skill at doing sth: *His mastery of the violin was quite exceptional for a child.* **2 mastery (of/over sb/sth)** control over sb/sth: *The battle was fought for mastery of the seas.*

masturbate /ˈmæstəbeɪt/ *verb* [I,T] to make yourself or sb else feel sexually excited by touching and rubbing the sex organs ▶ **masturbation** /ˌmæstəˈbeɪʃn/ *noun* [U]

mat /mæt/ *noun* [C] **1** a piece of carpet or other thick material that you put on the floor: *a doormat* ➲ look at **rug** **2** a small piece of material that you put under sth on a table: *a table mat* ◆ *a beer mat* ◆ *a mouse mat*

🔑 **match¹** /mætʃ/ *noun* **1** [C] a small stick of wood, cardboard, etc. that you use for starting a fire, lighting a cigarette, etc: *to light/strike a match* ◆ *a box of matches* **2** [C] an organized game or sports event: *a tennis/football match* **3** [sing] **a match for sb; sb's match** a person or thing that is as good as or better than sb/sth else: *Charo is **no match for** her mother when it comes to cooking* (= she doesn't cook as well as her mother). ◆ *I think you've **met your match** in Dave—you won't beat him.* **4** [sing] **a match (for sb/sth)** something that looks good with sth else: *Those shoes aren't a very good match with your dress.*

🔑 **match²** /mætʃ/ *verb* **1** [I,T] to have the same colour or pattern as sth else; to look good with sth else: *Your shirt and jacket don't match.* ◆ *That shirt doesn't match your jacket.* **2** [T] to find sb/sth that is like or suitable for sb/sth else: *The agency tries to match single people with suitable partners.* ◆ *In this exercise, match the words with the pictures.* **3** [T] to be as good as or better than sb/sth else: *The two teams are very evenly matched.* ◆ *Taiwan produces the goods at a price that Europe cannot match.*

PHR V **match up** to be the same: *The statements of the two witnesses don't match up.*

match sth up (with sth) to fit or put sth together (with sth else): *What you have to do is match up each star with his or her pet.*

M

match up to sb/sth to be as good as sb/sth: *The film didn't match up to my expectations.*

matchbox /ˈmætʃbɒks/ *noun* [C] a small box for matches ➲ picture at **container**

matching /ˈmætʃɪŋ/ *adj* [only *before* a noun] (used about clothes, objects, etc.) having the same colour, pattern, style, etc. and therefore looking attractive together: *a pine table with four matching chairs*

matchstick /ˈmætʃstɪk/ *noun* [C] the thin wooden part of a match

🔑 **mate**[1] /meɪt/ *noun* [C] **1** (*informal*) a friend or sb you live, work or do an activity with: *He's an old mate of mine.* ◆ *a flatmate/classmate/team-mate/playmate* ➲ note at **friend** **2** (*BrE slang*) used when speaking to a man: *Can you give me a hand, mate?* **3** one of a male and female pair of animals, birds, etc: *The female sits on the eggs while her mate hunts for food.* **4** an officer on a ship **5** = **checkmate**

🔑 **mate**[2] /meɪt/ *verb* **1** [I] (used about animals and birds) to have sex and produce young: *Pandas rarely mate in zoos.* **2** [T] to bring two animals together so that they can **mate** SYN for both meanings **breed**

🔑 **material**[1] /məˈtɪəriəl/ *noun* **1** [C,U] cloth (for making clothes, etc.): *Is there enough material for a dress?* **2** [C,U] a substance that can be used for making or doing sth: *raw materials* ◆ *writing/teaching/building materials* ◆ *This new material is strong but it is also very light.* **3** [U] facts or information that you collect before you write a book, article, etc: *She's collecting material for her latest novel.*

🔑 **material**[2] /məˈtɪəriəl/ *adj* **1** [only *before* a noun] connected with real or physical things rather than the spirit or emotions: *We should not value material comforts too highly.* ➲ look at **spiritual** **2** important and needing to be considered: *material evidence*

HELP This meaning of the word is not common. Look at **immaterial**.

▶ **materially** /-riəli/ *adv*

materialism /məˈtɪəriəlɪzəm/ *noun* [U] the belief that money and possessions are the most important things in life ▶ **materialist** /-ɪst/ *noun* [C] ▶ **materialistic** /məˌtɪəriəˈlɪstɪk/ *adj*

materialize (also **-ise**) /məˈtɪəriəlaɪz/ *verb* [I] to become real; to happen: *The pay rise that they had promised never materialized.*

maternal /məˈtɜːnl/ *adj* **1** behaving as a mother would behave; connected with being a mother: *maternal love/instincts* **2** [only *before* a noun] related through your mother's side of the family: *your maternal grandfather* ➲ look at **paternal**

maternity /məˈtɜːnəti/ *adj* connected with women who are going to have or have just had a baby: *maternity clothes* ◆ *the hospital's maternity ward* ➲ look at **paternity**

mathematician /ˌmæθəməˈtɪʃn/ *noun* [C] a person who studies or is an expert in mathematics

🔑 **mathematics** /ˌmæθəˈmætɪks/ *noun* [U] (*formal*) the science or study of numbers, quantities or shapes: *the school mathematics curriculum* ➲ look at **algebra, arithmetic, geometry**

HELP The British abbreviation is **maths**, in American English it is **math**: *Maths is my favourite subject.*

▶ **mathematical** /-ɪkl/ *adj*: *mathematical calculations/problems* ▶ **mathematically** /-kli/ *adv*

matinee (also **matinée**) /ˈmætɪneɪ/ *noun* [C] an afternoon performance of a play, film, etc.

matrimony /ˈmætrɪməni/ *noun* [U] (*formal*) the state of being married ▶ **matrimonial** /ˌmætrɪˈməʊniəl/ *adj*

matron /ˈmeɪtrən/ *noun* [C] **1** a woman who works as a nurse in a school **2** (*old-fashioned*) a nurse who is in charge of the other nurses in a hospital (now usually called a **senior nursing officer**)

matt (*AmE* also **matte**) /mæt/ *adj* not shiny: *This paint gives a matt finish.* ➲ look at **gloss**

matted /ˈmætɪd/ *adj* (used especially about hair) forming a thick mass, especially because it is wet and/or dirty

🔑 **matter**[1] /ˈmætə(r)/ *noun* **1** [C] a subject or situation that you must think about and give your attention to: *It's a personal matter and I don't want to discuss it with you.* ◆ *Finding a job will be* ***no easy matter.*** ◆ *to simplify/complicate matters* **2** [sing] **the matter (with sb/sth)** the reason sb/sth has a problem or is not good: *She looks sad.* ***What's the matter*** *with her?* ◆ *There seems to be* ***something the matter*** *with the car.* ◆ *Eat that food! There's* ***nothing the matter*** *with it.* **3** [U] all physical substances; a substance of a particular kind: *reading matter* ◆ *waste matter* ◆ *organic matter*

IDM **another/a different matter** something much more serious, difficult, etc: *I can speak a little Japanese, but reading it is quite another matter.*

as a matter of fact to tell the truth; in reality: *I like him very much, as a matter of fact.*

for that matter in addition; now that I think about it: *Mick is really fed up with his course. I am too, for that matter.*

(be) a matter of sth/doing sth a situation in which sth is needed: *Learning a language is largely a matter of practice.*

a matter of course something that you always do; the usual thing to do: *Goods leaving the factory are checked as a matter of course.*

a matter of hours, minutes, etc.; a matter of inches, metres, etc. only a few hours, minutes, etc: *The fight lasted a matter of seconds.*

a matter of life and/or death extremely urgent and important

a matter of opinion a subject on which people do not agree: *'I think the government is doing a good job.' 'That's a matter of opinion.'*

no matter who, what, where, etc. it is not important who, what, where, etc: *They never listen, no matter what you say.*

to make matters/things worse ➲ **worse**

M

matter[2] /ˈmætə(r)/ *verb* [I] [not used in the continuous tenses] matter (to sb) to be important: ***It doesn't*** *really* ***matter*** *how much it costs.* ◆ *Nobody's hurt, and* ***that's all that matters.*** ◆ *Some things matter more than others.* ◆ *It doesn't matter to me what he does in his free time.*

> **HELP** Compare **it doesn't matter** and **I don't mind**: *'I've broken a cup!' 'It was an old one. It doesn't matter* (= it is not important).*'* ◆ *'What shall we have for dinner?' 'I don't mind* (= I will be happy with any type of dinner).*'*

ˌmatter-of-ˈfact *adj* said or done without showing any emotion, especially when it would seem more normal to express your feelings: *He was very matter-of-fact about his illness.*

mattress /ˈmætrəs/ *noun* [C] the soft part of a bed that you lie on ➲ picture at **bed**

mature /məˈtʃʊə(r)/ *adj* **1** behaving in a sensible adult way: *Is she mature enough for such responsibility?* **2** fully grown or fully developed: *a mature tree/bird/animal* **OPP** for both meanings **immature** ▶ **mature** *verb* [I]: *He matured a lot during his two years at college.* ▶ **maturity** /məˈtʃʊərəti/ *noun* [U]

maul /mɔːl/ *verb* [T] (usually used about a wild animal) to attack and injure sb

mauve /məʊv/ *adj, noun* [U] (of) a pale purple colour

max /mæks/ *abbr* = **maximum**: *max temp 21°C* **OPP min.**

maxim /ˈmæksɪm/ *noun* [C] a few words that express a rule for good or sensible behaviour: *Our maxim is: 'If a job's worth doing, it's worth doing well.'*

maximize (also -ise) /ˈmæksɪmaɪz/ *verb* [T] to increase sth as much as possible: *to maximize profits* **OPP minimize**

maximum /ˈmæksɪməm/ *noun* [sing] (*abbr* max) the greatest amount or level of sth that is possible, allowed, etc: *The bus can carry a maximum of 40 people.* ◆ *That is the maximum we can afford.* **OPP minimum** ▶ **maximum** *adj* [only *before* a noun]: *a maximum speed of 120 miles per hour*

May /meɪ/ *noun* [U,C] the 5th month of the year, coming after April ➲ note at **January**

may /meɪ/ *modal verb* (*negative* may not; *pt* might /maɪt/; *negative* might not) **1** used for saying that sth is possible: *'Where's Sue?' 'She may be in the garden.'* ◆ *You may be right.* ◆ *I may be going to China next year.* ◆ *They may have forgotten the meeting.* **2** used for contrasting two facts: *He may be very clever but he can't do anything practical.* **3** used as a polite way of asking for and giving permission: *May I use your phone?* ◆ *You may not take photographs in the museum.* **4** (*formal*) used for expressing wishes and hopes: *May you both be very happy.* ℹ For more information about modal verbs, look at the **Reference Section** at the back of this dictionary.
IDM may/might as well (do sth) ➲ **well**[1]

maybe /ˈmeɪbi/ *adv* perhaps; possibly: *'Are you going to come?' 'Maybe.'* ◆ *There were three, maybe four armed men.* ◆ *Maybe I'll accept the invitation and maybe I won't.* ➲ note at **perhaps**

ˈMay Day *noun* [C] 1st May

> **CULTURE**
> **May Day** is traditionally celebrated as a spring festival, and in some countries as a holiday in honour of working people.

mayonnaise /ˌmeɪəˈneɪz/ *noun* [U] a thick cold white sauce made with eggs and oil

mayor /meə(r)/ *noun* [C] a person who is elected to be the leader of a group of people who manage the affairs of a town or city: *the Lord Mayor of London*

mayoress /meəˈres/ *noun* [C] a woman **mayor**, or a woman who is married to or helps a **mayor**

maze /meɪz/ *noun* [C] a system of paths which is designed to confuse you so that it is difficult to find your way out: (*figurative*) *a maze of winding streets* **SYN labyrinth**

MB *abbr* = **megabyte**: *512MB of memory*

Mb (also Mbit) *abbr* = **megabit**

MBA /ˌem biː ˈeɪ/ *abbr* **Master of Business Administration**; an advanced university degree in business

MD /ˌem ˈdiː/ *abbr* **Doctor of Medicine**

me /miː/ *pron* (used as an object) the person who is speaking or writing: *He telephoned me yesterday.* ◆ *She wrote to me last week.* ◆ *Hello, is that Frank? It's me, Sadiq.*

meadow /ˈmedəʊ/ *noun* [C] a field of grass ➲ picture on **page P10**

meagre (*AmE* meager) /ˈmiːɡə(r)/ *adj* too small in amount: *a meagre salary*

meal /miːl/ *noun* [C] the time when you eat or the food that is eaten at that time: *Shall we* ***go out for a meal*** *on Friday?* ◆ *a heavy/light meal* ◆ *What time do you have your evening meal?* ➲ note at **lunch, restaurant**
IDM a square meal ➲ **square**[1]

> **TOPIC**
> **Meals**
> The main **meals** of the day are **breakfast, lunch** and **dinner. Tea** and **supper** are usually smaller meals, but some people use these words to talk about the main evening meal. The midday meal can be called **dinner**. Before a meal you **lay the table** by putting a **tablecloth, cutlery** (= knives, forks and spoons), etc. on it. After the meal you **clear the table** and **wash up/wash the dishes.** If you don't want to cook, you can **go out for a meal/eat out** (= go to a restaurant) or you can get a **takeaway** (= a meal that you collect and take home). A **picnic** is a meal that you prepare at home and take to eat outdoors. Something small that you eat between meals is a **snack**.

mealtime /ˈmiːltaɪm/ *noun* [C] the time at which a meal is usually eaten

mean[1] /miːn/ *verb* [T] (*pt, pp* **meant** /ment/)
➤HAVE AS MEANING **1** [not used in the continuous tenses] to express, show or have as a meaning: ***What does** this word **mean**? ◆ The bell means that the lesson has ended. ◆ Does the name 'Kate Wallace' **mean anything to you*** (= do you know who she is)?

HELP Although this verb is not used in the continuous tenses, it is common to see the present participle (= *-ing* form): *The weather during filming was terrible, meaning that several scenes had to be shot again later.*

➤WANT TO SAY **2** to want or intend to say sth; to refer to sb/sth: *Well, she said 'yes' but I think she really meant 'no'. ◆ **What do you mean by** 'a lot of money'? ◆ I only meant that I couldn't come tomorrow—any other day would be fine. ◆ **I see what you mean,** but I'm afraid it's not possible.* ➲ note at **think**

HELP Note that **mean** cannot be used when we want to say 'to have the opinion that'. We say: *I think that ...* or *In my opinion ...*: *I think that she'd be silly to buy that car.* **I mean** is often used in conversation when you want to explain something you have just said or to add more information: *What a terrible summer—I mean it's rained almost all the time.* **I mean** is also used to correct something you have just said: *We went there on Tuesday, I mean Thursday.*

➤INTEND TO DO **3** [often passive] **mean (sb) to do sth; mean sth (as/for sth/sb); mean sb/sth to be sth** to intend sth; to be supposed to be/do sth: *I'm sure she didn't mean to upset you. ◆ She meant the present to be for both of us. ◆ I didn't mean you to cook the whole meal! ◆ It was only meant as a joke. ◆ What's this picture meant to be?*
➤BE SERIOUS **4** to be serious or sincere about sth: *He said he loved me but I don't think he meant it!*
➤CAUSE **5** to make sth likely; to cause: *The shortage of teachers means that classes are larger.*
➤BE IMPORTANT **6** **mean sth (to sb)** to be important to sb: *This job **means a lot to me.** ◆ Money **means nothing to her.***
IDM **be meant to be sth** to be considered or said to be sth: *That restaurant is meant to be excellent.*
mean well to want to be kind and helpful but usually without success: *My mother means well but I wish she'd stop treating me like a child.*

mean[2] /miːn/ *adj* (**meaner**; **meanest**) **1** **mean (with sth)** wanting to keep money, etc. for yourself rather than let other people have it: *It's no good asking him for any money—he's much too mean. ◆ They're mean with the food in the canteen.* **OPP** **generous** **2** **mean (to sb)** (used about people or their behaviour) unkind: *It was mean of him not to invite you too.* **3** [only *before* a noun] average: *the mean temperature* ▶ **meanness** *noun* [U]

meander /miˈændə(r)/ *verb* [I] **1** (used about a river, road, etc.) to have a lot of curves and bends ➲ picture on **page P10** **2** to walk or travel slowly or without any definite direction ▶ **meander** *noun* [C]: *The town is situated on a meander of the river.*

meaning /ˈmiːnɪŋ/ *noun* **1** [C,U] the thing or idea that sth represents; what sb is trying to communicate: *This word has two different meanings in English. ◆ What do you think the meaning is of the last line of the poem?* **2** [U] the purpose or importance of an experience: *Having a child gave new meaning to their lives.*

meaningful /ˈmiːnɪŋfl/ *adj* **1** useful, important or interesting: *Most people need a meaningful relationship with another person.* **2** (used about a look, expression, etc.) trying to express a certain feeling or idea: *They kept giving each other meaningful glances across the table.* ▶ **meaningfully** /-fəli/ *adv*

meaningless /ˈmiːnɪŋləs/ *adj* without meaning, reason or sense: *The figures are meaningless if we have nothing to compare them with.*

means /miːnz/ *noun* **1** [C] (*pl* **means**) **a means (of doing sth)** a method of doing sth: *Do you have any **means of transport** (= a car, bicycle, etc.)? ◆ Is there any means of contacting your husband?* **2** [pl] (*formal*) all the money that sb has: *This car is **beyond the means of** most people.*
IDM **by all means** used to say that you are happy for sb to have or do sth: *'Can I borrow your newspaper?' 'By all means.'*
by means of by using: *We got out of the hotel by means of the fire escape.*
by no means; not by any means (used to emphasize sth) not at all: *I'm by no means sure that this is the right thing to do.*
a means to an end an action or thing that is not important in itself but is a way of achieving sth else: *I don't enjoy my job, but it's a means to an end.*

meant *past tense, past participle of* **mean**[1]

meantime /ˈmiːntaɪm/ *noun*
IDM **in the meantime** in the time between two things happening: *Our house isn't finished so in the meantime we're living with my mother.*

meanwhile /ˈmiːnwaɪl/ *adv* during the same time or during the time between two things happening: *Peter was at home studying. Omar, meanwhile, was out with his friends.*

measles /ˈmiːzlz/ *noun* [U] a common infectious disease, especially among children, in which your body feels hot and your skin is covered in small red spots

GRAMMAR **Measles** looks like a plural noun but is used with a singular verb: *Measles **is** a very dangerous disease.*

measly /ˈmiːzli/ *adj* (*informal*) much too small in size, amount or value: *All that work for this measly amount of money!*

measure[1] /ˈmeʒə(r)/ *verb* **1** [I,T] to find the size, weight, quantity, etc. of sb/sth in standard units by using an instrument: *to measure the height/width/length/depth of something ◆ Could you measure how wide the table is to see if it will fit into our room?* **2** [T] to be a certain height, width, length, etc: *The room measures five metres across.* **3** [T] **measure sth (against sth)** to judge the value or effect of sth: *Our*

M

sales do not look good when measured against those of our competitors.

PHR V **measure up (sb/sth)** to measure sb/sth **measure up (to sth)** to be as good as you need to be or as sb expects you to be: *Did the holiday measure up to your expectations?*

measure² /ˈmeʒə(r)/ *noun* **1** [C, usually pl] an official action that is done for a special reason: *The government is to* **take** *new* **measures** *to reduce inflation.* ♦ *As a temporary measure, the road will have to be closed.* **2** [sing] (*formal*) **a/some measure of sth** a certain amount of sth; some: *The play achieved a measure of success.* **3** [sing] a way of understanding or judging sth: *The school's popularity is a measure of the teachers' success.* **4** [C] a way of describing the size, amount, etc. of sth: *A metre is a measure of length.* ➲ look at **tape measure**

IDM **for good measure** in addition to sth, especially to make sure that there is enough: *He made a few extra sandwiches for good measure.*

made to measure specially made or perfectly suitable for a particular person, use, etc: *I'm getting a suit made to measure for the wedding.*

measurement /ˈmeʒəmənt/ *noun* **1** [U] the act or process of measuring sth: *the metric system of measurement* **2** [C] a size, amount, etc. that is found by measuring: *What are the exact measurements of the room?* (= how wide, long, etc. is it?)

ˈmeasuring tape = **tape measure**

meat /miːt/ *noun* [U] the parts of animals or birds that people eat: *meat and two vegetables* ♦ *meat-eating animals* ♦ *a* **piece/slice of meat**

TOPIC

Meat

We get **pork, ham** or **bacon** from a pig, **beef** from a cow and **veal** from a calf (= a young cow). **Mutton** comes from a sheep, but we get **lamb** from a lamb (= a young sheep). We often call beef, mutton and lamb **red meat**. Pale-coloured meat such as chicken is called **white meat**. We can **fry, grill, roast** or **stew** meat. We **carve** a **joint** of meat. Meat can be described as **tough** or **tender, lean** or **fatty**. Uncooked meat is **raw**. You buy meat at **the butcher's**. A person who does not eat meat is a **vegetarian**.

meaty /ˈmiːti/ *adj* (**meatier; meatiest**) **1** like meat, or containing a lot of meat: *meaty sausages* **2** containing a lot of important or good ideas: *a meaty topic for discussion* **3** large and fat: *meaty tomatoes*

mebibit /ˈmebibɪt/ (*abbr* **Mib; Mibit**) = **megabit**(2)

mebibyte /ˈmebibaɪt/ (*abbr* **MiB**) = **megabyte**(2)

Mecca /ˈmekə/ *noun* **1** [sing] the city in Saudi Arabia where the Prophet Muhammad was born, which is the centre of Islam **2 mecca** [C, usually sing] a place that many people wish to visit because of a particular interest: *Italy is a mecca for art lovers.*

mechanic /məˈkænɪk/ *noun* **1** [C] a person whose job is to repair and work with machines: *a car mechanic* **2 mechanics** [U] the science of how machines work **3 the mechanics** [pl] the way in which sth works or is done: *Don't ask me—I don't understand the mechanics of the legal system.*

mechanical /məˈkænɪkl/ *adj* **1** connected with or produced by machines: *a mechanical pump* ♦ *mechanical engineering* **2** (used about sb's behaviour) done like a machine as if you are not thinking about what you are doing: *He played the piano in a dull and mechanical way.* ▶ **mechanically** /-kli/ *adv*

mechanism /ˈmekənɪzəm/ *noun* [C] **1** a set of moving parts in a machine that does a certain task: *Our car has an automatic locking mechanism.* **2** the way in which sth works or is done: *I'm afraid there is no mechanism for dealing with your complaint.*

mechanize (also **-ise**) /ˈmekənaɪz/ *verb* [T] to use machines instead of people to do work: *We have mechanized the entire production process.* ▶ **mechanization** (also **-isation**) /ˌmekənaɪˈzeɪʃn/ *noun* [U]

the Med /med/ (*informal*) = **the Mediterranean**

med *abbr* = **medium²**(2)

medal /ˈmedl/ *noun* [C] a small flat piece of metal, usually with a design and words on it, which is given to sb who has shown courage or as a prize in a sport: *to win a gold/silver/bronze medal in the Olympics*

medallion /məˈdæliən/ *noun* [C] a small round piece of metal on a chain which is worn as jewellery around the neck

medallist (*AmE* **medalist**) /ˈmedəlɪst/ *noun* [C] a person who has won a **medal**, especially in sport: *an Olympic gold medallist*

meddle /ˈmedl/ *verb* [I] **meddle (in/with sth)** to take too much interest in sb's private affairs or to touch sth that does not belong to you: *She hated her mother meddling in her private life.*

media /ˈmiːdiə/ *noun* [U, with sing or pl verb] TV, radio, newspapers and the Internet used as a means of communication: *The reports* ***in the media*** *have been greatly exaggerated.* ➲ note at **newspaper** ➲ look at **mass media**

GRAMMAR **Media** is used with a singular or plural verb: *The media always take/takes a great interest in the royal family.*

mediaeval = **medieval**

mediate /ˈmiːdieɪt/ *verb* [I,T] **mediate (in sth) (between A and B)** to try to end a disagreement between two or more people or groups: *As a supervisor she had to mediate between her colleagues and the management.* ▶ **mediation** /ˌmiːdiˈeɪʃn/ *noun* [U] ▶ **mediator** /ˈmiːdieɪtə(r)/ *noun* [C]

medical¹ /ˈmedɪkl/ *adj* connected with medicine and the treatment of illness: *medical treatment/care* ◆ *the* ***medical profession*** ▶ **medically** /-kli/ *adv*: *medically fit/unfit for work*

medical² /ˈmedɪkl/ *noun* [C] an examination of your body by a doctor to check your state of health: *to have a medical*

medication /ˌmedɪˈkeɪʃn/ *noun* [C,U] medicine that a doctor has given to you: *Are you* ***on*** *any medication?*

medicinal /məˈdɪsɪnl/ *adj* useful for curing illness or infection: *medicinal plants*

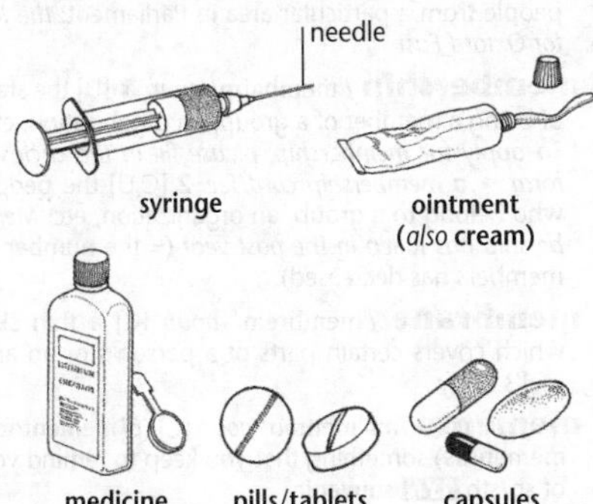

medicine /ˈmedsn; ˈmedɪsn/ *noun* **1** [U] the science of preventing and treating illness: *to study medicine* **2** [C,U] a substance, especially a liquid, that you take in order to cure an illness: ***Take*** *this* ***medicine*** *three times a day.* ◆ *cough medicine* ➲ note at **doctor**

medieval (also **mediaeval**) /ˌmediˈiːvl/ *adj* connected with **the Middle Ages** (= the period in history between about 1000 AD and 1450 AD)

mediocre /ˌmiːdiˈəʊkə(r)/ *adj* of not very high quality: *He gave a mediocre performance* ▶ **mediocrity** /ˌmiːdiˈɒkrəti/ *noun* [U]

meditate /ˈmedɪteɪt/ *verb* [I] **meditate (on/upon sth)** to think carefully and deeply, especially for religious reasons or to make your mind calm: *I've been meditating on what you said last week.* ▶ **meditation** /ˌmedɪˈteɪʃn/ *noun* [U]

the Mediterranean /ˌmedɪtəˈreɪniən/ (also *informal* **the Med**) *noun* [sing], *adj* [only *before* a noun] (of) the Mediterranean Sea or the countries around it: *Mediterranean cookery*

medium¹ /ˈmiːdiəm/ *adj* **1** in the middle between two sizes, lengths, temperatures, etc.; average: *She was of medium height.* ◆ *Would you like the small, medium or large packet?* ◆ *a medium-sized car/town/dog* **2** (used about meat) cooked until it is brown all the way through ➲ look at **rare**, **well done**

medium² /ˈmiːdiəm/ *noun* **1** [C] (*pl* **media** or **mediums**) a means you can use to express or communicate sth: *The Internet is the modern* ***medium of communication.*** ◆ *English is the* ***medium of instruction*** *in the school.* ◆ *the* ***medium of radio/television*** ➲ look at **media**, **mass media** **2** [C,U] (*abbr* **med**) **medium** size: *Have you got this shirt in (a) medium?* **3** [C] (*pl* **mediums**) a person who says that they can speak to the spirits of dead people

medley /ˈmedli/ *noun* [C] **1** a piece of music consisting of several tunes or songs played one after the other without a break **2** a mixture of different things: *a medley of styles/flavours*

meek /miːk/ *adj* (**meeker**; **meekest**) (used about people) quiet, and doing what other people say without asking questions ▶ **meekly** *adv* ▶ **meekness** *noun* [U]

meet /miːt/ *verb* (*pt*, *pp* **met** /met/)
➤COME TOGETHER **1** [I,T] to come together by chance or because you have arranged it: *What time shall we meet for lunch?* ◆ *I just met Kareem on the train.* **2** [T] to go to a place and wait for sb/sth to arrive: *I'll come and meet you at the station.*
➤FOR THE FIRST TIME **3** [I,T] to see and know sb for the first time: *Have you two met before?* ◆ *Where did you first meet your husband?* ➲ note at **know**
➤IN COMPETITION **4** [I,T] to play, fight, etc. together as opponents in a sports competition: *These two teams met in last year's final.* ◆ *Yamada will meet Suzuki in the second round.*
➤EXPERIENCE STH **5** [T] to experience sth, often sth unpleasant: *We will never know how he met his death.*
➤JOIN **6** [I,T] to touch, join or make contact with: *The two roads meet not far from here.* ◆ *His eyes met hers.*
➤BE ENOUGH **7** [T] to be enough for sth; to be able to deal with sth: *The money that I earn is enough to* ***meet*** *our* ***basic needs.*** ◆ *to* ***meet a challenge***
IDM **make ends meet** ➲ **end¹**
there is more to sb/sth than meets the eye sb/sth is more interesting or complicated than he/she/it seems: *Do you think there's more to their relationship than meets the eye?*
PHR V **meet up (with sb)** (*informal*) to meet sb, especially after a period of being apart: *I have a few things I need to do now, but let's meet up later.* ➲ look at **get together**
meet with sb (*especially AmE*) to meet sb, especially

for discussion: *The President met with his advisers early this morning.*
meet with sth to get a particular answer, reaction or result: *to meet with success/failure/opposition*

meeting /ˈmiːtɪŋ/ *noun* **1** [C] an organized occasion when a number of people come together in order to discuss or decide sth: *The group* ***hold*** *regular* ***meetings*** *all year.* ◆ *We need to* ***have a meeting*** *to discuss these matters.*

> **MORE** We **call, arrange** or **organize** a meeting. We can also **cancel** or **postpone** a meeting.

2 [sing] the people at a meeting: *The meeting was in favour of the new proposals.* **3** [C] the coming together of two or more people: *Christmas is a time of family meetings and reunions.*

meg /meg/ (*informal*) = **megabyte**: *more than 512 megs of memory* ◆ *a 24-meg broadband*

megabit /ˈmegəbɪt/ *noun* [C] (*abbr* Mb; Mbit) **1** a unit of computer memory, equal to 10^6 (= 1 000 000) **bits** (= the smallest units of information) **2** (also mebibit) a unit of computer memory, equal to 2^{20} (= 1 048 576) **bits** (= the smallest units of information)

M

megabyte /ˈmegəbaɪt/ *noun* [C] (*abbr* MB) (also *informal* meg) **1** a unit of computer memory, equal to 10^6 (= 1 000 000) **bytes** (= small units of information): *a 512-megabyte flash drive* **2** (also mebibyte) a unit of computer memory, equal to 2^{20} (= 1 048 576) **bytes** (= small units of information): *a 40-megabyte hard disk*

megaphone /ˈmegəfəʊn/ *noun* [C] a piece of equipment that you speak through to make your voice sound louder when speaking to a crowd

melancholy /ˈmelənkəli; -kɒli/ *noun* [U] (*formal*) a feeling of sadness which lasts for a long time ▶ **melancholy** *adj*

mellow /ˈmeləʊ/ *adj* (mellower; mellowest) **1** (used about colours or sounds) soft and pleasant: *mellow autumn colours* **2** (used about people) calm and relaxed: *My dad's grown mellower as he's got older.* ▶ **mellow** *verb* [I,T]: *Experience had mellowed her views about many things.*

melodic /məˈlɒdɪk/ *adj* **1** [only *before* a noun] connected with the main tune in a piece of music: *The melodic line is carried by the clarinets.* **2** = **melodious**

melodious /məˈləʊdiəs/ (also melodic) *adj* pleasant to listen to, like music: *a rich melodious voice* ▶ **melodiously** *adv*

melodrama /ˈmelədrɑːmə/ *noun* [C,U] a story, play or film in which a lot of exciting things happen and in which people's emotions are stronger than in real life

melodramatic /ˌmelədrəˈmætɪk/ *adj* (often disapproving) making things seem more exciting or serious than they really are: *Don't be so melodramatic, Simon—of course you're not going to die!* ◆ *a melodramatic plot full of deceit and murder*

melody /ˈmelədi/ *noun* [C] (*pl* melodies) a song or tune; the main tune of a piece of music

melon /ˈmelən/ *noun* [C,U] a large round fruit with a thick yellow or green skin and a lot of seeds ➲ picture on **page P14**

melt /melt/ *verb* **1** [I,T] to change or make sth change from a solid to a liquid by means of heat: *When we got up in the morning the snow had melted.* ◆ *First melt the butter in a saucepan.* ➲ look at **thaw** **2** [I] (used about sb's feelings, etc.) to become softer or less strong: *My heart melted when I saw the baby.*
PHR V **melt away** to disappear: *The crowd slowly melted away when the speaker had finished.*
melt sth down to heat a metal or glass object until it becomes liquid

meltdown /ˈmeltdaʊn/ *noun* [U,C] a serious accident in which the central part of a nuclear **reactor** (= a very large machine that produces nuclear energy) melts, causing harmful substances to escape: (*figurative*) *The country is* ***in*** *economic* ***meltdown.***

ˈmelting pot *noun* [C] a place where a lot of different cultures, ideas, etc. come together: *New York is a melting pot of different cultures.*

member /ˈmembə(r)/ *noun* [C] a person, animal or thing that belongs to a group, a club, an organization, etc: *All the members of the family were there.* ◆ *to become a member of a club* ◆ *a member of staff*

ˌMember of ˈParliament *noun* [C] (*abbr* MP) a person who has been elected to represent people from a particular area in Parliament: *the MP for Oxford East*

membership /ˈmembəʃɪp/ *noun* **1** [U] the state of being a member of a group, an organization, etc: *To* ***apply for membership****, please fill in the enclosed form.* ◆ *a membership card/fee* **2** [C,U] the people who belong to a group, an organization, etc: *Membership has fallen in the past year* (= the number of members has decreased).

membrane /ˈmembreɪn/ *noun* [C] a thin skin which covers certain parts of a person's or an animal's body

memento /məˈmentəʊ/ *noun* [C] (*pl* mementoes; mementos) something that you keep to remind you of sb/sth **SYN** **souvenir**

memo /ˈmeməʊ/ *noun* [C] (*pl* memos) (also *formal* memorandum) a note sent from one person or office to another within an organization

memoirs /ˈmemwɑːz/ *noun* [pl] sb's written account of their own life and experiences **SYN** **autobiography**

memorabilia /ˌmemərəˈbɪliə/ *noun* [U] things that people buy because they are connected with a famous person, event, etc: *Beatles/Titanic/war memorabilia*

memorable /ˈmemərəbl/ *adj* worth remembering or easy to remember: *The concert was a memorable experience.* **SYN** **unforgettable** ▶ **memorably** /-əbli/ *adv*

memorandum /ˌmeməˈrændəm/ *noun* (*pl* memoranda /-də/) (*formal*) = **memo**

memorial /məˈmɔːriəl/ *noun* [C] a memorial (to sb/sth) something that is built or done to remind people of an event or a person: *a memorial to the victims of the bombing* ◆ *a war memorial* ◆ *a memorial service*

memorize (also -ise) /ˈmeməraɪz/ *verb* [T] to learn sth so that you can remember it exactly: *Actors have to memorize their lines.*

memory /ˈmeməri/ *noun* (*pl* memories) **1** [C] sb's ability to remember things: *to have a good/bad memory* ◆ *The drug can affect your short-term memory.* **2** [C,U] the part of your mind in which you store things that you remember: *That day remained firmly* ***in my memory*** *for the rest of my life.* ◆ *Are you going to do your speech* ***from memory****, or are you going to use notes?* **3** [C] something that you remember: *That is one of my happiest memories.* ◆ *childhood memories* **4** [C,U] the part of a computer where information is stored: *This computer has a 640k memory/640k of memory.*
IDM **in memory of sb** in order to remind people of sb who has died: *A service was held in memory of the dead.*
jog sb's memory ➲ **jog**[1]
refresh your memory ➲ **refresh**

ˈ**memory card** *noun* [C] an electronic device that can be used to store data, used especially with cameras, mobile phones, music players, etc.

ˈ**memory stick** = **flash drive**

men *plural* of **man**[1]

menace /ˈmenəs/ *noun* **1** [C] a menace (to sb/sth) a danger or threat: *The new road is a menace to everyone's safety.* **2** [U] a quality, feeling, etc. that is threatening or frightening: *He spoke with menace in his voice.* **3** [C] a person or thing that causes trouble ▸ **menace** *verb* [T] ▸ **menacing** *adj*

mend[1] /mend/ *verb* [T] to repair sth that is damaged or broken: *Can you mend the hole in this jumper for me?* ◆ (*figurative*) *They tried to mend their differences.* SYN **repair**

mend[2] /mend/ *noun*
IDM **be on the mend** (*informal*) to be getting better after an illness or injury: *She's been in bed for a week but she's on the mend now.*

menial /ˈmiːniəl/ *adj* (used about work) not skilled or important: *a menial job*

meningitis /ˌmenɪnˈdʒaɪtɪs/ *noun* [U] a dangerous illness which affects the brain and the **spinal cord** (= the inside of the bones in your back)

the menopause /ˈmenəpɔːz/ *noun* [sing] the time when a woman stops **menstruating** and can no longer have children. This usually happens around the age of 50.

menstrual /ˈmenstruəl/ *adj* connected with the time when a woman **menstruates** each month: *The average length of a woman's* ***menstrual cycle*** *is 28 days.*

menstruate /ˈmenstrueɪt/ *verb* [I] (*formal*) (used about women) to lose blood once a month from the **womb** (= the part of the body where a baby grows)
➲ A more common way of saying this is **have a period.** ▸ **menstruation** /ˌmenstruˈeɪʃn/ *noun* [U]

mental /ˈmentl/ *adj* [only *before* a noun] **1** of or in the mind; involving the process of thinking: *It's fascinating to watch a child's mental development.* ◆ *mental arithmetic* (= counting with numbers done in your head) **2** connected with illness of the mind: *a* ***mental illness/hospital*** ◆ ***mental health***

mentality /menˈtæləti/ *noun* [C] (*pl* mentalities) a type of mind or way of thinking: *I just can't understand his mentality!* ◆ *the criminal mentality*

mentally /-təli/ *adv* connected with or happening in the mind: *She's mentally ill.* ◆ *The baby is very mentally alert.*

mention /ˈmenʃn/ *verb* [T] to say or write sth about sb/sth without giving much information: *He mentioned (to me) that he might be late.* ◆ *Did she mention what time the film starts?*
IDM **don't mention it** used as a polite reply when sb thanks you for sth: *'Thank you for all your help.' 'Don't mention it.'*
not to mention (used to emphasize sth) and also; as well as: *This is a great habitat for birds, not to mention other wildlife.*
▸ **mention** *noun* [C,U]: *It was odd that there wasn't even a mention of the riots in the newspaper.*

menu /ˈmenjuː/ *noun* [C] **1** a list of the food that you can choose at a restaurant: *Could we have/see the menu, please?* ◆ *I hope there's soup* ***on the menu****.* ◆ *They do a special lunchtime menu here.* ➲ note at **restaurant 2** a list of choices in a computer program which is shown on the screen: *a pull-down menu*

ˈ**menu bar** *noun* [C] a horizontal bar at the top of a computer screen that contains **drop-down menus** (= lists of possible choices) such as 'File', 'Edit' and 'Help'

MEP /ˌem iː ˈpiː/ *abbr* **Member of the European Parliament**

mercenary[1] /ˈmɜːsənəri/ *noun* [C] (*pl* mercenaries) a soldier who fights for any group or country that will pay them

mercenary[2] /ˈmɜːsənəri/ *adj* interested only in making money: *I know his motives are entirely mercenary.*

merchandise /ˈmɜːtʃəndaɪs; -daɪz/ *noun* [U] (*formal*) goods that are for sale

merchant /ˈmɜːtʃənt/ *noun* [C] a person whose job is to buy and sell goods, usually of one particular type, in large amounts

the ˌmerchant ˈnavy *noun* [C, with sing or pl verb] a country's commercial ships and the people who work on them

merciful /ˈmɜːsɪfl/ *adj* feeling or showing **mercy**: *His death was a merciful release from pain.* ▸ **mercifully** /-fəli/ *adv*

merciless /ˈmɜːsɪləs/ *adj* showing no **mercy** ▸ **mercilessly** *adv*

M

Mercury /ˈmɜːkjəri/ *noun* [sing] the planet that is nearest to the sun

mercury /ˈmɜːkjəri/ *noun* [U] (*symbol* **Hg**) a heavy silver-coloured metal that is usually in liquid form. Mercury is used in **thermometers** (= instruments that measure temperature).

mercy /ˈmɜːsi/ *noun* [U] kindness shown by sb/sth who has the power to make sb suffer: *The prisoners begged for mercy from the king.* ♦ *The rebels were* ***shown no mercy****. They were taken out and shot.*
IDM at the mercy of sb/sth having no power against sb/sth that is strong: *The climbers spent the night on the mountain at the mercy of the wind and rain.*

⚷ **mere** /mɪə(r)/ *adj* (**merest**) [no comparative] [only *before* a noun] **1** (used for emphasizing how small or unimportant sth is) nothing more than: *90% of the country's land is owned by a mere 2% of the population.* **2** used to say that just the fact that sb/sth is present in a situation is enough to have an influence: *The mere thought of giving a speech in public makes me feel sick.*
IDM the merest even a very small amount of sth: *The merest smell of the fish market made her feel ill.*

M

⚷ **merely** /ˈmɪəli/ *adv* (*formal*) only; just: *I don't want to place an order. I am merely making an enquiry.*

merge /mɜːdʒ/ *verb* **1** [I] **merge (with/into sth); merge (together)** to become part of sth larger: *This stream merges with the river a few miles downstream.* ♦ *Three small companies merged into one large one.* ♦ *Fact and fiction merge together in his latest book.* **2** [T] to join things together so that they become one: *We have merged the two classes into one.* **SYN amalgamate**

merger /ˈmɜːdʒə(r)/ *noun* [C,U] **a merger (with sb/sth); a merger (between/of A and B)** the act of joining two or more companies together

meridian /məˈrɪdiən/ *noun* [C] a line that we imagine on the surface of the earth that joins the North Pole to the South Pole and passes through a particular place: *the prime meridian* ➲ look at **longitude**

meringue /məˈræŋ/ *noun* [C,U] a mixture of sugar and egg white that is cooked in the oven; a cake made from this

merit¹ /ˈmerɪt/ *noun* **1** [U] the quality of being good: *There is a lot of merit in her ideas.* ♦ *He got the job* ***on merit****, not because he's the manager's son.* **2** [C, usually pl] an advantage or a good quality of sb/sth: *Each case must be judged separately on its own merits* (= not according to general principles).

merit² /ˈmerɪt/ *verb* [T] (*formal*) to be good enough for sth; to deserve: *This suggestion merits further discussion.*

mermaid /ˈmɜːmeɪd/ *noun* [C] (in stories) a woman who has the tail of a fish instead of legs and who lives in the sea

merriment /ˈmerimənt/ *noun* [U] happiness, fun and the sound of people laughing **SYN mirth**

merry /ˈmeri/ *adj* (**merrier; merriest**) **1** happy: *merry laughter* ♦ ***Merry Christmas*** (= used to say you hope sb has a happy holiday) **2** (*especially BrE informal*) slightly drunk ► **merrily** *adv*: *She was singing merrily.*

ˈmerry-go-round (*BrE also* **roundabout**; *AmE also* **carousel**) *noun* [C] a big round platform that turns round and round and has model animals, etc. on it for children to ride on

merry-go-round

mesh /meʃ/ *noun* [C,U] material made of threads that are twisted together like a net: *a fence made of wire mesh*

mesmerize (also **-ise**) /ˈmezməraɪz/ *verb* [T] to hold sb's attention completely: *The audience seemed to be mesmerized by the speaker's voice.*

⚷ **mess¹** /mes/ *noun* **1** [C, usually sing] the state of being dirty or untidy; a person or thing that is dirty or untidy: *The kitchen's* ***in a*** *terrible* ***mess!*** ♦ *My hair is a mess.* ♦ *You can paint the door, but don't* ***make a mess!*** **2** [sing] the state of having problems or troubles: *The company is* ***in a*** *financial* ***mess.*** ♦ *to* ***make a mess of*** *your life*

mess² /mes/ *verb* [T] (*AmE informal*) to make sth dirty or untidy: *Don't mess your hands.*
PHR V mess about/around 1 to behave in a silly and annoying way **2** to spend your time in a relaxed way without any real purpose: *We spent Sunday just messing around at home.*
mess sb about/around to treat sb in a way that is not fair or reasonable, for example by changing your plans without telling them
mess about/around with sth to touch or use sth in a careless way: *It is dangerous to mess about with fireworks.*
mess sth up 1 to make sth dirty or untidy **2** to do sth badly or spoil sth: *I really messed up the last question in the exam.*
mess with sb/sth to deal or behave with sb/sth in a way that you should not: *You shouldn't mess with people's feelings.*

⚷ **message** /ˈmesɪdʒ/ *noun* **1** [C] a written or spoken piece of information that you send to or leave for a person when you cannot speak to them: *Mr Vos is not here at the moment. Can I* ***take a message?*** ♦ *Could you* ***give a message*** *to Kate, please?* ♦ *If he's not in I'll* ***leave a message*** *on his answering machine.* **2** [C] a piece of information that is sent in electronic form: *an email message* ♦ *There were six messages in my inbox.* **3** [sing] an important idea that a book, speech, etc. is trying to communicate: *It was a funny film but it also had a serious message.* ♦ *The advertising campaign is trying to* ***get the message across*** *that smoking kills.* ♦ *The advertising campaign is trying to* ***get the message across*** *that recycling is important.*
IDM get the message (*informal*) to understand

what sb means even if it is not clearly stated: *He finally got the message and went home.*

ˈmessage board *noun* [C] a place on a website where a user can write or read messages: *I posted a question on the message board.* ➲ note at **Internet**

messenger /ˈmesɪndʒə(r)/ *noun* [C] a person who carries a message

Messiah (also **messiah**) /məˈsaɪə/ *noun* [C] a person, for example Jesus Christ, who is expected to come and save the world

messy /ˈmesi/ *adj* (**messier**; **messiest**) **1** dirty or untidy: *a messy room* **2** that makes sb/sth dirty: *Painting the ceiling is a messy job.* **3** having or causing problems or trouble: *a messy divorce*

met *past tense* of **meet**

metabolism /məˈtæbəlɪzəm/ *noun* [U, sing] the chemical processes in the body that change food, etc. into energy: *The body's metabolism is slowed down by extreme cold.* ▶ **metabolic** /ˌmetəˈbɒlɪk/ *adj*: *a high/low metabolic rate*

⚷ **metal** /ˈmetl/ *noun* [C,U] a type of solid substance that is usually hard and shiny and that heat and electricity can travel through: *metals such as tin, iron, gold and steel* ◆ *to recycle scrap metal* ◆ *a metal bar/pipe*

metallic /məˈtælɪk/ *adj* looking like metal or making a noise like one piece of metal hitting another: *a metallic blue car* ◆ *harsh metallic sounds*

metamorphosis /ˌmetəˈmɔːfəsɪs/ *noun* [C] (*pl* **metamorphoses** /-əsiːz/) (*formal*) a complete change of form (as part of natural development): *the metamorphosis of a tadpole into a frog*

metaphor /ˈmetəfə(r)/ *noun* [C,U] a word or phrase that is used to show that one thing has the same qualities as another; a way of making a comparison: *'Her words were a knife in his heart' is a metaphor.* ➲ look at **simile** ▶ **metaphorical** /ˌmetəˈfɒrɪkl/ *adj* ▶ **metaphorically** /-kli/ *adv*

mete /miːt/ *verb*
PHR V **mete sth out (to sb)** (*formal*) to give sb a punishment; to make sb suffer bad treatment: *Severe penalties were meted out by the court.*

meteor /ˈmiːtiə(r); -iɔː(r)/ *noun* [C] a small piece of rock, etc. in space. When a **meteor** enters the earth's atmosphere it makes a bright line in the night sky.

meteoric /ˌmiːtiˈɒrɪk/ *adj* very fast or successful: *a meteoric rise to fame*

meteorite /ˈmiːtiəraɪt/ *noun* [C] a piece of rock from space that hits the earth's surface

meteorologist /ˌmiːtiəˈrɒlədʒɪst/ *noun* [C] a person who studies the weather

meteorology /ˌmiːtiəˈrɒlədʒi/ *noun* [U] the study of the weather and climate ▶ **meteorological** /ˌmiːtiərəˈlɒdʒɪkl/ *adj*

meter /ˈmiːtə(r)/ *noun* [C] **1** a piece of equipment that measures the amount of gas, water, electricity, etc. you have used: *a parking meter* **2** (*AmE*) = **metre** ▶ **meter** *verb* [T]: *Is your water metered?*

⚷ **method** /ˈmeθəd/ *noun* [C] a way of doing sth: *What method of payment do you prefer? Cash, credit or debit card?* ◆ *modern teaching methods*

methodical /məˈθɒdɪkl/ *adj* having or using a well organized and careful way of doing sth: *Paul is a very methodical worker.* ▶ **methodically** /-kli/ *adv*

methodology /ˌmeθəˈdɒlədʒi/ *noun* [C,U] (*pl* **methodologies**) (*formal*) a way of doing sth based on particular principles and methods: *language teaching methodologies* ▶ **methodological** /ˌmeθədəˈlɒdʒɪkl/ *adj*

meticulous /məˈtɪkjələs/ *adj* giving or showing great attention to detail; very careful: *meticulous checking* ▶ **meticulously** *adv*

⚷ **metre** (*AmE* **meter**) /ˈmiːtə(r)/ *noun* [C] (*abbr* **m**) a measure of length; 100 centimetres: *a two-metre high wall* ◆ *Who won the 100 metres?*

metric /ˈmetrɪk/ *adj* using the system of measurement that is based on metres, grams, litres, etc: *the metric system* ➲ look at **imperial**

metropolis /məˈtrɒpəlɪs/ *noun* [C] a very large city ▶ **metropolitan** /ˌmetrəˈpɒlɪtən/ *adj*

mg *abbr* = **milligram**

MHz /ˈmegəhɜːts/ *abbr* **megahertz**; (used in radio) a measure of **frequency** (= the rate at which a sound wave moves up and down)

miaow /miˈaʊ/ *noun* [C] the sound that a cat makes ▶ **miaow** *verb* [I] ➲ look at **purr**

MiB *abbr* = **mebibyte**

Mib (also **Mibit**) *abbr* = **mebibit**

mice *plural* of **mouse**

microbe /ˈmaɪkrəʊb/ *noun* [C] an extremely small living thing that you can only see under a **microscope** (= a piece of equipment that makes small objects look bigger) and that may cause disease

microblogging /ˈmaɪkrəʊblɒgɪŋ/ *noun* [U] the activity of sending regular short messages over the Internet to tell people what you are doing or what interests you ➲ note at **blog**

microchip /ˈmaɪkrəʊtʃɪp/ (also **chip**) *noun* [C] a very small piece of **silicon** (= a chemical element) that is used inside a computer, etc. to make it work

microcosm /ˈmaɪkrəʊkɒzəm/ *noun* [C] **a microcosm (of sth)** something that is a small example of sth larger: *Our little village is a microcosm of society as a whole.*

microphone /ˈmaɪkrəfəʊn/ (also *informal* **mike**) *noun* [C] a piece of electrical equipment that is used for making sounds louder or for recording them

microprocessor /ˌmaɪkrəʊˈprəʊsesə(r)/ *noun* [C] a small unit of a computer that controls all the other parts of the system

microscope /ˈmaɪkrəskəʊp/ *noun* [C] a piece of equipment that makes very small objects look big enough for you to be able to see them: *to examine something* ***under a microscope***

M

microscopic /ˌmaɪkrəˈskɒpɪk/ *adj* too small to be seen without a **microscope**

microwave /ˈmaɪkrəweɪv/ *noun* [C] **1** (also ˌmicrowave ˈoven) a type of oven that cooks or heats food very quickly using **microwaves** **2** a short electric wave that is used for sending radio messages and for cooking food ▶ **microwave** *verb* [T] ➲ note at **cook**

mid- /mɪd/ [in compounds] (in nouns and adjectives) in the middle of: *mid-morning coffee* ◆ *a mid-air collision* ◆ *She's in her mid-thirties.*

midday /ˌmɪdˈdeɪ/ *noun* [U] at or around 12 o'clock in the middle of the day: *We arranged to meet **at midday**.* ◆ *the heat of the midday sun* **SYN** **noon** ➲ look at **midnight**

middle[1] /ˈmɪdl/ *noun* **1** [sing] **the middle (of sth)** the part, point or position that is at about the same distance from the two ends or sides of sth: *the white line **in the middle of** the road* ◆ *Here's a photo of me with my two brothers. I'm the one **in the middle**.*

> **HELP** **Middle** or **centre**? **Centre** and **middle** are often very similar in meaning, but centre is used when you mean the exact middle of something: *How do you find the centre of a circle?* ◆ *There was a large table in the middle of the room.* ◆ *The bee stung me **right in the middle** of my back.* When you are talking about a period of time only **middle** may be used: *in the middle of the night* ◆ *the middle of July*

2 [C] (*informal*) your waist: *I want to lose weight around my middle.*

IDM **be in the middle of sth/doing sth** to be busy doing sth: *Can you call back in five minutes—I'm in the middle of feeding the baby.*

in the middle of nowhere a long way from any town

middle[2] /ˈmɪdl/ *adj* [only *before* a noun] in the middle: *I wear my ring on my **middle finger*** (= the longest finger). ◆ *Pens are in the middle drawer.*

ˌmiddle ˈage *noun* [U] the time when you are about 40 to 60 years old: *in **early/late middle age*** ▶ **ˌmiddle-ˈaged** *adj*: *a middle-aged man*

the ˌMiddle ˈAges *noun* [pl] the period of European history from about 1100 to 1450 AD

ˌmiddle ˈclass *noun* [sing, with sing or pl verb] (also **the ˌmiddle ˈclasses** [pl]) the group of people in society whose members are neither very rich nor very poor and that includes professional and business people: *the **upper/lower middle class*** ◆ *the growth of the middle classes* ➲ look at **upper class**, **working class** ▶ **ˌmiddle-ˈclass** *adj*: *a middle-class background* ◆ *a middle-class attitude* (= traditional views, typical of the middle class)

the ˌMiddle ˈEast *noun* [sing] an area that covers SW Asia and NE Africa ▶ **ˌMiddle ˈEastern** *adj*

middleman /ˈmɪdlmæn/ *noun* [C] (*pl* **-men** /-men/) **1** a person or company who buys goods from the company that makes them and then sells them to sb else **2** a person who helps to arrange things between two people who do not want to talk directly to each other

ˈmiddle school *noun* [C] (in Britain) a school for children aged between 9 and 13

midge /mɪdʒ/ *noun* [C] a very small flying insect that can bite people **SYN** **gnat**

midget /ˈmɪdʒɪt/ *noun* [C] a very small person

> **HELP** Be careful. This word is considered offensive.

the Midlands /ˈmɪdləndz/ *noun* [sing, with sing or pl verb] the central part of England around Birmingham and Nottingham

midnight /ˈmɪdnaɪt/ *noun* [U] 12 o'clock at night: *They left the party **at midnight**.* ◆ *The clock struck midnight.* ➲ look at **midday**

midriff /ˈmɪdrɪf/ *noun* [C] the part of your body between your chest and your waist

midst /mɪdst/ *noun* [U] the middle of sth; among a group of people or things: *The country is **in the midst of** a recession.* ◆ *They realized with a shock that there was an enemy **in their midst**.*

midway /ˌmɪdˈweɪ/ *adj, adv* in the middle of a period of time or between two places: *The village lies midway between two large towns.* **SYN** **halfway**

midweek /ˌmɪdˈwiːk/ *noun* [U] the middle of the week (= Tuesday, Wednesday and Thursday) ▶ **midweek** *adv*: *If you travel midweek it will be less crowded.*

the Midwest /ˌmɪdˈwest/ *noun* [sing] the northern central part of the US

midwife /ˈmɪdwaɪf/ *noun* [C] (*pl* **midwives** /-waɪvz/) a person who is trained to help women give birth to babies

might[1] /maɪt/ *modal verb* (*negative* **might not**; *short form* **mightn't** /ˈmaɪtnt/) **1** used as the form of 'may' when you report what sb has said: *He said he might be late* (= his words were, 'I may be late'). **2** used for saying that sth is possible: *'Where's Vinay?' 'He might be upstairs.'* ◆ *I think I might have forgotten the tickets.* ◆ *She might not come if she's very busy.* **3** (*BrE formal*) used to ask for sth or suggest sth very politely: *I wonder if I might go home half an hour early today?* ⓘ For more information about modal verbs, look at the **Reference Section** at the back of this dictionary.

IDM **I might have known** used for saying that you are not surprised that sth has happened: *I might have known he wouldn't help.*

may/might as well (do sth) ➲ **well**[1]

you, etc. might do sth used when you are angry to say what sb could or should have done: *They might at least have phoned if they're not coming.*

might[2] /maɪt/ *noun* [U] (*formal*) great strength or power: *I pushed **with all** my **might**, but the rock did not move.*

mighty[1] /ˈmaɪti/ *adj* (**mightier**; **mightiest**) very strong or powerful

mighty² /ˈmaɪti/ *adv* (*AmE informal*) very: *That's mighty kind of you.*

migraine /ˈmiːɡreɪn/ *noun* [C,U] a terrible pain in your head that makes you feel sick

migrant /ˈmaɪɡrənt/ *noun* [C] a person who goes from one place to another, especially in order to find work

migrate /maɪˈɡreɪt/ *verb* [I] **1** (used about animals and birds) to travel from one part of the world to another at the same time every year **2** (used about a large number of people) to go and live and work in another place: *Country people were forced to migrate to the cities to find work.* ➲ look at **emigrate** ▶ **migration** /maɪˈɡreɪʃn/ *noun* [C,U] ▶ **migratory** /ˈmaɪɡrətri; maɪˈɡreɪtəri/ *adj*: *migratory flights/birds*

mike /maɪk/ (*informal*) = **microphone**

milage = **mileage**

⚷ **mild** /maɪld/ *adj* (**milder**; **mildest**) **1** not strong; not very bad: *a mild soap* ◆ *a mild winter* ◆ *a mild punishment* **2** kind and gentle: *He's a very mild man —you never see him get angry.* **3** (used about food) not having a strong taste: *mild cheese* ▶ **mildness** *noun* [U]

mildly /ˈmaɪldli/ *adv* **1** not very; slightly: *mildly surprised* **2** in a gentle way: *He spoke mildly to the child.*

⚷ **mile** /maɪl/ *noun* **1** [C] a measure of length; 1.6 kilometres. There are 1 760 yards in a **mile**: *The nearest beach is seven miles away.* ◆ *It's a seven-mile drive to the beach.* ℹ For more information about measurements, look at the section on using numbers at the back of this dictionary. **2 miles** [pl] a long way: *How much further is it? We've walked miles already.* ◆ *From the top of the hill you can see* **for miles**. **3** [C] a lot: *He missed the target by a mile.* ◆ *I'm feeling miles better this morning.*

IDM **see, hear, tell, spot, etc. sb/sth a mile off** (*informal*) used to say that sb/sth is very obvious: *He's lying—you can tell that a mile off.*

mileage (also **milage**) /ˈmaɪlɪdʒ/ *noun* **1** [C,U] the distance that has been travelled, measured in **miles**: *The car is five years old but it has a low mileage.* **2** [U] (*informal*) the amount of use that you get from sth: *The newspapers got a lot of mileage out of the scandal.*

mileometer = **milometer**

milestone /ˈmaɪlstəʊn/ *noun* [C] a very important event: *The concert was a milestone in the band's history.*

militant /ˈmɪlɪtənt/ *adj* ready to use force or strong pressure to get what you want: *The workers were in a very militant mood.* ▶ **militant** *noun* [C] ▶ **militancy** /-ənsi/ *noun* [U]

⚷ **military** /ˈmɪlətri/ *adj* [only *before* a noun] connected with soldiers or the army, navy, etc: *All men in that country have to do two years'* ***military service***. ◆ *to take military action*

militia /məˈlɪʃə/ *noun* [C, with sing or pl verb] a group of people who are not professional soldiers but who have had military training

⚷ **milk¹** /mɪlk/ *noun* [U] **1** a white liquid that is produced by some animals as food for their young. People drink milk and use it to make butter and cheese: *skimmed/long-life/low-fat milk* ◆ *a carton of milk* **2** a white liquid that is produced by women and female animals to feed their babies **3** the juice of some plants or trees that looks like milk: *coconut milk* ➲ picture on **page P14**

milk² /mɪlk/ *verb* [T] **1** to take milk from an animal such as a cow **2** to get as much money, advantage, etc. for yourself from sb/sth as you can, without caring about others: *He milked the company of a small fortune.*

milkman /ˈmɪlkmən/ *noun* [C] (*pl* **-men** /-mən/) a person who takes milk to people's houses every day

milkshake /ˈmɪlkʃeɪk/ *noun* [C,U] a drink made of milk with an added flavour of fruit or chocolate ➲ picture on **page P16**

milky /ˈmɪlki/ *adj* like milk, or made with milk: *milky white skin* ◆ *milky coffee*

the ˌMilky ˈWay = **the Galaxy**(2)

mill¹ /mɪl/ *noun* [C] **1** a building that contains a large machine that was used in the past for making grain into flour ➲ look at **windmill** **2** a factory that is used for making certain kinds of material: *a cotton/paper/steel mill* **3** a kitchen tool that is used for making sth into powder: *a pepper mill*

mill² /mɪl/ *verb* [T] to produce sth in a **mill**

PHR V **mill about/around** (*informal*) (used about a large number of people or animals) to move around in a place with no real purpose

millennium /mɪˈleniəm/ *noun* [C] (*pl* **millennia** /-niə/ *or* **millenniums**) a period of 1 000 years: *How did you celebrate the millennium?*

millet /ˈmɪlɪt/ *noun* [U] a plant with a lot of small seeds that are used as food for people and birds

milli- /ˈmɪli/ [in compounds] (used in units of measurement) one thousandth: *a millisecond*

⚷ **milligram** (also **milligramme**) /ˈmɪliɡræm/ *noun* [C] (*abbr* **mg**) a measure of weight. There are 1 000 **milligrams** in a gram.

millilitre (*AmE* **milliliter**) /ˈmɪliliːtə(r)/ *noun* [C] (*abbr* **ml**) a measure of liquid. There are 1 000 **millilitres** in a litre.

⚷ **millimetre** (*AmE* **millimeter**) /ˈmɪlimiːtə(r)/ *noun* [C] (*abbr* **mm**) a measure of length. There are 1 000 **millimetres** in a metre.

millinery /ˈmɪlɪnəri/ *noun* [U] the business of making or selling women's hats

⚷ **million** /ˈmɪljən/ *number* (*abbr* **m**) **1** 1 000 000: *Nearly 60 million people live in Britain.* ◆ *Millions of people are at risk from the disease.*

> **HELP** Notice that you use **million** without 's' when talking about more than one million: *six million people*

2 a million; **millions (of)** (*informal*) a very large amount: *I still have a million things to do.* ♦ *There are millions of reasons why you shouldn't go.* ℹ For more information about numbers, look at the section on using numbers at the back of this dictionary.

millionaire /ˌmɪljəˈneə(r)/ *noun* [C] a person who has a million pounds, dollars, etc.; a very rich person

millionth[1] /ˈmɪljənθ/ *ordinal number* 1 000 000th

millionth[2] /ˈmɪljənθ/ *noun* [C] one of a million equal parts of sth: *a millionth of a second*

milometer (also **mileometer**) /maɪˈlɒmɪtə(r)/ (*AmE* **odometer**, *informal* **clock**) *noun* [C] an instrument in a vehicle that measures the distance it has travelled

mime /maɪm/ (also **pantomime**) *noun* [U,C] the use of movements of your hands and body and the expression on your face to tell a story or to act sth without speaking; a performance using this method of acting: *The performance consisted of dance, music and mime.* ▶ **mime** *verb* [I,T]

mimic[1] /ˈmɪmɪk/ *verb* [T] (**mimicking**; **mimicked**) to copy sb's behaviour, movements, voice, etc. in an amusing way: *She's always mimicking the teachers.*

mimic[2] /ˈmɪmɪk/ *noun* [C] a person who can copy sb's behaviour, movements, voice, etc. in an amusing way: *He is a gifted mimic.* ▶ **mimicry** /ˈmɪmɪkri/ *noun* [U]

M

min. *abbr* **1** = **minute[1]** (1): *fastest time: 6 min.* **2** = **minimum[2]**: *min. temp tomorrow 2°* OPP **max**

minaret /ˌmɪnəˈret/ *noun* [C] a tall thin tower, usually part of a **mosque** (= a religious building), from which Muslims are called to come and say prayers

mince /mɪns/ (*AmE* **ground ˈbeef**; **hamburger**) *noun* [U] meat that has been cut into very small pieces with a special machine ▶ **mince** *verb* [T]

ˌmince ˈpie *noun* [C] a small round **pastry** (= a mixture of flour, fat and water) filled with **mincemeat** (= a mixture of dried fruit, sugar, etc.), traditionally eaten in Britain at Christmas time

mind[1] /maɪnd/ *noun* [C,U] the part of your brain that thinks and remembers; your thoughts, feelings and intelligence: *There were all sorts of thoughts running through my mind.* ♦ *My mind wandered as the teacher went on talking.* ♦ *He has a brilliant mind.* ♦ *Not everybody has the right sort of mind for this work.* ♦ *the* ***conscious/unconscious mind***

IDM **at/in the back of your mind** ➲ **back[1]**

be in two minds (about sth/ doing sth) ➲ **two**

be/go out of your mind (*informal*) to be or become crazy or very worried: *I was going out of my mind when Tina didn't come home on time.*

bear in mind (that); **bear/keep sb/sth in mind** to remember or consider (that); to remember sb/sth: *We'll bear/keep your suggestion in mind for the future.*

bring/call sb/sth to mind to be reminded of sb/sth; to remember sb/sth

cast your mind back ➲ **cast[1]**

change your mind ➲ **change[1]**

come/spring to mind if sth comes/springs to mind, you suddenly remember or think of it

cross your mind ➲ **cross[2]**

ease sb's mind ➲ **ease[2]**

frame of mind ➲ **frame[1]**

give sb a piece of your mind ➲ **piece[1]**

go clean out of your mind ➲ **clean[3]**

have sb/sth in mind (for sth) to be considering sb/sth as suitable for sth; to have a plan: *Who do you have in mind for the job?*

have/keep an open mind ➲ **open[1]**

keep your mind on sth to continue to pay attention to sth: *Keep your mind on the road while you're driving!*

make up your mind to decide: *I can't make up my mind which sweater to buy.*

on your mind worrying you: *Don't bother her with that. She's got enough on her mind already.*

prey on sb's mind ➲ **prey[2]**

put/set your/sb's mind at rest to make sb stop worrying: *The results of the blood test set his mind at rest.*

slip your mind ➲ **slip[1]**

speak your mind ➲ **speak**

state of mind ➲ **state[1]**

take sb's mind off sth to help sb not to think or worry about sth

to my mind in my opinion: *To my mind, this is a complete waste of time!*

mind[2] /maɪnd/ *verb* **1** [I,T] [usually in questions, answers, and negative sentences] to feel annoyed, upset or uncomfortable about sth/sb: *I'm sure Simon won't mind if you don't invite him.* ♦ *I don't mind what you do—it's your decision.* ♦ *Do you mind having to travel so far to work every day?* ♦ *Are you sure your parents won't mind me coming?* ♦ *'Would you like tea or coffee?' 'I don't mind.'* (= I'm happy to have either) ♦ *I wouldn't mind a break right now* (= I would like one). ➲ note at **matter[2]** **2** [T] (used in a question as a polite way of asking sb to do sth or for permission to do sth) could you ...?; may I ...?: *Would you mind closing the window for me?* ♦ *Do you mind driving? I'm feeling rather tired.* **3** [T] used to tell sb to be careful of sth or to pay attention to sb/sth: *It's a very low doorway so mind your head.* ♦ *Mind that step!* ♦ *Don't mind me! I won't disturb you.* **4** [T] (*especially BrE*) to look after or watch sb/sth for a short time: *Could you mind my bag while I go and get us some drinks?*

IDM **mind you** used for attracting attention to a point you are making or for giving more information: *Paul seems very tired. Mind you, he has been working very hard recently.*

mind your own business to pay attention to your own affairs, not other people's: *Stop asking me personal questions and mind your own business!*

never mind do not worry; it does not matter: *'I forgot to post your letter.' 'Never mind, I'll do it later.'*

PHR V **mind out** (*informal*) Get out of the way!: *Mind out! There's a car coming.*

ˈmind-boggling *adj* (*informal*) difficult to imagine, understand or believe: *Mind-boggling amounts of money were being discussed.*

minded /ˈmaɪndɪd/ *adj* [in compounds] **1** having the type of mind mentioned: *a strong-minded/open-minded/narrow-minded person* **2** interested in the thing mentioned: *money-minded*

minder /ˈmaɪndə(r)/ *noun* [C] a person whose job is to look after and protect sb/sth: *a star surrounded by her minders*

mindful /ˈmaɪndfl/ *adj* (*formal*) **mindful of sb/sth; mindful that** ... remembering sb/sth and considering them or it when you do sth: *Mindful of the danger of tropical storms, I decided not to go out.*

mindless /ˈmaɪndləs/ *adj* **1** done or acting without thought and for no particular reason: *mindless violence* **2** not needing thought or intelligence: *a mindless and repetitive task*

ˈ**mind map** (also spidergram) *noun* [C] a diagram that you make in order to plan a project, an essay, etc. You write down as many words and ideas as you can think of that are linked to the main topic.

WRITING TIP

Preparing to write

Making a mind map is a good way to **brainstorm** (= think of as many ideas as you can in a short time) your ideas before you start to write. You can then use this diagram as the basis of a plan for your writing.

ⓘ For more help with writing, look at **Wordpower Writing Tutor** at the back of this dictionary.

mine[1] /maɪn/ *pron* of or belonging to me: *'Whose is this jacket?' 'It's mine.'* ♦ *She wanted one like mine.* ♦ *May I introduce a friend of mine* (= one of my friends)? ➲ look at **my**

mine[2] /maɪn/ *noun* [C] **1** a deep hole, or a system of passages under the ground where minerals such as coal, tin, gold, etc. are dug: *a coal/salt/gold mine* ➲ look at **quarry** **2** a bomb that is hidden under the ground or underwater and explodes when sb/sth touches it: *The car went over a mine and blew up.*

mine[3] /maɪn/ *verb* **1** [I,T] to dig in the ground for minerals such as coal, tin, gold, etc: *Diamonds are mined in South Africa.* ➲ look at **mining** **2** [T] to put **mines**[2](2) in an area of land or sea

minefield /ˈmaɪnfiːld/ *noun* [C] **1** an area of land or sea where **mines**[2](2) have been hidden **2** a situation that is full of hidden dangers or difficulties: *a political minefield*

miner /ˈmaɪnə(r)/ *noun* [C] a person whose job is to work in a **mine**[2](1) to get coal, salt, tin, etc.

mineral /ˈmɪnərəl/ *noun* [C] a natural substance such as coal, salt, oil, etc., especially one that is found in the ground. Some minerals are also present in food and drink and are very important for good health: *a country rich in minerals* ♦ *the recommended daily intake of vitamins and minerals*

ˈ**mineral water** *noun* [U] water from a spring in the ground that contains minerals or gases and is thought to be good for your health

mingle /ˈmɪŋgl/ *verb* [I,T] **mingle A and B (together); mingle (A) (with B)** to mix with other things or people: *The colours slowly mingled together to make a muddy brown.* ♦ *His excitement was mingled with fear.* ♦ *to mingle with the rich and famous*

mini- /ˈmɪni/ [in compounds] very small: *a miniskirt* ♦ *minigolf*

miniature /ˈmɪnətʃə(r)/ *noun* [C] a small copy of sth which is much larger: *a miniature camera*
IDM **in miniature** exactly the same as sb/sth else but in a very small form

minibeast /ˈmɪnibiːst/ *noun* [C] (*BrE*) (used especially in schools) any small animal that does not have a **backbone** (= the row of bones in the middle of your back): *minibeasts such as worms, snails, centipedes, ants and spiders*

minibus /ˈmɪnibʌs/ *noun* [C] (*especially BrE*) a small bus with seats for about twelve people

minimal /ˈmɪnɪməl/ *adj* very small in amount, size or level; as little as possible: *The project must be carried out at minimal cost.*

minimize (also -ise) /ˈmɪnɪmaɪz/ *verb* [T] **1** to make sth as small as possible (in amount or level): *We shall try to minimize the risks to the public.* **2** to try to make sth seem less important than it really is **3** to make sth small on a computer screen OPP **maximize**

minimum[1] /ˈmɪnɪməm/ *adj* [only *before* a noun] the smallest possible or allowed; extremely small: *to introduce a national **minimum wage*** (= the lowest amount of money that an employer is legally allowed to pay workers) OPP **maximum** ▸ **minimum** *adv*: *We'll need £200 minimum for expenses.*

minimum[2] /ˈmɪnɪməm/ *noun* [sing] (*abbr* min.) the smallest amount or level that is possible or allowed: *I need a minimum of seven hours' sleep.* ♦ *We will try and **keep** the cost of the tickets **to a minimum**.* OPP **maximum**

mining /ˈmaɪnɪŋ/ *noun* [U] [in compounds] the process or industry of getting minerals, metals, etc. out of the ground by digging: *coal/tin/gold mining*

minister /ˈmɪnɪstə(r)/ *noun* [C] **1** (*BrE*) Minister a member of the government, often the head of a government department: *the Minister for Transport* ➲ look at **cabinet, prime minister, secretary** **2** a priest in some Protestant churches ➲ look at **vicar**

ministerial /ˌmɪnɪˈstɪəriəl/ *adj* connected with a government minister or department

ministry /ˈmɪnɪstri/ *noun* [C] (*pl* ministries) (*BrE*) (also department) a government department that has a particular area of responsibility: *the Ministry of Defence*

HELP **Department** is the only word used in American English.

mink /mɪŋk/ *noun* [C] a small wild animal that is kept for its thick brown fur which is used to make expensive coats

minor[1] /ˈmaɪnə(r)/ *adj* **1** not very big, serious or important (when compared with others): *It's only a minor problem. Don't worry.* ♦ *She's gone into*

M

hospital for a minor operation. **OPP** **major** **2** of one of the two types of **key**[1] (4) in which music is usually written: *a symphony in F minor* ➲ look at **major**

minor[2] /ˈmaɪnə(r)/ *noun* [C] (used in law) a person who is not legally an adult

MORE In Britain you are a minor until you are eighteen, which is when you **come of age**.

minority /maɪˈnɒrəti/ *noun* [C] (*pl* **minorities**) **1** [usually sing, with sing or pl verb] the smaller number or part of a group; less than half: *Only a minority of students become/becomes involved in politics.* **OPP** **majority** **2** a small group of people who are of a different race or religion to most of the people in the community or country where they live: *Schools in Britain need to do more to help children of* ***ethnic minorities****.*

IDM **be in a/the minority** to be the smaller of two groups: *Men are in the minority in the teaching profession.* ➲ look at **in a/the majority**

mint /mɪnt/ *noun* **1** [U] a **herb** (= a type of plant) whose leaves are used to give flavour to food, drinks, etc: *lamb with mint sauce* ➲ picture on **page P14** **2** [C] a type of sweet with a strong fresh flavour **3** [sing] the place where money in the form of coins and notes is made by the government ▶ **mint** *verb* [T]: *freshly minted coins*

minus[1] /ˈmaɪnəs/ *prep* **1** (used in sums) less; take away: *Six minus two is four (6–2 = 4).* **OPP** **plus** ➲ look at **subtract** **2** (used about a number) below zero: *The temperature will fall to minus 10.* **3** (*informal*) without sth that was there before: *We're going to be minus a car for a while.*

minus[2] /ˈmaɪnəs/ *noun* [C] **1** (also ˈ**minus sign**) the symbol (–) used in mathematics **2** (also ˈ**minus point**) (*informal*) a negative quality; a disadvantage: *Let's consider the pluses and minuses of moving out of the city.* **OPP** for both meanings **plus**

minus[3] /ˈmaɪnəs/ *adj* **1** (used in mathematics) lower than zero: *a minus figure* **2** [not before a noun] (used in a system of grades given for school work) slightly lower than: *I got A minus (A–) for my essay.* **OPP** for both meanings **plus**

minuscule /ˈmɪnəskjuːl/ *adj* extremely small

ˈ**minus point** = **minus**[2](2)

ˈ**minus sign** = **minus**[2](1)

minute[1] /ˈmɪnɪt/ *noun* **1** [C] (*abbr* min.) one of the 60 parts that make up one hour; 60 seconds: *It's twelve minutes to nine.* ◆ *He telephoned ten minutes ago.* ◆ *The programme lasts for about fifty minutes.* **2** [sing] (*spoken*) a very short time; a moment: ***Just/Wait a minute*** (= wait)! *You've forgotten your notes.* ◆ *Have you got a minute?—I'd like to talk to you.* **3 the minutes** [pl] a written record of what is said and decided at a meeting: *to take the minutes* (= to write them down)

IDM **(at) any minute/moment (now)** (*informal*) very soon: *The plane should be landing any minute now.*

in a minute very soon: *I'll be with you in a minute.*

the last minute/moment ➲ **last**[1] (1)

the minute/moment (that) as soon as: *I'll tell him you rang the minute (that) he gets here.*

this minute immediately; now: *I don't know what I'm going to do yet—I've just this minute found out.*

up to the minute (*informal*) having the most recent information: *For up to the minute information on flight times, phone this number ...*

minute[2] /maɪˈnjuːt/ *adj* (**minutest**) [no comparative] **1** very small: *I couldn't read his writing. It was minute!* **SYN** **tiny** **2** very exact or accurate: *She was able to describe the man* ***in minute/the minutest detail****.*

miracle /ˈmɪrəkl/ *noun* **1** [C] a wonderful event that seems impossible and that is believed to be caused by God or a god **2** [sing] a lucky thing that happens that you did not expect or think was possible: *It's a miracle (that) nobody was killed in the crash.*

IDM **work/perform miracles** to achieve very good results: *The new diet and exercise programme has worked miracles for her.*

miraculous /mɪˈrækjələs/ *adj* completely unexpected and very lucky: *She's made a miraculous recovery.* ▶ **miraculously** *adv*

mirage /ˈmɪrɑːʒ; mɪˈrɑːʒ/ *noun* [C] something that you think you see in very hot weather, for example water in a desert, but which does not really exist

mirror /ˈmɪrə(r)/ *noun* [C] a piece of special flat glass that you can look into in order to see yourself or what is behind you: *to look* ***in the mirror*** ◆ *a rear-view mirror* (= in a car, so that the driver can see what is behind) ➲ picture at **car** ➲ picture on **page P8**

MORE A mirror **reflects** images. What you see in a mirror is a **reflection**.

▶ **mirror** *verb* [T]: *The trees were mirrored in the lake.*

mirth /mɜːθ/ *noun* [U] (*written*) happiness, fun and the sound of people laughing: *There was much mirth in the audience.* **SYN** **merriment**

misapprehension /ˌmɪsæprɪˈhenʃn/ *noun* [U, C] (*formal*) to have the wrong idea about sth or to believe sth is true when it is not: *I was* ***under the misapprehension*** *that this course was for beginners.*

misbehave /ˌmɪsbɪˈheɪv/ *verb* [I] to behave badly **OPP** **behave** ▶ **misbehaviour** (*AmE* **misbehavior**) /ˌmɪsbɪˈheɪvjə(r)/ *noun* [U]

miscalculate /ˌmɪsˈkælkjuleɪt/ *verb* [I,T] to make a mistake in calculating or judging a situation, an amount, etc: *The driver totally miscalculated the speed at which the other car was travelling.* ▶ **miscalculation** /ˌmɪskælkjuˈleɪʃn/ *noun* [C,U]

miscarriage /ˈmɪskærɪdʒ/ *noun* [C,U] giving birth to a baby a long time before it is ready to be born, with the result that it cannot live ➲ look at **abortion**

IDM **a miscarriage of justice** an occasion when sb is punished for a crime that they did not do

miscarry /ˌmɪsˈkæri/ *verb* [I] (**miscarrying**; **miscarries**; *pt, pp* **miscarried**) to give birth to a baby before it is ready to be born, with the result that it cannot live

miscellaneous /ˌmɪsəˈleɪniəs/ *adj* consisting of many different types or things: *a box of miscellaneous items for sale*

mischief /ˈmɪstʃɪf/ *noun* [U] bad behaviour (usually of children) that is not very serious: *The children are always **getting into mischief**.*

mischievous /ˈmɪstʃɪvəs/ *adj* (usually used about children) liking to behave badly and embarrassing or annoying people ▶ **mischievously** *adv*

misconception /ˌmɪskənˈsepʃn/ *noun* [C] a wrong idea or understanding of sth: *It is a popular misconception* (= many people wrongly believe) *that people need meat to be healthy.*

misconduct /ˌmɪsˈkɒndʌkt/ *noun* [U] (*formal*) unacceptable behaviour, especially by a professional person: *The doctor was dismissed for **gross*** (= very serious) ***misconduct**.*

misconstrue /ˌmɪskənˈstruː/ *verb* [T] (*formal*) misconstrue sth (as sth) to understand sb's words or actions wrongly ➲ look at **construe**

misdemeanour (*AmE* misdemeanor) /ˌmɪsdɪˈmiːnə(r)/ *noun* [C] something slightly bad or wrong that a person does; a crime that is not very serious ➲ look at **felony**

miser /ˈmaɪzə(r)/ *noun* [C] a person who loves having a lot of money but hates spending it ▶ **miserly** *adj*

miserable /ˈmɪzrəbl/ *adj* **1** very unhappy: *Oh dear, you look miserable. What's wrong?* **2** unpleasant; making you feel unhappy: *What miserable weather!* (= grey, cold and wet) **SYN** **dismal** **3** too small or of bad quality: *I was offered a miserable salary so I didn't take the job.* ▶ **miserably** /-əbli/ *adv*: *I stared miserably out of the window.* ♦ *He **failed miserably** as an actor.*

misery /ˈmɪzəri/ *noun* [U,C] (*pl* miseries) great unhappiness or suffering: *I couldn't bear to see him in such misery.* ♦ *the miseries of war*

IDM **put sb out of their misery** (*informal*) to stop sb worrying about sth by telling the person what they want to know: *Put me out of my misery—did I pass or not?*

put sth out of its misery to kill an animal because it has an illness or injury that cannot be treated

misfire /ˌmɪsˈfaɪə(r)/ *verb* [I] to fail to have the intended result or effect: *The plan misfired.*

misfit /ˈmɪsfɪt/ *noun* [C] a person who is not accepted by other people, especially because their behaviour or ideas are very different

misfortune /ˌmɪsˈfɔːtʃuːn/ *noun* [C,U] (*formal*) (an event, accident, etc. that brings) bad luck or disaster: *I hope I don't ever **have the misfortune to** meet him again.*

misgiving /ˌmɪsˈɡɪvɪŋ/ *noun* [C,U] a feeling of doubt or worry: *I **had serious misgivings** about leaving him on his own.*

misguided /ˌmɪsˈɡaɪdɪd/ *adj* wrong because you have understood or judged a situation badly: *She only moved the victim in a misguided effort to help.*

mishap /ˈmɪshæp/ *noun* [C,U] a small accident or piece of bad luck that does not have serious results: *to have a slight mishap*

misinform /ˌmɪsɪnˈfɔːm/ *verb* [T] (*formal*) to give sb the wrong information: *I think you've been misinformed—no one is going to lose their job in the near future.*

misinterpret /ˌmɪsɪnˈtɜːprɪt/ *verb* [T] misinterpret sth (as sth) to understand sth wrongly: *His comments were misinterpreted as a criticism of the project.* **OPP** **interpret** ▶ **misinterpretation** /ˌmɪsɪntɜːprɪˈteɪʃn/ *noun* [C,U]: *Parts of the speech were **open to misinterpretation*** (= easy to understand wrongly).

misjudge /ˌmɪsˈdʒʌdʒ/ *verb* [T] **1** to form a wrong opinion of sb/sth, usually in a way which is unfair to them or it **2** to guess time, distance, etc. wrongly: *He misjudged the speed of the other car and almost crashed.* ▶ **misjudgement** (also misjudgment) *noun* [C,U]

mislay /ˌmɪsˈleɪ/ *verb* [T] (mislaying; mislays; *pt, pp* mislaid /-ˈleɪd/) to lose sth, usually for a short time, because you cannot remember where you put it

mislead /ˌmɪsˈliːd/ *verb* [T] (*pt, pp* misled /-ˈled/) to make sb have the wrong idea or opinion about sb/sth ▶ **misleading** *adj*: *a misleading advertisement*

M

mismanage /ˌmɪsˈmænɪdʒ/ *verb* [T] to manage or organize sth badly ▶ **mismanagement** *noun* [U]

misplaced /ˌmɪsˈpleɪst/ *adj* given to sb/sth that is not suitable or good enough to have it: *misplaced loyalty*

misprint /ˈmɪsprɪnt/ *noun* [C] a mistake in printing or typing

mispronounce /ˌmɪsprəˈnaʊns/ *verb* [T] to say a word or letter wrongly: *People always mispronounce my surname.* ▶ **mispronunciation** /ˌmɪsprəˌnʌnsiˈeɪʃn/ *noun* [C,U]

misread /ˌmɪsˈriːd/ *verb* [T] (*pt, pp* misread /-ˈred/) misread sth (as sth) to read or understand sth wrongly: *He misread my silence as a refusal.*

misrepresent /ˌmɪsˌreprɪˈzent/ *verb* [T, usually passive] to give a wrong description of sb/sth: *In the newspaper article they were misrepresented as uncaring parents.* ▶ **misrepresentation** /ˌmɪsˌreprɪzenˈteɪʃn/ *noun* [C,U]

🔑 **Miss** /mɪs/ used as a title before the family name of a young woman or a woman who is not married: *Dear Miss Holland, ...* ♦ *That's all, thank you, Miss Dawson.*

HELP **Miss**, **Mrs**, **Ms** and **Mr** are all titles that we use in front of sb's family name, NOT his/her first name, unless it is included with the family name: *Is there a Miss (Emma) Hudson here?* NOT: *Miss Emma*

🔑 **miss**[1] /mɪs/ *verb*

➤NOT HIT/CATCH **1** [I,T] to fail to hit, catch, etc. sth: *She tried to catch the ball but she missed.* ♦ *The bullet narrowly missed his heart.*

➤NOT SEE/HEAR **2** [T] to not see, hear, understand, etc.

sb/sth: *The house is on the corner, so **you can't miss it**.* ◆ *They completely **missed the point** of what I was saying.* ◆ *My Mum will know there's something wrong. She **doesn't miss much**.*

➤NOT GO **3** [T] to fail to go to or do sth: *Of course I'm coming to your wedding. I **wouldn't miss it for the world*** (= used to emphasize that you really want to do sth). ◆ *You can't afford to miss meals* (= not eat meals) *now you're pregnant.*

➤BE LATE **4** [T] to arrive too late for sb/sth: *Hurry up or you'll miss the train!*

➤FEEL SAD **5** [T] to feel sad because sb is not with you any more, or because you have not got or cannot do sth that you once had or did: *I'll miss you terribly when you go away.* ◆ *What did you miss most when you lived abroad?*

➤NOTICE STH NOT THERE **6** [T] to notice that sb/sth is not where they or it should be: *When did you first miss your handbag?*

➤AVOID STH BAD **7** [T] to avoid sth unpleasant: *If we leave now, we'll miss the rush-hour traffic.*

PHR V **miss sb/sth out** to not include sb/sth: *You've missed out several important points in your report.*

miss out (on sth) to not have a chance to have or do sth: *You'll miss out on all the fun if you stay at home.*

M

🔑 **miss[2]** /mɪs/ *noun* [C] a failure to hit, catch or reach sth: *After several misses he finally managed to hit the target.*

IDM **give sth a miss** (*especially BrE informal*) to decide not to do or have sth: *I think I'll give aerobics a miss tonight.*

a near miss ➲ **near[1]**

missile /ˈmɪsaɪl/ *noun* [C] **1** a powerful exploding weapon that can be sent long distances through the air: *nuclear missiles* **2** an object that is thrown at sb in order to hurt them: *The rioters threw missiles such as bottles and stones.*

🔑 **missing** /ˈmɪsɪŋ/ *adj* **1** lost, or not in the right or usual place: *a missing person* ◆ *Two files have **gone missing** from my office.* **2** (used about a person) not present after a battle, an accident, etc. but not known to have been killed: *Many soldiers were listed as **missing in action**.* **3** not included, often when it should have been: *Fill in the missing words in the text.*

mission /ˈmɪʃn/ *noun* [C]

➤OFFICIAL JOB/GROUP **1** an important official job that sb is sent somewhere to do, especially to another country: *Your mission is to send back information about the enemy's movements.* **2** a group of people who are sent to a foreign country to perform a special task: *a British trade mission to China*

➤PLACE **3** a place where people are taught about the Christian religion, given medical help, etc. by **missionaries**

➤YOUR DUTY **4** a particular task which you feel it is your duty to do: *Her work with the poor was more than just a job—it was her **mission in life**.*

➤JOURNEY **5** a special journey made by a **spacecraft** (= a vehicle that travels in space) or military aircraft: *a mission to the moon*

missionary /ˈmɪʃənri/ *noun* [C] (*pl* **missionaries**) a person who is sent to a foreign country to teach about the Christian religion

misspell /ˌmɪsˈspel/ *verb* [T] (*pt, pp* **misspelled** *or* **misspelt** /ˌmɪsˈspelt/) to spell sth wrongly

mist[1] /mɪst/ *noun* [C,U] a cloud made of very small drops of water in the air just above the ground, that makes it difficult to see: *The fields were covered in mist.* ➲ note at **fog, weather** ▶ **misty** *adj*: *a misty morning* ➲ look at **foggy**

mist[2] /mɪst/ *verb*

PHR V **mist (sth) up/over** to cover or be covered with very small drops of water that make it difficult to see: *My glasses misted up when I came in from the cold.*

🔑 **mistake[1]** /mɪˈsteɪk/ *noun* [C] something that you think or do that is wrong: *Try not to **make** any **mistakes** in your essays.* ◆ *a **spelling mistake*** ◆ *It was a big mistake to trust her.* ◆ ***I made the mistake of** giving him my address.*

IDM **by mistake** as a result of being careless: *The terrorists shot the wrong man by mistake.*

> OTHER WORDS FOR
>
> **mistake**
>
> **Error** is more formal than **mistake**: *a computing error.* When you **make a mistake** you **do** sth **wrong**: *I got the answer wrong.* ◆ *You must have the wrong number* (= on the phone). **Fault** indicates who is responsible for sth bad: *The accident wasn't my fault. The other driver pulled out in front of me.* **Fault** is also used to describe a problem or weakness that sb/sth has: *a technical fault.*

🔑 **mistake[2]** /mɪˈsteɪk/ *verb* [T] (*pt* **mistook** /mɪˈstʊk/; *pp* **mistaken** /mɪˈsteɪkən/) to be wrong about sth: *I think you've mistaken my meaning.* ◆ ***There was no mistaking*** (= it was impossible to mistake) *his anger.*

PHR V **mistake sb/sth for sb/sth** to think wrongly that sb/sth is sb/sth else: *I'm sorry, I mistook you for a friend of mine.*

🔑 **mistaken** /mɪˈsteɪkən/ *adj* wrong; not correct: *I thought the film was a comedy but I must have been mistaken.* ◆ *a case of mistaken identity* ◆ *a mistaken belief/idea* ▶ **mistakenly** *adv*

mistletoe /ˈmɪsltəʊ/ *noun* [U] a plant with white **berries** (= small round fruit) and green leaves. **Mistletoe** grows on trees.

> CULTURE
>
> Mistletoe is used as a decoration inside houses in Britain at Christmas time. There is a tradition of kissing people 'under the mistletoe'.

mistook *past tense* of **mistake[2]**

mistreat /ˌmɪsˈtriːt/ *verb* [T] to be cruel to a person or an animal: *The owner of the zoo was accused of mistreating the animals.* ▶ **mistreatment** *noun* [U]

mistress /ˈmɪstrəs/ *noun* [C] **1** a woman who is having a secret sexual relationship with a married man **2** (*formal*) a woman who is in authority or control: *She is the mistress of plain speech.*

mistrust /ˌmɪsˈtrʌst/ *verb* [T] to have no confidence in sb/sth because you think they or it may be harmful: *I always mistrust politicians who smile too much.* ➲ look at **distrust** ▶ **mistrust** *noun* [U, sing]: *She has a deep mistrust of strangers.*

misty /ˈmɪsti/ ➲ **mist**[1]

misunderstand /ˌmɪsʌndəˈstænd/ *verb* [I,T] (*pt, pp* **misunderstood** /-ˈstʊd/) to understand sb/sth wrongly: *I misunderstood the instructions and answered too many questions.*

misunderstanding /ˌmɪsʌndəˈstændɪŋ/ *noun* **1** [C,U] a situation in which sb/sth is not understood correctly: *The contract is written in both languages to avoid any misunderstanding.* **2** [C] a disagreement or an argument

misuse /ˌmɪsˈjuːz/ *verb* [T] to use sth in the wrong way or for the wrong purpose: *These chemicals can be dangerous if misused.* ▶ **misuse** /ˌmɪsˈjuːs/ *noun* [C,U]

mitigate /ˈmɪtɪgeɪt/ *verb* [T] (*formal*) to make sth less serious, painful, unpleasant, etc. ▶ **mitigating** *adj*: *Because of the* ***mitigating circumstances*** (= that made the crime seem less bad) *the judge gave her a lighter sentence.*

mitten /ˈmɪtn/ (*also* **mitt** /mɪt/) *noun* [C] a type of glove that has one part for the thumb and another part for all four fingers ➲ look at **glove** ➲ picture at **glove**

⚷ **mix**[1] /mɪks/ *verb* **1** [I,T] mix (A) (with B); mix (A and B) (together) if two or more substances mix or if you mix them, they combine to form a new substance: *Oil and water don't mix.* ◆ *Mix all the ingredients together in a bowl.* ◆ *to mix a cocktail* (= by mixing various drinks) **2** [I] mix (with sb) to be with and talk to other people: *He mixes with all types of people at work.* **3** [T] to combine different recordings of voices and/or instruments to produce a single piece of music

IDM **be/get mixed up in sth** (*informal*) to be/become involved in sth bad or unpleasant

PHR V **mix sth up** to put sth in the wrong order: *He was so nervous that he dropped his speech and got the pages all mixed up.*

mix sb/sth up (with sb/sth) to confuse sb/sth with sb/sth else: *I always get him mixed up with his brother.*

⚷ **mix**[2] /mɪks/ *noun* **1** [C, usually sing] a group of different types of people or things: *We need a good racial mix in the police force.* **2** [C,U] a special powder that contains all the substances needed to make sth. You add water or another liquid to this powder: *cake mix*

⚷ **mixed** /mɪkst/ *adj* **1** being both good and bad: *I* ***have mixed feelings*** *about leaving my job.* **2** made or consisting of different types of person or thing: *Was your school mixed or single-sex?* ◆ *a mixed salad*

ˌmixed ˈmarriage *noun* [C] a marriage between people of different races or religions

ˌmixed-ˈup *adj* (*informal*) confused because of emotional problems: *He has been very mixed-up since his parents' divorce.*

mixers

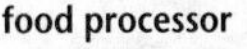

food processor

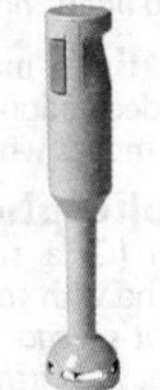

hand-held blender

blender (*BrE also* **liquidizer**)

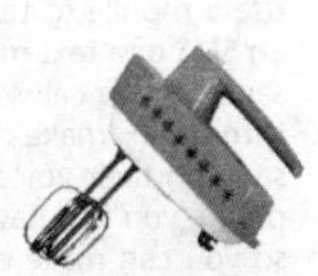

electric whisk

mixer /ˈmɪksə(r)/ *noun* [C] a machine that is used for mixing sth: *a food/cement mixer*

⚷ **mixture** /ˈmɪkstʃə(r)/ *noun* **1** [sing] a combination of different things: *Monkeys eat a mixture of leaves and fruit.* ◆ *I stood and stared with a mixture of amazement and horror.* **2** [C,U] a substance that is made by mixing other substances together: *cake mixture* ◆ *a mixture of eggs, flour and milk*

ˈmix-up *noun* [C] (*informal*) a mistake in the planning or organization of sth: *There was a mix-up and we were given the wrong ticket.*

ml *abbr* = **millilitre**: *contents 75ml*

mm *abbr* = **millimetre**: *a 35mm camera*

mo *abbr* (*AmE*) (*pl* **mos**) = **month**

moan /məʊn/ *verb* [I] **1** to make a low sound because you are in pain, very sad, etc: *to moan with pain* **2** (*informal*) to keep saying what is wrong about sth; to complain: *The English are always moaning about the weather.* ▶ **moan** *noun* [C]

moat /məʊt/ *noun* [C] a hole that was dug around a castle and filled with water to make it difficult for enemies to attack

mob[1] /mɒb/ *noun* [C, with sing or pl verb] a large crowd of people that may become violent or cause trouble

mob[2] /mɒb/ *verb* [T] (**mobbing**; **mobbed**) to form a large crowd around sb, for example in order to see or touch them: *The band was mobbed by fans as they left the hotel.*

⚷ **mobile**[1] /ˈməʊbaɪl/ *adj* able to move or be moved easily: *My daughter is much more mobile now she has*

M

her own car. ♦ *a mobile shop/library* ▶ **mobility** /məʊˈbɪləti/ *noun* [U]

mobile² /ˈməʊbaɪl/ *noun* [C] **1** = **mobile phone** **2** a decoration that you hang from the ceiling and that moves when the air around it moves

ˈmobile phone (*BrE* **mobile**; *AmE* **cellphone**) *noun* [C] a small telephone that you can carry around with you ➲ note at **telephone**: *In most countries it's illegal to drive while using a mobile phone.* ♦ *Please switch off your mobile before the performance begins.*

TOPIC

Mobile phones

Calling from a **mobile phone/cellphone** can be more convenient than from a **landline** (= a normal telephone), because **mobiles** can be used anywhere where there is a **signal**. You can also use a mobile to **text** somebody/**send** somebody an **SMS** or a **text message** (= a short written message). If you call somebody, but you cannot **get through** (= make contact), you can leave a message on their **voicemail**. To use a **pay-as-you-go** phone you first have to buy **credit** (= pay money so you can make calls and send text messages), and then **top up** your phone (= pay more money) when the credit **runs out**. You also need to **recharge** your phone when its **battery** is **flat** (= not producing electricity).

mobilize (also -ise) /ˈməʊbəlaɪz/ *verb* **1** [T] to organize people or things to do sth: *They mobilized the local residents to oppose the new development.* **2** [I,T] (used about the army, navy, etc.) to get ready for war

mock¹ /mɒk/ *verb* [I,T] (*formal*) to laugh at sb/sth in an unkind way or to make other people laugh at them or it ➲ Less formal and more common expressions are **laugh at** and **make fun of**.

mock² /mɒk/ *adj* [only *before* a noun] not real or genuine: *He held up his hands in mock surprise.* ♦ *a mock interview/examination*

mock³ /mɒk/ *noun* [usually pl] (in Britain) a practice exam that you do before the official one

EXAM TIP

Mock exams

A mock exam gives you the chance to work under exam conditions, to discover your strengths and weaknesses and whether you can complete the exam in the time allowed. When you get the results of your mock exam, pay special attention to what you got wrong, so that you can practise and improve for the real exam.

mockery /ˈmɒkəri/ *noun* [U] comments or actions that make sb/sth look silly or stupid: *She couldn't stand any more of their mockery.* SYN **ridicule**

IDM **make a mockery of sth** to make sth seem silly or useless: *The trial made a mockery of justice* (= the trial was not fair).

ˈmock-up *noun* [C] a model of sth that shows what it will look like or how it will work

modal /ˈməʊdl/ (also **modal ˈverb**) *noun* [C] a verb, for example 'might', 'can' or 'must' that is used with another verb for expressing possibility, permission, intention, etc. ⓘ For more information about modal verbs, look at the **Reference Section** at the back of this dictionary.

mode /məʊd/ *noun* [C] **1** a type of sth or way of doing sth: *a mode of transport/life* **2** one of the ways in which a machine can work: *Switch the camera to automatic mode.*

model¹ /ˈmɒdl/ *noun* [C]
➤COPY **1** a copy of sth that is usually smaller than the real thing: *a model aeroplane* ♦ *a working model* (= one in which the parts move) ➲ picture on **page P3**
➤MACHINE **2** one of the machines, vehicles, etc. that is made by a particular company: *The latest models are on display at the show.*
➤GOOD EXAMPLE **3** a person or thing that is a good example to copy: *a model student* ♦ *Children often use older brothers or sisters as* ***role models*** (= copy the way they behave).
➤FASHION **4** a person who is employed to wear clothes at a fashion show or for magazine photographs: *a fashion/male model*
➤FOR ARTIST **5** a person who is painted, drawn or photographed by an artist: *Gwen John was Rodin's model.*

model² /ˈmɒdl/ *verb* (**modelling**; **modelled**, (*AmE*) **modeling**; **modeled**) **1** [I,T] to wear and show clothes at a fashion show or for photographs: *to model swimsuits* **2** [I,T] to make a model of sth: *This clay is difficult to model.*

PHR V **model sth/yourself on sb/sth** to make sth/yourself similar to sth/sb else: *The house is modelled on a Roman villa.*

modelling (*AmE* **modeling**) /ˈmɒdəlɪŋ/ *noun* [U] the work of a fashion model

modem /ˈməʊdem/ *noun* [C] a piece of equipment that connects two or more computers together by means of a telephone line so that information can go from one to the other ➲ note at **Internet**

moderate¹ /ˈmɒdərət/ *adj* **1** being, having, using, etc. neither too much nor too little of sth: *a moderate speed* ♦ *We've had a moderate amount of success.* **2** having or showing opinions, especially about politics, that are not extreme: *moderate policies/views* ➲ look at **extreme, radical** ▶ **moderately** *adv*: *His career has been moderately successful.*

moderate² /ˈmɒdəreɪt/ *verb* [I,T] to become or to make sth less strong or extreme: *The union moderated its original demands.* ▶ **moderator** *noun* [C] a person who prevents offensive material from being published on a website: *A moderator had removed the message.* ➲ note at **chat room**

moderate³ /ˈmɒdərət/ *noun* [C] a person whose opinions, especially about politics, are not extreme ➲ look at **extremist**

moderation /ˌmɒdəˈreɪʃn/ *noun* [U] the quality of being reasonable and not being extreme: *Alcohol can harm unborn babies even if it's taken* ***in moderation****.*

🔑 **modern** /ˈmɒdn/ *adj* **1** of the present or recent times: *Pollution is one of the major problems in the modern world.* **2** [only *before* a noun] (used about styles of art, music, etc.) new and different from traditional styles: *modern jazz/architecture/art* **3** having all the newest methods, equipment, designs, etc: *It is one of the most modern hospitals in the country.* **SYN** **up to date** ➲ look at **old-fashioned**

modernize (also -ise) /ˈmɒdənaɪz/ *verb* [T] to make sth suitable for use today using new methods, styles, etc. ▸ **modernization** (also -isation) /ˌmɒdənaɪˈzeɪʃn/ *noun* [U]: *The house is large but is in need of modernization.*

ˌmodern ˈlanguage *noun* [usually pl] a language that is spoken now and that you study at school or college

modest /ˈmɒdɪst/ *adj* **1** not very large: *a modest pay increase* **2** not talking too much about your own abilities, good qualities, etc: *She got the best results in the exam but she was too modest to tell anyone.* ➲ look at **humble, proud 3** (used about a woman's clothes) not showing much of the body ▸ **modesty** *noun* [U] ▸ **modestly** *adv*

modify /ˈmɒdɪfaɪ/ *verb* [T] (modifying; modifies; *pt*, *pp* modified) to change sth slightly: *We shall need to modify the existing plan.* ▸ **modification** /ˌmɒdɪfɪˈkeɪʃn/ *noun* [C,U]

modular /ˈmɒdjələ(r)/ *adj* **1** (used about a course of study, especially at a British university or college) consisting of separate units from which students may choose several: *a modular course* **2** (used about machines, buildings, etc.) consisting of separate parts or units that can be joined together

module /ˈmɒdjuːl/ *noun* [C] a unit that forms part of sth bigger: *You must complete three modules* (= courses that you study) *in your first year.*

mohair /ˈməʊheə(r)/ *noun* [U] very soft wool that comes from a **goat** (= a small animal with horns that lives in mountain areas): *a mohair jumper*

Mohammed = **Muhammad**

moist /mɔɪst/ *adj* slightly wet: *Her eyes were moist with tears.* ◆ *Keep the soil moist or the plant will die.* ➲ note at **wet** ▸ **moisten** /ˈmɔɪsn/ *verb* [I,T]

moisture /ˈmɔɪstʃə(r)/ *noun* [U] water in small drops on a surface, in the air, etc.

moisturize (*BrE also* -ise) /ˈmɔɪstʃəraɪz/ *verb* [I,T] to put a special cream on your skin to make it less dry ▸ **moisturizer** (*BrE also* -iser /-raɪzə(r)/) *noun* [C,U]

molar /ˈməʊlə(r)/ *noun* [C] one of the large teeth at the back of your mouth

molasses /məˈlæsɪz/ (*AmE*) = **treacle**

mold, moldy (*AmE*) = **mould, mouldy**

mole /məʊl/ *noun* [C] **1** a small animal with dark fur that lives underground and is almost unable to see **2** a small dark spot on sb's skin that never goes away ➲ look at **freckle 3** (*informal*) a person who works in one organization and gives secret information to another organization ➲ look at **spy**

molecule /ˈmɒlɪkjuːl/ *noun* [C] the smallest unit into which a substance can be divided without changing its chemical nature ➲ look at **atom**

molest /məˈlest/ *verb* [T] to attack sb, especially a child, in a sexual way

mollusc (*AmE* mollusk) /ˈmɒləsk/ *noun* [C] any creature with a soft body that is not divided into different sections, and usually a hard outer shell. **Snails** and **slugs** are **molluscs**. ➲ look at **shellfish**

molt (*AmE*) = **moult**

molten /ˈməʊltən/ *adj* (used about metal or rock) made liquid by very great heat

🔑 **mom** /mɒm/ (*AmE*) = **mum**

🔑 **moment** /ˈməʊmənt/ *noun* **1** [C] a very short period of time: *One moment, please* (= please wait). ◆ *Joe left just a few moments ago.* **2** [sing] a particular point in time: *Just at that moment my mother arrived.* ◆ *the moment of birth/death* ◆ *I'm waiting for* ***the right moment*** *to give him the news.*

IDM **(at) any minute/moment (now)** ➲ **minute**[1]

at the moment now: *I'm afraid she's busy at the moment. Can I take a message?* ➲ note at **actually**

for the moment/present for a short time; for now: *This coat is fine for the moment, but I'll need a new one next winter.*

in a moment very soon: *Just wait here. I'll be back in a moment.*

the last minute/moment ➲ **last**[1]

the minute/moment (that) ➲ **minute**[1]

on the spur of the moment ➲ **spur**[1]

momentary /ˈməʊməntri/ *adj* lasting for a very short time: *a momentary lack of concentration* ▸ **momentarily** /-trəli/ *adv*

momentous /məˈmentəs/ *adj* very important: *a momentous decision/event/change*

momentum /məˈmentəm/ *noun* [U] the ability to keep increasing or developing; the force that makes sth move faster and faster: *The environmental movement is* ***gathering momentum****.*

mommy /ˈmɒmi/ (*AmE*) = **mummy**(1)

Mon. *abbr* = **Monday**: *Mon. 6 June*

monarch /ˈmɒnək/ *noun* [C] a king or queen

monarchy /ˈmɒnəki/ *noun* (*pl* monarchies) **1** [sing,U] the system of government or rule by a king or queen **2** [C] a country that is governed by a king or queen ➲ look at **republic**

monastery /ˈmɒnəstri/ *noun* [C] (*pl* monasteries) a place where **monks** (= religious men) live together in a religious community ➲ look at **convent**

🔑 **Monday** /ˈmʌndeɪ; -di/ *noun* [C,U] (*abbr* Mon.) the day of the week after Sunday: *I visit my grandparents every Monday after school.*

M

HELP Days of the week are always written with a capital letter. Note how we use them in sentences: *I'm going to see her* **on Monday**. ◆ *(informal) I'll see you Monday.* ◆ *I finish work a bit later* **on Mondays/on a Monday**. ◆ *Monday morning/afternoon/evening/night* ◆ *last/next Monday* ◆ *a week on Monday/Monday week* (= not next Monday, but the Monday after that) ◆ *The museum is open Monday to Friday, 10 till 4.30.* ◆ *Did you see that article about Italy in Monday's paper?*

monetary /ˈmʌnɪtri/ *adj* [only *before* a noun] connected with money: *the government's monetary policy*

money

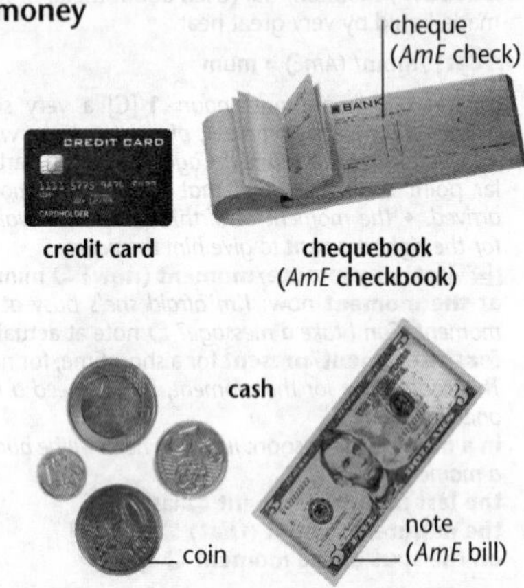

TOPIC

Money

You can **save** money in a bank **account**, and this money is called your **savings**. You can spend **cash** (= notes and coins) to buy things, or you can write a **cheque**. If you use a **debit card**, the money comes straight out of your bank account. If you use a **credit card**, you pay later. If you have a **cash card**, you can **withdraw** (= take out) money from your bank account at a **cash machine**. If you spend more money than is in your account you are **overdrawn**.

Some people **invest** money, for example in the **stock exchange**, and make a **fortune** (= a large amount of money). People who have a lot of money are **rich/wealthy**, and someone who often **gives** money **away**, for example to **charity**, is **generous**.

🔑 **money** /ˈmʌni/ *noun* [U] the means of paying for sth or buying sth (= coins or notes): *Will you* **earn** *more* **money** *in your new job?* ◆ *The new road will* **cost** *a lot of* **money**. ◆ *If we do the work ourselves we will* **save money**. ◆ *The government* **make** *a huge amount of* **money** *out of tobacco tax.* ➲ note at **pay** ➲ look at **pocket money**

IDM **be rolling in money/in it** ➲ **roll²**

get your money's worth to get full value for the money you have spent

to put money on sth to bet money on sth: *He put all his money on a horse.* **SYN** **bet** ➲ note at **loan**

money order (*AmE*) = **postal order**

mongrel /ˈmʌŋɡrəl/ *noun* [C] a dog that has parents of different breeds ➲ look at **pedigree**

🔑 **monitor¹** /ˈmɒnɪtə(r)/ *noun* [C] **1** a machine that shows information or pictures on a screen like a TV: *a PC with a 17-inch colour monitor* ➲ picture at **computer** **2** a machine that records or checks sth: *A monitor checks the baby's heartbeat.*

🔑 **monitor²** /ˈmɒnɪtə(r)/ *verb* [T] to check, record or test sth regularly for a period of time: *Pollution levels in the lake are closely monitored.*

monk /mʌŋk/ *noun* [C] a member of a religious group of men who live in a **monastery** (= a special building) and do not get married or have possessions ➲ look at **nun**

monkey

gorilla

monkey /ˈmʌŋki/ *noun* [C] an animal with a long tail that lives in hot countries and can climb trees ➲ look at **ape**

MORE **Chimpanzees** and **gorillas** are **apes**, although people sometimes call them monkeys.

IDM **monkey business** silly or dishonest behaviour

mono /ˈmɒnəʊ/ *adj* (used about recorded music or a system for playing it) having the sound coming from one direction only ➲ look at **stereo**

mono- /ˈmɒnəʊ/ [combining form] (in nouns and adjectives) one; single: *monorail* ◆ *monogamy*

monochrome /ˈmɒnəkrəʊm/ *adj* (used about a photograph or picture) using only black, white and shades of grey

monoculture /ˈmɒnəkʌltʃə(r)/ *noun* [U] the practice of growing only one type of crop on a certain area of land

monogamy /məˈnɒɡəmi/ *noun* [U] the fact or custom of being married to, or having a sexual relationship with, only one person at a particular time ➲ look at **bigamy, polygamy** ▶ **monogamous** /məˈnɒɡəməs/ *adj*: *a monogamous relationship* ◆ *Most birds are monogamous.*

monolingual /ˌmɒnəˈlɪŋgwəl/ *adj* using only one language: *This is a monolingual dictionary.* ➲ look at **bilingual**

monologue (*AmE* also **monolog**) /ˈmɒnəlɒg/ *noun* [C] a long speech by one person, for example in a play

monopolize (also -ise) /məˈnɒpəlaɪz/ *verb* [T] to control sth so that other people cannot share it: *She completely monopolized the conversation. I couldn't get a word in.*

monopoly /məˈnɒpəli/ *noun* [C] (*pl* **monopolies**) **a monopoly (on/in sth) 1** the control of an industry or service by only one company; a type of goods or a service that is controlled in this way: *The company has a monopoly on broadcasting international football.* **2** the complete control, possession or use of sth; something that belongs to only one person or group and is not shared

monorail /ˈmɒnəʊreɪl/ *noun* [C] a railway in which the train runs on a single track, usually high above the ground

monosyllabic /ˌmɒnəsɪˈlæbɪk/ *adj* **1** having only one syllable: *a monosyllabic word* **2** saying very little, in a way that seems rude to other people

monosyllable /ˈmɒnəsɪləbl/ *noun* [C] a short word, such as 'leg', that has only one syllable

monotonous /məˈnɒtənəs/ *adj* never changing and therefore boring: *monotonous work* ♦ *a monotonous voice* ▶ **monotonously** *adv*

monotony /məˈnɒtəni/ *noun* [U] the state of being always the same and therefore boring: *the monotony of working on a production line*

monsoon /ˌmɒnˈsuːn/ *noun* [C] the season when it rains a lot in Southern Asia; the rain that falls during this period

monster /ˈmɒnstə(r)/ *noun* [C] (in stories) a creature that is large, ugly and frightening: *a monster with three heads* ♦ (*figurative*) *The murderer was described as a dangerous monster.*

monstrosity /mɒnˈstrɒsəti/ *noun* [C] (*pl* **monstrosities**) something that is very large and ugly, especially a building

monstrous /ˈmɒnstrəs/ *adj* **1** that people think is shocking and unacceptable because it is morally wrong or unfair: *It's monstrous that she earns less than he does for the same job!* **2** very large (and often ugly or frightening): *a monstrous creature*

⚷ **month** /mʌnθ/ *noun* [C] (*abbr* **mth**) **1** one of the twelve periods of time into which the year is divided: *They are starting work next month.* ♦ *Have you seen this month's 'Vogue'?* **2** the period of about 30 days from a certain date in one month to the same date in the next, for example 13 May to 13 June: *'How long will you be away?' 'For about a month.'* ♦ *a six-month course*

monthly¹ /ˈmʌnθli/ *adj, adv* (happening or produced) once every month: *a monthly meeting/magazine/visit* ♦ *Are you paid weekly or monthly?*

monthly² /ˈmʌnθli/ *noun* [C] (*pl* **monthlies**) a magazine that is published once a month

monument /ˈmɒnjumənt/ *noun* [C] **a monument (to sb/sth) 1** a building or statue that is built to remind people of a famous person or event **2** an old building or other place that is of historical importance

monumental /ˌmɒnjuˈmentl/ *adj* [only *before* a noun] very great, large or important: *a monumental success/task/achievement*

moo /muː/ *noun* [C] the sound that a cow makes ➲ note at **cow** ▶ **moo** *verb* [I]

⚷ **mood** /muːd/ *noun* **1** [C,U] the way that you are feeling at a particular time: *to be in a bad/good mood* (= to feel angry/happy) ♦ *Turn that music down a bit—I'm not* ***in the mood for*** *it.* ♦ *Are you* ***in the mood to*** *go and see a film tonight?* **2** [C] a time when you are angry or bad-tempered: *Becky's in one of her moods again.* **SYN** **temper 3** [sing] the way that a group of people feel about sth: *The mood of the crowd suddenly changed and violence broke out.*

moody /ˈmuːdi/ *adj* (**moodier; moodiest**) **1** often changing moods in a way that people cannot predict: *You never know where you are with Andy because he's so moody.* **2** bad-tempered or unhappy, often for no particular reason ▶ **moodily** *adv* ▶ **moodiness** *noun* [U]

⚷ **moon** /muːn/ *noun* **1 the moon** [sing] the object that shines in the sky at night and that moves round the earth once every 28 days: *The moon's very bright tonight.* ➲ picture at **eclipse**

> **MORE** The moon as it appears at its different stages, can be called a **new moon**, a **full moon**, a **half-moon** or a **crescent moon**.

➲ *adjective* **lunar 2** [C] an object like the moon that moves around another planet: *How many moons does Neptune have?*

IDM **once in a blue moon** ➲ **once**

over the moon (*informal*) (*especially BrE*) extremely happy and excited about sth

moonlight /ˈmuːnlaɪt/ *noun* [U] light that comes from the moon: *The lake looked beautiful in the moonlight.*

moonlit /ˈmuːnlɪt/ *adj* lit by the moon

moor¹ /mɔː(r); mʊə(r)/ (also **moorland**) *noun* [C, U] a wild open area of high land that is covered with grass and **heather** (= a low plant that has small purple, pink or white flowers): *We walked across* ***the moors.*** ➲ look at **heath**

moor² /mɔː(r); mʊə(r)/ *verb* [I,T] **moor (sth to sth)** to fasten a boat to the land or to an object in the water with a rope or chain

mooring /ˈmɔːrɪŋ/ *noun* [C, usually pl] a place where a boat is tied; the ropes, chains, etc. used to fasten a boat

moorland /ˈmɔːlənd/ = **moor¹**

moose /muːs/ (*AmE*) = **elk**

M

mop[1] /mɒp/ *noun* [C] a tool for washing floors that has a long handle with a bunch of thick strings or soft material at the end ➲ picture at **bucket**

mop[2] /mɒp/ *verb* [T] (mopping; mopped) **1** to clean a floor with water and a **mop** **2** to remove liquid from sth using a dry cloth: *to mop your forehead with a handkerchief*

PHR V **mop sth up** to get rid of liquid from a surface with a **mop** or dry cloth: *Mop up that tea you've spilt or it'll leave a stain!*

mope /məʊp/ *verb* [I] mope (about/around) to spend your time doing nothing and feeling sorry for yourself because you are unhappy: *Moping around the house all day won't make the situation any better.*

moped /ˈməʊped/ *noun* [C] a type of small, not very powerful motorbike

⚷ **moral**[1] /ˈmɒrəl/ *adj* **1** [only *before* a noun] concerned with what is right and wrong: *Some people refuse to eat meat* ***on moral grounds*** (= because they believe it to be wrong). ♦ *a moral dilemma/issue/question* **2** having a high standard of behaviour that is considered good and right by most people: *She has always led a very moral life.* OPP **immoral** ➲ look at **amoral**

IDM **moral support** help or confidence that you give to sb who is nervous or worried: *I went to the dentist's with him just to give him some moral support.*

moral[2] /ˈmɒrəl/ *noun* **1** morals [pl] standards of good behaviour: *These people appear to have no morals.* **2** [C] a lesson in the right way to behave that can be learnt from a story or an experience: *The moral of the play is that friendship is more important than money.*

morale /məˈrɑːl/ *noun* [U] how happy, sad, confident, etc. a group of people feels at a particular time: *The team's morale was low/high before the match* (= they felt worried/confident). ♦ *to boost/raise/improve morale*

morality /məˈræləti/ *noun* [U] principles concerning what is good and bad or right and wrong behaviour: *a debate about the morality of abortion* SYN **ethics** OPP **immorality**

moralize (also -ise) /ˈmɒrəlaɪz/ *verb* [I] moralize (about/on sth) to tell other people what the right or wrong way to behave is

⚷ **morally** /ˈmɒrəli/ *adv* connected with standards of what is right or wrong: *Parents should be morally responsible for their children.* ♦ *morally right/wrong*

morbid /ˈmɔːbɪd/ *adj* showing interest in unpleasant things, for example disease and death

⚷ **more**[1] /mɔː(r)/ *determiner, pron* a larger number or amount of people or things; something extra as well as what you have: *There were* ***more*** *people* ***than*** *I expected.* ♦ *We had more time than we thought.* ♦ *There's room for three more people.* ♦ *I couldn't eat any more.* ♦ *I can't stand much more of this.* ♦ *Tell me more about your job.* OPP **less, fewer**

IDM **more and more** an increasing amount or number: *There are more and more cars on the road.*

what's more (used for adding another fact) also; in addition: *The hotel was awful and what's more it was miles from the beach.*

⚷ **more**[2] /mɔː(r)/ *adv* **1** used to form the comparative of many adjectives and adverbs: *She was* ***far/much more*** *intelligent* ***than*** *her sister.* ♦ *a course for more advanced students* ♦ *Please write more carefully.* OPP **less** **2** to a greater degree than usual or than sth else: *I like him* ***far/much more*** *than his wife.* OPP for both meanings **less**

IDM **more or less** approximately; almost: *We are more or less the same age.*

the more, less, etc. ... the more, less, etc. ... used to show that two things change to the same degree: *The more she thought about it, the more depressed she became.*

not any more not any longer: *She doesn't live here any more.*

⚷ **moreover** /mɔːrˈəʊvə(r)/ *adv* (*written*) (used for adding another fact) also; in addition: *This firm did the work very well. Moreover, the cost was not too high.*

morgue /mɔːg/ *noun* [C] a building where dead bodies are kept until they are buried or burned ➲ look at **mortuary**

⚷ **morning** /ˈmɔːnɪŋ/ *noun* [C,U] **1** the early part of the day between the time when the sun rises and midday: *Pat's going to London* ***tomorrow morning.*** ♦ *Bye, see you* ***in the morning*** (= tomorrow morning). ♦ *I've been studying hard* ***all morning.*** ♦ *Dave makes breakfast* ***every morning.*** ♦ *She only works* ***in the mornings.*** **2** the part of the night that is after midnight: *I was woken by a noise in* ***the early hours of the morning.*** ♦ *He didn't come home until three* ***in the morning.***

> **HELP** Note that when we are talking about a particular morning, we say **on Monday, Tuesday, Wednesday, etc. morning,** but when we are talking generally about doing sth at the time of day we say **in the morning.** 'Afternoon' and 'evening' are used in the same way.
> When you use the adjectives *early* or *late* before 'morning', 'afternoon' or 'evening' you must use the preposition **in:** *The accident happened in the early morning.* ♦ *We arrived in the late afternoon.* With other adjectives, use **on:** *They set out on a cold, windy afternoon.* ♦ *School starts on Monday morning.* No preposition is used before *this, tomorrow, yesterday*: *Let's go swimming this morning.* ♦ *I'll phone Liz tomorrow evening.* ♦ *What did you do yesterday afternoon?*

IDM **Good morning** (*formal*) used when you see sb for the first time in the morning

> **HELP** Often we just say **Morning:** *Morning Kay, how are you today?*

moron /ˈmɔːrɒn/ *noun* [C] (*informal*) a rude way of referring to sb who you think is very stupid: *Stop treating me like a moron!* ▶ **moronic** /məˈrɒnɪk/ *adj*

morose /məˈrəʊs/ *adj* bad-tempered, and not saying much to other people ▶ **morosely** *adv*

morphine /ˈmɔːfiːn/ *noun* [U] a powerful drug that is used for reducing pain

morsel /ˈmɔːsl/ *noun* [C] a very small piece of sth, usually food

mortal[1] /ˈmɔːtl/ *adj* **1** that cannot live for ever and must die: *We are all mortal.* OPP **immortal** **2** (*written*) that will result in death: *a mortal wound/blow* ◆ *to be in mortal danger* ➲ look at **fatal** **3** very great or extreme: *They were in mortal fear of the enemy.* ▶ **mortally** /-təli/ *adv*

mortal[2] /ˈmɔːtl/ *noun* [C] (*formal*) a human being

mortality /mɔːˈtæləti/ *noun* [U] **1** the fact that you will die: *He didn't like to think about his own mortality.* **2** the number of deaths in one period of time or in one place: *Infant mortality is high in the region.*

mortar /ˈmɔːtə(r)/ *noun* **1** [U] a mixture of **cement** (= a grey powder), sand and water used in building for holding bricks and stones together **2** [C] a type of heavy gun that fires a type of bomb high into the air **3** [C] a small hard bowl in which you can crush some foods or substances into powder with a **pestle** (= a heavy tool with a round end) ➲ picture at **squeeze**

mortgage /ˈmɔːgɪdʒ/ *noun* [C] money that you borrow in order to buy a house or flat: *We took out a £100 000 mortgage.* ➲ note at **loan**

mortician /mɔːˈtɪʃn/ (*AmE*) = **undertaker**

mortify /ˈmɔːtɪfaɪ/ *verb* [I,T] (**mortifying**; **mortifies**; *pt, pp* **mortified**) [usually passive] to feel or to make sb feel very embarrassed: *She was mortified to realize he had heard every word she said.* ▶ **mortification** /ˌmɔːtɪfɪˈkeɪʃn/ *noun* [U] ▶ **mortifying** *adj*: *How mortifying to have to apologize to him!*

mortuary /ˈmɔːtʃəri/ *noun* [C] (*pl* **mortuaries**) a room, usually in a hospital, where dead bodies are kept before they are buried or burned ➲ look at **morgue**

mosaic /məʊˈzeɪɪk/ *noun* [C,U] a picture or pattern that is made by placing together small coloured stones, pieces of glass, etc.

Moslem /ˈmɒzləm/ = **Muslim**

mosque /mɒsk/ *noun* [C] a building where Muslims meet and worship

mosquito /məˈskiːtəʊ; mɒˈs-/ *noun* [C] (*pl* **mosquitoes**) a small flying insect that lives in hot countries and bites people or animals to drink their blood. Some types of **mosquito** spread **malaria** (= a very serious disease). ➲ picture on **page P13**

moss /mɒs/ *noun* [C,U] a small soft green plant, with no flowers, that grows in wet places, especially on rocks or trees ▶ **mossy** *adj*

most[1] /məʊst/ *determiner, pron* **1** [used as the superlative of *many* and *much*] greatest in number or amount: *Who got the most points?* ◆ *The children had the most fun.* ◆ *We all worked hard but I did the most.* OPP **least**, **fewest** **2** nearly all of a group of people or things: *Most people in this country have a TV.* ◆ *I like most Italian food.*

> **HELP** When **most** is followed by a noun which has **the, this, my**, etc. before it, we must use **most of**: *Most of my friends were able to come to the wedding.* ◆ *It rained most of the time we were in England.*

IDM **at (the) most** not more than a certain number, and probably less: *There were 20 people there, at the most.*

for the most part usually or mostly

make the most of sth to get as much pleasure, profit, etc. as possible from sth: *You won't get another chance—make the most of it!*

most[2] /məʊst/ *adv* **1** used to form the superlative of many adjectives and adverbs: *It's the most beautiful house I've ever seen.* ◆ *I work most efficiently in the morning.* OPP **least** **2** more than anyone/anything else: *What do you miss most when you're abroad?* OPP **least** **3** (*formal*) very: *We heard a most interesting talk about Japan.*

mostly /ˈməʊstli/ *adv* in almost every case; almost all the time: *Our students come mostly from Japan.*

MOT /ˌem əʊ ˈtiː/ *abbr* (also **MOˈT test**) a test in the UK to make sure that vehicles over a certain age are safe to drive: *My car failed its MOT.*

motel /məʊˈtel/ *noun* [C] a hotel near a main road for people who are travelling by car ➲ note at **hotel**

moth /mɒθ/ *noun* [C] an insect with wings that usually flies at night. Some **moths** eat cloth and leave small holes in your clothes. ➲ picture on **page P13**

mothball /ˈmɒθbɔːl/ *noun* [C] a small ball made of a chemical substance that protects clothes in cupboards from **moths**

mother[1] /ˈmʌðə(r)/ *noun* [C] the female parent of a person or an animal: *a mother and baby group* ◆ *a mother-to-be* (= a woman who is pregnant) ◆ *a mother of two* (= a woman with two children) ◆ *I saw your mother in town yesterday.* ➲ look at **mum**, **mummy**, **stepmother**

mother[2] /ˈmʌðə(r)/ *verb* [T] to look after sb as a mother does: *Stop mothering me—I can look after myself!*

motherhood /ˈmʌðəhʊd/ *noun* [U] the state of being a mother

ˈmother-in-law *noun* [C] (*pl* **mothers-in-law**) the mother of your husband or wife

motherland /ˈmʌðəlænd/ *noun* [C] (*formal*) the country where you or your family were born and which you feel a strong emotional connection with

motherly /ˈmʌðəli/ *adj* having the qualities of a good mother: *motherly love/instincts/advice*

ˈMother's Day *noun* [C] a day when mothers receive cards and gifts from their children, celebrated in Britain on the fourth Sunday in Lent and in the US on the 2nd Sunday in May

ˈ**mother tongue** *noun* [C] the first language that you learnt to speak as a child

motif /məʊˈtiːf/ *noun* [C] a picture or pattern on sth: *a flower motif*

motion¹ /ˈməʊʃn/ *noun* **1** [U] movement or a way of moving: *The motion of the ship made us all feel sick.* ♦ *Pull the lever to **set** the machine **in motion*** (= make it start moving). ➲ look at **slow motion** **2** [C] a formal suggestion at a meeting that you discuss and vote on: *The motion was carried/rejected by a majority of eight votes.*

motion² /ˈməʊʃn/ *verb* [I,T] **motion to sb (to do sth); motion (for) sb (to do sth)** to make a movement, usually with your hand, that tells sb what to do: *I motioned to the waiter.* ♦ *The manager motioned for me to sit down.*

motionless /ˈməʊʃnləs/ *adj* not moving

motivate /ˈməʊtɪveɪt/ *verb* [T] **1** [usually passive] to cause sb to act in a particular way: *Her reaction was motivated by fear.* **2** to make sb want to do sth, especially sth that involves hard work and effort: *Our new teacher certainly knows how to motivate his classes.* ♦ *I just can't motivate myself to do anything this morning.* ▶ **motivated** *adj*: *highly motivated students* ▶ **motivation** /ˌməʊtɪˈveɪʃn/ *noun* [C,U]: *He's clever enough, but he lacks motivation.*

M

motive /ˈməʊtɪv/ *noun* [C,U] (a) **motive (for sth/doing sth)** a reason for doing sth, often sth bad: *The police couldn't discover a motive for the murder.*

motor¹ /ˈməʊtə(r)/ *noun* [C] a device that uses petrol, gas, electricity, etc. to produce movement and makes a machine, etc. work: *The washing machine doesn't work. I think something is wrong with the motor.*

MORE **Engine**, not **motor**, is usually used in connection with cars and motorbikes.

motor² /ˈməʊtə(r)/ *adj* [only *before* a noun] **1** having or using the power of an engine or a motor: *a motor vehicle* **2** (*especially BrE*) connected with vehicles that have engines, especially cars: *the motor industry* ♦ *motor racing*

motorbike /ˈməʊtəbaɪk/ (also *formal* **motorcycle**) *noun* [C] a vehicle that has two wheels and an engine: *He rides a classic Harley Davidson motorbike.* ♦ *Simon comes to work on a motorbike.* ➲ picture on **page P7**

motorboat /ˈməʊtəbəʊt/ *noun* [C] a small fast boat that has a motor

ˈ**motor car** (*BrE formal*) = **car**(1)

motorcycle /ˈməʊtəsaɪkl/ (*formal*) = **motorbike**

motorcyclist /ˈməʊtəsaɪklɪst/ *noun* [C] a person who rides a motorbike

motoring /ˈməʊtərɪŋ/ *noun* [U] driving in a car: *a motoring holiday*

motorist /ˈməʊtərɪst/ *noun* [C] a person who drives a car ➲ note at **driving** ➲ look at **pedestrian**

motorized (also **-ised**) /ˈməʊtəraɪzd/ *adj* [only *before* a noun] that has an engine: *a motorized wheelchair*

motorway /ˈməʊtəweɪ/ (*AmE* **expressway**; **freeway**) *noun* [C] (*abbr* **M**) a wide road where traffic can travel fast for long distances between large towns ➲ note at **road**

motto /ˈmɒtəʊ/ *noun* [C] (*pl* **mottoes** *or* **mottos**) a short sentence or phrase that expresses the aims and beliefs of a person, a group, an organization, etc: *'Live and let live.' That's my motto.*

mould¹ (*AmE* **mold**) /məʊld/ *noun* **1** [C] a container that you pour a liquid or substance into. The liquid then becomes solid in the same shape as the container, for example after it has cooled or cooked: *Pour the chocolate into the heart-shaped mould.* **2** [C, usually sing] a particular type: *She doesn't fit into the usual mould of sales directors.* **3** [U] a soft green or black substance like fur that grows in wet places or on old food ➲ look at **fungus** ▶ **mouldy** (*AmE* **moldy**) *adj*: *The cheese had gone mouldy.*

mould² (*AmE* **mold**) /məʊld/ *verb* [T] **mould A (into B); mould B (from/out of A)** to make sth into a particular shape or form by pressing it or by putting it into a **mould¹**(1): *First mould the dough into a ball.* ♦ *a bowl moulded from clay*

moult (*AmE* **molt**) /məʊlt/ *verb* [I] (used about an animal or a bird) to lose hairs or feathers before growing new ones

mound /maʊnd/ *noun* [C] **1** a large pile of earth or stones; a small hill **2** (*spoken*) **a mound (of sth)** a pile or a large amount of sth: *I've got a mound of work to do.* **SYN** for both meanings **heap**

mount¹ /maʊnt/ *verb* **1** [T] to organize sth: *to mount a protest/a campaign/an exhibition/an attack* **2** [I] to increase gradually in level or amount: *The tension mounted as the end of the match approached.* **3** [T] (*written*) to go up sth or up on to sth: *He mounted the platform and began to speak.* **4** [I,T] to get on a horse or bicycle: *He mounted his horse and rode away.* **OPP** **dismount** **5** [T] **mount sth (on/onto/in sth)** to fix sth firmly on sth else: *The gas boiler was mounted on the wall.*

PHR V **mount up** to increase (often more than you want): *When you're buying food for six people the cost soon mounts up.*

mount² /maʊnt/ *noun* [C] **Mount** (*abbr* **Mt**) (used in names) a mountain: *Mt Everest/Vesuvius/Fuji*

mountain /ˈmaʊntən/ *noun* [C] **1** a very high hill: *Which is the highest mountain in the world?* ♦ *mountain roads/scenery/villages* ♦ *a mountain range* ➲ picture on **page P10** **2 a mountain (of sth)** a large amount of sth: *I've got a mountain of work to do.*

ˈ**mountain bike** *noun* [C] a bicycle with a strong frame, wide tyres and many different gears (= speeds) designed for riding on rough ground

HELP We usually use **go mountain biking** to talk about riding a mountain bike for pleasure.

mountaineering /ˌmaʊntəˈnɪərɪŋ/ *noun* [U] the sport of climbing mountains ▶ **mountaineer** *noun* [C]

mountainous /ˈmaʊntənəs/ *adj* **1** having many mountains: *a mountainous region* **2** very large in size or amount: *The mountainous waves made sailing impossible.* SYN **huge**

mountainside /ˈmaʊntənsaɪd/ *noun* [C] the land on the side of a mountain

mounted /ˈmaʊntɪd/ *adj* [only *before* a noun] riding a horse: *mounted police*

mounting /ˈmaʊntɪŋ/ *adj* [only *before* a noun] increasing: *mounting unemployment/tension/concern*

mourn /mɔːn/ *verb* [I,T] **mourn (for/over) sb/sth** to feel and show great sadness, especially because sb has died: *He is still mourning (for) his wife.* ▶ **mourning** *noun* [U]: *He wore a black armband to show he was* ***in mourning***.

mourner /ˈmɔːnə(r)/ *noun* [C] a person who goes to a funeral as a friend or relative of the person who has died

mournful /ˈmɔːnfl/ *adj* (*written*) very sad: *a mournful song* ▶ **mournfully** /-fəli/ *adv*

⚷ **mouse** /maʊs/ *noun* [C] (*pl* mice /maɪs/) **1** a very small animal with fur and a long thin tail: *Mice, rats and hamsters are members of the rodent family.* **2** a piece of equipment, connected to a computer, for moving around the screen and entering commands without touching the keys: *Use the mouse to drag the icon to a new position.* ➲ picture at **computer**

ˈ**mouse mat** (*AmE* ˈmouse pad) *noun* [C] a small piece of material that is the best kind of surface on which to use a computer mouse

mousse /muːs/ *noun* [C,U] **1** a cold **dessert** (= a sweet food) made with cream and egg whites and flavoured with fruit, chocolate, etc.; a similar dish flavoured with fish, vegetables, etc: *a chocolate/strawberry mousse* ◆ *salmon mousse* **2** a substance that is used on hair to make it stay in a particular style

moustache (*AmE* mustache) /məˈstɑːʃ/ *noun* [C] hair that grows on a man's top lip, between the mouth and nose ➲ picture at **hair**

⚷ **mouth¹** /maʊθ/ *noun* [C] (*pl* mouths /maʊðz/) **1** the part of your face that you use for eating and speaking: *to open/close your mouth* ➲ picture at **body** **2** the place where a river enters the sea **3** -mouthed /-maʊðd/ [in compounds] having a particular type of mouth or a particular way of speaking: *We stared open-mouthed in surprise.* ◆ *He's a loud-mouthed bully.*

IDM **keep your mouth shut** (*informal*) to not say sth to sb because it is a secret or because it will upset or annoy them

mouth² /maʊð/ *verb* [I,T] to move your mouth as if you were speaking but without making any sound: *Vinay was outside the window, mouthing something to us.*

mouthful /ˈmaʊθfʊl/ *noun* **1** [C] the amount of food or drink that you can put in your mouth at one time **2** [sing] a word or phrase that is long or difficult to say: *Her name is a bit of a mouthful.*

ˈ**mouth organ** = **harmonica**

mouthpiece /ˈmaʊθpiːs/ *noun* [C] **1** the part of a telephone, musical instrument, etc. that you put in or near your mouth ➲ picture at **music** **2** a person, newspaper, etc. that a particular group uses to express its opinions: *Pravda was the mouthpiece of the Soviet government.*

ˈ**mouth-watering** *adj* (used about food) that looks or smells very good

movable /ˈmuːvəbl/ *adj* that can be moved OPP **fixed** ➲ look at **portable, mobile**

⚷ **move¹** /muːv/ *verb*

➤CHANGE POSITION **1** [I,T] to change position or to put sth in a different position: *The station is so crowded you* ***can hardly move***. ◆ *Please move your car. It's blocking the road.* ◆ *The meeting has been moved to Thursday.* **2** [I,T] **move along, down, over, up, etc.** to move (sth) further in a particular direction in order to make space for sb/sth else: *If we move up a bit, Rob can sit here too.* ◆ *Move your head down—I can't see the screen.*

➤MAKE PROGRESS **3** [I] **move (on/ahead)** to make progress: *When the new team of builders arrived, things started moving very quickly.*

➤TAKE ACTION **4** [I] to take action: *Unless we move quickly lives will be lost.*

➤CHANGE HOUSE, JOB, ETC. **5** [I,T] to change the place where you live, work, study, etc: *Our neighbours are moving to Exeter next week.* ◆ *to* ***move house*** ◆ *Yuka's moved down to the beginners' class.*

➤CAUSE STRONG FEELINGS **6** [T] to cause sb to have strong feelings, especially of sadness: *Many people were* ***moved to tears*** *by reports of the massacre.*

IDM **get moving** to go, leave or do sth quickly

get sth moving to cause sth to make progress

PHR V **move in (with sb)** to start living in a new home (with sb)

move off (used about a vehicle) to start a journey; to leave

move on (to sth) to start doing or discussing sth new

move out to leave your old home

⚷ **move²** /muːv/ *noun* [C] **1** a change of place or position: *She was watching every move I made.* **2** a change in the place where you live or work: *a move to a bigger house* **3** action that you take because you want to achieve a particular result: *Both sides want to negotiate but neither is prepared to* ***make the first move***. ◆ *Asking him to help me was* ***a good move***. **4** (in **chess** and other games) a change in the position of a piece: *It's your move.*

IDM **be on the move** to be going somewhere: *We've been on the move for four hours so we should stop for a rest.*

get a move on (*informal*) to hurry: *I'm late. I'll have to get a move on.*

make a move to start to go somewhere: *It's time to go home. Let's make a move.*

M

movement /ˈmuːvmənt/ *noun*
➤CHANGING POSITION **1** [C,U] an act of moving: *The dancer's movements were smooth and controlled.* ◆ *The seat belt doesn't allow much freedom of movement.* ◆ *I could see some movement* (= sb/sth moving) *in the trees.* **2** [C,U] an act of moving or being moved from one place to another: *the slow movement of the clouds across the sky*
➤GROUP OF PEOPLE **3** [C] a group of people who have the same aims or ideas: *I support the peace movement.*
➤SB'S ACTIVITIES **4 movements** [pl] sb's actions or plans during a period of time: *Detectives have been watching the man's movements for several weeks.*
➤CHANGE OF IDEAS/BEHAVIOUR **5** [C, usually sing] a movement (away from/towards sth) a general change in the way people think or behave: *There's been a movement away from the materialism of the 1980s.*
➤MUSIC **6** [C] one of the main parts of a long piece of music: *a symphony in four movements*

movie /ˈmuːvi/ *noun (especially AmE)* **1** = **film**[1](1): *Shall we go and* ***see a movie****?* ◆ *a science fiction/horror movie* ◆ *a movie director/star* ◆ *a movie theater* (= a cinema) **2 the movies** [pl] = **cinema**(1): *Let's* ***go to the movies.***

M

moving /ˈmuːvɪŋ/ *adj* **1** causing strong feelings, especially of sadness: *a deeply moving speech/story* **2** [only *before* a noun] that moves: *It's a computerized machine with few moving parts.*

mow /məʊ/ *verb* [I,T] (*pt* **mowed**; *pp* **mown** /məʊn/ *or* **mowed**) to cut grass using a **mower**: *to mow the lawn*
PHR V **mow sb down** to kill sb with a gun or a car

mower /ˈməʊə(r)/ *noun* [C] a machine for cutting grass: *a lawnmower* ◆ *an electric mower*

mown *past participle of* **mow**

MP /ˌem ˈpiː/ *abbr (especially BrE)* = **Member of Parliament**

MP3 /ˌem piː ˈθriː/ *noun* [C,U] a method of reducing the size of a computer file containing sound, or a file that is reduced in size in this way

MPˈ3 player *noun* [C] a small piece of equipment that can store information taken from the Internet and that you carry with you, for example so that you can listen to music. An **MP3 player** can open and play **MP3** files. ➲ note at **iPod**™, **listen, podcast**

mpg /ˌem piː ˈdʒiː/ *abbr* **miles per gallon**: *This car does 40 mpg* (= you can drive 40 miles on one gallon of petrol).

mph /ˌem piː ˈeɪtʃ/ *abbr* **miles per hour**: *a 70 mph speed limit*

MPV /ˌem piː ˈviː/ *noun* [C] **multi-purpose vehicle**; a large car that can carry a number of people

Mr /ˈmɪstə(r)/ *abbr* used as a title before the name of a man: *Mr (Matthew) Wallace* ◆ *I'd like to speak to Mr Wallace.* ➲ note at **Miss**

Mrs /ˈmɪsɪz/ *abbr* used as a title before the name of a married woman: *Mrs (Belinda) Allan* ◆ *Good morning, Mrs Allan.* ➲ note at **Miss**

MS /ˌem ˈes/ *abbr* = **multiple sclerosis**

Ms /mɪz; məz/ used as a title before the family name of a woman who may or may not be married: *Ms (Keiko) Harada* ◆ *Dear Ms Harada, ...* ➲ note at **Miss**

> **MORE** Some women prefer the title **Ms** to **Mrs** or **Miss**. We can also use it if we do not know whether or not a woman is married.

MSc /ˌem es ˈsiː/ *abbr* **Master of Science**; a second degree that you receive when you complete a more advanced course or piece of research in a science subject at university or college ➲ look at **BSc, MA**

Mt *abbr* = **Mount**[2]: *Mt Everest*

mth *abbr (pl* **mths**) = **month**

much /mʌtʃ/ *determiner, pron, adv* **1** [used with uncountable nouns, mainly in negative sentences and questions, or after *as, how, so, too*] a large amount of sth: *I haven't got much money.* ◆ *Did she say much?* ◆ *You've given me* ***too much*** *food.* ◆ ***How much*** *time have you got?* ◆ *I can't carry* ***that much****!* ◆ *Eat* ***as much as*** *you can.* ◆ *How much is it* (= what does it cost)?

> **HELP** In positive statements we usually use **a lot of** NOT **much**: *I've got a lot of experience.*

2 to a great degree: *I don't like her very much.* ◆ *Do you see Sashi much?* (= very often) ◆ *Do you see much of Sashi?* ◆ *much taller/prettier/harder* ◆ *much more interesting/unusual* ◆ *much more quickly/happily* ◆ *You ate* ***much more*** *than me.* **3** [with past participles used as adjectives] very: *a much-needed rest*
IDM **much the same** very similar: *Softball is much the same as baseball.*
not much good (at sth) not skilled (at sth): *I'm not much good at singing.*
not much of a ... not a good ...: *She's not much of a cook.*
not up to much ➲ **up**
nothing much ➲ **nothing**

muck[1] /mʌk/ *noun* [U] **1** the waste from farm animals, used to make plants grow better ➲ A more common word is **manure**. **2** (*BrE informal*) dirt or mud

muck[2] /mʌk/ *verb (informal)*
PHR V **muck about/around** to behave in a silly way or to waste time: *Stop mucking around and come and help me!*
muck sth up to do sth badly; to spoil sth: *I was so nervous that I completely mucked up my interview.*

mucus /ˈmjuːkəs/ *noun* [U] *(formal)* a sticky substance that is produced in some parts of the body, especially the nose

mud /mʌd/ *noun* [U] soft, wet earth: *He came home from the football match* ***covered in mud.***

muddle /ˈmʌdl/ *verb* [T] **1** muddle sth (up) to put things in the wrong place or order or to make them untidy: *Try not to* ***get*** *those papers* ***muddled up.*** **2** muddle sb (up) to confuse sb: *I do my homework* *and schoolwork in separate books so that I don't* ***get muddled up.*** ▶ **muddle** *noun* [C,U]: *If you* ***get in a muddle****, I'll help you.* ▶ **muddled** *adj*

muddy /ˈmʌdi/ *adj* (**muddier**; **muddiest**) full of or covered in mud: *muddy boots* ◆ *It's very muddy down by the river.*

mudguard /ˈmʌdɡɑːd/ *noun* [C] a curved cover over the wheel of a bicycle or motorbike

muesli /ˈmjuːzli/ *noun* [U] food made of grains, nuts, dried fruit, etc. that you eat with milk for breakfast

muezzin /muːˈezɪn; mjuː-/ *noun* [C] a man who calls Muslims to come to a **mosque** (= a religious building) to pray

muffin /ˈmʌfɪn/ *noun* [C] **1** (*AmE* ˌEnglish ˈmuffin) a type of bread roll often eaten hot with butter **2** a type of small cake ➲ picture at **cake**

muffle /ˈmʌfl/ *verb* [T] to make a sound quieter and more difficult to hear: *He put his hand over his mouth to muffle his laughter.* ▶ **muffled** *adj*: *I heard muffled voices outside.*

muffler /ˈmʌflə(r)/ (*AmE*) = **silencer**

mug¹ /mʌɡ/ *noun* [C] **1** a large cup with straight sides and a handle: *a coffee mug* ◆ *a mug of tea* ◆ *a beer mug* (= a large glass with a handle) ➲ picture at **cup, glass 2** (*informal*) a person who seems stupid

mug² /mʌɡ/ *verb* [T] (**mugging**; **mugged**) to attack and steal from sb in the street: *Keep your wallet out of sight or you'll* ***get mugged****.* ▶ **mugger** *noun* [C] ➲ note at **thief** ▶ **mugging** *noun* [C,U]: *The mugging took place around midnight.*

muggy /ˈmʌɡi/ *adj* (used about the weather) warm and slightly wet in an unpleasant way

Muhammad (also **Mohammed**) /məˈhæmɪd/ *noun* [sing] the **prophet** (= a person who is chosen by God to give his message to people) who started the religion of Islam

mule /mjuːl/ *noun* [C] an animal that is used for carrying heavy loads and whose parents are a horse and a **donkey** (= an animal like a small horse with long ears)

mull /mʌl/ *verb*

PHR V mull sth over to think about sth carefully and for a long time: *Don't ask me for a decision right now. I'll have to mull it over.*

multi- /ˈmʌlti/ [in compounds] more than one; many: *multicoloured* ◆ *a multimillionaire* ◆ *a multi-ethnic society*

multicultural /ˌmʌltiˈkʌltʃərəl/ *adj* for or including people of many different races, languages, religions and customs: *a multicultural society*

multiculturalism /ˌmʌltiˈkʌltʃərəlɪzəm/ *noun* [U] the practice of giving importance to all cultures in a society

multilateral /ˌmʌltiˈlætərəl/ *adj* involving more than two groups of people, countries, etc: *They signed a multilateral agreement.* ➲ look at **bilateral, unilateral**

multimedia /ˌmʌltiˈmiːdiə/ *adj* [only *before* a noun] using sound, pictures and film on a computer in addition to text on the screen: *multimedia systems/products*

multinational¹ /ˌmʌltiˈnæʃnəl/ *adj* existing in or involving many countries: *multinational companies*

multinational² /ˌmʌltiˈnæʃnəl/ *noun* [C] a large and powerful company that operates in several different countries: *The company is owned by Ford, the US multinational.*

multiple¹ /ˈmʌltɪpl/ *adj* [only *before* a noun] involving many people or things or having many parts: *a multiple pile-up* (= a crash involving many vehicles)

multiple² /ˈmʌltɪpl/ *noun* [C] a number that contains another number an exact number of times: *12, 18 and 24 are multiples of 6.*

ˌmultiple-ˈchoice *adj* (used about exam questions) showing several different answers from which you have to choose the right one

EXAM TIP

Multiple-choice

Part of your exam might be a multiple-choice paper. Each question has three or four possible answers. You need to select the correct one by putting a mark in the box next to the answer you have chosen. Don't spend too long on any one question, and always give an answer. Even if you don't know the answer you can guess, and, who knows, you might be right!

multiple sclerosis /ˌmʌltɪpl skləˈrəʊsɪs/ *noun* [U] (*abbr* **MS**) a serious disease which causes you to slowly lose control of your body and become less able to move

multiplex /ˈmʌltɪpleks/ *noun* [C] a large cinema with several separate rooms with screens

multiply /ˈmʌltɪplaɪ/ *verb* (**multiplying**; **multiplies**; *pt, pp* **multiplied**) **1** [I,T] **multiply A by B** to increase a number by the number of times mentioned: *2 multiplied by 4 makes 8* (2 x 4 = 8) **OPP divide 2** [I,T] to increase or make sth increase by a very large amount: *We've multiplied our profits over the last two years.* ▶ **multiplication** /ˌmʌltɪplɪˈkeɪʃn/ *noun* [U] ➲ look at **division, addition, subtraction**

multi-purpose /ˌmʌlti ˈpɜːpəs/ *adj* that can be used for several different purposes: *a multi-purpose tool/machine*

multi-storey ˈcar park (also ˌmulti-ˈstorey; *AmE* ˈparking garage) *noun* [C] a large building with several floors for parking cars in

multitasking /ˌmʌltiˈtɑːskɪŋ/ *noun* [U] **1** the ability of a computer to operate several programs at the same time **2** the activity of doing several things at the same time

multitude /ˈmʌltɪtjuːd/ *noun* [C] (*formal*) a very large number of people or things

mum /mʌm/ (*AmE* **mom**) *noun* [C] (*informal*) mother: *Is that your mum?* ◆ *Can I have a drink, Mum?* ➲ look at **mummy**

mumble /ˈmʌmbl/ *verb* [I,T] to speak quietly without opening your mouth properly, so that people cannot hear the words: *I can't hear if you mumble.* ➲ look at **mutter**

mummy /ˈmʌmi/ *noun* [C] (*pl* **mummies**) **1** (*AmE* **mommy**) (*informal*) a child's word for mother: *Here comes your mummy now.* **2** the dead body of a person or an animal which has been kept by rubbing it with special oils and covering it in cloth

mumps /mʌmps/ *noun* [U] an infectious disease, especially of children, that causes the neck to swell: *to have/catch (the) mumps*

munch /mʌntʃ/ *verb* [I,T] **munch (on sth)** to bite and eat sth noisily: *He sat there munching (on) an apple.*

mundane /mʌnˈdeɪn/ *adj* ordinary; not interesting or exciting: *a mundane job*

municipal /mjuːˈnɪsɪpl/ *adj* connected with a town or city that has its own local government: *municipal buildings* (= the town hall, public library, etc.)

M

munitions /mjuːˈnɪʃnz/ *noun* [pl] military supplies, especially bombs and guns

mural /ˈmjʊərəl/ *noun* [C] a large picture painted on a wall

murder /ˈmɜːdə(r)/ *noun* **1** [C,U] the crime of killing a person illegally and on purpose: *to **commit murder*** ◆ *a vicious murder* ◆ *the murder victim/weapon* ➲ note at **crime** ➲ look at **manslaughter** **2** [U] (*informal*) a very difficult or unpleasant experience: *It's murder trying to work when it's so hot.*

IDM get away with murder to do whatever you want without being stopped or punished: *He lets his students get away with murder.*

▶ **murder** *verb* [I,T] ➲ note at **kill** ▶ **murderer** *noun* [C]

murderous /ˈmɜːdərəs/ *adj* intending or likely to murder

murky /ˈmɜːki/ *adj* (**murkier**; **murkiest**) dark and unpleasant or dirty: *The water in the river looked very murky.* ◆ (*figurative*) *According to rumours, the new boss had a murky past.*

murmur /ˈmɜːmə(r)/ *verb* [I,T] to say sth in a low quiet voice: *He murmured a name in his sleep.* ▶ **murmur** *noun* [C]

muscle /ˈmʌsl/ *noun* [C,U] one of the parts inside your body that you can make tight or relax in order to produce movement: *Riding a bicycle is good for developing the leg muscles.* ◆ *Lifting weights builds muscle.*

muscular /ˈmʌskjələ(r)/ *adj* **1** connected with the muscles: *muscular pain/tissue* **2** having large strong muscles: *a muscular body*

museum /mjuˈziːəm/ *noun* [C] a building where collections of valuable and interesting objects are kept and shown to the public: *Have you been to the Science Museum in London?* ➲ look at **gallery** ➲ picture on **page P11**

mushroom /ˈmʌʃrʊm; -ruːm/ *noun* [C] a type of plant which grows very quickly, has a flat or round top and can be eaten as a vegetable ➲ picture on **page P15**

> **MORE** A mushroom is a type of **fungus**. Some, but not all, **fungi** can be eaten. **Toadstool** is a name for some types of poisonous fungi.

music /ˈmjuːzɪk/ *noun* [U] **1** an arrangement of sounds in patterns to be sung or played on instruments: *What sort of music do you like?* ◆ *classical/pop/rock music* ◆ *to write/compose music* ◆ *a music lesson/teacher* ➲ note at **instrument**, **pop** **2** the written signs that represent the sounds of music: *Can you read music?*

> **TOPIC**
>
> **Music**
>
> A large group of **musicians** playing **classical music** together on different **instruments** is an **orchestra**. They are directed by a **conductor**. Music is **composed** (= written) by a **composer** and musicians learn to **read music** in order to play it. There are different types of classical **composition**, for example a **symphony** (= a long piece of music for an orchestra) or an **opera** (= a piece for the theatre where the words are sung). Note that we usually say 'play **the** violin, the piano, etc.': *I've been learning the flute for four years.* When talking about modern music such as pop, rock, etc. it is possible to say 'play drums, guitar, etc.', without *the*: *He plays bass in a band.*

musical¹ /ˈmjuːzɪkl/ *adj* **1** [only *before* a noun] connected with music: *Can you play a musical instrument* (= the piano, the violin, the trumpet, etc.)? **2** interested in or good at music: *He's very musical.* **3** having a pleasant sound like music: *a musical voice* ▶ **musically** /-kli/ *adv*: *She is musically gifted.*

musical² /ˈmjuːzɪkl/ *noun* [C] a play or film which has singing and dancing in it ➲ look at **opera**

musician /mjuˈzɪʃn/ *noun* [C] a person who plays a musical instrument or writes music, especially as a job ➲ note at **music**

Muslim (also **Moslem**) /ˈmʊzlɪm/ *noun* [C] a person whose religion is Islam ▶ **Muslim** (also **Moslem**) *adj*: *Muslim traditions/beliefs*

muslin /ˈmʌzlɪn/ *noun* [U] a type of thin cotton cloth

mussel /ˈmʌsl/ *noun* [C] a **shellfish** (= a creature with a shell that lives in water) that you can eat, with a black shell in two parts ➲ picture at **shellfish**

must¹ /məst; *strong form* mʌst/ *modal verb* (*negative* **must not**; *short form* **mustn't** /ˈmʌsnt/) **1** used for saying that it is necessary that sth happens: *I must remember to go to the bank today.* ◆ *You mustn't take photographs in here. It's forbidden.*

Musical Instruments

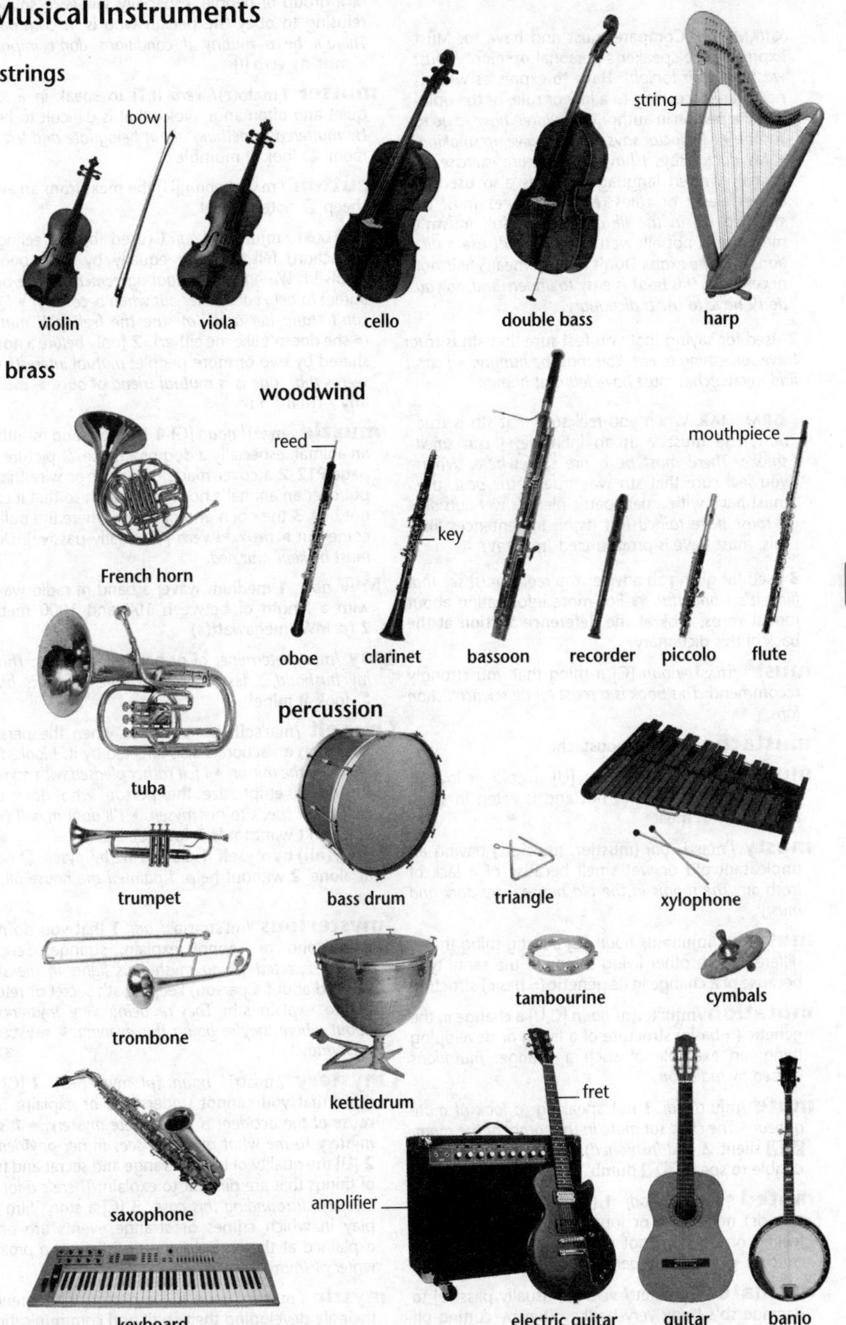

GRAMMAR Compare **must** and **have to. Must** expresses the speaker's personal opinion: *I must wash my hair tonight.* **Have to** expresses what is necessary according to a law or rule, or the opinion of a person in authority: *Children have to go to school.* ◆ *My doctor says I have to give up smoking.* ◆ *My doctor says I have to get more exercise.* In formal, written language **must** is also used to express laws or rules: *Mobile phones must be switched off in the library.* Be careful: **mustn't** means 'it is not allowed': *You mustn't use a dictionary in the exam.* **Don't have to** means 'it is not necessary': *This book is easy to understand, so you don't have to use a dictionary.*

2 used for saying that you feel sure that sth is true: *Have something to eat. You must be hungry.* ◆ *I can't find my watch. I must have left it at home.*

GRAMMAR When you feel sure that sth is true *now*, use **must** with an infinitive: *I can smell smoke. There must be a fire somewhere.* When you feel sure that sth was true *in the past*, use **must have** with a past participle: *It's wet outside. It must have rained last night.* In sentences like this, **must have** is pronounced /mʌstəv/.

M

3 used for giving sb advice: *You really must see that film. It's wonderful.* ℹ For more information about modal verbs, look at the **Reference Section** at the back of this dictionary.

must² /mʌst/ *noun* [C] a thing that you strongly recommend: *This book is a must for all science fiction fans.*

mustache (*AmE*) = **moustache**

mustard /ˈmʌstəd/ *noun* [U] a cold yellow or brown sauce that tastes hot and is eaten in small amounts with meat

musty /ˈmʌsti/ *adj* (**mustier**; **mustiest**) having an unpleasant old or wet smell because of a lack of fresh air: *The rooms in the old house were dark and musty.*

mutant /ˈmjuːtənt/ *noun* [C] a living thing that is different from other living things of the same type because of a change in its **genetic** (= basic) structure

mutation /mjuːˈteɪʃn/ *noun* [C,U] a change in the **genetic** (= basic) structure of a living or developing thing; an example of such a change: *mutations caused by radiation*

mute /mjuːt/ *adj* **1** not speaking: *a look of mute appeal* ◆ *The child sat mute in the corner of the room.* **SYN** **silent** **2** (*old-fashioned*) (used about a person) unable to speak **SYN** **dumb**

muted /ˈmjuːtɪd/ *adj* **1** (used about colours or sounds) not bright or loud; soft **2** (used about a feeling or reaction) not strongly expressed: *muted criticism* ◆ *a muted response*

mutilate /ˈmjuːtɪleɪt/ *verb* [T, usually passive] to damage sb's body very badly, often by cutting off parts ▶ **mutilation** /ˌmjuːtɪˈleɪʃn/ *noun* [C,U]

mutiny /ˈmjuːtəni/ *noun* [C,U] (*pl* **mutinies**) an act of a group of people, especially sailors or soldiers, refusing to obey the person who is in command: *There'll be a mutiny if conditions don't improve.* ▶ **mutiny** *verb* [I]

mutter /ˈmʌtə(r)/ *verb* [I,T] to speak in a low, quiet and often angry voice that is difficult to hear: *He muttered something about being late and left the room.* ➲ look at **mumble**

mutton /ˈmʌtn/ *noun* [U] the meat from an adult sheep ➲ note at **meat**

mutual /ˈmjuːtʃuəl/ *adj* **1** (used about a feeling or an action) felt or done equally by both people involved: *We have* ***a mutual agreement*** (= we both agree) *to help each other out when necessary.* ◆ *I just can't stand her and I'm sure* ***the feeling is mutual*** (= she doesn't like me either). **2** [only *before* a noun] shared by two or more people: *mutual interests* ◆ *It seems that Jane is* ***a mutual friend*** *of ours.* ▶ **mutually** /-tʃuəli/ *adv*

muzzle /ˈmʌzl/ *noun* [C] **1** the nose and mouth of an animal, especially a dog or a horse ➲ picture on **page P12** **2** a cover made of leather or wire that is put over an animal's nose and mouth so that it cannot bite **3** the open end of a gun where the bullets come out ▶ **muzzle** *verb* [T, usually passive]: *Dogs must be kept muzzled.*

MW *abbr* **1** **medium wave**; a band of radio waves with a length of between 100 and 1000 metres **2** (*pl* **MW**) **megawatt(s)**

🔑 **my** /maɪ/ *determiner* of or belonging to me: *This is my husband, Giles.* ◆ *My favourite colour is blue.* ➲ look at **mine¹**

🔑 **myself** /maɪˈself/ *pron* **1** used when the person who does an action is also affected by it: *I looked at myself in the mirror.* ◆ *I felt rather pleased with myself.* **2** used to emphasize the person who does the action: *I'll speak to her myself.* ◆ *I'll do it myself* (= if you don't want to do it for me).

IDM **(all) by myself** **1** alone: *I live by myself.* ➲ note at **alone** **2** without help: *I painted the house all by myself.*

🔑 **mysterious** /mɪˈstɪəriəs/ *adj* **1** that you do not understand or cannot explain; strange: *Several people reported seeing mysterious lights in the sky.* **2** (used about a person) keeping sth secret or refusing to explain sth: *They're being very mysterious about where they're going this evening.* ▶ **mysteriously** *adv*

🔑 **mystery** /ˈmɪstri/ *noun* (*pl* **mysteries**) **1** [C] a thing that you cannot understand or explain: *The cause of the accident is a complete mystery.* ◆ ***It's a mystery to me*** *what my sister sees in her boyfriend.* **2** [U] the quality of being strange and secret and full of things that are difficult to explain: *There's a lot of mystery surrounding this case.* **3** [C] a story, film or play in which crimes or strange events are only explained at the end: *Agatha Christie was a prolific writer of (murder) mysteries.*

mystic /ˈmɪstɪk/ *noun* [C] a person who spends their life developing their spirit and communicating with God or a god

mystical /ˈmɪstɪkl/ (also **mystic**) *adj* connected with the spirit; strange and wonderful: *Watching the sun set over the island was an almost mystical experience.*

mysticism /ˈmɪstɪsɪzəm/ *noun* [U] the belief that you can reach complete truth and knowledge of God or gods by prayer, thought and development of the spirit: *Eastern mysticism*

mystify /ˈmɪstɪfaɪ/ *verb* [T] (**mystifying**; **mystifies**; *pt, pp* **mystified**) to make sb confused because they cannot understand sth: *I was mystified by the strange note he'd left behind.*

mystique /mɪˈstiːk/ *noun* [U,sing] the quality of being mysterious or secret that makes sb/sth seem interesting or attractive

myth /mɪθ/ *noun* [C] **1** a story from past times, especially one about gods and men of courage. **Myths** often explain natural or historical events. SYN **legend** **2** an idea or story which many people believe but that does not exist or is false: *The idea that money makes you happy is a myth.*

mythical /ˈmɪθɪkl/ *adj* **1** existing only in **myths** (1): *mythical beasts/heroes* **2** not real or true; existing only in the imagination

mythology /mɪˈθɒlədʒi/ *noun* [U] very old stories and the beliefs contained in them: *Greek and Roman mythology* ▶ **mythological** /ˌmɪθəˈlɒdʒɪkl/ *adj*: *mythological figures/stories*

N, n /en/ *noun* [C,U] (*pl* **Ns**; **N's**; **n's** /enz/) the 14th letter of the English alphabet: *'Nicholas' begins with (an) 'N'.*

N (*AmE* **No.**) *abbr* **north**[1], **northern**: *N Yorkshire*

naff /næf/ *adj* (*BrE informal*) lacking style, taste or quality: *There was a naff band playing.*

nag /næg/ *verb* (**nagging**; **nagged**) **1** [I,T] **nag (at) sb** to continuously complain to sb about their behaviour or to ask them to do sth many times: *My parents are always nagging (at) me to work harder.* **2** [I,T] to worry or trouble sb continuously: *a nagging doubt/headache*

nail[1] /neɪl/ *noun* [C] **1** the thin hard layer that covers the ends of your fingers and toes: *Don't bite your nails!* ◆ *fingernails/toenails* ➲ picture at **body** **2** a small thin piece of metal that is used for holding pieces of wood together, hanging pictures on, etc: *to hammer in a nail* ➲ picture at **bolt**

IDM **hit the nail on the head** ➲ **hit**[1]

nail[2] /neɪl/ *verb* [T] to fasten sth to sth with a nail or nails

PHR V **nail sb down (to sth)** to make a person say clearly what they want or intend to do: *She says she'll visit us in the summer but I can't nail her down to a definite date.*

ˈ**nail-biting** *adj* [usually before a noun] making you feel very excited or anxious because you do not know what is going to happen: *It's been a nail-biting couple of weeks waiting for my results.*

ˈ**nail brush** *noun* [C] a small brush for cleaning your nails ➲ picture at **brush**

ˈ**nail file** *noun* [C] a small metal tool with a rough surface that you use for shaping your nails

ˈ**nail polish** (*BrE also* ˈ**nail varnish**) *noun* [U] a liquid that people paint on their nails to give them colour

naive (also **naïve**) /naɪˈiːv/ *adj* without enough experience of life and too ready to believe or trust other people: *I was too naive to realize what was happening.* ◆ *a naive remark/question/view* SYN **innocent** ▶ **naively** (also **naïvely**) *adv*: *She naively accepted the first price he offered.* ▶ **naivety** (also **naïvety** /naɪˈiːvəti/) *noun* [U]

naked /ˈneɪkɪd/ *adj* **1** not wearing any clothes: *He came to the door naked except for a towel.* ◆ *naked shoulders/arms* ➲ look at **bare**, **nude** **2** [only *before* a noun] (used about sth that is usually covered) not covered: *a naked flame/bulb/light* **3** [only *before* a noun] (used about emotions, etc.) clearly shown or expressed in a way that is often shocking: *naked aggression/ambition/fear*

IDM **the naked eye** the normal power of your eyes without the help of glasses, a machine, etc: *Bacteria are too small to be seen with the naked eye.*

TOPIC

Names

Your **first name** is the name your parents choose for you when you are born. In Christian countries this is sometimes called your **Christian name**. Your parents may give you one or more other names after your first name, called your **middle name**, which you rarely use except on formal, official documents, where all names are referred to as your **forenames. Surname** is the word usually used for your **family name** which you are born with. When a woman marries, she may change her surname to be the same as her husband's. Her surname before marriage is then called her **maiden name**.

name[1] /neɪm/ *noun* **1** [C] a word or words by which sb/sth is known: *What's your name, please?* ◆ *Do you know the name of this flower?* **2** [sing] an opinion that people have of a person or thing: *That area of London has rather a bad name.* SYN **reputation** **3** [C] a famous person: *All the big names in show business were invited to the party.*

IDM **by name** using the name of sb/sth: *It's a big school but the head teacher knows all the children by name.*

call sb names ➲ **call**[1]

in the name of sb; **in sb's name** for sb/sth; officially belonging to sb: *The contract is in my name.*

in the name of sth used to give a reason or excuse for an action, even when what you are doing might be wrong: *They acted in the name of democracy.*

make a name for yourself; **make your name** to

become well known and respected: *She made a name for herself as a journalist.*

name² /neɪm/ *verb* [T] **1** **name sb/sth (after sb)** to give sb/sth a name: *Columbia was named after Christopher Columbus.*

HELP When you are saying what someone's name is, you can use **be called**: *Their youngest son is called Mark.*

2 to say what the name of sb/sth is: *The journalist refused to name the person who had given her the information.* ♦ *Can you name all the planets?* **3** to state sth exactly: *Name your price—we'll pay it!*

nameless /ˈneɪmləs/ *adj* **1** without a name or with a name that you do not know **2** whose name is kept a secret: *a well-known public figure who shall* ***remain nameless*** **SYN** **anonymous**

namely /ˈneɪmli/ *adv* (used for giving more detail about what you are saying) that is to say: *There is only one person who can overrule the death sentence, namely the President.*

namesake /ˈneɪmseɪk/ *noun* [C] a person who has the same name as another

nan /næn/ (also **nana, nanna**) *noun* [C] (*informal*) (used by children) grandmother: *my nan and grandad*

nanny /ˈnæni/ *noun* [C] (*pl* **nannies**) a woman whose job is to look after a family's children and who usually lives in the family home

nanometre (*AmE* **nanometer**) /ˈnænəʊmiːtə(r)/ *noun* [C] (*abbr* **nm**) one thousand millionth of a metre

nanotechnology /ˌnænəʊtekˈnɒlədʒi/ *noun* [U] the branch of technology that deals with structures that are less than 100 **nanometres** long. Scientists often build these structures using individual **molecules** (= the smallest units into which a substance can be divided without changing its chemical nature) of substances.

nap /næp/ *noun* [C] a short sleep that you have during the day ➲ look at **snooze** ▶ **nap** *verb* [I] (**napping; napped**)

nape /neɪp/ *noun* [sing] the back part of your neck

napkin /ˈnæpkɪn/ *noun* [C] a piece of cloth or paper that you use when you are eating to protect your clothes or for cleaning your hands and mouth: *a paper napkin* **SYN** **serviette**

nappy /ˈnæpi/ *noun* [C] (*pl* **nappies**) (*AmE* **diaper**) a piece of soft thick cloth or paper that a baby or very young child wears around its bottom and between its legs: *Does his nappy need changing?* ♦ *disposable nappies* (= that you throw away when they have been used)

narcotic /nɑːˈkɒtɪk/ *noun* [C] **1** a powerful illegal drug that affects your mind in a harmful way **2** a substance or drug that relaxes you, stops pain, or makes you sleep ▶ **narcotic** *adj*

narrate /nəˈreɪt/ *verb* [T] (*formal*) to tell a story ▶ **narration** /nəˈreɪʃn/ *noun* [C,U]

narrative /ˈnærətɪv/ *noun* (*formal*) **1** [C] the description of events in a story **2** [U] the process or skill of telling a story

narrator /nəˈreɪtə(r)/ *noun* [C] the person who tells a story or explains what is happening in a play, film, etc.

narrow¹ /ˈnærəʊ/ *adj* (**narrower; narrowest**) **1** having only a short distance from side to side: *The bridge is too narrow for two cars to pass.* **OPP** **wide, broad** **2** by a small amount: *That was a very narrow escape. You were lucky.* ♦ *a narrow defeat/victory* **3** not large: *a narrow circle of friends* ▶ **narrowness** *noun* [U]

narrow² /ˈnærəʊ/ *verb* [I,T] to become or make sth narrower: *The road narrows in 50 metres.* ♦ *He narrowed his eyes at her.*

PHR V **narrow sth down** to make a list of things smaller: *The police have narrowed down their list of suspects to three.*

narrowly /ˈnærəʊli/ *adv* only by a small amount

ˌnarrow-ˈminded *adj* not willing to listen to new ideas or to the opinions of other people **OPP** **broad-minded, open-minded**

nasal /ˈneɪzl/ *adj* **1** connected with the nose: *a nasal spray* **2** (used about sb's voice) produced partly through the nose

nasty /ˈnɑːsti/ *adj* (**nastier; nastiest**) very bad or unpleasant: *a nasty accident* ♦ *I had a nasty feeling he would follow me.* ♦ *When she was asked to leave she* ***got/turned nasty.*** ♦ *a nasty bend in the road* ♦ *What's that nasty smell in this cupboard?* ▶ **nastily** *adv* ▶ **nastiness** *noun* [U]

nation /ˈneɪʃn/ *noun* [C] a country or all the people in a country: *a summit of the leaders of seven nations* ➲ note at **country**

national¹ /ˈnæʃnəl/ *adj* connected with all of a country; typical of a particular country: *Here is today's national and international news.* ♦ *a national newspaper* ♦ *national costume* ➲ look at **international, regional, local** ▶ **nationally** /-nəli/ *adv*

national² /ˈnæʃnəl/ *noun* [C] (*formal*) a citizen of a particular country

ˌnational ˈanthem *noun* [C] the official song of a country that is played at public events

the ˌNational ˈHealth Service *noun* [sing] (*abbr* **NHS**) the system that provides free or cheap medical care for everyone in Britain and that is paid for by taxes ➲ look at **health service**

ˌNational Inˈsurance *noun* [U] (*abbr* **NI**) (in Britain) the system of payments that have to be made by employers and employees to the government to help people who are ill, unemployed, old, etc: *to pay National Insurance contributions*

nationalise = **nationalize**

nationalism /ˈnæʃnəlɪzəm/ *noun* [U] **1** the desire of a group of people who share the same race, culture, language, etc. to form an independent country **2** a feeling of love or pride for your own

N

country; a feeling that your country is better than any other

nationalist /ˈnæʃnəlɪst/ *noun* [C] a person who wants their country or region to become independent: *a Welsh nationalist*

nationalistic /ˌnæʃnəˈlɪstɪk/ *adj* having strong feelings of love for or pride in your own country so that you think it is better than any other

> **HELP** **Nationalistic** is usually used in a critical way, meaning that a person's feelings of pride are too strong.

nationality /ˌnæʃəˈnæləti/ *noun* [C,U] (*pl* **nationalities**) the state of being legally a citizen of a particular country: *to have French nationality* ◆ *students of many nationalities* ◆ *to have* ***dual nationality*** (= of two countries)

nationalize (also **-ise**) /ˈnæʃnəlaɪz/ *verb* [T] to put a company or an organization under the control of the government **OPP** **privatize** ▶ **nationalization** (also **-isation**) /ˌnæʃnəlaɪˈzeɪʃn/ *noun* [U]

ˌnational ˈpark *noun* [C] a large area of beautiful land that is protected by the government so that the public can enjoy it

nationwide /ˌneɪʃnˈwaɪd/ *adj, adv* over the whole of a country: *The police launched a nationwide hunt for the killer.*

native[1] /ˈneɪtɪv/ *adj* **1** [only *before* a noun] connected with the place where you were born or where you have always lived: *your native language/country/city* ◆ *native Londoners* **2** [only *before* a noun] connected with the people who originally lived in a country before other people, especially white people, came to live there: *native art/dance*

> **HELP** Be careful. This sense of **native** is sometimes considered offensive

3 native (to ...) (used about an animal or plant) living or growing naturally in a particular place: *This plant is native to South America.* ◆ *a native species/habitat*

native[2] /ˈneɪtɪv/ *noun* [C] **1** a person who was born in a particular place: *a native of New York* **2** [usually pl] (*old-fashioned*) the people who were living in Africa, America, etc. originally, before the Europeans arrived there

> **HELP** Be careful. This sense of **native** is now considered offensive.

ˌNative AˈmericanORTH (also **AˌmericanˈIndian**) *adj, noun* [C] (of) a member of the race of people who were the original people to live in America

ˌnative ˈspeaker *noun* [C] a person who speaks a language as their first language and has not learnt it as a foreign language: *All our Spanish teachers are native speakers.*

NATO (also **Nato**) /ˈneɪtəʊ/ *abbr* **North Atlantic Treaty Organization**; a group of European countries, Canada and the US, who agree to give each other military help if necessary

natural /ˈnætʃrəl/ *adj* **1** [only *before* a noun] existing in nature; not made or caused by humans: *I prefer to see animals in their* ***natural habitat*** *rather than in zoos.* ◆ *Britain's* ***natural resources*** *include coal, oil and gas.* ◆ *She died of* ***natural causes*** (= of old age or illness). **2** usual or normal: *It's natural to feel nervous before an interview.* **OPP** **unnatural** **3** that you had from birth or that was easy for you to learn: *a natural gift for languages* **4** [only *before* a noun] (used about parents or their children) related by blood: *She's his stepmother, not his natural mother.*

ˌnatural ˈhistory *noun* [U] the study of plants and animals

naturalist /ˈnætʃrəlɪst/ *noun* [C] a person who studies plants and animals

naturalize (also **-ise**) /ˈnætʃrəlaɪz/ *verb* [T, usually passive] to make sb a citizen of a country where they were not born ▶ **naturalization** (also **-isation**) /ˌnætʃrəlaɪˈzeɪʃn/ *noun* [U]

naturally /ˈnætʃrəli/ *adv* **1** of course; as you would expect: *The team was naturally upset about its defeat.* **2** in a natural way; not forced or artificial: *naturally wavy hair* ◆ *He is naturally a very cheerful person.* **3** in a way that is relaxed and normal: *Don't try and impress people. Just* ***act naturally.***

nature /ˈneɪtʃə(r)/ *noun* **1** [U] all the plants, animals, etc. in the universe and all the things that happen in it that are not made or caused by people: *the forces of nature* (for example volcanoes, hurricanes, etc.) ◆ *the wonders/beauties of nature* ➲ note at **scenery**

> **HELP** You cannot say 'the nature' with this meaning. Use another word: *I love walking in* ***the countryside.*** ◆ *We have to protect* ***the environment.***

2 [C,U] the qualities or character of a person or thing: *It's* ***not in his nature*** *to be unkind.* ◆ *It's* ***human nature*** *never to be completely satisfied.* ◆ *She's basically honest* ***by nature.*** **3** [sing] a type of sth: *I'm not very interested in things of that nature.* ◆ *books of a scientific nature* **4 -natured** [in compounds] having a particular quality or type of character: *a kind-natured man*

IDM **second nature** ➲ **second**[1]

naughty /ˈnɔːti/ *adj* (**naughtier**; **naughtiest**) (*especially BrE*) (used when you are talking to or about a child) not obeying: *It was very naughty of you to wander off on your own.* **SYN** **badly behaved** ▶ **naughtily** *adv* ▶ **naughtiness** *noun* [U]

nausea /ˈnɔːziə/ *noun* [U] the feeling that you are going to **vomit** (= bring up food from the stomach) ➲ look at **sick**

nauseate /ˈnɔːzieɪt/ *verb* [T] to cause sb to feel sick or disgusted ▶ **nauseating** *adj*

nautical /ˈnɔːtɪkl/ *adj* connected with ships, sailors or sailing

naval /ˈneɪvl/ *adj* connected with the navy: *a naval base/officer/battle*

navel /ˈneɪvl/ (also *informal* ˈbelly button) *noun* [C] the small hole or lump in the middle of your stomach

navigable /ˈnævɪɡəbl/ *adj* (used about a river or narrow area of sea) that boats can sail along

navigate /ˈnævɪɡeɪt/ *verb* **1** [I] to use a map, etc. to find your way to somewhere: *If you drive, I'll navigate.* ➲ look at **satnav** **2** [T] to sail a boat along a river or across a sea **3** [I,T] to find your way around on the Internet or on a website ▶ **navigator** /ˈnævɪɡeɪtə(r)/ *noun* [C] ▶ **navigation** /ˌnævɪˈɡeɪʃn/ *noun* [U]

navy /ˈneɪvi/ *noun* [C, with sing or pl verb] (*pl* navies) the part of a country's armed forces that fights at sea in times of war: *to join the navy/the Navy* ◆ *Their son is in* **the navy/the Navy**. ➲ note at **war** ➲ look at **air force, army, merchant navy** ➲ *adjective* **naval**

GRAMMAR In the singular, **navy** is used with a singular or plural verb: *The Navy is/are introducing a new warship this year.*

ˌnavy ˈblue (also navy) *adj, noun* [U] (of) a very dark blue colour

N

NB (also nb) /ˌen ˈbiː/ *abbr* (from Latin) **nota bene**; (used before a written note) take special notice of: *NB There is a charge for reservations.*

NE *abbr* = **north-east**[1]: *NE Scotland*

near[1] /nɪə(r)/ *adj* (nearer; nearest) *adv, prep* **1** not far away in time or distance; close: *Let's walk to the library. It's quite near.* ◆ *We're hoping to move to Wales* **in the near future** (= very soon). ◆ *Where's the nearest Post Office?* ◆ *The day of the interview was getting nearer.* ◆ *It's a little village near Cardiff.* ➲ note at **nearby, next**

HELP **Near or close? Close** and **near** are often the same in meaning but in some phrases, such as the following, only one of them may be used: *a close friend/relative* ◆ *the near future* ◆ *a close contest*

2 near- [in compounds] almost: *a near-perfect performance* **3** [usually **nearest**] similar; most similar: *He was* **the nearest thing to** (= the person most like) *a father she had ever had.* ➲ look at **o.n.o.**

IDM **close/dear/near to sb's heart** ➲ **heart**

a near miss a situation where sth nearly hits you or where sth bad nearly happens: *The bullet flew past his ear. It was a very near miss.*

a near thing a situation in which you are successful, but which could also have ended badly: *Phew! That was a near thing! It could have been a disaster.*

nowhere near ➲ **nowhere**

to the nearest ... followed by a number when you are calculating or measuring approximately: *We worked out the cost to the nearest 50 dollars.*

near[2] /nɪə(r)/ *verb* [T,I] to get closer to sth in time or distance: *At last we were nearing the end of the project.*

nearby /ˌnɪəˈbaɪ/ *adj, adv* not far away in distance: *A new restaurant has opened nearby.* ◆ *We went out to a nearby restaurant.*

HELP **Nearby** or **near**? Notice that **nearby** as an adjective is only used before the noun. **Near** cannot be used before a noun in this way: *We went out to a nearby restaurant.* ◆ *The restaurant we went to is quite near.*

nearly /ˈnɪəli/ *adv* almost; not completely or exactly: *It's nearly five years since I've seen him.* ◆ *Linda was so badly hurt she very nearly died.* ◆ *It's not far now. We're nearly there.*

IDM **not nearly** much less than; not at all: *It's not nearly as warm as it was yesterday.*

nearsighted /ˌnɪəˈsaɪtɪd/ (*especially AmE*) = **short-sighted**(1)

neat /niːt/ *adj* (neater; neatest) **1** arranged or done carefully; tidy and in order: *Please keep your room* **neat and tidy**. ◆ *neat rows of figures* **2** (used about a person) liking to keep things tidy and in order: *The new secretary was very neat and efficient.* **3** simple but clever: *a neat solution/explanation/idea/trick* **4** (*AmE informal*) good; nice: *That's a really neat car!* **5** (*AmE* straight) (used about an alcoholic drink) on its own, without ice, water or any other liquid: *a neat whisky* ▶ **neatly** *adv*: *neatly folded clothes* ▶ **neatness** *noun* [U]

necessarily /ˈnesəsərəli; ˌnesəˈserəli/ *adv* used to say that sth cannot be avoided or has to happen: *The number of tickets available is necessarily limited.*

IDM **not necessarily** used to say that sth might be true but is not definitely or always true

necessary /ˈnesəsəri/ *adj* necessary (for sb/sth) (to do sth) that is needed for a purpose or a reason: *A good diet is necessary for a healthy life.* ◆ *It's not necessary for you all to come.* ◆ *If necessary, I can pick you up after work that day.* **SYN** **essential** **OPP** **unnecessary**

necessitate /nəˈsesɪteɪt/ *verb* [T] (*formal*) to make sth necessary

necessity /nəˈsesəti/ *noun* (*pl* necessities) **1** [U] necessity (for sth/to do sth) the need for sth; the fact that sth must be done or must happen: *Is there any necessity for change?* ◆ *There's no necessity to write every single name down.* ◆ *They sold the car* **out of necessity** (= because they had to). **2** [C] something that you must have: *Clean water is an absolute necessity.*

neck /nek/ *noun* [C] **1** the part of your body that joins your head to your shoulders: *She wrapped a scarf around her neck.* ◆ *Giraffes have long necks.* ➲ picture at **body** **2** the part of a piece of clothing that goes round your neck: *a polo-neck/V-neck sweater* ◆ *The neck on this shirt is too tight.* ➲ picture on **page P1** **3** -necked [in compounds] having the type of neck mentioned: *a round-necked sweater* **4** [C] the long narrow part of sth: *the neck of a bottle*

IDM **by the scruff (of the/sb's neck)** ➲ **scruff**

neck and neck (with sb/sth) equal or level with sb in a race or competition
up to your neck in sth having a lot of sth to deal with: *We're up to our necks in work at the moment.*

necklace /ˈnekləs/ *noun* [C] a piece of jewellery that you wear around your neck ➲ picture at **jewellery**

necktie /ˈnektaɪ/ (*AmE*) = **tie**²(1)

nectar /ˈnektə(r)/ *noun* [U] a sweet liquid that is produced by flowers and collected by **bees** (= black and yellow insects) to make **honey** (= a sweet substance that we eat)

née /neɪ/ *adj* used in front of the family name that a woman had before she got married: *Louise Mitchell, née Greenan* ➲ look at **maiden name**

⚷ **need**¹ /niːd/ *verb* [T] [not usually used in the continuous tenses] **1** need sb/sth (for sth/to do sth) if you need sb/sth, you want or must have them or it: *All living things need water.* ◆ *I need a new bag. The strap's broken on this one.* ◆ *Does Roshni need any help?* ◆ *I need to find a doctor.* ◆ *I need you to go to the shop for me.* **2** to have to: *Do we need to buy the tickets in advance?* ◆ *I need to ask some advice.* ◆ *You didn't need to bring any food but it was very kind of you.*

> **GRAMMAR** Note that the question form of the main verb **need** is **do I need**?, etc. and the past tense is **needed** (question form **did you need**?, etc.; negative **didn't need**).

3 need (sth) doing if sth needs doing, it is necessary or must be done: *This jumper needs washing.* ◆ *He needed his eyes testing.*

⚷ **need**² /niːd/ *modal verb*

> **GRAMMAR** The forms of **need** as a modal verb are: present tense **need** in all persons; negative **need not (needn't** /ˈniːdnt/**)**, question form **need I**?, etc.

[not used in the continuous tenses; used mainly in questions or negative sentences after *if* and *whether*, or with words like *hardly*, *only*, *never*] to have to: *Need we pay the whole amount now?* ◆ *You needn't come to the meeting if you're too busy.* ◆ *I **hardly need** remind you* (= you already know) *that this is very serious.*

> **GRAMMAR** When talking about the past, **needn't have** with a past participle shows that you *did* something but discovered after doing it that it was *not* necessary: *I needn't have gone to the hospital* (= I went but it wasn't necessary). **Didn't need to** with an infinitive usually means that you did *not* do something because you *already* knew that it was not necessary: *I didn't need to go to the hospital* (= I didn't go because it wasn't necessary).

ⓘ For more information about modal verbs, look at the **Reference Section** at the back of this dictionary.

⚷ **need**³ /niːd/ *noun* **1** [U,sing] need (for sth); need (for sb/sth) to do sth a situation in which you must have or do sth: *We are all **in need of** a rest.* ◆ *There is a growing need for new books in schools.* ◆ *There's **no need for** you to come if you don't want to.* ◆ *Do phone me if you **feel the need** to talk to someone.* **2** [C, usually pl] the things that you must have: *He doesn't earn enough to pay for his basic needs.* ◆ *Parents must consider their children's emotional as well as their physical needs.* **3** [U] the state of not having enough food, money or support: *a campaign to help families **in need***

⚷ **needle** /ˈniːdl/ *noun* [C]
➤FOR SEWING **1** a small thin piece of metal with a point at one end and an **eye** (= a hole) at the other that is used for sewing: *to thread a needle with cotton* ➲ look at **pins and needles** ➲ picture at **sew**
➤FOR KNITTING **2** (also ˈ**knitting needle**) one of two long thin pieces of metal or plastic with a point at one end that are used for knitting: *knitting needles* ➲ picture at **sew**
➤FOR DRUGS **3** the sharp metal part of a **syringe** (= an instrument that is used for putting drugs into sb's body or for taking blood out): *a hypodermic needle* ➲ picture at **medicine**
➤ON INSTRUMENT **4** a thin metal part on a scientific instrument that moves to point to the correct measurement or direction: *The needle on the petrol gauge showed 'empty'.*
➤ON TREE **5** the thin, hard pointed leaf of certain trees that stay green all year: *pine needles* ➲ picture at **tree**

needless /ˈniːdləs/ *adj* that is not necessary and that you can easily avoid: *We had gone through a lot of needless worry. He was safe at home.* ▶ **needlessly** *adv*

needlework /ˈniːdlwɜːk/ *noun* [U] something that you sew by hand, especially for decoration

needy /ˈniːdi/ *adj* (needier; neediest) **1** not having enough money, food, clothes, etc. **2** the needy *noun* [pl] people who do not have enough money, food, clothes, etc.

⚷ **negative**¹ /ˈnegətɪv/ *adj* **1** bad or harmful: *The effects of the new rule have been rather negative.* OPP **positive** **2** only thinking about the bad qualities of sb/sth: *I'm feeling very negative about my job —in fact I'm thinking about leaving.* ◆ *If you go into the match with a negative attitude, you'll never win.* OPP **positive** **3** (used about a word, phrase or sentence) meaning 'no' or 'not': *a negative sentence* ◆ *His reply was negative/He gave a negative reply* (= he said 'no'). OPP **affirmative** **4** (*abbr* neg.) (used about a medical or scientific test) showing that sth has not happened or has not been found: *The results of the pregnancy test were negative.* OPP **positive** **5** (used about a number) less than zero OPP **positive** ▶ **negatively** *adv*

negative² /ˈnegətɪv/ *noun* [C] **1** a word, phrase or sentence that says or means 'no' or 'not': *Roger answered **in the negative*** (= he said no). ◆ *'Never', 'neither' and 'nobody' are all negatives.* OPP **affirmative** **2** a piece of film from which we can make a photograph. The light areas of a negative

N

are dark on the final photograph and the dark areas are light.

neglect /nɪˈɡlekt/ *verb* [T] **1** to give too little or no attention or care to sb/sth: *Don't neglect your health.* ♦ *The old house had stood neglected for years.* **2** (*formal*) **neglect to do sth** to fail or forget to do sth: *He neglected to mention that he had spent time in prison.* ▸ **neglect** *noun* [U]: *The garden was like a jungle after years of neglect.* ▸ **neglected** *adj*: *neglected children*

negligence /ˈneɡlɪdʒəns/ *noun* [U] not being careful enough; lack of care: *The accident was a result of negligence.* ▸ **negligent** /ˈneɡlɪdʒənt/ *adj* ▸ **negligently** *adv*

negligible /ˈneɡlɪdʒəbl/ *adj* very small and therefore not important

negotiable /nɪˈɡəʊʃiəbl/ *adj* that can be decided or changed by discussion: *The price is not negotiable/non-negotiable.*

negotiate /nɪˈɡəʊʃieɪt/ *verb* **1** [I] **negotiate (with sb) (for/about sth)** to talk to sb in order to decide or agree about sth: *The unions are still negotiating with management about this year's pay claim.* **2** [T] to decide or agree sth by talking about it: *to negotiate an agreement/a deal/a settlement* **3** [T] to get over, past or through sth difficult: *To escape, prisoners would have to negotiate a five-metre wall.* ▸ **negotiator** /-tə(r)/ *noun* [C]

negotiation /nɪˌɡəʊʃiˈeɪʃn/ *noun* [pl, U] discussions at which people try to decide or agree sth: *to enter into/break off negotiations* ♦ *The pay rise is still **under negotiation**.*

neigh /neɪ/ *noun* [C] the long high sound that a horse makes ▸ **neigh** *verb* [I]

⚷ **neighbour** (*AmE* **neighbor**) /ˈneɪbə(r)/ *noun* [C] **1** a person who lives near you: *My neighbours are very friendly.* ♦ *our **next-door neighbours*** **2** a person or thing that is near or next to another: *Britain's nearest neighbour is France.* ♦ *Discuss the answers with your neighbour.*

⚷ **neighbourhood** (*AmE* **neighborhood**) /ˈneɪbəhʊd/ *noun* [C] a particular part of a town and the people who live there: *a friendly neighbourhood*

neighbouring (*AmE* **neighboring**) /ˈneɪbərɪŋ/ *adj* [only *before* a noun] near or next to: *Farmers from neighbouring villages come into town each week for the market.*

neighbourly (*AmE* **neighborly**) /ˈneɪbəli/ *adj* friendly and helpful

⚷ **neither** /ˈnaɪðə(r); ˈniːðə(r)/ *determiner, pron, adv* **1** (used about two people or things) not one and not the other: *Neither team played very well.* ♦ *Neither of the teams played very well.* ♦ *'Would you like tea or juice?' 'Neither, thank you. I'm not thirsty.'*

> **GRAMMAR** Notice that **neither** is followed by a singular noun and verb: *Neither day was suitable.* The noun or pronoun that follows **neither of** is in the plural but the verb may be singular or plural: *Neither of the days is/are suitable.*

2 also not; not either: *I don't eat meat and neither does Carlos.* ♦ *'I don't like fish.' 'Neither do I.'* ♦ (*informal*) *'I don't like fish.' 'Me neither.'*

> **GRAMMAR** In this sense **nor** can be used in the same way: *'I don't like fish.' 'Nor do I.'* Notice that when you use **not … either** the order of words is different: *I don't eat meat and Carlos doesn't either.* ♦ *'I haven't seen that film.' 'I haven't either.'*

3 neither … nor not … and not: *Neither Carlos nor I eat meat.* ➲ look at **either**

> **GRAMMAR** **Neither … nor** can be used with a singular or a plural verb: *Neither Stella nor Meena was/were at the meeting.*

neon /ˈniːɒn/ *noun* [U] (*symbol* **Ne**) a type of gas that is used for making bright lights and signs

⚷ **nephew** /ˈnefjuː; ˈnevjuː/ *noun* [C] the son of your brother or sister; the son of your husband's or wife's brother or sister ➲ look at **niece**

nepotism /ˈnepətɪzəm/ *noun* [U] giving unfair advantages to your own family if you are in a position of power, especially by giving them jobs

Neptune /ˈneptjuːn/ *noun* [sing] the planet that is 8th in order from the sun

nerd /nɜːd/ *noun* [C] (*informal*) a person who spends a lot of time on a particular interest and who is not always popular or fashionable: *a computer nerd* **SYN** **geek** ▸ **nerdy** *adj*

⚷ **nerve** /nɜːv/ *noun* **1** [C] one of the long thin threads in your body that carry feelings or other messages to and from your brain: *nerve endings* **2 nerves** [pl] worried, nervous feelings: *Breathing deeply should help to **calm/steady** your **nerves**.* ♦ *I was **a bag of nerves** before my interview.* **3** [U] the courage that you need to do sth difficult or dangerous: *Racing drivers need a lot of nerve.* ♦ *He didn't **have the nerve** to ask Maria to go out with him.* ♦ *Some pilots **lose** their **nerve** and can't fly any more.* **4** [sing, U] (*informal*) a way of behaving that people think is not acceptable: *You've got a nerve, calling me lazy!*

IDM **get on sb's nerves** (*informal*) to annoy sb or make sb angry

ˈ**nerve-racking** *adj* making you very nervous or worried

⚷ **nervous** /ˈnɜːvəs/ *adj* **1 nervous (about/of sth/doing sth)** worried or afraid: *I'm a bit nervous about travelling on my own.* ♦ *I always **get nervous** just before a match.* ♦ *a nervous laugh/smile/voice* ♦ *She was nervous of giving the wrong answer.* **OPP** **confident** **2** connected with the nerves of the body: *a nervous disorder* ▸ **nervously** *adv* ▸ **nervousness** *noun* [U]

ˌ**nervous** ˈ**breakdown** (also **breakdown**) *noun* [C] a time when sb suddenly becomes so unhappy that they cannot continue living and working normally: *to have a nervous breakdown*

the ˈnervous system *noun* [C] your brain and all the nerves in your body

nest /nest/ *noun* [C] **1** a structure that a bird builds to keep its eggs and babies in ➲ picture on **page P12** **2** the home of certain animals or insects: *a wasps' nest* ▶ **nest** *verb* [I]

ˈnest egg *noun* [C] (*informal*) an amount of money that you save to use in the future

nestle /ˈnesl/ *verb* [I,T] to be or go into a position where you are comfortable, protected or hidden: *The baby nestled her head on her mother's shoulder.*

net¹ /net/ *noun* **1** [U] material that has large, often square, spaces between the threads: *net curtains* **2** [C] a piece of net that is used for a particular purpose: *a tennis/fishing/mosquito net* ➲ look at **safety net** ➲ picture on **page P4** **3 the Net** (*informal*) = **the Internet**

net² (also **nett**) /net/ *adj* **net (of sth)** (used about a number or amount) from which nothing more needs to be taken away: *I earn about £15000 net* (= after tax, etc. has been paid). ♦ *The net weight of the biscuits is 350g* (= not including the box). ♦ *a net profit* ➲ look at **gross**

net³ /net/ *verb* [T] (**ne<u>tt</u>ing**; **ne<u>tt</u>ed**) **1** to gain sth as a profit **2** to catch sth with a net; to kick a ball into a net

netball /ˈnetbɔːl/ *noun* [U] a game that is played by two teams of seven players, usually women. Players score by throwing the ball through a high net hanging from a ring.

netbook /ˈnetbʊk/ *noun* [C] a **laptop** (= a small computer) designed especially for using the Internet and email ➲ note at **computer**

netiquette /ˈnetɪket/ *noun* [U] (*informal*) the rules of correct or polite behaviour among people using the Internet

TOPIC

Netiquette

When you take part in an **online discussion** on a **message board/bulletin board** (= a place where you can read or write messages on the Internet), it is important to follow the rules of **netiquette**. When you **post a message** or **follow a thread** (= add your comments), you should not **go off-topic** (= talk about things that are not connected to the topic of the discussion), or write everything in capital letters. As in real life, you should be polite and show respect to the other people taking part.

ˈNet surfer = **surfer**(2)

netting /ˈnetɪŋ/ *noun* [U] material that is made of long pieces of string, thread, wire, etc. that are tied together with spaces between them

nettle /ˈnetl/ *noun* [C] a wild plant with large leaves. Some **nettles** make your skin red and painful if you touch them.

network¹ /ˈnetwɜːk/ *noun* [C] **1** a system of roads, railway lines, nerves, etc. that are connected to each other: *an underground railway network* **2** a group of people or companies that work closely together: *We have a network of agents who sell our goods all over the country.* **3** a number of computers that are connected together so that information can be shared: *The network allows users to share files.* **4** a group of TV or radio companies that are connected and that send out the same programmes at the same time in different parts of a country: *the four big US television networks*

network² /ˈnetwɜːk/ *verb* **1** [T] to connect a number of computers together in order to share information **2** [I] to talk to people who may be useful to you in your work: *Conferences are a good place to network.* ▶ **networking** *noun* [U] ➲ look at **social networking**

neurologist /njʊəˈrɒlədʒɪst/ *noun* [C] a doctor who studies and treats diseases of the nerves

neurology /njʊəˈrɒlədʒi/ *noun* [U] the scientific study of nerves and their diseases ▶ **neurological** /ˌnjʊərəˈlɒdʒɪkl/ *adj*: *He suffered severe neurological damage.*

neuron /ˈnjʊərɒn/ (*especially BrE* **neurone** /ˈnjʊərəʊn/) *noun* [C] a cell that carries information within the brain and between the brain and other parts of the body; a nerve cell

neurosis /njʊəˈrəʊsɪs/ *noun* [C] (*pl* **neuroses** /-əʊsiːz/) a mental illness that causes strong feelings of fear and worry

neurotic /njʊəˈrɒtɪk/ *adj* **1** suffering from a **neurosis** **2** worried about things in a way that is not normal

neuter¹ /ˈnjuːtə(r)/ *adj* (used about a word in some languages) not **masculine** or **feminine** according to the rules of grammar ➲ note at **masculine**

neuter² /ˈnjuːtə(r)/ *verb* [T] to remove the sexual parts of an animal ➲ look at **castrate**

neutral¹ /ˈnjuːtrəl/ *adj* **1** not supporting or belonging to either side in an argument, war, etc: *I don't take sides when my brothers argue—I* ***remain neutral.*** ♦ *The two sides agreed to meet on neutral ground.* ♦ *They escaped to Switzerland, which was a neutral country during the Second World War.* **2** having or showing no strong qualities, emotions or colour: *neutral colours* ♦ *a neutral tone of voice*

neutral² /ˈnjuːtrəl/ *noun* [U] the position of the gears (= a part of the machinery in a vehicle) when no power is sent from the engine to the wheels

neutrality /njuːˈtræləti/ *noun* [U] the state of not supporting either side in an argument, war, etc.

neutralize (also **-ise**) /ˈnjuːtrəlaɪz/ *verb* [T] to take away the effect of sth: *to neutralize a threat*

neutron /ˈnjuːtrɒn/ *noun* [C] part of the **nucleus** (= the central part) of an atom that carries no electric charge ➲ look at **electron**, **proton**

never /ˈnevə(r)/ *adv* **1** at no time; not ever: *I've never been to Portugal.* ♦ *He never ever eats meat.* ♦ (*formal*) *Never before has such a high standard been achieved.* **2** used for emphasizing a negative

N

statement: *I never realized she was so unhappy.* ♦ *Roy never so much as looked at us* (= he didn't even look at us). ♦ *'I got the job!' 'Never!'* (= expressing surprise)
IDM **never mind** ➲ **mind**[2]
you never know ➲ **know**[1]

nevertheless /ˌnevəðəˈles/ *adv* (*formal*) in spite of that: *It was a cold, rainy day. Nevertheless, more people came than we had expected.* SYN **nonetheless** ➲ note at **contrast**

new /njuː/ *adj* (newer; newest) **1** that has recently been built, made, discovered, etc: *a new design/film/hospital* ♦ *a new method of treating mental illness* ♦ *new evidence* OPP **old** **2** different or changed from what was before: *I've just started reading a new book.* ♦ *to make new friends* OPP **old** **3** new (to sb) that you have not seen, learnt, etc. before: *This type of machine is new to me.* ♦ *to learn a new language* **4** new (to sth) having just started being or doing sth: *a new parent* ♦ *She's new to the job and needs a lot of help.* ♦ *a new member of the club*
IDM **a (whole) new/different ball game** ➲ **ball game**
break fresh/new ground ➲ **ground**[1]
▸ **newness** *noun* [U]

ˈ**New Age** *adj* connected with a way of life that rejects modern Western values and is based on spiritual ideas and beliefs: *a New Age festival* ♦ ***New Age travellers*** (= people in Britain who reject the values of modern society and travel from place to place living in their vehicles)

newborn /ˈnjuːbɔːn/ *adj* [only *before* a noun] (used about a baby) that has been born very recently

newcomer /ˈnjuːkʌmə(r)/ *noun* [C] a person who has just arrived in a place

newfangled /ˌnjuːˈfæŋgld/ *adj* new or modern in a way that the speaker does not like

newly /ˈnjuːli/ *adv* [usually before a past participle] recently: *the newly appointed Minister of Health*

ˈ**newly-wed** *noun* [C, usually pl] a person who has recently got married

news /njuːz/ *noun* **1** [U] information about sth that has happened recently: *Write and tell me all your news.* ♦ *Have you had any news from Susie recently?* ♦ *That's news to me* (= I didn't know that). ♦ *I've got some good news: you've passed the exam!*

> GRAMMAR **News** is uncountable. When we are talking about a single item we say **a piece of news** (not 'a news'). **News** is followed by a singular verb: *The news is very depressing.*

2 the news [sing] a regular programme giving the most recent news on the radio or TV: *We always watch the 10 o'clock news on TV.* ♦ *I heard about the accident* ***on the news***.
IDM **break the news (to sb)** to be the first to tell sb about sth important that has happened

newsagent /ˈnjuːzeɪdʒənt/ (*AmE* newsdealer /ˈnjuːzdiːlə(r)/) *noun* **1** [C] a person who owns or works in a shop that sells newspapers and magazines, etc. **2 the newsagent's** [sing] a shop that sells newspapers, magazines, etc.

newscaster /ˈnjuːzkɑːstə(r)/ = **newsreader**

newsgroup /ˈnjuːzgruːp/ *noun* [C] a place in a computer network, especially the Internet, where people can discuss a particular subject and exchange information about it

newsletter /ˈnjuːzletə(r)/ *noun* [C] a report about an organization that is sent regularly to members and other people who may be interested

newspaper /ˈnjuːzpeɪpə(r)/ *noun* **1** (also paper) [C] large folded pieces of paper printed with news, advertisements and articles on various subjects. Newspapers are printed and sold either every day or every week and some also appear online: *a daily/weekly/Sunday newspaper* ♦ *an online newspaper* ♦ *a newspaper article* ♦ *I read about it* ***in the newspaper***. ♦ *She works for the local newspaper* (= the company that produces it) **2** [U] the paper on which newspapers are printed: *We wrapped the plates in newspaper.* ➲ look at **media**

> TOPIC
>
> **Newspapers**
>
> Newspapers and the **journalists/reporters** who write **articles** for them are called **the press**. The **editor** decides what is printed. **Quality** newspapers deal with the news in a serious way. **Tabloids** have small pages, and some of them have **sensational** (= shocking) stories and **gossip columns** (= reports about famous people's private lives). Photographers who follow famous people in order to take photographs of them are called **paparazzi**. You can buy **newspapers** and **magazines** at **the newsagent's** or you might have them delivered to your house by a **paper boy** or **paper girl**. Many **newspapers** are also available online.

newsreader /ˈnjuːzriːdə(r)/ (also newscaster) *noun* [C] a person who reads the news on the radio or TV

ˈ**news-stand** (*AmE*) = **bookstall**

the ˌNew ˈTestament *noun* [sing] the second part of the Bible that describes the life and teachings of Jesus Christ ➲ look at **the Old Testament**

new ˈyear (also New Year) *noun* [U, sing] the first few days of January: *Happy New Year!* ♦ *We will get in touch in the new year.* ♦ ***New Year's Eve*** (= 31 December) ♦ ***New Year's Day*** (= 1 January)

next /nekst/ *adj, adv* **1** [usually with *the*] coming immediately after sth in order, space or time; closest: *The next bus leaves in twenty minutes.* ♦ *The next name on the list is Paulo.* ♦ *Who is next?*

> HELP **Next or nearest? The next** means 'the following' in a series of events or places: *When is your next appointment?* ♦ *Turn left at the next traffic lights.* **The nearest** means 'the closest' in time or place: *Where's the nearest supermarket?*

N

2 [used without *the* before days of the week, months, seasons, years, etc.] the one immediately following the present one: *See you again next Monday.* ◆ *Let's go camping next weekend.* ◆ *next summer/next year/next Christmas* **3** after this or after that; then: *I wonder what will happen next.* ◆ *I know Joe arrived first, but who came next?* ◆ *It was ten years until I next saw her.* ➲ note at **then** **4** **the next** *noun* [sing] the person or thing that is next: *If we miss this train, we'll have to wait two hours for the next.*
IDM **last/next but one, two, etc.** ➲ **last**[1]

ˌnext ˈdoor *adj, adv* in or into the next house or building: *our* ***next-door neighbours*** ◆ *Who lives next door?* ◆ *The school is* ***next door to*** *an old people's home.*

ˌnext of ˈkin *noun* [C] (*pl* **next of kin**) your closest living relative or relatives: *My husband is my next of kin.*

⚷ **next to** *prep* **1** at the side of sb/sth; beside: *He sat down next to Gita.* ◆ *There's a cafe next to the cinema.* **2** in a position after sth: *Next to English my favourite subject is Maths.*
IDM **next to nothing** almost nothing: *We took plenty of money but we've got next to nothing left.*

NGO /ˌen dʒiː ˈəʊ/ *noun* [C] (*pl* **NGOs**) **non-governmental organization**; a charity, association, etc. that is independent of government and business

NHS /ˌen eɪtʃ ˈes/ *abbr* (*BrE*) = **National Health Service**

NI *abbr* = **National Insurance**

nib /nɪb/ *noun* [C] the metal point of a pen, where the ink comes out ➲ picture at **stationery**

nibble /ˈnɪbl/ *verb* [I,T] to eat sth by taking small bites: *The bread had been nibbled by mice.* ▶ **nibble** *noun* [C]

⚷ **nice** /naɪs/ *adj* (**nicer**; **nicest**) **1** pleasant, enjoyable or attractive: *a nice place/feeling/smile* ◆ *I'm not eating this—it doesn't taste very nice.* ◆ *Did you* ***have a nice time?*** ◆ *You look very nice.* ◆ *It would be nice to spend more time at home.* ◆ *'Hi, I'm Kate.' 'I'm Fergus—****nice to meet you.****'* ◆ *Have a nice day!* (a friendly way of saying goodbye, especially to customers) **2** (*informal*) used before adjectives and adverbs to emphasize how pleasant or suitable sth is: *It's nice and warm by the fire.* ◆ *a nice long chat* **3** **nice (to sb); nice (of sb) (to do sth); nice (about sth)** kind; friendly: *What a nice girl!* ◆ *Everyone was very nice to me when I felt ill.* ◆ *It was really nice of Donna to help us.* ◆ *The neighbours were very nice about it when I hit their car.* OPP **nasty** ▶ **nicely** *adv* ▶ **niceness** *noun* [U]

OTHER WORDS FOR

nice

In informal English you can say **great**, **lovely** or **wonderful** instead of 'nice' or 'very nice': *The party was great.* ◆ *We had a lovely weekend.* When you want to talk about a person, you can say 'He/She is **lovely**' or 'He/She is very **friendly**'. We also say: *a* ***cosy*** */an* ***attractive*** *room* ◆ ***beautiful/lovely*** *weather* ◆ ***expensive/fashionable/smart*** *clothes.*

niche /niːʃ; nɪtʃ/ *noun* [C] **1** a job, position, etc. that is suitable for you: *to find your niche in life* **2** (in business) an opportunity to sell a particular product to a particular group of people **3** a place in a wall that is further back, where a statue, etc. can be put

nick[1] /nɪk/ *noun* [C] a small cut in sth
IDM **in good/bad nick** (*BrE slang*) in a good/bad state or condition
in the nick of time only just in time

nick[2] /nɪk/ *verb* [T] **1** to make a very small cut in sb/sth **2** (*BrE slang*) to steal sth **3** (*BrE slang*) to arrest sb

nickel /ˈnɪkl/ *noun* **1** [U] (*symbol* **Ni**) a hard silver-white metal that is often mixed with other metals **2** [C] an American or Canadian coin that is worth five cents

nickname /ˈnɪkneɪm/ *noun* [C] an informal name that is used instead of your real name, usually by your family or friends ▶ **nickname** *verb* [T]

nicotine /ˈnɪkətiːn/ *noun* [U] the poisonous substance in **tobacco** (= the dried leaves used for making cigarettes)

⚷ **niece** /niːs/ *noun* [C] the daughter of your brother or sister; the daughter of your husband's or wife's brother or sister: *My niece Jenny will be two next month.* ➲ look at **nephew**

niggle /ˈnɪɡl/ *verb* **1** [I,T] **niggle (at) sb** to annoy or worry sb: *His untidy habits really niggled her.* **2** [I] **niggle (about/over sth)** to complain or argue about things that are not important ▶ **niggle** *noun*: *There were no major problems, just a few niggles*

niggling /ˈnɪɡlɪŋ/ *adj* not very serious (but that does not go away): *niggling doubts* ◆ *a niggling injury*

⚷ **night** /naɪt/ *noun* [C,U] **1** the part of the day when it is dark and when most people sleep: *I had a strange dream last night.* ◆ *The baby cried* ***all night.*** ◆ *It's a long way home. Why don't you* ***stay the night?*** ◆ *We will be away for a few nights.* **2** the time between late afternoon and when you go to bed: *Let's go out on Saturday night.* ◆ *He doesn't get home until 8 o'clock* ***at night.*** ◆ *I went out with Kate* ***the other night*** (= a few nights ago).

HELP Note the use of different prepositions with **night**. **At** is most common: *I'm not allowed out after 11 o'clock at night.* **By** is used about something that you usually do in the night-time: *These animals sleep by day and hunt by night.* **In/during** the night is usually used for the night that has just passed: *I woke up twice in the night.* **On** is used when you are talking about one particular night: *On the night of Saturday 30 June.* **Tonight** means the night or evening of today: *Where are you staying tonight?*

IDM **an early/a late night** an evening when you go to bed earlier/later than usual: *Try to have an early night before the exam.*

N

in/at the dead of night ➲ **dead²**
a night out an evening that you spend out of the house enjoying yourself

nightclub /ˈnaɪtklʌb/ *noun* [C] = **club¹**(2)

nightdress /ˈnaɪtdres/ (also *informal* **nightie** /ˈnaɪti/) *noun* [C] a loose dress that a girl or woman wears in bed

nightingale /ˈnaɪtɪŋgeɪl/ *noun* [C] a small brown bird that has a beautiful song

nightlife /ˈnaɪtlaɪf/ *noun* [U] the entertainment that is available in the evenings in a particular place: *It's a small town with very little nightlife.*

nightly /ˈnaɪtli/ *adj, adv* happening every night: *a nightly news bulletin*

nightmare /ˈnaɪtmeə(r)/ *noun* [C] **1** a frightening or unpleasant dream: *I had a terrible nightmare about being stuck in a lift last night.* **2** (*informal*) an experience that is very unpleasant or frightening: *Travelling in the rush hour can be a real nightmare.*

ˈ**night-time** *noun* [U] the time when it is dark

nightwatchman /naɪtˈwɒtʃmən/ *noun* [C] (*pl* **-men** /-mən/) a man who guards a building at night

nil /nɪl/ *noun* [U] the number 0 (especially as the score in some games): *We won two-nil/by two goals to nil.* ➲ note at **zero**

N

nimble /ˈnɪmbl/ *adj* (**nimbler**; **nimblest**) able to move quickly and lightly ▶ **nimbly** /ˈnɪmbli/ *adv*

⚷ **nine** /naɪn/ *number* 9 ➲ note at **six**
IDM **nine to five** the hours that you work in most offices: *a nine-to-five job*

⚷ **nineteen** /ˌnaɪnˈtiːn/ *number* 19 ➲ note at **six** ▶ **nineteenth** /ˌnaɪnˈtiːnθ/ *ordinal number, noun* ➲ note at **sixth**

⚷ **ninety** /ˈnaɪnti/ *number* 90 ➲ note at **sixty** ▶ **ninetieth** /ˈnaɪntiəθ/ *ordinal number, noun* ➲ note at **sixth**

⚷ **ninth¹** /naɪnθ/ *ordinal number* 9th ➲ note at **sixth**

⚷ **ninth²** /naɪnθ/ *noun* [C] ⅑; one of nine equal parts of sth

nip /nɪp/ *verb* (**nipping**; **nipped**) **1** [I,T] to give sb/sth a quick bite or to quickly squeeze a piece of sb's skin between your thumb and finger: *She nipped him on the arm.* **2** [I] (*BrE spoken*) to go somewhere quickly and/or for a short time
IDM **nip sth in the bud** to stop sth bad before it develops or gets worse
▶ **nip** *noun* [C]

nipple /ˈnɪpl/ *noun* [C] **1** either of the two small dark circles on either side of your chest. A baby can suck milk from his or her mother's breast through the **nipples**. **2** (*AmE*) = **teat**(1)

niqab /nɪˈkɑːb/ *noun* [C] a piece of cloth that covers the face but not usually the eyes, worn in public by some Muslim women

nit /nɪt/ *noun* [C] the egg of a small insect that lives in the hair of people or animals

ˈ**nit-picking** *noun* [U] the habit of finding small mistakes in sb's work or paying too much attention to small, unimportant details ▶ ˈ**nit-picking** *adj*

nitrogen /ˈnaɪtrədʒən/ *noun* [U] (*symbol* N) a gas that has no colour, taste or smell. **Nitrogen** forms about 80% of the air around the earth.

the nitty-gritty /ˌnɪti ˈgrɪti/ *noun* [sing] (*informal*) the most important facts, not the small or unimportant details

nm *abbr* = **nanometre**

No. (also **no.**) *abbr* **1** (*pl* **Nos**; **nos**) (*AmE* #) = **number¹**(2): *No. 10 Downing Street* ◆ *tel no. 512364* **2** (*AmE*) = **North, Northern**

⚷ **no¹** /nəʊ/ *exclam* **1** used for giving a negative reply: *'Are you ready?' 'No, I'm not.'* ◆ *'Would you like something to eat?'* ***'No, thank you.'*** ◆ *'Can I borrow the car?' 'No, you can't.'* OPP **yes**

> **HELP** You can also use **no** when you want to agree with a negative statement: *'This programme's not very good.' 'No, you're right. It isn't.'*

2 used for expressing surprise or shock: *'Mike's had an accident.' 'Oh, no!'*

⚷ **no²** /nəʊ/ *determiner, adv* **1** not any; not a: *I have no time to talk now.* ◆ *No visitors may enter without a ticket.* ◆ *He's no friend of mine.* ◆ *Alice is feeling no better this morning.* **2** used for saying that sth is not allowed: *No smoking.* ◆ *No flash photography.* ◆ *No parking.*

nobility /nəʊˈbɪləti/ *noun* **1** **the nobility** [sing, with sing or pl verb] people of high social position who have titles such as that of Duke or Duchess SYN **aristocracy** **2** [U] (*formal*) the quality of having courage and honour

noble¹ /ˈnəʊbl/ *adj* (**nobler**; **noblest**) **1** honest; full of courage and care for others: *a noble leader* ◆ *noble ideas/actions* **2** belonging to the highest social class: *a man of noble birth* ▶ **nobly** /ˈnəʊbli/ *adv*: *He nobly sacrificed his own happiness for that of his family.*

noble² /ˈnəʊbl/ *noun* [C] (in past times) a person who belonged to the highest social class and had a special title ➲ A more common word nowadays is **peer**.

⚷ **nobody¹** /ˈnəʊbədi/ (also ˈ**no one**) *pron* no person; not anyone: *He screamed but nobody came to help him.* ◆ *No one else was around.* ◆ *There was nobody at home.*

> **HELP** **None of**, not **nobody**, must be used before words like *the, his, her, those,* etc. or before a pronoun: *None of my friends remembered my birthday.* ◆ *I've asked all my classmates but none of them are free.*

nobody² /ˈnəʊbədi/ *noun* [C] (*pl* **nobodies**) a person who is not important or famous: *She rose from being a nobody to being a superstar.*

nocturnal /nɒkˈtɜːnl/ *adj* **1** (used about animals and birds) awake and active at night and asleep during the day: *Owls are nocturnal birds.* **2** (*formal*) happening in the night: *a nocturnal adventure*

nod

He nodded his head.

nod /nɒd/ *verb* [I,T] (**nodding**; **nodded**) to move your head up and down as a way of saying 'yes' or as a sign to sb to do sth: *Everybody at the meeting nodded in agreement.* ◆ *Nod your head if you understand what I'm saying and shake it if you don't.*
PHR V **nod off** (*informal*) to go to sleep for a short time
▶ **nod** *noun* [C]

ˌ**no-'frills** *adj* [only *before* a noun] (used especially about a service or product) including only the basic features, without anything that is unnecessary, especially things added to make sth more attractive or comfortable: *a no-frills airline*

ˌ**no-'go area** *noun* [sing] a place, especially part of a city, where it is very dangerous to go because there is a lot of violence or crime

noise /nɔɪz/ *noun* [C,U] a sound, especially one that is loud or unpleasant: *Did you hear a noise downstairs?* ◆ *Try not to* **make a noise** *if you come home late.* ◆ *What an awful noise!* ◆ *Why is the engine making so much noise?*

noiseless /ˈnɔɪzləs/ *adj* making no sound ▶ **noiselessly** *adv*

noisy /ˈnɔɪzi/ *adj* (**noisier**; **noisiest**) making a lot of or too much noise; full of noise: *The clock was so noisy that it kept me awake.* ◆ *noisy children/traffic/crowds* ◆ *The classroom was very noisy.* ➲ note at **loud** ▶ **noisily** *adv*

nomad /ˈnəʊmæd/ *noun* [C] a member of a community that moves with its animals from place to place ▶ **nomadic** /nəʊˈmædɪk/ *adj*

ˈ**no-man's-land** *noun* [U, sing] an area of land between the borders of two countries or between two armies during a war and which is not controlled by either

nominal /ˈnɒmɪnl/ *adj* **1** being sth in name only but not in reality: *the nominal leader of the country* (= sb else is really in control) **2** (used about a price, sum of money, etc.) very small; much less than normal: *Because we are friends he only charges me* ***a nominal rent.*** ▶ **nominally** /-nəli/ *adj*: *He was nominally in charge of the company.*

nominate /ˈnɒmɪneɪt/ *verb* [T] **nominate sb/sth (for/as sth)** to formally suggest that sb/sth should be given a job, role, prize, etc: *I would like to nominate Bob Fry as chairman.* ◆ *The film has been nominated for three Oscars.* ◆ *You may nominate a representative to speak for you.* ▶ **nomination** /ˌnɒmɪˈneɪʃn/ *noun* [C,U]

nominee /ˌnɒmɪˈniː/ *noun* [C] a person who is suggested for an important job, role, prize, etc.

non- /nɒn/ [in compounds] not: *non-biodegradable* ◆ *non-flammable*

ˌ**non-acaˈdemic** *adj* connected with technical or practical subjects rather than subjects of interest to the mind

ˌ**non-alcoˈholic** *adj* (used about drinks) not containing any alcohol: *non-alcoholic drinks*

nonchalant /ˈnɒnʃələnt/ *adj* behaving in a calm and relaxed way and not appearing to be worried or excited ▶ **nonchalance** /-ləns/ *noun* [U] ▶ **nonchalantly** *adv*

ˌ**non-coˈmmittal** *adj* not saying or showing exactly what your opinion is or which side of an argument you agree with

nonconformist /ˌnɒnkənˈfɔːmɪst/ *noun* [C] a person who behaves or thinks differently from most other people in society **OPP** **conformist** ▶ **nonconformist** *adj*

ˌ**non-count** = **uncountable**

ˌ**non-deˈfining** *adj* (used about clauses) giving extra information about a noun phrase, inside commas in writing or in a particular **intonation** (= the rise and fall of your voice) in speech ℹ For more information, look at the **Reference Section** at the back of this dictionary.

nondescript /ˈnɒndɪskrɪpt/ *adj* not having any interesting or unusual qualities

none[1] /nʌn/ *pron* **none (of sb/sth)** not any, not one (of a group of three or more): *They gave me a lot of information but none of it was very helpful.* ◆ *I've got four brothers but none of them live/lives nearby.* ◆ *'Have you brought any books to read?' 'No, none.'* ◆ *I went to several shops but none had what I was looking for.*

GRAMMAR With uncountable nouns **none of** means 'not any of' and we use a singular verb: *None of our money goes towards illegal activities.* With countable nouns **none of** means 'not one of' and can be used with a singular verb (less formal) or a plural verb (more formal): *None of the children likes/like spinach.*

When we are talking about two people or things we use **neither**, not **none**: *Neither of my brothers lives nearby.* Note the difference between **none** and **no**. **No** must go in front of a noun, but **none** replaces the noun: *I told him that I had* ***no money*** *left.* ◆ *When he asked me how much money I had left, I told him that I had* ***none***.

none[2] /nʌn/ *adv*
IDM **none the wiser/worse** knowing no more

than before; no worse than before: *We talked for a long time but I'm still* ***none the wiser****.*

none too happy, clean, pleased, etc. (*informal*) not very happy, clean, pleased, etc.

nonetheless /ˌnʌnðəˈles/ *adv* (*formal*) in spite of this fact: *It won't be easy but they're going to try nonetheless.* **SYN** **nevertheless** ➲ note at **contrast**

ˌnon-eˈxistent *adj* not existing or not available

ˌnon-ˈfiction *noun* [U] writing that is about real people, events and facts: *You'll find biographies in the non-fiction section of the library.* **OPP** **fiction**

nonplussed /ˌnɒnˈplʌst/ *adj* confused; not able to understand

ˌnon-reˈnewable *adj* (used about natural sources of energy such as gas or oil) that cannot be replaced after use

⚿ **nonsense** /ˈnɒnsns/ *noun* [U] **1** ideas, statements or beliefs that you think are ridiculous or not true: *Don't* ***talk nonsense****!* ♦ *It's nonsense to say you aren't good enough to go to university!* **SYN** **rubbish 2** silly or unacceptable behaviour: *The head teacher won't stand for any nonsense.*

nonsensical /nɒnˈsensɪkl/ *adj* ridiculous; without meaning

ˌnon-ˈsmoker *noun* [C] a person who does not smoke cigarettes, etc. **OPP** **smoker** ▶ **ˌnon-ˈsmoking** *adj*: *You can request a non-smoking room at the hotel.*

ˌnon-ˈstarter *noun* [C] (*informal*) a person, plan or idea that has no chance of success

ˌnon-ˈstick *adj* (used about a pan, etc.) covered with a substance that prevents food from sticking to it

ˌnon-ˈstop *adj, adv* without a stop or a rest: *a non-stop flight to Mumbai* ♦ *He talked non-stop for two hours about his holiday.*

ˌnon-ˈviolence *noun* [U] fighting for political or social change without using force, for example by not obeying laws ▶ **ˌnon-ˈviolent** *adj*: *a non-violent protest*

noodle /ˈnuːdl/ *noun* [C, usually pl] long thin pieces of food made of flour, egg and water that are cooked in boiling water or used in soups ➲ picture on **page P16**

nook /nʊk/ *noun* [C] a small quiet place or corner (in a house, garden, etc.)

IDM **every nook and cranny** (*informal*) every part of a place

noon /nuːn/ *noun* [U] 12 o'clock in the middle of the day; midday: ***At noon*** *the sun is at its highest point in the sky.* **SYN** **midday** ➲ look at **midnight**

⚿ **ˈno one** = **nobody**[1]

noose /nuːs/ *noun* [C] a circle that is tied in the end of a rope and that gets smaller as one end of the rope is pulled: *a hangman's noose*

ˈno place (*especially AmE*) = **nowhere**: *I have no place else to go*

⚿ **nor** /nɔː(r)/ *conj, adv* **1** neither ... nor ... and not: *I have neither the time nor the inclination to listen to his complaints again.* **2** [used before a positive verb to agree with sth negative that has just been said] also not; neither: *'I don't like golf.' 'Nor do I.'* ♦ *'We haven't been to America.' 'Nor have we.'*

> **MORE** In this sense **neither** can be used in the same way: *'I won't be here tomorrow.' 'Nor/Neither will I.'*

3 [used after a negative statement to add some more information] also not: *Michael never forgot her birthday. Nor their wedding anniversary for that matter.*

norm /nɔːm/ *noun* [C] [often with *the*] a situation or way of behaving that is usual or expected: *Storing photos on computers has become the norm.* ♦ *social/cultural norms*

⚿ **normal**[1] /ˈnɔːml/ *adj* typical, usual or ordinary; what you expect: *I'll meet you at the normal time.* ♦ *It's quite normal to feel angry in a situation like this.* **OPP** **abnormal**

⚿ **normal**[2] /ˈnɔːml/ *noun* [U] the usual or average state, level or standard: *temperatures above/below normal* ♦ *Things are* ***back to normal*** *at work now.*

normality /nɔːˈmæləti/ (*AmE* also **normalcy** /ˈnɔːmlsi/) *noun* [U] the state of being normal

normalize (also **-ise**) /ˈnɔːməlaɪz/ *verb* [I,T] (*formal*) to become or make sth become normal again or return to how it was before: *The two countries agreed to normalize relations* (= return to a normal, friendly relationship, for example after a disagreement or a war).

⚿ **normally** /ˈnɔːməli/ *adv* **1** usually: *I normally leave the house at 8 o'clock.* ♦ *Normally he takes the bus.* **2** in the usual or ordinary way: *The man wasn't behaving normally.*

⚿ **north**[1] /nɔːθ/ *noun* [U, sing] (*abbr* N; No.) **1** (also **the north**) the direction that is on your left when you watch the sun rise; one of the **points of the compass** (= the main directions that we give names to): *cold winds from the north* ♦ *Which way is north?* ♦ *I live* ***to the north of*** (= further north than) *Chicago.* ➲ picture at **compass 2 the north; the North** the northern part of a country, a city, a region or the world: *Houses are less expensive in the North of England than in the South.* ♦ *I live in the north of Athens.* ➲ look at **south, east, west**

⚿ **north**[2] /nɔːθ/ *adj, adv* **1** [only *before* a noun] in the north: *The new offices will be in North London.* ♦ *The north wing of the hospital was destroyed in a fire.* **2** (used about a wind) coming from the north **3** to or towards the north: *We got onto the motorway going north instead of south.* ♦ *The house faces north.* ♦ *Is Rouen north of Paris?*

northbound /ˈnɔːθbaʊnd/ *adj* travelling or leading towards the north: *northbound traffic*

ˌnorth-ˈeast[1] (also **the north-east**) *noun* [sing] (*abbr* NE) the direction or a region that is an equal distance between north and east ➲ picture at **compass**

ˌnorth-ˈeast² *adj, adv* in, from or to the **north-east** of a place or country: *the north-east coast of Australia* ◆ *If you look north-east you can see the mountains.*

ˌnorth-ˈeasterly *adj* **1** [only *before* a noun] towards the north-east: *in a north-easterly direction* **2** (used about a wind) coming from the north-east

ˌnorth-ˈeastern *adj* (*abbr* NE) [only *before* a noun] connected with the north-east of a place or country

ˌnorth-ˈeastwards (also ˌnorth-ˈeastward) *adv* towards the north-east: *Follow the A619 north-eastward.*

northerly /ˈnɔːðəli/ *adj* **1** [only *before* a noun] to, towards or in the north: *Keep going in a northerly direction.* **2** (used about a wind) coming from the north

🔑 **northern** (also Northern) /ˈnɔːðən/ *adj* (*abbr* N) of, in or from the north of a place: *She has a northern accent.* ◆ *in northern Australia*

northerner /ˈnɔːðənə(r)/ *noun* [C] a person who was born in or who lives in the northern part of a country

northernmost /ˈnɔːðənməʊst/ *adj* furthest north: *the northernmost island of Japan*

the North ˈPole *noun* [sing] the point on the Earth's surface which is furthest north ➲ picture at **earth**

northwards /ˈnɔːθwədz/ (also northward) *adv* towards the north: *Continue northwards out of the city for about five miles.* ▶ **northward** *adj*: *in a northward direction*

ˌnorth-ˈwest¹ (also the north-west) *noun* [sing] (*abbr* NW) the direction or a region that is an equal distance between north and west ➲ picture at **compass**

ˌnorth-ˈwest² *adj, adv* in, from or to the **north-west** of a place or country: *the north-west coast of Scotland* ◆ *Our house faces north-west.*

ˌnorth-ˈwesterly *adj* **1** [only *before* a noun] towards the north-west: *in a north-westerly direction* **2** (used about a wind) coming from the north-west

ˌnorth-ˈwestern *adj* (*abbr* NW) [only *before* a noun] connected with the north-west of a place or country

ˌnorth-ˈwestwards (also ˌnorth-ˈwestward) *adv* towards the north-west: *Follow the A40 north-westward for ten miles.*

🔑 **nose¹** /nəʊz/ *noun* [C] **1** the part of your face, above your mouth, that is used for breathing and smelling: *Breathe in through your nose and out through your mouth.* ➲ picture at **body** **2 -nosed** [in compounds] having the type of nose mentioned: *red-nosed* ◆ *big-nosed* **3** the front part of a plane, etc: *The nose of the plane was badly damaged.*

IDM **blow your nose** ➲ **blow¹**

follow your nose ➲ **follow**

look down your nose at sb/sth ➲ **look¹**

poke/stick your nose into sth (*informal*) to be interested in or try to become involved in sth which does not concern you

turn your nose up at sth (*informal*) to refuse sth because you do not think it is good enough for you

nose² /nəʊz/ *verb* [I] (used about a vehicle) to move forward slowly and carefully

PHR V **nose about/around** (*informal*) to look for sth, especially private information about sb

nosebleed /ˈnəʊzbliːd/ *noun* [C] a sudden flow of blood that comes from your nose

nosedive /ˈnəʊzdaɪv/ *noun* [C] a sudden sharp fall or drop: *Oil prices* ***took a nosedive*** *in the crisis.* ▶ **nosedive** *verb* [I]: *All of a sudden the plane nosedived.*

nostalgia /nɒˈstældʒə/ *noun* [U] a feeling of pleasure, mixed with sadness, when you think of happy times in the past: *She was suddenly filled with* ***nostalgia for*** *her university days.* ▶ **nostalgic** /nɒˈstældʒɪk/ *adj* ▶ **nostalgically** /-kli/ *adv*

nostril /ˈnɒstrəl/ *noun* [C] one of the two openings at the end of your nose that you breathe through ➲ picture at **body**

nosy (also nosey) /ˈnəʊzi/ *adj* (*informal*) too interested in other people's personal affairs: *a nosy neighbour*

🔑 **not** /nɒt/ *adv* **1** used to form the negative with **auxiliary verbs** (= the verbs 'be', 'do' and 'have') and with **modal verbs** (= verbs such as 'can', 'must' and 'will'). *Not* is often pronounced or written *n't* in informal situations: *It's not/it isn't raining now.* ◆ *I cannot/can't see from here.* ◆ *He didn't invite me.* ◆ *Don't you like spaghetti?* ◆ *I hope she will not/won't be late.* ◆ *You're German, aren't you?* **2** used to give the following word or phrase a negative meaning: *He told me not to phone.* ◆ *She accused me of not telling the truth.* ◆ *Not one person replied to my advertisement.* ◆ *It's not easy.* ◆ *He's not very tall.* **3** used to give a short negative reply: *'Do you think they'll get divorced?' 'I hope not.'* (= I hope they will not.) ◆ *'Can I borrow £20?'* ***'Certainly not!'*** ◆ *'Whose turn is it to do the shopping?' 'Not mine.'* **4** used with or to give a negative possibility: *Shall we tell her* ***or not****?* ◆ *I don't know if/whether he's telling the truth or not.*

IDM **not at all 1** used as a way of replying when sb has thanked you: *'Thanks for the present.' 'Not at all, don't mention it.'* **2** used as a way of saying 'no' or 'definitely not': *'Do you mind if I come too?' 'Not at all.'* ◆ *The instructions are not at all clear.*

not only ... (but) also used for emphasizing the fact that there is sth more to add: *They not only have two houses in London, they also have one in France.*

notable /ˈnəʊtəbl/ *adj* notable (for sth) interesting or important enough to receive attention: *The area is notable for its wildlife.*

notably /ˈnəʊtəbli/ *adv* used for giving an especially important example of what you are talking about: *Several politicians, most notably the Prime Minister and the Home Secretary, have given the proposal their full support.*

notation /nəʊˈteɪʃn/ *noun* [U,C] a system of signs or symbols used to represent information, especially in mathematics, science and music

N

notch[1] /nɒtʃ/ *noun* [C] **1** a level on a scale of quality: *This meal is certainly* ***a notch above*** *the last one we had here.* **2** a cut in an edge or surface, often in the shape of a V, sometimes used to help you count sth

notch[2] /nɒtʃ/ *verb*
PHR V **notch sth up** to score or achieve sth: *Lewis notched up his best ever time in the 100 metres.*

note[1] /nəʊt/ *noun*
➤TO REMIND YOU **1** [C] some words that you write down quickly to help you remember sth: *I'd better* ***make a note of*** *your name and address.* ♦ ***Keep a note of*** *who has paid and who hasn't.* ♦ *The lecturer advised the students to* ***take notes*** *while he was speaking.*

EXAM TIP

Revision notes
Write down the key words and phrases that you want to learn on small pieces of paper. Stick them in places where you will see them every day, such as your mirror, computer or fridge.

➤SHORT LETTER **2** [C] a short letter: *This is just a note to thank you for having us to dinner.* ♦ *If Mark's not at home we'll leave a note for him.* ♦ *a sick note from your doctor*
➤IN BOOK **3** [C] a short explanation or extra piece of information that is given at the back of a book, etc. or at the bottom or side of a page: *See note 5, page 340.* ➲ look at **footnote**
➤MONEY **4** [C] (also **banknote**; *AmE* **bill**) a piece of paper money: *I'd like the money in £10 notes, please.* ➲ picture at **money**
➤IN MUSIC **5** [C] a single musical sound made by a voice or an instrument; a written sign that represents a musical sound: *I can only remember the first few notes of the song.*
➤QUALITY **6** [sing] something that shows a certain quality or feeling: *The meeting ended on a rather unpleasant note.*
IDM **compare notes (with sb)** ➲ **compare**
take note (of sth) to pay attention to sth and be sure to remember it

note[2] /nəʊt/ *verb* [T] **1** to notice or pay careful attention to sth: *He noted a slight change in her attitude towards him.* ♦ *Please note that this office is closed on Tuesdays.* **2** to mention sth: *I'd like to note that the project has so far been extremely successful.*
PHR V **note sth down** to write sth down so that you remember it

notebook /ˈnəʊtbʊk/ *noun* [C] **1** a small book in which you write down things that you want to remember **2** (also ˌ**notebook comˈputer**) a **laptop** (= a small computer) that can work with a battery and be easily carried ➲ note at **computer 3** (*AmE*) = **exercise book**

noted /ˈnəʊtɪd/ *adj* (*formal*) **noted (for/as sth)** well known; famous: *The hotel is noted for its food.*

notepad /ˈnəʊtpæd/ *noun* [C] sheets of paper in a block that are used for writing things on

notepaper /ˈnəʊtpeɪpə(r)/ *noun* [U] paper that you write letters on

noteworthy /ˈnəʊtwɜːði/ *adj* interesting or important; that is worth noticing

nothing /ˈnʌθɪŋ/ *pron* not anything; no thing: *There's nothing in this suitcase.* ♦ *I'm bored—there's* ***nothing to do*** *here.* ♦ *There was* ***nothing else*** *to say.* ♦ *'What's the matter?' 'Oh, nothing.'* ♦ *'Thank you so much for all your help.' 'It was nothing.'* ♦ *The doctor said there's nothing wrong with me.* ➲ note at **zero**
IDM **be/have nothing to do with sb/sth** to have no connection with sb/sth: *That question has nothing to do with what we're discussing.* ♦ *Keep out of this—it's nothing to do with you.*
come to nothing ➲ **come**
do nothing/not do anything by halves ➲ **half**[1]
for nothing 1 for no payment; free: *Children under four are allowed in for nothing.* **2** for no good reason or with no good result: *His hard work was all for nothing.*
next to nothing ➲ **next to**
nothing but only: *We've had nothing but trouble with this car.*
nothing like 1 not at all like: *She looks nothing like either of her parents.* **2** not at all; not nearly: *There's nothing like enough food for all of us.*
nothing much not a lot of sth; nothing of importance: *It's a nice town but there's nothing much to do in the evenings.* ♦ *'What did you do at the weekend?' 'Nothing much.'*
(there's) nothing to it (it's) very easy: *You'll soon learn—there's nothing to it really.*
stop at nothing ➲ **stop**[1]
there is/was nothing (else) for it (but to do sth) there is/was no other action possible: *There was nothing for it but to resign.*

notice[1] /ˈnəʊtɪs/ *noun* **1** [U] the act of paying attention to sth or knowing about sth: *The protests are finally making the government* ***take notice.*** ♦ ***Take no notice of*** *what he said—he was just being silly.* ♦ *Some people don't take any notice of* (= choose to ignore) *speed limits.* ♦ *It has* ***come to*** *my* ***notice*** *that you have missed a lot of classes.* **2** [C] a piece of paper or a sign giving information, a warning, etc. that is put where everyone can read it: *There's a notice on the board saying that the meeting has been cancelled.* ♦ *The notice said 'No dogs allowed'.* **3** [U] a warning that sth is going to happen: *I can't produce a meal* ***at*** *such* ***short notice!*** ♦ *I wish you'd* ***give*** *me more* ***notice*** *when you're going to be off work.* ♦ *The swimming pool is closed* ***until further notice*** (= until we are told that it will open again). ♦ *She's* ***handed in her notice*** (written a letter to say that she is leaving her job).

notice[2] /ˈnəʊtɪs/ *verb* [I,T] [not usually used in the continuous tenses] to see and become conscious of sth: *'What kind of car was the man driving?' 'I'm afraid I didn't notice.'* ♦ *I noticed (that) he was carrying a black briefcase.* ♦ *Did you notice which direction she went in?* ♦ *We didn't notice him leave/him leaving.*

noticeable /ˈnəʊtɪsəbl/ *adj* easy to see or notice: *The scar from the accident was hardly noticeable.* ► **noticeably** /-əbli/ *adv*

noticeboard /ˈnəʊtɪsbɔːd/ (*AmE* ˈbulletin board) *noun* [C] a board on a wall for putting written information where everyone can read it

notify /ˈnəʊtɪfaɪ/ *verb* [T] (**notifying; notifies**; *pt, pp* **notified**) **notify sb (of sth)** to tell sb about sth officially ▸ **notification** /ˌnəʊtɪfɪˈkeɪʃn/ *noun* [C,U]

notion /ˈnəʊʃn/ *noun* [C] **a notion (that ... /of sth)** something that you have in your mind; an idea: *I had a vague notion that I had seen her before.*

notional /ˈnəʊʃənl/ *adj* existing only in the mind; not based on facts or reality

notoriety /ˌnəʊtəˈraɪəti/ *noun* [U] the state of being well known for sth bad

notorious /nəʊˈtɔːriəs/ *adj* **notorious (for/as sth)** well known for sth bad: *a notorious criminal* ◆ *This road is notorious for the number of accidents on it.* **SYN** **infamous** ▸ **notoriously** *adv*

notwithstanding /ˌnɒtwɪθˈstændɪŋ/ *prep, adv* (*formal*) in spite of sth

nought /nɔːt/ (*especially AmE* **zero**) *noun* [C] the figure 0: *A million is written with six noughts.* ◆ *We say 0.1 'nought point one'.*

ˌnoughts and ˈcrosses (*AmE* **tic-tac-ˈtoe**) *noun* [U] a game for two players in which each person tries to win by writing three 0s or three Xs in a line.

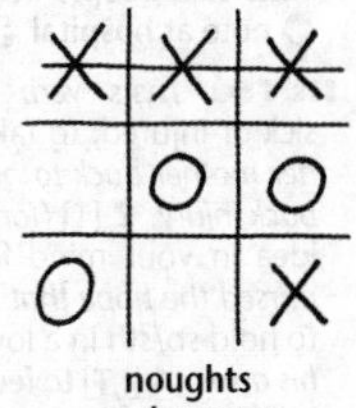
noughts and crosses

noun /naʊn/ *noun* [C] a word that is the name of a thing, an idea, a place or a person: *'Water', 'happiness', 'France' and 'James' are all nouns.* ➲ look at **countable, uncountable**

nourish /ˈnʌrɪʃ/ *verb* [T] **1** to give sb/sth the right kind of food so that they or it can grow and be healthy **2** (*formal*) to allow a feeling, an idea, etc. to grow stronger ▸ **nourishment** *noun* [U]

Nov. *abbr* = **November**: *17 Nov. 2012*

novel[1] /ˈnɒvl/ *noun* [C] a book that tells a story about people and events that are not real: *a romantic/historical/detective novel* ➲ note at **book**

novel[2] /ˈnɒvl/ *adj* new and different: *That's a novel idea! Let's try it.*

novelist /ˈnɒvəlɪst/ *noun* [C] a person who writes novels

novelty /ˈnɒvlti/ *noun* (*pl* **novelties**) **1** [U] the quality of being new and different: *The novelty of her new job soon wore off.* **2** [C] something new and unusual: *It was quite a novelty not to have to get up early.* **3** [C] a small, cheap object that is sold as a toy or decoration

November /nəʊˈvembə(r)/ *noun* [U,C] (*abbr* **Nov.**) the 11th month of the year, coming after October ➲ note at **January**

novice /ˈnɒvɪs/ *noun* [C] a person who is new and without experience in a certain job, situation, etc. **SYN** **beginner**

now /naʊ/ *adv, conj* **1** (at) the present time: *We can't go for a walk now—it's raining.* ◆ *Where are you living now?* ◆ ***From now on** I'm going to work harder.* ◆ ***Up till now** we haven't been able to afford a house of our own.* ◆ *He will be on his way home **by now**.* ◆ *I can manage **for now** but I might need some help later.* **2** immediately: *Go now before anyone sees you.* ◆ *You must go to the doctor **right now**.* **3** used to introduce or to emphasize what you are saying, or while pausing to think: *Now listen to what he's saying.* ◆ *What does he want now?* ◆ *Now, let me think.*

MORE Now then is also used: *Now then, what was I saying?*

4 now (that) ... because of the fact that: *Now (that) the children have left home we can move to a smaller house.*

IDM **any moment, day, minute, second, etc. (now)** ➲ **any**

just now ➲ **just**[1]

(every) now and again/then from time to time: *We see each other now and then, but not very often.* **SYN** **occasionally**

now what? 1 used when you are annoyed because sb keeps interrupting you: *'Dad?' 'Now what?'* **2** used to say that you do not know what to do next in a particular situation

right now ➲ **right**[2]

nowadays /ˈnaʊədeɪz/ *adv* at the present time (when compared with the past): *I don't go to London much nowadays* (= but I did in the past). **SYN** **today**

nowhere /ˈnəʊweə(r)/ *adv* not in or to any place; not anywhere: *I'm afraid there's nowhere to stay in this village.* ◆ *I don't like it here, but there's **nowhere else** for us to sit.*

IDM **get somewhere/nowhere (with sb/sth)** ➲ **get**

in the middle of nowhere ➲ **middle**[1]

nowhere near far from: *We've sold nowhere near enough tickets to make a profit.*

noxious /ˈnɒkʃəs/ *adj* (*formal*) harmful or poisonous: *noxious gases*

nozzle /ˈnɒzl/ *noun* [C] a narrow tube that is put on the end of a pipe to control the liquid or gas coming out

nr *abbr* (*BrE*) = **near**[1](1): *Masham, nr Ripon*

nuance /ˈnjuːɑːns/ *noun* [C] a very small difference in meaning, feeling, sound, etc.

nuclear /ˈnjuːkliə(r)/ *adj* **1** using, producing or resulting from the energy that is produced when the **nucleus** of an atom is split: *nuclear energy* ◆ *a nuclear power station* ◆ *nuclear war/weapons* ➲ look at **atomic** **2** connected with the **nucleus** of an atom: *nuclear physics*

ˌnuclear reˈactor (also **reactor**) *noun* [C] a very large machine that produces nuclear energy

N

nucleus /ˈnjuːkliəs/ *noun* [C] (*pl* **nuclei** /-kliaɪ/) **1** the central part of an atom or of certain cells **2** the central or most important part of sth

nude[1] /njuːd/ *adj* not wearing any clothes ➲ look at **bare, naked** ▸ **nudity** /ˈnjuːdəti/ *noun* [U]: *This film contains scenes of nudity.*

nude[2] /njuːd/ *noun* [C] a picture or photograph of a person who is not wearing any clothes
IDM in the nude not wearing any clothes

nudge /nʌdʒ/ *verb* [T] to touch or push sb/sth gently, especially with your elbow ➲ picture at **elbow** ▸ **nudge** *noun* [C]: *to give somebody a nudge*

nudist /ˈnjuːdɪst/ *noun* [C] a person who does not wear any clothes because they believe this is more natural and healthy: *a nudist beach/camp* ▸ **nudism** /ˈnjuːdɪzəm/ *noun* [U]

nuisance /ˈnjuːsns/ *noun* [C] a person, thing or situation that annoys you or causes you trouble: *It's a nuisance having to queue for everything.*

numb /nʌm/ *adj* not able to feel anything; not able to move: *My fingers were numb with cold.* ♦ *I'll give you an injection and the tooth will* ***go numb.*** ▸ **numb** *verb* [T]: *We were numbed by the dreadful news.* ▸ **numbness** *noun* [U]

number[1] /ˈnʌmbə(r)/ *noun*
➤WORD/SYMBOL **1** [C] a word or symbol that indicates a quantity: *Choose a number between ten and twenty.* ♦ *2, 4, 6, etc. are* ***even numbers*** *and 1, 3, 5, etc. are* ***odd numbers.*** ♦ *a three-figure number* (= from 100 to 999)
➤POSITION **2** [C] (*abbr* **No.**; **no.**) (*AmE abbr* **#**) used before a number to show the position of sth in a series: *We live at number 32 Moorland Road.* ♦ *room No 347*
➤TELEPHONE, ETC. **3** [C] a group of numbers that is used to identify sb/sth: *a telephone number* ♦ *a code number*
➤QUANTITY **4** [C,U] **a number (of sth)** a quantity of people or things: *a large number of visitors* ♦ *We must reduce the number of accidents on the roads.* ♦ *Pupils in the school have doubled* ***in number*** *in recent years.* ♦ *There are* ***a number of*** (= several) *things I don't understand.*
➤MAGAZINE **5** [C] (*BrE*) a copy of a magazine, newspaper, etc: *Back numbers of 'New Scientist' are available from the publishers.*
➤SONG **6** [C] (*informal*) a song or dance: *They sang a slow romantic number.*
IDM any number of very many: *There could be any number of reasons why she isn't here.*
in round figures/numbers ➲ **round**[1]
your opposite number ➲ **opposite**

number[2] /ˈnʌmbə(r)/ *verb* [T] **1** to give a number to sth: *The houses are numbered from 1 to 52.* **2** used for saying how many people or things there are: *Our forces number 40 000.*

ˈ**number plate** (*AmE* ˈ**license plate**) *noun* [C] the sign on the front and back of a vehicle that shows the **registration number** (= the particular combination of numbers and letters belonging to that vehicle)

numeracy /ˈnjuːmərəsi/ *noun* [U] a good basic knowledge of mathematics; the ability to understand and work with numbers: *standards of numeracy and literacy* ➲ look at **literacy**

numeral /ˈnjuːmərəl/ *noun* [C] a sign or symbol that represents a quantity: *Roman numerals* (= I, II, III, IV, etc.)

numerate /ˈnjuːmərət/ *adj* having a good basic knowledge of mathematics ➲ look at **literate**

numerical /njuːˈmerɪkl/ *adj* of or shown by numbers: *to put something* ***in numerical order***

numerous /ˈnjuːmərəs/ *adj* (*formal*) existing in large numbers; many

nun /nʌn/ *noun* [C] a member of a religious group of women who live together in a **convent** (= a special building) and do not marry or have possessions ➲ look at **monk**

nurse[1] /nɜːs/ *noun* [C] a person who is trained to look after sick or injured people: *a male nurse* ♦ *a psychiatric nurse* ♦ *a community/district nurse* (= who visits sick people in their homes to care for them) ➲ note at **hospital** ➲ picture on **page P2**

nurse[2] /nɜːs/ *verb* **1** [T] to take care of sb who is sick or injured; to take care of an injury: *She nursed her mother back to health.* ♦ *Ahmed is still nursing a back injury.* **2** [T] (*formal*) to have a strong feeling or idea in your mind for a long time: *Tim had long nursed the hope that Sharon would marry him.* **3** [T] to hold sb/sth in a loving way: *He nursed the child in his arms.* **4** [I,T] to feed a baby or young animal with milk from the breast; to drink milk from the mother's breast

nursery /ˈnɜːsəri/ *noun* (*pl* **nurseries**) **1** [C,U] a place where small children and babies are looked after so that their parents can go to work ➲ look at **crèche 2** [C] a place where young plants are grown and sold

ˈ**nursery rhyme** *noun* [C] a traditional poem or song for young children

ˈ**nursery school** *noun* [C] a school for children aged from about 2 to 5 **SYN kindergarten**

nursing /ˈnɜːsɪŋ/ *noun* [U] the job of being a nurse

ˈ**nursing home** *noun* [C] a small private hospital, often for old people

nurture /ˈnɜːtʃə(r)/ *verb* [T] (*formal*) **1** to take special care of sth/sb that is growing and developing: *These delicate plants need careful nurturing.* ♦ *children nurtured by loving parents* **2** to help sth to develop and be successful: *It's important to nurture a good working relationship.* ▸ **nurture** *noun* [U] (*formal*)

nut /nʌt/ *noun* [C] **1** a dry fruit that consists of a hard shell with a seed inside. Many types of nut can be eaten: *to* ***crack a nut*** (= to open it) **2** a small piece of metal with a round hole in the middle through which you put a **bolt** (= long round piece of metal) to fasten things together: *to tighten a nut* ➲ picture at **bolt**

nuts

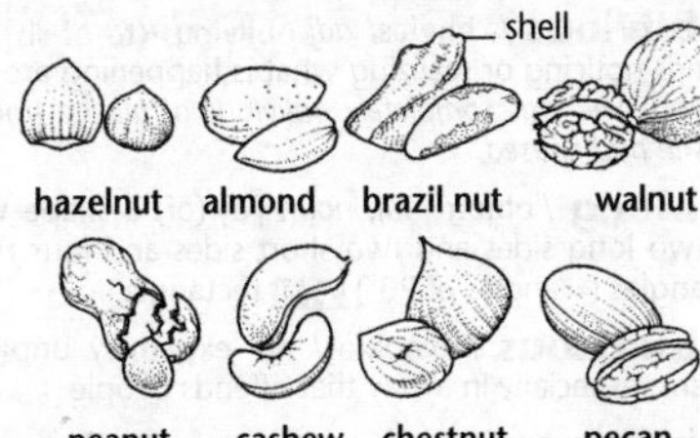

nutcracker /ˈnʌtkrækə(r)/ [C] (*BrE also* **nutcrackers** [pl]) *noun* a tool that you use for breaking open the shell of a nut

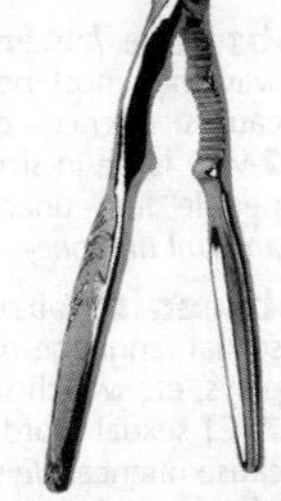
nutcracker

nutmeg /ˈnʌtmeg/ *noun* [C,U] a type of hard seed that is often made into powder and used as a spice in cooking

nutrient /ˈnjuːtriənt/ *noun* [C] a substance that is needed to keep a living thing alive and healthy: *Plants take minerals and other nutrients from the soil.*

nutrition /njuˈtrɪʃn/ *noun* [U] the food that you eat and the way that it affects your health: *Good nutrition is essential for children's growth.* ▶ **nutritional** /-ʃənl/ *adj*

nutritious /njuˈtrɪʃəs/ *adj* (used about a food) very good for you

nuts /nʌts/ *adj* [not before a noun] (*informal*) crazy: *I'll **go nuts** if that phone doesn't stop ringing.* ◆ *She's **driving me nuts** with all her stupid questions.*

nutshell /ˈnʌtʃel/ *noun*
IDM **in a nutshell** using few words

nutty /ˈnʌti/ *adj* (**nuttier**; **nuttiest**) containing or tasting of nuts

nuzzle /ˈnʌzl/ *verb* [I,T] to press or rub sb/sth gently with the nose

NW *abbr* = **north-west**[1], **north-western**: *NW Australia*

nylon /ˈnaɪlɒn/ *noun* [U] a very strong artificial material that is used for making clothes, rope, brushes, etc.

nymph /nɪmf/ *noun* [C] (in ancient Greek and Roman stories) a spirit of nature in the form of a young woman that lives in rivers, woods, etc.

O, o /əʊ/ *noun* [C,U] (*pl* Os; O's; o's /əʊz/) **1** the 15th letter of the English alphabet: *'Orange' begins with (an) 'O'.* **2** (used when you are speaking) zero: *My number is five O nine double four (= 50944).* ➲ note at **zero**

O = **oh**

oak /əʊk/ *noun* **1** (also ˈ**oak tree**) [C] a type of large tree with hard wood that is common in many northern parts of the world **2** [U] the wood from the **oak** tree: *a solid oak table* ➲ look at **acorn**

OAP /ˌəʊ eɪ ˈpiː/ *abbr* (*BrE*) = **old-age pensioner**

oar /ɔː(r)/ *noun* [C] a long pole that is flat and wide at one end and that you use for **rowing** (= moving a small boat through water) ➲ look at **paddle** ➲ picture at **boat**

oasis /əʊˈeɪsɪs/ *noun* [C] (*pl* **oases** /-siːz/) a place in the desert where there is water and where plants grow

oath /əʊθ/ *noun* [C] **1** a formal promise: *They have to **swear/take an oath** of loyalty.* **2** (*old-fashioned*) = **swear word**
IDM **be on/under oath** to have made a formal promise to tell the truth in a court of law

oats /əʊts/ *noun* [pl] a type of grain that is used as food for animals and for making flour, etc.

obedient /əˈbiːdiənt/ *adj* **obedient (to sb/sth)** doing what you are told to do: *As a child he was always obedient to his parents.* OPP **disobedient** ▶ **obedience** *noun* [U] ▶ **obediently** *adv*

obese /əʊˈbiːs/ *adj* (used about people) very fat, in a way that is not healthy ➲ note at **fat** ▶ **obesity** /əʊˈbiːsəti/ *noun* [U]

⚷ **obey** /əˈbeɪ/ *verb* [I,T] to do what you are told to do: *Soldiers are trained to obey orders.* OPP **disobey**

obituary /əˈbɪtʃuəri/ *noun* [C] (*pl* **obituaries**) a piece of writing about sb's life that is printed in a newspaper soon after they have died

⚷ **object**[1] /ˈɒbdʒɪkt/ *noun* [C] **1** a thing that can be seen and touched, but is not alive: *The shelves were filled with objects of all shapes and sizes.* ◆ *everyday/household objects* **2 the object of sth** a person or thing that causes a feeling, interest, thought, etc: *the object of his desire/affections* **3** the noun or phrase describing the person or thing that is affected by the act of a verb ➲ look at **subject** **4** an aim or purpose: *Making money is his sole object in life.*

> **GRAMMAR** In the sentences: *I sent a letter to Eva.* ◆ *I sent Eva a letter.* 'a letter' is the **direct object** of the verb and 'Eva' is the **indirect object**.

IDM **money, etc. is no object** money, etc. is not important or is no problem: *They always want the best. Expense is no object.*

object² /əbˈdʒekt/ *verb* **1** [I] object (to sb/sth); object (to doing sth/to sb doing sth) to not like or to be against sb/sth: *Many people object to the new tax.* ♦ *I object to companies trying to sell me things over the phone.* **2** [T] to say a reason why you think sth is wrong: *'I think that's unfair,' he objected.* SYN for both meanings **protest** ▸ **objector** *noun* [C]

objection /əbˈdʒekʃn/ *noun* [C] an objection (to sb/sth); an objection (to doing sth/to sb doing sth) a reason why you do not like or are against sb/sth: *We listed our objections to the proposed new road.* ♦ *I **have no objection** to you using my desk while I'm away.*

objectionable /əbˈdʒekʃənəbl/ *adj* very unpleasant

objective¹ /əbˈdʒektɪv/ *noun* [C] something that you are trying to achieve; an aim: *Our objective is to finish by the end of the year.* ♦ *to achieve your objective* SYN **goal**

objective² /əbˈdʒektɪv/ *adj* not influenced by your own personal feelings; considering only facts: *Please try and give an objective report of what happened.* ♦ *It's hard to be objective about your own family.* OPP **subjective** ▸ **objectively** *adv*: *He is too upset to see things objectively.* ▸ **objectivity** /ˌɒbdʒekˈtɪvəti/ *noun* [U]

obligation /ˌɒblɪˈɡeɪʃn/ *noun* [C,U] (an) obligation (to sb) (to do sth) the state of having to do sth because it is a law or duty, or because you have promised: *Unfortunately the shop is **under no obligation** to give you your money back.* ♦ *We **have an obligation** to help people who are in need.* ♦ *By refusing to examine the animal, the vet failed to fulfil his professional obligations.*

obligatory /əˈblɪɡətri/ *adj* (*formal*) that you must do: *It is obligatory to get insurance before you drive a car.* OPP **optional**

oblige /əˈblaɪdʒ/ *verb* **1** [T, usually passive] to force sb to do sth: *Parents are obliged by law to send their children to school.* ♦ *Although I wasn't hungry, I felt obliged to eat something.* **2** [I,T] (*formal*) to do what sb asks; to be helpful: *If you ever need any help, I'd be happy to oblige.* ▸ **obliged** *adj* [not before a noun] (*formal*): *Thanks for your help. I'm **much obliged** to you.* ▸ **obliging** *adj* (*formal*): *I asked my neighbour for advice and he was very obliging.*

oblique /əˈbliːk/ *adj* **1** not expressed or done in a direct way: *an oblique reference/approach/comment* SYN **indirect** **2** (used about a line) at an angle; sloping ▸ **obliquely** *adv*: *He referred only obliquely to their recent problems.* ♦ *Always cut stems obliquely to enable flowers to absorb more water.*

obliterate /əˈblɪtəreɪt/ *verb* [T, often passive] (*formal*) to remove all signs of sth by destroying or covering it completely

oblivion /əˈblɪviən/ *noun* [U] **1** a state in which you do not realize what is happening around you, usually because you are unconscious or asleep: *I was in a state of complete oblivion.* **2** the state in which sb/sth has been forgotten and is no longer famous or important: *His work **faded into oblivion** after his death.*

oblivious /əˈblɪviəs/ *adj* oblivious (to/of sb/sth) not noticing or realizing what is happening around you: *She was completely oblivious of all the trouble she had caused.*

oblong /ˈɒblɒŋ/ *adj, noun* [C] (of) a shape with two long sides and two short sides and four **right angles** (= angles of 90°) SYN **rectangle**

obnoxious /əbˈnɒkʃəs/ *adj* extremely unpleasant, especially in a way that offends people

oboe /ˈəʊbəʊ/ *noun* [C] a musical instrument made of wood that you play by blowing through it ➲ picture at **music**

obscene /əbˈsiːn/ *adj* **1** connected with sex in a way that most people find disgusting and which causes offence: *obscene books/gestures/language* **2** very large in size or amount in a way that some people find unacceptable: *He earns an obscene amount of money.*

obscenity /əbˈsenəti/ *noun* (*pl* obscenities) **1** [U] sexual language or behaviour, especially in books, plays, etc. which shocks people and causes offence **2** [C] sexual words or acts that shock people and cause offence: *He shouted a string of obscenities out of the car window.*

obscure¹ /əbˈskjʊə(r)/ *adj* **1** not well known: *an obscure Spanish poet* **2** not easy to see or understand: ***For some obscure reason**, he decided to give up his well-paid job, to become a writer.* ▸ **obscurity** /əbˈskjʊərəti/ *noun* [U]

obscure² /əbˈskjʊə(r)/ *verb* [T] to make sth difficult to see or understand: *A high fence obscured our view.*

observance /əbˈzɜːvəns/ *noun* [U,sing] observance (of sth) the practice of obeying or following a law, custom, etc.

observant /əbˈzɜːvənt/ *adj* good at noticing things around you: *An observant passer-by gave the police a full description of the men.*

observation /ˌɒbzəˈveɪʃn/ *noun* **1** [U] the act of watching sb/sth carefully, especially to learn sth: *My research involves the observation of animals in their natural surroundings.* ♦ *The patient is being kept **under observation**.* **2** [U] the ability to notice things: *Scientists need good **powers of observation**.* **3** [C] an observation (about/on sth) (*formal*) something that you say or write about sth: *He began by making a few general observations about the sales figures.* ➲ More common words are **remark** and **comment**.

observatory /əbˈzɜːvətri/ *noun* [C] (*pl* observatories) a building from which scientists can watch the stars, the weather, etc.

observe /əbˈzɜːv/ *verb* [T] **1** (*formal*) to see or notice sb/sth: *A man and a woman were observed leaving by the back door.* **2** to watch sb/sth carefully, especially to learn more about them or it: *We observed the birds throughout the breeding season.* **3** (*formal*) to make a comment: *'We're late,' she observed.* **4** (*formal*) to obey a law, rule, etc: *to observe the speed limit*

observer /əbˈzɜːvə(r)/ *noun* [C] **1** a person who watches sb/sth: *According to observers, the plane exploded shortly after take-off.* **2** a person who attends a meeting, lesson, etc. to watch and listen but who does not take part

obsess /əbˈses/ *verb* [I,T] [usually passive] to completely fill your mind so that you cannot think of anything else: *He became obsessed with getting his revenge.* ♦ *He's obsessed by computers.*

obsession /əbˈseʃn/ *noun* **obsession (with sb/sth)** **1** [U] the state in which you can only think about one person or thing so that you cannot think of anything else: *The media's obsession with the prince continues.* **2** [C] a person or thing that you think about too much

obsessive /əbˈsesɪv/ *adj* thinking too much about one particular person or thing; behaving in a way that shows this: *He's obsessive about not being late.* ♦ *obsessive cleanliness*

obsolete /ˈɒbsəliːt/ *adj* no longer useful because sth better has been invented

obstacle /ˈɒbstəkl/ *noun* [C] **1** an **obstacle (to sth/doing sth)** something that makes it difficult for you to do sth or go somewhere: *Not speaking a foreign language was a major obstacle to her career.* **2** an object that is in your way and that makes it difficult for you to move forward

obstetrician /ˌɒbstəˈtrɪʃn/ *noun* [C] a hospital doctor who looks after women who are pregnant

obstinate /ˈɒbstɪnət/ *adj* refusing to change your opinions, way of behaving, etc. when other people try to persuade you to: *an obstinate refusal to apologize* SYN **stubborn** ▶ **obstinacy** /ˈɒbstɪnəsi/ *noun* [U] ▶ **obstinately** *adv*

obstruct /əbˈstrʌkt/ *verb* [T] to stop sb/sth from happening or moving either by accident or deliberately: *Could you move on, please? You're obstructing the traffic if you park there.*

obstruction /əbˈstrʌkʃn/ *noun* **1** [U] the act of stopping sth from happening or moving **2** [C] a thing that stops sb/sth from moving or doing sth: *This car is **causing an obstruction**.*

obstructive /əbˈstrʌktɪv/ *adj* trying to stop sb/sth from moving or doing sth

obtain /əbˈteɪn/ *verb* [T] (*formal*) to get sth: *to obtain advice/information/permission* ♦ *Where can I obtain tickets for the play?*

obtainable /əbˈteɪnəbl/ *adj* that you can get: *Full details are obtainable from our website.*

obtuse /əbˈtjuːs/ *adj* (*formal*) slow to understand sth: *Are you being deliberately obtuse?* ▶ **obtuseness** *noun* [U]

obˌtuse ˈangle *noun* [C] an angle between 90° and 180° ➲ look at **acute angle**, **reflex angle**, **right angle**

obvious /ˈɒbviəs/ *adj* **obvious (to sb)** easily seen or understood: ***For obvious reasons**, I'd prefer not to give my name.* ♦ *His disappointment was obvious to everyone.* SYN **clear** ▶ **obviously** *adv*: *There has obviously been a mistake.*

occasion /əˈkeɪʒn/ *noun* **1** [C] a particular time when sth happens: *I have met Bill on two occasions.* **2** [C] a special event, ceremony, etc: *Their wedding was a memorable occasion.* **3** [sing] the suitable or right time (for sth): *I shall tell her what I think if the occasion arises* (= if I get the chance).

> **HELP** **Occasion** or **opportunity**? You use **occasion** when you mean the time is right or suitable for something: *I saw them at the funeral, but it was not a suitable occasion for discussing holiday plans.* You use **opportunity** or **chance** when you mean that it is possible to do something: *I was only in Paris for one day and I didn't get the opportunity/chance to visit the Louvre.*

IDM **on occasion(s)** sometimes but not often

occasional /əˈkeɪʒənl/ *adj* [only *before* a noun] done or happening from time to time but not very often: *We have the occasional argument but most of the time we get on.* ▶ **occasionally** /əˈkeɪʒnəli/ *adv*: *We see each other occasionally.*

occult /əˈkʌlt; ˈɒkʌlt/ *adj* **1** [only *before* a noun] connected with magic powers and things that cannot be explained by reason or science **2** **the occult** /əˈkʌlt/ *noun* [sing] magic powers, ceremonies, etc.

occupant /ˈɒkjəpənt/ *noun* [C] a person who is in a building, car, etc. at a particular time

occupation /ˌɒkjuˈpeɪʃn/ *noun* **1** [C] (*formal*) a job or profession; the way in which you spend your time: *Please state your occupation on the form.* ➲ note at **work²** **2** [U] the act of the army of one country taking control of another country; the period of time that this situation lasts: *the Roman occupation of Britain* **3** [U] the act of living in or using a room, building, etc.

occupational /ˌɒkjuˈpeɪʃənl/ *adj* [only *before* a noun] connected with your work: *Accidents are an **occupational hazard** (= a risk connected with a particular job) on building sites.*

occupied /ˈɒkjupaɪd/ *adj* **1** [not before a noun] being used by sb: *Is this seat occupied?* **2** busy doing sth: *Looking after the children keeps me fully occupied.* ➲ look at **preoccupied** **3** (used about a country or a piece of land) under the control of another country: *His country had been occupied for many years.*

occupier /ˈɒkjupaɪə(r)/ *noun* [C] (*formal*) a person who owns, lives in or uses a house, piece of land, etc.

occupy /ˈɒkjupaɪ/ *verb* [T] (**occupying**; **occupies**; *pt, pp* **occupied**) **1** to fill a space or period of time: *The large table occupied most of the room.* SYN **take up** **2** (*formal*) to live in or use a house, piece of land, etc: *The house next door has not been occupied for some months.* **3** to take control of a building, country, etc. by force: *The rebel forces have occupied the TV station.* **4** **occupy sb/yourself** to keep sb/yourself busy: *How does he occupy himself now that he's retired?*

occur /əˈkɜː(r)/ *verb* [I] (**occurring**; **occurred**) **1** (*formal*) to happen, especially in a way that has

O

not been planned: *The accident occurred late last night.* ➲ note at **happen** **2** to exist or be found somewhere: *The virus occurs more frequently in children.*
PHR V occur to sb (used about an idea or a thought) to come into your mind: *It never occurred to John that his wife might be unhappy.*

occurrence /əˈkʌrəns/ *noun* [C] something that happens or exists

ocean /ˈəʊʃn/ *noun* **1** [U] (*especially AmE*) the mass of salt water that covers most of the surface of the earth: *Two thirds of the earth's surface is covered by ocean.*

MORE Ocean is used in science and geography in British English, but the more general word is sea: *I swam in the sea.* In American English it is more usual to say **ocean**: *I swam in the ocean.*

2 Ocean [C] one of the five main areas into which the water is divided: *the Atlantic/Indian/Pacific Ocean* ➲ look at sea
IDM a drop in the ocean ➲ **drop**[2]
▶ **oceanic** /ˌəʊʃiˈænɪk/ *adj*: *oceanic fish*

ochre (*AmE* also ocher) /ˈəʊkə(r)/ *noun* [U] a pale brownish-yellow colour ▶ **ochre** *adj*

o'clock /əˈklɒk/ *adv* used after the numbers one to twelve for saying what the time is: *Lunch is at 12 o'clock.*

HELP Be careful. **o'clock** can only be used with full hours: *We arranged to meet at 5 o'clock. It's 5.30 already and he's still not here.*

Oct. *abbr* = **October**: *13 Oct. 2012*

octagon /ˈɒktəgən/ *noun* [C] a shape that has eight straight and equal sides ▶ **octagonal** /ɒkˈtægənl/ *adj*

octave /ˈɒktɪv/ *noun* [C] the set of eight musical notes that western music is based on

October /ɒkˈtəʊbə(r)/ *noun* [U,C] (*abbr* **Oct.**) the 10th month of the year, coming after September ➲ note at **January**

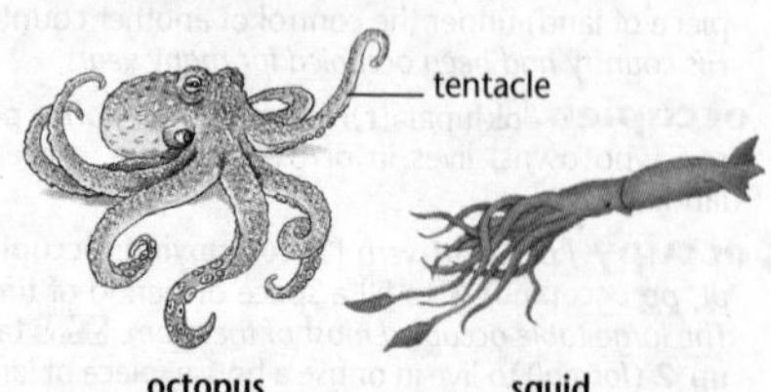

octopus /ˈɒktəpəs/ *noun* [C] a sea animal with a soft body and eight **tentacles** (= long thin parts like arms)

odd /ɒd/ *adj* (**odder**; **oddest**)
➤STRANGE **1** strange; unusual: *There's something odd about him.* ♦ *It's a bit odd that she didn't phone to say she couldn't come.* **SYN peculiar** **2 odd-** [in compounds] strange or unusual in the way mentioned: *an odd-sounding name*
➤NOT REGULAR **3** [only *before* a noun] not regular or fixed; happening sometimes: *He makes the odd mistake, but nothing very serious.*
➤VARIOUS **4** [only *before* a noun] that is left after other similar things have been used: *He made the bookshelves out of a few odd bits of wood.*
➤NOT MATCHING **5** not with the pair or set it belongs to; not matching: *You're wearing odd socks.*
➤NUMBER **6** (of a number) that cannot be divided by two: *One, three, five and seven are all odd numbers.* **OPP even**
➤APPROXIMATELY **7** (usually used after a number) a little more than: *'How old do you think he is?' 'Well, he must be thirty odd, I suppose.'*
IDM the odd man/one out one that is different from all the others in a group: *Her brothers and sisters were much older than she was. She was always the odd one out.*
▶ **oddly** *adv*: ***Oddly enough**, the most expensive tickets sold fastest.* ▶ **oddness** *noun* [U]

oddity /ˈɒdəti/ *noun* [C] (*pl* **oddities**) a person or thing that is unusual

ˌodd ˈjobs *noun* [pl] small jobs or tasks of various types

oddments /ˈɒdmənt/ *noun* [pl] (*especially BrE*) **1** pieces of cloth, wood, etc. that is left after the rest has been used **2** small items that are not part of a set

odds /ɒdz/ *noun* [pl] **the odds (on/against sth/sb)** (used for saying how probable sth is) the degree to which sth is likely to happen: *The odds on him surviving are very slim* (= he will probably die). ♦ *The odds are against you* (= you are not likely to succeed). ♦ *The odds are in your favour* (= you are likely to succeed).
IDM against (all) the odds happening although it seemed impossible
be at odds (with sb) (over sth) to disagree with sb about sth
be at odds (with sth) to be different from sth, when the two things should be the same
odds and ends (*informal*) small things of little value or importance

ode /əʊd/ *noun* [C] a poem that is written to or about a person or thing or to celebrate a special event: *Keats's 'Ode to a Nightingale'*

odometer /əʊˈdɒmɪtə(r)/ (*AmE*) = **milometer**

odour (*AmE* odor) /ˈəʊdə(r)/ *noun* [C] (*formal*) a smell (often an unpleasant one) ➲ note at **smell**[2]

odourless (*AmE* odorless) /ˈəʊdələs/ *adj* without a smell

of /əv; *strong form* ɒv/ *prep* **1** belonging to, connected with, or part of sth/sb: *the roof of the house* ♦ *the result of the exam* ♦ *the back of the book* ♦ *the leader of the party* ♦ *a friend of mine* (= one of my friends) **2** made, done or produced by sb: *the poems of Milton* **3** showing sb/sth: *a map of York* ♦ *a photograph of my parents* **4** used for saying what sb/sth is or what a thing contains or is made of: *a woman of intelligence* ♦ *the city of Paris* ♦ *a glass of milk* ♦ *a crowd of people* ♦ *It's made of silver.* ♦ *a*

feeling of anger **5** with measurements, directions and expressions of time and age: *a litre of milk* ◆ *the fourth of July* ◆ *a girl of 12* ◆ *an increase of 2.5%* ◆ *five miles north of Leeds* **6** showing that sb/sth is part of a larger group: *some of the people* ◆ *three of the houses* **7** indicating the reason for or cause of sth: *He died of pneumonia.* **8** used after a noun describing an action to show either who did the action or who it happened to: *the arrival of the president* (= he arrives) ◆ *the murder of the president* (= he is murdered) **9** with some verbs: *This perfume smells of roses.* ◆ *Think of a number.* ◆ *It reminds me of you.* **10** with some adjectives: *I'm proud of you.* ◆ *She's jealous of her.*
IDM of course ➲ course

off[1] /ɒf/ *adv, prep* **1** down or away from a place or a position on sth: *to fall off a ladder/motorbike/wall* ◆ *We got off the bus.* ◆ *I shouted to him but he just walked off.* ◆ ***I must be off*** (= I must leave here). *It's getting late.* ◆ *When are you off to Spain?* ◆ *(figurative) We've got off the subject.* **2** used with verbs that mean 'remove' or 'separate': *She took her coat off.* ◆ *He shook the rain off his umbrella.* **OPP on** **3** joined to and leading away from: *My street is off the Cowley Road.* **4** at some distance from sth: *The island of Elba is just off the west coast of Italy.* ◆ *Christmas is still a long way off* (= it is a long time until then). **5** (used about a plan or arrangement) not going to happen; cancelled: *The meeting/wedding/trip is off.* **OPP on** **6** (used about a machine, a light, etc.) not connected, working or being used: *Please make sure the TV/light/heating is off.* **7** not present at work, school, etc: *She's **off work/off sick** with a cold.* ◆ *I'm having **a day off*** (= a day's holiday) *next week.* **8** cheaper; less by a certain amount: *cars with £600 off* ◆ *£600 off the price of a car* **9** not eating or using sth: *The baby's off his food.* ℹ For special uses with many verbs, for example **go off**, look at the verb entries.
IDM off and on; on and off sometimes; starting and stopping: *It has been raining on and off all day.*
well/badly off having/not having a lot of money: *They don't seem too badly off—they have smart clothes and a nice house.*

off[2] /ɒf/ *adj (informal)* [not before a noun] **1** (used about food or drink) no longer fresh enough to eat or drink: *The milk's off.* **2** *(spoken)* unfriendly: *My neighbour was rather off with me today.*

offal /ˈɒfl/ *noun* [U] the heart and other organs of an animal, used as food

ˈoff chance *noun* [sing] a slight possibility: *She popped round **on the off chance** of finding him at home.*

ˈoff day *noun* [C] *(informal)* a day when things go badly or you do not work well: *Even the best players have off days occasionally.*

ˌoff-ˈduty *adj* not at work: *an off-duty police officer*

offence (*AmE* offense) /əˈfens/ *noun* **1** [C] *(formal)* **an offence (against sth)** a crime; an illegal action: *to commit an offence* ◆ *a criminal/minor/serious/sexual offence* **2** [U] **offence (to sb/sth)** the act of upsetting or insulting sb: *I didn't mean to **cause** you any **offence**.*
IDM take offence (at sth) to feel upset or hurt by sb/sth

offend /əˈfend/ *verb* **1** [T, often passive] to hurt sb's feelings; to upset sb: *I hope they won't be offended if I don't come.* ◆ *He felt offended that she hadn't written for so long.* **2** [I] *(formal)* to do sth illegal; to commit a crime: *The prisoner had offended again within days of his release from jail.*

offender /əˈfendə(r)/ *noun* [C] **1** *(formal)* a person who breaks the law or commits a crime: ***Young offenders** should not be sent to adult prisons.* ◆ *a first offender* (= sb who has committed a crime for the first time) **2** a person or thing that does sth wrong

offensive[1] /əˈfensɪv/ *adj* **1** **offensive (to sb)** unpleasant; insulting: *offensive behaviour/language/remarks* **OPP inoffensive** **2** [only *before* a noun] *(formal)* used for or connected with attacking: *offensive weapons* **OPP defensive** ▶ **offensively** *adv*

offensive[2] /əˈfensɪv/ *noun* [C] a military attack
IDM be on the offensive to be the first to attack sb/sth, rather than waiting for them to attack you

offer[1] /ˈɒfə(r)/ *verb* **1** [T] **offer sth (to sb) (for sth)**; **offer (sb) sth** to ask if sb would like sth or to give sb the chance to have sth: *He offered his seat on the bus to an old lady.* ◆ *I've been offered a job in London.* ◆ *He offered (me) £2000 for the car and I accepted.* **2** [I] **offer (to do sth)** to say or show that you will do sth for sb if they want: *I don't want to do it but I suppose I'll have to offer.* ◆ *My brother's offered to help me paint the house.* **3** [T] to make sth available or to provide the opportunity for sth: *The job offers plenty of opportunity for travel.*

offer[2] /ˈɒfə(r)/ *noun* [C] **1** **an offer (of sth)**; **an offer (to do sth)** a statement offering to do sth or give sth to sb: *She accepted my offer of help.* ◆ *Thank you for your kind offer to help.*

> **MORE** We can **make, accept, refuse, turn down** or **withdraw** an offer.

2 **an offer (of sth) (for sth)** an amount of money that you say you will give for sth: *They've made an offer for the house.* ◆ *We've turned down* (= refused) *an offer of £150 000.* ➲ look at **o.n.o.** **3** a low price for sth in a shop, usually for a short time: *See below for details of our special holiday offer.*
IDM on offer **1** for sale or available: *The college has a wide range of courses on offer.* **2** *(especially BrE)* for sale at a lower price than usual for a certain time: *This cheese is on offer until next week.*

offering /ˈɒfərɪŋ/ *noun* [C] something that is given or produced for other people to watch, enjoy, etc.

offhand[1] /ˌɒfˈhænd/ *adj* (used about behaviour) not showing any interest in sb/sth in a way that seems rude: *an offhand manner/voice*

offhand[2] /ˌɒfˈhænd/ *adv* without having time to think; immediately: *I can't tell you what it's worth offhand.*

O

office /ˈɒfɪs/ *noun* **1** [C] a room, set of rooms or a building where people work, usually sitting at desks: *I usually get to the office at about 9 o'clock.* ♦ *The firm's* ***head office*** (= the main branch of the company) *is in Cairo.* ♦ *Please phone again during* ***office hours.***

HELP In the US doctors and dentists have **offices**. In Britain they have **surgeries**.

2 [C] [in compounds] a room or building that is used for a particular purpose, especially for providing a service: *the tax/ticket/tourist office* ➲ look at **booking office**, **box office**, **post office** **3** Office [sing] a government department, including the people who work there and the work they do: *the Foreign/Home Office* **4** [C,U] an official position, often as part of a government or other organization: *The Labour party was* ***in office*** *from 1997 to 2010.*

TOPIC

Office work

I work as a **secretary** for a large **firm** of lawyers. The **company** employs over 50 **members of staff**. I work in an **open-plan office** so I share a large room with my **colleagues** (= the people I work with). On my desk I have a **PC** (= personal computer) and a **printer**. My **duties** include **typing** letters and emails for my boss, **filing** (= putting documents into files), answering the phone and doing the **photocopying**. I go to **meetings** and take the **minutes** (= write down what is said). I am also responsible for **ordering stationery** (= pens, paper, envelopes, etc.) and making **travel arrangements** for my boss's business trips. I work **nine to five** and have twenty days' holiday a year.

ˈ**office block** *noun* [C] a large building that contains offices, usually belonging to more than one company ➲ picture on **page P11**

officer /ˈɒfɪsə(r)/ *noun* [C] **1** a person who is in a position of authority in the armed forces: *an army/air-force officer* **2** a person who is in a position of authority in the government or a large organization: *a prison/customs/welfare officer* **3** = **police officer**

official[1] /əˈfɪʃl/ *adj* **1** [only *before* a noun] connected with the position of sb in authority: *official duties/responsibilities* **2** accepted and approved by the government or some other authority: *The scheme has not yet received official approval.* ♦ *The country's official language is Spanish.* **3** that is told to the public, but which may or may not be true: *The official reason for his resignation was that he wanted to spend more time with his family.* **OPP** for all meanings **unofficial**

official[2] /əˈfɪʃl/ *noun* [C] a person who has a position of authority: *The reception was attended by MPs and high-ranking officials.*

MORE An **office worker** is a person who works in an office, at a desk. An **official** is a person who has a position of responsibility in an organization, often the government: *senior government officials*. An **officer** is either a person who gives orders to others in the armed forces or is a member of the police force. However the word is sometimes used like **official**: *She's a tax officer in the Civil Service.*

officialdom /əˈfɪʃldəm/ *noun* [U] groups of people in positions of authority in large organizations who seem more interested in following the rules than in being helpful

officially /əˈfɪʃəli/ *adv* **1** publicly and by sb in a position of authority: *The new school was officially opened last week.* **2** according to a particular set of laws, rules, etc: *Officially we don't accept children under six, but we'll make an exception in this case.*

officious /əˈfɪʃəs/ *adj* too ready to tell other people what to do and use the power you have to give orders

offing /ˈɒfɪŋ/ *noun*
IDM **in the offing** (*informal*) likely to appear or happen soon

ˈ**off-licence** *noun* [C] (*AmE* ˈ**liquor store**) a shop which sells alcoholic drinks in bottles and cans

offline /ˌɒfˈlaɪn/ *adj, adv* not directly controlled by or connected to a computer or the Internet: *For offline orders, call this number.* ♦ *Could you tell me how to write an email offline?* ➲ look at **online**

offload /ˌɒfˈləʊd/ *verb* [T] (*informal*) **offload sth (on/onto sb)** to give away sth that you do not want to sb else: *It's nice to have someone you can offload your problems onto.*

ˌ**off-ˈpeak** *adj, adv* [only *before* a noun] available, used or done at a less popular or busy time: *an off-peak train ticket/bus pass/phone call* ♦ *It's cheaper to travel off-peak.* ➲ look at **peak**

ˌ**off-ˈputting** *adj* unpleasant in a way that stops you from liking sb/sth

offset /ˈɒfset/ *verb* [T] (**offsetting**; *pt, pp* **offset**) to make the effect of sth less strong or noticeable: *The disadvantages of the scheme are more than offset by the advantages.*

offshoot /ˈɒfʃuːt/ *noun* [C] a thing that develops from sth else, especially a small organization that develops from a larger one

offshore /ˌɒfˈʃɔː(r)/ *adj, adv* in the sea but not very far from the land: *an offshore oil rig* ♦ *a ship anchored offshore*

offside *adj* **1** /ˌɒfˈsaɪd/ (used about a player in football and other sports) in a position that is not allowed by the rules of the game **2** /ˈɒfsaɪd/ (*BrE*) (used about a part of a vehicle) on the side that is furthest away from the edge of the road

offspring /ˈɒfsprɪŋ/ *noun* [C] (*pl* **offspring**) (*formal*) a child or children; the young of an animal: *to produce/raise offspring*

ˌ**off-ˈwhite** *adj* not pure white

often /ˈɒfn; ˈɒftən/ *adv* **1** many times: *We often go swimming at the weekend.* ♦ *I'm sorry I didn't write very often.* ♦ ***How often*** *should you go to the dentist?*

SYN **frequently** **2** in many cases: *Old houses are often damp.* SYN **commonly**
IDM **every so often** sometimes; from time to time **more often than not** usually

ogre /ˈəʊɡə(r)/ *noun* [C] **1** (in children's stories) a very large, cruel and frightening creature that eats people **2** a person who is unpleasant and frightening

oh (also **O**) /əʊ/ *exclam* **1** used for reacting to sth that sb has said: *'I'm a teacher.' 'Oh? Where?'* **2** used to express surprise, fear, joy, etc: *'Oh no!' she cried as she began to read the letter.*

ˌoh well = well³(2)

oil /ɔɪl/ *noun* [U] **1** a thick dark liquid that comes from under the ground and is used as a fuel or to make machines work smoothly: *Britain obtains oil from the North Sea.* **2** a thick liquid that comes from animals or plants and is used in cooking: *cooking/vegetable/sunflower/olive oil* ▸ **oil** *verb* [T]

oilfield /ˈɔɪlfiːld/ *noun* [C] an area where there is oil under the ground or under the sea

ˈoil painting *noun* [C] a picture that has been painted using paint made with oil

ˈoil rig (also **rig**) *noun* [C] a large platform in the sea with equipment for getting oil out from under the sea

ˈoil slick (also **slick**) *noun* [C] an area of oil that floats on the sea, usually after a ship carrying oil has crashed

ˈoil well (also **well**) *noun* [C] a hole that is made deep in the ground or under the sea in order to obtain oil

oily /ˈɔɪli/ *adj* (**oilier**; **oiliest**) covered with oil or like oil: *Mechanics always have oily hands.* ♦ *oily food*

ointment /ˈɔɪntmənt/ (also **cream**) *noun* [C,U] a smooth substance that you put on sore skin or on an injury to help it get better ➲ picture at **medicine**

OK¹ (also **okay**) /əʊˈkeɪ/ *adj, adv, exclam* (*informal*) **1** all right; good or well enough: *'Did you have a nice day?' 'Well, it was OK, I suppose.'* ♦ *Is it okay if I come at about 7?* **2** yes; all right: *'Do you want to come with us?' 'OK.'*

OK² (also **okay**) /əʊˈkeɪ/ *noun* [sing] agreement or permission: *As soon as my parents* ***give me the OK****, I'll come and stay with you.*

old /əʊld/ *adj* (**older**; **oldest**)
➤AGE **1** [used with a period of time or with *how*] of a particular age: *That building is 500 years old.* ♦ *The book is aimed at eight- to ten-year-olds.* ♦ *How old are you?* ➲ note at **age¹**
➤NOT YOUNG **2** having lived a long time: *My mother wasn't very old when she died.* ♦ *He's only 50 but he looks older.* ♦ *to* ***get/grow*** *old* OPP **young** **3** **the old** *noun* [pl] old people: *The old feel the cold more than the young.* ➲ look at **the elderly**, **the aged**
➤NOT NEW **4** that has existed for a long time; connected with past times: *This house is quite old.* ♦ *old ideas/traditions* ♦ *In the old days, people generally had larger families than nowadays.* OPP **new**, **modern** **5** having been used a lot: *I got rid of all my old clothes.* OPP **new** ➲ look at **second-hand** **6** [only *before* a noun] former: *I earn more now than I did in my old job.* SYN **previous** **7** [only *before* a noun] known for a long time: *She's a very old friend of mine. We knew each other at school.*

> **GRAMMAR** **Older** and **oldest** are the usual comparative and superlative forms of **old**: *My father's older than my mother.* ♦ *I'm the oldest in the class.* **Elder** and **eldest** can be used when comparing the ages of people, especially members of a family. However, it is only used in phrases like: *elder brother* and: *eldest daughter* It is not used with *than*, so it is not correct to say, 'My sister is elder than me.'

➤NOT IMPORTANT **8** [only *before* a noun] (*informal*) used for emphasizing that sth has little importance or value: *I write any old rubbish in my diary.*
IDM **be an old hand (at sth)** to be good at sth because you have done it often before: *She's an old hand at dealing with the press.*

ˌold ˈage *noun* [U] the part of your life when you are old: *He's enjoying life* ***in his old age****.* ➲ look at **youth**

ˌold-age ˈpension *noun* [U] (*BrE*) money paid by the state to people above a certain age ▸ **ˌold-age ˈpensioner** (also **pensioner**) *noun* [C] (*abbr* **OAP**) ➲ look at **pension**

> **HELP** The expression **senior citizen** is more polite and is more common nowadays.

ˌOld ˈEnglish = Anglo-Saxon(3)

ˌold-ˈfashioned *adj* **1** usual in the past but not now: *old-fashioned clothes/ideas* ♦ *That word sounds a bit old-fashioned.* **2** (used about people) believing in old ideas, customs, etc: *My parents are quite old-fashioned about some things.* ➲ look at **modern**, **unfashionable**

the ˌOld ˈTestament *noun* [sing] the first part of the Bible that tells the history of the Jewish people before the birth of Christ ➲ look at **the New Testament**

oligarch /ˈɒlɪɡɑːk/ *noun* [C] **1** a member of a government in which only a small group of people hold all the power **2** an extremely rich and powerful person

olive /ˈɒlɪv/ *noun* **1** [C] a small green or black fruit with a bitter taste, used for food and oil: *Fry the onions in a little olive oil.* **2** (also **ˌolive ˈgreen**) [U] a colour between yellow and green ▸ **olive** *adj*

the Olympic Games /əˌlɪmpɪk ˈɡeɪmz/ (also **the Oˈlympics**) *noun* [pl] an international sports competition which is organized every four years in a different country: *to win a medal at/in the Olympics* ♦ *the Winter/Summer Olympics* ▸ **Olympic** *adj* [only *before* a noun]: *Who holds the Olympic record for the 1500 metres?*

ombudsman /ˈɒmbʊdzmən; -mæn/ *noun* [sing] an official whose job is to examine and report on complaints made by ordinary people about public organizations

omelette (*AmE* omelet) /ˈɒmlət/ *noun* [C] a dish made of eggs that have been beaten and fried

omen /ˈəʊmən/ *noun* [C] a sign of sth that will happen in the future: *a good/bad omen for the future*

ominous /ˈɒmɪnəs/ *adj* suggesting that sth bad is going to happen: *Those black clouds look ominous.*

omission /əˈmɪʃn/ *noun* [C,U] something that has not been included; the act of not including sb/sth: *There were several omissions on the list of names.*

omit /əˈmɪt/ *verb* [T] (**omitting**; **omitted**) **1** to not include sth; to leave sth out: *Several verses of the song can be omitted.* **2** (*formal*) **omit to do sth** to forget or choose not to do sth

on /ɒn/ *adv, prep* **1** (also *formal* **upon**) supported by, fixed to or touching sth, especially a surface: *on the table/ceiling/wall* ◆ *We sat on the beach/grass/floor.* ◆ *She was carrying the baby on her back.* ◆ *Write it down on a piece of paper.* ◆ *The ball hit me on the head.* **2** in a place or position: *on a farm/housing estate/campsite* ◆ *a house on the river/seafront/border* ◆ *I live on the other side of town.* **3** used with ways of travelling and types of travel: *on the bus/train/plane* ◆ *We came* **on foot** (= we walked). ◆ *Eddie went past on his bike.* ◆ *to go on a trip/journey/excursion*

HELP Note that we say **in the car**.

4 with expressions of time: *on August 19th* ◆ *on Monday* ◆ *on Christmas Day* ◆ *on your birthday* **5** showing that sth continues: *The man shouted at us but we walked on.* ◆ *The speeches went* **on and on** *until everyone was bored.* **6** wearing sth; carrying sth in your pocket or bag: *What did she* **have on**? ◆ *to* **put** *your shoes/coat/hat/make-up* **on** ◆ *I've got no money on me.* ◆ *You should carry ID on you at all times.* **7** working; being used: *All the lights were on.* ◆ **Switch** *the TV* **on**. **8** immediately or soon after: *He telephoned her on his return from New York.* **9** about sth: *We've got a test on irregular verbs tomorrow.* ◆ *a talk/a book/an article on Japan* **10** happening or arranged to happen: *What's on at the cinema?* ◆ *Is the meeting still on, or has it been cancelled?* **11** using drugs or medicine; using a particular kind of food or fuel: *to be on medication/antibiotics/heroin* ◆ *Gorillas live on leaves and fruit.* ◆ *Does this car run on petrol or diesel?* **12** showing direction: *on the right/left* ◆ *on the way to school* **13** showing the reason for or starting point of sth: *She doesn't eat meat* **on principle**. ◆ *The film is* **based on** *a true story.* **14** receiving a certain amount of money: *What will you be on* (= how much will you earn) *in your new job?* ◆ *He's been (living) on unemployment benefit since he lost his job.* **15** paid for by sb: *The drinks are on me!* **16** using sth; by means of sth: *I was (talking)* **on the phone** *to Laura.* ◆ *I saw it* **on TV**. ◆ *I cut my hand on some glass.* ◆ *Dave spends most evenings* **on the Internet**. **17** showing the thing or person that is affected by an action or is the object of an action: *Divorce can have a bad effect on children.* ◆ *He spends a lot on clothes.* ◆ *Don't waste your time on that.* **18** compared to: *Sales are up 10% on last year.* ⓘ For special uses with many verbs and nouns, for example **get on**, **on holiday**, see the verb and noun entries.

IDM **from now/then on** starting from this/that time and continuing: *From then on she never spoke to him again.*

not on (*informal*) not acceptable: *No, you can't stay out that late. It's just not on.*

off and on; on and off ➲ **off**[1]

PHR V **be/go on at sb** ➲ **go**[1]

once /wʌns/ *adv, conj* **1** one time only; on one occasion: *I've only been to France once.* ◆ *once a week/month/year* ◆ *I visit them about once every six months.* **2** at some time in the past: *This house was once the village school.* **SYN** **formerly** **3** as soon as; when: *Once you've practised a bit you'll find that it's quite easy.*

IDM **all at once** all at the same time or suddenly: *People began talking all at once.* ◆ *All at once she got up and left the room.*

at once 1 immediately; now: *Come here at once!* **2** at the same time: *I can't understand if you all speak at once.*

just this once; (just) for once on this occasion only: *Just this once, I'll help you with your homework.*

once again/more again, as before: *Spring will soon be here once again.*

once and for all now and for the last time: *You've got to make a decision once and for all.*

once in a blue moon (*informal*) almost never

once in a while sometimes but not often

once more one more time: *Let's listen to that track once more, shall we?*

once upon a time (used at the beginning of a children's story) a long time ago; in the past: *Once upon a time there was a princess ...*

oncoming /ˈɒnkʌmɪŋ/ *adj* [only *before* a noun] coming towards you: *oncoming traffic*

one[1] /wʌn/ *number, determiner* **1** the number 1: *There's only one biscuit left.* ◆ *The journey takes one hour.* ◆ *If you take one from ten it leaves nine.* ➲ note at **six** ➲ look at **first** **2** used with *the other, another* or *other(s)* to make a contrast: *The twins are so alike that it's hard to tell one from the other.* **3 the one** used for emphasizing that there is only one of sth: *She's the one person I trust.* ◆ *We can't all get in the one car.* **4** (used when you are talking about a time in the past or future without actually saying when) a certain: *He came to see me one evening last week.* ◆ *We must go and visit them one day.*

IDM **(all) in one** all together or combined: *It's a printer and scanner all in one.*

the odd man/one out ➲ **odd**

one after another/the other first one, then the next, etc: *One after another the winners went up to get their prizes.*

one at a time separately: *I'll deal with the problems one at a time.* **SYN** **individually**

one by one separately: *One by one, people began to arrive at the meeting.*

one or two a few: *I've borrowed one or two new books from the library.*

one[2] /wʌn/ *pron* [C] **1** used instead of repeating a noun: *I think I'll have an apple. Would you like one?* **2** used after *this, that, which* or after an adjective instead of a noun: *'Which dress do you like?' 'This one.'* ♦ *'Can I borrow some books of yours?' 'Yes. Which ones?'* ♦ *'This coat's a bit small. You need a bigger one.'* ♦ *That idea is a very good one.* **3 the one/the ones** used before a group of words that show which person or thing you are talking about: *My house is the one after the post office.* ♦ *If you find some questions difficult, leave out the ones you don't understand.* **4 one of** a member (of a certain group): *He's staying with one of his friends.* ♦ *One of the children is crying.*

GRAMMAR **One of** is always followed by a plural noun. The verb is singular because the subject is **one**: *One of our assistants is ill.* ♦ *One of the buses was late.*

5 (*formal*) used for referring to people in general, including the speaker or writer: *One must be sure of one's facts before criticizing other people.*

HELP This use of **one** is very formal and now sounds old-fashioned. It is much more usual to say **you**.

ˌone aˈnother *pron* used when you are saying that each member of a group does sth to or for the other people in the group: *We exchanged news with one another.*

ˌone-ˈoff *adj* [only *before* a noun] something that is made or that happens only once: *a one-off payment/opportunity* ▶ **one-off** *noun* [C]: *It was just a one-off; it won't happen again.*

ˌone-on-ˈone (*AmE*) = **one-to-one**

onerous /ˈəʊnərəs/ *adj* (*formal*) needing great effort; causing trouble or worry: *an onerous duty/task/responsibility* **SYN** **taxing**

oneself /wʌnˈself/ *pron* (*formal*) **1** used when the person who does an action is also affected by it: *One can teach oneself to play the piano but it is easier to have lessons.* **2** used to emphasize the person who does the action: *One could easily arrange it all oneself.*

IDM **(all) by oneself** **1** alone ➲ note at **alone** **2** without help

ˌone-ˈsided *adj* **1** (used about an opinion, an argument, etc.) showing only one point of view; not balanced: *Some newspapers give a very one-sided view of politics.* **2** (used about a relationship or a competition) not equal: *The match was very one-sided—we lost 12-1.*

ˌone-to-ˈone (*AmE usually* ˌone-on-ˈone) *adj, adv* between only two people: *one-to-one English lessons* (= one teacher to one student)

ˌone-ˈway *adv, adj* **1** (used about roads) that you can only drive along in one direction: *a one-way street* **2** (*especially AmE*) (used about a ticket) that you can use to travel somewhere but not back again: *a one-way ticket* **SYN** **single**

ongoing /ˈɒŋɡəʊɪŋ/ *adj* [usually *before* a noun] continuing to exist now: *It's an ongoing problem.*

onion /ˈʌnjən/ *noun* [C,U] a white or red vegetable with many layers. Onions are often used in cooking and have a strong smell: *a kilo of onions* ♦ *onion soup* ➲ picture on **page P15**

online /ˌɒnˈlaɪn/ *adj, adv* controlled by or connected to a computer or to the Internet: *an online ticket booking system* ♦ *I'm studying French online.* ➲ note at **Internet** ➲ look at **offline**

TOPIC

Online

Many people like to **shop online**. You can **browse the website** or use the **search box** of a shop or **online retailer** (= a company that sells things on the Internet) to find what you want. When you want to buy something, you **add it to your basket** (= click a button by the item). When you have finished shopping, you **go to a checkout** (= click another button) to pay for your purchases, using a credit or debit card. You can also buy or sell things on **eBay™** (= a website where people can sell goods to the person who offers the most money for them).

onlooker /ˈɒnlʊkə(r)/ *noun* [C] a person who watches sth happening without taking part in it

only /ˈəʊnli/ *adj* [only *before* a noun] *adv, conj* **1** with no others existing or present: *This is the only dress we have in your size.* ♦ *I was the only woman in the room.* **2** and nobody or nothing else; no more than: *She only likes pop music.* ♦ *I've only asked a few friends to the party.* ♦ *It's only 1 o'clock.* **3** the most suitable or the best: *She's the only person for the job.*

GRAMMAR In written English **only** is usually placed *before* the word it refers to. In spoken English we can use stress to show which word it refers to and **only** does not have to change position: *I only kissed ˈJane* (= I kissed Jane and no one else). ♦ *I only ˈkissed Jane* (= I kissed Jane but I didn't do anything else).

4 (*informal*) except that; but: *The film was very good, only it was a bit too long.*

IDM **if only** ➲ **if**

not only … but also ➲ **not**

only just **1** not long ago: *I've only just started this job.* **2** almost not: *We only just had enough money to pay for the meal.* **SYN** **hardly**

ˌonly ˈchild *noun* [C] a child who has no brothers or sisters

o.n.o. (also **ono**) *abbr* (*BrE*) or near/nearest offer (used in small advertisements to show that sth may be sold at a lower price than the price that has been asked): *Motorbike for sale. £750 o.n.o.*

onset /ˈɒnset/ *noun* [sing] **the onset (of sth)** the beginning (often of sth unpleasant): *the onset of winter/a headache*

onslaught /ˈɒnslɔːt/ *noun* [C] **an onslaught (on/against sb/sth)** a violent or strong attack: *an onslaught on government policy*

onto (also on to) /ˈɒntə; *before vowels* ˈɒntu/ *prep* to a position on sth: *The cat jumped onto the sofa.* ◆ *The bottle fell off the table onto the floor.* ◆ *The crowd ran onto the pitch.*

IDM **be onto sb** (*informal*) to have found out about sth illegal that sb is doing: *The police were onto the car thieves.*

be onto sth to have some information, etc. that could lead to an important discovery

onwards /ˈɒnwədz/ (also **onward** /ˈɒnwəd/) *adv* **1 from ... onwards** continuing from a particular time: *From September onwards it usually begins to get colder.* **2** (*formal*) forward: *The road stretched onwards into the distance.*

ooze /uːz/ *verb* [I,T] **ooze from/out of sth; ooze (with) sth** to flow slowly out or to allow sth to flow slowly out: *Blood was oozing from a cut on his head.* ◆ *The fruit was oozing juice.*

op /ɒp/ (*informal*) = **operation**(1)

opaque /əʊˈpeɪk/ *adj* **1** that you cannot see through: *opaque glass in the door* **2** (*formal*) difficult to understand; not clear OPP for both meanings **transparent**

OPEC /ˈəʊpek/ *abbr* **Organization of Petroleum Exporting Countries**

the ˈopen *noun* [sing] outside; the countryside: *After working in an office all week, I like to be* **out in the open** *at weekends.*

IDM **bring sth out into the open; come out into the open** to make sth known publicly; to be known publicly: *I'm glad our secret has come out into the open at last.*

open¹ /ˈəʊpən/ *adj*

➤NOT CLOSED **1** not closed or covered: *Don't leave the door open.* ◆ *an open window* ◆ *I can't get this bottle of wine open.* ◆ *She stared at me with her eyes wide open.* ◆ *The diary was lying open on her desk.* ◆ *The curtains were open so that we could see into the room.* ◆ *His shirt was open at the neck.*

➤OF LAND/SEA **2** [only *before* a noun] away from towns and buildings; at a distance from the land: *open country* ◆ *on the open sea*

➤FOR VISITORS/CUSTOMERS **3 open (to sb/sth); open (for sth)** available for people to enter, visit, use, etc.; not closed to the public: *The bank isn't open till 9.30.* ◆ *The new shopping centre will soon be open.* ◆ *The competition is open to everyone.* ◆ *The gardens are* **open to the public** *in the summer.* ◆ *The hotel damaged by the bomb is now* **open for business** *again.* OPP **closed, shut**

➤OF CHARACTER **4** not keeping feelings and thoughts hidden: *Elena doesn't mind talking about her feelings —she's a very open person.* ◆ *He looked at him with open dislike.*

➤NOT DECIDED **5** [not before a noun] not finally decided; still being considered: *Let's leave the details open.*

IDM **have/keep an open mind (about/on sth)** to be ready to listen to or consider new ideas and suggestions

in the open air outside: *Somehow, food eaten in the open air tastes much better.*

keep an eye open/out (for sb/sth) ➲ **eye¹**

open to sth willing to receive sth: *I'm always open to suggestions.*

with your eyes open ➲ **eye¹**

with open arms in a friendly way that shows that you are pleased to see sb or have sth: *The unions welcomed the government's decision with open arms.*

open² /ˈəʊpən/ *verb* **1** [I,T] to move sth or part of sth so that it is no longer closed; to move so as to be no longer closed: *This window won't open—it's stuck.* ◆ *The parachute failed to open and he was killed.* ◆ *The book opened at the very page I needed.* ◆ *Open the curtains, will you?* ◆ *to open your eyes/hand/mouth* ◆ *to open a bag/letter/box* OPP **close, shut** **2** [I,T] to make it possible for people to enter a place: *Does that shop open on Sundays?* ◆ *The museum opens at 10.* ◆ *The company is opening two new branches soon.* ◆ *Police finally opened the road six hours after the accident.* OPP **close, shut** **3** [I,T] to start (sth): *The play opens in London next month.* ◆ *The chairman opened the meeting by welcoming everybody.* ◆ *I'd like to open a bank account.* OPP **close** **4** [T] to start a computer program or file so that you can use it on the screen

IDM **open fire (at/on sb/sth)** to start shooting: *He ordered his men to open fire.*

PHR V **open into/onto sth** to lead to another room, area or place: *This door opens onto the garden.*

open out to become wider

open up 1 to talk about what you feel and think **2** to open a door: *'Open up,' shouted the police to the man inside.*

open (sth) up 1 to become available or to make sth available: *When I left school all sorts of opportunities opened up for me.* **2** to start business: *The restaurant opened up last year.*

ˌopen-ˈair *adj* [only *before* a noun] not inside a building: *an open-air swimming pool*

ˈopen day *noun* [C] a day when the public can visit a place that they cannot usually go into: *The school is having an open day next month.*

opener /ˈəʊpnə(r)/ *noun* [C] [in compounds] a thing that takes the lid, etc. off sth: *a tin opener* ◆ *a bottle opener*

opening /ˈəʊpnɪŋ/ *noun* [C]

➤SPACE/HOLE **1** a space or hole that sb/sth can go through: *We were able to get through an opening in the hedge.*

➤BEGINNING **2** the beginning or first part of sth: *The film is famous for its dramatic opening.*

➤CEREMONY **3** a ceremony to celebrate the first time a public building, road, etc. is used: *the opening of the new hospital*

➤JOB **4** a job which is available: *We have an opening for a sales manager at the moment.*

➤OPPORTUNITY **5** a good opportunity: *I'm sure she'll be a great journalist—all she needs is an opening.*

▶ **opening** *adj* [only *before* a noun]: *the opening chapter of a book* ◆ *the opening ceremony of the Olympic Games*

openly /ˈəʊpənli/ *adv* honestly; not keeping anything secret: *I think you should discuss your feelings openly with each other.*

ˌopen-ˈminded *adj* ready to consider new ideas and opinions OPP **narrow-minded**

openness /ˈəʊpənnəs/ *noun* [U] the quality of being honest and ready to talk about your feelings

ˌopen-ˈplan *adj* (used about a large area inside a building) not divided into separate rooms: *an open-plan office*

the ˌOpen Uniˈversity *noun* [sing] (in Britain) a university whose students study mainly at home. Their work is sent to them by post or email and there are special television, radio and online programmes for them.

opera /ˈɒprə/ *noun* [C,U] a play in which most of the words are sung to music; works of this kind performed as entertainment: *an opera by Mozart* ◆ *Do you like opera?* ◆ *a comic opera* ➲ look at **musical**, **soap opera**

ˈopera house *noun* [C] a theatre where **operas** are performed

operate /ˈɒpəreɪt/ *verb* **1** [I,T] to work, or to make sth work: *I don't understand how this machine operates.* ◆ *These switches here operate the central heating.* SYN **function** **2** [I] to act or to have an effect: *Several factors were operating to our advantage.* **3** [I, T] to do business; to manage sth: *The firm operates from its central office in Delhi.* **4** [I] operate (on sb/sth) (for sth) to cut open sb's body in hospital in order to deal with a part that is damaged, infected, etc: *The surgeon is going to operate on her in the morning.* ◆ *He was operated on for appendicitis.*

operatic /ˌɒpəˈrætɪk/ *adj* connected with **opera**: *operatic music*

ˈoperating system *noun* [C] a computer program that organizes a number of other programs at the same time

ˈoperating theatre (also theatre, *AmE* ˈoperating room) *noun* [C] a room in a hospital where medical operations are performed

operation /ˌɒpəˈreɪʃn/ *noun*
➤MEDICAL **1** [C] (also *informal* op) the process of cutting open a patient's body in order to deal with a part inside: *He* ***had an operation*** *to remove his appendix.* ➲ note at **hospital**
➤ACTIVITY **2** [C] an organized activity that involves many people doing different things: *A rescue operation was mounted to find the missing children.*
➤BUSINESS **3** [C] a business or company involving many parts: *a huge international operation*
➤COMPUTING **4** [C] an act performed by a machine, especially a computer: *The computer can perform millions of operations per second.*
➤MACHINE/SYSTEM **5** [U] the way in which you make sth work: *The operation of these machines is extremely simple.*
IDM **be in operation; come into operation** to be/start working or having an effect: *The new tax system will come into operation in the spring.*

operational /ˌɒpəˈreɪʃənl/ *adj* **1** connected with the way a business, machine, system, etc. works **2** ready for use: *The new factory is now fully operational.* **3** [only *before* a noun] connected with military operations

operative /ˈɒpərətɪv/ *adj* (*formal*) **1** working, able to be used; in use: *The new law will be operative from 1 May.* **2** [only *before* a noun] connected with a medical operation

operator /ˈɒpəreɪtə(r)/ *noun* [C] **1** a person whose job is to work a particular machine or piece of equipment: *a keyboard operator* **2** a person whose job is to connect telephone calls, for the public or in a particular building: *Dial 100 for the operator.* ◆ *a switchboard operator* **3** a person or company that does certain types of business: *a tour operator*

opinion /əˈpɪnjən/ *noun* **1** [C] an opinion (of sb/sth); an opinion (on/about sth) what you think about sb/sth: *She asked me for my opinion of her new hairstyle and I told her.* ◆ *He has very strong opinions on almost everything.* ◆ ***In my opinion****, you're making a terrible mistake.* ➲ note at **point of view**, **think** **2** [U] what people in general think about sth: *Public opinion is in favour of a change in the law.*
IDM **be of the opinion that ...** (*formal*) to think or believe that ...
have a good, high, etc. opinion of sb/sth; have a bad, low, poor, etc. opinion of sb/sth to think that sb/sth is good/bad
a matter of opinion ➲ **matter**[1]

oˈpinion poll = **poll**[1] (1)

opium /ˈəʊpiəm/ *noun* [U] a powerful drug that is made from the juice of a type of **poppy** (= a type of flower)

opp. *abbr* = **opposite**

opponent /əˈpəʊnənt/ *noun* [C] **1** (in sport or competitions) a person who plays against sb: *They are the toughest opponents we've played against.* **2** an opponent (of sth) a person who disagrees with sb's actions, plans or beliefs and tries to stop or change them: *the President's political opponents*

opportune /ˈɒpətjuːn/ *adj* (*formal*) **1** (used about a time) suitable for doing a particular thing, so that it is likely to be successful: *The offer could not have come at a more opportune moment.* SYN **favourable** **2** (used about an action or event) done or happening at the right time to be successful: *an opportune remark* OPP for both meanings **inopportune**

opportunism /ˌɒpəˈtjuːnɪzəm/ *noun* [U] making use of a situation for your own good and not caring about other people

opportunist /ˌɒpəˈtjuːnɪst/ (also **opportunistic** /ˌɒpətjuːˈnɪstɪk/) *adj* not done in a planned way; making use of an opportunity: *an opportunist crime* ▶ **opportunist** *noun* [C]: *80% of burglaries are committed by casual opportunists.*

opportunity /ˌɒpəˈtjuːnəti/ *noun* [C,U] (*pl* opportunities) an opportunity (for sth/to do sth) a

O

chance to do sth that you would like to do; a situation or a time in which it is possible to do sth that you would like to do: *There will be plenty of opportunity for asking questions later.* ♦ *I have a* ***golden opportunity*** *to go to America now that my sister lives there.* ♦ *When we're finally alone, I'll* ***take the opportunity*** *to ask him a few personal questions.* ♦ *I'll give Steve your message if I* ***get the opportunity****.* SYN chance ➲ note at **occasion**

oppose /ə'pəʊz/ *verb* [T] to disagree with sb's beliefs, actions or plans and to try to change or stop them: *They opposed the plan to build a new road.*

opposed /ə'pəʊzd/ *adj* **opposed to sth** disagreeing with a plan, action, etc.; believing that sth is wrong: *She has always been strongly opposed to experiments on animals.*

IDM **as opposed to** (used to emphasize the difference between two things) rather than; and not: *Your work will be judged on quality, as opposed to quantity.*

opposing /ə'pəʊzɪŋ/ *adj* [only *before* a noun] **1** (used about teams, armies, etc.) playing, fighting, working, etc. against each other: *a player from the opposing side* **2** (used about opinions, attitudes, etc.) very different from each other: *They have opposing views.*

opposite

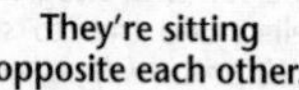

They're sitting opposite each other.

She's sitting in front of him.

opposite /'ɒpəzɪt; -sɪt/ *adj, adv, prep* (*abbr* **opp.**) **1** in a position on the other side of sb/sth; facing: *The old town and the new town are on opposite sides of the river.* ♦ *You sit there and I'll sit opposite.*

> **HELP** Sometimes **opposite** is used after a noun: *Write your answer in the space opposite.*

2 completely different: *I can't walk with you because I'm going in the opposite direction.* ♦ *the opposite sex* (= the other sex)

IDM **your opposite number** a person who does the same job or has the same position as you in a different company, organization, team, etc: *The Prime Minister met his Italian opposite number.*

▶ **opposite** *noun* [C]: *'Hot' is* ***the opposite of*** *'cold'.*

opposition /ˌɒpə'zɪʃn/ *noun* **1** [U] **opposition (to sb/sth)** the feeling of disagreeing with sth and the act of trying to change it: *He expressed strong opposition to the plan.* **2 the opposition** [sing, with sing or pl verb] the person or team who you compete against in sport, business, etc: *We need to find out what the opposition is doing.* **3 the Opposition** [sing, with sing or pl verb] the politicians or the political parties that are in a parliament but not in the government: *the leader of the Opposition* ♦ *Opposition MPs*

oppress /ə'pres/ *verb* [T, usually passive] to treat a group of people in a cruel and unfair way by not allowing them the same freedom and rights as others ▶ **oppressed** *adj*: *an oppressed minority* ▶ **oppression** /ə'preʃn/ *noun* [U]: *a struggle against oppression*

oppressive /ə'presɪv/ *adj* **1** allowing no freedom; controlling by force **2** (used especially about heat or the atmosphere) causing you to feel very uncomfortable

opt /ɒpt/ *verb* [I] **opt to do sth/for sth** to choose to do or have sth after thinking about it: *She opted for a career in music.*

PHR V **opt out (of sth)** to choose not to take part in sth: *Employees may opt out of the company's pension plan.*

optical /'ɒptɪkl/ *adj* connected with the sense of sight: *optical instruments*

ˌoptical ilˈlusion *noun* [C] an image that tricks the eye and makes you think you can see sth that you cannot

optical illusions

Are there two prongs or three?

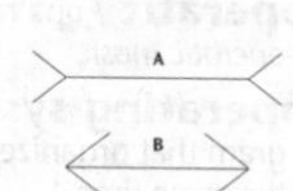

Which line is longer, A or B?

optician /ɒp'tɪʃn/ *noun* [C] a person whose job is to test eyes, sell glasses, etc: *I have to go to the optician's* (= the shop) *for an eye test.*

optimal /'ɒptɪməl/ = **optimum**

optimism /'ɒptɪmɪzəm/ *noun* [U] the feeling that the future will be good or successful: *There is considerable optimism that the economy will improve.* OPP **pessimism** ▶ **optimist** /-ɪst/ *noun* [C]

optimistic /ˌɒptɪ'mɪstɪk/ *adj* **optimistic (about sth/that ...)** expecting good things to happen or sth to be successful; showing this feeling: *I've applied for the job but I'm not very optimistic that I'll get it.* SYN **positive** OPP **pessimistic** ▶ **optimistically** /-kli/ *adv*

optimum /'ɒptɪməm/ (also **optimal**) *adj* [only *before* a noun] the best possible; producing the best possible results: *optimum growth* ♦ *the optimum conditions for effective learning*

option /'ɒpʃn/ *noun* [U,C] something that you can choose to do; the freedom to choose: *She looked carefully at all the options before deciding on a career.* ♦ *Students* ***have the option*** *of studying part-time or full-time.* ♦ *If you're late again, you will give us* ***no option but to*** *dismiss you.* SYN **choice**

optional /ˈɒpʃənl/ *adj* that you can choose or not choose: *an optional subject at school* OPP **compulsory, obligatory**

or /ɔː(r)/ *conj* **1** used in a list of possibilities or choices: *Would you like to sit here or next to the window?* ◆ *Are you interested or not?* ◆ *For the main course, you can have lamb, beef or fish.* ➲ look at **either 2** [after a negative] and neither; and not: *Alexi hasn't phoned or emailed me for weeks.* ◆ *I've never been either to Italy or Spain.* ➲ look at **neither 3** if not; otherwise: *Don't drive so fast or you'll have an accident!* SYN **or else 4** used between two numbers to show approximately how many: *I've been there five or six times.* **5** used before a word or phrase that explains or comments on what has been said before: *20% of the population, or one in five*
IDM **or something/somewhere; someone/something/somewhere or other** (*spoken*) used for showing that you are not sure, cannot remember or do not know which thing or place: *She's a computer programmer or something.* ◆ *He muttered something or other about having no time and disappeared.*

oral¹ /ˈɔːrəl/ *adj* **1** spoken, not written: *an oral test* **2** [only *before* a noun] concerning or using the mouth: *oral hygiene* ➲ look at **aural** ▸ **orally** /ˈɔːrəli/ *adv*: *You can ask the questions orally or in writing.* ◆ *This medicine is taken orally* (= is swallowed).

oral² /ˈɔːrəl/ *noun* [C] a spoken exam: *I've got my German oral next week.*

EXAM TIP

Oral/Speaking exams

Check what the time limits are for the exam. Practise speaking for the necessary amount of time, to get used to how much you can say in that time. In the exam, never stop and say 'I've finished' or 'That's all'; continue speaking until you are told to stop.

orange¹ /ˈɒrɪndʒ/ *noun* **1** [C,U] a round fruit with a thick skin that is divided into sections inside and is a colour between red and yellow: *orange juice/peel* ◆ *an orange tree* ➲ picture on **page P14 2** [U,C] a drink made from oranges or with the taste of oranges; a glass of this drink: *freshly squeezed orange* **3** [U,C] the colour of this fruit, between red and yellow

orange² /ˈɒrɪndʒ/ *adj* having the colour orange: *orange paint*

ˌorange ˈsquash *noun* [C,U] (*BrE*) a drink made by adding water to a liquid that tastes of orange

orang-utan /ɔːˌræŋ uːˈtæn; əˈræŋ uːtæn/ *noun* [C] a large animal that has long arms and reddish hair, like a **monkey** (= an animal that lives in hot countries and can climb trees) with no tail and that lives in South East Asia ➲ look at **ape**

orator /ˈɒrətə(r)/ *noun* [C] (*formal*) a person who is good at making public speeches

orbit /ˈɔːbɪt/ *noun* [C,U] a curved path taken by a planet or another object as it moves around another planet, star, moon, etc: *the earth's orbit around the sun* ▸ **orbit** *verb* [I,T]

orbital /ˈɔːbɪtl/ *adj* [only *before* a noun] **1** connected with the **orbit** of a planet or another object in space **2** (*BrE*) (used about a road) built around the outside of a city or town to reduce the amount of traffic travelling through the centre ▸ **orbital** *noun* [C, usually sing]

orchard /ˈɔːtʃəd/ *noun* [C] a piece of land on which fruit trees are grown: *a cherry orchard* ➲ picture on **page P11**

orchestra /ˈɔːkɪstrə/ *noun* [C] a large group of musicians who play various musical instruments together, led by a **conductor**: *a symphony orchestra* ➲ note at **music** ▸ **orchestral** /ɔːˈkestrəl/ *adj*

orchid /ˈɔːkɪd/ *noun* [C] a beautiful and sometimes rare type of plant that has flowers of unusual shapes and bright colours

ordain /ɔːˈdeɪn/ *verb* [T, usually passive] **ordain sb (as) (sth)** to make sb a priest or minister: *He was ordained (as) a priest last year.* ➲ look at **ordination**

ordeal /ɔːˈdiːl; ˈɔːdiːl/ *noun* [C, usually sing] a very unpleasant or difficult experience

order¹ /ˈɔːdə(r)/ *noun*
➤ARRANGEMENT **1** [U, sing] the way in which people or things are arranged in relation to each other: *a list of names in* ***alphabetical order*** ◆ *Try to put the things you have to do* ***in order of importance.*** ◆ *What's the order of events today?* **2** [U] an organized state, where everything is in its right place: *I really must* ***put*** *my notes* ***in order****, because I can never find what I'm looking for.* OPP **disorder**
➤CONTROLLED STATE **3** [U] the situation in which laws, rules, authority, etc. are obeyed: *Following last week's riots, order has now been restored.* ➲ look at **disorder**
➤INSTRUCTION **4** [C] **an order (for sb) (to do sth)** something that you are told to do by sb in a position of authority: *In the army, you have to* ***obey orders*** *at all times.* ◆ *She* ***gave the order*** *for the work to be started.*
➤GOODS **5** [C,U] **an order (for sth)** a request asking for sth to be made, supplied or sent: *The company has just received a major export order.* ◆ *The book I need is* ***on order*** (= they are waiting for it to arrive).
➤FOOD/DRINKS **6** [C] a request for food or drinks in a hotel, restaurant, etc.; the food or drinks you asked for: *Can I* ***take your order*** *now, sir?*
IDM **in order to do sth** with the purpose or intention of doing sth; so that sth can be done: *We left early in order to avoid the traffic.*
in/into reverse order ➲ **reverse³**
in working order ➲ **working**
law and order ➲ **law**
out of order 1 (used about a machine, etc.) not working properly or not working at all: *I had to walk up to the tenth floor because the lift was out of order.* **2** (*BrE informal*) (used about sb's behaviour) unacceptable, because it is rude, etc: *That comment was completely out of order!*

order² /ˈɔːdə(r)/ *verb* **1** [T] **order sb (to do sth)** to use your position of authority to tell sb to do sth or to say that sth must happen: *I'm not asking you to do*

O

your homework, I'm ordering you! ◆ The company was ordered to pay compensation to its former employees. **2** [T] to ask for sth to be made, supplied or sent somewhere: *The shop didn't have the book I wanted so I ordered it.* **3** [I,T] order (sb) (sth); order (sth) (for sb) to ask for food or drinks in a restaurant, hotel, etc: *Are you ready to order yet, madam?* ◆ *Can you order me a sandwich while I make a phone call?* ◆ *Could you order a sandwich for me?*

PHR V **order sb about/around** to keep telling sb what to do and how to do it: *Stop ordering me about! You're not my father.*

orderly[1] /ˈɔːdəli/ *adj* **1** arranged or organized in a tidy way: *an orderly office/desk* **2** peaceful; behaving well OPP for both meanings **disorderly**

orderly[2] /ˈɔːdəli/ *noun* [C] (*pl* **orderlies**) a worker in a hospital, usually doing jobs that do not need special training

ordinal /ˈɔːdɪnl/ (also ˌordinal ˈnumber) *noun* [C] a number that shows the order or position of sth in a series: *'First', 'second', and 'third' are ordinals.* ➲ look at **cardinal**

ordinarily /ˈɔːdnrəli/ *adv* usually; generally: *Ordinarily, I don't work as late as this.* SYN **normally**

ordinary /ˈɔːdnri/ *adj* normal; not unusual or different from others: *It's interesting to see how ordinary people live in other countries.* ◆ *Simon was wearing a suit, but I was in my ordinary clothes.*

IDM **out of the ordinary** unusual; different from normal

ordination /ˌɔːdɪˈneɪʃn/ *noun* [U,C] the act or ceremony of making sb a priest, etc. ➲ look at **ordain**

ore /ɔː(r)/ *noun* [C,U] rock or earth from which metal can be taken: *iron ore*

organ /ˈɔːɡən/ *noun* [C] **1** one of the parts inside your body that have a particular function: ***vital organs*** (= those such as the heart and liver which help to keep you alive) ◆ *sexual/reproductive organs* ➲ picture at **body** **2** a large musical instrument like a piano with pipes through which air is forced. Organs are often found in churches: *organ music* ▶ **organist** /-nɪst/ *noun* [C]: *the church organist*

organic /ɔːˈɡænɪk/ *adj* **1** (used about food or farming methods) produced by or using natural materials, without artificial chemicals: *organic vegetables* ◆ *organic farming* **2** produced by or from living things: *organic compounds/molecules* OPP **inorganic** ▶ **organically** /-kli/ *adv*: *organically grown/produced*

organism /ˈɔːɡənɪzəm/ *noun* [C] a living thing, especially one that is so small that you can only see it with a **microscope** (= a piece of equipment that makes small objects look bigger)

organization (also -isation) /ˌɔːɡənaɪˈzeɪʃn/ *noun* **1** [C] a group of people who form a business, club, etc. together in order to achieve a particular aim: *She works for a voluntary organization helping homeless people.* **2** [U] the activity of making preparations or arrangements for sth: *An enormous amount of organization went into the festival.* **3** [U] the way in which sth is organized, arranged or prepared: *Your written work lacks organization.* OPP **disorganization** ▶ **organizational** (also -isational) /-ʃənl/ *adj*: *The job requires a high level of organizational ability.*

organize (also -ise) /ˈɔːɡənaɪz/ *verb* **1** [T] to plan or arrange an event, activity, etc: *The school organizes trips to various places of interest.* **2** [I,T] to put or arrange things into a system or logical order: *Can you decide what needs doing? I'm hopeless at organizing.* ◆ *You need to organize your work more carefully.* ▶ **organizer** (also -iser) *noun* [C]: *The organizers of the concert said that it had been a great success.*

organized (also -ised) /ˈɔːɡənaɪzd/ *adj* **1** [only *before* a noun] involving a large number of people working together to do sth in a way that has been carefully planned: *an organized campaign against cruelty to animals* ◆ *organized crime* (= done by a large group of professional criminals) **2** arranged or planned in the way mentioned: *a carefully/badly/well-organized trip* OPP **disorganized** **3** (used about a person) able to plan your work, life, etc. well: *I wish I were as organized as you!* OPP **disorganized**

orgasm /ˈɔːɡæzəm/ *noun* [U,C] the point of greatest sexual pleasure: *to have an orgasm*

orgy /ˈɔːdʒi/ *noun* [C] (*pl* **orgies**) **1** a party, involving a lot of eating, drinking and sexual activity **2** an orgy (of sth) a period of doing sth in a wild way, without control: *The gang went on an orgy of destruction.*

the Orient /ˈɔːriənt/ *noun* [sing] (*formal*) the eastern part of the world, especially China and Japan

orient /ˈɔːrient/ (*BrE also* **orientate**) *verb* [T] **orient yourself** to find out where you are; to become familiar with a place ➲ look at **disorientate**

oriental /ˌɔːriˈentl/ *adj* **Oriental** coming from or belonging to the East or Far East: *oriental languages*

HELP Be careful. When it refers to a person, this word is offensive. It is better to say 'Asian'.

orientate /ˈɔːriənteɪt/ (*BrE*) = **orient**

orientation /ˌɔːriənˈteɪʃn/ *noun* [U] the feelings, beliefs or interests that a person or an organization has: *a person's **religious/political/sexual** orientation*

oriented /ˈɔːrientɪd/ (also **orientated** /ˈɔːrɪənteɪtɪd/) *adj* for or interested in a particular type of person or thing: *a company selling male-oriented products* ◆ *She's very career orientated.*

orienteering /ˌɔːriənˈtɪərɪŋ/ *noun* [U] a sport in which you find your way across country on foot, as quickly as possible, using a map and a **compass** (= an instrument that shows direction)

origami /ˌɒrɪˈɡɑːmi/ *noun* [U] the Japanese art of folding paper into attractive shapes

origin /ˈɒrɪdʒɪn/ *noun* [C, usually pl, U] **1** the point from which sth starts; the cause of sth: *This particular tradition **has its origins in** Wales.* ◆ *Many English words are **of** Latin **origin**.* **2** the country, race, culture, etc. that a person comes from: *people of African origin*

original[1] /ə'rɪdʒənl/ *adj* **1** [only *before* a noun] first; earliest (before any changes or developments): *The original meaning of this word is different from the meaning it has nowadays.* **2** new and interesting; different from others of its type: *There are no original ideas in his work.* **3** made or created first, before copies: *'Is that the original painting?' 'No, it's a copy.'*

original[2] /ə'rɪdʒənl/ *noun* [C] the first document, painting, etc. that was made; not a copy: *Could you make a photocopy of my birth certificate and give the original back to me?*

originality /əˌrɪdʒə'næləti/ *noun* [U] the quality of being new and interesting

originally /ə'rɪdʒənəli/ *adv* in the beginning, before any changes or developments: *I'm from London originally, but I left when I was young.*

originate /ə'rɪdʒɪneɪt/ *verb* [I] (*formal*) to happen or appear for the first time in a particular place or situation

ornament /'ɔːnəmənt/ *noun* [C] an object that you have because it is attractive, not because it is useful. **Ornaments** are used to decorate rooms, etc.

ornamental /ˌɔːnə'mentl/ *adj* made or put somewhere in order to look attractive, not for any practical use

ornate /ɔː'neɪt/ *adj* covered with a lot of small complicated designs as decoration

ornithology /ˌɔːnɪ'θɒlədʒi/ *noun* [U] the study of birds ▶ **ornithologist** /-dʒɪst/ *noun* [C]

orphan /'ɔːfn/ *noun* [C] a child whose parents are dead ▶ **orphan** *verb* [T, usually passive]: *She was orphaned when she was three and went to live with her grandparents.* ➲ note at **child**

orphanage /'ɔːfənɪdʒ/ *noun* [C] a home for children whose parents are dead ➲ A more common word is **children's home**.

orthodox /'ɔːθədɒks/ *adj* **1** that most people believe, do or accept; usual: *orthodox opinions/methods* OPP **unorthodox** **2** (in certain religions) closely following the old, traditional beliefs, ceremonies, etc: *an orthodox Jew* ◆ *the Greek Orthodox Church*

orthopaedics (*AmE* **orthopedics**) /ˌɔːθə'piːdɪks/ *noun* [U] the area of medicine connected with injuries and diseases of the bones or muscles ▶ **orthopaedic** (*AmE* **orthopedic**) *adj*: *an orthopaedic surgeon/hospital*

ostentatious /ˌɒsten'teɪʃəs/ *adj* **1** expensive or noticeable in a way that is intended to impress other people: *ostentatious gold jewellery* **2** behaving in a way that is intended to impress people with how rich or important you are ▶ **ostentatiously** *adv*

osteopath /'ɒstiəpæθ/ *noun* [C] a person whose job is treating some diseases and physical problems by pressing and moving the bones and muscles ▶ **osteopathy** /ˌɒsti'ɒpəθi/ *noun* [U]

ostracize (also **-ise**) /'ɒstrəsaɪz/ *verb* [T] (*formal*) to refuse to allow sb to be a member of a social group; to refuse to meet or talk to sb

ostrich /'ɒstrɪtʃ/ *noun* [C] a very large African bird with a long neck and long legs, which can run very fast but which cannot fly

other /'ʌðə(r)/ *adj, pron* **1** in addition to or different from the one or ones that have already been mentioned: *I hadn't got any other plans that evening so I accepted their invitation.* ◆ *If you're busy now, I'll come back some other time.* ◆ *I like this jumper but not the colour. Have you got any others?* ◆ *Some of my friends went to university, others didn't.* ◆ *She doesn't care what other people think.* ➲ look at **another**

HELP **Other** cannot be used after 'an'.

2 [after *the, my, your, his, her*, etc. with a singular noun] the second of two people or things, when the first has already been mentioned: *I can only find one sock. Have you seen the other one?* **3** [after *the, my, your, his, her*, etc. with a plural noun] the rest of a group or number of people or things: *Their youngest son still lives with them but their other children have left home.* ◆ *I'll have to wear this shirt because all my others are dirty.* ◆ *Mick and I got a taxi there, the others walked.*

IDM **in other words** used for saying sth in a different way: *My boss said she would have to let me go. In other words, she sacked me.*

one after another/the other ➲ **one**[1]

the other day, morning, week, etc. recently, not long ago: *An old friend rang me the other day.*

other than [usually after a negative] apart from; except (for): *The plane was a little late, but other than that the journey was fine.*

the other way round in the opposite way or order: *My appointment's at 3 and Lella's is at 3.15—or was it the other way round?*

somebody/something/somewhere or other ➲ **or**

otherwise /'ʌðəwaɪz/ *adv, conj* **1** (used for stating what would happen if you do not do sth or if sth does not happen) if not: *You have to press the red button, otherwise it won't work.* **2** apart from that: *I'm a bit tired but otherwise I feel fine.* **3** in a different way to the way mentioned; differently: *I'm afraid I can't see you next weekend, I'm* **otherwise engaged** (= I will be busy doing sth else).

otter /'ɒtə(r)/ *noun* [C] a river animal that has brown fur and eats fish

otter

ouch /aʊtʃ/ (also **ow**) *exclam* used when reacting to a sudden feeling of pain

ought to /'ɔːt tə; *before vowels and in final position* 'ɔːt tu/ *modal verb* (*negative* **ought not to**; *short form* **oughtn't to** /'ɔːtnt tə/ *before vowels*

O

and in final position /ˈɔːtnt tu/) **1** used to say what sb should do: *You ought to visit your parents more often.* ♦ *She oughtn't to make private phone calls in work time.* ♦ *He oughtn't to have been driving so fast.* **2** used to say what should happen or what you expect: *She ought to pass her test.* ♦ *They ought to be here by now. They left at six.* ♦ *There ought to be more buses in the rush hour.* **3** used for asking for and giving advice about what to do: *You ought to read this book. It's really interesting.* ℹ For more information about modal verbs, look at the **Reference Section** at the back of this dictionary.

ounce /aʊns/ *noun* **1** [C] (*abbr* oz) a measure of weight; 28.35 grams. There are 16 **ounces** in a pound: *For this recipe you need four ounces of flour.* ℹ For more information about weights, look at the section on using numbers at the back of this dictionary. **2** [sing] [usually in negative statements] **an ounce of sth** a very small amount of sth: *That boy hasn't got an ounce of imagination.*

⚷ **our** /ɑː(r); ˈaʊə(r)/ *determiner* of or belonging to us: *Our house is at the bottom of the road.* ♦ *This is our first visit to Britain.*

⚷ **ours** /ɑːz; ˈaʊəz/ *pron* the one or ones belonging to us: *Their garden is quite nice but I prefer ours.*

⚷ **ourselves** /ɑːˈselvz; ˌaʊəˈs-/ *pron* **1** used when the people who do an action are also affected by it: *Let's forget all about work and just enjoy ourselves.* ♦ *They asked us to wait so we sat down and made ourselves comfortable.* ♦ *We built the house ourselves.* **2** used to emphasize the people who do the action: *Do you think we should paint the flat ourselves* (= or should we ask sb else to do it for us)?

IDM **(all) by ourselves** **1** alone: *Now that we're by ourselves, could I ask you a personal question?* ➲ note at **alone** **2** without help: *We managed to move all our furniture into the new flat by ourselves.*

oust /aʊst/ *verb* [T] **oust sb (from sth/as sth)** to force sb out of a job or position of power, especially in order to take their place: *The rebels finally managed to oust the government from power.* ♦ *He was ousted as chairman.*

⚷ **out¹** /aʊt/ *adj, adv* **1** away from the inside of a place: *He opened the drawer and took a fork out.* ♦ *She opened the window and put her head out.* ♦ *Can you show me the way out?* **2** not at home or in your place of work: *My manager was out when she called.* ♦ *I'd love a night out—I'm bored with staying at home.* **3** a long distance away from a place, for example from land or your country: *The current is quite strong so don't swim too far out.* **4** (used about the sea) when the water is furthest away from the land: *Don't swim when the tide is on the way out.* **5** used for showing that sth is no longer hidden: *I love the spring when all the flowers are out.* ♦ *The secret's out now. There's no point pretending any more.* **6** made available to the public; published: *There'll be a lot of controversy when her book comes out next year.* **7** in a loud voice; clearly: *She cried out in pain.* **8** (used about a player in a game or sport) not allowed to continue playing: *If you get three answers wrong, you're out.* **9** (used about a ball, etc. in a game or sport) not inside the playing area and therefore not allowed: *Although the player argued with the umpire, the ball was clearly out.* **10** (used when you are calculating sth) making or containing a mistake; wrong: *My guess was only out by a few centimetres.* **11** (*informal*) not possible or acceptable: *I'm afraid Friday is out. I've got a meeting that day.* **12** not in fashion: *Short skirts are out this season.* **13** (used about a light or a fire) not on; not burning: *The lights are out. They must be in bed.* ♦ *Once the fire was completely out, experts were sent in to inspect the damage.* ℹ For special uses with many verbs, for example **look out**, look at the verb entries.

IDM **be out for sth; be out to do sth** to try hard to get or do sth: *I'm not out for revenge.*

down and out ➲ **down¹**

out-and-out complete: *It was out-and-out war between us.*

ˌout ˈloud = **aloud**

⚷ **ˈout²** *prep* **out (of sth)** **1** (used with verbs expressing movement) away from the inside of sth: *She took her purse out of her bag.* ♦ *to get out of bed* OPP **into** **2** away from or no longer in a place or situation: *He's out of the country on business.* ♦ *The doctors say she's* ***out of danger.*** **3** at a distance from a place: *We live a long way out of London.* **4** used for saying which feeling causes you to do sth: *We were only asking out of curiosity.* **5** used for saying what you use to make sth else: *What is this knife* ***made out of***? ♦ *to be made out of wood/metal/plastic/gold* **6** from among a number or set: *Nine out of ten people prefer this model.* **7** from; having sth as its source: *I copied the recipe out of a book.* ♦ *I paid for it out of the money I won on the lottery.* **8** used for saying that you no longer have sth: *to be* ***out of milk/sugar/coffee*** ♦ *He's been* ***out of work*** *for months.* **9** used for saying that sth is not as it should be: *My notes are all* ***out of order*** *and I can't find the right page.*

IDM **be/feel out of it** to be/feel lonely and unhappy because you are not included in sth: *I don't speak French so I felt rather out of it at the meeting.*

out³ /aʊt/ *verb* [T] to say publicly that sb is **homosexual** (= sexually attracted to people of the same sex), especially when they would rather keep it a secret: *The politician was eventually outed by a tabloid newspaper.*

the outback /ˈaʊtbæk/ *noun* [sing] the part of a country (especially Australia) which is a long way from the coast and towns, and where few people live

outboard motor /ˌaʊtbɔːd ˈməʊtə(r)/ *noun* [C] an engine that can be fixed to a boat

outbox /ˈaʊtbɒks/ *noun* [C] the place on a computer where new email messages that you write are stored before you send them

outbreak /ˈaʊtbreɪk/ *noun* [C] the sudden start of sth unpleasant (especially a disease or violence): *an outbreak of cholera/fighting*

outburst /ˈaʊtbɜːst/ *noun* [C] a sudden expression of a strong feeling, especially anger: *Afterwards, she apologized for her outburst.*

outcast /ˈaʊtkɑːst/ *noun* [C] a person who is no longer accepted by society or by a group of people: *a social outcast*

outclass /ˌaʊtˈklɑːs/ *verb* [T, often passive] to be much better than sb/sth, especially in a game or competition

outcome /ˈaʊtkʌm/ *noun* [C] the result or effect of an action or an event

outcrop /ˈaʊtkrɒp/ *noun* [C] a large mass of rock that stands above the surface of the ground

outcry /ˈaʊtkraɪ/ *noun* [C, usually sing] (*pl* outcries) a strong protest by a large number of people because they disagree with sth: *The public outcry forced the government to change its mind about the new tax.*

outdated /ˌaʊtˈdeɪtɪd/ *adj* not useful or common any more; old-fashioned: *A lot of the computer equipment is getting outdated.*

outdo /ˌaʊtˈduː/ *verb* [T] (outdoing; outdoes /-ˈdʌz/; *pt* outdid /-ˈdɪd/; *pp* outdone /-ˈdʌn/) to do sth better than another person; to be more successful than sb else: ***Not to be outdone*** (= not wanting anyone else to do better), *she tried again.*

⚷ **outdoor** /ˈaʊtdɔː(r)/ *adj* [only *before* a noun] happening, done, or used outside, not in a building: *an outdoor swimming pool* ♦ *outdoor clothing/activities* OPP **indoor**

⚷ **outdoors** /ˌaʊtˈdɔːz/ *adv* outside a building: *It's a very warm evening so why don't we eat outdoors?* SYN **out of doors** OPP **indoors** ➲ look at **outside**

⚷ **outer** /ˈaʊtə(r)/ *adj* [only *before* a noun] **1** on the outside of sth: *the outer layer of skin on an onion* **2** far from the inside or the centre of sth: *the outer suburbs of a city* OPP for both meanings **inner**

outermost /ˈaʊtəməʊst/ *adj* [only *before* a noun] furthest from the inside or centre OPP **innermost**

ˌouter ˈspace = space[1] (2)

outfit /ˈaʊtfɪt/ *noun* [C] a set of clothes that are worn together for a particular occasion or purpose: *I'm going to buy a whole new outfit for the party.*

outgoing /ˈaʊtgəʊɪŋ/ *adj* **1** friendly and interested in other people and new experiences SYN **sociable 2** [only *before* a noun] leaving a job or a place: *the outgoing president/government* ♦ *Put all the outgoing mail in a pile on that table.* OPP **incoming**

outgoings /ˈaʊtgəʊɪŋz/ *noun* [pl] (*BrE*) an amount of money that you spend regularly, for example every week or month OPP **income**

outgrow /ˌaʊtˈgrəʊ/ *verb* [T] (*pt* outgrew /-ˈgruː/; *pp* outgrown /-ˈgrəʊn/) to become too old or too big for sth

outing /ˈaʊtɪŋ/ *noun* [C] a short trip for pleasure: *to **go on an outing** to the zoo*

outlandish /aʊtˈlændɪʃ/ *adj* very strange or unusual: *outlandish clothes*

outlast /ˌaʊtˈlɑːst/ *verb* [T] to continue to exist or to do sth for a longer time than sb/sth

outlaw[1] /ˈaʊtlɔː/ *verb* [T] to make sth illegal

outlaw[2] /ˈaʊtlɔː/ *noun* [C] (used in past times) a person who has done sth illegal and is hiding to avoid being caught

outlay /ˈaʊtleɪ/ *noun* [C, usually sing] outlay (on sth) money that is spent, especially in order to start a business or project

outlet /ˈaʊtlet/ *noun* [C] **1** an outlet (for sth) a way of expressing and making good use of strong feelings, ideas or energy: *Gary found an outlet for his aggression in boxing.* **2** a shop, business, etc. that sells goods made by a particular company or of a particular type: *fast food/retail outlets* **3** a pipe through which a gas or liquid can escape OPP **inlet**

⚷ **outline**[1] /ˈaʊtlaɪn/ *verb* [T] outline sth (to sb) to tell sb or give the most important facts or ideas about sth

⚷ **outline**[2] /ˈaʊtlaɪn/ *noun* [C] **1** a description of the most important facts or ideas about sth: *a brief outline of Indian history* **2** a line that shows the shape or outside edge of sb/sth: *She could see the outline of a person through the mist.*

outlive /ˌaʊtˈlɪv/ *verb* [T] to live or exist longer than sb/sth

outlook /ˈaʊtlʊk/ *noun* [C] **1** an outlook (on sth) your attitude to or feeling about life and the world: *an optimistic outlook on life* **2** outlook (for sth) what will probably happen: *The outlook for the economy is not good.*

outlying /ˈaʊtlaɪɪŋ/ *adj* [only *before* a noun] far away from the centre of a town or city: *The bus service to the outlying villages is very poor.*

outmoded /ˌaʊtˈməʊdɪd/ *adj* no longer common or fashionable

outnumber /ˌaʊtˈnʌmbə(r)/ *verb* [T, often passive] to be greater in number than an enemy, another team, etc: *The enemy troops outnumbered us by three to one.* ♦ *We were completely outnumbered.*

ˌout of ˈdate *adj* **1** old-fashioned: *Her ideas were out of date.* **2** no longer valid ➲ look at **up to date**

ˌout-of-ˈwork *adj* [only *before* a noun] unable to find a job; unemployed: *an out-of-work actor*

outpatient /ˈaʊtpeɪʃnt/ *noun* [C] a person who goes to a hospital for treatment but who does not stay there during the night

outpost /ˈaʊtpəʊst/ *noun* [C] a small town or camp that is away from other places: *a remote outpost* ♦ *the last outpost of civilization*

⚷ **output** /ˈaʊtpʊt/ *noun* [U,C] **1** the amount that a person or machine produces: *Output has increased in the past year.* **2** the information that a computer produces: *data output* ➲ look at **input**

outrage /ˈaʊtreɪdʒ/ *noun* **1** [U] great anger: *a feeling of outrage* **2** [C] something that is very bad or wrong and that causes you to feel great anger: *It's an outrage that such poverty should exist in the 21st century.* ▶ **outrage** *verb* [T]

O

outrageous /aʊtˈreɪdʒəs/ *adj* that makes you very angry or shocked: *outrageous behaviour/prices* ▶ **outrageously** *adv*

outright /ˈaʊtraɪt/ *adj* [only *before* a noun] *adv* **1** open and direct; in an open and direct way: *She told them outright what she thought about it.* **2** complete and clear; completely and clearly: *an outright victory* ◆ *to win outright* **3** not gradually; immediately: *They were able to buy the house outright.*

outset /ˈaʊtset/ *noun* [sing]
IDM at/from the outset (of sth) at/from the beginning (of sth)

outside¹ /ˌaʊtˈsaɪd/ *noun* **1** [C,usually sing] the outer side or surface of sth: *There is a list of all the ingredients on the outside of the packet.* **2** [sing] the area that is near or round a building, etc: *We've only seen the church from the outside.* **3** [sing] the part of a road, a track, etc. that is away from the side that you usually drive on, run on, etc: *The other runners all overtook him on the outside.* **OPP** for all meanings **inside**
IDM at the outside at the most: *It will take us 3 days at the outside.*

outside² /ˈaʊtsaɪd/ *adj* [only *before* a noun] **1** of or on the outer side or surface of sth: *the outside walls of a building* **SYN external** **2** not part of the main building: *an outside toilet* **SYN external** **3** not connected with or belonging to a particular group or organization: *We can't do all the work by ourselves. We'll need outside help.* **4** (used about a chance or possibility) very small: *an **outside chance** of winning*
IDM the outside world people, places, activities, etc. that are away from the area where you live and your own experience of life

outside³ /ˌaʊtˈsaɪd/ *adv, prep* **1** in, at or to a place that is not in a room or not in a building: *Please wait outside for a few minutes.* ◆ *Leave your muddy boots outside the door.*

> **MORE** When we mean 'outside a building', we can also say **outdoors** and **out of doors**.

2 not in: *You may do as you wish outside office hours.* ◆ *a small village just outside Stratford*

outsider /ˌaʊtˈsaɪdə(r)/ *noun* [C] **1** a person who is not accepted as a member of a particular group **2** a person or an animal in a race or competition that is not expected to win **OPP favourite**

outsize /ˈaʊtsaɪz/ *adj* (often used about clothes) larger than usual

outskirts /ˈaʊtskɜːts/ *noun* [pl] the parts of a town or city that are furthest from the centre: *They live **on the outskirts** of Athens.*

outspoken /aʊtˈspəʊkən/ *adj* saying exactly what you think or feel although you may shock or upset other people: *Linda is very outspoken in her criticism.*

outstanding /aʊtˈstændɪŋ/ *adj* **1** extremely good; excellent: *The results in the exams were outstanding.* **2** not yet paid, done or dealt with: *A large amount of the work is still outstanding.* ◆ *outstanding debts/issues*

outstandingly /aʊtˈstændɪŋli/ *adv* very well; extremely: *outstandingly good/successful*

outstretched /ˌaʊtˈstretʃt/ *adj* reaching as far as possible: *He came towards her with his arms outstretched.*

outward /ˈaʊtwəd/ *adj* [only *before* a noun] **1** connected with the way things seem to be rather than what is actually true: *Despite her cheerful outward appearance, she was in fact very unhappy.* **2** (used about a journey) going away from the place that you will return to later **OPP return** **3** away from the centre or from a particular point: *outward movement/pressure* **OPP inward** ▶ **outwardly** *adv*: *He remained outwardly calm so as not to frighten the children.*

outwards /ˈaʊtwədz/ (*especially AmE* outward) *adv* towards the outside or away from the place where you are: *This door opens outwards.*

outweigh /ˌaʊtˈweɪ/ *verb* [T] to be more in amount or importance than sth: *The advantages outweigh the disadvantages.*

outwit /ˌaʊtˈwɪt/ *verb* [T] (**outwitting**; **outwitted**) to gain an advantage over sb by doing sth clever

oval /ˈəʊvl/ *adj, noun* [C] shaped like an egg; a shape like that of an egg ➲ picture at **shape**

ovary /ˈəʊvəri/ *noun* [C] (*pl* **ovaries**) one of the two parts of the female body that produce eggs

ovation /əʊˈveɪʃn/ *noun* [C] an enthusiastic reaction given by an audience when they like sb/sth very much: *The dancers got **a standing ovation** (= the audience stood up) at the end of the performance.*

oven /ˈʌvn/ *noun* [C] the part of a cooker shaped like a box with a door on the front. You put food in the oven to cook or heat it: *Cook in a hot oven for 50 minutes.* ◆ *a microwave oven*

over /ˈəʊvə(r)/ *adv, prep* **1** covering sth: *She put a blanket over the sleeping child.* ◆ *She hung her coat over the back of the chair.* **2** straight above sth, but not touching it: *There's a painting over the bookcase.* ◆ *We watched the plane fly over.* ➲ look at **above** **3** across to the other side of sth: *The horse jumped over the fence.* ◆ *a bridge over the river* ➲ note at **across** **4** on or to the other side: *The student turned the paper over and read the first question.* **5** down or sideways from a vertical position: *I fell over in the street this morning.* ◆ *He leaned over to speak to the woman next to him.* **6** above or more than a number, price, etc: *She lived in Athens for over ten years.* ◆ *suitable for children aged 10 and over* **7** used for expressing distance: *He's over in America at the moment.* ◆ *Sit down **over there**.* ◆ *Come **over here**, please.* **8** not used: *There are a lot of cakes **left over** from the party.* **9** finished: *The exams are all over now.* **10** [used with *all*] everywhere: *There was blood **all over the place**.* ◆ *I can't find my glasses. I've looked all over for them.* **11** used for saying that sth is repeated: *You'll have to start **all over again** (= from the beginning).* ◆ *She kept saying the same thing **over and over again**.* **12** about; on the subject of: *We quarrelled over money.* **13** during: *We met several times over the Christmas holiday.* ℹ For special uses with many verbs, for example **get over sth**, look at the verb entries.

over- /ˈəʊvə(r)/ [in compounds] **1** more than usual; too much: *to oversleep* ♦ *over-optimistic* ♦ *overactive* **2** completely: *overjoyed* **3** upper; outer; extra: *overcoat* ♦ *overtime* **4** over; above: *overcast* ♦ *to overhang*

⚷ **overall¹** /ˌəʊvərˈɔːl/ *adv, adj* [only *before* a noun] **1** including everything; total: *What will the overall cost of the work be?* **2** generally; when you consider everything: *Overall, I can say that we are pleased with the year's work.*

overalls (*AmE* **coveralls**) **dungarees** (*AmE* **overalls**) **apron**

overall² /ˈəʊvərɔːl/ *noun* **1** [C] (*BrE*) a piece of clothing like a coat that you wear over your clothes to keep them clean when you are working **2** **overalls** (*AmE* **coveralls**) [pl] a piece of clothing that covers your legs and body (and sometimes your arms) that you wear over your clothes to keep them clean when you are working **3** (*AmE*) **overalls** = **dungarees**

overawe /ˌəʊvərˈɔː/ *verb* [T, usually passive] to impress sb so much that they feel nervous or frightened

overbalance /ˌəʊvəˈbæləns/ *verb* [I] to lose your balance and fall

overbearing /ˌəʊvəˈbeərɪŋ/ *adj* trying to control other people in an unpleasant way: *an overbearing manner* **SYN** **domineering**

overboard /ˈəʊvəbɔːd/ *adv* over the side of a boat or ship into the water

IDM **go overboard (on/about/for sb/sth)** to be too excited or enthusiastic about sb/sth

overcame *past tense* of **overcome**

overcast /ˌəʊvəˈkɑːst/ *adj* (used about the sky) covered with cloud

overcharge /ˌəʊvəˈtʃɑːdʒ/ *verb* [I,T] to ask sb to pay too much money for sth: *The taxi driver overcharged me.* ➲ look at **charge**

overcoat /ˈəʊvəkəʊt/ *noun* [C] a long thick coat that you wear in cold weather

⚷ **overcome** /ˌəʊvəˈkʌm/ *verb* [T] (*pt* **overcame** /-ˈkeɪm/; *pp* **overcome**) **1** to manage to control or defeat sb/sth: *She tried hard to overcome her fear of flying.* **2** [usually passive] to be extremely strongly affected by sth: *He was overcome with emotion and had to leave the room.*

overcrowded /ˌəʊvəˈkraʊdɪd/ *adj* (used about a place) with too many people inside: *The trains are overcrowded on Friday evenings.*

overdo /ˌəʊvəˈduː/ *verb* [T] (**overdoing**; **overdoes** /-ˈdʌz/; *pt* **overdid** /-ˈdɪd/; *pp* **overdone** /-ˈdʌn/) **1** to use or do too much of sth **2** to cook sth too long: *The meat was overdone.*

IDM **overdo it/things** to work, etc. too hard: *Exercise is fine but don't overdo it.*

overdose /ˈəʊvədəʊs/ *noun* [C] an amount of a drug or medicine that is too large and so is not safe: *to take an overdose* ➲ look at **dose**

overdraft /ˈəʊvədrɑːft/ *noun* [C] an amount of money that you have spent that is greater than the amount you have in your bank account; an arrangement that allows you to borrow this money

overdrawn /ˌəʊvəˈdrɔːn/ *adj* having spent more money than you have in your bank account: *I checked my balance and discovered I was overdrawn.*

overdue /ˌəʊvəˈdjuː/ *adj* late in arriving, happening, being paid, returned, etc: *an overdue library book* ♦ *Her baby is a week overdue.*

overestimate /ˌəʊvərˈestɪmeɪt/ *verb* [T] to guess that sb/sth is bigger, better, more important, etc. than he/she/it really is: *I overestimated how much we could manage to do in a weekend.* **OPP** **underestimate**

overflow

'Oh no! The bath's overflowing!'

overflow /ˌəʊvəˈfləʊ/ *verb* **1** [I,T] **overflow (with sth)** to be so full that the contents go over the sides: *The tap was left on and the bath overflowed.* ♦ *The roads are overflowing with cars.* **2** [I] **overflow (into sth)** to be forced out of a place or a container that is too full: *The crowd overflowed into the street.*

overgrown /ˌəʊvəˈgrəʊn/ *adj* covered with plants that have grown too big and untidy

overhang /ˌəʊvəˈhæŋ/ *verb* [I,T] (*pt, pp* **overhung**) to stick out, over and above sth else: *The overhanging trees kept the sun off us.* ➲ picture at **overlap**

O

overhaul /ˌəʊvəˈhɔːl/ *verb* [T] to look at sth carefully and change or repair it if necessary: *to overhaul an engine* ▸ **overhaul** /ˈəʊvəhɔːl/ *noun* [C]

overhead *adj* /ˈəʊvəhed/ , *adv* /ˌəʊvəˈhed/ above your head: *overhead electricity cables* ◆ *A helicopter flew overhead.*

overheads /ˈəʊvəhedz/ *noun* [pl] (*AmE* overhead [U]) money that a company must spend on things like heat, light, rent, etc.

overhear /ˌəʊvəˈhɪə(r)/ *verb* [T] (*pt, pp* overheard /-ˈhɜːd/) to hear what sb is saying by accident, when they are speaking to sb else and not to you

overhung *past tense, past participle* of **overhang**

overjoyed /ˌəʊvəˈdʒɔɪd/ *adj* [not before a noun] overjoyed (at sth/to do sth) very happy

overland /ˈəʊvəlænd/ *adj* not by sea or by air: *an overland journey* ▸ **overland** *adv*

overlap

overlapping tiles **overlapping dates** **overhanging branches**

overlap /ˌəʊvəˈlæp/ *verb* [I,T] (overlapping; overlapped) **1** when two things **overlap**, part of one covers part of the other: *Make sure that the two pieces of material overlap.* **2** to be partly the same as sth: *Our jobs overlap to some extent.* ▸ **overlap** /ˈəʊvəlæp/ *noun* [C,U]

overleaf /ˌəʊvəˈliːf/ *adv* on the other side of the page: *Full details are given overleaf.*

overload /ˌəʊvəˈləʊd/ *verb* [T] **1** [often passive] to put too many people or things into or onto sth: *an overloaded vehicle* **2** overload sb (with sth) to give sb too much of sth: *to be overloaded with work/information* **3** to put too much electricity through sth: *If you use too many electrical appliances at one time you may overload the system.*

overlook /ˌəʊvəˈlʊk/ *verb* [T] **1** to fail to see or notice sth: *to overlook a spelling mistake* ◆ *She felt that her opinion had been completely overlooked.* **2** to see sth wrong but decide to forget it: *I will overlook your behaviour this time but don't let it happen again.* **3** to have a view over sth: *My room overlooks the sea.*

overnight /ˌəʊvəˈnaɪt/ *adj* [only *before* a noun] *adv* **1** for one night: *an overnight bag* (= containing the things you need for one night away from home) ◆ *We stayed overnight in Hamburg.* **2** (happening) very suddenly: *She became a star overnight.*

overpass /ˈəʊvəpɑːs/ (*AmE*) = **flyover**

overpay /ˌəʊvəˈpeɪ/ *verb* [T] (*pt, pp* overpaid) [usually passive] to pay sb too much; to pay sb more than their job is worth **OPP** **underpay**

overpower /ˌəʊvəˈpaʊə(r)/ *verb* [T] to be too strong for sb: *The fireman was overpowered by the heat and smoke.* ▸ **overpowering** *adj*: *an overpowering smell*

overran *past tense* of **overrun**

overrate /ˌəʊvəˈreɪt/ *verb* [T, often passive] to think that sth/sb is better than he/she/it really is **OPP** **underrate**

overreact /ˌəʊvəriˈækt/ *verb* [I] overreact (to sth) to react too strongly, especially to sth unpleasant ▸ **overreaction** *noun* [sing,U]

override /ˌəʊvəˈraɪd/ *verb* [T] (*pt* overrode /-ˈrəʊd/; *pp* overridden /-ˈrɪdn/) **1** to use your authority to reject sb's decision, order, etc: *They overrode my protest and continued with the meeting.* **2** to be more important than sth

overriding /ˌəʊvəˈraɪdɪŋ/ *adj* [only *before* a noun] more important than anything else: *Our overriding concern is safety.*

overrode *past tense* of **override**

overrule /ˌəʊvəˈruːl/ *verb* [T] to use your authority to change what sb else has already decided or done: *The Appeal Court overruled the judge's decision.*

overrun /ˌəʊvəˈrʌn/ *verb* (*pt* overran /-ˈræn/; *pp* overrun) **1** [T, often passive] to spread all over an area in great numbers: *The city was completely overrun by rats.* **2** [I,T] to use more time or money than expected: *The meeting overran by 30 minutes.*

oversaw *past tense* of **oversee**

overseas /ˌəʊvəˈsiːz/ *adj* [only *before* a noun] *adv* in, to or from another country that you have to cross the sea to get to: *overseas students studying in Britain* ◆ *Frank has gone to live overseas.*

oversee /ˌəʊvəˈsiː/ *verb* [T] (*pt* oversaw /-ˈsɔː/; *pp* overseen /-ˈsiːn/) to watch sth to make sure that it is done properly

overshadow /ˌəʊvəˈʃædəʊ/ *verb* [T] **1** to cause sb/sth to seem less important or successful: *Connor always seemed to be overshadowed by his sister.* **2** to cause sth to be less enjoyable

oversight /ˈəʊvəsaɪt/ *noun* [C,U] something that you do not notice or do (that you should have noticed or done)

oversimplify /ˌəʊvəˈsɪmplɪfaɪ/ *verb* [I,T] (oversimplifying; oversimplifies; *pt, pp* oversimplified) to explain sth in such a simple way that its real meaning is lost

oversleep /ˌəʊvəˈsliːp/ *verb* [I] (*pt, pp* overslept /-ˈslept/) to sleep longer than you should have done: *I overslept and was late for school.* ➲ look at **lie in**, **sleep in**

overstate /ˌəʊvəˈsteɪt/ *verb* [T] to say sth in a way that makes it seem more important than it really is **OPP** **understate**

overstep /ˌəʊvəˈstep/ *verb* [T] (overstepping; overstepped) to go further than what is normal or allowed: *to overstep your authority* ◆ *He tends to **overstep the boundaries** of good taste.*

IDM **overstep the mark/line** to behave in a way that people think is not acceptable

overt /əʊˈvɜːt; ˈəʊvɜːt/ *adj* (*formal*) done in an open way and not secretly: *There was little overt support for the project.* OPP **covert** ▶ **overtly** *adv*: *overtly political activities*

overtake /ˌəʊvəˈteɪk/ *verb* [I,T] (*pt* overtook /-ˈtʊk/; *pp* overtaken /-ˈteɪkən/) **1** to go past another person, car, etc. because you are moving faster: *The lorry overtook me on the bend.* **2** to become greater in number, amount or importance than sth else: *Nuclear energy may overtake oil as the main fuel.*

overthrow /ˌəʊvəˈθrəʊ/ *verb* [T] (*pt* overthrew /-ˈθruː/; *pp* overthrown /-ˈθrəʊn/) to remove a leader or government from power, by using force ▶ **overthrow** /ˈəʊvəθrəʊ/ *noun* [sing]

overtime /ˈəʊvətaɪm/ *noun* [U] time that you spend at work after your usual working hours; the money that you are paid for this: *Betty did ten hours' overtime last week.* ▶ **overtime** *adv*: *I have been working overtime for weeks.*

overtone /ˈəʊvətəʊn/ *noun* [C, usually pl] something that is suggested but not expressed in an obvious way: *Some people claimed there were racist overtones in the advertisement.*

overtook *past tense* of **overtake**

overture /ˈəʊvətʃʊə(r); -tjʊə(r)/ *noun* **1** [C] a piece of music that is the introduction to a musical play such as an **opera** or a **ballet** **2** [C, usually pl] (*formal*) an act of being friendly towards sb, especially because you want to be friends, to start a business relationship, etc.

overturn /ˌəʊvəˈtɜːn/ *verb* **1** [I,T] to turn over or turn sth over so that the top is at the bottom: *The car overturned but the driver escaped unhurt.* **2** [T] to officially decide that a decision is wrong and change it

overview /ˈəʊvəvjuː/ *noun* [C] a general description that gives the most important facts about sth

overweight /ˌəʊvəˈweɪt/ *adj* too heavy or fat: *I'm a bit overweight—I think I might go on a diet.* OPP **underweight** ➲ note at **fat**

overwhelm /ˌəʊvəˈwelm/ *verb* [T, usually passive] **1** to cause sb to feel such a strong emotion that they do not know how to react: *The new world champion was overwhelmed by all the publicity.* **2** to be so powerful, big, etc., that sb cannot deal with it: *He overwhelmed his opponent with his superb technique.* ◆ *The TV company was overwhelmed by complaints.*

overwhelming /ˌəʊvəˈwelmɪŋ/ *adj* extremely great or strong: *Anne-Marie had an overwhelming desire to return home.* ▶ **overwhelmingly** *adv*

overwork /ˌəʊvəˈwɜːk/ *verb* [I,T] to work or make sb work too hard: *They are overworked and underpaid.* ▶ **overwork** *noun* [U]

ovulate /ˈɒvjuleɪt/ *verb* [I] (of a woman or female animal) to produce an egg from the **ovary** (= part of the female body) ▶ **ovulation** /ˌɒvjuˈleɪʃn/ *noun* [U]: *when ovulation takes place*

ow /aʊ/ = **ouch**

🔑 **owe** /əʊ/ *verb* [T] **1** owe sth (to sb); owe sb for sth to have to pay money to sb for sth that they have done or given: *I owe Katrina a lot of money.* ◆ *I owe a lot of money to Katrina.* ◆ *I still owe you for that bread you bought yesterday.* ➲ note at **loan** ➲ look at **debt** **2** owe sb sth; owe sth to sb to feel that you should do sth for sb or give sth to sb, especially because they have done sth for you: *Claudia owes me an explanation.* ◆ *I owe you an apology.* **3** owe sth to sb/sth to have sth (for the reason given): *She said she owes her success to hard work and determination.*

owing /ˈəʊɪŋ/ *adj* [not before a noun] owing (to sb) not yet paid: *How much is still owing to you?*

ˈowing to *prep* because of: *The match was cancelled owing to bad weather.*

owl /aʊl/ *noun* [C] a bird with large eyes that hunts small animals at night

owl

🔑 **own¹** /əʊn/ *adj, pron* **1** used to emphasize that sth belongs to a particular person: *I saw him do it with **my own** eyes.* ◆ *This is **his own** house.* ◆ *This house is his own.* ◆ *Rachel would like her own room/a room **of her own**.* **2** used to show that sth is done or made without help from another person: *The children are old enough to get their own breakfast.*

IDM **come into your own** to have the opportunity to show your special qualities

get/have your own back (on sb) (*informal*) to hurt sb who has hurt you

hold your own (against sb/sth) to be as strong, good, etc. as sb/sth else

(all) on your, etc. own **1** alone: *John lives all on his own.* ➲ note at **alone** **2** without help: *I managed to repair the car all on my own.*

🔑 **own²** /əʊn/ *verb* [T] to have sth belonging to you: *We don't own the house. We just rent it.* ◆ *a privately owned company*

PHR V **own up (to sth)** (*informal*) to tell sb that you have done sth wrong: *None of the children owned up to breaking the window.* ➲ A more formal word is **confess**.

🔑 **owner** /ˈəʊnə(r)/ *noun* [C] a person who owns sth: *a house/dog owner*

ownership /ˈəʊnəʃɪp/ *noun* [U] the state of owning sth: *in private/public **ownership***

ox /ɒks/ *noun* [C] (*pl* oxen /ˈɒksn/) a **bull** (= male cow) that has been **castrated** (= had part of its sex organs removed) and is used for pulling or carrying heavy loads ➲ note at **cow** ➲ look at **bull**

O

oxygen /ˈɒksɪdʒən/ *noun* [U] (*symbol* O) a gas that you cannot see, taste or smell. Plants and animals cannot live without **oxygen**.

oyster /ˈɔɪstə(r)/ *noun* [C] a type of **shellfish** (= a creature with a shell that lives in water) that you can eat. Some **oysters** produce **pearls** (= small hard round white objects used to make jewellery). ➲ picture at **shellfish**

oz *abbr* = **ounce**(1): *Add 4oz flour.*

ozone /ˈəʊzəʊn/ *noun* [U] a poisonous gas which is a form of **oxygen**

ˌozone-ˈfriendly *adj* (used about cleaning products, etc.) not containing chemicals that could harm the **ozone layer**

the ˈozone layer *noun* [sing] the layer of **ozone** high up in the atmosphere that helps to protect the earth from the harmful effects of the sun: *a hole in the ozone layer* ➲ note at **environment** ➲ look at **CFC**

P, p /piː/ *noun* [C,U] (*pl* Ps; P's; p's /piːz/) the 16th letter of the English alphabet: *'Pencil' begins with (a) 'P'.*

p *abbr* **1** (*pl* pp) = **page**[1]: *See p.94 and pp.63-96.* **2** (*BrE informal*) = **penny**(1), **pence**: *a 46p stamp* **3** P (on a road sign) parking

P

PA /ˌpiː ˈeɪ/ *abbr, noun* [C] (*especially BrE*) **personal assistant**; a person who types letters, answers the telephone, arranges meetings, etc. for just one manager

p.a. *abbr* (from Latin) **per annum**; in or for a year: *salary: £25 000 p.a.*

pace[1] /peɪs/ *noun* **1** [U, sing] pace (of sth) the speed at which you walk, run, etc. or at which sth happens: *to run at a steady/gentle pace* ◆ *I can't stand the pace of life in London.* ◆ *Students are encouraged to work* ***at their own pace*** (= as fast or as slowly as they like). **2** [C] the distance that you move when you take one step: *Take two paces forward and then stop.* SYN **step**

IDM **keep pace (with sb/sth)** to move or do sth at the same speed as sb/sth else; to change as quickly as sth else is changing: *Wages are not keeping pace with inflation.*

set the pace to move or do sth at the speed that others must follow: *Pinto set the pace for the first three miles.*

pace[2] /peɪs/ *verb* [I,T] to walk up and down in the same area many times, especially because you are nervous or angry

pacemaker /ˈpeɪsmeɪkə(r)/ *noun* [C] **1** a machine that helps to make sb's heart beat regularly or more strongly **2** a person in a race who sets the speed that the others try to follow

pacifier /ˈpæsɪfaɪə(r)/ (*AmE*) = **dummy**(4)

pacifism /ˈpæsɪfɪzəm/ *noun* [U] the belief that all wars are wrong and that you should not fight in them ▶ **pacifist** /-ɪst/ *noun* [C]

pacify /ˈpæsɪfaɪ/ *verb* [T] (pacifying; pacifies; *pt, pp* pacified) to make sb who is angry or upset be calm or quiet

pack[1] /pæk/ *verb* **1** [I,T] to put your things into a suitcase, etc. before you go away or go on holiday: *Have you packed yet?* ◆ *Have you packed your toothbrush?* ◆ *I'll have to pack my suitcase in the morning.*

HELP The expression **do your packing** means the same.

OPP **unpack** **2** [T] to put things into containers so they can be stored, transported or sold: *I packed all my books into boxes.* OPP **unpack** **3** [T, often passive] (*informal*) to fill with people or things until crowded or full: *The train was absolutely packed.* ◆ *The book is* ***packed with*** *useful information.* ◆ *People packed the pavements, waiting for the president to arrive.*

PHR V **pack sth in** (*informal*) to stop doing sth: *I've packed in my job.* ◆ *I've had enough of you boys arguing—just pack it in, will you!*

pack sth in/into sth to do a lot in a short time: *They packed a lot into their three days in Rome.*

pack sth out [usually passive] to fill sth with people: *The bars* ***are packed out*** *every night.*

pack up (*BrE informal*) **1** (used about a machine, engine, etc.) to stop working: *My old car packed up last week so now I cycle to work.* **2** to finish working or doing sth: *There was nothing else to do so we packed up and went home.*

pack[2] /pæk/ *noun* [C]

➤CONTAINER **1** (*especially AmE*) a small box, bag, etc. in which things are packed to be sold in a shop

➤SET OF THINGS **2** a set of things that are supplied together for a particular purpose: *an information pack* ◆ *These batteries are sold in packs of four.* ◆ (*figurative*) *Everything she told me was* ***a pack of lies.*** ➲ look at **package, packet, parcel**

➤BAG **3** = **backpack**[1]: *It was hard to walk fast with the heavy pack on my back.*

➤OF ANIMALS **4** [with sing or pl verb] a group of wild animals that hunt together: *a pack of dogs/wolves*

➤OF PEOPLE **5** a large group of similar people or things, especially one that you do not like or approve of: *a pack of journalists*

➤OF CARDS **6** (*AmE* deck) a complete set of playing cards: *a pack of cards* ➲ note at **card** ➲ picture at **card**

package /ˈpækɪdʒ/ *noun* [C] **1** (*AmE*) = **parcel, packet**(1) **2** (*BrE*) something, or a number of things, covered in paper or in a box: *There's a large package on the table for you.* ➲ look at **pack, packet, parcel** **3** a number of things that must be bought or accepted together: *a software package* ◆ *a financial aid package* ▶ **package** *verb* [T]: *Goods that are attractively packaged sell more quickly.*

ˈpackage holiday (*AmE* ˈpackage tour) *noun* [C] a holiday that is organized by a company for a fixed price that includes the cost of travel, hotels, etc. ➲ note at **holiday**

packaging /ˈpækɪdʒɪŋ/ *noun* [U] all the materials (boxes, bags, paper, etc.) that are used to cover or protect goods before they are sold: *Attractive packaging can help to sell a product.* ➲ picture at **container**

packed /pækt/ *adj* **1** extremely full of people: *The restaurant was packed.* **SYN** **crowded** **2** containing a lot of a particular thing: *a book packed with information*

packed ˈlunch *noun* [C] (*BrE*) food that you prepare at home and take with you to eat at work or school

packer /ˈpækə(r)/ *noun* [C] a person, company or machine that puts goods, especially food, into boxes, plastic, paper, etc. to be sold

packet /ˈpækɪt/ *noun* **1** (*abbr* pkt) (*AmE* pack; package) [C] a small box, bag, etc. in which things are packed to be sold in a shop: ***a packet of** sweets/biscuits/crisps* ◆ *a cigarette packet* ➲ look at **pack, package, parcel** ➲ picture at **container** **2** [sing] (*informal*) a large amount of money: *That new kitchen must have cost them a packet.*

packing /ˈpækɪŋ/ *noun* [U] **1** the act of putting your clothes, possessions, etc. into boxes or cases in order to take or send them somewhere: *We're going on holiday tomorrow so I'll **do my packing** tonight.* **2** soft material that you use to stop things from being damaged or broken when you are sending them somewhere: *The price includes **postage and packing**.*

pact /pækt/ *noun* [C] (a) pact between A and B a formal agreement between two or more people, groups or countries

pad¹ /pæd/ *noun* [C] **1** a thick piece of soft material, used for cleaning or protecting sth or to make sth a different shape: *Remove eye make-up with cleanser and a cotton-wool pad.* ◆ *a jacket with shoulder pads* ➲ picture at **football** **2** a number of pieces of paper that are fastened together at one end: *a notepad* **3** the soft part on the bottom of the feet of some animals, for example dogs and cats **4** the place where a **spacecraft** (= a vehicle that travels in space) takes off: *a launch pad*

pad² /pæd/ *verb* (pa<u>dd</u>ing; pa<u>dd</u>ed) **1** [T, usually passive] pad sth (with sth) to fill or cover sth with soft material in order to protect it, make it larger or more comfortable, etc: *I sent the photograph frame in a padded envelope.* **2** [I] pad about, along, around, etc. to walk quietly, especially because you are not wearing shoes: *He got up and padded into the bathroom.*

PHR V **pad sth out** to make a book, speech, etc. longer by adding things that are not necessary

padding /ˈpædɪŋ/ *noun* [U] soft material that is put inside sth to protect it or to make it larger, more comfortable, etc.

paddle¹ /ˈpædl/ *noun* [C] a short pole that is flat and wide at one or both ends and that you use for moving a small boat through water ➲ look at **oar** ➲ picture at **kayak**

paddle² /ˈpædl/ *verb* **1** [I,T] to move a small boat through water using a short pole that is flat and wide at one or both ends: *We paddled down the river.* ➲ look at **row** **2** [I] to walk in water that is not very deep: *We paddled in the stream.*

paddock /ˈpædək/ *noun* [C] a small field where horses are kept

paddy /ˈpædi/ (also ˈ**paddy field**) *noun* [C] (*pl* paddies) a field in which rice is grown: *a rice paddy*

padlock /ˈpædlɒk/ *noun* [C] a type of lock that you can use for fastening gates, bicycles, etc. ▶ **padlock** *verb* [T] padlock sth (to sth): *I padlocked my bicycle to a lamp post.*

paediatrician (*AmE* pediatrician) /ˌpiːdiəˈtrɪʃn/ *noun* [C] a doctor who deals with the diseases of children

paediatrics (*AmE* pediatrics) /ˌpiːdiˈætrɪks/ *noun* [U] the area of medicine connected with the diseases of children ▶ **paediatric** (*AmE* pediatric) *adj*

paella /paɪˈelə/ *noun* [U,C] a Spanish dish made with rice, meat, fish and vegetables

pagan /ˈpeɪgən/ *adj* having religious beliefs that do not belong to any of the main religions ▶ **pagan** *noun* [C]

page¹ /peɪdʒ/ *noun* [C] (*abbr* p) **1** one or both sides of a piece of paper in a book, magazine, etc: *The letter was three pages long.* ◆ *Turn over the page.* ◆ *Turn to page 12 of your book.* ◆ ***the front page** of a newspaper* **2** a section of data that can be shown on a computer screen at any one time: *Go to our home page* (= the main page of an organization).

page² /peɪdʒ/ *verb* [T] to call sb by sending a message to a **pager**, or by calling their name through a **loudspeaker** (= a piece of equipment fixed to a wall in a public place)

pageant /ˈpædʒənt/ *noun* [C] **1** a type of public entertainment at which people dress in clothes from past times and give outdoor performances of scenes from history **2** (*especially AmE*) a beauty competition for young women

pageantry /ˈpædʒəntri/ *noun* [U] impressive public events or ceremonies with many people wearing special clothes: *the pageantry of royal occasions*

pager /ˈpeɪdʒə(r)/ *noun* [C] a small machine that you carry, that makes a sound when sb sends you a message **SYN** **bleeper**

pagoda /pəˈgəʊdə/ *noun* [C] a religious building in South or East Asia in the form of a tall tower with several levels, each with a roof

paid¹ *past tense, past participle of* **pay¹**

P

paid² /peɪd/ *adj* (of work, etc.) for which people receive money: *Neither of them is currently in paid employment.*

ˌpaid-ˈup *adj* [only *before* a noun] having paid all the money that you owe, for example to become a member of a club: *He's a fully paid-up member of Friends of the Earth.*

pain¹ /peɪn/ *noun* **1** [C,U] the unpleasant feeling that you have when a part of your body has been hurt or when you are ill: *to* ***be in pain*** ◆ *He screamed with pain.* ◆ *chest pains*

HELP **Pain** or **ache**? We use **ache** for a long, continuous pain and **pain** for sudden, short, sharp periods of pain. Therefore we usually say: *I've got earache/backache/toothache/a headache* but: *He was admitted to hospital with pains in his chest.* For the use of 'a' or 'an' with **ache**, look at the note at **ache**.

2 [U] sadness that you feel because sth bad has happened: *the pain of losing a parent*
IDM **a pain (in the neck)** (*informal*) a person, thing or situation that makes you angry or annoyed

pain² /peɪn/ *verb* [T] (*formal*) to make sb feel sad or upset: ***It pains me*** *to think how much money we've wasted.* **SYN** **hurt**

pained /peɪnd/ *adj* showing that you are sad or upset: *a pained expression*

painful /ˈpeɪnfl/ *adj* painful (for sb) (to do sth) **1** that causes pain: *A wasp sting can be very painful.* ◆ *painful joints* ◆ *My ankle is still too painful to walk on.* **2** making you feel upset or embarrassed: *a painful experience/memory* ▶ **painfully** /-fəli/ *adv*

painkiller /ˈpeɪnkɪlə(r)/ *noun* [C] a drug that is used for reducing pain

painless /ˈpeɪnləs/ *adj* that does not cause pain: *The animals' death is quick and painless.* ▶ **painlessly** *adv*

pains /peɪnz/ *noun*
IDM **be at/take (great) pains to do sth; take (great) pains (with/over sth)** to make a special effort to do sth well: *He was at pains to hide his true feelings.*

painstaking /ˈpeɪnzteɪkɪŋ/ *adj* very careful and taking a long time: *The painstaking search of the wreckage gave us clues as to the cause of the crash.* **SYN** **thorough** ▶ **painstakingly** *adv*

paint¹ /peɪnt/ *noun* **1** [U] coloured liquid that you put onto a surface to decorate or protect it: *green/orange/yellow paint* ◆ *The door will need another* ***coat of paint****.* **2** [U] coloured liquid that you can use to make a picture: *oil paint* ◆ *watercolour paint* **3 paints** [pl] a collection of tubes or blocks of paint that an artist uses for painting pictures: *oil paints*

paint² /peɪnt/ *verb* [I,T] **1** to put paint onto a surface or an object: *We painted the fence.* ◆ *The walls were painted pink.* **2** to make a picture of sb/sth using paints: *I'm painting a picture of some flowers.*

paintbox /ˈpeɪntbɒks/ *noun* [C] a box that contains blocks or tubes of paint of many colours

paintbrush /ˈpeɪntbrʌʃ/ *noun* [C] a brush that you use for painting with ➲ picture at **brush**

painter /ˈpeɪntə(r)/ *noun* [C] **1** a person whose job is to paint buildings, walls, etc: *a painter and decorator* **2** a person who paints pictures: *a famous painter* ➲ note at **art**

painting /ˈpeɪntɪŋ/ *noun* **1** [C] a picture that sb has painted: *a famous painting by Van Gogh*

MORE A **drawing** is not done with paints, but with pencils, pens, etc.

2 [U] the act of painting pictures or buildings: *painting and decorating* ➲ note at **art** ➲ picture on page P3

paintwork /ˈpeɪntwɜːk/ *noun* [U] a painted surface, especially on a vehicle

pair¹ /peə(r)/ *noun* [C] **1** two things of the same type that are used or worn together: *a pair of shoes/gloves/earrings* **2** a thing that consists of two parts that are joined together: *a pair of scissors/glasses/trousers* ➲ picture at **glasses** **3** [with sing or pl verb] two people or animals that are doing sth together: *These boxers have fought several times, and tonight the pair meet again.*

MORE We use **couple** to refer to two people who are married or in a relationship together.

IDM **in pairs** two at a time: *These earrings are only sold in pairs.* ◆ *The students were working in pairs.*

pair² /peə(r)/ *verb*
PHR V **pair (sb/sth) off (with sb)** to come together, especially to form a romantic relationship; to bring two people together for this purpose: *She's always trying to pair me off with her brother.*
pair up (with sb) to join together with another person or group to work, play a game, etc: *I paired up with another student and we did the project together.*

pajamas (*AmE*) = **pyjamas**

palace /ˈpæləs/ *noun* [C] a large house that is or was the home of a king or queen: *Did you visit Buckingham Palace?* ◆ *a royal palace*

palate /ˈpælət/ *noun* [C] the top part of the inside of your mouth

pale /peɪl/ *adj* (**paler**; **palest**) **1** (used about a person or their face) having skin that is light in colour, often because of fear or illness: *She has a pale complexion.* ◆ *I felt myself* ***go/turn pale*** *with fear.* ➲ look at **pallid** ➲ *noun* **pallor** **2** not bright or strong in colour: *a pale yellow dress* **OPP** **dark** ▶ **pale** *verb* [I]

pall /pɔːl/ *verb* [I] to become less interesting or important: *After a few months, the excitement of his new job began to pall.*

pallid /ˈpælɪd/ *adj* (used about a person or their face) light in colour, especially because of illness: *His pallid complexion made him look unhealthy.* ➲ look at **pale**

pallor /ˈpælə(r)/ *noun* [U] pale colouring of the face, especially because of illness or fear

palm¹ /pɑːm/ *noun* [C] **1** the flat, inner surface of your hand: *She held the coins tightly in the palm of her hand.* ➲ picture at **body** **2** (also ˈ**palm tree**) a tall straight type of tree that grows in hot countries. **Palms** have a lot of large leaves at the top but no branches.

palm² /pɑːm/ *verb*

PHR V **palm sb off (with sth)** (*informal*) to persuade sb to believe sth that is not true in order to stop them asking questions or complaining

palm sth off (on sb) (*informal*) to persuade sb to accept sth that they do not want: *She's always palming off the worst jobs on her assistant.*

palmtop /ˈpɑːmtɒp/ *noun* [C] a very small computer that can be held in one hand

paltry /ˈpɔːltri/ *adj* too small to be considered important or useful: *a paltry sum of money*

pamper /ˈpæmpə(r)/ *verb* [T] to take care of sb very well and make them feel as comfortable as possible

pamphlet /ˈpæmflət/ *noun* [C] a very thin book with a paper cover containing information about a particular subject

pan /pæn/ *noun* [C] a metal container with a handle or handles that is used for cooking food in; the contents of a pan: *Cook the spaghetti in a pan of boiling water.*

pancake /ˈpænkeɪk/ *noun* [C] a type of very thin round cake that is made by frying a mixture of flour, milk and eggs ➲ picture on **page P16**

ˈ**Pancake Day** *noun* [U,C] (*informal*) a Tuesday in February when people in Britain traditionally eat **pancakes**. Pancake Day is the day before the period of Lent begins. ➲ look at **Shrove Tuesday**

panda /ˈpændə/ *noun* [C] a large black and white animal that comes from China

panda

pandemic /pænˈdemɪk/ *noun* [C] a disease that spreads over a whole country or the whole world

pandemonium /ˌpændəˈməʊniəm/ *noun* [U] a state of great noise and confusion SYN **chaos**

pander /ˈpændə(r)/ *verb*

PHR V **pander to sb/sth** to do or say exactly what sb wants especially when this is not reasonable: *He refuses to pander to his boss's demands.*

p. and p. (also **p. & p.**) *abbr* (*BrE*) **postage and packing**: *price: £29 incl. p. and p.*

pane /peɪn/ *noun* [C] a piece of glass in a window, etc: *a windowpane*

panel /ˈpænl/ *noun* [C] **1** a square or long thin piece of wood, metal or glass that forms part of a door or wall: *They smashed one of the glass panels in the front door.* **2** [with sing or pl verb] a group of people who give their advice or opinions about sth; a group of people who discuss topics of interest on TV or radio: *a panel of judges* (= in a competition) ◆ *a panel game* (= a TV game show with two teams) **3** a flat surface that contains the equipment for controlling a vehicle, machine, etc: *a control/display panel*

panelling (*AmE* **paneling**) /ˈpænəlɪŋ/ *noun* [U] large flat pieces of wood used to cover and decorate walls, ceilings, etc.

panellist (*AmE* **panelist**) /ˈpænəlɪst/ *noun* [C] a member of a **panel**(2)

pang /pæŋ/ *noun* [C, usually pl] a sudden strong feeling of emotional or physical pain: *a pang of jealousy* ◆ *hunger pangs*

panic /ˈpænɪk/ *noun* [C,U] a sudden feeling of fear that cannot be controlled and stops you from thinking clearly: *There was a mad panic when the alarm went off.* ◆ *People fled* **in panic** *as the fire spread.* ▶ **panic** *verb* [I] (**panicking**; **panicked**): *Stay calm and don't panic.*

ˈ**panic-stricken** *adj* very frightened in a way that stops you from thinking clearly

panorama /ˌpænəˈrɑːmə/ *noun* [C] a view over a wide area of land ▶ **panoramic** /ˌpænəˈræmɪk/ *adj*

pant /pænt/ *verb* [I] to breathe quickly, for example after running or because it is very hot ▶ **pant** *noun* [C]

panther /ˈpænθə(r)/ *noun* [C] a large wild animal of the cat family with black fur ➲ picture at **lion**

panties /ˈpæntiz/ (*AmE*) = **knickers**

pantomime /ˈpæntəmaɪm/ *noun* [C,U] **1** (also *informal* **panto** /ˈpæntəʊ/) (*in Britain*) a type of play for children, with music, dancing and jokes

> **CULTURE**
>
> Pantomimes are usually performed at Christmas and are based on traditional children's stories.

2 = **mime**

pantry /ˈpæntri/ *noun* [C] (*pl* **pantries**) a small room where food is kept SYN **larder**

pants /pænts/ **1** (*BrE*) = **underpants**: *a pair of pants* **2** (*AmE*) = **trousers**: *ski pants*

pantyhose /ˈpæntihəʊz/ (*AmE*) = **tights**

paparazzi /ˌpæpəˈrætsi/ *noun* [pl] photographers who follow famous people around in order to get pictures of them to sell to a newspaper or magazine

papaya /pəˈpaɪə/ (also **pawpaw**) *noun* [C] a large tropical fruit which is sweet and orange inside and has small black seeds ➲ picture on **page P14**

paper /ˈpeɪpə(r)/ *noun*

➤FOR WRITING, ETC. **1** [U] material made in thin sheets that you use for writing or drawing on, covering things, etc: *a piece/sheet of paper* ◆ *a paper handkerchief* ➲ picture on **page 528**

MORE Types of paper include **filter paper, tissue paper, toilet paper** and **writing paper**.

➤NEWSPAPER **2** [C] a newspaper: *Where's today's paper?* ➲ note at **newspaper**
➤DOCUMENTS **3 papers** [pl] important letters or pieces of paper that have information written on them: *The document you want is somewhere in the pile of papers on her desk.*
➤EXAM **4** [C] a set of exam questions; the answers that people write to the questions: *The history exam is divided into three papers.*
➤PIECE OF WRITING **5** [C] a piece of writing on a particular subject that is written for people who know a lot about the subject: *At the conference, the Professor presented a paper on Sri Lankan poetry.*
IDM on paper 1 in writing: *I've had nothing on paper to say that I've been accepted.* **2** as an idea, but not in a real situation: *The scheme seems fine on paper, but would it work in practice?* **SYN in theory**

paperback /ˈpeɪpəbæk/ *noun* [C,U] a book that has a paper cover: *The novel is available* ***in paperback.*** ➲ look at **hardback**

ˈpaper boy, ˈpaper girl *noun* [C] a boy or girl who takes newspapers to people's houses

ˈpaper clip *noun* [C] a small piece of bent wire that is used for holding pieces of paper together ➲ picture at **stationery**

paperwork /ˈpeɪpəwɜːk/ *noun* [U] **1** the written work that is part of a job, such as writing letters and reports and filling in forms, etc: *I hate doing paperwork.* **2** documents that need to be prepared, collected, etc. in order for a piece of business to be completed: *Some of the paperwork is missing from this file.*

papier mâché /ˌpæpieɪ ˈmæʃeɪ/ *noun* [U] paper mixed with glue or flour and water, that is used to make decorative objects

paprika /ˈpæprɪkə/ *noun* [U] a red powder that you can use in cooking as a mild spice

papyrus /pəˈpaɪrəs/ *noun* (*pl* papyri /pəˈpaɪriː/) **1** [U] a tall plant that grows in water **2** [C,U] paper made from the **stems** (= the central part) of the **papyrus** plant, used in ancient Egypt for writing and drawing on

par /pɑː(r)/ *noun* [U] (in the sport of **golf**) the standard number of times a good player should hit the ball in order to complete a particular hole or series of holes
IDM below par (*informal*) not as good or as well as usual
on a par with sb/sth of an equal level, standard, etc. to sb/sth else: *Is a teacher's salary on a par with a doctor's?*

par. (also para.) *abbr* = **paragraph**

parable /ˈpærəbl/ *noun* [C] a short story that teaches a lesson, especially one told by Jesus in the Bible

parabola /pəˈræbələ/ *noun* [C] a curve like the path of an object that is thrown through the air and falls back to earth

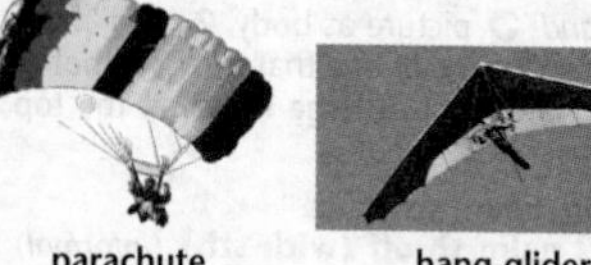
parachute hang-glider

parachute /ˈpærəʃuːt/ *noun* [C] a piece of equipment made of thin cloth, that opens and lets a person fall to the ground slowly when they jump from a plane ► **parachute** *verb* [I]

parade /pəˈreɪd/ *noun* [C] **1** a celebration of a special day or event, usually with bands in the streets and decorated vehicles: *the Lord Mayor's parade* **2** an occasion when a group of people stand or walk in a line so that people can look at them: *a military parade* ♦ *a fashion parade*

paradise /ˈpærədaɪs/ *noun* **1 Paradise** [U] [without *a* or *the*] the place where some people think that good people go after they die **SYN heaven 2** [C] a perfect place: *This beach is a paradise for windsurfers.*

paradox /ˈpærədɒks/ *noun* [C] a situation or statement with two or more parts that seem strange or impossible together: *It's a paradox that some countries produce too much food while in many other countries people are starving.* ► **paradoxical** /ˌpærəˈdɒksɪkl/ *adj* ► **paradoxically** /-kli/ *adv*

paraffin /ˈpærəfɪn/ (*AmE* **kerosene**) *noun* [U] a type of oil that is burned to produce heat or light

paragliding /ˈpærəglaɪdɪŋ/ *noun* [U] a sport in which you wear a special piece of equipment like a **parachute** (a piece of thin cloth that opens when you jump from a plane), jump from a high place and are carried along by the wind before coming down to earth

paragraph /ˈpærəgrɑːf/ *noun* [C] (*abbr* par., para.) a part of a piece of writing that usually consists of several sentences.

EXAM TIP

Paragraphs

When you write an essay, it is important to organize your writing into paragraphs to show how your ideas develop. Each paragraph should contain a separate idea and include at least two sentences that relate to this idea. You start each paragraph on a new line.

🔑 **parallel¹** /ˈpærəlel/ *adj, adv* **1 parallel** (to sth) (used about two lines, etc.) with the same distance between them for all their length: *parallel lines* ♦ *The railway runs parallel to the road.* ➲ picture at **line 2** similar and happening at the same time: *The two brothers followed parallel careers in different companies.*

parallel² /ˈpærəlel/ *noun* [C,U] a person, thing or situation that is similar to another one in a different situation, place or time: *The party's huge election victory is **without parallel** in its history.*

paralyse (*AmE* paralyze) /ˈpærəlaɪz/ *verb* [T] **1** to make a person unable to move their body or a part of it: *She is paralysed from the waist down.* **2** to make sb/sth unable to work in a normal way ▶ **paralysis** /pəˈræləsɪs/ *noun* [U]: *The disease can cause paralysis or even death.* ◆ *There has been complete paralysis of the country's railway system.*

paramedic /ˌpærəˈmedɪk/ *noun* [C] a person who has had special training in treating people who are hurt or ill, but who is not a doctor or nurse

paramilitary /ˌpærəˈmɪlətri/ *adj* organized in the same way as, but not belonging to, an official army: *a paramilitary group* ▶ **paramilitary** *noun* [C, usually pl] (*pl* **paramilitaries**)

paramount /ˈpærəmaʊnt/ *adj* (*formal*) most important: *Safety is paramount in car design.*

paranoia /ˌpærəˈnɔɪə/ *noun* [U] **1** a type of mental illness in which you wrongly believe that other people want to harm you **2** (*informal*) a feeling that other people want to harm you or are saying bad things about you, when you have no evidence for this

paranoid /ˈpærənɔɪd/ *adj* wrongly believing that other people are trying to harm you or are saying bad things about you

paraphernalia /ˌpærəfəˈneɪliə/ *noun* [U] a large number of different objects that you need for a particular purpose

paraphrase /ˈpærəfreɪz/ *verb* [T] to express sth again using different words so that it is easier to understand ▶ **paraphrase** *noun* [C]

parasite /ˈpærəsaɪt/ *noun* [C] a plant or an animal that lives in or on another plant or animal and gets its food from it

parasol /ˈpærəsɒl/ *noun* [C] an object like an umbrella that is used to create shade and protect you from the sun

paratroops /ˈpærətruːps/ *noun* [pl] soldiers who are trained to jump from a plane with a **parachute** (= a piece of equipment on their backs that opens and allows them to fall slowly)

parcel /ˈpɑːsl/ (*AmE* also **package**) *noun* [C] something that is covered in paper or put into a thick envelope and sent or given to sb ➲ look at **pack**, **package**, **packet**

parched /pɑːtʃt/ *adj* very hot and dry, or very thirsty: *Nothing would grow in the parched soil.* ◆ *Can I have a drink? I'm parched!*

pardon¹ /ˈpɑːdn/ (also **pardon ˈme**) *exclam* **1** used for asking sb to repeat what they have just said because you did not hear or understand it **2** used by some people to mean *sorry* or *excuse me*

pardon² /ˈpɑːdn/ *noun* [C,U] an official decision not to punish sb for a crime ▶ **pardon** *verb* [T] pardon sb (for sth/doing sth)

> **MORE** **I beg your pardon** is a formal way of saying 'sorry': *Oh, I beg your pardon. I had no idea this was your seat.*

pare /peə(r)/ *verb* [T] **1 pare sth (off/away)** to remove the thin outer layer of sth: *First, pare the skin away.* ◆ *She pared the apple.* **2 pare sth (back/down)** to gradually reduce the size or amount of sth: *The training budget has been pared back to a minimum.*

⚷ **parent** /ˈpeərənt/ *noun* [C] **1** a person's mother or father: *He's still living with his parents.*

> **MORE** A **single parent** is a mother or father who is bringing up their child or children alone, without the other parent. A **foster parent** is a person who looks after a child who is not legally their own.

2 a company that owns smaller companies of the same type: *a parent company*

parental /pəˈrentl/ *adj* [only *before* a noun] of a parent or parents: *parental support/advice*

parenthesis /pəˈrenθəsɪs/ (*pl* **parentheses** /pəˈrenθəsiːz/) (*especially AmE*) = **bracket¹**(1)

parenthood /ˈpeərənthʊd/ *noun* [U] the state of being a parent

parish /ˈpærɪʃ/ *noun* [C] an area or district which has its own church; the people who live in this area: *the parish church* ▶ **parishioner** /pəˈrɪʃənə(r)/ *noun* [C]

⚷ **park¹** /pɑːk/ *noun* [C] **1** an open area in a town, often with grass or trees, where people can go to walk, play, etc: *Let's go for a walk in the park.* ➲ picture on **page P11** **2** [in compounds] a large area of land that is used for a special purpose: *a national park* ◆ *a business park* ◆ *a theme park*

⚷ **park²** /pɑːk/ *verb* [I,T] to leave the vehicle that you are driving somewhere for a period of time: *It's very expensive to park in the centre of town.* ◆ *Somebody's parked their car in front of the exit.*

parking /ˈpɑːkɪŋ/ *noun* [U] **1** the act of leaving a car, lorry, etc. somewhere for a time: *The sign said 'No Parking'.* **2** a space or an area for leaving cars, lorries, etc: *There is ample free parking behind the hotel.*

> **MORE** A place where many cars can be parked and left is called a **car park**. A place where one car can be parked is called a **parking space**. If you **park** where you are not allowed to, a **traffic warden** might give you a **parking ticket**.

ˈparking brake (*AmE*) = **handbrake**

ˈparking garage (*AmE*) = **multi-storey car park**

ˈparking lot (*AmE*) = **car park**

ˈparking meter *noun* [C] a machine that you put coins into to pay for parking a car in the space beside it for a period of time

ˈparking ticket *noun* [C] a piece of paper that orders you to pay money as a punishment for parking your car where it is not allowed

P

parliament /ˈpɑːləmənt/ *noun* **1** [C, with sing or pl verb] the group of people who are elected to make and change the laws of a country: *the German parliament* **2 Parliament** [U, with sing or pl verb] the parliament of the United Kingdom: *a Member of Parliament (MP)*

CULTURE

The UK Parliament consists of **the House of Lords**, whose members have been appointed rather than elected, and **the House of Commons**, whose members have been elected by the people to represent areas of the country (called **constituencies**).

parliamentary /ˌpɑːləˈmentri/ *adj* [only *before* a noun] connected with a parliament

parody /ˈpærədi/ *noun* [C,U] (*pl* **parodies**) a piece of writing, speech or music that copies the style of sb/sth in a funny way: *a parody of a spy novel* ▶ **parody** *verb* [T] (**parodying; parodies;** *pt, pp* **parodied**)

parole /pəˈrəʊl/ *noun* [U] permission that is given to a prisoner to leave prison early on the condition that he or she behaves well: *He's going to be released **on parole**.*

parrot /ˈpærət/ *noun* [C] a type of tropical bird with a curved beak and usually with very bright feathers. **Parrots** that are kept as pets can be trained to copy what people say.

ˈ**parrot-fashion** *adv* (*BrE*) without understanding the meaning of something: *to learn something parrot-fashion*

P

parsley /ˈpɑːsli/ *noun* [U] a **herb** (= a type of plant) with small curly leaves that are used in cooking or for decorating food ➲ picture on **page P14**

parsnip /ˈpɑːsnɪp/ *noun* [C] a long thin white vegetable, that grows under the ground ➲ picture on **page P15**

part[1] /pɑːt/ *noun*
- ›SOME **1** [U] **part of sth** some, but not all of sth: *Part of the problem is lack of information.* ◆ *Part of the building was destroyed in the fire.*
- ›PIECE **2** [C] one of the pieces, areas, periods, things, etc. that together with others forms the whole of sth: *Which part of Spain do you come from?* ◆ *The film is good **in parts**.* ◆ ***spare parts** for a car* ◆ *a part of the body* ◆ *I enjoy being part of a team.*
- ›REGION **3 parts** [pl] (*old-fashioned, informal*) a region or area: *Are you from these parts?* ➲ note at **area**
- ›OF BOOK/SERIES **4** [C] a section of a book, TV series, etc: *You can see part two of this series at the same time next week.*
- ›IN FILM/PLAY **5** [C] a role or character in a play, film, etc: *He played the part of Macbeth.* ◆ *I had a small part in the school play.*
- ›EQUAL AMOUNT **6** [C] an amount or quantity (of a liquid or substance): *Use one part cleaning fluid to ten parts water.*
- ›HAIR **7** (*AmE*) = **parting**

IDM **the best/better part of sth** most of sth; more than half of sth, especially a period of time: *They've lived here for the best part of forty years.*

for the most part ➲ **most**[1]

for my, his, their, etc. part in my, his, their, etc. opinion; personally

have/play a part (in sth) to be involved in sth

in part not completely: *The accident was, in part, the fault of the driver.*

on the part of sb/on sb's part made, done or felt by sb: *There is concern on the part of the teachers that class sizes will increase.* ◆ *I'm sorry. It was a mistake on my part.*

take part (in sth) to join with other people in an activity: *We all took part in the discussion.*

part[2] /pɑːt/ *verb* **1** [I,T] (*formal*) **part (sb) (from sb)** to leave or go away from sb; to separate people or things: *We exchanged telephone numbers when we parted.* ◆ *He hates being parted from his children for long.* **2** [I,T] to move apart; to make things or people move apart: *Her lips were slightly parted.* **3** [T] to separate the hair on your head so as to make a clear line that goes from the back of your head to the front: *She parts her hair in the middle.* ➲ look at **parting**

IDM **part company (with sb/sth)** to go different ways or to separate after being together

PHR V **part with sth** to give or sell sth to sb: *When we went to live in Italy, we had to part with our horses.*

part[3] /pɑːt/ *adv* not completely one thing and not completely another: *She's part Russian and part Chinese.*

ˌ**part exˈchange** *noun* [U] (*BrE*) a way of buying sth, such as a car, in which you give your old one as some of the payment for a more expensive one

partial /ˈpɑːʃl/ *adj* **1** not complete: *The project was only a partial success.* **2 partial to sth** (*old-fashioned*) liking sth very much: *He's very partial to ice cream.* ▶ **partially** /-ʃəli/ *adv*

partiality /ˌpɑːʃiˈæləti/ *noun* [U] (*formal*) the unfair support of one person, team, etc. above another: *The referee was accused of partiality towards the home team.* OPP **impartiality** ➲ look at **impartial**

participant /pɑːˈtɪsɪpənt/ *noun* [C] a person who takes part in sth

participate /pɑːˈtɪsɪpeɪt/ *verb* [I] **participate (in sth)** to take part or become involved in sth: *Students are encouraged to participate in the running of the college.* ▶ **participation** /pɑːˌtɪsɪˈpeɪʃn/ *noun* [U]

participle /pɑːˈtɪsɪpl/ *noun* [C] a word that is formed from a verb and that ends in *-ing* (present participle) or *-ed*, *-en*, etc. (past participle). Participles are used to form tenses of the verb, or as adjectives: *'Hurrying' and 'hurried' are the present and past participles of 'hurry'.*

particle /ˈpɑːtɪkl/ *noun* [C] **1** a very small piece: *dust particles* **2** a small word that is not as important as a noun, verb or adjective: *In the phrasal verb 'break down', 'down' is an adverbial particle.*

particular /pəˈtɪkjələ(r)/ *adj* **1** [only *before* a noun] used to emphasize that you are talking about one person, thing, time, etc. and not about others: *Is* *there any particular dish you enjoy making?* **2** connected with one person or thing and not with others: *Everybody has their own particular problems.* **3** [only *before* a noun] greater than usual; special: *This article is of particular interest to me.* **4** [not before a noun] **particular (about/over sth)** difficult to please: *Some people are extremely particular about what they eat.* ➲ look at **fussy**

IDM in particular especially: *Is there **anything in particular** you'd like to do tomorrow?*

particularly /pəˈtɪkjələli/ *adv* especially; more than usual or more than others: *I'm particularly interested in Indian history.* ◆ *The match was excellent, particularly the second half.*

particulars /pəˈtɪkjələz/ *noun* [pl] (*formal*) facts or details about sb/sth: *The police took down all the particulars about the missing child.*

parting /ˈpɑːtɪŋ/ *noun* **1** [C,U] saying goodbye to, or being separated from, another person (usually for quite a long time) **2** (*AmE* **part**) [C] the line in sb's hair where it is divided in two with a **comb** (= a flat piece of metal or plastic with teeth): *a side/centre parting* ➲ look at **part**[2] ➲ picture at **hair**

partisan[1] /ˌpɑːtɪˈzæn; ˈpɑːtɪzæn/ *adj* showing too much support for one person, group or idea, especially without considering it carefully: *Most newspapers are politically partisan.* **SYN one-sided**

partisan[2] /ˌpɑːtɪˈzæn; ˈpɑːtɪzæn/ *noun* [C] **1** a person who strongly supports a particular leader, group or idea **SYN follower** **2** a member of an armed group that is fighting secretly against enemy soldiers who have taken control of its country

partition /pɑːˈtɪʃn/ *noun* **1** [C] something that divides a room, office etc. into two or more parts, especially a thin or temporary wall **2** [U] the division of a country into two or more countries ▸ **partition** *verb* [T]

partly /ˈpɑːtli/ *adv* not completely: *She was only partly responsible for the mistake.*

partner /ˈpɑːtnə(r)/ *noun* [C] **1** the person that you are married to or live with as if you are married: *a marriage partner* ◆ *All members of staff and their partners are invited.* **2** one of the people who owns a business: *business partners* **3** a person that you are doing an activity with as a team, for example dancing or playing a game: *a tennis partner* **4** a country or an organization that has an agreement with another: *Britain's EU partners* ▸ **partner** *verb* [T]: *Hales partnered his brother in the doubles, and they won the gold medal.*

partnership /ˈpɑːtnəʃɪp/ *noun* **1** [U] the state of being a partner in business: *Simona went into partnership with her sister and opened a shop in Rome.* **2** [C,U] a relationship between two people, organizations, etc: *Marriage is a partnership for life.* ◆ *a **civil partnership*** (= between two people of the same sex) **3** [C] a business owned by two or more people: *a junior member of the partnership*

ˌpart of ˈspeech *noun* [C] one of the groups that words are divided into, for example noun, verb, adjective, etc.

EXAM TIP

Parts of speech

When you do a **gap-fill exercise** (= where you choose the correct word to fill a gap in a sentence), it is important to know whether you need a noun, verb, adjective, etc. You also need to know whether to use a singular or plural noun, what tense a verb should be, whether to use the definite or indefinite article, etc.

ˌpart-ˈtime *adj, adv* for only a part of the working day or week: *She's got a part-time job.* ➲ look at **full-time**

party /ˈpɑːti/ *noun* [C] (*pl* **parties**) **1** (also **Party**) a group of people who have the same political aims and ideas and who are trying to win elections to parliament, etc: *Which party are you going to vote for in the next election?* ◆ *a **political party*** ➲ note at **politics**

CULTURE

The two main political parties in Great Britain are the **Labour** Party (left-wing) and the **Conservative** (or **Tory**) Party (right-wing). There is also a centre party called the **Liberal Democrats** and some other smaller parties. In the United States the main political parties are the **Republican Party** and the **Democratic Party**.

2 a social occasion to which people are invited in order to eat, drink and enjoy themselves: *When we've moved into our new house we're going to **have a party**.* ◆ *a birthday/dinner party* **3** a group of people who are working, travelling, etc. together: *a party of tourists* **4** (*formal*) one of the people or groups of people involved in a legal case: *the guilty/innocent party* ➲ look at **third party**

pass[1] /pɑːs/ *verb*

➤MOVE **1** [I,T] to move past or to the other side of sb/sth: *The street was crowded and the two buses couldn't pass.* ◆ *I passed him in the street but he didn't say hello.*

HELP **Passed** or **past**? **Passed** is a verb and **past** is an adjective or preposition: *The summer months passed slowly.* ◆ *The past week was very hot.* ◆ *Our house is just past the church.*

2 [I,T] **pass (sth) along, down, through, etc. (sth)** to go or move, or make sth move, in the direction mentioned: *A plane passed overhead.* ◆ *We'll have to pass the wire through the window.*

➤GIVE **3** [T] **pass sth (to sb)** to give sth to sb: *Could you pass (me) the salt, please?*

➤BALL **4** [I,T] **pass (sth) (to sb)** to kick, hit or throw the ball to sb on your own team: *He passed (the ball) to Walcott.*

➤TIME **5** [I] to go by: *At least a year had passed since she had last seen them.* ◆ *It was a long journey but the time passed very quickly.* **6** [T] to spend time, especially when you are bored or waiting for sth: *I'll have to think of something to do to **pass the time** in hospital.*

P

➤EXAM **7** [I,T] to achieve the necessary standard in an exam, test, etc: *Good luck in the exam! I'm sure you'll pass.* **OPP** **fail**

HELP Be careful. **Pass an exam** does NOT mean 'do an exam'. Use **take/sit an exam** to mean this.

8 [T] to test sb/sth and say that he/she/it is good enough: *The examiner passed most of the students.*
➤LAW **9** [T] to officially approve a law, etc. by voting: *One of the functions of Parliament is to* ***pass*** *new* ***laws****.*
➤BE ALLOWED **10** [I] to be allowed or accepted: *I didn't like what he was saying but I* ***let it pass****.*
➤GIVE OPINION **11** [T] **pass sth (on sb/sth)** to give an opinion, judgement, etc: *The judge* ***passed sentence*** *on the young man* (= said what his punishment would be).
IDM **pass the buck (to sb)** to make sb else responsible for a difficult situation
pass water (*formal*) to get rid of waste liquid from your body
PHR V **pass away** used as a polite way of saying 'die'
pass by (sb/sth) to go past: *I pass by your house on the way to work.*
pass sth down to give or teach sth to people who will live after you have died
pass for sb/sth to be accepted as sb/sth that he/she/it is not: *His mother looks so young she'd pass for his sister.*
pass sb/sth off (as sb/sth) to say that a person or a thing is sth that he/she/it is not: *He tried to pass the work off as his own.*
pass sth on (to sb) to give sth to sb else, especially after you have been given it or used it yourself: *Could you pass the message on to Mr Roberts?*
pass out to become unconscious **SYN** **faint** **OPP** **come round/to**

pass² /pɑːs/ *noun* [C] **1** a successful result in an exam: *The pass mark is 50%.* ♦ *Grades A, B and C are passes.* **OPP** **fail** **2** an official piece of paper that gives you permission to enter or leave a building, travel on a bus or train, etc: *Show your student pass when you buy a ticket.* ➲ look at **boarding pass** **3** the act of kicking, hitting or throwing the ball to sb on your own team in some sports **4** a road or way over or through mountains: *a mountain pass*

passable /ˈpɑːsəbl/ *adj* **1** good enough but not very good: *My French is not brilliant but it's passable.* **2** [not before a noun] (used about roads, rivers, etc.) possible to use or cross; not blocked **OPP** **impassable**

⚷ **passage** /ˈpæsɪdʒ/ *noun* **1** [C] (also **passageway** /ˈpæsɪdʒweɪ/) a long, narrow way with walls on either side that connects one place with another: *a secret underground passage* **2** [C] a tube in your body which air, liquid, etc. can pass through: *the nasal passages* **3** [C] a short part of a book, a speech or a piece of music: *The students were given a passage from the novel to study.* **4** [sing] the process of passing: *His painful memories faded with* ***the passage of time****.*

⚷ **passenger** /ˈpæsɪndʒə(r)/ *noun* [C] a person who is travelling in a car, bus, train, plane, etc. but who is not driving it or working on it: *The plane was carrying 200 passengers.*

ˌ**passer-ˈby** *noun* [C] (*pl* **passers-by**) a person who is walking past sb/sth

⚷ **passing¹** /ˈpɑːsɪŋ/ *noun* [U] the process of going by: *the passing of time*
IDM **in passing** done or said quickly, while you are thinking or talking about sth else: *He mentioned the house in passing but he didn't give any details.*

⚷ **passing²** /ˈpɑːsɪŋ/ *adj* [only *before* a noun] **1** lasting for only a short time: *a passing phase/thought/interest* **SYN** **brief** **2** going past: *I stopped a passing car and asked for help.*

passion /ˈpæʃn/ *noun* **1** [C,U] (a) very strong feeling, especially of love, hate or anger: *He was a very violent man, controlled by his passions.* **2** [sing] a **passion (for sb)** very strong sexual love or attraction: *He longed to tell Sashi of his passion for her.* **3** [sing] a **passion for sth** a very strong liking for or interest in sth: *She has a passion for history.*

passionate /ˈpæʃənət/ *adj* **1** showing or feeling very strong love or sexual attraction: *a passionate kiss* **2** showing or caused by very strong feelings: *The president gave a passionate speech about crime.* ▶ **passionately** *adv*: *He believes passionately in democracy.*

passive /ˈpæsɪv/ *adj* **1** showing no reaction, feeling or interest; not active: *Some people prefer to play a passive role in meetings.* **2** used about the form of a verb or a sentence when the subject of the sentence is affected by the act of the verb: *In the sentence 'He was bitten by a dog', the verb is passive.* ➲ look at **active**

HELP You can also say: 'The verb is in the passive'.

▶ **passively** *adv*

ˌ**passive ˈsmoking** *noun* [U] the act of breathing in smoke from other people's cigarettes

Passover /ˈpɑːsəʊvə(r)/ *noun* [sing] the most important Jewish festival, which takes place in spring and lasts seven or eight days

⚷ **passport** /ˈpɑːspɔːt/ *noun* [C] **1** an official document that identifies you as a citizen of a particular country and that you have to show when you enter or leave a country: *You have to go through* ***passport control*** (= where passports are checked) *at the airport.* ♦ *a passport photo*

MORE You **apply for** or **renew** your passport at the **passport office**. This office **issues** new passports.

2 a **passport to sth** a thing that makes it possible to achieve sth: *a passport to success*

password /ˈpɑːswɜːd/ *noun* [C] **1** a secret word or phrase that you need to know in order to be allowed into a place **2** a series of letters and/or numbers that you must type into a computer or computer system in order to be able to use it: *Please enter your password.*

past[1] /pɑːst/ *adj* **1** [only *before* a noun] just finished; last: *He's had to work very hard during the past year.* **2** already gone; belonging to a time before the present: *in past centuries/times* ♦ *I'd rather forget some of my past mistakes.*

past[2] /pɑːst/ *noun* **1 the past** [sing] the time that has gone by; things that happened in an earlier time: *the* ***recent/distant past*** ♦ *Writing letters seems to be* ***a thing of the past.*** **2** [C] a person's life or career before now: *We don't know anything about his past.* **3 the past; the ˌpast ˈtense** [sing] the form of a verb used to describe actions in the past: *The past tense of 'take' is 'took'.* ⓘ For more information about the past tenses, look at the **Reference Section** at the back of this dictionary.

past[3] /pɑːst/ *prep, adv* **1** (used when telling the time) after; later than: *It's ten (minutes) past three.* ♦ *It was past midnight when we got home.* ♦ *A week went past and nothing had happened.* **2** from one side to the other of sb/sth; further than or on the other side of sb/sth: *He walked straight past me.* ♦ *She looked right past me without realizing who I was.* **3** above or further than a certain point, limit or age: *Unemployment is now past the 2 million mark.* ♦ *I'm so tired that I'm* ***past caring*** (= I don't care any more) *what we eat.*

IDM not put it past sb (to do sth) [used with *would*] to think sb is capable of doing sth bad: *I wouldn't put it past him to do a thing like that.*

past it (*BrE informal*) too old

pasta /ˈpæstə/ *noun* [U] an Italian food made from flour, water and sometimes eggs, formed into different shapes, cooked, and usually served with a sauce ➲ picture on **page P16**

GRAMMAR **Pasta** is uncountable. If we are talking about one piece, we say **a bit of pasta** (not 'a pasta').

paste[1] /peɪst/ *noun* **1** [C,U] a soft, wet mixture, usually made of a powder and a liquid and sometimes used for sticking things: *wallpaper paste* ♦ *Mix the flour and milk into a paste.* **2** [U] [in compounds] a soft mixture of food that you can spread onto bread, etc: *fish/chicken paste*

paste[2] /peɪst/ *verb* [T] **1** to stick sth to sth else using **paste**: *He pasted the picture into his book.* **2** (in computing) to copy or move text into a document from somewhere else: *This function allows you to* ***cut and paste*** *text.*

pastel /ˈpæstl/ *adj* (used about colours) pale; not strong

pasteurized (also -ised) /ˈpɑːstʃəraɪzd/ *adj* (used about milk or cream) free from bacteria because it has been heated and then cooled

pastime /ˈpɑːstaɪm/ *noun* [C] something that you enjoy doing when you are not working **SYN hobby**

pastoral /ˈpɑːstərəl/ *adj* **1** (connected with the work of a priest or a teacher) giving help and advice on personal matters rather than on matters of religion or education **2** connected with pleasant country life

ˌpast ˈparticiple *noun* [C] the form of the verb that ends in *-ed, -en,* etc. ⓘ For more information about the use of tenses, look at the **Reference Section** at the back of this dictionary.

ˌpast ˈperfect (also **pluperfect**) *noun* [sing] the tense of a verb that describes an action that was finished before another event happened ⓘ For more information about the past perfect, look at the **Reference Section** at the back of this dictionary.

pastry /ˈpeɪstri/ *noun* (*pl* **pastries**) **1** [U] a mixture of flour, fat and water that is rolled out flat and cooked as a base or covering for **pies** (= a type of baked food), etc. **2** [C] a small cake made with **pastry**

ˌpast ˈtense (also **the past**) *noun* [sing] the tense of a verb that describes an action that happened in the past: *The past tense of 'take' is 'took'.* ⓘ For more information about the past perfect, look at the **Reference Section** at the back of this dictionary.

pasture /ˈpɑːstʃə(r)/ *noun* [C,U] a field or land covered with grass, where cows, etc. can feed

pasty /ˈpæsti/ *noun* [C] (*pl* **pasties**) (*BrE*) a small **pie** (= a type of baked food) containing meat and/or vegetables

pat[1] /pæt/ *verb* [T] (**patting; patted**) to touch sb/sth gently with a flat hand, especially as a sign of friendship, care, etc. ➲ picture at **stroke**

pat[2] /pæt/ *noun* [C] a gentle friendly touch with a flat hand: *He gave her knee an affectionate pat.*

IDM a pat on the back (for sth/doing sth) approval for sth good that a person has done: *She deserves a pat on the back for all her hard work.*

pat[3] /pæt/ *adj* [only *before* a noun] *adv* (used about an answer, comment, etc.) said in a quick or simple way that does not sound natural or realistic

patch[1] /pætʃ/ *noun* [C] **1 a patch (of sth)** a part of a surface that is different in some way from the area around it: *Drive carefully. There are patches of ice on the roads.* ♦ *a bald patch* **2** a piece of material that you use to cover a hole in clothes, etc: *I sewed patches on the knees of my jeans.* **3** a small piece of cloth that you wear over one eye, usually because the eye is damaged **4** a small piece of land, especially for growing vegetables or fruit: *a vegetable patch*

IDM go through a bad patch (*informal*) to experience a difficult or unhappy period of time

not a patch on sb/sth (*especially BrE informal*) not nearly as good as sb/sth: *Her new book isn't a patch on her others.*

patch[2] /pætʃ/ *verb* [T] to cover a hole in clothes, etc. with a piece of cloth in order to repair it: *patched jeans*

PHR V patch sth up **1** to repair sth, especially in a temporary way by adding a new piece of material **2** to stop arguing with sb and to be friends again: *Have you tried to* ***patch things up*** *with her?*

P

patchwork /ˈpætʃwɜːk/ *noun* [U] a type of sewing in which small pieces of cloth of different colours and patterns are sewn together

patchy /ˈpætʃi/ *adj* **1** existing or happening in some places but not others: *patchy fog/clouds/rain* **2** not complete; good in some parts but not in others: *My knowledge of German is rather patchy.*

pâté /ˈpæteɪ/ *noun* [U] food that is made by making meat, fish or vegetables into a smooth, thick mixture that is served cold and spread on bread, etc: *liver pâté*

patent[1] /ˈpætnt; ˈpeɪtnt/ *noun* [C,U] the official right to be the only person to make, use or sell a new product; the document that proves this ▸ **patent** *verb* [T]

patent[2] /ˈpeɪtnt/ *adj* [only *before* a noun] (*formal*) clear; obvious: *a patent lie* ▸ **patently** *adv*

patent leather /ˌpeɪtnt ˈleðə(r)/ *noun* [U] a type of leather with a hard, shiny surface, used especially for making shoes and bags

paternal /pəˈtɜːnl/ *adj* **1** behaving as a father would behave; connected with being a father **2** [only *before* a noun] related through the father's side of the family: *my paternal grandparents* ➲ look at **maternal**

paternity /pəˈtɜːnəti/ *noun* [U] the fact of being the father of a child: *paternity leave* (= time that the father of a new baby is allowed to have away from work) ➲ look at **maternity**

P

path /pɑːθ/ *noun* [C] **1** a way across a piece of land that is made by or used by people walking: *the garden path* ◆ *Keep to the path or you may get lost.* ➲ look at **footpath** ➲ picture on **page P8**

MORE Pathway is similar in meaning: *There was a narrow pathway leading down the cliff.*

2 the line along which sb/sth moves; the space in front of sb/sth as he/she/it moves: *the **flight path** of an aeroplane*

pathetic /pəˈθetɪk/ *adj* **1** causing you to feel pity or sadness: *the pathetic cries of the hungry children* **2** (*informal*) very bad, weak or useless: *What a pathetic performance! The team deserved to lose.* ▸ **pathetically** /-kli/ *adv*

pathological /ˌpæθəˈlɒdʒɪkl/ *adj* **1** caused by feelings that you cannot control; not reasonable or sensible: *He's a pathological liar* (= he cannot stop lying). ◆ *pathological fear/hatred/violence* **2** caused by or connected with disease or illness: *pathological depression* **3** connected with **pathology** ▸ **pathologically** /-kli/ *adv*

pathologist /pəˈθɒlədʒɪst/ *noun* [C] a doctor who is an expert in **pathology**, and examines dead bodies to find out why a person has died

pathology /pəˈθɒlədʒi/ *noun* [U] the scientific study of diseases of the body

pathos /ˈpeɪθɒs/ *noun* [U] (in writing, speech and plays) a quality that produces feelings of sadness and pity

patience /ˈpeɪʃns/ *noun* [U] **1** **patience (with sb/sth)** the quality of being able to stay calm and not get angry, especially when there is a difficulty or you have to wait a long time: *I've got no patience with people who don't even try.* ◆ *to **lose patience** with somebody* **OPP** **impatience** **2** (*AmE* **solitaire**) a card game for only one player

patient[1] /ˈpeɪʃnt/ *noun* [C] a person who is receiving medical treatment: *a hospital patient* ➲ note at **hospital**

patient[2] /ˈpeɪʃnt/ *adj* **patient (with sb/sth)** able to stay calm and not get angry, especially when there is a difficulty or you have to wait a long time: *He's very patient with young children.* **OPP** **impatient** ▸ **patiently** *adv*: *She sat patiently waiting for her turn.*

patio /ˈpætiəʊ/ *noun* [C] (*pl* **patios** /-əʊz/) a flat, hard area, usually behind a house, where people can sit, eat, etc. outside ➲ look at **terrace**, **veranda**

patriot /ˈpeɪtriət; ˈpæt-/ *noun* [C] a person who loves their country and is ready to defend it against an enemy ▸ **patriotism** /ˈpeɪtriətɪzəm; ˈpæt-/ *noun* [U]

patriotic /ˌpeɪtriˈɒtɪk; ˌpæt-/ *adj* having or showing great love for your country ▸ **patriotically** /-kli/ *adv*

patrol[1] /pəˈtrəʊl/ *verb* [I,T] (**patrolling**; **patrolled**) to go round an area, building, etc. at regular times to make sure that it is safe and that nothing is wrong

patrol[2] /pəˈtrəʊl/ *noun* **1** [C,U] the act of going round an area, building, etc. at regular times to make sure that it is safe and that nothing is wrong: *a police car **on patrol** in the area* **2** [C] a group of soldiers, vehicles, etc. that **patrol** sth: *a naval/police patrol* ◆ *a patrol car/boat*

patron /ˈpeɪtrən/ *noun* [C] **1** a person who gives money and support to artists, writers and musicians: *a patron of the arts* **2** a famous person who supports an organization such as a charity and whose name is used in advertising it ➲ look at **sponsor** **3** (*formal*) a person who uses a particular shop, theatre, restaurant, etc: *This car park is for patrons only.*

patronage /ˈpætrənɪdʒ; ˈpeɪt-/ *noun* [U] the support, especially financial, that is given to a person or an organization by a **patron**: *Patronage of the arts comes from businesses and private individuals.*

patronize (also **-ise**) /ˈpætrənaɪz/ *verb* [T] **1** to treat sb in a way that shows that you think you are better, more intelligent, experienced, etc. than they are **2** (*formal*) to be a regular customer of a shop, restaurant, etc. ▸ **patronizing** (also **-ising**) *adj*: *I hate that patronizing smile of hers.* ▸ **patronizingly** (also **-isingly**) *adv*

ˌpatron ˈsaint *noun* [C] a religious person who is believed by Christians to protect a particular place or people doing a particular activity: *St David is the patron saint of Wales.*

patter /ˈpætə(r)/ *noun* [sing] the sound of many quick light steps or knocks on a surface: *the patter of the children's feet on the stairs* ▶ **patter** *verb* [I]

pattern /ˈpætn/ *noun* [C] **1** the regular way in which sth happens, develops, or is done: *Her days all seemed to follow the same pattern.* ♦ *changing patterns of behaviour/work/weather* **2** a regular arrangement of lines, shapes, colours, etc. as a design: *a shirt with a floral pattern on it* SYN **design** ➲ picture on **page P1** **3** a design, a set of instructions or a shape to cut around that you use in order to make sth: *a dress/sewing pattern*

patterned /ˈpætənd/ *adj* decorated with a pattern(2) ➲ picture on **page P1**

pause¹ /pɔːz/ *verb* [I] pause (for sth) to stop talking or doing sth for a short time before continuing: *He paused for a moment before answering my question.*

pause² /pɔːz/ *noun* **1** [C] a pause (in sth) a short period of time during which sb stops talking or stops what they are doing: *He continued playing for twenty minutes without a pause.* ➲ note at **interval** **2** (also ˈpause button) [C,U] a control that allows you to stop a CD, DVD, etc. for a short time: *Can you press pause while I go and make a cup of tea?*

pave /peɪv/ *verb* [T, often passive] pave sth (with sth) to cover an area of ground with **paving stones** or bricks

pavement /ˈpeɪvmənt/ (*AmE* **sidewalk**) *noun* [C] a hard flat area at the side of a road for people to walk on ➲ picture at **roundabout** ➲ picture on **page P11**

pavilion /pəˈvɪliən/ *noun* [C] (*BrE*) **1** a building at a sports ground where players can change their clothes **2** a temporary building used at public events and exhibitions

ˈpaving stone *noun* [C] a flat piece of stone that is used for covering the ground

paw¹ /pɔː/ *noun* [C] the foot of animals such as dogs, cats, bears, etc. ➲ picture on **page P12**

paw² /pɔː/ *verb* [I,T] paw (at) sth (used about an animal) to touch or scratch sb/sth several times with a paw: *The dog pawed at my sleeve.*

pawn¹ /pɔːn/ *noun* [C] **1** (in the game of **chess**) one of the eight pieces that are of least value and importance **2** a person who is used or controlled by other more powerful people

pawn² /pɔːn/ *verb* [T] to leave a valuable object with a **pawnbroker**, in return for money. If you cannot pay back the money after a certain period, the object can be sold or kept.

pawnbroker /ˈpɔːnbrəʊkə(r)/ *noun* [C] a person who lends money to people when they leave sth of value with them

pawpaw /ˈpɔːpɔː/ = **papaya**

pay¹ /peɪ/ *verb* (*pt, pp* **paid**) **1** [I,T] pay (sb) (for sth); pay (sb) sth (for sth) to give sb money for work, goods, services, etc: *She is very* ***well paid.*** ♦ *The work's finished but we haven't paid for it yet.* ♦ *We paid the dealer £3 000 for the car.* **2** [T] pay sth (to sb) to give the money that you owe for sth: *Have you paid her the rent yet?* ♦ *to pay a bill/fine* **3** [I,T] to be worth doing: *It would pay you to get professional advice before making a decision.* **4** [I,T] to make a profit: *It's hard to make farming pay.* **5** [I] pay (for sth) to suffer or be punished because of your beliefs or actions: *You'll pay for that remark!*

IDM **charge/pay the earth** ➲ **earth¹**

pay attention (to sb/sth) to listen carefully to or to take notice of sb/sth

pay sb a compliment; pay a compliment to sb to say that you like sth about sb

pay your respects (to sb) (*formal*) to visit sb as a sign of respect: *Hundreds came to* ***pay their last respects*** *to her* (= went to her funeral).

pay tribute to sb/sth to say good things about sb/sth and show your respect for sb/sth

put paid to sth to destroy or finish sth: *The bad weather put paid to our picnic.*

PHR V **pay sb/sth back** to give money back to sb that you borrowed from them: *Can you lend me £5? I'll pay you back/I'll pay it back to you on Friday.*

pay sb back (for sth) to punish sb for making you or sb else suffer: *What a mean trick! I'll pay you back one day.*

pay off (*informal*) to be successful: *All her hard work has paid off! She passed her exam.*

pay sth off to pay all the money that you owe for sth: *to pay off a debt/mortgage*

pay up (*informal*) to pay the money that you owe: *If you don't pay up, we'll take you to court.*

pay² /peɪ/ *noun* [U] money that you get regularly for work that you have done: *It's a boring job but the pay is good.* ♦ *a pay increase/rise*

> TOPIC
>
> **Pay**
>
> Pay is the general word for money that you earn (= get regularly for work that you have done). Wages are paid weekly or daily in cash. A **salary** is paid monthly, directly into a bank account. When your wages or salary are increased, you get a **pay rise**. Your **income** is all the money you get regularly, both for work you have done, and as interest on money you have saved. **Payment** is money for work that you do once or not regularly. You pay a **fee** for professional services, for example to a doctor, lawyer, etc. The money that you have to pay to the government is called tax.

payable /ˈpeɪəbl/ *adj* [not before a noun] that should or must be paid: *A 10% deposit is payable in advance.* ♦ ***Please make the cheque payable to*** *Helena Braun.*

ˌpay-as-you-ˈgo *adj* connected with a system of paying for a service before you use it, rather than paying for it later: *pay-as-you-go mobile phones* ➲ note at **mobile phone**

payee /ˌpeɪˈiː/ *noun* [C] a person that money, especially a cheque, is paid to

payment /ˈpeɪmənt/ *noun* payment (for sth) **1** [U] the act of paying sb or of being paid: *payment*

P

of a bill ◆ *I did the work last month but I haven't had any payment for it yet.* ➲ note at **pay²** **2** [C] an amount of money that you must pay: *They asked for a payment of £100 as a deposit.*

ˌpay-per-ˈview *noun* [U] a system of receiving television programmes in which you pay an extra sum of money to watch a particular programme, such as a film or a sports event

payslip /ˈpeɪslɪp/ *noun* [C] (*BrE*) a piece of paper that your employer gives you each month to show how much money you have been paid and how much tax, etc. has been taken off: *There seems to be a mistake on my payslip.*

PC /ˌpiː ˈsiː/ *abbr* **1 personal computer**; a computer that is designed for one person to use at work or at home ➲ note at **computer** ➲ look at **mainframe** ➲ picture at **computer** **2** (*BrE*) = **police constable** **3** = **politically correct**

PE /ˌpiː ˈiː/ *abbr* **physical education**; the school subject of sport and exercise: *a PE lesson*

pea /piː/ *noun* [C] a small round green seed that is eaten as a vegetable. A number of **peas** grow together in a **pod** (= a long thin case). ➲ picture on **page P15**

⚷ **peace** /piːs/ *noun* [U] **1** a situation or a period of time in which there is no war or violence in a country or area: *The two communities now manage to live **in peace** together.* ◆ *A UN force has been sent in to **keep the peace**.* **2** the state of being calm or quiet: *He longed to escape from the city to the **peace and quiet** of the countryside.* ◆ *I'm tired—can't you just **leave** me **in peace*** (= stop disturbing me)?

⚷ **peaceful** /ˈpiːsfl/ *adj* **1** not wanting or involving war, violence or argument: *a peaceful protest/demonstration* **2** calm and quiet: *a peaceful village* ▶ **peacefully** /-fəli/ *adv*: *The siege ended peacefully and nobody was hurt.* ▶ **peacefulness** *noun* [U]

peacetime /ˈpiːstaɪm/ *noun* [U] a period when a country is not at war

peach /piːtʃ/ *noun* **1** [C] a soft round fruit with reddish-orange skin and a large stone in its centre ➲ picture on **page P14** **2** [U] a pinkish-orange colour ▶ **peach** *adj*

peacock /ˈpiːkɒk/ *noun* [C] a large bird with beautiful long blue and green tail feathers that it can lift up and spread out

⚷ **peak¹** /piːk/ *noun* [C] **1** the point at which sth is the highest, best, strongest, etc: *a man **at the peak of** his career* **2** the pointed top of a mountain: *snow-covered peaks* ➲ picture on **page P10** **3** the stiff front part of a cap which sticks out above your eyes ➲ picture at **hat**

peak² /piːk/ *verb* [I] to reach the highest point or value: *Sales peak just before Christmas.*

peak³ /piːk/ *adj* [only *before* a noun] used to describe the highest level of sth, or a time when the greatest number of people are doing or using sth: *The athletes are all in peak condition.* ◆ *Summer is the peak period for most hotels.* ➲ look at **off-peak**

peal /piːl/ *noun* [C] the loud ringing of a bell or bells: (*figurative*) *peals of laughter* ▶ **peal** *verb* [I]

peanut /ˈpiːnʌt/ *noun* **1** (*BrE also* **groundnut**) [C] a nut that grows underground in a thin shell ➲ picture at **nut** **2** **peanuts** [pl] (*informal*) a very small amount of money: *We get paid peanuts for doing this job.*

ˌpeanut ˈbutter *noun* [U] a thick soft substance made from very finely chopped **peanuts**, usually eaten spread on bread

pear /peə(r)/ *noun* [C] a fruit that has a yellow or green skin and is white inside. **Pears** are wider at the bottom than at the top. ➲ picture on **page P14**

pearl /pɜːl/ *noun* [C] a small hard round white object that grows inside the shell of an **oyster** (= a type of creature that lives in water). Pearls are used to make jewellery: *pearl earrings*

peasant /ˈpeznt/ *noun* [C] (used especially in past times) a person who owns or rents a small piece of land on which they grow food and keeps animals in order to feed their family

HELP Be careful. This word is considered offensive nowadays.

peat /piːt/ *noun* [U] a soft black or brown natural substance that is formed from dead plants just under the surface of the ground in cool, wet places. It can be burned as a fuel or used in the garden to make plants grow better.

pebble /ˈpebl/ *noun* [C] a smooth round stone that is found in or near water ➲ picture on **page P10**

pecan /ˈpiːkən/ *noun* [C] a type of nut that you can eat, with a smooth pinkish-brown shell ➲ picture at **nut**

peck /pek/ *verb* [I,T] **1** **peck (at) sth** (used about a bird) to eat or bite sth with its beak **2** (*informal*) to kiss sb quickly and lightly: *She pecked him on the cheek and then left.* ▶ **peck** *noun* [C]

peckish /ˈpekɪʃ/ *adj* (*BrE informal*) hungry

peculiar /pɪˈkjuːliə(r)/ *adj* **1** unusual or strange: *There's a very peculiar smell in here.* **SYN** **odd** **2** **peculiar to sb/sth** only belonging to one person or found in one place: *a species of bird peculiar to South East Asia*

peculiarity /pɪˌkjuːliˈærəti/ *noun* (*pl* **peculiarities**) **1** [C] a strange or unusual characteristic, quality or habit: *There are some peculiarities in her behaviour.* **2** [C] a characteristic or a quality that only belongs to one particular person, thing or place: *the cultural peculiarities of the English* **3** [U] the quality of being strange or unusual

peculiarly /pɪˈkjuːliəli/ *adv* **1** especially; very: *Lilian's laugh can be peculiarly annoying.* **2** in a way that is especially typical of one person, thing or place: *a peculiarly Italian custom* **3** in a strange and unusual way: *Luke is behaving very peculiarly.*

pedagogic /ˌpedəˈɡɒdʒɪk/ (also **pedagogical** /-ɪkl/) *adj* connected with ways of teaching

pedal /ˈpedl/ *noun* [C] the part of a bicycle, car or other machine that you push with your foot in order to make it move or work ➲ picture at **bicycle, piano** ▸ **pedal** *verb* [I,T] (**pedalling; pedalled**, (*AmE*) **pedaling; pedaled**): *She had to pedal hard to get up the hill.*

pedantic /pɪˈdæntɪk/ *adj* too worried about small rules or details ▸ **pedantically** /-kli/ *adv*

pedestal /ˈpedɪstl/ *noun* [C] the base on which a column, statue, etc. stands

pedestrian /pəˈdestriən/ *noun* [C] a person who is walking in the street (not travelling in a vehicle) ➲ look at **motorist**

peˌdestrian ˈcrossing (*AmE* crosswalk) *noun* [C] a place where vehicles must stop to allow **pedestrians** to cross the road ➲ look at **zebra crossing**

pediatrician, pediatrics (*AmE*) = **paediatrician, paediatrics**

pedigree¹ /ˈpedɪgriː/ *noun* [C] **1** an official record of the animals from which a particular animal has been bred ➲ look at **mongrel** **2** a person's family history, especially when this is impressive

pedigree² /ˈpedɪgriː/ *adj* [only *before* a noun] (used about an animal) of high quality because the family of animals that it comes from are all of the same breed and specially chosen

pee /piː/ *verb* [I] (*informal*) to get rid of waste water from your body **SYN** **urinate** ▸ **pee** *noun* [U, sing]

peek /piːk/ *verb* [I] (*informal*) **peek (at sth)** to look at sth quickly and secretly because you should not be looking at it: *No peeking at your presents before your birthday!* ▸ **peek** *noun* [sing]: *to have a quick peek*

peel¹ /piːl/ *verb* **1** [T] to take the skin off a fruit or vegetable: *Could you peel the potatoes, please?* **2** [I, T] **peel (sth) (off/away/back)** to come off or to take sth off a surface in one piece or in small pieces: *I peeled off the price label before handing her the book.*
IDM **keep your eyes peeled/skinned (for sb/sth)** ➲ **eye¹**

peel² /piːl/ *noun* [U] the skin of a fruit or vegetable: *apple/potato peel* ➲ look at **rind, skin** ➲ picture on page P14

peeler /ˈpiːlə(r)/ *noun* [C] a special knife for taking the skin off fruit and vegetables: *a potato peeler* ➲ picture at **kitchen**

peep¹ /piːp/ *verb* [I] **1** **peep (at sth)** to look at sth quickly and secretly, especially through a small opening **2** to be just able to be seen: *The moon is peeping out from behind the clouds.*

peep² /piːp/ *noun* [sing] (*informal*) **1** a quick look: *Have a peep in the bedroom and see if the baby is asleep.* **2** a sound: *There hasn't been a peep out of the children for hours.*

peer¹ /pɪə(r)/ *noun* [C] **1** a person who is of the same age or position in society as you: *Children hate to look stupid in front of their peers.* **2** (in Britain) a member of the **nobility** (= people of the highest social class, who have special titles)

peer² /pɪə(r)/ *verb* [I] **peer (at sb/sth)** to look closely or carefully at sb/sth, for example because you cannot see very well: *He peered at the photo, but it was blurred.*

peerage /ˈpɪərɪdʒ/ *noun* **1** [sing] all the **peers¹** (2) as a group **2** [C] the position of a **peer¹** (2)

ˈpeer group *noun* [C] a group of people who are all of the same age and social position

peeved /piːvd/ *adj* (*informal*) quite angry or annoyed

pegs

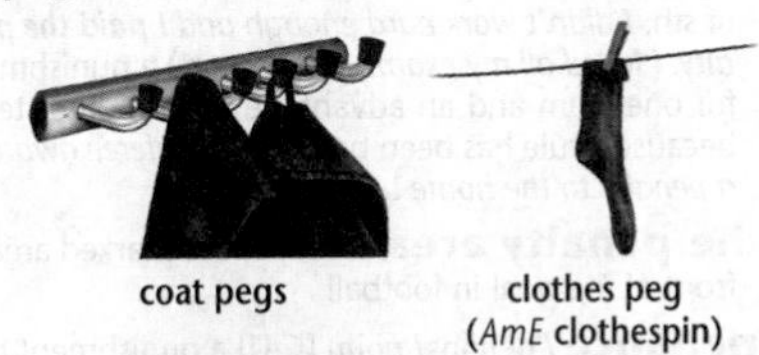

coat pegs

clothes peg (*AmE* clothespin)

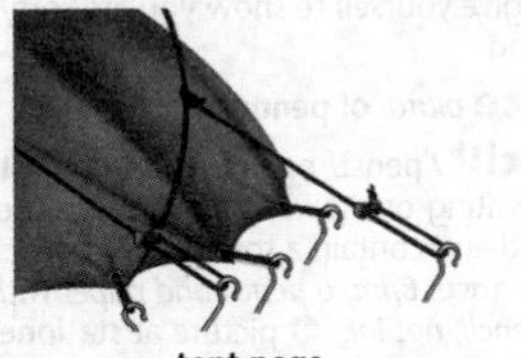

tent pegs

peg¹ /peg/ *noun* [C] **1** a piece of wood, metal, etc. on a wall or door that you hang your coat on **2** (also **tent peg**) a piece of metal that you push into the ground to keep one of the ropes of a tent in place **3** (also **ˈclothes peg**; *AmE* **ˈclothes pin**) a type of small wooden or plastic object used for fastening wet clothes to a clothes line

peg² /peg/ *verb* [T] (**pegging; pegged**) **1** **peg sth (out)** to fasten sth with a **peg** **2** **peg sth (at/to sth)** to fix or keep sth at a certain level: *Wage increases were pegged at 5%.*

pelican /ˈpelɪkən/ *noun* [C] a large bird that lives near water in warm countries. A **pelican** has a large beak that it uses for catching and holding fish.

pellet /ˈpelɪt/ *noun* [C] **1** a small hard ball of any substance, often of soft material that has become hard **2** a very small metal ball that is fired from a gun: *shotgun pellets*

pelt /pelt/ *verb* **1** [T] **pelt sb (with sth)** to attack sb/sth by throwing things **2** [I] **pelt (down)** (used about rain) to fall very heavily: *It's absolutely pelting down.* **3** [I] (*informal*) to run very fast: *Some kids pelted past us.*

pelvis /ˈpelvɪs/ *noun* [C] the set of wide bones at the bottom of your back, to which your leg bones are joined ➲ picture at **body** ▸ **pelvic** /ˈpelvɪk/ *adj*

🔑 **pen** /pen/ *noun* [C] **1** an object that you use for writing in ink: *a ballpoint/felt-tip/marker/fountain pen* **2** a small piece of ground with a fence around it that is used for keeping animals in: *a sheep pen*

P

penal /ˈpiːnl/ *adj* [only *before* a noun] connected with punishment by law: *the penal system*

penalize (also -ise) /ˈpiːnəlaɪz/ *verb* [T] **1** to punish sb for breaking a law or rule **2** to cause sb to have a disadvantage: *Children should not be penalized because their parents cannot afford to pay.*

penalty /ˈpenəlti/ *noun* [C] (*pl* penalties) **1** a punishment for breaking a law, rule or contract: *the death penalty* ◆ *What's the maximum penalty for using your mobile phone while driving?* **2** a disadvantage or sth unpleasant that happens as the result of sth: *I didn't work hard enough and I* ***paid the penalty****. I failed all my exams.* **3** (in sport) a punishment for one team and an advantage for the other team because a rule has been broken: *The referee awarded a penalty to the home team.*

the ˈpenalty area *noun* [C] the marked area in front of the goal in football

penance /ˈpenəns/ *noun* [C,U] a punishment that you give yourself to show you are sorry for doing sth wrong

pence *plural* of **penny**

pencil[1] /ˈpensl/ *noun* [C,U] an object that you use for writing or drawing. Pencils are usually made of wood and contain a thin stick of a black or coloured substance: *Bring a pencil and paper with you.* ◆ *Write* ***in pencil****, not ink.* ➲ picture at **stationery**

pencil[2] /ˈpensl/ *verb* [T] (pencilling; pencilled, (*AmE*) penciling; penciled) to write or draw with a pencil

PHR V pencil sth/sb in to write down the details of an arrangement that might have to be changed later: *Shall we pencil the next meeting in for the fourteenth?*

ˈpencil case *noun* [C] a small bag or box that you keep pens, pencils, etc. in

ˈpencil sharpener *noun* [C] a small device that you use for making pencils sharp ➲ picture at **stationery**

pendant /ˈpendənt/ *noun* [C] a small attractive object that you wear on a chain around your neck

pending /ˈpendɪŋ/ *adj, prep* (*formal*) **1** waiting to be done or decided: *The judge's decision is still pending.* **2** until sth happens: *He took over the leadership pending the elections.*

ˈpen drive = **flash drive**

pendulum /ˈpendjələm/ *noun* [C] **1** a chain or stick with a heavy weight at the bottom that moves regularly from side to side to work a clock **2** a way of describing a situation that changes from one thing to its opposite: *Since last year's election, the pendulum of public opinion has swung against the government.*

penetrate /ˈpenɪtreɪt/ *verb* [I,T] **1** to go through or into sth, especially when this is difficult: *The knife penetrated ten centimetres into his chest.* **2** to manage to understand sth difficult: *Scientists have still not penetrated the workings of the brain.* **3** to be understood or realized: *I was back at home when the meaning of her words finally penetrated.* ▶ **penetration** /ˌpenɪˈtreɪʃn/ *noun* [U]

penetrating /ˈpenɪtreɪtɪŋ/ *adj* **1** (used about sb's eyes or of a way of looking) making you feel uncomfortable because it seems sb knows what you are thinking: *a penetrating look/stare/gaze* ◆ *penetrating blue eyes* **2** showing that you have understood sth completely and quickly: *a penetrating question/comment* **3** loud and hard **4** spreading deeply or widely: *penetrating cold*

penfriend /ˈpenfrend/ (*especially AmE* ˈpen pal) *noun* [C] a person that you become friendly with by exchanging letters or emails, often a person who you have never met

penguin /ˈpeŋgwɪn/ *noun* [C] a black and white bird that cannot fly and that lives in the Antarctic

penguin

penicillin /ˌpenɪˈsɪlɪn/ *noun* [U] a substance that is used as a drug for preventing and treating infections caused by bacteria

peninsula /pəˈnɪnsjələ/ *noun* [C] an area of land that is almost surrounded by water

penis /ˈpiːnɪs/ *noun* [C] the male sex organ that is used for getting rid of waste liquid and for having sex

penitent /ˈpenɪtənt/ *adj* (*formal*) sorry for having done sth wrong

penitentiary /ˌpenɪˈtenʃəri/ *noun* [C] (*pl* penitentiaries) (*AmE*) a prison

penknife /ˈpennaɪf/ *noun* [C] (*pl* penknives /ˈpennaɪvz/) a small knife with one or more blades that fold away when not being used

penknife

penniless /ˈpeniləs/ *adj* having no money; poor

penny /ˈpeni/ *noun* [C] (*pl* pence /pens/ *or* pennies) **1** (*abbr* p) a small brown British coin. There are a hundred pence in a pound: *a fifty-pence piece/coin* **2** (*AmE*) a cent

> **MORE** In sense 1, **pennies** is used to refer to the coins, and **pence** to refer to an amount of money. In sense 2, the plural is **pennies**.

ˈpen pal (*especially AmE*) = **penfriend**

pension /ˈpenʃn/ *noun* [C] money that is paid regularly by a government or company to sb who has stopped working because of old age or who cannot work because they are ill: *The state pension age for men and women is 65.* ◆ *She lives on her pension and her savings.* ◆ *a disability/widow's* pension ◆ *a retirement/old-age pension* ➲ note at **retire** ▸ **pensioner** = **old-age pensioner**

pentagon /ˈpentəgən/ *noun* **1** [C] a shape that has five straight and equal sides **2 the Pentagon** [sing] a large government building near Washington DC in the US that contains the main offices of the US military forces; the military officials who work there

pentathlon /penˈtæθlən/ *noun* [C] a sports competition in which you have to take part in five different events ➲ look at **triathlon**

penthouse /ˈpenthaʊs/ *noun* [C] an expensive flat at the top of a tall building

pent-up /ˈpent ʌp/ *adj* [only *before* a noun] (used about feelings) that you hold inside and do not express: *pent-up anger*

penultimate /penˈʌltɪmət/ *adj* [only *before* a noun] (in a series) the one before the last one: *'Y' is the penultimate letter of the alphabet.*

⚷ **people** /ˈpiːpl/ *noun* **1** [pl] more than one person: *How many people are coming to the party?*

> **HELP** **People** or **persons**? **People** is almost always used instead of the plural form **persons**. **Persons** is very formal and is usually used in legal language: *Persons under the age of eighteen are not permitted to buy cigarettes.*

2 [C] (*pl* **peoples**) (*formal*) all the men, women and children who belong to a particular place or race: *The President addressed the American people.* ◆ *the French-speaking peoples of the world* **3 the people** [pl] the ordinary citizens of a country: *The President is popular because he listens to the people.* **4** [pl] men and women who work in a particular activity: *business/sports people*

⚷ **pepper¹** /ˈpepə(r)/ *noun* **1** [U] a black or white powder with a hot taste that is used for flavouring food: *salt and pepper* **2** [C] a green, red or yellow vegetable that is almost empty inside: *stuffed green peppers* ➲ picture on **page P15**

pepper² /ˈpepə(r)/ *verb* [T, usually passive] **pepper sb/sth with sth** to hit sb/sth with a series of small objects, especially bullets: *The wall had been peppered with bullets.*

peppermint /ˈpepəmɪnt/ *noun* **1** [U] a natural substance with a strong fresh flavour that is used in sweets and medicines **2** [C] (also **mint**) a sweet with a **peppermint** flavour ➲ look at **spearmint**

pep talk /ˈpep tɔːk/ *noun* [C] (*informal*) a speech that is given to encourage people or to make them work harder

⚷ **per** /pə(r); *strong form* pɜː(r)/ *prep* for each: *The speed limit is 110 kilometres per hour.* ◆ *Rooms cost 60 dollars per person per night.*

perceive /pəˈsiːv/ *verb* [T] (*formal*) **1** to notice or realize sth: *Scientists failed to perceive how dangerous the level of pollution had become.* **2** to understand or think of sth in a particular way: *I perceived his comments as a criticism.* **SYN** see ➲ *noun* **perception**

⚷ **per ˈcent** (*AmE* **percent**) *adj, adv, noun* [C, with sing or pl verb] (*pl* **per cent**) (*symbol* %) in or of each hundred; one part in every hundred: *There is a ten per cent service charge.* ◆ *You get 10% off if you pay cash.* ◆ *90% of the population owns a TV.* ◆ *The price of bread has gone up **by 50 per cent** in two years.*

percentage /pəˈsentɪdʒ/ *noun* [C, with sing or pl verb] the number, amount, rate, etc. of sth, expressed as if it is part of a total which is a hundred; a part or share of a whole: *What percentage of people voted in the last election?*

perceptible /pəˈseptəbl/ *adj* (*formal*) that can be seen or felt: *a barely perceptible change in colour* **OPP** **imperceptible** ▸ **perceptibly** /-əbli/ *adv*

perception /pəˈsepʃn/ *noun* (*formal*) **1** [U] the ability to notice or understand sth **2** [C] a particular way of looking at or understanding sth; an opinion: *What is your perception of the situation?* ➲ *verb* **perceive**

perceptive /pəˈseptɪv/ *adj* (*formal*) quick to notice or understand things: *She is very perceptive.* ▸ **perceptively** *adv*

perch¹ /pɜːtʃ/ *verb* **1** [I] (used about a bird) to sit on a branch, etc. **2** [I,T] to sit or be put on the edge of sth: *The house was perched on the edge of a cliff.*

perch² /pɜːtʃ/ *noun* [C] a place where a bird sits, especially a branch or a bar for this purpose

percussion /pəˈkʌʃn/ *noun* [U] drums and other instruments that you play by hitting them ➲ note at **instrument** ➲ picture at **music**

perennial /pəˈreniəl/ *adj* that happens often or that lasts for a long time: *a perennial problem*

⚷ **perfect¹** /ˈpɜːfɪkt/ *adj* **1** completely good; without faults or weaknesses: *The car is two years old but it is still in perfect condition.* **OPP** **imperfect** **2** **perfect (for sb/sth)** exactly suitable or right: *Ken would be perfect for the job.* **3** [only *before* a noun] complete; total: *What she was saying made perfect sense to me.* ◆ *a perfect stranger* **4** used to describe the tense of a verb that is formed with *has/have/had* and the past participle: *the present perfect tense* ▸ **perfectly** *adv*: *Laura understood perfectly what I meant.* ◆ *He played the piece of music perfectly.*

perfect² /pəˈfekt/ *verb* [T] to make sth perfect: *Vinay is spending a year in France to perfect his French.*

the ˈperfect = **the perfect tense**

perfection /pəˈfekʃn/ *noun* [U] the state of being perfect or without fault: *The steak was cooked **to perfection**.*

perfectionist /pəˈfekʃənɪst/ *noun* [C] a person who always does things as well as they possibly can and who expects others to do the same

the ˈperfect tense (also **the ˈperfect**) *noun* [sing] the tense of a verb that is formed with *has/have/had* and the past participle: *'I have finished' is in the present perfect tense.* ⓘ For more information about the perfect tense, look at the **Reference Section** at the back of this dictionary.

perforate /ˈpɜːfəreɪt/ *verb* [T] to make a hole or holes in sth

perforation /ˌpɜːfəˈreɪʃn/ *noun* **1** [C] a series of small holes in paper, etc. that make it easy for you to tear it **2** [U] the act of making a hole or holes in sth

perform /pəˈfɔːm/ *verb* **1** [T] (*formal*) to do a piece of work or sth that you have been ordered to do: *to perform an operation/an experiment/a task* **2** [I,T] to take part in a play or to sing, dance, etc. in front of an audience: *She is currently performing at the National Theatre.* **3** [I] perform (well/badly/poorly) to work or function well or badly: *The company has not been performing well recently.*
IDM **work/perform miracles** ➲ **miracle**

performance /pəˈfɔːməns/ *noun* **1** [C] the act of performing sth in front of an audience; something that you perform: *What time does the performance start?* **2** [C] the way a person performs in a play, concert, etc: *His moving performance in the film won him an Oscar.* **3** [C,U] the way in which you do sth, especially how successful you are: *The company's performance was disappointing last year.* **4** [U] (used about a machine, etc.) how well or badly sth works: *a car with outstanding performance* **5** [U, sing] (*formal*) the act or process of doing a task, an action, etc: *the performance of your duties*

performer /pəˈfɔːmə(r)/ *noun* [C] **1** a person who performs for an audience: *a brilliant performer* **2** a person or thing that behaves or works in the way mentioned: *Diana is a poor performer in exams.*

the perˌforming ˈarts *noun* [pl] arts such as music, dance and drama which are performed for an audience

P

perfume /ˈpɜːfjuːm/ *noun* [C,U] **1** (*BrE also* scent) a liquid with a sweet smell that you put on your body to make yourself smell nice: *Are you wearing perfume?* **2** a pleasant, often sweet, smell: *The flowers had a delicate perfume.* ➲ note at **smell²**

perhaps /pəˈhæps; præps/ *adv* (used when you are not sure about sth) possibly: *Perhaps he's forgotten.* • *She was, perhaps, one of the most famous writers of the time.* SYN **maybe**

> HELP **Perhaps** and **maybe** are often used to make something sound more polite: *Perhaps/Maybe it would be better if you came back tomorrow* (= Please come back tomorrow).

peril /ˈperəl/ *noun* (*formal*) **1** [U] great danger: *A lack of trained nurses is putting patients' lives* ***in peril.*** **2** [C] something that is very dangerous: *the perils of drug abuse* ▶ **perilous** /ˈperələs/ *adj* ➲ More common words are **danger** and **dangerous**.

perimeter /pəˈrɪmɪtə(r)/ *noun* [C] the outside edge or limit of an area of land: *the perimeter fence of the army camp*

period /ˈpɪəriəd/ *noun* [C] **1** a length of time: *The scheme will be introduced for a six-month trial period.* • *Her son is going through a difficult period at the moment.* • *What period of history are you most interested in?* **2** a lesson in school: *We have five periods of English a week.* **3** the time every month when a woman loses blood from her body: *When did you last have a period?* **4** (*especially AmE*) = **full stop**

periodic /ˌpɪəriˈɒdɪk/ (also **periodical**) *adj* happening regularly and fairly often: *We have periodic meetings to check on progress.* ▶ **periodically** /-kli/ *adv*: *All machines need to be checked periodically.*

periodical /ˌpɪəriˈɒdɪkl/ *noun* [C] (*formal*) a magazine that is produced regularly

peripheral¹ /pəˈrɪfərəl/ *adj* **1** (*formal*) peripheral (to sth) not as important as the main aim, part, etc. of sth: *peripheral information* • *Fund-raising is peripheral to their main activities.* **2** (*technical*) connected with the edge of a particular area: *the peripheral nervous system* • *peripheral vision*

peripheral² /pəˈrɪfərəl/ *noun* [C] a piece of equipment that is connected to a computer: *monitors, printers and other peripherals*

periphery /pəˈrɪfəri/ *noun* [C, usually sing] (*pl* peripheries) (*formal*) **1** the outer edge of a particular area: *industrial development* ***on the periphery of*** *the town* **2** the less important part of sth, for example of a particular activity or of a social or political group: *minor parties* ***on the periphery of*** *American politics*

periscope /ˈperɪskəʊp/ *noun* [C] a device like a long tube, containing mirrors, used especially in a **submarine** (= a type of ship that can travel underwater) to see above the surface of the sea

perish /ˈperɪʃ/ *verb* [I] (*formal*) to die or be destroyed: *Thousands perished in the war.*

perishable /ˈperɪʃəbl/ *adj* (used about food) that will go bad quickly

perjury /ˈpɜːdʒəri/ *noun* [U] (*formal*) the act of telling a lie in a court of law ▶ **perjure** /ˈpɜːdʒə(r)/ *verb* [T] perjure yourself: *She admitted that she had perjured herself while giving evidence.*

perk¹ /pɜːk/ *noun* [C] (*informal*) something extra that you get from your employer in addition to money: *Travelling abroad is one of the perks of the job.*

perk² /pɜːk/ *verb*
PHR V **perk (sb/sth) up** (*informal*) to become happier; to make sb/sth become happier and have more energy

perm /pɜːm/ *noun* [C] the treatment of hair with special chemicals in order to make it curly ➲ look at **wave** ▶ **perm** *verb* [T]: *She has had her hair permed.*

permanent /ˈpɜːmənənt/ *adj* lasting for a long time or for ever; that will not change: *The accident left him with a permanent scar.* • *Are you looking for a permanent or a temporary job?* ▶ **permanence** *noun* [U] ▶ **permanently** *adv*: *Has she left permanently?*

permissible /pəˈmɪsəbl/ *adj* (*formal*) permissible (for sb) (to do sth) that is allowed by law or by a set of rules: *It is not permissible for banks to release their customers' personal details.*

permission /pəˈmɪʃn/ *noun* [U] permission (for sth); permission (for sb) (to do sth) the act of allowing sb to do sth, especially when this is done by sb in a position of authority: *I'm afraid you can't leave* *without permission.* ◆ *to* ***ask/give permission*** *for something*

HELP Be careful. **Permission** is uncountable. A document which says that you are allowed to do something is a **permit**.

permissive /pəˈmɪsɪv/ *adj* having, allowing or showing a lot of freedom that many people do not approve of, especially in sexual matters

permit[1] /pəˈmɪt/ *verb* (permitting; permitted) **1** [T] (*formal*) to allow sb to do sth or to allow sth to happen: *You are not permitted to smoke in the hospital.* ◆ *You are not permitted to use mobile phones in the hospital.* ◆ *His visa does not permit him to work.* ➲ note at **allow** **2** [I,T] to make sth possible: *Let's have a barbecue at the weekend,* ***weather permitting.***

permit[2] /ˈpɜːmɪt/ *noun* [C] an official document that says you are allowed to do sth, especially for a limited period of time: *Next month I'll have to apply for a new* ***work permit.***

perpendicular /ˌpɜːpənˈdɪkjələ(r)/ *adj* **1** at an angle of 90° to sth: *Are the lines perpendicular to each other?* ➲ look at **horizontal**, **vertical** **2** pointing straight up: *The path was almost perpendicular* (= it was very steep).

perpetrate /ˈpɜːpətreɪt/ *verb* [T] (*formal*) perpetrate sth (against/upon/on sb) to commit a crime or do sth wrong or evil: *to perpetrate a crime/fraud/massacre* ◆ *violence perpetrated against women and children*

perpetual /pəˈpetʃuəl/ *adj* **1** continuing for a long period of time without stopping: *They lived in perpetual fear of losing their jobs.* **2** repeated many times in a way which is annoying: *How can I work with these perpetual interruptions?* ▶ **perpetually** /-tʃuəli/ *adv*

perpetuate /pəˈpetʃueɪt/ *verb* [T] (*formal*) to cause sth to continue for a long time: *to perpetuate an argument*

perplexed /pəˈplekst/ *adj* not understanding sth; confused

persecute /ˈpɜːsɪkjuːt/ *verb* [T] **1** [often passive] persecute sb (for sth) to treat sb in a cruel and unfair way, especially because of race, religion or political beliefs: *persecuted minorities* **2** to deliberately annoy sb and make their life unpleasant ▶ **persecution** /ˌpɜːsɪˈkjuːʃn/ *noun* [C,U]: *the persecution of minorities* ▶ **persecutor** /ˈpɜːsɪkjuːtə(r)/ *noun* [C]

persevere /ˌpɜːsɪˈvɪə(r)/ *verb* [I] persevere (at/in/with sth) to continue trying to do or achieve sth that is difficult: *The treatment is painful but I'm going to persevere with it.* ▶ **perseverance** *noun* [U]

persist /pəˈsɪst/ *verb* [I] **1** persist (in sth/doing sth) to continue doing sth even though other people say that you are wrong or that you should not do it: *If you persist in making so much noise, I shall call the police.* **2** to continue to exist: *If your symptoms persist you should consult your doctor.* ▶ **persistence** *noun* [U]: *Finally her persistence was rewarded and she got exactly what she wanted.*

persistent /pəˈsɪstənt/ *adj* **1** determined to continue doing sth even though people say that you are wrong or that you should not do it: *Some salesmen can be very persistent.* **2** lasting for a long time or happening often: *a persistent cough* ▶ **persistently** *adv*

person /ˈpɜːsn/ *noun* [C] (*pl* **people**) **1** a man or woman; a human being: *I would like to speak to the person in charge.* ◆ *He's just the person we need for the job.* ➲ note at **people**

HELP In very formal or official cases the plural of *person* can be **persons**.

2 -person [in compounds] a person doing the job mentioned: *a salesperson/spokesperson* **3** one of the three types of pronoun in grammar. *I/we* are the first person, *you* is the second person and *he/she/it/they* are the third person.

IDM **in person** seeing or speaking to sb face to face (not speaking on the telephone or writing a letter, etc.): *I went to apologise to her in person.*

personal /ˈpɜːsənl/ *adj*

➤YOUR OWN **1** [only *before* a noun] of or belonging to one particular person: *personal belongings* ◆ *Judges should not let their* ***personal feelings*** *influence their decisions.*

➤FEELINGS, ETC. **2** connected with your feelings, health or relationships with other people: *I should like to speak to you in private. I have something personal to discuss.* ◆ *Do you mind if I ask you a* ***personal question****?*

➤NOT OFFICIAL **3** not connected with sb's job or official position: *Please keep personal phone calls to a minimum.* ◆ *I try not to let work interfere with my* ***personal life.***

➤DONE BY PERSON **4** [only *before* a noun] done by a particular person rather than by sb who is acting for them: *The Prime Minister made a personal visit to the victims in hospital.*

➤FOR EACH PERSON **5** [only *before* a noun] made or done for one particular person rather than for a large group of people or for people in general: *We offer a personal service to all our customers.*

➤APPEARANCE/CHARACTER **6** speaking about sb's appearance or character in an unpleasant or unfriendly way: *It started as a general discussion but then people started to* ***get personal*** *and an argument began.* **7** [only *before* a noun] connected with the body: *personal hygiene* ◆ *She's always worrying about her personal appearance.*

ˌpersonal asˈsistant = PA

ˌpersonal comˈputer = PC(1)

personality /ˌpɜːsəˈnæləti/ *noun* (*pl* **personalities**) **1** [C,U] the different qualities of sb's character that make them different from other people: *The children all have very different personalities.* **2** [U] the quality of having a strong, interesting and attractive character: *A good entertainer needs a lot of personality.* **3** [C] a famous person (especially in sport, on TV, etc.): *a TV personality* **SYN** **celebrity**

P

personalize (also -ise) /ˈpɜːsənəlaɪz/ *verb* [T] to mark sth in some way to show that it belongs to you: *Their towels were personalized with their initials.*

personally /ˈpɜːsənəli/ *adv* **1** used to show that you are expressing your own opinion: *Personally, I think that nurses deserve more money.* **2** done by you yourself, not by sb else acting for you: *I will deal with this matter personally.* **3** in a way that is connected with one particular person rather than a group of people: *I wasn't talking about you personally—I meant all teachers.* **4** in a way that is intended to offend: *Please don't* ***take it personally****, but I would just rather be alone this evening.* **5** in a way that is connected with sb's private life, rather than their job: *Have you had any dealings with any of the suspects, either personally or professionally?*

ˌpersonal ˈpronoun *noun* [C] any of the pronouns *I, me, she, her, he, him, we, us, you, they, them*

ˌpersonal ˈstereo *noun* [C] a small piece of equipment with **headphones** (= a piece of equipment worn over or in the ears) that you can carry with you in order to listen to music

ˌpersonal ˈtrainer *noun* [C] a person who is paid by sb to help them exercise, especially by deciding what types of exercise are best for them

personify /pəˈsɒnɪfaɪ/ *verb* [T] (personifying; personifies; *pt, pp* personified) **1** to be an example in human form of a particular quality: *She is kindness personified.* **2** to describe an object or a feeling as if it were a person: *The river was personified as a goddess.* ▶ **personification** /pəˌsɒnɪfɪˈkeɪʃn/ *noun* [C,U]

P

personnel /ˌpɜːsəˈnel/ *noun* **1** [pl] the people who work for a large organization or one of the armed forces: *sales/medical/technical personnel* **2** (also personˈnel department) [U, with sing or pl verb] the department of a large company or organization that deals with employing and training people: *Personnel is/are currently reviewing pay scales.* SYN **human resources**

perspective /pəˈspektɪv/ *noun* **1** [C] your opinion or attitude towards sth: *Try and look at this from my perspective.* **2** [U] the ability to think about problems and decisions in a reasonable way without exaggerating them: *Hearing about others' experiences often helps to* ***put*** *your own problems* ***into perspective*** (= makes them seem less important than you thought). ◆ *Try to* ***keep*** *these issues* ***in perspective*** (= do not exaggerate them). **3** [U] the art of drawing on a flat surface so that some objects appear to be further away than others

perspire /pəˈspaɪə(r)/ *verb* [I] (*formal*) to lose liquid through your skin when you are hot ▶ **perspiration** /ˌpɜːspəˈreɪʃn/ *noun* [U] ➲ A more common word is **sweat**.

persuade /pəˈsweɪd/ *verb* [T] **1** persuade sb (to do sth); persuade sb (into sth/doing sth) to make sb do sth by giving them good reasons: *It was difficult to persuade Louise to change her mind.* ◆ *We eventually persuaded Sanjay into coming with us.* OPP **dissuade** **2** (*formal*) persuade sb that ...; persuade sb (of sth) to make sb believe sth: *She had persuaded herself that she was going to fail.* ◆ *The jury was not persuaded of her innocence.* ➲ look at **convince**

persuasion /pəˈsweɪʒn/ *noun* **1** [U] the act of persuading sb to do sth or to believe sth: *It took a lot of persuasion to get Alan to agree.* **2** [C] (*formal*) a religious or political belief: *politicians of all persuasions*

persuasive /pəˈsweɪsɪv/ *adj* able to persuade sb to do or believe sth: *the persuasive power of advertising* ▶ **persuasively** *adv* ▶ **persuasiveness** *noun* [U]

pertinent /ˈpɜːtɪnənt/ *adj* (*formal*) closely connected with the subject being discussed: *to ask a pertinent question*

perturb /pəˈtɜːb/ *verb* [T] (*formal*) to make sb worried or upset ▶ **perturbed** *adj*

pervade /pəˈveɪd/ *verb* [T] (*formal*) to spread through and be noticeable in every part of sth: *A sadness pervades most of her novels.*

pervasive /pəˈveɪsɪv/ *adj* that is present in all parts of sth: *a pervasive mood of pessimism*

perverse /pəˈvɜːs/ *adj* (*formal*) liking to behave in a way that is not acceptable or reasonable or that most people think is wrong: *Derek gets perverse pleasure from shocking his parents.* ▶ **perversely** *adv* ▶ **perversity** /pəˈvɜːsəti/ *noun* [U]

perversion /pəˈvɜːʃn/ *noun* [U,C] **1** sexual behaviour that is not considered normal or acceptable by most people **2** the act of changing sth from right to wrong or from good to bad: *That statement is a perversion of the truth.*

pervert[1] /pəˈvɜːt/ *verb* [T] **1** to change a system, process, etc. in a bad way: *to pervert the course of justice* (= to deliberately prevent the police from finding out the truth about a crime) **2** to cause sb to think or behave in a way that is not moral or acceptable

pervert[2] /ˈpɜːvɜːt/ *noun* [C] a person whose sexual behaviour is not thought to be natural or normal by most people

pessimism /ˈpesɪmɪzəm/ *noun* [U] pessimism (about/over sth) the state of expecting or believing that bad things will happen and that things will not be successful OPP **optimism** ▶ **pessimistic** /ˌpesɪˈmɪstɪk/ *adj* ▶ **pessimistically** /-kli/ *adv*

pessimist /ˈpesɪmɪst/ *noun* [C] a person who always thinks that bad things will happen or that things will be not be successful OPP **optimist**

pest /pest/ *noun* [C] **1** an insect or an animal that destroys plants, food, etc. **2** (*informal*) a person or thing that annoys you: *That child is such a pest!*

pester /ˈpestə(r)/ *verb* [T] pester sb (for sth); pester sb (to do sth) to annoy sb, for example by asking them sth many times: *to pester somebody for money* ◆ *The kids kept pestering me to take them to the park.*

pesticide /ˈpestɪsaɪd/ *noun* [C,U] a chemical substance that is used for killing animals, especially insects, that eat food crops ➲ look at **insecticide**

pestle /ˈpesl/ *noun* [C] a small heavy tool with a round end used for crushing some foods or substances in a **mortar** (= a hard bowl) ➲ picture at **squeeze**

pet /pet/ *noun* [C] **1** an animal or bird that you keep in your home for pleasure rather than for food or work: *a pet dog/cat/hamster* • *a pet shop* (= where pets are sold) **2** a person who is treated better because they are liked more than any others: *She's the teacher's pet.*

TOPIC

Pets

Dogs, cats, rabbits, hamsters and **guinea pigs** are all popular pets. **Goldfish** are kept in **tanks**, and **budgerigars** (= a type of bird) in **cages**. Some people keep **exotic** pets, such as **snakes**. Some pets love being **stroked**, but they might **scratch** or **bite** if they are frightened. If you **have a pet**, you need to **look after** it. You should **feed** it, **groom** it and take it to the **vet** (= animal doctor). If an animal is very ill, the vet might have to **put** it **down** (= kill it) to stop it suffering.

petal /ˈpetl/ *noun* [C] one of the thin soft coloured parts of a flower ➲ picture at **plant**

ˌpet ˈhate *noun* [C] something that you particularly do not like: *Filling in forms is one of my pet hates.*

petition /pəˈtɪʃn/ *noun* [C] a written document, signed by many people, that asks a government, etc. to do or change sth: *More than 50 000 people signed the petition protesting about the new road.* • *I signed an* ***online petition*** *against changes to the health service.* ▶ **petition** *verb* [I,T]

petrified /ˈpetrɪfaɪd/ *adj* very frightened

petrol /ˈpetrəl/ (*AmE* **gas**; **gasoline**) *noun* [U] the liquid that is used as fuel for vehicles such as cars and motorbikes ➲ note at **car** ➲ look at **diesel**

petroleum /pəˈtrəʊliəm/ *noun* [U] mineral oil that is found under the ground or sea and is used to make petrol, plastic and other types of chemical substances

ˈpetrol station (also ˈ**service station**; *AmE* **gas station**) *noun* [C] a place where you can buy petrol and other things for your car ➲ look at **garage**

petty /ˈpeti/ *adj* **1** small and unimportant: *He didn't want to get involved with the petty details.* • *petty crime/theft* (= that is not very serious) SYN **minor 2** unkind or unpleasant to other people (for a reason that does not seem very important): *petty jealousy/revenge*

pew /pjuː/ *noun* [C] a long wooden seat in a church

pewter /ˈpjuːtə(r)/ *noun* [U] a grey metal made by mixing tin with **lead** (= a soft heavy metal), used especially in the past for making cups, dishes, etc.; objects made from this metal

PG /ˌpiː ˈdʒiː/ *abbr* (*BrE*) (used about films which are not suitable for children to watch without an adult) **parental guidance**

pH /ˌpiː ˈeɪtʃ/ *noun* [sing] a measurement of the level of acid or **alkali** in a substance. In the pH range of 0 to 14 a reading of below 7 shows an acid and one of above 7 shows an **alkali**.

phantom /ˈfæntəm/ *noun* [C] **1** (*written*) the spirit of a dead person that is seen or heard by sb who is still living ➲ A more common word is **ghost**. **2** something that you think exists, but that is not real

pharmaceutical /ˌfɑːməˈsuːtɪkl; -ˈsjuː-/ *adj* [only *before* a noun] connected with the production of medicines and drugs: *pharmaceutical companies*

pharmacist /ˈfɑːməsɪst/ = **chemist**(1)

pharmacy /ˈfɑːməsi/ *noun* (*pl* **pharmacies**) **1** [C] a shop or part of a shop where medicines and drugs are prepared and sold

MORE A shop that sells medicine is also called a **chemist's (shop)** in British English or a **drugstore** in American English.

2 [U] the preparation of medicines and drugs

phase¹ /feɪz/ *noun* [C] a stage in the development of sb/sth: *Julie went through a difficult phase when she started school.*

phase² /feɪz/ *verb*

PHR V **phase sth in** to introduce or start using sth gradually in stages over a period of time: *The tax system was phased in over two years.*

phase sth out to stop using sth gradually in stages over a period of time: *The older machines are gradually being phased out and replaced by new ones.*

PhD /ˌpiː eɪtʃ ˈdiː/ *abbr* **Doctor of Philosophy**; an advanced university degree that you receive when you complete a piece of research into a special subject: *She has a PhD in History.*

pheasant /ˈfeznt/ *noun* [C] (*pl* **pheasants** or **pheasant**) a type of bird with a long tail. The males have brightly coloured feathers. **Pheasants** are often shot for sport and eaten.

phenomenal /fəˈnɒmɪnl/ *adj* very great or impressive: *phenomenal success* ▶ **phenomenally** /-nəli/ *adv*

phenomenon /fəˈnɒmɪnən/ *noun* [C] (*pl* **phenomena** /-ɪnə/) a fact or an event in nature or society, especially one that is not fully understood: *Acid rain is not a natural phenomenon. It is caused by pollution.*

phew /fjuː/ *exclam* a sound which you make to show that you are hot, tired or happy that sth bad did not happen or has finished: *Phew, it's hot!* • *Phew, I'm glad that interview's over!*

philanthropist /fɪˈlænθrəpɪst/ *noun* [C] a rich person who helps the poor and those in need, especially by giving money

philanthropy /fɪˈlænθrəpi/ *noun* [U] the practice of helping the poor and those in need, especially by giving money ▶ **philanthropic** /ˌfɪlənˈθrɒpɪk/ *adj*: *philanthropic work*

philosopher /fəˈlɒsəfə(r)/ *noun* [C] a person who has developed a set of ideas and beliefs about the meaning of life: *the Greek philosopher Aristotle*

P

philosophical /ˌfɪləˈsɒfɪkl/ (also **philosophic**) *adj* **1** connected with **philosophy**: *a philosophical debate* **2 philosophical (about sth)** staying calm and not getting upset or worried about sth bad that happens: *He is quite philosophical about failing the exam and says he will try again next year.* ▶ **philosophically** /-kli/ *adv*

philosophy /fəˈlɒsəfi/ *noun* (*pl* **philosophies**) **1** [U] the study of ideas and beliefs about the meaning of life: *a degree in philosophy* **2** [C] a set of beliefs that tries to explain the meaning of life or give rules about how to behave: *Her philosophy is 'If a job's worth doing, it's worth doing well'.*

phishing /ˈfɪʃɪŋ/ *noun* [U] the activity of tricking people by getting them to give their identity, bank account numbers, etc. over the Internet or by email, and then using these to steal money from them ➲ note at **cybercrime**

phlegm /flem/ *noun* [U] the thick substance that is produced in your nose and throat when you have a cold

phlegmatic /flegˈmætɪk/ *adj* (*formal*) not easily made angry or upset; calm

phobia /ˈfəʊbiə/ *noun* [C] a very strong fear or hatred that you cannot explain: *She **has a phobia about** flying.* ◆ *arachnophobia* (= fear of spiders)

phone /fəʊn/ *noun* (*informal*) **1** [U] = **telephone** (1): *a phone conversation* ◆ *You can book the tickets by phone/over the phone.* **2** [C] = **telephone**(2): *The phone is ringing—could you answer it?* ◆ *Could everyone switch off their phones before we start?* ➲ note at **telephone, mobile phone, smartphone**

IDM on the phone/telephone 1 using the telephone: *He's been on the phone to Kate for more than an hour.* **2** having a phone in your home: *They're not on the phone at their holiday cottage.*

▶ **phone** *verb* [I,T]: *Did anybody phone while I was out?* ◆ *Could you phone the restaurant and book a table?* ◆ *I'm busy at the moment, so can I phone you back later?* **SYN ring, call**

ˈphone book = **telephone directory**

ˈphone box = **telephone box**

ˈphone call = **call**[2](1)

phonecard /ˈfəʊnkɑːd/ *noun* [C] a small plastic card that you can use in some telephones instead of money

ˈphone hacking *noun* [U] the practice of secretly looking at or listening to information on sb else's mobile phone: *The journalist admitted five charges of phone hacking while working for the paper.* ◆ *the phone hacking scandal*

ˈphone-in *noun* [C] a radio or TV programme during which you can ask a question or give your opinion by telephone

phonetic /fəˈnetɪk/ *adj* **1** (used about spelling) having a close relationship with the sounds represented: *Spanish spelling is phonetic, unlike English spelling.* **2** connected with the sounds of human speech; using special symbols to represent these sounds: *the phonetic alphabet* ▶ **phonetically** /-kli/ *adv*

phonetics /fəˈnetɪks/ *noun* [U] the study of the sounds of human speech

phoney (*AmE* **phony**) /ˈfəʊni/ *adj* (*informal*) (**phonier; phoniest**) not real: *She spoke with a phoney Russian accent.* **SYN fake** ▶ **phoney** (*AmE* **phony**) *noun* [C]

photo /ˈfəʊtəʊ/ (*pl* **photos** /-təʊz/) = **photograph**: *Shall I **take your photo**?* ◆ *a photo album*

photocopier /ˈfəʊtəʊkɒpiə(r)/ (*especially AmE* **copier**) *noun* [C] a machine that makes copies of documents by photographing them

photocopy /ˈfəʊtəʊkɒpi/ *noun* [C] (*pl* **photocopies**) a copy of a document, a page in a book, etc. that is made by a **photocopier** **SYN Xerox™** ➲ look at **copy** ▶ **photocopy** *verb* (also **copy**) [I,T] (**photocopying; photocopies**; *pt, pp* **photocopied**)

photograph /ˈfəʊtəgrɑːf/ (also **photo**) *noun* [C] a picture that is taken with a camera: *to take a photograph* ◆ *She looks younger in real life than she did **in the photograph**.* ➲ note at **camera** ➲ look at **negative, slide** ▶ **photograph** *verb* [T]

photographer /fəˈtɒgrəfə(r)/ *noun* [C] a person who takes photographs: *a fashion/wildlife photographer* ➲ look at **cameraman**

photographic /ˌfəʊtəˈgræfɪk/ *adj* connected with photographs or **photography**

photography /fəˈtɒgrəfi/ *noun* [U] the skill or process of taking photographs: *wildlife photography* ➲ picture on **page P3**

photosynthesis /ˌfəʊtəʊˈsɪnθəsɪs/ *noun* [U] the process by which green plants turn **carbon dioxide** (= a gas) and water into food using energy obtained from light from the sun

phrasal verb /ˌfreɪzl ˈvɜːb/ *noun* [C] a verb that is combined with an adverb or a preposition to give a new meaning, such as 'look after' or 'put off' ➲ look at **verb**

phrase[1] /freɪz/ *noun* [C] a group of words that are used together. A phrase does not contain a full verb: *'First of all' and 'a bar of chocolate' are phrases.* ➲ look at **sentence**

phrase[2] /freɪz/ *verb* [T] to express sth in a particular way: *The statement was phrased so that it would offend no one.*

ˈphrase book *noun* [C] a book that gives common words and useful phrases in a foreign language. People often use phrase books when they travel to another country whose language they do not know.

physical /ˈfɪzɪkl/ *adj* **1** connected with your body rather than your mind: *physical fitness/strength/disabilities* **2** [only *before* a noun] connected with real things that you can touch, or with the laws of nature: *physical geography* (= the natural features on the face of the earth) **3** [only *before* a noun] connected with physics: *physical chemistry/laws* ▶ **physically** /-kli/ *adv*: *to be physically fit* ◆ *It will be physically impossible to get to London before ten.*

ˌ**physical ˈtherapy** (*AmE*) = **physiotherapy**

physician /fɪˈzɪʃn/ (*especially AmE formal*) = **doctor**[1] (1)

physicist /ˈfɪzɪsɪst/ *noun* [C] a person who studies or is an expert in physics

⚷ **physics** /ˈfɪzɪks/ *noun* [U] the scientific study of natural forces such as light, sound, heat, electricity, pressure, etc. ➲ note at **science**: *the laws of physics* ◆ *a school physics department*

physiology /ˌfɪziˈɒlədʒi/ *noun* [U] **1** the scientific study of the normal functions of living things: *the department of anatomy and physiology* **2** the way in which a particular living thing functions: *the physiology of the horse* ◆ *plant physiology* ▶ **physiological** /ˌfɪziəˈlɒdʒɪkl/ *adj*: *the physiological effect of space travel* ▶ **physiologically** /-kli/ *adv*

physiotherapist /ˌfɪziəʊˈθerəpɪst/ *noun* [C] a person who is trained to use **physiotherapy**

physiotherapy /ˌfɪziəʊˈθerəpi/ (*AmE* ˌphysical ˈtherapy) *noun* [U] the treatment of disease or injury by exercise, light, heat, **massage** (= rubbing the muscles), etc.

physique /fɪˈziːk/ *noun* [C] the size and shape of sb's body: *a strong muscular physique* **SYN** **build**

pianist /ˈpɪənɪst/ *noun* [C] a person who plays the piano

pianos

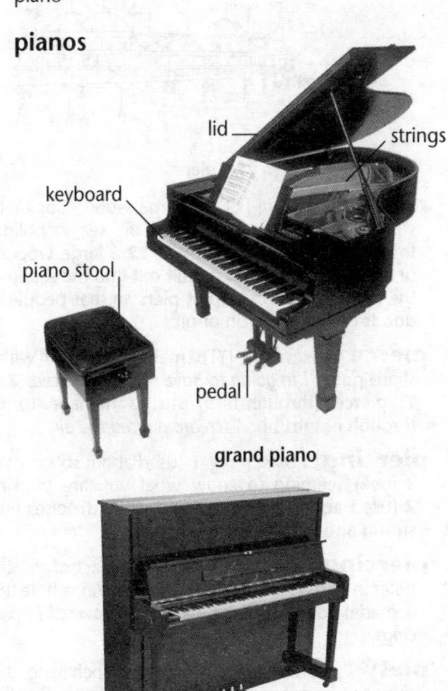

grand piano

upright piano

⚷ **piano** /piˈænəʊ/ *noun* [C] (*pl* **pianos** /-nəʊz/) a large musical instrument that you play by pressing down black and white keys: *an upright piano* ◆ *a grand piano*

piccolo /ˈpɪkələʊ/ *noun* [C] (*pl* **piccolos**) a small **flute** (= a musical instrument that you hold sideways and blow into) that plays high notes ➲ picture at **music**

⚷ **pick**[1] /pɪk/ *verb* [T] **1** to choose sb/sth from a group of people or things: *They picked Giles as their captain.* ◆ *Have I picked a bad time to visit?* ➲ look at **select** **2** to take a flower, fruit or vegetable from the place where it is growing: *to pick flowers/grapes/cotton* **3** to remove a small piece or pieces of sth with your fingers: *Don't pick your nose!* ◆ *She picked a hair off her jacket.*

IDM **have a bone to pick with sb** ➲ **bone**[1]

pick and choose to choose only the things that you like or want very much

pick a fight (with sb) to start a fight with sb deliberately

pick a lock to open a lock without using a key

pick sb's pocket to steal money, etc. from sb's pocket or bag

pick your way across, over, through, etc. sth to walk carefully, choosing the best places to put your feet: *She picked her way over the rough ground.*

PHR V **pick at sth** **1** to eat only small amounts of food because you are not hungry **2** to touch sth many times with your fingers

pick on sb to behave unfairly or in a cruel way towards sb

pick sb/sth out to choose or recognize sb/sth from a number of people or things; identify: *I immediately picked Jean out in the photo.*

pick up to become better; to improve

pick up speed to get faster

pick sb up to collect sb, in a car, etc: *We've ordered a taxi to pick us up at ten.*

pick sb/sth up to take hold of and lift sb/sth: *Lucy picked up the child and gave him a cuddle.*

pick sth up **1** to learn sth without formal lessons: *Joe picked up a few words of Spanish on holiday.* **2** to go and get sth; to collect sth: *I have to pick up my jacket from the cleaner's.* **3** to get or find sth: *I picked up this book at the market.* **4** to receive an electronic signal, sound or picture: *We were able to pick up the BBC World Service in Delhi.*

pick[2] /pɪk/ *noun* **1** [sing] the one that you choose; your choice: *You can have whichever cake you like. Take your pick.* **2** [sing] the best of a group: *You can see **the pick of** the new films at this year's festival.* **3** = **pickaxe** **4** = **plectrum**

pickaxe /ˈpɪkæks/ (*AmE* **pickax**, **pick**) *noun* [C] a tool that consists of a curved iron bar with sharp points at both ends, fixed onto a wooden handle. **Pickaxes** are used for breaking stones or hard ground.

picket /ˈpɪkɪt/ *noun* [C] a worker or group of workers who stand outside the entrance to a building to protest about sth, especially in order to stop people entering a factory, etc. during a strike ▶ **picket** *verb* [I,T]

P

pickle /ˈpɪkl/ *noun* **1** [C, usually pl] a vegetable that is cooked and put in salt water or **vinegar** (= a liquid with a strong sharp taste), served cold with meat, salads, etc. **2** [U] (*BrE*) a cold thick sauce made from fruit and vegetables, that is served with meat, cheese, etc: *a cheese and pickle sandwich* ▶ **pickle** *verb* [T]: *pickled onions*

pickpocket /ˈpɪkpɒkɪt/ *noun* [C] a person who steals things from other people's pockets or bags in public places

pickup /ˈpɪkʌp/ (also ˈ**pickup truck**) *noun* [C] a type of vehicle that has an open part with low sides at the back

picky /ˈpɪki/ *adj* (*informal*) (used about a person) liking only certain things and difficult to please ➲ look at **fussy**

picnic /ˈpɪknɪk/ *noun* [C] a meal that you take with you to eat outdoors: *We had a picnic on the beach.* ➲ note at **meal** ▶ **picnic** *verb* [I] (picnicking; picnicked)

pictorial /pɪkˈtɔːriəl/ *adj* expressed in pictures: *pictorial representations of objects*

picture[1] /ˈpɪktʃə(r)/ *noun* [C] **1** a painting, drawing or photograph: *Who painted the picture in the hall?* ◆ *The teacher asked us to* ***draw a picture*** *of our families.* ◆ *Have you got any pictures of your trip?* ➲ picture on **page P8** **2** an image on a TV screen: *They showed pictures of the crash on the news.* **3** a description of sth that gives you a good idea of what it is like: *The police are trying to build up a picture of exactly what happened.*

picture[2] /ˈpɪktʃə(r)/ *verb* [T] **1 picture sb/sth (as sth)** to imagine sb/sth in your mind: *I can't picture Ivan as a father.* **2** [usually passive] to show sb/sth in a photograph or picture: *She is pictured here with her parents.*

picturesque /ˌpɪktʃəˈresk/ *adj* (usually used about an old building or place) attractive: *a picturesque fishing village*

pie /paɪ/ *noun* [C,U] meat, vegetables or fruit baked in a dish with **pastry** (= a mixture of flour, fat and water) on the bottom, sides and top: *apple pie* ◆ *meat pie* ➲ picture on **page P16**

piece[1] /piːs/ *noun* [C]
➤SEPARATE AMOUNT **1** an amount or example of sth: *a piece of paper* ◆ *a piece of furniture* ◆ *a good piece of work* ◆ *a piece of information/advice/news*
➤PART OF STH **2** one of the parts that sth is made of: *We'll have to* ***take*** *the engine* ***to pieces*** *to find the problem.* **3** one of the parts into which sth breaks: *The plate fell to the floor and smashed* ***to pieces.*** ◆ *The vase lay* ***in pieces*** *on the floor.*
➤ART, MUSIC ETC. **4** a single work of art, music, etc: *He played a piece by Chopin.*
➤NEWS ARTICLE **5 a piece (on/about sb/sth)** an article in a newspaper or magazine: *There's a good piece on China in today's paper.*
➤COIN **6** a coin of the value mentioned: *a fifty-pence piece*
➤IN GAMES **7** one of the small objects that you use when you are playing games such as **chess**
IDM **bits and pieces** ➲ **bit**[1]
give sb a piece of your mind to speak to sb angrily because of sth they have done
go to pieces to be no longer able to work or behave normally because of a difficult situation: *When his wife died he seemed to go to pieces.*
in one piece not broken or injured: *I've only been on a motorbike once, and I was just glad to get home in one piece.*
a piece of cake (*informal*) something that is very easy

piece[2] /piːs/ *verb*
PHR V **piece sth together 1** to discover the truth about sth from different pieces of information: *Detectives are trying to piece together the last few days of the man's life.* **2** to put sth together from several pieces

piecemeal /ˈpiːsmiːl/ *adj, adv* (done or happening) a little at a time

ˈ**pie chart** *noun* [C] a diagram consisting of a circle divided into parts to show the size of particular parts in relation to the whole ➲ picture at **graph**

pier

pier /pɪə(r)/ *noun* [C] **1** a large wooden or metal structure that is built out into the sea in holiday towns, where people can walk **2** a large wooden or metal structure that is built out into the sea from the land. Boats can stop at **piers** so that people or goods can be taken on or off.

pierce /pɪəs/ *verb* **1** [T] to make a hole in sth with a sharp point: *I'm going to* ***have my ears pierced.*** **2** [I, T] **pierce (through/into) sth** to manage to go through or into sth: *A scream pierced the air.*

piercing[1] /ˈpɪəsɪŋ/ *adj* **1** (used about sb's eyes or a look) seeming to know what you are thinking **2** (used about the wind, pain, a loud noise, etc.) strong and unpleasant

piercing[2] /ˈpɪəsɪŋ/ *noun* [U,C] the act of making holes in parts of the body as a decoration; a hole that is made: *body piercing* ◆ *Her face is covered in piercings.*

piety /ˈpaɪəti/ *noun* [U] a way of behaving that shows a deep respect for God and religion ➲ *adjective* **pious**

pig[1] /pɪɡ/ *noun* [C] **1** an animal with pink, black or brown skin, short legs, a wide nose and a curly tail, and that is kept on farms for **pork** (= its meat): *a pig farmer* ➲ note at **meat**

MORE **Pig** is often used for both males and females. A male pig is a **boar**, a female pig is a **sow** and a young pig is a **piglet**. When they make a noise, piglets **squeal** and pigs **grunt**.

2 (*informal*) an unpleasant person or a person who eats too much: *She* ***made a pig of herself*** *with the ice cream* (= ate too much).

pig² /pɪɡ/ *verb* [T] (**pigging**; **pigged**) (*informal*) **pig yourself** to eat too much
PHR V **pig out (on sth)** (*informal*) to eat too much of sth

pigeon /ˈpɪdʒɪn/ *noun* [C] a fat grey bird that often lives in towns

pigeonhole /ˈpɪdʒɪnhəʊl/ *noun* [C] one of a set of small open boxes that are used for putting papers or letters in

piggyback /ˈpɪɡibæk/ *noun* [C] the way of carrying sb, especially a child, on your back: *to give somebody a piggyback*

ˈpiggy bank *noun* [C] a small box, often shaped like a pig, that children save money in

ˌpig-ˈheaded *adj* (*informal*) not prepared to change your mind or say that you are wrong ➲ look at **stubborn, obstinate**

piglet /ˈpɪɡlət/ *noun* [C] a young pig

pigment /ˈpɪɡmənt/ *noun* [C,U] a substance that gives colour to things: *The colour of your skin depends on the amount of pigment in it.*

pigsty /ˈpɪɡstaɪ/ (also **sty**; *AmE* **ˈpigpen** /ˈpɪɡpen/) *noun* [C] (*pl* **pigsties**) a small building where pigs are kept

pigtail /ˈpɪɡteɪl/ (*AmE* **braid**) *noun* [C] hair that is tied together in one or two lengths made by **plaiting** (= crossing three pieces of hair over and under each other) ➲ picture at **hair**

pile¹ /paɪl/ *noun* [C] **1** a number of things lying on top of each other, or an amount of sth lying in a mass: *a pile of books/sand* ◆ *He put the coins* ***in*** *neat piles.* ◆ *She threw the clothes* ***in a pile*** *on the floor.*

HELP **Pile** or **heap**? A **pile** may be tidy or untidy. A **heap** is always untidy.

2 [usually plural] (*informal*) **piles of sth** a lot of sth: *I've got piles of work to do this evening.*

pile² /paɪl/ *verb* [T] **1** **pile sth (up)** to put things one on top of the other to form a pile: *We piled the boxes in the corner.* **2** **pile A on(to) B; pile B with A** to put a lot of sth on top of sth: *She piled the papers on the desk.* ◆ *The desk was piled with papers.*
PHR V **pile into, out of, off, etc. sth** (*informal*) to go into, out of, off, etc. sth quickly and all at the same time: *The children piled onto the train.*
pile up (used about sth bad) to increase in quantity: *Our problems are really piling up.*

piles /paɪlz/ = **haemorrhoids**

ˈpile-up *noun* [C] a crash that involves several cars, etc.

pilgrim /ˈpɪlɡrɪm/ *noun* [C] a person who travels a long way to visit a religious place

pilgrimage /ˈpɪlɡrɪmɪdʒ/ *noun* [C,U] a long journey that a person makes to visit a religious place

pill /pɪl/ *noun* **1** [C] a small round piece of medicine that you swallow: *Take one pill, three times a day after meals.* ◆ *a sleeping pill* ➲ look at **tablet** ➲ picture at **medicine** **2** **the pill**; **the Pill** [sing] a **pill** that some women take regularly so that they do not become pregnant: *She is* ***on the pill.***

pillar /ˈpɪlə(r)/ *noun* [C] **1** a column of stone, wood or metal that is used for supporting part of a building **2** a person who has a strong character and is important to sb/sth: *Dave was a* ***pillar of strength*** *to his sister when she was ill.*

ˈpillar box *noun* [C] (*old-fashioned*) (in Britain) a tall round red box in a public place into which you can post letters, which are then collected by sb from the post office ➲ look at **postbox, letter box**

pillion /ˈpɪliən/ *noun* [C] a seat for a passenger behind the driver on a motorbike ▶ **pillion** *adv*: *to ride pillion on a motorbike*

pillow /ˈpɪləʊ/ *noun* [C] a large cloth bag filled with soft material that you put under your head when you are in bed ➲ picture at **bed**

pillowcase /ˈpɪləʊkeɪs/ *noun* [C] a thin soft cover for a **pillow**

pilot¹ /ˈpaɪlət/ *noun* [C] a person who flies an aircraft: *an airline pilot* ➲ picture on **page P2**

pilot² /ˈpaɪlət/ *verb* [T] **1** to fly an aircraft or guide a ship **2** to lead sb/sth through a difficult situation: *The booklet pilots you through the process of starting your own business.* **3** to test a new product, idea, etc. that will be used by everyone: *The new exam is being piloted in schools in Italy.*

pilot³ /ˈpaɪlət/ *adj* [only *before* a noun] done as an experiment or to test sth that will be used by everyone: *The pilot scheme will run for six months.*

pimple /ˈpɪmpl/ *noun* [C] a small spot on your skin ➲ look at **goose pimples**

PIN /pɪn/ (also **ˈPIN number**) *noun* [C, usually sing] **personal identification number**; a number given to you, for example by a bank, so that you can use a plastic card to take out money from a **cash machine** (= a special machine in or outside a bank): *I've forgotten my PIN.*

pin¹ /pɪn/ *noun* [C] **1** a short thin piece of metal with a round head at one end and a sharp point at the other. Pins are used for fastening together pieces of cloth, paper, etc. **2** a thin piece of wood or metal that is used for a particular purpose: *a hairpin* ◆ *a two-pin plug* ➲ picture at **plug**

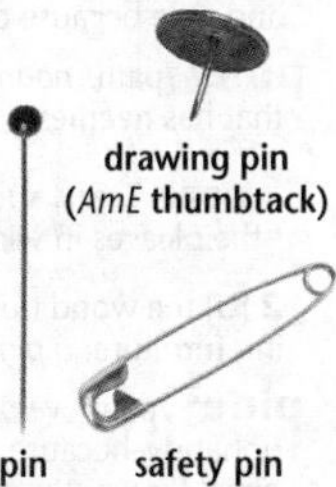

pin² /pɪn/ *verb* [T] (**pinning**; **pinned**) **1** **pin sth to/on sth; pin sth together** to fasten sth with a pin or

P

pins: *Could you pin this notice on the board, please?* **2** pin sb/sth against, to, under, etc. sth to make sb/sth unable to move by holding or pressing down on them or it: *They pinned him against a wall and stole his wallet.* ◆ *He was pinned under the fallen tree.*

IDM **pin (all) your hopes on sb/sth** to believe completely that sb/sth will help you or will succeed

PHR V **pin sb down 1** to hold sb so they cannot move **2** to force sb to decide sth or to say exactly what they are going to do: *Can you pin her down to what time she'll be coming?*

pin sth down to describe or explain exactly what sth is

pinafore /ˈpɪnəfɔː(r)/ *noun* [C] (*especially BrE*) a loose dress with no sleeves, usually worn over other clothes

pincer /ˈpɪnsə(r)/ *noun* **1 pincers** [pl] a tool made of two crossed pieces of metal that is used for holding things, pulling nails out of wood, etc. **2** [C] one of the two sharp, curved front legs of some **shellfish** (= creatures with shells that live in water) that are used for holding things ➲ picture on **page P13**

pinch¹ /pɪntʃ/ *verb* **1** [T] to hold a piece of sb's skin tightly between your thumb and first finger, especially in order to hurt them: *Paul pinched his brother and made him cry.* **2** [I,T] to hold sth too tight, often causing pain: *I've got a pinched nerve in my neck.* **3** [T] (*informal*) to steal: *Who's pinched my pen?*

pinch

PHR V **pinch in** (on some small computer devices) to make the screen smaller using your finger and thumb **OPP** **zoom** ➲ note at **touch screen**

pinch² /pɪntʃ/ *noun* [C] **1** the holding of sb's skin tightly between your finger and thumb: *She gave him a little pinch on the arm.* **2** the amount of sth that you can pick up with your thumb and first finger: *a pinch of salt*

IDM **at a pinch** used to say that sth can be done if it is really necessary: *We can fit six people round this table at a pinch.*

take sth with a pinch of salt to think that sth is probably not true or accurate

pinched /pɪntʃt/ *adj* (used about sb's face) thin and pale because of illness or cold

pine¹ /paɪn/ *noun* **1** [C] (also ˈ**pine tree**) a tall tree that has **needles**(= thin pointed leaves)

MORE Trees, such as the **pine**, that do not lose their leaves in winter are called **evergreens**.

2 [U] the wood from **pine** trees, often used for making furniture: *a pine table*

pine² /paɪn/ *verb* [I] **pine (for sb/sth)** to be very unhappy because sb has died or gone away: *She pined for months after he'd gone.*

pineapple /ˈpaɪnæpl/ *noun* [C,U] a large sweet fruit that is yellow inside and has a thick brown skin with sharp points. **Pineapples** grow in hot countries. ➲ picture on **page P14**

ˈ**pine tree** = **pine¹**(1)

ping /pɪŋ/ *noun* [C] a short high noise that is made by a small bell or by a metal object hitting against sth: *The lift went ping and the doors opened.* ▶ **ping** *verb* [I]

ˈ**ping-pong** (*informal*) = **table tennis**

pink /pɪŋk/ *adj, noun* [U] (of) a pale red colour: *She was dressed in pink.*

pinnacle /ˈpɪnəkl/ *noun* [C] **1** the most important or successful part of sth: *Celia is at the pinnacle of her career.* **2** a high pointed rock on a mountain

pinpoint /ˈpɪnpɔɪnt/ *verb* [T] **1** to find the exact position of sth: *to pinpoint a place on the map* **2** to describe or explain exactly what sth is: *First we have to pinpoint the cause of the failure.*

ˌ**pins and** ˈ**needles** *noun* [U] a strange, sometimes painful feeling that you get in a part of your body after it has been in one position for too long and when the blood is returning to it

pint /paɪnt/ *noun* [C] **1** (*abbr* **pt**) a measure of liquid; 0.57 of a litre: *a pint of milk*

MORE There are 8 **pints** in a gallon. An American pint is 0.47 of a litre.

ℹ For more information about measurements, look at the section on using numbers at the back of this dictionary. **2** (*BrE informal*) a pint of beer: *We had a pint and a sandwich at the local pub.*

ˈ**pin-up** *noun* [C] (*informal*) a picture of an attractive person, made to be put on a wall; a person who appears in these pictures

pioneer /ˌpaɪəˈnɪə(r)/ *noun* [C] **1 a pioneer (in/of sth)** a person who is one of the first to develop an area of human knowledge, culture, etc: *Yuri Gagarin was one of the pioneers of space exploration.* **2** a person who is one of the first to go and live in a particular area: *the pioneers of the American West* ▶ **pioneer** *verb* [T]: *a technique pioneered in the US*

pious /ˈpaɪəs/ *adj* having or showing a deep belief in religion ▶ **piously** *adv* ➲ *noun* **piety**

pip /pɪp/ *noun* [C] (*BrE*) the small seed of an apple, a lemon, an orange, etc. ➲ picture on **page P14**

pipe¹ /paɪp/ *noun* [C] **1** a tube that carries gas or liquid: *a gas/water pipe* **2** a tube with a small bowl at one end that is used for smoking **tobacco** (= the dried leaves used for making cigarettes): *to smoke a pipe* **3** a simple musical instrument that consists of a tube with holes in it. You blow into it to play it.

pipe² /paɪp/ *verb* [T] to carry liquid or gas in pipes: *Water is piped to all the houses in the town.*

PHR V **pipe up** (*informal*) to suddenly say sth: *Suddenly Shirin piped up with a question.*

pipeline /ˈpaɪplaɪn/ *noun* [C] a line of pipes that are used for carrying liquid or gas over a long distance

IDM **in the pipeline** being planned or prepared

piper /ˈpaɪpə(r)/ *noun* [C] a person who plays music on a pipe, or who plays the **bagpipes** (= a typically Scottish musical instrument)

piracy /ˈpaɪrəsi/ *noun* [U] **1** the crime of attacking ships in order to steal from them **2** the illegal copying of books, CDs, etc.

pirate[1] /ˈpaɪrət/ *noun* [C] **1** a criminal who attacks ships in order to steal from them **2** a person who copies books, CDs, computer programs, etc. in order to sell them illegally

pirate[2] /ˈpaɪrət/ *verb* [T] to make an illegal copy of a book, CD, etc. in order to sell it

Pisces /ˈpaɪsiːz/ *noun* [C,U] the 12th sign of the **zodiac** (= 12 signs which represent the positions of the sun, moon and planets), the Fishes; a person born under this sign: *I'm a Pisces.* ➲ picture at **zodiac**

pistachio /pɪˈstæʃiəʊ; -ˈstɑːʃiəʊ/ *noun* [C] (*pl* pistachios) (also piˈstachio nut) the small green nut of an Asian tree

pistol /ˈpɪstl/ *noun* [C] a small gun that you hold in one hand ➲ note at **gun**

piston /ˈpɪstən/ *noun* [C] a piece of metal in an engine, etc. that fits tightly inside a metal tube. The piston is moved up and down inside the tube and causes other parts of the engine to move.

pit[1] /pɪt/ *noun* **1** [C] a large hole that is made in the ground: *They dug a large pit to bury the dead animals.* **2** [C] = **coal mine** **3** the pits [pl] the place on a motor racing track where cars stop for fuel, new tyres, etc. during a race **4** [C] (*AmE*) = **stone**(4)
IDM **be the pits** (*informal*) to be very bad: *The food in that restaurant is the pits!*

pit[2] /pɪt/ *verb* [T] (pitting; pitted) to make small holes in the surface of sth: *The front of the building was pitted with bullet marks.*
PHR V **pit A against B** to test one person or thing against another in a fight or competition: *The two strongest teams were pitted against each other in the final.*

pitch[1] /pɪtʃ/ *noun* **1** [C] (*BrE*) a special area of ground where you play certain sports: *a football/hockey/cricket pitch* ➲ look at **court, field** **2** [sing] the strength or level of feelings, activity, etc: *The children's excitement almost reached fever pitch.* **3** [U] how high or low a sound is, especially a musical note: *I think somebody's singing **off pitch**.* **4** [C] talk or arguments used by sb who is trying to sell sth or persuade sb to do sth: *a sales pitch* ◆ *to make a pitch for something*

pitch[2] /pɪtʃ/ *verb* **1** [I,T] to throw; to be thrown: *Doug pitched his empty can into the bushes.* **2** [T] to set sth at a particular level: *The talk was pitched at people with far more experience than me.* ◆ *a high-pitched voice* **3** [T] pitch sth (at sb) to try to sell a product to a particular group of people or in a particular way: *This new breakfast cereal is being pitched at kids.* **4** [T] to put up a tent or tents: *We could pitch our tents in that field.*
PHR V **pitch in** (*informal*) to join in and work together with other people: *Everybody pitched in to clear up the flood damage.*

ˌpitch-ˈblack *adj* completely dark; with no light at all

pitcher /ˈpɪtʃə(r)/ *noun* [C] **1** a large container for holding and pouring liquids ➲ picture at **jug** **2** (in the sport of **baseball**) the player who throws the ball to a player from the other team, who tries to hit it **3** (*AmE*) = **jug**

piteous /ˈpɪtiəs/ *adj* (*formal*) that makes you feel pity or sadness ▶ **piteously** *adv*

pitfall /ˈpɪtfɔːl/ *noun* [C] a danger or difficulty, especially one that is hidden or not obvious

pith /pɪθ/ *noun* [U] the white substance inside the skin of an orange, lemon, etc.

pithy /ˈpɪθi/ *adj* (pithier; pithiest) (used about a comment, piece of writing, etc.) short but expressed in a clear, direct way: *a pithy comment*

pitiful /ˈpɪtɪfl/ *adj* causing you to feel pity or sadness: *the pitiful groans of the wounded soldiers* ▶ **pitifully** /-fəli/ *adv*

pitiless /ˈpɪtiləs/ *adj* having or showing no pity for other people's suffering ▶ **pitilessly** *adv*

pitta (*AmE* pita) /ˈpiːtə; ˈpɪtə/ *noun* [U,C] a type of flat bread in the shape of an **oval** that can be split open and filled: *pitta bread with hummus*

pity[1] /ˈpɪti/ *noun* **1** [U] a feeling of sadness that you have for sb/sth that is suffering or in trouble: *The situation is his fault so I don't feel any pity for him.* **2** [sing] something that makes you feel a little sad or disappointed: *'You're too late. Emily left five minutes ago.' 'Oh, **what a pity**!'* ◆ *It's **a pity** that Bina couldn't come.* SYN **shame**
IDM **take pity on sb** to help sb who is suffering or in trouble because you feel sorry for them

pity[2] /ˈpɪti/ *verb* [T] (pitying; pities; *pt, pp* pitied) to feel pity or sadness for sb who is suffering or in trouble

pivot[1] /ˈpɪvət/ *noun* [C] **1** the central point on which sth turns or balances **2** the central or most important person or thing: *West Africa was the pivot of the cocoa trade.*

pivot[2] /ˈpɪvət/ *verb* [I] to turn or balance on a central point

pixel /ˈpɪksl/ *noun* [C] any of the very small individual areas on a computer, TV or camera screen, which together form the whole image

pixelate (also pixellate) /ˈpɪksəleɪt/ *verb* [T] to divide an image into **pixels**, sometimes in order to hide sb's identity, especially on television

pixie /ˈpɪksi/ *noun* [C] (in children's stories) a creature like a small person with pointed ears that has magic powers

pizza /ˈpiːtsə/ *noun* [C,U] an Italian dish consisting of a flat round bread base with vegetables, cheese, meat, etc. on top, which is cooked in an oven ➲ picture on **page P16**

pkt *abbr* = **packet**(1)

pl. *abbr* = **plural**

P

placard banner

placard /ˈplækɑːd/ *noun* [C] a large written or printed notice that is put in a public place or carried on a stick in a protest march

placate /pləˈkeɪt/ *verb* [T] (*formal*) to make sb feel less angry about sth

🔑 **place**[1] /pleɪs/ *noun* [C]

➤POSITION/AREA **1** [C] a particular position or area: *Show me the exact place where it happened.* ◆ *This would be a good place to sit down and have a rest.* ◆ *The wall was damaged in several places.*

➤TOWN/BUILDING **2** [C] a particular village, town, country, etc: *Which places did you go to in Italy?* ◆ *Vienna is a very beautiful place.* **3** [C] a building or area that is used for a particular purpose: *The square is a popular* ***meeting place*** *for young people.* ◆ *The town is full of inexpensive eating places.*

➤SEAT **4** [C] a seat or position that can be used by sb/sth: *They went into the classroom and sat down in their places.* ◆ *Go on ahead and* ***save me a place*** *in the queue.*

HELP **Place, space** or **room**? A **place** is a seat or position for someone/something. A place where you can park your car is also called a **space**. You use **space** and **room** when you are talking about empty areas: *This piano* ***takes up*** *too much* ***space***. ◆ *There is enough* ***room for*** *three people in the back of the car.*

➤ROLE **5** [sing] your position in society; your role: *I feel* ***it is not my place*** *to criticize my boss.*

➤IN COLLEGE/TEAM **6** [C] an opportunity to study at a college, play for a team, etc: *Abina has got a place to study law at Oxford University.* ◆ *Laila is now sure of a place on the team.*

➤CORRECT POSITION **7** [C] the usual or correct position or occasion for sth: *The room was tidy. Everything had been put away* ***in its place***. ◆ *A funeral is not the place to discuss business.*

➤SB'S HOME **8** [sing] (*spoken*) sb's home: *Her parents have got a place on the coast.*

➤IN COMPETITION **9** [C, usually sing] the position that you have at the end of a race, competition, etc: *Cara finished* ***in second place***.

➤IN NUMBERS **10** [C] the position of a number after the **decimal point** (= a small round mark used to separate the parts of a number): *Your answer should be correct to three decimal places.*

IDM **all over the place** everywhere

change/swap places (with sb) to take sb's seat, position, etc. and let them have yours: *Let's change places so that you can look out of the window.*

fall/slot into place (used about sth that is complicated or difficult to understand) to become organized or clear in your mind: *After two weeks in my new job, everything suddenly started to fall into place.*

in the first, second, etc. place (*informal*) used when you are giving a list of reasons for sth or explaining sth **SYN** **firstly, secondly**, etc.

in place **1** in the correct or usual position: *Use tape to hold the picture in place.* **2** (used about plans or preparations) finished and ready to be used: *All the preparations for the trip are now in place.*

in sb's place/shoes in sb's situation or position: *If I were in your place I would wait a year before getting married.*

in place of sb/sth; **in sb/sth's place** instead of sb/sth

out of place **1** not in the correct or usual place **2** not suitable for a particular situation: *I felt very out of place among all those clever people.*

put sb in his/her place to show that sb is not as clever, important, etc. as they believe: *It really put her in her place when she failed to qualify for the race.*

put yourself in sb's place to imagine that you are in the same situation as sb else: *Put yourself in Steve's place and you will realize how worried he must be.*

take place (used about a meeting, an event, etc.) to happen: *The ceremony took place in glorious sunshine.* ➲ note at **happen**

🔑 **place**[2] /pleɪs/ *verb* [T]

➤INTO POSITION **1** (*formal*) to put sth carefully or deliberately in a particular position: *The chairs had all been placed in neat rows.* ◆ *The poster was placed where everyone could see it.* **2** to put sb in a particular position or situation: *His behaviour placed me in a difficult situation.* ◆ *to place somebody in charge* ◆ *Rhoda was placed third in the competition.*

➤ATTITUDE **3** used to express the attitude that sb has to sb/sth: *We placed our trust in you and you failed us.* ◆ *The blame for the disaster was placed firmly on the company.*

➤RECOGNIZE **4** [usually in negative statements] to recognize sb/sth and be able to identify them or it: *Her face is familiar but I just can't quite place her.*

➤ORDER/BET **5** to give instructions about sth or to ask for sth to happen: *to place a bet on something* ◆ *to place an order for something*

ˈplace name *noun* [C] the name of a city, town, etc.

placid /ˈplæsɪd/ *adj* (used about a person or an animal) calm and not easily excited: *a placid baby/horse* ▶ **placidly** *adv*

plagiarize (also **-ise**) /ˈpleɪdʒəraɪz/ *verb* [T,I] to copy another person's ideas, words or work and pretend that they are your own: *He was accused of plagiarizing his colleague's results.* ▶ **plagiarism** /ˈpleɪdʒərɪzəm/ *noun* [U,C]: *accusations of plagiarism* ◆ *The text was full of plagiarisms.*

plague[1] /pleɪɡ/ *noun* **1** **the plague** [U] an infectious disease spread by **rats** (= animals like a large mice) that makes large spots form on the body, causes a very high temperature and often results in death **2** [C,U] any infectious disease that spreads quickly and kills many people **3** [C] a plague of sth a large number of unpleasant animals or insects that come into an area at one time: *a plague of ants/ locusts*

plague² /pleɪg/ *verb* [T] to cause sb/sth a lot of trouble: *The project was plagued by a series of disasters.*

plaice /pleɪs/ *noun* [C,U] (*pl* plaice) a type of flat sea fish that we eat

plain¹ /pleɪn/ *adj* (plainer; plainest) **1** easy to see, hear or understand; clear: *It was plain that he didn't want to talk about it.* ◆ *She* ***made it plain that*** *she didn't want to see me again.* **2** (used about people, thoughts, actions, etc.) saying what you think; direct and honest: *I'll be plain with you. I don't like the idea.* **3** simple in style; not decorated or complicated: *My father likes plain English cooking.* **4** [only *before* a noun] all one colour; without a pattern on it: *a plain blue jumper* ➲ picture on **page P1** **5** (used especially about a woman or girl) not beautiful or attractive: *She's a rather plain child.*

plain² /pleɪn/ *noun* [C] (also plains [pl]) a large area of flat land with few trees

plain³ /pleɪn/ *adv* (*informal*) completely: *That's plain silly.*

ˌplain-ˈclothes *adj* [only *before* a noun] (used about a police officer) in ordinary clothes, not uniform: *a plain-clothes detective*

ˌplain ˈflour *noun* [U] flour that does not contain **baking powder** (= powder that makes cakes, etc. rise) ➲ look at **self-raising flour**

plainly /ˈpleɪnli/ *adv* **1** clearly: *He was plainly very upset.* **2** using simple words to say sth in a direct and honest way: *She told him plainly that he was not doing his job properly.* **3** in a simple way, without decoration: *She was plainly dressed and wore no make-up.*

plaintiff /ˈpleɪntɪf/ *noun* [C] a person who starts a legal action against sb in a court of law ➲ look at **defendant**

plaintive /ˈpleɪntɪv/ *adj* sounding sad, especially in a weak complaining way: *a plaintive cry/voice* ▶ **plaintively** *adv*

plait /plæt/ (*AmE* braid) *verb* [T] to cross three or more long pieces of hair, rope, etc. over and under each other to make one thick piece ▶ **plait** (*AmE* braid) *noun* [C] ➲ picture at **plait**

plan¹ /plæn/ *noun* **1** [C] a plan (for sth/to do sth) an idea or arrangement for doing or achieving sth in the future: *We usually* ***make*** *our holiday* ***plans*** *in January.* ◆ *The firm has no plans to employ more people.* ◆ *There has been* ***a change of plan***—*we're meeting at the restaurant.* ◆ *If everything* ***goes according to plan*** (= happens as we planned) *we should be home by midnight.* **2** [C] a detailed map of a building, town, etc: ***a street plan*** *of Berlin* **3** plans [pl] detailed drawings of a building, machine, road, etc. that show its size, shape and measurements: *We're getting an architect to* ***draw up*** *some* ***plans*** *for a new kitchen.* **4** [C] a diagram that shows how sth is to be organized or arranged: *Before you start writing an essay, you should make a brief plan.*

EXAM TIP

Planning your answer

It is very important to plan your answers in a writing exam. Always make some notes about what you want to say before you start, and write down some key vocabulary. Look at the **Writing Tutor** for help with writing different types of essay.

plan² /plæn/ *verb* (planning; planned) **1** [I,T] plan (sth) (for sth) to decide, organize or prepare for sth you want to do in the future: *to plan for the future* ◆ *You need to plan your work more carefully.* ◆ *We're planning a surprise for Gwen's 50th birthday.* **2** [I] plan (on sth/doing sth); plan (to do sth) to intend or expect to do sth: *I'm planning on having a holiday in July.* ◆ *We plan to arrive at about 4 o'clock.* **3** [T] to make a diagram or a design of sth: *You need an expert to help you plan the garden.* ▶ **planning** *noun* [U]: *The project requires careful planning.*

plane¹ /pleɪn/ (also aeroplane; *AmE* airplane) *noun* [C] **1** a vehicle with wings and one or more engines that can fly through the air: *Has her plane landed yet?* ◆ *a plane ticket* ◆ *a plane crash* ◆ *Have you ever been on a plane?* ➲ picture on **page P6** **2** (*technical*) a flat surface: *the horizontal/vertical plane* **3** a tool used for making the surface of wood smooth by taking very thin pieces off it ➲ picture at **tool**

TOPIC

Travelling by plane

A large **airport** may have more than one **terminal**. You go to the **check-in desk** and **check in** (= say that you have arrived). You might be able to choose an **aisle** seat or a **window** seat. There is often an **online check-in** so that you can do this before you go to the airport. You **check in** the **baggage** that will go into the **hold** (= the part of the plane where goods are stored) but you carry your **hand luggage** with you onto the plane. You wait in the **departure lounge**, and when your flight is called you go to the correct **gate**. You need to show your **boarding pass** in order to get on the plane. The plane **takes off** from the **runway**. The **flight attendants/cabin crew** look after you during the flight. If you are taking an international flight (= travelling to a different country), you will have to show your **passport** at **immigration** when you land. Then you collect your luggage from **baggage reclaim** and exit through **customs**.

plane² /pleɪn/ *verb* [T] to make the surface of a piece of wood flat and smooth using a **plane¹**(3)

planet /ˈplænɪt/ *noun* **1** [C] a very large round object in space that moves around the sun or another star: *the planets of our solar system* ➲ note at **space** **2** the planet [sing] the world we live in;

P

the Earth, especially when talking about the environment: *the battle to save the planet*

planetarium /ˌplænɪˈteəriəm/ *noun* [C] a building with a curved ceiling that represents the sky at night. It is used for showing the positions and movements of the planets and stars for education and entertainment.

plank /plæŋk/ *noun* [C] a long flat thin piece of wood that is used for building or making things

plankton /ˈplæŋktən/ *noun* [U, with sing or pl verb] very small forms of plant and animal life that live in water

plant

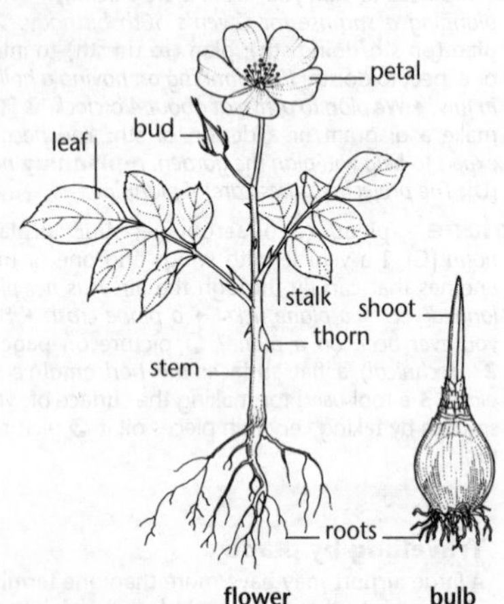

plant¹ /plɑːnt/ *noun* [C] **1** a living thing that grows in the ground and usually has leaves, a **stem** (= the central part) and roots: *a tomato plant* ◆ *a plant pot* (= a container for plants) **2** a very large factory: *a car plant* ◆ *a nuclear reprocessing plant*

plant² /plɑːnt/ *verb* [T] **1** to put plants, seeds, etc. in the ground to grow: *Bulbs should be planted in the autumn.* **2 plant sth (with sth)** to cover or supply a garden, area of land, etc. with plants: *The field's been planted with wheat this year.* **3** to put yourself/sth firmly in a particular place or position: *He planted himself in the best seat.* **4 plant sth (on sb)** to hide sth, especially sth illegal, in sb's clothing, property, etc. in order to make them seem guilty of a crime: *The women claimed that the stolen money had been planted on them.* **5 plant sth** to hide sth such as a bomb in a place where it will not be found: *The police think that terrorists may have* ***planted the bomb****.*

plantation /plɑːnˈteɪʃn/ *noun* [C] **1** a large area of land, especially in a hot country, where **tobacco** (= the plant used for making cigarettes), tea, cotton, etc. are grown: *a coffee plantation* **2** an area of land where trees are grown to produce wood

plaque /plɑːk/ *noun* **1** [C] a flat piece of stone or metal, usually with names and dates on it, that is fixed on a wall in memory of a famous person or event **2** [U] a harmful substance that forms on your teeth

plasma /ˈplæzmə/ (also **plasm** /ˈplæzəm/) *noun* [U] the clear liquid part of blood, in which the blood cells, etc., float

ˌplasma screen *noun* [C] a type of television or computer screen that is larger and thinner than most screens and produces a very clear image

plaster¹ /ˈplɑːstə(r)/ *noun* **1** [U] a mixture of a special powder and water that becomes hard when it is dry. **Plaster** is put on walls and ceilings to form a smooth surface. **2** (also ˌ**plaster of ˈParis**) [U] a white powder that is mixed with water and becomes hard when dry. It is then used especially for making copies of statues or for holding broken bones in place: *a plaster bust of Julius Caesar* ◆ *When Alan broke his leg it was* ***in plaster*** *for six weeks.* **3** (also ˈ**sticking plaster**) [C] a small piece of sticky material that is used to cover a cut, etc. on the body

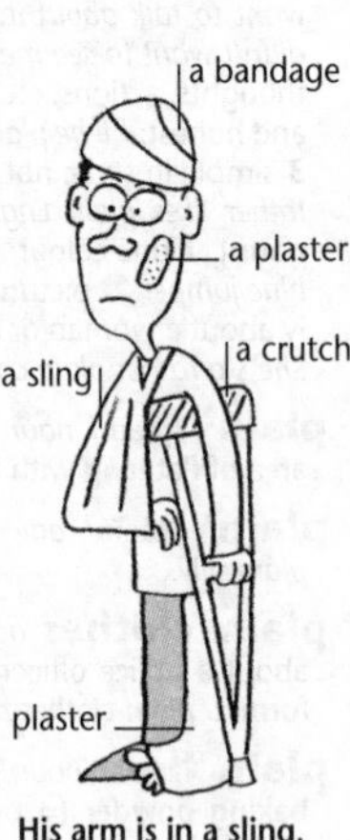

His arm is in a sling. His leg is in plaster.

plaster² /ˈplɑːstə(r)/ *verb* [T] **1** to cover a wall, etc. with **plaster¹**(1) to make the surface smooth **2 plaster sb/sth (in/with sth)** to cover sb/sth with a large amount of sth: *He plastered his walls with posters.*

plastic¹ /ˈplæstɪk/ *noun* [C,U] a light, strong material that is made with chemicals and is used for making many different kinds of objects: *A lot of kitchen utensils are made of plastic.* ◆ *Plastics and other synthetic materials are commonly used today.*

plastic² /ˈplæstɪk/ *adj* made of plastic: *plastic cups* ◆ *a plastic bag*

ˌplastic ˈsurgery *noun* [U] a medical operation to repair or replace damaged skin or to improve the appearance of sb's face or body ➲ look at **facelift**, **surgery**

plate /pleɪt/ *noun* **1** [C] a flat, usually round, dish for eating or serving food from: *a plastic/paper/china plate* ◆ *a plate of food*

MORE You eat your main course from a **dinner plate**. You may put bread, etc. on a **side plate**. You eat cereal or a pudding from a **bowl**.

2 [C] a thin flat piece of metal or glass: *a steel/metal plate* **3** [C] a flat piece of metal with sth written on it: *The brass plate beside the door said 'Dr Dawson'.* **4** [U] metal that has a thin covering of gold or silver: *gold/silver plate*

plateau /ˈplætəʊ/ *noun* [C] (*pl* **plateaus** /-təʊz/ *or* **plateaux** /-təʊ/) **1** a large high area of flat land **2** a state where there is little development or change: *House prices seem to have* ***reached a plateau****.*

plateful /ˈpleɪtfʊl/ *noun* [C] the amount of food that a plate can hold

platform /ˈplætfɔːm/ *noun* [C] **1** the place where you get on or off trains at a railway station: *Which platform does the train to York leave from?* **2** a flat surface, higher than the level of the floor or ground, on which people stand when they are speaking or performing, so that the audience can see them: *Coming onto the platform now is tonight's conductor, Jane Glover.* **3** [usually sing] the ideas and aims of a political party that wants to be elected: *They fought the election on a platform of low taxes.* **4** the type of computer system or the software that is used: *an IBM platform* ◆ *a multimedia platform*

platinum /ˈplætɪnəm/ *noun* [U] (*symbol* **Pt**) a silver-coloured metal that is often used for making expensive jewellery: *a platinum wedding ring*

platonic /pləˈtɒnɪk/ *adj* (used about a relationship between two people) friendly but not sexual

platoon /pləˈtuːn/ *noun* [C] a small group of soldiers

plausible /ˈplɔːzəbl/ *adj* that you can believe; reasonable: *a plausible excuse* **OPP** **implausible**

play[1] /pleɪ/ *verb*

➤HAVE FUN **1** [I] **play (with sb/sth)** to do sth to enjoy yourself; to have fun: *The children have been playing on the beach all day.* ◆ *Emma's found a new friend to play with.*

➤GAMES/SPORTS **2** [I,T] to take part in a game or sport: *to play football/tennis/hockey* ◆ *I usually play against Bill.* ◆ *She played him at table tennis and won.* ◆ *Do you know how to play chess?* ◆ *Who's Brazil playing next in the World Cup?*

➤MUSICAL INSTRUMENT **3** [I,T] **play (sth) (on sth)** to make music with a musical instrument: *to play the piano/guitar/trumpet* ◆ *My son's learning the piano. He plays very well.* ◆ *She played a few notes on the violin.* ➲ note at **music**

➤CDS, DVDS, ETC. **4** [I,T] to make a CD, DVD, etc. produce sound: *My favourite song was playing on the radio.* ◆ *Shall I play the DVD for you again?*

➤ACT/PERFORM **5** [I,T] to act in a play, film, TV programme, etc.; to act the role of sb: *Richard is going to play Romeo.*

> **HELP** Play a **part**, **role**, etc. is often used in a figurative way: *Britain has played an active part in the recent discussions.* ◆ *John played a key role in organizing the protest.*

➤OF LIGHT **6** [I] (*formal*) to move quickly and lightly: *Sunlight played on the surface of the sea.* ℹ For idioms containing **play**, look at the entries for the nouns, adjectives, etc. For example **play it by ear** is at **ear**.

PHR V **play at sth/being sth** to do sth with little interest or effort: *He's only playing at studying. He'd prefer to get a job now.* ◆ *What is that driver playing at* (= doing)?

play sth back (to sb) to turn on and watch or listen to a film, music, etc. that you have recorded: *Play that last scene back to me again.*

play sth down to make sth seem less important than it really is: *to play down a crisis*

play A off against B to make people compete or argue with each other, especially for your own advantage: *I think she enjoys playing one friend off against another.*

play on sth to use and take advantage of sb's fears or weaknesses: *This advertising campaign plays on people's fears of illness.*

play (sb) up (*informal*) to cause sb trouble or pain: *The car always plays up in wet weather.*

play[2] /pleɪ/ *noun* **1** [U] activity done for enjoyment only, especially by children: *Young children learn through play.* ◆ *the happy sound of children* ***at play*** **2** [C] a piece of writing performed by actors in the theatre, or on TV or radio: *Would you like to see a play while you're in London?* ◆ *a radio/TV play* ➲ note at **theatre** **3** [U] the playing of a game or sport: *Bad weather stopped play yesterday.*

> **HELP** We **play** tennis, football, etc. but we CANNOT say **a play** of tennis. We have **a game** of tennis.

4 [U] a control on a CD or DVD player, etc. that you press to start the tape, etc. running: *Put the DVD into the machine then* ***press play****.*

IDM **fair play** ➲ **fair**[1]

playboy /ˈpleɪbɔɪ/ *noun* [C] a rich man who spends his time enjoying himself

player /ˈpleɪə(r)/ *noun* [C] **1** a person who plays a game or sport: *a game for four players* ◆ *She's an excellent tennis player.* ➲ picture at **football** **2** [in compounds] a machine on which you can watch pictures or listen to sound that has been recorded on CD, DVD, etc: *a CD/DVD player* **3** a person who plays a musical instrument: *a piano player*

playful /ˈpleɪfl/ *adj* **1** full of fun; wanting to play: *a playful puppy* **2** done or said in fun; not serious: *a playful remark*

playground /ˈpleɪɡraʊnd/ *noun* [C] an area of land where children can play: *the school playground*

playgroup /ˈpleɪɡruːp/ (also **playschool**) a place where very young children go to play and learn ➲ look at **nursery school**

playhouse /ˈpleɪhaʊs/ *noun* **1** [sing] used in the name of some theatres: *the Liverpool Playhouse* **2** [C] a model of a house for children to play in

ˈ**playing card** = **card**(4)

ˈ**playing field** *noun* [C] a large field used for sports

IDM **a level playing field** ➲ **level**[2]

playlist /ˈpleɪlɪst/ *noun* [C] a list of songs and pieces of music that sb chooses and puts together, for example to play at a party or on a radio programme

P

ˈ**play-off** *noun* [C] a match between two teams or players who have equal scores to decide the winner: *They lost to Chicago in the play-offs.*

playschool /ˈpleɪskuːl/ = **playgroup**

plaything /ˈpleɪθɪŋ/ *noun* [C] (*old-fashioned*) a toy

playtime /ˈpleɪtaɪm/ *noun* [C,U] (*BrE*) a period of time between lessons when children at school can go outside to play

playwright /ˈpleɪraɪt/ *noun* [C] a person who writes plays for the theatre, TV or radio SYN **dramatist** ➲ note at **literature**

plc (also PLC) /ˌpiː el ˈsiː/ *abbr* (*BrE*) **Public Limited Company**; used after the name of a company

plea /pliː/ *noun* [C] **1** (*formal*) a plea (for sth) an important and emotional request: *a plea for help* **2** a plea of sth a statement made by or for sb in a court of law: *a plea of guilty/not guilty*

plead /pliːd/ *verb* **1** [I] plead (with sb) (to do/for sth) to ask sb for sth in a very strong and serious way: *She pleaded with him not to leave her.* ◆ *He pleaded for mercy.* ➲ look at **beg** **2** [I] to state in a court of law that you did or did not do a crime: *The defendant* ***pleaded not guilty*** *to the charge of theft.* **3** [T] plead sth (for sth) to give sth as an excuse or explanation for sth: *He pleaded family problems for his lack of concentration.* **4** [I,T] plead (sth) (for sb/sth) (used especially about a lawyer in a court of law) to support sb's case: *He needs the very best lawyer to plead (his case) for him.*

P

⚷ **pleasant** /ˈpleznt/ *adj* (**pleasanter**; **pleasantest**) [**More pleasant** and **most pleasant** are more common.] nice, enjoyable or friendly: *a pleasant evening/climate/place/view* ◆ *a pleasant smile/voice/manner* OPP **unpleasant** ▸ **pleasantly** *adv*

⚷ **please**[1] /pliːz/ *exclam* used as a polite way of asking for sth or telling sb to do sth: *Come in, please.* ◆ *Please don't spend too much money.* ◆ *Sit down, please.* ◆ *Two cups of coffee, please.*

IDM **yes, please** used when you are accepting an offer of sth politely: *'Sugar?' 'Yes, please.'* OPP **No, thank you**

⚷ **please**[2] /pliːz/ *verb* **1** [I,T] to make sb happy: *There's just no pleasing some people* (= some people are impossible to please). SYN **satisfy** **2** [I] [not used as the main verb in a sentence; used after words like *as, what, whatever, anything*, etc.] to want; to choose: *You can't always* ***do as you please.*** ◆ *She has so much money she can buy anything she pleases.*

IDM **please yourself** to be able to do whatever you want: *Without anyone else to cook for, I can please myself what I eat.*

⚷ **pleased** /pliːzd/ *adj* [not before a noun] pleased (with sb/sth); pleased to do sth; pleased that ... happy or satisfied about sth: *John seems very pleased with his new car.* ◆ *Aren't you pleased to see me?* ◆ *We're* ***only too pleased*** (= very happy) *to help.* ◆ *I'm so pleased that you've decided to stay another week.* ➲ note at **happy**

⚷ **pleasing** /ˈpliːzɪŋ/ *adj* giving you pleasure and satisfaction: *The exam results are very pleasing this year.*

pleasurable /ˈpleʒərəbl/ *adj* (*formal*) enjoyable: *a pleasurable experience*

⚷ **pleasure** /ˈpleʒə(r)/ *noun* **1** [U] the feeling of being happy or satisfied: *Parents* ***get*** *a lot of* ***pleasure out of*** *watching their children grow up.* ◆ ***It gives me great pleasure*** *to introduce our next speaker.* **2** [U] enjoyment (rather than work): *What brings you to Paris—business or pleasure?* **3** [C] an event or activity that you enjoy or that makes you happy: *It's been a pleasure to work with you.* ◆ *'Thanks for your help.'* ***'It's a pleasure.'***

IDM **take (no) pleasure in sth/doing sth** to enjoy/not enjoy (doing) sth

with pleasure used as a polite way of saying that you are happy to do sth: *'Could you give me a lift into town?' 'Yes, with pleasure.'*

pleat /pliːt/ *noun* [C] a permanent fold that is sewn or pressed into a piece of cloth: *a skirt with pleats at the front*

plectrum /ˈplektrəm/ (also *informal* pick) *noun* [C] a small piece of metal, plastic, etc. that you use to play a musical instrument such as a **guitar**

pledge /pledʒ/ *noun* [C] a pledge (to do sth) a formal promise or agreement ▸ **pledge** *verb* [T] pledge sth (to sb/sth): *The Government has pledged £5 million to help the victims of the disaster.*

plentiful /ˈplentɪfl/ *adj* available in large amounts or numbers: *Fruit is plentiful at this time of year.* OPP **scarce**

⚷ **plenty** /ˈplenti/ *pron, adv* **1** plenty (of sb/sth) as much or as many of sth as you need: *'Shall I get some more coffee?' 'No, we've still got plenty.'* ◆ *There's still plenty of time to get there.* ◆ *Have you brought plenty to drink?* **2** [before *more*] a lot: *There's plenty more ice cream.* **3** [with *big, long, tall*, etc. followed by *enough*] (*informal*) easily: *'This shirt's too small.' 'Well, it looks plenty big enough to me.'*

pliable /ˈplaɪəbl/ (also pliant /ˈplaɪənt/) *adj* **1** easy to bend or shape **2** (used about a person) easy to influence

pliers /ˈplaɪəz/ *noun* [pl] a metal tool with handles, that is used for holding things firmly and for cutting wire: *a pair of pliers* ➲ picture at **tool**

plight /plaɪt/ *noun* [sing] (*formal*) a bad or difficult state or situation

plimsoll /ˈplɪmsəl/ *noun* [C] (*BrE*) a light shoe made of **canvas** (= strong cloth) that is especially used for sports, etc: *a pair of plimsolls* ➲ look at **trainer**

plod /plɒd/ *verb* [I] (plo<u>dd</u>ing; plo<u>dd</u>ed) plod (along/on) to walk slowly and in a heavy or tired way: *We plodded on through the rain for nearly an hour.*

PHR V **plod along/on** to make slow progress,

especially with difficult or boring work: *I just plod on with my work and never seem to get anywhere.*

plonk /plɒŋk/ *verb* [T] (*informal*) **1** plonk sth (down) to put sth down on sth, especially noisily or carelessly: *Just plonk your bag down anywhere.* **2** plonk (yourself) (down) to sit down heavily and carelessly: *He just plonked himself down in front of the TV.*

plop¹ /plɒp/ *noun* [C, usually sing] a sound like that of a small object dropping into water

plop² /plɒp/ *verb* [I] (plopping; plopped) to fall making a **plop**: *The frog plopped back into the water.*

plot¹ /plɒt/ *noun* [C] **1** the series of events which form the story of a novel, film, etc: *The play had a very weak plot.* ◆ *I can't follow the plot of this novel.* **2** a plot (to do sth) a secret plan made by several people to do sth wrong or illegal: *a plot to kill the president* **3** a small piece of land, used for a special purpose: *a plot of land*

plot² /plɒt/ *verb* (plotting; plotted) **1** [I,T] plot (with sb) (against sb) to make a secret plan to do sth wrong or illegal: *They were accused of plotting against the government.* ◆ *The terrorists had been plotting this campaign for years.* **2** [T] to mark sth on a map, diagram, etc: *to plot the figures on a graph*

plough (*AmE* plow) /plaʊ/ *noun* [C] a large piece of equipment which is pulled by a **tractor** (= a large vehicle that is used on farms) or by an animal. A plough turns the soil over ready for seeds to be planted. ➲ look at **snowplough** ▶ **plough** (*AmE* plow) *verb* [I,T] (*figurative*): *The book was long and boring but I managed to plough through it* (= read it with difficulty).

ploy /plɔɪ/ *noun* [C] a ploy (to do sth) something that you say or do in order to get what you want or to persuade sb to do sth

pluck¹ /plʌk/ *verb* [T] **1** pluck sth/sb (from sth/out) to remove or take sth/sb from a place: *He plucked the letter from my hands.* **2** to pull the feathers out of a bird in order to prepare it for cooking **3** to play a musical instrument, especially a **guitar** by pulling the strings with your fingers
IDM **pluck up courage** to try to get enough courage to do sth
PHR V **pluck at sth** to pull sth gently several times

pluck² /plʌk/ *noun* [U] (*informal*) courage and determination ▶ **plucky** *adj* (pluckier; pluckiest)

plug¹ /plʌg/ *noun* [C] **1** a plastic or rubber object with two or three metal pins, which connects a piece of electrical equipment to the electricity supply: *I'll have to change the plug on the kettle.* **2** a round piece of rubber or plastic that you use to block the hole in a sink, bath, etc: *She* ***pulled out the plug*** *and let the water drain away.* **3** (*informal*) a mention that sb makes of a new book, film, etc. in order to encourage people to buy or see it: *He managed to get in a plug for his new book.*

plug² /plʌg/ *verb* [T] (plugging; plugged) **1** to fill or block a hole with sth that fits tightly into it: *He managed to plug the leak in the pipe.* **2** (*informal*) to say good things about a new book, film, etc. in order to make people buy or see it: *They're really plugging that song on the radio at the moment.*
PHR V **plug sth in** to connect a piece of electrical equipment to the electricity supply or to another piece of equipment: *Is the microphone plugged in?* OPP **unplug**

plugs

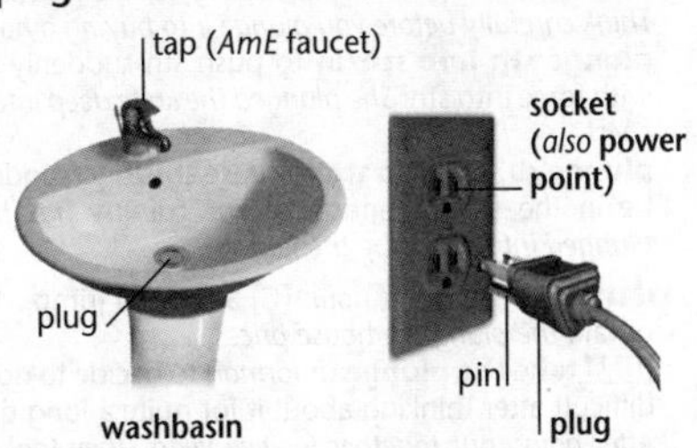

plughole /ˈplʌghəʊl/ *noun* [C] (*BrE*) a hole in a bath, etc. where the water flows away

plum /plʌm/ *noun* [C] a soft, round fruit with red or yellow skin and a stone in the middle ➲ picture on **page P14**

plumage /ˈpluːmɪdʒ/ *noun* [U] a bird's feathers

plumber /ˈplʌmə(r)/ *noun* [C] a person whose job is to put in or repair water pipes, baths, toilets, etc. ➲ note at **house** ➲ picture on **page P2**

plumbing /ˈplʌmɪŋ/ *noun* [U] **1** all the pipes, taps, etc. in a building **2** the work of a person who puts in and repairs water pipes, taps, etc.

plume /pluːm/ *noun* [C] **1** a narrow cloud of smoke that rises in the air **2** a large feather or group of feathers, often worn as a decoration

plummet /ˈplʌmɪt/ *verb* [I] to fall suddenly and quickly from a high level or position: *Share prices have plummeted to an all-time low.* SYN **plunge**

plump¹ /plʌmp/ *adj* (plumper; plumpest) (used about a person or an animal) pleasantly fat: *the baby's plump cheeks*

plump² /plʌmp/ *verb*
PHR V **plump for sb/sth** (*informal*) to choose or decide to have sb/sth: *I think I'll plump for the roast chicken, after all.*

plunder /ˈplʌndə(r)/ *noun* [U] the act of stealing from people or places, especially during war or fighting; the goods that are stolen ▶ **plunder** *verb* [I,T]

plunge¹ /plʌndʒ/ *verb* **1** [I,T] to move or make sb/sth move suddenly forwards and/or downwards: *She lost her balance and plunged 100 feet to her death.* ◆ *The earthquake plunged entire towns over the edge of the cliffs.* **2** [I] to decrease suddenly and quickly: *Share prices plunged overnight.*
PHR V **plunge into sth/in 1** to jump into sth, especially with force: *He ran to the river and plunged*

P

in. **2** to start doing sth with energy and enthusiasm: *Think carefully before you plunge into buying a house.*
plunge sth into sth/in to push sth suddenly and with force into sth: *She plunged the knife deep into his chest.*
plunge sb/sth into sth to cause sb/sth to suddenly be in the state mentioned: *The country has been plunged into chaos by the floods.*

plunge² /plʌndʒ/ *noun* [C] a sudden jump, drop or fall: *the plunge in house prices*
IDM **take the plunge** (*informal*) to decide to do sth difficult after thinking about it for quite a long time: *After going out together for five years, they took the plunge and got married.*

pluperfect /ˌpluːˈpɜːfɪkt/ = **past perfect**

plural /ˈplʊərəl/ *noun* [C] (*abbr* **pl.**) the form of a noun, verb, etc. which refers to more than one person or thing: *The plural of 'boat' is 'boats'.* ◆ *The verb should be* ***in the plural.*** ▶ **plural** *adj* ➲ look at **singular**

⚷ **plus¹** /plʌs/ *prep* **1** and; added to: *Two plus two is four (2 + 2 = 4).* OPP **minus** **2** in addition to; and also: *You have to work five days a week plus every other weekend.*

⚷ **plus²** /plʌs/ *noun* [C] **1** an advantage of a situation: *My work is five minutes from my house, which is a definite plus.* **2** the symbol (+) used in mathematics: *He put a plus instead of a minus.* OPP **minus**

⚷ **plus³** /plʌs/ *adj* [only *after* a noun] **1** or more: *I'd say there were 30 000 plus at the match.* **2** [not before a noun] (used for marking work done by students) slightly above: *I got a B plus (= B+) for my homework.* OPP **minus**

P

plush /plʌʃ/ *adj* (*informal*) comfortable and expensive: *a plush hotel*

Pluto /ˈpluːtəʊ/ *noun* [sing] the name of a large round object in space which **orbits** (= goes around) the sun

> **CULTURE**
>
> Pluto was known as the ninth planet in the **solar system** until 2006.

plutonium /pluːˈtəʊniəm/ *noun* [U] (*symbol* Pu) a chemical element that is used in nuclear weapons and in producing nuclear energy

ply /plaɪ/ *verb* [I,T] (**plying**; **plies**; *pt, pp* **plied**) to try to sell services or goods to people, especially on the street: *Boat owners were* ***plying*** *their* ***trade*** *to passing tourists.* ◆ *to ply for business*
PHR V **ply sb with sth** to keep giving sb food and drink, or asking sb questions: *They plied us with food from the moment we arrived.*

plywood /ˈplaɪwʊd/ *noun* [U] board made by sticking several thin layers of wood together

PM *abbr* = **prime minister**

⚷ **p.m.** (*AmE* also **P.M.**) /ˌpiː ˈem/ *abbr* (from Latin) **post meridiem**; after midday: *The appointment is at 3 p.m.* ➲ look at **a.m.**

pneumatic /njuːˈmætɪk/ *adj* **1** filled with air: *a pneumatic tyre* **2** worked by air under pressure: *a pneumatic drill*

pneumonia /njuːˈməʊniə/ *noun* [U] a serious illness of the lungs which makes breathing difficult

PO /ˌpiː ˈəʊ/ *abbr* [in compounds] = **post office**: *a PO box*

poach /pəʊtʃ/ *verb* [T] **1** to cook food gently in liquid: *poached eggs/fish* **2** to hunt animals illegally on sb else's land: *The men were caught poaching elephants.* **3** to take an idea from sb else and use it as though it is your own **4** to take workers from another company in an unfair way

poacher /ˈpəʊtʃə(r)/ *noun* [C] a person who hunts animals illegally on sb else's land

ˈPO box *noun* [C] a place in a post office where letters, packages, etc. are kept until they are collected by the person they were sent to: *The address is PO Box 4287, Nairobi, Kenya.*

⚷ **pocket¹** /ˈpɒkɪt/ *noun* [C] **1** a piece of cloth like a small bag that is sewn inside or on a piece of clothing and is used for carrying things in: *He always walks with his hands in his trouser pockets.* ◆ *a pocket dictionary/calculator* (= one small enough to fit in your pocket) ➲ picture on **page P1** **2** a small bag or container that is fixed to the inside of a car door, suitcase, etc. and used for putting things in: *There are safety instructions in the pocket of the seat in front of you.* ➲ picture at **pool** **3** used to talk about the amount of money that you have to spend: *They sell cars to suit every pocket.* ◆ *He had no intention of paying for the meal* ***out of*** *his* ***own pocket.*** **4** a small area or group that is different from its surroundings: *a pocket of warm air*
IDM **pick sb's pocket** ➲ **pick¹**

pocket² /ˈpɒkɪt/ *verb* [T] **1** to put sth in your pocket: *He took the letter and pocketed it quickly.* **2** to steal or win money

ˈpocket money *noun* [U] (*especially AmE* allowance) an amount of money that parents give a child to spend, usually every week

pod /pɒd/ *noun* [C] the long, green part of some plants, such as **peas** and **beans**, that contains the seeds ➲ picture on **page P15**

podcast /ˈpɒdkɑːst/ *noun* [C] a recording of a radio broadcast or a video that can be taken from the Internet: *I download podcasts of radio shows and listen to them in the car.* ➲ note at **iPod™**

> **TOPIC**
>
> **Podcasts**
>
> You can **download a podcast** to your computer or **portable MP3 player** and watch or listen to it whenever you want to. If you **subscribe to a podcast** (= say that you want to receive regular broadcasts), your computer will **download** each new **episode** (= part) in a series.

podiatrist /pəˈdaɪətrɪst/ = **chiropodist**

podiatry /pəˈdaɪətri/ = **chiropody**

podium /ˈpəʊdiəm/ *noun* [C] a small platform for people to stand on when they are speaking, performing, etc. in public

poem /ˈpəʊɪm/ *noun* [C] a piece of writing arranged in short lines. Poems try to express thoughts and feelings with the help of sound and rhythm: *He wrote poems about the beauty of the countryside.* ♦ *She read the poem aloud.*

poet /ˈpəʊɪt/ *noun* [C] a person who writes poems

poetic /pəʊˈetɪk/ (also **poetical** /-ɪkl/) *adj* connected with poetry or like a poem ▶ **poetically** /-kli/ *adv*

poetry /ˈpəʊətri/ *noun* [U] a collection of poems; poems in general: *Shakespeare's poetry and plays* ♦ *Do you like poetry?* **SYN** **verse** ➲ note at **literature** ➲ look at **prose**

poignant /ˈpɔɪnjənt/ *adj* causing sadness or pity: *a poignant memory* ▶ **poignancy** /-jənsi/ *noun* [U] ▶ **poignantly** /-jəntli/ *adv*

point[1] /pɔɪnt/ *noun*

➤FACT/OPINION **1** [C] a particular fact, idea or opinion that sb expresses: *You* ***make*** *some interesting* ***points*** *in your essay.* ♦ *I see your point but I don't agree with you.*

> **MORE** We can **bring up, raise, make, argue, emphasize** and **illustrate** a point.

➤IMPORTANT IDEA **2 the point** [sing] the most important part of what is being said; the main piece of information: *It makes no difference how much it costs—**the point is** we don't have any money!* ♦ *She always talks and talks and takes ages to **get to the point**.* **3** [C] an important idea or thought that needs to be considered: *'Have you checked what time the last bus back is?' 'That's a point—no, I haven't.'*

➤PURPOSE **4** [sing] **the point (of/in sth/doing sth)** the meaning, reason or purpose of sth: *She's said no, so **what's the point** of telephoning her again?* ♦ ***There's no point** in talking to my parents—they never listen.*

➤QUALITY **5** [C] a detail, characteristic or quality of sb/sth: *Make a list of your **strong points** and your **weak points*** (= good and bad qualities).

➤PLACE/TIME **6** [C] a particular place, position or moment: *The library is a good **starting point** for that sort of information.* ♦ *He has reached the **high point** of his career.* ♦ *the boiling/freezing point of water* ♦ *He waved to the crowd and it was **at that point** that the shot was fired.* ♦ ***At one point** I thought I was going to laugh.*

➤DIRECTION **7** [C] one of the marks of direction around a **compass**: *the points of the compass* (= North, South, East, West, etc.)

➤IN COMPETITION **8** [C] (*abbr* **pt**) a single mark in some games, sports, etc. that you add to others to get the score: *to score a point* ♦ *Rios needs two more points to win the match.*

➤MEASUREMENT **9** [C] a unit of measurement for certain things: *The value of the dollar has fallen by a few points.*

➤IN NUMBERS **10** [C] a small round mark used when writing parts of numbers: *She ran the race in 11.2 (eleven point two) seconds.*

➤SHARP END **11** [C] the thin sharp end of sth: *the point of a pin/needle/pencil*

IDM **be on the point of doing sth** be just going to do sth: *I was on the point of going out when the phone rang.*

beside the point ➲ **beside**

have your, etc. (good) points to have some good qualities: *Bill has his good points, but he's very unreliable.*

make a point of doing sth to make sure you do sth because it is important or necessary: *He made a point of locking all the doors and windows before leaving the house.*

point of view a way of looking at a situation; an opinion: *From my point of view, it would be better to wait a little longer.* **SYN** **viewpoint, standpoint** ➲ note at **think**

> **HELP** **Point of view** or **opinion**? Do not confuse **from my point of view** with **in my opinion.** The first means 'from my position in life' (= as a student, business person, teacher, etc.). The second means 'I think': *From an advertiser's point of view, TV is a wonderful medium.* ♦ *In my opinion, people watch too much TV.*

a sore point ➲ **sore**[1]

sb's strong point ➲ **strong**

take sb's point to understand and accept what sb is saying

to the point connected with what is being discussed: *His speech was short and to the point.* **SYN** **relevant**

up to a point partly: *I agree with you up to a point.*

point[2] /pɔɪnt/ *verb* **1** [I] **point (at/to sb/sth)** to show where sth is or to draw attention to sth using your finger, a stick, etc: *'I'll have that one,' she said, pointing to a chocolate cake.* **2** [I,T] **point (sth) (at/towards sb/sth)** to aim (sth) in the direction of sb/sth: *She pointed the gun at the target and fired.* **3** [I] to face in a particular direction or to show that sth is in a particular direction: *The sign pointed towards the motorway.* ♦ *Turn round until you're pointing north.* **4** [I] **point to sth** to show that sth is likely to exist, happen or be true: *Research points to a connection between diet and cancer.*

PHR V **point sth out (to sb)** to make sb look at sth; to make sth clear to sb: *The guide pointed out all the places of interest to us on the way.* ♦ *I'd like to point out that we haven't got much time left.*

ˌpoint-ˈblank *adj* [only *before* a noun], *adv* **1** (used about a shot) from a very close position: *He was shot in the leg **at point-blank range**.* **2** (used about sth that is said) very direct and not polite; not allowing any discussion: *He told her point-blank to get out of the house and never come back.*

pointed /ˈpɔɪntɪd/ *adj* **1** having a sharp end: *a pointed stick/nose* **2** said in a critical way: *She made a pointed comment about people who are always late.* ▶ **pointedly** *adv*

pointer /ˈpɔɪntə(r)/ *noun* [C] **1** a piece of helpful advice or information: *Could you* ***give*** *me some*

P

pointers on how best to tackle the problem? **2** a stick that is used to point to things on a map, etc. **3** a small arrow on a computer screen that you move by moving the mouse

pointless /ˈpɔɪntləs/ *adj* without any use or purpose: *It's pointless to try and make him agree.* ▶ **pointlessly** *adv* ▶ **pointlessness** *noun* [U]

poise /pɔɪz/ *noun* [U] a calm, confident way of behaving

poised /pɔɪzd/ *adj* [not before a noun] **1** not moving but ready to move: *'Shall I call the doctor or not?' he asked, his hand poised above the telephone.* **2** **poised (to do sth)** ready to act; about to do sth: *The government is poised to take action if the crisis continues.* **3** calm and confident

poison¹ /ˈpɔɪzn/ *noun* [C,U] a substance that kills or harms you if you eat or drink it: *rat poison* ◆ *poison gas* ◆ *a deadly poison*

poison² /ˈpɔɪzn/ *verb* [T] **1** to kill, harm or damage sb/sth with poison: *The police confirmed that the murder victim had been poisoned.* **2** to put poison in sth: *The cup of coffee had been poisoned.* **3** to spoil or ruin sth: *The quarrel had poisoned their relationship.* ▶ **poisoned** *adj*: *a poisoned drink*

poisoning /ˈpɔɪzənɪŋ/ *noun* [U] the giving or taking of poison or a dangerous substance: *He got* ***food poisoning*** *from eating fish that wasn't fresh.*

poisonous /ˈpɔɪzənəs/ *adj* **1** causing death or illness if you eat or drink it: *a poisonous plant* **2** (used about animals, etc.) producing and using poison to attack its enemies: *He was bitten by a poisonous snake.* **3** very unpleasant and intended to upset sb: *She wrote him a poisonous letter criticizing his behaviour.*

poke /pəʊk/ *verb* **1** [T] to push sb/sth with a finger, stick or other long, thin object: *Be careful you don't poke yourself in the eye with that stick!* **2** [I,T] **poke (sth) into, through, out of, down, etc. sth** to push or move sth quickly into sth or in a certain direction: *He poked the stick down the hole to see how deep it was.* ◆ *A child's head poked up from behind the wall.* **3** to send a short message to a friend on a **social networking** site (= a service on the Internet for people who share your interests) ➲ note at **social networking**

poke

She poked the fire.

IDM **poke fun at sb/sth** to make jokes about sb/sth, often in an unkind way

poke/stick your nose into sth ➲ **nose¹**

▶ **poke** *noun* [C]

poker /ˈpəʊkə(r)/ *noun* **1** [U] a type of card game usually played to win money **2** [C] a metal stick for moving the coal or wood in a fire ➲ picture at **fireplace**

poky /ˈpəʊki/ *adj* (**pokier**; **pokiest**) (*BrE informal*) (used about a house, room, etc.) too small: *a poky little office*

polar /ˈpəʊlə(r)/ *adj* [only *before* a noun] of or near the North or South Pole: *the polar regions*

ˌpolar ˈbear *noun* [C] a large white bear that lives in the area near the North Pole

polarize (also **-ise**) /ˈpəʊləraɪz/ *verb* [I,T] (*formal*) to separate or make people separate into two groups with completely opposite opinions: *Public opinion has polarized on this issue.* ◆ *The issue has polarized public opinion.*

pole /pəʊl/ *noun* [C] **1** a long, thin piece of wood or metal, used especially to hold sth up: *a flagpole* ◆ *a tent pole* **2** either of the two points at the exact top and bottom of the earth: *the North/South Pole* ➲ picture at **earth**

the ˈpole vault *noun* [sing] the sport of jumping over a high bar with the help of a long pole

police¹ /pəˈliːs/ *noun* [pl] the official organization whose job is to make sure that people obey the law, and to prevent and solve crime; the people who work for this organization: *Dial 999 if you need to* ***call the police.*** ◆ *a police car* ◆ *Kamal wants to join* ***the police force*** *when he finishes school.* ◆ *the local* ***police station***

> **HELP** You CANNOT say 'a police' meaning one man or woman. We usually refer to 'police officers'. When we are talking about the organization, we always use **the**: *There were over 100 police on duty.* ◆ *The police are investigating the murder.*

police² /pəˈliːs/ *verb* [T] to keep control in a place by using the police or a similar official group: *The cost of policing football games is extremely high.*

poˌlice ˈconstable (also **constable**) *noun* [C] (*abbr* PC) (in Britain) a police officer of the lowest level

policeman /pəˈliːsmən/ *noun* [C] (*pl* **policemen**) a male police officer

poˈlice officer (also **officer**) *noun* [C] a member of the police ➲ note at **official²** ➲ picture on **page P2**

policewoman /pəˈliːswʊmən/ *noun* [C] (*pl* **policewomen**) a female police officer

policy /ˈpɒləsi/ *noun* (*pl* **policies**) **1** [C,U] **policy (on sth)** a plan of action agreed or chosen by a government, a company, etc: *The Conservatives have a new set of policies on health.* ◆ *It is company policy not to allow children on the premises.* **2** [C,U] a way of behaving that you think is best in a particular situation: *It's my policy only to do business with people I like.* **3** [C] a document that shows an agreement that you have made with an insurance company: *an insurance policy*

polio /ˈpəʊliəʊ/ *noun* [U] a serious disease which can cause you to lose the power in certain muscles

polish¹ /ˈpɒlɪʃ/ *noun* **1** [U] a cream, liquid, etc. that you put on sth to clean it and make it shine: *a* *tin of shoe polish* ➲ picture at **bucket** **2** [sing] the act of polishing sth: *I'll **give** the glasses **a polish** before the guests arrive.*

polish² /ˈpɒlɪʃ/ *verb* [T] to make sth shine by rubbing it and often by putting a special cream or liquid on it: *to polish your shoes/a table*
PHR V **polish sth off** (*informal*) to finish sth quickly: *The two of them polished off a whole chicken for dinner!*

polished /ˈpɒlɪʃt/ *adj* **1** shiny because of polishing: *polished wood floors* **2** (used about a performance, etc.) of a high standard: *Most of the actors gave **a polished performance**.*

polite /pəˈlaɪt/ *adj* (**politer**; **politest**) [**More polite** and **most polite** are also common.] having good manners and showing respect for others: *The assistants in that shop are always very helpful and polite.* ♦ *He gave me a polite smile.* **OPP** **impolite** ▸ **politely** *adv* ▸ **politeness** *noun* [U]

political /pəˈlɪtɪkl/ *adj* **1** connected with politics and government: *a political leader/debate/party* ♦ *She has very strong political opinions.* **2** (used about people) interested in politics: *She became very political at university.* **3** concerned with competition for power inside an organization: *I suspect he was dismissed for political reasons.* ▸ **politically** /-kli/ *adv*: *Politically he's fairly right wing.*

poˌlitical aˈsylum *noun* [U] protection given by a state to a person who has left their own country for political reasons

poˌlitically corˈrect *adj* (*abbr* **PC**) used to describe language or behaviour that carefully avoids offending particular groups of people ▸ **poˌlitical corˈrectness** *noun* [U]

poˌlitical ˈscience = **politics**(4)

politician /ˌpɒləˈtɪʃn/ *noun* [C] a person whose job is in politics, especially one who is a member of parliament or of the government: *Politicians of all parties supported the war.*

TOPIC

Politics

In **democratic** countries, **the government** (= the people who control the country) are chosen in **elections**. People **vote for** (= choose) a **candidate** (= a person who wants to be elected). Most **politicians** belong to a **political party**. **Left-wing** parties desire equality (= everyone having the same rights and advantages) and believe that the government should own the main industries. **Right-wing** parties support the system in which industries are owned by individual people and not the state. In the United Kingdom, the person who leads the government is called the **Prime Minister**, and the people who make and change laws are called **Parliament**. In the United States, this group of people is called **Congress** and the head of the government is the **President**.

politics /ˈpɒlətɪks/ *noun* **1** [U, with sing or pl verb] the work and ideas that are connected with governing a country, a town, etc: *to go into politics* ♦ *Politics has/have never been of great interest to me.* **2** [pl] a person's political opinions and beliefs: *His politics are extreme.* **3** [U, with sing or pl verb] matters concerned with competition for power between people in an organization: *office politics* **4** (also **Poˌlitical ˈScience**) [U] the scientific study of government: *a degree in Politics* ➲ note at **congress, election, parliament, party**

poll¹ /pəʊl/ *noun* [C] **1** (also **opinion poll**) a way of finding out public opinion by asking a number of people their views on sth: *This was voted best drama series in a viewers' poll.* **2** the process of voting in a political election; the number of votes given: *The country will **go to the polls** (= vote) in June.*

poll² /pəʊl/ *verb* [T] **1** to receive a certain number of votes in an election: *The Liberal Democrat candidate polled over 3 000 votes.* **2** to ask members of the public their opinion on a subject: *Of those polled, only 20 per cent were in favour of changing the law.*

pollen /ˈpɒlən/ *noun* [U] a fine, usually yellow, powder which is formed in flowers. It makes other flowers of the same type produce seeds when it is carried to them by the wind or by insects, etc.

pollinate /ˈpɒləneɪt/ *verb* [T] to put **pollen** into a flower or plant so that it produces seeds: *flowers pollinated by bees/the wind* ▸ **pollination** /ˌpɒləˈneɪʃn/ *noun* [U]

polling /ˈpəʊlɪŋ/ *noun* [U] the process of voting in an election

pollutant /pəˈluːtənt/ *noun* [C] a substance that **pollutes** air, rivers, etc.

pollute /pəˈluːt/ *verb* [T] to make air, rivers, etc. dirty and dangerous: *Traffic fumes are polluting our cities.* ♦ *The beach has been polluted with oil.*

pollution /pəˈluːʃn/ *noun* [U] **1** the act of making the air, water, etc. dirty and dangerous: *Major steps are being taken to control the pollution of beaches.* **2** substances that **pollute**: *The rivers are full of pollution.* ➲ note at **environment**

polo /ˈpəʊləʊ/ *noun* [U] a game for two teams of players riding horses. The players try to score goals by hitting a ball with **mallets** (= long wooden hammers).

ˈ**polo neck** *noun* [C] a high round **collar** (= the part around the neck) on a piece of clothing that is rolled over and that covers most of your neck; a piece of clothing with a **polo neck**

polyester /ˌpɒliˈestə(r)/ *noun* [U] an artificial cloth that is used for making clothes, etc.

polygamy /pəˈlɪgəmi/ *noun* [U] the custom of having more than one wife or husband at the same time ➲ look at **bigamy, monogamy** ▸ **polygamist** /-mɪst/ *noun* [C] ▸ **polygamous** /pəˈlɪgəməs/ *adj*: *a polygamous society*

polystyrene /ˌpɒliˈstaɪriːn/ *noun* [U] a light firm plastic substance that is used for packing things so that they do not get broken

polythene /ˈpɒlɪθiːn/ (*AmE* **polyethylene** /ˌpɒliˈeθəliːn/) *noun* [U] a type of very thin plastic material

P

often used to make bags for food, etc. or to keep things dry

pomp /pɒmp/ *noun* [U] the impressive nature of a large official occasion or ceremony

pompous /ˈpɒmpəs/ *adj* showing that you think you are more important than other people, for example by using long words that sound impressive

pond /pɒnd/ *noun* [C] an small area of still water ➲ note at **lake** ➲ picture on **page P11**

ponder /ˈpɒndə(r)/ *verb* [I,T] (*formal*) **ponder (on/over) sth** to think about sth carefully or for a long time: *The teacher gave us a question to ponder over before the next class.*

pong /pɒŋ/ *noun* [C] (*BrE informal*) a strong unpleasant smell: *a terrible pong* ➲ note at **smell**[2] ▶ **pong** *verb* [I]

pony /ˈpəʊni/ *noun* [C] (*pl* **ponies**) a small horse

ponytail /ˈpəʊniteɪl/ *noun* [C] long hair that is tied at the back of the head and that hangs down in one piece ➲ picture at **hair**

ˈ**pony-trekking** *noun* [U] the activity of riding horses for pleasure in the country

poo /puː/ *noun* [C,U] a child's word for the solid waste material that you get rid of from your body when you go to the toilet ▶ **poo** *verb* [I]

poodle /ˈpuːdl/ *noun* [C] a type of dog with thick curly fur that is sometimes cut into a special pattern

pooh /puː/ *exclam* (*BrE informal*) said when you smell sth unpleasant

P

pool

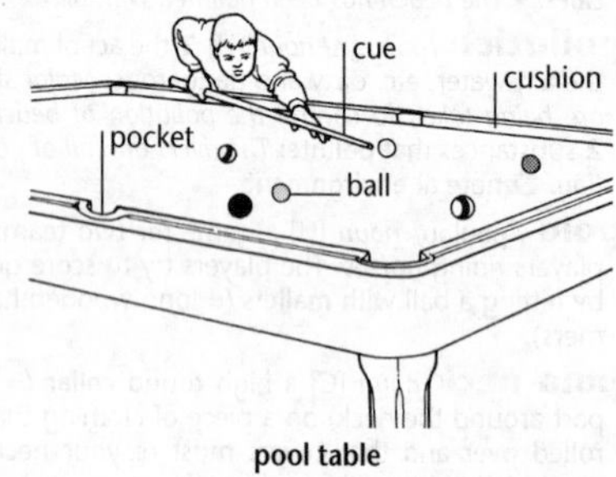

pool table

⚷ **pool**[1] /puːl/ *noun*

➤FOR SWIMMING **1** [C] = **swimming pool**: *She swims ten lengths of the pool every morning.*

➤OF LIQUID **2** a small amount of water, especially one that has formed naturally: *a rock pool* (= between rocks by the sea) ➲ picture on **page P10** **3** [C] a **pool (of sth)** a small amount of liquid lying on a surface: *There's a huge pool of water on the kitchen floor.* ➲ note at **lake**

➤OF LIGHT **4** [C] a small area of light: *a pool of light*

➤GROUP OF THINGS/PEOPLE **5** [C] a quantity of money, goods, etc. that is shared between a group of people: *There is a pool of cars that anyone in the company can use.*

➤GAME **6** [U] a game for two people played with 16 balls on a table. Players use **cues** (= long sticks) to try to hit the balls into pockets at the edge of the table: *a pool table* ➲ look at **billiards, snooker**

pool[2] /puːl/ *verb* [T] to collect money, ideas, etc. together from a number of people: *If we pool our ideas we should come up with a good plan.*

⚷ **poor** /pɔː(r); pʊə(r)/ *adj* (**poorer**; **poorest**) **1** not having enough money to have a comfortable life: *The family was too poor to buy new clothes.* ◆ *Richer countries could do more to help poorer countries.* OPP **rich** **2** **the poor** *noun* [pl] people who do not have enough money to have a comfortable life: *They provided food and shelter for the poor.* **3** [only *before* a noun] used when you are showing that you feel sorry for sb: *Poor Dan! He's very upset!* **4** of low quality or in a bad condition: *Paul is in very poor health.* ◆ *The industry has a poor safety record.*

poorly[1] /ˈpɔːli; ˈpʊəli/ *adv* not well; badly: *a poorly paid job*

poorly[2] /ˈpɔːli/ *adj* (*BrE informal*) not well; ill: *I'm feeling a bit poorly.*

⚷ **pop**[1] /pɒp/ *noun* **1** [U] (also ˈ**pop music**) modern music that is most popular among young people: *a pop group* ➲ look at **jazz, rock, classical** **2** [C] a short sudden sound like a small explosion: *There was a loud pop as the champagne cork came out of the bottle.*

TOPIC

Pop music

I like most kinds of music, including **pop**, **rock**, **hip hop** and **reggae**. I love going to **gigs** (= concerts). My favourite **band/group** is 'Alphagarden'. I'm one of their biggest **fans**. I love the **singer** because he has such a great **voice**! The **drummer** and **guitarist** play well, too. All their **songs** have good **lyrics** (= words) and the **tunes/melodies** are very **catchy** (= easy to remember). Last year they released an **album** (= a collection of songs on one CD) which became a big **hit** (= was very successful). They don't often **play live** (= with people watching), but next year they are going **on tour** (= performing in various places). I already have tickets to **go to a concert**.

⚷ **pop**[2] /pɒp/ *verb* (**popping**; **popped**) **1** [I,T] to make a short sudden sound like a small explosion; to cause sth to do this: *The balloon popped.* ◆ *He popped the balloon.* **2** [I] **pop across, down, out, etc.** to come or go somewhere quickly or suddenly: *I'm just popping out to the shops.* **3** [T] **pop sth in, into, etc. sth** to put or take sth somewhere quickly or suddenly: *She popped the note into her bag.*

PHR V **pop in** to make a quick visit: *Why don't you pop in for a cup of tea?*

pop out to come out (of sth) suddenly or quickly: *A window opened and a man's head popped out.*

pop up (*informal*) to appear or happen when you are not expecting it

pop. *abbr* = **population**: *pop. 12m*

popcorn /ˈpɒpkɔːn/ *noun* [U] a type of food made from **maize** (= a tall plant with yellow grains) that is heated until it bursts and forms light white balls that are eaten with salt or sugar on them

pope /pəʊp/ *noun* [C] the head of the Roman Catholic Church

poplar /ˈpɒplə(r)/ *noun* [C] a tall thin straight tree with soft wood

ˈ**pop music** = **pop**[1](1)

ˈ**popper** /ˈpɒpə(r)/ = **press stud**

poppy /ˈpɒpi/ *noun* [C] (*pl* **poppies**) a bright red wild flower that has small black seeds

Popsicle™ /ˈpɒpsɪkl/ (*AmE*) = **ice lolly**

🔑 **popular** /ˈpɒpjələ(r)/ *adj* **1 popular (with sb)** liked by many people or by most people in a group: *a popular holiday resort* ◆ *That teacher has always been very popular with his pupils.* **OPP unpopular** **2** made for the tastes and knowledge of ordinary people: *The popular newspapers seem more interested in scandal than news.* **3** [only *before* a noun] of or for a lot of people: *The programme is being repeated **by popular demand**.*

popularity /ˌpɒpjuˈlærəti/ *noun* [U] the quality or state of being liked by many people: *The band's popularity is growing.*

popularize (also -ise) /ˈpɒpjələraɪz/ *verb* [T] to make a lot of or most people like sth: *The film did a lot to popularize her novels.*

popularly /ˈpɒpjələli/ *adv* by many people; generally: *The Conservatives are popularly known as the Tories.*

populate /ˈpɒpjuleɪt/ *verb* [T, usually passive] to fill a particular area with people: *Hong Kong is very densely populated.*

🔑 **population** /ˌpɒpjuˈleɪʃn/ *noun* (*abbr* **pop.**) **1** [C,U] the number of people who live in a particular area, city or country: *What is the population of your country?* ◆ *an increase/a fall in population* **2** [C] all the people who live in a particular place or all the people or animals of a particular type that live somewhere: *the local population* ◆ *the male/female population* ◆ *The prison population has increased in recent years.*

ˈ**pop-up** *adj* [only *before* a noun] **1** (used about a computer menu, etc.) that can be brought to the screen quickly while you are working on another document: *a **pop-up** menu/window* **2** (used about a book, etc.) containing a picture that stands up when the pages are opened

porcelain /ˈpɔːsəlɪn/ *noun* [U] a hard white substance that is used for making expensive cups, plates, etc.

porch /pɔːtʃ/ *noun* [C] **1** a small covered area at the entrance to a house or church ➲ picture on **page P8** **2** (*AmE*) = **veranda**

pore[1] /pɔː(r)/ *noun* [C] one of the small holes in your skin through which sweat can pass

pore[2] /pɔː(r)/ *verb*

PHR V pore over sth to study or read sth very carefully

pork /pɔːk/ *noun* [U] meat from a pig ➲ note at **meat** ➲ look at **bacon, gammon, ham**

pornography /pɔːˈnɒɡrəfi/ (also *informal* **porn** /pɔːn/) *noun* [U] magazines, films, websites, etc. that describe or show sexual acts in order to cause sexual excitement ▶ **pornographic** /ˌpɔːnəˈɡræfɪk/ *adj*

porous /ˈpɔːrəs/ *adj* having many small holes that allow water or air to pass through slowly: *porous material/rocks/surfaces*

porpoise /ˈpɔːpəs/ *noun* [C] a sea animal that looks like a large fish with a pointed nose and that lives in groups ➲ look at **dolphin**

porridge /ˈpɒrɪdʒ/ *noun* [U] a soft, thick, white food that is made from **oats** (= a type of grain) boiled with milk or water and eaten hot, especially for breakfast

🔑 **port** /pɔːt/ *noun* **1** [C] a town or city that has a large area of water where ships load goods, etc: *Hamburg is a major port.* **2** [C,U] an area where ships stop to let goods and passengers on and off: *a naval port* ◆ *The damaged ship reached port safely.* **3** [U] a strong sweet red wine **4** [U] the side of a ship that is on your left when you are facing towards the front of the ship: *the port side* **OPP starboard** ➲ note at **boat**

portable /ˈpɔːtəbl/ *adj* that can be moved or carried easily: *a portable TV* ➲ look at **movable, mobile**

portal /ˈpɔːtl/ *noun* [C] a website which is used as a point to enter the Internet, giving links to information that will be useful to a person interested in particular kinds of things: *a business/news/shopping portal*

porter /ˈpɔːtə(r)/ *noun* [C] **1** a person whose job is to carry suitcases, etc. at a railway station, airport, etc. **2** a person whose job is to be in charge of the entrance of a hotel or other large building

portfolio /pɔːtˈfəʊliəʊ/ *noun* [C] (*pl* **portfolios**) **1** a thin flat case used for carrying documents, drawings, etc. **2** a collection of photographs, drawings, etc. that you use as an example of your work, especially when applying for a job

porthole /ˈpɔːthəʊl/ *noun* [C] a small round window in a ship

portion /ˈpɔːʃn/ *noun* [C] **a portion (of sth)** **1** a part or share of sth: *What portion of your salary goes on tax?* ◆ *We must both accept a portion of the blame.* **2** an amount of food for one person (especially in a restaurant): *Could we have two extra portions of chips, please?* ➲ look at **helping**

portrait /ˈpɔːtreɪt; -trət/ *noun* **1** [C] a picture, painting or photograph of a person: *to paint somebody's portrait* **2** [C] a description of sb/sth in words **3** [U] (*technical*) the way of printing a document in which the top of the page is one of the shorter sides ➲ look at **landscape** ➲ picture at **computer**

portray /pɔːˈtreɪ/ *verb* [T] **1** to show sb/sth in a picture; to describe sb/sth in a piece of writing: *Zola portrayed life in 19th-century France.* **2 portray sb/sth as sth** to describe sb/sth in a particular way: *In many of his novels life is portrayed as being hard.* **3** to act the part of sb in a play or film: *In this film*

P

she portrays a very old woman. ▶ **portrayal** /pɔːˈtreɪəl/ *noun* [C,U]

pose¹ /pəʊz/ *verb* **1** [T] to create or give sb sth that they have to deal with: *to pose a problem/threat/challenge/risk* ♦ *to pose* (= ask) *a question* **2** [I] to sit or stand in a particular position for a painting, photograph, etc: *After the wedding we all posed for photographs.* **3** [I] **pose as sb/sth** to pretend to be sb/sth: *The robbers got into the house by posing as telephone engineers.* **4** [I] to behave in a way that is intended to impress people who see you: *They hardly swam at all. They just sat posing at the side of the pool.*

pose² /pəʊz/ *noun* [C] **1** a position in which sb stands, sits, etc. especially in order to be painted or photographed: *He adopted a relaxed pose for the camera.* **2** a way of behaving that is intended to impress people who see you: *His show of interest is just a pose.*

posh /pɒʃ/ *adj* (**posher**; **poshest**) (*informal*) **1** fashionable and expensive: *We went for a meal in a really posh hotel.* SYN **stylish** **2** (*BrE*) (used about people) belonging to or typical of a high social class

position¹ /pəˈzɪʃn/ *noun*

➤PLACE **1** [C,U] the place where sb/sth is or should be: *Are you happy with the position of the chairs?* ♦ *All the dancers were* ***in position*** *waiting for the music to begin.*

➤OF BODY, ETC. **2** [C,U] the way in which sb/sth sits, sleeps or stands, or the direction that sth is pointing in: *My leg hurts when I* ***change position****.* ♦ *Turn the switch to the off position.*

➤SITUATION **3** [C, usually sing] the state or situation that sb/sth is in: *I'm in a very* ***difficult position****.* ♦ *I'm sorry, I'm not* ***in a position*** *to help you financially.*

➤OPINION **4** [C] **a position (on sth)** what you think about sth; your opinion: *What is your position on school uniform?*

➤LEVEL OF IMPORTANCE **5** [C,U] the place or level of a person, company, team, etc. compared to others: *the position of women in society* ♦ *Max finished the race in second position.* ♦ *Wealth and position are very important to some people.*

➤JOB **6** [C] (*formal*) a job: *There have been over a hundred applications for the position of Sales Manager.* SYN **post**

➤IN SPORT **7** [C] the part you play in a team game: *Danny can play any position except goalkeeper.*

position² /pəˈzɪʃn/ *verb* [T] to put sb/sth in a particular place or position: *Mary positioned herself near the door so she could get out quickly.*

positive /ˈpɒzətɪv/ *adj*

➤CONFIDENT **1** thinking or talking mainly about the good things in a situation; feeling confident and sure that sth good will happen: *Their reaction to my idea was generally positive.* ♦ *I* ***feel*** *very* ***positive*** *about our team's chances this season.* ♦ ***Positive thinking*** *will help you to succeed.* OPP **negative**

➤CERTAIN/DEFINITE **2** **positive (about sth/that …)** certain; sure: *Are you positive that this is the woman you saw?* **3** clear; definite: *There is no positive evidence that he is guilty.* ♦ *to take positive action*

➤SCIENTIFIC TEST **4** showing that sth has happened or is present: *The result of the pregnancy test was positive.* ♦ *Two athletes tested positive for steroids.* OPP **negative**

➤NUMBER **5** more than zero OPP **negative**

positively /ˈpɒzətɪvli/ *adv* **1** (used for emphasizing sth) really; extremely: *He wasn't just annoyed—he was positively furious!* **2** in a way that shows you are thinking about the good things in a situation, not the bad: *Thinking positively helps many people deal with stress.* **3** with no doubt; firmly: *I was positively convinced that I was doing the right thing.*

possess /pəˈzes/ *verb* [T] [not used in the continuous tenses] **1** (*formal*) to have or own sth: *They lost everything they possessed in the fire.* ♦ *Paola possesses a natural ability to make people laugh.* **2** to influence sb or to make sb do sth: *What possessed you to say a thing like that!*

> **HELP** Although this verb is not used in the continuous tenses, it is common to see the present participle (= *-ing* form): *Any student possessing the necessary qualifications will be considered for the course.*

possession /pəˈzeʃn/ *noun* **1** [U] (*formal*) the state of having or owning sth: *The gang were caught* ***in possession of*** *stolen goods.* ♦ *Enemy forces* ***took possession of*** *the town.* **2** [C, usually pl] something that you have or own: *Bud packed all his possessions and left.*

possessive /pəˈzesɪv/ *adj* **1** **possessive (of/about sb/sth)** not wanting to share sb/sth: *Dan is so possessive about his toys—he won't let other children play with them.* **2** used to describe words that show who or what a person or thing belongs to: *'My', 'your' and 'his' are possessive adjectives.* ♦ *'Mine', 'yours' and 'his' are possessive pronouns.*

possessor /pəˈzesə(r)/ *noun* [C] (*formal*) a person who has or owns sth

possibility /ˌpɒsəˈbɪləti/ *noun* (*pl* **possibilities**) **1** [U,C] **(a) possibility (of sth/doing sth); (a) possibility that …** the fact that sth might exist or happen, but is not likely to: *There's not much possibility of the letter reaching you before Saturday.* ♦ *There is a* ***strong possibility*** *that the fire was started deliberately.* **2** [C] one of the different things that you can do in a particular situation or in order to achieve sth: *There is a wide range of possibilities open to us.*

possible /ˈpɒsəbl/ *adj* **1** that can happen or be done: *I'll phone you back* ***as*** *soon* ***as possible****.* ♦ *Could you give me your answer today,* ***if possible****?* ♦ *The doctors did* ***everything possible*** *to save his life.* ♦ *You were warned of all the possible dangers.* OPP **impossible** **2** that might exist or happen but is not certain to: *the possible side effects of the drug* **3** reasonable or acceptable in a particular situation: *There are several possible explanations.* ➲ look at **probable** **4** used after adjectives to emphasize that sth is the best, worst, etc. of its type: *Alone and with no job or money, I was in the worst possible situation.*

P

possibly /ˈpɒsəbli/ *adv* **1** perhaps: *'Will you be free on Sunday?' 'Possibly.'* ◆ *Could you possibly give me some help tomorrow?* SYN **maybe** **2** (used for emphasizing sth) according to what is possible: *I will leave as soon as I possibly can.* ◆ *I can't possibly finish this work today.*

post[1] /pəʊst/ *noun*
▸LETTERS **1** (*especially AmE* mail) [U] the system or organization for collecting and dealing with letters, packages, etc: *The document is too valuable to send by post.* ◆ *If you hurry you might* ***catch the post*** (= post it before everything is collected). **2** (*AmE* mail) [U] letters, packages, etc. that are collected or brought to your house: *Has the post come yet this morning?* ◆ *There wasn't any post for you.*
▸JOB **3** [C] (*formal*) a job: *The post was advertised in the local newspaper.* SYN **position**
▸SOLDIER/GUARD **4** [C] a place where sb is on duty or is guarding sth: *The soldiers had to remain at their posts all night.*
▸METAL/WOOD **5** [C] a vertical piece of metal or wood that is put in the ground to mark a position or to support sth: *a goal post* ◆ *Can you see a signpost anywhere?* **6** (also posting) [C] a message sent to a discussion group on the Internet: *The forum doesn't allow posts from non-members.* ➲ note at **chat room, netiquette**
IDM **by return (of post)** ➲ **return**[2]

post[2] /pəʊst/ *verb* **1** (*especially AmE* mail) [T] to send a letter, package, etc. by post: *This letter was posted in Edinburgh yesterday.* **2** [T] to send sb to go and work somewhere: *After two years in London, Angela was posted to the Tokyo office.* **3** [T] to put sb on guard or on duty in a particular place: *Policemen were posted outside the building.* **4** [T, often passive] to put a notice where everyone can see it: *The exam results will be posted on the main noticeboard.* **5** [I,T] to put information or pictures on a website: *The winners' names will be posted on our website.* ◆ *The photos have been provided by fans who post on the message board.*

TOPIC

Posting letters

Post (noun and verb) is more commonly used in British English and **mail** in American English. However, the noun **mail** is often used in British English, for example in the official name of the Post Office organization, the **Royal Mail**. When you have written a **letter** you put it in an **envelope, address** it, **put/stick a stamp** on it and put it in a **postbox** (*US* **mailbox**). The address should include the **postcode** (*US* **zip code**). You can choose to send **parcels** and letters by **airmail** or **surface mail**. If it is urgent, you might send it by **courier**. You can order goods to be delivered by mail, using a **mail-order** service.

postage /ˈpəʊstɪdʒ/ *noun* [U] the amount that you must pay to send a letter, package etc.

ˈ**postage stamp** = **stamp**[1] (1)

postal /ˈpəʊstl/ *adj* [only *before* a noun] connected with the sending and collecting of letters, packages, etc.

ˈ**postal order** (*AmE* ˈmoney order) *noun* [C] a piece of paper that you can buy at a post office that represents a certain amount of money. A **postal order** is a safe way of sending money by post.

postbox (*BrE*)

mailbox (*AmE*)

postbox /ˈpəʊstbɒks/ (also ˈletter box; *AmE* mailbox) *noun* [C] a box in a public place where you put letters, etc. that you want to send ➲ look at **pillar box**

postcard /ˈpəʊstkɑːd/ *noun* [C] a card that you write a message on and send to sb. **Postcards** have a picture on one side and are usually sent without an envelope. ➲ picture at **letter**

postcode /ˈpəʊstkəʊd/ (*AmE* zip code) *noun* [C] a group of letters and/or numbers that you put at the end of an address

poster /ˈpəʊstə(r)/ *noun* [C] **1** a large printed picture or a notice in a public place, often used to advertise sth **2** a large picture printed on paper that is put on a wall for decoration

posterity /pɒˈsterəti/ *noun* [U] (*formal*) the future and the people who will be alive then: *We should all look after our environment for the sake of posterity.*

postgraduate /ˌpəʊstˈɡrædʒuət/ *noun* [C] a person who is doing further studies at a university after taking their first degree ➲ look at **graduate, undergraduate**

posthumous /ˈpɒstjʊməs/ *adj* given or happening after sb has died: *a posthumous medal for bravery* ▸ **posthumously** *adv*

posting /ˈpəʊstɪŋ/ *noun* [C] **1** a job in another country that you are sent to do by your employer: *an overseas posting* **2** = **post**[1] (6)

ˈ**Post-it**™ (also ˈPost-it note) *noun* [C] a small piece of coloured, sticky paper that you use for writing a note on, and that can be easily removed

postman /ˈpəʊstmən/ (*AmE* mailman) *noun* [C] (*pl* -men /-mən/) a person whose job is to take letters, packages, etc. to people's houses

postmark /ˈpəʊstmɑːk/ *noun* [C] an official mark over a stamp on a letter, package, etc. that says when and where it was posted ➲ picture at **letter**

post-mortem /ˌpəʊst ˈmɔːtəm/ *noun* [C] a medical examination of a dead body to find out how the person died

P

post-natal /ˌpəʊst ˈneɪtl/ *adj* [only *before* a noun] connected with the period after the birth of a baby **OPP** **antenatal**

ˈpost office *noun* [C] (*abbr* PO) **1** a place where you can buy stamps, post packages, etc: *Where's the main post office?* **2 the Post Office** [sing] the national organization that is responsible for collecting and dealing with letters, packages, etc: *He works for the Post Office.*

postpone /pəˈspəʊn/ *verb* [T] to arrange that sth will happen at a later time than the time you had planned; to delay: *The match was postponed because of water on the pitch.* ➲ look at **cancel** ▸ **postponement** *noun* [C,U]

postscript /ˈpəʊstskrɪpt/ = **PS**

posture /ˈpɒstʃə(r)/ *noun* [C,U] the way that a person sits, stands, walks, etc: *Poor posture can lead to backache.*

ˌpost-ˈwar *adj* existing or happening in the period after the end of a war, especially the Second World War

pot¹ /pɒt/ *noun* [C] **1** a round container that is used for cooking food in: *pots and pans* **2** a container that you use for a particular purpose: *a flowerpot* ◆ *a pot of paint* **3** the amount that a pot contains: *We drank two pots of tea.*

pot² /pɒt/ *verb* [T] (potting; potted) **1** to put a plant into a pot filled with soil **2** to hit a ball into one of the pockets in the table in the game of **pool**, **billiards** or **snooker** (= games that are played on special tables): *He potted the black ball into the corner pocket.*

P

potassium /pəˈtæsiəm/ *noun* [U] (*symbol* K) a chemical element that exists as a soft, silver-white metal and is used combined with other elements in industry and farming

potato /pəˈteɪtəʊ/ *noun* [C,U] (*pl* potatoes) a round vegetable that grows under the ground with a brown, yellow or red skin. Potatoes are white or yellow inside: *mashed potato* ◆ *to peel potatoes* ➲ note at **recipe** ➲ picture on **page P15**

poˌtato ˈcrisp (*AmE* poˈtato chip) = **crisp²**

potent /ˈpəʊtnt/ *adj* strong or powerful: *a potent drug* ▸ **potency** /ˈpəʊtnsi/ *noun* [U]

potential¹ /pəˈtenʃl/ *adj* [only *before* a noun] that may possibly become sth, happen, be used, etc: *Wind power is a potential source of energy.* ◆ *potential customers* **SYN** **possible** ▸ **potentially** /-ʃəli/ *adv*

potential² /pəˈtenʃl/ *noun* [U] the qualities or abilities that sb/sth has but that may not be fully developed yet: *That boy **has great potential** as an athlete.*

pothole /ˈpɒthəʊl/ *noun* [C] **1** a hole in the surface of a road that is formed by traffic and bad weather **2** a deep hole in rock that is formed by water over thousands of years

potholing /ˈpɒthəʊlɪŋ/ *noun* [U] the sport of climbing down inside **potholes**(2) and walking through underground tunnels: *to go potholing*

potion /ˈpəʊʃn/ *noun* [C] **1** a drink of medicine or poison **2** (in stories) a liquid with magic powers: *a magic/love potion*

ˈpot plant *noun* [C] (*BrE*) a plant that you grow in a pot and keep inside a building

potter¹ /ˈpɒtə(r)/ (*AmE* putter /ˈpʌtə(r)/) *verb* [I] potter (about/around) to spend your time doing small jobs or things that you enjoy without hurrying: *Grandpa spends most of the day pottering about in the garden.*

potter² /ˈpɒtə(r)/ *noun* [C] a person who makes **pottery** from baked **clay** (= a type of earth)

pottery /ˈpɒtəri/ *noun* (*pl* potteries) **1** [U] pots, dishes, etc. that are made from baked **clay** (= a type of earth) **2** [U] the activity or skill of making dishes, etc. from **clay**: *a pottery class* **3** [C] a place where **clay** pots and dishes are made

potty¹ /ˈpɒti/ *adj* (pottier; pottiest) (*BrE old-fashioned informal*) **1** crazy or silly **2** potty about sb/sth liking sb/sth very much: *Penny's potty about Mark.*

potty² /ˈpɒti/ *noun* [C] (*pl* potties) a plastic bowl that young children use when they are too small to use a toilet

pouch /paʊtʃ/ *noun* [C] **1** a small bag: *a leather pouch* **2** a pocket of skin on the stomach of some female animals, for example **kangaroos**, in which they carry their babies ➲ picture at **kangaroo**

poultry /ˈpəʊltri/ *noun* **1** [pl] birds, for example chickens, **ducks**, etc. that are kept for their eggs or their meat **2** [U] the meat from these birds: *Eat plenty of fish and poultry.*

pounce /paʊns/ *verb* [I] pounce (on sb/sth) to attack sb/sth by jumping suddenly on them or it: *The cat sat motionless, waiting to pounce on the mouse.* ◆ (*figurative*) *He was quick to pounce on any mistakes I made.*

pound¹ /paʊnd/ *noun* **1** [C] (also ˌpound ˈsterling) (*symbol* £) the unit of money in the UK; one hundred pence (100p): *Melissa earns £26 000 a year.* ◆ *Can you change a ten-pound note?* ◆ *a pound coin* **2 the pound** [sing] the value of the UK pound on international money markets: *The pound has fallen against the dollar.* ◆ *How many yen are there **to the pound**?* **3** [C] (*abbr* lb) a measure of weight; equal to 0.454 of a kilogram: *The carrots cost 45p a pound.* ◆ *Half a pound of mushrooms, please.* ℹ For more information about weights, look at the section on using numbers at the back of this dictionary.

pound² /paʊnd/ *verb* **1** [I,T] pound (at/against/on) sth to hit sth hard many times making a lot of noise: *Great waves pounded the rocks.* ◆ *She pounded on the door with her fists.* **2** [I] pound along, down, up, etc. to walk with heavy, noisy steps in a particular direction: *Jason went pounding up the stairs three at a time.* **3** [I] (used about your heart, blood, etc.) to beat quickly and loudly: *Her heart was pounding with fear.* **4** [T] to hit sth many times to break it into smaller pieces

pour /pɔː(r)/ *verb* **1** [T] to make a liquid or other substance flow steadily out of or into a container: *Pour the sugar into a bowl.* **2** [I] (used about a liquid, smoke, light, etc.) to flow out of or into sth quickly and steadily, and in large quantities: *Tears were pouring down her cheeks.* ◆ *She opened the curtains and sunlight poured into the room.* **3** [T] pour sth (out) to serve a drink to sb by letting it flow from a container into a cup or glass: *Have you poured out the tea?* **4** [I] pour (down) (with rain) to rain heavily: *The rain poured down all day long.* ◆ *I'm not going out. It's pouring with rain.* **5** [I] to come or go somewhere continuously in large numbers: *People were pouring out of the station.*

IDM **pour your heart out (to sb)** to tell sb all your personal problems, feelings, etc.

PHR V **pour sth out** to speak freely about what you think or feel about sth that has happened to you: *to pour out all your troubles*

pout /paʊt/ *verb* [I] to push your lips, or your bottom lip, forward to show that you are annoyed about sth or to look sexually attractive ▶ **pout** *noun* [C]

poverty /ˈpɒvəti/ *noun* [U] the state of being poor: *There are millions of people in this country who are living* ***in poverty***.

poverty-stricken /ˈpɒvəti strɪkən/ *adj* very poor

powder /ˈpaʊdə(r)/ *noun* [U,C] a dry substance that is in the form of very small grains: *washing powder* ◆ *Grind the spices into a fine powder.* ▶ **powder** *verb* [T]

powdered /ˈpaʊdəd/ *adj* (used about a substance that is usually liquid) dried and made into powder: *powdered milk/soup*

power[1] /ˈpaʊə(r)/ *noun*

➤CONTROL **1** [U] power (over sb/sth) ; power (to do sth) the ability to control people or things or to do sth: *The aim is to give people more power over their own lives.* ◆ *to have somebody* ***in your power*** ◆ ***It's not in my power*** (= I am unable) *to help you.* **2** [U] political control of a country or area: *When did this government* ***come to power***? ◆ *to take/seize power*

➤ABILITY **3** powers [pl] a particular ability of the body or mind: *He has great powers of observation.* ◆ *She had to use all her powers of persuasion on him.*

➤AUTHORITY **4** [C] the power (to do sth) the right or authority to do sth: *Do the police have the power to stop cars without good reason?*

➤COUNTRY **5** [C] a country with a lot of influence in world affairs or that has great military strength: *Britain is no longer* ***a world power***. ◆ *a military/economic power*

➤ENERGY **6** [U] the energy or strength that sb/sth has: *The ship was helpless against the power of the storm.* ◆ *He hit the ball with as much power as he could.*

➤ELECTRICITY **7** [U] energy that can be collected and used for operating machines, making electricity, etc: *nuclear/wind/solar power*

power[2] /ˈpaʊə(r)/ *verb* [T] to supply energy to sth to make it work: *What powers the motor in this machine?* ▶ **-powered** *adj*: *a solar-powered calculator* ◆ *a high-powered engine*

ˈpower cut *noun* [C] a time when the supply of electricity stops, for example during a storm

powerful /ˈpaʊəfl/ *adj* **1** having a lot of control or influence over other people: *a powerful nation* ◆ *a rich and powerful businessman* **2** having great strength or force: *a powerful car/engine/telescope* ◆ *a powerful swimmer* **3** having a strong effect on your mind or body: *The Prime Minister made a powerful speech.* ◆ *a powerful drug* ▶ **powerfully** /-fəli/ *adv*

powerless /ˈpaʊələs/ *adj* **1** without strength, influence or control **2** powerless to do sth completely unable to do sth: *I stood and watched him struggle, powerless to help.*

ˈpower plant (*AmE*) = **power station**

ˈpower point (*BrE*) = **socket**(1)

ˈpower station (*AmE* ˈpower plant) *noun* [C] a place where electricity is produced

pp *abbr* **1** pp. *plural* of **p.**(1) **2** p.p. (before the name at the end of a letter) instead of: *pp Mark Dilks* (= from Mark Dilks, but signed by sb else because Mark Dilks is away)

PR /ˌpiː ˈɑː(r)/ *abbr* **1** = **public relations 2** = **proportional representation**

practicable /ˈpræktɪkəbl/ *adj* (*formal*) (used about an idea, a plan or a suggestion) able to be done successfully: *The scheme is just not practicable.*

practical[1] /ˈpræktɪkl/ *adj*

➤ACTION NOT IDEAS **1** concerned with actually doing sth rather than with ideas or thought: *Have you got any* ***practical experience*** *of working on a farm?* ➲ look at **theoretical**

➤LIKELY TO WORK **2** that is likely to succeed; right or sensible: *We need to find a practical solution to the problem.* OPP **impractical**

➤USEFUL **3** very suitable for a particular purpose; useful: *a practical little car, ideal for the city* OPP **impractical**

➤SENSIBLE **4** (used about people) making sensible decisions and good at dealing with problems: *We must be practical. It's no good buying a house we cannot afford.* OPP **impractical**

➤GOOD WITH HANDS **5** (used about a person) good at making and repairing things: *Brett's very practical and has made a lot of improvements to their new house.*

practical[2] /ˈpræktɪkl/ *noun* [C] (*BrE informal*) a lesson or exam where you do or make sth rather than just writing: *He passed the theory paper but failed the practical.*

practicality /ˌpræktɪˈkæləti/ *noun* **1** [U] the quality of being suitable and realistic, or likely to succeed: *I am not convinced of the practicality of the scheme.* **2** practicalities [pl] the real facts rather than ideas or thoughts: *Let's look at the practicalities of the situation.*

ˌpractical ˈjoke *noun* [C] a trick that you play on sb that makes them look silly and makes other people laugh ➲ note at **humour**

practically /ˈpræktɪkli/ *adv* **1** almost; very nearly: *My essay is practically finished now.* **2** in a realistic or sensible way: *Practically speaking, we can't afford it.*

practice /ˈpræktɪs/ *noun*
➤ACTION NOT IDEAS **1** [U] action rather than ideas or thought: *Your suggestion sounds fine in theory, but would it work* ***in practice****?* ◆ *I can't wait to* ***put*** *what I've learnt* ***into practice****.* ➲ look at **theory**
➤WAY OF DOING STH **2** [C,U] (*formal*) the usual or expected way of doing sth in a particular organization or situation; a habit or custom: *It is standard practice not to pay bills until the end of the month.*
➤FOR IMPROVING SKILL **3** [C,U] (a period of) doing an activity many times or training regularly so that you become good at it: *piano/football practice* ◆ *His accent should improve* ***with practice****.*
➤OF DOCTOR/LAWYER **4** [U] the work or the place of work of a doctor or lawyer: *Dr Roberts doesn't work in a hospital. He's in* ***general practice*** (= he's a family doctor). **5** [C] the business of a doctor, dentist or lawyer: *a successful medical/dental practice*
IDM **be/get out of practice** to find it difficult to do sth because you have not done it for a long time: *I'm not playing very well at the moment. I'm really out of practice.*
in practice in reality

practise (*AmE* practice) /ˈpræktɪs/ *verb* [I,T] **1** practise for sth; practise (sth) (on sb/sth) to do an activity or train regularly so that you become very good at sth: *She's practising for her flute exam.* ◆ *If you want to play a musical instrument well, you must practise every day.* ◆ *He likes to* ***practise*** *his English* ***on*** *me.* **2** to do sth or take part in sth regularly or publicly: *a practising Catholic/Jew/Muslim* **3** practise (sth/as sth) to work as a doctor or lawyer: *He was banned from practising medicine.* ◆ *She's practising as a barrister in Leeds.*

practised (*AmE* practiced) /ˈpræktɪst/ *adj* practised (in sth) very good at sth, because you have done it a lot or often: *He was practised in the art of inventing excuses.*

practitioner /prækˈtɪʃənə(r)/ *noun* [C] a person who works in a profession, especially medicine or law: *a dental practitioner* ➲ look at **GP**

pragmatic /prægˈmætɪk/ *adj* dealing with problems in a practical way rather than by following ideas or principles

prairie /ˈpreəri/ *noun* [C] a very large area of flat land covered in grass with few trees (especially in North America)

praise¹ /preɪz/ *noun* [U] what you say when you are expressing admiration for sb/sth: *The survivors were full of praise for the paramedics.*

praise² /preɪz/ *verb* [T] praise sb/sth (for sth) to say that sb/sth is good and should be admired: *The firefighters were praised for their courage.*

praiseworthy /ˈpreɪzwɜːði/ *adj* that should be admired and recognized as good

pushchair (*AmE* **stroller**)

pram (*AmE* **baby carriage**)

pram /præm/ (*AmE* ˈbaby carriage) *noun* [C] a small vehicle on four wheels for a young baby, pushed by a person on foot

prance /prɑːns/ *verb* [I] to move about with quick, high steps, often because you feel proud or pleased with yourself

prank /præŋk/ *noun* [C] a trick that is played on sb as a joke: *a childish prank*

prat /præt/ *noun* [C] (*BrE slang*) a stupid person: *What a prat!*

prawn /prɔːn/ (*AmE* **shrimp**) *noun* [C] a small **shellfish** (= a creature with a shell that lives in water) that you can eat, which becomes pink when cooked ➲ picture on **page P13**

pray /preɪ/ *verb* [I,T] pray (to sb) (for sb/sth) **1** to speak to God or a god in order to give thanks or to ask for help: *They knelt down and prayed for peace.* ◆ *They prayed that the war would end soon.* **2** to hope very much that sth will happen: *We're praying for good weather on Saturday.*

prayer /preə(r)/ *noun* **1** [C] a prayer (for sb/sth) the words that you use when you speak to God or a god: *Let's* ***say a prayer*** *for all the people who are ill.* ◆ *a prayer book* **2** [U] the act of speaking to God or a god: *to kneel* ***in prayer***

preach /priːtʃ/ *verb* **1** [I,T] to give a **sermon** (= a talk on a religious subject), especially in a church **2** [T] to say that sth is good and persuade other people to accept it: *I always preach caution in situations like this.* **3** [I] to give sb advice on moral behaviour, in a way which they find boring or annoying: *I'm sorry, I didn't mean to preach.*

preacher /ˈpriːtʃə(r)/ *noun* [C] a person who gives **sermons** (= talks on religious subjects), for example in a church

precarious /prɪˈkeəriəs/ *adj* not safe or certain; dangerous: *That ladder looks very precarious.* ▶ **precariously** *adv*

precaution /prɪˈkɔːʃn/ *noun* [C] a precaution (against sth) something that you do now in order to avoid danger or problems in the future: *precautions against fire/theft* ◆ *You should always* ***take the precaution of*** *locking your valuables in the hotel safe.* ▶ **precautionary** /prɪˈkɔːʃənəri/ *adj*

precede /prɪˈsiːd/ *verb* [I,T] (*formal*) to happen, come or go before sb/sth: *Look at the table on the preceding page.*

precedence /ˈpresɪdəns/ *noun* [U] **precedence (over sb/sth)** the right that sb/sth has to come before sb/sth else because he/she/it is more important: *In business, making a profit seems to* ***take precedence*** *over everything else.*

precedent /ˈpresɪdənt/ *noun* [C,U] an official action or decision that has happened in the past and that is considered as an example or rule to follow in the same situation later: *We don't want to* ***set a precedent*** *by allowing one person to come in late or they'll all want to do it.* ◆ *Such protests are* ***without precedent*** *in recent history.* ➲ look at **unprecedented**

precinct /ˈpriːsɪŋkt/ *noun* **1** [C] (*BrE*) a special area of shops in a town where cars are not allowed: *a shopping precinct* **2** [C] (*AmE*) one of the parts into which a town or city is divided **3 precincts** [pl] (*formal*) the area near or around a building: *the hospital and its precincts*

precious /ˈpreʃəs/ *adj* **1** of great value (usually because it is rare or difficult to find): *In overcrowded Hong Kong, every small piece of land is precious.* **2** loved very much: *The painting was very precious to her.*

ˌprecious ˈmetal *noun* [C] a metal which is very rare and valuable and often used in jewellery: *Gold and silver are precious metals.*

ˌprecious ˈstone (also **stone**) *noun* [C] a stone which is very rare and valuable and often used in jewellery: *diamonds and other precious stones*

precipice /ˈpresəpɪs/ *noun* [C] a very steep side of a high mountain or rock

precis /ˈpreɪsiː/ *noun* [C,U] (*pl* **precis** /-siːz/) a short version of a speech or a piece of writing that gives the main points or ideas: *to* ***write/give/make a precis*** *of a report* SYN **summary**

⚷ **precise** /prɪˈsaɪs/ *adj* **1** clear and accurate: *precise details/instructions/measurements* ◆ *He's in his forties —well, forty-four,* ***to be precise.*** ◆ *She couldn't be very precise about what her attacker was wearing.* OPP **imprecise** **2** [only *before* a noun] exact; particular: *I'm sorry. I can't come just* ***at this precise moment.*** **3** (used about a person) taking care to get small details right: *He's very precise about his work.*

⚷ **precisely** /prɪˈsaɪsli/ *adv* **1** exactly: *The time is 10.03 precisely.* **2** used to emphasize that sth is very true or obvious: *It's precisely because I care about you that I got so angry when you stayed out late.* **3** (*spoken*) (used for agreeing with a statement) yes, that is right: *'So, if we don't book now, we probably won't get a flight?' 'Precisely.'*

precision /prɪˈsɪʒn/ *noun* [U] the quality of being clear or exact: *The plans were drawn with great precision.*

preclude /prɪˈkluːd/ *verb* [T] (*formal*) **preclude sth; preclude sb from doing sth** to prevent sth from happening or sb from doing sth; to make sth impossible: *Lack of time precludes any further discussion.*

precocious /prɪˈkəʊʃəs/ *adj* (used about children, often in a critical way) having developed certain abilities and ways of behaving at a much younger age than usual: *a precocious child who started her acting career at the age of 5*

preconceived /ˌpriːkənˈsiːvd/ *adj* [only *before* a noun] (used about an idea or opinion) formed before you have enough information or experience

preconception /ˌpriːkənˈsepʃn/ *noun* [C] an idea or opinion that you have formed about sb/sth before you have enough information or experience

predator /ˈpredətə(r)/ *noun* [C] an animal that kills and eats other animals

predatory /ˈpredətri/ *adj* **1** (used about animals) living by killing and eating other animals **2** (used about people) using weaker people for their own financial or sexual advantage: *a predatory insurance salesman* ◆ *a predatory look*

predecessor /ˈpriːdɪsesə(r)/ *noun* [C] **1** the person who was in a job or position before the person who is in it now: *The new head teacher is much better than her predecessor.* **2** a thing such as a machine, that has been followed or replaced by sth else: *This computer is faster than its predecessors.* ➲ look at **successor**

predicament /prɪˈdɪkəmənt/ *noun* [C] an unpleasant and difficult situation that is hard to get out of

predicative /prɪˈdɪkətɪv/ *adj* (used about an adjective) not used before a noun: *You cannot say 'an asleep child' because 'asleep' is a predicative adjective.*

> **MORE** An adjective that *can* be used before a noun is called **attributive**. Most adjectives, for example 'big', can be either predicative or attributive: *The house is big.* ◆ *It's a big house.*

▶ **predicatively** *adv*

⚷ **predict** /prɪˈdɪkt/ *verb* [T] to say that sth will happen in the future: *Scientists still cannot predict exactly when earthquakes will happen.*

> EXAM TIP
>
> **Predicting listening**
>
> In a **listening exam** you can often predict something about what the speakers may say about a topic, and some of the vocabulary that they will use, before you listen. Read the questions and see if you can predict what type of information you need to be listening for. Is the answer going to be a number, a date, a time, an occupation, a sport, a musical instrument, etc.? It will also help to think about what part of speech is needed to fill the gap.

predictable /prɪˈdɪktəbl/ *adj* **1** that was or could be expected to happen: *a predictable result* **2** (used about a person) always behaving in a way that you would expect and therefore rather boring: *I knew you were going to say that—you're so predictable.* OPP for both meanings **unpredictable** ▶ **predictably** /-əbli/ *adv*

P

prediction /prɪˈdɪkʃn/ *noun* [C,U] saying what will happen; what sb thinks will happen: *The exam results confirmed my predictions.*

predictive /prɪˈdɪktɪv/ *adj* [usually before a noun] **1** (*formal*) connected with the ability to show what will happen in the future **2** (used about a computer program) allowing you to enter text on a computer or a mobile phone more quickly by using the first few letters of each word to predict what you want to say: ***predictive messaging***

predominance /prɪˈdɒmɪnəns/ *noun* [sing] the state of being more important or greater in number than other people or things: *There is a predominance of Japanese tourists in Hawaii.*

predominant /prɪˈdɒmɪnənt/ *adj* most noticeable, powerful or important: *The predominant colour was blue.*

predominantly /prɪˈdɒmɪnəntli/ *adv* mostly; mainly: *The population of the island is predominantly Spanish.*

predominate /prɪˈdɒmɪneɪt/ *verb* [I] (*formal*) predominate (over sb/sth) to be most important or greatest in number

pre-empt /priˈempt/ *verb* [T] **1** to prevent sth from happening by taking action to stop it: *Her departure pre-empted any further questions.* **2** to do or say sth before sb else does: *She was just about to apologize when he pre-empted her.*

pre-emptive /priˈemptɪv/ *adj* done to stop sb taking action, especially action that will be harmful to you: *a **pre-emptive attack/strike** on the military base*

P

preface /ˈprefəs/ *noun* [C] a written introduction to a book that explains what it is about or why it was written

prefect /ˈpriːfekt/ *noun* [C] (in some British schools) a student who has special duties and responsibilities. **Prefects** often help to make sure that the younger students behave properly.

🔑 **prefer** /prɪˈfɜː(r)/ *verb* [T] (preferring; preferred) [not used in the continuous tenses] prefer sb/sth (to sb/sth); prefer to do sth; prefer doing sth to choose sth rather than sth else; to like sb/sth better: *Would you prefer tea or coffee?* ♦ *Marianne prefers not to walk home on her own at night.* ♦ *My parents would prefer me to study law at university.*

> **GRAMMAR** Notice the different ways that **prefer** can be used: *Helen **prefers going** by train to flying* (= generally or usually). ♦ *Helen **would prefer to go** by train rather than (to) fly* (= on this occasion). Although this verb is not used in the continuous tenses, it is common to see the present participle (= *-ing* form): *Their elder son had gone to work in London, preferring not to join the family firm.*

> **HELP** **Prefer** is generally rather formal. Instead of: *I prefer skating to skiing* we can say: *I like skating better than skiing.*

preferable /ˈprefrəbl/ *adj* preferable (to sth/doing sth) better or more suitable: *Going anywhere is preferable to staying at home for the weekend.*

preferably /ˈprefrəbli/ *adv* used to show which person or thing would be better or preferred, if you are given a choice: *Give me a ring tonight–preferably after 7 o'clock.*

🔑 **preference** /ˈprefrəns/ *noun* [C,U] (a) preference (for sth) an interest in or desire for one thing more than another: *What you wear is entirely a matter of **personal preference**.* ♦ *Please list your choices **in order of preference*** (= put the things you want most first on the list).

IDM **give (a) preference to sb/sth** to give special treatment to one person or group rather than to others: *When allocating accommodation, we will give preference to families with young children.*

preferential /ˌprefəˈrenʃl/ *adj* [only *before* a noun] giving or showing special treatment to one person or group rather than to others: *I don't see why he should get **preferential treatment**–I've worked here just as long as he has!*

prefix /ˈpriːfɪks/ *noun* [C] a letter or group of letters that you put at the beginning of a word to change its meaning, such as **un-** in **unhappy** ➲ look at **suffix**

pregnancy /ˈpregnənsi/ *noun* [U,C] (*pl* pregnancies) the state of being pregnant

🔑 **pregnant** /ˈpregnənt/ *adj* (used about a woman or female animal) having a baby developing in her body: *Liz is five months pregnant.* ♦ *to get pregnant* ➲ note at **baby**

> **MORE** It is also possible to say: *Liz is expecting a baby* or: *Liz is going to have a baby.*

prehistoric /ˌpriːhɪˈstɒrɪk/ *adj* from the time in history before events were written down

prejudice[1] /ˈpredʒudɪs/ *noun* [C,U] prejudice (against sb/sth) a strong unreasonable feeling of not liking or trusting sb/sth, especially when it is based on their race, religion or sex: *a victim of **racial prejudice***

prejudice[2] /ˈpredʒudɪs/ *verb* [T] **1** prejudice sb (against sb/sth) to influence sb so that they have an unreasonable or unfair opinion about sb/sth: *The newspaper stories had prejudiced the jury against him.* **2** to have a harmful effect on sb/sth: *Continuing to live with her violent father may prejudice the child's welfare.*

prejudiced /ˈpredʒədɪst/ *adj* not liking or trusting sb for no other reason than their race, religion or sex

preliminary[1] /prɪˈlɪmɪnəri/ *adj* coming or happening before sth else that is more important: *After a few preliminary remarks the discussions began.*

preliminary[2] /prɪˈlɪmɪnəri/ *noun* [C, usually pl] (*pl* preliminaries) an action or event that is done before and in preparation for another event: *Once the preliminaries are over, we can get down to business.*

prelude /ˈpreljuːd/ *noun* [C] **1** a short piece of music, especially an introduction to a longer piece **2** (*formal*) prelude (to sth) an action or event that happens before sth else or that forms an introduction to sth

premature /ˈpremətʃə(r)/ *adj* **1** happening before the normal or expected time: *Her baby was premature* (= born before the expected time). **2** acting or happening too soon: *I think our decision was premature. We should have thought about it for longer.* ▶ **prematurely** *adv*

premeditated /priːˈmedɪteɪtɪd/ *adj* (used about a crime) planned in advance

premier[1] /ˈpremiə(r)/ *adj* [only *before* a noun] most important; best: *a premier chef* ◆ *the Premier League* (= in football)

premier[2] /ˈpremiə(r)/ *noun* [C] (used especially in newspapers) the leader of the government of a country SYN **prime minister**

premiere /ˈpremieə(r)/ *noun* [C] the first public performance of a film or play: *the* ***world premiere*** *of his new play* ◆ *The film will have its premiere in July.* ▶ **premiere** *verb* [I,T]: *His new movie premieres in New York this week.*

⚷ **premises** /ˈpremɪsɪz/ *noun* [pl] the building and the land around it that a business owns or uses: *The health club is moving to larger premises.* ◆ *Children are not allowed* ***on the premises.***

premium /ˈpriːmiəm/ *noun* [C] **1** an amount of money that you pay regularly to a company for insurance against accidents, damage, etc: *a monthly premium of £25* **2** an extra payment: *You must pay a premium for express delivery.*

premonition /ˌpriːməˈnɪʃn; ˌprem-/ *noun* [C] a premonition (of sth) a feeling that sth unpleasant is going to happen in the future: *a premonition of disaster*

preoccupation /priˌɒkjuˈpeɪʃn/ *noun* [U,C] preoccupation (with sth) the state of thinking and/or worrying continuously about sth: *She was irritated by his preoccupation with money.*

preoccupied /priˈɒkjupaɪd/ *adj* preoccupied (with sth) not paying attention to sb/sth because you are thinking or worrying about sb/sth else: *Sarah is very preoccupied with her work at present.* ➲ look at **occupied**

preoccupy /priˈɒkjupaɪ/ *verb* [T] (preoccupying; preoccupies; *pt, pp* preoccupied) to fill sb's mind so that they do not think about anything else; to worry sb

⚷ **preparation** /ˌprepəˈreɪʃn/ *noun* **1** [U] getting sb/sth ready: *The team has been training hard* ***in preparation for*** *the big game.* ◆ *exam preparation* **2** [C, usually pl] preparation (for sth/to do sth) something that you do to get ready for sth: *We started to* ***make preparations*** *for the wedding six months ago.*

preparatory /prɪˈpærətri/ *adj* (*formal*) done in order to get ready for sth

preˈparatory school (also ˈprep school) *noun* [C] **1** (in Britain) a private school for children aged between 7 and 13 **2** (in the US) a private school that prepares students for college

⚷ **prepare** /prɪˈpeə(r)/ *verb* [I,T] prepare (sb/sth) (for sb/sth) to get ready or to make sb/sth ready: *Bo helped me prepare for the exam.* ◆ *The course prepares foreign students for studying at university.* ◆ *to prepare a meal*

IDM **be prepared for sth** to be ready for sth difficult or unpleasant

be prepared to do sth to be ready and happy to do sth: *I am not prepared to stay here and be insulted.*

preposition /ˌprepəˈzɪʃn/ *noun* [C] a word or phrase that is used before a noun or pronoun to show place, time, direction, etc: *'In', 'for', 'to' and 'out of' are all prepositions.*

preposterous /prɪˈpɒstərəs/ *adj* (*formal*) silly; ridiculous; not to be taken seriously

ˈprep school = preparatory school

prerequisite /ˌpriːˈrekwəzɪt/ *noun* [C] (*formal*) a prerequisite (for/of sth) something that is necessary for sth to happen or exist: *Is a good education a prerequisite of success?* ➲ look at **requisite**

prerogative /prɪˈrɒɡətɪv/ *noun* [C] (*formal*) a special right that sb/sth has: *It is the Prime Minister's prerogative to fix the date of the election.*

prescribe /prɪˈskraɪb/ *verb* [T] **1** to say what medicine or treatment sb should have: *Can you prescribe something for my cough please, doctor?* **2** (*formal*) (used about a person or an organization with authority) to say that sth must be done: *The law prescribes that the document must be signed in the presence of two witnesses.*

prescription /prɪˈskrɪpʃn/ *noun* [C,U] an official piece of paper on which a doctor has written the name of the medicine that you need; the medicine itself: *a prescription for sleeping pills* ◆ *Some medicines are only available from the chemist* ***on prescription*** (= with a prescription from a doctor). ➲ note at **doctor**

⚷ **presence** /ˈprezns/ *noun* **1** [U] the fact of being in a particular place: *He apologized to her* ***in the presence of*** *the whole family.* ◆ *an experiment to test for the presence of oxygen* OPP **absence** **2** [sing] a number of soldiers or police officers who are in a place for a special reason: *There was a huge police presence at the demonstration.*

⚷ **present[1]** /ˈpreznt/ *adj* **1** [only *before* a noun] existing or happening now: *We hope to overcome our present difficulties very soon.* **2** [not before a noun] being in a particular place: *There were 200 people present at the meeting.* OPP **absent**

IDM **the present day** modern times: *In some countries traditional methods of farming have survived to the present day.*

⚷ **present[2]** /ˈpreznt/ *noun* **1** [C] something that you give to sb or receive from sb: *a birthday/wedding/leaving/Christmas present* SYN **gift** **2** *usually* the present [sing] the time now: *We live* ***in the pre-***

P

sent but we must learn from the past. ♦ *I'm rather busy* ***at present****. Can I call you back later?* ➲ note at **actually** **3** the present [sing] = **the present tense**
IDM **for the moment/present** ➲ **moment**

present³ /prɪˈzent/ *verb* [T] **1** present sb with sth; present sth (to sb) to give sth to sb, especially at a formal ceremony: *All the dancers were presented with flowers.* ♦ *Flowers were presented to all the dancers.* **2** present sth (to sb) to show sth that you have prepared to people: *Good teachers try to present their material in an interesting way.* **3** present sb with sth; present sth (to sb) to give sb sth that has to be dealt with: *The manager presented us with a bill for the broken chair.* ♦ *Learning English presented no problem to him.* **4** to introduce a TV or radio programme: *She used to present a gardening programme on TV.* **5** to show a play, etc. to the public: *The Theatre Royal is presenting a new production of 'Ghosts'.* **6** present sb (to sb) to introduce sb to a person in a formal ceremony: *The teams were presented to the President before the game.*

presentable /prɪˈzentəbl/ *adj* good enough to be seen by people you do not know well

presentation /ˌpreznˈteɪʃn/ *noun* **1** [C,U] the act of giving or showing sth to sb: *The head will now* ***make a presentation*** *to the winners of the competition.* **2** [U] the way in which sth is shown, explained, offered, etc. to people: *Untidy presentation of your work may lose you marks.* **3** [C] a formal talk at which sth is shown or explained to a group of people: *Each student has to* ***give a*** *short* ***presentation*** *on a subject of his/her choice.* **4** [C] a formal ceremony at which a prize, etc. is given to sb

P

presenter /prɪˈzentə(r)/ *noun* [C] (*BrE*) a person who introduces a TV or radio programme

presently /ˈprezntli/ *adv* **1** (*especially AmE*) now: *The management are presently discussing the matter.* SYN **currently** **2** (*written*) after a short time: *Presently I heard the car door shut.* **3** soon: *I'll be finished presently.* SYN **shortly**

HELP Notice that when **presently** means 'soon' it usually comes at the end of the sentence. When it means 'after a short time' it usually comes at the beginning of the sentence. When it means 'now' it goes with the verb.

ˌpresent ˈparticiple *noun* [C] the form of the verb that ends in *-ing* ℹ For more information about the use of tenses, look at the **Reference Section** at the back of this dictionary.

the ˌpresent ˈperfect *noun* [sing] the form of a verb that expresses an action done in a time period from the past to the present, formed with the present tense of *have* and the past participle of the verb: *'I've finished', 'She hasn't arrived' and 'I've been studying' are all* ***in the present perfect****.*

the ˌpresent ˈtense (also the present) *noun* [sing] the tense of the verb that you use when you are talking about what is happening or what exists now

preservative /prɪˈzɜːvətɪv/ *noun* [C,U] a substance that is used for keeping food, etc. in good condition

preserve /prɪˈzɜːv/ *verb* [T] to keep sth safe or in good condition: *They've managed to preserve most of the wall paintings in the caves.* ▶ **preservation** /ˌprezəˈveɪʃn/ *noun* [U]

preside /prɪˈzaɪd/ *verb* [I] to be in charge of a discussion, meeting, etc.
PHR V **preside over sth** to be in control of or responsible for sth

presidency /ˈprezɪdənsi/ *noun* (*pl* presidencies) **1** the presidency [sing] the position of being president **2** [C] the period of time that sb is president

president /ˈprezɪdənt/ *noun* [C] **1** (also President) the leader of a **republic** (= a country with an elected government and no king or queen): *the president of France* ♦ *President Obama* ♦ *the US president* **2** the person with the highest position in some organizations ▶ **presidential** /ˌprezɪˈdenʃl/ *adj*: *presidential elections*

press¹ /pres/ *noun*
➤NEWSPAPERS **1** *usually* the press [sing, with sing or pl verb] newspapers and the journalists who work for them: *The story has been reported on TV and* ***in the press****.* ♦ *the local/national press* ♦ *The press support/supports government policy.* ➲ note at **newspaper** **2** [sing, U] the type or amount of reports that newspapers write about sb/sth: *This company has had* ***a bad press*** *recently.* ♦ *The strike got very little press.*
➤PRINTING MACHINE **3** [C,U] a machine for printing books, newspapers, etc.; the process of printing them: *All details were correct at the time of* ***going to press****.*
➤BUSINESS **4** [C] a business that prints books, etc: *Oxford University Press*
➤ACT OF PUSHING **5** [C, usually sing] an act of pushing sth firmly: ***Give*** *that button* ***a press*** *and see what happens.*

press² /pres/ *verb*
➤PUSH/SQUEEZE **1** [I,T] to push sth firmly: *Just press that button and the door will open.* ♦ *He pressed the lid firmly shut.* ♦ *Press here to open.* ➲ picture at **squeeze** **2** [T] to put weight onto sth, for example in order to get juice out of it: *to press grapes* **3** [T] to hold sb/sth firmly in a loving way: *She pressed the photo to her chest.* **4** [I] press across, against, around, etc. (sth) to move in a particular direction by pushing: *The crowd pressed against the line of policemen.*
➤TRY TO PERSUADE **5** [T] press (sb) (for sth/to do sth) to try to persuade or force sb to do sth: *to press somebody for an answer* ♦ *I pressed them to stay for dinner.*
➤SAY/REPEAT STH **6** [T] to express or repeat sth in an urgent way: *I don't want to press the point, but you still owe me money.*
➤MAKE SMOOTH **7** [T] to make a piece of clothing smooth by using an iron: *This shirt needs pressing.*
IDM **be hard pressed/pushed/put to do sth** ➲ **hard²**

be pressed for sth to not have enough of sth: *I must hurry. I'm really pressed for time.*
bring/press charges (against sb) ➲ **charge**[1]
PHR V **press ahead/forward/on (with sth)** to continue doing sth even though it is difficult or hard work: *They pressed on with the building work in spite of the bad weather.*

ˈpress conference *noun* [C] a meeting when a famous or important person answers questions from newspaper and TV journalists: *to hold a press conference*

pressing /ˈpresɪŋ/ *adj* that must be dealt with immediately SYN **urgent**

ˈpress stud (also popper; *AmE* snap) *noun* [C] two round pieces of metal or plastic that you press together in order to fasten a piece of clothing ➲ picture at **button**

ˈpress-up (*AmE* ˈpush-up) *noun* [C] a type of exercise in which you lie on your front on the floor and push your body up with your arms: *I do 50 press-ups every morning.* ➲ picture at **exercise**

pressure /ˈpreʃə(r)/ *noun* **1** [U] the force that is produced when you press on or against sth: *Apply pressure to the cut and it will stop bleeding.* ◆ *The pressure of the water caused the dam to crack.* **2** [C, U] the force that a gas or liquid has when it is contained inside sth: *high/low blood pressure* ◆ *You should check your tyre pressures regularly.* **3** [U] worries or difficulties that you have because you have too much to deal with: *financial pressures* ◆ *I find it difficult to cope with pressure at work.* SYN **stress**
IDM **put pressure on sb (to do sth)** to force sb to do sth: *His boss is putting pressure on him to resign.*
under pressure **1** (used about liquid or gas) contained inside sth or sent somewhere using force: *Water is forced out through the hose under pressure.* **2** being forced to do sth: *Anna was under pressure from her parents to leave school and get a job.* **3** worried or in difficulty because you have too much to deal with: *I perform poorly under pressure, so I hate exams.*
▶ **pressure** *verb* = **pressurize**

ˈpressure group *noun* [C, with sing or pl verb] a group of people who are trying to influence what a government or other organization does

pressurize (also -ise) /ˈpreʃəraɪz/ (also pressure) *verb* [T] pressurize sb (into sth/doing sth) to use force or influence to make sb do sth: *Some workers were pressurized into taking early retirement.*

pressurized (also -ised) /ˈpreʃəraɪzd/ *adj* (used about air in an aircraft) kept at the pressure at which people can breathe

prestige /preˈstiːʒ/ *noun* [U] the respect and admiration that people feel for a person because they have a high social position or have been very successful: *jobs in supermarkets with low prestige*
▶ **prestigious** /preˈstɪdʒəs/ *adj*: *a prestigious prize/school/job*

presumably /prɪˈzjuːməbli/ *adv* I imagine; I suppose: *Presumably this rain means the match will be cancelled?*

presume /prɪˈzjuːm/ *verb* [T] to think that sth is true even if you do not know for sure; to suppose: *The house looks empty so I presume they are away on holiday.* SYN **assume** ▶ **presumption** /prɪˈzʌmpʃn/ *noun* [C]

presumptuous /prɪˈzʌmptʃuəs/ *adj* confident that sth will happen or that sb will do sth without making sure first, in a way that annoys people: *It was very presumptuous of him to say that I would help without asking me first.*

presuppose /ˌpriːsəˈpəʊz/ *verb* [T] (*formal*) to accept sth as true or existing and act on that belief, before it has been proved to be true: *Teachers sometimes presuppose a fairly high level of knowledge by the students.* SYN **presume**

pretence (*AmE* pretense) /prɪˈtens/ *noun* [U, sing] an action that makes people believe sth that is not true: *She was unable to keep up the pretence that she loved him.*
IDM **on/under false pretences** ➲ **false**

pretend /prɪˈtend/ *verb* [I,T] **1** to behave in a particular way in order to make other people believe sth that is not true: *You can't just pretend that the problem doesn't exist.* ◆ *Paul's not really asleep. He's just pretending.* **2** (used especially about children) to imagine that sth is true as part of a game: *The kids were under the bed pretending to be snakes.*

pretentious /prɪˈtenʃəs/ *adj* trying to appear more serious or important than you really are: *I think it sounds pretentious to use a lot of foreign words.*

pretext /ˈpriːtekst/ *noun* [C] a reason that you give for doing sth that is not the real reason: *Tariq left* ***on the pretext of*** *having an appointment at the dentist's.*

pretty[1] /ˈprɪti/ *adv* (*informal*) quite; fairly: *The film was pretty good but not fantastic.* ◆ *I'm pretty certain that Alex will agree.* ➲ note at **rather**
IDM **pretty much/nearly/well** almost; very nearly: *I won't be long. I've pretty well finished.*

pretty[2] /ˈprɪti/ *adj* (prettier; prettiest) attractive and pleasant to look at or hear: *a pretty girl/smile/dress/garden/name* ➲ note at **beautiful** ▶ **prettily** *adv*: *The room is prettily decorated.* ▶ **prettiness** *noun* [U]

prevail /prɪˈveɪl/ *verb* [I] (*formal*) **1** to exist or be common in a particular place or at a particular time: *In some areas traditional methods of farming still prevail.* **2** prevail (against/over sb/sth) to win or be accepted, especially after a fight or discussion: *In the end justice prevailed and the men were set free.*

prevailing /prɪˈveɪlɪŋ/ *adj* [only *before* a noun] **1** existing or most common at a particular time: *the prevailing climate of opinion* **2** (used about the wind) most common in a particular area: *The prevailing wind is from the south-west.*

prevalent /ˈprevələnt/ *adj* (*formal*) most common in a particular place at a particular time: *The prevalent atmosphere was one of fear.* ▶ **prevalence**

P

noun [U]: *an increase in the prevalence of heart disease*

prevent /prɪˈvent/ *verb* [T] **prevent sb/sth (from) (doing sth)** to stop sth happening or to stop sb doing sth: *This accident could have been prevented.* ◆ *Her parents tried to prevent her from going to live with her boyfriend.* ➲ **Prevent** is more formal than **stop**. ▶ **prevention** *noun* [U]: *accident/crime prevention*

preventable /prɪˈventəbl/ *adj* that can be prevented: *Many accidents are preventable.*

preventive /prɪˈventɪv/ (also **preventative** /prɪˈventətɪv/) *adj* [only *before* a noun] intended to stop or prevent sth from happening: *preventative medicine*

preview /ˈpriːvjuː/ *noun* [C] a chance to see a play, film, etc. before it is shown to the general public

previous /ˈpriːviəs/ *adj* [only *before* a noun] coming or happening before or earlier: *Do you have previous experience of this type of work?* ◆ *Matt has two children from his previous marriage.* ◆ *the previous day* ▶ **previously** *adv*: *Before I moved to Spain, I had previously worked in Italy.*

prey[1] /preɪ/ *noun* [U] an animal or bird that is killed and eaten by another animal or bird: *The eagle is a bird of prey* (= it kills and eats other birds or small animals).

prey[2] /preɪ/ *verb* [I]

IDM **prey on sb's mind** to cause sb to worry or think about sth: *The thought that he was responsible for the accident preyed on the train driver's mind.*

PHR V **prey on sth** (used about an animal or bird) to kill and eat other animals or birds: *Owls prey on mice and other small animals.*

price[1] /praɪs/ *noun* **1** [C] the amount of money that you must pay in order to buy sth: *What's the price of petrol now?* ◆ *We can't afford to buy the car at that price.* ◆ *There's no price on* (= written on) *this jar of coffee.*

MORE A shop may **raise/increase, reduce/bring down** or **freeze** its prices. The prices **rise/go up** or **fall/go down.**

2 [sing] unpleasant things that you have to experience in order to achieve sth or as a result of sth: *Sleepless nights are a small price to pay for having a baby.*

IDM **at any price** even if the cost is very high or if it will have unpleasant results: *Richard was determined to succeed at any price.*

at a price costing a lot of money or involving sth unpleasant: *He'll help you get a job—at a price.*

not at any price never; not for any reason

price[2] /praɪs/ *verb* [T] to fix the price of sth or to write the price on sth: *The books were all priced at between £5 and £10.*

OTHER WORDS FOR

price

A **charge** is the amount of money that you must pay for using something: *Is there a charge for parking here?* ◆ *admission charges.* You use **cost** when you are talking about paying for services or about prices in general without mentioning an actual sum of money: *The cost of electricity is going up.* ◆ *the cost of living.* The **price** of something is the amount of money that you must pay in order to buy it.

priceless /ˈpraɪsləs/ *adj* of very great value: *priceless jewels and antiques* ➲ look at **worthless, valuable, invaluable**

ˈprice list *noun* [C] a list of the prices of the goods that are on sale

pricey /ˈpraɪsi/ *adj* (**pricier; priciest**) (*informal*) expensive

prick[1] /prɪk/ *verb* [T] to make a small hole in sth or to cause sb pain with a sharp point: *She pricked her finger on a needle.*

IDM **prick up your ears** (used about an animal) to hold up the ears in order to listen carefully to sth: (*figurative*) *Mike pricked up his ears when he heard Emma's name mentioned.*

prick[2] /prɪk/ *noun* [C] the sudden pain that you feel when sth sharp goes into your skin

prickle[1] /ˈprɪkl/ *noun* [C] one of the sharp points on some plants and animals: *Hedgehogs are covered in prickles.* ➲ look at **spine**

prickle[2] /ˈprɪkl/ *verb* [I] to have or make sb/sth have an uncomfortable feeling on the skin: *I don't like that shirt—it prickles.* ◆ *His skin prickled with fear.*

prickly /ˈprɪkli/ *adj* (**pricklier; prickliest**) **1** covered with sharp points: *a prickly bush* **2** causing an uncomfortable feeling on the skin: *That T-shirt makes my skin go all prickly.* **3** (*informal*) (used about a person) easily made angry: *Don't mention his accident—he's a bit prickly about it.*

pride[1] /praɪd/ *noun* **1** [U, sing] **pride (in sth/doing sth)** the feeling of pleasure that you have when you or people who are close to you do sth good or own sth good: *I **take a** great **pride** in my work.* ◆ *Jane's parents watched with pride as she went up to collect her prize.* ◆ *You should **feel pride** in your achievement.* ◆ *We take great pride in offering the best service in town.* **2** [sing] **the pride of sth/sb** a person or thing that is very important or of great value to sth/sb: *The new stadium was the pride of the whole town.* **3** [U] the respect that you have for yourself: *You'll hurt his pride if you refuse to accept the present.* **4** [U] the feeling that you are better than other people: *Male pride forced him to suffer in silence.* ➲ *adjective* **proud**

IDM **sb's pride and joy** a thing or person that gives sb great pleasure or satisfaction

pride[2] /praɪd/ *verb*

PHR V **pride yourself on sth/doing sth** to feel pleased about sth good or clever that you can do: *Fabio prides himself on his ability to cook.*

priest /priːst/ *noun* [C] a person who performs religious ceremonies in some religions: *The priest gave a* blessing at the end of the service. ♦ *the ordination of women priests*

MORE In some religions a female priest is called a **priestess**.

prim /prɪm/ *adj* (**primmer**; **primmest**) (used about a person) always behaving in a careful or formal way and easily shocked by anything that is rude ▶ **primly** *adv*

primaeval = **primeval**

primarily /ˈpraɪmərəli; praɪˈmerəli/ *adv* more than anything else; mainly: *The course is aimed primarily at beginners.*

primary¹ /ˈpraɪməri/ *adj* [only *before* a noun] **1** most important; main: *Smoking is one of the primary causes of lung cancer.* **2** connected with the education of children between about 4 and 11 years old

primary² /ˈpraɪməri/ (also ˌ**primary eˈlection**) *noun* [C] (*pl* **primaries**) (in the US) an election in which a political party chooses the person who will represent the party for a later important election, such as for president

ˌ**primary ˈcolour** *noun* [C] any of the colours red, yellow or blue. You can make any other colour by mixing **primary colours** in different ways.

ˌ**primary eˈlection** = **primary²**

ˌ**primary school** *noun* [C,U] (in Britain) a school for children between the ages of 4 and 11: *a local primary school*

MORE **Primary school** consists of **infant school** and **junior school**. Children attend **infant school** from the age of four and **junior school** from the age of seven. When they leave **primary school** at the age of eleven, they go on to **secondary school**.

➲ note at **school**

primate /ˈpraɪmeɪt/ *noun* [C] any animal that belongs to the group that includes humans, and animals such as **monkeys** and **apes**

prime¹ /praɪm/ *adj* [only *before* a noun] **1** main; the first example of sth that sb would think of or choose: *She is a prime candidate as the next team captain.* **2** of very good quality; best: *prime pieces of beef* **3** having all the typical qualities: *That's a **prime example** of what I was talking about.*

prime² /praɪm/ *noun* [sing] the time when sb is strongest, most beautiful, most successful, etc: *Several of the team are **past their prime**.* ♦ ***In his prime**, he was a fine actor.* ♦ *to be **in the prime of life***

prime³ /praɪm/ *verb* [T] **prime sb (for/with sth)** to give sb information in order to prepare them for sth: *The politician had been well primed with all the facts before the interview.*

ˌ**prime minister** *noun* [C] (*abbr* **PM**) the leader of the government in some countries, for example Britain ➲ look at **minister**: *The games were opened by the prime minister of Thailand.*

primeval (also **primaeval**) /praɪˈmiːvl/ *adj* from the earliest period of the history of the world; very ancient: *primeval forests*

primitive /ˈprɪmətɪv/ *adj* **1** very simple and not developed: *The washing facilities in the camp were very primitive.* **2** [only *before* a noun] connected with a very early stage in the development of humans or animals: *Primitive man lived in caves and hunted wild animals.*

primrose /ˈprɪmrəʊz/ *noun* [C] a yellow spring flower

prince /prɪns/ *noun* [C] **1** a son or other close male relative of a king or queen: *the Prince of Wales* **2** the male ruler of a small country

princess /ˌprɪnˈses/ *noun* [C] **1** a daughter or other close female relative of a king or queen: *Princess Anne* **2** the wife of a **prince**

principal¹ /ˈprɪnsəpl/ *adj* [only *before* a noun] most important; main: *the principal characters in a play* ▶ **principally** /-pli/ *adv*: *Our products are designed principally for the European market.*

principal² /ˈprɪnsəpl/ (also **head, head teacher**) *noun* [C] the head of some schools, colleges, etc.

principle /ˈprɪnsəpl/ *noun* **1** [C,U] a rule for good behaviour, based on what a person believes is right: *He doesn't eat meat **on principle**.* ♦ *She refuses to wear fur. It's **a matter of principle** with her.* ♦ *a person of high moral principles* **2** [C] a basic general law, rule or idea: *The system works **on the principle that** heat rises.* ♦ *The course teaches the basic principles of car maintenance.*

IDM **in principle** in general, but possibly not in detail: *His proposal sounds fine in principle, but there are a few points I'm not happy about.*

print¹ /prɪnt/ *verb*

➤LETTERS/PICTURES **1** [T] to put words, pictures, etc. onto paper by using a special machine: *How much did it cost to print the posters?* ♦ *Print your work on both sides.*

➤BOOKS, ETC. **2** [T] to produce books, newspapers, etc. in this way: *50 000 copies of the textbook were printed.*

➤PUBLISH **3** [T] to include sth in a book, newspaper, etc: *The newspaper should not have printed the photographs of the crash.*

➤PHOTOGRAPH **4** [T] to make a photograph from a digital image or a piece of film: *She printed the children's portraits.*

➤WRITE **5** [I,T] to write with letters that are not joined together: *Please print your name clearly at the top of the paper.*

➤MAKE DESIGN **6** [T] to put a pattern onto cloth, paper, etc: *printed cotton/wallpaper*

PHR V **print (sth) out** to print information from a computer onto paper: *I'll just print out this file.*

print² /prɪnt/ *noun*

➤LETTERS/WORDS **1** [U] the letters, words, etc. in a book, newspaper, etc: *The print is too small for me to read without my glasses.*

P

➤NEWSPAPERS/BOOKS **2** [U] used to refer to the business of producing newspapers, books, etc: *the print unions/workers*
➤MARK **3** [C] a mark that is made by sth pressing onto sth else: *His prints were found at the scene of the crime.* ➲ look at **fingerprint, footprint**
➤PICTURE **4** [C] a picture that was made by printing: *a framed set of prints*
➤PHOTOGRAPH **5** [C] a photograph (when it has been printed from a digital file): *I ordered an extra set of prints for my friends.*
IDM in print 1 (used about a book) still available from the company that published it **2** (used about sb's work) published in a book, newspaper, etc.
out of print (used about a book) no longer available from the company that published it; not being printed any more

printer /ˈprɪntə(r)/ *noun* [C] **1** a machine that prints out information from a computer onto paper: *a laser printer* ➲ picture at **computer 2** a person or company that prints books, newspapers, etc.

printing /ˈprɪntɪŋ/ *noun* [U] **1** the act of producing letters, pictures, patterns, etc. on sth by pressing a surface covered with ink against it: *the invention of printing by Gutenberg* **2** the act of printing a number of copies of a book at one time: *The book is in its sixth printing.*

ˈprinting press (also **press**) *noun* [C] a machine that is used for printing books, newspapers, etc.

printout /ˈprɪntaʊt/ *noun* [C,U] information from a computer that is printed onto paper

prior /ˈpraɪə(r)/ *adj* [only *before* a noun] existing before or earlier: *She was unable to attend because of a prior engagement.*

priority /praɪˈɒrəti/ *noun* (*pl* **priorities**) **1** [C] something that is most important or that you must do before anything else: *Our* ***top priority*** *is to get food and water to the refugee camps.* ◆ *I'll* ***make it*** *my* ***priority*** *to sort out your problem.* **2** [U] **priority (over sb/sth)** the state of being more important than sb/sth or of coming before sb/sth else: *We* ***give priority*** *to families with small children.* ◆ *Emergency cases* ***take priority*** *over other patients in hospital.*
▶ **prioritize** (also **-ise**) /praɪˈɒrətaɪz/ *verb* [I,T]: *You should make a list of all the jobs you have to do and prioritize them.*

ˈprior to *prep* (*formal*) before: *Prepare the surface prior to applying the first coat of paint.*

prise /praɪz/ (*especially AmE* **prize, pry**) *verb* [T] **prise sth off, apart, open, etc.** to use force to open sth, remove a lid, etc: *He prised the door open with an iron bar.*

prism /ˈprɪzəm/ *noun* [C] **1** a solid figure with ends that are parallel and of the same size and shape, and with sides whose opposite edges are equal and parallel **2** a piece of glass or plastic in the shape of a triangle, which separates light that passes through it into seven colours

prison /ˈprɪzn/ (also **jail**) *noun* [C,U] a building where criminals are kept as a punishment: *The terrorists were* ***sent to prison*** *for twenty-five years.* ◆ *He will be* ***released from prison*** *next month.* **SYN jail** ➲ note at **court** ➲ look at **imprison**

HELP If a person goes **to prison** or is **in prison** (without **'the'**), he/she has to stay there as a prisoner: *He was sent to prison for two years.* 'The prison' refers to a particular prison, or indicates that a person is only visiting the building temporarily: *The politician visited the prison and said that conditions were poor.*

prisoner /ˈprɪznə(r)/ *noun* [C] a person who is being kept in prison: *a political prisoner*
IDM hold/take sb captive/prisoner ➲ **captive**[1]

ˌprisoner of ˈwar *noun* [C] a soldier, etc. who is caught by the enemy during a war and who is kept in prison until the end of the war

privacy /ˈprɪvəsi/ *noun* [U] **1** the state of being alone and not watched or disturbed by other people: *There is not much privacy in large hospital wards.* **2** the state of being free from the attention of the public: *The star claimed that the photographs were an* ***invasion of privacy***.

private[1] /ˈpraɪvət/ *adj* **1** belonging to or intended for one particular person or group and not to be shared by others: *This is private property. You may not park here.* ◆ *a private letter/conversation* **2** with nobody else present: *I would like a private interview with the personnel manager.* **3** not wanting to share thoughts and feelings with other people: *He's a very private person.* **4** owned, done or organized by a person or company, and not by the government: *a private hospital/school* (= you pay to go there) ◆ *a private detective* (= one who is not in the police) **OPP public 5** not connected with work or business: *He never discusses his* ***private life*** *with his colleagues at work.* **6** (used about classes, lessons, etc.) given by a teacher to one student or a small group for payment: *Claire gives private English lessons at her house.*
▶ **privately** *adv*

private[2] /ˈpraɪvət/ *noun* [C] a soldier of the lowest level
IDM in private with nobody else present: *May I speak to you in private?*

privatize (also **-ise**) /ˈpraɪvətaɪz/ *verb* [T] to sell a business or an industry that was owned by the government to a private company: *The electricity industry was privatized several years ago.* **OPP nationalize**
▶ **privatization** (also **-isation**) /ˌpraɪvətaɪˈzeɪʃn/ *noun* [U]

privilege /ˈprɪvəlɪdʒ/ *noun* **1** [C,U] a special right or advantage that only one person or group has: *Prisoners who behave well* ***enjoy*** *special* ***privileges***. **2** [sing] a special advantage or opportunity that gives you great pleasure: *It was a great privilege to hear her sing.*

privileged /ˈprɪvəlɪdʒd/ *adj* having an advantage or opportunity that most people do not have: *Only* ***a privileged few*** *are allowed to enter this room.* ◆ *I feel very privileged to be playing for the national team.* ➲ look at **underprivileged**

prize[1] /praɪz/ *noun* [C] something of value that is given to sb who is successful in a race, competition, game, etc: *She won* ***first prize*** *in the competition.* ♦ *a prize-winning novel*

prize[2] /praɪz/ *adj* [only *before* a noun] winning, or good enough to win, a prize: *a prize flower display*

prize[3] /praɪz/ *verb* [T] **1** to consider sth to be very valuable: *This picture is one of my most prized possessions.* **2** (*especially AmE*) = **prise**

pro /prəʊ/ (*pl* pros) (*informal*) **1** = **professional**[2](2): *a golf pro* **2** = **professional**[2](3)

IDM **the pros and cons** the reasons for and against doing sth: *We should consider all the pros and cons before reaching a decision.* ➲ look at **advantage**

pro- /prəʊ/ [in compounds] in favour of; supporting: *pro-democracy* ➲ look at **anti-**

proactive /ˌprəʊˈæktɪv/ *adj* controlling a situation by making things happen, rather than waiting for things to happen and then reacting to them

probability /ˌprɒbəˈbɪləti/ *noun* (*pl* probabilities) **1** [U,sing] how likely sth is to happen: *At that time there seemed little probability of success.* **2** [C] something that is likely to happen: *Closure of the factory now seems a probability.*

probable /ˈprɒbəbl/ *adj* that you expect to happen or to be true; likely: *I suppose it's possible that they might still come but it doesn't seem very probable.* OPP **improbable** ➲ look at **possible**

> **HELP** **Probable** or **likely**? Notice that **probable** and **likely** mean the same but are used differently: ***It's probable that*** *he will be late.* ♦ *He* ***is likely to*** *be late.*

probably /ˈprɒbəbli/ *adv* almost certainly: *I will phone next week, probably on Wednesday.*

probation /prəˈbeɪʃn/ *noun* [U] **1** a system that allows sb who has committed a crime not to go to prison if they go to see to a **probation** officer regularly for a fixed period of time: *Jamie is* ***on probation*** *for two years.* **2** a period of time at the start of a new job when you are tested to see if you are suitable: *a three-month probation period*

probe[1] /prəʊb/ *verb* [I,T] **1** probe (into sth) to ask questions in order to find out secret or hidden information: *The newspapers are now probing into the President's past.* **2** to examine or look for sth, especially with a long thin instrument: *The doctor probed the cut for pieces of broken glass.* ▶ **probing** *adj*: *to ask probing questions*

probe[2] /prəʊb/ *noun* [C] **1** the process of asking questions, collecting facts, etc. in order to find out hidden information about sth: *a police probe into illegal financial dealing* **2** a long thin tool that you use for examining sth that is difficult to reach, especially a part of the body

problem /ˈprɒbləm/ *noun* [C] **1** something that causes difficulty or trouble: *social/family/financial/technical problems* ♦ *You won't* ***solve the problem*** *if you ignore it.* ♦ *The company will* ***face problems*** *from unions if it sacks workers.* ♦ *It's going to* ***cause problems*** *if Donna brings her husband.* ♦ *I can't play because I've got* ***a problem with*** *my knee.* ♦ *'Can you fix this for me?'* ***'No problem.'*** ♦ *It's a great painting—****the problem is*** *I've got nowhere to put it.* **2** a question that you have to solve by thinking about it: *a maths/logic problem*

problematic /ˌprɒbləˈmætɪk/ (also **problematical** /-ɪkl/) *adj* difficult to deal with; full of problems

procedure /prəˈsiːdʒə(r)/ *noun* [C,U] the usual or correct way for doing sth: *What's the procedure for making a complaint?*

proceed /prəˈsiːd/ *verb* [I] **1** proceed (with sth) to continue doing sth; to continue being done: *The building work was proceeding according to schedule.* **2** proceed to do sth to do sth next, after having done sth else first: *Once he had calmed down he proceeded to tell us what had happened.*

proceedings /prəˈsiːdɪŋz/ *noun* [pl] (*formal*) **1** proceedings (against sb/for sth) legal action: *to start divorce proceedings* **2** events that happen, especially at a formal meeting, ceremony, etc: *The proceedings were interrupted by demonstrators.*

proceeds /ˈprəʊsiːdz/ *noun* [pl] proceeds (of/from sth) money that you get when you sell sth: *The proceeds from the sale will go to charity.*

process[1] /ˈprəʊses/ *noun* [C] **1** a series of actions that you do for a particular purpose: *We've just begun the complicated process of selling the house.* **2** a series of changes that happen naturally: *Mistakes are a normal part of the learning process.*

IDM **in the process** while you are doing sth else: *We washed the dog yesterday—and we all got very wet in the process.*

in the process of sth/doing sth in the middle of doing sth: *They are in the process of moving house.*

process[2] /ˈprəʊses/ *verb* [T] **1** to treat sth, for example with chemicals, in order to preserve it, change it, etc: *Cheese is processed so that it lasts longer.* **2** to deal with information, for example on a computer: *It will take about ten days to process your application.*

procession /prəˈseʃn/ *noun* [C,U] a number of people, vehicles, etc. that move slowly in a line, especially as part of a ceremony: *to walk* ***in procession*** ♦ *a funeral procession*

processor /ˈprəʊsesə(r)/ *noun* [C] a machine or person that **processes** sth ➲ look at **food processor**, **word processor**

proclaim /prəˈkleɪm/ *verb* [T] (*formal*) to make sth known officially or publicly: *The day has been proclaimed a national holiday.* ▶ **proclamation** /ˌprɒkləˈmeɪʃn/ *noun* [C,U]: *to make a proclamation of war*

procure /prəˈkjʊə(r)/ *verb* [T] (*formal*) procure sth (for sb) to obtain sth, especially with difficulty: *I managed to procure two tickets for the match.*

prod /prɒd/ *verb* [I,T] (prodding; prodded) to push or press sb/sth with your finger or a pointed object: (*figurative*) *Ruth works quite hard but she does need*

P

prodding occasionally. ▶ **prod** *noun* [C]: *to give the fire a prod with a stick* ▶ **prodding** *noun* [U]

prodigious /prəˈdɪdʒəs/ *adj* (*formal*) very large or powerful and surprising: *He seemed to have a prodigious amount of energy.*

prodigy /ˈprɒdədʒi/ *noun* [C] (*pl* **prodigies**) a child who is unusually good at sth: *Mozart was a* ***child prodigy.*** ➲ look at **genius**

🔑 **produce**[1] /prəˈdjuːs/ *verb* [T]
➤GOODS **1** to make sth to be sold, especially in large quantities: *The factory produces 20000 cars a year.* SYN **manufacture**
➤MAKE NATURALLY **2** to grow or make sth by a natural process: *This region produces most of the country's wheat.* ◆ *(figurative) He's the greatest athlete this country has produced.*
➤MAKE WITH SKILL **3** to create sth using skill: *The children have produced some beautiful pictures for the exhibition.*
➤EFFECT/RESULT **4** to cause a particular effect or result: *Her remarks produced roars of laughter.*
➤SHOW **5** to show sth so that sb else can look at or examine it: *to produce evidence in court*
➤FILM/PLAY **6** to be in charge of preparing a film, play, etc. so that it can be shown to the public: *She is producing 'Romeo and Juliet' at the local theatre.*

produce[2] /ˈprɒdjuːs/ *noun* [U] food, etc. that is grown on a farm and sold: *fresh farm produce*

🔑 **producer** /prəˈdjuːsə(r)/ *noun* [C] **1** a person, company or country that makes or grows sth: *Brazil is a major producer of coffee.* **2** a person who deals with the business side of organizing a play, film, etc: *Hollywood screenwriters, actors and producers* **3** a person who arranges for sb to make a programme for TV or radio, or a record, CD, etc: *an independent television producer*

🔑 **product** /ˈprɒdʌkt/ *noun* [C] **1** something that is made in a factory or that is formed naturally: *dairy/meat/pharmaceutical/software products* ◆ *The company has just launched a new product.* ◆ *Carbon dioxide is one of the waste products of this process.* **2** product of sth the result of sth: *The industry's problems are the product of government policy.*

🔑 **production** /prəˈdʌkʃn/ *noun* **1** [U] the making or growing of sth, especially in large quantities: *The latest model will be* ***in production*** *from April.* ◆ *This farm specializes in the production of organic vegetables.* ◆ *mass production* **2** [U] the amount of sth that is made or grown: *a rise/fall in production* ◆ *a high level of production* **3** [C] a play, film or programme that has been made for the public
IDM **on production of sth** when you show sth: *You can get a ten per cent discount on production of your membership card.*

productive /prəˈdʌktɪv/ *adj* **1** that makes or grows sth, especially in large quantities: *The company wants to sell off its less productive factories.* **2** useful (because results come from it): *a productive discussion* ▶ **productivity** /ˌprɒdʌkˈtɪvəti/ *noun* [U]

Prof. /prɒf/ *abbr* = **professor**

profess /prəˈfes/ *verb* [T] (*formal*) **1** to say that sth is true or correct, even when it is not: *Marianne professed to know nothing at all about it, but I did not believe her.* **2** to state openly that you have a particular belief, feeling, etc: *He professed his hatred of war.*

🔑 **profession** /prəˈfeʃn/ *noun* [C] **1** a job that needs a high level of training and/or education: *the medical/legal/teaching profession* ◆ *She's thinking of entering the nursing profession.* ➲ note at **work**[2] **2 the ... profession** [with sing or pl verb] all the people who work in a particular profession: *The legal profession is/are trying to resist the reforms.*
IDM **by profession** as your job: *George is an accountant by profession.*

🔑 **professional**[1] /prəˈfeʃənl/ *adj* **1** [only *before* a noun] connected with a job that needs a high level of training and/or education: *Get professional advice from your lawyer before you take any action.* ◆ *professional qualifications* **2** doing sth in a way that shows skill, training or care: *The police are trained to deal with every situation in a calm and professional manner.* ◆ *Her application was neatly typed and looked very professional.* **3** (used about a sport, etc.) done by people who are paid; doing a sport, etc. as a job or for money: *He's planning to* ***turn professional*** *after the Olympics.* ◆ *professional football* OPP **amateur**

🔑 **professional**[2] /prəˈfeʃənl/ *noun* [C] **1** a person who works in a job that needs a high level of training and/or education: *doctors and other health professionals* **2** (also *informal* **pro**) a person who plays or teaches a sport, etc. for money: *a top golf professional* **3** (also *informal* **pro**) a person who has a lot of skill and experience: *This was clearly a job for a professional.*

professionalism /prəˈfeʃənəlɪzəm/ *noun* [U] a way of doing a job that shows great skill and experience: *We were impressed by the professionalism of the staff.*

professionally /prəˈfeʃənəli/ *adv* **1** in a way that shows great skill and experience **2** for money; by a professional person: *Rob plays the saxophone professionally.*

🔑 **professor** /prəˈfesə(r)/ *noun* [C] (*abbr* **Prof.**) **1** (*especially BrE*) a university teacher of the highest level: *She's professor of English at Bristol University.* **2** (*AmE*) a teacher at a college or university: *a chemistry professor*

proficient /prəˈfɪʃnt/ *adj* **proficient (in/at sth/doing sth)** able to do a particular thing well; skilled: *We are looking for someone who is proficient in French.* ▶ **proficiency** /prəˈfɪʃnsi/ *noun* [U] **proficiency (in sth/doing sth)**: *a certificate of proficiency in English*

profile /ˈprəʊfaɪl/ *noun* [C] **1** a person's face or head seen from the side, not the front: *I did a sketch of him* ***in profile.*** **2** a short description of sb/sth that gives useful information: *We're building up a profile of our average customer.* ◆ *You should be careful what you put on your* ***Facebook profile*** (= a description and photograph(s) of yourself on an Internet site), *as it isn't always private.*
IDM **a high/low profile** a way of behaving that

does/does not attract other people's attention: *I don't know much about the subject—I'm going to keep a low profile at the meeting tomorrow.*

profit[1] /ˈprɒfɪt/ *noun* [C,U] the money that you make when you sell sth for more than it cost you: *Did you **make a profit on** your house when you sold it?* ◆ *I'm hoping to sell my shares **at a profit**.* **OPP** **loss**

profit[2] /ˈprɒfɪt/ *verb* [I,T] (*formal*) **profit (from/by sth)** to get an advantage from sth; to give sb an advantage: *Who will profit most from the tax reforms?*

profitable /ˈprɒfɪtəbl/ *adj* **1** that makes money: *a profitable business* **2** helpful or useful: *We had a profitable discussion yesterday.* ▸ **profitably** /-əbli/ *adv*: *to spend your time profitably* ▸ **profitability** /ˌprɒfɪtəˈbɪləti/ *noun* [U]

profound /prəˈfaʊnd/ *adj* **1** very great; that you feel very strongly: *The experience had a profound influence on her.* **2** needing or showing a lot of knowledge or thought: *He's always making profound statements about the meaning of life.* **SYN** **deep** ▸ **profoundly** *adv*: *I was profoundly relieved to hear the news.*

profuse /prəˈfjuːs/ *adj* (*formal*) given or produced in great quantity: *profuse apologies* ▸ **profusely** *adv*: *She apologized profusely for being late.*

profusion /prəˈfjuːʒn/ *noun* [sing, with sing or pl verb, U] (*formal*) a very large quantity of sth: *a profusion of colours* ◆ *Roses grew **in profusion** against the old wall.* **SYN** **abundance**

program[1] /ˈprəʊɡræm/ *noun* [C] **1** a set of instructions that you give to a computer so that it will do a particular task: *to write a program*

HELP When we are talking about computers, both the American and the British spelling is **program.** For every other meaning the British spelling is **programme** and the American spelling is **program.**

2 (*AmE*) = **programme[1]**

program[2] /ˈprəʊɡræm/ *verb* [I,T] (**programming**; **programmed**) to give a set of instructions to a computer: *In this class, students will learn how to program.*

programme[1] (*AmE* **program**) /ˈprəʊɡræm/ *noun* [C] **1** a plan of things to do: *What's (on) your programme today?* (= what are you going to do today?) ◆ *The leaflet outlines the government's programme of educational reforms.* **2** a show or other item that is sent out on the radio or TV: *a TV/radio programme* ◆ *We've just missed an interesting programme on elephants.* ➲ note at **television** **3** a little book or piece of paper which you get at a concert, a sports event, etc. that gives you information about what you are going to see: *a theatre programme* ➲ note at **program**

programme[2] (*AmE* **program**) /ˈprəʊɡræm/ *verb* [T] (**programming**; **programmed**, (*AmE* also) **programing**; **programed**) [usually passive] **1** to plan for sth to happen at a particular time: *The road is programmed for completion next May.* **2** to make sb/sth work or act automatically in a particular way: *The lights are programmed to come on as soon as it gets dark.*

programmer /ˈprəʊɡræmə(r)/ *noun* [C] a person whose job is to write programs for a computer

progress[1] /ˈprəʊɡres/ *noun* [U] **1** movement forwards or towards achieving sth: *Anna's **making progress** at school.* ◆ *to make slow/steady/rapid/good progress* **2** change or improvement in society: *scientific progress*

IDM **in progress** happening now: *Silence! Examination in progress.*

progress[2] /prəˈɡres/ *verb* [I] **1** to become better; to develop (well): *Medical knowledge has progressed rapidly in the last twenty years.* **SYN** **advance** **2** to move forward; to continue: *I got more and more tired as the evening progressed.* **SYN** **go on**

progression /prəˈɡreʃn/ *noun* [C,U] (a) **progression (from sth) (to sth)** movement forward or a development from one stage to another: *You've made the progression from beginner to intermediate level.*

progressive /prəˈɡresɪv/ *adj* **1** using modern methods and ideas: *a progressive school* **2** happening or developing steadily: *a progressive reduction in the number of staff*

progressively /prəˈɡresɪvli/ *adv* steadily; a little at a time: *The situation became progressively worse.*

the proˌgressive ˈtense = **the continuous tense**

prohibit /prəˈhɪbɪt/ *verb* [T] (*formal*) **prohibit sb/sth (from doing sth)** to say that sth is not allowed by law: *English law prohibits anyone under 18 from buying cigarettes.* **SYN** **forbid, prevent**

prohibition /ˌprəʊɪˈbɪʃn/ *noun* **1** [U] the act of stopping sth being done or used, especially by law: *the prohibition of smoking in public places* **2** [C] (*formal*) **a prohibition (on/against sth)** a law or rule that stops sth being done or used: *There is a prohibition on the carrying of knives.*

prohibitive /prəˈhɪbətɪv/ *adj* (used about a price or cost) so high that it prevents people from buying sth or doing sth: *The price of houses in the centre of town is prohibitive.* ▸ **prohibitively** *adv*

project[1] /ˈprɒdʒekt/ *noun* [C] **1** a piece of work, often involving many people, that is planned and organized carefully: *a major project to reduce pollution in our rivers* ◆ *a housing project* **2** a piece of school work in which the student has to collect information about a certain subject and then write about it: *Our group chose to do a project on rainforests.*

project[2] /prəˈdʒekt/ *verb*

➤PLAN **1** [T, usually passive] to plan sth that will happen in the future: *the band's projected world tour*

➤GUESS **2** [T, usually passive] to guess or calculate the size, cost or amount of sth: *a projected increase of 10%* **SYN** **forecast**

➤LIGHT/IMAGE **3** [T] **project sth (on/onto sth)** to make light, a picture from a film, etc. appear on a flat

P

surface or screen: *Images are projected onto the retina of the eye.*

➤SOUND **4** [T] to make a sound so that it can be heard at a distance: *Actors must learn to project their voices.*

➤STICK OUT **5** [I] (*formal*) to stick out: *The balcony projects one metre out from the wall.*

➤PRESENT YOURSELF **6** [T] to show or represent sb/sth/yourself in a certain way: *The government is trying to project a more caring image.*

projection /prəˈdʒekʃn/ *noun* **1** [C] a guess about a future amount, situation, etc. based on the present situation: *sales projections for the next five years* **2** [U] the act of making light, a picture from a film, a computer image, etc. appear on a surface

projector /prəˈdʒektə(r)/ *noun* [C] a piece of equipment that **projects** images, pictures or films onto a screen or wall: *a film/data/overhead projector*

proliferate /prəˈlɪfəreɪt/ *verb* [I] (*formal*) to increase quickly in number ▶ **proliferation** /prəˌlɪfəˈreɪʃn/ *noun* [U, sing]

prolific /prəˈlɪfɪk/ *adj* (used especially about a writer, artist, etc.) producing a lot: *a prolific goal scorer* ◆ *Picasso was extremely prolific all through his life.*

prologue /ˈprəʊlɒɡ/ *noun* [C] a piece of writing or a speech that introduces a play, poem, etc. ➲ look at **epilogue**

prolong /prəˈlɒŋ/ *verb* [T] to make sth last longer

prolonged /prəˈlɒŋd/ *adj* continuing for a long time: *There was a prolonged silence before anybody spoke.*

P

prom /prɒm/ *noun* [C] **1** = **promenade** **2** a dance that is held at the end of a school year

promenade /ˌprɒməˈnɑːd/ (also **prom**) *noun* [C] a wide path where people walk beside the sea in a town on the coast

prominent /ˈprɒmɪnənt/ *adj* **1** important or famous: *a prominent political figure* **2** noticeable; easy to see: *The church is the most prominent feature of the village.* ▶ **prominence** *noun* [U, sing]: *The newspaper gave the affair great prominence.* ▶ **prominently** *adv*

promiscuous /prəˈmɪskjuəs/ *adj* having sexual relations with many people ▶ **promiscuity** /ˌprɒmɪˈskjuːəti/ *noun* [U]

⚷ **promise**[1] /ˈprɒmɪs/ *verb* **1** [I,T] **promise (to do sth); promise (sb) that ...** to say definitely that you will do or not do sth or that sth will happen: *She promised to phone every week.* ◆ *She promised (me) that she would write.* **2** [T] **promise sth (to sb); promise sb sth** to say definitely that you will give sth to sb: *Can you promise your support?* ◆ *You have to give him the money if you promised it to him.* ◆ *My dad has promised me a bicycle.* **3** [T] to show signs of sth, so that you expect it to happen: *It promises to be an exciting occasion.*

⚷ **promise**[2] /ˈprɒmɪs/ *noun* **1** [C] **a promise (to do sth/that ...)** a written or spoken statement or agreement that you will or will not do sth: *You should never **break a promise**.* ◆ *Make sure you **keep** your **promise** to always do your homework.* ◆ *I want you to **make a promise** that you won't do that again.* ◆ *I **give** you my **promise** that I won't tell anyone.* **2** [U] signs that you will be able to do sth well or be successful: *He **showed** great **promise** as a musician.*

promising /ˈprɒmɪsɪŋ/ *adj* showing signs of being very good or successful: *a promising young writer*

⚷ **promote** /prəˈməʊt/ *verb* [T] **1** to encourage sth; to help sth to happen or develop: *to promote good relations between countries* **2 promote sth (as sth)** to advertise sth in order to increase its sales or make it popular: *The new face cream is being promoted as a miracle cure for wrinkles.* **3** [often passive] **promote sb (from sth) (to sth)** to give sb a higher position or more important job: *He's been promoted from assistant manager to manager.* OPP **demote** ➲ note at **job**

promoter /prəˈməʊtə(r)/ *noun* [C] a person who organizes or provides the money for an event

⚷ **promotion** /prəˈməʊʃn/ *noun* **1** [C,U] **promotion (to sth)** a move to a higher position or more important job: *The new job is a promotion for her.* OPP **demotion** **2** [C,U] things that you do in order to advertise a product and increase its sales: *It's all part of a special promotion of the new book.* **3** [U] (*formal*) **promotion (of sth)** the activity of trying to make sth develop or become accepted by people: *We need to work on the promotion of health, not the treatment of disease.*

⚷ **prompt**[1] /prɒmpt/ *adj* **1** immediate; done without delay: *We need a prompt decision on this matter.* **2** [not before a noun] **prompt (in doing sth/to do sth)** (used about a person) quick; acting without delay: *We are always prompt in paying our bills.* ◆ *She was prompt to point out my mistake.*

⚷ **prompt**[2] /prɒmpt/ *verb* **1** [T] to cause sth to happen; to make sb decide to do sth: *What prompted you to give up your job?* **2** [I,T] to encourage sb to speak by asking questions or to remind an actor of his or her words in a play: *The speaker had to be prompted several times.* ▶ **prompting** *noun* [U]: *He apologized without any prompting.*

prompt[3] /prɒmpt/ *noun* [C] **1** a word or words said to an actor to remind them of what to say next: *When she forgot her lines I had to give her a prompt.* **2** a sign on a computer screen that shows that the computer has finished what it was doing and is ready for more instructions: *Wait for the prompt to come up, then type in your password.*

⚷ **promptly** /ˈprɒmptli/ *adv* **1** immediately; without delay: *I invited her to dinner and she promptly accepted.* **2** (also **prompt**) at exactly the time that you have arranged: *We arrived promptly at 12 o'clock.* ◆ *I'll pick you up at 7 o'clock prompt.* SYN **punctually**

prone /prəʊn/ *adj* **prone to sth/to do sth** likely to suffer from sth or to do sth bad: *prone to infection/injury/heart attacks* ◆ *Working without a break makes you more prone to error.* ◆ *to be **accident-prone*** (= to have a lot of accidents)

prong /prɒŋ/ *noun* [C] **1** each of the two or more long pointed parts of a fork **2** each of the separate parts of an attack, argument, etc. that sb uses to achieve sth **3 -pronged** [in compounds] having the number or type of **prongs** mentioned: *a three-pronged attack*

pronoun /ˈprəʊnaʊn/ *noun* [C] a word that is used in place of a noun or a phrase that contains a noun: *'He', 'it', 'hers', 'me', 'them', etc. are all pronouns.* ➲ look at **personal pronoun**

pronounce /prəˈnaʊns/ *verb* **1** [T] to make the sound of a word or letter in a particular way: *You don't pronounce the 'b' at the end of 'comb'.* ♦ *How do you pronounce your surname?* ➲ *noun* **pronunciation** **2** [T] (*formal*) to say or give sth formally, officially or publicly: *The judge will pronounce sentence today.* **3** [I,T] (*formal*) **pronounce (on sth)** to give your opinion on sth, especially formally: *The play was pronounced 'brilliant' by all the critics.*

pronounced /prəˈnaʊnst/ *adj* very noticeable; obvious: *His English is excellent although he speaks with a pronounced French accent.*

pronunciation /prəˌnʌnsiˈeɪʃn/ *noun* **1** [U,C] the way in which a language or a particular word or sound is said: *American pronunciation* ➲ *verb* **pronounce** **2** [U] sb's way of speaking a language: *His grammar is good but his pronunciation is awful!*

EXAM TIP

Pronunciation

Make sure you know how to pronounce important words for the topics you will have to talk about in your **oral/speaking exam**. Use the **phonetic transcription** (= the special symbols that show you how to say a word) to help you, or listen to the sound on the Wordpower CD-ROM to get the pronunciation right. You can practise your pronunciation using the 'Record your pronunciation' feature on the CD-ROM.

proof /pruːf/ *noun* **1** [U] **proof (of sth); proof that ...** information, documents, etc. which show that sth is true: *'We need some* **proof of identity**,*' the shop assistant said.* ♦ *You've got no proof that John took the money.* ➲ look at **evidence** ➲ *verb* **prove** **2** [C, usually pl] (*technical*) a first copy of printed material that is produced so that mistakes can be corrected: *She was checking the proofs of her latest novel.*

-proof /pruːf/ *adj* [in compounds] able to protect against the thing mentioned: *a soundproof room* ♦ *a waterproof/windproof jacket*

prop¹ /prɒp/ *noun* [C] **1** a stick or other object that you use to support sth or to keep sth in position: *Rescuers used props to stop the roof of the tunnel collapsing.* **2** [usually pl] an object that is used in a play, film, etc: *He's responsible for all the stage props, machinery and lighting.*

prop² /prɒp/ *verb* [T] (**propping**; **propped**) to support sb/sth or keep sb/sth in position by putting them or it against or on sth: *I'll use this book to prop the window open.* ♦ *He propped his bicycle against the wall.*

PHR V **prop sth up** to support sth that would otherwise fall or fail

propaganda /ˌprɒpəˈɡændə/ *noun* [U] information and ideas that may be exaggerated or false, which are used to gain support for a political leader, party, etc: *political propaganda*

propagate /ˈprɒpəɡeɪt/ *verb* **1** [T] (*formal*) to spread an idea, a belief or a piece of information among many people: *TV advertising propagates a false image of the ideal family.* **2** [I,T] to produce new plants from a parent plant: *Mum propagated many of her own plants every summer.* ▶ **propagation** /ˌprɒpəˈɡeɪʃn/ *noun* [U]

propel /prəˈpel/ *verb* [T] (**propelling**; **propelled**) to move, drive or push sb/sth forward or in a particular direction

propeller /prəˈpelə(r)/ *noun* [C] a device with several blades that turn round very fast in order to make a ship or a plane move

propensity /prəˈpensəti/ *noun* [C] (*pl* **propensities**) (*formal*) **propensity (for sth); propensity (for doing sth); propensity (to do sth)** a habit of or a liking for behaving in a particular way: *He showed a propensity for violence.* ♦ *She has a propensity to exaggerate.* SYN **inclination**

proper /ˈprɒpə(r)/ *adj* **1** [only *before* a noun] (*especially BrE*) right, suitable or correct: *If you're going skiing you must have the proper clothes.* ♦ *I've got to get these pieces of paper in the proper order.* **2** [only *before* a noun] that you consider to be real or good enough: *I didn't see much of the flat yesterday. I'm going to go today and have a proper look.* **3** (*formal*) socially and morally acceptable: *I think it would be only proper for you to apologize.* OPP **improper** **4** [only *after* a noun] real or main: *We travelled through miles of suburbs before we got to the city proper.*

properly /ˈprɒpəli/ *adv* **1** (*especially BrE*) correctly; in an acceptable way: *The teacher said I hadn't done my homework properly.* ♦ *These shoes don't fit properly.* **2** in a way that is socially and morally acceptable; politely: *If you two children can't behave properly, then we'll have to go home.* OPP **improperly**

ˌproper ˈnoun (also **ˌproper ˈname**) *noun* [C] a word which is the name of a particular person or place and begins with a capital letter: *'Mary' and 'Rome' are proper nouns.*

property /ˈprɒpəti/ *noun* (*pl* **properties**) **1** [U] a thing or things that belong to sb: *The sack contained* **stolen property**. ♦ *Is this bag your property?* ♦ *This file is government property.* ➲ look at **lost property** **2** [U] land and buildings: *Property prices vary enormously from area to area.* **3** [C] one building and the land around it: *There are a lot of empty properties in the area.* **4** [C, usually pl] (*formal*) a special quality or characteristic that a substance, etc. has: *Some plants have healing properties.*

ˈproperty developer = **developer**

P

prophecy /ˈprɒfəsi/ *noun* [C] (*pl* prophecies) a statement about what is going to happen in the future: *to fulfil a prophecy* (= to make it come true)

prophesy /ˈprɒfəsaɪ/ *verb* [T] (prophesying; prophesies; *pt, pp* prophesied) to say what you think will happen in the future: *to prophesy disaster/war*

prophet /ˈprɒfɪt/ *noun* [C] **1** (also Prophet) (in the Christian, Jewish and Muslim religions) a person who is sent by God to teach the people and give them messages from God **2** a person who tells what is going to happen in the future ▶ **prophetic** /prəˈfetɪk/ *adj*

⚷ **proportion** /prəˈpɔːʃn/ *noun* **1** [C] a part or share of a whole: *A large proportion of the earth's surface is covered by sea.* **2** [U] proportion (of sth to sth) the relationship between the size or amount of two things: *The proportion of men to women in the college has changed dramatically over the years.* **3** proportions [pl] the size or shape of sth: *a room of fairly generous proportions* ◆ *Political unrest is reaching alarming proportions.*

IDM **in proportion** the right size in relation to other things: *to draw something in proportion* ◆ *She's so upset that it's hard for her to keep the problem in proportion* (= to her it seems more important or serious than it really is).

in proportion to sth by the same amount or number as sth else; relative to: *Salaries have not risen in proportion to inflation.* ◆ *The room is very long in proportion to its width.*

out of proportion (to sth) **1** too big, small, etc. in relation to other things **2** too great, serious, important, etc. in relation to sth: *His reaction was completely out of proportion to the situation.*

proportional /prəˈpɔːʃənl/ *adj* proportional (to sth) of the right size, amount or degree compared with sth else: *Salary is proportional to years of experience.*

proˌportional ˌrepresenˈtation *noun* [U] (*abbr* PR) a system that gives each political party in an election a number of seats in a parliament in direct relation to the number of votes it receives ➲ look at **representation**

⚷ **proposal** /prəˈpəʊzl/ *noun* [C] **1** a proposal (for/to do sth); a proposal that … a plan that is formally suggested: *a new proposal for raising money* ◆ *a proposal to build more student accommodation* ◆ *May I* ***make a proposal*** *that we all give an equal amount?* **2** an act of formally asking sb to marry you

⚷ **propose** /prəˈpəʊz/ *verb* **1** [T] to formally suggest sth as a possible plan or action: *At the meeting a new advertising campaign was proposed.* **2** [T] to intend to do sth; to have sth as a plan: *What do you propose to do now?* **3** [I,T] propose (to sb) to ask sb to marry you: *to propose marriage* **4** [T] propose sb for/as sth to suggest sb for an official position: *I'd like to propose Anna Marsh as Chairperson.*

proposition /ˌprɒpəˈzɪʃn/ *noun* [C] **1** an idea, a plan or an offer, especially in business; a suggestion: *A month's holiday in Spain is a very* ***attractive proposition.*** **2** an idea or opinion that sb expresses about sth: *That's a very interesting proposition. But can you prove it?*

proprietor /prəˈpraɪətə(r)/ (*fem* proprietress /prəˈpraɪətres/) *noun* [C] (*formal*) the owner of a business, a hotel, etc.

prose /prəʊz/ *noun* [U] written language that is not poetry: *to write* ***in prose*** ➲ look at **poetry**

prosecute /ˈprɒsɪkjuːt/ *verb* [I,T] prosecute sb (for sth) to officially charge sb with a crime and try to show that they are guilty, in a court of law: *the prosecuting counsel/lawyer/attorney* ◆ *He was prosecuted for theft.* ➲ look at **defend**

prosecution /ˌprɒsɪˈkjuːʃn/ *noun* **1** [U,C] the process of officially charging sb with a crime and of trying to show that they are guilty, in a court of law: *Failure to pay your parking fine will result in prosecution.* ◆ *to bring a prosecution against somebody* **2** the prosecution [sing, with sing or pl verb] the person or group of people who try to show that sb is guilty of a crime in a court of law: *The prosecution claim/claims that Lloyd was driving at 100 miles per hour.* ➲ note at **court** ➲ look at **the defence**

prosecutor /ˈprɒsɪkjuːtə(r)/ *noun* [C] **1** a public official who charges sb officially with a crime and **prosecutes** them in court: *the public/state prosecutor* **2** a lawyer who leads the case against the person who is accused of a crime

⚷ **prospect** /ˈprɒspekt/ *noun* **1** [U, sing] prospect (of sth/of doing sth) the possibility that sth will happen: *There's little prospect of better weather before next week.* **2** [sing] prospect (of sth/of doing sth) a thought about what may or will happen in the future: *The prospect of becoming a father filled James with horror.* **3** prospects [pl] chances of being successful in the future: *good job/career/promotion prospects*

prospective /prəˈspektɪv/ *adj* likely to be or to happen; possible: *They are worried about prospective changes in the law.*

prospectus /prəˈspektəs/ *noun* [C] a small book which gives information about a school or college in order to advertise it

prosper /ˈprɒspə(r)/ *verb* [I] to develop in a successful way; to be successful, especially with money

prosperity /prɒˈsperəti/ *noun* [U] the state of being successful, and having a lot of money: *Tourism has brought prosperity to many parts of Spain.*

prosperous /ˈprɒspərəs/ *adj* rich and successful

prostitute /ˈprɒstɪtjuːt/ *noun* [C] a person, especially a woman, who earns money by having sex with people

prostitution /ˌprɒstɪˈtjuːʃn/ *noun* [U] the work of a **prostitute**

prostrate /ˈprɒstreɪt/ *adj* (*formal*) lying flat on the ground, facing downwards

protagonist /prəˈtægənɪst/ *noun* [C] (*formal*) the main character in a play, film or book ➲ look at **hero**

P

protect /prəˈtekt/ *verb* [T] protect sb/sth (against/from sth) to keep sb/sth safe; to defend sb/sth: *Parents try to protect their children from danger as far as possible.* ◆ *Bats are a* ***protected species*** (= they must not be killed).

protection /prəˈtekʃn/ *noun* [U] protection (against/from sth) the act of keeping sb/sth safe so that he/she/it is not harmed or damaged: *Vaccination gives protection against diseases.* ◆ *After the attack the man was put* ***under*** *police* ***protection***.

protective /prəˈtektɪv/ *adj* **1** [only *before* a noun] that prevents sb/sth from being damaged or harmed: *In certain jobs workers need to wear protective clothing.* **2** protective (of/towards sb/sth) wanting to keep sb/sth safe: *Female animals are very protective of their young.*

protector /prəˈtektə(r)/ *noun* [C] a person who protects sb/sth

protein /ˈprəʊtiːn/ *noun* [C,U] a substance found in food such as meat, fish and eggs. It is important for helping people and animals to grow and be healthy.

protest[1] /ˈprəʊtest/ *noun* [U,C] protest (against sth) a statement or action that shows that you do not like or approve of sth: *He resigned* ***in protest*** *against the decision.* ◆ *The trade union organized a protest against the redundancies.*

IDM **under protest** not happily and after expressing disagreement: *Fiona agreed to pay in the end but only under protest.*

protest[2] /prəˈtest/ *verb* **1** [I,T] protest (about/against/at sth) to say or show that you do not approve of or agree with sth, especially publicly: *Students have been protesting against the government's decision.*

HELP In American English **protest** is used without a preposition: *They protested the government's handling of the situation.*

2 [T] to say sth firmly, especially when others do not believe you: *She has always* ***protested*** *her* ***innocence***.

HELP **Protest or complain? Protest** is stronger and usually used about more serious things than **complain**. You **protest** about something that you feel is not right or fair, you **complain** about the quality of something or about a less serious action: *to protest about a new tax* ◆ *to complain about the poor weather*

▶ **protester** *noun* [C]: *Protesters blocked the road outside the factory.*

Protestant /ˈprɒtɪstənt/ *noun* [C] a member of the Christian church that separated from the Catholic church in the 16th century ▶ **Protestant** *adj*: *a Protestant church* ➲ look at **Roman Catholic**

protocol /ˈprəʊtəkɒl/ *noun* [U] a system of fixed rules and formal behaviour used in official meetings or other very formal situations: *a breach of protocol (= a failure to follow it)* ◆ *the protocol of diplomatic visits*

proton /ˈprəʊtɒn/ *noun* [C] part of the **nucleus** (= the central part) of an atom that carries a positive electric charge ➲ look at **electron, neutron**

prototype /ˈprəʊtətaɪp/ *noun* [C] the first model or design of sth from which other forms will be developed

protrude /prəˈtruːd/ *verb* [I] (*formal*) protrude (from sth) to stick out from a place or surface: *protruding eyes/teeth*

protrusion /prəˈtruːʒn/ *noun* [C,U] (*formal*) a thing that sticks out from a place or surface; the fact of doing this: *a protrusion on the rock face*

proud /praʊd/ *adj* (**prouder; proudest**) **1** proud (of sb/sth); proud to do sth/that ... feeling pleased and satisfied about sth that you own or have done: *They are very proud of their new house.* ◆ *I feel very proud to be part of such a successful organization.* ◆ *You should feel very proud that you have been chosen.* **2** feeling that you are better and more important than other people: *Now she's at university she'll be much too proud to talk to us!* **3** having respect for yourself and not wanting to lose the respect of others: *He was too proud to ask for help.* ➲ *noun* **pride** ▶ **proudly** *adv*: *'I did all the work myself,' he said proudly.*

prove /pruːv/ *verb* (*pp* **proved**, *AmE* **proven**) **1** [T] prove sth (to sb) to use facts and evidence to show that sth is true: *It will be difficult to prove that she was lying.* ◆ *She tried to prove her innocence to the court.* ◆ *He felt he needed* ***to prove a point*** (= show other people that he was right). ➲ *noun* **proof** **2** [I] to show a particular quality over a period of time: *The job proved more difficult than we'd expected.* **3** [T] prove yourself (to sb) to show other people how good you are at doing sth and/or that you are capable of doing sth: *He constantly feels that he has to prove himself to others.*

proven /ˈprəʊvn; ˈpruːvn/ *adj* [only *before* a noun] that has been shown to be true: *a proven fact*

proverb /ˈprɒvɜːb/ *noun* [C] a short well-known sentence or phrase that gives advice or says that sth is generally true in life: *'All's fair in love and war' is a proverb.* ➲ look at **saying**

proverbial /prəˈvɜːbiəl/ *adj* [only *before* a noun] used to show that you are referring to a particular **proverb** or well-known phrase: *He drinks like the proverbial fish.* ▶ **proverbially** /-biəli/ *adv*

provide /prəˈvaɪd/ *verb* [T] provide sb (with sth); provide sth (for sb) to give sth to sb or make sth available for sb to use: *This book will provide you with all the information you need.* ◆ *We are able to provide accommodation for two students.* **SYN** **supply** ➲ *noun* **provision**

PHR V **provide for sb** to give sb all that they need to live, for example food and clothing: *Robin has four children to provide for.*

provide for sth to make preparations to deal with sth that might happen in the future: *We did not provide for such a large increase in prices.*

P

provided /prəˈvaɪdɪd/ (also **providing**) *conj* **provided/providing (that)** only if; on condition that: *She agreed to go and work abroad provided (that) her family could go with her.*

province /ˈprɒvɪns/ *noun* **1** [C] one of the main parts into which some countries are divided, that has its own local government: *Canada has ten provinces.* ➲ look at **county, state** **2 the provinces** [pl] all the parts of a country except the capital city

provincial /prəˈvɪnʃl/ *adj* **1** [only *before* a noun] connected with one of the large areas that some countries are divided into: *provincial governments/elections* **2** connected with the parts of a country that do not include its most important city: *a provincial town/newspaper* **3** (used about a person or their ideas) not wanting to consider new or different ideas or fashions: *provincial attitudes*

provision /prəˈvɪʒn/ *noun* (*formal*) **1** [U] the giving or supplying of sth to sb or making sth available for sb to use: *The council is responsible for the provision of education and social services.* **2** [U] **provision for sb/sth** preparations that you make to deal with sth that might happen in the future: *She **made provision for*** (= planned for the financial future of) *the children in the event of her death.* **3 provisions** [pl] supplies of food and drink, especially for a long journey ➲ *verb* **provide**

provisional /prəˈvɪʒənl/ *adj* only for the present time; that is likely to be changed in the future: *The provisional date for the next meeting is 18 November.* ◆ *a **provisional driving licence*** (= that you use when you are learning to drive) SYN **temporary** ▸ **provisionally** /-nəli/ *adv*: *I've only repaired the bike provisionally—we'll have to do it properly later.*

provocation /ˌprɒvəˈkeɪʃn/ *noun* [U,C] the act of doing or saying sth deliberately to try to make sb angry or upset; something that is said or done to cause this: *You should never hit children, even **under** extreme **provocation**.* ➲ *verb* **provoke**

provocative /prəˈvɒkətɪv/ *adj* **1** intended to make sb angry or upset or to cause an argument: *He made a provocative remark about a woman's place being in the home.* **2** intended to cause sexual excitement: *a provocative look* ▸ **provocatively** *adv*

provoke /prəˈvəʊk/ *verb* [T] **1** to cause a particular feeling or reaction: *an article intended to provoke discussion* **2 provoke sb (into sth/into doing sth)** to say or do sth that you know will make a person angry or upset: *The lawyer claimed his client was provoked into acts of violence.* ➲ *noun* **provocation**

prow /praʊ/ *noun* [C] (*formal*) the pointed front part of a ship or boat OPP **stern**

prowess /ˈpraʊəs/ *noun* [U] (*formal*) great skill at doing sth: *academic/sporting prowess*

prowl /praʊl/ *verb* [I,T] **prowl (about/around)** (used about an animal that is hunting or a person who is waiting for a chance to steal sth or do sth bad) to move around an area quietly so that you are not seen or heard: *I could hear someone prowling around outside so I called the police.* ▸ **prowl** *noun* [sing]: *an intruder **on the prowl*** ▸ **prowler** *noun* [C]: *The police have arrested a prowler outside the hospital.*

proximity /prɒkˈsɪməti/ *noun* [U] (*formal*) **proximity (of sb/sth) (to sb/sth)** the state of being near to sb/sth in distance or time: *The proximity of the new offices to the airport is a great advantage.*

proxy /ˈprɒksi/ *noun* [U] the authority that you give to sb to act for you if you cannot do sth yourself: *to vote **by proxy***

prude /pruːd/ *noun* [C] a person who is easily shocked by anything connected with sex ▸ **prudish** *adj*

prudent /ˈpruːdnt/ *adj* (*formal*) sensible and careful when making judgements and decisions; avoiding unnecessary risks: *It would be prudent to get some more advice before you invest your money.* ▸ **prudence** *noun* [U] ▸ **prudently** *adv*

prune¹ /pruːn/ *noun* [C] a dried **plum** (= a soft round fruit with a stone inside)

prune² /pruːn/ *verb* [T] to cut branches or parts of branches off a tree or bush in order to give it a better shape

pry /praɪ/ *verb* (**prying**; **pries**; *pt, pp* **pried**) **1** [I] **pry (into sth)** to try to find out about other people's private affairs: *I'm sick of you prying into my personal life.* **2** [T] (*especially AmE*) = **prise**

PS (also **ps**) /ˌpiː ˈes/ *noun* [C], *abbr* **postscript** an extra message or extra information that is added at the end of an email, a note, etc: *Love Tessa. PS I'll bring the car.*

pseudonym /ˈsuːdənɪm; ˈsjuː-/ *noun* [C] a name used by sb, especially a writer, instead of their real name

psych /saɪk/ *verb*

PHR V **psych yourself up** (*informal*) to prepare yourself in your mind for sth difficult: *I've got to psych myself up for this interview.*

psyche /ˈsaɪki/ *noun* [C] (*formal*) the mind; your deepest feelings and attitudes: *the human/female/national psyche*

psychedelic /ˌsaɪkəˈdelɪk/ *adj* (used about art, music, clothes, etc.) having bright colours or patterns or strange sounds

psychiatrist /saɪˈkaɪətrɪst/ *noun* [C] a doctor who is trained to treat people with mental illness

psychiatry /saɪˈkaɪətri/ *noun* [U] the study and treatment of mental illness ➲ look at **psychology** ▸ **psychiatric** /ˌsaɪkiˈætrɪk/ *adj*: *a psychiatric hospital/unit/nurse*

psychic /ˈsaɪkɪk/ *adj* (used about a person or their mind) seeming to have unusual powers that cannot be explained, for example knowing what sb else is thinking or being able to see into the future

psycho /ˈsaɪkəʊ/ (*informal*) = **psychopath**

psychoanalysis /ˌsaɪkəʊəˈnæləsɪs/ (also **analysis**) *noun* [U] a method of treating sb with mental illness by asking about their past experiences, feelings, dreams, etc. in order to find out what is making them unhappy ▸ **psychoanalyse** (*AmE* psychoanalyze) /ˌsaɪkəʊˈænəlaɪz/ *verb* [T]

psychoanalyst /ˌsaɪkəʊˈænəlɪst/ *noun* [C] a person who treats sb with a mental illness by using **psychoanalysis**

psychological /ˌsaɪkəˈlɒdʒɪkl/ *adj* **1** connected with the mind or the way that it works: *Has her ordeal caused her long-term psychological damage?* **2** [only *before* a noun] connected with **psychology** ▸ **psychologically** /-kli/ *adv*: *Psychologically, it was a bad time to be starting a new job.*

psychologist /saɪˈkɒlədʒɪst/ *noun* [C] a scientist who studies the mind and the way that people behave

psychology /saɪˈkɒlədʒi/ *noun* **1** [U] the scientific study of the mind and the way that people behave: *child psychology* ➲ look at **psychiatry** **2** [sing] the type of mind that a person or group of people has: *If we understood the psychology of the killer we would have a better chance of catching him.*

psychopath /ˈsaɪkəpæθ/ (also *informal* psycho) *noun* [C] a person who has a serious mental illness that may cause them to hurt or kill other people

psychosis /saɪˈkəʊsɪs/ *noun* [C,U] (*pl* psychoses) a very serious mental illness that affects your whole character ▸ **psychotic** /saɪˈkɒtɪk/ *adj, noun* [C]: *a psychotic patient/individual*

psychotherapy /ˌsaɪkəʊˈθerəpi/ *noun* [U] the treatment of mental illness by discussing sb's feelings rather than by giving them drugs

pt *abbr* (*pl* pts) **1** = **pint**(1): *2 pts milk* **2** = **point**[1](7): *Laura 5pts, Arthur 4pts*

PTO (also pto) /ˌpiː tiː ˈəʊ/ *abbr* (at the bottom of a page) **please turn over**

⚷ **pub** /pʌb/ (also *formal* public house) *noun* [C] a place where people go to buy and drink alcohol and that also often serves food: *a pub lunch* ◆ *a quiz at the local pub* ◆ *Are you coming to the pub tonight?*

puberty /ˈpjuːbəti/ *noun* [U] the time when a child's body is changing and becoming physically like that of an adult: *to reach puberty* SYN **adolescence**

pubic /ˈpjuːbɪk/ *adj* [only *before* a noun] of the area around the sexual organs: *pubic hair*

⚷ **public**[1] /ˈpʌblɪk/ *adj* **1** [only *before* a noun] connected with ordinary people in general: ***Public opinion*** *was in favour of the war.* ◆ *How much public support is there for the government's policy?* **2** provided for the use of people in general: *a public library/telephone* ◆ *public spending* (= money that the government spends on education, health care, etc.) **3** known, seen or heard by many people: *We're going to* ***make*** *the news* ***public*** *soon.* ◆ *It was the band's last* public appearance. OPP for all meanings **private**

IDM **be common/public knowledge** ➲ knowledge

go public **1** to tell people about sth that is a secret: *The sacked employee went public with his stories of corruption inside the company.* **2** (used about a company) to start selling shares to the public

in the public eye often appearing on TV, in magazines, etc.

▸ **publicly** /-kli/ *adv*: *The company refused to admit publicly that it had acted wrongly.*

⚷ **public**[2] /ˈpʌblɪk/ *noun* [sing, with sing or pl verb] **1** **the public** people in general: *The university swimming pool is* ***open to the public*** *in the evenings.* ◆ *The police have asked for help from* ***members of the public.*** ◆ *The public is/are generally in favour of the new law.* **2** a group of people who are all interested in sth or who have sth in common: *the travelling public*

IDM **in public** when other people are present: *This is the first time that Miss Potter has spoken about her experience in public.*

publican /ˈpʌblɪkən/ *noun* [C] (*BrE*) a person who owns or manages a pub

⚷ **publication** /ˌpʌblɪˈkeɪʃn/ *noun* **1** [U] the act of preparing a book, magazine, etc. and making it available to the public in print or on the Internet: *His latest book has just been accepted for publication.* **2** [C] a book, magazine, etc. that has been published: *specialist publications* **3** [U] the act of making sth known to the public: *the publication of exam results*

ˌpublic ˈcompany (also ˌpublic ˌlimited ˈcompany) *noun* [C] (*BrE*) (*abbr* plc) a large company that sells its shares to the public

ˌpublic conˈvenience *noun* [C] (*BrE*) a toilet in a public place that anyone can use

ˌpublic ˈhouse (*formal*) = **pub**

⚷ **publicity** /pʌbˈlɪsəti/ *noun* [U] **1** notice or attention from newspapers, TV, etc: *to seek/avoid publicity* **2** the business of attracting people's attention to sth/sb; advertising: *There has been a lot of publicity for this film.*

publicize (also -ise) /ˈpʌblɪsaɪz/ *verb* [T] to attract people's attention to sth: *The event has been well publicized and should attract a lot of people.*

ˌpublic ˌlimited ˈcompany = **public company**

ˌpublic reˈlations *noun* (*abbr* PR) **1** [U] the job of giving information to the public about an organization or person in order to create a good impression: *a Public Relations Officer* **2** [pl] the state of the relationship between an organization and the public: *Giving money to local charities is good for public relations.*

ˌpublic ˈschool *noun* [C] **1** (in Britain, especially in England) a private school for children aged between 13 and 18

CULTURE

Parents have to pay to send their children to one of these schools. Many public schools are boarding schools (= schools where children can live while they are studying). Famous public schools are Eton and Rugby.

2 (in the US, Australia, Scotland and other

P

countries) a local school that any child can go to that provides free education

ˌpublic-ˈspirited *adj* always ready to help other people and the public in general

ˌpublic ˈtransport *noun* [U] (the system of) buses, trains, etc. that run according to a series of planned times and that anyone can use: *to travel by/on public transport*

publish /ˈpʌblɪʃ/ *verb* **1** [I,T] to prepare a book, magazine, etc. and make it available to the public in print or on the Internet: *This dictionary was published by Oxford University Press.* **2** [T] (used about a writer, etc.) to have your work put in a book, magazine, etc: *Dr Wreth has published several articles on the subject.* **3** [T] to make sth known to the public: *Large companies must publish their accounts every year.*

publisher /ˈpʌblɪʃə(r)/ *noun* [C] a person or company that publishes books, magazines, etc.

publishing /ˈpʌblɪʃɪŋ/ *noun* [U] the business of preparing books, magazines, etc. to be sold in print or on the Internet: *a career in publishing* ◆ *digital publishing*

puck /pʌk/ *noun* [C] a small flat rubber object that is used as a ball in **ice hockey** (= a sport) ➲ note at **hockey**

pudding /ˈpʊdɪŋ/ *noun* [C,U] (*BrE*) **1** any sweet food that is eaten at the end of a meal: *What's for pudding today?* ➲ look at **sweet** ➲ A more formal word is **dessert. 2** a type of sweet food that is made from bread, flour or rice with eggs, milk, etc: *rice pudding*

puddle /ˈpʌdl/ *noun* [C] a small pool of water or other liquid, especially rain, that has formed on the ground ➲ note at **lake**

puff[1] /pʌf/ *verb* **1** [I,T] to smoke a cigarette, pipe etc: *to puff on a cigarette* **2** [I,T] (used about air, smoke, wind, etc.) to blow or come out in clouds: *Smoke was puffing out of the chimney.* **3** [I] to breathe loudly or quickly, for example when you are running: *He was puffing hard as he ran up the hill.* **4** [I] **puff along, in, out, up, etc.** to move in a particular direction with loud breaths or small clouds of smoke: *The train puffed into the station.*

PHR V puff sth out/up to cause sth to become larger by filling it with air: *The trumpet player was puffing out his cheeks.*

puff up (used about part of the body) to become swollen: *Her arm puffed up when she was stung by a wasp.*

puff[2] /pʌf/ *noun* [C] (*BrE informal*) **1** one breath that you take when you are smoking a cigarette or pipe: *to take/have a puff on a cigarette* **2** a small amount of air, smoke, wind, etc. that is blown or sent out: *a puff of smoke*

puffed /pʌft/ (also ˌ**puffed ˈout**) *adj* [not before a noun] finding it difficult to breathe, for example because you have been running

puffin /ˈpʌfɪn/ *noun* [C] a black and white bird with a large, brightly coloured beak that lives near the sea, common in the North Atlantic

puffy /ˈpʌfi/ *adj* (**puffier; puffiest**) (used about a part of sb's body) looking soft and swollen: *Your eyes look a bit puffy. Have you been crying?*

puke /pju:k/ *verb* [I,T] (*informal*) to be sick **SYN vomit** ▶ **puke** *noun* [U]

pull/push

She's pulling the dog.

He's pushing the car.

pull[1] /pʊl/ *verb* **1** [I,T] to use force to move sb/sth towards yourself: *I pulled on the rope to make sure that it was secure.* ◆ *to pull the trigger of a gun* ◆ *I felt someone pull at my sleeve and turned round.* ◆ *They managed to pull the child out of the water just in time.* **2** [T] **pull sth on, out, up, down, etc.** to move sth in the direction that is described: *She pulled her sweater on/She pulled on her sweater.* ◆ *He pulled up his trousers/He pulled his trousers up.* ◆ *I switched off the TV and pulled out the plug.* ◆ *It's dark–pull the curtains* (= close them). ◆ *He felt in his pocket and pulled out a pen.* **3** [T] to hold or be fastened to sth and move it along behind you in the direction that you are going: *That cart is too heavy for one horse to pull.* **4** [I,T] to move your body or a part of your body away with force: *She pulled away as he tried to kiss her.* ◆ *I pulled back my fingers just as the door slammed.* **5** [T] to damage a muscle, etc. by using too much force: *I've **pulled a muscle** in my thigh.*

IDM make/pull faces/a face (at sb/sth) ➲ **face**[1]

pull sb's leg (*informal*) to play a joke on sb by trying to make them believe sth that is not true

pull out all the stops (*informal*) to make the greatest possible effort to achieve sth

pull (your) punches [usually used in negative sentences] (*informal*) to be careful about what you say or do in order not to shock or upset anyone: *The film pulls no punches in its portrayal of urban violence.*

pull your socks up (*BrE*) to start working harder or better than before

pull strings to use your influence to gain an advantage

pull your weight to do your fair share of the work

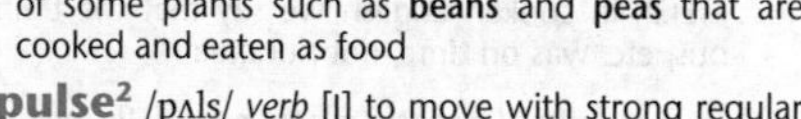

PHR V **pull away (from sb/sth)** to start moving forward, leaving sb/sth behind: *We waved as the bus pulled away.*
pull sth down to destroy a building
pull in (to sth); **pull into sth** **1** (used about a train) to enter a station **2** (used about a car, etc.) to move to the side of the road and stop
pull sth off (*informal*) to succeed in sth: *to pull off a business deal*
pull out (used about a car, etc.) to move away from the side of the road: *I braked as a car suddenly pulled out in front of me.*
pull out (of sth) (used about a train) to leave a station
pull (sb/sth) out (of sth) (to cause sb/sth) to leave sth: *The Americans have pulled their team out of the competition.* ♦ *We've pulled out of the deal.*
pull over (used about a vehicle or its driver) to slow down and move to the side of the road: *I pulled over to let the ambulance past.*
pull through (sth) to survive a dangerous illness or a difficult time
pull together to do sth or work together with other people in an organized way and without fighting
pull yourself together to control your feelings and behave in a calm way: *Pull yourself together and stop crying!*
pull up (to cause a car, etc.) to stop

pull[2] /pʊl/ *noun* **1** [C] **a pull (at/on sth)** the act of moving sb/sth towards you using force: *I gave a pull on the rope to check it was secure.* **2** [sing] a physical force or an attraction that makes sb/sth move in a particular direction: *the earth's gravitational pull* ♦ (*figurative*) *He couldn't resist the pull of the city.*

pulley /ˈpʊli/ *noun* [C] a piece of equipment, consisting of a wheel and a rope, that is used for lifting heavy things

load

pulley

pullover /ˈpʊləʊvə(r)/ *noun* [C] (*especially BrE*) a knitted piece of clothing for the upper part of the body, made of wool, with long sleeves and no buttons SYN **jersey**, **jumper** ➲ note at **sweater**

ˈ**pull tab** (*AmE*) = **ring pull**

pulp /pʌlp/ *noun* **1** [sing,U] a soft substance that is made especially by crushing sth: *Mash the beans to a pulp.* **2** [U] the soft inner part of some fruits or vegetables

pulsate /pʌlˈseɪt/ *verb* [I] to move or shake with strong regular movements: *a pulsating rhythm*

pulse[1] /pʌls/ *noun* **1** [C, usually sing] the regular beating in your body as blood is pushed around it by your heart. You can feel your **pulse** at your wrist, neck, etc: *Your pulse rate increases after exercise.* ♦ *to feel/take somebody's pulse* (= to count how many times it beats in one minute) **2 pulses** [pl] the seeds of some plants such as **beans** and **peas** that are cooked and eaten as food

pulse[2] /pʌls/ *verb* [I] to move with strong regular movements

pulverize (also -ise) /ˈpʌlvəraɪz/ *verb* [T] **1** (*formal*) to crush sth into a fine powder **2** (*especially BrE informal*) to defeat or destroy sb/sth completely: *We pulverized the opposition.* SYN for both meanings **crush**

pump[1] /pʌmp/ *noun* [C] **1** a machine that is used for forcing a gas or liquid in a particular direction: *Have you got a bicycle pump?* ♦ *a petrol pump* ➲ picture at **bicycle** **2** [usually pl] a flat woman's shoe with no fastening: *ballet pumps*

pump[2] /pʌmp/ *verb* **1** [T] to force a gas or liquid to go in a particular direction: *Your heart pumps blood around your body.* **2** [I] (used about a liquid) to flow in a particular direction as if forced by a **pump**: *Blood was pumping out of the wound.* **3** [I, T] to be moved or to move sth very quickly up and down or in and out: *He pumped his arms up and down to keep warm.*
PHR V **pump sth into sth/sb** to put a lot of sth into sth/sb: *He pumped all his savings into the business.*
pump sth up to fill sth with air, for example by using a **pump**: *to pump up a car tyre*

pumpkin /ˈpʌmpkɪn/ *noun* [C,U] a very large round vegetable with thick orange skin that is cooked and eaten ➲ picture on **page P15**

pun /pʌn/ *noun* [C] an amusing use of a word that can have two meanings or of different words that sound the same: *We're banking on them lending us the money—no pun intended!*

punch[1] /pʌntʃ/ *verb* [T] **1 punch sb (in/on sth)** to hit sb/sth hard with your **fist** (= closed hand): *He punched Mike hard in the stomach and ran away.* ♦ *to punch somebody on the nose* ♦ *She punched the air when she heard the good news.* ➲ note at **hit** **2** to make a hole in sth with a **punch[2]**(2): *He punched a hole in the ticket.*

punch

punch[2] /pʌntʃ/ *noun* **1** [C] a hard hit with your **fist** (= closed hand): *She gave him a hard punch on the arm.* **2** [C] a machine or tool that you use for making holes in sth: *a ticket punch* ♦ *a hole punch* ➲ picture at **stationery** **3** [U] a drink made from wine, fruit juice and sugar
IDM **pull (your) punches** ➲ **pull[1]**

punchline /ˈpʌntʃlaɪn/ *noun* [C] the last and most important words of a joke or story

ˈ**punch-up** *noun* [C] (*BrE informal*) a fight in which people hit each other

punctual /ˈpʌŋktʃuəl/ *adj* doing sth or happening at the right time; not late: *It is important to be punctual for your classes.*

P

HELP In spoken English we say that the train, bus, etc. was **on time**, not punctual.

▶ **punctuality** /ˌpʌŋktʃuˈæləti/ *noun* [U]: *Japanese trains are famous for their punctuality.* ▶ **punctually** /ˈpʌŋktʃuəli/ *adv*

punctuate /ˈpʌŋktʃueɪt/ *verb* **1** [T] **punctuate sth (with sth)** to interrupt sth many times: *Her speech was punctuated with bursts of applause.* **2** [I, T] to divide writing into sentences and phrases by adding full stops, question marks, etc.

punctuation /ˌpʌŋktʃuˈeɪʃn/ *noun* [U] the marks used for dividing writing into sentences and phrases: ***Punctuation marks*** *include full stops, commas and question marks.*

puncture /ˈpʌŋktʃə(r)/ *noun* [C] a small hole made by a sharp point, especially in a bicycle or car tyre ▶ **puncture** *verb* [I,T]

pungent /ˈpʌndʒənt/ *adj* (used about a smell) very strong

punish /ˈpʌnɪʃ/ *verb* [T] **punish sb (for sth/for doing sth)** to make sb suffer because they have done sth bad or wrong: *The children were severely punished for telling lies.*

punishable /ˈpʌnɪʃəbl/ *adj* **punishable (by sth)** (used about a crime, etc.) that you can be punished for doing: *a punishable offence* ◆ *In some countries drug smuggling is punishable by death.* ◆ *In some countries murder is punishable by death.*

punishing /ˈpʌnɪʃɪŋ/ *adj* that makes you very tired or weak: *The Prime Minister had a punishing schedule, visiting five countries in five days.*

P

punishment /ˈpʌnɪʃmənt/ *noun* [C,U] the action or way of punishing sb: *He was excluded from school for a week as a punishment.* ◆ ***capital punishment*** (= punishment by death)

punitive /ˈpjuːnətɪv/ *adj* (*formal*) **1** intended as a punishment: *to take punitive measures against somebody* **2** (used about taxes, etc.) very severe and that people find very difficult to pay: *punitive taxation*

punk /pʌŋk/ *noun* **1** [U] a type of loud music that was popular in Britain in the late 1970s and early 1980s. **Punk** musicians deliberately tried to offend people with traditional opinions. **2** [C] a person who likes **punk** music and often has brightly coloured hair and unusual clothes

punt /pʌnt/ *noun* [C] a long boat with a flat bottom and square ends which you move by pushing the end of a long pole against the bottom of the river ▶ **punt** *verb* [I]: *We spent the day punting on the river.* ◆ *to go punting*

puny /ˈpjuːni/ *adj* (**punier**; **puniest**) very small and weak

pup /pʌp/ *noun* [C] **1** = **puppy** **2** the young of some animals: *a seal pup*

pupil /ˈpjuːpl/ *noun* [C] **1** (*especially BrE*) a child in school: *There are 28 pupils in my class.* ➲ note at **school**

HELP **Pupil** is starting to become old-fashioned, so now we often use **student**, especially when talking about older children.

2 a person who is taught art, music, etc. by an expert: *He was a pupil of Liszt.* **3** the round black hole in the middle of your eye

puppet /ˈpʌpɪt/ *noun* [C] **1** a model of a person or an animal that you can move by pulling the strings which are tied to it or by putting your hand inside it and moving your fingers **2** a person or an organization that is controlled by sb else: *The occupying forces set up a puppet government.*

puppy /ˈpʌpi/ (also **pup**) *noun* [C] (*pl* **puppies**) a young dog ➲ note at **dog**

purchase /ˈpɜːtʃəs/ *noun* (*formal*) **1** [U] the act of buying sth: *to take out a loan for the purchase of a car* **2** [C] something that you buy: *These shoes were a poor purchase—they're falling apart already.* ◆ *to make a purchase* ▶ **purchase** *verb* [T]: *Many employees have the opportunity to purchase shares in the company they work for.*

purchaser /ˈpɜːtʃəsə(r)/ *noun* [C] (*formal*) a person who buys sth: *The purchaser of the house agrees to pay a deposit of 10%.* ➲ look at **vendor**

pure /pjʊə(r)/ *adj* (**purer**; **purest**)
➤NOT MIXED **1** not mixed with anything else: *pure orange juice* ◆ *pure silk*
➤CLEAN **2** clean and not containing any harmful substances: *pure air/water* **OPP** **impure**
➤COMPLETE **3** [only *before* a noun] complete and total: *We met by pure chance.*
➤MORALLY GOOD **4** not doing or knowing anything evil or anything that is connected with sex: *a young girl still pure in mind and body* **OPP** **impure**
➤SOUND/COLOUR/LIGHT **5** very clear; perfect: *She was dressed in pure white.*
➤SUBJECT **6** [only *before* a noun] (used about an area of learning) concerned only with increasing knowledge rather than having practical uses: *pure mathematics* **OPP** **applied**

purée /ˈpjʊəreɪ/ *noun* [C,U] a food that you make by cooking a fruit or vegetable and then pressing and mixing it until it is smooth and liquid: *apple/tomato purée* ▶ **purée** *verb* [T]

purely /ˈpjʊəli/ *adv* only or completely: *It's not purely a question of money.*

purge /pɜːdʒ/ *verb* [T] **purge sth (of sb)**; **purge sb (from sth)** to remove people that you do not want from a political party or other organization ▶ **purge** *noun* [C]: *The General carried out a purge of his political enemies.*

purify /ˈpjʊərɪfaɪ/ *verb* [T] (**purifying**; **purifies**; *pt, pp* **purified**) to remove dirty or harmful substances from sth: *purified water*

puritan /ˈpjʊərɪtən/ *noun* [C] a person who thinks that it is wrong to enjoy yourself ▶ **puritan** (also **puritanical** /ˌpjʊərɪˈtænɪkl/) *adj*: *a puritan attitude to life*

purity /ˈpjʊərəti/ *noun* [U] the state of being pure: *the purity of the water* ➲ look at **impurity**

purple /ˈpɜːpl/ *adj, noun* [U] (having) the colour of blue and red mixed together: *His face was purple with rage.*

purpose /ˈpɜːpəs/ *noun* **1** [C] the aim or intention of sth: *The main purpose of this meeting is to decide what we should do next.* ◆ *You may only use the telephone for business purposes.* **2 purposes** [pl] what is needed in a particular situation: ***For the purposes of** this demonstration, I will use model cars.* **3** [U] a meaning or reason that is important to you: *A good leader inspires people with a **sense of purpose**.* **4** [U] the ability to plan sth and work hard to achieve it: *I was impressed by his **strength of purpose**.* ➲ look at **cross purposes**

IDM on purpose not by accident; with a particular intention: *'You've torn a page out of my book!' 'I'm sorry, I didn't do it on purpose.'* **SYN deliberately**

to/for all intents and purposes ➲ **intent**²

purposeful /ˈpɜːpəsfl/ *adj* having a definite aim or plan: *Greg strode off down the street looking purposeful.* ▶ **purposefully** /-fəli/ *adv*

purposely /ˈpɜːpəsli/ *adv* with a particular intention: *I purposely waited till everyone had gone so that I could speak to you in private.* **SYN deliberately**

purr /pɜː(r)/ *verb* [I] (used about a cat) to make a continuous low sound that shows pleasure ➲ look at **miaow**

purse¹ /pɜːs/ *noun* [C] **1** a small bag made of leather, etc., for carrying coins and often also paper money, used especially by women ➲ look at **wallet** **2** (*AmE*) = **handbag** ➲ picture at **bag**

purse² /pɜːs/ *verb*

IDM purse your lips to press your lips together to show that you do not like sth: *He frowned and pursed his lips.*

pursue /pəˈsjuː/ *verb* [T] (*formal*) **1** to try to achieve sth or to continue to do sth over a period of time: *to pursue a career in banking* ◆ *She didn't seem to want to pursue the discussion so I changed the subject.* **2** to follow sb/sth in order to catch them or it: *The robber ran off pursued by two policemen.* ➲ A less formal word is **chase**.

pursuer /pəˈsjuːə(r)/ *noun* [C] a person who is following and trying to catch sb/sth

pursuit /pəˈsjuːt/ *noun* **1** [U] the act of trying to achieve or get sth: *the pursuit of pleasure* **2** [C] an activity that you do either for work or for pleasure: *outdoor/leisure pursuits* **3** the act of following or chasing sb

IDM in hot pursuit ➲ **hot**¹

in pursuit (of sb/sth) trying to catch or get sb/sth: *He neglected his family in pursuit of his own personal ambitions.*

pus /pʌs/ *noun* [U] a thick yellowish liquid that may form in a part of your body that has been hurt

push¹ /pʊʃ/ *verb*

▸MOVE STH **1** [I,T] to use force to move sb/sth forward or away from you: *She pushed him into the water.* ◆ *to push a pram* ◆ *She pushed the door shut with her foot.* ➲ picture at **pull** **2** [I,T] to move forward by pushing sb/sth: *John pushed his way through the crowd.* ◆ *to push past somebody* ◆ *People were **pushing and shoving** to try to get to the front.*

▸SWITCH/BUTTON **3** [I,T] to press a switch, button, etc., for example in order to start a machine: *Push the red button if you want the bus to stop.*

▸PERSUADE/FORCE **4** [T] **push sb (to do sth /into doing sth); push sb (for sth)** to try to make sb do sth that they do not want to do: *My friend pushed me into entering the competition.* ◆ *Ella will not work hard unless you push her.*

▸NEW PRODUCT **5** [T] (*informal*) to try to make sth seem attractive, for example so that people will buy it: *They are launching a major publicity campaign to push their new product.*

IDM be hard pressed/pushed/put to do sth ➲ **hard**²

be pushed for sth (*BrE informal*) to not have enough of sth: *Hurry up. We're really **pushed for** time.*

push your luck; push it/things (*informal*) to take a risk because you have successfully avoided problems in the past: *You didn't get caught last time, but don't push your luck!*

PHR V push sb about/around to give orders to sb in a rude and unpleasant way: *Don't let your boss push you around.*

push ahead/forward (with sth) to continue with sth

push for sth to try hard to get sth: *Jim is pushing for a pay rise.*

push in to join a line of people waiting for sth by standing in front of others who were there before you

push on to continue a journey: *Although it was getting dark, we decided to push on.*

push sb/sth over to make sb/sth fall down by pushing them or it

push² /pʊʃ/ *noun* [C] an act of pushing: *Can you help me **give** the car **a push** to get it started?* ◆ *The car windows opened at the push of a button.*

IDM at a push (*BrE informal*) if it is really necessary (but only with difficulty): *We can get ten people round the table at a push.*

give sb the push (*BrE informal*) to tell sb you no longer want them in a relationship, or in a job

ˈpush-button *adj* [only *before* a noun] (used about a machine, etc.) that you work by pressing a button: *a radio with push-button controls*

pushchair /ˈpʊʃtʃeə(r)/ (*BrE also* **buggy**; *AmE* **stroller**) *noun* [C] a chair on wheels that you use for pushing a young child in ➲ picture at **pram**

pusher /ˈpʊʃə(r)/ *noun* [C] (*informal*) a person who sells illegal drugs

pushover /ˈpʊʃəʊvə(r)/ *noun* [C] (*informal*) **1** something that is easy to do or win **2** a person who is easy to persuade to do sth

push-up (*AmE*) = **press-up**

pushy /ˈpʊʃi/ *adj* (**pushier**; **pushiest**) (*informal*) (used about a person) trying hard to get what you want, in a way that seems rude: *You need to be pushy to be successful in show business.*

P

put /pʊt/ *verb* [T] (**putting**; *pt, pp* **put**)
➤IN PLACE/POSITION **1** to move sb/sth into a particular place or position: *She put the book on the table.* ◆ *Did you put sugar in my tea?* ◆ *When do you put the children to bed?*
➤FIX **2** to fix sth to or in sth else: *Can you put (= sew) a button on this shirt?* ◆ *We're going to put a picture on this wall.*
➤WRITE **3** to write sth: *12.30 on Friday? I'll put it in my diary.* ◆ *What did you put for question 2?*
➤INTO STATE/CONDITION **4 put sb/sth in/into sth** to bring sb/sth into the state or condition mentioned: *This sort of weather always puts me in a bad mood.* ◆ *I was* **put in charge** *of the project.* ◆ *It was time to* **put** *our ideas* **into practice**.
➤AFFECT SB/STH **5** to make sb/sth feel sth or be affected by sth: *This will* **put pressure on** *them to finish the job quickly.* ◆ *Don't* **put the blame on** *me!* ◆ *The new teacher soon* **put a stop to** *cheating in tests.*
➤GIVE VALUE **6** to give or fix a particular value or importance to sb/sth: *We'll have to* **put a limit on** *how much we spend.* ◆ *I'd put him in my top five favourite writers.*
➤EXPRESS **7** to say or express sth: *I don't know exactly how to put this, but ...* ◆ ***To put it another way****, you're sacked.* ◆ ***Put simply****, he just wasn't good enough.*
IDM put it to sb that ... (*formal*) to suggest to sb that sth is true: *I put it to you that this man is innocent.* ⓘ For other idioms containing **put**, look at the entries for the nouns, adjectives, etc. For example, **put an end to sth** is at **end**.
PHR V put sth/yourself across/over to say what you want to say clearly, so that people can understand it: *He didn't put his ideas across very well at the meeting.*
put sth aside 1 to save sth, especially money, to use later **2** to ignore or forget sth: *We agreed to put aside our differences and work together.*
put sb away (*informal*) to send sb to prison
put sth away 1 to put sth where you usually keep it because you have finished using it: *Put the tools away if you've finished with them.* **2** to save money to spend later: *She puts part of her wages away in the bank every week.*
put sth back 1 to return sth to its place: *to put books back on the shelf* **2** to move sth to a later time: *The meeting's been put back until next week.* **OPP bring sth forward 3** to change the time shown on a clock to an earlier time: *We have to put the clocks back tonight.* **OPP put sth forward**
put sb/sth before/above sb/sth to treat sb/sth as more important than sb/sth else: *He puts his children before anything else.*
put sth by to save money to use later: *Her grandparents had put some money by for her wedding.*
put sb down (*informal*) **1** to say things to make sb seem stupid or silly: *He's always putting his wife down.* **2** to put a baby to bed
put sth down 1 to stop holding sth and put it on the floor, a table, etc: *She put her book down to answer the phone.* **2** to write sth: *I'll put that down in my diary.* **3** to pay part of the cost of sth: *We put down a 10% deposit on a car.* **4** (used about a government, an army or the police) to stop sth by force: *to put down a rebellion* **5** to kill an animal because it is old, sick or dangerous: *The dog was very sick and had to be put down.*
put sth down to sth to believe that sth is caused by sth: *I put his bad exam results down to laziness rather than a lack of ability.*
put yourself/sb forward to suggest that you or another person should be considered for a job, etc: *His name was put forward for the position of chairman.*
put sth forward 1 to change the time shown on a clock to a later time: *We put the clocks forward in spring.* **OPP put sth back 2** to move sth to an earlier time or date **3** to suggest sth: *She put forward a plan to help the homeless.*
put sth in 1 to fix equipment or furniture in position so that it can be used: *We're having a shower put in.* **SYN install 2** to include a piece of information, etc. in sth that you write: *In your letter, you forgot to put in the time your plane would arrive.* **3** to ask for sth officially: *to put in an invoice/request*
put sth in; put sth into sth/into doing sth to spend time, etc. on sth: *She puts all her time and energy into her business.*
put sb off (sb/sth/doing sth) 1 to say to a person that you can no longer do what you had agreed: *They were coming to stay last weekend but I had to put them off at the last moment.* **2** to make sb not like sb/sth or not want to do sth: *The accident put me off driving for a long time.* **3** to make sb unable to give their attention to sth: *Don't stare at me—you're putting me off!*
put sth off to turn or switch a light off: *She put off the light and went to sleep.*
put sth off; put off doing sth to move sth to a later time: *She put off writing her essay until the last minute.* **SYN delay**
put sth on 1 to dress yourself in sth: *Put on your coat!* ◆ *I'll have to put my glasses on.* **OPP take sth off 2** to cover an area of your skin with sth: *You'd better put some sun cream on.* **3** to switch on a piece of electrical equipment: *It's too early to put the lights on yet.* **4** to make a tape, a CD, etc. begin to play: *Let's put some music on.* **5** to become heavier: *I put* **on weight** *very easily.* **OPP lose 6** to organize or prepare sth for people to see or use: *The school is putting on 'Macbeth'.* ◆ *They put on extra trains in the summer.* **7** to pretend to be feeling sth; to pretend to have sth: *He's not angry with you really: he's just putting it on.*
put sth on sth 1 to add an amount of money, etc. to the cost or value of sth: *The government want to put more tax on the price of a packet of cigarettes.* **2** to bet money on sth: *He put £10 on a horse.* **SYN bet**
put sb out 1 to give sb trouble or extra work: *He put his hosts out by arriving very late.* **SYN inconvenience 2** to make sb upset or angry: *I was quite put out by their selfish behaviour.*
put sth out 1 to take sth out of your house and leave it: *to put the rubbish out* **2** to make sth stop burning: *to put out a fire* **SYN extinguish 3** to switch off a piece of electrical equipment: *They put out the lights and locked the door.* **4** to give or tell the public sth, often on the TV or radio or in newspapers: *The police put out a warning about the escaped prisoner.*

P

put yourself out to do sth for sb, even though it brings you trouble or extra work: *'I'll give you a lift home.' 'I don't want you to put yourself out. I'll take a taxi.'*
put sth/yourself over = **put sth/yourself across/over**
put sb through sth to make sb experience sth unpleasant
put sb/sth through to make a telephone connection that allows sb to speak to sb: *Could you put me through to Jeanne, please?*
put sth to sb to suggest sth to sb; to ask sb sth: *I put the question to her.*
put sth together to build or repair sth by joining its parts together: *The furniture comes with instructions on how to put it together.*
put sth towards sth to give money to pay part of the cost of sth: *We all put a pound towards a leaving present for Joe.*
put sb up to give sb food and a place to stay: *She had missed the last train home, so I offered to put her up for the night.*
put sth up 1 to lift or hold sth up: *Put your hand up if you know the answer.* **2** to build sth: *to put up a fence/tent* **3** to fix sth to a wall, etc. so that everyone can see it: *to put up a notice* **4** to increase sth: *Some shops put up their prices just before Christmas.*
put up sth to try to stop sb attacking you: *The old lady put up a struggle against her attacker.*
put up with sb/sth to suffer sb/sth unpleasant and not complain about it: *I don't know how they put up with this noise.*

putrid /ˈpjuːtrɪd/ *adj* (used about dead animals or plants) smelling very bad: *the putrid smell of rotten meat* **SYN** **foul**

putt /pʌt/ *verb* [I,T] (in the sport of **golf**) to hit the ball gently when it is near the hole

putter /ˈpʌtə(r)/ (*AmE*) = **potter**[1]

putty /ˈpʌti/ *noun* [U] a soft substance that is used for fixing glass into windows that becomes hard when dry

puzzle[1] /ˈpʌzl/ *noun* [C] **1** a game or toy that makes you think a lot: *a book of* ***crossword puzzles*** ♦ *a* ***jigsaw puzzle*** ♦ *I like to* ***do puzzles.*** **2** [usually sing] something that is difficult to understand or explain: *The reasons for his actions have remained a puzzle to historians.* **SYN** **mystery**

puzzle[2] /ˈpʌzl/ *verb* [T] to make sb feel confused because they do not understand sth: *Her strange illness puzzled all the experts.*
PHR V **puzzle over sth** to think hard about sth in order to understand or explain it: *to puzzle over a mathematical problem*
puzzle sth out to find the answer to sth by thinking hard: *The letter was in Italian and it took us an hour to puzzle out what it said.*

puzzled /ˈpʌzld/ *adj* not able to understand or explain sth: *a puzzled expression*

PVC /ˌpiː viː ˈsiː/ *noun* [U] a strong plastic material used to make a wide variety of products, such as clothing, pipes, floor coverings, etc.

pyjamas (*AmE* **pajamas**) /pəˈdʒɑːməz/ *noun* [pl] loose trousers and a loose shirt that you wear in bed ➲ picture on **page P1**

HELP Notice that you use **pyjama** (without an 's') before another noun: *pyjama trousers*

pylon /ˈpaɪlən/ *noun* [C] a tall metal tower that supports heavy electrical wires

pyramid /ˈpɪrəmɪd/ *noun* [C] **1** a shape with a flat base and three or four sides in the shape of triangles ➲ picture at **cube** **2** a large building in the shape of a **pyramid**. The ancient Egyptians built stone **pyramids** as places to bury their kings and queens.

python /ˈpaɪθən/ *noun* [C] a large snake that kills animals by squeezing them very hard

Q, q /kjuː/ *noun* [C,U] (*pl* Qs; Q's; q's /kjuːz/) the 17th letter of the English alphabet: *'Queen' begins with (a) 'Q'.*

Q *abbr* = **question**[1](1): *Qs 1-5 are compulsory.*

QR code /ˌkjuː ˈɑː kəʊd/ *noun* [C] **quick response code**; a pattern of black and white squares that contains information, such as timetables, links to websites, etc. You can read this information using the camera on your **smartphone** (= a mobile phone with some computer functions).

QR code

qt *abbr* = **quart**

quack /kwæk/ *noun* [C] the sound made by a **duck** (= a bird that lives on or near water) ▸ **quack** *verb* [I] ➲ note at **duck**

quad bike /ˈkwɒd baɪk/ (*AmE* ˌ**four-ˈwheeler**) *noun* [C] a motorbike with four large wheels, used for riding over rough ground, often for fun

quadrangle /ˈkwɒdræŋgl/ (also **quad**) *noun* [C] a square open area with buildings round it in a school, college, etc.

quadruple /kwɒˈdruːpl/ *verb* [I,T] to multiply or be multiplied by four

quaint /kweɪnt/ *adj* attractive or unusual because it seems to belong to the past

quake /kweɪk/ *verb* [I] (used about a person, the earth or a building) to shake: *to quake with fear* ▸ **quake** *noun* [C] (*informal*) = **earthquake**

qualification /ˌkwɒlɪfɪˈkeɪʃn/ *noun* **1** [C] an exam that you have passed or a course of study that you have completed: *to* ***have a*** *teaching/nursing*

Q

qualification ♦ *She left school at 16 with no formal qualifications.* ➔ note at **degree** **2** [C] a skill or quality that you need to do a particular job: *Is there a height qualification for the police force?* **3** [C,U] something that limits the meaning of a general statement or makes it weaker: *I can recommend him for the job **without qualification**.* ♦ *She accepted the proposal with only a few qualifications.* **4** [U] the fact of doing what is necessary in order to be able to do a job, play in a competition, etc: *Italy achieved qualification for the championships with their win over Wales.*

qualified /ˈkwɒlɪfaɪd/ *adj* **1** qualified (for sth/to do sth) having passed an exam or having the knowledge, experience, etc. in order to be able to do sth: *Duncan is well qualified for this job.* ♦ *a fully qualified doctor* ♦ *I don't feel qualified to comment—I know nothing about the subject.* **2** not complete; limited: *My boss gave only qualified approval to the plan.* **OPP** for both meanings **unqualified**

qualify /ˈkwɒlɪfaɪ/ *verb* (qualifying; qualifies; *pt, pp* qualified) **1** [I] qualify (as sth) to pass the examination that is necessary to do a particular job: *It takes five years to qualify as a vet.* **2** to have the qualities that are necessary for sth: *A cup of coffee and a sandwich doesn't really qualify as a meal.* **3** [I, T] qualify (sb) (for sth/to do sth) to have or give sb the right to have or do sth: *How many years must you work to qualify for a pension?* ♦ *This exam will qualify me to teach music.* **4** [I] qualify (for sth) to win the right to enter a competition or continue to the next part: *Our team has qualified for the final.* **5** [T] to limit the meaning of a general statement or make it weaker: *I must qualify what I said earlier—it wasn't quite true.*

Q

qualitative /ˈkwɒlɪtətɪv/ *adj* connected with how good sth is, rather than with how much of it there is: *qualitative analysis/research* ➔ look at **quantitative**

quality /ˈkwɒləti/ *noun* (*pl* qualities) **1** [U, sing] how good or bad sth is: *This paper isn't very good quality.* ♦ *to be of good/poor/top quality* ♦ *goods of a high quality* ♦ *high-quality goods* ♦ *the **quality of life** in our cities* **2** [U] a high standard or level: *Aim for quality rather than quantity in your writing.* **3** [C] something that is typical of a person or thing: *Vicky has all the qualities of a good manager.*

qualm /kwɑːm/ *noun* [C, usually pl] a feeling of doubt or worry that what you are doing may not be morally right: *I don't **have** any **qualms about** asking them to lend us some money.*

quandary /ˈkwɒndəri/ *noun* [C, usually sing] a state of not being able to decide what to do; a difficult situation: *I'm **in a quandary**—should I ask her or not?*

quantify /ˈkwɒntɪfaɪ/ *verb* [T] (quantifying; quantifies; *pt, pp* quantified) to describe or express sth as an amount or a number: *The risks to health are impossible to quantify.*

quantitative /ˈkwɒntɪtətɪv/ *adj* connected with the amount or number of sth rather than with how good it is: *quantitative research* ➔ look at **qualitative**

quantity /ˈkwɒntəti/ *noun* [C,U] (*pl* quantities) **1** a number or an amount of sth: *Add a small quantity of salt.* ♦ *It's cheaper to buy goods **in large quantities**.* **2** a large number or amount of sth: *It's usually cheaper to buy goods **in quantity**.*
IDM **an unknown quantity** ➔ **unknown[1]**

quarantine /ˈkwɒrəntiːn/ *noun* [U] a period of time when a person or an animal that has or may have an infectious disease must be kept away from other people or animals

quark /kwɑːk/ *noun* [C] a very small part of matter (= a substance). There are several types of **quark** and it is thought that **protons** (= parts of an atom that carry a positive electric charge), **neutrons** (= parts of an atom that carry no electric charge), etc. are formed from them.

quarrel[1] /ˈkwɒrəl/ *noun* **1** [C] a quarrel (about/over sth) an angry argument or disagreement: *We sometimes **have a quarrel** about who should do the washing-up.* ➔ note at **argument** ➔ look at **fight** **2** [U] quarrel with sb/sth a reason for complaining about or disagreeing with sb/sth: *I have no quarrel with what has just been said.*

quarrel[2] /ˈkwɒrəl/ *verb* [I] (quarrelling; quarrelled, (*AmE*) quarreling; quarreled) **1** quarrel (with sb) (about/over sth) to have an angry argument or disagreement: *The children are always quarrelling!* ♦ *I don't want to quarrel with you about it.* ➔ look at **argue**, **fight** **2** quarrel with sth to disagree with sth

quarrelsome /ˈkwɒrəlsəm/ *adj* (used about a person) liking to argue with other people **SYN** **argumentative**

quarry[1] /ˈkwɒri/ *noun* (*pl* quarries) **1** [C] a place where large amounts of sand, stone, etc. are dug out of the ground ➔ look at **mine** **2** [sing] a person or an animal that is being hunted

quarry[2] /ˈkwɒri/ *verb* [I,T] (quarrying; quarries; *pt, pp* quarried) to dig, stone, sand, etc. out of the ground: *to quarry for marble*

quart /kwɔːt/ *noun* [C] (*abbr* qt) a measure of liquid; 1.14 litres. There are 2 pints in a **quart**.

HELP An American quart is 0.94 of a litre.

quarter /ˈkwɔːtə(r)/ *noun*
➤ 1 OF 4 PARTS **1** [C] one of four equal parts of sth: *The programme lasts for three quarters of an hour.* ♦ *a mile and a quarter* ♦ *to cut an apple into quarters*
➤ 15 MINUTES **2** [sing] 15 minutes before or after every hour: *I'll meet you at **(a) quarter past** six.* ♦ *It's **(a) quarter to** three.*

HELP In American English you say '(a) quarter **after**' and '(a) quarter **of**': *I'll meet you at (a) quarter after six.* ♦ *It's a quarter of three.*

➤ 3 MONTHS **3** [C] a period of three months: *You get a gas bill every quarter.*
➤ PART OF TOWN **4** [C] a part of a town, especially a

part where a particular group of people live: *the Chinese quarter of the city*

➤PERSON/GROUP **5** [C] a person or group of people who may give help or information or who have certain opinions: *Jim's parents haven't got much money so he can't expect any help from that quarter.*

➤25 CENTS **6** [C] (in the US or Canada) a coin that is worth 25 cents (¼ dollar)

➤PLACE TO LIVE **7 quarters** [pl] a place that is provided for people, especially soldiers, to live in

➤WEIGHT **8** [C] four **ounces** (= a measure of weight) of sth; ¼ of a pound: *a quarter of mushrooms*

IDM **at close quarters** ➲ **close**[3]

ˌquarter-ˈfinal *noun* [C] one of the four matches between the eight players or teams left in a competition ➲ look at **semi-final**

quarterly /ˈkwɔːtəli/ *adj, adv* (produced or happening) once every three months: *a quarterly magazine*

quartet /kwɔːˈtet/ *noun* [C] **1** four people who sing or play music together **2** a piece of music for four people to sing or play together

quartz /kwɔːts/ *noun* [U] a type of hard rock that is used in making very accurate clocks or watches

quash /kwɒʃ/ *verb* [T] (*formal*) **1** to say that an official decision is no longer true or legal **2** to stop or defeat sth by force: *to quash a rebellion*

quaver /ˈkweɪvə(r)/ *verb* [I] if sb's voice **quavers**, it shakes, usually because the person is nervous or afraid: *'I'm not safe here, am I?' she asked in a quavering voice.*

quay /kiː/ *noun* [C] a platform where goods and passengers are loaded on and off boats

quayside /ˈkiːsaɪd/ *noun* [sing] the area of land that is near a **quay**

queasy /ˈkwiːzi/ *adj* feeling sick; wanting to **vomit** (= bring up food from the stomach)

🔑 **queen** /kwiːn/ *noun* [C] **1** (also **Queen**) the female ruler of a country: *Queen Elizabeth II* (= the second) ➲ look at **king, prince, princess 2** (also **Queen**) the wife of a king **3** (in the game of **chess**) the most powerful piece, that can move any distance and in all directions **4** one of the four playing cards in a pack with a picture of a queen: *the queen of hearts* ➲ note at **card** ➲ picture at **card 5** the largest and most important female in a group of insects: *the queen bee*

queer /kwɪə(r)/ *adj* (**queerer**; **queerest**) (*old-fashioned*) strange or unusual: *She had a queer feeling that she was being watched.* SYN **odd**

quell /kwel/ *verb* [T] (*formal*) to end sth

quench /kwentʃ/ *verb* [T] **quench your thirst** to drink so that you no longer feel thirsty

query /ˈkwɪəri/ *noun* [C] (*pl* **queries**) a question, especially one asking for information or expressing a doubt about sth: *Does anyone have any queries?*
▶ **query** *verb* [T] (**querying**; **queries**; *pt, pp* **queried**): *We queried the bill but were told it was correct.*

quest /kwest/ *noun* [C] (*formal*) a long search for sth that is difficult to find: *the quest for happiness/knowledge/truth*

🔑 **question**[1] /ˈkwestʃən/ *noun* **1** [C] (*abbr* **Q**) a **question (about/on sth)** a sentence or phrase that asks for an answer: *Put up your hand if you want to* ***ask a question***. ◆ *In the examination, you must* ***answer*** *five* ***questions*** *in one hour.* ◆ *What's the answer to Question 5?* ◆ *There will be a Q and A* (= question and answer) *session at the end of the talk.* **2** [C] a problem or difficulty that needs to be discussed or dealt with: *The resignations* ***raise the question*** *of who will take over.* ◆ ***The question is,*** *how are we going to raise the money?* **3** [U] doubt or confusion about sth: *There is no question about her enthusiasm for the job.* ◆ *His honesty is* ***beyond question***. ◆ *The results of the report were accepted* ***without question***.

IDM **in question** that is being considered or talked about: *The lawyer asked where she was on the night in question.*

no question of no possibility of: *There is no question of him leaving hospital yet.*

out of the question impossible: *A new car is out of the question. It's just too expensive.*

(be) a question of sth/of doing sth a situation in which sth is needed: *It's not difficult—it's just a question of finding the time to do it.*

🔑 **question**[2] /ˈkwestʃən/ *verb* [T] **1 question sb (about/on sth)** to ask sb a question or questions: *The police questioned him for several hours.* **2** to express or feel doubt about sth: *She told me she was from the council so I didn't question her right to be there.* ◆ *to question somebody's sincerity/honesty*

questionable /ˈkwestʃənəbl/ *adj* **1** that you have doubts about; not certain: *It's questionable whether we'll finish in time.* **2** likely to be dishonest or morally wrong: *questionable motives* OPP for both meanings **unquestionable**

ˈquestion mark *noun* [C] the sign (?) that you use when you write a question

questionnaire /ˌkwestʃəˈneə(r)/ *noun* [C] a list of questions that are answered by many people. A **questionnaire** is used to collect information about a particular subject: *to complete/fill in a questionnaire*

ˈquestion tag (also **tag**) *noun* [C] a short phrase such as 'isn't it?' or 'did you?' at the end of a sentence that changes it into a question and is often used to ask sb to agree with you

queue /kjuː/ (*AmE* **line**) *noun* [C] a line of people, cars, etc. that are waiting for sth or to do sth: *We had to* ***wait in a queue*** *for hours to get tickets.* ◆ *to* ***join*** *the end of* ***a queue*** ◆ *We were told to* ***form a queue*** *outside the doors.*

IDM **jump the queue** ➲ **jump**[1]

▶ **queue** *verb* [I] **queue (up) (for sth)**: *to queue for a bus*

quiche /kiːʃ/ *noun* [C,U] a type of food made of **pastry** (= a mixture of flour, fat and water) filled with egg and milk with cheese, onion, etc. and cooked in the oven. You can eat **quiche** hot or cold. ➲ picture on **page P16**

🔑 **quick**[1] /kwɪk/ *adj* (**quicker**; **quickest**) **1** done with speed; taking or lasting a short time: *May I make a*

Q

quick telephone call? ♦ *This dish is quick and easy to make.* ♦ *His quick thinking saved her life.* ♦ *We need to make a quick decision.* **2** quick (to do sth) doing sth at speed or in a short time: *It's quicker to travel by train.* ♦ *She is a quick worker.* ♦ *She was quick to point out the mistakes I had made.*

HELP **Quick** or **fast**? **Fast** is more often used for describing a person or thing that moves or can move at great speed: *a fast horse/car/runner.* **Quick** is more often used for describing something that is done in a short time: *a quick decision/visit*

3 used to form adjectives: *quick-thinking* ♦ *quick-drying paint*
IDM **quick/slow on the uptake** ➲ **uptake**

quick[2] /kwɪk/ *adv* (*informal*) quickly: *Come over here quick!*
IDM **(as) quick as a flash** very quickly: *Quick as a flash, he grabbed my money and ran.*

quicken /ˈkwɪkən/ *verb* [I,T] (*formal*) to become quicker or make sth quicker: *She felt her heartbeat quicken as he approached.* ♦ *He quickened his pace to catch up with them.*

⚷ **quickly** /ˈkwɪkli/ *adv* fast; in a short time: *He quickly undressed and got into bed.* ♦ *I'd like you to get here as quickly as possible.*

quicksand /ˈkwɪksænd/ *noun* [U] deep wet sand that you sink into if you walk on it

quid /kwɪd/ *noun* [C] (*pl* quid) (*BrE informal*) a pound (in money); £1: *Can you lend me a couple of quid until tomorrow?*

⚷ **quiet**[1] /ˈkwaɪət/ *adj* (quieter; quietest) **1** with very little or no noise: *Be quiet!* ♦ *His voice was quiet but firm.* ♦ *Go into the library if you want to work. It's much quieter in there.* **OPP** **loud** **2** without much activity or many people: *The streets are very quiet on Sundays.* ♦ *Business is quiet at this time of year.* ♦ *a quiet country village* ♦ *We lead a quiet life.* **3** (used about a person) not talking very much: *You're very quiet today. Is anything wrong?* ♦ *He's very quiet and shy.*
IDM **keep quiet about sth; keep sth quiet** to say nothing about sth: *Would you keep quiet about me leaving until I've told the boss?*
▶ **quietly** *adv*: *Try and shut the door quietly!*
▶ **quietness** *noun* [U]

quiet[2] /ˈkwaɪət/ *noun* [U] the state of being calm and without much noise or activity: *the **peace and quiet** of the countryside*
IDM **on the quiet** secretly: *She's given up chocolate but she still has an occasional piece on the quiet.*

quieten /ˈkwaɪətn/ *verb* [T] to make sb/sth quiet
PHR V **quieten (sb/sth) down** to become quiet or to make sb/sth quiet: *When you've quietened down, I'll tell you what happened.*

quilt /kwɪlt/ *noun* [C] a cover for a bed that has a thick warm material, for example feathers, inside it ➲ look at **duvet**

quintet /kwɪnˈtet/ *noun* [C] **1** a group of five people who sing or play music together **2** a piece of music for five people to sing or play together

quirk /kwɜːk/ *noun* [C] **1** an aspect of sb's character or behaviour that is strange: *You'll soon get used to the boss's little quirks.* **2** a strange thing that happens by chance: *By **a** strange **quirk of fate** they met again several years later.* ▶ **quirky** *adj*: *Some people don't like his quirky sense of humour.*

⚷ **quit** /kwɪt/ *verb* (qui**tt**ing; *pt, pp* quit) **1** [I,T] quit (as sth) to leave a job, etc. or to go away from a place: *She quit as manager of the volleyball team.* **2** [T] (*especially AmE informal*) to stop doing sth: *to quit smoking* **3** [I,T] to close a computer program

⚷ **quite** /kwaɪt/ *adv* **1** not very; to a certain degree; rather: *The film's quite good.* ♦ *It's quite a good film.* ♦ *I quite enjoy cooking.* ♦ *They had to wait quite a long time.* ♦ *It's quite cold today.* ♦ *We still meet up quite often.* ➲ note at **rather** **2** (used for emphasizing sth) completely; very: *Are you quite sure you don't mind?* ♦ *I quite agree—you're quite right.* ♦ *To my surprise, the room was quite empty.* **SYN** **absolutely** **3** (*BrE*) used for showing that you agree with or understand sth: *'We didn't win, but at least we tried.' 'Yes, quite.'*
IDM **not quite** used for showing that there is almost enough of sth, or that it is almost suitable: *There's not quite enough bread for breakfast.* ♦ *These shoes don't quite fit.*
quite a used for showing that sth is unusual: *That's quite a problem.*
quite enough used for emphasizing that no more of sth is wanted or needed: *I've had quite enough of listening to you two arguing!* ♦ *That's quite enough wine, thanks.*
quite a few; quite a lot (of) a fairly large amount or number: *We've received quite a few enquiries.*

quits /kwɪts/ *adj*
IDM **be quits (with sb)** (*informal*) if two people are **quits**, it means that neither of them owes the other anything: *You buy me a drink and then we're quits.*

quiver /ˈkwɪvə(r)/ *verb* [I] to shake slightly: *to quiver with rage/excitement/fear* **SYN** **tremble**

quiz[1] /kwɪz/ *noun* [C] (*pl* quizzes) a game or competition in which you have to answer questions: *a general knowledge quiz* ♦ *a television quiz show*

quiz[2] /kwɪz/ *verb* [T] (qui**zz**ing; qui**zz**es; *pt, pp* qui**zz**ed) to ask sb a lot of questions in order to get information

quizzical /ˈkwɪzɪkl/ *adj* (used about a look, smile, etc.) seeming to ask a question ▶ **quizzically** /-kli/ *adv*

quorum /ˈkwɔːrəm/ *noun* [sing] the smallest number of people that must be at a meeting before it can make official decisions

quota /ˈkwəʊtə/ *noun* [C] the number or amount of sth that is allowed or that you must do: *We have a fixed quota of work to get through each day.*

quotation /kwəʊˈteɪʃn/ (also quote) *noun* [C] **1** a phrase from a book, speech, play, etc., that sb repeats because it is interesting or useful: *a* *quotation from Shakespeare* **2** a statement that says how much a piece of work will probably cost: *You should get quotations from three different builders.* ➲ look at **estimate**

quo'tation marks (also *informal* quotes; *BrE also* inverted commas) *noun* [pl] the signs ('...') or ("...") that you put around a word, a sentence, etc. to show that it is what sb said or wrote, that it is a title or that you are using it in a special way

⚷ **quote** /kwəʊt/ *verb* **1** [I,T] quote (sth) (from sb/sth) to repeat exactly sth that sb else has said or written before: *The minister asked the newspaper not to quote him.* **2** [T] to give sth as an example to support what you are saying: *She quoted several reasons why she was unhappy about the decision.* **3** [T] to say what the cost of a piece of work, etc. will probably be: *How much did they quote you for repairing the roof?*

quotes /kwəʊts/ (*informal*) = **quotation marks**

the Qur'an = the Koran

R, r /ɑː(r)/ *noun* [C,U] (*pl* Rs; R's; r's /ɑː(r)z/) the 18th letter of the English alphabet: *'Rabbit' begins with an 'R'.*

R. *abbr* = **river**: *R. Thames*

R & B /ˌɑːr ən ˈbiː/ *noun* [U] **rhythm and blues**; a type of music that is a mixture of **blues** (= slow sad music) and **jazz** (= music with a strong rhythm)

rabbi /ˈræbaɪ/ *noun* [C] (*pl* rabbis) a Jewish religious leader and teacher of Jewish law

rabbit

hare

rabbit /ˈræbɪt/ *noun* [C] a small animal with long ears: *a wild rabbit* ♦ *a rabbit hutch* (= a cage for rabbits) ➲ note at **pet**

MORE The children's word for a rabbit is **bunny**.

'rabbit warren (also warren) *noun* [C] **1** a system of holes and underground tunnels where wild **rabbits** live **2** a building or part of a city with many narrow passages or streets: *The council offices were a real rabbit warren.*

rabble /ˈræbl/ *noun* [C] a noisy crowd of people who are or may become violent

rabies /ˈreɪbiːz/ *noun* [U] a very dangerous disease that a person can get if they are bitten by an animal that has the disease

⚷ **race¹** /reɪs/ *noun* **1** [C] a race (against/with sb/sth); a race for sth/to do sth a competition between people, animals, cars, etc. to see which is the fastest or to see which can achieve sth first: *to run/win/lose a race* ♦ *to come first/second/last* ***in a race*** ♦ *Rescuing victims of the earthquake is now* ***a race against time.*** ♦ *the race for the presidency* ♦ *the race to find a cure for AIDS* **2 the races** [pl] (*BrE*) an occasion when a number of horse races are held in one place: *We're going to the races for the day.* **3** [C,U] one of the groups into which people can be divided according to the colour of their skin, their hair type, the shape of their face, etc: *a child of mixed race* ➲ look at **human race** **4** [C] a group of people who have the same language, customs, history, etc: *the Spanish race*

IDM the rat race ➲ **rat**

⚷ **race²** /reɪs/ *verb* **1** [I,T] race (against/with) (sb/sth) to have a competition with sb/sth to find out who is the fastest or to see who can do sth first: *I'll race you home.* **2** [T] to make an animal or a vehicle take part in a race: *He races pigeons as a hobby.* **3** [I,T] to go very fast or to move sb/sth very fast: *We raced up the stairs.* ♦ *The child had to be raced to hospital.*

racecourse /ˈreɪskɔːs/ (*AmE* racetrack) *noun* [C] a place where horse races take place

racehorse /ˈreɪshɔːs/ *noun* [C] a horse that is trained to run in races

ˌrace reˈlations *noun* [pl] the relations between people of different races who live in the same town, area, etc.

racetrack /ˈreɪstræk/ = **racecourse**

racial /ˈreɪʃl/ *adj* connected with people's race; happening between people of different races: *racial tension/discrimination* ▶ **racially** /-ʃəli/ *adv*: *a racially mixed school*

⚷ **racing** /ˈreɪsɪŋ/ *noun* [U] **1** = **horse racing** **2** the sport of taking part in races: *motor racing* ♦ *a racing driver/car*

racism /ˈreɪsɪzəm/ *noun* [U] the belief that some races of people are better than others; unfair ways of treating people that show this belief: *to take measures to combat racism* ▶ **racist** /-ɪst/ *noun* [C], *adj*: *He's a racist.* ♦ *racist beliefs/views/remarks*

rack¹ /ræk/ *noun* [C] [in compounds] a piece of equipment, usually made of bars, that you can put things in or on: *I got on the train and put my bags up in the luggage rack.* ♦ *We need a roof rack on the car for all this equipment.* ➲ picture on **page 594**

IDM go to rack and ruin to be in or get into a bad state because of a lack of care

rack² /ræk/ *verb*

IDM rack your brains to try hard to think of sth or remember sth

R

racks

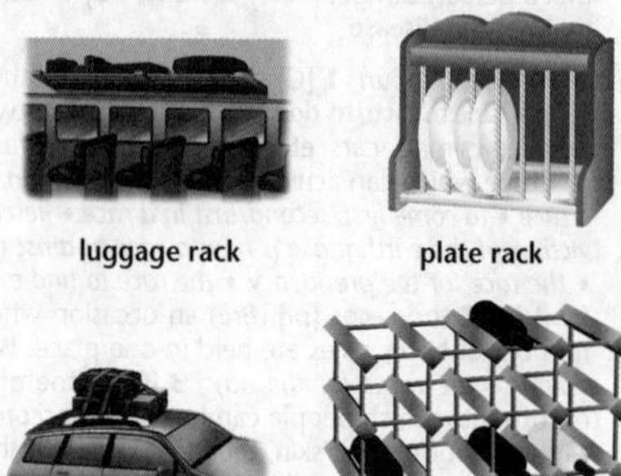

racket /ˈrækɪt/ *noun* **1** [sing] (*informal*) a loud noise: *Stop making that terrible racket!* **2** [C] an illegal way of making money: *a drugs racket* **3** (also racquet) [C] a piece of sports equipment that you use to hit the ball in sports such as **tennis** and **badminton** ➲ picture at **badminton** ➲ picture on **page P4**

MORE Rackets have **strings**, but **bats** do not.

racy /ˈreɪsi/ *adj* (racier; raciest) (used especially about writing) having a style that is exciting and amusing, sometimes in a way that is connected with sex: *a racy novel*

radar /ˈreɪdɑː(r)/ *noun* [U] a system that uses radio waves for finding the position of moving objects, for example ships and planes: *This plane is hard to detect by radar.*

R

radiant /ˈreɪdiənt/ *adj* **1** showing great happiness: *a radiant smile* **2** sending out light or heat: *the radiant heat/energy of the sun*

radiate /ˈreɪdieɪt/ *verb* **1** [T] (used about people) to clearly show a particular quality or emotion in your appearance or behaviour: *She radiated self-confidence in the interview.* **2** [T] to send out light or heat **3** [I] to go out in all directions from a central point: *Narrow streets radiate from the village square.*

radiation /ˌreɪdiˈeɪʃn/ *noun* [U] **1** powerful and very dangerous rays that are sent out from certain substances. You cannot see or feel **radiation** but it can cause serious illness or death. ➲ look at **radioactive** **2** heat, light or energy that is sent out from sth: *ultraviolet radiation*

radiator /ˈreɪdieɪtə(r)/ *noun* [C] **1** a piece of equipment that is usually fixed to the wall and is used for heating a room. **Radiators** are made of metal and filled with hot water. ➲ picture on **page P8** **2** a piece of equipment that is used for keeping a vehicle cool

radical¹ /ˈrædɪkl/ *adj* **1** (used about changes in sth) very great; complete: *The tax system needs radical reform.* ◆ *radical change* **2** wanting great social or political change: *to have radical views* ➲ look at **moderate, extreme** ▶ **radically** /-kli/ *adv*: *The First World War radically altered the political map of Europe.*

radical² /ˈrædɪkl/ *noun* [C] a person who wants great social or political change ➲ look at **moderate, extremist**

radii *plural of* **radius**

radio /ˈreɪdiəʊ/ *noun* (*pl* radios) **1** *often* **the radio** [U, sing] the activity of sending out programmes for people to listen to; the programmes that are sent out: *I always* **listen to the radio** *in the car.* ◆ *I heard an interesting report* **on the radio** *this morning.* ◆ *a radio station/programme* ◆ *national/local radio* ➲ look at **media** **2** [C] a piece of equipment that is used for receiving and/or sending radio messages or programmes (on a ship, plane, etc. or in your house): *a car radio*

MORE You **put, switch** or **turn** a radio **on** or **off**. You may also **turn it up** or **down** to make it louder or quieter. To choose a particular **station**, you **tune in to** it.

3 [U] the sending or receiving of messages through the air by electrical signals: *to keep in radio contact* ◆ *radio signals/waves* ▶ **radio** *verb* [I,T] (*pt, pp* radioed)

radioactive /ˌreɪdiəʊˈæktɪv/ *adj* sending out powerful and very dangerous energy that is produced when atoms are broken up. This energy cannot be seen or felt but can cause serious illness or death: *the problem of the disposal of* **radioactive waste** *from power stations* ➲ look at **radiation** ▶ **radioactivity** /ˌreɪdiəʊækˈtɪvəti/ *noun* [U]

radiographer /ˌreɪdiˈɒɡrəfə(r)/ *noun* [C] a person in a hospital who is trained to take **X-rays** (= pictures of your bones, etc.) or to use **X-rays** for the treatment of certain illnesses

radish /ˈrædɪʃ/ *noun* [C] a small red vegetable that is white inside with a strong taste. You eat **radishes** in salads. ➲ picture on **page P15**

radium /ˈreɪdiəm/ *noun* [U] (*symbol* Ra) a chemical element that is used in the treatment of diseases such as cancer

radius /ˈreɪdiəs/ *noun* [C] (*pl* radii) /-diaɪ/ **1** the distance from the centre of a circle to the outside edge ➲ look at **diameter, circumference** ➲ picture at **circle** **2** a round area that is measured from a point in its centre: *The wreckage of the plane was scattered over a radius of several miles.*

raffle /ˈræfl/ *noun* [C] a way of making money for a charity or a project by selling tickets with numbers on them. Later some numbers are chosen and the tickets with these numbers on them win prizes.

raft /rɑːft/ *noun* [C] **1** a flat structure made of pieces of wood tied together and used as a boat or a floating platform **2** a small boat made of rubber or plastic that is filled with air ➲ look at **white-water rafting**

rafter /ˈrɑːftə(r)/ *noun* [C] one of the long pieces of wood that support a roof

rag /ræg/ *noun* **1** [C,U] a small piece of old cloth that you use for cleaning **2 rags** [pl] clothes that are very old and torn

rage¹ /reɪdʒ/ *noun* [C,U] a feeling of violent anger that is difficult to control: *to fly into a rage* ◆ *He was trembling with rage.*

rage² /reɪdʒ/ *verb* [I] **1 rage (at/against/about sb/sth)** to show great anger about sth, especially by shouting: *He raged against the injustice of it all.* **2** (used about a battle, disease, storm, etc.) to continue with great force: *The battle raged for several days.* ▶ **raging** *adj* [only *before* a noun]: *a raging headache*

ragged /ˈrægɪd/ *adj* **1** (used about clothes) old and torn **2** not straight; untidy: *a ragged edge/coastline*

raid /reɪd/ *noun* [C] **a raid (on sth) 1** a short surprise attack on an enemy by soldiers, ships or aircraft: *an air raid* **2** a surprise visit by the police looking for criminals or illegal goods **3** a surprise attack on a building in order to steal sth: *a bank raid* ▶ **raid** *verb* [T]: *Police raided the club at dawn this morning.*

🔑 **rail** /reɪl/ *noun* **1** [C] a bar fixed to a wall, which you can hang things on: *a towel/curtain/picture rail* ➲ picture at **curtain** ➲ picture on **page P8** **2** [C] a wooden or metal bar placed round sth to stop you falling: *She leaned on the ship's rail and gazed out to sea.* **3** [C, usually pl] each of the two metal bars that form the track that trains run on **4** [U] the railway system; trains as a means of transport: *rail travel/services/fares*

railcard /ˈreɪlkɑːd/ *noun* [C] (*BrE*) a special card that allows you to buy train tickets at a lower price if you are an old person, a young person, student, etc.

railing /ˈreɪlɪŋ/ *noun* [C, usually pl] a fence (around a park, garden, etc.) that is made of metal bars ➲ picture on **page P11**

ˈrailroad crossing (*AmE*) = **level crossing**

🔑 **railway** /ˈreɪlweɪ/ (*AmE* **railroad** /ˈreɪlrəʊd/) *noun* [C] **1** (*BrE* **ˈrailway line**) the metal lines on which trains travel between one place and another: *In Canada there is a railway which goes right across the Rocky Mountains.* **2** the whole system of tracks, the trains and the organization and people needed to operate them: *He works on the railways.* ◆ *a railway engine/company*

ˈrailway station = **station¹**(1)

🔑 **rain¹** /reɪn/ *noun* **1** [U] the water that falls from the sky: *Take your umbrella, **it looks like rain*** (= as if it is going to rain). ◆ *It's **pouring with rain*** (= the rain is very heavy). ➲ note at **weather** ➲ look at **shower**, **acid rain** **2 rains** [pl] (in tropical countries) the time of the year when there is a lot of rain: *When the rains come in July, the people move to higher ground.*
IDM **(as) right as rain** ➲ **right¹**

🔑 **rain²** /reɪn/ *verb* **1** [I] [used with *it*] to fall as rain: *Oh no! **It's raining** again!* ◆ *Is it **raining hard**?* ◆ *We'll go out when it stops raining.* **2** [I,T] **rain (sth) (down) (on sb/sth)** to fall or make sth fall on sb/sth in large quantities: *Bombs rained down on the city.*
PHR V **be rained off** to be cancelled or to have to stop because it is raining: *The tennis was rained off.*

rainbow /ˈreɪnbəʊ/ *noun* [C] a curved band of many colours that sometimes appears in the sky when the sun shines through rain

ˈrain check *noun*
IDM **take a rain check on sth** (*spoken*) to refuse an invitation or offer but say that you might accept it later

raincoat /ˈreɪnkəʊt/ *noun* [C] a long light coat which keeps you dry in the rain

raindrop /ˈreɪndrɒp/ *noun* [C] a single drop of rain

rainfall /ˈreɪnfɔːl/ *noun* [U, sing] the total amount of rain that falls in a particular place during a month, year, etc.

rainforest /ˈreɪnfɒrɪst/ *noun* [C] a thick forest in tropical parts of the world that have a lot of rain: *the Amazon rainforest*

rainy /ˈreɪni/ *adj* (**rainier**; **rainiest**) having or bringing a lot of rain: *a rainy day* ◆ *floods during the rainy season*
IDM **keep/save sth for a rainy day** to save sth, especially money, for a time when you really need it

🔑 **raise¹** /reɪz/ *verb* [T]
➤ MOVE UPWARDS **1** to lift sth/sb/yourself up: *If you want to leave the room, raise your hand.* ◆ *He raised himself up on one elbow.* **OPP** **lower** ➲ note at **rise²**
➤ INCREASE **2 raise sth (to sth)** to increase the level of sth or to make sth better or stronger: *to raise taxes/salaries/prices* ◆ *The hotel needs to **raise** its **standards**.* ◆ *There's no need to **raise your voice*** (= speak loudly or angrily). **OPP** **lower** ➲ note at **rise²**
➤ COLLECT MONEY **3** to get money from people for a particular purpose: *We are doing a sponsored walk to **raise money** for charity.* ◆ *a **fund-raising** event*
➤ INTRODUCE TOPIC **4** to introduce a subject that needs to be talked about or dealt with: *I would like to **raise the subject** of money.* ◆ *This **raises the question** of why nothing was done before.*
➤ CAUSE **5** to cause a particular reaction or emotion: *The neighbours **raised the alarm*** (= told everyone there was a fire/an emergency) *when they saw smoke coming out of the window.* ◆ *to **raise hopes/fears/suspicions** in people's minds*
➤ CHILD/ANIMAL **6** to look after a child or an animal until they are an adult: *You can't **raise a family** on what I earn.* ➲ look at **bring sb up**
➤ FARM ANIMALS/PLANTS **7** to breed animals or grow a type of plant for a particular purpose: *Sheep are raised for meat and wool.*
IDM **raise your eyebrows** to show that you are surprised or that you do not approve of sth

raise² /reɪz/ *noun* [C] (*AmE*) = **rise¹**(2)

raisin /ˈreɪzn/ *noun* [C] a dried **grape** (= a small fruit that grows in bunches), used in cakes, etc. ➲ look at **sultana**

rake /reɪk/ *noun* [C] a garden tool with a long handle and a row of metal teeth, used for collecting

R

leaves or making the earth smooth ➲ picture at **garden**
PHR V **rake sth in** (*informal*) to earn a lot of money, especially when it is done easily: *She's been **raking it in** since she got promoted.*
rake sth up (*informal*) to start talking about sth that it would be better to forget: *Don't rake up all those old stories again.*
▸ **rake** *verb* [T]: *to rake up the leaves*

rally[1] /ˈræli/ *noun* [C] (*pl* **rallies**) **1** a large public meeting, especially one held to support a political idea: *a peace rally* **2** a race for cars or motorbikes on public roads **3** (in **tennis** and similar sports) a series of hits of the ball before a point is won

rally[2] /ˈræli/ *verb* (**rallying**; **rallies**; *pt, pp* **rallied**) **1** [I,T] **rally (sb/sth) (around/behind/to sb)** to come together or to bring people together in order to help or support sb/sth: *The cabinet rallied behind the Prime Minister.* **2** [I] to get stronger, healthier, etc. after an illness or a period of weakness: *He never really rallied after the operation.* **SYN** **recover**
PHR V **rally round** to come together to help sb: *When I was in trouble, my family all rallied round.*

RAM /ræm/ *noun* [U] **random-access memory**; computer memory in which data can be changed or removed and can be looked at in any order: *32 megabytes of RAM* ➲ look at **ROM**

ram[1] /ræm/ *verb* [T] (**ramming**; **rammed**) to crash into sth or push sth with great force

ram[2] /ræm/ *noun* [C] a male sheep ➲ note at **sheep** ➲ picture at **goat**

Ramadan /ˈræmədæn; ˌræməˈdæn/ *noun* [C,U] the 9th month of the Muslim year, when Muslims do not eat or drink anything from when the sun rises in the morning to when it goes down in the evening ➲ look at **Eid**

ramble[1] /ˈræmbl/ *verb* [I] **1** to walk in the countryside for pleasure, especially as part of an organized group: *to **go rambling*** **2** **ramble (on) (about sth)** to talk for a long time in a confused way: *Halfway through his speech he began to ramble.*

ramble[2] /ˈræmbl/ *noun* [C] a long, organized walk in the country for pleasure ▸ **rambler** *noun* [C]

rambling /ˈræmblɪŋ/ *adj* **1** (used about a building) spreading in many directions: *a rambling old house in the country* **2** (used about a speech or piece of writing) very long and confused

ramp /ræmp/ *noun* [C] **1** a slope that joins two parts of a road, path, building, etc. when one is higher than the other: *There are ramps at both entrances for wheelchair access.* **2** (*AmE*) = **slip road**

rampage[1] /ˈræmpeɪdʒ/ *noun*
IDM **be/go on the rampage** to move through a place in a violent group, usually breaking things and attacking people

rampage[2] /ræmˈpeɪdʒ/ *verb* [I] to move through a place in a violent group, usually breaking things and attacking people: *The football fans rampaged through the town.*

rampant /ˈræmpənt/ *adj* (used about sth bad) existing or spreading everywhere in a way that is very difficult to control: *Car theft is rampant in this town.*

ramshackle /ˈræmʃækl/ *adj* (usually used about a building) old and needing repair

ran *past tense* of **run**[1]

ranch /rɑːntʃ/ *noun* [C] a large farm, especially in the US or Australia, where cows, horses, sheep, etc. are kept

rancid /ˈrænsɪd/ *adj* if food containing fat is **rancid**, it tastes or smells unpleasant because it is no longer fresh: *rancid butter*

random /ˈrændəm/ *adj* **1** chosen by chance: *For the survey they interviewed **a random selection** of people in the street.* **2** [only *before* a noun] (*informal*) (used especially about a person) not known or not identified: *Some random guy gave me fifty pounds.* **3** (*informal*) a thing or a person that is **random** is strange and does not make sense, often in a way that amuses or interests you: *Mum, you're so random!*
IDM **at random** without thinking or deciding in advance what is going to happen: *The competitors were chosen at random from the audience.*
▸ **randomly** *adv*

ˌrandom-ˌaccess ˈmemory *noun* [U] = **RAM**

randy /ˈrændi/ *adj* (**randier**; **randiest**) (*BrE informal*) sexually excited

rang *past tense* of **ring**[2]

range[1] /reɪndʒ/ *noun* **1** [C, usually sing] **a range (of sth)** a variety of things that belong to the same group: *The course will cover a **whole range** of topics.* ◆ *This shop has a very **wide range** of clothes.* **2** [C] the limits between which sth can vary: *That car is outside my **price range**.* ◆ *I don't think this game is suitable for all **age ranges**.* **3** [C,U] the distance that it is possible for sb/sth to travel, see, hear, etc: *Keep **out of range of** the cameras.* ◆ *The gunman shot the policeman **at close range**.* ◆ *They can pick up signals **at a range of** 400 metres.* **4** [C] a line of mountains or hills: *the great mountain range of the Alps* ➲ picture on **page P10**

range[2] /reɪndʒ/ *verb* [I] **1** **range between A and B; range from A to B** to vary between two amounts, sizes, etc., including all those between them: *The ages of the students range from 15 to 50.* **2** **range (from A to B)** to include a variety of things in addition to those mentioned: *She's had a number of different jobs, ranging from chef to swimming instructor.*

ranger /ˈreɪndʒə(r)/ *noun* [C] a person whose job is to take care of a park, a forest or an area of the countryside

rank[1] /ræŋk/ *noun* **1** [C,U] the position, especially a high position, that sb has in an organization such as the army, or in society: *General is one of the highest ranks in the army.* ◆ *She's much higher in rank than I am.* **2** **the ranks** [pl] the ordinary soldiers in the army; the members of any large group: *At the age of 43, he was forced to **join the ranks of** the unemployed.* **3** [C] a group or line of things or people: *a taxi rank*

IDM the rank and file the ordinary soldiers in the army; the ordinary members of an organization

rank² /ræŋk/ *verb* [I,T] [not used in the continuous tenses] **rank (sb/sth) (as sth)** to give sb/sth a particular position on a scale according to importance, quality, success, etc.; to have a position of this kind: *She's ranked as one of the world's top players.* ◆ *a high-ranking police officer*

ransack /ˈrænsæk/ *verb* [T] **ransack sth (for sth)** to make a place untidy, causing damage, because you are looking for sth: *The house had been ransacked by burglars.*

ransom /ˈrænsəm/ *noun* [C,U] the money that you must pay to free sb who has been captured illegally and who is being kept as a prisoner: *The kidnappers demanded a ransom of $500 000 for the boy's release.*
IDM hold sb to ransom to keep sb as a prisoner and say that you will not free them until you have received a certain amount of money ➲ look at **hostage**
▶ **ransom** *verb* [I,T]

rant /rænt/ *verb* [I,T] **rant (on) (about sth); rant at sb** to speak or complain about sth in a loud and/or angry way ▶ **rant** *noun* [C]

rap¹ /ræp/ *noun* **1** [C] a quick, sharp hit or knock on a door, window, etc: *There was a sharp rap on the door.* **2** [C,U] a style or a piece of music with a fast strong rhythm, in which the words are spoken fast, not sung ➲ look at **rapper**

rap² /ræp/ *verb* (**rapping**; **rapped**) **1** [I,T] to hit a hard object or surface several times quickly and lightly, making a noise: *She rapped angrily on/at the door.* **2** [T] (*informal*) (used mainly in newspapers) to criticize sb strongly: *Minister raps police over rise in crime.* **3** [I] to speak the words of a **rap¹**(2)

rape¹ /reɪp/ *verb* [T] to force a person to have sex when they do not want to, using threats or violence

rape² /reɪp/ *noun* **1** [U,C] the crime of forcing sb to have sex when they do not want to: *to commit rape* **2** [sing] (*formal*) **the rape (of sth)** the act of destroying sth beautiful

rapid /ˈræpɪd/ *adj* happening very quickly or moving with great speed: *She made rapid progress and was soon the best in the class.* ▶ **rapidity** /rəˈpɪdəti/ *noun* (*formal*): *The rapidity of economic growth has astonished most people.* ▶ **rapidly** *adv*

rapids /ˈræpɪdz/ *noun* [pl] a part of a river where the water flows very fast over rocks

rapist /ˈreɪpɪst/ *noun* [C] a person who forces sb to have sex when they do not want to ➲ look at **rape**

rappel /ræˈpel/ (*AmE*) = **abseil**

rapper /ˈræpə(r)/ *noun* [C] a person who performs a **rap¹**(2) (= a piece of music with a strong fast rhythm, in which the words are spoken, not sung)

rapport /ræˈpɔː(r)/ *noun* [sing,U] **rapport (with sb); rapport (between A and B)** a friendly relationship in which people understand each other very well: *She has established a close rapport with clients.*

rapt /ræpt/ *adj* so interested in one particular thing that you are not conscious of anything else: *a rapt audience* ◆ *She listened with rapt attention.*

rapture /ˈræptʃə(r)/ *noun* [U] a feeling of extreme happiness
IDM go into raptures (about/over sb/sth) to feel and show that you think that sb/sth is very good: *I didn't like the film much but my boyfriend went into raptures about it.*

rare /reə(r)/ *adj* (**rarer**; **rarest**) **1 rare (for sb/sth to do sth); rare (to do sth)** not done, seen, happening, etc. very often: *a rare bird/flower/plant* **2** (used about meat) not cooked for very long so that the inside is still red: *a rare steak* ➲ look at **medium**, **well done** ▶ **rarely** *adv*: *Human beings rarely live to be over 100 years old.*

raring /ˈreərɪŋ/ *adj* **raring to do sth** wanting to start doing sth very much: *They were raring to try out the new computer.*

rarity /ˈreərəti/ *noun* (*pl* **rarities**) **1** [C] a thing or a person that is unusual and is therefore often valuable or interesting: *Women in senior positions should not be a rarity.* **2** [U] the quality of being rare: *The rarity of this stamp increases its value a lot.*

rascal /ˈrɑːskl/ *noun* [C] (*informal*) a person, especially a child or man, who shows little respect for other people and enjoys playing jokes on them: *Come here, you little rascal!*

rash¹ /ræʃ/ *noun* **1** [C, usually sing] an area of small red spots that appear on your skin when you are ill or have a reaction to sth: *He **came out in a rash** where the plant had touched him.* **2** [sing] **a rash (of sth)** a series of unpleasant events of the same kind happening over a short period of time

rash² /ræʃ/ *adj* (used about people) doing things that might be dangerous or bad without thinking about the possible results first; (used about actions) done in this way: *a rash decision/promise* ▶ **rashly** *adv*

rasher /ˈræʃə(r)/ *noun* [C] (*BrE*) a slice of **bacon** (= meat from a pig)

raspberry /ˈrɑːzbəri/ *noun* [C] (*pl* **raspberries**) a small, soft, red fruit which grows on bushes: *raspberry jam* ➲ picture on **page P14**

rat /ræt/ *noun* [C] an animal like a large mouse: *Rats belong to the family of animals that are called rodents.*
IDM the rat race the way of life in which everyone is only interested in being better or more successful than everyone else

rate¹ /reɪt/ *noun* [C] **1** a measurement of the speed at which sth happens or the number of times sth happens or exists during a particular period: *The **birth rate** (= the number of children born each year) is falling.* ◆ *The population is increasing **at the rate of** less than 0.5% a year.* ◆ *an **exchange rate** of one pound to 1.5 dollars* **2** a fixed amount of money that sth costs or that sb is paid: *The basic **rate of pay** is £10 an hour.* ◆ *We offer special reduced rates for students.* ➲ look at **first-rate**, **second-rate**
IDM at any rate (*spoken*) **1** whatever else might happen: *Well, that's one good piece of news at any rate.* **2** used when you are giving more exact

R

information about sth: *He said that they would be here by ten. At any rate, I think that's what he said.*
the going rate (for sth) ➲ **going²**

rate² /reɪt/ *verb* [not used in the continuous tenses] **1** [T, usually passive] to say how good you think sb/sth is: *She's rated among the best tennis players of all time.* **2** [I,T] to be good, important, etc. enough to be treated in a particular way: *The accident wasn't very serious—it didn't rate a mention in the local newspaper.* ◆ *The match rated as one of their worst defeats.*

rather /ˈrɑːðə(r)/ *adv* quite: *It was a rather nice day.* ◆ *It was rather a nice day.* ◆ *It cost rather a lot of money.* ◆ *I was rather hoping that you'd be free on Friday.*

HELP If you use **rather** with a positive word, it sounds as if you are surprised and pleased: *My teacher doesn't look very friendly, but he is actually rather nice.* You can use **rather** with a negative word to criticize sth: *This room's rather untidy.* **Rather**, **quite** and **fairly** can all mean 'not very'. **Rather** is the strongest and **fairly** is the weakest. **Pretty** has the same meaning as **rather** but is informal.

IDM or rather used as a way of correcting sth you have said, or making it more exact: *She lives in London, or rather she lives in a suburb of London.*
rather than instead of; in place of: *I think I'll just have a sandwich rather than a full meal.*
would rather ... (than) would prefer to: *I'd rather go to the cinema than watch TV.*

ratify /ˈrætɪfaɪ/ *verb* [T] (**ratifying**; **ratifies**; *pt, pp* **ratified**) to make an agreement officially valid by voting for or signing it: *The treaty was ratified by all the member states.* ▶ **ratification** /ˌrætɪfɪˈkeɪʃn/ *noun* [U]

R

rating /ˈreɪtɪŋ/ *noun* **1** [C] a measurement of how popular, important, good, etc. sth is **2 the ratings** [pl] a set of figures showing the number of people who watch a particular TV programme, etc., used to show how popular the programme is

ratio /ˈreɪʃiəʊ/ *noun* [C] (*pl* **ratios**) **ratio (of A to B)** the relation between two numbers which shows how much bigger one quantity is than another: *The ratio of boys to girls in this class is three to one* (= there are three times as many boys as girls).

ration /ˈræʃn/ *noun* [C] a limited amount of food, petrol, etc. that you are allowed to have when there is not enough for everyone to have as much as they want ▶ **ration** *verb* [T]: *In the desert water is strictly rationed.* ▶ **rationing** *noun* [U]

rational /ˈræʃnəl/ *adj* **1** based on reason; sensible or logical: *There must be a rational explanation for why he's behaving like this.* **2** (used about a person) able to use logical thought rather than emotions to make decisions **SYN** **reasonable** **OPP** **irrational** ▶ **rationally** /-nəli/ *adv*

rationale /ˌræʃəˈnɑːl/ *noun* [C] (*formal*) **rationale (behind/for/of sth)** the principles or reasons which explain a particular decision, plan, belief, etc: *What is the rationale behind these new exams?* **SYN** **reasoning**

rationalize (also **-ise**) /ˈræʃnəlaɪz/ *verb* **1** [I,T] to find reasons that explain why you have done sth (perhaps because you do not like the real reason) **2** [T] to make a business or a system better organized ▶ **rationalization** (also **-isation**) /ˌræʃnəlaɪˈzeɪʃn/ *noun* [C,U]

rattle¹ /ˈrætl/ *verb* **1** [I,T] to make a noise like hard things hitting each other, or to shake sth so that it makes this noise: *The windows were rattling all night in the wind.* ◆ *He rattled the money in the tin.* **2** [T] (*informal*) to make sb suddenly become worried: *The news of his arrival really rattled her.*
PHR V rattle sth off to say a list of things you have learnt very quickly: *She rattled off the names of every player in the team.*

rattle² /ˈrætl/ *noun* [C] **1** [usually sing] a noise made by hard things hitting each other **2** a toy that a baby can shake to make a noise

raucous /ˈrɔːkəs/ *adj* (used about people's voices) loud and unpleasant: *raucous laughter*

ravage /ˈrævɪdʒ/ *verb* [T] to damage sth very badly; to destroy sth: *The forests were ravaged by the winter storms.*

rave¹ /reɪv/ *verb* [I] **1** (*informal*) **rave (about sb/sth)** to say very good things about sb/sth: *Everyone's raving about her latest album!* **2** to speak angrily or in a wild way

rave² /reɪv/ *noun* [C] a large party held outside or in an empty building, at which people dance to electronic music

raven /ˈreɪvn/ *noun* [C] a large black bird that makes an unpleasant sound

ravenous /ˈrævənəs/ *adj* very hungry ▶ **ravenously** *adv*

ˌrave reˈview *noun* [C] an article in a newspaper, etc. that says very good things about a new book, film, play, etc.

ravine /rəˈviːn/ *noun* [C] a narrow deep valley with steep sides

raving /ˈreɪvɪŋ/ *adj* [only *before* a noun] *adv* (*informal*) talking or behaving in a way that shows they are crazy: *Have you gone raving mad?*

raw /rɔː/ *adj* **1** not cooked: *Raw vegetables are good for your teeth.* **2** in the natural state; not yet made into anything: *raw materials* (= that are used to make things in factories, etc.) **3** used about an injury where the skin has come off from being rubbed: *There's a nasty raw place on my heel where my shoes have rubbed.*

ray /reɪ/ *noun* [C] a line of light, heat or energy: *the sun's rays* ◆ *ultraviolet rays* ➲ look at **X-ray**
IDM a ray of hope a small chance that things will get better

razor /ˈreɪzə(r)/ *noun* [C] a sharp instrument which people use to shave with: *an electric razor* ◆ *a disposable razor*

ˈrazor blade *noun* [C] the thin sharp piece of metal that you put in a **razor**

Rd *abbr* = **road**(2): *21 Hazel Rd*

RE /ˌɑːr ˈiː/ *noun* [U] **religious education**; a school subject in which students learn about different religions: *an RE teacher*

re /riː/ *prep* about or concerning sth; used at the beginning of a business letter or an email to introduce the subject: *Re your letter of 1 September ...* ◆ *Re: travel expenses*

re- /riː/ [in compounds] again: *reapply* ◆ *reappearance* ◆ *reassuring*

⚷ **reach¹** /riːtʃ/ *verb* **1** [T] to arrive at a place or condition that you have been going towards: *We won't reach Dover before 12.* ◆ *The two sides hope to* ***reach an agreement*** *sometime today.* ◆ *Sometimes the temperature reaches 45°C.* ◆ *The team reached the semi-final last year.* ◆ *to reach a decision/conclusion/compromise* **2** [I,T] reach (out) (for sb/sth); reach (sth) (down) to stretch out your arm to try and touch or get sth: *The child reached out for her mother.* ◆ *She reached into her bag for her purse.* **3** [I,T] to be able to touch sth: *Can you get me that book off the top shelf? I can't reach.* ◆ *He couldn't reach the light switch.* ◆ *I need a longer ladder. This one won't reach.* **4** [T] to communicate with sb, especially by telephone; contact: *You can reach me at this number.*

reach² /riːtʃ/ *noun* [sing] the distance that you can stretch your arm

IDM **beyond/out of (sb's) reach** **1** outside the distance that you can stretch your arm: *Keep this medicine out of the reach of children.* **2** not able to be got or done by sb: *A job like that is completely beyond his reach.*

within (sb's) reach **1** inside the distance that you can stretch your arm **2** able to be achieved by sb: *We were one goal ahead with ten minutes left and so could sense that victory was within our reach.*

within (easy) reach of sth not far from sth

⚷ **react** /riˈækt/ *verb* [I] **1** react (to sth) (by doing sth) to do or say sth because of sth that has happened or been said: *He reacted to the news by jumping up and down and shouting.* ◆ *The players reacted angrily to the decision.* **2** react (to sth) to become ill after eating, breathing, etc. a particular substance: *He reacted badly to the drug and had to go to hospital.* **3** react (with sth/together) (used about a chemical substance) to change after coming into contact with another substance: *Iron reacts with water and air to produce rust.*

PHR V **react against sb/sth** to behave or talk in a way that shows that you do not like the influence of sb/sth (for example authority, your family, etc.)

⚷ **reaction** /riˈækʃn/ *noun*

➤TO EVENT **1** [C,U] (a) reaction (to sb/sth) something that you do or say because of sth that has happened: *Could we have your reaction to the latest news, Prime Minister?* ◆ *I shook him to try and wake him up but there was no reaction.*

➤TO SB/SITUATION **2** [C,U] (a) reaction (against sb/sth) behaviour that shows that you do not like the influence of sb/sth (for example authority, your family, etc.): *Her strange clothes are a reaction against the conservative way she was brought up.*

➤TO FOOD, DRUGS, ETC. **3** [C] a reaction (to sth) a bad effect that your body experiences because of sth that you have eaten, touched or breathed: *She had an* ***allergic reaction*** *to something in the food.*

➤TO DANGER **4** [C, usually pl] the physical ability to act quickly when sth happens: *If the other driver's reactions hadn't been so good, there would have been an accident.*

➤IN CHEMISTRY **5** [C,U] (*technical*) a chemical change produced by two or more substances coming into contact with each other: *a nuclear reaction*

reactionary /riˈækʃənri/ *noun* [C] (*pl* reactionaries) a person who tries to prevent political or social change ▶ **reactionary** *adj*: *reactionary views/politics/groups*

reactor /riˈæktə(r)/ = **nuclear reactor**

⚷ **read¹** /riːd/ *verb* (*pt, pp* read /red/) **1** [I,T] to look at words or symbols and understand them: *He never learnt to read and write.* ◆ *Have you read any good books lately?* ◆ *Can you read music?* **2** [I,T] read (sb) (sth); read sth (to sb) to say written words to sb: *My father used to read me stories when I was a child.* ◆ *I hate reading out loud.* **3** to discover or find out about sb/sth by reading: *I read about the accident in the local paper.* **4** [T] to be able to understand sth from what you can see: *A man came to read the gas meter.* ◆ *Profoundly deaf people often learn to* ***read lips***. ◆ *I've no idea what he'll say—I can't* ***read*** *his* ***mind***! **5** [T] to show words or a sign of sth: *The sign read 'Keep Left'.* **6** [T] (*formal*) to study a subject at university: *She read Modern Languages at Cambridge.*

PHR V **read sth into sth** to think that there is a meaning in sth that may not really be there

read on to continue reading; to read the next part of sth

read sth out to read sth to other people

read sth through to read sth to check details or to look for mistakes: *I read my essay through a few times before handing it in.*

read up on sth to read a lot about a subject

read² /riːd/ *noun* [sing] (*informal*) a period or the act of reading: *I generally* ***have a*** *quick* ***read*** *of the newspaper over breakfast.* ◆ *Her detective novels are usually* ***a good read***.

readable /ˈriːdəbl/ *adj* **1** easy or interesting to read **2** able to be read: *machine-readable data* ➲ look at **legible**

⚷ **reader** /ˈriːdə(r)/ *noun* [C] **1** a person who reads sth (a particular newspaper, magazine, type of book, etc.): *She's an avid reader of science fiction.* **2** [with an adjective] a person who reads in a particular way: *a fast/slow reader* **3** a book for practising reading: *a series of English graded readers*

readership /ˈriːdəʃɪp/ *noun* [sing] the number of people who regularly read a particular newspaper, magazine, etc: *The newspaper has a readership of 200 000.*

readily /ˈredɪli/ *adv* **1** easily, without difficulty: *Most vegetables are* ***readily available*** *at this time of year.* **2** without pausing; without being forced: *He readily admitted that he was wrong.*

R

readiness /ˈredinəs/ *noun* [U] **1** readiness (for sth) the state of being ready or prepared **2** readiness (to do sth) the state of being prepared to do sth without arguing or complaining: *The bank have indicated their readiness to lend him the money.*

reading /ˈriːdɪŋ/ *noun* **1** [U] what you do when you read: *I haven't had time to do much reading lately.* ♦ *Her hobbies include painting and reading.* **2** [U] books, articles, etc. that are intended to be read: *The information office gave me a pile of* ***reading matter*** *to take away.* **3** [C] the particular way in which sb understands sth: *What's your reading of the situation?* **4** [C] the number or measurement that is shown on an instrument: *a reading of 20°*

readjust /ˌriːəˈdʒʌst/ *verb* **1** [I] readjust (to sth) to get used to a different or new situation: *After her divorce, it took her a long time to readjust to being single again.* **2** [T] to change or move sth slightly ▶ **readjustment** *noun* [C,U]

ˌread-only ˈmemory *noun* [U] = ROM

ready /ˈredi/ *adj* (readier; readiest) **1** ready to do sth; ready (with/for sth) prepared and happy to do sth: *You know me—I'm always ready to help.* ♦ *Charlie's always ready with advice.* ♦ *The men were angry and ready for a fight.* ♦ *I know it's early, but I'm* ***ready for bed.*** **2** ready (for sb/sth); ready (to do sth) prepared and able to do sth or to be used: *The car will be ready for you to collect on Friday.* ♦ *He isn't ready to take his driving test—he hasn't had enough lessons.* ♦ *I'm meeting him at 7, so I don't have long to* ***get ready.*** ♦ *I'll go and* ***get*** *the dinner* ***ready.*** ♦ ***Have*** *your money* ***ready*** *before you get on the bus.* **3** *adv* [in compounds] already made or done; not done especially for you: *ready-cooked food* ♦ *There are no* ***ready-made*** *answers to this problem—we'll have to find our own solution.*

R

real[1] /ˈriːəl; rɪəl/ *adj*

➤NOT IMAGINED **1** actually existing, not imagined: *The film is based on real life.* ♦ *This isn't a real word, I made it up.* ♦ *We have a real chance of winning.* ♦ *Closure of the factory is a very real danger.*

➤NATURAL **2** natural, not artificial: *This shirt is real silk.*

➤TRUE **3** actually true; not only what people think is true: *The name he gave to the police wasn't his real name.*

➤GENUINE **4** [only *before* a noun] having all, not just some, of the qualities necessary to really be sth: *She was my first real girlfriend.*

➤BIG **5** [only *before* a noun] (used to emphasize a state, feeling or quality) strong or big: *Money is a real problem for us at the moment.* ♦ *He made a real effort to be polite.*

IDM **for real** genuine or serious: *Her tears weren't for real.* ♦ *Was he for real when he offered you the job?*

the real thing (*informal*) something genuine, not a copy: *This painting is just a copy. The real thing is in a gallery.* ♦ *She's had boyfriends before but this time she says it's the real thing* (= real love).

real[2] /ˈriːəl; rɪəl/ *adv* (*AmE informal*) very; really

ˈreal estate *noun* [U] (*especially AmE*) property in the form of land and buildings

ˈreal estate agent (*AmE*) = estate agent

realise = realize

realism /ˈriːəlɪzəm/ *noun* [U] **1** behaviour that shows that you accept the facts of a situation and are not influenced by your feelings ➲ look at **idealism** **2** (in art, literature, etc.) showing things as they really are

realist /ˈriːəlɪst/ *noun* [C] **1** a person who accepts the facts of a situation, and does not try to pretend that it is different: *I'm a realist—I don't expect the impossible.* **2** an artist or writer who shows things as they really are

realistic /ˌriːəˈlɪstɪk/ *adj* **1** sensible and understanding what it is possible to achieve in a particular situation: *We have to be realistic about our chances of winning.* **2** showing things as they really are: *a realistic drawing/description* **3** not real but appearing to be real: *The monsters in the film were very realistic.* OPP for all meanings **unrealistic** ▶ **realistically** /-kli/ *adv*

reality /riˈæləti/ *noun* (*pl* realities) **1** [U] the way life really is, not the way it may appear to be or how you would like it to be: *I enjoyed my holiday, but now it's back to reality.* ♦ *We have to* ***face reality*** *and accept that we've failed.* **2** [C] a thing that is actually experienced, not just imagined: *Films portray war as heroic and exciting, but the reality is very different.*

IDM **in reality** in fact, really (not the way sth appears or has been described): *People say this is an exciting city but in reality it's rather boring.*

reˈality check *noun* [usually sing] (*informal*) an occasion when you are reminded of how things are in the real world, rather than how you would like things to be: *It's time for a reality check—you're never going to finish that book!*

reˌality TˈV *noun* [U] television shows that are based on real people (not actors) in real situations, presented as entertainment

realize (also -ise) /ˈriːəlaɪz/ *verb* [T] **1** to know and understand that sth is true or that sth has happened: *I'm sorry I mentioned it; I didn't realize how much it upset you.* ♦ *Didn't you realize (that) you needed to bring money?* **2** to become conscious of sth or that sth has happened, usually some time later: *When I got home, I realized that I had left my keys at the office.* **3** to make sth that you imagined become reality: *His worst fears were realized when he saw the damage caused by the fire.* ▶ **realization** (also -isation) /ˌriːəlaɪˈzeɪʃn; ˌrɪəl-/ *noun* [U]

really /ˈrɪəli/ *adv* **1** actually; in fact: *I couldn't believe it was really happening.* ♦ *He said he was sorry but I don't think he really meant it.* ♦ *She wasn't really angry, she was only pretending.* ♦ *Is it really true?* **2** very; very much: *I'm really tired.* ♦ *I really hope you enjoy yourself.* ♦ *I really tried but I couldn't do it.* **3** used in negative sentences to make what you are saying less strong: *I don't really agree with that.* **4** used in questions when you are expecting sb to answer 'No': *You don't really expect me to believe that, do you?* **5** used as a question for expressing surprise, interest, doubt, etc: *'She's left her husband.' 'Really? When did that happen?'*

Realtor™ /ˈriːəltə(r)/ (*AmE*) = **estate agent**

reap /riːp/ *verb* [T] **1** to obtain sth, especially sth good, as a direct result of sth that you have done: *If you work hard now, you'll* ***reap the benefits*** *later on.* **2** to cut and collect a crop, especially **corn, wheat** (= types of plant grown for their grain), etc., from a field

reappear /ˌriːəˈpɪə(r)/ *verb* [I] to appear again or be seen again ▶ **reappearance** *noun* [C,U]

reappraisal /ˌriːəˈpreɪzl/ *noun* [C,U] the new examination of a situation, way of doing sth, etc. in order to decide if any changes are necessary

rear¹ /rɪə(r)/ *noun* **1** [sing] **the rear** the back part: *There are toilets at the rear of the plane.* **2** [C, usually sing] the part of your body that you sit on; your bottom

IDM **bring up the rear** to be the last one in a race, a line of people, etc.

▶ **rear** *adj* [only *before* a noun]: *the rear window/lights of a car* ➲ picture on **page P7**

rear² /rɪə(r)/ *verb* **1** [T] to care for young children or animals until they are fully grown: *She reared a family of five on her own.* **2** [T] to breed and look after animals on a farm, etc: *to rear cattle/poultry* **3** [I] **rear (up)** (used about horses) to stand only on the back legs

rearrange /ˌriːəˈreɪndʒ/ *verb* [T] **1** to change the position or order of things: *We've rearranged the living room to make more space.* **2** to change a plan, meeting, etc. that has been fixed

reason¹ /ˈriːzn/ *noun* **1** [C] **a reason (for sth/for doing sth); a reason why .../that ...** a cause or an explanation for sth that has happened or for sth that sb has done: *What's your reason for being so late?* ♦ *Is there any reason why you couldn't tell me this before?* ♦ *He said he couldn't come but he didn't* ***give a reason.*** ♦ *The reason (that) I'm phoning you is to ask a favour.* ♦ ***For some reason*** *they can't give us an answer until next week.* ♦ *She left the job for personal reasons.* **2** [C,U] **(a) reason (to do sth); (a) reason (for sth/for doing sth)** something that shows that it is right or fair to do sth: *I* ***have reason*** *to believe that you've been lying.* ♦ *I think we have reason for complaint.* ♦ *You* ***have every reason*** *(= you are completely right) to be angry, considering how badly you've been treated.* **3** [U] the ability to think and to make sensible decisions: *Only human beings are capable of reason.* **4** [U] what is right or acceptable: *I tried to persuade him not to drive but he just wouldn't* ***listen to reason.*** ♦ *I'll pay anything* ***within reason*** *for a ticket.*

IDM **it stands to reason** (*informal*) it is obvious if you think about it

reason² /ˈriːzn/ *verb* [I,T] to form a judgement or opinion about sth, after thinking about it in a logical way

PHR V **reason with sb** to talk to sb in order to persuade them to behave or think in a more reasonable way

reasonable /ˈriːznəbl/ *adj* **1** fair, practical and sensible: *I think it's reasonable to expect people to keep their promises.* ♦ *I tried to be reasonable even though I was very angry.* **OPP** **unreasonable** **2** acceptable and appropriate in a particular situation: *It was a lovely meal and the bill was very reasonable!* **3** quite good, high, big, etc. but not very: *His work is of a reasonable standard.*

reasonably /ˈriːznəbli/ *adv* **1** fairly or quite (but not very): *The weather was reasonably good but not brilliant.* **2** in a sensible and fair way: *If you think about my suggestion reasonably, you'll realize that I'm right.*

reasoning /ˈriːzənɪŋ/ *noun* [U] the process of thinking about sth and making a judgement or decision: *What's the reasoning behind his sudden decision to leave?*

reassurance /ˌriːəˈʃʊərəns; -ˈʃɔːr-/ *noun* [U,C] advice or help that you give to sb to stop them worrying or being afraid: *I need some reassurance that I'm doing things the right way.*

reassure /ˌriːəˈʃʊə(r); -ˈʃɔː(r)/ *verb* [T] to say or do sth in order to stop sb worrying or being afraid: *The mechanic reassured her that the engine was fine.* ▶ **reassuring** *adj* ▶ **reassuringly** *adv*

rebate /ˈriːbeɪt/ *noun* [C] a sum of money that is given back to you because you have paid too much: *to get a tax rebate*

rebel¹ /ˈrebl/ *noun* [C] **1** a person who fights against their country's government because they want things to change **SYN** **insurgent** **2** a person who refuses to obey people in authority or to accept rules: *At school he had a reputation as a rebel.*

rebel² /rɪˈbel/ *verb* [I] (**rebelling; rebelled**) **rebel (against sb/sth)** to fight against authority, society, a law, etc: *She rebelled against her parents by marrying a man she knew they didn't approve of.*

rebellion /rɪˈbeljən/ *noun* [C,U] **1** an occasion when some of the people in a country try to change the government, using violence **2** the act of fighting against authority or refusing to accept rules: *Voting against the leader of the party was an act of open rebellion.*

rebellious /rɪˈbeljəs/ *adj* not doing what authority, society, etc. wants you to do: *rebellious teenagers*

reboot /ˌriːˈbuːt/ *verb* [I,T] if you **reboot** a computer or if it **reboots**, you turn it off and then turn it on again immediately

rebound /rɪˈbaʊnd/ *verb* [I] **rebound (from/off sth)** to hit sth/sb and then go in a different direction: *The ball rebounded off Cole and went into the goal.* ▶ **rebound** /ˈriːbaʊnd/ *noun* [C]

rebuff /rɪˈbʌf/ *noun* [C] an unkind refusal of an offer or suggestion ▶ **rebuff** *verb* [T]

rebuild /ˌriːˈbɪld/ *verb* [T] (*pt, pp* **rebuilt** /ˌriːˈbɪlt/) to build sth again: *Following the storm, a great many houses will have to be rebuilt.*

rebuke /rɪˈbjuːk/ *verb* [T] (*formal*) to speak angrily to sb because they have done sth wrong ▶ **rebuke** *noun* [C]

R

recall /rɪˈkɔːl/ *verb* [T] (*formal*) **1** to remember sth (a fact, an event, an action, etc.) from the past: *I don't recall exactly when I first met her.* ♦ *She couldn't recall meeting him before.* **2** to order sb to return; to ask for sth to be returned: *The company has recalled all the faulty hairdryers.*

recap /ˈriːkæp/ (recapping; recapped) (*informal*) (also *formal* recapitulate /ˌriːkəˈpɪtʃuleɪt/) *verb* [I,T] to repeat or look again at the main points of sth to make sure that they have been understood: *Let's quickly recap what we've done in today's lesson, before we finish.*

recapture /ˌriːˈkæptʃə(r)/ *verb* [T] **1** to win back sth that was taken from you by an enemy: *Government troops have recaptured the city.* **2** to catch a person or an animal that has escaped **3** to create or experience again sth from the past: *The film brilliantly recaptures life in the 1930s.*

recede /rɪˈsiːd/ *verb* [I] **1** to move away and begin to disappear: *The coast began to recede into the distance.* **2** (used about a hope, fear, chance, etc.) to become smaller or less strong **3** (used about a man's hair) to fall out and stop growing at the front of the head: *He's got a **receding hairline**.*

receipt /rɪˈsiːt/ *noun* **1** [C] a receipt (for sth) a piece of paper that is given to show that you have paid for sth: *Keep the receipt in case you want to exchange the shirt.* **2** [U] (*formal*) receipt (of sth) the receiving of sth: *Payment must be made within seven days of receipt of the goods.*

receive /rɪˈsiːv/ *verb* [T] **1** receive sth (from sb/sth) to get or accept sth that sb sends or gives to you: *I received a letter from an old friend last week.* ♦ *to receive a phone call/a prize* **2** to experience a particular kind of treatment or injury: *We received a warm welcome from our hosts.* ♦ *He received several cuts and bruises in the accident.* **3** [often passive] to react to sth new in a particular way: *The film has been well received by the critics.*

R

receiver /rɪˈsiːvə(r)/ *noun* [C] **1** (also handset) the part of a telephone that is used for listening and speaking ➲ note at **telephone** **2** a piece of TV or radio equipment that changes electronic signals into sounds or pictures

recent /ˈriːsnt/ *adj* that happened or began only a short time ago: ***In recent years** there have been many changes.* ♦ *This is a recent photograph of my daughter.*

> **HELP** **Recently** or **lately**? **Recently** can refer to both a point in time and a period of time. If it refers to a point in time, use the past simple tense: *He got married recently.* If it refers to a period, use the present perfect or present perfect continuous tense: *I haven't done anything interesting recently.* ♦ *She's been working hard recently.* **Lately** can only refer to a period of time. It is used only with the present perfect or present perfect continuous tense: *I've seen a lot of films lately.* ♦ *I've been spending too much money lately.*

recently /ˈriːsntli/ *adv* not long ago: *She worked here until quite recently.* ♦ *Have you seen Paul recently?*

receptacle /rɪˈseptəkl/ *noun* [C] (*formal*) a container

reception /rɪˈsepʃn/ *noun* **1** [U] the place inside the entrance of a hotel or office building where guests or visitors go when they first arrive: *Leave your key **at/in reception** if you go out, please.* ♦ *the reception desk* **2** [C] a formal party to celebrate sth or to welcome an important person: *Their **wedding reception** was held at a local hotel.* ♦ *There will be an official reception at the embassy for the visiting ambassador.* **3** [sing] the way people react to sth: *The play got a mixed reception* (= some people liked it, some people didn't). **4** [U] the quality of radio, TV or mobile phone signals: *TV reception is very poor where we live.*

receptionist /rɪˈsepʃənɪst/ *noun* [C] a person who works in a hotel, a doctor's surgery, an office, etc. answering the telephone and dealing with visitors and guests when they arrive: *a hotel receptionist*

receptive /rɪˈseptɪv/ *adj* receptive (to sth) ready to listen to new ideas, suggestions, etc.

recess /rɪˈses; ˈriːses/ *noun* **1** [C,U] a period of time when parliament or other groups that meet for official discussions do not meet **2** [U] (*AmE*) a short break during a trial in a court of law ➲ note at **interval** **3** [C] part of a wall that is further back than the rest, forming a space **4** [C] a part of a room that receives very little light

recession /rɪˈseʃn/ *noun* [C,U] a period when the business and industry of a country is not successful: *The country is now **in recession**.* ♦ *How long will the recession last?*

recharge /ˌriːˈtʃɑːdʒ/ *verb* [I,T] to fill a battery with electrical power; to fill up with electrical power: *He plugged the drill in to recharge it.* ➲ look at **charge** ▶ **rechargeable** *adj*: *rechargeable batteries*

recipe /ˈresəpi/ *noun* [C] **1** a recipe (for sth) the instructions for cooking or preparing sth to eat: *a recipe for chocolate cake* **2** a recipe for sth the way to get or produce sth: *Putting Dave in charge of the project is **a recipe for disaster**.*

> TOPIC
>
> **A recipe**
>
> **Shepherd's pie**
>
> **Peel** four potatoes, then **cut** them in pieces and **boil** them in a **saucepan** of water. When they are cooked, **strain** them in a **colander** to remove the water, then **mash** them with some butter and milk. Next **slice** an onion, and **fry** it in a **frying pan**. Add some **minced** meat, some **chopped** tomatoes and herbs (= special leaves used in cooking), and put the mixture in a **casserole** dish, with the **mashed potato** on top. **Grate** some cheese on the potato, and then **bake** in the **oven** for half an hour.

recipient /rɪˈsɪpiənt/ *noun* [C] (*formal*) a person who receives sth

reciprocal /rɪˈsɪprəkl/ *adj* involving two or more people or groups who agree to help each other or to behave in the same way towards each other: *The arrangement is reciprocal. They help us and we help them.*

reciprocate /rɪˈsɪprəkeɪt/ *verb* [I,T] **reciprocate (sth) (with sth)** to behave or feel towards sb in the same way as they behave or feel towards you: *Her love for him was not reciprocated.* ♦ *I wasn't sure whether to laugh or to reciprocate with a remark of my own.* ▶ **reciprocation** /rɪˌsɪprəˈkeɪʃn/ *noun* [U]

recital /rɪˈsaɪtl/ *noun* [C] a formal public performance of music or poetry: *a piano recital* ➲ look at **concert**

recite /rɪˈsaɪt/ *verb* [I,T] to say a poem, piece of literature, etc. that you have learned, especially to an audience: *Each child had to recite a poem to the class*

reckless /ˈrekləs/ *adj* not thinking about possible bad or dangerous results that could come from your actions: *reckless driving* ♦ *a reckless disregard for safety* ▶ **recklessly** *adv*

⚷ **reckon** /ˈrekən/ *verb* [T] **1** (*informal*) to think; to have an opinion about sth: *She's very late now. I reckon (that) she isn't coming.* ♦ *I think she's forgotten. What do you reckon?* **2** to calculate sth approximately: *The journey was reckoned to take half an hour.*

PHR V **reckon on sth** to expect sth to happen and therefore to base a plan or action on it: *I didn't book in advance because I wasn't reckoning on tickets being so scarce.*

reckon (sth) up to calculate the total amount or number of sth

reckon with sb/sth to think about sb/sth as a possible problem: *They were a political force* ***to be reckoned with.*** ♦ *I didn't reckon with there being so much traffic.*

reckoning /ˈrekənɪŋ/ *noun* [U,C] the act of calculating sth, especially in a way that is not very exact: ***By my reckoning*** *you still owe me £5.*

reclaim /rɪˈkleɪm/ *verb* [T] **1 reclaim sth (from sb/sth)** to get back sth that has been lost or taken away: *Reclaim your luggage after you have been through passport control.* **2** to make wet land suitable for use **3** to get back useful materials from waste products ▶ **reclamation** /ˌrekləˈmeɪʃn/ *noun* [U]: *land reclamation*

recline /rɪˈklaɪn/ *verb* [I,T] to sit or lie back in a relaxed and comfortable way ▶ **reclining** *adj*: *The car has* ***reclining seats*** *at the front.*

recluse /rɪˈkluːs/ *noun* [C] a person who lives alone and likes to avoid other people ▶ **reclusive** /rɪˈkluːsɪv/ *adj*: *a reclusive millionaire*

⚷ **recognition** /ˌrekəgˈnɪʃn/ *noun* **1** [U] the fact that you can identify sb/sth that you see: *She looked at me with no sign of recognition on her face.* **2** [U, sing] the act of accepting that sth exists, is true or is official: *There is a growing recognition that older people are important in the workplace.* **3** [U] a public show of respect for sb's work or actions: *She has* ***received*** *public* ***recognition*** *for her services to charity.* ♦ *Please accept this gift* ***in recognition of*** *the work you have done.*

recognizable (also **-isable**) /ˈrekəgnaɪzəbl; ˌrekəgˈnaɪzəbl/ *adj* **recognizable (as sb/sth)** that can be identified as sb/sth: *He was barely recognizable with his new short haircut.* ▶ **recognizably** (also **-isably**) /-əbli/ *adv*

⚷ **recognize** (also **-ise**) /ˈrekəgnaɪz/ *verb* [T] **1** to know again sb/sth that you have seen or heard before: *I recognized him but I couldn't remember his name.* **2** to accept that sth exists or is true: *I recognize that some of my ideas are unrealistic.* **3** to accept sth officially: *My qualifications are not recognized in other countries.* **4** to show officially that you think sth that sb has done is good: *The company gave her a special present to recognize her long years of service.*

recoil /rɪˈkɔɪl/ *verb* [I] to quickly move away from sb/sth unpleasant: *She recoiled in horror at the sight of the rat.*

recollect /ˌrekəˈlekt/ *verb* [I,T] to remember sth, especially by making an effort: *I don't recollect exactly when it happened.*

recollection /ˌrekəˈlekʃn/ *noun* **1** [U] **recollection (of sth/doing sth)** the ability to remember: *I* ***have no recollection*** *of promising to lend you money.* **2** [C, usually pl] something that you remember: *I have only vague recollections of the town where I spent my early years.* **SYN** for both meanings **memory**

⚷ **recommend** /ˌrekəˈmend/ *verb* [T] **1 recommend sb/sth (to sb) (for/as sth)** to say that sb/sth is good and that sb should try or use them or it: *Which film would you recommend?* ♦ *Could you recommend me a good hotel?* ♦ *We hope that you'll recommend this restaurant to all your friends.* ♦ *Doctors don't always recommend drugs as the best treatment for every illness.* **2** to tell sb what you strongly believe they should do: *I recommend that you get some legal advice.* ♦ *I wouldn't recommend (your) travelling on your own. It could be dangerous.* ♦ ***It is recommended that*** *machines are checked every year.*

recommendation /ˌrekəmenˈdeɪʃn/ *noun* **1** [C] a statement about what should be done in a particular situation: *In their report on the crash, the committee* ***make*** *several* ***recommendations*** *on how safety could be improved.* **2** [C,U] saying that sth is good and should be tried or used: *I visited Seville* ***on*** *a friend's* ***recommendation*** *and I really enjoyed it.*

recompense /ˈrekəmpens/ *verb* [T] (*formal*) **recompense sb (for sth)** to give money, etc. to sb for special efforts or work or because you are responsible for a loss they have suffered: *The airline has agreed to recompense us for the damage to our luggage.* ▶ **recompense** *noun* [sing,U]: *Please accept this cheque* ***in recompense for*** *our poor service.*

reconcile /ˈrekənsaɪl/ *verb* [T] **1 reconcile sth (with sth)** to find a way of dealing with two ideas, situations, statements, etc. that seem to be opposite to each other: *She finds it difficult to reconcile her career ambitions with her responsibilities to her*

R

children. **2** [often passive] reconcile sb (with sb) to make people become friends again after an argument: *After years of not speaking to each other, she and her parents were eventually reconciled.* **3** reconcile yourself to sth to accept an unpleasant situation because there is nothing you can do to change it ▶ **reconciliation** /ˌrekənsɪli'eɪʃn/ *noun* [sing,U]: *The negotiators are hoping to bring about a reconciliation between the two sides.*

reconnaissance /rɪ'kɒnɪsns/ *noun* [C,U] the study of a place or area for military reasons: *The plane was shot down while on a reconnaissance mission over enemy territory.*

reconsider /ˌri:kən'sɪdə(r)/ *verb* [I,T] to think again about sth, especially because you may want to change your mind: *Public protests have forced the government to reconsider their policy.*

reconstruct /ˌri:kən'strʌkt/ *verb* [T] **1** to build again sth that has been destroyed or damaged **2** to get a full description or picture of sth using the facts that are known: *The police are trying to reconstruct the victim's movements on the day of the murder.*

reconstruction /ˌri:kən'strʌkʃn/ *noun* [C,U] **1** the activity of building again sth that has been damaged or destroyed **2** a short film showing events that are known to have happened, made in order to try and get more information or better understanding: *a reconstruction of the crime using actors*

⚷ **record[1]** /'rekɔ:d/ *noun* **1** [C] a record (of sth) a written account of what has happened, been done, etc: *The teachers* ***keep records*** *of the children's progress.* ◆ *medical records* ◆ *It's* ***on record*** *that he was out of the country at the time of the murder.* **2** [C] the best performance or the highest or lowest level, etc. ever reached in sth, especially in sport: *Who* ***holds*** *the world* ***record for*** *high jump?* ◆ *She's hoping to* ***break the record*** *for the 100 metres.* ◆ *He did it* ***in record time*** (= very fast). **3** [C] the facts, events, etc. that are known (and sometimes written down) about sb/sth: *The police said that the man had* ***a criminal record*** (= he had been found guilty of crimes in the past). ◆ *This airline has a bad safety record.* **4** [C] a thin, round piece of plastic on which music is recorded: *a record collection*

IDM **off the record** (used about sth a person says) not to be treated as official; not intended to be made public: *She told me off the record that she was going to resign.*

put/set the record straight to correct a mistake by telling sb the true facts

⚷ **record[2]** /rɪ'kɔ:d/ *verb* **1** [T] to write down or film facts or events so that they can be referred to later and will not be forgotten: *He recorded everything in his diary.* ◆ *At the inquest the coroner* ***recorded a verdict*** *of accidental death.* **2** [I,T] to put music, a film, a programme, etc. onto a CD or DVD so that it can be listened to or watched again later: *Quiet, please! We're recording.* ◆ *The band has recently recorded a new album.* ◆ *There's a concert I would like to record from the radio this evening.*

'record-breaker *noun* [C] a person or thing that achieves a better result or higher level than has ever been achieved before ▶ **'record-breaking** *adj* [only *before* a noun] the best, fastest, highest, etc. ever: *We did the journey in record-breaking time.*

recorder /rɪ'kɔ:də(r)/ *noun* [C] **1** a machine for recording sound and/or pictures: *a tape/DVD/video recorder* **2** a type of musical instrument that is often played by children. You play it by blowing through it and covering the holes in it with your fingers. ➲ picture at **music**

⚷ **recording** /rɪ'kɔ:dɪŋ/ *noun* **1** [C] sound or pictures that have been put onto a CD, video, etc: *the Berlin Philharmonic's recording of Mahler's Sixth symphony* **2** [U] the process of making a CD, film, etc: *a recording session/studio*

'record label = **label[1]** (2)

'record player *noun* [C] a machine that you use for playing records in order to listen to music, etc. on them

recount /rɪ'kaʊnt/ *verb* [T] (*formal*) to tell a story or describe an event

recourse /rɪ'kɔ:s/ *noun* [U] (*formal*) the fact of having to use sth or ask sb for help in a difficult situation: *She made a complete recovery* ***without recourse to*** *surgery.*

⚷ **recover** /rɪ'kʌvə(r)/ *verb* **1** [I] recover (from sth) to become well again after you have been ill: *It took him two months to recover from the operation.* **2** [I] recover (from sth) to get back to normal again after a bad experience, etc: *The old lady never really recovered from the shock of being mugged.* **3** [T] recover sth (from sb/sth) to find or get back sth that was lost or stolen: *Police recovered the stolen goods from a warehouse in South London.* **4** [T] to get back the use of your senses, control of your emotions, etc: *He needs daily exercise if he's going to recover the use of his legs.*

recovery /rɪ'kʌvəri/ *noun* **1** [C,usually sing] recovery (from sth) a return to good health after an illness or to a normal state after a difficult period of time: *to* ***make a*** *good/quick/speedy/slow* ***recovery*** ◆ *She's* ***on the road to recovery*** (= getting better all the time) *now.* ◆ *the prospects of* ***economic recovery*** **2** [U] recovery (of sth/sb) getting back sth that was lost, stolen or missing

recreation /ˌrekri'eɪʃn/ *noun* [U,sing] the fact of enjoying yourself and relaxing when you are not working; a way of doing this: ***recreation activities*** *such as swimming or reading* ▶ **recreational** *adj*

recreˌational 'vehicle (*AmE*) = **camper**(2)

recrimination /rɪˌkrɪmɪ'neɪʃn/ *noun* [C,usually pl,U] an angry statement accusing sb of sth, especially in answer to a similar statement from them: *bitter recriminations*

recruit[1] /rɪ'kru:t/ *verb* [I,T] to find new people to join a company, an organization, the armed forces, etc: *to recruit young people to the teaching profession* ▶ **recruitment** *noun* [U]

recruit[2] /rɪ'kru:t/ *noun* [C] a person who has just joined the army or another organization

rectangle /ˈrektæŋgl/ *noun* [C] a shape with four straight sides and four **right angles** (= angles of 90°). Two of the sides are longer than the other two. SYN **oblong** ➲ picture at **shape** ▶ **rectangular** /rekˈtæŋgjələ(r)/ *adj*

rectify /ˈrektɪfaɪ/ *verb* [T] (rectifying; rectifies; *pt, pp* rectified) (*formal*) to correct sth that is wrong

rectum /ˈrektəm/ *noun* [C] the end section of the tube where solid food waste collects before leaving the body

recuperate /rɪˈkuːpəreɪt/ *verb* [I] (*formal*) recuperate (from sth) to get well again after an illness or injury ▶ **recuperation** /rɪˌkuːpəˈreɪʃn/ *noun* [U]

recur /rɪˈkɜː(r)/ *verb* [I] (recurring; recurred) to happen again or many times: *a recurring problem/nightmare* ▶ **recurrence** /rɪˈkʌrəns/ *noun* [C,U] ▶ **recurrent** /rɪˈkʌrənt/ *adj*

recycle /ˌriːˈsaɪkl/ *verb* [T] **1** to put used objects and materials through a process so that they can be used again: *recycled paper* ◆ *Aluminium cans can be recycled.* ➲ note at **environment** **2** to keep used objects and materials and use them again: *Don't throw away your plastic carrier bags—recycle them!* ▶ **recyclable** *adj*: *Most plastics are recyclable.* ▶ **recycling** *noun* [U]: *the recycling of glass* ◆ *a recycling bin*

red /red/ *adj, noun* [C,U] (redder; reddest) **1** (of) the colour of blood: *red wine* ◆ *She was dressed in red.* ➲ look at **crimson, maroon, scarlet** **2** a colour that some people's faces become when they are embarrassed, angry, shy, etc: *He went bright red when she spoke to him.* ◆ *to turn/be/go red in the face* **3** (used about sb's hair or an animal's fur) (of) a colour between red, orange and brown: *She's got red hair and freckles.*

IDM **be in the red** (*informal*) to have spent more money than you have in the bank, etc: *I'm £500 in the red at the moment.* OPP **be in the black**

catch sb red-handed ➲ **catch**[1]

a red herring an idea or subject which takes people's attention away from what is really important

see red ➲ **see**

ˌred ˈcard *noun* [C] (in football) a card that is shown to a player who is being sent off the field for doing sth wrong ➲ look at **yellow card**

the ˌred ˈcarpet *noun* [sing] a piece of red carpet that is put outside to receive an important visitor; a special welcome for an important visitor: *I didn't expect to be given the red carpet treatment!*

redcurrant /ˌredˈkʌrənt/ *noun* [C] a small round red fruit that you can eat: *redcurrant jelly*

redden /ˈredn/ *verb* [I,T] to become red or to make sth red ➲ **Go red** (or when talking about a person's face, **blush**) is more common.

reddish /ˈredɪʃ/ *adj* fairly red in colour

redeem /rɪˈdiːm/ *verb* [T] **1** to prevent sth from being completely bad: *The **redeeming feature** of the job is the good salary.* **2** redeem yourself to do sth to improve people's opinion of you, especially after you have done sth bad

redemption /rɪˈdempʃn/ *noun* [U] the act of being saved from evil

IDM **beyond redemption** too bad to be saved or improved

redevelop /ˌriːdɪˈveləp/ *verb* [T] to build or arrange an area, a town, a building, etc. in a different and more modern way: *They're redeveloping the city centre.* ▶ **redevelopment** *noun* [U]

redhead /ˈredhed/ *noun* [C] a person who has red hair

ˌred-ˈhot *adj* (used about a metal) so hot that it turns red

redial /ˌriːˈdaɪəl/ *verb* [I,T] to call the same telephone number again

redistribute /ˌriːdɪˈstrɪbjuːt; ˌriːˈdɪs-/ *verb* [T] to share sth out among people in a different way from before ▶ **redistribution** /ˌriːdɪstrɪˈbjuːʃn/ *noun* [U]

ˌred ˈpepper = **pepper**[1] (2)

ˌred ˈtape *noun* [U] official rules that must be followed which seem unnecessary and often cause delay and difficulty in achieving sth

reduce /rɪˈdjuːs/ *verb* [T] reduce sth (from sth) (to sth); reduce sth (by sth) to make sth less or smaller in quantity, price, size, etc: *The sign said 'Reduce speed now'.* ◆ *I bought this shirt because the price was reduced from £50 to £25.* OPP **increase**

PHR V **reduce sb/sth (from sth) to sth** [often passive] to force sb/sth into a particular state or condition, usually a bad one: *One of the older boys **reduced** the small child **to tears**.*

reduction /rɪˈdʌkʃn/ *noun* **1** [C,U] reduction (in sth) the act of becoming or making sth less or smaller: *a sharp reduction in the number of students* **2** [C] the amount by which sth is made smaller, especially in price: *There were massive reductions in the June sales.*

redundant /rɪˈdʌndənt/ *adj* **1** (*BrE*) (used about employees) no longer needed for a job and therefore out of work: *When the factory closed 800 people were **made redundant**.* ➲ note at **job** **2** not necessary or wanted ▶ **redundancy** /rɪˈdʌndənsi/ *noun* [C,U] (*pl* redundancies): *redundancy pay*

reed /riːd/ *noun* [C] **1** a tall plant, like grass, that grows in or near water **2** a thin piece of wood, metal or plastic at the end of some musical instruments which produces a sound when you blow through it ➲ picture at **music**

reef /riːf/ *noun* [C] a long line of rocks, plants, etc. just below or above the surface of the sea: *a coral reef*

reek /riːk/ *verb* [I] reek (of sth) to smell strongly of sth unpleasant: *His breath reeked of tobacco.* ▶ **reek** *noun* [sing]

reel[1] /riːl/ *noun* [C] a round object that thread, wire, film for cameras, etc. is put around: *a cotton reel* ◆ *a reel of film* ➲ look at **spool** ➲ picture at **garden, sewing**

R

reel² /riːl/ *verb* [I] **1** to walk without being able to control your legs, for example because you are drunk or you have been hit **2** to feel very shocked or upset about sth: *His mind was still reeling from the shock of seeing her again.*
PHR V **reel sth off** to say or repeat sth from memory quickly and without having to think about it: *She reeled off a long list of names.*

ref /ref/ (*informal*) = **referee**(1)

ref. /ref/ *abbr* = **reference**(3): *ref. no. 3456*

refer /rɪˈfɜː(r)/ *verb* (**referring; referred**)
PHR V **refer to sb/sth (as sth)** to mention or talk about sb/sth: *When he said 'some students', do you think he was referring to us?* ◆ *She always referred to Ben as 'that nice man'.*
refer to sb/sth 1 to describe or be connected with sb/sth: *The term 'adolescent' refers to young people between the ages of 12 and 17.* **2** to find out information by asking sb or by looking in a book, etc: *If you don't understand a word you may refer to your dictionaries.*
refer sb/sth to sb/sth to send sb/sth to sb/sth else for help or to be dealt with: *The doctor has referred me to a specialist.*

referee /ˌrefəˈriː/ *noun* [C] **1** (also *informal* **ref**) the official person in sports such as football who controls the match and prevents players from breaking the rules ➲ look at **umpire 2** (*BrE*) a person who gives information about your character and ability, usually in a letter, for example when you are hoping to be chosen for a job: *Her teacher agreed to **act as her referee**.* ▶ **referee** *verb* [I,T]

reference /ˈrefrəns/ *noun*
➤MENTIONING SB/STH **1** [C,U] (a) **reference (to sb/sth)** a written or spoken comment that mentions sb/sth: *The article **made a** direct **reference** to a certain member of the royal family.*
➤LOOKING FOR INFORMATION **2** [U] looking at sth for information: *The guidebook might be useful **for future reference**.*
➤IN BUSINESS **3** [C] (*abbr* **ref.**) a special number that identifies a letter, etc: *Please quote our reference when replying.*
➤FOR NEW JOB **4** [C] a statement or letter describing sb's character and ability that is given to a possible future employer: *My boss gave me a good reference.* ➲ note at **job**

TOPIC

References

When you apply for a job you are usually asked to **give references**.These are the job titles, names and addresses of two or more people who know you well. The new employer can contact them to check that you are suitable for new job.You can ask a teacher or a previous employer to give you a reference, but not a friend or a member of your family.

➤IN BOOK **5** [C] a note, especially in a book, that tells you where certain information came from or can be found: *There is a list of references at the end of each chapter.*
IDM **with reference to sb/sth** (*formal*) about or concerning sb/sth: *I am writing with reference to your letter of 10 April ...*

ˈreference book *noun* [C] a book that you use to find a piece of information: *dictionaries, encyclopedias and other reference books*

referendum /ˌrefəˈrendəm/ *noun* [C,U] (*pl* **referendums** *or* **referenda** /-də/) an occasion when all the people of a country can vote on a particular political question: *The government will hold a referendum on the issue.*

refill /ˌriːˈfɪl/ *verb* [T] to fill sth again: *Can I refill your glass?* ▶ **refill** /ˈriːfɪl/ *noun* [C]: *I'd like to buy a refill for my pen.*

refine /rɪˈfaɪn/ *verb* [T] **1** to make a substance pure and free from other substances: *to refine sugar/oil* **2** to improve sth by changing little details: *to refine a theory*

refined /rɪˈfaɪnd/ *adj* **1** (used about a substance) that has been made pure by having other substances taken out of it: *refined sugar/oil/flour* OPP **unrefined 2** (used about a person) polite; having very good manners **3** improved and therefore producing a better result

refinement /rɪˈfaɪnmənt/ *noun* **1** [C] a small change that improves sth: *The new model has electric windows and other refinements.* **2** [U] good manners and polite behaviour

refinery /rɪˈfaɪnəri/ *noun* [C] (*pl* **refineries**) a factory where a substance is made pure by having other substances taken out of it: *an oil/sugar refinery*

reflect /rɪˈflekt/ *verb* **1** [T, usually passive] **reflect sb/sth (in sth)** to show an image of sb/sth on the surface of sth such as a mirror, water or glass: *She caught sight of herself reflected in the shop window.* **2** [T] to send back light, heat or sound from a surface: *The windows reflected the bright morning sunlight.* **3** [T] to show or express sth: *His music reflects his interest in African culture.* **4** [I] **reflect (on/upon sth)** to think, especially deeply and carefully, about sth: *I really need some time to reflect on what you've said.*
PHR V **reflect (well, badly, etc.) on sb/sth** to give a particular impression of sb/sth: *It reflects badly on the whole school if some of its pupils misbehave in public.*

reflection /rɪˈflekʃn/ *noun* **1** [C] an image that you see in a mirror, in water or on a shiny surface: *He admired his reflection in the mirror.* **2** [U] the sending back of light, heat or sound from a surface **3** [C] a thing that shows what sb/sth is like: *Your clothes are a reflection of your personality.* **4** [sing] **a reflection on/upon sb/sth** something that causes people to form a good or bad opinion about sb/sth: *Parents often feel that their children's behaviour is a reflection on themselves.* **5** [U,C] careful thought about sth: *A week off would give her time for reflection.*
IDM **on reflection** after thinking again: *I think, on reflection, that we were wrong.*

reflective /rɪˈflektɪv/ *adj* **1** (*formal*) (used about a person, mood, etc.) thinking deeply about things: *a reflective expression* **2** (used about a surface) sending back light or heat: *Wear reflective strips when you're cycling at night.* **3** reflective (of sth) showing what sth is like

reflector /rɪˈflektə(r)/ *noun* [C] **1** a surface that **reflects** light, heat or sound that hits it **2** a small piece of glass or plastic on a bicycle or on clothing that can be seen at night when light shines on it

reflex /ˈriːfleks/ *noun* **1** [C] (also ˈreflex action) a sudden movement or action that you make without thinking: *She put her hands out as a reflex to stop her fall.* **2** reflexes [pl] the ability to act or move quickly when necessary: *A good tennis player needs to have excellent reflexes.*

ˌreflex ˈangle *noun* [C] an angle of more than 180° ➲ look at **acute angle**, **obtuse angle**, **right angle**

reflexion (*BrE*) = **reflection**

reflexive /rɪˈfleksɪv/ *adj* [C] (of a word or verb form) showing that the person who performs an action is also affected by it: *In 'He cut himself', 'cut' is a* ***reflexive verb*** *and 'himself' is a* ***reflexive pronoun****.*

reflexology /ˌriːfleksˈɒlədʒi/ *noun* [U] a type of treatment in which sb's feet are rubbed in a particular way in order to heal other parts of their body or to make them feel relaxed ▸ **reflexologist** /ˌriːfleksˈɒlədʒɪst/ *noun* [C]

⚷ **reform** /rɪˈfɔːm/ *verb* **1** [T] to change a system, the law, etc. in order to make it better: *to reform the examination system* **2** [I,T] to improve your behaviour; to make sb do this: *Our prisons aim to reform criminals, not simply to punish them.* ▸ **reform** *noun* [C,U]: *a major reform to the system*

reformer /rɪˈfɔːmə(r)/ *noun* [C] a person who tries to change society and make it better

refrain¹ /rɪˈfreɪn/ *verb* [I] (*formal*) refrain (from sth/doing sth) to stop yourself doing sth; to not do sth: *Please refrain from eating in the classroom.*

refrain² /rɪˈfreɪn/ *noun* [C] the part of a song that is repeated, usually at the end of each **verse** (= a group of lines that is not repeated) SYN **chorus**

refresh /rɪˈfreʃ/ *verb* **1** [T] to make sb/sth feel less tired or less hot and full of energy again: *He looked refreshed after a good night's sleep.* **2** [T,I] to get the most recent information, for example on an Internet page, usually by clicking on a button: *Click here to refresh this document.* ◆ *The page refreshes automatically.*

IDM **refresh your memory** to remind sb/yourself about sth: *Could you refresh my memory about what we said on this point last week?*

refreshing /rɪˈfreʃɪŋ/ *adj* **1** pleasantly new or different: *It makes* ***a refreshing change*** *to meet somebody who is so enthusiastic.* **2** making you feel less tired or hot: *a refreshing swim/shower/drink*

refreshment /rɪˈfreʃmənt/ *noun* **1** refreshments [pl] light food and drinks that are available at a cinema, theatre or other public place **2** [U] (*formal*) the fact of making sb feel stronger and less tired or hot; food or drink that helps to do this

refrigerate /rɪˈfrɪdʒəreɪt/ *verb* [T] to make food, etc. cold in order to keep it fresh ▸ **refrigeration** /rɪˌfrɪdʒəˈreɪʃn/ *noun* [U]: *Keep all meat products under refrigeration.*

refrigerator /rɪˈfrɪdʒəreɪtə(r)/ (*formal*) = **fridge**: *This dessert can be served straight from the refrigerator.*

refuge /ˈrefjuːdʒ/ *noun* [U,C] refuge (from sb/sth) protection from danger, trouble, etc.; a place that is safe: *We had to* ***take refuge*** *from the rain under a tree.* ◆ *a refuge for the homeless* SYN **shelter**

refugee /ˌrefjuˈdʒiː/ *noun* [C] a person who has been forced to leave their country for political or religious reasons, or because there is a war, not enough food, etc: *a refugee camp* ➲ look at **fugitive**, **exile**

refund /ˈriːfʌnd/ *noun* [C] a sum of money that is paid back to you, especially because you have paid too much or you are not happy with sth you have bought: *to claim/demand/get a refund* ➲ note at **shopping** ▸ **refund** /rɪˈfʌnd; ˈriːfʌnd/ *verb* [T] ▸ **refundable** /riːˈfʌndəbl/ *adj*: *The deposit is not refundable.*

refurbish /ˌriːˈfɜːbɪʃ/ *verb* [T] to clean and decorate a room, building, etc. in order to make it more attractive, more useful, etc. ▸ **refurbishment** *noun* [U,C]: *The hotel is now closed for refurbishment.*

⚷ **refusal** /rɪˈfjuːzl/ *noun* [U,C] (a) refusal (of sth); (a) refusal (to do sth) the act of saying or showing that you will not do, give or accept sth: *I can't understand her refusal to see me.*

⚷ **refuse¹** /rɪˈfjuːz/ *verb* [I,T] to say or show that you do not want to do, give or accept sth: *He refused to listen to what I was saying.* ◆ *My application for a grant has been refused.*

refuse² /ˈrefjuːs/ *noun* [U] (*formal*) things that you throw away; rubbish: *the refuse collection* (= when dustbins are emptied)

regain /rɪˈɡeɪn/ *verb* [T] to get sth back that you had lost: *to regain consciousness*

regal /ˈriːɡl/ *adj* very impressive; typical of or suitable for a king or queen

⚷ **regard¹** /rɪˈɡɑːd/ *verb* [T] **1** regard sb/sth as sth; regard sb/sth (with sth) to think of sb/sth (in the way mentioned): *Do you regard this issue as important?* ◆ *Her work is highly regarded* (= people have a high opinion of it). ◆ *In some villages newcomers are regarded with suspicion.* **2** (*formal*) to look at sb/sth for a while: *She regarded us with interest.*

IDM **as regards sb/sth** (*formal*) in connection with sb/sth: *What are your views as regards this proposal?*

⚷ **regard²** /rɪˈɡɑːd/ *noun* **1** [U] regard to/for sb/sth attention to or care for sb/sth: *He shows little regard for other people's feelings.* **2** [U, sing] (a) regard (for sb/sth) a feeling of admiration for sb/sth; respect: *She obviously* ***has*** *great* ***regard*** *for your ability.* **3** regards [pl] (used especially to end a letter

R

politely) kind thoughts; best wishes: *Please **give my regards to** your parents.* ◆ ***Kind regards,** Cecily*
IDM in/with regard to sb/sth; in this/that/one regard (*formal*) about sb/sth; connected with sb/sth: *With regard to the details—these will be finalized later.*

regarding /rɪˈɡɑːdɪŋ/ *prep* (*formal*) about or in connection with: *Please write if you require further information regarding this matter.*

regardless /rɪˈɡɑːdləs/ *adv, prep* **regardless (of sb/sth)** paying no attention to sb/sth; treating problems and difficulties as unimportant: *I suggested she should stop but she **carried on regardless**.* ◆ *Everybody will receive the same, regardless of how long they've worked here.*

regatta /rɪˈɡætə/ *noun* [C] an event at which there are boat races

regenerate /rɪˈdʒenəreɪt/ *verb* [I,T] to grow again; to make sth grow or grow strong again: *Once they have been destroyed, brain cells do not regenerate.* ◆ *The money will be used to regenerate the old part of the town.* ▶ **regeneration** /rɪæs:dʒenəˈreɪʃn/ *noun* [U]

reggae /ˈreɡeɪ/ *noun* [U] a type of West Indian music with a strong rhythm

regime /reɪˈʒiːm/ *noun* [C] a method or system of government: *a military/fascist regime*

regiment /ˈredʒɪmənt/ *noun* [C,with sing or pl verb] a group of soldiers in the army who are commanded by a **colonel** (= an officer of a high level) ▶ **regimental** /ˌredʒɪˈmentl/ *adj*

regimented /ˈredʒɪmentɪd/ *adj* (*formal*) (too) strictly controlled

region /ˈriːdʒən/ *noun* [C] **1** a part of the country or the world; a large area of land: *desert/tropical/polar regions* ◆ *This region of France is very mountainous.* ➲ note at **area** **2** an area of your body: *He's been having pains in the region of his heart.*
IDM in the region of sth about or approximately: *There were somewhere in the region of 30 000 people at the rally.*

regional /ˈriːdʒənl/ *adj* connected with a particular region: *regional accents* ➲ look at **local, international, national**

register¹ /ˈredʒɪstə(r)/ *verb*
➤ PUT NAME ON LIST **1** [I,T] to put a name on an official list: *You should register with a doctor nearby.* ◆ *All births, deaths and marriages must be registered.*
➤ MEASUREMENT **2** [I,T] to show sth or to be shown on a measuring instrument: *The thermometer registered 32°C.* ◆ *The earthquake registered 6.4 on the Richter scale.*
➤ SHOW FEELING **3** [T] to show feelings, opinions, etc: *Her face registered intense dislike.*
➤ NOTICE STH **4** [I,T] [often used in negative sentences] to notice sth and remember it; to be noticed and remembered: *He barely registered our presence.* ◆ *He told me his name but it didn't register.*
➤ LETTER **5** [T] to send a letter or package by registered mail: *Parcels containing valuable goods should be registered.*

register² /ˈredʒɪstə(r)/ *noun* **1** [C] an official list of names, etc. or a book that contains this kind of list: *The teacher calls the register first thing in the morning.* ◆ *the electoral register* (= of people who are able to vote in an election) **2** [C,U] the type of language (formal or informal) that is used in a piece of writing: *The essay suddenly switches from a formal to an informal register.*

ˌregistered ˈmail (*BrE also* **ˌregistered ˈpost**) *noun* [U] a method of sending a letter or package in which the person sending it can claim money if it arrives late or if it is lost or damaged

ˈregister office = **registry office**

registrar /ˌredʒɪˈstrɑː(r); ˈredʒɪstrɑː(r)/ *noun* [C] **1** a person whose job is to keep official lists, especially of births, marriages and deaths **2** a person who is responsible for keeping information about the students at a college or university

registration /ˌredʒɪˈstreɪʃn/ *noun* [U] putting sb/sth's name on an official list: *Registration for evening classes will take place on 8 September.*

ˌregiˈstration number *noun* [C] the numbers and letters on the front and back of a vehicle that are used to identify it

registry /ˈredʒɪstri/ *noun* [C] (*pl* **registries**) a place where official lists are kept

ˈregistry office (*also* **register office**) *noun* [C] an office where a marriage can take place and where births, marriages and deaths are officially written down ➲ note at **wedding**

regret¹ /rɪˈɡret/ *verb* [T] (**regretting**; **regretted**) **1** to feel sorry that you did sth or that you did not do sth: *I hope you won't regret your decision later.* ◆ *Do you regret not taking the job?* **2** (*formal*) used as a way of saying that you are sorry for sth: *I regret to inform you that your application has been unsuccessful.*

regret² /rɪˈɡret/ *noun* [C,U] a feeling of sadness about sth that cannot now be changed: *Do you **have any regrets** about not going to university?* ▶ **regretful** /-fl/ *adj*: *a regretful look/smile* ▶ **regretfully** /-fəli/ *adv*

regrettable /rɪˈɡretəbl/ *adj* that you should feel sorry or sad about: *It is deeply regrettable that we were not informed sooner.* ▶ **regrettably** /-əbli/ *adv*

regular¹ /ˈreɡjələ(r)/ *adj*
➤ AT SAME TIME **1** having the same amount of space or time between each thing or part: *a regular heartbeat* ◆ *Nurses checked her blood pressure **at regular intervals**.* ◆ *The fire alarms are tested **on a regular basis**.* ◆ *We have regular meetings every Thursday.* **OPP irregular**
➤ FREQUENT **2** done or happening often: *The doctor advised me to take regular exercise.* ◆ *Accidents are **a regular occurrence** on this road.* **3** [only *before* a noun] going somewhere or doing sth often: *a regular customer* ◆ *We're regular visitors to Britain.*
➤ USUAL **4** [only *before* a noun] normal or usual: *Who is your regular dentist?*
➤ SAME SHAPE **5** not having any individual part that is

different from the rest: *regular teeth/features* ♦ *a regular pattern* **OPP irregular**

➤PERMANENT **6** fixed or permanent: *a regular income/job* ♦ *a regular soldier/army*

➤ORDINARY **7** (*especially AmE*) standard, average or normal: *Regular or large fries?*

➤GRAMMAR **8** (used about a noun, verb, etc.) having the usual or expected plural, verb form, etc: *'Walk' is a regular verb.* **OPP irregular** ▶ **regularly** *adv*: *to have a car serviced regularly* ♦ *Ravi regularly takes part in competitions but this is the first one that he has won.* ▶ **regularity** /ˌregjuˈlærəti/ *noun* [U,C]: *My car breaks down with increasing regularity.*

regular² /ˈregjələ(r)/ *noun* [C] **1** (*informal*) a person who goes to a particular shop, bar, restaurant, etc. very often **2** a person who usually does a particular activity or sport **3** a permanent member of the army, navy, etc.

regulate /ˈregjuleɪt/ *verb* [T] **1** to control sth by using laws or rules **2** to control a machine, piece of equipment, etc: *You can regulate the temperature in the car with this dial.*

🔑 **regulation** /ˌregjuˈleɪʃn/ *noun* **1** [C, usually pl] an official rule that controls how sth is done: *to observe/obey the safety regulations* ♦ *The plans must comply with EU regulations.* **2** [U] the control of sth by using rules: *state regulation of imports and exports*

rehabilitate /ˌriːəˈbɪlɪteɪt/ *verb* [T] to help sb to live a normal life again after an illness, being in prison, etc. ▶ **rehabilitation** /ˌriːəˌbɪlɪˈteɪʃn/ *noun* [U]: *a rehabilitation centre for drug addicts*

rehearsal /rɪˈhɜːsl/ *noun* [C,U] the time when you practise a play, dance, piece of music, etc. before you perform it to other people: *a dress rehearsal* (= when all the actors wear their stage clothes) ▶ **rehearse** /rɪˈhɜːs/ *verb* [I,T]

reign /reɪn/ *verb* [I] **1** reign (over sb/sth) (used about a king or queen) to rule a country **2** reign (over sb/sth) to be the best or most important in a particular situation: *the reigning world champion* **3** to be present as the most important quality of a particular situation: *Chaos reigned after the first snow of winter.* ▶ **reign** *noun* [C]

reimburse /ˌriːɪmˈbɜːs/ *verb* [T] (*formal*) to pay money back to sb: *The company will reimburse you in full for your travelling expenses.*

rein /reɪn/ *noun* [C, usually pl] a long narrow leather band that is attached to a metal bar in a horse's mouth and is held by the rider in order to control the horse ➲ picture at **horse**

reincarnation /ˌriːɪnkɑːˈneɪʃn/ *noun* **1** [U] the belief that people who have died can live again in a different body: *Do you believe in reincarnation?* **2** [C] a person or an animal whose body is believed to contain the spirit of a dead person: *He believes he is the reincarnation of an Egyptian princess.* ➲ look at **incarnation**

reindeer

reindeer /ˈreɪndɪə(r)/ *noun* [C] (*pl* reindeer) a type of large brown wild animal with **antlers** (= horns shaped like branches), that lives in cold northern regions

reinforce /ˌriːɪnˈfɔːs/ *verb* [T] to make sth stronger: *Concrete can be reinforced with steel bars.* ♦ *She reinforced her argument with plenty of evidence.*

reinforcement /ˌriːɪnˈfɔːsmənt/ *noun* **1** reinforcements [pl] extra people who are sent to make an army, navy, etc. stronger **2** [U] the act of making sth stronger: *The sea wall is weak in places and needs reinforcement.*

reinstate /ˌriːɪnˈsteɪt/ *verb* [T] **1** reinstate sb (in/as sth) to give back a job or position that was taken from sb: *He was cleared of the charge of theft and reinstated as Head of Security.* **2** to return sth to its former position or role ▶ **reinstatement** *noun* [U]

🔑 **reject¹** /rɪˈdʒekt/ *verb* [T] to refuse to accept sb/sth: *The plan was rejected as being impractical.* ♦ *I've rejected all the candidates for the job except one.* ▶ **rejection** *noun* [C,U]: *Gargi got a rejection from Leeds University.* ♦ *There has been total rejection of the new policy.*

reject² /ˈriːdʒekt/ *noun* [C] a person or thing that is not accepted because he/she/it is not good enough: *Rejects are sold at half price.*

rejoice /rɪˈdʒɔɪs/ *verb* [I] (*formal*) rejoice (at/over sth) to feel or show great happiness ▶ **rejoicing** *noun* [U]: *There were scenes of rejoicing when the war ended.*

rejuvenate /rɪˈdʒuːvəneɪt/ *verb* [T, often passive] to make sb/sth feel or look younger ▶ **rejuvenation** /rɪˌdʒuːvəˈneɪʃn/ *noun* [U]

relapse /rɪˈlæps/ *verb* [I] to become worse again after an improvement: *to relapse into bad habits* ▶ **relapse** /ˈriːlæps/ *noun* [C]: *The patient had a relapse and then died.*

🔑 **relate** /rɪˈleɪt/ *verb* [T] **1** relate A to/with B to show or make a connection between two or more things: *The report relates heart disease to high levels of stress.* **2** (*formal*) relate sth (to sb) to tell a story to sb: *He related his side of the story to a journalist.*

PHR V relate to sb/sth 1 to be concerned or involved with sth: *That question is very interesting but it doesn't really relate to the subject that we're discussing.* **2** to be able to understand how sb feels: *Some teenagers find it hard to relate to their parents.*

🔑 **related** /rɪˈleɪtɪd/ *adj* related (to sb/sth) **1** connected with sb/sth: *The rise in the cost of living is directly related to the price of oil.* **2** of the same family: *We are related by marriage.*

🔑 **relation** /rɪˈleɪʃn/ *noun* **1** relations [pl] relations (with sb); relations (between A and B) the way that people, groups, countries, etc. feel about or behave towards each other: *The police officer stressed that good relations with the community were essential.* **2** [C,U] relation (between sth and sth); relation (to sth) the connection between two or more things: *There seems to be little relation between the cost of the houses and their size.* ♦ *Their salaries* ***bear no relation*** *to the number of hours they work.* **3** [C] a

R

member of your family: *a near/close/distant relation* **SYN relative**

HELP Note the expressions: *What relation are you to each other? (= Are you sisters, cousins, etc.?)* and *Are you any relation to each other?*

IDM in/with relation to sb/sth 1 concerning sb/sth: *Many questions were asked, particularly in relation to the cost of the new buildings.* **2** compared with: *Prices are low in relation to those in other parts of Europe.*

relationship /rɪˈleɪʃnʃɪp/ *noun* **1** [C] a relationship (with sb/sth); a relationship (between A and B) the way that people, groups, countries, etc. feel about or behave towards each other: *The relationship between the parents and the school has improved greatly.* **2** [C] a relationship (with sb); a relationship (between A and B) a friendly or loving connection between people: *to **have a relationship** with somebody* ◆ *He'd never been **in a** serious **relationship** before he got married.* ◆ *The film describes the relationship between a young man and an older woman.* ◆ *Do you have a close relationship with your brother?* **3** [C,U] a relationship (to sth); a relationship (between A and B) the way in which two or more things are connected: *Is there a relationship between violence on TV and the increase in crime?* **4** [C,U] a relationship (to sb); a relationship (between A and B) a family connection: *'What is your relationship to Bruce?' 'He's married to my cousin.'*

relative¹ /ˈrelətɪv/ *adj* **1** relative (to sth) when compared to sb/sth else: *the position of the earth relative to the sun* ◆ *They live in relative luxury.* **2** referring to an earlier noun, phrase or sentence: *In the phrase 'the lady who lives next door', 'who' is a relative pronoun.* ℹ For more information about relative pronouns and clauses, look at the **Reference Section** at the back of this dictionary.

relative² /ˈrelətɪv/ *noun* [C] a member of your family: *a close/distant relative* **SYN relation**

relatively /ˈrelətɪvli/ *adv* to quite a large degree, especially when compared to others: *Spanish is a relatively easy language to learn.*

relax /rɪˈlæks/ *verb* **1** [I] to rest while you are doing sth enjoyable, especially after work or effort: *This holiday will give you a chance to relax.* ◆ *They spent the evening relaxing in front of the TV.* **SYN unwind** **2** [I] to become calmer and less worried: *Relax—everything's going to be OK!*

MORE In informal English **chill out** and **take it easy** can be used instead of **relax**.

3 [I,T] to become or make sb/sth become less hard or tight: *You should be able to feel all your muscles relaxing.* ◆ *A hot bath will relax you after a hard day's work.* ◆ *Don't relax your grip on the rope!* **4** [T] to make rules or laws less strict: *The regulations on importing animals have been relaxed.*

relaxation /ˌriːlækˈseɪʃn/ *noun* **1** [C,U] a way or ways to rest and enjoy yourself, especially after work or effort: *Everyone needs time for rest and relaxation.* **2** [U] making sth less strict, tight or strong

relaxed /rɪˈlækst/ *adj* not worried or tense: *I felt surprisingly relaxed before my interview.* ◆ *The relaxed atmosphere made everyone feel at ease.* **SYN calm** ➲ look at **stressed**

relaxing /rɪˈlæksɪŋ/ *adj* pleasant, helping you to rest and become less worried: *a quiet relaxing holiday*

relay¹ /rɪˈleɪ; ˈriːleɪ/ *verb* [T] (*pt, pp* **relayed**) **1** to receive and then pass on a signal or message: *Instructions were relayed to us by phone.* **2** to put a programme on the radio or TV

relay² /ˈriːleɪ/ (also ˈ**relay race**) *noun* [C] a race in which each member of a team runs, swims, etc. one part of the race

release¹ /rɪˈliːs/ *verb* [T]
➤ SET FREE **1** release sb/sth (from sth) to allow sb/sth to be free: *He's been released from prison.* ◆ *(figurative) His firm released him for two days a week to go on a training course.*
➤ STOP HOLDING STH **2** to stop holding sth so that it can move, fly, fall, etc. freely: *1 000 balloons were released at the ceremony.* ◆ *(figurative) Crying is a good way to release pent-up emotions.*
➤ MOVE STH **3** to move sth from a fixed position: *He released the handbrake and drove off.*
➤ MAKE PUBLIC **4** to allow sth to be known by the public: *The identity of the victim has not been released.* **5** to make a film, CD, etc. available so the public can see or hear it: *Their new album is due to be released next week.*

release² /rɪˈliːs/ *noun* [C,U] **1** (a) release (of sb/sth) (from sth) the freeing of sb/sth or the state of being freed: *The release of the hostages took place this morning.* ◆ *the release of carbon dioxide into the atmosphere* ◆ *I had a great feeling of release when my exams were finished.* **2** a book, film, CD, piece of news, etc. that has been made available to the public; the act of making sth available to the public: *a press release* ◆ *The band played their latest release.* ◆ *The film won't **be/go on release** until March.*

relegate /ˈrelɪɡeɪt/ *verb* [T] to put sb/sth into a lower level or position: *She was relegated to the role of assistant.* ◆ *The football team finished bottom and were relegated to the second division.* ▶ **relegation** /ˌrelɪˈɡeɪʃn/ *noun* [U]

relent /rɪˈlent/ *verb* [I] **1** to finally agree to sth that you had refused: *Her parents finally relented and allowed her to go to the concert.* **2** to become less determined, strong, etc: *The heavy rain finally relented and we went out.*

relentless /rɪˈlentləs/ *adj* not stopping or changing: *the relentless fight against crime* ▶ **relentlessly** *adv*: *The sun beat down relentlessly.*

relevant /ˈreləvənt/ *adj* relevant (to sb/sth) **1** connected with what is happening or being talked about: *Much of what was said was not directly relevant to my case.* **2** important and useful: *Many people feel that poetry is no longer relevant in today's world.* **OPP** for both meanings **irrelevant** ▶ **relevance** *noun* [U]: *I honestly can't see the relevance of what he said.*

R

EXAM TIP

Relevant information

When you are writing or speaking in an exam, it is important to only include relevant information in your answers. If you give information that is not relevant, you risk wasting time and losing marks.

reliable /rɪˈlaɪəbl/ *adj* that you can trust: *Japanese cars are usually very reliable.* ♦ *Is he a reliable witness?* OPP **unreliable** ➲ *verb* **rely** ▸ **reliability** /rɪˌlaɪəˈbɪləti/ *noun* [U] ▸ **reliably** /rɪˈlaɪəbli/ *adv*: *I have been reliably informed that there will be no trains tomorrow.*

reliance /rɪˈlaɪəns/ *noun* [U] **reliance on sb/sth** **1** being able to trust sb/sth: *Don't* ***place*** *too much* ***reliance*** *on her promises.* **2** the fact of not being able to live or work without sb/sth: *the country's reliance on imported oil* SYN **dependence** ➲ *verb* **rely**

reliant /rɪˈlaɪənt/ *adj* **reliant on sb/sth** not able to live or work without sb/sth: *They are totally reliant on the state for financial support.* SYN **dependent** ➲ look at **self-reliant** ➲ *verb* **rely**

relic /ˈrelɪk/ *noun* [C] an object, custom, etc. from the past that still survives today

relief /rɪˈliːf/ *noun* **1** [U,sing] **relief (from sth)** the feeling that you have when sth unpleasant stops or becomes less strong: *The drugs brought him some relief from the pain.* ♦ ***What a relief!*** *That awful noise has stopped.* ♦ *It was a great relief to know they were safe.* ♦ *to breathe* ***a sigh of relief*** ♦ ***To my relief***, *he didn't argue with my suggestion at all.* **2** [U] the act of removing or reducing pain, worry, etc: *These tablets provide pain relief for up to four hours.* **3** [U] money or food that is given to help people who are in trouble or difficulty: *disaster relief for the flood victims* SYN **aid** **4** [U] a reduction in the amount of tax you have to pay

relieve /rɪˈliːv/ *verb* [T] to make an unpleasant feeling or situation stop or get better: *This injection should* ***relieve the pain.*** ♦ *We played cards to relieve the boredom.*

PHR V **relieve sb of sth** (*formal*) to take sth away from sb: *General Scott was relieved of his command.*

relieved /rɪˈliːvd/ *adj* pleased because your fear or worry has been taken away: *I was very relieved to hear that you weren't seriously hurt.*

religion /rɪˈlɪdʒən/ *noun* **1** [U] the belief in a god or gods and the activities connected with this: *I never discuss politics or religion.* **2** [C] one of the systems of beliefs that is based on a belief in a god or gods: *the Christian/Hindu/Muslim/Sikh religion*

religious /rɪˈlɪdʒəs/ *adj* **1** [only *before* a noun] connected with religion: *religious faith* **2** having a strong belief in a religion: *a deeply religious person*

religiously /rɪˈlɪdʒəsli/ *adv* **1** very carefully or regularly: *She stuck to the diet religiously.* **2** in a religious way

relinquish /rɪˈlɪŋkwɪʃ/ *verb* [T] (*formal*) to stop having or doing sth ➲ A more common expression is **give up**.

relish¹ /ˈrelɪʃ/ *verb* [T] to enjoy sth very much or wait with pleasure for sth to happen: *I don't* ***relish the prospect*** *of getting up early tomorrow.*

relish² /ˈrelɪʃ/ *noun* **1** [U] (*written*) great enjoyment: *She accepted the award with obvious relish.* **2** [U,C] a thick, cold sauce made from fruit and vegetables

relive /ˌriːˈlɪv/ *verb* [T] to remember sth and imagine that it is happening again

reload /ˌriːˈləʊd/ *verb* [I,T] to put sth into a machine again: *The shooting stopped while he reloaded.* ♦ *to reload a disk into a computer*

reluctant /rɪˈlʌktənt/ *adj* **reluctant (to do sth)** not wanting to do sth because you are not sure it is the right thing to do ▸ **reluctance** *noun* [U]: *Tony left* ***with obvious reluctance.*** ▸ **reluctantly** *adv*

rely /rɪˈlaɪ/ *verb* [I] (**relying**; **relies**; *pt, pp* **relied**)

PHR V **rely on/upon sb/sth (to do sth)** **1** to need sb/sth and not be able to live or work properly without them or it: *The old lady had to rely on other people to do her shopping for her.* **2** to trust sb/sth to work or behave well: *Can I rely on you to keep a secret?* ➲ look at **reliable, reliant** ➲ *noun* **reliance**

remain /rɪˈmeɪn/ *verb* [I] **1** to stay or continue in the same place or condition: *to remain silent/standing/seated* ♦ *Josef went to live in America but his family remained behind in Europe.* ➲ note at **stay** **2** to be left after other people or things have gone: *Today only a few stones remain of the castle.* ♦ *to remain behind after class* **3** to still need to be done, said or dealt with: *It* ***remains to be seen*** (= we do not know yet) *whether we've made the right decision.* ♦ *Although he seems very pleasant,* ***the fact remains*** *that I don't trust him.*

remainder /rɪˈmeɪndə(r)/ *noun* [sing, with sing or pl verb] *usually* **the remainder** the people, things, etc. that are left after the others have gone away or been dealt with; the rest

remaining /rɪˈmeɪnɪŋ/ *adj* [only *before* a noun] still needing to be done or dealt with: *The remaining twenty patients were transferred to another hospital.* ♦ *Any remaining tickets for the concert will be sold on the door.*

remains /rɪˈmeɪnz/ *noun* [pl] **1** what is left behind after other parts have been used or taken away: *The builders found the remains of a Roman mosaic floor.* **2** (*formal*) a dead body (sometimes one that has been found somewhere a long time after death): *Human remains were discovered in the wood.*

remand /rɪˈmɑːnd/ *noun* [U] the time before a prisoner's trial takes place: *a remand prisoner*

IDM **on remand** (used about a prisoner) waiting for the trial to take place

▸ **remand** *verb* [T]: *The man was* ***remanded in custody*** (= kept in prison until the trial).

remark¹ /rɪˈmɑːk/ *verb* [I,T] **remark (on/upon sb/sth)** to say or write sth: *A lot of people have remarked*

R

on the similarity between them. SYN **comment** ➲ look at **observation**

remark² /rɪˈmɑːk/ *noun* [C] something that you say or write about sb/sth: *The teacher added a few personal remarks at the bottom of the page.* ◆ *He made a number of rude remarks about the food.*

remarkable /rɪˈmɑːkəbl/ *adj* unusual and surprising in a way that people notice: *That is a remarkable achievement for someone so young.* SYN **astonishing** ▶ **remarkably** /-əbli/ *adv*

remedial /rɪˈmiːdiəl/ *adj* [only *before* a noun] **1** aimed at improving or correcting a situation **2** helping people who are slow at learning sth: *remedial English classes*

remedy¹ /ˈremədi/ *noun* [C] (*pl* **remedies**) **a remedy (for sth) 1** a way of solving a problem: *There is no easy remedy for unemployment.* SYN **solution 2** something that makes you better when you are ill or in pain: *Hot lemon with honey is a good remedy for colds.*

remedy² /ˈremədi/ *verb* [T] (**remedying; remedies;** *pt, pp* **remedied**) to change or improve sth that is wrong or bad: *to remedy an injustice*

remember /rɪˈmembə(r)/ *verb* [I,T] **1 remember (sb/sth); remember (doing sth); remember that …** to have sb/sth in your mind or to bring sb/sth back into your mind: *We arranged to go out tonight—remember?* ◆ ***As far as I can remember,*** *I haven't seen him before.* ◆ *I'm sorry. I don't remember your name.* ◆ *Do you remember meeting him for the first time?* ◆ *Remember that we're having visitors tonight.* ◆ *Can you remember when we bought the stereo?* **2 remember (sth/to do sth)** to not forget to do what you have to do: *Did you remember your camera?* ◆ *Remember to turn the lights off before you leave.*

R

GRAMMAR If you **remember to do sth**, you don't forget to do it: *It's my mother's birthday. I must remember to phone her.* If you **remember doing sth**, you have a picture or memory in your mind of doing it: *Do you remember going to the cinema for the first time?*

IDM **remember me to sb** used when you want to send good wishes to a person you have not seen for a long time: *Please remember me to your parents.* ➲ note at **remind**

remembrance /rɪˈmembrəns/ *noun* [U] (*formal*) thinking about and showing respect for sb who is dead: *a service* ***in remembrance of*** *those killed in the war*

remind /rɪˈmaɪnd/ *verb* [T] **1 remind sb (about/of sth); remind sb (to do sth/that …)** to help sb to remember sth, especially sth important that they have to do: *Can you remind me of your address?* ◆ *He reminded the children to wash their hands.* ◆ *Remind me what we're supposed to be doing tomorrow.* **2 remind sb of sb/sth** to cause sb to remember sb/sth: *That smell reminds me of school.* ◆ *You remind me of your father.*

HELP You **remember** something by yourself. If somebody or something **reminds** you of something, he/she/it causes you to remember it: *Did you remember to phone Ali last night?* ◆ *Please remind me to phone Ali later.*

reminder /rɪˈmaɪndə(r)/ *noun* [C] something that makes you remember sth: *We received a reminder that we hadn't paid the electricity bill.*

reminisce /ˌremɪˈnɪs/ *verb* [I] **reminisce (about sb/sth)** to talk about pleasant things that happened in the past

reminiscent /ˌremɪˈnɪsnt/ *adj* [not before a noun] that makes you remember sb/sth; similar to: *His suit was strongly reminiscent of an old army uniform.*

remnant /ˈremnənt/ *noun* [C] a piece of sth that is left after the rest has gone: *These few trees are the remnants of a huge forest.*

remorse /rɪˈmɔːs/ *noun* [U] **remorse (for sth/doing sth)** a feeling of sadness because you have done sth wrong: *She was filled with remorse for what she had done.* ➲ look at **guilt** ▶ **remorseful** /-fl/ *adj* ▶ **remorsefully** /-fəli/ *adv*

remorseless /rɪˈmɔːsləs/ *adj* **1** not stopping or becoming less strong: *a remorseless attack on somebody* **2** showing no pity: *a remorseless killer* ▶ **remorselessly** *adv*

remote /rɪˈməʊt/ *adj* (**remoter; remotest**) **1 remote (from sth)** far away from where other people live: *a remote island in the Pacific* **2** [only *before* a noun] far away in time: *the remote past/future* **3** not very friendly or interested in other people: *He seemed rather remote.* **4** not very great: *I haven't* ***the remotest*** *idea who could have done such a thing.* ◆ *a remote possibility* ▶ **remoteness** *noun* [U]

reˌmote conˈtrol *noun* **1** [U] a system for controlling sth from a distance: *The doors can be opened by remote control.* **2** (also **remote**) [C] a piece of equipment for controlling sth from a distance

remotely /rɪˈməʊtli/ *adv* (used in negative sentences) to a very small degree; at all: *I'm not remotely interested in your problems.*

removal /rɪˈmuːvl/ *noun* **1** [U] the act of taking sb/sth away: *the removal of restrictions/regulations/rights* **2** [C,U] the activity of moving from one house to live in another: *a removal van*

remove /rɪˈmuːv/ *verb* [T] (*formal*) **1 remove sb/sth (from sth)** to take sb/sth off or away: *Remove the saucepan from the heat.* ◆ *This washing powder will remove most stains.* ◆ *to remove doubts/fears/problems* ◆ *I would like you to remove my name from your mailing list.* ◆ *He had an operation to remove the tumour.* ➲ Less formal expressions are **take off, out, etc.**. **2 remove sb (from sth)** to make sb leave their job or position: *The person responsible for the error has been removed from his post.*

removed /rɪˈmuːvd/ *adj* [not before a noun] far or different from sth: *Hospitals today are* ***far removed from*** *what they were fifty years ago.*

remover /rɪˈmuːvə(r)/ *noun* [C,U] a substance that cleans off paint, dirty marks, etc: *make-up remover*

the Renaissance /rɪˈneɪsns/ *noun* [sing] the period in Europe during the 14th, 15th and 16th centuries when people became interested in the ideas and culture of ancient Greece and Rome, and used these influences in their own art, literature, etc: *Renaissance art*

render /ˈrendə(r)/ *verb* [T] (*formal*) **1** to cause sb/sth to be in a certain condition: *She was rendered speechless by the criticism.* **2** to give help, etc. to sb: *to render somebody a service/render a service to somebody*

rendezvous /ˈrɒndɪvuː; -deɪ-/ *noun* [C] (*pl* rendezvous /-vuːz/) **1** a rendezvous (with sb) a meeting that you have arranged with sb: *He had a secret rendezvous with Daniela.* **2** a place where people often meet: *The cafe is a popular rendezvous for students.*

rendition /renˈdɪʃn/ *noun* [C] the performance of sth, especially a song or piece of music; the particular way in which it is performed

renegade /ˈrenɪgeɪd/ *noun* [C] [often used as an adjective] (*formal*) (usually used in a critical way) a person who leaves one political, religious, etc. group to join another that has very different views or beliefs

renew /rɪˈnjuː/ *verb* [T] **1** to start sth again: *renewed outbreaks of violence* ◆ *to renew a friendship* **2** to do sth with new strength or energy: *After a break he set to work with renewed enthusiasm.* **3** to make sth valid for a further period of time: *to renew a contract/passport/library book* ▶ **renewal** /rɪˈnjuːəl/ *noun* [C,U]: *When is your passport due for renewal?*

renewable /rɪˈnjuːəbl/ *adj* **1** (used about sources of energy) that can be replaced naturally: *renewable resources such as wind and solar power* **OPP** **non-renewable** ➲ note at **environment** **2** that can be continued or replaced with a new one for another period of time: *The contract is for two years but it is renewable.*

renounce /rɪˈnaʊns/ *verb* [T] (*formal*) to say formally that you no longer want to have sth or to be connected with sb/sth ➲ *noun* **renunciation**

renovate /ˈrenəveɪt/ *verb* [T] to repair an old building and put it back into good condition ➲ note at **house** ▶ **renovation** /ˌrenəˈveɪʃn/ *noun* [C,U]: *The house is in need of renovation.*

renown /rɪˈnaʊn/ *noun* [U] (*formal*) fame and respect that you get for doing sth especially well ▶ **renowned** *adj* renowned (for/as sth): *The region is renowned for its food.*

rent¹ /rent/ *noun* [U,C] money that you pay regularly for the use of land, a house or a building: *a high/low rent* ◆ *She was allowed to live there* ***rent-free*** *until she found a job.* ◆ *Is this house* ***for rent*** (= available to rent)?

rent² /rent/ *verb* [T] **1** rent sth (from sb) to pay money for the use of land, a building, a machine, etc: *Do you own or rent your flat?* ◆ *to rent a car* ➲ note at **flat**, **hire** **2** rent sth (out) (to sb) to allow sb to use land, a building, a machine, etc. for money: *We could rent out the small bedroom to a student.* ➲ look at **hire 3** (*AmE*) = **hire¹**(1) ▶ **rented** *adj*: *a rented house*

rental /ˈrentl/ *noun* [C,U] money that you pay when you rent a telephone, car, etc.

renunciation /rɪˌnʌnsiˈeɪʃn/ *noun* [U] (*formal*) saying that you no longer want sth or believe in sth ➲ *verb* **renounce**

reorganize (also -ise) /riˈɔːgənaɪz/ *verb* [I,T] to organize sth again or in a new way ▶ **reorganization** (also -isation) /riˌɔːgənaɪˈzeɪʃn/ *noun* [C,U]: *reorganization of the school system*

Rep. *abbr* = **Republican**(2)

rep /rep/ (also *formal* representative) *noun* [C] a person whose job is to travel round a particular area and visit companies, etc., to sell the products of a particular firm: *a sales rep for a drinks company*

repair¹ /rɪˈpeə(r)/ *verb* [T] to put sth old or damaged back into good condition: *These cars can be expensive to repair.* ◆ *How much will it cost to have the TV repaired?* **SYN** **fix, mend** ➲ look at **irreparable**

repair² /rɪˈpeə(r)/ *noun* [C,U] something that you do to fix sth that is damaged: *The school is closed for repairs to the roof.* ◆ *The road is* ***in need of repair.*** ◆ *The bridge is* ***under repair.*** ◆ *The bike was damaged* ***beyond repair*** *so I threw it away.*

IDM **in good, bad, etc. repair** in a good, bad, etc. condition

repatriate /ˌriːˈpætrieɪt/ *verb* [T] to send or bring sb back to their own country ▶ **repatriation** /ˌriːˌpætriˈeɪʃn/ *noun* [C,U]

repay /rɪˈpeɪ/ *verb* [T] (*pt, pp* repaid /rɪˈpeɪd/) **1** repay sth (to sb); repay (sb) sth to pay back money that you owe to sb: *to repay a debt/loan* ◆ *When will you repay the money to them?* ◆ *When will you repay them the money?* **2** repay sb (for sth) to give sth to sb in return for help, kindness, etc: *How can I ever repay you for all you have done for me?*

repayable /rɪˈpeɪəbl/ *adj* that you can or must pay back: *The loan is repayable over three years.*

repayment /rɪˈpeɪmənt/ *noun* **1** [U] paying sth back: *the repayment of a loan* **2** [C] money that you must pay back to sb/sth regularly: *I make monthly repayments on my loan.*

repeal /rɪˈpiːl/ *verb* [T] (*formal*) to officially make a law no longer valid

repeat¹ /rɪˈpiːt/ *verb* **1** [I,T] repeat (sth/yourself) to say, write or do sth again or more than once: *Don't repeat the same mistake again.* ◆ *Could you repeat what you just said?* ◆ *The essay is quite good, but you repeat yourself several times.* ◆ *Raise your left leg ten times, then repeat with the right.* **2** [T] repeat sth (to sb) to say or write sth that sb else has said or written or that you have learnt: *Please don't repeat what you've heard here to anyone.* ◆ *Repeat each sentence after me.* ➲ *noun* **repetition**

R

repeat² /rɪˈpiːt/ *noun* [C] something that is done, shown, given, etc. again: *I think I've seen this programme before—it must be a repeat.*

repeated /rɪˈpiːtɪd/ *adj* [only *before* a noun] done or happening many times: *There have been repeated accidents on this stretch of road.* ▶ **repeatedly** *adv*: *I've asked him repeatedly not to leave his bicycle there.*

repel /rɪˈpel/ *verb* [T] (repelling; repelled) **1** to send or push sb/sth back or away **2** to make sb feel disgusted: *The dirt and smell repelled her.* ➲ *adjective* **repulsive**

repellent¹ /rɪˈpelənt/ *adj* (*formal*) causing a strong feeling of disgust: *a repellent smell*

repellent² /rɪˈpelənt/ *noun* [C,U] a chemical substance that is used to keep insects, etc. away: *a mosquito repellent*

repent /rɪˈpent/ *verb* [I,T] (*formal*) repent (sth/of sth) to feel and show that you are sorry about sth bad that you have done: *He later repented his hasty decision.* ◆ *to repent of your sins* ▶ **repentance** *noun* [U] ▶ **repentant** *adj*

repercussion /ˌriːpəˈkʌʃn/ *noun* [C, usually pl] an unpleasant effect or result of sth you do: *His resignation will* ***have*** *serious* ***repercussions****.*

repertoire /ˈrepətwɑː(r)/ *noun* [C] **1** all the plays or music that an actor or a musician knows and can perform: *He must have sung every song in his repertoire last night.* **2** all the things that a person is able to do

repetition /ˌrepəˈtɪʃn/ *noun* [U,C] the action of doing sth again; something that you do or that happens again: *to learn by repetition* ◆ *Let's try to avoid a repetition of what happened last Friday.* ▶ **repetitious** /ˌrepəˈtɪʃəs/ *adj*: *a long and repetitious speech* ➲ *verb* **repeat**

repetitive /rɪˈpetətɪv/ *adj* not interesting because the same thing is repeated many times

rephrase /ˌriːˈfreɪz/ *verb* [T] to say or write sth using different words in order to make the meaning clearer

replace /rɪˈpleɪs/ *verb* [T] **1** to take the place of sb/sth; to use sb/sth in place of another person or thing: *Teachers will never be replaced by computers in the classroom.* **2** replace sb/sth (with/by sb/sth) to exchange sb/sth for sb/sth that is better or newer: *We will replace any goods that are damaged.* **3** to put sth back in the place where it was before: *Please replace the books on the shelves when you have finished with them.* ➲ A more common and less formal expression is **put back**.

replaceable /rɪˈpleɪsəbl/ *adj* that can be replaced OPP **irreplaceable**

replacement /rɪˈpleɪsmənt/ *noun* **1** [U] exchanging sb/sth for sb/sth that is better or newer: *The carpets are in need of replacement.* **2** [C] a person or thing that will take the place of sb/sth: *Mary is leaving next month so we must advertise for a replacement for her.*

replay¹ /ˈriːpleɪ/ *noun* [C] **1** a sports match that is played again because neither team won the first time **2** something on TV, on a DVD, etc. that you watch or listen to again: *Now let's see* ***an action replay*** *of that tremendous goal!*

replay² /ˌriːˈpleɪ/ *verb* [T] **1** to play a sports match, etc. again because neither team won the first time **2** to play again sth that you have recorded: *They kept replaying the goal over and over again.*

replenish /rɪˈplenɪʃ/ *verb* [T] replenish sth (with sth) (*formal*) to make sth full again by replacing what has been used: *to replenish food and water supplies*

replica /ˈreplɪkə/ *noun* [C] a replica (of sth) an exact copy of sth

replicate /ˈreplɪkeɪt/ *verb* [T] (*formal*) to copy sth exactly SYN **duplicate** ▶ **replication** /ˌreplɪˈkeɪʃn/ *noun* [U]

reply /rɪˈplaɪ/ *verb* [I,T] (replying; replies; *pt, pp* replied) reply (to sb/sth) (with sth) to say, write or do sth as an answer to sb/sth: *I wrote to Sue but she hasn't replied.* ◆ *'Yes, I will,' she replied.* ◆ *to reply to a question* ◆ *Brazil replied to Chile's early goal with a penalty.* ➲ note at **answer²** ▶ **reply** *noun* [C,U] (*pl* replies): *Al nodded* ***in reply to*** *my question.*

report¹ /rɪˈpɔːt/ *verb* **1** [I,T] report (to sb/sth)(on sb/sth); report sth (to sb) to give people information about what you have seen, heard, done, etc: *The research team will report to the committee on their findings next month.* ◆ *The company reported huge profits last year.* ◆ *Several people reported seeing/having seen the boy.* ◆ *Several people reported that they had seen the boy.* ◆ *Call me if you have anything new to report.* **2** [I,T] report (on) sth (in a newspaper or on the TV or radio) to write or speak about sth that has happened: *The paper sent a journalist to report on the events.* **3** [T] (*formal*) be reported to be/as sth used to say that you have heard sth said, but you are not sure if it is true: *The 70-year-old actor is reported to be/as being comfortable in hospital.* **4** [T] report sb/sth (to sb) (for sth) to tell a person in authority about an accident, a crime, etc. or about sth wrong that sb has done: *Someone reported her to the head teacher for cheating.* ◆ *The boy was reported missing early this morning.* ◆ *All accidents must be reported to the police.* **5** [I] report (to sb/sth) for sth to tell sb that you have arrived: *On your arrival, please report to the reception desk.*

PHR V **report back (on sth) (to sb)** to give information to sb about sth they have asked you to find out about: *One person in each group will then report back on what you've decided to the class.*

report to sb [not used in the continuous tenses] to have sb as your manager in the company or organization that you work for

report² /rɪˈpɔːt/ *noun* [C] **1** a report (on/of sth) a written or spoken description of what you have seen, heard, done, studied, etc: *newspaper reports* ◆ *a report on the company's finances* ◆ *a first-hand report* (= from the person who saw what happened) **2** a written statement about the work of a student at school, college, etc: *to get a good/bad report*

re͵ported ˈspeech (also ͵indirect ˈspeech) *noun* [U] the fact of reporting what sb has said, not using the actual words. If sb says *'I'll phone again later'*, this becomes *She said that she would phone again later* in reported speech. ➲ look at **direct speech** ℹ For more information about reported speech, look at the **Reference Section** at the back of this dictionary.

reporter /rɪˈpɔːtə(r)/ *noun* [C] a person who writes about the news in a newspaper or speaks about it on the TV or radio ➲ note at **newspaper** ➲ look at **journalist**

🔑 **represent** /͵reprɪˈzent/ *verb* [T] **1** to act or speak in the place of sb else; to be the **representative** of a group or country: *You will need a lawyer to represent you in court.* ◆ *It's an honour for an athlete to represent his or her country.* **2** to be equal to sth; to be sth: *These results represent a major breakthrough in our understanding of cancer.* **3** to be a picture, sign, example, etc. of sb/sth: *The yellow lines on the map represent minor roads.* **4** to describe sb/sth in a particular way: *In the book Billy is represented as a very cruel person.*

representation /͵reprɪzenˈteɪʃn/ *noun* **1** [U,C] the way that sb/sth is shown or described; something that shows or describes sth: *The article complains about the representation of women in advertising.* ➲ look at **proportional representation** **2** [U] (*formal*) having sb to speak for you

🔑 **representative**[1] /͵reprɪˈzentətɪv/ *noun* [C] **1** a person who has been chosen to act or speak for sb else or for a group: *a union representative* **2** (*formal*) = rep

🔑 **representative**[2] /͵reprɪˈzentətɪv/ *adj* representative (of sb/sth) typical of a larger group to which sb/sth belongs: *Tonight's audience is not representative of national opinion.*

repress /rɪˈpres/ *verb* [T] **1** to control an emotion or to try to prevent it from being shown or felt: *She tried to repress her anger.* **2** to limit the freedom of a group of people ▶ **repression** /rɪˈpreʃn/ *noun* [U]: *protests against government repression*

repressed /rɪˈprest/ *adj* **1** (used about a person) having emotions and desires that they do not show or express **2** (used about an emotion) that you do not show: *repressed anger/desire*

repressive /rɪˈpresɪv/ *adj* that limits people's freedom: *a repressive government*

reprieve /rɪˈpriːv/ *verb* [T] **1** to stop or delay the punishment of a prisoner who was going to be punished by death **2** to officially cancel or delay plans to close sth or end sth ▶ **reprieve** *noun* [C]: *The judge granted him a last-minute reprieve.*

reprimand /ˈreprɪmɑːnd/ *verb* [T] (*formal*) reprimand sb (for sth) to tell sb officially that they have done sth wrong ▶ **reprimand** *noun* [C]: *a severe reprimand*

reprisal /rɪˈpraɪzl/ *noun* [C,U] a violent or aggressive act towards sb because of sth bad that they have done towards you

reproach /rɪˈprəʊtʃ/ *verb* [T] reproach sb (for/with sth) to tell sb that they are responsible for sth bad that has happened: *You've nothing to reproach yourself for. It wasn't your fault.* SYN **blame** ▶ **reproach** *noun* [C,U]: *His behaviour is **beyond reproach*** (= cannot be criticized). ◆ *Alison felt her manager's reproaches were unfair.* ▶ **reproachful** /-fl/ *adj*: *a reproachful look* ▶ **reproachfully** /-fəli/ *adv*

🔑 **reproduce** /͵riːprəˈdjuːs/ *verb* **1** [T] to produce a copy of sth: *It is very hard to reproduce a natural environment in the laboratory.* **2** [I,T] (used about people, animals and plants) to produce young: *Fish reproduce by laying eggs.*

reproduction /͵riːprəˈdʌkʃn/ *noun* **1** [U] the process of producing babies or young: *sexual reproduction* **2** [U] the production of copies of sth: *Digital recording gives excellent sound reproduction.* **3** [C] a copy of a painting, etc.

reproductive /͵riːprəˈdʌktɪv/ *adj* [only *before* a noun] connected with the production of young animals, plants, etc: *the male reproductive organs*

reproof /rɪˈpruːf/ *noun* [C,U] (*formal*) something that you say to sb when you do not approve of what they have done

reptile /ˈreptaɪl/ *noun* [C] an animal that has cold blood and a skin covered in scales, and whose young come out of eggs: *Crocodiles, turtles and snakes are all reptiles.* ➲ look at **amphibian** ➲ picture on **page P13**

republic /rɪˈpʌblɪk/ *noun* [C] a country that has an elected government and a president: *the Republic of Ireland* ➲ look at **monarchy**

republican /rɪˈpʌblɪkən/ *noun* [C] **1** a person who supports the system of an elected government with no king or queen **2** Republican (*abbr* Rep.) a member of the Republican Party of the US ➲ look at **Democrat** ▶ **republican** *adj*

the Reˈpublican Party *noun* [sing] one of the two main political parties of the US ➲ look at **the Democratic Party**

repudiate /rɪˈpjuːdieɪt/ *verb* [T] (*formal*) to say that you refuse to accept or believe sth: *to repudiate a suggestion/an accusation/responsibility*

repugnant /rɪˈpʌgnənt/ *adj* (*formal*) repugnant (to sb) making you feel disgust: *We found his suggestion absolutely repugnant.* ◆ *The idea of eating meat was totally repugnant to her.* SYN **repulsive**

repulsive /rɪˈpʌlsɪv/ *adj* that causes a strong feeling of disgust ➲ *verb* **repel** ▶ **repulsion** /rɪˈpʌlʃn/ *noun* [U]

reputable /ˈrepjətəbl/ *adj* honest and providing a good service OPP **disreputable**

🔑 **reputation** /͵repjuˈteɪʃn/ *noun* [C] a reputation (for/as sth) the opinion that people in general have about what sb/sth is like: *to **have a good/bad reputation*** ◆ *Adam has a reputation for being late.* SYN **name**

repute /rɪˈpjuːt/ *noun* [U] (*formal*) the opinion that people in general have of sb/sth: *She's a writer of*

R

international repute (= having a good reputation in many countries).

reputed /rɪˈpjuːtɪd/ *adj* generally said to be sth, although it is not certain: *She's reputed to be the highest-paid sportswoman in the world.* ▶ **reputedly** *adv*

request¹ /rɪˈkwest/ *noun* [C,U] request (for sth/that ...) an act of asking for sth: *a request for help* ◆ *I'm going to* ***make a request*** *for a larger desk.* ◆ *to grant/turn down a request* ◆ *Single rooms are available* ***on request****.*

request² /rɪˈkwest/ *verb* [T] (*formal*) request sth (from/of sb) to ask for sth: *Passengers are requested not to bring hot drinks onto the coach.* ◆ *to request a loan from the bank* ➲ **Request** is more formal than **ask**.

require /rɪˈkwaɪə(r)/ *verb* [T] **1** to need sth: *a situation that requires tact and diplomacy* ➲ **Require** is more formal than **need**. **2** [often passive] to officially demand or order sth: *Passengers are required by law to wear seat belts.*

requirement /rɪˈkwaɪəmənt/ *noun* [C] something that you need or that you must do or have: *university entrance requirements*

requisite /ˈrekwɪzɪt/ *adj* [only *before* a noun] (*formal*) necessary for a particular purpose: *She lacks the requisite experience for this job.* ▶ **requisite** *noun* [C]: *A university degree has become a requisite for entry into most professions.* ➲ look at **prerequisite**

rescue /ˈreskjuː/ *verb* [T] rescue sb/sth (from sb/sth) to save sb/sth from a situation that is dangerous or unpleasant: *He rescued a child from drowning.* ▶ **rescue** *noun* [C,U]: *Ten fishermen were saved in a daring sea rescue.* ◆ *Blow the whistle if you're in danger, and someone should* ***come to your rescue****.* ◆ *rescue workers/boats/helicopters* ▶ **rescuer** *noun* [C]

research /rɪˈsɜːtʃ; ˈriːsɜːtʃ/ *noun* [U] research (into/on sth) detailed and careful study of sth to find out more information about it: *to do research into something* ◆ *scientific/medical/historical research* ◆ *We are carrying out* ***market research*** *to find out who our typical customer is.* ▶ **research** *verb* [I,T] research (into/in/on) (sth): *Scientists are researching into the possible causes of childhood diseases.* ◆ *They're researching ways of reducing traffic in the city centre.*

researcher /rɪˈsɜːtʃə(r)/ *noun* [C] a person who does research

resemble /rɪˈzembl/ *verb* [T] to be or look like sb/sth else: *Laura closely resembles her brother.* ▶ **resemblance** /rɪˈzembləns/ *noun* [C,U] (a) resemblance (to sb/sth); (a) resemblance (between A and B): *a family resemblance* ◆ *The boys* ***bear*** *no* ***resemblance*** *to their father.*

resent /rɪˈzent/ *verb* [T] to feel angry about sth because you think it is unfair: *I resent his criticism.* ◆ *Louise bitterly resented being treated differently from the men.* ▶ **resentful** /-fl/ *adj* ▶ **resentfully** /-fəli/ *adv* ▶ **resentment** *noun* [sing,U]: *She felt deep resentment at the way she'd been treated.*

reservation /ˌrezəˈveɪʃn/ *noun* **1** [C] a seat, table, room, etc. that you have **reserved**: *We have reservations in the name of Dvorak.* ◆ *I'll phone the restaurant to* ***make a reservation****.* **2** [C,U] a feeling of doubt about sth (such as a plan or an idea): *I have some* ***reservations*** *about letting Julie go out alone.* **3** (also reserve) [C] an area of land in the US that is kept separate for Native Americans to live in

reserve¹ /rɪˈzɜːv/ *verb* [T] reserve sth (for sb/sth) **1** to keep sth for a special reason or to use at a later time: *The car park is reserved for hotel guests only.* **2** to ask for a seat, table, room, etc. to be available at a future time: *to reserve theatre tickets* SYN **book**

reserve² /rɪˈzɜːv/ *noun* **1** [C, usually pl] something that you keep for a special reason or to use at a later date: *oil reserves* **2** [C] an area of land where the plants, animals, etc. are protected by law: *a nature reserve* ◆ *He works as a warden on a* ***game reserve*** *in Kenya.* **3** [U] the quality of being shy or keeping your feelings hidden: *It took a long time to break down her reserve and get her to relax.* **4** [C] (in sport) a person who will play in a game if one of the usual members of the team cannot play **5** [C] = **reservation**(3)

IDM **in reserve** that you keep and use only if you need to: *Keep some money in reserve for emergencies.*

reserved /rɪˈzɜːvd/ *adj* shy and keeping your feelings hidden OPP **unreserved**

reservoir /ˈrezəvwɑː(r)/ *noun* [C] a large lake where water is stored to be used by a particular area, city, etc.

reside /rɪˈzaɪd/ *verb* [I] (*formal*) reside (in/at ...) to have your home in or at a particular place

residence /ˈrezɪdəns/ *noun* **1** [C] (*formal*) a house, especially an impressive or important one **2** [U] the state of having your home in a particular place: *The family applied for permanent residence in the United States.* ◆ *a* ***hall of residence*** *for college students* ◆ *Some birds have taken up residence in our roof.*

resident /ˈrezɪdənt/ *noun* [C] **1** a person who lives in a place: *local residents* **2** a person who is staying in a hotel: *The hotel bar is open only to residents.* ▶ **resident** *adj*

residential /ˌrezɪˈdenʃl/ *adj* **1** (used about a place or an area) that has houses rather than offices, large shops or factories: *They live in a quiet residential area.* **2** that provides a place for sb to live: *This home provides residential care for the elderly.*

residual /rɪˈzɪdjuəl/ *adj* [only *before* a noun] (*formal*) still present at the end of a process: *There are still a few residual problems with the computer program.*

residue /ˈrezɪdjuː/ *noun* [C, usually sing] (*formal*) what is left after the main part of sth is taken or used: *The washing powder left a white residue on the clothes.*

resign /rɪˈzaɪn/ *verb* [I,T] resign (as sth); resign (from sth) to leave your job or position: *He's resigned as chairman of the committee.* ➲ note at **job**

PHR V resign yourself to sth/doing sth to accept sth that is unpleasant but that you cannot change: *Jamie resigned himself to the fact that she was not coming back to him.*

resignation /ˌrezɪgˈneɪʃn/ *noun* **1** [C,U] resignation (from sth) a letter or statement that says you want to leave your job or position: *to hand in your resignation* ♦ *a letter of resignation* ➲ note at **job 2** [U] the state of accepting sth unpleasant that you cannot change: *They accepted their defeat with resignation.*

resigned /rɪˈzaɪnd/ *adj* resigned (to sth/doing sth) accepting sth that is unpleasant but that you cannot change: *Ben was resigned to the fact that he would never be an athlete.*

resilient /rɪˈzɪliənt/ *adj* strong enough to deal with illness, a shock, change, etc. ▶ **resilience** *noun* [U]

resin /ˈrezɪn/ *noun* [C,U] **1** a sticky substance that is produced by some trees and plants **2** an artificial substance used in making plastics

⚷ **resist** /rɪˈzɪst/ *verb* [I,T] **1** to try to stop sth happening or to stop sb from doing sth; to fight back against sth/sb: *The government are resisting pressure to change the law.* ♦ *to resist arrest* **SYN oppose 2** to stop yourself from having or doing sth that you want to have or do: *I couldn't resist telling Nadia what we'd bought for her.*

⚷ **resistance** /rɪˈzɪstəns/ *noun* [U] **1** resistance (to sb/sth) trying to stop sth from happening or to stop sb from doing sth; fighting back against sb/sth: *The government troops overcame the resistance of the rebel army.* **2** resistance (to sth) the power in sb's body not to be affected by disease: *People with AIDS have very little resistance to infection.*

resistant /rɪˈzɪstənt/ *adj* resistant (to sth) **1** not harmed or affected by sth: *plants that are resistant to disease* ♦ *This watch is water-resistant.* **2** not wanting sth and trying to prevent sth happening: *resistant to change*

resolute /ˈrezəluːt/ *adj* having or showing great determination: *resolute leadership* ♦ *a resolute refusal to change* ➲ A more common word is **determined**. ▶ **resolutely** *adv*

resolution /ˌrezəˈluːʃn/ *noun* **1** [C] a formal decision that is taken after a vote by a group of people: *The UN resolution condemned the invasion.* **2** [U] solving or settling a problem, disagreement, etc. **3** [U] the quality of being firm and determined **4** [C] a firm decision to do or not to do sth: *Alison made a New Year's resolution to walk to school every day.*

⚷ **resolve** /rɪˈzɒlv/ *verb* (*formal*) **1** [T] to find an answer to a problem: *Most of the difficulties have been resolved.* **SYN settle 2** [I,T] to decide sth and be determined not to change your mind: *He resolved never to repeat the experience.*

resonant /ˈrezənənt/ *adj* (*formal*) deep, clear and continuing for a long time: *a deep resonant voice* ▶ **resonance** *noun* [U]: *Her voice had a thrilling resonance.*

⚷ **resort**[1] /rɪˈzɔːt/ *noun* [C] a place where a lot of people go to on holiday: *a seaside/ski resort* ➲ note at **holiday**
IDM in the last resort; (as) a last resort ➲ **last**[1]

resort[2] /rɪˈzɔːt/ *verb* [I] resort to sth/doing sth to do or use sth bad or unpleasant because you feel you have no choice: *After not sleeping for three nights I finally resorted to sleeping pills.*

resounding /rɪˈzaʊndɪŋ/ *adj* [only *before* a noun] **1** very great: *a resounding victory/win/defeat/success* **2** very loud: *resounding cheers*

⚷ **resource** /rɪˈsɔːs; -ˈzɔːs/ *noun* [C, usually pl] a supply of sth, a piece of equipment, etc. that is available for sb to use: *Russia is rich in* ***natural resources*** *such as oil and minerals.*

resourceful /rɪˈsɔːsfl; -ˈzɔːs-/ *adj* good at finding ways of doing things

⚷ **respect**[1] /rɪˈspekt/ *noun* **1** [U] respect (for sb/sth) the feeling that you have when you admire or have a high opinion of sb/sth: *I* ***have*** *little* ***respect*** *for people who are arrogant.* ♦ *to win/lose somebody's respect* ➲ look at **self-respect 2** [U] respect (for sb/sth) polite behaviour or care towards sb/sth that you think is important: *We should all* ***treat*** *older people* ***with respect.*** ♦ *He has no respect for her feelings.* **OPP disrespect 3** [C] a detail or point: ***In what respects*** *do you think things have changed in the last ten years?* ♦ *Her performance was brilliant* ***in every respect.***
IDM pay your respects ➲ **pay**[1]
with respect to sth (*formal*) about or concerning sth: *The groups differ with respect to age.*

⚷ **respect**[2] /rɪˈspekt/ *verb* [T] **1** respect sb/sth (for sth) to admire or have a high opinion of sb/sth: *I respect him for his honesty.* **2** to show care for or pay attention to sb/sth: *We should respect other people's cultures and values.* ▶ **respectful** /-fl/ *adj* respectful (to/towards sb): *They are not always respectful towards their teacher.* **OPP disrespectful** ▶ **respectfully** /-fəli/ *adv*

respectable /rɪˈspektəbl/ *adj* **1** considered by society to be good, proper or correct: *a respectable family* ♦ *He combed his hair and tried to look respectable for the interview.* **2** quite good or large: *a respectable salary* ▶ **respectability** /rɪˌspektəˈbɪləti/ *noun* [U]

respective /rɪˈspektɪv/ *adj* [only *before* a noun] belonging separately to each of the people who have been mentioned: *Helen and Sue's respective start times are 8.15 and 9.00.*

respectively /rɪˈspektɪvli/ *adv* in the same order as sb/sth that was mentioned

respiration /ˌrespəˈreɪʃn/ *noun* [U] (*formal*) breathing

respite /ˈrespaɪt/ *noun* [sing, U] respite (from sth) a short period of rest from sth that is difficult or unpleasant: *There was a brief respite from the fighting.*

R

respond /rɪˈspɒnd/ *verb* [I] **1** (*formal*) respond (to sb/sth) (with/by sth) to say or do sth as an answer or reaction to sth: *He responded to my question with a nod.* ◆ *Gerrard responded to the manager's criticism by scoring two goals.* ➲ note at **answer** ➲ **Respond** is more formal than **answer** or **reply**. **2** respond (to sb/sth) to have or show a good or quick reaction to sb/sth: *The patient did not respond very well to the new treatment.*

response /rɪˈspɒns/ *noun* [C,U] (a) response (to sb/sth) an answer or reaction to sb/sth: *I've sent out 20 letters of enquiry but I've had no responses yet.* ◆ *The government acted* ***in response to*** *economic pressure.*

responsibility /rɪˌspɒnsəˈbɪləti/ *noun* (*pl* responsibilities) **1** [U,C] responsibility (for sb/sth); responsibility (to do sth) a duty to deal with sth so that it is your fault if sth goes wrong: *I refuse to* ***take responsibility*** *if anything goes wrong.* ◆ *Who* ***has responsibility*** *for the new students?* ◆ *It is John's responsibility to make sure the orders are sent out on time.* ◆ *I feel that I* ***have a responsibility*** *to help them—after all, they did help me.* **2** [U] the fact of sth being your fault: *No group has yet admitted responsibility for planting the bomb.* SYN **blame**
IDM **shift the blame/responsibility (for sth) (onto sb)** ➲ **shift**[1]

responsible /rɪˈspɒnsəbl/ *adj*
➤HAVING DUTY **1** [not before a noun] responsible (for sb/sth); responsible (for doing sth) having the job or duty of dealing with sb/sth, so that it is your fault if sth goes wrong: *The school is responsible for the safety of the children in school hours.* ◆ *The manager is responsible for making sure the shop is run properly.*
➤CAUSING STH **2** [not before a noun] responsible (for sth) being the thing or person whose caused sth to happen: *Who was responsible for the accident?*
➤REPORTING TO SB **3** [not before a noun] responsible (to sb/sth) having to report to sb/sth with authority, or to sb who you are working for, about what you are doing: *Members of Parliament are responsible to the electors.*
➤RELIABLE **4** (used about a person) that you can trust to behave well and in a sensible way: *Mai is responsible enough to take her little sister to school.* OPP **irresponsible**
➤JOB **5** (used about a job) that is important and that should be done by a person who can be trusted

responsibly /rɪˈspɒnsəbli/ *adv* in a sensible way that shows you can be trusted

responsive /rɪˈspɒnsɪv/ *adj* paying attention to sb/sth and reacting in a suitable or positive way: *By being responsive to changes in the market, the company has had great success.*

rest[1] /rest/ *verb* **1** [I] to relax, sleep or stop after a period of activity or because of illness: *We've been walking for hours. Let's rest here for a while.* **2** [T] to not use a part of your body for a period of time because it is tired or painful: *Your knee will get better as long as you rest it as much as you can.* **3** [I,T] rest (sth) on/against sth to place sth in a position where it is supported by sth else; to be in such a position: *She rested her head on his shoulder and went to sleep.*
IDM **let sth rest** to not talk about sth any longer
PHR V **rest on sb/sth** to depend on sb/sth or be based on sth: *The whole theory rests on a very simple idea.*

rest[2] /rest/ *noun* **1** [sing, with sing or pl verb] the rest (of sb/sth) the part that is left; the ones that are left: *We had lunch and spent the rest of the day on the beach.* ◆ *She takes no interest in what happens in the rest of the world.* ◆ *They were the first people to arrive. The rest came later.* ◆ *The rest of our bags are still in the car.* **2** [C,U] a period of relaxing, sleeping or doing nothing: *I can't walk any further! I need a rest.* ◆ *I'm going upstairs to* ***have a rest*** *before we go out.* ◆ *Try not to worry now.* ***Get some rest*** *and think about it tomorrow.* ◆ *I sat down to* ***give*** *my bad leg* ***a rest****.*
IDM **at rest** (*formal*) not moving: *Do not open the door until the vehicle is at rest.*
come to rest to stop moving: *The car crashed through a wall and came to rest in a field.*
put/set your/sb's mind at rest ➲ **mind**[1]
the rest is history used when you are telling a story to say that you are not going to tell the end of the story, because everyone knows it already

ˈrest area (also ˈrest stop) (*AmE*) = **lay-by**

restart /ˈriːstɑːt/ *verb* [I,T] to start again or make sth start again after it has stopped: *Restart your computer to see if this solves the problem.*

restaurant /ˈrestrɒnt/ *noun* [C] a place where you can buy and eat a meal: *a fast food/hamburger restaurant* ◆ *a Chinese restaurant* ➲ look at **cafe**, **takeaway**

TOPIC

Restaurants

A **cafe**, a **sandwich bar**, a **takeaway** or a **fast-food restaurant** is often a good place to **have a snack** or eat cheaply, but for a special occasion you can go to a **restaurant**. If it is popular, you should **reserve/book a table** in advance. You choose from the **menu** and a **waiter** or **waitress** takes your **order**. A **set menu** gives a limited choice of **courses** or **dishes** at a **fixed price**. An **à la carte** menu lists all the separate dishes available. You can **order** a **starter** (= a light first course), a **main course** and a **pudding/dessert**. If you want alcoholic drinks, you can ask to see the **wine list**. At the end of the meal you must pay the **bill**. Friends often **split the bill** (= each pays for a share of the meal). If **service** is not included in the bill, people usually leave a **tip** (= a small amount of extra money).

restful /ˈrestfl/ *adj* giving a relaxed, peaceful feeling: *I find this piece of music very restful.*

restless /ˈrestləs/ *adj* **1** unable to relax or be still because you are bored, nervous or impatient: *The children always get restless on long journeys.* **2** (used about a period of time) without sleep or rest ▶ **restlessly** *adv*

restoration /ˌrestəˈreɪʃn/ *noun* **1** [C,U] the return of sth to its original condition; the things that

R

are done to achieve this: *The house is in need of restoration.* **2** [U] the return of sth to its original owner: *the restoration of stolen property to its owner*

restore /rɪˈstɔː(r)/ *verb* [T] **1** restore sb/sth (to sb/sth) to put sb/sth back into their or its former condition or position: *She restores old furniture as a hobby.* ♦ *In the recent elections, the former president was restored to power.* **2** (*formal*) restore sth to sb to give sth that was lost or stolen back to sb: *The police have now restored the painting to its rightful owner.*

restrain /rɪˈstreɪn/ *verb* [T] restrain sb/sth (from sth/doing sth) to keep sb or sth under control; to prevent sb or sth from doing sth: *I had to restrain myself from saying something rude.*

restrained /rɪˈstreɪnd/ *adj* not showing strong feelings

restraint /rɪˈstreɪnt/ *noun* **1** [C] a restraint (on sb/sth) a limit or control on sth: *Are there any restraints on what the newspapers are allowed to publish?* **2** [U] the quality of behaving in a calm or controlled way: *It took a lot of restraint on my part not to hit him.* ♦ *Soldiers have to exercise **self-restraint** even when provoked.* SYN **self-control**

restrict /rɪˈstrɪkt/ *verb* [T] restrict sb/sth (to sth/doing sth) to put a limit on sb/sth: *There is a plan to restrict the use of cars in the city centre.*

restricted /rɪˈstrɪktɪd/ *adj* controlled or limited: *There is only restricted parking available.*

restriction /rɪˈstrɪkʃn/ *noun* restriction (on sth) **1** [C] something (sometimes a rule or law) that limits the number, amount, size, freedom, etc. of sb/sth: *parking restrictions in the city centre* ♦ *The government is to **impose** tighter **restrictions** on the number of immigrants permitted to settle in this country.* **2** [U] the act of limiting the freedom of sb/sth: *This ticket permits you to travel anywhere, without restriction.*

restrictive /rɪˈstrɪktɪv/ *adj* limiting; preventing people from doing what they want

restroom /ˈrestruːm; -rʊm/ *noun* [C] (*AmE*) a room with a toilet in a public place such as a hotel, shop, etc. ➲ note at **toilet**

ˈrest stop (*AmE*) = **lay-by**

result¹ /rɪˈzʌlt/ *noun*

➤CAUSED BY STH **1** [C] something that happens because of sth else; the final situation at the end of a series of actions: *The traffic was very heavy and **as a result** I arrived late.* ♦ *This wasn't really the result that I was expecting.*

➤OF COMPETITION **2** [C] the score at the end of a game, competition or election: *Do you know today's football results?* ♦ *The results of this week's competition will be published next week.* ♦ *The result of the by-election was a win for the Liberal Democrats.*

➤OF EXAM **3** [C, usually pl] the mark given for an exam or test: *When do you **get** your exam **results**?*

➤OF MEDICAL TEST **4** [C] something that is discovered by a medical test: *I'm still waiting for the result of my X-ray.* ♦ *The result of the test was negative.*

➤SUCCESS **5** [C,U] a good effect of an action: *He has tried very hard to find a job, until now without result.* ♦ *The treatment is beginning to show results.*

result² /rɪˈzʌlt/ *verb* [I] result (from sth) to happen or exist because of sth: *Ninety per cent of the deaths resulted from injuries to the head.*
PHR V **result in sth** to cause sth to happen; to produce as an effect: *There has been an accident on the motorway, resulting in long delays.*

resume /rɪˈzuːm; -ˈzjuː-/ *verb* [I,T] (*formal*) to begin again or continue after a pause or interruption: *Normal service will resume as soon as possible.*

résumé /ˈrezjumeɪ/ (*AmE*) = **CV**

resumption /rɪˈzʌmpʃn/ *noun* [sing, U] (*formal*) beginning again or continuing after a pause or interruption

resurrect /ˌrezəˈrekt/ *verb* [T] to bring back sth that has not been used or has not existed for a long time: *From time to time they resurrect old programmes and show them again on TV.*

resurrection /ˌrezəˈrekʃn/ *noun* **1** the Resurrection [sing] (in the Christian religion) the return to life of Jesus Christ **2** [U] the action of bringing back sth that has not existed or not been used for a long time

resuscitate /rɪˈsʌsɪteɪt/ *verb* [T] to make sb start breathing again after they have almost died: *Unfortunately, all efforts to resuscitate the patient failed.* ▶ **resuscitation** /rɪˌsʌsɪˈteɪʃn/ *noun* [U]: *mouth-to-mouth resuscitation*

retail /ˈriːteɪl/ *noun* [U] the selling of goods to the public in shops, etc. ➲ look at **wholesale**

retailer /ˈriːteɪlə(r)/ *noun* [C] a person or company that sells goods to the public: *local retailers* ♦ *an online retailer*

retain /rɪˈteɪn/ *verb* [T] (*formal*) to keep or continue to have sth; not to lose sth: *Despite all her problems, she has managed to retain a sense of humour.* ➲ *noun* **retention**

retaliate /rɪˈtælieɪt/ *verb* [I] retaliate (against sb/sth) to react to sth unpleasant that sb does to you by doing sth unpleasant in return: *They have announced that they will retaliate against anyone who attacks their country.* ▶ **retaliation** /rɪˌtæliˈeɪʃn/ *noun* [U] retaliation (against sb/sth) (for sth): *The terrorist group said that the shooting was **in retaliation** for the killing of one of its members.*

retarded /rɪˈtɑːdɪd/ *adj* (*old-fashioned*) slower to develop than normal

HELP Be careful. Many people find this word offensive.

retention /rɪˈtenʃn/ *noun* [U] the act of keeping sth or of being kept ➲ *verb* **retain**

rethink /ˌriːˈθɪŋk/ *verb* [I,T] (*pt, pp* rethought /-ˈθɔːt/) to think about sth again because you probably need to change it: *The government has been forced to rethink its economic policy.*

reticent /ˈretɪsnt/ *adj* (*formal*) reticent (about sth) not willing to tell people about things: *She was shy*

R

and reticent. ♦ *He was extremely reticent about his personal life.* ▶ **reticence** *noun* [U]

retina /ˈretɪnə/ *noun* [C] the area at the back of your eye that is sensitive to light and sends signals to the brain about what is seen

retire /rɪˈtaɪə(r)/ *verb* [I] **1 retire (from sth)** to leave your job and stop working, usually because you have reached a certain age: *She retired from the company at the age of 60.* ➲ note at **job** ➲ look at **old-age pension**

> **MORE** After someone **retires**, we say that he/she is **retired**. A **pension** is the money that retired people receive regularly from their former employer and/or the government.

2 (*formal*) to leave and go to a quiet or private place: *to retire to bed*

retired /rɪˈtaɪəd/ *adj* having stopped work permanently: *a retired teacher*

retirement /rɪˈtaɪəmənt/ *noun* **1** [C,U] the act of stopping working permanently: *She has decided to* ***take early retirement****.* ♦ *The former world champion has announced his retirement from the sport.* **2** [sing, U] the situation or period after **retiring** from work: *We all wish you a long and happy retirement.* ➲ look at **old-age pensioner, senior citizen**

retiring /rɪˈtaɪərɪŋ/ *adj* (used about a person) shy and quiet

retort /rɪˈtɔːt/ *verb* [T] to reply quickly to what sb says, in an angry or amusing way: *'Who asked you for your opinion?' she retorted.* ▶ **retort** *noun* [C]: *an angry retort*

retrace /rɪˈtreɪs/ *verb* [T] to repeat a past journey, series of events, etc: *If you* ***retrace*** *your* ***steps****, you might see where you dropped the ticket.*

retract /rɪˈtrækt/ *verb* [I,T] (*formal*) to say that sth you have said is not true: *When he appeared in court, he retracted the confession he had made to the police.*

retreat[1] /rɪˈtriːt/ *verb* [I] **1** (used about an army, etc.) to move backwards in order to leave a battle or in order not to become involved in a battle: *The order was given to retreat.* **OPP advance** **2** to move backwards; to go to a safe or private place: (*figurative*) *She seems to retreat into a world of her own sometimes.*

retreat[2] /rɪˈtriːt/ *noun* **1** [C,U] the act of moving backwards, away from a difficult or dangerous situation: *The invading forces are now in retreat.* **OPP advance** **2** [C] a private place where you can go when you want to be quiet or to rest: *a religious retreat*

retribution /ˌretrɪˈbjuːʃn/ *noun* [U] (*formal*) **retribution (for sth)** punishment for a crime

retrieve /rɪˈtriːv/ *verb* [T] **1 retrieve sth (from sb/sth)** to get sth back from the place where it was left or lost: *Police divers retrieved the body from the canal.* **2** to find information that has been stored on a computer: *The computer can retrieve all the data about a particular customer.* **3** to make a bad situation or a mistake better; to put sth right: *The team was losing two-nil at half-time but they managed to* ***retrieve the situation*** *in the second half.* ▶ **retrieval** /rɪˈtriːvl/ *noun* [U]

retro /ˈretrəʊ/ *adj* using styles or fashions from the recent past: *She dresses in a 1980s retro style.*

retrospect /ˈretrəspekt/ *noun*

IDM in retrospect thinking about sth that happened in the past, often seeing it differently from the way you saw it at the time: *In retrospect, I can see what a stupid mistake it was.*

retrospective /ˌretrəˈspektɪv/ *adj* **1** looking again at the past: *a retrospective analysis of historical events* **2** (used about laws, decisions, payments, etc.) intended to take effect from a date in the past: *Is this new tax law retrospective?* ▶ **retrospectively** *adv*

return[1] /rɪˈtɜːn/ *verb*

➤GO/COME BACK **1** [I] **return (to/from ...)** to come or go back to a place: *I leave on the 10th July and return on the 25th.* ♦ *I shall be returning to this country in six months.* ♦ *When did you return from Italy?* ♦ *He left his home town when he was 18 and never returned.*

➤TO EARLIER STATE **2** [I] **return (to sth/doing sth)** to go back to the former or usual activity, situation, condition, etc: *The strike is over and they will* ***return to work*** *on Monday.* ♦ *It is hoped that train services will* ***return to normal*** *soon.*

➤HAPPEN AGAIN **3** [I] to come back; to happen again: *If the pain returns, make another appointment to see me.*

➤GIVE BACK **4** [T] **return sth (to sb/sth)** to give, send, put or take sth back: *I've stopped lending him things because he never returns them.* ♦ *Application forms must be returned by 14 March.*

➤DO THE SAME **5** [T] to react to sth that sb does, says or feels by doing, saying, or feeling sth similar: *I've phoned them several times and left messages but they haven't returned any of my calls.* ♦ *We'll be happy to return your hospitality if you ever come to our country.*

➤IN TENNIS **6** [T] to hit or throw the ball back: *to return a service/shot*

return[2] /rɪˈtɜːn/ *noun*

➤COMING BACK **1** [sing] **a return (to/from ...)** coming or going back to a place or to a former activity, situation or condition: *I'll contact you* ***on*** *my* ***return*** *from holiday.* ♦ *He has recently made a return to form* (= started playing well again).

➤GIVING BACK **2** [U] giving, sending, putting or taking sth back: *I demand the immediate return of my passport.*

➤TICKET **3** [C] (*BrE also* **reˌturn ˈticket**; *AmE* **ˌround ˈtrip**; **ˌround-trip ˈticket**) a ticket to travel to a place and back again: *A* ***day return*** *to Oxford, please.* ♦ *Is the* ***return fare*** *cheaper than two singles?* **OPP single, one-way**

➤ON COMPUTER **4** [sing] (*also* **the reˈturn key**) the button on a computer that you press when you reach the end of a line or of an instruction: *To exit this option, press return.*

➤PROFIT **5** [C,U] **(a) return (on sth)** the profit from a business, etc: *This account offers high returns on all investments.*

➤IN TENNIS **6** [C] the act of hitting or throwing the ball back: *She hit a brilliant return.*
IDM **by return (of post)** (*BrE*) immediately; by the next post
in return (for sth) as payment or in exchange (for sth); as a reaction to sth: *Please accept this present in return for all your help.*

returnable /rɪˈtɜːnəbl/ *adj* that can or must be given or taken back: *a non-returnable deposit*

the reˈturn key = return²(5)

reˌturn ˈticket = return²(4)

retweet /riːˈtwiːt/ *verb* [I,T] to send a message that someone has sent you on the Twitter™ **social networking service** (= short communications using the Internet) to other people: *People love to retweet job ads.*

reunion /riːˈjuːniən/ *noun* **1** [C] a social occasion or party attended by a group of people who have not seen each other for a long time: *The college holds an annual reunion for former students.* **2** [C,U] a reunion (with sb/between A and B) coming together again after being apart: *The released hostages had an emotional reunion with their families at the airport.*

reunite /ˌriːjuːˈnaɪt/ *verb* [I,T] reunite (A with/and B) to join two or more people, groups, etc. together again; to come together again: *The missing child was found by the police and reunited with his parents.*

reuse /ˌriːˈjuːz/ *verb* [T] to use sth that has been used before: *Save money by reusing envelopes.*

Rev. *abbr* = **reverend**: *Rev. Jesse Jackson*

rev¹ /rev/ *verb* [I,T] (revving; revved) rev (sth) (up) when an engine **revs** or when you **rev** it, it runs quickly and noisily

rev² /rev/ *noun* [C] (*informal*) (used when talking about an engine's speed) one complete turn: *4000 revs per minute* ➲ look at **revolution**

⚷ **reveal** /rɪˈviːl/ *verb* [T] **1** reveal sth (to sb) to make sth known that was secret or unknown before: *He refused to reveal any names to the police.* **2** to show sth that was hidden before: *The X-ray revealed a tiny fracture in her right hand.*

revealing /rɪˈviːlɪŋ/ *adj* **1** allowing sth to be known that was secret or unknown before: *This book provides a revealing insight into the world of politics.* **2** allowing sth to be seen that is usually hidden, especially sb's body: *a very revealing swimsuit*

revel /ˈrevl/ *verb* (revelling; revelled, (*AmE*) reveling; reveled)
PHR V **revel in sth/doing sth** to enjoy sth very much: *He likes being famous and revels in the attention he gets.*

revelation /ˌrevəˈleɪʃn/ *noun* **1** [C] something that is made known that was secret or unknown before, especially sth surprising: *This magazine is full of revelations about the private lives of the stars.* **2** [sing] a thing or a person that surprises you and makes you change your opinion about sb/sth

revenge /rɪˈvendʒ/ *noun* [U] revenge (on sb) (for sth) something that you do to punish sb who has hurt you, made you suffer, etc: *He made a fool of me and now I want to* **get** *my* **revenge**. ♦ *He wants to* **take revenge** *on the judge who sent him to prison.* ♦ *The shooting was* **in revenge** *for an attack by the nationalists.* ➲ look at **vengeance** ▶ **revenge** *verb* [T] revenge yourself on sb: *She revenged herself on her enemy.* ➲ look at **avenge**

revenue /ˈrevənjuː/ *noun* [U] (also [pl] revenues) money regularly received by a government, company, etc: *Revenue from income tax rose last year.*

reverberate /rɪˈvɜːbəreɪt/ *verb* [I] (used about a sound) to be repeated several times as it hits and is sent back from different surfaces: *Her voice reverberated around the hall.* ▶ **reverberation** /rɪˌvɜːbəˈreɪʃn/ *noun* [C,U]

reverence /ˈrevərəns/ *noun* [U] (*formal*) reverence (for sb/sth) a feeling of great respect

reverend /ˈrevərənd/ *adj* [only *before* a noun] (*abbr* Rev.) the title of a Christian priest

reverent /ˈrevərənt/ *adj* (*formal*) showing great respect

reversal /rɪˈvɜːsl/ *noun* [U,C] the act of changing sth to the opposite of what it was before; an occasion when this happens: *The government insists that there will be no reversal of policy.* ♦ *The decision taken yesterday was a complete reversal of last week's decision.*

⚷ **reverse¹** /rɪˈvɜːs/ *verb* **1** [T] to put sth in the opposite position to normal or to how it was before: *Today's results have reversed the order of the top two teams.* **2** [T] to exchange the positions or functions of two things or people: *Jane and her husband have reversed roles—he stays at home now and she goes to work.* **3** [I,T] to go backwards in a vehicle, etc.; to make a vehicle go backwards: *It will probably be easier to reverse into that parking space.* ♦ *He reversed his brand new car into a wall.*
IDM **reverse (the) charges** (*BrE*) to make a telephone call that will be paid for by the person who receives it: *Phone us when you get there, and reverse the charges.*

HELP The American expression is to **call collect**.

⚷ **reverse²** /rɪˈvɜːs/ *noun* **1** [sing] the reverse (of sth) the complete opposite of what was said just before, or of what is expected: *Of course I don't dislike you—quite the reverse* (= I like you very much). ♦ *This course is the exact reverse of what I was expecting.* **2** (also reˌverse ˈgear) [U] the control in a car, etc. that allows it to move backwards: *Leave the car* **in reverse** *while it's parked on this hill.* ♦ *Where's reverse in this car?*
IDM **in reverse** in the opposite order, starting at the end and going back to the beginning SYN **backwards**

reverse³ /rɪˈvɜːs/ *adj* [only *before* a noun] opposite to what is expected or has just been described
IDM **in/into reverse order** starting with the last one and going backwards to the first one: *The results will be announced in reverse order.*

R

reversible /rɪˈvɜːsəbl/ *adj* (used about clothes) that can be worn with either side on the outside: *a reversible coat*

revert /rɪˈvɜːt/ *verb* [I] revert (to sth) to return to a former state or activity: *The land will soon revert to jungle if it is not farmed.* ♦ *If this is unsuccessful we will revert to the old system.*

review[1] /rɪˈvjuː/ *noun* **1** [C,U] the examining or considering again of sth in order to decide if changes are necessary: *There will be a review of your contract after the first six months.* ♦ *The system is in need of review.* **2** [C] a newspaper or magazine article, or an item on TV or radio, in which sb gives an opinion on a new book, film, play, etc: *The film got bad reviews.* **3** [C] a look back at sth in order to check, remember, or be clear about sth: *a review of the major events of the year*

review[2] /rɪˈvjuː/ *verb* [T] **1** to examine or consider sth again in order to decide if changes are necessary: *Your salary will be reviewed after one year.* **2** to look at or think about sth again to make sure that you understand it: *Let's review what we've done in class this week.* **3** to write an article or to talk on TV or radio, giving an opinion on a new book, film, play, etc: *In this week's edition our film critic reviews the latest films.*

reviewer /rɪˈvjuːə(r)/ *noun* [C] a person who writes about new books, films, etc.

revise /rɪˈvaɪz/ *verb* **1** [T] to make changes to sth in order to correct or improve it: *The book has been revised for this new edition.* ♦ *I revised my opinion of him when I found out that he had lied.* **2** [I,T] (*BrE*) revise (sth/for sth) to read or study again sth that you have learnt, especially when preparing for an exam: *I can't come out tonight. I'm revising for my exam.* ♦ *Let's revise the past perfect.* ♦ *None of the things I had revised came up in the exam.*

revision /rɪˈvɪʒn/ *noun* **1** [C,U] the changing of sth in order to correct or improve it: *It has been suggested that the whole system is in need of revision.* **2** [U] (*BrE*) the work of reading or studying again sth you have learnt, especially when preparing for an exam: *I'm going to have to* ***do*** *a lot of* ***revision*** *for History.*

EXAM TIP

Revision

It is very important to prepare for exams by revising. Do not leave all your revision until the night before the exam, but try to revise little and often. That way you can build up your knowledge gradually, making sure that you have learnt everything that you need to know for the exam.

revival /rɪˈvaɪvl/ *noun* **1** [C,U] the act of becoming or making sth strong or popular again: *economic revival* ♦ *a revival of interest in traditional farming methods* **2** [C] a new performance of a play that has not been performed for some time: *a revival of the musical 'The Sound of Music'*

revive /rɪˈvaɪv/ *verb* [I,T] **1** to become, or to make sb/sth become, conscious or strong and healthy again: *Hopes have revived for an early end to the fighting.* ♦ *I'm very tired but I'm sure a cup of coffee will revive me.* ♦ *Attempts were made to revive him but he was already dead.* **2** to become or to make sth popular again; to begin to do or use sth again: *Public interest in athletics has revived now that the national team is doing well.* ♦ *to revive an old custom*

revoke /rɪˈvəʊk/ *verb* [T] (*formal*) to officially cancel sth so that it is no longer valid

revolt /rɪˈvəʊlt/ *verb* **1** [I] revolt (against sb/sth) to protest in a group, often violently, against the person or people in power: *A group of generals revolted against the government.* **2** to behave in a way that is the opposite of what sb expects of you: *Teenagers often revolt against parental discipline.* **3** [T] to make sb feel disgusted or ill: *The sight and smell of the meat revolted him.* ➲ *noun* **revulsion** ▶ **revolt** *noun* [C,U]: *The people rose* ***in revolt*** *against the corrupt government.*

revolting /rɪˈvəʊltɪŋ/ *adj* extremely unpleasant: *What a revolting smell!* SYN **disgusting**

revolution /ˌrevəˈluːʃn/ *noun* **1** [C,U] action taken by a large group of people to try to change the government of a country, especially by violent action: *the French Revolution of 1789* ♦ *a country on the brink of revolution* **2** [C] a revolution (in sth) a complete change in methods, opinions, etc., often as a result of progress: *the Industrial Revolution* **3** [C, U] a movement around sth; one complete turn around a central point (for example in a car engine): *400 revolutions per minute* ➲ look at **rev**

revolutionary[1] /ˌrevəˈluːʃənəri/ *adj* **1** connected with or supporting political **revolution**: *the revolutionary leaders* **2** producing great changes; very new and different: *revolutionary advances in medicine*

revolutionary[2] /ˌrevəˈluːʃənəri/ *noun* [C] (*pl* revolutionaries) a person who starts or supports action to try to change the government of a country, especially by using violence

revolutionize (also -ise) /ˌrevəˈluːʃənaɪz/ *verb* [T] to change sth completely, usually improving it: *a discovery that could revolutionize the treatment of mental illness*

revolve /rɪˈvɒlv/ *verb* [I] to move in a circle around a central point: *The earth revolves around the sun.* PHR V **revolve around sb/sth** to have sb/sth as the most important part: *Her life revolves around the family.*

revolver /rɪˈvɒlvə(r)/ *noun* [C] a type of small gun with a container for bullets that turns round ➲ note at **gun**

revolving /rɪˈvɒlvɪŋ/ *adj* that goes round in a circle: *revolving doors*

revulsion /rɪˈvʌlʃn/ *noun* [U] a feeling of disgust (because sth is extremely unpleasant) ➲ *verb* **revolt**

reward[1] /rɪˈwɔːd/ *noun* reward (for sth/for doing sth) **1** [C,U] something that you achieve or are given because you have done sth good, worked hard, etc: *Winning the match was* ***just reward*** *for all* *the effort.* **2** [C] an amount of money that is given in exchange for helping the police, returning sth that was lost, etc: *Police are offering a reward for information leading to a conviction.*

reward² /rɪˈwɔːd/ *verb* [T, often passive] **reward sb (for sth/for doing sth)** to give sth to sb because they have done sth good, worked hard, etc: *Victoria was rewarded for all her hard work with a rise in salary.*

rewarding /rɪˈwɔːdɪŋ/ *adj* (used about an activity, a job, etc.) giving satisfaction; making you happy because you think it is important, useful, etc.

rewind /ˌriːˈwaɪnd/ *verb* [T] (*pt, pp* **rewound**) to make a video or tape go backwards ▶ **rewind** *noun* [U] ➲ look at **fast forward**

rewrite /ˌriːˈraɪt/ *verb* [T] (*pt* **rewrote** /-ˈrəʊt/; *pp* **rewritten** /-ˈrɪtn/) to write sth again in a different or better way

rhetoric /ˈretərɪk/ *noun* [U] (*formal*) a way of speaking or writing that is intended to impress or influence people but is not always sincere ▶ **rhetorical** /rɪˈtɒrɪkl/ *adj* ▶ **rhetorically** /-kli/ *adv*

rheˌtorical ˈquestion *noun* [C] a question that does not expect an answer

rheumatism /ˈruːmətɪzəm/ *noun* [U] an illness that causes pain in your muscles and where your bones are connected

rhinoceros /raɪˈnɒsərəs/ *noun* [C] (*pl* **rhinoceros** *or* **rhinoceroses**) (also *informal* **rhino**) a large animal from Africa or Asia, with thick skin and with either one or two horns on its nose ➲ picture at **hippopotamus**

rhubarb /ˈruːbɑːb/ *noun* [U] a plant with red **stalks** (= the long thin parts) that can be cooked and eaten as fruit

rhyme¹ /raɪm/ *noun* **1** [C] a word that has the same sound as another **2** [C] a short piece of writing, or sth spoken, in which the word at the end of each line sounds the same as the word at the end of the line before it ➲ look at **nursery rhyme** **3** [U] the use of words in a poem or song that have the same sound, especially at the ends of lines: *All of his poetry was written* ***in rhyme.***

rhyme² /raɪm/ *verb* **1** [I] **rhyme (with sth)** to have the same sound as another word; to contain lines that end with words that sound the same: *'Tough' rhymes with 'stuff'.* **2** [T] **rhyme sth (with sth)** to put together words that have the same sound

rhythm /ˈrɪðəm/ *noun* [C,U] a regular repeated pattern of sound or movement: *I'm not keen on the tune but I love the rhythm.* ◆ *He's a terrible dancer because he has no* ***sense of rhythm.*** ◆ *He tapped his foot* ***in rhythm*** *with the music.* ▶ **rhythmic** /ˈrɪðmɪk/ (also **rhythmical** /ˈrɪðmɪkl/) *adj*: *the rhythmic qualities of African music* ▶ **rhythmically** /-kli/ *adv*

rib /rɪb/ *noun* [C] **1** one of the curved bones that go round your chest: *He's so thin that you can see his ribs.* ➲ picture at **body** **2** a piece of meat with one or more bones from the ribs of an animal

ribbon /ˈrɪbən/ *noun* [C,U] a long, thin piece of cloth that is used for tying or decorating sth: *a present wrapped in a blue ribbon* ➲ picture at **medal**, **wrap**

rice /raɪs/ *noun* [U] short, thin, white or brown grain from a plant that grows on wet land in hot countries. We cook and eat rice: *boiled/fried/steamed rice*

rich /rɪtʃ/ *adj* (**richer**; **richest**)

➤WITH A LOT OF MONEY **1** having a lot of money or property; not poor: *a rich family/country* ◆ *one of the richest women in the world* **SYN** **wealthy, well-to-do** **OPP** **poor** **2 the rich** *noun* [pl] people with a lot of money or property: *the rich and famous*

➤FULL OF STH **3 rich in sth** containing a lot of sth: *Oranges are rich in vitamin C.* **4** very interesting and full of variety: *the region's rich history and culture*

➤FOOD **5** containing a lot of fat, oil, sugar or cream and making you feel full quickly: *a rich chocolate cake*

➤SOIL **6** containing the substances that make it good for growing plants in: *a rich well-drained soil*

➤COLOUR/SOUND/SMELL **7** strong and deep: *a rich purple* ▶ **richness** *noun* [U]

riches /ˈrɪtʃɪz/ *noun* [pl] (*formal*) a lot of money or property **SYN** **wealth**

richly /ˈrɪtʃli/ *adv* **1** in a generous way: *She was richly rewarded for her hard work.* **2** in a way that people think is right: *His promotion was* ***richly deserved.***

rickety /ˈrɪkəti/ *adj* likely to break; not strongly made: *a rickety old fence* ◆ *rickety furniture*

rickshaw /ˈrɪkʃɔː/ *noun* [C] a small light vehicle with two wheels, used especially in some Asian countries to carry passengers. It is pulled by sb walking or riding a bicycle.

ricochet /ˈrɪkəʃeɪ/ *verb* [I] (*pt, pp* **ricocheted** /ˈrɪkəʃeɪd/) **ricochet (off sth)** (used about a moving object) to fly away from a surface after hitting it: *The bullet ricocheted off the wall and grazed his shoulder.*

rid /rɪd/ *verb* [T] (ridding; *pt, pp* rid)

IDM **get rid of sb/sth** to make yourself free of sb/sth that is annoying you or that you do not want; to throw sth away: *Let's get rid of that old chair and buy a new one.*

be rid of sb/sth (*formal*) to be free of sb/sth that is annoying you or that you do not want: *He was a nuisance and we're* ***well rid*** *of him* (= it will be much better without him).

PHR V **rid yourself/sb/sth of sb/sth** (*formal*) to make yourself/sb/sth free from sb/sth that is unpleasant or not wanted: *He was unable to rid himself of his fears and suspicions.*

riddance /ˈrɪdns/ *noun*

IDM **good riddance (to sb/sth)** used for expressing pleasure or satisfaction that sb/sth that you do not like has gone

ridden¹ *past participle of* **ride¹**

ridden² /ˈrɪdn/ *adj* [often in compounds] (*formal*) full of: *She was guilt-ridden.* ◆ *She was ridden with guilt.*

R

riddle /ˈrɪdl/ *noun* [C] **1** a difficult question that you ask people for fun that has a clever or amusing answer **2** a person, a thing or an event that you cannot understand or explain

riddled /ˈrɪdld/ *adj* **riddled with sth** full of sth, especially sth unpleasant: *This essay is riddled with mistakes.*

ride¹ /raɪd/ *verb* (*pt* **rode** /rəʊd/; *pp* **ridden** /ˈrɪdn/) **1** [I,T] to sit on a horse and control it as it moves: *We rode through the woods and over the moor.* ◆ *Which horse is Dettori riding in the next race?*

> **HELP** **Go riding** is a common way of talking about riding a horse for pleasure in British English: *She goes riding every weekend.* In American English **go horseback riding** is used.

2 [I,T] to sit on a bicycle, motorbike, etc. and control it as it moves: *She jumped onto her motorbike and rode off* (= went away). ◆ *Can John ride a bicycle yet?* **3** [I,T] (*especially AmE*) to travel as a passenger in a bus, car, etc: *She rode the bus to school every day.* ▶ **rider** *noun* [C]: *She's an experienced rider.* ◆ *three horses and their riders*

ride² /raɪd/ *noun* [C] **1** a short journey on a horse or bicycle, or in a car, bus, etc: *We went for a bike ride on Saturday.* ◆ *It's only a short bus/train ride into town.* **2** used to describe what a journey or trip is like: *a smooth/bumpy/comfortable ride* **3** a large moving machine which you pay to go on for fun or excitement; an occasion when you go on one of these: *My favourite* ***fairground ride*** *is the roller coaster.*
IDM **take sb for a ride** (*informal*) to cheat or trick sb

ridge /rɪdʒ/ *noun* [C] **1** a long, narrow piece of high land along the top of a line of hills or mountains **2** a line where two surfaces meet at an angle: *the ridge of the roof*

ridicule /ˈrɪdɪkjuːl/ *noun* [U] unkind behaviour or comments that make sb/sth look silly: *He had become an object of ridicule.* ▶ **ridicule** *verb* [T]: *The idea was ridiculed by everybody.*

ridiculous /rɪˈdɪkjələs/ *adj* very silly or unreasonable: *They're asking a ridiculous* (= very high) *price for that house.* **SYN** **absurd** ▶ **ridiculously** *adv*

riding /ˈraɪdɪŋ/ (also **horse riding**; *AmE* ˈ**horseback riding**) *noun* [U] the sport or hobby of riding a horse: *Kate* ***goes riding*** *every weekend.* ◆ *riding boots* ◆ *a riding school* ➲ picture at **horse**

rife /raɪf/ *adj* [not before a noun] (*formal*) (used especially about bad things) very common: *Rumours are rife that his wife has left him.*

rifle¹ /ˈraɪfl/ *noun* [C] a long gun that you hold against your shoulder to shoot with: *She fired the rifle.* ➲ note at **gun**

rifle² /ˈraɪfl/ *verb* [I,T] **rifle (through) sth** to search sth, usually in order to steal sth from it: *I caught him rifling through the papers on my desk.*

rift /rɪft/ *noun* [C] **1** a serious disagreement between friends, groups, etc. that stops their relationship from continuing: *a growing rift between the brothers* **2** a very large crack or opening in the ground, a rock, etc.

rig¹ /rɪg/ *verb* [T] (**rigging**; **rigged**) to arrange or control an event, etc. in an unfair way, in order to get the result you want: *They claimed that the competition had been rigged.*
PHR V **rig sth up** to make sth quickly, using any materials you can find: *We tried to rig up a shelter using our coats.*

rig² /rɪg/ = **oil rig**

rigging /ˈrɪgɪŋ/ *noun* [U] the ropes, etc. that support a ship's sails

right¹ /raɪt/ *adj*
➤ MORALLY GOOD **1** (used about behaviour, actions, etc.) fair; morally and socially correct: *It's not right to pay people so badly.* ◆ *What do you think is* ***the right thing*** *to do?* **OPP** **wrong**
➤ CORRECT **2** correct; true: *I'm afraid that's not the right answer.* ◆ *Have you got* ***the right time****?* ◆ *You're quite right—the film does start at 7 o'clock.* ◆ *You were right about the weather—it did rain.* ◆ *'You're Chinese, aren't you?' 'Yes,* ***that's right****.'* **OPP** **wrong**
➤ MOST SUITABLE **3** **right (for sb/sth)** best; most suitable: *I hope I've made* ***the right decision****.* ◆ *I'm sure we've chosen* ***the right person*** *for the job.* ◆ *I would help you to wash the car, but I'm not wearing the right clothes.* **OPP** **wrong**
➤ NORMAL **4** healthy or normal; as it should be: *The car exhaust doesn't sound right—it's making a funny noise.* ◆ *I don't know what it is, but something's just not right.* **OPP** **wrong**
➤ NOT LEFT **5** [only *before* a noun] on or of the side of the body that faces east when a person is facing north: *Most people write with their right hand.* ◆ *He's blind in his right eye.* **OPP** **left**
➤ COMPLETE **6** [only *before* a noun] (*BrE spoken*) (used for emphasizing sth bad) real or complete: *I'll look a right idiot in that hat!*
IDM **get/start off on the right/wrong foot (with sb)** ➲ **foot¹**
get on the right/wrong side of sb ➲ **side¹**
on the right/wrong track ➲ **track¹**
put sth right to correct sth or deal with a problem: *There's something wrong with the lawnmower. Do you think you'll be able to put it right?*
right (you are)! (*spoken*) 'yes, I will' or 'yes, I agree': *'See you later.' 'Right you are!'* **SYN** **OK**
(as) right as rain completely healthy and normal
▶ **rightness** *noun* [U]

right² /raɪt/ *adv, exclam*
➤ EXACTLY **1** directly: *The train was right on time.* ◆ *He was sitting right beside me.*
➤ COMPLETELY **2** all the way: *Did you watch the film right to the end?* ◆ *There's a high wall that goes right round the house.*
➤ IMMEDIATELY **3** immediately: *Wait here a minute—I'll* ***be right back****.*
➤ CORRECTLY **4** in the way that it should happen or should be done: *Have I spelt your name right?* ◆ *Nothing seems to be going right for me at the moment.* **OPP** **wrong**

➤NOT LEFT **5** to the right side: *Turn right at the traffic lights.* OPP **left**

➤TO GET ATTENTION **6** (*spoken*) (used for preparing sb for sth that is about to happen) get ready; listen: *Have you got your seat belts on? Right, off we go!*

IDM **right/straight away** ➲ **away**

right now at this moment; exactly now: *We can't discuss this right now.*

serve sb right ➲ **serve**

right³ /raɪt/ *noun* **1** [U] what is morally good and fair: *Does a child of ten really understand the difference between right and wrong?* ♦ *You* ***did right*** *to tell me what happened.* OPP **wrong 2** [U,C] **the right (to sth/to do sth)** a thing that you are allowed to do according to the law; a moral authority to do sth: *Freedom of speech is one of the basic* ***human rights.*** ♦ ***civil rights*** (= the rights each person has to political and religious freedom, etc.) ♦ *animal rights campaigners* ♦ *Everyone has the right to a fair trial.* ♦ *You* ***have no right*** *to tell me what to do.* **3** [sing] the right side or direction: *We live in the first house* ***on the right.*** ♦ *Take the first right and then the second left.* OPP **left 4 the Right** [sing, with sing or pl verb] the people or political parties who believe in individual responsibility, rather than state support: *The Right in British politics is represented by the Conservative Party.* ➲ look at **right wing**

IDM **be in the right** to be correct and fair: *You don't need to apologize. You were in the right and he was in the wrong.*

by rights according to what is fair or correct: *By rights, half the profit should be mine.*

in your own right because of what you are yourself and not because of other people

within your rights (to do sth) acting in a reasonable or legal way: *You are quite within your rights to demand to see your lawyer.*

right⁴ /raɪt/ *verb* [T] to put sb/sth/yourself back into a normal position: *The boat tipped over and then righted itself again.*

IDM **right a wrong** to do sth to correct an unfair situation or sth bad that you have done

ˈright angle *noun* [C] an angle of 90°: *A square has four right angles.* ➲ look at **acute angle, obtuse angle, reflex angle** ➲ picture at **angle**

ˈright-angled *adj* having or consisting of a **right angle**: *a right-angled triangle*

ˌright-ˈclick *verb* [I,T] **right-click (on) sth** to press the button on a mouse that is on the right side, in order to choose a particular function on a computer screen

righteous /ˈraɪtʃəs/ *adj* (*formal*) that you think is morally good or fair: *righteous anger/indignation* ➲ look at **self-righteous**

rightful /ˈraɪtfl/ *adj* [only *before* a noun] (*formal*) legally or morally correct; fair ▶ **rightfully** /-fəli/ *adv*

ˈright-hand *adj* [only *before* a noun] of or on the right of sb/sth: *The postbox is on the right-hand side of the road.* ♦ *in the top right-hand corner of the screen* OPP **left-hand**

ˌright-ˈhanded *adj* using the right hand for writing, etc. and not the left OPP **left-handed**

ˌright-hand ˈman *noun* [sing] the person you depend on most to help and support you in your work: *the President's right-hand man*

rightly /ˈraɪtli/ *adv* correctly or fairly: *He's been sacked and* ***quite rightly****, I believe.*

ˌright of ˈway *noun* (*pl* **rights of way**) **1** [C,U] (*especially BrE*) a path across private land that the public may use; legal permission to go into or through another person's land: *Walkers have right of way through the farmer's field.* **2** [U] (used in road traffic) the fact that a vehicle in a particular position is allowed to drive into or across a road before another vehicle in a different position: *He should have stopped—I had the right of way.*

ˌright ˈwing *noun* [sing, with sing or pl verb] the people or political parties who believe in individual responsibility, rather than state support ▶ **right-wing** *adj*: *a right-wing government* OPP **left wing**

rigid /ˈrɪdʒɪd/ *adj* **1** not able or not wanting to change or be changed SYN **inflexible 2** difficult to bend; stiff: *a rucksack with a rigid frame* ♦ *She was rigid with fear.* ▶ **rigidity** /rɪˈdʒɪdəti/ *noun* [U] ▶ **rigidly** *adv*: *The speed limit must be rigidly enforced.*

rigorous /ˈrɪɡərəs/ *adj* done very carefully and with great attention to detail: *Rigorous tests are carried out on drinking water.* ▶ **rigorously** *adv*: *The country's press is rigorously controlled.*

rigour (*AmE* **rigor**) /ˈrɪɡə(r)/ *noun* (*formal*) **1** [U] doing sth carefully with great attention to detail: *The tests were carried out with rigour.* **2** [U] the quality of being strict: *the full rigour of the law* **3** [C, usually pl] difficult conditions

rim /rɪm/ *noun* [C] an edge at the top or outside of sth that is round: *the rim of a cup* ♦ *She wore spectacles with gold rims.*

rind /raɪnd/ *noun* [C,U] the thick hard skin on the outside of some fruits, some types of cheese, meat, etc.

> MORE We say the **rind** or **peel** of a lemon or an orange. The soft covering on a fruit like a banana can be called a **peel** or a **skin**.

ring¹ /rɪŋ/ *noun*

➤JEWELLERY **1** [C] a piece of jewellery that you wear on your finger: *a gold/wedding ring* ♦ *an engagement ring* ♦ *A diamond ring glittered on her finger.* ➲ picture at **jewellery**

➤CIRCLE **2** [C] [in compounds] a round object of any material with a hole in the middle: *curtain rings* ♦ *a key ring* (= for holding keys) **3** [C] a round mark or shape: *The coffee cup left a ring on the table top.* ♦ *Stand in a ring and hold hands.*

➤FOR PERFORMANCE **4** [C] the space with seats all around it where a performance, etc. takes place: *a boxing ring*

➤FOR COOKING **5** (*AmE* **burner**) [C] one of the round parts on the top of an electric or gas cooker on which you can put pans: *an electric cooker with an oven, a grill and four rings*

›GROUP OF PEOPLE **6** [C] a number of people who are involved in sth that is secret or not legal: *a spy/drugs ring*

›OF BELL **7** [C] the sound made by a bell; the act of ringing a bell: *There was a ring at the door.*

›QUALITY **8** [sing] **a ring of sth** a particular quality that words or sounds have: *What the man said* ***had a ring of truth*** *about it* (= sounded true).

IDM **give sb a ring** (*BrE informal*) to telephone sb: *I'll give you a ring in the morning.*

ring² /rɪŋ/ *verb* (*pt* **rang** /ræŋ/; *pp* **rung** /rʌŋ/)

›TELEPHONE **1** [I,T] (*especially AmE* **call**) **ring (sb/sth) (up)** to telephone sb/sth: *What time will you ring tomorrow?* ◆ *I rang up yesterday and booked the hotel.* ◆ *Ring the station and ask what time the next train leaves.* SYN **phone** ➲ note at **telephone**

›BELL **2** [I,T] to make a sound like a bell or to cause sth to make this sound: *Is that the phone ringing?* ◆ *We rang the door bell but nobody answered.* **3** [I] **ring (for sb/sth)** to ring a bell in order to call sb, ask for sth, etc: *'Did you ring, sir?' asked the stewardess.* ◆ *Ring for the nurse if you need help.*

›WITH SOUND **4** [I] **ring (with sth)** to be filled with loud sounds: *The music was so loud it made my ears ring.*

›WITH QUALITY **5** [I] (used about words or sounds) to have a certain effect when you hear them: *Her words didn't* ***ring true*** (= you felt that you could not believe what she said).

›SURROUND **6** [T] (*pt, pp* **ringed**) [often passive] to surround sb/sth: *The whole area was ringed with police.*

›DRAW CIRCLE **7** [T] (*pt, pp* **ringed**) (*especially BrE*) to draw a circle around sth: *Ring the correct answer in pencil.* SYN **circle**

IDM **ring a bell** to sound familiar or to remind you, not very clearly, of sb/sth: *'Do you know Josef Vos?' 'Well, the name rings a bell.'*

PHR V **ring (sb) back** (*BrE*) to telephone sb again or to telephone sb who has telephoned you: *I can't talk now—can I ring you back?*

ring in (*BrE*) to telephone a TV or radio show, or the place where you work: *Mandy rang in sick this morning.*

ring off to put down the telephone, because you have finished speaking

ring out to sound loudly and clearly

ringleader /ˈrɪŋliːdə(r)/ *noun* [C] a person who leads others in crime or in causing trouble: *The ringleaders were jailed for 15 years.*

ˈring pull (*AmE* **ˈpull tab**) *noun* [C] a small piece of metal with a ring which you pull to open cans of food, drink, etc.

ˈring road *noun* [C] (*BrE*) a road that is built all around a town so that traffic does not have to go into the town centre ➲ look at **bypass**

ringtone /ˈrɪŋtəʊn/ *noun* [C] the sound that your phone makes when sb is calling you. **Ringtones** are often short tunes.

rink /rɪŋk/ = **skating rink**

rinse /rɪns/ *verb* [T] to wash sth in water in order to remove soap or dirt: *Rinse your hair thoroughly after each shampoo.* ▶ **rinse** *noun* [C]

riot /ˈraɪət/ *noun* [C] a situation in which a group of people behave in a violent way in a public place, often as a protest: *Further riots have broken out in the city.*

IDM **run riot 1** to behave in a wild way without any control: *At the end of the match, the crowd ran riot.* **2** if your imagination, a feeling, etc. **runs riot** you allow it to develop and continue without trying to control it

▶ **riot** *verb* [I]: *There is a danger that the prisoners will riot if conditions do not improve.* ▶ **rioter** *noun* [C]

riotous /ˈraɪətəs/ *adj* **1** wild or violent; lacking in control **2** wild and full of fun: *a riotous party* ◆ *riotous laughter*

ˈriot shield = **shield¹** (2)

RIP /ˌɑːr aɪ ˈpiː/ *abbr* (written on the stones where dead people are buried) **rest in peace**

rip¹ /rɪp/ *verb* (**ripping**; **ripped**) **1** [I,T] to tear or be torn quickly and suddenly: *Oh no! My dress has ripped!* ◆ *He* ***ripped*** *the letter* ***in half/two*** *and threw it in the bin.* ◆ *The blast of the bomb ripped the house apart.* **2** [T] to remove sth quickly and violently, often by pulling it: *He ripped the poster from the wall.* **3** [T] to copy sound or video files from a website or CD onto a computer

PHR V **rip sb off** (*informal*) to cheat sb by charging too much money for sth

rip through sth to move very quickly and violently through sth: *The house was badly damaged when fire ripped through the first floor.*

rip sth up to tear sth into small pieces

rip² /rɪp/ *noun* [C] a long tear (in cloth, etc.)

ripe /raɪp/ *adj* (**riper**; **ripest**) **1** (used about fruit, grain, etc.) ready to be picked and eaten **2 ripe (for sth)** ready for sth or in a suitable state for sth ▶ **ripen** /ˈraɪpən/ *verb* [I,T]

ˈrip-off *noun* [C] (*informal*) something that costs a lot more than it should: *The food in that restaurant is a complete rip-off!*

ripple

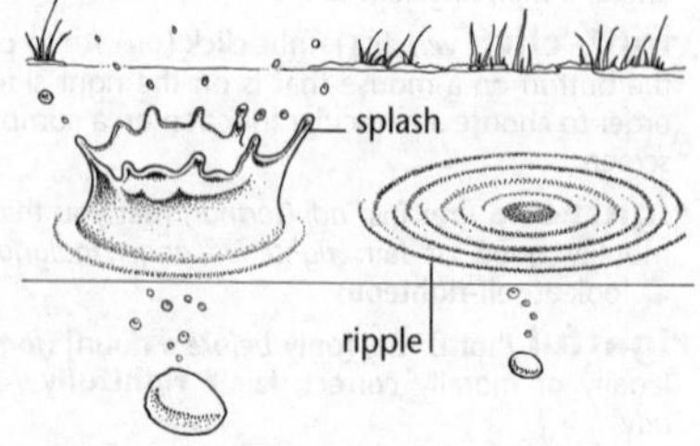

ripple /ˈrɪpl/ *noun* [C] **1** a very small wave or movement on the surface of water **2** [usually sing] **a ripple (of sth)** a sound that gradually becomes louder and then quieter again; a feeling that gradually spreads through a person or a group of people: *a ripple of laughter* ▶ **ripple** *verb* [I,T]

R

rise[1] /raɪz/ *noun* **1** [C] a rise (in sth) an increase in an amount, a number or a level: *There has been a **sharp rise** in the number of people out of work.* OPP **drop, fall 2** [C] (*AmE* raise) an increase in the money you are paid for the work you do: *I'm hoping to **get a rise** next April.* ◆ *a 10% **pay rise*** **3** [sing] the rise (of sth) the process of becoming more powerful or important: *the rise of fascism in Europe* ◆ *her rapid **rise to fame/power***

IDM **give rise to sth** (*formal*) to cause sth to happen or exist

rise[2] /raɪz/ *verb* [I] (*pt* rose /rəʊz/; *pp* risen /ˈrɪzn/)

➤MOVE UPWARDS **1** to move upwards; to become higher, stronger or to increase: *Smoke was rising from the chimney.* ◆ *The temperature has risen to nearly forty degrees.* OPP **fall**

> **HELP** **Rise or raise? Rise** does not have an object. When people or things **rise**, they move upwards: *The helicopter rose into the air.* ◆ *The river has risen (by) several metres.* **Rise** can also mean 'increase': *Prices are always rising.* **Raise** must have an object. When you **raise** something, you lift it up or increase it: *He raised his head from the pillow.* ◆ *Shops are always raising prices.*

➤GET UP **2** (*formal*) to get up from a chair, bed, etc: *The audience rose and applauded the singers.*

➤SUN/MOON **3** to appear above the **horizon** (= the line where the earth meets the sky): *The sun rises in the east and sets in the west.* OPP **set**

➤BECOME POWERFUL **4** to become more successful, powerful, important, etc: *He **rose through the ranks** to become the company director.* ◆ *She **rose to power** in the 90s.*

➤COME FROM **5** to come from: *Shouts of protest rose from the crowd.*

➤FIGHT **6** (*formal*) rise (up) (against sb/sth) to start fighting against your ruler, government, etc: *The people were afraid to rise up against the dictator.*

➤BE SEEN **7** (*formal*) to be seen above or higher than sth else: *A range of mountains rose in the distance.*

IDM **an early riser** ➲ early

rise to the occasion, challenge, task, etc. to show that you are able to deal with a problem, etc. successfully

▶ **rising** *adj*: *the rising cost of living* ◆ *a rising young rock star*

risk[1] /rɪsk/ *noun* **1** [C,U] (a) risk (of sth/that ...); (a) risk (to sb/sth) a possibility of sth dangerous or unpleasant happening; a situation that could be dangerous or have a bad result: *Don't **take** any **risks** when you're driving.* ◆ *You could drive a car without insurance, but it's **not worth the risk**.* ◆ *Scientists say these pesticides **pose a risk** to wildlife.* ◆ *If we don't leave early enough, we **run the risk** of missing the plane.* ◆ *Small children are most **at risk** from the disease.* **2** [sing] a person or thing that might cause danger: *If he knows your real name, he's a security risk.*

IDM **at your own risk** having the responsibility for whatever may happen: *This building is in a dangerous condition—enter at your own risk.*

at the risk of sth/doing sth even though there could be a bad effect: *He rescued the girl at the risk of his own life.*

risk[2] /rɪsk/ *verb* [T] **1** to put sth or yourself in a dangerous position: *The man **risked** his **life** to save the little boy.* **2** to do sth that may mean that you get into a situation which is unpleasant for you: *If you don't work hard now, you risk failing your exams.*

risky /ˈrɪski/ *adj* (riskier; riskiest) involving the possibility of sth bad happening SYN **dangerous**: *a risky investment*

rite /raɪt/ *noun* [C] a ceremony performed by a particular group of people, often for religious purposes: *funeral rites*

ritual /ˈrɪtʃuəl/ *noun* [C,U] a series of actions that is always done in the same way: *(a) religious ritual* ▶ **ritual** *adj* [only *before* a noun] ▶ **ritually** /-tʃuəli/ *adv*

rival[1] /ˈraɪvl/ *noun* [C] a person or thing that is competing with you: *It seems that we're rivals for the sales manager's job.* ▶ **rival** *adj*: *rival companies*

rival[2] /ˈraɪvl/ *verb* [T] (rivalling; rivalled, (*AmE*) rivaling; rivaled) rival sb/sth (for/in sth) to be as good as sb/sth: *Nothing rivals skiing for sheer excitement.*

rivalry /ˈraɪvlri/ *noun* [C,U] (*pl* rivalries) rivalry (between A and B); rivalry (with sb) competition between people, groups, etc: *There was a lot of rivalry between the sisters.*

river /ˈrɪvə(r)/ *noun* [C] (*abbr* R.) a large, natural flow of water that goes across land and into the sea: *the River Nile* ◆ *He sat down on the bank of the river to fish.* ➲ picture on **page P10**

> **MORE** A river **flows** into the sea. The place where it joins the sea is the river **mouth**. A boat sails **on** the river. We sail **up** or **down river** and walk **along** the river (= by the side of it). The ground by the side of a river is the **bank**.

R

riverside /ˈrɪvəsaɪd/ *noun* [sing] the land next to a river: *a riverside hotel*

rivet[1] /ˈrɪvɪt/ *noun* [C] a metal pin for fastening two pieces of metal together

rivet[2] /ˈrɪvɪt/ *verb* [T, usually passive] to keep sb very interested: *I was riveted by her story.* ▶ **riveting** *adj*

roach /rəʊtʃ/ (*AmE*) = **cockroach**

road /rəʊd/ *noun* [C] **1** a hard surface built for vehicles to travel on: *Turn left off the **main** (= important) **road**.* ◆ *road signs* **2** Road (*abbr* Rd) used in names of roads, especially in towns: *60 Marylebone Road, London* ➲ note on next page

IDM **by road** in a car, bus, etc: *It's going to be a terrible journey by road—let's take the train.*

on the road travelling: *We were on the road for 14 hours.*

roadblock /ˈrəʊdblɒk/ *noun* [C] a barrier put across a road by the police or army to stop traffic

ˈroad rage *noun* [U] a situation in which a driver becomes extremely angry or violent with the driver of another car because of the way they are driving

OTHER WORDS FOR

road
Roads connect towns and cities. A **street** is a road that is in a town or city and has buildings at the side: *a street map of York*. Streets often have the word **Road** in their name: *Abbey Road*. **Motorways** (*AmE* **freeways/expressways**) are large roads for traffic travelling fast over long distances, avoiding towns. A **lane** is a narrow road in the country. It can also be one section of a motorway: *He passed me in the fast lane.*

roadside /ˈrəʊdsaɪd/ *noun* [C, usually sing] the edge of a road: *a roadside cafe*

ˈ**road tax** *noun* [C,U] (*BrE*) a tax which the owner of a vehicle has to pay to be allowed to drive it on public roads

the roadway /ˈrəʊdweɪ/ *noun* [sing] a road or the part of a road used by vehicles

roadworks /ˈrəʊdwɜːks/ *noun* [pl] work that involves repairing or building roads

roadworthy /ˈrəʊdwɜːði/ *adj* in good enough condition to be driven on the road

roam /rəʊm/ *verb* [I,T] to walk or travel with no particular plan or aim: *Gangs of youths were roaming the streets looking for trouble.*

roaming /ˈrəʊmɪŋ/ *noun* [U] using a mobile phone by connecting to a different company's network, for example when you are in a different country

roar /rɔː(r)/ *verb* **1** [I] to make a loud, deep sound: *She* ***roared with laughter*** *at the joke.* ◆ *The lion opened its huge mouth and roared.* **2** [I,T] to shout sth very loudly **3** [I] **roar along, down, past, etc.** to move in the direction mentioned, making a loud, deep sound: *A motorbike roared past us.* ▶ **roar** *noun* [C]: *the roar of heavy traffic on the motorway* ◆ *roars of laughter*

roaring /ˈrɔːrɪŋ/ *adj* [only *before* a noun] **1** making a very loud noise **2** (used about a fire) burning very well **3** very great: *a roaring success*

roast[1] /rəʊst/ *verb* **1** [I,T] to cook or be cooked in an oven or over a fire: *a smell of roasting meat* ◆ *to roast a chicken* **2** [T] to heat and dry sth: *roasted peanuts* ➲ note at **cook** ▶ **roast** *adj* [only *before* a noun]: *roast beef/potatoes/chestnuts*

roast[2] /rəʊst/ *noun* **1** [C,U] a piece of meat that has been cooked in an oven **2** [C] (*especially AmE*) an outdoor meal at which food is cooked over a fire ➲ look at **barbecue**

rob /rɒb/ *verb* [T] (**robbing**; **robbed**) **rob sb/sth (of sth)** to take money, property, etc. from a person or place illegally: *to rob a bank* ➲ note at **steal**
PHR V **rob sb/sth (of sth)** to take sth away from sb/sth that they or it should have: *His illness robbed him of the chance to play for his country.*

robber /ˈrɒbə(r)/ *noun* [C] a person who steals from a place or a person, especially using violence or threats ➲ note at **thief**

robbery /ˈrɒbəri/ *noun* [C,U] (*pl* **robberies**) the crime of stealing from a place or a person, especially using violence or threats: *They were found guilty of* ***armed robbery*** (= using a weapon).

robe /rəʊb/ *noun* [C] **1** a long, loose piece of clothing, especially one that is worn at ceremonies **2** (*AmE*) = **dressing gown**

robin /ˈrɒbɪn/ *noun* [C] a small brown bird with a bright red chest

robot /ˈrəʊbɒt/ *noun* [C] a machine that works automatically and can do some tasks that a human can do: *These cars are built by robots.*

robust /rəʊˈbʌst/ *adj* (**robuster**; **robustest**) strong and healthy

rock[1] /rɒk/ *noun*
➤HARD MATERIAL **1** [U] the hard, solid material that forms part of the surface of the earth: *layers of rock formed over millions of years* **2** [C, usually pl] a large mass of rock that sticks out of the sea or the ground: *The ship hit the rocks and started to sink.* **3** [C] a single large piece of rock: *The beach was covered with rocks that had broken away from the cliffs.*
➤STONE **4** [C] (*AmE*) a small piece of rock that can be picked up: *The boy threw a rock at the dog.* ➲ picture on **page P10**
➤MUSIC **5** (also ˈ**rock music**) [U] a type of music with a very strong beat, played on musical instruments such as electric **guitars**, drums, etc: *I prefer jazz to rock.* ◆ *a rock singer/band* ➲ look at **classical, jazz, pop**
➤SWEET **6** [U] (*BrE*) a type of hard sweet made in long, round sticks: *a stick of rock*
IDM **on the rocks 1** (used about a marriage, business, etc.) having problems and likely to fail **2** (used about drinks) served with ice but no water: *whisky on the rocks*

rock[2] /rɒk/ *verb* **1** [I,T] to move backwards and forwards or from side to side; to make sb/sth do this: *boats rocking gently on the waves* ◆ *He rocked the baby in his arms to get her to sleep.* **2** [T] to shake sth violently: *The city was rocked by a bomb blast.* **3** [T] to shock sb
IDM **rock the boat** (*informal*) to do sth that causes problems or upsets people: *They employ mainly quiet people who won't complain and rock the boat.*

ˌ**rock and** ˈ**roll** (also **rock 'n' roll**) *noun* [U] a type of music with a strong beat that was most popular in the 1950s

ˌ**rock** ˈ**bottom** *noun* [U] (*informal*) the lowest point: *He* ***hit rock bottom*** *when he lost his job and his wife left him.* ◆ *rock-bottom prices*

ˈ**rock climbing** *noun* [U] the sport of climbing rocks and mountains with ropes, etc.

rocket[1] /ˈrɒkɪt/ *noun* [C] **1** a vehicle that is used for travel into space: *a space rocket* ◆ *to launch a rocket* **2** a weapon that travels through the air and that carries a bomb SYN **missile 3** a type of **firework** (= an object that explodes in a beautiful way when you light it with a flame) that shoots high into the air

rocket² /ˈrɒkɪt/ *verb* [I] to increase or rise very quickly: *Prices have rocketed recently.*

ˈ**rock music** = rock¹(5)

ˌ**rock ʼnʼ** ˈ**roll** = rock and roll

rocky /ˈrɒki/ *adj* (**rockier**; **rockiest**) covered with or made of rocks: *a rocky coastline*

rod /rɒd/ *noun* [C] [often in compounds] a thin straight piece of wood, metal, etc: *a fishing rod*

rode *past tense of* **ride¹**

rodent /ˈrəʊdnt/ *noun* [C] a type of small animal, such as a **rat**, a **rabbit**, a mouse, etc. which has strong sharp front teeth

rodeo /ˈrəʊdiəʊ; rəʊˈdeɪəʊ/ *noun* [C] (*pl* **rodeos**) (especially in the US) a competition or performance in which people show their skill in riding wild horses, catching cows, etc.

roe /rəʊ/ *noun* [U] the eggs of a fish, that can be eaten

rogue /rəʊg/ *adj* [only *before* a noun] behaving differently from other similar people or things, often causing damage: *a rogue gene/program*

role /rəʊl/ *noun* [C] **1** the position or function of sb/sth in a particular situation: *Parents **play a** vital **role** in their children's education.* ♦ *a **role model*** (= a person that you admire and try to copy) **2** a person's part in a play, film, etc: *She was chosen to **play the role** of Cleopatra.* ♦ *a **leading role** in the film*

ˈ**role-play** *noun* [C,U] an activity used especially in teaching in which a person acts a part

rolls

toilet roll

bread rolls

roll of tape

roll¹ /rəʊl/ *noun*

➤OF PAPER, ETC. **1** [C] something made into the shape of a tube by turning it round and round itself: *a roll of film/wallpaper*

➤BREAD **2** [C] bread baked in a round shape for one person to eat: *a cheese roll* (= filled with cheese) ➲ picture at **bread**

➤MOVEMENT **3** [C] an act of moving or making sth move by turning over and over: *Everything depended on one roll of the dice.* **4** a movement from side to side: *the roll of a ship*

➤LIST OF NAMES **5** [C] an official list of names: *the electoral roll* (= the list of people who can vote in an election)

➤SOUND **6** [C] a long, low sound: *a roll of drums*

roll² /rəʊl/ *verb*

➤TURN OVER **1** [I,T] to move by turning over and over; to make sth move in this way: *The apples fell out of the bag and rolled everywhere.* ♦ *He tried to roll the rock up the hill.* **2** [I,T] **roll (sth) (over)** to turn over and over; to make sth do this: *The horse was rolling in the dirt.* ♦ *The car rolled over in the crash.* ♦ *We rolled the log over to see what was underneath.*

➤MOVE SMOOTHLY **3** [I] to move smoothly, often on wheels: *The car began to roll back down the hill.* ♦ *Tears were rolling down her cheeks.*

➤MAKE BALL/TUBE **4** [I,T] **roll (sth) (up)** to make sth into the shape of a ball or tube: *I rolled the string into a ball.* ♦ *The insect rolled up when I touched it.* OPP **unroll**

➤MAKE FLAT **5** [T] **roll sth (out)** to make sth become flat by moving sth heavy over it: *Roll out the pastry thinly.*

➤OF SHIP, ETC. **6** [I] to move from side to side: *The ship began to roll in the storm.*

IDM **be rolling in money/in it** (*informal*) to have a lot of money

PHR V **roll in** (*informal*) to arrive in large numbers or amounts: *Offers of help have been rolling in.*

roll up (*informal*) (used about a person or a vehicle) to arrive, especially late

roller /ˈrəʊlə(r)/ *noun* [C] **1** a piece of equipment or part of a machine that is shaped like a tube and used, for example, to make sth flat or to help sth move: *a roller blind on a window* ➲ picture at **curtain** **2** [usually pl] a small plastic tube that hair is rolled around to give it curls

Rollerblade™ /ˈrəʊləbleɪd/ *noun* [C] a boot with one row of narrow wheels on the bottom: *a pair of Rollerblades* ➲ picture at **skate** ▶ **rollerblade** *verb* [I] ▶ **rollerblading** *noun* [U]

HELP **Go rollerblading** is a common way of talking about rollerblading for pleasure: *We go rollerblading every weekend.*

ˈ**roller coaster** *noun* [C] a narrow metal track that goes up and down and round tight bends, and that people ride on in a small train for fun and excitement

ˈ**roller skate** (also **skate**) *noun* [C] a type of shoe with two pairs of small wheels on the bottom: *a pair of roller skates* ➲ picture at **skate** ▶ **roller skate** *verb* [I] ▶ ˈ**roller skating** *noun* [U]

ˈ**rolling pin** *noun* [C] a piece of wood, etc. in the shape of a tube, that you use for making **pastry** (= a mixture of flour, fat and water) flat and thin before cooking it ➲ picture at **kitchen**

ROM /rɒm/ *abbr* **read-only memory**; computer memory that contains instructions or data that cannot be changed or removed ➲ look at **CD-ROM**, **RAM**

the Roma /ˈrəʊmə/ *noun* [pl] the **Romani** people

Roman /ˈrəʊmən/ *adj* **1** connected with ancient Rome or the Roman Empire: *Roman coins* ♦ *the*

R

Roman invasion of Britain **2** connected with the modern city of Rome ▶ **Roman** *noun* [C]

the ˌRoman ˈalphabet *noun* [sing] the letters A to Z, used in most western European languages

ˌRoman ˈCatholic (also **Catholic**) *noun* [C], *adj* (a member) of the Christian Church which has the Pope as its head: *She's (a) Roman Catholic.* ➲ look at **Protestant**

ˌRoman Caˈtholicism (also **Catholicism**) *noun* [U] the beliefs of the Roman Catholic Church

romance /rəʊˈmæns; ˈrəʊmæns/ *noun* **1** [C] a relationship between two people who are in love with each other: *The film was about a teenage romance.* **2** [U] a feeling or atmosphere of love or of sth new, special and exciting **3** [C] a novel about a love affair: *historical romances*

Romani (also **Romany**) /ˈrɒməni; ˈrəʊm-/ *noun* (*pl* -ies) **1** [C] a member of a race of people who traditionally spend their lives travelling around from place to place, living in **caravans** (= homes with wheels that can be pulled by a car or by a horse) ➲ look at **Gypsy**, **traveller** **2** [U] the language of the **Romani** people

ˌRoman ˈnumeral *noun* [pl] one of the letters used by the ancient Romans as numbers

HELP Roman numerals, for example IV (= 4) and X (= 10), are still used sometimes. For example, they may be found numbering the pages and chapters of books, or on some clocks.

romantic¹ /rəʊˈmæntɪk/ *adj* **1** having a quality that strongly affects your emotions or makes you think about love; showing feelings of love: *a romantic candlelit dinner* ◆ *She isn't very romantic—she never says she loves me.* **2** involving a relationship between two people who are in love with each other: *Reports of a romantic relationship between the two film stars have been strongly denied.* **3** having or showing ideas about life that are emotional rather than real or practical: *He has a romantic idea that he'd like to live on a farm in Scotland.* ▶ **romantically** /-kli/ *adv*

romantic² /rəʊˈmæntɪk/ *noun* [C] a person who has ideas that are not based on real life or that are not very practical

romanticize (also -ise) /rəʊˈmæntɪsaɪz/ *verb* [I, T] to make sth seem more interesting, exciting, etc. than it really is

romp /rɒmp/ *verb* [I] (used about children and animals) to play in a happy and noisy way

IDM **romp home/to victory** to win easily: *United romped to a 4-0 victory over Juventus.*

▶ **romp** *noun* [C]

roof /ruːf/ *noun* [C] (*pl* **roofs**) **1** the part of a building, vehicle, etc. which covers the top of it: *a flat/sloping/tiled roof* ◆ *the roof of a car* ◆ *The library and the sports hall are* ***under one roof*** (= in the same building). ➲ picture on **page P9** **2** the highest part of the inside of sth: *The roof of the cave had collapsed.* ◆ *The soup burned the roof of my mouth.*

IDM **hit the roof** ➲ **hit¹**

a roof over your head somewhere to live: *I might not have any money, but at least I've got a roof over my head.*

ˈroof rack *noun* [C] a structure that you fix to the roof of a car and use for carrying luggage or other large objects ➲ picture at **rack**

rooftop /ˈruːftɒp/ *noun* [C, usually pl] the outside of the roof of a building: *From the tower we looked down over the rooftops of the city.*

room /ruːm; rʊm/ *noun* **1** [C] a part of a house or building that has its own walls, floor and ceiling: *a sitting/dining/living room* ◆ *I sat down in the waiting room until the doctor called me.* ◆ *I'd like to book a double room for two nights next month.* **2** [U] **room (for sb/sth); room (to do sth)** space; enough space: *These chairs* ***take up*** *too much* ***room.*** ◆ *I threw away my old clothes to* ***make room*** *in the wardrobe for some new ones.* ◆ *There were so many people that there wasn't any room to move.* ➲ note at **place¹** ➲ look at **space** **3** [U] **room for sth** the opportunity or need for sth: *There's* ***room for improvement*** *in your work* (= it could be much better). ◆ *The lack of time gives us very little* ***room for manoeuvre.***

roomful /ˈruːmfʊl; ˈrʊm-/ *noun* [C] a large number of people or things in a room

ˈroommate *noun* [C] a person that you share a room with in a flat, etc.

roomy /ˈruːmi/ *adj* (**roomier**; **roomiest**) having plenty of space: *a roomy house/car* **SYN** **spacious**

roost /ruːst/ *noun* [C] a place where birds rest or sleep ▶ **roost** *verb* [I]

rooster /ˈruːstə(r)/ (*AmE*) = **cock¹** (1)

root¹ /ruːt/ *noun* **1** [C] the part of a plant that grows under the ground and takes in water and food from the soil: *The deep roots of these trees can cause damage to buildings.* ◆ ***root vegetables*** *such as carrots and parsnips* ➲ picture at **plant**, **tree** **2** [C] the part of a hair or tooth that is under the skin and that fixes it to the rest of the body **3** **roots** [pl] the feelings or connections that you have with a place because you or your family have lived there **4** [C] the basic cause or origin of sth: *Let's try and get to the* ***root of the problem.*** ➲ look at **square root**

root² /ruːt/ *verb*

PHR V **root about/around (for sth)** to search for sth by moving things: *What are you rooting around in my bag for?*

root for sb (*informal*) to give support to sb who is in a competition, etc.

root sth out to find and destroy sth bad completely

rope¹ /rəʊp/ *noun* [C,U] very thick, strong string that is used for tying or lifting heavy things, climbing up, etc: *The rope broke and she fell.* ◆ *We need some rope to tie up the boat with.*

IDM **show sb/know/learn the ropes** to show sb/know/learn how a job should be done

rope² /rəʊp/ *verb* [T] **rope A to B/A and B together** to tie sb/sth with a rope

PHR V **rope sb in (to do sth)** (*informal*) to per-

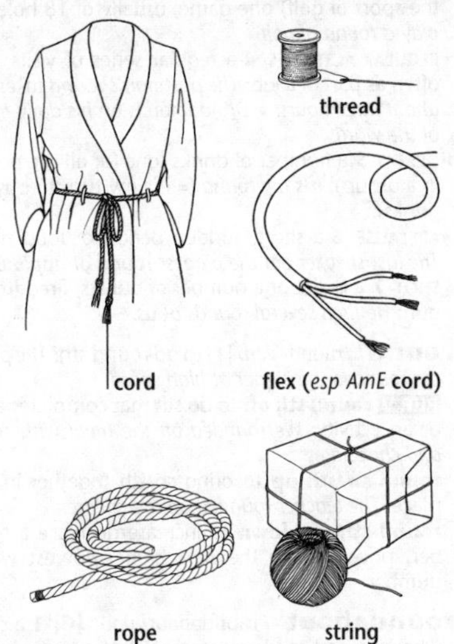

suade sb to help in an activity, especially when they do not want to: *I've been roped in to help with the school play.*

rope sth off to put ropes round or across an area in order to keep people out of it

rosary /ˈrəʊzəri/ *noun* [C] (*pl* **rosaries**) a string of small round pieces of wood, etc. used for counting prayers

rose¹ *past tense* of **rise²**

rose² /rəʊz/ *noun* [C] a flower with a sweet smell, that grows on a bush that usually has **thorns** (= sharp points) growing on it

rosé /ˈrəʊzeɪ/ *noun* [U] pink wine

rosemary /ˈrəʊzməri/ *noun* [U] a **herb** (= a type of plant) with small narrow leaves that smell sweet and are used in cooking

rosette /rəʊˈzet/ *noun* [C] a round decoration made from **ribbons** (= long pieces of coloured cloth) that you wear on your clothes. Rosettes are given as prizes or worn to show that sb supports a particular political party. ➲ picture at **medal**

roster /ˈrɒstə(r)/ (*AmE*) = **rota**

rostrum /ˈrɒstrəm/ *noun* [C] a platform that sb stands on to make a public speech, etc.

rosy /ˈrəʊzi/ *adj* (**rosier**; **rosiest**) **1** pink and pleasant in appearance: *rosy cheeks* **2** likely to be good or successful: *The future was looking rosy.*

rot /rɒt/ *verb* [I,T] (**rotting**; **rotted**) to go bad or make sth go bad as part of a natural process: *Too many sweets will rot your teeth!* **SYN** **decay** ▶ **rot** *noun* [U]

rota /ˈrəʊtə/ (*AmE* **roster**) *noun* [C] a list of people who share a certain job or task and the times that they are each going to do it: *We organize the cleaning* ***on a rota.***

rotary /ˈrəʊtəri/ *adj* [only *before* a noun] moving in circles round a central point

rotate /rəʊˈteɪt/ *verb* [I,T] **1** to turn in circles round a central point; to make sth do this: *The earth rotates on its axis.* **2** to happen in turn or in a particular order; to make sth do this: *We rotate the duties so that nobody is stuck with a job they don't like.*

rotation /rəʊˈteɪʃn/ *noun* [C,U] **1** movement in a circle round a central point: *one rotation every 24 hours* **2** happening or making things happen in a particular order: *The company is chaired by all the members* ***in rotation.***

rotor /ˈrəʊtə(r)/ *noun* [C] a part of a machine that turns round, for example the blades that go round on top of a **helicopter** (= a small aircraft that can go straight up in the air)

rotten /ˈrɒtn/ *adj* **1** (used about food and other substances) old and not fresh enough or good enough to use: *rotten vegetables* **2** (*informal*) very unpleasant: *That was a rotten thing to say!* **3** [only *before* a noun] (*spoken*) used to emphasize that you are angry: *You can keep your rotten job!*

rouge /ruːʒ/ *noun* [U] (*old-fashioned*) a red powder or cream used for giving more colour to the cheeks

🔑 **rough¹** /rʌf/ *adj* (**rougher**; **roughest**) **1** not smooth or level: *rough ground* **OPP** **smooth** **2** made or done quickly or without much care: *a rough estimate* ◆ *Can you give me a rough idea of what time you'll be arriving?* **SYN** **approximate** **3** violent; not calm or gentle: *You can hold the baby, but don't be rough with him.* ◆ *The sea was rough and half the people on the boat were seasick.* **4** (*BrE informal*) looking or feeling ill: *You look a bit rough—are you feeling all right?* **5** difficult and unpleasant **SYN** **tough**: *He's had a really* ***rough time*** *recently* (= he's had a lot of problems) ▶ **roughness** *noun* [U]

rough² /rʌf/ *noun*

IDM **in rough** (*BrE*) done quickly without worrying about mistakes, as a preparation for the finished piece of work or drawing

take the rough with the smooth to accept difficult or unpleasant things in addition to pleasant things

rough³ /rʌf/ *verb*

IDM **rough it** (*informal*) to live without all the comfortable things that you usually have: *You have to rough it a bit when you go camping.*

rough⁴ /rʌf/ *adv* using force or violence: *Does the team always* ***play*** *this* ***rough****?*

IDM **live/sleep rough** (*BrE*) to live or sleep outdoors, usually because you have no home or money

roughage /ˈrʌfɪdʒ/ *noun* [U] the part of food that helps food and waste products to pass through the body **SYN** **fibre**

roughen /ˈrʌfn/ *verb* [T] to make sth less smooth or soft

🔑 **roughly** /ˈrʌfli/ *adv* **1** not exactly; approximately: *It took roughly three hours, I suppose.* **2** in a violent way; not gently: *He grabbed her roughly by her arm.*

roulette /ruːˈlet/ *noun* [U] a gambling game in which a ball is dropped onto a moving wheel that has holes with numbers on them. The players bet on which number hole the ball will be in when the wheel stops.

round¹ /raʊnd/ (**rounder; roundest**) *adj* having the shape of a circle or a ball: *a round table*
IDM in round figures/numbers given to the nearest 10, 100, 1 000, etc.; not given in exact numbers

round² /raʊnd/ *adv, prep* **1** in a full circle: *The wheels spun* ***round and round*** *but the car wouldn't move.* ♦ *How long would it take to walk round the world?* **2** on, to or from the other side of sth: *We were just talking about Ravi and he came* ***round the corner.*** ♦ (*figurative*) *It wasn't easy to see a way round the problem* (= a way of solving it). **3** on all sides of sb/sth; surrounding sb/sth: *He had a bandage right round his head.* ♦ *We sat round the table, talking late into the night.* **4** from one place, person, etc. to another: ***Pass*** *the photographs* ***round*** *for everyone to see.* ♦ *I've been rushing round all day.* **5** in or to a particular area or place: *Do you live round here?* ♦ *I'll come round to see you at about 8 o'clock.* **6** turning to look or go in the opposite direction: *Don't* ***look round*** *but the teacher's just come in.* ♦ *She* ***turned*** *the car* ***round*** *and drove off.* **7** in or to many parts of sth: *Let me* ***show*** *you* ***round*** *the house.* ♦ *He spent six months travelling round Europe.*

HELP **Around** has the same meaning as **round** and is more common in American English.

ⓘ For special uses with many verbs, for example **come round, get round, go round,** etc. see the verb entries.
IDM the other way round ➲ **other**
round about (sth) 1 approximately: *We hope to arrive round about 6.00.* **2** in the area near a place: *I know all the good places to eat round about here.*
round the bend (*BrE informal*) crazy: *His behaviour is* ***driving me round the bend*** (= annoying me very much). **SYN mad**

round³ /raʊnd/ *noun* [C]
➤EVENTS **1** a number or series of events, etc: *a further round of talks with other European countries*
➤IN SPORT **2** one part of a game or competition: *Parma will play Real Madrid in the next round.* **3** (in the sport of **golf**) one game, usually of 18 holes: *to play a round of golf*
➤REGULAR ACTIVITIES **4** a regular series of visits, etc., often as part of a job: *The postman's round takes him about three hours.* ♦ *Dr Adamou is on his daily round of the wards.*
➤DRINKS **5** a number of drinks (one for all the people in a group): *It's my round* (= it's my turn to buy the drinks).
➤APPLAUSE **6** a short, sudden period of loud noise: *The last speaker got the biggest* ***round of applause.***
➤SHOT **7** a bullet or a number of bullets, fired from a gun: *He fired several rounds at us.*

round⁴ /raʊnd/ *verb* [T] to go round sth: *The police car rounded the corner at high speed.*
PHR V round sth off to do sth that completes a job or an activity: *We rounded off the meal with coffee and chocolates.*
round sb/sth up to bring sb/sth together in one place: *The teacher rounded up the children.*
round sth up/down to increase/decrease a number, price, etc. to the next highest/lowest whole number

roundabout¹ /ˈraʊndəbaʊt/ *noun* [C] **1** a circle where several roads meet, that all the traffic has to go round in the same direction **2** (*AmE* **merry-go-round**) a round platform made for children to play on. They sit or stand on it and sb pushes it round. ➲ picture at **swing 3** (*BrE*) = **merry-go-round**

roundabout² /ˈraʊndəbaʊt/ *adj* longer than is necessary or usual; not direct: *We got lost and came by rather a roundabout route.*

rounded /ˈraʊndɪd/ *adj* **1** having a round shape: *a surface with rounded edges* ♦ *rounded shoulders* **2** having a wide variety of qualities that combine to produce sth pleasant, complete and balanced: *a fully rounded education*

rounders /ˈraʊndəz/ *noun* [U] a British game played especially in schools by two teams using a **bat** and ball. Each player tries to hit the ball and then run around the four sides of a square before the other team can return the ball.

ˌround ˈtrip *noun* [C] **1** a journey to a place and back again: *It's a four-mile round trip to the centre of town.* **2** (also ˌ**round-trip ˈticket**) (*AmE*) = **return²**(4)

rouse /raʊz/ *verb* [T] (*formal*) **1** to make sb wake up: *She was sleeping so soundly that I couldn't rouse*

roundabout

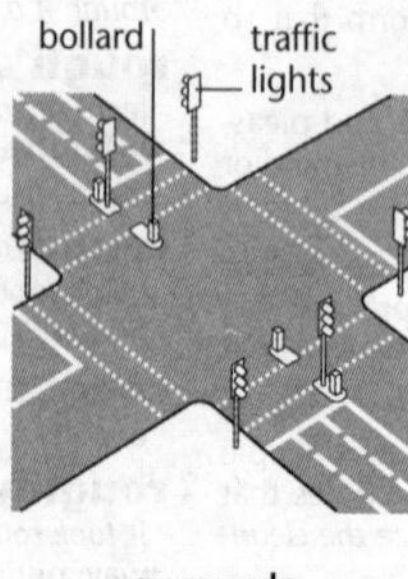

crossroads

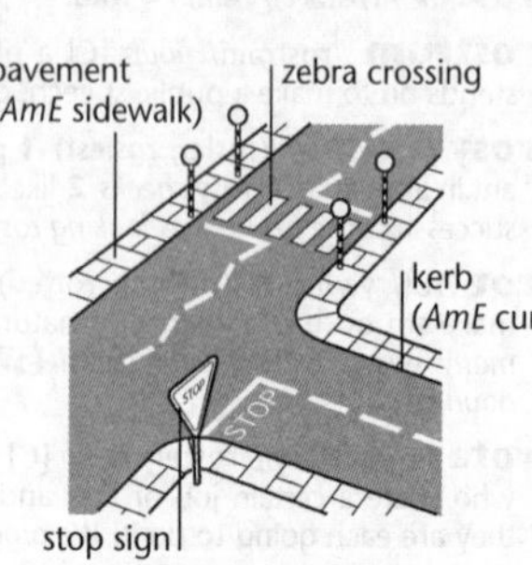

T-junction

her. **2** to make sb/sth very angry, excited, interested, etc.

rousing /ˈraʊzɪŋ/ *adj* exciting and powerful: *a rousing speech*

rout /raʊt/ *verb* [T] to defeat sb completely ▶ **rout** *noun* [C]

route /ru:t/ *noun* [C] **1** a route (from A) (to B) a way from one place to another: *What is the most direct route from Bordeaux to Lyon?* ◆ *I got a leaflet about the bus routes from the information office.* **2** a route to sth a way of achieving sth: *Hard work is the only route to success.* **3** used before the number of a main road in the US

router /ˈru:tə(r)/ *noun* [C] a device which sends data to the parts of a computer network. You can use a router to connect your computer or laptop to the Internet.

routine¹ /ru:ˈti:n/ *noun* **1** [C,U] the usual order and way in which you regularly do things: *Make exercise part of your daily routine.* **2** [U] tasks that have to be done again and again and so are boring: *I gave up the job because I couldn't stand the routine.* **3** [C] a series of movements, jokes, etc. that are part of a performance: *a dance/comedy routine*

TOPIC

Daily routine

On weekdays (= Monday to Friday), I **wake up** when the alarm goes off and **get up** at 7.30. If I **oversleep** (= sleep too long), I know that I will be late for work. I **have a shower** and wash my hair. I **blow-dry** my hair with a hairdryer and **get dressed**. I have breakfast at about 8.00, while listening to the radio. I **brush my teeth** and then at 8.30 I leave the house to walk to the station. The train is very crowded with other commuters because it is rush hour. I work from **nine to five**, with a **lunch hour** from one until two. After work I like spending time with friends. We go to the cinema, or to a bar or cafe for a drink. **Twice a week** I go to the gym because I like to keep fit. I **get home** some time after 7.00 and have dinner. In the evening I **relax** and watch TV or read the paper. I **go to bed** at 11.00 and **fall asleep** straight away.

routine² /ru:ˈti:n/ *adj* **1** normal and regular; not unusual or special: *The police would like to ask you some routine questions.* **2** boring; not exciting: *It's a very routine job, really.*

routinely /ru:ˈti:nli/ *adv* regularly; as part of a **routine**: *The machines are routinely checked every two months.*

row¹ /rəʊ/ *noun* [C] **1** a line of people or things: *a row of books* ◆ *The children were all standing* ***in a row*** *at the front of the class.* **2** a line of seats in a theatre, cinema, etc: *Our seats were in the back row.* ◆ *a front-row seat*

IDM in a row one after another; without a break: *It rained solidly for four days in a row.*

row² /rəʊ/ *verb* **1** [I,T] to move a boat through the water using **oars** (= long thin pieces of wood with flat parts at the end): *We often go rowing on the lake.* **2** [T] to carry sb/sth in a boat that you row: *Could you row us over to the island?* ➲ look at **paddle** ▶ **row** *noun* [sing]

row³ /raʊ/ *noun* (*especially BrE*) **1** [C] a row (about/over sth) a noisy argument or a serious disagreement between two or more people, groups, etc: *When I* ***have a row*** *with my girlfriend, I always try to make up as soon as possible.* ◆ *A row has broken out between the main parties over education.* ➲ note at **argument** **2** [sing] a loud noise: *What a row! Could you be a bit quieter?* ▶ **row** *verb* [I] row (with sb) (about/over sth): *Pete and I are always rowing about money.*

HELP Be careful when you use the word **row** that you use the correct pronunciation, as **row** /rəʊ/ and **row** /raʊ/ have different meanings.

rowboat /ˈrəʊbəʊt/ (*AmE*) = **rowing boat**

rowdy /ˈraʊdi/ *adj* (rowdier; rowdiest) noisy and likely to cause trouble: *The football fans soon got rowdy.* ▶ **rowdily** *adv* ▶ **rowdiness** *noun* [U]

ˈrowing boat (*AmE* rowboat) *noun* [C] a small boat that you move through the water using **oars** (= long thin pieces of wood with flat parts at the end) ➲ note at **boat** ➲ picture at **boat**

royal /ˈrɔɪəl/ *adj* [only *before* a noun] **1** connected with a king or queen or a member of their family: *the royal family* **2** (used in the names of organizations) supported by a member of the royal family: *the Royal Society for the Protection of Birds* ▶ **royal** *noun* (*informal*): *the Queen, the Princes and other royals*

ˌRoyal ˈHighness *noun* [C] used when you are speaking to or about a member of the royal family

royalty /ˈrɔɪəlti/ *noun* (*pl* royalties) **1** [U] members of the royal family **2** [C, usually pl] an amount of money that is paid to the person who wrote a book, piece of music, etc. every time their work is sold or performed: *The author earns a 2% royalty on each copy sold.*

rpm /ˌɑ: pi: ˈem/ *abbr* **revolutions per minute**: *engine speed 2500 rpm*

RSI /ˌɑ:r es ˈaɪ/ *noun* [U] **repetitive strain injury**; pain and swelling, especially in the wrists and hands, caused by doing the same movement many times in a job or an activity

RSVP /ˌɑ:r es vi: ˈpi:/ *abbr* (from French) **répondez s'il vous plaît**; (used on invitations) please reply

Rt Hon *abbr* **Right Honourable**; a title used in Britain about people of high social rank and the most important ministers in the government

rub /rʌb/ *verb* (rubbing; rubbed) **1** [I,T] to move your hand, a cloth, etc. backwards and forwards on the surface of sth while pressing firmly: *Ralph rubbed his hands together to keep them warm.* ◆ *The cat rubbed against my leg.* **2** [T] rub sth in (to sth) to put a cream, liquid, etc. onto a surface by rubbing: *Apply a little of the lotion and rub it into the skin.* **3** [I, T] rub (on/against sth) to press on/against sth, often

R

causing pain or damage: *These new shoes are rubbing against my heels.*

IDM **rub salt into the wound/sb's wounds** to make sb who feels bad feel even worse

rub shoulders with sb to meet and spend time with famous people: *As a journalist you rub shoulders with the rich and famous.*

PHR V **rub it/sth in** to keep reminding sb of sth embarrassing that they want to forget: *I know it was a stupid mistake, but there's no need to rub it in!*

rub off (on/onto sb) (used about a good quality) to be passed from one person to another: *Let's hope some of her enthusiasm rubs off onto her brother.*

rub sth off (sth) to remove sth from a surface by rubbing: *He rubbed the dirt off his boots.*

rub sth out (*BrE*) to remove the marks made by a pencil, etc. using a rubber, etc: *That answer is wrong. Rub it out.*

▸ **rub** *noun* [C, usually sing]

rubber /ˈrʌbə(r)/ *noun* **1** [U] a strong substance that can be stretched and does not allow water to pass through it, used for making tyres, boots, etc. Rubber is made from the juice of a tropical tree or is produced using chemicals: *a rubber ball* ◆ *rubber gloves* ◆ *foam rubber* **2** [C] (*especially AmE* **eraser**) a small piece of rubber that you use for removing pencil marks from paper; a piece of soft material used for removing **chalk** (= soft stone that you use for writing or drawing) marks from a board ➲ picture at **stationery** **3** (*informal*) (*especially AmE*) = **condom**

ˌrubber ˈband (also eˌlastic ˈband) *noun* [C] a thin round piece of rubber that is used for holding things together: *a pile of envelopes with a rubber band round them* ➲ picture at **stationery**

ˌrubber ˈstamp *noun* [C] **1** a small tool that you use for printing a name, date, etc. on a document ➲ picture at **stationery** **2** a person or group who gives official approval to sth without thinking about it first ▸ **ˌrubber-ˈstamp** *verb* [T]: *The committee have no real power—they just rubber-stamp the chairman's ideas.*

rubbery /ˈrʌbəri/ *adj* like rubber: *This meat is rubbery.*

rubbish /ˈrʌbɪʃ/ (*especially AmE* **garbage**; *AmE* **trash**) *noun* [U] **1** things that you do not want any more; waste material: *The dustmen collect the rubbish every Monday.* ◆ *a rubbish bin* ◆ *It's only rubbish —throw it away.* ➲ look at **waste** **2** something that you think is bad, silly or wrong: *I thought that film was absolute rubbish.* ◆ *Don't talk such rubbish.* SYN **nonsense**

ˈrubbish tip = **tip**[1] (4)

rubble /ˈrʌbl/ *noun* [U] pieces of broken brick, stone, etc., especially from a damaged building

rubella /ruːˈbelə/ = **German measles**

ruby /ˈruːbi/ *noun* [C] (*pl* **rubies**) a red **precious stone** (= one that is rare and valuable)

rucksack /ˈrʌksæk/ *noun* [C] (*BrE*) = **backpack**[1]

rudder /ˈrʌdə(r)/ *noun* [C] a piece of wood or metal that is used for controlling the direction of a boat or plane

rude /ruːd/ *adj* (**ruder**; **rudest**) **1 rude (to sb) (about sb/sth)** not polite: *She was very rude to me about my new jacket.* ◆ *It's rude to interrupt when people are speaking.* ◆ *I think it was rude of them not to phone and say that they weren't coming.* SYN **impolite** **2** connected with sex, using the toilet, etc. in a way that might offend people: *a rude joke/word/gesture* SYN **offensive** **3** [only *before* a noun] sudden and unpleasant: *If you're expecting any help from him, you're in for a rude shock.* ▸ **rudely** *adv* ▸ **rudeness** *noun* [U]

rudimentary /ˌruːdɪˈmentri/ *adj* (*formal*) very basic or simple

rudiments /ˈruːdɪmənts/ *noun* [pl] (*formal*) the **rudiments (of sth)** the most basic facts of a particular subject, skill, etc.

ruffle /ˈrʌfl/ *verb* [T] **1 ruffle sth (up)** to make sth untidy or no longer smooth: *to ruffle somebody's hair* **2** [often passive] to make sb annoyed or confused

rug /rʌg/ *noun* [C] **1** a piece of thick material that covers a small part of a floor ➲ look at **carpet, mat** ➲ picture on **page P8** **2** (*BrE*) a large piece of thick cloth that you put over your legs to keep warm

rugby /ˈrʌgbi/ *noun* [U] a game that is played by two teams of 13 or 15 players with a ball shaped like an egg that can be carried, kicked or thrown ➲ look at **league** ➲ picture on **page P4**

MORE **Rugby League** is played with 13 players in a team, **Rugby Union** with 15 players.

rugged /ˈrʌgɪd/ *adj* **1** (used about land) rough, with a lot of rocks and not many plants **2** (used about a man) strong and attractive **3** strong and made for difficult conditions

ruin[1] /ˈruːɪn/ *verb* [T] **1** to damage sth so badly that it loses all its value, pleasure, etc: *The bad news ruined my week.* ◆ *That one mistake ruined my chances of getting the job.* **2** to cause sb to lose all their money, hope of being successful, etc: *The cost of the court case nearly ruined them.*

ruin[2] /ˈruːɪn/ *noun* **1** [U] the state of being destroyed or very badly damaged: *The city was in a state of ruin.* **2** [U] the fact of having no money, of having lost your job, position, etc: *Many small companies are facing **financial ruin**.* **3** [U] something that causes a person, company, etc. to lose all their money, job, position, etc. **4** [C] (also **ruins**) the parts of a building that are left standing after it has been destroyed or badly damaged: *the ruins of the ancient city of Pompeii*

IDM **go to rack and ruin** ➲ **rack**[1]

in ruin(s) badly damaged or destroyed: *After the accident her life seemed to be in ruins.*

ruined /ˈruːɪnd/ *adj* [only *before* a noun] destroyed or severely damaged so that only parts remain: *a ruined building*

ruinous /ˈruːɪnəs/ *adj* (*formal*) causing serious problems, especially with money

rule[1] /ruːl/ *noun*
➤OF ACTIVITY/GAME **1** [C] an official statement that tells you what you must or must not do in a particular situation or when playing a game: *to **obey/break a rule** ◆ Do you know the rules of chess? ◆ It's **against the rules** to talk during the exam. ◆ The company have strict **rules and regulations** governing employees' dress.*

HELP Rule or law? A law is stronger. You can be punished by the legal system if you break it.

➤ADVICE **2** [C] a piece of advice about what you should do in a particular situation: *There are no **hard and fast rules** for planning healthy meals.*
➤NORMAL SITUATION **3** [sing] what is usual: *Large families are the exception rather than the rule nowadays. ◆ **As a general rule**, women live longer than men. ◆ I don't read much **as a rule**.*
➤OF LANGUAGE **4** [C] a description of what is usual or correct in a language: *What is the rule for forming the past tense?*
➤GOVERNMENT **5** [U] government; control: *The country is **under** military **rule**.*
IDM **bend the rules** ➲ **bend**[1]
the golden rule (of sth) ➲ **golden**
a rule of thumb a simple piece of practical advice, not involving exact details or figures
work to rule ➲ **work**[1]

rule[2] /ruːl/ *verb* [I,T] **1 rule (over sb/sth)** to have power over a country, group of people, etc: *Julius Caesar ruled over a vast empire. ◆ (figurative) His whole life was ruled by his ambition to become President.* **2 rule (on sth); rule (in favour of/against sb/sth)** to make an official decision: *The judge will rule on whether or not the case can go ahead.*
PHR V **rule sb/sth out** to say that sb/sth is not possible, cannot do sth, etc.; to prevent sth: *The government has ruled out further increases in train fares next year.*

ruler /ˈruːlə(r)/ *noun* [C] **1** a person who rules a country, etc: *The country was finally united under one ruler.* **2** a straight piece of wood, plastic, etc. marked with centimetres, that you use for measuring sth or for drawing straight lines ➲ picture at **stationery**

ruling[1] /ˈruːlɪŋ/ *adj* [only *before* a noun] with the most power in an organization, a country, etc: *the ruling political party*

ruling[2] /ˈruːlɪŋ/ *noun* [C] an official decision

rum /rʌm/ *noun* [U,C] a strong alcoholic drink that is made from the juice of **sugar cane** (= a plant from which sugar is made)

rumble /ˈrʌmbl/ *verb* [I] to make a long deep sound: *I was so hungry that my stomach was rumbling.* ▶ **rumble** *noun* [sing]: *a rumble of thunder*

rummage /ˈrʌmɪdʒ/ *verb* [I] to move things and make them untidy while you are looking for sth: *Nina rummaged through the drawer looking for the tin opener.*

ˈ**rummage sale** (*AmE*) = **jumble sale**

rumour (*AmE* **rumor**) /ˈruːmə(r)/ *noun* [C,U] (a) **rumour (about/of sb/sth)** (a piece of) news or information that many people are talking about but that is possibly not true: *I didn't start the rumour about Barry's operation. ◆ **Rumour has it** (= people are saying) that Lena has resigned. ◆ to confirm/deny a rumour* (= to say that it is true/not true)

rumoured (*AmE* **rumored**) /ˈruːməd/ *adj* reported or said, but perhaps not true: *They are rumoured to be getting divorced.*

rump /rʌmp/ *noun* [C] the back end of an animal: *rump steak* (= meat from the rump)

run[1] /rʌn/ *verb* (**running**; *pt* **ran** /ræn/; *pp* **run**)
➤ON FOOT **1** [I,T] to move using your legs, going faster than a walk: *I had to run to catch the bus. ◆ I often **go running** in the evenings* (= as a hobby). *◆ I ran nearly ten kilometres this morning. ◆ to run a marathon*
➤MANAGE **2** [T] to organize or be in charge of sth; to provide a service: *She runs a restaurant. ◆ They run English courses all the year round.*
➤VEHICLE **3** [T] to use and pay for a vehicle: *It costs a lot to run a car.*
➤OF MACHINE **4** [I,T] to operate or function; to make sth do this: *The engine is running very smoothly now. ◆ We're running a new computer program today.*
➤MOVE SOMEWHERE **5** [I,T] to move, or move sth, quickly in a particular direction: *I've been running around after the kids all day. ◆ The car ran off the road and hit a tree. ◆ She ran her finger down the list of passengers.*
➤LEAD **6** [I] to lead from one place to another; to be in a particular position: *The road runs along the side of a lake.*
➤CONTINUE **7** [I] to continue for a time: *My contract has two months left to run. ◆ The play ran for nearly two years in a London theatre.*
➤HAPPEN **8** [I] to operate at a particular time: *All the trains are **running late** this morning. ◆ We'd better hurry up—we're running behind schedule.*
➤LIQUID **9** [I,T] to flow; to make water flow: *When it's really cold, my nose runs. ◆ I can hear a tap running somewhere. ◆ to run a bath/a tap* **10** [I] **run with sth** to be covered with flowing water: *My face was running with sweat.*
➤COLOUR **11** [I] to spread, for example when clothes are washed: *Don't put that red shirt in the washing machine. It might run.*
➤IN NEWSPAPER **12** [T] to publish sth in a newspaper or magazine: *'The Independent' is running a series of articles on pollution.*
➤TEST **13** [T] **run a test/check (on sth)** to do a test or check on sth: *They're running checks on the power supply to see what the problem is.*
➤IN ELECTION **14** [I] **run (for sth)** to be one of the people who hopes to be chosen in an election: *He's running for president.*
IDM **be running at sth** to be at or near a certain level: *Inflation was running at 26%.*
run for it to run in order to escape ❶ For other idioms containing **run**, look at the entries for the nouns, adjectives, etc. For example, **run in the family** is at **family**.

R

PHR V **run across sb/sth** to meet or find sb/sth by chance
run after sb/sth to try to catch sb/sth
run away to escape from somewhere: *He's run away from home.*
run (sth) down to stop functioning gradually; to make sth do this: *Turn the lights off or you'll run the battery down.*
run sb/sth down **1** to hit a person or an animal with your vehicle: *She was run down by a bus.* **2** to criticize sb/sth: *He's always running her down in front of other people.*
run into sb (*informal*) to meet sb by chance
run into sth to have difficulties or a problem: *If you run into any problems, just let me know.*
run (sth) into sb/sth to hit sb/sth with a car, etc: *He ran his car into a brick wall.*
run sth off to copy sth, using a machine
run off with sth to take or steal sth
run out (of sth) to finish your supply of sth; to come to an end: *We've run out of coffee.* ◆ *Time is running out.* ◆ *My passport runs out next month.*
run sb/sth over to hit a person or an animal with your vehicle: *The child was run over as he was crossing the road.*
run through sth to discuss or read sth quickly: *She ran through the names on the list.*

run² /rʌn/ *noun*
➤ON FOOT **1** [C] an act of running on foot: *I go for a three-mile **run** every morning.* ◆ *The prisoner tried to **make a run for it** (= to escape on foot).*
➤IN CAR, ETC. **2** [C] a journey by car, train, etc: *The bus was picking up kids on the school run.*
➤OF SUCCESS/FAILURE **3** [sing] a series of similar events or sth that continues for a very long time: *We've had a run of bad luck recently.*
➤SUDDEN DEMAND **4** [sing] **a run on sth** a sudden great demand for sth: *There's always a run on sunglasses in hot weather.*
➤IN SPORTS **5** [C] a point in the sports of **baseball** and **cricket**: *Our team won by two runs.* **6** (*AmE*) = **ladder**(2)
IDM **in the long run** ➲ **long¹**
on the run hiding or trying to escape from sb/sth: *The escaped prisoner is still on the run.*

runaway¹ /ˈrʌnəweɪ/ *adj* [only *before* a noun] **1** out of control: *a runaway horse/car/train* **2** happening very easily: *a runaway victory*

runaway² /ˈrʌnəweɪ/ *noun* [C] a person, especially a child, who has left or escaped from somewhere

ˌrun-ˈdown *adj* **1** (used about a building or place) in bad condition: *a run-down block of flats* **2** [not before a noun] very tired and not healthy

rung¹ /rʌŋ/ *noun* [C] one of the bars that form the steps of a **ladder** (= a piece of equipment that is used for climbing up sth) ➲ picture at **ladder**

rung² *past participle of* **ring²**

runner /ˈrʌnə(r)/ *noun* [C] **1** a person or an animal that runs, especially in a race: *a cross-country/long-distance runner* **2** a person who takes guns, drugs, etc. illegally from one country to another: *a drug runner*

ˌrunner-ˈup *noun* [C] (*pl* **runners-up**) the person or team that finished second in a race or competition

running¹ /ˈrʌnɪŋ/ *noun* [U] **1** the action or sport of running: *How often do you **go running**?* ◆ *running shoes* **2** the process of managing a business or other organization: *She's not involved in the day-to-day running of the office.* ◆ *the **running costs** of a car* (= petrol, insurance, repairs, etc.)
IDM **in/out of the running (for sth)** (*informal*) having/not having a good chance of getting or winning sth

running² /ˈrʌnɪŋ/ *adj* **1** used after a number and a noun to say that sth has happened a number of times in the same way without a change: *Our school has won the competition for four years running.* **2** [only *before* a noun] (used about water) flowing or available from a tap: *There is no running water in the cottage.* **3** [only *before* a noun] not stopping; continuous: *a running battle between two rival gangs*

ˌrunning ˈcommentary *noun* [C] a spoken description of sth while it is happening

runny /ˈrʌni/ *adj* (**runnier**; **runniest**) **1** (used about your eyes or nose) producing too much liquid: *Their children always seem to have runny noses.* **2** containing more liquid than is usual or than you expected: *runny jam*

ˈrun-up *noun* [sing] **1** the period of time before a certain event: *the run-up to the election* **2** (in sport) a run that people do in order to be going fast enough to do an action, such as jumping or throwing

runway /ˈrʌnweɪ/ *noun* [C] a long piece of ground with a hard surface where aircraft take off and land at an airport

rupture /ˈrʌptʃə(r)/ *noun* [C,U] **1** a sudden bursting or breaking **2** (*formal*) the sudden ending of good relations between two people or groups **3** = **hernia** ▶ **rupture** *verb* [I,T]: *Her appendix ruptured and she had to have emergency surgery.*

rural /ˈrʊərəl/ *adj* connected with the country, not the town: *This part of France is very rural.* ➲ look at **urban**, **rustic**

ruse /ruːz/ *noun* [C] a trick or clever plan

rush¹ /rʌʃ/ *verb* **1** [I,T] to move or do sth with great speed, often too fast: *I rushed back home when I got the news.* ◆ *Don't rush off–I want to talk to you.* ◆ *The public rushed to buy shares in the company.* ◆ *She rushed her lunch, so that she could get back to work as soon as possible.* **2** [T] to take sb/sth to a place very quickly: *He suffered a heart attack and **was rushed to hospital**.* **3** [I,T] **rush (sb) (into sth/into doing sth)** to do sth or make sb do sth without thinking about it first: *Don't let yourself be rushed into marriage.* ◆ *Please don't rush me–I'm thinking!*
IDM **be rushed/run off your feet** ➲ **foot¹**

rush² /rʌʃ/ *noun*
➤HURRY **1** [sing] a sudden quick movement: *At the end of the match there was a rush for the exits.* ◆ *I was so nervous, all my words came out **in a rush**.* **2** [sing,U] a situation in which you are in a hurry

and need to do things quickly: *I can't stop now. I'm **in a** terrible **rush**.* ♦ *Don't hurry your meal. There's no rush.*

➤BUSY SITUATION **3** [sing] a time when there is a lot of activity and people are very busy: *We'll leave early to avoid the rush.*

➤SUDDEN DEMAND **4** [sing] a rush (on sth) a time when many people try to get sth: *There's always a rush on umbrellas when it rains.*

➤PLANT **5** [C] a type of tall grass that grows near water

ˈrush hour *noun* [C] the time each day when there is a lot of traffic because people are travelling to or from work: *rush-hour traffic*

rust /rʌst/ *noun* [U] a reddish-brown substance that forms on the surface of iron, etc., caused by the action of air and water ▶ **rust** *verb* [I,T]: *Some parts of the car had rusted.*

rustic /ˈrʌstɪk/ *adj* typical of the country or of country people; simple: *The whole area is full of rustic charm.* ➲ look at **rural**, **urban**

rustle /ˈrʌsl/ *verb* [I,T] to make a sound like dry leaves or paper moving: *There was a rustling noise in the bushes.*

PHR V **rustle sth up (for sb)** (*informal*) to make or find sth quickly for sb and without planning it: *to rustle up a quick snack*

▶ **rustle** *noun* [sing]

rusty /ˈrʌsti/ *adj* (**rustier**; **rustiest**) **1** (used about metal objects) covered with **rust** as a result of being in contact with water and air: *rusty tins* **2** (used about a skill) not as good as it was because you have not used it for a long time: *My French is rather rusty.*

rut /rʌt/ *noun* [C] **1** a deep track that a wheel makes in soft ground **2** a boring way of life that is difficult to change: *I felt I was **stuck in a rut** in my old job.*

ruthless /ˈruːθləs/ *adj* (used about people and their behaviour) hard and cruel; determined to get what you want and showing no pity to others: *a ruthless dictator* ▶ **ruthlessly** *adv* ▶ **ruthlessness** *noun* [U]

RV /ˌɑː ˈviː/ (*AmE*) **recreational vehicle** = **camper**(2)

rye /raɪ/ *noun* [U] a plant that is grown in colder countries for its grain, which is used to make flour and also **whisky** (= a strong alcoholic drink)

S, s /es/ *noun* [C,U] (*pl* **Ss**; **S's**; **s's** /ˈesɪz/) the 19th letter of the English alphabet: *'School' begins with (an) 'S'.*

S *abbr* **1** = **small**(1) **2** = **south**[1], **southern**: *S Yorkshire* **3** = **saint**

sabbath /ˈsæbəθ/ *often* **the Sabbath** *noun* [sing] the day of the week for rest and prayer in certain religions (Sunday for Christians, Saturday for Jews)

sabotage /ˈsæbətɑːʒ/ *noun* [U] damage that is done on purpose and secretly in order to prevent an enemy being successful, for example by destroying machinery, roads, bridges, etc: *industrial/economic/military sabotage* ▶ **sabotage** *verb* [T]

saccharin /ˈsækərɪn/ *noun* [U] a very sweet substance that can be used instead of sugar

sachet /ˈsæʃeɪ/ *noun* [C] a closed plastic or paper package that contains a very small amount of liquid or powder: *a sachet of shampoo/sugar/coffee* ➲ picture at **container**

sack[1] /sæk/ *noun* [C] a large bag made from a rough heavy material, paper or plastic, used for carrying or storing things: *sacks of flour/potatoes*

IDM **get the sack** (*BrE*) to be told by your employer that you can no longer continue working for them (usually because you have done sth wrong): *Tony **got the sack** for poor work.*

give sb the sack (*BrE*) to tell an employee that they can no longer continue working for you (because of bad work, behaviour, etc.): *Tony's work wasn't good enough and he was given the sack.* ➲ note at **job**

sack[2] /sæk/ (*especially AmE* **fire**) *verb* [T] to tell an employee that they can no longer work for you (because of bad work, bad behaviour, etc.): *Her boss has threatened to sack her if she's late again.*

sacred /ˈseɪkrɪd/ *adj* **1** connected with God, a god or religion: *The Koran is the sacred book of Muslims.* **2** too important and special to be changed or harmed: *a sacred tradition*

sacrifice[1] /ˈsækrɪfaɪs/ *noun* [U,C] **1** the act of giving up sth that is important or valuable to you in order to get or do sth that seems more important; something that you give up in this way: *If we're going to have a holiday this year, we'll have to **make** some **sacrifices**.* **2** **sacrifice (to sb)** the act of offering sth to a god, especially an animal that has been killed in a special way; an animal, etc. that is offered in this way

sacrifice[2] /ˈsækrɪfaɪs/ *verb* **1** [T] **sacrifice sth (for sb/sth)** to give up sth that is important or valuable to you in order to get or do sth that seems more important: *She is not willing to sacrifice her career in order to have children.* **2** [I,T] to kill an animal and offer it to a god, in order to please the god

sacrilege /ˈsækrəlɪdʒ/ *noun* [U, sing] treating a religious object or place without the respect that it deserves

sad /sæd/ *adj* (**sadder**; **saddest**) **1** **sad (to do sth)**; **sad (that ...)** unhappy or causing sb to feel unhappy: *We are very sad to hear that you are leaving.* ♦ *I'm very sad that you don't trust me.* ♦ *That's one of the saddest stories I've ever heard!* ♦ *a sad poem/song/film* **2** bad or unacceptable: *It's a sad state of affairs when your best friend doesn't trust you.* ▶ **sadden** /ˈsædn/ *verb* [T] (*formal*): *The news of your father's death saddened me greatly.* ▶ **sadness** *noun* [C,U]

S

OTHER WORDS FOR

sad

If something **upsets** you, you feel **unhappy** about it: *This will upset a lot of people.* **Upset** is also an adjective: *I felt upset about what they had said.* If you feel **miserable**, you are very sad. If you feel **depressed**, you feel very sad and without hope. This feeling often lasts for a long period of time: *He's been very depressed since he lost his job.* You can describe sad things that happen as **depressing**: *depressing news.*

saddle[1] /ˈsædl/ *noun* [C] **1** a seat, usually made of leather, that you put on a horse so that you can ride it ➲ picture at **horse** **2** a seat on a bicycle or motorbike ➲ picture at **bicycle**

saddle[2] /ˈsædl/ *verb* [T] to put a **saddle** on a horse: *Their horses were saddled and waiting.*

PHR V **saddle sb with sth** to give sb a responsibility or task that they do not want

sadism /ˈseɪdɪzəm/ *noun* [U] getting pleasure, especially sexual pleasure, from hurting other people ➲ look at **masochism**

sadist /ˈseɪdɪst/ *noun* [C] a person who gets pleasure, especially sexual pleasure, from hurting other people ▶ **sadistic** /səˈdɪstɪk/ *adj* ▶ **sadistically** /-kli/ *adv*

sadly /ˈsædli/ *adv* **1** unfortunately: *Sadly, after eight years of marriage they had grown apart.* **2** in a way that shows unhappiness: *She shook her head sadly.* **3** in a way that is wrong: *If you think that I've forgotten what you did, you're **sadly mistaken**.*

sae /ˌes eɪ ˈiː/ *abbr* (*BrE*) = **stamped addressed envelope**: *Please enclose an sae.*

safari /səˈfɑːri/ *noun* [C,U] (*pl* **safaris**) a trip to see or hunt wild animals, especially in East Africa: *to be/go **on safari*** ➲ note at **holiday**

S

safe[1] /seɪf/ *adj* (**safer**; **safest**) **1** [not before a noun] **safe (from sb/sth)** free from danger; not able to be hurt: *She didn't **feel safe** in the house on her own.* ◆ *Do you think my car will be safe in this street?* ◆ *Keep the papers where they will be safe from fire.* **2** **safe (to do sth)**; **safe (for sb)** not likely to cause danger, harm or risk: *Don't sit on that chair, it isn't safe.* ◆ *I left my suitcase in a **safe place** and went for a cup of coffee.* ◆ *She's a very safe driver.* ◆ *It's not safe to walk alone in the streets at night here.* ◆ *Is it safe to drink the water here?* ◆ *Is this drug safe for children?* ◆ *I think **it's safe to say** that the situation is unlikely to change for some time.* **3** [not before a noun] not hurt, damaged or lost: *After the accident he checked that all the passengers were safe.* ◆ *After five days the child was found, **safe and sound**.*

IDM **in safe hands** with sb who will take good care of you

on the safe side not taking risks; being very careful

▶ **safely** *adv*: *I rang my parents to tell them I had arrived safely.*

safe[2] /seɪf/ *noun* [C] a strong metal box or cupboard with a special lock that is used for keeping money, jewellery, documents, etc. in

safeguard /ˈseɪfɡɑːd/ *noun* [C] a **safeguard (against sb/sth)** something that protects against possible dangers ▶ **safeguard** *verb* [T]: *to safeguard somebody's interests/rights/privacy*

safety /ˈseɪfti/ *noun* [U] the state of being safe; the state of not being dangerous or in danger: *In the interests of safety, smoking is forbidden.* ◆ *In the interests of safety, please stay behind the yellow line.* ◆ ***road safety*** (= preventing road accidents) ◆ *New **safety measures** have been introduced on trains.*

ˈ**safety belt** = seat belt

ˈ**safety net** *noun* [C] **1** a net that is placed underneath sb who is high above the ground to catch them if they fall **2** an arrangement that helps to prevent disaster (usually with money) if sth goes wrong

ˈ**safety pin** *noun* [C] a metal pin with a point that is bent back towards the head, which is covered so that it cannot be dangerous ➲ picture at **pin**

ˈ**safety valve** *noun* [C] a device in a machine that allows steam, gas, etc. to escape if the pressure becomes too great

sag /sæɡ/ *verb* [I] (**sagging**; **sagged**) to hang or to bend down, especially in the middle

saga /ˈsɑːɡə/ *noun* [C] a very long story; a long series of events

sage /seɪdʒ/ *noun* [U] a **herb** (= a type of plant) with flat, light green leaves that have a strong smell and are used in cooking

Sagittarius /ˌsædʒɪˈteəriəs/ *noun* [C,U] the 9th sign of the **zodiac** (= 12 signs which represent the positions of the sun, moon and planets), the Archer; a person born under this sign: *I'm (a) Sagittarius.* ➲ picture at **zodiac**

said *past tense, past participle of* **say**[1]

sail[1] /seɪl/ *verb* **1** [I,T] (used about a boat or ship and the people on it) to travel on water in a ship or boat of any type: *I stood at the window and watched the ships sailing by.* ◆ *to sail round the world* ◆ *to sail the seas* **2** [I,T] to travel in and control a boat with sails, especially as a sport: *My father is teaching me to sail.* ◆ *I've never sailed this kind of yacht before.*

HELP When we are talking about spending time sailing a boat for pleasure, we say **go sailing**: *We often go sailing at weekends.*

3 [I] to begin a journey on water: *When does the ship sail?* ◆ *We sail for Santander at 6 o'clock tomorrow morning.* **4** [I] to move somewhere quickly in a smooth or proud way: *The ball sailed over the fence and into the neighbour's garden.* ◆ *Mary sailed into the room, completely ignoring all of us.*

IDM **sail through (sth)** to pass a test or exam easily

sail[2] /seɪl/ *noun* **1** [C] a large piece of strong cloth that is fixed onto a ship or boat. The wind blows against the sail and moves the ship along. ➲ picture on **page P6** **2** [sing] a trip on water in a ship or boat with a sail: *Would you like to **go for a sail** in my boat?* **3** [C] a set of boards that the wind moves round that are fixed to a **windmill** (= a building used for making flour from grain) or **wind turbine** (= a building used to make electricity) ➲ picture at **windmill**

IDM set sail (*formal*) to begin a journey by sea: *Columbus set sail for India.*

sailboard /ˈseɪlbɔːd/ = **windsurfer**(1)

sailboat /ˈseɪlbəʊt/ (*AmE*) = **sailing boat**

⚷ **sailing** /ˈseɪlɪŋ/ *noun* [U] the sport of being in, and controlling, small boats with sails: *They do a lot of sailing.* ➲ picture on **page P3**

ˈ**sailing boat** (*AmE* sailboat) *noun* [C] a boat with a sail or sails

⚷ **sailor** /ˈseɪlə(r)/ *noun* [C] a person who works on a ship or a person who sails a boat: *a ship with four sailors on board*

saint /seɪnt; snt/ *noun* [C] **1** (*abbr* S; St) a very good or religious person who is given special respect after death by the Christian Church ➲ look at **patron saint**

> **HELP** When it is used as a title, **saint** is written with a capital letter: *Saint Patrick.* In the names of places, churches, etc. the short form **St** is usually used: *St Andrew's Church.* Before names **saint** is pronounced /snt/.

2 a very good, kind person

sake /seɪk/ *noun* [C]

IDM for Christ's/God's/goodness'/Heaven's/pity's sake (*spoken*) used to emphasize that it is important to do sth, or to show that you are annoyed: *For goodness' sake, hurry up!* ♦ *Why have you taken so long, for God's sake?*

> **HELP** Be careful. **For God's sake** and especially **for Christ's sake** may offend some people.

for the sake of sb/sth; for sb's/sth's sake in order to help sb/sth: *Don't go to any trouble for my sake.* ♦ *They only stayed together for the sake of their children/for their children's sake.*

for the sake of sth/of doing sth in order to get or keep sth; for the purpose of sth: *She gave up her job for the sake of her health.*

⚷ **salad** /ˈsæləd/ *noun* [C,U] a mixture of vegetables, usually not cooked, that you often eat together with other foods: *All main courses are served with salad.* ➲ picture on **page P16**

salami /səˈlɑːmi/ *noun* [U,C] (*pl* salamis) a type of large spicy **sausage** (= meat that is made into a long thin shape) served cold in thin slices

⚷ **salary** /ˈsæləri/ *noun* [C,U] (*pl* salaries) the money that a person receives (usually every month) for the work they have done: *My salary is paid directly into my bank account.* ♦ *a high/low salary* ➲ note at **pay**[2]

⚷ **sale** /seɪl/ *noun* **1** [C,U] the act of selling or being sold; the occasion when sth is sold: *She raised the money through the sale of her house..* ♦ *a sale of used toys* **2 sales** [pl] the number of items sold: *Sales of smartphones have increased rapidly.* ♦ *The company reported excellent sales figures.* **3 sales** [U] (also ˈsales department) the part of a company that deals with selling its products: *Jodie works in sales/in the sales department.* ♦ *a sales representative/sales rep* **4** [C] a time when shops sell things at prices that are lower than usual: *The sale starts on December 28th.* ♦ *I got several bargains **in the sales**.* ➲ look at **car boot sale, jumble sale**

IDM for sale offered for sb to buy: *This painting is not for sale.* ♦ *I see our neighbours have **put** their house **up for sale**.*

on sale 1 available for sb to buy, especially in shops: *This week's edition is on sale now at your local newsagents.* **2** (*AmE*) offered at a lower price than usual

ˈ**sales clerk** (*AmE*) = **shop assistant**

ˈ**sales department** = sale(3)

salesman /ˈseɪlzmən/, **saleswoman** /ˈseɪlzwʊmən/, **salesperson** /ˈseɪlzpɜːsn/ *noun* [C] (*pl* -men /-mən/, -women /-wɪmɪn/, -persons *or* -people /-piːpl/) a person whose job is selling things to people

salient /ˈseɪliənt/ *adj* [only *before* a noun] most important or noticeable

saliva /səˈlaɪvə/ *noun* [U] the liquid that is produced in the mouth ➲ look at **spit**

salmon /ˈsæmən/ *noun* [C,U] (*pl* salmon) a large fish with silver skin and pink meat that we eat: *smoked salmon*

salmonella /ˌsælməˈnelə/ *noun* [U] a type of bacteria that makes people sick if they eat infected food; an illness caused by this bacteria

salon /ˈsælɒn/ *noun* [C] **1** a shop where you can have beauty or hair treatment or where you can buy expensive clothes **2** (*old-fashioned*) a room in a large house that is used for receiving guests **3** (in the past) a regular meeting of writers, artists and other guests at the house of a famous or important person

saloon /səˈluːn/ (*AmE* sedan) *noun* [C] a car with a fixed roof and a **boot** (= a space in the back for luggage)

⚷ **salt**[1] /sɔːlt/ (*BrE also* /sɒlt/) *noun* [U] a common white substance that is found in sea water and the earth. Salt is used in cooking for flavouring food: *Season with **salt and pepper**.* ♦ *Add a pinch (= a small amount) of salt.*

IDM rub salt into the wound/sb's wounds ➲ **rub**

take sth with a pinch of salt ➲ **pinch**[2]

▸ **salt** *adj* [only *before* a noun]: *salt water*

salt[2] /sɔːlt/ *verb* [T, usually passive] to put salt on or in sth: *salted peanuts*

saltwater /ˈsɔːltwɔːtə(r)/ *adj* living in the sea: *a saltwater fish*

> **MORE** Fish that live in rivers are **freshwater** fish.

S

salty /ˈsɔːlti/ *adj* (**saltier**; **saltiest**) having the taste of or containing salt: *I didn't like the soup; it was too salty.*

salute /səˈluːt/ *noun* [C] **1** an action that a soldier, etc. does to show respect, by touching the side of his or her head with the right hand: *to give a salute* **2** something that shows respect for sb: *The next programme is **a salute to** a great film star.* ▶ **salute** *verb* [I,T]: *The soldiers saluted as they marched past the general.*

salvage¹ /ˈsælvɪdʒ/ *noun* [U] the action of saving things that have been or are likely to be lost or damaged, especially in an accident or a disaster; the things that are saved: *a salvage operation/company/team*

salvage² /ˈsælvɪdʒ/ *verb* [T] **salvage sth (from sth)** to manage to rescue sth from being lost or damaged; to rescue sth or a situation from disaster: *They salvaged as much as they could from the house after the fire.*

salvation /sælˈveɪʃn/ *noun* **1** [U] (in the Christian religion) being saved from the power of evil **2** [U, sing] a thing or person that rescues sb/sth from danger, disaster, etc.

same /seɪm/ *adj, adv, pron* **1 the same ... (as sb/sth); the same ... that ...** not different, not another or other; exactly the one or ones that you have mentioned before: *My brother and I had the same teacher at school.* ♦ *They both said the same thing.* ♦ *I'm going to wear the same clothes as/that I wore yesterday.* ♦ *This one looks **exactly the same** as that one.* **2 the same ... (as sb/sth); the same ... that ...** exactly like the one already mentioned: *I wouldn't buy the same car again* (= the same model of car). ♦ *We treat all the children in the class the same.* ♦ *I had the same experience as you some time ago.* ♦ *All small babies look the same.* ♦ *Is there another word that means the same as this?*

HELP We cannot say 'a same ...' To express this idea we use **the same sort of**: *I'd like the same sort of job as my father.*

IDM all/just the same used when saying or writing sth which contrasts in some way with what has gone before: *I understand what you're saying. All the same, I don't agree with you.* ♦ *I don't need to borrow any money, but thanks all the same for offering.*
at the same time 1 together; at one time: *I can't think about more than one thing at the same time.* **2** on the other hand; however: *It's a very good idea but at the same time it's rather risky.*
much the same ➲ **much**
on the same wavelength ➲ **wavelength**
(the) same again (*spoken*) a request to be served or given the same drink as before
same here (*spoken*) the same thing is also true for me: *'I'm bored.' 'Same here.'*
(the) same to you (*spoken*) used as an answer when sb says sth rude to you or wishes you sth: *'You idiot!' 'Same to you!'* ♦ *'Have a good weekend.' 'The same to you.'*

sample /ˈsɑːmpl/ *noun* [C] **1** a small number or amount of sb/sth that is looked at, tested, examined, etc. to find out what the rest is like: *The interviews were given to a **random sample** of shoppers.* ♦ *to take a blood sample* ♦ *a free sample of shampoo* ➲ look at **specimen 2** a piece of recorded music or sound that is used in a new piece of music: *'Candy' includes a sample from a Walker Brothers song.* ▶ **sample** *verb* [T]: *You are welcome to sample any of our wines before making a purchase.*

sanatorium /ˌsænəˈtɔːriəm/ (*especially AmE* **sanitarium**) *noun* [C] a type of hospital where patients who need a long period of treatment for an illness can stay

sanction¹ /ˈsæŋkʃn/ *noun* **1** [C, usually pl] **sanctions (against sb)** an official order that limits business, contact, etc. with a particular country, in order to make it do sth, such as obey international law: *The sanctions against those countries have now been lifted.* **2** [U] (*formal*) official permission to do or change sth **3** [C] a punishment for breaking a rule or law

sanction² /ˈsæŋkʃn/ *verb* [T] to give official permission for sth

sanctuary /ˈsæŋktʃuəri/ *noun* (*pl* **sanctuaries**) **1** [C] a place where birds or animals are protected from being hunted **2** [C,U] a place or area where sb can be safe from enemies, the police, etc.

sand /sænd/ *noun* **1** [U] a powder consisting of very small grains of rock, found in deserts and on beaches: *a grain of sand* ➲ picture on **page P10** **2** [U,C, usually pl] a large area of sand: *miles of golden sands*

sandal /ˈsændl/ *noun* [C] a type of light, open shoe that people wear when the weather is warm ➲ picture at **shoe**

sandcastle /ˈsændkɑːsl/ *noun* [C] a pile of sand that looks like a castle, made by children playing on a beach

ˈsand dune = **dune**

sandpaper /ˈsændpeɪpə(r)/ *noun* [U] strong paper with a rough surface on it that is used for rubbing surfaces in order to make them smooth

sandwich¹ /ˈsænwɪtʃ; -wɪdʒ/ *noun* [C] two slices of bread with food between them: *a ham/cheese sandwich* ➲ picture on **page P16**

sandwich² /ˈsænwɪtʃ; -wɪdʒ/
PHR V sandwich sb/sth (between sb/sth) to place sb/sth in a very narrow space between two other things or people

sandy /ˈsændi/ *adj* (**sandier**; **sandiest**) covered with or full of sand

sane /seɪn/ *adj* (**saner**; **sanest**) **1** (used about a person) mentally normal; not crazy: *No sane person would do anything like that.* **2** (used about a person or an idea, a decision, etc.) sensible; showing good judgement **OPP** for both meanings **insane** ➲ *noun* **sanity**

sang *past tense* of **sing**

sanitarium /ˌsænəˈteəriəm/ (*AmE*) = **sanatorium**

sanitary /ˈsænətri/ *adj* [only *before* a noun] connected with the protection of health, for example how human waste is removed: *Sanitary conditions in the refugee camps were terrible.* ➲ look at **insanitary**

ˈ**sanitary towel** (*AmE* ˈsanitary napkin) *noun* [C] a thick piece of soft material that women use to absorb blood lost during their period (3) ➲ look at **tampon**

sanitation /ˌsænɪˈteɪʃn/ *noun* [U] the equipment and systems that keep places clean, especially by removing human waste

sanity /ˈsænəti/ *noun* [U] **1** the state of having a normal healthy mind **2** the state of being sensible and reasonable OPP for both meanings **insanity** ➲ *adjective* **sane**

sank *past tense* of **sink**[1]

Santa Claus /ˈsæntə klɔːz/ Santa = **Father Christmas**

sap[1] /sæp/ *noun* [U] the liquid in a plant or tree

sap[2] /sæp/ *verb* [T] (sapping; sapped) sap (sb of) sth to make sb/sth weaker; to destroy sth gradually: *Years of failure have sapped (him of) his confidence.*

sapling /ˈsæplɪŋ/ *noun* [C] a young tree

sapphire /ˈsæfaɪə(r)/ *noun* [C,U] a bright blue **precious** (= rare and valuable) stone

sarcasm /ˈsɑːkæzəm/ *noun* [U] the use of words or expressions to mean the opposite of what they actually say. People use **sarcasm** in order to criticize other people or to make them look silly. ➲ look at **ironic** ▶ **sarcastic** /sɑːˈkæstɪk/ *adj*: *He's always making sarcastic comments.* ▶ **sarcastically** /-kli/ *adv*

sardine /ˌsɑːˈdiːn/ *noun* [C] a type of very small silver fish that we cook and eat: *a tin of sardines*

sari /ˈsɑːri/ *noun* [C] a dress that consists of a long piece of silk or cotton that women, particularly Indian women, wear around their bodies

sari

sash /sæʃ/ *noun* [C] a long piece of cloth that is worn round the waist or over the shoulder, often as part of a uniform

Sat. *abbr* = **Saturday**: *Sat 2 May*

sat *past tense, past participle* of **sit**

Satan /ˈseɪtn/ *noun* a name for the Devil ➲ look at **devil**

satchel /ˈsætʃəl/ *noun* [C] a bag, often carried over the shoulder, used by children for taking books to and from school

satellite /ˈsætəlaɪt/ *noun* [C] **1** an electronic device that is sent into space and moves round the earth or another planet for a particular purpose: *a weather/communications satellite* **2** a natural object that moves round a bigger object in space

ˈ**satellite dish** (also dish) *noun* [C] a large round piece of equipment on the outside of houses that receives signals from a **satellite**(1), so that people can watch **satellite TV** ➲ picture on **page P8**

ˈ**satellite television** (also ˈsatellite TV) *noun* [U] TV programmes that are sent out using a **satellite**(1)

satin /ˈsætɪn/ *noun* [U] a type of cloth that is smooth and shiny: *a satin dress/ribbon*

satire /ˈsætaɪə(r)/ *noun* **1** [U] the use of humour to attack a person, an organization, an idea, etc. that you think is bad or silly ➲ note at **humour** **2** [C] a satire (on sb/sth) a piece of writing or a play, film, etc. that uses **satire**: *a satire on political life* ▶ **satirical** /səˈtɪrɪkl/ *adj*: *a satirical magazine* ▶ **satirically** /-kli/ *adv*

satirize (also -ise) /ˈsætəraɪz/ *verb* [T] to use **satire** to show the faults in a person, an organization, an idea, etc.

🔑 **satisfaction** /ˌsætɪsˈfækʃn/ *noun* [U] the feeling of pleasure that you have when you have done, got or achieved what you wanted; something that gives you this feeling: *Roshni stood back and looked at her work with a sense of satisfaction.* ◆ *We finally found a solution that was* **to everyone's satisfaction**. ◆ *She was about to* **have the satisfaction of** *seeing her book in print.* OPP **dissatisfaction**

satisfactory /ˌsætɪsˈfæktəri/ *adj* good enough for a particular purpose; acceptable: *This piece of work is not satisfactory. Please do it again.* OPP **unsatisfactory** ▶ **satisfactorily** /ˌsætɪsˈfæktərəli/ *adv*: *Work is progressing satisfactorily.*

🔑 **satisfied** /ˈsætɪsfaɪd/ *adj* satisfied (with sb/sth) pleased because you have had or done what you wanted: *a satisfied customer* ◆ *a satisfied smile* OPP **dissatisfied**

🔑 **satisfy** /ˈsætɪsfaɪ/ *verb* [T] (satisfying; satisfies; *pt, pp* satisfied) **1** to make sb pleased by doing or giving them what they want: *No matter how hard I try, my piano teacher is never satisfied.* **2** to have or do what is necessary for sth: *Make sure you* **satisfy** *the entry* **requirements** *before you apply to the university.* ◆ *I had a quick look inside the parcel just to* **satisfy** *my* **curiosity**. **3** satisfy sb (that ...) (*formal*) to show or give proof to sb that sth is true or has been done: *Once the police were satisfied that they were telling the truth, they were allowed to go.*

🔑 **satisfying** /ˈsætɪsfaɪɪŋ/ *adj* pleasing, giving satisfaction: *I find it satisfying to see people enjoying something I've cooked.*

satnav /ˈsætnæv/ *noun* [C,U] (*BrE*) **satellite navigation**; a computer system that uses information obtained from **satellites** (= electronic devices that move round the earth) to guide the driver of a vehicle: *All our company's drivers have satnav.* ◆ *Have you got a satnav?* ➲ look at **GPS** ➲ picture at **car**

S

satsuma /sæt'suːmə/ *noun* [C] a type of small orange

saturate /'sætʃəreɪt/ *verb* [T] **1** to make sth extremely wet: *The continuous rain had saturated the soil.* **2** [often passive] to fill sth so completely that it is impossible to add any more: *The market is saturated with cheap imports.* ▶ **saturated** *adj*: *Her clothes were saturated.* ▶ **saturation** /ˌsætʃə'reɪʃn/ *noun* [U]

Saturday /'sætədeɪ; -di/ *noun* [C,U] (*abbr* **Sat.**) the day of the week after Friday ➲ note at **Monday**

Saturn /'sætɜːn; -tən/ *noun* [sing] the planet that is 6th in order from the sun and that has rings around it

sauce /sɔːs/ *noun* [C,U] a thick hot or cold liquid that you eat on or with food: *The chicken was served in a delicious sauce.* ◆ *spaghetti with tomato sauce* ➲ look at **gravy** ➲ picture on **page P16**

saucepan /'sɔːspən/ *noun* [C] a round metal pot with a handle that is used for cooking things on top of a cooker

saucer /'sɔːsə(r)/ *noun* [C] a small round plate that a cup stands on ➲ picture at **cup**

sauna /'sɔːnə/ *noun* [C] **1** a type of bath where you sit in a room that is very hot: *to have a sauna* **2** the room that you sit in to have a **sauna**

saunter /'sɔːntə(r)/ *verb* [I] to walk without hurrying

sausage /'sɒsɪdʒ/ *noun* [C,U] a mixture of meat cut into very small pieces and spices, etc. that is made into a long thin shape. Some **sausage** is eaten cold in slices; other types are cooked and then served whole: *liver sausage* ◆ *We had sausages and chips for lunch.*

savage /'sævɪdʒ/ *adj* very cruel or violent: *He was the victim of a savage attack.* ◆ *The book received savage criticism.* ▶ **savage** *verb* [T] to attack sb violently: *The boy died after being savaged by a dog.* ▶ **savagely** *adv* ▶ **savagery** /'sævɪdʒri/ *noun* [U]

S

save[1] /seɪv/ *verb*

➤KEEP SAFE **1** [T] **save sb/sth (from sth/from doing sth)** to keep sb/sth safe from death, harm, loss, etc: *to **save** somebody's **life*** ◆ *to save somebody from drowning* ◆ *We are trying to save the school from closure.*

➤MONEY **2** [I,T] **save (sth) (up) (for sth)** to keep or not spend money so that you can use it later: *I'm saving up for a new bike.* ◆ *Do you manage to save any of your wages?* ➲ note at **money**

➤FOR FUTURE **3** [T] to keep sth for future use: *I'll be home late, so please save me some dinner.* ◆ *Save that box. It might come in useful.* ◆ *If you get there first, please save me a seat.*

➤NOT WASTE **4** [I,T] **save (sb) (sth) (on) sth** to avoid wasting time, money, etc: *It will save you twenty minutes on the journey if you take the express train.* ◆ *You can save on petrol by getting a smaller car.* ◆ *This car will save you a lot on petrol.*

➤AVOID STH BAD **5** [T] **save (sb) sth/doing sth** to avoid, or make sb able to avoid, doing sth unpleasant or difficult: *If you make an appointment, it will save you waiting.*

➤IN SPORT **6** [I,T] (in games such as football, **hockey**, etc.) to stop a goal being scored: *to save a penalty*

➤COMPUTING **7** [I,T] to store information in a computer by giving a special instruction: *Don't forget to save the file before you close it.*

IDM keep/save sth for a rainy day ➲ **rainy**

save face to prevent yourself losing the respect of other people

save[2] /seɪv/ *noun* [C] (in football, etc.) the act of preventing a goal from being scored: *The goalkeeper made a great save.*

saver /'seɪvə(r)/ *noun* [C] **1** a person who saves money for future use: *The rise in interest rates is good news for savers.* **2** [in compounds] a thing that helps you save time, money, or the thing mentioned: *a great time-saver*

saving /'seɪvɪŋ/ *noun* **1** [C] **a saving (of sth) (on sth)** an amount of time, money, etc. that you do not have to use or spend: *The sale price represents a saving of 25% on the usual price.* **2 savings** [pl] money that you have saved for future use: *All our savings are in the bank.* ◆ *I opened a **savings account** at my local bank.*

saviour (*AmE* savior) /'seɪvjə(r)/ *noun* [C] a person who rescues or saves sb/sth from danger, loss, death, etc.

savoury (*AmE* savory) /'seɪvəri/ *adj* (used about food) having a taste that is not sweet ➲ look at **sweet**

saw[1] *past tense* of **see**

saw[2] /sɔː/ *noun* [C] a tool that is used for cutting wood, etc. A saw has a blade with sharp teeth on it, and a handle at one or both ends. ➲ picture at **tool** ▶ **saw** *verb* [I,T] (*pt* **sawed**; *pp* **sawn** /sɔːn/; *AmE* **sawed**): *to saw through the trunk of a tree* ◆ *He sawed the log up into small pieces.*

sawdust /'sɔːdʌst/ *noun* [U] very small pieces of wood that fall like powder when you are cutting a large piece of wood

sawn *past participle* of **saw**

saxophone /'sæksəfəʊn/ (also *informal* **sax** /sæks/) *noun* [C] a metal musical instrument that you play by blowing into it. **Saxophones** are especially used for playing modern music, for example **jazz**: *This track features Dexter Gordon on sax.* ➲ picture at **music**

say[1] /seɪ/ *verb* [T] (**says** /sez/; *pt, pp* **said** /sed/)

➤SPEAK **1 say sth (to sb); say that ...; say sth (about sb)** to speak or tell sb sth, using words: *'Please come back,' she said.* ◆ *I said goodbye to her at the station.* ◆ *We can ask him, but I'm sure he'll say no.* ◆ *The teacher said we should hand in our essays on Friday.* ◆ *He said to his mother that he would phone back later.* ◆ *They just sat there without saying anything.* ◆ *'This isn't going to be easy,' she said to herself* (= she thought). ◆ *'What time is she coming?' 'I don't know—she didn't say.'* ◆ ***It is said that** cats can sense the presence of ghosts.*

HELP Say or tell? **Say** is often used with the actual words that were spoken or before **that** in reported speech: *'I'll catch the 9 o'clock train,' he said.* ♦ *He said that he would catch the 9 o'clock train.* Notice that you say something **to** somebody: *He said to me that he would catch the 9 o'clock train.* **Tell** is always followed by a noun or pronoun, showing who you were speaking to: *He told me that he would catch the 9 o'clock train.* **Tell**, not **say**, can also be used when you are talking about giving orders or advice: *I told them to hurry up.* ♦ *She's always telling me what I ought to do.*

➤EXPRESS OPINION **2** to express an opinion on sth: *I wouldn't say she's unfriendly—just shy.* ♦ *What is the artist trying to say in this painting?* ♦ *Well, **what do you say**? Do you think it's a good idea?* ♦ *It's **hard to say** what I like about the book.* ♦ *'When will it be finished?' **'I couldn't say** (= I don't know)'.*
➤IMAGINE **3** to imagine or guess sth about a situation; to suppose: *We will need, say, £5000 for a new car.* ♦ *Say you don't get a place at university, what will you do then?*
➤SHOW FEELINGS **4** say sth (to sb) to show a feeling, a situation, etc. without using words: *His angry look said everything about the way he felt.*
➤WRITTEN INFORMATION **5** to give written information: *What time does it say on that clock?* ♦ *The map says the hotel is just past the railway bridge.* ♦ *The sign clearly says 'No dogs'.*

IDM easier said than done ➲ easy

go without saying to be clear, so that you do not need to say it: *It goes without saying that the children will be well looked after at all times.*

have a lot, nothing, etc. to say for yourself to have a lot, nothing, etc. to say in a particular situation: *Late again! What have you got to say for yourself?*

I dare say ➲ dare[1]

I must say (*spoken*) used to emphasize your opinion: *I must say, I didn't believe him at first.*

let's say for example: *You could work two mornings a week, let's say Tuesday and Friday.*

say no (to sth) to refuse an offer, a suggestion, etc: *If you don't go to Madrid, you're saying no to a great opportunity.*

say when (*spoken*) used to tell sb to say when you have poured enough drink in their glass or put enough food on their plate

that is to say ... which means ...: *We're leaving on Friday, that's to say in a week's time.*

to say the least used to say that sth is in fact much worse, more serious, etc. than you are saying: *Adam's going to be annoyed, to say the least, when he sees his car.*

say[2] /seɪ/ *noun* [sing,U] (a) say (in sth) the authority or right to decide sth: *I'd like to have some say in the arrangements for the party.*

IDM have your say to express your opinion: *Thank you for your comments. Now let somebody else have their say.*

saying /ˈseɪɪŋ/ *noun* [C] a well-known phrase that gives advice about sth or says sth that many people believe is true: *'Love is blind' is an old saying.* ➲ look at proverb

scab /skæb/ *noun* [C,U] a mass of dried blood that forms over a part of the body where the skin has been cut or broken ➲ look at **scar**

scaffold /ˈskæfəʊld/ *noun* [C] a platform on which criminals were killed in past times by hanging

scaffolding /ˈskæfəldɪŋ/ *noun* [U] long metal poles and wooden boards that form a structure which is put next to a building so that people who are building, painting, etc. can stand and work on it

scald /skɔːld/ *verb* [T] to burn sb/sth with very hot liquid: *I scalded my arm badly when I was cooking.* ▶ **scald** *noun* [C] ▶ **scalding** *adj*: *scalding hot water*

scales

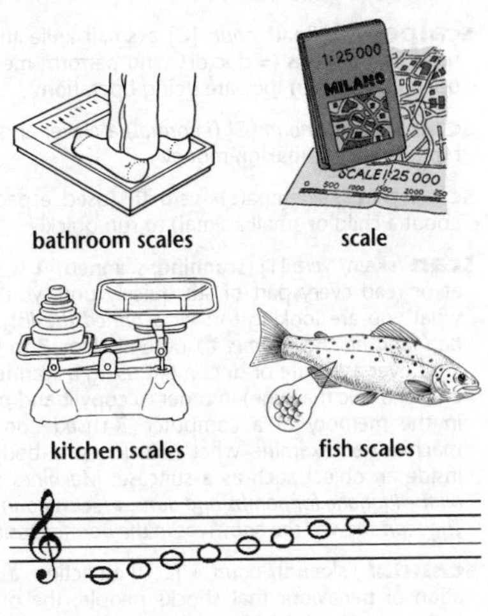

bathroom scales — scale — kitchen scales — fish scales — the scale of C

scale[1] /skeɪl/ *noun*
➤SIZE **1** [C,U] the size of sth, especially when compared to other things: *We shall be making the product **on a large scale** next year.* ♦ *At this stage it is impossible to estimate **the full scale of** the disaster.*
➤FOR MEASURING **2** [C] a series of numbers, amounts, etc. that are used for measuring or fixing the level of sth: *The earthquake measured 6.5 on the Richter scale.* ♦ *the new pay scale for nurses*
➤FOR MEASURING **3** [C] a series of marks on a tool or piece of equipment that you use for measuring sth: *The ruler has one scale in centimetres and one scale in inches.*
➤OF MAP/DRAWING **4** [C] the relationship between the actual size of sth and its size on a map or plan: *The map has a scale of one centimetre to a kilometre.* ♦ *a scale of 1:50000 (= one to fifty thousand)* ♦ *We need a map with a larger scale.* ♦ *a scale model*
➤FOR WEIGHING **5 scales** [pl] a piece of equipment that is used for weighing sb/sth: *I weighed it on the kitchen scales.*
➤IN MUSIC **6** [C] a series of musical notes which go up

S

or down in a fixed order. People play or sing scales to improve their technical ability: *the scale of C major* ➤ON FISH **7** [C] one of the small flat pieces of hard material that cover the body of fish and some animals: *the scales of a snake*

scale² /skeɪl/ *verb* [T] (*formal*) to climb to the top of sth very high and steep
PHR V scale sth up/down to increase/decrease the size, number, importance, etc. of sth: *Police have scaled up their search for the missing boy.*

scallop /ˈskɒləp/ *noun* [C] a **shellfish** (= a creature with a shell that lives in water) that you can eat, with two flat round shells that fit together

scalp /skælp/ *noun* [C] the skin on the top of your head that is under your hair

scalpel /ˈskælpəl/ *noun* [C] a small knife that is used by **surgeons** (= doctors who perform medical operations) when they are doing operations

scam /skæm/ *noun* [C] (*informal*) a clever and dishonest plan for making money

scamper /ˈskæmpə(r)/ *verb* [I] (used especially about a child or small animal) to run quickly

scan /skæn/ *verb* [T] (scanning; scanned) **1** to look at or read every part of sth quickly until you find what you are looking for: *Vic scanned the list until he found his own name.* ➲ note at **skim** **2** to pass light over a picture or document using a **scanner** (= an electronic machine) in order to copy it and put it in the memory of a computer **3** (used about a machine) to examine what is inside sb's body or inside an object such as a suitcase: *Machines scan all the luggage for bombs and guns.* ▶ **scan** *noun* [C]: *The scan showed the baby was in the normal position.*

scandal /ˈskændl/ *noun* **1** [C,U] an action, a situation or behaviour that shocks people; the public feeling that is caused by such behaviour: *The chairman resigned after being involved in a financial scandal.* ◆ *There was no suggestion of scandal in his private life.* ◆ *The poor state of school buildings is a real scandal.* **2** [U] talk about sth bad or wrong that sb has or may have done: *to spread scandal about somebody*

scandalize (also -ise) /ˈskændəlaɪz/ *verb* [T] to cause sb to feel shocked by doing sth that they think is bad or wrong

scandalous /ˈskændələs/ *adj* very shocking or wrong: *It is scandalous that so much money is wasted.*

Scandinavia /ˌskændɪˈneɪviə/ *noun* [sing] the group of countries in northern Europe that consists of Denmark, Norway and Sweden. Sometimes Finland and Iceland are also said to be part of Scandinavia. ▶ **Scandinavian** *adj, noun* [C]

scanner /ˈskænə(r)/ *noun* [C] **1** a machine used for looking at or recording images: *The scanner can detect cancer at an early stage.* **2** a device which copies pictures and documents so that they can be stored on a computer: *I used the scanner to send the document by email.*

scant /skænt/ *adj* [only *before* a noun] not very much; not as much as necessary

scanty /ˈskænti/ *adj* (scantier; scantiest) too small in size or amount: *We didn't learn much from the scanty information they gave us.* ▶ **scantily** *adv*: *I realized I was too scantily dressed for the cold weather.*

scapegoat /ˈskeɪpgəʊt/ *noun* [C] a person who is punished for things that are not their fault: *When Alison was sacked she felt she had been* ***made a scapegoat*** *for all of the company's problems.*

scar /skɑː(r)/ *noun* [C] a mark on the skin that is caused by a wound that has healed: *The operation didn't leave a very big scar.* ➲ look at **scab** ▶ **scar** *verb* [I,T] (scarring; scarred): *William's face was* ***scarred for life*** *in the accident.*

scarce /skeəs/ *adj* not existing in large quantities; hard to find: *Food for birds and animals is scarce in the winter.* **OPP plentiful** ▶ **scarcity** /ˈskeəsəti/ *noun* [C,U] (*pl* scarcities): *(a) scarcity of food/jobs/resources*

scarcely /ˈskeəsli/ *adv* **1** only just; almost not: *There was scarcely a car in sight.* ◆ *She's not a friend of mine. I scarcely know her.* ➲ look at **hardly** **2** used to suggest that sth is not reasonable or likely: *You can scarcely expect me to believe that after all you said before.*

scare¹ /skeə(r)/ *verb* **1** [T] to make a person or an animal frightened: *The sudden noise scared us all.* ◆ *It scares me to think what might happen.* **2** [I] to become frightened: *I don't scare easily, but when I saw the snake I was terrified.*
PHR V scare sb/sth away/off to make a person or an animal leave or stay away by frightening them or it: *Don't make any noise or you'll scare the birds away.*

scare² /skeə(r)/ *noun* [C] **1** a situation where many people are afraid or worried about sth: *Last night there was a* ***bomb scare*** *in the city centre.* **2** a feeling of being frightened: *It wasn't a serious heart attack but it gave him a scare.*

scarecrow /ˈskeəkrəʊ/ *noun* [C] a very simple model of a person that is put in a field in order to frighten away the birds

scared /skeəd/ *adj* scared (of sb/sth); scared (of doing sth/to do sth) frightened: *Are you scared of the dark?* ◆ *She's scared of walking home alone.* ◆ *Everyone was too scared to move.*

scarf /skɑːf/ *noun* [C] (*pl* scarves /skɑːvz/ or scarfs /skɑːfs/) **1** a long thin piece of cloth, usually made of wool, that you wear around your neck to keep warm **2** a piece of cloth that women wear around their neck or over their head or shoulders to keep warm or for decoration

scarlet /ˈskɑːlət/ *adj, noun* [U] (of) a bright red colour

scary /ˈskeəri/ *adj* (scarier; scariest) (*informal*) frightening: *a scary ghost story* ◆ *It was a bit scary driving in the mountains at night.*

scathing /ˈskeɪðɪŋ/ *adj* **scathing (about sb/sth)** expressing a very strong negative opinion about sb/sth; very critical: *a scathing attack on the new leader* ◆ *scathing criticism*

scatter /ˈskætə(r)/ *verb* **1** [T] to drop or throw things in different directions over a wide area: *The wind scattered the papers all over the room.* **2** [I] (used about a group of people or animals) to move away quickly in different directions

scattered /ˈskætəd/ *adj* spread over a large area or happening several times during a period of time: *There will be sunny intervals with scattered showers today.*

scavenge /ˈskævɪndʒ/ *verb* [I,T] to look for food, etc. among waste and rubbish ▶ **scavenger** *noun* [C]: *Scavengers steal the food that the lion has killed.*

SCE /ˌes siː ˈiː/ *abbr* **Scottish Certificate of Education**. Students in Scotland take the **SCE** at Standard grade at the age of about 16 and at Higher grade at about 17.

scenario /səˈnɑːriəʊ/ *noun* [C] (*pl* **scenarios**) **1** one way that things may happen in the future: *A likely scenario is that the company will get rid of some staff.* **2** a description of what happens in a play or film

scene /siːn/ *noun*

➤PLACE **1** [C] the place where sth happened: *the scene of a crime/an accident* ◆ *An ambulance was* ***on the scene*** *in minutes.*

➤IN PLAY, FILM, ETC. **2** [C] one part of a book, play, film, etc. in which the events happen in one place: *The first scene of 'Hamlet' takes place on the castle walls.*

➤AREA OF ACTIVITY **3 the scene** [sing] the way of life or the present situation in a particular area of activity: *The political scene in that part of the world is very confused.* ◆ *the fashion scene*

➤VIEW **4** [C,U] what you see around you in a particular place: *Her new job was no better, but at least it would be a* ***change of scene****.*

➤ARGUMENT **5** [C] an occasion when sb expresses great anger or another strong emotion in public: *There was quite a scene when she refused to pay the bill.*

IDM **set the scene (for sth)** **1** to create a situation in which sth can easily happen or develop: *His arrival set the scene for another argument.* **2** to give sb the information and details they need in order to understand what comes next: *The first part of the programme was just setting the scene.*

scenery /ˈsiːnəri/ *noun* [U] **1** the natural beauty that you see around you in the country: *The scenery is superb in the mountains.* ➲ note at **nature** **2** the furniture, painted cloth, boards, etc. that are used on the stage in a theatre: *The scenery is changed during the interval.*

scenic /ˈsiːnɪk/ *adj* having beautiful **scenery**

scent /sent/ *noun* **1** [C,U] a pleasant smell: *This flower has no scent.* ➲ note at **smell²** **2** [C,U] the smell that an animal leaves behind and that some other animals can follow **3** [U] (*BrE old-fashioned*) = **perfume**(1) **4** [sing] the feeling that sth is going to happen: *The scent of victory was in the air.* ▶ **scent** *verb* [T]: *The dog scented a rabbit and ran off.* ▶ **scented** *adj*

OTHER WORDS FOR

scenery

Country and **countryside** both mean land away from towns and cities. We use the word **countryside** if we want to emphasize the natural features such as hills, rivers, trees, etc. that are found there: *beautiful countryside* ◆ *the destruction of the countryside by new roads*. We say that an area of the country has beautiful **scenery** when it is attractive to look at. The **landscape** of a particular area is the way the features of it are arranged: *Trees and hedges are a typical feature of the British landscape.* ◆ *an urban landscape* (= in a city or town). You have a **view** of something when you look out of a window or down from a high place: *There was a marvellous view of the sea from our hotel room.*

sceptic (*AmE* **skeptic**) /ˈskeptɪk/ *noun* [C] a person who doubts that sth is true, right, etc. ▶ **sceptical** (*AmE* **skeptical**) /-kl/ *adj* **sceptical (of/about sth)**: *Many doctors are sceptical about the value of alternative medicine.*

scepticism (*AmE* **skepticism**) /ˈskeptɪsɪzəm/ *noun* [U] a general feeling of doubt about sth; a feeling that you are not likely to believe sth

schedule¹ /ˈʃedjuːl/ *noun* **1** [C,U] a plan of things that will happen or of work that must be done: *Max has a busy schedule for the next few days.* ◆ *to be ahead of/behind schedule* (= to have done more/less than was planned) **2** (*AmE*) = **timetable**

schedule² /ˈʃedjuːl/ *verb* [T] **schedule sth (for sth)** to arrange for sth to happen or be done at a particular time: *We've scheduled the meeting for Monday morning.* ◆ *The train was scheduled to arrive at 10.07.* ◆ *Is it a* ***scheduled flight****?* (= one that leaves at a regular time each day or week)

scheme¹ /skiːm/ *noun* [C] (*BrE*) **1 a scheme (to do sth/for doing sth)** an official plan or system for doing or organizing sth: *a new scheme to provide houses in the area* ◆ *a local scheme for recycling newspapers* **2** a clever plan to do sth: *He's thought of a new scheme for making money fast.* ➲ look at **colour scheme**

scheme² /skiːm/ *verb* [I,T] to make a secret or dishonest plan: *She felt that everyone was scheming to get rid of her.*

schizophrenia /ˌskɪtsəˈfriːniə/ *noun* [U] a serious mental illness in which a person confuses the real world and the world of the imagination and often behaves in strange and unexpected ways ▶ **schizophrenic** /ˌskɪtsəˈfrenɪk/ *adj, noun* [C]

scholar /ˈskɒlə(r)/ *noun* [C] **1** a person who studies and has a lot of knowledge about a particular subject **2** a person who has passed an exam or won a competition and has been given a **scholarship**(1) to help pay for their studies: *He has*

S

come here as a British Council scholar. ➲ look at **student**

scholarly /ˈskɒləli/ *adj* **1** (used about a person) spending a lot of time studying and having a lot of knowledge about an academic subject ➲ look at **studious 2** connected with academic study: *a scholarly journal* SYN **academic**

scholarship /ˈskɒləʃɪp/ *noun* **1** [C] an amount of money that is given to a person who has passed an exam or won a competition, in order to help pay for their studies: *to win a scholarship to Yale* **2** [U] serious study of an academic subject

🔑 **school** /skuːl/ *noun*
➤EDUCATION **1** [C] the place where children go to be educated: *Where did you* ***go to school****? ◆ They're building a new school in our area. ◆ Do you have to wear a school uniform? ◆ Was your school co-educational* (= for boys and girls) *or single-sex?* **2** [U] the time you spend at a school; the process of being educated in a school: *Their children are still* ***at school****. ◆ Children* ***start school*** *at 5 years old in Britain and can* ***leave school*** *at 17. ◆ School starts at 9 o'clock and finishes at about 3.30. ◆ After school we usually have homework to do.*

> **HELP** You say **school** (without **'the'**) when you are talking about going there for the usual reasons (that is, as a student or teacher): *Where do your children go to school? ◆ I enjoyed being at school. ◆ Do you walk to school?* You say **the school** if you are talking about going there for a different reason (for example, as a parent): *I have to go to the school on Thursday to talk to John's teacher.* You must also use **a** or **the** when more information about the school is given: *Rahul goes to the school in the next village. ◆ She teaches at a special school for children with learning difficulties.*

3 [sing, with sing or pl verb] all the students and teachers in a school: *The whole school is/are going on a trip tomorrow.* **4** [in compounds] connected with school: *children* ***of school age*** *◆ The bus was full of* ***schoolchildren****. ◆ It is getting increasingly difficult for* ***school-leavers*** *to find jobs. ◆* ***Schoolteachers*** *have been awarded a 2% pay rise. ◆ I don't have many good memories of my* ***schooldays****. ◆ I went skating with some of my* ***school friends****.*
➤FOR PARTICULAR SKILL **5** [C] a place where you go to learn a particular subject: *a language/driving/drama/business school*
➤COLLEGE/UNIVERSITY **6** [C,U] (*AmE*) a college or university: *famous schools like Yale and Harvard ◆ He's still in school.* **7** [C] a department of a university that teaches a particular subject: *the school of geography at Leeds University*
➤ARTISTS **8** [C] a group of writers, artists, etc. who have the same ideas or style: *the Flemish school of painting*
➤FISH **9** [C] a large group of fish, etc., swimming together: *a school of dolphins*
IDM **a school of thought** the ideas or opinions that one group of people share: *There are various schools of thought on this matter.*

> TOPIC
> ### Schools
> Children go to **primary** and **secondary** schools. These can be **private** or **state** schools (= paid for by the government), and sometimes they are also **boarding** schools (= where students live and sleep). A school for very young children is a **nursery school**. Schools have **classrooms** and every **pupil/student** is a member of a **class**. During **lessons** pupils study **subjects**, and after school they can do **extra-curricular** activities, such as sport or drama. Some **teachers** are **strict** while others are **lenient**, and sometimes they give pupils a lot of **homework**. It is important to get good **marks**, especially in **exams** at the end of **term**. Students who **bully** their **classmates** or **skip school/play truant** (= do not go to school when they should) usually **get into trouble** with the **head teacher**.

schoolchild /ˈskuːltʃaɪld/ *noun* [C] (*pl* schoolchildren /-tʃɪldrən/) a child who goes to school

schooling /ˈskuːlɪŋ/ *noun* [U] the time that you spend at school; your education

🔑 **science** /ˈsaɪəns/ *noun* **1** [U] the study of and knowledge about the physical world and natural laws: *Modern science has discovered a lot about the origin of life. ◆ Fewer young people are studying science at university.* **2** [C] one of the subjects into which science can be divided ➲ look at **art**

> **MORE** **Chemistry, physics** and **biology** are all sciences. **Scientists** do **research** and **experiments** in a **laboratory** to see what happens and to try to discover new information. The study of people and society is called **social science**.

ˌscience ˈfiction *noun* [U] books, films, etc. about imaginary events that take place in the future, often involving travel in space

🔑 **scientific** /ˌsaɪənˈtɪfɪk/ *adj* **1** connected with or involving science: *We need more funding for scientific research. ◆ scientific instruments* **2** (used about a way of thinking or of doing sth) careful and logical: *a scientific study of the way people use language* ▶ **scientifically** /-kli/ *adv*: *Sorting out the files won't take long if we do it scientifically.*

🔑 **scientist** /ˈsaɪəntɪst/ *noun* [C] a person who studies or teaches science, especially biology, chemistry or physics: *a research scientist ◆ nuclear scientists*

scintillating /ˈsɪntɪleɪtɪŋ/ *adj* very clever, amusing and interesting: *The lead actor gave a scintillating performance.*

🔑 **scissors** /ˈsɪzəz/ *noun* [pl] a tool for cutting paper or cloth, that has two sharp blades with handles, joined together in the middle

GRAMMAR **Scissors** are plural: *These scissors are blunt.* We say **a pair of scissors**, NOT 'a scissors'.

scoff /skɒf/ *verb* **1** [I] **scoff (at sb/sth)** to speak about sb/sth in a way that shows you think that he/she/it is stupid or ridiculous **2** [T] (*BrE informal*) to eat a lot of sth quickly

scold /skəʊld/ *verb* [I,T] **scold sb (for sth/for doing sth)** to speak angrily to sb because they have done sth bad or wrong ➲ A more common expression is **tell sb off**.

scone /skɒn; skəʊn/ *noun* [C] a small round cake that you cut in half and eat with butter, cream and jam on it

scoop¹ /sku:p/ *noun* [C] **1** a tool like a spoon used for picking up flour, grain, etc. **2** the amount that one **scoop** contains: *a scoop of ice cream* **3** an exciting piece of news that is reported by one newspaper, TV or radio station before it is reported anywhere else

scoop² /sku:p/ *verb* [T] **1 scoop sth (out/up)** to make a hole in sth or to take sth out by using a **scoop** or sth similar: *Scoop out the middle of the pineapple.* **2 scoop sb/sth (up)** to move or lift sb/sth using a continuous action: *He scooped up the child and ran.* **3** to get a story before all other newspapers, TV stations, etc. **4** to win money or a big or important prize: *The film has scooped all the awards this year.*

scooter /ˈsku:tə(r)/ *noun* [C] **1** a light motorbike with a small engine ➲ picture on **page P7** **2** a child's toy with two wheels that you stand on and move by pushing one foot against the ground

scope /skəʊp/ *noun* **1** [U] **scope (for sth/to do sth)** the chance or opportunity to do sth: *The job offers plenty of scope for creativity.* **2** [sing] the variety of subjects that are being discussed or considered: *The government was unwilling to extend the scope of the inquiry.*

scorch /skɔ:tʃ/ *verb* [T] to burn sth so that its colour changes but it is not destroyed: *I scorched my blouse when I was ironing it.*

scorching /ˈskɔ:tʃɪŋ/ *adj* (*informal*) very hot: *It was absolutely scorching on Tuesday.*

⚷ **score¹** /skɔ:(r)/ *noun* **1** [C] the number of points, goals, etc. that sb/sth gets in a game, a competition, an exam, etc: *What was the final score?* ♦ *The score is 3-2 to Liverpool.* ♦ *The top score in the test was 80%.* **2** [C] the written form of a piece of music: *an orchestral score* **3 scores** [pl] very many: *Scores of people have written to offer their support.*

IDM on that score as far as that is concerned: *Lan will be well looked after. Don't worry on that score.*

⚷ **score²** /skɔ:(r)/ *verb* [I,T] to get points, goals, etc. in a game, a competition, an exam, etc: *The team still hadn't scored by half-time.* ♦ *Louise scored the highest marks in the exam.*

scoreboard /ˈskɔ:bɔ:d/ *noun* [C] a large board that shows the score during a game, competition, etc.

scorn¹ /skɔ:n/ *noun* [U] **scorn (for sb/sth)** the strong feeling that you have when you do not respect sb/sth

scorn² /skɔ:n/ *verb* [T] **1** to feel or show a complete lack of respect for sb/sth: *The President scorned his critics.* **2** to refuse to accept help or advice, especially because you are too proud: *The old lady scorned all offers of help.* ▶ **scornful** /ˈskɔ:nfl/ *adj*: *a scornful look/smile/remark* ▶ **scornfully** /-fəli/ *adv*

Scorpio /ˈskɔ:piəʊ/ *noun* [C,U] (*pl* **Scorpios**) the 8th sign of the **zodiac** (= 12 signs which represent the positions of the sun, moon and planets), the **Scorpion**; a person born under this sign: *I'm a Scorpio.* ➲ picture at **zodiac**

scorpion /ˈskɔ:piən/ *noun* [C] a creature which looks like a large insect and lives in hot countries. A **scorpion** has a long curved tail with a poisonous sting in it.

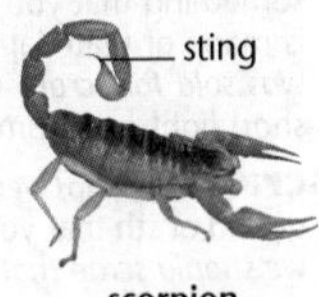

scorpion

Scot /skɒt/ *noun* [C] a person who comes from Scotland

Scotch /skɒtʃ/ *noun* [U,C] a type of **whisky** (= a strong alcoholic drink) that is made in Scotland; a glass of this

Scotch tape™ (*AmE*) = **Sellotape™**

Scots /skɒts/ *adj* of or connected with people from Scotland

Scottish /ˈskɒtɪʃ/ *adj* of or connected with Scotland, its people, culture, etc.

scoundrel /ˈskaʊndrəl/ *noun* [C] (*old-fashioned*) a man who behaves very badly towards other people, especially by being dishonest

scour /ˈskaʊə(r)/ *verb* [T] **1** to search a place very carefully because you are looking for sb/sth **2** to clean sth by rubbing it hard with sth rough: *to scour a dirty pan*

scourge /skɜ:dʒ/ *noun* [C] a person or thing that causes a lot of trouble or suffering: *Inflation was the scourge of the 1970s.*

scout /skaʊt/ *noun* [C] **1 Scout** a member of the **Scouts** (= an organization that teaches young people how to look after themselves and encourages them to help others). Scouts do sport, learn useful skills, go camping, etc. ➲ look at **Guide** **2** a soldier who is sent on in front of the rest of the group to find out where the enemy is or which is the best route to take

scowl /skaʊl/ *noun* [C] a look on your face that shows you are angry or in a bad mood ➲ look at **frown** ▶ **scowl** *verb* [I]

scrabble /ˈskræbl/ *verb* [I] (*especially BrE*) to move your fingers or feet around quickly, trying to find sth or get hold of sth: *She scrabbled about in her purse for some coins.*

scramble /ˈskræmbl/ *verb* [I] **1** to climb quickly up or over sth using your hands to help you; to move somewhere quickly: *He scrambled up the hill and over the wall.* ♦ *He* **scrambled to his feet** (= off the

S

ground) *and ran off into the trees.* ♦ *The children scrambled into the car.* **2** scramble (for sth/to do sth) to fight or move quickly to get sth which a lot of people want: *People stood up and began scrambling for the exits.* ♦ *Everyone was scrambling to get the best bargains.* ▶ **scramble** *noun* [sing]

ˌ**scrambled** ˈ**eggs** *noun* [U,C] eggs mixed together with milk and then cooked in a pan

scrap¹ /skræp/ *noun* **1** [C] a small piece of sth: *a scrap of paper/cloth* ♦ *scraps of food* SYN **bit** **2** [U] something that you do not want any more but that is made of material that can be used again: *The car was sold* **for scrap**. ♦ *scrap paper* **3** [C] (*informal*) a short fight or argument

scrap² /skræp/ *verb* [T] (scrapping; scrapped) to get rid of sth that you do not want any more: *I think we should scrap that idea.*

scrapbook /ˈskræpbʊk/ *noun* [C] a large book with empty pages that you can stick pictures, newspaper articles, etc. in

scrape¹ /skreɪp/ *verb* **1** [T] scrape sth (down/out/off) to remove sth from a surface by moving a sharp edge across it firmly: *Scrape all the mud off your boots before you come in.* **2** [T] scrape sth (against/along/on sth) to damage or hurt sth by rubbing it against sth rough or hard: *Mark fell and scraped his knee.* ♦ *Sunita scraped the car against the wall.* **3** [I,T] scrape (sth) against/along/on sth to rub (sth) against sth and make a sharp unpleasant noise: *The branches scraped against the window.* **4** [T] (*BrE*) to manage to get or win sth with difficulty: *I just scraped a pass in the maths exam.*

PHR V **scrape by (on sth)** to manage to live on the money you have, but with difficulty: *We can just scrape by on my salary.*

scrape through (sth) to succeed in doing sth with difficulty: *to scrape through an exam* (= just manage to pass it)

scrape sth together/up to get or collect sth together with difficulty

S

scrape² /skreɪp/ *noun* [C] **1** the action or unpleasant sound of one thing rubbing hard against another **2** damage or an injury caused by rubbing against sth rough: *I got a nasty scrape on my knee.* **3** (*informal*) a difficult situation that was caused by your own stupid behaviour

ˈ**scrapheap** *noun* [C] a large pile of objects, especially metal, that are no longer wanted

IDM **on the scrapheap** (*informal*) not wanted any more: *Many of the unemployed feel that they are on the scrapheap.*

scrappy /ˈskræpi/ *adj* (*informal*) (scrappier; scrappiest) not organized or tidy and so not pleasant to see: *a scrappy essay/football match*

⚷ **scratch¹** /skrætʃ/ *verb* **1** [I,T] scratch (at sth) to rub your skin with your nails: *Don't scratch at your insect bites or they'll get worse.* ♦ *Could you scratch my back for me?* ♦ *She sat and scratched her head as she thought about the problem.* **2** [I,T] to make a mark on a surface or a slight cut on sb's skin with sth sharp: *The cat will scratch if you annoy it.* ♦ *The table was badly scratched.* **3** [T] to use sth sharp to make or remove a mark: *He scratched his name on the top of his desk.* ♦ *I tried to scratch the paint off the table.* **4** [I] to make a sound by rubbing a surface with sth sharp: *The dog was scratching at the door to go outside.*

⚷ **scratch²** /skrætʃ/ *noun* **1** [C] a cut, mark or sound that was made by sth sharp rubbing a surface: *There's a scratch on the car door.* **2** [sing] an act of scratching part of the body: *The dog had a good scratch.*

IDM **from scratch** from the very beginning: *I'm learning Spanish from scratch.*

(be/come) up to scratch (*informal*) (to be/become) good enough

scrawl /skrɔːl/ *verb* [I,T] to write sth quickly in an untidy and careless way: *He scrawled his name across the top of the paper.* ▶ **scrawl** *noun* [sing]: *Her signature was just a scrawl.* ➲ look at **scribble**

scrawny /ˈskrɔːni/ *adj* (*informal*) (scrawnier; scrawniest) very thin in a way that is not attractive

⚷ **scream¹** /skriːm/ *verb* [I,T] scream (sth) (out) (at sb) to cry out loudly in a high voice because you are afraid, excited, angry, in pain, etc: *She saw a rat and screamed out.* ♦ *'Don't touch that,' he screamed.* ♦ *She screamed at the children to stop.* ♦ *He screamed with pain.* ♦ *He clung to the edge of the cliff, screaming for help.* ♦ *Cathy screamed his name.* ➲ look at **shout**

⚷ **scream²** /skriːm/ *noun* **1** [C] a loud cry in a high voice: *a scream of pain* **2** [sing] (*informal, old-fashioned*) a person or thing that is very funny: *Mel's a real scream.*

screech /skriːtʃ/ *verb* [I,T] to make an unpleasant loud, high sound: *'Get out of here,' she screeched at him.* ➲ look at **shriek** ▶ **screech** *noun* [sing]: *the screech of brakes*

⚷ **screen¹** /skriːn/ *noun* **1** [C] the glass surface of a TV or computer where the picture or information appears: *They were staring at the television screen.* ♦ *Move your cursor to the top of the screen.* ➲ picture at **camera**, **computer** **2** [C] the large flat surface on which films are shown **3** [sing,U] films and TV: *Some actors look better in real life than on screen.* **4** [C] a flat vertical surface that is used for dividing a room or keeping sb/sth out of sight: *The nurse pulled the screen round the bed.*

screen² /skriːn/ *verb* [T] **1** screen sb/sth (off) (from sb/sth) to hide or protect sb/sth from sb/sth else: *The bed was screened off while the doctor examined him.* ♦ *to screen your eyes from the sun* **2** screen sb (for sth) to examine or test sb to find out if they have a particular disease or if they are suitable for a particular job: *All women over 50 should be screened for breast cancer.* ♦ *The Ministry of Defence screens all job applicants.* **3** to show sth on TV or in a cinema

screenplay /ˈskriːnpleɪ/ *noun* [C] the words that are written for a film, together with instructions for how it is to be acted and made into a film ➲ note at **film**

ˈ**screen saver** *noun* [C] a computer program that replaces what is on the screen with a moving image if the computer is not used for a certain amount of time

screenshot /ˈskriːnʃɒt/ *noun* [C] an image of the display on a screen, used when showing how a program works

screenwriter /ˈskriːnraɪtə(r)/ *noun* [C] a person who writes instructions about what happens in a film and the words the actors say

screw¹ /skruː/ *noun* [C] a thin pointed piece of metal used for fixing two things, for example pieces of wood, together. You turn a screw with a **screwdriver**: *One of the screws is loose.* ➲ picture at **bolt**

screw² /skruː/ *verb* **1** [T] screw sth (on, down, etc.) to fasten sth with a screw or screws: *The bookcase is screwed to the wall.* ◆ *The lid is screwed down so you can't remove it.* **2** [I,T] to fasten sth, or to be fastened, by turning: *The legs screw into holes in the underside of the seat.* ◆ *Make sure that you screw the top of the jar on tightly.* **3** [T] screw sth (up) (into sth) to squeeze sth, especially a piece of paper, into a tight ball: *He screwed the letter up into a ball and threw it away.*

PHR V **screw (sth) up** (*slang*) to make a mistake and cause sth to fail: *You'd better not screw up this deal.*

screw your eyes, face, etc. up to change the expression on your face by nearly closing your eyes, in pain or because the light is strong

screwdriver /ˈskruːdraɪvə(r)/ *noun* [C] a tool that you use for turning **screws** ➲ picture at **tool**

scribble /ˈskrɪbl/ *verb* [I,T] **1** to write sth quickly and carelessly: *to scribble a note down on a pad* ➲ look at **scrawl** **2** to make marks with a pen or pencil that are not letters or pictures: *The children had scribbled all over the walls.* ▶ **scribble** *noun* [C,U]

script /skrɪpt/ *noun* **1** [C] the written form of a play, film, speech, etc: *Who wrote the script for the movie?* **2** [C,U] a system of writing: *Arabic/Cyrillic/Roman script*

scripture /ˈskrɪptʃə(r)/ (also the scriptures) *noun* [U, pl] the books of a religion, such as the Bible

scroll¹ /skrəʊl/ *noun* [C] a long roll of paper with writing on it

scroll² /skrəʊl/ *verb* [I] scroll (up/down/across) to move text up and down or left and right on a computer screen: *Scroll down to the bottom of the page.*

ˈscroll bar *noun* [C] a strip at the edge of a computer screen that you use to move the text up and down or left and right

scrounge /skraʊndʒ/ *verb* [I,T] (*informal*) scrounge (sth) (from/off sb) to get sth by asking another person to give it to you instead of making an effort to get it for yourself: *Lucy is always scrounging money off her friends.*

scrub¹ /skrʌb/ *verb* [I,T] (scrubbing; scrubbed) **1** scrub (sth) (down/out) to clean sth with soap and water by rubbing it hard, often with a brush: *to scrub (down) the floor/walls* **2** scrub (sth) (off/out); scrub (sth) (off sth/out of sth) to remove sth or be removed by **scrubbing**: *to scrub the dirt off the walls* ◆ *I hope these coffee stains will scrub out.*

scrub² /skrʌb/ *noun* **1** [sing] an act of cleaning sth by rubbing it hard, often with a brush: *This floor needs a good scrub.* **2** [U] small trees and bushes that grow in an area that has very little rain

scruff /skrʌf/ *noun*

IDM **by the scruff (of the/sb's neck)** by the back of an animal's or person's neck: *She picked up the puppy by the scruff of the neck.*

scruffy /ˈskrʌfi/ *adj* (scruffier; scruffiest) dirty and untidy: *He always looks so scruffy.* ◆ *scruffy jeans*

scrum /skrʌm/ *noun* [C] (in the sport of **rugby**) when several players put their heads down in a circle and push against each other to try to get the ball

scruples /ˈskruːplz/ *noun* [pl] a feeling that stops you from doing sth that you think is morally wrong: *I've got no scruples about asking them for money* (= I don't think it's wrong).

scrupulous /ˈskruːpjələs/ *adj* **1** very careful or paying great attention to detail: *a scrupulous investigation into the causes of the disaster* **2** careful to be honest and do what is right OPP **unscrupulous** ▶ **scrupulously** *adv*: *scrupulously clean/honest/tidy*

scrutinize (also -ise) /ˈskruːtənaɪz/ *verb* [T] to look at or examine sth carefully: *The immigration official scrutinized every page of my passport.* ▶ **scrutiny** /ˈskruːtəni/ *noun* [U]: *The police kept all the suspects **under close scrutiny**.*

scuba-diving /ˈskuːbə daɪvɪŋ/ *noun* [U] the activity of swimming underwater using special equipment for breathing: *to go scuba-diving* ➲ picture at **snorkel**

scuff /skʌf/ *verb* [T] to make a mark on your shoes or with your shoes, for example by kicking sth or by rubbing your feet along the ground

scuffle /ˈskʌfl/ *noun* [C] a short, not very violent, fight

sculptor /ˈskʌlptə(r)/ *noun* [C] a person who makes **sculptures** from stone, wood, etc. ➲ note at **art**

sculpture /ˈskʌlptʃə(r)/ *noun* **1** [C,U] a work of art that is a figure or an object made from stone, wood, metal, etc. **2** [U] the art of making **sculptures** ➲ note at **art**

scum /skʌm/ *noun* [U] **1** a dirty or unpleasant substance on the surface of a liquid **2** (*slang*) an insulting word for people that you have no respect for: *Drug dealers are scum.*

scurry /ˈskʌri/ *verb* [I] (scurrying; scurries; *pt, pp* scurried) to run quickly with short steps; to hurry

scuttle /ˈskʌtl/ *verb* [I] to run quickly with short steps: *The spider scuttled away when I tried to catch it.*

scythe /saɪð/ *noun* [C] a tool with a long handle and a long, curved blade. You use a **scythe** to cut long grass, etc.

SE *abbr* = **south-east¹**, **south-eastern**: *SE Asia*

S

sea /siː/ *noun* **1** *often* **the sea** [U] the salt water that covers large parts of the surface of the earth: *The sea is quite calm/rough today.* ◆ *Do you live* **by the sea**? ◆ *to travel* **by sea** ◆ *There were several people swimming* **in the sea**. ➲ picture on **page P10** ➲ note at **ocean** **2** *often* **Sea** [C] a particular large area of salt water. A sea may be part of a larger area of water or may be surrounded by land: *the Mediterranean Sea* ◆ *the Black Sea* ➲ look at **ocean** **3** [C] (also **seas** [pl]) the state or movement of the waves of the sea: *The boat sank in heavy* (= rough) *seas off the Scottish coast.* **4** [sing] a large amount of sb/sth close together: *The pavement was just a sea of people.*

IDM **at sea** **1** sailing in a ship: *They spent about three weeks at sea.* **2** not understanding or not knowing what to do: *When I first started this job, I was completely at sea.*

the ˈseabed *noun* [sing] the floor of the sea

seafood /ˈsiːfuːd/ *noun* [U] fish and sea creatures that we eat, especially **shellfish** (= creatures with shells that live in water)

the seafront /ˈsiːfrʌnt/ *noun* [sing] the part of a town facing the sea: *The hotel is right* **on the seafront**. ◆ *to walk* **along the seafront**

seagull /ˈsiːɡʌl/ = **gull**

seal[1] /siːl/ *verb* [T] **1** **seal sth (up/down)** to close or fasten a package, an envelope, etc: *The parcel was sealed with tape.* ◆ *to seal (down) an envelope* **2** **seal sth (up)** to fill a hole or cover sth so that air or liquid does not get in or out: *The food is packed in sealed bags to keep it fresh.* **3** (*formal*) to make sth sure, so that it cannot be changed or argued about: *to seal an agreement*

PHR V **seal sth off** to stop any person or thing from entering or leaving an area or building: *The building was sealed off by the police.*

seal[2] /siːl/ *noun* [C] **1** an official design or mark that is put on a document, an envelope, etc. to show that it is genuine or that it has not been opened: *The letter bore the President's seal.* **2** something that stops air or liquid from getting in or out of sth: *The seal has worn and oil is escaping.* **3** a small piece of paper, metal, plastic, etc. on a bottle, box, etc. that you must break before you can open it: *Check the seal isn't broken.* **4** a grey animal with short fur that lives in and near the sea and that eats fish. Seals have no legs and swim with the help of **flippers** (= short flat arms): *a colony of seals*

seal

ˈsea level *noun* [U] the average level of the sea, used for measuring the height of places on land: *The town is 500 metres above sea level.*

ˈsea lion *noun* [C] a large **seal** that lives by the Pacific Ocean

seam /siːm/ *noun* [C] **1** the line where two pieces of cloth are sewn together **2** a layer of coal under the ground

seaman /ˈsiːmən/ *noun* [C] (*pl* **-men** /-mən/) a sailor

seamless /ˈsiːmləs/ *adj* with no spaces or pauses between one part and the next: *a seamless flow of talk* ▶ **seamlessly** *adv*

seance /ˈseɪɒ̃s/ *noun* [C] a meeting at which people try to talk to the spirits of dead people

search[1] /sɜːtʃ/ *verb* [I,T] **search (sb/sth) (for sb/sth); search (through sth) (for sth)** to examine sb/sth carefully because you are looking for sth; to look for sth that is missing: *The men were arrested and searched for drugs.* ◆ *Were your bags searched at the airport?* ◆ *They are still searching for the missing child.* ◆ *She searched through the papers on the desk, looking for the letter.*

search[2] /sɜːtʃ/ *noun* [C,U] the act of looking for sth: *the search for the missing boy* ◆ *She walked round for hours* **in search of** *her missing dog.* ◆ *to do a search on the Internet*

ˈsearch engine *noun* [C] a computer program that searches the Internet for information ➲ note at **Internet**

searcher /ˈsɜːtʃə(r)/ *noun* [C] **1** a person who is looking for sb/sth **2** a program that allows you to look for particular information on a computer

searching /ˈsɜːtʃɪŋ/ *adj* (used about a look, question, etc.) trying to find out the truth: *The customs officers asked a lot of searching questions about our trip.*

ˈsearch party *noun* [C] an organized group of people who are looking for sb/sth that is lost or missing

ˈsearch warrant *noun* [C] an official piece of paper that gives the police the right to search a building, etc.

seashell /ˈsiːʃel/ *noun* [C] the empty shell of a small animal that lives in the sea

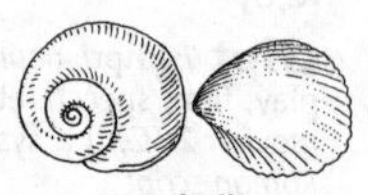
seashells

seashore /ˈsiːʃɔː(r)/ *noun* [U] *usually* **the seashore** the part of the land that is next to the sea: *We were looking for shells* **on the seashore**.

seasick /ˈsiːsɪk/ *adj* feeling sick or **vomiting** (= bringing up food from the stomach) because of the movement of a boat or ship: *to feel/get/be seasick* ➲ look at **airsick, carsick, travel-sick**

seaside /ˈsiːsaɪd/ *noun* [sing] *often* **the seaside** an area on the coast, especially one where people go on holiday: *to go to the seaside* ◆ *a seaside town*

season[1] /ˈsiːzn/ *noun* [C] **1** one of the four main periods of the year: *In cool countries, the four seasons are spring, summer, autumn and winter.* ◆ *the dry/rainy season* **2** the period of the year when sth is common or popular or when sth usually happens or is done: *the football season*

IDM **in season** **1** (used about fresh foods) available in large quantities because it is the right time of the year: *Tomatoes are cheapest when they are in season.* **2** (used about a female animal) ready to have sex

out of season **1** (used about fresh foods) not available in large quantities because it is the wrong time of the year **2** (used about a place where people go on holiday) at the time of year when it is least popular with tourists: *This hotel is much cheaper out of season.*

season² /ˈsiːzn/ *verb* [T] to add salt, spices, etc. to food in order to make it taste better ▸ **seasoning** *noun* [C,U]: *Add seasoning to the soup and serve with bread.*

seasonal /ˈsiːzənl/ *adj* happening or existing at a particular time of the year: *There are a lot of seasonal jobs in the summer.*

seasoned /ˈsiːznd/ *adj* having a lot of experience of sth: *a seasoned traveller*

ˈseason ticket *noun* [C] a ticket that allows you to make a particular journey by bus, train, etc. or to go to a theatre or watch a sports team as often as you like for a fixed period of time

seat¹ /siːt/ *noun* [C] **1** something that you sit on: *Please* ***take a seat*** (= sit down). ♦ *the back/driving/passenger seat of a car* ➲ picture at **bicycle**, **car** **2** the part of a chair, etc. that you sit on: *a steel chair with a plastic seat* **3** a place in a theatre, on a plane, etc. where you pay to sit: *There are no seats left on that flight.* **4** an official position as a member of a parliament, etc: *to win/lose a seat*
IDM **be in the driving seat** ➲ **driving¹**
take a back seat ➲ **back²**

seat² /siːt/ *verb* [T] **1** [often passive] (*formal*) to give sb a place to sit; to sit down: *Please be seated.* **2** to have seats or chairs for a particular number of people

ˈseat belt (also ˈ*safety belt*) *noun* [C] a long narrow piece of cloth that is fixed to the seat in a car or plane and that you wear around your body, so that you are not thrown forward if there is an accident: *to fasten/unfasten your seat belt* ➲ look at **belt** ➲ picture at **car**

seating /ˈsiːtɪŋ/ *noun* [U] the seats or chairs in a place or the way that they are arranged: *The conference hall has seating for 500 people.*

seaweed /ˈsiːwiːd/ *noun* [U] a plant that grows in the sea. There are many different types of **seaweed**. ➲ picture on **page P10**

sec /sek/ (*informal*) = **second²**(2)

secluded /sɪˈkluːdɪd/ *adj* far away from other people, roads, etc.; very quiet: *a secluded beach/garden* ▸ **seclusion** /sɪˈkluːʒn/ *noun* [U]

second¹ /ˈsekənd/ *determiner, ordinal number, adv* 2nd: *We are going on holiday in the second week in July.* ♦ *Birmingham is the second largest city in Britain after London.* ♦ *She poured herself a second cup of coffee.* ♦ *Our team finished second.* ♦ *I* ***came second*** *in the competition.* ♦ *Queen Elizabeth the Second* ♦ ***the second of*** *January* ♦ *January* ***the second*** ➲ note at **sixth**
IDM **second nature (to sb)** something that has become a habit or that you can do easily because you have done it so many times: *With practice, driving becomes second nature.*
second thoughts a change of mind or opinion about sth; doubts that you have when you are not sure if you have made the right decision: ***On second thoughts****, let's go today, not tomorrow.* ♦ *I'm starting to* ***have second thoughts*** *about accepting their offer.*

second² /ˈsekənd/ *noun*
›SHORT TIME **1** [C] (*abbr* **sec**) one of the 60 parts into which a minute is divided: *She can run 100 metres in just over 11 seconds.* **2** (also *informal* **sec**) [C] a short time: *Wait a second, please.* SYN **moment**
›PRODUCT **3** [C, usually pl] something that has a small fault and that is sold at a lower price: *The clothes are all seconds.*
›IN CAR **4** [U] the second of the **gears** (= speeds) that a vehicle can move forward in: *Once the car's moving, put it* ***in second****.*
›UNIVERSITY **5** [C] **a second (in sth)** the second highest level of degree given by a British university: *to get an upper/a lower second in physics*

second³ /ˈsekənd/ *verb* [T] to support sb's suggestion or idea at a meeting so that it can then be discussed and voted on

second⁴ /sɪˈkɒnd/ *verb* [T, usually passive] (*especially BrE*) **second sb (from sth) (to sth)** to send an employee to another department, office, etc. in order to do a different job for a short period of time ▸ **secondment** *noun* [U,C]: *They met while she was* ***on secondment*** *from the Foreign Office.*

secondary /ˈsekəndri/ *adj* **1** less important than sth else: *Other people's opinions are secondary—it's my opinion that counts.* **2** caused by or developing from sth else: *She developed a secondary infection following a bad cold.*

ˈsecondary school *noun* [C] a school for children aged from 11 to 18 ➲ note at **primary school**

ˌsecond ˈbest¹ *adj* not quite the best but the next one after the best: *the second-best time in the 100 metres race* ➲ look at **best**

ˌsecond ˈbest² *noun* [U] something that is not as good as the best, or not as good as you would like: *I'm not prepared to accept second best.*

ˌsecond ˈclass *noun* [U] **1** (also ˈ*standard class*) the ordinary, less expensive seats on a train, ship, etc: *You can never get a seat in second class.* **2** (in Britain) the way of sending letters, etc. that costs less but takes longer to arrive than **first class**

ˌsecond-ˈclass *adj* **1** of little importance: *Old people should not be treated as* ***second-class citizens****.* **2** [only *before* a noun] used about the ordinary, less expensive seats on a train, ship, etc. **3** [only *before* a noun] (in Britain) used about the way of sending letters, etc. that costs less but takes longer to arrive than **first class** **4** [only *before* a noun] (used about a British university degree) of the level that is next after **first-class** ▸ **ˌsecond-ˈclass** *adv*

ˌsecond ˈcousin *noun* [C] the child of your mother's or father's cousin

ˌsecond ˈfloor *noun* [C] the floor in a building that is two floors above the lowest floor: *I live on the second floor.* ♦ *a second-floor flat*

S

HELP In American English the second floor is next above the lowest.

the ˈsecond hand *noun* [C] the hand on some clocks and watches that shows seconds

ˌsecond-ˈhand *adj* **1** already used or owned by sb else: *a second-hand car* ➲ look at **old** **2** (used about news or information) that you heard from sb else, and did not see or experience yourself ➲ look at **first-hand** ▸ **second-hand** *adv*: *I bought this bike second-hand.*

ˌsecond ˈlanguage *noun* [C] a language that sb learns to speak well and that they use for work or at school, but that is not the language they learned first: *ESL is short for English as a Second Language.*

secondly /ˈsekəndli/ *adv* (used when you are giving your second reason or opinion) also: *Firstly, I think it's too expensive and secondly, we don't really need it.*

ˈsecond name *noun* [C] (*especially BrE*) **1** = **surname** **2** a second personal name: *His second name is Prabhakar, after his father.*

ˌsecond-ˈrate *adj* of poor quality: *a second-rate poet*

secrecy /ˈsiːkrəsi/ *noun* [U] the fact of being secret or keeping sth secret: *I must stress the importance of secrecy in this matter.*

⚷ **secret¹** /ˈsiːkrət/ *adj* **1** **secret (from sb)** that is not or must not be known by other people: *We have to **keep** the party **secret** from Carmen.* ◆ *a secret address* ◆ *a secret love affair* **2** [only *before* a noun] used to describe actions that you do not tell anyone about: *a secret drinker* ◆ *She's got a secret admirer.* ▸ **secretly** *adv*: *The government secretly agreed to pay the kidnappers.*

⚷ **secret²** /ˈsiːkrət/ *noun* **1** [C] something that is not or must not be known by other people: *to **keep a secret*** ◆ *to let somebody in on/tell somebody a secret* ◆ *I can't tell you where we're going—it's a secret.* ◆ ***It's no secret that** they don't like each other* (= everyone knows). **2** [sing] **the secret (of/to sth/doing sth)** the only way or the best way of doing or achieving sth: *What is the secret of your success* (= how did you become so successful)?

IDM **in secret** without other people knowing: *to meet in secret*

ˌsecret ˈagent (also **agent**) *noun* [C] a person who tries to find out secret information, especially about the government of another country ➲ look at **spy**

secretarial /ˌsekrəˈteəriəl/ *adj* involving or connected with the work that a **secretary** does: *secretarial skills/work*

⚷ **secretary** /ˈsekrətri/ *noun* [C] (*pl* **secretaries**) **1** a person who works in an office. A **secretary** types letters, answers the telephone, keeps records, etc: *the director's personal secretary* ➲ note at **office** **2** an official of a club or society who is responsible for keeping records, writing letters, etc: *the membership secretary* **3** **Secretary** (in the US) the head of a government department, chosen by the President: *Secretary of the Treasury* ➲ look at **minister** **4** **Secretary** (*BrE*) = **Secretary of State**(1)

ˌSecretary of ˈState *noun* [C] **1** (also **Secretary**) (in Britain) the head of one of the main government departments: *the Secretary of State for Defence* **2** (in the US) the head of the government department that deals with foreign affairs

secrete /sɪˈkriːt/ *verb* [T] **1** (used about a part of a plant, animal or person) to produce a liquid **2** (*formal*) to hide sth in a secret place

secretion /sɪˈkriːʃn/ *noun* [C,U] (*formal*) a liquid that is produced by a plant or an animal; the process by which the liquid is produced: *The frog covers its skin in a poisonous secretion for protection.*

secretive /ˈsiːkrətɪv/ *adj* liking to keep things secret from other people: *Wendy is very secretive about her private life.* ▸ **secretively** *adv* ▸ **secretiveness** *noun* [U]

the ˌsecret ˈservice *noun* [sing] the government department that tries to find out secret information about other countries and governments

sect /sekt/ *noun* [C] a group of people who have a particular set of religious or political beliefs. A **sect** has often broken away from a larger group.

sectarian /sekˈteəriən/ *adj* connected with the differences that exist between groups of people who have different religious views: *sectarian attacks/violence*

⚷ **section** /ˈsekʃn/ *noun* [C] **1** one of the parts into which sth is divided: *the string section of an orchestra* ◆ *the financial section of a newspaper* ◆ *The library has an excellent reference section.* **2** a view or drawing of sth as if it was cut from the top to the bottom so that you can see the inside: *The illustration shows a section through a leaf.*

⚷ **sector** /ˈsektə(r)/ *noun* [C] **1** a part of the business activity of a country: *The manufacturing sector has declined in recent years.* ◆ *the public/private sector* **2** a part of a particular area, especially an area under military control: *the occupied sector of the city*

secular /ˈsekjələ(r)/ *adj* not concerned with religion or the church

⚷ **secure¹** /sɪˈkjʊə(r)/ *adj* **1** free from worry or doubt; confident: *Children need to **feel secure**.* ◆ *to be financially secure* **OPP** **insecure** **2** not likely to be lost: *Business is good so his job is secure.* ◆ *a secure investment* **SYN** **safe** **3** not likely to fall or be broken; firmly fixed: *That ladder doesn't look very secure.* **SYN** **stable** **4** **secure (against/from sb/sth)** well locked or protected: *Make sure the house is secure before you go to bed.* ▸ **securely** *adv*: *All doors and windows must be securely fastened.*

⚷ **secure²** /sɪˈkjʊə(r)/ *verb* [T] **1** **secure sth (to sth)** to fix or lock sth firmly: *The load was secured with ropes.* ◆ *Secure the rope to a tree or a rock.* **2** **secure sth (against/from sth)** to make sth safe: *The sea wall needs strengthening to secure the town against flooding.* **3** to obtain or achieve sth, especially by having to make a big effort: *The company has secured a contract to build ten planes.*

S

security /sɪˈkjʊərəti/ *noun* (*pl* **securities**) **1** [U] things that you do to protect sb/sth from attack, danger, thieves, etc: *Security was tightened at the airport before the President arrived.* ◆ *The robbers were caught on the bank's* ***security cameras.*** **2** [U] the section of a large company or organization that deals with the protection of buildings, equipment and workers: *If you see a suspicious bag, contact airport security immediately.* **3** [U] the state of feeling safe and being free from worry; protection against the difficulties of life: *Children need the security of a stable home environment.* ◆ *financial/job security* OPP **insecurity** **4** [C,U] something of value that you use when you borrow money. If you cannot pay the money back then you lose the thing you gave as **security**: *You may need to use your house* ***as security for*** *the loan.*

sedan /sɪˈdæn/ (*AmE*) = **saloon**

sedate¹ /sɪˈdeɪt/ *adj* quiet, calm and well behaved

sedate² /sɪˈdeɪt/ *verb* [T] to give a person or animal a drug to make them feel calm or want to sleep: *The lion was sedated and treated by a vet.* ▶ **sedation** /sɪˈdeɪʃn/ *noun* [U]: *The doctor put her* ***under sedation.***

sedative /ˈsedətɪv/ *noun* [C] a drug that makes you feel calm or want to sleep ➲ look at **tranquillizer**

sedentary /ˈsedntri/ *adj* involving a lot of sitting down; not active: *a sedentary lifestyle/job*

sediment /ˈsedɪmənt/ *noun* [U] a thick substance that forms at the bottom of a liquid

seduce /sɪˈdjuːs/ *verb* [T] **1** to persuade sb to have sex with you **2** **seduce sb (into sth/doing sth)** to persuade sb to do sth they would not usually agree to do: *Special offers seduce customers into spending their money.* ▶ **seduction** /sɪˈdʌkʃn/ *noun* [C,U]

seductive /sɪˈdʌktɪv/ *adj* **1** sexually attractive: *a seductive smile* **2** attractive in a way that makes you want to have or do sth: *The idea of retiring to the coast is highly seductive.*

see /siː/ *verb* (*pt* **saw** /sɔː/; *pp* **seen** /siːn/)
➤USE EYES **1** [I,T] to become conscious of sth, using your eyes; to use the power of sight: *It was so dark that we couldn't see.* ◆ *On a clear day you can see for miles.* ◆ *Have you seen my wallet anywhere?* ◆ *I've just seen a mouse run under the cooker.* ◆ *He looked for her but couldn't see her in the crowd.* ➲ note at **look¹**, **smell¹**
➤FILM, TV, ETC. **2** [T] to look at or watch a film, play, TV programme, etc: *Did you see that programme on sharks last night?* ◆ *Have you seen Spielberg's latest film?*
➤VISIT **3** [T] to spend time with sb; to visit sb: *I saw Alan at the weekend; we had dinner together.* ◆ *You should see a doctor about that cough.*
➤UNDERSTAND **4** [I,T] to understand sth; to realize sth: *Do you* ***see what I mean?*** ◆ *She doesn't* ***see the point in*** *spending so much money on a car.* ◆ *'You have to key in your password first.' 'Oh,* ***I see.'***
➤HAVE OPINION **5** [T] to have an opinion about sth: *How do you see the situation developing?*
➤IMAGINE **6** [T] to imagine sth as a future possibility: *I can't see her changing her mind.*
➤FIND OUT **7** [T] to find out sth by looking, asking or waiting: ***Go and see*** *if the postman has been yet.* ◆ *We'll* ***wait and see*** *what happens before making any decisions.* ◆ *'Can we go swimming today, Dad?' 'I'll see.'* ◆ *I saw in the paper that they're building a new theatre.*
➤MAKE SURE **8** [T] to do what is necessary in a situation; to make sure that sb does sth: *I'll see that he gets the letter.*
➤HAPPEN **9** [T] to be the time when an event happens: *Last year saw huge changes in the education system.*
➤HELP **10** [T] to go with sb, for example to help or protect them: *He asked me if he could see me home, but I said no.* ◆ *I'll see you to the door.*
IDM **as far as the eye can see** ➲ **far²**
let me see; let's see (*informal*) used when you are thinking or trying to remember sth: *Where did I put the car keys? Let's see. I think I left them by the telephone.*
see eye to eye (with sb) to agree with sb; to have the same opinion as sb: *We don't always see eye to eye on political matters.*
see if ... to try to do sth: *I'll see if I can find time to do it.* ◆ *See if you can undo this knot.*
see the joke to understand what is funny about a joke or trick
see red (*informal*) to become very angry
see you (later) (*informal*) used for saying goodbye to sb you expect to see soon or later that day
see you around (*informal*) used for saying goodbye to sb you have made no arrangement to see again
you see (*formal*) used for giving a reason: *She's very unhappy. He was her first real boyfriend, you see.*
PHR V **see about sth/doing sth** to deal with sth: *I've got to go to the station to see about changing my ticket.*
see sb off to go with sb to the railway station, the airport, etc. in order to say goodbye to them
see through sb/sth to be able to see that sb/sth is not what he/she/it appears: *The police immediately saw through his story.*
see to sb/sth to do what is necessary in a situation; to deal with sb/sth: *I'll see to the travel arrangements and you book the hotel.*

seed /siːd/ *noun* **1** [C,U] the small hard part of a plant from which a new plant of the same kind can grow: *a packet of sunflower seeds* ◆ *Grass seed should be sown in the spring.* ➲ picture on **page P14** **2** [C] the start of a feeling or an event that continues to grow: *Her answer* ***planted the seeds of*** *doubt in my mind.* **3** [C] a player in a sports competition, especially **tennis**, who is expected to finish in a high position: *the number one seed*

seeded /ˈsiːdɪd/ *adj* (used about a player or a team in a sports competition) expected to finish in a high position

seedless /ˈsiːdləs/ *adj* having no seeds: *seedless grapes*

seedling /ˈsiːdlɪŋ/ *noun* [C] a very young plant or tree that has grown from a seed

S

seedy /ˈsiːdi/ *adj* (**seedier**; **seediest**) dirty and unpleasant; possibly connected with illegal or immoral activities: *a seedy hotel/neighbourhood*

seeing /ˈsiːɪŋ/ (also **seeing that**; **seeing as**) *conj* (*informal*) because; as: *Seeing as we're going the same way, I'll give you a lift.*

seek /siːk/ *verb* [T] (*pt, pp* **sought** /sɔːt/) (*formal*) **1** to try to find or get sth: *Politicians are still seeking a peaceful solution.* **2 seek sth (from sb)** to ask sb for sth: *You should seek advice from a solicitor about what to do next.* **3 seek (to do sth)** to try to do sth: *They are still seeking to find a peaceful solution to the conflict.* SYN **attempt** **4 -seeking** [in compounds] looking for or trying to get the thing mentioned: *attention-seeking behaviour* ◆ *a heat-seeking missile*

seeker /ˈsiːkə(r)/ *noun* [C] [often in compounds] a person who is trying to find or get sth: *an attention seeker* ◆ *asylum seekers*

seem /siːm/ *verb* [I] [not used in the continuous tenses] **seem (to sb) (to be) sth; seem (like) sth** to give the impression of being or doing sth: *Emma seems (like) a very nice girl.* ◆ *Emma seems to be a very nice girl.* ◆ *It seems to me that we have no choice.* ◆ *You seem happy today.* ◆ *This machine doesn't seem to work.* SYN **appear**

seeming /ˈsiːmɪŋ/ *adj* (*formal*) [only *before* a noun] appearing to be sth: *Despite her seeming enthusiasm, Sandra didn't really help very much.* SYN **apparent** ▶ **seemingly** *adv*: *a seemingly endless list of complaints*

seen *past participle* of **see**

seep /siːp/ *verb* [I] (used about a liquid) to flow very slowly through sth: *Water started seeping in through small cracks.*

ˈsee-saw *noun* [C] an outdoor toy for children that consists of a long piece of wood that is balanced in the middle. One child sits on each end of the **see-saw** and one goes up while the other is down.

seethe /siːð/ *verb* [I] **1** to be very angry but to try not to show it: *I was seething with frustration.* **2** (*formal*) **seethe (with sth)** to be very crowded: *The streets were seething with people.*

segment /ˈsegmənt/ *noun* [C] **1** a section or part of sth: *I've divided the sheet of paper into three segments.* ◆ *a segment of the population* **2** one of the parts into which an orange can be divided ➲ picture on **page P14**

segregate /ˈsegrɪgeɪt/ *verb* [T] **segregate sb/sth (from sb/sth)** to separate one group of people or things from the rest: *The two groups of football fans were segregated to avoid trouble.* ➲ look at **integrate** ▶ **segregation** /ˌsegrɪˈgeɪʃn/ *noun* [U]: *racial segregation* (= separating people of different races)

seismic /ˈsaɪzmɪk/ *adj* [only *before* a noun] connected with or caused by **earthquakes** (= violent movements of the earth's surface)

seize /siːz/ *verb* [T] **1** to take hold of sb/sth suddenly and firmly: *The thief seized her handbag and ran off with it.* ◆ (*figurative*) *to seize a chance/an opportunity* SYN **grab** **2** to take control or possession of sb/sth: *The police seized 50 kilos of illegal drugs.* **3** [usually passive] (used about an emotion) to affect sb suddenly and very strongly: *I felt myself seized by panic.* PHR V **seize (on/upon) sth** to make use of a good and unexpected chance: *He seized on a mistake by the goalkeeper and scored.*

seize up (used about a machine) to stop working because it is too hot, does not have enough oil, etc.

seizure /ˈsiːʒə(r)/ *noun* **1** [U] using force or legal authority to take control or possession of sth: *the seizure of 30 kilos of heroin by police* **2** [C] a sudden strong attack of an illness, especially one affecting the brain

seldom /ˈseldəm/ *adv* not often: *There is seldom snow in Athens.* ◆ *I very seldom go to the theatre.* SYN **rarely**

select[1] /sɪˈlekt/ *verb* [T] to choose sb/sth from a number of similar things: *The best candidates will be selected for interview.*

> **HELP** **Select** or **choose**? **Select** is more formal than **choose** and suggests that a lot of care is taken when making the decision.

select[2] /sɪˈlekt/ *adj* (*formal*) **1** [only *before* a noun] carefully chosen as the best of a group: *A university education is no longer the privilege of* ***a select few.*** **2** used or owned by rich people

selection /sɪˈlekʃn/ *noun* **1** [U] the process of choosing or being chosen: *The manager is responsible for team selection.* **2** [C] a number of people or things that have been chosen: *a selection of hits from the fifties and sixties* **3** [C] a number of things from which you can choose: *This shop has a very good selection of toys.* SYN **choice, range**

selective /sɪˈlektɪv/ *adj* **1** concerning only some people or things; not general: *a selective school* (= one that chooses which students to admit, often according to ability) **2** careful when choosing: *She's very selective about who she invites to her parties.* ▶ **selectively** *adv*

self /self/ *noun* [C] (*pl* **selves** /selvz/) a person's own nature or qualities: *It's good to see you back to* ***your old self*** *again* (= feeling well or happy again). ◆ *Her spiteful remark revealed her* ***true self*** (= what she was really like).

self- /self/ [in compounds] of, to or by yourself or itself: *self-assessment* ◆ *self-taught*

ˌself-addressed ˈenvelope = **stamped addressed envelope**

ˌself-asˈsurance = **assurance**(2)

ˌself-asˈsured = **assured**

ˌself-ˈcatering *adj* (*BrE*) (used about a holiday or a place to stay) where meals are not provided for you so you cook them yourself

ˌself-ˈcentred (*AmE* **ˌself-ˈcentered**) *adj* thinking only about yourself and not about other people ➲ look at **selfish**

ˌself-conˈfessed *adj* [only *before* a noun] admitting that you are sth or do sth that most people consider to be bad

ˌself-ˈconfident *adj* feeling sure about your own value and abilities ➲ look at **confident** ▶ **ˌself-ˈconfidence** *noun* [U]: *Many women lack the self-confidence to apply for senior jobs.*

ˌself-ˈconscious *adj* too worried about what other people think about you: *He's self-conscious about being short.* ▶ **ˌself-ˈconsciously** *adv* ▶ **ˌself-ˈconsciousness** *noun* [U]

ˌself-conˈtained *adj* **1** not needing or depending on other people **2** (*BrE*) (used about a flat, etc.) having its own private entrance, kitchen and bathroom: *self-contained accommodation*

ˌself-conˈtrol *noun* [U] the ability to control your emotions and appear calm even when you are angry, afraid, excited, etc: *to lose/keep your self-control*

ˌself-deˈfence (*AmE* ˌself-deˈfense) *noun* [U] the use of force to protect yourself or your property: *Lee is learning karate for self-defence.* ◆ *to shoot somebody* ***in self-defence*** (= because they are going to attack you)

ˌself-deˈstruct *verb* [I] (used about a machine, etc.) to destroy itself ▶ **self-destructive** *adj*

ˌself-ˈdiscipline *noun* [U] the ability to make yourself do sth difficult or unpleasant: *It takes a lot of self-discipline to give up smoking.* ◆ *It takes a lot of self-discipline to train for a marathon.*

ˌself-emˈployed *adj* working for yourself and earning money from your own business

ˌself-esˈteem *noun* [U] a good opinion of your own character and abilities: *a man with high/low self-esteem*

ˌself-ˈevident *adj* that does not need any proof or explanation; clear

ˌself-exˈplanatory *adj* clear and easy to understand; not needing to be explained: *The book's title is self-explanatory.*

ˌself-imˈportant *adj* thinking that you are more important than other people **SYN** **arrogant** ▶ **ˌself-imˈportance** *noun* [U] ▶ **ˌself-imˈportantly** *adv*

ˌself-inˈdulgent *adj* allowing yourself to have or do things you enjoy (sometimes when it would be better to stop yourself) ▶ **ˌself-inˈdulgence** *noun* [U]

ˌself-ˈinterest *noun* [U] thinking about what is best for yourself rather than for other people

selfish /ˈselfɪʃ/ *adj* thinking only about your own needs or wishes and not about other people's: *a selfish attitude* ◆ *I'm sick of your selfish behaviour!* **OPP** **unselfish, selfless** ➲ look at **self-centred** ▶ **selfishly** *adv* ▶ **selfishness** *noun* [U]

selfless /ˈselfləs/ *adj* thinking more about other people's needs or wishes than your own **OPP** **selfish** ➲ look at **unselfish**

ˌself-ˈmade *adj* having become rich or successful by your own efforts: *a self-made millionaire*

ˌself-ˈpity *noun* [U] the state of thinking too much about your own problems or troubles and feeling sorry for yourself

ˌself-ˈportrait *noun* [C] a picture that you draw or paint of yourself

ˌself-raising ˈflour (*AmE* ˌself-rising ˈflour) *noun* [U] flour that contains **baking powder** (= a substance that makes cakes, etc. rise during cooking) ➲ look at **plain flour**

ˌself-reˈliant *adj* not depending on help from anyone else ➲ look at **reliant**

ˌself-reˈspect *noun* [U] a feeling of confidence and pride in yourself: *Old people need to keep their dignity and self-respect.* ➲ look at **respect** ▶ **ˌself-reˈspecting** *adj* [often in negative sentences]: *No self-respecting language student* (= nobody who is serious about learning a language) *should be without this book.*

ˌself-ˈrighteous *adj* believing that you are always right and other people are wrong, so that you are better than other people ➲ look at **righteous** ▶ **ˌself-ˈrighteously** *adv* ▶ **ˌself-ˈrighteousness** *noun* [U]

ˌself-rising ˈflour (*AmE*) = **self-raising flour**

ˌself-ˈsacrifice *noun* [U] giving up what you need or want in order to help others

ˌself-ˈservice *adj* (used about a shop, petrol station, restaurant, etc.) where you serve yourself and then pay for the goods

ˌself-sufˈficient *adj* able to produce or provide everything that you need without help from other people or having to buy from other people

sell /sel/ *verb* (*pt, pp* **sold** /səʊld/)

➤EXCHANGE FOR MONEY **1** [I,T] **sell (sb) (sth) (at/for sth); sell (sth) (to sb) (at/for sth)** to give sth to sb who pays for it and is then the owner of it: *We are going to sell our car.* ◆ *I sold my guitar to my neighbour for £200.* ◆ *Would you sell me your ticket?* ◆ *I offered them a lot of money but they wouldn't sell.* **2** [T] to offer sth for people to buy: *Excuse me, do you sell stamps?* ◆ *to sell insurance/advertising space*

➤BE BOUGHT **3** [I,T] to be bought by people in the way or in the numbers mentioned; to be offered at the price mentioned: *Her books sell well abroad.* ◆ *These watches sell at £1 000 each in the shops but you can have this one for £500.* ◆ *This paper sells over a million copies a day.*

➤PERSUADE **4** [T] to make people want to buy sth: *They rely on advertising to sell their products.* **5** [T] **sell sth/yourself to sb** to persuade sb to accept sth; to persuade sb that you are the right person for a job, position, etc: *Now we have to try and sell the idea to the management.* ➲ *noun for senses* **1** *to* **4** *is* **sale**

IDM **be sold on sth** (*informal*) to be very enthusiastic about sth

PHR V **sell sth off** to sell sth in order to get rid of it, often at a low price: *The shops sell their remaining winter clothes off in the spring sales.*

sell out; be sold out (used about tickets for a

S

concert, football game, etc.) to be all sold: *All the tickets sold out within two hours.* ♦ *The concert was sold out weeks ago.*

sell out (of sth); be sold out (of sth) to sell all of sth so that no more is/are available to be bought: *I'm afraid we've sold out of bread.*

sell up to sell everything you own, especially your house, your business, etc. (in order to start a new life, move to another country, etc.)

ˈ**sell-by date** *noun* [C] (*BrE*) the date printed on food packages after which the food should not be sold: *This milk is past its sell-by date.*

seller /ˈselə(r)/ *noun* [C] **1** [in compounds] a person or business that sells: *a bookseller* ♦ *a flower seller* OPP **buyer** **2** something that is sold, especially in the amount or way mentioned: *This magazine is a big seller in the 25-40 age group.* ➲ look at **bestseller**

Sellotape™ /ˈseləteɪp/ (*BrE* ˈsticky tape, *AmE* ˈScotch tape™) *noun* [U] a type of clear sticky tape that is sold in rolls and used for sticking things ➲ look at **tape** ➲ picture at **stationery** ▶ **sellotape** *verb* [T]

ˈ**sell-out** *noun* [C, usually sing] a play, concert, etc. for which all the tickets have been sold: *Next week's final is likely to be a sell-out.* ♦ *The band are on a sell-out tour.*

selves *plural* of **self**

semantic /sɪˈmæntɪk/ *adj* connected with the meaning of words and sentences ▶ **semantically** /-kli/ *adv*

semblance /ˈsembləns/ *noun* [sing, U] (*formal*) (a) **semblance of sth** the appearance of being sth or of having a certain quality

semen /ˈsiːmen/ *noun* [U] the liquid that is produced by the male sex organs containing **sperm** (= the seed necessary for making babies)

semester /sɪˈmestə(r)/ *noun* [C] one of the two periods of time that the school or college year is divided into: *the spring/fall semester* ➲ look at **term**

semi /ˈsemi/ *noun* [C] (*pl* **semis** /ˈsemiz/) (*BrE informal*) a house that is joined to another one with a shared wall between them, forming a pair of houses

semi- /ˈsemi/ [in compounds] half; partly: *semicircular* ♦ *semi-final*

semicircle /ˈsemisɜːkl/ *noun* [C] one half of a circle; something that is arranged in this shape: *Please sit* ***in a semicircle****.* ➲ picture at **circle** ▶ **semicircular** /ˌsemiˈsɜːkjələ(r)/ *adj*: *a semicircular driveway*

semicolon /ˌsemiˈkəʊlən/ *noun* [C] the mark (;) used in writing for separating parts of a sentence or items in a list

ˌ**semi-deˈtached** *adj* (used about a house) joined to another house with a shared wall on one side forming a pair of houses ➲ picture on **page P9**

ˌ**semi-ˈfinal** *noun* [C] one of the two games in a sports competition that decide which players or teams will play each other in the final: *He's through to the semi-finals.* ➲ look at **quarter-final, final** ▶ ˌ**semi-ˈfinalist** *noun* [C]

seminar /ˈsemɪnɑː(r)/ *noun* [C] **1** a class at a university, college, etc. in which a small group of students discuss or study a subject with a teacher: *I've got a seminar on Goethe this morning.* **2** a meeting for business people in which working methods, etc. are taught or discussed: *a one-day management seminar*

Sen. *abbr* = **Senator**

⚷ **senate** /ˈsenət/ *noun* [C, with sing or pl verb] often **the Senate** one of the two groups of elected politicians who make laws in the government in some countries, for example the US ➲ look at **Congress, the House of Representatives**

⚷ **senator** /ˈsenətə(r)/ *noun* [C] often **Senator** (*abbr* **Sen.**) a member of **the Senate**: *Senator McCarthy*

⚷ **send** /send/ *verb* [T] (*pt, pp* **sent** /sent/) **1 send sth (to sb/sth); send (sb) sth** to make sth go or be taken somewhere, especially by post, radio, etc: *to send a letter/parcel/message/email to somebody* ♦ *Don't forget to send me a postcard.* **2** to tell sb to go somewhere or to do sth; to arrange for sb to go somewhere: *My company is sending me on a training course next month.* ♦ *She* ***sent*** *the children* ***to bed*** *early.* ♦ *to* ***send somebody to prison*** ♦ *I'll send someone round to collect you at ten o' clock.* **3** to cause sb/sth to move in a particular direction, often quickly or as a reaction that cannot be prevented: *I accidentally pushed the table and* ***sent*** *all the drinks* ***flying****.* **4 send sb (to/into sth)** to make sb have a particular feeling or enter a particular state: *The movement of the train* ***sent*** *me* ***to sleep****.*

IDM **give/send sb your love** ➲ **love**[1]

PHR V **send for sb/sth** to ask for sb to come to you; to ask for sth to be brought or sent to you: *Quick! Send for an ambulance!*

send sth in to send sth to a place where it will be officially dealt with: *I sent my application in three weeks ago but I still haven't had a reply.*

send away (to sb) (for sth); send off (for sth) to write to sb and ask for sth to be sent to you: *Let's send off for some holiday brochures.*

send sb off (*BrE*) (used in a sports match) to order a player who has broken a rule to leave the field and not to return: *Jones was sent off for a foul in the first half.*

send sth off to post sth: *I'll send the information off today.*

send sth out 1 to send sth to a lot of different people or places: *We sent out the invitations two months before the wedding.* **2** to produce sth, for example light, heat, sound, etc: *The sun sends out light and heat.*

send sb/sth up (*informal*) to make sb/sth look ridiculous or silly, especially by copying them or it in a way that is intended to be amusing

senile /ˈsiːnaɪl/ *adj* behaving in a confused and strange way, and unable to remember things because of old age: *I think she's* ***going senile****.* ▶ **senility** /səˈnɪləti/ *noun* [U]

⚷ **senior**[1] /ˈsiːniə(r)/ *adj* **1 senior (to sb)** having a high or higher position in a company, an organization, etc: *a senior lecturer/officer/manager* ♦ *He's* senior to me. OPP junior **2** *often* Senior (*abbr* Snr; Sr) (*especially AmE*) used after the name of a man who has the same name as his son, to avoid confusion OPP junior **3** (*BrE*) (used in schools) older: *This common room is for the use of senior pupils only.* **4** (*AmE*) connected with the final year at high school or college: *the senior prom*

senior² /ˈsiːniə(r)/ *noun* [C] **1** a person who is older or of a higher position (than one or more other people): *My oldest sister is* ***ten years my senior.*** ◆ *She felt undervalued, both by her colleagues and her seniors.* OPP **junior** **2** (*BrE*) one of the older students at a school **3** (*AmE*) a student in the final year of school, college or university: *high school seniors*

ˌsenior ˈcitizen *noun* [C] an older person, especially sb who has retired from work ➲ look at **old-age pensioner**

ˌsenior ˈhigh school (also ˌsenior ˈhigh) *noun* [C,U] (in the US) a school for young people between the ages of 14 and 18 ➲ look at **junior high school**

seniority /ˌsiːniˈɒrəti/ *noun* [U] the position or importance that a person has in a company, an organization, etc. in relation to others: *The names are listed below* ***in order of seniority.***

sensation /senˈseɪʃn/ *noun* **1** [C] a feeling that is caused by sth affecting your body or part of your body: *a pleasant/an unpleasant/a tingling sensation* SYN **feeling** **2** [U] the ability to feel when touching or being touched: *For some time after the accident he had no sensation in his legs.* SYN **feeling** **3** [C, usually sing] a general feeling or impression that is difficult to explain: *I had the peculiar sensation that I was floating in the air.* SYN **feeling** **4** [C, usually sing] great excitement, surprise or interest among a group of people; sb/sth that causes this excitement: *The young American* ***caused a sensation*** *by beating the top player.*

sensational /senˈseɪʃənl/ *adj* **1** causing, or trying to cause, a feeling of great excitement, surprise or interest among people: *This magazine specializes in sensational stories about the rich and famous.* ➲ note at **newspaper** **2** (*informal*) extremely good or beautiful; very exciting SYN **fantastic** ▶ **sensationally** /-ʃənəli/ *adv*

sense¹ /sens/ *noun*

➤SIGHT, HEARING, ETC. **1** [C] one of the five natural physical powers of sight, hearing, smell, taste and touch, that people and animals have: *I've got a cold and I've lost my* ***sense of smell.*** ◆ *Dogs have an acute* ***sense of hearing.***

➤FEELING **2** [sing] a feeling of sth: *I felt a tremendous* ***sense of relief*** *when the exams were finally over.* ◆ *She only visits her family out of a* ***sense of duty.***

➤NATURAL ABILITY **3** [U, sing] the ability to understand sth; the ability to recognize what sth is or what its value is: *She seems to have lost all* ***sense of reality.*** ◆ *I like him—he's got a great* ***sense of humour.*** ◆ *I'm always getting lost. I've got absolutely no* ***sense of direction.*** **4** [U, sing] a natural ability to do or produce sth well: *Good* ***business sense*** *made her a millionaire.* ◆ *He's got absolutely no* ***dress sense*** (= he dresses very badly).

➤JUDGEMENT **5** [U] the ability to think or act in a reasonable or sensible way; good judgement: *At least he* ***had the sense*** *to stop when he realized he was making a mistake.* ◆ *I think there's a lot of sense in what you're saying.* ➲ look at **common sense**

➤REASON **6** [U] **sense (in doing sth)** the reason for doing sth; purpose: ***What's the sense*** *in making the situation more difficult for yourself?* ◆ *There's no sense in going any further—we're obviously lost.*

➤MEANING **7** [C] (used about a word, phrase, etc.) a meaning: *This word has two senses.*

IDM **come to your senses** to finally realize that you should do sth because it is the most sensible thing to do

in a sense in one particular way but not in other ways; partly: *In a sense you're right, but there's more to the matter than that.*

make sense **1** to be possible to understand; to have a clear meaning: *What does this sentence mean? It doesn't make sense to me.* **2** (used about an action) to be sensible or logical: *I think it would make sense to wait for a while before making a decision.*

make sense of sth to manage to understand sth that is not clear or is difficult to understand: *I can't make sense of these instructions.*

talk sense ➲ **talk¹**

sense² /sens/ *verb* [T] [not used in the continuous tenses] to realize or become conscious of sth; to get a feeling about sth even though you cannot see it, hear it, etc: *I sensed that something was wrong as soon as I went in.*

> **HELP** Although this verb is not used in the continuous tenses, it is common to see the present participle (= *-ing* form): *Sensing a scandal, the tabloid photographers rushed to the star's hotel.*

senseless /ˈsensləs/ *adj* **1** having no meaning or purpose **2** [not before a noun] unconscious: *He was beaten senseless.*

sensibility /ˌsensəˈbɪləti/ *noun* (*pl* **sensibilities**) **1** [U,C] the ability to understand and experience deep feelings, for example in art, literature, etc. **2** **sensibilities** [pl] sb's feelings, especially when they are easily offended

sensible /ˈsensəbl/ *adj* (used about people and their behaviour) able to make good judgements based on reason and experience; practical: *a sensible person/decision/precaution* ◆ *Stop joking and give me a sensible answer.* ◆ *I think it would be sensible to leave early, in case there is a lot of traffic.* OPP **silly, foolish** ▶ **sensibly** /-əbli/ *adv*: *Let's sit down and discuss the matter sensibly.*

> **HELP** **Sensible or sensitive? Sensible** is connected with common sense, reasonable action and good judgement. **Sensitive** is connected with feelings and emotions and with the five senses of sight, hearing, touch, smell and taste.

sensitive /ˈsensətɪv/ *adj*

➤THINKING OF FEELINGS **1** **sensitive (to sth)** showing that you are conscious of and able to understand people's feelings, problems, etc: *It wasn't very*

S

sensitive of you to mention her boyfriend. You know they've just split up. ◆ *She always tries to be sensitive to other people's feelings.* OPP **insensitive** ➲ note at **sensible**

➤EASILY UPSET **2** sensitive (about/to sth) easily upset, offended or annoyed, especially about a particular subject: *She's still a bit sensitive about her divorce.* ◆ *He's very sensitive to criticism.* OPP **insensitive**

➤SUBJECT/SITUATION **3** needing to be dealt with carefully because it is likely to cause anger or trouble: *This is a sensitive period in the negotiations between the two countries.*

➤TO PAIN, COLD, ETC. **4** sensitive (to sth) easily hurt or damaged; painful, especially if touched: *a new cream for sensitive skin* ◆ *My teeth are very sensitive to hot or cold food.*

➤SCIENTIFIC INSTRUMENT **5** able to measure very small changes: *a sensitive instrument*

▶ **sensitively** *adv*: *The investigation will need to be handled sensitively.* ▶ **sensitivity** /ˌsensəˈtɪvəti/ *noun* [U]: *I think your comments showed a complete lack of sensitivity.*

sensual /ˈsenʃuəl/ *adj* connected with physical or sexual pleasure: *the sensual rhythms of Latin music* ▶ **sensuality** /ˌsenʃuˈæləti/ *noun* [U]

sensuous /ˈsenʃuəs/ *adj* giving pleasure to the mind or body through the senses: *the sensuous feel of pure silk* ▶ **sensuously** *adv* ▶ **sensuousness** *noun* [U]

sent *past tense, past participle* of **send**

⚷ **sentence[1]** /ˈsentəns/ *noun* [C] **1** a group of words containing a subject and a verb, that expresses a statement, a question, etc. When a sentence is written, it begins with a capital letter and ends with a full stop: *You don't need to write a long letter. A couple of sentences will be enough.* ➲ note at **paragraph** ➲ look at **phrase** **2** the punishment given by a judge to sb who has been found guilty of a crime: *20 years in prison was a very harsh sentence.* ➲ note at **court**

sentence[2] /ˈsentəns/ *verb* [T] sentence sb (to sth) (used about a judge) to tell sb who has been found guilty of a crime what the punishment will be: *The judge sentenced her to three months in prison for shoplifting.*

sentiment /ˈsentɪmənt/ *noun* **1** [C,U] (*formal*) an attitude or opinion that is often caused or influenced by emotion: *His comments expressed my sentiments exactly.* **2** [U] feelings such as pity, romantic love, sadness, etc. that influence sb's actions or behaviour (sometimes in situations where this is not appropriate): *There's no room for sentiment in business.*

sentimental /ˌsentɪˈmentl/ *adj* **1** producing or connected with emotions such as romantic love, pity, sadness, etc. which may be too strong or not appropriate: *How can you be sentimental about an old car!* ◆ *a sentimental love song* **2** connected with happy memories or feelings of love rather than having any financial value: *The jewellery wasn't worth much but it had great* ***sentimental value*** *to me.*

▶ **sentimentality** /ˌsentɪmenˈtæləti/ *noun* [U] [disapproving] ▶ **sentimentally** /ˌsentɪˈmentəli/ *adv*

sentry /ˈsentri/ *noun* [C] (*pl* **sentries**) a soldier who stands outside a building and guards it

separable /ˈsepərəbl/ *adj* able to be separated OPP **inseparable**

⚷ **separate[1]** /ˈseprət/ *adj* **1** different; not connected: *We stayed in separate rooms in the same hotel.* **2** separate (from sth/sb) apart; not together: *You should always keep your cash and credit cards separate.*

⚷ **separate[2]** /ˈsepəreɪt/ *verb* **1** [T] separate sb/sth (from sb/sth) to keep people or things apart; to be between people or things with the result that they are apart: *The two sides of the city are separated by the river.* SYN **divide** **2** [I,T] separate (sb/sth) (from sb/sth) to stop being together; to cause people or things to stop being together: *I think we should separate into two groups.* ◆ *The friends separated at the airport.* ◆ *I got separated from my friends in the crowd.* ◆ *The police were called to separate the two men.* **3** [I] to stop living together as a couple with your wife, husband or partner: *His parents separated when he was still a baby.*

⚷ **separated** /ˈsepəreɪtɪd/ *adj* not living together as a couple any more: *My wife and I are separated.*

⚷ **separately** /ˈseprətli/ *adv* apart; not together: *Shall we pay separately or all together?*

⚷ **separation** /ˌsepəˈreɪʃn/ *noun* **1** [C,U] the act of separating or being separated; a situation or period of being apart: *Separation from family and friends made me very lonely.* **2** [C] an agreement where a couple decide not to live together any more: *a trial separation*

Sept. *abbr* = **September**: *2 Sept. 1920*

⚷ **September** /sepˈtembə(r)/ *noun* [U,C] (*abbr* Sept.) the 9th month of the year, coming after August ➲ note at **January**

septic /ˈseptɪk/ *adj* infected with poisonous bacteria: *The wound* ***went septic***.

sequel /ˈsiːkwəl/ *noun* [C] a sequel (to sth) **1** a book, film, etc. that continues the story of the one before **2** something that happens after, or is the result of, an earlier event

sequence /ˈsiːkwəns/ *noun* **1** [C] a number of things (actions, events, etc.) that happen or come one after another: *Complete the following sequence: 1, 4, 8, 13, …* **2** [C,U] the order in which a number of things happen or are arranged: *The photographs are* ***in sequence***.

sequin /ˈsiːkwɪn/ *noun* [C] a small flat shiny circle that is sewn onto clothing as decoration ▶ **sequinned** *adj*

serene /səˈriːn/ *adj* calm and peaceful: *Her smile was serene.* ▶ **serenely** *adv* ▶ **serenity** /səˈrenəti/ *noun* [U]

sergeant /ˈsɑːdʒənt/ *noun* [C] (*abbr* Sgt) **1** a member of one of the middle ranks in the army or air force **2** an officer with a middle position in the police force

S

serial /ˈsɪəriəl/ *noun* [C] a story in a magazine or on TV or radio that is told in a number of parts over a period of time: *the first part of a sixteen-part drama serial* ➲ note at **series** ▶ **serialize** (also **-ise**) /ˈsɪəriəlaɪz/ *verb* [T]: *The novel was serialized on TV in six parts.*

ˈ**serial number** *noun* [C] the number put on sth in order to identify it

⚷ **series** /ˈsɪəriːz/ *noun* [C] (*pl* **series**) **1** a number of things that happen one after another and are of the same type or connected: *a series of events* ◆ *There has been a series of burglaries in this district recently.* **2** a number of programmes on radio or TV which have the same main characters and each tell a complete story

> **HELP** Series or serial? In a **series** each part is a different, complete story involving the same main characters. In a **serial** the same story continues in each part.

⚷ **serious** /ˈsɪəriəs/ *adj* **1** bad or dangerous: *a serious accident/illness/offence* ◆ *Pollution is a very serious problem.* ◆ *Her condition is serious and she's likely to be in hospital for some time.* **2** needing to be treated as important, not just for fun: *Don't laugh, it's a serious matter.* ◆ *a serious discussion* **3 serious (about sth/about doing sth)** (used about a person) not joking; thinking deeply: *Are you serious about starting your own business* (= are you really going to do it)? ◆ *He's terribly serious. I don't think I've ever seen him laugh.* ◆ *You're looking very serious. Was it bad news?* ▶ **seriousness** *noun* [U]

⚷ **seriously** /ˈsɪəriəsli/ *adv* **1** in a serious way: *Three people were seriously injured in the accident.* ◆ *My mother is seriously ill.* ◆ *It's time you started to think seriously about the future.* **2** used at the beginning of a sentence to show that you are not joking or that you really mean what you are saying: *Seriously, I do appreciate all your help.* ◆ *Seriously, you've got nothing to worry about.* **3** used for expressing surprise at what sb has said and asking if it is really true: *'I'm 40 today.' 'Seriously? You look a lot younger.'*
IDM take sb/sth seriously to treat sb or sth as important: *You take everything too seriously! Relax and enjoy yourself.*

sermon /ˈsɜːmən/ *noun* [C] a speech on a religious or moral subject that is usually given by a religious leader as part of a service in church

serpent /ˈsɜːpənt/ *noun* [C] (in literature) a snake, especially a large one

serrated /səˈreɪtɪd/ *adj* having a row of points in V-shapes along the edge: *a knife with a serrated edge*

⚷ **servant** /ˈsɜːvənt/ *noun* [C] a person who is paid to work in sb's house, doing work such as cooking, cleaning, etc: *They treat their mother like a servant.* ➲ look at **civil servant**

⚷ **serve**[1] /sɜːv/ *verb*
➤FOOD/DRINK **1** [T] to give food or drink to sb during a meal; to take an order and then bring food or drink to sb in a restaurant, bar, etc: *Breakfast is served from 7.30 to 9.00 a.m.* **2** [T] (used about an amount) to be enough for a certain number of people: *According to the recipe, this dish serves four.*
➤IN SHOP **3** [I,T] to take a customer's order; to give help, sell goods, etc: *There was a long queue of people waiting to be served.*
➤BE USEFUL **4** [I,T] to be useful or suitable for a particular purpose: *The judge said the punishment would serve as a warning to others.* ◆ *It's an old car but it will* ***serve our purpose*** *for a few months.*
➤PERFORM DUTY **5** [I,T] to perform a duty or provide a service for the public or for an organization: *During the war, he served in the army.* ◆ *She became a nurse because she wanted to serve the community.*
➤IN PRISON **6** [T] to spend a period of time in prison as a punishment: *He is currently* ***serving a*** *ten-year* ***sentence*** *for fraud.*
➤IN TENNIS, ETC. **7** [I,T] to start play by hitting the ball: *She served an ace.*
IDM first come, first served ➲ **first**[2]
serve sb right used when sth unpleasant happens to sb and you do not feel sorry for them because you think it is their own fault: *'I feel sick.' 'It serves you right for eating so much.'*

serve[2] /sɜːv/ *noun* [C] = **service**[1] (8)

server /ˈsɜːvə(r)/ *noun* [C] a computer that stores information that a number of computers can share ➲ look at **client**

⚷ **service**[1] /ˈsɜːvɪs/ *noun*
➤PROVIDING STH **1** [C] a system or an organization that provides the public with sth that it needs; the job that an organization does: *There is a regular bus service to the airport.* ◆ *the postal service* ◆ *the National Health Service* ◆ *We offer a number of financial services.* ➲ look at **civil service**
➤IN RESTAURANT, HOTEL, ETC. **2** [U] the work or the quality of work done by sb when serving a customer: *I enjoyed the meal but the service was terrible.* ◆ *Is service included in the bill?*
➤WORK/HELP **3** [U,C] work done for sb; help given to sb: *He left the police force after thirty years' service.*
➤OF VEHICLE/MACHINE **4** [C,U] the checks, repairs, etc. that are necessary to make sure that a machine is working properly: *We take our car for a service every six months.*
➤ARMY, NAVY, ETC. **5** [U] (also **the services** [pl]) the armed forces; the army, navy or air force; the work done by the people in them: *They both joined the services when they left school.* ◆ *Do you have to do* ***military service*** *in your country?*
➤RELIGIOUS CEREMONY **6** [C] a religious ceremony, usually including prayers, singing, etc: *a funeral service*
➤AT SIDE OF ROAD **7 services** [pl] (also ˈ**service station**) a place at the side of a **motorway** (= a wide road for fast traffic) where there is a petrol station, a shop, toilets, a restaurant, etc: *It's five miles to the next services.*
➤IN TENNIS, ETC. **8** (also **serve**) [C] the first hit of the ball at the start of play; a player's turn to serve(7): *She's not a bad player but her service is weak.*

S

service² /ˈsɜːvɪs/ *verb* [T] to examine and, if necessary, repair a car, machine, etc: *All cars should be serviced at regular intervals.*

serviceman /ˈsɜːvɪsmən/, **servicewoman** /ˈsɜːvɪswʊmən/ *noun* [C] (*pl* **-men** /-mən/, **-women** /-wɪmɪn/) a person who is a member of the armed forces

ˈ**service station** **1** = **petrol station** **2** = **service¹** (7)

serviette /ˌsɜːviˈet/ *noun* [C] a square of cloth or paper that you use when you are eating to keep your clothes clean and to clean your mouth or hands on **SYN** **napkin**

sesame /ˈsesəmi/ *noun* [U] a tropical plant grown for its seeds and their oil, which are used in cooking

session /ˈseʃn/ *noun* **1** [C] a period of doing a particular activity: *The whole album was recorded in one session.* ◆ *She has a session at the gym every week.* **2** [C,U] a formal meeting or series of meetings of a court of law, parliament, etc: *This court is now* ***in session.***

set¹ /set/ *verb* (**setting**; *pt, pp* **set**)
➤PUT IN PLACE **1** [T] to put sb/sth in a particular place or position: *I set the box down carefully on the floor.*
➤CAUSE/START **2** [T] to cause sb/sth to be in a particular state; to start sth happening: *The new government* ***set*** *the prisoners* ***free.*** ◆ *The rioters* ***set*** *a number of cars* ***on fire.***
➤PLAY/BOOK/FILM **3** [T, often passive] to make the action of a book, play, film, etc. take place in a particular time, situation, etc: *The film is set in 16th-century Spain.*
➤PREPARE/ARRANGE **4** [T] to prepare or arrange sth for a particular purpose: *I set my alarm for 6.30.* ◆ *to* ***set the table*** (= to put the plates, knives, forks, etc. on it) **5** [T] to decide or arrange sth: *Can we* ***set a limit*** *of two hours for the meeting?* ◆ *They haven't* ***set the date*** *for their wedding yet.*
➤JEWELLERY **6** [T] to fix a **precious stone** (= one that is rare and valuable), etc. in a piece of jewellery: *The brooch had three diamonds set in gold.*
➤EXAMPLE/STANDARD **7** [T] to do sth good that people have to try to copy or achieve: *Try to* ***set a good example*** *to the younger children.* ◆ *He has* ***set a*** *new world* ***record.*** ◆ *They set high standards of customer service.*
➤WORK/TASK **8** [T] to give sb a piece of work or a task: *We've been* ***set*** *a lot of* ***homework*** *this weekend.* ◆ *I've* ***set*** *myself* ***a target*** *of four hours' study every evening.*
➤BECOME HARD **9** [I] to become firm or hard: *The concrete will* ***set solid/hard*** *in just a few hours.*
➤BONE **10** [T] to fix a broken bone in the correct position so that it can get better: *The doctor set her broken leg.*
➤SUN/MOON **11** [I] to go down below the **horizon** (= the line where the earth meets the sky) in the evening: *We sat and watched the sun setting.* **OPP** **rise**
ℹ For idioms containing **set**, look at the entries for the nouns, adjectives, etc. For example, **set sail** is at **sail**.
PHR V **set about doing sth** to start doing sth, especially dealing with a problem or task: *How would you set about tackling this problem?*
set sth aside to keep sth to use later: *I try to set aside part of my wages every week.*
set sb/sth back to delay sb/sth: *The bad weather has set our plans back six weeks.*
set forth (*formal*) to start a journey
set in to arrive and remain for a period of time: *I'm afraid that the bad weather has set in.*
set off to leave on a journey: *We set off at 3 o'clock this morning.*
set sth off to do sth which starts a reaction: *When this door is opened, it sets off an alarm.*
set on/upon sb [usually passive] to attack sb suddenly: *I opened the gate, and was immediately set on by a large dog.*
set out to leave on a journey
set out to do sth to decide to achieve sth: *He set out to prove that his theory was right.*
set (sth) up to start a business, an organization, a system, etc: *The company has set up a new branch in Wales.*

set² /set/ *noun* [C] **1** a number of things that belong together: *a set of kitchen knives* ◆ *In the first set of questions, you have to fill in the gaps.* ◆ *a set of instructions* ◆ *a spare set of keys* ◆ *a chess set* **2** a piece of equipment for receiving TV or radio signals: *a TV set* **3** the furniture, painted cloth, boards, etc. that are made to be used in a play or film: *a musical with spectacular sets* **4** (in sports such as **tennis**) a group of games forming part of a match: *She won in* ***straight sets*** (= without losing a set).

set³ /set/ *adj* **1** placed in a particular position: *deep-set eyes* ◆ *Our house is quite set back from the road.* **2** fixed and not changing; firm: *There are no set hours in my job.* ◆ *I'll have the set menu* (= with a fixed price and limited choice of dishes). **3** that everyone must study for an exam: *We have to study three set texts for French.* **4** **set (for sth)**; **set (to do sth)** ready, prepared or likely to do sth: *Okay, I'm set —let's go!* ◆ *I was all set to leave when the phone rang.* ◆ *The Swiss team look set for victory.*
IDM **be set against sth/doing sth** to be determined that sth will not happen or that you will not do sth
be set on sth/doing sth to be determined to do or have sth: *She's set on a career in acting.*

setback /ˈsetbæk/ *noun* [C] a difficulty or problem that stops you progressing as fast as you would like: *She suffered a major setback when she missed the exams through illness.*

ˈ**set square** (*AmE* **triangle**) *noun* [C] an instrument for drawing straight lines and angles, made from a flat piece of plastic or metal in the shape of a triangle with one angle of 90°

settee /seˈtiː/ *noun* [C] a long soft seat with a back and arms that more than one person can sit on **SYN** **sofa**

setting /ˈsetɪŋ/ *noun* [C] **1** the position sth is in; the place and time in which sth happens: *The hotel is in a beautiful setting, close to the sea.* **2** one of the positions of the controls of a machine: *Cook it in the oven on a low setting.*

S

settle /ˈsetl/ *verb*
➤END ARGUMENT **1** [I,T] to put an end to an argument or a disagreement: *They settled the dispute without going to court.* ♦ *They settled out of court.* ♦ *We didn't speak to each other for years, but we've **settled our differences** now.*
➤DECIDE/ARRANGE **2** [T] to decide or arrange sth finally: *Everything's settled. We leave on the 9 o'clock flight on Friday.*
➤PERMANENT HOME **3** [I] to go and live permanently in a new country, area, town, etc: *A great many immigrants have settled in this country.*
➤BECOME COMFORTABLE **4** [I,T] to put yourself or sb else into a comfortable position: *I settled in front of the TV for the evening.* ♦ *She settled herself beside him on the sofa.* **5** [I,T] to become or to make sb/sth calm or relaxed: *The baby wouldn't settle.*
➤COME TO REST **6** [I] to land on a surface and stop moving: *A flock of birds settled on the roof.*
➤PAY MONEY **7** [I,T] to pay money that you owe: *to settle a bill/a debt*
PHR V **settle down 1** to get into a comfortable position, sitting or lying: *I made a cup of tea and settled down with the newspapers.* **2** to start having a quieter way of life, especially by staying in the same place or getting married: *She had a number of jobs abroad before she eventually settled down.* **3** to become calm and quiet: *Settle down! It's time to start the lesson.*
settle down to sth to start doing sth which involves all your attention: *Before you settle down to your work, could I ask you something?*
settle for sth to accept sth that is not as good as what you wanted: *We're going to have to settle for the second prize.*
settle in/into sth to start feeling comfortable in a new home, job, etc: *How are the children settling in at their new school?*
settle on sth to choose or decide sth after considering many different things
settle up (with sb) to pay money that you owe to sb

settled /ˈsetld/ *adj* **1** not changing or not likely to change: *More settled weather is forecast for the next few days.* **2** comfortable; feeling that you belong (in a home, a job, a way of life, etc.): *We feel very settled here.*

settlement /ˈsetlmənt/ *noun* [C,U] **1** an official agreement that ends an argument; the act of reaching an agreement: *a divorce settlement* ♦ *the settlement of a dispute* **2** a place that a group of people have built and live in, where few or no people lived before; the process of people starting to live in a place: *There is believed to have been a prehistoric settlement on this site.* ♦ *the settlement of the American West*

settler /ˈsetlə(r)/ *noun* [C] a person who goes to live permanently in a place where not many people live: *the first white settlers in Australia*

ˌset-ˌtop ˈbox *noun* [C] a device that changes a **digital** (= using a particular electronic system) television signal into a form which can be seen on an ordinary television

ˈset-up *noun* [usually sing] (*informal*) a way of organizing sth; a system: *I've only been here a couple of weeks and I don't really know the set-up.*

seven /ˈsevn/ *number* **1** 7 ➲ note at **six** **2** [in compounds] having seven of the thing mentioned: *a seven-sided coin*

seventeen /ˌsevnˈtiːn/ *number* 17 ➲ note at **six**
▶ **seventeenth** /ˌsevnˈtiːnθ/ *ordinal number, noun* ➲ note at **sixth**

seventh¹ /ˈsevnθ/ *ordinal number* 7th ➲ note at **sixth**

seventh² /ˈsevnθ/ *noun* [C] ⅐; one of seven equal parts of sth

seventy /ˈsevnti/ *number* 70 ➲ note at **sixty**
▶ **seventieth** /ˈsevntiəθ/ *ordinal number, noun* ➲ note at **sixth**

sever /ˈsevə(r)/ *verb* [T] (*formal*) **1** to cut sth into two pieces; to cut sth off: *The builders accidentally severed a water pipe.* ♦ *His hand was almost severed in the accident.* **2** to end a relationship or communication with sb: *He has severed all links with his former friends.*

several /ˈsevrəl/ *pron, determiner* more than two but not very many; a few: *It took her several days to recover from the shock.* ♦ *There were lots of applications for the job—several of them from very well-qualified people.* ♦ *I don't think it's a good idea for several reasons.*

severe /sɪˈvɪə(r)/ *adj* (**severer**; **severest**) **1** extremely bad or serious: *The company is in severe financial difficulty.* ♦ *He suffered severe injuries in the fall.* ♦ *severe weather conditions* **2** causing sb to suffer, be upset or have difficulties: *Such terrible crimes deserve the severest punishment.* ♦ *I think your criticism of her work was too severe.* ➲ look at **harsh**
▶ **severely** *adv*: *The roof was severely damaged in the storm.* ♦ *The report severely criticizes the Health Service.* ▶ **severity** /sɪˈverəti/ *noun* [U]: *I don't think you realize the severity of the problem.*

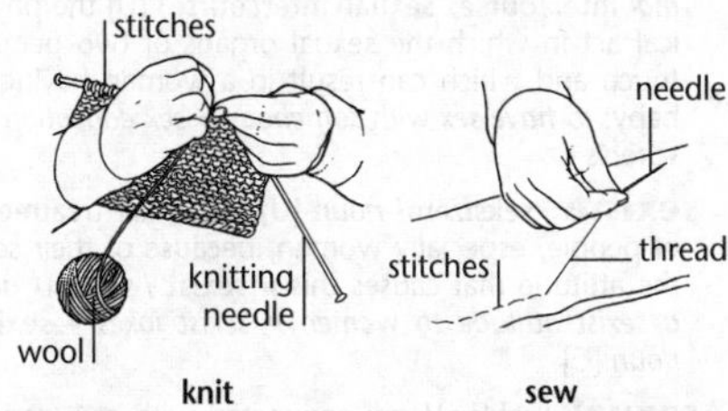

sew /səʊ/ *verb* [I,T] (*pt* **sewed**; *pp* **sewn** /səʊn/ *or* **sewed**) **sew (sth) (on)** to join pieces of cloth, or to join sth to cloth, using a needle and thread and forming **stitches** (= lines of thread): *I can't sew.* ♦ *A button's come off my shirt—I'll have to sew it back on.*
PHR V **sew sth up 1** to join two things by sewing; to repair sth by sewing two things together: *to sew up a hole* **2** (*informal*) to arrange sth so that it is

S

certain to happen or be successful: *I think we've got the deal sewn up.*

sewage /ˈsuːɪdʒ/ *noun* [U] the waste material from people's bodies that is carried away from their homes through special pipes

sewed *past tense* of **sew**

sewer /ˈsuːə(r)/ *noun* [C] an underground pipe that carries human waste to a place where it can be treated

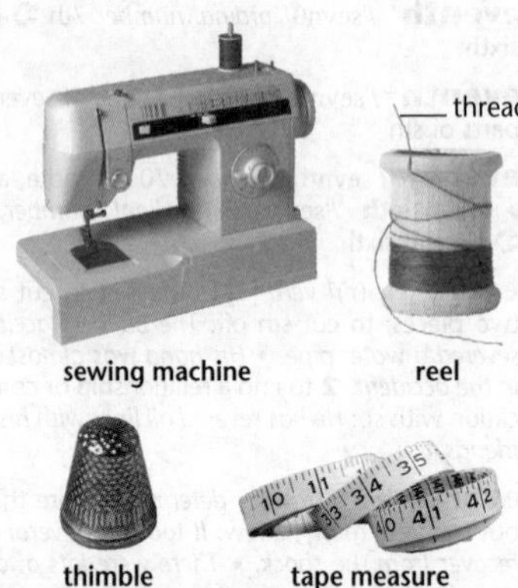

sewing /ˈsəʊɪŋ/ *noun* [U] **1** using a needle and thread to make or repair things: *I always take a sewing kit when I travel.* ♦ *a **sewing machine*** ➲ picture on **page P3** **2** something that is being sewn: *Have you seen my sewing?*

sewn *past participle* of **sew**

sex /seks/ *noun* **1** [U] the state of being either male or female: *Applications are welcome from anyone, regardless of sex or race.* ♦ *Do you mind what sex your baby is?* SYN **gender** **2** [C] one of the two groups consisting of all male people or all female people: *the male/female sex* ♦ *He's always found it difficult to get on with **the opposite sex*** (= women). **3** (*also formal* **intercourse**; ˌ**sexual ˈintercourse**) [U] the physical act in which the sexual organs of two people touch and which can result in a woman having a baby: *to **have sex** with somebody* ♦ *sex education in schools*

sexism /ˈseksɪzəm/ *noun* [U] the unfair treatment of people, especially women, because of their sex; the attitude that causes this ▶ **sexist** /ˈseksɪst/ *adj*: *a sexist attitude to women* ♦ *sexist jokes* ▶ **sexist** *noun* [C]

sexual /ˈsekʃuəl/ *adj* connected with sex: *sexual problems* ♦ *the sexual organs* ♦ *a campaign for sexual equality* (= to get fair and equal treatment for both men and women) ➲ look at **sexy** ▶ **sexually** /ˈsekʃəli/ *adv*: *to be sexually attracted to somebody*

ˌ**sexual ˈintercourse** (*formal*) = **sex**(3)

sexuality /ˌsekʃuˈæləti/ *noun* [U] the nature of sb's sexual activities or desires

sexy /ˈseksi/ *adj* (**sexier**; **sexiest**) (*informal*) sexually attractive or exciting: *Do you find the lead singer sexy?* ♦ *a sexy dress*

Sgt *abbr* = **sergeant**

sh (*also* **shh**) /ʃ/ *exclam* used to tell sb to stop making noise: *Sh! People are trying to sleep in here.*

shabby /ˈʃæbi/ *adj* (**shabbier**; **shabbiest**) **1** in bad condition because of having been used or worn too much: *a shabby suit* **2** (used about people) dressed in an untidy way; wearing clothes that are in bad condition **3** (used about the way that sb is treated) unfair; not generous ▶ **shabbily** *adv*: *a shabbily dressed man* ♦ *She felt she'd been treated shabbily by her employers.*

shack /ʃæk/ *noun* [C] a small building, usually made of wood or metal, that has not been built well

shade[1] /ʃeɪd/ *noun*

➤OUT OF SUN **1** [U] an area that is not in direct light from the sun and is darker and cooler than areas in the sun: *It was so hot that I had to go and sit **in the shade**.* ➲ picture at **shadow**

➤ON LAMP, ETC. **2** [C] something that keeps out light or makes it less bright: *a lampshade*

➤COLOUR **3** [C] **a shade (of sth)** a type of a particular colour: *a shade of green*

➤IN PICTURE **4** [C] the dark areas in a picture, especially the use of these to produce variety: *Your painting needs more **light and shade**.*

➤OF OPINION/FEELING **5** [C, usually pl] a small difference in the form or nature of sth: *a word with various shades of meaning*

➤SLIGHTLY **6** [sing] **a shade** a little; slightly: *I feel a shade more optimistic now.*

➤GLASSES **7 shades** [pl] (*informal*) = **sunglasses**

shade[2] /ʃeɪd/ *verb* [T] **1** to protect sth from direct light; to give shade to sth: *The sun was so bright that I had to shade my eyes.* **2 shade sth (in)** to make an area of a drawing darker, for example with a pencil: *The trees will look more realistic once you've shaded them in.*

shadow shade

shadow[1] /ˈʃædəʊ/ *noun* **1** [C] a dark shape on a surface that is caused by sth being between the light and that surface: *The dog was chasing its own shadow.* ♦ *The shadows lengthened as the sun went down.* **2** [U] an area that is dark because sth prevents direct light from reaching it: *His face was **in shadow**.* **3** [sing] a very small amount of sth: *I know without **a shadow of doubt** that he's lying.*

IDM **cast a shadow (across/over sth)** ➲ **cast**[1]

shadow[2] /ˈʃædəʊ/ *verb* [T] to follow sb and watch their actions: *The police shadowed the suspect for three days.*

shadow[3] /ˈʃædəʊ/ *adj* [only *before* a noun] (in British politics) belonging to the biggest political party that is not in power, with special responsibility for a particular subject, for example education or defence. **Shadow** ministers would probably become government ministers if their party won the next election: *the shadow Cabinet*

shadowy /ˈʃædəʊi/ *adj* **1** dark and full of shadows: *a shadowy forest* **2** difficult to see because there is not much light: *A shadowy figure was coming towards me.* **3** that not much is known about SYN **mysterious**

shady /ˈʃeɪdi/ *adj* (**shadier**; **shadiest**) **1** giving shade; giving protection from the sun: *I found a shady spot under the trees and sat down.* **2** (*informal*) not completely honest or legal

shaft /ʃɑːft/ *noun* [C] **1** a long, narrow hole in which sth can go up and down or enter or leave: *a lift shaft* ♦ *a mine shaft* **2** a bar that connects parts of a machine so that power can pass between them

shaggy /ˈʃægi/ *adj* (**shaggier**; **shaggiest**) **1** (used about hair, material, etc.) long, thick and untidy **2** covered with long, thick, untidy hair: *a shaggy dog*

shake

They shook hands.

He shook his head.

shake[1] /ʃeɪk/ *verb* (*pt* **shook** /ʃʊk/; *pp* **shaken** /ˈʃeɪkən/) **1** [I,T] to move or move sb/sth from side to side or up and down with short, quick movements: *I was so nervous that I was shaking.* ♦ *The whole building shakes when big trucks go past.* ♦ (*figurative*) *His voice shook with emotion as he described the accident.* ♦ *Shake the bottle before taking the medicine.* ♦ *She shook him to wake him up.* **2** [T] to disturb or upset sb/sth: *The scandal has shaken the whole country.* **3** [T] to cause sth to be less certain; to cause doubt about sth: *Nothing seems to shake her belief that she was right.*

IDM **shake sb's hand/shake hands (with sb)/shake sb by the hand** to take sb's hand and move it up and down (when you meet sb, to show that you have agreed on sth, etc.) ➲ note at **introduce**

shake your head to move your head from side to side, as a way of saying no

PHR V **shake sb/sth off** to get rid of sb/sth: *I don't seem to be able to shake off this cold.*

shake sth off (sth) to remove sth by shaking: *Shake the crumbs off the tablecloth.*

shake[2] /ʃeɪk/ *noun* [C] the act of shaking sth or being shaken: *a shake of the head* ♦ *You'll have to give the bottle a few shakes.*

ˈshake-up *noun* [C] a complete change in the structure or organization of sth

shaky /ˈʃeɪki/ *adj* (**shakier**; **shakiest**) **1** shaking or feeling weak because you are frightened or ill **2** not firm; weak or not very good: *The table's a bit shaky so don't put anything heavy on it.* ♦ *They've had a* ***shaky start*** *to the season, losing most of their games.* ▶ **shakily** *adv*

shall /ʃəl; *strong form* ʃæl/ *modal verb* (*negative* **shall not**; *short form* **shan't** /ʃɑːnt/; *pt* **should** /ʃʊd/; *negative* **should not**; *short form* **shouldn't** /ˈʃʊdnt/) **1** (*formal*) used with 'I' and 'we' in future tenses, instead of 'will': *I shall be very happy to see him again.* ♦ *We shan't be arriving until 10 o'clock.* ♦ *At the end of this year, I shall have been working here for five years.* **2** used for asking for information or advice: *What time shall I come?* ♦ *Where shall we go for our holiday?* **3** used for offering to do sth: *Shall I help you carry that box?* ♦ *Shall we drive you home?* **4 shall we** used for suggesting that you do sth with the person or people that you are talking to: *Shall we go out for a meal this evening?* **5** (*formal*) used for saying that sth must happen or will definitely happen: *In the rules it says that a player shall be sent off for using bad language.* ⓘ For more information about modal verbs, look at the **Reference Section** at the back of this dictionary.

shallot /ʃəˈlɒt/ *noun* [C] a vegetable like a small onion

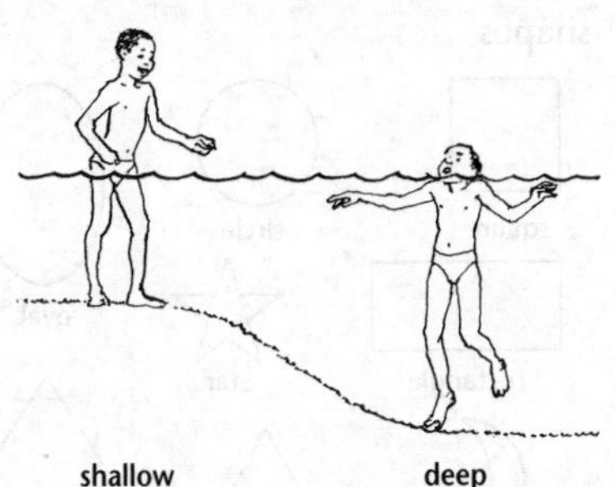

shallow deep

shallow /ˈʃæləʊ/ *adj* (**shallower**; **shallowest**) **1** not deep; with not much distance between top and bottom: *The sea is very shallow here.* ♦ *a shallow dish* **2** not having or showing serious or deep thought: *a shallow person/book* OPP **deep** ▶ **shallowness** *noun* [U]

shame[1] /ʃeɪm/ *noun* **1** [U] the unpleasant feelings such as embarrassment and sadness that you get when you have done sth stupid or wrong; the ability to have these feelings: *She was* ***filled with shame*** *at the thought of how she had lied to her mother.* ♦ *His actions have* ***brought shame on*** *his whole family.* ♦ *He doesn't care how he behaves in public. He's got no shame!* ➲ *adjective* **ashamed** **2 a shame** [sing] a fact or situation that makes you feel disappointed: ***It's a shame*** *about Adam failing his exams, isn't it?* ♦ ***What a shame*** *you have to leave so soon.* ♦ *It would be a shame to miss an opportunity like this.*

shame[2] /ʃeɪm/ *verb* [T] to make sb feel **shame** for sth bad that they have done

shameful /ˈʃeɪmfl/ *adj* that sb should feel bad about; shocking: *a shameful waste of public money* ▶ **shamefully** /-fəli/ *adv*

shameless /ˈʃeɪmləs/ *adj* not feeling embarrassed about doing sth bad; having no **shame**: *a shameless display of greed and bad manners* ▶ **shamelessly** *adv*

shampoo /ʃæmˈpuː/ *noun* (*pl* shampoos) **1** [C,U] a liquid that you use for washing your hair; a similar liquid for cleaning carpets, cars, etc: *shampoo for greasy/dry/normal hair* **2** [C, usually sing] the act of washing sth with **shampoo** ▶ **shampoo** *verb* [T] (shampooing; shampoos; *pt, pp* shampooed)

shamrock /ˈʃæmrɒk/ *noun* [C,U] a plant with three leaves, which is the national symbol of Ireland

shandy /ˈʃændi/ *noun* [C,U] (*especially BrE*) (*pl* shandies) a drink that is a mixture of beer and **lemonade** (= a sweet lemon drink with bubbles) ➲ note at **beer**

shan't /ʃɑːnt/ *short for* **shall not**

shanty town /ˈʃænti taʊn/ *noun* [C] an area, usually on the edge of a big city, where poor people live in bad conditions in buildings that they have made themselves

shapes

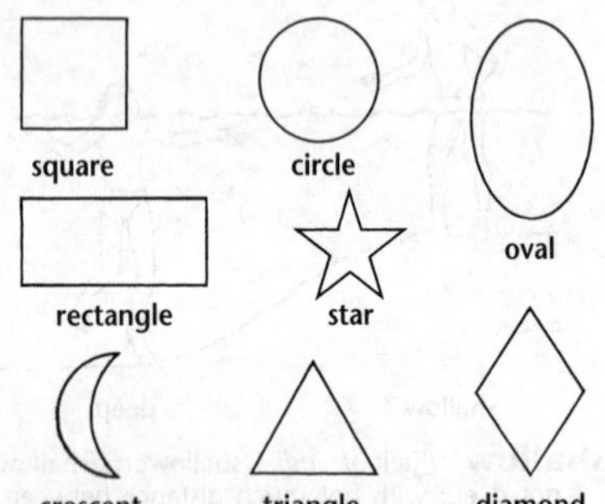

shape¹ /ʃeɪp/ *noun* **1** [C,U] the form of the outer edges or surfaces of sth; an example of sth that has a particular form: *a round/square/rectangular shape* ◆ *a cake* ***in the shape of*** *a heart* ◆ *clothes to fit people of* ***all shapes and sizes*** ◆ *Squares, circles and triangles are all different shapes.* ◆ *I could just make out a dark shape in the distance.* ◆ *The country is roughly square* ***in shape***. **2** [U] the physical condition of sb/sth; the good or bad state of sb/sth: *She was* ***in such bad shape*** (= so ill) *that she had to be taken to hospital.* ◆ *I go swimming regularly to keep* ***in shape***. **3** [sing] the shape (of sth) the organization, form or structure of sth: *Recent developments have changed the shape of the company.*

IDM **out of shape 1** not in the usual or correct shape: *My sweater's gone out of shape now that I've washed it.* **2** not physically fit: *You're out of shape. You should get more exercise.*

take shape to start to develop well: *Plans to expand the company are beginning to take shape.*

shape² /ʃeɪp/ *verb* [T] **1** shape sth (into sth) to make sth into a particular form: *Shape the mixture into small balls.* **2** to influence the way in which sth develops; to cause sth to have a particular form or nature: *His political ideas were shaped by his upbringing.*

shaped /ʃeɪpt/ *adj* [in compounds] having the shape mentioned: *an L-shaped room*

shapeless /ˈʃeɪpləs/ *adj* not having a clear shape: *a shapeless dress*

share¹ /ʃeə(r)/ *verb* **1** [T] share sth (out) to divide sth between two or more people: *We shared the pizza out between the four of us.* **2** [I,T] share (sth) (with sb) to have, use, do or pay sth together with another person or other people: *I share a flat with four other people.* ◆ *I shared my sandwiches with Jim.* ◆ *We share the same interests.* **3** [T] share sth (with sb) to tell sb about sth; to allow sb to know sth: *Sometimes it helps to share your problems.*

share² /ʃeə(r)/ *noun* **1** [sing] share (of sth) a part or an amount of sth that has been divided between several people: *We each pay a share of the household bills.* ◆ *I'm willing to* ***take*** *my* ***share*** *of the blame.* **2** [C, usually pl] shares (in sth) one of many equal parts into which the value of a company is divided, that can be sold to people who want to own part of the company: *a fall in share prices*

IDM **(more than) your fair share of sth** ➲ **fair¹**
the lion's share (of sth) ➲ **lion**

shareholder /ˈʃeəhəʊldə(r)/ *noun* [C] an owner of shares in a company

shark /ʃɑːk/ *noun* [C] (*pl* sharks or shark) a large, often dangerous, sea fish that has a lot of sharp teeth ➲ picture at **dolphin**

sharp¹ /ʃɑːp/ *adj* (sharper; sharpest)
➤EDGE/POINT **1** having a very thin but strong edge or point; that can cut or make a hole in sth easily: *a sharp knife* ◆ *sharp teeth* OPP **blunt**
➤CHANGE **2** (used about a change of direction or level) very great and sudden: *a sharp rise/fall in inflation* ◆ *This is a sharp bend, so slow down.*
➤CLEAR **3** clear and definite: *the sharp outline of the hills* ◆ *a sharp contrast between the lives of the rich and the poor*
➤MIND, EYES, EARS **4** able to think, act, understand, see or hear quickly: *a sharp mind* ◆ *to have sharp eyes*
➤WORDS/COMMENTS **5** said in an angry way; intended to upset sb or be critical: *During the debate there was a sharp exchange of views between the two parties.*
➤ACTIONS/MOVEMENTS **6** quick and sudden: *One short sharp blow was enough to end the fight.*
➤PAIN **7** very strong and sudden: *a sharp pain in the chest* OPP **dull**
➤TASTE/FEELING **8** (used about sth that affects the senses) strong; not mild or gentle, often causing an unpleasant feeling: *a sharp taste* ◆ *a sharp wind*
➤IN MUSIC **9** (*symbol* ♯) half a note higher than the stated note: *in the key of C sharp minor* OPP **flat** **10** slightly higher than the correct note: *That last note was sharp. Can you sing it again?* OPP **flat**
▶ **sharply** *adv*: *The road bends sharply to the left.*

◆ *Share prices fell sharply this morning.* ▶ **sharpness** *noun* [U]

sharp² /ʃɑːp/ *adv* **1** exactly on time: *Be here at 3 o'clock sharp.* **2** turning suddenly: *Go to the traffic lights and turn sharp right.* **3** slightly higher than the correct note ➲ look at **flat**

sharp³ /ʃɑːp/ *noun* [C] (*symbol* ♯) (in music) a note that is half a note higher than the note with the same letter ➲ look at **flat**

sharpen /ˈʃɑːpən/ *verb* [I,T] to become or to make sth sharp or sharper: *to sharpen a knife* ◆ *This knife won't sharpen.*

sharpener /ˈʃɑːpnə(r)/ *noun* [C] an object or a tool that is used for making sth sharp: *a pencil/knife sharpener*

shatter /ˈʃætə(r)/ *verb* **1** [I,T] (used about glass, etc.) to break or break sth into very small pieces: *I dropped the glass and it shattered on the floor.* ◆ *The force of the explosion shattered the windows.* **2** [T] to destroy sth completely: *Her hopes were shattered by the news.*

shattered /ˈʃætəd/ *adj* **1** very shocked and upset **2** (*informal*) very tired: *I'm absolutely shattered.*

⚷ **shave¹** /ʃeɪv/ *verb* [I,T] **shave (sth) (off)** to remove hair from the face or another part of the body with a **razor** (= a very sharp piece of metal): *I cut myself shaving this morning.* ◆ *When did you shave off your moustache?* ◆ *to shave your legs*

PHR V **shave sth off (sth)** to cut a very small amount from sth: *We'll have to shave a bit off the door to make it close properly.*

shave² /ʃeɪv/ *noun* [C, usually sing] the act of shaving: *to have a shave* ◆ *I need a shave.*

IDM **a close shave/thing** ➲ close³

shaven /ˈʃeɪvn/ *adj* having been shaved: *clean-shaven* (= not having a beard or moustache)

shaver /ˈʃeɪvə(r)/ (also eˌlectric ˈrazor) *noun* [C] an electric tool that is used for removing hair from the face or another part of the body

shawl /ʃɔːl/ *noun* [C] a large piece of cloth that is worn by a woman round her shoulders or head, or that is put round a baby

⚷ **she** /ʃiː/ *pron* (the subject of a verb) the female person who has already been mentioned: *'What does your sister do?' 'She's a dentist.'* ◆ *I asked her a question but she didn't answer.* ➲ note at **he**

shear /ʃɪə(r)/ *verb* [T] (*pt* **sheared**; *pp* **sheared** or **shorn**) to cut the wool off a sheep

shears /ʃɪəz/ *noun* [pl] a tool that is like a very large pair of scissors and that is used for cutting things in the garden: *a pair of shears* ➲ picture at **garden**

sheath /ʃiːθ/ *noun* [C] (*pl* **sheaths** /ʃiːðz/) a cover for a knife or other sharp weapon ➲ picture at **sword**

she'd /ʃiːd/ *short for* **she had; she would**

shed¹ /ʃed/ *noun* [C] a small building that is used for keeping things in: *a garden shed* ◆ *a bicycle shed*

shed² /ʃed/ *verb* [T] (**shedding**; *pt, pp* **shed**) **1** to get rid of or remove sth that is not wanted **2** to lose sth because it falls off: *This snake sheds its skin every year.* ◆ *Autumn is coming and the trees are beginning to shed their leaves.*

IDM **shed blood** (*formal*) to kill or injure people

shed light on sth to make sth clear and easy to understand

shed tears to cry

⚷ **sheep** /ʃiːp/ *noun* [C] (*pl* **sheep**) an animal that is kept on farms and used for its wool or meat ➲ note at **meat** ➲ picture at **goat**

> **MORE** A male sheep is a **ram**; a female sheep is a **ewe** and a young sheep is a **lamb**. When sheep make a noise they **bleat**. This is written as **baa**. The meat from sheep is called **lamb** or **mutton**.

sheepdog /ˈʃiːpdɒg/ *noun* [C] a dog that has been trained to control sheep

sheepish /ˈʃiːpɪʃ/ *adj* feeling or showing embarrassment because you have done sth silly: *a sheepish grin* ▶ **sheepishly** *adv*

sheepskin /ˈʃiːpskɪn/ *noun* [U] the skin of a sheep, including the wool, from which coats, etc. are made: *a sheepskin rug/jacket*

sheer /ʃɪə(r)/ *adj* **1** [only *before* a noun] used to emphasize the size, degree or amount of sth: *It's sheer stupidity to drink and drive.* ◆ *It was* ***sheer luck*** *that I happened to be in the right place at the right time.* ◆ *Her success is due to sheer hard work.* ◆ *I only agreed out of sheer desperation.* **2** very steep; almost vertical: *Don't walk near the edge. It's* ***a sheer drop*** *to the sea.*

⚷ **sheet** /ʃiːt/ *noun* [C] **1** a large piece of cloth used on a bed: *I've just changed the sheets on the bed.* ➲ picture at **bed** **2** a piece of paper that is used for writing, printing, etc. on: *a sheet of notepaper* ◆ *Write each answer on a separate sheet.* ➲ look at **balance sheet** **3** a flat, thin piece of any material: *a sheet of metal/glass* **4** a wide, flat area of sth: *The road was covered with* ***a sheet of ice.***

sheikh (also **sheik**) /ʃeɪk/ *noun* [C] an Arab prince or leader

⚷ **shelf** /ʃelf/ *noun* [C] (*pl* **shelves** /ʃelvz/) a long flat piece of wood, glass, etc. that is fixed to a wall or in a cupboard, used for putting things on: *I put up a shelf in the kitchen.* ◆ *I reached up and took down the book from the top shelf.* ◆ *a bookshelf* ➲ picture on **page P8**

she'll /ʃiːl/ *short for* **she will**

⚷ **shell¹** /ʃel/ *noun* **1** [C,U] a hard covering that protects eggs, nuts and some animals: *Some children were collecting shells on the beach.* ◆ *a piece of eggshell* ◆ *Tortoises have a hard shell.* ➲ picture at **nut, shellfish, snail** ➲ picture on **page P10, page P13, page P14** **2** [C] a metal container that explodes when it is fired from a large gun **3** [C] the walls or hard outer structure of sth: *The body shell of the car is made in another factory.*

IDM **come out of your shell** to become less shy and more confident when talking to other people

S

go, retreat, etc. into your shell to suddenly become shy and stop talking

shell² /ʃel/ *verb* [T] **1** to fire **shells¹**(2) from a large gun **2** to take the **shell¹**(1) off a nut or another kind of food: *to shell peas*

shellfish

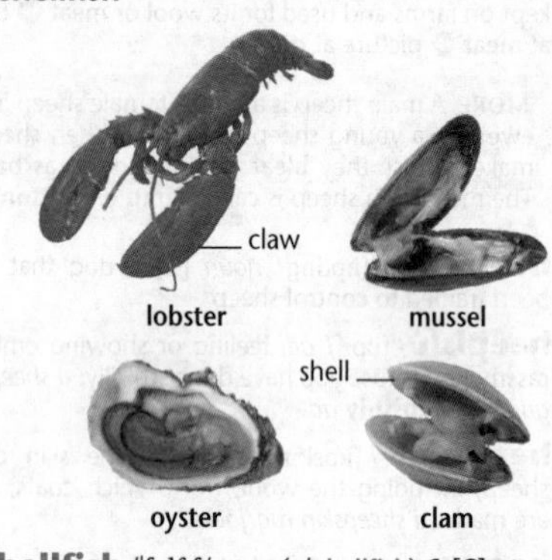

shellfish /ˈʃelfɪʃ/ *noun* (*pl* **shellfish**) **1** [C] a type of animal that lives in water and has a shell ➲ picture on **page P13** **2** [U] these animals eaten as food

shelter¹ /ˈʃeltə(r)/ *noun* **1** the fact of having a place to live or stay: *to give somebody food and shelter* **2** [U] **shelter (from sth)** protection from danger or bad weather: *We looked around for somewhere to* ***take shelter*** *from the storm.* **3** [C] a small building that gives protection, for example from bad weather or attack: *a bus shelter* ◆ *an air-raid shelter* **4** [C] a building, usually owned by a charity, where people or animals can stay if they do not have a home, or have been badly treated: *an animal shelter* **SYN** **refuge**

shelter² /ˈʃeltə(r)/ *verb* **1** [T] **shelter sb/sth (from sb/sth)** to protect sb/sth; to provide a safe place away from harm or danger: *The trees shelter the house from the wind.* **2** [I] **shelter (from sth)** to find protection or a safe place: *Let's shelter from the rain under that tree.*

sheltered /ˈʃeltəd/ *adj* **1** (used about a place) protected from bad weather **2** protected from unpleasant things in your life: *We had a sheltered childhood, living in the country.*

shelve /ʃelv/ *verb* [T] to decide not to continue with a plan, etc., either for a short time or permanently: *Plans for a new motorway have been shelved.*

shelves *plural* of **shelf**

shelving /ˈʃelvɪŋ/ *noun* [U] a set of shelves

shepherd¹ /ˈʃepəd/ *noun* [C] a person whose job is to look after sheep

shepherd² /ˈʃepəd/ *verb* [T] to lead and look after people so that they do not get lost

sheriff /ˈʃerɪf/ *noun* [C] (in the US) an officer of the law who is responsible for a particular town or part of a state

sherry /ˈʃeri/ *noun* [C,U] (*pl* **sherries**) a type of strong Spanish wine; a glass of this wine

she's /ʃiːz; ʃiz/ *short for* **she is; she has**

shield¹ /ʃiːld/ *noun* [C] **1** (in past times) a large piece of metal or wood that soldiers carried to protect themselves **2** (also ˈ**riot shield**) a piece of equipment made of strong plastic, that the police use to protect themselves from angry crowds **3** a person or thing that is used to protect sb/sth, especially by forming a barrier: *The metal door acted as a shield against the explosion.* **4** an object or a drawing in the shape of a **shield**, sometimes used as a prize in a sports competition ➲ picture at **medal**

shield² /ʃiːld/ *verb* [T] **shield sb/sth (against/from sb/sth)** to protect sb/sth from danger or damage: *I shielded my eyes from the bright light with my hand.*

shift¹ /ʃɪft/ *verb* [I,T] **1** to move or be moved from one position or place to another: *She shifted uncomfortably in her chair.* ◆ *He shifted his desk closer to the window.* **2** to change your opinion of or attitude towards sb/sth: *Public attitudes towards marriage have shifted over the years.*

IDM **shift the blame/responsibility (for sth) (onto sb)** to make sb else responsible for sth you should do or for sth bad you have done

shift² /ʃɪft/ *noun* **1** [C] **a shift (in sth)** a change in your opinion of or attitude towards sth: *There has been a shift in public opinion away from supporting the strikes.* **2** [C, with sing or pl verb] (in a factory, etc.) one of the periods that the working day is divided into; the group who work during this period: *The night shift has/have just gone off duty.* ◆ *to work* ***in shifts*** ◆ *shift work/workers* ◆ *to be on the day/night shift* **3** [sing] one of the keys that you use for writing on a computer, etc., that allows you to write a capital letter: *the shift key*

shifty /ˈʃɪfti/ *adj* (*informal*) (**shiftier; shiftiest**) seeming to be dishonest; looking guilty about sth: *shifty eyes*

shilling /ˈʃɪlɪŋ/ *noun* [C] **1** a British coin worth five pence that was used in past times **2** the basic unit of money in some countries, for example Kenya

shimmer /ˈʃɪmə(r)/ *verb* [I] to shine with a soft light that seems to be moving: *Moonlight shimmered on the sea.*

shin /ʃɪn/ *noun* [C] the bone down the front part of your leg from your knee to your ankle ➲ picture at **body**

shine¹ /ʃaɪn/ *verb* (*pt, pp* **shone** /ʃɒn/) **1** [I] to send out or send back light; to be bright: *I could see a light shining in the distance.* ◆ *The sea shone in the light of the moon.* **2** [T] to direct a light at sb/sth: *The policeman shone a torch on the stranger's face.*

shine² /ʃaɪn/ *noun* [sing] **1** a bright effect caused by light hitting a polished surface **2** the act of polishing sth so that it shines

shingle /ˈʃɪŋɡl/ *noun* [U] small pieces of stone lying in a mass on a beach

ˈ**shin guard** (*BrE also* ˈshin pad) *noun* [C] a thick piece of material used to protect the **shin** when playing some sports

shiny /ˈʃaɪni/ *adj* (**shinier**; **shiniest**) causing a bright effect when in the sun or in light: *The shampoo leaves your hair soft and shiny.* ♦ *a shiny new car*

ship[1] /ʃɪp/ *noun* [C] a large boat used for carrying passengers or goods by sea: *to travel* ***by ship*** ♦ *to launch a ship* ➲ note at **boat**

ship[2] /ʃɪp/ *verb* [T] (**shipping**; **shipped**) to send or carry sth by ship or by another type of transport

shipbuilder /ˈʃɪpbɪldə(r)/ *noun* [C] a person or company who makes or builds ships ▸ **shipbuilding** *noun* [U]

shipment /ˈʃɪpmənt/ *noun* **1** [U] the carrying of goods from one place to another **2** [C] a quantity of goods that are sent from one place to another

shipping /ˈʃɪpɪŋ/ *noun* [U] **1** ships in general or considered as a group **2** the carrying of goods from one place to another: *a shipping company*

shipwreck /ˈʃɪprek/ *noun* [C,U] an accident at sea in which a ship is destroyed by a storm, rocks, etc. and sinks; a ship which is destroyed in this way ▸ **shipwrecked** *adj*: *a shipwrecked sailor* ♦ *a shipwrecked vessel*

shipyard /ˈʃɪpjɑːd/ *noun* [C] a place where ships are repaired or built

shirk /ʃɜːk/ *verb* [I,T] to avoid doing sth that is difficult or unpleasant, especially because you are too lazy: *to shirk your responsibilities*

shirt /ʃɜːt/ *noun* [C] a piece of clothing made of cotton, etc. worn on the upper part of the body: *to wear a shirt and tie* ♦ *Nigel wears a crisp white shirt to the office every day.* ➲ picture on **page P1**

> **MORE** A shirt usually has a **collar** at the neck, long or short **sleeves**, and **buttons** down the front.

shiver /ˈʃɪvə(r)/ *verb* [I] to shake slightly, especially because you are cold or frightened: *shivering with cold/fright* ▸ **shiver** *noun* [C]: *The thought sent a shiver down my spine.*

shoal /ʃəʊl/ *noun* [C] a large group of fish that feed and swim together

shock[1] /ʃɒk/ *noun* **1** [C,U] the feeling that you get when sth unpleasant happens suddenly; the situation that causes this feeling: *The sudden noise* ***gave*** *him* ***a shock.*** ♦ *The bad news* ***came as a shock*** *to her.* ♦ *I'm still suffering from shock at the news.* ♦ *His mother is* ***in a state of shock.*** **2** [U] a serious medical condition of extreme weakness caused by damage to the body: *He* ***was in/went into shock*** *after the accident.* **3** [C] a violent shaking movement (caused by a crash, an explosion, etc.): *the shock of the earthquake* **4** [C] = **electric shock**

shock[2] /ʃɒk/ *verb* **1** [T] to cause an unpleasant feeling of surprise in sb: *We were shocked by his death.* ♦ *I'm sorry, I didn't mean to shock you when I came in.* **2** [I,T] to make sb feel disgusted or offended: *These films deliberately set out to shock.* ▸ **shocked** *adj*: *a shocked expression/look*

shocking /ˈʃɒkɪŋ/ *adj* **1** that offends or upsets people; that is morally wrong: *a shocking accident* ♦ *shocking behaviour/news* **2** (*BrE informal*) very bad: *The weather has been absolutely shocking.*

shod *past tense, past participle of* **shoe**[2]

shoddy /ˈʃɒdi/ *adj* (**shoddier**; **shoddiest**) **1** made carelessly or with poor quality materials: *shoddy goods* **2** dishonest or unfair ▸ **shoddily** *adv*

shoes

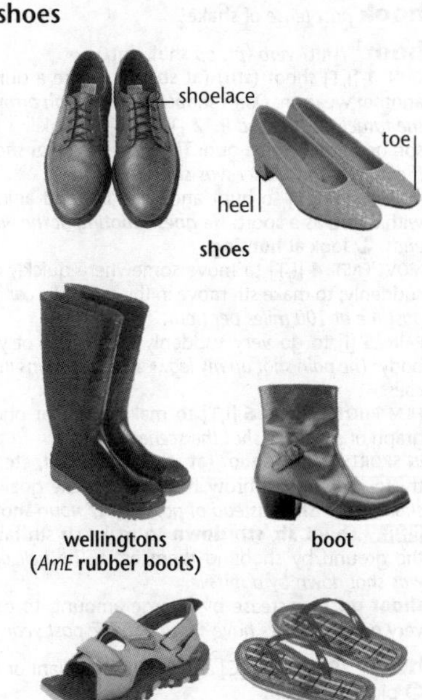

shoes

wellingtons (*AmE* **rubber boots**)

boot

sandal

flip-flops (*AmE* **thongs**)

trainers (*AmE* **sneakers**)

slippers

shoe[1] /ʃuː/ *noun* [C] **1** a type of covering for the foot, usually made of leather or plastic: *a pair of shoes* ♦ *running shoes* ♦ *What size are your shoes/What is your shoe size?* ♦ *I tried on a nice pair of shoes but they didn't fit.* ➲ picture on **page P1** **2** = **horseshoe**

IDM **in sb's place/shoes** ➲ **place**[1]

shoe[2] /ʃuː/ *verb* [T] (*pt, pp* **shod** /ʃɒd/) to fit a **horseshoe** (= a piece of metal in the shape of a U) on a horse

shoelace /ˈʃuːleɪs/ (also lace, *AmE* also shoestring /ˈʃuːstrɪŋ/) *noun* [C] a long thin piece of material like string used to fasten a shoe: *to tie/untie a shoelace* ➲ picture at **shoe**

shone *past tense, past participle* of **shine**[1]

shoo[1] /ʃuː/ *exclam* used to tell a child or animal to go away

shoo[2] /ʃuː/ *verb* [T] (*pt, pp* shooed) shoo sb/sth away, off, out, etc. to make sb/sth go away by saying '**shoo**' and waving your hands

shook *past tense* of **shake**[1]

shoot[1] /ʃuːt/ *verb* (*pt, pp* shot /ʃɒt/)
➤GUN **1** [I,T] shoot (sth) (at sb/sth) to fire a gun or another weapon: *Don't shoot!* ◆ *She shot an arrow at the target, but missed it.* **2** [T] to injure or kill a person or animal with a gun: *The policeman was shot in the arm.* ◆ *The soldier was* ***shot dead***.
➤ANIMALS **3** [I,T] to hunt and kill birds and animals with a gun as a sport: *He* ***goes shooting*** *at the weekends.* ➲ look at **hunting**
➤MOVE FAST **4** [I,T] to move somewhere quickly and suddenly; to make sth move in this way: *The car shot past me at 100 miles per hour.*
➤PAIN **5** [I] to go very suddenly along part of your body: *The pain shot up my leg.* ◆ *shooting pains in the chest*
➤FILM/PHOTOGRAPH **6** [I,T] to make a film or photograph of sth: *They shot the scene ten times.*
➤IN SPORTS **7** [I,T] shoot (at sth) (in football, etc.) to try to kick, hit or throw the ball into the goal: *He should have shot instead of passing.* ➲ *noun* **shot**
PHR V **shoot sb/sth down** to make sb/sth fall to the ground by shooting them or it: *The helicopter was shot down by a missile.*
shoot up to increase by a large amount; to grow very quickly: *Prices have shot up in the past year.*

shoot[2] /ʃuːt/ *noun* [C] a new part of a plant or tree ➲ picture at **plant**

shooting *noun* **1** [C] a situation in which a person is shot with a gun: *Terrorist groups claimed responsibility for the shootings.* **2** [U] the sport of shooting animals and birds with guns: *pheasant shooting* **3** [U] the process of filming a film: *Shooting began early this year.*

ˌshooting ˈstar *noun* [C] a piece of rock that burns with a bright light as it travels through space ➲ look at **comet**

shop[1] /ʃɒp/ (*AmE* store) *noun* [C] a building or part of a building where things are bought and sold: *a cake/shoe/sports/toy shop* ◆ *a corner shop* (= a local shop, usually at the corner of a street) ◆ *When do the shops open?*

> MORE The **butcher**, the **baker**, etc. is the person who sells a particular thing. We usually call their shop **the butcher's, the baker's** etc. instead of 'the butcher's shop', etc.

IDM **talk shop** ➲ **talk**[1]

> TOPIC
> **Shops**
> Before I **go shopping**, I make a **shopping list**. I buy bread and cakes **at the baker's**, where a **shop assistant serves** me. I buy meat at the **butcher's**, fish at the **fishmonger's**, fruit and vegetables at the **greengrocer's** and flowers at the **florist's**. If I want to buy everything in one shop, I go to the **supermarket**. There's a **market** in town on Fridays, and once a month there's a **farmer's market**, where you can buy local and **organic produce** (= food grown without chemicals).

shop[2] /ʃɒp/ *verb* [I] (shopping; shopped) shop (for sth) to go to a shop or shops in order to buy things: *He's shopping for some new clothes.*

> HELP **Go shopping** is more common than **shop**: *We go shopping every Saturday.*

PHR V **shop around (for sth)** to look at the price and quality of an item in different shops before you decide where to buy it
▶ **shopper** *noun* [C]

shopaholic /ˌʃɒpəˈhɒlɪk/ *noun* [C] (*informal*) a person who enjoys shopping very much and spends too much time or money doing it

ˈshop assistant (*AmE* ˈsales clerk; clerk) *noun* [C] a person who works in a shop ➲ picture on **page P2**

ˌshop ˈfloor *noun* [sing] (*BrE*) an area of a factory where things are made; the people who make things in a factory

shopkeeper /ˈʃɒpkiːpə(r)/ (*AmE* storekeeper) *noun* [C] a person who owns or manages a small shop

shoplifter /ˈʃɒplɪftə(r)/ *noun* [C] a person who steals sth from a shop while pretending to be a customer ➲ note at **thief**

shoplifting /ˈʃɒplɪftɪŋ/ *noun* [U] the crime of stealing goods from a shop while pretending to be a customer: *He was arrested for shoplifting.*

shopping /ˈʃɒpɪŋ/ *noun* [U] **1** the activity of going to the shops and buying things: *We always* ***do the shopping*** *on a Friday night.* ◆ *a shopping basket/bag/trolley* ➲ note at **supermarket** **2** (*especially BrE*) the things that you have bought in a shop: *Can you help me to put the shopping in the car?*

> TOPIC
> **Shopping**
> If you **go shopping** in the **sales**, you can often get good **bargains** (= things at a cheaper **price** than usual). You might spend time **browsing** (= looking at lots of things), or **window-shopping** (= looking in shop windows without intending to **buy** anything). If you are buying clothes, you **try** them **on** in the **fitting room**. You pay at the **cash desk**, where the **shop assistant** will give you a **receipt** (= a piece of paper). If you are not satisfied with a **product** you have bought, **take it back** to the shop. There you can **exchange** it or ask for a **refund** (= your money back).

ˈshopping centre (*AmE* ˈshopping center) *noun* [C] a place where there are many shops, either outside or in a covered building ➲ look at **mall** ➲ picture on **page P11**

shore¹ /ʃɔː(r)/ *noun* [C,U] the land at the edge of a sea or lake ➲ look at **ashore** ➲ picture on **page P10**

shore² /ʃɔː(r)/ *verb*

PHR V **shore sth up 1** to support part of a building or other large structure by placing large pieces of wood or metal against or under it so that it does not fall down **2** to help to support sth that is weak or going to fail: *The measures were aimed at shoring up the economy.*

shorn *past participle* of **shear**

🔑 **short¹** /ʃɔːt/ *adj* (**shorter**; **shortest**) *adv*

➤LENGTH/DISTANCE **1** not measuring much from one end to the other: *a short line/distance/dress* ◆ *This essay is rather short.* ◆ *short hair* OPP **long** ➲ picture at **hair** ➲ *verb* **shorten**

➤HEIGHT **2** less than the average height: *a short, fat man* OPP **tall**

➤TIME **3** not lasting a long time: *a short visit/film* ◆ *She left a short time ago.* ◆ *to have a short memory* (= to only remember things that have happened recently) OPP **long** ➲ *verb* **shorten**

➤NOT ENOUGH **4 short (of/on sth)** not having enough of what is needed: *Because of illness, the team is two players short.* ◆ *Good secretaries are* ***in short supply*** (= there are not enough of them). ◆ *We're a bit short of money at the moment.* ◆ *Your essay is a bit short on detail.* ➲ *noun* **shortage**

➤NAME/WORD **5 short for sth** used as a shorter way of saying sth: *'Bill' is short for 'William'.*

➤IMPATIENT **6 short (with sb)** (used about a person) speaking in an impatient and angry way to sb: *What's the matter with Michael? He was really short with me just now.* ➲ *adverb* **shortly**

➤SUDDENLY **7** suddenly: *She* ***stopped short*** *when she saw the accident.*

IDM **cut sb short** to not allow sb to finish speaking; to interrupt sb

fall short (of sth) ➲ **fall¹**

for short as a short form: *She's called 'Diana', or 'Di' for short.*

go short (of sth) to be without enough (of sth): *He made sure his family never went short of food.*

in the long/short term ➲ **term¹**

in short in a few words

run short (of sth) to have used up most of sth so there is not much left: *We're running short of coffee.*

short of sth/doing sth apart from; except for: *Nothing short of a miracle will save us now.*

stop short of sth/doing sth ➲ **stop¹**

short² /ʃɔːt/ *noun* [C] **1** (*BrE*) a small strong alcoholic drink: *I prefer wine to shorts.* **2** (*informal*) = **short circuit**

shortage /ˈʃɔːtɪdʒ/ *noun* [C] a situation where there is not enough of sth: *a food/housing/water shortage* ◆ *a shortage of trained teachers*

ˌshort ˈcircuit (also *informal* **short**) *noun* [C] a bad electrical connection that causes a machine to stop working ▶ **ˌshort-ˈcircuit** (also *informal* **short**) *verb* [I,T]: *The lights short-circuited.*

shortcoming /ˈʃɔːtkʌmɪŋ/ *noun* [C, usually pl] a fault or weakness

ˌshort ˈcut *noun* [C] a quicker, easier or more direct way to get somewhere or to do sth: *He* ***took a short cut*** *to school through the park.*

shorten /ˈʃɔːtn/ *verb* [I,T] to become shorter or to make sth shorter OPP **lengthen**

shortfall /ˈʃɔːtfɔːl/ *noun* [C] **shortfall (in sth)** the amount by which sth is less than you need or expect

shorthand /ˈʃɔːthænd/ *noun* [U] a method of writing quickly that uses signs or short forms of words: *to write* ***in shorthand*** ◆ *a shorthand typist*

shortlist /ˈʃɔːtlɪst/ *noun* [C, usually sing] a list of the best people for a job, etc. who have been chosen from all the people who want the job: *She's one of the four people on the shortlist.* ▶ **shortlist** *verb* [T]: *Six candidates were shortlisted for the post.*

ˌshort-ˈlived *adj* lasting only for a short time

🔑 **shortly** /ˈʃɔːtli/ *adv* **1** soon; not long: *The manager will see you shortly.* **2** in an impatient, angry way: *She spoke rather shortly to the customer.*

shorts /ʃɔːts/ *noun* [pl] **1** a type of short trousers ending above the knee that you wear in hot weather, while playing sports, etc. **2** (*AmE*) = **boxer shorts**

> **GRAMMAR** Shorts are plural, so we cannot say, for example, 'a new short'. The following are possible: *I need some shorts/a pair of shorts.* ◆ *These shorts are too small.*

ˌshort-ˈsighted *adj* **1** (*AmE* usually **near-sighted**) able to see things clearly only when they are very close to you: *I have to wear glasses because I'm short-sighted.* OPP **long-sighted 2** not considering what will probably happen in the future: *a short-sighted attitude/policy*

ˌshort-ˈstaffed *adj* (used about an office, a shop, etc.) not having enough people to do the work

ˌshort ˈstory *noun* [C] a piece of writing that is shorter than a novel

ˌshort ˈtemper *noun* [sing] a tendency to become angry very quickly and easily: *He has a short temper.* ▶ **ˌshort-ˈtempered** *adj*: *She's rather short-tempered when she's tired.*

ˌshort-ˈterm *adj* lasting for a short period of time from the present: *short-term plans/memory*

🔑 **shot¹** /ʃɒt/ *noun*

➤WITH GUN **1** [C] **a shot (at sb/sth)** an act of firing a gun, etc., or the noise that this makes: *to* ***take a shot*** *at the target* ◆ *The policeman fired* ***a warning shot*** *into the air.*

➤TRY **2** [C, usually sing] (*informal*) **a shot (at sth/at doing sth)** an attempt at doing sth: *Let me* ***have a shot*** *at it* (= let me try to do it). ◆ ***Just give it your best shot*** (= try as hard as you can). SYN **attempt**

➤IN SPORT **3** [C] the act of kicking, throwing or hitting a ball in order to score a point or a goal: *Giggs scored with a low shot into the corner of the net.* ◆ *Good*

S

shot! **4** *often* **the shot** [sing] the heavy ball that is used in the sports competition called the **shot-put**
➤PHOTOGRAPH **5** [C] a photograph or a picture in a film: *I got some good shots of the runners as they crossed the line.*
➤DRUG **6** [C] a small amount of a drug that is put into your body using a needle: *a shot of penicillin/morphine*
IDM **call the shots/tune** ➲ **call**[1]
like a shot (*informal*) very quickly; without stopping to think about it: *If someone invited me on a free holiday, I'd go like a shot.*
a long shot ➲ **long**[1]

shot[2] *past tense, past participle of* **shoot**[1]

shotgun /ˈʃɒtɡʌn/ *noun* [C] a long gun that is used for shooting small animals and birds ➲ note at **gun**

the ˈshot-put *noun* [sing] the event or sport of throwing a heavy metal ball as far as possible

⚿ **should** /ʃəd; *strong form* ʃʊd/ *modal verb* (*negative* **should not**; *short form* **shouldn't** /ˈʃʊdnt/) **1** (used for saying that it is right or appropriate for sb to do sth, or for sth to happen) ought to: *The police should do something about street crime in this area.* ◆ *Children shouldn't be left on their own.* ◆ *I'm tired. I shouldn't have gone to bed so late/I should have gone to bed earlier.* **2** used for giving or asking for advice: *You should try that new restaurant.* ◆ *Do you think I should phone him?* ◆ *What should I do?* **3** used for saying that you expect sth is true or will happen: *It's 4.30. They should be in New York by now.* ◆ *It should stop raining soon.* **4** (*BrE formal*) used with 'I/we' instead of 'would' in 'if' sentences: *I should be most grateful if you could send me ...* **5** (*formal*) used after 'if' and 'in case' to refer to a possible event or situation: *If you should decide to accept, please phone us.* ◆ *Should you decide to accept ...* **6** used as the past tense of 'shall' when we report what sb says: *He asked me if he should come today* (= he asked 'Shall I come today?'). **7** **I should imagine, say, think, etc.** used to give opinions that you are not certain about: *This picture is worth a lot of money, I should think.* ℹ For more information about modal verbs, look at the **Reference Section** at the back of this dictionary.

⚿ **shoulder**[1] /ˈʃəʊldə(r)/ *noun* [C] **1** the part of your body between your neck and the top of your arm: *I asked him why he'd done it but he just* ***shrugged his shoulders*** (= raised his shoulders to show that he did not know or care). ◆ *She fell asleep with her head on his shoulder.* ➲ picture at **body** **2** **-shouldered** [in compounds] having the type of shoulders mentioned: *a broad-shouldered man* **3** a part of a dress, coat, etc. that covers the shoulders: *a jacket with padded shoulders* **4** (*AmE*) = **hard shoulder**
IDM **have a chip on your shoulder** ➲ **chip**[1]
rub shoulders with sb ➲ **rub**
a shoulder to cry on used to describe a person who listens to your problems and understands how you feel

shoulder[2] /ˈʃəʊldə(r)/ *verb* [T] **1** to accept the responsibility for sth: *to* ***shoulder the blame/responsibility*** *for something* **2** to push sb/sth with your shoulder

ˈshoulder bag *noun* [C] a type of bag that you carry over one shoulder with a long narrow piece of cloth, leather, etc. ➲ picture on **page P1**

ˈshoulder blade *noun* [C] either of the two large flat bones on each side of your back, below your shoulders ➲ picture at **body**

⚿ **shout** /ʃaʊt/ *verb* **1** [I,T] **shout sth (at/to sb); shout sth out** to say sth in a loud voice: *'Careful,' she shouted.* ◆ *The captain shouted instructions to his team.* **2** [I] **shout (at/to sb); shout out** to speak or cry out in a very loud voice: *There's no need to shout—I can hear you.* ◆ *The teacher shouted angrily at the boys.* ◆ *to shout out in pain/excitement* ➲ look at **scream**
PHR V **shout sb down** to shout so that sb who is speaking cannot be heard: *The speaker was shouted down by a group of protesters.*
shout sth out to say sth in a loud voice: *The students kept shouting out the answers, so we stopped playing in the end.*
▶ **shout** *noun* [C]

shove /ʃʌv/ *verb* [I,T] (*informal*) to push with a sudden, rough movement: *Everybody in the crowd was* ***pushing and shoving.*** ◆ *The policeman shoved the thief into the back of the police car.* ▶ **shove** *noun* [C, usually sing]: *to give somebody/something a shove*

shovel /ˈʃʌvl/ *noun* [C] a tool used for picking up and moving earth, snow, sand, etc. ➲ look at **spade** ➲ picture at **garden** ▶ **shovel** *verb* [I,T] (**shovelling; shovelled**, (*AmE*) **shoveling; shoveled**): *to shovel snow*

⚿ **show**[1] /ʃəʊ/ *verb* (*pt* **showed**; *pp* **shown** /ʃəʊn/ *or* **showed**)
➤MAKE CLEAR **1** [T] to make sth clear; to give information about sth: *Research shows that most people get too little exercise.* ◆ *This graph shows how prices have gone up in the last few years.*
➤LET SB SEE **2** [T] **show sb/sth (to sb); show sb (sth)** to let sb see sb/sth: *I showed the letter to him.* ◆ *I showed him the letter.* ◆ *She showed me what she had bought.* ◆ *They're showing his latest film at our local cinema.* ◆ *She was showing signs of stress.* ◆ *This white T-shirt really shows the dirt.* ◆ *The picture showed him arguing with a photographer.*
➤TEACH **3** [T] to help sb to do sth by doing it yourself; to explain sth: *Can you show me how to make pancakes?*
➤GUIDE **4** [T] to lead sb to or round a place; to explain how to go to a place: *I'll come with you and show you the way.* ◆ *Shall I show you to your room?* ◆ *A guide showed us round the museum.*
➤BE SEEN **5** [I] to be able to be seen; to appear: *I tried not to let my disappointment show.*
IDM **show sb/know/learn the ropes** ➲ **rope**[1]
PHR V **show off** (*informal*) to try to impress people by showing them how clever you are: *John was showing off in front of his sister's friends.*
show sth off to show people sb/sth that you are proud of
show up (*informal*) to arrive, especially when sb is

S

expecting you: *Where have you been? I thought you'd never show up.*
show (sth) up to allow sth to be seen: *The sunlight shows up those dirty marks on the window.*
show sb up (*informal*) to make sb embarrassed about your behaviour or appearance: *He showed her up by shouting at the waiter.*

🔑 **show²** /ʃəʊ/ *noun* **1** [C] a type of entertainment performed for an audience: *a TV comedy show* ◆ *a quiz show* **2** [C,U] an occasion when a collection of things are brought together for people to look at: *a dog show* ◆ *a fashion show* ◆ *Paintings by local children will be* **on show** *at the town hall next week.* **3** [sing] an occasion when you let sb see sth: *a show of emotion/gratitude/temper* **4** [C,U] something that a person does or has in order to make people believe sth that is not true: *Although she hated him, she* **put on a show of** *politeness.* ◆ *His self-confidence is* **all show** (= he is not as confident as he pretends to be).

ˈ**show business** (also *informal* **showbiz** /ˈʃəʊbɪz/) *noun* [U] the business of entertaining people in the theatre, in films, on TV, etc: *He's been* **in show business** *since he was five years old.*

showdown /ˈʃəʊdaʊn/ *noun* [C, usually sing] a final argument, meeting or fight at the end of a long disagreement: *The management are preparing for a showdown with the union.*

🔑 **shower¹** /ˈʃaʊə(r)/ *noun* [C] **1** a piece of equipment that produces a spray of water that you stand under to wash; the small room or part of a room that contains a shower: *The shower doesn't work.* ◆ *She's in the shower.* ◆ *I'd like a room with a shower, please.* ➲ picture on **page P8** **2** an act of washing yourself by standing under a shower: *I'll just* **have a** *quick* **shower** *then we can go out.* **3** a short period of rain: *a heavy shower* ➲ look at **rain, acid rain** **4** a lot of very small objects that fall or fly through the air together: *a shower of sparks/broken glass*

shower² /ˈʃaʊə(r)/ *verb* **1** [I] to wash yourself under a shower: *I came back from my run, showered and got changed.* **2** [I,T] **shower (down) on sb/sth; shower sb with sth** to cover sb/sth with a lot of small falling objects: *Ash from the volcano showered down on the town.* ◆ *People suffered cuts after being showered with broken glass.*

showing /ˈʃəʊɪŋ/ *noun* **1** [C] an act of showing a film, etc: *The second showing of the film begins at 8 o'clock.* **2** [sing] how sb/sth behaves; how successful sb/sth is: *On its present showing, the party should win the election.*

showjumping /ˈʃəʊdʒʌmpɪŋ/ *noun* [U] a competition in which a person rides a horse over a series of jumps

shown *past participle* of **show¹**

ˈ**show-off** *noun* [C] (*informal*) a person who tries to impress others by showing them how clever he/she is, or by showing them sth he/she is proud of: *She's such a show-off, always boasting about how good she is at this and that.*

showroom /ˈʃəʊruːm; -rʊm/ *noun* [C] a type of large shop where customers can look at goods such as cars, furniture and electrical items that are on sale

shrank *past tense* of **shrink**

shrapnel /ˈʃræpnəl/ *noun* [U] small pieces of metal that fly around when a bomb explodes

shred¹ /ʃred/ *verb* [T] (**shredding**; **shredded**) to tear or cut sth into **shreds**: *shredded cabbage*

shred² /ʃred/ *noun* **1** [C] a small thin piece of material that has been cut or torn off: *His clothes were torn to shreds by the rose bushes.* **2** [sing] [in negative sentences] **not a shred of sth** a very small amount of sth: *There wasn't a shred of truth in her story.*

shrewd /ʃruːd/ *adj* (**shrewder**; **shrewdest**) able to make good decisions because you understand a situation well: *a shrewd thinker/decision* ▶ **shrewdly** *adv*

shriek /ʃriːk/ *verb* **1** [I] to make a short, loud, noise in a high voice: *She shrieked in fright.* ◆ *The children were shrieking with laughter.* **2** [T] to say sth loudly in a high voice: *'Stop it!' she shrieked.* ➲ look at **screech** ▶ **shriek** *noun* [C]

shrill /ʃrɪl/ *adj* (**shriller**; **shrillest**) (used about a sound) high and unpleasant: *a shrill cry*

shrimp /ʃrɪmp/ *noun* [C] **1** a small sea creature with a shell and a lot of legs that turns pink when you cook it. **Shrimps** are smaller than **prawns**. **2** (*AmE*) = **prawn**

shrine /ʃraɪn/ *noun* [C] a place that is important to a particular person or group of people for religious reasons or because it is connected with a special person

shrink

'Oh no! My T-shirt has shrunk!'

shrink /ʃrɪŋk/ *verb* (*pt* **shrank** /ʃræŋk/ *or* **shrunk** /ʃrʌŋk/; *pp* **shrunk**) **1** [I,T] to become smaller or make sth smaller: *My T-shirt shrank in the wash.* ◆ (*figurative*) *TV has shrunk the world.* ◆ *The rate of*

inflation has shrunk to 4%. **2** [I] to move back because you are frightened or shocked: *We shrank back against the wall when the dog appeared.*
PHR V **shrink from sth/doing sth** to not want to do sth because you find it unpleasant

shrivel /ˈʃrɪvl/ *verb* [I,T] (**shrivelling**; **shrivelled**, (*AmE*) **shriveling**; **shriveled**) **shrivel (sth) (up)** to become or make sth become smaller, especially because of dry conditions: *The plants shrivelled up and died in the hot weather.*

shroud[1] /ʃraʊd/ *noun* [C] a cloth or sheet that is put round a dead body before it is buried

shroud[2] /ʃraʊd/ *verb* [T, usually passive] **shroud sth (in sth)** to cover or hide sth

Shrove Tuesday /ˌʃrəʊv ˈtjuːzdeɪ; -di/ *noun* [C] the day before **Lent** (= a period of 40 days during which some Christians do not eat certain foods) ➲ look at **Pancake Day**

CULTURE

In some countries people celebrate the period before Shrove Tuesday as **carnival**. In Britain many people eat **pancakes** (= very thin round cakes made of flour, milk and eggs) on this day.

shrub /ʃrʌb/ *noun* [C] a small bush

shrubbery /ˈʃrʌbəri/ *noun* [C] (*pl* **shrubberies**) an area where a lot of small bushes have been planted

shrug /ʃrʌg/ *verb* [I,T] (**shrugging**; **shrugged**) to lift your shoulders as a way of showing that you do not know sth or are not interested: *'Who knows?' she said and shrugged.* ♦ *'It doesn't matter to me,' he said, **shrugging his shoulders**.*

shrug

PHR V **shrug sth off** to not allow sth to affect you in a bad way: *An actor has to learn to shrug off criticism.*
▶ **shrug** *noun* [C, usually sing]: *I asked him if he was sorry and he just answered with a shrug.*

shrunk *past tense, past participle of* **shrink**

shrunken /ˈʃrʌŋkən/ *adj* that has become smaller (and less attractive)

shudder /ˈʃʌdə(r)/ *verb* [I] to suddenly shake hard, especially because of an unpleasant feeling or thought: *Just thinking about the accident makes me shudder.* ♦ *The engine shuddered violently and then stopped.* ▶ **shudder** *noun* [C]

shuffle[1] /ˈʃʌfl/ *verb* **1** [I] to walk by sliding your feet along instead of lifting them off the ground: *The child shuffled past, wearing her mother's shoes.* **2** [I, T] to move your body or feet around because you are uncomfortable or nervous: *The audience were so bored that they began to shuffle in their seats.* **3** [I,T] to mix a pack of playing cards before a game: *It's your turn to shuffle.* ♦ *She shuffled the cards carefully.*

shuffle[2] /ˈʃʌfl/ *noun* [C, usually sing] **1** a way of walking without lifting your feet off the ground **2** an act of **shuffling** cards

shun /ʃʌn/ *verb* [T] (**shunning**; **shunned**) to avoid sb/sth; to keep away from sb/sth: *She was shunned by her family when she married him.*

shunt /ʃʌnt/ *verb* [T] **1** to push a train from one track to another **2** to move sb/sth to a different place, especially a less important one: *John was shunted sideways to a job in sales.*

🔑 **shut**[1] /ʃʌt/ *verb* (**shutting**; *pt, pp* **shut**) **1** [I,T] to make sth close; to become closed: *Could you shut the door, please?* ♦ *I can't shut my suitcase.* ♦ *Shut your books, please.* ♦ *He shut his eyes and tried to go to sleep.* ♦ *This window won't shut properly.* ♦ *The doors open and shut automatically.* **2** [I,T] (*BrE*) (used about a shop, restaurant, etc.) to stop doing business for the day; to close: *What time do the shops shut on Saturday?*
PHR V **shut sb/sth away** to keep sb/sth in a place where people cannot find or see them or it
shut (sth) down (used about a factory, etc.) to close, or close sth, for a long time or for ever: *Financial problems forced the business to shut down.*
shut sb/yourself in (sth) to put sb in a room and keep them there; to go to a room and stay there: *She shut herself in her room and refused to come out.*
shut sth in sth to trap sth by closing a door, lid, etc. on it: *Tony shut his fingers in the door of the car.*
shut sb/sth/yourself off (from sth) to keep sb/sth/yourself apart from sth: *He shuts himself off from the rest of the world.*
shut sb/sth out to stop yourself from having particular feelings: *He tried to shut out all thoughts of the accident.*
shut (sb) up (*informal*) to stop or make sb stop talking: *I wish you'd shut up!* ♦ *Nothing can shut him up once he's started.*
shut sb/sth up (in sth) to put sb/sth somewhere and stop them leaving: *He was shut up in prison for nearly ten years.*

🔑 **shut**[2] /ʃʌt/ *adj* [not before a noun] **1** in a closed position: *Make sure the door is shut properly before you leave.*

HELP **Shut** or **closed**? We can use **closed** before a noun: *a closed door*, but not **shut**.

2 (*BrE*) not open to the public: *The restaurant was shut so we went to one round the corner.*
IDM **keep your mouth shut** ➲ **mouth**[1]

shutter /ˈʃʌtə(r)/ *noun* [C] **1** a wooden or metal cover that is fixed outside a window and that can be opened or shut. A shop's **shutter** usually slides down from the top of the shop window. ➲ picture at **curtain** **2** the part at the front of a camera that opens for a very short time to let light in so that a photograph can be taken

shuttle /ˈʃʌtl/ *noun* [C] a plane, bus or train that travels regularly between two places

shuttlecock /ˈʃʌtlkɒk/ *noun* [C] (in the sport of **badminton**) the small, light object that is hit over the net ➲ picture at **badminton**

S

🔑 **shy**[1] /ʃaɪ/ *adj* (**shyer; shyest**) **1** nervous and uncomfortable about meeting and speaking to people; showing that sb feels like this: *She's very shy with strangers.* ◆ *a shy smile* **2** [not before a noun] **shy (of/about sth/doing sth)** frightened to do sth or to become involved in sth: *She's not shy of telling people what she thinks.* ▶ **shyly** *adv* ▶ **shyness** *noun* [U]: *He didn't overcome his shyness till he had left school.*

shy[2] /ʃaɪ/ *verb* [I] (**shying; shies;** *pt, pp* **shied**) (used about a horse) to suddenly move back or sideways in fear
PHR V **shy away from sth/from doing sth** to avoid doing sth because you are afraid

sibling /ˈsɪblɪŋ/ *noun* [C] (*formal*) a brother or a sister

> **HELP** In everyday language we use **brother(s)** and **sister(s)**: *Have you got any brothers and sisters?*

🔑 **sick**[1] /sɪk/ *adj*
➤ILL **1** not well: *a sick child* ◆ *Do you get paid for days when you're* **off sick** (= away from work)? ◆ *You're too ill to work today—you should* **phone in sick**.

> **HELP** Note that **be sick** in British English usually means 'to bring up food from the stomach; vomit'.

2 the sick *noun* [pl] people who are ill: *All the sick and wounded were evacuated.*
➤WANTING TO VOMIT **3** feeling ill in your stomach so that you may **vomit** (= bring up food from the stomach): *I feel sick—I think it was that fish I ate.* ◆ *Don't eat any more or you'll make yourself sick.* ➲ look at **airsick, carsick, nausea, seasick, travel-sick**
➤BORED/ANGRY **4 sick of sb/sth** (*informal*) feeling bored or annoyed because you have had too much of sb/sth: *I'm sick of my job.* ◆ *I'm sick of tidying up your mess!* **5 sick (at/about sth)** very annoyed or disgusted by sth: *He felt sick at the sight of so much waste.*
➤CRUEL **6** (*informal*) mentioning disease, suffering, death, etc. in a cruel or disgusting way: *He offended everyone with a sick joke about blind people.*
IDM **be sick** (*BrE*) to bring up food from the stomach: *It's common for women to be sick in the first months of pregnancy.* **SYN** **vomit**
make sb sick to make sb very angry: *Oh, stop complaining. You make me sick!*
sick to death of sb/sth feeling tired of or annoyed by sb/sth: *I'm sick to death of his grumbling.*

sick[2] /sɪk/ *noun* [U] (*BrE informal*) food that sb has brought up from their stomach: *There was sick all over the car seat.* **SYN** **vomit**

sicken /ˈsɪkən/ *verb* [T] to make sb feel disgusted: *The level of violence in the film sickens me.* ▶ **sickening** *adj*: *His head made a sickening sound as it hit the road.*

sickle /ˈsɪkl/ *noun* [C] a tool with a curved blade and a short handle, used for cutting grass, etc.

ˈ**sick leave** *noun* [U] a period spent away from work, etc. because of illness: *Mike's been off* **on sick leave** *since March.*

sickly /ˈsɪkli/ *adj* (**sicklier; sickliest**) **1** (used about a person) weak and often ill: *a sickly child* **2** unpleasant; causing you to feel ill: *the sickly smell of rotten fruit*

sickness /ˈsɪknəs/ *noun* **1** [U] the state of being ill: *A lot of workers are absent because of sickness.* **2** [C, U] a particular type of illness: *pills for seasickness* ◆ *Sleeping sickness is carried by the tsetse fly.* **3** [U] (*BrE*) a feeling in your stomach that may make you bring up food through your mouth: *Symptoms of the disease include sickness and diarrhoea.*

🔑 **side**[1] /saɪd/ *noun* [C]
➤LEFT/RIGHT **1** the area to the left or right of sth; the area in front of or behind sth: *We live (on)* **the other side** *of the main road.* ◆ *It's more expensive to live on the north side of town.* ◆ *In Japan they drive on* **the left-hand side** *of the road.* ◆ *She sat at the side of his bed/at his bedside.*
➤NOT TOP OR BOTTOM **2** one of the surfaces of sth except the top, bottom, front or back: *I went round to the side of the building.* ◆ *The side of the car was damaged.*
➤EDGE **3** the edge of sth, away from the middle: *Make sure you stay* **at the side** *of the road when you're cycling.* ◆ *We moved* **to one side** *to let the doctor get past.*
➤OF BODY **4** the right or the left part of your body, especially from under your arm to the top of your leg: *She lay on her side.* ◆ *The soldier stood with his hands by his sides.*
➤NEAR TO SB/STH **5** a place or position very near to sb/sth: *Her mother stood at her side.*
➤OF STH FLAT/THIN **6** either of the two flat surfaces of sth thin: *Write on both sides of the paper.*
➤SURFACE **7** one of the flat outer surfaces of sth: *A cube has six sides.*
➤-SIDED **8 -sided** [in compounds] having the number of sides mentioned: *a six-sided coin*
➤IN FIGHT/COMPETITION **9** either of two or more people or groups who are fighting, playing, arguing, etc. against each other: *The two sides agreed to stop fighting.* ◆ *the winning/losing side* ◆ *Whose side are you on?* (= Who do you want to win?)
➤OF STORY **10** what is said by one person or group that is different from what is said by another: *I don't know whose* **side of the story** *to believe.*
➤OF FAMILY **11** your mother's or your father's family: *There is no history of illness* **on** *his mother's* **side**.
IDM **err on the side of sth** ➲ **err**
get on the right/wrong side of sb to please/annoy sb: *He tried to get on the right side of his new boss.*
look on the bright side ➲ **look**[1]
on/from all sides; on/from every side in/from all directions
on the big, small, high, etc. side (*informal*) slightly too big, small, high, etc.
on the safe side ➲ **safe**[1]
put sth on/to one side; leave sth on one side to

S

leave or keep sth so that you can use it or deal with it later: *You should put some money to one side for the future.*

side by side next to each other; close together: *They walked side by side along the road.*

take sides (with sb) to show that you support one person rather than another in an argument: *Parents should never take sides when their children are quarrelling.*

side² /saɪd/ *verb*

PHR V side with sb (against sb) to support sb in an argument

sideboard /ˈsaɪdbɔːd/ *noun* [C] a type of low cupboard about as high as a table, that is used for storing plates, etc. in a **dining room** (= a room that is used for eating in) ➲ picture on **page P8**

sideburns /ˈsaɪdbɜːnz/ *noun* [pl] hair that grows down a man's face in front of his ears

ˈ**side dish** *noun* [C] a small amount of food, for example a salad, served with the main course of a meal: *a side dish of vegetables*

ˈ**side effect** *noun* [C] **1** an unpleasant effect that a drug may have in addition to its useful effects: *Side effects of the drug include nausea and dizziness.* **2** an unexpected effect of sth that happens in addition to the intended effect: *One of the side effects when the chemical factory closed was that fish returned to the river.*

sideline /ˈsaɪdlaɪn/ *noun* **1** [C] something that you do in addition to your regular job, especially to earn extra money: *He's an engineer, but he repairs cars* ***as a sideline.*** **2 sidelines** [pl] the lines that mark the two long sides of the area used for playing sports such as football, **tennis**, etc.; the area behind this

IDM on the sidelines not involved in an activity; not taking part in sth

sidelong /ˈsaɪdlɒŋ/ *adj* [only *before* a noun] directed from the side; sideways: *a sidelong glance*

ˈ**side order** *noun* [C] a small amount of food ordered in a restaurant to go with the main dish, but served separately: *a side order of chips* ➲ look at **side dish**

ˈ**side road** *noun* [C] a small road which joins a bigger main road

ˈ**side street** *noun* [C] a narrow or less important street near a main street

sidetrack /ˈsaɪdtræk/ *verb* [T] **sidetrack sb (into doing sth)** [usually passive] to make sb forget what they are doing or talking about and start doing or talking about sth less important

sidewalk /ˈsaɪdwɔːk/ (*AmE*) = **pavement**

🔑 **sideways** /ˈsaɪdweɪz/ *adv, adj* **1** to, towards or from one side: *He jumped sideways to avoid being hit.* ◆ *She gave him a sideways look.* **2** with one of the sides at the top: *We'll have to turn the sofa sideways to get it through the door.*

siding /ˈsaɪdɪŋ/ *noun* [C] **1** a short track beside a main railway line, where trains can stand when they are not being used **2** (*AmE*) material used to cover and protect the outside walls of buildings

sidle /ˈsaɪdl/ *verb* [I] **sidle up/over (to sb/sth)** to move towards sb/sth in a nervous way, as if you do not want anyone to notice you

siege /siːdʒ/ *noun* [C,U] a situation in which an army surrounds a town for a long time or the police surround a building so that nobody can get in or out

siesta /siˈestə/ *noun* [C] a short sleep or rest that people take in the afternoon, especially in hot countries: *to have/take a siesta*

sieve /sɪv/ *noun* [C] a type of kitchen tool that has a metal or plastic net, used for separating solids from liquids or very small pieces of food from large pieces: *Pour the soup through a sieve to get rid of any lumps.* ➲ picture at **kitchen** ▶ **sieve** *verb* [T]: *to sieve flour*

sift /sɪft/ *verb* **1** [T] to pass flour, sugar or a similar substance through a **sieve** in order to remove any lumps: *to sift flour/sugar* **2** [I,T] **sift (through) sth** to examine sth very carefully: *It took weeks to sift through all the evidence.*

sigh /saɪ/ *verb* **1** [I] to let out a long, deep breath that shows you are tired, sad, disappointed, etc: *She sighed with disappointment at the news.* **2** [T] to say sth with a **sigh**: *'I'm so tired,' he sighed.* **3** [I] to make a long sound like a **sigh** ▶ **sigh** *noun* [C]

IDM heave a sigh ➲ **heave¹**

🔑 **sight¹** /saɪt/ *noun*

➤ABILITY TO SEE **1** [U] the ability to see: *He lost his sight in the war* (= he became blind). ◆ *My grandmother has very poor sight.*

➤ACT OF SEEING **2** [sing] **the sight of sb/sth** the act of seeing sb/sth: *I feel ill* ***at the sight of*** *blood.*

➤HOW FAR YOU CAN SEE **3** [U] a position where sb/sth can be seen: *They waited until the plane was* ***in/within sight*** *and then fired.* ◆ *When we get over this hill the town should* ***come into sight.*** ◆ *She didn't let the child* ***out of*** *her* ***sight.***

➤WHAT YOU CAN SEE **4** [C] something that you see: *The burned-out building was a terrible sight.*

➤INTERESTING PLACES **5 sights** [pl] places of interest that are often visited by tourists: *When you come to New York I'll show you the sights.*

➤PERSON/THING **6 a sight** [sing] (*informal*) a person or thing that looks strange or amusing: *You should have seen Anna in my jacket—she did look a sight!*

➤ON GUN **7** [C,usually pl] the part of a gun that you look through in order to aim it: *He had the deer in his sights now.*

➤-SIGHTED **8** [in compounds] having eyes that are weak in a particular way ➲ look at **long-sighted, short-sighted**

IDM at first glance/sight ➲ **first¹**

catch sight of sb/sth ➲ **catch¹**

in sight likely to happen or come soon: *A peace settlement is in sight.*

lose sight of sb/sth ➲ **lose**

on sight as soon as you see sb/sth: *The soldiers were ordered to shoot the enemy on sight.*

sight² /saɪt/ *verb* [T] (*formal*) to see sb/sth, especially after looking out for them or it

S

sighting /ˈsaɪtɪŋ/ *noun* [C] an occasion when sb/sth is seen: *the first sighting of a new star*

sightseeing /ˈsaɪtsiːɪŋ/ *noun* [U] visiting the sights of a city, etc. as a tourist: *We did some sightseeing in Rome.* ➲ note at **holiday**

sightseer /ˈsaɪtsiːə(r)/ *noun* [C] a person who visits the sights of a city, etc. as a tourist ➲ look at **tourist**

⚷ **sign**[1] /saɪn/ *noun* [C]

➤SHOWING STH **1 sign (of sth)** something that shows that sb/sth is present, exists or may happen: *The patient was* ***showing*** *some* ***signs*** *of improvement.* ◆ *As we drove into the village there wasn't a sign of life anywhere* (= we couldn't see anyone).

➤FOR INFORMATION/WARNING **2** a piece of wood, paper, metal, etc. that has writing or a picture on it that gives you a piece of information, an instruction or a warning: *What does that sign say?* ◆ *a road sign* ◆ *Follow the signs to Banbury.* ➲ picture at **roundabout**

➤MOVEMENT **3** a movement that you make with your head, hands or arms that has a particular meaning: *I* ***made a sign*** *for him to follow me.* ◆ *I'll* ***give you a sign*** *when it's time for you to speak.*

➤SYMBOL **4** a type of shape, mark or symbol that has a particular meaning: *In mathematics, a cross is a plus sign.*

➤STAR SIGN **5 = star sign**

⚷ **sign**[2] /saɪn/ *verb* **1** [I,T] to write your name on a letter, document, etc. to show that you have written it or that you agree with what it says: *'Could you sign here, please?'* ◆ *I forgot to sign the cheque.* ◆ *The two presidents signed the treaty.* ➲ *noun* **signature 2** [I,T] **sign (sb) (up)** to get sb to sign a contract to work for you: *Real Madrid have signed two new players.* **3** [I] to communicate using sign language: *Dave's deaf friend taught him to sign.*

PHR V **sign in/out** to write your name to show you have arrived at or left a hotel, club, etc.

sign up (for sth) to agree formally to do sth: *I've signed up for evening classes.*

⚷ **signal** /ˈsɪɡnəl/ *noun* [C] **1** a sign, an action or a sound that sends a particular message: *When I give (you) the signal, run!* **2** an event, an action or a fact that shows that sth exists or is likely to happen: *The fall in unemployment is a clear signal that the economy is improving.* **3** a set of lights used to give information to drivers: *a stop signal* **4** a series of radio waves, etc. that are sent out or received: *a signal from a satellite* ◆ *I can't get a signal on my mobile phone here.* ▶ **signal** *verb* [I,T] (**signalling; signalled**, (*AmE*) **signaling; signaled**): *She was signalling wildly that something was wrong.*

signatory /ˈsɪɡnətri/ *noun* [C] (*pl* **signatories**) **signatory (to sth)** one of the people or countries that sign an agreement, etc.

⚷ **signature** /ˈsɪɡnətʃə(r)/ *noun* [C] a person's name, written by that person and always written in the same way: *I couldn't read his signature.* ➲ *verb* **sign**

significance /sɪɡˈnɪfɪkəns/ *noun* [U] the importance or meaning of sth: *Few people realized the significance of the discovery.*

⚷ **significant** /sɪɡˈnɪfɪkənt/ *adj* **1** important or large enough to be noticed or to have an effect: *There has been a significant improvement in your work.* **2** having a particular meaning: *It could be significant that he took out life insurance shortly before he died.* ◆ *Police said that the time of the murder was extremely significant.* ▶ **significantly** *adv*: *Attitudes have changed significantly since the 1980s.*

signify /ˈsɪɡnɪfaɪ/ *verb* [T] (**signifying; signifies**; *pt, pp* **signified**) (*formal*) **1** to be a sign of sth: *What do those lights signify?* SYN **mean 2** to express or indicate sth: *They signified their agreement by raising their hands.*

ˈsign language *noun* [U] a language used especially by people who cannot hear or speak, using their hands to make signs instead of using spoken words

signpost /ˈsaɪnpəʊst/ *noun* [C] a sign at the side of a road that gives information about directions and distances to towns ➲ picture at **roundabout** ➲ picture on **page P11**

Sikh /siːk/ *noun* [C] a member of a religion called **Sikhism** (= a religion that developed from Hinduism in India, but that teaches that there is only one god)

⚷ **silence** /ˈsaɪləns/ *noun* **1** [U] no noise or sound at all: *There must be silence during examinations.* SYN **quiet 2** [C,U] a period when nobody speaks or makes a noise: *My question was met with an awkward silence.* ◆ *We ate* ***in silence****.* **3** [U] not making any comments about sth: *I can't understand his silence on the matter.* ▶ **silence** *verb* [T]

silencer /ˈsaɪlənsə(r)/ *noun* [C] **1** (*AmE* **muffler**) a device which is fixed to the **exhaust pipe** (= the long tube under a vehicle) to reduce the noise made by the engine **2** a device which is fixed to a gun to reduce the noise that it makes when it is fired

⚷ **silent** /ˈsaɪlənt/ *adj* **1** where there is no noise; making no noise: *The house was empty and silent.* SYN **quiet 2** [only *before* a noun] not using spoken words: *a silent prayer/protest* **3 silent (on/about sth)** refusing to speak about sth: *The policeman told her she had the right to* ***remain silent****.* **4** (used about a letter) not pronounced: *The 'b' in 'comb' is silent.* ▶ **silently** *adv*: *She crept silently away.*

silhouette /ˌsɪluˈet/ *noun* [C] the dark solid shape of sb/sth seen against a light background ▶ **silhouetted** *adj*

silicon /ˈsɪlɪkən/ *noun* [U] (*symbol* Si) a chemical element that exists as a grey solid or a brown powder, and is found in rocks and sand. It is used in making glass and electronic equipment.

ˌsilicon ˈchip *noun* [C] a piece of **silicon** that is used in computers, etc.

⚷ **silk** /sɪlk/ *noun* [U] the soft smooth cloth that is made from threads produced by a **silkworm** (= a very small creature): *a silk shirt/dress*

silky /ˈsɪlki/ *adj* (**silkier; silkiest**) smooth, soft and shiny; like silk: *silky hair*

S

sill /sɪl/ *noun* [C] a shelf that is at the bottom of a window, either inside or outside: *a windowsill* ➲ picture on **page P8**

⚷ **silly** /ˈsɪli/ *adj* (**sillier**; **silliest**) **1** not showing thought or understanding; stupid: *a silly mistake* ◆ *Don't be so silly!* SYN **foolish** OPP **sensible** **2** appearing ridiculous, so that people will laugh: *I'm not wearing that hat—I'd look silly in it.* ▶ **silliness** *noun* [U]

silt /sɪlt/ *noun* [U] sand, soil or mud that collects at the sides or on the bottom of a river

⚷ **silver¹** /ˈsɪlvə(r)/ *noun* [U] **1** (*symbol* Ag) a valuable greyish-white metal that is used for making jewellery, coins, etc: *a silver spoon/necklace* ◆ *That's a nice ring. Is it silver?* **2** [U] coins made from silver or sth that looks like silver: *I need £2 in silver for the parking meter.* **3** [U] objects that are made of silver, for example knives, forks, spoons and dishes: *The thieves stole some jewellery and some valuable silver.* **4** [C] = **silver medal**

IDM **every cloud has a silver lining** ➲ **cloud¹**

⚷ **silver²** /ˈsɪlvə(r)/ *adj* **1** having the colour of silver: *a silver sports car* **2** celebrating the 25th anniversary of sth: *the silver jubilee of the Queen's accession in 1977* ➲ look at **diamond, golden**

ˌsilver ˈmedal (also **silver**) *noun* [C] a small flat round piece of silver that is given to the person or team that comes second in a sports competition: *to win a silver medal at the Olympic Games* ➲ look at **bronze medal, gold medal** ▶ **ˌsilver ˈmedallist** *noun* [C]

silverware /ˈsɪlvəweə(r)/ *noun* [U] **1** objects that are made of or covered with silver, especially knives, forks, dishes, etc. that are used for eating and serving food: *a piece of silverware* **2** (*AmE*) = **cutlery**

S

silvery /ˈsɪlvəri/ *adj* having the appearance or colour of silver: *an old lady with silvery hair*

SIM card /ˈsɪm kɑːd/ *noun* [C] a plastic card inside a mobile phone that stores phone numbers, etc.

⚷ **similar** /ˈsɪmələ(r)/ *adj* **similar (to sb/sth)**; **similar (in sth)** like sb/sth but not exactly the same: *Our houses are very similar in size.* ◆ *My teaching style is similar to that of many other teachers.* OPP **different, dissimilar** ▶ **similarly** *adv*: *The plural of 'shelf' is 'shelves'. Similarly, the plural of 'wolf' is 'wolves'.*

similarity /ˌsɪməˈlærəti/ *noun* (*pl* **similarities**) **1** [U, sing] **similarity (to sb/sth)**; **similarity (in sth)** the state of being like sb/sth but not exactly the same: *She **bears a** remarkable/striking **similarity** to her mother.* **2** [C] **a similarity (between A and B)**; **a similarity (in/of sth)** a characteristic that people or things have which makes them similar: *Although there are some similarities between the two towns, there are a lot of differences too.* ◆ *similarities in/of style* OPP **difference**

WRITING TIP

How to compare similar things

To say that two people, things, etc. are equal or identical in some way, use **as + adjective/adverb + as**: *John is as tall as Sarah* or: *Sarah is as tall as John* (= they are both the same height): *Jim ran as fast as Frank* or: *Frank ran as fast as Jim* (= they both ran at the same speed).

You can also compare two people or things using **Both X and Y ..., Like X, Y ...** or **X, like Y, ...**: *Both Jane and Fred play football for the school team.* ◆ *Like his father, Joe is very intelligent.* ◆ *Oxford, like Bologna, is an ancient university town.* ➲ note at **difference**

ⓘ For more help with writing, look at **Wordpower Writing Tutor** at the back of this dictionary.

simile /ˈsɪməli/ *noun* [C,U] a word or phrase that compares sth to sth else, using the words 'like' or 'as'; the use of such words and phrases. For example, 'a face like a mask' and 'as white as snow' are similes. ➲ look at **metaphor**

simmer /ˈsɪmə(r)/ *verb* [I,T] to cook sth gently in a liquid that is almost boiling

⚷ **simple** /ˈsɪmpl/ *adj* (**simpler**; **simplest**) [You can also use **more simple** and **most simple**.] **1** easy to understand, do or use; not difficult or complicated: *This dictionary is written in simple English.* ◆ *a simple task/method/solution* ◆ *I can't just leave the job. It's not as simple as that.* SYN **easy** **2** without decoration or unnecessary extra things: *a simple black dress* ◆ *The food is simple but perfectly cooked.* SYN **basic** OPP **fancy** **3** used for saying that the thing you are talking about is the only thing that is important or true: *I'm not going to buy it **for the simple reason that*** (= only because) *I haven't got enough money.* **4** (used about a person or a way of life) natural and not complicated: *a simple life in the country* **5** (*old-fashioned*) not intelligent; slow to understand

simplicity /sɪmˈplɪsəti/ *noun* [U] **1** the quality of being easy to understand, do or use: *We all admired the simplicity of the plan.* **2** the quality of having no decoration or unnecessary extra things; being natural and not complicated: *I like the simplicity of her paintings.*

simplify /ˈsɪmplɪfaɪ/ *verb* [T] (**simplifying**; **simplifies**; *pt, pp* **simplified**) to make sth easier to do or understand; to make sth less complicated: *The process of applying for visas has been simplified.* ▶ **simplification** /ˌsɪmplɪfɪˈkeɪʃn/ *noun* [C,U]

simplistic /sɪmˈplɪstɪk/ *adj* (disapproving) making a problem, situation, etc. seem less difficult and complicated than it really is

⚷ **simply** /ˈsɪmpli/ *adv* **1** used to emphasize how easy or basic sth is: *Simply add hot water and stir.* **2** (used to emphasize an adjective) completely: *That meal was simply excellent.* SYN **absolutely** **3** in a way that makes sth easy to understand: *Could you explain it more simply?* **4** in a simple, basic way; without decoration or unnecessary extra things: *They live simply, with very few luxuries.* **5** only:

There's no need to get angry. The whole problem is simply a misunderstanding. SYN **just**

simulate /ˈsɪmjuleɪt/ *verb* [T] to create certain conditions that exist in real life using computers, models, etc., usually for study or training purposes: *The astronauts trained in a machine that simulates conditions in space.* ▶ **simulation** /ˌsɪmjuˈleɪʃn/ *noun* [C,U]: *a computer simulation of a nuclear attack*

simultaneous /ˌsɪmlˈteɪniəs/ *adj* happening or done at exactly the same time as sth else ▶ **simultaneously** *adv*

sin /sɪn/ *noun* [C,U] an action or way of behaving that is not allowed by a religion: *He believes it is a sin for two people to live together without being married.* ▶ **sin** *verb* [I] (**sinning**; **sinned**) ▶ **sinner** *noun* [C]

since /sɪns/ *adv, conj, prep* **1** from a particular time in the past until a later time in the past or until now: *My parents bought this house in 1985 and we've been living here ever since.* ◆ *I've been working in a bank ever since I left school.* ◆ *It was the first time they'd won since 1998.* ◆ *I haven't seen him since last Tuesday.* ◆ *She has had a number of jobs since leaving university.*

> **GRAMMAR** We use both **since** and **for** to talk about how long something has been happening. We use **since** when we are talking about the *beginning* of the period of time, and **for** when we are talking about the *length* of the period of time: *I've known her since 2009.* ◆ *I've known him for three years.*

2 because; as: *Since they've obviously forgotten to phone me, I'll have to phone them.* **3** at a time after a particular time in the past: *We were divorced two years ago and she has since married someone else.*

sincere /sɪnˈsɪə(r)/ *adj* (**sincerest**) [no comparative] **1** (used about sb's feelings, beliefs or behaviour) true; showing what you really mean or feel: *Please accept our sincere thanks/apologies.* SYN **genuine** **2** (used about a person) really meaning or believing what you say; not pretending: *Do you think she was being sincere when she said she admired me?* SYN **honest** OPP for both meanings **insincere** ▶ **sincerely** *adv*: *I am sincerely grateful to you for all your help.* ◆ *Yours sincerely, ...* (= at the end of a formal letter) ➲ note at **dear**

> WRITING TIP
>
> **How to end a letter**
>
> Use **Yours sincerely** at the end of a letter, if you know the name of the person you are writing to. If you do not know their name, use **Yours faithfully**. Use **Sincerely, Sincerely yours** or **Yours truly** in American English.

ℹ For more help with writing, look at **Wordpower Writing Tutor** at the back of this dictionary. ▶ **sincerity** /sɪnˈserəti/ *noun* [U] OPP **insincerity**

sinful /ˈsɪnfl/ *adj* breaking a religious law; immoral

sing /sɪŋ/ *verb* [I,T] (*pt* **sang** /sæŋ/; *pp* **sung** /sʌŋ/) to make musical sounds with your voice: *He always sings when he's in the bath.* ◆ *The birds were singing outside my window.* ◆ *She sang all her most popular songs at the concert.* ▶ **singing** *noun* [U]: *singing lessons*

singe /sɪndʒ/ *verb* [I,T] (**singeing**) to burn the surface of sth slightly, usually by accident; to be burned in this way

singer /ˈsɪŋə(r)/ *noun* [C] a person who sings, or whose job is singing, especially in public: *an opera singer*

single[1] /ˈsɪŋgl/ *adj*

➤ONE **1** [only *before* a noun] only one: *He gave her a single red rose.* ◆ *I managed to finish the whole job in a single afternoon.* ◆ *I went to a* **single-sex school** (= for boys only or girls only).

➤FOR EMPHASIS **2** [only *before* a noun] used to emphasize that you are talking about each individual item in a group or series: *You answered* ***every single*** *question correctly. Well done!*

➤NOT MARRIED **3** not married or in a relationship: *Are you married or single?* ◆ *a single man/woman*

➤FOR ONE PERSON **4** [only *before* a noun] for the use of only one person: *I'd like to book a single room, please.* ➲ note at **bed**[1] ➲ picture at **bed**

➤TICKET **5** (*AmE* ˌ**one-ˈway**) [only *before* a noun] (used about a ticket or the price of a ticket) for a journey to a particular place, but not back again: *How much is the single fare to York?* ➲ look at **return**

IDM **in single file** in a line, one behind the other

single[2] /ˈsɪŋgl/ *noun*

➤TICKET **1** [C] a ticket for a journey to a particular place, but not back again: *Two singles to Hull, please.* ➲ look at **return**

➤CD **2** [C] a piece of recorded music, usually popular music, that consists of one song; a CD that a **single** is recorded on: *Adele's new single* ➲ look at **album**

➤ROOM **3** [C] a bedroom for one person in a hotel, etc. ➲ look at **double**

➤UNMARRIED PEOPLE **4 singles** [pl] people who are not married and do not have a romantic relationship with sb else

➤IN SPORT **5 singles** [pl] (in sports such as **tennis**) a game in which one player plays against one other player ➲ look at **double**

single[3] /ˈsɪŋgl/ *verb*

PHR V **single sb/sth out (for sth)** to give special attention or treatment to one person or thing from a group: *She was singled out for criticism.*

ˌ**single-ˈhanded** *adj, adv* on your own with nobody helping you

ˌ**single-ˈminded** *adj* having one clear aim or goal which you are determined to achieve ▶ **single-ˈmindedness** *noun* [U]

ˌ**single ˈparent** *noun* [C] a person who looks after their child or children without a husband, wife or partner: *a single-parent family*

singly /ˈsɪŋgli/ *adv* one at a time; alone: *You can buy the pens either singly or in packs of three.* SYN **individually**

singular /ˈsɪŋgjələ(r)/ *adj* **1** in the form that is used for talking about one person or thing only: *'Table' is a singular noun; 'tables' is its plural.* ➲ look

S

at **plural** **2** (*written*) unusual ▶ **singular** *noun* [sing]: *The word 'clothes' has no singular.* ◆ *What's the singular of 'people'?*

singularly /ˈsɪŋgjələli/ *adv* (*formal*) very; in an unusual way: *He chose a singularly inappropriate moment to make his request.* ◆ *singularly beautiful*

sinister /ˈsɪnɪstə(r)/ *adj* seeming evil or dangerous; making you feel that sth bad will happen: *There's something sinister about him. He frightens me.*

⚷ **sink**[1] /sɪŋk/ *verb* (*pt* **sank** /sæŋk/; *pp* **sunk** /sʌŋk/) **1** [I,T] to go down or make sth go down under the surface of liquid or a soft substance: *If you throw a stone into water, it sinks.* ◆ *The boat sank to the bottom of the sea.* ◆ *My feet sank into the mud.* ➲ picture at **float** **2** [I] (used about a person) to move downwards, usually by falling or sitting down: *I came home and sank into a chair, exhausted.* **3** [I] to get lower; to fall to a lower position or level: *We watched the sun sink slowly below the horizon.* **4** [I] to decrease in value, number, amount, strength, etc.

IDM **your heart sinks** ➲ **heart**

PHR V **sink in** (used about information, an event, an experience, etc.) to be completely understood or realized: *It took a long time for the terrible news to sink in.*

sink in; **sink into sth** (used about a liquid) to go into sth solid; to be absorbed

sink[2] /sɪŋk/ *noun* [C] a large open container in a kitchen or bathroom, with taps to supply water, where you wash things ➲ look at **washbasin** ➲ picture on **page P8**

sinus /ˈsaɪnəs/ *noun* [C, often plural] one of the spaces in the bones of your face that are connected to your nose: *I've got a terrible cold and my sinuses are blocked.* ◆ *a sinus infection*

sip /sɪp/ *verb* [I,T] (**sipping**; **sipped**) to drink, taking only a very small amount of liquid into your mouth at a time: *We sat in the sun, sipping lemonade.* ▶ **sip** *noun* [C]

siphon (also **syphon**) /ˈsaɪfn/ *verb* [T] **1** **siphon sth into/out of sth**; **siphon sth off/out** to remove a liquid from a container, often into another container, through a tube **2** **siphon sth off**; **siphon sth (from/out of sth)** to take money from a company illegally over a period of time

⚷ **sir** /sɜː(r)/ *noun* **1** [sing] used as a polite way of speaking to a man whose name you do not know, for example in a shop or restaurant, or to show respect: *I'm afraid we haven't got your size, sir.* ➲ look at **madam** **2** **Sir** [C] used at the beginning of a formal letter to a male person or male people: *Dear Sir ...* ◆ *Dear Sirs ...* ➲ look at **madam** **3** /sə(r)/ [sing] the title that is used in front of the name of a man who has received one of the highest British honours: *Sir Tom Jones*

siren /ˈsaɪrən/ *noun* [C] a device that makes a long, loud sound as a warning or signal: *an air-raid siren* ◆ *Three fire engines raced past, sirens wailing.*

⚷ **sister** /ˈsɪstə(r)/ *noun* [C] **1** a girl or woman who has the same parents as another person: *I've got one brother and two sisters.* ◆ *We're sisters.* ➲ look at **half-sister, stepsister**

> **HELP** **Siblings** means 'both brothers and sisters' but it is very formal, so we usually say: *Have you got any brothers and sisters?* ◆ *I haven't got any brothers or sisters.*

2 (*informal*) a woman who you feel close to because she is a member of the same society, group, etc. as you **3** *often* **Sister** (*BrE*) a female nurse who has responsibility for part of a hospital **4** **Sister** a **nun** (= a member of a religious group of women): *Sister Mary-Theresa* **5** [usually used as an adjective] a thing that belongs to the same type or group as sth else: *We have a sister company in Japan.*

ˈsister-in-law *noun* [C] (*pl* **sisters-in-law**) **1** the sister of your husband or wife **2** the wife of your brother

⚷ **sit** /sɪt/ *verb* (**sitting**; *pt, pp* **sat** /sæt/)

➤ON CHAIR, ETC. **1** [I] to rest your weight on your bottom, for example in a chair: *We sat in the garden all afternoon.* ◆ *She was sitting on the sofa, talking to her mother.* **2** [T] **sit sb (down)** to put sb into a sitting position; to make sb sit down: *He picked up his daughter and sat her down on a chair.* ◆ *She sat me down and offered me a cup of tea.*

➤OF THINGS **3** [I] to be in a particular place or position: *The letter sat on the table for several days before anybody opened it.*

➤PARLIAMENT, ETC. **4** [I] (*formal*) (used about an official group of people) to have a meeting or series of meetings: *Parliament was still sitting at 3 o'clock in the morning.*

➤EXAM **5** [T] (*BrE*) to take an exam: *If I fail, will I be able to sit the exam again?*

IDM **sit on the fence** to avoid saying which side of an argument you support

PHR V **sit about/around** (*informal*) to spend time doing nothing active or useful: *We just sat around chatting all afternoon.*

sit back to relax and not take an active part in what other people are doing: *Sit back and take it easy while I make dinner.*

sit down to lower your body into a sitting position: *He sat down in an armchair.*

sit sth out **1** to stay in a place and wait for sth unpleasant or boring to finish: *We sat out the storm in a cafe.* **2** to not take part in a dance, game, etc: *I think I'll sit this one out.*

sit through sth to stay in your seat until sth boring or long has finished

sit up **1** to move into a sitting position when you have been lying down, or to make your back straight: *Sit up straight and concentrate!* **2** to not go to bed although it is very late: *We sat up all night talking.*

sitcom /ˈsɪtkɒm/ (also *formal* ˌ**situation** ˈ**comedy**) *noun* [C,U] a funny programme on TV that shows the same characters in different amusing situations each week

⚷ **site** /saɪt/ *noun* [C] **1** a piece of land where a building was, is or will be: *a building/construction site* ◆ *The company is looking for a site for its new offices.* **2** a place where sth has happened or that is used for sth: *the site of a famous battle* **3** = **website** ▶ **site** *verb* [T] (*formal*): *The castle is magnificently sited on top of the mountain.*

sitting /ˈsɪtɪŋ/ *noun* [C] **1** a period of time during which a court of law or a parliament meets and does its work **2** a time when a meal is served in a school, hotel, etc. to a number of people at the same time: *Dinner will be in two sittings.*

ˈsitting room (*BrE*) = **living room**

situated /ˈsɪtʃueɪtɪd/ *adj* [not before a noun] in a particular place or position: *The hotel is conveniently situated close to the beach.*

situation /ˌsɪtʃuˈeɪʃn/ *noun* [C] **1** the things that are happening in a particular place or at a particular time: *The situation in the north of the country is extremely serious.* ◆ *Tim is* ***in a*** *difficult* ***situation*** *at the moment.* ◆ *the economic/financial/political situation* **2** (*formal*) the position of a building, town, etc. in relation to the area around it: *The house is in a beautiful situation on the edge of a lake.* **3** (*old-fashioned or formal*) a job: *Situations Vacant* (= the part of a newspaper where jobs are advertised)

ˌsituation ˈcomedy (*formal*) = **sitcom**

ˈsit-up *noun* [C] an exercise for the stomach muscles in which you lie on your back with your legs bent, then lift the top half of your body from the floor: *to* ***do sit-ups*** ➲ picture at **exercise**

six /sɪks/ *number* **1** 6 **2** **six-** [in compounds] having six of the thing mentioned: *She works a six-day week.*

HELP Note how numbers are used in sentences: *The answers are on page six.* ◆ *There are six of us for dinner tonight.* ◆ *Sally has six cats.* ◆ *My son is six (years old) next month.* ◆ *She lives at 6 Elm Drive.* ◆ *a birthday card with a big six on it*

ℹ For more information about numbers, look at the section on using numbers at the back of this dictionary.

sixteen /ˌsɪksˈtiːn/ *number* 16 ➲ note at **six** ▶ **sixteenth** /ˌsɪksˈtiːnθ/ *ordinal number, noun* ➲ note at **sixth**

sixth¹ /sɪksθ/ *ordinal number* 6th

HELP Note how ordinal numbers are used in sentences: *Today is March the sixth.* ◆ *My office is on the sixth floor.* ◆ *This is the sixth time I've tried to phone him.*

ℹ For more information about numbers, look at the section on using numbers at the back of this dictionary.

sixth² /sɪksθ/ *noun* [C] ⅙; one of six equal parts of sth

ˈsixth form *noun* [C, with sing or pl verb] (in Britain) the final two years at secondary school for students from the age of 16 to 18 who are studying for A level exams ▶ **ˈsixth-former** *noun* [C]

sixty /ˈsɪksti/ *number* **1** 60 ➲ note at **six**

HELP Note how numbers are used in sentences: *Sixty people went to the meeting.* ◆ *There are sixty pages in the book.* ◆ *He retired* ***at (the age of) sixty.***

2 the sixties [pl] the numbers, years or temperatures between 60 and 69; the 60s: *I don't know the exact number of members, but it's in the sixties.* ◆ *The most famous pop group of the sixties was The Beatles.* ◆ *The temperature tomorrow will be in the high sixties.*
IDM **in your sixties** between the age of 60 and 69: *I'm not sure how old she is but I should think she's in her sixties.* ◆ *in your* ***early/mid/late sixties***
▶ **sixtieth** /ˈsɪkstiəθ/ *ordinal number, noun* ➲ note at **sixth**

size¹ /saɪz/ *noun* **1** [C,U] how big or small sth is: *I was surprised at the size of the hotel. It was enormous!* ◆ *The planet Uranus is about four times the size of* (= as big as) *Earth.*

HELP When we ask about the size of something, we usually say, 'How big …?': *How big is your house?* We say, 'What size …?' when we ask about the size of something that is produced in a number of fixed measurements: ***What size*** *shoes* ***do you take?*** ◆ *What size are you?* (= when buying clothes)

2 [C] one of a number of fixed measurements in which sth is made: *Have you got this dress* ***in a*** *bigger* ***size?*** ◆ *I'm a size 12.* ◆ *What size pizza would you like? Medium or large?* **3** **-sized**; **-size** [in compounds] of the size mentioned: *a medium-sized flat* ◆ *a king-size bed*

size² /saɪz/ *verb*
PHR V **size sb/sth up** to form an opinion or a judgement about sb/sth

sizeable (also **sizable**) /ˈsaɪzəbl/ *adj* quite large: *a sizeable sum of money*

sizzle /ˈsɪzl/ *verb* [I] to make the sound of food frying in hot fat

skate¹ /skeɪt/ *verb* [I] **1** (also ˈ**ice-skate**) to move on ice wearing **skates**: *Can you skate?* ◆ *They skated across the frozen lake.*

HELP **Go skating** is a common way of talking about skating for pleasure.

2 = **roller skate** ▶ **skater** *noun* [C]

skates

ice skates

Rollerblades™

roller skates

skateboard

skate² /skeɪt/ *noun* [C] **1** (also ˈ**ice skate**) a boot with a thin sharp metal part on the bottom that is

S

used for moving on ice **2** = **roller skate** **3** a large flat sea fish that you can eat

skateboard /ˈskeɪtbɔːd/ *noun* [C] a short narrow board with small wheels at each end that you can stand on and ride as a sport ➲ picture at **skate** ▸ **skateboarder** *noun* [C] ▸ **skateboarding** *noun* [U]: *When we were children we used to* ***go skateboarding*** *in the park.*

skating /ˈskeɪtɪŋ/ *noun* [U] **1** (also ˈ**ice skating**) the activity or sport of moving on ice wearing special boots: *Would you like to* ***go skating*** *this weekend?* ➲ picture on **page P4** **2** = **roller skating**

ˈ**skating rink** (also **rink**) **1** = **ice rink** **2** an area or a building where you can **roller skate** (=move using a type of shoe with wheels on the bottom)

skeleton¹ /ˈskelɪtn/ *noun* [C] the structure formed by all the bones in a human or animal body: *the human skeleton* ◆ *a dinosaur skeleton* ➲ picture at **body**

skeleton² /ˈskelɪtn/ *adj* (used about an organization, a service, etc.) having the smallest number of people that is necessary for it to operate

skeptic, skepticism (*AmE*) = **sceptic, scepticism**

sketch /sketʃ/ *noun* [C] **1** a simple, quick drawing without many details: *He drew a* ***rough sketch*** *of the new building on the back of an envelope.* **2** a short funny scene on TV, in the theatre, etc: *The drama group did a sketch about a couple buying a new house.* **3** a short description without any details ▸ **sketch** *verb* [I,T]: *I sat on the grass and sketched the castle.*

sketchy /ˈsketʃi/ *adj* (**sketchier**; **sketchiest**) not having many or enough details

skewer /ˈskjuːə(r)/ *noun* [C] a long thin pointed piece of metal or wood that is pushed through pieces of meat, vegetables, etc. to hold them together while they are cooking or to check that they are completely cooked ➲ picture on **page P16** ▸ **skewer** *verb* [T]

ski¹ /skiː/ *verb* [I] (**skiing**; *pt, pp* **skied**) to move over snow on **skis**: *When did you learn to ski?* ◆ *They* ***go skiing*** *every year.* ▸ **ski** *adj* [only *before* a noun]: *a ski resort/instructor/slope/suit* ▸ **skiing** *noun* [U]: *alpine/downhill/cross-country skiing* ➲ picture on **page P4**

ski² /skiː/ *noun* [C] one of a pair of long, flat, narrow pieces of wood or plastic that are fastened to boots and used for sliding over snow: *a pair of skis*

skid /skɪd/ *verb* [I] (**skidding**; **skidded**) (often used about a vehicle) to suddenly slide forwards or sideways without any control: *The lorry skidded to a halt just in time.* ▸ **skid** *noun* [C]: *The car went into a skid and came off the road.*

skier /ˈskiːə(r)/ *noun* [C] a person who **skis**: *Dita's a good skier.* ➲ picture on **page P4**

⚷ **skilful** (*AmE* **skillful**) /ˈskɪlfl/ *adj* **1** (used about a person) very good at doing sth: *a skilful painter/politician* ◆ *He's very skilful with his hands.* **2** done very well: *skilful guitar playing* ▸ **skilfully** /-fəli/ *adv*

⚷ **skill** /skɪl/ *noun* **1** [U] the ability to do sth well, especially because of training, practice, etc: *It takes great skill to make such beautiful jewellery.* ◆ *This is an easy game to play. No skill is required.* **2** [C] an ability that you need in order to do a job, an activity, etc. well: *The course will help you to develop your reading and listening skills.* ◆ *management skills* ◆ *Typing is a skill I have never mastered.*

⚷ **skilled** /skɪld/ *adj* **1** (used about a person) having skill; skilful: *a skilled worker* **2** (used about work, a job, etc.) needing skill or skills; done by people who have been trained: *a highly skilled job* ◆ *Skilled work is difficult to find in this area.* **OPP** for both meanings **unskilled**

skim /skɪm/ *verb* (**skimming**; **skimmed**) **1** [T] **skim sth (off/from sth)** to remove sth from the surface of a liquid: *to skim the cream off the milk* **2** [I,T] to move quickly over or past sth, almost touching it or touching it slightly: *The plane flew very low, skimming the tops of the buildings.* **3** [I,T] **skim (through/over) sth** to read sth quickly in order to get the main idea, without paying attention to the details and without reading every word: *I usually just skim through the newspaper in the morning.*

EXAM TIP

Skimming

For a **reading comprehension** it is a good idea to skim the text first, to get a general idea of what it is about. If you do this, it will be easier to understand when you read it for a second time. Next, read the questions, then **scan** the text (= read it quickly), looking only for the relevant information to answer the questions.

ˌ**skimmed** ˈ**milk** *noun* [U] milk from which the cream has been removed

skimp /skɪmp/ *verb* [I] **skimp (on sth)** to use or provide less of sth than is necessary

skimpy /ˈskɪmpi/ *adj* (**skimpier**; **skimpiest**) using or having less than is necessary; too small or few

⚷ **skin¹** /skɪn/ *noun* [C,U]

➤ON BODY **1** the natural outer covering of a human or animal body: *to have (a) fair/dark/sensitive skin* ◆ *skin cancer*

➤-SKINNED **2** **-skinned** [in compounds] having the type of skin mentioned: *a dark-skinned/fair-skinned woman*

➤OF DEAD ANIMAL **3** [in compounds] the skin of a dead animal, with or without its fur, used for making things: *a sheepskin jacket* ◆ *a bag made of crocodile skin*

➤OF FRUIT/VEGETABLES **4** the natural outer covering of some fruits or vegetables; the outer covering of a **sausage** (= meat formed in a long thin shape): *(a) banana/tomato skin* ➲ note at **rind** ➲ picture on **page P14**

➤ON LIQUIDS **5** the thin solid layer that can form on a liquid: *A skin had formed on top of the milk.*

IDM **by the skin of your teeth** (*informal*) (used to show that sb almost failed to do sth) only just: *I ran*

into the airport and caught the plane by the skin of my teeth.
have a thick skin ➲ **thick**[1]

skin[2] /skɪn/ *verb* [T] (skinning; skinned) to remove the skin from sth
IDM **keep your eyes peeled/skinned (for sb/sth)** ➲ **eye**[1]

ˌ**skin-ˈdeep** *adj* (used about a feeling or an attitude) not as important or as strongly felt as it appears to be; only on the surface: *His concern for me was only skin-deep.* SYN **superficial**

skinny /ˈskɪni/ *adj* (*informal*) (skinnier; skinniest) (used about a person) too thin ➲ note at **thin**

skintight /skɪnˈtaɪt/ *adj* (used about a piece of clothing) fitting very tightly and showing the shape of the body

skip[1] /skɪp/ *verb* (skipping; skipped) **1** [I] to move along quickly and lightly in a way that is similar to dancing, with little jumps and steps, from one foot to the other: *A little girl came skipping along the road.* ◆ *Lambs were skipping about in the field.* **2** [I] to jump over a rope that you or two other people hold at each end, turning it round and round over your head and under your feet: *Some girls were skipping in the playground.* **3** [T] to not do sth that you usually do or should do: *I got up rather late, so I skipped breakfast.* **4** [T] to miss the next thing that you would normally read, do, etc: *I accidentally skipped one of the questions in the test.*

skip[2] /skɪp/ *noun* [C] **1** a small jumping movement **2** a large, open metal container for rubbish, often used during building work

skipper /ˈskɪpə(r)/ *noun* [C] (*informal*) the captain of a boat or ship, or of a sports team

ˈ**skipping rope** *noun* [C] a rope, often with handles at each end, that you turn over your head and then jump over, for fun or for exercise

skirmish /ˈskɜːmɪʃ/ *noun* [C] a short fight between groups of people

⚷ **skirt**[1] /skɜːt/ *noun* [C] a piece of clothing that is worn by women and girls and that hangs down from the waist ➲ picture on **page P1**

skirt[2] /skɜːt/ *verb* [I,T] to go around the edge of sth: *The road skirts the lake.*
PHR V **skirt round sth** to avoid talking about sth in a direct way: *The manager skirted round the subject of our pay increase.*

skittles /ˈskɪtlz/ *noun* [U] (in Britain) a game in which players roll a ball at nine **skittles** (= objects shaped like bottles) and try to knock over as many of them as possible

skive /skaɪv/ *verb* [I] (*BrE informal*) skive (off) to not work when you should

skulk /skʌlk/ *verb* [I] to stay somewhere quietly and secretly, hoping that nobody will notice you, especially because you are planning to do sth bad: *He was skulking in the bushes.*

skull /skʌl/ *noun* [C] the bone structure of a human or animal head: *She suffered a fractured skull in the fall.* ➲ picture at **body**

⚷ **sky** /skaɪ/ *noun* [C,U] (*pl* skies) the space that you can see when you look up from the earth, and where you can see the sun, moon and stars: *a cloudless sky* ◆ *a clear blue sky* ◆ *I saw a bit of blue sky between the clouds.* ◆ *I saw a plane high up* ***in the sky.***

skydiving /ˈskaɪdaɪvɪŋ/ *noun* [U] a sport in which you jump from a plane and fall for as long as you safely can before opening your **parachute** (= a piece of thin cloth that opens and lets you fall to the ground slowly): *to go skydiving* ▶ **skydiver** *noun* [C]

ˌ**sky-ˈhigh** *adj, adv* very high

skylight /ˈskaɪlaɪt/ *noun* [C] a small window in a roof ➲ picture on **page P8**

skyline /ˈskaɪlaɪn/ *noun* [C] the shape that is made by tall buildings, etc. against the sky: *the Manhattan skyline*

Skype™ /skaɪp/ *noun* [U] a telephone system that works by direct communication between users' computers on the Internet ▶ **skype** *verb* [I,T]: *When she was working in Turkey, Amy skyped her parents every week.*

skyscraper /ˈskaɪskreɪpə(r)/ *noun* [C] an extremely tall building ➲ picture on **page P11**

slab /slæb/ *noun* [C] a thick, flat piece of sth: *huge concrete slabs*

slack /slæk/ *adj* (slacker; slackest) **1** loose; not tightly stretched: *Leave the rope slack.* **2** (used about a period of business) not busy; not having many customers: *Trade is very slack here in winter.* **3** not carefully or properly done: *Slack security made terrorist attacks possible.* **4** (used about a person) not doing sth carefully or properly: *You've been rather slack about your homework lately.*

slacken /ˈslækən/ *verb* [I,T] **1** to become or make sth less tight: *The rope slackened and he pulled his hand free.* **2** slacken (sth) (off) to become or make sth slower or less active: *He slackened off his pace towards the end of the race.*

slag[1] /slæg/ *noun* [U] the waste material that is left after metal has been removed from rock

slag[2] /slæg/ *verb*
PHR V **slag sb off** (*slang*) to say cruel or critical things about sb

ˈ**slag heap** *noun* [C] a hill made of **slag**

slain *past participle* of **slay**

slalom /ˈslɑːləm/ *noun* [C] (in sports such as **skiing, canoeing**, etc.) a race along a course on which you have to move from side to side between poles

slam /slæm/ *verb* (slamming; slammed) **1** [I,T] to shut or make sth shut very loudly and with great force: *I heard the front door slam.* ◆ *She slammed her book shut and rushed out of the room.* **2** [T] to put sth somewhere very quickly and with great force: *He slammed the book down on the table and stormed out.* ➲ look at **grand slam**

slander /ˈslɑːndə(r)/ *noun* [C,U] a spoken statement about sb that is not true and that is intended

S

to damage the good opinion that other people have of them; the legal offence of making this kind of statement ▸ **slander** *verb* [T] ▸ **slanderous** /ˈslɑːndərəs/ *adj*

slang /slæŋ/ *noun* [U] very informal words and expressions that are more common in spoken than written language. Slang is sometimes used only by a particular group of people (for example students, young people or criminals) and often stays in fashion for a short time. Some slang is not polite: *'Hop it!' is slang for 'Go away!'*

slant¹ /slɑːnt/ *verb* **1** [I] to be at an angle, not vertical or horizontal: *My handwriting slants backwards.* ◆ *That picture isn't straight–it's slanting to the right.* **2** [T, usually passive] to describe information, events, etc. in a way that supports a particular group or opinion ▸ **slanting** *adj*: *She has beautiful slanting eyes.*

slant² /slɑːnt/ *noun* **1** [sing] a position at an angle, not horizontal or vertical: *The sunlight fell on the table* ***at a slant***. **2** [C] a way of thinking, writing, etc. about sth, that sees things from a particular point of view

slap¹ /slæp/ *verb* [T] (slapping; slapped) **1** to hit sb/sth with the inside of your hand when it is flat: *She slapped her really hard across the face.* ◆ *People slapped him on the back and congratulated him on winning.* **2** to put sth onto a surface quickly and carelessly ▸ **slap** *noun* [C]: *I gave him a slap across the face.*

slap

slap² /slæp/ (also ˌslap ˈbang) *adv* (*informal*) straight, and with great force: *I hurried round the corner and walked slap into someone coming the other way.*

slapdash /ˈslæpdæʃ/ *adj* careless, or done quickly and carelessly: *slapdash building methods* ◆ *He's a bit slapdash about doing his homework on time.*

slapstick /ˈslæpstɪk/ *noun* [U] a type of humour that is based on simple physical jokes, for example people falling over or hitting each other ➲ note at **humour**

ˈ**slap-up** *adj* (*BrE*) [only *before* a noun] (*informal*) (used about a meal) very large and very good

slash¹ /slæʃ/ *verb* **1** [I,T] slash (at) sb/sth to make or try to make a long cut in sth with a violent movement **2** [T] (*informal*) to reduce an amount of money, etc. very much: *The price of coffee has been slashed by 20%.*

slash² /slæʃ/ *noun* [C] **1** a sharp movement made with a knife, etc. in order to cut sb/sth **2** a long narrow wound or cut: *a slash across his right cheek* **3** the symbol (/) used to show alternatives, as in *lunch and/or dinner*, and in Internet addresses to separate the different parts of the address ➲ look at **forward slash, backslash**

slat /slæt/ *noun* [C] one of a series of long, narrow pieces of wood, metal or plastic, used in furniture, fences, etc.

slate /sleɪt/ *noun* **1** [U] a type of dark grey rock that can easily be split into thin flat pieces **2** [C] one of the thin flat pieces of **slate** that are used for covering roofs

slaughter /ˈslɔːtə(r)/ *verb* [T] **1** to kill an animal, usually for food **2** to kill a large number of people at one time, especially in a cruel way ➲ note at **kill** ▸ **slaughter** *noun* [U]

slaughterhouse /ˈslɔːtəhaʊs/ (*BrE also* abattoir) *noun* [C] a place where animals are killed for food

slave¹ /sleɪv/ *noun* [C] (especially in past times) a person who was owned by another person and had to work for them ▸ **slavery** /ˈsleɪvəri/ *noun* [U]: *the abolition of slavery in America*

slave² /sleɪv/ *verb* [I] slave (away) to work very hard

slay /sleɪ/ *verb* [T] (*pt* **slew** /sluː/; *pp* **slain** /sleɪn/) (*old-fashioned*) to kill sb/sth violently; to murder sb/sth

sleazy /ˈsliːzi/ *adj* (**sleazier**; **sleaziest**) (*informal*) (used about a place or a person) unpleasant and probably connected with criminal activities: *a sleazy nightclub*

sledge /sledʒ/ (also sled /sled/) *noun* [C] a vehicle without wheels that is used for travelling on snow. Large **sledges** are often pulled by dogs, and smaller ones are used for going down hills, for fun or as a sport ➲ look at **bobsleigh, toboggan** ➲ picture at **sleigh** ▸ **sledge** *verb* [I]

sleek /sliːk/ *adj* (**sleeker**; **sleekest**) **1** (used about hair or fur) smooth and shiny because it is healthy **2** (used about a vehicle) having an elegant, smooth shape: *a sleek new sports car*

🔑 **sleep¹** /sliːp/ *verb* (*pt, pp* **slept** /slept/) **1** [I] to rest with your eyes closed and your mind and body not active: *Did you sleep well?* ◆ *I only slept for a couple of hours last night.* ◆ *I slept solidly from 10 last night till 11 this morning.* ➲ note at **asleep, routine 2** [T] (used about a place) to have enough beds for a particular number of people: *an apartment that sleeps four people*

IDM live/sleep rough ➲ **rough⁴**

PHR V sleep in to sleep until later than usual in the morning because you do not have to get up ➲ look at **oversleep**

sleep together; sleep with sb to have sex with sb (usually when you are not married to or living with that person)

🔑 **sleep²** /sliːp/ *noun* **1** [U] the natural condition of rest when your eyes are closed and your mind and body are not active or conscious: *Most people need at least seven hours' sleep every night.* ◆ *I didn't get much sleep last night.* ◆ *Do you ever talk in your sleep?* ◆ *I couldn't* ***get to sleep*** *last night.* **2** [sing] a period of sleep: *You'll feel better after a good night's sleep.* ◆ *I sometimes have a short sleep in the afternoon.*

IDM go to sleep 1 to start sleeping: *He got into bed*

and went to sleep. **2** (used about an arm, a leg, etc.) to lose the sense of feeling in a part of your body **put (an animal) to sleep** to kill an animal that is ill or injured because you want to stop it suffering

TOPIC

Sleep

When we feel **tired** or **sleepy**, we usually **yawn** (= open our mouth wide and breathe in deeply). **Go to sleep** is the expression we use to mean 'start to sleep': *I was reading in bed last night, and I didn't go to sleep until about 1 o'clock.* Some people **snore** (= breathe noisily through their nose and mouth) when they are **asleep**. Most people **dream** (= see pictures in their mind). Frightening dreams are called **nightmares**. Some people **sleepwalk** (= get out of bed and move about while they are asleep). If you **wake up** later than you had planned to, you **oversleep**: *I'm sorry I'm late. I overslept.* Sometimes we don't have to **get up**, so we **have a lie-in** (= stay in bed longer than usual). A short sleep that you have in the day is called a **nap**.

sleeper /ˈsliːpə(r)/ *noun* [C] **1** [with an adjective] a person who sleeps in a particular way, for example if you are a **light sleeper** you wake up easily: *a light/heavy sleeper* **2** a bed on a train; a train with beds

ˈsleeping bag *noun* [C] a large soft bag that you use for sleeping in when you go camping, etc.

ˈsleeping pill *noun* [C] a medicine in solid form that you swallow to help you sleep: *to take a sleeping pill*

sleepless /ˈsliːpləs/ *adj* [only *before* a noun] (used about a period, usually the night) without sleep ▸ **sleeplessness** *noun* [U] ➲ look at **insomnia**

sleepover /ˈsliːpəʊvə(r)/ (*AmE* also ˈ**slumber party**) *noun* [C] a party for children or young people when a group of them spend the night at one house

sleepwalk /ˈsliːpwɔːk/ *verb* [I] to walk around while you are asleep

sleepy /ˈsliːpi/ *adj* (**sleepier**; **sleepiest**) **1** tired and ready to go to sleep: *These pills might make you feel a bit sleepy.* **2** (used about a place) very quiet and not having much activity ▸ **sleepily** *adv*: *She yawned sleepily.*

sleet /sliːt/ *noun* [U] a mixture of rain and snow ➲ note at **weather**

⚷ **sleeve** /sliːv/ *noun* [C] **1** one of the two parts of a piece of clothing that cover the arms or part of the arms: *a blouse with long sleeves* ➲ picture on **page P1** **2 -sleeved** [in compounds] with sleeves of a particular kind: *a short-sleeved shirt*

sleeveless /ˈsliːvləs/ *adj* without sleeves: *a sleeveless sweater*

sleigh /sleɪ/ *noun* [C] a vehicle without wheels that is used for travelling on snow and that is usually pulled by horses ➲ look at **bobsleigh**

sleight of hand /ˌslaɪt əv ˈhænd/ *noun* [U] skilful movements of your hand that other people cannot see: *The trick is done simply by sleight of hand.*

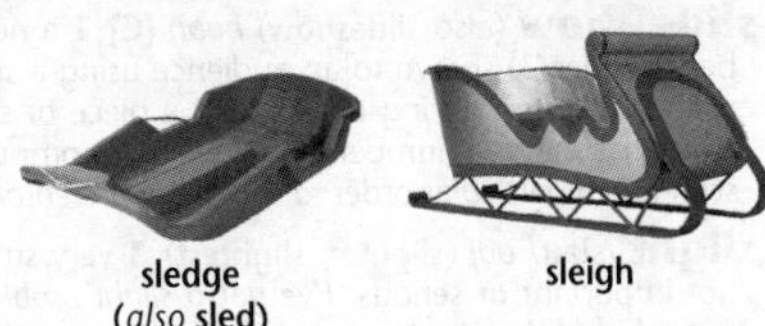

sledge (*also* **sled**) **sleigh**

slender /ˈslendə(r)/ *adj* (**slenderer**; **slenderest**) [You can also use **more slender** and **most slender**.] **1** (used about a person or part of sb's body) thin in an attractive way: *long slender fingers* **2** smaller in amount or size than you would like: *My chances of winning are very slender.*

slept *past tense, past participle* of **sleep**[1]

slew *past tense* of **slay**

⚷ **slice**[1] /slaɪs/ *noun* [C] **1** a flat piece of food that is cut from a larger piece: *a thick/thin slice of bread* ◆ *Cut the meat into thin slices.* ➲ picture at **cake** **2** a part of sth: *The directors have taken a large slice of the profits.*

⚷ **slice**[2] /slaɪs/ *verb* **1** [T] to cut into thin flat pieces: *Peel and slice the apples.* ◆ *a loaf of sliced bread* **2** [I, T] to cut sth easily with sth sharp: *He sliced through the rope with a knife.* ◆ *The glass sliced her hand.* **3** [T] (in ball sports) to hit the ball on the bottom or side so that it does not travel in a straight line

slick[1] /slɪk/ *adj* (**slicker**; **slickest**) **1** done smoothly and well, and seeming to be done without any effort **2** clever at persuading people but perhaps not completely honest

slick[2] /slɪk/ = **oil slick**

⚷ **slide**[1] /slaɪd/ *verb* (*pt, pp* **slid** /slɪd/) **1** [I,T] to move or make sth move smoothly along a surface: *She fell over and slid along the ice.* ◆ *The doors slide open automatically.* ◆ *You can slide the front seat forward* **2** [I,T] to move or make sth move quietly without being noticed: *I slid out of the room when nobody was looking.* ◆ *She slid her hand into her pocket and took out a sweet.* **3** [I] (used about prices, values, etc.) to go down slowly and continuously: *The Euro is sliding against the dollar.* **4** [I] to move gradually towards a worse situation: *The company slid into debt and eventually closed.*

slide[2] /slaɪd/ *noun* [C] **1** a continuous slow fall, for example of prices, values, levels, etc. **2** a large toy consisting of steps and a long piece of metal, plastic, etc. Children climb up the steps then slide down the other part. ➲ picture at **swing** **3** one page of an electronic presentation that is usually viewed on a computer screen or projected onto a larger screen **4** a small photograph on a piece of film in a frame that can be shown on a screen when you shine a light through it ➲ look at **transparency** **5** a small piece of glass that you put sth on when you want to examine it under a **microscope** (= a piece of equipment that makes small objects look bigger) **6** = **hairslide**

S

ˈ**slide show** (also **slideshow**) *noun* [C] **1** a number of **slides**(3) shown to an audience using a **slide projector**, often during a lecture **2** a piece of software that shows a number of images on a computer screen in a particular order: *a slideshow presentation*

slight /slaɪt/ *adj* (**slighter**; **slightest**) **1** very small; not important or serious: *I've got a slight problem, but it's nothing to get worried about.* ◆ *a slight change/difference/increase/improvement* ◆ *I haven't the slightest idea* (= no idea at all) *what you're talking about.* **2** (used about sb's body) thin and light: *His slight frame is perfect for a long-distance runner.*

IDM **not in the slightest** not at all: *'Are you angry with me?' 'Not in the slightest.'*

slightly /ˈslaɪtli/ *adv* **1** a little: *I'm slightly older than her.* **2** a **slightly built** person is small and thin

slim¹ /slɪm/ *adj* (**slimmer**; **slimmest**) **1** thin in an attractive way: *a tall, slim woman* ➲ note at **thin** **2** not as big as you would like: *Her chances of success are very slim.*

slim² /slɪm/ *verb* [I] (**slimming**; **slimmed**) to become or try to become thinner and lighter by eating less food, taking exercise, etc. ➲ look at **diet**

slime /slaɪm/ *noun* [U] a thick unpleasant liquid: *The pond was covered with slime and had a horrible smell.* SYN **goo** ➲ look at **sludge**

slimy /ˈslaɪmi/ *adj* (**slimier**; **slimiest**) **1** covered with **slime** **2** (*informal*) (used about a person) pretending to be friendly, in a way that you do not trust or like

sling¹ /slɪŋ/ *verb* [T] (*pt, pp* **slung**) **1** to put or throw sth somewhere in a rough or careless way **2** to put sth into a position where it hangs in a loose way

sling² /slɪŋ/ *noun* [C] a piece of cloth that you put under your arm and tie around your neck to support a broken arm, wrist, etc. ➲ picture at **plaster**

slingshot /ˈslɪŋʃɒt/ (*AmE*) = **catapult¹**

slink /slɪŋk/ *verb* [I] (*pt, pp* **slunk**) to move somewhere slowly and quietly because you do not want anyone to see you, often when you feel guilty or embarrassed

slip¹ /slɪp/ *verb* (**slipping**; **slipped**)

➤SLIDE/FALL **1** [I] **slip (over); slip (on sth)** to slide accidentally and fall or nearly fall: *She slipped over on the wet floor.* ◆ *His foot slipped on the top step and he fell down the stairs.*

➤OUT OF POSITION **2** [I] to slide accidentally out of the correct position or out of your hand: *This hat's too big. It keeps slipping down over my eyes.* ◆ *The glass slipped out of my hand and smashed on the floor.*

➤GO/PUT QUIETLY **3** [I] to move or go somewhere quietly, quickly, and often without being noticed: *While everyone was dancing we slipped away and went home.* **4** [T] **slip sth to sb/into sth; slip sb sth** to put sth somewhere or give sth to sb quietly and often without being noticed: *She picked up the money and slipped it into her pocket.*

➤CLOTHES **5** [I,T] **slip into/out of sth; slip sth on/off** to put on or take off a piece of clothing quickly and easily: *I slipped off my shoes.*

➤BECOME WORSE **6** [I] to fall a little in value, level, etc: *Sales have been slipping slightly over the last few months.*

IDM **let sth slip** to accidentally say sth that you should keep secret

slip your mind to be forgotten: *I'm sorry, the meeting completely slipped my mind.*

PHR V **slip out** when sth slips out, you say it without really intending to: *I'm sorry I said that. It just slipped out.*

slip up (*informal*) to make a mistake

slip² /slɪp/ *noun* [C] **1** a small mistake, usually made by being careless or not paying attention: *to make a slip* **2** a small piece of paper ➲ look at **payslip**: *I made a note of her name on **a slip of paper**.* **3** an act of sliding accidentally and falling or nearly falling **4** a thin piece of clothing that is worn by a woman under a dress or skirt

IDM **give sb the slip** (*informal*) to escape from sb who is following or trying to catch you

a slip of the tongue something that you say that you did not mean to say

ˌ**slipped ˈdisc** *noun* [C] a painful injury caused when one of the **discs** (= flat things between the bones in your back) moves out of its correct position

slipper /ˈslɪpə(r)/ *noun* [C] a light soft shoe that is worn inside the house: *a pair of slippers* ➲ picture at **shoe**

slippery /ˈslɪpəri/ (also *informal* **slippy** /ˈslɪpi/) *adj* (used about a surface or an object) difficult to walk on or hold because it is smooth, wet, etc: *a slippery floor*

ˈ**slip road** (*AmE* **ramp**) *noun* [C] a road that leads onto or off a large road such as a **motorway**

slit¹ /slɪt/ *noun* [C] a long narrow cut or opening: *a long skirt with a slit up the back*

slit² /slɪt/ *verb* [T] (**slitting**; *pt, pp* **slit**) to make a long narrow cut in sth: *She slit the envelope open with a knife.*

slither /ˈslɪðə(r)/ *verb* [I] to move by sliding from side to side along the ground like a snake: *I saw a snake slithering down a rock.*

slob /slɒb/ *noun* [C] (*informal*) (used as an insult) a very lazy or untidy person

slog¹ /slɒg/ *verb* [I] (**slogging**; **slogged**) (*informal*) **1** **slog (away) (at sth); slog (through sth)** to work hard for a long period at sth difficult or boring: *I've been slogging away at this homework for hours.* **2** **slog down, up, along, etc.** to walk or move in a certain direction with a lot of effort

slog² /slɒg/ *noun* [sing] a period of long, hard, boring work or a long, tiring journey

slogan /ˈsləʊgən/ *noun* [C] a short phrase that is easy to remember and that is used in politics or advertising: *Anti-government slogans had been painted all over the walls.* ◆ *an advertising slogan*

slop /slɒp/ *verb* [I,T] (**slopping**; **slopped**) (used about a liquid) to pour over the edge of its

S

container; to make a liquid do this: *He filled his glass too full and beer slopped onto the table.*

slope /sləʊp/ *noun* **1** [C] a surface or piece of land that goes up or down: *The village is built* ***on a slope.*** ♦ *a steep/gentle slope* ♦ *The best* ***ski slopes*** *are in the Alps.* ➲ picture on **page P10** **2** [sing] the amount that a surface is not level; the fact of not being level: *The slope of the football pitch makes it quite difficult to play on.* ▶ **slope** *verb* [I]: *The road slopes down to the river.* ♦ *a sloping roof*

sloppy /ˈslɒpi/ *adj* (**sloppier**; **sloppiest**) **1** that shows a lack of care, thought or effort; untidy: *a sloppy worker/writer/dresser* ♦ *a sloppy piece of work* **2** (used about clothes) not tight and without much shape **3** (*BrE informal*) showing emotions in a silly and embarrassing way: *I can't stand sloppy love songs.* ➲ A more formal word is **sentimental**.

slosh /slɒʃ/ *verb* (*informal*) **1** [I] (used about a liquid) to move around noisily inside a container **2** [T] to pour or drop liquid somewhere in a careless way

sloshed /slɒʃt/ *adj* (*slang*) drunk

slot¹ /slɒt/ *noun* [C] **1** a straight narrow opening in a machine, etc: *Put your money into the slot and take the ticket.* **2** a place in a list, a system, an organization, etc: *The single has occupied the Number One slot for the past two weeks.*

slot² /slɒt/ *verb* [I,T] (**slotting**; **slotted**) to put sth into a particular space that is designed for it; to fit into such a space: *He slotted a disc into the CD player.* ♦ *The disc slotted in easily.*
IDM **fall/slot into place** ➲ **place¹**

ˈ**slot machine** *noun* [C] a machine with an opening for coins that sells drinks, cigarettes, etc., or on which you can play games

slouch /slaʊtʃ/ *verb* [I] to sit, stand or walk in a lazy way, with your head and shoulders hanging down

slovenly /ˈslʌvnli/ *adj* (*old-fashioned*) lazy, careless and untidy

slow¹ /sləʊ/ *adj* (**slower**; **slowest**) *adv*
➤NOT FAST **1** moving, doing sth or happening without much speed; not fast: *The traffic is always very slow in the city centre.* ♦ *Haven't you finished your homework yet? You're being very slow!* ♦ *Progress was slower than expected.* ♦ *a slow driver/walker/reader*
OPP **fast**

> **GRAMMAR** It is possible to use **slow** as an adverb, but **slowly** is much more common. However, **slow** is often used in compounds: *slow-moving traffic.* The comparative forms **slower** and **more slowly** are both common: *Could you drive a bit slower/more slowly, please?*

➤WITH DELAY **2** slow to do sth; slow (in/about) doing sth not doing sth immediately: *She was rather slow to realize what was going on.* ♦ *They've been rather slow in replying to my letter!*
➤NOT CLEVER **3** not quick to learn or understand: *He's the slowest student in the class.*
➤NOT BUSY **4** not very busy; with little action: *Business is very slow at the moment.*
➤WATCH/CLOCK **5** [not before a noun] showing a time that is earlier than the real time: *That clock is five minutes slow* (= it says it is 8.55 when the correct time is 9.00). OPP **fast**
IDM **quick/slow on the uptake** ➲ **uptake**
▶ **slowness** *noun* [U]

slow² /sləʊ/ *verb* [I,T] to start to move, do sth or happen at a slower speed; to cause sth to do this: *He slowed his pace a little.*
PHR V **slow (sb/sth) down/up** to start to move, do sth or happen at a slower speed; to cause sb/sth to do this: *Can't you slow down a bit? You're driving much too fast.* ♦ *These problems have slowed up the whole process.*

slowly /ˈsləʊli/ *adv* at a slow speed; not quickly: *He walked slowly along the street.*

ˌ**slow** ˈ**motion** *noun* [U] (in a film or on TV) a method of making action appear much slower than in real life: *They showed the winning goal again, this time* ***in slow motion.***

sludge /slʌdʒ/ *noun* [U] thick, soft, wet mud or a substance that looks like it ➲ look at **slime**

slug /slʌg/ *noun* [C] a small black or brown creature with a soft body and no legs, that moves slowly along the ground and eats garden plants ➲ picture at **snail**

sluggish /ˈslʌgɪʃ/ *adj* moving or working more slowly than normal in a way that seems lazy

slum /slʌm/ *noun* [C] an area of a city where living conditions are extremely bad, and where the buildings are dirty and have not been repaired for a long time

slumber /ˈslʌmbə(r)/ *noun* [U,C] (*formal*) sleep; a time when sb is asleep: *She fell into a deep and peaceful slumber.* ▶ **slumber** *verb* [I]

ˈ**slumber party** (*AmE*) = **sleepover**

slump¹ /slʌmp/ *verb* [I] **1** (used about economic activity, prices, etc.) to fall suddenly and by a large amount: *Shares in BP* ***slumped*** *33p* ***to*** *181p yesterday.* ♦ *The newspaper's circulation has* ***slumped by*** *30%.* SYN **drop** **2** to fall or sit down suddenly when your body feels heavy and weak, usually because you are tired or ill

slump² /slʌmp/ *noun* [C] **1** a slump (in sth) a sudden large fall in sales, prices, the value of sth, etc: *a slump in house prices* SYN **decline** **2** a period when a country's economy is doing very badly and a lot of people do not have jobs: *The car industry is* ***in a*** *slump.* ➲ look at **boom**

slung *past tense, past participle of* **sling¹**

slunk *past tense, past participle of* **slink**

slur¹ /slɜː(r)/ *verb* [T] (**slurring**; **slurred**) to pronounce words in a way that is not clear, often because you are drunk

slur² /slɜː(r)/ *noun* [C] a slur (on sb/sth) an unfair comment or an insult that could damage people's opinion of sb/sth SYN **insult**

slurp /slɜːp/ *verb* [I,T] (*informal*) to drink noisily

S

slush /slʌʃ/ *noun* [U] **1** snow that has been on the ground for a time and that is now a dirty mixture of ice and water **2** (*informal*) films, books, feelings, etc. that are considered to be silly because they are too romantic and emotional ▶ **slushy** *adj*

sly /slaɪ/ *adj* **1** acting or done in a secret or dishonest way, often intending to trick people **SYN** **cunning** **2** suggesting that you know sth secret: *a sly smile/look* ▶ **slyly** *adv*

smack /smæk/ *verb* [T] to hit sb with the inside of your hand when it is flat, especially as a punishment: *I never smack my children.* ➲ note at **hit**
PHR V **smack of sth** to make you think that sb/sth has an unpleasant attitude or quality
▶ **smack** *noun* [C]

small /smɔːl/ *adj* (**smaller**; **smallest**) **1** not large in size, number, amount, etc: *a small car/flat/town* ◆ *a small group of people* ◆ *a small amount of money* ◆ *That dress is too small for you.* **2** young: *He has a wife and three small children.* ◆ *When I was small we lived in a big old house.* **3** not important or serious; slight: *Don't worry. It's only a small problem.*
IDM **in a big/small way** ➲ **way**[1]
▶ **small** *adv*: *She's painted the picture far too small.*

OTHER WORDS FOR

small

Small is the most usual opposite of **big** or **large**. **Little** is often used with another adjective to express an emotion, as well as the idea of smallness: *a horrible little man* ◆ *a lovely little girl* ◆ *a nice little house.* The comparative and superlative forms **smaller** and **smallest** are common, and small is often used with words like 'rather', 'quite' and 'very': *My flat is smaller than yours.* ◆ *The village is quite small.* ◆ *a very small car.* **Little** is not often used with these words and does not usually have a comparative or superlative form. **Tiny** and **minute** /maɪˈnjuːt/ both mean 'very small'.

S

ˈsmall ad (*BrE informal*) = **classified advertisement**

ˌsmall ˈchange *noun* [U] coins that have a low value

the ˈsmall hours *noun* [pl] the early morning hours soon after midnight

smallpox /ˈsmɔːlpɒks/ *noun* [U] a serious infectious disease that causes a high temperature and leaves marks on the skin. In past times many people died from **smallpox**.

the ˌsmall ˈprint (*AmE* **the ˌfine ˈprint**) *noun* [U] the important details of a legal document, contract, etc. that are usually printed in small type and are therefore easy to miss: *Make sure you read the small print before you sign anything.*

ˌsmall-ˈscale *adj* (used about an organization or activity) not large; limited in what it does

ˈsmall talk *noun* [U] polite conversation, for example at a party, about unimportant things: *We had to* ***make small talk*** *for half an hour.*

smart[1] /smɑːt/ *adj* (**smarter**; **smartest**) **1** (*especially BrE*) (used about a person) having a clean and tidy appearance: *You look smart. Are you going somewhere special?* **2** (*especially BrE*) (used about a piece of clothing, etc.) good enough to wear on a formal occasion: *a smart suit* **3** (*especially AmE*) clever; intelligent: *He's not smart enough to be a politician.* ➲ note at **intelligent** **4** (*especially BrE*) fashionable and usually expensive: *a smart restaurant/hotel* **5** (used about a movement or action) quick and usually done with force: *We set off at a smart pace.* ▶ **smartly** *adv*: *She's always smartly dressed.*

smart[2] /smɑːt/ *verb* [I] **1** **smart (from sth)** to feel a stinging pain in your body: *Her cheek smarted from the blow.* **2** **smart (from/over sth)** to feel upset or offended because of a criticism, failure, etc.

ˈsmart card *noun* [C] a small plastic card on which information can be stored in electronic form

smarten /ˈsmɑːtn/ *verb*
PHR V **smarten (yourself/sb/sth) up** to make yourself/sb/sth look tidy and more attractive

smartphone /ˈsmɑːtfəʊn/ *noun* [C] a mobile phone that also has some of the functions of a computer: *You can play games on your smartphone.*

TOPIC

Smartphones

You can use a smartphone to **access the Internet**, **browse web pages**, and **send** and **receive mail**. You can also **stream videos** and **music** (= view or listen via the Internet without buying or owning the files) to keep you entertained. There are **apps** (= special applications) that you can **download** that will make it possible to do more with your smartphone, such as play games, organize your **contacts** (= list of addresses, telephone numbers, etc. that belong to people you know), read books, etc. Don't forget to **charge the battery** using the **charger**, or your phone will **go dead** (= not work).

smash[1] /smæʃ/ *verb* **1** [I,T] to break sth, or to be broken violently and noisily into many pieces: *The police had to smash the door open.* ◆ *The glass smashed into a thousand pieces.* **2** [I,T] **smash (sth) against, into, through, etc.** to move with great force in a particular direction; to hit sth very hard: *The car smashed into a tree.* ◆ *He smashed his fist through the window.* **3** [T] **smash sth (up)** to crash a vehicle, usually causing a lot of damage: *I smashed up my father's car.* **4** [T] (in sports such as **tennis**) to hit a ball that is high in the air downwards very hard over the net

smash[2] /smæʃ/ *noun* **1** [sing] the action or the noise of sth breaking violently: *I heard the smash of breaking glass.* **2** [C] (in sports such as **tennis**) a way of hitting a ball that is high in the air downwards very hard over the net **3** (also **smash ˈhit**) [C] (*informal*) a song, play, film, etc. that is very successful: *her latest chart smash*

smashing /ˈsmæʃɪŋ/ *adj* (*BrE old-fashioned informal*) very good or enjoyable: *We had a smashing time.*

smear¹ /smɪə(r)/ *verb* [T] **smear sth on/over sth/sb; smear sth/sb with sth** to spread a sticky substance across sth/sb: *Her face was smeared with blood.*

smear² /smɪə(r)/ *noun* [C] **1** a dirty mark made by spreading a substance across sth: *a smear of oil* **2** something that is not true that is said or written about an important person and that is intended to damage people's opinion about them, especially in politics: *He was the victim of a* ***smear campaign****.*

smell¹ /smel/ *verb* (*pt, pp* **smelt** /smelt/ *or* **smelled** /smeld/) **1** [I] **smell (of sth)** to have a particular smell: *Dinner smells good!* ♦ *This perfume smells of roses.* ♦ *His breath smelt of whisky.* **2** [T] to notice or recognize sb/sth by using your nose: *He could smell something burning.* ♦ *Can you smell gas?* ♦ *I could still smell her perfume in the room.*

> **HELP** **Touch** can be used in the continuous tenses, but the other verbs of the senses **smell, taste, see** and **hear** cannot. Instead we often use **can**: *I can smell smoke.*

3 [T] to put your nose near sth and breathe in so that you can discover or identify its smell: *I smelt the milk to see if it had gone off.* **4** [I] to have a bad smell: *Your feet smell.* **5** [I] to be able to smell: *I can't smell properly because I've got a cold.*

smell² /smel/ *noun* **1** [C] the impression that you get of sth by using your nose; the thing that you smell: *What's that smell?* ♦ *a sweet/musty/fresh/sickly smell* ♦ *a strong/faint smell of garlic* **2** [sing] an unpleasant smell: *Ugh! What's that smell?* **3** [U] the ability to sense things with the nose: *Dogs have a very good* ***sense of smell****.* **4** [C] the act of putting your nose near sth to smell it: *Have a smell of this milk; is it all right?*

> **OTHER WORDS FOR**
> **smell**
> **Stink, stench, odour** and **pong** (*slang*) are all words for unpleasant smells. **Aroma, fragrance, perfume** and **scent** refer to pleasant smells.

smelly /ˈsmeli/ *adj* (**smellier; smelliest**) (*informal*) having a bad smell: *smelly feet*

smile¹ /smaɪl/ *verb* **1** [I] **smile (at sb/sth)** to make a smile appear on your face: *to smile sweetly/faintly/broadly* ♦ *She smiled at the camera.* **2** [T] to say or express sth with a smile: *I smiled a greeting to them.*

smile² /smaɪl/ *noun* [C] an expression on your face in which the corners of your mouth turn up, showing happiness, pleasure, etc: *to have a smile on your face* ♦ *'It's nice to see you,' he said with a smile.* ➲ look at **beam, grin, smirk**

smirk /smɜːk/ *noun* [C] an unpleasant smile which you have when you are pleased with yourself or think you are very clever ▶ **smirk** *verb* [I]

smog /smɒg/ *noun* [U] dirty, poisonous air that can cover a whole city ➲ note at **fog**

smoke¹ /sməʊk/ *noun* **1** [U] the grey, white or black gas that you can see in the air when sth is burning: *Thick smoke poured from the chimney.* ♦ *a room full of cigarette smoke* **2** [C, usually sing] an action of smoking a cigarette, etc: *He went outside for a quick smoke.*

smoke² /sməʊk/ *verb* **1** [I,T] to breathe in smoke through a cigarette, etc. and let it out again; to use cigarettes, etc. in this way, as a habit: *Do you mind if I smoke?* ♦ *I used to smoke 20 cigarettes a day.* **2** [I] to send out smoke: *The oil in the pan started to smoke.* ▶ **smoker** *noun* [C]: *She's a* ***chain smoker*** (= she finishes one cigarette and then immediately lights another). OPP **non-smoker** ▶ **smoking** *noun* [U]: *My doctor has advised me to give up smoking.* ♦ *All our rooms are non-smoking.*

smoked /sməʊkt/ *adj* (used of certain types of food) given a special taste by being hung for a period of time in smoke from wood fires: *smoked salmon/ham/cheese*

smoky /ˈsməʊki/ *adj* (**smokier; smokiest**) **1** full of smoke; producing a lot of smoke: *a smoky room/fire* **2** with the smell, taste or appearance of smoke

smolder (*AmE*) = **smoulder**

smooth¹ /smuːð/ *adj* (**smoother; smoothest**) **1** having a completely flat surface with no lumps or holes or rough areas: *smooth skin* ♦ *a smooth piece of wood* OPP **rough** **2** (used about a liquid mixture) without lumps: *Stir the sauce until it is smooth.* OPP **lumpy** **3** without difficulties: *The transition from the old method to the new has been very smooth.* **4** (used about a journey in a car, etc.) with an even, comfortable movement: *You get a very smooth ride in this car.* OPP **bumpy** **5** (used in a critical way, usually about a man) too pleasant or polite to be trusted: *I don't like him. He's far too smooth.*
IDM **take the rough with the smooth** ➲ **rough²**
▶ **smoothness** *noun* [U]

smooth² /smuːð/ *verb* [T] **smooth sth (away, back, down, out, etc.)** to move your hands in the direction mentioned over a surface to make it smooth

smoothie /ˈsmuːði/ *noun* [C] a drink made of fruit or fruit juice, sometimes mixed with milk or ice cream

smoothly /ˈsmuːðli/ *adv* without any difficulty: *My work has been going quite smoothly.*

smother /ˈsmʌðə(r)/ *verb* [T] **1 smother sb (with sth)** to kill sb by covering their face so that they cannot breathe: *She was smothered with a pillow.* **2 smother sth/sb in/with sth** to cover sth/sb with too much of sth: *The salad was smothered in oil.* **3** to stop a feeling, etc. from being expressed **4** to stop sth burning by covering it: *to smother the flames with a blanket*

smoulder (*AmE* **smolder**) /ˈsməʊldə(r)/ *verb* [I] to burn slowly without a flame: *The bonfire was still smouldering the next day.*

S

SMS /ˌes em ˈes/ *noun* [U] **short message service**; a system for sending short written messages from one mobile phone to another SYN **text** ▶ **SMS** *verb* [I,T]

smudge /smʌdʒ/ *verb* **1** [I] to become untidy, without a clean line around it: *Her lipstick smudged when she kissed him.* **2** [T] to make sth dirty or untidy by touching it: *Leave your painting to dry or you'll smudge it.* ▶ **smudge** *noun* [C]

smug /smʌg/ *adj* too happy or satisfied with yourself: *Don't look so smug.* ▶ **smugly** *adv*: *He smiled smugly as the results were announced.* ▶ **smugness** *noun* [U]

smuggle /ˈsmʌgl/ *verb* [T] to take things into or out of a country secretly in a way that is not allowed by the law; to take a person or a thing secretly into or out of a place: *The drugs had been smuggled through customs.* ▶ **smuggler** *noun* [C]: *a drug smuggler*

snack /snæk/ *noun* [C] food that you eat quickly between main meals: *I had a snack on the train.* ➲ note at **meal** ▶ **snack** *verb* [I] (*informal*) **snack** (on sth)

ˈ**snack bar** *noun* [C] a place where you can buy a small quick meal, such as a **sandwich** (= two slices of bread with food between them)

snag¹ /snæg/ *noun* [C] a small difficulty or disadvantage that is often unexpected or hidden: *His offer is very generous–are you sure there isn't a snag?*

snag² /snæg/ *verb* [T] (**snagging**; **snagged**) to catch a piece of clothing, etc. on sth sharp and tear it

snail /sneɪl/ *noun* [C] a type of animal with a soft body and no legs that is covered by a shell. **Snails** move very slowly.

ˈ**snail mail** *noun* [U] (*informal*) used by people who use email to describe the system of sending letters by ordinary post

snake¹ /sneɪk/ *noun* [C] a type of long thin animal with no legs that slides along the ground by moving its body from side to side: *a poisonous snake* ➲ picture on **page P13**

snake² /sneɪk/ *verb* [I] (*written*) to move like a snake in long curves from side to side

snap¹ /snæp/ *verb* (**snapping**; **snapped**)
➤BREAK **1** [I,T] to break or be broken suddenly, usually with a sharp noise: *The top has snapped off my pen.* ◆ *The branch snapped.* ◆ *He snapped a twig off a bush.*
➤MOVE INTO POSITION **2** [I,T] to move or be moved into a particular position, especially with a sharp noise: *She snapped the bag shut and walked out.*
➤SPEAK ANGRILY **3** [I,T] **snap (sth) (at sb)** to speak or say sth in a quick angry way: *Why do you always snap at me?*
➤OF ANIMAL **4** [I] to try to bite sb/sth: *The dog snapped at the child's hand.*
➤TAKE PHOTOGRAPH **5** [I,T] (*informal*) to take a quick photograph of sb/sth: *A tourist snapped the plane as it crashed.*
➤LOSE CONTROL **6** [I] to suddenly be unable to control your feelings any longer: *Suddenly something just snapped and I lost my temper with him.*
IDM **snap your fingers** to make a sharp noise by moving your middle finger quickly against your thumb, especially when you want to attract sb's attention
PHR V **snap sth up** to buy or take sth quickly, especially because it is very cheap

snap² /snæp/ *noun* **1** [C] a sudden sharp sound of sth breaking **2** (also **snapshot** /ˈsnæpʃɒt/) [C] a photograph that is taken quickly and in an informal way: *I showed them some holiday snaps.* **3** [U] a card game where players call out **'Snap'** when two cards that are the same are put down by different players **4** [C] (*AmE*) = **press stud**

snap³ /snæp/ *adj* [only *before* a noun] (*informal*) done quickly and suddenly, often without any careful thought: *a snap decision/judgement*

snare /sneə(r)/ *noun* [C] a piece of equipment used to catch birds or small animals ▶ **snare** *verb* [T]

snarl /snɑːl/ *verb* [I] **snarl (sth) (at sb)** (used about an animal) to make an angry sound while showing its teeth: *The dog snarled at the stranger.* ▶ **snarl** *noun* [C, usually sing]

snatch¹ /snætʃ/ *verb* **1** [I,T] to take sth with a quick rough movement: *A boy snatched her handbag and ran off.*

MORE **Grab** is similar in meaning.

2 [T] to take or get sth quickly using the only time or chance that you have: *I managed to snatch some sleep on the train.*
PHR V **snatch at sth** to try to take hold of sth suddenly: *The man snatched at my wallet but I didn't let go of it.*

snatch² /snætʃ/ *noun* **1** [C, usually pl] a short part or period of sth: *I heard snatches of conversation from the next room.* **2** [sing] a sudden movement that sb makes when trying to take hold of sth

sneak¹ /sniːk/ *verb* **1** [I] **sneak into, out of, past, etc. sth; sneak in, out, away, etc.** to go very quietly in the direction mentioned, so that nobody can see or hear you: *The prisoner sneaked past the guards.* ◆ *Instead of working, he sneaked out to play football.* **2** [T] (*informal*) to do or take sth secretly: *I tried to **sneak a look** at the test results in the teacher's bag.*
PHR V **sneak up (on sb/sth)** to go near sb very quietly, especially so that you can surprise them

sneak² /sniːk/ *noun* [C] (*informal*) (used in a critical way) a person, especially a child, who tells sb about the bad things sb else has done

sneaker /ˈsniːkə(r)/ (*AmE*) = **trainer**(1)

sneaking /ˈsniːkɪŋ/ *adj* [only *before* a noun] (used about feelings) not expressed; secret: *I've a sneaking suspicion that he's lying.*

sneer /snɪə(r)/ *verb* [I] **sneer (at sb/sth)** to show that you have no respect for sb/sth by the expression on your face or the way that you speak: *She sneered at his attempts to speak French.* ▶ **sneer** *noun* [C]

sneeze /sni:z/ *verb* [I] to make air come out of your nose suddenly and noisily in a way that you cannot control, for example because you have a cold: *Dust makes me sneeze.* ➲ picture at **cough** ▶ **sneeze** *noun* [C]

snide /snaɪd/ *adj* (*informal*) (used about an expression or a comment) critical in an unpleasant way

sniff /snɪf/ *verb* **1** [I] to breathe air in through the nose in a way that makes a sound, especially because you have a cold or you are crying: *Stop sniffing and blow your nose.* **2** [I,T] **sniff (at) sth** to smell sth by **sniffing**: *'I can smell gas,' he said, sniffing the air.* ◆ *The dog sniffed at the bone.* ▶ **sniff** *noun* [C]: *Have a sniff of this milk and tell me if it's still OK.*

sniffle /ˈsnɪfl/ *verb* [I] to make noises by breathing air suddenly up your nose, especially because you have a cold or you are crying

snigger /ˈsnɪɡə(r)/ *verb* [I] **snigger (at sb/sth)** to laugh quietly and secretly in an unpleasant way ▶ **snigger** *noun* [C]

snip[1] /snɪp/ *verb* [I,T] (**snipping**; **snipped**) **snip (sth) (off, out, in, etc.)** to cut using scissors, with a short quick action: *He sewed on the button and snipped off the ends of the cotton.* ◆ *to snip a hole in something*

snip[2] /snɪp/ *noun* **1** [C] a small cut made with scissors: *She made a row of small snips in the cloth.* **2** [sing] (*BrE informal*) something that is much cheaper than expected

sniper /ˈsnaɪpə(r)/ *noun* [C] a person who shoots at sb from a hidden position

snippet /ˈsnɪpɪt/ *noun* [C] a small piece of sth, especially information or news

snivel /ˈsnɪvl/ *verb* [I] (**snivelling**; **snivelled**, (*AmE*) **sniveling**; **sniveled**) to keep crying quietly in a way that is annoying

snob /snɒb/ *noun* [C] a person who thinks they are better than people of a lower social class and who admires people who have a high social position: *He's such a snob—he looks down on all my friends.* ▶ **snobbish** *adj* ▶ **snobbishly** *adv* ▶ **snobbishness** *noun* [U]

snobbery /ˈsnɒbəri/ *noun* [U] behaviour or attitudes typical of people who think they are better than other people in society, for example because they have more money, better education, etc: *To say that 'all pop music is rubbish' is just snobbery.*

snog /snɒɡ/ *verb* [I,T] (**snogging**; **snogged**) (*BrE informal*) (used about a couple) to kiss each other for a long period of time ▶ **snog** *noun* [sing]

snooker /ˈsnu:kə(r)/ *noun* [U] a game in which two players try to hit a number of coloured balls into pockets at the edges of a large table using a **cue** (= a long thin stick): *to play snooker* ➲ look at **billiards**, **pool**

snoop /snu:p/ *verb* [I] **snoop (around)**; **snoop (on sb)** to look around secretly and without permission in order to find out information, etc: *She suspected that her neighbours visited just to snoop on her.*

snooty /ˈsnu:ti/ *adj* (**snootier**; **snootiest**) (*informal*) acting in a rude way because you think you are better than other people

snooze /snu:z/ *verb* [I] (*informal*) to have a short sleep, especially during the day ▶ **snooze** *noun* [C, usually sing]: *I had a bit of a snooze on the train.* ➲ look at **nap**

snore /snɔ:(r)/ *verb* [I] to breathe noisily through your nose and mouth while you are asleep: *She heard her father snoring in the next room.* ▶ **snore** *noun* [C]: *He has the loudest snore I've ever heard.*

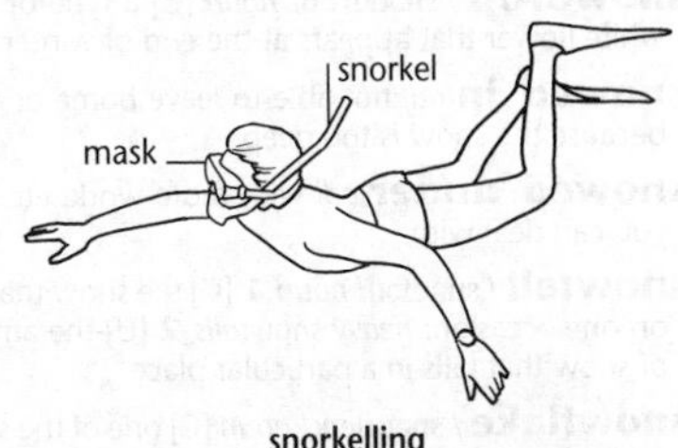

snorkelling

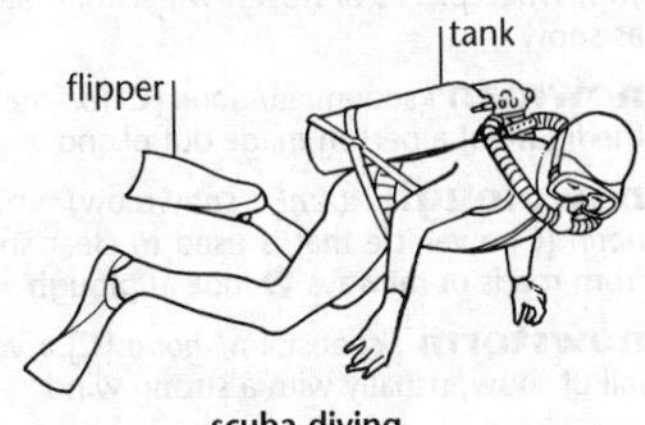

scuba-diving

snorkel /ˈsnɔ:kl/ *noun* [C] a short tube that a person swimming just below the surface of the water can use to breathe through ▶ **snorkelling** (*AmE* **snorkeling**) *noun* [U]: *to go snorkelling*

snort /snɔ:t/ *verb* [I] **1** (used about animals) to make a noise by blowing air through the nose and mouth: *The horse snorted in fear.* **2** (used about people) to blow out air noisily as a way of showing that you do not like sth, or that you are impatient ▶ **snort** *noun* [C]: *She gave a snort of disgust when I got the answer wrong.*

snot /snɒt/ *noun* [U] (*informal*) the liquid produced by the nose

snout /snaʊt/ *noun* [C] the long nose of certain animals: *a pig's snout* ➲ picture at **badger**

snow[1] /snəʊ/ *noun* [U] small, soft, white pieces of frozen water that fall from the sky in cold weather: *Three inches of snow fell during the night.* ◆ *The snow melted before it could settle* (= stay on the ground). ➲ note at **weather** ➲ picture on **page P10**

snow[2] /snəʊ/ *verb* [I] (used about snow) to fall from the sky: *It snowed all night.*

S

snowball¹ /ˈsnəʊbɔːl/ *noun* [C] a lump of snow that is pressed into the shape of a ball and used by children for throwing

snowball² /ˈsnəʊbɔːl/ *verb* [I] to quickly grow bigger and bigger or more and more important

snowboard /ˈsnəʊbɔːd/ *noun* [C] a type of board that you fasten to both your feet and use for moving down mountains that are covered with snow ▶ **snowboarder** *noun* [C] ▶ **snowboarding** *noun* [U]: *Have you ever been snowboarding?*

snowdrift /ˈsnəʊdrɪft/ *noun* [C] a deep pile of snow that has been made by the wind: *The car got stuck in a snowdrift.*

snowdrop /ˈsnəʊdrɒp/ *noun* [C] a type of small white flower that appears at the end of winter

ˌsnowed ˈin *adj* not able to leave home or travel because the snow is too deep

ˌsnowed ˈunder *adj* with more work, etc. than you can deal with

snowfall /ˈsnəʊfɔːl/ *noun* **1** [C] the snow that falls on one occasion: *heavy snowfalls* **2** [U] the amount of snow that falls in a particular place

snowflake /ˈsnəʊfleɪk/ *noun* [C] one of the small, soft, white pieces of frozen water that fall together as snow

snowman /ˈsnəʊmæn/ *noun* [C] (*pl* **-men** /-men/) the figure of a person made out of snow

snowplough (*AmE* **snowplow**) /ˈsnəʊplaʊ/ *noun* [C] a vehicle that is used to clear snow away from roads or railways ➲ look at **plough**

snowstorm /ˈsnəʊstɔːm/ *noun* [C] a very heavy fall of snow, usually with a strong wind

snowy /ˈsnəʊi/ *adj* (**snowier**; **snowiest**) with a lot of snow: *snowy weather* ◆ *a snowy scene*

S

Snr *abbr* (*especially AmE*) = **Senior¹** (2)

snub /snʌb/ *verb* [T] (**snubbing**; **snubbed**) to treat sb rudely, for example by refusing to look at or speak to them ▶ **snub** *noun* [C]: *When they weren't invited to the party, they felt it was a snub.*

snuff /snʌf/ *noun* [U] **tobacco** (= the dried leaves used for making cigarettes) in the form of a powder which people breathe up into their noses

snuffle /ˈsnʌfl/ *verb* [I] (used about people and animals) to make a noise through your nose: *The dog snuffled around the lamp post.*

snug /snʌg/ *adj* **1** warm and comfortable: *a snug little room* ◆ *The children were snug in bed.* **2** fitting sb/sth closely: *Adjust the safety belt to give a snug fit.* ▶ **snugly** *adv*

snuggle /ˈsnʌgl/ *verb* [I] **snuggle (up to sb)**; **snuggle (up/down)** to get into a position that makes you feel safe, warm and comfortable, usually next to another person: *She snuggled up to her mother.* ◆ *I snuggled down under the blanket to get warm.*

So. *abbr* (*AmE*) = **South¹**, **Southern**

so¹ /səʊ/ *adv* **1** used to emphasize an adjective or adverb, especially when this produces a particular result: *She's so ill (that) she can't get out of bed.* ◆ *He was driving so fast that he couldn't stop.* ◆ *You've been so kind. How can I thank you?* ➲ note at **such** **2** used in negative sentences for comparing people or things: *She's not so clever as we thought.* **3** used in place of sth that has been said already, to avoid repeating it: *Are you coming by plane? If so,* (= if you are coming by plane) *I can meet you at the airport.* ◆ *'I failed, didn't I?' 'I'm afraid so.'* ◆ *'Did you lock the door?' 'I think so.'* ◆ *'Can you come out tonight?' 'I hope so.'*

HELP In formal language, you can refer to actions that somebody has mentioned using **do** with **so**: *He asked me to write to him and **I did so*** (= I wrote to him).

4 [not with verbs in the negative] also; too: *He's a teacher and **so is** his wife.* ◆ *'I've been to New York.' '**So have I**.'* ◆ *I like singing and **so does** Helen.*

HELP In negative sentences we use **neither**: *I don't eat meat, and neither does Sarah.*

5 used to show that you agree that sth is true, especially when you are surprised: *'It's getting late.' 'So it is. We'd better go.'* **6** (*formal*) (used when you are showing sb sth) in this way; like this: *It was a black insect, about so big* (= using your hands to show the size). ◆ *Fold the paper in two diagonally, **like so**.*

IDM and so on (and so forth) used at the end of a list to show that it continues in the same way: *They sell pens, pencils, paper and so on.*

I told you so ➲ **tell**

it (just) so happens (used to introduce a surprising fact) by chance: *It just so happened that we were going the same way, so he gave me a lift.*

just so ➲ **just¹**

or so (used to show that a number, time, etc. is not exact) approximately; about: *A hundred or so people came to the meeting.*

so as to do sth with the intention of doing sth; in order to do sth

so much for used for saying that sth was not helpful or successful: *So much for that diet! I didn't lose any weight at all.*

that is so (*formal*) that is true

so² /səʊ/ *conj* **1 so (that)** with the purpose that; in order that: *She wore dark glasses so (that) nobody would recognize her.* **2** with the result that; therefore: *She felt very tired, so she went to bed early.* ➲ note at **because, therefore** **3** used to show how one part of a story follows another: *So what happened next?*

IDM so what? (*informal*) (showing that you think sth is not important) Who cares?: *'It's late.' 'So what? We don't have to go to school tomorrow.'*

soak /səʊk/ *verb* **1** [I,T] to become or make sb/sth completely wet: *Leave the dishes to soak for a while.* ◆ *The dog came out of the river and shook itself, soaking everyone.* **2** [I] **soak into/through sth**; **soak in** (used about a liquid) to pass into or through sth: *Blood had soaked right through the bandage.*

PHR V **soak sth up** to take sth in (especially a liquid): *I soaked the water up with a cloth.*

soaked /səʊkt/ *adj* [not before a noun] extremely wet: *I **got soaked** waiting for my bus in the rain.*

soaking /ˈsəʊkɪŋ/ (also ˌsoaking ˈwet) *adj* extremely wet

ˈso-and-so *noun* [C] (*pl* so-and-sos) (*informal*) **1** a person who is not named: *Imagine a Mrs So-and-so telephones. What would you say?* **2** a person that you do not like: *He's a bad-tempered old so-and-so.*

🔑 **soap** /səʊp/ *noun* **1** [U,C] a substance that you use for washing and cleaning: *He washed his hands with soap.* ◆ *a bar of soap* ◆ *soap powder* (= for washing clothes) ➲ picture at **bar** **2** [C] (*informal*) = **soap opera** ▶ **soapy** *adj*

ˈsoap opera (also *informal* soap /səʊp/) *noun* [C] a story about the lives and problems of a group of people, which continues several times a week on TV or radio ➲ look at **opera**

soar /sɔː(r)/ *verb* [I] **1** to rise very fast: *Prices are soaring because of inflation.* **2** to fly high in the air: *an eagle soaring above us*

sob /sɒb/ *verb* [I] (so**bb**ing; so**bb**ed) to cry while taking in sudden, sharp breaths; to speak while you are crying: *The child was sobbing because he'd lost his toy.* ▶ **sob** *noun* [C]: *It was heartbreaking to listen to her sobs.*

sober¹ /ˈsəʊbə(r)/ *adj* **1** (used about a person) not affected by alcohol: *He'd been drunk the first time he'd met her, but this time he was **stone-cold sober**.* **2** not funny; serious: *a sober expression* ◆ *Her death is a sober reminder of just how dangerous drugs can be.* ◆ *Her death is a sober reminder of just how dangerous extreme sports can be.* **3** (used about a colour) not bright or likely to be noticed: *a sober grey suit*

sober² /ˈsəʊbə(r)/ *verb*

PHR V **sober (sb) up** to become or make sb become normal again after being affected by alcohol: *There's no point talking to him until he's sobered up.*

sobering /ˈsəʊbərɪŋ/ *adj* making you feel serious: *It is **a sobering thought** that over 25 million people have been killed in car accidents.*

Soc. *abbr* = **Society**(2): *the Amateur Dramatic Soc.*

ˌso-ˈcalled *adj* **1** [only *before* a noun] used to show that the words you describe sb/sth with are not correct: *She realized that her so-called friends only wanted her money.* **2** used to show that a special name has been given to sb/sth

soccer /ˈsɒkə(r)/ (*especially AmE*) = **football**(1)

sociable /ˈsəʊʃəbl/ *adj* enjoying being with other people; friendly

🔑 **social** /ˈsəʊʃl/ *adj* [only *before* a noun] **1** connected with society and the way it is organized: *social problems/issues/reforms* **2** connected with the position of people in society: *We share the same social background.* **3** connected with meeting people and enjoying yourself: *a social club* ◆ *She has a busy **social life**.* ◆ *Children have to develop their **social skills** when they start school.* **4** (used about animals) living in groups: *Lions are social animals.* ▶ **socially** /-ʃəli/ *adv*: *We work together but I don't know him socially.*

socialism /ˈsəʊʃəlɪzəm/ *noun* [U] the political idea that is based on the belief that everyone has an equal right to a share of a country's wealth and that the government should own and control the main industries ➲ look at **capitalism, communism, Marxism** ▶ **socialist** /-ɪst/ *adj, noun* [C]: *socialist beliefs/policies/writers* ◆ *Tony was a socialist when he was younger.*

socialize (also -ise) /ˈsəʊʃəlaɪz/ *verb* [I] **socialize (with sb)** to meet and spend time with people in a friendly way, in order to enjoy yourself: *I enjoy socializing with the other students.* ➲ look at **go out**

ˌsocial ˈnetworking *noun* [U] communication with people who share your interests using a website or other service on the Internet

> TOPIC
>
> **Social networking**
>
> You can **access** social networking sites from your computer. First you need to **register**, then you can **create a personal profile** (= give details about yourself and your interests), and exchange messages with other **users**. If you are **on Facebook™**, you can **add** somebody **as a friend**, **post** photos and messages, **poke** somebody (= say hello) or **unfriend** somebody (= delete them from your list of contacts). Friends can post messages on your **wall** (= a space where you can share photos, messages, etc.) Your **status** tells people where you are and what you are doing. If you **like** a page on a website, you give positive feedback or make a connection with things you care about.

ˌsocial ˈscience *noun* [C,U] the study of people in society

ˌsocial seˈcurity (*AmE* **welfare**) *noun* [U] money paid regularly by the government to people who are poor, old, ill, or who have no job: *to live on social security*

ˌsocial ˈservices *noun* [pl] a group of services organized by local government to help people who have money or family problems

ˈsocial work *noun* [U] work that involves giving help and advice to people with money or family problems ▶ **ˈsocial worker** *noun* [C]

🔑 **society** /səˈsaɪəti/ *noun* (*pl* **societies**) **1** [C,U] the people in a country or an area, thought of as a group, who have shared customs and laws: *a civilized society* ◆ *Society's attitude to women has changed considerably this century.* ◆ *The role of men **in society** is changing.* **2** [C] (*abbr* **Soc.**) an organization of people who share a particular interest or purpose; a club: *a drama society*

sociologist /ˌsəʊsiˈɒlədʒɪst/ *noun* [C] a student of or an expert in **sociology**

sociology /ˌsəʊsiˈɒlədʒi/ *noun* [U] the study of human societies and social behaviour ▶ **sociological** /ˌsəʊsiəˈlɒdʒɪkl/ *adj*

S

sock /sɒk/ *noun* [C] a piece of clothing that you wear on your foot and lower leg, inside your shoe: *a pair of socks*
IDM **pull your socks up** ➲ **pull**[1]

socket /ˈsɒkɪt/ *noun* [C] **1** (also ˈ**power point**) (*BrE*) a place in a wall where a piece of electrical equipment can be connected to the electricity supply ➲ picture at **plug** **2** a hole in a piece of electrical equipment where another piece of equipment can be connected **3** a hole that sth fits into: *your eye socket*

soda /ˈsəʊdə/ *noun* **1** (also ˈ**soda water**) [U] water that has bubbles in it and is usually used for mixing with other drinks: *a whisky and soda* **2** [C] (*AmE*) = **fizzy drink**

sodium /ˈsəʊdiəm/ *noun* [U] (*symbol* Na) a chemical element that exists as a soft, silver-white metal and combines with other elements, for example to make salt

sofa /ˈsəʊfə/ *noun* [C] a comfortable seat with a back and arms for two or more people to sit on: *a sofa bed* (= a sofa that you can open out to make a bed) SYN **settee** ➲ picture at **chair**

soft /sɒft/ *adj* (**softer**; **softest**)
➤NOT HARD **1** not hard or firm: *a soft bed/seat* ◆ *The ground is very soft after all that rain.* OPP **hard**
➤NOT ROUGH **2** smooth and pleasant to touch: *soft skin/hands* ◆ *a soft towel* OPP **rough**
➤LIGHT/COLOURS **3** gentle and pleasant: *The room was decorated in soft pinks and greens.* OPP **bright**
➤NOT LOUD **4** (used about sounds, voices, words, etc.) quiet or gentle; not angry: *She spoke in a soft whisper.* OPP **loud, harsh**
➤NOT STRICT **5** (used about people) kind and gentle, sometimes too much so: *A good manager can't afford to be too soft.* OPP **hard, strict**
➤DRUGS **6** less dangerous and serious than the type of illegal drugs which can kill people: *soft drugs such as marijuana* ➲ look at **hard drug**
IDM **have a soft spot for sb/sth** (*informal*) to have positive or loving feelings towards sb/sth
▶ **softly** *adv*: *He closed the door softly behind him.*
▶ **softness** *noun* [U]

softball /ˈsɒftbɔːl/ *noun* [U] a team game similar to **baseball** but played on a smaller field with a larger, softer ball

ˌ**soft ˈdrink** *noun* [C] a cold drink that contains no alcohol ➲ look at **alcoholic**

soften /ˈsɒfn/ *verb* **1** [I,T] to become softer or gentler; to make sb/sth softer or gentler: *a lotion to soften the skin* **2** [T] to make sth less shocking and unpleasant: *Her letter sounded too angry so she softened the language.* ◆ *The airbag softened the impact of the crash.*

ˌ**soft-ˈhearted** *adj* kind and good at understanding other people's feelings OPP **hard-hearted**

ˌ**soft ˈoption** *noun* [C] the easier thing to do of two or more possibilities, but not the best one: *The government has taken the soft option of agreeing to their demands.*

ˌ**soft-ˈspoken** (also **softly-spoken**) *adj* having a gentle, quiet voice: *He was a kind, soft-spoken man.*

software /ˈsɒftweə(r)/ *noun* [U] the programs, etc. used to operate a computer: *There's a lot of new educational software available now.* ◆ *to install/run a piece of software* ➲ look at **hardware**

soggy /ˈsɒgi/ *adj* (**soggier**; **soggiest**) very wet and soft and so unpleasant

soil[1] /sɔɪl/ *noun* **1** [C,U] the substance that plants, trees, etc. grow in; earth: *poor/dry/acid/sandy soil* ➲ note at **ground**[1] **2** [U] (*written*) the land that is part of a country: *to set foot on British soil* (= to arrive in Britain)

soil[2] /sɔɪl/ *verb* [T, often passive] (*formal*) to make sth dirty

solace /ˈsɒləs/ *noun* [U,sing] (*formal*) **solace** (**in sth**) a feeling of comfort when you are sad or disappointed; a person or thing that gives you this feeling: *to find/seek solace in somebody/something* SYN **comfort**

solar /ˈsəʊlə(r)/ *adj* [only *before* a noun] **1** connected with the sun: *a solar eclipse* (= when the sun cannot be seen because the moon is passing in front of it) **2** using the sun's energy: *solar power* ➲ note at **environment**

the ˈsolar system *noun* [sing] the sun and the planets that move around it

sold *past tense, past participle* of **sell**

soldier /ˈsəʊldʒə(r)/ *noun* [C] a member of an army: *The soldiers marched past.*

sole[1] /səʊl/ *adj* [only *before* a noun] **1** only; single: *His sole interest is football.* **2** belonging to one person only; not shared ▶ **solely** *adv*: *I agreed to come solely because of your mother.*

sole[2] /səʊl/ *noun* **1** [C] the bottom surface of your foot ➲ picture at **body, shoe** **2** [C] the part of a shoe or sock that covers the bottom surface of your foot **3** [C,U] (*pl* **sole**) a flat sea fish that we eat

solemn /ˈsɒləm/ *adj* **1** (used about a person) very serious; not happy or smiling: *Her solemn face told them that the news was bad.* OPP **cheerful** **2** sincere; done or said in a formal way: *to make a solemn promise* SYN **serious** ▶ **solemnity** /səˈlemnəti/ *noun* [U] ▶ **solemnly** *adv*: *'I have something very important to tell you,' she began solemnly.*

solicit /səˈlɪsɪt/ *verb* **1** [T] (*formal*) to ask sb for money, help, support, etc: *They tried to solicit support for the proposal.* **2** [I,T] (used about a person who has sex for money) to go to sb, especially in a public place, and offer sex in return for money

solicitor /səˈlɪsɪtə(r)/ *noun* [C] (in Britain) a lawyer whose job is to give legal advice, prepare legal documents and arrange the buying and selling of land, etc. ➲ note at **lawyer**

solid[1] /ˈsɒlɪd/ *adj*
➤NOT LIQUID/GAS **1** hard and firm; not in the form of liquid or gas: *It was so cold that the village pond had frozen solid.*
➤WITHOUT HOLES **2** having no holes or empty spaces inside: *a solid mass of rock*
➤STRONG **3** strong, firm and well made: *a solid little*

car ◆ (*figurative*) *They built up a solid friendship over the years.*

➤STH YOU CAN TRUST **4** of good enough quality; that you can trust: *The police cannot make an arrest without solid evidence.*

➤MATERIAL **5** [only *before* a noun] made completely of one substance, both on the inside and outside: *a **solid gold** chain*

➤PERIOD OF TIME **6** (*informal*) without a break or pause: *I was so tired that I slept for twelve solid hours/twelve hours solid.* ▶ **solidity** /səˈlɪdəti/ *noun* [U]

solid² /ˈsɒlɪd/ *noun* [C] **1** a substance or object that is hard; not a liquid or gas: *Liquids become solids when frozen.* ◆ *The baby is not yet on solids* (= solid food). **2** an object that has length, width and height, not a flat shape: *A cube is a solid.*

solidarity /ˌsɒlɪˈdærəti/ *noun* [U] **solidarity (with sb)** the support of one group of people for another, because they agree with their aims: *Many local people expressed solidarity with the strikers.*

solidify /səˈlɪdɪfaɪ/ *verb* [I] (**solidifying**; **solidifies**; *pt, pp* **solidified**) to become hard or solid

solidly /ˈsɒlɪdli/ *adv* **1** strongly: *a solidly built house* **2** without stopping: *It rained solidly all night.*

solitaire /ˌsɒlɪˈteə(r)/ *noun* [U] **1** (*BrE*) a game for one person in which you remove pieces from a special board by moving other pieces over them until you have only one piece left **2** (*AmE*) = **patience**(2)

solitary /ˈsɒlətri/ *adj* **1** done alone, without other people: *Writing novels is a solitary occupation.* **2** (used about a person or an animal) enjoying being alone; often spending time alone: *She was always a solitary child.* **3** [only *before* a noun] alone; with no others around: *a solitary figure walking up the hillside* **SYN** **lone** **4** [only *before* a noun] [usually in negative sentences or questions] only one; single: *I can't think of a solitary example* (= not even one).

ˌsolitary conˈfinement *noun* [U] a punishment in which a person in prison is kept completely alone in a separate cell away from the other prisoners

solitude /ˈsɒlɪtjuːd/ *noun* [U] the state of being alone, especially when you find this pleasant: *She longed for peace and solitude.* ➲ look at **loneliness**, **isolation**

solo¹ /ˈsəʊləʊ/ *adj* [only *before* a noun] *adv* **1** (done) alone; by yourself: *a solo flight* ◆ *to fly solo* **2** connected with or played as a musical **solo**: *a solo artist* (= a singer who is not part of a group)

solo² /ˈsəʊləʊ/ *noun* [C] (*pl* **solos**) a piece of music for only one person to play or sing ➲ look at **duet** ▶ **soloist** /-ɪst/ *noun* [C]

solstice /ˈsɒlstɪs/ *noun* [C] the longest or the shortest day of the year: *the summer/winter solstice*

soluble /ˈsɒljəbl/ *adj* **1 soluble (in sth)** that will dissolve in liquid: *These tablets are soluble in water.* **2** (*formal*) (used about a problem, etc.) that has an answer; that can be solved **OPP** for both meanings **insoluble**

solution /səˈluːʃn/ *noun* **1** [C] **a solution (to sth)** a way of solving a problem, dealing with a difficult situation, etc: *a solution to the problem of unemployment* **2** [C] **the solution (to sth)** the answer (to a game, competition, etc.): *The solution to the quiz will be published next week.* **3** [C,U] (a) liquid in which sth solid has been dissolved: *saline solution*

solve /sɒlv/ *verb* [T] **1** to find a way of dealing with a problem or difficult situation: *The government is trying to solve the problem of inflation.* **2** to find the correct answer or explanation for sth: *to solve a puzzle/an equation/a riddle* ◆ *The police have not managed to solve the crime.* ◆ *to solve a mystery* ➲ *noun* **solution** ➲ *adjective* **soluble**

solvent /ˈsɒlvənt/ *noun* [C,U] a liquid that can dissolve another substance

sombre (*AmE* **somber**) /ˈsɒmbə(r)/ *adj* **1** dark in colour **SYN** **dull** **2** sad and serious: *a sombre occasion* ▶ **sombrely** *adv*

some /səm; *strong form* sʌm/ *determiner, pron* **1** [before uncountable nouns and plural countable nouns] a certain amount of or a number of: *We need some butter and some potatoes.* ◆ *I don't need any more money—I've still got some.*

> **HELP** In negative sentences and in questions we use **any** instead of **some**: *Do we need any butter?* ◆ *I need some more money. I haven't got any.* Look at sense 2 for examples of questions where **some** is used.

2 used in questions when you expect or want the answer 'yes': *Would you like some more cake?* ◆ *Can I take some of this paper?* **3 some (of sb/sth)** used when you are referring to certain members of a group or certain types of a thing, but not all of them: *Some pupils enjoy this kind of work, some don't.* ◆ *Some of his books are very exciting.* ◆ *Some of us are going to the park.* **4** used with singular nouns for talking about a person or thing without saying any details: *I'll see you again some time, I expect.* ◆ *There must be some mistake.* ◆ *I read about it in **some** newspaper **or other**.*

somebody /ˈsʌmbədi/ (also **someone**) *pron* a person who is not known or not mentioned by name: *How are you? Somebody said that you'd been ill.* ◆ *She's getting married to someone she met at work.* ◆ *There's somebody at the door.* ◆ *I think you should talk to **someone else*** (= another person) *about this problem.*

> **GRAMMAR** **Somebody, anybody** and **everybody** are used with a singular verb but are often followed by a plural pronoun (except in formal language, where 'his/her' or 'him/her' must be used): *Somebody has left **their** coat behind.* ◆ *Has anyone not brought **their** books?* ◆ *I'll see everybody concerned and tell **them** the news.*
>
> The difference between **somebody** and **anybody** is the same as the difference between **some** and **any**.

S

ˈ**some day** (also **someday**) *adv* at a time in the future that is not yet known: *I hope you'll come and visit me some day.*

🔑 **somehow** /ˈsʌmhaʊ/ *adv* **1** in a way that is not known or certain: *The car's broken down but I'll get to work somehow.* ◆ *Somehow we had got completely lost.* **2** for a reason you do not know or understand: *I somehow get the feeling that I've been here before.*

🔑 **someone** /ˈsʌmwʌn/ = **somebody**

someplace /ˈsʌmpleɪs/ (*AmE*) = **somewhere**

somersault /ˈsʌməsɔːlt/ *noun* [C] a movement in which you roll right over with your feet going over your head

🔑 **something** /ˈsʌmθɪŋ/ *pron* **1** a thing that is not known or not named: *I've got something in my eye.* ◆ *Wait a minute—I've forgotten something.* ◆ *Would you like* **something else** (= another thing) *to drink?*

> **HELP** The difference between **something** and **anything** is the same as the difference between **some** and **any**. Look at the note at **some**.

2 a thing that is important, useful or worth considering: *There's* **something in** *what your mother says.* ◆ *I think you've got something there—I like that idea.* **3** (*informal*) used to show that a description, an amount, etc. is not exact: *a new comedy series aimed at* **thirty-somethings** (= people between 30 and 40 years old). ◆ *'What's his job?' 'I think he's a plumber,* **or something**.*'* ◆ *The cathedral took* **something like** *200 years to build.* ◆ *A loganberry is* **something like** *a raspberry.* ◆ *The programme's* **something to do with** (= in some way about) *the environment.*

sometime (also **some time**) /ˈsʌmtaɪm/ *adv* at a time that you do not know exactly or have not yet decided: *I'll phone you sometime this evening.* ◆ *I must go and see her sometime.*

S

🔑 **sometimes** /ˈsʌmtaɪmz/ *adv* on some occasions; now and then: *Sometimes I drive to work and sometimes I go by bus.* ◆ *I sometimes watch TV in the evenings.*

🔑 **somewhat** /ˈsʌmwɒt/ *adv* rather; to some degree: *We missed the train, which was somewhat unfortunate.*

🔑 **somewhere** /ˈsʌmweə(r)/ (*AmE* also **someplace**) *adv* at, in, or to a place that you do not know or do not mention by name: *I've seen your glasses somewhere downstairs.* ◆ *'Have they gone to France?' 'No, I think they've gone* **somewhere else** (= to another place) *this year.'*

> **HELP** The difference between **somewhere** and **anywhere** is the same as the difference between **some** and **any**. Look at the note at **some**.

IDM get somewhere/nowhere (with sb/sth) ➲ **get**

somewhere along/down the line at some time; sooner or later

somewhere around used when you do not know an exact time, number, etc: *Your ideal weight should probably be* **somewhere around** *70 kilos.*

🔑 **son** /sʌn/ *noun* [C] a male child ➲ look at **daughter**: *They have a son and two daughters.*

sonata /səˈnɑːtə/ *noun* [C] a piece of music written for the piano, or for another instrument together with the piano

🔑 **song** /sɒŋ/ *noun* **1** [C] a piece of music with words that you sing: *a folk/love/pop song* ➲ note at **pop** **2** [U] songs in general; music for singing: *to burst/break into song* (= to suddenly start singing) **3** [U,C] the musical sounds that birds make: *birdsong*

songwriter /ˈsɒŋraɪtə(r)/ *noun* [C] a person who writes songs

sonic /ˈsɒnɪk/ *adj* (*technical*) connected with sound waves

ˈ**son-in-law** *noun* [C] (*pl* **sons-in-law**) the husband of your daughter

sonnet /ˈsɒnɪt/ *noun* [C] a type of poem that has 14 lines that **rhyme** (= end with the same sound) in a fixed pattern: *Shakespeare's sonnets*

🔑 **soon** /suːn/ *adv* **1** in a short time from now; a short time after sth else has happened: *It will soon be dark.* ◆ *He left soon after me.* ◆ *We should arrive at your house soon after twelve.* ◆ (*informal*) *See you soon.* **2** early; quickly: *Don't leave so soon. Stay for tea.* ◆ *How soon can you get here?*

IDM as soon as at the moment (that); when: *Phone me as soon as you hear some news.* ◆ *I'd like your reply* **as soon as possible** (= at the earliest possible moment).

no sooner ... than immediately when or after: *No sooner had I shut the door than I realized I'd left my keys inside.*

> **HELP** Note the word order here. The verb follows immediately after 'No sooner', and the subject comes after that.

sooner or later at some time in the future; one day

the sooner the better very soon; as soon as possible

soot /sʊt/ *noun* [U] black powder that is produced when wood, coal, etc. is burnt

soothe /suːð/ *verb* [T] **1** to make sb calmer or less upset **SYN comfort** **2** to make a part of the body or a feeling less painful: *The doctor gave me some skin cream to soothe the irritation.* ▶ **soothing** *adj*: *soothing music* ◆ *a soothing massage* ▶ **soothingly** *adv*

sophisticated /səˈfɪstɪkeɪtɪd/ *adj* **1** having or showing a lot of experience of the world and social situations; knowing about fashion, culture, etc. **2** (used about machines, systems, etc.) advanced and complicated **3** able to understand difficult or complicated things: *Voters are much more sophisticated these days.* ▶ **sophistication** /səˌfɪstɪˈkeɪʃn/ *noun* [U]

soppy /ˈsɒpi/ *adj* (**soppier**; **soppiest**) (*informal*) full of unnecessary emotion; silly: *a soppy romantic film*

soprano /səˈprɑːnəʊ/ *noun* [C] (*pl* sopranos /-nəʊz/) the highest singing voice; a woman, girl, or boy with this voice

sordid /ˈsɔːdɪd/ *adj* **1** unpleasant; not honest or moral: *We discovered the truth about his sordid past.* **2** very dirty and unpleasant

sore[1] /sɔː(r)/ *adj* (used about a part of the body) painful and often red: *to have a sore throat* ◆ *My feet were sore from walking so far.*
IDM **a sore point** a subject that is likely to make sb upset or angry when mentioned
stand/stick out like a sore thumb to be extremely obvious, especially in a negative way: *A big new office block would stand out like a sore thumb in the old part of town.*
▶ **soreness** *noun* [U]: *a cream to reduce soreness and swelling*

sore[2] /sɔː(r)/ *noun* [C] a painful, often red place on your body where the skin is cut or infected

sorely /ˈsɔːli/ *adv* (*formal*) very much; seriously: *You'll be* ***sorely missed*** *when you leave.*

sorrow /ˈsɒrəʊ/ *noun* (*formal*) **1** [U] a feeling of great sadness because sth bad has happened **2** [C] a very sad event or situation ▶ **sorrowful** /-fl/ *adj* ▶ **sorrowfully** /-fəli/ *adv*

sorry[1] /ˈsɒri/ *adj* (sorrier; sorriest) **1** [not before a noun] sorry (to see, hear, etc.); sorry that ... sad or disappointed: *I was sorry to hear that you've been ill.* ◆ *I am sorry that we have to leave so soon.* ◆ *'Simon's mother died last week.' 'Oh, I am sorry.'* **2** [not before a noun] sorry (for/about sth); sorry (to do sth/that ...) used for excusing yourself for sth that you have done: *I'm awfully sorry for spilling that coffee.* ◆ *I'm sorry I've kept you all waiting.* ◆ *I'm sorry to disturb you so late in the evening, but I wonder if you can help me.* **3** [only before a noun] very bad: *The house was in a* ***sorry state*** *when we first moved in.* ◆ *They were a* ***sorry sight*** *when they finally got home.*
IDM **be/feel sorry for sb** to feel sadness or pity for sb: *I feel very sorry for the families of the victims.* ◆ *Stop feeling sorry for yourself!*
I'm sorry used for politely saying 'no' to sth, disagreeing with sth or introducing bad news: *'Would you like to come to dinner on Friday?' 'I'm sorry, I'm busy that evening.'* ◆ *I'm sorry, I don't agree with you. I think we should accept the offer.* ◆ *I'm sorry to tell you that your application has been unsuccessful.*

sorry[2] /ˈsɒri/ *exclam* **1** used for making excuses, apologizing, etc: *Sorry, I didn't see you standing behind me.* ◆ *Sorry I'm late—the bus didn't come on time.* ◆ *He didn't even* ***say sorry*** (= apologize). **2** (*especially BrE*) (used for asking sb to repeat sth that you have not heard correctly): *'My name's Dave Harries.' 'Sorry? Dave who?'* **3** (used for correcting yourself when you have said sth wrong): *Take the second turning, sorry, the third turning on the right.*

sort[1] /sɔːt/ *noun* **1** [C] a sort of sb/sth a type or kind: *What sort of music do you like?* ◆ *She's got* ***all sorts of*** *problems at the moment.* ◆ *There were snacks —peanuts, olives,* ***that sort of thing****.* **2** [sing] (*especially BrE*) a particular type of character; a person: *My brother would never cheat on his wife; he's not that sort.* SYN for both meanings **kind**
IDM **a sort of sth** (*informal*) a type of sth; something that is similar to sth: *Can you hear a sort of ticking noise?*
sort of (*spoken*) rather; in a way: *'Do you see what I mean?' 'Sort of.'* ◆ *I'd sort of like to go, but I'm not sure.*

sort[2] /sɔːt/ *verb* [T] **1** sort sth (into sth) to put things into different groups or places, according to their type, etc.; to separate things of one type from others: *I'm just sorting these papers into the correct files.* ◆ *The computer will sort the words into alphabetical order.* **2** [often passive] (*especially BrE informal*) to find an answer to a problem or difficult situation; to organize sth/sb: *I'll have more time when I've* ***got things sorted*** *at home.*
PHR V **sort sth out** **1** to tidy or organize sth: *The toy cupboard needs sorting out.* **2** to find an answer to a problem; to organize sth: *I haven't found a flat yet but I hope to sort something out soon.*
sort through sth to look through a number of things, in order to find sth that you are looking for or to put them in order

ˌso-ˈso *adj, adv* (*informal*) all right but not particularly good/well: *'How are you feeling today?' 'So-so.'*

soufflé /ˈsuːfleɪ/ *noun* [C,U] a type of food made mainly from egg whites, flour and milk, beaten together and baked until it rises

sought *past tense, past participle* of **seek**

ˈsought after *adj* that people want very much, because it is of high quality or rare

soul /səʊl/ *noun*
➤ SPIRIT OF PERSON **1** [C] the spiritual part of a person that is believed to continue to exist after the body is dead: *Christians believe that your soul goes to heaven when you die.*
➤ INNER CHARACTER **2** [C] the inner part of a person containing their deepest thoughts and feelings: *There was a feeling of restlessness deep in her soul.* ➲ look at **spirit**
➤ PERSON **3** [C] [used with adjectives] (*old-fashioned*) a particular type of person: *She's a kind old soul.* **4** [sing] [in negative sentences] a person: *There wasn't a soul in sight* (= there was nobody). ◆ *Promise me you won't tell a soul.*
➤ MUSIC **5** (also ˈ**soul music**) [U] a type of music made popular by African American musicians: *a soul singer*
IDM **heart and soul** ➲ **heart**

soulful /ˈsəʊlfl/ *adj* having or showing deep feeling: *a soulful expression*

soulless /ˈsəʊlləs/ *adj* without feeling, warmth or interest: *They live in soulless concrete blocks.* SYN **depressing**

ˈsoul music = **soul**(5)

sound[1] /saʊnd/ *noun* **1** [C,U] something that you hear or that can be heard: *the sound of voices* ◆ *a clicking/buzzing/scratching sound* ◆ *After that, he didn't* ***make a sound****.* ◆ *She opened the door without a sound.* ◆ *Light travels faster than sound.* ◆ *sound waves* SYN **noise** **2** [U] what you can hear coming

S

from a TV, radio, etc: *Can you turn the sound up/down* (= make it louder/quieter)?

IDM **by the sound of it/that/things** judging from what sb has said or what you have read about sb/sth: *She must be an interesting person, by the sound of it.*

like the look/sound of sb/sth ➲ **like²**

sound² /saʊnd/ *verb* **1** [I] [not usually used in the continuous tenses] to give a particular impression when heard or read about; to seem: *That* ***sounds like*** *a child crying.* ◆ *She sounded upset and angry on the phone.* ◆ *You sound like your father when you say things like that!* ◆ *He sounds a very nice person from his letter.* ◆ *Does she sound like the right person for the job?* ◆ *It doesn't* ***sound as if/though*** *he's very reliable.*

HELP In spoken English, people often use 'like' instead of 'as if' or 'as though', especially in American English: *It sounds like you had a great time.* This is considered incorrect in written British English.

2 -sounding [in compounds] seeming to be of the type mentioned, from what you have heard or read: *a Spanish-sounding surname* ◆ *They had a very unromantic-sounding dinner at a fast food restaurant.* **3** [T] to cause sth to make a sound; to give a signal by making a sound: *to sound the horn of your car* ◆ *A student on one of the upper floors* ***sounded the alarm***.

PHR V **sound sb out (about sth)** to ask sb questions in order to find out what they think or intend to do

sound³ /saʊnd/ *adj* (sounder; soundest) *adv* **1** sensible; that you can depend on and that will probably give good results: *sound advice* ◆ *a sound investment* **2** healthy and strong; in good condition: *The structure of the bridge is basically sound.* OPP for both meanings **unsound**

IDM **be sound asleep** to be deeply asleep

▶ **soundness** *noun* [U]

ˈsound bite *noun* [C] a short phrase or sentence taken from a longer speech, especially a speech made by a politician, that is particularly effective or appropriate

ˈsound effect *noun* [C, usually pl] a sound, for example the sound of the wind, that is made in an artificial way and used in a play, film or computer game to make it more realistic

soundly /ˈsaʊndli/ *adv* completely or deeply: *The children were sleeping soundly.*

soundproof /ˈsaʊndpruːf/ *adj* made so that no sound can get in or out: *a soundproof room*

soundtrack /ˈsaʊndtræk/ *noun* [C] the recorded sound and music from a film or computer game ➲ note at **film** ➲ look at **track**

soup /suːp/ *noun* [U,C] liquid food made by cooking meat, vegetables, etc. in water: *a tin of chicken soup* ➲ picture on **page P16**

sour /ˈsaʊə(r)/ *adj* **1** having a sharp taste like that of a lemon: *This sauce is quite sour.* ➲ look at **bitter**, **sweet** **2** (used especially about milk) tasting or smelling unpleasant because it is no longer fresh: *This cream has* ***gone sour***. **3** (used about people) angry and unpleasant: *a sour expression* ◆ *a* ***sour-faced*** *old woman*

IDM **go/turn sour** to stop being pleasant or friendly: *Their relationship turned sour after a few months.*

sour grapes used to show that you think sb is jealous and is pretending that sth is not important

▶ **sour** *verb* [T] (*formal*): *The disagreement over trade tariffs has soured relations between the two countries.*

▶ **sourly** *adv* ▶ **sourness** *noun* [U]

source /sɔːs/ *noun* [C] a place, person or thing where sth comes or starts from or where sth is obtained: *Tourism in Cornwall is an important* ***source of income***. ◆ *The TV is a great source of entertainment.* ◆ *Police have refused to reveal the source of their information.* ◆ *He set out to discover the source of the river* ➲ picture on **page P10** ▶ **source** *verb* [T]

south¹ /saʊθ/ *noun* [U, sing] (*abbr* S; So.) **1** (also **the south**) the direction that is on your right when you watch the sun rise; one of the **points of the compass** (= the main directions that we give names to): *warm winds from the south* ◆ *Which way is south?* ◆ *We live to the south of* (= further south than) *London.* ➲ picture at **compass** **2 the south; the South** the southern part of a country, a city, a region or the world: *Nice is in the South of France.* ➲ look at **north**, **east**, **west**

south² /saʊθ/ *adj, adv* **1** [only *before* a noun] in the south: *the south coast of Cornwall* **2** (used about a wind) coming from the south **3** to or towards the south: *The house faces south.* ◆ *We live just south of Birmingham.*

southbound /ˈsaʊθbaʊnd/ *adj* travelling or leading towards the south

ˌsouth-ˈeast¹ (also **the ˌsouth-ˈeast**) *noun* [sing] (*abbr* SE) the direction or a region that is an equal distance between south and east ➲ picture at **compass**

ˌsouth-ˈeast² *adj, adv* in, from or to the **south-east** of a place or country: *the south-east coast of Spain*

ˌsouth-ˈeasterly *adj* **1** [only *before* a noun] towards the south-east: *in a south-easterly direction* **2** (used about a wind) coming from the south-east

ˌsouth-ˈeastern *adj* (*abbr* SE) [only *before* a noun] connected with the south-east of a place or country: *the south-eastern states of the US*

ˌsouth-ˈeastwards (also **ˌsouth-ˈeastward**) *adv* towards the south-east

southerly /ˈsʌðəli/ *adj* **1** [only *before* a noun] to, towards or in the south: *Keep going in a southerly direction.* **2** (used about a wind) coming from the south

southern (also **Southern**) /ˈsʌðən/ *adj* (*abbr* S; So.) of, in or from the south of a place: *a man with a southern accent* ◆ *Greece is in Southern Europe.*

southerner (also **Southerner**) /ˈsʌðənə(r)/ *noun* [C] a person who was born in or lives in the southern part of a country

the ˌSouth ˈPole *noun* [sing] the point on the Earth's surface which is furthest south ➲ picture at **earth**

southwards /ˈsaʊθwədz/ (also southward) *adv* towards the south: *We're flying southwards at the moment.* ▶ **southward** *adj*: *in a southward direction*

ˌsouth-ˈwest¹ (also the ˌSouth-ˈWest) *noun* [sing] (*abbr* SW) the direction or a region that is an equal distance between south and west ➲ picture at **compass**

ˌsouth-ˈwest² *adj, adv* in, from or to the **south-west** of a place or country: *the south-west coast of France* ♦ *Our garden faces south-west.*

ˌsouth-ˈwesterly *adj* **1** [only *before* a noun] towards the south-west: *in a south-westerly direction* **2** (used about a wind) coming from the south-west

ˌsouth-ˈwestern *adj* (*abbr* SW) [only *before* a noun] connected with the south-west of a place or country

ˌsouth-ˈwestwards (also ˌsouth-ˈwestward) *adv* towards the south-west: *Follow the B409 south-westwards for twenty miles.*

souvenir /ˌsuːvəˈnɪə(r)/ *noun* [C] something that you buy or keep to remind you of somewhere you have been on holiday or of a special event: *I brought back a menu as a souvenir of my trip.* SYN **memento**

sovereign¹ /ˈsɒvrɪn/ *noun* [C] a king or queen

sovereign² /ˈsɒvrɪn/ *adj* **1** [only *before* a noun] (used about a country) not controlled by any other country; independent **2** having the highest possible authority

sovereignty /ˈsɒvrənti/ *noun* [U] the power that a country has to control its own government

sow¹ /səʊ/ *verb* [T] (*pt* sowed; *pp* sown /səʊn/ or sowed) sow A (in B); sow B (with A) to plant seeds in the ground: *to sow seeds in pots* ♦ *to sow a field with wheat*

sow² /saʊ/ *noun* [C] an adult female pig ➲ note at **pig**

soya bean /ˈsɔɪə biːn/ (*AmE* soy bean) *noun* [C] a type of **bean** (= a seed from a plant) that can be cooked and eaten or used to make many different types of food, for example flour, oil and a type of milk

soy sauce /ˌsɔɪ ˈsɔːs/ (also ˌsoya ˈsauce) *noun* [U] a dark brown sauce that is made from **soya beans** and that you add to food to make it taste better

spa /spɑː/ *noun* [C] **1** a place where mineral water comes out of the ground and where people go to drink this water because it is considered to be healthy **2** a place where people can relax and improve their health: *a superb* ***health spa*** *which includes sauna, Turkish bath and fitness rooms*

🔑 **space¹** /speɪs/ *noun* **1** [C,U] space (for sb/sth) (to do sth) a place or an area that is empty or not used: *Is there enough space for me to park the car there?* ♦ *Shelves would* ***take up*** *less* ***space*** *than a cupboard.* ♦ *a parking space* ♦ *We're a bit short of space.* ♦ *There's a space here for you to write your name.* ♦ *Leave a space after the comma.* SYN **room** ➲ note at **place¹** **2** [U] (also ˌouter ˈspace) the area which surrounds the planet Earth and the other planets and stars: *space travel* ♦ *a spaceman/spacewoman* (= a person who travels in space) **3** [C, usually sing] a period of time: *Priti had been ill three times* ***in/within the space of*** *four months.* ♦ *He's achieved a lot in* ***a short space of time.*** **4** [U] time and freedom to think and do what you want: *I need some space to think.*

TOPIC

Space

The **Earth** and other **planets** form the **solar system.** The Earth **orbits** (= goes round) the **sun,** and the **moon** orbits the Earth. Everything beyond the Earth's **atmosphere** is **outer space** and the Earth, the planets and the whole of space make up the **universe. Astronomers** study the sun, planets and stars; the subject is called **astronomy. Astronauts** travel into space in a **spaceship** or **space shuttle. Satellites** are **launched** (= sent) into space and are used to send back information, television pictures, etc.

Some people believe that there is life on other planets and that these **aliens** are trying to contact us. Some people who see **UFOs** (= unidentified flying objects) think that they may be alien **spaceships.**

space² /speɪs/ *verb* [T] space sth (out) to arrange things so that there are empty spaces between them

ˈspace bar *noun* [C] a bar on the keyboard of a computer that you press to make spaces between words ➲ picture at **computer**

spacecraft /ˈspeɪskrɑːft/ *noun* [C] (*pl* spacecraft) a vehicle that travels in space

ˌspaced ˈout *adj* (*informal*) not completely conscious of what is happening around you, often because of taking drugs

spaceship /ˈspeɪsʃɪp/ *noun* [C] a vehicle that travels in space, carrying people

ˈspace shuttle *noun* [C] a vehicle that can travel into space and land like a plane when it returns to Earth

spacious /ˈspeɪʃəs/ *adj* having a lot of space; large in size: *a spacious flat* SYN **roomy** ▶ **spaciousness** *noun* [U]

spade /speɪd/ *noun* **1** [C] a tool that you use for digging ➲ look at **shovel** ➲ picture at **dig, garden** **2** spades [pl] in a pack of playing cards, the **suit** (= one of the four sets) with pointed black symbols on them: *the king of spades* ➲ note at **card** ➲ picture at **card** **3** [C] one of the cards from this suit: *Have you got a spade?*

spaghetti /spəˈgeti/ *noun* [U] a type of **pasta** (= Italian food made from flour and water) that looks like long strings: *How long does spaghetti take to cook?* ➲ note at **pasta** ➲ picture on **page P16**

S

spam /spæm/ *noun* [U] advertising material sent by email to people who have not asked for it ➲ look at **junk mail**

span¹ /spæn/ *noun* [C] **1** the length of time that sth lasts or continues: *Young children have a short attention span.* **2** the length of sth from one end to the other: *the wingspan of a bird*

span² /spæn/ *verb* [T] (spa**nn**ing; spa**nn**ed) **1** to form a bridge over sth **2** to last or continue for a particular period of time

spank /spæŋk/ *verb* [T] to hit sb several times on their bottom with an open hand as a punishment

spanner /ˈspænə(r)/ (*AmE* **wrench**) *noun* [C] a metal tool with an end shaped for turning **nuts** (= small metal rings) and **bolts** (= pins that are used for holding things together) ➲ picture at **tool**

🔑 **spare¹** /speə(r)/ *adj* **1** [only *before* a noun] not needed now but kept because it may be needed in the future: *The spare tyre is kept in the boot.* ◆ *a spare room* **2** not being used; free: *There were no seats spare so we had to stand.* **3** not used for work: *What do you do in your **spare time**?* ▶ **spare** *noun* [C]: *The fuse has blown. Where do you keep your spares?*

spare² /speə(r)/ *verb* [T] **1** **spare sth (for sb); spare (sb) sth** to be able to give sth to sb: *I suppose I can spare you a few minutes.* **2** **spare sb (from) sth/doing sth** to save sb from having an unpleasant experience: *You could spare yourself waiting if you book in advance.* **3** **spare sb/sth (from sth)** to not hurt or damage sb/sth **4** **spare no effort, expense,** etc. to do sth as well as possible without limiting the time, money, etc. involved: *No expense was spared at the wedding.* ◆ *He spared no effort in trying to find a job.*

IDM **to spare** more than is needed: *There's no time to spare. We must leave straight away.*

ˌspare ˈpart *noun* [C] a part for a machine, an engine, etc. that you can use to replace an old part which is damaged or broken

sparing /ˈspeərɪŋ/ *adj* (*formal*) using only a little of sth; careful ▶ **sparingly** *adv*

spark¹ /spɑːk/ *noun* **1** [C] a very small bright piece of burning material: *A spark set fire to the carpet.* **2** [C] a flash of light that is caused by electricity: *A spark ignites the fuel in a car engine.* **3** [C,U] an exciting quality that sb/sth has

spark² /spɑːk/ *verb* [T] **spark (sth) off** to cause sth to start or develop: *Eric's comments sparked off a tremendous argument.*

sparkle /ˈspɑːkl/ *verb* [I] to shine with many small points of light: *The river sparkled in the sunlight.* ▶ **sparkle** *noun* [C,U]

sparkler /ˈspɑːklə(r)/ *noun* [C] a type of small **firework** (= a small object that burns or explodes with coloured lights and loud sounds) that you hold in your hand and light. It burns with many bright **sparks**.

sparkling /ˈspɑːklɪŋ/ *adj* **1** shining with many small points of light: *sparkling blue eyes* **2** (used about a drink) containing bubbles of gas: *sparkling wine/mineral water* **SYN** **fizzy**

ˈspark plug *noun* [C] a small piece of equipment in an engine that produces a **spark** of electricity to make the fuel burn and start the engine

sparrow /ˈspærəʊ/ *noun* [C] a small brown and grey bird that is common in many parts of the world

sparse /spɑːs/ *adj* small in quantity or amount: *a sparse crowd* ◆ *He just had a few sparse hairs on his head.* ▶ **sparsely** *adv*: *a sparsely populated area* ▶ **sparseness** *noun* [U]

spartan /ˈspɑːtn/ *adj* (*formal*) very simple and not comfortable: *spartan living conditions*

spasm /ˈspæzəm/ *noun* [C,U] a sudden movement of a muscle that you cannot control: *He had painful muscular spasms in his leg.*

spat *past tense, past participle* of **spit¹**

spate /speɪt/ *noun* [sing] a large number or amount of sth happening at one time: *There has been a spate of burglaries in the area recently.*

spatial /ˈspeɪʃl/ *adj* (*formal*) connected with the size or position of sth

spatter /ˈspætə(r)/ *verb* [T] **spatter sb/sth (with sth); spatter sth (on sb/sth)** to cover sb/sth with small drops of sth wet

spatula /ˈspætʃələ/ *noun* [C] a tool with a wide flat part, used in cooking for mixing and spreading things ➲ picture at **kitchen**

🔑 **speak** /spiːk/ *verb* (*pt* **spoke** /spəʊk/; *pp* **spoken** /ˈspəʊkən/) **1** [I] **speak (to sb) (about sb/sth); speak (of sth)** to talk or say things: *I'd like to speak to the manager, please.* ◆ *Could you speak more slowly?* ◆ *I was so angry I could hardly speak.*

> **HELP** **Speak** or **talk**? **Speak** and **talk** have almost the same meaning but we use **talk** more informally, to show that two or more people are having a conversation, and **speak** to show that only one person is saying something, especially in a formal situation: *I'd like to speak to the manager, please.* ◆ *We talked all night.* ◆ *The head teacher spoke to the class about university courses.*

2 [I,T] [not used in the continuous tenses] to know and be able to use a language: *Does anyone here speak German?* ◆ *She speaks (in) Greek to her parents.* ◆ *a French-speaking guide* **3** [I] **speak (on/about sth)** to make a speech to a group of people: *Professor Hurst has been invited to speak on American foreign policy.*

IDM **be on speaking terms (with sb)** to be friendly with sb again after an argument: *Thankfully they are back on speaking terms again.*

be speaking (to sb) (*informal*) to be friendly with sb again after an argument

so to speak used when you are describing sth in a way that sounds strange: *She turned green, so to speak, after watching a TV programme about the environment.*

speak for itself to be very clear so that no other explanation is needed: *The statistics speak for themselves.*

speak/talk of the devil ➲ **devil**

speak your mind to say exactly what you think, even though you might offend sb
strictly speaking ➲ **strictly**
PHR V **speak for sb** to express the thoughts or opinions of sb else
speak out (against sth) to say publicly that you think sth is bad or wrong
speak up to speak louder

speaker /ˈspiːkə(r)/ *noun* [C] **1** a person who makes a speech to a group of people: *Tonight's speaker is a well-known writer and journalist.* **2** a person who speaks a particular language: *She's a fluent Russian speaker.* **3** (also **loudspeaker**) the part of a radio, computer or piece of musical equipment that the sound comes out of

spear /spɪə(r)/ *noun* [C] a long pole with a sharp point at one end, used for hunting or fighting ➲ picture at **sword**

spearhead /ˈspɪəhed/ *noun* [C, usually sing] a person or group that begins or leads an attack ▶ **spearhead** *verb* [T]

spearmint /ˈspɪəmɪnt/ *noun* [U] a type of leaf with a strong fresh taste that is used in sweets, etc: *spearmint chewing gum* ➲ look at **peppermint**

special[1] /ˈspeʃl/ *adj* **1** not usual or ordinary; important for some particular reason: *a special occasion* ◆ *Please take special care of it.* ◆ *Are you doing anything special tonight?* **2** [only *before* a noun] for a particular purpose: *Andy goes to a special school for the deaf.* ◆ *There's a special tool for doing that.*

special[2] /ˈspeʃl/ *noun* [C] something that is not of the usual or ordinary type: *an all-night election special on TV* ◆ *I'm going to cook one of my specials tonight.*

specialist /ˈspeʃəlɪst/ *noun* [C] a person with special knowledge of a particular subject: *She's a specialist in diseases of cattle.* ◆ *I have to see a heart specialist.* ◆ *to give specialist advice*

speciality /ˌspeʃiˈæləti/ *noun* [C] (*pl* **specialities**) (*AmE* **specialty**, *pl* **specialties**) **1** something made by a person, place, business, etc. that is very good and that he/she/it is known for: *The cheese is a speciality of the region.* **2** an area of study or a subject that you know a lot about

specialize (also **-ise**) /ˈspeʃəlaɪz/ *verb* [I] **specialize (in sth)** to give most of your attention to one subject, type of product, etc: *This shop specializes in clothes for taller men.* ▶ **specialization** (also **-isation**) /ˌspeʃəlaɪˈzeɪʃn/ *noun* [U]

specialized (also **-ised**) /ˈspeʃəlaɪzd/ *adj* **1** to be used for a particular purpose: *a specialized system* **2** having or needing special knowledge of a particular subject: *We have specialized staff to help you with any problems.*

specially /ˈspeʃəli/ (also **especially**) *adv* **1** for a particular purpose or reason: *I made this specially for you.* **2** (*informal*) particularly; very; more than usual: *The restaurant has a great atmosphere but the food is not specially good.* ◆ *I hate homework. Specially history.*

specialty /ˈspeʃəlti/ (*AmE*) = **speciality**

species /ˈspiːʃiːz/ *noun* [C] (*pl* **species**) a group of plants or animals that are all similar and that can breed together: *This conservation group aims to protect endangered species.* ◆ *a rare species of frog*

specific /spəˈsɪfɪk/ *adj* **1 specific (about sth)** detailed or exact: *You must give the class specific instructions on what they have to do.* ◆ *Can you be more specific about what the man was wearing?* **2** particular; not general: *Everyone has been given a specific job to do.* ▶ **specifically** /-kli/ *adv*: *a play written specifically for radio* ◆ *I specifically asked you to write in pencil, not pen.*

specification /ˌspesɪfɪˈkeɪʃn/ *noun* [C,U] detailed information about how sth is or should be built or made

specify /ˈspesɪfaɪ/ *verb* [T] (**specifying**; **specifies**; *pt, pp* **specified**) to say or name sth clearly or in detail: *The fire regulations specify the maximum number of people allowed in.*

specimen /ˈspesɪmən/ *noun* [C] **1** a small amount of sth that is tested for medical or scientific purposes: *Specimens of the patient's blood were tested in the hospital laboratory.* **2** an example of a particular type of thing, especially sth intended to be studied by experts or scientists SYN for both meanings **sample**

speck /spek/ *noun* [C] a very small spot or mark: *a speck of dust/dirt*

specs /speks/ (*informal*) = **glasses**

spectacle /ˈspektəkl/ *noun* [C] something that is impressive or shocking to look at

spectacles /ˈspektəklz/ (*formal*) = **glasses**

spectacular /spekˈtækjələ(r)/ *adj* very impressive to see: *The view from the top of the hill is quite spectacular.* ▶ **spectacularly** *adv*

spectator /spekˈteɪtə(r)/ *noun* [C] a person who is watching an event, especially a sports event

spectre (*AmE* **specter**) /ˈspektə(r)/ *noun* [C] **1** something unpleasant that people are afraid might happen in the future: *the spectre of unemployment* **2** (*old-fashioned*) = **ghost**

spectrum /ˈspektrəm/ *noun* [C, usually sing] (*pl* **spectra** /ˈspektrə/) **1** the set of seven colours into which white light can be separated: *You can see the colours of the spectrum in a rainbow.* **2** all the possible varieties of sth: *The speakers represented the whole spectrum of political opinions.*

speculate /ˈspekjuleɪt/ *verb* **1** [I,T] **speculate (about/on sth)**; **speculate that …** to make a guess about sth: *to speculate about the result of the next election* **2** [I] to buy and sell with the aim of making money but with the risk of losing it: *to speculate on the stock market* ▶ **speculation** /ˌspekjuˈleɪʃn/ *noun* [U,C] ▶ **speculator** /ˈspekjuleɪtə(r)/ *noun* [C]

speculative /ˈspekjələtɪv/ *adj* **1** based on guessing or on opinions that have been formed without knowing all the facts **2** (used in business) done in

S

the hope of making money, but involving the risk of losing it

sped *past tense, past participle of* **speed**[2]

speech /spiːtʃ/ *noun* **1** [C] a formal talk that you give to a group of people: *The Chancellor is going to* ***make a speech*** *to City businessmen.* **2** [U] the ability to speak: *He lost the* ***power of speech*** *after the accident.* ◆ *freedom of speech* (= being allowed to express your opinions in an open way) **3** [U] the particular way of speaking of a person or group of people: *She's doing a study of children's speech.* **4** [C] a group of words that one person must say in a play: *This character has the longest speech in the play.*

speechless /ˈspiːtʃləs/ *adj* not able to speak, for example because you are shocked, angry, etc: *He was speechless with rage.*

speed[1] /spiːd/ *noun* **1** [U] fast movement: *She started the race slowly, but she gradually* ***picked up speed.*** ◆ *The bus was travelling* ***at speed*** *when it hit the wall.* **2** [C,U] the rate at which sb/sth moves or travels: *The car was travelling* ***at a speed of*** *140 kilometres an hour.* ◆ *to travel* ***at top/high/full/maximum speed***

speed[2] /spiːd/ *verb* [I] (*pt, pp* **speeded** /ˈspiːdɪd/ *or* **sped** /sped/) **1** to go or move very quickly: *He sped round the corner on his bicycle.* **2** [only used in the continuous tenses] to drive a car, etc. faster than the legal speed limit: *The police said she had been speeding.*

PHR V speed (sth) up to go or make sth go faster: *The new computer system should speed up production in the factory.*

speedboat /ˈspiːdbəʊt/ *noun* [C] a small fast boat with an engine

speeding /ˈspiːdɪŋ/ *noun* [U] driving a car, etc. faster than the legal speed limit

ˈspeed limit *noun* [C, usually sing] the highest speed that you are allowed to drive without breaking the law on a particular road: *He was going way* ***over the speed limit*** *when the police stopped him.* ◆ *to* ***break/exceed the speed limit*** (= go faster than you are allowed to by law) ➲ note at **driving**

speedometer /spiːˈdɒmɪtə(r)/ *noun* [C] a piece of equipment in a vehicle that tells you how fast you are travelling ➲ picture at **car**

speedway /ˈspiːdweɪ/ *noun* [U] the sport of racing cars or motorbikes around a special track

speedy /ˈspiːdi/ *adj* (**speedier**; **speediest**) fast; quick: *a speedy response/reply* ▶ **speedily** *adv* ▶ **speediness** *noun* [U]

spell[1] /spel/ *verb* (*pt, pp* **spelled** /speld/ *or* **spelt** /spelt/) **1** [I,T] to write or say the letters of a word in the correct order: *I could never spell very well at school.* ◆ ***How do you spell*** *your surname?* ◆ *His name is spelt P-H-I-L-I-P.* **2** [T] (used about a set of letters) to form a particular word: *If you add an 'e' to 'car' it spells 'care'.* **3** [T] to mean sth; to have sth as a result: *Another poor harvest would* ***spell disaster*** *for the region.*

PHR V spell sth out 1 to express sth in a very clear and direct way: *Although she didn't spell it out, it was obvious she wasn't happy.* **2** to write or say the letters of a word or name in the correct order: *I have an unusual name, so I always have to spell it out to people.*

spell[2] /spel/ *noun* [C] **1** a short period of time: *a spell of cold weather* **2** (especially in stories) magic words that cause sb to be in a particular state or condition: *The witch* ***put/cast a spell on*** *the prince.*

spellchecker /ˈspeltʃekə(r)/ (*also* **spellcheck**) *noun* [C] a computer program that checks your writing to see if your spelling is correct

spelling /ˈspelɪŋ/ *noun* **1** [U] the ability to write the letters of a word correctly: *Roger is very poor at spelling.* **2** [C,U] the way that letters are arranged to make a word: *'Center' is the American spelling of 'centre'.*

EXAM TIP

Spelling mistakes

Keep a list of all the words that you have got wrong more than once in your homework. Before the exam, go through your list and learn the correct spellings. Work with a friend and test each other.

spelt *past tense, past participle of* **spell**[1]

spend /spend/ *verb* (*pt, pp* **spent** /spent/) **1** [I,T] **spend (sth) (on sth)** to give or pay money for sth: *You shouldn't go on spending like that.* ◆ *How much do you spend on food each week?* **2** [T] **spend sth (on sth/doing sth)** to pass time: *I spent a whole evening writing letters.* ◆ *I'm spending the weekend at my parents' house.* ◆ *He spent two years in Brno.* ◆ *I don't want to spend too much time on this project.*

spending /ˈspendɪŋ/ *noun* [U] the amount of money that is spent by a government or an organization

spent *past tense, past participle of* **spend**

sperm /spɜːm/ *noun* **1** [C] (*pl* **sperm** *or* **sperms**) a cell that is produced in the sex organs of a male and that can join with a female egg to produce young **2** [U] the liquid that contains **sperms** **SYN** **semen**

SPF /ˌes piː ˈef/ *abbr* **sun protection factor**; a number that tells you how much protection a particular cream or liquid gives you from the harmful effects of the sun

sphere /sfɪə(r)/ *noun* [C] **1** any round object shaped like a ball ➲ picture at **cube** **2** an area of interest or activity ▶ **spherical** /ˈsferɪkl/ *adj*

spice[1] /spaɪs/ *noun* **1** [C,U] a substance, especially a powder, that is made from a plant and used to give flavour to food: *I use a lot of herbs and spices in my cooking.* ◆ *There isn't enough spice in the sauce.* ➲ look at **herb** ➲ picture on **page P14** **2** [U] excitement and interest: *to* ***add spice*** *to a situation* ▶ **spicy** *adj* (**spicier**; **spiciest**): *Do you like spicy food?*

spice[2] /spaɪs/ *verb* [T] **spice sth (up) (with sth) 1** to add spice to food: *He always spices his cooking with lots of chilli powder.* **2** to add excitement to sth

spider /ˈspaɪdə(r)/ *noun* [C] a small creature with eight thin legs

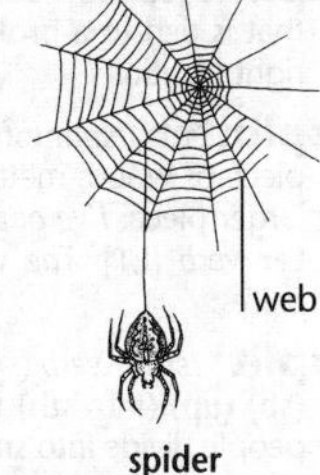

spider

spidergram /ˈspaɪdəgræm/ = **mind map**

spike /spaɪk/ *noun* [C] a piece of metal, wood, etc. that has a sharp point at one end

spill /spɪl/ *verb* (*pt, pp* **spilt** /spɪlt/ *or* **spilled**) **1** [I,T] (used especially about a liquid) to accidentally come out of a container; to make a liquid, etc. do this: *Some water had spilled out of the bucket onto the floor.* ◆ *The bag split, and sugar spilled everywhere.* ◆ *I've spilt some coffee on the desk.* **2** [I] **spill out, over, into, etc.** to come out of a place suddenly and go in different directions: *The train stopped and everyone spilled out.*
IDM spill the beans (*informal*) to tell a person about sth that should be a secret
▸ **spill** *noun* [C]: *Many seabirds died as a result of the oil spill.*

spill

spin¹ /spɪn/ *verb* (**spinning**; *pt, pp* **spun** /spʌn/) **1** [I,T] **spin (sth) (round)** to turn or to make sth turn round quickly: *Mary spun round when she heard someone call her name.* ◆ *to spin a ball/coin/wheel* **2** [I,T] to make thread from a mass of wool, cotton, etc: *She spun and dyed the wool herself.* **3** [T] to remove water from clothes that have just been washed in a machine that turns them round and round very fast
PHR V spin sth out to make sth last as long as possible

spin² /spɪn/ *noun* [C,U] **1** an act of making sth **spin¹**(1): *She **put** a lot of **spin on** the ball.* **2** (especially in politics) a way of talking publicly about a difficult situation, a mistake, etc. that makes it sound positive for you
IDM go/take sb for a spin to go/take sb out in a car or other vehicle

spinach /ˈspɪnɪtʃ; -ɪdʒ/ *noun* [U] a plant with large dark green leaves that can be cooked and eaten as a vegetable ➲ picture on **page P15**

spinal /ˈspaɪnl/ *adj* connected with the **spine** (= the bones of your back)

ˈ**spin doctor** *noun* [C] (especially in politics) a person who finds ways of talking about difficult situations, mistakes, etc. in a positive way

ˌ**spin** ˈ**dryer** *noun* [C] (*BrE*) a machine that removes water from wet clothes by turning them round and round very fast ➲ look at **tumble dryer**
▸ ˌ**spin-ˈdry** *verb* [T]

spine /spaɪn/ *noun* [C] **1** the row of small bones that are connected together down the middle of your back **SYN backbone** ➲ picture at **body** **2** one of the sharp points like needles on some plants and animals: *Porcupines use their spines to protect themselves.* ➲ look at **prickle** ➲ picture at **hedgehog** **3** the narrow part of the cover of a book that you can see when it is on a shelf

spineless /ˈspaɪnləs/ *adj* weak and easily frightened

ˈ**spin-off** *noun* [C] **a spin-off (from/of sth)** something unexpected and useful that develops from sth else

spinster /ˈspɪnstə(r)/ *noun* [C] (*old-fashioned*) a woman, especially an older woman, who has never been married ➲ look at **bachelor**

> **MORE** Nowadays **single** is the most usual word for describing a woman who is not married: *a single woman.*

spiral /ˈspaɪrəl/ *noun* [C] a long curved line that moves round and round away from a central point ▸ **spiral** *adj*: *a spiral staircase* ▸ **spiral** *verb* [I] (**spiralling**; **spiralled**, (*AmE*) **spiraling**; **spiraled**): *The plane spiralled to the ground.*

spiral

spiral staircase

spire /ˈspaɪə(r)/ *noun* [C] a tall pointed structure on the top of a building, especially a church

spirit¹ /ˈspɪrɪt/ *noun*
▸ **MIND/FEELINGS** **1** [sing] the part of a person that is not physical; your thoughts and feelings, not your body: *the power of the human spirit to overcome difficulties* **2 spirits** [pl] the mood, attitude or state of mind of sb/sth: *to be **in high/low spirits*** (= in a happy/sad mood)
▸ **-SPIRITED** **3 -spirited** [in compounds] having the mood or attitude of mind mentioned: *a group of high-spirited teenagers*
▸ **DETERMINATION** **4** [U] energy, strength of mind or determination: *The group had plenty of **team spirit**.*
▸ **QUALITY** **5** [sing] the typical or most important quality of sth: *the pioneer spirit* ◆ *The painting perfectly captures the spirit of the times.*
▸ **SOUL** **6** [C] a being without a body; the part of a person that many people believe still exists after their body is dead: *It was believed that people could be possessed by **evil spirits**.* ➲ look at **ghost**, **soul**
▸ **ALCOHOL** **7 spirits** [pl] (*especially BrE*) strong alcoholic drinks: *She didn't drink whisky or brandy or any other spirits.*

spirit² /ˈspɪrɪt/ *verb*
PHR V spirit sb/sth away/off to take sb/sth away secretly

spirited /ˈspɪrɪtɪd/ *adj* full of energy, determination and courage

spiritual /ˈspɪrɪtʃuəl/ *adj* **1** connected with deep thoughts, feelings or emotions rather than the body or physical things: *spiritual development/growth/needs* ➲ look at **material** **2** connected with religion: *a spiritual leader* ▸ **spiritually** /-tʃuəli/ *adv*

spiritualism /ˈspɪrɪtʃuəlɪzəm/ *noun* [U] the belief that people who have died can send messages to living people, usually through a **medium** (= a person who has special powers) ▸ **spiritualist** /-ɪst/ *noun* [C]

spit¹ /spɪt/ *verb* [I,T] (spitting; *pt, pp* spat /spæt/) **HELP** In American English the past tense and past participle can also be **spit**. spit (sth) (out) to force liquid, food, etc. out from your mouth: *He took one sip of the wine and spat it out.* ◆ *She spat in his face.*

spit² /spɪt/ *noun* **1** [U] (*informal*) the liquid in your mouth ➲ look at **saliva** **2** [C] a long thin piece of land that sticks out into the sea, a lake, etc. **3** [C] a long thin metal stick that you put through meat to hold it when you cook it over a fire: *chicken roasted on a spit*

spite /spaɪt/ *noun* [U] the desire to hurt or annoy sb: *He stole her letters* ***out of spite***.
IDM **in spite of** used to show that sth happened although you did not expect it: *In spite of all her hard work, Sue failed her exam.* ◆ *I slept well in spite of the noise.* ➲ note at **despite**
▸ **spite** *verb* [T]

spiteful /ˈspaɪtfl/ *adj* behaving in a cruel or unkind way in order to hurt or upset sb: *He's been saying a lot of spiteful things about his ex-girlfriend.* ▸ **spitefully** /-fəli/ *adv*

splash¹ /splæʃ/ *verb* [I,T] (used about a liquid) to fall or to make liquid fall noisily or fly in drops onto a person or thing: *Rain splashed against the windows.* ◆ *The children were splashing each other with water.* ◆ *Be careful not to splash paint onto the floor.*
PHR V **splash out (on sth)** (*BrE informal*) to spend money on sth that is expensive and that you do not really need

splash² /splæʃ/ *noun* [C] **1** the sound of liquid hitting sth or of sth hitting liquid: *Paul jumped into the pool with a big splash.* **2** a small amount of liquid that falls onto sth: *splashes of oil on the cooker* ➲ picture at **ripple** **3** a small bright area of colour: *Flowers add* ***a splash of colour*** *to a room.*

splatter /ˈsplætə(r)/ *verb* [I,T] (used about a liquid) to fly about in large drops and hit sb/sth noisily: *Heavy rain splattered on the roof.* ◆ *The paint was splattered all over the floor.* ◆ *The walls were splattered with blood.*

splay /spleɪ/ *verb* [I,T] splay (sth) (out) (to cause sth) to spread out or become wide apart at one end: *splayed fingers*

splendid /ˈsplendɪd/ *adj* (*old-fashioned*) **1** very good; excellent: *What a splendid idea!* **SYN** **great** **2** very impressive: *the splendid royal palace* ▸ **splendidly** *adv*

splendour (*AmE* splendor) /ˈsplendə(r)/ *noun* [U] very impressive beauty

splint /splɪnt/ *noun* [C] a piece of wood or metal that is tied to a broken arm or leg to keep it in the right position

splinter /ˈsplɪntə(r)/ *noun* [C] a small thin sharp piece of wood, metal or glass that has broken off a larger piece: *I've got a splinter in my finger.* ▸ **splinter** *verb* [I,T]: *The vase splintered into a thousand pieces.*

split¹ /splɪt/ *verb* (splitting; *pt, pp* split) **1** [I,T] split (sb) (up) (into sth) to divide or to make a group of people divide into smaller groups: *Let's split into two groups.* ◆ *A debate that has* ***split*** *the country* ***down the middle***. **2** [T] split sth (between sb/sth); split sth (with sb) to divide or share sth: *We split the cost of the meal between the six of us.* **3** [I,T] split (sth) (open) to break or make sth break along a straight line: *My jeans have split.*
IDM **split the difference** (used when discussing a price) to agree on an amount that is at an equal distance between the two amounts that have been suggested
split hairs (usually used in a critical way) to pay too much attention in an argument to details that are very small and not important
PHR V **split up (with sb)** to end a marriage or relationship: *He's split up with his girlfriend.*

split² /splɪt/ *noun* [C] **1** a disagreement that divides a group of people: *Disagreement about European policy led to a split within the Conservative party.* **2** a long cut or hole in sth: *There's a big split in the tent.* **3** a division between two or more things: *He demanded a 50–50 split of the profits.*

split ˈsecond *noun* [C] a very short period of time

splutter /ˈsplʌtə(r)/ *verb* **1** [I,T] to speak with difficulty, for example because you are very angry or embarrassed: *'How dare you!' she spluttered indignantly.* **2** [I] to make a series of sounds like a person coughing ▸ **splutter** *noun* [C]

spoil /spɔɪl/ *verb* [T] (*pt, pp* spoilt /spɔɪlt/ *or* spoiled /spɔɪld/) **1** to change sth good into sth bad, unpleasant, useless, etc.; to ruin sth: *The new office block will spoil the view.* ◆ *Our holiday was spoilt by bad weather.* ◆ *Eating between meals will* ***spoil*** *your* ***appetite***. **2** to do too much for sb, especially a child, so that you have a bad effect on their character: *a spoilt child* **3** spoil sb/yourself to do sth special or nice to make sb/yourself happy: *Why not spoil yourself with one of our new range of beauty products?* (= in an advertisement)

spoils /spɔɪlz/ *noun* [pl] (*formal*) things that have been stolen by thieves, or taken in a war or battle: *the spoils of war*

spoilsport /ˈspɔɪlspɔːt/ *noun* [C] (*informal*) a person who tries to stop other people enjoying themselves, for example by not taking part in an activity

spoilt *past tense, past participle of* **spoil**

spoke¹ /spəʊk/ *noun* [C] one of the thin pieces of metal that connect the centre of a wheel to the outside edge ➲ picture at **bicycle**

spoke² *past tense of* **speak**

S

spoken¹ /ˈspəʊkən/ *adj* involving speaking rather than writing; expressed in speech rather than in writing: *spoken English* ➲ look at **written**

spoken² *past participle* of **speak**

spokesman /ˈspəʊksmən/, **spokeswoman** /ˈspəʊkswʊmən/, **spokesperson** /ˈspəʊkspɜːsn/ *noun* [C] (*pl* -men /-mən/, -women /-wɪmɪn/, -persons *or* -people /-piːpl/) a person who is chosen to speak for a group or an organization

MORE **Spokesperson** is now often preferred to 'spokesman' or 'spokeswoman' because it can be used for a man or a woman.

sponge¹ /spʌndʒ/ *noun* [C,U] **1** a piece of artificial or natural material that is soft and light and full of holes and can hold water easily, used for washing yourself or cleaning sth ➲ picture at **bucket** **2** = **sponge cake**

sponge² /spʌndʒ/ *verb* [T] to remove or clean sth with a wet **sponge¹** (1) or cloth

PHR V **sponge off sb** (*informal*) to get money, food, etc. from sb without paying or doing anything in return

ˈ**sponge bag** (*BrE* ˈ**toilet bag**; (*AmE* ˈ**toiletry bag**) *noun* [C] a small bag that you use when travelling to carry the things you need to wash with, clean your teeth with, etc.

ˈ**sponge cake** (also **sponge**) *noun* [C,U] a light cake made from eggs, flour and sugar, with or without fat

sponsor /ˈspɒnsə(r)/ *noun* [C] **1** a person or an organization that helps to pay for a special sports event, etc. (usually so that it can advertise its products) ➲ look at **patron** **2** a person who agrees to pay money to a charity if sb else completes a particular activity ▶ **sponsor** *verb* [T]: *a sponsored walk to raise money for children in need* ▶ **sponsorship** *noun* [U]: *Many theatres depend on industry for sponsorship.*

spontaneous /spɒnˈteɪniəs/ *adj* done or happening suddenly; not planned: *a spontaneous burst of applause* ▶ **spontaneously** *adv* ▶ **spontaneity** /ˌspɒntəˈneɪəti/ *noun* [U]

spoof /spuːf/ *noun* [C] (*informal*) an amusing copy of a film, TV programme, etc. that exaggerates its main characteristics: *It's a spoof on horror movies.*

spooky /ˈspuːki/ *adj* (**spookier**; **spookiest**) (*informal*) strange and frightening: *It's spooky being in the house alone at night.* SYN **creepy**

spool /spuːl/ *noun* [C] a round object which thread, film, wire, etc. is put around ➲ look at **reel**

spoon /spuːn/ *noun* [C] an object with a round end and a long handle that you use for eating, mixing or serving food: *Give each person a* ***knife, fork and spoon.*** ◆ *a wooden spoon for cooking* ➲ look at **cutlery** ▶ **spoon** *verb* [T]: *Next, spoon the mixture onto a baking tray.*

spoonful /ˈspuːnfʊl/ *noun* [C] the amount that one spoon can hold: *Add two spoonfuls of sugar.*

spoons

sporadic /spəˈrædɪk/ *adj* not done or happening regularly ▶ **sporadically** /-kli/ *adv*

sport /spɔːt/ *noun* **1** [U] a physical game or activity that you do for exercise or because you enjoy it: *John* ***did*** *a lot of* ***sport*** *when he was at school.* ◆ *Do you like sport?* ➲ picture on **page P4** **2** [C] a particular game or type of sport: *What's your favourite sport?* ◆ ***winter sports*** (= skiing, skating, etc.) ◆ ***team sports*** ▶ **sporting** *adj* [only *before* a noun]: *a major sporting event*

TOPIC

Sport

You can **play** particular sports (without 'the'): *I play football every Saturday.* In **team sports,** one team **plays** or **plays against** another team: *Who are you playing against next week?* Other sports and activities can take the verbs **do** or **go**: *I do gymnastics and yoga.* ◆ *I go swimming twice a week.*

Sports that are played outside on a grass field, like **football, cricket** and **rugby,** are played on a **pitch**. Some other sports, for example **tennis** and **basketball,** are played on a **court**. **Athletics** is made up of **track events** (= sports that involve running on a track, such as **sprinting** and **hurdling**) and **field events** (= sports that involve jumping and throwing, such as the **high jump** and **javelin**). Sports that take place on snow or ice, such as **skiing, snowboarding** and **skating,** are called **winter sports**. Dangerous activities, such as **bungee jumping,** are often called **extreme sports**.

A person who trains people to compete in certain sports is a **coach**. The person who controls a **match** and makes sure that players do not break the rules is a **referee** (in football, rugby, etc.) or an **umpire** (in tennis, cricket, etc.)

ˈ**sports car** *noun* [C] a low, fast car often with a roof that you can open ➲ picture on **page P7**

sportsman /ˈspɔːtsmən/ *noun* [C] (*pl* -men /-mən/) a man who does a lot of sport or who is good at sport: *a keen sportsman*

sportsmanlike /ˈspɔːtsmənlaɪk/ *adj* behaving in a fair, generous and polite way when you are playing a game or doing sport

sportsmanship /ˈspɔːtsmənʃɪp/ *noun* [U] the quality of being fair, generous and polite when you are playing a game or doing sport

sportswoman /ˈspɔːtswʊmən/ *noun* [C] (*pl* -women /-wɪmɪn/) a woman who does a lot of sport or who is good at sport

sporty /ˈspɔːti/ *adj* (sportier; sportiest) (*especially BrE informal*) liking or good at sport: *I'm not very sporty.*

spot¹ /spɒt/ *noun* [C]
➤SMALL MARK **1** a small round mark on a surface: *Leopards have dark spots.* ◆ *a blue skirt with red spots on it* ➲ *adjective* **spotted** **2** a small dirty mark on sth: *grease/rust spots*
➤ON SKIN **3** a small red or yellow lump that appears on your skin: *Many teenagers* ***get spots.*** ➲ *adjective* **spotty**
➤PLACE **4** a particular place or area: *a quiet/lonely/secluded spot*
➤SMALL AMOUNT **5** [usually sing] (*BrE informal*) a spot of sth a small amount of sth: *Can you help me? I'm having a spot of trouble.*
➤LIGHT **6** = **spotlight**(1)
IDM **have a soft spot for sb/sth** ➲ **soft**
on the spot **1** immediately: *Paul was caught stealing money and was dismissed on the spot.* **2** at the place where sth happened or where sb/sth is needed: *The fire brigade were on the spot within five minutes.*
put sb on the spot to make sb answer a difficult question or make a difficult decision without having much time to think

spot² /spɒt/ *verb* [T] (spotting; spotted) [not used in the continuous tenses] to see or notice sb/sth, especially suddenly or when it is not easy to do: *I've spotted a couple of spelling mistakes.*

> **HELP** Although this verb is not used in the continuous tenses, it is common to see the present participle (= *-ing* form): *Spotting a familiar face in the crowd, he began to push his way towards her.*

S

ˌspot ˈcheck *noun* [C] a check that is made suddenly and without warning on a few things or people chosen from a group

spotless /ˈspɒtləs/ *adj* perfectly clean

spotlight /ˈspɒtlaɪt/ *noun* **1** (also **spot**) [C] a lamp that can send a single line of bright light onto a small area. **Spotlights** are often used in theatres. **2 the spotlight** [U] the centre of public attention or interest: *to be* ***in the spotlight***

ˌspot ˈon *adj* [not before a noun] (*BrE informal*) exactly right: *Your estimate was spot on.*

spotted /ˈspɒtɪd/ *adj* (used about clothes, cloth, etc.) having a regular pattern of round dots on it: *a red spotted blouse*

spotty /ˈspɒti/ *adj* having small red or yellow lumps on your skin

spouse /spaʊs/ *noun* [C] (*formal*) your husband or wife

> **HELP** **Spouse** is a formal or official word, used on forms, documents, etc.

spout¹ /spaʊt/ *noun* [C] a tube or pipe through which liquid comes out: *the spout of a teapot* ➲ picture at **teapot**

spout² /spaʊt/ *verb* [I,T] **1** (of a liquid) to come out with great force; to make a liquid do this **2** (*informal*) **spout (on/off) (about sth)** to say sth, using a lot of words, in a way that is boring or annoying

sprain /spreɪn/ *verb* [T] to injure part of your body, especially your wrist or your ankle, by suddenly bending or turning it: *I've sprained my ankle.* ▶ **sprain** *noun* [C]

sprang *past tense of* **spring²**

sprawl /sprɔːl/ *verb* [I] **1** to sit or lie with your arms and legs spread out in an untidy way: *People lay sprawled out in the sun.* **2** to cover a large area of land ▶ **sprawling** *adj*: *the sprawling city suburbs*

spray¹ /spreɪ/ *noun* **1** [U] liquid in very small drops that is sent through the air: *clouds of spray from the waves* **2** [C,U] liquid in an **aerosol** (= a special container) that is forced out under pressure when you push a button: *hairspray* ◆ *a body spray*

spray² /spreɪ/ *verb* [I,T] (used about a liquid) to be forced out of a container or sent through the air in very small drops; to send a liquid out in this way: *The crops are regularly sprayed with pesticide.*

spread¹ /spred/ *verb* (*pt, pp* **spread**) **1** [T] **spread sth (out) (on/over sth)** to open sth that has been folded so that it covers a larger area; to move things so that they cover a larger area: *Spread the map out on the table so we can all see it!* **2** [I,T] to affect a larger area or a bigger group of people; to make sth do this: *The fire spread rapidly because of the strong wind.* ◆ *Rats and flies* ***spread disease.*** ◆ *to* ***spread rumours*** *about somebody* **3** [T] **spread A on/over B; spread B with A** to cover a surface with a layer of a soft substance: *to spread jam on bread* ◆ *to spread bread with jam* **4** [T] **spread sth (out) (over sth)** to separate sth into parts and divide them between different times or people: *You can spread your repayments over a period of three years.*
PHR V **spread (sb/yourself) out** to move away from other people in a group in order to cover a larger area: *The police spread out to search the whole area.*

spread² /spred/ *noun* **1** [U] an increase in the amount or number of sth that there is, or in the area that is affected by sth: *Dirty drinking water encourages* ***the spread of disease.*** **2** [C,U] a soft food that you put on bread **3** [C] a newspaper or magazine article that covers one or more pages: *a double-page spread* **4** [C] a range or variety of people or things: *a broad spread of opinions*

spreadsheet /ˈspredʃiːt/ *noun* [C] a computer program for working with rows of numbers, used especially for doing accounts

spree /spriː/ *noun* [C] (*informal*) a short time that you spend doing sth you enjoy, often doing too much of it: *to **go on a** shopping/spending **spree***

sprig /sprɪg/ *noun* [C] a small piece of a plant with leaves on it

spring[1] /sprɪŋ/ *noun* **1** [C,U] the season of the year between winter and summer when the weather gets warmer and plants begin to grow: *Daffodils bloom **in spring**.* **2** [C] a long piece of thin metal or wire that is bent round and round. After you push or pull a spring it goes back to its original shape and size: *bed springs* ➲ picture at **coil 3** [C] a place where water comes up naturally from under the ground: *a hot spring* **4** [C] a sudden jump upwards or forwards

spring[2] /sprɪŋ/ *verb* [I] (*pt* **sprang** /spræŋ/; *pp* **sprung** /sprʌŋ/) **1** to jump or move quickly: *When the alarm went off, Ray sprang out of bed.* ♦ *to spring to your feet* (= stand up suddenly) ♦ (*figurative*) *to spring to somebody's defence/assistance* (= to quickly defend or help sb) **2** (used about an object) to move suddenly and violently: *The branch sprang back and hit him in the face.* **3** to appear or come somewhere suddenly: *Tears sprang to her eyes.* ♦ *Where did you just spring from?*

IDM **come/spring to mind** ➲ **mind**[1]

PHR V **spring from sth** (*formal*) to be the result of sth: *The idea for the book sprang from an experience she had while travelling in India.*

spring sth on sb to do or say sth that sb is not expecting

spring up to appear or develop quickly or suddenly: *Play areas for children are springing up everywhere.*

springboard /ˈsprɪŋbɔːd/ *noun* [C] **1** a low board that bends and that helps you jump higher, for example before you jump into a swimming pool **2 a springboard (for/to sth)** something that helps you start an activity, especially by giving you ideas

ˌspring-ˈclean *verb* [T] to clean a house, room, etc. very well, including the parts that you do not usually clean

ˌspring ˈonion *noun* [C,U] a type of small onion with a long green central part and leaves ➲ picture on **page P15**

springtime /ˈsprɪŋtaɪm/ *noun* [U] (*formal*) the season of spring

springy /ˈsprɪŋi/ *adj* (**springier**; **springiest**) going quickly back to its original shape or size after being pushed, pulled, etc: *soft springy grass*

sprinkle /ˈsprɪŋkl/ *verb* [T] **sprinkle A (on/onto/over B)**; **sprinkle B (with A)** to throw drops of water or small pieces of sth over a surface: *to sprinkle sugar on a cake* ♦ *to sprinkle a cake with sugar*

sprinkler /ˈsprɪŋklə(r)/ *noun* [C] a device with holes in it that sends out water in small drops. **Sprinklers** are used in gardens to keep the grass green, and in buildings to stop fires from spreading.

sprint /sprɪnt/ *verb* [I,T] to run a short distance as fast as you can ▸ **sprint** *noun* [C]: *a 100-metre sprint* ▸ **sprinter** *noun* [C]

sprout[1] /spraʊt/ *verb* [I,T] (used about a plant) to begin to grow or to produce new leaves: *The seeds are sprouting.*

sprout[2] /spraʊt/ *noun* [C] **1** = **Brussels sprout 2** a new part that has grown on a plant

spruce /spruːs/ *verb*

PHR V **spruce (sb/yourself) up** to make sb/yourself clean and tidy

sprung *past participle* of **spring**[2]

spud /spʌd/ *noun* [C] (*informal*) a potato

spun *past tense, past participle* of **spin**[1]

spur[1] /spɜː(r)/ *noun* [C] **1** a piece of metal that some riders wear on the back of their boots to encourage their horses to go faster ➲ picture at **horse 2 a spur (to sth)** something that encourages you to do sth or that makes sth happen more quickly: *My poor exam results acted as a spur to make me study harder.*

IDM **on the spur of the moment** without planning; suddenly

spur[2] /spɜː(r)/ *verb* [T] (**spurring**; **spurred**) **spur sb/sth (on/onto sth)** to encourage sb or make them work harder or faster: *The letter spurred me into action.* ♦ *We were spurred on by the positive feedback from customers.*

spurn /spɜːn/ *verb* [T] (*formal*) to refuse sth that sb has offered to you: *She spurned his offer of friendship.*

spurt /spɜːt/ *verb* **1** [I,T] (used about a liquid) to come out quickly with great force; to make a liquid do this: *Blood spurted from the wound.* **2** [I] to suddenly increase your speed or effort ▸ **spurt** *noun* [C]

spy[1] /spaɪ/ *noun* [C] (*pl* **spies**) a person who tries to get secret information about another country, person or organization

spy[2] /spaɪ/ *verb* (**spying**; **spies**; *pt, pp* **spied**) **1** [I] to try to get secret information about sb/sth ➲ look at **espionage 2** [T] (*formal*) to see sb/sth

IDM **spy on sb/sth** to watch sb/sth secretly: *The man next door is spying on us.*

sq *abbr* **1** = **square**[1](3): *10 sq cm* **2 Sq** = **square**[2](2): *6 Hanover Sq*

squabble /ˈskwɒbl/ *verb* [I] **squabble (over/about sth)** to argue in a noisy way about sth that is not very important ▸ **squabble** *noun* [C]

squad /skwɒd/ *noun* [C, with sing or pl verb] a group of people who work as a team: *He's a policeman with the fraud squad.*

squadron /ˈskwɒdrən/ *noun* [C, with sing or pl verb] a group of military aircraft or ships

squalid /ˈskwɒlɪd/ *adj* very dirty, untidy and unpleasant: *squalid housing conditions*

squall /skwɔːl/ *noun* [C] a sudden storm with strong winds

squalor /ˈskwɒlə(r)/ *noun* [U] the state of being very dirty, untidy or unpleasant: *to live **in squalor***

S

squander /ˈskwɒndə(r)/ *verb* [T] **squander sth (on sth)** to waste time, money, etc: *He squanders his time on TV and computer games.*

square[1] /skweə(r)/ *adj, adv*
➤SHAPE **1** having four straight sides of the same length and corners of 90°: *a square tablecloth* **2** shaped like a square or forming an angle of about 90°: *a square face* ◆ *square shoulders*
➤MEASUREMENT **3** (*abbr* sq) used for talking about the area of sth: *If a room is 5 metres long and 4 metres wide, its area is 20 square metres.* **4** (used about sth that is square in shape) having sides of a particular length: *The picture is twenty centimetres square* (= each side is twenty centimetres long).
➤WITH MONEY **5** [not before a noun] (*informal*) not owing any money: *Here is the money I owe you. Now we're (all) square.*
➤IN SPORT **6** [not before a noun] having equal points (in a game, etc.): *The teams were **all square** at half-time.*
➤HONEST **7** fair or honest, especially in business matters: *a square deal*
➤DIRECTLY **8** (also squarely) in an obvious and direct way: *to look somebody square in the eye* ◆ *I think the blame falls squarely on her.*
IDM **a square meal** a good meal that makes you feel satisfied

square[2] /skweə(r)/ *noun* [C] **1** a shape that has four sides of the same length and four **right angles** (= angles of 90°): *There are 64 squares on a chess board.* ➲ picture at **shape** **2** (also Square) (*abbr* Sq) an open space in a town or city that has buildings all around it: *Protesters gathered in the town square.* ◆ *Trafalgar Square* **3** the number that you get when you multiply another number by itself: *Four is the square of two.* ➲ look at **square root**

square[3] /skweə(r)/ *verb* [I,T] **square (sth) with sb/sth** to agree with sth; to make sure that sb/sth agrees with sth: *Your conclusion doesn't really square with the facts.* ◆ *If you want time off, you'll have to square it with the boss.*
PHR V **square up (with sb)** to pay sb the money that you owe them

S

squared /skweəd/ *adj* (used about a number) multiplied by itself: *Four squared is sixteen.* ➲ look at **square root**

squarely /ˈskweəli/ = **square**[1](8)

ˌsquare ˈroot *noun* [C] a number that produces another particular number when it is multiplied by itself: *The square root of sixteen is four.* ➲ look at **square**[2](3), **squared**, **root**

squash[1] /skwɒʃ/ *verb* **1** [T] to press sth so that it is damaged, changes shape or becomes flat: *The fruit at the bottom of the bag will **get squashed**.* ◆ *Move up—you're squashing me!* ➲ picture at **squeeze** **2** [I,T] to go into a place, or move sb/sth to a place, where there is not much space: *We all squashed into the back of the car.* **3** [T] to destroy sth because it is a problem: *to squash somebody's suggestion/plan/idea*

squash[2] /skwɒʃ/ *noun* **1** [C, usually sing] a lot of people in a small space: *We can get ten people around the table, but it's **a bit of a squash**.* **2** [U,C] (*BrE*) a drink that is made from fruit juice and sugar. You add water to **squash** before you drink it: *orange squash* **3** [U] a game for two people, played in a area surrounded by four walls using **rackets** (= types of bat) and a small rubber ball **4** a type of vegetable that grows on the ground and has yellow, orange or green skin

squat[1] /skwɒt/ *verb* [I] (squa**tt**ing; squa**tt**ed) **1** to rest with your weight on your feet, your legs bent and your bottom just above the ground ➲ picture at **kneel** **2** to go and live in an empty building without permission from the owner

squat[2] /skwɒt/ *adj* short and fat or thick: *a squat ugly building*

squatter /ˈskwɒtə(r)/ *noun* [C] a person who is living in an empty building without the owner's permission

squawk /skwɔːk/ *verb* [I,T] (used especially about a bird) to make a loud unpleasant noise ▶ **squawk** *noun* [C]

squeak /skwiːk/ *noun* [C] a short high noise that is not very loud: *the squeak of a mouse* ◆ *She gave a little squeak of surprise.* ▶ **squeak** *verb* [I,T] ▶ **squeaky** *adj*: *a squeaky floorboard* ◆ *a squeaky voice*

squeal /skwiːl/ *verb* [I,T] to make a loud high noise because of pain, fear or enjoyment: *The baby squealed in delight at the new toy.* ▶ **squeal** *noun* [C]

squeamish /ˈskwiːmɪʃ/ *adj* easily upset by unpleasant sights, especially blood

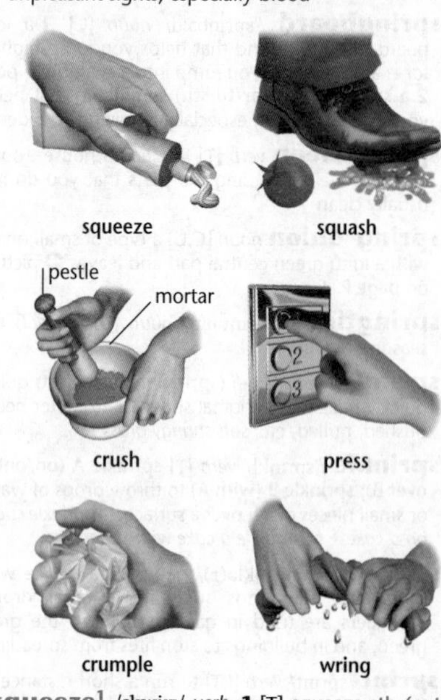

squeeze[1] /skwiːz/ *verb* **1** [T] **squeeze sth (out); squeeze sth (from/out of sth)** to press sth hard: *She* *squeezed his hand as a sign of affection.* ◆ *to squeeze a tube of toothpaste* **2** [T] to get liquid out of sth by pressing it hard: *Squeeze a lemon/the juice of a lemon into a glass.* ◆ *I squeezed the water out of the cloth.* **3** [I,T] **squeeze (sb/sth) into, through, etc. sth; squeeze (sb/sth) through, in, past, etc.** to force sb/sth into or through a small space: *We can squeeze another person into the back of the car.* ◆ *There was just room for the bus to squeeze past.*

squeeze² /skwi:z/ *noun* **1** [C] an act of pressing sth firmly: *He gave her hand a squeeze and told her he loved her.* **2** [C] the amount of liquid that you get from squeezing an orange, a lemon, etc: *a squeeze of lemon* **3** [sing] a situation where there is not much space: *It was **a tight squeeze** to get twelve people around the table.* **4** [C, usually sing] a reduction in the amount of money, jobs, etc. available; a difficult situation caused by this: *a government squeeze on spending*

squelch /skweltʃ/ *verb* [I] to make a wet sucking sound: *The mud squelched as I walked through it.*

squid /skwɪd/ *noun* [C,U] (*pl* **squid** *or* **squids**) a sea animal that you can eat, with a long soft body, eight arms and two **tentacles** (= long thin parts like arms) ➲ picture at **octopus**

squiggle /ˈskwɪgl/ *noun* [C] (*informal*) a quickly drawn line that goes in all directions

squint /skwɪnt/ *verb* [I] **1 squint (at sth)** to look at sth with your eyes almost closed: *to squint in bright sunlight* **2** to have eyes that appear to look in different directions at the same time ▶ **squint** *noun* [C]

squirm /skwɜ:m/ *verb* [I] to move around a lot because you are nervous, uncomfortable, etc.

squirrel /ˈskwɪrəl/ *noun* [C] a small animal with a long thick tail and red, grey or black fur, that lives in trees and eats nuts

squirrel

squirt /skwɜ:t/ *verb* [I, T] If a liquid **squirts** or if you **squirt** it, it is suddenly forced out of sth in a particular direction: *I cut the orange and juice squirted out.* ◆ *She squirted water on the flames.* ◆ *He squirted me with water.* ▶ **squirt** *noun* [C]: *a squirt of lemon juice*

Sr *abbr* = **Senior¹**(2)

St *abbr* **1** = **street**(2): *20 Swan St* **2** = **saint**(1): *St Peter*

st *abbr* = **stone**(5)

stab¹ /stæb/ *verb* [T] (**stabbing**; **stabbed**) to push a knife or other pointed object into sb/sth: *The man had been stabbed in the back.* ◆ *He stabbed a potato with his fork.*

stab² /stæb/ *noun* [C] **1** an injury that was caused by a knife, etc: *He received stab wounds to his neck and back.* **2** a sudden sharp pain

IDM have a stab at sth/doing sth (*informal*) to try to do sth

stabbing¹ /ˈstæbɪŋ/ *noun* [C] an occasion when sb is injured or killed with a knife or other sharp object

stabbing² /ˈstæbɪŋ/ *adj* [only *before* a noun] (used about a pain) sudden and strong

stability /stəˈbɪləti/ *noun* [U] the state or quality of being steady and not changing: *After so much change we now need a period of stability.* ◆ *The ladder is slightly wider at the bottom for greater stability.* **OPP instability** ➲ *adjective* **stable**

stabilize (also -ise) /ˈsteɪbəlaɪz/ *verb* [I,T] to become or to make sth firm, steady and unlikely to change: *The patient's condition has stabilized.* ➲ look at **destabilize**

stable¹ /ˈsteɪbl/ *adj* steady, firm and unlikely to change: *This ladder doesn't seem very stable.* ◆ *The patient is **in a stable condition**.* **OPP unstable** ➲ *noun* **stability**

stable² /ˈsteɪbl/ *noun* [C] a building where horses are kept ➲ picture on **page P11**

stack¹ /stæk/ *noun* [C] **1** a tidy pile of sth: *a stack of plates/books/chairs* **2** [often plural] (*informal*) a lot of sth: *I've still got stacks of work to do.*

stack² /stæk/ *verb* [T] **stack sth (up)** to put sth into a tidy pile: *Could you stack those chairs?*

stacked /stækt/ *adj* full of piles of things: *The room was stacked high with books.*

stadium /ˈsteɪdiəm/ *noun* [C] (*pl* **stadiums** *or* **stadia** /-diə/) a large structure, usually with no roof, where people can sit and watch sport

staff /stɑ:f/ *noun* [C, usually sing, U] the group of people who work for a particular organization: *hotel/library/medical staff* ◆ *Two **members of staff** will accompany the students on the school trip.* ◆ *The hotel has over 200 people **on its staff**.* ◆ *full-time/part-time staff*

> **GRAMMAR** We usually use **staff** in the singular but with a plural verb: *The staff are all English.*

▶ **staff** *verb* [T, usually passive]: *The office is staffed 24 hours a day.*

staffroom /ˈstɑ:fru:m; -rʊm/ *noun* [C] (*BrE*) a room in a school where teachers can go when they are not teaching

stag /stæg/ *noun* [C] a male **deer** (= a large wild animal) with **antlers** (= horns shaped like branches) on its head ➲ note at **deer** ➲ picture on **page P12**

stage¹ /steɪdʒ/ *noun* **1** [C] one part of the progress or development of sth: *The first stage of the course lasts for three weeks.* ◆ *I suggest we do the journey **in** two **stages**.* ◆ ***At this stage** it's too early to say what will happen.* **2** [C,U] a platform in a theatre, concert hall, etc. on which actors, musicians, etc. perform: *There were more than 50 people on stage in one scene.* **3** [sing,U] the world of theatre; the profession of acting: *Her parents didn't want her to **go on the stage**.* ◆ *an actor of stage and screen*

S

stage² /steɪdʒ/ *verb* [T] **1** to organize a performance of a play, concert, etc. for the public **2** to organize an event: *They have decided to stage a 24-hour strike.*

ˌstage ˈmanager *noun* [C] the person who is responsible for the stage, lights, etc. during a theatre performance

stagger /ˈstæɡə(r)/ *verb* [I] to walk with short steps as if you could fall at any moment, for example because you are ill, drunk or carrying sth heavy: *He staggered across the finishing line and collapsed.*

staggered /ˈstæɡəd/ *adj* **1** [not before a noun] (*informal*) very surprised: *I was absolutely staggered when I heard the news.* **2** (used about a set of times, payments, etc.) arranged so that they do not all happen at the same time: *staggered working hours* (= when people start and finish work at different times)

staggering /ˈstæɡərɪŋ/ *adj* that you find difficult to believe ▸ **staggeringly** *adv*

stagnant /ˈstæɡnənt/ *adj* **1** (used about water) not flowing and therefore dirty and having an unpleasant smell **2** (used about business, etc.) not active; not developing: *a stagnant economy*

stagnate /stæɡˈneɪt/ *verb* [I] **1** to stop developing, changing or being active: *a stagnating economy* **2** (used about water) to be or become **stagnant** ▸ **stagnation** /stæɡˈneɪʃn/ *noun* [U]

ˈstag night (also ˈstag party) *noun* [C] a party for men only that is given for a man just before his wedding day ➲ look at **hen party**

staid /steɪd/ *adj* serious, old-fashioned and rather boring

stain /steɪn/ *verb* [I,T] to leave a mark that is difficult to remove: *Don't spill any of that juice—it'll stain the carpet.* ▸ **stain** *noun* [C]: *The blood had left a stain on his shirt.*

ˌstained ˈglass *noun* [U] pieces of coloured glass that are used in church windows, etc: *a stained-glass window*

ˌstainless ˈsteel *noun* [U] a type of steel that does not **rust** (= get damaged by water or air and change colour): *a stainless steel pan*

⚷ **stair** /steə(r)/ *noun* **1 stairs** [pl] a series of steps inside a building that lead from one level to another: *a* ***flight of stairs*** ♦ *I heard somebody coming* ***down the stairs.*** ♦ *She ran* ***up the stairs.*** ➲ picture on **page P8** ➲ look at **downstairs, upstairs**

HELP **Stairs** or **steps**? **Stairs** or **flights of stairs** are usually inside buildings. **Steps** are usually outside buildings and made of stone or concrete.

2 [C] one of the steps in a series inside a building: *She sat down on the bottom stair to read the letter.*

staircase /ˈsteəkeɪs/ (also **stairway** /ˈsteəweɪ/) *noun* [C] a set of stairs with rails on each side that you can hold on to ➲ look at **escalator**

stake¹ /steɪk/ *noun* [C] **1** a wooden or metal pole with a point at one end that you push into the ground **2** a part of a company, etc. that you own, usually because you have put money into it: *Foreign investors now* ***have a 20% stake in*** *the company.* **3** something, especially money, that you might win or lose in a game or in a particular situation: *We play cards for money, but never for very* ***high stakes.***

IDM at stake in danger of being lost; at risk: *He thought very carefully about the decision because he knew his future was at stake.*

stake² /steɪk/ *verb* [T] **stake sth (on sth)** to put your future, etc. in danger by doing sth, because you hope that it will bring you a good result: *He is staking his political reputation on this issue.* **SYN bet**

IDM stake a/your claim (to sth) to say that you have a right to have sth

PHR V stake sth out 1 to clearly mark an area of land that you are going to use **2** to make your position, opinion, etc. clear to everyone: *In his speech, the President staked out his position on tax reform.* **3** to watch a place secretly for a period of time: *The police had been staking out the house for months.*

stale /steɪl/ *adj* **1** (used about food or air) old and not fresh any more: *The bread will* ***go stale*** *if you don't put it away.* **2** not interesting or exciting any more ➲ look at **fresh**

stalemate /ˈsteɪlmeɪt/ *noun* [sing,U] **1** a situation in an argument in which neither side can win or make any progress **2** (in the game of **chess**) a position in which a game ends without a winner because neither side can move

stalk¹ /stɔːk/ *noun* [C] one of the long thin parts of a plant which the flowers, leaves or fruit grow on ➲ picture at **plant** ➲ picture on **page P14**

stalk² /stɔːk/ *verb* **1** [T] to move slowly and quietly towards an animal in order to catch or kill it: *a lion stalking its prey* **2** [T] to follow a person over a period of time in a frightening or annoying way: *The actress claimed the man had been stalking her for two years.* **3** [I] to walk in an angry way

stall¹ /stɔːl/ *noun* **1** [C] a small shop with an open front or a table with things for sale: *a market stall* ♦ *a bookstall at the station* ➲ picture on **page P11** **2 stalls** [pl] the seats nearest the front in a theatre or cinema **3** [C, usually sing] a situation in which a vehicle's engine suddenly stops because it is not receiving enough power: *The plane went into a stall and almost crashed.*

stall² /stɔːl/ *verb* [I,T] **1** (used about a vehicle) to stop suddenly because the engine is not receiving enough power; to make a vehicle do this accidentally: *The bus often stalls on this hill.* ♦ *I kept stalling the car.* **2** to avoid doing sth or to try to stop sth happening until a later time

stallion /ˈstæliən/ *noun* [C] an adult male horse, especially one that is kept for breeding ➲ note at **horse**

stalwart /ˈstɔːlwət/ *adj* always loyal to the same organization, team, etc: *a stalwart supporter of the club* ▸ **stalwart** *noun* [C]

S

stamen /ˈsteɪmən/ *noun* [C] a small thin male part in the middle of a flower that produces **pollen** (= a fine yellow powder)

stamina /ˈstæmɪnə/ *noun* [U] the ability to do sth that involves a lot of physical or mental effort for a long time: *You need a lot of stamina to run long distances.*

stammer /ˈstæmə(r)/ *verb* [I,T] to speak with difficulty, repeating sounds and pausing before saying things correctly: *He stammered an apology and left quickly.* ▶ **stammer** *noun* [sing]: *to have a stammer*

stamp[1] /stæmp/ *noun* [C] **1** (also ˈ**postage stamp**) a small piece of paper that you stick onto a letter or package to show that you have paid for it to be posted: *a first-class/second-class stamp* ◆ *John's hobby is collecting stamps.* ➲ note at **post** ➲ look at **first class** ➲ picture at **letter** ➲ picture on **page P3**

> **MORE** In the British postal system, there are two types of stamp for posting letters, etc. to other parts of Britain: **first-class** stamps and **second-class** stamps. It costs more to send letters first-class, and they arrive more quickly.

2 a small object that prints some words, a design, the date, etc. when you press it onto a surface: *a date stamp* **3** the mark made by stamping sth onto a surface: *Have you got any visa stamps in your passport?* ◆ (*figurative*) *The government has given the project its* ***stamp of approval***. **4** [usually sing] **the stamp of sth** something that shows a particular quality or that sth was done by a particular person: *Her novels have the stamp of genius.*

stamp[2] /stæmp/ *verb* **1** [I,T] **stamp (on sth)** to put your foot down very heavily and noisily: *He stamped on the spider and squashed it.* ◆ *It was so cold that I had to stamp my feet to keep warm.* ◆ *She stamped her foot in anger.* **2** [I] to walk with loud heavy steps: *She stamped around the room, shouting angrily.* **3** [T] **stamp A (on B); stamp B (with A)** to print some words, a design, the date, etc. by pressing a **stamp**[1] (2) onto a surface: *to stamp a passport*
PHR V stamp sth out to put an end to sth completely: *The police are trying to stamp out this kind of crime.*

ˌ**stamped addressed** ˈ**envelope** *noun* [C] (*abbr* **SAE**) an empty envelope with your own name and address and a stamp on it that you send to a company, etc. when you want sth to be sent back to you

stampede /stæmˈpiːd/ *noun* [C] a situation in which a large number of animals or people start running in the same direction, for example because they are frightened or excited ▶ **stampede** *verb* [I,T]

stance /stæns; stɑːns/ *noun* [C, usually sing] **1 stance (on sth)** the opinions that sb expresses publicly about sth: *the prime minister's stance on foreign affairs* **2** the position in which sb stands, especially when playing a sport

stand[1] /stænd/ *verb* (*pt, pp* **stood** /stʊd/)
➤ON FEET **1** [I] to be on your feet, not sitting or lying down; to be in a vertical position: *He was standing near the window.* ◆ ***Stand still****—I'm trying to draw you!* ◆ *Only a few houses were left standing after the earthquake.* **2** [I] **stand (up)** to rise to your feet from another position: *He stood up when I entered the room.*
➤IN POSITION **3** [T] to put sb/sth in a particular place or position: *We stood the mirror against the wall while we decided where to hang it.* **4** [I] to be or to stay in a particular position or situation: *The castle stands on a hill.* ◆ *The house has stood empty for ten years.*
➤HEIGHT, LEVEL, ETC. **5** [I] **stand (at sth)** to be of a particular height, level, amount, etc: *The world record stands at 6.59 metres.* ◆ *The building stands nearly 60 metres high.*
➤STAY THE SAME **6** [I] to stay the same as before, without being changed: *Does your decision still stand?* ◆ *The world record has stood for ten years.*
➤HAVE OPINION **7** [I] **stand (on sth)** to have an opinion or view about sth: *Where do you stand on euthanasia?*
➤BE LIKELY TO **8** [I] **stand to do sth** to be in a situation where you are likely to do sth: *If he has to sell the company, he stands to lose a lot of money.*
➤NOT LIKE **9** [T] [in negative sentences and questions, with *can/could*] to not like sb/sth at all; to hate sb/sth: *I can't stand that woman—she's so rude.* ◆ *I couldn't* ***stand the thought of*** *waiting another two hours so I went home.* ➲ note at **dislike**
➤SURVIVE **10** [T] [used especially with *can/could*] to be able to survive difficult conditions: *Camels can stand extremely hot and cold temperatures.* **SYN bear, take**
➤IN ELECTION **11** [I] **stand (for/as sth)** to be one of the people who hopes to be chosen in an election: *She's standing for the European Parliament.* ℹ For idioms containing **stand**, look at the entries for the nouns, adjectives, etc. For example, **it stands to reason** is at **reason**.
PHR V stand around to stand somewhere not doing anything: *A lot of people were just standing around outside.*
stand aside to move to one side: *People stood aside to let the police pass.*
stand back to move back: *The policeman told everybody to stand back.*
stand by 1 to be present, but do nothing in a situation: *How can you stand by and let them treat their animals like that?* **2** to be ready to act: *The police are standing by in case there's trouble.*
stand by sb to help sb or be friends with them, even in difficult times
stand for sth 1 to be a short form of sth: *What does BBC stand for?* **2** to support sth (such as an idea or opinion): *I hate everything that the party stands for.*
stand in (for sb) to take sb's place for a short time
stand out to be easily seen or noticed
stand up to be or become vertical: *You'll look taller if you stand up straight.*
stand sb up (*informal*) to not appear when you have arranged to meet sb, especially a boyfriend or girlfriend
stand up for sb/sth to say or do sth which shows that you support sb/sth: *I admire him. He really stands up for his rights.*

S

stand up to sb/sth to defend yourself against sb/sth that is stronger or more powerful

stand² /stænd/ *noun* [C] **1** [usually sing] **a stand (on/against sth)** a strong effort to defend yourself or sth that you have a strong opinion about: *The head teacher has been praised for his tough stand on bullying.* ◆ *The workers have decided to* ***take/make a stand*** *against further job losses.* **2** a table or an object that holds or supports sth, often so that people can buy it or look at it: *a newspaper/hamburger stand* ◆ *a company stand at a trade fair* **3** a large structure with rows where people sit or stand to watch a sports event

standard¹ /ˈstændəd/ *noun* **1** [C,U] a level of quality, especially one that people think is acceptable: *By European* ***standards*** *this is a very expensive city.* ◆ *He is a brilliant player* ***by any standard.*** ◆ *We complained about the low standard of service in the hotel.* **2** [pl] a level of behaviour that is morally acceptable: *Many people are worried about falling standards in modern society.*

standard² /ˈstændəd/ *adj* **1** normal or average; not special or unusual: *He's got long arms, so standard sizes of shirt don't fit him.* **2** that people generally accept as normal and correct: *standard English*

ˈstandard class = **second class**(1)

standardize (also -ise) /ˈstændədaɪz/ *verb* [T] to make things that are different the same: *Safety tests on old cars have been standardized throughout Europe.* ▶ **standardization** (also -isation) /ˌstændədaɪˈzeɪʃn/ *noun* [U]

ˌstandard of ˈliving *noun* [C] (*pl* **standards of living**) the amount of money and level of comfort that a particular person or group has: *There is a higher standard of living in the north than in the south.*

MORE An expression with a similar meaning is **living standards**. This is used in the plural: *Living standards have improved.*

standby /ˈstændbaɪ/ *noun* **1** [C] (*pl* **standbys**) a thing or person that can be used if needed, for example if sb/sth is not available or in an emergency: *We always keep candles* ***as a standby*** *in case there is a power cut.* **2** [U] the state of being ready to do sth immediately if needed, or if a ticket becomes available: *Ambulances were* ***on standby*** *along the route of the marathon.* ◆ *We were* ***put on standby*** *for the flight to Beirut.* ▶ **standby** *adj* [only *before* a noun]: *a standby ticket/passenger*

standing¹ /ˈstændɪŋ/ *adj* [only *before* a noun] that always exists; permanent

standing² /ˈstændɪŋ/ *noun* [U] **1** the position that sb/sth has, or how people think of them or it: *The agreement has no legal standing.* **SYN** **status** **2** the amount of time during which sth has continued to exist

ˌstanding ˈorder *noun* [C] an instruction to your bank to make a regular payment to sb from your account

standpoint /ˈstændpɔɪnt/ *noun* [C] a particular way of thinking about sth **SYN** **point of view**

standstill /ˈstændstɪl/ *noun* [sing] a situation when there is no movement, progress or activity: *The traffic* ***is at/has come to a complete standstill.***
IDM **grind to a halt/standstill** ➲ **grind¹**

stank *past tense* of **stink**

stanza /ˈstænzə/ *noun* [C] a group of lines that form a unit in some types of poem **SYN** **verse**

staple /ˈsteɪpl/ *noun* [C] a small thin piece of bent wire that you push through pieces of paper using a **stapler** (= a special tool) to fasten them together ▶ **staple** *verb* [T]: *Staple the letter to the application form.* ▶ **stapler** *noun* [C] ➲ picture at **stationery**

ˌstaple ˈdiet *noun* [C, usually sing] the main food that a person or an animal normally eats: *a staple diet of rice and fish*

star¹ /stɑː(r)/ *noun*
➤IN SKY **1** [C] a large ball of burning gas in space that you see as a small point of light in the sky at night: *It was a clear night and the stars were shining brightly.*
➤SHAPE **2** [C] a shape, decoration, mark, etc. with five or six points sticking out in a regular pattern: *I've marked the possible candidates on the list with a star.* ➲ picture at **shape**
➤FOR HOTEL, ETC. **3** [C] a mark that represents a star that is used for telling you how good sth is, especially a hotel or restaurant: *a five-star hotel*
➤PERSON **4** [C] a famous person in acting, music or sport: *a pop/rock/film/movie star* ◆ *a football/tennis star*
➤BEST **5** [C] a person or thing that is the best: *a star student* ◆ *She was the star of many popular television series.* ◆ *A green parrot was the* ***star of the show.***
➤PREDICTING SB'S FUTURE **6 stars** [pl] = **horoscope**

star² /stɑː(r)/ *verb* (**starring**; **starred**) **1** [I] **star (in sth)** to be one of the main actors in a play, film, etc: *Anne Hathaway is to star in a new romantic comedy.* **2** [T] to have sb as a star: *The film stars Elio Germano as the son of a journalist.*

starboard /ˈstɑːbəd/ *noun* [U] the side of a ship that is on the right when you are facing towards the front of it **OPP** **port** ➲ note at **boat**

starch /stɑːtʃ/ *noun* **1** [C,U] a white substance that is found in foods such as potatoes, rice and bread **2** [U] a substance that is used for making cloth stiff

stardom /ˈstɑːdəm/ *noun* [U] the state of being a famous person in acting, music or sport: *She* ***shot to stardom*** *in a Broadway musical.*

stare /steə(r)/ *verb* [I] **stare (at sb/sth)** to look at sb/sth for a long time because you are surprised, shocked, etc: *Everybody stared at his hat.* ◆ *He didn't reply, he just stared into the distance.* ▶ **stare** *noun* [C]: *She gave him a blank stare.*

stark¹ /stɑːk/ *adj* (**starker**; **starkest**) **1** very empty and without decoration and therefore not attractive: *a stark landscape* **2** unpleasant and impossible to

S

avoid: *He now faces the* ***stark reality*** *of life in prison.* **3** very different to sth in a way that is easy to see

stark² /stɑːk/ *adv* completely; extremely: *stark naked* ◆ *Have you gone stark raving mad?*

starlight /ˈstɑːlaɪt/ *noun* [U] the light that is sent out by stars in the sky

starry /ˈstɑːri/ *adj* full of stars: *a starry night*

ˈstar sign (also *informal* **sign**) one of the twelve divisions of the **zodiac** (= symbols which represent the positions of the sun, moon and planets): *'What's your star sign?' 'Leo.'*

start¹ /stɑːt/ *verb*

➤BEGIN **1** [I,T] **start (sth/to do sth/doing sth)** to begin doing sth: *Turn over your exam papers and start now.* ◆ *We'll have to start (*= leave*) early if we want to be in Dover by 10.30.* ◆ *Prices start at £5.* ◆ *After waiting for an hour, the customers started to complain.* ◆ *She started playing the piano when she was six.* ◆ *What time do you have to* ***start work*** *in the morning?* **2** [I,T] to begin or to make sth begin to happen: *What time does the concert start?* ◆ *I'd like to start the meeting now.* ◆ *The police think a young woman may have started the fire.* ➲ note at **begin**

➤MACHINE/VEHICLE **3** [I,T] **start (sth) (up)** to make an engine, a car, etc. begin to work: *The car won't start.* ◆ *We heard an engine starting up in the street.* ◆ *He got onto his motorbike, started the engine and rode away.*

➤ORGANIZATION **4** [I,T] **start (sth) (up)** to create a company, an organization, etc.; to begin to exist: *There are a lot of new companies starting up in that area now.* ◆ *They've decided to start their own business.*

➤MOVE SUDDENLY **5** [I] to make a sudden, quick movement because you are surprised or afraid: *A loud noise outside made me start.*

IDM **get/start off on the right/wrong foot (with sb)** ➲ **foot¹**

set/start the ball rolling ➲ **ball**

to start (off) with 1 used for giving your first reason for sth: *'Why are you so angry?' 'Well, to start off with, you're late, and secondly you've lied to me.'* **2** in the beginning; at first: *Everything was fine to start with, but the marriage quickly deteriorated.*

PHR V **start off** to begin in a particular way: *I'd like to start off by welcoming you all to Leeds.*

start on sth to begin doing sth that needs to be done

start out (to do sth) to have a particular intention when you begin sth: *I started out to tidy my desk but ended up tidying the whole room.*

start over (*AmE*) to begin again

start² /stɑːt/ *noun*

➤BEGINNING **1** [C, usually sing] the point at which sth begins: *The chairman made a short speech* ***at the start of*** *the meeting.* ◆ *I told you it was a bad idea* ***from the start.*** **2** [C, usually sing] the action or process of starting: *to make a fresh start (*= do sth again in a different way*)*

➤IN RACE **3 the start** [sing] the place where a race begins: *The athletes are now lining up at the start.* **4** [C, usually sing] an amount of time or distance that you give to a weaker person at the beginning of a race, game, etc: *I gave the younger children a start.* ➲ look at **head start**

➤SUDDEN MOVEMENT **5** [C, usually sing] a sudden quick movement that your body makes because you are surprised or afraid: *She woke up* ***with a start.***

IDM **for a start** (*informal*) (used to emphasize your first reason for sth): *'Why can't we go on holiday?' 'Well, for a start we can't afford it ...'*

get off to a flying start ➲ **flying**

get off to a good, bad, etc. start to start well, badly, etc.

starter /ˈstɑːtə(r)/ (*AmE usually* **appetizer**) *noun* [C] a small amount of food that is served before the main course of a meal ➲ note at **restaurant**

ˈstarting point *noun* [C] **starting point (for sth) 1** an idea or a topic that you use to begin a discussion **2** the place where you begin a journey

startle /ˈstɑːtl/ *verb* [T] to surprise sb/sth in a way that slightly shocks or frightens them or it: *The noise startled the horses.* ▶ **startled** *adj* ▶ **startling** *adj*

starvation /stɑːˈveɪʃn/ *noun* [U] suffering or death because there is not enough food: *to die of starvation*

starve /stɑːv/ *verb* [I,T] to suffer or die because you do not have enough food to eat; to make sb/sth suffer or die in this way: *Millions of people are starving in the poorer countries of the world.* ◆ *That winter many animals* ***starved to death.***

IDM **be starved of sth** to suffer because you are not getting enough of sth that you need: *The children had been starved of love and affection for years.*

be starving (*informal*) to be extremely hungry

state¹ /steɪt/ *noun*

➤CONDITION **1** [C] the mental, emotional or physical condition that sb/sth is in at a particular time: *the state of the economy* ◆ *He is in a* ***state of shock.*** ◆ *The house is in a terrible state.*

➤COUNTRY **2** (also **State**) [C] a country considered as an organized political community controlled by one government: *Pakistan has been an independent state since 1947.* ➲ note at **country**

➤PART OF COUNTRY **3** (also **State**) [C] an organized political community forming part of a country: *the southern States of the US* ➲ look at **county, province**

➤GOVERNMENT **4** *often* **(the) State** [U, sing] the government of a country: *affairs/matters of state* ◆ *the relationship between the Church and the State* ◆ *a state-owned company* ◆ *heads of State (*= government leaders*)*

➤OFFICIAL CEREMONY **5** [U] the formal ceremonies connected with high levels of government or with the leaders of countries: *The president was driven* ***in state*** *through the streets.*

➤USA **6 the States** [pl] (*informal*) the United States of America: *We lived in the States for about five years.*

IDM **be in/get into a state** (*especially BrE informal*) **1** to be or become very nervous or upset: *Now don't get into a state! I'm sure everything will be all right.* **2** (*informal*) to be or become dirty or untidy

state of affairs a situation: *This state of affairs must not be allowed to continue.*

S

state of mind mental condition: *She's in a very confused state of mind.*

state² *adj* [only *before* a noun] **1** provided or controlled by the government of a country: *She went to a state school.* **2** connected with the leader of a country attending an official ceremony: *The Queen is on a **state visit** to Moscow.* **3** connected with a particular state of a country, especially in the US: *a state prison/hospital/university*

state³ /steɪt/ *verb* [T] to say or write sth, especially formally: *Your letter states that you sent the goods on 31 March, but we have not received them.*

stately /ˈsteɪtli/ *adj* formal and impressive: *a stately old building*

ˌstately ˈhome *noun* [C] (*BrE*) a large old house that has historical interest and can be visited by the public ➲ picture on **page P9**

statement /ˈsteɪtmənt/ *noun* [C] **1** something that you say or write, especially formally: *The Prime Minister will **make a statement** about the defence cuts today.* **2** = **bank statement**

ˌstate of the ˈart *adj* using the most modern or advanced methods; as good as it can be at the present time: *The system was state of the art.* ◆ *a state-of-the-art system*

statesman /ˈsteɪtsmən/ *noun* [C] (*pl* -men /-mən/) an important and experienced politician who has earned public respect

static¹ /ˈstætɪk/ *adj* not moving, changing or developing: *House prices are static.*

static² /ˈstætɪk/ *noun* [U] **1** sudden noises that disturb radio or TV signals, caused by electricity in the atmosphere **2** (also ˌstatic elecˈtricity) electricity that collects on a surface: *My hair gets full of static when I brush it.*

S

station¹ /ˈsteɪʃn/ *noun* [C] **1** a building on a railway line where trains stop so that passengers can get on and off: *I get off at the next station.* ◆ *a railway station* ◆ *a train station* ◆ (*BrE*) *a tube/underground station* ◆ (AmE) *a subway station* ➲ note at **train** **2** [in compounds] a building from which buses begin and end journeys: *The coach leaves the bus/coach station at 9.30 a.m.* **3** [in compounds] a building where a particular service or activity is based: *a police/fire station* ◆ *a petrol station* ◆ *a power station* (= where electricity is produced) **4** [usually in compounds] a radio or TV company and the programmes it sends out: *a local radio/TV station* ◆ *He tuned in to another station.* ➲ look at **channel**

station² /ˈsteɪʃn/ *verb* [T, often passive] to send sb, especially a member of the armed forces, to work in a place for a period of time

stationary /ˈsteɪʃənri/ *adj* not moving: *He crashed into the back of a stationary vehicle.*

stationer's /ˈsteɪʃənəz/ *noun* [sing] a shop that sells writing equipment, such as paper, pens, envelopes, etc.

stationery /ˈsteɪʃənri/ *noun* [U] writing equipment, for example pens, pencils, paper, envelopes, etc.

ˈstation wagon (*AmE*) = **estate car**

statistics /stəˈtɪstɪks/ *noun* (also *informal* stats) **1** [pl] a piece or a collection of information shown in numbers: *Statistics indicate that 90% of homes in this country have a TV.* ◆ *crime statistics* **2** [U] the science of collecting and studying these numbers ▸ **statistical** /stəˈtɪstɪkl/ *adj*: *statistical information* ▸ **statistically** /-kli/ *adv*

stats (*informal*) = **statistics**

statue /ˈstætʃuː/ *noun* [C] a figure of a person or an animal that is made of stone or metal and usually put in a public place: *the Statue of Liberty in New York* ➲ picture on **page P11**

stature /ˈstætʃə(r)/ *noun* [U] (*formal*) **1** the importance and respect that sb has because people have a high opinion of their skill or of what they have done **2** the height of a person: *He's quite small **in stature**.*

status /ˈsteɪtəs/ *noun* **1** [U] the legal position of a person, group or country: *Please indicate your name, age and **marital status*** (= if you are married or single). ◆ *They were granted refugee status.* **2** [sing] your social or professional position in relation to other people: *Teachers don't have a very high status in this country.* **3** [U] a high social position: *The new job gave him much more status.*

the status quo /ˌsteɪtəs ˈkwəʊ/ *noun* [sing] the situation as it is now, or as it was before a recent change

ˈstatus symbol *noun* [C] something that a person owns that shows that they have a high position in society and a lot of money

statute /ˈstætʃuːt/ *noun* [C] (*formal*) a law or a rule

statutory /ˈstætʃətri/ *adj* (*formal*) decided by law: *a statutory right*

staunch /stɔːntʃ/ *adj* (**staunchest**) [no comparative] believing in sb/sth or supporting sb/sth very strongly; loyal

stave /steɪv/ *verb*

PHR V **stave sth off** to stop sth unpleasant from happening now, although it may happen at a later time; to delay sth: *to stave off hunger/illness/inflation/bankruptcy*

stay¹ /steɪ/ *verb* [I] **1** to continue to be somewhere and not go away: *Patrick stayed in bed until 11 o'clock.* ◆ *I can't stay long.* ◆ *Stay on this road until you get to Wells.* ◆ *Pete's staying late at the office tonight.* ◆ *Can you stay for lunch?* **2** to continue to be in a particular state or situation without change: *I can't **stay awake** any longer.* ◆ *I don't know why they stay together* (= continue to be married or in a relationship).

> **HELP** Stay or **remain**? **Remain** and **stay** are similar in meaning but **remain** is more formal.

3 to live in a place temporarily as a visitor or guest: *We stayed with friends in France.* ◆ *Which hotel are you **staying at**?* ◆ *Why don't you **stay the night**?*

IDM **keep/stay/steer clear (of sb/sth)** ➲ clear³

stay put (*informal*) to continue in one place; to not leave

PHR V **stay behind** to not leave a place after other people have gone: *I'll stay behind and help you wash up.*

stay in to remain at home and not go out: *I'm going to stay in and watch TV.*

stay on (at ...) to continue studying, working, etc. somewhere for longer than expected or after other people have left

stay out to continue to be away from your house, especially late at night

stay out of sth to avoid or not become involved in sth: *to stay out of trouble*

stay up to go to bed later than usual: *I'm going to stay up to watch the late film.*

stay² /steɪ/ *noun* [C] a period of time that you spend somewhere as a visitor or guest: *Did you enjoy your stay in Crete?*

staycation /ˌsteɪˈkeɪʃn/ *noun* [C] a holiday that you spend at or near your home: *Turn off your phone and computer—you're on staycation, remember?*

STD /ˌes tiː ˈdiː/ *abbr* **1 sexually transmitted disease**; any disease that is spread through having sex **2** (*BrE*) **subscriber trunk dialling**; the system by which you can make direct telephone calls over long distances

steady¹ /ˈstedi/ *adj* (**steadier**; **steadiest**) **1** developing, growing or happening gradually and at a regular rate: *a steady increase/decline* **2** staying the same; not changing and therefore safe: *a steady job/income* ◆ *a **steady boyfriend/girlfriend*** (= one that has lasted a long time) **3** firmly fixed, supported or balanced; not shaking or likely to fall down: *You need **a steady hand** to take good photographs.* ◆ *He held the ladder steady as she climbed up it.* ▶ **steadily** *adv*: *Unemployment has risen steadily since April 2011.*

steady² /ˈstedi/ *verb* [I,T] (**steadying**; **steadies**; *pt, pp* **steadied**) to stop yourself/sb/sth from moving, shaking or falling; to stop moving, shaking or falling: *She thought she was going to fall, so she put out a hand to steady herself.* ◆ *He had to **steady** his **nerves/voice** before beginning his speech.*

steak /steɪk/ *noun* [C,U] a thick flat piece of meat or fish: *a piece of steak* ◆ *a cod/salmon steak* ➲ look at **chop**

steal /stiːl/ *verb* (*pt* **stole** /stəʊl/; *pp* **stolen** /ˈstəʊlən/) **1** [I,T] **steal (sth) (from sb/sth)** to take sth from a person, shop, etc. without permission and without intending to return it or pay for it: *We found out she had been stealing from us for years.* ◆ *The terrorists were driving a stolen car.* ➲ note at **thief**

stationery

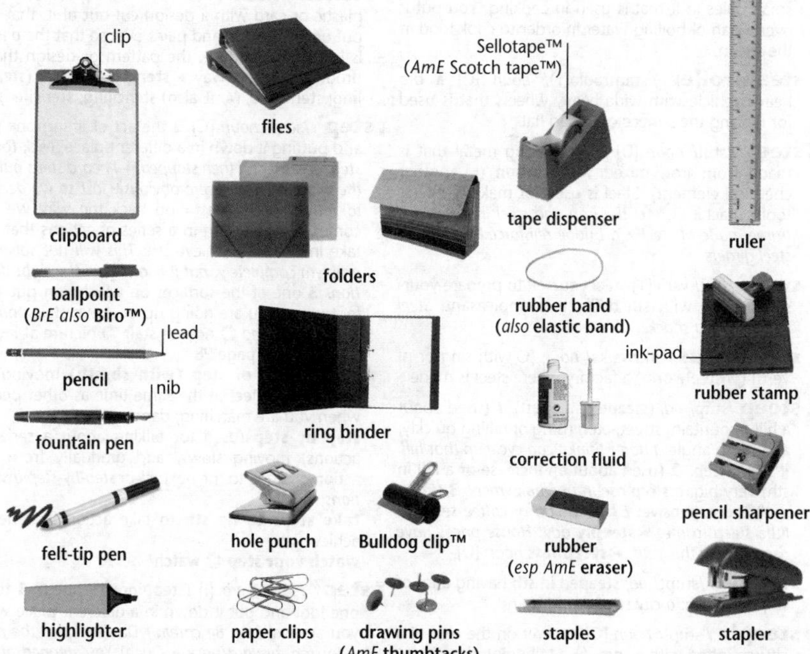

HELP **Steal** or **rob**? You **steal** things, but you **rob** a person or place: *My camera has been stolen!* ♦ *I've been robbed!* ♦ *to rob a bank*

2 [I] steal away, in, out, etc. to move somewhere secretly and quietly: *She stole out of the room.*

stealth /stelθ/ *noun* [U] (*formal*) behaviour that is secret or quiet ▶ **stealthy** *adj*: *a stealthy approach/movement* ▶ **stealthily** *adv*

steam¹ /sti:m/ *noun* [U] the hot gas that water changes into when it boils: *Steam was rising from the coffee.* ♦ *a steam engine* (= that uses the power of steam)

IDM **let off steam** (*informal*) to get rid of energy or express strong feeling by behaving in a noisy or wild way

run out of steam (*informal*) to gradually lose energy or enthusiasm

steam² /sti:m/ *verb* **1** [I] to send out steam: *a bowl of steaming hot soup* **2** [I,T] to place food over boiling water so that it cooks in the steam; to cook in this way: *Leave the potatoes to steam for 30 minutes.* ♦ *steamed vegetables/fish* ➲ note at **cook**

IDM **be/get steamed up** (*informal*) to be or become very angry or worried about sth

PHR V **steam (sth) up** to cover sth or become covered with steam: *As he walked in, his glasses steamed up.*

steamer /ˈsti:mə(r)/ *noun* [C] **1** a boat or ship driven by steam power **2** a metal container with small holes in it that is used in cooking. You put it over a pan of boiling water in order to cook food in the steam.

steamroller /ˈsti:mrəʊlə(r)/ *noun* [C] a big heavy vehicle with wide heavy wheels that is used for making the surface of a road flat

steel¹ /sti:l/ *noun* [U] a very strong metal that is made from iron mixed with **carbon** (= another chemical element). Steel is used for making knives, tools, machines, etc: *the iron and steel industry* ♦ *a frame made of steel* ♦ *a bridge reinforced with huge steel girders*

steel² /sti:l/ *verb* [T] steel yourself to prepare yourself to deal with sth difficult or unpleasant: *Steel yourself for a shock.*

steelworks /ˈsti:lwɜ:ks/ *noun* [C, with sing or pl verb] (*pl* steelworks) a factory where steel is made

steep /sti:p/ *adj* (steeper; steepest) **1** (used about a hill, mountain, street, etc.) rising or falling quickly; at a sharp angle: *I don't think I can cycle up that hill. It's too steep.* **2** (used about an increase or a fall in sth) very big: *a steep rise in unemployment* **3** (*informal*) too expensive: *£3 for a cup of coffee seems a little steep to me.* ▶ **steeply** *adv*: *House prices have risen steeply this year.* ▶ **steepness** *noun* [U]

steeped /sti:pt/ *adj* steeped in sth having a lot of sth; full of sth: *a city steeped in history*

steeple /ˈsti:pl/ *noun* [C] a tower on the roof of a church, often with a **spire** (= a tall pointed top)

steer /stɪə(r)/ *verb* **1** [I,T] to control the direction that a vehicle is going in: *Can you push the car while I steer?* ♦ *to steer a boat/ship/bicycle/motorbike* **2** [T] to take control of a situation and try to influence the way it develops: *She tried to steer the conversation away from the subject of money.*

IDM **keep/stay/steer clear (of sb/sth)** ➲ **clear³**

steering /ˈstɪərɪŋ/ *noun* [U] the parts of a vehicle that control the direction that it moves in: *the power steering in a car*

ˈsteering wheel (also wheel) *noun* [C] the wheel that the driver turns in a vehicle to control the direction that it moves in ➲ picture at **car**

stem¹ /stem/ *noun* [C] **1** the main central part of a plant above the ground from which the leaves or flowers grow ➲ picture at **plant** **2** the main part of a word onto which other parts are added: *'Writ-' is the stem of the words 'write', 'writing', 'written' and 'writer'.*

stem² /stem/ *verb* [T] (stemming; stemmed) to stop sth that is increasing or spreading

PHR V **stem from sth** [not used in the continuous tenses] to be the result of sth

ˈstem cell *noun* [C] a basic type of cell which can divide and develop into cells with particular functions. All the different kinds of cells in the human body develop from **stem cells**: *Tests suggest that stem cells could be used to regenerate damaged body parts.* ♦ *stem cell research*

stench /stentʃ/ *noun* [sing] a very unpleasant smell ➲ note at **smell²**

stencil /ˈstensl/ *noun* [C] a thin piece of metal, plastic or card with a design cut out of it, that you put onto a surface and paint over so that the design is left on the surface; the pattern or design that is produced in this way ▶ **stencil** *verb* [I,T] (stencilling; stencilled, (*AmE* also) stenciling; stenciled)

step¹ /step/ *noun* [C] **1** the act of lifting one foot and putting it down in a different place: *Nick* ***took a step*** *forward and then stopped.* ♦ *I heard steps outside the window.* ♦ *We were obviously lost so we decided to* ***retrace*** *our* ***steps*** (= go back the way we had come). **2** one action in a series of actions that you take in order to achieve sth: *This will not solve the problem completely, but it is* ***a step in the right direction.*** **3** one of the surfaces on which you put your foot when you are going up or down stairs: *on the top/bottom step* ➲ note at **stair** ➲ picture at **ladder** ➲ picture on **page P8**

IDM **in/out of step (with sb/sth)** moving/not moving your feet at the same time as other people when you are marching, dancing, etc.

step by step (used for talking about a series of actions) moving slowly and gradually from one action or stage to the next: *clear step-by-step instructions*

take steps to do sth to take action in order to achieve sth

watch your step ➲ **watch¹**

step² /step/ *verb* [I] (stepping; stepped) **1** to lift one foot and put it down in a different place when you are walking: *Be careful! Don't step in the mud.* ♦ *to step forward/back* ♦ *Ouch! You stepped on my* foot! **2** to move a short distance; to go somewhere: *Could you step out of the car please, sir?* ♦ *I stepped outside for a minute to get some air.*

PHR V step down to leave an important job or position and let sb else take your place

step in to help sb in a difficult situation or to become involved in a disagreement

step sth up to increase the amount, speed, etc. of sth: *The Army has decided to step up its security arrangements.*

step- /step-/ [in compounds] related as a result of one parent marrying again

stepbrother /ˈstepbrʌðə(r)/ *noun* [C] the son from an earlier marriage of sb who has married your mother or father ➲ look at **half-brother**

stepchild /ˈsteptʃaɪld/ *noun* [C] (*pl* **stepchildren**) the child from an earlier marriage of your husband or wife ➲ note at **child**

stepdaughter /ˈstepdɔːtə(r)/ *noun* [C] the daughter from an earlier marriage of your husband or wife

stepfather /ˈstepfɑːðə(r)/ *noun* [C] the man who has married your mother when your parents are divorced or your father is dead

stepladder /ˈsteplædə(r)/ *noun* [C] a short **ladder** (= a piece of equipment that is used for climbing up sth) with two parts, one with steps. The parts are joined together at the top so that it can stand on its own and be folded up when you are not using it. ➲ picture at **ladder**

stepmother /ˈstepmʌðə(r)/ *noun* [C] the woman who has married your father when your parents are divorced or your mother is dead

ˈ**stepping stone** *noun* [C] **1** one of a line of flat stones that you can step on in order to cross a river **2** something that allows you to make progress or helps you to achieve sth

stepsister /ˈstepsɪstə(r)/ *noun* [C] the daughter from an earlier marriage of sb who has married your mother or father ➲ look at **half-sister**

stepson /ˈstepsʌn/ *noun* [C] the son from an earlier marriage of your husband or wife

stereo /ˈsteriəʊ/ *noun* (*pl* **stereos**) **1** (also ˈ**stereo system**) [C] a machine that plays CDs, etc., sometimes with a radio, that has two separate speakers so that you hear sounds from each: *a car/personal stereo* ➲ note at **listen 2** [U] the system for playing recorded music, speech, etc. in which the sound is divided into two parts: *This programme is broadcast in stereo.* ➲ look at **mono** ▸ **stereo** *adj* [only *before* a noun]: *a stereo TV*

stereotype /ˈsteriətaɪp/ *noun* [C] a fixed idea about a particular type of person or thing, which is often not true in reality ▸ **stereotype** *verb* [T]: *In advertisements, women are often stereotyped as housewives.* ▸ **stereotypical** /ˌsteriəˈtɪpɪkl/ *adj*: *stereotypical views of accountants* ▸ **stereotypically** /-kli/ *adv*

sterile /ˈsteraɪl/ *adj* **1** not able to produce young animals or babies **2** completely clean and free from bacteria: *All equipment used during a medical operation must be sterile.* **3** not producing any useful result: *a sterile discussion/argument* ▸ **sterility** /stəˈrɪləti/ *noun* [U]

sterilize (also **-ise**) /ˈsterəlaɪz/ *verb* [T] **1** to make sb/sth completely clean and free from bacteria **2** [usually passive] to perform an operation on a person or an animal so that they or it cannot have babies ▸ **sterilization** (also **-isation**) /ˌsterəlaɪˈzeɪʃn/ *noun* [C,U]

sterling[1] /ˈstɜːlɪŋ/ *noun* [U] the system of money used in the UK, that uses the pound as its basic unit

sterling[2] /ˈstɜːlɪŋ/ *adj* of very high quality: *sterling work*

stern[1] /stɜːn/ *adj* (**sterner**; **sternest**) very serious; not smiling: *a stern expression/warning* ▸ **sternly** *adv*

stern[2] /stɜːn/ *noun* [C] the back end of a ship or boat **OPP bow** ➲ note at **boat** ➲ picture on **page P6**

steroid /ˈsterɔɪd/ *noun* [C] a chemical substance produced naturally in the body. There are many different **steroids** and they can be used to treat diseases and are sometimes used illegally by people playing sports.

stethoscope /ˈsteθəskəʊp/ *noun* [C] the piece of equipment that a doctor uses for listening to your breathing and heart

stew /stjuː/ *noun* [C,U] a type of food that you make by cooking meat and/or vegetables in liquid for a long time ▸ **stew** *verb* [I,T]

steward /ˈstjuːəd/ *noun* [C] **1** a man whose job is to look after passengers on an aircraft, a ship or a train **2** (*BrE*) a person who helps to organize a large public event, for example a race

stewardess /ˌstjuːəˈdes; ˈstjuːə-/ *noun* [C] **1** (*old-fashioned*) a woman whose job is to look after passengers on an aircraft **2** a woman who looks after the passengers on a ship or train

stick[1] /stɪk/ *verb* (*pt*, *pp* **stuck** /stʌk/)

➤ PUSH STH IN **1** [I,T] **stick (sth) in/into (sth)** to push a pointed object into sth; to be pushed into sth: *I found a nail sticking in the tyre.* ♦ *Stick a fork into the meat to see if it's ready.*

➤ FIX **2** [I,T] to fix sth to sth else by using a sticky substance; to become fixed to sth else: *I stuck a stamp on the envelope.* ♦ *We used glue to stick the pieces together.*

➤ PUT **3** [T] (*informal*) to put sth somewhere, especially quickly or carelessly: *Stick your bags in the bedroom.* ♦ *Just at that moment James stuck his head round the door.*

➤ BECOME FIXED **4** [I] **stick (in sth)** (used about sth that can usually be moved) to become fixed in one position so that it cannot be moved: *The car was stuck in the mud.* ♦ *This drawer keeps sticking.*

➤ DIFFICULT SITUATION **5** [T] [often in negative sentences and questions] (*informal*) to stay in a difficult or unpleasant situation: *I can't stick this job much longer.*

S

IDM poke/stick your nose into sth ➲ **nose**[1]
put/stick your tongue out ➲ **tongue**
stand/stick out like a sore thumb ➲ **sore**[1]
PHR V stick around (*informal*) to stay somewhere, waiting for sth to happen or for sb to arrive
stick at sth (*informal*) to continue working at sth even when it is difficult
stick by sb (*informal*) to continue to give sb help and support even in difficult times
stick out (*informal*) to be very noticeable and easily seen: *The new office block really sticks out from the older buildings around it.*
stick out (of sth) to be further out than sth else: *The boy's head was sticking out of the window.*
stick it/sth out (*informal*) to stay in a difficult or unpleasant situation until the end
stick to sth (*informal*) to continue with sth and not change to anything else
stick together (*informal*) (used about a group of people) to stay friendly and loyal to each other
stick up to point upwards: *You look funny. Your hair's sticking up!*
stick up for yourself/sb/sth (*informal*) to support or defend yourself/sb/sth: *Don't worry. I'll stick up for you if there's any trouble.*

🔑 **stick**[2] /stɪk/ *noun* [C] **1** a small thin piece of wood from a tree: *We collected dry sticks to start a fire.* **2** (*especially BrE*) = **walking stick 3** a long thin piece of wood that you use for hitting the ball in some sports: *a hockey stick* ➲ note at **bat 4** a long thin piece of sth: *a stick of celery/dynamite*

sticker /ˈstɪkə(r)/ *noun* [C] a piece of paper with writing or a picture on one side that you can stick onto sth

ˈ**sticking plaster** = **plaster**[1] (3)

🔑 **sticky** /ˈstɪki/ *adj* (**stickier**; **stickiest**) **1** used for describing a substance that easily becomes joined to things that it touches, or sth that is covered with this kind of substance: *These sweets are very sticky.* **2** (*informal*) (used about a situation) difficult or unpleasant: *There were a few sticky moments in the meeting.*

ˈ**sticky tape** = **Sellotape™**

🔑 **stiff**[1] /stɪf/ *adj* (**stiffer**; **stiffest**)
➤DIFFICULT TO BEND **1** (used about material, paper, etc.) firm and difficult to bend or move: *My new shoes feel rather stiff.* ♦ *The door handle is stiff and I can't turn it.*
➤PARTS OF BODY **2** if a person is stiff, their muscles hurt when they move them: *My arm feels really stiff after playing tennis yesterday.*
➤LIQUID **3** very thick; almost solid: *Beat the egg whites until they are stiff.*
➤DIFFICULT/STRONG **4** more difficult or stronger than usual: *The firm faces stiff competition from its rivals.* ♦ *a stiff breeze/wind*
➤BEHAVIOUR **5** not relaxed or friendly; formal: *The speech he made to welcome them was stiff and formal.*
➤ALCOHOLIC DRINK **6** [only *before* a noun] strong: *a stiff whisky* ▶ **stiffness** *noun* [U]

stiff[2] /stɪf/ *adv* (*informal*) extremely: *to be bored/frozen/scared/worried stiff*

stiffen /ˈstɪfn/ *verb* **1** [I] (used about a person) to suddenly stop moving and hold your body very straight, usually because you are afraid or angry **2** [I,T] to become, or to make sth become, difficult to bend or move

🔑 **stiffly** /ˈstɪfli/ *adv* in an unfriendly formal way: *He smiled stiffly.*

stifle /ˈstaɪfl/ *verb* **1** [T] to stop sth happening, developing or continuing: *Her strict education had stifled her natural creativity.* ♦ *to stifle a yawn/cry/giggle* **2** [I,T] to be or to make sb unable to breathe because it is very hot and/or there is no fresh air: *Fergus was almost stifled by the smoke.* ▶ **stifling** *adj*: *The heat was stifling.*

stigma /ˈstɪɡmə/ *noun* [C,U] bad and often unfair feelings that people in general have about a particular illness, way of behaving, etc: *There is still a lot of stigma attached to being unemployed.*

stiletto /stɪˈletəʊ/ *noun* [C] (*pl* -**os** *or* -**oes**) **1** a woman's shoe with a very high narrow heel **2** (also ˌ**stiletto** ˈ**heel**) the heel on such a shoe

🔑 **still**[1] /stɪl/ *adv* **1** continuing until now or until the time you are talking about and not finishing: *Do you still live in London?* ♦ *It's still raining.* ♦ *I've eaten all the food but I'm still hungry.* ♦ *In 2009 Zoran was still a student.* **2** in spite of what has just been said: *He had a bad headache but he still went to the party.* **3** used for making a comparative adjective stronger: *It was very cold yesterday, but today it's colder still.* ♦ *There was still more bad news to come.* **4** in addition; more: *There are still ten days to go until my holiday.*

🔑 **still**[2] /stɪl/ *adj* **1** not moving: *Stand still! I want to take a photograph!* ♦ *Children find it hard to* ***keep/stay still*** *for long periods.* **2** quiet or calm: *The water was perfectly still.* **3** (used about a drink) not containing gas: *still mineral water* ➲ look at **fizzy**, **sparkling** ▶ **stillness** *noun* [U]

still[3] /stɪl/ *noun* [C] a single photograph that is taken from a film or video

stillborn /ˈstɪlbɔːn/ *adj* (used about a baby) dead when it is born

stilt /stɪlt/ *noun* [C] **1** one of two long pieces of wood, with places to rest your feet on, on which you can walk above the ground: *Have you tried walking* ***on stilts****?* **2** one of a set of poles that supports a building above the ground or water

stilted /ˈstɪltɪd/ *adj* (used about a way of speaking or writing) not natural or relaxed; too formal

stimulant /ˈstɪmjələnt/ *noun* [C] a drug or medicine that makes you feel more active

stimulate /ˈstɪmjuleɪt/ *verb* [T] **1** to make sth active or more active: *Exercise stimulates the blood circulation.* ♦ *The government has decided to cut taxes in order to stimulate the economy.* **2** to make sb feel interested and excited about sth: *The lessons don't really stimulate him.* ▶ **stimulation** /ˌstɪmjuˈleɪʃn/ *noun* [U]

stimulating /ˈstɪmjuleɪtɪŋ/ *adj* interesting and exciting: *a stimulating discussion*

stimulus /ˈstɪmjələs/ *noun* [C,U] (*pl* **stimuli** /-laɪ/) something that causes activity, development or interest: *Books provide children with ideas and a stimulus for play.*

🔑 **sting¹** /stɪŋ/ *verb* [I,T] (*pt, pp* **stung** /stʌŋ/) **1** (used about an insect, a plant, etc.) to make a person or an animal feel a sudden pain by pushing sth sharp into their skin and sending poison into them: *Be careful. Those plants sting.* ◆ *Ow! I've been stung by a bee!* ➲ look at **bite** **2** to make sb/sth feel a sudden, sharp pain: *Soap stings if it gets in your eyes.* **3** to make sb feel very hurt and upset because of sth you say: *Kate was stung by her father's criticism.*

🔑 **sting²** /stɪŋ/ *noun* **1** [C] the sharp pointed part of some insects and animals that is used for pushing into the skin of a person or an animal and putting in poison: *the sting of a bee* ➲ picture at **scorpion** ➲ picture on **page P13** **2** [C] a wound that is made when an animal or insect pushes its sting into you: *I got a wasp sting on the leg.* **3** [C,U] a sharp pain that feels like a sting: *the sting of soap in your eyes*

stink /stɪŋk/ *verb* [I] (*pt* **stank** /stæŋk/ *or* **stunk** /stʌŋk/; *pp* **stunk**) (*informal*) **stink (of sth)** **1** to have a very strong and unpleasant smell: *It stinks in here—open a window!* ◆ *to stink of fish* ➲ note at **smell²** **2** to seem to be very bad, unpleasant or dishonest: *The whole business stinks of corruption.* ▶ **stink** *noun* [C]

stint /stɪnt/ *noun* [C] a fixed period of time that you spend doing sth: *He did a brief stint in the army after leaving school.*

stipulate /ˈstɪpjuleɪt/ *verb* [T] (*formal*) to say exactly and officially what must be done: *The law stipulates that all schools must be inspected every three years.* ▶ **stipulation** /ˌstɪpjuˈleɪʃn/ *noun* [C,U]

🔑 **stir¹** /stɜː(r)/ *verb* (**stirring**; **stirred**) **1** [T] to move a liquid, etc. round and round, using a spoon, etc: *She stirred her coffee with a teaspoon.* **2** [I,T] to move or make sb/sth move slightly: *She heard the baby stir in the next room.* **3** [T] to make sb feel a strong emotion: *The story stirred Carol's imagination.* ◆ *a stirring speech*

PHR V **stir sth up** to cause problems, or to make people feel strong emotions: *He's always trying to* ***stir up trouble.*** ◆ *The article stirred up a lot of anger among local residents.*

stir² /stɜː(r)/ *noun* **1** [sing] excitement, anger or shock that is felt by a number of people **2** [C] the act of **stirring¹**(1): *Give the soup a stir.*

ˈ**stir-fry** *verb* [T] to cook thin strips of vegetables or meat quickly in a small amount of very hot oil ▶ ˈ**stir-fry** *noun* [C]

stirrup /ˈstɪrəp/ *noun* [C] one of the two metal objects that you put your feet in when you are riding a horse ➲ picture at **horse**

stitch¹ /stɪtʃ/ *noun* [C] **1** one of the small lines of thread that you can see on a piece of cloth after it has been sewn ➲ picture at **sew** **2** one of the small circles of wool that you put round a needle when you are knitting **3** one of the small pieces of thread that a doctor uses to sew your skin together if you cut yourself very badly, or after an operation: *How many stitches did you have in your leg?* **4** [usually sing] a sudden pain that you get in the side of your body when you are running

IDM **in stitches** (*informal*) laughing so much that you cannot stop

stitch² /stɪtʃ/ *verb* [I,T] to sew

🔑 **stock¹** /stɒk/ *noun* [C,U] **1** the supply of things that a shop, etc. has for sale: *We'll have to order extra stock if we sell a lot more this week.* ◆ *I'm afraid that book's* ***out of stock*** *at the moment. Shall I order it for you?* ◆ *I'll see if we have your size* ***in stock.*** **2** an amount of sth that has been kept ready to be used: *Food stocks in the village were very low.* **3** a share that sb has bought in a company, or the value of a company's shares: *to invest in stocks and shares* **4** a liquid that is made by boiling meat, bones, vegetables, etc. in water, used especially for making soups and sauces: *vegetable/chicken stock*

IDM **take stock (of sth)** to think about sth very carefully before deciding what to do next

stock² /stɒk/ *verb* [T] **1** (usually used about a shop) to have a supply of sth: *They stock food from all over the world.* **2** to fill a place with sth: *a well-stocked library*

PHR V **stock up (on/with sth)** to collect a large supply of sth for future use: *to stock up with food for the winter*

stock³ /stɒk/ *adj* [only *before* a noun] (used for describing sth that sb says) used so often that it does not have much meaning: *He always gives the same stock answers.*

stockbroker /ˈstɒkbrəʊkə(r)/ (*also* **broker**) *noun* [C] a person whose job is to buy and sell shares in companies for other people

ˈ**stock exchange** *noun* [C] **1** a place where shares in companies are bought and sold: *the Tokyo Stock Exchange* **2** (*also* ˈ**stock market**) the business or activity of buying and selling shares in companies ➲ note at **money** ➲ look at **exchange**

stocking /ˈstɒkɪŋ/ *noun* [C] one of a pair of thin pieces of clothing that fit tightly over a woman's feet and legs: *a pair of stockings* ➲ look at **tights**

stockist /ˈstɒkɪst/ *noun* [C] a shop that sells goods made by a particular company

ˈ**stock market** = **stock exchange**(2)

stockpile /ˈstɒkpaɪl/ *verb* [T] to collect and keep a large supply of sth ▶ **stockpile** *noun* [C]: *a stockpile of weapons*

stocktaking /ˈstɒkteɪkɪŋ/ *noun* [U] the activity of counting the total supply of things that a shop or business has at a particular time: *They close for an hour a month to do the stocktaking.*

stocky /ˈstɒki/ *adj* (**stockier**; **stockiest**) (used about sb's body) short but strong and heavy

stoic /ˈstəʊɪk/ (*also* **stoical** /-kl/) *adj* (*formal*) suffering pain or difficulty without complaining ▶ **stoically** /-kli/ *adv* ▶ **stoicism** /ˈstəʊɪsɪzəm/ *noun* [U]

S

stoke /stəʊk/ *verb* [T] **1** **stoke sth (up) (with sth)** to add fuel to a fire: *to stoke up a fire with more coal* ◆ *to stoke a furnace* **2** **stoke sth (up)** to make people feel sth more strongly: *to stoke up envy*

stole *past tense* of **steal**

stolen *past participle* of **steal**

stolid /ˈstɒlɪd/ *adj* (used about a person) showing very little emotion or excitement ▶ **stolidly** *adv*

stomach¹ /ˈstʌmək/ (also *informal* **tummy**) *noun* [C] **1** the organ in your body where food goes after you have eaten it: *He went to the doctor with stomach pains.* ➲ picture at **body** **2** the front part of your body below your chest and above your legs: *She turned over onto her stomach.* ➲ picture at **body**

stomach² /ˈstʌmək/ *verb* [T] [usually in negative sentences and questions] (*informal*) to be able to watch, listen to, accept, etc. sth that you think is unpleasant: *I can't stomach too much violence in films.*

ˈ**stomach ache** *noun* [C,U] a pain in your stomach: *I've got terrible stomach ache.* ➲ note at **ache**

stomp /stɒmp/ *verb* [I] (*informal*) to walk with heavy steps

stone /stəʊn/ *noun*
➤ HARD SUBSTANCE **1** [U] a hard solid substance that is found in the ground: *The house was built of grey stone.* ◆ *a stone wall* **2** [C] a small piece of rock: *The boy picked up a stone and threw it into the river.*
➤ JEWEL **3** [C] = **precious stone**
➤ IN FRUIT **4** (*AmE* **pit**) [C] the hard seed inside some types of fruit: *Peaches, plums, cherries and olives all have stones.* ➲ picture on **page P14**
➤ WEIGHT **5** [C] (*pl* **stone**) (*abbr* **st**) (in Britain) a measure of weight; 6.35 kilograms. There are 14 pounds in a stone: *I weigh eleven stone two* (= 2 pounds).
IDM **kill two birds with one stone** ➲ **kill¹**

S

stoned /stəʊnd/ *adj* (*slang*) not behaving or thinking normally because of drugs or alcohol

stony /ˈstəʊni/ *adj* (**stonier**; **stoniest**) **1** (used about the ground) having a lot of stones in it, or covered with stones **2** not friendly: *There was a stony silence as he walked into the room.*

stood *past tense, past participle* of **stand¹**

stool /stuːl/ *noun* [C] a seat that does not have a back or arms: *a piano stool* ➲ picture at **chair, piano**

stoop /stuːp/ *verb* [I] to bend your head and shoulders forwards and downwards: *He had to stoop to get through the low doorway.*
PHR V **stoop to sth/doing sth** to do sth bad or wrong that you would normally not do
▶ **stoop** *noun* [sing]: *to walk with a stoop*

stop¹ /stɒp/ *verb* (**stopping**; **stopped**) **1** [I,T] to finish moving or make sb/sth finish moving: *He walked along the road for a bit, and then stopped.* ◆ *Does this train stop at Didcot?* ◆ *My watch has stopped.* ◆ *I stopped someone in the street to ask the way to the station.* **2** [I,T] to no longer continue or to make sb/sth not continue: *I think the rain has stopped.* ◆ *It's stopped raining now.* ◆ *Stop making that terrible noise!* ◆ *The bus service stops at midnight.* ◆ *We tied a bandage round his arm to stop the bleeding.*

> **GRAMMAR** If you **stop to do sth**, you stop in order to do it: *On the way home I stopped to buy a newspaper.* If you **stop doing sth**, you do not now do something that you did in the past: *I stopped smoking 3 months ago.*

3 [T] **stop sb/sth (from) doing sth** to make sb/sth end or finish an activity; to prevent sb/sth from doing sth: *They've built a fence to stop the dog getting out.* ◆ *I'm going to go and you can't stop me.* **4** [I,T] **stop (for sth); stop (and do/to do sth)** to end an activity for a short time in order to do sth: *Shall we stop for lunch now?* ◆ *Let's stop and look at the map.* ◆ *We stopped work for half an hour to have a cup of coffee.*
IDM **stop at nothing** to do anything to get what you want, even if it is wrong or dangerous
stop short of sth/doing sth to almost do sth, but then decide not to do it at the last minute
PHR V **stop off (at/in …)** to stop during a journey to do sth
stop over (at/in …) to stay somewhere for a short time during a long journey

stop² /stɒp/ *noun* [C] **1** an act of stopping or the state of being stopped: *Our first stop will be in Edinburgh.* ◆ *Production at the factory will* ***come to a stop*** *at midnight tonight.* ◆ *I managed to* ***bring*** *the car* ***to a stop*** *just in time.* **2** the place where a bus, train, etc. stops so that people can get on and off: *a bus stop* ◆ *I'm getting off at the next stop.* ➲ picture on **page P11**
IDM **pull out all the stops** ➲ **pull¹**
put a stop to sth to prevent sth bad or unpleasant from continuing

stopgap /ˈstɒpgæp/ *noun* [C] aperson or a thing that does a job for a short time until sb/sth permanent can be found

stopover /ˈstɒpəʊvə(r)/ *noun* [C] a short stay between two parts of a journey

stoppage /ˈstɒpɪdʒ/ *noun* [C] **1** a situation in which people stop working as part of a protest **2** (in sport) an interruption in a game for a particular reason

stopper /ˈstɒpə(r)/ *noun* [C] an object that you put into the top of a bottle in order to close it

stopwatch /ˈstɒpwɒtʃ/ *noun* [C] a watch which can be started and stopped by pressing a button, so that you can measure exactly how long sth takes

storage /ˈstɔːrɪdʒ/ *noun* [U] the process of keeping things until they are needed; the space where they are kept: *This room is being used for storage at the moment.*

store¹ /stɔː(r)/ *noun* [C] **1** a large shop: *She's a sales assistant in a large department store.* ◆ *a furniture store* ➲ look at **chain store** **2** (*AmE*) = **shop¹** **3** a supply of sth that you keep for future use; the place where it is kept: *a good store of food for the winter* ◆ *Police discovered a weapons store in the house.*
IDM **in store (for sb/sth)** going to happen in the

future: *There's a surprise in store for you when you get home!*

set ... store by sth to consider sth to be important: *Nick sets great store by his mother's opinion.*

store² /stɔː(r)/ *verb* [T] to keep sth or a supply of sth for future use: *to store information on a computer*

storekeeper /ˈstɔːkiːpə(r)/ (*AmE*) = **shopkeeper**

storeroom /ˈstɔːruːm; -rʊm/ *noun* [C] a room where things are kept until they are needed

storey (*AmE* story) /ˈstɔːri/ *noun* [C] (*pl* storeys, (*AmE*) stories) one floor or level of a building: *The building will be five storeys high.* ◆ *a two-storey house* ◆ *a multi-storey car park*

stork /stɔːk/ *noun* [C] a large black and white bird with a long beak, neck and legs. **Storks** often make their nests on the top of buildings.

storm¹ /stɔːm/ *noun* [C] very bad weather with strong winds and rain: *Look at those black clouds. I think there's going to be a storm.* ◆ *a hailstorm* (= a storm when hail falls from the sky) ◆ *a sandstorm* (= a storm in the desert when sand is blown into the air) ➲ note at **weather**

OTHER WORDS FOR

storm

During a **thunderstorm** you hear **thunder** and see flashes of **lightning** in the sky. Large, violent storms with very strong winds are called **cyclones. Hurricanes** (or **typhoons**) are a type of cyclone. A storm with a very strong circular wind is called a **tornado**. A **blizzard** is a very bad **snowstorm.**

storm² /stɔːm/ *verb* **1** [T] to attack a building, town, etc. suddenly and violently in order to take control of it **2** [I] to enter or leave somewhere in a very angry and noisy way: *He threw down the book and stormed out of the room.*

stormy /ˈstɔːmi/ *adj* (stormier; stormiest) **1** used for talking about very bad weather, with strong winds, heavy rain, etc: *a stormy night* ◆ *stormy weather* **2** involving a lot of angry argument and strong feeling: *a stormy relationship*

story /ˈstɔːri/ *noun* [C] (*pl* stories) **1** a story (about sb/sth) a description of people and events that are not real: *I'll **tell** you **a story** about the animals that live in that forest.* ◆ *I always read the children **a bedtime story**.* ◆ *a detective/fairy/ghost/love story* ➲ note at **history** **2** an account, especially a spoken one, of sth that has happened: *The police didn't believe his story.* **3** a description of true events that happened in the past: *He's writing his life story.* **4** an article or a report in a newspaper or a magazine: *The plane crash was the front-page story in most newspapers.* **5** (*AmE*) = **storey**

stout /staʊt/ *adj* (stouter; stoutest) **1** (used about a person) rather fat **2** strong and thick: *stout walking boots*

stove /stəʊv/ *noun* [C] **1** a piece of equipment that can burn wood, coal, etc. to heat a room: *a wood-burning stove* **2** (*especially AmE*) = **cooker**: *He put a pan of water to boil on the stove.*

stovetop /ˈstəʊvtɒp/ (*AmE*) = **hob**

stow /stəʊ/ *verb* [T] stow sth (away) to put sth away in a particular place until it is needed

stowaway /ˈstəʊəweɪ/ *noun* [C] a person who hides in a ship or plane so that they can travel without paying

straddle /ˈstrædl/ *verb* [T] **1** (used about a person) to sit or stand with your legs on each side of sth: *to straddle a chair* **2** (used about a building, bridge, etc.) to be on both sides of sth

straggle /ˈstræɡl/ *verb* [I] **1** to grow, spread or move in an untidy way or in different directions: *Her wet hair straggled across her forehead.* **2** to walk, etc. more slowly than the rest of the group: *The children straggled along behind their parents.* ▸ **straggler** *noun* [C] ▸ **straggly** *adj*: *long straggly hair*

straight¹ /streɪt/ *adv* (straighter; straightest) **1** not in a curve or at an angle; in a straight line: *Go **straight on** for about two miles until you come to some traffic lights.* ◆ *He was looking **straight ahead**.* ◆ *to sit up straight* (= with a straight back) **2** without stopping: *I took the children straight home after school.* ◆ *to walk straight past somebody/something* ◆ *I'm going straight to bed when I get home.* ◆ *He joined the army straight from school.* **3** in an honest and direct way: *Tell me straight, doctor—is it serious?*

IDM **go straight** (*informal*) to become honest after being a criminal

right/straight away ➲ **away**

straight out (*informal*) in an honest and direct way: *I told Asif straight out that I didn't want to see him any more.*

straight² /streɪt/ *adj* (straighter; straightest)

›WITHOUT BENDS **1** with no bends or curves; going in one direction only: *a straight line* ◆ *He's got straight dark hair.* ◆ *Keep your back straight!* ◆ *He was so tired he couldn't walk **in a straight line**.* ➲ picture at **hair, line**

›HORIZONTAL/VERTICAL **2** [not before a noun] in an exactly horizontal or vertical position: *That picture isn't straight.*

›TIDY **3** tidy or organized as it should be: *It took ages to **put** the room **straight** after we'd decorated it.*

›HONEST **4** honest and direct: *Politicians never give **a straight answer**.* ◆ *Are you being straight with me?*

›ALCOHOLIC DRINK **5** (*AmE*) = **neat**(5)

›BORING **6** (*informal*) used to describe a person who you think is too serious and boring

›SEX **7** (*informal*) attracted to people of the opposite sex SYN **heterosexual** OPP **gay**

IDM **get sth straight** to make sure that you understand sth completely

keep a straight face to stop yourself from smiling or laughing

put/set the record straight ➲ **record¹**

straighten /ˈstreɪtn/ *verb* [I,T] straighten (sth) (up/out) to become straight or to make sth straight: *The road straightens out at the bottom of the hill.* ◆ *to straighten your tie*

S

a strange town ♦ Do not talk to strange men. ➲ look at **foreign**

PHR V **straighten sth out** to remove the confusion or difficulties from a situation
straighten up to make your body straight and vertical

straightforward /ˌstreɪtˈfɔːwəd/ *adj* **1** easy to do or understand; simple: *straightforward instructions* **2** honest and open: *a straightforward person*

straightjacket = straitjacket

strain¹ /streɪn/ *noun*
➤WORRY **1** [C,U] worry or pressure caused by having too much to deal with: *to be* ***under*** *a lot of* ***strain*** *at work* **2** [C] something that makes you feel worried and tense: *I always find exams a terrible strain.*
➤PRESSURE **3** [U] pressure that is put on sth when it is pulled or pushed by a physical force: *Running downhill puts strain on the knees.* ♦ *The rope finally broke* ***under the strain.***
➤INJURY **4** [C,U] an injury to part of your body that is caused by using it too much: *He is out of today's game with a back strain.*
➤TYPE OF ANIMAL, ETC. **5** [C] one type of animal, plant or disease that is slightly different from the other types: *This new strain of the disease is particularly dangerous.*

strain² /streɪn/ *verb* **1** [T] to injure a part of your body by using it too much: *Don't read in the dark. You'll strain your eyes.* ♦ *I think I've strained a muscle in my neck.* **2** [I,T] to make a great effort to do sth: *I was straining to see what was happening.* ♦ *Bend down as far as you can without straining.* **3** [T] to put a lot of pressure on sth: *Money problems have strained their relationship.* **4** [T] to separate a solid and a liquid by pouring them into a special container with small holes in it: *to strain tea/vegetables/spaghetti*

strained /streɪnd/ *adj* **1** worried because of having too much to deal with: *Martin looked tired and strained.* **2** not natural or friendly: *Relations between the two countries are strained.*

strait /streɪt/ *noun* **1** [C] (also **straits** [pl]) a narrow piece of sea that joins two larger seas: *the Strait(s) of Gibraltar* **2** **straits** [pl] a very difficult situation, especially one caused by having no money: *The company is in desperate financial straits.*
IDM **be in dire straits** ➲ **dire**

straitjacket (also **straightjacket**) /ˈstreɪtdʒækɪt/ *noun* [C] a piece of clothing like a jacket with long arms which are tied to prevent people who are considered dangerous from behaving violently

strand /strænd/ *noun* [C] **1** a single piece of cotton, wool, hair, etc. **2** one part of a story, a situation or an idea

stranded /ˈstrændɪd/ *adj* left in a place that you cannot get away from: *We were left stranded when our car broke down in the mountains.*

strange /streɪndʒ/ *adj* (**stranger**; **strangest**) **1** unusual or unexpected: *A very strange thing happened to me on the way home.* ♦ *a strange noise* **2** that you have not seen, visited, met, etc. before: *a strange town* ♦ *Do not talk to strange men.* ➲ look at **foreign**

> **HELP** **Strange** does not mean 'from another country'.

▶ **strangely** *adv*: *The streets were strangely quiet.* ♦ *He's behaving very strangely at the moment.* ▶ **strangeness** *noun* [U]

stranger /ˈstreɪndʒə(r)/ *noun* [C] **1** a person that you do not know: *I had to ask a* ***complete stranger*** *to help me with my suitcase.* ➲ look at **foreigner**

> **HELP** **Stranger** DOES NOT mean 'someone who comes from a different country'.

2 a person who is in a place that they do not know: *I'm a stranger to this part of the country.*

strangle /ˈstræŋɡl/ *verb* [T] **1** to kill sb by squeezing their neck or throat with your hands, a rope, etc. **SYN** **throttle** ➲ look at **choke** **2** to prevent sth from developing

strap /stræp/ *noun* [C] a long narrow piece of leather, cloth, plastic, etc. that you use for carrying sth or for keeping sth in position: *a watch with a leather strap* ➲ picture at **bag**, **clock** ▶ **strap** *verb* [T] (**strapping**; **strapped**): *The racing driver was securely strapped into the car.*

strategic /strəˈtiːdʒɪk/ (also **strategical** /-kl/) *adj* **1** helping you to achieve a plan; giving you an advantage: *They made a strategic decision to sell off part of the company.* **2** connected with a country's plans to achieve success in a war or in its defence system **3** (used about bombs and other weapons) intended to be fired at the enemy's country rather than be used in battle ▶ **strategically** /-kli/ *adv*: *The island is strategically important.*

strategy /ˈstrætədʒi/ *noun* (*pl* **strategies**) **1** [C] a plan that you use in order to achieve sth: *What's your strategy for this exam?* **2** [U] the act of planning how to do or achieve sth: *military strategy*

straw /strɔː/ *noun* **1** [U] the long thin parts of some plants, for example **wheat** (= a plant grown for its grain), which are dried and then used for animals to sleep on or for making hats, covering a roof, etc: *a straw hat* **2** [C] one piece of **straw** **3** [C] a long plastic or paper tube that you can use for drinking through
IDM **the last/final straw** the last in a series of bad things that happen to you and that makes you decide that you cannot accept the situation any longer

strawberry /ˈstrɔːbəri/ *noun* [C] (*pl* **strawberries**) a small soft red fruit with small white seeds on it: *strawberries and cream* ➲ picture on **page P14**

stray¹ /streɪ/ *verb* [I] **1** to go away from the place where you should be: *The sheep had strayed onto the road.* **2** to not keep to the subject you should be thinking about or discussing: *My thoughts strayed for a few moments.*

stray² /streɪ/ *noun* [C] a dog, cat, etc. that does not have a home ▶ **stray** *adj* [only *before* a noun]: *a stray dog*

streak[1] /striːk/ *noun* [C] **1** streak (of sth) a thin line or mark: *The cat had brown fur with streaks of white in it.* **2** a part of sb's character that sometimes shows in the way they behave: *Vesna's a very caring girl, but she does have a selfish streak.* **3** a continuous period of bad or good luck in a game or sport: *The team is* ***on a losing/winning streak*** *at the moment.*

streak[2] /striːk/ *verb* [I] (*informal*) to run fast

streaked /striːkt/ *adj* streaked (with sth) having lines of a different colour: *black hair streaked with grey*

stream[1] /striːm/ *noun* [C] **1** a small river: *I waded across the shallow stream.* ➲ picture on **page P10**, **page P11** **2** the continuous movement of a liquid or gas: *a stream of blood* **3** a continuous movement of people or things: *a stream of traffic* **4** a large number of things which happen one after another: *a stream of letters/telephone calls/questions*

stream[2] /striːm/ *verb* **1** [I] (used about a liquid, gas or light) to flow in large amounts: *Tears were streaming down his face.* ◆ *Sunlight was streaming in through the windows.* **2** [I] (used about people or things) to move somewhere in a continuous flow: *People were streaming out of the station.* **3** [T] to play video or sound on a computer by receiving it as a continuous stream, from the Internet for example ➲ note at **touch screen**

streamer /ˈstriːmə(r)/ *noun* [C] a long piece of coloured paper that you use for decorating a room before a party, etc.

streamline /ˈstriːmlaɪn/ *verb* [T] **1** to give a vehicle, etc. a long smooth shape so that it will move easily through air or water **2** to make an organization, a process, etc. work better by making it simpler ▸ **streamlined** *adj*

street /striːt/ *noun* [C] **1** a public road in a city or town that has houses and buildings on one side or both sides: *to walk* ***along/down the street*** ◆ *to cross* ***the street*** ◆ *I met Ian* ***in the street*** *this morning.* ◆ *a narrow street* ◆ *a street map of Oporto* ➲ note at **road** **2** Street (*abbr* St) used in the names of streets: *64 High Street* ◆ *The post office is in Sheep Street.*

IDM **the man in the street** ➲ **man**[1]

streets ahead (of sb/sth) (*BrE informal*) much better than sb/sth

(right) up your street (*informal*) (used about an activity, a subject, etc.) exactly right for you because you know a lot about it, like it very much, etc.

streetcar /ˈstriːtkɑː(r)/ (*AmE*) = **tram**

ˈ**street light** (*BrE also* ˈstreet lamp) *noun* [C] a light at the top of a tall post in the street ➲ look at **lamp post**

strength /streŋθ/ *noun*

➤PHYSICAL POWER **1** [U] the quality of being physically strong; the amount of this quality that you have: *He pulled with all his strength but the rock would not move.* ◆ *I didn't have the strength to walk any further.* **2** [U] the ability of an object to hold heavy weights or to not break or be damaged easily: *All our suitcases are tested for strength before they leave the factory.*

➤INFLUENCE **3** [U] the power and influence that sb has: *Germany's economic strength*

➤OF FEELING/OPINION **4** [U] how strong a feeling or opinion is: *The government has misjudged the strength of public feeling on this issue.*

➤GOOD QUALITY **5** [C,U] a good quality or ability that sb/sth has: *His greatest strength is his ability to communicate with people.* ◆ *the strengths and weaknesses of a plan* ◆ *He showed great* ***strength of character***.

OPP **weakness**

IDM **at full strength** ➲ **full**[1]

below strength (used about a group) not having the number of people it needs or usually has

on the strength of as a result of information, advice, etc.

strengthen /ˈstreŋθn/ *verb* [I,T] to become stronger or to make sth stronger: *exercises to strengthen your muscles* OPP **weaken**

strenuous /ˈstrenjuəs/ *adj* needing or using a lot of effort or energy: *Don't do* ***strenuous exercise*** *after eating.* ▸ **strenuously** *adv*

stress[1] /stres/ *noun* **1** [C,U] worry and pressure that is caused by problems and by having too much to deal with: *He's been* ***under*** *a lot of* ***stress*** *since his wife went into hospital.* ➲ look at **trauma** **2** [C,U] a physical force that may cause sth to bend or break: *Heavy lorries* ***put*** *too much* ***stress*** *on this bridge.* **3** [U] stress (on sth) the special attention that you give to sth because you think it is important: *We should* ***put*** *more* ***stress*** *on preventing crime.* **4** [C,U] (a) stress (on sth) the force that you put on a particular word or part of a word when you speak: *In the word 'dictionary' the stress is on the first syllable, 'dic'.*

stress[2] /stres/ *verb* [T] to give sth special force or attention because it is important: *The minister stressed the need for a peaceful solution.* ◆ *You stress the first syllable in this word.* SYN **emphasize**

stressed /strest/ *adj* [not before a noun] (*informal*) (also ˌstressed ˈout) too anxious and tired to be able to relax: *He was feeling very stressed and tired.*

stressful /ˈstresfl/ *adj* causing worry and pressure: *a stressful job*

stretch[1] /stretʃ/ *verb* **1** [I,T] to pull sth so that it becomes longer or wider; to become longer or wider in this way: *The artist stretched the canvas tightly over the frame.* ◆ *My T-shirt stretched when I washed it.* **2** [I,T] stretch (sth) (out) to push out your arms, legs, etc. as far as possible: *He switched off the alarm clock, yawned and stretched.* ◆ *She stretched out on the sofa and fell asleep.* ◆ *She stretched out her arm to take the book.* ➲ picture at **exercise** **3** [I] to cover a large area of land or a long period of time: *The long white beaches stretch for miles along the coast.* **4** [T] to make use of all the money, ability, time, etc. that sb has available for use: *The test has been designed to really stretch students' knowledge.*

IDM **stretch your legs** (*informal*) to go for a walk after sitting down for a long time

stretch[2] /stretʃ/ *noun* [C] **1** a stretch (of sth) an area of land or water: *a dangerous stretch of road* **2** [usually sing] the act of making the muscles in

S

your arms, legs, back, etc. as long as possible: *Stand up, everybody, and have a good stretch.*
IDM **at full stretch** ➲ **full[1]**
at a stretch without stopping: *We travelled for six hours at a stretch.*

stretcher /ˈstretʃə(r)/ *noun* [C] a piece of cloth supported by two poles that is used for carrying a person who has been injured

stretchy /ˈstretʃi/ *adj* (**stretchier**; **stretchiest**) that can easily be made longer or wider without tearing or breaking: *stretchy fabric*

⚷ **strict** /strɪkt/ *adj* (**stricter**; **strictest**) **1** that must be obeyed completely: *I gave her strict instructions to be home before 9.00.* **2** not allowing people to break rules or behave badly: *Samir's very strict with his children.* ◆ *I went to an extremely strict school.* **3** obeying the rules of a particular religion or belief exactly: *a strict Muslim* **4** exactly correct; accurate: *a strict interpretation of the law*

⚷ **strictly** /ˈstrɪktli/ *adv* **1** with a lot of control and rules that must be obeyed: *She was brought up very strictly.* **2** used to emphasize that sth happens or must happen in all circumstances: *Smoking is strictly forbidden.* ◆ *Chewing gum is strictly forbidden in the classroom.*
IDM **strictly speaking** to be exactly correct or accurate: *Strictly speaking, the tomato is not a vegetable. It's a fruit.*

stride[1] /straɪd/ *verb* [I] (*pt* **strode** /strəʊd/) [not used in the perfect tenses] to walk with long steps, often because you feel very confident or determined: *He strode up to the house and knocked on the door.*

stride[2] /straɪd/ *noun* [C] a long step
IDM **get into your stride** to start to do sth well and in a confident way after an uncertain beginning
make great strides ➲ **great[1]**
take sth in your stride to deal with a new or difficult situation easily and without worrying

strident /ˈstraɪdnt/ *adj* (used about a voice or a sound) loud and unpleasant

strife /straɪf/ *noun* [U] (*formal*) trouble or fighting between people or groups

⚷ **strike[1]** /straɪk/ *verb* (*pt, pp* **struck** /strʌk/)
➤HIT SB/STH **1** [T] (*formal*) to hit sb/sth: *The stone struck her on the head.* ◆ *The boat struck a rock and began to sink.* ➲ note at **hit**
➤ATTACK **2** [I,T] to attack and harm sb/sth suddenly: *The earthquake struck Haiti in 2010.* ◆ *The building had been **struck by lightning**.*
➤OF THOUGHT **3** [T] to come suddenly into sb's mind: *It suddenly struck me that she would be the ideal person for the job.*
➤GIVE IMPRESSION **4** [T] **strike sb (as sth)** to give sb a particular impression: *Does anything here strike you as unusual?* ◆ *He strikes me as a very caring man.*
➤OF WORKERS **5** [I] to stop work as a protest: *The workers voted to strike for more money.*
➤MAKE FIRE **6** [T] to produce fire by rubbing sth, especially a match, on a surface: *She struck a match and lit the candle.*
➤OF CLOCK **7** [I,T] to ring a bell so that people know what time it is: *The church clock struck three.*
➤GOLD, OIL, ETC. **8** [T] to discover gold, oil, etc. in the ground: *They had struck oil!*
IDM **strike a balance (between A and B)** to find a middle way between two extremes
strike a bargain (with sb) to make an agreement with sb
within striking distance near enough to be reached or attacked easily
PHR V **strike back** to attack sb/sth that has attacked you
strike up sth (with sb) to start a conversation or friendship with sb

⚷ **strike[2]** /straɪk/ *noun* [C] **1** a period of time when people refuse to go to work, usually because they want more money or better working conditions: *a one-day strike* ◆ *Union members voted to **go on strike**.* **2** a sudden military attack, especially by aircraft: *an air strike*

striker /ˈstraɪkə(r)/ *noun* [C] **1** a person who has stopped working as a protest **2** (in football) a player whose job is to score goals

⚷ **striking** /ˈstraɪkɪŋ/ *adj* very noticeable; making a strong impression: *There was a striking similarity between the two men.* ▶ **strikingly** *adv*: *She is strikingly beautiful.*

⚷ **string[1]** /strɪŋ/ *noun*
➤FOR TYING THINGS **1** [C,U] a piece of long, strong material like very thin rope, that you use for tying things: *a ball/piece/length of string* ◆ *The key is hanging on a string.* ➲ picture at **rope**
➤LINE OF THINGS **2** [C] **a string of sth** a line of things that are joined together on the same piece of thread: *a string of beads*
➤SERIES **3** [C] **a string of sth** a series of people, things or events that follow one after another: *a string of visitors*
➤MUSICAL INSTRUMENTS **4** [C] one of the pieces of thin wire, etc. that produce the sound on some musical instruments: *A guitar has six strings.* ➲ picture at **music**, **piano** **5 the strings** [pl] (in an **orchestra**) the instruments that have strings: *Listen to the melody in the strings.* ➲ note at **instrument** ➲ picture at **music**
➤ON RACKET **6** [C] one of the pieces of thin material that is stretched across a **racket** (= the thing you use to hit the ball in some sports)
IDM **(with) no strings attached; without strings** with no special conditions
pull strings ➲ **pull[1]**

string[2] /strɪŋ/ *verb* [T] (*pt, pp* **strung** /strʌŋ/) **string sth (up)** to hang or tie sth in place, especially as a decoration: *Coloured lights were strung up along the front of the hotel.*
PHR V **string sb/sth out** to make people or things form a line with spaces between each person or thing
string sth together to put words or phrases together to make a sentence, speech, etc: *I can barely string two words together in Japanese.*

stringent /ˈstrɪndʒənt/ *adj* (used about a law, rule, etc.) very strict

⚷ **strip**[1] /strɪp/ *verb* (**stripping**; **stripped**) **1** [I,T] **strip (sth) (off)** to take off your clothes; to take off sb else's clothes: *The doctor asked him to strip to the waist.* ◆ *She was stripped and searched at the airport by two customs officers.* **2** [T] **strip sth (off)** to remove sth that is covering a surface: *to strip the paint off a door* ◆ *to strip wallpaper* **3** [T] **strip sb/sth (of sth)** to take sth away from sb/sth: *They stripped the house of all its furniture.*

⚷ **strip**[2] /strɪp/ *noun* [C] **1** a long narrow piece of sth: *a strip of paper* ◆ *a tiny strip of garden* **2** the uniform that is worn by the members of a sports team when they are playing

ˌstrip carˈtoon = **comic strip**

⚷ **stripe** /straɪp/ *noun* [C] a long narrow line of colour: *Zebras have black and white stripes.* ▶ **striped** *adj*: *a red and white striped dress* ➲ picture on **page P1**

stripper /ˈstrɪpə(r)/ *noun* [C] a person whose job is to take off their clothes in order to entertain people

striptease /ˈstrɪptiːz/ *noun* [C,U] entertainment in which sb takes off their clothes, usually to music

strive /straɪv/ *verb* [I] (*pt* **strove** /strəʊv/; *pp* **striven** /ˈstrɪvn/) (*formal*) **strive (for sth/to do sth)** to try very hard to do or get sth: *to strive for perfection*

strode *past tense* of **stride**[1]

⚷ **stroke**[1] /strəʊk/ *noun*

➤IN SPORT **1** [C] one of the movements that you make when you are swimming, **rowing** (= in a boat), etc: *Rose won by three strokes* (= hits of the ball in golf). **2** [C,U] [in compounds] one of the styles of swimming: *I can do backstroke and breaststroke, but not front crawl.* ➲ look at **crawl** ➲ picture at **swim**

➤WITH PEN/BRUSH **3** [C] one of the movements that you make when you are writing or painting: *a brush stroke*

➤LUCK **4** [sing] **a stroke of sth** a sudden successful action or event: *It was **a stroke of luck** finding your ring on the beach, wasn't it?*

➤ILLNESS **5** [C] a sudden illness which attacks the brain and can leave a person unable to move part of their body, speak clearly, etc: *to **have a stroke***

IDM **at a/one stroke** with a single action

not do a stroke (of work) to not do any work at all

⚷ **stroke**[2] /strəʊk/ *verb* [T] **1** to move your hand gently over sb/sth: *She stroked his hair affectionately.* ◆ *to stroke a dog* **2** to move sth somewhere with a smooth movement: *He stroked the ball just wide of the hole.*

stroke

He's stroking the dog.

He's patting the dog.

stroll /strəʊl/ *noun* [C] a slow walk for pleasure: *to **go for a stroll** along the beach* ▶ **stroll** *verb* [I]

stroller /ˈstrəʊlə(r)/ (*AmE*) = **pushchair**

⚷ **strong** /strɒŋ/ *adj* (**stronger**; **strongest**)

➤POWERFUL **1** (used about a person) able to lift or carry heavy things: *I need someone strong to help me move this bookcase.* ◆ *to have strong arms/muscles* OPP **weak** **2** powerful: *strong winds/currents/sunlight*

➤HAVING BIG EFFECT **3** having a big effect on the mind, body or senses: *a **strong smell** of garlic* ◆ *strong coffee* ◆ *a strong drink* (= with a lot of alcohol in it) ◆ *I have the **strong impression** that they don't like us.*

➤OPINION/BELIEF **4** difficult to fight against: *There was **strong opposition** to the idea.* ◆ ***strong support** for the government's plan* SYN **firm**

➤NOT EASILY BROKEN **5** (used about an object) not easily broken or damaged: *That chair isn't strong enough for you to stand on.* ➲ look at **fragile**

➤LIKELY TO SUCCEED **6** powerful and likely to succeed: *She's a strong candidate for the job.* ◆ *a strong team* ◆ *He's got a very strong will.* OPP **weak**

➤NUMBER OF PEOPLE **7** [used after a noun] having a particular number of people: *The army was 50 000 strong.* **8** great in number: *a strong police presence at the demonstration* ➲ *noun* **strength**

IDM **going strong** (*informal*) continuing, even after a long time: *The company was formed in 1851 and is still going strong.*

sb's strong point something that a person is good at: *Maths is not my strong point.*

▶ **strongly** *adv*: *The directors are strongly opposed to the idea.* ◆ *to feel very strongly about something*

ˈstrong form *noun* [C] used to describe the way some words are pronounced when they have stress OPP **weak form**

ˌstrong-ˈminded *adj* having firm ideas or beliefs SYN **determined**

stroppy /ˈstrɒpi/ *adj* (**stroppier**; **stroppiest**) (*BrE informal*) (used about a person) easily annoyed and difficult to deal with

strove *past tense* of **strive**

struck *past tense, past participle* of **strike**[1]

⚷ **structure**[1] /ˈstrʌktʃə(r)/ *noun* **1** [C,U] the way that the parts of sth are put together or organized: *the political and social structure of a country* ◆ *the grammatical structures of a language* **2** [C] a building or sth that has been built or made from a number of parts: *The old office block had been replaced by a modern glass structure.* **3** [C,U] the state of being well organized or planned; a careful plan: *Your essay needs (a) structure.* ▶ **structural** /ˈstrʌktʃərəl/ *adj*

structure[2] /ˈstrʌktʃə(r)/ *verb* [T] to arrange sth in an organized way: *a carefully structured English course*

⚷ **struggle**[1] /ˈstrʌɡl/ *verb* [I] **1 struggle (with sth/for sth/to do sth)** to try very hard to do sth, especially when it is difficult: *We struggled up the stairs with our heavy suitcases.* ◆ *Maria was struggling with her English homework.* ◆ *The country is struggling for independence.* ◆ *They struggled just to pay their bills.* **2 struggle (with sb/sth); struggle (against sth)** to fight in order to prevent sth or to escape from sb/sth: *He shouted and struggled but he couldn't get free.*

S

♦ *A passer-by was struggling with one of the robbers on the ground.* ♦ *He has been struggling against cancer for years.*

PHR V **struggle on** to continue to do sth although it is difficult: *I felt terrible but managed to struggle on to the end of the day.*

struggle² /ˈstrʌgl/ *noun* **1** [C] a fight in which sb tries to do or get sth when this is difficult: *All countries should join together in the struggle against terrorism.* ♦ *He will not give up the presidency without a struggle.* ♦ *a struggle for independence* **2** [sing] something that is difficult to achieve: *It will be a struggle to get there on time.* **SYN** **effort**

strum /strʌm/ *verb* [I,T] (**strumming**; **strummed**) to play a **guitar** (= a musical instrument with strings) by moving your hand up and down over the strings

strung *past tense, past participle of* **string²**

strut /strʌt/ *verb* [I] (**strutting**; **strutted**) to walk in a proud way

stub /stʌb/ *noun* [C] the short piece of a cigarette or pencil that is left after the rest of it has been used

stubble /ˈstʌbl/ *noun* [U] **1** the short parts of crops such as **wheat** (= a plant grown for its grain) that are left standing after the rest has been cut **2** the short hairs that grow on a man's face when he has not shaved for some time

stubborn /ˈstʌbən/ *adj* not wanting to do what other people want you to do; refusing to change your plans or decisions: *She's too stubborn to admit that she's wrong.* **SYN** **obstinate** ➲ look at **pig-headed** ▶ **stubbornly** *adv*: *He stubbornly refused to apologize so he was sacked.* ▶ **stubbornness** *noun* [U]

stuck¹ *past tense, past participle of* **stick²**

stuck² /stʌk/ *adj* [not before a noun] **1** not able to move: *This drawer's stuck. I can't open it at all.* ♦ *We were stuck in traffic for over two hours.* **2** not able to continue with an exercise, etc. because it is too difficult: *If you* **get stuck***, ask your teacher for help.*

stud /stʌd/ *noun* **1** [C] a small, round, solid piece of metal that you wear through a hole in your ear or other part of the body **2** [C] a small piece of metal that sticks out from the rest of the surface that it is fixed to: *a black leather jacket with studs all over it* **3** [C] one of the pieces of plastic or metal that stick out from the bottom of football boots, etc. and that help you stand up on wet ground **4** [C,U] a number of high quality horses or other animals that are kept for breeding young animals; the place where these animals are kept: *a stud farm*

studded /ˈstʌdɪd/ *adj* **1** covered or decorated with small pieces of metal that stick out from the rest of the surface **2** **studded (with sth)** containing a lot of sth

student /ˈstjuːdnt/ *noun* [C] a person who is studying at a school, college or university: *Paola is a medical student at Bristol University.* ♦ *a full-time/part-time student* ♦ *a postgraduate/research student* ♦ *a first-year student at Cherwell School* ➲ note at **school**, **university** ➲ look at **pupil**, **scholar**

studied /ˈstʌdid/ *adj* [only *before* a noun] (*formal*) carefully planned or done, especially when you are trying to give a particular impression

studio /ˈstjuːdiəʊ/ *noun* [C] (*pl* **studios**) **1** a room or building where films or TV programmes are made, or where music, radio programmes, etc. are recorded: *a film/TV/recording studio* **2** a room where an artist or a photographer works: *a sculptor's studio*

studious /ˈstjuːdiəs/ *adj* (used about a person) spending a lot of time studying

studiously /ˈstjuːdiəsli/ *adv* with great care

study¹ /ˈstʌdi/ *noun* (*pl* **studies**) **1** [U] the activity of learning about sth: *One hour every afternoon is left free for individual study.* ♦ *Physiology is the study of how living things work.* **2** **studies** [pl] the subjects that you study: *business/media/Japanese studies* **3** [C] a piece of research that examines a question or a subject in detail: *They are doing a study of the causes of heart disease.* **4** [C] a room in a house where you go to read, write or study

study² /ˈstʌdi/ *verb* (**studying**; **studies**; *pt, pp* **studied**) **1** [I,T] **study (sth/for sth)** to spend time learning about sth: *Leon has been studying hard for his exams.* ♦ *to study French at university* **2** [T] to look at sth very carefully: *to study a map*

TOPIC

Studying

If you want to **study** something or **learn about** something, you can **teach yourself** or you can take a **course**. This will be **full-time** or **part-time**, perhaps with **evening classes**. You will need to **take notes**, and you might have to **write essays** or **do a project**. You should **hand** these **in** to your **teacher/tutor** before the **deadline**. Before you take **exams**, you'll need to **revise** (= study again what you have learnt).

stuff¹ /stʌf/ *noun* [U] (*informal*) **1** used to refer to sth without using its name: *What's that green stuff at the bottom of the bottle?* ♦ *The shop was burgled and a lot of stuff was stolen.* ♦ *They sell stationery and stuff (like that).* ♦ *I'll put the swimming stuff in this bag.* **2** used to refer in general to things that people do, say, think, etc: *I've got lots of stuff to do tomorrow so I'm going to get up early.* ♦ *I don't believe all that stuff about him being robbed.* ♦ *I like reading and stuff.*

stuff² /stʌf/ *verb* [T] **1** **stuff sth (with sth)** to fill sth with sth: *The pillow was stuffed with feathers.* ♦ *red peppers stuffed with rice* **2** (*informal*) **stuff sth into sth** to put sth into sth else quickly or carelessly: *He quickly stuffed a few clothes into a suitcase.* **3** (*informal*) **stuff yourself (with sth)** to eat too much of sth: *Barry just sat there stuffing himself with sandwiches.* **4** to fill the body of a dead bird or animal with special material so that it looks as if it is alive: *They've got a stuffed crocodile in the museum.*

stuffing /ˈstʌfɪŋ/ *noun* [U] **1** a mixture of small pieces of food that you put inside a chicken,

S

vegetable, etc. before you cook it **2** the material that you put inside **cushions** (= soft bags which you put on chairs, etc. to make them more comfortable), soft toys, etc.

stuffy /ˈstʌfi/ *adj* (**stuffier**; **stuffiest**) **1** (used about a room) too warm and having no fresh air **2** (*informal*) (used about a person) formal and old-fashioned

stumble /ˈstʌmbl/ *verb* [I] **1 stumble (over/on sth)** to hit your foot against sth when you are walking or running and almost fall over **SYN** **trip** **2 stumble (over/through sth)** to make a mistake when you are speaking, playing music, etc: *The newsreader stumbled over the name of the Russian tennis player.*
PHR V **stumble across/on sb/sth** to meet or find sb/sth by chance

ˈ**stumbling block** *noun* [C] something that causes trouble or a problem, so that you cannot achieve what you want: *Money is still the stumbling block to settling the dispute.*

stump[1] /stʌmp/ *noun* [C] the part that is left after sth has been cut down, broken off, etc: *a tree stump*

stump[2] /stʌmp/ *verb* [T] (*informal*) to cause sb to be unable to answer a question or find a solution to a problem: *I was completely stumped by question 14.*

stun /stʌn/ *verb* [T] (**stunning**; **stunned**) **1** to make a person or an animal unconscious or confused by hitting them or it on the head **2** to make a person very surprised by telling them some unexpected news: *His sudden death stunned his friends.* **SYN** **astound** ▶ **stunned** *adj*: *a stunned silence*

stung *past tense, past participle of* **sting**[1]

stunk *past participle of* **stink**

stunning /ˈstʌnɪŋ/ *adj* (*informal*) very attractive, impressive or surprising: *a stunning view*

stunt[1] /stʌnt/ *noun* [C] **1** a very difficult or dangerous thing that sb does to entertain people or as part of a film: *Some actors do their own stunts; others use a stunt man.* **2** something that you do to get people's attention: *a publicity stunt*

stunt[2] /stʌnt/ *verb* [T] to stop sb/sth growing or developing properly: *A poor diet can stunt a child's growth.*

stuntman /ˈstʌntmæn/, **stuntwoman** /ˈstʌntwʊmən/ *noun* [C] (*pl* **-men** /-men/, **-women** /-wɪmɪn/) a person who does sth dangerous in a film in the place of an actor

stupendous /stjuːˈpendəs/ *adj* very large or impressive: *a stupendous achievement*

⚷ **stupid** /ˈstjuːpɪd/ *adj* (**stupider**; **stupidest**) [More **stupid** and **most stupid** are also common.] **1** not intelligent or sensible: *Don't be so stupid. Of course I'll help you!* ◆ *He was stupid to trust her.* ◆ *a stupid mistake/suggestion/question* **SYN** **silly** **2** [only before a noun] (*informal*) used to show that you are angry or do not like sb/sth: *I'm tired of hearing about his stupid car.* ▶ **stupidity** /stjuːˈpɪdəti/ *noun* [U] ▶ **stupidly** *adv*

stupor /ˈstjuːpə(r)/ *noun* [sing, U] the state of being nearly unconscious or being unable to think properly

sturdy /ˈstɜːdi/ *adj* (**sturdier**; **sturdiest**) strong and healthy; that will not break easily: *sturdy legs* ◆ *sturdy shoes* ▶ **sturdily** *adv* ▶ **sturdiness** *noun* [U]

sturgeon /ˈstɜːdʒən/ *noun* [C,U] (*pl* **sturgeon** *or* **sturgeons**) a large fish that we eat. The eggs (called **caviar**) are also eaten.

stutter /ˈstʌtə(r)/ *verb* [I,T] to have difficulty when you speak, so that you keep repeating the first sound of a word ▶ **stutter** *noun* [sing]: *to have a stutter*

sty /staɪ/ *noun* [C] **1** (*pl* **sties**) = **pigsty** **2** (also **stye**) (*pl* **sties** *or* **styes**) a painful spot on your **eyelid** (= the skin that covers your eye)

⚷ **style** /staɪl/ *noun* **1** [C,U] the way that sth is done, built, etc: *a new style of architecture* ◆ *The writer's style is very clear and simple.* ◆ *an American-style education system* **2** [C,U] the fashion, shape or design of sth: *We stock all the latest styles.* ➲ look at **hairstyle** **3** [U] the ability to do things in a way that other people admire: *He's got no sense of style.* ◆ *They don't have many parties but when they do, they do it* ***in style***.

stylish /ˈstaɪlɪʃ/ *adj* fashionable and attractive: *She's a stylish dresser.* ▶ **stylishly** *adv*

stylist /ˈstaɪlɪst/ *noun* [C] a person whose job is cutting and shaping people's hair

suave /swɑːv/ *adj* (usually used about a man) confident, elegant and polite, sometimes in a way that does not seem sincere

subconscious /ˌsʌbˈkɒnʃəs/ *noun* **the subconscious** [sing] the hidden part of your mind that can affect the way that you behave without you realizing ▶ **subconscious** *adj*: *the subconscious mind* ◆ *Many advertisements work on a subconscious level.* ▶ **subconsciously** *adv*

subcontinent /ˌsʌbˈkɒntɪnənt/ *noun* [sing] a large area of land that forms part of a continent, especially the part of Asia that includes India, Pakistan and Bangladesh: *the Indian subcontinent*

subdivide /ˌsʌbdɪˈvaɪd/ *verb* [I,T] to divide or be divided into smaller parts ▶ **subdivision** /ˌsʌbdɪˈvɪʒn/ *noun* [C,U]

subdue /səbˈdjuː/ *verb* [T] to defeat sb/sth or bring sb/sth under control

subdued /səbˈdjuːd/ *adj* **1** (used about a person) quieter and with less energy than usual **2** not very loud or bright: *subdued laughter/lighting*

⚷ **subject**[1] /ˈsʌbdʒɪkt/ *noun* [C] **1** a person or thing that is being considered, shown or talked about: *What subject is the lecture on?* ◆ *What are your views on this subject?* ◆ *I've tried several times to* ***bring up/raise the subject*** *of money.* **2** an area of knowledge that you study at school, university, etc: *My favourite subjects at school are Biology and French.* **3** the person or thing that does the action described by the verb in a sentence: *In the sentence 'The cat sat on the*

S

mat', 'the cat' is the subject. ➲ look at **object 4** a person from a particular country, especially one with a king or queen; a citizen: *a British subject*
IDM change the subject ➲ **change**[1]

subject[2] /ˈsʌbdʒekt/ *adj* **subject to sth 1** likely to be affected by sth: *The area is subject to regular flooding.* ♦ *Smokers are more subject to heart attacks than non-smokers.* ♦ *People who eat a lot of fatty foods are more subject to heart attacks.* **2** depending on sth as a condition: *The plan for new housing is still subject to approval by the minister.* **3** controlled by or having to obey sb/sth

subject[3] /səbˈdʒekt/ *verb*
PHR V subject sb/sth to sth to make sb/sth experience sth unpleasant: *He was subjected to verbal and physical abuse from the other boys.*

subjective /səbˈdʒektɪv/ *adj* based on your own tastes and opinions instead of on facts: *Try not to be so subjective in your essays.* **OPP objective** ▶ **subjectively** *adv*

ˈ**subject matter** *noun* [U] the ideas or information contained in a book, speech, painting, etc: *I don't think the* ***subject matter*** *of this programme is suitable for children.*

subjunctive /səbˈdʒʌŋktɪv/ *noun* [sing] the form of a verb in certain languages that expresses doubt, possibility, a wish, etc. ▶ **subjunctive** *adj*

sublime /səˈblaɪm/ *adj* (*formal*) of extremely high quality that makes you admire sth very much ▶ **sublimely** *adv*

submarine /ˌsʌbməˈriːn/ *noun* [C] a type of ship that can travel under the water as well as on the surface ➲ picture on **page P6**

submerge /səbˈmɜːdʒ/ *verb* [I,T] to go or make sth go underwater: *The fields were submerged by the floods.* ▶ **submerged** *adj*

S

submission /səbˈmɪʃn/ *noun* **1** [U] the accepting of sb else's power or control because they have defeated you **2** [U,C] the act of giving a plan, document, etc. to an official organization so that it can be studied and considered; the plan, document, etc. that you send

submissive /səbˈmɪsɪv/ *adj* ready to obey other people and do whatever they want

submit /səbˈmɪt/ *verb* (**submitting**; **submitted**) **1** [T] **submit sth (to sb/sth)** to give a plan, document, etc. to an official organization so that it can be studied and considered: *to submit an application/a complaint/a claim* **2** [I] **submit (to sb/sth)** to accept sb/sth's power or control because they have defeated you

subordinate[1] /səˈbɔːdɪnət/ *adj* **subordinate (to sb/sth)** having less power or authority than sb else; less important than sth else ▶ **subordinate** *noun* [C]: *the relationship between superiors and their subordinates*

subordinate[2] /səˈbɔːdɪneɪt/ *verb* [T] to treat one person or thing as less important than another

suˌbordinate ˈclause *noun* [C] a group of words that is not a sentence but that adds information to the main part of the sentence: *In the sentence 'We left early because it was raining', 'because it was raining' is the subordinate clause.*

subscribe /səbˈskraɪb/ *verb* [I] **subscribe (to sth)** to pay an amount of money regularly in order to receive or use sth: *Do you subscribe to 'Marie Claire'?* ♦ *We subscribe to several sports channels* (= on TV).
PHR V subscribe to sth to agree with an idea, a belief, etc: *I don't subscribe to the view that all war is wrong.*

subscriber /səbˈskraɪbə(r)/ *noun* [C] a person who pays to receive a newspaper or magazine regularly or to use a particular service: *subscribers to satellite and cable TV*

subscription /səbˈskrɪpʃn/ *noun* [C] an amount of money that you pay, usually once a year, to receive a newspaper or magazine regularly or to belong to an organization

subsequent /ˈsʌbsɪkwənt/ *adj* [only *before* a noun] (*formal*) coming after or later: *I thought that was the end of the matter but subsequent events proved me wrong.* ▶ **subsequently** *adv*: *The rumours were subsequently found to be untrue.*

subservient /səbˈsɜːviənt/ *adj* **1 subservient (to sb/sth)** too ready to obey other people **2** (*formal*) **subservient (to sth)** considered to be less important than sb/sth else ▶ **subservience** *noun* [U]

subside /səbˈsaɪd/ *verb* [I] **1** to become calmer or quieter: *The storm seems to be subsiding.* **2** (used about land, a building, etc.) to sink down into the ground ▶ **subsidence** /ˈsʌbsɪdns; səbˈsaɪdns/ *noun* [U]: *The road was closed because of subsidence.*

subsidiary[1] /səbˈsɪdiəri/ *adj* connected with sth but less important than it

subsidiary[2] /səbˈsɪdiəri/ *noun* [C] (*pl* **subsidiaries**) a business company that belongs to and is controlled by another larger company

subsidize (also **-ise**) /ˈsʌbsɪdaɪz/ *verb* [T] to give money to sb or an organization to help pay for sth: *Public transport should be subsidized.*

subsidy /ˈsʌbsədi/ *noun* [C,U] (*pl* **subsidies**) money that the government, etc. pays to help an organization or to keep the cost of a service low: *agricultural/state/housing subsidies*

subsist /səbˈsɪst/ *verb* [I] (*formal*) **subsist (on sth)** to manage to live with very little food or money ▶ **subsistence** *noun* [U]

⚷ **substance** /ˈsʌbstəns/ *noun* **1** [C] a solid or liquid material: *poisonous substances* ♦ *The cloth is coated in a new waterproof substance.* **2** [U] importance, value or truth: *The manager's report* ***gives substance to*** *these allegations.* ♦ *It was unkind gossip, completely* ***without substance***. **3** [U] the most important or main part of sth: *What was the substance of his argument?*

substandard /ˌsʌbˈstændəd/ *adj* of poor quality; not as good as usual or as it should be

⚷ **substantial** /səbˈstænʃl/ *adj* **1** large in amount: *The storms caused substantial damage.* ♦ *a* *substantial sum of money* **2** large and/or strongly built: *The furniture was cheap and not very substantial.* OPP for both meanings **insubstantial**

substantially /səbˈstænʃəli/ *adv* **1** very much: *House prices have fallen substantially.* SYN **greatly** **2** generally; in most points: *The landscape of Wales has remained substantially the same for centuries.*

substitute /ˈsʌbstɪtjuːt/ *noun* [C] a substitute (for sb/sth) a person or thing that takes the place of sb/sth else: *One player was injured so the substitute was sent on to play.* ▸ **substitute** *verb* [T] substitute sb/sth (for sb/sth): *You can substitute margarine for butter.* ▸ **substitution** /ˌsʌbstɪˈtjuːʃn/ *noun* [C,U]

subterranean /ˌsʌbtəˈreɪniən/ *adj* (*formal*) under the ground: *a subterranean cave*

subtitle /ˈsʌbtaɪtl/ *noun* [C, usually pl] the words at the bottom of the picture on TV or at the cinema. The **subtitles** translate the words that are spoken, or show them to help people with hearing problems: *a Polish film with English subtitles* ➲ look at **dub**

subtle /ˈsʌtl/ *adj* (**subtler**; **subtlest**) **1** not very noticeable; not very strong or bright: *subtle colours* ◆ *I noticed a subtle difference in her.* **2** very clever, and using indirect methods to achieve sth: *Advertisements persuade us to buy things in very subtle ways.* ▸ **subtlety** /ˈsʌtlti/ *noun* [C,U] (*pl* **subtleties**) ▸ **subtly** /ˈsʌtli/ *adv*

subtract /səbˈtrækt/ *verb* [T] subtract sth (from sth) to take one number or quantity away from another: *If you subtract five from nine, you get four.* OPP **add** ▸ **subtraction** /səbˈtrækʃn/ *noun* [C,U]

suburb /ˈsʌbɜːb/ *noun* [C] an area where people live that is outside the central part of a town or city: *Most people live* ***in the suburbs*** *and work in the centre of town.* ▸ **suburban** /səˈbɜːbən/ *adj*

> **MORE** People often think of life in the suburbs as dull, so **suburban** sometimes means 'uninteresting'.

▸ **suburbia** /səˈbɜːbiə/ *noun* [U]

subversive /səbˈvɜːsɪv/ *adj* trying to destroy or damage a government, religion or political system by attacking it secretly and in an indirect way: *subversive literature* ▸ **subversive** *noun* [C]

subvert /səbˈvɜːt/ *verb* [T] (*formal*) to try to destroy or damage a government, religion or political system by attacking it secretly and in an indirect way ▸ **subversion** /səbˈvɜːʃn/ *noun* [U]

subway /ˈsʌbweɪ/ *noun* [C] **1** (*BrE*) a tunnel under a busy road or railway that people can walk through to cross to the other side **2** (*AmE*) = **underground**[3]

succeed /səkˈsiːd/ *verb* **1** [I] succeed (in sth/doing sth) to manage to achieve what you want; to do well: *Our plan succeeded.* ◆ *A good education will help you succeed in life.* ◆ *to succeed in passing an exam* OPP **fail** **2** [I,T] to have a job or important position after sb else: *David Cameron succeeded Gordon Brown as British Prime Minister in 2010.*

success /səkˈses/ *noun* **1** [U] the fact that you have achieved what you want; doing well and becoming famous, rich, etc: *Hard work is* ***the key to success.*** ◆ *Her attempts to get a job for the summer have not* ***met with*** *much* ***success*** (= she hasn't managed to do it). ◆ *What's the secret of your success?* **2** [C] the thing that you achieve; something that becomes very popular: *He really tried to* ***make a success of*** *the business.* ◆ *The film 'War Horse' was a huge success.* OPP for both meanings **failure**

successful /səkˈsesfl/ *adj* having achieved what you wanted; having become popular, rich, etc: *a successful attempt to climb Mount Everest* ◆ *a successful actor* OPP **unsuccessful** ▸ **successfully** /-fəli/ *adv*

succession /səkˈseʃn/ *noun* **1** [C] a number of people or things that follow each other in time or order; a series: *a succession of events/problems/visitors* **2** [U] the right to have an important position after sb else

IDM **in succession** following one after another: *There have been three deaths in the family in quick succession.*

successive /səkˈsesɪv/ *adj* [only *before* a noun] following immediately one after the other: *This was their fourth successive win.* ◆ *Successive governments have tried to tackle the problem.* SYN **consecutive**

successor /səkˈsesə(r)/ *noun* [C] a person or thing that comes after sb/sth else and takes their or its place ➲ look at **predecessor**

succinct /səkˈsɪŋkt/ *adj* said clearly, in a few words ▸ **succinctly** *adv*

succulent /ˈsʌkjələnt/ *adj* (used about fruit, vegetables and meat) containing a lot of juice and tasting very good

succumb /səˈkʌm/ *verb* [I] (*formal*) succumb (to sth) to not be able to fight an attack, an illness, etc.

such /sʌtʃ/ *determiner, pron* **1** (used for referring to sb/sth that you mentioned earlier) of this or that type: *I don't believe in ghosts. There's* ***no such thing.*** ◆ *The economic situation is such that we all have less money to spend.* **2** used to describe the result of sth: *The statement was worded* ***in such a way that*** *it did not upset anyone.* **3** used for emphasizing the degree of sth: *It was such a fascinating book that I couldn't put it down.* ◆ *It seems such a long time since we last saw each other.*

> **GRAMMAR** You use **such** before a noun or before a noun that has an adjective in front of it: *Simon is such a bore!* ◆ *Susan is such a boring woman.* You use **so** before an adjective that is used without a noun: *Don't be so boring.* Compare: *It was so cold that we stayed at home.* ◆ *It was such a cold night that we stayed at home.*

IDM **as such** as the word is usually understood; exactly: *It's not a promotion as such, but it will mean more money.*

such as for example: *Fatty foods such as chips are bad for you.* ➲ note at **example**

suck /sʌk/ *verb* **1** [I,T] to pull a liquid into your mouth: *to suck milk up through a straw* ➲ picture

S

at **blow** **2** [I,T] to have sth in your mouth and keep touching it with your tongue: *He was noisily sucking (on) a sweet.* **3** [T] to pull sth in a particular direction, using force: *Vacuum cleaners suck up the dirt.*

sucker /ˈsʌkə(r)/ *noun* [C] **1** (*informal*) a person who believes everything that you tell them and who is easy to trick or persuade to do sth **2** a part of some plants, animals or insects that is used for helping them stick onto a surface

suction /ˈsʌkʃn/ *noun* [U] the act of removing air or liquid from a space or container so that sth else can be pulled into it or so that two surfaces can stick together: *A vacuum cleaner works by suction.*

sudden /ˈsʌdn/ *adj* done or happening quickly, or when you do not expect it: *a sudden decision/change* IDM **all of a sudden** quickly and unexpectedly: *All of a sudden the lights went out.*

sudden death a way of deciding who wins a game where the score is equal by continuing to play until one side gains the lead

▶ **suddenly** *adv*: *It all happened so suddenly.*
▶ **suddenness** *noun* [U]

WRITING TIP

Using adverbs

If you are writing a story, use adverbs and phrases that make it lively and interesting. Here are some common adverbs: ***Suddenly**, everybody started shouting.* ◆ ***All of a sudden**, there was a bang.* ◆ *His new neighbours were **amazingly** helpful.* ◆ ***Luckily**, she escaped with only minor injuries.* ◆ ***Unfortunately**, no one heard her cries for help.*

ⓘ For more help with writing, look at **Wordpower Writing Tutor** at the back of this dictionary.

sudoku /suˈdəʊkuː/ *noun* [U,C] a number puzzle with nine squares, each containing nine smaller squares in which you have to write the numbers 1 to 9 in a particular pattern: *I'm addicted to sudoku.* ◆ *a sudoku puzzle* ➲ picture at **crossword**

suds /sʌdz/ *noun* [pl] the bubbles that you get when you mix soap and water

sue /suː/ *verb* [I,T] **sue (sb) (for sth)** to go to a court of law and ask for money from sb because they have done sth bad to you, or said sth bad about you: *to sue somebody for libel/breach of contract/damages*

suede /sweɪd/ *noun* [U] a type of soft leather which does not have a smooth surface and feels a little like cloth

suet /ˈsuːɪt/ *noun* [U] a type of hard animal fat that is used in cooking

suffer /ˈsʌfə(r)/ *verb* **1** [I,T] **suffer (from sth); suffer (for sth)** to experience sth unpleasant, for example pain, sadness, difficulty, etc: *Mary often suffers from severe headaches.* ◆ *He made a rash decision and now he's suffering for it.* ◆ *Our troops suffered heavy losses.* **2** [I] to become worse in quality: *My work is suffering as a result of problems at home.* ▶ **sufferer** *noun* [C]: *asthma sufferers* ▶ **suffering** *noun* [U]: *The famine caused great hardship and suffering.*

sufficient /səˈfɪʃnt/ *adj* (*formal*) as much as is necessary; enough: *We have sufficient oil reserves to last for three months.* OPP **insufficient** ▶ **sufficiently** *adv*

suffix /ˈsʌfɪks/ *noun* [C] a letter or group of letters that you add at the end of a word, and that changes the meaning of the word or the way it is used: *To form the noun from the adjective 'sad', add the suffix 'ness'.* ➲ look at **prefix**

suffocate /ˈsʌfəkeɪt/ *verb* [I,T] to die because there is no air to breathe; to kill sb by not letting them breathe air ▶ **suffocating** *adj* ▶ **suffocation** /ˌsʌfəˈkeɪʃn/ *noun* [U]

sugar /ˈʃʊɡə(r)/ *noun* **1** [U] a sweet substance that you get from certain plants: *Do you **take sugar** in tea?* **2** [C] (in a cup of tea, coffee, etc.) the amount of sugar that a small spoon can hold; a lump of sugar: *Two sugars, please.*

sugary /ˈʃʊɡəri/ *adj* very sweet

suggest /səˈdʒest/ *verb* [T] **1** **suggest sth (to sb); suggest doing sth; suggest that ...** to mention a plan or an idea that you have for sb to discuss or consider: *Can anybody suggest ways of raising more money?* ◆ *Kate suggested going out for a walk.* ◆ *Kate suggested (that) we go out for a walk.* ◆ *Kate suggested a walk.* **2** **suggest sb/sth (for/as sth)** to say that a person, thing or place is suitable: *Who would you suggest for the job?* SYN **recommend**

HELP You CANNOT say 'suggest sb sth'.

3 to say or show sth in an indirect way: *Are you suggesting the accident was my fault?* **4** to put an idea into sb's mind; to make sb think that sth is true: *What do these results suggest to you?*

suggestion /səˈdʒestʃən/ *noun* **1** [C] a plan or idea that sb mentions for sb else to discuss and consider: *May I **make a suggestion**?* ◆ *Has anyone got any suggestions for how to solve this problem?* **2** [sing] a slight amount or sign of sth: *He spoke with **a suggestion of** a Scottish accent.* SYN **hint** **3** [U] putting an idea into sb's mind; giving advice about what to do: *I came **at** Tim's **suggestion*** (= because he suggested it).

suggestive /səˈdʒestɪv/ *adj* **1** **suggestive (of sth)** making you think of sth; being a sign of sth: *Your symptoms are more suggestive of an allergy than a virus.* **2** making you think about sex: *a suggestive dance/remark/posture* ▶ **suggestively** *adv*

suicidal /ˌsuːɪˈsaɪdl/ *adj* **1** people who are **suicidal** want to kill themselves: *to be/feel suicidal* **2** likely to have a very bad result; extremely dangerous: *Changing jobs at this point would be a suicidal career move.*

suicide /ˈsuːɪsaɪd/ *noun* [U,C] the act of killing yourself deliberately: *Ben has tried to **commit suicide** several times.* ◆ *There have been three suicides by university students this year.*

suit[1] /suːt/ *noun* [C] **1** a formal set of clothes that are made of the same cloth, consisting of a jacket and either trousers or a skirt: *He always wears a suit*

S

and tie to work. ➲ picture on **page P1** **2** a piece of clothing or set of clothes that you wear for a particular activity: *a diving suit* ♦ *a suit of armour* ➲ look at **swimsuit, tracksuit** **3** one of the 4 sets of 13 playing cards that form a pack: *The four suits are hearts, clubs, diamonds and spades.* ➲ note at **card** ➲ picture at **card**
IDM **follow suit** ➲ **follow**

suit² /suːt/ *verb* [T] [not used in the continuous tenses] **1** to be convenient or useful for sb/sth: *Would Thursday at 9.30 suit you?* ♦ *He will help around the house, but only when it suits him.* **2** (used about clothes, colours, etc.) to make you look attractive: *That dress really suits you.*

suitable /ˈsuːtəbl/ *adj* **suitable (for sb/sth); suitable (to do sth)** right or appropriate for sb/sth: *The film isn't suitable for children.* ♦ *I've got nothing suitable to wear for a wedding.* **OPP** **unsuitable** ▶ **suitability** /ˌsuːtəˈbɪləti/ *noun* [U] ▶ **suitably** /-əbli/ *adv*

suitcase /ˈsuːtkeɪs/ (also **case**) *noun* [C] a box with a handle that you use for carrying your clothes, etc. in when you are travelling ➲ picture at **bag**: *to pack/unpack a suitcase* ♦ *The suitcase was too heavy to lift.*

suite /swiːt/ *noun* [C] **1** a set of rooms, especially in a hotel: *the honeymoon/penthouse suite* ♦ *a suite of rooms/offices* ➲ look at **en suite** **2** a set of two or more pieces of furniture of the same style or covered in the same material: *a three-piece suite* (= a sofa and two armchairs)

suited /ˈsuːtɪd/ *adj* **suited (for/to sb/sth)** appropriate or right for sb/sth: *She and her husband are very well suited.*

sulk /sʌlk/ *verb* [I] to refuse to speak or smile because you want people to know that you are angry about sth ▶ **sulky** *adj* ▶ **sulkily** /-ɪli/ *adv*

sullen /ˈsʌlən/ *adj* looking bad-tempered and not wanting to speak to people: *a sullen face/expression/glare* ▶ **sullenly** *adv*

sulphur (*AmE* **sulfur**) /ˈsʌlfə(r)/ *noun* [U] (*symbol* S) a natural yellow substance with a strong unpleasant smell

sultan (also **Sultan**) /ˈsʌltən/ *noun* [C] the title of the ruler in some Muslim countries

sultana /sʌlˈtɑːnə/ *noun* [C] a dried **grape** (= a small fruit that grows in bunches) with no seeds in it that is used in cooking ➲ look at **raisin**

sultry /ˈsʌltri/ *adj* (**sultrier; sultriest**) **1** (used about the weather) hot and uncomfortable **2** (used about a woman) behaving in a way that makes her sexually attractive

sum¹ /sʌm/ *noun* [C] **1** an amount of money: *The industry has spent huge* ***sums of money*** *modernizing its equipment.* **2** [usually sing] **the sum (of sth)** the amount that you get when you add two or more numbers together: *The sum of two and five is seven.* **3** a simple problem that involves calculating numbers: *to* ***do sums*** *in your head*

sum² /sʌm/ *verb* (**summing; summed**)
PHR V **sum (sth) up** to describe in a few words the main ideas of what sb has said or written: ***To sum up****, there are three options here ...*

sum sb/sth up to form an opinion about sb/sth: *He summed the situation up immediately.*

summary¹ /ˈsʌməri/ *noun* [C] (*pl* **summaries**) a short description of the main ideas or points of sth but without any details: *A brief summary of the experiment is given at the beginning of the report.* **SYN** **precis** ▶ **summarize** (also **-ise**) /ˈsʌməraɪz/ *verb* [T]: *Could you summarize the story so far?*

summary² /ˈsʌməri/ *adj* [only *before* a noun] (*formal*) done quickly and without taking time to consider if it is the right thing to do or following the right process: *a summary judgment*

summer /ˈsʌmə(r)/ *noun* [C,U] one of the four seasons of the year, after spring and before autumn. Summer is the warmest season of the year: *Is it very hot here* ***in summer****?* ♦ *a summer's day* ▶ **summery** /ˈsʌməri/ *adj*: *summery weather* ♦ *a summery dress*

summertime /ˈsʌmətaɪm/ *noun* [U] the season of summer: *It's busy here in the summertime.*

ˌsumming-ˈup *noun* [C] (*pl* **summings-up**) a speech in which a judge gives a **summary** of what has been said in a court of law before a **verdict** (= a decision) is reached

summit /ˈsʌmɪt/ *noun* [C] **1** the top of a mountain **2** an important meeting or series of meetings between the leaders of two or more countries

summon /ˈsʌmən/ *verb* [T] **1** (*formal*) to order a person to come to a place: *The boys were summoned to the head teacher's office.* **2** **summon sth (up)** to find strength, courage or some other quality that you need even though it is difficult to do so: *She couldn't summon up the courage to leave him.*

summons /ˈsʌmənz/ *noun* [C] an order to appear in a court of law

sumptuous /ˈsʌmptʃuəs/ *adj* (*formal*) very expensive and looking very impressive: *We dined in sumptuous surroundings.* ▶ **sumptuously** *adv*

Sun. *abbr* = **Sunday**: *Sun. 5 April*

sun¹ /sʌn/ *noun* **1 the Sun** [sing] the star that shines in the sky during the day and that gives the earth heat and light: *The sun rises in the east and sets in the west.* ♦ *the rays of the sun* ➲ note at **space** ➲ picture at **eclipse** **2** [sing,U] light and heat from the sun: *Don't sit* ***in the sun*** *too long.* ♦ *Too much sun can be harmful.*
IDM **catch the sun** ➲ **catch¹**

sun² /sʌn/ *verb* [T] (**sunning; sunned**) **sun yourself** to sit or lie outside when the sun is shining in order to enjoy the heat

sunbathe /ˈsʌnbeɪð/ *verb* [I] to take off most of your clothes and sit or lie in the sun in order to get a **tan** (= darker skin) ➲ look at **bathe**

sunbeam /ˈsʌnbiːm/ *noun* [C] a line of light from the sun

sunbed /ˈsʌnbed/ *noun* [C] a bed for lying on under a **sunlamp** (= a lamp that can turn the skin brown) ➲ look at **sunlounger**

S

sunburn /ˈsʌnbɜːn/ *noun* [U] red painful skin caused by spending too long in the sun ▶ **sunburned** (also **sunburnt**) *adj*

suncream /ˈsʌnkriːm/ *noun* [C,U] (*especially BrE*) cream that you put on your skin to protect it from the harmful effects of the sun: *Make sure the children have plenty of suncream on.* ➲ look at **sunscreen**

⚷ **Sunday** /ˈsʌndeɪ; -di/ *noun* [C,U] (*abbr* **Sun.**) the day of the week after Saturday ➲ note at **Monday**

sundial /ˈsʌndaɪəl/ *noun* [C] a type of clock used in past times that uses the sun and the shadow from a pointed piece of metal to show what the time is

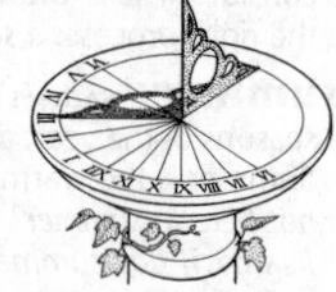
sundial

sundry /ˈsʌndri/ *adj* [only *before* a noun] of various kinds that are not important enough to be named separately IDM **all and sundry** (*informal*) everyone

sunflower /ˈsʌnflaʊə(r)/ *noun* [C] a very tall plant with large yellow flowers, often grown for its seeds and their oil which are used in cooking

sung *past participle of* **sing**

sunglasses /ˈsʌŋɡlɑːsɪz/ (also **dark ˈglasses**; *informal* **shades**) *noun* [pl] a pair of dark glasses which you wear to protect your eyes from bright **sunlight**

sunk *past participle of* **sink**[1]

sunken /ˈsʌŋkən/ *adj* **1** [only *before* a noun] below the water: *a sunken ship* **2** (used about cheeks or eyes) very far into the face as a result of illness or age **3** at a lower level than the surrounding area: *a sunken bath/garden*

sunlamp /ˈsʌnlæmp/ *noun* [C] a lamp that produces **ultraviolet** light that has the same effect as the sun and can turn the skin brown

sunlight /ˈsʌnlaɪt/ *noun* [U] the light from the sun: *a ray/pool of sunlight*

sunlit /ˈsʌnlɪt/ *adj* having bright light from the sun: *a sunlit terrace*

sunlounger /ˈsʌnlaʊndʒə(r)/ *noun* [C] a chair with a long seat that supports your legs, used for sitting or lying on in the sun

sunny /ˈsʌni/ *adj* (**sunnier**; **sunniest**) having a lot of light from the sun: *a sunny garden* ◆ *a sunny day*

sunrise /ˈsʌnraɪz/ *noun* [C,U] the time when the sun comes up in the morning: *to get up **at sunrise*** ➲ look at **dawn**, **sunset**

sunscreen /ˈsʌnskriːn/ *noun* [C,U] a cream or liquid that you put on your skin to protect it from the harmful effects of the sun: *I need to put some sunscreen on or I'll burn.* ◆ *factor 10 sunscreen* ➲ look at **suncream**

sunset /ˈsʌnset/ *noun* [C,U] the time when the sun goes down in the evening: *The park closes **at sunset**.* ◆ *a beautiful sunset*

sunshine /ˈsʌnʃaɪn/ *noun* [U] heat and light from the sun: *We sat down **in the sunshine** and had lunch.*

sunstroke /ˈsʌnstrəʊk/ *noun* [U] an illness that is caused by spending too much time in very hot, strong sun: *Keep your head covered or you'll **get sunstroke**.*

suntan /ˈsʌntæn/ (also **tan**) *noun* [C] when you have a **suntan**, your skin is darker than usual because you have spent time in the sun: *to have/get a suntan* ◆ *suntan lotion* ▶ **suntanned** (also **tanned**) *adj*

super /ˈsuːpə(r)/ *adj* **1** (*old-fashioned*) very good; wonderful: *We had a super time.* **2** [in compounds] bigger, better, stronger, etc. than other things of the same type: *super-rich* ◆ *superglue*

superb /suːˈpɜːb; sjuː-/ *adj* extremely good, excellent ▶ **superbly** *adv*

supercilious /ˌsuːpəˈsɪliəs; ˌsjuː-/ *adj* showing that you think that you are better than other people: *She gave a supercilious smile.* ▶ **superciliously** *adv*

superficial /ˌsuːpəˈfɪʃl/ *adj* **1** not studying or thinking about sth in a deep or complete way: *a superficial knowledge of the subject* **2** only on the surface, not deep: *a superficial wound/cut/burn* **3** (used about people) not caring about serious or important things: *He's a very superficial sort of person.* ▶ **superficiality** /ˌsuːpəˌfɪʃiˈæləti/ *noun* [U] ▶ **superficially** /-ʃəli/ *adv*

superfluous /suːˈpɜːfluəs; sjuː-/ *adj* more than is wanted; not needed

superhuman /ˌsuːpəˈhjuːmən; ˌsjuː-/ *adj* much greater than is normal: *superhuman strength*

superimpose /ˌsuːpərɪmˈpəʊz/ *verb* [T] **superimpose sth (on sth)** to put sth on top of sth else so that what is underneath can still be seen: *The old street plan was superimposed on a map of the modern city.*

superintendent /ˌsuːpərɪnˈtendənt/ *noun* [C] **1** a police officer with a high position: *Detective Superintendent Waters* **2** (*AmE*) a person who looks after a large building

⚷ **superior**[1] /suːˈpɪəriə(r); sjuː-/ *adj* **1** **superior (to sb/sth)** better than usual or than sb/sth else: *He is clearly superior to all the other candidates.* OPP **inferior** **2** **superior (to sb)** having a more important position: *his superior officer* **3** thinking that you are better than other people: *There's no need to be so superior.* ▶ **superiority** /suːˌpɪəriˈɒrəti; sjuː-/ *noun* [U]

superior[2] /suːˈpɪəriə(r)/ *noun* [C] a person of higher position: *Report any accidents to your superior.* OPP **inferior**

superlative /suˈpɜːlətɪv; sjuː-/ *noun* [C] the form of an adjective or adverb that expresses its highest degree: *'Most beautiful', 'best' and 'fastest' are all superlatives.*

⚷ **supermarket** /ˈsuːpəmɑːkɪt; ˈsjuː-/ *noun* [C] a very large shop that sells food, drink, goods used in the home, etc: *More and more of us are doing all our shopping in supermarkets.*

MORE At a supermarket, you put your **shopping** in a **basket** or a **trolley**. Then you **queue** (/kjuː/) at the **checkout**, where you **pack** everything into **shopping bags** or **carrier bags** and pay.

supermodel /ˈsuːpəmɒdl/ *noun* [C] a very famous and highly paid fashion model

supernatural /ˌsuːpəˈnætʃrəl; ˌsjuː-/ *adj* **1** that cannot be explained by the laws of science: *a creature with supernatural powers* **2 the supernatural** *noun* [sing] events, forces or powers that cannot be explained by the laws of science: *I don't believe in the supernatural.*

superpower /ˈsuːpəpaʊə(r); ˈsjuː-/ *noun* [C] one of the countries in the world that has very great military or economic power, for example the US

supersede /ˌsuːpəˈsiːd; ˌsjuː-/ *verb* [T] to take the place of sb/sth which existed or was used before and which has become old-fashioned: *The old software has been superseded by a new package.*

supersonic /ˌsuːpəˈsɒnɪk; ˌsjuː-/ *adj* faster than the speed of sound

superstar /ˈsuːpəstɑː(r); ˈsjuː-/ *noun* [C] a singer, film star, etc. who is very famous and popular

superstition /ˌsuːpəˈstɪʃn; ˌsjuː-/ *noun* [C,U] a belief that cannot be explained by reason or science: *According to superstition, it's unlucky to open an umbrella indoors.* ▶ **superstitious** /ˌsuːpəˈstɪʃəs; ˌsjuː-/ *adj*: *I never do anything important on Friday 13th—I'm superstitious.*

superstore /ˈsuːpəstɔː(r); ˈsjuː-/ *noun* [C] a very large shop that sells food or a wide variety of one particular type of goods

supervise /ˈsuːpəvaɪz; ˈsjuː-/ *verb* [I,T] to watch sb/sth to make sure that work is being done properly or that people are behaving correctly: *Your job is to supervise the building work.* ▶ **supervision** /ˌsuːpəˈvɪʒn; ˌsjuː-/ *noun* [U]: *Children should not play here without supervision.* ▶ **supervisor** /ˈsuːpəvaɪzə(r)/ *noun* [C]

supper /ˈsʌpə(r)/ *noun* [C,U] the last meal of the day, either the main meal of the evening or a small meal that you eat quite late, not long before you go to bed ➲ note at **meal**

supple /ˈsʌpl/ *adj* that bends or moves easily; not stiff: *Children are generally far more supple than adults.* ▶ **suppleness** *noun* [U]

supplement /ˈsʌplɪmənt/ *noun* [C] something that is added to sth else: *You have to pay a small supplement if you travel on a Saturday.* ♦ *I take a vitamin supplement every day.* ▶ **supplement** /ˈsʌplɪment/ *verb* [T] **supplement sth (with sth)**: *to supplement your diet with vitamins* ▶ **supplementary** /ˌsʌplɪˈmentri/ *adj*: *supplementary exercises at the back of the book*

supplier /səˈplaɪə(r)/ *noun* [C] a person or company that supplies goods

⚷ **supply**[1] /səˈplaɪ/ *noun* [C,U] (*pl* **supplies**) a store or an amount of sth that is provided or available to be used: *The water supply was contaminated.* ♦ *Food supplies were dropped by helicopter.* ♦ *In many parts of the country water is* ***in short supply*** (= there is not much of it).

⚷ **supply**[2] /səˈplaɪ/ *verb* [T] (**supplying**; **supplies**; *pt, pp* **supplied**) **supply sth (to sb)**; **supply sb (with sth)** to give or provide sth: *The farmer supplies eggs to the surrounding villages.* ♦ *He supplies the surrounding villages with eggs.*

⚷ **support**[1] /səˈpɔːt/ *verb* [T]

➤HELP SB/STH **1** to help sb/sth by saying that you agree with them or it, and sometimes giving practical help such as money: *Several large companies are supporting the project.* ♦ *Which political party do you support?*

➤GIVE MONEY **2** to give sb the money they need for food, clothes, etc: *Jim has to support two children from his previous marriage.*

➤CARRY WEIGHT **3** to carry the weight of sb/sth: *Large columns support the roof.*

➤SHOW STH IS TRUE **4** to show that sth is true or correct: *What evidence do you have to support what you say?*

➤SPORTS TEAM **5** to have a particular sports team that you like more than any other: *Which football team do you support?*

⚷ **support**[2] /səˈpɔːt/ *noun* **1** [U] **support (for sb/sth)** help and confidence that you give, especially in order to encourage a person or thing: *public support for the campaign* ♦ *Steve spoke* ***in support of*** *the proposal.* **2** [U] money to buy food, clothes, etc: *She has no home and no means of support.* **3** [C,U] something that carries the weight of sb/sth or holds sth firmly in place: *a roof support* ♦ *She held on to his arm for support.* **4** a band or singer who performs in a concert before the main performer

IDM moral support ➲ **moral**[1]

⚷ **supporter** /səˈpɔːtə(r)/ *noun* [C] a person who supports a political party, sports team, etc: *football supporters*

supportive /səˈpɔːtɪv/ *adj* giving help or support to sb in a difficult situation: *Everyone was very supportive when I lost my job.*

⚷ **suppose** /səˈpəʊz/ *verb* [T] **1** to think that sth is probable: *What do you suppose could have happened?* ♦ *I don't suppose that they're coming now.* **2** to pretend that sth will happen or is true: *Suppose you won the lottery. What would you do?* **3** used to make a suggestion, request or statement less strong: *I don't suppose you'd lend me your car tonight, would you?* **4** used when you agree with sth, but are not very happy about it: *'Can we give Andy a lift?' 'Yes, I suppose so, if we must.'*

IDM be supposed to do sth **1** to be expected to do sth or to have to do sth: *The train was supposed to arrive ten minutes ago.* ♦ *This is secret and I'm not supposed to talk about it.* **2** (*informal*) to be considered or thought to be sth: *This is supposed to be the oldest building in the city.*

S

not supposed to do sth to not be allowed to do sth: *This is secret and I'm not supposed to talk about it.*

supposedly /sə'pəʊzɪdli/ *adv* according to what many people believe

supposing /sə'pəʊzɪŋ/ *conj* if sth happens or is true; what if: *Supposing the plan goes wrong, what will we do then?*

supposition /ˌsʌpə'zɪʃn/ *noun* [C,U] (*formal*) an idea that a person thinks is true but which has not been shown to be true

suppress /sə'pres/ *verb* [T] **1** to stop sth by using force **2** to stop sth from being seen or known: *to suppress the truth* **3** to stop yourself from expressing your feelings, etc: *to suppress laughter/a yawn* ▶ **suppression** /sə'preʃn/ *noun* [U]

supremacy /su:'preməsi/ *noun* [U] **supremacy (over sb/sth)** the state of being the most powerful

supreme /su:'pri:m/ *adj* the highest or greatest possible

supremely /su:'pri:mli/ *adv* extremely

surcharge /'sɜ:tʃɑ:dʒ/ *noun* [C] an extra amount of money that you have to pay for sth

sure /ʃʊə(r); ʃɔ:(r)/ *adj* (**surer**; **surest**) [You can also use **more sure** and **most sure**, especially in sense 1.] *adv* **1** [not before a noun] having no doubt about sth; certain: *You must be sure of your facts before you make an accusation.* ◆ *I'm not sure what to do next.* ◆ *Craig was sure that he'd made the right decision.* ◆ *I think I had my bag when I got off the bus but I'm not sure.* **OPP** **unsure**

HELP **Sure** or **certain**? **Sure** and **certain** are very similar in meaning but are used differently: ***It is certain that*** *there will be an election next year.* ◆ ***There is sure to be*** *an election next year.*

2 [not before a noun] **sure of sth; sure to do sth** certain that you will receive sth or that sth will happen: *If you go and see them you can be sure of a warm welcome.* ◆ *If you work hard you are sure to pass the exam.* **3** that you can be certain of: *A noise like that is a sure sign of engine trouble.* **4** (*informal*) used to say 'yes' to sb: *'Can I have a look at your newspaper?' 'Sure.'*

IDM **be sure to do sth** (used for telling sb to do sth) do not forget to do sth: *Be sure to text and tell me what happens.*

for sure without doubt: *Nobody knows for sure what happened.* ◆ (*especially AmE*) *'Will you be there?' 'For sure!'*

make sure 1 to take the action that is necessary: *Make sure you are back home by 11 o'clock.* **2** to check that sth is in a particular state or has been done: *I must go back and make sure I closed the window.*

sure thing (*AmE informal*) yes: *'Can I borrow this book?' 'Sure thing.'*

sure enough as was expected: *I expected him to be early, and sure enough he arrived five minutes before the others.*

sure of yourself confident about your opinions, or about what you can do

surely /'ʃʊəli; 'ʃɔ:li/ *adv* **1** without doubt: *This will surely cause problems.* **2** used for expressing surprise at sb else's opinions, plans, actions, etc: *Surely you're not going to walk home in this rain?* ◆ *'Jo's looking for another job.' 'Surely not!'* **3** (*AmE old-fashioned informal*) yes; of course

surf¹ /sɜ:f/ *noun* [U] the white part on the top of waves in the sea

surf² /sɜ:f/ *verb* [I] **1** to stand or lie on a **surfboard** and ride on a wave towards the beach ➲ picture on **page P11**

HELP **Go surfing** is a common way of talking about this activity: *Let's go surfing in Cornwall this weekend.*

2 surf the net/ Internet to use the Internet

surface¹ /'sɜ:fɪs/ *noun* **1 the surface** [sing] the top part of an area of water: *leaves floating on the surface of a pond* **2** [C] the outside part of sth: *the earth's surface* ◆ *Teeth have a hard surface called enamel.* ◆ *This tennis court has a very uneven surface.* **3** [C] the flat top part of a piece of furniture, used for working on: *a work surface* ◆ *kitchen surfaces* **4** [sing] the qualities of sb/sth that you see or notice, that are not hidden: *Everybody seems very friendly but there are a lot of tensions **below/beneath the surface**.*

surface² /'sɜ:fɪs/ *verb* **1** [I] to come up to the surface of water **2** [I] to appear again: *All the old arguments surfaced again in the discussion.* **3** [T] to put a surface on a road, etc.

'surface mail *noun* [U] letters, packages, etc. that go by road, rail or sea, not by air ➲ look at **airmail**

surfboard /'sɜ:fbɔ:d/ *noun* [C] a long narrow board used for **surfing** ➲ picture on **page P5**

surfeit /'sɜ:fɪt/ *noun* [sing] (*formal*) **a surfeit (of sth)** too much of sth

surfer /'sɜ:fə(r)/ *noun* [C] **1** a person who rides on waves standing on a special board ➲ picture on **page P5** **2** (*informal*) a person who spends a lot of time using the Internet

surfing /'sɜ:fɪŋ/ *noun* [U] **1** the sport of riding on waves while standing or lying on a **surfboard**: *to go surfing* ➲ picture on **page P5** **2** the activity of looking at different things on the Internet, or of looking quickly at different TV programmes, in order to find sth interesting ➲ picture on **page P3**

surge /sɜ:dʒ/ *noun* [C, usually sing] **a surge (of/in sth)** **1** a sudden strong movement in a particular direction by a large number of people or things: *a surge of interest* ◆ *a surge (= an increase) in the demand for electricity* **2** a sudden strong feeling ▶ **surge** *verb* [I]: *The crowd surged forward.*

surgeon /'sɜ:dʒən/ *noun* [C] a doctor who performs medical operations: *a brain surgeon*

surgery /'sɜ:dʒəri/ *noun* (*pl* **surgeries**) **1** [U] medical treatment in which your body is cut open so that part of it can be removed or repaired: *to undergo*

S

surgery ➲ look at **operation, plastic surgery** **2** [C,U] the place or time when a doctor or dentist sees patients: *Surgery hours are from 9.00 to 11.30.* ➲ note at **doctor**

surgical /ˈsɜːdʒɪkl/ *adj* [only *before* a noun] connected with medical operations: *surgical instruments* ▶ **surgically** /-kli/ *adv*

surly /ˈsɜːli/ *adj* (**surlier**; **surliest**) unfriendly and rude: *a surly expression*

surmount /səˈmaʊnt/ *verb* [T] (*formal*) to deal successfully with a problem or difficulty ➲ look at **insurmountable**

surname /ˈsɜːneɪm/ (also ˈ**last name**; ˈ**second name**) *noun* [C] the name that you share with other people in your family: *'What's your surname?' 'Jones.'* ➲ note at **name**

surpass /səˈpɑːs/ *verb* [T] (*formal*) to do sth better than sb/sth else or better than expected: *The success of the film surpassed all expectations.*

surplus /ˈsɜːpləs/ *noun* [C,U] an amount that is extra or more than you need: *the food surplus in Western Europe* ▶ **surplus** *adj*: *They sell their surplus grain to other countries.*

surprise[1] /səˈpraɪz/ *noun* **1** [C] something that you did not expect or know about: *What a pleasant surprise to see you again!* ◆ *The news came as a complete surprise.* ◆ *a surprise visit/attack/party* **2** [U] the feeling that you have when sth happens that you do not expect: *They looked up* ***in surprise*** *when she walked in.* ◆ ***To my surprise*** *they all agreed with me.*

IDM **take sb by surprise** to happen or do sth when sb is not expecting it

surprise[2] /səˈpraɪz/ *verb* [T] **1** to make sb feel surprised: *It wouldn't surprise me if you get the job.* **2** to attack or find sb suddenly and unexpectedly

surprised /səˈpraɪzd/ *adj* feeling or showing surprise: *I was very surprised to see Cara there. I thought she was still abroad.*

surprising /səˈpraɪzɪŋ/ *adj* that causes surprise: *It's surprising how many adults can't read or write.* ▶ **surprisingly** *adv*: *Surprisingly few people got the correct answer.*

surreal /səˈriːəl/ (also **surrealistic** /səˌriːəˈlɪstɪk/) *adj* very strange; with images mixed together in a strange way like in a dream: *a surreal film/painting/situation*

surrender /səˈrendə(r)/ *verb* **1** [I,T] **surrender (yourself) (to sb)** to stop fighting and admit that you have lost SYN **yield** **2** [T] (*formal*) **surrender sb/sth (to sb)** to give sb/sth to sb else when you are forced to: *The police ordered them to surrender their weapons.* ▶ **surrender** *noun* [C,U]

surreptitious /ˌsʌrəpˈtɪʃəs/ *adj* done secretly: *I had a surreptitious look at what she was writing.* ▶ **surreptitiously** *adv*

surrogate /ˈsʌrəgət/ *noun* [C], *adj* (a person or thing) that takes the place of sb/sth else: *a* ***surrogate mother*** (= a woman who has a baby and gives it to another woman who cannot have children)

surround /səˈraʊnd/ *verb* [T] **surround sb/sth (by/with sth)** to be or go all around sb/sth: *The garden is surrounded by a high wall.* ◆ *Troops have surrounded the parliament building.*

surrounding /səˈraʊndɪŋ/ *adj* [only *before* a noun] that is near or around sth: *Oxford and the surrounding area*

surroundings /səˈraʊndɪŋz/ *noun* [pl] everything that is near or around you; the place where you live: *to live in pleasant surroundings* ◆ *animals living in their natural surroundings* (= not in zoos) ➲ look at **environment**

surveillance /sɜːˈveɪləns/ *noun* [U] the careful watching of sb who may have done sth wrong: *The building is protected by surveillance cameras.*

survey[1] /ˈsɜːveɪ/ *noun* [C] **1** a study of the opinions, behaviour, etc. of a group of people: *Surveys have shown that more and more people are getting into debt.* ◆ *to carry out/conduct/do a survey* **2** the act of examining an area of land and making a map of it: *a geological survey* **3** the act of examining a building in order to find out if it is in good condition

survey[2] /səˈveɪ/ *verb* [T] **1** to look carefully at the whole of sth: *We stood at the top of the hill and surveyed the countryside.* **2** to carefully measure and make a map of an area of land **3** to examine a building carefully in order to find out if it is in good condition

surveyor /səˈveɪə(r)/ *noun* [C] **1** a person whose job is to examine and record the details of a piece of land **2** (*AmE* **inspector**) a person whose job is to examine a building to make sure it is in good condition, usually done for sb who wants to buy it

survive /səˈvaɪv/ *verb* **1** [I,T] to continue to live or exist in or after a difficult or dangerous situation: *More than a hundred people were killed in the crash and only five passengers survived.* ◆ *How can she survive on such a small salary?* ◆ *to survive a plane crash* ◆ *Not many buildings survived the bombing.* **2** [T] to live longer than sb/sth: *The old man survived all his children.* ▶ **survival** /səˈvaɪvl/ *noun* [U]: *A heart transplant was his only chance of survival.* ▶ **survivor** /səˈvaɪvə(r)/ *noun* [C]: *There were five survivors of the crash.*

susceptible /səˈseptəbl/ *adj* [not before a noun] **susceptible to sth** easily influenced, damaged or affected by sb/sth: *The young are susceptible to advertising.* ◆ *Some of these plants are more susceptible to frost damage than others.*

suspect[1] /səˈspekt/ *verb* [T] **1** to believe that sth may happen or be true, especially sth bad: *The situation is worse than we first suspected.* ◆ *Nobody suspected that she was thinking of leaving.* ➲ look at **unsuspecting** **2** to not be sure that you can trust sb or believe sth: *I rather suspect his motives for offering to help.* **3 suspect sb (of sth/of doing sth)** to believe that sb is guilty of sth, although you do not have any proof: *I suspect Laura of taking the money.* ◆ *She strongly suspected that he was lying.* ▶ **suspected** *adj*: *suspected terrorists* ➲ *noun* **suspicion**

S

suspect² /ˈsʌspekt/ *noun* [C] a person who is thought to be guilty of a crime: *The suspects are being questioned by police.* ➲ note at **crime**

suspect³ /ˈsʌspekt/ *adj* possibly not true or not to be trusted: *to have suspect motives* ◆ *a suspect package* (= that may contain a bomb)

suspend /səˈspend/ *verb* [T] **1 suspend sth (from sth) (by/on sth)** to hang sth from sth else: *The huge skeleton is suspended from the museum's ceiling on chains.* **2** to stop or delay sth for a time: *Some rail services were suspended during the strike.* ◆ *The young man was given a **suspended sentence*** (= he will go to prison only if he commits another crime). **3 suspend sb (from sth)** to send sb away from their school, job, position, etc. for a period of time, usually as a punishment: *He was suspended from school for a week for stealing.* ➲ *noun* **suspension**

suspender /səˈspendə(r)/ *noun* **1** [C, usually pl] (*BrE*) a short piece of **elastic** (= material that can stretch) that women use to hold up their **stockings** (= thin pieces of clothing that fit closely over a woman's legs and feet) **2 suspenders** [pl] (*AmE*) = **brace¹** (2)

suspense /səˈspens/ *noun* [U] the feeling of excitement or worry that you have when you feel sth is going to happen, when you are waiting for news, etc: *Don't keep us **in suspense**. Tell us what happened.*

suspension /səˈspenʃn/ *noun* **1** [C,U] not being allowed to do your job or go to school for a period of time, usually as a punishment: *suspension on full pay* **2** [U] delaying sth for a period of time ➲ *verb* **suspend 3 the suspension** [U] the parts that are connected to the wheels of a car, etc. that make it more comfortable to ride in

suspicion /səˈspɪʃn/ *noun* **1** [C,U] a feeling or belief that sth is wrong or that sb has done sth wrong: *I always treat smiling politicians with suspicion.* ◆ *She was arrested **on suspicion of** murder.* ◆ *He is **under suspicion** of being involved in organized crime.* ◆ *It's time to confront him with our suspicions.* **2** [C] a feeling that sth may happen or be true: *I have a suspicion that he's forgotten he invited us.* ➲ *verb* **suspect**

suspicious /səˈspɪʃəs/ *adj* **1 suspicious (of/about sb/sth)** feeling that sb has done sth wrong, dishonest or illegal: *We became suspicious of his behaviour and alerted the police.* **2** that makes you feel that sth is wrong, dishonest or illegal: *The old man died **in suspicious circumstances**.* ◆ *It's very suspicious that she was not at home on the evening of the murder.* ◆ *a suspicious-looking person* ▸ **suspiciously** *adv*: *to behave suspiciously*

sustain /səˈsteɪn/ *verb* [T] **1** to keep sb/sth alive or healthy: *Oxygen sustains life.* **2** to make sth continue for a long period of time without becoming less: *It's hard to sustain interest for such a long time.* **3** (*formal*) to experience sth bad: *to sustain damage/an injury/a defeat*

sustainable /səˈsteɪnəbl/ *adj* **1** involving the use of natural products and energy in a way that does not harm the environment: *sustainable forest management* **2** that can continue or be continued for a long time: *sustainable economic growth* ▸ **sustainability** /səˌsteɪnəˈbɪləti/ *noun* [U]: *environmental sustainability*

SW *abbr* = **south-west¹**, **south-western**: *SW Australia*

swab /swɒb/ *noun* [C] **1** a piece of soft material used by a doctor, nurse, etc. for cleaning wounds or taking a small amount of a substance from sb's body for testing **2** an act of taking a small amount of a substance from sb's body, with a **swab**: *to take a throat swab* ▸ **swab** *verb* [T] (**swabbing**; **swabbed**)

swagger /ˈswæɡə(r)/ *verb* [I] to walk in a way that shows that you are too confident or proud ▸ **swagger** *noun* [sing]

swallow /ˈswɒləʊ/ *verb*

▸FOOD/DRINK **1** [T] to make food, drink, etc. go down your throat to your stomach: *It's easier to swallow pills if you take them with water.* ➲ picture at **lick**

▸IN FEAR, ETC. **2** [I] to make a movement in your throat, often because you are afraid or surprised, etc: *She swallowed hard and tried to speak, but nothing came out.*

▸USE ALL **3** [T] **swallow sth (up)** to use all of sth, especially money: *The rent swallows up most of our monthly income.*

▸ACCEPT/BELIEVE **4** [T] to accept or believe sth too easily: *You shouldn't swallow everything they tell you!* **5** [T] to accept an insult, etc. without complaining: *I find her criticisms very **hard to swallow**.* ▸ **swallow** *noun* [C]

swam *past tense* of **swim**

swamp¹ /swɒmp/ *noun* [C,U] an area of soft wet land

swamp² /swɒmp/ *verb* [T] **1** [usually passive] **swamp sb/sth (with sth)** to give sb so much of sth that they cannot deal with it: *We've been swamped with applications for the job.* SYN **inundate 2** to cover or fill sth with water: *The fishing boat was swamped by enormous waves.*

swan /swɒn/ *noun* [C] a large, usually white, bird with a very long neck that lives on lakes and rivers

swan

swap (also **swop**) /swɒp/ *verb* [I,T] (**swapping**; **swapped**) **swap (sth) (with sb)**; **swap A for B** to give sth for sth else; to exchange: *When we finish these books shall we swap* (= you have my book and I'll have yours)? ◆ *Would you swap seats with me?* ◆ *I'd swap my job for hers any day.*

goose

IDM **change/swap places (with sb)** ➲ **place¹**

▸ **swap** (also **swop**) *noun* [sing]: *Let's **do a swap**.*

swarm¹ /swɔːm/ *noun* [C] **1** a large group of insects moving around together: *a swarm of bees/locusts/flies* **2** a large number of people together

swarm² /swɔːm/ *verb* [I] to fly or move in large numbers
PHR V **swarm with sb/sth** to be full of people or things

swat /swɒt/ *verb* [T] (swatting; swatted) to hit sth, especially an insect, with sth flat

sway /sweɪ/ *verb* **1** [I] to move slowly from side to side: *The trees were swaying in the wind.* **2** [T] to influence sb: *Many people were swayed by his convincing arguments.*

swear /sweə(r)/ *verb* (*pt* swore /swɔː(r)/; *pp* sworn /swɔːn/) **1** [I] swear (at sb/sth) to use rude or bad language: *He hit his thumb with the hammer and swore loudly.* ♦ *There's no point in swearing at the car just because it won't start!* ➲ look at **curse** **2** [I,T] swear (to do sth); swear that ... to make a serious promise: *When you give evidence in court you have to swear to tell the truth.* ♦ *Will you swear not to tell anyone?*
PHR V **swear by sth** to believe completely in the value of sth
swear sb in [usually passive] to make sb say officially that they will accept the responsibility of a new position: *The President will be sworn in next week.*

swearing /ˈsweərɪŋ/ *noun* [U] rude language that may offend people: *I was shocked at the swearing.*

ˈswear word (also *old-fashioned* oath) *noun* [C] a word that is considered rude or bad and that may offend people

sweat /swet/ *verb* [I] **1** to produce liquid through your skin because you are hot, ill or afraid: *to sweat heavily* **2** sweat (over sth) to work hard: *I've been sweating over that problem all day.* ▶ **sweat** *noun* [C, U]: *He stopped digging and wiped the sweat from his forehead.* ♦ *He woke up* **in a sweat**. ➲ look at **perspiration**

sweater /ˈswetə(r)/ *noun* [C] a warm piece of clothing with long sleeves, often made of wool, which you wear on the top half of your body ➲ picture on **page P1**

> OTHER WORDS FOR
>
> **sweater**
>
> In British English, **sweater**, **jumper**, **pullover** and **jersey** are all words for the same piece of clothing. A **cardigan** is similar but fastens at the front. A **fleece** is made from a type of soft warm cloth that feels like sheep's wool. A **sweatshirt** is made from thick cotton and is often worn for sports.

sweatshirt /ˈswetʃɜːt/ *noun* [C] a piece of cotton clothing with long sleeves, which you wear on the top half of your body ➲ note at **sweater**

sweatshop /ˈswetʃɒp/ *noun* [C] a place where people work for low wages in poor conditions

sweaty /ˈsweti/ *adj* (sweatier; sweatiest) **1** wet with sweat: *I was hot and sweaty after the match and needed a shower.* **2** [only *before* a noun] causing you to sweat: *a hot sweaty day*

swede /swiːd/ *noun* [C,U] a large, round, yellow vegetable that grows under the ground

sweep¹ /swiːp/ *verb* (*pt, pp* swept /swept/)
➤WITH BRUSH **1** [I,T] to clean the floor, etc. by moving dust, dirt, etc. away with a brush: *to sweep the floor* ♦ *I'm going to sweep the leaves off the path.* ➲ note at **clean²**
➤WITH HAND **2** [T] to remove sth from a surface using your hand, etc: *He swept the books angrily off the table.*
➤MOVE WITH FORCE **3** [T] to move or push sb/sth with a lot of force: *The huge waves swept her overboard.* ♦ *He was swept along by the huge crowd.*
➤MOVE FAST **4** [I,T] to move quickly and smoothly over the area or in the direction mentioned: *Fire swept through the building.* **5** [I] to move in a way that impresses or is intended to impress people: *Five big black Mercedes swept past us.*
➤SEARCH **6** [I,T] to move over an area, especially in order to look for sth: *His eyes swept quickly over the page.* ♦ *The army were sweeping the fields for mines.*
PHR V **sweep sb/sth aside** to not allow sb/sth to affect your progress or plans
sweep sth out to remove dirt and dust from the floor of a room or building using a brush
sweep over sb (used about a feeling) to suddenly affect sb very strongly
sweep (sth) up/away to remove dirt, dust, leaves, etc. using a brush

sweep² /swiːp/ *noun* [C] **1** [usually sing] the act of moving dirt and dust from a floor or surface using a brush: *I'd better give the floor a sweep.* **2** a long, curving shape or movement: *He showed us which way to go with a sweep of his arm.* **3** a movement over an area, especially in order to look for sth **4** = **chimney sweep**
IDM **a clean sweep** ➲ **clean¹**

sweeper /ˈswiːpə(r)/ *noun* [C] **1** a person or thing that cleans surfaces with a brush: *He's a road sweeper.* ♦ *Do you sell carpet sweepers?* **2** (in football) the defending player who plays behind the other defending players

sweeping /ˈswiːpɪŋ/ *adj* **1** having a great and important effect: *sweeping reforms* **2** (used about statements, etc.) too general and not accurate enough: *He made a sweeping statement about all politicians being dishonest.*

sweet¹ /swiːt/ *adj* (sweeter; sweetest) **1** containing, or tasting as if it contains, a lot of sugar: *Children usually like sweet things.* ♦ *This cake's too sweet.* ➲ look at **savoury**, **sour** **2** (used about a smell or a sound) pleasant: *the sweet sound of children singing* **3** (used especially about children and small things) attractive: *a sweet little kitten* ♦ *Isn't that little girl sweet?* **SYN** **cute** **4** having or showing a kind character: *a sweet smile*
IDM **have a sweet tooth** (*informal*) to like eating sweet things
▶ **sweetness** *noun* [U]

sweet² /swiːt/ *noun* **1** [C, usually pl] (*AmE* candy) a small piece of boiled sugar, chocolate, etc., eaten between meals: *He was sucking a sweet.* ♦ *a sweet shop* **2** [C,U] sweet food served at the end of a meal: *As a sweet/For sweet there is ice cream or chocolate mousse.* ➲ look at **pudding**, **dessert**

S

sweetcorn /ˈswiːtkɔːn/ (*AmE* **corn**) *noun* [U] the yellow grains of a type of **maize** (= a tall plant) that you cook and eat as a vegetable: *tinned sweetcorn* ➲ picture on **page P15**

sweeten /ˈswiːtn/ *verb* [T] to make sth sweet by adding sugar, etc.

sweetener /ˈswiːtnə(r)/ *noun* [C,U] a substance used instead of sugar for making food or drink sweet: *artificial sweeteners*

sweetheart /ˈswiːthɑːt/ *noun* **1** [sing] used when speaking to sb, especially a child, in a very friendly way: *Do you want a drink, sweetheart?* **2** [C] (*old-fashioned*) a boyfriend or girlfriend

sweetly /ˈswiːtli/ *adv* in an attractive, kind or pleasant way: *She smiled sweetly.* ◆ *sweetly scented flowers*

swell¹ /swel/ *verb* (*pt* **swelled** /sweld/; *pp* **swollen** /ˈswəʊlən/ *or* **swelled**) **1** [I,T] **swell (up)** to become or to make sth bigger, fuller or thicker: *After the fall her ankle began to swell up.* ◆ *Heavy rain had swollen the rivers.* **2** [I,T] to increase or make sth increase in number or size: *The crowd swelled to 600 by the end of the evening.* **3** [I] (*formal*) (used about feelings or sound) to suddenly become stronger or louder: *Hatred swelled inside him.*

swell² /swel/ *noun* [sing] the slow movement up and down of the surface of the sea

swelling /ˈswelɪŋ/ *noun* **1** [U] the process of becoming swollen: *The disease often causes swelling of the ankles and knees.* **2** [C] a place on your body that is bigger or fatter than usual because of an injury or illness: *I've got a nasty swelling under my eye.*

sweltering /ˈsweltərɪŋ/ *adj* (*informal*) much too hot: *It was sweltering in the office today.*

swept *past tense, past participle of* **sweep¹**

swerve /swɜːv/ *verb* [I] to change direction suddenly: *The car swerved to avoid the child.* ▶ **swerve** *noun* [C]

swift /swɪft/ *adj* (**swifter**; **swiftest**) happening without delay; quick: *a swift reaction/decision/movement* ◆ *a swift runner* ▶ **swiftly** *adv*

swig /swɪg/ *verb* [I,T] (**swigging**; **swigged**) (*informal*) to take a quick drink of sth ▶ **swig** *noun* [C]

swill /swɪl/ *verb* [T] **swill sth (out/down)** to wash sth by pouring large amounts of water, etc. into, over or through it

swim /swɪm/ *verb* (**swimming**; *pt* **swam** /swæm/; *pp* **swum** /swʌm/) **1** [I,T] to move your body through water: *How far can you swim?* ◆ *Hundreds of tiny fish swam past.* ◆ *I swam 25 lengths of the pool.*

> **HELP** **Go swimming** is a common way of talking about swimming for pleasure: *We go swimming every Saturday.* We can also say **go for a swim** when we are talking about one particular occasion: *I went for a swim this morning.*

swimming

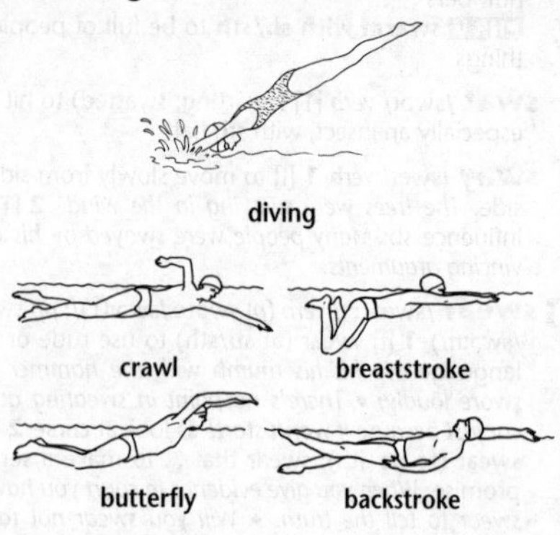

2 [I] **be swimming (in/with sth)** to be covered with a lot of liquid: *The salad was swimming in oil.* **3** [I] to seem to be moving or turning: *The floor began to swim before my eyes and I fainted.* **4** [I] (used about your head) to feel confused: *My head was swimming with so much new information.* ▶ **swim** *noun* [sing]: *to* **go for/have a swim** ▶ **swimmer** *noun* [C]: *a strong/weak swimmer*

swimming /ˈswɪmɪŋ/ *noun* [U] the sport or activity of swimming: *Swimming is a good form of exercise.*

ˈswimming bath *noun* [C] (*also* **swimming baths** [pl]) (*old-fashioned*) a public swimming pool, usually inside a building

ˈswimming costume (*BrE*) = **swimsuit**

ˈswimming pool (*also* **pool**) *noun* [C] a pool that is built especially for people to swim in; the building that contains this pool: *an indoor/outdoor/open-air swimming pool*

ˈswimming trunks *noun* [pl] a piece of clothing like short trousers that a man wears to go swimming: *a pair of swimming trunks*

swimsuit /ˈswɪmsuːt/ (*BrE also* **ˈswimming costume**; **costume**) *noun* [C] a piece of clothing that a woman wears to go swimming ➲ look at **bikini**

swindle /ˈswɪndl/ *verb* [T] **swindle sb/sth (out of sth)** to trick sb in order to get money, etc. ▶ **swindle** *noun* [C]: *a tax swindle*

swine /swaɪn/ *noun* **1** [C] (*informal*) a very unpleasant person **2** [pl] (*old-fashioned*) pigs

swing¹ /swɪŋ/ *verb* (*pt, pp* **swung** /swʌŋ/) **1** [I,T] to move backwards and forwards or from side to side while hanging from sth; to make sb/sth move in this way: *The rope was swinging from a branch.* ◆ *She sat on the wall, swinging her legs.* **2** [I] to move or change from one position or situation towards the opposite one: *She swung round when she heard the door open.* ◆ *His moods swing from one extreme to the other.* **3** [I,T] to move or make sb/sth move in a curve: *The door swung open and Rudi walked in.* ◆ *He swung the child up onto his shoulders.* **4** [I,T] **swing (sth) (at sb/sth)** to try to hit sb/sth: *He swung violently at the other man but missed.*

swing² /swɪŋ/ *noun* **1** [sing] a **swinging** movement or rhythm: *He took a swing at the ball.* **2** [C] a change from one position or situation towards the opposite one: *Opinion polls indicate a significant swing towards the right.* **3** [C] a seat, a piece of rope, etc. that is hung from above so that you can **swing** backwards and forwards on it: *Some children were playing on the swings.*
IDM in full swing ➲ **full¹**

swipe /swaɪp/ *verb* **1** [I,T] (*informal*) **swipe (at) sb/sth** to hit or try to hit sb/sth by moving your arm in a curve: *He swiped at the wasp with a newspaper but missed.* **2** [T] (*informal*) to steal sth **3** [T] to pass the part of a plastic card on which information is stored through a special machine for reading it: *The cash register only opens once the card has been swiped.* **4** [I] (on some small computer devices) to move content across a screen using your finger ➲ note at **touch screen** ▸ **swipe** *noun* [C]: *She took a swipe at him with her handbag.*

ˈswipe card *noun* [C] a small plastic card on which information is stored which can be read by an electronic machine

swirl /swɜːl/ *verb* [I,T] to move or to make sth move around quickly in a circle: *Her long skirt swirled round her legs as she danced.* ◆ *He swirled some water round in his mouth and spat it out.* ▸ **swirl** *noun* [C]: *a pattern of blue swirls*

switch¹ /swɪtʃ/ *noun* [C] **1** a small button or sth similar that you press up or down in order to turn on electricity: *a light switch* **2** a sudden change: *a switch in policy*

switch² /swɪtʃ/ *verb* [I,T] **1 switch (sth) (over) (from sth) (to sth); switch (between A and B)** to change or be changed from one thing to another: *I'm fed up with my glasses—I'm thinking of switching over to contact lenses.* ◆ *Press these two keys to switch between documents on screen.* ◆ *The match has been switched from Saturday to Sunday.* **2 switch (sth) (with sb/sth); switch (sth) (over/round)** to exchange positions, activities, etc: *This week you can have the car and I'll go on the bus, and next week we'll switch over.* ◆ *Someone switched the signs round and everyone went the wrong way.*
PHR V switch off to stop thinking about sth or paying attention to sth: *When I hear the word 'football', I switch off* (= because I'm not interested in it).
switch (sth) off/on to press a switch in order to stop/start electric power: *Don't forget to switch off the cooker.*
switch (sth) over to change to a different TV programme

switchboard /ˈswɪtʃbɔːd/ *noun* [C] the place in a large company, etc. where all the telephone calls are connected

swivel /ˈswɪvl/ *verb* [I,T] (**swivelling; swivelled**, (*AmE*) **swiveling; swiveled**) **swivel (sth) (round)** to turn around a central point; to make sth do this: *She swivelled round to face me.* ◆ *He swivelled his chair towards the door.*

swollen¹ *past participle* of **swell¹**

swollen² /ˈswəʊlən/ *adj* thicker or wider than usual: *Her ankle was badly swollen after she twisted it.*

swoop /swuːp/ *verb* [I] **1** to fly or move down suddenly: *The bird swooped down on its prey.* **2** (used especially about the police or the army) to visit or capture sb/sth without warning: *Police swooped at dawn and arrested the man at his home.* ▸ **swoop** *noun* [C] **a swoop (on sb/sth)**

swop = **swap**

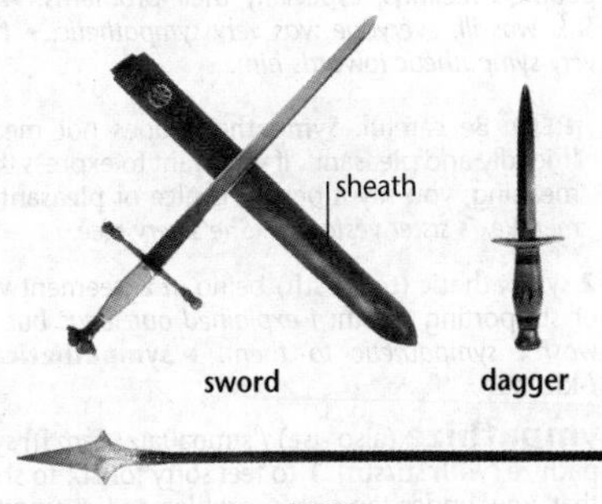

sword /sɔːd/ *noun* [C] a long, very sharp metal weapon, like a large knife

swore *past tense of* **swear**

sworn *past participle* of **swear**

swot¹ /swɒt/ *noun* [C] (*informal*) a person who studies too hard

swot² /swɒt/ *verb* [I,T] (*informal*) (**swotting; swotted**) **swot (up) (for/on sth); swot sth up** to study sth very hard, especially to prepare for an exam: *She's swotting for her final exams.*

swum *past participle* of **swim**

swung *past tense, past participle* of **swing¹**

syllable /ˈsɪləbl/ *noun* [C] a word or part of a word which contains one vowel sound: *'Mat' has one syllable and 'mattress' has two syllables.* ◆ *The stress in 'international' is on the third syllable.*

syllabus /ˈsɪləbəs/ *noun* [C] (*pl* **syllabuses**) a list of subjects, etc. that are included in a course of study ➲ look at **curriculum**

symbol /ˈsɪmbl/ *noun* [C] **1 a symbol (of sth)** a person, sign, object, etc. which represents sth: *The cross is the symbol of Christianity.* **2 a symbol (for sth)** a letter, number or sign that has a particular meaning: *O is the symbol for oxygen.*

S

symbolic /sɪmˈbɒlɪk/ (also symbolical /-kl/) *adj* used or seen to represent sth: *The white dove is symbolic of peace.* ▶ **symbolically** /-kli/ *adv*

symbolism /ˈsɪmbəlɪzəm/ *noun* [U] the use of symbols to represent things, especially in art and literature

symbolize (also -ise) /ˈsɪmbəlaɪz/ *verb* [T] to represent sth: *The deepest notes in music are often used to symbolize danger or despair.*

symmetric /sɪˈmetrɪk/ (also symmetrical /-rɪkl/) *adj* having two halves that match each other exactly in size, shape, etc. ▶ **symmetrically** /-kli/ *adv*

symmetry /ˈsɪmətri/ *noun* [U] the state of having two halves that match each other exactly in size, shape, etc.

sympathetic /ˌsɪmpəˈθetɪk/ *adj* **1** sympathetic (to/towards sb) showing that you understand other people's feelings, especially their problems: *When Suki was ill, everyone was very sympathetic.* ♦ *I felt very sympathetic towards him.*

> **HELP** Be careful. **Sympathetic** does not mean 'friendly and pleasant'. If you want to express this meaning, you say a person is **nice** or **pleasant**: *I met Alex's sister yesterday. She's very nice.*

2 sympathetic (to sb/sth) being in agreement with or supporting sb/sth: *I explained our ideas but she wasn't sympathetic to them.* ▶ **sympathetically** /-kli/ *adv*

sympathize (also -ise) /ˈsɪmpəθaɪz/ *verb* [I] sympathize (with sb/sth) **1** to feel sorry for sb; to show that you understand sb's problems: *I sympathize with her, but I don't know what I can do to help.* **2** to support sb/sth: *I find it difficult to sympathize with his opinions.*

S

sympathizer (also -iser) /ˈsɪmpəθaɪzə(r)/ *noun* [C] a person who agrees with and supports an idea or aim

sympathy /ˈsɪmpəθi/ *noun* (*pl* sympathies) **1** [U] sympathy (for/towards sb) an understanding of other people's feelings, especially their problems: *Everyone* ***feels*** *great* ***sympathy*** *for the victims of the attack.* ♦ *I don't expect any sympathy from you.* ♦ *I* ***have*** *no* ***sympathy*** *for Mark—it's his own fault.* **2** sympathies [pl] feelings of support or agreement: *Some members of the party have nationalist sympathies.*

IDM in sympathy (with sb/sth) in agreement, showing that you support or approve of sb/sth: *Train drivers stopped work in sympathy with the striking bus drivers.*

symphony /ˈsɪmfəni/ *noun* [C] (*pl* symphonies) a long piece of music written for a large **orchestra** (= a group of musicians who play together)

symptom /ˈsɪmptəm/ *noun* [C] **1** a change in your body that is a sign of illness: *The symptoms of flu include a headache, a high temperature and aches in the body.* ➲ note at **ill** **2** a sign (that sth bad is happening or exists) ▶ **symptomatic** /ˌsɪmptəˈmætɪk/ *adj*

synagogue /ˈsɪnəgɒg/ *noun* [C] a building where Jewish people go to worship or to study their religion

synchronize (also -ise) /ˈsɪŋkrənaɪz/ *verb* [T] to make sth happen or work at the same time or speed: *We synchronized our watches to make sure we agreed what the time was.*

syndicate /ˈsɪndɪkət/ *noun* [C] a group of people or companies that work together in order to achieve a particular aim

syndrome /ˈsɪndrəʊm/ *noun* [C] **1** a group of signs or changes in the body that are typical of an illness: *Down's syndrome* ♦ *Acquired Immune Deficiency Syndrome (AIDS)* **2** a set of opinions or a way of behaving that is typical of a particular type of person, attitude or social problem

synonym /ˈsɪnənɪm/ *noun* [C] a word or phrase that has the same meaning as another word or phrase in the same language: *'Big' and 'large' are synonyms.* ▶ **synonymous** /sɪˈnɒnɪməs/ *adj* synonymous (with sth) (*figurative*): *Wealth is not always synonymous with happiness.* ➲ look at **antonym**

> EXAM TIP
> **Synonyms**
> In an exam, your writing will be more interesting and you will make a better impression if you avoid repeating the same words again and again. Look at the **Other words for** notes in the dictionary to build up a good choice of words that you can use. In some exams, one of the tasks may be to find other words to express something.

synopsis /sɪˈnɒpsɪs/ *noun* [C] (*pl* synopses /-siːz/) a short description of a piece of writing, a play, etc: *The programme gives a brief synopsis of the plot.* **SYN** summary

syntax /ˈsɪntæks/ *noun* [U] the system of rules for the structure of sentences in a language

synthesis /ˈsɪnθəsɪs/ *noun* (*pl* syntheses /-siːz/) **1** [C,U] synthesis (of sth) the act of combining separate ideas, beliefs, styles, etc.; a mixture or combination of ideas, beliefs, styles, etc: *the synthesis of art with everyday life* ♦ *a synthesis of traditional and modern values* **2** [U] (*technical*) the natural chemical production of a substance in animals and plants, or the artificial production of such a substance: *protein synthesis* **3** [U] (*technical*) the production of sounds, music or speech using electronic equipment: *speech synthesis* ▶ **synthesize** (also -ise) /ˈsɪnθəsaɪz/ *verb* [T]

synthesizer (also -iser) /ˈsɪnθəsaɪzə(r)/ *noun* [C] an electronic musical instrument that can produce a wide variety of different sounds

synthetic /sɪnˈθetɪk/ *adj* made by a chemical process; not natural: *synthetic materials/fibres* ▶ **synthetically** /-kli/ *adv*

syphon = **siphon**

syringe /sɪˈrɪndʒ/ *noun* [C] a plastic or glass tube with a needle that is used for taking a small amount of blood out of the body or for putting drugs into the body ➲ picture at **medicine**

syrup /ˈsɪrəp/ *noun* [U] a thick sweet liquid, often made by boiling sugar with water or fruit juice: *peaches in syrup* ➲ look at **treacle**

⚷ **system** /ˈsɪstəm/ *noun* **1** [C] a set of ideas or rules for organizing sth; a particular way of doing sth: *a new system for assessing tax bills* ♦ *The government is planning to reform the education system.* **2** [C] a group of things or parts that work together: *a central heating system* ♦ *a transport system* ♦ *a computer operating system* **3** [C] the body of a person or an animal; parts of the body that work together: *the central nervous system* **4 the system** [sing] (*informal*) the traditional methods and rules of a society: *You can't **beat the system*** (= you must accept these rules).

IDM get sth out of your system (*informal*) to do sth to free yourself of a strong feeling or emotion

systematic /ˌsɪstəˈmætɪk/ *adj* done using a fixed plan or method: *a systematic search* ▶ **systematically** /-kli/ *adv*

ˈ**system unit** *noun* [C] the main part of a computer, separate from the keyboard, monitor and mouse, that contains all the other parts of the system ➲ picture at **computer**

T, t /tiː/ *noun* [C,U] (*pl* Ts; T's; t's /tiːz/) the 20th letter of the English alphabet: *'Table' begins with (a) 'T'.*

t *abbr* = **ton**(1), **tonne**: *5t coal*

ta /tɑː/ *exclam* (*BrE informal*) thank you

tab /tæb/ *noun* [C] **1** a small piece of cloth, metal or paper that is fixed to the edge of sth to help you open, hold or identify it: *You open the tin by pulling the metal tab.* **2** the money that you owe for food, drink, etc. that you receive in a bar, restaurant, etc. but pay for later **3** one of a number of small areas at the edge of a computer window that allows you to change the section of the website or piece of software that you are looking at: *Click on the tab at the top of this window to see another section of today's paper.* ♦ *Use the tab key.*

IDM keep tabs on sb/sth (*informal*) to watch sb/sth carefully; to check sth

⚷ **table** /ˈteɪbl/ *noun* [C] **1** a piece of furniture with a flat top supported by legs: *a dining/bedside/coffee/kitchen table* ♦ *Could you **lay/set the table** for lunch?* (= put the knives, forks, plates, etc. on it) ♦ *Let me help you **clear the table*** (= remove the dirty plates, etc. at the end of a meal). ♦ *Can I reserve a table, please* (= in a restaurant)? ➲ picture on **page P8**

HELP We put things **on the table** but we sit **at the table** (= around the table).

2 a list of facts or figures, usually arranged in rows and columns down a page: *Table 3 shows the results.*

tablecloth /ˈteɪblklɒθ/ *noun* [C] a piece of cloth that you use for covering a table, especially when having a meal

ˈ**table manners** *noun* [pl] behaviour that is considered correct while you are having a meal at a table with other people

tablespoon /ˈteɪblspuːn/ *noun* [C] **1** a large spoon used for serving or measuring food **2** (also **tablespoonful** /-fʊl/) (*abbr* **tbsp**) the amount that a **tablespoon** holds: *Add two tablespoons of sugar.* ➲ picture at **spoon**

⚷ **tablet** /ˈtæblət/ *noun* [C] **1** a small amount of medicine in solid form that you swallow: ***Take** two tablets with water before meals.* **SYN pill** ➲ picture at **medicine** **2** a small amount of a substance in solid form: *dishwasher tablets* **3** (also ˌ**Tablet P**ˈ**C**™) a very small, flat computer that you can carry with you and that you work by touching the screen

ˈ**table tennis** (also *informal* **ping-pong**) *noun* [U] a game with rules like **tennis** in which you hit a light plastic ball across a table with a small round **bat** (= a piece of wood) ➲ picture on **page P5**

tabloid /ˈtæblɔɪd/ *noun* [C] a newspaper with small pages, often with a lot of pictures and short articles, especially ones about famous people ➲ note at **newspaper**

taboo /təˈbuː/ *noun* [C] (*pl* **taboos**) something that you must not say or do because it might shock, offend or embarrass people ▶ **taboo** *adj*: *a taboo subject/word*

tacit /ˈtæsɪt/ *adj* (*formal*) understood but not actually said ▶ **tacitly** *adv*

tack[1] /tæk/ *noun* **1** [sing] a way of dealing with a particular situation: *If people won't listen we'll have to try a different tack.* **2** [C] a small nail with a sharp point and a flat head

tack[2] /tæk/ *verb* [T] **1** to fasten sth in place with **tacks**[1](2) **2** to fasten cloth together temporarily with long **stitches** (= lines of thread) that can be removed easily

PHR V tack sth on (to sth) to add sth extra on the end of sth

⚷ **tackle**[1] /ˈtækl/ *verb* **1** [T] to make an effort to deal with a difficult situation or problem: *The government must tackle the problem of rising unemployment.* ♦ *Firemen were brought in to tackle the blaze.* **2** [T] **tackle sb about sth** to speak to sb about a difficult subject: *I'm going to tackle Henry about the money he owes me.* **3** [I,T] (in football, etc.) to try to take the ball from sb in the other team: *He was tackled just outside the penalty area.* **4** [T] to stop sb running away by pulling them down: *The police officer tackled one of the robbers as he ran out.*

⚷ **tackle**[2] /ˈtækl/ *noun* **1** [C] the act of trying to get the ball from another player in football, etc. **2** [U] the equipment you use in some sports, especially fishing: *fishing tackle*

tacky /ˈtæki/ *adj* (**tackier**; **tackiest**) (*informal*) **1** cheap and of poor quality and/or not in good

T

taste: *a shop selling tacky souvenirs* **2** (used about paint, etc.) not quite dry; sticky

tact /tækt/ *noun* [U] the ability to deal with people without offending or upsetting them: *She handled the situation with great tact and diplomacy.*

tactful /ˈtæktfl/ *adj* careful not to say or do things that could offend people **SYN** **diplomatic** **OPP** **tactless** ▶ **tactfully** /-fəli/ *adv*

tactic /ˈtæktɪk/ *noun* **1** [C, usually pl] the particular method you use to achieve sth: *We must decide what our tactics are going to be at the next meeting.* ♦ *I don't think this tactic will work.* **2** **tactics** [pl] the skilful arrangement and use of military forces in order to win a battle

tactical /ˈtæktɪkl/ *adj* **1** connected with the particular method you use to achieve sth: *I made a tactical error.* ♦ *tactical planning* **2** designed to bring a future advantage: *a tactical decision* ▶ **tactically** /-kli/ *adv*

tactless /ˈtæktləs/ *adj* saying and doing things that are likely to offend and upset other people: *It was rather tactless of you to ask her how old she was.* **OPP** **tactful** ▶ **tactlessly** *adv*

tadpole /ˈtædpəʊl/ *noun* [C] a young form of a frog (= a small animal that lives in or near water, with long back legs that it uses for jumping) with a black head and a long tail ➲ picture on **page P13**

tag¹ /tæg/ *noun* [C] **1** [in compounds] a small piece of card, cloth, etc. fastened to sth to give information about it: *How much is this dress? There isn't a* ***price tag*** *on it.* ➲ picture at **label** **2** = **question tag**

tag² /tæg/ *verb* [T] (**tagging**; **tagged**) to fasten a **tag** onto sb/sth

PHR V **tag along** to follow or go somewhere with sb, especially when you have not been invited

tail¹ /teɪl/ *noun*

➤OF ANIMAL, BIRD **1** [C] the part at the end of the body of an animal, bird, fish, etc: *The dog barked and wagged its tail.* ➲ picture on **page P12, page P13**

➤OF PLANE **2** [C] the back part of an aircraft, etc: *the tail wing*

➤JACKET **3** **tails** [pl] a man's formal coat that is short at the front but with a long, divided piece at the back, worn especially at weddings: *The men all wore top hat and tails.*

➤SIDE OF COIN **4** **tails** [U] the side of a coin that does not have the head of a person on it: *'We'll toss a coin to decide,' said my father.* ***'Heads or tails?'***

➤PERSON **5** [C] (*informal*) a person who is sent to follow sb secretly to get information about them: *The police have* ***put a tail on*** *him.*

IDM **make head or tail of sth** ➲ **head¹**

tail² /teɪl/ *verb* [T] to follow sb closely, especially to watch where they go

PHR V **tail away/off** (*especially BrE*) to become less or weaker

tailor¹ /ˈteɪlə(r)/ *noun* [C] a person whose job is to make clothes, especially for men

tailor² /ˈteɪlə(r)/ *verb* [T, usually passive] **1** **tailor sth to/for sb/sth** to make or design sth for a particular person or purpose: *programmes tailored to the needs of specific groups* **2** to make clothes: *a well-tailored coat*

ˌtailor-ˈmade *adj* **tailor-made (for sb/sth)** made for a particular person or purpose and therefore very suitable

tailpipe /ˈteɪlpaɪp/ (*AmE*) = **exhaust¹** (2)

taint /teɪnt/ *noun* [C, usually sing] (*formal*) the effect of sth bad or unpleasant that spoils the quality of sb/sth: *the taint of corruption.* ▶ **taint** *verb* [T, usually passive]: *Her reputation was tainted by the scandal.*

take /teɪk/ *verb* [T] (*pt* **took** /tʊk/; *pp* **taken** /ˈteɪkən/)

➤CARRY/MOVE **1** to carry or move sb/sth; to go with sb from one place to another: *Take your coat with you—it's cold.* ♦ *Could you take this letter home to your parents?* ♦ *The ambulance took him to hospital.* ♦ *I'm taking the children swimming this afternoon.* ♦ *Her energy and talent took her to the top of her profession.* ➲ picture at **bring**

➤IN YOUR HAND **2** to put your hand round sth and hold it (and move it towards you): *She held out the keys, and I took them.* ♦ *He took a sweater out of the drawer.* ♦ *She took my hand/me by the hand* (= held my hand).

➤REMOVE **3** to remove sth from a place or a person, often without permission: *Who's taken my pen?* ♦ *My name had been taken off the list.* ♦ *The burglars took all my jewellery.*

➤CONTROL **4** to capture a place by force; to get control of sb/sth: *The state will* ***take control of*** *the company.*

➤EAT/DRINK **5** to swallow sth: ***Take*** *two* ***tablets*** *four times a day.* ♦ *Do you* ***take sugar*** *in tea?*

➤WRITE DOWN **6** to write or record sth: *She* ***took notes*** *during the lecture.* ♦ *The police officer took my name and address.*

➤PHOTOGRAPH **7** to photograph sth: *I* ***took*** *some nice* ***photos*** *of the wedding.*

➤MEASUREMENT **8** to measure sth: *The doctor* ***took*** *my* ***temperature****/pulse/blood pressure.*

➤ACCEPT **9** to accept or receive sth: *If you* ***take*** *my* ***advice*** *you'll forget all about him.* ♦ *Do you take credit cards?* ♦ *What coins does the machine take?* ♦ *I'm not going to* ***take the blame*** *for the accident.* ♦ *She's not going to* ***take the job.*** ♦ *We took a room at the hotel for two nights.* **10** to understand sth or react to sth in a particular way: *She took what he said as a compliment.* ♦ *I wish you would* ***take*** *things more* ***seriously.***

➤DEAL WITH STH BAD **11** to be able to deal with sth difficult or unpleasant: *I can't take much more of this heat.* **SYN** **stand**

➤HAVE FEELING **12** to get a particular feeling from sth: *He* ***takes*** *great* ***pleasure in*** *his grandchildren.* ♦ *When she failed the exam she* ***took comfort from*** *the fact that it was only by a few marks.*

➤ACTION **13** used with nouns to say that sb is performing an action: ***Take a look*** *at this article* (= look at it). ♦ *We have to* ***take a decision*** (= decide).

➤NEED **14** to need sth/sb: *How long did the journey*

take? ♦ *It took a lot of courage to say that.* ♦ *It took three people to move the piano.*

➤SIZE **15** [not used in the continuous tenses] to have a certain size of shoes or clothes: *What size shoes do you take?*

➤CONTAIN **16** [not used in the continuous tenses] to have enough space for sb/sth: *How many passengers can this bus take?*

➤TEACH **17** **take sb (for sth)** to give lessons to sb: *Who takes you for History* (= who is your teacher)?

➤EXAM **18** to study a subject for an exam; to do an exam: *I'm taking the advanced exam this summer.*

➤TRANSPORT **19** to use a form of transport; to use a particular route: *I always* **take the train** *to York.* ♦ *Which road do you take to Lille?* ♦ *Take the second turning on the right.*

➤GRAMMAR **20** [not used in the continuous tenses] to have or need a word to go with it in a sentence or other structure: *The verb 'depend' takes the preposition 'on'.*

IDM **be taken with sb/sth** to find sb/sth attractive or interesting

I take it (that ...) (used to show that you understand sth from a situation, even though you have not been told) I suppose: *I take it that you're not coming?*

take it from me believe me

take a lot of/some doing to need a lot of work or effort

take a lot out of sb to make sb very tired ℹ For other idioms containing **take**, look at the entries for the nouns, adjectives, etc. For example, **take place** is at **place**.

PHR V **take sb aback** to surprise or shock sb

take after sb [not used in the continuous tenses] to look or behave like an older member of your family, especially a parent

take sth apart to separate sth into the different parts it is made of

take away (used in sums) less: *Six take away two is four (6–2 = 4).*

take sb/sth away (from sb) to remove sb/sth: *She took the scissors away from the child.*

take sth away **1** to cause a feeling, etc. to disappear: *These aspirins will take the pain away.* **2** (*AmE* **take sth out**) to buy cooked food at a restaurant, etc. and carry it out to eat somewhere else, for example at home ➲ *noun* **takeaway**

take sth back **1** to return sth to the place that you got it from: *I took the dress back because it didn't go with my shoes.* ➲ note at **shopping** **2** to admit that sth you said was wrong

take sth down **1** to remove a structure by separating it into the pieces it is made of: *They took the tent down and started the journey home.* **2** to write down sth that is said

take sb in **1** to invite sb who has no home to live with you: *Her parents were killed in a crash so she was taken in by her grandparents.* **2** to make sb believe sth that is not true: *I was completely taken in by her story.*

take sth in to understand what you see, hear or read: *There was too much in the museum to take in at one go.*

take off **1** (used about an aircraft) to leave the ground and start flying: *The plane took off an hour late.* OPP **land** **2** (used about an idea, a product, etc.) to become successful or popular very quickly or suddenly

take sb off to copy the way sb speaks or behaves in an amusing way

take sth off **1** to remove sth, especially clothes: *Come in and take your coat off.* OPP **put sth on** **2** to have the period of time mentioned as a holiday: *I'm going to take a week off.*

take sb on to start to employ sb: *The firm is taking on new staff.*

take sth on to accept a responsibility or decide to do sth: *He's taken on a lot of extra work.*

take sb out to go out with sb (for a social occasion): *I'm taking Angela out for a meal tonight.*

take sth out **1** to remove sth from inside a person's body: *He's having two teeth taken out.* **2** to obtain a service: *to take out a mortgage/loan*

take sth out (of sth) to remove sth from sth: *He took a notebook out of his pocket.* ♦ *I need to take some money out of the bank.*

take it out on sb to behave badly towards sb because you are angry or upset about sth, even though it is not this person's fault

take (sth) over to get control of sth or responsibility for sth: *The firm is being taken over by a large company.* ♦ *Who's going to take over as assistant when Tim leaves?*

take to sb/sth to start liking sb/sth or doing sth well

take to sth/doing sth to begin doing sth regularly as a habit

take sth up to start doing sth regularly (for example as a hobby): *I've taken up yoga recently.*

take up sth to use or fill an amount of time or space: *All her time is taken up looking after the new baby.* SYN **occupy**

take sb up on sth **1** to say that you disagree with sth that sb has just said, and ask them to explain it: *I must take you up on that last point.* **2** (*informal*) to accept an offer that sb has made: *'Come and stay with us any time.' 'We'll take you up on that!'*

take sth up with sb to ask or complain about sth: *I'll take the matter up with my MP.*

takeaway /ˈteɪkəweɪ/ (*AmE* **takeout; carryout**) *noun* [C] **1** a restaurant that sells food that you can eat somewhere else **2** the food that such a restaurant sells: *Let's have a takeaway.* ➲ note at **meal**

taken *past participle of* **take**

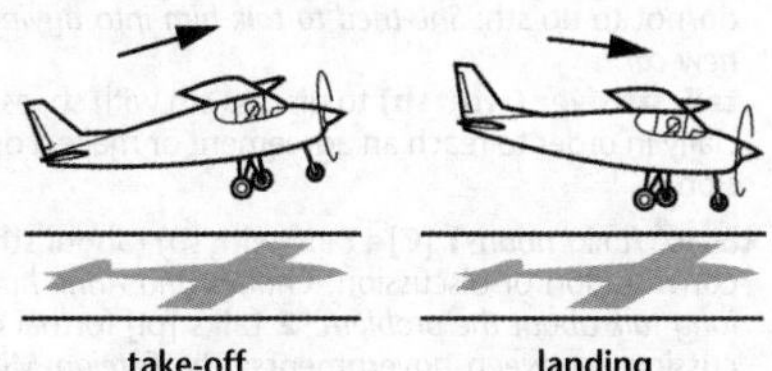

ˈ**take-off** *noun* [U,C] the moment when an aircraft leaves the ground and starts to fly: *The plane is ready for take-off.* OPP **landing**

takeout /ˈteɪkaʊt/ (*AmE*) = **takeaway**

takeover /ˈteɪkəʊvə(r)/ *noun* [C] the act of taking control of sth: *They made a takeover bid for the company.* ♦ *a military takeover of the government*

ˈ**take-up** *noun* [U,sing] the rate at which people accept sth that is offered or made available to them: *The take-up of foreign language courses has been disappointing.* ♦ *The take-up rate rose to 80%.*

takings /ˈteɪkɪŋz/ *noun* [pl] the amount of money that a shop, theatre, etc. gets from selling goods, tickets, etc.

talcum powder /ˈtælkəm paʊdə(r)/ (also **talc** /tælk/) *noun* [U] a soft powder which smells nice. People often put it on their skin after a bath.

tale /teɪl/ *noun* [C] **1** a story about events that are not real: *fairy tales* **2** a report or description of sb/sth that may not be true: *I've heard tales of people seeing ghosts in that house.*

talent /ˈtælənt/ *noun* [C,U] (a) **talent** (for sth) a natural skill or ability: *She has a talent for painting.* ♦ *His work shows great talent.* ♦ *a talent show* ▶ **talented** *adj*: *a talented musician*

⚷ **talk**[1] /tɔːk/ *verb* **1** [I] **talk (to/with sb) (about/of sb/sth)** to say things; to speak in order to give information or to express feelings, ideas, etc: *The baby is just starting to talk.* ♦ *I could hear them talking downstairs.* ♦ *Can I talk to you for a minute?* ♦ *Nasreen is not an easy person to talk to.* ♦ *We need to talk about the plans for the weekend.* ♦ *He's been talking of going to Australia for some time now.* ♦ *Dr Impey will be talking about Japanese Art in his lecture.* ➲ note at **speak** **2** [I,T] to discuss sth serious or important: *We can't go on like this. We need to talk.* ♦ *Could we* **talk business** *after dinner?* **3** [I] to discuss people's private lives: *His strange lifestyle and appearance started the local people talking.* **SYN** **gossip** **4** [I] to give information to sb, especially when you do not want to: *The police questioned him for hours but he refused to talk.*

IDM **know what you are talking about** ➲ **know**[1]
speak/talk of the devil ➲ **devil**
talk sense to say things that are correct or sensible: *He's the only politician who talks any sense.*
talk shop to talk about your work with the people you work with, outside working hours

PHR V **talk down to sb** to talk to sb as if they are less intelligent or important than you
talk sb into/out of doing sth to persuade sb to do/not to do sth: *She tried to talk him into buying a new car.*
talk sth over (with sb) to discuss sth with sb, especially in order to reach an agreement or make a decision

⚷ **talk**[2] /tɔːk/ *noun* **1** [C] **a talk (with sb) (about sth)** a conversation or discussion: *Charles and Anne had a long talk about the problem.* **2 talks** [pl] formal discussions between governments: *The Foreign Ministers of the two countries will meet for talks next week.* ♦ *arms/peace talks* **3** [C] **a talk (on sth)** a formal speech on a particular subject: *He's giving a talk on 'Our changing world'.* **SYN** **lecture** **4** [U] (*informal*) things that people say that are not based on facts or reality: *He says he's going to resign but it's just talk.* ➲ look at **small talk**

talkative /ˈtɔːkətɪv/ *adj* liking to talk a lot

⚷ **tall** /tɔːl/ *adj* (**taller**; **tallest**) **1** (used about people or things) of more than average height; not short: *a tall young man* ♦ *a tall tree/tower/chimney* ♦ *Nick is taller than his brother.* **OPP** **short** **2** used to describe the height of sb/sth: *Claire is five feet tall.* ♦ *How tall are you?* ➲ *noun* **height**

> **HELP** **Tall** or **high**? **Tall** and **high** have similar meanings. We use **tall** to describe the height of people, trees and other narrow objects: *He is six foot three inches tall.* ♦ *A tall oak tree stands in the garden.* ♦ *I saw the tall skyscrapers of Manhattan.* We use **high** to describe things that are not narrow: *high mountains* ♦ *The wall is two metres high.* and the distance of something from the ground: *a room with high ceilings*

talon /ˈtælən/ *noun* [C] a long sharp curved nail on the feet of some birds, used to catch other animals for food ➲ picture on **page P12**

tambourine /ˌtæmbəˈriːn/ *noun* [C] a musical instrument that has a round frame covered with plastic or skin, with small flat pieces of metal around the edge. To play it, you hit it or shake it with your hand. ➲ picture at **music**

tame[1] /teɪm/ *adj* (**tamer**; **tamest**) **1** (used about animals or birds) not wild or afraid of people: *The birds are so tame they will eat from your hand.* **2** boring; not interesting or exciting: *After the big city, you must find village life very tame.*

tame[2] /teɪm/ *verb* [T] to bring a wild animal under your control; to make sth easy to control

tamper /ˈtæmpə(r)/ *verb*
PHR V **tamper with sth** to make changes to sth without permission, especially in order to damage it

tampon /ˈtæmpɒn/ *noun* [C] a piece of cotton material that a woman puts inside her body to absorb the blood that she loses once a month ➲ look at **sanitary towel**

tan[1] /tæn/ *verb* [I,T] (**tanning**; **tanned**) (used about sb's skin) to become brown as a result of spending time in the sun: *Do you tan easily?* ▶ **tanned** *adj*: *You're looking very tanned—have you been on holiday?*

tan[2] /tæn/ *noun* **1** [U] a colour between yellow and brown **2** [C] = **suntan** ▶ **tan** *adj*

tandem /ˈtændəm/ *noun* [C] a bicycle with seats for two people, one behind the other
IDM **in tandem (with sb/sth)** working together with sth/sb else; happening at the same time as sth else

tangent /ˈtændʒənt/ *noun* [C] a straight line that touches a curve but does not cross it
IDM **go off at a tangent**; (*AmE*) **go off on a tangent** to suddenly start saying or doing sth that seems to have no connection with what has gone before

T

tangerine /ˌtændʒəˈriːn/ *noun* **1** [C] a fruit like a small sweet orange with a skin that is easy to take off **2** [U] a deep orange colour ▶ **tangerine** *adj*

tangible /ˈtændʒəbl/ *adj* that can be clearly seen to exist: *There are tangible benefits in the new system.* **OPP** **intangible**

tangle /ˈtæŋgl/ *noun* [C] a confused mass, especially of threads, hair, branches, etc. that cannot easily be separated from each other: *My hair's full of tangles.* ◆ *This string's* ***in a tangle.*** ▶ **tangled** *adj*: *The wool was all tangled up.*

tango /ˈtæŋgəʊ/ *noun* [C] (*pl* **tangos** /-gəʊz/) a fast South American dance with a strong beat, in which two people hold each other closely; a piece of music for this dance ▶ **tango** *verb* [I] (**tangoing**; **tangoes**; *pt, pp* **tangoed**)

🔑 **tank** /tæŋk/ *noun* [C] **1** a container for holding liquids or gas; the amount that a tank will hold: *a water/fuel/petrol/fish tank* ◆ *We drove there and back on one tank of petrol.* ➲ picture at **snorkel** **2** a large, heavy military vehicle covered with strong metal and armed with guns, that moves on special wheels

tanker /ˈtæŋkə(r)/ *noun* [C] a ship or lorry that carries oil, petrol, etc. in large amounts: *an oil tanker* ➲ picture on **page P6**

Tannoy™ /ˈtænɔɪ/ *noun* [C] a system used for giving spoken information in a public place: *They announced* ***over the Tannoy*** *that our flight was delayed.*

tantalizing (also **-ising**) /ˈtæntəlaɪzɪŋ/ *adj* making you want sth that you cannot have or do: *A tantalizing aroma of cooking was coming from the kitchen next door.* ▶ **tantalizingly** (also **-isingly**) *adv*

tantrum /ˈtæntrəm/ *noun* [C] a sudden explosion of anger, especially in a child

🔑 **tap**[1] /tæp/ *verb* (**tapping**; **tapped**) **1** [I,T] **tap (at/on sth)**; **tap sb/sth (on/with sth)** to touch or hit sb/sth quickly and lightly: *He tapped at the window.* ◆ *Their feet were tapping in time to the music.* ◆ *She tapped me on the shoulder.* **2** [I,T] **tap (into) sth** to make use of a source of energy, knowledge, etc. that already exists: *to tap the skills of young people* **3** [T] to fit a device to sb's telephone so that their calls can be listened to secretly: *She was convinced that the police had tapped her phone.*

🔑 **tap**[2] /tæp/ *noun* [C] **1** (*AmE* **faucet**) a type of handle that you turn to let water, gas, etc. out of a pipe or container: *Turn the hot/cold tap on/off.* ➲ picture at **plug** **2** a light hit with your hand or fingers: *a tap on the shoulder* **3** a device that is fitted to sb's telephone so that their calls can be listened to secretly: *a phone tap*

ˈ**tap dance** *noun* [C] a style of dancing in which you tap the rhythm of the music with your feet, wearing special shoes with pieces of metal on them ▶ ˈ**tap dance** *verb* [I] ▶ **tap-dancing** (also **tap**) *noun* [U]

🔑 **tape**[1] /teɪp/ *noun*

➤ FOR MUSIC **1** [U] a long thin band of plastic material used for recording sound, pictures or information: *I've got the whole concert* ***on tape*** (= recorded). **2** [C] a small flat plastic case containing tape for playing or recording music or sound: *a* ***blank tape*** (= a tape which is empty) ◆ *to rewind a tape*

➤ FOR STICKING **3** [U] a long narrow band of plastic, etc. with a sticky substance on one side that is used for sticking things together, covering electric wires, etc: *sticky/adhesive tape* ➲ look at **Sellotape™** ➲ picture at **roll**

➤ FOR TYING **4** [C,U] a narrow piece of cloth that is used for tying things together: *The papers were in a pile, bound with blue tape.* ➲ look at **red tape**

➤ IN RACE **5** [C] a piece of material stretched across a race track to mark where the race finishes: *the finishing tape*

tape[2] /teɪp/ *verb* [T] **1** to record sound, music, TV programmes, etc. using tape **2** **tape sth (up)** to fasten sth by sticking or tying sth with **tape**[1] (3)

ˈ**tape measure** (also ˈ**measuring tape**) *noun* [C] a long thin piece of plastic, cloth or metal with centimetres, etc. marked on it. It is used for measuring things. ➲ picture at **sewing**

ˈ**tape recorder** *noun* [C] a machine that is used for recording and playing sounds on tape

tapestry /ˈtæpəstri/ *noun* [C,U] (*pl* **tapestries**) a piece of heavy cloth with pictures or designs sewn on it in coloured thread

ˈ**tap water** *noun* [U] water that comes through pipes and out of taps, not water sold in bottles

tar /tɑː(r)/ *noun* [U] **1** a thick black sticky liquid that becomes hard when it is cold. **Tar** is obtained from coal and is used for making roads, etc. ➲ look at **Tarmac™** **2** a similar substance formed by burning **tobacco** (= the dried leaves used for making cigarettes): *low-tar cigarettes*

tarantula /təˈræntʃələ/ *noun* [C] a large spider covered with hair that lives in hot countries

🔑 **target**[1] /ˈtɑːgɪt/ *noun* [C] **1** a result that you try to achieve: *Our target is to finish the job by Friday.* ◆ *So far we're right* ***on target*** (= making the progress we expected). ◆ *a target area/audience/group* (= the particular area, audience, etc. that a product, programme, etc. is aimed at) **2** a person, place or thing that you try to hit when shooting or attacking: *They bombed military and civilian targets.* ◆ *Doors and windows are* ***an easy target*** *for burglars.* **3** a person or thing that people criticize, laugh at, etc: *The education system has been the target of heavy criticism.* **4** an object, often a round board with circles on it, that you try to hit in shooting practice: *to aim at/hit/miss a target*

target[2] /ˈtɑːgɪt/ *verb* [T, usually passive] **target sb/sth**; **target sth at/on sb/sth** to try to have an effect on a particular group of people; to try to attack sb/sth: *The advertising campaign is targeted at teenagers.*

tariff /ˈtærɪf/ *noun* [C] **1** a tax that has to be paid on goods coming into a country **2** a list of prices, especially in a hotel

Tarmac™ /ˈtɑːmæk/ *noun* **1** [U] a black material used for making the surfaces of roads ➲ look at **tar**

2 the tarmac [sing] an area covered with a Tarmac™ surface, especially at an airport

tarnish /ˈtɑːnɪʃ/ *verb* **1** [I,T] (used about metal, etc.) to become or to make sth less bright and shiny **2** [T] to spoil the good opinion people have of sb/sth

tarpaulin /tɑːˈpɔːlɪn/ *noun* [C,U] a piece of strong material that water cannot pass through, which is used for covering things to protect them from the rain

tart¹ /tɑːt/ *noun* **1** [C,U] an open **pie** (= a type of baked food) filled with sweet food such as fruit or jam **2** [C] (*BrE informal*) a woman who dresses or behaves in a way that people think is immoral

tart² /tɑːt/ *verb*
PHR V tart sb/sth up (*BrE informal*) to decorate and improve the appearance of sb/sth

tartan /ˈtɑːtn/ *noun* [U,C] **1** a traditional Scottish pattern of coloured squares and lines that cross each other **2** cloth made from wool with this pattern on it

task /tɑːsk/ *noun* [C] a piece of work that has to be done, especially an unpleasant or difficult one: *Your first task will be to type these letters.* ◆ *to perform/carry out/undertake a task*

tassel /ˈtæsl/ *noun* [C] a bunch of threads that are tied together at one end and hang from curtains, clothes, etc. as a decoration

taste¹ /teɪst/ *noun*
➤FLAVOUR **1** [C,U] the particular quality of different foods or drinks that allows you to recognize them when you put them in your mouth; flavour: *I don't like the taste of this coffee.* ◆ *a sweet/bitter/sour/salty taste*
➤SENSE **2** [U] the ability to recognize the flavour of food or drink: *I've got such a bad cold that I seem to have lost my sense of taste.*
➤SMALL QUANTITY **3** [C, usually sing] **a taste (of sth)** a small amount of sth to eat or drink that you have in order to see what it is like: *Have a taste of this cheese to see if you like it.*
➤SHORT EXPERIENCE **4** [sing] a short experience of sth: *That was my* ***first taste*** *of success.*
➤RECOGNIZING QUALITY **5** [U] the ability to decide if things are suitable, of good quality, etc: *He has excellent* ***taste in*** *music.*
➤WHAT YOU LIKE **6** [sing] **a taste (for sth)** what a person likes or prefers: *She has developed a taste for modern art.*
IDM (be) in bad, poor, etc. taste (used about sb's behaviour) (to be) unpleasant and not suitable: *Some of his comments were in very bad taste.*

taste² /teɪst/ *verb* **1** [I] **taste (of sth)** to have a particular flavour: *The pudding tasted of oranges.* ◆ *to taste sour/sweet/delicious* **2** [T] to notice or recognize the flavour of food or drink: *Can you taste the garlic in this soup?* ➲ note at **smell¹** **3** [T] to try a small amount of food and drink; to test the flavour of sth: *Can I taste a piece of that cheese to see what it's like?*

tasteful /ˈteɪstfl/ *adj* (used especially about clothes, furniture, decorations, etc.) attractive and well chosen **OPP tasteless** ▶ **tastefully** /-fəli/ *adv*

tasteless /ˈteɪstləs/ *adj* **1** having little or no flavour: *This sauce is rather tasteless.* **OPP tasty** **2** likely to offend people: *His joke about the funeral was particularly tasteless.* **3** (used especially about clothes, furniture, decorations, etc.) not attractive; not well chosen **OPP tasteful**

tasty /ˈteɪsti/ *adj* (**tastier; tastiest**) having a good flavour: *spaghetti with a tasty sauce*

tattered /ˈtætəd/ *adj* old and torn; in bad condition: *a tattered coat*

tatters /ˈtætəz/ *noun*
IDM in tatters badly torn or damaged: *Her dress was in tatters.*

tattoo /təˈtuː/ *noun* [C] (*pl* **tattoos**) a picture or pattern that is marked permanently with ink on sb's skin ▶ **tattoo** *verb* [T] (**tattooing; tattoos;** *pt, pp* **tattooed**): *She had a butterfly tattooed on her back.*

tatty /ˈtæti/ *adj* (**tattier; tattiest**) (*informal*) in bad condition: *tatty old clothes*

taught *past tense, past participle of* **teach**

taunt /tɔːnt/ *verb* [T] to try to make sb angry or upset by saying unpleasant or cruel things ▶ **taunt** *noun* [C]

Taurus /ˈtɔːrəs/ *noun* [C,U] the 2nd sign of the **zodiac** (= 12 signs which represent the positions of the sun, moon and planets), the Bull; a person born under this sign: *I'm a Taurus.* ➲ picture at **zodiac**

taut /tɔːt/ *adj* (used about rope, wire, etc.) stretched very tight; not loose

tavern /ˈtævən/ *noun* [C] (*old-fashioned*) a pub or bar

tax /tæks/ *noun* [C,U] **(a) tax (on sth)** the money that you have to pay to the government so that it can provide public services: *income tax* ◆ *There used to be a tax on windows.* ▶ **tax** *verb* [T, often passive]: *Petrol is heavily taxed.*

taxable /ˈtæksəbl/ *adj* on which you have to pay tax: *taxable income*

taxation /tækˈseɪʃn/ *noun* [U] **1** the amount of money that people have to pay in tax: *to increase/reduce taxation* ◆ *high/low taxation* **2** the system by which a government takes money from people so that it can pay for public services: *direct/indirect taxation*

tax-free *adj* on which you do not have to pay tax: *a tax-free allowance*

taxi¹ /ˈtæksi/ (also **ˈtaxicab** /ˈtæksikab/ *especially AmE* **cab**) *noun* [C] (*pl* **taxis**) a car with a driver whose job is to take you somewhere in exchange for money: *Shall we go by bus or* ***get/take a taxi****?* ➲ picture on **page P7**

MORE You **hail** a taxi to stop it so that you can get in. The amount of money that you have to pay (your **fare**) is shown on a **meter**.

taxi² /ˈtæksi/ (taxiing; taxies; *pt, pp* taxied) *verb* [I] (used about an aircraft) to move slowly along the ground before or after flying

taxing /ˈtæksɪŋ/ *adj* difficult; needing a lot of effort: *a taxing exam*

ˈtaxi rank *noun* [C] a place where taxis park while they are waiting for customers

taxpayer /ˈtækspeɪə(r)/ *noun* [C] a person who pays tax to the government, especially on the money that they earn

TB /ˌtiː ˈbiː/ *abbr* = **tuberculosis**

tbsp *abbr* = **tablespoon**(2): *Add 3 tbsp sugar.*

tea /tiː/ *noun* **1** [U] the dried leaves of the tea plant: *a packet of tea* **2** [C,U] a hot drink made by pouring boiling water onto the dried leaves of the tea plant or of some other plants; a cup of this drink: *a cup/pot of tea* ◆ *weak/strong tea* ◆ *herbal/mint/camomile tea* ◆ *Three teas and one coffee, please.* ➲ picture on **page P16** **3** [C,U] (*especially BrE*) a small afternoon meal of **sandwiches** (= two slices of bread with food between them), cakes, etc. and tea to drink, or a cooked meal eaten at 5 or 6 o'clock: *The kids have their tea as soon as they get home from school.* ➲ note at **meal**
IDM **not sb's cup of tea** ➲ **cup¹**

ˈtea bag *noun* [C] a small paper bag with tea leaves in it, that you use for making tea ➲ picture on **page P10**

teach /tiːtʃ/ *verb* (*pt, pp* taught /tɔːt/) **1** [I,T] **teach (sb/sth/to do sth)**; **teach sth (to sb)** to give sb lessons or instructions so that they know how to do sth: *My mother taught me to play the piano.* ◆ *He is teaching his son how to ride a bike.* ◆ *Jeremy teaches English to foreign students.* ◆ *I teach in a primary school.* **2** [T] to make sb believe sth or behave in a certain way: *The story teaches us that history often repeats itself.* ◆ *My parents taught me always to tell the truth.* **3** [T] to make sb have a bad experience so that they are careful not to do the thing that caused it again: *Lost all your money? That'll teach you to gamble!* ◆ *The accident* ***taught me a lesson*** *I'll never forget.*

teacher /ˈtiːtʃə(r)/ *noun* [C] a person whose job is to teach, especially in a school or college: *He's a teacher at a primary school.* ◆ *a chemistry/music teacher* ◆ *She's a* ***head teacher*** (= the teacher in charge of a school) *who knows the name of every student.* ➲ note at **school** ➲ look at **head¹**(5) ➲ picture on **page P2**

teaching /ˈtiːtʃɪŋ/ *noun* **1** [U] the work of a teacher: *My son went into teaching.* ◆ *teaching methods* **2** [C, usually pl] ideas and beliefs that are taught by sb/sth: *the teachings of Gandhi*

ˈtea cloth = **tea towel**

teacup /ˈtiːkʌp/ *noun* [C] a cup that you drink tea from

teak /tiːk/ *noun* [U] the strong hard wood of a tall Asian tree, used for making furniture

ˈtea leaves *noun* [pl] the small leaves that are left in a cup after you have drunk the tea

team¹ /tiːm/ *noun* [C, with sing or pl verb] **1** a group of people who play a sport or game together against another group: *a football team* ◆ *Are you* ***in/on the team?*** **2** a group of people who work together: *a team of doctors*

> **GRAMMAR** In the singular, **team** is used with a singular or plural verb: *The team play/plays two matches every week.*

team² /tiːm/ *verb*
PHR V **team up (with sb)** to join sb in order to do sth together: *I teamed up with Irena to plan the project.*

teammate /ˈtiːmmeɪt/ *noun* [C] a member of the same team or group as yourself

teamwork /ˈtiːmwɜːk/ *noun* [U] the ability of people to work together: *Teamwork is a key feature of the training programme.*

teapot /ˈtiːpɒt/ *noun* [C] a container that you use for making tea in and for serving it

teapot

tear¹ /tɪə(r)/ *noun* [C, usually pl] a drop of water that comes from your eye when you are crying, etc: *I was* ***in tears*** (= crying) *at the end of the film.* ◆ *The little girl* ***burst into tears*** (= suddenly started to cry).
IDM **shed tears** ➲ **shed²**

tear² /teə(r)/ *verb* (*pt* tore /tɔː(r)/; *pp* torn /tɔːn/) **1** [T,I] to damage sth by pulling it apart or into pieces; to become damaged in this way: *I tore my shirt on that nail.* ◆ *She tore the letter in half.* ◆ *I tore a page out of my notebook.* ◆ *This material doesn't tear easily.* **SYN** **rip** **2** [T] to make a hole in sth by force: *The explosion tore a hole in the wall.* **SYN** **rip** **3** [T] to remove sth by pulling violently and quickly: *Paul tore the poster down from the wall.* ◆ *He tore the bag out of her hands.* **SYN** **rip** **4** [I] **tear along, up, down, past, etc.** to move very quickly in a particular direction: *An ambulance went tearing past.*
IDM **wear and tear** ➲ **wear²**
PHR V **tear sth apart 1** to pull sth violently into pieces: *The bird was torn apart by the two dogs.* **2** to destroy sth completely: *The country has been torn apart by the war.*
tear yourself away (from sb/sth) to make yourself leave sb/sth or stop doing sth
be torn between A and B to find it difficult to choose between two things or people
tear sth down to pull or knock down a building, wall, etc: *They tore down the old houses and built a shopping centre.*
tear sth up to pull sth into pieces, especially sth made of paper: *'I hate this photograph,' she said, tearing it up.*
▸ **tear** *noun* [C]: *You've got a tear in the back of your trousers.*

tearful /ˈtɪəfl/ *adj* crying or nearly crying

T

tear gas /ˈtɪə gæs/ *noun* [U] a type of gas that hurts the eyes and throat, and is used by the police, etc. to control large groups of people

tease /tiːz/ *verb* [I,T] to laugh at sb either in a friendly way or in order to upset them: *Don't pay any attention to those boys. They're only teasing.* ♦ *They teased her about being fat.*

teaspoon /ˈtiːspuːn/ *noun* [C] **1** a small spoon used for putting sugar in tea, coffee, etc. **2** (also **teaspoonful** /-fʊl/) (*abbr* **tsp**) the amount that a **teaspoon** can hold ➲ picture at **spoon**

teat /tiːt/ *noun* [C] **1** (*AmE* **nipple**) the soft rubber part at the end of a baby's bottle **2** one of the parts of a female animal's body that the young animals suck in order to get milk ➲ look at **nipple**

ˈ**tea towel** (also ˈ**tea cloth**) (*BrE*) *noun* [C] a small piece of cloth that is used for drying plates, knives, forks, etc.

technical /ˈteknɪkl/ *adj* **1** connected with the practical use of machines, methods, etc. in science and industry: *The train was delayed due to a technical problem.* ♦ *All our software licences include **technical support**.* **2** connected with the skills involved in a particular activity or subject: *All the Brazilian team play with great technical skill.*

technicality /ˌteknɪˈkæləti/ *noun* [C] (*pl* **technicalities**) one of the details of a particular subject or activity

technically /ˈteknɪkli/ *adv* **1** according to the exact meaning, facts, etc: *Technically, you should pay by August 1st, but it doesn't matter if it's a few days late.* **2** used about sb's practical ability in a particular activity: *He's a technically brilliant dancer.* **3** in a way that involves detailed knowledge of the machines, etc. that are used in industry or science: *The country is technically not very advanced.*

technician /tekˈnɪʃn/ *noun* [C] a person whose work involves practical skills, especially in industry or science: *a laboratory technician*

technique /tekˈniːk/ *noun* **1** [C] a particular way of doing sth: *new techniques for teaching languages* ♦ *marketing/management techniques* **2** [U] the practical skill that sb has in a particular activity: *He's a naturally talented runner, but he needs to work on his technique.*

technology /tekˈnɒlədʒi/ *noun* [C,U] (*pl* **technologies**) the scientific knowledge and/or equipment that is needed for a particular industry, etc: *developments in computer technology* ▸ **technological** /ˌteknəˈlɒdʒɪkl/ *adj*: *technological developments* ▸ **technologist** /tekˈnɒlədʒɪst/ *noun* [C]: *Technologists are developing a computer that can perform surgery.*

tectonic /tekˈtɒnɪk/ *adj* [only *before* a noun] connected with the structure of the earth's surface

teddy bear /ˈtedi beə(r)/ (also **teddy**; *pl* **teddies**) *noun* [C] a soft toy that looks like a bear (= a large brown wild animal)

tedious /ˈtiːdiəs/ *adj* boring and lasting for a long time: *a tedious train journey* **SYN** **boring**

tee /tiː/ *noun* [C] (in the game of **golf**) a flat area where a player stands to hit the ball

teem /tiːm/ *verb* [I] **teem with sth** (used about a place) to have a lot of people or things moving about in it: *The streets were teeming with people.*

teenage /ˈtiːneɪdʒ/ *adj* [only *before* a noun] **1** between 13 and 19 years old: *teenage children* **2** typical of or suitable for people between 13 and 19 years old: *teenage magazines/fashion*

teenager /ˈtiːneɪdʒə(r)/ *noun* [C] a person aged between 13 and 19 years old: *The group's music is very popular with teenagers.* ➲ look at **adolescent**

teens /tiːnz/ *noun* [pl] the period of sb's life between the ages of 13 and 19: *to be **in your** early/late **teens***

ˈ**tee shirt** = **T-shirt**

teeth *plural* of **tooth**

teethe /tiːð/ *verb* [I] [usually in the *-ing* forms] (used about a baby) to start growing its first teeth

ˈ**teething troubles** (also ˈ**teething problems**) *noun* [pl] the problems that can develop when a person, system, etc. is new: *We've just installed this new software and are having a few teething troubles with it.*

teetotal /ˌtiːˈtəʊtl/ *adj* [not before a noun] (used about a person) never drinking alcohol ▸ **teetotaller** (*AmE* **teetotaler**) *noun* [C] ➲ look at **alcoholic**

TEFL /ˈtefl/ *abbr* **Teaching English as a Foreign Language**

tel. (also Tel.) *abbr* **telephone** (number): *tel. 01865 56767*

telecommunications /ˌtelikəˌmjuːnɪˈkeɪʃnz/ *noun* [pl] the technology of sending signals, images and messages over long distances by radio, telephone, TV, etc.

telegram /ˈtelɪgræm/ *noun* [C] (in the past) a message that is sent by a system that uses electrical signals and that is then printed and given to sb

telegraph /ˈtelɪgrɑːf/ *noun* [U] a method of sending messages over long distances, using wires that carry electrical signals

ˈ**telegraph pole** *noun* [C] a tall wooden pole that is used for supporting telephone wires

telemarketing /ˈtelimɑːkɪtɪŋ/ = **telesales**

telepathy /təˈlepəθi/ *noun* [U] the communication of thoughts between people's minds without using speech, writing or other normal methods

telephone /ˈtelɪfəʊn/ (also *informal* **phone**) *noun* **1** [U] an electrical system for talking to sb in another place by speaking into a special piece of equipment: *Can I contact you **by telephone**?* ♦ *to **make a telephone call*** ♦ *What's your **telephone number**?* **2** [C] the piece of equipment that you use when you talk to sb by telephone: *Could I use your telephone?* ♦ *Where's the nearest public telephone?*

HELP It is more common to use **phone** rather than **telephone**, especially when you are speaking.

IDM **on the phone/telephone** ➲ **phone** ➲ note at **mobile phone**

▸ **telephone** (also **phone**) *verb* [I,T]: *He telephoned to say he'd be late.*

TOPIC

Using the telephone

When you **call** somebody or **phone** somebody (NOT *to* somebody), his/her phone **rings** and he/she **answers** it. Sometimes the phone is **engaged** (= he/she is already talking to somebody on it) or there is **no answer**. You might need to **leave a message**, either on an **answering machine**, or with somebody else: *Could you please ask her to call me back?* Introduce yourself by saying **'It's ...'** or **'This is ...'** (NOT *'Here is ...'*). If you phone somebody by mistake you can say, 'I'm sorry, I've **dialled** the **wrong number**.' The number that you dial before the telephone number if you are telephoning a different area or country is called the **code**: *'What's the code for Spain?'* When you finish speaking you **put the phone down/hang up**. You can use a telephone line to send a copy of a letter, etc. using a **fax machine**.

ˈtelephone box (also ˈ**phone box**; ˈ**call box**) *noun* [C] a small covered place in a street, etc. that contains a telephone for public use

ˈtelephone directory (also ˈ**phone book**) *noun* [C] a book or website that gives a list of the names, addresses and telephone numbers of the people in a particular area

ˈtelephone exchange (also **exchange**) *noun* [C] a place belonging to a telephone company where telephone lines are connected to each other

telesales /ˈteliseɪlz/ (also **telemarketing**) *noun* [U] a method of selling things by telephone: *He works in telesales.*

telescope /ˈtelɪskəʊp/ *noun* [C] an instrument in the shape of a tube with **lenses** (= special pieces of glass) inside it. You look through it to make things that are far away appear bigger and nearer. ➲ picture at **binoculars**

televise /ˈtelɪvaɪz/ *verb* [T] to show sth on TV: *a televised concert*

⚷ **television** /ˈtelɪvɪʒn/ (also **TV**) *noun* **1** (also ˈ**television set**) (*BrE informal* **telly**) [C] a piece of electrical equipment with a screen on which you can watch programmes with moving pictures and sounds: *to switch/turn the television on/off* ♦ *a plasma/flat-screen television* ➲ picture on **page P8** **2** (*BrE informal* **telly**) [U] the programmes that are shown on a television set: *Paul's watching television.* **3** [U] the system, process or business of sending out television programmes: *a television presenter/series/documentary* ♦ *cable/satellite/digital television* ♦ *She works in television.*

IDM **on television** being shown by television; appearing in a television programme: *What's on television tonight?* ➲ look at **media**

TOPIC

Television

If you have **digital**, **cable** or **satellite TV**, you can watch **programmes** on lots of different **channels**. You use the **remote control** to change channels without having to leave your seat. **Independent** TV channels have a lot of **commercials/adverts** (= advertisements). They **broadcast** programmes that get good **ratings** (= have a lot of viewers). These include **dramas**, **quiz programmes** and **soap operas**. A TV **serial** has a number of **episodes** (= parts) which tell one story over a period of time.

⚷ **tell** /tel/ *verb* (*pt, pp* **told** /təʊld/)

▸GIVE INFORMATION **1** [T] **tell sb (sth/that ...)**; **tell sb (about sth)**; **tell sth to sb** to give information to sb by speaking or writing: *She told me her address but I've forgotten it.* ♦ *He wrote to tell me that his mother had died.* ♦ *Tell us about your holiday.* ♦ *to* ***tell the truth/a lie*** ♦ *to* ***tell a story*** ♦ *Excuse me, could you tell me where the station is?* ♦ *He tells that story to everyone he sees.* ➲ note at **say** **2** [T] (used about a thing) to give information to sb: *This book will tell you all you need to know.*

▸SECRET **3** [I] to not keep a secret: *Promise you won't tell!*

▸ORDER **4** [T] **tell sb to do sth** to order or advise sb to do sth: *The policewoman told us to get out of the car.*

▸KNOW **5** [I,T] to know, see or judge (sth) correctly: *'What do you think Jenny will do next?'* ***'It's hard to tell.'*** ♦ *I could tell that he had enjoyed the evening.* ♦ ***You can never tell*** *what he's going to say next.* ♦ *I can't* ***tell the difference between*** *Dan's sisters.*

▸HAVE EFFECT **6** [I] **tell (on sb/sth)** to have a noticeable effect: *I can't run as fast as I could—my age is beginning to tell!*

▸SEE DIFFERENCE **7** **tell A and B apart**; **tell A from B** to see the difference between one thing or person and another: *It's very difficult to tell Tom and James apart.* ♦ *Can you tell Tom from his twin brother?*

IDM **all told** with everyone or everything counted and included

(I'll) tell you what (*informal*) used to introduce a suggestion: *I'll tell you what—let's ask Diane to take us.*

I told you so (*informal*) I warned you that this would happen: *'I missed the bus.' 'I told you so. I said you needed to leave earlier.'*

tell the time to read the time from a clock or watch

PHR V **tell sb off (for sth/for doing sth)** to speak to sb angrily because they have done sth wrong: *The teacher told me off for not doing my homework.*

tell on sb to tell a parent, teacher, etc. about sth bad that sb has done

telling /ˈtelɪŋ/ *adj* **1** having a great effect: *That's quite a telling argument.* **2** showing, without intending to, what sb/sth is really like: *The number of homeless people is a telling comment on today's society.*

telltale /ˈtelteɪl/ *adj* [only *before* a noun] giving information about sth secret or private: *He said he*

T

was fine, but there were telltale signs of worry on his face.

telly /ˈteli/ *noun* (*pl* **tellies**) (*BrE informal*) = **television**

temp¹ /temp/ *noun* [C] (*informal*) a temporary employee, especially in an office, who works somewhere for a short period of time when sb else is ill or on holiday ▶ **temp** *verb* [I]

temp² (also **temp.**) *abbr* = **temperature**: *temp 15°C*

temper /ˈtempə(r)/ *noun* **1** [C,U] if you have a **temper**, you get angry very easily: *Be careful of Paul. He's got quite a temper!* ◆ *You must learn to control your temper.* **2** [C] the way you are feeling at a particular time: *It's no use talking to him when he's* ***in a bad temper.*** **SYN** **mood**

IDM **in a temper** feeling very angry and not controlling your behaviour

keep/lose your temper to stay calm/to become angry ➲ look at **bad-tempered**

temperament /ˈtemprəmənt/ *noun* [C,U] a person's character, especially as it affects the way they behave and feel: *to have an artistic/a fiery/a calm temperament* **SYN** **disposition**

temperamental /ˌtemprəˈmentl/ *adj* often and suddenly changing the way you behave or feel: *a temperamental character*

temperate /ˈtempərət/ *adj* (used about a climate) not very hot and not very cold

temperature /ˈtemprətʃə(r)/ *noun* (*abbr* **temp**) **1** [C,U] how hot or cold sth is: *Heat the oven to a temperature of 200°C.* ◆ *a high/low temperature* ◆ *an increase in temperature* ➲ note at **cold** **2** [C] how hot or cold sb's body is: *to take somebody's temperature* (= measure the temperature of sb's body)

IDM **have a temperature** to be hotter than normal because you are ill

> **MORE** In American English you can *take sb's temperature*, but in the other examples the word **fever** is used.

➲ look at **fever** ➲ note at **ill**

tempest /ˈtempɪst/ *noun* [C] (*formal*) a violent storm

temple /ˈtempl/ *noun* [C] **1** a building where people worship: *a Buddhist/Hindu temple* **2** one of the flat parts on each side of your head, at the same level as your eyes and higher ➲ picture at **body**

tempo /ˈtempəʊ/ *noun* (*pl* **tempos** /ˈtempəʊz/) **1** [C,U] the speed of a piece of music: *a fast/slow tempo* **2** [sing,U] the speed of an activity or event

temporary /ˈtemprəri/ *adj* lasting for a short time: *a temporary job* ◆ *This arrangement is only temporary.* **OPP** **permanent** ▶ **temporarily** /ˈtemprərəli/ *adv*

tempt /tempt/ *verb* [T] **tempt sb (into sth/into doing sth); tempt sb (to do sth)** to try to persuade or attract sb to do sth, even if it is wrong: *His dream of riches had tempted him into a life of crime.* ◆ *She was tempted to stay in bed all day.*

temptation /tempˈteɪʃn/ *noun* **1** [U] a feeling that you want to do sth, even if you know that it is wrong: *I managed to* ***resist the temptation*** *to tell him what I really thought.* ◆ *She wanted a cream cake badly, but didn't* ***give in to temptation.*** **2** [C] a thing that attracts you to do sth wrong or silly: *All that money is certainly a big temptation.*

tempting /ˈtemptɪŋ/ *adj* attractive in a way that makes you want to do or have sth: *a tempting offer*

ten /ten/ *number* 10 ➲ note at **six**

tenacious /təˈneɪʃəs/ *adj* (*formal*) not likely to give up or let sth go; determined ▶ **tenacity** /təˈnæsəti/ *noun* [U]

tenancy /ˈtenənsi/ *noun* [C,U] (*pl* **tenancies**) the use of a room, flat, building or piece of land, for which you pay rent to the owner: *a six-month tenancy* ◆ *It says in the tenancy agreement that you can't keep pets.*

tenant /ˈtenənt/ *noun* [C] a person who pays rent to the owner of a room, flat, building or piece of land so that they can live in it or use it ➲ look at **landlord**

tend /tend/ *verb* **1** [I] **tend to do sth** to usually do or be sth: *Women tend to live longer than men.* ◆ *There tends to be a lot of heavy traffic on that road.* ◆ *My brother tends to talk a lot when he's nervous.* **2** [I] used for giving your opinion in a polite way: *I* ***tend to think*** *that we shouldn't interfere.* **3** [I,T] (*formal*) **tend (to) sb/sth** to look after sb/sth: *Paramedics tended (to) the injured.*

tendency /ˈtendənsi/ *noun* [C] (*pl* **tendencies**) a **tendency (to do sth/towards sth)** something that a person or thing usually does; a way of behaving: *They both* ***have a tendency*** *to be late for appointments.* ◆ *The dog began to show vicious tendencies.* ◆ *She seems to have a tendency towards depression.*

tender¹ /ˈtendə(r)/ *adj* (**tenderer**; **tenderest**) [**More tender** and **most tender** are also common.] **1** kind and loving: *tender words/looks/kisses* **2** (used about food) soft and easy to cut or bite: *The meat should be nice and tender.* **OPP** **tough** **3** (used about a part of the body) painful when you touch it

IDM **at a tender age; at the tender age of …** when still young and without much experience: *She went to live in London at the tender age of 15.*

▶ **tenderly** *adv*

▶ **tenderness** *noun* [U]

tender² /ˈtendə(r)/ *verb* [I,T] (*formal*) to offer or give sth formally: *After the scandal the Foreign Minister was forced to tender her resignation.* ◆ *Five different companies tendered for the building contract* (= stated a price for doing the work). ▶ **tender** (*especially AmE* **bid**) *noun* [C]: *Several firms submitted a tender for the catering contract.*

tendon /ˈtendən/ *noun* [C] a strong, thin part inside the body that joins a muscle to a bone ➲ look at **ligament**

tenement /ˈtenəmənt/ *noun* [C] a large building that is divided into small flats, especially in a poor area of a city

tenner /ˈtenə(r)/ *noun* [C] (*BrE informal*) £10 or a ten-pound note: *You can have it for a tenner.*

tennis /ˈtenɪs/ *noun* [U] a game for two or four players who hit a ball over a net using a **racket** (= a piece of equipment that is held in the hand): *Let's play tennis.* ♦ *to have a game of tennis* ♦ *a tennis match* ♦ *a tennis court* ➲ note at **sport** ➲ picture on **page P4**

> **MORE** In tennis you can play **singles** (a game between two people) or **doubles** (a game between two teams of two people).

tenor /ˈtenə(r)/ *noun* [C] a fairly high singing voice for a man; a man with this voice: *José Carreras is a famous tenor.*

> **MORE** Tenor is between **alto** and **baritone**.

▶ **tenor** *adj* [only *before* a noun]: *a tenor saxophone/trombone*

tenpin bowling /ˌtenpɪn ˈbəʊlɪŋ/ *noun* [U] a game in which you roll a heavy ball towards ten **tenpins** (= objects shaped like bottles) and try to knock them down ➲ picture on **page P3**

tense[1] /tens/ *adj* **1** (used about a person) not able to relax because you are worried or nervous: *She looked pale and tense.* **2** (used about an atmosphere or a situation) in which people feel worried and not relaxed **3** (used about a muscle or a part of the body) tight; not relaxed

tense[2] /tens/ *noun* [C,U] a form of a verb that shows if sth happens in the past, present or future

> EXAM TIP
>
> **Irregular verb forms**
>
> Remember that the dictionary tells you when the past tense and past participle of a verb are irregular. There is a list in the back of the dictionary that you can work through, learning a few each day before the exam.

ℹ For more information about verb tenses, look at the **Reference Section** at the back of this dictionary.

tense[3] /tens/ *verb* [I,T] **tense (up)** to have muscles that have become hard and not relaxed

⚷ **tension** /ˈtenʃn/ *noun* **1** [C,U] bad feeling and lack of trust between people, countries, etc: *There are signs of growing tensions between the two countries.* **2** [U] the condition of not being able to relax because you are worried or nervous: *I could hear the tension in her voice as she spoke.* **3** [U] (used about a rope, muscle, etc.) the state of being stretched tight; how tightly sth is stretched: *The massage relieved the tension in my neck.*

⚷ **tent** /tent/ *noun* [C] a small structure made of cloth that is held up by poles and ropes. You use a tent to sleep in when you go camping: *to put up/take down a tent* ➲ picture at **camping**

tentacle /ˈtentəkl/ *noun* [C] one of the long thin soft parts like legs that some sea animals have: *An octopus has eight tentacles.* ➲ picture at **octopus**

tentative /ˈtentətɪv/ *adj* **1** (used about plans, etc.) uncertain; not definite **2** (used about a person or their behaviour) not confident about what you are saying or doing: *a tentative smile/suggestion* ▶ **tentatively** *adv*

tenterhooks /ˈtentəhʊks/ *noun*
IDM (be) on tenterhooks (to be) in a very nervous or excited state because you are waiting to find out what is going to happen

⚷ **tenth**[1] /tenθ/ *ordinal number* 10th ➲ note at **sixth**

⚷ **tenth**[2] /tenθ/ *noun* [C] $\frac{1}{10}$; one of ten equal parts of sth

ˈ**tent peg** = **peg**[1] (2)

tenuous /ˈtenjuəs/ *adj* very weak or uncertain: *The connection between Joe's story and what actually happened was tenuous.*

tenure /ˈtenjə(r)/ *noun* [U] a legal right to live in a place, hold a job, use land, etc. for a certain time

tepid /ˈtepɪd/ *adj* (used about liquids) only slightly warm

⚷ **term**[1] /tɜːm/ *noun* **1** [C] a word or group of words with a particular meaning: *What exactly do you mean by the term 'racist'?* ♦ *a technical term in computing* **2 terms** [pl] **in terms of ...; in ... terms** used for showing which particular way you are thinking about sth or from which point of view: *The flat would be ideal in terms of size, but it is very expensive.* ♦ *I'll explain in simple terms.* **3 terms** [pl] the conditions of an agreement: ***Under the terms of** the contract you must give a week's notice.* ♦ *Both sides agreed to the peace terms.* **4** [C] a period of time that the school or university year is divided into: *the autumn/spring/summer term* ♦ *an end-of-term test* ➲ look at **semester** **5** [C] a period of time for which sth lasts: *He faces a prison term of 25 years.* ♦ *The US President is now in his second term of office.*
IDM be on equal terms (with sb) ➲ **equal**[1]
be on good, friendly, etc. terms (with sb) to have a friendly relationship with sb
be on speaking terms (with sb) ➲ **speak**
come to terms with sth to accept sth unpleasant or difficult
in the long/short term over a long/short period of time in the future

term[2] /tɜːm/ *verb* [T] to describe sb/sth by using a particular word or expression: *the period of history that is often termed the 'Dark Ages'*

terminal[1] /ˈtɜːmɪnl/ *noun* [C] **1** a large railway station, bus station or building at an airport where journeys begin and end: *the bus terminal* ♦ *Which terminal are you flying from?* **2** the computer that one person uses for getting information from a central computer or for putting information into it

terminal[2] /ˈtɜːmɪnl/ *adj* (used about an illness) slowly causing death: *terminal cancer* ▶ **terminally** /-nəli/ *adv*: *a terminally ill patient*

terminate /ˈtɜːmɪneɪt/ *verb* [I,T] (*formal*) to end or to make sth end: *This train terminates at London*

T

Victoria. ♦ *to terminate a contract/an agreement* ▸ **termination** /ˌtɜːmɪˈneɪʃn/ *noun* [U]

terminology /ˌtɜːmɪˈnɒlədʒi/ *noun* [U] the special words and expressions that are used in a particular profession, subject or activity

terminus /ˈtɜːmɪnəs/ *noun* [C] the last stop or station at the end of a bus route or railway line

termite /ˈtɜːmaɪt/ *noun* [C] an insect that lives in hot countries and does a lot of damage by eating the wood of trees and buildings

terrace /ˈterəs/ *noun* **1** (*BrE*) [C] a line of similar houses that are all joined together **2** [C] a flat area of stone next to a restaurant or large house where people can have meals, sit in the sun, etc. ➲ look at **patio, veranda 3 terraces** [pl] the wide steps that people stand on to watch a football match **4** [C, usually pl] one of a series of steps that are cut into the side of a hill so that crops can be grown there

terraced /ˈterəst/ *adj* **1** (*BrE*) (used about a house) forming part of a line of similar houses that are all joined together ➲ picture on **page P9 2** (used about a hill) having steps cut out of it so that crops can be grown there

terrain /təˈreɪn/ *noun* [U] land of the type mentioned: *mountainous/steep/rocky terrain*

terrestrial /təˈrestriəl/ *adj* **1** connected with, or living on, the earth **2** (used about television, etc.) operating on earth rather than from a **satellite** (= an electronic device that is sent into space)

⚷ **terrible** /ˈterəbl/ *adj* **1** ill or very upset: *I feel terrible. I think I'm going to be sick.* ♦ *He felt terrible when he realized what he had done.* **2** very unpleasant; causing great shock or injury: *a terrible accident* ♦ *terrible news* ♦ *What a terrible thing to do!* **3** very bad; of poor quality: *a terrible hotel/book/memory/driver* ➲ note at **bad 4** [only *before* a noun] used to emphasize how bad sth is: *in terrible pain/trouble* ♦ *The room was in a terrible mess.*

⚷ **terribly** /ˈterəbli/ *adv* **1** very: *I'm terribly sorry.* **2** very badly: *I played terribly.* ♦ *The experiment went terribly wrong.*

T

terrier /ˈteriə(r)/ *noun* [C] a type of small dog

terrific /təˈrɪfɪk/ *adj* (*informal*) **1** extremely nice or good; excellent: *You're doing a terrific job!* ➲ note at **good 2** [only *before* a noun] very great: *I've got a terrific amount of work to do.* ▸ **terrifically** /-kli/ *adv*: *terrifically expensive*

terrified /ˈterɪfaɪd/ *adj* **terrified (of sb/sth)** very afraid: *I'm absolutely terrified of snakes.* ♦ *What's the matter? You look terrified.*

terrify /ˈterɪfaɪ/ *verb* [T] (**terrifying; terrifies;** *pt, pp* **terrified**) to frighten sb very much

territorial /ˌterəˈtɔːriəl/ *adj* [only *before* a noun] connected with the land or area of sea that belongs to a country: *territorial waters*

territory /ˈterətri/ *noun* (*pl* **territories**) **1** [C,U] an area of land that belongs to one country: *to fly over enemy territory* **2** [C,U] an area that an animal has as its own **3** [U] an area of knowledge or responsibility: *Computer programming is Frank's territory.*

terror /ˈterə(r)/ *noun* **1** [U] very great fear: *He screamed* **in terror** *as the rats came towards him.* **2** [C] a person or thing that makes you feel afraid: *the terrors of the night* **3** [U] violence and the killing of ordinary people for political purposes: *a campaign of terror* **4** [C] (*informal*) a person (especially a child) or an animal that is difficult to control: *Joey's a little terror.*

terrorism /ˈterərɪzəm/ *noun* [U] the use of violence for political purposes: *an act of terrorism* ▸ **terrorist** /-ɪst/ *noun* [C], *adj*: *a terrorist attack/bomb/group* ➲ note at **crime**

terrorize (also **-ise**) /ˈterəraɪz/ *verb* [T] to make sb feel frightened by using or threatening to use violence against them: *The gang has terrorized the neighbourhood for months.*

terse /tɜːs/ *adj* said in few words and in a not very friendly way: *a terse reply*

tertiary /ˈtɜːʃəri/ *adj* (*BrE*) (used about education) at university or college level: *a tertiary college*

TESL /ˈtesl/ *abbr* **Teaching English as a Second Language**

⚷ **test**[1] /test/ *noun* [C] **1** a short exam to measure sb's knowledge or skill in sth: *We have a spelling test every Friday.* ➲ note at **exam** ➲ look at **driving 2** a short medical examination of a part of your body: *to have an eye test* **3** an experiment to find out if sth works or to find out more information about it: *Tests show that the new drug is safe and effective.* ♦ *to carry out/perform/do a test* **4** a situation or event that shows how good, strong, etc. sb/sth is: *The local elections will be a good test of the government's popularity.*

IDM put sb/sth to the test to do sth to find out how good, strong, etc. sb/sth is

⚷ **test**[2] /test/ *verb* [T] **1 test sb (on sth)** to examine sb's knowledge or skill in sth: *We're being tested on irregular verbs this morning.* **2** to examine a part of the body to find out if it is healthy: *to have your eyes tested* **3 test sb/sth (for sth); test sth (on sb/sth)** to try, use or examine sth carefully to find out if it is working properly or what it is like: *These cars have all been tested for safety.* ♦ *Do you think it's right to test cosmetics on animals?*

EXAM TIP

Test yourself

If you just read through a list of words, it is difficult to be sure whether or not you really know them. Before an exam, test yourself and your friends. Can you write the words without making a spelling mistake? Do you know what they mean? Can you put them into a sentence correctly?

testament /ˈtestəmənt/ *noun* [C, usually sing] (*formal*) **a testament (to sth)** something that shows that sth exists or is true

testicle /ˈtestɪkl/ *noun* [C] one of the two male sex organs that produce **sperm** (= the seed necessary for making babies)

testify /ˈtestɪfaɪ/ *verb* [I,T] (**testifying**; **testifies**; *pt*, *pp* **testified**) to make a formal statement that sth is true, especially in a court of law

testimony /ˈtestɪməni/ *noun* (*pl* **testimonies**) **1** [U,sing] (*formal*) something that shows that sth else exists or is true **2** [C,U] a formal statement that sth is true, especially one that is made in a court of law

testing /ˈtestɪŋ/ *noun* [U] the activity of testing sb/sth in order to find sth out, see if it works, etc: *testing and assessment in education*

ˈ**test tube** *noun* [C] a thin glass tube that is used in chemical experiments

tetanus /ˈtetənəs/ *noun* [U] a serious disease that makes your muscles, especially the muscles of your face, hard and impossible to move. You can get **tetanus** by cutting yourself on sth dirty.

tether[1] /ˈteðə(r)/ *verb* [T] to tie an animal to sth with a rope, etc.

tether[2] /ˈteðə(r)/ *noun*
IDM at the end of your tether ➲ **end[1]**

⚷ **text[1]** /tekst/ *noun* **1** [U] the main written part of a book, newspaper, etc. (not the pictures, notes, etc.): *My job is to lay out the text on the page.* **2** [C] the written form of a speech, etc: *The newspaper printed the complete text of the interview.* **3** [C] = **text message 4** [C] a book or a short piece of writing that people study as part of a literature or language course: *a set text* (= one that has to be studied for an examination)

text[2] /tekst/ (also ˈ**text-message**) *verb* [T,I] to send sb a written message using a mobile phone: *I texted him to say we were home.* ➲ look at **SMS** ➲ note at **mobile phone**

textbook /ˈtekstbʊk/ *noun* [C] a book that teaches a particular subject and that is used especially in schools: *a history textbook*

textile /ˈtekstaɪl/ *noun* [C] any cloth made in a factory: *cotton textiles* ♦ *the textile industry*

ˈ**text message** (also **text**) *noun* [C] a written message that you send using a mobile phone: *Send a text message to this number to vote for the winner.* ➲ look at **SMS** ➲ note at **mobile phone** ▶ ˈ**text-messaging** (also **texting** /ˈtekstɪŋ/) *noun* [U]

texture /ˈtekstʃə(r)/ *noun* [C,U] the way that sth feels when you touch it: *a rough/smooth/coarse texture* ♦ *cheese with a very creamy texture*

⚷ **than** /ðən; *strong form* ðæn/ *conj*, *prep* **1** used when you are comparing two things: *He's taller than me.* ♦ *He's taller than I am.* ♦ *London is more expensive than Madrid.* ♦ *You speak French much better than she does/than her.* ♦ *I'd rather play tennis than football.* **2** used with 'more' and 'less' before numbers, expressions of time, distances, etc: *I've worked here for more than three years.*

⚷ **thank** /θæŋk/ *verb* [T] **thank sb (for sth/for doing sth)** to tell sb that you are grateful: *I'm writing to thank you for the present you sent me.* ♦ *I'll go and thank him for offering to help.*

HELP **Thank you** and **thanks** are both used for telling somebody that you are grateful for something. **Thanks** is more informal: *Thank you very much for your letter.* ♦ *'How are you, Rachel?' 'Much better, thanks.'* You can also use **thank you** and **thanks** to accept something that somebody has offered to you: *'Stay for dinner.' 'Thank you. That would be nice.'* When you want to refuse something you can say **no, thank you** or **no, thanks**: *'Would you like some more tea?' 'No, thanks.'*

IDM thank God, goodness, heavens, etc. used for expressing happiness that sth unpleasant has stopped or will not happen: *Thank goodness it's stopped raining!* ➲ note at **god**

thankful /ˈθæŋkfl/ *adj* [not before a noun] **thankful (for sth/to do sth/that ...)** pleased and grateful: *I was thankful to hear that you got home safely.* ♦ *I was thankful for my thick coat when it started to snow.*

thankfully /ˈθæŋkfəli/ *adv* **1** used for expressing happiness that sth unpleasant did not or will not happen **SYN** **fortunately**: *Thankfully, no one was injured in the accident.* **2** in a pleased or grateful way: *I accepted her offer thankfully.* **SYN** **gratefully**

thankless /ˈθæŋkləs/ *adj* involving hard work that other people do not notice or thank you for

⚷ **thanks** /θæŋks/ *noun* [pl] **1** words which show that you are grateful: *I'd like to express my thanks to all of you for coming here today.* ♦ *Thanks!* **2 no thanks** a polite way of refusing sth that sb has offered you: *'Would you like some more cake?' 'No thanks.'*
IDM thanks to sb/sth because of sb/sth: *We're late, thanks to you!*
a vote of thanks ➲ **vote[1]**

Thanksgiving (Day) /ˌθæŋksˈɡɪvɪŋ deɪ/ *noun* [U,C] a public holiday in the US and in Canada

CULTURE
Thanksgiving Day is on the fourth Thursday in November in the US and on the second Monday in October in Canada. It was originally a day when people thanked God for the **harvest** (= food from the land or sea, especially that which is produced by farmers).

⚷ ˈ**thank you** *noun* [C] an expression of thanks: *Thank you!* ♦ *'How are you?' 'I'm fine, thank you.'* ♦ *I'd like to say a big thank you to everybody who worked so hard.*

⚷ **that** /ðæt/ *determiner*, *pron*, *conj*, *adv* **1** (*pl* **those** /ðəʊz/) used to refer to a person or thing, especially when he/she/it is not near the person speaking: *I like that house over there.* ♦ *What's that in the road?* ♦ *'Could you pass me the book?' 'This one?' 'No, that one over there.'* ♦ *How much are those apples at the back?* **2** (*pl* **those**) used for talking about a person or thing already known or mentioned: *That was the year we went to Spain, wasn't it?* ♦ *Can you give me back that money I lent you last week?* **3** /ðət; *strong* form ðæt/ [used for introducing a relative clause] the person or thing already mentioned: *I'm reading the book that won the Booker prize.* ♦ *The people that live next door are French.* ➲ note at **which**

GRAMMAR When **that** is the object of the verb in the relative clause, it is often left out: *I want to see the doctor (that) I saw last week.* ♦ *She wore the dress (that) she bought in Paris.*

4 /ðət; *strong form* ðæt/ used after certain verbs, nouns and adjectives to introduce a new part of the sentence: *She told me that she was leaving.* ♦ *I hope that you feel better soon.* ♦ *I'm certain that he will come.* ♦ *It's funny that you should say that.*

GRAMMAR **That** is often left out in this type of sentence: *I thought you would like it.*

5 [used with adjectives and adverbs] as much as that: *30 miles? I can't walk that far.*
IDM **that is (to say)** used when you are giving more information about sb/sth: *I'm on holiday next week. That's to say, from Tuesday.*
that's that there is nothing more to say or do: *I'm not going and that's that.*

thatched /θætʃt/ *adj* (used about a building) having a roof made of **straw** (= dried grass) ➲ picture on **page P9**

thaw /θɔː/ *verb* [I,T] **thaw (sth) (out)** to become or to make sth become soft or liquid again after freezing: *Is the snow thawing?* ♦ *Always thaw chicken thoroughly before you cook it.* ➲ look at **melt** ▸ **thaw** *noun* [C, usually sing]

⚷ **the** /ðə; ði; *strong form* ðiː/ *definite article* **1** used for talking about a person or thing that is already known or that has already been mentioned: *I took the children to the dentist.* ♦ *We met the man who bought your house.* ♦ *The milk is in the fridge.* **2** used when there is only one of sth: *The sun is very strong today.* ♦ *Who won the World Cup?* ♦ *the government* **3** used with numbers and dates: *This is the third time I've seen this film.* ♦ *Friday the thirteenth* ♦ *I grew up in the 1980s.* **4** (*formal*) used with a singular noun when you are talking generally about sth: *The dolphin is an intelligent animal.* **5** with musical instruments: *Do you play the piano?* **6** used with adjectives to name a group of people: *the French* ♦ *the poor* **7** with units of measurement, meaning 'every': *Our car does forty miles to the gallon.* **8** the well-known or important one: *'My best friend at school was Adele.' 'You mean **the** Adele?'*

HELP 'The' is pronounced /ðiː/ in this sense.

9 **the ... the ...** used for saying that the way in which two things change is connected: *The more you eat, the fatter you get.* ℹ For more information about articles, look at the **Reference Section** at the back of this dictionary.

⚷ **theatre** (*AmE* **theater**) /ˈθɪətə(r)/ *noun* **1** [C] a building where you go to see plays, shows, etc: *How often do you **go to the theatre**?* **2** [U] plays in general: *He's studying modern Russian theatre.* **SYN** **drama** **3** [sing, U] the work of acting in or producing plays: *He's worked in (the) theatre for thirty years.* **4** [C,U] = **operating theatre**: *He's still **in theatre**.* ♦ *a theatre nurse* (= a nurse with special training who helps during operations)

TOPIC

Theatre

A **play** is performed in a **theatre**, on a flat area called **the stage**. The furniture, etc. on the stage is the **scenery**. If an **actor/actress** wants a **part** in a play, he/she must have an **audition**, so the **director** can decide if he/she is suitable. Before they **put on** a play, **the cast** (= all of the actors) practise by having **rehearsals**. If the **audience** like the play, they **clap/applaud** (= hit their hands together) at the end of the **performance**.

theatrical /θiˈætrɪkl/ *adj* **1** [only *before* a noun] connected with the theatre **2** (used about behaviour) exaggerated or showing feelings, etc. in a very obvious way because you want people to notice you

theft /θeft/ *noun* [C,U] the crime of stealing sth: *There have been a lot of thefts in this area recently.* ♦ *The woman was arrested for theft.* ➲ note at **thief**

⚷ **their** /ðeə(r)/ *determiner* **1** of or belonging to them: *The children picked up their books and left.* **2** used instead of *his* or *her*: *Has everyone got their book?* ➲ note at **he**

⚷ **theirs** /ðeəz/ *pron* of or belonging to them: *Our flat isn't as big as theirs.*

⚷ **them** /ðəm; *strong form* ðem/ *pron* [the object of a verb or preposition] **1** the people or things mentioned earlier: *I'll phone them now.* ♦ *'I've got the keys here.' 'Oh good. Give them to me.'* ♦ *We have students from several countries but **most of them** are Italian.* ♦ *They asked for your address so I gave it to them.* **2** him or her: *If anyone phones, tell them I'm busy.* ➲ note at **he**

⚷ **theme** /θiːm/ *noun* [C] the subject of a talk, a piece of writing or a work of art: *The theme of today's discussion will be 'Our changing cities'.*

ˈ**theme park** *noun* [C] a park where people go to enjoy themselves, for example by riding on **roller coasters** (= large machines that go very fast), and where much of the entertainment is connected with one subject or idea

⚷ **themselves** /ðəmˈselvz/ *pron* **1** used when the people or things who do an action are also affected by it: *Susie and Angela seem to be enjoying themselves.* ♦ *People often talk to themselves when they are worried.* **2** used to emphasize the people who do the action: *They themselves say that the situation cannot continue.* ♦ *Did they paint the house themselves?* (= or did sb else do it for them?)
IDM **(all) by themselves** **1** alone: *The boys are too young to go out by themselves.* ➲ note at **alone** **2** without help: *The children cooked the dinner all by themselves.*

⚷ **then** /ðen/ *adv* **1** (at) that time: *In 2009? I was at university then.* ♦ *I spoke to him on Wednesday, but I haven't seen him **since then**.* ♦ *They met in 1961 and

remained close friends **from then on.** ♦ *I'm going tomorrow. Can you wait* **until then**? ♦ *Phone me tomorrow—I will have decided* **by then**. **2** next; after that: *I'll have a shower and get changed, then we'll go out.* ♦ *There was silence for a minute. Then he replied.* **3** used to show the logical result of a statement or situation: *'I don't feel at all well.' 'Why don't you go to the doctor, then?'* ♦ *If you don't do any work then you'll fail the exam.* **4** used after words like *now, right, well,* etc. to show the beginning or end of a conversation or statement: *Now then, are we all ready to go?* ♦ *OK then, I'll see you tomorrow.*
IDM **then/there again** ➲ again
there and then; **then and there** ➲ there

WRITING TIP

Order of events

When you tell a story, you need to show how events follow one another. It is better not to use **then** every time: *I watched TV for a bit, and* **then** *I went to bed.* ♦ ***After a while,*** *I heard a strange noise.* ♦ ***Next,*** *somebody turned on the lights.* ♦ ***After that,*** *I heard people talking.* ♦ ***Later on,*** *everything went quiet.*

ⓘ For more help with writing, look at **Wordpower Writing Tutor** at the back of this dictionary.

thence /ðens/ *adv* (*old-fashioned*) from there

theology /θiˈɒlədʒi/ *noun* [U] the study of religion ▸ **theological** /ˌθiːəˈlɒdʒɪkl/ *adj*

theoretical /ˌθɪəˈretɪkl/ *adj* **1** based on ideas and principles, not on practical experience: *A lot of university courses are still far too theoretical.* **2** that may possibly exist or happen, although it is unlikely: *There is a theoretical possibility that the world will end tomorrow.* ➲ look at **practical** ▸ **theoretically** /-kli/ *adv*

⚷ **theory** /ˈθɪəri/ *noun* (*pl* **theories**) **1** [C] an idea or set of ideas that try to explain sth: *the theory about how life on earth began* **2** [U] the general idea or principles of a particular subject: *political theory* ♦ *the theory and practice of language teaching* **3** [C] an opinion or a belief that has not been shown to be true: *He has this theory that drinking tea helps you live longer.*
IDM **in theory** as a general idea which may not be true in reality: *Your plan sounds fine in theory, but I don't know if it'll work in practice.* ➲ look at **practice**

therapeutic /ˌθerəˈpjuːtɪk/ *adj* **1** helping to cure an illness: *therapeutic drugs* **2** helping you to relax and feel better: *I find listening to music very therapeutic.*

therapy /ˈθerəpi/ *noun* [U] treatment to help or cure a mental or physical illness, often without drugs or medical operations: *to have/undergo therapy* ♦ *She's* **in therapy** (= having psychotherapy). ▸ **therapist** /-pɪst/ *noun* [C]: *a speech therapist*

⚷ **there** /ðeə(r)/ *adv, pron* **1** used as the subject of 'be', 'seem', 'appear', etc. to say that sth exists: *Is there a god?* ♦ *There's a man at the door.* ♦ *There wasn't much to eat.* ♦ *There's somebody singing outside our house.* ♦ *There seems to be a mistake here.* **2** in, at or to that place: *Could you put the table there, please?* ♦ *I like Milan. My husband and I met there.* ♦ *Have you been to Bonn? We're going there next week.* ♦ *Have you looked under there?* **3** available if needed: *Her parents are always there if she needs help.* **4** at that point (in a conversation, story, etc.): *Could I interrupt you there for a minute?* **5** used for calling attention to sth: *Oh look, there's Kate!* ♦ *Hello there! Can anyone hear me?*
IDM **be there for sb** to be available to help and support sb when they have a problem: *Whenever I'm in trouble, my sister is always there for me.*
then/there again ➲ again
there and then; **then and there** at that time and place; immediately
there you are; **there you go 1** used when you give sth to sb: *There you are. I've bought you a newspaper.* **2** used when you are explaining sth to sb: *Just press the switch and there you are!*

thereabouts /ˌðeərəˈbaʊts/ *adv* [usually after or] somewhere near a number, time or place: *There are 100 students, or thereabouts.* ♦ *She lives in Sydney, or thereabouts.*

thereafter /ˌðeərˈɑːftə(r)/ *adv* (*formal*) after that

thereby /ˌðeəˈbaɪ/ *adv* (*formal*) in that way

⚷ **therefore** /ˈðeəfɔː(r)/ *adv* for that reason: *The new trains have more powerful engines and are therefore faster.*

WRITING TIP

Describing results

In formal writing you can use **therefore, as a result** or **consequently** to talk about the result of an action: *No one provided any money, and* **therefore** *the youth club closed.* ♦ *There was no money, and* **as a result***, the youth club closed.* ♦ *The money ran out, and consequently, the youth club closed.* A very formal way of saying **therefore** is **thus**: *There was no money, and thus the youth club could continue no longer.* In spoken and informal English it is more common to use **so**: *There was no money, so the youth club closed.*

ⓘ For more help with writing, look at **Wordpower Writing Tutor** at the back of this dictionary.

therein /ˌðeərˈɪn/ *adv* (*formal*) because of sth that has just been mentioned

thereupon /ˌðeərəˈpɒn/ *adv* (*formal*) immediately after that and often as the result of sth

thermal[1] /ˈθɜːml/ *adj* [only *before* a noun] **1** connected with heat: *thermal energy* **2** (used about clothes) made to keep you warm in cold weather: *thermal underwear*

thermal[2] /ˈθɜːml/ *noun* **1** [C] a flow of rising warm air **2** **thermals** [pl] clothes, especially underwear, made to keep you warm in cold weather

thermometer /θəˈmɒmɪtə(r)/ *noun* [C] an instrument for measuring the temperature of the air or of sb's body

T

Thermos™ /ˈθɜːməs/ (also ˈ**Thermos flask**; *BrE also* **flask**) *noun* [C] a type of container used for keeping a liquid hot or cold ➲ look at **vacuum**

thermostat /ˈθɜːməstæt/ *noun* [C] a device that controls the temperature in a house or machine by switching the heat on and off as necessary

thesaurus /θɪˈsɔːrəs/ *noun* [C] a book that contains lists of words with similar meanings in groups

these *plural* of **this**

thesis /ˈθiːsɪs/ *noun* [C] (*pl* **theses** /ˈθiːsiːz/) **1** a long piece of writing on a particular subject that you do as part of a university degree: *He did his thesis on Japanese investment in Europe.* ➲ look at **dissertation 2** an idea that is discussed and presented with evidence in order to show that it is true

⚷ **they** /ðeɪ/ *pron* [the subject of a verb] **1** the people or things that have been mentioned: *We've got two children. They're both boys.* ◆ *'Have you seen my keys?' 'Yes, they are on the table.'* **2** used instead of *he* or *she*: *Somebody phoned for you but they didn't leave their name.* ➲ note at **he 3** people in general or people whose identity is not known or stated: *They say it's going to be a mild winter.*

they'd /ðeɪd/ *short for* **they had; they would**

they'll /ðeɪl/ *short for* **they will**

they're /ðeə(r)/ *short for* **they are**

they've /ðeɪv/ *short for* **they have**

⚷ **thick¹** /θɪk/ *adj* (**thicker; thickest**)

➤NOT THIN **1** (used about sth solid) having a large distance between its opposite sides; not thin: *a thick black line* ◆ *a thick coat/book* ◆ *These walls are very thick.* OPP **thin 2** used for saying what the distance is between the two opposite sides of sth: *The ice was six centimetres thick.*

➤TREES/HAIR **3** growing closely together in large numbers: *a thick forest* ◆ *thick hair* OPP **thin**

➤LIQUID **4** that does not flow easily: *thick cream* ◆ *This paint is too thick.* OPP **thin**

➤CLOUD, FOG, ETC. **5** difficult to see through: *There'll be a thick fog tonight.* ◆ *thick clouds of smoke*

➤WITH LARGE AMOUNT **6 thick (with sth)** containing a lot of sth/sb close together: *The air was thick with dust.* ◆ *The streets were thick with shoppers.*

➤STUPID **7** (*informal*) slow to learn or understand; stupid: *Are you thick, or what?*

➤ACCENT **8** easily recognized as being from a particular country or area: *a thick Brooklyn accent* SYN **strong**

IDM **have a thick skin** to be not easily upset or worried by what people say about you

▶ **thick** *adv*: *Snow lay thick on the ground.* ▶ **thickly** *adv*: *Spread the butter thickly.* ◆ *a thickly wooded area*

thick² /θɪk/ *noun*

IDM **in the thick of sth** in the most active or crowded part of sth; very involved in sth

through thick and thin all the time, even when there are difficult times and situations

thicken /ˈθɪkən/ *verb* [I,T] to become or to make sth thicker

⚷ **thickness** /ˈθɪknəs/ *noun* [C,U] the quality of being thick or how thick sth is ➲ look at **width**

ˌ**thick-ˈskinned** *adj* not easily worried or upset by what other people say about you: *Politicians have to be thick-skinned.*

⚷ **thief** /θiːf/ *noun* [C] (*pl* **thieves** /θiːvz/) a person who steals things from another person ➲ note at **steal**: *'Stop thief!' she cried.* ◆ *A thief snatched her handbag containing her wages.*

> OTHER WORDS FOR
>
> **thief**
>
> A **thief** is a general word for a person who steals things, usually secretly and without violence. The name of the crime is **theft**. A **robber** steals from a bank, shop, etc. and often uses violence or threats. A **burglar** steals things by breaking into a house, shop, etc., often at night, and a **shoplifter** goes into a shop when it is open and takes things without paying. A **mugger** steals from somebody in the street and uses violence or threats.

thigh /θaɪ/ *noun* [C] the top part of your leg, above your knee ➲ picture at **body**

thimble /ˈθɪmbl/ *noun* [C] a small metal or plastic object that you wear on the end of your finger to protect it when you are sewing ➲ picture at **sewing**

⚷ **thin¹** /θɪn/ *adj* (**thinner; thinnest**) **1** (used about sth solid) having a small distance between the opposite sides: *a thin book/shirt* ◆ *a thin slice of meat* OPP **thick 2** having very little fat on the body: *You need to eat more. You're too thin!* OPP **fat 3** that flows easily; not thick: *a thin sauce* OPP **thick 4** not growing closely together or in large amounts: *thin grey hair* OPP **thick 5** not difficult to see through: *They fought their way through where the smoke was thinner.* OPP **thick**

IDM **thin on the ground** difficult to find; not common: *Jobs for people with my skills are fairly thin on the ground these days.*

through thick and thin ➲ **thick**

vanish, etc. into thin air to disappear completely

wear thin ➲ **wear¹**

> OTHER WORDS FOR
>
> **thin**
>
> **Thin** is the most general word for describing people who have very little fat on their bodies. **Slim** is used about people who are thin in an attractive way: *You're so slim! How do you do it?* If you say a person is **skinny**, you mean that he/she is too thin and not attractive. **Underweight** is a formal word, and is often used in a medical context: *The doctor says I'm underweight.*

▶ **thin** *adv*: *Don't slice the onion too thin.*

▶ **thinly** *adv*: *thinly sliced bread* ◆ *thinly populated areas*

thin² /θɪn/ *verb* [I,T] (**thinning; thinned**) **thin (sth) (out)** to become thinner or fewer in number; to make sth thinner: *The trees thin out towards the edge of the forest.* ◆ *Thin the sauce by adding milk.*

T

thing /θɪŋ/ *noun*

›OBJECT **1** [C] an object that is not named: *What's that red thing on the table?* ◆ *A pen is a thing you use for writing with.* ◆ *I need to get a few things at the shops.*

›EQUIPMENT **2 things** [pl] clothes or tools that belong to sb or are used for a particular purpose: *I'll just go and pack my things.* ◆ *We keep all the cooking things in this cupboard.*

›ACTION/EVENT **3** [C] an action, event or statement: *When I get home the first thing I do is have a cup of tea.* ◆ *A strange thing happened to me yesterday.* ◆ *What a nice thing to say!*

›FACT **4** [C] a fact, subject, etc: *He told me a few things that I didn't know before.*

›QUALITY/STATE **5** [C] a quality or state: *There's* ***no such thing as*** *a ghost* (= it doesn't exist). ◆ *The best thing about my job is the way it changes all the time.*

›YOUR LIFE **6 things** [pl] the situation or conditions of your life: *How are things with you?*

›WHAT IS NEEDED **7 the thing** [sing] exactly what is wanted or needed: *That's just the thing I was looking for!*

›PERSON/ANIMAL **8** [C] used for expressing how you feel about a person or an animal: *You've broken your finger? You poor thing!*

IDM **a close shave/thing** ➲ close[3]

be a good thing (that) to be lucky that: *It's a good thing you remembered your umbrella.*

do your own thing (*informal*) to do what you want to do, without thinking about other people: *I like to spend time alone, just doing my own thing.*

first/last thing as early/late as possible: *I'll phone her first thing tomorrow morning.* ◆ *I saw him last thing on Friday evening.*

for one thing used for introducing a reason for sth: *I think we should go by train. For one thing it's cheaper.*

have a thing about sb/sth (*informal*) to have strong feelings about sb/sth

to make matters/things worse ➲ worse

the real thing ➲ real[1]

take it/things easy ➲ easy[2]

think /θɪŋk/ *verb* (*pt, pp* thought /θɔːt/)

›HAVE OPINION **1** [I,T] **think (sth) (of/about sb/sth); think that ...** to have a particular idea or opinion about sth/sb; to believe sth: *'Do you think (that) we'll win?' 'No, I* ***don't think so.****'* ◆ *'Jay's coming tomorrow, isn't he?' 'Yes, I* ***think so.****'* ◆ *I think (that) they've moved to York but I'm not sure.* ◆ *What did you think of the film?* ◆ *What do you think about going out tonight?*

›USE MIND **2** [I] **think (about sth)** to use your mind to consider sth or to form connected ideas: *Think before you speak.* ◆ *What are you thinking about?* ◆ *He had to think hard* (= a lot) *about the question.*

›IMAGINE **3** [T] to form an idea of sth; to imagine sth: ***Just think*** *what we could do with all that money!*

›EXPECT **4** [T] to expect sth: *I never thought that I'd see her again.*

›IN A PARTICULAR WAY **5** [I] to think in a particular way: *If you want to be successful, you have to* ***think big.*** ◆ *We've got to* ***think positive.***

›INTEND **6** [I,T] **think of/about doing sth; think (that)...** to intend or plan to do sth: *We're thinking of moving house.* ◆ *I think (that) I'll go for a swim.*

›REMEMBER **7** [T] to remember sth; to have sth come into your mind: *Can you think where you left the keys?* ◆ *I didn't think to ask him his name.*

IDM **think better of (doing) sth** to decide not to do sth; to change your mind

think highly, a lot, not much, etc. of sb/sth to have a good, bad, etc. opinion of sb/sth: *I didn't think much of that film.*

think the world of sb/sth to love and admire sb/sth very much

PHR V **think about/of sb** to consider the feelings of sb else: *She never thinks about anyone but herself.*

think of sth to create an idea in your imagination: *Who first thought of the plan?*

think sth out to consider carefully all the details of a plan, idea, etc: *a well-thought-out scheme*

think sth over to consider sth carefully: *I'll think your offer over and let you know tomorrow.*

think sth through to consider every detail of sth carefully: *He made a bad decision because he didn't think it through.*

think sth up (*informal*) to create sth in your mind; to invent sth: *to think up a new advertising slogan*

OTHER WORDS FOR

think

If you want to give your opinion, you can say **'I think** (that) ...', or **'Personally, I think** (that) ...', or use another phrase: ***In my opinion/As far as I'm concerned/It seems to me that*** .... In informal conversation we often use **reckon** to say that something is true or possible: *I reckon (that) I'm going to get that job.* You can use **believe** to talk about something that you feel is morally right or wrong: *She believes (that) killing animals is wrong.* In a formal discussion with somebody you can ask 'What is your opinion of/on/about ...?', or 'How do you feel about ...?'

▸ **think** *noun* (*informal*): *I'm not sure. I'll have to* ***have a think*** *about it.*

thinker /ˈθɪŋkə(r)/ *noun* [C] **1** a person who thinks about serious and important subjects **2** a person who thinks in a particular way: *a quick/creative/clear thinker*

thinking[1] /ˈθɪŋkɪŋ/ *noun* [U] **1** using your mind to think about sth: *We're going to have to do some quick thinking.* **2** ideas or opinions about sth: *This accident will make them change their thinking on safety matters.* ➲ look at **wishful thinking**

thinking[2] /ˈθɪŋkɪŋ/ *adj* [only *before* a noun] intelligent and using your mind to think about important subjects

ˈthink tank *noun* [C] a group of experts who provide advice and ideas on political, social or economic matters

third[1] /θɜːd/ *ordinal number* 3rd ➲ note at **sixth**

third[2] /θɜːd/ *noun* [C] **1** ⅓; one of three equal parts of sth **2** (*BrE*) a result in final university exams, below first and second class degrees

T

thirdly /ˈθɜːdli/ *adv* used to introduce the third point in a list: *We have made savings in three areas: firstly, defence, secondly, education and thirdly, health.*

ˌthird ˈparty *noun* [C] a person who is involved in a situation in addition to the two main people involved

the ˌThird ˈWorld *noun* [sing] a way of referring to the poorer countries of Asia, Africa and South America, which is sometimes considered offensive

> **MORE** Many people now prefer to talk about **developing countries** or **the developing world**.

thirst /θɜːst/ *noun* **1** [U, sing] the feeling that you have when you want or need a drink: *Iced tea really quenches your thirst.* ◆ *to die of thirst* **2** [sing] a thirst for sth a strong desire for sth ➲ look at **hunger**

thirsty /ˈθɜːsti/ *adj* (**thirstier**; **thirstiest**) wanting or needing a drink: *I'm thirsty. Can I have a drink of water, please?* ➲ look at **hungry** ▶ **thirstily** *adv*

thirteen /ˌθɜːˈtiːn/ *number* 13 ➲ note at **six** ▶ **thirteenth** /ˌθɜːˈtiːnθ/ *ordinal number, noun* ➲ note at **sixth**

thirty /ˈθɜːti/ *number* 30 ➲ note at **sixty** ▶ **thirtieth** /ˈθɜːtiəθ/ *ordinal number, noun* ➲ note at **sixth**

this /ðɪs/ *determiner, pron* (*pl* **these** /ðiːz/) **1** used for talking about sb/sth that is close to you in time or space: *Have a look at this photo.* ◆ *These boots are really comfortable. My old ones weren't.* ◆ *Is this the book you asked for?* ◆ *These are the letters to be filed, not those over there.* ◆ *This chair's softer than that one, so I'll sit here.* **2** used for talking about sth that was mentioned or talked about earlier: *Where did you hear about this?* **3** used for introducing sb or showing sb sth: *This is my wife, Claudia, and these are our children, David and Vicky.* ◆ *It's easier if you do it like this.* **4** (used with days of the week or periods of time) of today or the present week, year, etc: *Are you busy this afternoon?* ◆ *this Friday* (= the Friday of this week) **5** (*informal*) (used when you are telling a story) a certain: *Then this woman said ...*
IDM this and that; this, that and the other (*informal*) various things: *We chatted about this and that.*
▶ **this** *adv*: *The road is not usually this busy.*

thistle /ˈθɪsl/ *noun* [C] a wild plant with purple flowers and sharp points on its leaves, which is the national symbol of Scotland

thong /θɒŋ/ (*AmE*) = **flip-flop**

thorn /θɔːn/ *noun* [C] one of the hard sharp points on some plants and bushes, for example on rose bushes ➲ picture at **plant**

thorny /ˈθɔːni/ *adj* (**thornier**; **thorniest**) **1** causing difficulty or disagreement: *a thorny problem/question* **2** having **thorns**

thorough /ˈθʌrə/ *adj* **1** careful and complete: *The police made a thorough search of the house.* **2** doing things in a very careful way, making sure that you look at every detail: *Pam is slow but she is very thorough.* ▶ **thoroughness** *noun* [U]: *I admire his thoroughness.*

thoroughbred /ˈθʌrəbred/ *noun* [C] an animal, especially a horse, of high quality, that has parents that are both of the same breed ▶ **thoroughbred** *adj*: *a thoroughbred mare*

thoroughly /ˈθʌrəli/ *adv* **1** completely; very much: *We thoroughly enjoyed our holiday.* **2** in a careful and complete way: *to study a subject thoroughly*

those *plural of* **that**

though /ðəʊ/ *conj, adv* **1** in spite of the fact that: *Though he had very little money, Neil always managed to dress smartly.* ◆ *She still loved him* **even though** *he had treated her so badly.* **SYN although** **2** but: *I'll come as soon as I can, though I can't promise to be on time.* **3** however: *I quite like him. I don't like his wife, though.* ➲ note at **although**
IDM as though ➲ **as**

thought[1] *past tense, past participle of* **think**

thought[2] /θɔːt/ *noun*
➤ IDEA/OPINION **1** [C] an idea or opinion: *What are your thoughts on this subject?* ◆ *The thought of living alone filled her with fear.* ◆ *I've just had a thought* (= an idea).
➤ MIND **2 thoughts** [pl] a person's mind and all the ideas that are in it: *You are always* **in my thoughts**.
➤ ACT OF THINKING **3** [U] the power or process of thinking: *I need to* **give** *this problem* **some thought**. ◆ *You haven't put enough thought into this work.*
➤ FEELING OF CARE **4** [C] a feeling of care or worry: *They sent me flowers. What a kind thought!*
➤ IN POLITICS, SCIENCE ETC. **5** [U] particular ideas or a particular way of thinking: *a change in medical thought on the subject*
IDM deep in thought/conversation ➲ **deep**[1]
a school of thought ➲ **school**
second thoughts ➲ **second**[1]

thoughtful /ˈθɔːtfl/ *adj* **1** thinking deeply: *a thoughtful expression* **2** thinking about what other people want or need: *It was very thoughtful of you to send her some flowers.* **SYN kind** ▶ **thoughtfully** /-fəli/ *adv* ▶ **thoughtfulness** *noun* [U]

thoughtless /ˈθɔːtləs/ *adj* not thinking about what other people want or need or what the result of your actions will be: *a thoughtless remark* **SYN inconsiderate** ▶ **thoughtlessly** *adv* ▶ **thoughtlessness** *noun* [U]

thousand /ˈθaʊznd/ *number* 1 000

> **HELP** Notice that you use **thousand** in the singular when you are talking about a number. You use **thousands** when you mean 'a lot': *There were over seventy thousand spectators at the match.* ◆ *Thousands of people took part in the protest march.*

ℹ For more information about numbers, look at the section on using numbers at the back of this dictionary.

thousandth[1] /ˈθaʊznθ/ *ordinal number* 1 000th: *the city's thousandth anniversary*

thousandth² /ˈθaʊznθ/ *noun* [C] ¹⁄₁₀₀₀; one of a thousand equal parts of sth: *one thousandth of a second*

thrash /θræʃ/ *verb* **1** [T] to hit sb/sth many times with a stick, etc. as a punishment **2** [I,T] **thrash (sth) (about/around)** to move or make sth move in a wild way without any control **3** [T] (*informal*) to defeat sb easily in a game, competition, etc: *I thrashed Leo at tennis yesterday.*
PHR V **thrash sth out** to talk about sth with sb until you reach an agreement

thrashing /ˈθræʃɪŋ/ *noun* [C] **1** the act of hitting sb/sth many times with a stick, etc. as a punishment **2** (*informal*) a bad defeat in a game

thread¹ /θred/ *noun* **1** [C,U] a long thin piece of cotton, wool, etc. that you use for sewing or making cloth: *a needle and thread* ➲ picture at **rope**, **sew**, **sewing** **2** [C] the connection between ideas, the parts of a story, etc: *I've lost the thread of this argument.* **3** [C] a series of connected messages on a **message board** (= a place where a user can write or read messages) on the Internet, which have been sent by different people

thread² /θred/ *verb* [T] **1** to put sth long and thin, especially thread, through a narrow opening or hole: *to thread a needle* ♦ *He threaded the belt through the loops on his trousers.* **2** to join things together by putting them onto a string, etc: *to thread beads onto a string*
IDM **thread your way through sth** to move through sth with difficulty, going around things or people that are in your way

threadbare /ˈθredbeə(r)/ *adj* (used about cloth or clothes) old and very thin

threat /θret/ *noun* **1** [C] a warning that sb may hurt, kill or punish you if you do not do what they want: *to **make threats** against somebody* ♦ *He keeps saying he'll resign, but he won't **carry out** his **threat**.* **2** [U, sing] the possibility of trouble or danger: *The forest is **under threat** from building developments.* **3** [C] a person or thing that may damage sth or hurt sb; something that indicates future danger: *a threat to national security*

threaten /ˈθretn/ *verb* **1** [T] **threaten sb (with sth)**; **threaten (to do sth)** to warn that you may hurt, kill or punish sb if they do not do what you want: *The boy threatened him with a knife.* ♦ *She was threatened with dismissal.* ♦ *The man threatened to kill her if she didn't tell him where the money was.* **2** [I,T] to seem likely to do sth unpleasant: *The strong wind was threatening to destroy the bridge.* ▶ **threatening** *adj*: *threatening behaviour* ♦ *I found a threatening message on my answering machine.* ▶ **threateningly** *adv*

three /θriː/ *number* **1** 3 ➲ note at **six** **2** [in compounds] having three of the thing mentioned: *a three-legged stool* ➲ look at **third**

ˌthree-diˈmensional (also ˌ**3-ˈD**) *adj* having, or appearing to have, length, width and height: *a three-dimensional model* ♦ *These glasses allow you to see the film in 3-D.*

threshold /ˈθreʃhəʊld/ *noun* [C] **1** the ground at the entrance to a room or building **2** the level at which sth starts to happen: *Young children have a low boredom threshold.* **3** the time when you are just about to start sth or find sth: *We could be **on the threshold of** a scientific breakthrough.*

threw *past tense of* **throw**

thrift /θrɪft/ *noun* [U] the quality of being careful not to spend too much money ▶ **thrifty** *adj*

thrill /θrɪl/ *noun* [C] a sudden strong feeling of pleasure or excitement ▶ **thrill** *verb* [T]: *His singing thrilled the audience.* ▶ **thrilled** *adj*: *He was thrilled with my present.* ▶ **thrilling** *adj*

thriller /ˈθrɪlə(r)/ *noun* [C] a play, film, book, etc. with a very exciting story, often about a crime

thrive /θraɪv/ *verb* [I] to grow or develop well ▶ **thriving** *adj*: *a thriving industry*

throat /θrəʊt/ *noun* [C] **1** the front part of your neck: *The attacker grabbed the man by the throat.* ➲ picture at **body** **2** the back part of your mouth and the passage down your neck through which air and food pass: *She got a piece of bread stuck in her throat.* ♦ *I've got a sore throat.* ➲ picture at **body**
IDM **clear your throat** ➲ **clear²**
have/feel a lump in your throat ➲ **lump¹**

throb /θrɒb/ *verb* [I] (**throbbing**; **throbbed**) to make strong regular movements or noises; to beat strongly: *Her finger throbbed with pain.* ▶ **throb** *noun* [C]

thrombosis /θrɒmˈbəʊsɪs/ *noun* [C,U] (*pl* **thromboses** /-siːz/) a serious condition caused by a blood **clot** (= a thick mass of blood) forming in the heart or in a tube that carries blood ➲ look at **deep vein thrombosis**

throne /θrəʊn/ *noun* **1** [C] the special chair where a king or queen sits **2 the throne** [sing] the position of being king or queen

throng¹ /θrɒŋ/ *noun* [C] (*formal*) a large crowd of people

throng² /θrɒŋ/ *verb* [I,T] (*formal*) (used about a crowd of people) to move into or fill a particular place: *Crowds were thronging into the square, keen to catch a glimpse of the band.*

throttle¹ /ˈθrɒtl/ *verb* [T] to hold sb tightly by the throat and stop them breathing SYN **strangle**

throttle² /ˈθrɒtl/ *noun* [C] the part in a vehicle that controls the speed by controlling how much fuel goes into the engine

through /θruː/ *prep, adv* **1** from one end or side of sth to the other: *We drove through the centre of London.* ♦ *to look through a telescope* ♦ *She cut through the rope.* ♦ *to push through a crowd of people* **2** from the beginning to the end of sth: *Food supplies will not last through the winter.* ♦ *We're halfway through the book.* ♦ *He read the letter through and handed it back.* **3** past a limit, stage or test: *He lifted the rope to let us through.* ♦ *She didn't get through the first interview.* **4** (also *informal* **thru**) (*AmE*) until, and including: *They are staying Monday through Friday.* **5** because of; with the help of: *Errors were*

made through bad organization. ♦ *David got the job through his uncle.* **6** (*BrE*) connected by telephone: *Can you put me through to extension 5678, please?*
PHR V **be through (with sb/sth)** to have finished with sb/sth

throughout /θruːˈaʊt/ *adv, prep* **1** in every part of sth: *The house is beautifully decorated throughout.* ♦ *The match can be watched live on TV throughout the world.* **2** from the beginning to the end of sth: *We didn't enjoy the holiday, because it rained throughout.*

throw /θrəʊ/ *verb* (*pt* threw /θruː/; *pp* thrown /θrəʊn/)
➤WITH HAND **1** [I,T] throw (sth) (to/at sb); throw sb sth to send sth from your hand through the air by moving your hand or arm quickly: *How far can you throw?* ♦ *Throw the ball to me.* ♦ *Throw me the ball.* ♦ *Don't throw stones at people.*
➤PUT CARELESSLY **2** [T] to put sth somewhere quickly or carelessly: *He threw his bag down in a corner.* ♦ *She threw on a sweater and ran out of the door.*
➤MOVE WITH FORCE **3** [T] to move your body or part of it quickly or suddenly: *Jenny threw herself onto the bed and sobbed.* ♦ *Lee threw back his head and roared with laughter.*
➤MAKE SB FALL **4** [T] to cause sb to fall down quickly or violently: *The bus braked and we were thrown to the floor.*
➤PUT IN SITUATION **5** [T] to put sb in a particular (usually unpleasant) situation: *We were thrown into confusion by the news.*
➤UPSET/CONFUSE **6** [T] (*informal*) to make sb feel upset, confused or surprised: *The question threw me and I didn't know what to reply.*
➤LIGHT/SHADE **7** [T] to send light or shade onto sth: *The tree threw a long shadow across the lawn in the late afternoon.*
PHR V **throw sth away 1** (also throw sth out) to get rid of rubbish or sth that you do not want: *I threw his letters away.* **2** to waste or not use sth useful: *to throw away an opportunity*
throw sth in (*informal*) to include sth extra without increasing the price
throw sb out to force sb to leave a place
throw sth out 1 to decide not to accept sb's idea or suggestion **2** = **throw sth away**(1)
throw up (*informal*) to be sick **SYN** **vomit**
throw sth up 1 (*informal*) to be sick: *The baby's thrown up her dinner.* **SYN** **vomit** **2** to produce or show sth: *Our research has thrown up some interesting facts.* **3** to leave your job, career, studies, etc.
▶ **throw** *noun* [C]: *It's your throw* (= it's your turn to throw the dice in a board game, etc.). ♦ *a throw of 97 metres*

thru (*AmE*) = **through**(4)

thrust¹ /θrʌst/ *verb* [I,T] (*pt, pp* thrust) **1** to push sb/sth suddenly or violently; to move quickly and suddenly in a particular direction: *The man thrust his hands deeper into his pockets.* ♦ *She thrust past him and ran out of the room.* **2** to make a sudden forward movement with a knife, etc.
PHR V **thrust sb/sth upon sb** to force sb to accept or deal with sb/sth

thrust² /θrʌst/ *noun* **1** the thrust [sing] the main part or point of an argument, policy, etc. **2** [C] a sudden strong movement forward

thud /θʌd/ *noun* [C] the low sound that is made when a heavy object hits sth else: *She fell to the ground and her head hit the floor with a dull thud.*
▶ **thud** *verb* [I] (thudding; thudded)

thug /θʌg/ *noun* [C] a violent person who may harm other people

thumb¹ /θʌm/ *noun* [C] **1** the short thick finger at the side of each hand: *She sucks her thumb.* ➲ note at **finger** ➲ picture at **body** **2** the part of a glove, etc. that covers your thumb
IDM **have green fingers/a green thumb** ➲ **green¹**
a rule of thumb ➲ **rule¹**
stand/stick out like a sore thumb ➲ **sore¹**
the thumbs up/down a sign or an expression that shows approval/disapproval
under sb's thumb (used about a person) completely controlled by sb: *She's got him under her thumb.*

thumb² /θʌm/ *verb* [I,T] thumb (through) sth to turn the pages of a book, etc. quickly
IDM **thumb a lift/ride** to hold out your thumb to cars going past, to ask sb to give you a free ride ➲ note at **hitchhike**

thumbtack /ˈθʌmtæk/ (*AmE*) = **drawing pin**

thump /θʌmp/ *verb* **1** [T] to hit sb/sth hard with sth, usually your **fist** (= closed hand): *He started coughing and Jo thumped him on the back.* **2** [I,T] to make a loud sound by hitting sth or by beating hard: *His heart was thumping with excitement.*
▶ **thump** *noun* [C]

thunder¹ /ˈθʌndə(r)/ *noun* [U] the loud noise in the sky that you can hear when there is a storm: *a clap/crash/roll of thunder* ➲ note at **storm** ➲ look at **lightning**

thunder² /ˈθʌndə(r)/ *verb* [I] **1** when **it thunders**, there is a loud noise in the sky during a storm: *The rain poured down and it started to thunder.* **2** to make a loud deep noise like **thunder**: *Traffic thundered across the bridge.*

thunderstorm /ˈθʌndəstɔːm/ *noun* [C] a storm with thunder and **lightning** (= flashes of light in the sky) ➲ note at **storm**

Thur. (also Thurs.) *abbr* = **Thursday**: *Thur. 26 September*

Thursday /ˈθɜːzdeɪ; -di/ *noun* [C,U] (*abbr* Thur.; Thurs.) the day of the week after Wednesday ➲ note at **Monday**

thus /ðʌs/ *adv* (*formal*) **1** like this; in this way: *Thus began the series of incidents which changed her life.* **2** because of or as a result of this: *He is the eldest son and thus heir to the throne.* ➲ note at **therefore**

thwart /θwɔːt/ *verb* [T] thwart sth; thwart sb (in sth) to stop sb doing what they planned to do; to prevent sth happening: *to thwart somebody's plans/ambitions/efforts* ♦ *She was thwarted in her attempt to gain control.*

T

thyme /taɪm/ *noun* [U] a **herb** (= a type of plant) that is used in cooking and has small leaves and a sweet smell ➲ picture on **page P14**

tic /tɪk/ *noun* [C] a sudden quick movement of a muscle, especially in your face or head, that you cannot control: *He has a nervous tic.*

tick¹ /tɪk/ *verb* **1** [I] (used about a clock or watch) to make regular short sounds **2** (*AmE* **check**) [T] to put a mark (✓) next to a name, an item on a list, etc. to show that sb/sth has been dealt with or chosen, or that sth is correct: *Please tick the appropriate box.*
IDM **what makes sb/sth tick** the reasons why sb behaves or sth works in the way he/she/it does: *He has a strong interest in people and what makes them tick.*
PHR V **tick away/by** (used about time) to pass
tick sb/sth off to put a mark (✓) next to a name, an item on a list, etc. to show that sth has been done or sb has been dealt with
tick over [usually used in the continuous tenses] (*informal*) **1** (used about an engine) to run slowly while the vehicle is not moving **2** to keep working slowly without producing or achieving very much

tick² /tɪk/ *noun* **1** [C] (*AmE* **check mark**; **check**) a mark (✓) next to an item on a list that shows that sth has been done or next to an answer to show that it is correct: *Put a tick after each correct answer.* **2** [U] (also **ticking**) the regular short sound that a watch or clock makes when it is working **3** (*BrE informal*) a moment

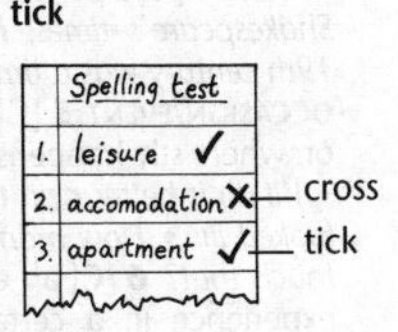

ticket /ˈtɪkɪt/ *noun* [C] **1 a ticket (for/to sth)** a piece of paper or card that shows you have paid for a journey, or allows you to enter a theatre, cinema, etc: *two tickets for the Cup Final* ◆ *I'd like a single/return ticket to London.* ◆ *a ticket office/machine/collector* ◆ *I always buy a lottery ticket* ➲ look at **season ticket** ➲ picture at **label 2** a piece of paper fastened to sth in a shop that shows its price, size, etc. **3** an official piece of paper that you get when you have parked illegally or driven too fast telling you that you must pay money as a punishment: *a parking ticket*
IDM **just the job/ticket** ➲ **job**

ticking /ˈtɪkɪŋ/ = **tick²**(2)

tickle /ˈtɪkl/ *verb* **1** [T] to touch sb lightly with your fingers or with sth soft so that they laugh: *She tickled the baby's toes.* **2** [I,T] to produce or to have an uncomfortable feeling in a part of your body: *The woollen scarf tickled her neck.* ◆ *My nose tickles/is tickling.* **3** [T] (*informal*) to amuse and interest sb: *That joke really tickled me.* ▶ **tickle** *noun* [C]

ticklish /ˈtɪklɪʃ/ *adj* if a person is **ticklish**, they laugh when sb **tickles** them: *Are you ticklish?*

tic-tac-toe /ˌtɪk tæk ˈtəʊ/ (*AmE*) = **noughts and crosses**

tidal /ˈtaɪdl/ *adj* connected with the **tides** of the sea: *tidal forces* ◆ *a tidal river*

ˈtidal wave *noun* [C] a very large wave in the sea which destroys things when it reaches the land, and is often caused by an **earthquake** (= a violent movement of the earth's surface) ➲ look at **tsunami**

tidbit /ˈtɪdbɪt/ (*AmE*) = **titbit**

tide¹ /taɪd/ *noun* **1** [C,U] the regular change in the level of the sea caused by the moon and the sun. At *high tide* the sea is closer to the land, at *low tide* it is further away and more of the beach can be seen: *The tide is **coming in/going out**.* ➲ note at **ebb 2** [C, usually sing] the way that most people think or feel about sth at a particular time: *It appears that **the tide has turned** in the government's favour.*

tide² /taɪd/ *verb*
PHR V **tide sb over** to give sb sth to help them through a difficult time

tidy¹ /ˈtaɪdi/ *adj* (**tidier**; **tidiest**) **1** (*especially BrE*) arranged with everything in good order: *If you keep your room tidy, it is easier to find things.* **2** (used about a person) liking to keep things in good order: *Mark is a very tidy boy.* **SYN** for both meanings **neat** **OPP** for both meanings **untidy** ▶ **tidily** *adv* ▶ **tidiness** *noun* [U]

tidy² /ˈtaɪdi/ *verb* [I,T] (**tidying**; **tidies**; *pt*, *pp* **tidied**) **tidy (sth) (up)** to make sth look in order and well arranged: *We must tidy this room up before the visitors arrive.*
PHR V **tidy sth away** to put sth into the drawer, cupboard, etc. where it is kept so that it cannot be seen

tie¹ /taɪ/ *verb* (**tying**; **ties**; *pt*, *pp* **tied**) **1** [T] to fasten sb/sth or fix sb/sth in position with rope, string, etc.; to make a knot in sth: *The prisoner was tied to a chair.* ◆ *Kay tied her hair back with a ribbon.* ◆ *to tie something in a knot* ◆ *to tie your shoelaces* **OPP** **untie** **2** [T, usually passive] **tie sb (to sth/to doing sth)** to limit sb's freedom and make them unable to do everything they want to: *I don't want to be tied to staying in this country permanently.* **3** [I] **tie (with sb) (for sth)** to have the same number of points as another player or team at the end of a game or competition: *England tied with Italy for third place.*
IDM **your hands are tied** ➲ **hand¹**
PHR V **tie sb/yourself down** to limit sb's/your freedom: *Having young children really ties you down.*
tie in (with sth) to agree with other facts or information that you have; to match: *The new evidence seems to tie in with your theory.*
tie sb/sth up **1** to fix sb/sth in position with rope, string, etc: *The dog was tied up in the back garden.* **OPP** **untie** **2** [usually passive] to keep sb busy: *Mr Jones is tied up in a meeting.*

tie² /taɪ/ *noun* [C] **1** (*AmE* also **necktie**) a long thin piece of cloth worn round the neck, especially by men, with a knot at the front. A tie is usually worn with a shirt: *a striped silk tie* ➲ look at **bow tie** ➲ picture on **page P1** **2** [usually pl] a strong connection between people or organizations: *personal/emotional ties* ◆ *family ties* **3** something that limits your freedom: *He never married because he didn't want any ties.* **4** a situation in a game or competi-

T

tion in which two or more teams or players get the same score: *There was a tie for first place.*

tier /tɪə(r)/ *noun* [C] one of a number of levels: *The seating is arranged in tiers.* ◆ *a wedding cake with three tiers*

tiger /ˈtaɪɡə(r)/ *noun* [C] a large wild cat that has yellow fur with black lines. **Tigers** live in parts of Asia. ➲ picture at **lion**

MORE A female tiger is called a **tigress** and a baby is called a **cub**.

tight /taɪt/ *adj* (**tighter**; **tightest**) *adv*

➤FIRM **1** fixed firmly in position and difficult to move or open: *a tight knot* ◆ *Keep a* ***tight grip/hold*** *on this rope.* ◆ ***Hold tight*** *so that you don't fall off.*

HELP **Tightly**, not **tight**, is used before a past participle: *The van was tightly packed with boxes.* ◆ *The van was packed tight with boxes.*

➤CLOTHES **2** fitting very closely in a way that is often uncomfortable: *These shoes hurt. They're too tight.* ◆ *a tight-fitting skirt* **OPP** **loose**

➤CONTROL **3** controlled very strictly and firmly: *Security is very tight at the airport.*

➤STRETCHED **4** stretched or pulled hard so that it cannot be stretched further: *The rope was stretched tight.*

➤BUSY/FULL **5** not having much free time or space: *My schedule this week is very tight.*

➤-TIGHT **6** **-tight** [in compounds] not allowing sth to get in or out: *an airtight/watertight container* ▶ **tightly** *adv*: *Screw the lid on tightly.* ◆ *She kept her eyes tightly closed.* ▶ **tightness** *noun* [U]

tighten /ˈtaɪtn/ *verb* [I,T] **tighten (sth) (up)** to become or to make sth tight or tighter: *His grip on her arm tightened.* ◆ *He tightened the screws as far as they would go.*

IDM **tighten your belt** to spend less money because you have less than usual available

PHR V **tighten up (on) sth** to cause sth to become stricter: *to tighten up security/a law*

tightrope /ˈtaɪtrəʊp/ *noun* [C] a rope or wire that is stretched high above the ground on which people walk, especially as a form of entertainment

tights /taɪts/ (*AmE* **pantyhose**) *noun* [pl] a piece of thin clothing, usually worn by women, that fits tightly from the waist over the legs and feet: *a pair of tights* ➲ look at **stocking** ➲ picture on **page P1**

tile /taɪl/ *noun* [C] one of the flat, usually square, objects that are arranged in rows to cover roofs, floors, bathroom walls, etc. ➲ picture on **page P8** ▶ **tile** *verb* [T]: *a tiled bathroom*

till[1] /tɪl/ (*informal*) = **until**: *We're open till 6 o'clock.* ◆ *Just wait till you see it. It's great.*

till[2] /tɪl/ (also ˈ**cash register**) *noun* [C] the machine or drawer where money is kept in a shop, etc: *Please pay at the till.*

tilt /tɪlt/ *verb* [I,T] to move, or make sth move, into a position with one end or side higher than the other: *The front seats of the car tilt forward.* ◆ *She tilted her head to one side.* ▶ **tilt** *noun* [sing]

timber /ˈtɪmbə(r)/ *noun* **1** (*especially AmE* **lumber**) [U] wood that is going to be used for building **2** [C] a large piece of wood: *roof timbers*

time[1] /taɪm/ *noun*

➤HOURS, YEARS, ETC. **1** [U, sing] a period of minutes, hours, days, etc: *As time passed and there was still no news, we got more worried.* ◆ *You're* ***wasting time****—get on with your work!* ◆ *I'll go by car to* ***save time****.* ◆ ***free/spare time*** ◆ *We haven't got time to stop now.* ◆ *I've been waiting* ***a long time****.* ◆ *Learning a language* ***takes time****.* **2** [U,C] **time (to do sth); time (for sth)** the time in hours and minutes shown on a clock; the moment when sth happens or should happen: *What's the time?/What time is it?* ◆ *Can you tell me the times of trains to Mumbai, please?* ◆ *It's time to go home.* ◆ ***By the time*** *I get home, Mark will have cooked the dinner.* ◆ ***This time tomorrow*** *I'll be on the plane.* ◆ *It's time for lunch.* ◆ *He never takes any* ***time off*** (= time spent not working). **3** [U] a system for measuring time in a particular part of the world: *11 o'clock* ***local time***

➤PERIOD **4** [C] a period in the past; a part of history: *In Shakespeare's times, few people could read.* ◆ *The 19th century was a time of great industrial change.*

➤OCCASION/EVENT **5** [C] an occasion when you do sth or when sth happens: *I phoned them three times.* ◆ *I'll do it better* ***next time****.* ◆ ***Last time*** *I saw him, he looked ill.* ◆ ***How many times*** *have I told you not to touch that?* **6** [C] an event or an occasion that you experience in a certain way: ***Have a good time*** *tonight.* ◆ *We had a terrible time at the hospital.*

➤FOR RACE **7** [C,U] the number of minutes, etc., taken to complete a race or an event: *What was his time in the hundred metres?*

IDM **(and) about time (too); (and) not before time** (*informal*) used to say that sth should already have happened

ahead of your time ➲ **ahead**

all the time/the whole time during the period that sb was doing sth or that sth was happening: *I searched everywhere for my keys and they were in the door all the time.*

at the same time ➲ **same**

at a time on each occasion: *The lift can hold six people at a time.* ◆ *She ran down the stairs two at a time.*

at one time in the past **SYN** **previously**

at the time at a particular moment or period in the past; then: *I agreed at the time but later changed my mind.*

at times sometimes: *At times I wish we'd never moved house.* **SYN** **occasionally**

before your time before you were born, or before you lived, worked, etc. somewhere

behind the times not modern or fashionable

bide your time ➲ **bide**

buy time ➲ **buy**[1]

for the time being just for the present; not for long

from time to time sometimes; not often

give sb a hard time ➲ **hard**[1]

have a hard time doing sth ➲ **hard**[1]

have no time for sb/sth to not like sb/sth: *I have no time for lazy people.*

have the time of your life (*informal*) to enjoy yourself very much
in the course of time ➲ **course**
in good time early; at the right time
in the nick of time ➲ **nick**[1]
in time (for sth/to do sth) not late; with enough time to be able to do sth: *Don't worry. We'll get to the station in time for your train.*
it's about/high time (*informal*) used to say that you think sb should do sth very soon: *It's about time you told him what's going on.*
on time not too late or too early: *The train left the station on time.*

HELP In time or on time? If you arrive **in time**, you arrive either before or at the correct time. If you arrive **on time**, you arrive at exactly the correct time: *I arrived at the station at 6.55, in time for the train, which left on time, at 7.00.*

once upon a time ➲ **once**
one at a time ➲ **one**[1]
take your time to do sth without hurrying
tell the time ➲ **tell**
time after time; time and (time) again again and again **SYN** **repeatedly**

time[2] /taɪm/ *verb* [T] **1** [often passive] to arrange to do sth or arrange for sth to happen at a particular time: *Their request was badly timed* (= it came at the wrong time). ◆ *She timed her arrival for shortly after three.* **2** to measure how long sb/sth takes: *Try timing yourself when you write your essay.*

EXAM TIP

Time yourself

A sure way to get a poor mark in an exam is not to answer enough questions. Make sure that you read through all the instructions at the beginning to find out how many questions you have to answer. Then you can work out how much time you can spend on each part.

ˈ**time-consuming** *adj* that takes or needs a lot of time

ˈ**time lag** = **lag**[2]

timeless /ˈtaɪmləs/ *adj* (*formal*) that does not seem to be changed by time or affected by changes in fashion

ˈ**time limit** *noun* [C] a time during which sth must be done: *We have to **set a time limit** for the work.*

timely /ˈtaɪmli/ *adj* happening at exactly the right time

timer /ˈtaɪmə(r)/ *noun* [C] a person or machine that measures time: *an oven timer*

times[1] /taɪmz/ *prep* (*symbol* ×) used when you are multiplying one figure by another: *Three times four is twelve.*

times[2] /taɪmz/ *noun* [pl] used for comparing amounts: *Cherries are **three times more** expensive in England than in Spain.*

⚷ **timetable** /ˈtaɪmteɪbl/ (*AmE* **schedule**) *noun* [C] **1** a list that shows the times at which sth happens: *a bus/train/school timetable* **2** a plan of when you hope or expect particular events to happen: *I have a busy timetable this week* (= I have planned to do many things).

timid /ˈtɪmɪd/ *adj* easily frightened; shy and nervous: *as timid as a rabbit* ▶ **timidity** /tɪˈmɪdəti/ *noun* [U] ▶ **timidly** *adv*

timing /ˈtaɪmɪŋ/ *noun* [U] **1** the time when sth is planned to happen: *The manager was careful about the timing of his announcement.* **2** the skill of doing sth at exactly the right time: *The timing of her speech was perfect.*

timpani /ˈtɪmpəni/ *noun* [pl] a set of large metal drums (also called **kettledrums**) ▶ **timpanist** /-nɪst/ *noun* [C]

⚷ **tin** /tɪn/ *noun* **1** [U] (*symbol* **Sn**) a soft silver-white metal that is often mixed with other metals: *a tin mine* **2** (also ˌ**tin** ˈ**can**; *especially AmE* **can**) [C] a closed metal container in which food, paint, etc. is stored and sold; the contents of one of these containers: *a tin of peas/beans/soup* ◆ *a tin of paint/varnish* ➲ note at **can**[2] ➲ picture at **container** **3** [C] a metal container with a lid for keeping food in: *a biscuit/cake tin* ▶ **tinned** *adj*: *tinned peaches/peas/soup*

tinfoil /ˈtɪnfɔɪl/ = **foil**[1]

tinge /tɪndʒ/ *noun* [C, usually sing] a small amount of a colour or a feeling: *a tinge of sadness* ▶ **tinged** *adj* **tinged (with sth)**: *Her joy at leaving was tinged with regret.*

tingle /ˈtɪŋɡl/ *verb* [I] (used about a part of the body) to feel as if a lot of small sharp points are pushing into it: *His cheeks tingled as he came in from the cold.* ▶ **tingle** *noun* [usually sing]: *a tingle of excitement/anticipation/fear*

tinker /ˈtɪŋkə(r)/ *verb* [I] **tinker (with sth)** to try to repair or improve sth without having the proper skill or knowledge

tinkle /ˈtɪŋkl/ *verb* [I] to make a light high ringing sound, like that of a small bell ▶ **tinkle** *noun* [C, usually sing]

ˈ**tin opener** (*especially AmE* ˈ**can opener**) *noun* [C] a tool that you use for opening a tin of food ➲ picture at **kitchen**

tinsel /ˈtɪnsl/ *noun* [U] long strings of material like metal, used as a decoration to hang on a Christmas tree

tint /tɪnt/ *noun* [C] a shade or a small amount of a colour: *white paint with a pinkish tint* ▶ **tint** *verb* [T]: *tinted glasses* ◆ *She had her hair tinted.*

⚷ **tiny** /ˈtaɪni/ *adj* (**tinier**; **tiniest**) very small: *the baby's tiny fingers*

⚷ **tip**[1] /tɪp/ *noun* [C]
➤ END OF STH **1** the thin or pointed end of sth: *the tips of your toes/fingers* ◆ *the tip of your nose* ◆ *the southernmost tip of South America*
➤ ADVICE **2** **a tip (on/for sth/doing sth)** a small piece of useful advice about sth practical: *useful tips on how to save money*

T

➤MONEY **3** a small amount of extra money that you give to sb who serves you, for example in a restaurant: *to leave a tip for the waiter* ◆ *I gave the porter a $5 tip.*

➤FOR RUBBISH **4** (*BrE*) (also ˈ**rubbish tip**) a place where you can take rubbish and leave it: *We took the old furniture to the tip.* **SYN** **dump**

➤UNTIDY PLACE **5** (*BrE informal*) a place that is very dirty or untidy: *The house was a tip!*

IDM **on the tip of your tongue** if a word or name is **on the tip of your tongue**, you are sure that you know it but you cannot remember it

the tip of the iceberg only a small part of a much larger problem

🔑 **tip**[2] /tɪp/ *verb* (**tipping**; **tipped**) **1** [I,T] **tip (sth) (up)** to move so that one side is higher than the other; to make sth move in this way: *When I stood up, the bench tipped up and the person on the other end fell off.* **2** [T] to make sth come out of a container by holding or lifting it at an angle: *Tip the dirty water down the drain.* ◆ *The child tipped all the toys onto the floor.* **3** [I,T] to give sb a small amount of extra money (in addition to the normal charge) to thank them for a service: *She tipped the taxi driver generously.* **4** [T] **tip sb/sth (as sth/to do sth)** to think or say that sb/sth is likely to do sth: *This horse is tipped to win the race.* ◆ *He is widely tipped as the next leader of the Labour Party.*

PHR V **tip sb off** (*informal*) to give sb secret information

tip (sth) up/over to fall or turn over; to make sth do this: *An enormous wave crashed into the little boat and it tipped over.*

ˈ**tip-off** *noun* [C] secret information that sb gives, for example to the police, about an illegal activity that is going to happen: *Acting on a tip-off, the police raided the house.*

tiptoe[1] /ˈtɪptəʊ/ *noun*

IDM **on tiptoe(s)** standing or walking on the ends of your toes with the back part of your foot off the ground, in order not to make any noise or to reach sth high up

tiptoe[2] /ˈtɪptəʊ/ *verb* [I] to walk on your toes with the back part of your foot off the ground

🔑 **tire**[1] /ˈtaɪə(r)/ *verb* [I,T] to feel that you need to rest or sleep; to make sb feel like this: *Now that he's over 60, he tires easily.*

PHR V **tire of sth/sb** to become bored or not interested in sth/sb any more: *I'll never tire of living here.*

tire sb/yourself out to make sb/yourself very tired: *The long country walk tired us all out.* **SYN** **exhaust**

🔑 **tire**[2] /ˈtaɪə(r)/ (*AmE*) = **tyre**

🔑 **tired** /ˈtaɪəd/ *adj* feeling that you need to rest or sleep: *She was tired after a hard day's work.* ◆ *They were cold, hungry and* ***tired out*** (= very tired). ➲ note at **sleep**

IDM **be tired of sb/sth/doing sth** to be bored with or annoyed by sb/sth/doing sth: *I'm tired of this game. Let's play something else.* ◆ *I'm* ***sick and tired*** *of listening to the same thing again and again.*

▶ **tiredness** *noun* [U]

tireless /ˈtaɪələs/ *adj* putting a lot of hard work and energy into sth over a long period of time without stopping or losing interest

tiresome /ˈtaɪəsəm/ *adj* (*formal*) that makes you angry or bored; annoying

🔑 **tiring** /ˈtaɪərɪŋ/ *adj* making you want to rest or sleep: *a tiring journey/job* **SYN** **exhausting**

tissue /ˈtɪʃuː; ˈtɪsjuː/ *noun* **1** (also **tissues**) [U,pl] the mass of cells that form the bodies of humans, animals and plants: *muscle/brain/nerve/scar tissue* ◆ *Radiation can destroy the body's tissues.* **2** [C] a thin piece of soft paper that you use to clean your nose and throw away after you have used it: *a box of tissues* ➲ note at **handkerchief** **3** (also ˈ**tissue paper**) [U] thin soft paper that you use for putting around things that may break

tit /tɪt/ *noun* [C] (*slang*) a woman's breast

> **HELP** Be careful. Some people find this word offensive.

IDM **tit for tat** something unpleasant that you do to sb because they have done sth to you

titbit /ˈtɪtbɪt/ (*AmE* **tidbit**) *noun* [C] **1** a small but very nice piece of food **2** an interesting piece of information

🔑 **title** /ˈtaɪtl/ *noun* [C] **1** the name of a book, play, film, picture, etc: *I know the author's name but I can't remember the title of the book.* **2** a word that shows sb's position, profession, etc: *'Lord', 'Doctor', 'Reverend', 'Mrs' and 'General' are all titles.* **3** the position of being the winner of a competition, especially a sports competition: *Sue is playing this match to defend her title* (= to remain the winner).

titled /ˈtaɪtld/ *adj* having a word, for example 'Lord', 'Lady', etc. before your name that shows that your family has an important position in society

ˈ**title-holder** *noun* [C] the person or team who won a sports competition the last time it took place

ˈ**title role** *noun* [C] the main role in a film, book, etc. whose name is the same as the title

titter /ˈtɪtə(r)/ *verb* [I] to laugh quietly, especially in an embarrassed or nervous way ▶ **titter** *noun* [C]

ˈ**T-junction** *noun* [C] a place where two roads join to form the shape of a T ➲ picture at **roundabout**

TM /ˌtiː ˈem/ *abbr* = **trademark**

🔑 **to** /tə; *before vowels* tu; *strong form* tuː/ *prep, adv* **1** in the direction of; as far as: *She's going to London.* ◆ *Turn to the left.* ◆ *Pisa is to the west of Florence.* ◆ *He has gone to school.* **2** reaching a particular state: *The meat was cooked to perfection.* ◆ *His speech reduced her to tears* (= made her cry). **3** used to show the end or limit of a series of things or period of time: ***from*** *Monday* ***to*** *Friday* ◆ *from beginning to end* **4** (used to say what time it is) before: *It's ten to three* (= ten minutes before 3 o'clock). **5** used to show the person or thing that receives sth or is affected by an action: *Give that to me.* ◆ *I am very grateful to my parents.* ◆ *What have you done to your hair?* ◆ *Sorry, I didn't realize you were talking to me.* **6** (nearly) touching sth; directed towards sth: *He put his hands* to his ears. ◆ *They sat back to back.* ◆ *She made no reference to her personal problems.* **7** used to introduce the second part of a comparison: *I prefer theatre to opera.* **8** (used for expressing quantity) for each unit of money, measurement, etc: *How many dollars are there to the euro?* **9** used for expressing a reaction or attitude to sth: *To my surprise, I saw two strangers coming out of my house.* ◆ *His paintings aren't really to my taste.* **10** used to express sb's opinion or feeling about sth: *To me, it was the wrong decision.* ◆ *It sounded like a good idea to me.* ◆ *I don't think our friendship means anything to him.* **11** used with verbs to form the infinitive: *I want to go home now.* ◆ *Don't forget to write.* ◆ *I didn't know what to do.* **12** /tuː/ (used about a door) in or into a closed position: *Push the door to.*

IDM **to and fro** backwards and forwards

toad /təʊd/ *noun* [C] a small animal with rough skin and long back legs that it uses for jumping, that lives both on land and in water ➲ picture on **page P13**

toadstool /ˈtəʊdstuːl/ *noun* [C] a plant without leaves, flowers or green colouring, with a flat or curved top. **Toadstools** are usually poisonous. ➲ note at **mushroom** ➲ look at **fungus**

toast /təʊst/ *noun* **1** [U] a thin piece of bread that is heated on both sides to make it brown

> **GRAMMAR** **Toast** in this meaning is uncountable. We say **a piece/slice of toast** (not 'a toast').

2 [C] **a toast (to sb/sth)** an occasion at which a group of people wish sb happiness, success, etc., by drinking a glass of wine, etc. at the same time: *I'd like to* ***propose a toast to*** *the happy couple.* ◆ *The committee* ***drank a toast to*** *the new project.* ➲ look at **drink** ▸ **toast** *verb* [T]

toaster /ˈtəʊstə(r)/ *noun* [C] an electrical machine for making bread turn brown by heating it on both sides

tobacco /təˈbækəʊ/ *noun* [U] the dried leaves of the **tobacco** plant that some people smoke in cigarettes and pipes

tobacconist /təˈbækənɪst/ *noun* **1** [C] a person who sells cigarettes, matches, etc. **2** (also **the tobacconist's**) [sing] a shop where you can buy cigarettes, matches, etc.

toboggan /təˈbɒgən/ *noun* [C] a type of plastic or board with flat pieces of metal underneath, that people use for travelling down hills on snow for fun ➲ look at **bobsleigh, sledge**

⚷ **today** /təˈdeɪ/ *noun* [U], *adv* **1** (on) this day: *Today is Monday.* ◆ *What shall we do today?* ◆ *School ends* ***a week today*** (= on this day next week). ◆ *Where is today's paper?* **2** (in) the present age; these days: *Young people today have far more freedom.* **SYN** **nowadays**

toddle /ˈtɒdl/ *verb* [I] **1** to walk with short, unsteady steps like a very young child **2** (*informal*) to walk or go somewhere

toddler /ˈtɒdlə(r)/ *noun* [C] a young child who has only just learnt to walk

⚷ **toe**[1] /təʊ/ *noun* [C] **1** one of the small parts like fingers at the end of each foot: *the big/little toe* (= largest/smallest toe) ➲ note at **finger** ➲ picture at **body** ➲ picture on **page P12** **2** the part of a sock, shoe, etc. that covers your toes ➲ picture at **shoe**

toe[2] /təʊ/ *verb* (**toeing**; **toed**)

IDM **toe the line** to do what sb in authority tells you to do, even if you do not agree with them

TOEFL /ˈtəʊfl/ *abbr* **Test of English as a Foreign Language**; the examination for foreign students who want to study at an American university

toenail /ˈtəʊneɪl/ *noun* [C] one of the hard flat parts that cover the end of your toes ➲ picture at **body**

toffee /ˈtɒfi/ *noun* [C,U] a hard sticky sweet that is made by cooking sugar and butter together

⚷ **together**[1] /təˈgeðə(r)/ *adv* **1** with or near each other: *Can we have lunch together?* ◆ *They walked home together.* ◆ *I'll get all my things together tonight because I want to leave early.* ◆ *Stand with your feet together.* **2** so that two or more things are mixed or joined to each other: *Mix the butter and sugar together.* ◆ *Tie the two ends together.* ◆ *Add these numbers together to find the total.* **3** at the same time: *Don't all talk together.*

IDM **get your act together** ➲ **act**[1]

put together [used after a noun or nouns referring to a group of people or things] combined; in total: *You got more presents than the rest of the family put together.*

put/get your heads together ➲ **head**[1]

together with in addition to; as well as: *I enclose my order together with a cheque for £15.*

together[2] /təˈgeðə(r)/ *adj* (*informal*) (used about a person) organized, capable: *I'm not very together this morning.*

togetherness /təˈgeðənəs/ *noun* [U] a feeling of friendship

toggle /ˈtɒgl/ *noun* [C] **1** a short piece of wood, plastic, etc. that is put through a **loop** (= a round piece) of thread to fasten sth, such as a coat or bag, instead of a button **2** (also ˈ**toggle switch**) a key on a computer that you press to change from one style or operation to another, and back again ▸ **toggle** *verb* [I,T] **toggle (between A and B)**; **toggle sth**: *He toggled between the two windows.*

toil /tɔɪl/ *verb* [I] (*formal*) to work very hard or for a long time at sth ▸ **toil** *noun* [U]

⚷ **toilet** /ˈtɔɪlət/ *noun* [C] a large bowl with a seat, connected to a water pipe, that you use when you need to get rid of waste material from your body; the room containing this: *I need to* ***go to the toilet*** (= use the toilet). ➲ picture on **page P8**

> **MORE** In their houses, people usually refer to the **toilet** or, informally, the **loo**. **Lavatory** and **WC** are formal and old-fashioned words. In public places the toilets are called the **Ladies** or the **Gents**. In American English, people talk about the **bathroom** in their houses and the **restroom, ladies' room** or **men's room** in public places.

ˈ**toilet bag** (*BrE*) = **sponge bag**

T

ˈtoilet paper (also ˈtoilet tissue) *noun* [U] soft, thin paper that you use to clean yourself after going to the toilet

toiletries /ˈtɔɪlətriz/ *noun* [pl] things such as soap or **toothpaste** that you use for washing, cleaning your teeth, etc. ➲ look at **sponge bag, toilet bag**

ˈtoilet roll *noun* [C] (*BrE*) a long piece of toilet paper rolled round a tube ➲ picture at **roll**

ˈtoiletry bag (*AmE*) = **sponge bag**

ˈtoilet tissue = **toilet paper**

token¹ /ˈtəʊkən/ *noun* [C] **1** a round piece of metal, plastic, etc. that you use instead of money to operate some machines or as a form of payment **2** (*BrE*) a piece of paper that you can use to buy sth of a certain value in a particular shop. **Tokens** are often given as presents: *a £10 book/CD/gift token* ➲ look at **voucher 3** something that represents or is a symbol of sth: *We would like you to accept this gift **as a token of** our gratitude.*

token² /ˈtəʊkən/ *adj* [only *before* a noun] **1** done, chosen, etc. in a very small quantity, and only in order not to be criticized: *There is a token woman on the board of directors.* **2** small, but done or given to show that you are serious about sth and will keep a promise or an agreement: *a token payment*

told *past tense, past participle* of **tell**

tolerable /ˈtɒlərəbl/ *adj* (*formal*) **1** quite good, but not of the best quality **2** of a level that you can accept or deal with, although unpleasant or painful: *Drugs can reduce the pain to a tolerable level.* **OPP intolerable**

tolerant /ˈtɒlərənt/ *adj* **tolerant (of/towards sb/sth)** able to allow or accept sth that you do not like or agree with: *As a society, we've become less tolerant of cruelty.* **OPP intolerant** ▶ **tolerance** (also **toleration**) *noun* [U] **tolerance (of/for sb/sth)**: *religious/racial tolerance* **OPP intolerance**

tolerate /ˈtɒləreɪt/ *verb* [T] **1** to allow or accept sth that you do not like or agree with: *In a democracy we must tolerate opinions that are different from our own.* **2** to accept or be able to deal with sb/sth unpleasant without complaining: *The noise was more than she could tolerate.* ▶ **toleration** /ˌtɒləˈreɪʃn/ = **tolerance**

toll /təʊl/ *noun* **1** [C] money that you pay to use a road or bridge: *motorway tolls* ♦ *a toll bridge* **2** [C, usually sing] the amount of damage done or the number of people who were killed or injured by sth: *The official death toll has now reached 5 000.*
IDM take a heavy toll/take its toll (on sth) to cause great loss, damage, suffering, etc.

tom /tɒm/ = **tomcat**

tomato /təˈmɑːtəʊ/ *noun* [C] (*pl* **tomatoes**) a soft red fruit that is often eaten without being cooked in salads, or cooked as a vegetable: *tomato juice/soup/sauce* ➲ picture on **page P15**

tomb /tuːm/ *noun* [C] a large grave, especially one built of stone above or below the ground: *the tombs of the Pharaohs* ➲ look at **grave**

tomboy /ˈtɒmbɔɪ/ *noun* [C] a young girl who likes games and activities that are traditionally considered to be for boys

tombstone /ˈtuːmstəʊn/ *noun* [C] a large flat stone that lies on or stands at one end of the place where sb is buried and shows the name, dates, etc. of the dead person **SYN gravestone, headstone**

tomcat /ˈtɒmkæt/ (also **tom**) *noun* [C] a male cat ➲ note at **cat**

tomorrow /təˈmɒrəʊ/ *noun* [U], *adv* **1** (on) the day after today: *Today is Friday so tomorrow is Saturday.* ♦ *See you tomorrow.* ♦ *I'm going to bed. I've got to get up early tomorrow morning.* ♦ *a week tomorrow* (= a week from tomorrow) ➲ note at **morning**

> **HELP** Notice that we say 'tomorrow morning', 'tomorrow afternoon', etc. NOT 'tomorrow in the morning', etc.

2 the future: *The schoolchildren of today are tomorrow's workers.*

ton /tʌn/ *noun* **1** [C] (*informal*) (*abbr* t) a measure of weight; 2240 pounds: *What have you got in this bag? It weighs a ton!*

> **HELP** Do not confuse **ton** and **tonne.** A ton is 1016.04 kilograms and a tonne is 1000 kilograms. In British English, a ton is 2240 pounds in the non-metric system, but in American English, a ton is 2000 pounds.

2 tons [pl] (*informal*) a lot: *I've got tons of homework to do.*

tone¹ /təʊn/ *noun* **1** [C,U] the quality of a sound or of sb's voice, especially expressing a particular emotion: *'Do you know each other?' she asked in a casual tone of voice.* **2** [sing] the general quality or style of sth: *The tone of the meeting was optimistic.* **3** [C] a shade of a colour: *warm tones of red and orange* **4** [C] a sound that you hear on the telephone: *Please speak after the tone* (= an instruction on an answering machine).

tone² /təʊn/ *verb* [T] **tone sth (up)** to make your muscles, skin, etc. firmer, especially by doing exercise
PHR V tone sth down to change sth that you have said, written, etc., to make it less likely to offend

ˌtone-ˈdeaf *adj* not able to sing or hear the difference between notes in music

tongs /tɒŋz/ *noun* [pl] a tool with two long parts that are joined at one end, that you use for picking up and holding things

tongue /tʌŋ/ *noun* **1** [C] the soft part inside your mouth that you can move. You use your tongue for speaking, tasting things, etc: *He ran his tongue nervously over his lips.* ➲ picture at **body 2** [C,U] the tongue of some animals, cooked and eaten: *a slice of ox tongue* **3** [C] (*formal*) a language: *your **mother tongue*** (= the language you learnt as a child)
IDM on the tip of your tongue ➲ **tip¹**
put/stick your tongue out to put your tongue outside your mouth as a rude sign to sb
a slip of the tongue ➲ **slip²**

(with) tongue in cheek done or said as a joke; not intended seriously

ˈtongue-tied *adj* not saying anything because you are shy or nervous

ˈtongue-twister *noun* [C] a phrase or sentence with many similar sounds that is difficult to say correctly when you are speaking quickly: *'Red lorry, yellow lorry' is a tongue-twister.*

tonic /ˈtɒnɪk/ *noun* **1** (also ˈtonic water) [U,C] a type of water with bubbles in it and a rather bitter taste that is often added to alcoholic drinks: *a gin and tonic* **2** [C,U] a medicine or sth you do that makes you feel stronger, healthier, etc., especially when you are very tired: *A relaxing holiday is a wonderful tonic.*

tonight /təˈnaɪt/ *noun* [U], *adv* (on) the evening or night of today: *Tonight is the last night of our holiday.* ◆ *What's on TV tonight?* ◆ *We are staying with friends tonight and going home tomorrow.*

tonne /tʌn/ *noun* [C] (*abbr* t) a measure of weight; 1 000 kilograms ➲ look at **ton**

tonsil /ˈtɒnsl/ *noun* [C] one of the two small soft parts in your throat at the back of your mouth: *She had to* **have** *her* **tonsils out** (= removed in a medical operation).

tonsillitis /ˌtɒnsəˈlaɪtɪs/ *noun* [U] an illness in which the **tonsils** become very sore and swollen

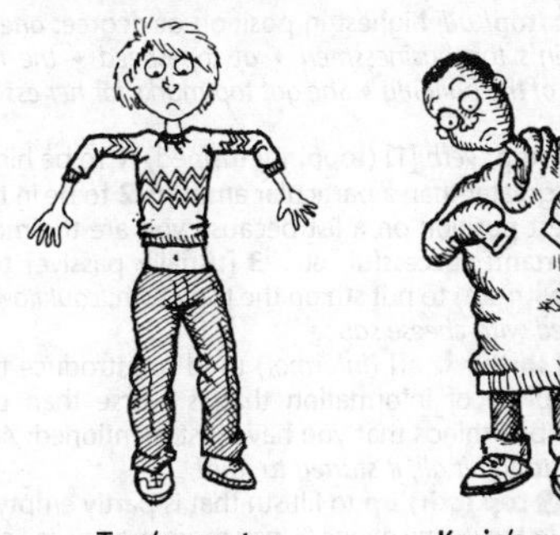

Tom's sweater is not big enough.

Kevin's sweater is too big.

too /tuː/ *adv* **1** [used before adjectives and adverbs] more than is good, allowed, possible, etc: *These boots are too small.* ◆ *It's far too cold to go out without a coat.* ◆ *It's too long a journey for you to make alone.*

HELP Notice that you cannot say 'It's a too long journey'.

2 [not with negative statements] in addition; also: *Red is my favourite colour but I like blue, too.* ◆ *Phil thinks you're right and I do too.* ➲ note at **also**

HELP Notice that at the end of a clause you use **too** for agreement with positive statements and **either** for agreement with negative statements: *I like eating out and Rakesh does too.* ◆ *I don't like cooking and Rakesh doesn't either.*

3 used to add sth which makes a situation even worse: *Her purse was stolen. And on her birthday, too.* **4** [usually used in negative sentences] very: *The weather is not too bad today.*

IDM be too much (for sb) to need more ability than you have; to be more difficult than you can bear

took *past tense* of **take**

tools

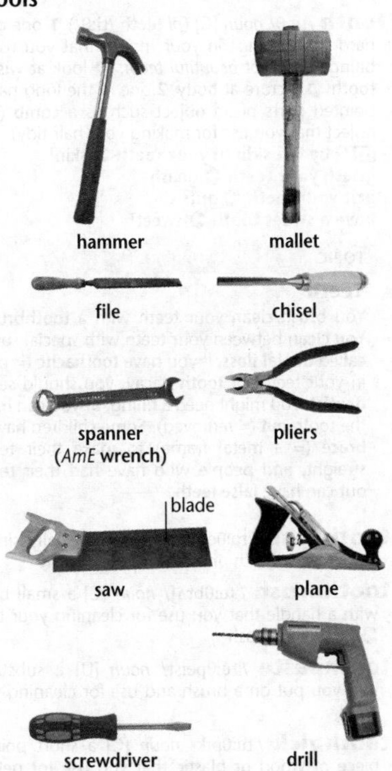

OTHER WORDS FOR

tool

A **tool** is usually something you can hold in your hand, for example a spanner or hammer. An **implement** is often used outside, for example for farming or gardening. A **machine** has moving parts and works by electricity, with an engine, etc. An **instrument** is often used for technical or delicate work: *a dentist's instruments.* A **device** is a more general word for a piece of equipment that you consider to be useful and that is designed to do one particular task: *The machine has a safety device which switches the power off if there is a fault.*

tool /tuːl/ *noun* [C] a piece of equipment such as a hammer, that you hold in your hand(s) and use to do a particular job: *Hammers, screwdrivers and saws are all carpenter's tools.* ♦ *garden tools* ♦ *a tool kit* (= a set of tools in a box or a bag)

toolbar /ˈtuːlbɑː(r)/ *noun* [C] a row of symbols on a computer screen that show the different things that the computer can do

toot /tuːt/ *noun* [C] the short high sound that a car horn makes ▶ **toot** *verb* [I,T] (*especially BrE*): *Toot your horn to let them know we're here.*

tooth /tuːθ/ *noun* [C] (*pl* **teeth** /tiːθ/) **1** one of the hard white things in your mouth that you use for biting: *She's got beautiful teeth.* ➲ look at **wisdom tooth** ➲ picture at **body** **2** one of the long narrow pointed parts of an object such as a **comb** (= an object that you use for making your hair tidy)
IDM **by the skin of your teeth** ➲ **skin**[1]
gnash your teeth ➲ **gnash**
grit your teeth ➲ **grit**[2]
have a sweet tooth ➲ **sweet**[1]

TOPIC

Teeth

You **brush/clean** your teeth with a **toothbrush**. You clean between your teeth with special string called **dental floss**. If you have **toothache** (= pain in your teeth) or **tooth decay**, you should see a **dentist**. You might need a **filling**, or you can **have** the tooth **out** (= removed). Some children have a **brace** (= a metal frame) to make their teeth straight, and people who have had their teeth out can have **false teeth**.

toothache /ˈtuːθeɪk/ *noun* [U,C, usually sing] a pain in your tooth or teeth ➲ note at **ache**

toothbrush /ˈtuːθbrʌʃ/ *noun* [C] a small brush with a handle that you use for cleaning your teeth ➲ picture at **brush**

toothpaste /ˈtuːθpeɪst/ *noun* [U] a substance that you put on a brush and use for cleaning your teeth

toothpick /ˈtuːθpɪk/ *noun* [C] a short pointed piece of wood or plastic that you use for getting pieces of food out from between your teeth

top[1] /tɒp/ *noun*
➤HIGHEST PART **1** [C] the highest part or point of sth: *The flat is* **at the top of** *the stairs.* ♦ *Snow was falling on the mountain tops.* ♦ *Start reading at the top of the page.* **OPP** **foot**
➤FARTHEST POINT **2** [sing] the end of a street, table, etc. that is farthest away from you or from where you usually come to it: *I'll meet you at the top of Broad Street.*
➤FLAT SURFACE **3** [C] the flat upper surface of sth: *a desk/table/bench top*
➤HIGHEST POSITION **4** [sing] **the top (of sth)** the highest or most important position: *to be at the top of your profession*
➤FOR PEN, ETC. **5** [C] the cover that you put onto sth in order to close it: *Put the tops back on the pens or they will dry out.* ➲ picture at **container**

HELP **Top, cap** or **lid**? A **top** or a **cap** is often small and round. You often take it off by turning: *a bottle top* ♦ *Unscrew cap to open.* A **lid** may be larger. You can lift it off: *a saucepan lid* ♦ *Put the lid back on the box.*

➤CLOTHING **6** [C] a piece of clothing that you wear on the upper part of your body: *a tracksuit/bikini/pyjama top* ♦ *I need a top to match my new skirt.* ➲ picture on **page P1**
➤TOY **7** [C] a child's toy that turns round very quickly on a point: *a spinning top*
IDM **at the top of your voice** as loudly as possible
get on top of sb (*informal*) to be too much for sb to manage or deal with: *I've got so much work to do. It's really getting on top of me.*
off the top of your head (*informal*) just guessing or using your memory without preparing or thinking about sth first
on top 1 on or onto the highest point: *a mountain with snow on top* **2** in control; in a leading position: *Josie always seems to come out on top.*
on top of sb/sth 1 on, over or covering sb/sth else: *Books were piled on top of one another.* ♦ *The remote control is on top of the TV.* **2** in addition to sb/sth else: *On top of everything else, the car's broken down.* **3** (*informal*) very close to sb/sth: *We were all living on top of each other in that tiny flat.*
over the top; OTT /ˌəʊ tiːˈtiː/ (*especially BrE spoken*) exaggerated or done with too much effort

top[2] /tɒp/ *adj* highest in position or degree: *one of Britain's top businessmen* ♦ *at top speed* ♦ *the top floor of the building* ♦ *She got top marks for her essay.*

top[3] /tɒp/ *verb* [T] (**topping; topped**) **1** to be higher or greater than a particular amount **2** to be in the highest position on a list because you are the most important, successful, etc. **3** [usually passive] **top sth (with sth)** to put sth on the top of sth: *cauliflower topped with cheese sauce*
IDM **to top it all** (*informal*) used to introduce the final piece of information that is worse than the other bad things that you have just mentioned: *And then, to top it all, it started to rain!*
PHR V **top (sth) up** to fill sth that is partly empty: *I need to top up my phone* (= pay more money so I can make more calls).

ˌtop ˈhat *noun* [C] the tall black or grey hat that a man wears on formal occasions ➲ picture at **hat**

ˌtop-ˈheavy *adj* heavier at the top than the bottom and likely to fall over

EXAM TIP

Topics

Revise vocabulary in related themes. The dictionary is a complete alphabetical list of words, but when you learn words, you will want to look at groups that belong together. Use the **Topic notes** to make sure you know the important words about each subject. If you have the **Wordpower CD-ROM**, choose a topic a day from the **Topic Dictionary** until you have revised all the topics you need to know for your exam.

T

🔑 **topic** /ˈtɒpɪk/ *noun* [C] a subject that you talk, write or learn about: *The main* ***topic of conversation*** *was Tim's new girlfriend.* ◆ *The topic for today's discussion is ...*

topical /ˈtɒpɪkl/ *adj* connected with sth that is happening now; that people are interested in at the present time

topless /ˈtɒpləs/ *adj, adv* (used about a woman) not wearing any clothes on the upper part of the body so that her breasts are not covered

topmost /ˈtɒpməʊst/ *adj* [only *before* a noun] highest: *the topmost branches of the tree*

topping /ˈtɒpɪŋ/ *noun* [C,U] something such as cream or a sauce that is put on the top of food to decorate it or make it taste nicer

topple /ˈtɒpl/ *verb* **1** [I] topple (over) to become less steady and fall down: *Don't add another book to the pile or it will topple over.* **2** [T] to cause a leader of a country, etc. to lose his or her position of power or authority

ˌtop ˈsecret *adj* that must be kept very secret, especially from other governments

ˈtop-up *noun* [C] (*BrE*) **1** a payment that you make to increase the amount of money, etc. to the level that is needed: *a phone top-up* **2** (*informal*) an amount of a drink that you add to a cup or glass in order to fill it again: *Can I give anyone a top-up?*

the Torah *noun* [sing] (in the Jewish religion) the law of God as given to Moses and recorded in the first five books of the Bible

torch /tɔːtʃ/ *noun* [C] **1** (*AmE* flashlight) a small electric light that you carry in your hand: *Shine the torch under the sofa and see if you can find my ring.* **2** a long piece of wood with burning material at the end that you carry to give light: *the Olympic torch*

torch

tore *past tense* of **tear²**

torment /ˈtɔːment/ *noun* [U,C] (*formal*) great pain and suffering in your mind or body; a person or thing that causes this: *to be* ***in torment*** ▶ **torment** /tɔːˈment/ *verb* [T]

torn *past participle* of **tear²**

tornado /tɔːˈneɪdəʊ/ *noun* [C] (*pl* tornados *or* tornadoes) a violent storm with very strong winds that move in a circle. **Tornadoes** form a tall column of air which is narrower at the bottom than at the top. ➲ note at **storm**

torpedo /tɔːˈpiːdəʊ/ *noun* [C] (*pl* torpedoes) a long narrow bomb that is fired under the water from a ship or **submarine** (= a type of ship that travels under the water) and explodes when it hits another ship

torrent /ˈtɒrənt/ *noun* [C] a strong fast flow of sth, especially water: *The rain was coming down* ***in torrents***.

torrential /təˈrenʃl/ *adj* (used about rain) very great in amount

torso /ˈtɔːsəʊ/ *noun* [C] (*pl* torsos) the main part of your body, not your head, arms and legs

tortoise /ˈtɔːtəs/ (*AmE* also turtle) *noun* [C] a small animal with a hard shell that moves very slowly. A **tortoise** can pull its head and legs into its shell to protect them. ➲ picture on **page P13**

tortuous /ˈtɔːtʃuəs/ *adj* (*formal*) **1** complicated, not clear and simple **2** (used about a road, etc.) with many bends

torture /ˈtɔːtʃə(r)/ *noun* [U,C] **1** the act of causing sb great pain either as a punishment or to make them say or do sth: *a confession extracted* ***under torture*** **2** mental or physical suffering: *It's torture having to sit here and listen to him complaining.* ▶ **torture** *verb* [T]: *Prisoners were tortured into making confessions.* ◆ *She was tortured by the thought that the accident was her fault.* ▶ **torturer** *noun* [C]

Tory /ˈtɔːri/ *noun* [C] (*pl* Tories) *adj* a member of, or sb who supports, the British Conservative Party; connected with this party: *the Tory Party conference*

toss /tɒs/ *verb* **1** [T] to throw sth lightly and carelessly: *Rhodri opened the letter and tossed the envelope into the bin.* **2** [T] to move your head back quickly, especially to show you are annoyed or impatient: *I tried to apologize but she just* ***tossed*** *her* ***head*** *and walked away.* **3** [I,T] to move, or make sb/sth move, up and down or from side to side: *He lay* ***tossing and turning*** *in bed, unable to sleep.* ◆ *The ship was tossed about by huge waves.* **4** [I,T] toss (up) (for sth) to throw a coin into the air in order to decide sth, by guessing which side of the coin will land facing upwards: *to toss a coin*

> **MORE** Look at **heads** and **tails**. These are the names of the two sides of a coin. We ask 'Heads or tails?' when we want someone to guess which side will face upwards.

▶ **toss** *noun* [C]

IDM **win/lose the toss** to guess correctly/wrongly which side of a coin will face upwards when it lands: *Ms Kvitova won the toss and chose to serve first.*

tot¹ /tɒt/ *noun* [C] **1** (*informal*) a very small child **2** (*especially BrE*) a small glass of a strong alcoholic drink

tot² /tɒt/ *verb* (totting; totted)

PHR V **tot (sth) up** (*informal*) to add numbers together to form a total

🔑 **total¹** /ˈtəʊtl/ *adj* **1** being the amount after everyone or everything is counted or added together: *What was the total number of people there?* **2** complete: *a total failure* ◆ *The couple ate in total silence.*

🔑 **total²** /ˈtəʊtl/ *noun* [C] the number that you get when you add two or more numbers or amounts together

IDM **in total** when you add two or more numbers or amounts together: *The appeal raised £4 million in total.*

▶ **total** *verb* [T] (totalling; totalled, (*AmE*) totaling; totaled): *His debts totalled more than £10000.*

T

totally /ˈtəʊtəli/ *adv* completely: *I totally agree with you.*

totter /ˈtɒtə(r)/ *verb* [I] to stand or move in a way that is not steady, as if you are going to fall, especially because you are drunk, ill or weak

touch¹ /tʌtʃ/ *verb* **1** [T] to put your hand or fingers onto sb/sth: *It's very delicate so don't touch it.* ◆ *He touched her gently on the cheek.* ◆ *The police asked us not to touch anything.* **2** [I,T] (used about two or more things, surfaces, etc.) to be or move so close together that there is no space between them: *They were sitting so close that their shoulders touched.* ◆ *This bicycle is too big. My feet don't* ***touch the ground.*** **3** [T] to make sb feel sad, sorry for sb, grateful, etc. ➲ look at **touched** **4** [T] [in negative sentences] to be as good as sb/sth in skill, quality, etc: *He's a much better player than all the others. No one else can touch him.*

IDM **knock on wood; touch wood** ➲ **wood**

PHR V **touch down** (used about an aircraft) to land

touch on/upon sth to mention or refer to a subject for only a short time

touch² /tʌtʃ/ *noun*

➤SENSE **1** [U] one of the five senses: the ability to feel things and know what they are like by putting your hands or fingers on them: *The* ***sense of touch*** *is very important to blind people.*

➤WITH HAND **2** [C, usually sing] the act of putting your hands or fingers onto sb/sth: *I felt the touch of her hand on my arm.* ➲ picture at **exercise**

➤WAY STH FEELS **3** [U] the way sth feels when you touch it: *Marble is cold* ***to the touch.***

➤DETAIL **4** [C] a small detail that is added to improve sth: *The flowers in our room were* ***a nice touch.*** ◆ *She's just* ***putting the finishing touches to*** *the cake.*

➤WAY OF DOING STH **5** [sing] a way or style of doing sth: *She prefers to write her letters by hand for a more* ***personal touch.***

➤SMALL AMOUNT **6** [sing] **a touch (of sth)** a small amount of sth: *He's not very ill. It's just a touch of flu.*

IDM **in/out of touch (with sb)** being/not being in contact with sb by speaking or writing to them: *During the year she was abroad, they* ***kept in touch*** *by email.*

in/out of touch with sth having/not having recent information about sth: *We're out of touch with what's going on.*

lose touch ➲ **lose**

lose your touch ➲ **lose**

touched /tʌtʃt/ *adj* [not before a noun] **touched (by sth); touched that …** made to feel sad, sorry for sb, grateful, etc: *We were very touched by the plight of the refugees.* ◆ *I was touched that he offered to help.*

touching /ˈtʌtʃɪŋ/ *adj* that makes you feel sad, sorry for sb, grateful, etc. **SYN** **moving**

ˈtouch pad (also **trackpad**) *noun* [C] a device which you touch in different places in order to operate a computer: *I use the touch pad on my laptop much more than the mouse.* ➲ picture at **computer**

ˈtouch screen *noun* [C] a computer screen which shows information when you touch it: *My satnav has a touch screen.* ◆ *a touch-screen phone*

TOPIC

Touch screens

With a **touch-screen phone** you can send and receive emails, **browse web pages** (= look for information), **stream music** and **videos** (= listen to them or view them via the Internet without buying or owning the files) or **download content**, as well as making calls. On a **touch-screen computer** you **swipe** to move across the screen, **zoom** to make the screen larger and see the details, and **pinch in** to make the screen smaller.

touchy /ˈtʌtʃi/ *adj* (**touchier; touchiest**) **1** **touchy (about sth)** easily upset or made angry: *He's a bit touchy about his weight.* **2** (used about a subject, situation, etc.) that may easily upset people or make them angry: *Don't mention the exam. It's a very touchy subject.* **SYN** for both meanings **sensitive**

tough /tʌf/ *adj* (**tougher; toughest**)

➤DIFFICULT **1** having or causing problems: *It will be a tough decision to make.* ◆ *He's had* ***a tough time of it*** *(= a lot of problems) recently.*

➤STRICT **2** **tough (on/with sb/sth)** not feeling sorry for anyone: *Don't be too tough on them—they were trying to help.* ◆ *The government plans to* ***get tough with*** *people who drink and drive.*

➤STRONG **3** strong enough to deal with difficult conditions or situations: *You need to be tough to go climbing in winter.* **4** not easily broken, torn or cut; very strong: *a tough pair of boots*

➤MEAT **5** difficult to cut and eat

➤BAD LUCK **6** (*informal*) **tough (on sb)** unfortunate for sb in a way that seems unfair: *It's tough on her that she lost her job.* ▶ **toughness** *noun* [U]

toughen /ˈtʌfn/ *verb* [I,T] **toughen (sb/sth) (up)** to make sb/sth **tough**

toupee /ˈtuːpeɪ/ *noun* [C] a small section of artificial hair, worn by a man to cover an area of his head where hair no longer grows

tour /tʊə(r); tɔː(r)/ *noun* **1** [C] **a tour (of/round/around sth)** a journey that you make for pleasure during which you visit many places: *to* ***go on a*** *ten-day coach* ***tour*** *of/around Scotland* ◆ *a sightseeing tour* ◆ *a tour operator* (= a person or company that organizes tours) ➲ note at **travel** **2** [C] a short visit around a city, famous building, etc: *a* ***guided tour*** *round St Paul's Cathedral* **3** [C,U] an official series of visits that singers, musicians, sports players, etc. make to different places to perform, play, etc: *The band is currently* ***on tour*** *in America.* ◆ *a concert/cricket tour* ▶ **tour** *verb* [I,T]: *We toured southern Spain for three weeks.*

tourism /ˈtʊərɪzəm; ˈtɔːr-/ *noun* [U] the business of providing and arranging holidays and services for people who are visiting a place: *The country's economy relies heavily on tourism.*

tourist /ˈtʊərɪst; ˈtɔːr-/ *noun* [C] a person who visits a place for pleasure: *The city is full of tourists* in summer. ♦ You can get more information at the local **tourist office**. ➲ look at **sightseer**

tournament /ˈtʊənəmənt; ˈtɔːn-/ *noun* [C] a competition in which many players or teams play games against each other

tourniquet /ˈtʊənɪkeɪ/ *noun* [C] a band of cloth that is tied tightly around an arm or a leg to stop the loss of blood from a wound

tousled /ˈtaʊzld/ *adj* (used about hair) untidy, often in an attractive way

tow /təʊ/ *verb* [T] to pull a car or boat behind another vehicle, using a rope or chain: *My car was towed away by the police.*
IDM **in tow** (*informal*) following closely behind: *He arrived with his wife and five children in tow.*
▶ **tow** *noun* [sing]

towards /təˈwɔːdz/ (also **toward** /təˈwɔːd/) *prep* **1** in the direction of sb/sth: *I saw Ken walking towards the station.* ♦ *She had her back towards me.* ♦ *a first step towards world peace* **2** near or nearer a time or date: *It gets cool towards evening.* ♦ *The shops get very busy towards Christmas.* **3** (used when you are talking about your feelings about sb/sth) in relation to: *Patti felt very protective towards her younger brother.* ♦ *What is your attitude towards this government?* **4** as part of the payment for sth: *The money will* ***go towards*** *the cost of a new minibus.*

towel /ˈtaʊəl/ *noun* [C] a piece of cloth or paper that you use for drying sb/sth/yourself: *a bath/hand/beach towel* ♦ *kitchen/paper towels* ➲ look at **sanitary towel, tea towel**

tower /ˈtaʊə(r)/ *noun* [C] a tall narrow building or part of a building such as a church or castle: *the Eiffel Tower* ♦ *a church tower* ▶ **tower** *verb* [T]
PHR V **tower over/above sb/sth** to be much higher or taller than the people or things that are near: *The cliffs towered above them.* ♦ *He towers over all his classmates.*

ˈtower block *noun* [C] (*BrE*) a very tall building consisting of flats or offices

town /taʊn/ *noun* **1** [C] a place with many streets and buildings. A town is larger than a village but smaller than a city: *Romsey is a small market town.* ♦ *After ten years away, she decided to move back to her* ***home town*** (= the town where she was born and lived when she was a child). **2 the town** [sing] all the people who live in a town: *The whole town is talking about it.* **3** [U] the main part of a town, where the shops, etc. are: *I've got to go into town this afternoon.*
IDM **go to town (on sth)** (*informal*) to do sth with a lot of energy and enthusiasm; to spend a lot of money on sth
(out) on the town (*informal*) going to restaurants, theatres, clubs, etc. for entertainment, especially at night

ˌtown ˈcouncil *noun* [C] (in the UK) a group of people who are responsible for the local government of a town

ˌtown ˈhall *noun* [C] a large building that contains the local government offices and often a large room for public meetings, concerts, etc. ➲ look at **hall**

toxic /ˈtɒksɪk/ *adj* poisonous

toy[1] /tɔɪ/ *noun* [C] an object for a child to play with: *The children were playing happily with their toys.* ♦ *a toyshop* ▶ **toy** *adj* [only *before* a noun]: *a toy soldier/farm*

toy[2] /tɔɪ/ *verb*
PHR V **toy with sth** **1** to think about doing sth, perhaps not very seriously: *She's* ***toying with the idea of*** *going abroad for a year.* **2** to move sth about without thinking about what you are doing, often because you are nervous or upset: *He toyed with his food but hardly ate any of it.*

trace[1] /treɪs/ *verb* [T] **1 trace sb/sth (to sth)** to find out where sb/sth is by following marks, signs or other information: *The wanted man was traced to an address in Amsterdam.* **2 trace sth (back) (to sth)** to find out where sth came from or what caused it; to describe the development of sth: *She traced her family tree back to the 16th century.* **3** to make a copy of a map, plan, etc. by placing a piece of **tracing paper** (= transparent paper) over it and drawing over the lines

trace[2] /treɪs/ *noun* **1** [C,U] a mark, an object or a sign that shows that sb/sth existed or happened: *traces of an earlier civilization* ♦ *The man* ***disappeared/vanished without trace.*** **2** [C] **a trace (of sth)** a very small amount of sth: *Traces of blood were found under her fingernails.*

track[1] /træk/ *noun*
➤PATH **1** [C] a natural path or rough road: *Follow the dirt track through the forest.* ➲ picture on **page P10**
➤MARKS ON GROUND **2** [C, usually pl] marks that are left on the ground by a person, an animal or a moving vehicle: *The hunter followed the tracks of a deer.* ♦ *tyre tracks* ➲ look at **footprint**
➤FOR TRAIN **3** [C,U] the two metal rails on which a train runs: *The train stopped because there was a tree across the track.*
➤FOR RACE **4** [C] a piece of ground, often in a circle, for people, cars, etc. to have races on: *a running track*
➤MUSIC **5** [C] one song or piece of music on a CD, record, etc: *the first track from her latest album* ➲ look at **soundtrack**
IDM **keep/lose track of sb/sth** to have/not have information about what is happening or where sb/sth is
off the beaten track ➲ **beat**[1]
on the right/wrong track having the right/wrong idea about sth: *That's not the answer but you're on the right track.*

track[2] /træk/ *verb* [T] to follow the movements of sb/sth: *to track enemy planes on a radar screen*
PHR V **track sb/sth down** to find sb/sth after searching for them or it

ˈtrack event *noun* [C] a sports event that consists of running round a track in a race, rather than throwing sth or jumping ➲ look at **field event**

trackpad /ˈtrækpæd/ = **touch pad**

ˈtrack record *noun* [sing] all the past successes or failures of a person or an organization

T

tracksuit /ˈtræksuːt/ *noun* [C] a warm pair of soft trousers and a matching jacket that you wear for sports practice

tractor /ˈtræktə(r)/ *noun* [C] a large vehicle that is used on farms for pulling heavy pieces of machinery

tractor

trade¹ /treɪd/ *noun* **1** [U] the buying or selling of goods or services between people or countries: *an international trade agreement* ◆ *Trade is not very good* (= not many goods are sold) *at this time of year.* **2** [C] a particular type of business: *the tourist/building/retail trade* **3** [C,U] a job for which you need special skill, especially with your hands: *Jeff is a plumber* ***by trade.*** ◆ *to learn a trade* ➲ note at **work**

trade² /treɪd/ *verb* **1** [I] trade (in sth) (with sb) to buy or sell goods or services: *We no longer trade with that country.* ◆ *to trade in luxury goods* ◆ *to trade in stocks and shares* **2** [T] trade sth (for sth) to exchange sth for sth else: *He traded his iPod for some concert tickets.*

PHR V **trade sth in (for sth)** to give sth old in part payment for sth new or newer: *We traded in our old car for a van.*

▶ **trading** *noun* [U]

trademark /ˈtreɪdmɑːk/ *noun* [C] (*abbr* TM) a special symbol, design or name that a company puts on its products and that cannot be used by any other company

trader /ˈtreɪdə(r)/ *noun* [C] a person who buys and sells things, especially goods in a market or company shares ➲ picture on **page P11**

tradesman /ˈtreɪdzmən/ *noun* [C] (*pl* -men /-mən/) a person who brings goods or services to people's homes or who has a shop

ˌtrade ˈunion = **union**

tradition /trəˈdɪʃn/ *noun* [C,U] a custom, belief or way of doing sth that has continued from the past to the present: *religious/cultural/literary traditions* ◆ ***By tradition****, the bride's family pays the costs of the wedding.* ▶ **traditional** /-ʃənl/ *adj*: *It is traditional in Britain to eat turkey at Christmas.* ▶ **traditionally** /-ʃənəli/ *adv*

traffic /ˈtræfɪk/ *noun* [U] **1** all the vehicles that are on a road at a particular time: *heavy/light traffic* ◆ *We got stuck* ***in traffic*** *and were late for the meeting.* **2** the movement of ships, aircraft, etc: *air traffic control* **3** traffic (in sth) the illegal buying and selling of sth: *the traffic in drugs/firearms*

ˈtraffic island (*BrE* island) *noun* [C] a higher area in the middle of the road, where you can stand and wait for the traffic to pass when you want to cross

ˈtraffic jam *noun* [C] a long line of cars, etc. that cannot move or that can only move very slowly: *We were stuck in a terrible traffic jam.* ➲ note at **driving**

trafficking /ˈtræfɪkɪŋ/ *noun* [U] the activity of buying and selling sth illegally: *drug trafficking* ▶ **trafficker** *noun* [C]: *a drugs trafficker*

ˈtraffic light *noun* [C, usually pl] a sign with red, orange and green lights that is used for controlling the traffic where two or more roads meet ➲ picture at **roundabout**

ˈtraffic warden *noun* [C] (*BrE*) a person whose job is to check that cars are not parked in the wrong place or for longer than is allowed ➲ note at **parking**

tragedy /ˈtrædʒədi/ *noun* (*pl* **tragedies**) [C,U] **1** a very sad event or situation, especially one that involves death: *It's a tragedy that he died so young.* **2** a serious play that has a sad ending; plays of this type: *Shakespeare's 'King Lear' is a tragedy.* ➲ look at **comedy**

tragic /ˈtrædʒɪk/ *adj* **1** that makes you very sad, especially because it involves death: *It's tragic that she lost her only child.* ◆ *a tragic accident* **2** [only before a noun] (used about literature) in the style of **tragedy**: *a tragic actor/hero* ▶ **tragically** /-kli/ *adv*

trail¹ /treɪl/ *noun* [C] **1** a series of marks in a long line that is left by sb/sth as he/she/it moves: *a trail of blood/footprints* **2** a track, sign or smell that is left behind and that you follow when you are hunting sb/sth: *The dogs ran off* ***on the trail of*** *the fox.* **3** a path through the country

trail² /treɪl/ *verb* **1** [I,T] to pull or be pulled along behind sb/sth: *The skirt was too long and trailed along the ground.* **2** [I] to move or walk slowly behind sb/sth else, usually because you are tired or bored: *It was impossible to do any shopping with the kids trailing around after me.* **3** [I,T] [usually used in the continuous tenses] trail (by/in sth) to be in the process of losing a game or a competition: *At half-time Liverpool were trailing by two goals to three.* **4** [I] (used about plants or sth long and thin) to grow over sth and hang downwards; to lie across a surface: *Computer wires trailed across the floor.*

PHR V **trail away/off** (used about sb's voice) to gradually become quieter and then stop

trailer /ˈtreɪlə(r)/ *noun* [C] **1** a type of container with wheels that is pulled by a vehicle: *a car towing a trailer with a boat on it* **2** (*AmE*) = **caravan**(1) **3** (*especially BrE*) a series of short pieces taken from a film and used to advertise it ➲ look at **clip**

train¹ /treɪn/ *noun* [C] **1** a type of transport that is pulled by an engine along a railway line. A train is divided into **carriages** and **coaches** (= sections for people) and **wagons** (= for goods): *a passenger/goods/freight train* ◆ *a fast/slow/express train* ◆ *to catch/take/get the train to London* ◆ *the 12 o'clock train to Bristol* ◆ *to get on/off a train* ◆ *Hurry up or we'll* ***miss the train.*** ◆ *You have to* ***change trains*** *at Reading.* ➲ picture on **page P7**

> **HELP** Note that we say **by train** when speaking in general. To talk about one particular train journey we say **on the train**: *Victoria travels to work by train.* ◆ *Yesterday she left her scarf on the train.*

2 [usually sing] a series of thoughts or events that

T

are connected: *A knock at the door interrupted my train of thought.*

TOPIC

Travelling by train

You go to the **station** to **catch** a train. You can buy a **single** (= to your destination but not back) or a **return** (= to your destination and back). In American English these are called a **one-way ticket** and a **round-trip ticket**. A **first-class** ticket is the most expensive type of ticket. A **timetable** is the list that shows the times when trains **arrive** and **depart** (= leave). You wait on the **platform** to get on your train. Sometimes it might be **delayed** (= late) or even **cancelled**. If you are late and the train is **on time**, you will **miss** it. If there is no **direct** service, you will have to **change** (= get off your train and get on another in order to continue your journey).

train² /treɪn/ *verb* **1** [T] train sb (as sth/to do sth) to teach a person to do sth which is difficult or which needs practice: *The organization trains guide dogs for the blind.* ♦ *There is a shortage of trained teachers.* **2** [I,T] train (as/in sth) (to do sth) to learn how to do a job: *She trained as an engineer.* ♦ *He's not trained in anything.* ♦ *He's training to be a doctor.* **3** [I,T] train (for sth) to prepare yourself, especially for a sports event, by practising; to help a person or an animal to do this: *I'm training for the London Marathon.* ♦ *to train racehorses*

PHR V **train sth at/on sb/sth** to point a gun, camera, etc. at sb/sth

ˈ**train driver** = engine driver

trainee /ˌtreɪˈniː/ *noun* [C] a person who is being taught how to do a particular job

trainer /ˈtreɪnə(r)/ *noun* [C] **1** (*AmE* sneaker) [usually pl] a shoe that you wear for doing sport or as informal clothing ➲ look at **plimsoll** ➲ picture at **shoe** ➲ picture on **page P1** **2** a person who teaches people or animals a skill or how to do a particular job well, or to do a particular sport: *teacher trainers* ♦ *a racehorse trainer*

training /ˈtreɪnɪŋ/ *noun* [U] **1** training (in sth/in doing sth) the process of learning the skills that you need to do a job: *Few candidates had received any training in management.* ♦ *a training course* **2** the process of preparing to take part in a sports competition by doing physical exercises: *to be **in training** for the Olympics*

trainspotter /ˈtreɪnspɒtə(r)/ *noun* [C] (*BrE*) **1** a person who collects the numbers of railway engines as a hobby **2** a person who has a boring hobby or who is interested in the details of a subject that other people find boring ▸ **trainspotting** *noun* [U]

trait /treɪt/ *noun* [C] a quality that forms part of your character

traitor /ˈtreɪtə(r)/ *noun* [C] a traitor (to sb/sth) a person who is not loyal to their country, friends, etc.

MORE A traitor **betrays** his/her friends, country, etc. and the crime against his/her country is called **treason**.

tram /træm/ (*AmE* streetcar; trolley) *noun* [C] a type of bus that works by electricity and that moves along special rails in the road carrying passengers ➲ picture on **page P7**

tramp¹ /træmp/ *noun* **1** [C] a person who has no home or job and who moves from place to place **2** [sing] the sound of people walking with heavy or noisy steps

tramp² /træmp/ *verb* [I,T] to walk with slow heavy steps, especially for a long time

trample /ˈtræmpl/ *verb* [I,T] trample on/over sb/sth to walk on sb/sth and damage or hurt them or it: *The boys trampled on the flowers.*

trampoline

trampoline /ˈtræmpəliːn/ *noun* [C] a piece of equipment for jumping up and down on, made of a piece of strong cloth fixed to a metal frame by springs ▸ **trampoline** *verb* [I] ▸ **trampolining** *noun* [U]

trance /trɑːns/ *noun* [C] a mental state in which you do not notice what is going on around you: *to go/fall into a trance*

tranquil /ˈtræŋkwɪl/ *adj* (*formal*) calm and quiet

tranquillizer (also -iser; *AmE* tranquilizer) /ˈtræŋkwəlaɪzə(r)/ *noun* [C] a drug that is used for making people or animals calm or unconscious ➲ look at **sedative** ▸ **tranquillize** (also -ise; *AmE* tranquilize) *verb* [T]

transaction /trænˈzækʃn/ *noun* [C] a piece of business that is done between people: *financial transactions*

transatlantic /ˌtrænzətˈlæntɪk/ *adj* [only *before* a noun] to or from the other side of the Atlantic Ocean; across the Atlantic: *a transatlantic flight/voyage*

transcend /trænˈsend/ *verb* [T] (*formal*) to go further than the usual limits of sth

transcribe /trænˈskraɪb/ *verb* [T] transcribe sth (into sth) to record thoughts, speech or data in a written form, or in a different written form from the original: *The interview was recorded and then transcribed.*

transcript /ˈtrænskrɪpt/ (also **transcription** /trænˈskrɪpʃn/) *noun* [C] a written or printed copy of what sb has said: *a transcript of the interview/trial*

transfer¹ /trænsˈfɜː(r)/ *verb* (**transferring**; **transferred**) **1** [I,T] **transfer (sb/sth) (from ...) (to ...)** to move, or to make sb/sth move, from one place to another: *He's transferring to our Tokyo branch next month.* ◆ *I'd like to transfer £1 000 from my deposit account* (= in a bank). ◆ *Transfer the data onto a disk.* **2** [T] to officially arrange for sth to belong to, or be controlled by, sb else: *She transferred the property to her son.* ▶ **transferable** *adj*: *This ticket is not transferable* (= may only be used by the person who bought it).

transfer² /ˈtrænsfɜː(r)/ *noun* **1** [C,U] moving or being moved from one place, job or state to another: *Paul is not happy here and has asked for a transfer.* **2** [U] changing to a different vehicle or route during a journey: *Transfer from the airport to the hotel is included.* **3** [C] (*AmE*) a ticket that allows you to continue your journey on another bus or train **4** [C] (*especially BrE*) a piece of paper with a picture or writing on it that you can stick onto another surface by pressing or heating it

transform /trænsˈfɔːm/ *verb* [T] **transform sb/sth (from sth) (into sth)** to change sb/sth completely, especially in a way which improves sb/sth: *Having a baby has transformed my life.* ▶ **transformation** /ˌtrænsfəˈmeɪʃn/ *noun* [C,U]: *Our lifestyles have **undergone a** complete **transformation** in the past decade.*

transformer /trænsˈfɔːmə(r)/ *noun* [C] a device for reducing or increasing the strength of a supply of electricity, usually to allow a particular piece of electrical equipment to be used

transfusion /trænsˈfjuːʒn/ *noun* [C] the act of putting new blood into sb's body because they are ill: *a blood transfusion*

T

transistor /trænˈzɪstə(r)/ *noun* [C] a small piece of electronic equipment that is used in computers, radios, TVs, etc.

transit /ˈtrænzɪt/ *noun* [U] **1** the act of being moved or carried from one place to another: *The goods had been damaged **in transit**.* **2** going through a place on the way to somewhere else

transition /trænˈzɪʃn/ *noun* [C,U] **(a) transition (from sth) (to sth)** a change from one state or form to another: *the transition from childhood to adolescence* ▶ **transitional** /-ʃənl/ *adj*: *a transitional stage/period*

transitive /ˈtrænsətɪv/ *adj* (used about a verb) that has a direct object. Transitive verbs are marked '[T]' in this dictionary. **OPP** **intransitive** ℹ For more information about transitive verbs, look at the **Reference Section** at the back of this dictionary.

translate /trænsˈleɪt; trænz-/ *verb* [I,T] **translate (sth) (from sth) (into sth)** to change sth written or spoken from one language to another: *This book has been translated from Czech into English.* ➲ look at **interpret** ▶ **translation** /trænsˈleɪʃn; trænz-/ *noun* [C,U]: *a word-for-word translation* ◆ *The book loses something **in translation**.*

translator /trænsˈleɪtə(r); trænz-/ *noun* [C] a person who changes sth that has been written or spoken from one language to another ➲ look at **interpreter**

translucent /trænsˈluːsnt; trænz-/ *adj* (*formal*) that light can pass through ➲ look at **opaque**, **transparent** ▶ **translucence** (also **translucency** /-snsi/) *noun* [U]

transmission /trænsˈmɪʃn; trænz-/ *noun* **1** [U] sending sth out or passing sth on from one person, place or thing to another: *the transmission of TV pictures by satellite* ◆ *the transmission of a disease/virus* **2** [C] a TV or radio programme **3** [U,C] the system in a car, etc. by which power is passed from the engine to the wheels

transmit /trænsˈmɪt; trænz-/ *verb* [T] (**transmitting**; **transmitted**) **1** to send out TV or radio programmes, electronic signals, etc: *The match was transmitted live all over the world.* **2** to send or pass sth from one person or place to another: *a sexually transmitted disease*

transmitter /trænsˈmɪtə(r); trænz-/ *noun* [C] a piece of equipment that sends out electronic signals, TV or radio programmes, etc.

transparency /trænsˈpærənsi/ *noun* [C] (*pl* **transparencies**) a picture printed on a piece of film, usually in a frame, that can be shown on a screen by shining light through the film: *a transparency for the overhead projector* ➲ look at **slide**

transparent /trænsˈpærənt/ *adj* that you can see through: *Glass is transparent.* **OPP** **opaque** ➲ look at **translucent**

transplant¹ /trænsˈplɑːnt; trænz-/ *verb* [T] **1** to take out an organ or other part of sb's body and put it into another person's body **2** to move a growing plant and plant it somewhere else ➲ look at **graft**

transplant² /ˈtrænsplɑːnt; ˈtrænz-/ *noun* [C] a medical operation in which an organ, etc. is taken out of sb's body and put into another person's body: *to have a heart/kidney transplant*

transport /ˈtrænspɔːt/ (*AmE usually* **transportation** /ˌtrænspɔːˈteɪʃn/) *noun* [U] **1** the act of carrying or taking people or goods from one place to another: *road/rail/sea transport* **2** vehicles that you travel in; a method of travel: *Do you have your own transport (for example a car)?* ◆ *I travel to school by **public transport**.* ◆ *His bike is his only **means of transport**.* ➲ picture on **page P6** ▶ **transport** /trænˈspɔːt/ *verb* [T]

transvestite /trænzˈvestaɪt/ *noun* [C] a person, especially a man, who enjoys dressing like a member of the opposite sex

trap¹ /træp/ *noun* [C] **1** a piece of equipment that you use for catching animals: *a mousetrap* ◆ *The rabbit's leg was caught in the trap.* **2** a clever plan that is designed to trick sb: *She **walked straight into the***

trap. **3** an unpleasant situation from which it is hard to escape: *He thought of marriage as a trap.*

trap² /træp/ *verb* [T] (**trapping**; **trapped**) **1** [often passive] to keep sb in a dangerous place or a bad situation from which they cannot escape: *The door closed behind them and they were trapped.* ◆ *Many people are trapped in low-paid jobs.* **2** to catch and keep or store sth: *Special glass panels trap heat from the sun.* **3** to force sb/sth into a place or situation from which they or it cannot escape: *Police believe this new evidence could help trap the killer.* **4** to catch an animal, etc. in a **trap**: *Raccoons used to be trapped for their fur.* **5** **trap sb (into sth/into doing sth)** to make sb do sth by tricking them: *She had been trapped into revealing her true identity.*

trapdoor /ˈtræpdɔː(r)/ *noun* [C] a small door in a floor or ceiling

trapeze /trəˈpiːz/ *noun* [C] a wooden or metal bar hanging from two ropes high above the ground, used by **acrobats** (= people who amuse an audience by performing difficult acts)

trappings /ˈtræpɪŋz/ *noun* [pl] (*formal*) clothes, possessions, etc. which are signs of a particular social position

trash /træʃ/ (*AmE*) = **rubbish**

ˈtrash can (*AmE*) = **dustbin, litter bin**

trashy /ˈtræʃi/ *adj* (*informal*) (**trashier**; **trashiest**) of poor quality: *trashy novels*

trauma /ˈtrɔːmə/ *noun* [C,U] (an event that causes) a state of great shock or sadness: *the trauma of losing your parents* ➲ look at **stress** ▶ **traumatic** /trɔːˈmætɪk/ *adj*

OTHER WORDS FOR

travel

The word **travel** is uncountable and you can only use it to talk about the general activity of moving from place to place: *Foreign travel is very popular these days.* When you talk about going from one particular place to another, you use **journey**. A journey can be long: *the journey across Canada* or short but repeated: *the journey to work.* A **tour** is a circular journey or walk during which you visit several places. You often use **trip** when you are thinking about the whole visit (including your stay in a place and the journeys there and back): *We're just back from a trip to Japan. We had a wonderful time.* A trip may be short: *a day trip*, or longer: *a trip round the world*, and can be for business or pleasure. An **excursion** is a short organized trip with a group of people. You **go on** a journey/tour/trip/excursion.

travel¹ /ˈtrævl/ *verb* (**travelling**; **travelled**, (*AmE*) **traveling**; **traveled**) **1** [I] to go from one place to another, especially over a long distance: *Charles travels a lot on business.* ◆ *to travel abroad* ◆ *to travel by sea/air/car* ◆ *to travel to work* ◆ *travelling expenses* ➲ note at **plane, train** **2** [I] to go or move at/in a particular speed, direction or distance: *News travels fast these days.* **3** [T] to make a journey of a particular distance: *They travelled 60 kilometres to come and see us.*

IDM **travel light** to take very few things with you when you travel

travel² /ˈtrævl/ *noun* **1** [U] the act of going from one place to another: *air/rail/space travel* ◆ *a travel bag/clock/iron* (= designed to be used when travelling) **2** **travels** [pl] time spent travelling, especially to places that are far away

ˈtravel agency *noun* [C] (*pl* **travel agencies**) a company that makes travel arrangements for people (arranging tickets, flights, hotels, etc.)

ˈtravel agent *noun* **1** [C] a person whose job is to make travel arrangements for people **2** **travel agent's** [sing] the shop where you can go to make travel arrangements, buy tickets, etc. ➲ note at **holiday**

traveller (*AmE* **traveler**) /ˈtrævələ(r)/ *noun* [C] **1** a person who is travelling or who often travels: *She is a frequent traveller to Belgium.* **2** (*BrE*) a person who travels around the country in a large vehicle and does not have a permanent home anywhere: *New Age travellers* ➲ note at **Gypsy**

ˈtraveller's cheque (*AmE* ˈ**traveler's check**) *noun* [C] a cheque that you can change into foreign money when you are travelling in other countries

ˈtravel-sick *adj* (*BrE*) feeling sick or **vomiting** (= bringing up food from the stomach) because of the movement of the vehicle you are travelling in ➲ look at **airsick, carsick, seasick**

trawl /trɔːl/ *verb* **1** [I,T] **trawl (through sth) (for sth/sb)**; **trawl sth (for sth/sb)** to search through a large amount of information or a large number of people, places, etc. looking for a particular thing or person: *The police are trawling through their files for similar cases.* ◆ *She trawled the shops for bargains.* **2** [I] **trawl (for sth)** to try to catch fish by pulling a large net with a wide opening through the water

trawler /ˈtrɔːlə(r)/ *noun* [C] a fishing boat that uses large nets that it pulls through the sea behind it

tray /treɪ/ *noun* [C] **1** a flat piece of wood, plastic, metal, etc. with slightly higher edges that you use for carrying food, drink, etc. on **2** a shallow plastic box, used for various purposes

treacherous /ˈtretʃərəs/ *adj* **1** (used about a person) that you cannot trust and who may do sth to harm you: *He was cowardly and treacherous.* **2** dangerous, although seeming safe: *The roads are treacherous this morning. There are icy patches.*

treachery /ˈtretʃəri/ *noun* [U] the act of causing harm to sb who trusts you

treacle /ˈtriːkl/ (*AmE* **molasses**) *noun* [U] a thick, dark, sticky liquid that is made from sugar ➲ look at **syrup**

tread¹ /tred/ *verb* (*pt* **trod** /trɒd/; *pp* **trodden** /ˈtrɒdn/) **1** [I] (*especially BrE*) **tread (on/in/over sb/sth)** to put your foot down while you are walking: *Don't tread in the puddle!* ◆ *He trod on my foot and didn't even say sorry!* **2** [T] **tread sth (in/into/down)** to press down on sth with your foot: *This wine is still made by treading grapes in the traditional way.*

T

tread² /tred/ *noun* **1** [sing] the sound you make when you walk; the way you walk **2** [C,U] the pattern on the surface of a tyre on a vehicle which is slightly higher than the rest of the surface

treason /ˈtriːzn/ *noun* [U] the criminal act of causing harm to your country, for example by helping its enemies ➲ note at **traitor**

treasure¹ /ˈtreʒə(r)/ *noun* **1** [U] a collection of very valuable objects, for example gold, silver, jewellery, etc: *to find buried treasure* **2** [C, usually pl] something that is very valuable

treasure² /ˈtreʒə(r)/ *verb* [T] to consider sb/sth to be very special or valuable: *I will treasure those memories forever.*

ˈtreasure hunt *noun* [C] a game in which people try to find a hidden prize by answering a series of questions that have been left in different places

treasurer /ˈtreʒərə(r)/ *noun* [C] the person who looks after the money and accounts of a club or an organization

the Treasury /ˈtreʒəri/ *noun* [sing, with sing or pl verb] the government department that controls public money

🔑 **treat¹** /triːt/ *verb* [T]

➤ BEHAVE TOWARDS SB/STH **1** **treat sb/sth (with/as/like sth)** to act or behave towards sb/sth in a particular way: *Teenagers hate being treated like children.* ◆ *They* ***treat*** *their workers* ***like dirt*** (= very badly). ◆ *You should treat older people with respect.* ◆ *to treat somebody badly/fairly/well*

➤ CONSIDER STH **2** **treat sth as sth** to consider sth in a particular way: *I decided to treat his comment as a joke.* **3** to deal with or discuss sth in a particular way: *The article treats this question in great detail.*

➤ GIVE MEDICAL CARE **4** **treat sb (for sth)** to use medicine or medical care to try to make a sick or injured person well again: *The boy was treated for burns at the hospital.*

➤ USE CHEMICAL **5** **treat sth (with sth)** to put a chemical substance onto sth in order to protect it from damage, clean it, etc: *Most vegetables are treated with insecticide.*

➤ PAY FOR STH SPECIAL **6** **treat sb/yourself (to sth)** to pay for sth or give sb/yourself sth that is very special or enjoyable: *Clare treated the children to ice creams* (= she paid for them).

treat² /triːt/ *noun* [C] something special or enjoyable that you pay for or give to sb/yourself: *I've brought some cream cakes as a treat.* ◆ *It's a real treat for me to stay in bed late.*

IDM **trick or treat** ➲ **trick**

🔑 **treatment** /ˈtriːtmənt/ *noun* **1** [U,C] **treatment (for sth)** the use of medicine or medical care to cure an illness or injury; something that is done to make sb feel and look good: *to require hospital/medical treatment* ◆ *The spa offers a wide range of beauty treatments.* **2** [U] the way that you behave towards sb or deal with sth: *The treatment of the prisoners of war was very harsh.* **3** [U,C] **treatment (for sth)** a process by which sth is cleaned, protected from damage, etc: *an effective treatment for dry rot*

treaty /ˈtriːti/ *noun* [C] (*pl* **treaties**) a written agreement between two or more countries: *to sign a peace treaty*

treble¹ /ˈtrebl/ *noun* [C] **1** a high singing voice, especially that of a young boy **2** a boy who has a high singing voice

treble² /ˈtrebl/ *verb* [I,T] to become or to make sth three times bigger: *Prices have trebled in the past ten years.* ▶ **treble** *determiner*: *This figure is treble the number five years ago.*

🔑 **tree** /triː/ *noun* [C] a tall plant that can live for a long time. Trees have a thick wooden central part from which branches grow: *an oak/apple/elm tree*

trek /trek/ *noun* [C] **1** a long hard walk, lasting several days or weeks, usually in the mountains **2** (*informal*) a long walk: *It's quite a trek to the shops from here.* ▶ **trek** *verb* [I] (**trekking**; **trekked**)

> **HELP** We use **go trekking** to talk about walking long distances for pleasure.

trellis /ˈtrelɪs/ *noun* [C,U] a light wooden frame used to support climbing plants

tremble /ˈtrembl/ *verb* [I] **tremble (with sth)** to shake, for example because you are cold, frightened, etc: *She was pale and trembling with shock.* ◆ *His hand was trembling as he picked up his pen to sign.* ▶ **tremble** *noun* [C, usually sing]

tremendous /trəˈmendəs/ *adj* **1** very large or great: *a tremendous amount of work* **SYN** **huge** **2** very good: *It was a tremendous experience.* **SYN** **great**

tremendously /trəˈmendəsli/ *adv* very; very much: *tremendously exciting* ◆ *Prices vary tremendously from one shop to another.*

tremor /ˈtremə(r)/ *noun* [C] a slight shaking movement: *There was a tremor in his voice.* ◆ *an earth tremor* (= a small earthquake)

trench /trentʃ/ *noun* [C] **1** a long narrow hole dug in the ground for water to flow along **2** a long deep hole dug in the ground for soldiers to hide in during enemy attacks: *life in the trenches during the First World War*

🔑 **trend** /trend/ *noun* [C] **a trend (towards sth)** a general change or development: *The current trend is towards smaller families.* ◆ *He always followed the latest trends in fashion.*

IDM **set a/the trend** to start a new style or fashion ▶ **trend** *verb* [I] **be trending**: *Find out what's trending on Twitter right now.*

trendy /ˈtrendi/ *adj* (**trendier**; **trendiest**) (*informal*) fashionable

trespass /ˈtrespəs/ *verb* [I] to go onto sb's land or property without permission ▶ **trespasser** *noun* [C]

🔑 **trial** /ˈtraɪəl/ *noun* [C,U] **1** the process in a court of law where a judge, and often a jury, listens to evidence and decides if sb is guilty of a crime or not: *a fair trial* ◆ *He was* ***on trial for*** *murder.* ➲ note at **court**

T

2 an act of testing sb/sth: *New drugs must go through extensive trials.* ♦ *a* ***trial period*** *of three months*

IDM trial and error trying different ways of doing sth until you find the best one

ˌtrial ˈrun *noun* [C] an occasion when you practise doing sth in order to make sure you can do it correctly later on

triangle /ˈtraɪæŋgl/ *noun* [C] **1** a shape that has three straight sides: *a right-angled triangle* ➲ picture at **shape 2** a metal musical instrument in the shape of a triangle that you play by hitting it with a metal stick ➲ picture at **music 3** (*AmE*) = **set square**

triangular /traɪˈæŋgjələ(r)/ *adj* shaped like a triangle

triathlon /traɪˈæθlən/ *noun* [C] a sports competition in which you have to take part in three different events, usually swimming, cycling and running ➲ look at **pentathlon**

tribe /traɪb/ *noun* [C] a group of people who have the same language and customs and who live in a particular area, often with one of the group as an official leader: *tribes living in the Amazonian rainforest* ▶ **tribal** /ˈtraɪbl/ *adj*: *tribal art*

tribunal /traɪˈbjuːnl/ *noun* [C] a type of court with the authority to decide who is right in particular types of disagreement: *an industrial tribunal*

tributary /ˈtrɪbjətri/ *noun* [C] (*pl* **tributaries**) a small river that flows into a larger river

tribute /ˈtrɪbjuːt/ *noun* **1** [C,U] **tribute (to sb/sth)** something that you say or do to show that you respect or admire sb/sth, especially sb who has died: *A special concert was held as a tribute to the composer.* **2** [sing] **a tribute to sb/sth** a sign of how good sb/sth is: *The success of the festival is a tribute to the organizers.*

IDM pay tribute to sb/sth ➲ **pay**[1]

trick /trɪk/ *noun* [C] **1** something that you do to make sb believe sth that is not true or a joke that you play to annoy sb: *The thieves used a trick to get past the security guards.* **2** something that confuses you so that you see, remember, understand, etc. things in the wrong way: *It was a* ***trick question*** (= one in which the answer looks easy, but actually is not). **3** an action that uses special skills to make people believe sth which is not true or real as a form of entertainment: *The magician* ***performed a trick*** *in which he made a rabbit disappear.* ♦ *a card trick* **4** [usually sing] a clever or the best way of doing sth: *I can't get the top off this jar.* ***Is there a trick to it?***

IDM do the job/trick ➲ **job**

play a joke/trick on sb ➲ **joke**[1]

trick or treat a custom in which children dress up in special clothes and go to people's houses on Halloween (= the evening of October 31st) and threaten to do sth bad to them if they do not give them sweets, etc: *to go trick or treating*

PHR V trick sb into sth/doing sth to persuade sb to do sth by making them believe sth that is not true: *He tricked me into lending him money.*

trick sb out of sth to get sth from sb by making them believe sth that is not true: *Stella was tricked out of her share of the money.*

▶ **trick** *verb* [T]: *I'd been tricked and I felt like a fool.*

trickery /ˈtrɪkəri/ *noun* [U] the use of dishonest methods to trick sb in order to get what you want

tree

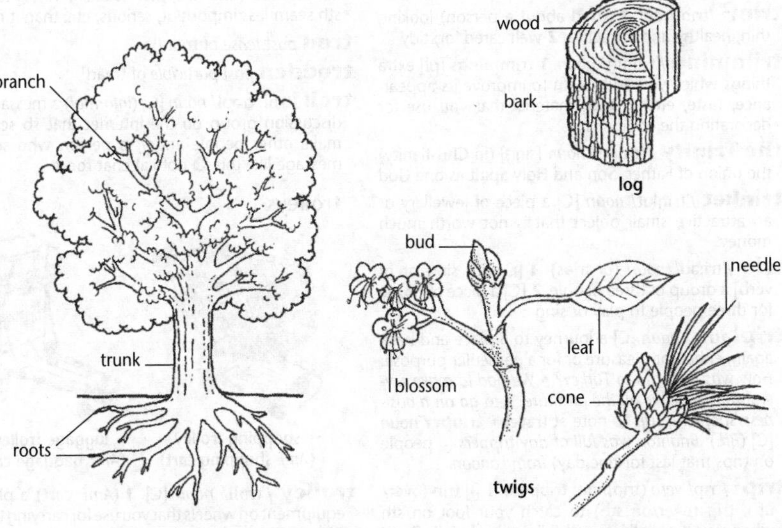

trickle /ˈtrɪkl/ *verb* [I] **1** (used about a liquid) to flow in a thin line: *Raindrops trickled down the window.* **2** to go somewhere slowly and gradually ▸ **trickle** *noun* [C,usually sing]: *a trickle of water*

tricky /ˈtrɪki/ *adj* (**trickier**; **trickiest**) difficult to do or deal with: *a tricky situation*

tricycle /ˈtraɪsɪkl/ *noun* [C] a bicycle that has one wheel at the front and two at the back

trifle /ˈtraɪfl/ *noun* **1** a **trifle** [sing] [used as an adverb] (*formal*) slightly; rather **2** [C] something that is of little value or importance **3** [C,U] (*BrE*) a type of cold **dessert** (= a sweet food) made from cake and fruit covered with **custard** (= a sweet yellow sauce) and cream

trifling /ˈtraɪflɪŋ/ *adj* (*formal*) very unimportant or small SYN **trivial**

trigger[1] /ˈtrɪɡə(r)/ *noun* [C] **1** the part of a gun that you press to fire it: *to pull the trigger* **2** the cause of a particular reaction or event, especially a bad one

trigger[2] /ˈtrɪɡə(r)/ *verb* [T] **trigger sth (off)** to make sth happen suddenly: *Smoke from the kitchen triggered off the fire alarm.*

trillion /ˈtrɪljən/ *number* one million million ⓘ For more information about numbers, look at the section on using numbers at the back of this dictionary.

trilogy /ˈtrɪlədʒi/ *noun* [C] (*pl* **trilogies**) a group of three novels, plays, films, etc. that form a set

trim[1] /trɪm/ *verb* [T] (**trimming**; **trimmed**) **1** to cut a small amount off sth so that it is tidy: *to trim your hair/fringe/beard* ◆ *The hedge needs trimming.* **2** **trim sth (off sth)** to cut sth off because you do not need it: *Trim the fat off the meat.* **3** **trim sth (with sth)** to decorate the edge of sth with sth ▸ **trim** *noun* [C,usually sing]: *My hair needs a trim.*

trim[2] /trɪm/ *adj* **1** (used about a person) looking thin, healthy and attractive **2** well cared for; tidy

trimming /ˈtrɪmɪŋ/ *noun* **1** **trimmings** [pl] extra things which you add to sth to improve its appearance, taste, etc. **2** [C,U] material that you use for decorating the edge of sth

the Trinity /ˈtrɪnəti/ *noun* [sing] (in Christianity) the union of Father, Son and Holy Spirit as one God

trinket /ˈtrɪŋkɪt/ *noun* [C] a piece of jewellery or an attractive small object that is not worth much money

trio /ˈtriːəʊ/ *noun* (*pl* **trios**) **1** [C,with sing or pl verb] a group of three people **2** [C] a piece of music for three people to play or sing

trip[1] /trɪp/ *noun* [C] a journey to a place and back again, either for pleasure or for a particular purpose: *How was your trip to Turkey?* ◆ *We had to make several trips to move all the furniture.* ◆ *to* **go on a** *business/shopping* **trip** ➲ note at **travel** ▸ **tripper** *noun* [C] (*BrE*): *Brighton was full of* **day trippers** (= people on trips that last for one day) *from London.*

trip[2] /trɪp/ *verb* (**tripping**; **tripped**) **1** [I] **trip (over/up)**; **trip (over/on sth)** to catch your foot on sth when you are walking and fall or nearly fall: *Don't leave your bag on the floor. Someone might trip over it.* ◆ *She tripped up on a loose paving stone.* **2** [T] **trip sb (up)** to catch sb's foot and make them fall or nearly fall: *Linda stuck out her foot and tripped Barry up.*

PHR V **trip (sb) up** to make a mistake; to make sb say sth that they did not want to say: *The journalist asked a difficult question to try to trip the politician up.*

triple /ˈtrɪpl/ *adj* [only *before* a noun] having three parts, happening three times or containing three times as much as usual: *You'll receive triple pay if you work over the New Year.* ▸ **triple** *verb* [I,T]

the ˈtriple jump *noun* [sing] a sporting event in which people try to jump as far forward as possible with three jumps. The first jump lands on one foot, the second on the other, and the third on both feet.

triplet /ˈtrɪplət/ *noun* [C] one of three children or animals that are born to one mother at the same time ➲ look at **twin**

tripod /ˈtraɪpɒd/ *noun* [C] a piece of equipment with three legs that you use for putting a camera, etc. on ➲ picture at **camera**

triumph[1] /ˈtraɪʌmf/ *noun* [C,U] a great success or victory; the feeling of happiness that you have because of this: *The team returned home* **in triumph**. ◆ *The new programme was a triumph with the public.*

triumph[2] /ˈtraɪʌmf/ *verb* [I] **triumph (over sb/sth)** to achieve success; to defeat sb/sth: *France triumphed over Brazil in the final.*

triumphant /traɪˈʌmfənt/ *adj* feeling or showing great happiness because you have won or succeeded at sth: *a triumphant cheer* ▸ **triumphantly** *adv*

trivial /ˈtrɪviəl/ *adj* of little importance; not worth considering: *a trivial detail/problem* ▸ **triviality** /ˌtrɪviˈæləti/ *noun* [C,U] (*pl* **trivialities**)

trivialize (also **-ise**) /ˈtrɪviəlaɪz/ *verb* [T] to make sth seem less important, serious, etc. than it really is

trod *past tense* of **tread**[1]

trodden *past participle* of **tread**[1]

troll /trɒl; trəʊl/ *noun* [C] (*informal*) a message to a discussion group on the Internet that sb sends to make other people angry; a person who sends a message like this ➲ note at **chat room**

trolleys

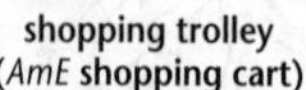

shopping trolley (*AmE* **shopping cart**)

luggage trolley (*AmE* **baggage cart**)

trolley /ˈtrɒli/ *noun* [C] **1** (*AmE* **cart**) a piece of equipment on wheels that you use for carrying things: *a supermarket/shopping/luggage trolley* **2** (*BrE*) a small table with wheels that is used for carrying or serving food and drinks: *a tea/sweet/drinks trolley* **3** (*AmE*) = **tram**

trombone /trɒmˈbəʊn/ *noun* [C] a large musical instrument made of **brass** (= a yellow metal) that you play by blowing into it and moving a long tube backwards and forwards ➲ picture at **music**

troop /truːp/ *noun* **1 troops** [pl] soldiers **2** [C] a large group of people or animals ▶ **troop** *verb* [I]: *When the bell rang everyone trooped into the hall.*

trophy /ˈtrəʊfi/ *noun* [C] (*pl* **trophies**) a large silver cup, etc. that you get for winning a competition or race ➲ picture at **medal**

tropic /ˈtrɒpɪk/ *noun* **1** [C, usually sing] one of the two imaginary lines around the earth that are 23° 26′ north and south of the **equator** (= the line around the middle of the earth). The lines are called the Tropic of Cancer (= north) and the Tropic of Capricorn (= south). ➲ picture at **earth 2 the tropics** [pl] the part of the world that is between these two lines, where the climate is hot and wet ▶ **tropical** /-kl/ *adj*: *tropical fruit* ◆ *tropical fish* ◆ *a tropical island*

trot[1] /trɒt/ *verb* [I] (**trotting**; **trotted**) **1** (used about a horse and its rider) to move forward at a speed that is faster than a walk ➲ look at **canter, gallop 2** (used about a person or an animal) to walk fast, taking short quick steps

PHR V trot sth out (*informal*) to repeat an old idea rather than thinking of sth new to say: *to trot out the same old story*

trot[2] /trɒt/ *noun* [sing] a speed that is faster than a walk

IDM on the trot (*BrE informal*) one after another; without stopping: *We worked for six hours on the trot.*

trouble[1] /ˈtrʌbl/ *noun* **1** [U,C] **trouble (with sb/sth)** (a situation that causes) a problem, difficulty or worry: *If I don't get home by 11 o'clock I'll* ***be in trouble.*** ◆ *I'm* ***having trouble*** *getting the car started.* ◆ *I'm having trouble with my car.* ◆ *financial troubles* ◆ *Marie is clever.* ***The trouble is*** *she's very lazy.* **2** [U] illness or pain: *back/heart trouble* **3** [U] a situation where people are fighting or arguing with each other: *There's often trouble in town on Saturday night after the bars have closed.* **4** [U] extra work or effort: *Let's eat out tonight. It will* ***save you the trouble*** *of cooking.* ◆ *Why don't you stay the night with us?* ***It's no trouble.*** ◆ *I'm sorry to* ***put you to*** *so much* ***trouble.***

IDM ask for trouble/it ➲ **ask**

get into trouble to get into a situation which is dangerous or in which you may be punished

go to a lot of trouble (to do sth) to put a lot of work or effort into sth: *They went to a lot of trouble to make us feel welcome.*

take trouble over/with sth; **take trouble to do sth/doing sth** to do sth with care

take the trouble to do sth to do sth even though it means extra work or effort

trouble[2] /ˈtrʌbl/ *verb* [T] **1** to make sb worried, upset, etc: *Is there something troubling you?* **2** (*formal*) **trouble sb (for sth)** (used when you are politely asking sb for sth or to do sth) to disturb sb: *I'm sorry to trouble you* **SYN** for both meanings **bother**

troublemaker /ˈtrʌblmeɪkə(r)/ *noun* [C] a person who often deliberately causes trouble

troubleshoot /ˈtrʌblʃuːt/ *verb* [I,T] **1** to analyse and solve serious problems for a company or other organization **2** to identify and correct faults in a computer system ▶ **troubleshooter** *noun* [C] ▶ **troubleshooting** *noun* [U]

troublesome /ˈtrʌblsəm/ *adj* causing trouble, pain, etc. over a long period of time **SYN annoying**

trough /trɒf/ *noun* [C] **1** a long narrow container from which farm animals eat or drink **2** a low area or point between two higher areas

trousers /ˈtraʊzəz/ (*AmE* **pants**) *noun* [pl] a piece of clothing that covers the body from the waist down and is divided into two parts to cover each leg separately ➲ picture on **page P1**

> **GRAMMAR** **Trousers** are plural, so we cannot say, for example, 'a new trouser'. The following are possible: *I need some trousers/a pair of trousers.* ◆ *These trousers are too tight.* Before another noun the form **trouser** is used: *a trouser suit* (= a woman's suit consisting of a jacket and trousers).

trout /traʊt/ *noun* [C,U] (*pl* **trout**) a type of fish that lives in rivers and that we eat

trowel /ˈtraʊəl/ *noun* [C] **1** a small garden tool used for lifting plants, digging small holes, etc. ➲ picture at **garden 2** a small tool with a flat blade, used in building

truant /ˈtruːənt/ *noun* [C] a child who stays away from school without permission

IDM play truant; *AmE* **play hooky** to stay away from school without permission

▶ **truancy** /-ənsi/ *noun* [U]

truce /truːs/ *noun* [C] an agreement to stop fighting for a period of time ➲ look at **ceasefire**

truck /trʌk/ *noun* [C] **1** (*especially AmE*) = **lorry**: *a truck driver* **2** (*AmE* **car**) a section of a train that is used for carrying goods or animals: *a cattle truck*

trudge /trʌdʒ/ *verb* [I] to walk with slow, heavy steps, for example because you are very tired

true /truː/ *adj* (**truer**; **truest**) **1** right or correct: *Is it true that Adam is leaving?* ◆ *I didn't think the film was at all* ***true to life*** (= it didn't show life as it really is). ◆ *Read the statements and decide if they are true or false.* **OPP untrue, false 2** real or genuine, often when this is different from how sth seems: *The novel was based on* ***a true story.*** **OPP false 3** having all the typical qualities of the thing mentioned: *How do you know when you have found* ***true love?*** **4 true (to sb/sth)** behaving as expected or as promised: *He was* ***true to his word*** (= he did what he had promised). ◆ *She has been a true friend to me.* ➲ *noun* **truth**

IDM come true to happen in the way you hoped or dreamed: *Winning was like a dream come true!*

too good to be true used to say that you cannot believe that sth is as good as it seems

true to form typical; as usual

T

truly /ˈtruːli/ *adv* **1** (used to emphasize a feeling, statement) really; completely: *We are truly grateful to you for your help.* ◆ *I'm* ***really and truly*** *sorry.* **2** used to emphasize that sth is correct or accurate: *I cannot truly say that I was surprised at the news.*

MORE **Yours truly** is often used at the end of a formal letter in American English.

➲ note at **sincere**
IDM **well and truly** ➲ **well**[1]

trump /trʌmp/ *noun* [C] (in some card games) a card of the chosen **suit** (= one of the four sets) that has a higher value than cards of the other three **suits** during a particular game: *Spades are trumps.*

ˈ**trump card** *noun* [C] a special advantage you have over other people that you keep secret until you can surprise them with it: *It was time for her to* ***play*** *her* ***trump card.***

trumpet /ˈtrʌmpɪt/ *noun* [C] a musical instrument made of **brass** (= a yellow metal) that you play by blowing into it. There are three buttons on it which you press to make different notes. ➲ note at **music** ➲ picture at **music**

truncheon /ˈtrʌntʃən/ (*especially BrE*) (also **baton**) *noun* [C] a short thick stick that a police officer carries as a weapon

trundle /ˈtrʌndl/ *verb* [I,T] to move, or make sth heavy move, slowly and noisily: *A lorry trundled down the hill.*

trunk /trʌŋk/ *noun*
➤TREE **1** [C] the thick central part of a tree that the branches grow from ➲ picture at **tree**
➤CAR **2** [C] (*AmE*) = **boot**[1](2)
➤ELEPHANT **3** [C] the long nose of an **elephant** (= a very large grey animal) ➲ picture at **elephant** ➲ picture on **page P12**
➤CLOTHING **4** **trunks** [pl] = **swimming trunks**
➤LARGE BOX **5** [C] a large box that you use for storing or transporting things ➲ picture on **page P8**
➤BODY **6** [usually sing] the main part of your body (not including your head, arms and legs)

trust[1] /trʌst/ *noun* **1** [U] **trust (in sb/sth)** the belief that sb/sth is good, honest, sincere, etc. and will not try to harm or trick you: *Our marriage is based on love and trust.* ◆ *I should never have* ***put my trust in*** *him.* ➲ look at **distrust, mistrust** **2** [C,U] a legal arrangement by which a person or an organization looks after money and property for sb else, usually until that person is old enough to control it: *The money was put into (a) trust for the children.*
IDM **take sth on trust** to believe what sb says without having proof that it is true: *I can't prove it. You must take it on trust.*

trust[2] /trʌst/ *verb* [T] **trust sb (to do sth)**; **trust sb (with sth)** to believe that sb/sth is good, sincere, honest, etc. and that they will not trick you or try to harm you: *He said the car was safe but I just don't trust him.* ◆ *You can't trust her with money.* ◆ *You can trust Penny to do the job well.* ➲ look at **distrust, mistrust**
IDM **trust you, him, her, etc. (to do sth)** (*spoken*) it is typical of sb to do sth: *Trust Alice to be late. She's never on time!*

trustee /trʌˈstiː/ *noun* [C] a person who looks after money or property for sb else

trusting /ˈtrʌstɪŋ/ *adj* believing that other people are good, sincere, honest, etc.

trustworthy /ˈtrʌstwɜːði/ *adj* that you can depend on to be good, sincere, honest, etc.

truth /truːθ/ *noun* (*pl* **truths** /truːðz/) **1 the truth** [sing] what is true; the facts: *Please* ***tell me the truth.*** ◆ *Are you telling me* ***the whole truth*** *about what happened?* ◆ ***The truth is,*** *we can't afford to live here any more.* **2** [U] the state or quality of being true: *There's a lot of truth in what she says.* **3** [C] a fact or an idea that is believed by most people to be true: *scientific/universal truths* ➲ *adjective* **true**

truthful /ˈtruːθfl/ *adj* **1** **truthful (about sth)** (used about a person) who tells the truth: *He was less than truthful about his part in the crime.* ◆ *I don't think you're being truthful with me.* **SYN** **honest** **2** (used about a statement) true or correct: *a truthful account*
▶ **truthfully** /-fəli/ *adv*

try[1] /traɪ/ *verb* (**trying**; **tries**; *pt, pp* **tried**) **1** [I,T] **try (to do sth)** to make an effort to do sth: *I tried to phone you but I couldn't get through.* ◆ *She was* ***trying hard*** *not to laugh.* ◆ *She'll* ***try her best*** *to help you.* ◆ *I'm sure you can do it if you try.*

HELP **Try and** is more informal than **try to.** It cannot be used in the past tense: *I'll try and get there on time.* ◆ *I tried to get there on time, but I was late.*

2 [T] **try (doing) sth** to do, use or test sth in order to see how good or successful it is: *'I've tried everything but I can't get the baby to sleep.' 'Have you tried taking her out in the car?'* ◆ *Have you ever tried raw fish?* ◆ *We tried the door but it was locked.*

GRAMMAR Compare **try to do sth** with **try doing sth**: *I tried to pick up the box, but it was too heavy* (= I attempted to pick it up, but I couldn't.) ◆ *'I've got a sore throat.' 'You should try taking some medicine.'* (= Medicine might help you feel better.)

3 [T] **try sb (for sth)** to examine sb in a court of law in order to decide if they are guilty of a crime or not: *He was tried for murder.*
IDM **try your hand at sth** to do sth such as an activity or a sport for the first time
PHR V **try sth on** to put on a piece of clothing to see if it fits you properly: *Can I try these jeans on, please?* ➲ note at **clothes**
try sb/sth out to test sb/sth to find out if he/she/it is good enough

try[2] /traɪ/ *noun* [C] (*pl* **tries**) an occasion when you try to do sth: *I don't know if I can move it by myself, but I'll* ***give it a try.*** **SYN** **attempt**

trying /ˈtraɪɪŋ/ *adj* that makes you tired or angry: *a trying journey*

tsar (also czar, tzar) /zɑː(r)/ *noun* [C] **1** the title of the ruler of Russia in the past: *Tsar Nicholas II* **2** an expert, usually chosen by a government, with responsibility for sth important: *the Government's social media tsar*

tsarina (also czarina, tzarina) /zɑːˈriːnə/ *noun* [C] the title of the female ruler of Russia in the past

ˈT-shirt (also teeshirt) *noun* [C] a shirt with short sleeves and without buttons or a **collar** (= a folded part around the neck)

tsp *abbr* = **teaspoon**(2): *Add 1 tsp salt.*

tsunami /tsuːˈnɑːmi/ *noun* [C] a very large wave in the sea caused, for example, by an **earthquake** (= a violent movement of the earth's surface) ➲ look at **tidal wave**

tub /tʌb/ *noun* [C] **1** a large round container: *On the terrace there were several tubs with flowers in them.* **2** a small plastic container with a lid that is used for holding food: *a tub of margarine/ice cream* **3** (*especially AmE informal*) = **bath**[1](1) ➲ picture at **container**

tuba /ˈtjuːbə/ *noun* [C] a large musical instrument made of **brass** (= a yellow metal) that makes a low sound ➲ picture at **music**

tube /tjuːb/ *noun* **1** [C] a long empty pipe: *Blood flowed along the tube into the bottle.* ◆ *the inner tube of a bicycle tyre* ➲ look at **test tube** **2** [C] a tube (of sth) a long thin container with a lid at one end made of soft plastic or metal. Tubes are used for holding thick liquids that can be squeezed out of them: *a tube of toothpaste* ➲ picture at **container** **3** the tube (also the Tube™) [sing] (*BrE informal*) = **underground**[3]: *We came **by tube**.*

tuberculosis /tjuːˌbɜːkjuˈləʊsɪs/ *noun* [U] (*abbr* TB) a serious disease that affects the lungs

tubing /ˈtjuːbɪŋ/ *noun* [U] a long piece of metal, rubber, etc. in the shape of a tube

TUC /ˌtiː juː ˈsiː/ *abbr* the **Trades Union Congress**; the association of British **trade unions** (= organizations for people who work in the same industry)

tuck /tʌk/ *verb* [T] **1** tuck sth in, under, round, etc. (sth) to put or fold the ends or edges of sth into or round sth else so that it looks tidy: *Tuck your shirt in—it looks untidy like that.* **2** tuck sth (away) to put sth into a small space, especially to hide it or to keep it safe: *The letter was tucked behind a pile of books.*

PHR V **tuck sth away** **1** [only in the passive form] to be hidden: *The house was tucked away among the trees.* **2** to hide sth somewhere; to keep sth in a safe place: *He tucked his wallet away in his inside pocket.*

tuck sb in/up to make sb feel comfortable in bed by pulling the covers up around them

tuck in; tuck into sth (*BrE informal*) to eat with pleasure

Tue. (also Tues.) *abbr* = **Tuesday**: *Tue. 9 March*

Tuesday /ˈtjuːzdeɪ; -di/ *noun* [C,U] (*abbr* Tue.; Tues.) the day of the week after Monday ➲ note at **Monday**

tuft /tʌft/ *noun* [C] a small amount of hair, grass, etc. growing together

tug[1] /tʌg/ *verb* [I,T] (tugging; tugged) tug (at/on sth) to pull sth hard and quickly, often several times: *The boy tugged at his father's trouser leg.*

tug[2] /tʌg/ *noun* [C] **1** (also tugboat /ˈtʌgbəʊt/) a small powerful boat that is used for pulling ships into a port, etc. **2** a sudden hard pull: *She gave the rope a tug.*

tuition /tjuˈɪʃn/ *noun* [U] tuition (in sth) teaching, especially to a small group of people: *private tuition in Italian* ◆ *tuition fees* (= the money that you pay to be taught, especially in a college or university)

tulip /ˈtjuːlɪp/ *noun* [C] a brightly coloured flower, shaped like a cup, that grows in the spring

tumble /ˈtʌmbl/ *verb* [I] **1** to fall down suddenly but without serious injury: *He tripped and tumbled all the way down the steps.* **2** to fall suddenly in value or amount: *House prices have tumbled.* **3** to move or fall somewhere in an untidy way: *She opened her bag and all her things tumbled out of it.*

PHR V **tumble down** to fall down: *The walls of the old house were tumbling down.*

▶ **tumble** *noun* [C, usually sing]

ˌtumble ˈdryer (also tumble-drier) *noun* [C] (*BrE*) a machine that dries clothes by moving them about in hot air

tumbler /ˈtʌmblə(r)/ *noun* [C] a glass for drinking out of with straight sides and no handle ➲ picture at **glass**

tummy /ˈtʌmi/ (*pl* tummies) (*informal*) = **stomach**[1]

tumour (*AmE* tumor) /ˈtjuːmə(r)/ *noun* [C] a mass of cells growing in or on a part of the body where they should not, usually causing medical problems: *a brain tumour*

tumultuous /tjuːˈmʌltʃuəs/ *adj* very noisy, because people are excited: *a tumultuous welcome* ◆ *tumultuous applause*

tuna /ˈtjuːnə/ (also ˈtuna fish) *noun* [C,U] (*pl* tuna) a large sea fish that we eat: *a tin of tuna*

tune[1] /tjuːn/ *noun* [C,U] a series of musical notes that are sung or played to form a piece of music: *The children **played us a tune** on their recorders.*

IDM **call the shots/tune** ➲ **call**[1]

change your tune ➲ **change**[1]

in/out of tune **1** (not) singing or playing the correct musical notes to sound pleasant: *You're singing out of tune.* **2** having/not having the same opinions, interests, feelings, etc. as sb/sth: *The President doesn't seem to be in tune with what ordinary people are thinking.*

tune[2] /tjuːn/ *verb* [T] **1** to make small changes to the sound a musical instrument makes so that it plays the correct notes: *to tune a piano/guitar* **2** to make small changes to an engine so that it runs well **3** [usually passive] tune sth (in) (to sth) to move the controls on a radio or TV so that you can receive a particular station: ***Stay tuned** to this station for the latest news.*

T

PHR V **tune in (to sth)** to listen to a radio programme or watch a TV programme

tune sth up to make small changes to a group of musical instruments so that they sound pleasant when played together

tuneful /ˈtjuːnfl/ *adj* (used about music) nice or pleasant to listen to

tunic /ˈtjuːnɪk/ *noun* [C] **1** a piece of women's clothing, usually without sleeves, that is long and not tight **2** (*BrE*) the jacket that is part of the uniform of police officers, soldiers, etc.

tunnel /ˈtʌnl/ *noun* [C] a passage built underground: *The train disappeared into a tunnel.* ▶ **tunnel** *verb* [I,T] (**tunnelling**; **tunnelled**, (*AmE*) **tunneling**; **tunneled**)

turban /ˈtɜːbən/ *noun* [C] a covering for the head worn especially by Muslim and Sikh men. A **turban** is made by folding a long piece of cloth around the head.

turbine /ˈtɜːbaɪn/ *noun* [C] a machine or an engine that receives its power from a wheel that is turned by the pressure of water, air or gas

turbulent /ˈtɜːbjələnt/ *adj* **1** in which there is a lot of sudden change, confusion, disagreement and sometimes violence **2** (used about water or air) moving in a violent way ▶ **turbulence** *noun* [U]

turf[1] /tɜːf/ *noun* [U,C] (a piece of) short thick grass and the layer of soil underneath it

turf[2] /tɜːf/ *verb* [T] to cover ground with **turf**

PHR V **turf sb out (of sth)** (*BrE informal*) to force sb to leave a place

turkey /ˈtɜːki/ *noun* [C, U] a large bird that is kept on farms for its meat. Turkeys are usually eaten at Christmas in Britain and at Thanksgiving in the US.

IDM **cold turkey** ➲ cold[1]

turkey

Turkish delight /ˌtɜːkɪʃ dɪˈlaɪt/ *noun* [U,C] a sweet made from a substance like jelly that is flavoured with fruit and covered with fine white sugar

turmoil /ˈtɜːmɔɪl/ *noun* [U,sing] a state of great noise or confusion: *Her mind was* ***in (a) turmoil.*** ◆ *His statement* ***threw*** *the court* ***into turmoil.***

turn[1] /tɜːn/ *verb*

➤MOVE ROUND **1** [I,T] to move or make sth move round a fixed central point: *The wheels turned faster and faster.* ◆ *She turned the key in the lock.* ◆ *Turn the steering wheel to the right.*

➤CHANGE POSITION/DIRECTION **2** [I,T] to move your body, or part of your body, so that you are facing in a different direction: *He turned round when he heard my voice.* ◆ *She* ***turned*** *her* ***back on*** *me* (= she deliberately moved her body to face away from me). **3** [T] to change the position of sth: *I turned the box upside down.* ◆ *He turned the page and started the next chapter.* **4** [I,T] to change direction when you are moving: *Go straight on and* ***turn left*** *at the church.* ◆ *The car* ***turned the corner.***

➤AIM **5** [T] to point or aim sth in a particular direction: *She turned her attention back to me.*

➤BECOME **6** [I,T] (to cause) to become: *He* ***turned*** *very* ***red*** *when I asked him about the money.* ◆ *These caterpillars will turn into butterflies.*

➤AGE/TIME **7** [T] [not used in the continuous tenses] to reach or pass a particular age or time: *It's turned midnight.*

ⓘ For idioms containing **turn**, look at the entries for the nouns, adjectives, etc. For example **turn a blind eye** is at **blind**.

PHR V **turn (sth) around/round** to change position or direction in order to face the opposite way, or to return the way you came; to make sth do this: *This road is a dead end. We'll have to turn round and go back to the main road.* ◆ *He turned the car around and drove off.*

turn away to stop looking at sb/sth: *She turned away in horror at the sight of the blood.*

turn sb away to refuse to allow a person to go into a place

turn back to return the same way that you came: *We've come so far already, we can't turn back now.*

turn sb/sth down to refuse an offer, etc. or the person who makes it: *Why did you turn that job down?* ◆ *He asked her to marry him, but she turned him down.*

turn sth down to reduce the sound or heat that sth produces: *Turn the TV down!*

turn off (sth) to leave one road and go on another

turn sth off to stop the flow of electricity, water, etc. by moving a switch, tap, etc: *He turned the TV off.*

turn sth on to start the flow of electricity, water, etc. by moving a switch, tap, etc: *to turn the lights on*

turn out (for sth) to be present at an event

turn out (to be sth) to be in the end: *The weather turned out fine.* ◆ *The house that they had promised us turned out to be a tiny flat.*

turn sth out to move the switch, etc. on a light or a source of heat to stop it: *Turn the lights out before you go to bed.*

turn over 1 to change position so that the other side is facing out or upwards: *He turned over and went back to sleep.* **2** (used about an engine) to start or to continue to run **3** (*BrE*) to change to another programme when you are watching TV: *This film's awful. Shall I turn over?*

turn sth over 1 to make sth change position so that the other side is facing out or upwards: *You may now turn over your exam papers and begin.* **2** to keep thinking about sth carefully: *She kept turning over what he'd said in her mind.*

turn to sb/sth to go to sb/sth to get help, advice, etc.

turn up 1 to arrive; to appear: *What time did they finally turn up?* **2** to be found, especially by chance: *I lost my glasses a week ago and they haven't turned up yet.*

turn sth up to increase the sound or heat that sth produces: *Turn the heating up—I'm cold.*

turn[2] /tɜːn/ *noun* [C]

➤MOVEMENT **1** the act of turning sb/sth round: *Give*

the screw another couple of turns to make sure it is really tight.
➤IN VEHICLE **2** a change of direction in a vehicle: *to make a* ***left/right turn*** ◆ *a U-turn* (= when you turn round in a vehicle and go back in the opposite direction)
➤IN ROAD **3** (*BrE also* **turning**) a bend or corner in a road, river, etc: *Take the next turn on the left.*
➤TIME **4** [usually sing] the time when sb in a group of people should or is allowed to do sth: *When it's your turn, take another card.* ◆ *Please wait in the queue until it is your turn.* ◆ *Whose turn is it to do the cleaning?*
➤CHANGE **5** an unusual or unexpected change: *The patient's condition has* ***taken a turn for the worse*** (= suddenly got worse).
IDM **(do sb) a good turn** (to do) sth that helps sb: *Well, that's my good turn for today.*
in turn one after the other: *I spoke to each of the children in turn.*
take turns (at sth); take it in turns to do sth one after the other to make sure it is fair
the turn of the century/year the time when a new century/year starts
wait your turn ➲ wait[1]

turning /ˈtɜːnɪŋ/ (*BrE* **turn**) *noun* [C] a place where one road leads off from another: *We must have taken a wrong turning.*

ˈ**turning point** *noun* [C] **a turning point (in sth)** a time when an important change happens, usually a good one

turnip /ˈtɜːnɪp/ *noun* [C,U] a round white vegetable that grows under the ground

ˈ**turn-off** *noun* [C] the place where a road leads away from a larger or more important road: *This is the turn-off for York.*

turnout /ˈtɜːnaʊt/ *noun* [C, usually sing] the number of people who go to a meeting, sports event, etc: *There was a good turnout despite the rain.*

turnover /ˈtɜːnəʊvə(r)/ *noun* [C, usually sing] **a turnover (of sth) 1** the amount of business that a company does in a particular period of time: *The firm has an annual turnover of $50 million.* **2** the rate at which workers leave a company and are replaced by new ones: *a high turnover of staff*

ˈ**turn signal** (*AmE*) = **indicator**(2)

turnstile /ˈtɜːnstaɪl/ *noun* [C] a metal gate that moves round in a circle when it is pushed, and allows one person at a time to enter a place

turntable /ˈtɜːnteɪbl/ *noun* [C] the round surface on a record player that you place the record on to be played

turpentine /ˈtɜːpəntaɪn/ *noun* [U] a clear liquid with a strong smell that you use for removing paint or for making paint thinner

turquoise /ˈtɜːkwɔɪz/ *noun* **1** [C,U] a blue or greenish-blue **precious stone** (= one that is rare and valuable) **2** [U] a greenish-blue colour ▶ **turquoise** *adj*

turret /ˈtʌrət/ *noun* [C] a small tower on the top of a large building

turtle /ˈtɜːtl/ *noun* [C] **1** an animal with a thick shell and a skin covered in scales that lives in the sea ➲ picture on **page P13 2** (*AmE*) = **tortoise**

tusk /tʌsk/ *noun* [C] one of the two very long pointed teeth of an **elephant** (= a large grey animal with a long nose), etc. **Elephants' tusks** are made of **ivory** (= a hard white substance like bone). ➲ picture at **elephant** ➲ picture on **page P12**

tussle /ˈtʌsl/ *noun* [C] (*informal*) **a tussle (for/over sth)** a fight, for example between two or more people who want to have the same thing

tut /tʌt/ (*also* ˌ**tut-**ˈ**tut**) *exclam* the way of writing the sound that people make to show disapproval of sb/sth

tutor /ˈtjuːtə(r)/ *noun* [C] **1** a private teacher who teaches one person or a very small group **2** (*BrE*) a teacher who is responsible for a small group of students at school, college or university. A **tutor** advises students on their work or helps them if they have problems in their private life.

tutorial /tjuːˈtɔːriəl/ *noun* [C] a lesson at a college or university for an individual student or a small group of students

tuxedo /tʌkˈsiːdəʊ/ *noun* (*pl* **tuxedos** /-dəʊz/) (*also informal* **tux** /tʌks/) (*especially AmE*) = **dinner jacket**

TV /ˌtiː ˈviː/ = **television**: *What's on TV tonight?* ◆ *cable/digital/satellite TV* ◆ *a TV programme/series/show*

twang /twæŋ/ *noun* [C] the sound that is made when you pull a tight string or wire, etc. and then let it go suddenly ▶ **twang** *verb* [I,T]

tweed /twiːd/ *noun* [U] a type of thick rough cloth that is made from wool and used for making clothes

tweet /twiːt/ *noun* [C] **1** the short high sound made by a small bird **2** (*also* **twitter**) a message sent using the Twitter™ **social networking service** (= short communications with people who share your interests using the Internet): *I've just sent a tweet about the match.* ▶ **tweet** *verb* [I,T] = **twitter**

tweezers /ˈtwiːzəz/ *noun* [pl] a small tool consisting of two pieces of metal that are joined at one end. You use **tweezers** for picking up or pulling out very small things: *a pair of tweezers*

twelve /twelv/ *number* 12 ➲ note at **six** ➲ look at **dozen** ▶ **twelfth** /twelfθ/ *ordinal number, noun* ➲ note at **sixth**

twenty /ˈtwenti/ *number* 20 ➲ note at **sixty** ▶ **twentieth** /ˈtwentiəθ/ *ordinal number, noun* ➲ note at **sixth**

twice /twaɪs/ *adv* two times: *I've been to Egypt twice—once last year and once in 1994.* ◆ *The film will be shown twice daily.* ◆ *Take the medicine twice a day.* ◆ *Prices have risen twice as fast in this country as in Japan.*

twiddle /ˈtwɪdl/ *verb* [I,T] (*BrE*) **twiddle (with) sth** to keep turning or moving sth with your fingers, often because you are nervous or bored

twig /twɪg/ *noun* [C] a small thin branch on a tree or bush ➲ picture at **tree**

twilight /ˈtwaɪlaɪt/ *noun* [U] the time after the sun has set and before it gets completely dark; the faint light at this time ➲ look at **dusk**

⚷ **twin** /twɪn/ *noun* [C] **1** one of two children or animals that are born to one mother at the same time: *They're very alike. Are they twins?* ♦ *a twin brother/sister* ♦ *identical twins* ➲ look at **triplet** **2** one of a pair of things that are the same or very similar: *twin engines* ♦ *twin beds* ➲ note at **bed**[1] ▶ **twin** *verb* [T]: *Oxford is twinned with Bonn in Germany.*

twinge /twɪndʒ/ *noun* [C] **1** a sudden short pain: *He kicked the ball and suddenly felt a twinge in his back.* **2** a twinge (of sth) a sudden short feeling of an unpleasant emotion

twinkle /ˈtwɪŋkl/ *verb* [I] **1** to shine with a light that seems to go on and off: *Stars twinkled in the sky.* **2** (used about your eyes) to look bright because you are happy ▶ **twinkle** *noun* [sing]

twin ˈtown *noun* [C] one of two towns in different countries that have a special relationship: *Bonn is Oxford's twin town.*

twirl /twɜːl/ *verb* [I,T] twirl (sb/sth) (around/round) to turn round and round quickly; to make sb/sth do this

⚷ **twist**[1] /twɪst/ *verb*

➤BEND **1** [I,T] to bend or turn sth into a particular shape, often one it does not go in naturally; to be bent in this way: *She twisted her long hair into a knot.* ♦ *Her face twisted in anger.* ♦ *He* ***twisted*** *his* ***ankle*** *while he was playing squash.*

➤TURN **2** [I,T] to turn a part of your body while the rest stays still: *She twisted round to see where the noise was coming from.* ♦ *He kept twisting his head from side to side.* **3** [T] to turn sth around in a circle with your hand: *She twisted the ring on her finger nervously.*

➤OF ROAD/RIVER **4** [I] to change direction often: *a narrow twisting lane* ♦ *The road* ***twists and turns*** *along the coast.*

➤PUT ROUND STH **5** [I,T] twist (sth) (round/around sth) to put sth round another object; to be round another object: *The telephone wire has* ***got twisted*** *round the table leg.*

➤WORDS/FACTS **6** [T] to change the meaning of what sb has said: *Journalists often* ***twist*** *your* ***words.***

IDM **twist sb's arm** (*informal*) to force or persuade sb to do sth

⚷ **twist**[2] /twɪst/ *noun* [C] **1** the act of turning sth with your hand, or of turning part of your body: *She killed the chicken with one twist of its neck.* **2** an unexpected change or development in a story or situation: *There's a brilliant twist at the end of the film.* **3** a place where a road, river, etc. bends or changes direction: *the* ***twists and turns*** *of the river* **4** something that has become or been bent into a particular shape: *Straighten out the wire so that there are no twists in it.*

twisted /ˈtwɪstɪd/ *adj* **1** bent or turned so that the original shape is lost: *After the crash the car was a mass of twisted metal.* ♦ *a twisted ankle* (= injured by being turned suddenly) **2** (used about a person's mind or behaviour) not normal; strange in an unpleasant way: *Her experiences had left her* ***bitter and twisted.***

twit /twɪt/ *noun* [C] (*especially BrE informal*) a stupid or annoying person

twitch /twɪtʃ/ *verb* [I,T] to make a quick sudden movement, often one that you cannot control; to cause sth to make a sudden movement: *The rabbit twitched and then lay still.* ♦ *He twitched his nose.* ▶ **twitch** *noun* [C]: *He has a nervous twitch.*

Twitter™ /ˈtwɪtə(r)/ *noun* [U] a service on the Internet that lets people send short messages to lots of people at the same time ➲ look at **microblogging, tweet**

twitter /ˈtwɪtə(r)/ *verb* [I] (also **tweet**) **1** (used about birds) to make a series of short high sounds **2** to send a message using **Twitter™**

⚷ **two** /tuː/ *number* **1** 2 ➲ note at **six** ➲ look at **second** **2** two- [in compounds] having two of the thing mentioned: *a two-week holiday*

IDM **be in two minds (about sth/doing sth)** to not feel sure of sth: *I'm in two minds about leaving Will alone in the house while we're away.*

in two in or into two pieces: *The plate fell on the floor and broke in two.*

tycoon /taɪˈkuːn/ *noun* [C] a person who is very successful in business or industry and who has become rich and powerful: *a business/property/media tycoon*

⚷ **type**[1] /taɪp/ *noun* **1** [C] a type (of sth) a group of people or things that share certain qualities and that are part of a larger group: *Which type of paint should you use on metal?* ♦ *Spaniels are a type of dog.* ♦ *You meet all types of people in this job.* ♦ *the first building of its type in the world* ♦ *I love this type/these types of movie.* SYN **kind, sort** **2** [C] a person of a particular kind: *He's the careful type.* ♦ *She's* ***not the type to*** *do anything silly.* ➲ look at **typical** **3** -type [in compounds] having the qualities, etc. of the group, person or thing mentioned: *a continental-type cafe* ♦ *a police-type badge* **4** [U] letters that are printed or typed: *The type is too small to read.*

⚷ **type**[2] /taɪp/ *verb* [I,T] to write sth using a computer or **typewriter**: *How fast can you type?* ♦ *Type (in) the filename, then press 'Return'.* ▶ **typing** *noun* [U]: *typing skills*

typewriter /ˈtaɪpraɪtə(r)/ *noun* [C] a machine that you use for writing in print

typewritten /ˈtaɪprɪtn/ *adj* written using a **typewriter** or computer

typhoid /ˈtaɪfɔɪd/ *noun* [U] a serious disease that can cause death. People get **typhoid** from bad food or water.

typhoon /taɪˈfuːn/ *noun* [C] a violent tropical storm with very strong winds ➲ note at **storm**

⚷ **typical** /ˈtɪpɪkl/ *adj* typical (of sb/sth) **1** having or showing the usual qualities of a particular person,

T

thing or type: *a typical Italian village* ◆ *There's no such thing as a typical American* (= they are all different). SYN **representative** OPP **atypical** **2** happening in the usual way; showing what sth is usually like: *On a typical day, I receive about 50 emails.* SYN **normal** OPP **untypical** **3** behaving in the way you expect: *It was absolutely typical of him not to reply to my letter.*

typically /ˈtɪpɪkli/ *adv* **1** in a typical case; that usually happens in this way: *Typically it is the girls who offer to help, not the boys.* **2** in a way that shows the usual qualities of a particular person, type or thing: *typically British humour*

typify /ˈtɪpɪfaɪ/ *verb* [T] (**typifying**; **typifies**; *pt, pp* **typified**) to be a typical mark or example of sb/sth: *This film typified the Hollywood westerns of that time.*

typist /ˈtaɪpɪst/ *noun* [C] a person who uses a computer keyboard to type letters, etc., especially sb who works in an office

tyranny /ˈtɪrəni/ *noun* [U] the cruel and unfair use of power by a person or small group to control a country or state ▸ **tyrannical** /tɪˈrænɪkl/ *adj*: *a tyrannical ruler* ▸ **tyrannize** (also **-ise**) /ˈtɪrənaɪz/ *verb* [I,T]

tyrant /ˈtaɪrənt/ *noun* [C] a cruel ruler who has complete power over the people in his or her country ➲ look at **dictator**

tyre (*AmE* **tire**) /ˈtaɪə(r)/ *noun* [C] the thick rubber ring that fits around the outside of a wheel: *a **flat tyre*** (= a tyre with no air in it) ➲ picture at **bicycle** ➲ picture on **page P7**

tzar, tzarina = **tsar, tsarina**

U, u /juː/ *noun* [C,U] (*pl* **Us**; **U's**; **u's** /juːz/) the 21st letter of the English alphabet: *'Understand' begins with (a) 'U'.*

U /juː/ *abbr* (*BrE*) (used about films that are suitable for anyone, including children) **universal**

ubiquitous /juːˈbɪkwɪtəs/ *adj* (*formal*) seeming to be everywhere or in several places at the same time; very common: *the ubiquitous mobile phone*

udder /ˈʌdə(r)/ *noun* [C] the part of a female cow, etc. that hangs under its body and produces milk ➲ picture at **cow**

UEFA /juˈeɪfə/ *abbr* the **Union of European Football Associations**: *the UEFA cup*

UFO (also **ufo**) /ˌjuː ef ˈəʊ; ˈjuːfəʊ/ *abbr* (*pl* **UFOs**) an **unidentified flying object**; a strange object that some people claim to have seen in the sky and believe is a **spacecraft** (= a vehicle from another planet) ➲ look at **flying saucer**

ugh /ɜː/ *exclam* used in writing to express the sound that you make when you think sth is disgusting

ugly /ˈʌgli/ *adj* (**uglier**; **ugliest**) **1** unpleasant to look at or listen to: *The burn left an ugly scar on her face.* ◆ *an ugly modern office block* SYN **unattractive** **2** (used about a situation) dangerous or threatening: *The situation **turned ugly** when people started throwing stones.* ▸ **ugliness** *noun* [U]

UHT /ˌjuː eɪtʃ ˈtiː/ *abbr* **ultra heat treated**; used about foods such as milk that are treated to last longer: *UHT milk*

UK /ˌjuː ˈkeɪ/ *abbr* = **United Kingdom**: *She is Kenyan by birth but is now a UK citizen*

ulcer /ˈʌlsə(r)/ *noun* [C] a painful area on your skin or inside your body, which may lose blood or produce a poisonous substance: *a mouth/stomach ulcer*

ulterior /ʌlˈtɪəriə(r)/ *adj* [only *before* a noun] that you keep hidden or secret: *Why is he suddenly being so nice to me? He must have an **ulterior motive**.*

ultimate¹ /ˈʌltɪmət/ *adj* [only *before* a noun] **1** being or happening at the end; last or final: *Our ultimate goal is complete independence.* **2** the greatest, best or worst: *For me the ultimate luxury is to stay in bed till 10 o'clock on a Sunday.*

ultimate² /ˈʌltɪmət/ *noun* [sing] (*informal*) **the ultimate (in sth)** the greatest or best: *This new car is the ultimate in comfort.*

ultimately /ˈʌltɪmətli/ *adv* **1** in the end: *Ultimately, the decision is yours.* **2** at the most basic level; most importantly: *Ultimately, this discussion is not about quality but about money.*

ultimatum /ˌʌltɪˈmeɪtəm/ *noun* [C] (*pl* **ultimatums**) a final warning to sb that, if they do not do what you ask, you will use force or take action against them: *I gave him an ultimatum—either he paid his rent or he was out.*

ultra- /ˈʌltrə/ [in compounds] extremely: *ultra-modern*

ultrasound /ˈʌltrəsaʊnd/ *noun* **1** [U] sound that is higher than humans can hear **2** [U,C] a medical process that produces an image of what is inside your body: *Ultrasound showed she was expecting twins.*

ultraviolet /ˌʌltrəˈvaɪələt/ *adj* (used about light) that causes your skin to turn darker and that can be dangerous in large amounts: *ultraviolet radiation* ➲ look at **infrared**

umbilical cord /ʌmˌbɪlɪkl ˈkɔːd/ *noun* [C] the tube that connects a baby to its mother before it is born

umbrella /ʌmˈbrelə/ (*BrE informal* **brolly**) *noun* [C] an object that you open and hold over your head to keep yourself dry when it is raining: *to put an umbrella up/down*

umpire /ˈʌmpaɪə(r)/ *noun* [C] a person who watches a game such as **tennis** or **cricket** to make sure that the players obey the rules ➲ look at **referee** ➲ picture on **page P4** ▸ **umpire** *verb* [I,T]

umpteen /ˌʌmpˈtiːn/ *pron, determiner* (*informal*) very many; a lot ▸ **umpteenth** /ˌʌmpˈtiːnθ/ *determiner*: *For the umpteenth time—phone if you're going to be late!*

U

UN /ˌjuː ˈen/ *abbr* = **United Nations**

unable /ʌnˈeɪbl/ *adj* **unable to do sth** not having the time, knowledge, skill, etc. to do sth; not able to do sth: *She lay there, unable to move.* OPP **able** ➲ *noun* **inability**

unacceptable /ˌʌnəkˈseptəbl/ *adj* that you cannot accept or allow: *Noise from the factory has reached unacceptable levels.* ◆ *Her behaviour was quite unacceptable.* OPP **acceptable** ▶ **unacceptably** /-əbli/ *adv*

unaccompanied /ˌʌnəˈkʌmpənid/ *adj* alone, without sb/sth else with you: *Unaccompanied children are not allowed in the building.*

unadulterated /ˌʌnəˈdʌltəreɪtɪd/ *adj* **1** used to emphasize that sth is complete or total: *For me, the holiday was sheer unadulterated pleasure.* **2** not mixed with other substances: *unadulterated foods* SYN **pure**

unaffected /ˌʌnəˈfektɪd/ *adj* **1** not changed by sth **2** behaving in a natural way without trying to impress anyone OPP for both meanings **affected**

unaffordable /ˌʌnəˈfɔːdəbl/ *adj* costing so much that people do not have enough money to pay for it: *Holidays abroad are unaffordable for many people.* OPP **affordable**

unafraid /ˌʌnəˈfreɪd/ *adj* [not before a noun] (*formal*) not afraid or nervous; not worried about what might happen: *She's unafraid of conflict.* ◆ *He's unafraid to speak his mind.* OPP **afraid**

unaided /ʌnˈeɪdɪd/ *adv* without any help

unanimous /juˈnænɪməs/ *adj* **1** (used about a decision, etc.) agreed by everyone: *The jury reached a unanimous verdict of guilty.* **2** (used about a group of people) all agreeing about sth: *The judges were unanimous in their decision.* ▶ **unanimously** *adv*

unarmed /ˌʌnˈɑːmd/ *adj* having no guns, knives, etc.; not armed OPP **armed**

unashamed /ˌʌnəˈʃeɪmd/ *adj* not feeling sorry or embarrassed about sth bad that you have done OPP **ashamed** ▶ **unashamedly** /ˌʌnəˈʃeɪmɪdli/ *adv*

unassuming /ˌʌnəˈsjuːmɪŋ/ *adj* not wanting people to notice how good, important, etc. you are SYN **modest**

unattached /ˌʌnəˈtætʃt/ *adj* **1** not married; without a regular partner SYN **single** **2** not connected to sb/sth else

unattended /ˌʌnəˈtendɪd/ *adj* not watched or looked after: *Do not leave bags unattended.*

unattractive /ˌʌnəˈtræktɪv/ *adj* **1** not attractive or pleasant to look at **2** not good, interesting or pleasant OPP for both meanings **attractive**

unauthorized /ʌnˈɔːθəraɪzd/ *adj* done without permission

unavoidable /ˌʌnəˈvɔɪdəbl/ *adj* that cannot be avoided or prevented OPP **avoidable** ▶ **unavoidably** /-əbli/ *adv*

unaware /ˌʌnəˈweə(r)/ *adj* [not before a noun] **unaware (of sb/sth)** not knowing about or not noticing sb/sth: *She seemed unaware of all the trouble she had caused.* OPP **aware**

unawares /ˌʌnəˈweəz/ *adv* by surprise; without expecting sth or being prepared for it: *I was **taken** completely **unawares** by his suggestion.*

unbalanced /ˌʌnˈbælənst/ *adj* **1** (used about a person) slightly crazy **2** not fair to all ideas or sides of an argument OPP **balanced**

unbearable /ʌnˈbeərəbl/ *adj* too unpleasant, painful, etc. for you to accept SYN **intolerable** OPP **bearable** ▶ **unbearably** /-əbli/ *adv*: *It was unbearably hot.*

unbeatable /ʌnˈbiːtəbl/ *adj* that cannot be defeated or improved on: *unbeatable prices*

unbeaten /ʌnˈbiːtn/ *adj* that has not been beaten or improved on

unbelievable /ˌʌnbɪˈliːvəbl/ *adj* very surprising; difficult to believe OPP **believable** ➲ look at **incredible** ▶ **unbelievably** /-əbli/ *adj*: *His work was unbelievably bad.*

unbiased (also **unbiassed**) /ʌnˈbaɪəst/ *adj* fair and not influenced by your own or sb else's opinions, desires, etc: *unbiased advice* ◆ *an unbiased judge* OPP **biased**

unblemished /ʌnˈblemɪʃt/ *adj* (*formal*) not spoiled, damaged or marked in any way: *The new party leader has an unblemished reputation.*

unborn /ˌʌnˈbɔːn/ *adj* not yet born: *She hasn't decided on a name for her unborn baby yet.*

unbroken /ʌnˈbrəʊkən/ *adj* **1** continuous; not interrupted: *a period of unbroken silence* **2** that has not been beaten: *His record for the 1500 metres remains unbroken.*

uncalled for /ʌnˈkɔːld fɔː(r)/ *adj* (used about sth sb says or does) not fair or appropriate: *His comments were uncalled for.* ◆ *uncalled-for comments* SYN **unnecessary**

uncanny /ʌnˈkæni/ *adj* very strange; that you cannot easily explain: *an uncanny coincidence*

uncertain /ʌnˈsɜːtn/ *adj* **1** **uncertain (about/of sth)** not sure; not able to decide: *She was still uncertain of his true feelings for her.* **2** not known exactly or not decided: *He's lost his job and his future seems very uncertain.* OPP for both meanings **certain** ▶ **uncertainly** *adv* ▶ **uncertainty** *noun* [C,U] (*pl* **uncertainties**): *Today's decision will put an end to all the uncertainty.* OPP **certainty**

unchanged /ʌnˈtʃeɪndʒd/ *adj* staying the same; not changed

uncharacteristic /ˌʌnˌkærəktəˈrɪstɪk/ *adj* not typical or usual OPP **characteristic** ▶ **uncharacteristically** /-kli/ *adv*

uncheck /ˌʌnˈtʃek/ *verb* [T] to click on a mark beside an answer or option on a computer in order to delete that mark: *Uncheck the box at the bottom of the page if you do not wish to receive our advertising material.*

U

unchecked /ˌʌnˈtʃekt/ *adj* (used about sth harmful) not controlled or stopped from getting worse: *The fire was allowed to burn unchecked.* ◆ *The rise in violent crime must not* ***go unchecked.*** ◆ *The plant will soon choke ponds and waterways if* ***left unchecked.***

uncle /ˈʌŋkl/ *noun* [C] the brother of your father or mother; the husband of your aunt: *Uncle Steven*

uncomfortable /ʌnˈkʌmftəbl/ *adj* **1** not pleasant to wear, sit in, lie on, etc: *uncomfortable shoes* **2** not able to sit, lie, etc. in a position that is pleasant: *I was very uncomfortable for most of the journey.* **3** feeling or causing worry or embarrassment: *I felt very uncomfortable when they started arguing in front of me.* OPP for all meanings **comfortable** ▶ **uncomfortably** /-əbli/ *adv*

uncommon /ʌnˈkɒmən/ *adj* unusual SYN **rare** OPP **common**

uncomplicated /ʌnˈkɒmplɪkeɪtɪd/ *adj* simple and without difficulties or problems: *an easy, uncomplicated routine*

uncompromising /ʌnˈkɒmprəmaɪzɪŋ/ *adj* refusing to discuss or change a decision

unconcerned /ˌʌnkənˈsɜːnd/ *adj* **unconcerned (about/by/with sth)** not interested in sth or not worried about it OPP **concerned**

unconditional /ˌʌnkənˈdɪʃənl/ *adj* without limits or conditions: *the unconditional surrender of military forces* OPP **conditional** ▶ **unconditionally** /-ʃənəli/ *adv*

unconscious /ʌnˈkɒnʃəs/ *adj* **1** in a state that is like sleep, for example because of injury or illness: *He was found lying unconscious on the kitchen floor.* **2 unconscious of sb/sth** not knowing about or not noticing sb/sth: *He seemed unconscious of everything that was going on around him.* SYN **unaware** **3** done, spoken, etc. without you thinking about it or realizing it: *The article was full of unconscious humour.* OPP for all meanings **conscious** **4 the unconscious** *noun* [sing] = **subconscious** ▶ **unconsciously** *adv* ▶ **unconsciousness** *noun* [U]

uncontrollable /ˌʌnkənˈtrəʊləbl/ *adj* that you cannot control: *I had an uncontrollable urge to laugh.* ▶ **uncontrollably** /-əbli/ *adv*

uncontrolled /ˌʌnkənˈtrəʊld/ *adj* **1** (used about emotions, behaviour, etc.) that sb cannot control or stop: *uncontrolled anger* **2** that is not limited or managed by law or rules: *the uncontrolled growth of cities* ◆ *uncontrolled dumping of toxic waste* ➲ look at **controlled**

uncountable /ʌnˈkaʊntəbl/ (also **non-count, uncount**) *adj* an uncountable noun cannot be counted and so does not have a plural. In this dictionary uncountable nouns are marked '[U]': *'Water', 'bread' and 'information' are all uncountable nouns.* OPP **countable** ℹ For more information about uncountable nouns, look at the **Reference Section** at the back of this dictionary.

uncouth /ʌnˈkuːθ/ *adj* rude or socially unacceptable: *an uncouth young man*

uncover /ʌnˈkʌvə(r)/ *verb* [T] **1** to remove the cover from sth OPP **cover** **2** to find out or discover sth: *Police have uncovered a plot to murder a top politician.*

undecided /ˌʌndɪˈsaɪdɪd/ *adj* **1** not having made a decision: *I'm still undecided about whether to take the job or not.* **2** without any result or decision

undeniable /ˌʌndɪˈnaɪəbl/ *adj* clear, true or certain ▶ **undeniably** /-əbli/ *adv*

under /ˈʌndə(r)/ *prep, adv* **1** in or to a position that is below sth: *We found him hiding under the table.* ◆ *The dog crawled under the gate and ran into the road.* **2** below the surface of sth; covered by sth: *Most of an iceberg is under the water.* ◆ *He was wearing a vest under his shirt.* **3** less than a certain number; younger than a certain age: *People working under 20 hours a week will pay no extra tax.* ◆ *Nobody under eighteen is allowed in the club.* **4** governed or controlled by sb/sth: *The country is now under martial law.* **5** according to a law, an agreement, a system, etc: *Under English law you are innocent until you are proved guilty.* **6** experiencing a particular feeling, process or effect: *She's been under a lot of stress recently.* ◆ *a building under construction* ◆ *The manager is* ***under pressure*** *to resign.* ◆ *I was* ***under the impression that*** *Bill was not very happy there.* **7** using a particular name: *to travel under a false name* **8** found in a particular part of a book, list, etc: *You'll find some information on rugby under 'team sports'.*

OTHER WORDS FOR

under

You use **under** to say that one thing is directly under another thing. There may be a space between the two things: *The cat is asleep under the table* or one thing may be touching or covered by the other thing: *I think your letter is under that book.* You can use **below** to say that one thing is in a lower position than another thing: *They live on the floor below us.* ◆ *The skirt comes down to just below the knee.* You use **under** (not **below**) to talk about movement from one side of something to the other side: *We swam under the bridge.* You can use **beneath** in formal writing to say that one thing is directly under another thing, but **under** is more common. You can use **underneath** in place of **under** when you want to emphasize that something is being covered or hidden by another thing: *Have you looked underneath the sofa as well as behind it?*

under- /ˈʌndə(r)/ [in compounds] **1** lower in level or position: *an under-secretary* **2** not enough: *undercooked food*

underarm /ˈʌndərɑːm/ *adj* [only *before* a noun] connected with the part of the body under the arm where it meets the shoulder: *underarm deodorant* ➲ look at **armpit**

undercarriage /ˈʌndəkærɪdʒ/ (also **landing gear**) *noun* [C] the part of an aircraft, including the wheels, that supports it when it is landing and taking off ➲ picture on **page P6**

U

underclothes /ˈʌndəkləʊðz/ *noun* [pl] (*formal*) = **underwear**

undercover /ˌʌndəˈkʌvə(r)/ *adj* working or happening secretly: *an undercover reporter/detective*

undercurrent /ˈʌndəkʌrənt/ *noun* [C] undercurrent (of sth) a feeling, especially a negative one, that is hidden but whose effects are felt: *I detect an undercurrent of resentment towards the new proposals.*

undercut /ˌʌndəˈkʌt/ *verb* [T] (undercutting; *pt*, *pp* undercut) to sell sth at a lower price than other shops, etc.

underdeveloped /ˌʌndədɪˈveləpt/ *adj* (used about a country, society, etc.) having few industries and a low standard of living ➲ look at **developed**, **developing** ▶ **underdevelopment** *noun* [U]

underdog /ˈʌndədɒg/ *noun* [C] a person, team, etc. who is weaker than others and not expected to be successful: *San Marino were the underdogs, but managed to win the game 2-1.*

underestimate /ˌʌndərˈestɪmeɪt/ *verb* [T] **1** to guess that the amount, etc. of sth will be less than it really is **2** to think that sb/sth is not as strong, good, etc. as he/she/it really is: *Don't underestimate your opponent. He's a really good player.* **OPP** for both meanings **overestimate** ▶ **underestimate** /-mət/ *noun* [C]

underfoot /ˌʌndəˈfʊt/ *adv* under your feet; where you are walking: *It's very wet underfoot.*

undergo /ˌʌndəˈgəʊ/ *verb* [T] (undergoing; undergoes /-ˈgəʊz/; *pt* underwent /-ˈwent/; *pp* undergone /-ˈgɒn/) to have a difficult or an unpleasant experience: *She underwent a five-hour operation.*

undergraduate /ˌʌndəˈgrædʒuət/ *noun* [C] a student at college or university who is studying for their first degree ➲ look at **graduate**, **postgraduate**

underground¹ /ˈʌndəgraʊnd/ *adj* [only *before* a noun] **1** under the surface of the ground: *an underground car park* **2** secret or illegal: *an underground radio station*

U

underground² /ˌʌndəˈgraʊnd/ *adv* **1** under the surface of the ground: *The cables all run underground.* **2** into a secret place: *She went underground to escape from the police.*

underground³ /ˈʌndəgraʊnd/ (*AmE* subway) *noun* [sing] a railway system under the ground ➲ picture on **page P7**

CULTURE

In London the underground railway is called **the underground** or **the tube**.

undergrowth /ˈʌndəgrəʊθ/ *noun* [U] bushes and plants that grow around and under trees

underhand /ˌʌndəˈhænd/ *adj* secret or not honest

underlie /ˌʌndəˈlaɪ/ *verb* [T] (underlying; underlies; *pt* underlay /ˌʌndəˈleɪ/; *pp* underlain /-ˈleɪn/) (*formal*) to be the reason for or cause of sth: *It is a principle that underlies all the party's policies.*

underline /ˌʌndəˈlaɪn/ (*especially AmE* underscore) *verb* [T] **1** to draw a line under a word, etc. **2** to show sth clearly or to emphasize sth: *This accident underlines the need for greater care.*

EXAM TIP

Underline key words

Underline the key words in questions to help you to focus on exactly what the question is asking you. When you are reading a text, underline words and phrases where you find answers. This way you can easily find these parts of the text again when you are checking your answers.

underlying /ˌʌndəˈlaɪɪŋ/ *adj* [only *before* a noun] important but hidden: *the underlying causes of the disaster*

undermine /ˌʌndəˈmaɪn/ *verb* [T] to make sth weaker: *The public's confidence in the government has been undermined by the crisis.*

underneath /ˌʌndəˈniːθ/ *prep*, *adv* under; below: *The coin rolled underneath the chair.* ➲ note at **under**

the underneath /ˌʌndəˈniːθ/ *noun* [sing] the bottom or lowest part of something: *There is a lot of rust on the underneath of the car.*

undernourished /ˌʌndəˈnʌrɪʃt/ *adj* in bad health because you do not have enough food or enough of the right type of food

underpaid *past tense, past participle* of **underpay**

underpants /ˈʌndəpænts/ (*BrE also* pants) *noun* [pl] a piece of clothing that men or boys wear under their trousers

underpass /ˈʌndəpɑːs/ *noun* [C] a road or path that goes under another road, railway, etc.

underpay /ˌʌndəˈpeɪ/ *verb* [T] (*pt*, *pp* underpaid) to pay sb too little **OPP** **overpay**

underprivileged /ˌʌndəˈprɪvəlɪdʒd/ *adj* having less money and fewer rights, opportunities, etc. than other people in society **OPP** **privileged**

underrate /ˌʌndəˈreɪt/ *verb* [T] to think that sb/sth is less clever, important, good, etc. than he/she/it really is **OPP** **overrate**

underscore¹ /ˌʌndəˈskɔː(r)/ *verb* [T] (*especially AmE*) = **underline**

underscore² /ˈʌndəskɔː(r)/ *noun* [C] the symbol (_) that is used to draw a line under a letter or word and used in computer commands and in Internet addresses

undershirt /ˈʌndəʃɜːt/ (*AmE*) = **vest**(1)

underside /ˈʌndəsaɪd/ *noun* [C] the side or surface of sth that is underneath **SYN** **bottom**

understand /ˌʌndəˈstænd/ *verb* (*pt*, *pp* understood /-ˈstʊd/) **1** [I,T] to know or realize the meaning of sth: *I'm not sure that I really understand.* ♦ *I didn't understand the instructions.* ♦ *Please speak more slowly. I can't understand you.* ♦ *Do you understand what I'm asking you?* **2** [T] to know how or

why sth happens or why it is important: *I can't understand why the engine won't start.* ◆ *As far as I understand it, the changes won't affect us.* **3** [T] to know sb's character and why they behave in a particular way: *It's easy to understand why she felt so angry.* **4** [T] (*formal*) to have heard or been told sth: *I understand that you have decided to leave.*
IDM **give sb to believe/understand (that)** ➲ **believe**
make yourself understood to make your meaning clear: *I can just about make myself understood in Russian.*

understandable /ˌʌndəˈstændəbl/ *adj* that you can understand: *It was an understandable mistake to make.* ▶ **understandably** /-əbli/ *adv*: *She was understandably angry at the decision.*

⚷ **understanding[1]** /ˌʌndəˈstændɪŋ/ *noun* **1** [U, sing] the knowledge that sb has of a particular subject or situation: *A basic understanding of physics is necessary for this course.* ◆ *He has little understanding of how computers work.* **2** [C, usually sing] an informal agreement: *I'm sure we can* ***come to/reach an understanding*** *about the money I owe him.* **3** [U] the ability to know why people behave in a particular way and to forgive them if they do sth wrong or bad: *She apologized for her actions and her boss showed great understanding.* **4** [U] the way in which you think sth is meant: *My understanding of the arrangement is that he will only phone if there is a problem.*
IDM **on the understanding that ...** (*formal*) only if ...; because it was agreed that ...: *We let them stay in our house on the understanding that it was only for a short period.*

understanding[2] /ˌʌndəˈstændɪŋ/ *adj* showing kind feelings towards sb SYN **sympathetic**

understate /ˌʌndəˈsteɪt/ *verb* [T] to say that sth is smaller or less important than it really is OPP **overstate** ▶ **understatement** *noun* [C]: *'Is she pleased?' 'That's an understatement. She's delighted.'*

understood *past tense, past participle of* **understand**

understudy /ˈʌndəstʌdi/ *noun* [C] (*pl* **understudies**) an actor who learns the role of another actor and replaces them if they are ill

undertake /ˌʌndəˈteɪk/ *verb* [T] (*pt* **undertook** /-ˈtʊk/; *pp* **undertaken** /-ˈteɪkən/) **1** to decide to do sth and start doing it: *The company is undertaking a major programme of modernization.* **2** to agree or promise to do sth

undertaker /ˈʌndəteɪkə(r)/ (also ˈ**funeral director**; *AmE* also **mortician**) *noun* [C] a person whose job is to prepare dead bodies to be buried and to arrange funerals

undertaking /ˌʌndəˈteɪkɪŋ/ *noun* [C, usually sing] **1** a piece of work or business: *Buying the company would be a very risky undertaking.* **2** **an undertaking (that .../to do sth)** a formal or legal promise to do sth

undertone /ˈʌndətəʊn/ *noun* [C] a feeling, quality or meaning that is not expressed in a direct way
IDM **in an undertone; in undertones** in a quiet voice

undertook *past tense of* **undertake**

undervalue /ˌʌndəˈvæljuː/ *verb* [T] to place too low a value on sb/sth

⚷ **underwater** /ˌʌndəˈwɔːtə(r)/ *adj, adv* (existing, happening or used) below the surface of water: *underwater exploration* ◆ *an underwater camera* ◆ *Can you swim underwater?*

⚷ **underwear** /ˈʌndəweə(r)/ *noun* [U] clothing that is worn next to the skin under other clothes: *She packed* ***a change of underwear.*** ◆ *Your clean underwear is in the top drawer.*

> MORE The word **underclothes** has the same meaning, but is more formal and is a plural noun.

underweight /ˌʌndəˈweɪt/ *adj* weighing less than is normal or correct OPP **overweight** ➲ note at **thin**

underwent *past tense of* **undergo**

the underworld /ˈʌndəwɜːld/ *noun* [sing] people who are involved in organized crime

undesirable /ˌʌndɪˈzaɪərəbl/ *adj* unpleasant or not wanted; likely to cause problems OPP **desirable**

undid *past tense of* **undo**

undignified /ʌnˈdɪɡnɪfaɪd/ *adj* causing you to look silly and to lose the respect of other people OPP **dignified**

undiscovered /ˌʌndɪsˈkʌvəd/ *adj* that has not been found or noticed; that has not been discovered: *a previously undiscovered talent*

undivided /ˌʌndɪˈvaɪdɪd/ *adj*
IDM **get/have sb's undivided attention** to receive all sb's attention
give your undivided attention (to sb/sth) to give all your attention to sb/sth

⚷ **undo** /ʌnˈduː/ *verb* [T] (**undoing**; **undoes** /ʌnˈdʌz/; *pt* **undid** /ʌnˈdɪd/; *pp* **undone** /ʌnˈdʌn/) **1** to open sth that was tied or fastened: *to undo a knot/zip/button* **2** to destroy the effect of sth that has already happened: *His mistake has undone all our good work.*

undone /ʌnˈdʌn/ *adj* **1** open; not fastened or tied: *I realized that my zip was undone.* **2** not done: *I left the housework undone.*

undoubted /ʌnˈdaʊtɪd/ *adj* definite; accepted as being true ▶ **undoubtedly** *adv*

undress /ʌnˈdres/ *verb* **1** [I] to take off your clothes ➲ **Get undressed** is more common than **undress**. **2** [T] to take off sb's clothes OPP for both meanings **dress** ▶ **undressed** *adj*

undue /ˌʌnˈdjuː/ *adj* (*formal*) [only *before* a noun] more than is necessary or reasonable: *The police try not to use undue force when arresting a person.* ▶ **unduly** *adv*: *She didn't seem unduly worried by their unexpected arrival.*

unearth /ʌnˈɜːθ/ *verb* [T] to dig sth up out of the ground; to discover sth that was hidden: *Archaeologists have unearthed a Roman tomb.*

U

unearthly /ʌnˈɜːθli/ *adj* strange or frightening: *an unearthly scream*
IDM **at an unearthly hour** (*informal*) extremely early in the morning

unease /ʌnˈiːz/ (also **uneasiness** /ʌnˈiːzinəs/) *noun* [U] a worried or an uncomfortable feeling SYN **anxiety** OPP **ease**

uneasy /ʌnˈiːzi/ *adj* **1** uneasy (about sth/doing sth) worried; not feeling relaxed or comfortable **2** not settled; unlikely to last: *an uneasy compromise* ▸ **uneasily** *adv*

uneconomic /ˌʌnˌiːkəˈnɒmɪk; ˌʌnˌek-/ *adj* (used about a company, etc.) not making or likely to make a profit OPP **economic**

uneconomical /ˌʌnˌiːkəˈnɒmɪkl; ˌʌnˌek-/ *adj* wasting money, time, materials, etc. OPP **economical** ▸ **uneconomically** /-kli/ *adv*

🔑 **unemployed** /ˌʌnɪmˈplɔɪd/ *adj* **1** not able to find a job; out of work: *She has been unemployed for over a year.* SYN **jobless** OPP **employed** ➲ look at **work** **2 the unemployed** *noun* [pl] people who cannot find a job: *the long-term unemployed*

🔑 **unemployment** /ˌʌnɪmˈplɔɪmənt/ *noun* [U] **1** the number of people who are unemployed: *The economy is doing very badly and unemployment is rising.* SYN **joblessness** ➲ look at **the dole** **2** the situation of not being able to find a job: *If the factory closes, many people face unemployment.* ◆ *The number of people claiming* ***unemployment benefit*** (= money given by the state) *has gone up.* OPP **employment**

unending /ʌnˈendɪŋ/ *adj* having or seeming to have no end

unequal /ʌnˈiːkwəl/ *adj* **1** not fair or balanced: *an unequal distribution of power* **2** different in size, amount, level, etc. OPP for both meanings **equal** ▸ **unequally** /ʌnˈiːkwəli/ *adv*

uneven /ʌnˈiːvn/ *adj* **1** not completely smooth, level or regular: *The sign was painted in rather uneven letters.* OPP **even** **2** not always of the same level or quality ▸ **unevenly** *adv*: *The country's wealth is unevenly distributed.*

🔑 **unexpected** /ˌʌnɪkˈspektɪd/ *adj* not expected and therefore causing surprise: *His death was completely unexpected.* ▸ **unexpectedly** *adv*: *I got there late because I was unexpectedly delayed.*

unfailing /ʌnˈfeɪlɪŋ/ *adj* that you can be sure will always be there and always be the same: *unfailing support* ▸ **unfailingly** *adv*

🔑 **unfair** /ˌʌnˈfeə(r)/ *adj* **1** unfair (on/to sb) not dealing with people as they deserve; not treating each person equally: *This law is unfair to women.* ◆ *The tax is unfair on people with low incomes.* **2** not following the rules and therefore giving an advantage to one person, team, etc: *The referee warned him for unfair play.* OPP for both meanings **fair** ▸ **unfairly** *adv* ▸ **unfairness** *noun* [U]

unfaithful /ʌnˈfeɪθfl/ *adj* unfaithful (to sb/sth) having a sexual relationship with sb who is not your husband, wife or partner OPP **faithful** ▸ **unfaithfulness** *noun* [U]

unfamiliar /ˌʌnfəˈmɪliə(r)/ *adj* **1** unfamiliar (to sb) that you do not know well: *an unfamiliar part of town* **2** unfamiliar (with sb/sth) not having knowledge or experience of sth: *I'm unfamiliar with this author.* OPP for both meanings **familiar**

unfashionable /ʌnˈfæʃnəbl/ *adj* that was popular in the past but is not popular now: *unfashionable ideas/clothes* OPP **fashionable** ➲ look at **old-fashioned**

unfasten /ʌnˈfɑːsn/ *verb* [T] to open sth that is fastened: *to unfasten a belt/button, etc.* OPP **fasten**

unfavourable (*AmE* **unfavorable**) /ʌnˈfeɪvərəbl/ *adj* **1** not good and likely to cause problems or make sth difficult **2** showing that you do not like or approve of sb/sth OPP for both meanings **favourable** ➲ look at **adverse**

unfinished /ʌnˈfɪnɪʃt/ *adj* not complete; not finished: *We have some* ***unfinished business*** *to settle.*

unfit /ʌnˈfɪt/ *adj* **1** unfit (for sth/to do sth) not suitable or not good enough for sth: *His criminal past makes him unfit to be a politician.* **2** not in good physical health, especially because you do not get enough exercise OPP for both meanings **fit**

unfold /ʌnˈfəʊld/ *verb* [I,T] **1** to open out and become flat; to open out sth that was folded: *The sofa unfolds into a spare bed.* ◆ *I unfolded the letter and read it.* OPP **fold (up)** **2** to become known, or to allow sth to become known, a little at a time

unforeseen /ˌʌnfɔːˈsiːn/ *adj* not expected: *an unforeseen problem*

unforgettable /ˌʌnfəˈgetəbl/ *adj* making such a strong impression that you cannot forget it SYN **memorable**

🔑 **unfortunate** /ʌnˈfɔːtʃənət/ *adj* **1** not lucky: *The unfortunate people who lived near the river lost their homes in the flood.* SYN **unlucky** **2** that you feel sorry about: *I would like to apologize for this unfortunate mistake.* ▸ **unfortunately** *adv*: *I'd like to help you but unfortunately there's nothing I can do.* ➲ note at **sudden**

unfounded /ʌnˈfaʊndɪd/ *adj* not based on or supported by facts: *unfounded allegations*

unfriend /ʌnˈfrend/ *verb* [T] to remove sb from your list of friends on a **social networking site** (= a website for people who share your interests) ➲ note at **social networking**

🔑 **unfriendly** /ʌnˈfrendli/ *adj* unfriendly (to/towards sb) unpleasant or not polite to sb: *There was an unfriendly atmosphere in the room.* OPP **friendly**

ungainly /ʌnˈgeɪnli/ *adj* moving in a way that is not smooth or elegant

ungrateful /ʌnˈgreɪtfl/ *adj* not feeling or showing thanks to sb OPP **grateful** ▸ **ungratefully** /-fəli/ *adv*

unguarded /ʌnˈgɑːdɪd/ *adj* **1** not protected or guarded **2** saying more than you wanted to OPP for both meanings **guarded**

U

unhappily /ʌnˈhæpɪli/ *adj* **1** in a sad way SYN sadly **2** unfortunately OPP for both meanings **happily**

unhappy /ʌnˈhæpi/ *adj* (**unhappier**; **unhappiest**) **1 unhappy (about sth)** sad: *She's terribly unhappy about losing her job.* ◆ *He had a very unhappy childhood.* ➲ note at **sad** **2 unhappy (about/at/with sth)** not satisfied or pleased; worried: *They're unhappy at being left out of the team.* OPP for both meanings **happy** ▶ **unhappiness** *noun* [U]

unhealthy /ʌnˈhelθi/ *adj* **1** not having or showing good health: *He looks pale and unhealthy.* **2** likely to cause illness or poor health: *unhealthy conditions* **3** not natural: *an unhealthy interest in death* OPP for all meanings **healthy**

unheard /ʌnˈhɜːd/ *adj* [not before a noun] not listened to or given any attention: *My suggestions went unheard.*

unˈheard-of *adj* not known; never having happened before

unhygienic /ˌʌnhaɪˈdʒiːnɪk/ *adj* not clean and therefore likely to cause disease or infection: *The animals were kept in cramped and unhygienic conditions* OPP **hygienic**

unicorn /ˈjuːnɪkɔːn/ *noun* [C] (in stories) an animal that looks like a white horse with a long straight horn on its head

unidentified /ˌʌnaɪˈdentɪfaɪd/ *adj* whose identity is not known: *An unidentified body has been found in the river.*

uniform[1] /ˈjuːnɪfɔːm/ *noun* [C,U] the set of clothes worn at work by the members of an organization or a group, or by children at school: *I didn't know he was a policeman because he wasn't **in uniform**.* ➲ note at **clothes** ▶ **uniformed** *adj*

uniform[2] /ˈjuːnɪfɔːm/ *adj* not varying; the same in all cases or at all times: *uniform rates of pay* ▶ **uniformity** /ˌjuːnɪˈfɔːməti/ *noun* [U]

unify /ˈjuːnɪfaɪ/ *verb* [T] (**unifying**; **unifies**; *pt, pp* **unified**) to join separate parts together to make one unit, or to make them similar to each other ▶ **unification** /ˌjuːnɪfɪˈkeɪʃn/ *noun* [U]

unilateral /ˌjuːnɪˈlætrəl/ *adj* done or made by one person, group or organization that is involved in sth without the agreement of the other person, group, etc: *a unilateral declaration of independence* ➲ look at **multilateral** ▶ **unilaterally** /-rəli/ *adv*

unimportant /ˌʌnɪmˈpɔːtnt/ *adj* not important: *unimportant details* ◆ *They dismissed the problem as unimportant.*

uninhabitable /ˌʌnɪnˈhæbɪtəbl/ *adj* not fit or possible to live in OPP **habitable**

uninhabited /ˌʌnɪnˈhæbɪtɪd/ *adj* (used about a place or a building) with nobody living in it

uninhibited /ˌʌnɪnˈhɪbɪtɪd/ *adj* behaving in a free and natural way, without worrying what other people think of you OPP **inhibited**

uninstall /ˌʌnɪnˈstɔːl/ *verb* [T] to remove a program from a computer: *Uninstall any programs that you no longer need.* OPP **install**

unintelligible /ˌʌnɪnˈtelɪdʒəbl/ *adj* impossible to understand OPP **intelligible**

unintentional /ˌʌnɪnˈtenʃənl/ *adj* not done deliberately, but happening by accident OPP **intentional** ▶ **unintentionally** /-ʃənəli/ *adv*: *He had unintentionally written the wrong date.*

uninterested /ʌnˈɪntrəstɪd/ *adj* **uninterested (in sb/sth)** having or showing no interest in sb/sth: *She seemed uninterested in anything I had to say.* OPP **interested**

> **HELP** Be careful. **Disinterested** has a different meaning.

union /ˈjuːniən/ *noun* **1** (also ˌtrade ˈunion; ˌtrades ˈunion) [C] an organization for people who all work in a particular industry. Unions try to get better pay and working conditions for their members. **2** [C] an organization for a particular group of people: *the Athletics Union* **3** [C] a group of states or countries that have joined together to form one country or group: *the European Union* **4** [U,sing] the act of joining or the situation of being joined: *the union of the separate groups into one organization*

the ˌUnion ˈJack *noun* [sing] the national flag of the United Kingdom, with red and white crosses on a dark blue background

unique /juˈniːk/ *adj* **1** not like anything else; being the only one of its type: *Everyone's fingerprints are unique.* **2** very unusual: *There's nothing unique about that sort of crime.* **3 unique to sb/sth** connected with only one place, person or thing: *This dance is unique to this region.*

unisex /ˈjuːnɪseks/ *adj* designed for and used by both sexes: *unisex fashions*

unison /ˈjuːnɪsn/ *noun*

IDM **in unison** saying, singing or doing the same thing at the same time as sb else: *'No, thank you,' they said **in unison**.*

unit /ˈjuːnɪt/ *noun* [C]

➤ SINGLE THING **1** a single thing which is complete in itself, although it can be part of sth larger: *The book is divided into ten units.*

➤ GROUP OF PEOPLE **2** a group of people who perform a certain function within a larger organization: *army/military units*

➤ MEASUREMENT **3** a fixed amount or number used as a standard of measurement: *a unit of currency*

➤ FURNITURE **4** a piece of furniture that fits with other pieces of furniture and has a particular use: *kitchen units*

➤ SMALL MACHINE **5** a small machine that performs a particular task or that is part of a larger machine: *The heart of a computer is the central processing unit.*

➤ DEPARTMENT **6** a department, especially in a hospital, that provides a particular type of care or treatment: *a maternity unit* ◆ *the intensive care unit*

unite /juˈnaɪt/ *verb* **1** [I] **unite (in sth/in doing sth)** to join together for a particular purpose: *We should all unite in seeking a solution to this terrible problem.*

U

2 [I,T] to join together and act in agreement; to make this happen: *Unless we unite, our enemies will defeat us.* ♦ *Italy was united in 1861.*

🔑 **united** /ju'naɪtɪd/ *adj* joined together by a common feeling or aim: *Throughout the crisis, the whole country remained united.*

the U,nited 'Kingdom *noun* [sing] (*abbr* (the) UK) England, Scotland, Wales and Northern Ireland (considered as a political unit)

CULTURE

The UK consists of England, Scotland, Wales and Northern Ireland, but *not* the Republic of Ireland (Eire), which is a separate country. **Great Britain** is England, Scotland and Wales only. **The British Isles** are a geographical unit including the Republic of Ireland and the UK.

the U,nited 'Nations *noun* [sing, with sing or pl verb] (*abbr* UN) the organization formed to encourage peace in the world and to deal with problems between countries

the U,nited 'States (of A'merica) *noun* [sing, with sing or pl verb] (*abbr* US; USA) a large country in North America made up of 50 states and the District of Columbia

unity /'ju:nəti/ *noun* [U] the situation in which people are in agreement and working together

universal /,ju:nɪ'vɜ:sl/ *adj* connected with, done by or affecting everyone in the world or everyone in a particular group: *The environment is a universal issue.* ▶ **universally** /-səli/ *adv*

🔑 **the universe** /'ju:nɪvɜ:s/ *noun* [sing] everything that exists, including the planets, stars, space, etc: *There are many theories of how the universe began.*

TOPIC

University

People who want to **go to university** in Britain have to **apply** and they often have to go for an **interview**. Some also apply for a **scholarship** in order to pay their **tuition fees**. University **students** attend classes such as **lectures, seminars** and **tutorials**. They are taught by **professors, lecturers** and **tutors**. They may have to **do research** and **write a thesis** (= a long piece of writing). People studying for their first degree are called **undergraduates** and those doing further studies after their first degree are called **postgraduates**. If undergraduates pass their **finals** (= final exams), they will **graduate** (/'grædʒueɪt/) with a **degree**. A person who has graduated is called a **graduate** (/'grædʒuət/).

🔑 **university** /,ju:nɪ'vɜ:səti/ *noun* [C] (*pl* universities) an institution that provides the highest level of education, in which students study for degrees and in which academic research is done: *Which university did you go to?* ♦ *I did History* ***at university.*** ♦ *a university lecturer* ➲ note at **study**

HELP We use the expressions **at university** and **go to university** without *a* or *the* when we mean that somebody attends the university as a student: *He's hoping to go to university next year* but not if somebody goes there for any other reason: *I'm going to a conference at the university in July.*

unkempt /,ʌn'kempt/ *adj* (especially of sb's hair or general appearance) not well cared for; not tidy: *greasy, unkempt hair* **SYN** **dishevelled**

🔑 **unkind** /,ʌn'kaɪnd/ *adj* unpleasant and not friendly: *That was an unkind thing to say.* ♦ *It would be unkind to go without him.* **OPP** **kind** ▶ **unkindly** *adv* ▶ **unkindness** *noun* [U]

🔑 **unknown**[1] /,ʌn'nəʊn/ *adj* **1** unknown (to sb) that sb does not know; without sb knowing: *Unknown to the boss, she went home early.* **2** not famous or familiar to other people: *an unknown actress* **OPP** **well known, famous**

IDM **an unknown quantity** a person or thing that you know very little about

unknown[2] /,ʌn'nəʊn/ *noun* **1** *usually* the unknown [sing] a place or thing that you know nothing about: *a fear of the unknown* **2** [C] a person who is not well known

unleaded /,ʌn'ledɪd/ *adj* not containing lead: *unleaded petrol*

unleash /ʌn'li:ʃ/ *verb* [T] unleash sth (on/upon sb/sth) to suddenly let a strong force, emotion, etc., be felt or have an effect: *The new government proposals unleashed a storm of protest in the press.*

🔑 **unless** /ən'les/ *conj* if ... not; except if: *I was told that unless my work improved, I would lose the job.* ♦ *'Would you like a cup of coffee?' 'Not unless you've already made some.'* ♦ *Unless anyone has anything else to say, the meeting is closed.* ♦ *Don't switch that on unless I'm here.*

🔑 **unlike** /,ʌn'laɪk/ *adj* [not before a noun] *prep* **1** in contrast to; different from: *He's extremely ambitious, unlike me.* ♦ *She's unlike anyone else I've ever met.* ♦ *This is an exciting place to live, unlike my home town.* ➲ note at **difference** **2** not typical of; unusual for: *It's unlike him to be so rude—he's usually very polite.* **OPP** for both meanings **like**

🔑 **unlikely** /ʌn'laɪkli/ *adj* (unlikelier; unlikeliest) **1** unlikely (to do sth/that ...) not likely to happen; not expected; not probable: *I suppose she might win but I think it's very unlikely.* ♦ *It's* ***highly unlikely*** *that I'll have any free time next week.* **OPP** **likely** **2** [only before a noun] difficult to believe: *an unlikely excuse* **SYN** for both meanings **improbable**

unlimited /ʌn'lɪmɪtɪd/ *adj* without limit; as much or as great as you want **OPP** **limited**

🔑 **unload** /,ʌn'ləʊd/ *verb* **1** [I,T] unload (sth) (from sth) to remove things from a vehicle or ship after it has taken them somewhere: *We unloaded the boxes from the back of the van.* ♦ *Parking here is restricted to vehicles that are loading or unloading.* **OPP** **load** **2** [T] (*informal*) unload sb/sth (on/onto sb) to get rid of sth you do not want or to pass it to sb else: *He shouldn't try and unload the responsibility onto you.*

unlock /ˌʌnˈlɒk/ *verb* [I,T] to open the lock on sth using a key; to be opened with a key: *I can't unlock this door.* ♦ *This door won't unlock.* OPP **lock**

⚷ **unlucky** /ʌnˈlʌki/ *adj* (**unluckier**; **unluckiest**) having or causing bad luck: *They were unlucky to lose because they played so well.* ♦ *Thirteen is often thought to be an unlucky number.* OPP **lucky** ▶ **unluckily** *adv*

unmanned /ˌʌnˈmænd/ *adj* if a machine, a vehicle, a place or an activity is **unmanned**, it does not have or need a person to control or operate it: *an unmanned spacecraft*

unmarried /ˌʌnˈmærid/ *adj* not married SYN **single** OPP **married**

unmistakable (also **unmistakeable**) /ˌʌnmɪˈsteɪkəbl/ *adj* that cannot be confused with anything else; easy to recognize: *She had an unmistakable French accent.* ▶ **unmistakably** (also **unmistakeably**) /-əbli/ *adv*

unmoved /ˌʌnˈmuːvd/ *adj* not affected in an emotional way: *The judge was unmoved by the man's sad story, and sent him to jail.*

unnatural /ʌnˈnætʃrəl/ *adj* different from what is normal or expected OPP **natural** ▶ **unnaturally** /-rəli/ *adv*: *It's unnaturally quiet in here.*

⚷ **unnecessary** /ʌnˈnesəsəri/ *adj* more than is needed or acceptable: *We should try to avoid all unnecessary expense.* OPP **necessary** ▶ **unnecessarily** /ʌnˈnesəsərəli; ˌʌnˌnesəˈserəli/ *adv*: *His explanation was unnecessarily complicated.*

unnerve /ˌʌnˈnɜːv/ *verb* [T] to make sb feel nervous or frightened or lose confidence: *His silence unnerved us.* ▶ **unnerving** *adj*

unnoticed /ˌʌnˈnəʊtɪst/ *adj* [not before a noun] not noticed or seen: *He didn't want his hard work to **go unnoticed**.*

unobtrusive /ˌʌnəbˈtruːsɪv/ *adj* (*formal*) avoiding being noticed; not attracting attention ▶ **unobtrusively** *adv*: *He tried to leave as unobtrusively as possible.*

unofficial /ˌʌnəˈfɪʃl/ *adj* not accepted or approved by a person in authority: *an unofficial strike* ♦ *Unofficial reports say that four people died in the explosion.* OPP **official** ▶ **unofficially** /-ʃəli/ *adv*

unorthodox /ʌnˈɔːθədɒks/ *adj* different from what is generally accepted, usual or traditional OPP **orthodox**

unpack /ˌʌnˈpæk/ *verb* [I,T] to take out the things that were in a bag, suitcase, etc: *When we arrived at the hotel we unpacked and went to the beach.* OPP **pack**

unpaid /ˌʌnˈpeɪd/ *adj* **1** not yet paid: *an unpaid bill* **2** (used about work) done without payment: *unpaid overtime* **3** not receiving money for work done: *an unpaid assistant*

⚷ **unpleasant** /ʌnˈpleznt/ *adj* **1** not pleasant or comfortable: *This news has come as an unpleasant surprise.* OPP **pleasant** **2** unfriendly; not polite: *There's no need to get unpleasant; we can discuss this in a friendly way.* ▶ **unpleasantly** *adv*

unplug /ˌʌnˈplʌg/ *verb* [T] (**unplugging**; **unplugged**) to remove a piece of electrical equipment from the electricity supply: *Could you unplug the printer, please?* OPP **plug sth in**

unpopular /ʌnˈpɒpjələ(r)/ *adj* **unpopular** (**with sb**) not liked by many people: *Her methods made her very unpopular with the staff.* OPP **popular** ▶ **unpopularity** /ˌʌnˌpɒpjuˈlærəti/ *noun* [U]

unprecedented /ʌnˈpresɪdentɪd/ *adj* never having happened or existed before ➲ look at **precedent**

unpredictable /ˌʌnprɪˈdɪktəbl/ *adj* that cannot be predicted because it changes a lot or depends on too many different things: *unpredictable weather* ♦ *The result is entirely unpredictable.* OPP **predictable** ▶ **unpredictability** /ˌʌnprɪˌdɪktəˈbɪləti/ *noun* [U] ▶ **unpredictably** /ˌʌnprɪˈdɪktəbli/ *adv*

unprovoked /ˌʌnprəˈvəʊkt/ *adj* (used especially about an attack) not caused by anything the person who is attacked has said or done OPP **provoked**

unqualified /ˌʌnˈkwɒlɪfaɪd/ *adj* **1** not having the knowledge or not having passed the exams that you need for sth: *I'm unqualified to offer an opinion on this matter.* OPP **qualified** **2** complete; total: *an unqualified success*

unquestionable /ʌnˈkwestʃənəbl/ *adj* certain; that cannot be doubted OPP **questionable** ▶ **unquestionably** /-əbli/ *adv*: *She is unquestionably the most famous opera singer in the world.*

unravel /ʌnˈrævl/ *verb* [I,T] (**unravelling**; **unravelled**, (*AmE*) **unraveling**; **unraveled**) **1** if you **unravel** threads that are twisted or they **unravel**, you separate them: *I unravelled the tangled string and wound it into a ball.* **2** (used about a complicated story, etc.) to become or to make sth become clear: *Eventually the mystery unravelled and the truth came out.*

unreal /ˌʌnˈrɪəl/ *adj* **1** very strange and seeming more like a dream than reality: *Her voice had an unreal quality about it.* **2** not connected with reality: *Some people have unreal expectations of marriage.*

unrealistic /ˌʌnrɪəˈlɪstɪk/ *adj* not showing or accepting things as they are: *unrealistic expectations* ♦ ***It is unrealistic to** expect them to be able to solve the problem immediately.* OPP **realistic** ▶ **unrealistically** /-kli/ *adv*

⚷ **unreasonable** /ʌnˈriːznəbl/ *adj* unfair; expecting too much: *I think she is being totally unreasonable about it.* ♦ *He makes unreasonable demands on his students.* OPP **reasonable** ▶ **unreasonably** /-əbli/ *adv*

unrelenting /ˌʌnrɪˈlentɪŋ/ *adj* (*formal*) continuously strong, not becoming weaker or less severe or stopping

unreliable /ˌʌnrɪˈlaɪəbl/ *adj* that cannot be trusted or depended on: *The trains are notoriously unreliable.* ♦ *an unreliable witness* ♦ *He's totally unreliable*

U

as a source of information. OPP **reliable** ▶ **unreliability** /ˌʌnrɪˌlaɪəˈbɪləti/ *noun* [U]

unreserved /ˌʌnrɪˈzɜːvd/ *adj* **1** (used about seats in a theatre, etc.) not kept for the use of a particular person OPP **reserved** **2** (*formal*) without limit; complete: *The government's action received the unreserved support of all parties.* ▶ **unreservedly** /ˌʌnrɪˈzɜːvɪdli/ *adv*: *We apologize unreservedly for our mistake and will refund your money.*

unrest /ʌnˈrest/ *noun* [U] a situation in which people are angry or not happy and likely to protest or fight: *political and social unrest*

unrivalled (*AmE* unrivaled) /ʌnˈraɪvld/ *adj* much better than any other of the same type: *His knowledge of Greek theology is unrivalled.*

unroll /ʌnˈrəʊl/ *verb* [I,T] to open from a rolled position: *He unrolled the poster and stuck it on the wall.* OPP **roll up**

unruly /ʌnˈruːli/ *adj* difficult to control; without discipline: *an unruly crowd* ▶ **unruliness** *noun* [U]

unsavoury (*AmE* unsavory) /ʌnˈseɪvəri/ *adj* unpleasant; not morally acceptable: *His friends are all unsavoury characters.*

unscathed /ʌnˈskeɪðd/ *adj* [not before a noun] not hurt, without injury: *He came out of the fight unscathed.*

unscrew /ˌʌnˈskruː/ *verb* [T] **1** to open or remove sth by turning it: *Could you unscrew the top of this bottle for me?* **2** to remove the screws from sth

unscrupulous /ʌnˈskruːpjələs/ *adj* being dishonest, cruel or unfair in order to get what you want OPP **scrupulous**

unselfish /ʌnˈselfɪʃ/ *adj* giving more time or importance to other people's needs or wishes than to your own OPP **selfish** ➲ look at **selfless**

unsettled /ʌnˈsetld/ *adj* **1** (used about a situation) that may change; making people uncertain about what might happen: *These were difficult and unsettled times.* ♦ *The weather has been very unsettled* (= it has changed a lot). **2** not calm or relaxed: *They all felt restless and unsettled.* **3** (used about an argument, etc.) that continues without any agreement being reached **4** (used about a bill, etc.) not yet paid

unsettling /ʌnˈsetlɪŋ/ *adj* making you feel upset, nervous or worried

unsightly /ʌnˈsaɪtli/ *adj* very unpleasant to look at: *an unsightly new building* SYN **ugly**

unskilled /ˌʌnˈskɪld/ *adj* not having or needing special skill or training: *an unskilled job/worker* OPP **skilled**

unsolicited /ˌʌnsəˈlɪsɪtɪd/ *adj* not asked for: *unsolicited praise/advice*

unsound /ˌʌnˈsaʊnd/ *adj* **1** based on wrong ideas and therefore not correct or sensible **2** in poor condition; weak: *The building is structurally unsound.* OPP for both meanings **sound**

unstable /ʌnˈsteɪbl/ *adj* **1** likely to change or fail: *a period of unstable government* **2** (used about sb's moods or behaviour) likely to change suddenly or often **3** likely to fall down or move; not firmly fixed OPP for all meanings **stable** ➲ *noun* **instability**

unsteady /ʌnˈstedi/ *adj* **1** not completely in control of your movements so that you might fall: *She is still a little* ***unsteady on her feet*** *after the operation.* **2** shaking or moving in a way that is not controlled: *His writing is untidy because he has an unsteady hand.* OPP for both meanings **steady** ▶ **unsteadily** *adv*

unstuck /ˌʌnˈstʌk/ *adj* no longer stuck together or stuck down: *The label on the parcel is about to* ***come unstuck.***

IDM **come unstuck** (*informal*) to fail badly; to go wrong: *His plan came unstuck when he realized he didn't have enough money.*

unsubscribe /ˌʌnsəbˈskraɪb/ *verb* [I,T] unsubscribe (from sth) to remove your email address from an Internet **mailing list** (= a list of the names and addresses of people to whom sth is sent)

unsuccessful /ˌʌnsəkˈsesfl/ *adj* not successful; not achieving what you wanted to: *His efforts to get a job proved unsuccessful.* ♦ *She made several unsuccessful attempts to see him.* OPP **successful** ▶ **unsuccessfully** /-fəli/ *adv*

unsuitable /ʌnˈsuːtəbl/ *adj* not right or appropriate for sb/sth: *This film is unsuitable for children under 12.* OPP **suitable**

unsure /ˌʌnˈʃʊə(r); -ˈʃɔː(r)/ *adj* **1** unsure (about/of sth) not certain; having doubts: *I didn't argue because I was unsure of the facts.* **2** unsure of yourself not feeling confident about yourself: *He's young and still quite unsure of himself.* OPP for both meanings **sure**

unsuspecting /ˌʌnsəˈspektɪŋ/ *adj* not realizing that there is danger ➲ look at **suspect**, **suspicious**

untangle /ˌʌnˈtæŋgl/ *verb* [T] to separate threads which have become tied together in a confused way: *The wires got mixed up and it took me ages to untangle them.*

unthinkable /ʌnˈθɪŋkəbl/ *adj* impossible to imagine or accept: *It was unthinkable that he would never see her again.*

unthinking /ʌnˈθɪŋkɪŋ/ *adj* (*formal*) done, said, etc. without thinking carefully ▶ **unthinkingly** *adv*

🔑 **untidy** /ʌnˈtaɪdi/ *adj* (untidier; untidiest) **1** not tidy or well arranged: *an untidy bedroom* ♦ *untidy hair* **2** (used about a person) not keeping things tidy or in good order: *My flatmate is so untidy!* OPP for both meanings **tidy**, **neat** ▶ **untidily** *adv* ▶ **untidiness** *noun* [U]

untie /ʌnˈtaɪ/ *verb* [T] (untying; unties; *pt, pp* untied) to remove a knot; to free sb/sth that is tied by a rope, etc. OPP **tie**, **tie up**, **fasten**

🔑 **until** /ənˈtɪl/ (also *informal* till) *prep, conj* up to the time or the event mentioned: *The restaurant is open until midnight.* ♦ *Until that moment she had been happy.* ♦ *She waited until he had finished.* ♦ *We won't* *leave until the police get here* (= we won't leave before they come).

OTHER WORDS FOR

until

We can use **until** in both formal and informal English. **Till** is more common in informal English and is not usually used at the beginning of a sentence. **Till/until** are used to talk about a time. We use **as far as** to talk about distance: *I walked as far as the shops.* We use **up to** to talk about a number: *You can take up to 20 kilos of luggage.*

untold /ˌʌn'təʊld/ *adj* [only *before* a noun] very great; so big, etc. that you cannot count or measure it: *untold suffering*

untoward /ˌʌntə'wɔːd/ *adj* (used about an event, etc.) unexpected and unpleasant: *The security guard noticed nothing untoward.*

untrue /ʌn'truː/ *adj* not true; not based on facts **SYN** **false** **OPP** **true**

untruth /ˌʌn'truːθ/ *noun* [C] (*pl* **untruths** /ˌʌn'truːðz/) (*formal*) something that is not true; a lie ▸ **untruthful** /-fl/ *adj* ▸ **untruthfully** /-fəli/ *adv*

untypical /ʌn'tɪpɪkl/ *adj* not typical or usual: *an untypical example* **OPP** **typical** ➲ look at **atypical**

unused¹ /ˌʌn'juːzd/ *adj* that has not been used

unused² /ʌn'juːst/ *adj* **unused to sth/to doing sth** not having any experience of sth: *She was unused to getting such a lot of attention.*

⚷ **unusual** /ʌn'juːʒuəl; -ʒəl/ *adj* **1** not expected or normal: *It's unusual for Joe to be late.* **OPP** **usual** **2** interesting because it is different: *What an unusual hat!*

⚷ **unusually** /ʌn'juːʒuəli; -ʒəli/ *adv* **1** more than is common; extremely: *an unusually hot summer* **2** in a way that is not normal or typical of sb/sth: *Unusually for her, she forgot his birthday.* **OPP** **usually**

unveil /ˌʌn'veɪl/ *verb* [T] to show sth new to the public for the first time: *The President unveiled a memorial to those who died in the war.*

unwanted /ˌʌn'wɒntɪd/ *adj* not wanted: *an unwanted gift*

unwarranted /ʌn'wɒrəntɪd/ *adj* (*formal*) that is not deserved or for which there is no good reason: *unwarranted criticism*

unwell /ʌn'wel/ *adj* [not before a noun] ill; sick: *to feel unwell* **OPP** **well**

unwieldy /ʌn'wiːldi/ *adj* difficult to move or carry because it is too big, heavy, etc.

⚷ **unwilling** /ʌn'wɪlɪŋ/ *adj* not wanting to do sth but often forced to do it by other people: *She was unwilling to give me any further details.* **OPP** **willing** ▸ **unwillingly** *adv*: *He handed over the money unwillingly.*

unwind /ˌʌn'waɪnd/ *verb* (*pt, pp* **unwound** /ˌʌn'waʊnd/) **1** [I,T] to undo sth that has been wrapped into a ball or around sth: *to unwind a ball of string* ◆ *The bandage had unwound.* **2** [I] (*informal*) to relax, especially after working hard: *After a busy day, it takes me a while to unwind.* ➲ look at **wind**

unwise /ˌʌn'waɪz/ *adj* showing a lack of good judgement; silly: *I think it would be unwise to tell anyone about our plan yet.* **OPP** **wise** ▸ **unwisely** *adv*

unwitting /ʌn'wɪtɪŋ/ *adj* [only *before* a noun] not realizing sth; not intending to do sth: *an unwitting accomplice to the crime* ▸ **unwittingly** *adv*

unwound *past tense, past participle* of **unwind**

unwrap /ʌn'ræp/ *verb* [T] (**unwrapping**; **unwrapped**) to take off the paper, etc. that covers or protects sth

unzip /ˌʌn'zɪp/ *verb* [I,T] (**unzipping**; **unzipped**) if a bag, piece of clothing, etc. **unzips**, or you **unzip** it, you open it by pulling on the **zip** (= the device that fastens the opening, with two rows of metal or plastic teeth) **OPP** **zip sth (up)**

⚷ **up** /ʌp/ *prep, adv* **1** at or to a high or higher level or position: *The monkey* ***climbed up*** *the tree.* ◆ *I carried her suitcase up to the third floor.* ◆ ***Put*** *your* ***hand up*** *if you know the answer.* ◆ *I walked up the hill.* **2** in or into a vertical position: ***Stand up****, please.* ◆ *Is he up* (= out of bed) *yet?* **3** used for showing an increase in sth: *Prices have* ***gone up****.* ◆ *Turn the volume up.* **4** to the place where sb/sth is: *She ran up to her mother and kissed her.* ◆ *A car drove up and two men got out.* **5** in or to the north: *My parents have just moved* ***up north****.* ◆ *When are you going up to Scotland?* **6** into pieces: *We chopped the old table up and used it for firewood.* ◆ *She* ***tore up*** *the letter and threw it away.* **7** used for showing that an action continues until it is completed: ***Eat up****, everybody, I want you to finish everything on the table.* ◆ *Can you help me* ***clean up*** *the kitchen?* **8** coming or being put together: *The teacher collected up our exam papers.* ◆ *Keiko and Jos teamed up in the doubles competition.* **9** (used about a period of time) finished: *Stop writing. Your time's up.* **10** used with verbs of closing or covering: ***Do up*** *your coat. It's cold.* ◆ *She tied the parcel up with string.* ◆ *I found some wood to* ***cover up*** *the hole.* **11** in a particular direction: *I live just* ***up the road****.* ◆ ***Move up*** *a little and let me sit down.* **12** (used about computers) working; in operation: *Are the computers back up yet?* **13** (*informal*) used for showing that sth is spoiled: *I really messed up when I told the interviewer I liked sleeping.* ℹ For special uses with many verbs, for example **pick sth up**, look at the verb entries.

IDM **be up for sth** **1** to be available to be bought or chosen: *That house is up for sale.* ◆ *How many candidates are up for election?* **2** (*informal*) to be willing to take part in an activity: *Is anyone up for a swim?*

be up to sb to be sb's responsibility: *I can't take the decision. It's not up to me.*

not up to much (*informal*) not very good: *The programme wasn't up to much.*

up against sth/sb (*informal*) facing sth/sb that causes problems

up and down backwards and forwards, or rising

U

and falling: *He was nervously walking up and down outside the interview room.*
up and running (used about sth new) working; being used
ups and downs ➲ **ups**
up to sth 1 as much/many as: *We're expecting up to 100 people at the meeting.* **2** as far as now: *Up to now, things have been easy.* **3** capable of sth: *I don't feel up to cooking this evening. I'm too tired.* **4** (*informal*) doing sth secret and perhaps bad: *What are the children up to? Go and see.*
what's up? (*informal*) what's the matter?

ˌup-and-ˈcoming *adj* likely to be successful and popular in the future: *up-and-coming young actors*

upbringing /ˈʌpbrɪŋɪŋ/ *noun* [sing] the way a child is treated and taught how to behave by their parents: *a strict upbringing*

update /ˌʌpˈdeɪt/ *verb* [T] **1** to make sth more modern **2** to put the most recent information into sth; to give sb the most recent information: *Our database of addresses is updated regularly.* ▶ **update** /ˈʌpdeɪt/ *noun* [C]: *an update on a news story* (= the latest information) ◆ *a **computer update*** (= the most recent improvements sent to a user of a program)

upgrade /ˌʌpˈgreɪd/ *verb* [T] to change sth so that it is of a higher standard: *Upgrading your computer software can be expensive.* ▶ **upgrade** /ˈʌpgreɪd/ *noun* [C]

upheaval /ʌpˈhiːvl/ *noun* [C,U] a sudden big change, especially one that causes a lot of trouble

upheld *past tense, past participle of* **uphold**

uphill /ˌʌpˈhɪl/ *adj, adv* **1** going towards the top of a hill **OPP** **downhill 2** needing a lot of effort: *It was an uphill struggle to find a job.*

uphold /ʌpˈhəʊld/ *verb* [T] (*pt, pp* **upheld** /-ˈheld/) to support a decision, etc. especially when other people are against it

upholstered /ʌpˈhəʊlstəd/ *adj* (used about a chair, etc.) covered with a soft thick material

upholstery /ʌpˈhəʊlstəri/ *noun* [U] the thick soft materials used to cover chairs, car seats, etc.

upkeep /ˈʌpkiːp/ *noun* [U] **1** the cost or process of keeping sth in a good condition: *The landlord pays for the upkeep of the building.* **2** the cost or process of providing children or animals with what they need to live

upland /ˈʌplənd/ *adj* [only *before* a noun] consisting of hills and mountains ▶ **upland** *noun* [C, usually pl]

uplifting /ˌʌpˈlɪftɪŋ/ *adj* producing a feeling of hope and happiness: *an uplifting speech*

upload /ˌʌpˈləʊd/ *verb* [T] to move data to a larger computer system from a smaller one **OPP** **download** ▶ **upload** /ˈʌpləʊd/ *noun* [C]

upmarket /ˌʌpˈmɑːkɪt/ *adj, adv* smart or expensive: *an upmarket restaurant* **OPP** **downmarket**

upon /əˈpɒn/ (*formal*) = **on**(1): *a castle upon a hill* ◆ *row upon row of seats* ◆ *Once upon a time there lived an old woman in the middle of a forest.*

upper /ˈʌpə(r)/ *adj* [only *before* a noun] in a higher position than sth else; above sth: *He had a cut on his upper lip.* **OPP** **lower**
IDM **get, have, etc. the upper hand** to get into a stronger position than another person; to gain control over sb

ˌupper ˈcase *noun* [U] letters that are written or printed in their large form: *'BBC' is written in upper case.* **SYN** **capital letters** **OPP** **lower case**

the ˌupper ˈclass *noun* [sing, with sing or pl verb] (*also* **the upper ˈclasses** [pl]) the groups of people that are considered to have the highest social position and that have more money and/or power than other people in society: *a member of the upper class/upper classes* ➲ look at **middle class, working class**
▶ **ˌupper ˈclass** *adj*: *Her family is very upper class.* ◆ *an upper-class accent*

uppermost /ˈʌpəməʊst/ *adj* in the highest or most important position: *Concern for her family was **uppermost in her mind**.*

upright /ˈʌpraɪt/ *adj, adv* **1** in or into a vertical position: *I was so tired I could hardly stay upright.* **SYN** **erect 2** honest and responsible
IDM **bolt upright** ➲ **bolt**[3]

uprising /ˈʌpraɪzɪŋ/ *noun* [C] a situation in which a group of people start to fight against the people in power in their country

uproar /ˈʌprɔː(r)/ *noun* [U, sing] a lot of noise, confusion, anger, etc.; an angry discussion about sth: *The meeting ended **in uproar**.*

uproot /ˌʌpˈruːt/ *verb* [T] to pull up a plant by the roots: *Strong winds had uprooted the tree.*

ups /ʌps/ *noun*
IDM **ups and downs** both good times and bad times: *We're happy together but we've had our ups and downs.*

upset[1] /ˌʌpˈset/ *verb* [T] (**upsetting**; *pt, pp* **upset**) **1** to make sb worry or feel unhappy: *The pictures of starving children upset her.* ➲ note at **sad 2** to make sth go wrong: *to upset someone's plans* **3** to make sb ill in the stomach: *Rich food usually upsets me.* **4** to knock sth over: *I upset a cup of tea all over the tablecloth.*

upset[2] /ˌʌpˈset/ *adj* **1** [not before a noun] worried and unhappy: *She was looking very upset about something.* ➲ note at **sad 2** slightly ill: *I've got an **upset stomach**.*

HELP Note that the adjective is pronounced /ˈʌpset/ when it comes before a noun and /ˌʌpˈset/ in other positions in the sentence.

upset[3] /ˈʌpset/ *noun* **1** [U] a situation in which there are unexpected problems or difficulties: *The company survived the recent upset in share prices.* **2** [C,U] a situation that causes worry and sadness: *She's had a few upsets recently.* ◆ *It had been the cause of much emotional upset.* **3** [C] a slight illness in your stomach: *a stomach upset*

upshot /ˈʌpʃɒt/ *noun* [sing] the upshot (of sth) the final result, especially of a conversation or an event

The painting is upside down.

🔑 **upside down** /ˌʌpsaɪd ˈdaʊn/ *adv* with the top part turned to the bottom: *You're holding the picture upside down.*
IDM **turn sth upside down 1** (*informal*) to make a place untidy when looking for sth: *I had to turn the house upside down looking for my keys.* **2** to cause large changes and confusion in sb's life: *His sudden death turned her world upside down.*
▸ **upside down** *adj*: *The painting is upside down.*

🔑 **upstairs** /ˌʌpˈsteəz/ *adv* to or on a higher floor of a building: *to* **go upstairs** ◆ *She's sleeping upstairs.* OPP **downstairs** ▸ **upstairs** /ˈʌpsteəz/ *adj* [only *before* a noun]: *an upstairs window* ▸ **upstairs** *noun* [sing]: *We're going to paint the upstairs.*

upstream /ˌʌpˈstriːm/ *adv, adj* in the direction that a river flows from: *He found it hard work swimming upstream.* OPP **downstream**

upsurge /ˈʌpsɜːdʒ/ *noun* [C,usually sing] an upsurge (in sth) a sudden increase of sth

uptake /ˈʌpteɪk/ *noun*
IDM **quick/slow on the uptake** (*informal*) quick/slow to understand the meaning of sth: *I gave him a hint but he's slow on the uptake.*

uptight /ˌʌpˈtaɪt/ *adj* (*informal*) nervous and not relaxed: *He gets uptight before an exam.*

ˌup to ˈdate *adj* **1** modern: *up-to-date fashions* **2** having the most recent information: *Is this information up to date?* ➲ look at **out of date**

ˌup-to-the-ˈminute *adj* having the most recent information possible

upturn /ˈʌptɜːn/ *noun* [C] an upturn (in sth) an improvement in sth: *an upturn in support for the government* OPP **downturn**

upturned /ˌʌpˈtɜːnd/ *adj* **1** pointing upwards: *an upturned nose* **2** with the top part turned to the bottom

🔑 **upward** /ˈʌpwəd/ *adj* [only *before* a noun] moving or directed towards a higher place: *an upward trend in exports* (= an increase) OPP **downward** ▸ **upwards** (also upward /ˈʌpwədz/) *adv*: *I looked upwards.*

ˈupwards of *prep* more than the number mentioned: *They've invited upwards of a hundred guests.*

uranium /juˈreɪniəm/ *noun* [U] (*symbol* U) a metal that can be used to produce nuclear energy: *Uranium is highly radioactive.*

Uranus /ˈjʊərənəs; jʊˈreɪnəs/ *noun* [sing] the planet that is 7th in order from the sun

🔑 **urban** /ˈɜːbən/ *adj* connected with a town or city: *urban development* ➲ look at **rural**

🔑 **urge¹** /ɜːdʒ/ *verb* [T] **1** urge sb (to do sth); urge sth to advise or try hard to persuade sb to do sth: *I urged him to fight the decision.* ◆ *Drivers are urged to take care on icy roads.* ◆ *Police urge caution on the icy roads.* **2** to force sb/sth to go in a certain direction: *He urged his horse over the fence.*
PHR V **urge sb on** to encourage sb: *The captain urged his team on.*

🔑 **urge²** /ɜːdʒ/ *noun* [C] a strong need or desire: *sexual/creative urges*

🔑 **urgent** /ˈɜːdʒənt/ *adj* needing immediate attention: *an urgent message* ▸ **urgency** /ˈɜːdʒənsi/ *noun* [U]: *a matter of the greatest urgency* ▸ **urgently** *adv*: *I must see you urgently.*

urinate /ˈjʊərɪneɪt/ *verb* [I] (*formal*) to pass **urine** from the body

urine /ˈjʊərɪn; -raɪn/ *noun* [U] the yellowish liquid that is passed from your body when you go to the toilet

URL /ˌjuː ɑːr ˈel/ *abbr* **uniform/universal resource locator**; the address of a World Wide Web page ➲ note at **Internet**

urn /ɜːn/ *noun* [C] **1** a special container, used especially to hold the **ashes** (= the powder) that is left when a dead person has been **cremated** (= burnt) **2** a large metal container used for making a large quantity of tea or coffee and for keeping it hot

US (also U.S.) /ˌjuː ˈes/ *abbr* the **United States** (of America)

🔑 **us** /əs; *strong form* ʌs/ *pron* [used as the object of a verb, or after *be*] me and another person or other people; me and you: *Come with us.* ◆ *Leave us alone.* ◆ *Will you write to us?*

USA (also U.S.A.) /ˌjuː es ˈeɪ/ *abbr* = **the United States of America**

usable /ˈjuːzəbl/ *adj* that can be used

usage /ˈjuːsɪdʒ/ *noun* **1** [U] the way that sth is used; the amount that sth is used **2** [C,U] the way that words are normally used in a language: *a guide to English grammar and usage*

USB /ˌjuː es ˈbiː/ *abbr* **universal serial bus**; the system for connecting other pieces of equipment to a computer: *All new PCs now have USB sockets.* ◆ *a USB port* ➲ picture at **computer**

USˈB drive (also *informal* ˌUSˈB stick) = **flash drive**

🔑 **use¹** /juːz/ *verb* [T] (using; *pt, pp* used /juːzd/) **1** use sth (as/for sth); use sth (to do sth) to do sth with a machine, an object, a method, etc. for a particular purpose: *Could I use your phone?* ◆ *The building was used as a shelter for homeless people.* ◆ *A pen is used*

U

for writing with. ♦ What's this used for? ♦ We used the money to buy a house. ♦ Use your imagination! ♦ That's a word I never use. **2** to need or to take sth: *Don't use all the milk.* ♦ *The heater uses a lot of electricity.* **3** to treat sb/sth in an unfair way in order to get sth that you want: *I felt used.*

PHR V **use sth up** to use sth until no more is left

use² /ju:s/ *noun* **1** [U] the act of using sth or of being used: *The use of car share schemes is now widespread.* ♦ *She kept the money for use in an emergency.* **2** [C,U] the purpose for which sth is used: *This machine has many uses.* **3** [U] the ability or permission to use sth: *He lost the use of his hand after the accident.* ♦ *She offered them the use of her car.* **4** [U] the advantage of sth; how useful sth is: ***It's no use** studying for an exam at the last minute.* ♦ ***What's the use of** trying?* ♦ *Will this jumper **be of use to** you or should I get rid of it?*

IDM **come into/go out of use** to start/stop being used regularly or by a lot of people: *When did this word come into common use?*

make use of sth/sb to use sth/sb in a way that will give you an advantage

used¹ /ju:zd/ *adj* that has had another owner before: *a garage selling used cars* SYN **second-hand**

used² /ju:st/ *adj* **used to sth/to doing sth** familiar with sth because you do it or experience it often: *He's used to the heat.* ♦ *I'll never **get used to** getting up so early.*

used to /'ju:st tə; *before a vowel and in final position* 'ju:st tu/ *modal verb* used for talking about sth that happened often or continuously in the past or about a situation which existed in the past: *She used to live with her parents, but she doesn't any more.* ♦ *You used to live in Glasgow, didn't you?* ♦ *Did you use to smoke?* ♦ *Did you use to believe in Father Christmas?* ♦ *He didn't use to speak to me.* ➲ look at **would**(8)

GRAMMAR To form questions we use **did** with **use to:** *Did she use to be in your class?* We form negatives with **didn't use to** or **never used to:** *I never used to like jazz.* Do not confuse **used to** + infinitive, which refers only to the past, with **be used to (doing) sth:** *I used to live with my parents, but now I live on my own.* ♦ *I'm used to living on my own* (= I am familiar with it), *so I don't feel lonely.* **Get used to (doing) sth** is for new situations that you are not yet familiar with: *I'm still getting used to my new job.*

U

useful /'ju:sfl/ *adj* having some practical use; helpful: *a useful tool* ♦ *useful advice*

IDM **come in useful** to be of practical help in a certain situation: *Don't throw that box away—it might come in useful for something.*

▶ **usefully** /-fəli/ *adv* ▶ **usefulness** *noun* [U]

useless /'ju:sləs/ *adj* **1** that does not work well, that does not achieve anything: *This new machine is useless.* ♦ *It's useless complaining/to complain—you won't get your money back.* **2** (*informal*) **useless (at sth/at doing sth)** (used about a person) weak or not successful at sth: *I'm useless at sport.* ▶ **uselessly** *adv* ▶ **uselessness** *noun* [U]

user /'ju:zə(r)/ *noun* [C] [in compounds] a person who uses a service, machine, place, etc: *users of public transport* ♦ *computer software users*

user-'friendly *adj* (used about computers, books, machines, etc.) easy to understand and use

username /'ju:zəneɪm/ *noun* [C] the name you use in order to be able to use a computer program or system: *Please enter your username.*

usher¹ /'ʌʃə(r)/ *noun* [C] a person who shows people to their seats in a theatre, church, etc.

usher² /'ʌʃə(r)/ *verb* [T] to take or show sb where to go: *I was ushered into an office.*

PHR V **usher sth in** (*formal*) to be the beginning of sth new or to make sth new begin: *The agreement ushered in a new period of peace for the two countries.*

usual /'ju:ʒuəl; -ʒəl/ *adj* **usual (for sb/sth) (to do sth)** happening or used most often: *It's usual for her to work at weekends.* ♦ *He got home later than usual.* ♦ *I sat in my usual seat.* OPP **unusual**

IDM **as usual** in the way that has often happened before: *Here's Dylan, late as usual!*

usually /'ju:ʒuəli; -ʒəli/ *adv* in the way that is usual; most often: *She's usually home by six.* ♦ *Usually, we go out on Saturdays.*

usurp /ju:'zɜ:p/ *verb* [T] (*formal*) to take sb's position and/or power without having the right to do this ▶ **usurper** *noun* [C]

UTC /ˌju: ti: 'si:/ *abbr* = **Coordinated Universal Time**

utensil /ju:'tensl/ *noun* [C] a type of tool that is used in the home: *kitchen/cooking utensils* ➲ picture at **kitchen**

uterus /'ju:tərəs/ *noun* [C] (*pl* **uteruses**; *in scientific use* **uteri** /-raɪ/) the part of a woman or female animal where a baby develops before it is born ➲ In everyday English we say **womb**.

utility /ju:'tɪləti/ *noun* (*pl* **utilities**) **1** [C] a service provided for the public, such as a water, gas or electricity supply: *the administration of **public utilities*** **2** [U] (*formal*) the quality of being useful **3** [C] a computer program or part of a program that does a particular task: *a utility program*

u'tility room *noun* [C] a small room in some houses, often next to the kitchen, where people keep large pieces of kitchen equipment, such as a washing machine

utilize (also **-ise**) /'ju:təlaɪz/ *verb* [T] (*formal*) to make use of sth: *to utilize natural resources*

utmost¹ /'ʌtməʊst/ *adj* [only *before* a noun] (*formal*) greatest: *a message **of the utmost importance***

utmost² /'ʌtməʊst/ *noun* [sing] the greatest amount possible: *Resources have been exploited **to the utmost**.* ♦ *I will **do my utmost** (= try as hard as possible) to help.*

utopia (also **Utopia**) /ju:'təʊpiə/ *noun* [C,U] a place or state that exists only in the imagination, where everything is perfect ▶ **utopian** (also **Utopian**) /ju:'təʊpiən/ *adj*

utter¹ /ˈʌtə(r)/ *adj* [only *before* a noun] complete; total: *He felt an utter fool.* ▸ **utterly** *adv*: *It's utterly impossible.*

utter² /ˈʌtə(r)/ *verb* [T] (*formal*) to say sth or make a sound with your voice: *She did not* ***utter a word*** (= she did not say anything) *in the meeting.* ▸ **utterance** /ˈʌtərəns/ *noun* [C] (*formal*)

U-turn /ˈjuː tɜːn/ *noun* [C] **1** a type of movement where a car, etc. turns round so that it goes back in the direction it came from **2** (*informal*) a sudden change from one plan or policy to a completely different or opposite one ➲ look at **about-turn**

V, v /viː/ *noun* [C,U] (*pl* V's; v's /viːz/) **1** the 22nd letter of the English alphabet: *'Velvet' begins with (a) 'V'.* **2** the shape of a V: *a V-neck sweater* ➲ picture on **page P1**

v *abbr* **1** (also vs) = **versus**(1): *Liverpool v Everton* **2** V = **volt**: *a 9V battery* **3** = **verse**(2) **4** (*informal*) = **very** (1): *v good*

vacancy /ˈveɪkənsi/ *noun* [C] (*pl* **vacancies**) **1** a **vacancy (for sb/sth)** a job that is available for sb to do: *We have a vacancy for a secretary.* **2** a room in a hotel, etc. that is available: *The sign outside the hotel said 'No Vacancies'.*

vacant /ˈveɪkənt/ *adj* **1** (used about a house, hotel room, seat, etc.) not being used; empty **2** (used about a job in a company, etc.) that is available for sb to take: *the* ***'Situations Vacant'*** *page* (= the page of a British newspaper where jobs are advertised) **3** showing no sign of intelligence or understanding: *a vacant expression* ▸ **vacantly** *adv*: *She stared at him vacantly.*

vacate /vəˈkeɪt; veɪˈk-/ *verb* [T] (*formal*) to leave a building, a seat, a job, a hotel room, etc. so that it is available for sb else

⚷ **vacation** /vəˈkeɪʃn/ *noun* **1** [C] (*BrE*) any of the periods of time when universities or courts of law are closed: *the Christmas/Easter vacation* **2** (*AmE*) = **holiday**(1): *The boss is* ***on vacation.***

vaccinate /ˈvæksɪneɪt/ *verb* [T, often passive] **vaccinate sb (against sth)** to give a person or an animal a **vaccine**, especially by **injecting** (= putting a substance under the skin using a needle) it, in order to protect them against a disease: *I was vaccinated against tetanus.* ➲ look at **immunize, inoculate** ▸ **vaccination** /ˌvæksɪˈneɪʃn/ *noun* [C,U]

vaccine /ˈvæksiːn/ *noun* [C,U] a substance that is put into the blood and that protects the body from a disease: *The polio vaccine has saved millions of lives.*

vacuum¹ /ˈvækjuəm/ *noun* [C] **1** a space that is completely empty of all substances, including air or other gases: *vacuum-packed foods* (= in a pack from which most of the air has been removed) ◆ *a vacuum flask* (= a bottle used for keeping liquids hot or cold) **2** [usually sing] a situation from which sth is missing or lacking **3** (*informal*) = **vacuum cleaner** **4** [usually sing] the act of cleaning sth with a **vacuum cleaner**: *to give a room a quick vacuum*

vacuum² /ˈvækjuəm/ *verb* [I,T] to clean sth using a **vacuum cleaner**

ˈvacuum cleaner (also *informal* **vacuum**) *noun* [C] an electric machine that cleans carpets, etc. by sucking up dirt ➲ look at **cleaner, Hoover™**

vacuum cleaner

vagina /vəˈdʒaɪnə/ *noun* [C] the passage in the body of a woman or female animal that connects the outer sex organs to the **womb** (= the part where a baby grows)

vagrant /ˈveɪgrənt/ *noun* [C] a person who has no home and no job, especially one who asks people for money

vague /veɪg/ *adj* (**vaguer**; **vaguest**) **1** not clear or definite: *He was very vague about how much money he'd spent.* ◆ *a vague shape in the distance* **2** (used about a person) not thinking or understanding clearly: *She looked a bit vague when I tried to explain.* ▸ **vagueness** *noun* [U]

vaguely /ˈveɪgli/ *adv* **1** in a way that is not clear; slightly: *Her name is vaguely familiar.* **2** without thinking about what is happening: *He smiled vaguely and walked away.*

vain /veɪn/ *adj* **1** failing to produce the result you want: *She turned away* ***in a vain attempt to*** *hide her tears.* 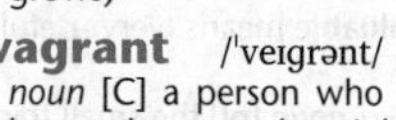 **SYN** **useless** **2** (used about a person) too proud of your own appearance, abilities, etc: *He's so vain–he looks in every mirror he passes.* ➲ *noun* **vanity**

IDM **in vain** without success: *The firemen tried in vain to put out the fire.*

▸ **vainly** *adv*

valentine /ˈvæləntaɪn/ *noun* [C] **1** (also ˈ**valentine card**) a card that you send, usually without putting your name on it, to sb you love

CULTURE

It is traditional to send these cards on **St Valentine's Day** (14 February).

2 the person you send this card to

valiant /ˈvæliənt/ *adj* (*formal*) full of courage and not afraid ▸ **valiantly** *adv*

⚷ **valid** /ˈvælɪd/ *adj* **1** **valid (for sth)** legally or officially acceptable: *This passport is valid for one year only.* **2** based on what is logical or true; acceptable: *I could raise no valid objections to the plan.* ◆ *Jeff's making a perfectly valid point.* **OPP** for both meanings **invalid** ▸ **validity** /vəˈlɪdəti/ *noun* [U]

validate /ˈvælɪdeɪt/ *verb* [T] (*formal*) **1** to prove that sth is true: *to validate a theory* OPP **invalidate** **2** to make sth legally or officially valid or acceptable: *to validate a contract* OPP **invalidate** **3** to state officially that sth is useful and of an acceptable standard: *Check that their courses have been validated by a reputable organization.* ▸ **validation** /ˌvælɪˈdeɪʃn/ *noun* [C,U]

valley /ˈvæli/ *noun* [C] the low land between two mountains or hills, which often has a river flowing through it: *a small town set in a valley* ➲ picture on **page P10**

valour (*AmE* valor) /ˈvælə(r)/ *noun* [U] (*formal, old-fashioned*) great courage, especially in war

valuable /ˈvæljuəbl/ *adj* **1** very useful: *a valuable piece of information* **2** worth a lot of money: *Is this ring valuable?* OPP for both meanings **valueless, worthless**

HELP Be careful. **Invaluable** means 'very useful'.

valuables /ˈvæljuəblz/ *noun* [pl] the small things that you own that are worth a lot of money, such as jewellery, etc: *Please put your valuables in the hotel safe.*

valuation /ˌvæljuˈeɪʃn/ *noun* [C] a professional judgement about how much money sth is worth

value¹ /ˈvæljuː/ *noun* **1** [U,C] the amount of money that sth is worth: *to go up/down in value* ◆ *The thieves stole goods with a total value of $10 000.* ➲ look at **face value** **2** [U] (*BrE*) how much sth is worth compared with its price: *The hotel was **good/excellent value*** (= well worth the money it cost). ◆ *Package holidays give the best **value for money**.* **3** [U] the importance of sth: *to be of great/little/no value to somebody* ◆ *This bracelet is of great **sentimental value** to me.* **4** values [pl] beliefs about what is the right and wrong way for people to behave; moral principles: *a return to traditional values* ◆ *Young people have a completely different **set of values** and expectations.*

value² /ˈvæljuː/ *verb* [T] (valuing) **1** value sb/sth (as sth) to think sb/sth is very important: *Sandra has always valued her independence.* ◆ *I really value her as a friend.* **2** [usually passive] value sth (at sth) to decide the amount of money that sth is worth: *The house was valued at $150 000.*

valueless /ˈvæljuːləs/ *adj* (*formal*) without value or use SYN **worthless** OPP **valuable**

valve /vælv/ *noun* [C] a device in a pipe or tube which controls the flow of air, liquid or gas, letting it move in one direction only: *a radiator valve* ◆ *the valve on a bicycle tyre* ➲ picture at **bicycle**

vampire /ˈvæmpaɪə(r)/ *noun* [C] (in stories) a dead person who comes out at night and drinks the blood of living people

van /væn/ *noun* [C] a road vehicle that is used for transporting things: *a delivery van* ◆ *a van driver* ➲ picture on **page P7**

HELP **Van** or **lorry**? A **van** is smaller than a **lorry** and is always covered.

vandal /ˈvændl/ *noun* [C] a person who damages sb else's property on purpose and for no reason ▸ **vandalism** /ˈvændəlɪzəm/ *noun* [U]: *acts of vandalism* ▸ **vandalize** (also -ise) /ˈvændəlaɪz/ *verb* [T, usually passive]: *All the garages in this area have been vandalized.* ➲ note at **crime**

vanilla /vəˈnɪlə/ *noun* [U] a substance from a plant that is used for giving flavour to sweet food: *vanilla ice cream*

vanish /ˈvænɪʃ/ *verb* [I] **1** to disappear suddenly or in a way that you cannot explain: *When he turned round, the two men had **vanished without trace**.* **2** to stop existing: *This species of plant is vanishing from our countryside.*

vanity /ˈvænəti/ *noun* [U] the quality of being too proud of your appearance or abilities ➲ *adjective* **vain**

vantage point /ˈvɑːntɪdʒ pɔɪnt/ *noun* [C] a place from which you have a good view of sth: (*figurative*) *From our modern vantage point, we can see why the Roman Empire collapsed.*

vapour (*AmE* vapor) /ˈveɪpə(r)/ *noun* [C,U] a mass of very small drops of liquid in the air, for example steam: *water vapour*

variable /ˈveəriəbl/ *adj* not staying the same; often changing ▸ **variable** *noun* [C] ▸ **variability** /ˌveəriəˈbɪləti/ *noun* [U]

variant /ˈveəriənt/ *noun* [C] a slightly different form or type of sth

variation /ˌveəriˈeɪʃn/ *noun* **1** [C,U] (a) variation (in sth) a change or difference in the amount or level of sth: *There was a lot of variation in the examination results.* ◆ *There may be a slight variation in price from shop to shop.* **2** [C] a variation (on/of sth) a thing that is slightly different from another thing in the same general group: *All her films are just variations on a basic theme.*

varied /ˈveərid/ *adj* having many different kinds of things or activities: *I try to make my classes as varied as possible.*

variety /vəˈraɪəti/ *noun* (*pl* varieties) **1** [sing] a variety (of sth) a number of different types of the same thing: *There is a **wide variety** of dishes to choose from.* **2** [U] the quality of not being or doing the same all the time: *There's so much variety in my new job. I do something different every day!* **3** [C] a variety (of sth) a type of sth: *a new variety of apple called 'Perfection'*

various /ˈveəriəs/ *adj* several different: *I decided to leave London for various reasons.*

varnish /ˈvɑːnɪʃ/ *noun* [U] a clear liquid that you paint onto hard surfaces, especially wood, to protect them and make them shine ➲ look at **nail polish** ▸ **varnish** *verb* [T]

vary /ˈveəri/ *verb* (varying; varies; *pt, pp* varied) **1** [I] vary (in sth) (used about a group of similar things) to be different from each other: *The hotel bedrooms vary in size from medium to very large.*

V

2 [I] vary (from ... to ...) to be different or to change according to the situation, etc: *The price of the holiday varies from £500 to £1 200, depending on the time of year.* **3** [T] to make sth different by changing it often in some way: *I try to vary my work as much as possible so I don't get bored.*

vase /vɑːz/ *noun* [C] a container that is used for holding cut flowers ➲ picture on **page P8**

vasectomy /vəˈsektəmi/ *noun* [C] (*pl* vasectomies) a medical operation to stop a man being able to make a woman pregnant

⚷ **vast** /vɑːst/ *adj* extremely big: *a vast sum of money* ♦ *a vast country* **SYN** **huge** ▸ **vastly** *adv*: *a vastly improved traffic system*

VAT (also Vat) /ˌviː eɪ ˈtiː; væt/ *abbr* **value added tax**; a tax that is added to the price of goods and services: *prices include VAT*

vault¹ /vɔːlt/ *noun* [C] **1** a room with a strong door and thick walls in a bank, etc. that is used for keeping money and other valuable things safe **2** a room under a church where dead people are buried: *a family vault* **3** a high roof or ceiling in a church, etc., made from a number of **arches** (= curved structures) joined together at the top **4** a jump made by **vaulting**

vault² /vɔːlt/ *verb* [I,T] vault (over) sth to jump over or onto sth in one movement, using your hands or a pole to help you: *The boy vaulted over the wall.*

VCR /ˌviː siː ˈɑː(r)/ *abbr* = **video cassette recorder**

VDU /ˌviː diː ˈjuː/ *noun* [C] **visual display unit**; a screen on which you can see information from a computer

veal /viːl/ *noun* [U] the meat from a **calf** (= a young cow) ➲ note at **meat**

veer /vɪə(r)/ *verb* [I] (used about vehicles) to change direction suddenly: *The car veered across the road and hit a tree.*

veg¹ /vedʒ/ (*BrE informal*) = **vegetable**: *a fruit and veg stall*

veg² /vedʒ/ *verb* (vegging; vegged)
PHR V **veg out** (*informal*) to relax and do nothing that needs thought or effort: *I'm just going to go home and veg out in front of the telly.*

vegan /ˈviːɡən/ *noun* [C] a person who does not eat meat or any other animal products at all ➲ look at **vegetarian** ▸ **vegan** *adj*

⚷ **vegetable** /ˈvedʒtəbl/ (also *informal* veg; veggie) *noun* [C] a plant or part of a plant that we eat: *Potatoes, beans and onions are all vegetables.* ♦ *vegetable soup* ➲ picture on **page P15**

vegetarian /ˌvedʒəˈteəriən/ (also *informal* veggie) *noun* [C] a person who does not eat meat or fish ➲ look at **vegan** ▸ **vegetarian** *adj*: *a vegetarian cookery book*

vegetation /ˌvedʒəˈteɪʃn/ *noun* [U] (*formal*) plants in general; all the plants that are found in a particular place: *tropical vegetation*

veggie /ˈvedʒi/ *noun* [C] (*informal*) **1** = **vegetarian** **2** = **vegetable** ▸ **veggie** *adj*: *a veggie burger*

vehement /ˈviːəmənt/ *adj* showing very strong (often negative) feelings, especially anger: *a vehement attack on the government*

⚷ **vehicle** /ˈviːəkl/ *noun* [C] **1** something which transports people or things from place to place, especially on land, for example cars, bicycles, lorries and buses: *Are you the owner of this vehicle?* **2** something which is used for communicating particular ideas or opinions: *This newspaper has become a vehicle for Conservative opinion.*

veil /veɪl/ *noun* [C] a piece of thin material for covering the head and face of a woman: *a bridal veil*

vein /veɪn/ *noun* **1** [C] one of the tubes which carry blood from all parts of your body to your heart ➲ look at **artery** **2** [sing, U] a particular style or quality: *After a humorous beginning, the programme continued in a more serious vein.*

Velcro™ /ˈvelkrəʊ/ *noun* [U] a material for fastening parts of clothes together. **Velcro™** is made of **nylon** (= a strong material) and is used in small pieces, one rough and one smooth, that can stick together and be pulled apart.

velocity /vəˈlɒsəti/ *noun* [U] (*technical*) the speed at which sth moves

velvet /ˈvelvɪt/ *noun* [U] a type of cloth made of cotton or other material, with a soft thick surface on one side only: *black velvet trousers*

vendetta /venˈdetə/ *noun* [C] a serious argument or disagreement between two people or groups which lasts for a long time

ˈ**vending machine** *noun* [C] a machine from which you can buy drinks, sweets, etc. by putting coins in it

vendor /ˈvendə(r)/ *noun* [C] (*formal*) a person who is selling sth ➲ look at **purchaser**

veneer /vəˈnɪə(r)/ *noun* **1** [C,U] a thin layer of wood or plastic that is stuck onto the surface of cheaper wood, to give it a better appearance **2** [sing] (*formal*) a veneer (of sth) a part of sb's behaviour or of a situation which hides what it is really like underneath: *a thin veneer of politeness*

venetian blind /vəˌniːʃn ˈblaɪnd/ *noun* [C] a covering for a window that is made of horizontal pieces of flat plastic, etc. which can be turned to let in as much light as you want ➲ picture at **curtain**

vengeance /ˈvendʒəns/ *noun* [U] (*formal*) vengeance (on sb) the act of punishing or harming sb in return for sth bad they have done to you, your friends or family: *He felt a terrible desire for vengeance on the people who had destroyed his career.* ➲ look at **revenge**
IDM **with a vengeance** to a greater degree than is expected or usual: *After a week of good weather winter returned with a vengeance.*

venison /ˈvenɪsn/ *noun* [U] the meat from a **deer** (= a large wild animal that eats grass) ➲ note at **deer**

venom /ˈvenəm/ *noun* [U] **1** the poisonous liquid that some snakes, spiders, etc. produce when they

V

bite or sting you **2** (*formal*) extreme anger or hatred and a desire to hurt sb: *a look of pure venom* ▶ **venomous** /ˈvenəməs/ *adj*

vent /vent/ *noun* [C] an opening in the wall of a room or machine which allows air to come in, and smoke, steam or smells to go out: *an air vent* ◆ *a heating vent*

ventilate /ˈventɪleɪt/ *verb* [T] to allow air to move freely in and out of a room or building: *The office is badly ventilated.* ▶ **ventilation** /ˌventɪˈleɪʃn/ *noun* [U]: *There was no ventilation in the room except for one tiny window.*

⚷ **venture[1]** /ˈventʃə(r)/ *noun* [C] a project which is new and possibly dangerous, because you cannot be sure that it will succeed: *a business venture*

⚷ **venture[2]** /ˈventʃə(r)/ *verb* [I] to do sth or go somewhere new and dangerous, when you are not sure what will happen: *He ventured out into the storm to look for the lost child.* ◆ *The company has decided to venture into computer production as well as design.*

venue /ˈvenjuː/ *noun* [C] the place where people meet for an organized event, for example a concert or a sports event

Venus /ˈviːnəs/ *noun* [sing] the planet that is second in order from the sun and nearest to the earth

veranda (also **verandah**) /vəˈrændə/ (*AmE* also **porch**) *noun* [C] a platform joined to the side of a house, with a roof and floor but no outside wall ➲ look at **patio, terrace**

verb /vɜːb/ *noun* [C] a word or group of words that expresses an action (such as *eat*), an event (such as *happen*) or a state (such as *exist*): *What's the main verb of the sentence?* ◆ *In this essay he has used the same verbs over and over again.* ➲ look at **phrasal verb**

verbal /ˈvɜːbl/ *adj* **1** connected with words or the use of words: *verbal skills* **2** spoken, not written: *a verbal agreement/warning* ▶ **verbally** /ˈvɜːbəli/ *adv*

verdict /ˈvɜːdɪkt/ *noun* [C] **1** the decision that is made by the **jury** (= a group of members of the public) in a court of law, which states if a person is guilty of a crime or not: *The jury* ***returned a verdict*** *of 'not guilty'.* ◆ *Has the jury* ***reached a verdict****?* ➲ note at **court 2** a verdict (on sb/sth) a decision that you make or an opinion that you give after testing sth or considering sth carefully: *The general verdict was that the restaurant was too expensive.*

verge[1] /vɜːdʒ/ *noun* [C] (*BrE*) the narrow piece of land at the side of a road, railway line, etc. that is usually covered in grass

IDM **on the verge of sth/doing sth** very near to doing sth, or to sth happening: *He was on the verge of a nervous breakdown.* ◆ *Scientists are on the verge of discovering a cure.*

verge[2] /vɜːdʒ/ *verb*

PHR V **verge on sth** to be very close to an extreme state or condition: *What they are doing verges on the illegal.*

verify /ˈverɪfaɪ/ *verb* [T] (**verifying**; **verifies**; *pt, pp* **verified**) (*formal*) to check or state that sth is true: *to verify a statement* ▶ **verification** /ˌverɪfɪˈkeɪʃn/ *noun* [U]

veritable /ˈverɪtəbl/ *adj* [only *before* a noun] (*formal*) used to emphasize that sb/sth can be compared to sb/sth else that is more exciting, more impressive, etc: *The meal he cooked was a veritable banquet.*

vermin /ˈvɜːmɪn/ *noun* [pl] small wild animals (for example mice) that carry disease and destroy plants and food

vernacular /vəˈnækjələ(r)/ *noun* [C] **the vernacular** [sing] the language spoken in a particular area or by a particular group, especially one that is not the official or written language

versatile /ˈvɜːsətaɪl/ *adj* **1** (used about a person) able to do many different things: *Gloria is so versatile! She can dance, sing, act and play the guitar!* **2** (used about an object) having many different uses: *a versatile tool that drills, cuts or polishes*

verse /vɜːs/ *noun* **1** [U] writing arranged in lines which have a definite rhythm and often **rhyme** (= end with the same sound): *He wrote his valentine's message in verse.* SYN **poetry 2** [C] (*abbr* v) a group of lines which form one part of a song or poem: *This song has five verses.* ➲ look at **chorus**

⚷ **version** /ˈvɜːʃn; -ʒn/ *noun* [C] **1** a thing which has the same basic content as sth else but which is presented in a different way: *Have you heard the live version of this song?* **2** a person's description of sth that has happened: *The two drivers gave very different versions of the accident.*

versus /ˈvɜːsəs/ *prep* **1** (*abbr* v; vs) used in sport for showing that two teams or people are playing against each other: *England versus Argentina* **2** used for showing that two ideas or things are opposite to each other, especially when you are trying to choose one of them: *It's a question of quality versus price.*

vertebra /ˈvɜːtɪbrə/ *noun* [C] (*pl* **vertebrae** /-reɪ; -riː/) any of the small bones that are connected together in a row down the middle of your back ➲ look at **spine**

⚷ **vertical** /ˈvɜːtɪkl/ *adj* going straight up at an angle of 90° from the ground: *a vertical line* ◆ *The cliff was almost vertical.* ➲ look at **horizontal, perpendicular** ➲ picture at **line** ▶ **vertically** /-kli/ *adv*

⚷ **very** /ˈveri/ *adv, adj* **1** (*abbr* v) used with an adjective or adverb to make it stronger: *very small* ◆ *very slowly* ◆ *I don't like milk very much.* ◆ *'Are you hungry?' 'No, not very.'*

> **GRAMMAR** We use **very** with superlative adjectives: *the very best, youngest, etc.* but with comparative adjectives we use **much** or **very much**: *much better; very much younger*

2 used to emphasize a noun: *We climbed to the very top of the mountain* (= right to the top). ◆ *You're the very person I wanted to talk to* (= exactly the right person).

V

vessel /ˈvesl/ *noun* [C] **1** (*formal*) a ship or large boat **2** (*old-fashioned*) a container for liquids, for example a bottle, cup or bowl: *ancient drinking vessels* ➲ look at **blood vessel**

vest /vest/ *noun* [C] **1** (*AmE* **undershirt**) a piece of clothing that you wear under your other clothes, on the top part of your body **2** (*AmE*) = **waistcoat**

vested interest /ˌvestɪd ˈɪntrest/ *noun* [C] a strong and often secret reason for doing sth that will bring you an advantage of some kind, for example more money or power

vestige /ˈvestɪdʒ/ *noun* [C] a small part of sth that is left after the rest of it has gone: *the last vestige of the old system* **SYN** **trace**

vet[1] /vet/ (*BrE formal* **ˈveterinary surgeon**; *AmE* **veterinarian**) *noun* [C] a doctor for animals: *We took the cat to the vet/to the vet's.* ➲ note at **pet**

vet[2] /vet/ *verb* [T] (**vetting**; **vetted**) to do careful and secret checks before deciding if sb/sth can be accepted or not: *All new employees at the Ministry of Defence are carefully vetted* (= sb examines the details of their past lives).

veteran /ˈvetərən/ *noun* [C] **1** a person who has very long experience of a particular job or activity **2** a person who has served in the army, navy or air force, especially during a war

veterinarian /ˌvetərɪˈneəriən/ (*AmE*) = **vet**[1]

veterinary /ˈvetnri; ˈvetrənəri/ *adj* [only *before* a noun] connected with the medical treatment of sick or injured animals: *a veterinary practice* ➲ look at **vet**

ˈveterinary surgeon (*BrE formal*) = **vet**[1]

veto /ˈviːtəʊ/ *verb* [T] (**vetoing**; **vetoes**; *pt, pp* **vetoed**) to refuse to give official permission for an action or a plan, when other people have agreed to it: *The Prime Minister vetoed the proposal to reduce taxation.* ▸ **veto** *noun* [C,U] (*pl* **vetoes**): *the right of veto*

vexed /vekst/ *adj* causing difficulty, worry and a lot of discussion: *the vexed question of our growing prison population*

⚷ **via** /ˈvaɪə/ *prep* **1** going through a place: *We flew from Paris to Sydney via Bangkok.* **2** by means of sth; using sth: *These pictures come to you via our satellite link.*

viable /ˈvaɪəbl/ *adj* that can be done; that will be successful: *I'm afraid your idea is not commercially viable.* ▸ **viability** /ˌvaɪəˈbɪləti/ *noun* [U]

viaduct /ˈvaɪədʌkt/ *noun* [C] a long, high bridge which carries a railway or road across a valley

vibrant /ˈvaɪbrənt/ *adj* **1** full of life and energy: *a vibrant city/atmosphere/personality* **SYN** **exciting** **2** (used about colours) bright and strong

vibrate /vaɪˈbreɪt/ *verb* [I] to make continuous very small and fast movements from side to side: *When a guitar string vibrates it makes a sound.* ▸ **vibration** /vaɪˈbreɪʃn/ *noun* [C,U]

vicar /ˈvɪkə(r)/ *noun* [C] a priest of the Anglican church. A **vicar** looks after a church and its **parish** (= the area around the church and the people in it). ➲ look at **minister**

vicarage /ˈvɪkərɪdʒ/ *noun* [C] the house where a vicar lives

vice /vaɪs/ *noun* **1** [U] criminal activities involving sex or drugs **2** [C] a moral weakness or bad habit: *Greed and envy are terrible vices.* ◆ *My only vice is smoking.* ➲ look at **virtue** **3** (*AmE* **vise**) [C] a tool that you use to hold a piece of wood, metal, etc. firmly while you are working on it: (*figurative*) *He held my arm in a vice-like* (= very firm) *grip.*

vice- /vaɪs/ [in compounds] having a position second in importance to the position mentioned: *vice-president* ◆ *the vice-captain*

vice versa /ˌvaɪs ˈvɜːsə; ˌvaɪsi/ *adv* in the opposite way to what has just been said: *Anna ordered fish and Maria chicken—or was it vice versa?*

vicinity /vəˈsɪnəti/ *noun*
IDM **in the vicinity (of sth)** in the surrounding area: *There's no bank in the immediate vicinity.*

vicious /ˈvɪʃəs/ *adj* **1** cruel; done in order to hurt sb/sth: *a vicious attack* **2** (used about an animal) dangerous; likely to hurt sb: *a vicious dog*
IDM **a vicious circle** a situation in which one problem leads to another and the new problem makes the first problem worse
▸ **viciously** *adv*

⚷ **victim** /ˈvɪktɪm/ *noun* [C] a person or an animal that is injured, killed or hurt by sb/sth: *a murder victim* ◆ *The children are often the innocent victims of a divorce.*

victimize (also **-ise**) /ˈvɪktɪmaɪz/ *verb* [T] to punish or make sb suffer unfairly ▸ **victimization** (also **-isation**) /ˌvɪktɪmaɪˈzeɪʃn/ *noun* [U]

victor /ˈvɪktə(r)/ *noun* [C] (*formal*) the person who wins a game, competition, battle, etc.

Victorian /vɪkˈtɔːriən/ *adj* **1** connected with the time of the British queen Victoria (1837–1901): *Victorian houses* **2** having attitudes that were typical in the time of Queen Victoria ▸ **Victorian** *noun* [C]

⚷ **victory** /ˈvɪktəri/ *noun* [C,U] (*pl* **victories**) success in winning a battle, a game, a competition, an election, etc: *Moyes led his team to victory in the final.*
IDM **romp home/to victory** ➲ **romp**
▸ **victorious** /vɪkˈtɔːriəs/ *adj*: *the victorious team*

⚷ **video** /ˈvɪdiəʊ/ *noun* (*pl* **videos**) **1** (also ˌ**video casˈsette**; **videotape**) [C] a tape used for recording moving pictures and sound; a plastic case containing this tape: *Have you got a blank video?* **2** = **video cassette recorder** **3** [U] a system of recording moving pictures and sound; a method of storing data: *My parents recorded their wedding* **on video**. ◆ *a* **music video** (= a short film made by a band to be shown with a song) **4** (also ˈ**video clip**) a short film or recording of an event that you watch on a computer: *Upload your videos and share them with friends and family online.* ▸ **video** *verb* [T] (**videoing**; **videos**; *pt, pp* **videoed**)

ˌ**video casˈsette recorder** (also **video**; ˈ**video recorder**) *noun* [C] (*abbr* **VCR**) a machine that is connected to a TV on which you can record or play back a film or TV programme

videoconferencing /ˈvɪdiəʊkɒnfərənsɪŋ/ *noun* [U] a system that people in different parts of the world can use to have a meeting, by watching and listening to each other using video screens ▸ **videoconference** *noun* [C] an official meeting conducted using **videoconferencing**: *We're having a videoconference this afternoon to discuss the budget.*

videotape /ˈvɪdiəʊteɪp/ *noun* [C] = **video**(1)

⚷ **view**[1] /vjuː/ *noun* **1** [C] a view (about/on sth) an opinion or a particular way of thinking about sth: *He expressed the view that standards were falling.* ◆ ***In my view**, she has done nothing wrong.* ◆ *She has **strong views** on the subject.* **2** [U, sing] the ability to see sth or to be seen from a particular place: *The garden was hidden from view behind a high wall.* ◆ *to come into view* ◆ *to disappear from view* **3** [C] what you can see from a particular place: *There are **breathtaking views** from the top of the mountain.* ◆ *a room with **a sea view*** ➲ note at **scenery**

IDM **have, etc. sth in view** (*formal*) to have sth as a plan or idea in your mind

in full view (of sb/sth) ➲ **full**[1]

in view of sth (*formal*) because of sth; as a result of sth: *In view of her apology, we decided to take no further action.*

point of view ➲ **point**[1]

with a view to doing sth (*formal*) with the aim or intention of doing sth

⚷ **view**[2] /vjuː/ *verb* [T] **1** view sb/sth (as sth) to think about sb/sth in a particular way: *She viewed holidays as a waste of time.* **2** to watch or look at sth: *Viewed from this angle, the building looks much taller than it really is.*

viewer /ˈvjuːə(r)/ *noun* [C] a person who watches TV

viewpoint /ˈvjuːpɔɪnt/ *noun* [C] a way of looking at a situation; an opinion: *Let's look at this problem from the customer's viewpoint.* SYN **point of view**

vigil /ˈvɪdʒɪl/ *noun* [C,U] a period when you stay awake all night for a special purpose: *All night she **kept vigil** over the sick child.*

vigilant /ˈvɪdʒɪlənt/ *adj* (*formal*) careful and looking out for danger ▸ **vigilance** *noun* [U]: *the need for constant vigilance*

vigilante /ˌvɪdʒɪˈlænti/ *noun* [C] a member of a group of people who try to prevent crime or punish criminals in a community, especially because they believe the police are not doing this

vigour (*AmE* **vigor**) /ˈvɪɡə(r)/ *noun* [U] strength or energy: *After the break we started work again with renewed vigour.* ▸ **vigorous** /ˈvɪɡərəs/ *adj*: *vigorous exercise* ▸ **vigorously** *adv*

vile /vaɪl/ *adj* (**viler**; **vilest**) very bad or unpleasant: *She's in a vile mood.* ◆ *a vile smell* SYN **terrible**

villa /ˈvɪlə/ *noun* [C] **1** a house that people rent and stay in on holiday **2** a large house in the country, especially in Southern Europe

⚷ **village** /ˈvɪlɪdʒ/ *noun* **1** [C] a group of houses with other buildings, for example a shop, school, etc., in a country area. A village is smaller than a town: *a small fishing village* ◆ *the village shop* ➲ picture on **page P11** **2** [sing, with sing or pl verb] all the people who live in a village: *All the village is/are taking part in the carnival.*

villager /ˈvɪlɪdʒə(r)/ *noun* [C] a person who lives in a village

villain /ˈvɪlən/ *noun* [C] **1** an evil person, especially in a book or play: *In most of his films he has played villains, but in this one he's a good guy.* ➲ look at **hero** **2** (*informal*) a criminal: *The police caught the villains who robbed the bank.*

vindicate /ˈvɪndɪkeɪt/ *verb* [T] (*formal*) **1** to prove that sth is true or that you were right to do sth, especially when other people had a different opinion: *I have every confidence that this decision will be fully vindicated.* **2** to prove that sb is not guilty when they have been accused of doing sth wrong or illegal: *New evidence emerged, vindicating him completely.*

vindictive /vɪnˈdɪktɪv/ *adj* wanting or trying to hurt sb without good reason: *a vindictive comment/person* ▸ **vindictiveness** *noun* [U]

vine /vaɪn/ *noun* [C] the climbing plant that **grapes** (= small green or purple fruit that grow in bunches) grow on

vinegar /ˈvɪnɪɡə(r)/ *noun* [U] a liquid with a strong sharp taste that is made from wine. **Vinegar** is often mixed with oil and put onto salads.

vineyard /ˈvɪnjəd/ *noun* [C] a piece of land where **grapes** (= small green or purple fruit that grow in bunches) are grown in order to produce wine

vintage[1] /ˈvɪntɪdʒ/ *noun* [C] the wine that was made in a particular year: *2010 was an excellent vintage.*

vintage[2] /ˈvɪntɪdʒ/ *adj* [only *before* a noun] **1** **vintage** wine is of very good quality and has been stored for several years: *a bottle of vintage champagne* **2** of very high quality: *a vintage performance by Robert De Niro*

vinyl /ˈvaɪnl/ *noun* [U] a strong plastic that can bend easily and is used to cover walls, floors, furniture, books, etc.

viola /viˈəʊlə/ *noun* [C] a musical instrument with strings, that you hold under your chin and play with a **bow** (= a long thin piece of wood with hair stretched across it): *A viola is like a large violin.* ➲ picture at **music**

violate /ˈvaɪəleɪt/ *verb* [T] (*formal*) **1** to break a rule, an agreement, etc: *to violate a peace treaty* **2** to not respect sth; to spoil or damage sth: *to violate somebody's privacy/rights* ▸ **violation** /ˌvaɪəˈleɪʃn/ *noun* [C,U]: *(a) violation of human rights*

⚷ **violence** /ˈvaɪələns/ *noun* [U] **1** behaviour which harms or damages sb/sth physically: *They threatened to **use violence** if we didn't give them the money.* ◆ *an* *act of violence* **2** great force or energy: *the violence of the storm*

violent /ˈvaɪələnt/ *adj* **1** using physical strength to hurt or kill sb; caused by this behaviour: *The demonstration started peacefully but later turned violent.* ◆ *a violent death* ◆ *violent crime* **2** very strong and impossible to control: *He has a violent temper.* ◆ *a violent storm/collision* ▶ **violently** *adv*: *The ground shook violently and buildings collapsed in the earthquake.*

violet /ˈvaɪələt/ *noun* **1** [C] a small plant that grows wild or in gardens and has purple or white flowers and a pleasant smell **2** [U] a bluish-purple colour ▶ **violet** *adj*

violin /ˌvaɪəˈlɪn/ *noun* [C] a musical instrument with strings, that you hold under your chin and play with a **bow** (= a long thin piece of wood with hair stretched across it) ➲ An informal word is **fiddle**. ➲ note at **music** ➲ picture at **music**

VIP /ˌviː aɪ ˈpiː/ *abbr* **very important person**: *the VIP lounge at the airport* ◆ *give someone the VIP treatment* (= treat sb especially well)

viral /ˈvaɪrəl/ *adj* like or caused by a virus: *a **viral infection*** ◆ *a **viral email*** (= that is sent on from one person to others, who then send it on again)

virgin¹ /ˈvɜːdʒɪn/ *noun* [C] a person who has never had sex

virgin² /ˈvɜːdʒɪn/ *adj* that has not yet been used, touched, damaged, etc: *virgin forest*

virginity /vəˈdʒɪnəti/ *noun* [U] the state of never having had sex: *to lose your virginity*

Virgo /ˈvɜːɡəʊ/ *noun* [C,U] (*pl* **Virgos**) the 6th sign of the **zodiac** (= 12 signs which represent the positions of the sun, moon and planets), the **Virgin**; a person born under this sign: *I'm a Virgo.* ➲ picture at **zodiac**

virile /ˈvɪraɪl/ *adj* (used about a man) strong and having great sexual energy

virility /vəˈrɪləti/ *noun* [U] a man's sexual power and energy

virtual /ˈvɜːtʃuəl/ *adj* [only *before* a noun] **1** being almost or nearly sth: *The country is in a state of virtual civil war.* **2** made to appear to exist by the use of computer software, for example on the Internet: *virtual reality* ▶ **virtually** /-ʃuəli/ *adv*: *The building is virtually finished.*

virtue /ˈvɜːtʃuː/ *noun* **1** [U] behaviour which shows high moral standards: *to lead a life of virtue* SYN **goodness** **2** [C] a good quality or habit: *Patience is a great virtue.* ➲ look at **vice** **3** [C,U] **the virtue (of sth/of being/doing sth)** an advantage or a useful quality of sth: *This new material **has the virtue** of being strong as well as very light.*

IDM **by virtue of sth** (*formal*) by means of sth or because of sth

virtuoso /ˌvɜːtʃuˈəʊsəʊ; -ˈəʊzəʊ/ *noun* [C] (*pl* **virtuosos** *or* **virtuosi** /-siː; -ziː/) a person who is extremely skilful at sth, especially playing a musical instrument

virtuous /ˈvɜːtʃuəs/ *adj* behaving in a morally good way

virulent /ˈvɪrələnt; -rjəl-/ *adj* **1** (used about a poison or a disease) very strong and dangerous: *a particularly virulent form of influenza* **2** (*formal*) very strong and full of anger: *a virulent attack on the leader*

virus /ˈvaɪrəs/ *noun* [C] **1** a living thing, too small to be seen without a **microscope** (= a piece of equipment that makes small objects look bigger), that causes disease in people, animals and plants: *HIV, the virus that can cause AIDS* ◆ *to catch a virus* ➲ look at **bacteria, germ** **2** a disease caused by a **virus**: *The doctor said I had a virus.* **3** instructions that are put into a computer program in order to stop it working properly and destroy information ➲ note at **cybercrime**

visa /ˈviːzə/ *noun* [C] an official mark or piece of paper that shows you are allowed to enter, leave or travel through a country: *His passport was full of visa stamps.* ◆ *a tourist/work/student visa*

vise (*AmE*) = **vice**(3)

visibility /ˌvɪzəˈbɪləti/ *noun* [U] the distance that you can see in particular light or weather conditions: *In the fog visibility was down to 50 metres.* ◆ *poor/good visibility*

visible /ˈvɪzəbl/ *adj* that can be seen or noticed: *The church tower was visible from the other side of the valley.* ◆ *a visible improvement in his work* OPP **invisible** ▶ **visibly** /-əbli/ *adv*: *Rosa was visibly upset.*

vision /ˈvɪʒn/ *noun*

➤SIGHT **1** [U] the ability to see; sight: *to have good/poor/normal/perfect vision*

➤PICTURE IN MIND **2** [C] a picture in your imagination: *They have a vision of a world without weapons.* ◆ *I **had visions of** being left behind, but in fact the others had waited for me.*

➤DREAM **3** [C] a dream or similar experience often connected with religion: *God appeared to Paul in a vision.*

➤PLANS FOR FUTURE **4** [U] the ability to make great plans for the future: *a leader of great vision*

➤TV/CINEMA **5** [U] the picture on a TV or cinema screen: *a temporary loss of vision*

visionary /ˈvɪʒənri/ *adj* having great plans for the future: *He was a visionary leader.* ▶ **visionary** *noun* [C] (*pl* **visionaries**)

visit /ˈvɪzɪt/ *verb* [I,T] **1** to go to see a person or place for a period of time: *I don't live here. I'm just visiting.* ◆ *We often visit relatives at the weekend.* ◆ *She's going to visit her son in hospital.* ◆ *When you go to London you must visit the Science Museum.* **2** to go to a website on the Internet: *For more information, visit our website.* ▶ **visit** *noun* [C]: *The Prime Minister is **on a visit** to Germany.* ◆ *We had a flying* (= very short) *visit from Richard on Sunday.*

visitor /ˈvɪzɪtə(r)/ *noun* [C] a person who visits sb/sth: *visitors to London from overseas*

visor /ˈvaɪzə(r)/ *noun* [C] **1** the part of a **helmet** (= a hard hat) that you can pull down to protect your eyes or face **2** a piece of plastic, cloth, etc. on a hat or in a car, which stops the sun shining into your eyes ➲ picture at **hat**

V

vista /ˈvɪstə/ *noun* [C] (*formal, written*) a beautiful view, for example of the countryside, a city, etc.

visual /ˈvɪʒuəl/ *adj* connected with seeing: *the visual arts* (= painting, sculpture, cinema, etc.) ▶ **visually** /ˈvɪʒuəli/ *adv*: *The film is visually stunning.*

ˌvisual ˈaid *noun* [C] a picture, film, map, etc. that helps a student to learn sth

visualize (also -ise) /ˈvɪʒuəlaɪz/ *verb* [T] to imagine or have a picture in your mind of sb/sth: *It's hard to visualize what this place looked like before the factory was built.*

vital /ˈvaɪtl/ *adj* **1** very important or necessary: *Practice is vital if you want to speak a language well.* ◆ *vital information* ➲ note at **important** **2** full of energy **SYN** **lively** ▶ **vitally** /-təli/ *adv*: *vitally important*

vitality /vaɪˈtæləti/ *noun* [U] the state of being full of energy

vitamin /ˈvɪtəmɪn/ *noun* [C] one of several natural substances in certain types of food that are important to help humans and animals grow and stay healthy: *Oranges are rich in vitamin C.*

vivacious /vɪˈveɪʃəs/ *adj* (used about a person, usually a woman) full of energy; happy **SYN** **lively**

vivid /ˈvɪvɪd/ *adj* **1** having or producing a strong, clear picture in your mind: *vivid dreams/memories* **2** (used about light or a colour) strong and very bright: *the vivid reds and yellows of the flowers* ▶ **vividly** *adv*

vivisection /ˌvɪvɪˈsekʃn/ *noun* [U] doing scientific experiments on live animals

vixen /ˈvɪksn/ *noun* [C] a female **fox** (= a wild animal like a dog, with reddish fur and a thick tail) ➲ note at **fox**

viz. /vɪz/ *abbr* (often read out as 'namely') used to introduce a list of things that explain sth more clearly or are given as examples: *four major colleges of surgery, viz. London, Glasgow, Edinburgh and Dublin*

VLE /ˌviː el ˈiː/ *noun* [C] (*BrE*) **virtual learning environment**; a software system for teaching and learning using the Internet

V

vocabulary /vəˈkæbjələri/ *noun* (*pl* vocabularies) **1** [C,U] all the words that sb knows or that are used in a particular book, subject, etc: *He has an amazing vocabulary for a five-year-old.* ◆ *Reading will increase your English vocabulary.* **2** [sing] all the words in a language: *New words are always entering the vocabulary.*

vocal /ˈvəʊkl/ *adj* **1** [only *before* a noun] connected with the voice: ***vocal cords*** (= the thin strips in the back of your throat that move to produce the voice) **2** expressing your ideas or opinions loudly or freely: *a small but vocal group of protesters*

vocalist /ˈvəʊkəlɪst/ *noun* [C] a singer, especially in a band: *a lead/backing vocalist*

vocation /vəʊˈkeɪʃn/ *noun* [C,U] a type of work or a way of life that you believe to be especially suitable for you: *Peter has finally found his vocation in life.*

vocational /vəʊˈkeɪʃənl/ *adj* connected with the skills, knowledge, etc. that you need to do a particular job: *vocational training*

vociferous /vəˈsɪfərəs/ *adj* (*formal*) expressing your opinions or feelings in a loud and confident way ▶ **vociferously** *adv*

vodka /ˈvɒdkə/ *noun* [C,U] a strong clear alcoholic drink originally from Russia

vogue /vəʊg/ *noun* [C,U] **a vogue (for sth)** a fashion for sth: *a vogue for large cars* ◆ *That hairstyle is **in vogue** at the moment.*

voice[1] /vɔɪs/ *noun*

➤SOUND FROM MOUTH **1** [C] the sounds that you make when you speak or sing; the ability to make these sounds: *He had a bad cold and **lost** his **voice*** (= could not speak for a period of time). ◆ *to speak in a loud/soft/low/hoarse voice* ◆ *to lower/raise your voice* (= speak more quietly/loudly) ◆ *Shh! **Keep your voice down!*** ◆ *Alan is 13 and his **voice is breaking*** (= becoming deep and low like a man's).

➤-VOICED **2** -**voiced** [in compounds] having a voice of the type mentioned: *husky-voiced*

➤OPINION **3** [sing] a voice (in sth) (the right to express) your ideas or opinions: *The workers want more of a voice in the running of the company.* **4** [C] a particular feeling, attitude or opinion that you have or express: *You should listen to the voice of reason and apologize.*

➤GRAMMAR **5** [sing] the form of a verb that shows if a sentence is active or passive: *'Keats wrote this poem' is in the **active voice**.* ◆ *'This poem was written by Keats' is in the **passive voice**.* ℹ For more information about the passive voice, look at the **Reference Section** at the back of this dictionary.

IDM **at the top of your voice** ➲ top[1]

voice[2] /vɔɪs/ *verb* [T] to express your opinions or feelings: *to voice complaints/criticisms*

voicemail /ˈvɔɪsmeɪl/ *noun* [U] an electronic system which can store telephone messages, so that you can listen to them later ➲ note at **mobile phone**

void[1] /vɔɪd/ *noun* [C, usually sing] (*formal*) a large empty space: *Her death left a void in their lives.*

void[2] /vɔɪd/ *adj* **1** (*formal*) **void (of sth)** completely lacking sth: *The sky was void of stars.* **2** (used about a ticket, contract, decision, etc.) that can no longer be accepted or used: *The agreement was declared void.*

vol. *abbr* (*pl* vols) = **volume**(1)(4): *The Complete Works of Byron, Vol. 2*

volatile /ˈvɒlətaɪl/ *adj* **1** that can change suddenly and unexpectedly: *a highly volatile situation which could easily develop into rioting* ◆ *a volatile personality* **2** (used about a liquid) that can easily change into a gas

volcano /vɒlˈkeɪnəʊ/ *noun* [C] (*pl* volcanoes; volcanos) a mountain with a **crater** (= a hole) at the top through which steam, **lava** (= hot

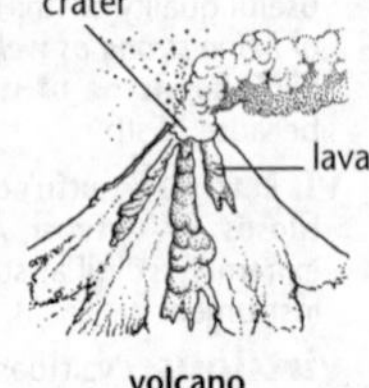

volcano

melted rock), fire, etc. sometimes come out: *an active/dormant/extinct volcano* ◆ *When did the volcano last erupt?* ▶ **volcanic** /vɒlˈkænɪk/ *adj*: *volcanic rock/ash*

volition /vəˈlɪʃn/ *noun* [U] (*formal*) the power to choose sth freely or to make your own decisions: *They left entirely* ***of their own volition*** (= because they wanted to).

volley /ˈvɒli/ *noun* [C] **1** (in sports such as football, tennis, etc.) a hit or kick of the ball before it touches the ground: *a forehand/backhand volley* **2** a number of stones, bullets, etc. that are thrown or shot at the same time: *The soldiers fired a volley over the heads of the crowd.* **3** a lot of questions, insults, etc. that are directed at one person very quickly, one after the other: *a volley of abuse* ▶ **volley** *verb* [I,T]: *Murray volleyed the ball into the net.*

volleyball /ˈvɒlibɔːl/ *noun* [U] a game in which two teams of six players hit a ball over a high net with their hands while trying not to let the ball touch the ground on their own side

volt /vəʊlt; vɒlt/ *noun* [C] (*abbr* V) a measure of electric force

voltage /ˈvəʊltɪdʒ/ *noun* [C,U] an electrical force measured in **volts**

⚷ **volume** /ˈvɒljuːm/ *noun* **1** [U,C] (*abbr* vol.) the amount of space that sth contains or fills: *What is the volume of this sphere?* ➲ look at **area** **2** [C,U] the large quantity or amount of sth: *the* ***sheer volume*** (= the large amount) *of traffic on the roads* ◆ *I've got volumes of work to get through.* **3** [U, sing] how loud a sound is: *to turn the volume on a radio up/down* ◆ *a low/high volume* ➲ note at **listen** **4** [C] (*abbr* vol.) a book, especially one of a set or series: *The dictionary comes in three volumes.*

voluminous /vəˈluːmɪnəs/ *adj* (*formal*) (used about clothing, furniture, etc.) very large; having plenty of space: *a voluminous skirt*

voluntary /ˈvɒləntri/ *adj* **1** done or given because you want to do it, not because you have to do it: *He took* ***voluntary redundancy*** *and left the firm last year.* OPP **compulsory** **2** done or working without payment: *She does some* ***voluntary work*** *at the hospital.* **3** (used about movements of the body) that you can control OPP **involuntary** ▶ **voluntarily** /ˈvɒləntrəli/ *adv*: *She left the job voluntarily; she wasn't sacked.*

volunteer[1] /ˌvɒlənˈtɪə(r)/ *noun* [C] **1** a person who offers or agrees to do sth without being forced or paid to do it: *Are there any volunteers to do the washing-up?* **2** a person who joins the armed forces without being ordered to ➲ look at **conscript**

volunteer[2] /ˌvɒlənˈtɪə(r)/ *verb* **1** [I,T] volunteer (sth); volunteer (to do sth) to offer sth or to do sth which you do not have to do or for which you will not be paid: *They volunteered their services free.* ◆ *She frequently volunteers for extra work because she really likes her job.* ◆ *One of my friends volunteered to take us all in his car.* **2** [T] to give information, etc. or to make a comment or suggestion without being asked to: *I volunteered a few helpful suggestions.* **3** [I] volunteer (for sth) to join the armed forces without being ordered

vomit /ˈvɒmɪt/ *verb* [I,T] to bring food, etc. up from the stomach and out of the mouth ➲ In everyday British English we say **be sick**. ▶ **vomit** *noun* [U]

⚷ **vote**[1] /vəʊt/ *noun* **1** [C] a vote (for/against sb/sth) a formal choice in an election or at a meeting in order to choose sb or decide sth: *The votes are still being counted.* ◆ *There were 10* ***votes for****, and 25* ***against****, the motion.* **2** [C] a vote (on sth) a method of deciding sth by asking people to express their choice and finding out what most people want: *The democratic way to decide this would be to* ***take a vote****.* ◆ *Let's* ***have a vote/put it to the vote****.* **3** the vote [sing] the total number of votes in an election: *She obtained 30% of the vote.* **4** the vote [sing] the legal right to vote in political elections: *Women did not get the vote in this country until the 1920s.*

IDM **cast a/your vote** ➲ **cast**[1]

a vote of thanks a short speech to thank sb, usually a guest at a meeting, etc: *The club secretary proposed a vote of thanks to the guest speaker.*

⚷ **vote**[2] /vəʊt/ *verb* **1** [I,T] vote (for/against sb/sth); vote (on sth); vote to do sth to show formally a choice or an opinion, for example by marking a piece of paper or by holding up your hand: *Who did you vote for in the last general election?* ◆ *46%* ***voted in favour of*** (= for) *the proposed change.* ◆ *Very few MPs voted against the new law.* ◆ *After the debate we'll vote on the motion.* ◆ *They voted to change the rules of the club.* ◆ *I voted Liberal Democrat.* ➲ note at **politics** **2** [T, usually passive] to choose sb for a particular position or prize: *He was voted best actor at the Oscars.* ▶ **voter** *noun* [C]

vouch /vaʊtʃ/ *verb*

PHR V **vouch for sb/sth** to say that a person is honest or good or that sth is true or genuine: *I can vouch for her ability to work hard.*

voucher /ˈvaʊtʃə(r)/ *noun* [C] a piece of paper that you can use instead of money to pay for all or part of sth ➲ look at **token**

vow /vaʊ/ *noun* [C] a formal and serious promise (especially in a religious ceremony): *to keep/break your* ***marriage vows*** ▶ **vow** *verb* [T]: *We vowed never to discuss the subject again.*

vowel /ˈvaʊəl/ *noun* [C] a letter that represents a **vowel** sound. In English the vowels are *a, e, i, o* or *u*. ➲ look at **consonant**

voyage /ˈvɔɪɪdʒ/ *noun* [C] a long journey by sea or in space: *a voyage to Jupiter* ➲ note at **journey** ▶ **voyager** *noun* [C]

vs *abbr* = **versus**(1)

VSO /ˌviː es ˈəʊ/ *abbr* **Voluntary Service Overseas**; a British organization that sends people to go to work in developing countries

vulgar /ˈvʌlgə(r)/ *adj* **1** not having or showing good judgement about what is attractive or appropriate; not polite or well behaved: *vulgar furnishings* ◆ *a vulgar man/woman* **2** rude or likely to offend people: *a vulgar joke* ▶ **vulgarity** /vʌlˈgærəti/ *noun* [C,U] (*pl* **vulgarities**)

vulnerable /ˈvʌlnərəbl/ *adj* **vulnerable (to sth/sb)** weak and easy to hurt in a physical or an emotional way: *Poor organization left the troops vulnerable to enemy attack.* ▶ **vulnerability** /ˌvʌlnərəˈbɪləti/ *noun* [U]

vulture /ˈvʌltʃə(r)/ *noun* [C] a large bird with no feathers on its head or neck that eats the flesh of animals that are already dead

vuvuzela™ /ˌvuːvuːˈzeɪlə/ *noun* [C] a long plastic instrument in the shape of a **trumpet** (= a musical instrument), that makes a very loud noise when you blow it and is popular with football fans in South Africa

W, w /ˈdʌbljuː/ *noun* [C,U] (*pl* Ws; W's; w's /ˈdʌbljuːz/) the 23rd letter of the English alphabet: *'Water' begins with (a) 'W'.*

W *abbr* **1** = **watt**: *a 60W light bulb* **2** = **west**[1], **western**[1](1): *W Africa*

wacky (also **whacky**) /ˈwæki/ *adj* (**wackier**; **wackiest**) (*informal*) amusing or funny in a slightly crazy way

wad /wɒd/ *noun* [C] **1** a large number of papers, paper money, etc. folded or rolled together: *He pulled a wad of £20 notes out of his pocket.* **2** a mass of soft material that is used for blocking sth or keeping sth in place: *The nurse used a wad of cotton wool to stop the bleeding.*

waddle /ˈwɒdl/ *verb* [I] to walk with short steps, moving the weight of your body from one side to the other, like a **duck** (= a common bird that lives near water)

wade /weɪd/ *verb* [I] to walk with difficulty through fairly deep water, mud, etc.
PHR V **wade through sth** to deal with or read sth that is boring and takes a long time

wafer /ˈweɪfə(r)/ *noun* [C] a very thin, dry biscuit often eaten with ice cream

W

waffle[1] /ˈwɒfl/ *noun* **1** [C] a flat cake with a pattern of squares on it that is often eaten warm with **syrup** (= a sweet sauce) ➲ picture on **page P16** **2** [U] (*BrE informal*) language that uses a lot of words but that does not say anything important or interesting: *The last two paragraphs of your essay are just waffle.*

waffle[2] /ˈwɒfl/ *verb* [I] (*BrE informal*) **waffle (on) (about sth)** to talk or write for much longer than necessary without saying anything important or interesting

waft /wɒft/ *verb* [I,T] to move, or make sth move, gently through the air: *The smell of her perfume wafted across the room.*

wag /wæg/ *verb* [I,T] (**wagging**; **wagged**) to shake up and down or move from side to side; to make sth do this: *The dog wagged its tail.*

wage[1] /weɪdʒ/ *noun* [sing] (also **wages** [pl]) the regular amount of money that you earn for a week's work: *a weekly wage of £200* ◆ *What's the national* ***minimum wage*** (= the lowest wage that an employer is allowed to pay by law)? ➲ note at **pay**[2]

> **HELP** **Wage** in the singular is mainly used to talk about the amount of money paid, or when the word is combined with another, for example 'wage packet', 'wage rise', etc. **Wages** in the plural means the money itself: *I have to pay the rent out of my wages.*

wage[2] /weɪdʒ/ *verb* [T] **wage sth (against/on sb/sth)** to begin and then continue a war, battle, etc: *to wage war on your enemy*

waggle /ˈwægl/ *verb* [I,T] (*informal*) to move up and down or from side to side with quick, short movements; to make sth do this

wagon /ˈwægən/ *noun* [C] **1** (*AmE* **freight car**) an open section of a train, used for carrying goods or animals: *coal transported in goods wagons* ➲ look at **truck** **2** (*BrE also* **waggon**) a vehicle with four wheels pulled by animals and used for carrying heavy loads

waif /weɪf/ *noun* [C] a small thin person, usually a child, who looks as if they do not have enough to eat

wail /weɪl/ *verb* **1** [I,T] to cry or complain in a loud, high voice, especially because you are sad or in pain **2** [I] (used about things) to make a sound like this: *sirens wailing in the streets outside* ▶ **wail** *noun* [C]: *a wail of anguish/despair/distress* ◆ *the wail of sirens*

waist /weɪst/ *noun* [C, usually sing] **1** the narrowest part around the middle of your body: *She put her arms around his waist.* ➲ picture at **body** **2** the part of a piece of clothing that goes round the waist: *The trousers are too baggy round the waist.*

waistband /ˈweɪstbænd/ *noun* [C] the narrow piece of cloth at the waist of a piece of clothing, especially trousers or a skirt

waistcoat /ˈweɪskəʊt/ (*AmE* **vest**) *noun* [C] a piece of clothing with buttons down the front and no sleeves that is often worn over a shirt and under a jacket as part of a man's suit

waistline /ˈweɪstlaɪn/ *noun* [C, usually sing] **1** (used to talk about how fat or thin a person is) the measurement or size of the body around the waist **2** the place on a piece of clothing where your waist is

wait[1] /weɪt/ *verb* [I] **1** **wait (for sb/sth) (to do sth)** to stay in a particular place and not do anything until sb/sth arrives or until sth happens: *Wait here. I'll be back in a few minutes.* ◆ *Have you been waiting long?* ◆ *If I'm a bit late, can you wait for me?* ◆ *I'm waiting to see the doctor.*

> **MORE** Compare **wait** and **expect**: *I was expecting him to be there at 7.30 but at 8 I was still waiting.* ◆ *I'm waiting for the exam results but*

I'm not expecting to pass. If you **wait for** somebody or something, you stay in one place and pass the time until somebody arrives or something happens: *I waited outside the theatre until they arrived.* If you **expect** something, you think that it will happen or is likely to happen: *I'm expecting you to get a good grade in your exam.* You use **hope**, not **expect**, to say that you want sth to happen: *I hope you have a good party.* You use **look forward to** when you are feeling happy and excited about something that you expect to happen: *I'm looking forward to your visit.*

2 to be left or delayed until a later time: *Is this matter urgent or* ***can it wait****?*
IDM can't wait/can hardly wait used when you are emphasizing that sb is very excited and enthusiastic about doing sth: *The kids can't wait to see their father again.*
keep sb waiting to make sb wait or be delayed, especially because you arrive late: *I'm sorry if I've kept you waiting.*
wait and see to be patient and find out what will happen later (perhaps before deciding to do sth): *We'll just have to wait and see—there's nothing more we can do.*
wait your turn to wait until the time when you are allowed to do sth
PHR V wait behind to stay in a place after others have left it: *She waited behind after class to speak to her teacher.*
wait in to stay at home because you are expecting sb to come or sth to happen
wait on sb to act as a servant to sb, especially by serving food to them
wait up (for sb) to not go to bed because you are waiting for sb to come home

wait² /weɪt/ *noun* [C, usually sing] **a wait (for sth/sb)** a period of time when you wait
IDM lie in wait (for sb) ➲ **lie²**

⚷ **waiter** /ˈweɪtə(r)/ *noun* [C] a man whose job is to serve customers at their tables in a restaurant, etc: *I'll ask the waiter for the bill.* ➲ picture on **page P2**

ˈwaiting list *noun* [C] a list of people who are waiting for sth, for example a service or medical treatment, that will be available in the future: *to put your name* ***on a waiting list***

ˈwaiting room *noun* [C] a room where people can sit while they are waiting, for example for a train, or to see a doctor or dentist

waitress /ˈweɪtrəs/ *noun* [C] a woman whose job is to serve customers at their tables in a restaurant, etc.

waive /weɪv/ *verb* [T] to say officially that a rule, etc. need not be obeyed; to say officially that you no longer have a right to sth: *In your case, we will waive your tuition fees.*

⚷ **wake¹** /weɪk/ *verb* [I,T] (*pt* **woke** /wəʊk/; *pp* **woken** /ˈwəʊkən/) **wake (sb) (up)** to stop sleeping; to make sb stop sleeping: *I woke early in the morning and got straight out of bed.* ♦ *Wake up! It's nearly 8 o'clock!* ♦ *Could you wake me at 7.30, please?* ➲ note at **sleep** ➲ *adjective* **awake**
PHR V wake sb up to make sb become more active or full of energy: *She always has a coffee to wake her up when she gets to work.*
wake up to sth to realize sth; to notice sth

wake² /weɪk/ *noun* [C] **1** an occasion before or after a funeral when people meet to remember the dead person, traditionally held at night to watch over the body before it is buried **2** the track that a moving ship leaves behind on the surface of the water ➲ picture on **page P10**
IDM in the wake of sb/sth following or coming after sb/sth: *The earthquake left a trail of destruction in its wake.*

waken /ˈweɪkən/ *verb* [I,T] (*old-fashioned, formal*) to stop sleeping or to make sb/sth stop sleeping: *She wakened from a deep sleep.*

⚷ **walk¹** /wɔːk/ *verb* **1** [I,T] to move or go somewhere by putting one foot in front of the other on the ground, but without running: *The door opened and Billy walked in.* ♦ *I walk to work every day.* ♦ *He walks with a limp.* ♦ *I've walked miles today.* ♦ *Are the shops* ***within walking distance*** (= near enough to walk to)*?* **2** [I,T] to move in this way for exercise or pleasure: *I walked across Scotland with a friend.* ➲ note at **walk² 3** [T] to go somewhere with sb/sth on foot, especially to make sure they get there safely: *I'll* ***walk you home*** *if you don't want to go on your own.* ♦ *He walked me to my car.* **4** [T] to take a dog out for exercise: *I'm just going to* ***walk the dog****.*
PHR V walk off with sth (*informal*) **1** to win sth easily: *She walked off with all the prizes.* **2** to steal sth; to take sth that does not belong to you by mistake: *When I got home I realized that I had walked off with her pen.*
walk out (of sth) to leave suddenly and angrily: *She walked out of the meeting in disgust.*
walk out on sb (*informal*) to leave sb for ever: *He walked out on his wife and children after 15 years of marriage.*
walk (all) over sb (*informal*) **1** to treat sb badly, without considering their needs or feelings: *I don't know why she lets her husband walk all over her like that.* **2** to defeat sb completely: *He played brilliantly and walked all over his opponent.*
walk up (to sb/sth) to walk towards sb/sth, especially in a confident way: *He walked up to her and asked her if she wanted to dance.*
▶ **walker** *noun* [C]: *She's a fast walker.* ♦ *This area is very popular with walkers.*

W

⚷ **walk²** /wɔːk/ *noun* **1** [C] an occasion when you go somewhere on foot for pleasure, exercise, etc: *We went for a walk in the country.* ♦ *I'm just going to take the dog for a walk.* ♦ *The beach is five minutes' walk/a five-minute walk from the hotel.*

HELP We use **go for a walk** when we are talking about a short walk that we take for pleasure. We use **go walking** to talk about a long walk that may last several hours or days.

2 [C] a path or route for walking for pleasure; an organized event when people walk for pleasure:

From here there's a lovely walk through the woods. ♦ *a charity walk* **3** [sing] a way or style of walking: *He has a funny walk.* **4** [sing] the speed of walking: *She slowed to a walk.*

IDM a walk of life a person's job or position in society: *She has friends from all walks of life.*

walkie-talkie /ˌwɔːki ˈtɔːki/ *noun* [C] (*informal*) a small radio that you can carry with you to send or receive messages

walking *noun* [U] the activity of going for walks in the countryside for exercise or pleasure: *to **go walking*** ♦ *walking boots* ♦ *We like to go walking in the Alps in the summer.*

ˈ**walking stick** (*especially BrE* **stick**) *noun* [C] a stick that you carry and use as a support to help you walk ➲ look at **crutch**

walkover /ˈwɔːkəʊvə(r)/ *noun* [C] an easy win or victory in a game or competition

wall /wɔːl/ *noun* [C] **1** a solid, vertical structure made of stone, brick, etc. that is built round an area of land to protect it or to divide it: *There is a high wall all around the prison.* **2** one of the sides of a room or building joining the ceiling and the floor: *He put the picture up **on the wall**.* ➲ picture at **fence**

IDM up the wall (*informal*) crazy or angry: *That noise is driving me up the wall.*

walled /wɔːld/ *adj* surrounded by a wall

wallet /ˈwɒlɪt/ (*AmE* **billfold**) *noun* [C] a small, flat, folding case in which you keep paper money, plastic cards, etc: *Don't forget your wallet and keys.* ➲ look at **purse** ➲ picture at **bag**

wallop /ˈwɒləp/ *verb* [T] (*informal*) to hit sb/sth very hard

wallow /ˈwɒləʊ/ *verb* [I] **wallow (in sth) 1** (used about people and large animals) to lie and roll around in water, etc. in order to keep cool or for pleasure: *I spent an hour wallowing in the bath.* **2** to take great pleasure in sth (a feeling, situation, etc.): *to wallow in self-pity* (= to think about your unhappiness all the time and seem to be enjoying it)

wallpaper /ˈwɔːlpeɪpə(r)/ *noun* [U] **1** paper that you stick to the walls of a room to decorate or cover them **2** the background pattern or picture that you choose to have on your computer screen ▸ **wallpaper** *verb* [I,T]

W

wall-to-ˈwall *adj* [only *before* a noun] **1** (used especially about a carpet) covering the floor of a room completely **2** (*informal*) continuous; happening all the time: *wall-to-wall TV sports coverage*

wally /ˈwɒli/ *noun* [C] (*pl* **wallies**) (*BrE slang*) a silly or stupid person

walnut /ˈwɔːlnʌt/ *noun* **1** [C] a nut that we eat, with a rough surface and a hard brown shell that is in two halves ➲ picture at **nut 2** (also ˈ**walnut tree**) [C] the tree on which these nuts grow **3** [U] the wood from the **walnut** tree, used in making furniture

walrus /ˈwɔːlrəs/ *noun* [C] a large animal with two tusks (= long teeth) that lives in or near the sea in Arctic regions

waltz¹ /wɔːls/ *noun* [C] an elegant dance that you do with a partner to music which has a rhythm of three beats; the music for this dance: *a Strauss waltz*

waltz² /wɔːls/ *verb* **1** [I,T] to dance a **waltz**: *They waltzed around the floor.* ♦ *He waltzed her round the room.* **2** [I] (*informal*) to go somewhere in a confident way: *You can't just waltz in and expect your meal to be ready for you.*

WAN /wæn/ *abbr* **wide area network**; a system in which computers in different places are connected, usually over a large area ➲ look at **LAN**

wan /wɒn/ *adj* looking pale and ill or tired

wand /wɒnd/ *noun* [C] a thin stick that people hold when they are doing magic tricks: *I wish I could **wave a magic wand** and make everything better.*

wander /ˈwɒndə(r)/ *verb* **1** [I,T] to walk somewhere slowly with no particular sense of direction or purpose: *We spent a pleasant day wandering around the town.* ♦ *He was found in a confused state, wandering the streets.* **2** [I] **wander (away/off) (from sb/sth)** to walk away from a place where you ought to be or the people you were with: *We must stay together while visiting the town so I don't want anybody to wander off.* ♦ *Don't wander away from the main road.* **3** [I] (used about sb's mind, thoughts, etc.) to stop paying attention to sth; to be unable to stay on one subject: *The lecture was so boring that my attention began to wander.* ▸ **wander** *noun* [sing]: *I went to the park for a wander.*

wane¹ /weɪn/ *verb* [I] **1** (*formal*) to become gradually weaker or less important: *My enthusiasm was waning rapidly.* **2** (used about the moon) to appear slightly smaller each day after being full and round

wane² /weɪn/ *noun*

IDM on the wane (*formal*) becoming smaller, less important or less common: *The singer's popularity seems to be on the wane these days.*

wangle /ˈwæŋgl/ *verb* [T] (*informal*) to get sth that you want by persuading sb or by having a clever plan: *Somehow he wangled a day off to meet me.*

wanna /ˈwɒnə/ a way of writing 'want to' or 'want a' to show that sb is speaking in an informal way: *I wanna go home now.* ➲ note at **contraction**

EXAM TIP

Do not write 'wanna' yourself (unless you are copying somebody's accent) because it might be marked as a mistake.

wannabe /ˈwɒnəbi/ *noun* [C] (*informal*) a person who behaves, dresses, etc. like a famous person because they want to be like them

want¹ /wɒnt/ *verb* [T] [not used in the continuous tenses]

➤WISH **1 want sth (for sth); want (sb) to do sth; want**

sth (to be) done to have a desire or a wish for sth: *He wants a new bike.* ◆ *What do they want for breakfast?* ◆ *I don't want to discuss it now.* ◆ *I want you to stop worrying about it.* ◆ *The boss wants this letter typed.* ◆ *I don't want Emma going out on her own at night.* ◆ *They want Bhanot as captain.*

HELP **Want** or **would like**? **Want** and **would like** are similar in meaning, but 'would like' is more polite: *'I want a drink!' screamed the child.* ◆ *'Would you like some more tea, Mrs Atwal?'*

➤NEED **2** (*informal*) used to say that sth needs to be done: *The button on my shirt wants sewing on.* ◆ *The house wants a new coat of paint.* **3** [usually passive] to need sb to be in a particular place or for a particular reason: *Mrs Dawson, you are wanted on the phone.* ◆ *She is* ***wanted by the police*** (= the police are looking for her because she may have committed a crime).

➤SHOULD/OUGHT TO **4** (*informal*) (used to give advice to sb) should or ought to: *He wants to be more careful about what he tells people.*

➤SEXUAL DESIRE **5** to feel sexual desire for sb

HELP Although this verb is not used in the continuous tenses, it is common to see the present participle (= *-ing* form): *She kept her head down, not wanting to attract attention.*

IDM **what do you want?** used to ask sb in a rude or angry way why they are there or what they want you to do

want² /wɒnt/ *noun* (*formal*) **1 wants** [pl] something you need or want: *All our wants were satisfied.* **2** [U, sing] a lack of sth: *a want of clean water*
IDM **for (the) want of sth** because of a lack of sth; because sth is not available: *I took the job for want of a better offer.*

wanting /ˈwɒntɪŋ/ *adj* (*formal*) [not before a noun] **wanting (in sth) 1** not having enough of sth; lacking: *The children were certainly not wanting in enthusiasm.* **2** not good enough: *The new system was* ***found wanting.***

wanton /ˈwɒntən/ *adj* (*formal*) (used about an action) done in order to hurt sb or damage sth for no good reason: *wanton vandalism*

WAP /wæp/ *abbr* **wireless application protocol**; a technology that connects devices such as mobile phones to the Internet: *a WAP-enabled phone*

🔑 **war** /wɔː(r)/ *noun* **1** [U,C] a state of fighting between different countries or groups within countries using armies and weapons: *The Prime Minister announced that the country was* ***at war.*** ◆ *to* ***declare war on*** *another country* (= say officially that a war has started) ◆ *When* ***war broke out*** (= started), *thousands of men volunteered for the army.* ◆ *a* ***civil war*** (= fighting between different groups in one country) ◆ *to* ***go to war*** *against somebody* ◆ *to fight a war* **2** [C,U] aggressive competition between groups of people, companies, countries, etc: *a price war among oil companies* **3** [U, sing] **war (against/on sb/sth)** efforts to end or get rid of sth: *We seem to be winning the war against organized crime.*

TOPIC

War

The three main parts of a country's **armed forces** are the **army**, the **navy** and the **air force**. **Officers** in the forces give orders to their **troops**. When a war **breaks out** (= starts), two or more countries are **at war**. A war between different groups in the same country is called a **civil war**. A country's **enemies** are the countries it is fighting against and its **allies** are countries which support it. If armed forces from one country enter another country, they **invade** it. If they stay there and take control of the country they **occupy** it. A country will try to **defend** itself against **attack** from another country. At the end of a war one country is **defeated** and **surrenders** (= stops fighting and says that it has lost).

ˈ**war crime** *noun* [C] a cruel act that is committed during a war and that is against the international rules of war

ward¹ /wɔːd/ *noun* [C] **1** a separate part or room in a hospital for patients with the same kind of medical condition: *the maternity/psychiatric/surgical ward* **2** one of the sections into which a town is divided for elections **3** a child who is under the protection of a court of law; a child whose parents are dead and who is cared for by a **guardian** (= sb who is legally responsible for their care): *The child was made a* ***ward of court.***

ward² /wɔːd/ *verb*
PHR V **ward sb/sth off** to protect or defend yourself against danger, illness, attack, etc.

warden /ˈwɔːdn/ *noun* [C] **1** a person whose job is to check that rules are obeyed or to look after a particular place: *a* ***traffic warden*** (= a person who checks that cars are not parked in the wrong place) **2** (*especially AmE*) the person in charge of a prison

warder /ˈwɔːdə(r)/ *noun* [C] (*BrE*) a person whose job is to guard prisoners in a prison ➲ look at **guard**

wardrobe /ˈwɔːdrəʊb/ *noun* **1** [C] a large cupboard in which you can hang your clothes ➲ picture on **page P8** **2** [usually sing] a person's collection of clothes: *I need a whole new summer wardrobe.*

ware /weə(r)/ *noun* **1** [U] [in compounds] things made from a particular type of material or suitable for a particular use: *glassware* ◆ *kitchenware* ➲ look at **hardware** **2 wares** [pl] (*old-fashioned*) goods offered for sale

warehouse /ˈweəhaʊs/ *noun* [C] a building where large quantities of goods are stored before being sent to shops

warfare /ˈwɔːfeə(r)/ *noun* [U] the activity of fighting a war; types of war: *guerrilla warfare*

warily, wariness ➲ **wary**

warlike /ˈwɔːlaɪk/ *adj* liking to fight or good at fighting: *a warlike nation*

🔑 **warm¹** /wɔːm/ *adj* (**warmer; warmest**) **1** having a pleasant temperature that is fairly high, between

W

cool and hot: *It's quite warm in the sunshine.* ◆ *I jumped up and down to keep my feet warm.* ➲ note at **cold**[1] **2** (used about clothes) preventing you from getting cold: *Take plenty of warm clothes.* **3** friendly, kind and pleasant: *I was given a very warm welcome.* **4** creating a pleasant, comfortable feeling: *warm colours* ▶ **the warm** *noun* [sing]: *It's awfully cold out here—I want to go back into the warm.* ▶ **warmly** *adv*: *warmly dressed* ◆ *She thanked him warmly for his help.*

warm[2] /wɔːm/ *verb* [I,T] **warm (sb/sth) (up)** to become or to make sb/sth become warm or warmer: *It was cold earlier but it's beginning to warm up now.* ◆ *I sat by the fire to warm up.*

PHR V **warm to/towards sb** to begin to like sb that you did not like at first

warm to sth to become more interested in sth

warm up to prepare to do an activity or sport by practising gently: *The team warmed up before the match.*

ˌwarm-ˈblooded *adj* (used about animals) having a warm blood temperature that does not change if the temperature around them changes ➲ look at **cold-blooded**

ˌwarm-ˈhearted *adj* kind and friendly

warmth /wɔːmθ/ *noun* [U] **1** a fairly high temperature or the effect created by this, especially when it is pleasant: *She felt the warmth of the sun on her face.* **2** the quality of being kind and friendly: *I was touched by the warmth of their welcome.*

warn /wɔːn/ *verb* [T] **1 warn sb (of sth); warn sb (about sb/sth)** to tell sb about sth unpleasant or dangerous that exists or might happen, so that they can avoid it: *When I saw the car coming I tried to warn him, but it was too late.* ◆ *The government is warning the public of possible terrorist attacks.* ◆ *He warned me about the danger of walking home alone at night.* **2 warn (sb) against doing sth; warn sb (not to do sth)** to advise sb not to do sth: *The radio warned people against going out during the storm.* ◆ *I warned you not to trust him.*

warning /ˈwɔːnɪŋ/ *noun* [C,U] something that tells you to be careful or tells you about sth, usually sth bad, before it happens: *Your employers can't dismiss you **without warning**.* ◆ *You could have given me some warning that your parents were coming to visit.*

W

warp /wɔːp/ *verb* **1** [I,T] to become bent into the wrong shape, for example as a result of getting hot or wet; to make sth become like this: *The window frame was badly warped and wouldn't shut.* **2** [T] to influence sb so that they start behaving in an unusual or shocking way: *His experiences in the war had warped him.* ▶ **warped** *adj*

warpath /ˈwɔːpɑːθ/ *noun*

IDM **(be/go) on the warpath** (*informal*) to be very angry and want to fight or punish sb

warrant[1] /ˈwɒrənt/ *noun* [C] an official written statement that gives sb permission to do sth: *a search warrant* (= a document that allows the police to search a house)

warrant[2] /ˈwɒrənt/ *verb* [T] (*formal*) to make sth seem right or necessary; to deserve sth: *Her behaviour does not warrant such criticism.*

warranty /ˈwɒrənti/ *noun* [C,U] (*pl* **warranties**) a written statement that you get when you buy sth, which promises to repair or replace it if it is broken or does not work: *Fortunately my washing machine is still **under warranty**.* ➲ look at **guarantee**

warren /ˈwɒrən/ = **rabbit warren**

warrior /ˈwɒriə(r)/ *noun* [C] (*old-fashioned*) a person who fights in a battle; a soldier

warship /ˈwɔːʃɪp/ *noun* [C] a ship for use in war

wart /wɔːt/ *noun* [C] a small hard dry lump that sometimes grows on the face or body

wartime /ˈwɔːtaɪm/ *noun* [U] a period of time during which there is a war

wary /ˈweəri/ *adj* (**warier**; *no superlative*) **wary (of sb/sth)** careful because you are uncertain or afraid of sb/sth: *Since becoming famous, she has grown wary of journalists.* ▶ **warily** *adv* ▶ **wariness** *noun* [U]

was /wəz; *strong form* wɒz/ ➲ **be**

wash[1] /wɒʃ/ *verb* **1** [I,T] to clean sb/sth/yourself with water and often soap: *to wash your hands/face/hair* ◆ *That shirt needs washing.* ◆ *Wash and dress quickly or you'll be late!* ◆ *I'll wash* (= wash the dishes), *you dry.* ➲ note at **clean**[2] **2** [I] to be able to be washed without being damaged: *Does this material wash well, or does the colour come out?* **3** [I,T] (used about water) to flow or carry sth/sb in the direction mentioned: *I let the waves wash over my feet.* ◆ *The current washed the ball out to sea.*

IDM **wash your hands of sb/sth** to refuse to be responsible for sb/sth any longer: *They washed their hands of their son when he was sent to prison.*

PHR V **wash sb/sth away** (used about water) to carry sb/sth away: *The floods had washed away the path.*

wash (sth) off to (make sth) disappear by washing: *The writing has washed off and now I can't read it.* ◆ *Go and wash that make-up off!*

wash out to be removed from a material by washing: *These grease marks won't wash out.*

wash sth out to wash sth or the inside of sth in order to remove dirt: *I'll just wash out this bowl and then we can use it.*

wash (sth) up 1 (*BrE*) to wash the plates, knives, forks, etc. after a meal: *Whose turn is it to wash up?* **2** (*AmE*) to wash your face and hands: *Go and wash up quickly and put on some clean clothes.* **3** [often passive] (used about water) to carry sth to land and leave it there: *Police found the girl's body washed up on the beach.*

wash[2] /wɒʃ/ *noun* **1** [C,usually sing] an act of cleaning or being cleaned with water: *I'd better go and **have a wash** before we go out.* **2** [sing] the waves caused by the movement of a ship through water

IDM **in the wash** (used about clothes) being washed: *'Where's my red T-shirt?' 'It's in the wash.'*

washable /ˈwɒʃəbl/ *adj* that can be washed without being damaged

washbasin /ˈwɒʃbeɪsn/ (also **basin**) *noun* [C] a large bowl for water that has taps and is fixed to a wall in a bathroom, etc. ➲ look at **sink** ➲ picture at **plug** ➲ picture on **page P8**

ˌwashed ˈout *adj* tired and pale: *They arrived looking washed out after their long journey.*

washer /ˈwɒʃə(r)/ *noun* [C] a small flat ring placed between two surfaces to make a connection tight ➲ picture at **bolt**

🔑 **washing** /ˈwɒʃɪŋ/ *noun* [U] **1** the act of cleaning clothes, etc. with water: *I usually* ***do the washing*** *on Mondays.* **2** clothes that need to be washed or are being washed: *Could you put the washing in the machine?* ◆ *a pile of dirty washing*

ˈwashing machine *noun* [C] an electric machine for washing clothes ➲ picture on **page P8**

ˈwashing powder *noun* [U] soap in the form of powder for washing clothes

ˌwashing-ˈup *noun* [U] **1** the work of washing the plates, knives, forks, etc. after a meal: *I'll* ***do the washing-up***. ◆ *washing-up liquid* **2** plates, etc. that need washing after a meal: *Put the washing-up next to the sink.*

washout /ˈwɒʃaʊt/ *noun* [C] (*informal*) an event that is a complete failure, especially because of rain

washroom /ˈwɒʃruːm; -rʊm/ *noun* [C] (*AmE*) a toilet, especially in a public building

wasn't /ˈwɒznt/ *short for* **was not**

wasp /wɒsp/ *noun* [C] a small black and yellow flying insect that can sting ➲ look at **bee** ➲ picture on **page P13**

wastage /ˈweɪstɪdʒ/ *noun* [U] (*formal*) using too much of sth in a careless way; the amount of sth that is wasted

🔑 **waste[1]** /weɪst/ *verb* [T] **1 waste sth (on sb/sth); waste sth (in doing sth)** to use or spend sth in a careless way or for sth that is not necessary: *She wastes a lot of money on magazines.* ◆ *He wasted his time at university because he didn't work hard.* ◆ *She wasted no time in decorating her new room* (= she did it immediately). **2** [usually passive] to give sth to sb who does not value it: *Expensive wine is wasted on me. I don't even like it.*

🔑 **waste[2]** /weɪst/ *noun* **1** [sing] **a waste (of sth)** using sth in a careless and unnecessary way: *The seminar was* ***a waste of time****—I'd heard it all before.* ◆ *It seems a waste to throw away all these old newspapers.* **2** [U] material, food, etc. that is not needed and is therefore thrown away: *nuclear waste* ◆ *A lot of household waste can be recycled and reused.* ➲ look at **rubbish** **3 wastes** [pl] (*formal*) large areas of land that are not lived in and not used: *the wastes of the Sahara desert*

IDM **go to waste** to not be used and so thrown away and wasted: *I can't bear to see good food going to waste!*

🔑 **waste[3]** /weɪst/ *adj* [only *before* a noun] **1** (used about land) not used or not suitable for use; not looked after: *There's an area of waste ground outside the town where people dump their rubbish.* **2** no longer useful; that is thrown away: *waste paper* ◆ *waste material*

wasted /ˈweɪstɪd/ *adj* **1** [only *before* a noun] not necessary or successful: *a wasted journey* **2** very thin, especially because of illness **3** (*slang*) suffering from the effects of drugs or alcohol

wasteful /ˈweɪstfl/ *adj* using more of sth than necessary; causing waste

ˌwaste-ˈpaper basket *noun* [C] a container in which you put paper, etc. that is to be thrown away

🔑 **watch[1]** /wɒtʃ/ *verb* **1** [I,T] to look at sb/sth for a time, paying attention to what happens: *I* ***watched in horror*** *as the car swerved and crashed.* ◆ *I'm watching to see how you do it.* ◆ *We* ***watch TV*** *most evenings.* ◆ *Watch what she does next.* ◆ *I watched him open the door and walk away.* ➲ note at **look** **2** [T] **watch sb/sth (for sth)** to take care of sth for a short time: *Could you watch my bag for a second while I go and get a drink?* **3** [T] to be careful about sb/sth; to pay careful attention to sth/sb: *You'd better* ***watch what you say*** *to her. She gets upset very easily.* ◆ *Watch that boy—he's acting suspiciously.*

IDM **watch your step** **1** to be careful about where you are walking: *The path's very slippery here so watch your step.* **2** to be careful about how you behave

PHR V **watch out** to be careful because of possible danger or trouble: *Watch out! There's a car coming.* ◆ *If you don't watch out you'll lose your job.*

watch out for sb/sth to look carefully and be ready for sb/sth: *Watch out for snakes if you walk through the fields.*

watch over sb/sth to look after or protect sb/sth: *For two weeks she watched over the sick child.*

🔑 **watch[2]** /wɒtʃ/ *noun* **1** [C] a type of small clock that you usually wear around your wrist: *a digital watch* ◆ *My watch is a bit fast/slow* (= shows a time that is later/earlier than the correct time). ➲ look at **clock** ➲ picture at **clock** **2** [sing, U] the act of watching sb/sth in case of possible danger or problems: *Tour companies have to* ***keep a close watch on*** *the political situation in the region.*

watchdog /ˈwɒtʃdɒg/ *noun* [C] a person or group whose job is to make sure that large companies respect people's rights: *a consumer watchdog*

watchful /ˈwɒtʃfl/ *adj* careful to notice things

🔑 **water[1]** /ˈwɔːtə(r)/ *noun* **1** [U] the clear liquid that falls as rain and is in rivers, seas and lakes: *a glass of water* ◆ *All the rooms have hot and cold running water.* ◆ *drinking water* ◆ *tap water* ➲ look at **freeze**, **steam** **2** [U] a large amount of water, especially the water in a lake, river or sea: *Don't go too near the edge or you'll fall in the water!* ◆ *After the heavy rain several fields were* ***under water***. **3 waters** [pl] the water in a particular sea, lake, etc. or near a particular country: *The ship was still in British waters.* **4** [U] the surface of an area of water: *Can you swim* ***under water***? ◆ *I can see my reflection in the water.*

W

IDM keep your head above water ➲ **head**[1]
pass water ➲ **pass**[1]

water[2] /ˈwɔːtə(r)/ *verb* **1** [T] to give water to plants **2** [I] (used about the eyes or mouth) to fill with liquid: *The smoke in the room was starting to* ***make my eyes water.*** ◆ *Chopping onions* ***makes*** *my* ***eyes water.*** ◆ *These menus will really* ***make*** *your* ***mouth water.***
PHR V water sth down 1 to add water to a liquid in order to make it weaker **2** to change a statement, report, etc. so that the meaning is less strong or direct

watercolour /ˈwɔːtəkʌlə(r)/ *noun* **1 watercolours** [pl] paints that are mixed with water, not oil **2** [C] a picture that has been painted with **watercolours**

watercress /ˈwɔːtəkres/ *noun* [U] a type of plant with small round green leaves which have a strong taste and are often eaten in salads

waterfall /ˈwɔːtəfɔːl/ *noun* [C] a river that falls from a high place, for example over a rock, etc. ➲ picture on **page P10**

waterhole /ˈwɔːtəhəʊl/ (also ˈ**watering hole**) *noun* [C] a place in a hot country, where animals go to drink

ˈ**watering can** *noun* [C] a container with a long tube on one side which is used for pouring water on plants ➲ picture at **garden**

waterlogged /ˈwɔːtəlɒgd/ *adj* **1** (used about the ground) extremely wet: *Our boots sank into the waterlogged ground.* **2** (used about a boat) full of water and likely to sink

watermelon /ˈwɔːtəmelən/ *noun* [C,U] a large, round fruit with a thick, green skin. It is pink or red inside with a lot of black seeds. ➲ picture on **page P14**

ˈ**water polo** *noun* [U] a game played by two teams of people swimming in a swimming pool. Players try to throw a ball into the other team's goal.

waterproof /ˈwɔːtəpruːf/ *adj* that does not let water go through: *a waterproof jacket*

watershed /ˈwɔːtəʃed/ *noun* [C] an event or a time which is important because it marks the beginning of sth new or different

waterski /ˈwɔːtəskiː/ *verb* [I] to move across the surface of water standing on **waterskis** (= narrow boards) and being pulled by a boat ➲ picture on **page P5**

watertight /ˈwɔːtətaɪt/ *adj* **1** made so that water cannot get in or out: *Store in a watertight container.* **2** (used about an excuse, opinion, etc.) impossible to prove wrong; without any faults: *His alibi was absolutely watertight.*

waterway /ˈwɔːtəweɪ/ *noun* [C] a river, **canal** (= an artificial river), etc. along which boats can travel

watery /ˈwɔːtəri/ *adj* **1** containing mostly water: *watery soup* ◆ *A watery liquid came out of the wound.* **2** weak and pale: *watery sunshine* ◆ *a watery smile*

watt /wɒt/ *noun* [C] (*abbr* W) a unit of electric power: *a 60-watt light bulb*

wave[1] /weɪv/ *noun* [C]
➤WATER **1** a line of water moving across the surface of water, especially the sea, that is higher than the rest of the surface: *We watched the waves roll in and break on the shore.* ➲ look at **tidal wave** ➲ picture on **page P10**
➤FEELING/BEHAVIOUR **2** a sudden increase or spread of a feeling or type of behaviour: *There has been a wave of sympathy for the refugees.* ◆ *a crime wave* ◆ *The pain came* ***in waves.*** ➲ look at **heatwave**
➤LARGE NUMBER **3** a large number of people or things suddenly moving or appearing somewhere: *There is normally a wave of tourists in August.*
➤MOVEMENT OF HAND **4** a movement of sth, especially your hand, from side to side in the air: *With a wave of his hand, he said goodbye and left.*
➤SOUND/LIGHT/HEAT **5** the form that some types of energy such as sound, light, heat, etc. take when they move: *sound waves* ◆ *shock waves from the earthquake* ➲ look at **LW, MW**
➤HAIR **6** a gentle curve in your hair ➲ look at **perm**

wave[2] /weɪv/ *verb* **1** [I, T] to move your hand from side to side in the air, usually to attract sb's attention or as you meet or leave sb: *She waved to her friends.* ◆ *He leant out of the window and* ***waved goodbye*** *to her as the train left the station.* **2** [T] wave sb/sth away, on, through, etc. to move your hand in a particular direction to show sb/sth which way to go: *There was a policeman in the middle of the road, waving us on.* **3** [T] **wave sth (at sb); wave sth (about)** to hold sth in the air and move it from side to side: *The crowd waved flags as the President came out.* ◆ *She was talking excitedly and waving her arms about.* **4** [I] to move gently up and down or from side to side: *The branches of the trees waved gently in the breeze.*
PHR V wave sth aside to decide not to pay attention to sb/sth because you think he/she/it is not important
wave sb off to wave to sb who is leaving

wave

They waved goodbye.

waveband /ˈweɪvbænd/ (also **band**) *noun* [C] a set of radio waves of similar length

wavelength /ˈweɪvleŋθ/ *noun* [C] **1** the distance between two sound waves **2** the length of wave on which a radio station sends out its programmes
IDM on the same wavelength able to understand sb because you have similar ideas and opinions

waver /ˈweɪvə(r)/ *verb* [I] **1** to become weak or uncertain, especially when making a decision or choice: *He never wavered in his support.* **2** to move

W

in a way that is not firm or steady: *His hand wavered as he reached for the money.*

wavy /ˈweɪvi/ *adj* (wavier; waviest) having curves; not straight: *wavy hair* ◆ *a wavy line* ➲ picture at **hair, line**

wax /wæks/ *noun* [U] **1** a substance made from fat or oil that melts easily and is used for making polish, **candles** (= tall sticks that you burn to give light), etc. **2** a yellow substance that is found in your ears

waxwork /ˈwæksw3:k/ *noun* [C] **1** a model of sb/sth, especially of a famous person, that is made of wax **2** waxworks [sing] a place where wax models of famous people are shown to the public

way[1] /weɪ/ *noun*

➤METHOD/STYLE **1** [C] a way (to do sth/of doing sth) a particular method, style or manner of doing sth: *What is* ***the best way*** *to learn a language?* ◆ *I've discovered a brilliant way of saving paper!* ◆ *They'll have to find the money* ***one way or another.*** ◆ *He always* ***does things*** *his* ***own way.*** ◆ *She smiled* ***in a*** *friendly* ***way.***

➤ROUTE **2** [C, usually sing] the route you take to reach somewhere; the route you would take if nothing were stopping you: *Can you tell me* ***the way to*** *James Street?* ◆ *Which way should I go to get to the town centre?* ◆ *If you* ***lose*** *your* ***way,*** *phone me.* ◆ *We stopped* ***on the way to*** *Leeds for a meal.* ◆ *Can I drive you home? It's* ***on my way.*** ◆ *Get out of my way!* ◆ *Can you move that box—it's* ***in my/the way.*** **3** [C] a path, road, route, etc. that you can travel along: *There's a way across the fields.* ➲ look at **highway, motorway, railway**

➤DIRECTION **4** [sing] a direction or position: *Look this way!* ◆ *That painting is* ***the wrong way up*** (= with the wrong edge at the top). ◆ *Shouldn't you be wearing that hat* ***the other way round?*** (= facing in the other direction) ◆ *He thought I was older than my sister but in fact it's* ***the other way round*** (= the opposite of what he thought). ➲ look at **back to front**

➤DISTANCE **5** [sing] a distance in space or time: ***It's a long way from*** *London* ***to*** *Edinburgh.* ◆ *The exams are still* ***a long way off.*** ◆ *We came all this way to see him and he's not at home!*

IDM be set in your ways to be unable to change your habits, attitudes, etc.

bluff your way in, out, through, etc. sth ➲ **bluff**[1]

by the way (used for adding sth to the conversation) on a new subject: *Oh, by the way, I saw Mario in town yesterday.*

change your ways ➲ **change**[1]

get/have your own way to get or do what you want, although others may want sth else

give way to break or fall down: *The branch of the tree suddenly gave way and he fell.*

give way (to sb/sth) 1 to stop or to allow sb/sth to go first: *Give way to traffic coming from the right.* ➲ picture at **roundabout 2** to allow sb to have what they want although you did not at first agree with it: *We shall not give way to the terrorists' demands.*

go a long way ➲ **long**[1]

go out of your way (to do sth) to make a special effort to do sth

have a long way to go ➲ **long**[1]

in a/one/any way; in some ways to a certain degree but not completely: *In some ways I prefer working in a small office.*

in a big/small way used for expressing the size or importance of an activity: *'Have you done any acting before?' 'Yes, but in a very small way* (= not very much).*'*

in the way 1 blocking the road or path: *I can't get past. There's a big lorry in the way.* **2** not needed or wanted: *I felt rather in the way at my daughter's party.*

learn the hard way ➲ **learn**

no way (*informal*) definitely not: *'Can I borrow your car?' 'No way!'*

on your/the/its ˈway coming or going: *I'd better be on my way* (= I must leave) *soon.*

the other way round ➲ **other**

out of harm's way ➲ **harm**[1]

out of the way no longer stopping sb from moving or doing sth: *I moved my legs out of the way so that she could get past.*

thread your way through sth ➲ **thread**[2]

under way having started and making progress: *Discussions between the two sides are now under way.*

a/sb's way of life the behaviour and customs that are typical of a person or group of people

way[2] /weɪ/ *adv* (*informal*) very far; very much: *I finally found his name way down the list.* ◆ *Matt's got way more experience than me.*

WC /ˌdʌblju: ˈsi:/ *abbr* **water closet;** toilet

we /wi:/ *pron* the subject of a verb; used for talking about the speaker and one or more other people: *We're going to the cinema.* ◆ *We are both going to the party.*

weak /wi:k/ *adj* (weaker; weakest)

➤NOT STRONG **1** (used about the body) having little strength or energy: *The child was weak with hunger.* ◆ *Her legs felt weak.* **2** that cannot support a lot of weight; likely to break: *That bridge is too weak to take heavy traffic.*

➤NOT POWERFUL **3** easy to influence; not firm: *He is too weak to be a good leader.* ◆ *a weak character*

➤ECONOMY **4** not having economic success: *a weak currency/economy/market*

➤NOT GOOD AT STH **5** weak (at/in/on sth) not very good at sth: *He's weak at maths.* ◆ *His maths is weak.* ◆ *a weak team* **OPP strong**

➤ARGUMENT/EXCUSE **6** not easy to believe: *She made some weak excuse about washing her hair tonight.*

➤VOICE/SMILE **7** not easy to see or hear; not definite or strong: *a weak voice* ◆ *She gave a weak smile.*

➤LIQUID **8** containing a lot of water, not strong in taste: *weak coffee* ◆ *I like my tea quite weak.* ▶ **weakly** *adv*

weaken /ˈwi:kən/ *verb* [I,T] **1** to become less strong; to make sb/sth less strong: *The illness had left her weakened.* ◆ *The building had been weakened by the earthquake.* **OPP strengthen 2** to become, or make sb become, less certain or firm about sth: *She eventually weakened and allowed him to stay.*

ˈweak form *noun* [C] a way of pronouncing a word when there is no stress on that word: *In the*

W

phrase 'bread and butter', 'and' is a weak form. OPP **strong form**

weakness /ˈwiːknəs/ *noun* **1** [U] the state of being weak: *He thought that crying was a sign of weakness.* OPP **strength** **2** [C] a fault or lack of strength, especially in sb's character: *It's important to know your own strengths and weaknesses.* OPP **strength** **3** [C, usually sing] a weakness for sth/sb a particular and often silly liking for sth/sb: *I have a weakness for chocolate.*

wealth /welθ/ *noun* **1** [U] a lot of money, property, etc. that sb owns; the state of being rich: *They were a family of enormous wealth.* SYN **riches** **2** [sing] a wealth of sth a large number or amount of sth: *a wealth of information/experience/talent*

wealthy /ˈwelθi/ *adj* (wealthier; wealthiest) having a lot of money, property, etc. SYN **rich, well-to-do** OPP **poor**

wean /wiːn/ *verb* [T] to gradually stop feeding a baby or young animal with its mother's milk and start giving it solid food

weapon /ˈwepən/ *noun* [C] an object which is used for fighting or for killing people, such as a gun, knife, bomb, etc.

wear[1] /weə(r)/ *verb* (*pt* wore /wɔː(r)/; *pp* worn /wɔːn/)

➤CLOTHES **1** [T] to have clothes, jewellery, etc. on your body: *He was wearing a suit and tie.* ♦ *I wear glasses for reading.* ➲ note at **carry**

➤EXPRESSION ON FACE **2** [T] to have a certain look on your face: *His face wore a puzzled look.*

➤DAMAGE WITH USE **3** [I,T] to become or make sth become thinner, smoother or weaker because of being used or rubbed a lot: *These tyres are badly worn.* ♦ *The soles of his shoes had worn smooth.* **4** [T] to make a hole, path, etc. in sth by rubbing, walking, etc: *Put some slippers on or you'll wear a hole in your socks!*

➤STAY IN GOOD CONDITION **5** [I] to last for a long time without becoming thinner or damaged: *This material wears well.*

IDM **wear thin** to have less effect because of being used too much: *We've heard that excuse so often that it's beginning to wear thin.*

PHR V **wear (sth) away** to damage sth or to make it disappear over a period of time, by using or touching it a lot; to disappear or become damaged in this way: *The wind had worn the soil away.*

wear (sth) down to become or to make sth smaller or smoother: *The heels on these shoes have worn right down.*

wear sb/sth down to make sb/sth weaker by attacking, persuading, etc: *They wore him down with constant arguments until he changed his mind.*

wear off to become less strong or to disappear completely: *The effects of the drug wore off after a few hours.*

wear (sth) out to become too thin or damaged to use any more; to cause sth to do this: *Children's shoes wear out very quickly.*

wear sb/yourself out to make sb/yourself very tired: *She wore herself out walking home with the heavy bags.* ➲ look at **worn out**

wear[2] /weə(r)/ *noun* [U] **1** wearing or being worn; use as clothing: *You'll need jeans and jumpers for everyday wear.* **2** [in compounds] used especially in shops to describe clothes for a particular purpose or occasion: *casual/evening/sports wear* ♦ *children's wear* **3** long use which damages the quality or appearance of sth: *The engine is checked regularly for signs of wear.*

IDM **wear and tear** the damage caused by ordinary use

the worse for wear ➲ **worse**

weary /ˈwɪəri/ *adj* (wearier; weariest) very tired, especially after you have been doing sth for a long time: *He gave a weary sigh.* ▶ **wearily** *adv* ▶ **weariness** *noun* [U]

weasel /ˈwiːzl/ *noun* [C] a small wild animal with reddish-brown fur, a long thin body and short legs

weather[1] /ˈweðə(r)/ *noun* [U] the condition of the atmosphere at a particular place and time, including how much wind, rain, sun, etc. there is, and how hot or cold it is: ***What's the weather like** where you are?* ♦ *hot/warm/sunny/fine weather* ♦ *cold/wet/windy/wintry weather* ♦ *I'm not going for a run **in this weather**!* ➲ note at **cold, fog, storm**

IDM **make heavy weather of sth** ➲ **heavy**

under the weather (*informal*) not very well

> TOPIC
>
> **Weather**
>
> Drops of water that fall from the sky are called **rain**. When it is raining a lot, it is **pouring**. When it is only raining slightly, it is **drizzling**. **Snow** is frozen rain that is soft and white. **Sleet** is rain that is not completely frozen. Small balls of ice that fall like rain are called **hail**. **Fog** is like a cloud close to the ground and is difficult to see through. When we talk about the weather, we often say 'It's a **lovely/beautiful/horrible/terrible** day (= the weather is good/bad), isn't it?' If you want to know what the weather is going to be like, you can watch or listen to the **weather forecast**.

weather[2] /ˈweðə(r)/ *verb* **1** [I,T] to change or make sth change in appearance because of the effect of the sun, air or wind: *The farmer's face was weathered by the sun.* **2** [T] to come safely through a difficult time or experience: *Their company managed to weather the recession and recover.*

ˈweather-beaten *adj* (used especially about sb's face or skin) made rough and damaged by the sun and wind

ˈweather forecast (also **forecast**) *noun* [C] a description of the weather that is expected for the next day or next few days

weave /wiːv/ *verb* [I,T] (*pt* wove /wəʊv/ *or in sense 2* weaved; *pp* woven /ˈwəʊvn/ *or in sense 2* weaved) **1** to make cloth, etc. by passing threads under and over a set of threads that is fixed to a **loom** (= a special frame or machine): *woven cloth* **2** to change direction often when you are moving so that you are

W

not stopped by anything: *The cyclist weaved in and out of the traffic.*

⚷ **web** /web/ *noun* **1** [C] a type of fine net that a spider makes in order to catch small insects: *A spider spins webs.* ➲ look at **cobweb** ➲ picture at **spider** **2 the Web** [sing] = **World Wide Web**: *I looked it up on the Web.*

webbed /webd/ *adj* [only *before* a noun] (used about the feet of some birds or animals) having the toes connected by pieces of skin ➲ picture on **page P12**

webcam (*AmE* Webcam™) /ˈwebkæm/ *noun* [C] a video camera that is connected to a computer so that what it records can be seen on a website as it happens

webcast /ˈwebkɑːst/ *noun* [C] a live broadcast that is sent out on the Internet: *We were able to watch a live webcast of the eclipse.*

webinar /ˈwebɪnɑː(r)/ *noun* [C] a live lecture, presentation, etc. that is sent out on the Internet and in which you can take part

weblog /ˈweblɒg/ = **blog**

ˈ**web page** *noun* [C] a document connected to the World Wide Web, usually forming part of a website, that anyone with an Internet connection can see: *We learned how to create and register a new web page.*

website /ˈwebsaɪt/ (also **site**) *noun* [C] a place connected to the Internet where a company, an organization or an individual person puts information: *I found it on their website.* ◆ *Visit our website to learn more.* ➲ note at **Internet**

Wed. (also **Weds.**) *abbr* = **Wednesday**: *Wed. 4 May*

we'd /wiːd/ *short for* **we had; we would**

⚷ **wedding** /ˈwedɪŋ/ *noun* [C] a marriage ceremony and often the **reception** (= the party that follows it): *I've been invited to their wedding.* ◆ *a wedding dress* ◆ *a wedding ring* (= one that is worn on the third finger to show that sb is married) ◆ *a wedding present*

TOPIC

Weddings

At a **wedding**, two people **get married**. The woman is called the **bride** and the man is the **groom** (or **bridegroom**). They are helped during the **wedding ceremony** by the **best man** and the **bridesmaids**. A wedding can take place in church (a **church wedding**) or in a **registry office**. After the ceremony there is usually a **wedding reception** (= a formal party). Many **couples** go on a **honeymoon** (= holiday) after getting married. **Marriage** refers to the relationship between a **husband** and **wife**: *They have a happy marriage.* A couple celebrate their **silver wedding anniversary** when they have been married for 25 years, their **golden wedding** after 50 years and their **diamond wedding** after 60.

wedge¹ /wedʒ/ *noun* [C] a piece of wood, etc. with one thick and one thin pointed end that you can push into a small space, for example to keep things apart: *The door was kept open with a wedge.*

wedge² /wedʒ/ *verb* [T] **1** to force sth/sb to fit into a small space: *The cupboard was wedged between the table and the door.* **2** to force sth apart or to prevent sth from moving by using a **wedge**: *to wedge a door open*

⚷ **Wednesday** /ˈwenzdeɪ; -di/ *noun* [C,U] (*abbr* **Wed.**) the day of the week after Tuesday ➲ note at **Monday**

wee /wiː/ (also ˈ**wee-wee**) *noun* [C,U] (*informal*) (used by young children or when you are talking to them) water that you pass from your body **SYN** **urine** ▸ **wee** (also ˈ**wee-wee**) *verb* [I]

weed¹ /wiːd/ *noun* **1** [C] a wild plant that is not wanted in a garden because it prevents other plants from growing properly **2** [U] a mass of very small green plants that floats on the surface of an area of water

weed² /wiːd/ *verb* [I,T] to remove **weeds** from a piece of ground, etc.

PHR V **weed sth/sb out** to remove the things or people that you do not think are good enough: *He weeded out all the letters with spelling mistakes in them.*

weedy /ˈwiːdi/ *adj* (**weedier**; **weediest**) (*informal*) small and weak: *a small weedy man*

⚷ **week** /wiːk/ *noun* [C] **1** (*abbr* **wk**) a period of seven days, especially from Monday to Sunday or from Sunday to Saturday: *We arrived* ***last week.*** ◆ *He left two weeks ago.* ◆ *I haven't seen her for a week.* ◆ *I go there twice a week.* ◆ *They'll be back in a week/in a week's time.*

MORE In British English, a period of two weeks is usually called a **fortnight**.

2 the part of the week when people go to work, etc. usually from Monday to Friday: *She works hard during the week so that she can enjoy herself at the weekend.* ◆ *I work a 40-hour week.*

IDM **today, tomorrow, Monday, etc. week** seven days after today, tomorrow, Monday, etc.

week in, week out every week without a rest or change: *He's played for the same team week in, week out for 20 years.*

a week yesterday, last Monday, etc. seven days before yesterday, Monday, etc.

weekday /ˈwiːkdeɪ/ *noun* [C] any day except Saturday or Sunday: *I only work on weekdays.* ➲ note at **routine**

⚷ **weekend** /ˌwiːkˈend/ *noun* [C] Saturday and Sunday: *What are you doing* ***at the weekend?***

HELP **At the weekend** is used in British English. In American English you say **on the weekend**.

⚷ **weekly**¹ /ˈwiːkli/ *adj, adv* happening or appearing once a week or every week: *a weekly report* ◆ *We are paid weekly.*

weekly² /ˈwiːkli/ *noun* [C] (*pl* **weeklies**) a newspaper or magazine that is published every week

W

weep /wiːp/ *verb* [I,T] (*pt, pp* **wept** /wept/) (*formal*) to let tears fall because of strong emotion; to cry: *She wept at the news of his death.*

🔑 **weigh** /weɪ/ *verb* **1** [T] to have or show a certain weight: *I weigh 56 kilos.* ◆ *How much does this weigh?* **2** [T] to measure how heavy sth is, especially by using **scales** (= a piece of equipment designed for this): *I weigh myself every week.* ◆ *Can you weigh this parcel for me, please?* **3** [T] **weigh sth (up)** to consider sth carefully: *You need to weigh up your chances of success.* **4** [T] **weigh sth (against sb/sth)** to consider if one thing is better, more important, etc. than another or not: *We shall weigh the advantages of the plan against the risks.* **5** [I] **weigh against (sb/sth)** to be considered as a disadvantage when sb/sth is being judged: *She didn't get the job because her lack of experience weighed against her.*

PHR V **weigh sb down** to make sb feel worried and sad: *He felt weighed down by all his responsibilities.*

weigh sb/sth down to make it difficult for sb/sth to move (by being heavy): *I was weighed down by heavy shopping.*

weigh on sb/sth to make sb worry: *The responsibilities* ***weigh heavily*** *on him.* ◆ *That problem has been* ***weighing on my mind*** *for a long time.*

weigh sb/sth up to consider sb/sth carefully and form an opinion: *I weighed up my chances and decided it was worth applying.*

🔑 **weight**[1] /weɪt/ *noun* (*abbr* **wt**) **1** [U] how heavy sth/sb is; the fact of being heavy: *The doctor advised him to* ***lose weight*** (= become thinner and less heavy). ◆ *He's* ***put on weight*** (= got fatter). ◆ *The weight of the snow broke the branch.* **2** [C] a heavy object: *The doctor has told me not to lift heavy weights.* **3** [C] a piece of metal that weighs a known amount that can be used to measure an amount of sth, or that can be lifted as a form of exercise: *a 500-gram weight* ◆ *She lifts weights in the gym as part of her daily training.* **4** [sing] something that you are worried about: *Telling her the truth took* ***a weight off*** *his* ***mind***.

IDM **carry weight** ➲ **carry**

pull your weight ➲ **pull**[1]

weight[2] /weɪt/ *verb* [T] **1** **weight sth (down) (with sth)** to hold sth down with a heavy object or objects: *to weight down a fishing net* **2** [usually passive] to organize sth so that a particular person or group has an advantage/disadvantage: *The system is* ***weighted in favour of/against*** *people with children.*

weightless /ˈweɪtləs/ *adj* having no weight, for example when travelling in space ▶ **weightlessness** *noun* [U]

weightlifting /ˈweɪtlɪftɪŋ/ *noun* [U] a sport in which heavy metal objects are lifted ➲ picture on page P4 ▶ **weightlifter** *noun* [C]

ˈ**weight training** *noun* [U] the activity of lifting weights as a form of exercise: *I* ***do weight training*** *to keep fit.*

weighty /ˈweɪti/ *adj* (**weightier; weightiest**) serious and important: *a weighty question*

weir /wɪə(r)/ *noun* [C] a type of wall that is built across a river to stop or change the direction of the flow of water

weird /wɪəd/ *adj* (**weirder; weirdest**) strange and unusual: *a weird noise/experience* **SYN** **bizarre, strange** ▶ **weirdly** *adv*

weirdo /ˈwɪədəʊ/ *noun* [C] (*pl* **weirdos** /-əʊz/) (*informal*) a person who looks strange and/or behaves in a strange way: *I wouldn't go into that bar—it's full of weirdos.*

🔑 **welcome**[1] /ˈwelkəm/ *verb* [T] **1** to be friendly to sb when they arrive somewhere: *Everyone came to the door to welcome us.* **2** to be pleased to receive or accept sth: *I've no idea what to do next, so I'd welcome any suggestions.* ▶ **welcome** *noun* [C]: *Let's give a warm welcome to our next guest.*

🔑 **welcome**[2] /ˈwelkəm/ *adj* **1** received with pleasure; giving pleasure: *You're always welcome here.* ◆ *welcome news* **2** **welcome to sth/to do sth** allowed to do sth: *You're welcome to use my bicycle.* **3** used to say that sb can have sth that you do not want yourself: *Take the car if you want. You're welcome to it. It's always breaking down.*

IDM **make sb welcome** to receive sb in a friendly way

you're welcome (*spoken*) you do not need to thank me: *'Thank you for your help.' 'You're welcome.'*

▶ **welcome** *exclam*: *Welcome to London!* ◆ *Welcome home!*

weld /weld/ *verb* [I,T] to join pieces of metal by heating them and pressing them together

welfare /ˈwelfeə(r)/ *noun* [U] **1** the general health, happiness and safety of a person, an animal or a group: *The doctor is concerned about the child's welfare.* **SYN** **well-being** **2** the help and care that is given to people who have problems with health, money, etc: *education and welfare services* **3** (*AmE*) = **social security**

ˌ**welfare ˈstate** *noun* [sing] a system organized by a government to provide free services and money for people who have no job, who are ill, etc.; a country that has this system

we'll /wiːl/ *short for* **we shall; we will**

🔑 **well**[1] /wel/ *adv* (**better; best**) **1** in a good way: *You speak English very well.* ◆ *I hope your work is* ***going well***. ◆ *You passed your exam!* ***Well done!*** ◆ *He took it well when I told him he wasn't on the team.* **OPP** **badly** **2** completely or fully: *Shake the bottle well before opening.* ◆ *How well do you know Henry?* **3** very much: *They arrived home well past midnight.* ◆ *She says she's 32 but I'm sure she's well over 40.* ◆ *This book is* ***well worth*** *reading.* **4** [used with *can, could, may* or *might*] probably or possibly: *He might well be right.* **5** [used with *can, could, may* or *might*] with good reason: *I can't very well refuse to help them after all they've done for me.* ◆ *'Where's Bill?' 'You may well ask!* (= I don't know either)*'*

IDM **as well (as sb/sth)** in addition to sb/sth: *Can I come as well?* ◆ *He's worked in Japan as well as Italy.* ➲ note at **also**

augur well/ill for sb/sth ➲ **augur**

bode well/ill (for sb/sth) ➲ **bode**

do well **1** to be successful: *Their daughter has done*

W

well at university. **2** to be getting better after an illness: *Mr Singh is doing well after his operation.*

do well to do sth used to say that sth is the right and sensible thing to do: *He would do well to check the facts before accusing people.*

it is just as well (that ...) ➲ **just**[1]

may/might as well (do sth) used for saying that sth is the best thing you can do in the situation, even though you may not want to do it: *I may as well tell you the truth—you'll find out anyway.*

mean well ➲ **mean**[1]

well and truly completely: *We were well and truly lost.*

well/badly off ➲ **off**[1]

⚷ **well**[2] /wel/ *adj* (**better** /ˈbetə(r)/, **best** /best/) [not before a noun] **1** in good health: *'How are you?' 'I'm very well, thanks.'* ◆ *This medicine will make you **feel better**.* ◆ ***Get well soon*** (= written in a card that you send to sb who is ill). **2** in a good state: *I hope all is well with you.*

IDM **all very well (for sb)** (*informal*) used for showing that you are not happy or do not agree with sth: *It's all very well for her to criticize* (= it's easy for her to criticize) *but it doesn't help the situation.*

be (just) as well (to do sth) to be sensible; to be a good idea: *It would be just as well to ask his permission.*

OTHER WORDS FOR

well

There are various answers to the question 'How are you?'. The most positive replies are: *I'm very well.* ◆ *I'm **great**.* ◆ *I'm **good**.* Other ways to say 'I'm well' are: *I'm **OK**.* ◆ *I'm **fine**.* If you are not feeling so well you can say: *I'm **not (too) bad**.* ◆ ***So-so**.*

⚷ **well**[3] /wel/ *exclam* **1** used for showing surprise: *Well, thank goodness you've arrived.* **2** (also **oh well**) used for showing that you know there is nothing you can do to change a situation: *Oh well, there's nothing we can do.* **3** used when you begin the next part of a story or when you are thinking about what to say next: *Well, the next thing that happened was ...* ◆ *Well now, let me see ...* **4** used when you feel uncertain about sth: *'Do you like it?' 'Well, I'm not really sure.'* **5** used to show that you are waiting for sb to say sth: *Well? Are you going to tell us what happened?* **6** used to show that you want to finish a conversation: *Well, it's been nice talking to you.*

well[4] /wel/ *noun* [C] **1** a deep hole in the ground from which water is obtained: *to draw water from a well* **2** = **oil well**

well[5] /wel/ *verb* [I] **well (out/up)** (used about a liquid) to come to the surface: *Tears welled up in her eyes.*

ˌwell ˈbalanced *adj* **1** (used about a meal, etc.) containing enough of the healthy types of food your body needs: *a well-balanced diet* **2** (used about a person) calm and sensible: *His response was well balanced.*

ˌwell beˈhaved *adj* behaving in a way that most people think is correct

ˈwell-being *noun* [U] a state of being healthy and happy

ˌwell ˈdone *adj* (used about meat, etc.) cooked for a long time ➲ look at **rare**, **medium**

ˌwell ˈdressed *adj* wearing attractive and fashionable clothes

ˌwell ˈearned *adj* that you deserve, especially because you have been working hard: *She's having a well-earned holiday.*

ˌwell ˈfed *adj* having good food regularly

ˌwell inˈformed *adj* knowing a lot about one or several subjects

wellington /ˈwelɪŋtən/ (also *informal* **welly**, *AmE* ˌ**rubber ˈboot**) *noun* [C] (*BrE*) one of a pair of long rubber boots that you wear to keep your feet and the lower part of your legs dry: *a pair of wellingtons* ◆ *It's very muddy—you'll need your wellingtons.* ➲ picture at **shoe**

ˌwell ˈkept *adj* looked after very carefully so that it has a tidy appearance: *a well-kept garden*

⚷ **ˌwell ˈknown** *adj* known by a lot of people **SYN** **famous** **OPP** **unknown**

ˌwell ˈmeaning *adj* (used about a person) wanting to be kind or helpful, but often not having this effect

ˌwell ˈmeant *adj* intended to be kind or helpful but not having this result

ˌwell ˈpaid *adj* earning or providing a lot of money: *well-paid doctors* ◆ *This job is not very well paid.*

ˌwell-to-ˈdo *adj* having a lot of money, property, etc. **SYN** **rich, wealthy**

ˈwell-wisher *noun* [C] a person who hopes that sb/sth will be successful: *She received lots of letters from well-wishers.*

welly /ˈweli/ (*pl* **wellies**) (*BrE informal*) = **wellington**

Welsh /welʃ/ *adj* from Wales ℹ For more information, look at the section on geographical names at the back of this dictionary.

went *past tense* of **go**[1]

wept *past tense, past participle* of **weep**

were /wə(r); *strong form* wɜː(r)/ ➲ **be**

we're /wɪə(r)/ *short for* **we are**

weren't /wɜːnt/ *short for* **were not**

⚷ **west**[1] /west/ *noun* [U, sing] (*abbr* W) **1** (also **the west**) the direction you look towards in order to see the sun go down; one of the four **points of the compass** (= the main directions that we give names to): *Which way is west?* ◆ *Rain is spreading from the west.* ◆ *There's a road **to the west of*** (= further west than) *here.* ➲ picture at **compass** **2 the West** the part of any country, city, etc. that is further to the west than other parts: *I live in the west of Scotland.* ◆ *The climate in the West is much wetter than the East.* **3 the West** [sing] the countries of North America

W

and Western Europe: *I was born in Japan, but I've lived in the West for some years now.*

west² /west/ *adj, adv* **1** (also West) [only *before* a noun] in the west: *West London* **2** (used about a wind) coming from the west **3** to or towards the west: *to travel west* ♦ *The island is five miles west of here.*

westbound /ˈwestbaʊnd/ *adj* travelling or leading towards the west: *the westbound carriageway of the motorway*

westerly /ˈwestəli/ *adj* **1** [only *before* a noun] to, towards or in the west: *in a westerly direction* **2** (used about winds) coming from the west

western¹ (also Western) /ˈwestən/ *adj* **1** [only *before* a noun] (*abbr* W) in or of the west: *western France* **2** from or connected with the western part of the world, especially Europe or North America: *Western art*

western² /ˈwestən/ *noun* [C] a film or book about life in the past in the west of the United States

westerner /ˈwestənə(r)/ *noun* [C] a person who was born or who lives in the western part of the world, especially Europe or North America: *Westerners arriving in China usually experience culture shock.*

westernize (also -ise) /ˈwestənaɪz/ *verb* [T, usually passive] to make a country or people more like Europe and North America: *Young people in our country are becoming westernized through watching American TV programmes.*

the West ˈIndies *noun* [pl] a group of islands in the Caribbean Sea that consists of the Bahamas, the Antilles and the Leeward and Windward Islands ▶ **West ˈIndian** *noun* [C]: *The West Indians won their match against Australia.* ▶ **West ˈIndian** *adj*

westwards /ˈwestwədz/ (also westward) *adv* towards the west: *to fly westwards* ▶ **westward** *adj*: *in a westward direction*

wet¹ /wet/ *adj* (wetter; wettest) **1** covered in a liquid, especially water: *wet clothes/hair/grass/roads* ♦ *Don't **get** your feet **wet**.* OPP **dry**

> MORE **Moist** means slightly wet. **Damp** is used to describe things that are slightly wet and feel unpleasant because of it: *Don't sit on the grass. It's damp.* **Humid** is used about weather or the air when it feels warm and damp.

2 (used about the weather, etc.) with a lot of rain: *a wet day* OPP **dry** **3** (used about paint, etc.) not yet dry or hard: *The ink is still wet.* OPP **dry** **4** (used about a person) without energy or enthusiasm: *'Don't be so wet,' she laughed.*

IDM **a wet blanket** (*informal*) a person who spoils other people's fun, especially because they refuse to take part in sth

wet through extremely wet

▶ **the wet** *noun* [sing]: *Come in out of the wet* (= the rain).

wet² /wet/ *verb* [T] (wetting; *pt, pp* wet or wetted) **1** to make sth wet **2** (used especially of young children) to make yourself or your bed, clothes, etc. wet by letting **urine** (= waste liquid) escape from your body

wetsuit /ˈwetsuːt/ *noun* [C] a piece of clothing made of rubber that fits the whole body closely, worn by people swimming underwater or sailing

wetted *past tense, past participle* of **wet²**

we've /wiːv/ *short for* **we have**

whack /wæk/ *verb* [T] (*informal*) to hit sb/sth hard

whacky = **wacky**

whale /weɪl/ *noun* [C] a very large animal that lives in the sea and looks like a very large fish ➲ picture on **page P12**

whaling /ˈweɪlɪŋ/ *noun* [U] the hunting of **whales**

wharf /wɔːf/ *noun* [C] (*pl* wharves /wɔːvz/) a platform made of stone or wood at the side of a river where ships and boats can be tied up

what /wɒt/ *determiner, pron* **1** used for asking for information about sb/sth: *What time is it?* ♦ *What kind of music do you like?* ♦ *She asked him what he was doing.* ♦ *What's their phone number?* ➲ note at **which** **2** the thing or things that have been mentioned or said: *What he says is true.* ♦ *I haven't got much, but you can borrow what money I have.* **3** used for emphasizing sth: *What strange eyes she's got!* ♦ *What a kind thing to do!* ♦ *What awful weather!*

IDM **how/what about ...?** ➲ **about²**

what? used to express surprise or to tell sb to say or repeat sth: *'I've asked Alice to marry me.' 'What?'*

what for? for what purpose or reason: *What's this little switch for?* ♦ *What did you say that for* (= why did you say that)*?*

what if ...? what would happen if ...?: *What if the car breaks down?*

what's up? ➲ **up**

whatever /wɒtˈevə(r)/ *determiner, pron, adv* **1** any or every; anything or everything: *You can say whatever you like.* ♦ *He took whatever help he could get.* **2** used to say that it does not matter what happens or what sb does, because the result will be the same: *I still love you, whatever you may think.* ♦ *Whatever she says, she doesn't really mean it.* **3** (used for expressing surprise or worry) what: *Whatever could have happened to them?* **4** (also whatsoever /wɒtsəʊˈevə(r)/) at all: *I've no reason whatever to doubt him.* ♦ *'Any questions?' 'None whatsoever.'*

IDM **or whatever** (*informal*) or any other or others of a similar kind: *You don't need to wear anything smart—jeans and a sweater or whatever.*

whatever you do used to emphasize that sb must not do sth: *Don't touch the red switch, whatever you do.*

wheat /wiːt/ *noun* [U] **1** a type of grain which can be made into flour **2** the plant which produces this grain: *a field of wheat* ➲ picture at **ear**

wheel¹ /wiːl/ *noun* [C] **1** one of the round objects under a car, bicycle, etc. that turns when it moves: *His favourite toy is a dog on wheels.* ♦ *By law, you* *have to carry a spare wheel in your car.* ➲ picture at **bicycle** ➲ picture on **page P7** **2** [usually sing] = **steering wheel**: *Her husband was* ***at the wheel*** (= he was driving) *when the accident happened.* **3** a flat round part in a machine: *gear wheels*

wheel² /wiːl/ *verb* **1** [T] to push along an object that has wheels; to move sb about in/on a vehicle with wheels: *He wheeled his bicycle up the hill.* ◆ *She was wheeled back to her bed on a trolley.* **2** [I] to fly round in circles: *Birds wheeled above the ship.* **3** [I] to turn round suddenly: *Eleanor wheeled round, with a look of horror on her face.*

wheelbarrow /ˈwiːlbærəʊ/ (also **barrow**) *noun* [C] a type of small open container with one wheel and two handles that you use outside for carrying things ➲ picture at **garden**

wheelchair /ˈwiːltʃeə(r)/ *noun* [C] a chair with large wheels that a person who cannot walk can move or be pushed about in ➲ picture at **chair**

ˈwheel clamp = **clamp²**(2)

wheeze /wiːz/ *verb* [I] to breathe noisily, for example if you have a chest illness

⚷ **when** /wen/ *adv, conj* **1** at what time: *When did she arrive?* ◆ *I don't know when she arrived.* **2** used for talking about the time at which sth happens or happened: *Sunday is the day when I can relax.* ◆ *I last saw her in May, when she was in London.* ◆ *He jumped up when the phone rang.*

> **GRAMMAR** Notice that we use the present tense after **when** if we are talking about a future time: *I'll call you when I'm ready.*

3 since; as; considering that: *Why do you want more money when you've got enough already?*

> **GRAMMAR** **When** is used for talking about something that you think or know will happen, but **if** is used for something you are not sure will happen. Compare: *I'll ask her when she comes* (= you are sure that she will come). ◆ *I'll ask her if she comes* (= you are not sure if she will come or not).

⚷ **whenever** /wenˈevə(r)/ *conj, adv* **1** at any time; no matter when: *You can borrow my car whenever you want.* ◆ *Don't worry. You can give it back the next time you see me, or whenever.* **2** (used in questions when you are showing that you are surprised or impatient) when: *Whenever did you find time to do all that cooking?*

⚷ **where** /weə(r)/ *adv, conj* **1** in or to what place or position: *Where can I buy a paper?* ◆ *I asked him where he lived.* **2** in or to the place or situation mentioned: *the town where you were born* ◆ *She ran to where they were standing.* ◆ *Where possible, you should travel by bus, not taxi.* ◆ *We came to a village, where we stopped for lunch.* ◆ ***Where*** *maths* ***is concerned,*** *I'm hopeless.*

whereabouts¹ /ˈweərəbaʊts/ *noun* [U, with sing or pl verb] the place where sb/sth is: *The whereabouts of the stolen painting is unknown.*

whereabouts² /ˌweərəˈbaʊts/ *adv* where; in or near what place: *Whereabouts did you lose your purse?*

⚷ **whereas** /ˌweərˈæz/ *conj* used for showing a fact that is different: *He eats meat, whereas she's a vegetarian.* **SYN** **while**

whereby /weəˈbaɪ/ *adv* (*formal*) by which; because of which: *These countries have an agreement whereby foreign visitors can have free medical care.*

whereupon /ˌweərəˈpɒn/ *conj* (*formal*) after which: *He fell asleep, whereupon she walked quietly from the room.*

⚷ **wherever** /weərˈevə(r)/ *conj, adv* **1** in or to any place: *You can sit wherever you like.* ◆ *She comes from Omiya, wherever that is* (= I do not know where it is). **2** everywhere, in all places that: *Wherever I go, he goes.* **3** used in questions for showing surprise: *Wherever did you learn to cook like that?*
IDM **or wherever** or any other place: *The students might be from Sweden, Denmark or wherever.*

whet /wet/ *verb* (**whetting**; **whetted**)
IDM **whet sb's appetite** to make sb want more of sth: *Our short stay in Prague whetted our appetite to spend more time there.*

⚷ **whether** /ˈweðə(r)/ *conj* **1** [used after verbs like *ask, doubt, know,* etc.] if: *He asked me whether we would be coming to the party.* **2** used for expressing a choice or doubt between two or more possibilities: *I can't make up my mind* ***whether*** *to go* ***or not***.

> **GRAMMAR** **Whether** and **if** can both be used in sense 1. Only **whether** can be used before 'to' + verb: *Have you decided* ***whether to*** *accept the offer yet?* Only **whether** can be used after a preposition: *the problem* ***of whether*** *to accept the offer.*

IDM **whether or not** used to say that sth will be true in either of the situations that are mentioned: *We shall play on Saturday whether it rains or not.* ◆ *Whether or not it rains, we shall play on Saturday.*

⚷ **which** /wɪtʃ/ *determiner, pron* **1** used in questions to ask sb to be exact, when there are a number of people or things to choose from: *Which hand do you write with?* ◆ *Which is your bag?* ◆ *She asked me which book I preferred.* ◆ *I can't remember which of the boys is the older.*

> **GRAMMAR** **Which** or **what**? We use **which** when there is only a limited group or number to choose from: *Which car is yours? The Toyota or the BMW?* (= there are only two cars there). We use **what** when the group is not limited: *What car would you choose* (= of all the makes of car that exist), *if you could have any one you wanted?* ◆ *What is your name?*

2 used for saying exactly what thing or things you are talking about: *Cars which use unleaded petrol are more eco-friendly.* ◆ *The situation* ***which*** *he found himself* ***in*** *was very difficult.*

W

HELP In formal English we write: *The situation* **in which** *he found himself was very difficult.*

GRAMMAR In the example above, the words 'which use unleaded petrol' give us *essential* (= necessary) information about the cars. This part of the sentence after **which** is called a **defining relative clause.** We can also use **that**: *Cars that use unleaded petrol ...* There is NO comma before **which** or **that** in these sentences.

ℹ For more information about defining relative clauses, look at the **Reference Section** at the back of this dictionary. **3** used for giving more information about a thing or an animal: *My first car, which I bought as a student, was a Renault.*

GRAMMAR In the example above, the words 'which I bought as a student' give us *extra* information about the car. This part of the sentence after **which** is called a **non-defining relative clause.** We CANNOT use **that** in sentences like this. Note that there is a comma (,) before 'which' and at the end of the part of the sentence which it introduces.

ℹ For more information about non-defining relative clauses, look at the **Reference Section** at the back of this dictionary. **4** used for making a comment on what has just been said: *We had to wait 16 hours for our plane, which was really annoying.*

HELP Note that there is a comma before 'which'.

whichever /wɪtʃˈevə(r)/ *determiner, pron* **1** used to say what feature or quality is important in deciding sth: *Whichever song gets the most votes will win.* ◆ *Pensions should be increased annually in line with earnings or prices, whichever is the higher.* **2** used to say that it does not matter which, as the result will be the same: *It takes three hours, whichever route you take.* **3** (used for expressing surprise) which: *You're very late. Whichever way did you come?*

whiff /wɪf/ *noun* [usually sing] **a whiff (of sth)** a smell, especially one which only lasts for a short time: *He* ***caught a whiff*** *of her perfume.*

⚷ **while¹** /waɪl/ (also *formal* **whilst** /waɪlst/) *conj* **1** during the time that; when: *He always phones while we're having lunch.* **2** at the same time as: *He always listens to the radio while he's driving to work.* **3** (*formal*) used when you are contrasting two ideas: *Some countries are rich, while others are extremely poor.* **SYN** **whereas** ➲ note at **difference**

⚷ **while²** /waɪl/ *noun* [sing] a (usually short) period of time: *Let's sit down here for a while.*
IDM **once in a while** ➲ **once**
worth sb's while ➲ **worth¹**

while³ /waɪl/ *verb*
PHR V **while sth away** to pass time in a lazy or relaxed way: *We whiled away the evening chatting and listening to music.*

whim /wɪm/ *noun* [C] a sudden idea or desire to do sth (often sth that is unusual or not necessary): *I bought a guitar* ***on a whim.***

whimper /ˈwɪmpə(r)/ *verb* [I] to make weak crying sounds, especially with fear or pain ▶ **whimper** *noun* [C]

whine /waɪn/ *verb* **1** [I,T] to complain about sth in an annoying, crying voice: *The children were whining all afternoon.* **2** [I] to make a long high unpleasant sound because you are in pain or unhappy: *The dog is whining to go out.* ▶ **whine** *noun* [C]

whip¹ /wɪp/ *noun* [C] **1** a long thin piece of leather, etc. with a handle, that is used for making animals go faster and for hitting people as a punishment: *He* ***cracked the whip*** *and the horse leapt forward.* **2** (in Britain and the US) an official of a political party who makes sure that all members vote in parliament on important matters

whip² /wɪp/ *verb* (**whipping**; **whipped**)
➤HIT PERSON/ANIMAL **1** [T] to hit a person or an animal hard with a **whip**, as a punishment or to make them or it go faster or work harder
➤MOVE QUICKLY **2** [I] (*informal*) to move quickly, suddenly or violently: *She whipped round to see what had made the noise behind her.* **3** [T] to remove or pull sth quickly and suddenly: *He whipped out a pen and made a note of the number.*
➤MIX **4** [T] **whip sth (up)** to mix the white part of an egg, cream, etc. until it is stiff: *whipped cream*
➤STEAL **5** [T] (*BrE informal*) to steal sth: *Who's whipped my pen?*
PHR V **whip through sth** (*informal*) to do or finish sth very quickly: *I whipped through my homework in ten minutes.*
whip sb/sth up to deliberately try to make people excited or feel strongly about sth: *to whip up excitement*
whip sth up (*informal*) to prepare food quickly: *to whip up a quick snack*

whir (*especially AmE*) = **whirr**

whirl¹ /wɜːl/ *verb* [I,T] to move, or to make sb/sth move, round and round very quickly in a circle: *The dancers whirled round the room.* ◆ (*figurative*) *I couldn't sleep. My mind was whirling after all the excitement.*

whirl² /wɜːl/ *noun* [sing] **1** the action or sound of sth moving round and round very quickly: *the whirl of the helicopter's blades* **2** a state of confusion or excitement: *My head's* ***in a whirl****—I'm so excited.* **3** a number of events or activities happening one after the other: *The next few days passed in a whirl of activity.*
IDM **give sth a whirl** (*informal*) to try sth to see if you like it or can do it

whirlpool /ˈwɜːlpuːl/ *noun* [C] a place in a river or the sea where currents in the water move very quickly round in a circle

whirlwind /ˈwɜːlwɪnd/ *noun* [C] a very strong wind that moves very fast in a circle **SYN** **tornado**

whirr (*especially AmE* **whir**) /wɜː(r)/ *verb* [I] to make a continuous low sound like the parts of a machine moving: *The noise of the fan whirring kept* *me awake.* ▶ **whirr** (*especially AmE* **whir**) *noun* [C, usually sing]

whisk¹ /wɪsk/ *verb* [T] **1** to beat or mix eggs, cream, etc. very fast using a fork or a **whisk**: *Whisk the egg whites until stiff.* **SYN** **beat** **2** to take sb/sth somewhere very quickly: *The prince was whisked away in a black limousine.*

whisk² /wɪsk/ *noun* [C] a tool that you use for beating eggs, cream, etc. very fast ➲ picture at **kitchen, mixer**

whisker /ˈwɪskə(r)/ *noun* [C] one of the long thick hairs that grow near the mouth of some animals such as a mouse, cat, etc. ➲ picture on **page P12**

whisky /ˈwɪski/ *noun* (*pl* **whiskies**) **HELP** In the US and Ireland the spelling is **whiskey**. **1** [U] a strong alcoholic drink that is made from grain and is sometimes drunk with water and/or ice: *Scotch whisky* **2** [C] a glass of **whisky**

⚷ **whisper** /ˈwɪspə(r)/ *verb* [I,T] to speak very quietly into sb's ear, so that other people cannot hear what you are saying: *She whispered something in his ear.* ♦ *What are you two whispering about?* ▶ **whisper** *noun* [C]: *to speak* ***in a whisper***

⚷ **whistle¹** /ˈwɪsl/ *noun* [C] **1** a small metal or plastic tube that you blow into to make a long high sound: *The referee blew his whistle to stop the game.* **2** the sound made by blowing a **whistle** or by blowing air out between your lips: *United scored just moments before* ***the final whistle.*** ♦ *He gave a low whistle of surprise.* **3** a sound made by air or steam being forced through a small opening, or by sth moving quickly through the air: *the whistle of a boiling kettle*

whistle

⚷ **whistle²** /ˈwɪsl/ *verb* **1** [I,T] to make a musical or a high sound by forcing air out between your lips or by blowing a **whistle**: *He whistled a tune to himself.* **2** [I] to move somewhere quickly making a sound like a **whistle**: *A bullet whistled past his head.*

⚷ **white¹** /waɪt/ *adj* (**whiter; whitest**) **1** having the very light colour of fresh snow or milk: *a white shirt* ♦ *white coffee* (= with milk) ♦ *white bread* **2** (used about a person) belonging to or connected with a race of people who have pale skin: *white middle-class families* **3 white (with sth)** (used about a person) very pale because you are ill, afraid, etc: *to be white with shock/anger/fear* ♦ *She went* ***white as a sheet*** *when they told her the news.*
IDM **black and white** ➲ **black¹**

⚷ **white²** /waɪt/ *noun* **1** [U] the very light colour of fresh snow or milk: *She was dressed* ***in white.*** **2** [C, usually pl] a member of a race of people with pale skin **3** [C,U] the part of an egg that surrounds the **yolk** (= the yellow part) and that becomes white when it is cooked: *Beat the whites of four eggs.* ➲ picture at **egg** **4** [C] the white part of the eye: *The whites of her eyes were bloodshot.*
IDM **in black and white** ➲ **black²**

whiteboard /ˈwaɪtbɔːd/ a large board with a smooth white surface that teachers, etc. write on with special pens ➲ look at **interactive whiteboard**

ˌwhite-ˈcollar *adj* (used about work) done in an office not a factory; (used about people) who work in an office ➲ look at **blue-collar**

ˌwhite ˈelephant *noun* [usually sing] something that you no longer need and that is not useful any more, although it cost a lot of money

the ˈWhite House *noun* [sing] **1** the large house in Washington D.C. where the US president lives and works **2** used to refer to the US president and the other people in the government who work with him or her

ˌwhite ˈlie *noun* [C] a lie that is not very harmful or serious, especially one that you tell because the truth would hurt sb

whitewash¹ /ˈwaɪtwɒʃ/ *noun* **1** [U] a white liquid that you use for painting walls **2** [sing] an attempt to try to hide unpleasant facts about sb/sth: *The opposition say the report is a whitewash.*

whitewash² /ˈwaɪtwɒʃ/ *verb* [T] **1** to paint **whitewash** onto a wall **2** to try to hide sth bad or wrong that you have done

ˌwhite-water ˈrafting *noun* [U] the sport of travelling in a rubber boat down a section of a river where water is moving very fast ➲ picture on **page P5**

whizz¹ (*especially AmE* **whiz**) /wɪz/ *verb* [I] (*informal*) to move very quickly, often making a high continuous sound: *The racing cars went whizzing past.*

whizz² (*especially AmE* **whiz**) /wɪz/ *noun* [C] (*informal*) a person who is very good and successful at sth: *She's a whizz at crosswords.* ♦ *He's our new marketing* ***whizz-kid*** (= a young person who is very good at sth).

⚷ **who** /huː/ *pron* **1** used in questions to ask sb's name, identity, position, etc: *Who was on the phone?* ♦ *Who's that woman in the grey suit?* ♦ *She wondered who he was.* **2** used for saying exactly which person or what kind of person you are talking about: *I like people who say what they think.* ♦ *That's the man who I met at Ann's party.* ♦ *The woman who I work for is very nice.*

> **GRAMMAR** In the last two examples (= when 'who' is the object, or when it is used with a preposition) 'who' is usually left out: *That's the man I met at Ann's party.* ♦ *The woman I work for is very nice.*

3 used for giving extra information about sb: *My grandmother, who's over 80, still drives a car.* ➲ note at **whom**

> **GRAMMAR** Note that the extra information you give is separated from the main clause by commas.

who'd /huːd/ *short for* **who had; who would**

W

whoever /huːˈevə(r)/ *pron* **1** the person or people who; any person who: *I want to speak to whoever is in charge.* **2** it does not matter who: *She doesn't want to see anybody—whoever it is.* **3** (used for expressing surprise) who: *Whoever could have done that?*

whole¹ /həʊl/ *adj* **1** [only *before* a noun] complete; full: *I drank a whole bottle of water.* ♦ *Let's just forget* ***the whole thing.*** ♦ *She wasn't telling me the* ***whole truth.*** **2** not broken or cut: *Snakes swallow their prey whole* (= in one piece). ➲ *adverb* **wholly**

whole² /həʊl/ *noun* [C] **1** a thing that is complete or full in itself: *Two halves make a whole.* **2 the whole of sth** all that there is of sth: *I spent the whole of the morning cooking.*

IDM **as a whole** as one complete thing or unit and not as separate parts: *This is true in Britain, but also in Europe as a whole.*

on the whole generally, but not true in every case: *On the whole I think it's a very good idea.*

wholefood /ˈhəʊlfuːd/ *noun* [U] (also [pl] **wholefoods**) food that is considered healthy because it does not contain artificial substances and is produced as naturally as possible

wholehearted /ˌhəʊlˈhɑːtɪd/ *adj* complete and enthusiastic: *to give somebody your wholehearted support* ▶ **wholeheartedly** *adv*

wholemeal /ˈhəʊlmiːl/ (also **wholewheat** /ˈhəʊlwiːt/) *adj* (made from flour) that contains all the grain including the outside layer: *wholemeal bread/flour*

wholesale /ˈhəʊlseɪl/ *adv, adj* [only *before* a noun] **1** connected with buying and selling goods in large quantities, especially in order to sell them again and make a profit: *They get all their building materials wholesale.* ♦ *wholesale goods/prices* ➲ look at **retail** **2** (usually about sth bad) very great; on a very large scale: *the wholesale slaughter of wildlife*

wholesome /ˈhəʊlsəm/ *adj* **1** good for your health: *simple wholesome food* **2** having a moral effect that is good: *clean wholesome fun*

who'll /huːl/ *short for* **who will**

wholly /ˈhəʊlli/ *adv* (*formal*) completely; fully: *George is not wholly to blame for the situation.*

W

whom /huːm/ *pron* (*formal*) used instead of 'who' as the object of a verb or preposition: *Whom did you meet there?* ♦ *He asked me whom I had met.* ♦ *To whom am I speaking?*

> **HELP** In very formal English we say 'He asked me **with whom** I had discussed it'. We usually say 'He asked me **who** I had discussed it **with**'.

whooping cough /ˈhuːpɪŋ kɒf/ *noun* [U] a serious disease, especially of children, which makes them cough loudly and not be able to breathe easily

whoops /wʊps/ *exclam* used when you have, or nearly have, a small accident, or say or do sth embarrassing: *Whoops! I nearly dropped the cup.*

whoosh /wʊʃ/ *noun* [C, usually sing] (*informal*) the sudden movement and sound of air or water going past very fast ▶ **whoosh** *verb* [I]

who're /ˈhuːə(r)/ *short for* **who are**

who's /huːz/ *short for* **who is; who has**

whose /huːz/ *determiner, pron* **1** (used in questions to ask who sth belongs to) of whom?: *Whose car is that?* ♦ *Whose is that car?* ♦ *Those are nice shoes —I wonder whose they are.* **2** (used to say exactly which person or thing you mean, or to give extra information about a person or thing) of whom; of which: *That's the boy whose mother I met.* ♦ *My neighbours, whose house is up for sale, are splitting up.*

> **GRAMMAR** When using 'whose' to give extra information about a person or thing, you should separate that part of the sentence from the main clause with commas.

who've /huːv/ *short for* **who have**

why /waɪ/ *adv* **1** for what reason: *Why was she so late?* ♦ *I wonder why they went.* ♦ *'I'm not staying any longer.' 'Why not?'* **2** used for giving or talking about a reason for sth: ***The reason why*** *I'm leaving you is obvious.* ♦ *I'm tired and* ***that's why*** *I'm in such a bad mood.*

IDM **why ever** used to show that you are surprised or angry: *Why ever didn't you phone?*

why not? used for making or agreeing to a suggestion: *Why not phone her tonight?* ♦ *'Shall we go out tonight?' 'Yes, why not?'*

wick /wɪk/ *noun* [C] the piece of string that burns in the middle of a **candle** (= a tall stick that you burn to give light) ➲ picture at **candle**

wicked /ˈwɪkɪd/ *adj* (**wickeder**; **wickedest**) [You can also use **more wicked** and **most wicked**.] **1** morally bad; evil **2** (*informal*) slightly bad but in a way that is amusing and/or attractive: *a wicked sense of humour* **3** (*slang*) very good: *This song's wicked.* ▶ **wickedly** *adv* ▶ **wickedness** *noun* [U]

wicker /ˈwɪkə(r)/ *noun* [U] thin sticks of wood that bend easily and are crossed over and under each other to make furniture and other objects: *a wicker basket* ➲ picture at **basket**

wicket /ˈwɪkɪt/ *noun* [C] **1** (in the sport of **cricket**) either of the two sets of three vertical sticks that the player throwing the ball tries to hit ➲ picture on **page P4** **2** (in the sport of **cricket**) the area of ground between the two **wickets**

wide /waɪd/ *adj* (**wider**; **widest**)

➤MEASUREMENT **1** measuring a lot from one side to the other: *The road was not wide enough for two cars to pass.* ♦ *a wide river* OPP **narrow** ➲ note at **broad** **2** measuring a particular distance from one side to the other: *The box was only 20 centimetres wide.* ♦ *How wide is the river?* ➲ *noun* **width**

➤LARGE NUMBER/AMOUNT **3** including a large number or variety of different people or things; covering a large area: *You're the nicest person in* ***the whole wide world!*** ♦ *a* ***wide range/choice/variety*** *of goods* ♦ *a manager with wide experience of industry*

➤OPEN **4** fully open: *The children's eyes were wide with excitement.*
➤NOT NEAR **5** not near what you wanted to touch or hit: *His first serve was wide* (for example in tennis). ▶ **wide** *adv*: *Open your mouth wide.* ◆ *It was late but she was still* ***wide awake.***

🔑 **widely** /ˈwaɪdli/ *adv* by a lot of people; in or to many places: *Steve travelled widely in his youth.* ◆ *Her books are* ***widely read*** (= a lot of people read them). ◆ *He's an educated,* ***widely-read*** *man* (= he has read a lot of books).

widen /ˈwaɪdn/ *verb* [I,T] to become wider; to make sth wider: *The road widens just up ahead.*

ˌwide-ˈranging *adj* covering a large area or many subjects: *a wide-ranging discussion*

widespread /ˈwaɪdspred/ *adj* found or happening over a large area; affecting a large number of people: *The storm has caused widespread damage.*

widget /ˈwɪdʒɪt/ *noun* [C] **1** (*informal*) used to refer to any small device that you do not know the name of **2** a small box on a web page that gives changing information, such as news items or weather reports, while the rest of the page remains the same: *This widget is a link to the latest news headlines.*

widow /ˈwɪdəʊ/ *noun* [C] a woman whose husband has died and who has not married again ▶ **widowed** *adj She's been widowed for ten years now.*

widower /ˈwɪdəʊə(r)/ *noun* [C] a man whose wife has died and who has not married again

🔑 **width** /wɪdθ/ *noun* **1** [C,U] the amount that sth measures from one side or edge to the other: *The room is eight metres* ***in width.*** ◆ *The carpet is available in two different widths.* ➲ *adjective* **wide** ➲ picture at **length** **2** [C] the distance from one side of a swimming pool to the other: *How many widths can you swim?* ➲ look at **length**, **breadth**

wield /wiːld/ *verb* [T] **1** to have and use power, authority, etc: *She wields enormous power in the company.* **2** to hold and be ready to use a weapon: *Some of the men were wielding knives.*

wiener /ˈwiːnə(r)/ (*AmE*) = **frankfurter**

🔑 **wife** /waɪf/ *noun* [C] (*pl* **wives** /waɪvz/) the woman to whom a man is married: *She's his second wife.* ◆ *a doctor's wife* ◆ *husband and wife*

Wi-Fi™ /ˈwaɪ faɪ/ *noun* [U] **wireless fidelity**; a system for sending data over computer networks using radio waves instead of wires: *Wi-Fi Internet access* ◆ *a Wi-Fi connection*

wig /wɪg/ *noun* [C] a covering made of real or false hair that you wear on your head

wiggle /ˈwɪgl/ *verb* [I,T] (*informal*) to move from side to side with small quick movements; to make sth do this: *You have to wiggle your hips in time to the music.* ▶ **wiggle** *noun* [C] ▶ **wiggly** /ˈwɪgli/ *adj*: *She drew a wiggly line.* **SYN** **wavy**

wigwam /ˈwɪgwæm/ *noun* [C] a type of tent that was used by some Native Americans in past times

wiki /ˈwɪki/ *noun* [C] a website that allows any user to change or add to the information it contains: *The company has a wiki where we can share ideas and information.* ◆ *a wiki page*

🔑 **wild¹** /waɪld/ *adj* (**wilder**; **wildest**)
➤ANIMAL/PLANT **1** living or growing in natural conditions, not looked after by people: *wild animals/flowers/strawberries*
➤LAND **2** in its natural state; not changed by people: *the wild plains of Siberia*
➤WITHOUT CONTROL **3** (used about a person or their behaviour or emotions) without control or discipline; slightly crazy: *The crowd* ***went wild*** *with excitement.* ◆ *They let their children* ***run wild*** (= behave in a free way, without enough control).
➤NOT SENSIBLE **4** not carefully planned; not sensible or accurate: *She made* ***a wild guess.*** ◆ *wild accusations/rumours*
➤LIKING STH/SB **5** (*informal*) **wild (about sb/sth)** liking sb/sth very much: *I'm not wild about the band's new album.*
➤WEATHER **6** with strong winds or storms: *It was a wild night last night.* ▶ **wildly** *adv* ▶ **wildness** *noun* [U]

wild² /waɪld/ *noun* **1** **the wild** [sing] a natural environment that is not controlled by people: *the thrill of seeing elephants* ***in the wild*** **2** **the wilds** [pl] places that are far away from towns, where few people live: *They live somewhere out in the wilds.*

wilderness /ˈwɪldənəs/ *noun* [C, usually sing] **1** a large area of land that has never been used for building on or for growing things: *The Antarctic is the world's last great wilderness.* **2** a place that people do not take care of or control: *Their garden is a wilderness.*

wildlife /ˈwaɪldlaɪf/ *noun* [U] animals, birds, insects, etc. that are wild and live in a natural environment

wilful (*AmE* also **willful**) /ˈwɪlfl/ *adj* **1** done deliberately although the person doing it knows that it is wrong: *wilful damage/neglect* **2** doing exactly what you want, no matter what other people think or say: *a wilful child* ▶ **wilfully** /-fəli/ *adv*

🔑 **will¹** /wɪl/ *modal verb* (*short form* **'ll** /l/; *negative* **will not**; *short form* **won't** /wəʊnt/; *pt* **would** /wəd; *strong form* wʊd/; *short form* **'d** /d/; *negative* **would not**; *short form* **wouldn't** /ˈwʊdnt/) **1** used in forming the future tenses: *He'll be here soon.* ◆ *I'm sure you'll pass your exam.* ◆ *I'll be sitting on the beach this time next week.* ◆ *Next Sunday, they will have been in England for a year.* **2** used for showing that sb is offering sth or wants to do sth, or that sth is able to do sth: *'We need some more milk.' 'OK, I'll get it.'* ◆ *Why won't you tell me where you were last night?* ◆ *My car won't start.* **3** used for asking sb to do sth: *Will you sit down, please?* **4** used for ordering sb to do sb: *Will you all be quiet!* **5** used for saying that you think sth is probably true: *That'll be the postman at the door.* ◆ *He'll have left work by now, I suppose.* **6** [only in positive sentences] used for

W

talking about habits: *She'll listen to music, alone in her room, for hours.*

HELP If you put extra stress on 'will' in this meaning, it shows that the habit annoys you: *He **will** keep interrupting me when I'm trying to work.*

ⓘ For more information about modal verbs, look at the **Reference Section** at the back of this dictionary.

will[2] /wɪl/ *verb* [T] to use the power of your mind to do sth or to make sth happen: *He willed himself to carry on to the end of the race.*

will[3] /wɪl/ *noun* **1** [C,U] the power of the mind to choose what to do; a feeling of strong determination: *Both her children have got very strong wills.* ♦ *My father seems to have lost **the will to live**.* **2** [sing] what sb wants to happen in a particular situation: *My mother doesn't want to sell the house and I don't want to **go against** her **will**.* **3** [C] a legal document in which you write down who should have your money and property after your death: *You really ought to **make a will**.* ♦ *Gran left us some money **in** her **will**.* **4 -willed** [in compounds] having the type of will mentioned: *a strong-willed/weak-willed person*
IDM of your own free will ➲ free[1]

willing /ˈwɪlɪŋ/ *adj* **1** [not before a noun] willing (to do sth) happy to do sth; having no reason for not doing sth: *Are you willing to help us?* ♦ *She's **perfectly** willing to lend me her car.* ♦ *I'm not willing to take any risks.* **2** ready or pleased to help and not needing to be persuaded; enthusiastic: *a willing helper/volunteer* **OPP** for both meanings **unwilling** ▶ **willingly** *adv* ▶ **willingness** *noun* [U, sing]

willow /ˈwɪləʊ/ (also ˈwillow tree) *noun* [C] a tree with long thin branches that hang down. Willows grow near water.

willpower /ˈwɪlpaʊə(r)/ *noun* [U] determination to do sth; strength of mind: *It takes a lot of willpower to give up smoking.* ♦ *It takes a lot of willpower to lose weight.*

willy /ˈwɪli/ *noun* [C] (*pl* willies) (*informal*) a word used by children to refer to the **penis** (= the male sexual organ)

willy-nilly /ˌwɪli ˈnɪli/ *adv* (*informal*) **1** if you want to or not **2** in a careless way without planning: *Don't spend your money willy-nilly.*

W

wilt /wɪlt/ *verb* [I,T] (used about a plant or person) to bend and become weak, often because of heat or a lack of water

wily /ˈwaɪli/ *adj* (wilier; wiliest) clever at getting what you want **SYN cunning**

wimp /wɪmp/ *noun* [C] (*informal*) a weak person who has no courage or confidence: *Don't be such a wimp!* ▶ **wimpish** *adj*

win /wɪn/ *verb* (winning; *pt, pp* won /wʌn/) **1** [I,T] to be the best, first or strongest in a race, game, competition, etc: *to win a game/match/championship* ♦ *I never win at table tennis.* ♦ *Which party do you think will win the next election?* **2** [T] to get money, a prize, etc. as a result of success in a competition, race, etc: *We won a trip to Australia.* ♦ *Who won the gold medal?* ♦ *He won the jackpot in the lottery.*

HELP Note that we **earn** (not **win**) money at our job: *I earn £25000 a year.*

3 [T] to get sth by hard work, great effort, etc: *Her brilliant performance won her a great deal of praise.* ♦ *to win support for a plan*
IDM you can't win (*informal*) there is no way of being completely successful or of pleasing everyone: *Whatever you do you will upset somebody. You can't win.*
win/lose the toss ➲ toss
PHR V win sb over/round (to sth) to persuade sb to support or agree with you: *They're against the proposal at the moment, but I'm sure we can win them over.*
▶ **win** *noun* [C]: *We have had two wins and a draw so far this season.* ➲ **winning**

wince /wɪns/ *verb* [I] to make a sudden quick movement (usually with a part of your face) to show you are feeling pain or embarrassment

winch /wɪntʃ/ *noun* [C] a machine that lifts or pulls heavy objects using a thick chain, rope, etc. ▶ **winch** *verb* [T]: *The injured climber was winched up into a helicopter.*

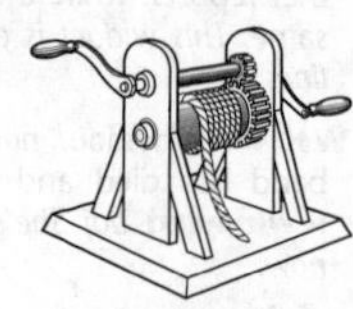
winch

wind[1] /wɪnd/ *noun* **1** [C,U] air that is moving across the surface of the earth: *There was a strong wind blowing.* ♦ *A **gust of wind** blew his hat off.* ♦ *gale-force/strong/high winds* ♦ *Listen to the wind.* **2** [U] gas that is formed in your stomach: *The baby cries when he has wind.* **3** [U] the breath that you need for doing exercise or playing a musical instrument: *She stopped running to get her wind back.* **4** [U] (in an **orchestra**) the group of instruments that you play by blowing into them: *the wind section*
IDM get wind of sth (*informal*) to hear about sth that is secret

wind[2] /wɪnd/ *verb* [T] **1** to cause sb to have difficulty in breathing: *The punch in the stomach winded her.* **2** to help a baby get rid of painful gas in the stomach by rubbing or gently hitting its back

wind[3] /waɪnd/ *verb* (*pt, pp* wound /waʊnd/) **1** [I] (used about a road, path, etc.) to have a lot of bends or curves in it: *The path winds down the cliff to the sea.* **2** [T] to put sth long round sth else several times: *She wound the bandage around his arm.* **3** [T] to make sth work or move by turning a key, handle, etc: *He wound the car window down.* ♦ *He had forgotten to wind his watch.*
PHR V wind down (about a person) to rest and relax after a period of hard work, worry, etc. ➲ look at **unwind**
wind up (*informal*) to find yourself in a place or situation that you did not intend to be in: *We got lost and wound up in a dangerous-looking part of town.*

wind sb up to annoy sb until they become angry
wind sth up to finish, stop or close sth: *The company was losing money and had to be wound up.*

windfall /ˈwɪndfɔːl/ *noun* [C] an amount of money that you win or receive unexpectedly

ˈ**wind farm** *noun* [C] an area of land on which there are a lot of **windmills** or **wind turbines** (= modern windmills) for producing electricity

winding /ˈwaɪndɪŋ/ *adj* with bends or curves in it: *a winding road through the hills*

ˈ**wind instrument** *noun* [C] a musical instrument that you play by blowing through it

windmill /ˈwɪndmɪl/ *noun* [C] a tall building or structure with long parts called **sails** that turn in the wind. In past times **windmills** were used for making flour from grain. ➲ look at **wind turbine**

windmill

🔑 **window** /ˈwɪndəʊ/ *noun* [C] **1** the opening in a building, car, etc. that you can see through and that lets light in. A window usually has glass in it: *Open the window. It's hot in here.* ◆ *a shop window* ◆ *These windows need cleaning.* ➲ picture on **page P8** **2** an area on a computer screen that has a particular type of information in it: *to open/close a window* **3** a time when you have not arranged to do anything and so are free to meet sb, etc: *I'm busy all Tuesday morning, but I've got a window from 2 until 3.*

ˈ**window box** *noun* a long narrow box outside a window, in which plants are grown ➲ picture on **page P8**

ˈ**window ledge** = **windowsill**

windowpane /ˈwɪndəʊpeɪn/ *noun* [C] one piece of glass in a window

ˈ**window-shopping** *noun* [U] looking at things in shop windows without intending to buy anything

windowsill /ˈwɪndəʊsɪl/ (also ˈ**window ledge**) *noun* [C] the narrow shelf at the bottom of a window, either inside or outside ➲ picture at **curtain** ➲ picture on **page P8**

windpipe /ˈwɪndpaɪp/ *noun* [C] the tube that takes air from the throat to the lungs

windscreen /ˈwɪndskriːn/ (*AmE* **windshield**) *noun* [C] the window in the front of a vehicle ➲ picture on **page P7**

ˈ**windscreen wiper** (also **wiper**; (*AmE* ˈ**windshield wiper**) *noun* [C] one of the two blades with rubber edges that move across a **windscreen** to make it clear of water, snow, etc. ➲ picture at **car**

windshield /ˈwɪndʃiːld/ (*AmE*) = **windscreen**

windshield wiper (*AmE*) = **windscreen wiper**

windsurf /ˈwɪndsɜːf/ *verb* [I] to move over water standing on a special board with a sail

HELP We usually say **go windsurfing**: *Have you ever been windsurfing?*

▶ **windsurfing** *noun* [U] ➲ picture on **page P5**

windsurfer /ˈwɪndsɜːfə(r)/ *noun* [C] **1** (also **sailboard**) a board with a sail that you stand on as it moves over the surface of the water, pushed by the wind **2** a person who rides on a board like this

windswept /ˈwɪndswept/ *adj* **1** (used about a place) that often has strong winds: *a windswept coastline* **2** looking untidy because you have been in a strong wind: *windswept hair*

ˈ**wind turbine** *noun* [C] a type of modern **windmill** (= a tall building with sails that turn in the wind) used for producing electricity

windy /ˈwɪndi/ *adj* (**windier**; **windiest**) with a lot of wind: *a windy day*

🔑 **wine** /waɪn/ *noun* [C,U] an alcoholic drink that is made from **grapes** (= small green or purple fruit that grow in bunches), or sometimes other fruit: *sweet/dry wine* ◆ *German wines* ➲ look at **beer**

MORE Wine is made in three colours: **red, white** and **rosé**. The grapes are grown in a **vineyard** (/ˈvɪnjəd/).

🔑 **wing** /wɪŋ/ *noun*
➤OF BIRD/INSECT **1** [C] one of the two parts that a bird, an insect, etc. uses for flying: *The goose ran around flapping its wings.* ➲ picture on **page P12, page P13**
➤OF PLANE **2** [C] one of the two long parts that stick out from the side of a plane and support it in the air ➲ picture on **page P6**
➤OF BUILDING **3** [C] a part of a building that sticks out from the main part or that was added on to the main part: *the maternity wing of the hospital*
➤OF CAR **4** (*AmE* **fender**) [C] the part of the outside of a car that covers the top of the wheels: *There was a dent in the wing.*
➤OF POLITICAL PARTY **5** [C, usually sing] a group of people in a political party that have particular beliefs or opinions: *He's on the right wing of the Conservative Party.* ➲ look at **left wing, right wing**
➤IN FOOTBALL, ETC. **6** [C] the part at each side of the area where the game is played: *to play on the wing* **7** (also **winger** /ˈwɪŋə(r)/) [C] a person who plays in an attacking position at one of the sides of the field
➤IN THEATRE **8 the wings** [pl] the area at the sides of the stage where the actors cannot be seen by the audience
IDM take sb under your wing to take care of and help sb who has less experience than you

wink /wɪŋk/ *verb* [I] **wink (at sb)** to close and open one eye very quickly, usually as a signal to sb ➲ picture at **blink**
IDM forty winks ➲ **forty**
▶ **wink** *noun* [C]: *He smiled and gave the little girl a wink.* ◆ *I didn't sleep a wink* (= not at all).

🔑 **winner** /ˈwɪnə(r)/ *noun* [C] **1** a person or an animal that wins a competition, game, race, etc: *The winner of the competition will be announced next*

W

week. **2** (*informal*) something that is likely to be successful: *I think your idea is a winner.* **3** (in sport) a goal that wins a match, a hit that wins a point, etc: *Henry scored the winner in the last minute.*

winning /ˈwɪnɪŋ/ *adj* [only before a noun] that wins or has won sth, for example a race or competition: *The winning ticket is number 65.* ◆ *He scored the winning goal in the final.*

winnings /ˈwɪnɪŋz/ *noun* [pl] money that you win in a competition or game

winter /ˈwɪntə(r)/ *noun* [C,U] the coldest season of the year between autumn and spring: *It snows a lot here* ***in winter.*** ◆ *a cold winter's day* ◆ *We went skiing in France last winter.* ▶ **wintry** /ˈwɪntri/ *adj*: *wintry weather*

ˌwinter ˈsports *noun* [pl] sports which take place on snow or ice, for example **skiing** and **skating**

wintertime /ˈwɪntətaɪm/ *noun* [U] the period or season of winter

wipe¹ /waɪp/ *verb* [T] **1** to clean or dry sth by rubbing it with a cloth, etc: *She stopped crying and wiped her eyes with a tissue.* ◆ *Could you wipe the table, please?* ➲ note at **clean²** **2** wipe sth from/off sth; wipe sth away/off/up to remove sth by rubbing it: *He wiped the sweat from his forehead.* ◆ *Wipe up the milk you spilled.* **3** wipe sth (off) (sth) to remove sound, information or images from sth: *I accidentally wiped the file.* ◆ *I tried to wipe the memory from my mind.*

PHR V **wipe sth out** to destroy sth completely: *Whole villages were wiped out in the bombing raids.*

wipe² /waɪp/ *noun* [C] **1** the act of **wiping**: *He gave the table a quick wipe.* **2** a piece of paper or thin cloth that has been made wet with a special liquid and is used for cleaning sth: *a box of baby wipes*

wiper /ˈwaɪpə(r)/ = **windscreen wiper**

wire¹ /ˈwaɪə(r)/ *noun* [C,U] **1** metal in the form of thin thread; a piece of this: *a piece of wire* ◆ *Twist those two wires together.* ◆ *a wire fence* **2** a piece of wire that is used to carry electricity: *telephone wires*

wire² /ˈwaɪə(r)/ *verb* [T] **1** wire sth (up) (to sth) to connect sth to a supply of electricity or to a piece of electrical equipment by using wires: *to wire a plug* ◆ *The microphone was wired up to a loudspeaker.* **2** wire sth (to sb); wire sb sth to send money to sb's bank account using an electronic system: *The bank's going to wire me the money.* **3** to join two things together using wire

wireless /ˈwaɪələs/ *adj* not using wires: *wireless technology/communications*

wiring /ˈwaɪərɪŋ/ *noun* [U] the system of wires that supplies electricity to rooms in a building or to parts of a machine

wiry /ˈwaɪəri/ *adj* (wirier; wiriest) (used about a person) small and thin but strong

wisdom /ˈwɪzdəm/ *noun* [U] the ability to make sensible decisions and judgements because of your knowledge or experience: *I don't see the wisdom of this plan* (= I do not think that it is a good idea). ➲ *adjective* **wise**

ˈwisdom tooth *noun* [C] one of the four teeth at the back of your mouth that do not grow until you are an adult

wise /waɪz/ *adj* (wiser; wisest) **1** (used about people) able to make sensible decisions and give good advice because of the experience and knowledge that you have: *a wise old man* **2** (used about actions) sensible; based on good judgement: *a wise decision* ◆ *It would be wiser to wait for a few days.*

IDM **none the wiser/worse** ➲ **none²**

▶ **wisely** *adv*

wish¹ /wɪʃ/ *verb* **1** [T] [often with a verb in the past tense] wish (that) to want sth that cannot now happen or that probably will not happen: *I wish I had listened more carefully.* ◆ *I wish that I knew what was going to happen.* ◆ *I wish I was taller.* ◆ *I wish I could help you.*

HELP In formal English we use **were** instead of **was** with 'I' or 'he/she': *I wish I were rich.* ◆ *She wishes she were in a different class.*

2 [I,T] (*formal*) wish (to do sth) to want to do sth: *I wish to make a complaint about one of the doctors.* **3** [I] wish for sth to think very hard that you want sth, especially sth that can only be achieved by good luck or magic: *She shut her eyes and wished for him to get better.* ◆ *It's no use wishing for the impossible.* **4** [T] to say that you hope sb will have sth: *I rang him up to* ***wish him a happy birthday.*** ◆ *We* ***wish*** *you* ***all the best*** *for your future career.*

wish² /wɪʃ/ *noun* **1** [C] a feeling that you want to have sth or that sth should happen: *I have no wish to see her ever again.* ◆ *Doctors should respect the patient's wishes.* **2** [C] a try at making sth happen by thinking hard about it, especially in stories when it often happens by magic: *Throw a coin into the fountain and* ***make a wish.*** ◆ *My* ***wish came true*** (= I got what I asked for). **3** wishes [pl] a hope that sb will be happy or have good luck: *Please* ***give*** *your parents* ***my best wishes.*** ◆ *Best Wishes* (= at the end of a letter)

ˌwishful ˈthinking *noun* [U] ideas that are based on what you would like, not on facts ➲ look at **thinking**

wisp /wɪsp/ *noun* [C] **1** a small, thin piece of hair, grass, etc. **2** a small amount of smoke ▶ **wispy** *adj*

wistful /ˈwɪstfl/ *adj* feeling or showing sadness because you cannot have what you want: *a wistful sigh* ▶ **wistfully** /-fəli/ *adv*

wit /wɪt/ *noun* [U] **1** the ability to use words in a clever and amusing way ➲ *adjective* **witty** **2** wits [pl] your ability to think quickly and clearly and to make good decisions: *The game of chess is essentially* ***a battle of wits.*** **3** -witted [in compounds] having a particular type of intelligence: *quick-witted* ◆ *slow-witted*

IDM **at your wits' end** not knowing what to do or say because you are very worried

keep your wits about you to be ready to act in a difficult situation

witch /wɪtʃ/ *noun* [C] (in past times and in stories) a woman who is thought to have magic powers ➲ look at **wizard**

witchcraft /ˈwɪtʃkrɑːft/ *noun* [U] the use of magic powers, especially evil ones

with /wɪð; wɪθ/ *prep* **1** in the company of sb/sth; in or to the same place as sb/sth: *I live with my parents.* ♦ *Are you coming with us?* ♦ *I talked about the problem with my tutor.* **2** having or carrying sth: *a girl with red hair* ♦ *a house with a garden* ♦ *the man with the suitcase* **3** using sth: *Cut it with a knife.* ♦ *I did it with his help.* **4** used for saying what fills, covers, etc. sth: *Fill the bowl with water.* ♦ *His hands were covered with oil.* **5** in competition with sb/sth; against sb/sth: *He's always arguing with his brother.* ♦ *I usually play tennis with my sister.* **6** towards, concerning or compared with sb/sth: *Is he angry with us?* ♦ *There's a problem with my visa.* ♦ *Compared with Canada, England has mild winters.* **7** including sth: *The price is for two people with all meals.* **8** used to say how sth happens or is done: *Open this parcel with care.* ♦ *to greet somebody with a smile* **9** because of sth; as a result of sth: *We were shivering with cold.* ♦ *With all the problems we've got, we're not going to finish on time.* **10** in the care of sb: *We left the keys with the neighbours.* **11** agreeing with or supporting sb/sth: *We've got everybody with us on this issue.* **OPP** **against** **12** at the same time as sth: *I can't concentrate with you watching me all the time.* **IDM** **be with me/you** (*informal*) to be able to follow what sb is saying: *I'm not quite with you. Say it again.*

withdraw /wɪðˈdrɔː/ *verb* (*pt* **withdrew** /-ˈdruː/; *pp* **withdrawn** /-ˈdrɔːn/) **1** [I,T] **withdraw (sb/sth) (from sth)** to move sb/sth or order sb to move back or away from a place: *The troops withdrew from the town.* **2** [T] to remove sth or take sth away: *to withdraw an offer/a statement* **3** [I] to decide not to take part in sth: *Jackson withdrew from the race at the last minute.* **4** [T] to take money out of a bank account: *How much would you like to withdraw?* ➲ note at **money** ➲ look at **deposit**

withdrawal /wɪðˈdrɔːəl/ *noun* **1** [C,U] moving or being moved back or away from a place: *the withdrawal of troops from the war zone* **2** [C] taking money out of your bank account; the amount of money that you take out: *to* ***make a withdrawal*** **3** [U] the act of stopping doing sth, especially taking a drug: *When he gave up alcohol he suffered severe withdrawal symptoms.*

withdrawn[1] *past participle of* **withdraw**

withdrawn[2] /wɪðˈdrɔːn/ *adj* (used about a person) very quiet and not wanting to talk to other people

withdrew *past tense of* **withdraw**

wither /ˈwɪðə(r)/ *verb* **1** [I,T] **wither (sth) (away)** (used about plants) to become dry and die; to make a plant do this: *The plants withered in the hot sun.* **2** [I] **wither (away)** to become weaker then disappear: *This type of industry will wither away in the years to come.*

withering /ˈwɪðərɪŋ/ *adj* done to make sb feel silly or embarrassed: *a withering look*

withhold /wɪðˈhəʊld; wɪθˈh-/ *verb* [T] (*pt, pp* **withheld** /-ˈheld/) (*formal*) **withhold sth (from sb/sth)** to refuse to give sth to sb: *to withhold information from the police*

within /wɪˈðɪn/ *prep, adv* **1** in a period not longer than a particular length of time: *I'll be back within an hour.* ♦ *She got married, found a job and moved house, all within a month.* **2** **within sth (of sth)** not further than a particular distance from sth: *The house is within a kilometre of the station.* **3** not outside the limits of sb/sth: *Each department must keep within its budget.* **4** (*formal*) inside sb/sth: *The anger was still there deep within him.* ♦ *Cleaner required. Apply within* (= come in and ask).

without /wɪˈðaʊt/ *prep, adv* **1** not having or showing sth: *Don't go out without a coat on.* ♦ *He spoke without much enthusiasm.* ♦ *If there's no salt, we'll have to manage without.* **2** not using or being with sb/sth: *I drink my coffee without milk.* ♦ *I can't see a thing without my glasses.* ♦ *Don't leave without me.* **3** used with a verb in the *-ing* form to mean 'not': *She left without saying goodbye.* ♦ *I used her phone without her knowing.*

withstand /wɪðˈstænd/ *verb* [T] (*pt, pp* **withstood** /-ˈstʊd/) (*formal*) to be strong enough not to break, give up, be damaged, etc: *These animals can withstand very high temperatures.*

witness[1] /ˈwɪtnəs/ *noun* [C] **1** (also **eyewitness**) a **witness (to sth)** a person who sees sth happen and who can tell other people about it later: *There were two witnesses to the accident.* **2** a person who appears in a court of law to say what they have seen or what they know about sb/sth: *a witness for the defence/prosecution* ➲ note at **court** **3** a person who sees sb sign an official document and who then signs it himself or herself: *Mary was one of the witnesses at our wedding.*
IDM **bear witness (to sth)** ➲ **bear**[1]

witness[2] /ˈwɪtnəs/ *verb* [T] **1** to see sth happen and be able to tell other people about it later: *to witness a murder* **2** to see sb sign an official document and then sign it yourself: *to witness a will*

ˈwitness box (*AmE* **ˈwitness stand**) *noun* [C] the place in a court of law where a **witness** stands when he or she is giving evidence

witty /ˈwɪti/ *adj* (**wittier**; **wittiest**) clever and amusing; using words in a clever way: *a very witty speech* ➲ note at **humour** ➲ *noun* **wit**

wives *plural of* **wife**

wizard /ˈwɪzəd/ *noun* [C] **1** (in stories) a man who is believed to have magic powers ➲ look at **witch**, **magician** **2** a person who is especially good at sth: *a computer/financial wizard*

wk *abbr* (*pl* **wks**) = **week**(1)

wobble /ˈwɒbl/ *verb* [I,T] to move from side to side in a way that is not steady; to make sb/sth do this: *Put something under the leg of the table. It's wobbling.* ♦ *Stop wobbling the desk. I can't write.*
▶ **wobbly** /ˈwɒbli/ *adj*

W

woe /wəʊ/ *noun* (*formal*) **1** woes [pl] the problems that sb has **2** [U] (*old-fashioned*) great unhappiness IDM **woe betide sb** used as a warning that there will be trouble if sb does/does not do a particular thing: *Woe betide anyone who yawns while the boss is talking.*

wok /wɒk/ *noun* [C] a large pan that is shaped like a bowl and used for cooking Chinese food

woke *past tense of* wake[1]

woken *past participle of* wake[1]

wolf /wʊlf/ *noun* [C] (*pl* wolves /wʊlvz/) a wild animal that looks like a dog and that lives and hunts in a group called a **pack** ➲ picture on **page P12**

⚷ **woman** /ˈwʊmən/ *noun* [C] (*pl* women /ˈwɪmɪn/) **1** an adult female person: *men, women and children* ♦ *Would you prefer to see a woman doctor?* **2** -woman [in compounds] a woman who does a particular activity: *a businesswoman*

womanhood /ˈwʊmənhʊd/ *noun* [U] (*formal*) the state of being a woman

womanly /ˈwʊmənli/ *adj* having qualities considered typical of a woman

womb /wuːm/ *noun* [C] the part of a woman or female animal where a baby grows before it is born ➲ A more formal word is **uterus**.

won *past tense, past participle of* win

⚷ **wonder**[1] /ˈwʌndə(r)/ *verb* **1** [I,T] wonder (about sth) to want to know sth; to ask yourself questions about sth: *I wonder what the new teacher will be like.* ♦ *Vesna's been gone a long time—I wonder if she's all right.* ♦ *It was something that she had been wondering about for a long time.* **2** [T] used as a polite way of asking a question or of asking sb to do sth: *I wonder if you could help me.* ♦ *I was wondering if you'd like to come to dinner at our house.* **3** [I,T] wonder (at sth) to feel great surprise or admiration: *We wondered at the speed with which he worked.* ♦ *'She was very angry.' 'I don't wonder* (= I'm not surprised). *She had a right to be.'*

wonder[2] /ˈwʌndə(r)/ *noun* **1** [U] a feeling of surprise and admiration: *The children just stared **in wonder** at the acrobats.* **2** [C] something that causes you to feel surprise or admiration: *the wonders of modern technology*
IDM **do wonders (for sb/sth)** to have a very good effect on sb/sth: *Working in Mexico did wonders for my Spanish.*
it's a wonder (that)... it's surprising that ...: *It's a wonder we managed to get here on time, with all the traffic.*
no wonder it is not surprising: *You've been out every evening this week. No wonder you're tired.*

⚷ **wonderful** /ˈwʌndəfl/ *adj* extremely good; great: *What wonderful weather!* ♦ *It's wonderful to see you again.* ➲ note at **good, nice** ▸ **wonderfully** /-fəli/ *adv*

won't *short for* **will not**

⚷ **wood** /wʊd/ *noun* **1** [U,C] the hard substance that trees are made of: *He chopped some wood for the fire.* ♦ *Pine is a soft wood.* ➲ picture at **tree** **2** [C, often plural] an area of land that is covered with trees. A wood is smaller than a forest: *a walk in the woods* ➲ note at **forest** ➲ picture on **page P11**
IDM **touch wood**; (*AmE*) **knock on wood** an expression that people use (often while touching a piece of wood) to prevent bad luck: *I've been driving here for 20 years and I haven't had an accident yet—touch wood!*

wooded /ˈwʊdɪd/ *adj* (used about an area of land) having a lot of trees growing on it

⚷ **wooden** /ˈwʊdn/ *adj* made of wood: *The toys are kept in a wooden box.*

woodland /ˈwʊdlənd/ *noun* [C,U] land that has a lot of trees growing on it: *The village is surrounded by woodland.* ♦ *woodland birds*

woodwind /ˈwʊdwɪnd/ *noun* [U, with sing or pl verb] the group of musical instruments that you play by blowing into them: *the woodwind section of the orchestra* ➲ note at **instrument** ➲ picture at **music**

woodwork /ˈwʊdwɜːk/ *noun* [U] **1** the parts of a building that are made of wood such as the doors, stairs, etc. **2** the activity or skill of making things out of wood

woof /wʊf/ *noun* [C] (*informal*) used for describing the sound that a dog makes ➲ look at **bark**

⚷ **wool** /wʊl/ *noun* [U] **1** the soft thick hair of sheep **2** thick thread or cloth that is made from wool: *The sweater is 50% wool and 50% acrylic.* ➲ look at **cotton wool** ➲ picture at **sew**

woollen (*AmE* woolen) /ˈwʊlən/ *adj* made of wool: *a warm woollen jumper*

woolly (*AmE* wooly) /ˈwʊli/ *adj* (woollier; woolliest (*AmE*) woollier; woolliest) like wool or made of wool: *The dog had a thick woolly coat.* ♦ *a warm woolly hat* ➲ picture at **hat**

⚷ **word**[1] /wɜːd/ *noun* **1** [C] a single unit of language that expresses a particular meaning: *What's the Greek word for 'mouth'?* ♦ *What does this word mean?* **2** [C] a thing that you say; a short statement or comment: *Could I **have a word** with you in private?* ♦ *Don't say a word about this to anyone.* **3** [sing] a promise: *I **give you my word** that I won't tell anyone.* ♦ *I **kept my word** and lent her the money.* ♦ *I trust him not to **go back on his word**.*
IDM **a dirty word** ➲ **dirty**[1]
(not) breathe a word (of/about sth) (to sb) ➲ **breathe**
not get a word in edgeways to not be able to interrupt when sb else is talking so that you can say sth yourself
have, etc. the last word ➲ **last**[1]
in other words ➲ **other**
lost for words ➲ **lost**[2]
put in a (good) word for sb to say sth good about sb to sb else: *If you could put in a good word for me I might stand a better chance of getting the job.*
take sb's word for it to believe what sb says without any proof
word for word **1** repeating sth exactly: *Sharon repeated word for word what he had told her.*

2 translating each word separately, not looking at the general meaning: *a word-for-word translation*

word² /wɜːd/ *verb* [T, often passive] to write or say sth using particular words: *The statement was carefully worded so that nobody would be offended by it.*

wording /ˈwɜːdɪŋ/ *noun* [sing] the words that you use to express sth: *The wording of the contract was vague.*

ˌword-ˈperfect *adj* able to say sth that you have learnt from memory, without making a mistake

ˈword processor *noun* [C] (*abbr* WP) a type of computer that you can use for writing letters, reports, etc. You can correct or change what you have written before you print it out. ▶ **ˈword processing** *noun* [U]

wordsearch /ˈwɜːdsɜːtʃ/ *noun* [C] a game consisting of letters arranged in a square, containing several hidden words that you must find: *The CD-ROM includes a wordsearch to help you learn new vocabulary.*

wore *past tense of* **wear¹**

work¹ /wɜːk/ *verb*

➤DO JOB/TASK **1** [I,T] **work (as sth) (for sb) ; work (at/on sth); work (to do sth)** to do sth which needs physical or mental effort, in order to earn money or to achieve sth: *She's working for a large firm in Glasgow.* ◆ *I'd like to work as a newspaper reporter.* ◆ *Doctors often work extremely long hours.* ◆ *My teacher said that I wouldn't pass the exam unless I worked harder.* ◆ *I hear she's working on a new novel.* ◆ *I'm going to stay in tonight and work at my project.* ➲ note at **job, office**

➤MAKE EFFORT **2** [T] to make yourself/sb work, especially very hard: *The coach works the players very hard in training.*

➤MACHINE **3** [I,T] to function; to make sth function; to operate: *Our telephone hasn't been working for several days.* ◆ *We still don't really understand how the brain works.* ◆ *Can you show me how to work the photocopier?*

➤HAVE RESULT **4** [I] to have the result or effect that you want; to be successful: *Your idea sounds good but I don't think it will really work.* ◆ *The heat today could work in favour of the African runners.*

➤USE MATERIALS **5** [I,T] to use materials to make a model, a picture, etc: *He worked the clay into the shape of a horse.* ◆ *She usually works in/with oils or acrylics.*

➤MOVE GRADUALLY **6** [I,T] to move gradually to a new position or state: *Engineers check the plane daily, because nuts and screws can* ***work loose.*** ◆ *I watched the snail* ***work its way*** *up the wall.*

IDM **work/perform miracles** ➲ **miracle**

work to rule to follow the rules of your job in a very strict way in order to cause delay, as a form of protest against your employer or your working conditions

PHR V **work out 1** to develop or progress, especially in a good way: *I hope things work out for you.* **2** to do physical exercises in order to keep your body fit: *We work out to music at my exercise class.*

work out (at) to come to a particular result or total after everything has been calculated: *If we divide the work between us, it'll work out at about four hours each.*

work sb out to understand sb: *I've never been able to work her out.*

work sth out 1 to find the answer to sth; to solve sth: *I can't work out how to do this.* **2** to calculate sth: *I worked out the total cost.* **3** to plan sth: *Have you worked out the route through France?*

work sth up to develop or improve sth with effort: *I'm trying to work up the energy to go out.*

work sb/yourself up (into sth) to make sb/yourself become angry, excited, upset, etc: *He had worked himself up into a state of anxiety about his interview.*

work up to sth to develop or progress to sth: *Start with 15 minutes' exercise and gradually work up to 30.*

work² /wɜːk/ *noun*

➤JOB **1** [U] the job that you do, especially in order to earn money; the place where you do your job: *It is very difficult to* ***find work*** *in this city.* ◆ *He's been* ***out of work*** (= without a job) *for six months.* ◆ *When do you* ***start work****?* ◆ *I'll ask if I can* ***leave work*** *early today.* ◆ ***I go to work*** *at 8 o'clock.* ◆ *The people* ***at work*** *gave me some flowers for my birthday.* ◆ *Police work is not as exciting as it looks on TV.* ➲ note at **job, routine** ➲ look at **employment** ➲ picture on **page P2**

> OTHER WORDS FOR
>
> **work**
>
> **Work** is uncountable in this meaning, so you CANNOT say 'a work' or 'works': *I've found work at the hospital.* **Job** is countable: *I've got a new job at the hospital.* **Employment** is the state of having a paid job and is more formal and official than **work** or **job**: *Many married women are in part-time employment.* **Occupation** is the word used on forms to ask what you are or what job you do: *Occupation—bus driver.* A **profession** is a job that needs special training and higher education: *the medical profession.* A **trade** is a job that you do with your hands and that needs special skill: *He's a carpenter by trade.*

➤EFFORT **2** [U] something that needs physical or mental effort that you do in order to achieve sth: *Her success is due to sheer* ***hard work.*** ◆ *I've got a lot of work to do today.* ◆ *We hope to* ***start work on*** *the project next week.*

➤PRODUCT OF WORK **3** [U] something that you are working on or have produced: *a piece of written work* ◆ *The teacher marked their work.* ◆ *Is this all your own work?*

➤ART **4** [C] a book, painting, piece of music, etc: *an early work by Picasso* ◆ *the complete works of Shakespeare*

➤BUILDING/REPAIRING **5 works** [pl] the act of building or repairing sth: *The roadworks are causing long traffic jams.*

➤FACTORY **6 works** [C, with sing or pl verb] [in compounds] a factory: *The steelworks is/are closing down.*

IDM **get/go/set to work (on sth)** to begin; to make a start (on sth)

workable /ˈwɜːkəbl/ *adj* that can be used successfully: *a workable idea/plan/solution* SYN **practical**

workaholic /ˌwɜːkəˈhɒlɪk/ *noun* [C] (*informal*) a person who loves work and does too much of it

workbench /ˈwɜːkbentʃ/ *noun* [C] a long heavy table used for doing practical jobs, working with tools, etc.

workbook /ˈwɜːkbʊk/ *noun* [C] a book with questions and exercises in it that you use when you are studying sth

worker /ˈwɜːkə(r)/ *noun* [C] **1** [in compounds] a person who works, especially one who does a particular kind of work: *factory/office/farm workers* ◆ *skilled/manual workers* **2** a person who is employed to do physical work rather than organizing things or managing people: *Workers' representatives will meet management today to discuss the pay dispute.* **3** a person who works in a particular way: *a slow/fast worker*

ˈwork experience *noun* [U] the knowledge and skills that you get from working in a particular job for a short period of time; the process of gaining this: *Students do unpaid work experience in local firms.* ◆ *Jill is* ***on work experience*** *at the local newspaper's offices for a month.*

workforce /ˈwɜːkfɔːs/ *noun* [C,with sing or pl verb] **1** the total number of people who work in a company, factory, etc. **2** the total number of people in a country who are able to work: *Ten per cent of the workforce is/are unemployed.*

working /ˈwɜːkɪŋ/ *adj* [only *before* a noun] **1** employed; having a job: *the problems of childcare for working mothers* **2** connected with your job: *He stayed with the same company for the whole of his* ***working life.*** ◆ *The company offers excellent working conditions.* **3** good enough to be used, although it could be improved: *We are looking for someone with* ***a working knowledge*** *of French.*

IDM **in working order** (used about machines, etc.) working properly, not broken

the ˌworking ˈclass *noun* [sing,with sing or pl verb] (also **the ˌworking ˈclasses** [pl]) the group of people in society who do not have much money or power and who usually do physical work, especially in industry: *unemployment among the working class* ➲ look at **middle class, upper class**
▶ **ˌworking-ˈclass** *adj*: *a working-class area/family*

workings /ˈwɜːkɪŋz/ *noun* [pl] the way in which a machine, an organization, etc. operates: *It's very difficult to understand the workings of the legal system.*

workload /ˈwɜːkləʊd/ *noun* [C] the amount of work that you have to do: *She often gets home late when she has a* ***heavy workload***.

workman /ˈwɜːkmən/ *noun* [C] (*pl* **-men** /-mən/) a man who works with his hands, especially at building or making things

workmanlike /ˈwɜːkmənlaɪk/ *adj* done, made, etc. very well, but not original or exciting: *a workmanlike performance*

workmanship /ˈwɜːkmənʃɪp/ *noun* [U] the skill with which sth is made

workmate /ˈwɜːkmeɪt/ *noun* [C] (*especially BrE*) a person that you work with, often doing the same job, in an office, a factory, etc. SYN **colleague**

ˌwork of ˈart *noun* [C] (*pl* **works of art**) a painting, book, piece of music, etc., usually one that is well-made ➲ look at **art**

workout /ˈwɜːkaʊt/ *noun* [C] a period of physical exercise, for example when you are training for a sport or keeping fit: *She does a twenty-minute workout every morning.*

workplace /ˈwɜːkpleɪs/ *noun* [C] *often* **the workplace** [sing] the office, factory, etc. where people work: *new technology in the workplace*

worksheet /ˈwɜːkʃiːt/ *noun* [C] a piece of paper with questions or exercises on it that you use when you are studying sth

workshop /ˈwɜːkʃɒp/ *noun* [C] **1** a place where things are made or repaired **2** a period of discussion and practical work on a particular subject, when people share their knowledge and experience: *a drama/writing workshop*

workstation /ˈwɜːksteɪʃn/ *noun* [C] the desk and computer at which a person works; one computer that is part of a system of computers

worktop /ˈwɜːktɒp/ (also **ˈwork surface**, *AmE* **counter**) *noun* [C] a flat surface in a kitchen, etc. that you use for preparing food, etc. on ➲ picture on **page P8**

world /wɜːld/ *noun*

➤ THE EARTH **1 the world** [sing] the earth with all its countries and people: *a map of the world* ◆ *the most beautiful place* ***in the world*** ◆ *I took a year off work to travel* ***round the world.*** ◆ *She is famous* ***all over the world.***

➤ COUNTRIES **2** [sing] a particular part of the earth or a group of countries: *the western world* ◆ *the Arab world* ◆ *the Third World*

➤ ANOTHER PLANET **3** [C] a planet with life on it: *Do you believe there are other worlds out there, like ours?*

➤ AREA OF ACTIVITY **4** [C] [in compounds] a particular area of activity or group of people or things: *the world of sport/fashion/politics* ◆ *the medical/business/animal/natural world*

➤ LIFE **5** [sing] the life and activities of people; their experience: *It's time you learned something about the real world!* ◆ *the modern world*

➤ PEOPLE **6** [sing] the people in the world: ***The whole world*** *was waiting for news of the astronauts.*

IDM **do sb a/the world of good** (*informal*) to have a very good effect on sb: *The holiday has done her the world of good.*

in the world used to emphasize what you are saying: *Everyone else is stressed but he doesn't seem to have a care in the world.* ◆ *There's no need to rush—we've got all the time in the world.* ◆ *What in the world are you doing?*

the outside world ➲ **outside**[2]

think the world of sb/sth ➲ **think**

ˌ**world-ˈclass** *adj* as good as the best in the world: *a world-class athlete*

ˌ**world-ˈfamous** *adj* known all over the world

worldly /ˈwɜːldli/ *adj* **1** [only *before* a noun] connected with ordinary life, not with the spirit: *He left all his worldly possessions to his nephew.* **2** having a lot of experience and knowledge of life and people: *a sophisticated and worldly man*

ˌ**world ˈwar** *noun* [C] a war that involves a lot of different countries: *the First World War/World War One* ◆ *the Second World War/World War Two*

worldwide /ˈwɜːldwaɪd/ *adj* happening in the whole world: *The situation has caused worldwide concern.* ▶ **worldwide** *adv* /ˌwɜːldˈwaɪd/: *The product will be marketed worldwide.*

the ˌWorld Wide ˈWeb (also **the Web**) *noun* [sing] (*abbr* **WWW**) the system for finding information on the Internet, in which documents are connected to other documents using special links ➲ look at **the Internet**

maggot

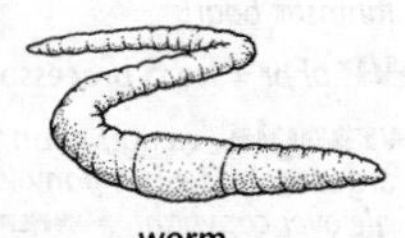
worm

worm¹ /wɜːm/ *noun* [C] **1** a small creature with a long thin body and no eyes, bones or legs: *an earthworm* **2 worms** [pl] one or more **worms** that live inside a person or an animal and may cause disease: *He's got worms.*

worm² /wɜːm/ *verb* [T] **worm your way/yourself along, through, etc.** to move slowly or with difficulty in the direction mentioned: *I managed to worm my way through the crowd.*

PHR V worm your way/yourself into sth to make sb like you or trust you, in order to dishonestly gain an advantage for yourself

worn *past participle* of **wear¹**

ˌ**worn ˈout** *adj* **1** too old or damaged to use any more: *My shoes are completely worn out.* **2** extremely tired: *I'm absolutely worn out. I think I'll go to bed early.* ➲ look at **wear**

🔑 **worried** /ˈwʌrid/ *adj* **worried (about sb/sth); worried (that ...)** thinking that sth bad might happen or has happened: *Don't look so worried. Everything will be all right.* ◆ *I'm* **worried sick** *about the exam.* ◆ *We were* **worried stiff** (= extremely worried) *that you might have had an accident.*

🔑 **worry¹** /ˈwʌri/ *verb* (**worrying; worries;** *pt, pp* **worried**) **1** [I] **worry (about sb/sth)** to think that sth bad might happen or has happened: *Don't worry—I'm sure everything will be all right.* ◆ *There's nothing to worry about.* ◆ *He worries if I don't phone every weekend.* **2** [T] **worry sb/yourself (about sb/sth)** to make sb/yourself think that sth bad might happen or has happened: *What worries me is how are we going to get home?* ◆ *She worried herself sick when he was away in the army.* **3** [T] **worry sb (with sth)** to disturb sb: *Don't keep worrying him with questions.*
SYN bother
IDM not to worry it is not important; it does not matter
▶ **worrying** *adj* /ˈwʌriɪŋ/: *a worrying situation* ◆ *It was a worrying time for us all.*

🔑 **worry²** /ˈwʌri/ *noun* (*pl* **worries**) **1** [U] the state of worrying about sth: *His son has caused him a lot of worry recently.* **2** [C] something that makes you worry; a problem: *Crime is a real worry for old people.* ◆ *financial worries*

🔑 **worse** /wɜːs/ *adj, adv* [the comparative of *bad* or of *badly*] **1** not as good or as well as sth else: *My exam results were* **far/much worse** *than I thought they would be.* ◆ *She speaks German* **even worse** *than I do.* **2** [not before a noun] more ill; less well: *If you* **get** *any* **worse**, *we'll call the doctor.*
IDM a change for the better/worse ➲ **change²**
none the wiser/worse ➲ **none²**
to make matters/things worse to make a situation, problem, etc. even more difficult or dangerous than before
the worse for wear (*informal*) damaged; not in good condition: *This suitcase looks a bit the worse for wear.*
worse luck (*spoken*) unfortunately: *The dentist says I need three fillings, worse luck!*
▶ **worse** *noun* [U]: *The situation was already bad but there was worse to come.*

worsen /ˈwɜːsn/ *verb* [I,T] to become worse or to make sth worse: *Relations between the two countries have worsened.*

🔑 **worship** /ˈwɜːʃɪp/ *verb* (**worshipping; worshipped,** (*AmE*) **worshiping; worshiped**) **1** [I,T] to show respect for God or a god, by saying prayers, singing with others, etc: *People travel from all over the world to worship at this shrine.* **2** [T] to love or admire sb/sth very much: *She worshipped her husband.* ▶ **worship** *noun* [U]: *Different religions have different forms of worship.* ▶ **worshipper** (*AmE* **worshiper**) *noun* [C]

🔑 **worst¹** /wɜːst/ *adj, adv* [the superlative of *bad* or of *badly*] the least pleasant or suitable; the least well: *It's been the worst winter that I can remember.* ◆ *A lot of the children behaved badly but my son behaved worst of all!*

worst² /wɜːst/ *noun* [sing] **the worst** the most serious or unpleasant thing that could happen: *My parents always expect the worst if I'm late.*
IDM at (the) worst if the worst happens or if you consider sb/sth in the worst way: *The problem doesn't look too serious. At worst we'll have to make a few small changes.*
bring out the best/worst in sb ➲ **best³**
if the worst comes to the worst if the worst possible situation happens

🔑 **worth¹** /wɜːθ/ *adj* [not before a noun] **1** having a particular value (in money): *How much do you think that house is worth?* **2 worth doing, etc.** used as a way of recommending or advising: *That museum's* **well worth** *visiting if you have time.* ◆ *The library closes in 5 minutes—it's* **not worth** *going in.*

W

HELP We can say either *It isn't worth repairing the car* or *The car isn't worth repairing.*

3 enjoyable or useful to do or have, even if it means extra cost, effort, etc: *It takes a long time to walk to the top of the hill but it's worth the effort.* ◆ *Don't bother cooking a big meal. It isn't* ***worth it****—we're not hungry.*
IDM **get your money's worth** ➲ **money**
worth sb's while helpful, useful or interesting to sb

worth² /wɜːθ/ *noun* [U] **1** the amount of sth that the money mentioned will buy: *twenty pounds' worth of petrol* **2** the amount of sth that will last for the time mentioned: *two days' worth of food* **3** the value of sb/sth; how useful sb/sth is: *She has proved her worth as a member of the team.*

worthless /ˈwɜːθləs/ *adj* **1** having no value or use: *It's worthless—it's only a bit of plastic!* **2** (used about a person) having bad qualities ➲ look at **priceless, valuable, invaluable**

worthwhile /ˌwɜːθˈwaɪl/ *adj* important, enjoyable or interesting enough to be worth the cost or effort: *Working for so little money just isn't worthwhile.*

worthy /ˈwɜːði/ *adj* (**worthier**; **worthiest**) **1** (*formal*) **worthy of sth/to do sth** good enough for sth or to have sth: *He felt he was not worthy to accept such responsibility.* **2** that should receive respect, support or attention: *a worthy leader* ◆ *a worthy cause*

⚷ **would** /wəd/ *strong form* /wʊd/ *modal verb* (*short form* **'d**; *negative* **would not**; *short form* **wouldn't** /ˈwʊdnt/) **1** used as the past form of 'will' when you report what sb says or thinks: *They said that they would help us.* ◆ *She didn't think that he would do a thing like that.* **2** used when talking about the result of an event that you imagine: *He would be delighted if you went to see him.* ◆ *She'd be stupid not to accept.* ◆ *I would have done more, if I'd had the time.* **3** used to describe sth that could have happened but did not: *If I had seen the advertisement in time, I would have applied for the job.* **4** used after 'wish': *I wish the sun would come out.* **5** to agree or be ready to do sth: *She just wouldn't do what I asked her.* **6** used when you are giving your opinion but are not certain that you are right: *I'd say she's about 40.* **7** used for asking sb politely to do sth: *Would you come this way, please?* **8** used with 'like' or 'love' as a way of asking or saying what sb wants: ***Would you like*** *to come with us?* ◆ ***I'd love*** *a piece of cake.* ➲ note at **want**

GRAMMAR **Would like** and **would love** are followed by the infinitive, not by the *-ing* form.

9 used for talking about things that often happened in the past: *When he was young he would often walk in these woods.* ➲ look at **used to** **10** used for commenting on behaviour that is typical of sb: *You would say that. You always support him.* ❶ For more information about modal verbs, look at the **Reference Section** at the back of this dictionary.

ˈ**would-be** *adj* [only *before* a noun] used to describe sb who is hoping to become the type of person mentioned: *a would-be actor* ◆ *advice for would-be parents*

⚷ **wound¹** /wuːnd/ *noun* [C] an injury to part of your body, especially a cut, often one received in fighting: *a bullet wound*
IDM **rub salt into the wound/sb's wounds** ➲ **rub**

⚷ **wound²** /wuːnd/ *verb* [T, usually passive] **1** to injure sb's body with a weapon: *He was wounded in the leg during the war.* ➲ note at **hurt** **2** to hurt sb's feelings deeply: *I was wounded by his criticism.* ▶ **wounded** *adj*: *a wounded soldier* ▶ **the wounded** *noun* [pl]: *Soldiers moved the wounded away from the battlefield.*

wound³ *past tense, past participle of* **wind³**

wove *past tense of* **weave**

woven *past participle of* **weave**

wow /waʊ/ *exclam* (*informal*) used for showing that you find sth impressive or surprising: *Wow! What a fantastic boat!*

WP *abbr* = **word processor, word processing**

wrangle /ˈræŋgl/ *noun* [C] a noisy or complicated argument: *The company is involved in* ***a legal wrangle*** *over copyright.* ▶ **wrangle** *verb* [I]

wrap

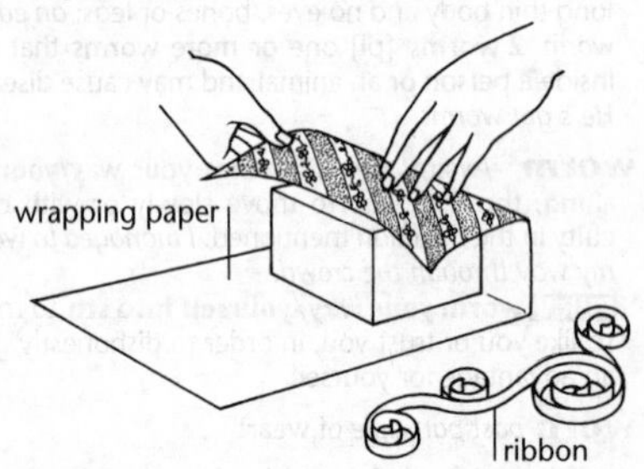

⚷ **wrap** /ræp/ *verb* [T] (**wrapping**; **wrapped**) **1** **wrap sth (up) (in sth)** to put paper or cloth around sb/sth as a cover: *to wrap up a present* ◆ *The baby was found wrapped in a blanket.* **2** **wrap sth round/around sb/sth** to tie sth such as paper or cloth around an object or a part of the body: *The man had a bandage wrapped round his head.*
IDM **be wrapped up in sb/sth** to be very involved and interested in sb/sth: *They were completely wrapped up in each other. They didn't notice I was there.*
PHR V **wrap (sb/yourself) up** to put warm clothes on sb/yourself

wrapper /ˈræpə(r)/ *noun* [C] the piece of paper or plastic which covers sth when you buy it: *a sweet/chocolate wrapper*

⚷ **wrapping** /ˈræpɪŋ/ *noun* [U] (also [pl] **wrappings**) paper, plastic, etc. that is used for covering sth in order to protect it: *She tore off the wrapping.*

wrapping paper *noun* [U] paper which is used for putting round presents ➲ picture at **wrap**

wrath /rɒθ/ *noun* [U] (*formal*) very great anger

wreak /riːk/ *verb* [T] (*formal*) **wreak sth (on sb/sth)** to cause great damage or harm to sb/sth: *Fierce storms* ***wreak havoc*** *at this time of year.*

wreath /riːθ/ *noun* [C] (*pl* **wreaths** /riːðz/) a circle of flowers and leaves placed on a grave, etc. as a sign of respect for sb who has died

wreck /rek/ *noun* **1** [C] a ship that has sunk or been badly damaged at sea: *Divers searched the wreck.* **2** [C] a car, plane, etc. which has been badly damaged, especially in an accident: *The car was a wreck but the lorry escaped almost without damage.* **3** [C, usually sing] (*informal*) a person or thing that is in a very bad condition: *He drove so badly I was* ***a nervous wreck*** *when we got there.* ▶ **wreck** *verb* [T]: *Vandals had wrecked the school hall.* ◆ *The strike wrecked all our holiday plans.*

wreckage /ˈrekɪdʒ/ *noun* [U] the broken pieces of sth that has been damaged or destroyed: *They searched the wreckage of the plane for evidence.*

wrench¹ /rentʃ/ *verb* [T] **1 wrench sb/sth (away, off, etc.)** to pull or turn sb/sth strongly and suddenly: *They had to wrench the door off the car to get the driver out.* ◆ (*figurative*) *The film was so exciting that I could hardly wrench myself away.* **2** to injure part of your body by turning it suddenly

wrench² /rentʃ/ *noun* **1** [C] (*AmE*) = **spanner** **2** [sing] the sadness you feel because you have to leave sb/sth **3** [C, usually sing] a sudden, violent pull or turn: *With a wrench I managed to open the door.*

wrestle /ˈresl/ *verb* [I] **1 wrestle (with) sb** to fight by trying to get hold of your opponent's body and throw them to the ground. People **wrestle** as a sport: *He managed to wrestle the man to the ground and take the knife from him.* **2 wrestle (with sth)** to try hard to deal with sth that is difficult

wrestling /ˈreslɪŋ/ *noun* [U] a sport in which two people fight and try to throw each other to the ground: *a wrestling match* ▶ **wrestler** *noun* [C]

wretch /retʃ/ *noun* [C] a poor, unhappy person: *The poor wretch was clearly starving.*

wretched /ˈretʃɪd/ *adj* **1** (of a person) very unhappy or ill **SYN** **awful** **2** [only *before* a noun] (*informal*) used for expressing anger: *That wretched dog has chewed up my slippers again!*

wriggle /ˈrɪgl/ *verb* [I,T] **1 wriggle (sth) (about / around)** to move about, or to move a part of your body, with short, quick movements, especially from side to side: *The baby was wriggling around on my lap.* ◆ *She wriggled her fingers about in the hot sand.* **2** to move in the direction mentioned by making quick turning movements: *The worm wriggled back into the soil.*
PHR V **wriggle out of sth/doing sth** (*informal*) to avoid sth by making clever excuses: *It's your turn to wash up—you can't wriggle out of it this time!*

wring /rɪŋ/ *verb* [T] (*pt, pp* **wrung** /rʌŋ/) **wring sth (out)** to press and squeeze sth in order to remove water from it ➲ picture at **squeeze**

wrinkle¹ /ˈrɪŋkl/ *noun* [C] a small line in sth, especially one on the skin of your face which you get as you grow older: *She's got fine wrinkles around her eyes.* ◆ *Smooth out the wrinkles in the fabric.* ➲ look at **furrow**

wrinkle² /ˈrɪŋkl/ *verb* [I,T] **wrinkle (sth) (up)** to form small lines and folds in sth: *She wrinkled her nose at the nasty smell.* ◆ *My skirt had wrinkled up on the journey.* ▶ **wrinkled** *adj*

He wrinkled his forehead.

⚷ **wrist** /rɪst/ *noun* [C] the narrow part at the end of your arm where it joins your hand ➲ picture at **body**: *She wore a silver bracelet on her wrist.*

wristband /ˈrɪstbænd/ *noun* [C] a strip of material worn around the wrist as a decoration, to absorb sweat during exercise or to show support for sth: *He was wearing an anti-nuclear wristband.*

wristwatch /ˈrɪstwɒtʃ/ *noun* [C] a watch that you wear on your wrist

writ /rɪt/ *noun* [C] a legal order to do or not to do sth, given by a court of law

⚷ **write** /raɪt/ *verb* (*pt* **wrote** /rəʊt/; *pp* **written** /ˈrɪtn/) [I,T] **1** to make words, letters, etc., especially on paper using a pen or pencil: *I can't write with this pen.* ◆ *Write your name and address on the form.* **2** to create a book, story, song, etc. in written form for people to read or use: *Tolstoy wrote 'War and Peace'.* ◆ *He wrote his wife a poem.* ◆ *Who wrote the music for that film?* **3 write (sth) (to sb); write (sb) sth** to write and send a letter, an email, etc. to sb: *She wrote that they were all well and would be home soon.* ◆ *She phones every week and writes occasionally.* ◆ *I've written a letter to my son./I've written my son a letter.* ◆ *I've written to him.*

HELP In American English we can say: *I've written him.*

4 [T] **write sth (out) (for sb)** to fill or complete a form, document, etc. with the necessary information: *I wrote out a receipt for £10.*
PHR V **write back (to sb)** to send a reply to sb **SYN** **reply**
write sth down to write sth on paper, especially so that you can remember it: *Did you write down Jon's address?*
write in (to sb/sth) (for sth) to write a letter to an organization, etc. to ask for sth, give an opinion, etc.
write off/away (to sb/sth) (for sth) to write a letter to an organization, etc. to order sth or ask for sth

W

write sb/sth off to accept or decide that sb/sth will not be successful or useful: *Don't write him off yet. He could still win.*
write sth off to accept that you will not get back an amount of money you have lost or spent: *to write off a debt*
write sth out to write the whole of sth on paper: *Can you write out that recipe for me?*
write sth up to write sth in a complete and final form, often using notes that you have made: *to write up lecture notes*

ˈ**write-off** *noun* [C] a thing, especially a vehicle, that is so badly damaged that it is not worth repairing

writer /ˈraɪtə(r)/ *noun* [C] a person who writes, especially one whose job is to write books, articles, stories, etc: *Charles Dickens was a famous writer.*

ˈ**write-up** *noun* [C] an article in a newspaper or magazine in which sb writes what they think about a new book, play, product, etc: *The performance got a good write-up in the local paper.*

writhe /raɪð/ *verb* [I] to turn and roll your body about: *She was writhing in pain.*

writing /ˈraɪtɪŋ/ *noun* [U] **1** the skill or activity of writing words: *He had problems with his reading and writing at school.* **2** the activity or job of writing books, etc: *It's difficult to earn much money from writing.* **3** the books, etc. that sb has written or the style in which sb writes: *Love is a common theme in his early writing.* **4** words that have been written or printed; the way a person writes: *This card's got no writing inside. You can put your own message.* ◆ *I can't read your writing, it's too small.*
IDM **in writing** in written form: *I'll confirm the offer in writing next week.*

ˈ**writing paper** *noun* [U] paper for writing letters on

written[1] /ˈrɪtn/ *adj* expressed in writing; not just spoken: *a written agreement* ◆ *Some expressions are only used in written English.* ◆ *a written test and an oral test* ➲ look at **spoken**

written[2] *past participle* of **write**

wrong[1] /rɒŋ/ *adj, adv* **1** not correct; in a way that is not correct: *the wrong answer* ◆ *I always pronounce that word wrong.* ◆ *You've got the wrong number* (= on the telephone). ◆ *I think you're wrong about Nicola—she's not lazy.* OPP **right** **2** [not before a noun] wrong (with sb/sth) causing problems or difficulties; not as it should be: *You look upset. Is something wrong?* ◆ ***What's wrong** with the car this time?* ◆ *She's got something wrong with her leg.* **3** not the best; not suitable: *That's the wrong way to hold the bat.* ◆ *I think she married the wrong man.* ◆ *I like him—I just think he's wrong for the job.* OPP right **4** wrong (to do sth) not morally right or honest: *It's wrong to tell lies.* ◆ *The man said that he had done nothing wrong.* OPP right
IDM **get/start off on the right/wrong foot (with sb)** ➲ **foot**[1]
get on the right/wrong side of sb ➲ **side**[1]
get sb wrong (*informal*) to not understand sb: *Don't get me wrong! I don't dislike him.*
go wrong 1 to make a mistake: *I'm afraid we've gone wrong. We should have taken the other road.* **2** to stop working properly or to stop developing well: *My computer keeps going wrong.*
on the right/wrong track ➲ **track**[1]

wrong[2] /rɒŋ/ *noun* **1** [U] things that are morally bad or dishonest: *Children quickly learn the difference between **right and wrong**.* **2** [C] an action or a situation which is not fair: *A terrible wrong has been done. Those men should never have gone to prison.*
IDM **in the wrong** (used about a person) having made a mistake
right a wrong ➲ **right**[4]

wrong[3] /rɒŋ/ *verb* [T] (*formal*) to do sth to sb which is bad or unfair: *I wronged her when I said she was lying.*

wrongful /ˈrɒŋfl/ *adj* [only *before* a noun] (*formal*) not fair, not legal or not moral: *He sued the company for wrongful dismissal.*

wrongly /ˈrɒŋli/ *adv* in a way that is wrong or not correct: *He was wrongly accused of stealing money.*

HELP Wrongly or **wrong**? The adverb **wrong** is used after a verb or the object of a verb, especially in conversation: *He's spelt my name wrong.* The adverb **wrongly** is especially used before a past participle or a 'that' clause: *My name's been wrongly spelt.*

wrote *past tense* of **write**

wrought iron /ˌrɔːt ˈaɪən/ *noun* [U] a form of iron used to make fences, gates, etc: *The gates were made of wrought iron.* ◆ *wrought-iron gates* ➲ look at **cast iron**

wrung *past tense, past participle* of **wring**

wry /raɪ/ *adj* showing that you are both disappointed and amused: *'Never mind,' she said with a wry grin. 'At least we got one vote.'* ▶ **wryly** *adv*

wt *abbr* = **weight**[1]: *net wt 500g*

WWW /ˌdʌblju: dʌblju: ˈdʌblju:/ *abbr* = **World Wide Web**

X, x /eks/ *noun* [C,U] (*pl* Xs; X's; x's /ˈeksɪz/) the 24th letter of the English alphabet: *'Xylophone' begins with (an) 'X'.*

HELP X is used by teachers to show that an answer is wrong. It is also used instead of the name of a person if you do not know or do not want to say his/her name: *Mr and Mrs X.* At the end of a letter it represents a kiss: *Lots of love, Mary XX.*

X

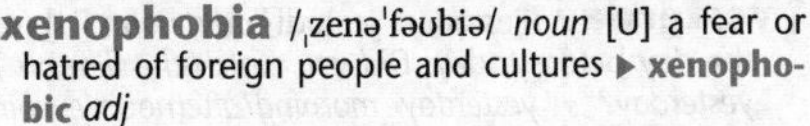

xenophobia /ˌzenəˈfəʊbiə/ *noun* [U] a fear or hatred of foreign people and cultures ▶ **xenophobic** *adj*

Xerox™ /ˈzɪərɒks/ *noun* **1** [U] a process for producing copies of letters, documents, etc. using a special machine **2** [C] a copy produced by **Xerox™** or a similar process **SYN** **photocopy** ▶ **xerox** *verb* [T]

X factor /ˈeks fæktə(r)/ *noun* [sing] a special quality, especially one that you need for success and that is difficult to describe: *She certainly has the X factor that all great singers have.*

XL *abbr* **extra large**; used for sizes of things, especially clothes

Xmas /ˈkrɪsməs; ˈeksməs/ *noun* [C,U] (*informal*) (used as a short form in writing) Christmas: *Happy Xmas* (= written message in a Christmas card)

ˈ**X-ray** *noun* [C] **1** [usually pl] a type of light that makes it possible to see inside solid objects, for example the human body, so that they can be examined and a photograph of them can be made **2** a photograph that is made with an **X-ray** machine: *The X-ray showed that the bone was not broken.* ➲ look at **ray** ▶ **X-ray** *verb* [T]: *She had her chest X-rayed.*

xylophone /ˈzaɪləfəʊn/ *noun* [C] a musical instrument that consists of two rows of wooden bars of different lengths. You play it by hitting these bars with a small hammer. ➲ picture at **music**

Y, y /waɪ/ *noun* [C,U] (*pl* **Ys**; **Y's**; **y's** /waɪz/) the 25th letter of the English alphabet: *'Yesterday' begins with (a) 'Y'.*

yacht /jɒt/ *noun* [C] **1** a boat with sails, often used for pleasure trips and racing: *a yacht race* ➲ note at **boat** ➲ picture on **page P6** **2** a large boat with a motor, used for pleasure ➲ look at **dinghy**

yachting /ˈjɒtɪŋ/ *noun* [U] the activity or sport of sailing or racing **yachts**

yachtsman /ˈjɒtsmən/, **yachtswoman** /ˈjɒtswʊmən/ *noun* [C] (*pl* **-men** /-mən/, **-women** /-wɪmɪn/) a person who sails a **yacht** in races or for pleasure

yank /jæŋk/ *verb* [I,T] (*informal*) to pull sth suddenly, quickly and hard: *She yanked at the door handle.* ▶ **yank** *noun* [C]

yap /jæp/ *verb* [I] (**yapping**; **yapped**) (used about dogs, especially small ones) to make short, loud noises in an excited way

🔑 **yard** /jɑːd/ *noun* [C] **1** an area outside a building, usually with a hard surface and a wall or fence around it: *a school/prison yard* ➲ look at **courtyard**, **churchyard** **2** (*AmE*) = **garden**[1](1) **3** [in compounds] an area, usually without a roof, used for a particular type of work or purpose: *a shipyard/boatyard* ◆ *a builder's yard*

> **HELP** In British English the piece of land belonging to a house is a **garden** if it has grass, flowers, etc., and a **yard** if it is made of concrete or stone. In American English this piece of land is a **yard** whether it has grass or is made of concrete or stone.

4 (*abbr* **yd**) a measure of length; 0.914 of a metre or 36 inches. There are 3 feet in a yard: *Our house is 100 yards from the supermarket.* ⓘ For more information about measurements, look at the section on using numbers at the back of this dictionary.

yardstick /ˈjɑːdstɪk/ *noun* [C] a standard with which things can be compared: *Exam results should not be the only yardstick by which pupils are judged.*

yarn /jɑːn/ *noun* **1** [C,U] thread (usually of wool or cotton) that is used for knitting, etc. **2** [C] (*informal*) a long story that sb tells, especially one that is invented or exaggerated

🔑 **yawn** /jɔːn/ *verb* [I] to open your mouth wide and breathe in deeply, especially when you are tired or bored: *I kept yawning all through the lecture.* ▶ **yawn** *noun* [C]: *'How much longer will it take?' he said with a yawn.*

yay /jeɪ/ *exclam* (*especially AmE informal*) used to show that you are very pleased about sth: *I won! Yay!*

yd *abbr* (*pl* **yds**) = **yard**(4)

🔑 **yeah** /jeə/ *exclam* (*informal*) yes: *Yeah, that's right.*

🔑 **year** /jɪə(r); jɜː(r)/ *noun* (*abbr* **yr**)

➤ 12 MONTHS **1** [C] (also ˈ**calendar year**) the period from 1 January to 31 December, 365 or 366 days divided into 12 months or 52 weeks: *last year/this year/next year* ◆ *The population of the country will be 70 million by the year 2014.* ◆ *Interest is paid on this account once a year.* ◆ *a* ***leap year*** (= one that has 366 days) ◆ *the* ***New Year*** (= the first days of January) **2** [C] any period of 12 months, measured from any date: *She worked here for twenty years.* ◆ *He left school just over a year ago.* ◆ *In a year's time, you'll be old enough to vote.* **3** [C] a period of 12 months in connection with schools, the business world, etc: *the academic/school year* ◆ *the tax/financial year*

➤ IN SCHOOL/UNIVERSITY **4** [C] (*especially BrE*) the level that a particular student is at: *My son is in year ten now.* ◆ *The first years* (= students in their first year at school/university, etc.) *do French as a compulsory subject.* ◆ *He was a year below me at school.*

➤ AGE **5** [C, usually pl] (used in connection with the age of sb/sth) a period of 12 months: *He's ten years old today.* ◆ *a six-year-old daughter* ◆ *This car is nearly five years old.* ◆ *The company is now in its fifth year.* ➲ note at **age**

> **HELP** that you say *He is ten, He's ten* or *He's ten years old*. You CANNOT say *He has ten years, He's ten years* or *a ten-years-old boy*.

➤ LONG TIME **6 years** [pl] a long time: *It happened years ago.* ◆ *I haven't seen him for years.*

IDM **all year round** for the whole year

Y

donkey's years ➲ donkey
the turn of the century/year ➲ turn²
year after year; year in year out every year for many years

yearbook /ˈjɪəbʊk/ *noun* [C] **1** a book published once a year, giving details of events, etc. of the previous year, especially those connected with a particular area of activity **2** a book that is produced by students in their final year of school or college, containing photographs of students and details of school activities

yearly /ˈjɪəli; ˈjɜːli/ *adj, adv* (happening) every year or once a year: *The conference is held yearly.*

yearn /jɜːn/ *verb* [I] (*formal*) yearn (for sb/sth); yearn (to do sth) to want sb/sth very much, especially sb/sth that you cannot have SYN **long**
▶ **yearning** *noun* [C,U]

yeast /jiːst/ *noun* [U] a substance used for making bread rise and for making beer, wine, etc.

yell /jel/ *verb* [I,T] yell (out) (sth); yell (sth) (at sb/sth) to shout very loudly, often because you are angry, excited or in pain: *She yelled out his name.* ◆ *There's no need to yell at me; I can hear you perfectly well.* ▶ **yell** *noun* [C]

yellow /ˈjeləʊ/ *adj* (yellower; yellowest) *noun* [C, U] (of) the colour of lemons or butter: *a pale/light yellow dress* ◆ *a bright shade of yellow* ◆ *the yellows and browns of the autumn leaves*

ˌyellow ˈcard *noun* [C] (in football) a card that is shown to a player as a warning that he or she will be sent off the field if he or she behaves badly again ➲ look at **red card**

yellowish /ˈjeləʊɪʃ/ *adj* (also yellowy) slightly yellow in colour

ˌyellow ˈline *noun* [C] (in Britain) a yellow line at the side of a road to show that you can only park there for a limited time: ***double yellow lines*** (= you must not park there at all)

ˌYellow ˈPages™ *noun* [pl] a website or telephone book (on yellow paper) that lists all the business companies, etc. in a certain area in sections according to the goods or services they provide

yellowy /ˈjeləʊi/ = **yellowish**

yelp /jelp/ *verb* [I] to give a sudden short cry, especially of pain ▶ **yelp** *noun* [C]

yes /jes/ *exclam* **1** used to give a positive answer to a question, for saying that sth is true or correct or for saying that you want sth: *'Are you having a good time?' 'Yes, thank you.'* ◆ *'You're married, aren't you?' 'Yes, I am.'* ◆ *'May I sit here?' 'Yes, of course.'* ◆ *'More coffee?' 'Yes, please.'* OPP **no** **2** used when saying that a negative statement that sb has made is not true: *'You don't care about anyone but yourself.' 'Yes I do.'* OPP **no** **3** used for showing you have heard sb or will do what they ask: *'Waiter!' 'Yes, madam.'* ▶ **yes** *noun* [C] (*pl* yesses or yeses): *Was that a yes or a no?*

yesterday /ˈjestədeɪ; ˈjestədi/ *adv, noun* [U] (on) the day before today: *Did you watch the film on TV yesterday?* ◆ *yesterday morning/afternoon/evening* ◆ *I posted the form* **the day before yesterday** (= if I am speaking on Wednesday, I posted it on Monday). ◆ *Have you still got yesterday's paper?* ◆ *I spent the whole of yesterday walking round the shops.*

yet /jet/ *adv* **1** used with negative verbs or in questions for talking about sth that has not happened but that you expect to happen: *Has it stopped raining yet?* ◆ *I haven't finished yet.* ◆ *I haven't seen that film yet.*

> **HELP** In American English you can say: *I didn't see that film yet.*

2 [used with negative verbs] now; as early as this: *You don't have to leave yet—your train isn't for another hour.* **3** from now until the period of time mentioned has passed: *She isn't that old; she'll live for years yet.* **4** [used especially with *may* or *might*] at some time in the future: *With a bit of luck, they may yet win.* **5** [used with superlatives] until now/until then; so far: *This is her best film yet.* **6** used with comparatives to emphasize an increase in the degree of sth: *a recent and yet more improbable theory*

IDM **as yet** until now: *As yet little is known about the disease.*

yet again (used for expressing surprise or anger that sth happens again) once more; another time: *I found out that he had lied to me yet again.*

yet another used for expressing surprise that there is one more of sth: *They're opening yet another fast food restaurant in the square.*

yet to do, etc. that has not been done and is still to do in the future: *The final decision has yet to be made.*

▶ **yet** *conj* but; in spite of that: *He seems pleasant, yet there's something about him I don't like.*

yew /juː/ *noun* **1** [C,U] (also ˈyew tree) a tree with dark green leaves and small round red fruit which are poisonous **2** [U] the wood from the yew tree

ˈY-fronts™ *noun* [pl] (*BrE*) a type of men's underwear with an opening in the front sewn in the shape of a Y upside-down

YHA /ˌwaɪ eɪtʃ ˈeɪ/ *abbr* **Youth Hostels Association**; an organization that provides cheap, simple accommodation

yield¹ /jiːld/ *verb*
➤PRODUCE STH **1** [T] to produce or provide crops, profits or results: *How much wheat does each field yield?* ◆ *Did the experiment yield any new information?*
➤STOP REFUSING **2** [I] (*formal*) yield (to sb/sth) to stop refusing to do sth or to obey sb: *The government refused to yield to the hostage-takers' demands.* ➲ A less formal expression is **give in**.
➤GIVE CONTROL **3** [T] yield sb/sth (up) (to sb/sth) to allow sb to have control of sth that you were controlling: *The army has yielded power to the rebels.*
➤MOVE UNDER PRESSURE **4** [I] (*formal*) to move, bend or break because of pressure: *The dam finally yielded under the weight of the water.* ➲ A less formal expression is **give way**.
➤IN VEHICLE **5** [I] (*AmE*) yield (to sb/sth) to allow

other vehicles on a bigger road to go first: *You have to yield to traffic from the left here.*

HELP Give way is used in British English.

PHR V **yield to sth** (*formal*) to be replaced by sth, especially sth newer: *Old-fashioned methods have yielded to new technology.* ➲ A less formal expression is **give way**.

yield² /jiːld/ *noun* [C] the amount that is produced: *Wheat yields were down 5% this year.* ♦ *This investment has an annual yield of 12%.*

yo /jəʊ/ *exclam* (*especially AmE slang*) used by some people when they see a friend; hello

yob /jɒb/ *noun* [C] (*BrE informal*) a boy or young man who is rude, loud and sometimes violent or aggressive ➲ look at **hooligan, lout** ▶ **yobbish** *adj* [usually before a noun]: *yobbish behaviour*

yoga /ˈjəʊgə/ *noun* [U] a system of exercises for the body that helps you control and relax both your mind and your body

yogurt (also **yoghurt**) /ˈjɒgət/ *noun* [C,U] a slightly sour, thick liquid food made from milk: *plain/banana/strawberry yogurt*

yoke /jəʊk/ *noun* **1** [C] a long piece of wood fixed across the necks of two animals so that they can pull heavy loads together **2** [sing] (*formal*) something that limits your freedom and makes your life difficult: *the yoke of parental control*

yolk /jəʊk/ *noun* [C,U] the yellow part in the middle of an egg ➲ picture at **egg**

⚷ **you** /ju; *strong form* juː/ *pron* **1** used as the subject or object of a verb, or after a preposition to refer to the person or people being spoken or written to: *You can play the guitar, can't you?* ♦ *I've told you about this before.* ♦ *Bring all your photos with you.* **2** used with a noun, adjective or phrase when calling sb sth: *You idiot! What do you think you're doing?* **3** used for referring to people in general: *The more you earn, the more tax you pay.*

you'd /juːd/ *short for* **you had; you would**

you'll /juːl/ *short for* **you will**

⚷ **young¹** /jʌŋ/ *adj* (**younger** /ˈjʌŋgə(r)/, **youngest** /ˈjʌŋgɪst/) not having lived or existed for very long; not old: *They have two young children.* ♦ *I'm a year younger than her.* ♦ *My father was the youngest of eight children.* ♦ *my younger brothers* **OPP** **old**
IDM **young at heart** behaving or thinking like a young person, although you are old

young² /jʌŋ/ *noun* [pl] **1** **the young** young people considered as a group: *The young of today are more ambitious than their parents.* **2** young animals: *Swans will attack to protect their young.*

youngish /ˈjʌŋɪʃ/ *adj* quite young

youngster /ˈjʌŋstə(r)/ *noun* [C] a young person: *There is very little entertainment for youngsters in this town.*

⚷ **your** /jɔː(r); jə(r)/ *determiner* **1** of or belonging to the person or people being spoken to: *What's your flat like?* ♦ *Thanks for all your help.* ♦ *How old are your children now?* **2** belonging to or connected with people in general: *When your life is as busy as mine, you have little time to relax.* **3** (*informal*) used for saying that sth is well known to people in general: *So this is your typical English summer, is it?* **4** (also **Your**) used in some titles: *your Highness*

you're /jʊə(r); jɔː(r)/ *short for* **you are**

⚷ **yours** /jɔːz/ *pron* **1** of or belonging to you: *Is this bag yours or mine?* ♦ *I was talking to a friend of yours the other day.* **2 Yours** used at the end of a letter: *Yours sincerely .../faithfully ...* ♦ *Yours ...* ➲ note at **sincere**

⚷ **yourself** /jɔːˈself; *weak form* jəˈself/ *pron* (*pl* **yourselves** /-ˈselvz/) **1** used when the person or people being spoken to both do an action and are also affected by the action: *Be careful or you'll hurt yourself.* ♦ *Here's some money. Buy yourselves a present.* ♦ *You're always talking about yourself!* ♦ *You don't look yourself today* (= you do not look well or do not look as happy as usual). **2** used to emphasize the person or people who do the action: *You yourself told me there was a problem last week.* ♦ *Did you repair the car yourselves?* (= or did sb else do it for you?) **3** (*informal*) you: *'How are you?' 'Not too bad, thanks. And yourself?'*
IDM **(all) by yourself/yourselves 1** alone: *Do you live by yourself?* ➲ note at **alone 2** without help: *You can't cook dinner for ten people by yourself.*

EXAM TIP

Talking about yourself

In a **speaking exam** you will be expected to talk about yourself. This could include talking about your daily routine, sports you like, travel and holidays, work experience or your hopes for the future. Before the exam, prepare some ideas and vocabulary for each of these topics, but do not be tempted to memorize complete answers. It is important to show that you can hold a conversation with someone.

⚷ **youth** /juːθ/ *noun* (*pl* **youths** /juːðz/) **1** [U] the period of your life when you are young, especially the time before a child becomes an adult: *He was quite a good sportsman* **in his youth**. **2** [U] the fact or state of being young: *I think that her youth will be a disadvantage in this job.* **3** [C] a young person (usually a young man, and often one that you do not have a good opinion of): *a gang of youths* **4 the youth** [U] young people considered as a group: *the youth of today* ➲ look at **age, old age**

youth club *noun* [C] a club where young people can meet each other and take part in various activities

youthful /ˈjuːθfl/ *adj* **1** typical of young people: *youthful enthusiasm* **2** seeming younger than you are: *She's a youthful fifty-year-old.*

ˈyouth hostel *noun* [C] a cheap and simple place to stay, especially for young people when they are travelling

you've /juːv/ *short for* **you have**

Y

ˈ**Yo Yo™** (also ˈyo-yo) *noun* [C] (*pl* Yo Yos; yo-yos) a toy which is a round piece of wood or plastic with a string round the middle. You put the string round your finger and can make the **yo-yo** go up and down it.

yr (also yr.) *abbr* (*pl* yrs) = **year**

yuck (also yuk) /jʌk/ *exclam* (*informal*) used for saying that you think sth is disgusting or very unpleasant: *It's filthy! Yuck!* ▶ **yucky** (also yukky) *adj*: *a yucky colour*

yummy /ˈjʌmi/ *adj* (*informal*) tasting very good: *a yummy cake* SYN **delicious**

yuppie (also yuppy) /ˈjʌpi/ *noun* [C] (*pl* yuppies) a successful young professional person who lives in a city, earns a lot of money and spends it on fashionable things

Z, z /zed/ *noun* [C,U] (*pl* Zs; Z's; z's /zedz/) the 26th letter of the English alphabet: *'Zero' begins with (a) 'Z'.*

zany /ˈzeɪni/ *adj* (*informal*) (zanier; zaniest) funny in an unusual and crazy way: *a zany comedian*

zap /zæp/ *verb* (zapping; zapped) (*informal*) **1** [T] zap sb/sth (with sth) to destroy, hit or kill sb, usually with a gun or other weapon: *It's a computer game where you have to zap aliens with a laser.* **2** [I,T] to change TV programmes very quickly using a **remote control** (= an electronic device)

zeal /ziːl/ *noun* [U] (*formal*) great energy or enthusiasm: *religious zeal*

zealous /ˈzeləs/ *adj* using great energy and enthusiasm ▶ **zealously** *adv*

zebra /ˈzebrə/ *noun* [C] (*pl* zebra *or* zebras) an African wild animal that looks like a horse, with black and white lines all over its body

zebra

ˌ**zebra** ˈ**crossing** *noun* [C] (*in Britain*) a place where the road is marked with black and white lines and people can cross safely because cars must stop to let them do this ➲ look at **pedestrian crossing** ➲ picture at **roundabout**

zenith /ˈzenɪθ/ *noun* [sing] **1** the highest point that the sun or moon reaches in the sky, directly above you: *The sun rose to its zenith.* **2** (*formal*) the time when sth is strongest and most successful

🔑 **zero¹** /ˈzɪərəʊ/ *number* (*pl* zeros) **1** [C] the figure 0 ➲ note at **six** **2** [U] freezing point in the Celsius system; 0°C: *The temperature is likely to fall to five degrees* ***below zero*** (= –5°C). **3** [U] the lowest possible amount or level; nothing at all: *zero growth/inflation/profit* ◆ *My chances of passing the exam are zero.*

> **OTHER WORDS FOR**
>
> **zero**
>
> The figure **0** has several different names in British English. **Zero** is most commonly used in scientific or technical contexts. **Nil** is most commonly used in scores in sport, especially football (when spoken). **Nought** is used when referring to the figure **0** as part of a larger number: *a million is one followed by six noughts.* **O** (pronounced /əʊ/) is most commonly used when saying numbers such as telephone or flight numbers.

zero² /ˈzɪərəʊ/ *verb* [T] (zeroing; zeroes; *pt, pp* zeroed) to turn an instrument, a control, etc. to zero PHR V **zero in on sb/sth 1** to fix all your attention on the person or thing mentioned: *They zeroed in on the key issues.* **2** to aim guns, etc. at the person or thing mentioned

ˌ**zero-**ˈ**carbon** *adj* in which the amount of **carbon dioxide** (= a gas) produced has been reduced to nothing or is balanced by actions that protect the environment: *a zero-carbon house that uses no energy from external sources* SYN **carbon neutral**

ˌ**zero** ˈ**tolerance** *noun* [U] the policy of applying laws very strictly so that people are punished even for offences that are not very serious

zest /zest/ *noun* [U,sing] zest (for sth) a feeling of enjoyment, excitement and enthusiasm: *She has a great* ***zest for life.***

zigzag /ˈzɪgzæg/ *noun* [C], *adj* [only *before* a noun] (consisting of) a line with left and right turns, like a lot of letter Ws, one after the other: *The skier came down the slope in a series of zigzags.* ◆ *a zigzag pattern/line* ➲ picture at **line** ➲ picture on **page P1** ▶ **zigzag** *verb* [I] (zigzagging; zigzagged): *We took a road that zigzagged through the mountains.*

zilch /zɪltʃ/ *noun* [U] (*informal*) nothing: *I arrived in this country with zilch.*

zillion /ˈzɪljən/ *noun* [C] (*especially AmE informal*) a very large number: *There were zillions of people waiting outside the theatre.*

zinc /zɪŋk/ *noun* [U] (*symbol* Zn) a silver-grey metal, often put on the surface of iron and steel as protection against water: *Brass is made from copper and zinc.*

zip /zɪp/ (*AmE* zipper) *noun* [C] a device consisting of two rows of metal or plastic teeth, that you use for fastening clothes, bags, etc: *to do up/undo a zip* ➲ picture at **button** ➲ picture on **page P1** ▶ **zip** *verb* [T] (zipping; zipped) zip sth (up): *There was so much in the bag that it was difficult to zip it up.* OPP **unzip**

ˈ**zip code** (also ZIP code) (*AmE*) = **postcode**

zipper /ˈzɪpə(r)/ (*AmE*) = **zip**

zit /zɪt/ *noun* [C] (*informal*) a spot on the skin, especially on the face

Z

the zodiac

the signs of the zodiac

the zodiac /ˈzəʊdiæk/ *noun* [sing] a diagram of the positions of the sun, moon and planets, which is divided into twelve equal parts, each with a special name and symbol called a **sign of the zodiac**

> **MORE** The signs of the zodiac are used in **astrology** and **horoscopes** (often called **the stars**) in newspapers and magazines. People often refer to the signs and to the influence that they think these have on a person's personality and future: *Which sign (of the zodiac) are you?*

zombie /ˈzɒmbi/ *noun* [C] (*informal*) a person who seems only partly alive, without any feeling or interest in what is happening

🔑 **zone** /zəʊn/ *noun* [C] an area that is different from those around it, for example because sth special happens there: *a war zone* ◆ *a flight crossing several **times zones**.* (= one of the 24 areas that the world is divided into, each with its own time)

zoo /zuː/ *noun* [C] (*pl* zoos) a park where many kinds of wild animals are kept so that people can look at them and where they are bred, studied and protected

zookeeper /ˈzuːkiːpə(r)/ *noun* [C] a person who works in a **zoo**, taking care of the animals

zoology /zuˈɒlədʒi/ *noun* [U] the scientific study of animals ➲ look at **biology, botany** ▶ **zoological** /ˌzuːəˈlɒdʒɪkl/ *adj*: *zoological illustrations* ▶ **zoologist** /-dʒɪst/ *noun* [C]

zoom /zuːm/ *verb* [I] **1** to move or go somewhere very fast: *Traffic zoomed past us.* **2** (on some small computer devices) to make the screen larger using your fingers, in order to see more detail **OPP** **pinch in** ➲ note at **touch screen**
PHR V **zoom in (on sb/sth)** (when taking a photograph) to give a closer view of the object/person being photographed by using a **zoom lens** on the camera: *The camera zoomed in on the actor's face.*

ˈ**zoom lens** (also zoom) *noun* [C] a device on a camera that makes an object being photographed appear gradually bigger or smaller so that it seems to be getting closer or further away ➲ picture at **camera**

zucchini /zuˈkiːni/ (*pl* zucchini *or* zucchinis) (*AmE*) = **courgette**

Z

Study section

WT1–WT16 **Wordpower Writing Tutor**
WT1 Using the Writing Tutor
WT4 Writing an argument essay
WT6 Writing a comparison essay
WT8 Writing a report
WT10 Writing a book or film review
WT12 Writing formal letters: a letter of complaint
WT14 Applying for a job 1: writing a CV
WT15 Applying for a job 2: writing a covering letter
WT16 Writing an informal email

P1–P16 **Colour pages**
P1 Clothes
P2 Work and jobs
P3 Leisure activities
P4 Sports
P6 Transport
P8 House
P9 Homes
P10 Landscape
P12 Animals
P14 Fruit
P15 Vegetables
P16 Food and drink

R1–R41 **Reference section**
R2 Grammar
R21 Other reference

R42–R55 **Wordpower Workout**
R56 Workout key
R60 List of illustrations in the dictionary
R62 List of notes in the dictionary

Wordpower Writing Tutor

Using the Oxford Wordpower Dictionary to improve your writing

In the Writing Tutor you will find examples of essays, letters and emails to help you with your writing in class and in exams. You will also find advice about planning and organizing your work, and tips about checking your writing.

The writing model
Look carefully at:
- the **content** (what is being said)
- the **language** and **style**
- the **layout** (the way the text is arranged on the page)

Before you write
This section will help you to think of ideas, to plan and organize your own writing.

Language Bank
This section gives you some useful words and phrases that you can use in each type of writing.

Notes in the dictionary
You can find notes in the main part of the dictionary to give you more help with your writing.

Checklist
Use this section to check and improve your work and correct mistakes.

Formal and informal writing

Your writing should not be informal unless you are writing an informal letter or email. When you check your work, think about these things:

Have you used any words that are too informal?
If you are not sure, check in the dictionary and do not use anything marked *informal*, *slang* or *spoken*.

Avoid short forms
For example, do not write *I'm* or *haven't*, but use *I am* or *have not*.

Sentences
Too many short sentences can sound very informal. To express your ideas you will need to use words like *which*, *that* (relative pronouns), *and*, *but*, *or* and *although*, *because*, *if* to join parts of sentences. Avoid very long sentences, as these can be difficult to understand.

Using 'I'
Try not to use 'I' too much in essays unless you are asked to give your own opinion. For example, instead of *I find my smartphone very useful*, write *Many people find smartphones very useful*.

Contents

Using the Writing Tutor	WT 1
Argument essay	WT 4
Comparison essay	WT 6
Report	WT 8
Book and film review	WT 10
Formal letters	WT 12
Applying for a job: CV and covering letter	WT 14
Email	WT 16

How to write well

When you have to write an essay, a letter or an email, whether it is for class, for an exam, or in real life, you will be more successful if you plan and write in an organized way.

1. Think

Before you start, ask yourself:
Who will read it?
Am I writing for a teacher or an examiner, other students, an employer?
The answer will help you to decide what information to include and how formal or informal your language should be.

2. Plan

Brainstorm
Think of as many ideas as possible about the topic. You can make lists, use a table or draw a mind map.
Organize
Choose your best ideas and organize them into paragraphs. Think about how many words you are asked to use.
Vocabulary and language
Additional notes in the dictionary, such as Topic and Writing Tips, will help you choose appropriate language. There is a list of notes on page R62.

3. Write

You are now ready to start writing.
Use your plan
Try to keep to your plan. Think about the content, the paragraphs and the sentences at this stage.
Language and style
Is this a formal or in informal piece of writing? You can use informal, slang or spoken words and phrases if you are writing to a friend, but you do not usually use them in an essay.
Layout
If you are writing a letter or an email, make sure you put names and addresses in the right place.

4. Check

Find and correct mistakes
It is very important to re-read your work and check it very carefully. If you make a lot of mistakes, people may find it difficult to understand and you can lose marks in an exam.

Check that you have used the right number of words
If you are told to write, for example, 170 – 200 words, you must not use fewer than 170 or more than 200. If you do, you may lose marks in an exam.

Checking your work

Using your dictionary

The main part of the dictionary can help you choose the right language to use. You can also use it to check that you have used the correct grammar and spelling.

Ask yourself:

Have I used the right word?
The dictionary has notes and illustrations that explain confusing words, for example *borrow/lend* (look at **borrow**) and *sympathetic/nice* (look at **sympathetic**). Sometimes learners choose the wrong word because they translate from their own language. Check any words that you are not sure about.

What about language and style?
Have you used any words that are too formal or informal in this type of writing? Check in the dictionary if you're not sure. The labels *formal, informal, spoken* and *slang* will help you.

Have I used the same word or phrase too many times?
Try to find different ways to say things. Use the **Other words for** notes in the dictionary. (For example, look at the note at **nice**.) See if there is a synonym for a word you use a lot.

Have I used the right words together?
Is it *make homework* or *do homework*? Look up the main word in the dictionary (**homework**) and see which word it is used with in the examples.

What about prepositions?
Is it *close to* or *close from*? Check prepositions after nouns, verbs or adjectives very carefully.

Have I used the correct verb patterns?
Is it *enjoy to do something* or *enjoy doing something*? Look at the example sentences for **enjoy**.

	Spelling test
1.	leisure ✓
2.	accomodation ✗
3.	apartment ✓

What about spelling?
Check the spelling of plurals, past tenses, -ing forms and comparative and superlative adjectives and adverbs. Words that are similar to words in your language may be spelled differently. You can find the names of countries, cities and nationalities in the list at the back of the dictionary.

Is the grammar correct?
Have you checked whether the nouns are countable or uncountable? Are the verbs irregular? There is a list of irregular verbs at the back of the dictionary.

Make your own checklist
Look carefully at the mistakes your teacher marks in your written work and make a list of the mistakes you often make. Use this list to check each piece of work you do – *before* you give it to the teacher.

Writing an argument essay

An argument essay needs to be clearly organized. You should give points for and against the argument. Use formal language and avoid using **I** too much.

A smartphone is an essential possession in modern society. Discuss. (170–200 words)

Paragraph 1 – Introduction
Show why the topic is important or interesting and give a basic plan for the rest of the essay.

Today's mobile devices allow us to receive email, chat online, and look at websites wherever we are. Smartphones offer a number of benefits, but they also have several disadvantages.

Paragraph 2 – Advantages
You may support your points with examples from your own experience.

Smartphones certainly have many advantages. For example, users can work, access information, and use services such as banking or shopping at any time. In addition, special software can provide directions and help if you get lost. Many people also like to play games, surf the web or watch videos while waiting for a bus or an appointment.

Paragraph 3 – Disadvantages
Try to balance the number of positive and negative points.

However, smartphones also have their drawbacks. First of all, many consumers cannot afford to buy them, and secondly, the monthly fees for service plans are quite high. Moreover, some people depend too much on their smartphones and feel uncomfortable when they are not able to use them.

Paragraph 4 – Conclusion
Summarize the main points. Give your own opinion on the topic.

In short, smartphones are not an essential part of modern life for everyone. Nevertheless, if you can afford one, and if you think you can control the amount of time you spend online, then a smartphone might be a convenient and enjoyable option for you.

Linking words and phrases help the reader to move easily from one point to the next.

Use formal language. *Allow* is more formal than *let*, and *receive* is more formal than *get*.

Use synonyms to avoid repeating key words and phrases. *Benefits* is a synonym for *advantages*, and *drawbacks* is a synonym for *disadvantages*.

Before you write

- Read the question carefully and make sure that you understand what it is asking before you begin to write.
- Brainstorm: Think of points for and against smartphones. For example:

advantages	disadvantages
• info and services whenever you need them (transfer money, etc.) • entertainment when bored (while waiting, etc.) ...	• expensive to buy • monthly fees are high ...

- Look again at your notes and choose the best points to include.
- Organize your ideas into paragraphs.
  1 Introduction 2 Advantages 3 Disadvantages 4 Conclusion

Language Bank: Linking expressions

You use all these words or phrases at the start of a sentence, except for *also* and *as well*.

Introduction
Today, Nowadays, These days,...

More information
In addition, Furthermore, Moreover, What is more, First of all, Firstly/ Secondly, Finally/Lastly, also, as well,...
➲ See NOTE at **also**

Contrast
However, Nevertheless, Despite this, In spite of this, Although, On the other hand,...
➲ See WRITING TIP at **contrast**

Consequences
Therefore, As a result, For this Reason, Consequently, So,...
➲ See WRITING TIP at **therefore**

Opinions
In my opinion, From my point of view,...
➲ See NOTE at **think**

Conclusion
In short, To sum up, In conclusion, To conclude,...

Checklist

Have I

- written about *exactly* what the task asked me to discuss? ☐
- written about both sides of the argument? ☐
- organized my ideas into logical paragraphs? ☐
- used linking words to help the reader follow what I've said? ☐
- given my opinion in the conclusion? ☐

Writing a comparison essay

When you are asked to compare two things, you should think about how they are similar to each other, as well as what makes them different.

Compare life for young people today with life before the invention of the Internet. Is it better to be a teenager today, or was it better in the past? (180–200 words)

Paragraph 1– Introduction
General comment about the two things

The Internet has brought important changes to the lives of young people. Teenagers today have a very different way of life from their parents, both at school and in their leisure time.

Paragraph 2
Differences and similarities at school

While their parents used to visit libraries and read books to research a school project, today's teenagers do research at home on their computers. They can find a much wider variety of up-to-date information. However, books are still used in lessons, so methods of teaching today are often quite similar to what their parents knew.

Paragraph 3
Differences and similarities in social life

Outside school, differences are greater. With the Internet, teenagers can chat to their friends more easily than when they had to use the family phone. They are also likely to have a wider circle of friends through social networking sites, although there is a danger that they may spend too much time alone with their computers. On the other hand, like their parents, teenagers today still enjoy spending time together.

Paragraph 4 – Conclusion
Summary and writer's opinion about which is better

In conclusion, the Internet has made life more interesting for today's teenagers. While any new technology should always be used with care, most of these changes have made life easier and more exciting.

Linking words and phrases help the reader to move easily from one point to the next.

These words and phrases show the reader the differences between the two things. Try to use a variety of ways of showing differences.

These words and phrases show the reader the similarities between the two things. Try to use a variety of phrases.

Before you write

- Make notes about the differences and similarities between the two things you are comparing:

Before Internet	Today	Similar or different?
• School: research in libraries for essays • teaching with books	• School: research on Internet • teaching mainly with books	• Different • Similar
• Social: used the family phone • Teenagers like to get together in person	• Social: chat via text/email • Social networking • Teenagers like to get together	• Different • Different • Similar

- Choose the best points to include.
- Choose a structure (A or B) and organize your ideas into paragraphs.
  A 1 Introduction 2 Differences and similarities of one aspect 3 Differences and similarities of a second aspect 4 Summary and your opinion
  B 1 Introduction 2 Similarities 3 Differences 4 Summary and opinion

Language Bank: Comparing two things

Similarities

as + adjective or adverb + as
X is as good/strong/fast as Y.
Both X and Y…
Both boys and girls follow fashion and music.
Like X, Y…
Like their parents, they enjoy meeting their friends.
➲ See WRITING TIP at similarity

Differences

Comparative adjectives and adverbs
X is better/stronger/faster than Y.
Unlike X, Y…
Unlike their parents, most teenagers have grown up using computers.
X is different from Y (in that…)
X…, while Y… / While X…, Y…
➲ See WRITING TIP at difference

Checklist

Have I

- written about *exactly* what the task asked me to discuss? ☐
- written about both similarities and differences? ☐
- organized my ideas into logical paragraphs? ☐
- used linking words to help the reader follow what I've said? ☐
- given my opinion in the conclusion? ☐

Writing a report

A report describes a project or a study of a situation or problem. It includes facts or the results of your research. It may also include your suggestions or opinions on these facts. The language in reports should be clear, accurate and formal. *We* and *I* are often used in reports, for example to describe research that you have carried out.

Your town council wants to improve the sports facilities for teenagers in your area. Your head teacher has asked you to write a report to describe the current situation and make suggestions on how improvements can be made.
(180 - 200 words)

Local Sports Facilities for Teenagers

The purpose of this report is to examine our town's sports facilities for teenagers and make suggestions for their improvement. I visited each of our five sports centres and conducted a survey of students at my school.

According to my survey, basketball and football are the most popular sports for boys, while swimming and tennis are the most popular for girls. Each centre has an indoor sports hall and swimming pool, as well as outdoor tennis courts, basketball courts and grass fields.

However, most students said that they do not visit the centres because they are in such poor condition. For example:

- All the outdoor courts need new fences and ground surfaces.
- The indoor facilities require new paint and flooring.
- The changing rooms are in poor condition and often dirty.
- Damaged equipment should be repaired.
- Each of the facilities is regularly short of equipment such as balls and nets.

From the evidence, I conclude that if the facilities were in a better state, they would be used more often. It is recommended that the council consider investing in these centres to make them safer and more appealing to young people.

Paragraph 1 – Introduction
Explains the purpose of the report and how you did your research.

Paragraph 2 and 3 – Results
Give the results of the research.

Paragraph 4 – Conclusion
Gives a general conclusion and makes some suggestions.

Before you write

Think about the reader:
Who will read this report and why?

Structure your writing
Title: Your title should tell the reader exactly what the report is about.
Introduction: This paragraph will give the reader some background.
Why are you writing this report?
What topics does it cover?
How did you get the information?
Results: Give precise information about your research and what you have learned from it. It is important to give facts here rather than opinions.
Conclusion: Make suggestions and give your opinion.

Language Bank: Useful phrases for reports

Stating the purpose of the report
The purpose/aim of this report is to…
This report aims to…

Outlining research
I visited…
I asked 10 students to…
We examined/looked at (e.g. several centres)
I conducted a survey (of)…

Presenting findings
According to my survey…
We found that, on the whole,…
Overall, people preferred…
50% of those surveyed said that…

Giving conclusions
From the evidence, I conclude that…
In conclusion,…
The research shows/demonstrates that…

Making suggestions
It is recommended that…
We recommend/suggest that…
The best solution is/would be to…

Checklist

Have I
- made the purpose of my report clear? ☐
- included the information asked for? ☐
- made suggestions in the conclusion? ☐
- used clear formal language? ☐

Writing a review of a book or a film

The main purpose of a review is to give information about the book or film so that your readers can decide if they would like to read it or see it. Many student magazines and websites use an informal tone. However, for exams it is best to use more formal vocabulary and sentence structures.

Your teacher has asked you to write a review for a film you have seen recently, to go on the school's website. Review the film, giving your opinion and saying whether or not you would recommend it. (180 - 200 words)

Harry Potter and the Deathly Hallows: Part 2

Paragraph 1 – Introduction
General comments about the film and your opinion.

Millions of people have watched the earlier Harry Potter films. Will the final film of this famous story live up to expectations? *Harry Potter and the Deathly Hallows: Part 2* is set in both modern Britain and a fantasy world. Although it is much darker than previous films in the series, fans will leave the cinema feeling satisfied.

Paragraph 2 – Plot or story
A summary of what happens. Do not spoil it for your readers by telling them the end of the story.

Harry and his friends, Hermione and Ron, continue their search for the last three special objects hidden by the evil Voldemort, which they must destroy. As they fight their enemies for the last time, they learn some surprising secrets about several of the other characters and Harry finally discovers what he must do.

Paragraph 3 – Characters
A comment on the characters in the film.

The three friends have now grown up, like the actors playing the parts. This makes these characters very convincing. In fact, the acting is as usual of a very high standard. Alan Rickman, playing the role of Severus Snape, skilfully shows us a hidden side of the wicked headmaster.

Paragraph 4 – Conclusion
Giving your opinion
Your conclusion and whether you think people should see the film or not.

The battle scenes are thrilling, and the audience will laugh and cry with Harry and his friends as the story comes to its emotional end. I thoroughly recommend this exciting and enjoyable film.

Starting with a question makes your readers interested.

Include the title in the first paragraph and the name of the author, if it is a book.

Use a variety of adjectives to make your review interesting.

Use the present tense to describe the story.

Before you write

- Think about the film or look at the book again.
- Make notes about: the **type** of book or film it is
  the **setting** (the time and place of the story)
  the **plot** (what happens)
  the **characters** (and the **acting**, if it is a film)
  your **opinion**, positive or negative, with reasons
- Choose the best points to include in your review.
- Organize your ideas into paragraphs.

TIP

Remember that the person who reads the review has NOT seen the film or read the book.

Language Bank: Adjectives

Try to use a good variety of adjectives in your review. Use your dictionary to find synonyms for words like 'interesting'.

*This is an **exciting**/a **fast-moving**/ **gripping** story...*
*This **dark**/**frightening** tale takes place in ...*
*A **funny**/an **amusing** scene shows ...*
*This **moving** account of... (e.g. a young man's experiences)*
*a **violent** film*
*an **interesting** situation*
*an **imaginary** world*
*a **romantic** relationship*
*a **tragic**/an **emotional** ending*

*The **principal**/My **favourite** characters are ...*
*an **unpleasant**/a **strange**/ **sympathetic** character*
*an **action**/a **battle**/**love**/**fight** scene*
*I thoroughly enjoyed this **rewarding** book.*
*I highly recommend this **action-packed** film.*

➲ See NOTE at **book**
➲ See NOTE at **film**

Checklist

Have I

- given the name of the film or book in the first paragraph? ☐
- written about the story without telling readers the ending? ☐
- written about the characters? ☐
- organized my ideas into logical paragraphs? ☐
- given my opinion in the conclusion? ☐

Writing formal letters: a letter of complaint

When you write a formal letter, think about **layout, style** and **content**.
Layout: how your letter looks on the page, where you put the addresses, etc.
Style: be polite. Avoid using 'you' or 'you didn't'.
Content: state the facts and say what you want to happen.

You have just returned from an English language course in England. You were not happy with the accommodation or activities arranged. Write a letter to the company complaining about this, and ask for compensation. (120 –150 words)

Carrer de Dali, 18
43740 Móra d'Ebre
Tarragona

Mrs Brigit Deakins
LearnFun Language Centres Ltd.
13 Erebos Road
London SW11 2AG
30th July 2012

Paragraph 1 – Reason for writing
Explain clearly why you are writing.

Dear Mrs Deakins

I am writing to complain about the English language course I took in Worcester from July 1st –22nd, organised by LearnFun Language Centres Ltd.

Paragraph 2 – Complaint
Explain the problem and how you were affected.

Firstly, I was very dissatisfied with the accommodation. The advertisement promised that each student would have 'their own private room with study facilities'. Not only did I have to share a room with two other students, but it was not possible for me to study. Furthermore, your advertisement mentioned that 'exciting excursions and activities' would be available every week. In fact there were only two trips, both to a nearby town where there was very little to do.

Paragraph 3 – Demand for action
State clearly what action you want the company to take.

I had been looking forward to my course. However, although the teaching was good, it was spoiled by these problems. I would therefore appreciate a refund of part of the cost of the course in compensation for my disappointment.

Paragraph 4 – Comment
A general comment saying you would like a quick reply.

I look forward to hearing from you.

Yours sincerely

Natalio Hidalgo

Mr N Hidalgo

Your address on the right.

The name and address of the person you are writing to on the left.

Date: usually under this address

Formal greeting and closing. If you do not know the person's name, use *Dear Sir or Madam* and finish with *Yours faithfully*.

Formal language.
Do not use contractions or abbreviations.

Linking words and phrases to help the reader move from one point to the next.

Before you write

- Make notes about the details you need to include.
- Organize your points into 3 or 4 paragraphs.
- Plan the layout.
- Think about the beginning and ending and the language you will use.

TIP
If you are writing for an exam, you do not usually need to include addresses.

Language Bank: Formal letters

Openings and closings
Dear Sir/Madam... ...Yours faithfully
Dear Mrs Dawson... ...Yours sincerely

Introducing the topic
I am writing to complain about...
I am writing to express my dissatisfaction with...

Describing the problem
Strong adjectives:
I am/was appalled, distressed, disgusted, shocked...
Less strong adjectives:
I am/was unhappy, disappointed, dissatisfied...

Consequences
Therefore, As a result, For this Reason, Consequently, So
➲ See NOTE at **therefore**

Listing items
Firstly,... Secondly,...
To begin with,...
In addition to this,...
Furthermore,...

What do you want?
A full/partial refund, a replacement, an apology, compensation

Endings
I look forward to your swift reply.
I look forward to hearing/ I hope to hear from you soon.

Checklist

Have I

- used the appropriate layout for a formal letter? ☐
- used a suitable greeting and close? ☐
- arranged my points into clear paragraphs? ☐
- explained the problem and the action I would like? ☐
- used formal, polite, clear language? ☐

Applying for a job 1: Writing a CV

A CV (*AmE résumé*) is a brief description of your education, work experience, skills and interests.

A good CV should be set out clearly so that the important facts and information are easy to find.

Name	Nicholas Woodward
Address	8 St Peter's Close, Bromyard, Herefordshire HR7 4PS
Telephone	01632 960531 Mobile 07700 900420
Email	nickw@zapmail.co.uk
Objective	To find a temporary position that will help me to gain work experience in the hotel business.
Profile	An outgoing and hard-working student.

Education and qualifications

2011–	The King's School, Hereford. Taking A levels in: German; History; Social Studies
2007–2011	Queen Mary High School, Bromyard. 9 GCSEs: English Language (A*); English Literature (A); German (A); ICT (B); History (B); Physics (B); Social Studies (B); Geography (C); Mathematics (C)

Work experience

July 2011-September 2011: Activities Assistant at Worton Sports Centre. Assisted with the summer programme for young people. Responsibilities included teaching football and swimming.

August 2010-July 2012: Saturday morning shop assistant at Pinsley News, Hereford. Served customers, handled money, and checked stock, often working alone.

Skills

Languages: German - good

IT: Good keyboard skills. Familiarity with Word and Excel.

First Aid: Junior First Aid Certificate (March 2010)

Interests

Football (I was captain of the school team last year), photography, Scouts (I have been a member of the local Scout group since 2008)

References – attached

You can omit these labels. You do not need to include other information or send a photo.

Your practical abilities. Mention any exams you have passed.

These sections are optional, but are useful for employers.

Keep this section short. Give the details of 2 people who know you well.

Put your most recent education first. Put your most recent work experience first. You do not need to use full sentences.

See NOTE at **job**
See NOTE at **reference**

Applying for a job 2: Writing a covering letter

When you apply for a job, you should send a covering letter (*AmE cover letter*) with your CV. Pay particular attention to the **layout**, **style** and **content**.

You have seen an advertisement for a hotel receptionist during the summer. Write to the hotel manager to apply for the job. Explain why you think you would be suitable. Give details of your skills and experience. (120 - 150 words)

8 St Peter's Close
Bromyard
Herefordshire HR7 4PS

Mrs Rachel Adams
The Lion Hotel
23 High Street
Hereford HR1 2LR

4th July 2012

Dear Mrs Adams

Paragraph 1: Give your reason for writing. Say why you are interested in the job.

I am writing to apply for the post of temporary receptionist, which I saw advertised in the local newspaper on 1st July. I enclose a copy of my CV. I have just finished the first year of my A level studies and am interested in gaining work experience within the hotel business during the summer, as I hope to apply to university to study Hotel Management.

Paragraph 2: Say what you can bring to the job.

As you will see from my CV, I have some experience in dealing with people. Although I lack direct experience as a receptionist, as a shop assistant I have dealt with all types of customers in a polite and helpful way. In addition, I can offer skills in IT, German and First Aid.

Paragraph 3: Say when you will be available for interview.

I would very much like to be a part of your team. I am available for interview next week, and I look forward to hearing from you.

Yours sincerely

N Woodward

Nick Woodward

Your address, but not your name, on the right. The name and address of the person you are writing to on the left. The date: usually under the address

Formal greeting and closing. If you do not know the person's name, use *Dear Sir or Madam* and finish with *Yours faithfully*.

Use formal language and full sentences. Do not use contractions or abbreviations.

See NOTE at dear
See NOTE at sincere

Writing an informal email

Emails can vary a lot in style. An email can be very informal if you are writing to somebody you know well. If you are writing about something serious, or if you do not know the person very well, you will need to use more formal language.

You have received an email from a friend who has moved to a new city and is very homesick. Reply to your friend and give her some advice about how she can make new friends and settle into her new surroundings. (120 – 150 words)

From: miguel@unimail.es

To: jules@informail.com

Subject: Feeling homesick

Hi Juliet

It was great to get your email, but I'm sorry to hear you're feeling homesick and missing us all. We miss you too!

I know it's lonely for you being in a new place - it was the same for me - but it takes time to make new friends. Why don't you try joining some local clubs or societies? You may be able to find people who have the same interests as you. I know you love rock climbing - maybe you can find some fellow climbers!

Another thing you should do is introduce yourself to your neighbours. It's always good to get to know the people who live around you. They may be able to help you settle in and find your way around.

I hope you'll start to feel better soon. Remember that you can always email me if you have any problems or just need to chat.

Love

Miguel

Write a subject line that says clearly what your email is about. You can use an informal greeting and close.

Use informal but polite language. You can use contractions and abbreviations. You do not need to use long or full sentences.

You can use exclamation marks, but not too many.

TIP

Do not use slang, emoticons (such as :-)) or texting abbreviations (such as **2nite** instead of **tonight**).

Language Bank: Informal emails

Opening

Dear, Hi , Hello + first name

Closing

Best wishes, All the best (friends and acquaintances)
Love, Take care, Speak to you soon (close friends)

Clothes

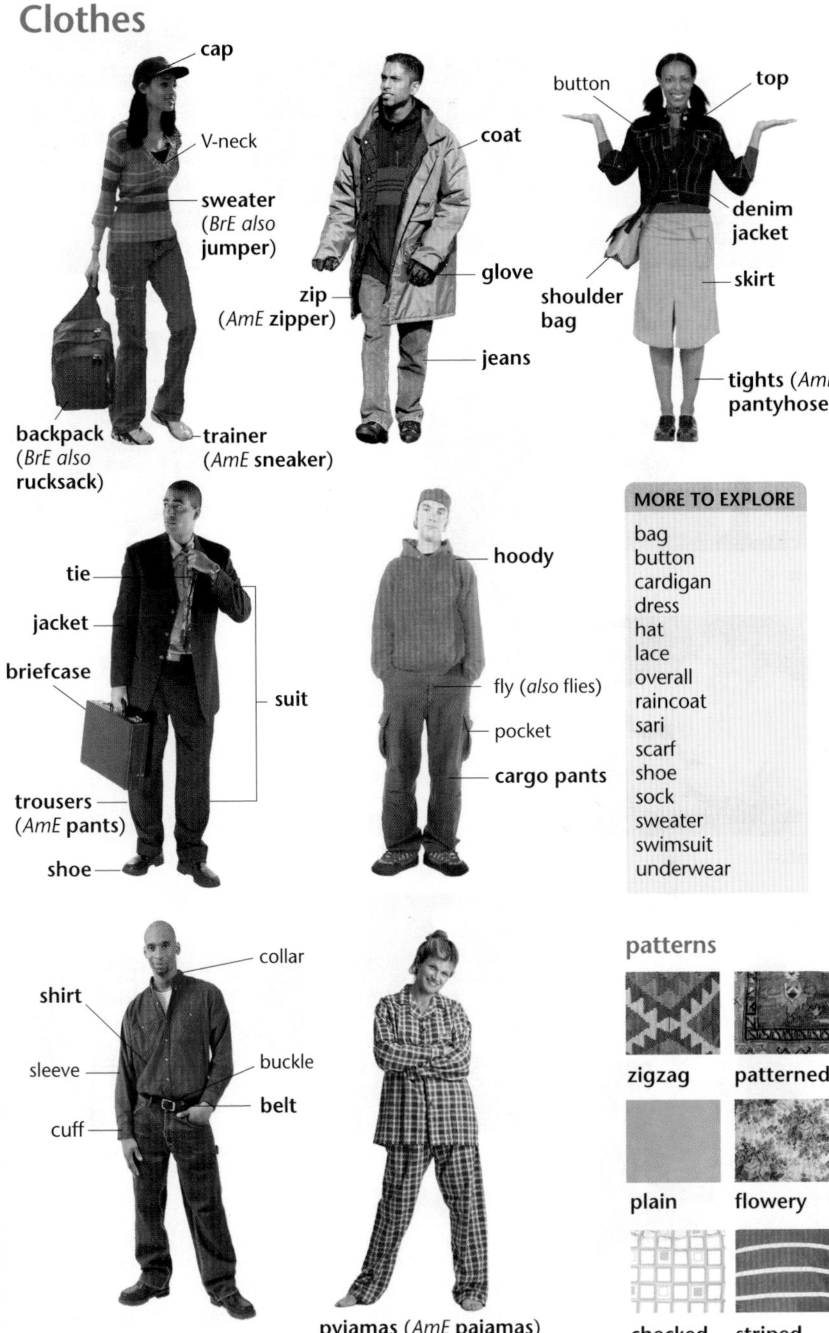

MORE TO EXPLORE

bag
button
cardigan
dress
hat
lace
overall
raincoat
sari
scarf
shoe
sock
sweater
swimsuit
underwear

patterns

zigzag **patterned**

plain **flowery**

checked **striped**

Work and jobs

farmer

carpenter

plumber

pilot

police officer

doctor

teacher

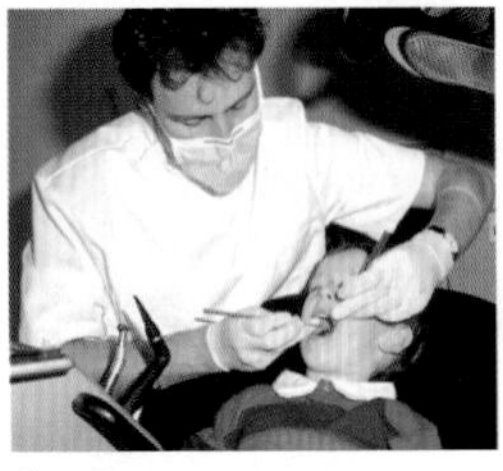
dentist

nurse

waiter

cook

shop assistant (*AmE* sales clerk)

MORE TO EXPLORE

accountant
chef
chemist
electrician
engineer
firefighter
hairdresser
job
journalist
lawyer
office
optician
pay
politician
programmer
secretary

Leisure activities

painting

tenpin bowling

playing computer games

model making

sewing

photography

stamp collecting

acting

sailing

going to the gym

surfing the Internet

climbing

MORE TO EXPLORE

aerobics
card
chess
domino
hiking
jigsaw
pool
snooker

Sports

rugby

baseball

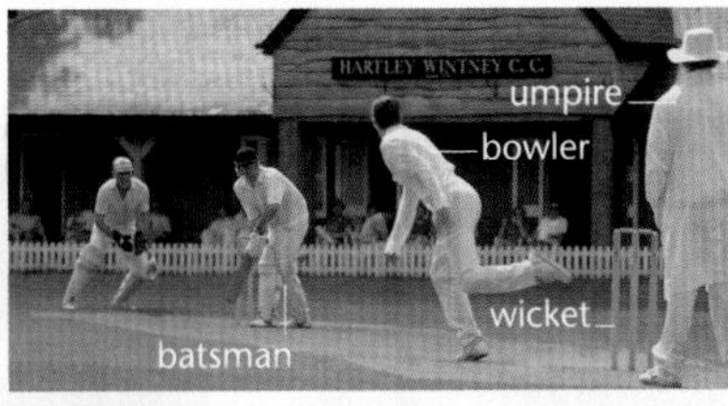

cricket

tennis

ice hockey
(*AmE* hockey)

hockey
(*AmE* field hockey)

basketball

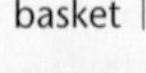

weightlifting

athletics

gymnastics

skating

skiing

horse racing

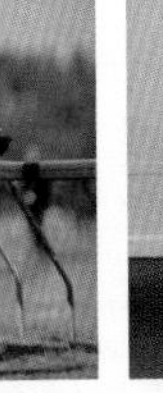

fencing

table tennis

karate

boxing

golf

MORE TO EXPLORE

badminton
football
horse
martial arts
netball
parachute
skate
sport
squash
swim
trampoline
volleyball
amateur
professional
exercise
score

Extreme sports

waterskiing

bungee jumping

surfing

abseiling
(*AmE* rappelling)

white-water
rafting

windsurfing

Transport

aircraft

plane

helicopter

glider

boats

oil tanker

liner

lifeboat

hovercraft

ferry

yacht

submarine

MORE TO EXPLORE

barge	bus	engine	sail
bicycle	car	motor	raft
bike	cruiser	parking	train
boat	driving	plane	travel

bus

tram

coach

taxi

van

lorry (*AmE* truck)

motorbike

scooter

cars

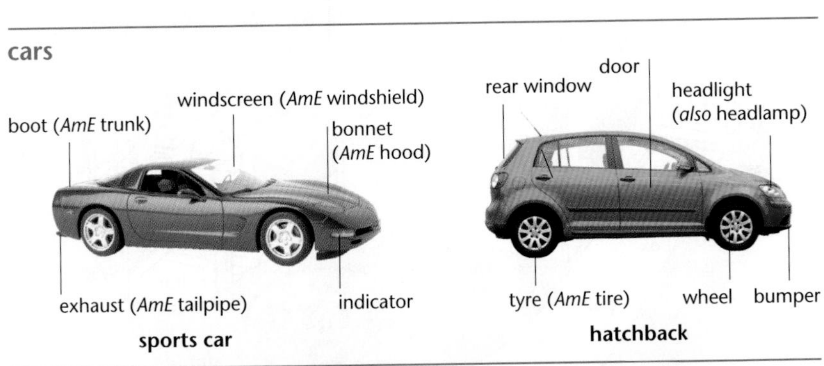

sports car

hatchback

underground (*AmE* **subway**)

train

House

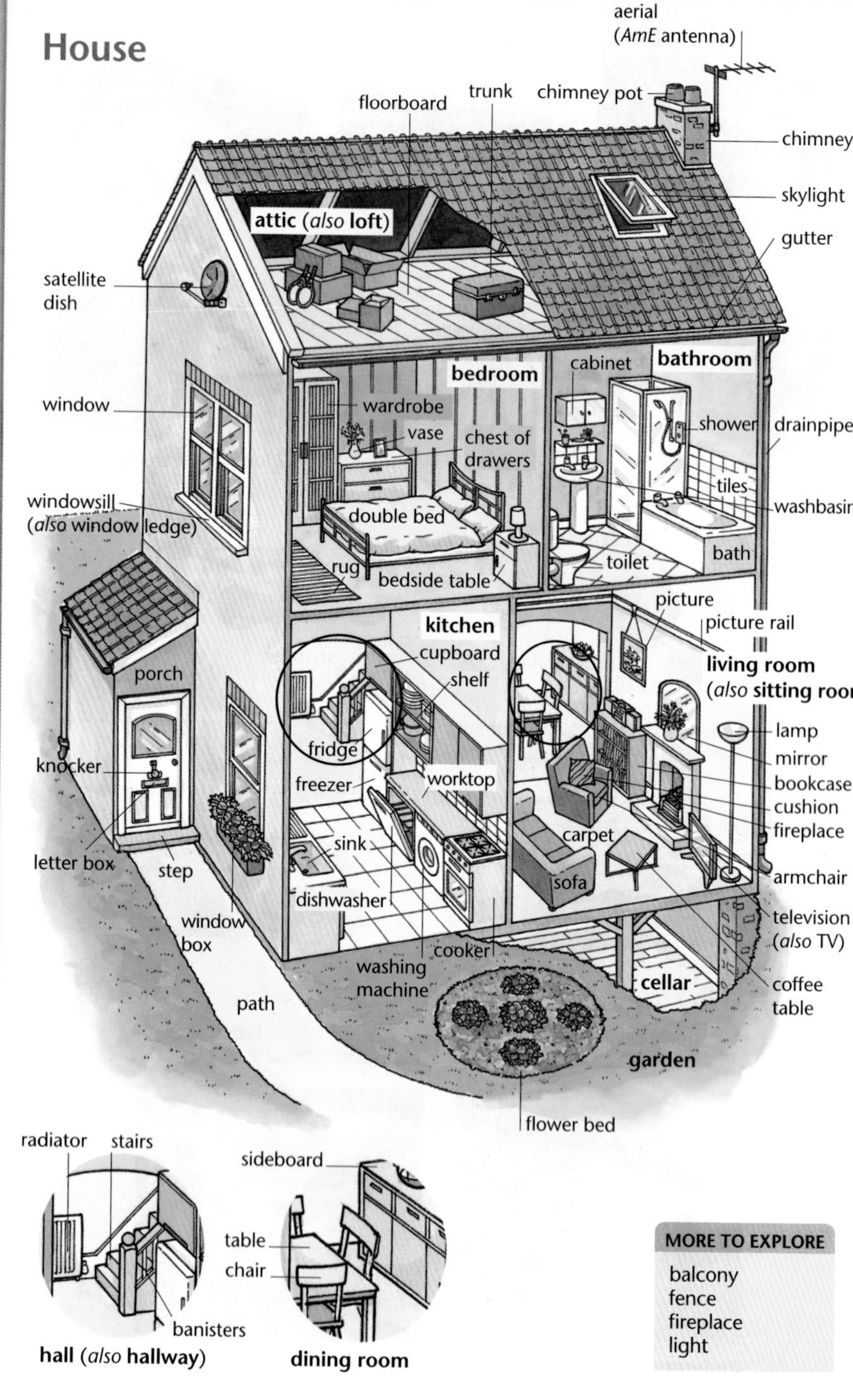

MORE TO EXPLORE

balcony
fence
fireplace
light

Homes

terraced houses

block of flats (*AmE* apartment block)

detached house

semi-detached houses

bungalow

thatched cottage

farm

stately home

MORE TO EXPLORE

castle	estate	palace	yard
chalet	flat	property	

Landscape

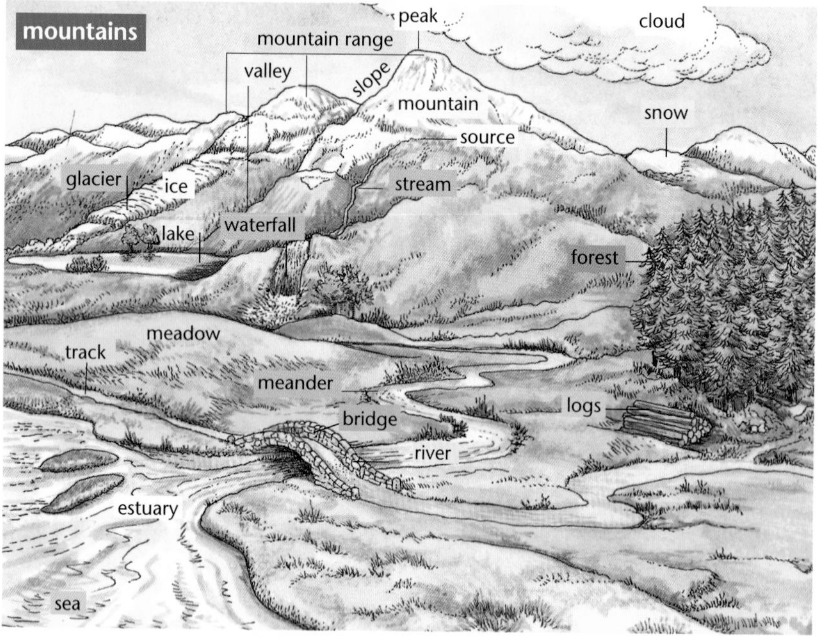

mountains

peak
cloud
mountain range
valley
slope
mountain
snow
source
glacier
ice
stream
lake
waterfall
forest
meadow
track
meander
logs
bridge
river
estuary
sea

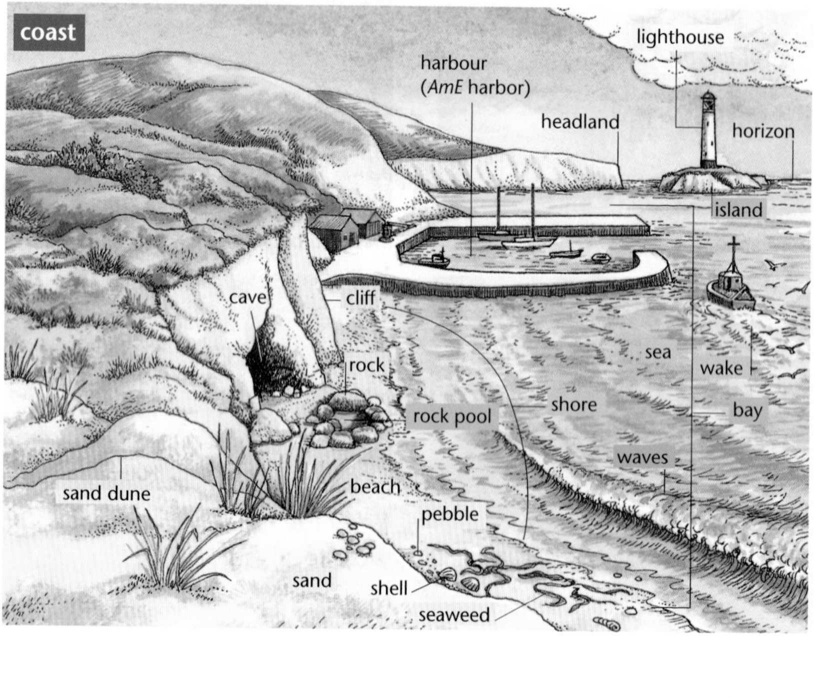

coast

lighthouse
harbour
(*AmE* harbor)
headland
horizon
island
cave
cliff
sea
wake
rock
shore
rock pool
bay
waves
sand dune
beach
pebble
sand
shell
seaweed

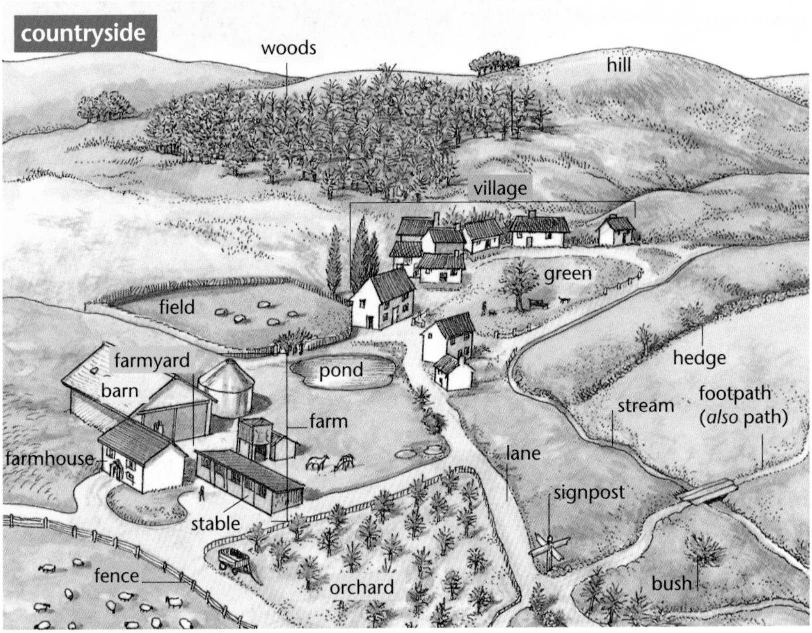

countryside

woods
hill
village
green
field
hedge
farmyard
pond
barn
footpath (*also* path)
stream
farm
farmhouse
lane
signpost
stable
fence
orchard
bush

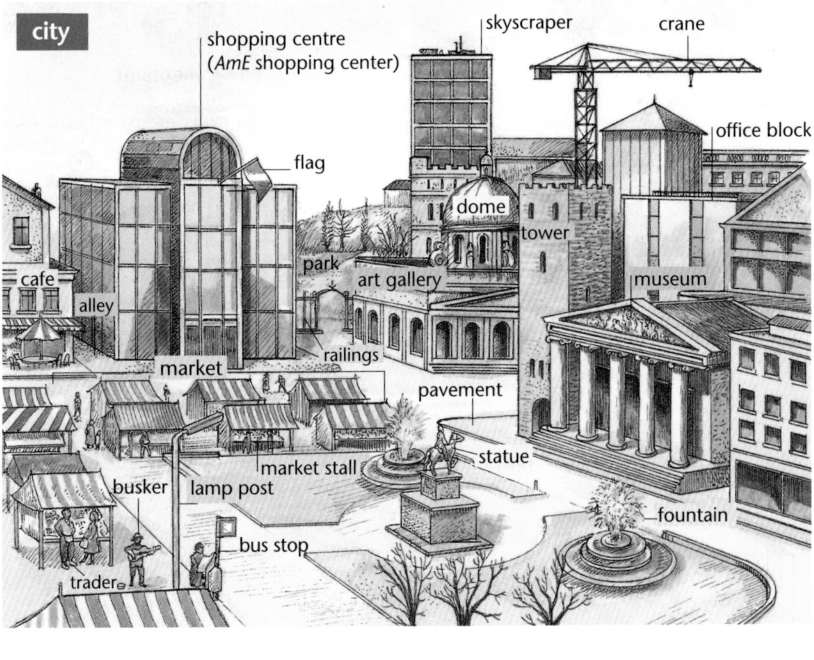

city

skyscraper
crane
shopping centre (*AmE* shopping center)
office block
flag
dome
tower
park
cafe
art gallery
museum
alley
railings
market
pavement
statue
market stall
busker
lamp post
fountain
bus stop
trader

Animals

mammals

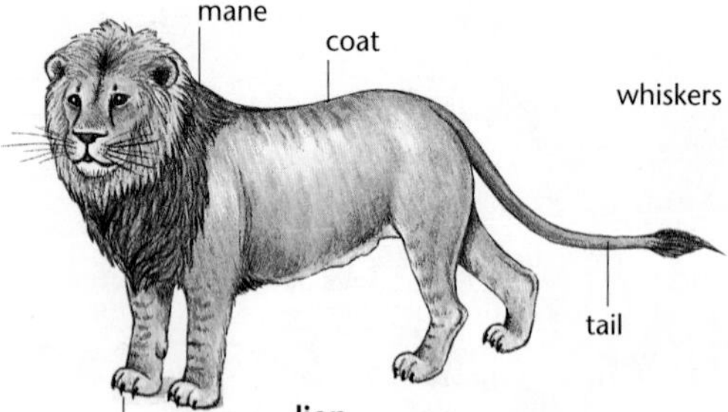

mane
coat
tail
claw
lion

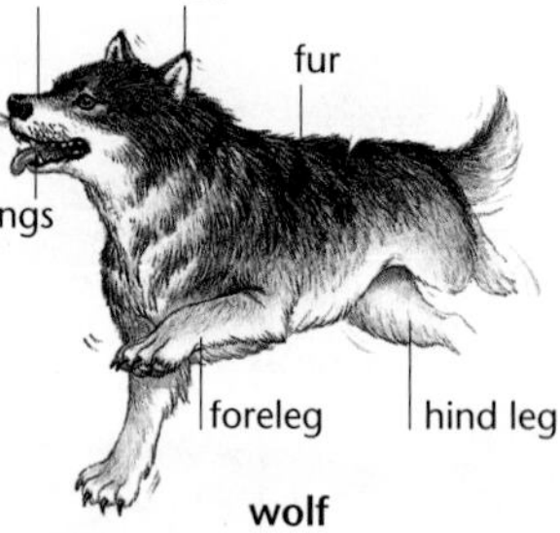

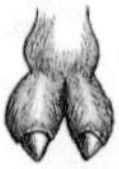

muzzle
ear
fur
whiskers
fangs
foreleg
hind leg
wolf

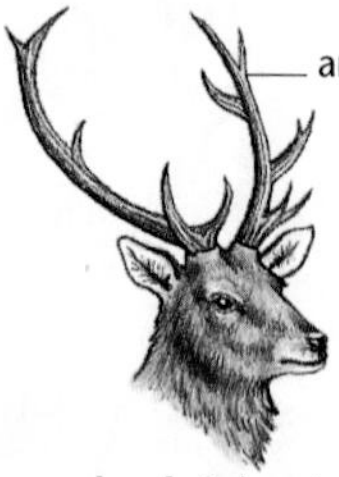

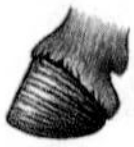

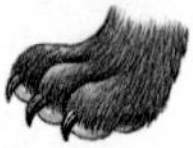

antler

hoof

toe

paw

horn
goat

buck (*also* **stag**)

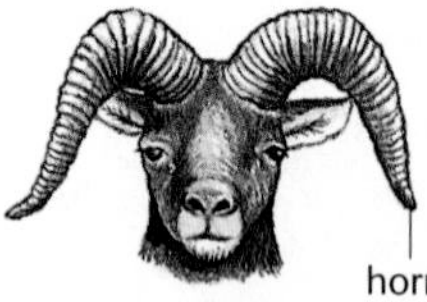

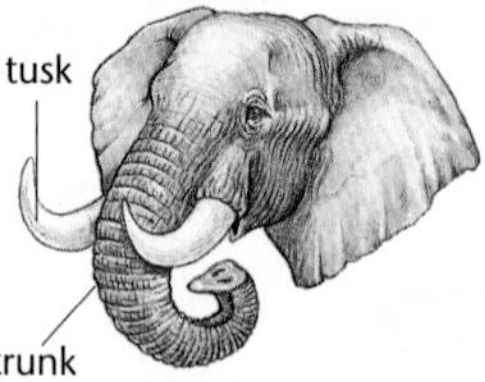

tusk
trunk
elephant

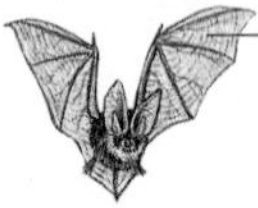

wing
bat

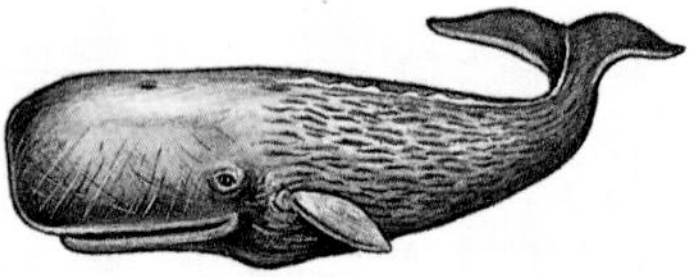

whale

MORE TO EXPLORE

bee	duck	pig
cat	fox	rabbit
chicken	horse	seal
cow	lion	sheep
deer	monkey	snail
dog	pet	worm

birds

beak
wing
breast
toe
tail
claw

talon

webbed foot

egg
nest

feather

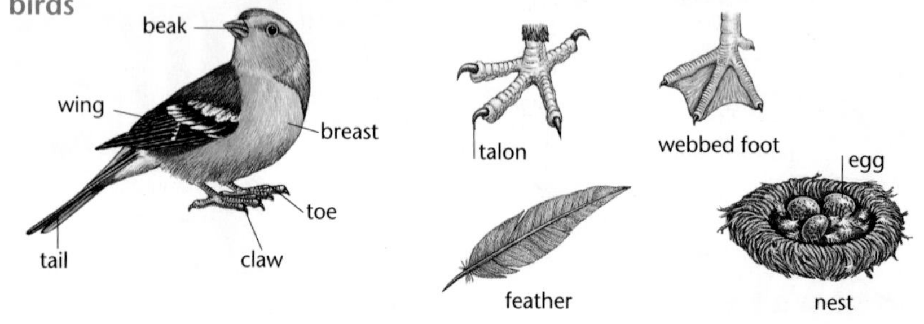

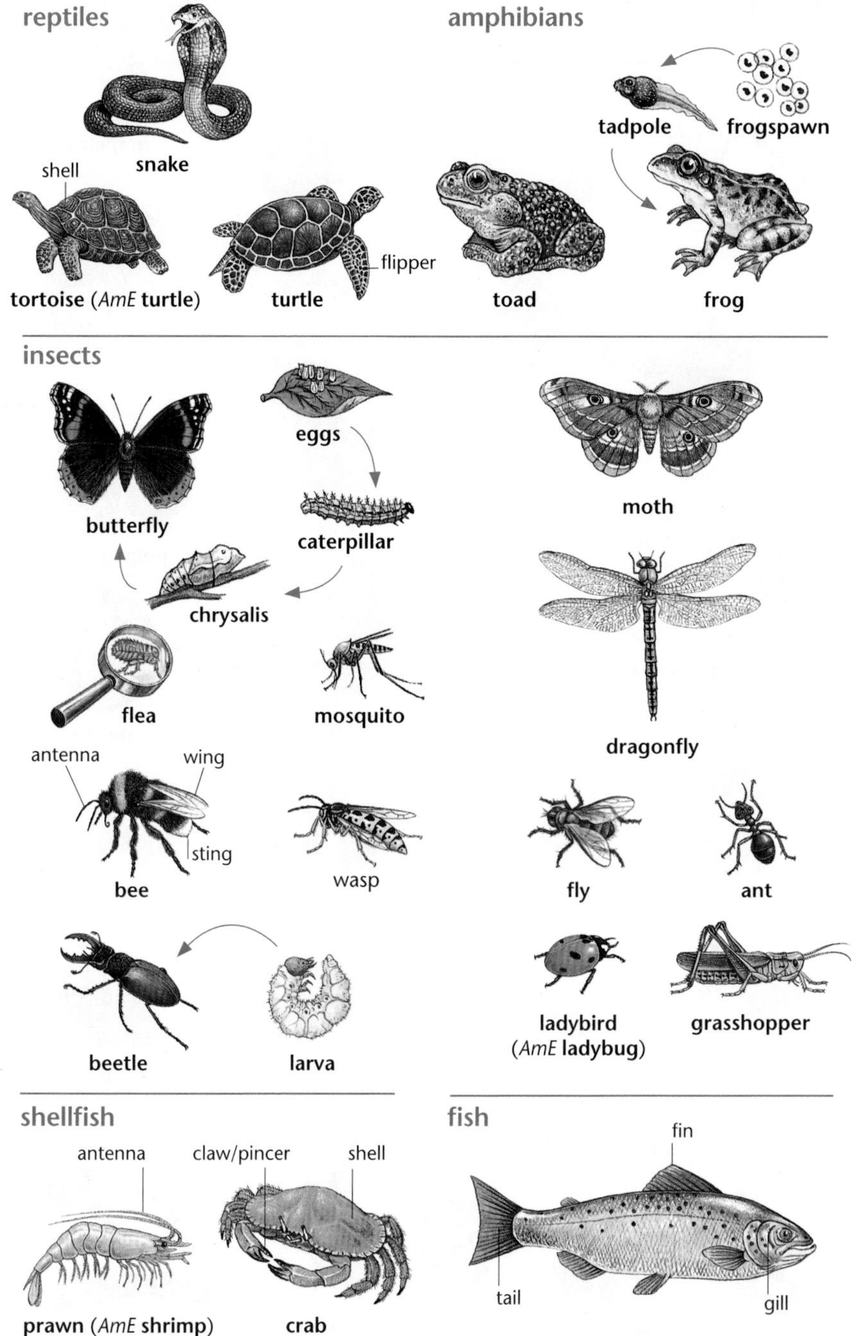
reptiles
snake
shell
tortoise (AmE turtle)
turtle
flipper
amphibians
tadpole
frogspawn
toad
frog
insects
eggs
butterfly
caterpillar
chrysalis
moth
dragonfly
flea
mosquito
antenna
wing
sting
bee
wasp
fly
ant
beetle
larva
ladybird
(AmE ladybug)
grasshopper
shellfish
antenna
claw/pincer
shell
prawn (AmE shrimp)
crab
fish
fin
tail
gill

Fruit

lime

lemon

orange

segment

grapefruit

pip

core

apple

pear

plum

stone

peach

skin

flesh

papaya (*also* pawpaw)

fig

apricot

kiwi fruit

seeds

pomegranate

shell

milk

coconut

mango

peel

banana

watermelon

melon

pineapple

stalk

cherries

strawberries

gooseberries

avocado

grapes

raspberries

blackberries

herbs and spices

thyme

parsley

basil

mint

ginger

cloves

cinnamon

Vegetables

asparagus

Brussels sprouts

parsnip

carrot

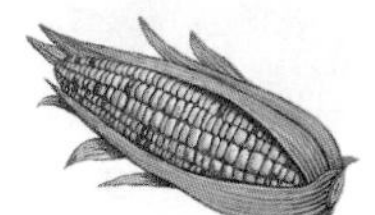
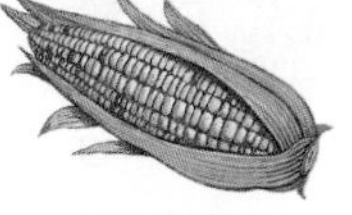
sweetcorn
(*AmE* corn)

potato

broccoli

artichoke

aubergine
(*AmE* eggplant)

cabbage

spinach

cauliflower

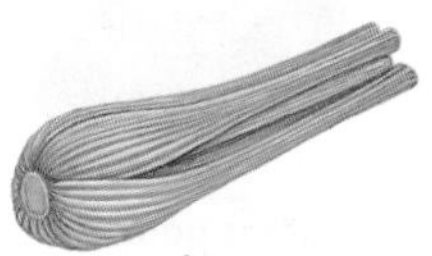
celery

pumpkin

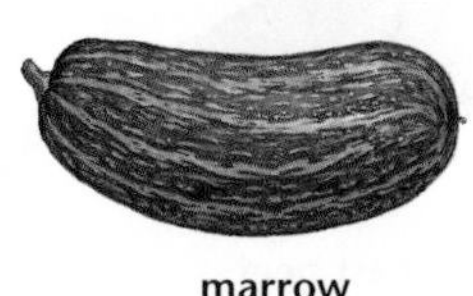
marrow

leek

courgette (*AmE* zucchini)

spring onions

mushrooms

peas

beans

onion

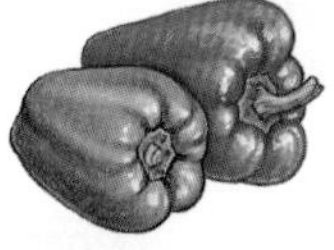
peppers

radishes

lettuce

garlic

chilli (*AmE* chili)

tomato

cucumber

Food and drink

salad

filling
sandwich

noodles

soup

burger
hot dog

pizza

skewer
kebab

pasta

fish and chips

roast beef

sauce
spaghetti

quiche

jacket potato (*also* baked potato)

apple pie

ice cream

pancake

cheese

bowl
cereal

eggs

jam (*AmE* jelly)

cream
waffle

honey

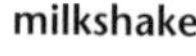
milkshake

cup of tea

black coffee

MORE TO EXPLORE

cake	nuts
coffee	porridge
drink	pudding
fish	sausage
fizzy	shellfish
meat	takeaway

Reference section

Contents

Grammar

R2 Irregular verbs
R5 Be, do, have
R6 The tenses of regular verbs
R8 Talking about the present, past and future
R10 Conditionals
R11 Modal verbs
R12 The passive
R13 Reported speech
R14 Verb patterns
R16 Phrasal verbs
R17 Nouns
R19 Adjectives
R20 Relative clauses

Other reference

R21 Prefixes
R22 Suffixes
R23 Expressions using numbers
R27 British and American English
R28 Map of the British Isles
R30 Map of Canada and the United States
R32 Geographical names
R37 Telephoning and texting
R38 Learning vocabulary
R40 Punctuation
R41 Pronunciation

Irregular verbs

In this list you will find the infinitive form of the verb followed by the past tense and the past participle. Where two forms are given, look up the verb in the main part of the dictionary to see whether there is a difference in the meaning.

Infinitive	Past tense	Past participle
arise	arose	arisen
awake	awoke	awoken
babysit	babysat	babysat
be	was/were	been
bear	bore	borne
beat	beat	beaten
become	became	become
befall	befell	befallen
begin	began	begun
bend	bent	bent
beset	beset	beset
bet	bet, betted	bet, betted
bid	bid	bid
bind	bound	bound
bite	bit	bitten
bleed	bled	bled
blow	blew	blown
break	broke	broken
breastfeed	breastfed	breastfed
breed	bred	bred
bring	brought	brought
broadcast	broadcast	broadcast
browbeat	browbeat	browbeaten
build	built	built
burn	burnt, burned	burnt, burned
burst	burst	burst
bust	bust, busted	bust, busted
buy	bought	bought
cast	cast	cast
catch	caught	caught
choose	chose	chosen
cling	clung	clung
come	came	come
cost	cost	cost
creep	crept	crept
cut	cut	cut
deal	dealt	dealt
dig	dug	dug

Infinitive	Past tense	Past participle
dive	dived; (*AmE*) dove	dived
do	did	done
draw	drew	drawn
dream	dreamt, dreamed	dreamt, dreamed
drink	drank	drunk
drive	drove	driven
dwell	dwelt, dwelled	dwelt, dwelled
eat	ate	eaten
fall	fell	fallen
feed	fed	fed
feel	felt	felt
fight	fought	fought
find	found	found
flee	fled	fled
fling	flung	flung
fly	flew	flown
forbid	forbade, forbad	forbidden
forecast	forecast	forecast
foresee	foresaw	foreseen
forget	forgot	forgotten
forgive	forgave	forgiven
forgo	forwent	forgone
forsake	forsook	forsaken
freeze	froze	frozen
get	got	got; (*AmE*) gotten
give	gave	given
go	went	gone
grind	ground	ground
grow	grew	grown
hang	hung, hanged	hung, hanged
have	had	had
hear	heard	heard
hide	hid	hidden
hit	hit	hit

Infinitive	Past tense	Past participle
hold	held	held
hurt	hurt	hurt
input	input, inputted	input, inputted
keep	kept	kept
kneel	knelt; (esp *AmE*) kneeled	knelt; (esp *AmE*) kneeled
know	knew	known
lay	laid	laid
lead	led	led
lean	leant, leaned	leant, leaned
leap	leapt, leaped	leapt, leaped
learn	learnt, learned	learnt, learned
leave	left	left
lend	lent	lent
let	let	let
lie	lay	lain
light	lighted, lit	lighted, lit
lose	lost	lost
make	made	made
mean	meant	meant
meet	met	met
mislay	mislaid	mislaid
mislead	misled	misled
misread	misread	misread
misspell	misspelt, misspelled	misspelt, misspelled
mistake	mistook	mistaken
misunderstand	misunderstood	misunderstood
mow	mowed	mown, mowed
outdo	outdid	outdone
outgrow	outgrew	outgrown
overcome	overcame	overcome
overdo	overdid	overdone
overhang	overhung	overhung
overhear	overheard	overheard
overpay	overpaid	overpaid
override	overrode	overridden
overrun	overran	overrun
oversee	oversaw	overseen
oversleep	overslept	overslept
overtake	overtook	overtaken
overthrow	overthrew	overthrown
pay	paid	paid
prove	proved	proved; (*AmE*) proven

Infinitive	Past tense	Past participle
put	put	put
quit	quit	quit
read	read	read
rebuild	rebuilt	rebuilt
repay	repaid	repaid
rethink	rethought	rethought
rewind	rewound	rewound
rewrite	rewrote	rewritten
rid	rid	rid
ride	rode	ridden
ring	rang	rung
rise	rose	risen
run	ran	run
saw	sawed	sawn; (*AmE*) sawed
say	said	said
see	saw	seen
seek	sought	sought
sell	sold	sold
send	sent	sent
set	set	set
sew	sewed	sewn, sewed
shake	shook	shaken
shear	sheared	shorn, sheared
shed	shed	shed
shine	shone	shone
shoe	shod	shod
shoot	shot	shot
show	showed	shown, showed
shrink	shrank, shrunk	shrunk
shut	shut	shut
sing	sang	sung
sink	sank	sunk
sit	sat	sat
slay	slew	slain
sleep	slept	slept
slide	slid	slid
sling	slung	slung
slink	slunk	slunk
slit	slit	slit
smell	smelt, smelled	smelt, smelled
sow	sowed	sown, sowed
speak	spoke	spoken
speed	sped, speeded	sped, speeded
spell	spelt, spelled	spelt, spelled

Infinitive	Past tense	Past participle
spend	spent	spent
spill	spilt, spilled	spilt, spilled
spin	spun	spun
spit	spat; (*AmE also*) spit	spat; (*AmE also*) spit
split	split	split
spoil	spoilt, spoiled	spoilt, spoiled
spread	spread	spread
spring	sprang	sprung
stand	stood	stood
steal	stole	stolen
stick	stuck	stuck
sting	stung	stung
stink	stank, stunk	stunk
stride	strode	—
strike	struck	struck
string	strung	strung
strive	strove	striven
swear	swore	sworn
sweep	swept	swept
swell	swelled	swollen, swelled
swim	swam	swum
swing	swung	swung
take	took	taken
teach	taught	taught
tear	tore	torn
tell	told	told

Infinitive	Past tense	Past participle
think	thought	thought
thrive	thrived, throve	thrived
throw	threw	thrown
thrust	thrust	thrust
tread	trod	trodden
undercut	undercut	undercut
undergo	underwent	undergone
underlie	underlay	underlain
underpay	underpaid	underpaid
understand	understood	understood
undertake	undertook	undertaken
undo	undid	undone
unwind	unwound	unwound
uphold	upheld	upheld
upset	upset	upset
wake	woke	woken
wear	wore	worn
weave	wove, weaved	woven, weaved
weep	wept	wept
wet	wet, wetted	wet, wetted
win	won	won
wind	wound	wound
withdraw	withdrew	withdrawn
withhold	withheld	withheld
withstand	withstood	withstood
wring	wrung	wrung
write	wrote	written

Be, do, have

Full forms	Short forms	Negative short forms
***be* present tense**		
I am	I'm	I'm not
you are	you're	you're not/you aren't
he is	he's	he's not/he isn't
she is	she's	she's not/she isn't
it is	it's	it's not/it isn't
we are	we're	we're not/we aren't
you are	you're	you're not/you aren't
they are	they're	they're not/they aren't
***be* past tense**		
I was	—	I wasn't
you were	—	you weren't
he was	—	he wasn't
she was	—	she wasn't
it was	—	it wasn't
we were	—	we weren't
you were	—	you weren't
they were	—	they weren't
***have* present tense**		
I have	I've	I haven't/I've not
you have	you've	you haven't/you've not
he has	he's	he hasn't/he's not
she has	she's	she hasn't/she's not
it has	it's	it hasn't/it's not
we have	we've	we haven't/we've not
you have	you've	you haven't/you've not
they have	they've	they haven't/they've not
***have* past tense (all persons)**		
had	I'd you'd etc.	hadn't
***do* present tense**		
I do	—	I don't
you do	—	you don't
he does	—	he doesn't
she does	—	she doesn't
it does	—	it doesn't
we do	—	we don't
you do	—	you don't
they do	—	they don't
***do* past tense (all persons)**		
did	—	didn't

	be	*do*	*have*
present participle	being	doing	having
past participle	been	done	had

- The negative full forms are formed by adding **not**.
- Questions in the present and past are formed by placing the verb before the subject:

▶ *am I?*	*isn't he?*
was I?	*weren't we?*
do I?	*didn't I?*
have I?	*hadn't they?*
etc.	

Auxiliary verbs

- **Do** is used to form questions and negatives in the present and past simple. Note that the auxiliary verb and not the main verb shows the negative past tense:
  - ▶ *She washed.*
  - ▶ *She didn't wash.*
- **Have** is used to form the perfect tenses:
  - ▶ *I haven't finished.*
  - ▶ *Has he arrived yet?*
  - ▶ *They hadn't seen each other for a long time.*
- **Be** is used to form the continuous tenses and the passive:
  - ▶ *I'm studying Italian.*
  - ▶ *We were watching TV.*
  - ▶ *It was painted by a famous artist.*

Verbs

Regular verbs: the simple tenses

Present simple		
I/we/you/they work	do not work (don't work)	Do **I** work?
he/she/it works	does not work (doesn't work)	Does **he** work?
Past simple		
I/we/you/they/he/she/it worked	did not work (didn't work)	Did **they** work?
Future simple		
I/we/you/they/he/she/it will work (**he**'ll work)	will not work (won't work)	Will **he** work?
Present perfect		
I/we/you/they have worked (**I**'ve worked)	have not worked (haven't worked)	Have **you** worked?
he/she/it has worked (**she**'s worked)	has not worked (hasn't worked)	Has **she** worked?
Past perfect		
I/we/you/they/he/she/it had worked (**they**'d worked)	had not worked (hadn't worked)	Had **they** worked?
Future perfect		
I/we/you/they/he/she/it will have worked (**we**'ll have worked)	will not have worked (won't have worked)	Will **we** have worked?
Conditional		
I/we/you/they/he/she/it would work (**I**'d work)	would not work (wouldn't work)	Would **you** work?
Conditional perfect		
I/we/you/they/he/she/it would have worked (would've worked)	would not have worked (wouldn't have worked)	Would **she** have worked?

Regular verbs: the continuous tenses

NOTE The continuous tenses are sometimes called the progressive tenses.

Present continuous

I am working (**I'm** working)	am not working (**I'm** not working)	Am **I** working?
you/we/they are working (**you're** working)	are not working (**aren't** working)	Are **you** working?
he/she/it is working (**he's** working)	is not working (**isn't** working)	Is **he** working?

Past continuous

I/he/she/it was working	was not working (**wasn't** working)	Was **he** working?
we/you/they were working	were not working (**weren't** working)	Were **you** working?

Future continuous

I/we/you/they/he/she/it will be working (**he'll** be working)	will not be working (**won't** be working)	Will **he** be working?

Present perfect continuous

I/we/you/they have been working (**you've** been working)	have not been working (**haven't** been working)	Have **I** been working?
he/she/it has been working (**she's** been working)	has not been working (**hasn't** been working)	Has **she** been working?

Past perfect continuous

I/we/you/they/he/she/it had been working (**he'd** been working)	had not been working (**hadn't** been working)	Had **he** been working?

Future perfect continuous

I/we/you/they/he/she/it will have been working (**she'll** have been working)	will not have been working (**won't** have been working)	Will **she** have been working?

Conditional continuous

I/we/you/they/he/she/it would be working (**he'd** be working)	would not be working (**wouldn't** be working)	Would **he** be working?

Conditional perfect continuous

I/we/you/they/he/she/it would have been working (**would've** been working)	would not have been working (**wouldn't** have been working)	Would **she** have been working?

Talking about the present

You use the **present continuous**

- to talk about an action that is happening now:
  - ▶ *We're **waiting** for a train.*
  - ▶ *What **are** you **doing**?*
  - ▶ *She's **listening** to the radio.*
- to talk about something that is not yet finished, even if you are not doing it at the moment when you are talking:
  - ▶ ***I'm learning** the guitar.*
  - ▶ *He's **writing** a book about fashion.*
- with **always**, to talk about something that happens often, and that you find annoying:
  - ▶ *He's always **asking** to borrow money.*
  - ▶ *She's always **phoning** her friends late at night.*

  NOTE Some verbs are not used in the continuous tenses, for example **need**, **want**, **know, hear, smell, agree, seem, appear, understand**, etc. These verbs refer to a state, not an action:
  - ▶ *I **need** a holiday.*
  - ▶ *She **hates** the new house.*
  - ▶ *They **love** Indian food.*
  - ▶ *He **wants** to be alone.*
  - ▶ *Do you **know** Lucy Johnston?*

Other verbs are used in the present continuous when they refer to an action, and the present simple when they refer to a state:

- ▶ *She's **tasting** the cheese.*
- ▶ *The cheese **tastes** salty.*
- ▶ *He's **being** noisy today.*
- ▶ *He's a noisy dog.*
- ▶ *What **are** you **thinking** about?*
- ▶ *Do you **think** I should leave?*

You use the **present simple**

- to talk about a permanent situation:
  - ▶ *He lives in Scotland.*
  - ▶ *She works in local government.*
- to talk about something that is always true:
  - ▶ *Oranges don't grow this far north.*
  - ▶ *What temperature does water freeze at?*
- to talk about things that happen regularly:
  - ▶ *She goes to yoga every Monday.*
  - ▶ *We don't often go to the theatre.*

Talking about the past

You use the **past simple**

- to talk about an action that took place in the past:
  - ▶ *He **turned** round, **dropped** the bag and **ran** away.*
  - ▶ ***I didn't write** to her, but I **rang** her.*
  - ▶ *Where **did** you **stay** in Glasgow?*

  NOTE Often a specific time is mentioned:
  - ▶ ***Did** you **see** Rory yesterday?*
- to talk about a state that continued for some time, but that is now finished:
  - ▶ *I **went** to school in Ireland.*
  - ▶ ***Did** she really **work** there for ten years?*
- to talk about actions that happened regularly in the past:
  - ▶ *They often **played** chess together. She always **won**.*
  - ▶ *We always **went** to Devon for our summer holidays when I was a child.*

You use the **present perfect**

- to talk about something that happened during a period of time that is not yet finished:
  - ▶ *The train **has been** late three times this week.*
  - ▶ *He still **hasn't visited** her.*

- when the time is not mentioned, or is not important:
  - ▶ *He's **written** a book.* (BUT *He **wrote** a book last year.*)
  - ▶ *I've **bought** a bike.* (BUT *I **bought** a bike on Saturday.*)
- when the action finished in the past, but the effect is still felt in the present:
  - ▶ *He's lost his wallet* (and he still hasn't found it).
- with **for** and **since** to show the duration of an action or state up until the present:
  - ▶ *She **hasn't bought** any new clothes for ages.*
  - ▶ *They **have lived** here for ten years, and they don't want to move.*
  - ▶ ***I've worked** here since 1998.*
- in British English with **just**, **ever**, **already** and **yet**:
  - ▶ *I've just **arrived**.*
  - ▶ ***Have** you ever **been** here before?*
  - ▶ *He's already **packed** his suitcases.*
  - ▶ ***Haven't** you **finished** yet?*

You use the **present perfect continuous**

- with **for** and **since** to talk about an activity that started in the past and is still happening:
  - ▶ ***I've been waiting** since ten o'clock.*
  - ▶ *They **haven't been learning** English for very long.*
- to talk about an activity that has finished and whose results are visible now:
  - ▶ *My hands are dirty because **I've been digging** the garden.*

You use the **past continuous**

- to talk about something that was already in progress when something else happened:
  - ▶ *The telephone rang while we **were having** dinner.*
  - ▶ ***Was it raining** when you left the house?*

  NOTE As with the present continuous, this tense cannot be used with 'state' verbs:
  - ▶ *Jamie's cake tasted delicious.* (NOT ~~*was tasting*~~)

You use the **past perfect**

- to talk about something that happened before another action in the past:
  - ▶ *When I got to the airport, the plane **had** already **left**.*
  - ▶ *They **had** just **bought** a flat when Joe lost his job.*

You use the **past perfect continuous**

- to talk about an activity that went on for a period of time further back in the past than something else:
  - ▶ *My hands were dirty because I **had been digging** the garden.*
  - ▶ *She **hadn't been working** at the shop very long when they sacked her.*

Talking about the future

There are several ways of talking about the future.

You use **be going to** with the **infinitive**

- to talk about what you intend to do in the future:
  - ▶ ***I'm going to see** a film tonight.*
  - ▶ *What **are you going to do** when you leave school?*
  - ▶ ***I'm** not **going to play** tennis this Saturday.*

You use the **future simple** (**will** with the **infinitive**)

- to talk about a decision that you make as you are speaking:
  - ▶ *It's warm in here. I'**ll open** a window.*
  - ▶ *I'**ll have** the salad, please.*
- to talk about what you know or think will happen in the future (but not about your own intentions or plans):
  - ▶ *She'**ll be** 25 on her next birthday.*
  - ▶ ***Will** he **pass** the exam, do you think?*
  - ▶ *This job **won't take** long.*

- for requests, promises, and offers:
  - ▶ ***Will** you **buy** some milk on your way home?*
  - ▶ *We'**ll be** back soon, don't worry.*
  - ▶ *I'**ll help** you with your homework.*

You use the **present continuous**

- to talk about future plans where the time is mentioned:
  - ▶ *He's **flying** to Thailand in June.*
  - ▶ *What **are** you **doing** this weekend?*
  - ▶ *I'**m** not **starting** my new job till next Monday.*

You use the **present simple**

- to talk about future plans where something has been officially arranged, for example on a timetable or programme:
  - ▶ *We **leave** Prague at 10 and **arrive** in London at 11.50.*
  - ▶ *School **starts** on 3rd September.*
- to refer to a future time after when, as soon as, before, until, etc.:
  - ▶ *Ring me as soon as you **hear** any news.*
  - ▶ *I'll look after Tim until you **get** back.*
  - ▶ *You'll remember Dita when you **see** her.*

You use **about to** with the **infinitive**

- to talk about the very near future:
  - ▶ *Hurry up! The train is **about to leave**.*

You use the **future continuous**

- to talk about actions that will continue for a period of time in the future:
  - ▶ *I'**ll be waiting** near the ticket office. I'**ll be wearing** a red scarf.*
  - ▶ *This time next week you'**ll be relaxing** in the sun!*
- to ask somebody about their plans or intentions:
  - ▶ *How many nights **will you be staying**?*
  - ▶ ***Will** you **be returning** by bus or by train?*

You use the **future perfect**:

- to talk about something that will be finished at a particular time in the future:
  - ▶ *I **will have finished** this work by 3 o'clock.*
  - ▶ *They'**ll have lived** here for four years in May.*

Conditionals

Sentences with *if* express possibilities. There are three main types:

1. possible – it might happen in the future:
   - ▶ *If I **win** £1000, I **will take** you to Paris.*
   - ▶ *If I **pass** the exam, I'**ll go** to medical school.*

   Present tense after *if*, **future tense** in the main clause.

2. improbable – it is unlikely to happen in the future:
   - ▶ *If I **won** £1000, I **would take** you to Paris.*
   - ▶ *If I **passed** the exam, I **would go** to medical school.*

   Past simple after *if*, **conditional tense** in the main clause.

3. impossible – it didn't happen in the past:
   - ▶ *If I **had won** £1000, I **would have taken** you to Paris.*
   - ▶ *If I **had passed** the exam, I **would have gone** to medical school.*

Past perfect after *if*, **conditional perfect** in the main clause.

Another type of *if* sentence expresses something that is always true or was always true in the past:

- ▶ *If you **pour** oil on water, it **floats**.*

Present simple in both parts of the sentence.

- ▶ *If I **asked** her to come with us, she always **said** no.*

Past simple in both parts of the sentence.

Modal verbs

Ability

can • could • be able to

- ▶ ***Can** he swim?*
- ▶ *My sister **could** read when she was four.*
- ▶ *I **couldn't** find my shoes this morning.*
- ▶ *I **could have** run faster, but I didn't want to get tired.*
- ▶ *She **has** not **been able to** walk since the accident.*
- ▶ *He **was able to** speak to Tracey before she left.*
- ▶ ***Will** people **be able to** live on the moon one day?*

➲ For the difference between 'could' and 'managed to', look at the note at the entry for **could**.

Possibility

could • may • might • can

- ▶ ***Could/Might** you **have** left it on the bus?*
- ▶ *She **may/might/could** be ill. I'll phone her.*
- ▶ *I **may have/might have** left my purse in the shop.*
- ▶ *Liz **might/may** know where it is.*
- ▶ *I **might/may** not go if I'm tired.*
- ▶ *He **might have** enjoyed the party if he'd gone.*
- ▶ *His wife **can** be very difficult at times.*

Permission

can • could • may

- ▶ ***Can** we come in?*
- ▶ ***Could** we possibly stay at your flat?*
- ▶ *Staff **may** take their break between 12 and 2.* (formal)
- ▶ ***May** I sit here?* (formal)

Prohibition

cannot • may not • must not

- ▶ *You **can't** get up until you're better.*
- ▶ *You **mustn't** tell anyone I'm here.*
- ▶ *Crockery **may not** be taken out of the canteen.* (written)
- ▶ *You **must not** begin until I tell you.* (formal)

Obligation

have (got) to • must

- ▶ *All visitors **must** report to reception on arrival.*
- ▶ *I **must** get that letter written today.*
- ▶ *Do you **have to** write your age on the form?*
- ▶ *She **had to** wait an hour for the bus.*
- ▶ *You **will have to** ring back later, I'm afraid.*

Advice and criticism

ought to • should

- ▶ ***Ought** I **to/Should** I wear a jacket?*
- ▶ *She **ought to/should** get her hair cut.*
- ▶ *You **ought to/should have** gone to bed earlier.*
- ▶ *You **ought not to/shouldn't** borrow the car without asking.*
- ▶ *I **ought to/should** go on a diet.*
- ▶ *I **ought to have/should have** asked her first.*

No necessity

don't have to • shouldn't have
didn't need to • needn't have

- ▶ *You **don't have to** cook, we can get a takeaway.*
- ▶ *They **didn't have to** show their passports.*
- ▶ *You **shouldn't have** bought me a present.*
- ▶ *He **didn't need to** have any fillings at the dentist's.*
- ▶ *They **needn't have** waited.*

➲ For the difference between 'didn't need to' and 'needn't have', look at the note at **need**[1].

Assumptions and deductions

will • should • must • can't

- ▶ *That **will** be Tanya – she's often early.*
- ▶ *The book **should** be interesting.*
- ▶ *There **must** be a leak – the floor's wet.*
- ▶ *You **must have** dialled the wrong number – there's no one called Pat living here.*
- ▶ *You **can't have** finished already!*

Requests

can • could • will • would

- ***Can** you help me lift this box?*
- ***Could** you pass me the salt?*
- ***Will** you buy me a puppy, Dad?*
- ***Would** you post this letter for me, please?*

Could and **would** are more formal than **can** and **will**.

Offers and suggestions

shall • will • can

- ***Shall** I make you a sandwich?*
- ***I'll** (I **will**) drive you to the station.*
- ***Shall** we go now?*
- ***Can** I help you?*

The passive

In an active sentence, the subject is the person or thing that performs the action:

- ***Masked thieves** stole a valuable painting from the museum last night.*

When you make this into a passive sentence, the object of the verb becomes the subject:

- ***A valuable painting** was stolen from the museum last night.*

The passive is made with the auxiliary verb **to be** and the **past participle** of the verb:

present simple	*The painting **is valued** by experts at 2 million dollars.*
present continuous	*The theft **is being investigated** by the police.*
present perfect	*Other museums **have been warned** to take extra care.*
past simple	*The painting **was kept** in a special room.*
past perfect	*The lock **had been broken**.*
past continuous	*This morning everything possible **was being done** to find the thieves.*
future	*Staff at the museum **will be questioned** tomorrow.*

You use the **passive**

- when you want to save new information until the end of the sentence for emphasis:
  - *The picture **was painted** by Turner.*
- when you do not know who performed the action, or when this information is not important. It is common in formal writing, for example scientific writing:
  - *The liquid **is heated** to 60° and then filtered.*

If you want to say who performed the action, you use **by** at the end of the sentence:

- *The painting was stolen **by** masked thieves.*

It is possible to put a verb that has two objects into the passive:

- *An American millionaire gave the museum the painting.*
- *The museum **was given** the painting by an American millionaire.*

NOTE Some verbs cannot be used in the passive, and this is shown at the entries.

Reported speech

Reported (or indirect) speech is the term used for the words that are used to report what someone has said.

If the reporting verb (say, ask, etc.) is in the present or present perfect, then the tense of the sentence does not change:

- ▶ *'I'm going home.'*
- ▶ *Bob says he's going home.*
- ▶ *Bob's just told me he's going home.*

Reporting statements in the past

When you report somebody's words using said, asked, etc., you usually change the tense to one further back in the past:

present simple	*'I **don't know** whether Nell **wants** an ice cream.'*
past simple	*He said he **didn't know** whether Nell **wanted** an ice cream.*
present continuous	*'She **is hoping** to rent a car tomorrow.'*
past continuous	*He said she **was hoping** to rent a car the following day.*
present perfect	***'Have** you **brought** your licence?'*
past perfect	*He asked whether she **had brought** her licence.*
past simple	*'I **passed** my driving test yesterday.'*
past perfect	*He said he **had passed** his driving test the day before.*
will	***'I'll ring** from the airport.'*
would	*She told me she **would ring** from the airport.*
can	*'I **can play** the flute.'*
could	*He said he **could play** the flute.*

- Other changes:
  I/you/we becomes **he/she/they**,
  my/your becomes **his/her**, etc.
- Time references change:
  tomorrow becomes **the following day**,
  yesterday becomes the **day before**,
  last week becomes **the week before/ the previous week**, etc.
- The modal verbs **should, would, might, could, must**, and **ought to** are not usually changed:
  - ▶ *'We **might** get a dog.'*
  - ▶ *They said they **might** get a dog.*
- The modal verb **may** changes to **might**.

Reporting requests and commands

When you report a request or an order, you usually use a to-infinitive:

- ▶ *'Please will you wash the dishes?'*
- ▶ *She asked me **to wash** the dishes.*
- ▶ *'Don't eat all the cake!'*
- ▶ *She told the children **not to eat** all the cake.*

Reporting questions

Notice that you use **if** or **whether** to report yes/no questions:

- ▶ *'Are you ready?'*
- ▶ *She asked **if/whether** I was ready.*

With **wh-** questions, the **wh-** word stays in the sentence:

- ▶ *'When are you leaving?'*
- ▶ *She asked me **when** I was leaving.*

The word order in these sentences is the same as a normal statement, not as in a question:

- ▶ *'Did you see them?'*
- ▶ *He asked me if I had seen them.*

Reporting verbs

Here are some useful reporting verbs. Look them up in the dictionary to see how you can use them:

admit	apologize	recommend
advise	complain	suggest
agree	deny	

Verb patterns

When one verb is followed by another, you need to know what form the second verb should take. Look at the entry for **promise** to see how this information is shown:

promise[1] /ˈprɒmɪs/ *verb* **1** [I,T] promise (to do sth); promise (sb) that ... to say definitely that you will do or not do sth or that sth will happen: *She promised to phone every week.* ♦ *She promised (me) that she would write.*

Every time you learn a new verb, write it down with the pattern that it uses. You will soon come to know which pattern looks or sounds right.

The meaning of the verb can sometimes make one pattern more likely than another. The following points can help you to make a good guess:

Many verbs that suggest that **an action will follow, or will be completed successfully**, are followed by **to do**:

(can) afford to do sth
agree to do sth
decide to do sth
hope to do sth
intend to do sth
manage to do sth
offer to do sth
plan to do sth
remember to do sth
try to do sth
(or try doing sth)
volunteer to do sth
ask (sb) to do sth
expect (sb) to do sth
help (sb) to do sth
need (sb) to do sth
wait (for sb) to do sth
want (sb) to do sth
would like (sb) to do sth
advise sb to do sth
allow sb to do sth
enable sb to do sth
encourage sb to do sth
get sb to do sth
persuade sb to do sth
remind sb to do sth
teach sb to do sth
tell sb to do sth

But note these verbs, which have a similar meaning but a different pattern:

let sb do sth
make sb do sth
consider doing sth
think about doing sth
suggest doing sth
recommend doing sth
look forward to doing sth
succeed in doing sth

Several verbs that suggest that **an action is unlikely to follow, or to be completed successfully**, are followed by an **-ing** form, sometimes with a preposition too:

avoid doing sth
resist doing sth
put sb off doing sth
save sb (from) doing sth
prevent sb from doing sth
dissuade sb from doing sth
advise sb against doing sth
(or *advise sb not to do sth*)

But note these verbs:

fail to do sth
forget to do sth
refuse to do sth

Several verbs that refer to **past events or actions** are followed by an **-ing** form, sometimes with a **preposition**:

admit doing sth
celebrate doing sth
miss doing sth
regret doing sth
remember doing sth
thank sb for doing sth

Verbs that refer to **starting, stopping or continuing** are often followed by an **-ing** form:

begin doing sth
continue doing sth
carry on doing sth
finish doing sth
go on doing sth
put off doing sth
start doing sth

But note that you can also say:

begin to do sth
continue to do sth
start to do sth

Verbs meaning **like** and **dislike** are usually followed by an **-ing** form:

like doing sth
love doing sth
prefer doing sth
hate doing sth
dread doing sth

But note that you can also say:

like to do sth
prefer to do sth
hate to do sth

Look at the entries for these verbs to see the slight difference in meaning that this pattern gives.

Transitive and intransitive

- ▶ *We arrived.*
- ▶ *He bought a jacket.*

Each of these sentences has a **subject** (we, he) and a **verb** (arrive, buy).

In the first sentence **arrive** stands alone. Verbs like this are called **intransitive**. They are marked [I] in this dictionary. In the second sentence **bought** has an object (a jacket). Verbs like this are called **transitive**. They are marked [T] in this dictionary.
Compare the following sentences:

- ▶ *Nobody spoke.*
- ▶ *Patrick speaks Japanese.*

In the first sentence the verb **speak** is used intransitively, without an object. In the second it is used transitively with the noun **Japanese** as the object. Many verbs can be both intransitive and transitive. In this dictionary they are marked [I,T]

Many verbs can have two objects, an **indirect object** and a **direct object**. The thing that is given, bought, etc. is the direct object and the person who receives it is the indirect object. The indirect object usually comes first.

Look up the verb **give** and notice the structures that are shown there:
give sb sth; give sth to sb
In a sentence you can say:

- ▶ *He gave his mother the eggs.*
- ▶ *He gave the eggs to his mother.*

Either or both of the objects can be pronouns:

- ▶ *He gave her the eggs.*
- ▶ *He gave the eggs to her.*
- ▶ *He gave them to his mother.*
- ▶ *He gave her them.*
- ▶ *He gave them to her.*

Phrasal verbs

Phrasal verbs are verbs that have two parts – a **verb** (sit, give, look, get, etc.) and a **particle** (down, up, after, etc.). Some phrasal verbs (come down with, put up with, etc.) have two particles.

sit down **give up**
look after **get along with**

Many phrasal verbs are easy to understand. For example, if you know the words **sit** and **down**, you can guess the meaning of **sit down**. But some phrasal verbs are more difficult because they have special meanings. For example, "**give up** smoking" means "stop smoking", but you can't guess this, even if you know the words **give** and **up**.

In Wordpower, phrasal verbs are listed after the ordinary meanings of the verb, in the sections marked PHR V (for example, to find **give up**, see **give**). The phrasal verbs are arranged alphabetically according to the particle (after, along, at, etc.).

The four types

There are four main types of phrasal verb:

Type 1
Phrasal verbs without an object

▶ *Please* ***sit down****.*
▶ *I have to* ***get up*** *early tomorrow.*

In the dictionary, these verbs are written like this: **sit down; get up.**

Type 2
Phrasal verbs that can be separated by an object

If the object is a noun, it can go either *after* both parts of the phrasal verb or *between* them:

▶ *She* ***tried on*** *the red sweater.*
▶ *She* ***tried*** *the red sweater* ***on****.*

If the object is a pronoun, it must go between the two parts of the phrasal verb:

▶ *She* ***tried*** *it* ***on****.* (NOT ~~*She tried on it.*~~)

In the dictionary, this verb is written like this: **try sth on**. When you see **sth** or **sb** between the two parts of the phrasal verb, you know that they can be separated by an object.

Type 3
Phrasal verbs that cannot be separated by an object

The two parts of the phrasal verb must go together:

▶ *Could you* ***look after*** *my dog while I'm on holiday?* (NOT ~~*Could you look my dog after while I'm on holiday?*~~)
▶ *Could you* ***look after*** *it while I'm on holiday?* (NOT ~~*Could you look it after while I'm on holiday?*~~)

In the dictionary, this verb is written like this: **look after sb/sth.** When you see **sb** or **sth** *after* the two parts of the phrasal verb, you know that they *cannot* be separated by an object.

Type 4
Phrasal verbs with three parts

The three parts of the phrasal verb must go together:

▶ *I can't* ***put up with*** *this noise anymore.*

In the dictionary, this verb is written like this: **put up with sb/sth**. Again, when you see **sb** or **sth** after the three parts of the phrasal verb, you know that they *cannot* be separated by an object.

Nouns

Countable and uncountable nouns

[C]

Countable nouns can be singular or plural:

▶ *a friend/two friends*
▶ *one book/five books*

In this dictionary they are marked [C].

[U]

Uncountable nouns cannot have a plural and are not used with **a/an**. They cannot be counted. In this dictionary they are marked [U].

➲ Look up the entries for:

advice **money**
furniture **rice**
information **water**

It is possible to say **some rice** but not **a rice** or **two rices**.

Abstract nouns like **happiness, importance** and **luck**, are usually uncountable.

[C,U]

Some nouns have both countable and uncountable meanings. In this dictionary they are marked [C,U] or [U,C].

Look up the entries for:

cheese coffee friendship paper

▶ [U] *Have some cheese!*
▶ [C] *They sell a variety of cheeses.* (= types of cheese)
▶ [U] *I don't drink much coffee.*
▶ [C] *She ordered two coffees.* (= cups of coffee)
▶ [U] *Friendship is more important than wealth.*
▶ [C] *None of these were lasting friendships.* (= relationships)
▶ [U] *I haven't got any more paper.*
▶ [C] *Can you buy me a paper?* (= a newspaper)

[sing]

Some nouns are only singular. They cannot be used in the plural. In this dictionary they are marked [sing].

➲ Look up the entries for:

the countryside **the doctor's** **a laugh**

▶ *We love walking in the countryside.*
▶ *I'm going to the doctor's today.*
▶ *The party was a good laugh.*

[pl]

Other words are only plural.
In this dictionary they are marked [pl].

➲ Look up the entries for:

jeans scissors sunglasses

You cannot say ~~a sunglasses~~. To talk about individual items, you say **a pair**:

▶ *a pair of sunglasses*
▶ *two pairs of sunglasses*

Words like **clothes, goods** and **headphones** can only be used in the plural:

▶ *I need to buy some new clothes.*

Nouns which describe groups of people, such as **the poor** are plural:

▶ *The poor are getting poorer and the rich are getting richer.*

Articles

The definite article

You use the definite article, **the**, when you expect the person who is listening to know which person or thing you are talking about:

▶ *Thank you for **the** flowers* (= the ones that you brought me).
▶ ***The** teacher said my essay was the best* (= our teacher).

You use **the** with the names of rivers and groups of islands:

▶ *Which is longer, **the** Rhine or **the** Danube?*
▶ *Where are **the** Seychelles?*
▶ *Menorca is one of **the** Balearic Islands.*

The indefinite article

You use the indefinite article, **a** (**an** before a vowel sound), when the other person does not know which person or thing you are talking about or when you are not referring to a particular thing or person:

▸ *He's got **a** new bike.*
(I haven't mentioned it before.)
▸ *Can I borrow **a** pen?*
(Any pen will be okay.)

You also use **a/an** to talk about a type or class of people or things, such as when you describe a person's job:

▸ *She's **an** accountant.*

You use **a/an** in prices, speeds, etc:

▸ *$100 **a** day*
▸ *50 cents **a** pack*
▸ *70 kilometres **an** hour*
▸ *three times **a** week*

No article

You do not use an article when you are talking in general:

▸ *I love flowers (all flowers).*
▸ *Honey is sweet (all honey).*
▸ *Lawyers are well paid (lawyers in general).*

You do not use **the** with most names of countries, counties, states, streets, or lakes:

▸ *I'm going to Turkey.*
▸ *a house in Walton Street*
▸ *She's from Yorkshire.*
▸ *Lake Louise*
▸ *They live in Iowa.*

or with a person's title when the name is mentioned:

▸ *President Kennedy*
BUT ***the** President of the United States*

➲ Look at the entries for **school, university, college, hospital, prison** and **music** for more information about the use of articles.

The possessive with 's

You can add **'s** to a word or a name to show possession. It is most often used with words for people, countries and animals:

▸ *Ann's job*
▸ *the children's clothes*
▸ *the manager's secretary*
▸ *the dog's basket*
▸ *my brother's computer*
▸ *Spain's beaches*

When the word already ends in a plural **s**, you add an apostrophe after it:

▸ *the boys' rooms*
▸ *the Smiths' house*

much, many, a lot, a little, a few

Much is used with **uncountable nouns,** usually in negative sentences and questions:

▸ *I haven't got **much** money left.*
▸ *Did you watch **much** television?*

Much is very formal in affirmative sentences:

▸ *There will be **much** discussion before a decision is made.*

Many is used with **countable nouns**, usually in negative sentences and questions:

▸ *There aren't **many** tourists here in December.*
▸ *Are there **many** opportunities for young people?*

In affirmative sentences, it is more formal than **a lot of**:

▸ ***Many** people prefer to stay at home.*

A lot of or (*informal*) **lots of** is used with countable and uncountable nouns:

▸ ***A lot of** tourists visit the castle.*
▸ *He's been here **lots of** times.*
▸ *I've spent **a lot of** money.*
▸ *You need **lots of** patience to make model aircraft.*

A little is used with **uncountable nouns**:

▸ *Add **a little** salt.*

A few is used with **countable nouns**:

▸ *I've got **a few** letters to write.*

Note that in these sentences, the meaning is positive. **Few** and **little** without **a** have a negative meaning.

Adjectives

Comparatives and superlatives

Look at this text. It contains several comparatives and superlatives.

▶ *Temperatures yesterday were **highest** in the south-east. The **sunniest** place was Brighton, and the **wettest** was Glasgow. Tomorrow will be **cooler** than today, but in Scotland it will be a **drier** day. **Better** weather is expected for the weekend, but it will become **more changeable** again next week.*

To form comparatives and superlatives:

- Adjectives of **one syllable** add -er, est:

cool	cooler	coolest
high	higher	highest

- Adjectives that already end in **-e** only add -r, -st:

nice	nicer	nicest

- Some words double the last letter:

wet	wetter	wettest
big	bigger	biggest

- Adjectives of three syllables or more take more, most:

changeable	more changeable most changeable
interesting	more interesting most interesting

- Some adjectives of **two syllables** are like **cool**, especially those that end in **-er**, **-y**, or **-ly**:

clever	cleverer	cleverest

- Words that end in -y change it to -i:

sunny	sunnier	sunniest
friendly	friendlier	friendliest

- Other adjectives of **two syllables** are like **interesting**:

harmful	more harmful most harmful

- Some adjectives have **irregular forms**:

good	better	best
bad	worse	worst

Adjectives with nouns

Most adjectives can be used **before** the noun that they describe or **after** a linking verb:

▶ *I need a **new** bike.*
▶ *This bike isn't **new**.*
▶ *It's an **interesting** book.*
▶ *She said the film sounded **interesting**.*

Some adjectives **cannot** come **before** a noun. ➲ Look at the entry for **asleep** and notice how this information is given in the dictionary. You can say:

▶ *Don't wake him – he's **asleep**.*
BUT NOT: *~~an asleep child~~*

➲ Look up the entries for **afraid** and **pleased**.

Some adjectives can **only** be used **before** a noun. ➲ Look at the entry for the adjective **chief** and notice how this information is given in the dictionary. You can say:

▶ *That was the **chief** disadvantage.*
BUT NOT: *~~This disadvantage was chief.~~*

➲ Look up the entries for **former** and **main**.

Relative clauses

Defining relative clauses

These phrases **define** or **identify** which person or thing we are talking about:

▶ *'Which of them is the boss?' 'The man **who came in late** is the boss.'*

When the **subject** is a person:

▶ *the man **who** came in late*
OR *the man **that** came in late*

When the **object** is a person:

▶ *the girl **that** I saw*
OR *the girl I saw*
OR *the girl **who** I saw*
OR *the girl **whom** I saw (formal)*

When the **subject** is a thing:

▶ *the chair **that** is in the corner*
OR *the chair **which** is in the corner*

When the **object** is a thing:

▶ *the book **that** I'm reading*
OR *the book I'm reading*
OR *the book **which** I'm reading*

whose shows that something belongs to somebody:

▶ *the woman **whose** car broke down*

▶ *the people **whose** house was burgled*

Whose is not usually used to refer to a thing:

▶ NOT ~~*the chair whose leg is broken*~~

It is more natural to say:

▶ *the chair with the broken leg*

Non-defining relative clauses

These phrases **add extra information** about somebody or something which could be left out and the sentence would still make sense. This extra information is separated from the main clause by commas:

▶ *The film, which was shot in Mexico, has won an Oscar.*

The pronouns that can be used in non-defining relative clauses are **who** for a person; **which** for a thing; **whose** to show belonging

▶ *My sister, who is a vegetarian, ordered a cheese salad.*

▶ *The tickets, which can be bought at the station, are valid for one day.*

▶ *Lucy, whose car had broken down, arrived by bus.*

Prefixes

a- not: *atypical*
ante- before: *antenatal* (= before birth)
anti- against: *anti-American, antisocial*
auto- self: *autobiography* (= the story of the writer's own life)
bi- two: *bicycle, bilingual* (= using two languages), *bimonthly* (= twice a month or every two months)
cent-, centi- hundred: *centenary* (= the hundredth anniversary), *centimetre* (= one hundredth of a metre)
circum- around: *circumnavigate* (= sail around)
co- with; together: *co-pilot, coexist, cooperation*
con- with; together: *context* (= the words or sentences that come before and after a particular word or sentence)
contra- against; opposite: *contradict* (= say the opposite)
counter- against; opposite: *counter-revolution, counterproductive* (= producing the opposite of the desired effect)
de- taking sth away; the opposite: *defrost* (= removing the layers of ice from a fridge, etc.), *decentralize*
deca- ten: *decathlon* (= a competition involving ten different sports)
deci- one tenth: *decilitre*
dis- reverse or opposite: *displeasure, disembark, discomfort*
e- using electronic communication: *e-commerce*
ex- former: *ex-wife, ex-president*
extra- **1** very; more than usual: *extra-thin, extra-special* **2** outside; beyond: *extraordinary, extraterrestrial* (= coming from somewhere beyond the earth)
fore- **1** before; in advance: *foreword* (= at the beginning of a book) **2** front: *foreground* (= the front part of a picture), *forehead*
hexa- six: *hexagon* (= a shape with six sides)
in-, il-, im-, ir- not: *incorrect, invalid, illegal, illegible, immoral, impatient, impossible, irregular, irrelevant*
inter- between; from one to another: *international, interracial*
kilo- thousand: *kilogram, kilowatt*
maxi- most; very large: *maximum*
mega- million; very large: *megabyte, megabucks* (= a lot of money)
micro- very small: *microchip*
mid- in the middle of: *mid-afternoon, mid-air*
milli- thousandth: *millisecond, millimetre*
mini- small: *miniskirt, miniseries*
mis- bad or wrong; not: *misbehave, miscalculate, misunderstand*
mono- one; single: *monolingual* (= using one language), *monorail*
multi- many: *multinational* (= involving many countries)
non- not: *non-alcoholic, nonsense, non-smoker, non-stop*
octa- eight: *octagon* (= a shape with eight sides)
out- more; to a greater degree: *outdo, outrun* (= run faster or better than sb)
over- more than normal; too much: *overeat, oversleep* (= sleep too long)
penta- five: *pentagon* (= a shape with five sides), *pentathlon* (= a competition involving five different sports)
post- after: *post-war*
pre- before: *pre-pay, preview*
pro- for; in favour of: *pro-democracy, pro-hunting*
quad- four: *quadruple* (= multiply by four), *quadruplet* (= one of four babies born at the same time)
re- again: *rewrite, rebuild*
self- of, to or by yourself: *self-taught*
semi- half: *semicircle, semiconscious*
sub- **1** below; less than: *sub-zero* **2** under: *subway, subtitles* (= translations under the pictures of a film)
super- extremely; more than: *superhuman* (= having greater power than humans normally have), *supersonic* (= faster than the speed of sound)
tele- far; over a long distance: *telecommunications, telephoto lens*
trans- across; through: *transatlantic, transcontinental*
tri- three: *triangle, tricycle*
ultra- extremely; beyond a certain limit: *ultra-modern*
un- not; opposite; taking sth away: *uncertain, uncomfortable, unsure, undo, undress*
under- not enough: *undercooked*
uni- one; single: *uniform* (= having the same form)
vice- the second most important: *vice-president*

Suffixes

-able, -ible, -ble (to make adjectives) possible to: *acceptable, noticeable, convertible, divisible* (= possible to divide), *irresistible* (= that you cannot resist)

-age (to make nouns) a process or state: *storage, shortage*

-al (to make adjectives) connected with: *experimental, accidental, environmental*

-ance, -ence, -ancy, -ency (to make nouns) an action, process or state: *appearance, performance, existence, intelligence, pregnancy, efficiency*

-ant, -ent (to make nouns) a person who does sth: *assistant, immigrant, student*

-ation (to make nouns) a state or an action: *examination, imagination, organization*

-ble → -able

-ed (to make adjectives) having a particular state or quality: *bored, patterned*

-ee (to make nouns) a person to whom sth is done: *employee* (= sb who is employed), *trainee* (= sb who is being trained)

-en (to make verbs) to give sth a particular quality; to make sth more ~: *shorten, widen, blacken, sharpen, loosen,* (but note: *lengthen*)

ence (-ency) → -ance

-ent → -ant

-er (to make nouns) a person who does sth: *rider, painter, banker, driver, teacher*

-ese (to make adjectives) from a place: *Japanese, Chinese, Viennese*

-ess (to make nouns) a woman who does sth as a job: *waitress, actress*

-ful (to make adjectives) having a particular quality: *helpful, useful, beautiful*

-hood (to make nouns) **1** a state, often during a particular period of time: *childhood, motherhood* **2** a group with sth in common: *sisterhood, neighbourhood*

-ian (to make nouns) a person who does sth as a job or hobby: *historian, comedian, politician*

-ible → -able

-ical (to make adjectives from nouns ending in -y or -ics) connected with: *economical, mathematical, physical*

-ify (to make verbs) to produce a state or quality: *beautify, simplify, purify*

-ing (to make adjectives) producing a particular state or effect: *interesting*

-ish (to make adjectives) **1** describing nationality or language: *English, Swedish, Polish* **2** like sth: *babyish, foolish* **3** fairly; sort of: *longish, youngish, brownish*

-ist (to make nouns) **1** a person who has studied sth or does sth as a job: *artist, scientist, economist* **2** a person who believes in sth or belongs to a particular group: *capitalist, pacifist, feminist*

-ion (to make nouns) a state or process: *action, connection, exhibition*

-ive (to make adjectives) having a particular quality: *attractive, effective*

-ize, -ise (to make verbs) producing a particular state: *magnetize, standardize, modernize, generalize*

-less (to make adjectives) not having sth: *hopeless, friendless*

-like (to make adjectives) similar to: *childlike*

-ly (to make adverbs) in a particular way: *badly, beautifully, completely*

-ment (to make nouns) a state, an action or a quality: *development, arrangement, excitement, achievement*

-ness (to make nouns) a state or quality: *kindness, happiness, weakness*

-ology (to make nouns) the study of a subject: *biology, psychology, zoology*

-or (to make nouns) a person who does sth, often as a job: *actor, conductor, sailor*

-ous (to make adjectives) having a particular quality: *dangerous, religious, ambitious*

-ship (to make nouns) showing status: *friendship, membership, citizenship*

-ward, -wards (to make adverbs) in a particular direction: *backward, upwards*

-wise (to make adverbs) in a particular way: *clockwise, edgewise*

-y (to make adjectives) having the quality of the thing mentioned: *cloudy, rainy, fatty, thirsty*

Expressions using numbers

The numbers

1	one	1st	first
2	two	2nd	second
3	three	3rd	third
4	four	4th	fourth
5	five	5th	fifth
6	six	6th	sixth
7	seven	7th	seventh
8	eight	8th	eighth
9	nine	9th	ninth
10	ten	10th	tenth
11	eleven	11th	eleventh
12	twelve	12th	twelfth
13	thirteen	13th	thirteenth
14	fourteen	14th	fourteenth
15	fifteen	15th	fifteenth
16	sixteen	16th	sixteenth
17	seventeen	17th	seventeenth
18	eighteen	18th	eighteenth
19	nineteen	19th	nineteenth
20	twenty	20th	twentieth
21	twenty-one	21st	twenty-first
22	twenty-two	22nd	twenty-second
30	thirty	30th	thirtieth
40	forty	40th	fortieth
50	fifty	50th	fiftieth
60	sixty	60th	sixtieth
70	seventy	70th	seventieth
80	eighty	80th	eightieth
90	ninety	90th	ninetieth
100	a/one hundred*	100th	hundredth
101	a/one hundred and one*	101st	hundred and first
200	two hundred	200th	two hundredth
1 000	a/one thousand*	1 000th	thousandth
10 000	ten thousand	10 000th	ten thousandth
100 000	a/one hundred thousand*	100 000th	hundred thousandth
1 000 000	a/one million*	1 000 000th	millionth

Examples
▶ 697: *six hundred and ninety-seven*
▶ 3 402: *three thousand, four hundred and two*
▶ 80 534: *eighty thousand, five hundred and thirty-four*

* You use **one hundred, one thousand**, etc., instead of **a hundred, a thousand**, when it is important to stress that you mean one (not two, for example). In numbers over a thousand, you use a comma or a small space: **1,200** or **1 200**

Telephone numbers

In telephone numbers you say each number separately, often with a pause after two or three numbers:

▶ 509236 *five oh nine – two three six*

You can say **six six** or **double six** for **66**:

▶ 02166 *oh two one – six six* or *oh two one – double six*

If you are phoning a number in a different town, you have to use the **area code** before the number:

▶ *01865 is the code for Oxford.*

If you are phoning somebody in a large firm, you can ask for their extension number.

▶ *(01865) 56767 x 4840 (extension 4840)*

Fractions and decimals

½	a half	⅓	a/one third
¼	a quarter	⅖	two fifths
⅛	an/one eighth	7/12	seven twelfths
1/10	a/one tenth	1½	one and a half
1/16	a/one sixteenth	2⅜	two and three eighths

0.1 (nought) point one
0.25 (nought) point two five
0.33 (nought) point three three
1.75 one point seven five
3.976 three point nine seven six

Percentages and proportions

▶ ***90%** of all households have a television.*
▶ ***Nine out of ten** households have a television.*
▶ ***Nine tenths of** all households have a television.*

Mathematical expressions

+ plus
– minus
× times or multiplied by
÷ divided by
= equals
% per cent
3^2 three squared
5^3 five cubed
6^{10} six to the power of ten

Examples
$7 + 6 = 13$ *seven plus six equals* (or *is*) *thirteen*
$5 \times 8 = 40$ *five times eight equals forty*
or *five eights are forty*
or *five multiplied by eight is forty*

Temperature

In Britain, temperatures are now usually given in **degrees Celsius**, (although many people are still more familiar with **Fahrenheit**). In the United States, **Fahrenheit** is used, except in science.

To convert **Fahrenheit** to **Celsius**, subtract 32 from the number, then multiply by 5 and divide by 9:

68 °F – 32
= 36 × 5
= 180 ÷ 9
= 20 °C

Examples
▶ *Water freezes at 32°F and boils at 212°F.*
▶ *The maximum temperature this afternoon will be 15°, and the minimum tonight may reach –5° (minus five).*
▶ *She had a temperature of 102° last night, and it's still above normal.*

Weight

		Non-metric	Metric
		1 ounce (oz)	= 28.35 grams (g)
16 ounces	=	1 pound (lb)	= 0.454 kilogram (kg)
14 pounds	=	1 stone (st)	= 6.356 kilograms
8 stone	=	1 hundredweight (cwt)	= 50.8 kilograms
20 hundredweight	=	1 ton (t)	= 1 016.04 kilograms

Examples
- ▶ *The baby weighed 8 lb 2oz (eight pounds two ounces).*
- ▶ *For this recipe you need 750g (seven hundred and fifty grams) of flour.*

Length and height

		Non-metric	Metric
		1 inch (in)	= 25.4 millimetres (mm)
12 inches	=	1 foot (ft)	= 30.48 centimetres (cm)
3 feet	=	1 yard (yd)	= 0.914 metre (m)
1 760 yards	=	1 mile	= 1.609 kilometres (km)

Examples
- ▶ *flying at 7 000 feet*
- ▶ *The speed limit is 30 mph (thirty miles per/an hour).*
- ▶ *The room is 11'x 9'6" (eleven feet by nine feet six* or *eleven foot by nine foot six).*
- ▶ *She's five feet four (inches).*
- ▶ *He's one metre sixty (centimetres).*

Area

		Non-metric	Metric
		1 square inch (sq in)	= 6.452 square centimetres (cm^2)
144 square inches	=	1 square foot (sq ft)	= 929.03 square centimetres
9 square feet	=	1 square yard (sq yd)	= 0.836 square metre (m^2)
4 840 square yards	=	1 acre	= 0.405 hectare
640 acres	=	1 square mile	= 2.59 square kilometres (km^2) or 259 hectares

Examples
- ▶ *an 80-acre country park*
- ▶ *160 000 square miles of the jungle have been destroyed.*

Cubic measurements

		Non-metric	Metric
		1 cubic inch (cu in)	= 16.39 cubic centimetres (cc)
1 728 cubic inches	=	1 cubic foot (cu ft)	= 0.028 cubic metre
27 cubic feet	=	1 cubic yard (cu yd)	= 0.765 cubic metre

Example
- ▶ *a car with a 1500 cc engine*

Capacity

		GB	US	Metric
20 fluid ounces (fl oz)	=	1 pint (pt)	= 1.201 pints	= 0.568 litre (l)
2 pints	=	1 quart (qt)	= 1.201 quarts	= 1.136 litres
4 quarts	=	1 gallon (gall)	= 1.201 gallons	= 4.546 litres

Examples
- ▶ *I drink a litre of water a day.*
- ▶ *a quart of orange juice*

Dates

- *8 April 2005 or 8th April 2005 (8/4/05) (BrE)*
- *Her birthday is on the thirteenth of July.*
- *Her birthday is on July the thirteenth.*
- *April 8, 2005 (4/8/05) (AmE)*
- *Her birthday is July 13th. (AmE)*

Years

1999 *nineteen ninety-nine*
1608 *sixteen oh eight*
1700 *seventeen hundred*
2000 *(the year) two thousand*
2002 *two thousand and two*
2015 *twenty fifteen*

Age

When saying a person's age, use only numbers:

- *Sue is ten and Tom is six.*
- *She left home at sixteen.*

You can say a … year-old/month-old/ week-old, etc.:

- *Youth training is available to all sixteen-year-olds.*
- *a ten-week-old baby*

To give the approximate age of a person:

13–19 *in his/her teens*
21–29 *in his/her twenties*
31–33 *in his/her early thirties*
34–36 *in his/her mid-thirties*
37–39 *in his/her late thirties*

Times

There is often more than one way of telling the time:

Half hours

6:30 *six thirty*
half past six
half six (informal)

Other times

5:45	*five forty-five*	*(a) quarter to six*
2:15	*two fifteen*	*(a) quarter past two*
1:10	*one ten*	*ten past one*
3:05	*three oh five*	*five past three*
1:55	*one fifty-five*	*five to two*

In American English, *after* is sometimes used instead of *past*, and *of* instead of *to*.

with 5, 10, 20 and 25 the word *minutes* is not necessary, but it is used with other numbers:

10.25 *twenty-five past ten*
10.17 *seventeen minutes past ten*

use *o'clock* only for whole hours:

- *It's three o'clock.*

Twenty-four hour clock

The twenty-four hour clock is used in official language:

13:52 *thirteen fifty-two (1:52 p.m.)*
22:30 *twenty-two thirty (10.30 p.m.)*

British and American English

There are some important differences between British and American English.

Vocabulary

Many everyday words are different in British and American English. For example:

- items of clothing: **dressing gown** (*AmE* **bathrobe**), **trainers** (*AmE* **sneakers**)
- words connected with cars: **boot** (*AmE* **trunk**), **motorway** (*AmE* **expressway**), **petrol** (*AmE* **gasoline**)

Some words have different meanings in British and American English. For example:

- *AmE* **pants** = a piece of clothing that covers the whole of both your legs (*BrE* **trousers**)
- *BrE* **pants** = a piece of clothing that men or boys wear under their trousers

Spelling

- Words which end in *-tre* are spelt *-ter* in American English: **centre** (*AmE* **center**)
- Words which end in *-our* are usually spelt *-or* in American English: **colour** (*AmE* **color**)
- Words which end in *-ogue* are usually spelt *-og* in American English: **dialogue** (*AmE* **dialog**)
- In British English many verbs can be spelt with either *-ize* or *-ise*. In American English only the spelling with *-ize* is possible: **realize, -ise**; (*AmE* **realize**)
- In verbs which end in *-l* and are not stressed on the final syllable, there is only one *-l-* in the *-ing* and *-ed* forms in American English: **cancelling** (*AmE* **canceling**)

Grammar

Past simple/Present perfect

American English often uses the past simple tense where British English uses the present perfect:

- *(BrE) I've just seen her.*
- *(AmE) I just saw her.*
- *(BrE) Have you heard the news?*
- *(AmE) Did you hear the news?*

Have/Have got

In American English **have** is always used instead of **have got** in questions and negative sentences:

- *(BrE) Have you got a dog?*
- *(BrE and AmE) Do you have a dog?*
- *(BrE) I haven't got a dog.*
- *(BrE and AmE) I don't have a dog.*

Prepositions and adverbs

Some prepositions and adverbs are used differently in British and American English, for example:

- *stay at home (AmE stay home)*
- *at the weekend (AmE on the weekend)*

Irregular verbs

In British English the past simple and past participle of many verbs can be formed with *-ed* or *-t*, for example **learned/learnt**. In American English only the forms ending in *-ed* are used:

- *(BrE) I learned/learnt English at school.*
- *(AmE) I learned English at school.*

Britain and Ireland

The UK (United Kingdom) consists of Great Britain and Northern Ireland. Great Britain (GB) is **England**/ˈɪŋɡlənd/, **Scotland** /ˈskɒtlənd/ and **Wales** /weɪlz/. The Republic of Ireland is a separate country.

The British Isles is a geographical term which includes the islands of Great Britain and Ireland, and the smaller islands around them.

Towns and cities in the UK and Ireland

Aberdeen /ˌæbəˈdiːn/
Bath /bɑːθ/
Belfast /ˈbelfɑːst; ˌbelˈfɑːst/
Berwick-upon-Tweed /ˌberɪk əpɒn ˈtwiːd/
Birmingham /ˈbɜːmɪŋəm/
Blackpool /ˈblækpuːl/
Bournemouth /ˈbɔːnməθ/
Bradford /ˈbrædfəd/
Brighton /ˈbraɪtn/
Bristol /ˈbrɪstl/
Caernarfon /kəˈnɑːvn/
Cambridge /ˈkeɪmbrɪdʒ/
Canterbury /ˈkæntəbəri/
Cardiff /ˈkɑːdɪf/
Carlisle /kɑːˈlaɪl/
Chester /ˈtʃestə(r)/
Colchester /ˈkəʊltʃɪstə(r)/
Cork /kɔːk/
Coventry /ˈkɒvəntri/
Derby /ˈdɑːbi/
Douglas /ˈdʌɡləs/
Dover /ˈdəʊvə(r)/
Dublin /ˈdʌblɪn/
Dundee /dʌnˈdiː/
Durham /ˈdʌrəm/
Eastbourne /ˈiːstbɔːn/
Edinburgh /ˈedɪnbrə/
Ely /ˈiːli/
Exeter /ˈeksɪtə(r)/
Galway /ˈɡɔːlweɪ/
Glasgow /ˈɡlɑːzɡəʊ/
Gloucester /ˈɡlɒstə(r)/
Hastings /ˈheɪstɪŋz/
Hereford /ˈherɪfəd/
Holyhead /ˈhɒlihed/
Inverness /ˌɪnvəˈnes/
Ipswich /ˈɪpswɪtʃ/
Keswick /ˈkezɪk/
Kingston upon Hull /ˌkɪŋstən əpɒn ˈhʌl/
Leeds /liːdz/
Leicester /ˈlestə(r)/
Limerick /ˈlɪmərɪk/
Lincoln /ˈlɪŋkən/
Liverpool /ˈlɪvəpuːl/
London /ˈlʌndən/
Londonderry /ˈlʌndənderi/
Luton /ˈluːtn/
Manchester /ˈmæntʃɪstə(r)/
Middlesbrough /ˈmɪdlzbrə/
Newcastle upon Tyne /ˌnjuːkɑːsl əpɒn ˈtaɪn/
Norwich /ˈnɒrɪdʒ/
Nottingham /ˈnɒtɪŋəm/
Oxford /ˈɒksfəd/
Plymouth /ˈplɪməθ/
Poole /puːl/
Portsmouth /ˈpɔːtsməθ/
Ramsgate /ˈræmzɡeɪt/
Reading /ˈredɪŋ/
Salisbury /ˈsɔːlzbəri/
Sheffield /ˈʃefiːld/
Shrewsbury /ˈʃrəʊzbəri/
Southampton /saʊˈθæmptən/
St Andrews /ˌsnt ˈændruːz/
Stirling /ˈstɜːlɪŋ/
Stoke-on-Trent /ˌstəʊk ɒn ˈtrent/
Stratford-upon-Avon /ˌstrætfəd əpɒn ˈeɪvn/
Swansea /ˈswɒnzi/
Taunton /ˈtɔːntən/
Warwick /ˈwɒrɪk/
Worcester /ˈwʊstə(r)/
York /jɔːk/

Map of Britain and Ireland

The United States of America and Canada

The provinces and territories of Canada

Alberta /æl'bɜ:tə/
British Columbia /ˌbrɪtɪʃ kə'lʌmbiə/
Manitoba /ˌmænɪ'təʊbə/
New Brunswick /ˌnju: 'brʌnzwɪk/
Newfoundland and Labrador /ˌnju:fəndlənd ən 'læbrədɔ:(r)/
Northwest Territories /ˌnɔ:θwest 'terətriz/
Nova Scotia /ˌnəʊvə 'skəʊʃə/
Nunavut /'nʊnəvʊt/
Ontario /ɒn'teəriəʊ/
Prince Edward Island /ˌprɪns 'edwəd aɪlənd/
Quebec /kwɪ'bek/
Saskatchewan /sə'skætʃəwən/
Yukon Territory /'ju:kɒn terətri/

The states of the USA

Alabama /ˌælə'bæmə/
Alaska /ə'læskə/
Arizona /ˌærɪ'zəʊnə/
Arkansas /'ɑ:kənsɔ:/
California /ˌkælə'fɔ:niə/
Colorado /ˌkɒlə'rɑ:dəʊ/
Connecticut /kə'netɪkət/
Delaware /'deləweə(r)/
Florida /'flɒrɪdə/
Georgia /'dʒɔ:dʒə/
Hawaii /hə'waii/
Idaho /'aɪdəhəʊ/
Illinois /ˌɪlə'nɔɪ/
Indiana /ˌɪndi'ænə/
Iowa /'aɪəwə/
Kansas /'kænzəs/
Kentucky /ken'tʌki/
Louisiana /luˌi:zi'ænə/
Maine /meɪn/
Maryland /'meərilənd/
Massachusetts /ˌmæsə'tʃu:sɪts/
Michigan /'mɪʃɪgən/
Minnesota /ˌmɪnɪ'səʊtə/
Mississippi /ˌmɪsɪ'sɪpi/
Missouri /mɪ'zʊəri/
Montana /mɒn'tænə/
Nebraska /nə'bræskə/
Nevada /nə'vɑ:də/
New Hampshire /ˌnju: 'hæmpʃə(r)/
New Jersey /ˌnju: 'dʒɜ:zi/
New Mexico /ˌnju: 'meksɪkəʊ/
New York /ˌnju: 'jɔ:k/
North Carolina /ˌnɔ:θ kærə'laɪnə/
North Dakota /ˌnɔ:θ də'kəʊtə/
Ohio /əʊ'haɪəʊ/
Oklahoma /ˌəʊklə'həʊmə/
Oregon /'ɒrɪgən/
Pennsylvania /ˌpensl'veɪniə/
Rhode Island /ˌrəʊd 'aɪlənd/
South Carolina /ˌsaʊθ kærə'laɪnə/
South Dakota /ˌsaʊθ də'kəʊtə/
Tennessee /ˌtenə'si:/
Texas /'teksəs/
Utah /'ju:tɑ:/
Vermont /və'mɒnt/
Virginia /və'dʒɪniə/
Washington /'wɒʃɪŋtən/
West Virginia /ˌwest və'dʒɪniə/
Wisconsin /wɪs'kɒnsɪn/
Wyoming /waɪ'əʊmɪŋ/

Cities in Canada and the USA

Anchorage /'æŋkərɪdʒ/
Atlanta /ət'læntə/
Baltimore /'bɔ:ltɪmɔ:(r)/
Boston /'bɒstən/
Chicago /ʃɪ'kɑ:gəʊ/
Cincinnati /ˌsɪnsɪ'næti/
Cleveland /'kli:vlənd/
Dallas /'dæləs/
Denver /'denvə(r)/
Detroit /dɪ'trɔɪt/
Honolulu /ˌhɒnə'lu:lu:/
Houston /'hju:stən/
Indianapolis /ˌɪndiə'næpəlɪs/
Kansas City /ˌkænzəs 'sɪti
Los Angeles /ˌlɒs 'ændʒəli:z/
Miami /maɪ'æmi/
Milwaukee /mɪl'wɔ:ki/
Minneapolis /ˌmɪni'æpəlɪs/
Montreal /ˌmɒntri'ɔ:l/
New Orleans /ˌnju: ɔ:'li:ənz/
New York /ˌnju: 'jɔ:k/
Ottawa /'ɒtəwə/
Philadelphia /ˌfɪlə'delfiə/
Pittsburgh /'pɪtsbɜ:g/
Quebec City /kwɪˌbek 'sɪti/
San Diego /ˌsæn di'eɪgəʊ/
San Francisco /ˌsæn frən'sɪskəʊ/
Seattle /si'ætl/
St Louis /ˌsnt 'lu:ɪs/
Toronto /tə'rɒntəʊ/
Vancouver /væn'ku:və(r)/
Washington D.C. /ˌwɒʃɪŋtən di: 'si:/
Winnipeg /'wɪnɪpeg/

Map of the United States of America and Canada

Geographical names

This list shows the English spelling and pronunciation of geographical names and the adjectives that go with them.

To talk in general about the people from a country, you can use the word **people**:

▶ *Moroccan people, French people, Italian people, Japanese people, etc.*

You can also add an **-s** to the adjective:

▶ *Moroccans, Italians, etc.*

If the adjective ends in a /s/, /z/ or /ʃ/ sound, use **the** and no **-s**:

▶ *the Swiss, the Chinese, the French, etc.*

To talk about a number of people from one country, add an **-s** to the adjective, unless it ends in an /s/, /z/ or /ʃ/ sound:

▶ *two Germans, some Pakistanis, a group of Japanese, a few Swiss, etc.*

Sometimes there is a special word for a person from a country, in which case this is shown after the adjective, for example **Denmark**: **Danish, a Dane**:

▶ *two Danes, several Turks, a roomful of Dutchwomen, etc.*

Inclusion in this list does not imply status as a sovereign nation.

Afghanistan /æfˈgænɪstɑːn/	**Afghan** /ˈæfgæn/
Africa /ˈæfrɪkə/	**African** /ˈæfrɪkən/
Albania /ælˈbeɪniə/	**Albanian** /ælˈbeɪniən/
Algeria /ælˈdʒɪəriə/	**Algerian** /ælˈdʒɪəriən/
America /əˈmerɪkə/	**American** /əˈmerɪkən/
Andorra /ænˈdɔːrə/	**Andorran** /ænˈdɔːrən/
Angola /æŋˈgəʊlə/	**Angolan** /æŋˈgəʊlən/
Antarctica /ænˈtɑːktɪkə/	**Antarctic** /ænˈtɑːktɪk/
Antigua and Barbuda /ænˌtiːgə ən bɑːˈbjuːdə/	**Antiguan** /ænˈtiːgən/ **Barbudan** /bɑːˈbjuːdən/
(the) Arctic /ˌɑːktɪk/	**Arctic** /ˈɑːktɪk/
Argentina /ˌɑːdʒənˈtiːnə/	**Argentinian** /ˌɑːdʒənˈtɪniən/ **Argentine** /ˈɑːdʒəntaɪn/
Armenia /ɑːˈmiːniə/	**Armenian** /ɑːˈmiːniən/
Asia /ˈeɪʒə/	**Asian** /ˈeɪʒn/
Australia /ɒˈstreɪliə/	**Australian** /ɒˈstreɪliən/
Austria /ˈɒstriə/	**Austrian** /ˈɒstriən/
Azerbaijan /ˌæzəbaɪˈdʒɑːn/	**Azerbaijani** /ˌæzəbaɪˈdʒɑːni/ **Azeri** /əˈzeəri/
(the) Bahamas /bəˈhɑːməz/	**Bahamian** /bəˈheɪmiən/
Bahrain /bɑːˈreɪn/	**Bahraini** /bɑːˈreɪni/
Bangladesh /ˌbæŋgləˈdeʃ/	**Bangladeshi** /ˌbæŋgləˈdeʃi/
Barbados /bɑːˈbeɪdɒs/	**Barbadian** /bɑːˈbeɪdiən/
Belarus /ˌbeləˈruːs/	**Belarusian** /ˌbeləˈruːsiən/ **Belorussian** /ˌbeləˈrʌʃn/
Belgium /ˈbeldʒəm/	**Belgian** /ˈbeldʒən/
Belize /bəˈliːz/	**Belizean** /bəˈliːziən/
Benin /beˈniːn/	**Beninese** /ˌbenɪˈniːz/
Bhutan /buːˈtɑːn/	**Bhutani** /buːˈtɑːni/ **Bhutanese** /ˌbuːtəˈniːz/
Bolivia /bəˈlɪviə/	**Bolivian** /bəˈlɪviən/
Bosnia and Herzegovina /ˌbɒzniə ən ˌhɜːtsəgəˈviːnə/	**Bosnian** /ˈbɒzniən/ **Herzegovinian** /ˌhɜːtsəgəˈvɪniən/
Botswana /bɒtˈswɑːnə/	**Botswanan** /bɒtˈswɑːnən/ person: a **Motswana** /mɒtˈswɑːnə/ people: **Batswana** /bætˈswɑːnə/

Brazil /brəˈzɪl/	**Brazilian** /brəˈzɪliən/
Brunei /bruːˈnaɪ/	**Bruneian** /bruːˈnaɪən/
Bulgaria /bʌlˈgeəriə/	**Bulgarian** /bʌlˈgeəriən/
Burkina /bɜːˈkiːnə/	**Burkinan** /ˌbɜːˈkiːnən/ **Burkinabe** /bɜːˌkiːnəˈbeɪ/
Burma /ˈbɜːmə/ (*see also* **Myanmar**)	**Burmese** /bɜːˈmiːz/
Burundi /bʊˈrʊndi/	**Burundian** /bʊˈrʊndiən/
Cambodia /kæmˈbəʊdiə/	**Cambodian** /kæmˈbəʊdiən/
Cameroon /ˌkæməˈruːn/	**Cameroonian** /ˌkæməˈruːniən/
Canada /ˈkænədə/	**Canadian** /kəˈneɪdiən/
Cape Verde /ˌkeɪp ˈvɜːd/	**Cape Verdean** /ˌkeɪp ˈvɜːdiən/
Central African Republic /ˌsentrəl ˌæfrɪkən rɪˈpʌblɪk/	**Central African** /ˌsentrəl ˈæfrɪkən/
Chad /tʃæd/	**Chadian** /ˈtʃædiən/
Chile /ˈtʃɪli/	**Chilean** /ˈtʃɪliən/
China /ˈtʃaɪnə/	**Chinese** /tʃaɪˈniːz/
Colombia /kəˈlɒmbiə/	**Colombian** /kəˈlɒmbiən/
Comoros /ˈkɒmərəʊz/	**Comoran** /kəˈmɔːrən/
Congo /ˈkɒŋgəʊ/	**Congolese** /ˌkɒŋgəˈliːz/
(the) Democratic Republic of the Congo (DR Congo) /ˌdeməˌkrætɪk rɪˌpʌblɪk əv ðə ˈkɒŋgəʊ/	**Congolese** /ˌkɒŋgəˈliːz/
Costa Rica /ˌkɒstə ˈriːkə/	**Costa Rican** /ˌkɒstə ˈriːkən/
Côte d'Ivoire /ˌkəʊt diːˈvwɑː(r)/ (*see also* **Ivory Coast**)	**Ivorian** /aɪˈvɔːriən/
Croatia /krəʊˈeɪʃə/	**Croatian** /krəʊˈeɪʃn/
Cuba /ˈkjuːbə/	**Cuban** /ˈkjuːbən/
Cyprus /ˈsaɪprəs/	**Cypriot** /ˈsɪpriət/
(the) Czech Republic /ˌtʃek rɪˈpʌblɪk/	**Czech** /tʃek/
Denmark /ˈdenmɑːk/	**Danish** /ˈdeɪnɪʃ/ **a Dane** /deɪn/
Djibouti /dʒɪˈbuːti/	**Djiboutian** /dʒɪˈbuːtiən/
Dominica /ˌdɒmɪˈniːkə/	**Dominican** /ˌdɒmɪˈniːkən/
(the) Dominican Republic /dəˌmɪnɪkən rɪˈpʌblɪk/	**Dominican** /dəˈmɪnɪkən/
East Timor /ˌiːst ˈtiːmɔː(r)/	**East Timorese** /ˌiːst tɪməˈriːz/
Ecuador /ˈekwədɔː(r)/	**Ecuadorian Ecuadorean** /ˌekwəˈdɔːriən/
Egypt /ˈiːdʒɪpt/	**Egyptian** /iˈdʒɪpʃn/
El Salvador /ˌel ˈsælvədɔː(r)/	**Salvadorean** /ˌsælvəˈdɔːriən/
England /ˈɪŋglənd/	**English** /ˈɪŋglɪʃ/ **an Englishman** /ˈɪŋglɪʃmən/ **an Englishwoman** /ˈɪŋglɪʃwʊmən/
Equatorial Guinea /ˌekwətɔːriəl ˈgɪni/	**Equatorial Guinean** /ˌekwətɔːriəl ˈgɪniən/
Eritrea /ˌerɪˈtreɪə/	**Eritrean** /ˌerɪˈtreɪən/
Estonia /eˈstəʊniə/	**Estonian** /eˈstəʊniən/
Ethiopia /ˌiːθiˈəʊpiə/	**Ethiopian** /ˌiːθiˈəʊpiən/
Europe /ˈjʊərəp/	**European** /ˌjʊərəˈpiːən/
Fiji /ˈfiːdʒiː/	**Fijian** /fiːˈdʒiːən/
Finland /ˈfɪnlənd/	**Finnish** /ˈfɪnɪʃ/ **a Finn** /fɪn/
France /frɑːns/	**French** /frentʃ/ **a Frenchman** /ˈfrentʃmən/ **a Frenchwoman** /ˈfrentʃwʊmən/

FYROM /ˈfaɪrɒm/ **(the) Former Yugoslav Republic of Macedonia** /ˌfɔːmə ˌjuːgəslɑːv rɪˌpʌblɪk əv ˌmæsəˈdəʊniə/	**Macedonian** /ˌmæsəˈdəʊniən/
Gabon /gæˈbɒn/	**Gabonese** /ˌgæbəˈniːz/
(the) Gambia /ˈgæmbiə/	**Gambian** /ˈgæmbiən/
Georgia /ˈdʒɔːdʒə/	**Georgian** /ˈdʒɔːdʒən/
Germany /ˈdʒɜːməni/	**German** /ˈdʒɜːmən/
Ghana /ˈgɑːnə/	**Ghanaian** /gɑːˈneɪən/
Great Britain /ˌgreɪt ˈbrɪtn/	**British** /ˈbrɪtɪʃ/ **a Briton** /ˈbrɪtn/
Greece /griːs/	**Greek** /griːk/
Grenada /grəˈneɪdə/	**Grenadian** /grəˈneɪdiən/
Guatemala /ˌgwɑːtəˈmɑːlə/	**Guatemalan** /ˌgwɑːtəˈmɑːlən/
Guinea /ˈgɪni/	**Guinean** /ˈgɪniən/
Guinea-Bissau /ˌgɪni bɪˈsaʊ/	**Guinean** /ˈgɪniən/
Guyana /gaɪˈænə/	**Guyanese** /ˌgaɪəˈniːz/
Haiti /ˈheɪti/	**Haitian** /ˈheɪʃn/
Honduras /hɒnˈdjʊərəs/	**Honduran** /hɒnˈdjʊərən/
Hungary /ˈhʌŋgəri/	**Hungarian** /hʌŋˈgeəriən/
Iceland /ˈaɪslənd/	**Icelandic** /aɪsˈlændɪk/ **an Icelander** /ˈaɪsləndə(r)/
India /ˈɪndiə/	**Indian** /ˈɪndiən/
Indonesia /ˌɪndəˈniːʒə/	**Indonesian** /ˌɪndəˈniːʒn/
Iran /ɪˈrɑːn/	**Iranian** /ɪˈreɪniən/
Iraq /ɪˈrɑːk/	**Iraqi** /ɪˈrɑːki/
(the) Republic of Ireland /rɪˌpʌblɪk əv ˈaɪələnd/	**Irish** /ˈaɪrɪʃ/ **an Irishman** /ˈaɪrɪʃmən/ **an Irishwoman** /ˈaɪrɪʃwʊmən/
Israel /ˈɪzreɪl/	**Israeli** /ɪzˈreɪli/
Italy /ˈɪtəli/	**Italian** /ɪˈtæliən/
(the) Ivory Coast /ˌaɪvəri ˈkəʊst/ (*see also* **Côte d'Ivoire**)	**Ivorian** /aɪˈvɔːriən/
Jamaica /dʒəˈmeɪkə/	**Jamaican** /dʒəˈmeɪkən/
Japan /dʒəˈpæn/	**Japanese** /ˌdʒæpəˈniːz/
Jordan /ˈdʒɔːdn/	**Jordanian** /dʒɔːˈdeɪniən/
Kazakhstan /ˌkæzəkˈstɑːn/	**Kazakh** /kəˈzæk/
Kenya /ˈkenjə/	**Kenyan** /ˈkenjən/
Kiribati /ˌkɪrɪˈbɑːti/	**Kiribati** /ˌkɪrɪˈbɑːti/
Kuwait /kʊˈweɪt/	**Kuwaiti** /kʊˈweɪti/
Kyrgyzstan /ˌkɜːgɪˈstaːn/	**Kyrgyz** /ˈkɜːgɪz/
Laos /laʊs/	**Laotian** /ˈlaʊʃn/
Latvia /ˈlætviə/	**Latvian** /ˈlætviən/
Lebanon /ˈlebənən/	**Lebanese** /ˌlebəˈniːz/
Lesotho /ləˈsuːtuː/	person: **a Mosotho** /məˈsuːtuː/ people: **Basotho** /bəˈsuːtuː/
Liberia /laɪˈbɪəriə/	**Liberian** /laɪˈbɪəriən/
Libya /ˈlɪbiə/	**Libyan** /ˈlɪbiən/
Liechtenstein /ˈlɪktənstaɪn/	**Liechtenstein a Liechtensteiner** /ˈlɪktenstaɪnə(r)/
Lithuania /ˌlɪθjuˈeɪniə/	**Lithuanian** /ˌlɪθjuˈeɪniən/
Luxembourg /ˈlʌksəmbɜːg/	**Luxembourg a Luxembourger** /ˈlʌksəmbɜːgə(r)/
Madagascar /ˌmædəˈgæskə(r)/	**Madagascan** /ˌmædəˈgæskən/ **Malagasy** /ˌmæləˈgæsi/

Malawi /mə'lɑːwi/	**Malawian** /mə'lɑːwiən/
Malaysia /mə'leɪʒə/	**Malaysian** /mə'leɪʒn/
(the) Maldives /'mɔːldiːvz/	**Maldivian** /mɔːl'dɪviən/
Mali /'mɑːli/	**Malian** /'mɑːliən/
Malta /'mɔːltə/	**Maltese** /mɔːl'tiːz/
Mauritania /ˌmɒrɪ'teɪniə/	**Mauritanian** /ˌmɒrɪ'teɪniən/
Mauritius /mə'rɪʃəs/	**Mauritian** /mə'rɪʃn/
Mexico /'meksɪkəʊ/	**Mexican** /'meksɪkən/
Moldova /mɒl'dəʊvə/	**Moldovan** /mɒl'dəʊvn/
Monaco /'mɒnəkəʊ/	**Monégasque** /ˌmɒnɪ'gæsk/
Mongolia /mɒŋ'gəʊliə/	**Mongolian** /mɒŋ'gəʊliən/ **Mongol** /'mɒŋgl/
Montenegro /ˌmɒntɪ'niːgrəʊ/	**Montenegrin** /ˌmɒntɪ'niːgrɪn/
Morocco /mə'rɒkəʊ/	**Moroccan** /mə'rɒkən/
Mozambique /ˌməʊzæm'biːk/	**Mozambican** /ˌməʊzæm'biːkən/
Myanmar /miˌæn'mɑː(r)/ (*see also* **Burma**)	
Namibia /nə'mɪbiə/	**Namibian** /nə'mɪbiən/
Nauru /'naʊruː/	**Nauruan** /naʊ'ruːən/
Nepal /nə'pɔːl/	**Nepalese** /ˌnepə'liːz/
(the) Netherlands /'neðələndz/	**Dutch** /dʌtʃ/ **a Dutchman** /'dʌtʃmən/ **a Dutchwoman** /'dʌtʃwʊmən/
New Zealand /ˌnjuː 'ziːlənd/	**New Zealand a New Zealander** /ˌnjuː 'ziːləndə(r)/
Nicaragua /ˌnɪkə'rægjuə/	**Nicaraguan** /ˌnɪkə'rægjuən/
Niger /niː'ʒeə(r)/	**Nigerien** /niː'ʒeəriən/
Nigeria /naɪ'dʒɪəriə/	**Nigerian** /naɪ'dʒɪəriən/
Northern Ireland /ˌnɔːðən 'aɪələnd/	**Northern Irish** /ˌnɔːðən 'aɪrɪʃ/
North Korea /ˌnɔːθ kə'riə/	**North Korean** /ˌnɔːθ kə'riən/
Norway /'nɔːweɪ/	**Norwegian** /nɔː'wiːdʒən/
Oman /əʊ'mɑːn/	**Omani** /əʊ'mɑːni/
Pakistan /ˌpɑːkɪ'stɑːn/	**Pakistani** /ˌpɑːkɪ'stɑːni/
Panama /'pænəmɑː/	**Panamanian** /ˌpænə'meɪniən/
Papua New Guinea /ˌpæpjuə ˌnjuː 'gɪni/	**Papua New Guinean** /ˌpæpjuə ˌnjuː 'gɪniən/
Paraguay /'pærəgwaɪ/	**Paraguayan** /ˌpærə'gwaɪən/
Peru /pə'ru/	**Peruvian** /pə'ruːviən/
(the) Philippines /'fɪlɪpiːnz/	**Philippine** /'fɪlɪpiːn/ **a Filipino** /ˌfɪlɪ'piːnəʊ/ **a Filipina** /ˌfɪlɪ'piːnə/
Poland /'pəʊlənd/	**Polish** /'pəʊlɪʃ/ **a Pole** /pəʊl/
Portugal /'pɔːtʃʊgl/	**Portuguese** /ˌpɔːtʃʊ'giːz/
Qatar /'kʌtɑː(r)/	**Qatari** /kʌ'tɑːri/
Romania /ru'meɪniə/	**Romanian** /ru'meɪniən/
Russia /'rʌʃə/	**Russian** /'rʌʃn/
Rwanda /ru'ændə/	**Rwandan** /ru'ændən/
Samoa /sə'məʊə/	**Samoan** /sə'məʊən/
San Marino /ˌsæn mə'riːnəʊ/	
São Tomé and Príncipe /ˌsaʊ təˌmeɪ ən 'prɪnsɪpeɪ/	
Saudi Arabia /ˌsaʊdi ə'reɪbiə/	**Saudi** /'saʊdi/ **Saudi Arabian** /ˌsaʊdi ə'reɪbiən/
Scotland /'skɒtlənd/	**Scottish** /'skɒtɪʃ/ **Scots** /skɒts/ **a Scot** /skɒt/ **a Scotsman** /'skɒtsmən/ **a Scotswoman** /'skɒtswʊmən/
Senegal /ˌsenɪ'gɔːl/	**Senegalese** /ˌsenɪgə'liːz/

Serbia /ˈsɜːbiə/	**Serbian** /ˈsɜːbiən/ **a Serb** /sɜːb/
(the) Seychelles /seɪˈʃelz/	**Seychellois** /ˌseɪʃelˈwɑː/
Sierra Leone /siˌerə liˈəʊn/	**Sierra Leonean** /siˌerə liˈəʊniən/
Singapore /ˌsɪŋəˈpɔː(r)/	**Singaporean** /ˌsɪŋəˈpɔːriən/
Slovakia /sləˈvækiə/	**Slovak** /ˈsləʊvæk/ **Slovakian** /sləˈvækiən/
Slovenia /sləˈviːniə/	**Slovene** /ˈsləʊviːn/ **Slovenian** /sləˈviːniən/
(the) Solomon Islands /ˈsɒləmən aɪləndz/	**a Solomon Islander** /ˈsɒləmən aɪləndə(r)/
Somalia /səˈmɑːliə/	**Somali** /səˈmɑːli/
South Africa /ˌsaʊθ ˈæfrɪkə/	**South African** /ˌsaʊθ ˈæfrɪkən/
South Korea /ˌsaʊθ kəˈriə/	**South Korean** /ˌsaʊθ kəˈriən/
South Sudan /ˌsaʊθ suˈdɑːn/	**South Sudanese** /ˌsaʊθ suːdəˈniːz /
Spain /speɪn/	**Spanish** /ˈspænɪʃ/ **a Spaniard** /ˈspænɪəd/
Sri Lanka /ˌsri ˈlæŋkə/	**Sri Lankan** /ˌsri ˈlæŋkən/
St Kitts and Nevis /snt ˌkɪts ən ˈniːvɪs/	**Kittitian** /kɪˈtɪʃn/, **Nevisian** /niːˈvɪsiən/
St Lucia /ˌsnt ˈluːʃə/	**St Lucian** /ˌsnt ˈluːʃən/
St Vincent and the Grenadines /snt ˌvɪnsnt ən ðə ˈgrenədiːnz/	**Vincentian** /vɪnˈsenʃn/
Sudan /suˈdɑːn/	**Sudanese** /ˌsuːdəˈniːz/
Suriname /ˌsʊərɪˈnɑːm/	**Surinamese** /ˌsʊərɪnəˈmiːz/
Swaziland /ˈswɑːzilænd/	**Swazi** /ˈswɑːzi/
Sweden /ˈswiːdn/	**Swedish** /ˈswiːdɪʃ/ **a Swede** /swiːd/
Switzerland /ˈswɪtsələnd/	**Swiss** /swɪs/
Syria /ˈsɪriə/	**Syrian** /ˈsɪriən/
Tajikistan /tæˌdʒiːkɪˈstɑːn/	**Tajik** /tæˈdʒiːk/
Tanzania /ˌtænzəˈniːə/	**Tanzanian** /ˌtænzəˈniːən/
Thailand /ˈtaɪlænd/	**Thai** /taɪ/
Togo /ˈtəʊgəʊ/	**Togolese** /ˌtəʊgəˈliːz/
Tonga /ˈtɒŋə/	**Tongan** /ˈtɒŋən/
Trinidad and Tobago /ˌtrɪnɪdæd ən təˈbeɪgəʊ/	**Trinidadian** /ˌtrɪnɪˈdædiən/ **Tobagan** /təˈbeɪgən/ **Tobagonian** /ˌtəʊbəˈgəʊniən/
Tunisia /tjuˈnɪziə/	**Tunisian** /tjuˈnɪziən/
Turkey /ˈtɜːki/	**Turkish** /ˈtɜːkɪʃ/ **a Turk** /tɜːk/
Turkmenistan /tɜːkˌmenɪˈstɑːn/	**Turkmen** /ˈtɜːkmen/
Tuvalu /tuːˈvɑːluː/	**Tuvaluan** /ˌtuːvɑːˈluːən/
Uganda /juːˈgændə/	**Ugandan** /juːˈgændən/
Ukraine /juːˈkreɪn/	**Ukrainian** /juːˈkreɪniən/
(the) United Arab Emirates (UAE) /juˌnaɪtɪd ˌærəb ˈemɪrəts/	**Emirati** /emɪˈrɑːti/
(the) United Kingdom (UK) /juˌnaɪtɪd ˈkɪŋdəm/	**British** /ˈbrɪtɪʃ/ **a Briton** /ˈbrɪtn/
(the) United States of America (USA) /juˌnaɪtɪd ˌsteɪts əv əˈmerɪkə/	**American** /əˈmerɪkən/
Uruguay /ˈjʊərəgwaɪ/	**Uruguayan** /ˌjʊərəˈgwaɪən/
Uzbekistan /ʊzˌbekɪˈstɑːn/	**Uzbek** /ˈʊzbek/
Vanuatu /ˌvænuːˈɑːtuː/	**Vanuatuan** /ˌvænwɑːˈtuːən/
Venezuela /ˌvenəˈzweɪlə/	**Venezuelan** /ˌvenəˈzweɪlən/
Vietnam /ˌvjetˈnæm/	**Vietnamese** /ˌvjetnəˈmiːz/
Wales /weɪlz/	**Welsh** /welʃ/ **a Welshman** /ˈwelʃmən/ **a Welshwoman** /ˈwelʃwʊmən/
Yemen /ˈjemən/	**Yemeni** /ˈjeməni/
Zambia /ˈzæmbiə/	**Zambian** /ˈzæmbiən/

Telephoning

Making an informal call

— Hi, can I speak to Martin, please?
— *Sorry, he's out at the moment. Can I take a message?*
— Can you tell him that Natasha called?
— *OK, Natasha. I'll let him know when he gets back.*

— Hello?
— *Hi, is that Tanya? It's Amy here.*
— Hi Amy! Sorry, the battery on my mobile is about to run out. Can you call me on the landline?
— *Sure, what's the number?*
— It's 258 440. (= two five eight, double four oh)

Finishing an informal call

...
— OK, then. So I'll see you next Saturday at 7 o'clock. I'm looking forward to it.
— *Yeah, me too. See you on Saturday, then. Thanks for calling.*
— No problem. Bye!

...
— Right, then, I'll find out how much the tickets cost and get back to you.
— *Thanks, that would be great. Speak to you later. Bye!*

Making a formal call

— Good morning, could I speak to Dr. McSweeney, please?
— *Yes, of course. May I ask who's calling?*
— It's Nigel Briggs.
— *OK, just a moment, please. I'll put you through.*

...
— *Hello, Mr Briggs? I'm afraid she's on the other line at the moment. Shall I ask her to call you back?*
— No, that's OK. I'll phone again later. Thank you. Goodbye.

— Good morning, this is Helen Randall. Could I talk to Simon Hooper, please?
— *I'm afraid he's away from his desk at the moment. Would you like to leave a message?*
— Yes, please. Could you ask him to call me when he gets back? My number is...

To find out more about telephoning, look at **mobile phone** and **telephone** in the dictionary.

Text messages

Mobile phone text messages, chat room messages and sometimes emails can be written using the smallest number of letters possible. These are some examples of how words might be shown in a message:

2day today
2moro tomorrow
2nite tonight
asap as soon as possible
b4 before
b4n bye for now
btw by the way
c see
cul8r see you later
gr8 great
ilu i love you
lol laughing out loud
msg message
pls please
soz sorry
spk speak
thx thanks
u you
wan2 want to
wknd weekend
x kiss

Learning vocabulary

You can easily remember a large number of new words if you organize your vocabulary learning.

Recording the meaning of new words

You can draw a picture:

▶ *snake*

You can explain the word in English:

▶ *salary = the money you receive from your job*

You can copy an example:

▶ *I've known her **since** 1997.*

And you can use the dictionary example sentence to help you write your own personal sentence:

▶ *I've been studying English **since** 2001.*

Vocabulary cards

You can record important new words on **cards**:

pronunciation | grammar information

happy /ˈhæpi/ (adjective) — meaning → *= feeling pleasure; pleased*

happy to do sth — example sentence → *I was really ________ to see my family again.*

OPP sad / unhappy ← related words — *OPP ________ / ________*

happiness (noun) — *________ (noun)*

(front of card) (back of card)

Carry the cards in your pocket or bag. When you have a few minutes, test yourself. Look at one side of the card and try to remember what is written on the other side.

Vocabulary notebooks

Write new vocabulary in a **notebook**:

Write the English words on the left, and the meaning, explanation, picture, etc. on the right. Then you can cover the left side and test yourself.

JOBS

employee /ɪmˈplɔɪiː/	*sb who works for an employer*
part-time (adj)	*OPP full-time* *She's got a ___ job.*
'What do you do?'	*'I'm a doctor.'*

Organizing words

You will remember new words more easily if you organize them into groups:

- topics ('*jobs*', '*the environment*', '*holidays*')
- word families (*happy, unhappy, happiness, happily*)
- opposite pairs (*happy/sad, rich/poor*)
- words with a similar meaning (*very good, great, wonderful, fantastic*)
- key words (*get up, get on well with sb, get your hair cut*)

Here are two more ways of grouping words:

Word tables

sport	person	place
football	footballer	pitch
athletics	athlete	track
golf	golfer	course
tennis	tennis player	court

Word diagrams

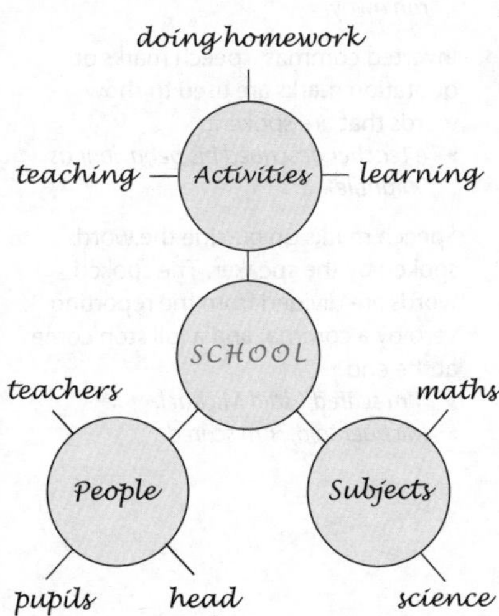

The most important words – The Oxford 3000™

There are thousands and thousands of words and phrases in this dictionary – you can't learn them all!

Start by learning the most important words. These are the **Oxford 3000™**. They are marked in the dictionary with a 🔑.

> 🔑 **progress** /ˈprəʊgres/ *noun* [U] movement forwards or towards achieving sth: *Anna's* ***making progress*** *at school.*

Remembering words

You will not remember words if you only write them down. You must also:

- **try** to remember them
- look at them **again** and **again**
- **start using** them when you speak or write English

Connecting words

One trick for remembering words is to connect the English word with a word in your language.

- For example, if a French student learning English wants to remember the verb **to chat** (= to talk to somebody in a friendly way), he/she can connect it to the French word **chat**, which means 'cat'. *Imagine a cat talking to its friends.*

It doesn't matter if the words are not exactly the same.

- For example, the Japanese verb *oyogu* (= swim) sounds a little like the English word *yogurt*. How could an English student remember this Japanese word? *Imagine a person swimming in a very big pot of yogurt.*

These connections may seem silly. But the sillier they are, the easier they will be to remember!

Punctuation

A A capital letter is used at the start of each new sentence. You also use capitals for proper nouns; names of people and places; titles of books, films, etc.:

▶ *Tessa and Don saw Finding Neverland at the Ritzy Cinema, Brixton when they were in England.*

. A full stop shows the end of a sentence. It is also often used after initials and abbreviations:

▶ *Peter Pan was written by J. M. Barrie.*

! An exclamation mark is used at the end of a sentence to show surprise, joy, anger or shock:

▶ *Don't speak to me like that!' she shouted.*

▶ *What a glorious day for a wedding!*

? A question mark is used at the end of a direct question:

▶ *'Can you drive?' asked Laura.*

, A comma separates parts of a sentence or words in a list, or shows additional information:

▶ *Peter refuses to leave Neverland, but Wendy returns to her family.*

▶ *It's a play about children, fairies and pirates.*

▶ *The crocodile, which was large and hungry, swam close to the ship.*

' An apostrophe replaces a missing letter or letters in contracted forms: *I'd* (= I had), *isn't* (= is not), *we'll* (= we will), *won't* (= will not). We also use apostrophes before or after the possessive with **s** (see Grammar Section R18).

( ) Brackets are used when the writer adds information, an explanation, a comment, etc. to something in the text. The text would still make sense if the information in brackets was removed:

▶ *Captain Hook (usually played by the same actor as Wendy's father) terrifies the children.*

— A dash is used when an additional comment or additional information is added to a sentence:

▶ *Peter is usually – but not always – played by a woman.*

- A hyphen is used in many cases where two words have been joined together to form one: *self-service*. It is also used to separate long words that will not fit on one line. As there are complicated rules about where you can correctly divide words, it is safer to start the word on the next line.

: A colon tells the reader that something is coming next, for example a list:

▶ *People go to the theatre for many reasons: to meet friends, to be entertained, to be educated.*

; A semicolon is used to divide two parts of a sentence:

▶ *She looked up and frowned; the boy ran away.*

“ ” ‘ ’ Inverted commas, speech marks or quotation marks are used to show words that are spoken:

▶ *A teacher described his behaviour as 'infantile'.*

Speech marks go outside the words spoken by the speaker. The spoken words are divided from the reporting verb by a comma, and a full stop comes at the end.

▶ *'I'm scared,' said Michael.*

▶ *Michael said, 'I'm scared.'*

Pronunciation

If two pronunciations for one word are given, both are acceptable. The first form given is considered to be more common.

/-/ A hyphen is used in alternative pronunciations when only part of the pronunciation changes. The part that remains the same is replaced by the hyphen.

accent /æksent; -sənt/

/ˈ/ This mark shows that the syllable after it is said with more force (stress) than other syllables in the word or group of words. For example **any** /ˈeni/ has a stress on the first syllable; **depend** /dɪˈpend/ has a stress on the second syllable.

/ˌ/ This mark shows that a syllable is said with more force than other syllables in a word but with a stress that is not as strong as for those syllables marked /ˈ/. So in the word **pronunciation** /prəˌnʌnsiˈeɪʃn/ the main stress is on the syllable /ˈeɪ/ and the secondary stress is on the syllable /ˌnʌn/.

Strong and weak forms

Some very common words, for example **an, as, that, of,** have two or more pronunciations: a **strong** form and one or more **weak** forms. In speech the weak forms are more common.

For example **from** is /frəm/ in *He comes **from** Spain.* The strong form occurs when the word comes at the end of a sentence or when it is given special emphasis. For example **from** is /frɒm/ in *Where are you **from**?* and in *The present's not **from** John, it's for him.*

Pronunciation in derivatives and compounds

Many **derivatives** are formed by adding a suffix to the end of a word. These are pronounced by simply saying the suffix after the word. For example **slowly** /ˈsləʊli/ is said by adding the suffix **-ly** /-li/ to the word **slow** /sləʊ/.

However, where there is doubt about how a derivative is pronounced, the phonetic spelling is given. The part that remains the same is represented by a hyphen.

accidental /ˌæksɪˈdentl/

accidentally /-təli/

In **compounds** (made up of two or more words) the pronunciation of the individual words is not repeated. The dictionary shows how the compound is stressed using the marks /ˈ/ and /ˌ/.

In ˈ**air force** the stress is on the first word. In ˌ**air**ˌ**traffic con**ˈ**troller** there are secondary stresses on **air** and on the first syllable of **traffic**, and the main stress is on the second syllable of **controller**.

Wordpower Workout

What is a Workout?

The **Wordpower Workout** will train you to use this dictionary in the best way. It will also help you to learn new vocabulary.

workout /ˈwɜːkaut/ *noun* [C] a period of physical exercise, for example when you are training for a sport or keeping fit: *She does a twenty-minute workout every morning.*

How to find words

The alphabet

A Put the words below into alphabetical order (a, b, c, etc.) by writing a number:

___ glasses	___ jellyfish
___ zodiac	___ windmill
___ ripple	___ sneeze
___ volcano	___ snorkel
2 blow	*1* arch
___ puddle	___ robot
___ snail	___ eclipse
___ duck	___ lick
___ hat	___ zebra

B Most of these words are **illustrations** (= pictures) in this dictionary. Do you know what these words mean? Check by looking at the illustrations.

C Two of these words are **not** illustrations in the dictionary. Which two?

Choosing the right meaning

Many words have more than one meaning.

A Look at the **bold** words below. They are all *nouns*. Find them in the dictionary and read the different meanings. Are these sentences true (T) or false (F)?

1 *F* A **mouse** is an animal and a piece of sports equipment.
(*A mouse is an animal and a piece of **computer** equipment.*)

2 ___ You can find a **mole** underground, or on your body.

3 ___ You can eat a Christmas **cracker**.

4 ___ Something that 'costs a **bomb**' is very cheap.

5 ___ It is polite to call somebody a **dummy**.

6 ___ A **school** is a large group of dogs.

7 ___ In British English, the season after summer and before winter is called **fall**.

8 ___ A piece of clothing that a man wears to go swimming is called **a trunk**.

9 ___ You can see **scenery** in the countryside and in the theatre.

B Fill the gaps with a verb in the correct form and write the sense number (= the number that shows which meaning of the verb it is). Each verb is used twice.

break	cut	drop	face
freeze	play	turn	

1 It's so cold that even the river has *frozen*. (*sense* *1*)

2 Tommy ________ the glass and it shattered on the floor. (*sense* ____)

3 He ________ the key in the lock. (*sense* ___)

4 Where do you get your hair ________? (*sense* ___)

5 When Jill ________ her leg it was in plaster for six weeks. (*sense* ___)

6 The hotel rooms all ________ the sea. (*sense* ___)

7 My favourite song was ________ on the radio. (*sense* ___)

8 The government wants to ________ taxes before the election. (*sense* ___)

9 She ________ the silence by coughing. (*sense* ___)

10 The weather has ________ cold. (*sense* ___)

11 She had to ________ the fact that her life had changed forever. (*sense* ___)

12 Can you ________ me near the station, please? (*sense* ___)

13 Parents ________ a vital role in their children's education. (*sense* ___)

14 She ________ with terror as the door slowly opened. (*sense* ___)

Finding phrasal verbs – fast!

Find **go** in the dictionary and look at the **PHR V** (= phrasal verbs) section.

A Complete the phrasal verbs by filling each gap with one word.

1 *go* away = leave home for a period of time, especially for a holiday

2 *go* ________ *with an illness* = become ill

3 *go* ________ *about sth* = talk about sth for a long time in an annoying way

4 *go* ________ *with sth* = continue doing sth

5 *go* ________ *for a meal / a walk*

6 *go* ________ / ________ *sth* = look at sth carefully, from beginning to end

7 *go* ________ *to sb's (home)* = visit sb

8 *go* ________ = become higher in price, level, etc.

9 *go* ________ *sth* = look good with sth else

B Complete the sentences using the verbs in part A.

1 Do you fancy going out for dinner tonight?

2 I went ________ with the flu when I was on holiday.

3 No, that shirt doesn't go ________ those trousers.

4 Let's go ________ / ________ your homework and correct the mistakes.

5 That's enough for now – let's go ________ with it tomorrow.

6 We went ________ to his house for dinner last night.

7 Prices in the shops keep going ________!

8 We're going ________ to the seaside for a week.

9 He's always going ________ about his health problems.

10 'Where's Tom?'
'He went ________ for a walk.'

Parts of speech (= nouns, verbs, etc.)

A Which **part of speech** is the word **light** in each of these sentences?
noun verb adjective adverb

1 Modern cameras are **light** and easy to carry. *adjective*
2 This room has big windows so there is lots of **light**. ____________
3 We had to **light** candles because there was no electricity. ____________
4 I always travel **light**. ____________

B Look at the **bold** words. Are they nouns, verbs, adjectives or adverbs? Find the word in the dictionary. Write the number of the part of speech.

1 What time is it? I don't have a **watch**. *noun* WATCH *2*
2 Do you **watch** much television? ____________ WATCH ____
3 We walked in the **park**. ____________ PARK ____
4 Where can I **park** my car? ____________ PARK ____
5 Do you live in a house or a **flat**? ____________ FLAT ____
6 People used to think the earth was **flat**. ____________ FLAT ____
7 I like travelling by **train**. ____________ TRAIN ____
8 You have to **train** to be a teacher. ____________ TRAIN ____
9 The exam was very **hard**. ____________ HARD ____
10 Students should work **hard**. ____________ HARD ____

C Use the words in part B to make your own sentences. They should include both parts of speech. Don't worry if they are funny or strange!

▶ *I **watched** a television programme about **watches**.*

▶ *You can't **park** your car in the **park**! You should **park** it in the car **park**.*

Finding the right word

The large blue words in the dictionary are called **headwords**.

Not all words are headwords. For example, if you want to find the word **happiness**, you should look at **happy**.

Types of words that may not be headwords include:

- derivatives (**happiness**, from **happy**)
- plural forms of nouns (**women**, from **woman**)
- comparative/superlative forms of adjectives (**noisier/noisiest**, from **noisy**)
- verb forms ending in -ing, -s, -ed (**studying, studies, studied**, from **study**)

Where can you find the words below?

1 inspection *inspect*
2 luckily ____________
3 spies ____________
4 thieves ____________
5 limo ____________
6 the jeweller's ____________
7 greedier ____________
8 clumsiest ____________
9 digging ____________
10 burgled ____________

Understanding words

Defining vocabulary

The **definitions** (= the meanings of words) in this dictionary are easy to understand because they use simple words. These 3 000 simple words are called the ***defining vocabulary***.

When a word that is not in the defining vocabulary is used in a definition, it is written in **bold** letters and explained with (= ...). For example:

> **octopus** /ˈɒktəpəs/ *noun* [C] a sea animal with a soft body and eight **tentacles** (= long thin parts like arms)

A Definitions puzzle

Look at the definitions. Which word is being defined? Write the word on the correct line in the puzzle below.

If you need help, look in your dictionary at the words in brackets.

1 a musical instrument with strings (Help? Look at *strum*)
2 a large wild animal with horns on its head (*stag*)
3 dried leaves used for making cigarettes (*cigarette*)
4 a mixture of flour, fat and water (*quiche*)
5 a vehicle that travels in space (*lift-off*)
6 a piece of equipment that makes small objects look bigger (*bacteria*)
7 small green or purple fruit that grow in bunches (*wine*)

When you have finished 1–6, read downwards to find the answer to 7

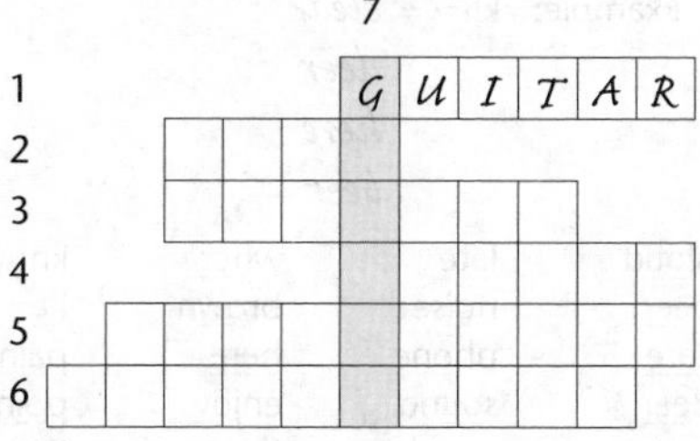

B Which word is different?

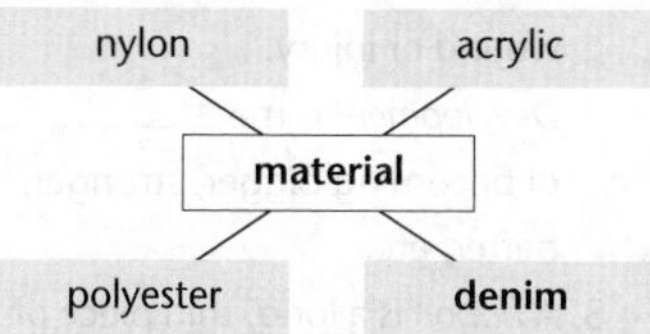

(Denim is a material made from ***cotton****. The others are* ***artificial materials****.)*

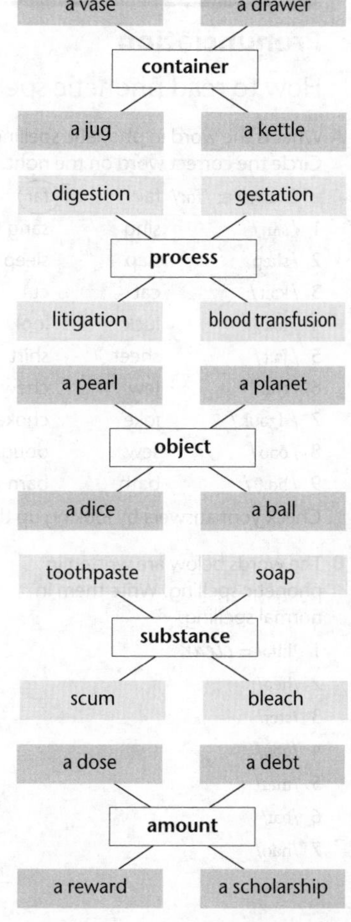

C Fill each space with one of the **bold** words from part B.

1 A *bandage* is a long piece of soft white *material* that you tie round a wound or injury.

2 *Development* is the ______ of becoming bigger, stronger, better, etc.

3 A *ribbon* is a long, thin piece of ______ that is used for tying or decorating something.

4 *Pocket money* is an ______ of money that parents give a child to spend, usually every week.

5 A *waste-paper basket* is a ______ in which you put paper, etc. that is to be thrown away.

6 *Salt* is a common white ______ that is found in sea water and the earth.

7 A *pencil* is an ______ that you use for writing or drawing.

Pronunciation

How to read phonetic spelling

A What is the word in phonetic spelling on the left? Circle the correct word on the right.

▶ Example: /fɑː/	fair	(far)	four	fur
1 /sʌŋ/	sing	sang	sung	song
2 /slæp/	slap	sleep	slip	slurp
3 /kɔːt/	cat	cut	kit	caught
4 /lʊk/	luck	look	lack	lick
5 /ʃɜːt/	sheet	shirt	shoot	feet
6 /tʃuː/	Jew	chew	dew	shoe
7 /dʒəʊk/	joke	choke	yolk	yoke
8 /ðəʊ/	sew	dough	toe	though
9 /bɑːθ/	bath	barn	bathe	back

Check your answers by looking up the words in the dictionary.

B The words below are written in phonetic spelling. Write them in normal spelling.

1 /klɪə/ = *clear*
2 /heə/
3 /steɪ/
4 /gəʊ/
5 /maɪ/
6 /bɔɪ/
7 /haʊ/

C How do we pronounce the words below? Put them into the correct group in part B according to the sound of the underlined part.

▶ Example: /klɪə/ = *clear*
deer
here
beer

aloud	late	where	know
~~beer~~	noise	brown	lie
care	phone	~~here~~	paint
~~deer~~	sound	enjoy	point
fair	weigh	five	though
high			

Stress

Word stress is shown in the dictionary like this:

Italy /ˈɪtəli/

The stress comes on the sound after ˈ. You can also mark stress like this:

Italy (• . .)

The adjective from *Italy* is *Italian*. The stress is like this:

Italian /ɪˈtaeliən/ Italian (. • . .)

A Write the adjectives. Mark the stress on the country and the adjective.

1 Italy *Italian*
2 Egypt
3 Peru
4 Canada
5 Brazil
6 Argentina
7 Turkey
8 Indonesia
9 Portugal
10 Japan

B Check your answers by looking at the list of **Geographical names** in the Reference Section.

C How is the name of your country pronounced in English? Is it the same in your language?

How to use words

Examples

Wordpower gives you lots of information in **examples.**

medal /ˈmedl/ *noun* [C] a small flat piece of metal, usually with a design and words on it, which is given to sb who has shown courage or as a prize in a sport: *to win a gold/silver/bronze medal in the Olympics*

Try to answer these questions *without* using the dictionary!

1 The best athlete usually wins a gold **medal**. What are the 2 other types of medal? *silver, bronze*

2 Name 3 sports that are played on a **court**, and 3 that are played on a **pitch**.

3 A place where a lot of people can go on holiday in order to **ski** is called a *ski* ________

4 Skating and skiing are types of ________ **sport**.

5 Is this example correct?
My brother is a very ***sporting*** *person.*

6 Which is correct? He is in **training** *to* / *for* / *of* the Olympics.

7 Complete the sentence: *Students are encouraged to* ***participate*** ________ *sporting activities.*

8 Where might you find a water **chute**?

9 Do these sentences mean the same thing?
He ***windsurfs*** *every summer.*
He ***goes windsurfing*** *every summer.*
Which is more usual?

10 In a sports match, who uses a **whistle**? What might he/she do with it?

11 Correct the mistake in this sentence:
This city has excellent sports ***facility****.*

Now find the **bold** words in the dictionary and look at the examples. Were your answers correct?

Collocation – Words that go together

Which is the correct word in these sentences?

- ▶ *I have to do / make an exam tomorrow.*
- ▶ *I'm sorry, I've done / made a mistake.*

Find the answers by looking at the examples in *Wordpower*.

> **exam** /ɪg'zæm/ (also *formal examination*) *noun* [C] a written, spoken or practical test of what you know or can do: *an English exam* ♦ *the exam results* ♦ *to* ***do/take/sit an exam*** ♦ *to* ***pass/fail an exam*** ♦ *to* ***revise for an exam*** ➲ note at **pass, study**

> **mistake** /mɪ'steɪk/ *noun* [C] something that you think or do that is wrong: *Try not to* ***make*** *any* ***mistakes*** *in your essays.*

We say **do an exam** and **make a mistake**. We never say *make an exam* or *do a mistake*.

Words which often go together (like **do + an exam**, and **make + a mistake**) are called **collocations**. They are very important in English.

Verb + noun collocations

A Match the verbs and nouns that usually go together.

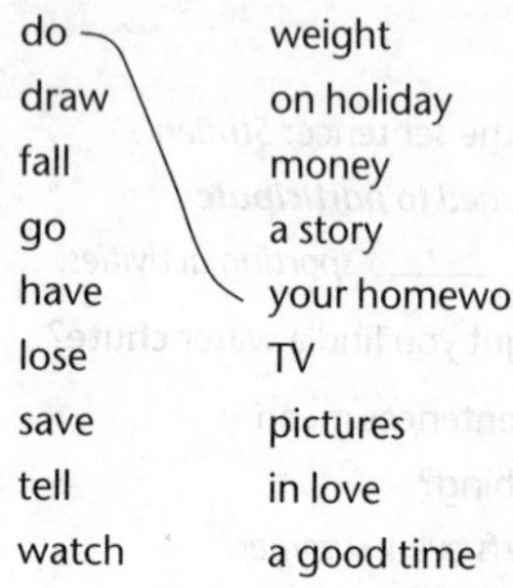

do	weight
draw	on holiday
fall	money
go	a story
have	your homework
lose	TV
save	pictures
tell	in love
watch	a good time

B Correct the mistakes below using a verb from the list in part A in the appropriate form.

1 Why haven't you ~~written~~ your homework? *done*
2 She became in love with him the moment she saw him.
3 If you hadn't seen so much TV, your eyes wouldn't be hurting now.
4 You look fabulous! Have you put off weight?
5 'Where is Eva?' 'She has left on holiday.'
6 The children love writing pictures.
7 I wish he wouldn't say the same stories over and over again.
8 Did you enjoy a good time at the party?
9 We need to keep more money if we want to buy a car.

Adjective + noun collocations

A Make collocations connected with **health** by matching the nouns from the box with the adjectives below. Use each noun only once.

headache	throat	~~back~~	recovery
ankle	illness	tooth	leg
nose	diet	disease	eye

1 a bad *back*
2 a balanced
3 a black
4 a broken
5 a contagious
6 a decayed
7 a runny
8 a serious
9 a sore
10 a speedy
11 a splitting
12 a twisted

B 10 of these expressions are types of illness or injury. In your opinion, which of the 10 is the most serious? Put them in order by writing a number from 1 (the most serious) to 10 (the least serious).

Prepositions

Wordpower gives you lots of information about **prepositions**.

> **good** /gud/ *adj* good at sth; good with sb/sth able to do sth or deal with sb/sth well

A Find the **bold** words in the dictionary. Fill the gaps below with the correct preposition.

1 Do you know anyone who is **afraid** ___of___ snakes, spiders, heights, etc?
2 Can you think of anything you have done that you are **proud** ______?
3 Are there any songs or smells that **remind** you ______ something?
4 Is there anything that you **dream** ______ / ______ doing one day?
5 Have you ever done something that you were **embarrassed** ______?
6 What kinds of things did you **worry** ______ when you were a teenager?
7 When you were at school, which subjects were you **bad** ______?
8 Do you **believe** ______ ghosts?
9 When did you last **receive** a present ______ somebody? What was it?

B Now answer the questions!

Verb patterns

A Find the **bold** words in the dictionary. Cross out the incorrect verb pattern.

1 What do you **enjoy** ~~do~~ / doing in your free time?
2 What are you **planning** doing / to do on your next holiday?
3 When you were a child, what did your parents / teachers **make** you to do / do? What were you not **allowed** do / to do?
4 Describe something that you are **looking forward** to do / to doing soon.
5 Do you know anyone who usually **puts off** doing / to do things that he / she **should to do / do**?
6 Have you ever **forgotten** to do / doing something important?
7 Describe something nice / terrible that you **remember** doing / to do when you were a child.

B Now answer the questions!

Irregular verbs

If you want to check the form of an irregular verb, look at the list of **Irregular verbs** at the back of this dictionary.

Complete the puzzle by writing the past tense and past participle forms of these irregular verbs. 'Sing' is already done for you as an example.

break	eat	take
do	fall	find
drink	run	write

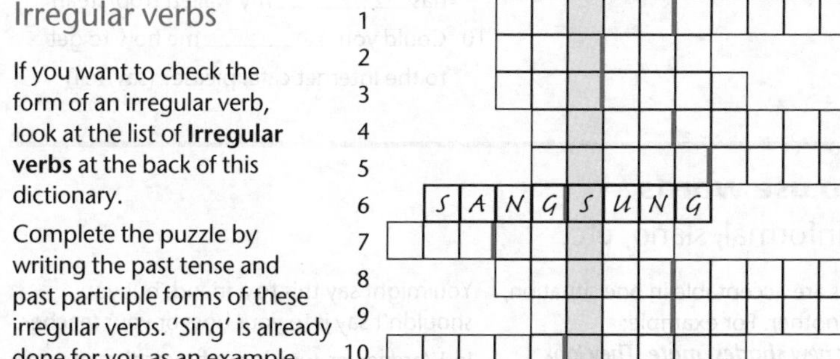

The letters in the blue boxes will reveal another word. Of which verb is it the irregular past tense and past participle?

GRAMMAR notes

These notes help you to avoid mistakes by explaining difficult or confusing grammar points.

Each of these sentences contains a mistake. Use the word in **bold** to help you find the GRAMMAR note in the dictionary. Then correct the sentence.

1 I never watch the **news** on TV because ~~they are~~ so depressing. *it is*
2 Thank you, it's delicious, but I can't eat **some** more.
3 I've been studying English **since** four years.
4 When I was a child I **must** to help my mother with the housework.
5 Could you give me some **informations** about your English courses, please?
6 **When** the weather will be good tomorrow, we can play tennis.
7 My twin brother **who** lives in Germany is called John.
8 I have a **so** boring teacher that I always fall asleep in lessons.
9 'Nice to meet you. When did you arrive in Oxford?' 'Two days **before**.'
10 I've visited Korea and Japan, but I've never **gone** to China.

HELP notes

These notes help you to avoid mistakes by explaining the difference between similar words.

Look up the words in brackets. Read the HELP notes and write the correct words in each sentence below. Change the form of the verb if necessary.

1 He drives ___*like*___ a maniac! (as/like)
2 My dog was sick so I stayed at home to ___________ it. (care about/take care of)
3 I'm sorry, but I ___________ my books at home this morning. (forget/leave)
4 Tom's jokes are not very ___________ (fun/funny)
5 Could you ___________ me some money? (lend/borrow)
6 I ___________ my towel on the sand, ___________ down on it and went to sleep. (lie/lay)
7 I like my colleagues. They are really ___________ people. (nice/sympathetic)
8 ___________ your hand if you know the answer. (rise/raise)
9 Help! I've been ___________! Somebody has ___________ my wallet! (rob/steal)
10 Could you ___________ me how to get to the Internet cafe, please? (say/tell)

When to use words

Formal, informal, slang, etc.

Some words are acceptable in one situation, but not in another. For example:

▸ *'I like your new* ***shades, mate****. They look really* ***cool****!'*

You might say this to a friend, but you shouldn't say it to your boss or your teacher.

In *Wordpower*, words or phrases that are only used in particular situations are marked using the terms *formal, informal*, etc.

Are the sentences true or false? Mark them with a ✓ or a ✗. Decide if the word in **bold** is *formal, informal, slang, figurative* or *spoken*. The first one has been done for you.

1 You wear a pair of **spectacles** on your feet.
✗ *formal*

2 'I beg your **pardon**' is another way of saying 'Thank you'.
___ __________

3 You give your friend a present. She says, 'This is **wicked**!' This means she doesn't like it.
___ __________

4 A **loony** is somebody who is **crazy**.
___ __________

5 A **half-baked** scheme is a type of dessert that you can buy in a bakery.
___ __________

6 Your **spouse** is the person to whom you are married.
___ __________

7 If somebody asks you, 'What is your **occupation**?', you should tell him/her where you live.
___ __________

8 If a person is **catapulted** to fame, he/she becomes famous very quickly.
___ __________

9 If an American says, 'Don't give me that **baloney**!', he/she thinks you are not telling the truth.
___ __________

10 You ask a friend if he wants to go to the cinema with you. He replies, 'You **bet**!' This means he doesn't want to go.
___ __________

British and American English

Wordpower shows you the difference between *British* and *American* words. For example:

boot /bu:t/ *noun* [C] (*AmE* **trunk**) the part of a car where you put luggage, usually at the back

Complete the balloons with the *British* or *American* words that mean the same:

A Write the *American* words.

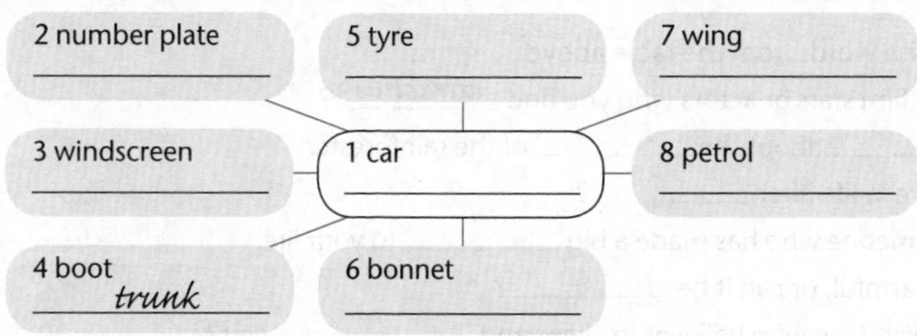

B Write the *British* words.

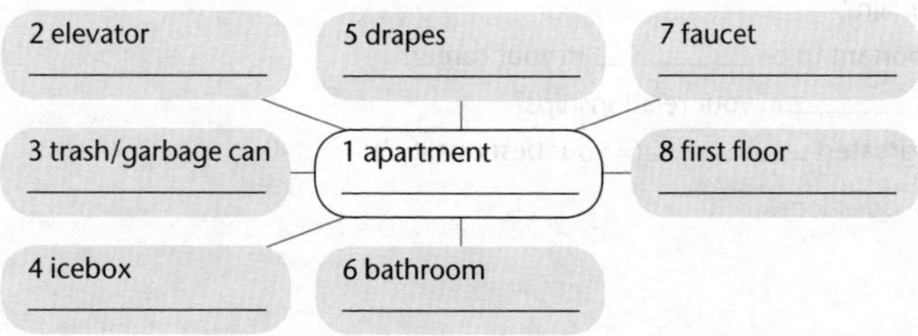

Build your vocabulary

Word families

You can improve your vocabulary fast by learning **word families** (for example, **happy, unhappy, happiness, happily**, etc.).

A Use the dictionary to fill in the missing words.

verb	noun	adjective
attract	*attraction*	(un) attractive
deepen		
	destruction	
		dead
differ		
	education	educated /
fly		
	fright	frightened /
	hope	(OPP)
satisfy		(dis)
		successful
		strong
	worry	/

B Fill the blanks with words from the table above.

1 Are there any film stars or actors who you find *attractive* ?
2 Do you ________ about the ________ of the rainforests?
3 Do you believe in life after ________?
4 Talk about someone who has made a big ________ to your life.
5 Is television harmful, or can it be ________?
6 Do you know anyone who believes in aliens and ________ saucers?
7 Have you ever been ________ with the service in a shop or restaurant? Did you complain?
8 Is it more important to be ________ in your career, or to have ________ in your relationships?
9 What is your greatest ________ (= your best quality?)

C Now answer the questions!

MORE notes

Look up the **bold** words in the dictionary. Use the MORE notes to find the answers.

Across

1 A **bruise** on your eye (5,3)
3 The children's word for a **rabbit** (5)
5 A **shirt** usually has one of these at the neck (6)
10 The opposite of a **saltwater** fish is a ____ fish (10)
11 A type of **jam** that is made from oranges or lemons (9)
13 If you ____ a **meeting**, you arrange that it will happen at a later time than you had planned (8)
14 Something that you have to do at the checkout in a **supermarket** (5)
15 The place where an **ambassador** lives and works (7)
17 A day when you choose to have a **holiday** and not go to work (3,3)
18 Things that **birds** build (5)

Down

2 Trees (such as the **pine**) which do not lose their leaves in winter are called ____ trees (9)
4 Cotton and wool are types of ____ **fibre** (7)
5 There are 100 of these in a **dollar** (5)
6 A **mirror** ____ images (8)
7 An **argument** or disagreement (7)
8 Another name for non-**alcoholic** drinks (4,6)
9 A type of ape, although people sometimes call it a **monkey** (10)
12 The signs of the **zodiac** are used in ____ (9)
13 The area of **science** concerned with natural forces such light, electricity, etc. (7)
16 When you close both **eyes** and open them again quickly, you ____ (5)

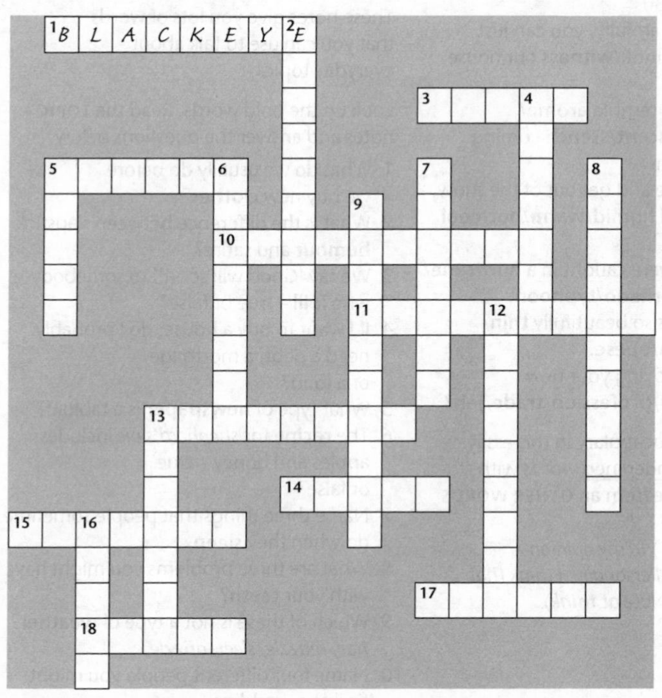

OTHER WORDS FOR notes

These notes help you to improve your vocabulary. They group similar words, and explain the differences between them.

A Choose the correct word in each sentence below. Find the **OTHER WORDS FOR** note that you need, and use it to help you.

1 It was his **mistake/error/fault/responsibility** that we were late. (*Note at **mistake***)
2 Tom and his sister are both very **pretty/good-looking/handsome/beautiful**.
3 If he wins this match, he will become the **largest/biggest/greatest/fattest** tennis player this country has ever known.
4 In our office, the lunch **interval/break/intermission/recess** is from 12.30 – 13.30.
5 If you look carefully, you can just **see/watch/look/witness** our house from here.
6 There was a terrible **aroma/fragrance/scent/stench** coming from the bin.
7 Come inside and get out of the snow. It's nice and **humid/warm/hot/cool** in here.
8 The skiers were caught in a **hurricane/blizzard/tornado/typhoon**.
9 Your sister is so beautifully **thin/skinny/slim/obese**.
10 Are you enjoying your new **occupation/profession/trade/job**?

B Improve the vocabulary in this essay. Replace the underlined words with a word or phrase from an **OTHER WORDS FOR** note.

▶ Example: (1) *In my opinion, Croatia . . . / Personally, I think that Croatia . . .* (*Note at **think***)

(1) I think that Croatia is a (2) very good place for a holiday. I had a (3) very good time there. When I arrived at my hotel, I was (4) very happy to discover that I had a (5) very good view of the sea. (6) I like swimming and (7) I also like water sports, so I went to the beach every day. I (8) also spent a lot of time looking at the scenery, because the (9) scenery in Croatia is so beautiful. The weather is also (10) nice. The restaurants served (11) good food. The breakfast in the hotel was also really (12) good, and the waitress was (13) nice. Nearly all of the Croatians I met were (14) nice. The only (15) bad experience I had was when I lost my backpack. That was (16) very bad! I felt (17) very sad because my camera was in it and I lost all my (18) nice photos.

TOPIC notes

These notes give you lots of words that you can use to talk about everyday topics.

Look up the bold words. Read the **TOPIC** notes and answer the questions below.

1 What do we usually do before we buy new **clothes**?
2 What is the difference between slapstick **humour** and satire?
3 We say 'Good will soon!' to somebody who is **ill** – true or false?
4 If I want to buy a house, do I probably need a debt, a mortgage or a **loan**?
5 What type of **newspaper** is a tabloid?
6 The **recipe** for *shepherd's pie* includes apples and honey – true or false?
7 Name three things that people sometimes do when they **sleep**.
8 What are three problems you might have with your **teeth**?
9 Which of these is not a type of **weather**? *hail, muzzle, sleet, drizzle*
10 Name four different people you might find at a **wedding**.

Colour pages

These pages are full of useful vocabulary arranged according to topic.

A Look at the definitions below.
Find the words on the colour pages.

1 a sweet brown powder that is used as a spice in cooking
2 a plant with a strong taste and smell that looks like a small onion and is used in cooking
3 trousers made of denim (= a strong, usually blue, cotton cloth)
4 a style of fighting originally from Japan in which the hands and feet are used as weapons
5 a small insect that is red or yellow with black spots
6 a person whose job is to put in or repair water pipes, baths, toilets etc.
7 a bag that you use for carrying things on your back
8 a piece of thick material that covers a small part of a floor
9 a mixture of vegetables, usually not cooked, that you often eat together with other foods
10 a light motorbike with a small engine
11 a type of animal, such as a crab or prawn, that lives in water
12 an extremely tall building
13 using a needle and thread to make or repair things
14 a male deer
15 a small river
16 flat, square objects that are arranged in rows to cover roofs, floors, bathroom walls, etc.
17 a tall narrow building or part of a building such as a church or castle
18 the long nose of an elephant
19 a river that falls from a high place, for example over a rock
20 a boat with sails, used for pleasure

B Circle the words in the wordsearch.

T	P	L	U	M	B	E	R	W	S	R	C
I	K	A	R	A	T	E	U	A	T	U	I
L	M	D	T	S	L	B	C	T	A	K	N
E	E	Y	A	C	H	T	K	E	G	S	N
S	O	B	K	O	R	O	S	R	P	H	A
K	W	I	S	O	G	W	A	F	O	E	M
S	Y	R	E	T	A	E	C	A	S	L	O
J	T	D	W	E	R	R	K	L	A	L	N
E	R	P	I	R	L	E	M	L	L	F	Y
A	U	U	N	D	I	J	A	P	A	I	A
N	N	T	G	E	C	L	F	M	D	S	R
S	K	Y	S	C	R	A	P	E	R	H	G

Workout key

How to find words

The alphabet

A 5 glasses
18 zodiac
10 ripple
15 volcano
2 blow
9 puddle
12 snail
3 duck
6 hat
7 jellyfish
16 windmill
13 sneeze
14 snorkel
1 arch
11 robot
4 eclipse
8 lick
17 zebra

Puddle and *robot* are not illustrations in *Wordpower*.

Choosing the right meaning

A 1 *F*
2 *T*
3 *F* A Christmas cracker is a cardboard tube covered in coloured paper.
4 *F* If something 'costs a bomb', it is expensive.
5 *F* A dummy is a stupid person.
6 *F* A school is a large group of fish.
7 *F* The season after summer and before winter is called **fall** in American English.
8 *F* A man wears trunks to go swimming.
9 *T*

B

1	frozen	sense 1
2	dropped	sense 1
3	turned	sense 1
4	cut	sense 4
5	broke	sense 1
6	faced/face	sense 1
7	playing	sense 4
8	cut	sense 6
9	broke	sense 5
10	turned	sense 6
11	face	sense 3
12	drop	sense 4
13	play	sense 5
14	froze	sense 4

Finding phrasal verbs – fast!

A 1 away
2 down
3 on
4 on
5 out
6 over/through
7 round
8 up
9 with

B 1 out
2 down
3 with
4 over/through
5 on
6 round
7 up
8 away
9 on
10 out

Parts of speech (= nouns, verbs, etc.)

A 1 adjective
2 noun
3 verb
4 adverb

B

1	noun	watch	2
2	verb	watch	1
3	noun	park	1
4	verb	park	2
5	noun	flat	2
6	adjective	flat	1
7	noun	train	1
8	verb	train	2
9	adjective	hard	1
10	adverb	hard	2

Finding the right word

1 inspect
2 lucky
3 spy
4 thief
5 limousine
6 jeweller
7 greedy
8 clumsy
9 dig
10 burglar

Understanding words

Defining vocabulary

A Definitions puzzle

1 guitar
2 deer
3 tobacco
4 pastry
5 spacecraft
6 microscope
7 grapes

B Which word is different?

drawer not a container for water
litigation not a process in the body
dice not a round object
scum not a substance used for cleaning
dose not an amount of money

C 1 material 5 container
2 process 6 substance
3 material 7 object
4 amount

Pronunciation

How to read phonetic spelling

A 1 sung 4 look 7 joke
2 slap 5 shirt 8 though
3 caught 6 chew 9 bath

B 1 clear 4 go 6 boy
2 hair 5 my 7 how
3 stay

C hair care fair where
stay late paint weigh
go know phone though
my five high lie
boy enjoy noise point
how aloud brown sound

Stress

A Check your answers by looking at the list of **Geographical names** at the back of the dictionary.

How to use words

Examples

2 court = badminton squash tennis
pitch = football hockey cricket
3 ski resort
4 winter sport
5 No. You cannot use **sporting** to describe people.
6 to be in training for
7 participate in
8 at a swimming pool
9 Yes, they do.
Goes windsurfing is more usual.
10 A referee. He/She blows it.
11 sports facilities

Collocation – Words that go together

Verb + noun collocations

A do your homework
draw pictures
fall in love
go on holiday
have a good time
lose weight
save money
tell a story
watch TV

B done your homework?
She fell in love with him…
If you hadn't watched so much…
Have you lost weight?
She has gone on holiday.
love drawing pictures.
tell the same stories…
have a good time…
save more money…

Adjective + noun collocations

1 a bad back
2 a balanced diet
3 a black eye
4 a broken leg
5 a contagious disease
6 a decayed tooth
7 a runny nose
8 a serious illness
9 a sore throat
10 a speedy recovery
11 a splitting headache
12 a twisted ankle

Prepositions

1 afraid of
2 proud of
3 remind you of
4 dream of/about
5 embarrassed about
6 worry about
7 bad at
8 believe in
9 receive a present from

Verb patterns

1 enjoy doing
2 planning to do
3 make you do/not allowed to do
4 looking forward to doing
5 puts off doing/should do
6 forgotten to do
7 remember doing

Irregular verbs

found / found
ran / run
did / done
fell / fallen
wrote / written
sang / sung
ate / eaten
broke / broken
took / taken
drank / drunk

mystery word = understood (past tense and past participle of understand)

GRAMMAR notes

1 it is so depressing (note at **news**)
2 I can't eat any more (note at **some**)
3 I've been studying English for four years (note at **since**)
4 I had to help (note at **must**)
5 some information about (note at **information**)
6 If the weather is good tomorrow (note at **when**)
7 My twin brother, who lives in Germany, is called (note at **who**)
8 I have such a boring teacher (note at **such**)
9 Two days ago (note at **ago**)
10 I've never been to China (note at **go**)

HELP notes

1 like
2 take care of
3 left
4 funny
5 lend
6 laid (= past simple of lay), lay (= past simple of lie)
7 nice
8 raise
9 robbed, stolen
10 tell

When to use words

Formal, informal, slang, etc.

1 ✗ formal
2 ✗ formal
3 ✗ slang
4 ✔ slang
5 ✗ informal
6 ✔ formal
7 ✗ formal
8 ✔ figurative
9 ✔ informal
10 ✗ spoken

British and American English

American words

1 automobile
2 license plate
3 windshield
4 trunk
5 tire
6 hood
7 fender
8 gas/gasoline

British words

1 flat
2 lift
3 dustbin/litter bin
4 fridge
5 curtains
6 toilet
7 tap
8 ground floor

Build your vocabulary

Word families

A

verb	noun	adjective
attract	**attraction**	(un)attractive
deepen	**depth**	**deep**
destroy	destruction	**destructive**
die	**death**	dead
differ	**difference**	**different**
educate	education	educated / **educational**
fly	**flight**	**flying**
frighten	fright	frightened / **frightening**
hope	hope	**hopeful** / (OPP **hopeless**)
satisfy	**satisfaction**	(dis)**satisfied**
succeed	**success**	successful
strengthen	**strength**	strong
worry	worry	**worried** / **worrying**

B

1 attractive
2 worry, destruction
3 death
4 difference
5 educational
6 flying
7 dissatisfied
8 successful, success
9 strength

MORE notes

across	down
1 black eye	2 evergreen
3 bunny	4 natural
5 collar	5 cents
10 freshwater	6 reflects
11 marmalade	7 quarrel
13 postpone	8 soft drinks
14 queue	9 chimpanzee
15 embassy	12 astrology
17 day off	13 physics
18 nests	16 blink

OTHER WORDS FOR notes

A 1 fault (note at **mistake**)
2 good-looking (note at **beautiful**)
3 greatest (note at **big**)
4 break (note at **interval**)
5 see (note at **look**)
6 stench (note at **smell**)
7 warm (note at **cold**)
8 blizzard (note at **storm**)
9 slim (note at **fat**)
10 job (note at **work**)

B Possible answers:
2 + 3 brilliant / an excellent / fantastic / great / wonderful
4 very glad / very pleased / delighted
5 brilliant / an excellent / fantastic / great / wonderful
6 I enjoy / I love / I'm really keen on / I'm really into
7 I also enjoy / I also love / I'm also really keen on / I'm also really into
8 spent a lot of time looking at the scenery as well / too
9 countryside
10 lovely
11+ 12 delicious / tasty
13 + 14 lovely / friendly
15 unpleasant
16 awful / dreadful / horrible / terrible
17 miserable / unhappy / upset
18 great / lovely / wonderful

TOPIC notes

1 We try them on to see if they fit.
2 **Slapstick** is the type of humour where people (such as clowns) fall over or cover other people with water. **Satire** is the type of humour which makes fun of people such as politicians.
3 False. We say 'Get well soon!'
4 You probably need a mortgage.
5 Tabloid newspapers have small pages. Some of them have shocking stories and reports about famous people's lives.
6 False. The recipe for shepherd's pie includes potatoes, butter, milk, an onion, minced meat, chopped tomatoes, herbs and cheese.
7 snore, dream, have nightmares or sleepwalk
8 You might have toothache, tooth decay, and you might need a brace to straighten your teeth. Some people need false teeth.
9 muzzle
10 the bride, the bridegroom, the bridesmaids and the best man

Colour pages

A

1 cinnamon	8 rug	15 stream
2 garlic	9 salad	16 tiles
3 jeans	10 scooter	17 tower
4 karate	11 shellfish	18 trunk
5 ladybird	12 skyscraper	19 waterfall
6 plumber	13 sewing	20 yacht
7 rucksack	14 stag	

B

List of illustrations in the dictionary

At or near these words in the dictionary, you will find pictures to help you to understand words and expand your vocabulary. Many of these pictures have different parts labelled, for example the picture at egg includes the items *eggshell*, *white* and *yolk*.

accordion
angle
antelope
arch
arm
back
badge
badger
badminton
bag
bagpipes
balcony
ballet
bar
basket
beaver
bed
bend
between
bicycle
bin
binoculars
blink
blow
boat
body
bolt
borrow
bread
bring
brush
bucket
bulldozer
button
cake
camel
camera
camp
candle
car
card
castle
catapult
chair
chess
chicken
chip[1]
chip[2]
circle
clock
cog
coil
compass
computer
concave
concentric
container
corner
corrugated
cough
cow
crawl
crinkle
cross-legged
crossword
cube
cup
curtain
cutlery
deer
dice
dig
dimple
dolphin
domino
donkey
drawer
drop
duck[1]
duck[2]
dummy
each other
eagle
ear
earth
eclipse
egg
elbow
elephant
elk
exercise
fan
fence
fireplace
firework
fist
flick
float
football
footprint
forklift
fox
frown
garden
glass
glasses
glove
goat
graffiti
graph
hair
handle
harmonica
hat
hedgehog
hinge
hippopotamus
hold
hook
hop
horse
iron
jellyfish
jewellery
jug
juggler

kangaroo
kayak
kettle
key
kitchen
kneel
koala
label
lace
ladder
lamp
lean
leapfrog
length
letter
lick
lighthouse
line
lion
lizard
loop
magnet
magnify
medal
medicine
merry-go-round
mixer
money
monkey
music
nod
noughts and crosses
nut
nutcracker
octopus
opposite
optical illusion
otter
overall
overflow
overlap
owl
padlock
panda
parachute
peg
penguin
penknife
piano
pier
pin
pinch
placard
plant
plaster
plug
poke
pool
postbox
pram
pull
pulley
punch
QR code
rabbit
rack
reindeer
ripple
roll
rope
roundabout
sari
scale
scissors
scorpion
seal
seashell
sew
sewing
shadow
shake
shallow
shape
shellfish
shoe
shrink
shrug
skate
slap
sleigh
snail
snorkel
spider
spill
spiral
spoon
spray
squeeze
squirrel
stationery
stroke
sundial
swan
swim
swing
sword
take-off
teapot
tick
too
tool
torch
tractor
trampoline
tree
trolley
turkey
upside down
vacuum
volcano
wave
whistle
winch
windmill
worm
wrap
wrinkle
zebra
zodiac

List of notes in the dictionary

Different types of note in the dictionary give you extra help with key aspects of English and support you with your studies. The words in blue show you where to find notes:

Culture

April Fool's Day
Bonfire Night
breakfast
cafe
clover
congress – US Congress
election – British elections
English – English, Scots, Welsh, British
fish – fish and chips
the Foreign and Commonwealth Office
form – the sixth form
Halloween
independence – Independence Day
May Day
mistletoe
pantomime
parliament – UK parliament
party – political parties
Pluto – the solar system
public school – types of school
Shrove Tuesday
Thanksgiving (Day)
underground – railway system
the United Kingdom
valentine – St. Valentine's Day

Exam tips

check	Checking your work
cloze test	Doing a cloze test
collocation	Collocations
contraction	Using contractions
copy	Copying
family	Word families
format	Exam format
gonna	gonna
last-minute	Last-minute learning
limit	Word limit
mock	Mock exams
multiple-choice	Multiple-choice
note	Revision notes
oral	Oral/Speaking exams
paragraph	Paragraphs
part	Parts of speech
plan	Planning your answer
predict	Predicting listening
pronunciation	Pronunciation
relevant	Relevant information
revision	Revision
skim	Skimming
spelling	Spelling mistakes
synonym	Synonyms
tense	Irregular verb forms
test	Test yourself
time	Time yourself
topic	Topics
underline	Underline key words
wanna	wanna
yourself	Talking about yourself

Other words for

allow	permit, let
alone	lonely, on your own, by yourself
also	too, as well
answer	reply, respond
area	district, region, part
bad	awful, dreadful, terrible, horrible
beautiful	pretty, good-looking, attractive, handsome, gorgeous
big	large, great
border	frontier, boundary
clean	wash, wipe, dust, brush, sweep, do the housework
cold	cool, freezing
country	nation, state, land

dislike	don't like, don't spend much time doing sth, not keen on, not interested in, hate, can't stand
fat	large, overweight, chubby, obese
good	brilliant, fantastic, great, excellent, wonderful, delicious, tasty, talented, outstanding
ground	the Earth, land, floor, earth, soil
happen	occur, take place
happy	glad, pleased, delighted, cheerful
hit	strike, beat, punch, smack
hurt	wounded, injured
important	essential, vital, play a vital/key role in…, historic
intelligent	bright, clever, smart
interval	intermission, break, recess, interlude, pause
kill	murder, assassinate, slaughter, massacre
lake	pond, pool, puddle
like	enjoy/spend a lot of time doing sth, keen on sth, be into sth, interested in
mistake	error, do sth wrong, fault
nice	great, lovely, wonderful, friendly, cosy, attractive, beautiful, expensive, fashionable, smart
price	charge, cost
road	street, motorway, freeway, expressway, lane
sad	upset, unhappy, miserable, depressed, depressing
scenery	country, countryside, landscape, view
small	little, tiny, minute
smell	stink, stench, odour, pong, aroma, fragrance, perfume, scent
storm	thunderstorm, cyclone, hurricane, typhoon, tornado, blizzard, snowstorm
sweater	jumper, pullover, cardigan, fleece, sweatshirt
thief	robber, burglar, shoplifter, mugger
thin	slim, skinny, underweight
think	In my opinion/As far as I'm concerned/It seems to me that…, reckon, believe
tool	implement, machine, instrument, device
travel	journey, tour, trip, excursion
under	below, beneath, underneath
until	till, as far as, up to
well	great, good, OK, fine, I'm not (too) bad
work	job, employment, occupation, profession, trade
zero	nil, nought, O

Topic notes

art	Art
baby	Babies
bed	Beds
birthday	Birthdays
blog	Blogs
boat	Boats
book	Books
bus	Travelling by bus
camera	Cameras
car	Cars
card	Playing cards
chat	Chat room
child	Children
city	City life
clothes	Clothes
coffee	Coffee
computer	Computers
cook	Cooking
court	Court
crime	Crime
cybercrime	Cybercrime
degree	Qualifications
direction	Asking for and giving directions
doctor	Going to the doctor
dog	Dogs
driving	Driving
eBay™	eBay

e-book	E-books
email	Email
environment	The environment
film	Films
flat	Living in a flat
friend	Friends
hair	Hair
hard drive	Hard drive
holiday	Holidays
hospital	Hospitals
hotel	Hotels
house	Houses
humour	Humour
ill	Feeling ill
instant messaging	Instant messaging
instrument	Musical instruments
Internet	The Internet
introduce	Introducing people
iPod™	iPods
job	Jobs
job	Leaving a job
listen	Listening to music
literature	Literature
loan	Loans
meal	Meals
meat	Meat
mobile phone	Mobile phones
money	Money
music	Music
name	Names
netiquette	Netiquette
newspaper	Newspapers
office	Office work
online	Online
pay	Pay
pet	Pets
plane	Travelling by plane
podcast	Podcasts
politics	Politics
pop	Pop music
post	Posting letters
recipe	A recipe
reference	References
restaurant	Restaurants
routine	Daily routine
school	Schools
shop	Shops
shopping	Shopping
sleep	Sleep
smartphone	Smartphones
social networking	Social networking
space	Space
sport	Sport
study	Studying
telephone	Using the telephone
television	Television
theatre	Theatre
tooth	Teeth
touch screen	Touch screens
train	Travelling by train
university	University
war	War
weather	Weather
wedding	Weddings

Writing tips

because	Giving a reason
contrast	How to show contrast 1
despite	How to show contrast 2
difference	How to compare different things
example	Giving examples
mind map	Preparing to write
similarity	How to compare similar things
sincere	How to end a letter
sudden	Using adverbs
then	Order of events
therefore	Describing results